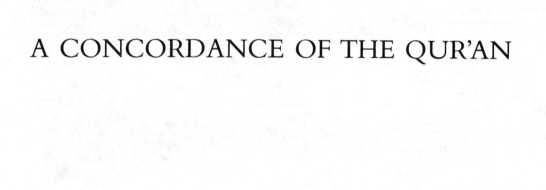

A CONCORDANCE OF THE QUR'AN

A CONCORDANCE OF THE QUR'AN

Hanna E. Kassis

Foreword by Fazlur Rahman

UNIVERSITY OF CALIFORNIA PRESS
Berkeley Los Angeles London

The University of California Press gratefully acknowledges
the assistance of the Andrew W. Mellon Foundation
in the publication of this volume.

University of California Press
Berkeley and Los Angeles, California
University of California Press, Ltd.
London, England

Printed in the United States of America

1 2 3 4 5 6 7 8 9

Library of Congress Cataloging in Publication Data

Kassis, H. E.
A concordance of the Qur'an.

Includes indexes.
1. Koran—Concordances. I. Koran. II. Title.
BP133.K37 297'.1225'21 82-40100
ISBN 0-520-04327-8
ISBN 0-520-04409-6 (pbk.)

For

Anne, Magdalena and Omar

CONTENTS

FOREWORD

This *Concordance of the Qur'an in English* satisfies a paramount need of those—and there are millions of them—who have no command of the Arabic language and yet desire to understand the Qur'an. The benefit derivable from English translations of the Sacred Book is, in principle, limited because, first, the Qur'an is not a "book" but a collection of passages revealed to Muḥammad over a period of about twenty-three years and, second, because the Qur'an is not really translatable. This does not mean that the Qur'an should not be translated. It does mean that translations lose much in tone and nuance, let alone the incommunicable beauty, grandeur, and grace of the original.

Realizing this, scholars have attempted to provide assistance to the reader of the Qur'an in translation. There are topical arrangements of the Qur'an which show, for example, what it has to say on God, man, or the universe. However, these works tend to be somewhat subjective because of the interpreter's inevitable point of view, his assumptions on given issues. Rudi Paret has produced a concordance of the Qur'an in German, an excellent piece of work in its way, in which under each verse or passage of the Qur'an, cross-references are given to other verses for the sake of comparison. The tool employed in Professor Paret's work, however, is the idea and not primarily the word. The user of the work depends, inevitably, on Professor Paret's decisions about how much of a given idea is to be found in a given word or set of words.

The main distinction of Hanna Kassis's concordance, in my view, is that it utilizes the semantic structure of Arabic vocabulary itself in revealing the meaning of the Qur'an on any given issue, point or concept. A reader who looks in the index of this concordance for a word which he has encountered in reading an English translation of the Qur'an—the word *pride*, for example—is directed immediately to the roots of the Arabic, Qur'anic terms for *pride*. At the entries for these Arabic roots, all the derivative forms are shown, and the verses of the Qur'an in which they appear are there listed in translation.

The author chose this procedure to overcome the subjectivity or relativity of translations. But the result is not only the faithful revelation of the original meaning of the Qur'anic terms but a whole conceptual field conveyed by those terms in their denotation, connotation, and association. This achievement goes beyond the performance of indices and concordances of the Qur'an in the original Arabic.

I am confident that any person who is sincerely interested in understanding the Qur'an and appreciating the nuances of its diction and shades of its meaning can satisfy his need more fully with this book than in any way short of developing a real command over the Arabic language itself.

Fazlur Rahman
Professor of Islamic Thought
University of Chicago

ACKNOWLEDGMENTS

The English text utilized in this work is that of A. J. Arberry, *The Koran Interpreted* (Oxford, 1964), which, in my opinion, is the best available translation to date of the Qur'an in English. For alternative definitions the following translations have been consulted: R. Bell, *The Qur'an* (Edinburgh, 1937), M. M. Pickthall, *The Meaning of the Glorious Koran* (New York, 1956) and Abdullah Yusuf Ali, *The Holy Qur'ān* (Lahore, 1934).

All Arabic entries in the Concordance are in romanized (transliterated) characters and are arranged alphabetically according to the order in the Table of Transliterations. The transliteration system of the Library of Congress as outlined in *Bulletin* 91 (September, 1970) of the Cataloging Service has been adopted. Two minor exceptions should be pointed out. In nouns derived from roots ending in *y*, the use of *-īy* instead of *-ī* has been adopted (contrary to the LC rules 6.b and c). Furthermore, a dot (.) is used, rather than a prime ('), between the *h* and the preceding letter, (*d*, *s* or *t*) when each letter is to have its distinct consonantal value (contrary to LC rule 21).

Particles (prepositions, conjunctions and particles of negation, affirmation, emphasis, etc.) have not been included in this work. Pronouns have also been excluded, with the exception of those occurrences of *huwa* (= he) that refer specifically to God. Most forms of the verbs *kāna* (= to be) and *qāla* (= to say) have been omitted, except where their occurrences are associated with or uttered by God.

In preparing this work I have benefited from the advice and assistance of many people. I wish to thank, in particular, Professors Charles Adams, Director of the Institute of Islamic Studies at McGill University, and Alford T. Welch of the Department of Religious Studies at Michigan State University for their counsel and advice. I alone must bear the responsibility for any errors and omissions.

Mrs. Anna Evans has generously granted me the permission to use the text of her late father's *Koran Interpreted* in the composition of the Concordance. Her kindness is duly acknowledged by the author and the publishers of this work.

Special thanks are due to my colleagues W. John Coulthard and Lewis R. James whose unfailing assistance over the past eight years in the preparation of the computer programmes brought this project to its conclusion. To them and to the staff of the Computing Centre of the University of British Columbia I shall remain indebted.

My thanks also go to Dr. John R. Miles, Editor of the University of California Press, to Mr. Czeslaw Jan Grycz, of the Production Department and to their staff for their efforts in producing and publishing this work.

Finally, I wish to acknowledge the financial support this project received from the Canada Council, the Social Sciences and Humanities Research Council of Canada, and the University of British Columbia.

H.E.K.

ABBREVIATIONS

act.	active (sec. C 9)
adj.	adjective (sec. C 17)
adv.	adverb (sec. C 18)
coll.	collective (noun)
com.	common gender (sec. C 15)
comp.	comparative adjective (sec. C 17)
du.	dual (sec. C 16)
f.	feminine (sec. C 11, 15)
impf.	imperfect (sec. C 7, 8, 10)
impv.	imperative (sec. C 7, 8, 10)
M	Meccan verse (see Appendix to Introduction)
m.	masculine (sec. C 11, 15)
ml.	Mysterious Letter of the Qur'an (see Index II.b)
n.	noun (sec. C 12–16)
n. prop.	proper noun
n. vb.	verbal noun (sec. C 19)
num.	numeral
pass.	passive (sec. C 9)
pcple.	participle (sec. C 20)
perf.	perfect (sec. C 7, 8, 10)
pl.	plural (sec. C 11, 16)
quad.	quadriliteral (sec. C 6, 10)
s.	singular (sec. C 11, 16)
vb.	verb (sec. C 5–10)
vs(s).	verse(s)
Y	Medinan verse (see Appendix to Introduction)
[Ali]	A. Yusuf Ali, *The Holy Qur'ān* (Lahore, 1934)
[Ar]	A. J. Arberry, *The Koran Interpreted* (Oxford, 1964)
[Bl]	R. Bell, *The Qur'an* (Edinburgh, 1937)
[Pk]	M. M. Pickthall, *The Meaning of the Glorious Koran* (New York, 1956)

[ ]	Reconstructed text (sec. B 3b)
( )	Contents to be excluded when considering the main entry (sec. B 3a)
< >	Contents represent meaning or position of verbal noun (sec. B 3c and sec. C 19)
*	Signifies the root (sec. C 3)
~	Signifies the meaning of the entry

TRANSLITERATIONS

The following list is arranged according to the English alphabetical order, with the insertion of the romanized Arabic consonants that have no phonemic or alphabetical equivalents in English. The order is that in which the entries are arranged in the Concordance.

CONSONANTS

LETTER	ARABIC NAME	COMMENTS
ʾ	*alif*	Also known as the *hamzah*. A glottal stop which at the beginning of a word is not transliterated but is implied in the vowel that follows it. In any other position it is transliterated as ʾ. (See "Vowels and Diphthongs", below)
ʿ	*ʿayn*	A laryngeal without equivalent in any Western language
b	*bā*	= English "b"
d	*dāl*	= English "d"
dh	*dhāl*	Pronounced as "th" in "that"
ḍ	*ḍāḍ*	A velarized "d"; no English equivalent
f	*fā*	= English "f"
gh	*ghayn*	Roughly equivalent to the French "r"
h	*hā*	= English "h"
ḥ	*ḥā*	A fricative "h"; no English equivalent
j	*jīm*	Pronounced as "j" in "just"

k	*kāf*	= English "k"
kh	*khā*	Roughly equivalent to the "ch" in "Bach"
l	*lām*	= French "l"
m	*mīm*	= English "m"
n	*nūn*	= English "n"
q	*qāf*	A velarized "k"; no English equivalent
r	*rā*	= Spanish "r"
s	*sīn*	= English "s"
sh	*shīn*	Pronounced as "sh"
ṣ	*ṣād*	A velarized "s"; no English equivalent
t	*tā*	= English "t"
th	*thā*	Pronounced as "th" in "thin"
ṭ	*ṭā*	A velarized "t", no English equivalent
w	*wāw*	Pronounced as "w" in "war". (See "Vowels and Diphthongs, below)
y	*yā*	Pronounced as "y" in "yarn". (See "Vowels and Diphthongs, below)
z	*zayn*	= English "z"
ẓ	*ẓā*	A velarized "dh"; no English equivalent

VOWELS AND DIPHTHONGS

a	*fat.ḥah*	Pronounced as "a" in "cattle"
i	*kasrah*	Pronounced as "i" in "fin"
u	*ḍammah*	Pronounced as "oo" in "foot"
ā	*alif mamdūdah*	Pronounced as "a" in "man" or "father", depending on letters that precede and follow it
á	*alif maqṣūrah*	Pronounced as "a" but occurs only at end of words
ī	*yā*	Pronounced as "ee" in "meet"
ū	*waw*	Pronounced as "oo" in "moon"
aw		Roughly equivalent to "ou" in "out"
ay		Roughly equivalent to the cockney "a" in "hate"

INTRODUCTION

A. THE QUR'AN: AN INTRODUCTORY COMMENT

The Qur'an is unique among sacred Books in style, unity of language and authorship, and significance in the life of the faith it governs. The Western reader should be prepared to receive it on its own terms. It is not too bold to suggest that the Qur'an is to the Muslim what Jesus Christ, and not the Bible, is to the believing Christian. No Muslim would question its divine revelation, and as a result, it has not been subjected to the same type of critical study as has the Bible. Unlike the Bible, it was revealed over a defined period of time and to one man, Muḥammad. According to tradition, its canon was established under Divine guidance by the Prophet, prior to his death, and not by believers at a later time, as is the case with the Old and New Testaments. Consequently, there is no accepted body of literature in the tradition of Islam equivalent to the Apocryphal Gospels (Christian) or the Books of the Apocrypha or Pseudepigrapha (Jewish).

The Qur'an contains 114 Chapters (*sūrah*, pl. *suwar*), each of which has a title. Some have more than one title. A title does not necessarily reflect the content of the Chapter, but may simply be one of the words occurring somewhere in that Chapter. With the exception of Chapter 1 (*al-Fātiḥah*), the Chapters are arranged, roughly speaking, according to length, the longest located at the beginning of the Qur'an and the shortest at the end. Readers of the Bible may note a similar practice in the arrangement of the books of the Prophets in the Old Testament, as well as of the Epistles in the New Testament.

Each Chapter, with the exception of Chapter 9, begins with the "invocation", the *basmalah*, "In the Name of God, the Merciful, the Compassionate". In some Chapters the *basmalah* is followed by one or more letters that have been described as "Mysterious Letters", whose exact meaning and function have defied scholarly ability throughout the centuries. The user finds them listed in the Index (II.B).

Each Chapter is divided into verses (*āyah*, pl. *āyāt*). There are two different senses to the word *āyah*. First, it is a "sign" of Divine authority in literary form, in the same sense that, according to Christian belief, the person of Jesus Christ, his words and his deeds are also "signs". Second, it is a literary device to identify smaller textual units within a larger literary context (as is a stanza, a pentad or a Biblical verse). In this respect, the verses of the Qur'an are identified, in Arabic, by rhyme or rhythm. Although this is apparent in the written Arabic text, it is more evident in the recitation of the Qur'an. This element, as well as other aspects of the linguistic beauty of the language of the Qur'an, is irretrievably lost in translation. Some translators, notably Arberry, have attempted to recover the rhythmic nature of the Arabic text by rounding and rhyming the translated verses. It should be noted that, governed by the rhyme, a verse may end and another may begin in the middle of a sentence. Thus, the end of a verse marks a pause in the recitation of the Qur'an rather than the termination of an idea, a sentence or a revelation.

The numerical order of the verses is recent. Originally, the end of each verse was indicated in the text by a mark (a decorative design) and not a number. As there are seven main traditions of transmission ("Readings") of the Qur'an, there are also variations in the identification of some verses. When enumeration began to replace the decorative identification of the verses, the variations remained. As a result, there are some editions of the Arabic Qur'an in circulation, each with a different verse enumeration. Recently, the enumeration system of the Cairo edition of the Qur'an (based on that of the school of Kūfa) has gained greater popularity over others, in the Muslim World. Gustav Fluegel, whose edition circulated widely among Western scholars, based his text on an edition (North African) other than that of Cairo. Arberry employed the verse enumeration of Fluegel, grouping his verses in pentads. For him, however, the numerical order of the verses is subordinate to his attempt to provide a glimpse of the rhyming of the Arabic original. Because Marmeduke Pickthall and Yusuf Ali used still other editions (Istanboul and Anjuman, respectively), there are some variations in the verse enumeration in their editions of the Qur'an. This variation in verse enumeration does not pose a problem for the Muslim who, wishing to refer to the Qur'an, will cite the text rather than refer to it by chapter and verse. Citation by page or chapter and verse is an innovation of modern Western scholarship which Muslim scholars have also adopted, without abandoning the traditional mode of reference.

The Qur'an was revealed to Muḥammad in two different places:

1) At Mecca where he first received the Faith (A.D. 610–622), and to which he returned triumphantly in A.D. 630 before his death (A.D. 632). These are commonly known as the "Meccan" revelations.

b) At Medīna, after his Migration (the *hijrah*, Latin "Hegira"), in A.D. 622, and the establishment of the Muslim state. These are known as the "Medīnan" revelations.

The tone and content of these revelations change as the community developed. One senses in the earliest Chapters—short, vibrant and rhapsodic—the mystery, fear and fascination (to borrow the vocabulary of Rudolph Otto) of the confrontation with and submission to the Divine Will. After the Migration and the establishment of the Muslim state, the Qur'an, while maintaining the initial themes, introduces revelations dealing with the various aspects (judicial, social and religious) of the daily life of the community under the rule of God. The Chapters, whatever their subject, become increasingly developed in style and structure. It would be wrong, however, to thus assume, as sometimes is done, that the rhapsodic language of the earlier period gave way entirely to the elaboration of legal formulations.

The revelations came to the Prophet in one or more verses at a time. According to Muslim belief, their content as well as the time and manner of their revelation, were determined by God and not by Muḥammad, who was simply the recipient and transmitter of the revelations. These revelations were memorized and written down by the believers as the Prophet conveyed them. When the "Authorized Version", the Qur'an in its present form, was redacted, during the lifetime of the first converts to Islam, more attention was paid to the authority of the text being assembled than to the logical or chronological sequence of the contents of the revelations. However, while the arrangement of the Chapters followed the traditions current in the Near East, the chronological and historical background of the revelations, as well as the location of these revelations (Mecca or Medīna) remain the subject of intense study in Muslim and Western scholarship. Muslim tradition, though without consensus, has established a chronological order of the Chapters and, in some cases, the verses, as well as the locus of their revelation. The dominant traditional chronological order (adopted in the Cairo edition, said to be based on the "reading" of ʿĀṣim as narrated by Ḥafṣ) is not in agreement with the results of Western scholarship, significant among which is the work of Th. Noeldeke (see Appendix to this Introduction).

While the language of the Qur'an is poetic, it is not poetry. It is prosodic but not exactly prose. Stylistically, it stands apart from any known body of literature in Arabic (or other languages of the Muslim community) and has remained inimitable. With the exception of Chapter 12, which has literary unity and narrative continuity, the style of the Qur'an is generally not that of didactic, folkloric or historical narrative, although these elements are present in it. As a result, one cannot use the Qur'an as one would the Bible. It cannot be reduced to the level of a child for religious instruction, nor be employed either as "source material" for the reconstruction of the biography of the Prophet and his companions, or as "church history". One may not find in it elaborate details of the practices, sagas, myths or history of the Arabs at the time of the rise of Islam. There are, however, Divine oracles regarding these and other matters.

The great degree to which the Qur'an shapes and governs the lives of millions of Muslims around the world is becoming increasingly evident. It is my conviction that in order to understand Islam and the Muslims, one should endeavour first to comprehend the "Word" that gave the faith its birth and continues to give the community of Islam its nourishment and sustenance. The Qur'an, according to Islam, is God's Word revealed to mankind in Arabic through the agency of the Prophet. Thus, in spite of their differing linguistic backgrounds, Muslims continue to the present day to recite the Scripture in the language of its revelation. While there is no doubt that it is the content of the Qur'an which is of paramount importance in the life of Islam and the Muslims, the language and the vocabulary of revelation, both divinely chosen, are also important. When the Muslim considers the Qur'an, three elements are of significance to him: what was revealed, the language in which it was revealed, and the vocabulary that was selected to convey the revelation. It follows, therefore, that the student of Islam should be able to read the Qur'an in Arabic. Unfortunately, this is an ideal which is not easily attainable, and translation must suffice. Although it is commonly and correctly argued that the Qur'an is neither translatable nor imitable, translations and interpretations do exist, even if none has claimed or received authenticity or the authority of Scripture. Translation tends to limit exegesis, to rigidify concepts and minimize or even obscure the different shades of meaning of a given word or text. But it would be quite wrong, in spite of these drawbacks, to limit the study of the Qur'an to those who have a command of Arabic.

This work, then, is a concordance of the Arabic vocabulary of the Qur'an for the use of the non-Arabist. A concordance, according to Samuel Johnson, is "a book which shows in how many texts of scripture any word occurs." This Concordance fits exactly Johnson's definition. It should be possible to locate in it all the texts in the Qur'an in which a given word occurs.

By listing English language entries in an alphabetic index rather than in some conceptual arrangement, I spare the user the imposition of the findings or opinions of any school of exegesis or interpretation. By grouping these entries according to Arabic root in the concordance proper (see sec. C. 3, below) I demonstrate the generic and semantic relationship of the vocabulary of the Qur'an. There is, for example, no visible relationship in English between the verb "to oppress" and the noun "darkness". By contrast, the semantic and generic relationship between their equivalent terms in Arabic is quite evident when one finds them listed under *ẓalama* and *ẓulmah*, respectively, and stemming from the same root **Ẓ L M*.

This may be sufficient to impress on the student of the Qur'an that a knowledge of Arabic, the language of the Qur'an, albeit a cursory one, is a necessity. If the Qur'an is the lifeline of Muslim life, thought and institutions, the Arabic language, in which it was revealed, is the fibre of that lifeline.

B. HOW TO USE THE CONCORDANCE

The Concordance consists of two major parts: the Concordance proper and the Index. The non-Arabist user of the Concordance is advised to begin with the Index in his search for the vocabulary, and hence the ideas, of the Qur'an. He should first draw up a list of the English vocabulary for the words or concepts he wishes to study in the Qur'an. He should then, a) refer to the Index (in its various parts) to locate the terms on his list, b) locate the derivative(s) and root(s) that are given for each English term, and c) refer to the Concordance proper to locate the Arabic vocabulary and the Qur'anic citations (see the examples given below).

1) THE INDEX

The Index is composed of all the English words that occur as translations of the Arabic vocabulary of the Qur'an. It comprises two main parts, corresponding to the two parts of the Concordance proper as follows:

I. The Divine Name (*Allāh*)	= Index I	Terms Associated with the Divine Name
II. The Remaining Vocabulary	= Index II.A	Divine Attributes
	Index II.B	Proper Nouns
	Index II.C	General Index

The Index is arranged alphabetically. Wherever there is more than one Arabic term (and root) listed against the English entry, the roots are also arranged alphabetically.

EXAMPLE:- Let us assume that the user wishes to find out what the Qur'an has to say about "pride". By looking up the word in the Index (II.C) he would come up with the following typical entry:

Pride, proud
ʿalā (*ʿ *l w*)
ʿatā (*ʿ *t w*)
kabura (**k b r*)
mukhtāl (**kh y l*)

He will learn immediately that the English term "pride" is a translation of four different Arabic words and constitutes four entries in the main part of the Concordance, to which he should now turn.

2) THE CONCORDANCE

The vocabulary of the Qur'an is listed in the Concordance under the roots (identified by an asterisk) from which it stems. The main part of the Concordance (other than the Index), is divided into two sections:

a) *The Divine Name (Allāh)*:- Because of the significance of the Divine Name and the number of times it is mentioned in the Qur'an, its occurrences are subdivided according to the root of the term with which the Divine Name is associated. For example, "God loves", "God creates", etc. are listed under the equivalent Arabic term(s), to "to love", "to create", etc. This subdivision should facilitate analysis of the texts in which the Name occurs and, through reference to the parallel root and derivative in the Concordance proper, of the terms with which it is associated.

b) *Concordance of the Remaining Vocabulary*:- The main part of the Concordance proper consists of the rest of the vocabulary of the Qur'an.

EXAMPLE (continued):-Having located the relevant entries for "pride" in the Index, the user should turn to the main part of the Concordance to locate the first term on his list, *ʿalā* under (*ʿ *L W*). There he would find the following entry (whose various elements are explained in Notes a–e which follow the Example):

a ——————*ᶜ L W

b c

ᶜ**ALĀ vb. (I)**~to ascend, to rise up, to be high, to exalt one's self. (n.vb.) ascent, height, exaltation, pride, exorbitance. (pcple. act.) one who is high, lofty, sublime; (adv) uppermost, upon

d —————————— *a)* perf. act.

e ———	17:7 (7)	destroy utterly that which they ascended to
	23:91 (91)	some of them would have risen up over others
	28:4 (3)	Pharaoh had exalted himself in the land

Notes:-

a) *ᶜ *L W*:- This is the root (sec. C 3, below). The entries in the Concordance are arranged alphabetically by root, following the order of the English alphabet with the modifications outlined in the Table of Transliterations, above. Each root is preceded by an asterisk (*).

b) ᶜ*ALĀ*:- This is the main entry in the Concordance. It is the derivative or the Arabic term derived from the root. The main entry could be a verb, a noun or possibly a particle, although particles have been largely excluded from the Concordance (see Acknowledgments). The derivatives are arranged under the root according to the following order:-

*Root	(sec. C 3)
Triliteral Verb, Form I	(sec. C 5)
Noun(s)	(sec. C 12–16)
Triliteral Verb, Form II–X	(sec. C 5, 10)
Quadriliteral Verb, Form I–IV	(sec. C 6)

c) *Notations:*- Each main entry, whether verb or noun, is followed by a notation. In the example above, this begins with "vb. (I) to ascend, to rise up", etc. The notation comprises the following: a) a grammatical abbreviation and b) the meaning(s) of the entry, preceded by the sign (~), in the translation cited (Arberry). Wherever consultation was necessary and alternative meanings or shades of meaning were found, these are included in the notations and are identified by the initials of the source within square brackets (thus [Ali], [Bl], and [Pk] in addition to [Ar]).

d) *"a) perf. act."*:- This element appears when the main entry is a verb. It is the abbreviatian of "Perfect active" (sec. C 7, 9) and is one of eight possible forms of the Arabic verb (see "The Grammatical Form of the Main Entries", below), one or more of which may occur.

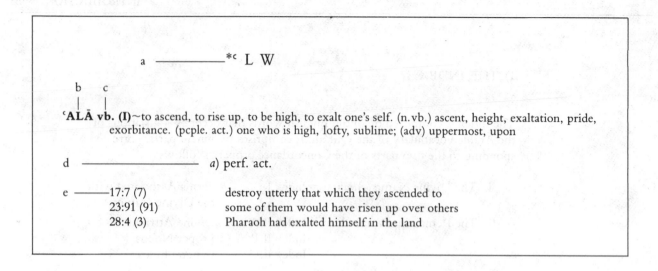

e) *Citation of the Qur'anic Text*:- The first citation in our example reads as follows:-

17:7 (7) destroy utterly that which they ascended to

The number "17" refers to the Chapter (or *Sūrah*) in the Qur'an. Numbering of the Chapters of the Qur'an is a recent innovation employed by both Muslims and non-Muslims (see Appendix to this Introduction). The numbers following the colon (:) are those of the verse (*āyah*). Two verse numbers are given, the second one in brackets. In our example, these are identical. They may be different in other citations. The first is that of the Cairo edition of the Qur'an, which is increasingly considered as the "standard" edition of the Arabic Qur'an. The second, within brackets, is that found in Fluegel's edition of the Arabic Qur'an, a text which, in spite of its variation from the accepted systems of enumeration, is still widely used in Western scholarly circles and has been followed by most English translators of the Qur'an. Thus 17:7 (7) refers to Chapter 17, verse 7 (in the Cairo edition) and 7 (in Fluegel's edition). In the third text cited in the Example, 28:4 (3) refers to Chapter 28, verse 4 (in the Cairo edition) but 3 (in Fluegel's edition). These references are followed by a brief citation of the Qur'anic text as interpreted by Arberry.

The user should notice that very often several entries may appear under the same root. Under the root *ᶜ *L W*, cited above, he will find the following additional derivatives:

ᶜALĪY

ᶜILĪYŪN

TAᶜĀLĀ

ISTAᶜLĀ

He should examine these entries in order to discover a truer sense of the Arabic term than that conveyed in the translations. Furthermore, he may detect possible semantic correlations between the term he is concerned with and others derived from the same root.

3) THE USE OF THE BRACKETS IN THE TEXT

The user may discover three types of brackets employed in the citation of the Qur'anic text: rounded ( ), squared [ ] or angular < >. This may be explained as follows:-

a) *The Use of the Rounded ( ) Brackets*:- Since the cited text is intended to illustrate only one entry at a time, the same citation is repeated as many times as the entry occurs in the same verse. In such cases, the English term that is *not* being referred to in that specific citation is placed within brackets ( ). An example of this is the following verse which is cited to refer to the term *yad* (= a hand) in which there are two occurrences of the term:

48:10 (10) God's hand is over their (hands)
48:10 (10) God's (hand) is over their hands

In addition, since the citation is intended to illustrate the occurrence of the *Arabic* word, it is not unusual to find the English translation of that word occurring more than once in a specific verse, while the original text of the Qur'an shows only one such occurrence. This may be due to stylistic reasons imposed by the exigencies of the English language. Or it may be due to the fact that the repeated English term is a translation of two different Arabic terms. In such cases also, the English term that is *not* applicable in that specific citation is placed within brackets ( ).

b) *The Use of the Squared* [ ] *Brackets*:- There are two situations in which these brackets may be used:-

i) In some cases the Arabic term of the entry may not appear in the English translation for stylistic reasons (which should not be construed as an alteration of the meaning of the Arabic text). In such cases squared brackets [ ] are used to enclose the word or words that would restore the missing Arabic term to the English text. An example of this is the following verse listed under the entry *Allāh* (= God):

33:39 (39) and were fearing Him, and fearing not any one except [God]

In this verse the Divine Name *Allāh* occurs in the Arabic text, while the English translation, for stylistic reasons, uses "Him". Consequently, the Divine Name is restored to the English text of the citation, and is enclosed within squared brackets.

ii) In other places, the entire text in which the term of the entry occurs is too lengthy to cite, or the verb or the subject of the sentence is quite removed from the term of the entry. Here also, the squared brackets [ ] are used to make the cited portion of the text more complete. An example is the following verse:

24:22 (22) Let not those of you who possess bounty and plenty swear off giving kinsmen and the poor and those who emigrate in the way of God

which in the citation, illustrating "poor", becomes:

24:22 (22) [let them not] swear off giving kinsmen and the poor and those who emigrate in the way of God

c) *The Use of the Angular* < > *Brackets*:- These are used to identify the English rendering of the verbal noun. The user should refer to the discussion of this complex structure below (sec. C 19). It should suffice here to give an example:-

17:4 (4) you shall ascend <exceeding> high

The bracketed term "exceeding" is used here to translate the sense of the action of the verb in the example cited above.

4) THE GRAMMATICAL FORM OF THE MAIN ENTRIES

The Verbs (sec. C 5–11) are always entered in the perfect active (third person, masculine, singular). They are arranged in the following order:-

a) Perfect active (sec. C 5, 7, 9)
b) Imperfect active (sec. C 7–10)
c) Imperative (sec. C 7, 8, 10)
d) Perfect passive (sec. C 7, 9, 10)
e) Imperfect passive (sec. C 7, 9, 10)
f) Verbal noun (sec. C 19)
g) Active participle (sec. C 20)
h) Passive participle (sec. C 20)

The tenses and nouns derived from the verb (items *b* to *h*, above) are always followed by the romanized form of the verb (third person, masculine, singular) or noun. If more than one verbal noun (sec. C 19) is derived from a specific verb, each is listed separately. The active and passive participles (sec. C 20) are normally listed in the masculine singular.

The Nouns (other than the verbal noun, which is listed under the verb from which it is derived) are arranged in alphabetical order and are entered after Form I of the verb (if it occurs). They are generally entered in the form in which they occur in the Qur'an. If both the singular and plural forms occur, then the main entry is that of the singular, followed in the notation by the plural. The plural is listed in the notation only if it occurs in the Qur'an and is a broken (irregular) plural that cannot be constructed according to the rules outlined below (sec. C 16). If only the plural form occurs in the Qur'an, then that form constitutes the main entry, followed in the notation by the singular of which it is the plural.

Having read this far, the researcher should be able to use the Concordance without difficulty. It would be worthwhile, however, for him to make a few trials to familiarize himself with the methodology employed. As he proceeds with his search, he might find it advantageous to acquire some understanding of the different parts of speech of Arabic, and for this purpose the section on the language of the Qur'an that follows should be of value.

C. THE LANGUAGE OF THE QUR'AN

While the non-Arabist user of the Concordance may find the following remarks on the language of the Qur'an of some benefit, it should be pointed out that the grammatical outline that follows is extremely oversimplified and should be supplemented, as the need arises, by reference to the relevant explanatory notes in some of the more complete grammars of the Arabic language.

1. GENERAL CONSIDERATIONS:

- Arabic, the language of the Qur'an, is a member of the so-called "Semitic" family of languages. This implies that it shares with other members of this "family" certain characteristics of structure and lexicography. Arabic stands closer than any other "Semitic" language to what has been hypothetically reconstructed by philologists as "proto-Semitic". In other words, Arabic, more than any other "Semitic" language, conserves phonological and morphological elements once common to all members of this linguistic family.

Whereas several forms of Arabic were current in the Arabian Peninsula during the period of revelation (*ca.* A.D. 610–632), the Qur'an was proclaimed in the Arabic of Koraish, the tribe to which the Prophet belonged. It is a matter of debate whether or not the Arabic of Koraish was written down in the period preceding Islam. It is notable that no written evidence survives from that period, although an oral corpus of poetry and prose was recollected and eventually written down during the first few centuries of Islam. The Qur'an, it may safely be said, is the earliest extant and complete text in the Arabic language.

2. THE ALPHABET:

- Arabic, which is written from right to left, has twenty-eight consonants and three vowels. The vowels have long and short values. In addition, there are two diphthongs (see Table of Transliterations, above).

3. THE ROOT:

- Arabic derives its vocabulary from "roots". These are triliteral or, rarely, quadriliteral clusters of consonants from which the words grow. The derivatives are, in most cases, constructed in accordance with established vocalic molds or patterns to which certain prefixes, infixes or suffixes are added. At the risk of oversimplification, the following illustration may demonstrate the point. In the hypothetical root *C C C* each radical *C* may represent any of the consonants in the language. The addition of the short vowel *a* after each consonant generates the ground form (or stem) *CaCaCa*. Certain roots take the short vowel *u* or *i* instead of the middle *a*. The resulting ground form (or stem) *CaCaCa*, *CaCuCa* or *CaCiCa* is a verb, perfect active, third person, masculine, singular. The meaning of this verb (rendered in English by the infinitive) is determined by the consonants. Other verbal forms (discussed below), as well as nouns, may be developed from the same root. Thus, the verbs *salima*, *sallama*, *aslama* and the nouns *islām*, *salām*, *silm*, *taslīm*, etc., are all developed from the same root **S L M*. While the roots of the greater proportion of Arabic vocabulary are triliteral, there are many words that are derived from quadriliteral roots. In rare cases, especially with loan words or foreign proper nouns, a root may be reconstructed, for lexicographical purposes, from all the consonants of the word. Arabic lexicons are arranged in the alphabetical order of the roots and not that of the vocabulary of the language, as is the case in English dictionaries.

Philologists have not always been in agreement on the roots of certain words. Difficulties have arisen in regard to loan words that were arabicized prior to the Qur'anic period as well as to defective roots (i.e., roots containing a *w* or *y* in the middle or final position).

4. PARTS OF SPEECH:

- Arab grammarians have traditionally divided the vocabulary of the language into three parts of speech: verbs, nouns and particles.

The Verb

5. TRILITERAL VERBS:

- In addition to the ground form (Form I or stem) discussed above, there are fourteen additional secondary forms, derived from triliteral roots, of which nine are in common use. These are constructed by adding to the stem specific vowels, prefixes or infixes or both, according to established patterns. Using the root **Q T L*, the ten most frequently used forms are:

Form I	*qatala*	The ground form (the stem)
Form II	*qattala*	Formed by doubling the middle consonant; generally intensive or causative in meaning
Form III	*qātala*	Formed by lengthening the first vowel; generally signifies reciprocity, effort to perform the action of the verb or an attempt to realize the action in another person
Form IV	*aqtala*	Formed by adding the prefix *a-* (consonant) and the loss of the first vowel; generally causative in meaning although, at times, it may also be declarative
Form V	*taqattala*	Formed by adding the prefix *ta-* to Form II; generally reflexive and, though more difficult to discern, intensive in meaning
Form VI	*taqātala*	Formed by adding the prefix *ta-* to Form III; generally reflexive and responsive in meaning. In the latter case it signifies someone doing an action already done in Form III
Form VII	*inqatala*	Formed by adding the prefix *in-* to Form I; generally reflexive in meaning
Form VIII	*iqtatala*	Formed by adding the prefix *i-* (consonant) and the infix *t* (the first of the two) to Form I; generally reflexive and, occasionally, passive in meaning

Form IX	*iqtalla*	Formed by adding the prefix *i-* to Form I, dropping the first vowel and doubling the final consonant. This form is rare and is used mainly to express colours or defects
Form X	*istaqtala*	Formed by adding the prefix *ista-* to Form I, and dropping the first vowel; generally converts a verb into a reflexive action, indicating, in particular, that the quality expressed in Form I is applicable to the speaker

6. QUADRILITERAL VERBS:

- There are, in addition, four forms that stem from quadriliteral roots. They occur only rarely in the language. They are:

Form I	*zaḥzaḥa*	(**Z Ḥ Z Ḥ*)	generally intensive or causative
Form II	*tajalbaba*	(**J L B B*)	generally reflexive and, though more difficult to detect, intensive in meaning
Form III	*iḥranjama*	(**Ḥ R J M*)	generally reflexive in meaning
Form IV	*iṭmaʾanna*	(**Ṭ M ʾ N*)	generally conveys a state or a quality

7. STATES (OR "TENSES") OF THE VERB:

- The verb appears in three states, two of which, the Perfect and the Imperfect, are "tenses", while the third, the Imperative, is a "mood". The Perfect usually signifies an action that is done and completed; the Imperfect signifies an action in the process of being done or completed, and the Imperative is simply an order or a command. This nomenclature does not necessarily refer to the time of the action (past, present or future), which is determined by the context rather than by the state of the verb. It should be noted that there are other "moods" in Arabic in addition to the Imperative (Indicative, Subjunctive, Jussive, Conditional and Energetic), but the user of the Concordance does not need to concern himself with these.

8. VOCALIZATION OF THE STATES (OR "TENSES") OF THE VERB:

- While the Perfect is constructed according to the patterns discussed above (sec. C 5), the Imperfect is formed by the addition of specific prefixes and

suffixes that indicate and are determined by the Form of the verb as well as by the gender and number of the doer of the action. The final vowel is determined by the "mood" of the verb, of which there are five in Arabic (but the user of the Concordance need not concern himself with these). Changes in the middle vowel of the stem are governed, in Forms II to X, by pre-established patterns (see sec. C 10). These changes, however, are unpredictable in Form I and the Arabist is compelled to consult the lexicon for them.
The Imperative is formed by replacing the prefix of the Imperfect with *i-* (or *u-*, if the middle vowel is *u*) and by dropping the final vowel altogether. The following table will illustrate this vowel variation in the ground Form (Form I):

PERFECT	IMPERFECT	IMPERATIVE	COMMENTS
fataḥa	*yaftaḥu*	*iftaḥ*	the middle *a* in the Perfect remains constant; *ya-* of the Imperfect is replaced by *i-* in the Imperative (= to open, etc.)
jalasa	*yajlisu*	*ijlis*	the middle vowel *a* in the Perfect changes unpredictably to *i* in the Imperfect (= to sit)
kataba	*yaktubu*	*uktub*	the middle vowel *a* in the Perfect changes unpredictably to *u* in the Imperfect; the initial *i* of the Imperative also changes to *u* (= to write, etc.)
shariba	*yashrabu*	*ishrab*	the middle vowel *i* in the Perfect changes unpredictably to *a* in the Imperfect (= to drink)
ṣaghura	*yaṣghuru*	*uṣghur*	the middle vowel *u* in the Perfect remains constant while the initial *i* of the Imperative changes to *u* (= to be small)

9. "VOICES" OF THE VERB:

- Arabic verbs have two "voices": active and passive. These appear only in the Perfect and Imperfect and are constructed according to established molds or patterns (see sec. C 10).

10. PARADIGM OF THE STRONG VERB:

- The following table lists the "states" and "voices" of the ten triliteral and four quadriliteral forms:

Triliteral Verbs
(Root **Q T L*)

FORM	PERFECT ACTIVE	IMPERFECT ACTIVE	IMPERATIVE	PERFECT PASSIVE	IMPERFECT PASSIVE
I	*qatala*	*yaqtulu*	*uqtul*	*qutila*	*yuqtalu*
II	*qattala*	*yuqattilu*	*qattil*	*quttila*	*yuqattalu*
III	*qātala*	*yuqātilu*	*qātil*	*qūtila*	*yuqātalu*
IV	*aqtala*	*yuqtilu*	*aqtil*	*uqtila*	*yuqtalu*
V	*taqattala*	*yataqattalu*	*taqattal*	*tuquttila*	*yutaqattalu*
VI	*taqātala*	*yataqātalu*	*taqātal*	*tuqūtila*	*yutaqātalu*
VII	*inqatala*	*yanqatilu*	*inqatil*	*inqutila*	*yunqatalu*
VIII	*iqtatala*	*yaqtatilu*	*iqtatil*	*iqtutila*	*yuqtatalu*
IX	*iqtalla*	*yaqtallu*	*iqtalil*		
X	*istaqtala*	*yastaqtilu*	*istaqtil*	*istuqtila*	*yustaqtalu*

Quadriliteral Verbs
(Root **Q M Ṭ R*)

FORM	PERFECT ACTIVE	IMPERFECT ACTIVE	IMPERATIVE	PERFECT PASSIVE	IMPERFECT PASSIVE
I	*qamṭara*	*yuqamṭiru*	*qamṭir*	*qumṭira*	*yuqamṭaru*
II	*taqamṭara*	*yataqamṭaru*	*taqamṭar*	*tuqumṭira*	*yutaqamṭaru*
III	*iqmanṭara*	*yaqmanṭiru*	*iqmanṭir*	*uqmunṭira*	*yuqmanṭaru*
IV	*iqmaṭarra*	*yaqmaṭirru*	*iqmaṭrir*	*uqmuṭirra*	*yuqmaṭarru*

11. PERSON, GENDER AND NUMBER (OF THE VERB):

- Arabic recognizes three persons: a first person (the speaker), a second person (the one who is addressed) and a third person (the one spoken about). The order in which these are listed, however, is the reverse: third, second and first. There are only two genders in Arabic: masculine and feminine. The neuter gender of other languages (signified by the pronoun "it") does not exist. Finally, there are three numbers in Arabic: singular, dual and plural. It should be noted that in the first person form of the verb there is no distinction between masculine and feminine genders, and the dual number does not exist.

THE NOUN

12. GENERAL CONSIDERATIONS:

- In addition to the primitive nouns (the Substantives) that are names of things or persons, Arabic has a class of derivative nouns (deverbal nouns). The latter are derived from verbs and may be adjectival or substantive in use. Notable among these are the verbal nouns and the participles (active and passive). Pronouns and numbers form a third class of nouns. While the construction of the verb is controlled by the different Forms, patterns or molds, there are, generally, no strict patterns for the formation of the nouns. This unpredictability does not, however, apply to the derivative (deverbal) nouns, nor to changes in number or gender.

13. THE DEFINITE ARTICLE:

- The definite article *al-* is always prefixed to the noun; thus *walad* (a boy) becomes *al-walad* (the boy). The "*l*" of the article is assimilated orally (but not in writing) to the consonant that follows it if the consonant is a dental, sibilant or liquid. Thus *al-* becomes *ad-*, *adh-*, *aḍ-*, *an- ar-*, *as-*, *ash-*, *aṣ-*, *at-*, *ath-*, *aṭ-*, *az-* or *aẓ-*. While the "*l*" has been preserved in the definite article in all cases, the user should endeavour to observe the rules of assimilation in pronouncing the Qur'anic vocabulary. He should, for example, pronounce the Divine epithet as *ar-raḥmān* rather than as *al-raḥmān*.

14. INDEFINITE NOUNS:

- While there is no indefinite article (such as the English "a" or "an"), the indefinite noun is terminated with a short vowel followed by the phoneme "n" (*-un*, *-an* and *-in*). This process, known as *tanwīn* or, sometimes, the "nunation", has been omitted except in the very few cases where terms or expressions are otherwise more difficult to comprehend.

15. GENDER:

- (See also sec. C 11). Nouns have only two genders in Arabic: masculine and feminine. A noun is masculine unless a) it is clearly a designation of a female, or b) it is identified (in the singular) by the ending *-at* or *-ah* (the pausal form of *-at*). There are a few exceptions to this rule. The words *arḍ* (= earth, land), *samā'* (= sky, heaven) or *yad* (= hand), for example, are feminine although they neither designate a female nor end with the feminine ending. It should be mentioned that there are some nouns that have a common gender and may be treated either as a masculine or as a feminine.

16. NUMBER:

- (See also sec. C 11). Nouns have three numbers: singular, dual and plural. The dual is formed by the addition of the suffix *-an* (in the nominative case) or *-ayn* (in the other cases). Thus, *walad* (= a boy) becomes *waladān* or *waladayn*, and *shafah* (= a lip) becomes *shafatān* or *shafatayn* (note that the pausal *-ah* reverts to *-at*).

The plural is more complex. The regular masculine plural has the ending *-ūn* (in the nominative case) or *-īn* (in other cases), while the regular feminine plural has the ending *-āt* (for all cases). The other, very common, type of plural is the so-called "broken" or irregular plural, which must be determined from the lexicon. Regular plurals have been listed only rarely in the Concordance; irregular plurals have been listed if they occur in the Qur'an.

17. THE ADJECTIVE:

- The adjective follows the noun it qualifies and agrees with it in number and gender as well as in being either definite or indefinite. Some nouns may function only as adjectives, expressing an inherent and permanent quality, such as *kabīr* (= big).

Substantive and deverbal nouns may sometimes function adjectivally. For example, *sayyid* (= a lord, a master) is a noun which in *rajul sayyid* is used adjectivally, qualifying the noun *rajul* (= a man) to give the meaning "a lordly man".

The Comparative and Superlative are expressed in Arabic by adapting the adjective to the mold or pattern *aqtal* (comparative) and *al-aqtal* (superlative). Thus the adjective *jamīl* (= beautiful) becomes *ajmal* (= more beautiful) or, with the addition of the definite article, *al-ajmal* (= the most beautiful). Although the same pattern is often used for both genders, the pattern *qutlá* is used for certain feminine adjectives.

18. THE ADVERB:

- The noun may be used as an adverb to determine the time, space, state, quality or quantity of the action of the verb. The same noun may be used both adjectivally or adverbially.

19. THE VERBAL NOUN:

- This noun, which is derived from the verb, is an abstract that conveys the idea of the action of the verb. Although it is basically a substantive noun, it may, nevertheless, be used adjectivally or adverbially. While there are at least forty patterns for constructing it from the ground form (Form I), the patterns for its derivation from the remaining verbal forms are more or less regular.

In some cases, more than one verbal noun of different patterns may be derived from the same verb. These may have similar or different meanings. Omitting the ground form, the main patterns for the verbal noun are listed below:

a) Patterns of the Verbal Nouns of Triliteral Verbs

FORM	PATTERN OF VERB	VERBAL NOUN
II	*qattala*	*taqtīl* *taqtilah*
III	*qātala*	*qitāl* *muqātalah*
IV	*aqtala*	*iqtāl*
V	*taqattala*	*taqattul*
VI	*taqātala*	*taqātul*
VII	*inqatala*	*inqitāl*
VIII	*iqtatala*	*iqtitāl*
IX	*iqtalla*	*iqtilāl*
X	*istaqtala*	*istiqtāl*

b) Patterns of the Verbal Nouns of Quadriliteral Verbs

FORM	PATTERN OF VERB	VERBAL NOUN
I	*qamṭara*	*qamṭarah* *qimṭār*
II	*taqamṭara*	*taqamṭur*
III	*iqmanṭara*	*iqminṭār*
IV	*iqmaṭarra*	*iqmiṭrār*

The verbal noun plays an important role in the Arabic language, but at the same time, it poses problems for the translator. It may be taken by a verb as a complement (in the accusative) to emphasize the action of the verb. For example, in the phrase *māta mawtan*, the first word is a verb (Perfect tense) while the second is the verbal noun taken by the verb as a complement. The phrase translates literally as "he died a dying" but more accurately as "he certainly died". In the Concordance this phrase would appear as, "he <certainly> died", the special brackets indicating that the term "certainly" stands for the verbal noun.

The verbal noun may be qualified by an adjective. In this case it may be translated as an ordinary noun or, depending on the context, both verbal noun and adjective may be translated as an adverb. In some other cases, the adjective may be translated as an adjective or adverb and, for reasons of style, the verbal noun not translated. In such cases, the special brackets <...> have been used to indicate the space occupied by the verbal noun in the Arabic text of the Qur'an.

Since the verbal noun conveys the idea of the action of the verb, it is often translated as a regular verb. Finally, it is frequently translated as either an infinitive ("to read", "to live", etc.), or a gerund ("reading", "living", etc.).

20. THE PARTICIPLES:

- The participles are derived from the verb to signify the doer (active participle) or recipient (passive participle) of the action. In addition, they signify an action which may be temporary, continuous or in a habitual state of being. And although adjectival in nature, they are also used as substantive nouns. The construction of the participles is very regular and follows a set of clear patterns in all forms of the verb. These patterns are:

Patterns of the Participles of Triliteral Verbs

FORM	PATTERN OF VERB	ACTIVE PCPLE.	PASSIVE PCPLE.
I	*qatala*	*qātil*	*maqtūl*
II	*qattala*	*muqattil*	*muqattal*
III	*qātala*	*muqātil*	*muqātal*
IV	*aqtala*	*muqtil*	*muqtal*
V	*taqattala*	*mutaqattil*	*mutaqattal*
VI	*taqātala*	*mutaqātil*	*mutaqātal*
VII	*inqatala*	*munqatil*	*munqatal*
VIII	*iqtatala*	*muqtatil*	*muqtatal*
IX	*iqtalla*	*muqtall*	
X	*istaqtala*	*mustaqtil*	*mustaqal*

Patterns of the Participles of Quadriliteral Verbs

FORM	PATTERN OF VERB	ACTIVE PCPLE.	PASSIVE PCPLE.
I	*qamṭara*	*muqamṭir*	*muqamṭar*
II	*taqamṭara*	*mutaqamṭir*	*mutaqamṭar*
III	*iqmanṭara*	*muqmanṭir*	*muqmanṭar*
IV	*iqmaṭarra*	*muqmaṭirr*	*muqmaṭarr*

Although they are more regular than the verbal nouns in their derivation, the participles pose similar difficulties for the translator, though to a lesser degree. The most common meaning of the active participle is that of the doer of the action. The term *qātil* (active participle of Form I) may be translated as "killer" or "he who kills". Not infrequently, however, it may appear as the infinitive "to kill". If prefixed with the particle *la-*, it may, at times, be translated as a verb with a future meaning.

The active participle is very frequently translated as an adjective or as a substantive noun. Thus *kātib* (active participle of Form I, *kataba*, "to write") may be translated, depending on the context, as either "writing" (adj) or "scribe" (n).

APPENDIX

APPENDIX

A NUMERICAL AND CHRONOLOGICAL LIST OF THE CHAPTERS OF THE QUR'AN

Below is a list of the Chapters of the Qur'an arranged as follows:- The conventional Chapter number is followed by the Arabic title(s), English translation(s), ordinal (chronological) position of the Chapter and its place of revelation according to Th. Noeldeke (*Geschichte des Qorans*) and the ordinal (chronological) position of the Chapter and its place of revelation according to the Cairo (A.H. 1337) edition. M stands for Mecca (hence, the Chapter is of the "Meccan" period) and Y stands for Medīna (hence, the Chapter is of the "Medīnan" period). Noeldeke divided the "Meccan" period into three: early (represented by M1), middle (represented by M2) and late (represented by M3). For the determination of the locus of revelation, the Cairo edition relies on the authority of the traditional Muslim (Arabic) works on the Qur'an, noting that these "are at times in disagreement with one another". While each Chapter is ascribed in Muslim tradition to either of the two loci of revelation, there are verses within many Chapters that were revealed at the alternative locus or, sometimes, at other loci (ʿArafāt, Ḥudaybīyah, Juḥfah or Miná). Thus, the Cairene order is followed by a notation indicating these variations, as well as the occasional disagreement with the Istanboul (Ottoman) edition on the locus of revelation.

CHAPTER NUMBER	ARABIC TITLE	ENGLISH TITLE	POSITION IN CHRONOLOGICAL ORDER NOELD.	CAIRO	REMARKS
1	al-Fātiḥah	The Opening	48 M1	5 M	
2	al-Baqarah	The Heifer [Ali] The Cow [Ar, Pk]	91 Y	87 Y	vs. 281 at Miná
3	Āl ʿImrān	The Family of Imrān [Ali, Pk] The House of Imrān [Ar]	97 Y	89 Y	
4	al-Nisāʾ	Women	100 Y	92 Y	
5	al-Māʾ idah	The Table Spread [Ali, Pk] The Table [Ar]	114 Y	112 Y	vs. 3 at ʿArafāt
6	al-Anʿām	Cattle	89 M3	55 M	vss. 20, 23, 91, 93, 114, 141, 151–153 (Y)

CHAPTER NUMBER	ARABIC TITLE	ENGLISH TITLE	POSITION IN CHRONOLOGICAL ORDER NOELD.	CAIRO	REMARKS
7	al-Aʿrāf	The Heights [Ali, Pk] The Battlements [Ar]	87 M3	39 M	vss. 163 170 (Y)
8	al-Anfāl	The Spoils of War [Ali, Pk] The Spoils [Ar]	95 Y	88 Y	vss. 30–36 (Y)
9	al-Tawbah al-Baraʾ ah	Repentance [all] Immunity [Ali]	113 Y	113 Y	vss. 128–129 (M)
10	Yūnus	Jonah	80 M3	51 M	vss. 40, 94–96 (M)
11	Hūd	Hud [Ali, Pk] Hood [Ar]	75 M3	52 M	vss. 12, 17, 114 (Y)
12	Yūsuf	Joseph	77 M3	53 M	vss. 1–3, 7 (M)
13	al-Ra ʿd	Thunder	90 M3	96 Y	
14	Ibrāhīm	Abraham	76 M3	72 M	vss. 28–29 (M)
15	al-Ḥijr	The Rocky Tract [Ali] El-Hijr [Ar, Pk]	57 M2	54 M	vs. 87 (M)
16	al-Naḥl	The Bee	73 M3	70 M	vss. 126–128 (M)
17	Banū Isrāʾ īl al-Isrāʾ	The Children of Israel [Ali, Pk] The Night Journey [Ar]	67 M2	50 M	vss. 26, 32–33, 57, 73–80 (Y)
18	al-Kahf	The Cave	69 M2	69 M	vss. 28, 83–101 (M)
19	Maryam	Mary	58 M2	44 M	vss. 58, 71 (Y)
20	Ṭāhā	Ta Ha	55 M2	45 M	vss. 130–131 (M)
21	al-Anbiyāʾ	The Prophets	65 M2	73 M	
22	al-Ḥajj	The Pilgrimage	107 Y	103 Y	vss. 52–55 between Mecca and Medina
23	al-Muʾ minūn	The Believers	64 M2	74 M	
24	al-Nūr	Light	105 Y	102 Y	
25	al-Furqān al-Khalāṣ	The Criterion [Ali, Pk] Salvation [Ar]	66 M2	42 M	
26	al-Shu ʿarāʾ	The Poets	56 M2	47 M	vss. 197, 224–227 (Y)
27	al-Naml	The Ant(s)	68 M2	48 M	
28	al-Qaṣaṣ	The Narration [Ali] The Story [Ar, Pk]	79 M3	49 M	vss. 52–55 (Y): vs. 85 at Juḥfah during the Migration
29	al- ʿAnkabūt	The Spider	81 M3	85 M	vss. 1–11 (Y)
30	al-Rūm	The Roman Empire [Ali] The Greeks [Ar] The Romans [Pk]	74 M3	84 M	vs. 17 (Y)
31	Luqmān	The Wise [Ali] Lokman (Luqman) [Ar. Pk]	82 M3	57 M	vss. 27–29 (Y)
32	al-Sajdah	The Adoration [Ali] Prostration [Ar, Pk]	70 M3	75 M	vss. 16–20 (Y)
33	al-Aḥzāb	The Confederates [Ali, Ar] The Clans [Pk]	103 Y	90 Y	
34	Sabaʾ	The City of Saba [Ali] Sheba [Ar] Saba [Pk]	85 M3	58 M	vs. 6 (Y)
35	al-Malāʾ ikah al-Fāṭir	The Angels [all] The Originator of Creation [Ali] The Creator [Pk]	86 M3	43 M	
36	Yā Sin	Ya Sin	60 M2	41 M	vs. 45 (Y)
37	al-Ṣāffāt	Those Ranged in Ranks [Ali] The Rangers [Ar] Those Who Sit in Ranks [Pk]	50 M2	56 M	
38	Ṣād	Sad	59 M2	38 M	
39	al-Zumar	The Crowds [Ali] The Companies [Ar] The Troops [Pk]	80 M3	59 M	vss. 52–54 (Y)
40	al-Muʾ min	The Believer	78 M3	60 M	vss. 56–57 (Y)
41	Fuṣṣilat as-Sajdah	Fusilat [Ali, Pk] Distinguished [Ar] The Prostration [Ari]	71 M3	616M	
42	al-Shūrá	Consultation [Ali] Counsel [Ar, Pk]	83 M3	62 M	23–25, 27 (Y)
43	al-Zukhruf	Ornaments of Gold [Ali, Pk] Ornaments [Ar]	61 M2	63 M	vs. 54 (Y)
44	al-Dukhān	Mist [Ali] Smoke [Ar, Pk]	53 M2	64 M	

CHAPTER NUMBER	ARABIC TITLE	ENGLISH TITLE	POSITION IN CHRONOLOGICAL ORDER NOELD.	CAIRO	REMARKS
45	al-Jāthiyah	Bowing the Knee [Ali] Hobbling [Ar] Crouching [Pk]	72 M3	65 M	vs. 14 (Y)
46	al-Aḥqāf	The Winding Sand-tracts [Ali] The Sand-Dunes [Ar] The Wind-Curved Sandhills [Pk]	88 M3	66 M	vss. 10, 15, 35 (Y)
47	Muḥammad	Muhammad	96 Y	95 Y	vs. 13 on the road during the Migration
48	al-Fatḥ	Victory	108 Y	111 Y	Entire Sūrah revealed on the road after departure from Ḥudaybīyah
49	al-Ḥujurāt	The Inner Apartments [Ali] Apartments [Ar] The Private Apartments [Pk]	112 Y	106 Y	
50	Qāf	Qaf	54 M2	34 M	vs. 38 (Y)
51	al-Dhāriyāt	The Winds that Scatter [Ali] The Scatterers [Ar] The Winnowing Winds [Pk]	39 M1	67 M	
52	al-Ṭūr	The Mount	40 M1	76 M	
53	al-Najm	The Star	28 M1	23 M	vs. 32 (Y)
54	al-Qamar	The Moon	49 M2	37 M	vss. 44–46 (Y)
55	al-Raḥmān	(God) Most Gracious [Ali] The All-Merciful [Ar] The Beneficent [Pk]	43 M1	97 Y	(M, according to Istanboul Edition)
56	al-Wāqi ʿah	The Inevitable Event [Ali] The Terror [Ar] The Event [Pk]	41 M1	46 M	vss. 81–82 (Y)
57	al-Ḥadid	Iron	99 Y	94 Y	
58	al-Mujādilah	The Woman Who Pleads [Ali] She that Disputeth [Ar] The Disputer [Pk]	106 Y	105 Y	
59	al-Ḥashr	The Gathering, The Banishment [Ali] The Mustering [Ar] The Exile [Pk]	102 Y	101 Y	
60	al-Mumtaḥanah	The Woman Examined [Ali] The Woman Tested [Ar] She that is to be Examined [Pk]	110 Y	91 Y	
61	al-Ṣaff	Battle Array [Ali] The Ranks [Ar, Pk]	98 Y	109 Y	
62	al-Jumu ʿah	The Assembly (Friday) Prayer [Ali] Congregation [A, Pk]	94 Y	110 Y	
63	al-Munāfiqūn	The Hypocrites	104 Y	104 Y	
64	al-Taghābun	Mutual Loss and Gain [Ali] Mutual Fraud [Ar] Mutual Disillusion [Pk]	93 Y	108 Y	
65	al-Ṭalāq	Divorce	101 Y	99 Y	
66	al-Taḥrīm	Holding Something be forbidden [Ali] The Forbidding [Ar] Banning [Pk]	109 Y	107 Y	
67	al-Mulk	Dominion [Ali] The Kingdom [Ar] Sovereignty [Pk]	63 M2	77 M	
68	al-Qalam	The Pen	18 M1	2 M	vss. 17–33, 48–50 (Y)
69	al-Ḥāqqah	Sure Reality [Ali] The Indubitable [Ar] The Reality [Pk]	38 M1	78 M	
70	al-Ma ʿārij	The Ways of Ascent [Ali] The Stairways [Ar] The Ascending Stairways [Pk]	42 M1	79 M	
71	Nūḥ	Noah	51 M2	71 M	
72	al-Jinn	The Spirits [Ali] The Jinn [Ar, Pk]	62 M2	40 M	

CHAPTER NUMBER	ARABIC TITLE	ENGLISH TITLE	POSITION IN CHRONOLOGICAL ORDER NOELD.	CAIRO	REMARKS
73	al-Muzzammil	Folded in Garments [Ali] The Enwrapped [Ar] The Enshrouded One [Pk]	23 M1	3 M	vss. 10–11, 20 (Y)
74	al-Muddaththir	One Wrapped [Ali] Shrouded [Ar] The Cloaked One [Pk]	2 M1	4 M	
75	al-Qiyāmah	The Resurrection [Ali, Ar] The Rising of the Dead [Pk]	36 M1	31 M	
76	al-Insān al-Dahr	Man [all] Time [Ali, Pk]	52 M2	98 Y	
77	al-Mursalāt	Those Sent Forth [Ali] The Loosed Ones [Ar] The Emissaries [Pk]	32 M1	33 M	vs. 48 (Y)
78	al-Naba'	The Great News [Ali] The Tiding(s) [Ar, Pk]	33 M1	80 M	
79	al-Nāzi ʿāt	Those Who Tear Out [Ali] The Pluckers [Ar] Those Who Drag Forth [Pk]	31 M1	81 M	
80	ʿAbasa	He Frowned	17 M1	24 M	
81	al-Takwīr	The Folding Up [Ali] The Darkening [Ar] The Overthrowing [Pk]	27 M1	7 M	
82	al-Infiṭār	The Cleaving Asunder [Ali] Splitting [Ar] The Cleaving [Pk]	26 M1	82 M	
83	al-Muṭaffifīn	Dealing in Fraud [Ali] The Stinters [Ar] Defrauding [Pk]	37 M1	86 M	Last Meccan Sūrah
84	al-Inshiqāq	Rending Asunder [Ali] The Rending [Ar] The Sundering [Pk]	29 M1	83 M	
85	al-Burūj	The Zodiacal Signs [Ali] The Constellations [Ar] The Mansions of the Stars [Pk]	22 M1	27 M	
86	al-Ṭāriq	The Night Visitant [Ali] The Night Star [Ar] The Morning Star [Pk]	15 M1	36 M	
87	al-Aʿlá	The Most High	19 M1	8 M	
88	al-Ghāshiyah	The Overwhelming Event [Ali] The Enveloper [Ar] The Overwhelming [Pk]	34 M1	68 M	
89	al-Fajr	The Break of Day [Ali] The Dawn [Ar, Pk]	35 M1	10 M	
90	al-Balad	The City [Ali, Pk] The Land [Ar]	11 M1	35 M	
91	al-Shams	The Sun	16 M1	26 M	
92	al-Layl	The Night	13 M1	9 M	
93	al-Ḍuḥá	The Glorious Morning Light [Ali] The Forenoon [Ar] The Morning Hours [Pk]	13 M1	11 M	
94	al-Inshirāḥ	The Expansion [Ali] The Expanding [Ar] Solace [Pk]	12 M1	12 M	
95	al-Tīn	The Fig	20 M1	28 M	
96	al- ʿAlaq	The Clot of Congealed Blood [Ali] The Blood Clot [Ar] The Clot [Pk]	.1 M	1 M	Also named Iqra', "Read, Proclaim"

CHAPTER NUMBER	ARABIC TITLE	ENGLISH TITLE	POSITION IN CHRONOLOGICAL ORDER NOELD.	CAIRO	REMARKS
97	al-Qadr	The Night of Power [Ali] Power [Ar, Pk]	14 M1	25 M	
98	al-Bayyinah	The Clear Evidence [Ali] The Clear Sign [Ar] The Clear Proof [Pk]	98 Y	100 Y	
99	al-Zilzāl	The Convulsion [Ali] The Earthquake [Ar, Pk]	25 M1	93 Y	
100	al- ʿĀdiyāt	Those That Run [Ali] The Chargers [Ar] The Coursers [Pk]	30 M1	14 M	
101	al-Qāri ʿah	The Day of Noise and Clamour [Ali] The Clatterer [Ar] The Calamity [Pk]	24 M1	30 M	
102	al-Takāthur	Piling Up [Ali] Rivalry [Ar] Rivalry in Worldly Increase [Pk]	8 M1	16 M	
103	al- ʿAṣr	Time Through the Ages [Ali] Afternoon [Ar] The Declining Day [Pk]	21 M1	13 M	
104	al-Humazah	The Scandal-monger [Ali] The Backbiter [Ar] The Traducer [Pk]	6 M1	32 M	
105	al-Fīl	The Elephant	9 M1	19 M	
106	Quraysh	Quraish [Ali] Koraish [Ar] Qureysh, Winter [Pk]	4 M1	29 M	
107	al-Mā ʿūn	Neighbourly Needs [Ali] Charity [Ar] Small Kindnesses [Pk]	7 M1	17 M	vss. 4–7 (Y)
108	al-Kawthar	Abundance	5 M1	15 M	
109	al-Kāfirūn	Those Who Reject Faith [Ali] The Unbelievers [Ar] The Disbelievers [Pk]	45 M1	18 M	
110	al-Naṣr	Help [Ali, Ar] Succour [Pk]	111 Y	114 Y	Entire Sūrah revealed at Miná
111	al-Lahab Tabbat Masad	The (Father) of Flame Perish [Ar] Palm Fibre [Pk]	3 M1	6 M	
112	al-Ikhlāṣ al-Tawḥīd	The Purity of Faith [Ali] Sincere Religion [Ar] The Unity [Pk]	44 M1	22 M	
113	al-Falaq	The Dawn [Ali] Daybreak [Ar, Pk]	46 M1	20 M	(Y, according to Istanboul Edition)
114	al-Nās	Mankind [Ali, Pk] Men [Ar]	47 M1	21 M	(Y, according to Istanboul Edition)

THE DIVINE NAME

ALLĀH

ALLĀH

*A DH N

ADHINA~to allow, to give leave. (n.vb.) the leave (of God)

a) perf. act.

10:59 (60)	has God given you leave?
24:36 (36)	temples God has allowed to be raised up

b) impf. act.

42:21 (20)	religion that for which God gave not leave
53:26 (27)	God gives leave to whomsoever He wills

f) n.vb.

2:97 (91)	he it was that brought it down upon thy heart by the leave of God
2:102 (96)	they did not hurt any man thereby, save by the leave of God
2:249 (250)	how often a little company has overcome a numerous company, by God's leave
2:251 (252)	and they routed them, by the leave of God
3:49 (43)	it will be a bird, by the leave of God
3:49 (43)	and bring to life the dead, by the leave of God
3:145 (139)	it is not given to any soul to die, save by the leave of God
3:166 (160)	the day the two hosts encountered, was by God's leave
4:64 (67)	he should be obeyed, by the leave of God
8:66 (67)	they will overcome two thousand by the leave of God
10:100 (100)	it is not for any soul to believe save by the leave of God
13:38 (38)	not for any Messenger to bring a sign, but by God's leave
14:11 (14)	save by the leave of God
35:32 (29)	some are outstrippers in good works by the leave of God
40:78 (78)	it was not for any Messenger to bring a sign, save by God's leave
58:10 (11)	not hurt them anything, except by the leave of God
59:5 (5)	left standing upon their roots, that was by God's leave
64:11 (11)	no affliction befalls, except it be by the leave of God

ADHĀN~proclamation

9:3 (3)		a proclamation, from God and His Messenger

*A DH Y

ĀDHÁ~to hurt

b) impf. act.

33:57 (57)	those who hurt God and His Messenger

d) perf. pass.

29:10 (9)	when such a man is hurt in God's cause

*A Ḥ D

AḤAD~one

112:1 (1)	He is God, One

*A J L

AJAL~term

29:5 (4)	whoso looks to encounter (God), God's term is coming
71:4 (4)	God's term, when it comes, cannot be deferred

*A J R

AJR~wage

4:100 (101)	his wage shall have fallen on God
10:72 (73)	my wage falls only on God
11:29 (31)	my wage falls only upon God
34:47 (46)	my wage falls only upon God
42:40 (38)	his wage falls upon God
48:16 (16)	if you obey, God will give you a goodly wage

*A KH DH

AKHADHA~to seize

a) perf. act.

3:11 (9)	God seized them because of their sins
6:46 (46)	what think you? If God seizes your hearing and sight
8:52 (54)	God seized them because of their sins
40:21 (22)	yet God seized them in their sins
40:22 (23)	so God seized them
79:25 (25)	God seized him with the chastisement

ĀKHADHA~to take to task

a) perf. act.

2:225 (225)	God will not take you to task for a slip in your oaths
5:89 (91)	God will not take you to task for a slip in your oaths

16:61 (63)	if God should take men to task for their evildoing
35:45 (44)	if God should take men to task for what they have earned

ITTAKHADHA~to take

a) perf. act.

2:116 (110)	they say, 'God has taken to Him a son'
4:125 (124)	and God took Abraham for a friend
10:68 (69)	they say, 'God has taken to Him a son'
18:4 (3)	those who say, 'God has taken to Himself a son'
23:91 (93)	God has not taken to Himself any son

b) impf. act.

19:35 (36)	it is not for God to take a son

*A KH R

AKHKHARA~to defer

b) impf. act.

63:11 (11)	God will never defer any soul

*A L F

ALLAFA~to bring together

a) perf. act.

8:63 (64)	God brought their hearts together

*A L H

ALLĀHUMMA~O God

3:26 (25)	O God, Master of the Kingdom
5:114 (114)	O God, our Lord, send down upon us a Table out of heaven
8:32 (32)	O God, if this be indeed the truth from Thee
10:10 (10)	glory to Thee, O God
39:46 (47)	O God, Thou originator of the heavens and the earth

ALLĀH~

"There is no god but God"

2:255 (256)	God there is no god but He
3:2 (1)	God there is no god but He
3:18 (16)	God bears witness that there is no god but He
3:62 (55)	there is no god but God
4:87 (89)	God — there is no god but He
20:8 (7)	God — there is no god but He
20:14 (14)	verily I am God; there is no god but I
20:98 (98)	your (God) is only the One God, there is no god, but He alone
27:26 (26)	God: there is no god but He
28:70 (70)	and He is God; there is no god but He
37:35 (34)	there is no god but God
38:65 (65)	there is not any god but God

47:19 (21)	there is no god but God
59:22 (22)	He is God; there is no god but He
59:23 (23)	He is God; there is no god but He
64:13 (13)	God— there is no god but He

"He is God, that is God"

6:3 (3)	He is God in the heavens and the earth
6:95 (95)	so that then is God
35:13 (14)	that is God, your Lord; to Him belongs the Kingdom
39:6 (8)	that then is God, your Lord

Belonging to God

2:115 (109)	to God belong the East and the West
2:142 (136)	to God belong the East and the West
2:284 (284)	to God belongs all that is in the heavens and earth
3:28 (27)	whoso does that belongs not to God
3:109 (105)	to God belongs all that is in the heavens and the earth
3:129 (124)	to God belongs all that is in the heavens and earth
3:180 (176)	to God belongs the inheritance of the heavens and earth
4:126 (125)	to God belongs all that is in the heavens and in the earth
4:131 (130)	to God belongs all that is in the heavens and in the earth
4:131 (130)	to God belongs all that is in the heavens and in the earth
4:132 (131)	to God belongs all that is in the heavens and in the earth
4:170 (168)	to God belongs all that is in the heavens and in the earth
6:12 (12)	[all that is in the heavens and earth] is God's
6:136 (137)	this is for God
6:136 (137)	what is for God reaches their associates
8:1 (1)	the spoils belong to God and the Messenger
8:41 (42)	whatever booty you take, the fifth of it is God's
10:55 (56)	to God belongs everything that is in the heavens and earth
10:66 (67)	to God belongs everyone that is in the heavens and in the earth
14:2 (2)	God, to whom belongs all that is in the heavens and all that is in the earth
23:85 (87)	they will say, 'God's'
23:87 (89)	they will say, 'God's'
23:89 (91)	they will say, 'God's'
24:64 (64)	to God belongs whatsoever is in the heavens and the earth
31:26 (25)	to God belongs all that is in the heavens and the earth
48:4 (4)	to God belong the hosts of the heavens and the earth
48:7 (7)	to God belong the hosts of the heavens and the earth
53:25 (25)	to God belongs the First and the Last
53:31 (32)	to God belongs whatsoever is in the heavens and whatsoever is in the earth
57:10 (10)	to God belongs the inheritance of the heavens and the earth
59:7 (7)	whatsoever spoils of war ... belongs to God, and His Messenger
63:7 (7)	unto God belong the treasuries of the heavens and of the earth

"By God!"

12:73 (73)	'By God,' they said
12:85 (85)	'By God,' they said
12:91 (91)	'By God,' they said
12:95 (95)	by God, thou art certainly in thy ancient error
16:56 (58)	by God, you shall be questioned
16:63 (65)	by God, assuredly We sent Messengers to nations
21:57 (58)	by God, I shall assuredly outwit your idols
26:97 (97)	by God, we were certainly in manifest error
37:56 (54)	by God, wellnigh thou didst destroy me

"With or from God; in God's sight" (*ʿind Allāh*)

2:79 (73)	this is from God
2:94 (88)	if the Last Abode with God is yours
2:110 (104)	you shall find it with God
2:217 (214)	that is more heinous in God's sight
2:282 (282)	that is more equitable in God's sight
3:14 (12)	but God — with Him is the fairest resort
3:37 (32)	'From God,' she said
3:78 (72)	it is from God
3:78 (72)	yet it is not from God
3:163 (157)	they are in ranks with God
3:198 (197)	a hospitality God Himself offers
3:198 (197)	that which is with God is better for the pious
4:78 (80)	this is from God
4:78 (80)	everything is from God
4:94 (96)	with God are spoils abundant
6:124 (124)	humiliation in God's sight shall befall the sinners
7:131 (128)	their ill augury was with God
7:187 (187)	the knowledge of it is only with God
8:22 (22)	the worst of beasts in God's sight are those that are deaf
8:28 (28)	and that with God is a mighty wage
8:55 (57)	the worst of beasts in God's sight are the unbelievers
9:19 (19)	not equal are they in God's sight
9:20 (20)	are mightier in rank with God
9:22 (22)	surely with God is a mighty wage
9:36 (36)	the number of the months, with God, is twelve
9:99 (100)	bringing them near to God
14:46 (47)	their devising is known to God
16:95 (97)	what is with God — that is better for you
16:96 (98)	what is with God abides
24:13 (13)	in God's sight they are the liars
24:15 (14)	and with God it was a mighty thing
24:61 (61)	greet one another with a greeting from God
27:47 (48)	your augury is with God
28:60 (60)	what is with God is better and more enduring
30:39 (38)	that it may increase upon the people's wealth, increases not with God
33:53 (53)	that would be, in God's sight, a monstrous thing
33:63 (63)	the knowledge of it is only with God
33:69 (69)	he was high honoured with God
40:35 (37)	very hateful is that in the sight of God and the believers
41:52 (52)	what think you? if it is from God
42:36 (34)	what is with God is better
46:10 (9)	if it be from God, and you disbelieve in it
48:5 (5)	that is in God's sight a mighty triumph
61:3 (3)	very hateful is it to God, that you say what you do not
62:11 (11)	what is with God is better than diversion and merchandise
64:15 (15)	with God is a mighty wage
73:20 (20)	you shall find it with God as better, and mightier a wage

"God is with"

9:40 (40)	sorrow not; surely God is with us
47:35 (37)	you shall be the upper ones, and God is with you

"Apart from God" (*dūn Allāh*)

2:23 (21)	call your witnesses, apart from God, if you are truthful
3:64 (57)	do not some of us take others as lords, apart from God

5:116 (116)	take me and my mother as gods, apart from God
9:16 (16)	apart from God and His Messenger and the believers
9:31 (31)	they have taken their rabbis and their monks as lords apart from God
10:18 (19)	they serve, apart from God, what hurts them not
10:37 (38)	this Koran could not have been forged apart from God
18:43 (41)	there was no host to help him, apart from God
19:81 (84)	they have taken to them other gods apart from God
27:24 (24)	I found her and her people prostrating to the sun, apart from God
28:81 (81)	there was no host to help him, apart from God
29:25 (24)	you have only taken to yourselves idols, apart from God
36:74 (74)	yet they have taken, apart from God, gods
37:86 (84)	gods apart from God
40:74 (74)	[where are those you associated] apart from God?
46:28 (27)	they had taken to themselves as mediators, gods apart from God
53:58 (58)	apart from God none can disclose it
71:25 (26)	they found not, apart from God, any to help them

"Other than God" (*ghayr Allāh*)

2:173 (168)	what has been hallowed to other than God
4:82 (84)	if it had been from other than God
5:3 (4)	what has been hallowed to other than God
6:14 (14)	shall I take to myself as protector other than God
6:19 (19)	do you indeed testify that there are other gods with God?
6:40 (40)	will you call upon any other than God
6:46 (46)	who is a god other than God
6:114 (114)	shall I seek after any judge but God?
6:145 (146)	an ungodly thing that has been hallowed to other than God
6:164 (164)	shall I seek after a Lord other than God
7:140 (136)	shall I seek a god for you other than God
15:96 (96)	those who set up with God another god
16:52 (54)	will you fear other than God?
16:115 (116)	what has been hallowed to other than God
17:22 (23)	set not up with God another god
17:39 (41)	set not up with God another god
21:22 (22)	were there gods in earth and heaven other than God
27:60 (61)	is there a god with God?
27:61 (62)	is there a god with God?
27:62 (63)	is there a god with God?
27:63 (64)	is there a god with God?
27:64 (65)	is there a god with God?
28:71 (71)	what god other than God shall bring you illumination?
28:72 (72)	what god other than God shall bring you night to repose in?
35:3 (3)	is there any creator, apart from God
39:64 (64)	is it other than God you bid me serve
50:26 (25)	who set up with God another god
51:51 (51)	set not up with God another god
52:43 (43)	or have they a god, other than God?

*A L W

ĀLĀ'~bounties

7:69 (67)	remember God's bounties
7:74 (72)	remember God's bounties

*A M N

ĀMANA~to believe. (n.vb.) faith, belief. (pcple. act.) believer

a) perf. act.

2:8 (7)	we believe in God and the Last Day
2:62 (59)	whoso believes in God and the Last Day
2:126 (120)	such of them as believe in God and the Last Day
2:136 (130)	we believe in God
2:177 (172)	true piety is this: to believe in God, and the Last Day
2:285 (285)	each one believes in God
3:52 (45)	we believe in God
3:84 (78)	we believe in God, and that which has been sent
4:39 (43)	what would it harm them, if they believed in God?
4:152 (151)	those who believe in God and His Messengers
4:175 (174)	as for those who believe in God
5:59 (64)	do you blame us for any other cause than that we believe in God?
5:69 (73)	whosoever believes in God and the Last Day
8:41 (42)	if you believe in God and that We sent down upon Our servant
9:18 (18)	who believes in God and the Last Day
9:19 (19)	the same as one who believes in God and the Last Day
10:84 (84)	if you believe in God, in Him put your trust
24:47 (46)	we believe in God and the Messenger, and we obey
24:62 (62)	those only are believers, who believe in God and His Messenger
29:10 (9)	we believe in God
40:84 (84)	we believe in God alone
49:15 (15)	the believers are those who believe in God and His Messenger
57:19 (18)	those who believe in God and His Messengers
57:21 (21)	made ready for those who believe in God and His Messengers

b) impf. act.

2:228 (228)	if they believe in God and the Last Day
2:232 (232)	whoso of you believes in God and the Last Day
2:256 (257)	whosoever disbelieves in idols and believes in God
2:264 (266)	and believes not in God and the Last Day
3:110 (106)	and believing in God
3:114 (110)	believing in God and in the Last Day
3:199 (198)	some there are of the People of the Book who believe in God
4:38 (42)	and believe not in God and the Last Day
4:59 (62)	if you believe in God and the Last Day
5:81 (84)	yet had they believed in God and the Prophet
5:84 (87)	why should we not believe in God and the truth
7:158 (158)	the Prophet of the common folk, who believes in God and His words
9:29 (29)	fight those who believe not in God and the Last Day
9:44 (44)	those who believe in God and the Last Day ask not leave
9:45 (45)	they only ask leave of thee who believe not in God
9:61 (61)	he believes in God, and believes the believers
9:99 (100)	some of the Bedouins believe in God and the Last Day
12:37 (37)	I have forsaken the creed of a people who believe not in God
12:106 (106)	the most part of them believe not in God
24:2 (2)	if you believe in God and the Last Day
24:62 (62)	they that believe in God and His Messenger
48:9 (9)	you may believe in God and His Messenger
48:13 (13)	whoso believes not in God and His Messenger
57:8 (8)	how is it with you, that you believe not in God

58:4 (5)	believe in God and His Messenger
58:22 (22)	thou shalt not find any people who believe in God
60:1 (1)	you believe in God your Lord
60:4 (4)	hatred for ever, until you believe in God alone
61:11 (11)	you shall believe in God and His Messenger
64:9 (9)	whosoever believes in God
64:11 (11)	whosoever believes in God
65:2 (2)	by this then is admonished whosoever believes in God
65:11 (11)	whosoever believes in God, and does righteousness
69:33 (33)	behold, he never believed in God the All-mighty
85:8 (8)	because they believed in God the All-mighty

c) impv.

3:179 (174)	believe you then in God
4:136 (135)	O believers, believe in God and His Messenger
4:171 (169)	so believe in God and His Messengers
7:158 (158)	believe then in God, and in His Messenger
9:86 (87)	believe in God, and struggle with His Messenger
57:7 (7)	believe in God and His Messenger
64:8 (8)	therefore believe in God and His Messenger

f) n.vb.

2:143 (138)	God would never leave your faith to waste
49:7 (7)	God has endeared to you belief, decking it fair in your hearts

g) pcple. act.

3:164 (158)	truly God was gracious to the believers
3:171 (165)	God leaves not to waste the wage of the believers
3:179 (173)	God will not leave the believers
4:146 (145)	God will certainly give the believers a mighty wage
4:162 (160)	those who believe in God
8:19 (19)	God is with the believers
48:18 (18)	God was well pleased with the believers

*A M R

AMARA~to command, to bid. (n.vb.) affair, issue, matter, purpose; command

a) perf. act.

2:27 (25)	such as cut what God has commanded should be joined
2:222 (222)	come unto them as God has commanded you
7:28 (27)	and God has commanded us to do it
13:21 (21)	who join what God has commanded shall be joined
13:25 (25)	who snap what God has commanded to be joined

b) impf. act.

2:67 (63)	God commands you to sacrifice a cow
4:58 (61)	God commands you to deliver trusts back to their owners
7:28 (27)	God does not command indecency
16:90 (92)	surely God bids to justice and good-doing

f) n.vb.

2:210 (206)	unto God all matters are returned
2:275 (276)	his affair is committed to God

3:109 (105)	unto Him all matters are returned
3:154 (148)	the affair belongs to God entirely
4:47 (50)	God's command is done
6:159 (160)	their affair is unto God
8:42 (43)	God might determine a matter that was done
8:44 (46)	God might determine a matter that was done
8:44 (46)	unto God all matters are returned
9:48 (48)	until the truth came, and God's command appeared
9:106 (107)	others are deferred to God's commandment
10:31 (32)	'Who directs the affair?' They will surely say, 'God'
11:43 (45)	there is no defender from God's command
11:73 (76)	dost thou marvel at God's command
12:21 (21)	God prevails in His purpose
13:11 (12)	watching over him by God's command
13:31 (30)	nay, but God's is the affair altogether
16:1 (1)	God's command comes; so seek not to hasten it
22:41 (42)	unto God belongs the issue
22:76 (75)	unto God all matters are returned
30:4 (3)	to God belongs the Command
31:22 (21)	unto God is the issue of all affairs
33:36 (36)	when God and His Messenger have decreed a matter
33:37 (37)	God's commandment must be performed
33:38 (38)	God's commandment is doom decreed
35:4 (4)	unto God all matters are returned
40:44 (47)	I commit my affair to God
40:78 (78)	when God's command comes, justly the issue shall be decided
42:53 (53)	surely unto God all things come home
49:9 (9)	fight the insolent one till it reverts to God's commandment
57:5 (5)	unto Him all matters are returned
57:14 (13)	and fancies deluded you, until God's commandment came
65:1 (1)	perchance after that God will bring something new to pass
65:3 (3)	God attains His purpose
65:5 (5)	that is God's command, that He has sent down
82:19 (19)	that day the Command shall belong unto God

*A R Ḍ

ARḌ~earth

4:97 (99)	was not God's earth wide
7:73 (71)	she may eat in God's earth
7:128 (125)	surely the earth is God's and He bequeaths it to whom He will
11:64 (67)	she may eat in God's earth
39:10 (13)	God's earth is wide

*A T Y

ATÁ~to come; to come upon; to bring

a) perf. act.

16:26 (28)	then God came upon their building from the foundations
26:89 (89)	except for him who comes to God with a pure heart
59:2 (2)	then God came upon them from whence they had not reckoned

b) impf. act.

2:109 (103)	yet do you pardon and be forgiving, till God brings His command

2:148 (143)	God will bring you all together
2:210 (206)	God shall come to them in the cloud-shadows
2:258 (260)	God brings the sun from the east
5:54 (59)	God will assuredly bring a people He loves, and who love Him
9:24 (24)	then wait till God brings His command
11:33 (35)	God will bring you it if He will
12:83 (83)	haply God will bring them all to me
17:92 (94)	or thou bringest God and the angels as a surety
31:16 (15)	God shall bring it forth

ĀTÁ~to give; to bring

a) perf. act.

2:251 (252)	God gave him the kingship, and Wisdom
2:258 (260)	that God had given him the kingship
3:170 (164)	rejoicing in the bounty that God has given
3:180 (175)	those who are niggardly with the bounty God has given them
9:59 (59)	were they well-pleased with what God and His Messenger have brought them
27:36 (36)	succour me with wealth, and what God gave me
28:77 (77)	seek, amidst that which God has given thee, the Last Abode
65:7 (7)	let him expend of what God has given him

b) impf. act.

2:247 (248)	God gives the kingship to whom He will
9:59 (59)	God will bring us of His bounty
11:31 (33)	God will not give them any good

*A TH R

ĀTHARA~to prefer

a) perf. act.

12:91 (91)	God has indeed preferred thee above us

*A Y W

ĀYAH~(God's) signs

2:61 (58)	that, because they had disbelieved the signs of God
2:219 (217)	so God makes clear His signs to you
2:231 (231)	take not God's signs in mockery
2:252 (253)	these are the signs of God We recite to thee
3:4 (3)	as for those who disbelieve in God's signs
3:19 (17)	whoso disbelieves in God's signs
3:21 (20)	those who disbelieve in the signs of God
3:70 (63)	why do you disbelieve in God's signs
3:98 (93)	People of the Book, why do you disbelieve in the signs of God
3:101 (96)	how can you disbelieve, seeing you have God's signs
3:108 (104)	these are the signs of God We recite to thee
3:112 (108)	that, because they disbelieved in God's signs
3:113 (109)	a nation upstanding, that recite God's signs
3:199 (198)	men humble to (God), not selling the signs of God
4:140 (139)	when you hear God's signs being disbelieved

4:155 (154)	for their breaking the compact, and disbelieving in the signs of God
6:33 (33)	it is the signs of God that they deny
6:109 (109)	signs are only with God
6:157 (158)	he who cries lies to God's signs
7:26 (25)	that is one of God's signs
8:52 (54)	who disbelieved in God's signs
9:9 (9)	they have sold the signs of God for a small price
10:71 (72)	and my reminding you of the signs of God
10:95 (95)	nor be of those who cry lies to God's signs
16:104 (106)	those that believe not in the signs of God
16:105 (107)	they only forge falsehood, who believe not in the signs of God
18:17 (16)	that was one of God's signs
28:87 (87)	let them not bar thee from the signs of God
29:23 (22)	those who disbelieve in God's signs
29:50 (49)	the signs are only with God
30:10 (9)	for that they cried lies to the signs of God
33:34 (34)	remember that which is recited in your houses of the signs of God
39:63 (63)	those who disbelieve in the signs of God
40:4 (4)	none but the unbelievers dispute concerning the signs of God
40:35 (37)	those who dispute concerning the signs of God
40:56 (58)	those who dispute concerning the signs of God
40:63 (65)	perverted are they who deny the signs of God
40:69 (71)	hast thou not regarded those who dispute concerning the signs of God
40:81 (81)	then which of God's signs do you reject?
45:6 (5)	those are the signs of God that We recite to thee
45:6 (5)	in what manner of discourse then, after God and His signs, will they believe?
45:8 (7)	who hears the signs of God being recited to him
45:35 (34)	that is for that you took God's signs in mockery
46:26 (25)	since they denied the signs of God
62:5 (5)	the people who have cried lies to God's signs
65:11 (11)	a Messenger reciting to you the signs of God

*ᶜ B D

ᶜABADA~to serve, to worship

b) impf. act.

2:83 (77)	you shall not serve any save God
3:64 (57)	that we serve none but God
25:17 (18)	He shall muster them and that they serve, apart from God
25:55 (57)	they serve, apart from God, what neither profits them nor hurts them
26:93 (93)	[where is that you were serving] apart from God?
27:43 (43)	that she served, apart from God, barred her
5:76 (80)	do you serve, apart from God, that which cannot hurt or profit you?
7:70 (68)	hast thou come to us that we may serve God alone
10:104 (104)	I serve not those you serve apart from God
10:104 (104)	but I serve God, who will gather you
11:2 (2)	serve you none but God
11:26 (28)	serve you none but God
13:36 (36)	I have only been commanded to serve God
16:73 (75)	do they serve, apart from God, that which has no power?
18:16 (15)	that they serve, excepting God
19:49 (50)	that they were serving, apart from God
21:66 (67)	do you serve, apart from God, that which profits you nothing

21:67 (67)	fie upon you and that you serve apart from God
21:98 (98)	you, and that you were serving apart from God, are fuel for Gehenna
22:11 (11)	there is such a one as serves God upon the very edge
22:71 (70)	they serve, apart from God
25:17 (18)	He shall muster them and that they serve, apart from God
25:55 (57)	they serve, apart from God, what neither profits them nor hurts them
26:93 (93)	[where is that you were serving] apart from God?
27:43 (43)	that she served, apart from God, barred her
29:17 (16)	you only serve, apart from God, idols
29:17 (16)	those you serve, apart from God, have no power
37:23 (23)	[that they were serving] apart from God
39:11 (14)	I have been commanded to serve God
39:14 (16)	God I serve
60:4 (4)	we are quit of you and that you serve, apart from God
98:5 (4)	they were commanded only to serve God

c) impv.

4:36 (40)	serve God, and associate naught with Him
5:72 (76)	Children of Israel, serve God, my Lord
5:117 (117)	serve God, my Lord and your Lord
7:59 (57)	O my people, serve God
7:65 (63)	O my people, serve God
7:73 (71)	O my people, serve God
7:85 (83)	O my people, serve God
11:50 (52)	O my people, serve God
11:61 (64)	O my people, serve God
11:84 (85)	O my people, serve God
16:36 (38)	serve you God, and eschew idols
23:23 (23)	O my people, serve God
23:32 (33)	serve God
27:45 (46)	serve you God
29:16 (15)	serve God, and fear Him
29:36 (35)	O my people, serve God
39:2 (2)	so worship God
39:66 (66)	nay, but God do thou serve
41:14 (13)	serve none but God
46:21 (20)	serve none but God
71:3 (3)	serve God, and fear Him

ʿABD~servant

3:79 (73)	be you servants to me apart from God
3:182 (178)	and for that God is never unjust unto his servants
4:172 (170)	the Messiah will not disdain to be a servant of God
8:51 (53)	God is never unjust unto His servants
19:30 (31)	lo, I am God's servant
22:10 (10)	and for that God is never unjust unto his servants
37:40 (39)	except for God's sincere servants
37:74 (72)	except for God's sincere servants
37:128 (128)	except for God's sincere servants
37:160 (160)	except for God's sincere servants
37:169 (169)	then were we God's sincere servants
44:18 (17)	deliver to me God's servants
72:19 (19)	when the servant of God stood calling
76:6 (6)	a fountain whereat drink the servants of God

*ᶜ D D

AᶜADDA~to prepare

a) perf. act.

4:102 (103) God has prepared for the unbelievers a humbling chastisement
9:89 (90) God has prepared for them gardens
33:29 (29) God has prepared for those amongst you such as do good
33:35 (35) for them God has prepared forgiveness
58:15 (16) God has made ready for them a chastisement
65:10 (10) God prepared for them a terrible chastisement

*ᶜ D W

ᶜADŪW~enemy

2:98 (92) whosoever is an enemy to God and His angels
8:60 (62) to terrify thereby the enemy of God and your (enemy)
9:114 (115) it became clear to him that he was an enemy of God
41:19 (18) the day when God's enemies are mustered to the Fire
41:28 (28) that is the recompense of God's enemies

*ᶜ DH B

ᶜADHĀB~chastisement

2:165 (160) God is terrible in chastisement
6:40 (40) what think you? If God's chastisement comes upon you
6:47 (47) what think you? If God's chastisement comes upon you
9:52 (52) we are awaiting in your case too, for God to visit you with chastisement
12:107 (107) there shall come upon them no enveloping of the chastisement of God
14:21 (24) will you avail us against the chastisement of God anything?
22:2 (2) God's chastisement is terrible
29:10 (9) he makes the persecution of men as it were God's chastisement
29:29 (28) then bring us the chastisement of God

ᶜADHDHABA~to chastise

b) impf. act.

8:33 (33) but God would never chastise them
8:34 (34) that God should not chastise them
9:14 (14) fight them, and God will chastise them at your hands
9:74 (75) God will chastise them with a painful chastisement
33:73 (73) that God may chastise the hypocrites
58:8 (9) why does God not chastise us for what we say?
88:24 (24) God shall chastise him with the greatest chastisement

g) pcple. act.

8:33 (33) God would never chastise them as they begged forgiveness

*ᶜ F W

ᶜAFĀ~to pardon, to efface

a) perf. act.

3:155 (149)	but God has pardoned them
5:95 (96)	God has pardoned what is past
5:101 (101)	God has effaced those things
9:43 (43)	God pardon thee

b) impf. act.

4:99 (100)	haply them God will yet pardon

ᶜAFŪW~All-pardoning

4:43 (46)	God is All-pardoning, All-forgiving
4:99 (100)	haply them (God) will yet pardon, for God is All-pardoning
4:149 (148)	surely God is All-pardoning, All-powerful
22:60 (59)	(God) will help him; surely God is All-pardoning
58:2 (3)	yet surely God is All-pardoning, All-forgiving

*ᶜ H D

ᶜAHIDA~to make covenant

a) perf. act.

3:183 (179)	God has made covenant

ᶜAHD~a covenant

2:27 (25)	such as break the covenant of God
2:80 (74)	have you taken with God a covenant
2:80 (74)	God will not fail in His covenant
3:77 (71)	those that sell God's covenant
6:152 (153)	and fulfil God's covenant
9:7 (7)	how should the idolaters have a covenant with God
9:111 (112)	who fulfils his covenant truer than God?
13:20 (20)	who fulfil God's covenant, and break not the compact
13:25 (25)	those who break the covenant of God
16:91 (93)	fulfil God's covenant
16:95 (97)	do not sell the covenant of God for a small price
33:15 (15)	covenants with God shall be questioned of

ᶜĀHADA~to make covenant

a) perf. act.

9:75 (76)	some of them have made covenant with God
33:15 (15)	they had made covenant with God before that
33:23 (23)	men who were true to their covenant with God
48:10 (10)	whoso fulfils his covenant made with God

*ᶜ J L

ᶜAJJALA~to hasten

b) impf. act.

10:11 (12)	if God should hasten unto men evil

*ᶜ J Z

AᶜJAZA~to frustrate

b) impf. act.

35:44 (43)	but God — there is naught ... that can frustrate Him
72:12 (12)	we thought that we should never be able to frustrate God

g) pcple. act.

9:2 (2)	know that you cannot frustrate the will of God
9:3 (3)	know that you cannot frustrate the will of God

*ᶜ L M

ᶜALIMA~to know. (n.vb.) knowledge

a) perf. act.

2:187 (183)	God knows that you have been betraying yourselves
2:235 (235)	God knows that you will be mindful of them
8:23 (23)	if God had known of any good in them

b) impf. act.

2:77 (72)	(know) they not that God knows what they keep secret?
2:197 (193)	whatever good you do, God knows it
2:216 (213)	God knows, and you (know) not
2:220 (219)	God knows well him who works corruption
2:232 (232)	God knows, and you (know) not
2:235 (236)	(know) that God knows what is in your hearts
2:270 (273)	whatever vow you vow, surely God knows it
3:7 (5)	none knows its interpretation, save only God
3:29 (27)	God knows it
3:66 (59)	God knows, and you (know) not
3:140 (134)	that God may know who are the believers
3:142 (136)	without God know who of you have struggled
4:63 (66)	those — God knows what is in their hearts
5:94 (95)	that God may know who fears Him in the Unseen
5:97 (98)	God knows all that is in the heavens and in the earth
5:99 (99)	God knows what you reveal and what you hide
7:62 (60)	I know from God that you (know) not
8:60 (62)	besides them that you (know) not; God knows them
8:70 (71)	if God knows of any good in your hearts
9:16 (16)	God knows not as yet those of you who have struggled
9:42 (42)	God knows that they are truly liars
9:78 (79)	did they not (know) that God knows their secret?

12:86 (86)	I know from God that you (know) not
12:96 (97)	did I not tell you I know from God
13:8 (9)	God knows what every female bears
14:9 (10)	those after them whom none knows but God
16:19 (19)	God knows what you keep secret
16:23 (24)	without a doubt God knows what they keep secret
16:74 (76)	surely God knows
16:91 (93)	surely God knows the things you do
22:70 (69)	didst thou not (know) that God knows all?
24:19 (19)	God knows, and you (know) not
24:29 (29)	God knows what you reveal and what you hide
24:63 (63)	God knows those of you who slip away surreptitiously
29:3 (2)	assuredly God knows those who speak truly
29:11 (10)	God surely knows the believers
29:42 (41)	God knows whatever thing they call upon
29:45 (44)	God knows the things you work
33:18 (18)	God would surely know those of you who hinder
33:51 (51)	God knows what is in your hearts
41:22 (21)	that God would never know much of the things that you were working
47:19 (21)	God knows your going to and fro
47:26 (28)	God knows their secrets
47:30 (32)	God knows your deeds
49:16 (16)	God knows what is in the heavens
57:25 (25)	so that God might know who helps Him
58:7 (8)	hast thou not seen that God knows whatsoever is in the heavens
63:1 (1)	God knows that thou art indeed His Messenger

f) n.vb.

11:14 (17)	know that it has been sent down with God's knowledge
31:34 (34)	surely God — He has knowledge of the Hour
46:23 (22)	knowledge is only with God
67:26 (26)	the knowledge is with God

AʿLAM~having greater knowledge, knowing very well

2:140 (134)	have you then greater knowledge, or God
3:36 (31)	God knew very well what she had given birth to
3:167 (161)	God knows very well the things they hide
4:25 (29)	God knows very well your faith
4:45 (47)	God knows well your enemies
5:61 (66)	God knows very well what they were hiding
6:53 (53)	knows not God very well the thankful?
6:124 (124)	God knows very well where to place His Message
11:31 (33)	God knows best what is in their hearts
12:77 (77)	God knows very well what you are describing
16:101 (103)	God knows very well what He is sending down
18:26 (25)	God knows very well how long they tarried
22:68 (67)	God knows very well what you are doing
29:10 (9)	does not God know very well what is in the breasts
60:10 (10)	God knows very well their belief
84:23 (23)	God knows very well what they are secreting

ʿALĪM~one who knows, one who has knowledge

"God is All-knowing, All-wise"

4:11 (12)	surely God is All-knowing, All-wise

4:17 (21)	God is All-knowing, All-wise
4:24 (28)	God is All-knowing, All-wise
4:26 (31)	God is All-knowing, All-wise
4:92 (94)	God is All-knowing, All-wise
4:104 (105)	God is All-knowing, All-wise
4:111 (111)	God is ever All-knowing, All-wise
4:170 (168)	God is All-knowing, All-wise
8:71 (72)	God is All-knowing, All-wise
9:15 (15)	God is All-knowing, All-wise
9:28 (28)	God is All-knowing, All-wise
9:60 (60)	God is All-knowing, All-wise
9:97 (98)	God is All-knowing, All-wise
9:106 (107)	God is All-knowing, All-wise
9:110 (111)	God is All-knowing, All-wise
22:52 (51)	surely God is All-knowing, All-wise
24:18 (17)	God is All-knowing, All-wise
24:58 (57)	God is All-knowing, All-wise
24:59 (58)	God is All-knowing, All-wise
33:1 (1)	God is All-knowing, All-wise
48:4 (4)	God is All-knowing, All-wise
49:8 (8)	God is All-knowing, All-wise
60:10 (10)	God is All-knowing, All-wise
76:30 (30)	surely God is ever All-knowing, All-wise

"God is All-knowing, All-clement"

4:12 (16)	God is All-knowing, All-clement
22:59 (58)	surely God is All-knowing, All-clement
33:51 (51)	God is All-knowing, All-clement

"God is All-knowing, All-aware"

4:35 (39)	surely God is All-knowing, All-aware
31:34 (34)	surely God is All-knowing, All-aware
49:13 (13)	God is All-knowing, All-aware

"God is All-knowing, All-powerful"

16:70 (72)	God is All-knowing, All-powerful

Other

2:95 (89)	God knows the evildoers
2:215 (211)	whatever good you may do, God has knowledge of it
2:231 (231)	know that God has knowledge of everything
2:246 (247)	God has knowledge of the evildoers
2:273 (274)	whatever good you expend, surely God has knowledge of it
2:282 (282)	God has knowledge of everything
2:283 (283)	God has knowledge of the things you do
3:63 (56)	assuredly God knows the workers of corruption
3:92 (86)	whatever thing you expend, God knows of it
3:119 (115)	God knows the thoughts in the breasts
3:154 (148)	God knows the thoughts in the breasts
4:32 (36)	God knows everything
4:70 (72)	God suffices as One who knows
4:39 (43)	God knows them
4:127 (126)	whatever good you do, God knows of it
4:176 (175)	God has knowledge of everything
5:7 (10)	surely God knows the thoughts in the breasts

5:97 (98)	God has knowledge of everything
8:75 (76)	surely God has knowledge of everything
9:47 (47)	God knows the evildoers
9:115 (116)	surely God knows everything
10:36 (37)	surely God knows the things they do
12:19 (19)	but God knew what they were doing
16:28 (30)	but surely God has knowledge of the things you did
24:28 (28)	God knows the things you do
24:35 (35)	God has knowledge of everything
24:41 (41)	God knows the things they do
24:64 (64)	God knows everything
29:62 (62)	God has knowledge of everything
31:23 (22)	surely God knows all the thoughts within the breasts
33:40 (40)	God has knowledge of everything
33:54 (54)	surely God has knowledge of everything
35:8 (9)	God has knowledge of the things they work
48:26 (26)	God has knowledge of everything
49:16 (16)	God has knowledge of everything
58:7 (8)	surely God has knowledge of everything
62:7 (7)	God knows the evildoers
64:4 (4)	God knows the thoughts within the breasts
64:11 (11)	God has knowledge of everything

ʿALLAMA~to teach

a) perf. act.

2:282 (282)	let not any writer refuse to write it down, as God has taught him
5:4 (6)	teaching them as God has taught you

b) impf. act.

2:282 (282)	God teaches you
49:16 (16)	what, would you teach God

*ʿ L W

ʿALĀ~to rise up

b) impf. act.

44:19 (18)	rise not up against God

ʿALĪY~All-high

4:34 (38)	God is All-high, All-great
22:62 (61)	and for that God is the All-high, the All-great
31:30 (29)	and for that God is the All-high, the All-great

TAʿĀLÁ~to be exalted

a) perf. act.

7:190 (190)	but God is high exalted above that they associate
20:114 (113)	so high exalted be God, the true King
23:116 (117)	then high exalted be God
27:63 (64)	high exalted be God, above that which they associate

*ᶜ Q B

ᶜIQĀB~retribution

2:196 (192)	know that God is terrible in retribution
2:211 (207)	after it has come to him, God is terrible in retribution
3:11 (9)	God is terrible in retribution
5:2 (3)	surely God is terrible in retribution
5:98 (98)	know God is terrible in retribution
8:13 (13)	surely God is terrible in retribution
8:25 (25)	know that God is terrible in retribution
8:48 (50)	God is terrible in retribution
59:4 (4)	God is terrible in retribution
59:7 (7)	surely God is terrible in retribution

*ᶜ Ṣ M

ᶜAṢAMA~to protect, to defend. (pcple. act.) defender, protector

a) perf. act.

5:67 (71)	God will protect thee from men
33:17 (17)	who is he that shall defend you from God

g) pcple. act.

10:27 (28)	neither have they any defender from God
40:33 (35)	having none to defend you from God

IᶜTAṢAMA~to hold fast

a) perf. act.

4:146 (145)	such as repent, and make amends, and hold fast to God

b) impf. act.

3:101 (96)	whosoever holds fast to God

c) impv.

22:78 (78)	hold you fast to God

*ᶜ Ṣ W

ᶜAṢÁ~to disobey

b) impf. act.

4:14 (18)	whoso disobeys God, and His Messenger
33:36 (36)	whosoever disobeys God and His Messenger has gone astray
66:6 (6)	disobey not God in what He commands them
72:23 (24)	whoso rebels against God and His Messenger

*ᶜ W DH

ᶜĀDHA~to take refuge

b) impf. act.

2:67 (63)	I take refuge with God

MAᶜĀDH~(*maᶜādh Allāh*) God forbid, God be my refuge

12:23 (23)	God be my refuge
12:79 (79)	God forbid that we should take any other

ISTAᶜĀDHA~to seek refuge

a) perf. act.

7:200 (199)	seek refuge in God
16:98 (100)	when thou recitest the Koran, seek refuge in God
40:56 (58)	so seek thou refuge in God
41:36 (36)	seek refuge in God

*ᶜ W N

ISTAᶜĀNA~to pray for succour. (pcple. pass.) one whose succour is sought

c) impv.

7:128 (125)	pray for succour to God, and be patient

h) pcple. pass.

12:18 (18)	it is God, whose succour is ever there to seek

*ᶜ Z Z

ᶜAZĪZ~great, mighty, All-mighty

"Not great for God"

11:92 (94)	is my tribe stronger against you than God?
14:20 (23)	that is surely no great matter for God
35:17 (18)	that is surely no great matter for God

"All-mighty, Vengeful"

3:4 (3)	God is All-mighty, Vengeful
5:95 (96)	God is All-mighty, Vengeful
14:47 (48)	surely God is All-mighty, Vengeful
39:37 (38)	is not God All-mighty, All-vengeful?

"All-mighty, All-wise"

2:209 (205)	know then that God is All-mighty, All-wise
2:220 (219)	surely God is All-mighty, All-wise
2:228 (228)	God is All-mighty, All-wise
2:240 (241)	God is All-mighty, All-wise
2:260 (262)	do thou know that God is All-mighty, All-wise

3:62 (55)	assuredly God is the All-mighty, the All-wise
3:126 (122)	help comes only from God, the All-mighty, the All-wise
4:56 (59)	surely God is All-mighty, All-wise
4:158 (156)	God is All-mighty, All-wise
4:165 (163)	God is All-mighty, All-wise
5:38 (42)	God is All-mighty, All-wise
8:10 (10)	surely God is All-mighty, All-wise
8:49 (51)	surely God is All-mighty, All-wise
8:67 (68)	God is All-mighty, All-wise
9:40 (40)	God is All-mighty, All-wise
9:71 (72)	God is All-mighty, All-wise
27:9 (9)	Moses, behold, it is I, God, the All-mighty, the All-wise
31:27 (26)	God is All-mighty, All-wise
34:27 (26)	No indeed; rather He is God, the All-mighty, the All-wise
39:1 (1)	The sending down of the Book is from God, the All-mighty, the All-wise
42:3 (1)	God, the All-mighty, the All-wise
45:2 (1)	the sending down of the Book is from God, the All-mighty, the All-wise
46:2 (1)	the sending down of the Book is from God, the All-mighty, the All-wise
48:7 (7)	God is All-mighty, All-wise
48:19 (19)	God is ever All-mighty, All-wise

"All-mighty, All-forgiving"

35:28 (25)	surely God is All-mighty, All-forgiving

ʿIZZAH~glory

4:139 (138)	glory altogether belongs to God
10:65 (66)	the glory belongs altogether to God
35:10 (11)	the glory altogether belongs to God
63:8 (8)	glory belongs unto God, and unto His Messenger

*B ʾ S

BAʾS~might

4:84 (86)	God is stronger in might, more terrible in punishing
40:29 (30)	who will help us against the might of God

*B ʿ TH

BAʿATHA~to send; to raise

a) perf. act.

2:213 (209)	then God sent forth the Prophets, good tidings to bear
2:247 (248)	God has raised up Saul for you as king
5:31 (34)	then God sent forth a raven, scratching into the earth
17:94 (96)	has God sent forth a mortal as Messenger?
25:41 (43)	is this he whom God sent forth as a Messenger?

b) impf. act.

6:36 (36)	God will raise them up
16:38 (40)	God will never raise up him who dies
22:7 (7)	God shall raise up whosoever is within the tombs
40:34 (36)	God will never send forth a Messenger after him

58:6 (7)	upon the day when God shall raise them up all
58:18 (19)	upon the day when God shall raise them up all
72:7 (7)	that God would never raise up anyone

*B D L

BADDALA~to change

b) impf. act.

25:70 (70)	those, God will change their evil deeds into good deeds

*B D W

BADĀ~to appear

a) perf. act.

39:47 (48)	there would appear to them from God that they never reckoned with

*B D Y

ABDÁ~(pcple. act.) one who reveals

g) pcple. act.

33:37 (37)	thou wast concealing within thyself what God should reveal

*B L GH

BALAGHA~(n.vb.) a deliverance

f) n.vb.

72:23 (24)	excepting a Deliverance from God

*B L W

BALĀ~to try

b) impf. act.

5:94 (95)	O believers, God will surely try you
16:92 (94)	God only tries you thereby

IBTALÁ~to try

b) impf. act.

3:154 (148)	and that God might try what was in your breasts

g) pcple. act.

2:249 (250)	God will try you with a river

*B N W

IBN~a son

5:18 (21)	we are the sons of God, and His beloved ones
9:30 (30)	Ezra is the Son of God
9:30 (30)	the Messiah is the Son of God

*B Q Y

BAQĪYAH~remainder

11:86 (87)	God's remainder is better for you

*B R ʾ

BARĀʾAH~acquittal

9:1 (1)	an acquittal, from God and His Messenger

BARĪʾ~quit, innocent

9:3 (3)	God is quit, and His Messenger, of the idolaters

BARRAʾA~to acquit

a) perf. act.

33:69 (69)	but God declared him quit of what they said

*B R K

TABĀRAKA~to be blessed

a) perf. act.

7:54 (52)	blessed be God, the Lord of all Being
23:14 (14)	so blessed be God, the fairest of creators
40:64 (66)	that then is God, your Lord, so blessed be God,

*B R Z

BARAZA~to sally forth

a) perf. act.

14:21 (24)	they sally forth unto God, all together
14:48 (49)	they sally forth unto God, the One, the Omnipotent

*B SH R

BUSHRÁ~a tiding

3:126 (122)	God wrought this not, save as good tiding to you
8:10 (10)	God wrought this not, save as good tidings

BASHSHARA~to give good tidings

b) impf. act.

3:39 (34)	lo, God gives thee good tidings
3:45 (40)	Mary, God gives thee good tidings
42:23 (22)	that is the good tidings God gives to His servants

*B Ṣ R

BAṢĪR~one who sees

2:96 (90)	God sees the things they do
2:110 (104)	assuredly God sees the things you do
2:233 (233)	know that God sees the things you do
2:237 (238)	surely God sees the things you do
2:265 (267)	God sees the things you do
3:15 (13)	God sees His servants
3:20 (19)	God sees His servants
3:156 (150)	God sees the things you do
3:163 (157)	God sees the things they do
5:71 (75)	God sees the things they do
8:39 (40)	surely God sees the things they do
8:72 (73)	God sees the things you do
33:9 (9)	God sees the things you do
35:45 (45)	surely God sees His servants
40:44 (47)	surely God sees His servants
48:24 (24)	God sees the things you do
49:18 (18)	God sees the things you do
57:4 (4)	God sees the things you do
60:3 (3)	God sees the things you do
64:2 (2)	God sees the things you do

*B Ṭ L

ABṬALA~to bring to naught

b) impf. act.

10:81 (81)	God will assuredly bring it to naught

*B Y ʿ

BĀYAʿA~to swear fealty

b) impf. act.

48:10 (10)	those who swear fealty to thee swear fealty in truth to God

*B Y N

BAYYANA~to make clear

b) impf. act.

2:187 (183)	so God makes clear His signs to men
2:219 (217)	so God makes clear His signs to you

2:242 (243)	so God makes clear His signs for you
2:266 (268)	so God makes clear the signs to you
3:103 (99)	even so God makes clear to you His signs
4:176 (175)	God makes clear to you, lest you go astray
5:89 (91)	so God makes clear to you His signs
24:18 (17)	God makes clear to you the signs
24:58 (57)	so God makes clear to you the signs
24:59 (58)	so God makes clear to you His signs
24:61 (61)	so God makes clear to you the signs

*D ᶜ W

DAᶜĀ~to call, to summon; to cry to, to call upon. (pcple. act.) a summoner

a) perf. act.

7:189 (189)	they cried to God their Lord
10:22 (23)	they call upon God
29:65 (65)	when they embark in the ships, they call on God
31:32 (31)	they call upon God
41:33 (33)	who speaks fairer than he who calls unto God?

b) impf. act.

2:221 (221)	God calls unto Paradise, and pardon, by His leave
6:56 (56)	I am forbidden to serve those you call on apart from God
6:71 (70)	shall we call, apart from God, on that which neither profits nor hurts us?
6:108 (108)	abuse not those to whom they pray, apart from God
7:37 (35)	where is that you were calling on, beside God?
7:194 (193)	those on whom you call apart from God
10:25 (26)	God summons to the Abode of Peace
10:66 (67)	who call upon associates, apart from God
10:106 (106)	do not call, apart from God
11:101 (103)	that they called upon, apart from God
12:108 (108)	I call to God with sure knowledge
16:20 (20)	those they call upon, apart from God, created nothing
17:110 (110)	call upon God
19:48 (49)	that you call upon, apart from God
22:12 (12)	he calls, apart from God
22:73 (72)	those upon whom you call, apart from God
23:117 (117)	whosoever calls upon another god with God
25:68 (68)	who call not upon another god with God
26:213 (213)	call thou not upon another god with God
28:88 (88)	call not upon another god with God
35:40 (38)	have you considered your associates on whom you call, apart from God?
39:38 (39)	that you call upon apart from God
40:66 (68)	I am forbidden to serve those you call on apart from God
46:4 (3)	have you considered that you call upon apart from God
46:5 (4)	who is further astray than he who calls, apart from God
72:18 (18)	so call not, along with God, upon anyone

c) impv.

10:38 (39)	call on whom you can, apart from God
11:13 (16)	call upon whom you are able, apart from God
34:22 (21)	call on those you have asserted apart from God
40:14 (14)	so call unto God, making your religion His sincerely

d) perf. pass.

24:48 (47)	when they are called to God and His Messenger
24:51 (50)	when they are called to God and His Messenger
40:12 (12)	when God was called to alone

g) pcple. act.

33:46 (45)	calling unto God by His leave
46:31 (30)	O our people, answer God's summoner
46:32 (31)	whosoever answers not God's summoner

*D F ᶜ

DAFAᶜA~(n.vb.) driving back

f) n.vb.

2:251 (252)	had God not driven back the people, some by the means of others
22:40 (41)	had God not driven back the people, some by the means of others

DĀFAᶜA~to defend

b) impf. act.

22:38 (39)	assuredly God will defend those

*D KH L

ADKHALA~to admit

b) impf. act.

22:14 (14)	God shall surely admit those who believe
22:23 (23)	God shall surely admit those who believe
47:12 (13)	God shall surely admit those who believe

*D M R

DAMMARA~to destroy

a) perf. act.

47:10 (11)	God destroyed them

*D Y N

DĪN~religion

2:193 (189)	the religion is God's
3:19 (17)	the true religion with God is Islam
3:83 (77)	do they desire another religion than God's?
4:146 (145)	and make their religion sincerely God's
8:39 (40)	and the religion is God's entirely
24:2 (2)	and in the matter of God's religion
39:3 (3)	belongs not sincere religion to God?
110:2 (2)	thou seest men entering God's religion in throngs

*DH H B

DHAHABA~to take away

a) perf. act.

2:17 (16) God took away their light, and left them in darkness

*DH K R

DHAKARA~to remember; to mention. (n.vb.) remembrance, mention

a) perf. act.

3:135 (129) themselves, remember God, and pray forgiveness
26:227 (227) and remember God oft
33:21 (21) whosoever hopes for (God) and the Last Day, and remembers God oft

b) impf. act.

3:191 (188) who remember God, standing and sitting
4:142 (141) and not remembering God save a little

c) impv.

2:198 (194) then remember God at the Holy Waymark
2:200 (196) when you have performed your holy rites remember God
2:203 (199) and remember God during certain days
2:239 (240) but when you are secure, then remember God
3:191 (188) who remember God, standing and sitting
4:103 (104) when you have performed the prayer, remember God
8:45 (47) remember God frequently
33:41 (41) O believers, remember God oft
62:10 (10) seek (God's) bounty, and remember God frequently

d) perf. pass.

8:2 (2) those only are believers who, when God is mentioned, their hearts quake
22:35 (36) who, when God is mentioned, their hearts quake
39:45 (46) when God is mentioned alone, then shudder the hearts

f) n.vb.

5:91 (93) and to bar you from the remembrance of God
13:28 (28) those who believe, their hearts being at rest in God's remembrance
13:28 (28) in God's remembrance are at rest the hearts
24:37 (37) neither commerce nor trafficking diverts from the remembrance of God
29:45 (44) God's remembrance is greater
39:22 (23) whose hearts are hardened against the remembrance of God
39:23 (24) their skins and their hearts soften to the remembrance of God
57:16 (15) who believe should be humbled to the Remembrance of God
58:19 (20) caused them to forget God's Remembrance
62:9 (9) hasten to God's remembrance
63:9 (9) neither your children divert you from God's remembrance

g) pcple. act.

33:35 (35) men and women who remember God oft

*DH W Q

ADHĀQA~to let someone taste

a) perf. act.

16:112 (113)	so God let it taste the garment of hunger and of fear
39:26 (27)	so God let them taste degradation

*Ḍ ᶜ F

ḌĀᶜAFA~to multiply

b) impf. act.

2:261 (263)	so God multiplies unto whom He will

*Ḍ L L

AḌALLA~to lead astray

a) perf. act.

4:88 (90)	do you desire to guide him whom God has led astray?
30:29 (28)	so who shall guide those whom God has led astray?
45:23 (22)	God has led him astray out of a knowledge

b) impf. act.

4:88 (90)	whom God leads astray, thou wilt not find for him a way
4:143 (142)	whom God leads astray, thou wilt not find for him a way
6:39 (39)	whomsoever God will, He leads astray
7:186 (185)	whomsoever God leads astray, no guide he has
9:115 (116)	God would never lead a people astray after that He has guided them
13:27 (27)	God leads astray whomsoever He will
13:33 (33)	whomsoever God leads astray, no guide has he
14:4 (4)	then God leads astray whomsoever He will
14:27 (32)	God leads astray the evildoers
35:8 (9)	God leads astray whomsoever He will
39:23 (24)	whomsoever God leads astray, no guide has he
39:36 (37)	whomsoever God leads astray, no guide has he
40:33 (35)	whomsoever God leads astray, no guide has he
40:34 (36)	even so God leads astray the prodigal
42:44 (42)	whomsoever God leads astray, he has no protector
42:46 (45)	whomsoever God leads astray, no way has he
74:31 (34)	so God leads astray whomsoever He will

*Ḍ R R

ḌARRA~to harm, to hurt

b) impf. act.

3:144 (138)	he will not harm God in any way
3:176 (170)	they will nothing hurt God
3:177 (171)	they will nothing hurt God
47:32 (34)	they will nothing hurt God

*F ᶜ L

FAᶜALA~to do

b) impf. act.

4:147 (146)	what would God do with chastising you?
14:27 (32)	God does what He will

*F Ḍ L

FAḌL~bounty; (*dhū faḍl*) bounteous, bountiful

2:64 (61)	but for the bounty and mercy of God towards you
2:105 (99)	God is of bounty abounding
2:243 (244)	truly God is bounteous to the people
2:251 (252)	but God is bounteous
3:73 (66)	surely bounty is in the hand of God
3:74 (67)	God is of bounty abounding
3:152 (146)	God is bounteous to the believers
3:174 (168)	God is of bounty abounding
4:32 (36)	and ask God of His bounty
4:37 (41)	themselves conceal the bounty that God has given them
4:54 (57)	the bounty that God has given them
4:70 (72)	that is the bounty from God
4:73 (75)	but if a bounty from God visits you
4:83 (85)	but for the bounty of God to you
4:113 (113)	but for God's bounty to thee and His mercy
4:113 (113)	God's bounty to thee is ever great
5:54 (59)	that is God's bounty
8:29 (29)	God is of bounty abounding
10:58 (59)	in the bounty of God, and His mercy
10:60 (61)	God is bountiful to men
12:38 (38)	that is of God's bounty to us, and to men
24:10 (10)	but for God's bounty to you and His mercy
24:14 (14)	but for God's bounty to you and His mercy
24:20 (20)	but for God's bounty to you and His mercy
24:21 (21)	but for God's bounty to you and His mercy
33:47 (46)	there awaits them with God great bounty
40:61 (63)	surely God is bountiful to men
48:29 (29)	bowing, prostrating, seeking bounty from God
49:8 (8)	by God's favour and blessing
57:21 (21)	that is the bounty of God
57:21 (21)	God is of bounty abounding
57:29 (29)	they have no power over anything of God's bounty
57:29 (29)	bounty is in the hand of God
57:29 (29)	God is of bounty abounding
59:8 (8)	seeking bounty from God
62:4 (4)	that is the bounty of God
62:4 (4)	God is of bounty abounding
62:10 (10)	seek God's bounty
73:20 (20)	seeking the bounty of God

FAḌḌALA~to prefer

a) perf. act.

4:32 (36) do not covet that whereby God in bounty has preferred one of you
4:34 (38) for that God has preferred in bounty one of them
4:95 (97) God has preferred in rank those who struggle
4:95 (97) God has preferred those who struggle
16:71 (73) God has preferred some of you over others

*F L Q

FALAQA~(pcple. act.) one who splits

g) pcple. act.

6:95 (95) it is God who splits the grain and the date-stone

*F Q R

FAQĪR~poor, in need

3:181 (177) those who said, 'Surely God is poor, and we are rich.'
35:15 (16) O men, you are the ones that have need of God

*F R Ḍ

FARAḌA~to ordain

a) perf. act.

33:38 (38) there is no fault in the Prophet, touching what God has ordained for him
66:2 (2) God has ordained for you the absolution of your oaths

FARĪḌAH~that which is ordained, apportioned

4:11 (12) so God apportions
9:60 (60) so God ordains

*F R Q

FARRAQA~to make division

b) impf. act.

4:150 (149) and desire to make division between God and His Messengers

*F R R

FARRA~to flee

c) impv.

51:50 (50) therefore flee unto God

*F R Ṭ

FARRAṬA~to neglect

a) perf. act.

39:56 (57) in that I neglected my duty to God

*F R Y

IFTARÁ~to forge (against God)

a) perf. act.

6:144 (145) who does greater evil than he who forges against God a lie

b) impf. act.

10:59 (60) or do you forge against God?

f) n.vb.

6:140 (141) forging against God

*F S Ḥ

FASAḤA~to make room

b) impf. act.

58:11 (12) and God will make room for you

*F Ṣ L

FAṢALA~to distinguish

b) impf. act.

22:17 (17) God shall distinguish between them on the Day of Resurrection

*F T Ḥ

FATAḤA~to open; to reveal. (n.vb.) victory

a) perf. act.

2:76 (71) do you speak to them of what God has revealed to you

b) impf. act.

35:2 (2) whatsoever mercy God opens to men, none can withhold

f) n.vb.

4:141 (140) if a victory comes to you from God
5:52 (57) it may be that God will bring the victory

*F T Y

AFATÁ~to pronounce (judgment)

b) impf. act.

4:127 (126)	God pronounces to you concerning them
4:176 (175)	God pronounces to you concerning the indirect heirs

*F Ṭ R

FIṬRAH~original

30:30 (29)	God's original upon which He originated mankind

*F Y ʾ

AFĀʾA~to give

a) perf. act.

33:50 (49)	spoils of war that God has given thee
59:6 (6)	whatever spoils of war God has given
59:7 (7)	whatsoever spoils of war God has given to His Messenger

*GH Ḍ B

GHAḌIBA~to be wroth, to be angry. (n.vb.) anger, wrath

a) perf. act.

4:93 (95)	God will be wroth with him
48:6 (6)	God is wroth with them, and has cursed them
58:14 (15)	a people against whom God is wrathful
60:13 (13)	take not for friends a people against whom God is wrathful

f) n.vb.

2:61 (58)	they were laden with the burden of God's anger
3:112 (108)	they will be laden with the burden of God's anger
8:16 (16)	he is laden with the burden of God's anger
16:106 (108)	upon them shall rest anger from God
24:9 (9)	the wrath of God shall be upon her

*GH F L

GHAFALA~(pcple. act.) one who is heedless

g) pcple. act.

2:74 (69)	God is not heedless of the things you do
2:85 (79)	God is not heedless of the things you do
2:140 (134)	God is not heedless of the things you do
2:144 (139)	God is not heedless of the things they do
2:149 (144)	God is not heedless of the things you do
3:99 (94)	God is not heedless of the things you do
14:42 (43)	deem not that God is heedless of what the evildoers work

*GH F R

GHAFARA~to forgive, to pardon

b) impf. act.

3:135 (129)	who shall forgive sins but God?
4:48 (51)	God forgives not that aught should be with Him associated
4:116 (116)	God forgives not that aught should be with Him associated
4:137 (136)	God is not likely to forgive them, neither to guide them
4:168 (166)	God would not forgive them, neither guide them
9:80 (81)	if thou askest pardon for them seventy times, God will not pardon them
12:92 (92)	God will forgive you
24:22 (22)	do you not wish that God should forgive you?
39:53 (54)	surely God forgives sins
47:34 (36)	them God will not forgive
48:2 (2)	that God may forgive thee thy former and thy latter sins
63:6 (6)	God will never forgive them

GHAFŪR~forgiving, All-forgiving

"All-forgiving, All-clement"

2:225 (225)	God is All-forgiving, All-clement
2:235 (236)	know that God is All-forgiving, All-clement
3:155 (149)	God is All-forgiving, All-clement
5:101 (101)	for God is All-forgiving, All-clement

"All-forgiving, All-compassionate"

2:173 (168)	God is All-forgiving, All-compassionate
2:182 (178)	surely God is All-forgiving, All-compassionate
2:192 (188)	surely God is All-forgiving, All-compassionate
2:199 (195)	God is All-forgiving, All-compassionate
2:218 (215)	God is All-forgiving, All-compassionate
2:226 (226)	God is All-forgiving, All-compassionate
3:31 (29)	God is All-forgiving, All-compassionate
3:89 (83)	God is All-forgiving, All-compassionate
3:129 (124)	God is All-forgiving, All-compassionate
4:23 (27)	God is All-forgiving, All-compassionate
4:25 (30)	God is All-forgiving All-compassionate
4:96 (98)	surely God is All-forgiving, All-compassionate
4:100 (101)	God is All-forgiving, All-compassionate
4:106 (106)	God is All-forgiving, All-compassionate
4:110 (110)	God is All-forgiving, All-compassionate
4:129 (128)	God is All-forgiving, All-compassionate
4:152 (151)	God is All-forgiving, All-compassionate
5:3 (5)	God is All-forgiving, All-compassionate
5:34 (38)	God is All-forgiving, All-compassionate
5:39 (43)	God is All-forgiving, All-compassionate
5:74 (78)	God is All-forgiving, All-compassionate
5:98 (98)	God is All-forgiving, All-compassionate
8:69 (70)	God is All-forgiving, All-compassionate
8:70 (71)	God is All-forgiving, All-compassionate
9:5 (5)	God is All-forgiving, All-compassionate
9:27 (27)	God is All-forgiving, All-compassionate
9:91 (92)	God is All-forgiving, All-compassionate

9:99 (100)	God is All-forgiving, All-compassionate
9:102 (103)	God is All-forgiving, All-compassionate
16:18 (18)	surely God is All-forgiving, All-compassionate
16:115 (116)	God is All-forgiving, All-compassionate
24:5 (5)	surely God is All-forgiving, All-compassionate
24:22 (22)	God is All-forgiving, All-compassionate
24:33 (33)	surely God, after their being constrained, is All-forgiving, All-compassionate
24:62 (62)	surely God is All-forgiving, All-compassionate
25:70 (70)	God is ever All-forgiving, All-compassionate
33:5 (5)	God is All-forgiving, All-compassionate
33:24 (24)	surely God is All-forgiving, All-compassionate
33:50 (50)	God is All-forgiving, All-compassionate
33:59 (59)	God is All-forgiving, All-compassionate
33:73 (73)	God is All-forgiving, All-compassionate
42:5 (3)	surely God - He is the All-forgiving, the All-compassionate
48:14 (14)	God is All-forgiving, All-compassionate
49:5 (5)	God is All-forgiving, All-compassionate
49:14 (14)	God is All-forgiving, All-compassionate
57:28 (28)	God is All-forgiving, All-compassionate
58:12 (13)	God is All-forgiving, All-compassionate
60:7 (7)	God is All-forgiving, All-compassionate
60:12 (12)	God is All-forgiving, All-compassionate
64:14 (14)	surely God is All-forgiving, All-compassionate
66:1 (1)	God is All-forgiving, All-compassionate
73:20 (20)	God is All-forgiving, All-compassionate

"All-forgiving, All-thankful"

42:23 (22)	surely God is All-forgiving, All-thankful

MAGHFIRAH~mercy, forgiveness

3:157 (151)	mercy from God
57:20 (20)	forgiveness from God

ISTAGHFARA~to pray for forgiveness

a) perf. act.

4:64 (67)	and prayed forgiveness of God

b) impf. act.

4:110 (110)	whosoever does evil, or wrongs himself, and then prays God's forgiveness
27:46 (47)	why do you not ask forgiveness of God

c) impv.

2:199 (195)	press on, and pray for God's forgiveness
4:106 (106)	pray forgiveness of God
24:62 (62)	and ask God's forgiveness
60:12 (12)	accept their fealty and ask God's forgiveness for them
73:20 (20)	and ask God's forgiveness

*GH N Y

GHANĪY~rich, All-sufficient; independent

2:263 (265)	God is All-sufficient, All-clement
2:267 (270)	know that God is All-sufficient, All-laudable

3:97 (92)	as for the unbeliever, God is All-sufficient
4:131 (130)	God is All-sufficient, All-laudable
14:8 (8)	yet assuredly God is All-sufficient
22:64 (63)	surely God — He is the All-sufficient, the All-laudable
29:6 (5)	surely God is All-sufficient nor needs any being
31:12 (11)	surely God is All-sufficient, All-laudable
31:26 (25)	surely God — He is the All-sufficient, the All-laudable
35:15 (16)	He is the All-sufficient, the All-laudable
39:7 (9)	if you are unthankful, God is independent of you
47:38 (40)	God is the All-sufficient; you are the needy ones
57:24 (24)	God is the All-sufficient, the All-laudable
60:6 (6)	surely God is the All-sufficient, the All-laudable
64:6 (6)	God is All-sufficient, All-laudable

AGHNÁ~to enrich; to avail against (God)

a) perf. act.

9:74 (75)	they took revenge only that God enriched them

b) impf. act.

3:10 (8)	will not avail them, neither their children, aught against God
3:116 (112)	their riches shall not avail them, neither their children, against God
4:130 (129)	God will enrich each of them of His plenty
9:28 (28)	God shall surely enrich you of His bounty
12:67 (67)	I cannot avail you anything against God
12:68 (68)	it availed them nothing against God
24:32 (32)	if they are poor, God will enrich them
24:33 (33)	let those who find not the means to marry be abstinent till God enriches them
45:19 (18)	surely they will not avail thee aught against God
58:17 (18)	shall avail them anything against God
66:10 (10)	they availed them nothing whatsoever against God

ISTAGHNÁ~to be in no need of (someone)

64:6 (6)	God was in no need of them

*GH R R

GHARRA~to delude

a) perf. act.

57:14 (13)	the Deluder deluded you concerning God

b) impf. act.

31:33 (33)	let not the Deluder delude you concerning God
35:5 (5)	let not the Deluder delude you concerning God

*GH W TH

ISTAGHĀTHA~to call for succour

b) impf. act.

46:17 (16)	while they call upon God for succour

*GH Y B

GHĀBA~(n.vb.) the unseen

f) n.vb.

9:78 (79)	God knows the things unseen
10:20 (21)	the Unseen belongs only to God
11:123 (123)	to God belongs the Unseen in the heavens and the earth
16:77 (79)	to God belongs the Unseen in the heavens and in the earth
27:65 (66)	none knows the Unseen in the heavens and earth except God
35:38 (36)	God knows the Unseen in the heavens and the earth
49:18 (18)	God knows the Unseen of the heavens and of the earth

*GH Y R

GHAYYARA~to change

b) impf. act.

8:53 (55)	that is because God would never change His favour
13:11 (12)	God changes not what is in a people, until they (change) what is in themselves

*H D Y

HADÁ~to guide. (n.vb.) guidance

a) perf. act.

2:143 (138)	save for those whom God has guided
2:213 (209)	then God guided those who believed to the truth
6:71 (70)	shall we be turned back on our heels after that God has guided us
6:90 (90)	those are they whom God has guided
7:43 (41)	had God not guided us, we had surely never been guided
14:21 (25)	if God had guided us
16:36 (38)	then some of them God guided
16:37 (39)	God guides not those whom He leads astray

b) impf. act.

2:213 (209)	and God guides whomsoever He will
2:258 (260)	God guides not the people of the evildoers
2:264 (266)	God guides not the people of the unbelievers
2:272 (274)	but God guides whomsoever He will
3:86 (80)	how shall God guide a people who have disbelieved?
3:86 (80)	God guides not the people of the evildoers
5:16 (18)	God guides whosoever follows His good pleasure in the ways of peace
5:51 (56)	God guides not the people of the evildoers
5:67 (71)	God guides not the people of the unbelievers
5:108 (107)	God guides not the people of the ungodly
6:144 (145)	God guides not the people of the evildoers
7:178 (177)	whomsoever God guides, he is rightly guided
9:19 (19)	God guides not the people of the evildoers
9:24 (24)	God guides not the people of the ungodly
9:37 (37)	God guides not the people of the unbelievers

9:80 (81)	God guides not the people of the ungodly
9:109 (110)	God guides not the people of the evildoers
10:35 (36)	God — He guides to the truth
12:52 (52)	God guides not the guile
16:104 (106)	God will not guide
16:107 (109)	God guides not the people of the unbelievers
17:97 (99)	whomsoever God guides, he is rightly guided
18:17 (16)	whomsoever God guides, he is rightly guided
24:35 (35)	God guides to His Light whom He will
24:46 (45)	God guides whomsoever He will
28:50 (50)	surely God guides not the people of the evildoers
28:56 (56)	but God guides whom He wills
39:3 (5)	surely God guides not him who is a liar
39:18 (19)	whom God has guided; those — they are men
39:37 (38)	but whomso God guides, none shall lead
39:57 (58)	if only God had guided me
40:28 (29)	God guides not him who is prodigal
45:23 (22)	who shall guide him after God
46:10 (9)	God guides not the people of the evildoers
61:5 (5)	God guides never the people of the ungodly
61:7 (7)	God guides never the people of the evildoers
62:5 (5)	God guides never the people of the evildoers
63:6 (6)	God guides not the people of the ungodly

f) n.vb.

2:120 (114)	God's guidance is the true (guidance)
3:73 (66)	the true (guidance) is God's guidance
6:71 (70)	God's guidance is the true (guidance)
6:88 (88)	that is God's guidance
28:50 (50)	follows his caprice without guidance from God
39:23 (24)	that is God's guidance

g) pcple. act.

22:54 (53)	God ever guides those who believe

*H J R

HĀJARA~to emigrate. (pcple. act.) an emigrant

a) perf. act.

16:41 (43)	those that emigrated in God's cause

g) pcple. act.

4:100 (101)	whoso goes forth from his house an emigrant to God and His Messenger

*H L K

AHLAKA~to destroy

a) perf. act.

28:78 (78)	did he not know that God had destroyed before?
67:28 (28)	what think you? If God destroys me

g) pcple. act.

7:164 (164)	why do you admonish a people God is about to destroy?

*H W N

AHĀNA~to abase

b) impf. act.

22:18 (19)	whom God abases, there is none to honour him

*H Z ʾ

ISTAHZAʾA~to mock

b) impf. act.

2:15 (14)	God shall mock them, and shall lead them on
9:65 (66)	then were you mocking God, and His signs

*Ḥ B B

ḤUBB~love

2:165 (160)	loving them as God is loved
2:165 (160)	those that believe love God more ardently
3:31 (29)	if you love God, follow me
9:24 (24)	if these are dearer to you than God and His Messenger

AḤABBA~to love, to like

b) impf. act.

"God loves"

2:222 (222)	truly, God loves those who repent
3:31 (29)	if you love (God) follow me, and God will love you
3:76 (70)	God loves the godfearing
3:146 (140)	God loves the patient
3:159 (153)	surely God loves those who put their trust
5:42 (46)	God loves the just
9:4 (4)	God loves the godfearing
9:7 (7)	God loves the godfearing
9:108 (109)	God loves those who cleanse themselves
49:9 (9)	God loves the just
60:8 (8)	God loves the just
61:4 (4)	God loves those who fight in His way

"God loves not"

2:190 (186)	God loves not the aggressors
2:205 (201)	God loves not corruption
2:276 (277)	God loves not any guilty ingrate
3:32 (29)	God loves not the unbelievers
3:57 (50)	God loves not the evildoers

3:140 (134)	God loves not the evildoers
4:36 (40)	surely God loves not the proud and boastful
4:107 (107)	surely God loves not the guilty traitor
4:148 (147)	God likes not the shouting of evil words
5:64 (69)	God loves not the workers of corruption
5:87 (89)	God loves not transgressors
8:58 (60)	surely God loves not the treacherous
22:38 (39)	surely God loves not any ungrateful traitor
28:76 (76)	God loves not those that exult
28:77 (77)	God loves not the workers of corruption
31:18 (17)	God loves not any man proud and boastful
57:23 (23)	God loves not any man proud and boastful

*Ḥ B L

ḤABL~a bond

3:103 (98)	hold you fast to God's bond
3:112 (108)	except they be in a bond of God

*Ḥ B Ṭ

AḤBAṬA~to cause to fail

a) perf. act.

33:19 (19)	God has made their works to fail

*Ḥ D D

ḤUDŪD~bounds

2:187 (183)	those are God's bounds; keep well within them
2:229 (229)	unless the couple fear they may not maintain God's bounds
2:229 (229)	if you fear they may not maintain God's bounds
2:229 (229)	those are God's bounds; do not transgress them
2:229 (229)	whosoever transgresses the bounds of God
2:230 (230)	if they suppose that they will maintain God's bounds
2:230 (230)	those are God's bounds
4:13 (17)	those are God's bounds
9:112 (113)	those who keep God's bounds
58:4 (5)	those are God's bounds
65:1 (1)	those are God's bounds
65:1 (1)	whosoever trespasses the bounds of God

ḤĀDDA~to oppose

a) perf. act.

58:22 (22)	anyone who opposes God and His Messenger

b) impf. act.

9:63 (64)	whosoever opposes God and His Messenger
58:5 (6)	those who oppose God and His Messenger
58:20 (21)	those who oppose God and His Messenger

*Ḥ DH R

ḤADHDHARA~to warn

b) impf. act.

3:28 (27) God warns you that you beware of Him
3:30 (28) God warns you that you beware of Him

*Ḥ F Ẓ

ḤAFIẒA~to guard. (pcple. act.) guardian

a) perf. act.

4:34 (38) (guarding) the secret for God's guarding

g) pcple. act.

12:64 (64) God is the best guardian

ḤAFĪẒ~warden

42:6 (4) God is Warden over them

*Ḥ J J

ḤAJJA~(n.vb.) pilgrimage

f) n.vb.

2:196 (192) fulfil the Pilgrimage and the Visitation unto God
3:97 (91) it is the duty of all men towards God to come to the House a pilgrim

ḤUJJAH~argument

4:165 (163) so that mankind might have no argument against God
6:149 (150) to God belongs the argument conclusive

ḤĀJJA~to dispute, to argue

b) impf. act.

2:139 (133) would you then dispute with us concerning God
6:80 (80) do you dispute with me concerning God
42:16 (15) those who argue concerning God

*Ḥ K M

ḤAKAMA~to decide, to judge. (n.vb.) judgment. (pcple. act.) a judge

a) perf. act.

40:48 (51) God already has passed judgment between His servants

b) impf. act.

2:113 (107)	God shall decide between them
4:141 (140)	God will judge between you on the Resurrection Day
5:1 (1)	God decrees whatsoever He desires
7:87 (85)	be patient till God shall judge between us
10:109 (109)	be thou patient until God shall judge
12:80 (80)	or God judges in my favour
13:41 (41)	God judges; none repels His judgment
22:69 (68)	God shall judge between you on the Day of Resurrection
39:3 (4)	surely God shall judge between them

f) n.vb.

5:43 (47)	seeing they have the Torah, wherein is God's judgment
5:50 (55)	yet who is fairer in judgment than God
6:57 (57)	the judgment is God's alone
12:40 (40)	judgment belongs only to God
12:67 (67)	judgment belongs not to any but God
40:12 (12)	judgment belongs to God, the All-high
42:10 (8)	the judgment thereof belongs to God
60:10 (10)	that is God's judgment; He judges between you

g) pcple. act.

95:8 (8)	is not God the justest of judges?

AḤKAMA~to confirm

b) impf. act.

22:52 (51)	God confirms His signs

*Ḥ L F

ḤALAFA~to swear (see also *Allāh* (d), above)

b) impf. act.

4:62 (65)	swearing by God
9:42 (42)	still they will swear by God
9:56 (56)	they swear by God that they belong with you
9:62 (63)	they swear to you by God, to please you
9:74 (75)	they swear by God that they said nothing
9:95 (96)	they will swear to you by God, when you turn back

*Ḥ L L

AḤALLA~to permit, to make lawful

a) perf. act.

2:275 (276)	God has permitted trafficking, and forbidden usury
5:87 (89)	forbid not such good things as God has permitted you
66:1 (1)	why forbiddest thou what God has made lawful to thee

*Ḥ M D

ḤAMADA~(n.vb.) praise

f) n.vb.

1:2 (1)	praise belongs to God, the Lord of all Being
6:1 (1)	praise belongs to God who created the heavens
6:45 (45)	praise belongs to God the Lord of all Being
7:43 (41)	praise belongs to God
10:10 (11)	praise belongs to God, the Lord of all Being
14:39 (41)	praise be to God
16:75 (77)	praise belongs to God
17:111 (111)	praise belongs to God
18:1 (1)	praise belongs to God
23:28 (29)	praise belongs to God
27:15 (15)	praise belongs to God who has preferred us
27:59 (60)	praise belongs to God
27:93 (95)	praise belongs to God
29:63 (63)	praise belongs to God
31:25 (24)	praise belongs to God
34:1 (1)	praise belongs to God
35:1 (1)	praise belongs to God, Originator of the heavens
35:34 (31)	praise belongs to God
37:182 (182)	praise belongs to God, the Lord of all Being
39:29 (30)	praise belongs to God
39:74 (74)	praise belongs to God, who has been true
39:75 (75)	praise belongs to God
40:65 (67)	praise belongs to God, the Lord of all Being
45:36 (35)	so to God belongs praise

*Ḥ N F

ḤANĪF~pure of faith

22:31 (32)	being men pure of faith unto God

*Ḥ Q Q

ḤAQQ~truth

22:6 (6)	that is because God — He is the Truth
22:62 (61)	that is because God — He is the Truth
24:25 (25)	they shall know that God is the manifest Truth
28:75 (75)	then will they know that Truth is God's
31:30 (29)	that is because God — He is the Truth

AḤAQQA~to verify

b) impf. act.

8:7 (7)	but God was desiring to verify the truth
10:82 (82)	God verifies the truth by His words

*Ḥ R B

ḤARABA~(n.vb.) war

f) n.vb.

2:279 (279) then take notice that God shall war with you

ḤĀRABA~to fight

a) perf. act.

9:107 (108) those who fought God and His Messenger aforetime

b) impf. act.

5:33 (37) this is the recompense of those who fight against God

*Ḥ R M

ḤURUMĀT~sacred things

22:30 (31) whosoever venerates the sacred things of God

ḤARRAMA~to prohibit, to hallow, to forbid

a) perf. act.

5:72 (76) God shall prohibit him entrance to Paradise
6:150 (151) those who testify God has forbidden this
6:151 (152) and that you slay not the soul God has forbidden
9:29 (29) do not forbid what God and His Messenger have forbidden
9:37 (37) hallow it another, to agree with the number that God has hallowed
9:37 (37) and so profane what God has hallowed
17:33 (35) slay not the soul God has forbidden, except by right
25:68 (68) nor slay the soul God has forbidden

*Ḥ S B

ḤASIBA~(n.vb.) enough, sufficient

f) n.vb.

3:173 (167) God is sufficient for us
8:62 (64) God is sufficient for thee
8:64 (65) O Prophet, God suffices thee, and the believers
9:59 (59) enough for us is God
9:129 (130) God is enough for me
39:38 (39) God is enough for me

ḤASĪB~a reckoner, one who keeps count

4:6 (7) God suffices for a reckoner
4:86 (88) surely God keeps a watchful count over everything
33:39 (39) God suffices as a reckoner

ḤISĀB~reckoning

2:202 (198) God is swift at the reckoning
3:19 (17) God is swift at the reckoning
3:199 (199) God is swift at the reckoning
5:4 (6) God is swift at the reckoning

14:51 (51)	God is swift at the reckoning
24:39 (39)	God is swift at the reckoning
40:17 (17)	surely God is swift at the reckoning

ḤĀSABA~to make a reckoning

b) impf. act.

2:284 (284)	God shall make reckoning with you for it

*Ḥ S N

ḤASANAH~good

4:79 (81)	whatever good visits thee, it is of God

AḤSANA~to do good to someone. (pcple. act.) a good-doer

a) perf. act.

28:77 (77)	do good, as God has been good to thee

g) pcple. act.

2:195 (191)	God loves the good-doers
3:134 (128)	God loves the good-doers
3:148 (141)	God loves the good-doers
5:13 (16)	surely God loves the good-doers
5:93 (94)	God loves the good-doers
9:120 (121)	God leaves not to waste the wage of the good-doers
11:115 (117)	God will not leave to waste the wage of the good-doers
12:90 (90)	God leaves not to waste the wage of the good-doers
29:69 (69)	God is with the good-doers

*Ḥ SH R

ḤASHARA~to muster

e) impf. pass.

3:158 (152)	it is unto God you shall be mustered

*Ḥ Ṣ Y

AḤṢÁ~to number

a) perf. act.

58:6 (7)	God has numbered it, and they have forgotten it

*Ḥ W L

ḤĀLA~to stand between

b) impf. act.

8:24 (24)	know that God stands between a man and his heart

*Ḥ W SH

ḤĀSHA~God save us (*ḥāsha li-Allāh*)

a) perf. act.

12:31 (31)	God save us
12:51 (51)	God save us

*Ḥ W Ṭ

AḤĀṬA~to encompass

a) perf. act.

48:21 (21)	God had encompassed them already
65:12 (12)	God encompasses everything in knowledge

g) pcple. act.

2:19 (18)	God encompasses the unbelievers
3:120 (116)	God encompasses the things they do
4:108 (108)	God encompasses the things they do
4:126 (125)	God encompasses everything
8:47 (49)	God encompasses the things they do
85:20 (20)	God is behind them, encompassing

*Ḥ Y F

ḤĀFA~to be unjust

b) impf. act.

24:50 (49)	do they fear that God may be unjust towards them

*Ḥ Y Y

ḤAYYĀ~to greet

b) impf. act.

58:8 (9)	they (greet) thee with a greeting God never greeted thee withal

AḤYĀ~to give life, to bring to life, to revive

b) impf. act.

2:73 (68)	God brings to life the dead
2:259 (261)	how shall God give life to this now it is dead
3:156 (150)	for God gives life, and He makes to die
45:26 (25)	God gives you life, then makes you die
57:17 (16)	know that God revives the earth

ISTAḤÁ~to be ashamed

b) impf. act.

33:53 (53)	but God is not ashamed before the truth

*Ḥ Z B

ḤIZB~a party

5:56 (61)	the believers — the party of God, they are the victors
58:22 (22)	those are God's party
58:22 (22)	surely God's party — they are the prosperers

*J ᶜ L

JAᶜALA~to make; to place, to set, to establish; to assign, to appoint, to give

a) perf. act.

4:5 (4)	do not give to fools their property that God has assigned to you to manage
5:97 (98)	God has appointed the Kaaba
5:103 (102)	God has not appointed cattle dedicated to idols
6:136 (137)	they appoint to God, of the tillage and cattle
16:72 (74)	God has appointed for you of yourselves wives
16:80 (82)	it is God who has appointed a place of rest
16:81 (83)	it is God who has appointed for you coverings
16:91 (93)	and you have made God your surety
28:71 (71)	what think you? If God should make the night unceasing
28:72 (72)	what think you? If God should make the day unceasing
33:4 (4)	God has not assigned to any man two hearts within
40:61 (63)	it is God who made for you the night
40:64 (66)	it is God who made for you the earth
40:79 (79)	it is God who appointed for you the cattle
65:3 (3)	God has appointed a measure for everything
71:19 (18)	God has laid the earth for you as a carpet

b) impf. act.

2:224 (224)	do not make God a hindrance, through your oaths
3:156 (150)	that God may make that an anguish in their hearts
4:19 (23)	you may be averse to a thing, and God set in it much good
4:144 (143)	do you desire to give God over you a clear authority?
6:125 (125)	so God lays abomination upon those who believe not
16:57 (59)	and they assign to God daughters
16:62 (64)	they assign to God that they themselves dislike
24:40 (40)	to whomsoever God assigns no light, no light has he
60:7 (7)	it may be God will yet establish between you and ... them ... love
65:7 (7)	God will assuredly appoint, after difficulty, easiness

*J B Y

IJTABÁ~to choose

b) impf. act.

3:179 (174)	but God chooses out of His Messengers
42:13 (12)	God chooses unto Himself whomsoever He will

*J D L

JĀDALA~to dispute

a) perf. act.

4:109 (109) who will dispute with God on their behalf

b) impf. act.

13:13 (14) yet they dispute about God
22:3 (3) among men there is such a one that disputes concerning God
22:8 (8) among men there is such a one that disputes concerning God
31:20 (19) among men there is such a one that disputes concerning God

*J H D

JĀHADA~to struggle

c) impv.

22:78 (77) struggle for God as is His due

*J M ᶜ

JAMAᶜA~to gather, to bring together

b) impf. act.

5:109 (108) the day when God shall gather the Messengers
42:15 (14) God shall bring us together

*J W B

ISTAJĀBA~to answer

a) perf. act.

3:172 (166) those who answered God and the Messenger

c) impv.

8:24 (24) O believers, respond to God and the Messenger

*J W R

AJĀRA~to protect

b) impf. act.

72:22 (22) from God shall protect me not anyone

*J Z Y

JAZÁ~to recompense

b) impf. act.

3:144 (138) God will recompense the thankful
9:121 (122) that God may recompense them the best of what they were doing

12:88 (88)	surely God recompenses the charitable
14:51 (51)	that God may recompense every soul for its earnings
24:38 (38)	that God may recompense them for their fairest works
33:24 (24)	that God may recompense the truthful ones

*K B R

KABBARA~to magnify

b) impf. act.

2:185 (181)	[that you] magnify God that He has guided you
22:37 (38)	that you may magnify God for that

*K DH B

KADHABA~to lie

a) perf. act.

9:90 (91)	those who lied to God and His Messenger
39:32 (33)	who does greater evil than he who lies against God
39:60 (61)	thou shalt see those who lied against God, their faces blackened

*K F F

KAFFA~to restrain

b) impf. act.

4:84 (86)	haply God will restrain the unbelievers' might

*K F R

KAFARA~to disbelieve. (pcple. act.) unbeliever

a) perf. act.

9:54 (54)	but that they believe not in God and His Messenger
9:80 (81)	that, because they disbelieved in God and His Messenger
9:84 (85)	they disbelieved in God and His Messenger
16:106 (108)	whoso disbelieves in God, after he has believed
29:52 (52)	those who believe in vanity and disbelieve in God

b) impf. act.

2:28 (26)	how do you disbelieve in God, seeing you were dead
4:136 (135)	whoso disbelieves in God and His angels
4:150 (149)	those who disbelieve in God and His Messengers
34:33 (32)	to disbelieve in God, and to set up compeers to Him
40:42 (45)	you call me to disbelieve in God

g) pcple. act.

2:98 (92)	surely God is an enemy to the unbelievers
4:140 (139)	God will gather the hypocrites and the unbelievers
4:141 (140)	God will not grant the unbelievers any way over the believers

7:50 (48)	God has forbidden them to the unbelievers
7:101 (99)	so God seals the hearts of the unbelievers
8:18 (18)	God weakens the unbelievers' guile
9:2 (2)	God degrades the unbelievers
33:64 (64)	God has cursed the unbelievers
40:74 (74)	even so God leads astray the unbelievers

KAFFARA~to acquit

b) impf. act.

39:35 (36)	that God may acquit them of the worst

*K F Y

KAFÁ~to suffice; to spare. (pcple. act.) one who suffices

a) perf. act.

29:52 (51)	God suffices as a witness between me and you
33:25 (25)	God spared the believers of fighting

b) impf. act.

2:137 (131)	God will suffice you for them

g) pcple. act.

39:36 (37)	shall not God suffice His servant

*K L F

KALLAFA~to charge

b) impf. act.

2:286 (286)	God charges no soul save to its capacity
65:7 (7)	God charges no soul save with what He has given him

*K L M

KALĀM~word, speech

2:75 (70)	there is a party of them that heard God's word
9:6 (6)	grant him protection till he hears the words of God
48:15 (15)	desiring to change God's words

KALIMAH~a word

3:39 (34)	who shall confirm a Word of God
6:34 (34)	no man can change the words of God
9:40 (40)	God's word is the uppermost
10:64 (65)	there is no changing the words of God
31:27 (26)	yet would the Words of God not be spent

KALLAMA~to speak

a) perf. act.

2:253 (254)	some there are to whom God spoke
4:164 (162)	and unto Moses God spoke directly

b) impf. act.

2:118 (112)	why does God not speak to us
2:174 (169)	God shall not speak to them on the Day of Resurrection
3:77 (71)	God shall not speak to them
42:51 (50)	it belongs not to any mortal that God should speak to him

*K R H

KARIHA~to be averse

a) perf. act.

9:46 (46)	but God was averse that they should be aroused

*K T B

KATABA~to write; to prescribe

a) perf. act.

2:187 (183)	seek what God has prescribed for you
5:21 (24)	enter the Holy Land which God has prescribed for you
9:51 (51)	naught shall visit us but what God has prescribed
58:21 (21)	God has written, 'I shall assuredly be the victor'
59:3 (3)	had God not prescribed dispersal for them

b) impf. act.

4:81 (83)	God writes down their meditations

KITĀB~book; what is prescribed

2:89 (83)	when there came to them a Book from God
2:101 (95)	a party of them that were given (the Book) reject the Book of God
2:174 (169)	those who conceal what of the Book God has sent down
2:176 (171)	that, because God has sent down the Book with the truth
3:23 (22)	being called to the Book of God
3:79 (73)	it belongs not to any mortal that God should give him the Book
4:24 (28)	so God prescribes for you
5:44 (48)	following such portion of God's Book as they were given to keep
8:68 (69)	had it not been for a prior prescription from God
8:75 (76)	by blood are nearer to one another in the Book of God
9:36 (36)	in the Book of God
28:49 (49)	bring a Book from God
30:56 (56)	you have tarried in God's Book till the Day of the Upraising
33:6 (6)	nearer to one another in the Book of God
35:29 (26)	those who recite the Book of God
39:23 (24)	God has sent down the fairest discourse
40:2 (1)	the sending down of the Book is from God
42:15 (14)	I believe in whatever Book God has sent down
42:17 (16)	God it is who has sent down the Book

*K T M

KATAMA~to conceal

b) impf. act.

4:42 (45)	they will not conceal from God one tiding

*KH B R

KHABĪR~aware

2:234 (234)	God is aware of the things you do
2:271 (273)	God is aware of the things you do
3:153 (147)	God is aware of the things you do
3:180 (176)	God is aware of the things you do
4:94 (96)	surely God is aware of the things you do
4:128 (127)	surely God is aware of the things you do
4:135 (134)	God is aware of the things you do
5:8 (11)	surely God is aware of the things you do
9:16 (16)	God is aware of what you do
24:30 (30)	God is aware of the things they work
24:53 (52)	surely God is aware of the things you do
31:29 (28)	and that God is aware of what you do?
33:2 (2)	surely God is aware of the things you do
35:31 (28)	God is aware of and sees His servants
48:11 (11)	God is ever aware of the things you do
57:10 (10)	God is aware of the things you do
58:3 (4)	God is aware of the things you do
58:11 (12)	God is aware of the things you do
58:13 (14)	God is aware of the things you do
59:18 (18)	God is aware of the things you do
63:11 (11)	God is aware of the things you do
64:8 (8)	God is aware of the things you do

*KH D ͨ

KHĀDAͨA~to trick

b) impf. act.

2:9 (8)	they would trick God and the believers
4:142 (141)	the hypocrites seek to trick God

*KH F F

KHAFFAFA~to lighten

a) perf. act.

8:66 (67)	now God has lightened it for you

b) impf. act.

4:28 (32)	God desires to lighten things for you

*KH F Y

KHAFÁ~to be hidden

b) impf. act.

3:5 (4)	from God nothing whatever is hidden in heaven and earth
14:38 (41)	from God nothing whatever is hidden in earth and heaven
40:16 (16)	the day they sally forth, and naught of theirs is hidden from God

ISTAKHFÁ~to hide

b) impf. act.

4:108 (108)	they (hide) themselves from men, but hide not themselves from God

*KH L F

AKHLAFA~to fail

a) perf. act.

9:77 (78)	they failed God in that they promised Him

b) impf. act.

3:9 (7)	verily God will not fail the tryst
13:31 (31)	God will not fail the tryst
39:20 (21)	God fails not the tryst

*KH L Q

KHALAQA~to create. (n.vb.) creation. (pcple. act.) creator

a) perf. act.

2:228 (228)	it is not lawful for them to hide what God has created
7:54 (52)	surely your Lord is God, who created the heavens and the earth
7:185 (184)	and what things God has created
10:3 (3)	surely your Lord is God, who created the heavens and the earth
10:5 (5)	God created that not save with the truth
10:6 (6)	what God has created in the heavens and the earth
14:19 (22)	God created the heavens and the earth in truth
14:32 (37)	it is God who created the heavens and the earth
16:48 (50)	have they not regarded all things that God has created
16:70 (72)	God created you
17:99 (101)	God, who created the heavens and earth, is powerful
24:45 (44)	God has created every beast of water
29:44 (43)	God created the heavens and the earth
29:61 (61)	'Who created the heavens and the earth ..?' they will say, 'God'
30:8 (7)	God created not the heavens and the earth ... save with the truth
30:40 (39)	God is He that created you
30:54 (53)	God is He that created you of weakness
31:25 (24)	'Who created the heavens and the earth?' they will say, 'God'
32:4 (3)	God is He that created the heavens and the earth
35:11 (12)	God created you of dust

37:96 (94)	God created you and what you make
39:38 (39)	'Who created the heavens and the earth?' they will say, 'God'
41:15 (14)	did they not see that God, who created them, was stronger than they?
43:87 (87)	'Who created you?' they will say, 'God'
45:22 (21)	God created the heavens and the earth
46:33 (32)	God who created the heavens and earth
65:12 (12)	it is God who created seven heavens
71:15 (14)	have you not regarded how God created seven heavens

b) impf. act.

3:47 (42)	God creates what He will
24:45 (44)	God creates whatever He will

f) n.vb.

4:119 (118)	they will alter God's creation
10:34 (35)	God — He originates creation
29:19 (18)	have they not seen how God originates creation
30:11 (10)	God originates creation
30:30 (29)	there is no changing God's creation
31:11 (10)	this is God's creation

g) pcple. act.

13:16 (17)	God is the Creator of everything
39:62 (63)	God is the Creator of every thing
40:62 (64)	that then is God, your Lord, the Creator of everything
59:24 (24)	He is God, the Creator, the Maker, the Shaper

*KH R J

AKHRAJA~to bring forth, to bring to light, to disclose

a) perf. act.

16:78 (80)	it is God who brought you forth, knowing nothing

b) impf. act.

47:29 (31)	that God would not bring to light

g) pcple. act.

2:72 (67)	God disclosed what you were hiding
9:64 (65)	God will bring forth what you fear

*KH S F

KHASAFA~to cause to swallow

b) impf. act.

16:45 (47)	that God will not cause the earth to swallow them

*KH SH ᶜ

KHASHAᶜA~(pcple. act.) humble

g) pcple. act.

3:199 (198)	men humble to God

*KH SH Y

KHASHIYA~to fear, to be afraid of. (n.vb.) fear

b) impf. act.

9:13 (13)	you would do better to be afraid of God
9:18 (18)	and pays the alms, and fears none but God alone
24:52 (51)	and fears God and has awe of Him
33:37 (37)	God has better right for thee to fear Him
33:39 (39)	and were fearing Him, and fearing not any one except [God]
35:28 (25)	only those of His servants fear God who have knowledge

f) n.vb.

2:74 (69)	others crash down in the fear of God
4:77 (79)	fearing the people as they would fear God
59:21 (21)	out of the fear of God

*KH T M

KHATAMA~to set a seal

a) perf. act.

2:7 (6)	God has set a seal on their hearts

*KH W F

KHĀFA~to fear

b) impf. act.

5:28 (31)	I fear God
8:48 (50)	I fear God
59:16 (16)	surely I fear God, the Lord of all Being

KHAWWAFA~to frighten

b) impf. act.

39:16 (18)	that it is wherewith God frightens His servants

*KH W N

KHĀNA~to betray, to trick

a) perf. act.

8:71 (72)	they have tricked God before

b) impf. act.

8:27 (27)	O believers, betray not God

*KH Y R

KHAYR~(with prep. *min*) better

20:73 (75)	God is better, and more abiding

*KH Z N

KHAZĀʾIN~treasuries

6:50 (50)	I possess the treasuries of God
11:31 (33)	I possess the treasuries of God

*L ʿ N

LAʿANA~to curse

a) perf. act.

2:88 (82)	God has cursed them for their unbelief
4:46 (49)	God has cursed them for their unbelief
4:52 (55)	those are they whom God has cursed
4:118 (118)	accursed by God
5:60 (65)	whomsoever God has cursed
9:68 (69)	God has cursed them
33:57 (57)	them God has cursed in the present world
47:23 (25)	those are they whom God has cursed

b) impf. act.

2:159 (154)	they shall be cursed by God and the cursers
4:52 (55)	he whom God has cursed

LAʿNAH~a curse

2:89 (83)	the curse of God is on the unbelievers
2:161 (156)	upon them shall rest the curse of God
3:61 (54)	so lay God's curse upon the ones who lie
3:87 (81)	their recompense is that there shall rest on them the curse of God
7:44 (42)	God's curse is on the evildoers
11:18 (21)	the curse of God shall rest upon the evildoers
24:7 (7)	the curse of God shall be upon him

*L J ʾ

MALJAʾ~a shelter

9:118 (119)	they thought that there was no shelter from God except in Him

*L Q Y

LAQIYA~(n.vb.) an encounter

f) n.vb.

6:31 (31)	lost indeed are they that cried lies to the encounter with God
10:45 (46)	lost will be those who cried lies to the encounter with God
29:5 (4)	whoso looks to encounter God

LĀQÁ~to meet

g) pcple. act.

2:249 (250)	those who reckoned they should meet God

*L Ṭ F

LAṬĪF~All-subtle, All-gentle

22:63 (62)	God is All-subtle, All-aware
31:16 (15)	surely God is All-subtle, All-aware
33:34 (34)	God is All-subtle, All-aware
42:19 (18)	God is All-gentle to His servants

*M Ḥ N

IMTAḤANA~to test

a) perf. act.

49:3 (3)	they whose hearts God has tested

*M Ḥ Q

MAḤAQA~to blot out

b) impf. act.

2:276 (277)	God blots out usury

*M Ḥ Ṣ

MAḤḤAṢA~to prove

b) impf. act.

3:141 (135)	and that God may prove the believers

*M Ḥ W

MAḤĀ~to blot out

b) impf. act.

13:39 (39)	God blots out, and He establishes
42:24 (23)	God blots out falsehood

*M K R

MAKARA~to devise. (n.vb.) devising. (pcple. act.) deviser

a) perf. act.

3:54 (47)	they devised, and God devised

b) impf. act.

8:30 (30)	and God was devising

f) n.vb.

7:99 (97)	do they feel secure against God's devising?
7:99 (97)	none feels secure against God's devising
10:21 (22)	God is swifter at devising
13:42 (42)	but God's is the devising altogether

g) pcple. act.

3:54 (47)	God is the best of devisers
8:30 (30)	God is the best of devisers

*M L K

MALAKA~to have power against God, to avail against God. (n.vb.) kingdom

b) impf. act.

5:17 (19)	who then shall overrule God in any way
5:41 (45)	thou canst not avail him anything with God
46:8 (7)	you have no power to help me against God
48:11 (11)	who can avail you aught against God
60:4 (4)	no power to do aught for thee against God

f) n.vb.

2:107 (101)	to God belongs the kingdom of the heavens and the earth
3:189 (186)	to God belongs the Kingdom of the heavens and of the earth
5:17 (20)	to God belongs the kingdom of the heavens and of the earth
5:18 (21)	to God belongs the kingdom of the heavens and of the earth
5:40 (44)	to God belongs the kingdom of the heavens and the earth
5:120 (120)	to God belongs the kingdom of the heavens and of the earth
9:116 (117)	to God belongs the kingdom of the heavens and of the earth
22:56 (55)	the Kingdom upon that day shall belong to God
24:42 (42)	to God belongs the Kingdom of the heavens and the earth
40:16 (16)	'Whose is the Kingdom today?' 'God's, the One, the Omnipotent'
42:49 (48)	to God belongs the Kingdom of the heavens and the earth
45:27 (26)	to God belongs the Kingdom of the heavens and the earth
48:14 (14)	to God belongs the Kingdom of the heavens and the earth

*M N ʿ

MANAʿA~to defend against

g) pcple. act.

59:2 (2)	that their fortresses would defend them against God

*M N N

MANNA~to be gracious, to confer a favour

a) perf. act.

4:94 (96)	but God has been gracious to you
6:53 (53)	are these the ones God has been gracious to among us
12:90 (90)	God has indeed been gracious unto us
28:82 (82)	had God not been gracious to us

b) impf. act.

14:11 (13)	God is gracious unto whomsoever He will of His servants
49:17 (17)	rather God confers a favour upon you

*M Q T

MAQATA~(n.vb.) hatred

f) n.vb.

40:10 (10)	surely God's hatred is greater than your (hatred)

*M S Ḥ

MASĪḤ~the Messiah

5:17 (19)	they are unbelievers who say, 'God is the Messiah'
5:72 (76)	they are unbelievers who say, 'God is the Messiah'

*M S K

AMSAKA~to hold

b) impf. act.

16:79 (81)	naught holds them but God
35:41 (39)	God holds the heavens and the earth

*M S S

MASSA~to touch, to visit (with affliction)

b) impf. act.

6:17 (17)	if God visits thee with affliction
10:107 (107)	if God visits thee with affliction

*M TH L

MATHAL~a similitude, a likeness

2:26 (24)	God is not ashamed to strike a similitude
3:59 (52)	truly, the likeness of Jesus, in God's sight
13:17 (18)	so God strikes both the true and the false
13:17 (18)	even so God strikes His similitudes

14:24 (29)	hast thou not seen how God has struck a similitude
14:25 (30)	so God strikes similitudes for men
16:60 (62)	God's is the loftiest likeness
16:74 (76)	so strike not any similitudes for God
16:75 (77)	God has struck a similitude: a servant
16:76 (78)	God has struck a similitude: two men
16:112 (113)	God has struck a similitude: a city
24:35 (35)	God strikes similitudes for men
39:29 (30)	God has struck a similitude — a man
47:3 (3)	even so God strikes their similitudes for men
66:10 (10)	God has struck a similitude for the unbelievers
66:11 (11)	God has struck a similitude for the believers
74:31 (33)	what did God intend by this as a similitude?

*M W L

MĀL~wealth

24:33 (33)	give them of the wealth of God

*M W Ṭ

AMĀTA~to cause to die

a) perf. act.

2:259 (261)	God made him die a hundred years, then He raised him up

*M Y Z

MĀZA~to distinguish

b) impf. act.

8:37 (38)	that God may distinguish the corrupt

*N ʿ M

NIʿMAH~blessing

2:211 (207)	whoso changes God's blessing
2:231 (231)	remember God's blessing
3:103 (98)	remember God's blessing upon you when you were enemies
3:171 (165)	joyful in blessing and bounty from God
3:174 (168)	they returned with blessing and bounty from God
5:7 (10)	remember God's blessing upon you
5:11 (14)	O believers, remember God's blessing upon you
5:20 (23)	O my people, remember God's blessing upon you
14:6 (6)	remember God's blessing upon you
14:28 (33)	those who exchanged the bounty of God with unthankfulness
14:34 (37)	if you count God's blessing, you will never number it
16:18 (18)	if you count God's blessing, you will never number it
16:53 (55)	whatsoever blessing you have, it comes from God
16:71 (73)	what, and do they deny God's blessing?
16:72 (74)	do they disbelieve in God's blessing?
16:83 (85)	they recognize the blessing of God

16:112 (113)	then it was unthankful for the blessings of God
16:114 (115)	be you thankful for the blessing of God
29:67 (67)	do they disbelieve in God's blessing?
31:31 (30)	the ships run upon the sea by the blessing of God
33:9 (9)	O believers, remember God's blessing upon you
35:3 (3)	O men, remember God's blessing upon you

ANʿAMA~to bless

a) perf. act.

4:69 (71)	they are with those whom God has blessed
4:72 (74)	God has blessed me
5:23 (26)	whom God had blessed
19:58 (59)	these are they whom God has blessed among the Prophets
33:37 (37)	when thou saidst to him whom God had blessed

*N B ʾ

NABĪY~prophet

2:91 (85)	why then were you slaying the Prophets of God
66:8 (8)	upon the day when God will not degrade the Prophet

NABBAʾA~to tell

a) perf. act.

9:94 (95)	God has already told us tidings of you

b) impf. act.

5:14 (17)	God will assuredly tell them of the things they wrought
10:18 (19)	will you tell God what He knows not

*N B T

ANBATA~to cause to grow

a) perf. act.

71:17 (16)	God caused you to grow out of the earth

*N D D

ANDĀD~compeers

2:22 (20)	so set not up compeers to God wittingly
2:165 (160)	there be men who take to themselves compeers apart from God
14:30 (35)	and they set up compeers to God
39:8 (11)	and sets up compeers to God

*N H Y

NAHÁ~to forbid

b) impf. act.

60:8 (8) God forbids you not, as regards those who have not fought you
60:9 (9) God only forbids you as to those who have fought you

*N J W

NAJJÁ~to deliver

a) perf. act.

7:89 (87) God delivered us from it

b) impf. act.

6:64 (64) God delivers you from them
39:61 (62) but God shall deliver those that were godfearing

ANJÁ~to deliver

a) perf. act.

29:24 (23) then God delivered him from the fire

*N K L

NAKĀL~a punishment
5:38 (42) a punishment exemplary from God

*N Q M

INTAQAMA~to take vengeance

b) impf. act.

5:95 (96) God will take vengeance on him

*N S KH

NASAKHA~to annul

b) impf. act.

22:52 (51) God annuls what Satan casts

*N S Y

NASIYA~to forget

a) perf. act.

9:67 (68) they have forgotten God, and He has (forgotten) them
59:19 (19) be not as those who forgot God

*N SH ʾ

ANSHAʾA~to cause to grow

b) impf. act.

29:20 (19)	then God causes the second growth to grow

*N Ṣ Ḥ

NAṢAḤA~to be true

a) perf. act.

9:91 (92)	those who find nothing to expend, if they are true to God

*N Ṣ R

NAṢARA~to help. (n.vb.) help

a) perf. act.

3:123 (119)	God most surely helped you at Badr
9:25 (25)	God has already helped you on many fields
9:40 (40)	if you do not help him, yet God has helped him

b) impf. act.

3:160 (154)	if God helps you, none can overcome you
11:30 (32)	who would help me against God
11:63 (66)	who shall help me against God if I rebel against Him?
22:15 (15)	whosoever thinks God will not help him
22:40 (41)	assuredly God will help him who (helps) Him
22:60 (59)	God will help him
47:7 (8)	if you help God, He will (help) you
48:3 (3)	and that God may help thee
59:8 (8)	and good pleasure, and helping God

f) n.vb.

2:214 (210)	when comes God's help
2:214 (210)	God's help is nigh
3:13 (11)	God confirms with His help whom He will
8:10 (10)	help comes only from God
30:5 (4)	[the believers shall rejoice] in God's help
61:13 (13)	other things you love, help from God and a nigh victory
110:1 (1)	when comes the help of God

NAṢĪR~a helper

3:52 (45)	who will be my helpers unto God
3:52 (45)	we will be helpers of God
4:45 (47)	God suffices as a helper
61:14 (14)	O believers, be you God's helpers
61:14 (14)	who will be my helpers unto God
61:14 (14)	we will be helpers of God

*N Ṭ Q

ANṬAQA~to give speech

a) perf. act.

41:21 (20) God gave us speech, as He gave everything speech

*N W B

ANĀBA~to turn penitent

a) perf. act.

39:17 (19) and turn penitent to God

*N W Q

NĀQAH~she-camel

7:73 (71) this is the She-camel of God, to be a sign for you
11:64 (67) this is the She-camel of God, to be a sign for you
91:13 (13) the She-camel of God; let her drink

*N W R

NĀR~fire

104:6 (6) the Fire of God kindled

NŪR~light

5:15 (18) there has come to you from God a light
9:32 (32) desiring to extinguish with their mouths God's light
9:32 (32) God refuses but to perfect His light
24:35 (35) God is the Light of the heavens and the earth
61:8 (8) they desire to extinguish with their mouths the light of God
61:8 (8) but God will perfect His light

*N Y L

NĀLA~to reach

b) impf. act.

22:37 (38) the flesh of them shall not reach God

*N Z L

NAZZALA~to send down

a) perf. act.

7:71 (69) touching which God has sent down never authority?
29:63 (63) 'who sends down out of heaven water?' they will say, 'God'
47:26 (28) averse to what God sent down
67:9 (9) God has not sent down anything

b) impf. act.

2:90 (84)	grudging that God should send down of His bounty on whomsoever He will
6:37 (37)	God is able to send down a sign

ANZALA~to send down

a) perf. act.

2:90 (84)	disbelieving in that which God sent down
2:91 (85)	believe in that God has sent down
2:164 (159)	the water God sends down from heaven
2:170 (165)	follow what God has sent down
4:61 (64)	come now to what God has sent down
4:113 (113)	God has sent down on thee the Book
5:44 (48)	whoso judges not according to what God has sent down
5:45 (49)	whoso judges not according to what God has sent down
5:47 (51)	let the People of the Gospel judge according to what God has sent down
5:47 (51)	whosoever judges not according to what God has sent down
5:48 (52)	judge between them according to what God has sent down
5:49 (54)	judge between them according to what God has sent down
5:49 (54)	lest they tempt thee away from any of what God has sent down
5:104 (103)	come now to what God has sent down
6:91 (91)	God has not sent down aught on any mortal
6:91 (91)	'Who sent down the Book that Moses brought..?' Say: 'God'
6:93 (93)	the like of what God has sent down
9:26 (26)	then God sent down upon His Messenger His Shechina
9:40 (40)	then God sent down on him His Shechina,
9:97 (98)	apter not to know the bounds of what God has sent down
12:40 (40)	God has sent down no authority touching them
16:65 (67)	it is God who sends down out of heaven water
22:63 (62)	hast thou not seen how that God has sent down out of heaven
31:21 (20)	follow what God has sent down
35:27 (25)	hast thou not seen how that God sends down out of heaven water
39:21 (22)	hast thou not seen how that God has sent down out of heaven water
47:9 (10)	they have been averse to what God has sent down
48:26 (26)	then God sent down His Shechina
53:23 (23)	God has sent down no authority touching them
65:10 (11)	God has sent down to you for a remembrance

*Q B Ḍ

QABAḌA~to grasp

b) impf. act.

2:245 (246)	God grasps, and outspreads

*Q D R

QADARA~to measure

a) perf. act.

6:91 (91)	they measured not God with His true measure
22:74 (73)	they measure not God with His true measure
39:67 (67)	they measure not God with His true measure

QADĪR~powerful, able

2:20 (19)	truly, God is powerful over everything
2:106 (100)	knowest thou not that God is powerful over everything?
2:109 (103)	truly God is powerful over everything
2:148 (143)	surely God is powerful over everything
2:259 (261)	I know that God is powerful over everything
2:284 (284)	God is powerful over everything
3:29 (27)	God is powerful over everything
3:165 (159)	surely God is powerful over everything
3:189 (186)	God is powerful over everything
4:133 (132)	surely God is powerful over that
5:17 (20)	God is powerful over everything
5:19 (22)	God is powerful over everything
5:40 (44)	God is powerful over everything
8:41 (42)	God is powerful over everything
9:39 (39)	for God is powerful over everything
16:77 (79)	surely God is powerful over everything
22:39 (40)	surely God is able to help them
24:45 (44)	God is powerful over everything
29:20 (19)	God is powerful over everything
33:27 (27)	God is powerful over everything
35:1 (1)	surely God is powerful over everything
48:21 (21)	God is powerful over everything
59:6 (6)	God is powerful over everything
60:7 (7)	God is All-powerful
65:12 (12)	God is powerful over everything

QADDARA~to determine

b) impf. act.

73:20 (20)	God determines the night and the day

IQTADARA~(pcple. act.) omnipotent

g) pcple. act.

18:45 (43)	God is omnipotent over everything

*Q Ḍ Y

QAḌÁ~to decide

b) impf. act.

40:20 (21)	God shall decide justly

*Q L B

QALLABA~to turn something about

b) impf. act.

24:44 (44)	God turns about the day and the night

*Q N T

QANATA~to be obedient. (pcple. act.) obedient

b) impf. act.

33:31 (31)	whosoever of you is obedient to God and His Messenger

g) pcple. act.

2:238 (239)	do you stand obedient to God
16:120 (121)	Abraham was a nation obedient unto God

*Q R B

QARRABA~to bring near

b) impf. act.

39:3 (4)	that they may bring us nigh in nearness to God

*Q R Ḍ

AQRAḌA~to lend

a) perf. act.

5:12 (15)	succour them, and lend to God a good loan
57:18 (17)	who make freewill offerings and have lent to God a good loan

b) impf. act.

2:245 (246)	who is he that will lend God a good loan
57:11 (11)	who is he that will lend to God a good loan?
64:17 (17)	if you lend to God a good loan

c) impv.

73:20 (20)	and lend to God a good loan

*Q S M

AQSAMA~to swear

a) perf. act.

5:53 (58)	the ones who swore by God most earnest oaths
6:109 (109)	they have sworn by God the most earnest oaths
16:38 (40)	they have sworn by God the most earnest oaths
35:42 (40)	they have sworn by God the most earnest oaths

b) impf. act.

5:106 (105)	they shall swear by God
5:107 (106)	and they shall swear by God
24:53 (52)	they have sworn by God the most earnest oaths

TAQĀSAMA~to swear to one another

c) impv.

27:49 (50) swear you, one to another, by God

*Q S Ṭ

AQSAṬ~(comp. adj.) more equitable

33:5 (5) that is more equitable in the sight of God

*Q T L

QATALA~to slay

a) perf. act.

8:17 (17) you did not (slay) them, but God slew them

QĀTALA~to assail

a) perf. act.

9:30 (30) God assail them
63:4 (4) God assail them

*Q W L

QĀLA~to say, to speak; to forge

"God said"

2:243 (244) God said to them, 'Die!'
3:55 (48) when God said, 'Jesus, I will take thee to Me'
5:12 (15) and God said, 'I am with you'
5:110 (109) when God said, 'Jesus Son of Mary'
5:115 (115) God said, 'Verily I do send it down on you'
5:116 (116) and when God said, 'O Jesus son of Mary'
5:119 (119) God said, 'This is the day the truthful shall be profited'
16:51 (53) God says: 'Take not to you two gods'
33:4 (4) but God speaks the truth
48:15 (15) you shall not follow us; so God said before

"To say or speak against God"

2:80 (74) or say you things against God of which you know nothing?
2:169 (164) and that you should speak against God such things
3:75 (69) they speak falsehood against God
3:78 (72) they speak falsehood against God
3:94 (88) whoso forges falsehood against God after that
4:50 (53) consider how they forge falsehood against God
4:171 (169) say not as to God but the truth
5:103 (102) but the unbelievers forge against God falsehood
6:21 (21) he who forges against God a lie

6:93 (93)	he who forges against God a lie
6:93 (93)	for what you said untruly about God
7:28 (27)	do you say concerning God such things as you know not?
7:33 (31)	and that you say concerning God such as you know not
7:37 (35)	he who forges against God a lie
7:89 (87)	we should have forged against God a lie
7:105 (103)	worthy to say nothing regarding God except the truth
7:169 (168)	should say concerning God nothing but the truth?
10:17 (18)	he who forges against God a lie
10:60 (61)	what will they think, who forge falsehood against God
10:68 (69)	do you say concerning God that you know not?
10:69 (70)	those who forge against God falsehood shall not prosper
11:18 (21)	he who forges against God a lie
16:116 (117)	so that you may forge against God falsehood
16:116 (117)	those who forge against God falsehood
18:15 (14)	he who forges against God a lie
20:61 (63)	forge not a lie against God
23:38 (40)	he is naught but a man who has forged against God a lie
29:68 (68)	he who forges against God a lie
34:8 (8)	what, has he forged against God a lie?
42:24 (23)	he has forged against God a lie
61:7 (7)	he who forges against God falsehood
72:4 (4)	the fool among us spoke against God
72:5 (5)	would never speak against God a lie

*Q W M

QĀMA~to stand

b) impf. act.

34:46 (45) that you stand unto God, two by two

QAWWĀM~securer; staunch, steadfast

5:8 (11) be you steadfast before God, witnesses for justice

*Q W T

AQĀTA~(pcple. act.) powerful

g) pcple. act.

4:85 (87) God has power over everything

*Q W Y

QAWĪY~strong, All-strong

8:52 (54)	God is strong, terrible in retribution
22:40 (41)	surely God is All-strong, All-mighty
22:74 (73)	surely God is All-strong, All-mighty
33:25 (25)	surely God is All-strong, All-mighty
57:25 (25)	surely God is All-strong, All-mighty
58:21 (21)	surely God is All-strong, All-mighty

QŪWAH~power

2:165 (160)	the power altogether belongs to God
18:39 (37)	there is no power except in God

*R ʾ F

RAʾŪF~gentle, All-gentle

2:143 (138)	truly, God is All-gentle with the people
2:207 (203)	God is gentle with His servants
3:30 (28)	God is gentle with His servants
22:65 (64)	surely God is All-gentle to men, All-compassionate
24:20 (20)	God is All-gentle, All-compassionate
57:9 (9)	surely God is to you All-gentle, All-compassionate

*R ʾ Y

RAʾÁ~to see

b) impf. act.

2:55 (52)	we will not believe thee till we see God openly
9:94 (95)	God will surely see your work
9:105 (106)	God will surely see your work
96:14 (14)	did he not know that God sees?

ARÁ~to show

a) perf. act.

4:105 (106)	thou mayest judge between the people by that God has shown thee
8:43 (45)	when God showed thee them in thy dream

b) impf. act.

2:167 (162)	even so God shall show them their works

c) impv.

4:153 (152)	show us God openly

*R B B

RABB~Lord

3:51 (44)	God is my Lord and your Lord
6:23 (23)	by God our Lord, we never associated other gods with Thee
6:102 (102)	that then is God your Lord
6:162 (163)	all belongs to God, the Lord of all Being
10:3 (3)	that then is God, your Lord
10:32 (33)	that then is God, your Lord, the True
13:16 (17)	'Who is the Lord of the heavens and of the earth?' Say: 'God'
18:38 (36)	He is God, my Lord
19:36 (37)	surely God is my Lord
22:40 (41)	our Lord is God
28:30 (30)	I am God, the Lord of all Being
37:126 (126)	God, your Lord

40:28 (29)	my Lord is God
40:64 (66)	that then is God, your Lord
41:30 (30)	our Lord is God
42:10 (8)	That then is God, my Lord
42:15 (14)	God is our Lord and your Lord
43:64 (64)	God is my Lord and your Lord
46:13 (12)	our Lord is God
70:3 (3)	God, the Lord of the Stairways

*R D D

RADDA~to refer; to send back; to restore

a) perf. act.

33:25 (25)	God sent back those that were unbelievers

b) impf. act.

4:59 (62)	if you should quarrel on anything, refer it to God

d) perf. pass.

6:62 (62)	then they are restored to God their Protector
10:30 (31)	shall be restored to God, their Protector, the True

MARADD~a return, a turning back

40:43 (46)	that to God we return
42:47 (46)	before there comes a day from God that cannot be turned back

*R Ḍ Y

RAḌIYA~to be well-pleased

a) perf. act.

5:119 (119)	God being well-pleased with them
9:100 (101)	God will be well-pleased with them
58:22 (22)	God being well-pleased with them, and they (well-pleased) with Him
98:8 (8)	God is well-pleased with them

b) impf. act.

9:96 (97)	God will surely not be well-pleased with the people of the ungodly

MARḌĀT~pleasure

2:207 (203)	desiring God's good pleasure
2:265 (267)	seeking God's good pleasure
4:114 (114)	whoso does that, seeking God's good pleasure

RIḌWĀN~pleasure

3:15 (13)	God's good pleasure
3:162 (156)	he who followsGod's good pleasure
3:174 (168)	they followed the good pleasure of God
9:72 (73)	Gardens of Eden; and greater, God's good pleasure
57:27 (27)	seeking the good pleasure of God

ARḌÁ~to please

b) impf. act.

9:62 (63) but God ... more right is it they should please Him

*R F ʿ

RAFAʿA~to raise

a) perf. act.

4:158 (156) God raised him up to Him
13:2 (2) God is He who raised up the heavens

b) impf. act.

58:11 (12) God will raise up in rank those of you who believe

*R GH B

RAGHIBA~to turn humbly

g) pcple. act.

9:59 (59) to God we humbly turn

*R H B

RAHIBA~(n.vb.) fear

f) n.vb.

59:13 (13) you arouse greater fear in their hearts than God

*R Ḥ M

RAḤIMA~to have mercy upon. (n.vb.) mercy

a) perf. act.

44:42 (42) save him upon whom God has mercy

b) impf. act.

9:71 (72) those — upon them God will have mercy

f) n.vb.

2:105 (99) God singles out for His mercy whom He will
2:218 (215) those have hope of God's compassion
3:107 (103) they shall be in God's mercy
3:159 (153) it was by some mercy of God that thou wast gentle to them
7:49 (47) are these the ones that you swore God would never reach with mercy?
7:56 (54) the mercy of God is nigh to the good-doers
9:99 (100) God will admit them into His mercy
11:73 (76) the mercy of God and His blessings be upon you

30:50 (49) so behold the marks of God's mercy
39:53 (54) do not despair of God's mercy
48:25 (25) that God may admit into His mercy whom He will

RAḤĪM~compassionate

4:29 (33) surely God is compassionate to you

*R J ʿ

RAJAʿA~to return

a) perf. act.

9:83 (84) if God returns thee to a party of them

e) impf. pass.

2:281 (281) fear a day wherein you shall be returned to God

MARJIʿ~a return

5:48 (53) unto God shall you return, all together
5:105 (104) unto God shall you return, all together
11:4 (4) to God shall you return

*R J W

RAJĀ~to hope for, to look for

b) impf. act.

4:104 (105) you are suffering, and you are hoping from God
33:21 (21) whosoever hopes for God and the Last Day
60:6 (6) whoever hopes for God and the Last Day
71:13 (12) what ails you, that you look not for majesty in God

*R K S

ARKASA~to overthrow

a) perf. act.

4:88 (90) God has overthrown them for what they earned

*R M Y

RAMÁ~to throw

a) perf. act.

8:17 (17) it was not thyself that threw, but God threw

*R Q B

RAQĪB~watchful

4:1 (1)	surely God ever watches over you
33:52 (52)	God is watchful over everything

*R S L

RASŪL~messenger, the Messenger (of God)

2:101 (95)	when there has come to them a Messenger from God
4:157 (156)	Jesus son of Mary, the Messenger of God
4:171 (169)	Jesus son of Mary, was only the Messenger of God
7:158 (157)	O mankind, I am the Messenger of God
9:61 (62)	those who hurt God's Messenger
9:81 (82)	tarrying behind the Messenger of God
9:120 (121)	to stay behind God's Messenger
33:21 (21)	you have had a good example in God's Messenger
33:40 (40)	Muhammad is not the father of any one of your men, but the Messenger of God
33:53 (53)	it is not for you to hurt God's Messenger
48:29 (29)	Muhammad is the Messenger of God
49:3 (3)	those who lower their voices in the presence of God's Messenger
49:7 (7)	know that the Messenger of God is among you
61:5 (5)	though you know I am the Messenger of God to you
61:6 (6)	Israel, I am indeed the Messenger of God to you
63:1 (1)	thou art indeed the Messenger of God
63:5 (5)	God's Messenger will ask forgiveness
63:7 (7)	do not expend on them that are with God's Messenger
91:13 (13)	then the Messenger of God said to them
98:2 (2)	a Messenger from God, reciting pages purified

RISĀLAH~message

33:39 (39)	who were delivering the Messages of God

RUSUL~messengers

6:124 (124)	until we are given the like of what God's Messengers were given
59:6 (6)	but God gives authority to His Messengers

ARSALA~to send, to loose

a) perf. act.

35:9 (10)	God is He that looses the winds

b) impf. act.

30:48 (47)	God is He that looses the winds

*R W D

ARĀDA~to desire

a) perf. act.

2:26 (24)	what did God desire by this for a similitude
13:11 (12)	whensoever God desires evil for a people

39:4 (6)	had God desired to take to Him a son
39:38 (39)	if God desires affliction for me

b) impf. act.

2:185 (181)	God desires ease for you, and desires not hardship for you
2:253 (254)	but God does whatsoever He desires
3:108 (104)	God desires not any injustice to living beings
3:176 (170)	God desires not to appoint for them a portion
4:26 (31)	God desires to make clear to you
4:27 (32)	God desires to turn towards you
5:6 (9)	God does not desire to make any impediment
5:41 (45)	whomsoever God desires to try
5:41 (45)	those are they whose hearts God desired not to purify
5:49 (54)	know that God desires only to smite them for some sin
6:125 (125)	whomsoever God desires to guide, He expands his breast to Islam
8:67 (68)	and God desires the world to come
9:55 (55)	God only desires thereby to chastise them
9:85 (86)	God only desires thereby to chastise them
11:34 (36)	if God desires to pervert you
22:14 (14)	surely God does that He desires
22:16 (16)	for that God guides whom He desires
33:29 (29)	but if you desire God and His Messenger
33:33 (33)	God only desires to put away from you abomination
40:31 (33)	God desires not wrong for His servants

*R W Ḥ

RĀḤA~(n.vb.) comfort

f) n.vb.

12:87 (87)	do not despair of God's comfort
12:87 (87)	of God's comfort no man despairs

*R Z Q

RAZAQA~to provide, to provision. (n.vb.) providing, provision. (pcple. act.) provider

a) perf. act.

4:39 (43)	if they ... expended of that God has provided them
5:88 (90)	eat of what God has provided you
6:140 (141)	and have forbidden what God has provided them
6:142 (143)	eat of what God has provided you
7:50 (48)	pour on us water, or of that God has provided you
16:114 (115)	so eat of what God has provided you
36:47 (47)	expend of that God has provided you

b) impf. act.

2:212 (208)	God provides whomsoever He will
3:37 (32)	truly God provisions whomsoever He will
22:58 (57)	God shall provide them
24:38 (38)	God provides whomsoever He will, without reckoning
29:60 (60)	but God provides for it and you
34:24 (23)	'Who provides for you out of the heavens and the earth?' Say: 'God'

f) n.vb.

2:60 (57)	eat and drink of God's providing
10:59 (60)	have you considered the provision God has sent down for you
11:6 (8)	no creature is there crawling on the earth, but its provision rests on God
13:26 (26)	God outspreads and straitens His provision
28:82 (82)	God outspreads and straitens His provision
29:17 (16)	so seek after your provision with God
29:62 (62)	God outspreads and straitens His provision
30:37 (36)	God outspreads and straitens His provision to whom He will
39:52 (53)	God outspreads and straitens His provision to whomsoever He will
42:27 (26)	had God expanded His provision to His servants
45:5 (4)	the provision God sends down from heaven
65:11 (11)	God has made for him a goodly provision

g) pcple. act.

22:58 (57)	surely God is the best of providers
62:11 (11)	God is the best of providers

RAZZĀQ~provider, All-provider

51:58 (58)	surely God is the All-provider

*S B B

SABBA~to abuse

b) impf. act.

6:108 (108)	they will abuse God in revenge without knowledge

*S B Ḥ

SUBḤĀN~glory be (to God)

12:108 (108)	to God be glory
21:22 (22)	so glory be to God, the Lord of the Throne
23:91 (93)	glory be to God
27:8 (8)	glory be to God, the Lord of all Being
28:68 (68)	glory be to God
30:17 (16)	so glory be to God
37:159 (159)	glory be to God
52:43 (43)	glory be to God, above that which they associate
59:23 (23)	glory be to God, above that they associate

SABBAḤA~to extol, to magnify

a) perf. act.

57:1 (1)	all that is in the heavens and the earth magnifies God
59:1 (1)	all that is in the heavens and the earth magnifies God
61:1 (1)	all that is in the heavens and the earth magnifies God

b) impf. act.

24:41 (41)	whatsoever is in the heavens and in the earth extols God
62:1 (1)	all that is in the heavens and the earth magnifies God
64:1 (1)	all that is in the heavens and the earth magnifies God

*S B L

SABĪL~way

2:154 (149)	those slain in God's way,
2:190 (186)	fight in the way of God
2:195 (191)	expend in the way of God
2:217 (214)	to bar from God's way
2:218 (215)	struggle in God's way
2:244 (245)	so fight in God's way
2:246 (247)	raise up for us a king, and we will fight in God's way
2:246 (247)	why should we not fight in God's way?
2:261 (263)	those who expend their wealth in the way of God
2:262 (264)	those who expend their wealth in the way of God
2:273 (274)	the poor who are restrained in the way of God
3:13 (11)	one company fighting in the way of God
3:99 (94)	why do you bar from God's way the believer?
3:146 (140)	for what smote them in God's way
3:157 (151)	if you are slain or die in God's way
3:167 (160)	come now, fight in the way of God, or repel
3:169 (163)	count not those who were slain in God's way as dead
4:15 (19)	or God appoints for them a way
4:74 (76)	let them fight in the way of God
4:74 (76)	whosoever fights in the way of God
4:75 (77)	how is it with you, that you do not fight in the way of God
4:76 (78)	the believers fight in the way of God
4:84 (86)	So do thou fight in the way of God
4:89 (91)	until they emigrate in the way of God
4:90 (92)	then God assigns not any way to you against them
4:94 (96)	when you are journeying in the path of God, be discriminating
4:95 (97)	those who struggle in the path of God
4:100 (101)	whoso emigrates in the way of God
4:160 (158)	for their barring from God's way many
4:167 (165)	those who disbelieve, and bar from the way of God
5:54 (59)	men who struggle in the path of God
6:116 (116)	they will lead thee astray from the path of God
7:45 (43)	who bar from God's way
7:86 (84)	and barring from God's way those who believe
8:36 (36)	the unbelievers expend their wealth to bar from God's way
8:47 (49)	to show off to men, and barring from God's way
8:60 (62)	whatsoever you expend in the way of God shall be repaid
8:72 (73)	struggled with their possessions and their selves in the way of God
8:74 (75)	and struggled in the way of God
9:19 (19)	and struggles in the way of God
9:20 (20)	and have struggled in the way of God with their possessions
9:34 (34)	consume the goods of the people in vanity and bar from God's way
9:34 (34)	do not expend them in the way of God
9:38 (38)	go forth in the way of God
9:41 (41)	struggle in God's way
9:60 (60)	the ransoming of slaves, debtors, in God's way, and the traveller
9:81 (82)	to struggle with their possessions and their selves in the way of God
9:111 (112)	they fight in the way of God
9:120 (121)	nor fatigue, nor emptiness in the way of God
11:19 (22)	who bar from God's way
14:3 (3)	and bar from God's way, desiring to make it crooked
16:9 (9)	God's it is to show the way

16:88 (90)	those that disbelieve and bar from the way of God
16:94 (96)	for that you barred from the way of God
22:9 (9)	turning his side to lead astray from God's way
22:25 (25)	those who disbelieve, and bar from God's way
22:58 (57)	those who emigrated in God's way
24:22 (22)	[let them not] swear off giving kinsmen and the poor and those who emigrate in the way of God
31:6 (5)	to lead astray from the way of God
38:26 (25)	lest it lead thee astray from the way of God
38:26 (25)	those who go astray from the way of God
47:1 (1)	those who disbelieve and bar from God's way
47:4 (5)	those who are slain in the way of God
47:32 (34)	those who disbelieve and bar from God's way
47:34 (36)	those who disbelieve and bar from God's way
47:38 (40)	to expend in God's way
49:15 (15)	and have struggled with their possessions and their selves in the way of God
57:10 (10)	how it is with you, that you expend not in the way of God
58:16 (17)	and barred from God's way
61:11 (11)	struggle in the way of God with your possessions
63:2 (2)	then they have barred from the way of God
73:20 (20)	and others fighting in the way of God

*S J D

SAJADA~to bow, to prostrate oneself

b) impf. act.

13:15 (16)	to God bow all who are in the heavens and the earth
16:49 (51)	to God bows everything in the heavens
22:18 (18)	hast thou not seen how to God bow all who are in the heavens
27:25 (25)	they prostrate not themselves to God

c) impv.

41:37 (37)	but bow yourselves to God who created them
53:62 (62)	so bow yourselves before God, and serve Him

g) pcple. act.

16:48 (50)	bowing themselves before God in all lowliness

MASJID~place of worship, mosque

2:114 (108)	he who bars God's places of worship
9:17 (17)	it is not for the idolaters to inhabit God's places of worship
9:18 (18)	only he shall inhabit God's places of worship
72:18 (18)	the places of worship belong to God

*S KH R

SAKHIRA~to deride

a) perf. act.

9:79 (80)	God derides them

SAKHKHARA~to subject

a) perf. act.

22:65 (64)	God has subjected to you all that is in the earth
31:20 (19)	have you not seen how that God has subjected to you
45:12 (11)	God is He who has subjected to you the sea

*S KH Ṭ

SAKHIṬA~to be angry. (n.vb.) anger

a) perf. act.

5:80 (83)	God is angered against them

f) n.vb.

3:162 (156)	him who is laden with the burden of God's anger

ASKHAṬA~to anger

a) perf. act.

47:28 (30)	that is because they have followed what angers God

*S L M

SALAM~surrender

16:87 (89)	they will offer God surrender that day

SALLAMA~to save

a) perf. act.

8:43 (45)	but God saved

ASLAMA~to submit, to surrender

a) perf. act.

2:112 (106)	whosoever submits his will to God
3:20 (18)	I have surrendered my will to God
4:125 (124)	he who submits his will to God
27:44 (45)	I surrender with Solomon to God, the Lord of all Being

b) impf. act.

31:22 (21)	whosoever submits his will to God

*S M ʿ

SAMIʿA~to hear

a) perf. act.

3:181 (177)	God has heard the saying of those who said
58:1 (1)	God has heard the words of her that disputes with thee

b) impf. act.

58:1 (1)	God hears the two of you conversing together

SAMĪʿ~hearing, All-hearing

2:181 (177)	surely God is All-hearing, All-knowing
2:224 (224)	surely God is All-hearing, All-knowing
2:227 (227)	surely God is All-hearing, All-knowing
2:244 (245)	know that God is All-hearing, All-knowing
2:256 (257)	God is All-hearing, All-knowing
3:34 (30)	God hears, and knows
3:121 (117)	God is All-hearing, All-knowing
4:58 (61)	God is All-hearing, All-seeing
4:134 (133)	God is All-hearing, All-seeing
4:148 (147)	God is All-hearing, All-knowing
5:76 (80)	God is the All-hearing, the All-knowing
8:17 (17)	surely God is All-hearing, All-knowing
8:42 (44)	surely God is All-hearing, All-knowing
8:53 (55)	God is All-hearing, All-knowing
9:98 (99)	God is All-hearing, All-knowing
9:103 (104)	God is All-hearing, All-knowing
22:61 (60)	God is All-hearing, All-seeing
22:75 (74)	surely God is All-hearing, All-seeing
24:21 (21)	God is All-hearing, All-knowing
24:60 (59)	God is All-hearing, All-knowing
31:28 (27)	God is All-hearing, All-seeing
40:20 (21)	surely God is the All-hearing, the All-seeing
49:1 (1)	God is All-hearing, All-knowing
58:1 (1)	God is All-hearing, All-seeing

ASMAʿA~to make to hear

b) impf. act.

35:22 (21)	God makes to hear whomsoever He will

*S M W

ISM~name

1:1 (1)	In the Name of God, the Merciful, the Compassionate
5:4 (6)	eat what they seize for you, and mention God's Name over it
6:118 (118)	eat of that over which God's Name has been mentioned
6:119 (119)	you do not eat of that over which God's Name has been mentioned
6:121 (121)	eat not of that over which God's Name has not been mentioned
6:138 (139)	over which they mention not the Name of God
7:180 (179)	to God belong the Names Most Beautiful
11:41 (43)	in God's Name shall be its course and its berthing
22:28 (29)	mention God's Name on days well-known
22:34 (35)	that they may mention God's Name over such beasts of the flocks
22:36 (37)	menion God's Name over them, standing in ranks
22:40 (41)	oratories and mosques, wherein God's Name is much mentioned
27:30 (30)	in the Name of God, the Merciful, the Compassionate

*S N N

SUNNAH~wont

33:38 (38)	God's wont with those who passed away before
33:62 (62)	God's wont with those who passed away
33:62 (62)	thou shalt find no changing the wont of God
35:43 (41)	thou shalt never find any changing the wont of God
35:43 (42)	thou shalt never find any altering the wont of God
40:85 (85)	the wont of God, as in the past, touching His servants
48:23 (23)	the wont of God, as in the past
48:23 (23)	thou shalt never find any changing the wont of God

*SH ᶜ R

SHAᶜĀʾIR~waymarks

2:158 (153)	Safa and Marwa are among the waymarks of God
5:2 (2)	O believers, profane not God's waymarks
22:32 (33)	whosoever venerates God's waymarks
22:36 (37)	We have appointed them for you as among God's waymarks

*SH F ᶜ

SHAFAᶜA~(n.vb.) intercession

f) n.vb.

39:44 (45)	to God belongs intercession altogether

SHAFĪᶜ~intercessor

10:18 (19)	these are our intercessors with God
39:43 (44)	have they taken intercessors apart from God?

*SH H D

SHAHIDA~to bear witness, to testify. (n.vb.) testimony. (pcple. act.) a witness

a) perf. act.

3:18 (16)	God bears witness that there is no god but He

b) impf. act.

4:166 (164)	God bears witness to that He has sent down
9:107 (108)	God testifies they are truly liars
24:8 (8)	if she testify by God four times
59:11 (11)	God bears witness that they are truly liars
63:1 (1)	God bears witness that the hypocrites are truly liars

f) n.vb.

2:140 (134)	he who conceals a testimony received from God
5:106 (105)	nor will we hide the testimony of God
24:6 (6)	the (testimony) of one of them shall be to testify by God four times
65:2 (2)	perform the witnessing to God Himself

g) pcple. act.

4:135 (134)	be you securers of justice, witnesses for God

SHAHĪD~a witness

3:98 (93)	surely God is witness of the things you do
4:33 (37)	God is witness over everything
4:79 (81)	God suffices for a witness
4:166 (164)	God suffices for a witness
6:19 (19)	God is witness between me and you
10:29 (30)	God is a sufficient witness between us and you
10:46 (47)	God is witness of the things they do
13:43 (43)	God suffices as a witness
17:96 (98)	God suffices as a witness between me and you
22:17 (17)	assuredly God is witness over everything
33:55 (55)	surely God is witness of everything
48:28 (28)	God suffices as a witness
58:6 (7)	God is witness over everything
85:9 (9)	God is Witness over everything

ASH.HADA~to call to witness

b) impf. act.

2:204 (200)	such a one calls on God to witness
11:54 (57)	I call God to witness

*SH K K

SHAKK~a doubt

14:10 (11)	is there any doubt regarding God?

*SH K R

SHAKARA~to give thanks. (pcple. act.) grateful, thankful

c) impv.

2:172 (167)	wherewith We have provided you, and give thanks to God
31:12 (11)	give thanks to God

g) pcple. act.

2:158 (153)	God is All-grateful, All-knowing
4:147 (146)	God is All-thankful, All-knowing

SHAKŪR~thankful

64:17 (17)	God is All-thankful, All-clement

*SH K W

SHAKĀ~to make complaint

b) impf. act.

12:86 (86)	I make complaint of my anguish and my sorrow unto God

ISHTAKÁ~to make complaint

b) impf. act.

58:1 (1) the words of her that disputes with thee and makes complaint unto God

*SH Q Q

SHĀQQA~to make a breach

a) perf. act.

8:13 (13) they had made a breach with God and with His Messenger
59:4 (4) that is because they made a breach with God

b) impf. act.

8:13 (13) whosoever makes a breach with God
59:4 (4) whosoever makes a breach with God

*SH R Ḥ

SHARAḤA~to expand

a) perf. act.

39:22 (23) he whose breast God has expanded unto Islam

*SH R K

SHARĪK~an associate

6:100 (100) yet they ascribe to God, as associates, the jinn
13:16 (17) have they ascribed to God associates who created as He created
13:33 (33) yet they ascribe to God associates

ASHRAKA~to associate (with God)

a) perf. act.

3:151 (144) for that they have associated with God
6:81 (81) seeing you fear not that you have associated with God

b) impf. act.

4:48 (51) whoso associates with God anything, has indeed forged a mighty sin
4:116 (116) whoso associates with God anything, has gone astray
5:72 (76) whoso associates with God anything
7:33 (31) and that you associate with God
12:38 (38) not ours is it to associate aught with God
22:31 (32) for whosoever associates with God anything
27:59 (60) is God better, or that they associate?
31:13 (12) O my son, do not associate others with God
60:12 (12) they will not associate with God anything

*SH R Y

ISHTARÁ~to buy

a) perf. act.

9:111 (112)	God has bought from the believers their selves

*SH Y ʾ

SHĀʾA~to will

a) perf. act.

2:20 (19)	had God willed, He would have taken away their hearing
2:70 (65)	if God will, we shall then be guided
2:220 (219)	had He willed He would have harassed you
2:253 (254)	had God willed, those who came after him would not have fought
2:253 (254)	had God willed they would not have fought
4:90 (92)	had God willed, He would have given them authority over you
5:48 (53)	if God had willed, He would have made you one nation
6:35 (35)	but had God willed, He would have gathered them to the guidance
6:107 (107)	had God willed, they were not idolaters
6:128 (128)	except as God will
6:137 (138)	had God willed, they would not have done so
6:148 (149)	had God willed, we would not have been idolaters
7:188 (188)	I have no power to profit for myself, or hurt, but as God will
10:16 (17)	had God willed I would not have recited it
10:49 (50)	I have no power to profit for myself, or hurt, but as God will
12:99 (100)	enter you into Egypt, if God will
16:35 (37)	if God had willed we would not have served
16:93 (95)	if God had willed, He would have made you one nation
18:39 (37)	Why when thou went into they garden, didst thou not say, 'As God will..?'
18:69 (68)	thou shalt find me, if God will, patient
23:24 (24)	if God willed, He would have sent down angels
27:87 (89)	excepting whom God wills
28:27 (27)	thou shalt assuredly find me, if God wills, one of the righteous
37:102 (102)	thou shalt find me, God willing, one of the steadfast
39:68 (68)	whosoever is in the earth shall swoon, save whom God wills
48:27 (27)	you shall enter the Holy Mosque, if God wills, in security
87:7 (7)	save what God wills

b) impf. act.

3:40 (35)	God does what He will
6:111 (111)	they would not have been the ones to believe, unless God willed
7:89 (87)	to return into it, unless God our Lord so will
12:76 (76)	except that God willed
13:31 (30)	if God had willed, He would have guided men all together
14:27 (32)	God confirms those who believe
18:24 (23)	[do not say, ... 'I am going to do that tomorrow,' but only,] 'If God will'
22:18 (19)	God does whatsoever He will
36:47 (47)	shall we feed such a one whom, if God willed, He would feed
42:8 (6)	if God have willed, He would have made them one nation
42:24 (23)	if God wills, He will set a seal on thy heart
47:4 (5)	if God had willed, He would have avenged Himself upon them

74:56 (55)	they will not remember, except that God wills
76:30 (30)	but you will not unless God wills
81:29 (29)	but (will) you shall not, unless God wills

*Ṣ B GH

ṢIBGHAH~baptism

2:138 (132)	the baptism of God
2:138 (132)	who is there that baptizes fairer than God?

*Ṣ B R

ṢABARA~(n.vb.) patience. (pcple. act.) patient

f) n.vb.

16:127 (128)	yet is thy patience only with the help of God

g) pcple. act.

2:153 (148)	surely God is with the patient
2:249 (250)	God is with the patient
8:46 (48)	surely God is with the patient
8:66 (67)	God is with the patient

*Ṣ D Q

ṢADAQA~to be true, to speak the truth. (pcple. act.) true

a) perf. act.

3:95 (89)	God has spoken the truth
3:152 (145)	God has been true in His promise towards you
33:22 (22)	God and His Messenger have spoken truly
47:21 (23)	when the matter is resolved, if they were true to God
48:27 (27)	God has indeed fulfilled the vision He vouchsafed to His Messenger truly

g) pcple. act.

4:87 (89)	who is truer in tidings than God?
4:122 (121)	who is truer in speech than God?

*Ṣ F W

IṢṬAFÁ~to choose

a) perf. act.

2:132 (126)	my sons, God has chosen for you the religion
2:247 (248)	God has chosen him over you
3:33 (30)	God chose Adam and Noah
3:42 (37)	Mary, God has chosen thee

b) impf. act.

22:75 (74)	God chooses of the angels Messengers

*Ṣ L Ḥ

AṢLAḤA~to set right

b) impf. act.

10:81 (81) God sets not right the work of those who do corruption

*Ṣ L W

ṢALLÁ~(with prep. ʿ*alá*) to bless

b) impf. act.

33:56 (56) God and His angels bless the Prophet

*Ṣ M D

ṢAMAD~everlasting refuge

112:2 (2) God, the Everlasting Refuge

*Ṣ N ʿ

ṢANAʿA~(n.vb.) handiwork

f) n.vb.

27:88 (90) passing by like clouds — God's handiwork

*Ṣ R F

ṢARAFA~to turn something away

a) perf. act.

9:127 (128) God has turned away their hearts

*Ṣ R Ṭ

ṢIRĀṬ~path

42:53 (53) [thou shalt guide unto a straight (path)] — the path of God

*Ṣ Y R

ṢĀRA~(n.vb.) homecoming

f) n.vb.

3:28 (27) and unto God is the homecoming
24:42 (42) and to Him is the homecoming
35:18 (19) to God is the homecoming

*T W B

TĀBA~(with prep. *ʿalá*) to turn towards, to return. (n.vb.) turning, a return

a) perf. act.

5:71 (75)	then God turned towards them
9:117 (118)	God has turned towards the Prophet and the Emigrants
58:13 (14)	God turns again unto you

b) impf. act.

4:17 (21)	God will return towards those
5:39 (43)	God will turn towards him
5:74 (78)	will they not turn to God and pray His forgiveness?
9:15 (15)	God turns towards whomsoever He will
9:27 (27)	then God thereafter turns towards whom He will
9:102 (103)	it may be that God will turn towards them
25:71 (71)	he truly turns to God in repentance
33:73 (73)	God may turn again unto the believers
66:4 (4)	if you two repent to God

c) impv.

24:31 (31)	turn all together to God, O you believers
66:8 (8)	believers, turn to God in sincere repentance

f) n.vb.

4:17 (21)	God shall turn only towards those who do evil in ignorance
4:92 (94)	let him fast two successive months — God's turning
9:104 (105)	God is He who accepts repentance from His servants

TAWWĀB~one who turns

4:16 (20)	God turns, and is All-compassionate
4:64 (67)	they would have found God turns, All-compassionate
9:104 (105)	God — He turns, and is All-compassionate
9:118 (119)	surely God turns, and is All-compassionate
24:10 (10)	God turns, and is All-wise
49:12 (12)	assuredly God turns

*TH L TH

THĀLITH~third (ordinal)

5:73 (77)	they are unbelievers who say, 'God is the Third of Three'

*TH W B

MATHŪBAH~a recompense

2:103 (97)	a recompense from God had been better
5:60 (65)	shall I tell you of a recompense with God, worse than that

THAWĀB~a reward

3:148 (141)	God gave them the reward of this world
3:195 (195)	a reward from God

3:195 (195) and God — with Him is the fairest reward
4:134 (133) with God is the reward of this world
28:80 (80) the reward of God is better for him who believes

ATHĀBA~to reward

a) perf. act.

5:85 (88) God rewards them for what they say

*Ṭ B ʿ

ṬABAʿA~to seal, to set a seal

a) perf. act.

4:155 (154) God sealed them for their unbelief, so they believe not
9:93 (94) God has set a seal on their hearts
16:108 (110) those — God has set a seal on their hearts
47:16 (18) those are they upon whose hearts God has set a seal

b) impf. act.

30:59 (59) even so God seals the hearts of those that know not
40:35 (37) so God sets a seal on every heart proud, arrogant

*Ṭ F ʾ

AṬFAʾA~to extinguish

a) perf. act.

5:64 (69) as often as they light a fire for war, God will extinguish it

*Ṭ L ʿ

AṬLAʿA~to inform

b) impf. act.

3:179 (174) God will not inform you of the Unseen

*Ṭ W ʿ

AṬĀʿA~to obey

a) perf. act.

33:66 (66) would we had obeyed God and the Messenger

b) impf. act.

4:13 (17) whoso obeys God and His Messenger
4:69 (71) whosoever obeys God, and the Messenger
4:80 (82) whosoever (obeys) the Messenger, thereby obeys God
9:71 (72) and they obey God and His Messenger

24:52 (51)	whoso obeys God and His Messenger
33:71 (71)	whosoever obeys God and His Messenger
48:17 (17)	whosoever obeys God and His Messenger
49:14 (14)	if you obey God and His Messenger

c) impv.

3:32 (29)	obey God, and the Messenger
3:132 (126)	and obey God and the Messenger
4:59 (62)	O believers, obey God, and (obey) the Messenger
5:92 (93)	and obey God
8:1 (1)	obey you God and His Messenger
8:20 (20)	O believers, obey God and His Messenger
8:46 (48)	obey God, and His Messenger
24:54 (53)	obey God, and (obey) the Messenger
33:33 (33)	and obey God and His Messenger
47:33 (35)	O believers, obey God
58:13 (14)	obey God and His Messenger
64:12 (12)	obey God, and (obey) the Messenger

*W ʿ D

WAʿADA~to promise. (n.vb.) a promise

a) perf. act.

4:95 (97)	God has promised the reward most fair
5:9 (12)	God has promised those that believe
9:68 (69)	God has promised the hypocrites, men and women, and the unbelievers
9:72 (73)	God has promised the believers, men and women, gardens
14:22 (26)	God surely promised you a true promise
22:72 (71)	the Fire — God has promised it to the unbelievers
24:55 (54)	God has promised those of you who believe
33:12 (12)	God and His Messenger promised us only delusion
33:22 (22)	this is what God and His Messenger promised us
48:20 (20)	God has promised you many spoils
48:29 (29)	God has promised those of them who believe
57:10 (10)	God has promised the reward most fair

b) impf. act.

2:268 (271)	God promises you His pardon and His bounty
8:7 (7)	when God promised you one of the two parties should be yours

f) n.vb.

4:122 (121)	God's promise in truth
10:4 (4)	God's promise, in truth
10:55 (56)	God's promise is true
13:31 (31)	until God's promise comes
14:47 (48)	do not deem that God will fail in His promise
18:21 (20)	that they might know that God's promise is true
22:47 (46)	God will not fail His promise
28:13 (12)	the promise of God is true
30:6 (5)	the promise of God

30:6 (5)	God fails not His promise
30:60 (60)	surely God's promise is true
31:9 (8)	therein to dwell forever — God's promise
31:33 (33)	surely God's promise is true
35:5 (5)	O men, God's promise is true
39:20 (21)	God's promise
40:55 (57)	surely God's promise is true
40:77 (77)	surely God's promise is true
45:32 (31)	God's promise is true
46:17 (16)	surely God's promise is true

*W ʿ Ẓ

WAʿAẒA~to admonish

b) impf. act.

4:58 (61)	good is the admonition God gives you
24:17 (16)	God admonishes you

*W F Q

WAFFAQA~to compose differences. (n.vb.) succour

b) impf. act.

4:35 (39)	God will compose their differences

f) n.vb.

11:88 (90)	my succour is only with God

*W F Y

WAFFÁ~to pay in full

b) impf. act.

24:25 (25)	upon that day God will pay them in full

TAWAFFÁ~to take

b) impf. act.

39:42 (43)	God takes the souls at the time of their death

*W Ḥ D

WĀḤID~one

4:171 (169)	God is only One (God)
12:39 (39)	which is better ... many lords at variance, or God the One
39:4 (6)	He is God, the One, the Omnipotent

*W J D

WAJADA~to find

a) perf. act.

24:39 (39)	there indeed he finds God

*W J H

WAJH~face

2:115 (109)	whithersoever you turn, there is the Face of God
2:272 (274)	for then you are expending, being desirous only of God's Face
30:38 (37)	that is better for those who desire God's Face
30:39 (38)	what you give in alms, desiring God's Face
76:9 (9)	we feed you only for the Face of God

*W K L

WAKĪL~a guardian

4:81 (83)	God suffices for a guardian
4:132 (131)	God suffices for a guardian
4:171 (169)	God suffices for a guardian
11:12 (15)	God is a Guardian over everything
12:66 (66)	God shall be Guardian over what we say
28:28 (28)	God is guardian of what we say
33:3 (3)	God suffices as a guardian
33:48 (47)	God suffices as a guardian

TAWAKKALA~to put one's trust

a) perf. act.

7:89 (87)	in God we have put our trust
10:71 (72)	in God have I put my trust
10:85 (85)	in God we have put our trust
11:56 (59)	truly, I have put my trust in God

b) impf. act.

3:122 (118)	in God let the believers put all their trust
3:160 (154)	in God let the believers put all their trust
5:11 (14)	in God let the believers put all their trust
8:49 (51)	whosoever puts his trust in God
9:51 (51)	in God let the believers put all their trust
14:11 (14)	in God let the believers put all their trust
14:12 (15)	why should we not put our trust in God
14:12 (15)	in God let all put their trust who put their trust
58:10 (11)	in God let the believers put all their trust
64:13 (13)	in God let the believers put their trust
65:3 (3)	whosoever puts his trust in God

c) impv.

3:159 (153)	put thy trust in God
4:81 (83)	put thy trust in God

5:23 (26)	put you all your trust in God, if you are believers
8:61 (63)	put thy trust in God
27:79 (81)	so put thy trust in God
33:3 (3)	and put thy trust in God
33:48 (47)	but put thy trust in God

*W L D

WALADA~to beget

a) perf. act.

37:152 (152)	'God has begotten?' They are truly liars

*W L J

AWLAJA~to make to enter

b) impf. act.

22:61 (60)	that is because God makes the night to enter into the day
31:29 (28)	God makes the night to enter into the day

*W L Y

WALÁ~(n.vb.) protection

f) n.vb.

18:44 (42)	thereover protection belongs only to God

AWLÁ~(comp. adj.) closest

4:135 (134)	God stands closest to either

MAWLÁ~protector

3:150 (143)	but God is your Protector
8:40 (41)	know that God is your Protector
47:11 (12)	that is because God is the Protector of the believers
66:2 (2)	God is your Protector
66:4 (4)	God is his Protector

WALĪY~protector; friend

2:107 (101)	you have none, apart from God, neither protector nor helper
2:120 (114)	thou shalt have against God neither protector nor helper
2:257 (258)	God is the Protector of the believers
3:68 (61)	God is the Protector of the believers
3:122 (118)	God was their Protector
4:45 (47)	God suffices as a protector
4:119 (118)	whoso takes Satan to him for a friend, instead of God
4:123 (122)	and will not find for him, apart from God, a friend or helper
4:173 (173)	they shall not find for them, apart from God, a friend or helper
5:55 (60)	your friend is only God, and His Messenger
6:70 (69)	apart from God, it has no protector
7:30 (28)	have taken Satans for friends instead of God

7:196 (195)	my protector is God
9:116 (117)	you have not, apart from God, either protector or helper
10:62 (63)	surely God's friends — no fear shall be on them
11:20 (22)	they have no protectors, apart from God
11:113 (115)	you have no protectors apart from God
29:22 (21)	you have not, apart from God, either protector or helper
29:41 (40)	those who have taken to them protectors, apart from God
33:17 (17)	they shall find for themselves, apart from God, neither protector nor helper
42:9 (7)	but God - He is the Protector
42:31 (30)	apart from God, you have neither protector nor helper
42:46 (45)	they have no protectors to help them, apart from God
45:10 (9)	nor those they took as protectors, apart from God
62:6 (6)	you of Jewry, if you assert that you are the friends of God

TAWALLÁ~to make someone a friend

b) impf. act.

5:56 (61) whoso makes God his friend

*W Q Y

WAQÁ~to guard. (pcple. act.) defender

a) perf. act.

40:45 (48)	so God guarded him against the evil
52:27 (27)	God was gracious to us, and guarded us
76:11 (11)	so God has guarded them from the evil

g) pcple. act.

13:34 (34)	they have none to defend them from God
13:37 (37)	thou shalt have no protector against God, and no defender
40:21 (22)	they had none to defend them from God

TAQWÁ~fear

9:109 (110) is he better who founded his building upon the fear of God?

ITTAQÁ~to fear. (pcple. act.) godfearing

a) perf. act.

2:189 (185) come to the houses by their doors, and fear God

b) impf. act.

2:282 (282)	and let him fear God his Lord
2:283 (283)	and let him fear God his Lord
4:9 (10)	let them fear God, and speak words hitting the mark
65:2 (2)	whosoever fears God, He will appoint for him a way out
65:4 (4)	whoso fears God, (God) will appoint for him ... easiness
65:5 (5)	whosoever fears God, He will acquit him

c) impv.

2:194 (190)	fear you God, and know that (God) is with the godfearing
2:196 (192)	fear God, and know that (God) is terrible in retribution

2:203 (199)	fear you God, and know that unto Him you shall be mustered
2:206 (202)	when it is said to him, 'Fear God'
2:223 (223)	fear God, and know that you shall meet Him
2:231 (231)	fear God, and know that (God) has knowledge of everything
2:233 (233)	fear God, and know that (God) sees the things you do
2:278 (278)	O believers, fear you God
2:282 (282)	if you do, that is ungodliness in you. And fear God
3:50 (44)	so fear you God, and obey you me
3:102 (97)	O believers, fear God as He should be (feared)
3:123 (119)	so fear God, and haply you will be thankful
3:130 (125)	fear you God; haply so you will prosper
3:200 (200)	fear you God; haply so you will prosper
4:1 (1)	fear God by whom you demand one of another
4:131 (130)	We have charged those who were given the Book before you, and you, 'Fear God'
5:2 (3)	fear God; surely (God) is terrible in retribution
5:4 (6)	fear God; (God) is swift at the reckoning
5:7 (10)	fear you God; surely (God) knows the thoughts in the breasts
5:8 (11)	fear God; surely (God) is aware of the things you do
5:11 (14)	fear God; and in (God) let the believers put all their trust
5:35 (39)	O believers, fear God, and seek the means to come to Him
5:57 (62)	fear God, if you are believers
5:88 (90)	fear God, in whom you are believers
5:96 (97)	fear God, unto whom you shall be mustered
5:100 (100)	so fear God, O men possessed of minds
5:108 (107)	fear God, and hearken; (God) guides not the people of the ungodly
5:112 (112)	fear you God, if you are believers
8:1 (1)	so fear you God, and set things right between you
8:29 (29)	O believers, if you fear God, He will assign you a salvation
8:69 (70)	and fear you God; surely (God) is All-forgiving, All-compassionate
9:119 (120)	O believers, fear God, and be with the truthful ones
11:78 (80)	so fear God, and do not degrade me in my guests
15:69 (69)	fear God, and do not degrade me
26:108 (108)	so fear you God, and obey you me
26:110 (110)	so fear you God, and obey you me
26:126 (126)	so fear you God, and obey you me
26:131 (131)	so fear you God, and obey you me
26:144 (144)	so fear you God, and obey you me
26:150 (150)	so fear you God, and obey you me
26:163 (163)	so fear you God, and obey you me
26:179 (179)	so fear you God, and obey you me
33:1 (1)	O Prophet, fear God, and obey not the unbelievers
33:37 (37)	keep thy wife to thyself, and fear God
33:55 (55)	and fear you God; surely (God) is witness of everything
33:70 (70)	O believers, fear God, and speak words hitting the mark
43:63 (63)	so fear you God and obey you me
49:1 (1)	advance not before (God) and His Messenger; and fear God
49:10 (10)	set things right between your two brothers, and fear God
49:12 (12)	and fear you God; assuredly (God) turns
57:28 (28)	O believers, fear God, and believe in His Messenger
58:9 (10)	fear God, unto whom you shall be mustered
59:7 (7)	fear God; surely (God) is terrible in retribution
59:18 (18)	O believers, fear God. Let every soul consider what it has forwarded for the morrow
59:18 (18)	let every soul consider what it has forwarded for the morrow. And fear God
60:11 (11)	fear God, in whom you believe
64:16 (16)	so fear God as far as you are able
65:1 (1)	count the period, and fear God your Lord
65:10 (10)	so fear God, O men possessed of minds

g) pcple. act.

2:194 (190)	know that God is with the godfearing
3:115 (111)	God knows the godfearing
5:27 (30)	God accepts only of the godfearing
9:36 (36)	know that God is with the godfearing
9:44 (44)	God knows the godfearing
9:123 (124)	know that God is with the godfearing
16:31 (33)	so God recompenses the godfearing
16:128 (128)	God is with those who are godfearing
45:19 (18)	God is the friend of the godfearing
49:13 (13)	among you in the sight of God is the most godfearing

*W S ʿ

WASIʿA~(pcple. act.) All-embracing

g) pcple. act.

2:115 (109)	God is All-embracing, All-knowing
2:247 (248)	God is All-embracing, All-knowing
2:261 (263)	God is All-embracing, All-knowing
2:268 (271)	God is All-embracing, All-knowing
3:73 (66)	God is All-embracing, All-knowing
4:130 (129)	God is All-embracing, All-wise
5:54 (59)	God is All-embracing, All-knowing
24:32 (32)	God is All-embracing, All-knowing

*W Ṣ L

WAṢALA~to reach

b) impf. act.

6:136 (137)	what is for their associates reaches not God

*W Ṣ Y

WAṢĪYAH~a charge

4:12 (16)	a charge from God

WAṢṢÁ~to charge someone

a) perf. act.

6:144 (145)	were you witnesses when God charged you

AWṢÁ~to charge someone

b) impf. act.

4:11 (12)	God charges you, concerning your children

*W TH Q

MAWTHIQ~a solemn pledge

12:66 (66)	until you bring me a solemn pledge by God
12:80 (80)	your father has taken a solemn pledge from you by God

MĪTHĀQ~a compact

3:81 (75)	when God took compact with the Prophets
3:187 (184)	when God took compact with those who had been given the Book
5:12 (15)	God took compact with the Children of Israel

*Y D Y

YAD~a hand; before (with prep. *bayna*)

5:64 (69)	the Jews have said, 'God's hand is fettered'
48:10 (10)	God's hand is over their hands
49:1 (1)	O believers, advance not before God

*Y S R

YASĪR~easy

4:30 (34)	that for God is an easy matter
4:169 (167)	that for God is an easy matter
22:70 (69)	surely that for God is an easy matter
29:19 (18)	surely that is an easy matter for God
33:19 (19)	that is easy for God
33:30 (30)	that is easy for God
35:11 (12)	surely that is easy for God
57:22 (22)	that is easy for God
64:7 (7)	that is easy for God

*Y W M

YAWM~a day

14:5 (5)	remind thou them of the Days of God
30:43 (42)	set thy face to the true religion before there comes a day from God
45:14 (13)	those who do not look for the days of God

*Z J W

AZJÁ~to drive

b) impf. act.

24:43 (43)	hast thou not seen how God drives the clouds, then composes them

*Z K Y

ZAKKÁ~to purify

b) impf. act.

4:49 (52)	only God purifies whom He will
24:21 (21)	but God purifies whom He will

*Z Y D

ZĀDA~to increase

a) perf. act.

2:10 (9)	God has increased their sickness

b) impf. act.

19:76 (78)	God shall increase those who were guided in guidance

*Z Y GH

AZĀGHA~to cause to swerve

a) perf. act.

61:5 (5)	God caused their hearts to swerve

*Z Y N

ZĪNAH~ornament

7:32 (30)	who has forbidden the ornament of God

*Ẓ H R

AẒHARA~to disclose

a) perf. act.

66:3 (3)	God disclosed that to him

*Ẓ L M

ẒALAMA~to wrong

a) perf. act.

3:117 (113)	God wronged them not

b) impf. act.

4:40 (44)	God shall not wrong so much as the weight of an ant
9:70 (71)	God would not wrong them
10:44 (45)	surely God wrongs not men anything
16:33 (35)	God wronged them not, but themselves they wronged
29:40 (39)	God would never wrong them
30:9 (8)	God would never wrong them

*Ẓ N N

ẒANNA~to think (evil thoughts)

b impf. act.

3:154 (148)	thinking of God thoughts that were not true
33:10 (10)	your hearts reached your throats, while you thought thoughts about God
48:6 (6)	men and women alike, and those who think evil thoughts of God

THE REMAINING VOCABULARY OF THE QUR'AN

ALIF

*A B B

ABB n.m.~pastures [Ar]; grass [Pk]; fodder [Ali]

80:31 (31)	and fruits, and pastures

*A B D

ABAD n.m.~(adv) ever, forever; never (whenever in negative construction)

2:95 (89)	But they will never long for it
4:57 (60)	therein dwelling forever and ever
4:122 (121)	therein dwelling for ever and ever
4:169 (167)	therein dwelling forever and ever
5:24 (27)	we will never enter it so long as they are in it
5:119 (119)	therein dwelling forever and ever
9:22 (22)	therein to dwell forever and ever
9:83 (84)	You shall not go forth with me ever
9:84 (85)	pray thou never over any one of them
9:100 (101)	therein to dwell forever and ever
9:108 (109)	Stand there never
18:3 (2)	therein to abide for ever
18:20 (19)	then you will not prosper ever
18:35 (33)	I do not think that this will ever perish
18:57 (56)	they will not be guided ever
24:4 (4)	do not accept any testimony of theirs ever
24:17 (16)	you shall never repeat the like of it again
24:21 (21)	not one of you would have been pure ever
33:53 (53)	neither to marry his wives after him, ever
33:65 (65)	therein to dwell for ever
48:12 (12)	the Messenger and the believers would never return
59:11 (11)	we will never obey anyone in regard to you
60:4 (4)	enmity has shown itself, and hatred for ever
62:7 (7)	But they will never long for it
64:9 (9)	therein to dwell for ever and ever

65:11 (11)	therein they shall dwell for ever and ever
72:23 (24)	therein they shall dwell forever
98:8 (7)	therein dwelling for ever and ever

*A B L

ABĀBĪL n.m.~flights (of birds) [Ar, Ali]; swarms [Pk]

105:3 (3)	And He loosed upon them birds in flights

IBIL n.m. (coll)~camel(s)

6:144 (145)	Of camels two, of oxen two
88:17 (17)	do they not consider how the camel was created

*A B Q

ABAQA vb. (I)~to run away

a) perf. act.

37:140 (140)	when he ran away to the laden ship

*A B R

IBRĀHĪM n.prop.~Abraham

2:124 (118)	And when his Lord tested Abraham
2:125 (119)	Take to yourselves Abraham's station
2:125 (119)	We made covenant with Abraham and Ishmael
2:126 (120)	Abraham said, 'My Lord, make this a land secure'
2:127 (121)	when Abraham … Raised up the foundations of the House
2:130 (124)	Who therefore shrinks from the religion of Abraham
2:132 (126)	And Abraham charged his sons with this
2:133 (127)	the God of thy fathers Abraham, Ishmael and Isaac
2:135 (129)	the creed of Abraham, a man of pure faith
2:136 (130)	and sent down on Abraham, Ishmael
2:140 (134)	or do you say, 'Abraham, Ishmael
2:258 (260)	him who disputed with Abraham
2:258 (260)	Abraham said, 'My Lord is He who gives life'
2:258 (260)	said Abraham, 'God brings the sun from the east'
2:260 (262)	and when Abraham said, 'My Lord, show me'
3:33 (30)	God chose Adam and Noah and the House of Abraham
3:65 (58)	why do you dispute concerning Abraham?
3:67 (60)	Abraham in truth was not a Jew
3:68 (61)	the people standing closest to Abraham
3:84 (78)	and sent down on Abraham and Ishmael
3:95 (89)	the creed of Abraham, a man of pure faith
3:97 (91)	Therein are clear signs — the station of Abraham
4:54 (57)	Yet We gave the people of Abraham
4:125 (124)	the creed of Abraham, a man of pure faith
4:125 (124)	And God took Abraham for a friend
4:163 (161)	and We revealed to Abraham, Ishmael
6:74 (74)	And when Abraham said to his father Azar
6:75 (75)	So We were showing Abraham the kingdom
6:83 (83)	Our argument, which We bestowed upon Abraham
6:161 (162)	the creed of Abraham, a man of pure faith

9:70 (71)	Thamood, the people of Abraham, the men of Midian
9:114 (115)	Abraham asked not pardon for his father
9:114 (115)	Abraham was compassionate, clement
11:69 (72)	Our messengers came to Abraham
11:74 (77)	So, when the awe departed from Abraham
11:75 (77)	Abraham was clement
11:76 (78)	O Abraham, turn away from this
12:6 (6)	He perfected it formerly on thy fathers Abraham and Isaac
12:38 (38)	the creed of my fathers, Abraham, Isaac and Jacob
14:35 (38)	Abraham said, 'My Lord, make this land secure
15:51 (51)	And tell them of the guests of Abraham
16:120 (121)	Surely, Abraham was a nation
16:123 (124)	the creed of Abraham, a man of pure faith
19:41 (42)	And mention in the Book Abraham
19:46 (47)	What, art thou shrinking from my gods, Abraham
19:58 (59)	and of the seed of Abraham and Israel
21:51 (52)	We gave Abraham aforetime his rectitude
21:60 (61)	and he was called Abraham
21:62 (63)	[art thou] who did this unto our gods, Abraham?
21:69 (69)	O fire, be coolness and safety for Abraham
22:26 (27)	We settled for Abraham the place of the House
22:43 (43)	and the people of Abraham
22:78 (77)	being the creed of your father Abraham
26:69 (69)	And recite to them the tiding of Abraham
29:16 (15)	And Abraham, when he said to his people
29:31 (30)	And when Our messengers came to Abraham
33:7 (7)	and from thee, and from Noah, and Abraham
37:83 (81)	Of his party was also Abraham
37:104 (104)	We called unto him, 'Abraham
37:109 (109)	Peace be upon Abraham
38:45 (45)	Remember also Our servants Abraham
42:13 (11)	that We charged Abraham with, Moses and Jesus
43:26 (25)	And when Abraham said to his father
51:24 (24)	the story of the honoured guests of Abraham
53:37 (38)	and Abraham, he who paid his debt in full
57:26 (26)	And We sent Noah, and Abraham
60:4 (4)	You have had a good example in Abraham
60:4 (4)	Except that Abraham said unto his father
87:19 (19)	the scrolls of Abraham and Moses

*A B W

AB n.m. (pl. *ābā'*)~father; (du) parents

2:133 (127)	We will serve thy God and the God of thy fathers
2:170 (165)	such things as we found our fathers doing
2:170 (165)	and if their fathers had no understanding
2:200 (196)	remember God, as you remember your fathers
4:11 (12)	to his parents to each one of the two the sixth
4:11 (12)	if he has no children, and his heirs are his parents
4:11 (12)	Your fathers and your sons
4:22 (26)	do not marry women that your fathers married
5:104 (103)	enough for us is what we found our fathers doing
5:104 (103)	even if their fathers had knowledge of naught
6:74 (74)	when Abraham said to his father Azar
6:87 (87)	and of their fathers, and of their seed

6:91 (91)	that you knew not, you and your fathers
6:148 (149)	we would not have been idolaters, neither our fathers
7:27 (26)	as he brought your parents out of the Garden
7:28 (27)	We found our fathers practising it
7:70 (68)	[that we may] forsake that our fathers served
7:71 (69)	you and your fathers
7:95 (93)	and happiness visited our fathers
7:173 (172)	Our fathers were idolaters
9:23 (23)	take not your fathers and brothers to be your friends
9:24 (24)	If your fathers, your sons, your brothers
9:114 (115)	Abraham asked not pardon for his father
10:78 (79)	turn us from that we found our fathers practising
11:62 (65)	to serve that our fathers served
11:87 (89)	that we should leave that our fathers served
11:109 (111)	they serve only as their fathers served before
12:4 (4)	When Joseph said to his father
12:4 (4)	Father, I saw eleven stars, and the sun and the moon
12:6 (6)	as He perfected it formerly on thy fathers
12:8 (8)	Joseph and his brother are dearer to our father than we
12:8 (8)	surely our father is in manifest error
12:9 (9)	that your father's face may be free for you
12:11 (11)	they said, 'Father, what ails thee
12:16 (16)	and they came to their father in the evening
12:17 (17)	they said, 'Father, we went running races
12:38 (38)	and I have followed the creed of my fathers
12:40 (40)	names yourselves have named, you and your fathers
12:59 (59)	a certain brother of yours from your father
12:61 (61)	We will solicit him of our father
12:63 (63)	So, when they had returned to their father
12:63 (63)	they said, 'Father, the measure was denied'
12:65 (65)	'Father,' they said, 'what more should we desire?'
12:68 (68)	after the manner their father commanded them
12:78 (78)	Mighty prince, he has a father
12:80 (80)	how your father has taken a solemn pledge
12:80 (80)	until my father gives me leave
12:81 (81)	Return you all to your father
12:81 (81)	Father, thy son stole
12:93 (93)	do you cast it on my father's face
12:94 (94)	when the caravan set forth, their father said
12:97 (98)	Our father, ask forgiveness
12:99 (100)	he took his father and mother into his arms
12:100 (101)	he lifted his father and mother upon the throne
12:100 (101)	'See, father,' he said
13:23 (23)	and those who were righteous of their fathers
14:10 (12)	to bar us from that our fathers served
16:35 (37)	we would not have served, apart from Him, anything, neither we nor our fathers
18:5 (4)	they have no knowledge of it, they nor their fathers
18:80 (79)	As for the lad, his parents were believers
18:82 (81)	Their father was a righteous man
19:28 (29)	thy father was not a wicked man
19:42 (43)	When he said to his father
19:42 (43)	Father, why worshippest thou that which neither hears nor sees
19:43 (44)	Father, there has come to me knowledge
19:44 (45)	Father, serve not Satan
19:45 (46)	Father, I fear that some chastisement from the All-merciful will smite thee

21:44 (45)	Ourselves gave these and their fathers enjoyment of days
21:52 (53)	when he said to his father and his people
21:53 (54)	We found our fathers serving them
21:54 (55)	and your fathers have been in manifest error
22:78 (77)	being the creed of your father Abraham
23:24 (24)	We never heard of this among our fathers, the ancients
23:68 (70)	that which came not upon their fathers, the ancients
23:83 (85)	We and our fathers have been promised this
24:31 (31)	or their fathers
24:31 (31)	or their husbands' fathers
24:61 (60)	eat of your houses, or your fathers' houses
25:18 (19)	Thou gavest them and their fathers enjoyment of days
26:26 (25)	and the Lord of your fathers, the ancients
26:70 (70)	when he said to his father and his people
26:74 (74)	but we found our fathers so doing
26:76 (76)	you and your fathers, the elders
26:86 (86)	forgive my father, for he is one of those astray
27:67 (69)	when we are dust, and our fathers
27:68 (70)	We have been promised this, and our fathers before
28:23 (23)	and our father is passing old
28:25 (25)	My father invites thee, that he may recompense thee
28:26 (26)	Said one of the two women, 'Father, hire him
28:36 (36)	we never heard of this among our fathers, the ancients
31:21 (20)	we will follow such things as we found our fathers doing
33:5 (5)	Call them after their true fathers
33:5 (5)	if you know not who their fathers were
33:40 (40)	Muhammad is not the father of any one of your men
33:55 (55)	no fault in the Prophet's wives touching their fathers
34:43 (42)	to bar you from that your fathers served
36:6 (5)	a people whose fathers were never warned
37:17 (17)	what, and our fathers, the ancients?
37:69 (67)	they found their fathers erring
37:85 (83)	when he said to his father and his folk
37:102 (102)	My father, do as thou art bidden
37:126 (126)	your Lord, and the Lord of your fathers
40:8 (8)	those who were righteous of their fathers
43:22 (21)	we found our fathers upon a community
43:23 (22)	indeed found our fathers upon a community
43:24 (23)	better guidance than you found your fathers upon
43:26 (25)	And when Abraham said to his father
43:29 (28)	Nay, but I gave these and their fathers
44:8 (7)	your Lord and the Lord of your fathers
44:36 (35)	bring us our fathers, if you speak truly
45:25 (24)	bring us our fathers, if you speak truly
53:23 (23)	names yourselves have named, and your fathers
56:48 (48)	what, and our fathers, the ancients?
58:22 (22)	though they were their fathers
60:4 (4)	except that Abraham said unto his father
80:35 (35)	his mother, his father

ABŪ LAHAB n.prop.~Abu Lahab (uncle of the Prophet)

111:1 (1)	Perish the hands of Abu Lahab, and perish he

*A B Y

ABÁ vb. (I)~to refuse

a) perf. act.

2:34 (32)	so they bowed themselves, save Iblis; he refused
15:31 (31)	save Iblis; he refused to be among those bowing
17:89 (91)	yet most men refuse all but unbelief
17:99 (101)	yet the unbelievers refuse all but unbelief
18:77 (76)	but they refused to receive them
20:56 (58)	but he cried lies, and refused
20:116 (115)	so they bowed themselves, save Iblis; he refused
25:50 (52)	yet most men refuse all but unbelief
33:72 (72)	but they refused to carry it

b) impf. act. (*ya'bá*)

2:282 (282)	let not any writer refuse to write it down
2:282 (282)	and let the witnesses not refuse
9:8 (8)	but in their hearts they refuse
9:32 (32)	and God refuses but to perfect His light

*A D D

IDD n.m. (adj)~hideous

19:89 (91)	You have indeed advanced something hideous

*A D M

ĀDAM n.prop.~Adam

2:31 (29)	And He taught Adam the names, all of them
2:33 (31)	Adam, tell them their names
2:34 (32)	bow yourselves to Adam
2:35 (33)	and We said, 'Adam, dwell thou, and thy wife
2:37 (35)	Thereafter Adam received certain words
3:33 (30)	God chose Adam and Noah
3:59 (52)	the likeness of Jesus, in God's sight, is as Adam's likeness
5:27 (30)	the story of the two sons of Adam
7:11 (10)	We said to the angels: 'Bow yourselves to Adam'
7:19 (18)	O Adam, dwell, thou and thy wife
7:26 (25)	Children of Adam! We have sent down on you
7:27 (26)	Children of Adam! Let not Satan tempt you
7:31 (29)	Children of Adam! Take your adornment
7:35 (33)	Children of Adam! If there should come to you
7:172 (171)	and when thy Lord took from the Children of Adam
17:61 (63)	We said to the angels, 'Bow yourselves to Adam'
17:70 (72)	We have honoured the Children of Adam
18:50 (48)	We said to the angels, 'Bow yourselves to Adam'
19:58 (59)	among the Prophets of the seed of Adam
20:115 (114)	And We made covenant with Adam before
20:116 (115)	We said to the angels, 'Bow yourselves to Adam'
20:117 (115)	Adam, surely this is an enemy to thee and thy wife
20:120 (118)	Adam, shall I point thee to
20:121 (119)	Adam disobeyed his Lord, and so he erred
36:60 (60)	Made I not covenant with you, Children of Adam

*A D Y

ADĀʾ n.m.~payment

2:178 (173) and let the payment be with kindliness

ADDÁ vb. (II)~to restore, to deliver

b) impf. act. (*yuʾaddī*)

2:283 (283) let him who is trusted deliver his trust
3:75 (68) he who, if thou trust him with a hundredweight, will restore it
3:75 (68) [he] will not restore it thee, unless ever thou standest over him
4:58 (61) God commands you to deliver trusts back to their owners

c) impv. (*addi*)

44:18 (17) Deliver to me God's servants

*A DH N

ADHINA vb. (I)~to allow, to give leave; to give ear, to take notice. (n.vb.) permission, leave

a) perf. act.

9:43 (43) God pardon thee! Why gavest thou them leave
10:59 (60) Has God given you leave
20:109 (108) him to whom the All-merciful gives leave
24:36 (36) in temples God has allowed to be raised up
34:23 (22) save for him to whom He gives leave
78:38 (38) him to whom the All-merciful has given leave
84:2 (2) and gives ear to its Lord, and is fitly disposed
84:5 (5) and gives ear to its Lord, and is fitly disposed

b) impf. act. (*yaʾdhanu*)

7:123 (120) You have believed in Him before I gave you leave
12:80 (80) until my father gives me leave
20:71 (74) have you believed him before I gave you leave?
26:49 (48) you have believed him before I gave you leave
42:21 (20) that for which God gave not leave
53:26 (27) that God gives leave to whomsoever He wills

c) impv. (*iʾdhan*)

2:279 (279) take notice that God shall war with you
9:49 (49) some of them there are that say, 'Give me leave
24:62 (62) give leave to whom thou wilt

d) perf. pass. (*udhina*)

22:39 (40) Leave is given to those who fight

e) impf. pass. (*yuʾdhanu*)

9:90 (91) [they] came with their excuses, that they may be given leave
16:84 (86) then to the unbelievers no leave shall be given
24:28 (28) enter it not until leave is given to you
33:53 (53) enter not the houses of the Prophet, except leave is given
77:36 (36) neither be given leave, and excuse themselves

f) n.vb. (*idhn*)

2:97 (91)	[he] brought it down upon thy heart by the leave of God
2:102 (96)	yet they did not hurt any man thereby, save by the leave of God
2:213 (209)	they were at variance, by His leave
2:221 (221)	and pardon, by His leave
2:249 (250)	How often a little company has overcome a numerous company, by God's leave
2:251 (252)	And they routed them, by the leave of God
2:255 (256)	who is there that shall intercede with Him save by His leave?
3:49 (43)	it will be a bird, by the leave of God
3:49 (43)	and bring to life the dead, by the leave of God
3:145 (139)	It is not given to any soul to die, save by the leave of God
3:152 (145)	when you blasted them by His leave
3:166 (160)	what visited you, the day the two hosts encountered, was by God's leave
4:25 (29)	So marry them, with their people's leave
4:64 (67)	that he should be obeyed, by the leave of God
5:16 (18)	and brings them forth from the shadows into the light by His leave
5:110 (110)	when thou createst out of clay, by My leave
5:110 (110)	and it is a bird, by My leave
5:110 (110)	and thou healest the blind and the leper by My leave
5:110 (110)	and thou bringest the dead forth by My leave
7:58 (56)	its vegetation comes forth by the leave of its Lord
8:66 (67)	they will overcome two thousand by the leave of God
10:3 (3)	Intercessor there is none, save after His leave
10:100 (100)	It is not for any soul to believe save by the leave of God
11:105 (107)	the day it comes, no soul shall speak save by His leave
13:38 (38)	it is not for any Messenger to bring a sign, but by God's leave
14:1 (1)	bring forth mankind from the shadows to the light by the leave of their Lord
14:11 (14)	save by the leave of God
14:23 (28)	therein dwelling forever, by the leave of their Lord
14:25 (30)	it gives its produce every season by the leave of its Lord
22:65 (64)	lest it should fall upon the earth, save by His leave
33:46 (45)	calling unto God by His leave
34:12 (11)	some worked before him by the leave of his Lord
35:32 (29)	and some are outstrippers in good works by the leave of God
40:78 (78)	it is not for any Messenger to bring a sign, save by God's leave
42:51 (51)	and he reveal whatsoever He will, by His leave
58:10 (11)	not hurt them anything, except by the leave of God
59:5 (5)	left standing upon their roots, that was by God's leave
64:11 (11)	No affliction befalls, except it be by the leave of God
97:4 (4)	in it the angels and the Spirit descend, by the leave of their Lord

ADHĀN n.m.~proclamation

9:3 (3)	A proclamation, from God and His Messenger

UDHUN n.f. (pl. *ādhān*)~ear

2:19 (18)	they put their fingers in their ears
4:119 (118)	they will cut off the cattle's ears
5:45 (49)	a nose for a nose, an ear for (an ear)
5:45 (49)	a nose for a nose, (an ear) for an ear
6:25 (25)	and in their ears heaviness
7:179 (178)	they have ears, but they hear not with them
7:195 (194)	or have they ears wherewith they give ear?
9:61 (61)	He is an ear
9:61 (61)	an ear of good for you

17:46 (48)	and in their ears heaviness
18:11 (10)	then We smote their ears many years in the Cave
18:57 (55)	and in their ears heaviness
22:46 (45)	[they have] ears to hear with
31:7 (6)	and in his ears were heaviness
41:5 (4)	and in our ears is a heaviness
41:44 (44)	in their ears is a heaviness
69:12 (12)	and for heeding ears to hold
71:7 (6)	they put their fingers in their ears

ADHDHANA vb. (II)~to proclaim. (pcple. act) a herald

a) perf. act.

7:44 (42)	And then a herald shall proclaim
12:70 (70)	Then a herald proclaimed

c) impv. (*adhdhin*)

22:27 (28)	and proclaim among men the Pilgrimage

g) pcple. act. (*mu'adhdhin*)

7:44 (42)	And then a herald shall proclaim
12:70 (70)	Then a herald proclaimed

ĀDHANA vb. (IV)~to proclaim to someone

a) perf. act.

21:109 (109)	I have proclaimed to you all equally
41:47 (47)	We proclaim to Thee, there is not a witness

TA'ADHDHANA vb. (V)~to proclaim, to cause to be proclaimed

a) perf. act.

7:167 (166)	And when thy Lord proclaimed He would send forth
14:7 (7)	And when your Lord proclaimed

ISTA'DHANA vb. (X)~to ask leave or permission

a) perf. act.

9:83 (84)	and they ask leave of thee to go forth
9:86 (87)	the affluent among them ask leave of thee, saying
24:59 (58)	as those before them asked leave
24:62 (62)	so, when they ask thy leave for some affair

b) impf. act. (*yasta'dhinu*)

9:44 (44)	Those who believe in God and the Last Day ask not leave of thee
9:45 (45)	They only ask leave of thee who believe not
9:93 (94)	The way is open only against those who ask leave of thee
24:58 (57)	those of you who have not reached puberty ask leave of you
24:59 (58)	when your children reach puberty, let them ask leave
24:62 (62)	go not away until they ask his leave
24:62 (62)	those who ask thy leave — those are they that believe in God
33:13 (13)	a part of them were asking leave of the Prophet

*A DH Y

ADHÁ n.m.~ailment, hurt, injury, molestation

2:196 (192)	[if any of you] has an ailment in his head
2:222 (222)	It is hurt, so let women alone
2:262 (264)	follow not up what they have expended with reproach and injury
2:263 (265)	a freewill offering followed by injury
2:264 (266)	void not your freewill offerings with reproach and injury
3:111 (107)	They will not harm you, except a little hurt
3:186 (183)	and from those who are idolaters, much hurt
4:102 (103)	if you suffer a molestation of rain, or you are sick
33:48 (47)	heed not their hurt

ĀDHÁ vb. (IV)~to hurt, to punish

a) perf. act.

14:12 (15)	We will surely endure patiently, whatever you hurt us
33:69 (69)	O believers, be not as those who hurt Moses

b) impf. act. (*yu'dhī*)

9:61 (61)	And some of them hurt the Prophet
9:61 (62)	Those who hurt God's Messenger — for them awaits a painful chastisement
33:53 (53)	that hurts the Prophet, and he is ashamed before you
33:53 (53)	It is not for you to hurt God's Messenger
33:57 (57)	Those who hurt God and His Messenger — them God has cursed
33:58 (58)	And those who hurt believing men and believing women
61:5 (5)	O my people, why do you hurt me

c) impv. (*ādhi*)

4:16 (20)	And when two of you commit indecency, punish them both

d) perf. pass. (*ūdhiya*)

3:195 (194)	those who suffered hurt in My way, and fought
6:34 (34)	they endured patiently that they were cried lies to, and were hurt
7:129 (126)	We have been hurt before thou camest to us
29:10 (9)	but when such a man is hurt in God's cause

e) impf. pass. (*yu'dhá*)

33:59 (59)	it is likelier they will be known, and not hurt

*A F F

AFFA vb. (I)~(n.vb.) fie!

f) n.vb. (*uff*)

17:23 (24)	say not to them 'Fie'
21:67 (67)	Fie upon you and that you serve apart from God
46:17 (16)	he who says to his father and his mother, 'Fie upon you!'

*A F K

AFAKA vb. (I)~to lie, to pervert

b) impf. act. (*ya'fiku*)

7:117 (114)	and lo, it forthwith swallowed up their lying invention
26:45 (44)	then Moses cast his staff and lo, it forthwith swallowed up their lying invention
46:22 (21)	hast thou come to pervert us from our gods?

d) perf. pass. (*ufika*)

51:9 (9)	and perverted therefrom are some

e) impf. pass. (*yu'faku*)

5:75 (79)	then behold, how they perverted are
6:95 (95)	so that then is God; then how are you perverted?
9:30 (30)	how they are perverted
10:34 (35)	so how are you perverted?
29:61 (61)	how then are they perverted?
30:55 (55)	they have not tarried above an hour; so they were perverted
35:3 (3)	how then are you perverted?
40:62 (64)	how then are you perverted?
40:63 (65)	even so perverted are they who deny the signs of God
43:87 (87)	how then are they perverted?
51:9 (9)	and perverted therefrom are some
63:4 (4)	God assail them! How they are perverted

AFFĀK n.m.~impostor

26:222 (222)	They come down on every guilty impostor
45:7 (6)	Woe to every guilty impostor

IFK n.m.~slander, calumny [Ar]; a lie [Ali, Pk]; fraud [Bl]

24:11 (11)	Those who came with the slander are a band of you
24:12 (12)	This is a manifest calumny
25:4 (5)	This is naught but a calumny he has forged
29:17 (16)	You only serve (...) idols and you create a calumny
34:43 (42)	This is nothing but a forged calumny
37:86 (84)	Is it a calumny, gods apart from God
37:151 (151)	Is it not of their own calumny
46:11 (10)	This is an old calumny
46:28 (27)	and that was their calumny

I'TAFAKA vb. (VIII)~(pcple. act.) subverted (city)

g) pcple. act. f. (*mu'tafikah*)

9:70 (71)	the men of Midian and the Subverted Cities
53:53 (54)	and the Subverted City He also overthrew
69:9 (9)	the people of Abraham, the men of Midian and the Subverted Cities

*A F L

AFALA vb. (I)~to set. (pcple. act.) setter

a) perf. act.

6:76 (76)	But when it set he said
6:77 (77)	But when it set he said
6:78 (78)	But when it set he said

g) pcple. act. (*āfil*)

6:76 (76)	I love not the setters

*A F Q

UFUQ n.m. (pl. *āfāq*)~horizon

41:53 (53)	We shall show them Our signs in the horizons
53:7 (7)	being on the higher horizon
81:23 (23)	he truly saw him on the clear horizon

*A H L

AHL (1) n.m. (coll)~people, family, folk, household, owner(s), inhabitant(s); (*ahl al-kitāb*) People of the Book

2:105 (99)	Those unbelievers of the People of the Book
2:109 (103)	many of the People of the Book wish they might restore you as unbelievers
2:196 (192)	him whose family are not present at the Holy Mosque
2:217 (214)	and to expel its people
3:64 (57)	People of the Book! Come now to a word common between us and you
3:65 (58)	People of the Book! Why do you dispute concerning Abraham?
3:69 (62)	there is a party of the People of the Book yearn to make you go astray
3:70 (63)	People of the Book! Why do you disbelieve in God's signs?
3:71 (64)	People of the Book! Why do you confound the truth with vanity?
3:72 (65)	there is a party of the People of the Book
3:75 (68)	And of the People of the Book is he who, if thou trust him with a hundredweight, will restore it
3:98 (93)	People of the Book, why do you disbelieve
3:99 (94)	People of the Book, why do you bar from God's way the believer
3:110 (106)	had the People of the Book believed, it were better for them
3:113 (109)	some of the People of the Book are a nation upstanding
3:121 (117)	When thou wentest forth at dawn from thy people
3:199 (198)	some there are of the People of the Book who believe in God
4:25 (29)	So marry them, with their people's leave
4:35 (39)	bring forth an arbiter from his people
4:35 (39)	and from her people an arbiter
4:58 (61)	God commands you to deliver trusts back to their owners
4:75 (77)	bring us forth from this city whose people are evildoers
4:92 (94)	and bloodwit is to be paid to his family
4:92 (94)	then bloodwit is to be paid to his family
4:123 (122)	It is not your fancies, nor the fancies of the People of the Book
4:153 (152)	The People of the Book will ask thee to bring down
4:159 (157)	There is not one of the People of the Book but will assuredly believe in him
4:171 (169)	People of the Book, go not beyond the bounds in your religion
5:15 (18)	People of the Book, now there has come to you Our Messenger
5:19 (22)	People of the Book, now there has come to you Our Messenger
5:47 (51)	let the People of the Gospel judge according to what God has sent down therein
5:59 (64)	People of the Book, do you blame us
5:65 (70)	but had the People of the Book believed
5:68 (72)	People of the Book, you do not stand on anything

5:77 (81)	People of the Book, go not beyond the bounds in your religion
5:89 (91)	the average of the food you serve to your families
6:131 (131)	while their inhabitants were heedless
7:83 (81)	So We delivered him and his family
7:94 (92)	but that We seized its people with misery
7:96 (94)	Yet had the peoples of the cities believed
7:97 (95)	Do the people of the cities feel secure
7:98 (96)	Do the people of the cities feel secure
7:100 (98)	those who inherit the earth after those who inhabited it
7:123 (120)	that you may expel its people from it
9:101 (102)	some of the people of the City are grown bold in hypocrisy
9:120 (121)	It is not for the people of the City
10:24 (25)	and its inhabitants think they have power over it
11:40 (42)	Embark in it two of every kind, and thy family
11:45 (47)	O my Lord, my son is of my family
11:46 (48)	Noah, he is not of thy family
11:73 (76)	His blessings be upon you, O people of the House
11:81 (83)	so set forth, thou with thy family
11:117 (119)	their people were putting things right
12:25 (25)	the recompense of him who purposes evil against thy folk
12:26 (26)	and a witness of her folk bore witness
12:62 (62)	when they have turned to their people
12:65 (65)	We shall get provision for our family
12:88 (88)	affliction has visited us and our people
12:93 (93)	then bring me your family all together
12:109 (109)	men We revealed to of the people living in the cities
15:65 (65)	So set forth, thou with thy family, in a watch of the night
15:67 (67)	And the people of the city came rejoicing
16:43 (45)	Question the people of the Remembrance
18:71 (70)	so as to drown the folk thereof
18:77 (76)	until, when they reached the people of a city
18:77 (76)	they asked the people for food
19:16 (16)	mention in the Book Mary when she withdrew from her people
19:55 (56)	He bade his people to pray
20:10 (9)	When he saw a fire, and said to his family
20:29 (30)	Appoint for me of my folk a familiar
20:40 (42)	Many years among the people of Midian thou didst sojourn
20:132 (132)	And bid thy family to pray
21:7 (7)	question the People of the Remembrance, if you do not know
21:76 (76)	[We] delivered him and his people from the great distress
21:84 (84)	We gave his people (...) mercy from Us
23:27 (28)	insert in it two of every kind and thy family
24:27 (27)	ask leave and salute the people thereof
26:169 (169)	My Lord, deliver me and my people
26:170 (170)	So We delivered him and his people
27:7 (7)	When Moses said to his people
27:34 (34)	and make the mighty ones of its inhabitants abased
27:49 (50)	We will attack him and his family
27:49 (50)	We were not witnesses of the destruction of his family
27:57 (58)	So We delivered him and his family
28:4 (3)	[he] had divided its inhabitants into sects
28:12 (11)	Shall I direct you to the people of a household
28:15 (14)	at a time when its people were unheeding
28:29 (29)	and [he] departed with his household
28:29 (29)	he said to his household, 'Tarry you here'

28:45 (45)	neither wast thou a dweller among the people of Midian
28:59 (59)	their inhabitants were evildoers
29:31 (30)	We shall destroy the people of this city
29:31 (30)	for its people are evildoers
29:32 (31)	We shall deliver him and his family
29:33 (32)	surely we shall deliver thee and thy family
29:34 (33)	We shall send down upon the people of this city wrath
29:46 (45)	Dispute not with the People of the Book
33:13 (13)	O people of Yathrib, there is no abiding here for you
33:26 (26)	He brought down those of the People of the Book
33:33 (33)	People of the House, God only desires to put away from you abomination
35:43 (41)	evil devising encompasses only the people who do it
36:50 (50)	nor will they return to their people
37:76 (74)	And We delivered him and his people
37:134 (134)	when We delivered him and his people
38:43 (42)	And We gave to him his family
38:64 (64)	the disputing of the inhabitants of the Fire
39:15 (17)	they who lose themselves and their families
42:45 (44)	they who lose themselves and their families
48:11 (11)	we were occupied by our possessions and our families
48:12 (12)	the believers would never return to their families
51:26 (26)	Then he turned to his household
52:26 (26)	we were before among our people, ever going in fear
57:29 (29)	that the People of the Book may know
59:2 (2)	the unbelievers among the People of the Book
59:7 (7)	God has given to His Messenger from the people of the cities
59:11 (11)	their brothers of the People of the Book
66:6 (6)	Believers, guard yourselves and your families
75:33 (33)	then he went to his household arrogantly
83:31 (31)	when they returned to their people they returned blithely
84:9 (9)	and he will return to his family joyfully
84:13 (13)	He once lived among his family joyfully
98:1 (1)	The unbelievers of the People of the Book
98:6 (5)	The unbelievers of the People of the Book
2:126 (120)	make this a land secure, and provide its people with fruits

AHL (2) n.m. (adj)~worthy

48:26 (26)	the word of godfearing to which they have better right and are worthy of
74:56 (55)	He is worthy to be feared
74:56 (55)	worthy to forgive

*A Ḥ D

AḤAD n.num. (f. *iḥdá*)~one; One (Divine attribute, in 112:1); any, anyone, any man; other

2:96 (90)	there is one of them wishes if he might be spared a thousand years
2:102 (96)	they taught not any man, without they said
2:102 (96)	yet they did not hurt any man thereby
2:136 (130)	we make no division between any of them
2:180 (176)	when any of you is visited by death
2:266 (268)	would any of you wish to have a garden of palms and vines
2:282 (282)	that if one of the two women errs
2:282 (282)	the other will remind her
2:285 (285)	we make no division between any one of His Messengers
3:73 (66)	that anyone should be given the like of what you have been given

3:84 (78)	we make no division between any of them
3:91 (85)	there shall not be accepted from any one of them
3:153 (147)	not twisting about for anyone
4:18 (22)	when one of them is visited by death
4:20 (24)	you have given to one a hundredweight
4:43 (46)	or if any of you comes from the privy
4:152 (151)	and make no division between any of them
5:6 (9)	or if any of you comes from the privy
5:20 (23)	such as He had not given to any being
5:27 (30)	it was accepted of one of them
5:106 (105)	when any of you is visited by death
5:115 (115)	a chastisement wherewith I chastise no other being
6:61 (61)	when any one of you is visited by death
7:80 (78)	you commit such indecency as never any being in all the world
8:7 (7)	when God promised you one of the two parties should be yours
9:4 (4)	neither lent support to any man against you
9:6 (6)	if any of the idolaters seeks of thee protection
9:52 (52)	aught to come to us but one of the two rewards most fair
9:84 (85)	pray thou never over any one of them when he is dead
9:127 (128)	does anyone see you?
11:81 (83)	let not any one of you turn round
12:36 (36)	Said one of them
12:41 (41)	as for one of you, he shall pour wine for his lord
12:78 (78)	so take one of us in his place
15:65 (65)	let not any one of you turn round
16:58 (60)	when any of them is given the good tidings of a girl, his face is darkened
16:76 (78)	two men, one of them dumb
17:23 (24)	you shall not serve any but Him
18:19 (18)	that they might question one another
18:19 (18)	let him be courteous, and apprise no man of you
18:22 (22)	ask not any of them for a pronouncement
18:26 (25)	He associates in His government no one
18:32 (31)	To one of them We assigned two gardens of vines
18:38 (36)	I will not associate with my Lord any one
18:42 (40)	would I had not associated with my Lord any one
18:47 (45)	so that We leave not so much as one of them behind
18:49 (47)	thy Lord shall not wrong anyone
18:110 (110)	[he does] not associate with his Lord's service anyone
19:26 (26)	if thou shouldst see any mortal
19:98 (98)	Dost thou perceive so much as one of them
23:99 (101)	till, when death comes to one of them, he says
24:6 (6)	the testimony of one of them shall be to testify by God four times
24:21 (21)	not one of you would have been pure ever
24:28 (28)	if you find not anyone therein, enter it not until leave is given
28:25 (25)	then came one of the two women to him
28:26 (26)	said one of the two women
28:27 (27)	I desire to marry thee to one of these my two daughters
29:28 (27)	you commit such indecency as never any being in all the world committed before you
33:32 (32)	Wives of the Prophet, you are not as other women
33:39 (39)	and [were] fearing not any one except Him
33:40 (40)	Muhammad is not the father of any one of your men
35:41 (39)	did they remove, none would hold them after Him
35:42 (40)	they would be more rightly guided than any one of the nations
38:35 (34)	give me a kingdom such as may not befall anyone after me

43:17 (16)	when any of them is given the good tidings
49:9 (9)	if one of them is insolent against the other, fight the insolent one
49:12 (12)	would any of you like to eat the flesh of his brother dead?
59:11 (11)	we will never obey anyone in regard to you
63:10 (10)	before that death comes upon one of you
69:47 (47)	and not one of you could have defended him
72:2 (2)	we will not associate with our Lord anyone
72:7 (7)	that God would never raise up anyone
72:18 (18)	so call not, along with God, upon anyone
72:20 (20)	and I do not associate with Him anyone
72:22 (22)	From God shall protect me not anyone
72:26 (26)	He discloses not His Unseen to anyone
74:35 (38)	surely it is one of the greatest things
89:25 (25)	Upon that day none shall chastise as He chastises
89:26 (26)	none shall bind as He binds
90:5 (5)	does he think none has power over him
90:7 (7)	what, does he think none has seen him?
92:19 (19)	and confers no favour on any man for recompense
112:1 (1)	say: 'He is God, One
112:4 (4)	and equal to Him is not any one

AḤADA ʿASHARA n.num.~eleven

12:4 (4)	Father, I saw eleven stars, and the sun and the moon

*A J J

UJĀJ n.m. (adj)~bitter

25:53 (55)	and this [is] salt, bitter to the tongue
35:12 (13)	and that is salt, bitter to the tongue
56:70 (69)	Did We will, We would make it bitter

*A J L

AJAL n.m.~a term

2:231 (231)	When you divorce women, and they have reached their term, then retain them honourably
2:232 (232)	When you divorce women, and they have reached their term, do not debar them from marrying
2:234 (234)	when they have reached their term then it is no fault in you what they may do
2:235 (236)	do not resolve on the knot of marriage until the book has reached its term
2:282 (282)	when you contract a debt one upon another for a stated term
2:282 (282)	And be not loth to write it down, whether it be small or great, with its term
4:77 (79)	why not defer us to a near term?
6:2 (2)	it is He who created you of clay, then determined a term
6:2 (2)	and a term is stated with Him
6:60 (60)	He raises you up therein, that a stated term may be determined
6:128 (128)	we have reached the term determined by Thee for us
7:34 (32)	to every nation a term
7:34 (32)	when their term comes they shall not put it back by a single hour
7:135 (131)	when We removed from them the wrath unto a term that they should come to
7:185 (184)	it may be their term is already nigh

10:11 (12)	as they would hasten good, their term would be already decided for them
10:49 (50)	to every nation a term
10:49 (50)	when their term comes they shall not put it back by a single hour
11:3 (3)	He will give you fair enjoyment unto a term stated
11:104 (106)	We shall not postpone it, save to a term reckoned
13:2 (2)	He subjected the sun and the moon, each one running to a term stated
13:38 (38)	Every term has a Book
14:10 (11)	that He may forgive you your sins, and defer you to a term stated
14:44 (45)	our Lord, defer us to a near term
15:5 (5)	and no nation outstrips its term
16:61 (63)	but He is deferring them to a term stated
16:61 (63)	when their term is come they shall not put it back by a single hour
17:99 (101)	He has appointed for them a term, no doubt of it
20:129 (129)	but for a word that preceded from thy Lord, and a stated term
22:5 (5)	and We establish in the wombs what We will, till a stated term
22:33 (34)	There are things therein profitable to you unto a stated term
23:43 (45)	no nation outstrips its term
28:28 (28)	Whichever of the two terms I fulfil
28:29 (29)	So when Moses had accomplished the term
29:5 (4)	Whoso looks to encounter God, God's term is coming
29:53 (53)	But for a stated term the chastisement would have come upon them
30:8 (7)	save with the truth and a stated term
31:29 (28)	He has subjected the sun and the moon, each of them running to a stated term
35:13 (14)	He has subjected the sun and the moon, each of them running to a stated term
35:45 (44)	but he is deferring them to a stated term
35:45 (45)	But when their term is come — surely God sees His servants
39:5 (7)	He has subjected the sun and the moon, each of them running to a stated term
39:42 (43)	but [He] looses the other till a stated term
40:67 (69)	and that you may reach a stated term
42:14 (13)	that preceded from thy Lord until a stated term
46:3 (2)	and what between them is, save with the truth and a stated term
63:10 (10)	Thou wouldst defer me unto a near term
63:11 (11)	But God will never defer any soul when its term comes
65:2 (2)	when they have reached their term, retain them honourably
65:4 (4)	their term is when they bring forth their burden
71:4 (4)	He will forgive you your sins, and defer you to a stated term
71:4 (4)	God's term, when it comes, cannot be deferred

AJL n.m.~sake; (*min ajl dhālik*) therefore

5:32 (35)	Therefore, We prescribed for the Children of Israel

AJJALA vb. (II)~to determine, to delay. (pcple. pass.) that which is appointed

a) perf. act.

6:128 (128)	we have reached the term which Thou hast determined

d) perf. pass. (*ujjila*)

77:12 (12)	to what day shall they be delayed?

h) pcple. pass. (*mu'ajjal*)

3:145 (139)	to die ... at an appointed time

*A J R

AJARA vb. (I)~to hire

b) impf. act. (*ya'juru*)

28:27 (27)	that thou hirest thyself to me for eight years

AJR n.m. (pl. *ujūr*)~wage [Ar]; reward [Ali, Pk]

2:62 (59)	their wage awaits them with their Lord
2:112 (106)	his wage is with his Lord
2:262 (264)	their wage is with their Lord
2:274 (275)	their wage awaits them with their Lord
2:277 (277)	their wage awaits them with their Lord
3:57 (50)	He will pay them in full their wages
3:136 (130)	how excellent is the wage of those who labour
3:171 (165)	God leaves not to waste the wage of the believers
3:172 (166)	[to] them who did good and feared God, shall be a mighty wage
3:179 (174)	there shall be for you a mighty wage
3:185 (182)	you shall surely be paid in full your wages
3:199 (199)	those — their wage is with their Lord
4:24 (28)	Such wives as you enjoy thereby, give them their wages apportionate
4:25 (29)	marry them, with their people's leave, and give them their wages honourably
4:40 (44)	He will double it, and give from Himself a mighty wage
4:67 (70)	We surely would have given them from Us a mighty wage
4:74 (76)	We shall bring him a mighty wage
4:95 (97)	for the bounty of a mighty wage
4:100 (101)	his wage shall have fallen on God
4:114 (114)	We shall surely give him a mighty wage
4:146 (145)	and God will certainly give the believers a mighty wage
4:152 (151)	those — We shall surely give them their wages
4:162 (160)	and the Last Day — them We shall surely give a mighty wage
4:173 (172)	He will pay them in full their wages
5:5 (7)	if you give them their wages, in wedlock
5:9 (12)	they shall have forgiveness and a mighty wage
6:90 (90)	I ask of you no wage for it
7:113 (110)	We shall surely have a wage
7:170 (169)	We leave not to waste the wage of those who set aright
8:28 (28)	that with God is a mighty wage
9:22 (22)	surely with God is a mighty wage
9:120 (121)	God leaves not to waste the wage of the good-doers
10:72 (73)	I have not asked you for any wage
10:72 (73)	my wage falls only on God
11:11 (14)	for them awaits forgiveness and a mighty wage
11:29 (31)	my wage falls only upon God
11:51 (53)	O my people, I do not ask of you a wage for this
11:51 (53)	my wage falls only upon Him who did originate me
11:115 (117)	God will not leave to waste the wage of the good-doers
12:56 (56)	We leave not to waste the wage of the good-doers
12:57 (57)	Yet is the wage of the world to come better
12:90 (90)	God leaves not to waste the wage of the good-doers
12:104 (104)	Thou askest of them no wage for it
16:41 (43)	and the wage of the world to come is greater
16:96 (98)	We shall recompense those who were patient their wage
16:97 (99)	We shall recompense them their wage

17:9 (10)	theirs shall be a great wage
18:2 (2)	theirs shall be a goodly wage
18:30 (29)	We leave not to waste the wage of him who does good works
18:77 (76)	thou couldst have taken a wage for that
25:57 (59)	I do not ask of you a wage for this
26:41 (40)	shall we indeed have a wage, if we should be the victors?
26:109 (109)	I ask of you no wage for this
26:109 (109)	my wage falls only upon the Lord of all Being
26:127 (127)	I ask of you no wage for this
26:127 (127)	my wage falls only upon the Lord of all Being
26:145 (145)	I ask of you no wage for this
26:145 (145)	my wage falls only upon the Lord of all Being
26:164 (164)	I ask of you no wage for this
26:164 (164)	my wage falls only upon the Lord of all Being
26:180 (180)	I ask of you no wage for this
26:180 (180)	my wage falls only upon the Lord of all Being
28:25 (25)	that he may recompense thee with the wage of thy drawing water for us
28:54 (54)	These shall be given their wage twice over
29:27 (26)	We gave him his wage in this world
29:58 (58)	and excellent is the wage of those who labour
33:29 (29)	for those amongst you such as do good a mighty wage
33:31 (31)	We shall pay her her wage twice over
33:35 (35)	for them God has prepared forgiveness and a mighty wage
33:44 (43)	He has prepared for them a generous wage
33:50 (49)	We have made lawful for thee thy wives whom thou hast given their wages
34:47 (46)	I have asked no wage of you
34:47 (46)	My wage falls only upon God
35:7 (8)	theirs shall be forgiveness and a great wage
35:30 (27)	that He may pay them in full their wages
36:11 (10)	give him the good tidings of forgiveness and a generous wage
36:21 (20)	Follow such as ask no wage of you
38:86 (86)	I ask of you no wage for it
39:10 (13)	the patient will be paid their wages in full
39:35 (36)	and recompense them with the wages of the fairest of what they were doing
39:74 (74)	How excellent is the wage of those that labour
41:8 (7)	those who believe, and do righteous deeds shall have a wage unfailing
42:23 (22)	I do not ask of you a wage for this
42:40 (38)	whoso pardons and puts things right, his wage falls upon God
47:36 (38)	He will give you your wages
48:10 (10)	God will give him a mighty wage
48:16 (16)	If you obey, God will give you a goodly wage
48:29 (29)	(He promised) forgiveness and a mighty wage
49:3 (3)	they shall have forgiveness and a mighty wage
52:40 (40)	Or askest thou them for a wage
57:7 (7)	those of you who believe and expend shall have a mighty wage
57:11 (11)	his shall be a generous wage
57:18 (17)	theirs shall be a generous wage
57:19 (18)	they have their wage, and their light
57:27 (27)	We gave those of them who believed their wage
60:10 (10)	to marry them when you have given them their wages
64:15 (15)	and with God is a mighty wage
65:5 (5)	and He will give him a mighty wage
65:6 (6)	If they suckle for you, give them their wages
67:12 (12)	there awaits them forgiveness and a great wage
68:3 (3)	Surely thou shalt have a wage unfailing

68:46 (46)	Or askest thou them for a wage
73:20 (20)	you shall find it with God as better, and mightier a wage
84:25 (25)	theirs shall be a wage unfailing
95:6 (6)	they shall have a wage unfailing

ISTA'JARA vb. (X)~to hire

a) perf. act.

28:26 (26)	the best man thou canst hire is the one strong and trusty

c) impv. (*ista'jir*)

28:26 (26)	Said one of the two women, 'Father, hire him'

*A K L

AKALA vb. (I)~to eat, to devour, to consume. (n.vb.) consuming, consumption, eating. (pcple. act.) one who eats. (pcple.pass.) eaten, devoured, consumed

a) perf. act.

5:3 (4)	and that devoured by beasts of prey
5:66 (70)	they would have eaten both what was above them
12:14 (14)	if the wolf eats him, and we a band, then we are losers
12:17 (17)	so the wolf ate him
20:121 (119)	So the two of them ate of it

b) impf. act. (*ya'kulu*)

2:174 (169)	they shall eat naught but the Fire in their bellies
2:188 (184)	Consume not your goods between you in vanity
2:188 (184)	that you may sinfully consume a portion of other men's goods
2:275 (276)	Those who devour usury shall not rise again
3:49 (43)	I will inform you too of what things you eat
3:130 (125)	O believers, devour not usury
3:183 (179)	until he brings to us a sacrifice devoured by fire
4:2 (2)	and devour not their property with your property
4:6 (5)	consume it not wastefully and hastily
4:6 (6)	if poor, let him consume in reason
4:10 (11)	Those who devour the property of orphans
4:10 (11)	devour Fire in their bellies
4:29 (33)	consume not your goods between you in vanity
5:75 (79)	they both ate food
5:113 (113)	we desire that we should eat of it
6:119 (119)	that you do not eat of that over which God's Name has been mentioned
6:121 (121)	eat not of that over which God's Name has not been mentioned
7:73 (71)	that she may eat in God's earth
9:34 (34)	many of the rabbis and monks indeed consume the goods of the people in vanity
10:24 (25)	the plants of the earth mingle with it whereof men and cattle eat
11:64 (67)	leave her that she may eat in God's earth
12:13 (13)	I fear the wolf may eat him
12:36 (36)	bread, that birds were eating of
12:41 (41)	he shall be crucified, and birds will eat of his head
12:43 (43)	seven fat kine, and seven lean ones devouring them
12:46 (46)	seven fat kine, that seven lean ones were devouring

12:47 (47)	leave [it] in the ear, excepting a little whereof you eat
12:48 (48)	seven hard years, that shall devour what you have laid up for them, all but a little
15:3 (3)	leave them to eat, and to take their joy
16:5 (5)	in them is warmth, and uses various, and of them you eat
16:14 (14)	It is He who subjected to you the sea, that you may eat of it
21:8 (8)	nor did We fashion them as bodies that ate not food
23:19 (19)	wherein are many fruits for you, and of them you eat
23:21 (21)	and many uses there are in them for you, and of them you eat
23:33 (34)	a mortal like yourselves, who eats
23:33 (34)	of what you eat
24:61 (60)	that you eat of your houses
24:61 (60)	that you eat all together, or in groups
25:7 (8)	what ails this Messenger that he eats food
25:8 (9)	why has he not a Garden to eat of?
25:20 (22)	We sent not before thee any Envoys, but that they ate food
32:27 (27)	whereof their cattle and themselves eat
34:14 (13)	but the Beast of the Earth devouring his staff
35:12 (13)	yet of both you eat fresh flesh
36:33 (33)	and brought forth from it grain, whereof they eat
36:35 (35)	that they might eat of its fruits
36:72 (72)	and some they eat
37:91 (89)	what do you eat?
40:79 (79)	and of some you eat
43:73 (73)	therein you have abundant fruits, whereof you may eat
47:12 (13)	they take their enjoyment and eat
47:12 (13)	as cattle eat
49:12 (12)	would any of you like to eat the flesh of his brother dead?
51:27 (27)	will you not eat?
69:37 (37)	none excepting the sinners eat
89:19 (20)	and you devour the inheritance greedily

c) impv. (*kul*)

2:35 (33)	dwell thou, and thy wife, in the Garden, and eat thereof easefully
2:57 (54)	Eat of the good things wherewith We have provided you
2:58 (55)	and eat easefully of it wherever you will
2:60 (57)	Eat and drink of God's providing
2:168 (163)	O men, eat of what is in the earth
2:172 (167)	eat of the good things wherewith We have provided you
2:187 (183)	eat and drink, until the white thread shows clearly
4:4 (3)	if they are pleased to offer you any of it, consume it
5:4 (6)	eat what they seize for you
5:88 (90)	Eat of what God has provided you
6:118 (118)	Eat of that over which God's Name has been mentioned
6:141 (142)	Eat of their fruits when they fructify
6:142 (143)	eat of what God has provided you
7:19 (18)	and eat of where you will
7:31 (29)	and eat and drink, but be you not prodigal
7:160 (160)	Eat of the good things wherewith We have supplied you
7:161 (161)	and eat of it wherever you will
8:69 (70)	Eat of what you have taken as booty
16:69 (71)	Then eat of all manner of fruit
16:114 (115)	So eat of what God has provided you
19:26 (26)	Eat therefore, and drink
20:54 (56)	Do you eat, and pasture your cattle

20:81 (83)	Eat of the good things wherewith We have provided you
22:28 (29)	So eat thereof, and feed the wretched poor
22:36 (37)	when their flanks collapse, eat of them
23:51 (53)	O Messengers, eat of the good things
34:15 (14)	Eat of your Lord's provision, and give thanks
52:19 (19)	Eat and drink, with wholesome appetite
67:15 (15)	walk in its tracts, and eat of His provision
69:24 (24)	Eat and drink with wholesome appetite
77:43 (43)	Eat and drink, with wholesome appetite
77:46 (46)	Eat and take your joy a little

f) n.vb. (*akl*)

4:161 (159)	and consuming the wealth of the people in vanity
5:62 (67)	and how they consume the unlawful
5:63 (68)	not forbid them to utter sin, and consume the unlawful
89:19 (20)	and your consuming theinheritance <greedily>

g) pcple. act. (*ākil*)

23:20 (20)	bears oil and seasoning for all to eat
37:66 (64)	and they eat of it
56:52 (52)	you shall eat of a tree called Zakkoum

h) pcple. pass. (*ma'kūl*)

105:5 (5)	and He made them like green blades devoured

AKKĀL n.m. (adj)~greedy, consumer

5:42 (46)	who listen to falsehood, and consume the unlawful

UKUL n.m.~produce

2:265 (267)	and it yields its produce twofold
6:141 (142)	palm-trees, and crops diverse in produce
13:4 (4)	some of them We prefer in produce above others
13:35 (35)	its produce is eternal, and its shade
14:25 (30)	it gives its produce every season
18:33 (31)	each of the two gardens yielded its produce
34:16 (15)	two gardens bearing bitter produce

*A KH DH

AKHADHA vb. (I)~to take, to seize, to lay hold of. (n.vb.) taking, seizing. (pcple. act.) taking, one who takes

a) perf. act.

2:55 (52)	the thunderbolt took you while you were beholding
2:63 (60)	And when We took compact with you
2:83 (77)	And when We took compact with the Children of Israel
2:84 (78)	And when We took compact with you: 'You shall not
2:93 (87)	And when We took compact with you
2:206 (202)	vainglory seizes him in his sin
3:11 (9)	God seized them because of their sins
3:81 (75)	God took compact with the Prophets
3:81 (75)	and do you take My load on you on that condition?
3:187 (184)	God took compact with those who had been given the Book

4:21 (25)	they have taken from you a solemn compact
4:153 (152)	the thunderbolt took them for their evildoing
4:154 (153)	We took from them a solemn compact
5:12 (15)	God took compact with the Children of Israel
5:14 (17)	with those who say 'We are Christians' We took compact
5:70 (74)	We took compact with the Children of Israel
6:42 (42)	and We seized them with misery and hardship
6:44 (44)	We seized them suddenly
6:46 (46)	if God seizes your hearing and sight
7:78 (76)	so the earthquake seized them
7:91 (89)	So the earthquake seized them
7:94 (92)	but that We seized its people with misery
7:95 (93)	So We seized them suddenly, unawares
7:96 (94)	We seized them for what they earned
7:130 (127)	Then seized We Pharaoh's people with years of dearth
7:150 (149)	[he] laid hold of his brother's head
7:154 (153)	when Moses' anger abated in him, he took the Tablets
7:155 (154)	when the earthquake seized them, he said
7:165 (165)	We seized the evildoers with evil chastisement
7:172 (171)	when thy Lord took from the Children of Adam, from their loins, their seed
8:52 (54)	God seized them because of their sins
8:68 (69)	there had afflicted you, for what you took, a mighty chastisement
9:50 (50)	we took our dispositions before
10:24 (25)	till, when the earth has taken on its glitter
11:67 (70)	And the Cry seized the evildoers
11:94 (97)	and the Cry seized the evildoers
11:102 (104)	when He seizes the cities that are evildoing
12:80 (80)	your father has taken a solemn pledge from you by God
13:32 (32)	I seized them — and how was my retribution?
15:73 (73)	and the Cry seized them at the sunrise
15:83 (83)	and the Cry seized them in the morning
16:113 (114)	the chastisement seized them
22:44 (43)	then I seized them; and how was My horror
22:48 (47)	I seized it, and to Me was the homecoming
23:41 (43)	And the Cry seized them justly
23:64 (66)	We seize with the chastisement the ones of them that live at ease
23:76 (78)	We already seized them with the chastisement
26:158 (158)	and the chastisement seized them
26:189 (189)	there seized them the chastisement of the Day of Shadow
28:40 (40)	Therefore We seized him and his hosts
29:14 (13)	the Flood seized them, while they were evildoers
29:37 (36)	so the earthquake seized them
29:40 (39)	Each We seized for his sin
29:40 (39)	and the Cry seized some of them
33:7 (7)	And when We took compact from the Prophets
33:7 (7)	We took from them a solemn compact
35:26 (24)	then I seized the unbelievers
40:5 (5)	Then I seized them; and how was My retribution
40:21 (22)	God seized them in their sins
40:22 (23)	so God seized them
41:17 (16)	the thunderbolt of the chastisement of humiliation seized them
43:48 (47)	and We seized them with chastisement
51:40 (40)	So We seized him and his hosts
51:44 (44)	and the thunderbolt took them
54:42 (42)	so We seized them with the seizing of One mighty

57:8 (8)	He has taken compact with you
69:10 (10)	He seized them with a surpassing grip
69:45 (45)	We would have seized him by the right hand
73:16 (16)	so We seized him remorselessly
79:25 (25)	God seized him with the chastisement of the Last World

b) impf. act. (*ya'khudhu*)

2:229 (229)	it is not lawful for you to take of what you have given them
2:255 (256)	Slumber seizes Him not, neither sleep
4:20 (24)	[if] you have given to one a hundredweight, take of it nothing
4:20 (24)	What, will you take it by way of calumny
4:21 (25)	How shall you take it, when each of you
4:102 (103)	and let them take their weapons
4:102 (103)	come and pray with thee, taking their precautions
7:73 (71)	lest a painful chastisement should seize you
7:145 (142)	command thy people to take the fairest of it
7:169 (168)	who inherited the Book, taking the chance goods of this lower world
7:169 (168)	if chance goods the like of them come to them, they will take them
9:104 (105)	[God] takes the freewill offerings
11:64 (67)	lest a nigh chastisement should seize you
12:76 (76)	he could not have taken his brother
12:79 (79)	God forbid that we should take any other
16:46 (48)	He will not seize them in their going to and fro
16:47 (49)	that He will not seize them, little by little
18:79 (78)	there was a king who was seizing every ship by brutal force
20:39 (39)	an enemy of Mine and his shall take him
20:94 (95)	take me not by the beard, or the head
24:2 (2)	in the matter of God's religion let no tenderness for them seize you
26:156 (156)	there seize you the chastisement of a dreadful day
36:49 (49)	they are awaiting only for one Cry to seize them
40:5 (5)	every nation purposed against their Messenger to seize him
48:15 (15)	when you set forth after spoils, to take them
48:19 (19)	and many spoils to take
48:20 (20)	God has promised you many spoils to take

c) impv. (*khudh*)

2:63 (60)	take forcefully what We have given you
2:93 (87)	take forcefully what We have given you
2:260 (262)	take four birds, and twist them to thee
4:71 (73)	O believers, take your precautions
4:89 (91)	take them, and slay them wherever you find them
4:91 (93)	restrain their hands, take them, and slay them
4:102 (103)	lay aside your weapons; but take your precautions
5:41 (45)	if you are given this, then take it
7:31 (29)	take your adornment at every place of worship
7:144 (141)	take what I have given thee
7:145 (142)	so take it forcefully
7:171 (170)	take forcefully what We have given you
7:199 (198)	Take the abundance, and bid to what is honourable
9:5 (5)	and take them, and confine them
9:103 (104)	Take of their wealth a freewill offering
12:78 (78)	take one of us in his place
19:12 (13)	O John, take the Book forcefully
20:21 (22)	Said He, 'Take it, and fear not

38:44 (43)	take in thy hand a bundle of rushes
44:47 (47)	take him, and thrust him into the midst of Hell
59:7 (7)	Whatever the Messenger gives you, take
69:30 (30)	Take him, and fetter him

d) perf. pass. (*ukhidha*)

8:70 (71)	He will give you better than what has been taken from you
33:61 (61)	wheresoever they are come upon they shall be seized
34:51 (50)	they are seized from a place near at hand

e) impf. pass. (*yu'khadhu*)

2:48 (45)	nor [shall] any counterpoise be taken
6:70 (69)	it shall not be taken from it
7:169 (168)	has not the compact of the Book been taken
55:41 (41)	they shall be seized by their forelocks and their feet
57:15 (14)	no ransom shall be taken from you

f) n.vb. (*akhdh*)

4:161 (159)	and for their taking usury, that they were prohibited
11:102 (104)	such is the seizing of thy Lord
11:102 (104)	surely His seizing is painful, terrible
54:42 (42)	We seized them with the seizing of One mighty
69:10 (10)	and He seized them <with a surpassing grip>
73:16 (16)	so We seized him <remorselessly>

g) pcple. act. (*ākhidh*)

2:267 (270)	you would never take it yourselves
11:56 (59)	there is no creature that crawls, but He takes it by the forelock
51:16 (16)	taking whatsoever their Lord has given them

ĀKHADHA vb. (III)~to take to task

b) impf. act. (*yu'ākhidhu*)

2:225 (225)	God will not take you to task for a slip in your oaths
2:225 (225)	He will take you to task for what your hearts have earned
2:286 (286)	Our Lord, take us not to task if we forget
5:89 (91)	God will not take you to task for a slip in your oaths
5:89 (91)	but He will take you to task for such bonds as you have made by oaths
16:61 (63)	If God should take men to task for their evildoing
18:58 (57)	if He should take them to task for that they have earned
18:73 (72)	do not take me to task that I forgot
35:45 (44)	If God should take men to task for what they have earned

ITTAKHADHA vb. (VIII)~to take (to one's self), to take as, to take for. (n.vb.) taking to oneself. (pcple. act.) one who takes to oneself

a) perf. act.

2:51 (48)	then you took to yourselves the Calf after him
2:80 (74)	have you taken with God a covenant?
2:92 (86)	then you took to yourselves the Calf after him
2:116 (110)	they say, 'God has taken to Him a son'
4:125 (124)	and God took Abraham for a friend

4:153 (152)	then they took to themselves the Calf
5:57 (62)	the unbelievers, who take your religion in mockery and as a sport
5:58 (63)	when you call to prayer, [they] take it in mockery and as a sport
5:81 (84)	they would not have taken them as friends
6:70 (69)	Leave alone those who take their religion for a sport and a diversion
7:30 (28)	they have taken Satans for friends instead of God
7:51 (49)	who have taken their religion as a diversion and a sport
7:148 (146)	the people of Moses took to them, after him, of their ornaments a Calf
7:148 (147)	yet they took it to them, and were evildoers
7:152 (151)	those who took to themselves the Calf — anger shall overtake them
9:31 (31)	they have taken their rabbis and their monks as lords
9:107 (108)	and those who have taken a mosque in opposition
10:68 (69)	they say, 'God has taken to Him a son'
11:92 (94)	have you taken Him as something to be thrust behind you?
13:16 (17)	then have you taken unto you others beside Him
17:40 (42)	[has He] taken to Himself from the angels females?
17:73 (75)	they would surely have taken thee as a friend
18:4 (3)	to warn those who say, 'God has taken to Himself a son'
18:15 (14)	these our people have taken to them other gods, apart from Him
18:56 (54)	they have taken My signs, and what they are warned of, in mockery
18:61 (60)	they forgot their fish, and it took its way into the sea, burrowing
18:63 (62)	it took its way into the sea in a manner marvellous
18:77 (76)	thou couldst have taken a wage for that
18:106 (106)	they were unbelievers and took My signs and My messengers in mockery
19:17 (17)	and she took a veil apart from them
19:78 (81)	[has he] taken a covenant with the All-merciful?
19:81 (84)	they have taken to them other gods apart from God
19:87 (90)	those who have taken with the All-merciful covenant
19:88 (91)	the All-merciful has taken unto Himself a son
21:17 (17)	We would have taken it to Us from Ourselves
21:21 (21)	or have they taken gods out of the earth
21:24 (24)	or have they taken gods apart from Him?
21:26 (26)	the All-merciful has taken to Him a son
23:91 (93)	God has not taken to Himself any son
23:110 (112)	but you took them for a laughing-stock
25:3 (3)	yet they have taken to them gods, apart from Him
25:27 (29)	would that I had taken a way along with the Messenger
25:30 (32)	my people have taken this Koran as a thing to be shunned
25:43 (45)	hast thou seen him who has taken his caprice to be his god?
26:29 (28)	if thou takest a god other than me
29:25 (24)	you have only taken to yourselves idols, apart from God
29:41 (40)	those who have taken to them protectors, apart from God
29:41 (40)	the spider that takes to itself a house
36:74 (74)	yet they have taken, apart from God, gods
38:63 (63)	did we take them for a laughing-stock?
39:3 (4)	and those who take protectors, apart from Him
39:43 (44)	or have they taken intercessors apart from God?
42:6 (4)	those who have taken to them protectors apart from Him
42:9 (7)	have they taken to them protectors apart from Him?
43:16 (15)	or has He taken to Himself, from that He creates, daughters
45:9 (8)	when he knows anything of Our signs, he takes them in mockery
45:10 (9)	nor those they took as protectors, apart from God
45:23 (22)	ast thou seen him who has taken his caprice to be his god
45:35 (34)	that is for that you took God's signs in mockery
46:28 (27)	they had taken to themselves as mediators, gods apart from God

58:16 (17)	they have taken their oaths as a covering
63:2 (2)	they have taken their oaths as a covering
72:3 (3)	He — exalted be our Lord's majesty! — has not taken to Himself either consort or a son
73:19 (19)	let him who will take unto his Lord a way
76:29 (29)	he who will, takes unto his Lord a way
78:39 (39)	whosoever wills takes unto his Lord a resort

b) impf. act. (*yattakhidhu*)

2:67 (63)	dost thou take us in mockery?
2:165 (160)	men who take to themselves compeers apart from God
2:231 (231)	take not God's signs in mockery
3:28 (27)	Let not the believers take the unbelievers for friends
3:64 (57)	some of us take others as Lords, apart from God
3:80 (74)	He would never order you to take the angels and the Prophets as Lords
3:118 (114)	O believers, take not for your intimates outside yourselves
3:140 (134)	that He may take witnesses from among you
4:89 (91)	take not to yourselves friends of them
4:89 (91)	take not to yourselves any one of them as friend or helper
4:118 (118)	I will take unto myself a portion
4:119 (118)	Whoso takes Satan to him for a friend, instead of God, has surely suffered
4:139 (138)	Those who take unbelievers for their friends
4:144 (143)	O believers, take not the unbelievers as friends instead of the believers
4:150 (149)	desiring to take between this and that a way
5:51 (56)	O believers, take not Jews and Christians as friends
5:57 (62)	O believers, take not as your friends those of them who were given the Book before you
6:14 (14)	shall I take to myself as protector other than God
6:74 (74)	takest thou idols for gods?
7:74 (72)	taking to yourselves castles of its plains
7:146 (143)	they will not take it for a way
7:146 (143)	they see the way of error, they will take it for a way
9:16 (16)	[have] taken not — apart from God and His Messenger and the believers
9:23 (23)	O believers, take not your fathers and brothers to be your friends
9:98 (99)	Some of the Bedouins take what they expend for a fine
9:99 (100)	[they] take what they expend for offerings
12:21 (21)	or we may take him for our own son
16:51 (53)	Take not to you two gods
16:67 (69)	of the fruits of the palms and the vines, you take therefrom an intoxicant
16:92 (94)	by taking your oaths as mere mutual deceit
16:94 (96)	Take not your oaths as mere mutual deceit
17:2 (2)	Take not unto yourselves any guardian apart from Me
17:111 (111)	Praise belongs to God, who has not taken to Him a son
18:21 (20)	We will raise over them a place of worship
18:50 (48)	do you take him and his seed to be your friends, apart from Me
18:86 (85)	or thou shalt take towards them a way of kindness
18:102 (102)	that they may take My servants as friends, apart from Me
19:35 (36)	it is not for God to take a son
19:92 (93)	it behoves not the All-merciful to take a son
21:17 (17)	had We desired to take to Us a diversion
21:36 (37)	when the unbelievers behold thee, they take thee only for mockery
25:2 (2)	He has not taken to Him a son
25:18 (19)	it did not behove us to take unto ourselves protectors apart from Thee
25:28 (30)	would that I had not taken So-and-so for a friend
25:41 (43)	when they see thee, they take thee in mockery only

25:57 (59)	except for him who wishes to take to his Lord a way
26:129 (129)	do you take to you castles, haply to dwell forever?
28:9 (8)	or we will take him for a son
31:6 (5)	and to take it in mockery
36:23 (22)	shall I take, apart from Him, gods
39:4 (6)	Had God desired to take to Him a son
43:32 (31)	some of them may take others in servitude
60:1 (1)	O believers, take not My enemy and your enemy for friends

c) impv. (*ittakhidh*)

2:125 (119)	Take to yourselves Abraham's station for a place of prayer
5:116 (116)	"Take me and my mother as gods, apart from God"
16:68 (70)	Take unto yourselves, of the mountains, houses
35:6 (6)	take him for an enemy
73:9 (9)	so take Him for a Guardian

f) n.vb. (*ittikhādh*)

2:54 (51)	you have done wrong against yourselves by your taking the Calf

g) pcple. act. (*muttakhidh*)

4:25 (29)	as women in wedlock, not as in licence or taking lovers
5:5 (7)	in wedlock and not in licence, or as taking lovers
18:51 (49)	I would not ever take those who lead others astray to be My supporters

*A KH R

ĀKHAR n.m. (adj., f. *ukhrá*)~other, another, last, second

2:184 (180)	then a number of other days
2:185 (181)	then a number of other days
2:282 (282)	the other will remind her
3:7 (5)	verses clear that are the Essence of the Book, and others ambiguous
3:13 (11)	one company fighting in the way of God and another unbelieving
4:91 (93)	you will find others desiring to be secure
4:102 (103)	let another party who have not prayed come and pray with thee
4:133 (132)	He can put you away, O men, and bring others
5:27 (30)	accepted of one of them, and not accepted of the other
5:41 (45)	who listen to falsehood, listen to other folk
5:106 (105)	two men of equity among you; or two others
5:107 (106)	then two others shall stand in their place
6:6 (6)	[We] raised up after them another generation
6:19 (19)	that there are other gods with God
6:133 (133)	from the seed of another people
6:164 (164)	no soul laden bears the load of another
7:38 (36)	the last of them shall say to the first of them
7:39 (37)	the first of them shall say to the last of them
8:60 (62)	and others besides them that you know not
9:102 (103)	and others have confessed their sins
9:102 (103)	they have mixed a righteous deed with another evil
9:106 (107)	and others are deferred to God's commandment
12:36 (36)	Said the other, 'I dreamed that I was carrying on my head
12:41 (41)	as for the other, he shall be crucified
12:43 (43)	seven green ears of corn, and seven [others] withered
12:46 (46)	seven green ears of corn, and seven [others] withered

15:96 (96)	those who set up with God another god
17:15 (16)	no soul laden bears the load of another
17:22 (23)	Set not up with God another god
17:39 (41)	set not up with God another god
17:69 (71)	He will not send you back into it a second time
20:18 (19)	other uses also I find in it
20:22 (23)	That is a second sign
20:37 (37)	already another time We favoured thee
20:55 (57)	and bring you forth from it a second time
21:11 (11)	[We have] set up after it another people
23:14 (14)	thereafter We produced him as another creature
23:31 (32)	Thereafter, after them, We produced another generation
23:42 (44)	Thereafter, after them, We produced other generations
23:117 (117)	whosoever calls upon another god with God
25:4 (5)	and other folk helped him to it
25:68 (68)	who call not upon another god with God
26:64 (64)	and there We brought the others on
26:66 (66)	then We drowned the others
26:172 (172)	then We destroyed the others
26:213 (213)	so call thou not upon another god
28:88 (88)	and call not upon another god with God
35:18 (19)	no soul laden bears the load of another
37:82 (80)	then afterwards We drowned the rest
37:136 (136)	then We destroyed the others
38:38 (37)	and others also, coupled in fetters
38:58 (58)	and other torments of the like kind
39:7 (9)	no soul laden bears the load of another
39:42 (43)	but looses the other till a stated term
39:68 (68)	then it shall be blown again
44:28 (27)	We bequeathed them upon another people
48:21 (21)	and other spoils you were not able to take
49:9 (9)	if one of them is insolent against the other, fight the insolent one
50:26 (25)	who set up with God another god
51:51 (51)	and set not up with God another god
53:13 (13)	indeed, he saw him another time
53:20 (20)	and Manat the third, the other
53:38 (39)	no soul laden bears the load of another
53:47 (48)	upon Him rests the second growth
61:13 (13)	and other things you love
62:3 (3)	and others of them who have not yet joined them
65:6 (6)	another woman shall suckle for him
73:20 (20)	and others journeying in the land
73:20 (20)	and others fighting in the way of God

ĀKHIR n.m. (adj., f. *ākhirah*; see also *ākhirah*, below)~last; Last (Divine attribute); end, late(r); (*al-yawm al-ākhir*) the Last Day; (*al-dār al-ākhirah*) the Last Abode

2:8 (7)	We believe in God and the Last Day
2:62 (59)	whoso believes in God and the Last Day
2:94 (88)	if the Last Abode with God is yours
2:126 (120)	such of them as believe in God and the Last Day
2:177 (172)	to believe in God, and the Last Day
2:228 (228)	if they believe in God and the Last Day
2:232 (232)	whoso of you believes in God and the Last Day
2:264 (266)	and believes not in God and the Last Day
3:72 (65)	who believe at beginning of the day, and disbelieve at the end of it

3:114 (110)	believing in God and in the Last Day
4:38 (42)	and [who] believe not in God and the Last Day
4:39 (43)	if they believed in God and the Last Day
4:59 (62)	if you believe in God and the Last Day
4:136 (135)	[whoso disbelieves in] the Last Day, has surely gone astray
4:162 (160)	those who believe in God and the Last Day
5:69 (73)	whosoever believes in God and the Last Day, and works righteousness
5:114 (114)	be for us a festival, the first and last of us
6:32 (32)	the Last Abode is better for those that are godfearing
7:169 (168)	the Last Abode is better for those who are godfearing
9:18 (18)	who believes in God and the Last Day
9:19 (19)	as one who believes in God and the Last Day
9:29 (29)	Fight those who believe not in God and the Last Day
9:44 (44)	Those who believe in God and the Last Day ask not leave of thee
9:45 (45)	They only ask leave of thee who believe not in God and the Last Day
9:99 (100)	some of the Bedouins believe in God and the Last Day
10:10 (11)	and the end of their cry is, 'Praise belongs to God
24:2 (2)	let no tenderness for them seize you if you believe in God and the Last Day
26:84 (84)	appoint me a tongue of truthfulness among the later folk
28:77 (77)	seek, amidst that which God has given thee, the Last Abode
28:83 (83)	That is the Last Abode
29:36 (35)	and look you for the Last Day
29:64 (64)	surely the Last Abode is Life
33:21 (21)	for whosoever hopes for God and the Last Day
33:29 (29)	if you desire God and His Messenger and the Last Abode
37:78 (76)	and left for him among the later folk
37:108 (108)	and left for him among the later folk
37:119 (119)	and left them among the later folk
37:129 (129)	and We left for him among the later folk
38:7 (6)	We have not heard of this in the last religion
43:56 (56)	We appointed them for an example to later folk
53:25 (25)	And to God belongs the First and the Last
56:14 (14)	and how few of the later folk
56:40 (39)	and a throng of the later folk
56:49 (49)	say: 'The ancients, and the later folk
57:3 (3)	He is the First and the Last, the Outward and the Inward
58:22 (22)	any people who believe in God and the Last Day
60:6 (6)	whoever hopes for God and the Last Day
65:2 (2)	whosoever believes in God and the Last Day
77:17 (17)	and then follow them with the later folk
79:25 (25)	God seized him with the chastisement of the Last World and the First
92:13 (13)	to Us belong the Last and the First
93:4 (4)	the Last shall be better for thee than the First

ĀKHIRAH n.f. (see also *ākhir*, above)~the Hereafter, the World to Come

2:4 (3)	and have faith in the Hereafter
2:86 (80)	those who have purchased the present life at the price of the world to come
2:102 (96)	[he] shall have no share in the world to come
2:114 (108)	and in the world to come a mighty chastisement
2:130 (124)	and in the world to come he shall be among the righteous
2:200 (196)	such men shall have no part in the world to come
2:201 (197)	give to us in this world good, and good in the world to come
2:217 (214)	their works have failed in this world and the next
2:220 (218)	in this world, and the world to come
3:22 (21)	their works have failed in this world and the next

3:45 (40)	high honoured shall he be in this world and the next
3:56 (49)	I will chastise them with a terrible chastisement in this world and the next
3:77 (71)	there shall be no share for them in the world to come
3:85 (79)	in the next world he shall be among the losers
3:145 (139)	and whoso desires the reward of the other world
3:148 (141)	the fairest reward of the world to come
3:152 (146)	and some of you there are desire the next world
3:176 (170)	God desires not to appoint for them a portion in the world to come
4:74 (76)	So let them fight in the way of God who sell the present life for the world to come
4:77 (79)	the world to come is better for him who fears God
4:134 (133)	with God is the reward of this world and of the world to come
5:5 (7)	in the world to come he shall be among the losers
5:33 (37)	in the world to come awaits them a mighty chastisement
5:41 (45)	in the world to come awaits them a mighty chastisement
6:92 (92)	those who believe in the world to come believe in it
6:113 (113)	that the hearts of those who believe not in the world to come may incline to it
6:150 (151)	who cried lies to Our signs, and who believe not in the world to come
7:45 (43)	disbelieving in the world to come
7:147 (145)	Those who cry lies to Our signs, and the encounter in the world to come
7:156 (155)	prescribe for us in this world good, and in the world to come
8:67 (68)	God desires the world to come
9:38 (38)	so content with this present life, rather than the world to come
9:38 (38)	the enjoyment of this present life, compared with the world to come, is a little thing
9:69 (70)	their works have failed in this world and in the world to come
9:74 (75)	God will chastise them with a painful chastisement in this world and the next
10:64 (65)	for them is good tidings in the present life and in the world to come
11:16 (19)	for whom in the world to come there is only the Fire
11:19 (22)	they disbelieve in the world to come
11:22 (24)	they without doubt will be the greatest losers in the world to come
11:103 (105)	a sign for him who fears the chastisement in the world to come
12:37 (37)	who moreover are unbelievers in the world to come
12:57 (57)	Yet is the wage of the world to come better
12:101 (102)	Thou art my Protector in this world and the next
12:109 (109)	the abode of the world to come is better for those that are godfearing
13:26 (26)	this present life, beside the world to come, is naught but passing enjoyment
13:34 (34)	the chastisement of the world to come is yet more grievous
14:3 (3)	such as prefer the present life over the world to come
14:27 (32)	God confirms those who believe with the firm word, in the present life and in the world to come
16:22 (23)	they who believe not in the world to come
16:30 (32)	the abode of the world to come is better
16:41 (43)	the wage of the world to come is greater
16:60 (62)	Those who believe not in the world to come
16:107 (109)	they have preferred the present life over the world to come
16:109 (110)	without a doubt, in the world to come they will be the losers
16:122 (123)	and in the world to come he shall be among the righteous
17:7 (7)	when the promise of the second came to pass
17:10 (11)	those who do not believe in the world to come
17:19 (20)	And whosoever desires the world to come
17:21 (22)	the world to come is greater in ranks
17:45 (47)	We place between thee, and those who do not believe in the world to come, a curtain
17:72 (74)	whosoever is blind in this world shall be blind in the world to come
17:104 (106)	when the promise of the world to come comes to pass
20:127 (127)	the chastisement of the world to come is more terrible
22:11 (11)	he loses this world and the world to come

22:15 (15)	Whosoever thinks God will not help him in the present world and the world to come
23:33 (34)	his people, who cried lies to the encounter of the world to come
23:74 (76)	they that believe not in the world to come are deviating
24:14 (14)	His mercy in the present world and the world to come
24:19 (19)	in the present world and the world to come
24:23 (23)	shall be accursed in the present world and the world to come
27:3 (3)	who perform the prayer, and pay the alms, and have sure faith in the Hereafter
27:4 (4)	Those who believe not in the Hereafter
27:5 (5)	they will be the greatest losers in the Hereafter
27:66 (68)	nay, but their knowledge fails as to the Hereafter
28:70 (70)	His is the praise in the former as in the latter
29:20 (19)	God causes the second growth to grow
29:27 (26)	in the world to come he shall be among the righteous
30:7 (6)	but of the Hereafter they are heedless
30:16 (15)	(who cried lies to) the encounter of the Hereafter
31:4 (3)	(who) have sure faith in the Hereafter
33:57 (57)	them God has cursed in the present world and the world to come
34:1 (1)	to Him belongs praise also in the Hereafter
34:8 (8)	those who believe not in the Hereafter are in chastisement
34:21 (20)	that We might know him who believed in the Hereafter from him who was in doubt
39:9 (12)	he being afraid of the world to come
39:26 (27)	the chastisement of the world to come is assuredly greater
39:45 (46)	shudder the hearts of those who believe not in the Hereafter
40:39 (42)	the world to come is the abode of stability
40:43 (46)	no call heard, in this world or in the world to come
41:7 (6)	who pay not the alms, and disbelieve in the world to come
41:16 (15)	the chastisement of the world to come is even more degrading
41:31 (31)	We are your friends in the present life and in the world to come
42:20 (19)	Whoso desires the tillage of the world to come, We shall give him increase
42:20 (19)	in the world to come he will have no share
43:35 (34)	and the world to come with thy Lord is for the godfearing
53:27 (28)	Those who do not believe in the world to come
57:20 (19)	in the world to come there is a terrible chastisement
59:3 (3)	there awaits them in the world to come the chastisement of the Fire
60:13 (13)	against whom God is wrathful, and who have despaired of the world to come
68:33 (33)	the chastisement of the world to come is assuredly greater
74:53 (53)	they do not fear the Hereafter
75:21 (21)	and leave be the Hereafter
87:17 (17)	the world to come is better, and more enduring

UKHRÁ n.f.~rear

3:153 (147)	the Messenger was calling you in your rear

AKHKHARA vb. (II)~to defer, to postpone

a) perf. act.

4:77 (79)	why not defer us to a near term?
11:8 (11)	and if We postpone the chastisement from them
17:62 (64)	if Thou deferrest me to the Day of Resurrection I shall assuredly master his seed
63:10 (10)	if only Thou wouldst defer me unto a near term, so that I may make freewill
75:13 (13)	what he has sent before and has deferred
82:5 (5)	a soul shall know what it has sent before and has deferred

b) impf. act. (*yu'akhkhiru*)

11:104 (106)	and We shall not postpone it
14:10 (11)	that He may forgive you your sins, and defer you to a term stated
14:42 (43)	He is only deferring them to a day when eyes shall stare
16:61 (63)	but He is deferring them to a term stated
35:45 (44)	He is deferring them to a stated term
63:11 (11)	But God will never defer any soul when its term comes
71:4 (4)	He will forgive you your sins, and defer you to a stated term

c) impv. (*akhkhir*)

14:44 (45)	Our Lord, defer us to a near term

e) impf. pass. (*yu'akhkharu*)

71:4 (4)	God's term, when it comes, cannot be deferred

TA'AKHKHARA vb. (V)~to delay, to come (later), to lag behind

a) perf. act.

2:203 (199)	and if any delays, it is not a sin
48:2 (2)	that God may forgive thee thy sin, the former and that which which is to come

b) impf. act. (*yata'akhkharu*)

74:37 (40)	whoever of you desires to go forward or lag behind

ISTA'KHARA vb. (X)~to put back. (pcple. act.) laggard

b) impf. act. (*yasta'khiru*)

7:34 (32)	they shall not put it back by a single hour
10:49 (50)	they shall not put it back by a single hour
15:5 (5)	no nation outstrips its term, nor do they put it back
16:61 (63)	they shall not put it back by a single hour
23:43 (45)	no nation outstrips its term, nor do they put it back
34:30 (29)	that you shall not put back by a single hour

g) pcple. act. (*musta'khir*)

15:24 (24)	We know the laggards

*A KH W

AKH n.m. (pl. *ikhwah, ikhwān*)~brother

2:178 (173)	if aught is pardoned a man by his brother
2:220 (219)	if you intermix with them, they are your brothers
3:103 (98)	by His blessing you became brothers
3:156 (150)	who say to their brothers, when they journey
3:168 (162)	who said of their brothers, and they themselves held back
4:11 (12)	if he has brothers, to his mother a sixth
4:12 (15)	[if they] have a brother or a sister
4:23 (27)	your brother's daughters
4:176 (175)	if there be brothers and sisters, the male shall receive

5:25 (28)	I rule no one except myself and my brother
5:30 (33)	his soul prompted him to slay his brother
5:31 (34)	how he might conceal the vile body of his brother
5:31 (34)	so conceal my brother's vile body
6:87 (87)	of their seed, and of their brethren
7:65 (63)	And to Ad their brother Hood
7:73 (71)	And to Thamood their brother Salih
7:85 (83)	And to Midian their brother Shuaib
7:111 (108)	put him and his brother off a while
7:142 (138)	Moses said to his brother Aaron
7:150 (149)	[he] laid hold of his brother's head
7:151 (150)	O my Lord, forgive me and my brother
7:202 (201)	and their brothers they lead on into error
9:11 (11)	then they are your brothers
9:23 (23)	take not your fathers and brothers to be your friends
9:24 (24)	if your fathers, your sons, your brothers
10:87 (87)	We revealed to Moses and his brother
11:50 (52)	And to Ad their brother Hood
11:61 (64)	And to Thamood their brother Salih
11:84 (85)	And to Midian their brother Shuaib
12:5 (5)	relate not thy vision to thy brothers
12:7 (7)	in Joseph and his brethren were signs
12:8 (8)	Joseph and his brother are dearer to our father
12:58 (58)	the brethren of Joseph came
12:59 (59)	bring me a certain brother of yours
12:63 (63)	so send with us our brother
12:64 (64)	as I entrusted before his brother to you
12:65 (65)	we shall be watching over our brother
12:69 (69)	taking his brother into his arms
12:69 (69)	I am thy brother; so do not despair
12:70 (70)	into the saddlebag of his brother
12:76 (76)	beginning with their sacks, before his brother's sack
12:76 (76)	he pulled it out of his brother's sack
12:76 (76)	he could not have taken his brother
12:77 (77)	a brother of his was a thief before
12:87 (87)	search out tidings of Joseph and his brother
12:89 (89)	are you aware of what you did with Joseph and his brother
12:90 (90)	This is my brother
12:100 (101)	Satan set at variance me and my brethren
15:47 (47)	as brothers they shall be upon couches
17:27 (29)	the squanderers are brothers of Satan
19:53 (54)	We gave him his brother Aaron
20:30 (31)	Aaron, my brother
20:42 (44)	go therefore, thou and thy brother
23:45 (47)	We sent Moses and his brother
24:31 (31)	or their brothers
24:31 (31)	or their brothers' sons
24:61 (60)	or your brothers' houses
25:35 (37)	[We] appointed with him his brother Aaron as minister
26:36 (35)	put him and his brother off a while
26:106 (106)	when their brother Noah said to them
26:124 (124)	when their brother Hood said to them
26:142 (142)	when their brother Salih said to them
26:161 (161)	when their brother Lot said to them

27:45 (46)	We sent to Thamood their brother Salih
28:34 (34)	my brother Aaron is more eloquent than I
28:35 (35)	We will strengthen thy arm by means of thy brother
29:36 (35)	And to Midian their brother Shuaib
33:5 (5)	then they are your brothers
33:18 (18)	those who say to their brothers
33:55 (55)	touching their fathers, their sons, their brothers
33:55 (55)	their brothers' sons, their sisters' sons
38:23 (22)	this my brother has ninety-nine ewes
46:21 (20)	remember the brother of Ad
49:10 (10)	the believers indeed are brothers
49:10 (10)	set things right between your two brothers
49:12 (12)	would any of you like to eat the flesh of his brother dead?
50:13 (13)	and Ad and Pharaoh, thebrothers of Lot
58:22 (22)	their brothers, or their clan
59:10 (10)	our Lord, forgive us and our brothers
59:11 (11)	saying to their brothers of the People of the Book
70:12 (12)	his companion wife, his brother
80:34 (34)	the day when a man shall flee from his brother

UKHT n.f. (pl. *akhawāt*)~sister

4:12 (15)	[if they] have a brother or a sister
4:23 (27)	forbidden to you are your mothers and daughters, your sisters
4:23 (27)	your brother's daughters, your sister's daughters
4:23 (27)	your suckling sisters, your wives' mothers
4:23 (27)	and that you should take to you two sisters
4:176 (175)	if a man perishes having no children, but he has a sister
7:38 (36)	it curses its sister-nation
19:28 (29)	Sister of Aaron, thy father was not a wicked man
20:40 (41)	when thy sister went out, saying
24:31 (31)	or their sisters' sons, or their women
24:61 (60)	or your sisters' houses
28:11 (10)	and she said to his sister
33:55 (55)	their brothers' sons, their sisters' sons
43:48 (47)	it was greater than its sister sign

*A L F

ALF n.m. (num)~thousand

2:96 (90)	if he might be spared a thousand years
2:243 (244)	who went forth from their habitations in their thousands
3:124 (120)	your Lord should reinforce you with three thousand angels
3:125 (121)	your Lord will reinforce you with five thousand swooping angels
8:9 (9)	I shall reinforce you with a thousand angels
8:65 (66)	they will overcome a thousand unbelievers
8:66 (67)	if there be of you a thousand
8:66 (67)	they will overcome two thousand
22:47 (46)	a day with thy Lord is as a thousand years
29:14 (13)	he tarried among them a thousand years
32:5 (4)	whose measure is a thousand years of your counting
37:147 (147)	We sent him unto a hundred thousand, or more
70:4 (4)	whereof the measure is fifty thousand years
97:3 (3)	The Night of Power is better than a thousand months

ALLAFA vb. (II)~to unite, to bring together, to compose; (pcple.pass.) brought together, united

a) perf. act.

3:103 (98)	He brought your hearts together
8:63 (64)	(He) brought their hearts together
8:63 (64)	thou couldst not have brought their hearts together
8:63 (64)	God brought their hearts together

b) impf. act. (*yuʾallifu*)

24:43 (43)	God drives the clouds, then composes them

h) pcple. pass. (*muʾallaf*)

9:60 (60)	those whose hearts are brought together

ĀLAFA vb. (IV)~(n.vb.) composing

f) n.vb. (*īlāf*)

106:1 (1)	For the composing of Koraish
106:2 (2)	their composing for the winter and summer caravan

*A L H

ALLĀH See separate entry

ILĀH n.m. (pl. *ālihah*)~God (see also *ALLĀH*); a god, a deity; (*lā ilāha illā Allāh* or *lā ilāha illā huwa*) there is no god but God, or but He

God

2:133 (127)	we will serve thy God
2:133 (127)	and the God of thy fathers
2:133 (127)	thy fathers Abraham, Ishmael and Isaac, One God
2:163 (158)	your God is One (God)
2:163 (158)	your (God) is One God
4:171 (169)	[He] is only One God
5:73 (77)	(no god is there but) One God
6:19 (19)	He is only One God
9:31 (31)	they were commanded to serve but One God
14:52 (52)	that they may know that He is One God
16:22 (23)	your God is One (God)
16:22 (23)	your (God) is One God
16:51 (53)	He is only One God
18:110 (110)	your God is One (God)
18:110 (110)	your (God) is One God
20:98 (98)	your God is only the One (God)
21:108 (108)	your God is One (God)
21:108 (108)	your (God) is One God
22:34 (35)	your God is One (God)
22:34 (35)	your (God) is One God
28:38 (38)	that I may mount up to Moses' God
29:46 (45)	our God and your (God) is One
29:46 (45)	our (God) and your God is One
37:4 (4)	surely your God is One

38:5 (4)	has he made the (gods) One God?
40:37 (39)	look upon Moses' God
41:6 (5)	to me it has been revealed that your God is One (God)
41:6 (5)	your (God) is One God
43:84 (84)	it is He who in heaven is God
43:84 (84)	and in earth is God
114:3 (3)	the God of men

Other (false) gods

2:163 (158)	there is no god but He
2:255 (256)	there is no god but He
3:2 (1)	there is no god but He
3:6 (4)	there is no god but He
3:18 (16)	there is no god but He
3:18 (16)	there is no god but He
3:62 (55)	there is no god but God
4:87 (89)	there is no god but He
5:73 (77)	no god is there but (one God)
5:116 (116)	take me and my mother as gods
6:19 (19)	that there are other gods with God
6:46 (46)	who is a god other than (God)
6:74 (74)	takest thou idols for gods?
6:102 (102)	there is no god but He
6:106 (106)	there is no god but He
7:59 (57)	you have no god other than He
7:65 (63)	you have no god other than He
7:73 (71)	you have no god other than He
7:85 (83)	you have no god other than He
7:127 (124)	and leave thee and thy gods
7:138 (134)	Moses, make for us a god
7:138 (134)	as they have gods
7:140 (136)	shall I seek a god for you other than (God)
7:158 (158)	there is no god but He
9:31 (31)	there is no god but He
9:129 (130)	there is no god but He
10:90 (90)	there is no god but He
11:14 (17)	there is no god but He
11:50 (52)	you have no god other than He
11:53 (56)	we will not leave our gods for what thou sayest
11:54 (57)	one of our gods has smitten thee with some evil
11:61 (64)	you have no god other than He
11:84 (85)	you have no god other than He
11:101 (103)	their gods availed them not
13:30 (29)	there is no god but He
15:96 (96)	those who set up with (God) another god
16:2 (2)	there is no god but I
16:51 (53)	take not to you two gods
17:22 (23)	set not up with (God) another god
17:39 (41)	set not up with (God) another god
17:42 (44)	if there had been other gods with Him
18:14 (13)	we will not call upon any god, apart from Him
18:15 (14)	our people have taken to them other gods
19:46 (47)	art thou shrinking from my gods, Abraham
19:81 (84)	they have taken to them other gods
20:8 (7)	there is no god but He

20:14 (14)	there is no god but I
20:88 (90)	this is your god
20:88 (90)	and the god of Moses
20:97 (97)	thy god, to whom all the day thou wast cleaving
20:98 (98)	there is no god, but He alone
21:21 (21)	or have they taken gods out of the earth
21:22 (22)	were there gods in earth and heaven
21:24 (24)	have they taken gods apart from Him
21:25 (25)	there is no god but I
21:29 (30)	I am a god apart from Him
21:36 (37)	the one who makes mention of your gods
21:43 (44)	have they gods that shall defend them
21:59 (60)	who has done this with our gods?
21:62 (63)	who did this unto our gods
21:68 (68)	burn him, and help your gods
21:87 (87)	there is no god but Thou
21:99 (99)	if those had been gods, they would never have gone down
23:23 (23)	you have no god other than He
23:32 (33)	you have no god other than He
23:91 (93)	nor is there any god with Him
23:91 (93)	each god would have taken off that he created
23:116 (117)	there is no god but He
23:117 (117)	whosoever calls upon another god
25:3 (3)	they have taken to them gods, apart from Him
25:42 (44)	wellnigh he had led us astray from our gods
25:43 (45)	hast thou seen him who has taken his caprice to be his god
25:68 (68)	who call not upon another god (with God)
26:29 (28)	if thou takest a god other than me
26:213 (213)	call thou not upon another god (with God)
27:26 (26)	there is no god but He
27:60 (61)	is there a god (with God)
27:61 (62)	is there a god (with God)
27:62 (63)	is there a god (with God)
27:63 (64)	is there a god (with God)
27:64 (65)	is there a god (with God)
28:38 (38)	I know not that you have any god but me
28:70 (70)	there is no god but He
28:71 (71)	what god other than (God) shall bring you illumination
28:72 (72)	what god other than (God) shall bring you night
28:88 (88)	call not upon another god with (God)
28:88 (88)	there is no god but He
35:3 (3)	there is no god but He
36:23 (22)	shall I take, apart from Him, gods
36:74 (74)	they have taken apart from (God) gods
37:35 (34)	there is no god but (God)
37:36 (35)	shall we forsake our gods for a poet possessed
37:86 (84)	is it a calumny, gods apart from (God) that you desire?
37:91 (89)	then he turned to their gods
38:5 (4)	has he made the gods One (God)?
38:6 (5)	be steadfast to your gods
38:65 (65)	there is not any god but (God)
39:6 (8)	there is no god but He
40:3 (3)	there is no god but He
40:62 (64)	there is no god but He
40:65 (67)	there is no god but He

43:45 (44)	have We appointed, apart from the All-merciful, gods to be served?
43:58 (58)	are our gods better, or he?
44:8 (7)	there is no god but He
45:23 (22)	hast thou seen him who has taken his caprice to be his god
46:22 (21)	hast thou come to pervert us from our gods?
46:28 (27)	they had taken to themselves as mediators, gods (apart from God)
47:19 (21)	there is no god (but God)
50:26 (25)	who set up (with God) another god
51:51 (51)	set not up (with God) another god
52:43 (43)	have they a god, other than (God)?
59:22 (22)	there is no god but He
59:23 (23)	there is no god but He
64:13 (13)	there is no god but He
71:23 (22)	do not leave your gods, and do not leave Wadd
73:9 (9)	there is no god but He

*A L L

ILL n.m.~bond, pact

9:8 (8)	they will not observe towards you any bond or treaty

*A L M

ALIF LĀM MĪM~ml

2:1 (1)	Alif Lam Mim
3:1 (1)	Alif Lam Mim
29:1 (1)	Alif Lam Mim
30:1 (1)	Alif Lam Mim
31:1 (1)	Alif Lam Mim
32:1 (1)	Alif Lam Mim

ALIMA vb. (I)~to suffer

b) impf. act. (*ya'lamu*)

4:104 (105)	if you are suffering
4:104 (105)	they are also suffering
4:104 (105)	as you are suffering

ALĪM n.m. (adj)~painful

2:10 (9)	and there awaits them a painful chastisement
2:104 (98)	for unbelievers awaits a painful chastisement
2:174 (169)	there awaits them a painful chastisement
2:178 (174)	for him there awaits a painful chastisement
3:21 (20)	give them the good tidings of a painful chastisement
3:77 (71)	for them awaits a painful chastisement
3:91 (85)	for them awaits a painful chastisement
3:177 (171)	there awaits them a painful chastisement
3:188 (185)	for them awaits a painful chastisement
4:18 (22)	for them We have prepared a painful chastisement
4:138 (137)	for them awaits a painful chastisement
4:161 (159)	We have prepared for the unbelievers among them a painful chastisement
4:173 (172)	them He will chastise with a painful chastisement
5:36 (40)	for them awaits a painful chastisement
5:73 (77)	there shall afflict those of them that disbelieve a painful chastisement

5:94 (95)	whoso thereafter commits transgression, there awaits him a painful chastisement
6:70 (69)	for them awaits a draught of boiling water and a painful chastisement
7:73 (71)	lest you be seized by a painful chastisement
8:32 (32)	rain down upon us stones out of heaven, or bring us a painful chastisement
9:3 (3)	give thou good tidings to the unbelievers of a painful chastisement
9:34 (34)	give them the good tidings of a painful chastisement
9:39 (39)	He will chastise you with a painful chastisement
9:61 (62)	for them awaits a painful chastisement
9:74 (75)	God will chastise them with a painful chastisement
9:79 (80)	for them awaits a painful chastisement
9:90 (91)	there shall befall the unbelievers of them a painful chastisement
10:4 (4)	for them awaits a draught of boiling water, and a painful chastisement
10:88 (88)	they do not believe, till they see the painful chastisement
10:97 (97)	though every sign come to them, till they see the painful chastisement
11:26 (28)	for you the chastisement of a painful day
11:48 (50)	there shall visit them from Us a painful chastisement
11:102 (104)	surely His seizing is painful, terrible
12:25 (25)	but that he should be imprisoned, or a painful chastisement
14:22 (27)	As for the evildoers, for them awaits a painful chastisement
15:50 (50)	and that My chastisement is the painful chastisement
16:63 (65)	there yet awaits them a painful chastisement
16:104 (106)	there awaits them a painful chastisement
16:117 (118)	then for them awaits a painful chastisement
17:10 (11)	We have prepared for them a painful chastisement
22:25 (26)	We shall let him taste a painful chastisement
24:19 (18)	there awaits them a painful chastisement
24:63 (63)	or there befall them a painful chastisement
25:37 (39)	We have prepared for the evildoers a painful chastisement
26:201 (201)	until they see the painful chastisement
29:23 (22)	there awaits them a painful chastisement
31:7 (6)	give him good tidings of a painful chastisement
33:8 (8)	He has prepared for the unbelievers a painful chastisement
34:5 (5)	theirs shall be a chastisement of painful wrath
36:18 (17)	there shall visit you from us a painful chastisement
37:38 (37)	you shall be tasting the painful chastisement
41:43 (43)	thy Lord is a Lord of forgiveness and of painful retribution
42:21 (20)	for the evildoers there awaits a painful chastisement
42:42 (40)	there awaits them a painful chastisement
43:65 (65)	because of the chastisement of a painful day
44:11 (10)	this is a painful chastisement
45:8 (7)	give him the good tidings of a painful chastisement
45:11 (10)	there awaits them a painful chastisement
46:24 (23)	a wind, wherein is a painful chastisement
46:31 (30)	[He will] protect you from a painful chastisement
48:16 (16)	He will chastise you with a painful chastisement
48:17 (17)	him He will chastise with a painful chastisement
48:25 (25)	We would have chastised the unbelievers among them with a painful chastisement
51:37 (37)	who fear the painful chastisement
58:4 (5)	for the unbelievers there awaits yet a painful chastisement
59:15 (15)	there awaits them a painful chastisement
61:10 (10)	commerce that shall deliver you from a painful chastisement
64:5 (5)	there yet awaits them a painful chastisement
67:28 (28)	who will protect the unbelievers from a painful chastisement?
71:1 (1)	warn thy people, ere there come on them a painful chastisement
73:13 (13)	food that chokes, and a painful chastisement

76:31 (31)	He has prepared for them a painful chastisement
84:24 (24)	give them good tidings of a painful chastisement

*A L M R

ALIF LĀM MĪM RĀ~ml

13:1 (1)	Alif Lam Mim Ra

*A L M Ṣ

ALIF LĀM MĪM ṢĀḌ~ml

7:1 (1)	Alif Lam Mim Sad

*A L R

ALIF LĀM RĀ~ml

10:1 (1)	Alif Lam Ra
11:1 (1)	Alif Lam Ra
12:1 (1)	Alif Lam Ra
14:1 (1)	Alif Lam Ra
15:1 (1)	Alif Lam Ra

*A L S

ILYĀS n.prop.~Elijah, Elias

6:85 (85)	Zachariah and John, Jesus and Elias
37:123 (123)	Elias too was one of the Envoys
37:130 (130)	Peace be upon Elias

*A L T

ALATA vb. (I)~to defraud, to deprive

a) perf. act.

52:21 (21)	We shall not defraud them of aught of their work

*A L W

ALĀ vb. (I)~to spare

b) impf. act. (*ya'lū*)

3:118 (114)	such men spare nothing to ruin you

ALÁ n.m. (pl. *ālā'*)~bounty [Ar, Pk]; benefit [Ali, Bl]

7:69 (67)	remember God's bounties
7:74 (72)	remember God's bounties
53:55 (56)	which of thy Lord's bounties disputest thou?
55:13 (12)	O which of your Lord's bounties will you and you deny?
55:16 (15)	O which of your Lord's bounties will you and you deny?
55:18 (18)	O which of your Lord's bounties will you and you deny?
55:21 (21)	O which of your Lord's bounties will you and you deny?
55:23 (23)	O which of your Lord's bounties will you and you deny?
55:25 (25)	O which of your Lord's bounties will you and you deny?
55:28 (28)	O which of your Lord's bounties will you and you deny?

55:30 (30)	O which of your Lord's bounties will you and you deny?
55:32 (32)	O which of your Lord's bounties will you and you deny?
55:34 (34)	O which of your Lord's bounties will you and you deny?
55:36 (36)	O which of your Lord's bounties will you and you deny?
55:38 (38)	O which of your Lord's bounties will you and you deny?
55:40 (40)	O which of your Lord's bounties will you and you deny?
55:42 (42)	O which of your Lord's bounties will you and you deny?
55:45 (45)	O which of your Lord's bounties will you and you deny?
55:47 (47)	O which of your Lord's bounties will you and you deny?
55:49 (49)	O which of your Lord's bounties will you and you deny?
55:51 (51)	O which of your Lord's bounties will you and you deny?
55:53 (53)	O which of your Lord's bounties will you and you deny?
55:55 (55)	O which of your Lord's bounties will you and you deny?
55:57 (57)	O which of your Lord's bounties will you and you deny?
55:59 (59)	O which of your Lord's bounties will you and you deny?
55:61 (61)	O which of your Lord's bounties will you and you deny?
55:63 (63)	O which of your Lord's bounties will you and you deny?
55:65 (65)	O which of your Lord's bounties will you and you deny?
55:67 (67)	O which of your Lord's bounties will you and you deny?
55:69 (69)	O which of your Lord's bounties will you and you deny?
55:71 (71)	O which of your Lord's bounties will you and you deny?
55:73 (73)	O which of your Lord's bounties will you and you deny?
55:75 (75)	O which of your Lord's bounties will you and you deny?
55:77 (77)	O which of your Lord's bounties will you and you deny?

ĀLÁ vb. (IV)~to forswear, to vow abstinence

b) impf. act. (*yuʾlī*)

2:226 (226)	for those who forswear their women

IʾTALÁ vb. (VIII)~to swear

b) impf. act. (*yaʾtali*)

24:22 (22)	let not those of you who possess bounty and plenty swear off giving kinsmen

*A M D

AMAD n.m.~term, space (in time)

3:30 (28)	it will wish if there were only a far space between it and that day
18:12 (11)	[which] would better calculate the while they had tarried [a long term]
57:16 (15)	the term seemed over long to them
72:25 (26)	whether my Lord will appoint for it a space

*A M L

AMAL n.m.~hope

15:3 (3)	[leave them] to be bemused by hope
18:46 (44)	[they] are better with God in reward, and better in hope

*A M M

AMMA vb. (I)~(pcple. act.) one who repairs to

g) pcple. act. (*āmm*)

5:2 (2)	nor those repairing to the Holy House

AMĀM n.m.~in front of, before, ahead

75:5 (5)	man would fain deny what is before him

IMĀM n.m. (pl. *a'immah*)~model, example, ensample; leader, guide; roadway; register, record, codex

2:124 (118)	I make you a leader for the people
9:12 (12)	fight the leaders of unbelief
11:17 (20)	before him is the Book of Moses for an ensample and a mercy
15:79 (79)	the two of them were upon a roadway manifest
17:71 (73)	the day when We shall call all men with their record
21:73 (73)	and appointed them to be leaders guiding by Our command
25:74 (74)	and make us a model to the godfearing
28:5 (4)	[We desired] to make them leaders
28:41 (41)	We appointed them leaders
32:24 (24)	We appointed from among them leaders guiding by Our command
36:12 (11)	We have numbered in a clear register
46:12 (11)	before it was the Book of Moses for a model and a mercy

UMM n.f. (pl. *ummahāt*)~mother, essence (as in "Essence of the Book," *umm al-kitāb*); abode (101:9)

3:7 (5)	wherein are verses clear that are the Essence of the Book
4:11 (12)	[if] his heirs are his parents, a third to his mother
4:11 (12)	if he has brothers, to his mother a sixth
4:23 (27)	forbidden to you are your mothers and daughters
4:23 (27)	your mothers who have given suck to you
4:23 (27)	your suckling sisters, your wives' mothers
5:17 (19)	if He desires to destroy the Messiah, Mary's son, and his mother
5:75 (79)	his mother was a just woman
5:116 (116)	take me and my mother as gods, apart from God
6:92 (92)	and for thee to warn the Mother of Cities
7:150 (149)	son of my mother, surely the people have abased me
13:39 (39)	with Him is the Essence of the Book
16:78 (80)	it is God who brought you forth, knowing nothing, from your mothers' wombs
19:28 (29)	nor was thy mother a woman unchaste
20:38 (38)	when We revealed what was revealed unto thy mother
20:40 (41)	so We returned thee to thy mother
20:94 (95)	'Son of my mother,' Aaron said
23:50 (52)	We made Mary's son, and his mother, to be a sign
24:61 (60)	or your mothers' houses, or your brothers' houses
28:7 (6)	so We revealed to Moses' mother
28:10 (9)	on the morrow the heart of Moses' mother became empty
28:13 (12)	so We returned him to his mother
28:59 (59)	until He sent in their mother-city a Messenger
31:14 (13)	his mother bore him in weakness
33:4 (4)	nor has He made your wives...your mothers
33:6 (6)	his wives are their mothers
39:6 (8)	He creates you in your mothers' wombs
42:7 (5)	that thou mayest warn the Mother of Cities
43:4 (3)	it is in the Essence of the Book, with Us
46:15 (14)	his mother bore him painfully
53:32 (33)	when you were yet unborn in your mothers' wombs
58:2 (2)	they are not truly their mothers
58:2 (2)	their mothers are only those who gave them birth

80:35 (35)	his mother, his father
101:9 (6)	the Pit shall be his abode

UMMAH n.f. (pl. *umam*)~nation; (also) community [Ar, Bl], a religion [Pk]; a time, a while (12:45)

2:128 (122)	and of our seed a nation submissive to Thee
2:134 (128)	that is a nation that has passed away
2:141 (135)	that is a nation that has passed away
2:143 (137)	thus We appointed you a midmost nation
2:213 (209)	the people were one nation
3:104 (100)	let there be one nation of you, calling to good
3:110 (106)	you are the best nation ever brought forth
3:113 (109)	some of the People of the Book are a nation upstanding
4:41 (45)	when We bring forward from every nation a witness
5:48 (53)	if God had willed, He would have made you one nation
5:66 (70)	some of them are a just nation
6:38 (38)	they are nations like unto yourselves
6:42 (42)	indeed We sent to nations before thee
6:108 (108)	We have decked out fair to every nation their deeds
7:34 (32)	to every nation a term
7:38 (36)	enter among nations that passed away before you
7:38 (36)	whenever any nation enters, it curses
7:159 (159)	of the people of Moses there is a nation who guide by the truth
7:160 (160)	We cut them up into twelve tribes, nations
7:164 (164)	when a certain nation of them said
7:168 (167)	We cut them up into nations in the earth
7:181 (180)	Of those We created are a nation who guide by the truth
10:19 (20)	mankind were only one nation
10:47 (48)	every nation has its Messenger
10:49 (50)	to every nation a term
11:8 (11)	if We postpone the chastisement from them till a reckoned moment they will say
11:48 (50)	blessings upon thee and on the nations of those with thee
11:48 (50)	and nations — We shall give them enjoyment
11:118 (120)	had thy Lord willed, He would have made mankind one nation
12:45 (45)	then said the one who had been delivered, remembering after a time
13:30 (29)	We have sent thee among a nation before
13:30 (29)	before which other nations have passed away
15:5 (5)	no nation outstrips its term
16:36 (38)	We sent forth among every nation a Messenger
16:63 (65)	We sent Messengers to nations before thee
16:84 (86)	the day We shall raise up from every nation a witness
16:89 (91)	the day We shall raise up from every nation a witness
16:92 (94)	one nation being more numerous
16:92 (94)	more numerous than another nation
16:93 (95)	if God had willed, He would have made you one nation
16:120 (121)	Abraham was a nation obedient unto God
21:92 (92)	this community of yours is one (community)
21:92 (92)	this (community) of yours is one community
22:34 (35)	We have appointed for every nation a holy rite
22:67 (66)	We have appointed for every nation a holy rite
23:43 (45)	no nation outstrips its term
23:44 (46)	whenever its Messenger came to a nation
23:52 (54)	this community of yours is one (community)
23:52 (54)	this (community) of yours is one community
27:83 (85)	We shall muster out of every nation a troop
28:23 (22)	he found a company of the people there
28:75 (75)	We shall draw out from every nation a witness
29:18 (17)	nations cried lies before you

35:24 (22)	not a nation there is, but there has passed away in it a warner
35:42 (40)	more rightly guided than any one of the nations
40:5 (5)	every nation purposed against their Messenger
41:25 (24)	against them has been realized the Word concerning nations that passed away
42:8 (6)	if God had willed, He would have made them one nation
43:22 (21)	we found our fathers upon a community
43:23 (22)	we indeed found our fathers upon a community
43:33 (32)	were it not that mankind would be one nation
45:28 (27)	thou shalt see every nation hobbling on their knees
45:28 (27)	every nation being summoned unto its Book
46:18 (17)	against whom has been realized the Word concerning nations that passed away

UMMĪY n.m. (adj)~one of the common folk [Ar, Bl]; unlettered, illiterate, one who can neither read nor write [Pk]; Meccans [Ali]

2:78 (73)	some there are of them that are common folk not knowing the Book
3:20 (19)	say to those who have been given the Book and to the common folk
3:75 (69)	there is no way over us as to the common folk
7:157 (156)	those who follow the Messenger, the Prophet of the common folk
7:158 (158)	[believe] in His Messenger, the Prophet of the common folk
62:2 (2)	it is He who has raised up from among the common folk a Messenger

*A M N

AMINA vb. (I)~to be secure; to trust, to entrust. (n.vb.) trust, security, a place of security (sanctuary). (pcple. act.) secure (adj); in security (adv). (pcple. pass.) that regarding which one feels secure

a) perf. act.

2:196 (192)	when you are secure, then whosoever enjoys the Visitation
2:239 (240)	when you are secure, then remember God
2:283 (283)	if one of you trusts another
7:97 (95)	do the people of the cities feel secure
7:98 (96)	do the people of the cities feel secure
7:99 (97)	do they feel secure against God's devising
12:64 (64)	as I entrusted before his brother to you
12:107 (107)	do they feel secure that there shall come upon them no enveloping
16:45 (47)	do they feel secure, those who devise
17:68 (70)	do you feel secure that He will not cause the shore to swallow you up
17:69 (71)	do you feel secure that He will not send you back into it a second time
67:16 (16)	do you feel secure that He who is in heaven will not cause the earth to swallow you
67:17 (17)	do you feel secure that He who is in heaven will not loose against you a squall of pebbles

b) impf. act. (*ya'manu*)

3:75 (68)	if thou trust him with a hundredweight, [he] will restore it thee
3:75 (68)	if thou trust him with one pound, [he] will not restore it thee
4:91 (93)	you will find others desiring to be secure from you
4:91 (93)	and secure from their people
7:99 (97)	none feels secure against God's devising
12:11 (11)	what ails thee, that thou trustest us not with Joseph
12:64 (64)	shall I entrust him to you

f) n.vb. (*amn*)

2:125 (119)	a place of visitation for the people, and a sanctuary
4:83 (85)	When there comes to them a matter, be it of security or fear, they broadcast it
6:81 (81)	which of the two parties has better title to security

6:82 (82)	to them belongs the true security
24:55 (54)	[He] will give them in exchange, after their fear, security

g) pcple. act. (*āmin*)

2:126 (120)	My Lord, make this a land secure
3:97 (91)	and whosoever enters it is in security
12:99 (100)	enter you into Egypt, if God will, in security
14:35 (38)	My Lord make this land secure
15:46 (46)	Enter you them, in peace and security
15:82 (82)	hewing the mountains into houses, therein dwelling securely
16:112 (113)	a city that was secure, at rest
26:146 (146)	Will you be left secure in this here
27:89 (91)	they shall be secure from terror that day
28:31 (31)	fear not; for surely thou art in security
28:57 (57)	Have We not established for them a sanctuary secure
29:67 (67)	Have they not seen that We have appointed a sanctuary secure
34:18 (17)	Journey among them by night and day in security
34:37 (36)	they shall be in the lofty chambers in security
41:40 (40)	he who comes on the Day of Resurrection in security
44:55 (55)	therein calling for every fruit, secure
48:27 (27)	you shall enter the Holy Mosque, if God wills, in security

h) pcple. pass. (*ma'mūn*)

70:28 (28)	from their Lord's chastisement none feels secure

AMANAH n.f.~security

3:154 (148)	Then He sent down upon you, after grief, security
8:11 (11)	causing slumber to overcome you as a security from Him

AMĀNAH n.f.~a trust, a deposit

2:283 (283)	let him who is trusted deliver his trust
4:58 (61)	God commands you to deliver trusts back to their owners
8:27 (27)	and betray not your trusts
23:8 (8)	and who preserve their trusts and their covenants
33:72 (72)	We offered the trust to the heavens and the earth
70:32 (32)	and who preserve their trusts and their covenant

AMĪN n.m. (adj)~faithful, trusty, trustworthy, secure

7:68 (66)	I am your adviser sincere, faithful
12:54 (54)	thou art established firmly in our favour and in our trust
26:107 (107)	I am for you a faithful Messenger
26:125 (125)	I am for you a faithful Messenger
26:143 (143)	I am for you a faithful Messenger
26:162 (162)	I am for you a faithful Messenger
26:178 (178)	I am for you a faithful Messenger
26:193 (193)	brought down by the Faithful Spirit
27:39 (39)	I have strength for it and I am trusty
28:26 (26)	the best man thou canst hire is the one strong and trusty
44:18 (17)	I am for you a faithful Messenger
44:51 (51)	the godfearing shall be in a station secure
81:21 (21)	obeyed, moreover trusty
95:3 (3)	and this land secure

MA'MAN n.m.~a place of security

9:6 (6)	do thou convey him to his place of security

ĀMANA vb. (IV)~to believe; (*alladhīna āmanū*) "those who believe", the believers. (n.vb.) faith, belief, the act of believing. (pcple act.) believer, believing; All- faithful (Divine attribute, in 59:23)

a) perf. act.

2:8 (7)	We believe in God and the Last Day
2:9 (8)	They would trick God and the believers
2:13 (12)	(Believe) as the people believe
2:13 (12)	(shall we believe) as fools believe?
2:14 (13)	when they meet those who believe, they say
2:14 (13)	they say, 'We believe'
2:25 (23)	give thou good tidings to those who believe
2:26 (24)	as for the believers, they know it is the truth
2:62 (59)	surely they that believe, and those of Jewry
2:62 (59)	whoso believes in God and the Last Day
2:76 (71)	when they meet those who believe, they say
2:76 (71)	they say, 'We believe'
2:82 (76)	those that believe, and do deeds of righteousness
2:103 (97)	had they believed, and been godfearing
2:104 (98)	O believers, do not say, 'Observe us'
2:126 (120)	such of them as believe in God and the Last Day
2:136 (130)	we believe in God
2:137 (131)	if they believe in the like of that you (believe) in
2:137 (131)	if they (believe) in the like of that you believe in
2:153 (148)	O all you who believe, seek you help in patience
2:165 (160)	those that believe love God more ardently
2:172 (167)	O believers, eat of the good things
2:177 (172)	True piety is this: to believe in God, and the Last Day
2:178 (173)	O believers, prescribed for you is retaliation
2:183 (179)	O believers, prescribed for you is the Fast
2:208 (204)	O believers, enter the peace, all of you
2:212 (208)	they deride the believers
2:213 (209)	God guided those who believed to the truth
2:214 (210)	the Messenger and those who believed with him said
2:218 (215)	But the believers, and those who emigrate
2:249 (250)	when he crossed it, and those who believed with him
2:253 (254)	some of them believed, and some disbelieved
2:254 (255)	O believers, expend of that wherewith We have provided you
2:257 (258)	God is the Protector of the believers
2:264 (266)	O believers, void not your freewill offerings
2:267 (269)	O believers, expend of the good things you have earned
2:277 (277)	Those who believe and do deeds of righteousness
2:278 (278)	O believers, fear you God
2:282 (282)	O believers, when you contract a debt
2:285 (285)	The Messenger believes in what was sent down to him from his Lord
2:285 (285)	each one believes in God and His angels
3:7 (5)	we believe in it; all is from our Lord
3:16 (14)	Our Lord, we believe; forgive us our sins
3:52 (45)	We will be helpers of God; we believe in God
3:53 (46)	Lord, we believe in that Thou hast sent down
3:57 (50)	as for the believers, who do deeds of righteousness

3:68 (61)	those who followed him, and this Prophet, and those who believe
3:72 (65)	those who believe at the beginning of the day
3:84 (78)	We believe in God, and that which has been sent down on us
3:99 (94)	why do you bar from God's way the believer
3:100 (95)	O believers, if you obey a sect of those
3:102 (97)	O believers, fear God as He should be feared
3:110 (106)	had the People of the Book believed, it were better for them
3:118 (114)	O believers, take not for your intimates outside yourselves
3:119 (115)	and when they meet you they say, 'We believe'
3:130 (125)	O believers, devour not usury
3:140 (134)	that God may know who are the believers
3:141 (135)	and that God may prove the believers
3:149 (142)	O believers, if you obey the unbelievers
3:156 (150)	O believers, be not as the unbelievers
3:193 (190)	and we believe
3:200 (200)	O believers, be patient
4:19 (23)	O believers, it is not lawful for you to inherit women against their will
4:29 (33)	O believers, consume not your goods between you in vanity
4:39 (43)	what would it harm them, if they believed in God and the Last Day
4:43 (46)	O believers, draw not near to prayer when you are drunken
4:51 (54)	these are more rightly guided on the way than the believers
4:55 (58)	some of them there are that believe
4:57 (60)	those that believe, and do deeds of righteousness
4:59 (62)	O believers, obey God, and obey the Messenger
4:60 (63)	those who assert that they believe in what has been sent down
4:71 (73)	O believers, take your precautions
4:76 (78)	the believers fight in the way of God
4:94 (96)	O believers, when you are journeying in the path of God, be discriminating
4:122 (121)	those that believe, and do deeds of righteousness
4:135 (134)	O believers, be you securers of justice
4:136 (135)	O believers, believe in God and His Messenger
4:137 (136)	those who believe, and then disbelieve
4:137 (136)	and then believe, and then disbelieve
4:144 (143)	O believers, take not the unbelievers as friends
4:147 (146)	what would God do with chastising you if you are thankful, and believe?
4:152 (151)	those who believe in God and His Messengers
4:173 (172)	As for the believers, who do deeds of righteousness
4:175 (174)	As for those who believe in God, and hold fast to Him
5:1 (1)	O believers, fulfil your bonds
5:2 (2)	O believers, profane not God's waymarks
5:6 (8)	O believers, when you stand up to pray wash your faces
5:8 (11)	O believers, be you steadfast before God
5:9 (12)	God has promised those that believe
5:11 (14)	O believers, remember God's blessing upon you
5:12 (15)	and believe in My Messengers and succour them
5:35 (39)	O believers, fear God
5:41 (45)	such men as say with their mouths 'We believe'
5:51 (56)	O believers, take not Jews and Christians as friends
5:53 (58)	and the believers will say
5:54 (59)	O believers, whosoever of you turns from his religion
5:55 (60)	and the believers who perform the prayer
5:56 (61)	Whoso makes God his friend , and His Messenger, and the believers
5:57 (62)	O believers, take not as your friends those of them, who were given the Book before you
5:59 (64)	do you blame us for any other cause than that we believe in God?

5:61 (66)	When they come to you, they say, 'We believe'
5:65 (70)	had the People of the Book believed and been godfearing
5:69 (73)	they that believe, and those of Jewry, and the Sabaeans, and those Christians
5:69 (73)	whosoever believes in God and the Last Day
5:82 (85)	Thou wilt surely find the most hostile of men to the believers are the Jews
5:82 (85)	the nearest of them in love to the believers are those who say 'We are Christians'
5:83 (86)	Our Lord we believe
5:87 (89)	O believers, forbid not such good things as God has permitted you
5:90 (92)	O believers, wine and arrow-shuffling, idols and divining-arrows are an abomination
5:93 (94)	there is no fault in those who believe and do deeds of righteousness
5:93 (94)	if they are godfearing, and believe, and do deeds of righteousness
5:93 (94)	and then are godfearing and believe
5:94 (95)	O believers, God will surely try you
5:95 (96)	O believers, slay not the game while you are in pilgrim sanctity
5:101 (101)	O believers, question not concerning things which ... would vex you
5:105 (104)	O believers, look after your own souls
5:106 (105)	O believers, the testimony between you when any of you is visited by death
5:111 (111)	We believe; witness Thou our submission
6:48 (48)	whoever believes and makes amends
6:82 (82)	Those who believe, and have not confounded their belief
6:158 (159)	(it shall not profit a soul to believe) that never believed before
7:32 (30)	exclusively for those who believed in this present life
7:42 (40)	those who believe, and do deeds of righteousness
7:75 (73)	[they said] to those of them who believed
7:76 (74)	we are unbelievers in the thing in which you believe
7:86 (84)	barring from God's way those who believe in Him
7:87 (85)	a party of you who believe in the Message I have been sent with
7:88 (86)	we will surely expel thee, O Shuaib, and those who believe with thee
7:96 (94)	Yet had the peoples of the cities believed
7:121 (118)	we believe in the Lord of all Being
7:123 (120)	you have believed in Him before I gave you leave
7:126 (123)	we have believed in the signs of our Lord
7:153 (152)	then [they] repent thereafter and believe
7:157 (156)	those who believe in him and succour him and help him
8:12 (12)	I am with you; so confirm the believers
8:15 (15)	O believers, when you encounter the unbelievers marching to battle
8:20 (20)	O believers, obey God and His Messenger
8:24 (24)	O believers, respond to God and the Messenger
8:27 (27)	O believers, betray not God and the Messenger
8:29 (29)	O believers, if you fear God, He will assign you a salvation
8:41 (42)	if you believe in God and that We sent down upon Our servant
8:45 (47)	O believers, whensoever you encounter a host, then stand firm
8:72 (73)	those who believe, and have emigrated
8:72 (73)	and those who believe, but have not emigrated
8:74 (75)	and those who believe, and have emigrated
8:75 (76)	those who have believed afterwards and emigrated
9:18 (18)	Only he shall inhabit God's places of worship who believes in God and the Last Day
9:19 (19)	as one who believes in God and the Last Day
9:20 (20)	Those who believe, and have emigrated
9:23 (23)	O believers, take not your fathers and brothers (...)
9:28 (28)	O believers, the idolaters are indeed unclean
9:34 (34)	O believers, many of the rabbis and monks indeed consume the goods of the people in vanity
9:38 (38)	O believers, what is amiss with you
9:61 (62)	he is a mercy to the believers among you

9:88 (89)	the Messenger, and the believers with him, have struggled
9:113 (114)	It is not for the Prophet and the believers to ask pardon for the idolaters
9:119 (120)	O believers, fear God, and be with the truthful ones
9:123 (124)	O believers, fight the unbelievers who are near to you
9:124 (125)	As for the believers, them it has increased in belief
10:2 (2)	give thou good tidings to the believers that they have a sure footing
10:4 (4)	that He may recompense those who believe
10:9 (9)	those who believe, and do deeds of righteousness, their Lord will guide them
10:51 (52)	will you then believe in it?
10:63 (64)	those who believe, and are godfearing
10:83 (83)	none believed in Moses, save a seed of his people
10:84 (84)	if you believe in God, in Him put your trust
10:90 (90)	I believe that there is no god but He
10:90 (90)	the Children of Israel believe
10:98 (98)	why was there never a city that believed
10:98 (98)	when they believed, We removed from them the chastisement
10:99 (99)	if thy Lord had willed, whoever is in the earth would have believed
10:103 (103)	Then We shall deliver Our Messengers and the believers
11:23 (25)	those who believe, and do righteous deeds
11:29 (31)	I will not drive away those who believe
11:36 (38)	but he who has already believed
11:40 (42)	[Embark in it two of every kind...] and whosoever believes
11:40 (42)	and there believed not with him except a few
11:58 (61)	when Our command came, We delivered Hood and those who believed with him
11:66 (69)	when Our command came, We delivered Salih and those who believed with him
11:94 (97)	when Our command came, We delivered Shuaib and those who believed with him
12:57 (57)	Yet is the wage of the world to come better for those who believe, and are godfearing
13:28 (28)	Those who believe, their hearts being at rest in God's remembrance
13:29 (28)	those who believe and do righteous deeds
13:31 (30)	Did not the believers know, if God had willed
14:23 (28)	as for those who believe, and do deeds of righteousness
14:27 (32)	God confirms those who believe with the firm word, in the present life
14:31 (36)	Say to My servants who believe, that they perform the prayer
16:99 (101)	he has no authority over those who believe
16:102 (104)	to confirm those who believe, and to be a guidance
18:13 (12)	they were youths who believed in their Lord
18:30 (29)	Surely those who believe, and do deeds of righteousness
18:88 (87)	But as for him who believes, and does righteousness
18:107 (107)	But those who believe, and do deeds of righteousness
19:60 (61)	save him who repents, and believes, and does a righteous deed
19:73 (74)	the unbelievers say to the believers
19:96 (96)	Surely those who believe and do deeds of righteousness
20:70 (73)	'We believe,' they said, 'in the Lord of Aaron and Moses'
20:71 (74)	have you believed him before I gave you leave?
20:73 (75)	we believe in our Lord, that He may pardon us
20:82 (84)	yet I am All-forgiving to him who repents and believes
21:6 (6)	not one city that We destroyed before them believed
22:14 (14)	God shall surely admit those who believe and do righteous deeds into gardens
22:17 (17)	surely they that believe, and those of Jewry
22:23 (23)	God shall surely admit those who believe and do righteous deeds into gardens
22:38 (39)	Assuredly God will defend those who believe
22:50 (49)	Those who believe, and do deeds of righteousness
22:54 (53)	God ever guides those who believe to a straight path
22:56 (55)	As for those who believe, and do deeds of righteousness
22:77 (76)	O believers bow you down and prostrate yourselves

23:109 (111)	Our Lord, we believe; therefore forgive us, and have mercy on us
24:19 (18)	Those who love that indecency should be spread abroad concerning them that believe
24:21 (21)	O believers, follow not the steps of Satan
24:27 (27)	O believers, do not enter houses other than your houses until you first ask leave
24:47 (46)	We believe in God and the Messenger, and we obey
24:55 (54)	God has promised those of you who believe and do righteous deeds
24:58 (57)	O believers, let those your right hands own
24:62 (62)	Those only are believers, who believe in God and His Messenger
25:70 (70)	save him who repents, and believes, and does righteous work
26:47 (46)	we believe in the Lord of all Being
26:49 (48)	you have believed him before I gave you leave
26:227 (227)	Save those that believe, and do righteous deeds
27:53 (54)	And We delivered those who believed
28:53 (53)	we believe in it; surely it is the truth
28:67 (67)	as for him who repents, and believes, and works righteousness
28:80 (80)	the reward of God is better for him who believes
29:2 (1)	do the people reckon that they will be left to say 'We believe,' and will not be tried?
29:7 (6)	those who believe, and do righteous deeds
29:9 (8)	those who believe, and do righteous deeds
29:10 (9)	some men there are who say, 'We believe in God'
29:11 (10)	God surely knows the believers
29:12 (11)	the unbelievers say to the believers
29:26 (25)	but Lot believed him
29:46 (45)	we believe in what has been sent down to us
29:52 (52)	Those who believe in vanity and disbelieve in God
29:56 (56)	O My servants who believe, surely My earth is wide
29:58 (58)	And those who believe, and do righteous deeds
30:15 (14)	as for those who believed, and did deeds of righteousness
30:45 (44)	that He may recompense those who believe and do righteous deeds of His bounty
31:8 (7)	those who believe, and do deeds of righteousness, there awaits them Gardens
32:19 (19)	those who believe, and do deeds of righteousness, there await them the Gardens
33:9 (9)	O believers, remember God's blessing upon you
33:41 (41)	O believers, remember God oft
33:49 (48)	O believers, when you marry believing women
33:53 (53)	O believers, enter not the houses of the Prophet, except leave is given you
33:56 (56)	O believers, do you also bless him, and pray him peace
33:69 (69)	O believers, be not as those who hurt Moses
33:70 (70)	O believers, fear God
34:4 (4)	that He may recompense those who believe
34:37 (36)	except for him who believes, and does righteousness
34:52 (51)	and they say, 'We believe in it'
35:7 (8)	those who believe, and do deeds of righteousness — theirs shall be forgiveness
36:25 (24)	Behold, I believe in your Lord
36:47 (47)	the (unbelievers) say to the believers, 'What, shall we feed such a one'
37:148 (148)	and they believed; so We gave them enjoyment
38:24 (23)	save those who believe, and do deeds of righteousness
38:28 (27)	Or shall We make those who believe and do righteous deeds as the workers of corruption
39:10 (13)	My servants who believe, fear your Lord
40:7 (7)	and they ask forgiveness for those who believe
40:25 (26)	slay the sons of those who believe with him
40:30 (31)	Then said he who believed
40:35 (37)	very hateful is that in the sight of God and the believers
40:38 (41)	Then said he who believed
40:51 (54)	We shall help Our Messengers and those who have believed

40:58 (60)	those who believe and do deeds of righteousness
40:84 (84)	We believe in God alone
41:8 (7)	those who believe, and do righteous deeds
41:18 (17)	We delivered those who believed and were godfearing
41:44 (44)	to the believers it is a guidance, and a healing
42:15 (14)	I believe in whatever Book God has sent down
42:18 (17)	those who believe in it go in fear of it
42:22 (21)	those who believe and do righteous deeds are in Meadows of Gardens
42:23 (22)	that is the good tidings God gives to His servants who believe
42:26 (25)	He answers those who believe and do righteous deeds
42:36 (34)	what is with God is better and more enduring for those who believe
42:45 (44)	and the believers shall say, 'Surely the losers
43:69 (69)	even those who believed in Our signs
45:14 (13)	Say unto those who believe, that they forgive
45:21 (20)	that We shall make them as those who believe
45:30 (29)	as for those who have believed and done deeds of righteousness
46:10 (9)	a witness from among the Children of Israel bears witness to its like, and believes
46:11 (10)	the unbelievers say, as regards the believers
47:2 (2)	but those who believe and do righteous deeds
47:2 (2)	and believe in what is sent down to Muhammad
47:3 (3)	and those who believe follow the truth from their Lord
47:7 (8)	O believers, if you help God, He will help you
47:11 (12)	God is the Protector of the believers
47:12 (13)	God shall surely admit those who believe and do righteous deeds into gardens
47:20 (22)	those who believe say, 'Why has a sura not been sent down?'
47:33 (35)	O believers, obey God, and obey the Messenger
48:29 (29)	God has promised those of them who believe
49:1 (1)	O believers, advance not before God and His Messenger
49:2 (2)	O believers, raise not your voices above the Prophet's voice
49:6 (6)	O believers, if an ungodly man comes to you with a tiding
49:11 (11)	O believers, let not any people scoff at another people
49:12 (12)	O believers, eschew much suspicion
49:14 (14)	the Bedouins say, 'We believe'
49:15 (15)	The believers are those who believe in God and His Messenger
52:21 (21)	And those who believed, and their seed followed them
57:7 (7)	those of you who believe and expend shall have a mighty wage
57:13 (13)	when the hypocrites, men and women, shall say to those who have believed
57:16 (15)	Is it not time that the hearts of those who believe should be humbled
57:19 (18)	those who believe in God and His Messengers — they are the just men
57:21 (21)	made ready for those who believe in God and His Messengers
57:27 (27)	We gave those of them who believed their wage
57:28 (28)	O believers, fear God
58:9 (10)	O believers, when you conspire secretly
58:10 (11)	that the believers may sorrow
58:11 (12)	O believers, when it is said to you 'Make room in the assemblies'
58:11 (12)	God will raise up in rank those of you who believe
58:12 (13)	O believers, when you conspire with the Messenger
59:10 (10)	put Thou not into our hearts any rancour towards those who believe
59:18 (18)	O believers, fear God
60:1 (1)	O believers, take not My enemy and your enemy for friends
60:10 (10)	O believers, when believing women come to you as emigrants, test them
60:13 (13)	O believers, take not for friends a people against whom God is wrathful
61:2 (2)	O you who believe, wherefore do you say what you do not?
61:10 (10)	O believers, shall I direct you to a commerce

61:14 (14) O believers, be you God's helpers
61:14 (14) and a party of the Children of Israel believed
61:14 (14) so We confirmed those who believed
62:9 (9) O believers, when proclamation is made for prayer
63:3 (3) because they have believed, then they have disbelieved
63:9 (9) O believers, let not your possessions neither your children divert you
64:14 (14) O believers, among your wives and children there is an enemy to you
65:10 (11) Believers, God has sent down to you for a remembrance
65:11 (11) that He may bring forth those who believe and do righteous deeds from the shadows
66:6 (6) Believers, guard yourselves and your families
66:8 (8) Believers, turn to God in sincere repentance
66:8 (8) God will not degrade the Prophet and those who believe with him
66:11 (11) God has struck a similitude for the believers
67:29 (29) We believe in Him, and in Him we put all our trust
72:2 (2) we believe in it, and we will not associate with our Lord anyone
72:13 (13) When we heard the guidance, we believed in it
74:31 (31) that those who believe may increase in belief
83:29 (29) Behold, the sinners were laughing at the believers
83:34 (34) today the believers are laughing at the unbelievers
84:25 (25) except those that believe, and do righteous deeds
85:11 (11) Those who believe, and do righteous deeds
90:17 (17) then that he become of those who believe
95:6 (6) save those who believe, and do righteous deeds
98:7 (6) But those who believe, and do righteous deeds
103:3 (3) save those who believe, and do righteous deeds
106:4 (4) and secured them from fear

b) impf. act. (*yuʾminu*)

2:3 (2) who believe in the Unseen, and perform the prayer
2:4 (3) who believe in what has been sent down to thee
2:6 (5) they do not believe
2:13 (12) shall we believe, (as fools believe?)
2:55 (52) Moses, we will not believe thee
2:75 (70) are you then so eager that they should believe you
2:85 (79) do you believe in part of the Book, and disbelieve in part?
2:88 (82) little will they believe
2:91 (85) we believe in what was sent down on us
2:100 (94) nay, but the most of them do not believe
2:121 (115) they believe in it
2:186 (182) let them believe in Me
2:221 (220) do not marry idolatresses, until they believe
2:221 (220) do not marry idolaters, until they believe
2:228 (228) if they believe in God and the Last Day
2:232 (232) that is an admonition for whoso of you believes in God and the Last Day
2:256 (257) [whosoever] believes in God, has laid hold of the most firm handle
2:260 (262) why, dost thou not believe?
2:264 (266) and believes not in God and the Last Day
3:73 (66) believe not any but him who follows your religion
3:81 (75) you shall believe in him and you shall help him
3:110 (106) forbidding dishonour, and believing in God
3:114 (110) believing in God and in the Last Day
3:119 (115) you believe in the Book, all of it
3:179 (174) if you believe and are godfearing, there shall be for you a mighty wage
3:183 (179) that we believe not any Messenger until he brings to us a sacrifice

3:199 (198)	some there are of the People of the Book who believe in God
4:38 (42)	[such as] believe not in God and the Last Day
4:46 (49)	so they believe not except a few
4:51 (54)	those who were given a share of the Book believing in demons
4:59 (62)	if you believe in God and the Last Day
4:65 (68)	they will not believe till they make thee the judge
4:150 (149)	We believe in part, and disbelieve in part
4:155 (154)	so they believe not except a few
4:159 (157)	There is not one of the People of the Book but will assuredly believe in him
4:162 (160)	believing in what has been sent down to thee
5:41 (45)	such men as say with their mouths 'We believe'
5:81 (84)	Yet had they believed in God and the Prophet
5:84 (87)	Why should we not believe in God and the truth that has come to us
6:12 (12)	those who have lost their souls, they do not believe
6:20 (20)	Those who have lost their own souls, they do not believe
6:25 (25)	if they see any sign whatever, they do not believe in it
6:54 (54)	when those who believe in Our signs come
6:92 (92)	those who believe in the world to come (believe) in it
6:92 (92)	those who (believe) in the world to come believe in it
6:99 (99)	in all this are signs for a people who do believe
6:109 (109)	if a sign comes to them they will believe in it
6:109 (109)	when it comes, they will not believe
6:110 (110)	even as they believed not in it the first time
6:111 (111)	they would not have been the ones to believe
6:113 (113)	that the hearts of those who believe not in the world to come may incline to it
6:124 (124)	We will not believe until we are given
6:125 (125)	So God lays abomination upon those who believe not
6:150 (151)	and who believe not in the world to come
6:154 (155)	haply they would believe in the encounter with their Lord
7:27 (26)	We have made the Satans the friends of those who do not believe
7:52 (50)	and a mercy unto a people that believe
7:87 (85)	and a party who believe not, be patient
7:101 (99)	but they were not the ones to believe in that
7:134 (131)	surely we will believe thee
7:146 (143)	though they see every sign, they will not believe in it
7:156 (155)	and those who indeed believe in Our signs
7:158 (158)	the Prophet of the common folk, who believes in God and His words
7:185 (184)	in what manner of discourse then will they after this believe?
7:188 (188)	I am only a warner, and a bearer of good tidings, to a people believing
7:203 (202)	guidance, and mercy for a people of believers
8:55 (57)	the worst of beasts in God's sight are the unbelievers, who will not believe
9:29 (29)	fight those who believe not in God and the Last Day
9:44 (44)	those who believe in God and the Last Day ask not leave of thee, that they may struggle
9:45 (45)	They only ask leave of thee who believe not in God and the Last Day
9:61 (61)	he believes in God and (believes) the believers
9:61 (61)	he (believes) in God and believes the believers
9:94 (95)	we will not believe you
9:99 (100)	some of the Bedouins believe in God and the Last Day
10:13 (14)	their Messengers came to them with the clear signs, but they would not believe
10:33 (34)	the word of they Lord is realized against the ungodly that they believe not
10:40 (41)	and some of them believe in it
10:40 (41)	and some believe not in it
10:74 (75)	but they were not men to believe
10:88 (88)	so that they do not believe, till they see the painful chastisement

10:96 (96)	Those against whom thy Lord's word is realized will not believe
10:100 (100)	It is not for any soul to believe save by the leave of God
10:101 (101)	nor warnings avail a people who do not believe
11:17 (20)	those believe in it
11:17 (20)	but most men do not believe
11:36 (38)	None of thy people shall believe
11:121 (122)	And say to those who do not believe
12:37 (37)	I have forsaken the creed of a people who believe not in God
12:106 (106)	And the most part of them believe not in God
12:111 (111)	and a guidance, and a mercy to a people who believe
13:1 (1)	but most men do not believe
15:13 (13)	they believe not in it
16:22 (23)	they who believe not in the world to come, their hearts deny
16:60 (62)	Those who believe not in the world to come, theirs is the evil likeness
16:64 (66)	as a guidance, and as a mercy to a people who believe
16:72 (74)	do they believe in vanity
16:79 (81)	surely in that are signs for a people who believe
16:104 (106)	Those that believe not in the signs of God, God will not guide
16:105 (107)	They only forge falsehood, who believe not in the signs of God
17:10 (11)	those who do not believe in the world to come
17:45 (47)	those who do not believe in the world to come
17:90 (92)	We will not believe thee till thou makest a spring to gush forth
17:93 (95)	we will not believe thy going up till thou bringest down on us a book
17:94 (96)	And naught prevented men from believing
17:107 (108)	believe in it, or believe not
18:6 (5)	if they believe not in this tiding, thou wilt consume thyself
18:29 (28)	so let whosoever will believe
18:55 (53)	and naught prevented men from believing
19:39 (40)	they yet heedless and do not believe
20:16 (17)	let none bar thee from it, that believes not in it
20:127 (127)	We recompense him who is prodigal and believes not in the signs of his Lord
21:6 (6)	what then, will they not believe?
21:30 (31)	will they not believe?
22:54 (53)	[they] may know that it is the truth from thy Lord and believe in it
23:44 (46)	so away with a people who do not believe
23:47 (49)	shall we believe two mortals like ourselves
23:58 (60)	those who believe in the signs of their Lord
23:74 (76)	they that believe not in the world to come are deviating
24:2 (2)	let no tenderness for them seize you if you believe in God and the Last Day
24:62 (62)	those are they that believe in God and His Messenger
26:111 (111)	shall we believe thee, whom the vilest follow?
26:201 (201)	who will not believe in it, until they see the painful chastisement
27:4 (4)	those who believe not in the Hereafter
27:81 (83)	neither shalt thou make any to hear, save such as believe in Our signs
27:86 (88)	surely in that is a sign for a people who believe
28:3 (2)	something of the tiding of Moses and Pharaoh truthfully, for a people who believe
28:52 (52)	those to whom We gave the Book before this believe in it
29:24 (23)	in that are signs for a people who believe
29:47 (46)	those to whom We have given the Book believe in it
29:47 (46)	and some of these believe in it
29:51 (50)	a mercy, and a reminder to a people who believe
29:67 (67)	what, do they believe in vanity?
30:37 (36)	surely in that are signs for a people who believe
30:53 (52)	except for such as believe in Our signs

32:15 (15)	Only those believe in Our signs who
33:19 (19)	those have never believed
34:8 (8)	those who believe not in the Hereafter are in chastisement
34:21 (20)	that We might know him who believed in the Hereafter
34:31 (30)	we will not believe in this Koran, nor in that before it
36:7 (6)	yet they do not believe
36:10 (9)	thou hast not warned them, they do not believe
39:45 (46)	then shudder the hearts of those who believe not in the Hereafter
39:52 (53)	Surely in that are signs for a people who believe
40:7 (7)	[they] proclaim the praise of their Lord, and believe in Him
40:12 (12)	if others are associated with Him, then you believe
40:27 (28)	who is proud, and believes not in the Day of Reckoning
40:59 (61)	The Hour is coming, no doubt of it, but most men do not believe
41:44 (44)	those who believe not, in their ears is a heaviness
42:18 (17)	Those that believe not therein seek to hasten it
43:88 (88)	these are a people who believe not
44:21 (20)	But if so be that you believe me not, go you apart from me
45:6 (5)	in what manner of discourse then, after God and His signs, will they believe?
47:36 (38)	if you believe and are godfearing, He will give you your wages
48:9 (9)	that you may believe in God and His Messenger
48:13 (13)	whoso believes not in God and His Messenger
49:14 (14)	you do not believe
52:33 (33)	nay, but they do not believe
53:27 (28)	those who do not believe in the world to come name the angels with the names of females
57:8 (8)	how is it with you, that you believe not in God
57:8 (8)	seeing that the Messenger is calling you to believe in your Lord
58:4 (5)	that you may believe in God and His Messenger
58:22 (22)	find any people who believe in God and the Last Day
60:1 (1)	because you believe in God your Lord
60:4 (4)	until you believe in God alone
61:11 (11)	You shall believe in God and His Messenger
64:9 (9)	whosoever believes in God, and does righteousness
64:11 (11)	whosoever believes in God, He will guide his heart
65:2 (2)	By this then is admonished whosoever believes in God and the Last Day
65:11 (11)	Whosoever believes in God, and does righteousness
69:33 (33)	he never believed in God the All-mighty
69:41 (41)	little do you believe
72:13 (13)	whosoever believes in his Lord, he shall fear neither paltriness nor vileness
77:50 (50)	in what discourse after this will they believe?
84:20 (20)	then what ails them, that they believe not
85:8 (8)	because they believed in God the All-mighty, the All-laudable

c) impv. (*āmin*)

2:13 (12)	when it is said to them, 'Believe
2:41 (38)	believe in that I have sent down
2:91 (85)	believe in that God has sent down
3:72 (65)	Believe in what has been sent down
3:179 (174)	Believe you then in God and His Messengers
3:193 (190)	Believe you in your Lord
4:47 (50)	believe in what We have sent down
4:136 (135)	O believers, believe in God and His Messenger
4:170 (168)	the Messenger has now come to you with the truth from your Lord; so believe
4:171 (169)	so believe in God and His Messengers
5:111 (111)	Believe in Me and My Messenger

7:158 (158)	Believe then in God, and in His Messenger
9:86 (87)	Believe in God, and struggle with His Messenger
17:107 (108)	believe in it
46:17 (16)	believe; surely God's promise is true
46:31 (30)	answer God's summoner, and believe in Him
57:7 (7)	believe in God and His Messenger
57:28 (28)	O believers, fear God, and believe in His Messenger
64:8 (8)	therefore believe in God and His Messenger

f) n.vb. (*īmān*)

2:93 (87)	Evil is the thing your faith bids you to
2:108 (102)	Whoso exchanges belief for unbelief has surely strayed from the right way
2:109 (103)	restore you as unbelievers, after your believing
2:143 (138)	God would never leave your faith to waste
3:86 (80)	How shall God guide a people who have disbelieved after their believing
3:90 (84)	Surely those who disbelieve after their believing
3:100 (95)	they will turn you, after your believing, into unbelievers
3:106 (102)	did you disbelieve after your believing?
3:167 (160)	they that day were nearer to unbelief than to belief
3:173 (167)	but it increased them in faith
3:177 (171)	those who buy unbelief at the price of faith
3:193 (190)	we have heard a caller calling us to belief
4:25 (29)	God knows very well your faith
5:5 (7)	whoso disbelieves in the faith, his work has failed
6:82 (82)	those who believe, and have not confounded their belief with evildoing
6:158 (159)	it shall not profit a soul to have faith that never believed before
6:158 (159)	or earned some good in his belief
8:2 (2)	when His signs are recited to them, it increases them in faith
9:23 (23)	if they prefer unbelief to belief
9:66 (67)	You have disbelieved after your believing
9:124 (125)	which of you has this increased in belief?
9:124 (125)	as for the believers, them it has increased in belief
10:9 (9)	their Lord will guide them for their belief
10:98 (98)	why was there never a city that believed, and its belief profited it
16:106 (108)	whoso disbelieves in God, after his believing
16:106 (108)	his heart is still at rest in his belief
30:56 (56)	those who have been given knowledge and faith shall say
32:29 (29)	On the Day of Victory their faith shall not profit the unbelievers
33:22 (22)	it only increased them in faith and surrender
40:10 (10)	when you were called unto belief, and disbelieved
40:28 (29)	of Pharaoh's folk that kept hidden his belief
40:85 (85)	But their belief when they saw Our might did not profit them
42:52 (52)	Thou knewest not what the Book was, nor belief
48:4 (4)	they might add faith to their (faith)
48:4 (4)	they might add (faith) to their faith
49:7 (7)	God has endeared to you belief
49:11 (11)	An evil name is ungodliness after belief
49:14 (14)	for belief has not yet entered your hearts
49:17 (17)	in that He has guided you to belief
52:21 (21)	and their seed followed them in belief
58:22 (22)	He has written faith upon their hearts
59:9 (9)	those who made their dwelling in the abode, and in belief
59:10 (10)	forgive us and our brothers, who preceded us in belief
60:10 (10)	God knows very well their belief
74:31 (31)	that those who believe may increase in belief

g) pcple. act. (*mu'min*)

2:8 (7)	but they are not believers
2:91 (85)	why then were you slaying the Prophets of God in former time, if you were believers?
2:93 (87)	evil is the thing your faith bids you to, if you are believers
2:97 (91)	a guidance and good tidings to the believers
2:221 (220)	a believing slavegirl is better than an idolatress
2:221 (220)	a believing slave is better than an idolater
2:223 (223)	Give thou good tidings to the believers
2:248 (249)	surely in that shall be a sign for you, if you are believers
2:278 (278)	give up the usury that is outstanding, if you are believers
2:285 (285)	The Messenger believes in what was sent down to him from his Lord, and the believers
3:28 (27)	let not the believers take the unbelievers for friends
3:28 (27)	rather than the believers
3:49 (43)	in that is a sign for you, if you are believers
3:68 (61)	God is the Protector of the believers
3:110 (106)	some of them are believers
3:121 (117)	to lodge the believers in their pitches for the battle
3:122 (118)	in God let the believers put all their trust
3:124 (120)	When thou saidst to the believers
3:139 (133)	you shall be the upper ones if you are believers
3:152 (146)	God is bounteous to the believers
3:160 (154)	in God let the believers put all their trust
3:164 (158)	Truly God was gracious to the believers
3:166 (160)	that He might know the believers
3:171 (165)	God leaves not to waste the wage of the believers
3:175 (169)	fear you Me, if you are believers
3:179 (173)	God will not leave the believers in the state in which you are
4:25 (29)	to be able to marry believing freewomen
4:25 (29)	let him take believing handmaids
4:84 (86)	and urge on the believers
4:92 (94)	it belongs not to a believer to slay
4:92 (94)	to slay a believer, except it be by error
4:92 (94)	if any slays a believer by error
4:92 (94)	let him set free a believing slave
4:92 (94)	if he belong to a people at enmity with you and is a believer
4:92 (94)	set free a believing slave
4:92 (94)	and the slayer shall set free a believing slave
4:93 (95)	and whoso slays a believer wilfully
4:94 (96)	Thou art not a believer
4:95 (97)	such believers as sit at home
4:103 (104)	the prayer is a timed prescription for the believers
4:115 (115)	and follows a way other than the believers
4:124 (123)	whosoever does deeds of righteousness, be it male or female, believing
4:139 (138)	those who take unbelievers for their friends instead of believers
4:141 (140)	did we not defend you from the believers?
4:141 (140)	God will not grant the unbelievers any way over the believers
4:144 (143)	take not the unbelievers as friends instead of the believers
4:146 (145)	those are with the believers
4:146 (145)	God will certainly give the believers a mighty wage
4:162 (160)	the believers who believe in what has been sent down to thee
4:162 (160)	those who believe in God and the Last Day
5:5 (7)	likewise believing women in wedlock
5:11 (14)	in God let the believers put all their trust

5:23 (26)	Put you all your trust in God, if you are believers
5:43 (47)	They are not believers
5:54 (59)	humble towards the believers
5:57 (62)	fear God, if you are believers
5:88 (90)	fear God, in whom you are believers
5:112 (112)	Fear you God, if you are believers
6:27 (27)	that we might be among the believers
6:118 (118)	if you are believers in His signs
7:2 (1)	to warn thereby, and as a reminder to believers
7:72 (70)	those who cried lies to Our signs and were not believers
7:75 (73)	In the Message he has been sent with we are believers
7:85 (83)	that is better for you, if you are believers
7:132 (129)	we will not believe thee
7:143 (140)	I am the first of the believers
8:1 (1)	obey you God and His Messenger, if you are believers
8:2 (2)	Those only are believers who, when God is mentioned, their hearts quake
8:4 (4)	those in truth are the believers
8:5 (5)	a part of the believers were averse to it
8:17 (17)	that He might confer on the believers a fair benefit
8:19 (19)	that God is with the believers
8:62 (64)	He has confirmed thee with His help, and with the believers
8:64 (65)	O Prophet, God suffices thee, and the believers
8:65 (66)	O Prophet, urge on the believers to fight
8:74 (75)	those in truth are the believers
9:10 (10)	observing neither bond nor treaty towards a believer
9:13 (13)	You would do better to be afraid of God, if you are believers
9:14 (14)	and bring healing to the breasts of a people who are believers
9:16 (16)	and taken not — apart from God and His Messenger and the believers — any intimate
9:26 (26)	God sent down upon His Messenger His Shechina, and upon the believers
9:51 (51)	in God let the believers put all their trust
9:61 (61)	he believes in God, and believes the believers
9:62 (63)	they should please Him, if they are believers
9:71 (72)	and the believers, the men and (the women), are friends
9:71 (72)	and the believers, (the men) and the women, are friends
9:72 (73)	God has promised the believers, men and (women)
9:72 (73)	God has promised the believers, (men) and women
9:79 (80)	those who find fault with the believers
9:105 (106)	God will surely see your work, and His Messenger, and the believers
9:107 (108)	and to divide the believers
9:111 (112)	God has bought from the believers their selves
9:112 (113)	give thou good tidings to the believers
9:122 (123)	It is not for the believers to go forth totally
9:128 (129)	anxious is he over you, gentle to the believers
10:57 (58)	a guidance, and a mercy to the believers
10:78 (79)	we are not believers in you
10:87 (87)	do thou give good tidings to the believers
10:99 (99)	then constrain the people, until they are believers
10:103 (103)	Our bounden duty, We shall deliver the believers
10:104 (104)	I am commanded to be of the believers
11:53 (56)	we are not believers in thee
11:86 (87)	God's remainder is better for you, if you are believers
11:120 (121)	an admonition, and a reminder to the believers
12:17 (17)	but thou wouldst never be one believing us
12:103 (103)	be thou ever so eager, the most part of men are not believers

14:11 (14)	in God let the believers put all their trust
14:41 (42)	forgive Thou me and my parents, and the believers
15:77 (77)	surely in that is a sign for believers
15:88 (88)	and lower thy wing unto the believers
16:97 (99)	whosoever does a righteous deed, be it male or female, believing
17:9 (9)	and gives good tidings to the believers
17:19 (20)	and strives after it as he should, being a believer
17:82 (84)	that which is a healing and a mercy to the believers
18:2 (2)	and to give good tidings unto the believers
18:80 (79)	As for the lad, his parents were believers
20:75 (77)	And whoso comes unto Him a believer
20:112 (111)	whosoever does deeds of righteousness, being a believer
21:88 (88)	even so do We deliver the believers
21:94 (94)	And whosoever does deeds of righteousness, being a believer
23:1 (1)	Prosperous are the believers
23:38 (40)	we will not be believing him
24:2 (2)	let a party of the believers witness their chastisement
24:3 (3)	that is forbidden to the believers
24:12 (12)	why, when you heard it, did the believing men and (women) not of their own account
24:12 (12)	why, when you heard it, did the believing (men) and women not of their own account
24:17 (16)	never repeat the like of it again, if you are believers
24:23 (23)	those who cast it up on women in wedlock that are heedless but believing
24:30 (30)	say to the believers, that they cast down their eyes
24:31 (31)	and say to the believing women, that they cast down their eyes
24:31 (31)	and turn all together to God, O you believers
24:47 (46)	those — they are not believers
24:51 (50)	All that the believers say
24:62 (62)	Those only are believers, who believe in God and His Messenger
26:3 (2)	thou consumest thyself that they are not believers
26:8 (7)	yet most of them are not believers
26:51 (51)	we are the first of the believers
26:67 (67)	yet most of them are not believers
26:102 (102)	O that we might return again, and be among the believers
26:103 (103)	yet most of them are not believers
26:114 (114)	I would not drive away the believers
26:118 (118)	and deliver me and the believers
26:121 (121)	yet most of them are not believers
26:139 (139)	yet most of them are not believers
26:158 (158)	yet most of them are not believers
26:174 (174)	yet most of them are not believers
26:190 (190)	yet most of them are not believers
26:199 (199)	they would not have been believers in it
26:215 (215)	Lower thy wing to those who follow thee, being believers
27:2 (2)	a guidance, and good tidings unto the believers
27:15 (15)	who has preferred us over many of His believing servants
27:77 (79)	it is a guidance, and a mercy unto the believers
28:10 (9)	that she might be among the believers
28:47 (47)	that we might follow Thy signs and so be among the believers
29:44 (43)	in that is a sign to the believers
30:4 (3)	and on that day the believers shall rejoice
30:47 (46)	ever a duty incumbent upon Us, to help the believers
32:18 (18)	is he who has been a believer like unto him who has been ungodly?
33:6 (6)	the Prophet is nearer to the believers than their selves

33:6 (6)	[they] are nearer to one another in the Book of God than the believers
33:11 (11)	there it was that the believers were tried
33:22 (22)	when the believers saw the Confederates
33:23 (23)	among the believers are men who were true
33:25 (25)	God spared the believers of fighting
33:35 (35)	believing men
33:35 (35)	and believing women
33:36 (36)	it is not for any believer, man or (woman)
33:36 (36)	it is not for any believer, (man) or woman
33:37 (37)	so that there should not be any fault in the believers
33:43 (42)	He is All-compassionate to the believers
33:47 (46)	Give good tidings to the believers
33:49 (48)	when you marry believing women
33:50 (49)	any woman believer, if she give herself to the Prophet
33:50 (49)	for thee exclusively, apart from the believers
33:58 (58)	those who hurt believing men and (believing women)
33:58 (58)	those who hurt (believing men) and believing women
33:59 (59)	and the believing women, that they draw veils
33:73 (73)	turn again unto the believers, men and (women) alike
33:73 (73)	turn again unto the believers, (men) and women alike
34:20 (19)	and they followed him, except a party of the believers
34:31 (30)	had it not been for you, we would have been believers
34:41 (40)	most of them were believers in them
37:29 (29)	on the contrary, you were not believers
37:81 (79)	he was among Our believeing servants
37:111 (111)	he was among Our believing servants
37:122 (122)	they were among Our believing servants
37:132 (132)	he was among Our believing servants
40:28 (29)	Then said a certain man, a believer
40:40 (43)	whosoever does a righteous deed, be it male or female, believing
44:12 (11)	remove Thou from us the chastisement; we are believers
45:3 (2)	in the heavens and earth there are signs for the believers
47:19 (21)	ask forgiveness for thy sin, and for the believers, men and (women)
47:19 (21)	ask forgiveness for thy sin, and for the believers, (men) and women
48:4 (4)	it is He who sent down the Shechina into the hearts of the believers
48:5 (5)	that He may admit the believers, men and (women) alike, into gardens
48:5 (5)	that He may admit the believers, (men) and women alike, into gardens
48:12 (12)	you thought that the Messenger and the believers would never return
48:18 (18)	God was well pleased with the believers
48:20 (20)	that it may be a sign to the believers
48:25 (25)	if it had not been for certain men believers
48:25 (25)	and certain women believers whom you knew not
48:26 (26)	then God sent down His Shechina upon His Messenger and the believers
49:9 (9)	if two parties of the believers fight
49:10 (10)	the believers indeed are brothers
49:15 (15)	the believers are those who believe in God and His Messenger
51:35 (35)	so We brought forth such believers as were in it
51:55 (55)	the Reminder profits the believers
57:8 (8)	He has taken compact with you, if you are believers
57:12 (12)	upon the day when thou seest the believers, men and (women)
57:12 (12)	upon the day when thou seest the believers, (men) and women
58:10 (11)	in God let the believers put all their trust
59:2 (2)	as they destroyed their houses with their own hands, and the hands of the believers
59:23 (23)	He is the King, the All-holy, the All-peaceable, the All-faithful, the All-preserver

60:10 (10)	when believing women come to you as emigrants, test them
60:10 (10)	if you know them to be believers, return them not to the unbelievers
60:11 (11)	And fear God, in whom you are believers
60:12 (12)	O Prophet, when believing women come to thee
61:13 (13)	Give thou good tidings to the believers
63:8 (8)	glory belongs unto God, and unto His Messenger and the believers
64:2 (2)	and one of you is a believer
64:13 (13)	And in God let the believers put their trust
66:4 (4)	and the righteous among the believers
66:5 (5)	women who have surrendered, believing, obedient, penitent, devout
71:28 (29)	and whosoever enters my house as a believer
71:28 (29)	and the believers, men and (women) alike
71:28 (29)	and the believers, (men) and women alike
74:31 (32)	and believers may not be in doubt
85:7 (7)	and were themselves witnesses of what they did with the believers
85:10 (10)	those who persecute the believers, men and (women)
85:10 (10)	those who persecute the believers, (men) and women

I'TAMANA vb. (VIII)~to trust

d) perf. pass. (*i'tumina*)

2:283 (283)	let him who is trusted deliver his trust

*A M R

AMARA vb. (I)~to command, to bid, to order. (n.vb.) a command, commandment, a bidding, task, matter, affair, a thing. (pcple. act.) one who commands, who bids, etc.

a) perf. act.

2:27 (25)	such as cut what God has commanded should be joined
2:222 (222)	then come unto them as God has commanded you
4:114 (114)	except for him who bids to freewill offering
5:117 (117)	I only said to them what Thou didst command me
7:12 (11)	what prevented thee to bow thyself, when I commanded thee?
7:28 (27)	and God has commanded us to do it
7:29 (28)	my Lord has commanded justice
12:40 (40)	He has commanded that you shall not serve any but Him
12:68 (68)	when they entered after the manner their father commanded them
13:21 (21)	who join what God has commanded shall be joined
13:25 (25)	who snap what God has commanded to be joined
17:16 (17)	We command its men who live at ease
22:41 (42)	pay the alms, and bid to honour
24:53 (52)	if thou commandest them they will go forth
66:6 (6)	who disobey not God in what He commands them
80:23 (23)	Man has not accomplished what He commanded him
96:12 (12)	or bade to godfearing

b) impf. act. (*ya'muru*)

2:44 (41)	Will you bid others to piety, and forget yourselves
2:67 (63)	God commands you to sacrifice a cow
2:93 (87)	Evil is the thing your faith bids you to
2:169 (164)	he only commands you to evil and indecency
2:268 (271)	Satan promises you poverty, and bids you unto indecency

3:21 (20)	[they] slay such men as bid to justice
3:80 (74)	He would never order you to take the angels and the Prophets as Lords
3:80 (74)	would He order you to disbelieve
3:104 (100)	bidding to honour, and forbidding dishonour
3:110 (106)	bidding to honour, and forbidding dishonour
3:114 (110)	bidding to honour and forbidding dishonour
4:37 (41)	such as are niggardly, and bid other men to be niggardly
4:58 (61)	God commands you to deliver trusts
4:119 (118)	I will command them and they will cut off the cattle's ears
4:119 (118)	I will command them and they will alter God's creation
7:28 (27)	God does not command indecency
7:110 (107)	what do you command?
7:157 (156)	bidding them to honour, and forbidding them dishonour
9:67 (68)	they bid to dishonour, and forbid honour
9:71 (72)	they bid to honour, and forbid dishonour
11:87 (89)	does thy prayer command thee that we should leave that our fathers served
12:32 (32)	if he will not do what I command him, he shall be imprisoned
16:76 (78)	is he equal to him who bids to justice
16:90 (92)	surely God bids to justice and good-doing
19:55 (56)	He bade his people to pray
24:21 (21)	assuredly he bids to indecency and dishonour
25:60 (61)	shall we bow ourselves to what thou biddest us?
26:35 (34)	what do you command?
27:33 (33)	so consider what thou wilt command
34:33 (32)	when you were ordering us to disbelieve in God
39:64 (64)	is it other than God you bid me serve
52:32 (32)	do their intellects bid them do this?
57:24 (24)	such as are niggardly, and bid men to be niggardly

c) impv. (*u'mur*)

7:145 (142)	command thy people to take the fairest
7:199 (198)	Take the abundance, and bid to what is honourable
20:132 (132)	And bid thy family to pray
31:17 (16)	and bid unto honour, and forbid dishonour

d) perf. pass. (*umira*)

4:60 (63)	yet they have been commanded to disbelieve
6:14 (14)	I have been commanded to be the first of them that surrender
6:71 (70)	and we are commanded to surrender to the Lord of all Being
6:163 (163)	even so I have been commanded
9:31 (31)	they were commanded to serve but One God
10:72 (73)	I have been commanded to be of those that surrender
10:104 (104)	I am commanded to be of the believers
11:112 (114)	So go thou straight, as thou hast been commanded
13:36 (36)	I have only been commanded to serve God
27:91 (93)	I have only been commanded to serve the Lord of this territory
27:91 (93)	and I have been commanded to be of those that surrender
39:11 (14)	I have been commanded to serve God
39:12 (14)	I have been commanded to be the first of those that surrender
40:66 (68)	I am commanded to surrender to the Lord of all Being
42:15 (14)	and go straight as thou hast been commanded
42:15 (14)	I have been commanded to be just
98:5 (4)	They were commanded only to serve God

e) impf. pass. (*yu'maru*)

2:68 (63)	so do that you are bidden
15:65 (65)	depart unto the place you are commanded
15:94 (94)	So shout that thou art commanded
16:50 (52)	and they do what they are commanded
37:102 (102)	My father, do as thou art bidden
66:6 (6)	do what they are commanded

f) n.vb. (*amr*)

2:109 (103)	be forgiving, till God brings His command
2:117 (111)	when He decrees a thing, He but says to it, 'Be,'and it is
2:210 (206)	the matter is determined
2:210 (206)	unto God all matters are returned
2:275 (276)	his affair is committed to God
3:47 (42)	when He decrees a thing He does but say to it 'Be'
3:109 (105)	unto Him all matters are returned
3:128 (123)	no part of the matter is thine
3:147 (141)	and that we exceeded in our affair
3:152 (145)	you lost heart, and quarrelled about the matter
3:154 (148)	have we any part whatever in the affair?
3:154 (148)	the affair belongs to God entirely
3:154 (148)	if we had had a part in the affair
3:159 (153)	take counsel with them in the affair
3:186 (183)	surely that is true constancy
4:47 (50)	God's command is done
4:59 (62)	and obey the Messenger and those in authority among you
4:83 (85)	when there comes to them a matter
4:83 (85)	if they had referred it to the Messenger and to those in authority among them
5:52 (57)	it may be that God will bring the victory, or some commandment
5:95 (96)	he may taste the mischief of his action
6:8 (8)	the matter would have been determined
6:58 (58)	the matter between you and me would be decided
6:159 (160)	their affair is unto God
7:54 (52)	the sun, and the moon, and the stars subservient, by His command
7:54 (52)	verily, His are the creation and the command
7:77 (75)	[they] turned in disdain from the commandment of their Lord
7:150 (149)	have you outstripped your Lord's commandment?
8:42 (43)	but that God might determine a matter that was done
8:43 (45)	you would have lost heart, and quarrelled about the matter
8:44 (46)	that God might determine a matter that was done
8:44 (46)	unto God all matters are returned
9:24 (24)	then wait till God brings His command
9:48 (48)	[they] turned things upside down for thee
9:48 (48)	and God's command appeared
9:50 (50)	We took our dispositions before
9:106 (107)	others are deferred to God's commandment
10:3 (3)	then sat Himself upon the Throne, directing the affair
10:24 (25)	Our command comes upon it
10:31 (32)	and who directs the affair?
10:71 (72)	so resolve on your affair
10:71 (72)	then let not your affair be a worry
11:40 (42)	until, when Our command came
11:43 (45)	there is no defender from God's command
11:44 (46)	the affair was accomplished

11:58 (61)	and when Our command came, We delivered
11:59 (62)	[they] followed the command of every froward tyrant
11:66 (69)	and when Our command came, We delivered
11:73 (76)	dost thou marvel at God's command?
11:76 (78)	thy Lord's command has surely come
11:82 (84)	when Our command came, We turned it uppermost nethermost
11:94 (97)	and when Our command came, We delivered
11:97 (99)	but they followed Pharaoh's command
11:97 (99)	and Pharaoh's command was not right-minded
11:101 (103)	when the command of thy Lord came
11:123 (123)	to Him the whole matter shall be returned
12:15 (15)	Thou shalt tell them of this deed of theirs
12:18 (18)	your spirits tempted you to do something
12:21 (21)	God prevails in His purpose
12:41 (41)	the matter is decided whereon you enquire
12:83 (83)	your spirits tempted you to do something
12:102 (103)	when they agreed upon their plan, devising
13:2 (2)	He directs the affair
13:11 (12)	watching over him by God's command
13:31 (30)	God's is the affair altogether
14:22 (26)	Satan says, when the issue is decided
14:32 (37)	He subjected to you the ships to run upon the sea at His commandment
15:66 (66)	We decreed for him that commandment
16:1 (1)	God's command comes
16:2 (2)	He sends down the angels with the Spirit of His command
16:12 (12)	and the stars are subjected by His command
16:33 (35)	or thy Lord's command shall come
16:77 (79)	And the matter of the Hour is as a twinkling of the eye
17:85 (87)	The Spirit is of the bidding of my Lord
18:10 (9)	and furnish us with rectitude in our affair
18:16 (15)	[He] will furnish you with a gentle issue of your affair
18:21 (20)	contending among themselves of their affair
18:21 (20)	said those who prevailed over their affair
18:28 (27)	and his affair has become all excess
18:50 (48)	[he] committed ungodliness against his Lord's command
18:69 (68)	I shall not rebel against thee in anything
18:73 (72)	neither constrain me to do a thing too difficult
18:82 (81)	I did it not of my own bidding
18:88 (87)	we shall speak to him, of our command, easiness
19:21 (21)	it is a thing decreed
19:35 (36)	when He decrees a thing, He but says to it 'Be'
19:39 (40)	when the matter shall be determined
19:64 (65)	we come not down, save at the commandment of thy Lord
20:26 (27)	and do Thou ease for me my task
20:32 (33)	and associate him with me in my task
20:62 (65)	and they disputed upon their plan between them
20:90 (92)	therefor follow me, and obey my commandment
20:93 (94)	didst thou then disobey my commandment?
21:27 (27)	[that] perform as He commands
21:73 (73)	and appointed them to be leaders guiding by Our command
21:81 (81)	that ran at his command unto the land
21:93 (93)	but they split up their affair between them
22:41 (42)	and unto God belongs the issue of all affairs
22:65 (64)	and the ships to run upon the sea at His commandment
22:67 (66)	Let them not therefore wrangle with thee upon the matter

22:76 (75)	and unto God all matters are returned
23:27 (27)	and then, when Our command comes and the Oven boils
23:53 (55)	But they split in their affair between them
24:62 (62)	when they are with him upon a common matter
24:63 (63)	let those who go against His command beware
26:151 (151)	obey not the commandment of the prodigal
27:32 (32)	O Council, pronounce to me concerning my affair
27:32 (32)	I am not used to decide an affair until you bear me witness
27:33 (33)	the affair rests with thee
28:44 (44)	when We decreed to Moses the commandment
30:4 (3)	to God belongs the Command before and after
30:25 (24)	is that the heaven and earth stand firm by His command
30:46 (45)	that the ships may run at His commandment
31:17 (16)	surely that is true constancy
31:22 (21)	unto God is the issue of all affairs
32:5 (4)	He directs the affair from heaven to earth
32:24 (24)	We appointed from among them leaders guiding by Our command
33:36 (36)	when God and His Messenger have decreed a matter
33:36 (36)	to have the choice in the affair
33:37 (37)	God's commandment must be performed
33:38 (38)	God's commandment is doom decreed
34:12 (11)	such of them as swerved away from Our commandment
35:4 (4)	unto God all matters are returned
36:82 (82)	His command, when He desires a thing, is to say to it 'Be,' and it is
38:36 (35)	So We subjected to him the wind, that ran at his commandment
40:15 (15)	casting the Spirit of His bidding upon whomever He will of His servants
40:44 (47)	I commit my affair to God
40:68 (70)	and when He decrees a thing, He but says to it 'Be,' and it is
40:78 (78)	When God's command comes, justly the issue shall be decided
41:12 (11)	[He] revealed its commandment in every heaven
42:38 (36)	their affair being counsel between them
42:43 (41)	surely that is true constancy
42:52 (52)	We have revealed to thee a Spirit of Our bidding
42:53 (53)	unto God all things come home
43:79 (79)	or have they contrived some matter?
44:4 (3)	therein every wise bidding determined
44:5 (4)	[determined] as a bidding from Us
45:12 (11)	the ships may run on it at His commandment
45:17 (16)	We gave them clear signs of the Command
45:18 (17)	then We set thee upon an open way of the Command
46:25 (24)	destroying everything by the commandment of its Lord
47:21 (23)	Then, when the matter is resolved
47:26 (28)	We will obey you in some of the affair
49:7 (7)	If he obeyed you in much of the affair, you would suffer
49:9 (9)	fight the insolent one till it reverts to God's commandment
50:5 (5)	when it came to them, and so they are in a case confused
51:4 (4)	and the partitioners [by command]
51:44 (44)	Then they turned in disdain from the commandment of their Lord
54:3 (3)	but every matter is settled
54:12 (12)	and the waters met for a matter decreed
54:50 (50)	Our commandment is but one word
57:5 (5)	and unto Him all matters are returned
57:14 (13)	and fancies deluded you, until God's commandment came
59:15 (15)	[those who] tasted the mischief of their action
64:5 (5)	[those that] tasted the mischief of their action

65:1 (1)	perchance after that God will bring something new to pass
65:3 (3)	God attains His purpose
65:4 (4)	Whoso fears God, God will appoint for him, of His command, easiness
65:5 (5)	That is God's command, that He has sent down
65:8 (8)	how many a city turned in disdain from the commandment of its Lord
65:9 (9)	so it tasted the mischief of its action
65:9 (9)	and the end of its affair was loss
65:12 (12)	between them the Command descending
79:5 (5)	by those that direct an affair
82:19 (19)	that day the Command shall belong unto God
97:4 (4)	by the leave of their Lord, upon every command

g) pcple. act. (*āmir*)

9:112 (113)	those who bid to honour and forbid dishonour

AMMĀR n.m.~one who incites, who enjoins, etc.

12:53 (53)	surely the soul of man incites to evil

IMR n.m. (adj)~grievous, dreadful

18:71 (70)	Thou hast indeed done a grievous thing

I'TAMARA vb. (VIII)~to consult, to conspire

b) impf. act. (*ya'tamiru*)

28:20 (19)	the Council are conspiring to slay thee

c) impv. (*i'tamir*)

65:6 (6)	and consult together honourably

*A M S

AMS n.m.~yesterday, the day before, the other day

10:24 (25)	as though yesterday it flourished not
28:18 (17)	the man who had sought his succour on the day before cried out to him
28:19 (18)	as thou slewest a living soul yesterday
28:82 (82)	those who had longed to be in his place the day before

*A M T

AMT n.m.~curving, ruggedness

20:107 (106)	wherein thou wilt see no crookedness neither any curving

*A M W

AMAH n.f.~slavegirl, handmaiden

2:221 (220)	a believing slavegirl is better than an idolatress
24:32 (32)	[marry] your handmaidens that are righteous

*A N F

ANF n.m.~nose

5:45 (49)	a nose for a (nose)
5:45 (49)	a (nose) for a nose

ĀNIF n.m.~(adv) lately, just now

47:16 (18)	what said he just now?

*A N M

ANĀM n.coll.~beings, creatures

55:10 (9)	and earth — He set it down for all beings

*A N S

INS n.m.~man, mankind

6:112 (112)	an enemy — Satans of men and jinn
6:128 (128)	Company of jinn, you have made much of mankind
6:128 (128)	then their friends among mankind will say
6:130 (130)	Company of jinn and mankind, did not Messengers come to you from among you
7:38 (36)	enter among nations that passed away before you, jinn and mankind
7:179 (178)	We have created for Gehenna many jinn and men
17:88 (90)	if men and jinn banded together to produce the like of this Koran
27:17 (17)	and his hosts were mustered to Solomon, jinn, men and birds
41:25 (24)	the Word concerning nations that passed away before them, men and jinn alike
41:29 (29)	show us those that led us astray, both jinn and men
46:18 (17)	the Word concerning nations that passed away before them, men and jinn alike
51:56 (56)	I have not created jinn and mankind except to serve Me
55:33 (33)	O tribe of jinn and of men
55:39 (39)	on that day none shall be questioned about his sin, neither man nor jinn
55:56 (56)	untouched before them by any man or jinn
55:74 (74)	untouched before them by any man or jinn
72:5 (5)	and we had thought that men and jinn would never speak against God
72:6 (6)	there were certain men of mankind who would take refuge with certain men of jinn

INSĀN n.m.~man, mankind

4:28 (32)	for man was created a weakling
10:12 (13)	When affliction visits a man, he calls Us
11:9 (12)	And if We let a man taste mercy from Us
12:5 (5)	surely Satan is to man a manifest enemy
14:34 (37)	surely man is sinful, unthankful
15:26 (26)	Surely We created man of a clay
16:4 (4)	He created man of a sperm-drop
17:11 (12)	man prays for evil, as he prays for good
17:11 (12)	man is ever hasty
17:13 (14)	And every man — We have fastened to him his bird of omen upon his neck
17:53 (55)	and Satan is ever a manifest foe to man
17:67 (69)	man is ever unthankful
17:83 (85)	and when We bless man, he turns
17:100 (102)	and man is ever niggardly
18:54 (52)	man is the most disputatious of things
19:66 (67)	man says, 'What, when I am dead shall I then be brought forth alive?'

19:67 (68)	will not man remember that We created him aforetime, when he was nothing?
21:37 (38)	man was created of haste
22:66 (65)	surely man is ungrateful
23:12 (12)	We created man of an extraction of clay
25:29 (31)	Satan is ever a forsaker of men
29:8 (7)	We have charged man, that he be kind to his parents
31:14 (13)	We have charged man concerning his parents
32:7 (6)	He originated the creation of man out of clay
33:72 (72)	and man carried it
36:77 (77)	has not man regarded how that We created him of a sperm-drop?
39:8 (11)	when some affliction visits a man, he calls upon his Lord, turning to Him
39:49 (50)	when some affliction visits a man, he calls unto Us
41:49 (49)	man wearies not of praying for good
41:51 (51)	and when We bless man, he turns away
42:48 (47)	and when We let man taste mercy from Us, he rejoices in it
42:48 (47)	then surely man is unthankful
43:15 (14)	man is clearly unthankful
46:15 (14)	We have charged man, that he be kind to his parents
50:16 (15)	We indeed created man
53:24 (24)	or shall man have whatever he fancies?
53:39 (40)	and that a man shall have to his account only as he has laboured
55:3 (2)	He created man
55:14 (13)	He created man of a clay like the potter's
59:16 (16)	like Satan, when he said to man, 'Disbelieve'
70:19 (19)	surely man was created fretful
75:3 (3)	what, does man reckon We shall not gather his bones?
75:5 (5)	nay, but man desires to continue on as a libertine
75:10 (10)	upon that day man shall say, 'Whither to flee?'
75:13 (13)	upon that day man shall be told his former deeds and his latter
75:14 (14)	nay, man shall be a clear proof against himself
75:36 (36)	what, does man reckon he shall be left to roam at will?
76:1 (1)	has there come on man a while of time when he was a thing unremembered?
76:2 (2)	We created man of a sperm-drop, a mingling
79:35 (35)	upon the day when man shall remember what he has striven
80:17 (16)	perish Man! How unthankful he is
80:24 (24)	let Man consider his nourishment
82:6 (6)	O Man! What deceived thee as to thy generous Lord
84:6 (6)	O Man! Thou art labouring unto thy Lord laboriously
86:5 (5)	so let man consider of what he was created
89:15 (14)	as for man, whenever his Lord tries him
89:23 (24)	man will remember
90:4 (4)	indeed, We created man in trouble
95:4 (4)	We indeed created man in the fairest stature
96:2 (2)	[He] created man of a blood-clot
96:5 (5)	[He] taught Man that he knew not
96:6 (6)	surely Man waxes insolent
99:3 (3)	and Man says, 'What ails her?'
100:6 (6)	surely Man is ungrateful to his Lord
103:2 (2)	surely Man is in the way of loss

INSĪY n.m. (pl. *anāsīy*)~a man

19:26 (27)	today I will not speak to any man
25:49 (51)	of that We created, cattle and men

UNĀS n.m. (pl. of *ins;* see also *N W S)~people, folk, men

2:60 (57) all the people knew now their drinking-place
7:82 (80) surely they are folk that keep themselves clean
7:160 (160) all the people knew now their drinking-place
17:71 (73) On the day when We shall call all men with their record
27:56 (57) Expel the folk of Lot from your city

ĀNASA vb. (IV)~to observe, to perceive

a) perf. act.

4:6 (5) if you perceive in them right judgment, deliver to them their property
20:10 (9) Tarry you here; I observe a fire
27:7 (7) I observe a fire
28:29 (29) he observed on the side of the Mount a fire
28:29 (29) tarry you here; I observe a fire

ISTA'NASA vb. (X)~to ask leave, to announce one's presence. (pcple. act.) one who lingers for idle talk (among familiar people)

b) impf. act. (*yasta'nisu*)

24:27 (27) until you first ask leave and salute the people thereof

g) pcple. act. (*musta'nis*)

33:53 (53) disperse, neither lingering for idle talk

*A N TH

UNTHÁ n.f. (pl. *ināth*)~female

2:178 (173) female for (female)
2:178 (173) (female) for female
3:36 (31) Lord, I have given birth to her, a female
3:36 (31) the male is not as the female
3:195 (193) be you male or female — the one of you is as the other
4:11 (12) to the male the like of the portion of two females
4:117 (117) they pray not except to female beings
4:124 (123) whosoever does deeds of righteousness, be it male or female
4:176 (175) the male shall receive the portion of two females
6:143 (144) is it the two males He has forbidden or the two females?
6:143 (144) or what the wombs of the two females contain
6:144 (145) is it the two males He has forbidden or the two females?
6:144 (145) or what the wombs of the two females contain
13:8 (9) God knows what every female bears
16:58 (60) when any of them is given the good tidings of the birth of a female his face is darkened
16:97 (99) and whosoever does a righteous deed, be it male or female
17:40 (42) [has He] taken to Himself from the angels females?
35:11 (12) no female bears or brings forth, save with His knowledge
37:150 (150) did We create the angels females, while they were witnesses?
40:40 (43) whosoever does a righteous deed, be it male or female
41:47 (47) no female bears or brings forth, save with His knowledge
42:49 (48) He gives to whom He will females
42:50 (49) He couples them, both males and females

43:19 (18)	who are themselves servants of the All-merciful, females
49:13 (13)	O mankind, We have created you male and female
53:21 (21)	what, have you males, and He females?
53:27 (28)	[they] name the angels with the names of females
53:45 (46)	that He Himself created the two kinds, male and female
75:39 (39)	and He made of him two kinds, male and female
92:3 (3)	and That which created the male and the female

*A N Y

ANÁ (1) vb. (I)~to be the time for

b) impf. act. (*ya'nī*)

57:16 (15)	Is it not time that the hearts of those who believe should be humbled

ANÁ (2) vb. (I)~(pcple. act.) boiling

g) pcple. act. (*ānī*)

55:44 (44)	they shall go round between it and between hot, boiling water
88:5 (5)	watered at a boiling fountain

INÁ n.m. (pl. *ānā'*)~hour, watch (of the night), time, season

3:113 (109)	recite God's signs in the watches of the night
20:130 (130)	proclaim thy Lord's praise in the watches of the night
33:53 (53)	without watching for its hour
39:9 (12)	he who is obedient in the watches of the night

INĀ' n.m. (pl. *āniyah*)~vessel

76:15 (15)	there shall be passed around them vessels of silver

*A R B

IRBAH n.f.~sexual desire, vigour

24:31 (31)	such men as attend them, not having sexual desire

MA'RAB n.m. (pl. *ma'ārib*)~a use

20:18 (19)	other uses also I find in it

*A R Ḍ

ARḌ n.f.~land, earth

2:11 (10)	Do not corruption in the land
2:22 (20)	who assigned to you the earth for a couch
2:27 (25)	and such as do corruption in the land
2:29 (27)	It is He who created for you all that is in the earth
2:30 (28)	I am setting in the earth a viceroy
2:33 (31)	the unseen things of the heavens and earth
2:36 (34)	in the earth a sojourn shall be yours
2:60 (57)	mischief not in the earth, doing corruption
2:61 (58)	that He may bring forth for us of that the earth produces
2:71 (66)	a cow not broken to plough the earth

2:107 (101)	to God belongs the kingdom of the heavens and the earth
2:116 (110)	to Him belongs all that is in the heavens and the earth
2:117 (111)	the Creator of the heavens and the earth
2:164 (159)	surely in the creation of the heavens and the earth
2:164 (159)	therewith reviving the earth after it is dead
2:164 (159)	and the clouds compelled between heaven and earth
2:168 (163)	O men, eat of what is in the earth
2:205 (201)	he hastens about the earth, to do corruption there
2:251 (252)	the earth had surely corrupted
2:255 (256)	to Him belongs all that is in the heavens and the earth
2:255 (256)	His Throne comprises the heavens and earth
2:267 (269)	and of that We have produced for you from the earth
2:273 (274)	[who] are unable to journey in the land
2:284 (284)	To God belongs all that is in the heavens and the earth
3:5 (4)	From God nothing whatever is hidden in heaven and earth
3:29 (27)	what is in the heavens and what is in the earth
3:83 (77)	to Him has surrendered whoso is in the heavens and the earth
3:91 (85)	there shall not be accepted from any one of them the whole earth full of gold
3:109 (105)	To God belongs all that is in the heavens and in the earth
3:129 (124)	To God belongs all that is in the heavens and earth
3:133 (127)	a garden whose breadth is as the heavens and earth
3:137 (131)	journey in the land, and behold how was the end of those that cried lies
3:156 (150)	when they journey in the land, or are upon expeditions
3:180 (176)	to God belongs the inheritance of the heavens and earth
3:189 (186)	To God belongs the Kingdom of the heavens and of the earth
3:190 (187)	Surely in the creation of the heavens and earth
3:191 (188)	[who] reflect upon the creation of the heavens and the earth
4:42 (45)	[they] will wish that the earth might be levelled with them
4:97 (99)	We were abased in the earth
4:97 (99)	but was not God's earth wide
4:100 (101)	[he] will find in the earth many refuges
4:101 (102)	and when you are journeying in the land
4:126 (125)	to God belongs all that is in the heavens and in the earth
4:131 (130)	to God belongs all that is in the heavens and in the earth
4:131 (130)	to God belongs all that is in the heavens and in the earth
4:132 (131)	to God belongs all that is in the heavens and in the earth
4:170 (168)	to God belongs all that is in the heavens and in the earth
4:171 (169)	to Him belongs all that is in the heavens and in the earth
5:17 (19)	and all those who are on earth
5:17 (20)	to God belongs the kingdom of the heavens and of the earth
5:18 (21)	to God belongs the kingdom of the heavens and of the earth
5:21 (24)	O my people, enter the Holy Land
5:26 (29)	while they are wandering in the earth
5:31 (34)	Then God sent forth a raven, scratching into the earth
5:32 (35)	nor for corruption done in the land
5:32 (36)	then many of them thereafter commit excesses in the earth
5:33 (37)	[who] hasten about the earth, to do corruption there
5:33 (37)	or they shall be banished from the land
5:36 (40)	though they possessed all that is in the earth
5:40 (44)	knowest thou not that to God belongs the kingdom of the heavens and the earth?
5:64 (69)	they hasten about the earth, to do corruption there
5:97 (98)	God knows all that is in the heavens and in the earth
5:106 (105)	if you are journeying in the land
5:120 (120)	to God belongs the kingdom of the heavens and of the earth
6:1 (1)	praise belongs to God who created the heavens and the earth

6:3 (3)	He is God in the heavens and the earth
6:6 (6)	many a generation We established in the earth
6:11 (11)	journey in the land
6:12 (12)	to whom belongs what is in the heavens and in the earth?
6:14 (14)	other than God, the Originator of the heavens and of the earth
6:35 (35)	if thou canst seek out a hole in the earth
6:38 (38)	No creature is there crawling on the earth
6:59 (59)	Not a grain in the earth's shadows
6:71 (70)	lured to bewilderment in the earth by Satans
6:73 (72)	It is He who created the heavens and the earth
6:75 (75)	So We were showing Abraham the kingdom of the heavens and earth
6:79 (79)	to Him who originated the heavens and the earth
6:101 (101)	The Creator of the heavens and the earth
6:116 (116)	If thou obeyest the most part of those on earth
6:165 (165)	It is He who has appointed you viceroys in the earth
7:10 (9)	We have established you in the earth
7:24 (23)	In the earth a sojourn shall be yours
7:54 (52)	Surely your Lord is God, who created the heavens and the earth in six days
7:56 (54)	Do not corruption in the land, after it has been set right
7:73 (71)	leave her that she may eat in God's earth
7:74 (72)	[He] lodged you in the land
7:74 (72)	and do not mischief in the earth
7:85 (83)	and do not corruption in the land
7:96 (94)	We would have opened upon them blessings from heaven and earth
7:100 (98)	a guidance to those who inherit the earth
7:110 (107)	who desires to expel you from your land
7:127 (124)	wilt thou leave Moses and his people to work corruption in the land
7:128 (125)	the earth is God's and He bequeaths it to whom He will
7:129 (126)	[He] will make you successors in the land
7:137 (133)	the east and the west of the land We had blessed
7:146 (143)	those who wax proud in the earth unjustly
7:158 (158)	Him to whom belongs the kingdom of the heavens and of the earth
7:168 (167)	And We cut them up into nations in the earth
7:176 (175)	but he inclined towards the earth
7:185 (184)	have they not considerred the dominion of the heaven and of the earth
7:187 (186)	Heavy is it in the heavens and the earth
8:26 (26)	And remember when you were few and abased in the land
8:63 (64)	Hadst thou expended all that is in the earth
8:67 (68)	until he make wide slaughter in the land
8:73 (74)	there will be persecution in the land
9:2 (2)	Journey freely in the land for four months
9:25 (25)	the land for all its breadth was strait for you
9:36 (36)	the day that He created the heavens and the earth
9:38 (38)	you sink down heavily to the ground
9:74 (75)	on the earth they have no protector or helper
9:116 (117)	Surely to God belongs the kingdom of the heavens and of the earth
9:118 (119)	when the earth became strait for them
10:3 (3)	who created the heavens and the earth in six days
10:6 (6)	what God has created in the heavens and the earth
10:14 (15)	Then We appointed you viceroys in the earth
10:18 (19)	will you tell God what He knows not either in the heavens or in the earth?
10:23 (24)	behold, they are insolent in the earth
10:24 (25)	and the plants of the earth mingle with it
10:24 (25)	when the earth has taken on its glitter
10:31 (32)	who provides you out of heaven and earth

10:54 (55)	if every soul that has done evil possessed all that is in the earth
10:55 (56)	to God belongs everything that is in the heavens and earth
10:61 (62)	not so much as the weight of an ant in earth or heaven escapes from thy Lord
10:66 (67)	to God belongs everyone that is in the heavens and in the earth
10:68 (69)	to Him belongs all that is in the heavens and in the earth
10:78 (79)	that the domination in the land might belong to you two
10:83 (83)	and Pharaoh was high in the land
10:99 (99)	whoever is in the earth would have believed
10:101 (101)	Behold what is in the heavens and in the earth
11:6 (8)	No creature is there crawling on the earth, but its provision rests on God
11:7 (9)	And it is He who created the heavens and the earth in six days
11:20 (22)	they are unable to frustrate Him on earth
11:44 (46)	Earth, swallow thy waters
11:61 (64)	It is He who produced you from the earth
11:64 (67)	leave her that she may eat in God's earth
11:85 (86)	and do not mischief in the land
11:107 (109)	so long as the heavens and earth abide
11:108 (110)	so long as the heavens and earth abide
11:116 (118)	men of a remainder forbidding corruption in the earth
11:123 (123)	To God belongs the Unseen in the heavens and the earth
12:9 (9)	Kill you Joseph, or cast him forth into some land
12:21 (21)	So We established Joseph in the land
12:55 (55)	Set me over the land's storehouses
12:56 (56)	So We established Joseph in the land
12:73 (73)	we came not to work corruption in the land
12:80 (80)	never will I quit this land
12:101 (102)	O Thou, the Originator of the heavens and earth
12:105 (105)	How many a sign there is in the heavens and in the earth
12:109 (109)	have they not journeyed in the land?
13:3 (3)	it is He who stretched out the earth
13:4 (4)	and on the earth are tracts neighbouring each to each
13:15 (16)	to God bow all who are in the heavens and the earth
13:16 (17)	who is the Lord of the heavens and of the earth?
13:17 (18)	and what profits men abides in the earth
13:18 (18)	if they possessed all that is in the earth
13:25 (25)	and who work corruption in the earth
13:31 (30)	whereby the mountains were set in motion, or the earth were cleft
13:33 (33)	will you tell Him what He knows not in the earth?
13:41 (41)	have they not seen how We come to the land
14:2 (2)	God, to whom belongs all that is in the heavens and all that is in the earth
14:8 (8)	if you are thankless, you and whoso is on earth
14:10 (11)	regarding God, the Originator of the heavens and the earth
14:13 (16)	we will assuredly expel you from our land
14:14 (17)	and We will surely make you to dwell in the land after them
14:19 (22)	hast thou not seen that God created the heavens and the earth in truth?
14:26 (31)	is as a corrupt tree — uprooted from the earth
14:32 (37)	It is God who created the heavens and the earth
14:38 (41)	from God nothing whatever is hidden in earth and heaven
14:48 (49)	upon the day the earth shall be changedto other than the (earth)
14:48 (49)	upon the day the (earth) shall be changed to other than the earth
15:19 (19)	and the earth — We stretched it forth
15:39 (39)	I shall deck all fair to them in the earth
15:85 (85)	We created not the heavens and the earth, and all that is between them, save in truth
16:3 (3)	He created the heavens and the earth in truth
16:13 (13)	that which He has multiplied for you in the earth

16:15 (15)	and He cast on the earth firm mountains
16:36 (38)	so journey in the land, and behold how was the end of them
16:45 (47)	that God will not cause the earth to swallow them
16:49 (51)	every creature crawling on the earth
16:52 (54)	To Him belongs all that is in the heavens and earth
16:65 (67)	and therewith revives the earth after it is dead
16:73 (75)	that which has no power to provide them anything from the heavens and the earth
16:77 (79)	To God belongs the Unseen in the heavens and in the earth
17:4 (4)	you shall do corruption in the earth twice
17:37 (39)	and walk not in the earth exultantly
17:37 (39)	thou wilt never tear the earth open
17:44 (46)	the seven heavens and the earth, and whosoever in them is, extol Him
17:55 (57)	thy Lord knows very well all who are in the heavens and the earth
17:76 (78)	indeed they were near to startling thee from the land
17:90 (92)	thou makest a spring to gush forth from the earth for us
17:95 (97)	had there been in the earth angels
17:99 (101)	God, who created the heavens and the earth
17:102 (104)	except the Lord of the heavens and earth
17:103 (105)	He desired to startle them from the land
17:104 (106)	dwell in the land
18:7 (6)	We have appointed all that is on the earth for an adornment for it
18:14 (13)	Our Lord is the Lord of the heavens and earth
18:26 (25)	To Him belongs the Unseen in the heavens and in the earth
18:45 (43)	the plants of the earth mingle with it
18:47 (45)	and thou seest the earth coming forth
18:51 (49)	I made them not witnesses of the creation of the heavens and earth
18:84 (83)	We established him in the land
18:94 (93)	Gog and Magog are doing corruption in the earth
19:40 (41)	We shall inherit the earth and all that are upon it
19:65 (66)	Lord He of the heavens and earth
19:90 (92)	and the earth is split asunder
19:93 (94)	None is there in the heavens and earth but he comes to the All-merciful
20:4 (3)	Him who created the earth and the high heavens
20:6 (5)	to Him belongs all that is in the heavens and the earth
20:53 (55)	He who appointed the earth to be a cradle for you
20:57 (59)	Hast thou come to expel us out of our land
20:63 (66)	their purpose is to expel you out of your land by their sorcery
21:4 (4)	My Lord knows what is said in the heavens and the earth
21:16 (16)	We created not the heaven and the earth
21:19 (19)	To Him belongs whosoever is in the heavens and the earth
21:21 (21)	or have they taken gods out of the earth who raise the dead?
21:30 (31)	that the heavens and the earth were a mass
21:31 (32)	and We set in the earth firm mountains
21:44 (45)	do they not see how We come to the land
21:56 (57)	your Lord is the Lord of the heavens and the earth
21:71 (71)	and We delivered him, and Lot, unto the land that We had blessed
21:81 (81)	[the wind] that ran at his command unto the land
21:105 (105)	The earth shall be the inheritance of My righteous servants
22:5 (5)	And thou beholdest the earth blackened
22:18 (18)	to God bow all who are in the heavens and all who are in the earth
22:41 (42)	who, if We establish them in the land, perform the prayer
22:46 (45)	have they not journeyed in the land
22:63 (62)	in the morning the earth becomes green
22:64 (63)	to Him belongs all that is in the heavens and in the earth
22:65 (64)	God has subjected to you all that is in the earth

22:65 (64)	He holds back heaven lest it should fall upon the earth
22:70 (69)	God knows all that is in heaven and earth
23:18 (18)	and [We] lodged it in the earth
23:71 (73)	the heavens and the earth and whosoever in them is had surely corrupted
23:79 (81)	It is He who scattered you in the earth
23:84 (86)	Whose is the earth, and whoso is in it
23:112 (114)	How long have you tarried in the earth
24:35 (35)	God is the Light of the heavens and the earth
24:41 (41)	whatsoever is in the heavens and in the earth extols God
24:42 (42)	To God belongs the Kingdom of the heavens and the earth
24:55 (54)	He will surely make you successors in the land
24:57 (56)	Think not the unbelievers able to frustrate God in the earth
24:64 (64)	to God belongs whatsoever is in the heavens and the earth
25:2 (2)	to whom belongs the Kingdom of the heavens and the earth
25:6 (7)	He sent it down, who knows the secret in the heavens and earth
25:59 (60)	[He] who created the heavens and the earth,
25:63 (64)	those who walk in the earth modestly
26:7 (6)	What, have they not regarded the earth
26:24 (23)	The Lord of the heavens and earth
26:35 (34)	who desires to expel you from your land by his sorcery
26:152 (152)	who do corruption in the earth
26:183 (183)	and do not mischief in the earth
27:25 (25)	to God, who brings forth what is hidden in the heavens and earth
27:48 (49)	there were nine persons who did corruption in the land
27:60 (61)	He who created the heavens and earth
27:61 (62)	He who made the earth a fixed place
27:62 (63)	[He] appoints you to be successors in the earth
27:64 (65)	[He] provides you out of heaven and earth
27:65 (66)	None knows the Unseen in the heavens and earth except God
27:69 (71)	Journey in the land
27:75 (77)	And not a thing is there hidden in heaven and earth
27:82 (84)	We shall bring forth for them out of the earth a beast
27:87 (89)	terrified is whosoever is in the heavens and earth
28:4 (3)	Now Pharaoh had exalted himself in the land
28:5 (4)	We desired to be gracious to those that were abased in the land
28:6 (5)	and to establish them in the land
28:19 (18)	thou only desirest to be a tyrant in the land
28:39 (39)	And he waxed proud in the land
28:57 (57)	we shall be snatched from our land
28:77 (77)	seek not to work corruption in the earth
28:81 (81)	We made the earth to swallow him and his dwelling
28:83 (83)	those who desire not exorbitance in the earth
29:20 (19)	Journey in the land
29:22 (21)	You are not able to frustrate Him either in the earth or in heaven
29:36 (35)	and do not mischief in the land
29:39 (38)	they waxed proud in the earth
29:40 (39)	and some We made the earth to swallow
29:44 (43)	God created the heavens and the earth with the truth
29:52 (52)	He knows whatsoever is in the heavens and earth
29:56 (56)	My earth is wide
29:61 (61)	Who created the heavens and the earth
29:63 (63)	and therewith revives the earth after it is dead
30:3 (2)	in the nearer part of the land
30:8 (7)	God created not the heavens and the earth
30:9 (8)	have they not journeyed in the land

30:9 (8)	they ploughed up the earth and cultivated it
30:18 (17)	His is the praise in the heavens and earth
30:19 (18)	and He revives the earth after it is dead
30:22 (21)	And of His signs is the creation of the heavens and earth
30:24 (23)	and He revives the earth after it is dead
30:25 (24)	and of His signs is that the heaven and earth stand firm
30:25 (24)	when He calls you once and suddenly, out of the earth
30:26 (25)	to Him belongs whosoever is in the heavens and the earth
30:27 (26)	His is the loftiest likeness in the heavens and the earth
30:42 (41)	journey in the land
30:50 (49)	how He quickens the earth after it was dead
31:10 (9)	He cast on the earth firm mountains
31:16 (15)	[though it be] in the earth, God shall bring it forth
31:18 (17)	and walk not in the earth exultantly
31:20 (19)	God has subjected to you whatsoever is in the heavens and earth
31:25 (24)	who created the heavens and the earth?
31:26 (25)	to God belongs all that is in the heavens and the earth
31:27 (26)	though all the trees in the earth were pens
31:34 (34)	no soul knows in what land it shall die
32:4 (3)	God is He that created the heavens and the earth
32:5 (4)	He directs the affair from heaven to earth
32:10 (9)	when we have gone astray in the earth
32:27 (27)	how We drive the water to the dry land
33:27 (27)	and He bequeathed upon you their lands
33:27 (27)	and a land you never trod
33:72 (72)	We offered the trust to the heavens and the earth
34:1 (1)	to whom belongs whatsoever is in the heavens and whatsoever is in the earth
34:2 (2)	He knows what penetrates into the earth
34:3 (3)	not so much as the weight of an ant in heaven and earth escapes from Him
34:9 (9)	and what lies behind them of heaven and earth
34:9 (9)	did We will, We would make the earth to swallow them
34:14 (13)	but the Beast of the Earth devouring his staff
34:22 (21)	they possess not so much as the weight of an ant in the heavens nor in the earth
34:24 (23)	who provides for you out of the heavens and the earth?
35:1 (1)	praise belongs to God, Originator of the heavens and earth
35:3 (3)	is there any creator, apart from God, who provides for you out of heaven and earth?
35:9 (10)	and therewith revive the earth, after it is dead
35:38 (36)	God knows the Unseen in the heavens and the earth
35:39 (37)	it is He who appointed you viceroys in the earth
35:40 (38)	show me what they have created in the earth
35:41 (39)	God holds the heavens and the earth, lest they remove
35:43 (41)	waxing proud in the land
35:44 (43)	have they not journeyed in the land
35:44 (43)	there is naught in the heavens or the earth that can frustrate Him
36:33 (33)	And a sign for them is the dead land, that We quickened
36:36 (36)	Glory be to Him, who created all the pairs of what the earth produces
36:81 (81)	Is not He, who created the heavens and earth
37:5 (5)	Lord of the heavens and the earth
38:10 (9)	Or is theirs the kingdom of the heavens and earth
38:26 (25)	We have appointed thee a viceroy in the earth
38:27 (26)	We have not created the heavens and earth, and what between them is, for vanity
38:28 (27)	as the workers of corruption in the earth
38:66 (66)	Lord of the heavens and earth

39:5 (7)	He created the heavens and the earth in truth
39:10 (13)	and God's earth is wide
39:21 (22)	[He has] threaded it as springs in the earth
39:38 (39)	who created the heavens and the earth?
39:44 (45)	His is the kingdom of the heavens and the earth
39:46 (47)	Thou originator of the heavens and the earth
39:47 (48)	if the evildoers possessed all that is in the earth
39:63 (63)	unto Him belong the keys of the heavens and the earth
39:67 (67)	the earth altogether shall be His handful
39:68 (68)	and whosoever is in the earth shall swoon, save whom God wills
39:69 (69)	And the earth shall shine with the light of its Lord
39:74 (74)	[God] has bequeathed upon us the earth
40:21 (22)	have they not journeyed in the land
40:21 (22)	[they] left firmer traces in the earth
40:26 (27)	that he may cause corruption to appear in the land
40:29 (30)	[you] who are masters in the land
40:57 (59)	the creation of the heavens and earth is greater than the creation of men
40:64 (66)	It is God who made for you the earth a fixed place
40:75 (75)	because you rejoiced in the earth without right
40:82 (82)	have they not journeyed in the land
40:82 (82)	[they] left firmer traces in the earth
41:9 (8)	do you disbelieve in Him who created the earth in two days
41:11 (10)	[He] said to it and to the earth
41:15 (14)	they waxed proud in the earth
41:39 (39)	thou seest the earth humble
42:4 (2)	To Him belongs whatsoever is in the heavens and whatsoever is in the earth
42:5 (3)	ask forgiveness for those on earth
42:11 (9)	The Originator of the heavens and the earth
42:12 (10)	To Him belong the keys of the heavens and the earth
42:27 (26)	they would have been insolent in the earth
42:29 (28)	And of His signs is the creation of the heavens and earth
42:31 (30)	You are not able to frustrate Him in the earth
42:42 (40)	[those who] are insolent in the earth wrongfully
42:49 (48)	To God belongs the Kingdom of the heavens and the earth
42:53 (53)	to whom belongs whatsoever is in the heavens, and whatsoever is in the earth
43:9 (8)	who created the heavens and earth?
43:10 (9)	He who appointed the earth to be a cradle for you
43:60 (60)	We would have appointed angels among you to be successors in the earth
43:82 (82)	glory be to the Lord of the heavens and the earth
43:84 (84)	and it is He who in heaven is God and in earth is God
43:85 (85)	glory be to Him, to whom belongs the Kingdom of the heavens and the earth
44:7 (6)	Lord of the heavens and earth
44:29 (28)	neither heaven nor earth wept for them
44:38 (38)	We created not the heavens and earth, and all that between them is, in play
45:3 (2)	surely in the heavens and earth there are signs
45:5 (4)	therewith revives the earth after it is dead
45:13 (12)	He has subjected to you what is in the heavens and what is in the earth
45:22 (21)	God created the heavens and the earth in truth
45:27 (26)	to God belongs the Kingdom of the heavens and the earth
45:36 (35)	the Lord of the heavens and the Lord of the earth
45:37 (36)	His is the Domination in the heavens and the earth
46:3 (2)	We have not created the heavens and the earth, and what between them is, save with the truth
46:4 (3)	Show me what they have created of the earth
46:20 (19)	you waxed proud in the earth without right

46:32 (31)	[he] cannot frustrate God in the earth
46:33 (32)	God who created the heavens and earth
47:10 (11)	have they not journeyed in the land
47:22 (24)	would you then haply work corruption in the land
48:4 (4)	to God belong the hosts of the heavens and the earth
48:7 (7)	To God belong the hosts of the heavens and the earth
48:14 (14)	To God belongs the kingdom of the heavens and of the earth
49:16 (16)	God knows what is in the heavens and what is in the earth
49:18 (18)	God knows the Unseen of the heavens and of the earth
50:4 (4)	We know what the earth diminishes of them
50:7 (7)	And the earth — We stretched it forth
50:38 (37)	We created the heavens and the earth
50:44 (43)	Upon the day when the earth is split asunder from about them
51:20 (20)	In the earth are signs for those having sure faith
51:23 (23)	So by the Lord of heaven and earth, it is as surely true
51:48 (48)	And the earth — We spread it forth
52:36 (36)	or did they create the heavens and earth?
53:31 (32)	to God belongs whatsoever is in the heavens and whatsoever is in the earth
53:32 (33)	when He produced you from the earth
54:12 (12)	[He] made the earth to gush with fountains
55:10 (9)	and earth — He set it down for all beings
55:29 (29)	whatsoever is in the heavens and the earth implore Him
55:33 (33)	if you are able to pass through the confines of heaven and earth
56:4 (4)	when the earth shall be rocked
57:1 (1)	All that is in the heavens and the earth magnifies God
57:2 (2)	to Him belongs the Kingdom of the heavens and the earth
57:4 (4)	it is He that created the heavens and the earth
57:4 (4)	He knows what penetrates into the earth
57:5 (5)	to Him belongs the Kingdom of the heavens and the earth
57:10 (10)	to God belongs the inheritance of the heavens and the earth
57:17 (16)	know that God revives the earth after it was dead
57:21 (21)	a Garden the breadth whereof is as the breadth of heaven and earth
57:22 (22)	no affliction befalls in the earth or in yourselves, but it is in a Book
58:7 (8)	God knows whatsoever is in the heavens, and whatsoever is in the earth
59:1 (1)	All that is in the heavens and the earth magnifies God
59:24 (24)	All that is in the heavens and the earth magnifies Him
61:1 (1)	All that is in the heavens and the earth magnifies God
62:1 (1)	All that is in the heavens and the earth magnifies God
62:10 (10)	Then, when the prayer is finished, scatter in the land
63:7 (7)	unto God belong the treasuries of the heavens and of the earth
64:1 (1)	All that is in the heavens and the earth magnifies God
64:3 (3)	He created the heavens and the earth with the truth
64:4 (4)	He knows whatever is in the heavens and the earth
65:12 (12)	It is God who created seven heavens, and of earth their like
67:15 (15)	It is He who made the earth submissive to you
67:16 (16)	[that He] will not cause the earth to swallow you
67:24 (24)	It is He who scattered you in the earth
69:14 (14)	and the earth and the mountains are lifted up
70:14 (14)	and whosoever is in the earth, all together
71:17 (16)	And God caused you to grow out of the earth
71:19 (18)	And God has laid the earth for you
71:26 (27)	leave not upon the earth of the unbelievers
72:10 (10)	we know not whether evil is intended for those in the earth
72:12 (12)	we thought that we should never be able to frustrate God in the earth
73:14 (14)	upon the day when the earth and the mountains shall quake

73:20 (20)	others [of you are] journeying in the land
77:25 (25)	Made We not the earth to be a housing
78:6 (6)	Have We not made the earth as a cradle
78:37 (37)	Lord of the heavens and earth
79:30 (30)	and the earth — after that He spread it out
80:26 (26)	then We split the earth in fissures
84:3 (3)	when earth is stretched out
85:9 (9)	to whom belongs the Kingdom of the heavens and the earth
86:12 (12)	by earth splitting with verdure
88:20 (20)	how the earth was outstretched
89:21 (22)	when the earth is ground to powder
91:6 (6)	and by the earth and That which extended it
99:1 (1)	when earth is shaken with a mighty shaking
99:2 (2)	and earth brings forth her burdens

*A R K

ARĪKAH n.f.~couch

18:31 (30)	therein reclining upon couches
36:56 (56)	they and their spouses, reclining upon couches
76:13 (13)	therein they shall recline upon couches
83:23 (23)	upon couches gazing
83:35 (35)	upon couches gazing

*A R M

IRAM n.prop.~Iram

89:7 (6)	Iram of the pillars

*A S F

ASIFA vb. (I)~(n.vb.) grief, woe

f) n.vb. (*asaf*)

12:84 (84)	ah, woe is me for Joseph
18:6 (5)	thou wilt consume thyself, following after them, of grief

ASIF n.m. (adj)~sorrowful, grieved

7:150 (149)	Moses returned to his people, angry and sorrowful
20:86 (88)	Then Moses returned very angry and sorrowful to his people

ĀSAFA vb. (IV)~to anger

a) perf. act.

43:55 (55)	So, when they had angered Us, We took vengenace on them

*A S M

ISMĀʿĪL n.prop.~Ishmael, Isma'il

2:125 (119)	We made covenant with Abraham and Ishmael
2:127 (121)	when Abraham, and Ishmael with him, raised up the foundations of the House

2:133 (127)	the God of thy fathers Abraham, Ishmael and Isaac
2:136 (130)	that which has been sent down on us and sent down on Abraham, Ishmael
2:140 (134)	Abraham, Ishmael, Isaac and Jacob, and the Tribes
3:84 (78)	and sent down on Abraham and Ishmael
4:163 (161)	We revealed to Abraham, Ishmael, Isaac, Jacob, and the Tribes
6:86 (86)	Ishmael and Elisha, Jonah and Lot — each one We preferred above all beings
14:39 (41)	Praise be to God, who has given me, though I am old, Ishmael and Isaac
19:54 (55)	mention in the Book Ishmael
21:85 (85)	Ishmael, Idris, Dhul Kifl — each was of the patient
38:48 (48)	remember also Our servants Ishmael, Elisha, and Dhul Kifl

*A S N

ASANA vb. (I)~(pcple. act.) staling, polluted

g) pcple. act. (*āsin*)

47:15 (16)	therein are rivers of water unstaling

*A S R

ASARA vb. (I)~to make captive

b) impf. act. (*ya'siru*)

33:26 (26)	some you made captive

ASĪR n.m. (pl. *asrá, asārá*)~captive, prisoner

2:85 (79)	if they come to you as captives, you ransom them
8:67 (68)	It is not for any Prophet to have prisoners
8:70 (71)	O Prophet, say to the prisoners in your hands
76:8 (8)	they give food, for the love of Him, to the needy, the orphan, the captive

ASR n.m.~a joint, a ligament, frame; (hence) vigour, energy

76:28 (28)	We created them, and We strengthened their joints

ISRĀ'ĪL n.prop.~Israel (Biblical people or person, prob. Jacob)

2:40 (38)	Children of Israel, remember My blessing wherewith I blessed you
2:47 (44)	Children of Israel, remember My blessing wherewith I blessed you
2:83 (77)	And when We took compact with the Children of Israel
2:122 (116)	Children of Israel, remember My blessing wherewith I blessed you
2:211 (207)	Ask the Children of Israel how many a clear sign We gave them
2:246 (247)	Hast thou not regarded the Council of the Children of Israel
3:49 (43)	to be a Messenger to the Children of Israel
3:93 (87)	All food was lawful to the Children of Israel
3:93 (87)	save what Israel forbade for himself
5:12 (15)	God took compact with the Children of Israel
5:32 (35)	We prescribed for the Children of Israel that whoso slays a soul not to retaliate
5:70 (74)	We took compact with the Children of Israel
5:72 (76)	Children of Israel, serve God
5:78 (82)	Cursed were the unbelievers of the Children of Israel by the tongue of David
5:110 (110)	I restrained from thee the Children of Israel
7:105 (103)	send forth with me the Children of Israel
7:134 (131)	[we will] send forth with thee the Children of Israel

7:137 (133)	was fulfilled the most fair word of thy Lord upon the Children of Israel
7:138 (134)	We brought the Children of Israel over the sea
10:90 (90)	We brought the Children of Israel over the sea
10:90 (90)	I believe that there is no god but He in whom the Children of Israel believe
10:93 (93)	We settled the Children of Israel in a sure settlement
17:2 (2)	We gave Moses the Book, and made it a guidance to the Children of Israel
17:4 (4)	We decreed for the Children of Israel in the Book
17:101 (103)	Ask the Children of Israel when he came to them
17:104 (106)	And We said to the Children of Israel
19:58 (59)	of those We bore with Noah, and of the seed of Abraham and Israel
20:47 (49)	send forth with us the Children of Israel
20:80 (82)	Children of Israel, We delivered you from your enemy
20:94 (95)	thou hast divided the Children of Israel
26:17 (16)	send forth with us the Children of Israel
26:22 (21)	having enslaved the Children of Israel
26:59 (59)	We bequeathed them upon the Children of Israel
26:197 (197)	it is known to the learned of the Children of Israel
27:76 (78)	this Koran relates to the Children of Israel
32:23 (23)	We appointed it for a guidance to the Children of Israel
40:53 (56)	We bequeathed upon the Children of Israel the Book
43:59 (59)	We made him to be an example to the Children of Israel
44:30 (29)	We delivered the Children of Israel from the humbling chastisement
45:16 (15)	We gave the Children of Israel the Book, the Judgment, and the Prophethood
46:10 (9)	a witness from among the Children of Israel bears witness to its like
61:6 (6)	Children of Israel, I am indeed the Messenger of God to you
61:14 (14)	And a party of the Children of Israel believed, and a party disbelieved

*A S S

ASSASA vb. (II)~to found, to establish

a) perf. act.

9:109 (110)	who founded his building upon the fear of God
9:109 (110)	who founded his building upon the brink of a crumbling bank

d) perf. pass. (*ussisa*)

9:108 (109)	A mosque that was founded upon godfearing

*A S W

USWAH n.f.~model, good example

33:21 (21)	You have had a good example in God's Messenger
60:4 (4)	You have had a good example in Abraham
60:6 (6)	You have had a good example in them

*A S Y

ASÁ vb. (I)~to grieve

b) impf. act. (*ya*ʾ*sá*)

5:26 (29)	grieve not for the people of the ungodly
5:68 (72)	grieve not for the people of the unbelievers
7:93 (91)	how should I grieve for a people of unbelievers?
57:23 (23)	that you may not grieve for what escapes you

*A SH R

ASHIR n.m. (adj)~impudent, rash

54:25 (25)	nay, rather he is an impudent liar
54:26 (26)	they shall surely know tomorrow who is the impudent liar

*A Ṣ L

AṢĪL n.m. (pl. *āṣāl*)~evening, eventide

7:205 (204)	not loud of voice, at morn and eventide
13:15 (16)	as do their shadows also in the mornings and the evenings
24:36 (36)	therein glorifying Him, in the mornings and the evenings
25:5 (6)	they are recited to him at the dawn and in the evening
33:42 (41)	and give Him glory at the dawn and in the evening
48:9 (9)	that you may give Him glory at the dawn and in the evening
76:25 (25)	And remember the Name of thy Lord at dawn and in the evening

AṢL n.m. (pl. *uṣūl*)~root

14:24 (29)	is as a good tree — its roots are firm
37:64 (62)	It is a tree that comes forth in the root of Hell
59:5 (5)	Whatever palm-trees you cut down, or left standing upon their roots

*A Ṣ R

IṢR n.m.~load, burden

2:286 (286)	Our Lord, charge us not with a load
3:81 (75)	do you take My load on you on that condition?
7:157 (156)	and relieving them of their loads

*A T Y

ATÁ vb. (I)~to come, to come to, to come upon, to approach; to go; to give; (with prep. *bi-*) to bring; to perform, to commit. (pcple. act.) one who comes, coming

a) perf. act.

2:145 (140)	if thou shouldst bring to those that have been given the Book every sign
3:188 (185)	those who rejoice in what they have brought
4:25 (30)	if they commit indecency, they shall be liable
6:34 (34)	until Our help came unto them
6:40 (40)	what think you? If God's chastisement comes upon you
6:40 (40)	or the Hour comes upon you
6:47 (47)	what think you? If God's chastisement comes upon you
7:138 (134)	they came upon a people cleaving to idols they had
9:70 (71)	Their Messengers came to them with the clear signs
9:92 (93)	who, when they came to thee, for thee to mount them
10:24 (25)	Our command comes upon it by night or day
10:50 (51)	if His chastisement comes upon you by night or day
15:64 (64)	We have come to thee with the truth
16:1 (1)	God's command comes
16:26 (28)	then God came upon their building from the foundations
16:26 (28)	the chastisement came upon them from whence they were not aware
18:77 (76)	when they came unto the people of a city
19:27 (28)	then she brought the child to her folk

20:9 (8)	hath there come unto thee the story of Moses?
20:11 (11)	When he came to it, a voice cried
20:60 (62)	Thereafter he came again
20:69 (72)	and the sorcerer prospers not, wherever he goes
20:126 (126)	Our signs came unto thee
21:47 (48)	We shall produce it, and sufficient are We for reckoners
23:71 (73)	Nay, We brought them their Remembrance
23:90 (92)	Nay, but We brought them the truth
25:40 (42)	Surely they have come by the city
26:89 (89)	except for him who comes to God with a pure heart
27:18 (18)	till, when they came on the Valley of Ants
27:87 (89)	every one shall come to Him, all utterly abject
28:30 (30)	When he came to it, a voice cried from the right bank
28:46 (46)	a people to whom no warner came before thee
32:3 (2)	a people to whom no warner came before thee
38:21 (20)	has the tiding of the dispute come to thee?
39:25 (26)	the chastisement came upon them
40:35 (37)	without any authority come to them
40:56 (58)	without any authority come to them
41:11 (10)	We come willingly
51:24 (24)	hath there come to thee the story of the honoured guests of Abraham?
51:42 (42)	that left nothing it came upon
51:52 (52)	not a Messenger came to those before them
59:2 (2)	then God came upon them from whence they had not reckoned
74:47 (48)	till the Certain came to us
76:1 (1)	has there come on man a while of time when he was a thing unremembered?
79:15 (15)	hathe there come to thee the story of Moses?
85:17 (17)	hathe there come to thee the story of the hosts
88:1 (1)	hath there come to thee the story of the Enveloper?

b) impf. act. (*ya'tī*)

2:38 (36)	yet there shall come to you guidance from Me
2:85 (79)	if they come to you as captives, you ransom them
2:106 (100)	We bring a better or the like of it
2:109 (103)	and be forgiving, till God brings His command
2:118 (112)	why does a sign not come to us?
2:148 (143)	God will bring you all together
2:189 (185)	it is not piety to come to the houses from the backs of them
2:210 (206)	what do they look for, but that God shall come to them in the cloud-shadows
2:214 (210)	without there had come upon you the like of those who passed away before you
2:248 (249)	the sign of his kingship is that the Ark will come to you
2:254 (255)	before there comes a day wherein shall be neither traffick, nor friendship
2:258 (260)	God brings the sun from the east
2:260 (262)	summon them, and they will come to thee
3:125 (121)	and [if] the foe come against you instantly
3:161 (155)	whoso defrauds shall bring the fruits of his fraud on the Day of Resurrection
3:183 (179)	until he brings to us a sacrifice
4:15 (19)	such of your women as commit indecency
4:16 (20)	and when two of you commit indecency
4:19 (23)	except when they commit a flagrant indecency
4:102 (103)	let another party who have not prayed come and pray with thee
4:133 (132)	if He will, He can put you away, O men, and bring others
5:41 (45)	who have not come to thee, perverting words
5:52 (57)	but it may be that God will bring the victory

5:54 (59)	God will assuredly bring a people He loves
5:108 (107)	it is likelier that they will bear testimony in proper form
6:4 (4)	not a sign of their Lord comes to them
6:5 (5)	there shall come to them news of that they were mocking
6:35 (35)	to bring them some sign
6:46 (46)	who is a god other than God to give it back to you?
6:130 (130)	did not Messengers come to you from among you
6:158 (159)	do they look for the angels to come to them
6:158 (159)	or that thy Lord should come
6:158 (159)	or that one of thy Lord's signs should come
6:158 (159)	on the day that one of thy Lord's signs comes
7:17 (16)	then I shall come on them from before them
7:35 (33)	If there should come to you Messengers from among you
7:53 (51)	the day its interpretation comes
7:80 (78)	what, do you commit such indecency
7:81 (79)	see, you approach men lustfully
7:97 (95)	Our might shall not come upon them at night
7:98 (96)	Our might shall not come upon them in daylight
7:112 (109)	to bring thee every cunning sorcerer
7:129 (126)	We have been hurt before thou camest to us
7:132 (129)	Whatsoever sign thou bringest to us, to cast a spell upon us
7:163 (163)	when their fish came to them on the day of their Sabbath
7:163 (163)	on the day they kept not Sabbath, they came not unto them
7:169 (168)	if chance goods the like of them come to them, they will take them
7:187 (186)	it will not come on you but — suddenly
7:203 (202)	when thou bringest them not a sign
9:24 (24)	then wait till God brings His command
9:54 (54)	and [they] perform not the prayer
9:70 (71)	Has there not come to you the tidings of those who were before you
10:39 (40)	whose interpretation has not yet come to them
11:8 (11)	the day it shall come to them, it shall not be turned aside from
11:33 (35)	God will bring you it if He will
11:39 (41)	to whom will come a chastisement degrading him
11:93 (96)	to whom will come the chastisement
11:105 (107)	the day it comes, no soul shall speak save by His leave
12:37 (37)	no food shall come to you
12:37 (37)	ere it comes to you I shall tell you its interpretation
12:48 (48)	there shall come upon you seven hard years
12:49 (49)	there shall come a year wherein the people will be succoured
12:60 (60)	but if you bring him not to me
12:66 (66)	that you will surely bring him back to me
12:83 (83)	haply God will bring them all to me
12:93 (93)	he shall recover his sight
12:107 (107)	that there shall come upon them no enveloping of the chastisement of God
12:107 (107)	that the Hour shall not come upon them suddenly
13:31 (31)	it alights nigh their habitation, until God's promise comes
13:38 (38)	it was not for any Messenger to bring a sign
13:41 (41)	Have they not seen how We come to the land
14:9 (9)	Has there not come to you the tidings of those who were before you
14:11 (13)	It is not for us to bring you an authority
14:17 (20)	and death comes upon him from every side
14:19 (22)	If He will, He can put you away and bring a new creation
14:31 (36)	before a day comes wherein shall be neither bargaining nor befriending
14:44 (44)	warn mankind of the day when the chastisement comes on them
15:7 (7)	Why dost thou not bring the angels unto us

15:11 (11)	not a single Messenger came to them
15:99 (99)	and serve thy Lord, until the Certain comes to thee
16:33 (35)	do they look for aught but that the angels shall come to them
16:33 (35)	or thy Lord's command shall come
16:45 (47)	or that the chastisement will not come upon them
16:76 (78)	wherever he despatches him, he brings no good
16:111 (112)	the day that every soul shall come disputing
16:112 (113)	that was secure, at rest, its provision coming to it easefully from every place
17:88 (90)	they would never produce its like
17:88 (90)	if men and jinn banded together to produce the like of this Koran
17:92 (94)	or thou bringest God and the angels as a surety
18:15 (14)	they would bring some clear authority
18:19 (18)	and [let him] bring you provision thereof
18:55 (53)	that the wont of the ancients should come upon them
18:55 (53)	or that the chastisement should come upon them
19:38 (39)	how well they will hear and see on the day they come to Us
19:43 (44)	such as came not to thee
19:80 (83)	and he shall come to Us alone
20:10 (10)	perhaps I shall bring you a brand from it
20:58 (60)	We shall assuredly bring thee sorcery the like of it
20:74 (76)	whosoever comes unto his Lord a sinner, for him awaits Gehenna
20:75 (77)	and whoso comes unto Him a believer
20:123 (121)	if there comes to you from Me guidance
20:133 (133)	why does he not bring us a sign from his Lord?
20:133 (133)	has there not come to them the clear sign of what is in the former scrolls
21:2 (2)	no Remembrance from their Lord comes to them
21:3 (3)	will you take to sorcery with your eyes open?
21:5 (5)	now therefore let him bring us a sign
21:40 (41)	but it shall come upon them suddenly
21:44 (45)	do they not see how We come to the land, diminishing it
22:27 (28)	and they shall come unto thee on foot
22:27 (28)	they shall come from every deep ravine
22:55 (54)	until the Hour comes on them suddenly
22:55 (54)	or there shall come upon them the chastisement of a barren day
23:68 (70)	that which came not upon their fathers, the ancients
24:4 (4)	those who cast it up on women in wedlock, and then bring not four witnesses
24:13 (13)	since they did not bring the witnesses
24:49 (48)	if they are in the right, they will come to him submissively
25:33 (35)	They bring not to thee any similitude
26:5 (4)	never fresh remembrance comes to them from the All-merciful
26:6 (5)	assuredly tidings will come to them
26:37 (36)	to bring thee every cunning sorcerer
26:165 (165)	What, do you come to male beings
26:202 (202)	so that it will come upon them suddenly
27:7 (7)	I observe a fire, and will bring you news of it
27:7 (7)	or I will bring you a flaming brand
27:21 (21)	or he bring me a clear authority
27:37 (37)	we shall assuredly come against them with hosts
27:38 (38)	which one of you will bring me her throne
27:38 (38)	before they come to me in surrender
27:39 (39)	I will bring it to thee
27:40 (40)	I will bring it to thee
27:54 (55)	what, do you commit indecency
27:55 (56)	what, do you approach men lustfully
28:29 (29)	perhaps I shall bring you news of it

28:71 (71)	what god other than God shall bring you illumination?
28:72 (72)	what god other than God shall bring you night to repose in?
29:28 (27)	surely you commit such indecency
29:29 (28)	what, do you approach men, and cut the way
29:29 (28)	and [do you] commit in your assembly dishonour?
29:53 (53)	but it shall come upon them suddenly
30:43 (42)	before there comes a day from God
31:16 (15)	God shall bring it forth
33:18 (18)	[those who] come to battle but little
33:20 (20)	if the Confederates come, they will wish that they were desert-dwellers
33:30 (30)	whosoever among you commits a flagrant indecency
34:3 (3)	the Hour will never come to us
34:3 (3)	it shall come to you, by Him who knows
35:16 (17)	if He will, He can put you away and bring a new creation
36:30 (29)	never comes unto them a Messenger, but they mock at him
36:46 (46)	yet never any sign of the signs of their Lord comes to them
37:28 (28)	why, you of old would come to us from the right hand
39:40 (41)	to whom will come a chastisement
39:54 (55)	ere the chastisement comes upon you, then
39:55 (56)	ere the chastisement comes upon you suddenly
39:71 (71)	Did not Messengers come to you
40:22 (23)	That was because their Messengers came to them with the clear signs
40:50 (53)	did not your Messengers bring you the clear signs?
40:78 (78)	it was not for any Messenger to bring a sign, save by God's leave
41:40 (40)	he who comes on the Day of Resurrection in security
41:42 (42)	falsehood comes not to it from before it
42:47 (46)	answer your Lord, before there comes a day from God that cannot be turned
43:7 (6)	but not a Prophet came to them, without they mocked at him
43:66 (66)	are they looking for aught but the Hour, that it shall come upon them suddenly
44:10 (9)	a day when heaven shall bring a manifest smoke
47:18 (20)	are they looking for aught but the Hour, that it shall come upon them suddenly?
52:34 (34)	then let them bring a discourse like it
52:38 (38)	then let any of them that has listened bring a clear authority
60:12 (12)	nor slay their children, nor bring a calumny
61:6 (6)	a Messenger who shall come after me
63:10 (10)	before that death comes upon one of you
64:5 (5)	has there not come to you the tidings of those that disbelieved before
64:6 (6)	that is because their Messengers came to them with the clear signs
65:1 (1)	except when they commit a flagrant indecency
67:8 (8)	came there no warner to you?
67:30 (30)	then who would bring you running water?
68:41 (41)	let them bring their associates
71:1 (1)	warn thy people, ere there come on them a painful chastisement
78:18 (18)	the day the Trumpet is blown, and you shall come in troops
98:1 (1)	till the Clear Sign came to them

c) impv. (*iʾti*)

2:23 (21)	then bring a sura like it
2:189 (185)	so come to the houses by their doors
2:222 (222)	then come unto them as God has commanded you
2:223 (223)	so come unto your tillage as you wish
2:258 (260)	so bring thou it from the west
3:93 (87)	Bring you the Torah now, and recite it
6:71 (70)	call him to guidance, 'Come to us'
7:70 (68)	Then bring us that thou promisest us

7:77 (75)	bring us that thou promisest us
7:106 (103)	If thou hast brought a sign, produce it
8:32 (32)	or bring us a painful chastisement
10:15 (16)	Bring a Koran other than this
10:38 (39)	then produce a sura like it
10:79 (80)	Bring me every cunning sorcerer
11:13 (16)	Then bring you ten suras the like of it
11:32 (34)	Then bring us that thou promisest us
12:50 (50)	bring him to me
12:54 (54)	bring him to me
12:59 (59)	bring me a certain brother of yours
12:93 (93)	then bring me your family all together
14:10 (12)	then bring us a manifest authority
20:47 (49)	so go you both to Pharaoh
20:64 (67)	then come in battle-line
21:61 (62)	Bring him before the people's eyes
26:10 (9)	Go to the people of the evildoers
26:16 (15)	So go you to Pharaoh, and say
26:31 (30)	Bring it then, if thou art of the truthful
26:154 (154)	then produce a sign, if thou art one of the truthful
27:31 (31)	Rise not up against me, but come to me in surrender
28:49 (49)	Bring a Book from God that gives better guidance than these
29:29 (28)	Then bring us the chastisement of God
37:157 (157)	Bring your Book, if you speak truly
41:11 (10)	Come willingly, or unwillingly
44:36 (35)	Bring us our fathers, if you speak truly
45:25 (24)	Bring us our fathers, if you speak truly
46:4 (3)	Bring me a Book before this
46:22 (21)	Then bring us that thou promisest us

d) perf. pass. (*utiya*)

2:25 (23)	that they shall be brought it in perfect semblance

g) pcple. act. (*ātī*)

6:134 (134)	The thing you are promised, that will surely come
11:76 (78)	there is coming upon them a chastisement
15:85 (85)	Surely the Hour is coming
19:93 (94)	None is there in the heavens and earth but he comes to the All-merciful
19:95 (95)	Every one of them shall come to Him
20:15 (15)	The Hour is coming
22:7 (7)	because the Hour is coming, no doubt of it
29:5 (4)	God's term is coming
40:59 (61)	The Hour is coming, no doubt of it
44:19 (18)	I come to you with a clear authority

h) pcple. pass. (*ma'tīy*)

19:61 (62)	His promise is ever performed

ĀTÁ vb. (IV)~to give (someone something); to bring; to do, to perform (esp. the prayer; see impv.). (n.vb.) giving, performing. (pcple. act.) one who performs or gives. (pcple.pass.) performed

a) perf. act.

2:53 (50)	and when We gave to Moses the Book
2:63 (60)	take forcefully what We have given you

2:87 (81)	and We gave to Moses the Book
2:87 (81)	and We gave Jesus son of Mary the clear signs
2:93 (87)	take forcefully what We have given you
2:121 (115)	those to whom We have given the Book
2:146 (141)	whom We have given the Book, and they recognize it
2:177 (172)	to give of one's substance, however cherished
2:177 (172)	to perform the prayer, to pay the alms
2:211 (207)	ask the Children of Israel how many a clear sign We gave them
2:229 (229)	it is not lawful for you to take of what you have given them
2:233 (233)	it is no fault in you provide you hand over what you have given
2:251 (252)	and God gave him the kingship, and Wisdom
2:253 (254)	and We gave Jesus son of Mary the clear signs
2:258 (260)	that God had given him the kingship
2:265 (267)	and it yields its produce twofold
2:277 (277)	and perform the prayer, and pay the alms
3:81 (75)	That I have given you of Book and Wisdom
3:148 (141)	And God gave them the reward of this world
3:170 (164)	rejoicing in the bounty that God has given them
3:180 (175)	those who are niggardly with the bounty God has given them
4:19 (23)	that you may go off with part of what you have given them
4:20 (24)	and [if] you have given to one a hundredweight, take of it nothing
4:37 (41)	and themselves conceal the bounty that God has given them
4:54 (57)	or are they jealous of the people for the bounty that God has given them?
4:54 (57)	yet We gave the people of Abraham the Book and the Wisdom
4:54 (57)	and We gave them a mighty kingdom
4:67 (70)	and then We surely would have given them from Us a mighty wage
4:153 (152)	that, and We bestowed upon Moses a clear authority
4:163 (161)	and We gave to David Psalms
5:5 (7)	if you give them their wages, in wedlock
5:12 (15)	if you perform the prayer, and pay the alms
5:20 (23)	and [He] gave you such as He had not given to any being
5:46 (50)	and We gave to him the Gospel
5:48 (53)	but that He may try you in what He has given you
6:20 (20)	Those to whom We have given the Book recognize it
6:83 (83)	That is Our argument, which We bestowed upon Abraham as against his people
6:89 (89)	Those are they to whom We gave the Book
6:114 (114)	those whom We have given the Book know it is sent down from thy Lord
6:154 (155)	Then We gave Moses the Book, complete
6:165 (165)	that He may try you in what He has given you
7:144 (141)	take what I have given thee, and be of the thankful
7:171 (170)	Take forcefully what We have given you
7:175 (174)	recite to them the tiding of him to whom We gave Our signs
7:189 (189)	If Thou givest us a righteous son, we indeed shall be of the thankful
7:190 (190)	when He gave them a righteous son, they assigned Him associates
7:190 (190)	they assigned Him associates in that He had given them
9:5 (5)	[if they] perform the prayer, and pay the alms
9:11 (11)	Yet if they repent, and perform the prayer, and pay the alms
9:18 (18)	[who] performs the prayer, and pays the alms
9:59 (59)	O were they well-pleased with what God and His Messenger have brought them
9:75 (76)	If He gives us of His bounty, we will make offerings
9:76 (77)	when He gave them of His bounty they were niggardly of it
10:88 (88)	Our Lord, Thou hast given to Pharaoh and his Council adornment
11:28 (30)	and He has given me mercy from Him
11:63 (66)	and He has given me mercy from Him
11:110 (112)	And We gave Moses the Book
12:22 (22)	And when he was fully grown, We gave him judgment and knowledge

12:31 (31)	then she gave to each one of them a knife
12:66 (66)	When they had brought him their solemn pledge
12:101 (102)	O my Lord, Thou hast given me to rule
13:36 (36)	And those to whom We have given the Book rejoice in what is sent down unto thee
14:34 (37)	and [He] gave you of all you asked Him
15:81 (81)	We brought them Our signs, and they turned away from them
15:87 (87)	We have given thee seven of the oft-repeated
16:55 (57)	that they may show unthankfulness for that We have given them
16:122 (123)	And We gave him in this world good
17:2 (2)	And We gave Moses the Book
17:55 (57)	and We gave to David Psalms
17:59 (61)	and We brought Thamood the She-camel visible
17:101 (103)	And We gave Moses nine signs
18:33 (31)	each of the two gardens yielded its produce
18:65 (64)	Then they found one of Our servants unto whom We had given mercy
18:84 (83)	and We gave him a way to everything
19:12 (13)	and We gave him judgment, yet a little child
19:30 (31)	God has given me the Book
20:99 (99)	and We have given thee a remembrance from Us
21:48 (49)	We gave Moses and Aaron the Salvation
21:51 (52)	We gave Abraham aforetime his rectitude — for We knew him
21:74 (74)	And Lot — to him We gave judgment
21:79 (79)	and unto each gave We judgment
21:84 (84)	and We gave his people, and the like of them with them, mercy from Us
22:41 (42)	who, if We establish them in the land, perform the prayer, and pay the alms
23:49 (51)	And We gave Moses the Book
23:60 (62)	and those (who give) what they give
24:33 (33)	of the wealth of God that He has given you
25:35 (37)	We gave Moses the Book
27:15 (15)	And We gave David and Solomon knowledge
27:36 (36)	what God gave me is better
27:36 (36)	better than what He has given you
28:14 (13)	We gave him judgment and knowledge
28:43 (43)	And We gave Moses the Book
28:52 (52)	Those to whom We gave the Book before this believe in it
28:76 (76)	We had given him treasures such that the very keys of them were too heavy
28:77 (77)	but seek, amidst that which God has given thee, the Last Abode
29:27 (26)	We gave him his wage in this world
29:47 (46)	Those to whom We have given the Book believe in it
29:66 (66)	that they may be ungrateful for what We have given them
30:34 (33)	that they may be ungrateful for what We have given them
30:39 (38)	and what you give in usury
30:39 (38)	but what you give in alms, desiring God's Face
31:12 (11)	indeed, We gave Lokman wisdom
32:13 (13)	We could have given every soul its guidance
32:23 (23)	indeed, We gave Moses the Book
33:14 (14)	[if] they had been asked to apostatise, they would have done so
33:50 (49)	thy wives whom thou hast given their wages
33:51 (51)	every one of them will be well-pleased with what thou givest her
34:10 (10)	And We gave David bounty from Us
34:44 (43)	We have not given them any Books to study
34:45 (44)	they reached not a tenth of what We gave them
35:40 (38)	Or have We given them a Book
37:117 (117)	and We gave them the Manifesting Book
38:20 (19)	We strengthened his kingdom, and gave him wisdom

40:53 (56)	We also gave Moses the guidance
41:45 (45)	And We gave Moses the Book
43:21 (20)	Or did We bring them a Book aforetime
44:33 (32)	and gave them signs wherein there was a manifest trial
45:16 (15)	We gave the Children of Israel the Book
45:17 (16)	We gave them clear signs of the Command
47:17 (19)	He increases in guidance, and gives them their godfearing
51:16 (16)	taking whatsoever their Lord has given them
52:18 (18)	rejoicing in that their Lord has given them
57:23 (23)	nor rejoice in what has come to you
57:27 (27)	and [We] gave unto him the Gospel
57:27 (27)	so We gave those of them who believed their wage
59:7 (7)	whatever the Messenger gives you, take
60:10 (10)	to marry them when you have given them their wages
65:7 (7)	let him expend of what God has given him
65:7 (7)	God charges no soul save with what He has given him

b) impf. act. (*yuʾtī*)

2:247 (248)	God gives the kingship to whom He will
2:269 (272)	He gives the Wisdom to whomsoever He will
2:271 (273)	but if you conceal them, and give them to the poor, that is better for you
3:26 (25)	Thou givest the Kingdom to whom Thou wilt
3:73 (66)	He gives it unto whomsoever He will
3:79 (73)	it belongs not to any mortal that God should give him the Book
3:145 (139)	whoso desires the reward of this world, We will give him of this
3:145 (139)	and whoso desires the reward of the other world, We will give him of that
4:5 (4)	but do not give to fools their property
4:40 (44)	He will double it, and give from Himself a mighty wage
4:53 (56)	they do not give the people a single date-spot
4:74 (76)	We shall bring him a mighty wage
4:114 (114)	We shall surely give him a mighty wage
4:127 (126)	the orphan women to whom you give not what is prescribed
4:146 (145)	and God will certainly give the believers a mighty wage
4:152 (151)	We shall surely give them their wages
4:162 (160)	them We shall surely give a mighty wage
5:20 (23)	such as He had not given to any being
5:54 (59)	He gives it unto whom He will
5:55 (60)	the believers who perform the prayer and pay the alms
7:156 (155)	I shall prescribe it for those who are godfearing and pay the alms
8:70 (71)	He will give you better than what has been taken
9:59 (59)	God will bring us of His bounty
9:71 (72)	they perform the prayer, and pay the alms
11:3 (3)	and He will give of His bounty to every man of grace
11:31 (33)	God will not give them any good
12:66 (66)	until you bring me a solemn pledge by God
14:25 (30)	it gives its produce every season
18:40 (38)	it may be that my Lord will give me better than thy garden
23:60 (62)	and those who give what (they give)
24:22 (22)	Let not those of you who possess bounty and plenty swear off giving kinsmen
27:3 (3)	who perform the prayer, and pay the alms
31:4 (3)	who perform the prayer, and pay the alms
33:31 (31)	We shall pay her her wage twice over
41:7 (6)	who pay not the alms
42:20 (19)	Whoso desires the tillage of the world to come, We shall give him increase
47:36 (38)	He will give you your wages

48:10 (10)	God will give him a mighty wage
48:16 (16)	If you obey, God will give you a goodly wage
57:21 (21)	He gives it unto whomsoever He will
57:28 (28)	He will give you a twofold portion of His mercy
57:29 (29)	He gives it unto whomsoever He will
62:4 (4)	That is the bounty of God; He gives it to whom He will
92:18 (18)	even he who gives his wealth to purify himself
98:5 (4)	and to perform the prayer, and pay the alms

c) impv. (*āti*)

2:43 (40)	And perform the prayer, and pay the alms
2:83 (77)	and perform the prayer, and pay the alms
2:110 (104)	And perform the prayer, and pay the alms
2:200 (196)	Our Lord, give to us in this world
2:201 (197)	Our Lord, give to us in this world good
3:194 (192)	Our Lord, give us what Thou hast promised us
4:2 (2)	Give the orphans their property
4:4 (3)	And give the women their dowries as a gift
4:24 (28)	give them their wages apportionate
4:25 (29)	and give them their wages honourably
4:33 (37)	So give to them their share
4:77 (79)	and perform the prayer, and pay the alms
6:141 (142)	pay the due thereof on the day of its harvest
7:38 (36)	so give them a double chastisement
17:26 (28)	And give the kinsman his right
18:10 (9)	Our Lord, give us mercy from Thee
18:62 (61)	bring us our breakfast
18:96 (95)	bring me ingots of iron
18:96 (95)	bring me, that I may pour molten brass on it
22:78 (78)	so perform the prayer, and pay the alms
24:33 (33)	and give them of the wealth of God
24:56 (55)	perform the prayer, and pay the alms
30:38 (37)	and give the kinsman his right
33:33 (33)	and perform the prayer, and pay the alms
33:68 (68)	Our Lord, give them chastisement twofold
58:13 (14)	then perform the prayer, and pay the alms
60:10 (10)	give the unbelievers what they have expended
60:11 (11)	give those whose wives have gone away the like of what they have expended
65:6 (6)	if they suckle for you, give them their wages
73:20 (20)	and perform the prayer, and pay the alms

d) perf. pass. (*ūtiya*)

2:101 (95)	a party of them that were given the Book reject the Book of God
2:136 (130)	and that which was given to Moses and Jesus
2:136 (130)	and [that which was given to] the Prophets, of their Lord
2:144 (139)	those who have been given the Book know it is the truth from their Lord
2:145 (140)	if thou shouldst bring to those that have been given the Book every sign
2:213 (209)	and only those who had been given it were at variance upon it
2:269 (272)	whoso is given the Wisdom, has been given much good
3:19 (17)	Those who were given the Book were not at variance
3:20 (19)	And say to those who have been given the Book
3:23 (22)	Hast thou not regarded those who were given a portion of the Book
3:73 (66)	the like of what you have been given
3:84 (78)	in that which was given to Moses and Jesus
3:100 (95)	a sect of those who have been given the Book

3:186 (183)	you shall hear from those who were given the Book before you
3:187 (184)	when God took compact with those who had been given the Book
4:44 (47)	Hast thou not regarded those who were given a share of the Book
4:47 (50)	You who have been given the Book, believe
4:51 (54)	Hast thou not regarded those who were given a share of the Book
4:131 (130)	We have charged those who were given the Book before you
5:5 (7)	the food of those who were given the Book is permitted to you
5:5 (7)	and in wedlock women of them who were given the Book before you
5:41 (45)	if you are given this, then take it
5:57 (62)	take not as your friends those of them, who were given the Book before you
6:44 (44)	when they rejoiced in what they were given
6:124 (124)	the like of what God's Messengers were given
9:29 (29)	being of those who have been given the Book
16:27 (29)	Those that were given the knowledge will say
17:71 (73)	and whoso is given his book in his right hand
17:85 (87)	You have been given of knowledge nothing
17:107 (108)	those who were given the knowledge before it
20:36 (36)	Thou art granted, Moses, thy petition
22:54 (53)	that they who have been given knowledge may know
27:16 (16)	we have been given of everything
27:23 (23)	and she has been given of everything
27:42 (42)	And we were given the knowledge before her
28:48 (48)	why has he not been given the like of
28:48 (48)	the like of that Moses was given
28:48 (48)	did they not disbelieve also in what Moses was given aforetime?
28:60 (60)	whatever thing you have been given is the enjoyment of the present life
28:78 (78)	what I have been given is only because of a knowledge that is in me
28:79 (79)	would that we possessed the like of that Korah has been given
28:80 (80)	those to whom knowledge had been given said
29:49 (48)	in the breasts of those who have been given knowledge
30:56 (56)	those who have been given knowledge and faith shall say
34:6 (6)	Those who have been given the knowledge see
39:49 (50)	I was given it only because of a knowledge
42:36 (34)	Whatever thing you have been given is the enjoyment of the present life
47:16 (18)	they say to those who have been given knowledge
57:16 (15)	they should not be as those to whom the Book was given aforetime
58:11 (12)	those of you who believe and have been given knowledge
59:9 (9)	not finding in their breasts any need for what they have been given
69:19 (19)	as for him who is given his book in his right hand
69:25 (25)	as for him who is given his book in his left hand
74:31(31)	that those who were given the Book may have certainty
74:31 (32)	that those who were given the Book [may not be in doubt]
84:7 (7)	as for him who is given his book in his right hand
84:10 (10)	as for him who is given his book behind his back
98:4 (3)	And they scattered not, those that were given the Book

e) impf. pass. (*yu'tá*)

2:247 (248)	seeing he has not been given amplitude of wealth
2:269 (272)	and whoso is given the Wisdom
3:73 (66)	that anyone should be given the like of what (you have been given)
5:41 (45)	if you are not given it, beware
6:124 (124)	We will not believe until we are given
19:77 (80)	I shall be given wealth and children
28:54 (54)	These shall be given their wage twice over
69:25 (25)	Would that I had not been given my book
74:52 (52)	every man of them desires to be given scrolls unrolled

f) n.vb. (*ītā'*)

16:90 (92)	God bids to justice and good-doing and giving to kinsmen
21:73 (73)	to perform the prayer, and to pay the alms
24:37 (37)	to perform the prayer, and to pay the alms

g) pcple. act. (*mu'tī*)

4:162 (160)	[those] that perform the prayer and pay the alms

*A TH L

ATHL n.m.~tamarisk-bushes

34:16 (15)	two gardens bearing bitter produce and tamarisk-bushes

*A TH M

ATHIMA vb. (I)~(pcple. act.) sinful, sinner

g) pcple. act. (*āthim*)

2:283 (283)	whoso conceals it, his heart is sinful
5:106 (105)	for then we would surely be among the sinful
76:24 (24)	and obey not one of them, sinner or unbeliever

ATHĀM n.m.~sin

25:68 (68)	for whosoever does that shall meet the price of sin

ATHĪM n.m. (adj)~guilty

2:276 (277)	God loves not any guilty ingrate
4:107 (107)	God loves not the guilty traitor
26:222 (222)	They come down on every guilty impostor
44:44 (44)	is the food of the guilty
45:7 (6)	Woe to every guilty impostor
68:12 (12)	hinderer of good, guilty aggressor
83:12 (12)	and none cries lies to it but every guilty aggressor

ITHM n.m.~sin

2:85 (79)	conspiring against them in sin and enmity
2:173 (168)	no sin shall be on him
2:181 (177)	the sin shall rest upon those who change it
2:182 (178)	if any man fears injustice or sin from one making testament
2:182 (178)	then sin shall not rest upon him
2:188 (184)	that you may sinfully consume a portion of other men's goods
2:203 (199)	if any man hastens on in two days, that is no sin in him
2:203 (199)	if any delays, it is not a sin in him, if he be godfearing
2:206 (202)	vainglory seizes him in his sin
2:219 (216)	in both is heinous sin, and uses for men
2:219 (216)	the sin in them is more heinous than the usefulness
3:178 (172)	We grant them indulgence only that they may increase in sin
4:20 (24)	will you take it by way of calumny and manifest sin?
4:48 (51)	whoso associates with God anything, has indeed forged a mighty sin
4:50 (53)	and that suffices for a manifest sin
4:111 (111)	and whosoever earns a sin, earns it against himself only
4:112 (112)	whosoever earns a fault or a sin and then casts it upon the innocent

4:112 (112)	thereby has laid upon himself calumny and manifest sin
5:2 (3)	do not help each other to sin and enmity
5:3 (5)	[whosoever is] not inclining purposely to sin
5:29 (32)	I desire that thou shouldest be laden with my sin
5:29 (32)	I desire that thou shouldest be laden with [my sin and] thy sin
5:62 (67)	Thou seest many of them vying in sin and enmity
5:63 (68)	Why do the masters and the rabbis not forbid them to utter sin
5:107 (106)	that both of them have merited the accusation of any sin
6:120 (120)	forsake the outward sin, and the inward
6:120 (120)	surely the earners of sin shall be recompensed
7:33 (31)	My Lord has only forbidden indecencies, the inward and the outward, and sin
24:11 (11)	every man of them shall have the sin that he has earned charged to him
33:58 (58)	have laid upon themselves calumny and manifest sin
42:37 (35)	And those who avoid the heinous sins
49:12 (12)	some suspicion is a sin
53:32 (33)	Those who avoid the heinous sins and indecencies
58:8 (9)	they converse secretly together in sin and enmity
58:9 (10)	conspire not together in sin and enmity

ATHTHAMA vb. (II)~(n.vb.) cause of sin, accusation of sinfulness

f) n.vb. (*ta'thīm*)

52:23 (23)	wherein is no idle talk, no cause of sin
56:25 (24)	Therein they shall hear no idle talk, no cause of sin

*A TH R

ATHARA vb. (I)~to stir up, to trump up

e) impf. pass. (*yu'tharu*)

74:24 (24)	This is naught but a trumped-up sorcery

ATHAR n.m. (pl. *āthār*)~footstep, mark, trace, track, that which is left behind; after

5:46 (50)	And We sent, following in their footsteps, Jesus son of Mary
18:6 (5)	thou wilt consume thyself, following after them, of grief
18:64 (63)	And so they returned upon their tracks
20:84 (86)	They are upon my tracks
20:96 (96)	I seized of dust from the messenger's track
30:50 (49)	So behold the marks of God's mercy
36:12 (11)	and write down what they have forwarded and what they have left behind
37:70 (68)	and they run in their footsteps
40:21 (22)	and [they] left firmer traces in the earth
40:82(82)	and [they] left firmer traces in the earth
43:22 (21)	and we are guided upon their traces
43:23 (22)	and we are following upon their traces
48:29 (29)	Their mark is on their faces, the trace of prostration
57:27 (27)	Then We sent, following in their footsteps, Our Messengers

ATHĀRAH n.f.~remnant, trace

46:4 (3)	Bring me a Book before this, or some remnant of a knowledge

ĀTHARA vb. (IV)~to prefer

a) perf. act.

12:91 (91) God has indeed preferred thee above us
79:38 (38) and preferred the present life

b) impf. act. (*yu'thiru*)

20:72 (75) We will not prefer thee over the clear signs that have come to us
59:9 (9) preferring others above themselves
87:16 (16) but you prefer the present life

*A TH TH

ATHĀTH n.m. (coll)~furniture, furnishing

16:80 (82) and of their hair furnishing and an enjoyment for a while
19:74 (75) who were fairer in furnishing and outward show

*A W B

ĀBA vb. (I)~(n.vb.) return

f) n.vb. (*iyāb*)

88:25 (25) Truly, to Us is their return

AWWĀB n.m. (adj)~penitent; (adj) reverting

17:25 (27) He is All-forgiving to those who are penitent
38:17 (16) Our servant David, the man of might; he was a penitent
38:19 (18) and the birds, duly mustered, every one to him reverting
38:30 (29) how excellent a servant he was! He was a penitent
38:44 (44) how excellent a servant he was! He was a penitent
50:32 (31) it is for every mindful penitent

MA'ĀB n.m.~a place of return, a resort

3:14 (12) but God — with Him is the fairest resort
13:29 (28) theirs is blessedness and a fair resort
13:36 (36) To Him I call, and to Him is my turning
38:25 (24) he has a near place in Our presence and a fair resort
38:40 (39) he had a near place in Our presence and a fair resort
38:49 (49) and for the godfearing is a fair resort
38:55 (55) but for the insolent awaits an ill resort
78:22 (22) for the insolent a resort
78:39 (39) so whosoever wills takes unto his Lord a resort

AWWABA vb. (II)~to sing the praises of God

c) impv. (*awwib*)

34:10 (10) O you mountains, echo God's praises with him, and you birds

*A W D

ĀDA vb. (I)~to oppress

b) impf. act. (*ya'ūdu*)

2:255 (256)	the preserving of them oppresses Him not

*A W H

AWWĀH n.m. (adj)~compassionate

9:114 (115)	Abraham was compassionate, clement
11:75 (77)	Abraham was clement, compassionate, penitent

*A W L

ĀL n.m. (coll)~folk, people, House (such as "House of Jacob")

2:49 (46)	when We delivered you from the folk of Pharaoh
2:50 (47)	[We] delivered you, and drowned Pharaoh's folk
2:248 (249)	a remnant of what the folk of Moses
2:248 (249)	and [of what] Aaron's folk left behind
3:11 (9)	like Pharaoh's folk, and the people before them
3:33 (30)	God chose Adam and Noah and the House of Abraham
3:33 (30)	and the House of Imran above all beings
4:54 (57)	We gave the people of Abraham the Book and the Wisdom
7:130 (127)	then seized We Pharaoh's people with years
7:141 (137)	We delivered you from the folk of Pharaoh
8:52 (54)	like Pharaoh's folk, and the people before him
8:54 (56)	like Pharaoh's folk, and the people before him
8:54 (56)	and We drowned the folk of Pharaoh
12:6 (6)	and [Hewill] perfect His blessing upon thee and upon the House of Jacob
14:6 (6)	when He delivered you from the folk of Pharaoh
15:59 (59)	excepting the folk of Lot; them we shall deliver
15:61 (61)	when the envoys came to the folk of Lot
19:6 (6)	[who shall be] the inheritor of the House of Jacob
27:56 (57)	Expel the folk of Lot from your city
28:8 (7)	then the folk of Pharaoh picked him out
34:13 (12)	Labour, O House of David, in thankfulness
40:28 (29)	a believer of Pharaoh's folk that kept hidden
40:45 (48)	there encompassed the folk of Pharaoh the evil chastisement
40:46 (49)	Admit the folk of Pharaoh into the most terrible chastisement
54:34 (34)	except the folk of Lot; We delivered them
54:41 (41)	The warnings came also to Pharaoh's folk

AWWAL n.num. (f. *ūlá*; see *awwalūn*, below)~first; First (Divine attribute in 57:3)

2:41 (38)	and be not the first to disbelieve in it
3:96 (90)	The first House established for the people was that at Bekka
5:114 (114)	that shall be for us a festival, the first and last of us
6:14 (14)	I have been commanded to be the first of them that surrender
6:94 (94)	as We created you upon the first time
6:110 (110)	even as they believed not in it the first time
6:163 (163)	I am the first of those that surrender
7:38 (36)	the last of them shall say to the first of them
7:39 (37)	the first of them shall say to the last of them
7:143 (140)	I am the first of the believers
9:13 (13)	beginning the first time against you

9:83 (84)	you were well-pleased to tarry the first time
9:108 (109)	founded upon godfearing from the first day
17:5 (5)	when the promise of the first of these came to pass
17:7 (7)	as they entered it the first time
17:51 (53)	He who originated you the first time
18:48 (46)	You have come to Us, as We created you upon the first time
20:21 (22)	We will restore it to its first state
20:51 (53)	and what of the former generations?
20:65 (68)	or we shall be the first to cast
20:133 (133)	has there not come to them the clear sign of what is in the former scrolls?
21:104 (104)	as We originated the first creation
26:51 (51)	we are the first of the believers
28:43 (43)	We had destroyed the former generations
28:70 (70)	His is the praise in the former as in the latter
33:33 (33)	display not your finery, as did the pagans of old
36:79 (79)	He shall quicken them, who originated them the first time
37:59 (57)	except for our first death
39:12 (14)	I have been commanded to be the first of those that surrender
41:21 (20)	He created you the first time
43:81 (81)	then I am the first to serve him
44:35 (34)	there is nothing but our first death
44:56 (56)	they shall not taste therein of death, save the first death
50:15 (14)	were We wearied by the first creation?
53:25 (25)	and to God belongs the First and the Last
53:50 (51)	and that He destroyed Ad, the ancient
53:56 (57)	This is a warner, of the warners of old
56:62 (62)	You have known the first growth
57:3 (3)	He is the First and the Last
59:2 (2)	the unbelievers among the People of the Book at the first mustering
79:25 (25)	God seized him with the chastisement of the Last World and the First
87:18 (18)	Surely this is in the ancient scrolls
92:13 (13)	to Us belong the Last and the First
93:4 (4)	the Last shall be better for thee than the First

AWWALŪN n.m. (pl. of *awwal*, above)~ancient ones

6:25 (25)	This is naught but the fairy-tales of the ancient ones
8:31 (31)	this is naught but the fairy-tales of the ancients
8:38 (39)	the wont of the ancients is already gone
9:100 (101)	And the Outstrippers, the first of the Emigrants
15:10 (10)	We sent Messengers before thee, among the factions of the ancients
15:13 (13)	the wont of the ancients is already gone
16:24 (26)	Fairy-tales of the ancients
17:59 (61)	but that the ancients cried lies to them
18:55 (53)	that the wont of the ancients should come upon them
21:5 (5)	as the ancient ones were sent as Messengers
23:24 (24)	We never heard of this among our fathers, the ancients
23:68 (70)	that which came not upon their fathers, the ancients
23:81 (83)	they said the like of what the ancients said
23:83 (85)	this is naught but the fairy-tales of the ancients
25:5 (6)	Fairy-tales of the ancients that he has had written down
26:26 (25)	Your Lord and the Lord of your fathers, the ancients
26:137 (137)	this is nothing but the habit of the ancients
26:184 (184)	Fear Him who created you, and the generations of the ancients
26:196 (196)	Truly it is in the Scriptures of the ancients
27:68 (70)	this is naught but the fairy-tales of the ancients
28:36 (36)	We never heard of this among our fathers, the ancients

35:43 (41)	So do they expect anything but the wont of the ancients
37:17 (17)	what, and our fathers, the ancients?
37:71 (69)	before them erred most of the ancients
37:126 (126)	God, your Lord, and the Lord of your fathers, the ancients
37:168 (168)	if only we had had a Reminder from the ancients
43:6 (5)	how many a Prophet We sent among the ancients
43:8 (7)	the example of the ancients passed away
44:8 (7)	your Lord and the Lord of your fathers, the ancients
46:17 (16)	this is naught but the fairy-tales of the ancients
56:13 (13)	a throng of the ancients
56:39 (38)	a throng of the ancients
56:48 (48)	what, and our fathers, the ancients?
56:49 (49)	the ancients, and the later folk
68:15 (15)	fairy-tales of the ancients
77:16 (16)	did We not destroy the ancients
77:38 (38)	We have joined you with the ancients
83:13 (13)	fairy-tales of the ancients

AWWALA vb. (II)~(n.vb.) interpretation, result, issue

f) n.vb. (*ta'wīl*)

3:7 (5)	desiring dissension, and desiring its interpretation
3:7 (5)	none knows its interpretation, save only God
4:59 (62)	that is better, and fairer in the issue
7:53 (51)	do they look for aught else but its interpretation?
7:53 (51)	the day its interpretation comes
10:39 (40)	whose interpretation has not yet come to them
12:6 (6)	[He will] teach thee the interpretation of tales
12:21 (21)	that We might teach him the interpretation of tales
12:36 (36)	Tell us its interpretation
12:37 (37)	I shall tell you its interpretation
12:44 (44)	We know nothing of the interpretation of nightmares
12:45 (45)	I will myself tell you its interpretation
12:100 (101)	this is the interpretation of my vision
12:101 (102)	Thou hast taught me the interpretation of tales
17:35 (37)	that is better and fairer in the issue
18:78 (77)	Now I will tell thee the interpretation
18:82 (81)	This is the interpretation of that thou couldst not bear patiently

*A W Y

AWÁ vb. (I)~to take refuge

a) perf. act.

18:10 (9)	When the youths took refuge in the Cave
18:63 (62)	When we took refuge in the rock

b) impf. act. (*ya'wī*)

11:43 (45)	I will take refuge in a mountain
11:80 (82)	or [that I] might take refuge in a strong pillar

c) impv. (*i'wi*)

18:16 (15)	take refuge in the Cave

MA'WÁ n.m.~lodging, refuge

3:151 (144)	their lodging shall be the Fire
3:162 (156)	whose refuge is Gehenna? An evil homecoming
3:197 (196)	their refuge is Gehenna — an evil cradling
4:97 (99)	their refuge shall be Gehenna — an evil homecoming
4:121 (120)	their refuge shall be Gehenna
5:72 (76)	his refuge shall be the Fire
8:16 (16)	his refuge is Gehenna — an evil homecoming
9:73 (74)	their refuge is Gehenna — an evil homecoming
9:95 (96)	their refuge is Gehenna
10:8 (8)	those — their refuge is the Fire
13:18 (18)	their refuge shall be Gehenna — an evil cradling
17:97 (99)	their refuge shall be Gehenna
24:57 (56)	their refuge is the Fire — an evil homecoming
29:25 (24)	and your refuge will be the Fire
32:19 (19)	there await them the Gardens of the Refuge
32:20 (20)	their refuge shall be the Fire
45:34 (33)	your refuge is the Fire
53:15 (15)	nigh which is the Garden of the Refuge
57:15 (14)	Your refuge is the Fire, that is your master — an evil homecoming
66:9 (9)	their refuge shall be Gehenna — an evil homecoming
79:39 (39)	surely Hell shall be the refuge
79:41 (41)	surely Paradise shall be the refuge

ĀWÁ vb. (IV)~to give refuge, to take into one's arms, to shelter, to take to one's self

a) perf. act.

8:26 (26)	but He gave you refuge, and confirmed you
8:72 (73)	and those who have given refuge and help
8:74 (75)	Those who have given refuge and help
12:69 (69)	he said, taking his brother into his arms
12:99 (100)	he took his father and mother into his arms
23:50 (52)	and [We] gave them refuge upon a height
93:6 (6)	did He not find thee an orphan, and shelter thee?

b) impf. act. (*yu'wī*)

33:51 (51)	and whom thou wilt thou mayest take to thee
70:13 (13)	his kin who sheltered him

*A Y B

AYYŪB n.prop.~Job

4:163 (161)	Jesus and Job, Jonah and Aaron
6:84 (84)	David and Solomon, Job and Joseph
21:83 (83)	And Job — when he called unto his Lord
38:41 (40)	Remember also Our servant Job

*A Y D

AYD n.m.~might, strength

38:17 (16)	remember Our servant David, the man of might
51:47 (47)	And heaven — We built it with might

AYYADA vb. (II)~to confirm, to support

a) perf. act.

2:87 (81)	and [We] confirmed him with the Holy Spirit
2:253 (254)	and [We] confirmed him with the Holy Spirit
5:110 (109)	when I confirmed thee with the Holy Spirit
8:26 (26)	and [He] confirmed you with His help
8:62 (64)	He has confirmed thee with His help
9:40 (40)	and [He] confirmed him with legions you did not see
58:22 (22)	He has confirmed them with a Spirit from Himself
61:14 (14)	So We confirmed those who believed against their enem

b) impf. act. (*yu'ayyidu*)

3:13 (11)	God confirms with His help whom He will

*A Y K

AYKAH n.f.~thicket, wood (a name for Midian)

15:78 (78)	the dwellers in the Thicket were evildoers
26:176 (176)	The men of the Thicket cried lies to the Envoys
38:13 (12)	the men of the Thicket — those were the parties
50:14 (13)	the men of the Thicket, the people of Tubba

*A Y M

AYĀMÁ n.f. (pl. of *ayyim*)~unmarried, spouseless (women)

24:32 (32)	Marry the spouseless among you

*A Y W

ĀYAH n.f. (pl. *āyāt, āy*)~sign [Ar, Bl]; a communication (from God) [Ali]; a revelation [Pk]; (also) a verse of the Koran, Ayah

2:39 (37)	As for the unbelievers who cry lies to Our signs
2:41 (38)	And sell not My signs for a little price
2:61 (58)	because they had disbelieved the signs of God
2:73 (68)	and He shows you His signs
2:99 (93)	We have sent down unto thee signs
2:106 (100)	And for whatever verse We abrogate
2:118 (112)	why does a sign not come to us?
2:118 (112)	We have made clear the signs unto a people who are sure
2:129 (123)	a Messenger, one of them, who shall recite to them Thy signs
2:145 (140)	if thou shouldst bring to [them] every sign, they will not follow
2:151 (146)	a Messenger, to recite Our signs to you
2:164 (159)	there are signs for a people having understanding
2:187 (183)	God makes clear His signs to men
2:211 (207)	how many a clear sign We gave them
2:219 (217)	So God makes clear His signs to you
2:221 (221)	He makes clear His signs to the people
2:231 (231)	take not God's signs in mockery
2:242 (243)	so God makes clear His signs for you
2:248 (249)	the sign of his kingship is that the Ark will come to you

2:248 (249)	surely in that shall be a sign for you
2:252 (253)	these are the signs of God We recite to thee in truth
2:259 (261)	so We would make thee a sign for the people
2:266 (268)	so God makes clear the signs to you
3:4 (3)	those who disbelieve in God's signs
3:7 (5)	the Book, wherein are verses clear
3:11 (9)	the people before them, who cried lies to Our signs
3:13 (11)	there has already been a sign for you
3:19 (17)	whoso disbelieves in God's signs
3:21 (20)	those who disbelieve in the signs of God
3:41 (36)	appoint to me a sign
3:41 (36)	thy sign is that thou shalt not speak, save by tokens
3:49 (43)	I have come to you with a sign from your Lord
3:49 (43)	in that is a sign for you
3:50 (44)	I have come to you with a sign from your Lord
3:58 (51)	This We recite to thee of signs and wise remembrance
3:70 (63)	Why do you disbelieve in God's signs
3:97 (91)	Therein are clear signs — the station of Abraham
3:98 (93)	why do you disbelieve in the signs of God
3:101 (96)	How can you disbelieve, seeing you have God's signs
3:103 (99)	God makes clear to you His signs
3:108 (104)	These are the signs of God We recite to thee in truth
3:112 (108)	because they disbelieved in God's signs
3:113 (109)	a nation upstanding, that recite God's signs
3:118 (114)	We have made clear to you the signs
3:164 (158)	to recite to them His signs
3:190 (187)	in the alternation of night and day there are signs
3:199 (198)	not selling the signs of God for a small price
4:56 (59)	those who disbelieve in Our signs
4:140 (139)	When you hear God's signs being disbelieved
4:155 (154)	and disbelieving in the signs of God
5:10 (13)	And the unbelievers, who cried lies to Our signs
5:44 (48)	and sell not My signs for a little price
5:75 (79)	Behold, how We make clear the signs to them
5:86 (88)	those who disbelieve, and cry lies to Our signs
5:89 (91)	God makes clear to you His signs
5:114 (114)	[it shall be for us a festival] and a sign from Thee
6:4 (4)	not a sign of ([the signs of]) their Lord comes to them
6:4 (4)	not a (sign) of [the signs of] Their Lord comes to them
6:21 (21)	or [he who] cries lies to His signs
6:25 (25)	if they see any sign whatever, they do not believe in it
6:27 (27)	[would that we] not cry lies to the signs of our Lord
6:33 (33)	it is the signs of God that they deny
6:35 (35)	or a ladder in heaven, to bring them some sign
6:37 (37)	why has no sign been sent down upon him from his Lord?
6:37 (37)	God is able to send down a sign
6:39 (39)	those who cry lies to Our signs are deaf and dumb
6:46 (46)	Behold how We turn about the signs
6:49 (49)	those who cry lies to Our signs, them the chastisement shall visit
6:54 (54)	when those who believe in Our signs come to thee
6:55 (55)	Thus We distinguish Our signs
6:65 (65)	Behold how We turn about the signs
6:68 (67)	When thou seest those who plunge into Our signs
6:93 (93)	waxing proud against His signs
6:97 (97)	We have distinguished the signs for a people who know

6:98 (98)	We have distinguished the signs for a people who understand
6:99 (99)	in all this are signs for a people who do believe
6:105 (105)	So We turn about the signs
6:109 (109)	if a sign comes to them they will believe in it
6:109 (109)	signs are only with God
6:118 (118)	if you believe in His signs
6:124 (124)	and when a sign came to them, they said
6:126 (126)	We have distinguished the signs to a people who remember
6:130 (130)	did not Messengers come to you from among you, relating to you My signs
6:150 (151)	the caprices of those who cried lies to Our signs
6:157 (158)	he who cries lies to God's signs
6:157 (158)	We shall surely recompense those who turn away from Our signs
6:158 (159)	that one of thy Lord's signs should come
6:158 (159)	on the day that one of thy Lord's signs comes
7:9 (8)	they have lost their souls for wronging Our signs
7:26 (25)	that is one of God's signs
7:32 (30)	So We distinguish the signs for a people who know
7:35 (33)	Messengers from among you, relating to you My signs
7:36 (34)	those that cry lies to Our signs
7:37 (35)	or [he who] cries lies to His signs
7:40 (38)	Those that cry lies to Our signs
7:51 (49)	that they denied Our signs
7:58 (56)	We turn about the signs for a people that are thankful
7:64 (62)	We drowned those who cried lies to Our signs
7:72 (70)	the last remnant of those who cried lies to Our signs
7:73 (71)	this is the She-camel of God, to be a sign for you
7:103 (101)	We sent, after them, Moses with Our signs
7:106 (103)	If thou hast brought a sign, produce it
7:126 (123)	we have believed in the signs of our Lord
7:132 (129)	Whatsoever sign thou bringest to us
7:133 (130)	the lice and the frogs, the blood, distinct signs
7:136 (132)	for that they cried lies to Our signs
7:146 (143)	I shall turn from My signs those who wax proud
7:146 (143)	though they see every sign, they will not believe in it
7:146 (144)	because they have cried lies to Our signs
7:147 (145)	Those who cry lies to Our signs
7:156 (155)	those who indeed believe in Our signs
7:174 (173)	So We distinguish the signs
7:175 (174)	the tiding of him to whom We gave Our signs
7:176 (175)	that people's likeness who cried lies to Our signs
7:177 (176)	the people who cried lies to Our signs
7:182 (181)	those who cry lies to Our signs
7:203 (202)	And when thou bringest them not a sign
8:2 (2)	when His signs are recited to them
8:31 (31)	when Our signs were being recited to them
8:52 (54)	who disbelieved in God's signs
8:54 (56)	who cried lies to the signs of their Lord,
9:9 (9)	They have sold the signs of God for a small price
9:11 (11)	We distinguish the signs for a people who know
9:65 (66)	then were you mocking God, and His signs
10:1 (1)	Those are the signs of the Wise Book
10:5 (5)	distinguishing the signs to a people who know
10:6 (6)	there are signs for a godfearing people
10:7 (7)	those who are heedless of Our signs
10:15 (16)	when Our signs are recited to them

10:17 (18)	[he who] cries lies to His signs
10:20 (21)	why has a sign not been sent down upon him from his Lord?
10:21 (22)	they have a device concerning Our signs
10:24 (25)	We distinguish the signs for a people who reflect
10:67 (68)	in that are signs for a people who have ears
10:71 (72)	and my reminding you of the signs of God
10:73 (74)	We drowned those who cried lies to Our signs
10:75 (76)	We sent forth, after them, Moses and Aaron to Pharaoh and his Council with Our signs
10:92 (92)	that thou mayest be a sign to those after thee
10:92 (92)	many men are heedless of Our signs
10:95 (95)	nor be of those who cry lies to God's signs
10:97 (97)	though every sign come to them
10:101 (101)	neither signs nor warnings avail a people who do not believe
11:1 (1)	A Book whose verses are set clear
11:59 (62)	they denied the signs of their Lord
11:64 (67)	this is the She-camel of God, to be a sign for you
11:96 (99)	And We sent Moses with Our signs
11:103 (105)	in that is a sign for him who fears the chastisement
12:1 (1)	Those are the signs of the Manifest Book
12:7 (7)	In Joseph and his brethren were signs for those who ask questions
12:35 (35)	Then it seemed good to them, after they had seen the signs
12:105 (105)	How many a sign there is in the heavens and in the earth that they pass by
13:1 (1)	Those are the signs of the Book
13:2 (2)	He distinguishes the signs
13:3 (3)	in that are signs for a people who reflect
13:4 (4)	in that are signs for a people who understand
13:7 (8)	Why has a sign not been sent down upon him from his Lord
13:27 (27)	why has a sign not been sent down upon him from his Lord?
13:38 (38)	it was not for any Messenger to bring a sign
14:5 (5)	and We sent Moses with Our signs
14:5 (5)	in that are signs for every man enduring, thankful
15:1 (1)	those are the signs of the Book
15:75 (75)	in that are signs for such as mark
15:77 (77)	in that is a sign for believers
15:81 (81)	We brought them Our signs
16:11 (11)	in that is a sign for a people who reflect
16:12 (12)	in that are signs for a people who understand
16:13 (13)	in that is a sign for a people who remember
16:65 (67)	in that is a sign for a people who have ears
16:67 (69)	in that is a sign for a people who understand
16:69 (71)	in that is a sign for a people who reflect
16:79 (81)	in that are signs for a people who believe
16:101 (103)	and when We exchange a verse
16:101 (103)	in the place of another verse
16:104 (106)	those that believe not in the signs of God
16:105 (107)	they only forge falsehood, who believe not in the signs of God
17:1 (1)	that We might show him some of Our signs
17:12 (13)	We have appointed the night and the day as two signs
17:12 (13)	then We have blotted out the sign of the night
17:12 (13)	and [We] made the sign of the day to see
17:59 (61)	naught prevented Us from sending the signs
17:59 (61)	We do not send the signs, except to frighten
17:98 (100)	because they disbelieved in Our signs
17:101 (103)	and We gave Moses nine signs

18:9 (8)	dost thou think the Men of the Cave and Er-Rakeem were among Our signs
18:17 (16)	that was one of God's signs
18:56 (54)	they have taken My signs, and what they are warned of, in mockery
18:57 (55)	who, being reminded of the signs of his Lord, turns away from them
18:105 (105)	those are they that disbelieve in the signs of their Lord
18:106 (106)	[they] took My signs and My messengers in mockery
19:10 (11)	Lord, appoint to me some sign
19:10 (11)	thy sign is that thou shalt not speak
19:21 (21)	that We may appoint him a sign unto men
19:58 (59)	when the signs of the All-merciful were recited to them
19:73 (74)	when Our signs are recited to them
19:77 (80)	hast thou seen him who disbelieves in Our signs
20:22 (23)	that is a second sign
20:23 (24)	We would show thee some of Our greatest signs
20:42 (44)	go therefore, thou and thy brother, with My signs
20:47 (49)	we have brought thee a sign from thy Lord
20:54 (56)	in that are signs for men possessing reason
20:56 (58)	We showed Pharaoh all Our signs,
20:126 (126)	Our signs came unto thee
20:127 (127)	[who] believes not in the signs of his Lord
20:128 (128)	Surely in that are signs for men possessing reaon
20:133 (133)	why does he not bring us a sign from his Lord?
20:134 (134)	so that we might have followed Thy signs
21:5 (5)	now therefore let him bring us a sign
21:32 (33)	still from Our signs they are turning away
21:37 (38)	I shall show you My signs
21:77 (77)	the people who cried lies to Our signs
21:91 (91)	[We] appointed her and her son to be a sign unto all beings
22:16 (16)	even so We have sent it down as signs
22:51 (50)	those who strive against Our signs
22:52 (51)	then God confirms His signs
22:57 (56)	the unbelievers, who cried lies to Our signs
22:72 (71)	when Our signs are recited to them
22:72 (71)	they rush upon those who recite to them Our signs
23:30 (31)	surely in that are signs
23:45 (47)	We sent Moses and his brother Aaron with Our signs
23:50 (52)	and We made Mary's son, and his mother, to be a sign
23:58 (60)	those who believe in the signs of their Lord
23:66 (68)	My signs were recited to you
23:105 (107)	were My signs not recited to you, and you cried them lies?
24:1 (1)	We have sent down in it signs
24:18 (17)	God makes clear to you the signs
24:34 (34)	now We have sent down to you signs
24:46 (45)	now We have sent down signs making all clear
24:58 (57)	so God makes clear to you the signs
24:59 (58)	so God makes clear to you His signs
24:61 (61)	So God makes clear to you the signs
25:36 (38)	Go to the people who have cried lies to Our signs
25:37 (39)	and [We] made them to be a sign to mankind
25:73 (73)	when they are reminded of the signs of their Lord
26:2 (1)	Those are the signs of the Manifest Book
26:4 (3)	We shall send down on them out of heaven a sign
26:8 (7)	Surely in that is a sign
26:15 (14)	go, both of you, with Our signs
26:67 (67)	Surely in that is a sign
26:103 (103)	Surely in that is a sign

26:121 (121)	Surely in that is a sign
26:128 (128)	do you build on every prominence a sign
26:139 (139)	Surely in that is a sign
26:154 (154)	then produce a sign, if thou art one of the truthful
26:158 (158)	Surely in that is a sign
26:174 (174)	Surely in that is a sign
26:190 (190)	Surely in that is a sign
26:197 (197)	Was it not a sign for them
27:1 (1)	Those are the signs of the Koran
27:12 (12)	among nine signs to Pharaoh and his people
27:13 (13)	when Our signs came to them
27:52 (53)	in that is a sign for a people who have knowledge
27:81 (83)	save such as believe in Our signs
27:82 (84)	Mankind had no faith in Our signs
27:83 (85)	a troop of those that cried lies to Our signs
27:84 (86)	Did you cry lies to My signs
27:86 (88)	in that is a sign for a people who are believers
27:93 (95)	He shall show you His signs
28:2 (1)	Those are the signs of the Manifest Book
28:35 (35)	they shall not reach you because of Our signs
28:36 (36)	when Moses came to them with Our signs
28:45 (45)	a dweller among the Midianites, reciting to them Our signs
28:47 (47)	that we might follow Thy signs
28:59 (59)	until He sent in their mother-city a Messenger, to recite Our signs
28:87 (87)	Let them not bar thee from the signs of God
29:15 (14)	and [We] appointed it for a sign unto all beings
29:23 (22)	those who disbelieve in God's signs
29:24 (23)	in that are signs for a people who believe
29:35 (34)	We have left thereof a sign
29:44 (43)	in that is a sign to the believers
29:47 (46)	none denies Our signs but the unbelievers
29:49 (48)	nay; rather it is signs
29:49 (48)	none denies Our signs but the evildoers
29:50 (49)	why have signs not been sent down upon him from his Lord?
29:50 (49)	the signs are only with God
30:10 (9)	for that they cried lies to the signs of God
30:16 (15)	?those who? Cried lies to Our signs
30:20 (19)	and of His signs is that He created you of dust
30:21 (20)	and of His signs is that He created for you, of yourselves, spouses
30:21 (20)	in that are signs for a people who consider
30:22 (21)	and of His signs is the creation of the heavens and earth
30:22 (21)	in that are signs for all living beings
30:23 (22)	and of His signs is your slumbering by night and day
30:23 (22)	in that are signs for a people who hear
30:24 (23)	and of His signs He shows you lightning
30:24 (23)	surely in that are signs for a people who understand
30:25 (24)	and of His signs is that the heaven and earth stand firm
30:28 (27)	so We distinguish the signs for a people who understand
30:37 (36)	in that are signs for a people who believe
30:46 (45)	and of His signs is that He looses the winds
30:53 (52)	except for such as believe in Our signs
30:58 (58)	if thou bringest them a sign
31:2 (1)	those are the signs of the Wise Book
31:7 (6)	when Our signs are recited to such a man he turns away

31:31 (30)	that He may show you some of His signs
31:31 (30)	in that are signs for every man enduring, thankful
31:32 (31)	and none denies Our signs
32:15 (15)	only those believe in Our signs
32:22 (22)	he who is reminded of the signs of his Lord
32:24 (24)	[they] had sure faith in Our signs
32:26 (26)	surely in that are signs
33:34 (34)	that which is recited in your houses of the signs of God
34:5 (5)	and those who strive against Our signs
34:9 (9)	in that is a sign to every penitent servant
34:15 (14)	for Sheba also there was a sign in their dwelling-place
34:19 (18)	in that are signs for every man enduring, thankful
34:38 (37)	and those who strive against Our signs
34:43 (42)	and when Our signs are recited to them
36:33 (33)	and a sign for them is the dead land
36:37 (37)	and a sign for them is the night
36:41 (41)	and a sign for them is that We carried their seed in the laden ship
36:46 (46)	never any sign (of the signs) of their Lord comes to them
36:46 (46)	never (any sign) of the signs of their Lord comes to them
37:14 (14)	when they see a sign, [they] would scoff
38:29 (28)	that men possessed of minds may ponder its signs
39:42 (43)	in that are signs for a people who reflect
39:52 (53)	in that are signs for a people who believe
39:59 (60)	My signs did come to thee
39:63 (63)	those who disbelieve in the signs of God
39:71 (71)	Did not Messengers come to you from among yourselves, reciting to you the signs of your Lord
40:4 (4)	None but the unbelievers dispute concerning the signs of God
40:13 (13)	It is He who shows you His signs
40:23 (24)	We also sent Moses with Our signs
40:35 (37)	Those who dispute concerning the signs of God, without any authority
40:56 (58)	Those who dispute concerning the signs of God, without any authority
40:63 (65)	Even so perverted are they who deny the signs of God
40:69 (71)	hast thou not regarded those who dispute concerning the signs of God
40:78 (78)	it was not for any Messenger to bring a sign, save by God's leave
40:81 (81)	and He shows you His signs
40:81 (81)	then which of God's signs do you reject?
41:3 (2)	a Book whose signs have been distinguished
41:15 (14)	and they denied Our signs
41:28 (28)	they denied Our signs
41:37 (37)	And of His signs are the night and the day
41:39 (39)	And of His signs is that thou seest the earth humble
41:40 (40)	Those who blaspheme Our signs are not hidden from Us
41:44 (44)	why are its signs not distinguished?
41:53 (53)	We shall show them Our signs in the horizons
42:29 (28)	And of His signs is the creation of the heavens and earth
42:32 (31)	And of His signs are the ships that run on the sea
42:33 (31)	in that are signs for every man enduring, thankful
42:35 (33)	those who dispute concerning Our signs
43:46 (45)	We also sent Moses with Our signs to Pharaoh and his Council
43:47 (46)	But when he brought them Our signs, lo, they laughed at them
43:48 (47)	And not a sign We showed them, but it was greater than its sister
43:69 (69)	even those who believed in Our signs
44:33 (32)	and gave them signs wherein there was a manifest trial

45:3 (2)	in the heavens and earth there are signs for the believers
45:4 (3)	there are signs for a people having sure faith
45:5 (4)	there are signs for a people who understand
45:6 (5)	those are the signs of God that We recite to thee in truth
45:6 (5)	in what manner of discourse then, after God and His signs, will they believe?
45:8 (7)	who hears the signs of God being recited to him,
45:9 (8)	and when he knows anything of Our signs, he takes them in mockery
45:11 (10)	those who disbelieve in the signs of their Lord
45:13 (12)	in that are signs for a people who reflect
45:25 (24)	and when Our signs are recited to them
45:31 (30)	Were not My signs recited to you
45:35 (34)	you took God's signs in mockery
46:7 (6)	And when Our signs are recited to them
46:26 (25)	since they denied the signs of God
46:27 (26)	and We turned about the signs
48:20 (20)	that it may be a sign to the believers
51:20 (20)	In the earth are signs for those having sure faith
51:37 (37)	therein We left a sign to those who fear the painful chastisement
53:18 (18)	he saw one of the greatest signs of his Lord
54:2 (2)	if they see a sign they turn away
54:15 (15)	And We left it for a sign
54:42 (42)	They cried lies to Our signs, all of them
57:9 (9)	It is He who sends down upon His servant signs
57:17 (16)	We have indeed made clear for you the signs
57:19 (18)	[those] who have cried lies to Our signs, they are the inhabitants of Hell
58:5 (6)	Now We have sent down signs
62:2 (2)	a Messenger from among them, to recite His signs to them
62:5 (5)	the people who have cried lies to God's signs
64:10 (10)	And those who disbelieved and cried lies to Our signs
65:11 (11)	a Messenger reciting to you the signs of God
68:15 (15)	When Our signs are recited to him
74:16 (16)	he is froward unto Our signs
78:28 (28)	they cried loud lies to Our signs
79:20 (20)	So he showed him the great sign
83:13 (13)	When our signs are recited to him
90:19 (19)	those who disbelieve in Our signs

*A Z F

AZIFA vb. (I)~to be imminent, to approach, to be nigh

a) perf. act.

53:57 (58)	The Imminent is imminent

ĀZIFAH n.f.~that which is imminent, the day of approaching doom, the threatened Hour

40:18 (18)	And warn them against the Day of the Imminent
53:57 (58)	The Imminent is imminent

*A Z R

ĀZAR n.prop.~Azar

6:74 (74)	And when Abraham said to his father Azar

AZR n.m.~strength

20:31 (32) by him confirm my strength

ĀZARA vb. (IV)~to strengthen

a) perf. act.

48:29 (29) as a seed that puts forth its shoot, and strengthens it

*A Z Z

AZZA vb. (I)~to prick. (n.vb.) pricking

b) impf. act. (*ya'uzzu*)

19:83 (86) how We sent the Satans against the unbelievers, to prick them

f) n.vb. (*azz*)

19:83 (86) against the unbelievers, to prick them *exceedingly*

ʿAYN

*ʿ B ʾ

ʿABAʾA vb. (I)~to esteem, to concern one's self with

b) impf. act. (*yaʿbaʾu*)

25:77 (77)	my Lord esteems you not at all

*ʿ B D

ʿABADA vb. (I)~to serve, to worship. (n.vb.) service, worship. (pcple. act.) one who serves, one who is devout, serving

a) perf. act.

5:60 (65)	apes and swine, and worshippers of idols
16:35 (37)	if God had willed we would not have served, apart from Him
43:20 (19)	we would not have served them
109:4 (4)	nor am I serving what you have served

b) impf. act. (*yaʿbudu*)

1:5 (4)	Thee only we serve
2:83 (77)	you shall not serve any save God
2:133 (127)	what will you serve after me?
2:133 (127)	we will serve thy God and the God of thy fathers
2:172 (167)	if it be Him that you serve
3:64 (57)	that we serve none but God
5:76 (80)	do you serve, apart from God, that which cannot hurt or profit you?
6:56 (56)	I am forbidden to serve those you call on
7:70 (68)	hast thou come to us that we may serve God alone
7:70 (68)	and forsake that our fathers served
9:31 (31)	they were commanded to serve but One God
10:18 (19)	they serve, apart from God, what hurts them not
10:28 (29)	not us you were serving
10:104 (104)	I serve not those you (serve) apart from God
10:104 (104)	I (serve) not those you serve apart from God
10:104 (104)	but I serve God
11:2 (2)	serve you none but God
11:26 (28)	serve you none but God
11:62 (65)	dost thou forbid us to serve that our fathers (served)?
11:62 (65)	dost thou forbid us to (serve) that our fathers served?
11:87 (89)	we should leave that our fathers served
11:109 (111)	be thou not in doubt concerning what these men serve
11:109 (111)	they serve only as their fathers (served) before
11:109 (111)	they (serve) only as their fathers served before
12:40 (40)	that which you serve, apart from Him
12:40 (40)	you shall not serve any but Him
13:36 (36)	I have only been commanded to serve God
14:10 (12)	bar us from that our fathers served
14:35 (38)	turn me and my sons away from serving idols
16:73 (75)	do they serve, apart from God, that which has no power?
16:114 (115)	if it be Him that you serve

17:23 (24)	you shall not serve any but Him
18:16 (15)	apart from them and that they serve
19:42 (43)	why worshippest thou that which neither hears nor sees
19:44 (45)	father, serve not Satan
19:49 (50)	he went apart from them and that they were serving
21:66 (67)	do you serve, apart from God
21:67 (67)	that you serve apart from God
21:98 (98)	surely you, and that you were serving
22:11 (11)	there is such a one as serves God
22:71 (70)	they serve, apart from God
24:55 (54)	They shall serve Me
25:17 (18)	He shall muster them and that they serve, apart from God
25:55 (57)	they serve, apart from God
26:70 (70)	what do you serve?
26:71 (71)	we serve idols, and continue cleaving to them
26:75 (75)	have you considered what you have been serving
26:92 (92)	where is that you were serving
27:43 (43)	she served, apart from God
27:91 (93)	I have only been commanded to serve the Lord
28:63 (63)	it was not us that they were serving
29:17 (16)	you only serve, apart from God, idols
29:17 (16)	those you serve, apart from God, have no power
34:40 (39)	was it you these were serving?
34:41 (40)	they were serving the jinn
34:43 (42)	to bar you from that your fathers served
36:22 (21)	why should I not serve Him
36:60 (60)	you should not serve Satan
37:22 (22)	their wives, and that they were serving
37:85 (83)	what do you serve?
37:95 (93)	do you serve what you hew
37:161 (161)	as for you, and that you serve
39:3 (4)	we only serve them that they may bring us nigh
39:11 (14)	I have been commanded to serve God
39:14 (16)	God I serve, making my religion His
39:17 (19)	those who eschew the serving of idols
39:64 (64)	is it other than God you bid me serve
40:66 (68)	I am forbidden to serve those you call on
41:14 (13)	serve none but God
41:37 (37)	bow yourselves to God who created them, if Him you serve
43:26 (25)	surely I am quit of that you serve
46:21 (20)	serve none but God
51:56 (56)	I have not created jinn and mankind except to serve Me
60:4 (4)	we are quit of you and that you serve
98:5 (4)	they were commanded only to serve God
106:3 (3)	so let them serve the Lord
109:2 (2)	I (serve) not what you serve
109:2 (2)	I serve not what you (serve)
109:3 (3)	you are not serving what I serve
109:5 (5)	neither are you serving what I serve

c) impv. (*uʿbud*)

2:21 (19)	serve your Lord Who created you
3:51 (44)	God is my Lord and your Lord; so serve Him
4:36 (40)	Serve God, and associate naught with Him
5:72 (76)	Children of Israel, serve God, my Lord

5:117 (117)	serve God, my Lord and your Lord
6:102 (102)	so serve Him, for He is Guardian
7:59 (57)	O my people, serve God
7:65 (63)	O my people, serve God
7:73 (71)	O my people, serve God
7:85 (83)	O my people, serve God
10:3 (3)	so serve Him
11:50 (52)	O my people, serve God
11:61 (64)	O my people, serve God
11:84 (85)	O my people, serve God
11:123 (123)	so serve Him
15:99 (99)	serve thy Lord, until the Certain comes to thee
16:36 (38)	serve you God, and eschew idols
19:36 (37)	God is my Lord, and your Lord; so serve you Him
19:65 (66)	So serve Him, and be thou patient in His service
20:14 (14)	there is no god but I; therefore serve Me
21:25 (25)	there is no god but I; so serve Me
21:92 (92)	I am your Lord; so serve Me
22:77 (76)	serve your Lord, and do good
23:23 (23)	O my people, serve God
23:32 (33)	serve God! You have no god other than He
27:45 (46)	serve you God
29:16 (15)	serve God, and fear Him
29:17 (16)	seek after your provision with God, and serve Him
29:36 (35)	O my people, serve God
29:56 (56)	My earth is wide; therefore Me do you serve
36:61 (61)	you should serve Me
39:2 (2)	so worship God, making thy religion His sincerely
39:15 (17)	serve what you will apart from Him
39:66 (66)	nay, but God do thou serve
43:64 (64)	God is my Lord and your Lord; therefore serve Him
53:62 (62)	bow yourselves before God, and serve Him
71:3 (3)	serve God, and fear Him

e) impf. pass. (*yuʿbadu*)

43:45 (44)	have We appointed, apart from the All-merciful, gods to be served?

f) n.vb. (*ʿibādah*)

4:172 (171)	whosoever disdains to serve Him
7:206 (205)	wax not too proud to serve Him
10:29 (30)	we were heedless of your service
18:110 (110)	not associate with his Lord's service anyone
19:65 (66)	and be thou patient in His service
19:82 (85)	they shall deny their service
21:19 (19)	wax not too proud to do Him service
40:60 (62)	who wax too proud to do Me service shall enter Gehenna
46:6 (5)	and shall deny their service

g) pcple. act. (*ʿābid*)

2:138 (132)	Him we are serving
9:112 (113)	those who repent, those who serve
21:53 (54)	we found our fathers serving them
21:73 (73)	Us they served
21:84 (84)	a Reminder to those who serve

21:106 (106)	a Message delivered unto a people who serve
23:47 (49)	whose people are our servants
43:81 (81)	I am the first to serve him
66:5 (5)	women who have surrendered, believing, obedient, penitent, devout
109:3 (3)	you are not serving what I serve
109:4 (4)	nor am I serving what you have served
109:5 (5)	neither are you serving what I serve

ʿABD n.m. (pl. *ʿibād, ʿabīd*)~servant, slave; people (39:53) [Ar]

2:23 (21)	concerning that We have sent down on Our servant
2:90 (84)	whomsoever He will of His servants
2:178 (173)	freeman for freeman, slave for (slave)
2:178 (173)	freeman for freeman, (slave) for slave
2:186 (182)	when My servants question thee concerning Me
2:207 (203)	God is gentle with His servants
2:221 (220)	a believing slave is better than an idolater
3:15 (13)	God sees His servants
3:20 (19)	God sees His servants
3:30 (28)	God is gentle with His servants
3:79 (73)	be you servants to me
3:182 (178)	God is never unjust unto His servants
4:118 (118)	take unto myself a portion appointed of Thy servants
4:172 (170)	The Messiah will not disdain to be a servant of God
5:118 (118)	they are Thy servants
6:18 (18)	He is Omnipotent over His servants
6:61 (61)	He is the Omnipotent over His servants
6:88 (88)	whom He will of His servants
7:32 (30)	ornament of God which He brought forth for His servants
7:128 (125)	He bequeaths it to whom He will among His servants
7:194 (193)	servants the likes of you
8:41 (42)	We sent down upon Our servant on the day
8:51 (53)	God is never unjust unto His servants
9:104 (105)	God is He who accepts repentance from His servants
10:107 (107)	whomsoever He will of His servants
12:24 (24)	he was one of Our devoted servants
14:11 (13)	God is gracious unto whomsoever He will of His servants
14:31 (36)	say to My servants who believe
15:40 (40)	Thy servants among them that are devoted
15:42 (42)	over My servants thou shalt have no authority
15:49 (49)	tell My servants I am the All-forgiving
16:2 (2)	upon whomsoever He will among His servants
16:75 (77)	a similitude: a servant possessed by his master
17:1 (1)	Glory be to Him, who carried His servant by night
17:3 (3)	he was a thankful servant
17:5 (5)	We sent against you servants of Ours
17:17 (18)	one who is aware of and sees the sins of His servants
17:30 (32)	He is aware of and sees His servants
17:53 (55)	say to My servants, that they say words that are kindlier
17:65 (67)	over My servants thou shalt have no authority
17:96 (98)	He is aware of and sees His servants
18:1 (1)	who has sent down upon His servant the Book
18:65 (64)	then they found one [servant] of Our (servants)
18:65 (64)	then they found one ([servant]) of Our servants
18:102 (102)	that they may take My servants as friends
19:2 (1)	the mention of thy Lord's mercy unto His servant Zachariah

19:30 (31)	lo, I am God's servant
19:61 (62)	Gardens of Eden that the All-merciful promised His servants
19:63 (64)	an inheritance to those of Our servants who are godfearing
19:93 (94)	but he comes to the All-merciful as a servant
20:77 (79)	Go with My servants by night
21:26 (26)	they are honoured servants
21:105 (105)	earth shall be the inheritance of My righteous servants
22:10 (10)	God is never unjust unto His servants
23:109 (111)	there is a party of My servants
24:32 (32)	marry the spouseless among you, and your slaves
25:1 (1)	who has sent down the Salvation upon His servant, that he may be a warner
25:17 (18)	was it you that led these My servants astray
25:58 (60)	is He aware of His servants' sins
25:63 (64)	the servants of the All-merciful
26:52 (52)	go with My servants by night
27:15 (15)	preferred us over many of His believing servants
27:19 (19)	amongst Thy righteous servants
27:59 (60)	peace be on His servants whom He has chosen
28:82 (82)	whomsoever He will of His servants
29:56 (56)	O My servants who believe
29:62 (62)	whomsoever He will of his servants
30:48 (47)	whomsoever of His servants
34:9 (9)	a sign to every penitent servant
34:13 (12)	among My servants
34:39 (38)	whomsoever He will of His servants
35:28 (25)	only those of His servants
35:31 (28)	God is aware of and sees His servants
35:32 (29)	those of Our servants We chose
35:45 (45)	surely God sees His servants
36:30 (29)	ah, woe for those servants
37:40 (39)	except for God's sincere servants
37:74 (72)	except for God's sincere servants
37:81 (79)	he was among Our believeing servants
37:111 (111)	he was among Our believing servants
37:122 (122)	they were among Our believing servants
37:128 (128)	except for God's sincere servants
37:132 (132)	he was among Our believing servants
37:160 (160)	except for God's sincere servants
37:169 (169)	then were we God's sincere servants
37:171 (171)	already Our Word has preceded to Our servants
38:17 (16)	remember Our servant David
38:30 (29)	how excellent a servant he was
38:41 (40)	remember also Our servant Job
38:44 (44)	how excellent a servant he was
38:45 (45)	remember also Our servants Abraham, Isaac and Jacob
38:83 (84)	excepting those Thy servants among them
39:7 (9)	He approves not unthankfulness in His servants
39:10 (13)	my servants who believe, fear your Lord
39:16 (18)	wherewith God frightens His servants
39:16 (18)	O My servants, so fear you Me
39:17 (19)	give thou good tidings to My servants
39:36 (37)	shall not God suffice His servant
39:46 (47)	Thou shalt judge between Thy servants
39:53 (54)	O my people who have been prodigal against yourselves
40:15 (15)	whomever He will of His servants
40:31 (33)	God desires not wrong for His servants

40:44 (47)	surely God sees His servants
40:48 (51)	God already has passed judgment between His servants
40:85 (85)	touching His servants
41:46 (46)	thy Lord wrongs not His servants
42:19 (18)	God is All-gentle to His servants
42:23 (22)	the good tidings God gives to His servants
42:25 (24)	He who accepts repentance from His servants
42:27 (26)	had God expanded His provision to His servants
42:27 (26)	surely He is aware of and sees His servants
42:52 (52)	We guide whom We will of Our servants
43:15 (14)	they have assigned to Him a part of His own servants
43:19 (18)	the angels, who are themselves servants
43:59 (59)	he is only a servant We blessed
43:68 (68)	O My servants, today no fear is on you
44:18 (17)	deliver to me God's servants
44:23 (22)	then set thou forth with My servants
50:8 (8)	a reminder to every penitent servant
50:29 (28)	I wrong not My servants
53:10 (10)	then revealed to his servant that he revealed
54:9 (9)	they cried lies to Our servant
57:9 (9)	He who sends down upon His servant signs
66:10 (10)	they were under two of Our righteous servants
50:11 (11)	a provision for the servants
66:10 (10)	they were under two of Our righteous servants
71:27 (28)	they will lead Thy servants astray
72:19 (19)	the servant of God stood calling on Him
76:6 (6)	a fountain whereat drink the servants of God
89:29 (29)	enter thou among My servants
96:10 (10)	a servant when he prays

ᶜABBADA vb. (II)~to enslave

a) perf. act.

26:22 (21)	having enslaved the Children of Israel

*ᶜ B Q R

ᶜABQARĪY n.m.~a drugget, a well-designed carpet

55:76 (76)	reclining upon green cushions and lovely druggets

*ᶜ B R

ᶜABARA vb. (I)~to traverse; to expound. (pcple. act.) one who traverses; traversing

b) impf. act. (*yaᶜburu*)

12:43 (43)	if you are expounders of dreams

g) pcple. act. (*ᶜābir*)

4:43 (46)	unless you are traversing a way

ᶜIBRAH n.f.~a lesson

3:13 (11)	surely in that is a lesson for men

12:111 (111) in their stories is surely a lesson to men
16:66 (68) in the cattle there is a lesson for you
23:21 (21) in the cattle there is a lesson for you
24:44 (44) in that is a lesson for those who have eyes
79:26 (26) in that is a lesson for him who fears

IʿTABARA vb. (VIII)~to take heed

c) impv. (*iʿtabir*)

59:2 (2) take heed, you who have eyes

*ʿ B S

ʿABASA vb. (I)~to frown

a) perf. act.

74:22 (22) then he frowned, and scowled
80:1 (1) He frowned and turned away

ʿABŪS n.m. (adj)~frowning

76:10 (10) we fear from our Lord a frowning day

*ʿ B TH

ʿABATHA vb. (I)~to sport. (n.vb.) a sport, playfulness

b) impf. act. (*yaʿbathu*)

26:128 (128) on every prominence a sign, sporting

f) n.vb. (*ʿabath*)

23:115 (117) did you think that We created you only for sport

*ʿ D D

ʿADDA vb. (I)~to count, to number, to reckon. (n.vb.) a number, a reckoning. (pcple. act.) one who numbers, a numberer. (pcple. pass.) numbered, counted, reckoned

a) perf. act.

19:94 (94) and He has numbered them

b) impf. act. (*yaʿuddu*)

14:34 (37) if you count God's blessing, (you will never number it)
16:18 (18) if you count God's blessing, (you will never number it)
19:84 (87) We are only numbering for them a number
22:47 (46) a thousand years of your counting
32:5 (4) a thousand years of your counting
38:62 (62) counted among the wicked

f) n.vb. (*ʿadd*)

19:84 (87) We are only numbering for them a number
19:94 (94) He has numbered them <exactly>

g) pcple. act. (*ʿādd*)

23:113 (115) ask the numberers

h) pcple. pass. (*maʿdūd*)

2:80 (74) Fire shall not touch us save a number of days
2:184 (180) for days numbered
2:203 (199) remember God during certain days numbered
3:24 (23) Fire shall not touch us, except for a number of days
11:8 (11) till a reckoned moment they will say
11:104 (106) We shall not postpone it, save to a term reckoned
12:20 (20) a handful of counted dirhams

ʿADAD n.m.~a number; (adv) many

10:5 (5) that you might know the number of the years
17:12 (13) that you may know the number of the years
18:11 (10) We smote their ears many years in the Cave
23:112 (114) how long have you tarried in the earth, by number of years?
72:24 (25) who is weaker in helpers and fewer in numbers
72:28 (28) He has numbered everything in numbers

ʿIDDAH n.f.~a number; a period

2:184 (180) a number of other days
2:185 (181) a number of other days
2:185 (181) you fulfil the number
9:36 (36) the number of the months, with God, is twelve
9:37 (37) to agree with the number that God has hallowed
18:22 (21) my Lord knows very well their number
33:49 (48) you have no period to reckon against them
65:1 (1) divorce them when they have reached their period
65:1 (1) count the period, and fear God your Lord
65:4 (4) their period shall be three months
74:31 (31) their number We have appointed only as a trial

ʿUDDAH n.f.~preparation, equipment

9:46 (46) they would have made some preparation for it

ʿADDADA vb. (II)~to count over, to recount; to arrange

a) perf. act.

104:2 (2) who has gathered riches and counted them over

AʿADDA vb. (IV)~to prepare, to make ready

a) perf. act.

4:93 (95) prepare for him a mighty chastisement
4:102 (103) God has prepared for the unbelievers

9:46 (46)	they would have made some preparation for it
9:89 (90)	God has prepared for them gardens
9:100 (101)	He has prepared for them gardens
33:8 (8)	He has prepared for the unbelievers
33:29 (29)	God has prepared for those amongst you
33:35 (35)	for them God has prepared forgiveness
33:44 (43)	He has prepared for them a generous wage
33:57 (57)	and has prepared for them a humbling chastisement
33:64 (64)	and prepared for them a Blaze
48:6 (6)	and has prepared for them Gehenna
58:15 (16)	God has made ready for them a chastisement
65:10 (10)	God prepared for them a terrible chastisement
76:31 (31)	He has prepared for them a painful chastisement

c) impv. (*aᶜidda*)

8:60 (62)	make ready for them whatever force

d) perf. pass. (*uᶜidda*)

2:24 (22)	Fire, whose fuel is men and stones, prepared for unbelievers
3:131 (126)	fear the Fire prepared for the unbelievers
3:133 (127)	prepared for the godfearing
57:21 (21)	made ready for those who believe in God

IᶜTADDA vb. (VIII)~to reckon (against)

b) impf. act. (*yaᶜtaddu*)

33:49 (48)	you have no period to reckon against them

*ᶜ D L

ᶜADALA vb. (I)~to proportion, to create in symmetry; to be just, to be equitable; to offer an eqivalent; to swerve; (with prep. *bi-*) to ascribe equals to (God)

a) perf. act.

82:7 (7)	who created thee and shaped thee and wrought thee in symmetry

b) impf. act. (*yaᶜdilu*)

4:3 (3)	if you fear that you will not act justly towards the orphans
4:129 (128)	you will not be able to be equitable between your wives
4:135 (134)	then follow not caprice, so as to swerve
5:8 (11)	move you not to be equitable; be equitable
6:1 (1)	the unbelievers ascribe equals to their Lord
6:70 (69)	though it offer any equivalent, it shall not be taken
6:150 (151)	ascribe equals to their Lord
7:159 (159)	by it act with justice
7:181 (180)	guide by the truth, and by it act with justice
27:60 (61)	a people who assign to Him equals
42:15 (14)	I have been commanded to be just between you

c) impv. (*iᶜdil*)

5:8 (11)	not to be equitable; be equitable
6:152 (153)	when you speak, be just

ᶜADL n.m.~counterpoise, equivalent; justice, equity; (adv) justly, equitably

2:48 (45)	nor any counterpoise be taken
2:123 (117)	no counterpoise shall be accepted from it
2:282 (282)	let a writer write it down between you justly
2:282 (282)	let his guardian dictate justly
4:58 (61)	when you judge between the people, that you judge with justice
5:95 (96)	as shall be judged by two men of equity
5:95 (96)	the equivalent of that in fasting
5:106 (105)	at the bequeathing, shall be two men of equity
6:70 (69)	though it offer any equivalent, it shall not be taken
6:115 (115)	perfect are the words of thy Lord in truthfulness and justice
16:76 (78)	is he equal to him who bids to justice
16:90 (92)	God bids to justice and good-doing
49:9 (9)	set things right between them equitably, and be just
65:2 (2)	call in to witness two men of equity

*ᶜ D N

ᶜADN n.prop.~Eden

9:72 (73)	goodly dwelling-places in the Gardens of Eden
13:23 (23)	Gardens of Eden which they shall enter
16:31 (33)	Gardens of Eden they shall enter
18:31 (30)	theirs shall be Gardens of Eden
19:61 (62)	Gardens of Eden that the All-merciful promised His servants
20:76 (78)	Gardens of Eden, underneath which rivers flow
35:33 (30)	Gardens of Eden they shall enter
38:50 (50)	Gardens of Eden, whereof the gates
40:8 (8)	admit them to the Gardens of Eden
61:12 (12)	dwelling-places goodly in Gardens of Eden
98:8 (7)	Gardens of Eden, underneath which rivers flow

*ᶜ D S

ᶜADAS n.m. (coll)~lentils

2:61 (58)	green herbs, cucumbers, corn, lentils, onions

*ᶜ D W

ᶜADÁ vb. (I)~to transgress, to turn away. (n.vb.) transgression, impetuousness, revenge; (adv) impetuously. (pcple. act.) transgressor, transgressing

b) impf. act. (*yaᶜdū*)

4:154 (153)	transgress not the Sabbath
7:163 (163)	when they transgressed the Sabbath
18:28 (27)	let not thine eyes turn away from them

f) n.vb. (*ᶜadw*)

6:108 (108)	they will abuse God in revenge without knowledge
10:90 (90)	Pharaoh and his hosts followed them insolently and impetuously

g) pcple. act. (*ʿādī*)

2:173 (168)	whoso is constrained, not desiring nor transgressing
6:145 (146)	whoso is constrained, not desiring nor transgressing
16:115 (116)	whoso is constrained, not desiring nor transgressing
23:7 (7)	whosoever seeks after more than that, those are the transgressors
26:166 (166)	you are a people of transgressors
70:31 (31)	whoso seeks after more than that, they are the transgressors

ʿADĀWAH n.f.~enmity

5:14 (17)	We have stirred up among them enmity
5:64 (69)	We have cast between them enmity
5:82 (85)	the most hostile of men to the believers are the Jews
5:91 (93)	Satan only desires to precipitate enmity and hatred
41:34 (34)	he between whom and thee there is enmity
60:4 (4)	between us and you enmity has shown itself

ʿĀDIYAH n.f. (pl. *ʿādiyāt*)~courser, charger

100:1 (1)	By the snorting chargers

ʿADŪW n.m. (pl. *aʿdāʾ*)~enemy, foe

2:36 (34)	each of you an enemy of each
2:97 (91)	whosoever is an enemy to Gabriel
2:98 (92)	whosoever is an enemy to God and His angels
2:98 (92)	God is an enemy to the unbelievers
2:168 (163)	he is a manifest foe to you
2:208 (204)	he is a manifest foe to you
3:103 (98)	remember God's blessing upon you when you were enemies
4:45 (47)	God knows well your enemies
4:92 (94)	if he belong to a people at enmity with you
4:101 (102)	the unbelievers are for you a manifest foe
6:112 (112)	We have appointed to every Prophet an enemy
6:142 (143)	he is a manifest foe to you
7:22 (21)	Satan is for you a manifest foe
7:24 (23)	each of you an enemy to each
7:129 (126)	perchance your Lord will destroy your enemy
7:150 (149)	make not my enemies to gloat over me
8:60 (62)	to terrify thereby the enemy of God and your (enemy)
8:60 (62)	to terrify thereby the (enemy) of God and your enemy
9:83 (84)	you shall not fight with me any enemy
9:114 (115)	it became clear to him that he was an enemy of God
9:120 (121)	nor gain any gain from any enemy
12:5 (5)	Satan is to man a manifest enemy
17:53 (55)	Satan is ever a manifest foe to man
18:50 (48)	and they an enemy to you
20:39 (39)	an enemy of Mine and his shall take him
20:39 (39)	and [an enemy] of his shall take him
20:80 (82)	We delivered you from your enemy
20:117 (115)	Adam, surely this is an enemy to thee
20:123 (121)	each of you an enemy to each
25:31 (33)	We have appointed to every Prophet an enemy
26:77 (77)	they are an enemy to me
28:8 (7)	the folk of Pharaoh picked him out to be an enemy
28:15 (14)	the other was of his enemies
28:15 (14)	the other that was of his enemies
28:15 (14)	he is surely an enemy

28:19 (18)	when he would have assaulted the man who was an enemy
35:6 (6)	Satan is an enemy to you
35:6 (6)	take him for an enemy
36:60 (60)	he is a manifest foe to you
41:19 (18)	when God's enemies are mustered to the Fire
41:28 (28)	that is the recompense of God's enemies
43:62 (62)	he is for you a manifest foe
43:67 (67)	friends on that day shall be foes
46:6 (5)	shall be enemies to them
60:1 (1)	take not My enemy and your (enemy)
60:1 (1)	take not My (enemy) and your enemy for friends
60:2 (2)	they will be enemies to you
61:14 (14)	We confirmed those who believed against their enemy
63:4 (4)	they are the enemy; so beware
64:14 (14)	among your wives and children there is an enemy

ʿUDWAH n.f.~a bank (of a valley)

8:42 (43)	when you were on the nearer bank
8:42 (43)	and they were on the farther bank

ʿUDWĀN n.m.~enmity, transgression

2:85 (79)	conspiring against them in sin and enmity
2:193 (189)	there shall be no enmity save for evildoers
4:30 (34)	whosoever does that in transgression
5:2 (3)	do not help each other to sin and enmity
5:62 (67)	thou seest many of them vying in sin and enmity
28:28 (28)	it shall be no injustice to me
58:8 (9)	they converse secretly together in sin and enmity
58:9 (10)	conspire not together in sin and enmity

ʿĀDÁ vb. (III)~to be at enmity with

a) perf. act.

60:7 (7)	those of them with whom you are at enmity

TAʿADDÁ vb. (V)~to transgress, to trespass

b) impf. act. (*yataʿaddá*)

2:229 (229)	do not transgress them. Whosoever transgresses the bounds of God
4:14 (18)	and transgresses His bounds
65:1 (1)	whosoever trespasses the bounds of God

IʿTADÁ vb. (VIII)~to commit aggression, to transgress, to be an aggressor. (pcple. act.) aggressor, transgressor [Ar, Pk]; one who shows enmity [Bl]; one who exceeds the limits [Ali]

a) perf. act.

2:65 (61)	those among you that transgressed the Sabbath
2:178 (174)	for him who commits aggression
2:194 (190)	whoso commits aggression against you
2:194 (190)	like as he has committed against you
5:94 (95)	whoso thereafter commits transgression
5:107 (106)	we have not transgressed

b) impf. act. (*yaʿtadī*)

2:61 (58) they disobeyed, and were transgressors
2:190 (186) who fight with you, but aggress not
2:229 (229) those are God's bounds; do not transgress them
2:231 (231) do not retain them by force, to transgress
3:112 (108) they acted rebelliously and were transgressors
5:2 (3) move you to commit aggression
5:78 (82) for their rebelling and their transgression
5:87 (89) and transgress not

c) impv. (*iʿtadi*)

2:194 (190) do you commit aggression against him

g) pcple. act. (*muʿtadī*)

2:190 (186) God loves not the aggressors
5:87 (89) God loves not transgressors
6:119 (119) thy Lord knows very well the transgressors
7:55 (53) He loves not transgressors
9:10 (10) they are the transgressors
10:74 (75) We seal the hearts of the transgressors
50:25 (24) every hinderer of the good, transgressor, disquieter
68:12 (12) hinderer of good, guilty aggressor
83:12 (12) none cries lies to it but every guilty aggressor

*ʿ DH B

ʿADHĀB n.m.~chastisement, punishment, torment, torture

2:7 (6) there awaits them a mighty chastisement
2:10 (9) there awaits them a painful chastisement
2:49 (46) who were visiting you with evil chastisement
2:85 (79) to be returned unto the most terrible of chastisement
2:86 (80) for them the chastisement shall not be lightened
2:90 (84) for unbelievers awaits a humbling chastisement
2:96 (90) his being spared alive shall not remove him from the chastisement
2:104 (98) for unbelievers awaits a painful chastisement
2:114 (108) in the world to come a mighty chastisement
2:126 (120) shall compel him to the chastisement of the Fire
2:162 (157) the chastisement shall not be lightened for them
2:165 (160) when they see the chastisement
2:165 (160) God is terrible in chastisement
2:166 (161) they see the chastisement, and their cords are cut
2:174 (169) there awaits them a painful chastisement
2:175 (170) chastisement at the price of pardon
2:178 (174) for him there awaits a painful chastisement
2:201 (197) guard us against the chastisement of the Fire
3:4 (3) for them awaits a terrible chastisement
3:16 (14) guard us against the chastisement of the Fire
3:21 (20) do thou give them the good tidings of a painful chastisement
3:56 (49) I will chastise them with a terrible chastisement
3:77 (71) for them awaits a painful chastisement
3:88 (82) the chastisement shall not be lightened for them
3:91 (85) for them awaits a painful chastisement
3:105 (101) there awaits a mighty chastisement

3:106 (102)	then taste the chastisement for that you disbelieved
3:176 (170)	there awaits them a mighty chastisement
3:177 (171)	there awaits them a painful chastisement
3:178 (172)	there awaits them a humbling chastisement
3:181 (177)	taste the chastisement of the burning
3:188 (185)	do not reckon them secure from chastisement
3:188 (185)	for them awaits a painful chastisement
3:191 (188)	guard us against the chastisement of the Fire
4:14 (18)	for him there awaits a humbling chastisement
4:18 (22)	for them We have prepared a painful chastisement
4:25 (30)	half the chastisement of freewomen
4:37 (41)	for the unbelievers a humbling chastisement
4:56 (59)	that they may taste the chastisement
4:93 (95)	and prepare for him a mighty chastisement
4:102 (103)	for the unbelievers a humbling chastisement
4:138 (137)	for them awaits a painful chastisement
4:147 (146)	what would God do with chastising you
4:151 (150)	for the unbelievers a humbling chastisement
4:161 (159)	for the unbelievers among them a painful chastisement
4:173 (172)	them He will chastise with a painful chastisement
5:33 (37)	in the world to come awaits them a mighty chastisement
5:36 (40)	to ransom themselves from the chastisement
5:36 (40)	for them awaits a painful chastisement
5:37 (41)	for them awaits a lasting chastisement
5:41 (45)	in the world to come awaits them a mighty chastisement
5:73 (77)	those of them that disbelieve a painful chastisement
5:80 (83)	in the chastisement they shall dwell forever
5:94 (95)	there awaits him a painful chastisement
5:115 (115)	chastise him with a chastisement wherewith I chastise no other
6:15 (15)	the chastisement of a dreadful day
6:30 (30)	then taste the chastisement for your unbelief
6:40 (40)	if God's chastisement comes upon you
6:47 (47)	if God's chastisement comes upon you
6:49 (49)	them the chastisement shall visit
6:65 (65)	He is able to send forth upon you chastisement
6:70 (69)	a draught of boiling water and a painful chastisement
6:93 (93)	you shall be recompensed with the chastisement
6:124 (124)	a terrible chastisement, for what they devised
6:157 (158)	an evil chastisement for their turning away
7:38 (36)	so give them a double chastisement
7:39 (37)	so taste the chastisement
7:59 (57)	I fear for you the chastisement
7:73 (71)	lest you be seized by a painful chastisement
7:141 (137)	who were visiting you with evil chastisement
7:156 (155)	my chastisement — I smite with it whom I will
7:164 (164)	or to chastise with a terrible chastisement
7:165 (165)	We seized the evildoers with evil chastisement
7:167 (166)	those who should visit them with evil chastisement
8:14 (14)	the chastisement of the Fire is for the unbelievers
8:32 (32)	bring us a painful chastisement
8:35 (35)	taste you now the chastisement
8:50 (52)	taste the chastisement of the burning
8:68 (69)	for what you took, a mighty chastisement
9:3 (3)	the unbelievers of a painful chastisement
9:34 (34)	give them the good tidings of a painful chastisement

9:39 (39)	He will chastise you with a painful chastisement
9:52 (52)	for God to visit you with chastisement from Him
9:61 (62)	for them awaits a painful chastisement
9:68 (69)	there awaits them a lasting chastisement
9:74 (75)	God will chastise them with a painful chastisement
9:79 (80)	for them awaits a painful chastisement
9:90 (91)	there shall befall the unbelievers of them a painful chastisement
9:101 (102)	they will be returned to a mighty chastisement
10:4 (4)	a draught of boiling water, and a painful chastisement
10:15 (16)	the chastisement of a dreadful day
10:50 (51)	if His chastisement comes upon you
10:52 (53)	taste the chastisement of eternity
10:54 (55)	they will be secretly remorseful when they see the chastisement
10:70 (71)	We shall let them taste the terrible chastisement
10:88 (88)	till they see the painful chastisement
10:97 (97)	till they see the painful chastisement
10:98 (98)	We removed from them the chastisement of degradation
11:3 (3)	I fear for you the chastisement
11:8 (11)	if We postpone the chastisement from them
11:20 (22)	for them the chastisement shall be doubled
11:26 (28)	I fear for you the chastisement of a painful day
11:39 (41)	to whom will come a chastisement degrading him
11:39 (41)	there shall alight a lasting chastisement
11:48 (50)	there shall visit them from Us a painful chastisement
11:58 (61)	and delivered them from a harsh chastisement
11:64 (67)	lest you be seized by a nigh chastisement
11:76 (78)	there is coming upon them a chastisement
11:84 (85)	I fear for you the chastisement
11:93 (96)	to whom will come the chastisement degrading him
11:103 (105)	in that is a sign for him who fears the chastisement
12:25 (25)	that he should be imprisoned, or a painful chastisement
12:107 (107)	upon them no enveloping of the chastisement
13:34 (34)	for them is chastisement in the present life
13:34 (34)	the chastisement of the world to come
14:2 (2)	woe to the unbelievers for a terrible chastisement
14:6 (6)	who were visiting you with evil chastisement
14:7 (7)	My chastisement is surely terrible
14:17 (20)	beyond him is a harsh chastisement
14:21 (24)	will you avail us against the chastisement of God
14:22 (27)	for them awaits a painful chastisement
14:44 (44)	warn mankind of the day when the chastisement comes
15:50 (50)	and that My chastisement is the painful (chastisement)
15:50 (50)	and that My (chastisement) is the painful chastisement
16:26 (28)	the chastisement came upon them
16:45 (47)	the chastisement will not come upon them
16:63 (65)	there yet awaits them a painful chastisement
16:85 (87)	when the evildoers behold the chastisement
16:88 (90)	them We shall give increase of chastisement upon (chastisement)
16:88 (90)	them We shall give increase of (chastisement) upon chastisement
16:94 (96)	lest there should await you a mighty chastisement
16:104 (106)	there awaits them a painful chastisement
16:106 (108)	there awaits them a mighty chastisement
16:113 (114)	they were seized by the chastisement
16:117 (118)	for them awaits a painful chastisement
17:10 (11)	we have prepared for them a painful chastisement

17:57 (59)	they hope for His mercy, and fear His chastisement
17:57 (59)	thy Lord's chastisement is a thing to beware of
17:58 (60)	We shall chastise it with a terrible chastisement
18:55 (53)	the chastisement should come upon them
18:58 (57)	He would hasten for them the chastisement
18:87 (86)	He shall chastise him with a horrible chastisement
19:45 (46)	I fear that some chastisement from the All-merciful
19:75 (77)	whether the chastisement, or the Hour
19:79 (82)	We shall prolong for him the chastisement
20:48 (50)	chastisement shall light upon him
20:61 (64)	lest He destroy you with a chastisement
20:71 (74)	which of us is more terrible in chastisement
20:127 (127)	the chastisement of the world to come
20:134 (134)	Had We destroyed them with a chastisement aforetime
21:46 (47)	a breath of thy Lord's chastisement
22:2 (2)	God's chastisement is terrible
22:4 (4)	he guides him to the chastisement of the burning
22:9 (9)	We shall let him taste the chastisement
22:18 (18)	many merit the chastisement
22:22 (22)	taste the chastisement of the burning
22:25 (26)	We shall let him taste a painful chastisement
22:47 (46)	they demand of thee to hasten the chastisement
22:55 (54)	there shall come upon them the chastisement
22:57 (56)	for them awaits a humbling chastisement
23:64 (66)	when We seize with the chastisement
23:76 (78)	We already seized them with the chastisement
23:77 (79)	a door of terrible chastisement
24:2 (2)	let a party of the believers witness their chastisement
24:8 (8)	it shall avert from her the chastisement
24:11 (11)	him there awaits a mighty chastisement
24:14 (14)	for your mutterings a mighty chastisement
24:19 (18)	there awaits them a painful chastisement
24:23 (23)	there awaits them a mighty chastisement
24:63 (63)	there befall them a painful chastisement
25:19 (21)	We shall let him taste a great chastisement
25:37 (39)	for the evildoers a painful chastisement
25:42 (44)	when they see the chastisement
25:65 (66)	turn Thou from us the chastisement of Gehenna
25:65 (66)	its chastisement is torment most terrible
25:69 (69)	doubled shall be the chastisement for him
26:135 (135)	I fear for you the chastisement
26:156 (156)	there seize you the chastisement of a dreadful day
26:158 (158)	and the chastisement seized them
26:189 (189)	then there seized them the chastisement
26:189 (189)	assuredly it was the chastisement
26:201 (201)	until they see the painful chastisement
26:204 (204)	do they seek to hasten Our chastisement?
27:5 (5)	those are they whom an evil chastisement awaits
27:21 (21)	I will chastise him with a terrible chastisement
28:64 (64)	they shall see the chastisement
29:10 (9)	he makes the persecution of men as it were God's chastisement
29:23 (22)	there awaits them a painful chastisement
29:29 (28)	then bring us the chastisement of God
29:53 (53)	they demand of thee to hasten the chastisement
29:53 (53)	the chastisement would have come upon them

29:54 (54)	they demand of thee to hasten the chastisement
29:55 (55)	the chastisement shall overwhelm them
30:16 (15)	they shall be arraigned into the chastisement
31:6 (5)	there awaits them a humbling chastisement
31:7 (6)	give him good tidings of a painful chastisement
31:21 (20)	though Satan were calling them to the chastisement
31:24 (23)	We compel them to a harsh chastisement
32:14 (14)	taste the chastisement of eternity
32:20 (20)	taste the chastisement of the Fire
32:21 (21)	We shall surely let them taste the nearer chastisement, before the greater ([chastisement])
32:21 (21)	We shall surely let them taste the nearer (chastisement), before the greater [chastisement]
33:8 (8)	for the unbelievers a painful chastisement
33:30 (30)	for her the chastisement shall be doubled
33:57 (57)	for them a humbling chastisement
33:68 (68)	give them chastisement twofold
34:5 (5)	theirs shall be a chastisement of painful wrath
34:8 (8)	are in chastisement and far error
34:12 (11)	We would let them taste the chastisement
34:14 (13)	they would not have continued in the humbling chastisement
34:33 (32)	remorseful when they see the chastisement
34:38 (37)	those shall be arraigned into the chastisement
34:42 (41)	taste the chastisement of the Fire, which you cried lies to
34:46 (45)	before a terrible chastisement
35:7 (7)	there awaits them a terrible chastisement
35:10 (11)	theirs shall be a terrible chastisement
35:36 (33)	nor shall its chastisement be lightened for them
36:18 (17)	there shall visit you from us a painful chastisement
37:9 (9)	theirs is an everlasting chastisement
37:33 (32)	are sharers in the chastisement
37:38 (37)	you shall be tasting the painful chastisement
37:176 (176)	do they seek to hasten Our chastisement?
38:8 (7)	they have not yet tasted My chastisement
38:26 (25)	there awaits them a terrible chastisement
38:41 (40)	Satan has visited me with weariness and chastisement
38:61 (61)	give him a double chastisement in the Fire
39:13 (15)	the chastisement of a dreadful day
39:19 (20)	against whom the word of chastisement is realized
39:24 (25)	against the evil of the chastisement
39:25 (26)	the chastisement came upon them
39:26 (27)	the chastisement of the world to come
39:40 (41)	to whom will come a chastisement degrading him
39:40 (41)	upon whom lights a lasting chastisement
39:47 (48)	ransom themselves from the evil of the chastisement
39:54 (55)	ere the chastisement comes upon you
39:55 (56)	ere the chastisement comes upon you
39:58 (59)	when it sees the chastisement
39:71 (71)	the word of the chastisement has been realized
40:7 (7)	guard them against the chastisement of Hell
40:45 (48)	encompassed the folk of Pharaoh the evil chastisement
40:46 (49)	the folk of Pharaoh into the most terrible chastisement
40:49 (52)	lighten for us one day of the chastisement
41:16 (15)	We might let them taste the chastisement
41:16 (15)	the chastisement of the world to come

41:17 (16)	the thunderbolt of the chastisement
41:27 (26)	We shall let the unbelievers taste a terrible chastisement
41:50 (50)	We shall let them taste a harsh chastisement
42:16 (15)	there awaits them a terrible chastisement
42:21 (20)	there awaits a painful chastisement
42:26 (25)	for them awaits a terrible chastisement
42:42 (40)	there awaits them a painful chastisement
42:44 (43)	when they see the chastisement
42:45 (44)	the evildoers are in lasting chastisement
43:39 (38)	you are partners in the chastisement
43:48 (47)	We seized them with chastisement
43:50 (49)	when We removed from them the chastisement
43:65 (65)	because of the chastisement of a painful day
43:74 (74)	the evildoers dwell forever in the chastisement of Gehenna
44:11 (10)	this is a painful chastisement
44:12 (11)	remove Thou from us the chastisement
44:15 (14)	We are removing the chastisement a little
44:30 (29)	We delivered the Children of Israel from the humbling chastisement
44:48 (48)	pour over his head the chastisement of boiling water
44:56 (56)	He shall guard them against the chastisement of Hell
45:8 (7)	give him the good tidings of a painful chastisement
45:9 (8)	for them awaits a humbling chastisement
45:10 (9)	for them awaits a mighty chastisement
45:11 (10)	there awaits them a painful chastisement
46:20 (19)	shall be recompensed with the chastisement
46:21 (20)	I fear for you the chastisement of a dreadful day
46:24 (23)	wherein is a painful chastisement
46:31 (30)	protect you from a painful chastisement
46:34 (33)	taste the chastisement of your unbelief
48:16 (16)	He will chastise you with a painful chastisement
48:17 (17)	him He will chastise with a painful chastisement
48:25 (25)	chastised the unbelievers among them with a painful chastisement
50:26 (25)	cast him into the terrible chastisement
51:37 (37)	a sign to those who fear the painful chastisement
52:7 (7)	thy Lord's chastisement is about to fall
52:18 (18)	their Lord shall guard them against the chastisement of Hell
52:27 (27)	and guarded us against the chastisement
52:47 (47)	there surely awaits the evildoers a chastisement
54:16 (16)	how then were My chastisement and My warnings?
54:18 (18)	how then were My chastisement and My warnings?
54:21 (21)	how then were My chastisement and My warnings?
54:30 (30)	how then were My chastisement and My warnings?
54:37 (37)	taste now My chastisement and My warnings
54:38 (38)	there came upon them a settled chastisement
54:39 (39)	taste now My chastisement and My warnings
57:13 (13)	against the outward thereof is chastisement
57:20 (19)	in the world to come there is a terrible chastisement
58:4 (5)	for the unbelievers there awaits yet a painful chastisement
58:5 (6)	for the unbelievers awaits a humbling chastisement
58:15 (16)	God has made ready for them a chastisement
58:16 (17)	there awaits them a humbling chastisement
59:3 (3)	in the world to come the chastisement of the Fire
59:15 (15)	there awaits them a painful chastisement
61:10 (10)	commerce that shall deliver you from a painful chastisement
64:5 (5)	there yet awaits them a painful chastisement

65:8 (8)	and chastised it with a horrible chastisement
65:10 (10)	God prepared for them a terrible chastisement
67:5 (5)	We have prepared for them the chastisement
67:6 (6)	there awaits the chastisement of Gehenna
67:28 (28)	who will protect the unbelievers from a painful chastisement?
68:33 (33)	such is the chastisement
68:33 (33)	and the chastisement of the world to come
70:1 (1)	a questioner asked of a chastisement
70:11 (11)	might ransom himself from the chastisement
70:27 (27)	go in fear of the chastisement of their Lord
70:28 (28)	(from their Lord's chastisement none feels secure)
71:1 (1)	ere there come on them a painful chastisement
72:17 (17)	He will thrust him into chastisement rigorous
73:13 (13)	food that chokes, and a painful chastisement
76:31 (31)	He has prepared for them a painful chastisement
78:30 (30)	We shall increase you not save in chastisement
78:40 (40)	We have warned you of a nigh chastisement
84:24 (24)	give them good tidings of a painful chastisement
85:10 (10)	there awaits them the chastisement of Gehenna
85:10 (10)	and there awaits them the chastisement of the burning
88:24 (24)	God shall chastise him with the greatest chastisement
89:13 (12)	thy Lord unloosed on them a scourge of chastisement
89:25 (25)	upon that day none shall chastise as He chastises

ʿADHB n.m. (adj)~sweet (usu. in reference to water)

25:53 (55)	it is He who let forth the two seas, this one sweet
35:12 (13)	not equal are the two seas; this is sweet

ʿADHDHABA vb. (II)~to chastise, to punish, to torment, to torture. (pcple. act.) one who chastises, torments, etc. (pcple. pass.) one who is chastised, tormented, etc.

a) perf. act.

9:26 (26)	He chastised the unbelievers
48:25 (25)	We would have chastised the unbelievers
59:3 (3)	He would have chastised them in this world
65:8 (8)	and chastised it with a horrible chastisement

b) impf. act. (*yuʿadhdhibu*)

2:284 (284)	and chastise whom He will
3:56 (49)	I will chastise them with a terrible chastisement
3:128 (123)	whether He turns towards them again, or chastises them
3:129 (124)	He forgives whom He will, and chastises whom He will
4:173 (172)	them He will chastise with a painful chastisement
5:18 (21)	why then does He chastise you for your sins?
5:18 (21)	He forgives whom He will, and He chastises whom He will
5:40 (44)	He chastises whom He will, and forgives whom He will
5:115 (115)	I shall chastise him with a chastisement
5:115 (115)	wherewith I chastise no other being
5:118 (118)	if Thou chastisest them, they are Thy servants
8:33 (33)	but God would never chastise them
8:34 (34)	what have they now, that God should not chastise them
9:14 (14)	God will chastise them at your hands
9:39 (39)	if you go not forth, He will chastise you
9:55 (55)	God only desires thereby to chastise them in this present life

9:66 (67)	We will chastise another party
9:74 (75)	God will chastise them with a painful chastisement
9:85 (86)	God only desires thereby to chastise them in this present world
9:101 (102)	We shall chastise them twice
9:106 (107)	He chastises them, or turns towards them
17:54 (56)	if He will, He will chastise you
18:86 (85)	either thou shalt chastise them
18:87 (86)	for the evildoer, him we shall chastise
18:87 (86)	He shall chastise him with a horrible chastisement
20:47 (49)	send forth with us the Children of Israel and chastise them not
27:21 (21)	assuredly I will chastise him
29:21 (20)	chastising whom He will
33:24 (24)	and chastise the hypocrites, if He will
33:73 (73)	that God may chastise the hypocrites
48:6 (6)	He may chastise the hypocrites
48:14 (14)	whomsoever He will He chastises
48:16 (16)	He will chastise you with a painful chastisement
48:17 (17)	him He will chastise with a painful chastisement
58:8 (9)	why does God not chastise us for what we say?
88:24 (24)	God shall chastise him with the greatest chastisement
89:25 (25)	upon that day none shall chastise as He chastises

g) pcple. act. (*muʿadhdhib*)

7:164 (164)	or to chastise with a terrible chastisement
8:33 (33)	God would never chastise them as they begged forgiveness
17:15 (16)	We never chastise, until We send forth a Messenger
17:58 (60)	We shall chastise it with a terrible chastisement

h) pcple. pass. (*muʿadhdhab*)

26:138 (138)	we shall not be chastised
26:213 (213)	lest thou shouldst be one of those that are chastised
34:35 (34)	we shall not be chastised
37:59 (57)	and are we not chastised?

*ᶜ DH R

ᶜUDHR n.m.~an excuse, excusing

18:76 (75)	thou hast already experienced excuse sufficient on my part
77:6 (6)	excusing or warning

MAᶜDHIRAH n.f. (pl. *maᶜādhīr*)~an excuse

7:164 (164)	as an excuse to your Lord
30:57 (57)	that day their excuses will not profit the evildoers
40:52 (55)	upon the day when their excuses shall not profit the evildoers
75:15 (15)	even though he offer his excuses

ᶜADHDHARA vb. (II)~(pcple. act.) one who has an excuse

g) pcple. act. (*muᶜadhdhir*)

9:90 (91)	the Bedouins came with their excuses

IʿTADHARA vb. (VIII)~to excuse one's self, to make excuses

b) impf. act. (*yaʿtadhiru*)

9:66 (67)	make no excuses. You have disbelieved
9:94 (95)	they will excuse themselves to you
9:94 (95)	do not excuse yourselves
66:7 (7)	do not excuse yourselves
77:36 (36)	neither be given leave, and excuse themselves

*ʿ Ḍ D

ʿAḌUD n.m.~arm; supporter, helper

18:51 (49)	to be My supporters
28:35 (35)	We will strengthen thy arm

*ʿ Ḍ Ḍ

ʿAḌḌA vb. (I)~to bite

3:119 (115)	they bite at you their fingers

b) impf. act. (*yaʿaḍḍu*)

25:27 (29)	upon the day the evildoer shall bite his hands

*ʿ Ḍ L

ʿAḌALA vb. (I)~to debar

b) impf. act. (*yaʿḍulu*)

2:232 (232)	do not debar them from marrying their husbands
4:19 (23)	neither debar them, that you may go off

*ʿ Ḍ W

ʿIḌAH n.f. (pl. *ʿiḍūn*)~a fragment

15:91 (91)	who have broken the Koran into fragments

*ʿ F F

TAʿAFFAFA vb. (V)~(n.vb.) abstinence, modesty, restraint

f) n.vb. (*taʿaffuf*)

2:273 (274)	supposes them rich because of their abstinence

ISTAʿAFFA vb. (X)~to be abstinent

b) impf. act. (*yastaʿiffu*)

4:6 (6)	if any man is rich, let him be abstinent
24:33 (33)	be abstinent till God enriches them
24:60 (59)	to abstain is better for them

*ᶜ F R

ᶜIFRĪT n.m.~"efreet," a demon, a stalwart

27:39 (39)	an efreet of the jinns said

*ᶜ F W

ᶜAFĀ vb. (I)~to pardon, to forgive, to remit, to efface; to multiply. (n.vb.) forgiveness; abundance, superfluity. (pcple. act.) one who pardons, etc.

a) perf. act.

2:52 (49)	then We pardoned you after that
2:187 (183)	and has turned to you and pardoned you
3:152 (146)	He has pardoned you
3:155 (149)	but God has pardoned them
4:153 (152)	yet We pardoned them
5:95 (96)	God has pardoned what is past
5:101 (101)	God has effaced those things
7:95 (93)	in the place of evil good, till they multiplied
9:43 (43)	God pardon thee
42:40 (38)	but whoso pardons and puts things right

b) impf. act. (*yaᶜfū*)

2:237 (238)	unless it be they make remission, or he makes (remission)
2:237 (238)	unless it be they make (remission), or he makes remission
2:237 (238)	yet that you should remit is nearer to godfearing
4:99 (100)	haply them God will yet pardon
4:149 (148)	if you do good openly or in secret or pardon an evil
5:15 (18)	you have been concealing of the Book, and effacing many things
9:66 (67)	if We forgive one party of you
24:22 (22)	let them pardon and forgive
42:25 (24)	He who accepts repentance from His servants, and pardons evil deeds
42:30 (29)	He pardons much
42:34 (32)	He pardons much
64:14 (14)	if you pardon, and overlook, and if you forgive

c) impv. (*uᶜfu*)

2:109 (103)	yet do you pardon and be forgiving
2:286 (286)	and pardon us, and forgive us
3:159 (153)	so pardon them, and pray forgiveness
5:13 (16)	yet pardon them, and forgive

d) perf. pass. (*ᶜufiya*)

2:178 (173)	if aught is pardoned a man by his brother

f) n.vb. (*ᶜafw*)

2:219 (217)	say: 'The abundance'
7:199 (198)	take the abundance, and bid

g) pcple. act. (*ᶜāfī*)

3:134 (128)	and [those who] pardon the offences of their fellowmen

ʿAFŪW n.m. (adj)~All-pardoning, Clement, Forgiving (Divine attribute)

4:43 (46)	God is All-pardoning, (All-forgiving)
4:99 (100)	for God is All-pardoning, (All-forgiving)
4:149 (148)	surely God is All-pardoning, All-powerful
22:60 (59)	surely God is All-pardoning, (All-forgiving)
58:2 (3)	yet surely God is All-pardoning, (All-forgiving)

*ʿ H D

ʿAHIDA vb. (I)~to stipulate, to make a covenant

a) perf. act.

2:125 (119)	We made covenant with Abraham and Ishmael
3:183 (179)	God has made covenant with us
7:134 (131)	by the covenant He has made with thee
20:115 (114)	We made covenant with Adam before
43:49 (48)	by the covenant He has made with thee

b) impf. act. (*yaʿhadu*)

36:60 (60)	made I not covenant with you, Children of Adam

ʿAHD n.m.~a covenant, a promise

2:27 (25)	such as break the covenant of God
2:40 (38)	and fulfil My covenant
2:40 (38)	I shall fulfil your covenant
2:80 (74)	have you taken with God a covenant?
2:80 (74)	God will not fail in His covenant
2:100 (94)	whensoever they have made a covenant
2:124 (118)	My covenant shall not reach the evildoers
2:177 (172)	they who fulfil their covenant
3:76 (70)	whoso fulfils his covenant and fears God
3:77 (71)	those that sell God's covenant
6:152 (153)	fulfil God's covenant
7:102 (100)	We found no covenant in the most part
8:56 (58)	they break their compact every time
9:4 (4)	with them fulfil your covenant
9:7 (7)	how should the idolaters have a covenant with God
9:12 (12)	if they break their oaths after their covenant
9:111 (112)	who fulfils his covenant truer than God?
13:20 (20)	who fulfil God's covenant
13:25 (25)	those who break the covenant of God
16:91 (93)	fulfil God's covenant
16:95 (97)	do not sell the covenant of God
17:34 (36)	fulfil the covenant
17:34 (36)	surely the covenant shall be questioned of
19:78 (81)	or taken a covenant with the All-merciful
19:87 (90)	those who have taken with the All-merciful covenant
20:86 (89)	did the time of the covenant seem so long
23:8 (8)	who preserve their trusts and their covenant
33:15 (15)	covenants with God shall be questioned of
70:32 (32)	who preserve their trusts and their covenant

ʿĀHADA vb. (III)~to make a covenant

a) perf. act.

2:100 (94)	whensoever they have made a covenant
2:177 (172)	when they have engaged in a covenant
8:56 (58)	those of them with whom thou hast made compact
9:1 (1)	the idolaters with whom you made covenant
9:4 (4)	excepting those of the idolaters with whom you made covenant
9:7 (7)	those with whom you made covenant at the Holy Mosque
9:75 (76)	some of them have made covenant with God
16:91 (93)	fulfil God's covenant, when you make covenant
33:15 (15)	yet they had made covenant with God before that
33:23 (23)	men who were true to their covenant with God
48:10 (10)	whoso fulfils his covenant made with God

*ʿ H N

ʿIHN n.m.~wool, wool-tufts

70:9 (9)	the mountains shall be as plucked wool-tufts
101:5 (4)	the mountains shall be like plucked wool-tufts

*ʿ J B

ʿAJIBA vb. (I)~to wonder, to marvel

a) perf. act.

7:63 (61)	do you wonder that a reminder from your Lord
7:69 (67)	do you wonder that a reminder from your Lord
37:12 (12)	thou marvellest; and they scoff
38:4 (3)	now they marvel that a warner has come to them
50:2 (2)	they marvel that a warner has come to them

b) impf. act. (*yaʿjabu*)

11:73 (76)	dost thou marvel at God's command?
13:5 (5)	if thou wouldst wonder, surely wonderful is their saying
53:59 (59)	do you then marvel at this discourse

ʿAJAB n.m.~wonder; (adj) wonderful, marvellous

10:2 (2)	was it a wonder to the people
13:5 (5)	if thou wouldst wonder, surely wonderful
18:9 (8)	Men of the Cave and Er-Rakeem were among Our signs a wonder
18:63 (62)	into the sea in a manner marvellous
72:1 (1)	we have indeed heard a Koran wonderful

ʿAJĪB n.m. (adj)~strange, marvellous

11:72 (75)	this assuredly is a strange thing
50:2 (2)	this is a marvellous thing

ʿUJĀB n.m. (adj)~marvellous, wonderful

38:5 (4)	this is indeed a marvellous thing

AʿJABA vb. (IV)~to please, to cause admiration, to admire

a) perf. act.

2:221 (220) though you may admire her
2:221 (220) though you may admire him
5:100 (100) though the abundance of the corrupt please thee
9:25 (25) when your multitude was pleasing to you
33:52 (52) though their beauty please thee
57:20 (19) a rain whose vegetation pleases the unbelievers

b) impf. act. (*yuʿjibu*)

2:204 (200) the present world pleases thee
9:55 (55) let not their possessions or their children please thee
9:85 (86) let not their possessions and their children please thee
48:29 (29) pleasing the sowers
63:4 (4) when thou seest them, their bodies please thee

*ʿ J F

ʿIJĀF n.f. (pl. of *ʿajfāʾ*)~lean

12:43 (43) seven fat kine, and seven lean ones
12:46 (46) pronounce to us regarding seven fat kine

*ʿ J L

ʿAJILA vb. (I)~to hasten, to outstrip. (pcple. act.) hasty, that which hastens away; (n) the transitory world

a) perf. act.

7:150 (149) have you outstripped your Lord's commandment?
20:84 (86) I have hastened, Lord

b) impf. act. (*yaʿjalu*)

19:84 (87) so hasten thou not against them
20:114 (113) hasten not with the Koran
75:16 (16) move not thy tongue with it to hasten it

g) pcple. act. f. (*ʿājilah*)

17:18 (19) whosoever desires this hasty world
75:20 (20) you love the hasty world
76:27 (27) surely these men love the hasty world

ʿAJAL n.m.~haste

21:37 (38) man was created of haste

ʿAJŪL n.m. (adj)~hasty

17:11 (12) man is ever hasty

ʿIJL n.m.~a calf

2:51 (48) then you took to yourselves the Calf
2:54 (51) you have done wrong against yourselves by your taking the Calf

2:92 (86)	then you took to yourselves the Calf
2:93 (87)	they were made to drink the Calf in their hearts
4:153 (152)	they took to themselves the Calf
7:148 (146)	people of Moses took to them, after him, of their ornaments a Calf
7:152 (151)	surely those who took to themselves the Calf
11:69 (72)	and presently he brought a roasted calf
20:88 (90)	he brought out for them a Calf
51:26 (26)	he turned to his household and brought a fattened calf

ʿAJJALA vb. (II)~to hasten

a) perf. act.

17:18 (19)	We hasten for him therein what We will
18:58 (57)	He would hasten for them the chastisement
48:20 (20)	these He has hastened to you

b) impf. act. (*yuʿajjilu*)

10:11 (12)	if God should hasten unto men evil

c) impv. (*ʿajjil*)

38:16 (15)	Lord, hasten to us our share

AʿJALA vb. (IV)~to cause to hasten, to speed (tr)

a) perf. act.

20:83 (85)	what has sped thee far from thy people

TAʿAJJALA vb. (V)~to be in a hurry, to hasten on

a) perf. act.

2:203 (199)	if any man hastens on in two days

ISTAʿJALA vb. (X)~to seek to hasten. (n.vb.) the desire to hasten

a) perf. act.

46:24 (23)	rather it is that you sought to hasten

b) impf. act. (*yastaʿjilu*)

6:57 (57)	not with me is that you seek to hasten
6:58 (58)	if what you seek to hasten were with me
10:50 (51)	what part of it will the sinners seek to hasten?
10:51 (52)	now, when already you seek to hasten it
13:6 (7)	they would have thee hasten the evil
16:1 (1)	so seek not to hasten it
21:37 (38)	so demand not that I make haste
22:47 (46)	they demand of thee to hasten the chastisement
26:204 (204)	do they seek to hasten Our chastisement?
27:46 (47)	why do you seek to hasten evil before good?
27:72 (74)	already is some part of that you seek to hasten on
29:53 (53)	they demand of thee to hasten the chastisement
29:54 (54)	they demand of thee to hasten the chastisement

37:176 (176)	do they seek to hasten Our chastisement?
42:18 (17)	those that believe not therein seek to hasten it
46:35 (34)	seek not to hasten it for them
51:14 (14)	this is that you were seeking to hasten
51:59 (59)	let them not hasten Me

f) n.vb. (*istiʿjāl*)

10:11 (12)	as they would hasten good

*ʿ J M

AʿJAMĪY n.m. (adj)~a barbarian, a non-Arab; barbarous, a foreign tongue

16:103 (105)	the speech of him at whom they hint is barbarous
26:198 (198)	if We had sent it down on a barbarian
41:44 (44)	if We had made it a barbarous Koran
41:44 (44)	what, barbarous and Arabic?

*ʿ J Z

ʿAJAZA vb. (I)~to be weak, to be unable

a) perf. act.

5:31 (34)	am I unable to be as this raven

AʿJĀZ n.m. (pl)~stumps of trees

54:20 (20)	men as if they were stumps of uprooted palm-trees
69:7 (7)	as if they were the stumps of fallen down palm-trees

ʿAJŪZ n.f.~old woman

11:72 (75)	shall I bear, being an old woman
26:171 (171)	save an old woman among those that tarried
37:135 (135)	save an old woman among those that tarried
51:29 (29)	An old woman, barren

ʿĀJAZA vb. (III)~(pcple. act.) one who strives to void, one who baffles

g) pcple. act. (*muʿājiz*)

22:51 (50)	those who strive against Our signs to void them
34:5 (5)	those who strive against Our signs to void them
34:38 (37)	those who strive against Our signs to void them

AʿJAZA vb. (IV)~to frustrate, to weaken. (pcple. act.) one who frustrates, one who weakens

b) impf. act. (*yuʿjizu*)

8:59 (61)	they cannot frustrate My will
35:44 (43)	naught in the heavens or the earth that can frustrate Him
72:12 (12)	we should never be able to frustrate God
72:12 (12)	neither be able to frustrate Him by flight

g) pcple. act. (*mu*ᶜ*jiz*)

6:134 (134)	you cannot frustrate it
9:2 (2)	you cannot frustrate the will of God
9:3 (3)	you cannot frustrate the will of God
10:53 (54)	you cannot frustrate Him
11:20 (22)	they are unable to frustrate Him on earth
11:33 (35)	you cannot frustrate Him
16:46 (48)	they will not be able to frustrate Him
24:57 (56)	think not the unbelievers able to frustrate God
29:22 (21)	you are not able to frustrate Him
39:51 (52)	they will not be able to frustrate it
42:31 (30)	you are not able to frustrate Him
46:32 (31)	whosoever answers not God's summoner cannot frustrate God

*ᶜ K F

ᶜAKAFA vb. (I)~to cleave to, to give one's self up to, to inhabit. (pcple. act.) one who cleaves to, one who inhabits. (pcple. pass.) one who is detained

b) impf. act. (*ya*ᶜ*kufu*)

7:138 (134)	they came upon a people cleaving to idols

g) pcple. act. (ᶜ*ākif*)

2:125 (119)	those that shall go about it and those that cleave to it
2:187 (183)	do not lie with them while you cleave to the mosques
20:91 (93)	'We will not cease,' they said, 'to cleave to it'
20:97 (97)	thy god, to whom all the day thou wast cleaving
21:52 (53)	what are these statues unto which you are cleaving?
22:25 (25)	alike him who cleaves to it
26:71 (71)	we serve idols, and continue cleaving to them

h) pcple. pass. (*ma*ᶜ*kūf*)

48:25 (25)	the offering, detained so as not to reach its place of sacrifice

*ᶜ L M

ᶜALIMA vb. (I)~to know; (*alladhīna lā ya*ᶜ*lamūn*) "those who do not know", the ignorant. (n.vb.) knowledge. (pcple. act.) one who has knowledge, one knowing, learned; Knower (Divine attribute); (an alternative vocalization occurs for 30:22, ᶜ*ālamīn*, instead of ᶜ*ālimīn*. In case of the former vocalization the term should be rendered, as below, "all beings"). (pcple. pass.) known, fixed

a) perf. act.

2:60 (57)	all the people knew now their drinking-place
2:65 (61)	well you know there were those among you
2:102 (96)	knowing well that whoso buys it
2:187 (183)	god knows that you have been betraying yourselves
2:235 (235)	God knows that you will be mindful of them
4:83 (85)	whose task it is to investigate would have known the matter
5:116 (116)	Thou knowest it, knowing
7:160 (160)	all the people knew now their drinking-place
8:23 (23)	if God had known of any good in them
8:66 (67)	knowing that there is weakness in you

11:79 (81)	Thou knowest we have no right
12:51 (51)	we know no evil against him
12:73 (73)	you know well that we came not to work corruption
12:81 (81)	we do not testify except that we know
12:89 (89)	are you aware of what you did with Joseph
15:24 (24)	We know the ones of you who press forward
15:24 (24)	We know the laggards
17:102 (104)	thou knowest that none sent these down
21:65 (66)	very well indeed thou knowest these do not speak
24:33 (33)	if you know some good in them
24:41 (41)	He knows its prayer and its extolling; and God knows
28:38 (38)	I know not that you have any god but me
28:75 (75)	then will they know that Truth is God's
33:50 (50)	We know what We have imposed upon them
37:158 (158)	the jinn know that they shall be arraigned
45:9 (8)	when he knows anything of Our signs
48:18 (18)	He knew what was in their hearts
48:27 (27)	He knew what you (knew not)
50:4 (4)	We know what the earth diminishes of them
56:62 (62)	you have known the first growth
60:10 (10)	if you know them to be believers
73:20 (20)	He knows that you will not number it
73:20 (20)	He knows that some of you are sick
81:14 (14)	then shall a soul know what it has produced
82:5 (5)	then a soul shall know its works

b) impf. act. (*yaᶜlamu*)

2:13 (12)	they are the foolish ones, but they do not know
2:22 (20)	set not up compeers to God wittingly
2:26 (24)	as for the believers, they know it is the truth
2:30 (28)	He said, 'Assuredly I know that you (know) not'
2:30 (28)	He said, 'Assuredly I (know) that you know not'
2:33 (31)	did I not tell you I know the unseen things
2:33 (31)	I know what things you reveal
2:42 (39)	do not conceal the truth wittingly
2:75 (70)	after they had comprehended it, wittingly
2:77 (72)	know they not that God (knows) what they keep secret
2:77 (72)	(know) they not that God knows what they keep secret
2:78 (73)	not knowing the Book, but only fancies
2:80 (74)	say you things against God of which you know nothing?
2:101 (95)	behind their backs, as though they knew not
2:102 (96)	if they had but known
2:103 (97)	if they had but known
2:106 (100)	knowest thou not that God is powerful
2:107 (101)	knowest thou not that to God belongs the kingdom
2:113 (107)	so too the ignorant say the like of them
2:118 (112)	and they that know not say
2:143 (138)	that We might know who followed the Messenger
2:144 (139)	those who have been given the Book know it is the truth
2:146 (141)	a party of them conceal the truth and that wittingly
2:151 (146)	and to teach you that you knew not
2:169 (164)	you should speak against God such things as you know not
2:184 (180)	you should fast is better for you, if you but know
2:188 (184)	consume a portion of other men's goods, and that wittingly
2:197 (193)	whatever good you do, God knows it

2:216 (213)	God knows and you (know) not
2:216 (213)	God (knows) and you know not
2:220 (219)	God knows well him who works corruption
2:230 (230)	He makes them clear unto a people that have knowledge
2:232 (232)	God knows and you (know) not
2:232 (232)	God (knows) and you know not
2:235 (236)	God knows what is in your hearts
2:239 (240)	He taught you the things that you knew not
2:255 (256)	He knows what lies before them
2:259 (261)	I know that God is powerful over everything
2:270 (273)	whatever vow you vow, surely God knows it
2:280 (280)	freewill offerings is better for you, did you but know
3:7 (5)	none knows its interpretation, save only God
3:29 (27)	whether you hide what is in your breasts or publish it, God knows it
3:29 (27)	God knows what is in the heavens
3:66 (59)	God knows and you (know) not
3:66 (59)	God (knows) and you know not
3:71 (64)	conceal the truth and that wittingly
3:75 (69)	they speak falsehood against God and that wittingly
3:78 (72)	they speak falsehood against God, and that wittingly
3:135 (129)	and do not persevere in the things they did and that wittingly
3:140 (134)	that God may know who are the believers
3:142 (136)	without God know who of you have struggled
3:142 (136)	and [without He know] who are patient
3:166 (160)	that He might know the believers
3:167 (160)	that He might also know the hypocrites
3:167 (160)	if only we knew how to fight
4:43 (46)	when you are drunken until you know what you are saying
4:63 (66)	God knows what is in their hearts
4:113 (113)	He has taught thee that thou knewest not
5:40 (44)	knowest thou not that to God belongs the kingdom
5:94 (95)	that God may know who fears Him in the Unseen
5:97 (98)	that you may know that God (knows) all
5:97 (98)	God knows all that is in the heavens
5:99 (99)	God knows what you reveal
5:104 (103)	even if their fathers had knowledge of naught
5:113 (113)	that we may know that thou hast spoken true
5:116 (116)	Thou knowest it, knowing what is within my soul
5:116 (116)	I know not what is within Thy soul
6:3 (3)	He knows your secrets
6:3 (3)	He knows what you are earning
6:33 (33)	We know indeed that it grieves thee
6:37 (37)	most of them know not
6:50 (50)	I know not the Unseen
6:59 (59)	none knows them but He
6:59 (59)	He knows what is in land and sea
6:59 (59)	not a leaf falls, but He knows it
6:60 (60)	He knows what you work by day
6:67 (66)	every tiding has its time appointed; you will surely know
6:81 (81)	if you have any knowledge
6:91 (91)	that you knew not, you and your fathers
6:97 (97)	We have distinguished the signs for a people who know
6:105 (105)	We may make it clear to a people having knowledge
6:114 (114)	those whom We have given the Book know it is sent
6:135 (135)	I am acting. And assuredly you will know

7:28 (27)	concerning God such things as you know not
7:32 (30)	We distinguish the signs for a people who know
7:33 (31)	and that you say concerning God such as you know not
7:38 (36)	Unto each a double, but you know not
7:62 (60)	for I know from God that you (know) not
7:62 (60)	for I (know) from God that you know not
7:75 (73)	do you know that Salih is an Envoy
7:123 (120)	now you shall know
7:131 (128)	the most of them knew not
7:182 (181)	We will draw them on little by little whence they know not
7:187 (187)	most men know not
7:188 (188)	had I knowledge of the Unseen
8:27 (27)	and betray not your trusts and that wittingly
8:34 (34)	most of them know not
8:60 (62)	others besides them that you know not
8:60 (62)	God knows them
8:70 (71)	if God knows of any good in your hearts
9:6 (6)	they are a people who do not know
9:11 (11)	We distinguish the signs for a people who know
9:16 (16)	God knows not as yet those of you
9:41 (41)	that is better for you, did you know
9:42 (42)	God knows that they are truly liars
9:43 (43)	thou knewest the liars
9:63 (64)	do they not know that whosoever opposes God
9:78 (79)	did they not know that God (knows) their secret
9:78 (79)	did they not (know) that God knows their secret
9:93 (94)	God has set a seal on their hearts, so they know not
9:97 (98)	and apter not to know the bounds of what God has sent down
9:101 (102)	thou knowest them not
9:101 (102)	but We know them, and We shall chastise them twice
9:104 (105)	do they not know that God is He who accepts repentance
10:5 (5)	that you might know the number of the years
10:5 (5)	distinguishing the signs to a people who know
10:18 (19)	will you tell God what He knows not
10:55 (56)	the most of them have no knowledge
10:68 (69)	what, do you say concerning God that you know not?
10:89 (89)	follow not the way of those that know not
11:5 (6)	their garments He knows what they secrete
11:6 (8)	He knows its lodging-place
11:31 (33)	I know not the Unseen
11:39 (40)	and you shall know
11:49 (51)	thou didst not know it, neither thy people
11:79 (81)	thou well knowest what we desire
11:93 (95)	certainly you will know
12:21 (21)	God prevails in His purpose, but most men know not
12:40 (40)	most men know not
12:46 (46)	haply I shall return to the men, haply they will know
12:52 (52)	so that he may know I betrayed him not
12:68 (68)	most men know not
12:80 (80)	do you not know how your father has taken a solemn pledge
12:86 (86)	I know from God
12:86 (86)	that you know not
12:96 (97)	did I not tell you I know from God
12:96 (97)	that you know not
13:8 (9)	God knows what every female bears

13:19 (19)	he who knows what is sent down to thee
13:33 (33)	will you tell Him what He knows not in the earth?
13:42 (42)	He knows what every soul earns
13:42 (42)	the unbelievers shall assuredly know whose will be the Ultimate
14:9 (10)	those after them whom none knows but God
14:38 (41)	Thou knowest what we keep secret
14:52 (52)	that they may know that He is One God
15:3 (3)	certainly they will soon know
15:96 (96)	certainly they will soon know
15:97 (97)	We know indeed thy breast is straitened
16:8 (8)	He creates what you know not
16:19 (19)	God knows what you keep secret
16:23 (24)	God knows what they keep secret
16:38 (40)	most men know not
16:39 (41)	the unbelievers may know that they were truly liars
16:41 (43)	the wage of the world to come is greater, did they but know
16:43 (45)	question the people of the Remembrance, if it should be that you do not know
16:55 (57)	certainly you will soon know
16:56 (58)	that We have provided them to what they know not
16:70 (72)	that after knowing somewhat, they may know nothing
16:74 (76)	surely God knows
16:74 (76)	and you know not
16:75 (77)	most of them know not
16:78 (80)	knowing nothing, from your mothers' wombs
16:91 (93)	surely God knows the things you do
16:95 (97)	that is better for you, did you but know
16:101 (103)	the most of them have no knowledge
16:103 (105)	We know very well that they say
17:12 (13)	that you may know the number of the years
18:12 (11)	that We might know which of the two parties
18:21 (20)	that they might know that God's promise is true
18:22 (21)	none knows them, except a few
19:65 (66)	knowest thou any that can be named with His Name?
19:75 (77)	they shall surely know who is worse in place
20:7 (6)	surely He knows the secret
20:71 (74)	you shall know of a certainty which of us is more terrible
20:110 (109)	He knows what is before them and behind them
20:135 (135)	assuredly you shall know who are the travellers
21:4 (4)	my Lord knows what is said in the heavens
21:7 (7)	question the People of the Remembrance, if you do not know
21:24 (24)	the most part of them know not the truth
21:28 (28)	He knows what is before them and behind them
21:39 (40)	if the unbelievers but knew when
21:110 (110)	surely He knows what is spoken aloud
21:110 (110)	He knows what you hide
22:5 (5)	that after knowing somewhat, they may know nothing
22:54 (53)	they who have been given knowledge may know
22:70 (69)	didst thou not know that God (knows) all
22:70 (69)	didst thou not (know) that God knows all
22:76 (75)	He knows whatsoever is before them and behind them
23:84 (86)	if you have knowledge
23:88 (90)	if you have knowledge
23:114 (116)	you have tarried but a little, did you know
24:19 (19)	God knows, and you (know) not
24:19 (19)	God (knows), and you know not

24:25 (25)	they shall know that God is the manifest Truth
24:29 (29)	God knows what you reveal
24:63 (63)	God knows those of you who slip away surreptitiously
24:64 (64)	He ever knows what state you are upon
25:6 (7)	He sent it down, who knows the secret
25:42 (44)	they shall know, when they see the chastisement
26:49 (48)	now you shall know
26:132 (132)	fear Him who has succoured you with what you know
26:197 (197)	was it not a sign for them, that it is known to the learned
26:227 (228)	those who do wrong shall surely know
27:25 (25)	He knows what you conceal
27:52 (53)	in that is a sign for a people who have knowledge
27:61 (62)	the most of them have no knowledge
27:65 (66)	none knows the Unseen in the heavens and earth except God
27:74 (76)	thy Lord knows what their hearts conceal
28:13 (12)	that she might know that the promise of God is true
28:13 (12)	the promise of god is true; but most of them do not know
28:57 (57)	most of them know not
28:69 (69)	thy Lord knows what their breasts conceal
28:78 (78)	did he not know that God had destroyed before him generations
29:3 (2)	assuredly God knows those who speak truly
29:3 (2)	assuredly He knows the liars
29:11 (10)	God surely knows the believers
29:11 (10)	and He knows the hypocrites
29:16 (15)	that is better for you, did you know
29:41 (40)	did they but know
29:42 (41)	God knows whatever thing they call upon
29:45 (44)	God knows the things you work
29:52 (52)	He knows whatsoever is in the heavens
29:64 (64)	the Last Abode is Life, did they but know
29:66 (66)	they will soon know
30:6 (5)	God fails not His promise, but most men do not know it
30:7 (6)	they know an outward part of the present life
30:30 (29)	most men know it not
30:34 (33)	certainly you will soon know
30:56 (56)	this is the Day of the Upraising, but you did not know
30:59 (59)	God seals the hearts of those that know not
31:25 (24)	most of them have no knowledge
31:34 (34)	He knows what is in the wombs
32:17 (17)	no soul knows what comfort is laid up
33:5 (5)	if you know not who their fathers were
33:18 (18)	God would surely know those of you who hinder
33:51 (51)	God knows what is in your hearts
34:2 (2)	He knows what penetrates into the earth
34:14 (13)	had they only known the Unseen, they would not have continued
34:21 (20)	that We might know him who believed in the Hereafter
34:28 (27)	most men do not know it
34:36 (35)	most men do not know it
36:16 (15)	Our Lord knows we are Envoys unto you
36:26 (25)	would that my people had knowledge
36:36 (36)	of themselves, and of what they know not
36:76 (76)	assuredly We know what they keep secret
37:170 (170)	soon they shall know
38:88 (88)	you shall surely know its tiding
39:9 (12)	are they equal — those who know

39:9 (12)	and those who know not
39:26 (27)	did they but know
39:29 (30)	but most of them do not know
39:39 (40)	soon you will know
39:49 (50)	most of them do not know it
39:52 (53)	do they know that God outspreads and straitens His provision
40:19 (20)	He knows the treachery of the eyes
40:57 (59)	but most men know it not
40:70 (72)	soon they will know
41:3 (2)	an Arabic Koran for a people having knowledge
41:22 (21)	you thought that God would never know much of the things
42:18 (17)	go in fear of it, knowing that it is the truth
42:25 (24)	He knows the things you do
42:35 (33)	those who dispute concerning Our signs may know they have no asylum
43:86 (86)	such as have testified to the truth, and that knowingly
43:89 (89)	soon they will know
44:39 (39)	most of them know it not
45:18 (17)	follow not the caprices of those who do not know
45:26 (25)	most men do not know
47:19 (21)	God knows your going to and fro
47:26 (28)	God knows their secrets
47:30 (32)	God knows your deeds
47:31 (33)	until We know those of you who struggle and are steadfast
48:25 (25)	believers and certain women believers whom you knew not
48:27 (27)	He knew what you knew not
49:16 (16)	God knows what is in the heavens
49:18 (18)	God knows the Unseen of the heavens
50:16 (15)	We know what his soul whispers within him
52:47 (47)	most of them know it not
54:26 (26)	they shall surely know tomorrow who is the impudent liar
56:61 (61)	to grow again in a fashion you know not
56:76 (75)	that is indeed a mighty oath, did you but know it)
57:4 (4)	He knows what penetrates into the earth
57:25 (25)	so that God might know who helps Him
57:29 (29)	that the People of the Book may know
58:7 (8)	hast thou not seen that God knows whatsoever is in the heavens
58:14 (15)	they swear upon falsehood, and that wittingly
61:5 (5)	though you know I am the Messenger
61:11 (11)	that is better for you, did you but know
62:9 (9)	that is better for you, did you but know
63:1 (1)	and God knows that thou art indeed His Messenger
63:8 (8)	the hypocrites do not know it
64:4 (4)	He knows whatever is in the heavens
64:4 (4)	He knows what you conceal
65:12 (12)	that you may know that God is powerful
67:14 (14)	shall He not know, who created?
67:17 (17)	then you shall know how My warning is
67:29 (29)	assuredly, you will soon know who is in manifest error
68:33 (33)	did they but know
68:44 (44)	We will draw them on little by little whence they know not
69:49 (49)	We know that some of you will cry lies
70:39 (39)	We have created them of what they know
71:4 (4)	did you but know
72:24 (25)	then they will know who is weaker
72:28 (28)	that He may know they have delivered the Messages

73:20 (20)	thy Lord knows that thou keepest vigil
74:31 (34)	none knows the hosts of thy Lord but He
78:4 (4)	they shall soon know
78:5 (5)	they shall soon know
82:12 (12)	who know whatever you do
87:7 (7)	surely He knows what is spoken aloud
96:5 (5)	taught Man that he knew not
96:14 (14)	did he not know that God sees?
100:9 (9)	knows he not that when that which is in the tombs is overthrown
102:3 (3)	but soon you shall know
102:4 (4)	but soon you shall know
102:5 (5)	did you know with the knowledge of certainty

c) impv. (*iʿlam*)

2:194 (190)	fear you God, and know that God is with the godfearing
2:196 (192)	know that God is terrible in retribution
2:203 (199)	know that unto Him you shall be mustered
2:209 (205)	know then that God is All-mighty, All-wise
2:223 (223)	know that you shall meet Him
2:231 (231)	know that God has knowledge of everything
2:233 (233)	know that God sees the things you do
2:235 (236)	know that God (knows) what is in your hearts
2:235 (236)	know that God is All-forgiving, All-clement
2:244 (245)	know that God is All-hearing, All-knowing
2:260 (262)	do thou know that God is All-mighty, All-wise
2:267 (270)	know that God is All-sufficient, All-laudable
5:34 (38)	know you that God is All-forgiving, All-compassionate
5:49 (54)	know that God desires only to smite them
5:92 (93)	know that it is only for Our Messenger to deliver the Message Manifest
5:98 (98)	know God is terrible in retribution
8:24 (24)	know that God stands between a man and his heart
8:25 (25)	know that God is terrible in retribution
8:28 (28)	know that your wealth and your children are a trial
8:40 (41)	know that God is your Protector
8:41 (42)	know that, whatever booty you take
9:2 (2)	know that you cannot frustrate the will of God
9:3 (3)	know that you cannot frustrate the will of God
9:36 (36)	know that God is with the godfearing
9:123 (124)	know that God is with the godfearing
11:14 (17)	know that it has been sent down with God's knowledge
28:50 (50)	know that they are only following their caprices
47:19 (21)	know thou therefore that there is no god but God
49:7 (7)	know that the Messenger of God is among you
57:17 (16)	know that God revives the earth after it was dead
57:20 (19)	know that the present life is but a sport

e) impf. pass. (*yuʿlamu*)

24:31 (31)	so that their hidden ornament may be known

f) n.vb. (*ʿilm*)

2:32 (30)	we know not save what Thou hast taught us
2:120 (114)	after the knowledge that has come to thee
2:145 (140)	after the knowledge that has come to thee
2:247 (248)	has increased him broadly in knowledge and body

2:255 (256)	they comprehend not anything of His knowledge
3:7 (5)	only God. And those firmly rooted in knowledge
3:18 (16)	the angels, and men possessed of knowledge
3:19 (17)	except after the knowledge came to them
3:61 (54)	after the knowledge that has come to thee
3:66 (59)	you are the ones who dispute on what you know
3:66 (59)	why then dispute you touching a matter of which you know not anything
4:157 (156)	they have no knowledge of him
4:162 (160)	those of them that are firmly rooted in knowledge
4:166 (164)	He has sent it down with His knowledge
5:109 (108)	we have no knowledge
6:80 (80)	my Lord embraces all things in His knowledge
6:100 (100)	sons and daughters without any knowledge
6:108 (108)	they will abuse God in revenge without knowledge
6:119 (119)	many lead astray by their caprices, without any knowledge
6:140 (141)	losers are they who slay their children in folly, without knowledge
6:143 (144)	tell me the knowledge, if you speak truly
6:144 (145)	may lead mankind astray without any knowledge
6:148 (149)	have you any knowledge, for you to bring forth
7:7 (6)	and We shall relate to them with knowledge; assuredly
7:52 (50)	a Book that We have well distinguished, resting on knowledge
7:89 (87)	our Lord embraces all things in His knowledge
7:187 (186)	the knowledge of it is only with my Lord
7:187 (187)	the knowledge of it is only with God
10:39 (40)	they have cried lies to that whereof they comprehended not the knowledge
10:93 (93)	they differed not until the knowledge came to them
11:14 (17)	sent down with God's knowledge
11:46 (48)	do not ask of Me that whereof thou hast no knowledge
11:47 (49)	lest I should ask of Thee that whereof I have no knowledge
12:22 (22)	We gave him judgment and knowledge
12:68 (68)	verily he was possessed of a knowledge
12:76 (76)	over every man of knowledge is One who knows
13:37 (37)	after the knowledge that has come to thee
13:43 (43)	whosoever possesses knowledge of the Book
16:25 (27)	those that they lead astray without any knowledge
16:27 (29)	those that were given the knowledge
16:70 (72)	after knowing somewhat, they may know nothing
17:36 (38)	pursue not that thou hast no knowledge of
17:85 (87)	you have been given of knowledge nothing except a little
17:107 (108)	those who were given the knowledge before it
18:5 (4)	they have no knowledge of it
18:65 (64)	We had taught him knowledge proceeding from Us
19:43 (44)	Father, there has come to me knowledge
20:52 (54)	the knowledge of them is with my Lord
20:98 (98)	who in His knowledge embraces everything
20:110 (109)	they comprehend Him not in knowledge
20:114 (113)	increase me in knowledge
21:74 (74)	to him We gave judgment and knowledge
21:79 (79)	unto each gave We judgment and knowledge
22:3 (3)	such a one that disputes concerning God without knowledge
22:5 (5)	after knowing somewhat, they may know nothing
22:8 (8)	such a one that disputes concerning God without knowledge
22:54 (53)	they who have been given knowledge
22:71 (70)	and that whereof they have no knowledge
24:15 (14)	speaking with your mouths that whereof you had no knowledge

26:112 (112)	what knowledge have I of that they have been doing?
27:15 (15)	We gave David and Solomon knowledge
27:40 (40)	said he who possessed knowledge of the Book
27:42 (42)	we were given the knowledge before her
27:66 (68)	their knowledge fails as to the Hereafter
27:84 (86)	my signs, not comprehending them in knowledge
28:14 (13)	We gave him judgment and knowledge
28:78 (78)	a knowledge that is in me
28:80 (80)	those to whom knowledge had been given
29:8 (7)	associate with Me that whereof thou hast no knowledge
29:49 (48)	those who have been given knowledge
30:29 (28)	the evildoers follow their own caprices, without knowledge
30:56 (56)	those who have been given knowledge and faith
31:6 (5)	to lead astray from the way of God without knowledge
31:15 (14)	associate with Me that whereof thou hast no knowledge
31:20 (19)	such a one that disputes concerning God without knowledge
31:34 (34)	He has knowledge of the Hour
33:63 (63)	the knowledge of it is only with God
34:6 (6)	those who have been given the knowledge
35:11 (12)	save with His knowledge
38:69 (69)	I had no knowledge of the High Council
39:49 (50)	I was given it only because of a knowledge
40:7 (7)	Thou embracest every thing in mercy and knowledge
40:42 (45)	to associate with Him that whereof I have no knowledge
40:83 (83)	they rejoiced in what knowledge they had
41:47 (47)	to Him is referred the knowledge of the Hour
41:47 (47)	save with His knowledge
42:14 (13)	save after knowledge had come to them
43:20 (19)	they have no knowledge of that
43:61 (61)	It is knowledge of the Hour; doubt not
43:85 (85)	with Him is the knowledge of the Hour
44:32 (31)	We chose them, out of a knowledge, above all beings
45:17 (16)	they differed not, except after the knowledge had come to them
45:23 (22)	God has led him astray out of a knowledge
45:24 (23)	of that they have no knowledge
46:4 (3)	bring me a Book before this, or some remnant of a knowledge
46:23 (22)	knowledge is only with God
47:16 (18)	to those who have been given knowledge
48:25 (25)	and there befall you guilt unwittingly on their account
53:28 (29)	they have not any knowledge thereof
53:30 (31)	that is their attainment of knowledge
53:35 (36)	does he possess the knowledge of the Unseen
58:11 (12)	those of you who believe and have been given knowledge
65:12 (12)	God encompasses everything in knowledge
67:26 (26)	the knowledge is with God
102:5 (5)	did you know with the knowledge of certainty

g) pcple. act. (*ʿālim*)

6:73 (73)	He is Knower of the Unseen
9:94 (95)	to Him who knows the unseen
9:105 (106)	to Him who knows the unseen
12:44 (44)	we know nothing of the interpretation of nightmares
13:9 (10)	the Knower of the unseen and the visible
21:51 (52)	for We knew him
21:81 (81)	We had knowledge of everything

23:92 (94)	who has knowledge of the Unseen
29:43 (42)	none understands them save those who know
30:22 (21)	surely in that are signs for all living beings
32:6 (5)	He is the knower of the Unseen
34:3 (3)	by Him who knows the Unseen
35:38 (36)	God knows the Unseen in the heavens
39:46 (47)	who knowest the Unseen and the Visible
59:22 (22)	He is the knower of the Unseen
62:8 (8)	the Knower of the Unseen
64:18 (18)	Knower He of the Unseen and the Visible
72:26 (26)	Knower He of the Unseen

h) pcple. pass. (*maʿlūm*)

2:197 (193)	the Pilgrimage is in months well-known
15:4 (4)	never a city have We destroyed, but it had a known decree
15:21 (21)	We send it not down but in a known measure
15:38 (38)	unto the day of a known time
22:28 (29)	mention God's Name on days well-known
26:38 (37)	the sorcerers were assembled for the appointed time of a fixed day
26:155 (155)	and to you a draught, on a day appointed
37:41 (40)	for them awaits a known provision
37:164 (164)	none of us is there, but has a known station
38:81 (82)	until the day of the known time
56:50 (50)	gathered to the appointed time of a known day
70:24 (24)	those in whose wealth is a right known
77:22 (22)	till a known term decreed

ʿĀLAMĪN n.m. (pl. of ʿ*ālam*)~all beings [Ar]; worlds [others]; (*rabb al-ʿālamīn*) the Lord of all Being

1:2 (1)	praise belongs to God, the Lord of all Being
2:47 (44)	I have preferred you above all beings
2:122 (116)	I have preferred you above all beings
2:131 (125)	I have surrendered me to the Lord of all Being
2:251 (252)	God is bounteous unto all beings
3:33 (30)	the House of Imran above all beings
3:42 (37)	He has chosen thee above all women
3:96 (90)	a place holy, and a guidance to all beings
3:97 (92)	God is All-sufficient nor needs any being
3:108 (104)	God desires not any injustice to living beings
5:20 (23)	gave you such as He had not given to any being
5:28 (31)	I fear God, the Lord of all Being
5:115 (115)	wherewith I chastise no other being
6:45 (45)	praise belongs to God the Lord of all Being
6:71 (70)	we are commanded to surrender to the Lord of all Being
6:86 (86)	each one We preferred above all beings
6:90 (90)	it is but a reminder unto all beings
6:162 (163)	all belongs to God, the Lord of all Being
7:54 (52)	blessed be God, the Lord of all Being
7:61 (59)	I am a Messenger from the Lord of all Being
7:67 (65)	I am a Messenger from the Lord of all Being
7:80 (78)	as never any being in all the world committed
7:104 (102)	I am a Messenger from the Lord of all Being
7:121 (118)	we believe in the Lord of all Being
7:140 (136)	who has preferred you above all beings
10:10 (11)	praise belongs to God, the Lord of all Being
10:37 (38)	the Book, wherein is no doubt, from the Lord of all Being

12:104 (104)	it is nothing but a reminder unto all beings
15:70 (70)	have we not forbidden thee all beings?
21:71 (71)	the land that We had blessed for all beings
21:91 (91)	a sign unto all beings
21:107 (107)	a mercy unto all beings
25:1 (1)	a warner to all beings
26:16 (15)	I am the Messenger of the Lord of all Being
26:23 (22)	what is the Lord of all Being?
26:47 (46)	we believe in the Lord of all Being
26:77 (77)	except the Lord of all Being
26:98 (98)	we made you equal with the Lord of all Being
26:109 (109)	my wage falls only upon the Lord of all Being
26:127 (127)	my wage falls only upon the Lord of all Being
26:145 (145)	my wage falls only upon the Lord of all Being
26:164 (164)	my wage falls only upon the Lord of all Being
26:165 (165)	do you come to male beings
26:180 (180)	my wage falls only upon the Lord of all Being
26:192 (192)	the revelation of the Lord of all Being
27:8 (8)	glory be to God, the Lord of all Being
27:44 (45)	I surrender with Solomon to God, the Lord of all Being
28:30 (30)	I am God, the Lord of all Being
29:6 (5)	God is All-sufficient nor needs any being
29:10 (9)	in the breasts of all beings
29:15 (14)	a sign unto all beings
29:28 (27)	as never any being in all the world
32:2 (1)	the Book, wherein no doubt is, from the Lord of all Being
37:79 (77)	peace be upon Noah among all beings
37:87 (85)	what think you then of the Lord of all Being?
37:182 (182)	praise belongs to God, the Lord of all Being
38:87 (87)	a reminder unto all beings
39:75 (75)	praise belongs to God, the Lord of all Being
40:64 (66)	blessed be God, the Lord of all Being
40:65 (67)	praise belongs to God, the Lord of all Being
40:66 (68)	I am commanded to surrender to the Lord of all Being
41:9 (8)	that is the Lord of all Being
43:46 (45)	I am the Messenger of the Lord of all Being
44:32 (31)	We chose them, out of a knowledge, above all beings
45:16 (15)	We preferred them above all beings
45:36 (35)	Lord of the earth, Lord of all Being
56:80 (79)	a sending down from the Lord of all Being
59:16 (16)	I fear God, the Lord of all Being
68:52 (52)	a Reminder unto all beings
69:43 (43)	a sending down from the Lord of all Being
81:27 (27)	a Reminder unto all beings
81:29 (29)	unless God wills, the Lord of all Being
83:6 (6)	mankind shall stand before the Lord of all Being

ʿALAM n.m. (pl. *aʿlām*)~a sign, a land-mark; (f. *ʿalāmah*) a waymark

16:16 (16)	and waymarks; and by the stars they are guided
42:32 (31)	are the ships that run on the sea like landmarks
55:24 (24)	raised up in the sea like land-marks

AʿLAM n.m. (comp. adj)~having greater knowledge, knowing very well

2:140 (134)	have you then greater knowledge, or God?
3:36 (31)	God knew very well what she had given birth to

3:167 (161)	God knows very well the things they hide
4:25 (29)	God knows very well your faith
4:45 (47)	God knows well your enemies
5:61 (66)	God knows very well what they were hiding
6:53 (53)	knows not God very well the thankful?
6:58 (58)	God knows very well the evildoers
6:117 (117)	thy Lord knows very well who goes astray
6:117 (117)	He knows very well the right-guided
6:119 (119)	thy Lord knows very well the transgressors
6:124 (124)	God knows very well where to place His Message
10:40 (41)	Thy Lord knows very well those who do corruption
11:31 (33)	God knows best what is in their hearts
12:77 (77)	God knows very well what you are describing
16:101 (103)	God knows very well what He is sending down
16:125 (126)	thy Lord knows very well those who have gone astray
16:125 (126)	He knows very well those who are guided
17:25 (26)	your Lord knows very well what is in your hearts
17:47 (50)	We know very well how they listen
17:54 (56)	your Lord knows you very well
17:55 (57)	thy Lord knows very well all who are in the heavens
17:84 (86)	your Lord knows very well what man is best guided
18:19 (18)	your Lord knows very well how long
18:21 (20)	their Lord knows of them very well
18:22 (21)	my Lord knows very well their number
18:26 (25)	God knows very well how long they tarried
19:70 (71)	We shall know very well those most deserving
20:104 (104)	We know very well what they will say
22:68 (67)	God knows very well what you are doing
23:96 (98)	we Ourselves know very well that they describe
26:188 (188)	my Lord knows very well what you are doing
28:37 (37)	my Lord knows very well who comes with the guidance
28:56 (56)	God guides whom He wills, and knows very well
28:85 (85)	my Lord knows very well who comes with guidance
29:10 (9)	does not God know very well what is in the breasts
29:32 (31)	We know very well who is in it
39:70 (70)	He knows very well what they do
46:8 (7)	He knows very well what you are pressing upon
50:45 (44)	We know very well what they say
53:30 (31)	thy Lord knows very well those who have gone astray
53:30 (31)	He knows very well those who are guided
53:32 (33)	very well He knows you
53:32 (33)	God knows very well him who is godfearing
60:1 (1)	I know very well what you conceal
60:10 (10)	God knows very well their belief
68:7 (7)	thy Lord knows very well those who have gone astray
68:7 (7)	He knows very well those who are guided
84:23 (23)	God knows very well what they are secreting

ʿALĪM n.m. (adj), (pl. *ʿulamā*ʾ)~one who has knowledge, knower, cunning; All-knowing (Divine attribute)

2:29 (27)	He has knowledge of everything
2:32 (30)	Thou art the All-knowing, the All-wise
2:95 (89)	God knows the evildoers
2:115 (109)	God is All-embracing, All-knowing
2:127 (121)	Thou art the All-hearing, the All-knowing
2:137 (131)	He is the All-hearing, the All-knowing

2:158 (153)	God is All-grateful, All-knowing
2:181 (177)	God is All-hearing, All-knowing
2:215 (211)	God has knowledge of it
2:224 (224)	God is All-hearing, All-knowing
2:227 (227)	God is All-hearing, All-knowing
2:231 (231)	God has knowledge of everything
2:244 (245)	God is All-hearing, All-knowing
2:246 (247)	God has knowledge of the evildoers
2:247 (248)	God is All-embracing, All-knowing
2:256 (257)	God is All-hearing, All-knowing
2:261 (263)	God is All-embracing, All-knowing
2:268 (271)	God is All-embracing, All-knowing
2:273 (274)	God has knowledge of it
2:282 (282)	God has knowledge of everything
2:283 (283)	God has knowledge of the things you do
3:34 (30)	God hears, and knows
3:35 (31)	Thou hearest, and knowest
3:63 (56)	God knows the workers of corruption
3:73 (66)	God is All-embracing, All-knowing
3:92 (86)	whatever thing you expend, God knows of it
3:115 (111)	God knows the godfearing
3:119 (115)	God knows the thoughts in the breasts
3:121 (117)	God is All-hearing, All-knowing
3:154 (148)	God knows the thoughts in the breasts
4:11 (12)	God is All-knowing, All-wise
4:12 (16)	God is All-knowing, All-clement
4:17 (21)	God is All-knowing, All-wise
4:24 (28)	God is All-knowing, All-wise
4:26 (31)	God is All-knowing, All-wise
4:32 (36)	God knows everything
4:35 (39)	God is All-knowing, All-aware
4:39 (43)	God knows them
4:70 (72)	God suffices as One who knows
4:92 (94)	God is All-knowing, All-wise
4:104 (105)	God is All-knowing, All-wise
4:111 (111)	God is ever All-knowing, All-wise
4:127 (126)	whatever good you do, God knows of it
4:147 (146)	God is All-thankful, All-knowing
4:148 (147)	God is All-hearing, All-knowing
4:170 (168)	God is All-knowing, All-wise
4:176 (175)	God has knowledge of everything
5:7 (10)	God knows the thoughts in the breasts
5:54 (59)	God is All-embracing, All-knowing
5:76 (80)	God is the All-hearing, the All-knowing
5:97 (98)	God has knowledge of everything
6:13 (13)	He is the All-hearing, the All-knowing
6:83 (83)	thy Lord is All-wise, All-knowing
6:96 (96)	that is the ordaining of the All-mighty, the All-knowing
6:101 (101)	He has knowledge of everthing
6:115 (115)	He is the All-hearing, the All-knowing
6:128 (128)	thy Lord is All-wise, All-knowing
6:139 (140)	He is All-wise, All-knowing
7:109 (106)	surely this man is a cunning sorcerer
7:112 (109)	to bring thee every cunning sorcerer
7:200 (199)	He is All-hearing, All-knowing

8:17 (17)	All-hearing, All-knowing
8:42 (44)	God is All-hearing, All-knowing
8:43 (45)	He knows the thoughts in the breasts
8:53 (55)	God is All-hearing, All-knowing
8:61 (63)	He is the All-hearing, the All-knowing
8:71 (72)	God is All-knowing, All-wise
8:75 (76)	God has knowledge of everything
9:15 (15)	God is All-knowing, All-wise
9:28 (28)	God is All-knowing, All-wise
9:44 (44)	God knows the godfearing
9:47 (47)	God knows the evildoers
9:60 (60)	God is All-knowing, All-wise
9:97 (98)	God is All-knowing, All-wise
9:98 (99)	God is All-hearing, All-knowing
9:103 (104)	God is All-hearing, All-knowing
9:106 (107)	God is All-knowing, All-wise
9:110 (111)	God is All-knowing, All-wise
9:115 (116)	God knows everything
10:36 (37)	God knows the things they do
10:65 (66)	He is the All-hearing, the All-knowing
10:79 (80)	bring me every cunning sorcerer
11:5 (7)	He knows all the thoughts within the breasts
12:6 (6)	thy Lord is All-knowing, All-wise
12:19 (19)	God knew what they were doing
12:34 (34)	He is the All-hearing, the All-knowing
12:50 (50)	my Lord has knowledge of their guile
12:55 (55)	I am a knowing guardian
12:76 (76)	over every man of knowledge is One who knows
12:83 (83)	He is the All-knowing, the All-wise
12:100 (101)	He is the All-knowing, the All-wise
15:25 (25)	He is All-wise, All-knowing
15:53 (53)	we give thee good tidings of a cunning boy
15:86 (86)	thy Lord, He is the All-creator, the All-knowing
16:28 (30)	God has knowledge of the things you did
16:70 (72)	God is All-knowing, All-powerful
21:4 (4)	He is the All-hearing, the All-knowing
22:52 (51)	God is All-knowing, All-wise
22:59 (58)	God is All-knowing, All-clement
23:51 (53)	surely I know the things you do
24:18 (17)	God is All-knowing, All-wise
24:21 (21)	God is All-hearing, All-knowing
24:28 (28)	God knows the things you do
24:32 (32)	God is All-embracing, All-knowing
24:35 (35)	God has knowledge of everything
24:41 (41)	God knows the things they do
24:58 (57)	God is All-knowing, All-wise
24:59 (58)	God is All-knowing, All-wise
24:60 (59)	God is All-hearing, All-knowing
24:64 (64)	God knows everything
26:34 (33)	this man is a cunning sorcerer
26:37 (36)	to bring thee every cunning sorcerer
26:197 (197)	was it not a sign for them, that it is known to the learned
26:220 (220)	He is the All-hearing, the All-knowing
27:6 (6)	the Koran from One All-wise, All-knowing
27:78 (80)	He is the All-mighty, the All-knowing

29:5 (4)	He is the All-hearing, the All-knowing
29:60 (60)	He is the All-hearer, the All-knower
29:62 (62)	God has knowledge of everything
30:54 (53)	He is the All-knowing, the All-powerful
31:23 (22)	God knows all the thoughts within the breasts
31:34 (34)	God is All-knowing, All-aware
33:1 (1)	God is All-knowing, All-wise
33:40 (40)	God has knowledge of everything
33:51 (51)	God is All-knowing, All-clement
33:54 (54)	God has knowledge of everything
34:26 (25)	He is the Deliverer, the All-knowing
35:8 (9)	God has knowledge of the things they work
35:28 (25)	only those of His servants fear God who have knowledge
35:38 (36)	He knows the thoughts within the breasts
35:44 (43)	He is All-knowing, All-powerful
36:38 (38)	the ordaining of the All-mighty, the All-knowing
36:79 (79)	He knows all creation
36:81 (81)	He is the All-creator, the All-knowing
39:7 (10)	He knows the thoughts within the breasts
40:2 (1)	the Book is from God the All-mighty, the All-knowing
41:12 (11)	the ordaining of the All-mighty, the All-knowing
41:36 (36)	He is the All-hearing, the All-knowing
42:12 (10)	He has knowledge of everything
42:24 (23)	He knows the thoughts within the breasts
42:50 (49)	He is All-knowing, All-powerful
43:9 (8)	The All-mighty, the All-knowing created them
43:84 (84)	He is the All-wise, the All-knowing
44:6 (5)	He is the All-hearing, the All-knowing
48:4 (4)	God is All-knowing, All-wise
48:26 (26)	God has knowledge of everything
49:1 (1)	God is All-hearing, All-knowing
49:8 (8)	God is All-knowing, All-wise
49:13 (13)	God is All-knowing, All-aware
49:16 (16)	God has knowledge of everything
51:28 (28)	they gave him good tidings of a cunning boy
51:30 (30)	He is the All-wise, the All-knowing
57:3 (3)	He has knowledge of everything
57:6 (6)	He knows the thoughts within the breasts
58:7 (8)	God has knowledge of everything
60:10 (10)	God is All-knowing, All-wise
62:7 (7)	God knows the evildoers
64:4 (4)	God knows the thoughts within the breasts
64:11 (11)	God has knowledge of everything
66:2 (2)	He is the All-knowing, the All-wise
66:3 (3)	I was told of it by the All-knowing, the All-aware
67:13 (13)	He knows the thoughts within the breasts
76:30 (30)	God is ever All-knowing, All-wise

ʿALLĀM n.m. (adj)~one who knows, knower

5:109 (108)	Thou art the Knower of the things unseen
5:116 (116)	Thou knowest the things unseen
9:78 (79)	God knows the things unseen
34:48 (47)	the Knower of the Unseen

ᶜALLAMA vb. (II)~to teach; to study (as in 3:79). (pcple. pass.) one who is taught or tutored

a) perf. act.

2:31 (29)	He taught Adam the names
2:32 (30)	we know not save what Thou hast taught us
2:239 (240)	remember God, as He taught you
2:251 (252)	He taught him such as He willed
2:282 (282)	as God has taught him
4:113 (113)	He has taught thee that thou knewest not
5:4 (6)	such hunting creatures as you teach
5:4 (6)	(teaching) them as God has taught you
5:110 (110)	when I taught thee the Book
12:37 (37)	what my Lord has taught me
12:68 (68)	for that We had taught him
12:101 (102)	Thou hast taught me the interpretation
18:65 (64)	We had taught him knowledge proceeding from Us
20:71 (74)	the same that taught you sorcery
21:80 (80)	We taught him the fashioning of garments
26:49 (48)	the same that taught you sorcery
36:69 (69)	We have not taught him poetry
53:5 (5)	taught him by one terrible in power
55:2 (1)	has taught the Koran
55:4 (3)	He has taught him the Explanation
96:4 (4)	who taught by the Pen
96:5 (5)	taught Man that he knew not

b) impf. act. (*yuᶜallimu*)

2:102 (96)	teaching the people sorcery
2:102 (96)	they taught not any man
2:129 (123)	and teach them the Book
2:151 (146)	and to teach you the Book
2:151 (146)	and to teach you that you knew not
2:282 (282)	God teaches you
3:48 (43)	He will teach him the Book
3:79 (73)	the Book, and in that you study
3:164 (158)	teach them the Book
5:4 (6)	teaching them as God has taught you
12:6 (6)	and teach thee the interpretation of tales
12:21 (21)	that We might teach him the interpretation
16:103 (105)	only a mortal is teaching him
18:66 (65)	shall I follow thee so that thou teachest me
49:16 (16)	would you teach God what your religion is
62:2 (2)	and to teach them the Book

d) perf. pass. (*ᶜullima*)

6:91 (91)	you were taught that you knew not
18:66 (65)	thou teachest me, of what thou hast been taught
27:16 (16)	we have been taught the speech of the birds

h) pcple. pass. (*muᶜallam*)

44:14 (13)	a man tutored, possessed

TAᶜALLAMA vb. (V)~to learn

b) impf. act. (*yataᶜallamu*)

2:102 (96)	from them they learned how
2:102 (96)	they learned what hurt them

*ᶜ L N

ᶜALĀNIYAH n.f. (adv)~in public, publicly

2:274 (275)	secretly and in public
13:22 (22)	secretly and in public
14:31 (36)	secretly and in public
35:29 (26)	secretly and in public

Aᶜ LANA vb. (IV)~to publish, to make manifest, to announce, to speak publicly

a) perf. act.

60:1 (1)	what you conceal and what you publish
71:9 (8)	I spoke publicly unto them

b) impf. act. (*yuᶜlinu*)

2:77 (72)	what they keep secret and what they publish
11:5 (6)	what they secrete and what they publish
14:38 (41)	what we keep secret and what we publish
16:19 (19)	what you keep secret and what you publish
16:23 (24)	what they keep secret and what they publish
27:25 (25)	what you conceal and what you publish
27:74 (76)	what their hearts conceal, and what they publish
28:69 (69)	what their breasts conceal and what they publish
36:76 (76)	what they keep secret and what they publish
64:4 (4)	what you conceal and what you publish

*ᶜ L Q

ᶜALAQAH n.f. (pl. *ᶜalaq***)**~blood-clot, a clot

22:5 (5)	then of a sperm-drop, then of a blood-clot
23:14 (14)	We created of the drop a clot
23:14 (14)	We created of the clot a tissue
40:67 (69)	then of a sperm-drop, then of a blood-clot
75:38 (38)	then he was a blood-clot
96:2 (2)	created Man of a blood-clot

ᶜALLAQA vb. (II)~(pcple. pass.) suspended

h) pcple. pass. f. (*muᶜallaqah*)

4:129 (128)	you leave her as it were suspended

*ᶜ L W

ᶜALĀ vb. (I)~to ascend, to rise up, to be high, to exalt one's self. (n.vb.) ascent, height; exaltation, pride, exorbitance. (pcple. act.) one who is high, lofty, sublime; (adv) uppermost, upon

a) perf. act.

17:7 (7)	destroy utterly that which they ascended to
23:91 (93)	some of them would have risen up over others
28:4 (3)	Pharaoh had exalted himself in the land

b) impf. act. (*yaʿlū*)

17:4 (4)	you shall ascend exceeding high
27:31 (31)	rise not up against me
44:19 (18)	rise not up against God

f) n.vb. (*ʿulūw*)

17:4 (4)	you shall ascend <exceeding> high
17:43 (45)	high indeed be He exalted above that they say
27:14 (14)	wrongfully and out of pride
28:83 (83)	those who desire not exorbitance in the earth

g) pcple. act. (*ʿālī*)

10:83 (83)	and Pharaoh was high in the land
11:82 (84)	We turned it uppermost nethermost
15:74 (74)	We turned it uppermost nethermost
23:46 (48)	they were a lofty people
38:75 (76)	hast thou waxed proud, or art thou of the lofty ones?
44:31 (30)	surely he was a high one
69:22 (22)	in a lofty Garden
76:21 (21)	upon them shall be green garments of silk
88:10 (10)	in a sublime Garden

ʿALĪY n.m. (adj), (f. *ʿulá*, comp. *aʿlá*)~high, sublime, lofty, upper one; All-high (Divine attribute)

2:255 (256)	He is the All-high, the All-glorious
3:139 (133)	you shall be the upper ones
4:34 (38)	God is All-high, All-great
9:40 (40)	God's word is the uppermost
16:60 (62)	God's is the loftiest likeness
19:50 (51)	a tongue of truthfulness, sublime
19:57 (58)	We raised him up to a high place
20:4 (3)	Him who created the earth and the high heavens
20:68 (71)	thou art the uppermost
20:75 (77)	for them await the most sublime degrees
22:62 (61)	God is the All-high, the All-great
30:27 (26)	His is the loftiest likeness in the heavens
31:30 (29)	God is the All-high, the All-great
34:23 (22)	He is the All-high, the All-great
37:8 (8)	they listen not to the High Council
38:69 (69)	I had no knowledge of the High Council
40:12 (12)	God, the All-high, the All-great
42:4 (2)	He is the All-high, the All-glorious
42:51 (51)	He is All-high, All-wise
43:4 (3)	the Essence of the Book, with Us; sublime indeed
47:35 (37)	you shall be the upper ones
53:7 (7)	being on the higher horizon
79:24 (24)	I am your Lord, the Most High
87:1 (1)	magnify the Name of thy Lord the Most High
92:20 (20)	the Face of his Lord the Most High

ʿILLĪYŪN n.prop.~Illiyun, probably the name of the highest place in Heaven

83:18 (18)	the book of the pious is in Illiyun
83:19 (19)	what shall teach thee what is Illiyun?

TAʿĀLÁ vb. (VI)~Although this is a regular verb, the perf. form is used, in the Koran, as an optative with the Name of God, or surrogate pronoun, "He". There is no negative form for this verb. to be high, to be exalted; (impv) come; (*taʿālá Allāhu*, or *taʿālá*) High exalted be God, be He exalted (optative). (pcple. act.) one who is exalted; All-exalted (Divine attribute)

a) perf. act. (optative)

6:100 (100)	high be He exalted above what they describe
7:190 (190)	God is high exalted above that they associate
10:18 (19)	high be He exalted above that they associate
16:1 (1)	high be He exalted above that they associate with Him
16:3 (3)	high be He exalted above that they associate with Him
17:43 (45)	high indeed be He exalted above that they say
20:114 (113)	so high exalted be God, the true King
23:92 (94)	high exalted be He, above that they associate
23:116 (117)	high exalted be God, the King, the True
27:63 (64)	high exalted be God, above that which they associate
28:68 (68)	high be He exalted above that they associate
30:40 (39)	high be He exalted above that they associate
39:67 (67)	high be He exalted above that they associate
72:3 (3)	exalted be our Lord's majesty

c) impv. (*taʿāla*)

3:61 (54)	come now, let us call our sons
3:64 (57)	come now to a word common between us
3:167 (160)	come now, fight in the way of God
4:61 (64)	come now to what God has sent down
5:104 (103)	come now to what God has sent down
6:151 (152)	come, I will recite what your Lord has forbidden you
33:28 (28)	if you desire the present life and its adornment, come now
63:5 (5)	when it is said to them, 'Come now'

g) pcple. act. (*mutaʿālī*)

13:9 (10)	the All-great, the All-exalted

ISTAʿLÁ vb. (X)~to gain the upper hand, to be uppermost

a) perf. act.

20:64 (67)	whoever today gains the upper hand

*ʿ M D

ʿIMĀD n.com. (pl. *ʿamad*)~pillar, column

13:2 (2)	God is He who raised up the heavens without pillars
31:10 (9)	He created the heavens without pillars
89:7 (6)	Iram of the pillars
104:9 (9)	in columns outstretched

TAʿAMMADA vb. (V)~to premeditate, to purpose. (pcple. act.) wilfully, on purpose

a) perf. act.

33:5 (5)	only in what your hearts premeditate

g) pcple. act. (*mutaʿammid*)

4:93 (95)	whoso slays a believer wilfully
5:95 (96)	whosoever of you slays it wilfully

*ʿ M H

ʿAMAHA vb. (I)~to wander blindly

b) impf. act. (*yaʿmahu*)

2:15 (14)	lead them on blindly wandering in their insolence
6:110 (110)	in their insolence wandering blindly
7:186 (185)	He leaves them in their insolence blindly wandering
10:11 (12)	in their insolence wandering blindly
15:72 (72)	they wandered blindly in their dazzlement
23:75 (77)	they would persist in their insolence wandering blindly
27:4 (4)	they wander blindly

*ʿ M L

ʿAMILA vb. (I)~to do, to make, to work, to act; (*mā ʿamilat aydīhum*) what their hands wrought, their hands' labour. (n.vb.) work, action, deed. (pcple. act.) one who works, who acts, who does, who labours, etc.

a) perf. act.

2:25 (23)	those who believe and do deeds
2:62 (59)	whoso believes in God and the Last Day, and works righteousness
2:82 (76)	those that believe, and do deeds of righteousness
2:277 (277)	those who believe and do deeds of righteousness
3:30 (28)	every soul shall find what it has done of good
3:30 (28)	and what it has done of evil
3:57 (50)	the believers, who do deeds of righteousness
4:57 (60)	those that believe, and do deeds of righteousness
4:122 (121)	those that believe, and do deeds of righteousness
4:173 (172)	the believers, who do deeds of righteousness
5:9 (12)	those that believe, and do deeds of righteousness
5:69 (73)	and works righteousness
5:93 (94)	those who believe and do deeds of righteousness
5:93 (94)	and believe, and do deeds of righteousness
6:54 (54)	whosoever of you does evil in ignorance
6:132 (132)	all have degrees according to what they have done
7:42 (40)	those who believe, and do deeds of righteousness
7:153 (152)	those who do evil deeds
10:4 (4)	those who believe and do deeds of righteousness
10:9 (9)	those who believe, and do deeds of righteousness
11:11 (14)	such as are patient, and do deeds of righteousness
11:23 (25)	those who believe, and do righteous deeds

13:29 (28)	those who believe and do righteous deeds
14:23 (28)	those who believe, and do deeds of righteousness
16:34 (36)	the evil things that they wrought smote them
16:97 (99)	whosoever does a righteous deed
16:111 (112)	every soul shall be paid in full for what it wrought
16:119 (120)	those who did evil in ignorance
18:30 (29)	those who believe, and do deeds of righteousness
18:49 (47)	they shall find all they wrought present
18:88 (87)	as for him who believes, and does righteousness
18:107 (107)	those who believe, and do deeds of righteousness
19:60 (61)	and does a righteous deed
19:96 (96)	those who believe and do deeds of righteousness
20:75 (77)	a believer having done deeds of righteousness
20:82 (84)	and does righteousness
22:14 (14)	those who believe and do righteous deeds
22:23 (23)	those who believe and do righteous deeds
22:50 (49)	those who believe, and do deeds of righteousness
22:56 (55)	those who believe, and do deeds of righteousness
24:38 (38)	God may recompense them for their fairest works
24:55 (54)	those of you who believe and do righteous deeds
24:64 (64)	He will tell them of what they did
25:23 (25)	what work they have done
25:70 (70)	and does righteous work
25:71 (71)	whosoever repents, and does righteousness
26:227 (227)	those that believe, and do righteous deeds
28:67 (67)	him who repents, and believes, and works righteousness
28:80 (80)	him who believes, and works righteousness
28:84 (84)	those who have done evil deeds
29:7 (6)	those who believe, and do righteous deeds
29:9 (8)	those who believe, and do righteous deeds
29:58 (58)	those who believe, and do righteous deeds
30:15 (14)	those who believed, and did deeds of righteousness
30:41 (40)	that which they have done
30:44 (43)	whosoever does righteousness
30:45 (44)	those who believe and do righteous deeds
31:8 (7)	those who believe, and do deeds of righteousness
31:23 (22)	We shall tell them what they did
32:19 (19)	those who believe, and do deeds of righteousness
34:4 (4)	those who believe, and do righteous deeds
34:37 (36)	except for him who believes, and does righteousness
34:37 (36)	those — there awaits them double recompense for that they did
35:7 (8)	those who believe, and do deeds of righteousness
36:35 (35)	that they might eat of its fruits and their hands' labour
36:71 (71)	We have created for them of that Our hands wrought
38:24 (23)	those who believe, and do deeds of righteousness
38:28 (27)	those who believe and do righteous deeds
39:35 (36)	the worst of what they did
39:70 (70)	paid in full for what it has wrought
40:40 (43)	whosoever does an evil deed
40:40 (43)	whosoever does a righteous deed
40:58 (60)	those who believe and do deeds of righteousness
41:8 (7)	those who believe, and do righteous deeds
41:33 (33)	he who calls unto God and does righteousness
41:46 (46)	whoso does righteousness
41:50 (50)	tell the unbelievers the things they have done

42:22 (21)	those who believe and do righteous deeds
42:23 (22)	servants who believe and do righteous deeds
42:26 (25)	those who believe and do righteous deeds
45:15 (14)	whoso does righteousness
45:21 (20)	those who believe and do righteous deeds
45:30 (29)	those who have believed and done deeds of righteousness
45:33 (32)	the evil deeds that they have done shall appear
46:16 (15)	the best of what they have done
46:19 (18)	according to what they have wrought
47:2 (2)	those who believe and do righteous deeds
47:12 (13)	those who believe and do righteous deeds
48:29 (29)	those of them who believe and do deeds of righteousness
53:31 (32)	those who do evil for what they have done
58:6 (7)	He shall tell them what they did
58:7 (8)	He shall tell them what they have done
64:7 (7)	you shall be told the things you did
65:11 (11)	those who believe and do righteous deeds
84:25 (25)	those that believe, and do righteous deeds
85:11 (11)	those who believe, and do righteous deeds
95:6 (6)	those who believe, and do righteous deeds
98:7 (6)	those who believe, and do righteous deeds
103:3 (3)	those who believe, and do righteous deeds

b) impf. act. (*yaᶜmalu*)

2:74 (69)	God is not heedless of the things you do
2:85 (79)	God is not heedless of the things you do
2:96 (90)	god sees the things they do
2:110 (104)	God sees the things you do
2:134 (128)	you shall not be questioned concerning the things they did
2:140 (134)	God is not heedless of the things you do
2:141 (135)	you shall not be questioned concerning the things they did
2:149 (144)	god is not heedless of the things you do
2:233 (233)	God sees the things you do
2:234 (234)	god is aware of the things you do
2:237 (238)	God sees the things you do
2:265 (267)	God sees the things you do
2:271 (273)	God is aware of the things you do
2:283 (283)	God has knowledge of the things you do
3:98 (93)	God is witness of the things you do
3:99 (94)	God is not heedless of the things you do
3:120 (116)	God encompasses the things they do
3:153 (147)	God is aware of the things you do
3:156 (150)	God sees the things you do
3:163 (157)	God sees the things they do
3:180 (176)	God is aware of the things you do
4:17 (21)	those who do evil in ignorance
4:18 (22)	those who do evil deeds
4:94 (96)	God is aware of the things you do
4:108 (108)	God encompasses the things they do
4:110 (110)	whosoever does evil
4:123 (122)	whosoever does evil
4:124 (123)	whosoever does deeds of righteousness
4:128 (127)	God is aware of the things you do
4:135 (134)	God is aware of the things you do

5:8 (11)	God is aware of the things you do
5:62 (67)	evil is the thing they have been doing
5:66 (70)	evil are the things they do
5:71 (75)	God sees the things they do
5:105 (104)	He will tell you what you were doing
6:43 (43)	Satan decked out fair to them what they were doing
6:60 (60)	He will tell you of what you have been doing
6:88 (88)	it would have failed them, the things they did
6:108 (108)	He will tell them what they have been doing
6:122 (122)	it is decked out fair to the unbelievers the things they have done
6:127 (127)	He is their Protector for that they were doing
6:132 (132)	thy Lord is not heedless of the things they do
7:43 (41)	your inheritance for what you did
7:53 (51)	shall we be returned, to do other than that we have (done)
7:53 (51)	shall we be returned, (to do) other than that we have done
7:118 (115)	false was proved what they were doing
7:129 (126)	He may behold how you shall do
7:139 (135)	void is what they have been doing
7:147 (145)	according to the things they have done
7:180 (179)	they shall assuredly be recompensed for the things they did
8:39 (40)	surely God sees the things they do
8:47 (49)	God encompasses the things they do
8:72 (73)	God sees the things you do
9:9 (9)	truly evil is that they have been doing
9:16 (16)	God is aware of what you do
9:94 (95)	He will tell you what you were doing
9:105 (106)	He will tell you what you were doing
9:121 (122)	God may recompense them the best of what they were doing
10:12 (13)	that they have been doing
10:14 (15)	We might behold how you would do
10:23 (24)	We shall tell you what you were doing
10:41 (42)	you are quit of what I do
10:41 (42)	and I am quit of what you do
10:61 (62)	nor do you any work
11:16 (19)	void will be their works
11:78 (80)	they had been doing evil deeds
11:92 (94)	My Lord encompasses the things you do
11:111 (113)	He is aware of the things they do
11:112 (114)	He sees the things you do
11:123 (123)	thy Lord is not heedless of the things you do
12:19 (19)	God knew what they were doing
12:69 (69)	do not dispair of that they have done
14:42 (43)	deem not that God is heedless of what the evildoers work
15:93 (93)	concerning that they were doing
16:28 (30)	we were doing nothing evil
16:28 (30)	God has knowledge of the things you did
16:32 (34)	enter Paradise for that you were doing
16:93 (95)	you will surely be questioned about the things you wrought
16:96 (98)	according to the best of what they did
16:97 (99)	according to the best of what they did
17:9 (10)	who do deeds of righteousness
17:84 (86)	every man works according to his own manner
18:2 (2)	unto the believers, who do righteous deeds
18:79 (78)	certain poor men, who toiled upon the sea
18:110 (110)	work righteousness, and not associate with his Lord's service anyone

20:112 (111)	whosoever does deeds of righteousness
21:27 (27)	and perform as He commands
21:74 (74)	the city that had been doing deeds of corruption
21:82 (82)	and did other work besides
21:94 (94)	whosoever does deeds of righteousness
22:68 (67)	God knows very well what you are doing
23:51 (53)	I know the things you do
23:100 (102)	haply I shall do righteousness
24:24 (24)	touching that they were doing
24:28 (28)	God knows the things you do
24:53 (52)	God is aware of the things you do
26:112 (112)	what knowledge have I of that they have been doing
26:169 (169)	deliver me and my people from that they do
26:188 (188)	my Lord knows very well what you are doing
26:216 (216)	I am quit of that you do
27:19 (19)	that I may do righteousness well-pleasing to Thee
27:84 (86)	or what have you been doing?
27:90 (92)	are you recompensed but for what you did?
27:93 (95)	thy Lord is not heedless of the things you do
28:84 (84)	be recompensed for that they were doing
29:4 (3)	those who do evil deeds
29:7 (6)	recompense them the best of what they were doing
29:8 (7)	I shall tell you what you were doing
29:55 (55)	taste now what you were doing
31:15 (14)	I shall tell you what you were doing
31:29 (28)	God is aware of what you do
32:12 (12)	that we may do righteousness
32:14 (14)	taste the chastisement of eternity for that you were doing
32:17 (17)	a recompense for that they were doing
32:19 (19)	in hospitality for that they were doing
33:2 (2)	God is aware of the things you do
33:9 (9)	God sees the things you do
33:31 (31)	and does righteousness
34:11 (10)	I see the things you do
34:12 (11)	of the jinn, some worked before him
34:13 (12)	fashioning for him whatsoever he would
34:25 (24)	shall we be questioned as to what you do
34:33 (32)	except for what they were doing
35:37 (34)	bring us forth, and we will do righteousness
35:37 (34)	righteousness, other than what we have done
36:54 (54)	according to what you have been doing
37:39 (38)	according to what you were doing
37:61 (59)	let the workers work
37:96 (94)	God created you and what you make
39:7 (9)	He will tell you what you have been doing
39:35 (36)	the wages of the fairest of what they were doing
41:20 (19)	concerning what they have been doing
41:22 (21)	much of the things that you were working
41:27 (27)	the worst of what they were working
41:40 (40)	He sees the things you do
43:72 (72)	the things that you were doing
45:28 (27)	you shall be recompensed for that you were doing
45:29 (28)	We have been registering all that you were doing
46:14 (13)	a recompense for that they have been doing
46:15 (14)	I may do righteousness well-pleasing to Thee

48:11 (11)	God is ever aware of the things you do
48:24 (24)	God sees the things you do
49:18 (18)	God sees the things you do
52:16 (16)	you are only being recompensed for that you were working
52:19 (19)	for that you were working
56:24 (23)	a recompense for that they laboured
57:4 (4)	God sees the things you do
57:10 (10)	God is aware of the things you do
58:3 (4)	God is aware of the things you do
58:11 (12)	God is aware of the things you do
58:13 (14)	God is aware of the things you do
58:15 (16)	evil are the things they have been doing
59:18 (18)	God is aware of the things you do
60:3 (3)	God sees the things you do
62:8 (8)	He will tell you that you have been doing
63:2 (2)	evil are the things they have been doing
63:11 (11)	God is aware of the things you do
64:2 (2)	God sees the things you do
64:8 (8)	God is aware of the things you do
64:9 (9)	whosoever believes in God, and does righteousness
65:11 (11)	whosoever believes in God, and does righteousness
66:7 (7)	you are only being recompensed for what you were doing
77:43 (43)	for that you were working
99:7 (7)	whoso has done an atom's weight of good
99:8 (8)	whoso has done an atom's weight of evil

c) impv. (*iʿmal*)

6:135 (135)	act according to your station
9:105 (106)	Work; and God will surely see your work
11:93 (95)	act according to your station
11:121 (122)	act you according to your station
23:51 (53)	eat of the good things and do righteousness
34:11 (10)	fashion wide coats of mail
34:11 (10)	do ye righteousness
34:13 (12)	labour, O House of David, in thankfulness
39:39 (40)	act according to your station; I am acting
41:5 (4)	so act; we are acting
41:40 (40)	do what you will

f) n.vb. (*ʿamal*, pl. *aʿmāl*)

2:139 (133)	our deeds belong to us
2:139 (133)	to you belong your deeds
2:167 (162)	God shall show them their works
2:217 (214)	their works have failed in this world
3:22 (21)	their works have failed in this world
3:195 (193)	I waste not the labour of any that labours among you
5:5 (7)	whoso disbelieves in the faith, his work has failed
5:53 (58)	their works have failed
5:90 (92)	some of Satan's work; so avoid it
6:108 (108)	We have decked out fair to every nation their deeds
7:147 (145)	their works have failed
8:48 (50)	Satan decked out their deeds fair to them
9:17 (17)	their works have failed them
9:37 (37)	decked out fair to them are their evil deeds

9:69 (70)	their works have failed in this world
9:94 (95)	God will surely see your work
9:102 (103)	they have mixed a righteous deed with another evil
9:105 (106)	God will surely see your work
9:120 (121)	a righteous deed is thereby written to their account
10:41 (42)	I have my work
10:41 (42)	and you have your work
10:61 (62)	nor do you any work
10:81 (81)	God sets not right the work of those who do corruption
11:7 (9)	He might try you, which one of you is fairer in works
11:15 (18)	pay them in full for their works therein
11:46 (48)	it is a deed not righteous
11:111 (113)	thy Lord will pay them in full for their works
14:18 (21)	their works are as ashes
16:63 (65)	Satan decked out fair to them their deeds
18:7 (6)	try which of them is fairest in works
18:30 (29)	the wage of him who does good works
18:103 (103)	who will be the greatest losers in their works
18:105 (105)	their works have failed
18:110 (110)	him, who hopes for the encounter with his Lord, work righteousness
21:82 (82)	some dived for him and did other work besides
23:63 (65)	they have deeds besides that that they are doing
24:39 (39)	their works are as a mirage in a spacious plain
25:23 (25)	We shall advance upon what work they have done
25:70 (70)	him who repents, and believes, and does righteous work
26:168 (168)	I am a detester of what you do
27:4 (4)	We have decked out fair for them their works
27:24 (24)	Satan has decked out fair their deeds to them
28:15 (14)	this is of Satan's doing
28:55 (55)	we have our deeds
28:55 (55)	and you your deeds
29:38 (37)	Satan decked out fair to them their works
33:19 (19)	God has made their works to fail
33:71 (71)	He will set right your deeds for you
35:8 (9)	the evil of whose deeds has been decked out fair to him
35:10 (11)	and the righteous deed — He uplifts it
39:65 (65)	thy work shall surely fail
40:37 (40)	the evil of his deeds was decked out fair to Pharaoh
42:15 (14)	we have our deeds
42:15 (14)	and you have your deeds
46:19 (18)	He may pay them in full for their works
47:1 (1)	God will send their works astray
47:4 (5)	He will not send their works astray
47:8 (9)	He will send their works astray
47:9 (10)	He has made their works to fail
47:14 (15)	unto whom his evil deeds have been decked out fair
47:28 (30)	He has made their works to fail
47:30 (32)	God knows your deeds
47:32 (34)	He will make their works to fail
47:33 (35)	do not make your own works vain
47:35 (37)	and will not deprive you of your works
49:2 (2)	lest your works fail while you are not aware
49:14 (14)	He will not diminish you anything of your works
52:21 (21)	We shall not defraud them of aught of their work
66:11 (11)	deliver me from Pharaoh and his work

67:2 (2)	He might try you which of you is fairest in works
99:6 (6)	men shall issue in scatterings to see their works

g) pcple. act. (*ʿāmil*)

3:136 (130)	how excellent is the wage of those who labour
3:195 (193)	I waste not the labour of any that labours among you
6:135 (135)	I am acting
9:60 (60)	those who work to collect
11:93 (95)	I am acting
11:121 (122)	we are acting
23:63 (65)	they have deeds besides that that they are doing
29:58 (58)	excellent is the wage of those who labour
37:61 (59)	for the like of this let the workers work
39:39 (40)	I am acting
39:74 (74)	how excellent is the wage of those that labour
41:5 (4)	we are acting
88:3 (3)	labouring, toilworn

*ʿ M M

ʿAMM n.m. (pl. *aʿmām*)~uncle paternal

24:61 (60)	the houses of your uncles or your aunts paternal
33:50 (49)	the daughters of thy uncles paternal and aunts paternal

ʿAMMAH n.f. (pl. *ʿammāt*)~aunt paternal

4:23 (27)	your sisters, your aunts paternal
24:61 (60)	the houses of your uncles or your aunts paternal
33:50 (49)	the daughters of thy uncles paternal and aunts paternal

*ʿ M Q

ʿAMĪQ n.m. (adj)~deep

22:27 (28)	they shall come from every deep ravine

*ʿ M R

ʿAMARA vb. (I)~to build upon; to inhabit; to cultivate; to perform the sacred visitation (to Mecca). (pcple. pass.) inhabited; visited frequently

a) perf. act.

30:9 (8)	they ploughed up the earth and cultivated it
30:9 (8)	they themselves have cultivated it

b) impf. act. (*yaʿmuru*)

9:17 (17)	it is not for the idolaters to inhabit God's places of worship
9:18 (18)	only he shall inhabit God's places of worship

h) pcple. pass. (*maʿmūr*)

52:4 (4)	by the House inhabited

ʿAMR n.m. (used usually in an oath formula, *la-ʿamrika*)~life

15:72 (72)	by thy life, they wandered blindly

ʿIMĀRAH n.f.~visiting; inhabiting; tendance

9:19 (19)	the inhabiting of the Holy Mosque

ʿIMRĀN n.prop.~Imran

3:33 (30)	the House of Abraham and the House of Imran
3:35 (31)	the wife of Imran said, 'Lord, I have vowed to Thee'
66:12 (12)	Mary, Imran's daughter, who guarded her virginity

ʿUMRAH n.f.~the sacred visitation (to Mecca)

2:196 (192)	fulfil the Pilgrimage and the Visitation unto God
2:196 (192)	whosoever enjoys the Visitation until the Pilgrimage

ʿUMUR n.m.~life, lifetime, age

10:16 (17)	I abode among you a lifetime
16:70 (72)	some of you will be kept back unto the vilest state of life
21:44 (45)	enjoyment of days, until their life had lasted
22:5 (5)	some of you are kept back unto the vilest state of life
26:18 (17)	didst thou not tarry among us years of thy life?
28:45 (45)	We raised up generations, and long their lives continued
35:11 (12)	neither is any diminished in his life

ʿAMMARA vb. (II)~to give one a long life, to spare one's life. (pcple. pass.) one who is given a long life

b) impf. act. (*yuʿammiru*)

35:37 (34)	did We not give you long life
36:68 (68)	to whomsoever We give long life

e) impf. pass. (*yuʿammaru*)

2:96 (90)	one of them wishes if he might be spared a thousand years
2:96 (90)	yet his being spared alive shall not remove him
35:11 (12)	none is given long life

h) pcple. pass. (*muʿammar*)

35:11 (12)	who is given long life

IʿTAMARA vb. (VIII)~to visit (Mecca)

a) perf. act.

2:158 (153)	whosoever makes the Pilgrimage to the House

ISTAʿMARA vb. (X)~to make one live, to settle someone

a) perf. act.

11:61 (64)	He who produced you from the earth and has given you to live therein

*ᶜ M Y

ᶜAMIYA vb. (I)~to be blind, to be in darkness or dimness, to be obscure

a) perf. act.

5:71 (75)	but blind they were, and deaf
5:71 (75)	then again blind they were
6:104 (104)	whoso is blind, it is to his own loss
28:66 (66)	the tidings will be darkened for them

b) impf. act. (*yaᶜmâ*)

22:46 (45)	it is not the eyes that are blind
22:46 (45)	but blind are the hearts within the breasts

ᶜAMÁ n.m.~blindness, blindness of heart

41:17 (16)	they preferred blindness above guidance
41:44 (44)	in their ears is a heaviness, and to them it is a blindness

AᶜMÁ n.m. (pl. *ᶜumī*)~blind, dark, blind at heart

2:18 (17)	deaf, dumb, blind
2:171 (166)	deaf, dumb, blind
6:50 (50)	are the blind and the seeing man equal?
10:43 (44)	wilt thou then guide the blind
11:24 (26)	as the man blind and deaf
13:16 (17)	are the blind and the seeing man equal
13:19 (19)	like him who is blind
17:72 (74)	whosoever is blind in this world
17:72 (74)	shall be blind in the world to come
17:97 (99)	blind, dumb, deaf
20:124 (124)	We shall raise him blind
20:125 (125)	why hast thou raised me blind
24:61 (60)	there is no fault in the blind
25:73 (73)	fall not down thereat deaf and blind
27:81 (83)	thou shalt not guide the blind out of their error
30:53 (52)	thou shalt not guide the blind out of their error
35:19 (20)	not equal are the blind and the seeing man
40:58 (60)	not equal are the blind and the seeing man
43:40 (39)	or shalt thou guide the blind
48:17 (17)	there is no fault in the blind
80:2 (2)	the blind man came to him

ᶜAMĪ n.m. (adj), (pl. *ᶜamūn*)~blind

7:64 (62)	they were a blind people
27:66 (68)	they are blind to it

ᶜAMMÁ vb. (II)~to blind, to hide from, to conceal, to keep in the dark

d) perf. pass. (*ᶜummiya*)

11:28 (30)	it has been obscured for you

AᶜMÁ vb. (IV)~to blind

a) perf. act.

47:23 (25)	and so made them deaf, and blinded their eyes

*ᶜ N B

ᶜINAB n.m. (pl. *aᶜnāb*)~vine, grapes

2:266 (268)	would any of you wish to have a garden of palms and vines
6:99 (99)	gardens of vines
13:4 (4)	gardens of vines
16:11 (11)	for you crops, and olives, and palms, and vines
16:67 (69)	of the fruits of the palms and the vines, you take therefrom an intoxicant
17:91 (93)	till thou possessest a garden of palms and vines
18:32 (31)	We assigned two gardens of vines
23:19 (19)	We produced for you therewith gardens of palms and vines
36:34 (34)	We made therein gardens of palms and vines
78:32 (32)	gardens and vineyards
80:28 (28)	and vines, and reeds

*ᶜ N D

ᶜANĪD n.m. (adj)~froward, stubborn, constumacious

11:59 (62)	and followed the command of every froward tyrant
14:15 (18)	then was disappointed every froward tyrant
50:24 (23)	into Gehenna every froward unbeliever
74:16 (16)	he is froward unto Our signs

*ᶜ N K B

ᶜANKABŪT n.com.~spider

29:41 (40)	as the likeness of the spider
29:41 (40)	the frailest of houses is the house of the spider

*ᶜ N Q

ᶜUNUQ n.com. (pl. *aᶜnāq*)~neck

8:12 (12)	so smite above the necks
13:5 (6)	those — on their necks are fetters
17:13 (14)	We have fastened to him his bird of omen upon his neck
17:29 (31)	keep not thy hand chained to thy neck
26:4 (3)	a sign, so their necks will stay humbled
34:33 (32)	We put fetters on the necks of the unbelievers
36:8 (7)	We have put on their necks fetters
38:33 (32)	he began to stroke their shanks and necks
40:71 (73)	when the fetters and chains are on their necks

*ᶜ N T

ᶜANITA vb. (I)~to be hampered, to suffer, to fall into misfortune or ruin. (n.vb.) fornication [Ar]; sin [Pk, Ali, Bl]

a) perf. act.

3:118 (114)	to ruin you; they yearn for you to suffer
9:128 (129)	grievous to him is your suffering
49:7 (7)	if he obeyed you in much of the affair, you would suffer

f) n.vb. (*ᶜanat*)

4:25 (30)	that provision is for those of you who fear fornication

AʿNATA vb. (IV)~to destroy, to cause hardship to befall, to overburden

a) perf. act.

2:220 (219)	had He willed He would have harassed you

*ʿ N W

ʿANĀ vb. (I)~to be humble

a) perf. act.

20:111 (110)	faces shall be humbled unto the Living

*ʿ Q B

ʿAQABAH n.f.~steep, ascent

90:11 (11)	yet he has not assaulted the steep
90:12 (12)	what shall teach thee what is the steep?

ʿAQIB n.com. (pl. *aʿqāb*)~posterity, heel; (*ʿalá ʿaqibihi*) upon his heels

2:143 (138)	who followed the Messenger from him who turned on his heels
3:144 (138)	will you turn about on your heels?
3:144 (138)	if any man should turn about on his heels
3:149 (142)	if you obey the unbelievers they will turn you upon your heels
6:71 (70)	and shall we be turned back on our heels
8:48 (50)	he withdrew upon his heels
23:66 (68)	upon your heels you withdrew
43:28 (27)	he made it a word enduring among his posterity

ʿĀQIBAH n.f.~end, result, issue

3:137 (131)	behold how was the end of those that cried lies
6:11 (11)	how was the end of them that cried lies
6:135 (136)	who shall possess the Abode Ultimate
7:84 (82)	so behold thou, how was the end of the sinners
7:86 (84)	how was the end of the workers of corruption
7:103 (101)	how was the end of the workers of corruption
7:128 (125)	the issue ultimate is to the godfearing
10:39 (40)	how was the end of the evildoers
10:73 (74)	how was the end of them that were warned
11:49 (51)	the issue ultimate is to the godfearing
12:109 (109)	how was the end of those before them
16:36 (38)	how was the end of them that cried lies
20:132 (132)	the issue ultimate is to godfearing
22:41 (42)	unto God belongs the issue of all affairs
27:14 (14)	how was the end of the workers of corruption
27:51 (52)	how was the end of their device
27:69 (71)	how was the end of the sinners
28:37 (37)	and shall possess the Ultimate Abode
28:40 (40)	how was the end of the evildoers
28:83 (83)	the issue ultimate is to the godfearing
30:9 (8)	and beheld how was the end of those before them
30:10 (9)	the end of those that did evil was evil
30:42 (41)	how was the end of those that were before

31:22 (21)	unto God is the issue of all affairs
35:44 (43)	how was the end of those before them?
37:73 (71)	how was the end of them that were warned
40:21 (22)	how was the end of those before them?
40:82 (82)	how was the end of those before them?
43:25 (24)	how was the end of them that cried lies
47:10 (11)	how was the end of those before them?
59:17 (17)	their end is
65:9 (9)	the end of its affair was loss

ʿIQĀB n.m. (see *ʿāqaba*, below)~retribution, punishment, requital

2:196 (192)	know that God is terrible in retribution
2:211 (207)	God is terrible in retribution
3:11 (9)	God is terrible in retribution
5:2 (3)	God is terrible in retribution
5:98 (98)	know God is terrible in retribution
6:165 (165)	thy Lord is swift in retribution
7:167 (166)	thy Lord is swift in retribution
8:13 (13)	God is terrible in retribution
8:25 (25)	God is terrible in retribution
8:48 (50)	God is terrible in retribution
8:52 (54)	God is strong, terrible in retribution
13:6 (7)	thy Lord is terrible in retribution
13:32 (32)	how was my retribution?
38:14 (13)	so My retribution was just
40:3 (2)	Accepter of penitence, Terrible in retribution
40:5 (5)	and how was My retribution
40:22 (23)	He is All-strong, terrible in retribution
41:43 (43)	thy Lord is a Lord of forgiveness and of painful retribution
59:4 (4)	God is terrible in retribution
59:7 (7)	God is terrible in retribution

ʿUQB n.m.~consequence, issue, success

18:44 (42)	He is best rewarding, best in the issue

ʿUQBÁ n.f.~end, issue, ultimate, requital, reward

13:22 (22)	theirs shall be the Ultimate Abode
13:24 (24)	fair is the Ultimate Abode
13:35 (35)	that is the requital of the godfearing
13:35 (35)	the requital of the unbelievers is — the Fire
13:42 (42)	whose will be the Ultimate Abode
91:15 (15)	He fears not the issue thereof

ʿAQQABA vb. (II)~to turn back, to retrace one's steps. (pcple. act.) one who puts off, reverses, repels or postpones; (*muʿaqqibāt*) Angels

b) impf. act. (*yuʿaqqibu*)

27:10 (10)	he turned about, retreating, and turned not back
28:31 (31)	he turned about retreating, and turned not back

g) pcple. act. (*muʿaqqib*)

13:11 (12)	he has attendant angels, before him and behind him
13:41 (41)	none repels His judgment

ʿĀQABA vb. (III)~to punish, to chastise, to retaliate

a) perf. act.

16:126 (127)	if you chastise, chastise even as you have been chastised
22:60 (59)	whosoever chastises after the manner that he was chastised
60:11 (11)	and then you retaliate

c) impv. (*ʿāqib*)

16:126 (127)	if you (chastise), chastise even as you have been (chastised)

d) perf. pass. (*ʿūqiba*)

16:126 (127)	if you (chastise), (chastise) even as you have been chastised
22:60 (59)	after the manner that he was chastised

AʿQABA vb. (IV)~to do as a consequence, to cause to follow

a) perf. act.

9:77 (78)	as a consequence He put hypocrisy into their hearts

*ᶜ Q D

ʿAQADA vb. (I)~to tie a knot; to make or swear a compact

a) perf. act.

4:33 (37)	those with whom you have sworn compact
5:89 (91)	He will take you to task for such bonds as you have made by oaths

ʿAQD n.m. (pl. *ʿuqūd*)~a compact, a bond

5:1 (1)	O believers, fulfil your bonds

ʿUQDAH n.f. (pl. *ʿuqad*)~a knot, a tie

2:235 (236)	do not resolve on the knot of marriage
2:237 (238)	he makes remission in whose hand is the knot of marriage
20:27 (28)	unloose the knot upon my tongue
113:4 (4)	the evil of the women who blow on knots

*ᶜ Q L

ʿAQALA vb. (I)~to understand, to comprehend; to be prudent, sagacious

a) perf. act.

2:75 (70)	and that after they had comprehended it, wittingly

b) impf. act. (*yaʿqilu*)

2:44 (41)	do you not understand?
2:73 (68)	that haply you may have understanding
2:76 (71)	have you no understanding?
2:164 (159)	there are signs for a people having understanding
2:170 (165)	if their fathers had no understanding

2:171 (166)	they do not understand
2:242 (243)	haply you will understand
3:65 (58)	have you no reason?
3:118 (114)	We have made clear to you the signs, if you understand
5:58 (63)	they are a people who have no understanding
5:103 (102)	most of them have no understanding
6:32 (32)	do you not understand?
6:151 (152)	haply you will understand
7:169 (168)	do you not understand?
8:22 (22)	those that are deaf and dumb and do not understand
10:16 (17)	will you not understand?
10:42 (43)	the deaf to hear, though they understand not
10:100 (100)	abomination upon those who have no understanding
11:51 (53)	will you not understand?
12:2 (2)	haply you will understand
12:109 (109)	do you not understand?
13:4 (4)	in that are signs for a people who understand
16:12 (12)	in that are signs for a people who understand
16:67 (69)	in that is a sign for a people who understand
21:10 (10)	will you not understand?
21:67 (67)	do you not understand?
22:46 (45)	they have hearts to understand with
23:80 (82)	will you not understand?
24:61 (61)	haply you will understand
25:44 (46)	deemest thou that most of them hear or understand?
26:28 (27)	if you have understanding
28:60 (60)	will you not understand?
29:35 (34)	a clear sign, unto a people who understand
29:43 (42)	none understands them save those who know
29:63 (63)	Nay, but most of them have no understanding
30:24 (23)	signs for a people who understand
30:28 (27)	the signs for a people who understand
36:62 (62)	did you not understand?
36:68 (68)	do they not understand?
37:138 (138)	will you not understand?
39:43 (44)	they have no power whatever and no understanding
40:67 (69)	haply you will understand
43:3 (2)	haply you will understand
45:5 (4)	there are signs for a people who understand
49:4 (4)	most of them do not understand
57:17 (16)	that haply you will understand
59:14 (14)	they are a people who have no sense
67:10 (10)	if we had only heard, or had understood

*ᶜ Q M

ᶜAQĪM n.m. (adj)~barren, withering

22:55 (54)	the chastisement of a barren day
42:50 (49)	He makes whom He will barren
51:29 (29)	an old woman, barren
51:41 (41)	We loosed against them the withering wind

*ᶜ Q R

ᶜAQARA vb. (I)~to wound, to hamstring

a) perf. act.

7:77 (75)	so they hamstrung the She-camel
11:65 (68)	they hamstrung her
26:157 (157)	they hamstrung her
54:29 (29)	he took in hand, and hamstrung her
91:14 (14)	they cried him lies, and hamstrung her

ᶜĀQIR n.f. (adj)~barren (woman)

3:40 (35)	I am an old man and my wife is barren
19:5 (5)	my wife is barren
19:8 (9)	shall I have a son, seeing my wife is barren

*ᶜ R B

AᶜRĀB n.m. (pl.; no sing)~nomads, bedouins

9:90 (91)	Bedouins came with their excuses
9:97 (98)	Bedouins are more stubborn in unbelief
9:98 (99)	some of the Bedouins take what they expend
9:99 (100)	some of the Bedouins believe in God
9:101 (102)	some of the Bedouins who dwell around you
9:120 (121)	for the Bedouins who dwell around them
33:20 (20)	they were desert-dwellers among the Bedouins
48:11 (11)	the Bedouins who were left behind
48:16 (16)	say to the Bedouins who were left
49:14 (14)	the Bedouins say, 'We believe'

ᶜARABĪY n.m. (adj)~Arabic

12:2 (2)	We have sent it down as an Arabic Koran
13:37 (37)	We have sent it down as an Arabic judgment
16:103 (105)	this is speech Arabic
20:113 (112)	We have sent it down as an Arabic Koran
26:195 (195)	in a clear, Arabic tongue
39:28 (29)	an Arabic Koran, wherein there is no crookedness
41:3 (2)	an Arabic Koran for a people having knowledge
41:44 (44)	what, barbarous and Arabic?
42:7 (5)	We have revealed to thee an Arabic Koran
43:3 (2)	We have made it an Arabic Koran
46:12 (11)	this is a Book confirming, in Arabic tongue

ᶜURUB n.f. (pl. of *ᶜarūb*)~beloved, loving, amorous

56:37 (36)	chastely amorous, like of age

*ᶜ R Ḍ

ᶜARAḌA vb. (I)~to present, to offer. (n.vb.) presenting, offering; breadth

a) perf. act.

2:31 (29)	He presented them unto the angels
18:100 (100)	We shall present Gehenna to the unbelievers
33:72 (72)	We offered the trust to the heavens

d) perf. pass. (*ʿuriḍa*)

18:48 (46) they shall be presented before their Lord
38:31 (30) in the evening were presented to him the standing steeds

e) impf. pass. (*yuʿraḍu*)

11:18 (21) those shall be presented before their Lord
40:46 (49) the Fire, to which they shall be exposed
42:45 (44) thou shalt see them, as they are exposed to it
46:20 (19) the day when the unbelievers are exposed to the Fire
46:34 (33) the day when the unbelievers are exposed to the Fire
69:18 (18) on that day you shall be exposed

f) n.vb. (*ʿarḍ*)

3:133 (127) a garden whose breadth is as the heavens
18:100 (100) We shall present Gehenna to the unbelievers
57:21 (21) a Garden the breadth whereof
57:21 (21) as the breadth of heaven

ʿARAḌ n.m.~temporal or chance goods, advantage

4:94 (96) seeking the chance goods of the present life
7:169 (168) taking the chance goods of this lower world
7:169 (168) if chance goods the like of them come to them
8:67 (68) you desire the chance goods of the present world
9:42 (42) were it a gain near at hand, and an easy journey
24:33 (33) seek the chance goods of the present life

ʿARĪḌ n.m. (adj)~full of, abounding

41:51 (51) he is full of endless prayers

ʿĀRIḌ n.m.~a sudden or passing cloud

46:24 (23) they saw it as a sudden cloud
46:24 (23) this is a cloud, that shall give us rain

ʿURḌAH n.f.~hindrance, impediment

2:224 (224) do not make God a hindrance

ʿARRAḌA vb. (II)~(with prep. *bi-*) to offer

a) perf. act.

2:235 (235) the proposal to women you offer

AʿRAḌA vb. (IV)~to turn away or aside, to swerve; to decline to do a thing; (also with prep. *ʿan*) to suffer someone to be. (n.vb.) turning away, aversion. (pcple. act.) one who turns away or aside from; turning or swerving aside

a) perf. act.

17:67 (69) when He delivers you to land, you turn away
17:83 (85) when We bless man, he turns away
18:57 (55) (who) turns away from them
20:100 (100) whosoever turns away from it
20:124 (123) whosoever turns away from My remembrance
28:55 (55) when they hear idle talk, they turn away from it
32:22 (22) then [he] turns away from them

34:16 (15)	but they turned away
41:4 (3)	most of them have turned away
41:13 (12)	but if they turn away
41:51 (51)	when We bless man, he turns away
42:48 (47)	but if they turn away
66:3 (3)	he made known part of it, and turned aside

b) impf. act. (*yuʿriḍu*)

4:135 (134)	if you twist or turn, God is aware of things you do
5:42 (46)	if thou turnest away from them
9:95 (96)	that you may turn aside from them
17:28 (30)	if thou turnest from them
54:2 (2)	if they see a sign they turn away
72:17 (17)	whosoever turns away from the Remembrance of his Lord

c) impv. (*aʿriḍ*)

4:16 (20)	punish them both; but if they repent and make amends, then suffer them to be
4:63 (66)	so turn away from them, and admonish them
4:81 (83)	so turn away from them
5:42 (46)	judge thou between them, or turn away from them
6:68 (67)	turn away from them until they plunge
6:106 (106)	turn thou away from the idolaters
7:199 (198)	turn away from the ignorant
9:95 (96)	so turn aside from them
11:76 (78)	O Abraham, turn away from this
12:29 (29)	Joseph, turn away from this
15:94 (94)	turn thou away from the idolaters
32:30 (30)	so turn thou away from them
53:29 (30)	turn thou from him who turns away from Our Remembrance

f) n.vb. (*iʿrāḍ*)

4:128 (127)	if a woman fear rebelliousness or aversion in her husband
6:35 (35)	if their turning away is distressful for thee

g) pcple. act. (*muʿriḍ*)

2:83 (77)	then you turned away, all but a few of you, swerving aside
3:23 (22)	then a party of them turned away, swerving aside
6:4 (4)	they turn away from it
8:23 (23)	they would have turned away, swerving aside
9:76 (77)	they were niggardly of it, and turned away, swerving aside
12:105 (105)	they pass by, turning away from it
15:81 (81)	they turned away from them
21:1 (1)	while they in heedlessness are yet turning away
21:24 (24)	so therefore they are turning away
21:32 (33)	yet still from Our signs they are turning away
21:42 (43)	from the Remembrance of their Lord they are turning away
23:3 (3)	from idle talk turn away
23:71 (73)	from their Remembrance they turned
24:48 (47)	a party of them are swerving aside
26:5 (4)	they turn away from it
36:46 (46)	they are turning away from it
38:68 (68)	from which you are turning away
46:3 (2)	unbelievers are turning away from that they were warned of
74:49 (50)	they turn away from the Reminder

*ᶜ R F

ᶜARAFA vb. (I)~to know, to recognize, to discern. (pcple. pass.) that which is known or recognized; reason; (adj) honourable

a) perf. act.

2:89 (83)	there came to them that they recognized
5:83 (86)	because of the truth they recognize
12:58 (58)	and [they] entered unto him, and he knew them
47:30 (32)	thou wouldst know them by their mark

b) impf. act. (*yaᶜrifu*)

2:146 (141)	We have given the Book, and they recognize it
2:146 (141)	as they recognize their sons
2:273 (274)	thou shalt know them by their mark
6:20 (20)	those to whom We have given the Book recognize it
6:20 (20)	([they] recognize it) as they recognize their sons
7:46 (44)	on the Ramparts are men knowing each by their mark
7:48 (46)	certain men they know by their sign
12:62 (62)	haply they will recognize it
16:83 (85)	they recognize the blessing of God
22:72 (71)	thou recognisest in the faces of the unbelievers denial
23:69 (71)	did they not recognise their Messenger
27:93 (95)	and you will recognise them
47:30 (32)	thou shalt certainly know them
83:24 (24)	thou knowest in their faces the radiancy of bliss

e) impf. pass. (*yuᶜrafu*)

33:59 (59)	so it is likelier they will be known
55:41 (41)	the sinners shall be known by their mark

h) pcple. pass. (*maᶜrūf*)

2:178 (173)	let the pursuing be honourable
2:180 (176)	to make testament in favour of his parents and kinsmen honourably
2:228 (228)	women have such honourable rights as obligations
2:229 (229)	divorce is twice; then honourable retention
2:231 (231)	then retain them honourably
2:231 (231)	or set them free honourably
2:232 (232)	when they have agreed together honourably
2:233 (233)	to provide them and clothe them honourably
2:233 (233)	what you have given honourably
2:234 (234)	what they may do with themselves honourably
2:235 (235)	do not make troth with them secretly without you speak honourable words
2:236 (237)	according to his means the needy man, honourably
2:240 (241)	what they may do with themselves honourably
2:241 (242)	there shall be for divorced women provision honourable
2:263 (265)	honourable words, and forgiveness, are better
3:104 (100)	[one nation] bidding to honour, and forbidding dishonour
3:110 (106)	best nation ever brought forth to men, bidding to honour
3:114 (110)	bidding to honour and forbidding dishonour
4:5 (4)	speak to them honourable words
4:6 (6)	if poor, let him consume in reason
4:8 (9)	speak to them honourable words
4:19 (23)	consort with them honourably

4:25 (29)	give them their wages honourably
4:114 (114)	him who bids to freewill offering, or honour
7:157 (156)	bidding them to honour, and forbidding them dishonour
9:67 (68)	they bid to dishonour, and forbid honour
9:71 (72)	they bid to honour, and forbid dishonour
9:112 (113)	those who bid to honour and forbid dishonour
22:41 (42)	bid to honour, and forbid dishonour
24:53 (52)	honourable obedience is sufficient
31:15 (14)	keep them company honourable in this world
31:17 (16)	bid unto honour, and forbid dishonour
33:6 (6)	you should act towards your friends honourably
33:32 (32)	speak honourable words
47:21 (22)	obedience, and words honourable
60:12 (12)	nor disobey thee in aught honourable
65:2 (2)	retain them **honourably** or part from them (honourably)
65:2 (2)	retain them (honourably) or part from them honourably
65:6 (6)	consult together honourably

AʿRĀF n.m. (pl. of *ʿurf*)~ramparts, battlements; (the "wall" that separates Heaven from Hell)

7:46 (44)	on the Ramparts are men knowing each by their mark
7:48 (46)	dwellers on the Battlements shall call

ʿARAFĀT n.prop.~Arafat (name of mountain near Mecca)

2:198 (194)	when you press on from Arafat

ʿURF n.m. (see pl. *aʿrāf*, with different meaning, above)~that which is honourable; (adv) successively

7:199 (198)	bid to what is honourable
77:1 (1)	by the loosed ones successively

ʿARRAFA vb. (II)~to make known, to acquaint

a) perf. act.

47:6 (7)	that He has made known to them
66:3 (3)	he made known part of it

TAʿĀRAFA vb. (VI)~to know or recognize one another

b) impf. act. (*yataʿārafu*)

10:45 (46)	mutually recognizing one another
49:13 (13)	that you may know one another

IʿTARAFA vb. (VIII)~(with prep. *bi-*) to confess

a) perf. act.

9:102 (103)	and other have confessed their sins
40:11 (11)	now we confess our sins
67:11 (11)	so they confess their sins

*ʿ R J

ʿARAJA vb. (I)~to mount, to go up, to ascend

b) impf. act. (*yaᶜruju*)

15:14 (14)	still they mounted through it
32:5 (4)	then it goes up to Him in one day
34:2 (2)	what comes down from heaven, and what goes up to it
57:4 (4)	what comes down from heaven, and what goes up unto it
70:4 (4)	to Him the angels and the Spirit mount up

AᶜRAJ n.m. (comp. in form)~lame

24:61 (60)	there is no fault in the lame
48:17 (17)	there is no fault in the lame

MAᶜĀRIJ n.m. (pl. of *maᶜraj*)~stairs, a ladder

43:33 (32)	and stairs whereon to mount
70:3 (3)	the Lord of the Stairways

*ᶜ R J N

ᶜURJŪN n.m.~an aged palm-bough, a dry date-stalk

36:39 (39)	till it returns like an aged palm-bough

*ᶜ R M

ᶜARIM n.prop.~Arim or Iram

34:16 (15)	We loosed on them the Flood of Arim

*ᶜ R R

MAᶜARRAH n.f.~a crime, guilt

48:25 (25)	there befall you guilt unwittingly

IᶜTARRA vb. (VIII)~(pcple. pass.) suppliant, the poor person who does not beg

h) pcple. pass. (*muᶜtarr*)

22:36 (37)	feed the beggar and the suppliant

*ᶜ R SH

ᶜARASHA vb. (I)~to build. (pcple. pass.) trellised

b) impf. act. (*yaᶜrishu*)

7:137 (133)	Pharaoh and his people, and what they had been building
16:68 (70)	the trees, and of what they are building

h) pcple. pass. (*maᶜrūsh*)

6:141 (142)	it is He who produces gardens trellised and (untrellised)
6:141 (142)	it is He who produces gardens (trellised), and untrellised

ᶜARSH n.m. (pl. *ᶜurūsh*)~turret, trellise, throne

2:259 (261)	a city that was fallen down upon its turrets
7:54 (52)	then sat Himself upon the Throne

9:129 (130)	He is the Lord of the Mighty Throne
10:3 (3)	then sat Himself upon the Throne
11:7 (9)	His Throne was upon the waters
12:100 (101)	he lifted his father and mother upon the throne
13:2 (2)	He sat Himself upon the Throne
17:42 (44)	the Lord of the Throne
18:42 (40)	it was fallen down upon its trellises
20:5 (4)	the All-merciful sat Himself upon the Throne
21:22 (22)	so glory be to God, the Lord of the Throne
22:45 (44)	now it is fallen down upon its turrets
23:86 (88)	the Lord of the mighty Throne
23:116 (117)	the Lord of the noble Throne
25:59 (60)	then sat Himself upon the Throne
27:23 (23)	she possesses a mighty throne
27:26 (26)	the Lord of the Mighty Throne
27:38 (38)	which one of you will bring me her throne
27:41 (41)	disguise her throne for her
27:42 (42)	is thy throne like this?
32:4 (3)	then seated Himself upon the Throne
39:75 (75)	angels encircling about the Throne
40:7 (7)	those who bear the Throne, and those round about it
40:15 (15)	Possessor of the Throne
43:82 (82)	the Lord of the Throne
57:4 (4)	then seated Himself upon the Throne
69:17 (17)	eight shall carry above them the Throne of thy Lord
81:20 (20)	having power, with the Lord of the Throne secure
85:15 (15)	Lord of the Throne, the All-glorious

*ᶜ R W

ᶜURWAH n.f.~handle, handhold

2:256 (257)	laid hold of the most firm handle
31:22 (21)	laid hold of the most firm handle

IᶜTARĀ vb. (VIII)~to smite, to afflict

a) perf. act.

11:54 (57)	one of our gods has smitten thee

*ᶜ R Y

ᶜARIYA vb. (I)~to be naked

b) impf. act. (*yaᶜrá*)

20:118 (116)	neither to hunger therein, nor to go naked

ᶜARĀʾ n.m.~wilderness

37:145 (145)	We cast him upon the wilderness
68:49 (49)	he would have been cast upon the wilderness

*ᶜ S L

ᶜASAL n.com.~honey

47:15 (17)	rivers, too, of honey purified

*ᶜ S Q

ᶜAYN SĪN QĀF~ml

42:2 (1)	Ain Sin Qaf

*ᶜ S R

ᶜASARA vb. (I)~(n.vb.) hardship, difficulty, a difficult thing

f) n.vb. (*ᶜusr*)

2:185 (181)	God desires ease for you, and desires not hardship
18:73 (72)	neither constrain me to do a thing too difficult
65:7 (7)	God will assuredly appoint, after difficulty, easiness
94:5 (5)	truly with hardship comes ease
94:6 (6)	truly with hardship comes ease

ᶜASĪR n.m. (adj)~difficult, harsh

25:26 (28)	a day harsh for the unbelievers
54:8 (8)	this is a hard day
74:9 (9)	that day will be a harsh day

ᶜUSRÁ n.f.~hardship, difficulty

92:10 (10)	We shall surely ease him to the Hardship

ᶜUSRAH n.f.~difficulty

2:280 (280)	if any man should be in difficulties
9:117 (118)	Helpers who followed him in the hour of difficulty

TAᶜĀSARA vb. (VI)~to be difficult, to make difficulties

a) perf. act.

65:6 (6)	if you both make difficulties

*ᶜ S S

ᶜASᶜASA vb. (quad I)~to close; to pass, to elapse; to swarm

a) perf. act.

81:17 (17)	by the night swarming

*ᶜ SH R

ᶜASHĪR n.m.~friend, companion

22:13 (13)	he, an evil friend

ʿASHĪRAH n.f.~kindred on the father's side, a clan, tribe

9:24 (24)	your brothers, your wives, your clan
26:214 (214)	warn thy clan, thy nearest kin
58:22 (22)	or their brothers, or their clan

ʿASHR n.m. (num.; f. *ʿasharah*)~ten

2:196 (192)	that is ten completely
2:234 (234)	by themselves for four months and ten nights
5:89 (91)	expiation is to feed ten poor persons
6:160 (161)	whoso brings a good deed shall have ten the like of it
7:142 (138)	We completed them with ten
11:13 (16)	then bring you ten suras the like of it
20:103 (103)	you have tarried only ten nights
28:27 (27)	if thou completest ten [years]
89:2 (1)	and ten nights

ʿISHĀR n.f. (pl. of *ʿushrāʾ*)~pregnant camels

81:4 (4)	when the pregnant camels shall be neglected

ʿISHRŪN n.m. (num)~twenty

8:65 (66)	if there be twenty of you, patient men

MAʿSHAR n.m.~company, assembly

6:128 (128)	company of jinn
6:130 (130)	company of jinn and mankind
55:33 (33)	company of jinn and of men

MIʿSHĀR n.m. (num)~one tenth

34:45 (44)	yet they reached not a tenth of what We gave

ʿĀSHARA vb. (III)~to consort with, to live with

c) impv. (*ʿāshir*)

4:19 (23)	consort with them honourably

*ʿ SH W

ʿASHĀ vb. (I)~to blind one's self

b) impf. act. (*yaʿshū*)

43:36 (35)	whoso blinds himself to the Remembrance of the All-merciful

ʿASHĪY n.m. (f. *ʿashīyah*)~evening

3:41 (36)	give glory at evening and dawn
6:52 (52)	those who call upon their Lord at morning and evening
18:28 (27)	those who call upon their Lord at morning and evening
19:11 (12)	give you glory at dawn and evening
19:62 (63)	they shall have their provision at dawn and evening
30:18 (17)	alike at the setting sun
38:18 (17)	We subjected the mountains to give glory at evening
38:31 (30)	in the evening were presented to him

40:46 (49)	the Fire, to which they shall be exposed morning and evening
40:55 (57)	proclaim the praise of thy Lord at evening
79:46 (46)	they have but tarried for an evening

ʿISHĀʾ n.m.~evening, commencement of evening

12:16 (16)	they came to their father in the evening
24:58 (57)	and after the evening prayer

*ʿ Ṣ B

ʿAṢĪB n.m. (adj)~fierce, heavy, grievous

11:77 (79)	this is a fierce day

ʿUṢBAH n.f. (coll)~a band, a company, a group of men

12:8 (8)	dearer to our father than we, though we are a band
12:14 (14)	if the wolf eats him, and we a band
24:11 (11)	those who came with the slander are a band of you
28:76 (76)	a company of men endowed with strength

*ʿ Ṣ F

ʿAṢAFA vb. (I)~(n.vb.) tempestuousness, (adv) tempestuously. (pcple. act.) (wind) that blows strongly, (adj) tempestuous

f) n.vb. (*ʿaṣf*)

77:2 (2)	storming tempestuously

g) pcple. act. (*ʿāṣif*)

10:22 (23)	there comes upon them a strong wind
14:18 (21)	whereon the wind blows strong upon a tempestuous day
21:81 (81)	to Solomon the wind, strongly blowing
77:2 (2)	storming tempestuously

ʿAṢF n.m.~a blade of wheat; grain

55:12 (11)	grain in the blade, and fragrant herbs
105:5 (5)	He made them like green blades devoured

*ʿ Ṣ M

ʿAṢAMA vb. (I)~to save from harm, to protect, to defend. (pcple. act.) defender, protector

b) impf. act. (*yaʿṣimu*)

5:67 (71)	God will protect thee from men
11:43 (45)	a mountain, that shall defend me from the water
33:17 (17)	who is he that shall defend you from God

g) pcple. act. (*ʿāṣim*)

10:27 (28)	neither have they any defender from God
11:43 (45)	today there is no defender from God's command
40:33 (35)	having none to defend you from God

ʿIṢAM n.f. (pl. of ʿ*iṣmah*)~tie, guardianship

60:10 (10)	do not hold fast to the ties of unbelieving women

IʿTAṢAMA vb. (VIII)~to take hold on, to cleave firmly to, to hold fast to

a) perf. act.

4:146 (145)	hold fast to God
4:175 (174)	as for those who believe in God, and hold fast to Him

b) impf. act. (*yaʿtaṣimu*)

3:101 (96)	whosoever holds fast to God

c) impv. (*iʿtaṣim*)

3:103 (98)	hold you fast to God's bond, together
22:78 (78)	hold you fast to God

ISTAʿṢAMA vb. (X)~to preserve one's self (from sin), to abstain

a) perf. act.

12:32 (32)	yes, I solicited him, but he abstained

*ʿ Ṣ R

ʿAṢARA vb. (I)~to press (grapes)

b) impf. act. (*yaʿṣiru*)

12:36 (36)	I dreamed that I was pressing grapes
12:49 (49)	people will be succoured and press in season

ʿAṢR n.m.~afternoon, declining day

103:1 (1)	by the afternoon

AʿṢARA vb. (IV)~(n.vb.) whirlwind. (pcple. act.) rain-emitting clouds

f) n.vb. (*iʿṣār*)

2:266 (268)	then a whirlwind with fire smites it

g) pcple. act. (*muʿṣir*)

78:14 (14)	out of the rain-clouds water cascading

*ʿ Ṣ W

ʿAṢĀ n.f. (pl. ʿ*iṣīy*)~staff, rod

2:60 (57)	strike with thy staff the rock
7:107 (104)	he cast his staff
7:117 (114)	cast thy staff
7:160 (160)	strike with thy staff the rock
20:18 (19)	it is my staff
20:66 (69)	their ropes and their staffs were sliding

26:32 (31)	he cast his staff
26:44 (43)	they cast their ropes and their staffs
26:45 (44)	then Moses cast his staff
26:63 (63)	strike with thy staff the sea
27:10 (10)	cast down thy staff
28:31 (31)	cast down thy staff

*ʿ Ṣ Y

ʿAṢÁ vb. (I)~to disobey, to rebel or act rebelliously. (n.vb.1) disobedience [Ar]; rebellion [Pk, Ali]; opposition [Bl]. (n.vb.2) disobedience [Ar, Ali]; rebellion [Pk]; opposition [Bl]

a) perf. act.

2:61 (58)	because they disobeyed, and were transgressors
2:93 (87)	we hear, and rebel
3:112 (108)	for that they acted rebelliously
3:152 (145)	and were rebellious, after He had shown you
4:42 (45)	those who have disobeyed the Messenger
4:46 (48)	we have heard and we disobey
5:78 (82)	for their rebelling and their transgression
6:15 (15)	I fear, if I should rebel against my Lord
10:15 (16)	I fear, if I should rebel against my Lord
10:91 (91)	before thou didst rebel
11:59 (62)	and rebelled against His Messengers
11:63 (66)	who shall help me against God if I rebel
14:36 (39)	whoso rebels against me
20:93 (94)	didst thou then disobey my commandment?
20:121 (119)	Adam disobeyed his Lord
26:216 (216)	if they disobey thee
39:13 (15)	I fear, if I should rebel against my Lord
69:10 (10)	they rebelled against the Messenger
71:21 (20)	they have rebelled against me
73:16 (16)	Pharaoh rebelled against the Messenger
79:21 (21)	he cried lies, and rebelled

b) impf. act. (*yaʿṣī*)

4:14 (18)	whoso disobeys God, and His Messenger
18:69 (68)	I shall not rebel against thee in anything
33:36 (36)	whosoever disobeys God and His Messenger
60:12 (12)	nor disobey thee in aught honourable
66:6 (6)	terrible angels who disobey not God
72:23 (24)	whoso rebels against God and His Messenger

f) n.vb. (1) (*ʿiṣyān*)

49:7 (7)	unbelief and ungodliness and disobedience

f) n.vb. (2) (*maʿṣiyah*)

58:8 (9)	in disobedience to the Messenger
58:9 (10)	conspire not together in sin and enmity and disobedience

ʿAṢĪY n.m. (adj)~disobedient, rebellious

19:14 (14)	not arrogant, rebellious
19:44 (45)	Satan is a rebel against the All-merciful

*ʿ T B

AʿTABA vb. (IV)~(pcple. act.) one to whom favour is shown, one to whom amends are made

g) pcple. act. (*muʿtab*)

41:24 (23) no amends shall be made to them

ISTAʿTABA vb. (X)~to ask for favour or amends

b) impf. act. (*yastaʿtibu*)

41:24 (23) if they ask amends

e) impf. pass. (*yustaʿtabu*)

16:84 (86) nor shall they be suffered to make amends
30:57 (57) nor will they be suffered to make amends
45:35 (34) nor will they be suffered to make amends

*ʿ T D

ʿATĪD n.m. (adj)~ready

50:18 (17) by him is an observer ready
50:23 (22) this is what I have, made ready

AʿTADA vb. (IV)~to prepare, to make ready

a) perf. act.

4:18 (22) for them We have prepared a painful chastisement
4:37 (41) We have prepared for the unbelievers
4:151 (150) We have prepared for the unbelievers
4:161 (159) We have prepared for the unbelievers
12:31 (31) and made ready for them a repast
17:10 (11) we have prepared for them a painful chastisement
18:29 (28) We have prepared for the evildoers a fire
18:102 (102) We have prepared Gehenna
25:11 (12) We have prepared for him who cries lies
25:37 (39) We have prepared for the evildoers
33:31 (31) We have prepared for her a generous provision
48:13 (13) We have prepared for the unbelievers
67:5 (5) We have prepared for them the chastisement
76:4 (4) We have prepared for the unbelievers

*ʿ T L

ʿATALA vb. (I)~to drag violently, to thrust

c) impv. (*uʿtul*)

44:47 (47) thrust him into the midst of Hell

ʿUTULL n.m. (adj)~violent, cruel, coarse-grained

68:13 (13) coarse-grained, moreover ignoble

*ᶜ T Q

ᶜATĪQ n.m. (adj)~old, ancient

22:29 (30)	and go about the Ancient House
22:33 (34)	place of sacrifice is by the Ancient House

*ᶜ T W

ᶜATĀ vb. (I)~to turn in disdain, to be proud or insolent. (n.vb.) insolence, disdain, pride. (pcple. act.) very violent, fierce roaring (wind)

7:77 (75)	and [they] turned in disdain from the commandment
7:166 (166)	when they turned in disdain from that forbidding
25:21 (23)	and become greatly disdainful
51:44 (44)	they turned in disdain from the commandment
65:8 (8)	how many a city turned in disdain

f) n.vb. (*ᶜutūw*)

25:21 (23)	and become <greatly> disdainful
67:21 (21)	they persist in disdain and aversion

g) pcple. act. (*ᶜātī*)

69:6 (6)	they were destroyed by a wind clamorous, violent

ᶜITĪY n.m.~old age; exceedingly disdainful

19:8 (9)	I have attained to the declining of old age
19:69 (70)	whichever of them was the most hardened in disdain

*ᶜ TH R

ᶜATHARA vb. (I)~to discover, to stumble upon (plus prep. *ᶜalá*)

d) perf. pass. (*ᶜuthira*)

5:107 (106)	if it be discovered that both of them

AᶜTHARA vb. (IV)~to cause to stumble

a) perf. act.

18:21 (20)	We made them stumble upon them

*ᶜ TH W

ᶜATHĀ vb. (I)~to do evil or mischief

b) impf. act. (*yaᶜthū*)

2:60 (57)	mischief not in the earth, doing corruption
7:74 (72)	do not mischief in the earth, working corruption
11:85 (86)	do not mischief in the land, working corruption
26:183 (183)	do not mischief in the earth, working corruption
29:36 (35)	do not mischief in the land, working corruption

*ᶜ Ṭ F

ᶜIṬF n.m.~side

22:9 (9)	turning his side to lead astray from God's way

*ᶜ Ṭ L

ᶜAṬṬALA vb. (II)~to neglect, to ruin. (pcple. pass.) neglected, ruined

d) perf. pass. (*ᶜuṭṭila*)

81:4 (4)	when the pregnant camels shall be neglected

h) pcple. pass. (*muᶜaṭṭal*)

22:45 (44)	how many a ruined well

*ᶜ Ṭ Y

ᶜAṬĀʾ n.m.~a gift

11:108 (110)	save as thy Lord will—for a gift unbroken
17:20 (21)	each We succour, these and those, from thy Lord's gift
17:20 (21)	thy Lord's gift is not confined
38:39 (38)	this is Our gift
78:36 (36)	from thy Lord, a gift, a reckoning

AᶜṬÁ vb. (IV)~to give; to pay (tribute)

20:50 (52)	Our Lord is He who gave everything its creation
53:34 (35)	and gives a little, and then grudgingly
92:5 (5)	for him who gives and is godfearing
108:1 (1)	We have given thee abundance

b) impf. act. (*yuᶜṭī*)

9:29 (29)	they pay the tribute out of hand
93:5 (5)	Thy Lord shall give thee, and thou shalt be satisfied

d) perf. pass. (*uᶜṭiya*)

9:58 (58)	if they are given a share of them they are well-pleased

e) impf. pass. (*yuᶜṭá*)

9:58 (58)	if they are given none then they are angry

TAᶜĀṬÁ vb. (VI)~to take in hand, to undertake

54:29 (29)	he took in hand, and hamstrung her

*ᶜ W D

ᶜĀDA vb. (I)~to return, to revert, to do something again, to retract. (pcple. act.) one who returns or reverts, etc.

a) perf. act.

2:275 (276)	whosoever reverts— those are the inhabitants of the Fire
5:95 (96)	whoever offends again, God will take vengeance on him

6:28 (28)	they would again commit the very thing they were prohibited
7:89 (87)	We should have forged against God a lie if we returned into your creed
17:8 (8)	if you return, We shall (return)
17:8 (8)	if you (return) We shall return
23:107 (109)	if we revert, we shall be evildoers indeed
36:39 (39)	till it returns like an aged palm-bough

b) impf. act. (*yaʿūdu*)

7:29 (28)	as He originated you so you will return
7:88 (86)	unless you return into our creed
7:89 (87)	it is not for us to return into it
8:19 (19)	but if you return We shall (return)
8:19 (19)	if you (return) We shall return
8:38 (39)	if they return, the wont of the ancients is already gone
14:13 (16)	you will surely return into our creed
24:17 (16)	you shall never repeat the like of it again
58:3 (4)	then retract what they have said
58:8 (9)	then they return to that they were forbidden

g) pcple. act. (*ʿāʾid*)

44:15 (14)	behold, you revert

ʿĀD n.prop.~Ad (an ancient tribe of Arabia)

7:65 (63)	to Ad their brother Hood
7:74 (72)	He appointed you successors after Ad
9:70 (71)	people of Noah, Ad
11:50 (52)	to Ad their brother Hood
11:59 (62)	that was Ad
11:60 (63)	Ad disbelieved in their Lord
11:60 (63)	so away with Ad, the people of Hood
14:9 (9)	people of Noah, Ad, Thamood
22:42 (43)	people of Noah cried lies, and Ad and Thamood
25:38 (40)	and Ad, and Thamood
26:123 (123)	Ad cried lies to the Envoys
29:38 (37)	and Ad, and Thamood
38:12 (11)	people of Noah, and Ad
40:31 (32)	the like of the case of Noah's people, Ad
41:13 (12)	a thunderbolt like to the thunderbolt of Ad and Thamood
41:15 (14)	as for Ad, they waxed proud in the earth
46:21 (20)	remember the brother of Ad
50:13 (13)	and Ad and Pharaoh, the brothers of Lot
51:41 (41)	also in Ad, when We loosed against them
53:50 (51)	He destroyed Ad, the ancient
54:18 (18)	Ad cried lies
69:4 (4)	Thamood and Ad cried lies to the Clatterer
69:6 (6)	as for Ad, they were destroyed by a wind clamorous
89:6 (5)	hast thou not seen how thy Lord did with Ad

MAʿĀD n.m.~a place of return or homing, a home, (here, probably a reference to Mecca)

28:85 (85)	[He] shall surely restore thee to a place of homing

AᶜĀDA vb. (IV)~to bring back, to cause to return

b) impf. act. (*yuᶜīdu*)

10:4 (4)	He originates creation, then He brings it back again
10:34 (35)	who originates creation, then brings it back again
10:34 (35)	He originates creation, then brings it back again
17:51 (53)	who will bring us back?
17:69 (71)	do you feel secure that He will not send you back into it
18:20 (19)	they will stone you, or restore you to their creed
20:21 (22)	We will restore it to its first state
20:55 (57)	We shall restore you into it
21:104 (104)	as We originated the first creation, so We shall bring it back again
27:64 (65)	who originates creation, then brings it back again
29:19 (18)	God originates creation, then brings it back again
30:11 (10)	God originates creation, then brings it back again
30:27 (26)	it is He who originates creation, then brings it back again
34:49 (48)	falsehood originates not, nor brings again
71:18 (17)	He shall return you into it
85:13 (13)	it is He who originates, and brings again

d) perf. pass. (*uᶜīda*)

22:22 (22)	they shall be restored into it
32:20 (20)	they shall be restored into it

*ᶜ W DH

ᶜĀDHA vb. (I)~to take refuge

a) perf. act.

40:27 (28)	I take refuge in my Lord and your Lord from every man
44:20 (19)	I take refuge in my Lord and your Lord

b) impf. act. (*yaᶜūdhu*)

2:67 (63)	I take refuge with God
11:47 (49)	my Lord, I take refuge with Thee
19:18 (18)	I take refuge in the All-merciful from thee
23:97 (99)	I take refuge in Thee from the evil suggestions
23:98 (100)	I take refuge in Thee, O my Lord
72:6 (6)	who would take refuge with certain men of the jinn
113:1 (1)	I take refuge with the Lord of the Daybreak
114:1 (1)	I take refuge with the Lord of men

MAᶜĀDH n.m.~refuge, shelter

12:23 (23)	God be my refuge
12:79 (79)	God forbid that we should take any other but him

AᶜĀDHA vb. (IV)~to commend to the protection (of God)

b) impf. act. (*yuᶜīdhu*)

3:36 (31)	commend her to Thee with her seed

ISTAʿĀDHA vb. (X)~to seek refuge

c) impv. (*istaʿidh*)

7:200 (199)	seek refuge in God
16:98 (100)	seek refuge in God
40:56 (58)	so seek thou refuge in God
41:36 (36)	seek refuge in God

*ʿ W J

ʿIWAJ n.m.~crookedness, crooked; curvature

3:99 (94)	why do you bar from God's way the believer, desiring to make it crooked
7:45 (43)	who bar from God's way, desiring to make it crooked
7:86 (84)	barring from God's way those who believe in Him, desiring to make it crooked
11:19 (22)	who bar from God's way, desiring to make it crooked
14:3 (3)	and bar from God's way, desiring to make it crooked
18:1 (1)	and has not assigned unto it any crookedness
20:107 (106)	wherein thou wilt see no crookedness neither any curving
20:108 (107)	the Summoner in whom is no crookedness
39:28 (29)	an Arabic Koran, wherein there is no crookedness

*ʿ W L

ʿĀLA vb. (I)~to swerve, to be partial

b) impf. act. (*yaʿūlu*)

4:3 (3)	so it is likelier you will not be partial

*ʿ W M

ʿĀM n.m.~a year

2:259 (261)	God made him die a hundred years
2:259 (261)	thou hast tarried a hundred years
9:28 (28)	let them not come near the Holy Mosque after this year of theirs
9:37 (37)	one year they make it profane
9:37 (37)	and hallow it another [year]
9:126 (127)	do they not see that they are tried every year
12:49 (49)	there shall come a year wherein the people will be succoured
29:14 (13)	he tarried among them a thousand years
31:14 (13)	his weaning was in two years

*ʿ W N

ʿAWĀN n.f. (adj)~middle-aged (f), middling

2:68 (63)	a cow neither old, nor virgin, middling between the two

AʿĀNA vb. (IV)~to assist, to help

a) perf. act.

25:4 (5)	other folk have helped him to it

c) impv. (*aᶜin*)

18:95 (94) so aid me forcefully

TAᶜĀWANA vb. (VI)~to co-operate, to help one another

b) impf. act. (*yataᶜāwanu*)

5:2 (3) help one another to piety and godfearing
5:2 (3) do not help each other to sin and enmity

ISTAᶜĀNA vb. (X)~to pray for succour. (pcple. pass.) one whose help or succour is being sought

b) impf. act. (*yastaᶜīnu*)

1:5 (4) Thee only we serve; to Thee alone we pray for succour

c) impv. (*istaᶜin*)

2:45 (42) seek you help in patience and prayer
2:153 (148) seek you help in patience and prayer
7:128 (125) pray for succour to God, and be patient

h) pcple. pass. (*mustaᶜān*)

12:18 (18) it is God, whose succour is ever there to seek
21:112 (112) His succour is ever to be sought against that you describe

*ᶜ W Q

ᶜAWWAQA vb. (II)~(pcple. act.) one who hinders or delays

g) pcple. act. (*muᶜawwiq*)

33:18 (18) God would surely know those of you who hinder

*ᶜ W R

ᶜAWRAH n.f.~nakedness; (adj) exposed, naked

24:31 (31) children who have not yet attained knowledge of women's private parts
24:58 (57) the evening prayer — three times of nakedness for you
33:13 (13) our houses are exposed
33:13 (13) yet they were not exposed

*ᶜ Y B

ᶜĀBA vb. (I)~to mar, to damage

b) impf. act. (*yaᶜību*)

18:79 (78) I desired to damage it

*ᶜ Y D

ᶜĪD n.m.~a festival, a feast

5:114 (114) out of heaven, that shall be for us a festival

*ᶜ Y L

ᶜĀLA vb. (I)~(pcple. act.) poor, needy

g) pcple. act. (*ᶜāʾil*)

93:8 (8) Did He not find thee needy, and suffice thee?

ᶜAYLAH n.f.~poverty

9:28 (28) if you fear poverty, God shall surely enrich you of His bounty

*ᶜ Y N

ᶜAYN (1) n.f. (pl. *ᶜuyūn*)~eye, sight; (*qarra ᶜaynan*) to be comforted, to rejoice

3:13 (11)	they saw them twice the like of them, as the eye sees
5:45 (49)	a life for a life, an eye for an (eye)
5:45 (49)	a life for a life, an (eye) for an eye
5:83 (86)	thou seest their eyes overflow with tears
7:116 (113)	they put a spell upon the people's eyes
7:179 (178)	they have eyes, but perceive not with them
7:195 (194)	have they eyes wherewith they see
8:44 (46)	God showed you them in your eyes as few
8:44 (46)	and [He] made you few in their eyes
9:92 (93)	they turned away, their eyes overflowing with tears
11:31 (33)	nor do I say to those your eyes despise
11:37 (39)	make thou the Ark under Our eyes
12:84 (84)	his eyes turned white because of the sorrow
15:88 (88)	stretch not thine eyes to that We have given
18:28 (27)	let not thine eyes turn away from them
18:101 (101)	whose eyes were covered against My remembrance
19:26 (26)	and be comforted; and if thou shouldst see
20:39 (40)	to be formed in My sight
20:40 (41)	We returned thee to thy mother that she might rejoice
20:131 (131)	stretch not thine eyes to that We have given
21:61 (62)	bring him before the people's eyes
23:27 (27)	make thou the Ark under Our eyes
25:74 (74)	give us refreshment of our wives and seed
28:9 (8)	he will be a comfort to me and thee
28:13 (12)	We returned him to his mother, that she might be comforted
32:17 (17)	no soul knows what comfort is laid up for them secretly
33:19 (19)	their eyes rolling like one who swoons
33:51 (51)	it is likelier they will be comforted, and not sorrow
36:66 (66)	We would have obliterated their eyes
40:19 (20)	He knows the treachery of the eyes
43:71 (71)	therein being whatever the souls desire, and the eyes delight in
52:48 (48)	thou art before Our eyes
54:14 (14)	running before Our eyes
54:37 (37)	We obliterated their eyes
90:8 (8)	have We not appointed to him two eyes
102:7 (7)	you shall surely see it with the eye of certainty

ᶜAYN (2) (pl. *aᶜyun*)~a spring, fountain

2:60 (57)	and there gushed forth from it twelve fountains
7:160 (160)	and there gushed forth from it twelve fountains

15:45 (45)	the godfearing shall be amidst gardens and fountains
18:86 (84)	he found it setting in a muddy spring
26:57 (57)	We expelled them from gardens and fountains
26:134 (134)	gardens and fountains
26:147 (147)	among gardens and fountains
34:12 (11)	We made the Fount of Molten Brass to flow for him
36:34 (34)	therein We caused fountains to gush forth
44:25 (24)	they left how many gardens and foutains
44:52 (52)	among gardens and fountains
51:15 (15)	the godfearing shall be among gardens and fountains
54:12 (12)	and made the earth to gush with fountains
55:50 (50)	therein two fountains of running water
55:66 (66)	therein two fountains of gushing water
76:6 (6)	a fountain whereat drink the servants of God
76:18 (18)	therein a fountain whose name is called Salsabil
77:41 (41)	the godfearing shall dwell amid shades and fountains
83:28 (28)	a fountain at which do drink those brought nigh
88:5 (5)	watered at a boiling fountain
88:12 (12)	therein a running fountain

ʿĪN n.f. (pl. of *aʿyan*)~wide-eyed, having large eyes

37:48 (47)	and with them wide-eyed maidens
44:54 (54)	We shall espouse them to wide-eyed houris
52:20 (20)	We shall espouse them to wide-eyed houris
56:22 (22)	and wide-eyed houris

MAʿĪN n.m.~a spring, running water

23:50 (52)	upon a height, where was a hollow and a spring
37:45 (44)	a cup from a spring being passed round to them
56:18 (18)	with goblets, and ewers, and a cup from a spring
67:30 (30)	then who would bring you running water?

*ʿ Y R

ʿĪR n.com.~caravan, cameleers

12:70 (70)	ho, cameleers, you are robbers
12:82 (82)	the caravan in which we approached
12:94 (94)	when the caravan set forth

*ʿ Y S

ʿĪSÁ n.prop.~Jesus

2:87 (81)	We gave Jesus son of Mary the clear signs
2:136 (130)	that which was given to Moses and Jesus
2:253 (254)	We gave Jesus son of Mary the clear signs
3:45 (40)	whose name is Messiah, Jesus, son of Mary
3:52 (45)	when Jesus perceived their unbelief
3:55 (48)	Jesus, I will take thee to Me
3:59 (52)	the likeness of Jesus, in God's sight
3:84 (78)	that which was given to Moses and Jesus
4:157 (156)	we slew the Messiah, Jesus son of Mary
4:163 (161)	Isaac, Jacob, and the Tribes, Jesus and Job
4:171 (169)	Jesus son of Mary, was only the Messenger of God
5:46 (50)	We sent, following in their footsteps, Jesus

5:78 (82)	by the tongue of David, and Jesus, Mary's son
5:110 (109)	Jesus Son of Mary, remember My blessing upon thee
5:112 (112)	O Jesus son of Mary, is thy Lord able
5:114 (114)	said Jesus son of Mary
5:116 (116)	O Jesus son of Mary, didst thou say unto men
6:85 (85)	Zachariah and John, Jesus and Elias
19:34 (35)	that is Jesus, son of Mary
33:7 (7)	Moses, and Jesus, Mary's son
42:13 (11)	that We charged Abraham with, Moses and Jesus
43:63 (63)	when Jesus came with the clear signs
57:27 (27)	We sent, following, Jesus son of Mary
61:6 (6)	when Jesus son of Mary said
61:14 (14)	be you God's helpers, as Jesus, Mary's son, said to the Apostles

*ᶜ Y SH

ᶜĪSHAH n.f.~life

69:21 (21)	he shall be in a pleasing life
101:7 (5)	shall inherit a pleasing life

MAᶜĀSH n.f.~a livelihood

78:11 (11)	We appointed day for a livelihood

MAᶜĪSHAH n.f. (pl. *maᶜāyish*)~livelihood, life

7:10 (9)	and there appointed for you livelihood
15:20 (20)	and there appointed for you livelihood
20:124 (123)	his shall be a life of narrowness
28:58 (58)	that [had its livelihood] in insolent ease
43:32 (31)	we have divided between them their livelihood

*ᶜ Y Y

ᶜAYÁ vb. (I)~to be weary

a) perf. act.

50:15 (14)	were We wearied by the first creation?

b) impf. act. (*yaᶜyá*)

46:33 (32)	not being wearied by creating them

*ᶜ Z B

ᶜAZABA vb. (I)~to escape, to be hidden from

b) impf. act. (*yaᶜzubu*)

10:61 (62)	not so much as the weight of an ant in earth or heaven escapes
34:3 (3)	not so much as the weight of an ant in heaven and earth escapes

*ᶜ Z L

ᶜAZALA vb. (I)~to set aside, to remove from place. (pcple. pass.) set aside, expelled

a) perf. act.

33:51 (51) if thou seekest any thou hast set aside

h) pcple. pass. (*maᶜzūl*)

26:212 (212) they are expelled from hearing

MAᶜZIL n.m.~a place apart

11:42 (44) Noah called to his son, who was standing [in a place] apart

IᶜTAZALA vb. (VIII)~to go apart, to withdraw

a) perf. act.

4:90 (92) if they withdraw from you, and do not fight you
18:16 (15) when you have gone apart from them and that they serve
19:49 (50) when he went apart from them

b) impf. act. (*yaᶜtazilu*)

4:91 (93) if they withdraw not from you, and offer you peace
19:48 (49) I will go apart from you and that you call upon

c) impv. (*iᶜtazil*)

2:222 (222) go apart from women during the monthly course
44:21 (20) go you apart from me

*ᶜ Z M

ᶜAZAMA vb. (I)~to resolve, to be determined on something. (n.vb.) constancy, steadfastness

a) perf. act.

2:227 (227) if they resolve on divorce
3:159 (153) when thou art resolved, put thy trust in God
47:21 (23) then, when the matter is resolved

b) impf. act. (*yaᶜzimu*)

2:235 (236) do not resolve on the knot of marriage

f) n.vb. (*ᶜazm*)

3:186 (183) surely that is true constancy
20:115 (114) We found in him no constancy
31:17 (16) surely that is true constancy
42:43 (41) surely that is true constancy
46:35 (34) the Messengers possessed of constancy were also patient

*ᶜ Z R

ᶜUZAYR n.prop.~Ezra

9:30 (30) Ezra is the Son of God

ᶜAZZARA vb. (II)~to assist, to succour, to support

a) perf. act.

5:12 (15)	believe in My Messengers and succour them
7:157 (156)	those who believe in him and succour him and help him

b) impf. act. (*yuᶜazziru*)

48:9 (9)	you may believe in God and His Messenger and succour Him

*ᶜ Z W

ᶜIZĪN n.f. (pl. of ᶜ*izah*)~group, knot

70:37 (37)	on the right hand and on the left hand in knots

*ᶜ Z Z

ᶜAZZA vb. (I)~to conquer, to overcome. (n.vb.) power, might, glory

a) perf. act.

38:23 (22)	he overcame me in the argument

f) n.vb. (*ᶜizz*)

19:81 (84)	that they might be for them a might

ᶜAZĪZ n.m. (adj., pl. *aᶜizzah*)~great, strong, mighty; All-mighty [Ar], Sublime [Bl] (Divine attribute); a prince, a governor; grievous, disdainful

2:129 (123)	Thou art the All-mighty
2:209 (205)	know then that God is All-mighty
2:220 (219)	surely God is All-mighty
2:228 (228)	God is All-mighty
2:240 (241)	God is All-mighty
2:260 (262)	do thou know that God is All-mighty
3:4 (3)	God is All-mighty
3:6 (4)	there is no god but He, the All-mighty
3:18 (16)	there is no god but He, the All-mighty
3:62 (55)	assuredly God is the All-mighty
3:126 (122)	help comes only from God the All-mighty
4:56 (59)	surely God is All-mighty
4:158 (156)	God is All-mighty
4:165 (163)	God is All-mighty
5:38 (42)	God is All-mighty
5:54 (59)	humble towards the believers, disdainful towards the unbelievers
5:95 (96)	God is All-mighty
5:118 (118)	Thou art the All-mighty
6:96 (96)	that is the ordaining of the All-mighty
8:10 (10)	surely God is All-mighty
8:49 (51)	surely God is All-mighty
8:63 (64)	surely He is All-mighty
8:67 (68)	God is All-mighty
9:40 (40)	God is All-mighty
9:71 (72)	God is All-mighty
9:128 (129)	grievous to him is your suffering
11:66 (69)	thy Lord is the All-strong, the All-mighty
11:91 (93)	thou art not strong against us

11:92 (94)	is my tribe stronger against you than God?
12:30 (30)	the Governor's wife has been soliciting her page
12:51 (51)	the Governor's wife said, 'Now the truth is at last discovered'
12:78 (78)	mighty prince, he has a father
12:88 (88)	O mighty prince, affliction has visited us
14:1 (1)	to the path of the All-mighty, the All-laudable
14:4 (4)	He is the All-mighty
14:20 (23)	that is surely no great matter for God
14:47 (48)	surely God is All-mighty, Vengeful
16:60 (62)	He is the All-mighty, the All-wise
18:34 (32)	mightier in respect of men
22:40 (41)	surely God is All-strong, All-mighty
22:74 (73)	surely God is All-strong, All-mighty
26:9 (8)	He is the All-mighty
26:68 (68)	thy Lord, He is the All-mighty
26:104 (104)	thy Lord, He is the All-mighty
26:122 (122)	thy Lord, He is the All-mighty
26:140 (140)	thy Lord, He is the All-mighty
26:159 (159)	thy Lord, He is the All-mighty
26:175 (175)	thy Lord, He is the All-mighty
26:191 (191)	thy Lord, He is the All-mighty
26:217 (217)	put thy trust in the All-mighty
27:9 (9)	behold, it is I, God, the All-mighty
27:34 (34)	make the mighty ones of its inhabitants abased
27:78 (80)	He is the All-mighty
29:26 (25)	He is the All-mighty
29:42 (41)	He is the All-mighty
30:5 (4)	He is the All-mighty
30:27 (26)	He is the All-mighty
31:9 (8)	He is the All-mighty
31:27 (26)	God is All-mighty
32:6 (5)	He is the knower of the Unseen and the Visible, the All-mighty
33:25 (25)	surely God is All-strong, All-mighty
34:6 (6)	the path of the All-mighty
34:27 (26)	rather He is God, the All-mighty
35:2 (2)	He is the All-mighty
35:17 (18)	that is surely no great matter for God
35:28 (25)	surely God is All-mighty
36:5 (4)	the sending down of the All-mighty
36:38 (38)	that is the ordaining of the All-mighty
38:9 (8)	they the treasuries of thy Lord's mercy, the All-mighty
38:66 (66)	Lord of the heavens and earth, and of what between them is, the All-mighty
39:1 (1)	the sending down of the Book is from God the All-mighty
39:5 (7)	is not He the All-mighty
39:37 (38)	is not God All-mighty
40:2 (1)	the sending down of the Book is from God the All-mighty
40:8 (8)	Thou art the All-mighty
40:42 (45)	I call you to the All-mighty
41:12 (11)	that is the ordaining of the All-mighty
41:41 (41)	surely it is a Book Sublime
42:3 (1)	God, the All-mighty
42:19 (18)	He is the All-strong, the All-mighty
43:9 (8)	the All-mighty, the All-knowing created them
44:42 (42)	He is the All-mighty
44:49 (49)	surely thou art the mighty, the noble

45:2 (1)	the sending down of the Book is from God, the All-mighty
45:37 (36)	He is the All-mighty
46:2 (1)	the sending down of the Book is from God, the All-mighty
48:3 (3)	that God may help thee with mighty help
48:7 (7)	God is All-mighty
48:19 (19)	God is ever All-mighty
54:42 (42)	We seized them with the seizing of One Mighty, Omnipotent
57:1 (1)	He is the All-mighty
57:25 (25)	surely God is All-strong, All-mighty
58:21 (21)	surely God is All-strong, All-mighty
59:1 (1)	He is the All-mighty
59:23 (23)	the All-faithful, the All-preserver, the All-mighty
59:24 (24)	He is the All-mighty
60:5 (5)	Our Lord, Thou art the All-mighty
61:1 (1)	He is the All-mighty
62:1 (1)	the King, the All-holy, the All-mighty
62:3 (3)	He is the All-mighty
63:8 (8)	if we return to the City, the mightier ones of it will expel
64:18 (18)	Knower He of the Unseen and the Visible, the All-mighty
67:2 (2)	He is the All-mighty
85:8 (8)	they believed in God the All-mighty

ʿIZZAH n.f.~might, glory, vainglory [Ar]; power [Pk]; honour [Bl]

2:206 (202)	vainglory seizes him in his sin
4:139 (138)	do they seek glory
4:139 (138)	glory altogether belongs to God
10:65 (66)	glory belongs altogether to God
26:44 (43)	by the might of Pharaoh we shall be the victors
35:10 (11)	whosoever desires glory
35:10 (11)	glory altogether belongs to God
37:180 (180)	glory be to thy Lord, the Lord of Glory
38:2 (1)	the unbelievers glory in their schism
38:82 (83)	by Thy glory, I shall pervert them all together
63:8 (8)	glory belongs unto God

ʿUZZÁ n.prop.~Al-ʿUzza

53:19 (19)	have you considered El-Lat and El-'Uzza

ʿAZZAZA vb. (II)~to strengthen, to reinforce

a) perf. act.

36:14 (13)	We sent a third as reinforcement

AʿAZZA vb. (IV)~to render powerful, to exalt

b) impf. act. (*yuʿizzu*)

3:26 (25)	Thou exaltest whom Thou wilt

*ʿ Ẓ M

ʿAẒĪM n.m. (adj)~mighty, glorious, a man of moment; All-mighty, All-glorious (Divine attribute); grievous; (*Allāhu dhū al-faḍl al-ʿaẓīm*) God is of bounty abounding

2:7 (6)	there awaits them a mighty chastisement

2:49 (46)	in that was a grievous trial from your Lord
2:105 (99)	God is of bounty abounding
2:114 (108)	in the world to come a mighty chastisement
2:255 (256)	He is the All-high, the All-glorious
3:74 (67)	God is of bounty abounding
3:105 (101)	those there awaits a mighty chastisement
3:172 (166)	of them who did good and feared God, shall be a mighty wage
3:174 (168)	God is of bounty abounding
3:176 (170)	there awaits them a mighty chastisement
3:179 (174)	there shall be for you a mighty wage
4:13 (17)	that is the mighty triumph
4:27 (32)	those who follow their lusts desire you to swerve away mightily
4:40 (44)	He will double it, and give from Himself a mighty wage
4:48 (51)	has indeed forged a mighty sin
4:54 (57)	We gave them a mighty kingdom
4:67 (70)	We surely would have given them from Us a mighty wage
4:73 (75)	to attain a mighty triumph
4:74 (76)	We shall bring him a mighty wage
4:93 (95)	and prepare for him a mighty chastisement
4:95 (97)	the ones who sit at home for the bounty of a mighty wage
4:113 (113)	God's bounty to thee is ever great
4:114 (114)	We shall surely give him a mighty wage
4:146 (145)	God will certainly give the believers a mighty wage
4:156 (155)	and their uttering against Mary a mighty calummy
4:162 (160)	them We shall surely give a mighty wage
5:9 (12)	they shall have forgiveness and a mighty wage
5:33 (37)	in the world to come awaits them a mighty chastisement
5:41 (45)	in the world to come awaits them a mighty chastisement
5:119 (119)	that is the mighty triumph
6:15 (15)	against my Lord, the chastisement of a dreadful day
7:59 (57)	I fear for you the chastisement of a dreadful day
7:116 (113)	and produced a mighty sorcery
7:141 (137)	in that was a grievous trial from your Lord
8:28 (28)	that with God is a mighty wage
8:29 (29)	God is of bounty abounding
8:68 (69)	for what you took, a mighty chastisement
9:20 (20)	are mightier in rank with God
9:22 (22)	surely with God is a mighty wage
9:63 (64)	that is the mighty degradation
9:72 (73)	that is the mighty triumph
9:89 (90)	that is the mighty triumph
9:100 (101)	that is the mighty triumph
9:101 (102)	they will be returned to a mighty chastisement
9:111 (112)	that is the mighty triumph
9:129 (130)	He is the Lord of the Mighty Throne
10:15 (16)	the chastisement of a dreadful day
10:64 (65)	that is the mighty triumph
12:28 (28)	surely your guile is great
14:6 (6)	that was a grievous trial from your Lord
15:87 (87)	We have given thee seven of the oft-repeated, and the mighty Koran
16:94 (96)	lest there should await you a mighty chastisement
16:106 (108)	there awaits them a mighty chastisement
17:40 (42)	surely it is a monstrous thing you are saying
19:37 (38)	woe to those who disbelieve for the scene of a dreadful day
21:76 (76)	and delivered him and his people from the great distress

22:1 (1)	surely the earthquake of the Hour is a mighty thing
23:86 (88)	who is the Lord of the seven heavens and the Lord of the mighty Throne?
24:11 (11)	him there awaits a mighty chastisement
24:14 (14)	for your mutterings a mighty chastisement
24:15 (14)	with God it was a mighty thing
24:16 (15)	this is a mighty calumny
24:23 (23)	there awaits them a mighty chastisement
26:63 (63)	each part was as a mighty mount
26:135 (135)	I fear for you the chastisement of a dreadful day
26:156 (156)	chastisement of a dreadful day
26:189 (189)	assuredly it was the chastisement of a dreadful day
27:23 (23)	she possesses a mighty throne
27:26 (26)	there is no god but He, the Lord of the Mighty Throne
28:79 (79)	surely he is a man of mighty fortune
31:13 (12)	to associate others with God is a mighty wrong
33:29 (29)	for those amongst you such as do good a mighty wage
33:35 (35)	God has prepared forgiveness and a mighty wage
33:53 (53)	surely that would be, in God's sight, a monstrous thing
33:71 (71)	has won a mighty triumph
37:60 (58)	this is indeed the mighty triumph
37:76 (74)	We delivered him and his people from the great distress
37:107 (107)	We ransomed him with a mighty sacrifice
37:115 (115)	We delivered them and their people from the great distress
38:67 (67)	it is a mighty tiding
39:13 (15)	chastisement of a dreadful day
40:9 (9)	that is indeed the mighty triumph
41:35 (35)	none shall receive it, except a man of mighty fortune
42:4 (2)	He is the All-high, the All-glorious
43:31 (30)	Why was this Koran not sent down upon some man of moment?
44:57 (57)	that is the mighty triumph
45:10 (9)	for them awaits a mighty chastisement
46:21 (20)	I fear for you the chastisement of adreadful day
48:5 (5)	that is in God's sight a mighty triumph
48:10 (10)	God will give him a mighty wage
48:29 (29)	forgiveness and a mighty wage
49:3 (3)	they shall have forgiveness and a mighty wage
56:46 (45)	and persisted in the Great Sin
56:74 (73)	magnify the Name of thy Lord, the All-mighty
56:76 (75)	that is indeed a mighty oath
56:96 (96)	magnify the Name of thy Lord, the All-mighty
57:10 (10)	those are mightier in rank
57:12 (12)	that is indeed the mighty triumph
57:21 (21)	God is of bounty abounding
57:29 (29)	God is of bounty abounding
61:12 (12)	that is the mighty triumph
62:4 (4)	God is of bounty abounding
64:9 (9)	that is the mighty triumph
64:15 (15)	and with God is a mighty wage
68:4 (4)	surely thou art upon a mighty morality
69:33 (33)	he never believed in God the All-mighty
69:52 (52)	then magnify the Name of thy Lord, the All-mighty
73:20 (20)	you shall find it with God as better, and mightier a wage
78:2 (2)	of the mighty tiding
83:5 (5)	unto a mighty day

ᶜAẒM n.m. (pl. ᶜ*iẓām*)~a bone

2:259 (261)	look at the bones, how We shall set them up
6:146 (147)	what is mingled with bone
17:49 (52)	when we are bones and broken bits
17:98 (100)	when we are bones and broken bits
19:4 (3)	behold the bones within me are feeble
23:14 (14)	then We created of the tissue bones
23:14 (14)	then We garmented the bones in flesh
23:35 (37)	when you are dead, and become dust and bones
23:82 (84)	when we are dead and become dust and bones
36:78 (78)	who shall quicken the bones when they are decayed
37:16 (16)	when we are dead and become dust and bones
37:53 (51)	when we are dead and become dust and bones
56:47 (47)	when we are dead and become dust and bones
75:3 (3)	does man reckon We shall not gather his bones?
79:11 (11)	when we are bones old and wasted

ᶜAẒẒAMA vb. (II)~to make great, to honour, to venerate

b) impf. act. (*yuᶜaẓẓimu*)

22:30 (31)	whosoever venerates the sacred things of God
22:32 (33)	whosoever venerates God's waymarks

AᶜẒAMA vb. (IV)~to magnify, to increase

b) impf. act. (*yuᶜẓimu*)

65:5 (5)	He will magnify his wage

BĀ

*B ʾ R

BIʾR n.f.~well, cistern

22:45 (44)	how many a ruined well

*B ʾ S

BAʾISA vb. (I)~(pcple. act.) needy, wretched

g) pcple. act. (*bāʾis*)

22:28 (29)	eat thereof, and feed the wretched poor

BIʾSA vb. (I) A unique type of verb which is not conjugated, belonging to a family of verbs known as the "verbs of praise and blame." Note that the vocalization is also changed from *faʿala* to *fiʿla*~to be evil (evil is...), to be miserable

a) perf. act.

2:90 (84)	evil is the thing they have sold themselves for
2:93 (87)	evil is the thing your faith bids you to
2:102 (96)	evil then was that they sold themselves for
2:126 (120)	how evil a homecoming
2:206 (202)	how evil a cradling
3:12 (10)	an evil cradling
3:151 (144)	evil is the lodging of the evildoers
3:162 (156)	an evil homecoming
3:187 (184)	how evil was that their selling
3:197 (196)	an evil cradling
5:62 (67)	evil is the thing they have been doing
5:63 (68)	evil is the thing they have been working
5:79 (82)	surely evil were the things they did
5:80 (83)	evil is that they have forwarded to their account
7:150 (149)	evilly have you done in my place, after me
8:16 (16)	an evil homecoming
9:73 (74)	an evil homecoming
11:98 (100)	evil the watering-place to be led down to
11:99 (101)	evil the offering to be offered
13:18 (18)	an evil cradling
14:29 (34)	an evil stablishment
16:29 (31)	evil is the lodging of those that wax proud
18:29 (28)	how evil a potion, and how evil a resting-place
18:50 (48)	how evil is that exchange for the evildoers
22:13 (13)	an evil protector indeed
22:13 (13)	an evil friend
22:72 (71)	an evil homecoming
24:57 (56)	an evil homecoming
38:56 (56)	an evil cradling
38:60 (60)	how evil a stablishment
39:72 (72)	how evil is the lodging of those that are proud
40:76 (76)	how evil is the lodging of those that are proud
43:38 (37)	an evil comrade

49:11 (11)	an evil name is ungodliness after belief
57:15 (14)	an evil homecoming
58:8 (9)	an evil homecoming
62:5 (5)	evil is the likeness of the people who have cried lies
64:10 (10)	an evil homecoming
66:9 (9)	an evil homecoming
67:6 (6)	an evil homecoming

BA'S n.m.~might, peril, battle [Ar]; prowess [Bl]; panic, fury, wrath [Ali]; stress, fear [Pk]

2:177 (172)	endure with fortitude misfortune, hardship and peril
4:84 (86)	haply God will restrain the unbelievers' might
4:84 (86)	God is stronger in might, more terrible
6:43 (43)	when Our might came upon them, they had been humble
6:65 (65)	to make you taste the violence of one another
6:147 (148)	His might will never be turned back from the people
6:148 (149)	people before them cried lies until they tasted Our might
7:4 (3)	Our might came upon it at night
7:5 (4)	they but cried, when Our might came upon them
7:97 (95)	Our might shall not come upon them at night
7:98 (96)	Our might shall not come upon them in daylight
12:110 (110)	Our might will never be turned back from the people
16:81 (83)	shirts to protect you from your own violence
17:5 (5)	servants of Ours, men of great might
18:2 (2)	to warn of great violence from Him
21:12 (12)	when they perceived Our might, behold, they ran headlong out of it
21:80 (80)	to fortify you against your violence
27:33 (33)	We possess force and we possess great might
33:18 (18)	come to battle but little
40:29 (30)	who will help us against the might of God
40:84 (84)	when they saw Our might
40:85 (85)	when they saw Our might did not profit them
48:16 (16)	a people possessed of great might
57:25 (25)	We sent down iron, wherein is great might
59:14 (14)	their valour is great, among themselves

BA'ĪS n.m. (adj)~evil, dreadful

7:165 (165)	We seized the evildoers with evil chastisement

BA'SĀ' n.f.~hardship, bodily misfortune, tribulation

2:177 (172)	endure with fortitude misfortune, hardship
2:214 (210)	they were afflicted by misery and hardship
6:42 (42)	We seized them with misery and hardship
7:94 (92)	We seized its people with misery and hardship

IBTA'ASA vb. (VIII)~to be grieved, to be distressed; to despair

b) impf. act. (*yabta'isu*)

11:36 (38)	be thou not distressed by that they may be doing
12:69 (69)	do not be dispair of that they have done

*B ʿ D

BAʿUDA vb. (I) (*baʿida*, in 11:95)~to be distant, to be removed afar, to be done away. (n.vb.) distance; away with (acc. followed by prep. *li-*)

a) perf. act.

9:42 (42)	the distance was too far for them
11:95 (98)	away with Midian, even as Thamood was done away

f) n.vb. (*buʿd*)

11:44 (46)	away with the people of the evildoers
11:60 (63)	away with Ad, the people of Hood
11:68 (71)	away with Thamood
11:95 (98)	away with Midian, even as Thamood was done away
23:41s34(43)	away with the people of the evildoers
23:44 (46)	away with a people who do not believe
43:38 (37)	would there had been between me and thee the distance of the two Easts

BAʿĪD n.m. (adj)~distant, far, wide, long

2:176 (171)	those that are at variance regarding the Book are in wide schism
3:30 (28)	if there were only a far space between it and that day
4:60 (63)	Satan desires to lead them astray into far error
4:116 (116)	with God anything, has gone astray into far error
4:136 (135)	has surely gone astray into far error
4:167 (165)	have gone astray into far error
11:83 (84)	marked with thy Lord, and never far from the evildoers
11:89 (91)	people of Lot are not far away from you
14:3 (3)	they are in far error
14:18 (21)	that is the far error
21:109 (109)	I know not whether near or far is that you are promised
22:12 (12)	that is indeed the far error
22:53 (52)	surely the evildoers are in wide schism
25:12 (13)	when it sees them from a far place
27:22 (22)	he tarried not long
34:8 (8)	are in chastisement and far error
34:52 (51)	how can they reach from a place far away
34:53 (52)	guessing at the Unseen from a place far away
41:44 (44)	they are called from a far place
41:52 (52)	who is further astray than he who is in wide schism?
42:18 (17)	those who are in doubt concerning the Hour are indeed in far error
50:3 (3)	that is a far returning
50:27 (26)	he was in far error
50:31 (30)	Paradise shall be brought forward to the godfearing, not afar
70:6 (6)	they see it as if far off

BĀʿADA vb. (III)~to cause a distance to be, to prolong

c) impv. (*bāʿid*)

34:19 (18)	Lord, prolong the stages of our travel

ABʿADA vb. (IV)~(pcple. pass.) that which is kept far off

h) pcple. pass. (*mubʿad*)

21:101 (101)	they shall be kept far from it

*B ʿ Ḍ

BAʿŪḌAH n.f.~a gnat

2:26 (24)	God is not ashamed to strike a similitude even of a gnat

*B ʿ L

BAʿL (1) n.m. (pl. *buʿūlah*)~husband, mate

2:228 (228)	in such time their mates have better right to restore them
4:128 (127)	if a woman fear rebelliousness or aversion in her husband
11:72 (75)	this my husband is an old man
24:31 (31)	not reveal their adornment save to their husbands
24:31 (31)	or their fathers, or their husbands' fathers
24:31 (31)	or their sons, or their husbands' sons

BAʿL (2)~Baal (a pre-Islamic deity)

37:125 (125)	do you call on Baal

*B ʿ R

BAʿĪR n.com.~a camel

12:65 (65)	we shall obtain an extra camel's load
12:72 (72)	whoever brings it shall receive a camel's load

*B ʿ TH

BAʿATHA vb. (I)~to raise up, to send forth. (n.vb.) upraising. (pcple. pass.) one who is raised up

a) perf. act.

2:56 (53)	We raised you up after you were dead
2:213 (209)	then God sent forth the Prophets
2:247 (248)	God has raised up Saul for you as king
2:259 (261)	God made him die a hundred years, then He raised him up
3:164 (158)	He raised up among them a Messenger
5:12 (15)	We raised up from among them twelve chieftains
5:31 (34)	then God sent forth a raven
7:103 (101)	then We sent, after them, Moses
10:74 (75)	then We sent forth, after him, Messengers
10:75 (76)	then We sent forth, after them, Moses
16:36 (38)	We sent forth among every nation a Messenger
17:5 (5)	We sent against you servants of Ours
17:94 (96)	has God sent forth a mortal as Messenger?
18:12 (11)	afterwards We raised them up again
18:19 (18)	even so We raised them up again
25:41 (43)	is this he whom God sent forth as a Messenger?
25:51 (53)	We would have raised up in every city a warner
36:52 (52)	who roused us out of our sleeping-place?
62:2 (2)	He who has raised up from among the common people

b) impf. act. (*yabʿathu*)

6:36 (36)	God will raise them up
6:60 (60)	He raises you up therein

6:65 (65)	He is able to send forth upon you chastisement
7:167 (166)	He would send forth against them
16:38 (40)	God will never raise up him who dies
16:84 (86)	We shall raise up from every nation a witness
16:89 (91)	We shall raise up from every nation a witness
17:15 (16)	We never chastise, until We send forth a Messenger
17:79 (81)	thy Lord will raise thee up to a laudable station
22:7 (7)	God shall raise up whosoever is within the tombs
28:59 (59)	He sent in their mother-city a Messenger
40:34 (36)	God will never send forth a Messenger after him
58:6 (7)	upon the day when God shall raise them up
58:18 (19)	upon the day when God shall raise them up
72:7 (7)	that God would never raise up anyone

c) impv. (*ibʿath*)

2:129 (123)	do Thou send among them a Messenger
2:246 (247)	raise up for us a king
4:35 (39)	bring forth an arbiter from his people
18:19 (18)	now send one of you forth with this silver
26:36 (35)	send among the cities musterers

e) impf. pass. (*yubʿathu*)

7:14 (13)	respite me till the day they shall be raised
15:36 (36)	respite me till the day they shall be raised
16:21 (22)	when they shall be raised
19:15 (15)	the day he is raised up alive
19:33 (34)	the day I am raised up alive
23:16 (16)	on the Day of Resurrection you shall surely be raised up
23:100 (102)	the day that they shall be raised up
26:87 (87)	degrade me not upon the day when they are raised up
27:65 (67)	when they shall be raised
37:144 (144)	until the day they shall be raised
38:79 (80)	respite me till the day they shall be raised
64:7 (7)	unbelievers assert that they will never be raised up
64:7 (7)	you shall be raised up

f) n.vb. (*baʿth*)

22:5 (5)	if you are in doubt as to the Upraising
30:56 (56)	till the Day of the Upraising
30:56 (56)	this is the Day of the Upraising
31:28 (27)	your creation and your upraising are as but as a single soul

h) pcple. pass. (*mabʿūth*)

6:29 (29)	we shall not be raised
11:7 (10)	you shall surely be raised up after death
17:49 (52)	shall we really be raised up again
17:98 (100)	shall we really be raised up again
23:37 (39)	we die, and we live, and we shall not be raised up
23:82 (84)	shall we be indeed raised up?
37:16 (16)	shall we indeed be raised up?
56:47 (47)	shall we indeed be raised up?
83:4 (4)	do those not think that they shall be raised up

INBAʿATHA vb. (VII)~to be upraised or aroused; to be sent. (n.vb.) arousing, apraising

a) perf. act.

91:12 (12) when the most wretched of them uprose

f) n.vb. (*inbiʿāth*)

9:46 (46) God was averse that they should be aroused

*B ʿ TH R

BAʿTHARA vb. (quad I)~to scatter abroad, to turn upside down, to overthrow

d) perf. pass. (*buʿthira*)

82:4 (4) when the tombs are overthrown
100:9 (9) that which is in the tombs is overthrown

*B B L

BĀBIL n.prop.~Babylon

2:102 (96) that which was sent down upon Babylon's two angels

*B D ʾ

BADAʾA vb. (I)~to begin, to originate (tr)

a) perf. act.

7:29 (28) as He originated you so you will return
9:13 (13) and purposed to expel the Messenger, beginning the first time against you
12:76 (76) he made beginning with their sacks
21:104 (104) as We originated the first creation
29:20 (19) behold how He originated creation
32:7 (6) He originated the creation of man

b) impf. act. (*yabdaʾu*)

10:4 (4) in truth. He originates creation
10:34 (35) is there any of your associates who originates creation
10:34 (35) God — He originates creation
27:64 (65) who originates creation
30:11 (10) God originates creation
30:27 (26) it is He who originates creation

ABDAʾA vb. (IV)~to originate (tr), to cause to begin

b) impf. act. (*yubdiʾu*)

29:19 (18) have they not seen how God originates creation
34:49 (48) truth has come; falsehood originates not
85:13 (13) it is He who originates

*B D ᶜ

BADĪᶜ n.m.~Creator (Divine attribute)

2:117 (111)	Creator of the heavens and the earth
6:101 (101)	Creator of the heavens and the earth

BIDᶜ n.m.~innovation, new

46:9 (8)	I am not an innovation among the Messengers

IBTADAᶜA vb. (VIII)~to invent

a) perf. act.

57:27 (27)	and monasticism they invented

*B D L

BADAL n.m.~an exchange

18:50 (48)	how evil is that exchange for the evildoers

BADDALA vb. (II)~to exchange, to substitute, to give in place of. (n.vb.) changing [Ar, Ali]; alteration [Bl]; substitute [Pk]. (pcple. act.) one who changes (tr)

a) perf. act.

2:59 (56)	then the evildoers substituted a saying
2:181 (177)	if any man changes it after hearing it
4:56 (59)	We shall give them in exchange other skins
7:95 (93)	We gave them in the place of evil good
7:162 (162)	then the evildoers of them substituted a saying
14:28 (33)	those who exchanged the bounty of God with unthankfulness
16:101 (103)	when We exchange a verse in the place of another
27:11 (11)	then, after evil, has changed into good
33:23 (23)	they have not changed in the least
34:16 (15)	We gave them, in exchange for their two gardens
76:28 (28)	when We will, We shall exchange their likes

b) impf. act. (*yubaddilu*)

2:181 (177)	sin shall rest upon those who change it
2:211 (207)	whoso changes God's blessing
10:15 (16)	it is not for me to alter it of my own accord
24:55 (54)	and will give them in exchange, after their fear, security
25:70 (70)	those, God will change their evil deeds
40:26 (27)	I fear that he may change your religion
48:15 (15)	desiring to change God's words
56:61 (61)	We may exchange the likes of you
70:41 (41)	to substitute a better than they

c) impv. (*baddil*)

10:15 (16)	bring a Koran other than this, or alter it

e) impf. pass. (*yubaddalu*)

14:48 (49)	upon the day the earth shall be changed
50:29 (28)	the Word is not changed with Me

f) n.vb. (*tabdīl*)

10:64 (65)	there is no changing the words of God
30:30 (29)	there is no changing God's creation
33:23 (23)	they have not changed <in the least>
33:62 (62)	thou shalt find no changing the wont of God
35:43 (41)	thou shalt never find any changing the wont of God
48:23 (23)	thou shalt never find any changing the wont of God
76:28 (28)	when We will, We shall exchange their likes <...>

g) pcple. act. (*mubaddil*)

6:34 (34)	no man can change the words of God
6:115 (115)	no man can change His words
18:27 (26)	no man can change His words

ABDALA vb. (IV)~to change, to cause to change (with double accus)

b) impf. act. (*yubdilu*)

18:81 (80)	their Lord should give to them in exchange one better
66:5 (5)	his Lord will give him in exchange wives
68:32 (32)	our Lord will give us in exchange a better than it

TABADDALA vb. (V)~to exchange, to take in exchange

a) perf. act.

33:52 (52)	neither for thee to take other wives in exchange

b) impf. act. (*yatabaddalu*)

2:108 (102)	whoso exchanges belief for unbelief
4:2 (2)	do not exchange the corrupt for the good

ISTABDALA vb. (X)~to substitute, to have in exchange. (n.vb.) exchanging, substituting

b) impf. act. (*yastabdilu*)

2:61 (58)	would you have in exchange what is meaner
9:39 (39)	instead of you He will substitute another people
47:38 (40)	if you turn away, He will substitute another people

f) n.vb. (*istibdāl*)

4:20 (24)	if you desire to exchange a wife

*B D N

BADAN n.m.~body

10:92 (92)	We shall deliver thee with thy body

BUDN n.m. (pl. of *badanah*)~beasts (prob. camels) of sacrifice

22:36 (37)	beasts of sacrifice — We have appointed them

*B D R

BADR n.prop.~Badr

3:123 (119)	God most surely helped you at Badr

BIDĀR n.m. (adv)~hastily

4:6 (5)	consume it not wastefully and hastily

*B D W

BADĀ vb. (I)~to appear, to be manifest, to seem; to show oneself; to reveal. (pcple. act.) desert-dweller; (*bādī ar-ra'y*) without reflection, inconsiderately

a) perf. act.

3:118 (114)	hatred has already shown itself of their mouths
6:28 (28)	that which they were concealing before has now appeared
7:22 (21)	their shameful parts revealed to them
12:35 (35)	it seemed good to them, after they had seen the signs
20:121 (119)	their shameful parts revealed to them
39:47 (48)	yet there would appear to them from God
39:48 (49)	there would appear to them the evils
45:33 (32)	evil deeds that they have done shall appear to them
60:4 (4)	between us and you enmity has shown itself

g) pcple. act. (*bādī*)

11:27 (29)	we see not any following thee but the vilest of us, inconsiderately
22:25 (25)	alike him who cleaves to it and the tent-dweller
33:20 (20)	they will wish that they were desert-dwellers among the Bedouins

BADW n.m.~a desert

12:100 (101)	when He brought you out of the desert

ABDÁ vb. (IV)~to reveal, to publish, to show, to do openly. (pcple. act.) one who reveals, who shows etc.

b) impf. act. (*yubdī*)

2:33 (31)	I know what things you reveal
2:271 (273)	if you publish your freewill offerings
2:284 (284)	whether you publish what is in your hearts
3:29 (27)	whether you hide what is in your breasts or publish it
3:154 (148)	they were concealing in their hearts that they show not to thee
4:149 (148)	if you do good openly or in secret
5:99 (99)	God knows what you reveal
6:91 (91)	you put it into parchments, revealing them
7:20 (19)	Satan whispered to them, to reveal to them
12:77 (77)	Joseph secreted it in his soul and disclosed it not
24:29 (29)	God knows what you reveal
24:31 (31)	and reveal not their adornment save such as is outward
24:31 (31)	and not reveal their adornment
28:10 (9)	she wellnigh disclosed him had We not strengthened her heart
33:54 (54)	whether you reveal anything

e) impf. pass. (*yubdá*)

5:101 (101) question not concerning things which, if they were revealed to you
5:101 (101) they will be revealed to you

g) pcple. act. (*mubdī*)

33:37 (37) thou wast concealing within thyself what God should reveal

*B DH R

BADHDHARA vb. (II)~to squander. (n.vb.) squandering. (pcple. act.) one who squanders, a squanderer

b) impf. act. (*yubadhdhiru*)

17:26 (28) and never squander

f) n.vb. (*tabdhīr*)

17:26 (28) and <never> squander

g) pcple. act. (*mubadhdhir*)

17:27 (29) squanderers are brothers of Satan

*B Ḍ ᶜ

BIḌᶜ n.m.~some, few, certain

12:42 (42) he continued in the prison for certain years
30:4 (3) in a few years

BIḌĀᶜAH n.f.~merchandise, goods

12:19 (19) they hid him as merchandise
12:62 (62) put their merchandise in their saddlebags
12:65 (65) when they opened their things, they found their merchandise
12:65 (65) our merchandise here is restored to us
12:88 (88) we come with merchandise of scant worth

*B GH Ḍ

BAGHḌĀʾ n.f.~hatred

3:118 (114) hatred has already shown itself of their mouths
5:14 (17) We have stirred up among them enmity and hatred
5:64 (69) We have cast between them enmity and hatred
5:91 (93) Satan only desires to precipitate enmity and hatred
60:4 (4) between us and you enmity has shown itself, and hatred

*B GH L

BAGHL n.m. (pl. *bighāl*)~a mule

16:8 (8) and horses, and mules, and asses, for you to ride

*B GH T

BAGHTAH n.f. (adv)~suddenly

6:31 (31)	when the Hour comes to them suddenly
6:44 (44)	We seized them suddenly
6:47 (47)	what think you? If God's chastisement comes upon you, suddenly
7:95 (93)	We seized them suddenly, unawares
7:187 (186)	it will not come on you but — suddenly
12:107 (107)	shall not come upon them suddenly
21:40 (41)	it shall come upon them suddenly
22:55 (54)	until the Hour comes on them suddenly
26:202 (202)	so that it will come upon them suddenly
29:53 (53)	it shall come upon them suddenly
39:55 (56)	chastisement comes upon you suddenly
43:66 (66)	it shall come upon them suddenly
47:18 (20)	that it shall come upon them suddenly

*B GH Y

BAGHÁ vb. (I)~to be insolent, to wrong, to injure, to encroach, to overpass, to oppress; to seek, to look for, to desire. (n.vb.) insolence; insolent, grudging [Ar]; oppressive treatment [Bl]; disobedience, contumacy [Ali]; wrong [Pk]. (pcple. act.) one who desires, desiring

a) perf. act.

28:76 (76)	he became insolent to them
38:22 (21)	one of us has injured the other
42:27 (26)	they would have been insolent in the earth
49:9 (9)	if one of them is insolent against the other

b) impf. act. (*yabghī*)

3:83 (77)	do they desire another religion than God's
3:99 (94)	why do you bar from God's way the believer, desiring to make it crooked
4:34 (38)	look not for any way against them
5:50 (55)	is it the judgment of pagandom then that they are seeking?
6:164 (164)	shall I seek after a Lord other than God
7:45 (43)	who bar from God's way, desiring to make it crooked
7:86 (84)	barring from God's way those who believe in Him, desiring to make it crooked
7:140 (136)	shall I seek a god for you other than God
9:47 (47)	seeking to stir up sedition between you
10:23 (24)	they are insolent in the earth
11:19 (22)	who bar from God's way, desiring to make it crooked
12:65 (65)	what more should we desire?
14:3 (3)	and bar from God's way, desiring to make it crooked
18:64 (63)	this is what we were seeking
18:108 (108)	desiring no removal out of them
28:77 (77)	seek not to work corruption in the earth
38:24 (23)	many intermixers do injury one against the other
42:42 (40)	and are insolent in the earth wrongfully
49:9 (9)	fight the insolent one till it reverts to God's commandment
55:20 (20)	between them a barrier they do not overpass

d) perf. pass. (*bughiya*)

22:60 (59) and then again is oppressed, assuredly God will help him

f) n.vb. (*baghy*)

2:90 (84) grudging that God should send down of His bounty
2:213 (209) being insolent one to another
3:19 (17) being insolent one to another
6:146 (147) We recompensed them for their insolence
7:33 (31) and unjust insolence, and that you associate
10:23 (24) your insolence is only against yourselves
10:90 (90) Pharaoh and his hosts followed them insolently
16:90 (92) He forbids indecency, dishonour, and insolence
42:14 (13) being insolent one to another
42:39 (37) who, when insolence visits them, do help themselves
45:17 (16) being insolent one to another

g) pcple. act. (*bāghī*)

2:173 (168) whoso is constrained, not desiring nor transgressing
6:145 (146) whoso is constrained, not desiring nor transgressing
16:115 (116) whoso is constrained, not desiring nor transgressing

BAGHĪY n.f.~a harlot, unchaste woman

19:20 (20) whom no mortal has touched, neither have I been unchaste
19:28 (29) nor was thy mother a woman unchaste

BIGHĀʾ n.m.~prostitution, fornication

24:33 (33) constrain not your slavegirls to prostitution

INBAGHÁ vb. (VII)~to behove, to be fit and proper, to be seemly, to befall or belong

b) impf. act. (*yanbaghī*)

19:92 (93) it behoves not the All-merciful to take a son
25:18 (19) it did not behove us to take unto ourselves protectors
26:211 (211) it behoves them not, neither are they able
36:40 (40) it behoves not the sun to overtake the moon
36:69 (69) We have not taught him poetry; it is not seemly for him
38:35 (34) give me a kingdom such as may not befall anyone

IBTAGHÁ vb. (VIII)~to seek, to desire. (n.vb.) seeking, desiring

a) perf. act.

9:48 (48) they sought to stir up sedition already
17:42 (44) they would have sought a way unto the Lord of the Throne
23:7 (7) whosoever seeks after more than that
33:51 (51) if thou seekest any thou hast set aside
70:31 (31) whoso seeks after more than that

b) impf. act. (*yabtaghī*)

2:198 (194) it is no fault in you, that you should seek bounty
3:85 (79) whoso desires another religion than Islam
4:24 (28) beyond all that, is that you may seek

4:94 (96) seeking the chance goods of the present life
4:139 (138) do they seek glory in them?
5:2 (2) nor those repairing to the Holy House seeking from their Lord bounty
6:35 (35) if thou canst seek out a hole in the earth
6:114 (114) shall I seek after any judge but God?
16:14 (14) and that you may seek of His bounty
17:12 (13) and that you may seek bounty from your Lord
17:57 (59) those they call upon are themselves seeking
17:66 (68) that you may seek His bounty
24:33 (33) those your right hands own who seek emancipation
24:33 (33) desire to live in chastity, that you may seek the chance goods
28:55 (55) We desire not the ignorant
28:73 (73) for you to repose in and seek after His bounty
30:46 (45) and that you may seek His bounty
35:12 (13) that you may seek of His bounty
45:12 (11) that you may seek His bounty
48:29 (29) seeking bounty from God and good pleasure
59:8 (8) seeking bounty from God and good pleasure
66:1 (1) seeking the good pleasure of thy wives
73:20 (20) others journeying in the land, seeking the bounty of God

c) impv. (*ibtaghi*)

2:187 (183) seek what God has prescribed for you
5:35 (39) fear God, and seek the means to come to Him
17:110 (110) seek thou for a way between that
28:77 (77) seek, amidst that which God has given thee, the Last Abode
29:17 (16) seek after your provision with God
62:10 (10) seek God's bounty, and remember God frequently

f) n.vb. (*ibtighā'*)

2:207 (203) other men there are that sell themselves desiring God's good pleasure
2:265 (267) those who expend their wealth, seeking God's good pleasure
2:272 (274) for then you are expending, being desirous only of God's Face
3:7 (5) they follow the ambiguous part, desiring dissension
3:7 (5) and desiring its interpretation
4:104 (105) faint not in seeking the heathen
4:114 (114) whoso does that, seeking God's good pleasure
13:17 (18) being desirous of ornament or ware
13:22 (22) patient men, desirous of the Face of their Lord
17:28 (30) if thou turnest from them, seeking mercy from thy Lord
30:23 (22) your seeking after His bounty
57:27 (27) seeking the good pleasure of God
60:1 (1) struggle in My way and seek My good pleasure
92:20 (20) only seeking the Face of his Lord

*B H J

BAHĪJ n.m. (adj)~joyous

22:5 (5) and puts forth herbs of every joyous kind
50:7 (7) We caused to grow therein of every joyous kind

BAHJAH n.f.~loveliness

27:60 (61) We caused to grow therewith gardens full of loveliness

*B H L

IBTAHALA vb. (VIII)~to beseech, to humbly pray

b) impf. act. (*yabtahilu*)

3:61 (54) then let us humbly pray

*B H M

BAHĪMAH n.f.~beast, animal

5:1 (1) permitted to you is the beast of the flocks
22:28 (29) over such beasts of the flocks as He has
22:34 (35) that they may mention God's Name over such beasts of the flocks

*B H T

BAHATA vb. (I)~to confound, to dumbfound

b) impf. act. (*yabhatu*)

21:40 (41) it shall come upon them suddenly, dumbfounding them

d) perf. pass. (*buhita*)

2:258 (260) then the unbeliever was confounded

BUHTĀN n.m.~calumny, slander

4:20 (24) will you take it by way of calumny and manifest sin?
4:112 (112) thereby has laid upon himself calumny
4:156 (155) against Mary a mighty calummy
24:16 (15) this is a mighty calummy
33:58 (58) have laid upon themselves calumny
60:12 (12) nor slay their children, nor bring a calumny

*B Ḥ R

BAḤR n.m. (pl. *biḥār* and *abḥur*)~sea

2:50 (47) when We divided for you the sea
2:164 (159) ship that runs in the sea with profit
5:96 (97) permitted to you is the game of the sea
6:59 (59) he knows what is in land and sea
6:63 (63) who delivers you from the shadows of land and sea?
6:97 (97) you might be guided in the shadows of land and sea
7:138 (134) We brought the Children of Israel over the sea
7:163 (163) the township which was bordering the sea
10:22 (23) it is He who conveys you on the land and the sea
10:90 (90) We brought the Children of Israel over the sea
14:32 (37) He subjected to you the ships to run upon the sea
16:14 (14) it is He who subjected to you the sea
17:66 (68) your Lord it is who drives for you the ships on the sea
17:67 (69) when affliction visits you upon the sea
17:70 (72) and carried them on land and sea
18:60 (59) I will not give up until I reach the meeting of the two seas

18:61 (60)	it took its way into the sea
18:63 (62)	it took its way into the sea in a manner marvellous
18:79 (78)	certain poor men, who toiled upon the sea
18:109 (109)	if the sea were ink for the Words of my Lord
18:109 (109)	the sea would be spent before the Words of my Lord
20:77 (79)	strike for them a dry path in the sea
22:65 (64)	the ships to run upon the sea at His commandment
24:40 (40)	they are as shadows upon a sea obscure
25:53 (55)	it is He who let forth the two seas
26:63 (63)	strike with thy staff the sea
27:61 (62)	and placed a partition between the two seas
27:63 (64)	He who guides you in the shadows of the land and the sea
30:41 (40)	corruption has appeared in the land and sea
31:27 (26)	and the sea — seven (seas) after it
31:27 (26)	and the (sea) — seven seas after it
31:31 (30)	hast thou not seen how that the ships run upon the sea
35:12 (13)	not equal are the two seas
42:32 (31)	of His signs are the ships that run on the sea
44:24 (23)	and leave the sea becalmed
45:12 (11)	God is He who has subjected to you the sea
52:6 (6)	and the sea swarming
55:19 (19)	He let forth the two seas that meet together
55:24 (24)	raised up in the sea like land-marks
81:6 (6)	when the seas shall be set boiling
82:3 (3)	when the seas swarm over

BAḤĪRAH n.prop.~Bahira (a camel dedicated to idols)

5:103 (102)	idols, such as Bahira

*B Ḥ TH

BAḤATHA vb. (I)~to scratch in the ground

b) impf. act. (*yabḥathu*)

5:31 (34)	God sent forth a raven, scratching into the earth

*B J S

INBAJASA vb. (VII)~to gush or burst forth

a) perf. act.

7:160 (160)	and there gushed forth from it twelve fountains

*B K K

BAKKAH n.prop.~Bekka (a name for Mecca)

3:96 (90)	first House established for the people was that at Bekka

*B K M

ABKAM n.m. (pl. *bukm*)~dumb

2:18 (17)	deaf, dumb, blind— so they shall not return
2:171 (166)	deaf, dumb, blind—they do not understand

6:39 (39)	those who cry lies to Our signs are deaf and dumb
8:22 (22)	those that are deaf and dumb
16:76 (78)	one of them dumb, having no power
17:97 (99)	upon their faces, blind, dumb, deaf

*B K R

BIKR n.f.~virgin

2:68 (63)	she is a cow neither old, nor virgin
56:36 (35)	We made them spotless virgins
66:5 (5)	given to fasting, who have been married and virgins too

BUKRAH n.f.~dawn, early morning

19:11 (12)	give you glory at dawn and evening
19:62 (63)	they shall have their provision at dawn
25:5 (6)	they are recited to him at the dawn
33:42 (41)	give Him glory at the dawn
48:9 (9)	that you may give Him glory at the dawn
54:38 (38)	in the morning early there came upon them a settled chastisement
76:25 (25)	remember the Name of thy Lord at dawn

ABKARA vb. (IV)~(n.vb.) dawn

f) n.vb. (*ibkār*)

3:41 (36)	give glory at evening and dawn
40:55 (57)	proclaim the praise of thy Lord at evening and dawn

*B K Y

BAKÁ vb. (I)~to weep

a) perf. act.

44:29 (28)	neither heaven nor earth wept for them

b) impf. act. (*yabkī*)

9:82 (83)	therefore let them laugh little, and weep much
12:16 (16)	and they were weeping
17:109 (109)	they fall down upon their faces weeping
53:60 (60)	and do you laugh, and do you not weep

BUKKĪY n.com. (adv)~weeping

19:58 (59)	they fell down prostrate, weeping

ABKÁ vb. (IV)~to cause to weep

a) perf. act.

53:43 (44)	it is He who makes to laugh, and that makes to weep

*B KH ᶜ

BAKHAᶜA vb. (I)~(pcple. act.) one who consumes himself with grief *g*) pcple. act. (*bākhiᶜ*)

18:6 (5) thou wilt consume thyself, following after them
26:3 (2) perchance thou consumest thyself

*B KH L

BAKHILA vb. (I)~to be a miser or niggardly. (n.vb.) avarice, stinginess, being niggardly

a) perf. act.

3:180 (176) that they were niggardly with they shall have hung about their necks
9:76 (77) they were niggardly of it, and turned away
92:8 (8) as for him who is a miser, and self-sufficient

b) impf. act. (*yabkhalu*)

3:180 (175) as for those who are niggardly with the bounty
4:37 (41) such as are niggardly, and bid other men
47:37 (39) you are niggardly
47:38 (40) some of you are niggardly
47:38 (40) whoso is niggardly
47:38 (40) is niggardly only to his own soul
57:24 (24) such as are niggardly

f) n.vb. (*bukhl*)

4:37 (41) and [such as] bid other men to be niggardly
57:24 (24) such as are niggardly, and bid men to be niggardly

*B KH S

BAKHASA vb. (I)~to defraud, to diminish (tr). (n.vb.) paltriness, paltry (adj)

b) impf. act. (*yabkhasu*)

2:282 (282) let him fear God his Lord and not diminish aught of it
7:85 (83) diminish not the goods of the people
11:85 (86) do not diminish the goods of the people
26:183 (183) diminish not the goods of the people

e) impf. pass. (*yubkhasu*)

11:15 (18) they shall not be defrauded there

f) n.vb. (*bakhs*)

12:20 (20) then they sold him for a paltry price
72:13 (13) he shall fear neither paltriness nor vileness

*B L ᶜ

BALAᶜA vb. (I)~to swallow

c) impv. (*iblaᶜ*)

11:44 (46) earth, swallow thy waters

*B L D

BALAD n.m. (f. *baldah*, pl. *bilād*)~land

2:126 (120)	make this a land secure
3:196 (196)	unbelievers go to and fro in the land
7:57 (55)	We drive it to a dead land
7:58 (56)	the good land — its vegetation comes forth
14:35 (38)	make this land secure
16:7 (7)	they bear your loads unto a land that you never would reach
25:49 (51)	We might revive a dead land
27:91 (93)	I have only been commanded to serve the Lord of this territory
34:15 (14)	and give thanks to Him; a good land, and a Lord
35:9 (10)	then We drive it to a dead land
40:4 (4)	let not their going to and fro in the land delude thee
43:11 (10)	We revived thereby a land that was dead
50:11 (11)	thereby We revived a land that was dead
50:36 (35)	they searched about in the land
89:8 (7)	the like of which was never created in the land
89:11 (10)	who all were insolent in the land
90:1 (1)	I swear by this land
90:2 (2)	thou art a lodger in this land
95:3 (3)	and this land secure

*B L GH

BALAGHA vb. (I)~to reach, to attain; (*balagha ashuddahu*) to be fully grown, to be or come of age. (n.vb.) delivering a message, deliverance. (pcple. act.) reaching, far- reaching, attaining, conclusive

a) perf. act.

2:231 (231)	when you divorce women, and they have reached their term
2:232 (232)	when you divorce women, and they have reached their term
2:234 (234)	when they have reached their term
3:40 (35)	how shall I have a son, [when I have reached old age]
4:6 (5)	test well the orphans, until they reach the age of marrying
6:19 (19)	that I may warn you thereby, and whomsoever it may reach
6:128 (128)	we have reached the term determined by Thee for us
12:22 (22)	when he was fully grown, We gave him judgment
18:61 (60)	then, when they reached their meeting
18:76 (75)	thou hast already experienced excuse sufficient on my part
18:86 (84)	when he reached the setting of the sun
18:90 (89)	when he reached the rising of the sun
18:93 (92)	when he reached between the two barriers
19:8 (9)	I have attained to the declining of old age
24:59 (58)	when your children reach puberty
28:14 (13)	when he was fully grown and in the perfection of his strength
33:10 (10)	your hearts reached your throats
34:45 (44)	they reached not a tenth of what We gave
37:102 (100)	when he had reached the age of running with him
46:15 (14)	when he is fully grown, and (reaches) forty
46:15 (14)	when he is (fully grown), and reaches forty
56:83 (82)	when the soul leaps to the throat of the dying
65:2 (2)	when they have reached their term
75:26 (26)	when it reaches the clavicles

b) impf. act. (*yablughu*)

2:196 (192) shave not your heads, till the offering reaches its place
2:235 (236) do not resolve on the knot of marriage until the book has reached its term
6:152 (153) until he is of age
13:14 (15) that it may reach his mouth
17:23 (24) whether one or both of them attains old age
17:34 (36) until he is of age
17:37 (39) nor attain the mountains in height
18:60 (59) I will not give up until I reach the meeting
18:82 (81) thy Lord desired that they should come of age
22:5 (5) We deliver you as infants, then that you may come of age
24:58 (57) those of you who have not reached puberty
40:36 (38) build for me a tower, that haply so I may reach the cords
40:67 (69) He delivers you as infants, then that you may come of age
40:67 (69) and that you may reach a stated term
40:80 (80) and that on them you may attain a need
48:25 (25) the offering, detained so as not to reach its place

f) n.vb. (*balāgh*)

3:20 (19) if they turn their backs, thine it is only to deliver the Message
5:92 (93) it is only for Our Messenger to deliver the Message Manifest
5:99 (99) it is only for the Messenger to deliver the Message
13:40 (40) thine only to deliver the Message, and Ours the reckoning
14:52 (52) this is a Message to be delivered to mankind
16:35 (37) is aught for the Messengers, but to deliver the manifest Message?
16:82 (84) thine it is only to deliver the manifest Message
21:106 (106) in this is a Message delivered unto a people
24:54 (53) it is only for the Messenger to deliver the manifest Message
29:18 (17) it is only for the Messenger to deliver the Manifest Message
36:17 (16) it is only for us to deliver the Manifest Message
42:48 (47) it is for thee only to deliver the Message
46:35 (35) a Message to be delivered
64:12 (12) it is only for the Messenger to deliver the Manifest Message
72:23 (24) excepting a Deliverance from God and His Messages

g) pcple. act. (*bāligh*)

5:95 (96) an offering to reach the Kaaba
6:149 (150) to God belongs the argument conclusive
7:135 (131) when We removed from them the wrath unto a term that they should come to
13:14 (15) and it reaches it not
16:7 (7) they bear your loads unto a land that you never would reach
40:56 (58) in their breasts is only pride, that they shall never attain
54:5 (5) a Wisdom far-reaching
65:3 (3) God attains His purpose
68:39 (39) have you oaths from Us, reaching to the Day of Resurrection?

BALĪGH n.m. (adj)~penetrating, eloquent

4:63 (66) say to them penetrating words about themselves

MABLAGH n.m.~attainment, sum

53:30 (31) that is their attainment of knowledge

BALLAGHA vb. (II)~to deliver (a message)

a) perf. act.

5:67 (71)	thou wilt not have delivered His Message

b) impf. act. (*yuballighu*)

7:62 (60)	I deliver to you the Messages of my Lord
7:68 (66)	I deliver to you the Messages of my Lord
33:39 (39)	who were delivering the Messages of God
46:23 (22)	I deliver to you the Message with which I was sent

c) impv. (*balligh*)

5:67 (71)	deliver that which has been sent down to thee from thy Lord

ABLAGHA vb. (IV)~to deliver (a message), to convey

a) perf. act.

7:79 (77)	I have delivered to you the Message of my Lord
7:93 (91)	I have delivered to you the Messages of my Lord
11:57 (60)	I have delivered to you that I was sent with
72:28 (28)	He may know they have delivered the Messages of their Lord

c) impv. (*abligh*)

9:6 (6)	then do thou convey him to his place of security

*B L S

ABLASA vb. (IV)~to be confounded, to despair. (pcple. act.) one who is seized with despair, confounded

b) impf. act. (*yublisu*)

30:12 (11)	sinners shall be confounded

g) pcple. act. (*mublis*)

6:44 (44)	We seized them suddenly, and behold, they were sore confounded
23:77 (79)	they are sore confounded at it
30:49 (48)	it was sent down on them before that they had been in despair
43:75 (75)	therein they are sore confounded

IBLĪS n.prop.~Iblis

2:34 (32)	so they bowed themselves, save Iblis; he refused
7:11 (10)	so they bowed themselves, save Iblis
15:31 (31)	save Iblis; he refused to be among those bowing
15:32 (32)	what ails thee, Iblis
17:61 (63)	so they bowed themselves, save Iblis
18:50 (48)	so they bowed themselves, save Iblis
20:116 (115)	so they bowed themselves, save Iblis
26:95 (95)	and the hosts of Iblis, all together
34:20 (19)	Iblis proved true his opinion of them
38:74 (74)	save Iblis; he waxed proud
38:75 (75)	iblis, what prevented thee to bow thyself before that I created

*B L W

BALĀ vb. (I)~to try (someone with), to test, to prove. (n.vb.) a trial, a test; a benefit

a) perf. act.

7:168 (167)	We tried them with good things and evil
68:17 (17)	now We have tried them
68:17 (17)	even as We tried the owners of the garden

b) impf. act. (*yablū*)

2:155 (150)	We will try you with something of fear
5:48 (53)	He may try you in what He has given you
5:94 (95)	o believers, God will surely try you
6:165 (165)	He may try you in what He has given you
7:163 (163)	We were trying them for their ungodliness
10:30 (31)	every soul shall prove its past deeds
11:7 (9)	that He might try you
16:92 (94)	God only tries you thereby
18:7 (6)	that We may try which of them is fairest in works
21:35 (36)	We try you with evil and good
27:40 (40)	He may try me, whether I am thankful
47:4 (5)	He may try some of you by means of others
47:31 (33)	We shall assuredly try you
47:31 (33)	those of you who struggle and are steadfast, and try your tidings
67:2 (2)	who created death and life, that He might try you

e) impf. pass. (*yublá*)

3:186 (183)	you shall surely be tried in your possessions
86:9 (9)	upon the day when the secrets are tried

f) n.vb. (*balā'*)

2:49 (46)	in that was a grievous trial from your Lord
7:141 (137)	in that was a grievous trial from your Lord
8:17 (17)	that He might confer on the believers a fair benefit
14:6 (6)	in that was a grievous trial from your Lord
37:106 (106)	this is indeed the manifest trial
44:33 (32)	signs wherein there was a manifest trial

ABLÁ vb. (IV)~to confer on someone [Ar]; to test [Pk, Ali]; to cause to experience [Bl]

b) impf. act. (*yublī*)

8:17 (17)	that He might confer on the believers a fair benefit

IBTALÁ vb. (VIII)~to try, to prove (by trial), to test. (pcple. act.) testing, trying; one who tries or tests

a) perf. act.

2:124 (118)	when his Lord tested Abraham with certain words
89:15 (14)	as for man, whenever his Lord tries him
89:16 (16)	but when he tries him and stints for him

b) impf. act. (*yabtalī*)

3:152 (146) that He might try you
3:154 (148) that God might try what was in your breasts
76:2 (2) We created man of a sperm-drop, a mingling, trying him

c) impv. (*ibtali*)

4:6 (5) test well the orphans

d) perf. pass. (*ibtuliya*)

33:11 (11) there it was that the believers were tried

g) pcple. act. (*mubtalī*)

2:249 (250) God will try you with a river
23:30 (31) in that are signs, and surely We put to the test

*B L Y

BALIYA vb. (I)~to decay

b) impf. act. (*yablá*)

20:120 (118) the Tree of Eternity, and a Kingdom that decays not

*B N N

BANĀN n.m. (coll)~finger(s)

8:12 (12) smite above the necks, and smite every finger
75:4 (4) We are able to shape again his fingers

*B N Y

BANÁ vb. (I)~to build. (n.vb.) building (the act); edifice (pcple. pass.) that which is built

a) perf. act.

9:110 (111) buildings they have built will not cease to be a point of doubt
50:6 (6) heaven above them, how We have built it
51:47 (47) heaven — We built it with might
78:12 (12) We have built above you seven strong ones
79:27 (27) are you stronger in constitution or the heaven He built?
91:5 (5) by the heaven and That which built it

b) impf. act. (*yabnī*)

26:128 (128) do you build on every prominence a sign

c) impv. (*ibni*)

18:21 (20) build over them a building
37:97 (95) build him a building
40:36 (38) Haman, build for me a tower
66:11 (11) Lord, build for me a house in Paradise

f) n.vb. (*binā*ʾ)

2:22 (20)	who assigned to you the earth for a couch, and heaven for an edifice
40:64 (66)	it is God who made for you the earth a fixed place and heaven for an edifice

h) pcple. pass. (*mabnīy*)

39:20 (21)	above which are built lofty chambers

BANNĀʾ n.m.~builder, architect

38:37 (36)	every builder and diver

BUNYĀN n.m.~a building

9:109 (110)	is he better who founded his building upon the fear of God
9:109 (110)	who founded his building upon the brink of a crumbling bank
9:110 (111)	buildings they have built will not cease to be a point of doubt
16:26 (28)	then God came upon their building from the foundations
18:21 (20)	build over them a building
37:97 (95)	build him a building
61:4 (4)	as though they were a building well-compacted

IBN n.m.~(pl. *abnā*ʾ) son; (pl., *banūn*) children; (*ibn al-sabīl*) a traveller; (*bunayya*) My son

Son (pl. *abnā*ʾ)

2:49 (46)	who were visiting you with evil chastisement, slaughtering your sons
2:146 (141)	they recognize it as they recognize their sons
2:246 (247)	who have been expelled from our habitations and our children
3:61 (54)	let us call our sons and your (sons)
3:61 (54)	our (sons) and your sons
4:11 (12)	your fathers and your sons
4:23 (27)	spouses of your sons who are of your loins
5:18 (21)	We are the sons of God, and His beloved ones
5:27 (30)	recite thou to them the story of the two sons
6:20 (20)	recognize it as they recognize their sons
7:127 (124)	We shall slaughter their sons
7:141 (137)	slaying your sons, and sparing your women
7:150 (149)	son of my mother
9:24 (24)	if your fathers, your sons, your brothers
9:30 (30)	the Jews say, 'Ezra is the Son of God'
9:30 (30)	the Christians say, 'The Messiah is the Son of God'
11:42 (44)	Noah called to his son, who was standing apart
11:45 (47)	my son is of my family
12:81 (81)	father, thy son stole
14:6 (6)	slaughtering your sons, and sparing your women
20:94 (95)	'son of my mother,' Aaron said
24:31 (31)	or their sons
24:31 (31)	or their husbands' sons
28:4 (3)	slaughtering their sons, and sparing their women
31:13 (12)	when Lokman said to his son
33:4 (4)	neither has He made your adopted sons your sons in fact
33:55 (55)	touching their fathers, their sons, their brothers
33:55 (55)	their brothers' sons
33:55 (55)	their sisters' sons
40:25 (26)	slay the sons of those who believe with him
58:22 (22)	though they were their fathers, or their sons

Jesus son of Mary

2:87 (81)	We gave Jesus son of Mary the clear signs
2:253 (254)	We gave Jesus son of Mary the clear signs
3:45 (40)	whose name is Messiah, Jesus, son of Mary
4:157 (156)	we slew the Messiah, Jesus son of Mary
4:171 (169)	the Messiah, Jesus son of Mary
5:17 (19)	they are unbelievers who say, 'God is the Messiah, Mary's son'
5:17 (19)	if He desires to destroy the Messiah, Mary's son, and his mother
5:46 (50)	We sent, following in their footsteps, Jesus son of Mary
5:72 (76)	they are unbelievers who say, 'God is the Messiah, Mary's son'
5:75 (79)	the Messiah, son of Mary, was only a Messenger
5:78 (82)	Jesus, Mary's son
5:110 (109)	Jesus Son of Mary, remember My blessing upon thee
5:112 (112)	Jesus son of Mary, is thy Lord able
5:114 (114)	said Jesus son of Mary
5:116 (116)	O Jesus son of Mary
9:31 (31)	apart from God, and the Messiah, Mary's son
19:34 (35)	that is Jesus, son of Mary
21:91 (91)	and appointed her and her son to be a sign
23:50 (52)	We made Mary's son, and his mother
33:7 (7)	Moses, and Jesus, Mary's son
43:57 (57)	when the son of Mary is cited as an example
57:27 (27)	We sent, following, Jesus son of Mary
61:6 (6)	when Jesus son of Mary said
61:14 (14)	be you God's helpers, as Jesus, Mary's son

The Traveller (*ibn al-sabil*)

2:177 (172)	the needy, the traveller, beggars
2:215 (211)	orphans, the needy, and the traveller
4:36 (40)	and to the traveller
8:41 (42)	and for the needy, and the traveller
9:60 (60)	debtors, in God's way, and the traveller
17:26 (28)	and the needy, and the traveller
30:38 (37)	and the needy, and the traveller
59:7 (7)	orphans, the needy and the traveller

Children, Sons (pl. *banūn*)

2:132 (126)	Abraham charged his sons with this
2:132 (126)	my sons, God has chosen for you the religion
2:133 (127)	he said to his sons, 'What will you serve after me?'
3:14 (12)	women, children, heaped-up heaps of gold
6:100 (100)	they impute to Him sons and daughters without any knowledge
12:67 (67)	o my sons, enter not by one door
12:87 (87)	depart, my sons, and search out tidings
14:35 (38)	turn me and my sons away from serving idols
16:72 (74)	He has appointed for you of your wives sons and grandsons
17:6 (6)	We succoured you with wealth and children
17:40 (42)	has your Lord favoured you with sons
18:46 (44)	wealth and sons are the adornment of the present world
23:55 (57)	do they think that We succour them with of wealth and children
24:31 (31)	or their brothers, or their brothers' sons
24:31 (31)	or their sisters' sons, or their women
26:88 (88)	the day when neither wealth nor sons shall profit
26:133 (133)	succoured you with flocks and sons

37:149 (149)	has thy Lord daughters, and they sons?
37:153 (153)	has He chosen daughters above sons?
43:16 (15)	has He taken to Himself, from that He creates, daughters, and favoured you with sons?
52:39 (39)	or has He daughters, and they sons?
68:14 (14)	because he has wealth and sons
70:11 (11)	might ransom himself from the chastisement of that day even by his sons
71:12 (11)	and will succour you with wealth and sons
74:13 (13)	and sons standing before him
80:36 (36)	his consort, his sons

Children of Israel (*banū isrāʾīl*)

2:40 (38)	Children of Israel, remember My blessing
2:47 (44)	Children of Israel, remember My blessing
2:83 (77)	when We took compact with the Children of Israel
2:122 (116)	Children of Israel, remember My blessing
2:211 (207)	ask the Children of Israel how many a clear sign
2:246 (247)	hast thou not regarded the Council of the Children of Israel
3:49 (43)	to be a Messenger to the Children of Israel
3:93 (87)	all food was lawful to the Children of Israel
5:12 (15)	god took compact with the Children of Israel
5:32 (35)	therefore We prescribed for the Children of Israel
5:70 (74)	We took compact with the Children of Israel
5:72 (76)	Children of Israel, serve God, my Lord
5:78 (82)	cursed were the unbelievers of the Children of Israel
5:110 (110)	when I restrained from thee the Children of Israel
7:105 (103)	so send forth with me the Children of Israel
7:134 (131)	and send forth with thee the Children of Israel
7:137 (133)	was fulfilled the most fair word of thy Lord upon the Children of Israel
7:138 (134)	We brought the Children of Israel over the sea
10:90 (90)	We brought the Children of Israel over the sea
10:90 (90)	no god but He in whom the Children of Israel believe
10:93 (93)	We settled the Children of Israel in a sure settlement
17:2 (2)	We gave Moses the Book, and made it a guidance to the Children of Israel
17:4 (4)	We decreed for the Children of Israel in the Book
17:101 (103)	Ask the Children of Israel
17:104 (106)	and We said to the Children of Israel
20:47 (49)	send forth with us the Children of Israel
20:80 (82)	Children of Israel, We delivered you
20:94 (95)	thou hast divided the Children of Israel
26:17 (16)	so send forth with us the Children of Israel
26:22 (21)	having enslaved the Children of Israel
26:59 (59)	We bequeathed them upon the Children of Israel
26:197 (197)	that it is known to the learned of the Children of Israel
27:76 (78)	surely this Koran relates to the Children of Israel
32:23 (23)	We appointed it for a guidance to the Children of Israel
40:53 (56)	We bequeathed upon the Children of Israel the Book
43:59 (59)	We made him to be an example to the Children of Israel
44:30 (29)	We delivered the Children of Israel
45:16 (15)	We gave the Children of Israel the Book
46:10 (9)	witness from among the Children of Israel
61:6 (6)	Children of Israel, I am indeed the Messenger of God
61:14 (14)	a party of the Children of Israel believed

Children of Adam (*banū ādam*)

7:26 (25)	Children of Adam! We have sent down on you a garment
7:27 (26)	Children of Adam! Let not Satan tempt you
7:31 (29)	Children of Adam! Take your adornment
7:35 (33)	Children of Adam! If there should come to you Messengers
7:172 (171)	when thy Lord took from the Children of Adam
17:70 (72)	We have honoured the Children of Adam
36:60 (60)	made I not covenant with you, Children of Adam

My Son (*bunayya*)

11:42 (44)	embark with us, my son
12:5 (5)	O my son, relate not thy vision
31:13 (12)	O my son, do not associate others with God
31:16 (15)	O my son, if it should be
31:17 (16)	O my son, perform the prayer
37:102 (101)	My son, I see in a dream

IBNAH n.f. (f. of *ibn*, pl. *banāt*)~daughter

4:23 (27)	forbidden to you are your mothers and daughters
4:23 (27)	your brother's daughters
4:23 (27)	your sister's daughters
6:100 (100)	they impute to Him sons and daughters without any knowledge
11:78 (80)	these are my daughters; they are cleaner for you
11:79 (81)	thou knowest we have no right to thy daughters
15:71 (71)	these are my daughters, if you would be doing
16:57 (59)	they assign to God daughters
28:27 (27)	I desire to marry thee to one of these my two daughters
33:50 (49)	God has given thee, and the daughters of thy uncles paternal
33:50 (49)	and [the daughters of your] aunts paternal
33:50 (49)	[the daughters of your] uncles maternal
33:50 (49)	and [the daughters of your] aunts maternal
33:59 (59)	say to thy wives and daughters
37:149 (149)	has thy Lord daughters, and they sons?
37:153 (153)	has He chosen daughters above sons?
43:16 (15)	has He taken to Himself, from that He creates, daughters
52:39 (39)	has He daughters, and they sons?
66:12 (12)	Mary, Imran's daughter, who guarded her virginity

*B Q ʿ

BUQʿAH n.f.~hollow, depression, a corner of ground

28:30 (30)	a voice cried from the right bank of the watercourse, in the sacred hollow

*B Q L

BAQL n.m.~herbs

2:61 (58)	green herbs, cucumbers, corn

*B Q R

BAQARAH n.f. (pl. *baqarāt* or *baqar*)~cow, kine, ox

2:67 (63)	God commands you to sacrifice a cow
2:68 (63)	he says she is a cow neither old, nor virgin

2:69 (64)	she shall be a golden cow
2:70 (65)	cows are much alike to us
2:71 (66)	she shall be a cow not broken to plough the earth
6:144 (145)	of camels two, of oxen two
6:146 (147)	of oxen and sheep We have forbidden them the fat of them
12:43 (43)	I saw in a dream seven fat kine, and seven lean ones
12:46 (46)	pronounce to us regarding seven fat kine, that seven lean ones

*B Q Y

BAQIYA vb. (I)~to remain, to be outstanding, to abide. (pcple. act.) that which remains or abides, the rest, remnant, abiding, enduring

a) perf. act.

2:278 (278)	give up the usury that is outstanding

b) impf. act. (*yabqá*)

55:27 (27)	abides the Face of thy Lord

g) pcple. act. (*bāqī*)

16:96 (98)	what is with God abides
18:46 (44)	the abiding things, the deeds of righteousness, are better with God
19:76 (79)	the abiding things, the deeds of righteousness, are better with thy Lord
20:71 (74)	which of us is more terrible in chastisement, and more abiding
20:73 (75)	God is better, and more abiding
20:127 (127)	chastisement of the world to come is more terrible and more enduring
20:131 (131)	thy Lord's provision is better, and more enduring
26:120 (120)	then afterwards We drowned the rest
28:60 (60)	God is better and more enduring
37:77 (75)	We made his seed the survivors
42:36 (34)	what is with God is better and more enduring
43:28 (27)	he made it a word enduring
69:8 (8)	now dost thou see any remnant of them?
87:17 (17)	world to come is better, and more enduring

BAQĪYAH n.f.~remainder, remnant

2:248 (249)	in it a Shechina from your Lord, and a remnant
11:86 (87)	God's remainder is better for you
11:116 (118)	men of a remainder forbidding corruption

ABQÁ vb. (IV)~to spare, to cause to remain

a) perf. act.

53:51 (52)	He did not spare them

b) impf. act. (*yubqī*)

74:28 (28)	it spares not, neither leaves alone

*B R ʾ

BARAʾA vb. (I)~to create. (pcple. act.) Creator (Divine attribute) *b*) impf. act. (*yabra'u*)

57:22 (22) — it is in a Book, before We create it

g) pcple. act. (*bāri'*)

2:54 (51) — now turn to your Creator
2:54 (51) — that will be better for you in your Creator's sight
59:24 (24) — He is God, the Creator, the Maker, the Shaper

BARĪYAH n.f.~creature(s)

98:6 (5) — those are the worst of creatures
98:7 (6) — those are the best of creatures

BARĀ' n.m.~innocent, free from guilt, sound, quit (same as *barī'*, below)

43:26 (25) — surely I am quit of that you serve
60:4 (4) — we are quit of you and that you serve, apart from God

BARĀ'AH n.f.~acquittal, immunity

9:1 (1) — an acquittal, from God and His Messenger
54:43 (43) — have you an immunity in the Scrolls?

BARĪ' n.m.~innocent, free from guilt, sound, quit (same as *barā'*, above)

4:112 (112) — whosoever earns a fault or a sin and then casts it upon the innocent
6:19 (19) — I am quit of that you associate
6:78 (78) — surely I am quit of that you associate
8:48 (50) — I am quit of you
9:3 (3) — God is quit, and His Messenger, of the idolaters
10:41 (42) — you are quit of what I do
10:41 (42) — and I am quit of what you do
11:35 (37) — I am quit of the sins you do
11:54 (57) — I am quit of that you associate
26:216 (216) — I am quit of that you do
59:16 (16) — I am quit of you

BARRA'A vb. (II)~to declare innocent or quit, to acquit, to absolve. (pcple. pass.) one who is declared innocent or quit, absolved

a) perf. act.

33:69 (69) — God declared him quit of what they said

b) impf. act. (*yubarri'u*)

12:53 (53) — I claim not that my soul was innocent

h) pcple. pass. (*mubarra'*)

24:26 (26) — these are declared quit of what they say

ABRA'A vb. (IV)~to cure, to heal

b) impf. act. (*yubri'u*)

3:49 (43) — I will also heal the blind and the leper
5:110 (110) — thou healest the blind and the leper

TABARRA'A vb. (V)~to clear oneself, to declare oneself innocent, to disown

a) perf. act.

2:166 (161)	when those that were followed disown their followers
2:167 (162)	return again and disown them, as they have disowned us
9:114 (115)	he declared himself quit of him
28:63 (63)	we declare our innocence unto Thee

b) impf. act. (*yatabarra'u*)

2:167 (162)	if only we might return again and disown them, as they have disowned

*B R D

BARADA vb. (I)~(n.vb.) coolness. (pcple. act.) that which is cool

f) n.vb. (*bard*)

21:69 (69)	O fire, be coolness and safety for Abraham
78:24 (24)	tasting therein neither coolness nor any drink

g) pcple. act. (*bārid*)

38:42 (41)	this is a laving-place cool, and a drink
56:44 (43)	neither cool, neither goodly

BARAD n.m.~hail

24:43 (43)	He sends down out of heaven mountains, wherein is hail

*B R H N

BURHĀN n.m.~a proof

2:111 (105)	produce your proof, if you speak truly
4:174 (174)	a proof has now come to you
12:24 (24)	he saw the proof of his Lord
21:24 (24)	bring your proof
23:117 (117)	[another god] whereof he has no proof
27:64 (65)	produce your proof, if you speak truly
28:32 (32)	these shall be two proofs from thy Lord
28:75 (75)	produce your proof

*B R Ḥ

BARAḤA vb. (I)~to quit, to give up, to leave, to cease

b) impf. act. (*yabraḥu*)

12:80 (80)	never will I quit this land
18:60 (59)	I will not give up
20:91 (93)	we will not cease

*B R J

BURŪJ n.m. (pl. of *burj*)~tower, constellation, sign of the zodiac

4:78 (80)	death will overtake you, though you should be in raised-up towers
15:16 (16)	We have set in heaven constellations
25:61 (62)	who has set in heaven constellations
85:1 (1)	by heaven of the constellations

TABARRAJA vb. (V)~to deck oneself, to display or flaunt one's finery. (n.vb.) decking oneself, displaying or flaunting one's finery. (pcple. act.) one who decks oneself; decking or flaunting oneself

b) impf. act. (*yatabarraju*)

33:33 (33)	display not your finery, as did the pagans of old

f) n.vb. (*tabarruj*)

33:33 (33)	display not your finery, <as did> the pagans of old

g) pcple. act. (*mutabarrij*)

24:60 (59)	so be it that they flaunt no ornament

*B R K

BARAKAH n.f.~blessing

7:96 (94)	We would have opened upon them blessings
11:48 (50)	peace from Us, and blessings upon thee
11:73 (76)	mercy of God and His blessings be upon you

BĀRAKA vb. (III)~to bless. (pcple. pass.) one who is blessed, holy

a) perf. act.

7:137 (133)	the east and the west of the land We had blessed
17:1 (1)	precincts of which We have blessed
21:71 (71)	land that We had blessed
21:81 (81)	land that We had blessed
34:18 (17)	between them and the cities that We have blessed
37:113 (113)	We blessed him, and Isaac
41:10 (9)	He set therein firm mountains over it, and He blessed it

d) perf. pass. (*būrika*)

27:8 (8)	blessed is He who is in the fire

h) pcple. pass. (*mubārak*)

3:96 (90)	Bekka, a place holy
6:92 (92)	this is a Book We have sent down, blessed
6:155 (156)	this is a Book We have sent down, blessed
19:31 (32)	blessed He has made me
21:50 (51)	this is a blessed Remembrance
23:29 (30)	do Thou harbour me in a blessed harbour
24:35 (35)	kindled from a Blessed Tree
24:61 (61)	a greeting from God, blessed and good
28:30 (30)	from the right bank of the watercourse, in the sacred hollow
38:29 (28)	Book We have sent down to thee, blessed
44:3 (2)	We have sent it down in a blessed night
50:9 (9)	We sent down out of heaven water blessed

TABĀRAKA vb. (VI)~to be blessed

a) perf. act.

7:54 (52)	blessed be God, the Lord of all Being
23:14 (14)	so blessed be God, the fairest of creators
25:1 (1)	blessed be He who has sent down the Salvation
25:10 (11)	blessed be He who, if He will, shall assign to thee
25:61 (62)	blessed be He who has set in heaven constellations
40:64 (66)	so blessed be God, the Lord of all Being
43:85 (85)	blessed be He,to whom belongs the Kingdom
55:78 (78)	blessed be the Name of thy Lord
67:1 (1)	blessed be He in whose hand is the Kingdom

*B R M

ABRAMA vb. (IV)~to contrive, to fix, to determine. (pcple. act.) one who contrives or determines, contriving, determining

a) perf. act.

43:79 (79)	have they contrived some matter?

g) pcple. act. (*mubrim*)

43:79 (79)	we too are contriving

*B R Q

BARIQA vb. (I)~to be dazed, to be astonished

a) perf. act.

75:7 (7)	when the sight is dazed

BARQ n.m.~lightning

2:19 (18)	in which is darkness, and thunder, and lightning
2:20 (19)	the lightning wellnigh snatches away their sight
13:12 (13)	it is He who shows you the lightning
24:43 (43)	the gleam of His lightning snatches away the sight
30:24 (23)	He shows you lightning, for fear and hope

IBRĪQ n.m.~ewer, jug

56:18 (18)	with goblets, and ewers, and a cup from a spring

ISTABRAQ n.m.~brocade

18:31 (30)	they shall be robed in green garments of silk and brocade
44:53 (53)	robed in silk and brocade, set face to face
55:54 (54)	reclining upon couches lined with brocade
76:21 (21)	upon them shall be green garments of silk and brocade

*B R R

BARRA vb. (I)~to be pious or just, to deal kindly. (pcple. act.) pious

b) impf. act. (*yabarru*)

2:224 (224)	do not make God a hindrance, through your oaths, to being pious
60:8 (8)	God forbids you not ... that you should be kindly to them

g) pcple. act. (*bārr*, pl. *bararah*)

80:16 (15)	noble, pious

BARR (1) n.m. (pl. *abrār*)~pious, beneficent, just, kind; All-benign (Divine attribute)

3:193 (191)	take us to Thee with the pious
3:198 (197)	that which is with God is better for the pious
19:14 (14)	and cherishing his parents, not arrogant, rebellious
19:32 (33)	and likewise to cherish my mother
52:28 (28)	He is the All-benign, the All-compassionate
76:5 (5)	surely the pious shall drink of a cup
82:13 (13)	surely the pious shall be in bliss
83:18 (18)	the book of the pious is in Illiyun
83:22 (22)	surely the pious shall be in bliss

BARR (2) n.m.~dry land (as opposed to the sea)

5:96 (97)	forbidden to you is the game of the land
6:59 (59)	He knows what is in land and sea
6:63 (63)	who delivers you from the shadows of land and sea?
6:97 (97)	you might be guided in the shadows of land and sea
10:22 (23)	it is He who conveys you on the land
17:67 (69)	when He delivers you to land, you turn away
17:68 (70)	He will not cause the shore to swallow you up
17:70 (72)	We have honoured the Children of Adam and carried them on land
27:63 (64)	He who guides you in the shadows of the land
29:65 (65)	when He has delivered them to the land
30:41 (40)	corruption has appeared in the land and sea
31:32 (31)	when He has delivered them to the land

BIRR n.m.~piety, kindness [Ar]; virtuous conduct [Bl, Ali]; righteousness [Pk, Ali]

2:44 (41)	will you bid others to piety, and forget yourselves
2:177 (172)	it is not piety, that you turn your faces
2:177 (172)	true piety is this
2:189 (185)	it is not piety to come to the houses from the backs of them
2:189 (185)	but piety is to be godfearing
3:92 (86)	you will not attain piety until you expend of what you love
5:2 (3)	help one another to piety and godfearing
58:9 (10)	conspire in piety and godfearing

*B R Ṣ

ABRAṢ n.m.~a leper

3:49 (43)	I will also heal the blind and the leper
5:110 (110)	thou healest the blind and the leper

*B R Z

BARAZA vb. (I)~to go or sally forth. (pcple. act.) one who goes or sallies forth

a) perf. act.

2:250 (251)	when they went forth against Goliath
3:154 (148)	those for whom slaying was appointed would have sallied forth
4:81 (83)	when they sally forth from thee
14:21 (24)	they sally forth unto God, all together
14:48 (49)	they sally forth unto God

g) pcple. act. (*bāriz*)

18:47 (45) thou seest the earth coming forth
40:16 (16) the day they sally forth

BARRAZA vb. (II)~to advance for, to make manifest to

d) perf. pass. (*burriza*)

26:91 (91) Hell advanced for the perverse
79:36 (36) Hell is advanced for whoever sees

*B R Z KH

BARZAKH n.m.~a barrier, a partition

23:100 (102) there, behind them, is a barrier until the day
25:53 (55) He set between them a barrier
55:20 (20) between them a barrier they do not overpass

*B S L

ABSALA vb. (IV)~to give up to destruction

d) perf. pass. (*ubsila*)

6:70 (69) those are they who are given up to destruction

e) impf. pass. (*yubsalu*)

6:70 (69) lest a soul should be given up to destruction

*B S M

TABASSAMA vb. (V)~to smile

a) perf. act.

27:19 (19) he smiled, laughing at its words

*B S Q

BĀSIQ n.m. (adj)~tall

50:10 (10) tall palm-trees with spathes compact

*B S R

BASARA vb. (I)~to scowl. (pcple. act.) one who scowls, scowling

a) perf. act.

74:22 (22) then he frowned, and scowled

g) pcple. act. (*bāsir*)

75:24 (24) upon that day faces shall be scowling

*B S S

BASSA vb. (I)~to crumble to dust. (n.vb.) crumbling

d) perf. pass. (*bussa*)

56:5 (5) and the mountains crumbled

f) n.vb. (*bass*)

56:5 (5) and the mountains crumbled <...>

*B S Ṭ

BASAṬA vb. (I)~to stretch out, expand, spread, outspread. (n.vb.) spreading, outspreading, expanding. (pcple. act.) one who stretches, expands, etc.; stretching, expanding, etc. (pcple. pass.) outspread, stretched out

a) perf. act.

5:28 (31) yet if thou stretchest out thy hand against me
42:27 (26) had God expanded His provision to His servants

b) impf. act. (*yabsuṭu*)

2:245 (246) God grasps, and outspreads
5:11 (14) when a certain people purposed to stretch against you
13:26 (26) God outspreads and straitens His provision
17:29 (31) nor outspread it widespread altogether
17:30 (32) thy Lord outspreads and straitens His provision
28:82 (82) God outspreads and straitens His provision
29:62 (62) God outspreads and straitens His provision
30:37 (36) have they not seen that God outspreads
30:48 (47) He spreads them in heaven how He will
34:36 (35) my Lord outspreads and straitens His provision
34:39 (38) my lord outspreads and straitens His provision
39:52 (53) do they know that God outspreads
42:12 (10) He outspreads and straitens His provision
60:2 (2) they will be enemies to you, and stretch against you

f) n.vb. (*basṭ*)

17:29 (31) nor outspread it <widespread> altogether

g) pcple. act. (*bāsiṭ*)

5:28 (31) I will not stretch out my hand against thee
6:93 (93) the angels are stretching out their hands
13:14 (15) it is as a man who stretches out his hands
18:18 (17) and their dog stretching its paws on the threshold

h) pcple. pass. (*mabsūṭ*)

5:64 (69) nay, but His hands are outspread

BASṬAH n.f.~an increase in stature

2:247 (248) and has increased him broadly in knowledge and body
7:69 (67) and increased you in stature broadly

BISĀṬ n.m.~carpet

71:19 (18)	God has laid the earth for you as a carpet

*B SH R

BASHAR n.com.~man, mankind, mortal

3:47 (42)	seeing no mortal has touched me
3:79 (73)	it belongs not to any mortal
5:18 (21)	you are mortals, of His creating
6:91 (91)	God has not sent down aught on any mortal
11:27 (29)	We see thee not other than a mortal
12:31 (31)	this is no mortal
14:10 (12)	you are nothing but mortals
14:11 (13)	we are nothing but mortals
15:28 (28)	I am creating a mortal of a clay
15:33 (33)	I would never bow myself before a mortal
16:103 (105)	only a mortal is teaching him
17:93 (95)	am I aught but a mortal
17:94 (96)	has God sent forth a mortal as Messenger?
18:110 (110)	I am only a mortal
19:17 (17)	that presented himself to her a man without fault
19:20 (20)	how shall I have a son whom no mortal has touched
19:26 (26)	if thou shouldst see any mortal
21:3 (3)	is this aught but a mortal like to yourselves?
21:34 (35)	We have not assigned to any mortal before thee
23:24 (24)	this is naught but a mortal like yourselves
23:33 (34)	this is naught but a mortal like yourselves
23:34 (36)	if you obey a mortal like yourselves
23:47 (49)	shall we believe two mortals like ourselves
25:54 (56)	it is He who created of water a mortal
26:154 (154)	thou art naught but a mortal, like us
26:186 (186)	thou art naught but a mortal, like us
30:20 (19)	you are mortals, all scattered abroad
36:15 (14)	you are naught but mortals like us
38:71 (71)	I am creating a mortal of a clay
41:6 (5)	I am only a mortal, like you are
42:51 (50)	it belongs not to any mortal that God should speak to him
54:24 (24)	shall we follow a mortal, one out of ourselves?
64:6 (6)	shall mortals be our guides?
74:25 (25)	this is nothing but mortal speech
74:29 (29)	scorching the flesh
74:31 (34)	it is naught but a Reminder to mortals
74:36 (39)	as a warner to mortals

BASHĪR n.m.~bearer of good tidings

2:119 (113)	We have sent thee with the truth, good tidings to bear
5:19 (22)	there has not come to us any bearer of good tidings
5:19 (22)	there has come to you a bearer of good tidings
7:188 (188)	I am only a warner, and a bearer of good tidings
11:2 (2)	a warner from Him and a bearer of good tidings
12:96 (96)	when the bearer of good tidings came to him
34:28 (27)	We have sent thee not, except to mankind entire, good tidings to bear
35:24 (22)	We have sent thee with the truth good tidings to bear
41:4 (3)	good tidings to bear, and warning

BUSHR n.m.~one who bears good tidings

7:57 (55)	He who looses the winds, bearing good tidings
25:48 (50)	He who has loosed the winds, bearing good tidings
27:63 (64)	and looses the winds, bearing good tidings

BUSHRÁ n.f.~good tidings

2:97 (91)	for a guidance and good tidings to the believers
3:126 (122)	God wrought this not, save as good tiding to you
8:10 (10)	God wrought this not, save as good tidings
10:64 (65)	for them is good tidings in the present life
11:69 (72)	Our messengers came to Abraham with the good tidings
11:74 (77)	when the awe departed from Abraham and the good tidings came to him
12:19 (19)	Good news
16:89 (91)	and as good tidings to those who surrender
16:102 (104)	and to be a guidance and good tidings
25:22 (24)	no good tidings that day for the sinners
27:2 (2)	a guidance, and good tidings unto the believers
29:31 (30)	when Our messengers came to Abraham with the good tidings
39:17 (19)	for them is good tidings! So give thou good tidings
46:12 (11)	and good tidings to the good-doers
57:12 (12)	good tidings for you today

BASHSHARA vb. (II)~to give good tidings. (pcple. act.) one who bears good tidings

a) perf. act.

11:71 (74)	We gave her the glad tidings of Isaac
15:54 (54)	do you give me good tidings
15:55 (55)	We give thee good tidings of truth
37:101 (99)	We gave him the good tidings of a prudent boy
37:112 (112)	We gave him the good tidings of Isaac
51:28 (28)	they gave him good tidings of a cunning boy

b) impf. act. (*yubashshiru*)

3:39 (34)	God gives thee good tidings of John
3:45 (40)	God gives thee good tidings of a Word from Him
9:21 (21)	their Lord gives them good tidings of mercy from Him
15:53 (53)	we give thee good tidings of a cunning boy
15:54 (54)	of what do you give me good tidings?
17:9 (9)	Koran guides to the way that is straightest and gives good tidings
18:2 (2)	and to give good tidings unto the believers
19:7 (7)	We give thee good tidings of a boy
19:97 (97)	that thou mayest bear good tidings thereby to the godfearing
42:23 (22)	that is the good tidings God gives to His servants

c) impv. (*bashshir*)

2:25 (23)	give thou good tidings to those who believe
2:155 (150)	give thou good tidings unto the patient
2:223 (223)	give thou good tidings to the believers
3:21 (20)	do thou give them the good tidings of a painful chastisement
4:138 (137)	give thou good tidings to the hypocrites
9:3 (3)	give thou good tidings to the unbelievers
9:34 (34)	give them the good tidings of a painful chastisement
9:112 (113)	give thou good tidings to the believers

10:2 (2)	give thou good tidings to the believers
10:87 (87)	do thou give good tidings to the believers
22:34 (35)	give thou good tidings unto the humble
22:37 (38)	give thou good tidings unto the good-doers
31:7 (6)	give him good tidings of a painful chastisement
33:47 (46)	give good tidings to the believers
36:11 (10)	give him the good tidings of forgiveness
39:17 (19)	give thou good tidings to My servants
45:8 (7)	give him the good tidings of a painful chastisement
61:13 (13)	give thou good tidings to the believers
84:24 (24)	give them good tidings of a painful chastisement

d) perf. pass. (*bushshira*)

16:58 (60)	when any of them is given the good tidings of a girl
16:59 (61)	the good tidings that have been given unto him
43:17 (16)	when any of them is given the good tidings

g) pcple. act. (*mubashshir*)

2:213 (209)	then God sent forth the Prophets, good tidings to bear
4:165 (163)	Messengers bearing good tidings
6:48 (48)	We do not send the Envoys, except good tidings to bear
17:105 (106)	We have sent thee not, except good tidings to bear
18:56 (54)	We send not the Envoys, but good tidings to bear
25:56 (58)	We have sent thee not, except good tidings to bear
30:46 (45)	He looses the winds, bearing good tidings
33:45 (44)	We have sent thee as a witness, and good tidings to bear
48:8 (8)	We have sent thee as a witness, good tidings to bear
61:6 (6)	giving good tidings of a Messenger

BĀSHARA vb. (III)~to lie with, to go in unto (a wife)

b) impf. act. (*yubāshiru*)

2:187 (183)	do not lie with them while you cleave to the mosques

c) impv. (*bāshir*)

2:187 (183)	so now lie with them

ABSHARA vb. (IV)~to rejoice (as a result of hearing good tidings)

c) impv. (*abshir*)

41:30 (30)	rejoice in Paradise that you were promised

ISTABSHARA vb. (X)~to rejoice (as a result of hearing good tidings). (pcple. act.) joyous

b) impf. act. (*yastabshiru*)

3:170 (164)	and joyful in those who remain behind
3:171 (165)	joyful in blessing and bounty from God
9:124 (125)	they are joyful
15:67 (67)	people of the city came rejoicing
30:48 (47)	they rejoice
39:45 (46)	when those apart from Him are mentioned behold, they rejoice

c) impv. (*istabshir*)

9:111 (112) so rejoice in the bargain you have made with Him

g) pcple. act. (*mustabshir*)

80:39 (39) laughing, joyous

*B Ṣ L

BAṢAL n.m.~onions

2:61 (58) green herbs, cucumbers, corn, lentils, onions

*B Ṣ R

BAṢURA vb. (I)~to behold, to perceive [Ar]; to see [Bl]; to observe [Pk]; to watch [Ali]

a) perf. act.

20:96 (96) I beheld what they (beheld) not
28:11 (10) and she perceived him from afar

b) impf. act. (*yabṣuru*)

20:96 (96) I (beheld) what they beheld not

BAṢAR n.m. (pl. *abṣār*)~sight, sense of seeing, eye-sight, eyes

2:7 (6) and on their eyes is a covering
2:20 (19) the lightning wellnigh snatches away their sight
2:20 (19) He would have taken away their hearing and their sight
3:13 (11) in that is a lesson for men possessed of eyes
6:46 (46) if God seizes your hearing and sight, and sets a seal
6:103 (103) the eyes attain Him not, but He attains the (eyes)
6:103 (103) the (eyes) attain Him not, but He attains the eyes
6:110 (110) We shall turn about their hearts and their eyes
7:47 (45) when their eyes are turned towards the inhabitants of the Fire
10:31 (32) or who possesses hearing and sight
14:42 (43) He is only deferring them to a day when eyes shall stare
15:15 (15) our eyes have been dazzled
16:77 (79) as a twinkling of the eye
16:78 (80) He appointed for you hearing, and sight
16:108 (110) God has set a seal on ... their eyes
17:36 (38) the hearing, the sight, the heart — all of those
21:97 (97) and behold, the eyes of the unbelievers staring
22:46 (45) it is not the eyes that are blind
23:78 (80) it is He who produced for you hearing, and eyes
24:30 (30) that they cast down their eyes
24:31 (31) that they cast down their eyes
24:37 (37) a day when hearts and eyes shall be turned about
24:43 (43) gleam of His lightning snatches away the sight
24:44 (44) in that is a lesson for those who have eyes
32:9 (8) He appointed for you hearing, and sight
33:10 (10) when your eyes swerved
38:45 (45) Isaac and Jacob—men of might they and of vision
38:63 (63) or have our eyes swerved away from them?
41:20 (19) their eyes and their skins bear witness against them

41:22 (21)	your eyes and your skins should not bear witness against you
45:23 (22)	and laid a covering on his eyes
46:26 (25)	We appointed for them hearing, and sight
46:26 (25)	their sight and their hearts availed them nothing
47:23 (25)	and so made them deaf, and blinded their eyes
50:22 (21)	thy sight today is piercing
53:17 (17)	his eye swerved not, nor swept astray
54:7 (7)	abasing their eyes, they shall come forth
54:50 (50)	as the twinkling of an eye
59:2 (2)	take heed, you who have eyes
67:3 (3)	return thy gaze; seest thou any fissure?
67:4 (4)	return thy gaze again, and again, and thy (gaze) comes back to thee dazzled
67:4 (4)	return thy (gaze) again, and again, and thy gaze comes back to thee dazzled
67:23 (23)	and appointed for you hearing and sight
68:43 (43)	humbled shall be their eyes
68:51 (51)	the unbelievers wellnigh strike thee down with their glances
70:44 (44)	humbled their eyes, overspreading them abasement
75:7 (7)	but when the sight is dazed
79:9 (9)	and their eyes shall be humbled

BAṢĪR n.m. (adj)~one who sees, who understands clearly; All-seeing (Divine attribute)

God is All-seeing, God sees

2:96 (90)	god sees the things they do
2:110 (104)	assuredly God sees the things you do
2:233 (233)	know that God sees the things you do
2:237 (238)	surely God sees the things you do
2:265 (267)	God sees the things you do
3:15 (13)	God sees His servants
3:20 (19)	God sees His servants
3:156 (150)	God sees the things you do
3:163 (157)	God sees the things they do
4:58 (61)	God is All-hearing, All-seeing
4:134 (133)	God is All-hearing, All-seeing
5:71 (75)	God sees the things they do
6:50 (50)	are the blind and the seeing man equal?
8:39 (40)	surely God sees the things they do
8:72 (73)	God sees the things you do
11:24 (26)	and the man who sees and hears; are they equal
11:112 (114)	surely He sees the things you do
17:1 (1)	He is the All-hearing, the All-seeing
17:17 (18)	who is aware of and sees the sins of His servants
17:30 (32)	surely He is aware of and sees His servants
17:96 (98)	surely He is aware of and sees His servants
20:35 (35)	surely Thou seest into us
22:61 (60)	God is All-hearing, All-seeing
22:75 (74)	surely God is All-hearing, All-seeing
25:20 (22)	thy Lord is ever All-seeing
31:28 (27)	God is All-hearing, All-seeing
33:9 (9)	God sees the things you do
34:11 (10)	surely I see the things you do
35:31 (28)	God is aware of and sees His servants
35:45 (45)	surely God sees His servants
40:20 (21)	surely God is the All-hearing, the All-seeing
40:44 (47)	surely God sees His servants

40:56 (58)	surely He is the All-hearing, the All-seeing
41:40 (40)	surely He sees the things you do
42:11 (9)	He is the All-hearing, the All-seeing
42:27 (26)	surely He is aware of and sees His servants
48:24 (24)	God sees the things you do
49:18 (18)	God sees the things you do
57:4 (4)	God sees the things you do
58:1 (1)	God is All-hearing, All-seeing
60:3 (3)	God sees the things you do
64:2 (2)	God sees the things you do
67:19 (19)	He sees everything
84:15 (15)	his Lord had sight of him

General Usage

12:93 (93)	and he shall recover his sight
12:96 (96)	forthwith he saw once again
13:16 (17)	are the blind and the seeing man equal
20:125 (125)	thou raised me blind, and I was wont to see
35:19 (20)	not equal are the blind and the seeing man
40:58 (60)	not equal are the blind and the seeing man
76:2 (2)	We made him hearing, seeing

BAṢĪRAH n.f. (pl. *baṣāʾir*)~clear evidence, clear proof, sure knowledge

6:104 (104)	clear proofs have come to you from your Lord
7:203 (202)	this is clear testimony from your Lord
12:108 (108)	I call to God with sure knowledge
17:102 (104)	none sent these down, except the Lord ..., as clear proofs
28:43 (43)	destroyed the former generations, to be examples and a guidance
45:20 (19)	this is clear proofs for men
75:14 (14)	man shall be a clear proof against himself

TABṢIRAH n.f.~insight, a matter of contemplation

50:8 (8)	for an insight and a reminder to every penitent servant

BAṢṢARA vb. (II)~to give sight to

e) impf. pass. (*yubaṣṣaru*)

70:11 (11)	as they are given sight of them

ABṢARA vb. (IV)~to see, to consider, having open eyes (to see), to perceive. (pcple. act.) one who sees, perceives; seeing, perceiving; visible

a) perf. act.

6:104 (104)	whoso sees clearly, it is to his own gain
32:12 (12)	our Lord, we have seen and heard

b) impf. act. (*yubṣiru*)

2:17 (16)	God took away their light, and left them in darkness unseeing
7:179 (178)	they have eyes, but perceive not with them
7:195 (194)	or have they eyes wherewith they see
7:198 (197)	thou seest them looking at thee, unperceiving
10:43 (44)	wilt thou then guide the blind, though they do not see?
11:20 (22)	they could not hear, neither did they see

19:42 (43)	why worshippest thou that which neither hears nor sees
21:3 (3)	will you take to sorcery with your eyes open?
27:54 (55)	do you commit indecency with your eyes open?
28:72 (72)	will you not see?
32:27 (27)	will they not see?
36:9 (8)	We have covered them, so they do not see
36:66 (66)	but how would they see?
37:175 (175)	soon they shall see
37:179 (179)	soon they shall see
43:51 (50)	what, do you not see?
51:21 (21)	what, do you not see?
52:15 (15)	is this magic, or is it you that do not see?
56:85 (84)	We are nigher him than you, but you do not see Us
68:5 (5)	so thou shalt see, and they will (see)
68:5 (5)	so thou shalt (see), and they will see
69:38 (38)	I swear by that you see
69:39 (39)	and by that you do not see

c) impv. (*abṣir*)

18:26 (25)	how well He sees
19:38 (39)	how well they will hear and see on the day they come to Us
37:175 (175)	and see them; soon they shall see
37:179 (179)	and see; soon they shall see

g) pcple. act. (*mubṣir*)

7:201 (200)	remember, and then see clearly
10:67 (68)	and the day, to see
17:12 (13)	and made the sign of the day to see
17:59 (61)	We brought Thamood the She-camel visible
27:13 (13)	when Our signs came to them visibly
27:86 (88)	and the day, to see
40:61 (63)	and the day, to see

ISTABṢARA vb. (X)~(pcple. act.) one who sees clearly

g) pcple. act. (*mustabṣir*)

29:38 (37)	though they saw clearly

*B T K

BATTAKA vb. (II)~to cut off

b) impf. act. (*yubattiku*)

4:119 (118)	they will cut off the cattle's ears

*B T L

BATTALA vb. (II)~(n.vb.) total devotion; (adv) very devoutly

f) n.vb. (*tabtīl*)

73:8 (8)	devote thyself unto Him very devoutly

TABATTALA vb. (V)~to devote oneself (to God)

c) impv. (*tabattal*)

73:8 (8) devote thyself unto Him

*B T R

ABTAR n.m. (adj)~one who is cut off, childless

108:3 (3) he that hates thee, he is the one cut off

*B TH TH

BATHTHA vb. (I)~to scatter abroad (tr), to disperse. (n.vb.) anguish. (pcple. pass.) scattered, outspread, dispersed

a) perf. act.

2:164 (159) and His scattering abroad in it all manner of crawling thing
4:1 (1) from the pair of them scattered abroad many
31:10 (9) He scattered abroad in it all manner of crawling thing
42:29 (28) and the crawling things He has scattered abroad in them

b) impf. act. (*yabuththu*)

45:4 (3) and the crawling things He scatters abroad

f) n.vb. (*bathth*)

12:86 (86) I make complaint of my anguish and my sorrow unto God

h) pcple. pass. (*mabthūth*)

88:16 (16) and carpets outspread
101:4 (3) the day that men shall be like scattered moths

INBATHTHA vb. (VII)~(pcple. pass.) scattered abroad, dispersed

h) pcple. pass. (*munbathth*)

56:6 (6) and become a dust scattered

*B Ṭ ʾ

BAṬṬAʾA vb. (II)~to be dilatory, to retard, to tarry

b) impf. act. (*yubaṭṭiʾu*)

4:72 (74) some of you there are that are dilatory

*B Ṭ L

BAṬALA vb. (I)~to be in vain, to perish, to prove false

a) perf. act.

7:118 (115) and false was proved what they were doing

BĀṬIL n.m.~vanity, falsehood, false, void, untrue (usually opp. *ḥaqq*)

2:42 (39)	do not confound the truth with vanity
2:188 (184)	consume not your goods between you in vanity
3:71 (64)	why do you confound the truth with vanity
3:191 (188)	Thou hast not created this for vanity
4:29 (33)	consume not your goods between you in vanity
4:161 (159)	prohibited, and consuming the wealth of the people in vanity
7:139 (135)	and void is what they have been doing
8:8 (8)	that He might verify the truth and prove untrue the untrue
9:34 (34)	many of the rabbis and monks indeed consume the goods of the people in vanity
11:16 (19)	and void will be their works
13:17 (18)	so God strikes both the true and the false
16:72 (74)	do they believe in vanity, and do they disbelieve
17:81 (83)	the truth has come, and falsehood has vanished away
17:81 (83)	surely falsehood is ever certain to vanish
18:56 (54)	yet do the unbelievers dispute with falsehood
21:18 (18)	We hurl the truth against falsehood and it prevails over it
22:62 (61)	that they call upon apart from Him — that is the false
29:52 (52)	those who believe in vanity and disbelieve in God
29:67 (67)	do they believe in vanity, and do they disbelieve
31:30 (29)	that they call upon apart from Him — that is the false
34:49 (48)	truth has come; falsehood originates not
38:27 (26)	what between them is, for vanity
40:5 (5)	and disputed with falsehood that they might rebut thereby the truth
41:42 (42)	falsehood comes not to it from before it nor from behind it
42:24 (23)	God blots out falsehood and verifies the truth
47:3 (3)	those who disbelieve follow falsehood

ABṬALA vb. (IV)~to prove untrue, to bring to naught, to frustrate. (pcple. act.) one who deals in falsehood, vain-doer

b) impf. act. (*yubṭilu*)

2:264 (266)	void not your freewill offerings with reproach and injury
8:8 (8)	He might verify the truth and prove untrue the untrue
10:81 (81)	God will assuredly bring it to naught
47:33 (35)	do not make your own works vain

g) pcple. act. (*mubṭil*)

7:173 (172)	wilt Thou then destroy us for the deeds of the vain-doers?
29:48 (47)	those who follow falsehood would have doubted
30:58 (58)	you do nothing but follow falsehood
40:78 (78)	then the vain-doers shall be lost
45:27 (26)	upon that day the vain-doers shall lose

*B Ṭ N

BATANA vb. (I)~to be within, to be inward. (pcple. act.) that which is hidden, that which is inward; Inward (Divine attribute)

a) perf. act.

6:151 (152)	and that you approach not any indecency outward or inward
7:33 (31)	my Lord has only forbidden indecencies, the inward and the outward

g) pcple. act. (*bāṭin*)

6:120 (120)	forsake the outward sin, and the inward
31:20 (19)	He has lavished on you His blessings, outward and inward
57:3 (3)	He is the First and the Last, the Outward and the Inward
57:13 (13)	having a door in the inward whereof is mercy

BAṬN n.m. (pl. *buṭūn*)~belly, hollow

2:174 (169)	they shall eat naught but the Fire in their bellies
3:35 (31)	I have vowed to Thee, in dedication, what is within my womb
4:10 (11)	those who devour the property of orphans unjustly, devour Fire in their bellies
6:139 (140)	what is within the bellies of these cattle is reserved for our males
16:66 (68)	We give you to drink of what is in their bellies
16:69 (71)	then comes there forth out of their bellies a drink
16:78 (80)	it is God who brought you forth, knowing nothing, from your mothers' wombs
22:20 (21)	whereby whatsoever is in their bellies
23:21 (21)	We give you to drink of what is in their bellies
24:45 (44)	and some of them go upon their bellies
37:66 (64)	and of it fill their bellies
37:144 (144)	he would have tarried in its belly
39:6 (8)	He creates you in your mothers' wombs
44:45 (45)	like molten copper, bubbling in the belly
48:24 (24)	in the hollow of Mecca
53:32 (33)	when you were yet unborn in your mothers' wombs
56:53 (53)	and you shall fill therewith your bellies

BIṬĀNAH n.f. (pl. *baṭāʾin*)~inner linings; intimate friend

3:118 (114)	take not for your intimates outside yourselves
55:54 (54)	reclining upon couches lined with brocade

*B Ṭ R

BAṬIRA vb. (I)~to be insolent, reckless, arrogant. (n.vb.) boasting, recklessness

a) perf. act.

28:58 (58)	a city We have destroyed that flourished in insolent ease

f) n.vb. (*baṭar*)

8:47 (49)	be not as those who went forth from their habitations swaggering boastfully

*B Ṭ SH

BAṬASHA vb. (I)~to lay hold, to seize by force. (n.vb.) assault, valour

a) perf. act.

26:130 (130)	when you assault, you (assault) like tyrants
26:130 (130)	when you (assault), you assault like tyrants

b) impf. act. (*yabṭishu*)

7:195 (194)	have they hands wherewith they lay hold
28:19 (18)	when he would have assaulted the man who was an enemy
44:16 (15)	the day when We shall assault most mightily

f) n.vb. (*baṭsh*)

43:8 (7)	We destroyed men stronger in valour than they
50:36 (35)	a generation We destroyed before them that was stronger in valour
85:12 (12)	surely thy Lord's assault is terrible

BAṬSHAH n.f.~assault; (adv) mightily

44:16 (15)	the day when We shall assault most mightily
54:36 (36)	He had warned them of Our assault

*B W ʾ

BĀʾA vb. (I)~to bring back, to bring down upon oneself, to be laden with a burden (of God's wrath)

a) perf. act.

2:61 (58)	they were laden with the burden of God's anger
2:90 (84)	they were laden with anger upon anger
3:112 (108)	they will be laden with the burden of God's anger
3:162 (156)	him who is laden with the burden of God's anger
8:16 (16)	he is laden with the burden of God's anger

b) impf. act. (*yabūʾu*)

5:29 (32)	I desire that thou shouldest be laden with my sin and thy sin

BAWWAʾA vb. (II)~to lodge, to prepare a dwelling for

a) perf. act.

7:74 (72)	and lodged you in the land
10:93 (93)	We settled the Children of Israel in a sure settlement
22:26 (27)	when We settled for Abraham the place of the House

b) impf. act. (*yubawwiʾu*)

3:121 (117)	to lodge the believers in their pitches for the battle

MUBAWWAʾ n.m.~a dwelling, a place of lodging, a settlement

10:93 (93)	We settled the Children of Israel in a sure settlement
16:41 (43)	We shall surely lodge them in this world in a goodly lodging
29:58 (58)	We shall surely lodge them in lofty chambers of Paradise

TABAWWAʾA vb. (V)~to take or make as one's dwelling, to occupy

a) perf. act.

59:9 (9)	those who made their dwelling in the abode

b) impf. act. (*yatabawwaʾu*)

12:56 (56)	We established Joseph in the land, to make his dwelling there
39:74 (74)	to make our dwelling wheresoever we will in Paradise

c) impv. (*tabawwaʾ*)

10:87 (87)	take you, for your people, in Egypt certain houses

*B W B

BĀB n.m. (pl. *abwāb*)~door, gate

2:58 (55)	enter in at the gate, prostrating
2:189 (185)	come to the houses by their doors
4:154 (153)	enter in at the gate, prostrating
5:23 (26)	enter against them the gate
6:44 (44)	We opened unto them the gates of everything
7:40 (38)	the gates of heaven shall not be opened
7:161 (161)	enter in at the gate, prostrating
12:23 (23)	[she] solicited him, and closed the doors on them
12:25 (25)	they raced to the door
12:25 (25)	they encountered her master by the door
12:67 (67)	my sons, enter not by one door
12:67 (67)	enter by separate doors
13:23 (23)	angels shall enter unto them from every gate
15:14 (14)	though We opened to them a gate in heaven
15:44 (44)	seven gates it has
15:44 (44)	and unto each gate a set portion
16:29 (31)	so enter the gates of Gehenna
23:77 (79)	when We open against them a door of terrible chastisement
38:50 (50)	Gardens of Eden, whereof the gates are open to them
39:71 (71)	when they have come thither, then its gates will be opened
39:72 (72)	enter the gates of Gehenna, to dwell therein
39:73 (73)	when they have come thither, and its gates are opened
40:76 (76)	enter the gates of Gehenna, to dwell therein
43:34 (33)	and doors to their houses, and couches
54:11 (11)	We opened the gates of heaven unto water torrential
57:13 (13)	having a door in the inward whereof is mercy
78:19 (19)	and heaven is opened, and become gates

*B W L

BĀL n.m.~mind; (*mā bāl*) what of, what is the case of

12:50 (50)	what of the women who cut their hands?
20:51 (53)	what of the former generations?
47:2 (2)	He will acquit them of their evil deeds, and dispose their minds aright
47:5 (6)	He will guide them, and dispose their minds aright

*B W R

BĀRA vb. (I)~to come to naught. (n.vb.) naught, ruin, perdition

b) impf. act. (*yabūru*)

35:10 (11)	and their devising shall come to naught
35:29 (26)	look for a commerce that comes not to naught

f) n.vb. (*bawār*)

14:28 (33)	and caused their people to dwell in the abode of ruin

BŪR n.m. (adj)~corrupt, wicked

25:18 (19)	until they forgot the Remembrance, and were a people corrupt
48:12 (12)	you thought evil thoughts, and you were a people corrupt

*B Y ᶜ

BĀᶜA vb. (I)~(n.vb.) selling, trafficking

f) n.vb. (*bayᶜ*)

2:254 (255)	there comes a day wherein shall be neither traffick, nor friendship
2:275 (276)	trafficking is like usury
2:275 (276)	God has permitted trafficking, and forbidden usury
9:111 (112)	so rejoice in the bargain you have made with Him
14:31 (36)	a day comes wherein shall be neither bargaining nor befriending
24:37 (37)	men whom neither commerce nor trafficking diverts
62:9 (9)	hasten to God's remembrance and leave trafficking aside

BIYAᶜ n.f. (pl. of *bīᶜah*)~church

22:40 (41)	there had been destroyed cloisters and churches

BĀYAᶜA vb. (III)~to make a bargain or a contract with someone, to swear fealty, to take oath of allegiance

a) perf. act.

9:111 (112)	so rejoice in the bargain you have made with Him

b) impf. act. (*yubāyiᶜu*)

48:10 (10)	those who swear fealty to thee
48:10 (10)	swear fealty in truth to God
48:18 (18)	the believers when they were swearing fealty to thee
60:12 (12)	when believing women come to thee, swearing fealty

c) impv. (*bāyiᶜ*)

60:12 (12)	nor disobey thee in aught honourable, accept their fealty

TABĀYAᶜA vb. (VI)~to sell, to traffick with one another

a) perf. act.

2:282 (282)	and take witnesses when you are trafficking one with another

*B Y D

BĀDA vb. (I)~to perish

b) impf. act. (*yabīdu*)

18:35 (33)	I do not think that this will ever perish

*B Y Ḍ

ABYAḌ n.m. (f., *bayḍāʾ*, pl., *bīḍ*), (adj)~white

2:187 (183)	eat and drink, until the white thread shows clearly
7:108 (105)	he drew forth his hand, and lo, it was white
20:22 (23)	it shall come forth white, without evil
26:33 (32)	it was white to the beholders
27:12 (12)	and it will come forth white
28:32 (32)	and it will come forth white without evil

35:27 (25)	in the mountains are streaks white and red
37:46 (45)	white, a delight to the drinkers

BAYḌ n.m.~pearls [Ar]; eggs [Pk, Ali, Bl]

37:49 (47)	as if they were hidden pearls

IBYAḌḌA vb. (XI)~to be whitened, to become white

a) perf. act.

3:107 (103)	as for those whose faces are whitened
12:84 (84)	his eyes turned white because of the sorrow

b) impf. act. (*yabyaḍḍu*)

3:106 (102)	the day when some faces are blackened, and some faces whitened

*B Y N

BAYYINAH n.f. (adj)~clear or manifest signs [Ar, Ali]; evidence [Bl]; clear proofs [Pk]

2:87 (81)	We gave Jesus son of Mary the clear signs
2:92 (86)	Moses came to you with the clear signs
2:99 (93)	We have sent down unto thee signs, clear signs
2:159 (154)	those who conceal the clear signs and the guidance
2:185 (181)	to be a guidance to the people, and as clear signs
2:209 (205)	if you slip, after the clear signs have come to you
2:211 (207)	how many a clear sign We gave them
2:213 (209)	after the clear signs had come to them
2:253 (254)	We gave Jesus son of Mary the clear signs
2:253 (254)	after the clear signs had come to them
3:86 (80)	and the clear signs came to them
3:97 (91)	therein are clear signs
3:105 (101)	be not as those who scattered and fell into variance after the clear signs
3:183 (180)	Messengers have come to you before me bearing clear signs
3:184 (181)	Messengers before thee, who came bearing clear signs
4:153 (152)	after the clear signs had come to them
5:32 (36)	Our Messengers have already come to them with the clear signs
5:110 (110)	when thou camest unto them with the clear signs
6:57 (57)	I stand upon a clear sign from my Lord
6:157 (158)	yet indeed a clear sign has come to you
7:73 (71)	there has now come to you a clear sign
7:85 (83)	there has now come to you a clear sign
7:101 (99)	their Messengers came to them with the clear signs
7:105 (103)	I have brought a clear sign to you from your Lord
8:42 (44)	whosoever perished might perish by a clear sign
8:42 (44)	by a clear sign he might live
9:70 (71)	their Messengers came to them with the clear signs
10:13 (14)	their Messengers came to them with the clear signs
10:15 (16)	when Our signs are recited to them, clear signs
10:74 (75)	they brought them the clear signs
11:17 (20)	what of him who stands upon a clear sign from his Lord
11:28 (30)	if I stand upon a clear sign from my Lord
11:53 (56)	Hood, thou hast not brought us a clear sign
11:63 (66)	if I stand upon a clear sign from my Lord
11:88 (90)	if I stand upon a clear sign from my Lord

14:9 (10)	their Messengers came to them with the clear signs
16:44 (46)	with the clear signs, and the Psalms
17:101 (103)	We gave Moses nine signs, clear signs
18:15 (14)	they would bring some clear authority regarding them
19:73 (74)	when Our signs are recited to them as clear signs
20:72 (75)	We will not prefer thee over the clear signs
20:133 (133)	has there not come to them the clear sign
22:16 (16)	even so We have sent it down as signs, clear signs
22:72 (71)	when Our signs are recited to them, clear signs
24:1 (1)	We have sent down in it signs, clear signs
28:36 (36)	when Moses came to them with Our signs, clear signs
29:35 (34)	We have left thereof a sign, a clear sign
29:39 (38)	Moses came to them with the clear signs
29:49 (48)	nay; rather it is signs, clear signs
30:9 (8)	their Messengers came to them with the clear signs
30:47 (46)	they brought them the clear signs
34:43 (42)	when Our signs are recited to them, clear signs
35:25 (23)	their Messengers came to them with the clear signs
35:40 (38)	so that they are upon a clear sign from it
40:22 (23)	their Messengers came to them with the clear signs
40:28 (29)	he has brought you the clear signs from your Lord
40:34 (36)	Joseph brought you the clear signs before
40:50 (53)	did not your Messengers bring you the clear signs?
40:66 (68)	since the clear signs came to me from my Lord
40:83 (83)	when their Messengers brought them the clear signs
43:63 (63)	when Jesus came with the clear signs
45:17 (16)	We gave them clear signs of the Command
45:25 (24)	when Our signs are recited to them, clear signs
46:7 (6)	when Our signs are recited to them, clear signs
47:14 (15)	is he who is upon a clear sign from his Lord like unto such a one
57:9 (9)	it is He who sends down upon His servant signs, clear signs
57:25 (25)	We sent Our Messengers with the clear signs
58:5 (6)	We have sent down signs, clear signs
61:6 (6)	when he brought them the clear signs, they said
64:6 (6)	their Messengers came to them with the clear signs
98:1 (1)	idolaters would never leave off, till the Clear Sign came to them
98:4 (3)	excepting after the Clear Sign came to them

TIBYĀN n.m.~an exposition that makes clear

16:89 (91)	We have sent down on thee the Book making clear everything

BAYYANA vb. (II)~to make clear, to make manifest, to show, to declare. (pcple. act.) that which makes clear; manifest, flagrant (sin)

a) perf. act.

2:118 (112)	yet We have made clear the signs unto a people
2:159 (154)	after We have shown them clearly in the Book
2:160 (155)	save such as repent and make amends, and show clearly
3:118 (114)	now We have made clear to you the signs
57:17 (16)	We have indeed made clear for you the signs

b) impf. act. (*yubayyinu*)

2:68 (63)	that He may make clear to us what she may be
2:69 (64)	that He make clear to us what her colour may be

2:70 (65)	that He make clear to us what she may be
2:187 (183)	so God makes clear His signs to men
2:219 (217)	so God makes clear His signs to you
2:221 (221)	He makes clear His signs to the people
2:230 (230)	He makes them clear unto a people that have knowledge
2:242 (243)	so God makes clear His signs for you
2:266 (268)	so God makes clear the signs to you
3:103 (99)	even so God makes clear to you His signs
3:187 (184)	you shall make it clear unto the people
4:26 (31)	God desires to make clear to you
4:176 (175)	god makes clear to you, lest you go astray
5:15 (18)	Our Messenger, making clear to you many things
5:19 (22)	Our Messenger, making things clear to you
5:75 (79)	behold, how We make clear the signs to them
5:89 (91)	so God makes clear to you His signs
6:105 (105)	that We may make it clear to a people having knowledge
9:115 (116)	He has guided them, until He makes clear to them
14:4 (4)	that he might make all clear to them
16:39 (41)	so that He may make clear to them
16:44 (46)	that thou mayest make clear to mankind
16:64 (66)	make clear to them that whereon they were at variance
16:92 (94)	He will make clear to you upon the Day of Resurrection
22:5 (5)	that We may make clear to you
24:18 (17)	God makes clear to you the signs
24:58 (57)	God makes clear to you the signs
24:59 (58)	so God makes clear to you His signs
24:61 (61)	so God makes clear to you the signs
43:63 (63)	I may make clear to you some of that whereon you are at variance

g) pcple. act. (*mubayyin*)

4:19 (23)	except when they commit a flagrant indecency
24:34 (34)	We have sent down to you signs making all clear
24:46 (45)	We have sent down signs making all clear
33:30 (30)	whosoever among you commits a flagrant indecency
65:1 (1)	nor let them go forth, except when they commit a flagrant indecency
65:11 (11)	a Messenger reciting to you the signs of God

ABĀNA vb. (IV)~to make things clear. (n.vb.) exposition, clear demonstration, argument, explanation. (pcple. act.) that which makes clear or plain; manifest, evident, plain; (43:18) be seen [Ar, Bl]; making oneself clear [Pk]; giving clear account [Ali]

b) impf. act. (*yubīnu*)

43:52 (52)	and scarcely makes things clear

f) n.vb. (*bayān*)

3:138 (132)	this is an exposition for mankind
55:4 (3)	He has taught him the Explanation
75:19 (19)	then Ours it is to explain it

g) pcple. act. (*mubīn*)

2:168 (163)	Satan; he is a manifest foe to you
2:208 (204)	he is a manifest foe to you
3:164 (158)	the Book and the Wisdom, though before they were in manifest error

4:20 (24)	will you take it by way of calumny and manifest sin?
4:50 (53)	that suffices for a manifest sin
4:91 (93)	against them We have given you a clear authority
4:101 (102)	unbelievers are for you a manifest foe
4:112 (112)	thereby has laid upon himself calumny and manifest sin
4:119 (118)	has surely suffered a manifest loss
4:144 (143)	do you desire to give God over you a clear authority?
4:153 (152)	We bestowed upon Moses a clear authority
4:174 (174)	We have sent down to you a manifest light
5:15 (18)	to you from God a light, and a Book Manifest
5:92 (93)	Our Messenger to deliver the Message Manifest
5:110 (110)	this is nothing but sorcery manifest
6:7 (7)	this is naught but manifest sorcery
6:16 (16)	that is the manifest triumph
6:59 (59)	it is in a Book Manifest
6:74 (74)	I see thee, and thy people, in manifest error
6:142 (143)	he is a manifest foe to you
7:22 (21)	Satan is for you a manifest foe
7:60 (58)	we see thee in manifest error
7:107 (104)	it was a serpent manifest
7:184 (183)	he is naught but a plain warner
10:2 (2)	this is a manifest sorcerer
10:61 (62)	is aught smaller than that, or greater, but in a Manifest Book
10:76 (77)	surely this is a manifest sorcery
11:6 (8)	all is in a Manifest Book
11:7 (10)	this is naught but a manifest sorcery
11:25 (27)	I am for you a [plain] warner, and a bearer of good tidings
11:96 (99)	We sent Moses with Our signs, and a manifest authority
12:1 (1)	those are the signs of the Manifest Book
12:5 (5)	Satan is to man a manifest enemy
12:8 (8)	our father is in manifest error
12:30 (30)	we see her in manifest error
14:10 (12)	then bring us a manifest authority
15:1 (1)	those are the signs of the Book and of a manifest Koran
15:18 (18)	he is pursued by a manifest flame
15:79 (79)	the two of them were upon a roadway manifest
15:89 (89)	surely, I am the manifest warner
16:4 (4)	he is a manifest adversary
16:35 (37)	aught for the Messengers, but to deliver the manifest Message
16:82 (84)	thine it is only to deliver the manifest Message
16:103 (105)	this is speech Arabic, manifest
17:53 (55)	Satan is ever a manifest foe to man
19:38 (39)	the evildoers even today are in error manifest
21:54 (55)	your fathers have been in manifest error
22:11 (11)	that is indeed the manifest loss
22:49 (48)	I am only for you a plain warner
23:45 (47)	We sent Moses and his brother Aaron with Our signs and a manifest authority
24:12 (12)	this is a manifest calumny
24:25 (25)	they shall know that God is the manifest Truth
24:54 (53)	it is only for the Messenger to deliver the manifest Message
26:2 (1)	those are the signs of the Manifest Book
26:30 (29)	even though I brought thee something manifest
26:32 (31)	it was a serpent manifest
26:97 (97)	we were certainly in manifest error
26:115 (115)	I am naught but a plain warner

26:195 (195)	in a clear, Arabic tongue
27:1 (1)	those are the signs of the Koran and a Manifest Book
27:13 (13)	this is a manifest sorcery
27:16 (16)	this is indeed the manifest bounty
27:21 (21)	or he bring me a clear authority
27:75 (77)	it is in a Manifest Book
27:79 (81)	thou art upon the manifest truth
28:2 (1)	those are the signs of the Manifest Book
28:15 (14)	he is surely an enemy misleading, manifest
28:18 (17)	clearly thou art a quarreller
28:85 (85)	who comes with guidance, and who is in manifest error
29:18 (17)	it is only for the Messenger to deliver the Manifest Message
29:50 (49)	I am only a plain warner
31:11 (10)	the evildoers are in manifest error
33:36 (36)	has gone astray into manifest error
33:58 (58)	have laid upon themselves calumny and manifest sin
34:3 (3)	but it is in a Manifest Book
34:24 (23)	either we or you are upon right guidance, or in manifest error
34:43 (42)	this is nothing but manifest sorcery
36:12 (11)	everything We have numbered in a clear regiser
36:17 (16)	it is only for us to deliver the Manifest Message
36:24 (23)	in that case I should be in manifest error
36:47 (47)	you are only in manifest error
36:60 (60)	surely he is a manifest foe to you
36:69 (69)	it is only a Remembrance and a Clear Koran
36:77 (77)	he is a manifest adversary
37:15 (15)	this is nothing but manifest sorcery
37:106 (106)	this is indeed the manifest trial
37:113 (113)	some are good-doers, and some manifest self-wrongers
37:156 (156)	or have you a clear authority?
38:70 (70)	that I am only a clear warner
39:15 (17)	is not that the manifest loss?
39:22 (23)	those are in manifest error
40:23 (24)	We also sent Moses with Our signs and a clear authority
43:2 (1)	by the Clear Book
43:15 (14)	man is clearly unthankful
43:18 (17)	and, when the time of altercation comes, [he] is not to be seen
43:29 (28)	until the truth came unto them, and a manifest Messenger
43:40 (39)	shalt thou guide the blind and him who is in manifest error?
43:62 (62)	he is for you a manifest foe
44:2 (1)	by the Clear Book
44:10 (9)	a day when heaven shall bring a manifest smoke
44:13 (12)	seeing a clear Messenger already came to them
44:19 (18)	I come to you with a clear authority
44:33 (32)	and gave them signs wherein there was a manifest trial
45:30 (29)	His mercy; that is the manifest triumph
46:7 (6)	this is manifest sorcery
46:9 (8)	I am only a clear warner
46:32 (31)	those are in manifest error
48:1 (1)	We have given thee a manifest victory
51:38 (38)	We sent him unto Pharaoh, with a clear authority
51:50 (50)	I am a clear warner from Him to you
51:51 (51)	I am a clear warner from Him to you
52:38 (38)	let any of them that has listened bring a clear authority
61:6 (6)	when he brought them the clear signs

62:2 (2)	though before that they were in manifest error
64:12 (12)	only for the Messenger to deliver the Manifest Message
67:26 (26)	I am only a clear warner
67:29 (29)	you will soon know who is in manifest error
71:2 (2)	I am unto you a clear warner
81:23 (23)	he truly saw him on the clear horizon

TABAYYANA vb. (V)~to make or become clear, evident

a) perf. act.

2:109 (103)	after the truth has become clear to them
2:256 (257)	rectitude has become clear from error
2:259 (261)	when it was made clear to him, he said
4:115 (115)	whoso makes a breach with the Messenger after the guidance has become clear to him
8:6 (6)	disputing with thee concerning the truth after it had become clear
9:113 (114)	after that it has become clear to them
9:114 (115)	and when it became clear to him that he was an enemy
14:45 (47)	it became clear to you how We did with them
29:38 (37)	it has become clear to you from their dwelling-places
34:14 (13)	and when he fell down, the jinn saw clearly that
47:25 (27)	after the guidance has become clear to them
47:32 (34)	after the guidance has become clear to them

b) impf. act. (*yatabayyanu*)

2:187 (183)	until the white thread shows clearly to you
9:43 (43)	till it was clear to thee which of them spoke the truth
41:53 (53)	till it is clear to them that it is the truth

c) impv. (*tabayyan*)

4:94 (96)	when you are journeying in the path of God, be discriminating
4:94 (96)	so be discriminating
49:6 (6)	make clear, lest you afflict a people

ISTABĀNA vb. (X)~to be manifest, clear. (pcple. act.) that which makes clear or manifest

b) impf. act. (*yastabīnu*)

6:55 (55)	that the sinners' way may be manifest

g) pcple. act. (*mustabīn*)

37:117 (117)	We gave them the Manifesting Book

*B Y T

BĀTA vb. (I)~to pass the night

b) impf. act. (*yabītu*)

25:64 (65)	who pass the night prostrate to their Lord and standing

BAYĀT n.m. (adv)~at night (usually in reference to an attack)

7:4 (3)	Our might came upon it at night
7:97 (95)	Our might shall not come upon them at night
10:50 (51)	have you considered? If His chastisement comes upon you by night

BAYT n.m. (pl. *buyūt*)~house, household, abode, family; temple, sanctuary, (specifically) The House (the Kaᶜba)

The House (Kaᶜba)

2:125 (119)	when We appointed the House to be a place of visitation
2:125 (119)	purify My House for those that shall go about it
2:127 (121)	when Abraham, and Ishmael with him, raised up the foundations of the House
2:158 (153)	whosoever makes the Pilgrimage to the House
3:96 (90)	the first House established for the people was that at Bekka
3:97 (91)	it is the duty of all men towards God to come to the House
5:2 (2)	those repairing to the Holy House seeking from their Lord bounty
5:97 (98)	God has appointed the Kaaba, the Holy House
8:35 (35)	their prayer at the House is nothing
11:73 (76)	His blessings be upon you, O people of the House
14:37 (40)	dwell in a valley where is no sown land by Thy Holy House
22:26 (27)	We settled for Abraham the place of the House
22:26 (27)	do thou purify My House for those that shall go about it
22:29 (30)	let them fulfil their vows, and go about the Ancient House
22:33 (34)	their lawful place of sacrifice is by the Ancient House
24:36 (36)	in temples God has allowed to be raised up
33:33 (33)	People of the House
52:4 (4)	by the House inhabited
106:3 (3)	let them serve the Lord of this House

General Usage

2:189 (185)	it is not piety to come to the houses from the backs of them
2:189 (185)	so come to the houses by their doors
3:49 (43)	what you treasure up in your houses
3:154 (148)	even if you had been in your houses
4:15 (19)	then detain them in their houses
4:100 (101)	whoso goes forth from his house an emigrant
7:74 (72)	and hewing its mountains into houses
8:5 (5)	as thy Lord brought thee forth from thy house
10:87 (87)	take you, for your people, in Egypt certain houses
10:87 (87)	and make your houses a direction for men to pray to
12:23 (23)	now the woman in whose house he was solicited him
15:82 (82)	they were hewing the mountains into houses
16:68 (70)	take unto yourselves, of the mountains, houses
16:80 (82)	it is God who has appointed a place of rest for you of your houses
16:80 (82)	and He has appointed for you of the skins of the cattle houses
17:93 (95)	or till thou possessest a house of gold
24:27 (27)	O believers, do not enter houses
24:27 (27)	other than your houses
24:29 (29)	there is no fault in you that you enter houses uninhabited
24:61 (60)	that you eat of your houses
24:61 (60)	or your father's houses
24:61 (60)	or your mothers' houses
24:61 (60)	or your brothers' houses
24:61 (60)	or your sisters' houses
24:61 (60)	or the houses of your uncles [paternal]
24:61 (60)	[or the houses of] your aunts paternal
24:61 (60)	or the houses of your uncles [maternal]
24:61 (60)	or [the houses of] your aunts maternal
24:61 (61)	when you enter houses, greet one another
26:149 (149)	will you still skilfully hew houses out of the mountains?

27:52 (53)	those are their houses, all fallen down
28:12 (11)	shall I direct you to the people of a household
29:41 (40)	the likeness of the spider that takes to itself a house
29:41 (40)	surely the frailest of houses is the (house) of the spider
29:41 (40)	surely the frailest of (houses) is the house of the spider
33:13 (13)	our houses are exposed
33:33 (33)	remain in your houses; and display not your finery
33:34 (34)	remember that which is recited in your houses
33:53 (53)	enter not the houses of the Prophet
43:33 (32)	roofs of silver to their houses, and stairs
43:34 (33)	and doors to their houses, and couches
51:36 (36)	We found not therein except one house
59:2 (2)	they destroyed their houses with their own hands
65:1 (1)	do not expel them from their houses
66:11 (11)	build for me a house in Paradise
71:28 (29)	forgive me and my parents and whosoever enters my house

BAYYATA vb. (II)~to meditate at night, to attack by night

a) perf. act.

4:81 (83)	a party of them meditate all night

b) impf. act. (*yubayyitu*)

4:81 (83)	God writes down their meditations
4:108 (108)	He is with them while they meditate at night
27:49 (50)	We will attack him and his family by night

*B Z GH

BAZAGHA vb. (I)~(pcple. act.) that which rises; rising

g) pcple. act. (*bāzigh*)

6:77 (77)	when he saw the moon rising, he said
6:78 (78)	when he saw the sun rising, he said

DĀL

*D ʾ B

DAʾABA vb. (I)~(pcple. act.) diligent, constant in one's work

g) pcple. act. (*dāʾib*)

14:33 (37) He subjected to you the sun and moon constant upon their courses

DAʾB n.m.~custom, manner, wont; (*ka-daʾb*) like

3:11 (9) like Pharaoh's folk, and the people before them
8:52 (54) like Pharaoh's folk, and the people before him
8:54 (56) like Pharaoh's folk, and the people before him
12:47 (47) you shall sow seven years after your wont
40:31 (32) the like of the case of Noah's people

*D ʿ ʿ

DAʿʿA vb. (I)~to push, to drive away with force, to repulse, to pitch into. (n.vb.) pitching into, driving away, thrusting

b) impf. act. (*yaduʿʿu*)

107:2 (2) that is he who repulses the orphan

e) impf. pass. (*yudaʿʿu*)

52:13 (13) the day when they shall be pitched into the fire of Gehenna

f) n.vb. (*daʿʿ*)

52:13 (13) the day when they shall be pitched <...> into the fire of Gehenna

*D ʿ W

DAʿĀ vb. (I)~to call to, to pray; to ascribe, to attribute. (n.vb.) a prayer, supplication, call, shout, petition. (pcple. act.) a caller, summoner, one who prays

a) perf. act.

2:186 (182) I am near to answer the call of the caller, when he calls to Me
3:38 (33) then Zachariah prayed to his Lord
7:189 (189) they cried to God their Lord, If Thou givest us
7:193 (192) equal it is to you whether you call them, or whether you are silent
8:24 (24) when He calls you unto that which will give you life
10:12 (13) when affliction visits a man, he calls Us on his side
10:22 (23) they call upon God, making their religion His sincerely
14:22 (27) that I called you, and you answered me
18:52 (50) then they shall call on them, but they will not answer them
19:91 (93) for that they have attributed to the All-merciful a son
25:13 (14) of that Fire, they will call out there for destruction
27:62 (63) He who answers the constrained, when he calls unto Him
28:64 (64) they will call upon them, but they shall not answer them
29:65 (65) when they embark in the ships, they call on God

30:25 (24)	then, when He calls you once and suddenly, out of the earth
30:33 (32)	when some affliction visits mankind, they call unto their Lord
31:32 (31)	when the waves cover them like shadows they call upon God
39:8 (11)	when some affliction visits a man, he calls upon his Lord
39:49 (50)	when some affliction visits a man, he calls unto Us
41:33 (33)	who speaks fairer than he who calls unto God
44:22 (21)	and he called to his Lord, saying
54:10 (10)	and so he called unto his Lord, saying
71:5 (5)	my Lord, I have called my people by night and by day
71:7 (6)	whenever I called them, that Thou mightest forgive them
71:8 (7)	then indeed I called them openly

b) impf. act. (*yadʿū*)

2:221 (221)	those call unto the Fire
2:221 (221)	and God calls unto Paradise, and pardon
3:61 (54)	come now, let us call our sons and your sons
3:104 (100)	let there be one nation of you, calling to good
3:153 (147)	the Messenger was calling you in your rear
4:117 (117)	they pray not except to female beings
4:117 (117)	they pray not except to a rebel Satan
6:40 (40)	will you call upon any other than God
6:41 (41)	upon Him you will call
6:41 (41)	remove that for which you call upon Him if He will
6:52 (52)	do not drive away those who call upon their Lord at morning
6:56 (56)	I am forbidden to serve those you call on apart from God
6:63 (63)	you call upon Him humbly and secretly
6:71 (70)	shall we call, apart from God
6:71 (70)	though he has friends who call him to guidance
6:108 (108)	abuse not those to whom they pray, apart from God
7:37 (35)	where is that you were calling on, beside God?
7:193 (192)	if you call them to guidance they will not follow you
7:194 (193)	those on whom you call apart from God, are servants
7:197 (196)	those on whom you call, apart from God, have no power
7:198 (197)	if you call them to the guidance they do not hear
10:12 (13)	he passes on, as if he never called Us to an affliction
10:25 (26)	and God summons to the Abode of Peace
10:66 (67)	they follow, who call upon associates, apart from God
10:106 (106)	and do not call, apart from God
11:62 (65)	we are in doubt, concerning what thou callest us to
11:101 (103)	their gods availed them not that they called upon, apart from God
12:33 (33)	my Lord, prison is dearer to me than that they call me to
12:108 (108)	I call to God with sure knowledge
13:14 (15)	those upon whom they call, apart from Him, answer them nothing
13:36 (36)	to Him I call, and to Him I turn
14:9 (10)	we are in doubt, concerning that you call us unto
14:10 (11)	who calls you so that He may forgive you your sins
16:20 (20)	those they call upon, apart from God, created nothing
16:86 (88)	these are our associates on whom we called apart from Thee
17:11 (12)	man prays for evil, as he prays for good
17:52 (54)	on the day when He will call you, and you will answer
17:57 (59)	those they call upon are themselves seeking the means to come
17:67 (69)	there go astray those on whom you call
17:71 (73)	on the day when We shall call all men with their record
17:110 (110)	whichsoever you call upon, to Him belong the Names
18:14 (13)	we will not call upon any god, apart from Him

18:28 (27)	restrain thyself with those who call upon their Lord
18:57 (56)	though thou callest them to the guidance, yet they will not be guided
19:48 (49)	now I will go apart from you and that you call upon
19:48 (49)	I will call upon my Lord
21:90 (90)	and called upon Us out of yearning and awe
22:12 (12)	he calls, apart from God, upon that which hurts him not
22:13 (13)	he calls upon him who is likelier to hurt him
22:62 (61)	He is the Truth, and that they call upon apart from Him
22:73 (72)	those upon whom you call, apart from God
23:73 (75)	assuredly thou art calling them to a straight path
23:117 (117)	whosoever calls upon another god with God, whereof he has no proof
25:14 (15)	call not out today for one destruction
25:68 (68)	who call not upon another god with God
26:72 (72)	do they hear you when you call
26:213 (213)	call thou not upon another god with God
28:25 (25)	my father invites thee, that he may recompense thee
28:41 (41)	We appointed them leaders, calling to the Fire
28:88 (88)	and call not upon another god with God
29:42 (41)	God knows whatever thing they call upon apart from Him
31:21 (20)	even though Satan were calling them to the chastisement of the burning
31:30 (29)	He is the Truth, and that they call upon apart from Him
32:16 (16)	their sides shun their couches as they call on their Lord in fear
35:6 (6)	He calls his party only that they may be among the inhabitants
35:13 (14)	those you call upon, apart from Him
35:14 (15)	if you call upon them, they will not hear your prayer
35:18 (19)	if one heavy-burdened calls for its load to be carried
35:40 (38)	have you considered your associates on whom you call
37:125 (125)	do you call on Baal, and abandon the Best of creators?
38:51 (51)	they call for fruits abundant
39:8 (11)	when some affliction visits a man, he calls upon his Lord
39:38 (39)	what think you? that you call upon apart from God
40:20 (21)	those the call on, apart from Him, shall not decide by any means
40:26 (27)	and let him call to his Lord
40:41 (44)	I call you to salvation
40:41 (44)	and you call me to the Fire
40:42 (45)	you call me to disbelieve in God
40:42 (45)	while I call you to the All-mighty
40:43 (46)	no doubt that what you call me to has no call heard
40:66 (68)	I am forbidden to serve those you call on apart from God
40:74 (74)	it was nothing at all that we called upon aforetime
41:5 (4)	our hearts are veiled from what thou callest us to
41:48 (48)	then that they called upon before will go astray from them
42:13 (12)	that thou callest them to
43:86 (86)	those they call upon, apart from Him, have no power
44:55 (55)	therein calling for every fruit, secure
46:4 (3)	have you considered that you call upon apart from God?
46:5 (4)	who is further astray than he who calls, apart from God
47:35 (37)	so do not faint and call for peace
52:28 (28)	we were before ever calling upon Him
54:6 (6)	the day when the Caller shall call unto a horrible thing
57:8 (8)	seeing that the Messenger is calling you to believe
70:17 (17)	calling him who drew back
72:18 (18)	so call not, along with God, upon anyone
72:19 (19)	when the servant of God stood calling on Him
72:20 (20)	I call only upon my Lord

84:11 (11)	he shall call for destruction
96:17 (17)	so let him call on his concourse
96:18 (18)	we shall call on the guards of Hell

c) impv. (*udʿu*)

2:23 (21)	call your witnesses, apart from God, if you are truthful
2:61 (58)	pray to thy Lord for us, that Hemay bring forth
2:68 (63)	pray to thy Lord for us, that He may make clear
2:69 (64)	pray to thy Lord for us, that He make clear
2:70 (65)	pray to thy Lord for us, that He make clear
2:260 (262)	then summon them, and they will come to thee
7:29 (28)	call on Him, making your religion sincerely His
7:55 (53)	call on your Lord, humbly and secretly
7:56 (54)	call on Him fearfully, eagerly
7:134 (131)	Moses, pray to thy Lord for us by the covenant He has made
7:180 (179)	to God belong the Names Most Beautiful; so call Him by them
7:194 (193)	call them and let them answer you, if you speak truly
7:195 (194)	call you then to your associates
10:38 (39)	call on whom you can, apart from God
11:13 (16)	call upon whom you are able, apart from God
16:125 (126)	call thou to the way of thy Lord
17:56 (58)	call on those you asserted apart from Him
17:110 (110)	call upon God
17:110 (110)	or call upon the Merciful
22:67 (66)	and do thou summon unto thy Lord
25:14 (15)	call not out today for one destruction
28:64 (64)	call you now upon your associates
28:87 (87)	call upon thy Lord, and be thou not of the idolaters
33:5 (5)	call them after their true fathers
34:22 (21)	call on those you have asserted apart from God
40:14 (14)	so call unto God, making your religion His sincerely
40:49 (52)	call on your Lord, to lighten for us one day of the chastisement
40:50 (53)	they shall say, 'Then do you call'
40:60 (62)	call upon Me and I will answer you
40:65 (67)	so call upon Him, making your religion His sincerely
42:15 (14)	therefore call thou, and go straight as thou hast been commanded
43:49 (48)	sorcerer, pray to thy Lord for us by the covenant

d) perf. pass. (*duʿiya*)

2:282 (282)	let the witnesses not refuse, whenever they are summoned
24:48 (47)	when they are called to God and His Messenger
24:51 (50)	when they are called to God and His Messenger
33:53 (53)	but when you are invited, then enter
40:12 (12)	that is because, when God was called to alone, you disbelieved

e) impf. pass. (*yudʿá*)

3:23 (22)	being called to the Book of God
40:10 (10)	when you were called unto belief, and disbelieved
45:28 (27)	every nation being summoned unto its Book
47:38 (40)	you are called upon to expend in God's way
48:16 (16)	you shall be called against a people possessed of great might
61:7 (7)	forges against God falsehood, when he is being called unto surrender
68:42 (42)	they shall be summoned to bow themselves
68:43 (43)	they had been summoned to bow themselves while they were whole

f) n.vb. (*duʿā'*)

2:171 (166)	one who shouts to that which hears nothing, save a call and a cry
3:38 (33)	yea, Thou hearest prayer
13:14 (15)	the prayer of the unbelievers goes only astray
14:39 (41)	surely my Lord hears the petition
14:40 (42)	and receive my petition
17:11 (12)	man prays for evil, as he prays for good
19:4 (4)	and in calling on Thee, my Lord
19:48 (49)	I shall not be, in calling upon my Lord, unprosperous
21:45 (46)	they that are deaf do not hear the call when they are warned
24:63 (63)	make not the calling of the Messenger
24:63 (63)	among yourselves like your calling one of another
25:77 (77)	my Lord esteems you not at all were it not for your prayer
27:80 (82)	neither shalt thou make the deaf to hear the call
30:52 (51)	neither shalt thou make the deaf to hear the call
35:14 (15)	if you call upon them, they will not hear your prayer
40:50 (53)	the calling of the unbelievers is only in error
41:49 (49)	man wearies not of praying for good
41:51 (51)	when evil visits him, he is full of endless prayers
46:5 (4)	such as are heedless of their calling
71:6 (5)	my calling has only increased them in flight

g) pcple. act. (*dāʿī*)

2:186 (182)	I am near to answer the call of the caller
20:108 (107)	on that day they will follow the Summoner
33:46 (45)	calling unto God by His leave
46:31 (30)	O our people, answer God's summoner
46:32 (31)	whosoever answers not God's summoner
54:6 (6)	the day when the Caller shall call unto a horrible thing
54:8 (8)	running with outstretched necks to the Caller

ADʿIYĀ' n.m. (pl. of *daʿīy*)~adopted son

33:4 (4)	neither has He made your adopted sons your sons in fact
33:37 (37)	there should not be any fault in the believers, touching the wives of their adopted sons

DAʿWÁ n.f.~a cry, call, prayer

7:5 (4)	and they but cried, when Our might came upon them
10:10 (10)	their cry therein, Glory to Thee, O God,'
10:10 (11)	and their cry ends, Praise belongs to God
21:15 (15)	so they ceased not to cry, until We made them

DAʿWAH n.f.~a prayer, call

2:186 (182)	I am near to answer the call
10:89 (89)	your prayer is answered
13:14 (15)	to Him is the call of truth
14:44 (46)	we will answer Thy call
30:25 (24)	when He calls you once and suddenly
40:43 (46)	what you call me to has no call heard

IDDAᶜÁ vb. (VIII)~to claim, call for

b) impf. act. (*yaddaᶜī*)

36:57 (57) they have all that they call for
41:31 (31) all that your souls desire, all that you call for
67:27 (27) this is that for which you used to call

*D B B

DĀBBAH n.f. (pl. *dawāb*)~beast, animal, crawling creature

2:164 (159) His scattering abroad in it all manner of crawling thing
6:38 (38) no creature is there crawling on the earth
8:22 (22) the worst of beasts in God's sight are those that are deaf
8:55 (57) the worst of beasts in God's sight are the unbelievers
11:6 (8) no creature is there crawling on the earth
11:56 (59) there is no creature that crawls
16:49 (51) to God bows everything in the heavens, and every creature crawling
16:61 (63) He would not leave on the earth one creature that crawls
22:18 (18) the stars and the mountains, the trees and the beasts
24:45 (44) God has created every beast of water
27:82 (84) We shall bring forth for them out of the earth a beast that shall speak
29:60 (60) how many a beast that bears not its own provision
31:10 (9) He scattered abroad in it all manner of crawling thing
34:14 (13) but the Beast of the Earth devouring his staff
35:28 (25) men too, and beasts and cattle — diverse are their hues
35:45 (44) He would not leave upon the face of the earth one creature that crawls
42:29 (28) the crawling things He has scattered abroad in them
45:4 (3) the crawling things He scatters abroad

*D B R

DĀBIR n.m.~extreme, last remnant

6:45 (45) so the last remnant of the people who did evil was cut off
7:72 (70) We cut off the last remnant of those who cried lies
8:7 (7) and to cut off the unbelievers to the last remnant
15:66 (66) that the last remnant of those should be cut off

DUBUR n.m. (pl. *adbār*)~back, hinder part, end; (*min dubur*) from behind; (*wallá al- adbār*) to turn one's back

3:111 (107) they fight with you, they will turn on you their backs
4:47 (50) before We obliterate faces, and turn them upon their backs
5:21 (24) turn not back in your traces, to turn about losers
8:15 (15) turn not your backs to them
8:16 (16) whoso turns his back that day to them
8:50 (52) take the unbelievers, beating their faces and their backs
12:25 (25) she tore his shirt from behind
12:27 (27) if it be that his shirt has been torn from behind
12:28 (28) when he saw his shirt was torn from behind
15:65 (65) and follow after the backs of them
17:46 (49) they turn in their traces in aversion
33:15 (15) they had made covenant with God before that, that they would not turn their backs
47:25 (27) those who have turned back in their traces
47:27 (29) beating their faces and their backs
48:22 (22) if the unbelievers had fought you, they would have turned their backs

50:40 (39)	proclaim thy Lord's praise in the night, and at the ends of the prostrations
54:45 (45)	certainly the host shall be routed, and turn their backs
59:12 (12)	they would surely turn their backs

DABBARA vb. (II)~to direct, to manage. (pcple. act.) one who directs or manages

b) impf. act. (*yudabbiru*)

10:3 (3)	then sat Himself upon the Throne, directing the affair
10:31 (32)	and who directs the affair?
13:2 (2)	He directs the affair
32:5 (4)	He directs the affair from heaven to earth

g) pcple. act. (*mudabbir*)

79:5 (5)	by those that direct an affair

ADBARA vb. (IV)~to draw back, retreat, turn away. (n.vb.) drawing back, retreating, declining. (pcple. act.) one who retreats, draws back or turns about; retreating, turning back

a) perf. act.

70:17 (17)	calling him who drew back
74:23 (23)	then he retreated, and waxed proud
74:33 (36)	and the night when it retreats
79:22 (22)	then he turned away hastily

f) n.vb. (*idbār*)

52:49 (49)	proclaim the praise of thy Lord in the night, and at the declining of the stars

g) pcple. act. (*mudbir*)

9:25 (25)	and you turned about, retreating
21:57 (58)	after you have gone away turning your backs
27:10 (10)	he turned about, retreating
27:80 (82)	neither shalt thou make the deaf to hear the call when they turn about, retreating
28:31 (31)	he turned about retreating, and turned not back
30:52 (51)	neither shalt thou make the deaf to hear the call when they turn about, retreating
37:90 (88)	they went away from him, turning their backs
40:33 (35)	the day you turn about, retreating

TADABBARA vb. (V)~to ponder, to meditate upon, to consider

b) impf. act. (*yatadabbaru*); also alternate form (*yaddabbaru*)

4:82 (84)	do they not ponder the Koran?
23:68 (70)	have they not pondered the saying
38:29 (28)	that men possessed of minds may ponder its signs
47:24 (26)	do they not ponder the Koran?

*D F ʾ

DIFʾ n.m.~warmth

16:5 (5)	He created them for you; in them is warmth

*D F ᶜ

DAFAᶜA vb. (I)~to deliver, to pay over; to push, to repel, to drive away. (n.vb.) driving back, repelling. (pcple. act.) one who averts

a) perf. act.

4:6 (7) when you deliver to them their property, take witnesses over them

c) impv. (*idfaᶜ*)

3:167 (160) come now, fight in the way of God, or repel
4:6 (5) deliver to them their property
23:96 (98) repel thou the evil with that which is fairer
41:34 (34) repel with that which is fairer

f) n.vb. (*dafᶜ*)

2:251 (252) had God not driven back the people
22:40 (41) had God not driven back the people

g) pcple. act. (*dāfiᶜ*)

52:8 (8) there is none to avert it
70:2 (2) for the unbelievers, which none may avert

DĀFAᶜA vb. (III)~(with prep. *ᶜan*) to defend

b) impf. act. (*yudāfiᶜu*)

22:38 (39) God will defend those who believe

*D F Q

DAFAQA vb. (I)~(pcple. act.) that which pours or gushes forth

g) pcple. act. (*dāfiq*)

86:6 (6) he was created of gushing water

*D H M

ID.HĀMMA vb. (XI)~(pcple. act.) that which is dark green

g) pcple. act. (*mud.hāmm*)

55:64 (64) green, green pastures

*D H N

DIHĀN n.m.~red leather

55:37 (37) when heaven is split asunder, and turns crimson like red leather

DUHN n.m.~oil, anointing oil, butter

23:20 (20) a tree issuing from the Mount of Sinai that bears oil and seasoning

AD.HANA vb. (IV)~to compromise. (pcple. act.) one who scorns, who holds (someone) in disdain

b) impf. act. (*yud.hinu*)

68:9 (9) they wish that thou shouldst compromise
68:9 (9) they would compromise

g) pcple. act. (*mud.hin*)

56:81 (80) what, do you hold this discourse in disdain

*D H Q

DIHĀQ n.m. (adj)~full, overflowing

78:34 (34) and a cup overflowing

*D H R

DAHR n.m.~time

45:24 (23) we die, and we live, and nothing but Time destroys us
76:1 (1) has there come on man a while of time when he was a thing unremembered?

*D H Y

AD.HÁ n.m. (comp. adj. of *dāhī* or *dahīy*)~more calamitous, wretched; smart, shrewd

54:46 (46) the Hour is very calamitous and bitter

*D Ḥ Ḍ

DAḤAḌA vb. (I)~(pcple. act.) that which is null and void or has no weight

g) pcple. act. (*dāḥiḍ*)

42:16 (15) their argument is null and void in the sight of their Lord

ADḤAḌA vb. (IV)~to rebut, to refute. (pcple. pass.) rebutted, refuted, condemned

b) impf. act. (*yudḥiḍu*)

18:56 (54) that they may rebut thereby the truth
40:5 (5) that they might rebut thereby the truth

g) pcple. pass. (*mudḥaḍ*)

37:141 (141) and cast lots, and was of the rebutted

*D Ḥ R

DAḤARA vb. (I)~(n.vb.) one who is rejected, repelled or outcast. (pcple. pass.) rejected, banished, repelled

f) n.vb. (*duḥūr*)

37:9 (9) rejected, and theirs is an everlasting chastisement

h) pcple. pass. (*madḥūr*)

7:18 (17) go thou forth from it, despised and banished
17:18 (19) Gehenna wherein he shall roast, condemned and rejected
17:39 (41) wilt be cast into Gehenna, reproached and rejected

*D Ḥ W

DAḤĀ vb. (I)~to spread out (tr)

a) perf. act.

79:30 (30) and the earth — after that He spread it out

*D K K

DAKKA vb. (I)~to crush, to ground to powder or dust. (n.vb.) crumbling to dust; dust, powder

d) perf. pass. (*dukka*)

69:14 (14) the earth and the mountains are lifted up and crushed with a single blow
89:21 (22) when the earth is ground to powder

f) n.vb. (*dakk*)

7:143 (139) He made it crumble to dust
89:21 (22) when the earth is ground to powder
89:21 (22) when the earth is ground to powder

DAKKĀʾ n.f. (adj)~flat mound or ground; dust or powder

18:98 (98) He will make it into powder

DAKKAH n.f.~a blow, a crash

69:14 (14) the earth and the mountains are lifted up and crushed with a single blow

*D K R

IDDAKARA vb. (V')~to remember. (pcple. act.) one who remembers

a) perf. act.

12:45 (45) then said the one who had been delivered, remembering after a time

g) pcple. act. (*muddakir*)

54:15 (15) is there any that will remember?
54:22 (22) is there any that will remember?
54:32 (32) is there any that will remember?
54:40 (40) is there any that will remember?
54:51 (51) is there any that will remember?

*D KH L

DAKHALA vb. (I)~to go in, to enter. (pcple. act.) one who enters

a) perf. act.

3:37 (32)	Zachariah went in to her in the Sanctuary
3:97 (91)	and whosoever enters it is in security
4:23 (27)	being born of your wives you have been in to
4:23 (27)	if you have not yet been in to them it is no fault in you
5:23 (26)	when you enter it, you will be victors
5:61 (66)	they have entered in unbelief, and so they have departed in it
7:38 (36)	whenever any nation enters, it curses its sister-nation
12:36 (36)	and there entered the prison with him two youths
12:58 (58)	the brethren of Joseph came, and entered unto him
12:68 (68)	when they entered after the manner their father commanded them
12:69 (69)	when they entered unto Joseph, he said
12:88 (88)	so, when they entered unto him, they said
12:99 (100)	so, when they entered unto Joseph, he took his father and mother into his arms
15:52 (52)	when they entered unto him, saying
17:7 (7)	Temple, as they entered it the first time
18:35 (33)	and he entered his garden
18:39 (37)	when thou wentest into thy garden
24:61 (61)	when you enter houses, greet one another
27:34 (34)	when they enter a city, disorder it
28:15 (14)	and he entered the city
38:22 (21)	when they entered upon David
51:25 (25)	when they entered unto him, saying
71:28 (29)	forgive me and my parents and whosoever enters my house

b) impf. act. (*yadkhulu*)

2:111 (105)	none shall enter Paradise except that they be Jews
2:114 (108)	such men might never enter them, save in fear
2:214 (210)	did you suppose you should enter Paradise
3:142 (136)	did you suppose you should enter Paradise
4:124 (123)	they shall enter Paradise, and not be wronged
5:22 (25)	we will not enter it until they depart from it
5:24 (27)	Moses, we will never enter it so long as they are in it
7:40 (38)	nor shall they enter Paradise until the camel passes through the eye
7:46 (44)	they have not entered it, for all their eagerness
12:67 (67)	O my sons, enter not by one door
13:23 (23)	Gardens of Eden which they shall enter
13:23 (23)	the angels shall enter unto them
16:31 (33)	Gardens of Eden they shall enter
17:7 (7)	and to enter the Temple, as they entered it the first time
19:60 (61)	those — they shall enter Paradise
24:27 (27)	do not enter houses other than your houses
24:28 (28)	enter it not until leave is given
24:29 (29)	there is no fault in you that you enter houses uninhabited
33:53 (53)	O believers, enter not the houses of the Prophet
35:33 (30)	Gardens of Eden they shall enter
40:40 (43)	be it male or female, believing — those shall enter Paradise
40:60 (62)	who wax too proud to do Me service shall enter Gehenna
48:27 (27)	you shall enter the Holy Mosque
49:14 (14)	belief has not yet entered your hearts
68:24 (24)	no needy man shall enter it today
110:2 (2)	thou seest men entering God's religion in throngs

c) impv. (*udkhul*)

2:58 (55)	Enter this township
2:58 (55)	and enter in at the gate, prostrating
2:208 (204)	O believers, enter the peace, all of you
4:154 (153)	We said to them, 'Enter in at the gate, prostrating'
5:21 (24)	O my people, enter the Holy Land
5:23 (26)	enter against them the gate
7:38 (36)	Enter among nations that passed away before you
7:49 (47)	enter Paradise; no fear upon you
7:161 (161)	and enter in at the gate, prostrating
12:67 (67)	by one door; enter by separate doors
12:99 (100)	enter you into Egypt, if God will
15:46 (46)	enter you them, in peace and security
16:29 (31)	so enter the gates of Gehenna, there to dwell forever
16:32 (34)	enter Paradise for that you were doing
27:18 (18)	Ants, enter your dwelling-places
27:44 (44)	it was said to her, 'Enter the pavilion'
33:53 (53)	when you are invited, then enter
36:26 (25)	it was said, 'Enter Paradise'
39:72 (72)	Enter the gates of Gehenna, to dwell therein
39:73 (73)	well you have fared; enter in, to dwell forever
40:76 (76)	enter the gates of Gehenna
43:70 (70)	enter Paradise, you and your wives, walking with joy
50:34 (33)	enter it in peace! This is the Day of Eternity
66:10 (10)	enter, you two, the Fire with
89:29 (29)	enter thou among My servants
89:30 (30)	enter thou My Paradise

d) perf. pass. (*dukhila*)

33:14 (14)	if entrance had been forced against them from those quarters

g) pcple. act. (*dākhil*)

5:22 (25)	if they depart from it then we will enter
66:10 (10)	enter, you two, the Fire with those who enter

DAKHAL n.m.~vice, corruption, mutual deceit

16:92 (94)	by taking your oaths as mere mutual deceit
16:94 (96)	take not your oaths as mere mutual deceit

MUDDAKHAL n.m.~a place or retreat, a place to creep into or enter

9:57 (57)	[if they could find] any place to creep into

MUDKHAL n.m.~a gate, ingoing

4:31 (35)	[We will] admit you by the gate of honour
17:80 (82)	lead me in with a just ingoing
22:59 (58)	He shall admit them by a gate that is well-pleasing to them

ADKHALA vb. (IV)~to cause to enter, to admit, to introduce

a) perf. act.

5:65 (70)	and admitted them to Gardens of Bliss
21:75 (75)	and We admitted him into Our mercy
21:86 (86)	and We admitted them into Our mercy

b) impf. act. (*yudkhilu*)

3:192 (189) whomsoever Thou admittest into the Fire
3:195 (194) I shall admit them to gardens underneath which rivers flow
4:13 (17) He will admit him to gardens underneath which rivers flow
4:14 (18) him He will admit to a Fire
4:31 (35) and admit you by the gate of honour
4:57 (60) them We shall admit to gardens underneath which rivers flow
4:57 (60) We shall admit them to a shelter of plenteous shade
4:122 (121) them We shall admit to gardens underneath which rivers flow
4:175 (174) to Him, He will surely admit them to mercy
5:12 (15) I will admit you to gardens underneath which rivers flow
5:84 (87) that our Lord should admit us with the righteous people
9:99 (100) and God will admit them into His mercy
22:14 (14) God shall surely admit those who believe
22:23 (23) God shall surely admit those who believe
22:59 (58) He shall admit them by a gate
29:9 (8) assuredly We shall admit them among the righteous
42:8 (6) He admits whomsoever He will into His mercy
45:30 (29) their Lord shall admit them into His mercy
47:6 (7) and He will admit them to Paradise
47:12 (13) God shall surely admit those who believe
48:5 (5) He may admit the believers, men and women alike
48:17 (17) He will admit him into gardens
48:25 (25) (that God may admit into His mercy whom He will)
58:22 (22) He shall admit them into gardens underneath which rivers flow
61:12 (12) He will forgive you your sins and admit you into gardens
64:9 (9) and admit him into gardens
65:11 (11) He will admit him to gardens
66:8 (8) and will admit you into gardens underneath which rivers flow
76:31 (31) He admits into His mercy whomsoever He will

c) impv. (*adkhil*)

7:151 (150) forgive me and my brother and enter us into Thy mercy
17:80 (82) lead me in with a just ingoing, and lead me out
27:12 (12) thrust thy hand in thy bosom and it will come forth white
27:19 (19) do Thou admit me, by Thy mercy, amongst Thy righteous servants
40:8 (8) and admit them to the Gardens of Eden
40:46 (49) when the Hour is come: Admit the folk of Pharaoh

d) perf. pass. (*udkhila*)

3:185 (182) whosoever is removed from the Fire and admitted to Paradise
14:23 (28) they shall be admitted to gardens underneath which rivers flow
71:25 (25) they were drowned, and admitted into a Fire

e) impf. pass. (*yudkhalu*)

70:38 (38) is every man of them eager to be admitted to a Garden of Bliss?

*D KH N

DUKHĀN n.m.~smoke

41:11 (10) He lifted Himself to heaven when it was smoke
44:10 (9) be on the watch for a day when heaven shall bring a manifest smoke

*D KH R

DAKHARA vb. (I)~(pcple. act.) that which is lowly, abject, humbled

g) pcple. act. (*dākhir*)

16:48 (50) bowing themselves before God in all lowliness
27:87 (89) every one shall come to Him, all utterly abject
37:18 (18) say: 'Yes, and in all lowliness'
40:60 (62) those who wax too proud to do Me service shall enter Gehenna utterly abject

*D L K

DALAKA vb. (I)~(n.vb.) sinking, going down

f) n.vb. (*dulūk*)

17:78 (80) perform the prayer at the sinking of the sun

*D L L

DALLA vb. (I)~to show, indicate; to direct, to point to

a) perf. act.

34:14 (13) naught indicated to them that he was dead

b) impf. act. (*yadullu*)

20:40 (41) shall I point you to one to have charge of him?
20:120 (118) Adam, shall I point thee to the Tree of Eternity
28:12 (11) shall I direct you to the people of a household who will take charge of him
34:7 (7) shall we point you to a man who will tell you
61:10 (10) shall I direct you to a commerce that shall deliver you

DALĪL n.m.~a guide

25:45 (47) then We appointed the sun, to be a guide to it

*D L W

DALW n.m.~a bucket

12:19 (19) they sent one of them, a water-drawer, who let down his bucket

DALLÁ vb. (II)~to let down, to lower; to lead

a) perf. act.

7:22 (21) so he led them on by delusion

ADLÁ vb. (IV)~to let down, to lower; to proffer

a) perf. act.

12:19 (19) they sent one of them, a water-drawer, who let down his bucket

b) impf. act. (*yudlī*)

2:188 (184) neither proffer it to the judges

TADALLÁ vb. (V)~to hang suspended, to go down

a) perf. act.

53:8 (8) then drew near and suspended hung

*D M ʿ

DAMAʿA vb. (I)~(n.vb.) tears

f) n.vb. (*damʿ*)

5:83 (86) thou seest their eyes overflow with tears because of the truth
9:92 (93) they turned away, their eyes overflowing with tears of sorrow

*D M D M

DAMDAMA vb. (quad I)~to destroy, to crush, to doom

a) perf. act.

91:14 (14) so their Lord crushed them for their sin, and levelled them

*D M GH

DAMAGHA vb. (I)~to prevail over [Ar]; to break the head [Pk]; to knock out the brain [Bl, Ali]

b) impf. act. (*yadmaghu*)

21:18 (18) We hurl the truth against falsehood and it prevails over it

*D M M

DAM n.m. (pl. *dimāʾ*)~blood

2:30 (28) who will do corruption there, and shed blood
2:84 (78) you shall not shed your own blood
2:173 (168) these things only has He forbidden you: carrion, blood
5:3 (4) forbidden to you are carrion, blood
6:145 (146) except it be carrion, or blood outpoured
7:133 (130) the lice and the frogs, the blood, distinct signs
12:18 (18) they brought his shirt with false blood on it
16:66 (68) between filth and blood, pure milk, sweet to drinkers
16:115 (116) these things only He has forbidden you: carrion, blood
22:37 (38) the flesh of them shall not reach God, neither their blood

*D M R

DAMMARA vb. (II)~to destroy. (n.vb.) destruction

a) perf. act.

7:137 (133) We destroyed utterly the works of Pharaoh and his people
17:16 (17) and We destroy it utterly

25:36 (38)	then We destroyed them utterly
26:172 (172)	then We destroyed the others
27:51 (52)	We destroyed them and their people
37:136 (136)	then We destroyed the others
47:10 (11)	God destroyed them

b) impf. act. (*yudammiru*)

46:25 (24)	destroying everything by the commandment of its Lord

f) n.vb. (*tadmīr*)

17:16 (17)	is realized against it, and We destroy it <utterly>
25:36 (38)	then We destroyed them <utterly>

*D N R

DĪNĀR n.m.~a Dinar (a unit of currency)

3:75 (68)	if thou trust him with one pound

*D N W

DANĀ vb. (I)~to draw near, to be low. (pcple. act.) one who draws near, that which is near, nigh, ready to the hand

a) perf. act.

53:8 (8)	then drew near and suspended hung

g) pcple. act. (*dānī*)

6:99 (99)	dates thick-clustered, ready to the hand
55:54 (54)	the fruits of the gardens nigh to gather
69:23 (23)	its clusters nigh to gather
76:14 (14)	near them shall be its shades, and its clusters hung

ADNÁ n.m. (comp. adj.; see also *dunyā*, below)~lower, nearer; fewer; likelier

2:61 (58)	would you have in exchange what is meaner for what is better?
2:282 (282)	more upright for testimony, and likelier that you will not be in doubt
4:3 (3)	so it is likelier you will not be partial
5:108 (107)	so it is likelier that they will bear testimony
7:169 (168)	taking the chance goods of this lower world
30:3 (2)	in the nearer part of the land
32:21 (21)	We shall surely let them taste the nearer chastisement
33:51 (51)	so it is likelier they will be comforted
33:59 (59)	so it is likelier they will be known, and not hurt
53:9 (9)	two bows'-length away, or nearer
58:7 (8)	neither fewer than that, neither more
73:20 (20)	thy Lord knows that thou keepest vigil nearly two-thirds of the night

DUNYĀ n.f. (also comp. adj.; see also *adná*, above)~(n) world, the present world; (adj) meaner, lower; nearer, likelier; (*al-ḥayāt al-dunyā*) the present life

2:85 (79)	degradation in the present life
2:86 (80)	those who have purchased the present life at the price of the world to come
2:114 (108)	for them is degradation in the present world
2:130 (124)	We chose him in the present world
2:200 (196)	Our Lord, give to us in this world

2:201 (197)	Our Lord, give to us in this world good
2:204 (200)	some men there are whose saying upon the present world pleases thee
2:212 (208)	decked out fair to the unbelievers is the present life
2:217 (214)	their works have failed in this world and the next
2:220 (218)	in this world, and the world to come
3:14 (12)	that is the enjoyment of the present life
3:22 (21)	their works have failed in this world and the next
3:45 (40)	high honoured shall he be in this world and the next
3:56 (49)	in this world and the next
3:117 (113)	the likeness of that they expend in this present life
3:145 (139)	whoso desires the reward of this world
3:148 (141)	God gave them the reward of this world
3:152 (146)	some of you there are that desire this world
3:185 (182)	the present life is but the joy of delusion
4:74 (76)	let them fight in the way of God who sell the present life for the world to come
4:77 (79)	the enjoyment of this world is little
4:94 (96)	seeking the chance goods of the present life
4:109 (109)	you have disputed on their behalf in the present life
4:134 (133)	whoso desires the reward of this world
4:134 (133)	with God is the reward of this world
5:33 (37)	that is a degradation for them in this world
5:41 (45)	for them is degradation in this world
6:29 (29)	there is only our present life
6:32 (32)	the present life is naught but a sport
6:70 (69)	whom the present life has deluded
6:130 (130)	they were deluded by the present life
7:32 (30)	for those who believed in this present life
7:51 (49)	whom the present life has deluded
7:152 (151)	and abasement in this present life
7:156 (155)	and prescribe for us in this world good
8:42 (43)	when you were on the nearer bank, and they were on the farther bank
8:67 (68)	you desire the chance goods of the present world
9:38 (38)	are you so content with this present life
9:38 (38)	the enjoyment of this present life, compared with the world to come
9:55 (55)	God only desires thereby to chastise them in this present life
9:69 (70)	their works have failed in this world and in the world to come
9:74 (75)	God will chastise them with a painful chastisement in this world
9:85 (86)	God only desires thereby to chastise them in this present world
10:7 (7)	and are well-pleased with the present life
10:23 (24)	the enjoyment of this present life
10:24 (25)	the likeness of this present life is as water
10:64 (65)	for them is good tidings in the present life
10:70 (71)	some enjoyment in this world
10:88 (88)	to Pharaoh and his Council adornment and possessions in this present life
10:98 (98)	degradation in this present life
11:15 (18)	whoso desires the present life and its adornment
11:60 (63)	there was sent following after them in this world a curse
12:101 (102)	Thou art my Protector in this world and the next
13:26 (26)	they rejoice in this present life
13:26 (26)	this present life, beside the world to come, is naught but passing enjoyment
13:34 (34)	for them is chastisement in the present life
14:3 (3)	such as prefer the present life over the world to come
14:27 (32)	God confirms those who believe with the firm word, in the present life
16:30 (32)	Good! For those who do good in this world good
16:41 (43)	We shall surely lodge them in this world in a goodly lodging

16:107 (109)	because they have preferred the present life over the world to come
16:122 (123)	We gave him in this world good
18:28 (27)	desiring the adornment of the present life
18:45 (43)	and strike for them the similitude of the present life
18:46 (44)	wealth and sons are the adornment of the present world
18:104 (104)	those whose striving goes astray in the present life
20:72 (75)	thou canst only decide touching this present life
20:131 (131)	the flower of the present life
22:9 (9)	for him is degradation in this world
22:11 (11)	he loses this world and the world to come
22:15 (15)	whosoever thinks God will not help him in the present world
23:33 (34)	to whom We had given ease in the present life
23:37 (39)	there is nothing but our present life
24:14 (14)	in the present world and the world to come
24:19 (19)	in the present world and the world to come
24:23 (23)	shall be accursed in the present world
24:33 (33)	live in chastity, that you may seek the chance goods of the present life
28:42 (42)	We pursued them in this world with a curse
28:60 (60)	whatever thing you have been given is the enjoyment of the present life
28:61 (61)	him to whom We have given the enjoyment of the present life
28:77 (77)	forget not thy portion of the present world
28:79 (79)	those who desired the present life said
29:25 (24)	a mark of mutual love between you in the present life
29:27 (26)	We gave him his wage in this world
29:64 (64)	this present life is naught but a diversion
30:7 (6)	they know an outward part of the present life
31:15 (14)	keep them company honourable in this world
31:33 (33)	let not the present life delude you
33:28 (28)	if you desire the present life and its adornment
33:57 (57)	them God has cursed in the present world
35:5 (5)	God's promise is true; so let not the present life delude you
37:6 (6)	We have adorned the lower heaven with the adornment of the stars
39:10 (13)	those who do good in this world
39:26 (27)	so God let them taste degradation in this present life
40:39 (42)	surely this present life is but a passing enjoyment
40:43 (46)	that what you call me to has no call heard, in this world
40:51 (54)	those who have believed, in the present life
41:12 (11)	We adorned the lower heaven with lamps
41:16 (15)	We might let them taste the chastisement of degradation in the present life
41:31 (31)	We are your friends in the present life
42:20 (19)	whoso desires the tillage of this world
42:36 (34)	whatever thing you have been given is the enjoyment of the present life
43:32 (31)	We have divided between them their livelihood in the present life
43:35 (34)	all this is but the enjoyment of the present life
45:24 (23)	there is nothing but our present life
45:35 (34)	and the present life deluded you
46:20 (19)	you dissipated your good things in your present life
47:36 (38)	the present life is naught but a sport
53:29 (30)	him who turns away from Our Remembrance, and desires only the present life
57:20 (19)	the present life is but a sport and a diversion
57:20 (20)	and the present life is but the joy of delusion
59:3 (3)	He would have chastised them in this world
67:5 (5)	We adorned the lower heaven with lamps
79:38 (38)	and preferred the present life
87:16 (16)	nay, but you prefer the present life

ADNÁ vb. (IV)~to draw something closer, to bring near

b) impf. act. (*yudnī*)

33:59 (59)	that they draw their veils close to them

*D R ʾ

DARAʾA vb. (I)~to avert, to drive off

b) impf. act. (*yadraʾu*)

13:22 (22)	and who avert evil with good — theirs shall be
24:8 (8)	it shall avert from her the chastisement if she testify
28:54 (54)	they patiently endured, and avert evil with good

c) impv. (*idraʾ*)

3:168 (162)	then avert death from yourselves, if you speak truly

IDDĀRAʾA vb. (VI)~to dispute, to strive one with the other

a) perf. act.

2:72 (67)	when you killed a living soul, and disputed thereon

*D R H M

DARĀHIM n.m. (pl. of *dirham*)~money (a unit of currency, smaller than *dīnār*)

12:20 (20)	then they sold him for a paltry price, a handful of counted dirhams

*D R J

DARAJAH n.f. (pl. *darajāt*)~degree, rank, step, grade (of honour)

2:228 (228)	their men have a degree above them
2:253 (254)	some there are to whom God spoke, and some He raised in rank
3:163 (157)	they are in ranks with God
4:95 (97)	God has preferred in rank those who struggle
4:96 (98)	in ranks standing before Him
6:83 (83)	We raise up in degrees whom We will
6:132 (132)	all have degrees according to what they have done
6:165 (165)	and has raised some of you in rank above others
8:4 (4)	they have degrees with their Lord, and forgiveness
9:20 (20)	are mightier in rank with God
12:76 (76)	whomsoever We will, We raise in rank
17:21 (22)	surely the world to come is greater in ranks
20:75 (77)	those — for them await the most sublime degrees
40:15 (15)	Exalter of ranks is He, Possessor of the Throne
43:32 (31)	and raised some of them above others in rank
46:19 (18)	all shall have their degrees, according to what they have wrought
57:10 (10)	those are mightier in rank than they who spent and fought
58:11 (12)	God will raise up in rank those of you who believe

ISTADRAJA vb. (X)~to draw on gradually, to lead (someone) step by step *b*) impf. act. (*yastadriju*)

7:182 (181) We will draw them on little by little whence they know not
68:44 (44) We will draw them on little by little whence they know not

*D R K

DARAKA vb. (I)~(n. vb.) overtaking

f) n. vb. (*darak*)

20:77 (80) fearing not overtaking, neither afraid

DARK n.m.~lowest reach, deep

4:145 (144) the hypocrites will be in the lowest reach of the Fire

ADRAKA vb. (IV)~to overtake, to attain. (pcple. pass.) overtaken

a) perf. act.

10:90 (90) when the drowning overtook him, he said

b) impf. act. (*yudriku*)

4:78 (80) wherever you may be, death will overtake you
4:100 (101) and then death overtakes him
6:103 (103) the eyes attain Him not, but He attains the eyes
6:103 (103) the eyes attain Him not, but He attains the eyes
36:40 (40) it behoves not the sun to overtake the moon

h) pcple. pass. (*mudrak*)

26:61 (61) the companions of Moses said, 'We are overtaken'

TADĀRAKA vb. (VI)~to overtake, to come successively, to follow one the other;

a) perf. act.

68:49 (49) had there not overtaken him a blessing from his Lord

IDDĀRAKA vb. (VI)~to come successively; (ūṭ:ḍḍ presents difficulties)

a) perf. act.

7:38 (36) when they have all successively come there, the last of them
27:66 (68) nay, but their knowledge fails as to the Hereafter

*D R R

DURRĪY n.m. (adj)~glittering, shining

24:35 (35) the glass as it were a glittering star

MIDRĀR n.m.~a torrent, an abundant rain

6:6 (6) how We loosed heaven upon them in torrents
11:52 (54) He will loose heaven in torrents upon you
71:11 (10) He will loose heaven upon you in torrents

*D R S

DARASA vb. (I)~to study, to read

a) perf. act.

6:105 (105)	Thou hast studied
7:169 (168)	they have studied what is in it

b) impf. act. (*yadrusu*)

3:79 (73)	be you masters in that you know the Book, and in that you study
34:44 (43)	We have not given them any Books to study
68:37 (37)	or have you a Book wherein you study?

DIRĀSAH n.f.~study, reading

6:156 (157)	we have indeed been heedless of their study

IDRĪS n.prop.~Idris, Enoch

19:56 (57)	and mention in the Book Idris
21:85 (85)	and Ishmael, Idris, Dhul Kifl

*D R Y

DARÁ vb. (I)~to know

b) impf. act. (*yadrī*)

4:11 (12)	you know not which out of them is nearer in profit
21:109 (109)	even though I know not whether near or far is that you are promised
21:111 (111)	I know not; haply it is a trial for you
31:34 (34)	no soul knows what it shall earn tomorrow
31:34 (34)	no soul knows in what land it shall die
42:52 (52)	thou knewest not what the Book was, nor belief
45:32 (31)	we know not what the Hour may be
46:9 (8)	I know not what shall be done with me or with you
65:1 (1)	thou knowest not, perchance after that God will bring something new to pass
69:26 (26)	and not known my reckoning
72:10 (10)	we know not whether evil is intended for those in the earth
72:25 (26)	I do not know whether that which you are promised is nigh

ADRÁ vb. (IV)~to cause to know, to teach, to convey; (*mā adrāka*) what will teach thee? what will convey unto thee?

a) perf. act.

10:16 (17)	neither would He have taught you it
69:3 (3)	and what will teach thee what is the Indubitable?
74:27 (27)	and what will teach thee what is Sakar?
77:14 (14)	and what shall teach thee what is the Day of Decision?
82:17 (17)	and what shall teach thee what is the Day of Doom?
82:18 (18)	again, what shall teach thee what is the Day of Doom?
83:8 (8)	and what shall teach thee what is Sijjin?
83:19 (19)	and what shall teach thee what is Illiyun?
86:2 (2)	and what shall teach thee what is the night-star?
90:12 (12)	and what shall teach thee what is the steep?
97:2 (2)	and what shall teach thee what is the Night of Power

101:3 (2)	and what shall teach thee what is the Clatterer?
101:10 (7)	and what shall teach thee what is the Pit?
104:5 (5)	and what shall teach thee what is the Crusher?

b) impf. act. (*yudrī*)

33:63 (63)	what shall make thee know?
42:17 (16)	and what shall make thee know?
80:3 (3)	and what should teach thee?

*D S R

DUSUR n.m. (pl. of *disār*)~oakum or fibres of palm trees used to caulk ships with; nails

54:13 (13)	We bore him upon a well-planked vessel well-caulked

*D S S

DASSA vb. (I)~to trample [Ar]; to bury [Pk, Ali]; to hide [Bl]

b) impf. act. (*yadussu*)

16:59 (61)	whether he shall preserve it in humiliation, or trample it into the dust

*D S W

DASSĀ vb. (II)~to corrupt, stunt, seduce

a) perf. act.

91:10 (10)	and failed has he who seduces it

*D TH R

DATHTHARA vb. (II)~(pcple. act.) one who shrouds or wraps himself up in a garment

g) pcple. act. (*mudaththir*)

74:1 (1)	O thou shrouded in thy mantle

*D W D

DĀWŪD n.prop.~David

2:251 (252)	and David slew Goliath
4:163 (161)	and We gave to David Psalms
5:78 (82)	cursed were the unbelievers of the Children of Israel by the tongue of David
6:84 (84)	and of his seed David and Solomon, Job and Joseph
17:55 (57)	and We gave to David Psalms
21:78 (78)	and David and Solomon — when they gave judgment
21:79 (79)	with David We subjected the mountains to give glory
27:15 (15)	We gave David and Solomon knowledge
27:16 (16)	and Solomon was David's heir
34:10 (10)	We gave David bounty from Us
34:13 (12)	labour, O House of David, in thankfulness
38:17 (16)	and remember Our servant David, the man of might
38:22 (21)	when they entered upon David, and he took fright at them
38:24 (23)	and David thought that We had only tried him

38:26 (25) David, behold, We have appointed thee a viceroy in the earth
38:30 (29) and We gave unto David Solomon

*D W L

DŪLAH n.f.~a commodity that is changes hands among people

59:7 (7) so that it be not a thing taken in turns among the rich of you

DĀWALA vb. (III)~to cause to alternate, to deal out in turn

b) impf. act. (*yudāwilu*)

3:140 (134) such days We deal out in turn among men

*D W M

DĀMA vb. (I)~to continue, to remain; to keep on doing something; (*mā dāma*) so long as. (pcple. act.) one that continues, eternal

a) perf. act.

3:75 (68) [he] will not restore it thee, unless ever thou standest over him
5:24 (27) Moses, we will never enter it so long as they are in it
5:96 (97) so long as you remain in pilgrim sanctity; and fear God
5:117 (117) I was a witness over them, while I remained among them
11:107 (109) therein dwelling forever, so long as the heavens and earth abide
11:108 (110) Paradise, therein dwelling forever, so long as the heavens and earth abide
19:31 (32) and to give the alms, so long as I live

g) pcple. act. (*dā'im*)

13:35 (35) its produce is eternal, and its shade
70:23 (23) and continue at their prayers

*D W R

DĀRA vb. (I)~to turn, to go round, to roll

b) impf. act. (*yadūru*)

33:19 (19) thou seest them looking at thee, their eyes rolling like one who swoons

DĀR n.f. (pl. *diyār*)~habitation, abode, dwelling; (*al-dār al-ākhirah*) the Last Abode, the Abode of the Hereafter

2:84 (78) neither expel your own from your habitations
2:85 (79) and expelling a party of you from their habitations
2:94 (88) if the Last Abode with God is yours exclusively
2:243 (244) those who went forth from their habitations in their thousands
2:246 (247) who have been expelled from our habitations
3:195 (194) those who emigrated, and were expelled from their habitations
4:66 (69) leave your habitations,'
6:32 (32) the Last Abode is better for those that are godfearing
6:127 (127) theirs is the abode of peace with their Lord
6:135 (136) who shall possess the Abode Ultimate
7:78 (76) morning found them in their habitation fallen prostrate
7:91 (89) morning found them in their habitation fallen prostrate

7:145 (142)	I shall show you the habitation of the ungodly
7:169 (168)	the Last Abode is better for those who are godfearing
8:47 (49)	be not as those who went forth from their habitations
10:25 (26)	God summons to the Abode of Peace
11:65 (68)	take your joy in your habitation
11:67 (70)	morning found them in their habitations fallen prostrate
11:94 (97)	morning found them in their habitations fallen prostrate
12:109 (109)	the abode of the world to come is better
13:22 (22)	theirs shall be the Ultimate Abode
13:24 (24)	fair is the Ultimate Abode
13:25 (25)	and theirs the Evil Abode
13:31 (31)	or it alights nigh their habitation
13:42 (42)	assuredly know whose will be the Ultimate Abode
14:28 (33)	and caused their people to dwell in the abode of ruin
16:30 (32)	the abode of the world to come is better
16:30 (32)	excellent is the abode of the godfearing
17:5 (5)	men of great might, and they went through the habitations
22:40 (41)	who were expelled from their habitations without right
28:37 (37)	who comes with the guidance from Him, and shall possess the Ultimate
28:77 (77)	amidst that which God has given thee, the Last Abode
28:81 (81)	We made the earth to swallow him and his dwelling
28:83 (83)	that is the Last Abode
29:37 (36)	morning found them in their habitation fallen prostrate
29:64 (64)	surely the Last Abode is Life
33:27 (27)	He bequeathed upon you their lands, their habitations
33:29 (29)	if you desire God and His Messenger and the Last Abode
35:35 (32)	who of His bounty has made us to dwell in the abode of everlasting life
38:46 (46)	We purified them with a quality most pure, the remembrance of the Abode
40:39 (42)	the world to come is the abode of stability
40:52 (55)	theirs shall be the curse, and theirs the evil abode
41:28 (28)	the Fire, wherein they shall have the Abode of Eternity as a recompense
59:2 (2)	it is He who expelled from their habitations the unbelievers
59:8 (8)	it is for the poor emigrants, who were expelled from their habitations
59:9 (9)	those who made their dwelling in the abode, and in belief
60:8 (8)	nor expelled you from your habitations
60:9 (9)	and expelled you from your habitations

DĀʾIRAH n.f. (pl. *dawāʾir*)~a turn, a turn or change of fortune

5:52 (57)	we fear lest a turn of fortune should smite us
9:98 (99)	the Bedouins take what they expend for a fine, and await the turns of fortune
9:98 (99)	theirs shall be the evil turn
48:6 (6)	against them shall be the evil turn of fortune

DAYYĀR n.m.~anyone

71:26 (27)	leave not upon the earth of the unbelievers even one

ADĀRA vb. (IV)~to transact (a business), to give and take

b) impf. act. (*yudīru*)

2:282 (282)	unless it be merchandise present that you give and take between you

*D Y N

DĀNA vb. (I)~to judge; to practise a religion. (pcple. pass.) indebted, (with negative) requited; at the disposal of another [Ar]; brought to book, one in bondage [Pk]; receiving rewards and punishment, brought to account [Ali]; judged, under judgment [Bl]

b) impf. act. (*yadīnu*)

9:29 (29) such men as practise not the religion of truth

h) pcple. pass. (*madīn*)

37:53 (51) when we are dead and become dust and bones, shall we indeed be requited?
56:86 (85) why, if you are not at Our disposal

DAYN n.m.~a debt

2:282 (282) when you contract a debt one upon another for a stated term
4:11 (12) after any bequest he may bequeath, or any debt
4:12 (13) they leave a fourth, after any bequest they may bequeath, or any debt
4:12 (14) you leave an eighth, after any bequest you may bequeath, or any debt
4:12 (15) equally a third, after any bequest he may bequeath, or any debt

DĪN n.m.~judgment, doom, (*yawm al-dīn*) Day of Doom; that which is due; religion

1:4 (3) the Master of the Day of Doom
2:132 (126) God has chosen for you the religion
2:193 (189) fight them, till there is no persecution and the religion is God's
2:217 (214) they will not cease to fight with you, till they turn you from your religion
2:217 (214) whosoever of you turns from his religion, and dies disbelieving
2:256 (257) no compulsion is there in religion
3:19 (17) the true religion with God is Islam
3:24 (23) the lies they forged has deluded them in their religion
3:73 (66) believe not any but him who follows your religion
3:83 (77) do they desire another religion than God's
3:85 (79) whoso desires another religion than Islam
4:46 (48) twisting with their tongues and traducing religion
4:125 (124) who is there that has a fairer religion than he who submits his will to God
4:146 (145) hold fast to God, and make their religion sincerely God's
4:171 (169) People of the Book, go not beyond the bounds in your religion
5:3 (4) today the unbelievers have despaired of your religion
5:3 (5) today I have perfected your religion for you
5:3 (5) I have approved Islam for your religion
5:54 (59) whosoever of you turns from his religion
5:57 (62) the unbelievers, who take your religion in mockery and as a sport
5:77 (81) People of the Book, go not beyond the bounds in your religion
6:70 (69) leave alone those who take their religion for a sport
6:137 (138) to destroy them, and to confuse their religion
6:159 (160) those who have made divisions in their religion and become sects
6:161 (162) my Lord has guided me to a straight path, a right religion
7:29 (28) call on Him, making your religion sincerely His
7:51 (49) who have taken their religion as a diversion and a sport
8:39 (40) fight them, till there is no persecution and the religion is God's entirely
8:49 (51) their religion has deluded them
8:72 (73) they ask you for help, for religion's sake
9:11 (11) pay the alms, then they are your brothers in religion
9:12 (12) if they break their oaths after their covenant and thrust at your religion
9:29 (29) such men as practise not the religion of truth
9:33 (33) He who has sent His Messenger with the guidance and the religion of truth
9:33 (33) He may uplift it above every religion
9:36 (36) that is the right religion. So wrong not each other
9:122 (123) why should not a party of every section of them go forth, to become learned in religion
10:22 (23) they call upon God, making their religion His sincerely

10:104 (104)	if you are in doubt regarding my religion
10:105 (105)	set thy face to the religion
12:40 (40)	that is the right religion
12:76 (76)	he could not have taken his brother, according to the king's doom
15:35 (35)	upon thee shall rest the curse, till the Day of Doom
16:52 (54)	His is the religion for ever
22:78 (77)	and has laid on you no impediment in your religion
24:2 (2)	in the matter of God's religion let no tenderness for them seize you
24:25 (25)	upon that day God will pay them in full their just due
24:55 (54)	He will surely establish their religion for them that He has approved for them
26:82 (82)	who I am eager shall forgive me my offence on the Day of Doom
29:65 (65)	they call on God, making their religion sincerely His
30:30 (29)	so set thy face to the religion
30:30 (29)	that is the right religion
30:32 (31)	those who have divided up their religion, and become sects
30:43 (42)	so set thy face to the true religion
31:32 (31)	they call upon God, making their religion sincerely His
33:5 (5)	then they are your brothers in religion, and your clients
37:20 (20)	Woe, alas for us! This is the Day of Doom
38:78 (79)	upon thee shall rest My curse, till the Day of Doom
39:2 (2)	so worship God, making thy religion His sincerely
39:3 (3)	Belongs not sincere religion to God?
39:11 (14)	I have been commanded to serve God making my religion His sincerely
39:14 (16)	God I serve, making my religion His sincerely
40:14 (14)	so call unto God, making your religion His sincerely
40:26 (27)	I fear that he may change your religion
40:65 (67)	so call upon Him, making your religion His sincerely
42:13 (11)	He has laid down for you as religion that He charged Noah with
42:13 (11)	perform the religion, and scatter not regarding it
42:21 (20)	have they associates who have laid down for them as religion that for which
48:28 (28)	He who has sent His Messenger with the guidance and the religion of truth
48:28 (28)	He may uplift it above every religion
49:16 (16)	What, would you teach God what your religion is
51:6 (6)	and surely the Doom is about to fall
51:12 (12)	When shall be the Day of Doom?
56:56 (56)	this shall be their hospitality on the Day of Doom
60:8 (8)	God forbids you not, as regards those who have not fought you in religion's cause
60:9 (9)	God only forbids you as to those who have fought you in religion's cause
61:9 (9)	He who has sent His Messenger with the guidance and the religion of truth
61:9 (9)	He may uplift it above every religion
70:26 (26)	who confirm the Day of Doom
74:46 (47)	and we cried lies to the Day of Doom
82:9 (9)	but you cry lies to the Doom
82:15 (15)	roasting therein on the Day of Doom
82:17 (17)	and what shall teach thee what is the Day of Doom?
82:18 (18)	again, what shall teach thee what is the Day of Doom?
83:11 (11)	who cry lies to the Day of Doom
95:7 (7)	what then shall cry thee lies as to the Doom?
98:5 (4)	they were commanded only to serve God, making the religion His sincerely
98:5 (4)	the prayer, and pay the alms — that is the religion of the True
107:1 (1)	hast thou seen him who cries lies to the Doom?
109:6 (6)	to you your religion, and to me my religion
109:6 (6)	to you your religion, and to me my religion
110:2 (2)	thou seest men entering God's religion in throngs

TADĀYANA vb. (VI)~to contract a debt

a) perf. act.

2:282 (282) when you contract a debt one upon another for a stated term

DHĀL

*DH ʾ B

DHIʾB n.m.~wolf

12:13 (13)	I fear the wolf may eat him
12:14 (14)	if the wolf eats him, and we a band, then are we losers
12:17 (17)	so the wolf ate him

*DH ʾ M

DHAʾAMA vb. (I)~(pcple. pass.) despised

h) pcple. pass. (*madhʾūm*)

7:18 (17)	go thou forth from it, despised and banished

*DH ʿ N

ADHʿANA vb. (IV)~(pcple. act.) one who is obedient, submissive

g) pcple. act. (*mudhʿin*)

24:49 (48)	they will come to him submissively

*DH B B

DHUBĀB n.m. (pl. of *dhubābah*)~a fly

22:73 (72)	whom you call, apart from God, shall never create a fly
22:73 (72)	if a fly should rob them of aught

*DH B DH B

DHABDHABA vb. (quad I)~(pcple. pass.) wavering, moving to and fro

h) pcple. pass. (*mudhabdhab*)

4:143 (142)	wavering all the time — not to these, not to those

*DH B Ḥ

DHABAḤA vb. (I)~to slaughter, slay, sacrifice

a) perf. act.

2:71 (66)	therefore they sacrificed her

b) impf. act. (*yadhbaḥu*)

2:67 (63)	God commands you to sacrifice a cow
27:21 (21)	or I will slaughter him
37:102 (101)	I see in a dream that I shall sacrifice thee

d) perf. pass. (*dhubiḥa*)

5:3 (4)	excepting that you have sacrificed duly

DHIBḤ n.m.~that which is slaughtered, a sacrifice

37:107 (107)	We ransomed him with a mighty sacrifice

DHABBAḤA vb. (II)~to slaughter, to massacre

b) impf. act. (*yudhabbiḥu*)

2:49 (46)	slaughtering your sons, and sparing your women
14:6 (6)	slaughtering your sons, and sparing your women
28:4 (3)	slaughtering their sons, and sparing their women

*DH H B

DHAHABA vb. (I)~to go, to depart; (with prep. *bi-*) to take or snatch away, to go off with; (with prep. *ʿalá*) to be wasted. (n.vb.) going away; (with prep. *bi*) taking away. (pcple. act.) one who goes; going

a) perf. act.

2:17 (16)	God took away their light, and left them in darkness
2:20 (19)	He would have taken away their hearing and their sight
11:10 (13)	the evils have gone from me
11:74 (77)	when the awe departed from Abraham
12:15 (15)	so when they went with him
12:17 (17)	we went running races
21:87 (87)	and Dhul Nun — when he went forth enraged
23:91 (93)	each god would have taken off that he created
33:19 (19)	when the fear departs, they flay you with sharp tongues
60:11 (11)	give those whose wives have gone away the like of what they have expended
75:33 (33)	then he went to his household arrogantly

b) impf. act. (*yadh.habu*)

4:19 (23)	that you may go off with part of what you have given them
8:46 (48)	so lose heart, and your power depart
12:13 (13)	it grieves me that you should go with him
13:17 (18)	as for the scum, it vanishes as jetsam

17:86 (88)	if We willed, We could take away that We have revealed to thee
20:63 (66)	and to extirpate your justest way
24:43 (43)	the gleam of His lightning snatches away the sight
24:62 (62)	go not away until they ask his leave
33:20 (20)	they think the Confederates have not departed
35:8 (9)	let not thy soul be wasted in regrets for them
43:41 (40)	whether We take thee away, We shall take vengenace
81:26 (26)	where then are you going?

c) impv. (*idh.hab*)

5:24 (27)	go forth, thou and thy Lord, and do battle
12:87 (87)	depart, my sons, and search out tidings
12:93 (93)	go, take this shirt, and do you cast it
17:63 (65)	Depart! Those of them that follow thee
20:24 (25)	go to Pharaoh; he has waxed insolent
20:42 (44)	go therefore, thou and thy brother
20:43 (45)	go to Pharaoh, for he has waxed insolent
20:97 (97)	'Depart!' said Moses. 'It shall be thine'
25:36 (38)	go to the people who have cried lies
26:15 (14)	but go, both of you, with Our signs
27:28 (28)	take this letter of mine, and cast it
79:17 (17)	go to Pharaoh; he has waxed insolent

f) n.vb. (*dhahāb*)

23:18 (18)	and We are able to take it away

g) pcple. act. (*dhāhib*)

37:99 (97)	I am going to my Lord

DHAHAB n.com.~gold

3:14 (12)	women, children, heaped-up heaps of gold
3:91 (85)	there shall not be accepted from any one of them the whole earth full of gold
9:34 (34)	those who treasure up gold and silver
18:31 (30)	therein they shall be adorned with bracelets of gold
22:23 (23)	they shall be adorned with bracelets of gold
35:33 (30)	they shall be adorned with bracelets of gold
43:53 (53)	why then have bracelets of gold not been cast on him
43:71 (71)	there shall be passed around them platters of gold

ADH.HABA vb. (IV)~to cause to go away, put or drive away, dissipate, remove

a) perf. act.

35:34 (31)	praise belongs to God who has put away all sorrow
46:20 (19)	you dissipated your good things in your present life

b) impf. act. (*yudh.hibu*)

4:133 (132)	if He will, He can put you away, O men
6:133 (133)	if He will, He can put you away
8:11 (11)	and to put away from you the defilement of Satan
9:15 (15)	He will remove the rage within their hearts
11:114 (116)	the good deeds will drive away the evil deeds
14:19 (22)	if He will, He can put you away

22:15 (15) whether his guile does away with what enrages him
33:33 (33) God only desires to put away from you abomination
35:16 (17) if He will, He can put you away

*DH H L

DHAHALA vb. (I)~to forget, neglect

b) impf. act. (*yadh.halu*)

22:2 (2) every suckling woman shall neglect the child she has suckled

*DH K R

DHAKARA vb. (I)~to remember, mention, be mindful of. (n.vb.) a remembrance, reminder, a mention, commemoration; a warning [Ar]; (also) reputation [Bl]; fame [Ar, Pk]; esteem [Ali]. (pcple. act.) one who remembers, mentions or is mindful. (pcple. pass.) that which is remembered

a) perf. act.

3:135 (129) who, when they commit an indecency or wrong themselves, remember God
17:46 (49) when thou mentionest thy Lord only in the Koran
26:227 (227) and do righteous deeds, and remember God oft
33:21 (21) whosoever hopes for God and the Last Day, and remembers God oft
74:55 (54) whoever wills shall remember it
80:12 (12) and whoso wills, shall remember it
87:15 (15) and mentions the Name of his Lord, and prays

b) impf. act. (*yadhkuru*)

2:152 (147) so remember Me, and I will remember you
2:235 (235) God knows that you will be mindful of them
3:191 (188) who remember God, standing and sitting
4:142 (141) and not remembering God save a little
6:138 (139) over which they mention not the Name of God
12:85 (85) thou wilt never cease mentioning Joseph till thou art consumed
18:63 (62) so that I should not remember it
19:67 (68) will not man remember that We created him aforetime
20:34 (34) and remember Thee abundantly
21:36 (37) is this the one who makes mention of your gods?
21:60 (61) we heard a young man making mention of them
22:28 (29) and mention God's Name on days well-known
22:34 (35) that they may mention God's Name over such beasts of the flocks
37:13 (13) and, when reminded, do not remember
40:44 (47) you will remember what I say to you
43:13 (12) and then remember your Lord's blessing
74:56 (55) and they will not remember, except that God wills

c) impv. (*udhkur*)

2:40 (38) Children of Israel, remember My blessing
2:47 (44) Children of Israel, remember My blessing

2:63 (60)	remember what is in it; haply you shall be godfearing
2:122 (116)	Children of Israel, remember My blessing
2:152 (147)	so remember Me, and I will remember
2:198 (194)	when you press on from Arafat, then remember God
2:198 (194)	remember Him as He has guided you
2:200 (196)	remember God, as you remember your fathers
2:203 (199)	and remember God during certain days
2:231 (231)	and remember God's blessing
2:239 (240)	remember God, as He taught you the things that you knew not
3:41 (36)	mention thy Lord oft, and give glory at evening
3:103 (98)	and do not scatter; remember God's blessing
4:103 (104)	when you have performed the prayer, remember God
5:4 (6)	mention God's Name over it
5:7 (10)	and remember God's blessing upon you
5:11 (14)	O believers, remember God's blessing
5:20 (23)	O my people, remember God's blessing
5:110 (109)	Jesus Son of Mary, remember My blessing upon thee
7:69 (67)	and remember when He appointed you as successors
7:69 (67)	remember God's bounties
7:74 (72)	remember when He appointed you successors after Ad
7:74 (72)	remember God's bounties
7:86 (84)	and remember when you were few
7:171 (170)	what We have given you, and remember what is in it
7:205 (204)	remember thy Lord in thy soul, humbly and fearfully
8:26 (26)	and remember when you were few
8:45 (47)	remember God frequently
12:42 (42)	Mention me in thy lord's presence
14:6 (6)	remember God's blessing upon you
18:24 (23)	and mention thy Lord, when thou forgettest, and say
19:16 (16)	and mention in the Book Mary
19:41 (42)	and mention in the Book Abraham
19:51 (52)	and mention in the Book Moses
19:54 (55)	and mention in the Book Ishmael
19:56 (57)	and mention in the Book Idris
22:36 (37)	so mention God's Name over them, standing in ranks
33:9 (9)	O believers, remember God's blessing upon you
33:34 (34)	and remember that which is recited in your houses
33:41 (41)	O believers, remember God oft
35:3 (3)	O men, remember God's blessing upon you
38:17 (16)	bear patiently what they say, and remember Our servant David
38:41 (40)	remember also Our servant Job
38:45 (45)	remember also Our servants Abraham, Isaac and Jacob
38:48 (48)	remember also Our servants Ishmael, Elisha, and Dhul Kifl
46:21 (20)	and remember the brother of Ad
62:10 (10)	and seek God's bounty, and remember God frequently
73:8 (8)	remember the Name of thy Lord, and devote thyself unto Him
76:25 (25)	and remember the Name of thy Lord

d) perf. pass. (*dhukira*)

6:118 (118)	eat of that over which God's Name has been mentioned
6:119 (119)	that over which God's Name has been mentioned
8:2 (2)	when God is mentioned, their hearts quake
22:35 (36)	who, when God is mentioned, their hearts quake
39:45 (46)	when God is mentioned alone
39:45 (46)	when those apart from Him are mentioned behold, they rejoice
47:20 (22)	sura is sent down, and therein fighting is mentioned

e) impf. pass. (*yudhkaru*)

2:114 (108)	so that His Name be not rehearsed in them
6:121 (121)	eat not of that over which God's Name has not been mentioned
22:40 (41)	oratories and mosques, wherein God's Name is much mentioned
24:36 (36)	and His Name to be commemorated therein

f) n.vb. (*dhikr*)

2:200 (196)	(remember) God, as you remember your fathers
2:200 (196)	as you (remember) your fathers or yet <more devoutly>
3:58 (51)	this We recite to thee of signs and wise remembrance
5:91 (93)	and to bar you from the remembrance of God
7:63 (61)	do you wonder that a reminder from your Lord should come to you
7:69 (67)	do you wonder that a reminder from your Lord should come to you
12:42 (42)	Satan caused him to forget to mention him to his master
12:104 (104)	it is nothing but a reminder unto all beings
13:28 (28)	their hearts being at rest in God's remembrance
13:28 (28)	in God's remembrance are at rest the hearts
15:6 (6)	thou, upon whom the Remembrance is sent down
15:9 (9)	it is We who have sent down the Remembrance
16:43 (45)	question the people of the Remembrance
16:44 (46)	We have sent down to thee the Remembrance
18:28 (27)	whose heart We have made neglectful of Our remembrance
18:70 (69)	until I myself introduce the mention of it to thee
18:83 (82)	I will recite to you a mention of him
18:101 (101)	whose eyes were covered against My remembrance
19:2 (1)	the mention of thy Lord's mercy unto His servant Zachariah
20:14 (14)	and perform the prayer of My remembrance
20:42 (44)	and neglect not to remember Me
20:99 (99)	We have given thee a remembrance from Us
20:113 (112)	or it may arouse in them remembrance
20:124 (123)	whosoever turns away from My remembrance
21:2 (2)	no Remembrance from their Lord comes to them
21:7 (7)	question the People of the Remembrance
21:10 (10)	We have sent down to you a Book wherein is your Remembrance
21:24 (24)	this is the Remembrance of him who is with me
21:24 (24)	and the Remembrance of those before me
21:36 (37)	they in the Remembrance of the All-merciful are unbelievers
21:42 (43)	from the Remembrance of their Lord they are turning away
21:48 (49)	We gave Moses and Aaron the Salvation and a Radiance, and a Remembrance
21:50 (51)	this is a blessed Remembrance
21:105 (105)	We have written in the Psalms, after the Remembrance
23:71 (73)	We brought them their Remembrance
23:71 (73)	but from their Remembrance they turned
23:110 (112)	till they made you forget My remembrance
24:37 (37)	men whom neither commerce nor trafficking diverts from the remembrance of God
25:18 (19)	until they forgot the Remembrance, and were a people corrupt
25:29 (31)	He indeed led me astray from the Remembrance
26:5 (4)	never fresh remembrance comes to them from the All-merciful
29:45 (44)	God's remembrance is greater; and God knows
33:41 (41)	O believers, remember God oft
36:11 (10)	Thou only warnest him who follows the Remembrance
36:69 (69)	it is only a Remembrance and a Clear Koran
37:3 (3)	and the reciters of a Remembrance
37:168 (168)	if only we had had a Reminder from the ancients

38:1 (1) by the Koran, containing the Remembrance
38:8 (7) what, has the Remembrance been sent down on him
38:8 (7) nay, but they are in doubt of My Remembrance
38:32 (31) I have loved the love of good things better than the remembrance of my Lord
38:49 (49) this is a Remembrance; and for the godfearing
38:87 (87) it is nothing but a reminder unto all beings
39:22 (23) woe to those whose hearts are hardened against the remembrance of God
39:23 (24) their skins and their hearts soften to the remembrance of God
41:41 (41) those who disbelieve in the Remembrance
43:5 (4) shall We turn away the Remembrance from you
43:36 (35) whoso blinds himself to the Remembrance
43:44 (43) surely it is a Reminder
53:29 (30) turn thou from him who turns away from Our Remembrance
54:17 (17) now We have made the Koran easy for Remembrance
54:22 (22) now We have made the Koran easy for Remembrance
54:25 (25) has the Reminder been cast upon him
54:32 (32) now We have made the Koran easy for Remembrance
54:40 (40) now We have made the Koran easy for Remembrance
57:16 (15) who believe should be humbled to the Remembrance of God
58:19 (20) and caused them to forget God's Remembrance
62:9 (9) hasten to God's remembrance
63:9 (9) neither your children divert you from God's remembrance
65:10 (11) God has sent down to you for a remembrance
68:51 (51) when they hear the Reminder, and they say
68:52 (52) it is nothing but a Reminder unto all beings
72:17 (17) whosoever turns away from the Remembrance of his Lord
77:5 (5) and those hurling a reminder
81:27 (27) it is naught but a Reminder
94:4 (4) did We not exalt thy fame?

g) pcple. act. (*dhākir*)

11:114 (116) that is a remembrance unto the mindful
33:35 (35) men and (women) who remember God oft
33:35 (35) (men) and women who remember God oft

h) pcple. pass. (*madhkūr*)

76:1 (1) has there come on man a while of time when he was a thing unremembered?

DHAKAR n.m. (pl. *dhukūr*)~male

3:36 (31) the male is not as the female
3:195 (193) be you male or female — the one of you is as the other
4:11 (12) to the male the like of the portion of two females
4:124 (123) whosoever does deeds of righteousness, be it male or female
4:176 (175) the male shall receive the portion of two females
6:139 (140) what is within the bellies of these cattle is reserved for our males
6:143 (144) say: 'Is it the two males He has forbidden'
6:144 (145) say: 'Is it the two males He has forbidden'
16:97 (99) whosoever does a righteous deed, be it male or female
26:165 (165) what, do you come to male beings
40:40 (43) whosoever does a righteous deed, be it male or female
42:49 (48) and He gives to whom He will males
42:50 (49) or He couples them, both males and females
49:13 (13) O mankind, We have created you male and female
53:21 (21) what, have you males, and He females?

53:45 (46)	He Himself created the two kinds, male and female
75:39 (39)	and He made of him two kinds, male and female
92:3 (3)	and That which created the male and the female

DHIKRÁ n.f.~reminder, warning

6:68 (67)	do not sit, after the reminding, with the people of the evildoers
6:69 (68)	nothing of their account falls upon those that are godfearing; but a reminding
6:90 (90)	no wage for it; it is but a reminder unto all beings
7:2 (1)	to warn thereby, and as a reminder to believers
11:114 (116)	that is a remembrance unto the mindful
11:120 (121)	and an admonition, and a reminder to the believers
21:84 (84)	mercy from Us, and a Reminder to those who serve
26:209 (209)	for a reminder; and never did We wrong
29:51 (50)	a mercy, and a reminder to a people who believe
38:43 (42)	from us, and a reminder unto men possessed of minds
38:46 (46)	We purified them with a quality most pure, the remembrance of the Abode
39:21 (22)	in that is a reminder for men possessed of minds
40:54 (56)	and for a reminder to men possessed of minds
44:13 (12)	how should they have the Reminder
47:18 (20)	how shall they have their Reminder?
50:8 (8)	and a reminder to every penitent servant
50:37 (36)	surely in that there is a reminder to him
51:55 (55)	the Reminder profits the believers
74:31 (34)	and it is naught but a Reminder to mortals
79:43 (43)	what art thou about, to mention it?
80:4 (4)	or yet remember, and the Reminder profit him
87:9 (9)	therefore remind, if the Reminder profits
89:23 (24)	and how shall the Reminder be for him?

TADHKIRAH n.f.~a reminder, warning, admonition

20:3 (2)	but only as a reminder to him who fears
56:73 (72)	We Ourselves made it for a reminder
69:12 (12)	that We might make it a reminder for you
69:48 (48)	surely it is a Reminder to the godfearing
73:19 (19)	surely this is a Reminder
74:49 (50)	what ails them, that they turn away from the Reminder
74:54 (54)	no indeed; surely it is a Reminder
76:29 (29)	surely this is a Reminder
80:11 (11)	no indeed; it is a Reminder

DHAKKARA vb. (II)~to remind, to warn. (n.vb.) reminding, warning. (pcple. act.) one who reminds, a warner

b) impf. act. (*yudhakkiru*)

2:282 (282)	if one of the two women errs the other will remind her

c) impv. (*dhakkir*)

6:70 (69)	remind hereby, lest a soul should be given up to destruction
14:5 (5)	and remind thou them of the Days of God
50:45 (45)	therefore remind by the Koran him who fears My threat
51:55 (55)	and remind; the Reminder profits the believers
52:29 (29)	therefore remind! By thy Lord's blessing thou art not a soothsayer
87:9 (9)	therefore remind, if the Reminder profits
88:21 (21)	then remind them! Thou art only a reminder

d) perf. pass. (*dhukkira*)

5:13 (16) they have forgotten a portion of that they were reminded of
5:14 (17) they have forgotten a portion of that they were reminded of
6:44 (44) so, when they forgot what they were reminded of
7:165 (165) so, when they forgot that they were reminded of
18:57 (55) who, being reminded of the signs of his Lord, turns away from them
25:73 (73) who, when they are reminded of the signs of their Lord, fall not down
32:15 (15) only those believe in Our signs who, when they are reminded of them, fall down
32:22 (22) who does greater evil than he who is reminded of the signs of his Lord, then turns away
36:19 (18) your augury is with you; if you are reminded
37:13 (13) and, when reminded, do not remember

f) n.vb. (*tadhkīr*)

10:71 (72) and my reminding you of the signs of God

g) pcple. act. (*mudhakkir*)

88:21 (21) then remind them! Thou art only a reminder

TADHAKKARA vb. (V)~to recollect, remember, be mindful

a) perf. act.

7:201 (200) when a visitation of Satan troubles them, remember, and then see clearly
35:37 (34) him who would remember

b) impf. act. (*yatadhakkaru*)

2:221 (221) haply they will remember
2:269 (272) yet none remembers but men possessed of minds
3:7 (5) yet none remembers, but men possessed of minds
6:80 (80) my Lord embraces all things in His knowledge; will you not remember?
6:126 (126) We have distinguished the signs to a people who remember
6:152 (153) haply you will remember
7:3 (2) follow no friends other than He; little do you remember
7:26 (25) that is one of God's signs; haply they will remember
7:57 (55) We shall bring forth the dead; haply you will remember
7:130 (127) that haply they might remember
8:57 (59) haply they will remember
9:126 (127) still they do not repent, nor do they remember
10:3 (3) will you not remember?
11:24 (26) will you not remember?
11:30 (32) will you not remember?
13:19 (19) only men possessed of minds remember
14:25 (30) so God strikes similitudes for men; haply they will remember
14:52 (52) and that all possessed of minds may remember
16:13 (13) surely in that is a sign for a people who remember
16:17 (17) will you not remember?
16:90 (92) admonishing you, so that haply you will remember
17:41 (43) We have turned about in this Koran, that they may remember
20:44 (46) speak gently to him, that haply he may be mindful
23:85 (87) say: 'Will you not then remember?'
24:1 (1) in it signs, clear signs, that haply you will remember
24:27 (27) that is better for you; haply you will remember
25:50 (52) so that they may remember; yet most men refuse all

25:62 (63)	He who made the night and day a succession for whom He desires to remember
27:62 (63)	little indeed do you remember
28:43 (43)	and a guidance and a mercy, that haply so they might remember
28:46 (46)	that haply they may remember
28:51 (51)	We have brought them the Word; haply they may remember
32:4 (3)	you have no protector neither intercessor; will you not remember?
35:37 (34)	did We not give you long life, enough to remember in
37:155 (155)	what, and will you not remember?
38:29 (28)	that men possessed of minds may ponder its signs and so remember
39:9 (12)	only men possessed of minds remember
39:27 (28)	haply they will remember
40:13 (13)	yet none remembers but he who repents
40:58 (60)	little do you reflect
44:58 (58)	that haply they may remember
45:23 (22)	what, will you not remember?
51:49 (49)	haply you will remember
56:62 (62)	so why will you not remember?
69:42 (42)	nor the speech of a soothsayer, little do you remember
79:35 (35)	upon the day when man shall remember what he has striven
80:4 (4)	or yet remember, and the Reminder profit him
87:10 (10)	and he who fears shall remember
89:23 (24)	man will remember; and how shall the Reminder be for him?

*DH K Y

DHAKKÁ vb. (II)~to slay lawfully, to sacrifice

a) perf. act.

5:3 (4)	excepting that you have sacrificed duly

*DH KH R

IDHDHAKHARA vb. (VIII)~to store up, to treasure up

b) impf. act. (*yadhdhakhiru*)

3:49 (43)	and what you treasure up in your houses

*DH L L

DHALLA vb. (I)~to be humiliated. (n.vb.) humiliation, humbleness

b) impf. act. (*yadhillu*)

20:134 (134)	we might have followed Thy signs before that we were humiliated

f) n.vb. (*dhull*)

17:24 (25)	and lower to them the wing of humbleness
17:111 (111)	nor any protector out of humbleness
42:45 (44)	thou shalt see them, as they are exposed to it, abject in humbleness

DHILLAH n.f.~abasement, humiliation

2:61 (58)	and abasement and poverty were pitched upon them
3:112 (108)	abasement shall be pitched on them
7:152 (151)	anger shall overtake them from their Lord, and abasement
10:26 (27)	neither dust nor abasement shall overspread their faces
10:27 (28)	abasement shall overspread them
68:43 (43)	and abasement shall overspread them
70:44 (44)	humbled their eyes, overspreading them abasement

DHALĪL n.m. (adj., pl. *adhillah*)~abject, humble, abased

3:123 (119)	God most surely helped you at Badr, when you were utterly abject
5:54 (59)	bring a people He loves, and who love Him, humble towards the believers
27:34 (34)	make the mighty ones of its inhabitants abased
27:37 (37)	we shall expel them from there, abased and utterly humbled
58:20 (21)	those are among the most abject
63:8 (8)	the mightier ones of it will expel the more abased

DHALŪL n.com. (adj., pl. *dhulul*)~submissive, well-trained, broken (to perform)

2:71 (66)	he says she shall be a cow not broken to plough the earth
16:69 (71)	and follow the ways of your Lord easy to go upon
67:15 (15)	it is He who made the earth submissive to you

DHALLALA vb. (II)~to subdue, to render submissive, to bring low. (n.vb.) subjugation, humiliation, bringing low; (adv) meekly

a) perf. act.

36:72 (72)	We have subdued them to them, and some of them they ride

d) perf. pass. (*dhullila*)

76:14 (14)	near them shall be its shades, and its clusters hung

f) n.vb. (*tadhlīl*)

76:14 (14)	near them shall be its shades, and its clusters hung meekly down

ADHALLA vb. (IV)~to abase

b) impf. act. (*yudhillu*)

3:26 (25)	Thou exaltest whom Thou wilt, and Thou abasest whom Thou wilt

*DH M M

DHAMMA vb. (I)~(pcple. pass.) one who is condemned

h) pcple. pass. (*madhmūm*)

17:18 (19)	wherein he shall roast, condemned and rejected
17:22 (23)	wilt sit condemned and forsaken
68:49 (49)	he would have been cast upon the wilderness, being condemned

DHIMMAH n.f.~treaty, pact

9:8 (8)	they will not observe towards you any bond or treaty
9:10 (10)	observing neither bond nor treaty towards a believer

*DH N B

DHANB n.m. (pl. *dhunūb*)~sin, fault, crime; portion

3:11 (9)	God seized them because of their sins
3:16 (14)	our Lord, we believe; forgive us our sins
3:31 (29)	and God will love you, and forgive you your sins
3:135 (129)	remember God, and pray forgiveness for their sins
3:135 (129)	and who shall forgive sins but God?
3:147 (141)	Lord, forgive us our sins
3:193 (191)	our Lord, forgive Thou us our sins
5:18 (21)	say: 'Why then does He chastise you for your sins?'
5:49 (54)	know that God desires only to smite them for some sin
6:6 (6)	then We destroyed them because of their sins
7:100 (98)	did We will, We would smite them because of their sins
8:52 (54)	God seized them because of their sins
8:54 (56)	so We destroyed them because of their sins
9:102 (103)	and other have confessed their sins
12:29 (29)	and thou, woman, ask forgiveness of thy crime
12:97 (98)	our father, ask forgiveness of our crimes for us
14:10 (11)	who calls you so that He may forgive you your sins
17:17 (18)	thy Lord suffices as one who is aware of and sees the sins of His servants
25:58 (60)	sufficiently is He aware of His servants' sins
26:14 (13)	they also have a sin against me
28:78 (78)	the sinners shall not be questioned concerning their sins
29:40 (39)	each We seized for his sin
33:71 (71)	He will set right your deeds for you and will forgive you your sins
39:53 (54)	surely God forgives sins
40:3 (2)	Forgiver of sins, Accepter of penitence
40:11 (11)	now we confess our sins
40:21 (22)	yet God seized them in their sins
40:55 (57)	and ask forgiveness for thy sin
46:31 (30)	believe in Him, and He will forgive you some of your sins
47:19 (21)	and ask forgiveness for thy sin
48:2 (2)	that God may forgive thee thy former and thy latter sins
51:59 (59)	the evildoers shall have their portion
51:59 (59)	like the portion of their fellows
55:39 (39)	on that day none shall be questioned about his sin
61:12 (12)	He will forgive you your sins and admit you into gardens
67:11 (11)	so they confess their sins
71:4 (4)	and He will forgive you your sins
81:9 (9)	for what sin she was slain
91:14 (14)	so their Lord crushed them for their sin

*DH Q N

ADHQĀN n.f. (pl. of *dhaqn*)~chin, face

17:107 (108)	when it is recited to them, fall down upon their faces
17:109 (109)	and they fall down upon their faces weeping
36:8 (7)	We have put on their necks fetters up to the chin

*DH R ʾ

DHARAʾA vb. (I)~to create, to multiply, to scatter broadcast

a) perf. act.

6:136 (137)	they appoint to God, of the tillage and cattle that He multiplied, a portion
7:179 (178)	We have created for Gehenna many jinn and men
16:13 (13)	that which He has multiplied for you in the earth
23:79 (81)	it is He who scattered you in the earth
67:24 (24)	it is He who scattered you in the earth

b) impf. act. (*yadhraʾu*)

42:11 (9)	and pairs also of the cattle, therein multiplying you

*DH R ʿ

DHARʿ n.m.~strength, power; (*ḍāqa dharʿan bi-*) to be distressed for; the length of an arm, cubit

11:77 (79)	he was troubled on their account and distressed for them
29:33 (32)	he was troubled on their account and distressed for them
69:32 (32)	then in a chain of seventy cubits' length insert him!

DHIRĀʿ n.com.~an arm, the length of an arm, a cubit, a paw

18:18 (17)	and their dog stretching its paws on the threshold
69:32 (32)	then in a chain of seventy cubits' length insert him!

*DH R R

DHARRAH n.f.~an ant (in weight), an atom; least degree [Ali]; a grain [Bl]

4:40 (44)	God shall not wrong so much as the weight of an ant
10:61 (62)	not so much as the weight of an ant in earth or heaven escapes from thy Lord
34:3 (3)	not so much as the weight of an ant in heaven and earth escapes from Him
34:22 (21)	they possess not so much as the weight of an ant in the heavens
99:7 (7)	whoso has done an atom's weight of good shall see it
99:8 (8)	whoso has done an atom's weight of evil shall see it

DHURRĪYAH n.f.~progeny, seed, offspring

2:124 (118)	said he, 'And of my seed?'
2:128 (122)	make us submissive to Thee, and of our seed a nation submissive
2:266 (268)	then old age smites him, and he has seed, but weaklings
3:34 (30)	the seed of one another
3:36 (31)	commend her to Thee with her seed, to protect them
3:38 (33)	give me of Thy goodness a goodly offspring

4:9 (10)	let those fear who, if they left behind them weak seed, would be afraid
6:84 (84)	and Noah We guided before; and of his seed
6:87 (87)	and of their fathers, and of their seed
6:133 (133)	as He produced you from the seed of another people
7:172 (171)	when thy Lord took from the Children of Adam, from their loins, their seed
7:173 (172)	our fathers were idolaters aforetime, and we were seed after them
10:83 (83)	so none believed in Moses, save a seed of his people
13:23 (23)	those who were righteous of their fathers, and their wives, and their seed
13:38 (38)	We assigned to them wives, and seed
14:37 (40)	I have made some of my seed to dwell in a valley where is no sown land
14:40 (42)	make me a performer of the prayer, and of my seed
17:3 (3)	the seed of those We bore with Noah
17:62 (64)	I shall assuredly master his seed, save a few
18:50 (48)	do you take him and his seed to be your friends
19:58 (59)	these are they whom God has blessed among the Prophets of the seed of Adam
19:58 (59)	We bore with Noah, and of the seed of Abraham
25:74 (74)	give us refreshment of our wives and seed
29:27 (26)	appointed the Prophecy and the Book to be among his seed
36:41 (41)	a sign for them is that We carried their seed
37:77 (75)	and We made his seed the survivors
37:113 (113)	and of their seed some are good-doers
40:8 (8)	those who were righteous of their fathers, and their wives, and their seed
46:15 (14)	and make me righteous also in my seed
52:21 (21)	those who believed, and their seed followed them
52:21 (21)	We shall join their seed with them
57:26 (26)	We appointed the Prophecy and the Book to be among their seed

*DH R W

DHARĀ vb. (I)~to scatter, to winnow. (n.vb.) scattering, winnowing. (pcple. act.) scatterer, one who winnows

b) impf. act. (*yadhrū*)

18:45 (43)	in the morning it is straw the winds scatter

f) n.vb. (*dharw*)

51:1 (1)	by the <swift> scatterers

g) pcple. act. (*dhārī*)

51:1 (1)	by the swift scatterers

*DH W D

DHĀDA vb. (I)~to hold or keep back

b) impf. act. (*yadhūdu*)

28:23 (23)	he found, apart from them, two women holding back their flocks

*DH W Q

DHĀQA vb. (I)~to taste, to experience. (pcple. act.) one who tastes; tasting

a) perf. act.

6:148 (149)	the people before them cried lies until they tasted Our might
7:22 (21)	when they tasted the tree, their shameful parts revealed
59:15 (15)	like those who a short time before them tasted the mischief of their action
64:5 (5)	that disbelieved before, then tasted the mischief of their action
65:9 (9)	so it tasted the mischief of its action

b) impf. act. (*yadhūqu*)

4:56 (59)	give them in exchange other skins, that they may taste the chastisement
5:95 (96)	he may taste the mischief of his action
16:94 (96)	it has stood firm, and you should taste evil
38:8 (7)	they have not yet tasted My chastisement
38:57 (57)	let them taste it — boiling water and pus
44:56 (56)	they shall not taste therein of death
78:24 (24)	tasting therein neither coolness nor any drink

c) impv. (*dhuq*)

3:106 (102)	then taste the chastisement
3:181 (177)	taste the chastisement of the burning
6:30 (30)	then taste the chastisement for your unbelief
7:39 (37)	taste the chastisement for what you have been earning
8:14 (14)	therefore taste it
8:35 (35)	taste you now the chastisement for your unbelief
8:50 (52)	taste the chastisement of the burning
9:35 (35)	taste you now what you were treasuring
10:52 (53)	taste the chastisement of eternity
22:22 (22)	taste the chastisement of the burning
29:55 (55)	taste now what you were doing
32:14 (14)	now taste, for that you forgot the encounter of this your day
32:14 (14)	taste the chastisement of eternity
32:20 (20)	taste the chastisement of the Fire
34:42 (41)	taste the chastisement of the Fire
35:37 (35)	so taste you now!
39:24 (25)	taste now that you were earning
44:49 (49)	Taste! Surely thou art the mighty, the noble
46:34 (33)	then taste the chastisement of your unbelief
51:14 (14)	Taste your trial!
54:37 (37)	taste now My chastisement and My warnings
54:39 (39)	taste now My chastisement and My warnings
54:48 (48)	Taste now the touch of Sakar
78:30 (30)	Taste! We shall increase you not

g) pcple. act. (*dhā'iq*)

3:185 (182)	every soul shall taste of death; you shall surely
21:35 (36)	every soul shall taste of death; and We try you
29:57 (57)	every soul shall taste of death; then unto Us
37:31 (30)	our Lord's Word is realised against us; we are tasting it
37:38 (37)	now certainly you shall be tasting the painful chastisement

ADHĀQA vb. (IV)~to cause to taste (with double accus.)

a) perf. act.

10:21 (22)	We let the people taste mercy after hardship has visited them
11:9 (12)	if We let a man taste mercy from Us
11:10 (13)	if We let him taste prosperity after hardship that has visited him
16:112 (113)	so God let it taste the garment of hunger
17:75 (77)	then would We have let thee taste the double of life
30:33 (32)	when He lets them taste mercy from Him
30:36 (35)	when We let men taste mercy
39:26 (27)	let them taste degradation in this present life
41:50 (50)	if We let him taste mercy from Us after hardship that has visited him
42:48 (47)	when We let man taste mercy from Us, he rejoices in it

b) impf. act. (*yudhīqu*)

6:65 (65)	and to make you taste the violence of one another
10:70 (71)	then We shall let them taste the terrible chastisement
22:9 (9)	We shall let him taste the chastisement of the burning
22:25 (26)	We shall let him taste a painful chastisement
25:19 (21)	We shall let him taste a great chastisement
30:41 (40)	that He may let them taste some part of that which they have done
30:46 (45)	and that He may let you taste of His mercy
32:21 (21)	We shall surely let them taste the nearer chastisement
34:12 (11)	We would let them taste the chastisement of the Blaze
41:16 (15)	We might let them taste the chastisement of degradation in the present life
41:27 (26)	We shall let the unbelievers taste a terrible chastisement
41:50 (50)	if We let him taste mercy from Us after hardship that has visited him

*DH Y ʿ

ADHĀʿA vb. (IV)~to broadcast, to noise abroad

a) perf. act.

4:83 (85)	when there comes to them a matter, be it of security or fear, they broadcast it

DĀD

*Ḍ ʾ N

ḌAʾN n.m. (pl. of *ḍāʾin*)~sheep

6:143 (144)	eight couples: two of sheep, of goats two

*Ḍ ʿ F

ḌAʿUFA vb. (I)~to be weak. (n.vb.) weakness, infirmity

a) perf. act.

3:146 (140)	for what smote them in God's way, neither weakened, nor did they humble themselves
22:73 (72)	feeble indeed alike are the seeker and the sought

f) n.vb. (*ḍaʿf*)

8:66 (67)	God has lightened it for you, knowing that there is weakness in you
30:54 (53)	God is He that created you of weakness
30:54 (53)	then He appointed after weakness strength
30:54 (53)	then after strength He appointed weakness and grey hairs

ḌAʿĪF n.m. (adj)~weak, weakling, feeble, infirm

2:266 (268)	then old age smites him, and he has seed, but weaklings
2:282 (282)	the debtor be a fool, or weak, or unable to dictate himself
4:9 (10)	let those fear who, if they left behind them weak seed, would be afraid
4:28 (32)	God desires to lighten things for you, for man was created a weakling
4:76 (78)	surely the guile of Satan is ever feeble
9:91 (92)	there is no fault in the weak and the sick
11:91 (93)	truly we see thee weak among us
14:21 (24)	then say the weak to those who waxed proud
19:75 (77)	who is worse in place, and who is weaker in hosts
40:47 (50)	the weak say unto those who waxed proud
72:24 (25)	then they will know who is weaker in helpers

ḌIʿF n.m. (pl. *aḍʿāf*)~the like, an equal portion, a double, twofold

2:245 (246)	and He will multiply it for him manifold
2:265 (267)	and it yields its produce twofold
3:130 (125)	O believers, devour not usury, doubled
7:38 (36)	so give them a double chastisement
7:38 (36)	unto each a double
17:75 (77)	then would We have let thee taste the double of life
17:75 (77)	and the double of death
33:30 (30)	for her the chastisement shall be doubled
33:68 (68)	give them chastisement twofold, and curse them with a mighty curse
34:37 (36)	those — there awaits them the double recompense for that they did
38:61 (61)	whoso forwarded this for us, give him a double chastisement in the Fire

ḌĀᶜAFA vb. (III)~to double, multiply. (pcple. pass.) multiplied, redoubled

b) impf. act. (*yuḍāᶜifu*)

2:245 (246)	and He will multiply it for him manifold
2:261 (263)	so God multiplies unto whom He will
4:40 (44)	if it be a good deed He will double it
57:11 (11)	and He will multiply it for him
64:17 (17)	if you lend to God a good loan, He will multiply it for you

e) impf. pass. (*yuḍāᶜafu*)

11:20 (22)	for them the chastisement shall be doubled
25:69 (69)	doubled shall be the chastisement for him
33:30 (30)	for her the chastisement shall be doubled
57:18 (17)	it shall be multiplied for them

h) pcple. pass. (*muḍāᶜaf*)

3:130 (125)	O believers, devour not usury, doubled and redoubled

AḌᶜAFA vb. (IV)~(pcple. act.) one who makes double, manifold

g) pcple. act. (*muḍᶜif*)

30:39 (38)	those — they receive recompense manifold

ISTAḌᶜAFA vb. (X)~to esteem one weak, to take advantage of one's weakness, to abase. (pcple. pass.) one who is abased (on account of his weakness), oppressed

a) perf. act.

7:150 (149)	surely the people have abased me

b) impf. act. (*yastaḍᶜifu*)

28:4 (3)	and had divided its inhabitants into sects, abasing one party of them

d) perf. pass. (*istuḍᶜifa*)

7:75 (73)	said the Council of those of his people who waxed proud to those that were abased
28:5 (4)	We desired to be gracious to those that were abased in the land
34:31 (30)	those that were abased will say to those that waxed proud
34:32 (31)	those that waxed proud will say to those that were abased
34:33 (32)	those that were abased will say to those that waxed proud

e) impf. pass. (*yustaḍᶜafu*)

7:137 (133)	We bequeathed upon the people that were abased all the east and the west

h) pcple. pass. (*mustaḍᶜaf*)

4:75 (77)	women, and children who, being abased, say
4:97 (99)	we were abased in the earth
4:98 (100)	except the men, women, and children who, being abased, can devise nothing
4:127 (126)	and yet desire to marry them, and the oppressed children
8:26 (26)	remember when you were few and abased in the land

*Ḍ B Ḥ

ḌABAḤA vb. (I)~(n.vb.) panting, snorting (adv)

f) n.vb. (*ḍabḥ*)

100:1 (1) by the snorting chargers

*Ḍ D D

ḌIDD n.m.~contrary, one pitted against, against

19:82 (85) and they shall be against them pitted

*Ḍ F Ḍ ᶜ

ḌAFĀDIᶜ n.m. (pl. of *ḍafdaᶜ*)~a frog

7:133 (130) We let loose upon them the flood and the locusts, the lice and the frogs

*Ḍ GH N

AḌGHĀN n.m. (pl. of *ḍaghn*)~ill-feeling, hatred, rancour

47:29 (31) that God would not bring to light their rancour
47:37 (39) He brings to light your rancour

*Ḍ GH TH

ḌIGHTH n.m. (pl. *aḍghāth*)~(s) a bundle of grass or rushes, a branch; (pl) a confusion, hotchpotch, jumble

12:44 (44) a hotchpotch of nightmares!
21:5 (5) nay, but they say: 'A hotchpotch of nightmares!'
38:44 (43) take in thy hand a bundle of rushes, and strike therewith

*Ḍ H Y

ḌĀHÁ vb. (III)~to resemble, to conform with

b) impf. act. (*yuḍāhiʾu*)

9:30 (30) that is the utterance of their mouths, conforming with the unbelievers before them

*Ḍ Ḥ K

ḌAḤIKA vb. (I)~to laugh. (pcple. act.) one who laughs, laughing

a) perf. act.

11:71 (74)	his wife was standing by; she laughed

b) impf. act. (*yaḍḥaku*)

9:82 (83)	therefore let them laugh little, and weep much
23:110 (112)	but you took them for a laughing-stock
43:47 (46)	when he brought them Our signs, lo, they laughed at them
53:60 (60)	and do you laugh, and do you not weep
83:29 (29)	behold, the sinners were laughing at the believers
83:34 (34)	today the believers are laughing at the unbelievers

g) pcple. act. (*ḍāḥik*)

27:19 (19)	but he smiled, laughing at its words
80:39 (39)	laughing, joyous

AḌḤAKA vb. (IV)~to cause to laugh

a) perf. act.

53:43 (44)	and that it is He who makes to laugh

*Ḍ Ḥ Y

ḌAḤIYA vb. (I)~to be exposed to or suffer from the heat of the sun

b) impf. act. (*yaḍḥá*)

20:119 (117)	neither to thirst therein, nor to suffer the sun

ḌUḤÁ n.com.~daytime, forenoon, high noon; daylight

7:98 (96)	Our might shall not come upon them in daylight
20:59 (61)	let the people be mustered at the high noon
79:29 (29)	and darkened its night, and brought forth its forenoon
79:46 (46)	they have but tarried for an evening, or its forenoon
91:1 (1)	by the sun and his morning brightness
93:1 (1)	by the white forenoon

*Ḍ J ᶜ

MAḌĀJIᶜ n.m. (pl. of *maḍjaᶜ*)~a sleeping or resting place, a couch

3:154 (148)	those for whom slaying was appointed would have sallied forth unto their last
4:34 (38)	banish them to their couches
32:16 (16)	their sides shun their couches as they call on their Lord

*Ḍ L L

ḌALLA vb. (I)~to wander away, to be lost, to go astray, to err. (n.vb.) the act of going astray, error. (pcple. act.) one who goes astray

a) perf. act.

2:108 (102)	whoso exchanges belief for unbelief has surely strayed from the right way
4:116 (116)	whoso associates with God anything, has gone astray into far error
4:136 (135)	and the Last Day, has surely gone astray into far error
4:167 (165)	those who disbelieve, and bar from the way of God, have gone astray into far error
5:12 (15)	whosoever of you thereafter disbelieves, surely he has gone astray from the right way
5:77 (81)	follow not the caprices of a people who went astray before
5:77 (81)	and now again have gone astray from the right way
5:105 (104)	He who is astray cannot hurt you
6:24 (24)	and how that which they were forging has gone astray from them
6:56 (56)	else I had gone astray, and would not be of the right-guided
6:94 (94)	which you ever asserted has now gone astray from you
6:140 (141)	they have gone astray, and are not right-guided
7:37 (35)	They have gone astray from us
7:53 (51)	that which they were forging has gone astray from them
7:149 (148)	when they smote their hands, and saw that they had gone astray
10:30 (31)	there shall go astray from them that they were forging
10:108 (108)	whosoever goes astray, it is only to his own loss
11:21 (23)	that they forged has gone astray from them
16:87 (89)	and there shall go astray from them that they were forging
16:125 (126)	thy Lord knows very well those who have gone astray from His way
17:15 (16)	whosoever goes astray, it is only to his own loss
17:48 (51)	behold, how they strike similitudes for thee, and go astray
17:67 (69)	there go astray those on whom you call except Him
18:104 (104)	those whose striving goes astray in the present life
20:92 (94)	what prevented thee, Aaron, when thou sawest them in error
25:9 (10)	behold, how they strike similitudes for thee, and go astray
25:17 (18)	or did they themselves err from the way?
27:92 (94)	whosoever goes astray, say: 'I am naught but a warner.'
28:75 (75)	there shall go astray from them that they were forging
32:10 (9)	when we have gone astray in the earth, shall we indeed be in a new creation?
33:36 (36)	whosoever disobeys God and His Messenger has gone astray
34:50 (49)	if I go astray, I (go astray) only to my own loss
37:71 (69)	before them erred most of the ancients
39:41 (42)	whosoever goes astray, it is only to his own loss
40:74 (74)	They have gone astray from us
41:48 (48)	then that they called upon before will go astray from them
46:28 (27)	not so; but they went astray from them
53:2 (2)	your comrade is not astray, neither errs
53:30 (31)	surely thy Lord knows very well those who have gone astray
60:1 (1)	whosoever of you does that, has gone astray from the right way
68:7 (7)	thy Lord knows very well those who have gone astray from His way

b) impf. act. (*yaḍillu*)

2:282 (282)	if one of the two women errs the other will remind her
4:44 (47)	and desiring that you should also err from the way
4:176 (175)	God makes clear to you, lest you go astray
6:117 (117)	thy Lord knows very well who goes astray from His path
10:108 (108)	whosoever goes astray, it is only to his own loss

17:15 (16)	whosoever goes astray, it is only to his own loss
20:52 (54)	my Lord goes not astray, nor forgets
20:123 (122)	whosoever follows My guidance shall not go astray
34:50 (49)	if I (go astray), I go astray only to my own loss
38:26 (25)	those who go astray from the way of God
39:41 (42)	whosoever goes astray, it is only to his own loss

f) n.vb. (*ḍalāl*)

3:164 (158)	to teach them the Book and the Wisdom, though before they were in manifest error
4:60 (63)	Satan desires to lead them astray into far error
4:116 (116)	whoso associates with God anything, has gone astray into far error
4:136 (135)	[he] has surely gone astray into far error
4:167 (165)	and bar from the way of God, have gone astray into far error
6:74 (74)	I see thee, and thy people, in manifest error
7:60 (58)	we see thee in manifest error
10:32 (33)	what is there, after truth, but error?
12:8 (8)	surely our father is in manifest error
12:30 (30)	he smote her heart with love; we see her in manifest error
12:95 (95)	by God, thou art certainly in thy ancient error
13:14 (15)	the prayer of the unbelievers goes only astray
14:3 (3)	they are in far error
14:18 (21)	they have no power over that they have earned — that is the far error
19:38 (39)	the evildoers even today are in error manifest
21:54 (55)	assuredly you and your fathers have been in manifest error
22:12 (12)	that is indeed the far error
26:97 (97)	by God, we were certainly in manifest error
28:85 (85)	my Lord knows very well who comes with guidance, and who is in manifest error
31:11 (10)	nay, but the evildoers are in manifest error
33:36 (36)	whosoever disobeys God and His Messenger has gone astray into manifest error
34:8 (8)	those who believe not in the Hereafter are in chastisement and far error
34:24 (23)	either we or you are upon right guidance, or in manifest error
36:24 (23)	in that case I should be in manifest error
36:47 (47)	you are only in manifest error
39:22 (23)	those are in manifest error
40:25 (26)	the guile of the unbelievers is ever in error
40:50 (53)	the calling of the unbelievers is only in error
42:18 (17)	those who are in doubt concerning the Hour are indeed in far error
43:40 (39)	shalt thou guide the blind and him who is in manifest error?
46:32 (31)	those are in manifest error
50:27 (26)	I made him not insolent, but he was in far error
54:24 (24)	then indeed we should be in error and insanity
54:47 (47)	surely the sinners are in error and insanity
62:2 (2)	before that they were in manifest error
67:9 (9)	you are only in great error
67:29 (29)	you will soon know who is in manifest error
71:24 (24)	increase Thou not the evildoers save in error

g) pcple. act. (*ḍāll*)

1:7 (7)	nor of those who are astray
2:198 (194)	He has guided you, though formerly you were gone astray
3:90 (84)	those are the ones who stray
5:60 (65)	and have gone further astray from the right way
6:77 (77)	I shall surely be of the people gone astray
7:179 (178)	they are like cattle; nay, rather they are further astray

15:56 (56)	who despairs of the mercy of his Lord, excepting those that are astray?
17:72 (74)	he shall be even further astray from the way
23:106 (108)	our adversity prevailed over us; we were an erring people
25:34 (36)	they shall be worse in place, and gone further astray from the way
25:42 (44)	they shall know, when they see the chastisement, who is further astray from the way
25:44 (46)	nay, they are further astray from the way
26:20 (19)	indeed I did it then, being one of those that stray
26:86 (86)	forgive my father, for he is one of those astray
28:50 (50)	who is further astray than he who follows his caprice without guidance
37:69 (67)	they found their fathers erring
41:52 (52)	who is further astray than he who is in wide schism?
46:5 (4)	who is further astray than he who calls, apart from God
56:51 (51)	then you erring ones, you that cried lies
56:92 (92)	and went astray
68:26 (26)	Surely we are gone astray
83:32 (32)	Lo, these men are astray
93:7 (7)	did He not find thee erring, and guide thee?

ḌALĀLAH n.f.~falsehood, error

2:16 (15)	those are they that have bought error at the price of guidance
2:175 (170)	those are they that have bought error at the price of guidance
4:44 (47)	hast thou not regarded those who were given a share of the Book purchasing error
7:30 (28)	a part He guided, and a part justly disposed to error
7:61 (59)	my people, there is no error in me
16:36 (38)	God guided, and some were justly disposed to error
19:75 (76)	whosoever is in error, let the All-merciful prolong his term for him
27:81 (83)	thou shalt not guide the blind out of their error
30:53 (52)	thou shalt not guide the blind out of their error

ḌALLALA vb. (II)~(n.vb.) going astray, going to naught

f) n.vb. (*taḍlīl*)

105:2 (2)	did He not make their guile to go astray?

AḌALLA vb. (IV)~to cause to go astray, to lead astray. (pcple. act.) one who leads astray

a) perf. act.

4:88 (90)	do you desire to guide him whom God has led astray?
5:77 (81)	who (went astray) before and led astray many
7:38 (36)	O our Lord, these led us astray
14:36 (39)	my Lord, they have led astray many men
20:79 (81)	Pharaoh had led his people astray, and was no guide to them
20:85 (87)	the Samaritan has misled them into error
25:17 (18)	was it you that led these My servants astray, or did they themselves err
25:29 (31)	He indeed led me astray from the Remembrance
26:99 (99)	it was naught but the sinners that led us astray
30:29 (28)	who shall guide those whom God has led astray?
33:67 (67)	and they led us astray from the way
36:62 (62)	He led astray many a throng of you; did you not understand?
41:29 (29)	show us those that led us astray
45:23 (22)	God has led him astray out of a knowledge
47:1 (1)	God will send their works astray

47:8 (9)	He will send their works astray
71:24 (24)	and they have led many astray

b) impf. act. (*yuḍillu*)

2:26 (24)	thereby He leads many astray, and thereby He guides many
2:26 (24)	thereby He leads none astray save the ungodly
3:69 (62)	there is a party of the People of the Book yearn to make you go astray
3:69 (62)	yet none they make to stray, except themselves
4:60 (63)	Satan desires to lead them astray into far error
4:88 (90)	whom God leads astray, thou wilt not find for him a way
4:113 (113)	a party of them purposed to lead thee astray
4:113 (113)	but they lead only themselves astray
4:119 (118)	I will lead them astray, and fill them with fancies
4:143 (142)	whom God leads astray, thou wilt not find for him a way
6:39 (39)	whomsoever God will, He leads astray
6:116 (116)	they will lead thee astray from the path of God
6:119 (119)	many lead astray by their caprices, without any knowledge
6:125 (125)	whomsoever He desires to lead astray, He makes his breast narrow, tight
6:144 (145)	in order that he may lead mankind astray without any knowledge
7:155 (154)	it is only Thy trial, whereby Thou leadest astray whom Thou wilt
7:178 (177)	whom He leads astray — they are the losers
7:186 (185)	whomsoever God leads astray, no guide he has
9:115 (116)	God would never lead a people astray after that He has guided them
10:88 (88)	our Lord, let them go astray from Thy way
13:27 (27)	God leads astray whomsoever He will
13:33 (33)	whomsoever God leads astray, no guide has he
14:4 (4)	then God leads astray whomsoever He will
14:27 (32)	and God leads astray the evildoers
14:30 (35)	they set up compeers to God, that they might lead astray from His way
16:25 (27)	some of the loads of those that they lead astray
16:37 (39)	God guides not those whom He leads astray
16:93 (95)	He leads astray whom He will, and guides whom He will
17:97 (99)	whom He leads astray — thou wilt not find for them protectors
18:17 (16)	whomsoever He leads astray, thou wilt not find for him a protector
22:4 (4)	whosoever takes him for a friend, him he leads astray
22:9 (9)	turning his side to lead astray from God's way
25:42 (44)	wellnigh he had led us astray from our gods
31:6 (5)	some men there are who buy diverting talk to lead astray from the way of God
35:8 (9)	God leads astray whomsoever He will
38:26 (25)	lest it lead thee astray from the way of God
39:8 (11)	and sets up compeers to God, to lead astray from His way
39:23 (24)	whomsoever God leads astray, no guide has he
39:36 (37)	whomsoever God leads astray, no guide has he
40:33 (35)	whomsoever God leads astray, no guide has he
40:34 (36)	God leads astray the prodigal and the doubter
40:74 (74)	even so God leads astray the unbelievers
42:44 (42)	whomsoever God leads astray, he has no protector
42:46 (45)	whomsoever God leads astray, no way has he
47:4 (5)	those who are slain in the way of God, He will not send their works astray
71:27 (28)	if Thou leavest them, they will lead Thy servants astray
74:31 (34)	God leads astray whomsoever He will

e) impf. pass. (*yuḍallu*)

9:37 (37)	the month postponed is an increase of unbelief whereby the unbelievers go astray

g) pcple. act. (*muḍill*)

18:51 (49) I would not ever take those who lead others astray to be My supporters
28:15 (14) this is of Satan's doing; he is surely an enemy misleading, manifest
39:37 (38) whomso God guides, none shall lead him astray

*Ḍ M M

ḌAMMA vb. (I)~to clasp, to press to one's self, to hug

c) impv. (*uḍmum*)

20:22 (23) now clasp thy hand to thy arm-pit
28:32 (32) and press to thee thy arm, that thou be not afraid

*Ḍ M R

ḌĀMIR n.m. (adj)~lean, slender

22:27 (28) they shall come unto thee on foot and upon every lean beast

*Ḍ N K

ḌANUKA vb. (I)~(n.vb.) narrowness

f) n.vb. (*ḍank*)

20:124 (123) his shall be a life of narrowness

*Ḍ N N

ḌANĪN n.m. (adj)~greedy, avid, avaricious, niggardly

81:24 (24) he is not niggardly of the Unseen

*Ḍ R ᶜ

ḌARĪᶜ n.m.~a plant of Hell, a thorn-fruit

88:6 (6) no food for them but cactus thorn

TAḌARRAᶜA vb. (V)~to humble or abase one's self. (n.vb.) humbleness; (adv) humbly

a) perf. act.

6:43 (43) if only, when Our might came upon them, they had been humble *b*) impf. act. (*yataḍarraᶜu*)

6:42 (42)	We seized them with misery and hardship that haply they might be humble
7:94 (92)	We seized its people with misery and hardship, that haply they might be humble
23:76 (78)	they abased not themselves to their Lord nor were they humble

f) n.vb. (*taḍarruᶜ*)

6:63 (63)	you call upon Him humbly and secretly
7:55 (53)	call on your Lord, humbly and secretly
7:205 (204)	remember thy Lord in thy soul, humbly and fearfully

*Ḍ R B

ḌARABA vb. (I)~to strike, smite, stamp, beat; to liken or strike (a parable or similitude), to cite (an example or a dispute); (*ḍaraba fī al-arḍ*) to journey; to draw or cast (a veil); (with prep. *ᶜalá*) to pitch on, to stamp; (with prep. *ᶜan*) to turn something away; (with prep. *bayn*) to set up between, to separate. (n.vb.) striking, smiting, etc.; (with prep. *fī*) journeying

a) perf. act.

3:156 (150)	who say to their brothers, when they journey in the land
4:94 (96)	when you are journeying in the path of God, be discriminating
4:101 (102)	when you are journeying in the land there is no fault in you
5:106 (105)	if you are journeying in the land and the affliction of death befalls you
14:24 (29)	hast thou not seen how God has struck a similitude?
14:45 (47)	and how We struck similitudes for you
16:75 (77)	God has struck a similitude: a servant
16:76 (78)	God has struck a similitude: two men
16:112 (113)	God has struck a similitude: a city
17:48 (51)	behold, how they strike similitudes
18:11 (10)	We smote their ears many years in the Cave
25:9 (10)	behold, how they strike similitudes
25:39 (41)	We struck similitudes, and each
30:28 (27)	He has struck for you a similitude
30:58 (58)	We have struck for the people in this Koran every manner of similitude
36:78 (78)	he has struck for Us a similitude
39:27 (28)	We have struck for the people in this Koran every manner of similitude
39:29 (30)	God has struck a similitude — a man
43:17 (16)	when any of them is given the good tidings of that he has likened to the All-merciful, his face is darkened
43:58 (58)	they cite not him to thee, save to dispute
66:10 (10)	God has struck a similitude for the unbelievers
66:11 (11)	God has struck a similitude for the believers

b) impf. act. (*yaḍribu*)

2:26 (24)	God is not ashamed to strike a similitude even of a gnat
8:50 (52)	if thou couldst only see when the angels take the unbelievers, beating their faces and their backs
13:17 (18)	God strikes both the true and the false
13:17 (18)	even so God strikes His similitudes
14:25 (30)	so God strikes similitudes for men
16:74 (76)	so strike not any similitudes for God
24:31 (31)	let them cast their veils over their bosoms

24:31 (31)	nor let them stamp their feet, so that their hidden ornament may be known
24:35 (35)	God strikes similitudes for men
29:43 (42)	those similitudes — We strike them for the people
43:5 (4)	shall We turn away the Remembrance from you
47:3 (3)	even so God strikes their similitudes for men
47:27 (29)	how shall it be, when the angels take them, beating their faces and their backs?
59:21 (21)	those similitudes — We strike them for men
73:20 (20)	and others journeying in the land, seeking the bounty of God

c) impv. (*iḍrib*)

2:60 (57)	Strike with thy staff the rock
2:73 (68)	Smite him with part of it
4:34 (38)	banish them to their couches, and beat them
7:160 (160)	strike with thy staff the rock'
8:12 (12)	so smite above the necks
8:12 (12)	and smite every finger of them
18:32 (31)	strike for them a similitude: two men
18:45 (43)	strike for them the similitude of the present life
20:77 (79)	strike for them a dry path in the sea
26:63 (63)	strike with thy staff the sea
36:13 (12)	strike for them a similitude
38:44 (43)	take in thy hand a bundle of rushes, and strike therewith

d) perf. pass. (*ḍuriba*)

2:61 (58)	abasement and poverty were pitched upon them
3:112 (108)	abasement shall be pitched on them
3:112 (108)	and poverty shall be pitched on them
22:73 (72)	O men, a similitude is struck
43:57 (57)	when the son of Mary is cited as an example, behold
57:13 (13)	a wall shall be set up between them, having a door in the inward

f) n.vb. (*ḍarb*)

2:273 (274)	in the way of God, and are unable to journey in the land
37:93 (91)	he turned upon them smiting them with his right hand
47:4 (4)	when you meet the unbelievers, smite their necks

*Ḍ R R

ḌARRA vb. (I)~to hurt, harm, injure. (n.vb.) harm, injury, affliction, hurt; (*mā malaka li-nafsihi ḍarran walā naf'an*) which cannot hurt or profit. (pcple. act.) one who hurts, hurting

b) impf. act. (*yaḍurru*)

2:102 (96)	and they learned what hurt them, and did not profit them
3:111 (107)	they will not harm you, except a little hurt
3:120 (116)	if you are patient and godfearing, their guile will hurt you nothing
3:144 (138)	if any man should turn about on his heels, he will not harm God
3:176 (170)	they will nothing hurt God
3:177 (171)	they will nothing hurt God
4:113 (113)	they do not hurt thee in anything
5:42 (46)	if thou turnest away from them, they will hurt thee nothing
5:105 (104)	he who is astray cannot hurt you

6:71 (70)	shall we call, apart from God, on that which neither profits nor hurts us
9:39 (39)	you will not hurt Him anything, for God is powerful
10:18 (19)	they serve, apart from God, what hurts them not
10:106 (106)	do not call, apart from God, on that which neither profits nor hurts thee
11:57 (60)	you will not hurt Him anything
21:66 (67)	that which profits you nothing, neither hurts you
22:12 (12)	he calls, apart from God, upon that which hurts him not
25:55 (57)	they serve, apart from God, what neither profits them nor hurts them
26:73 (73)	do they profit you, or harm?
47:32 (34)	they will nothing hurt God

f) n.vb. (*ḍarr*)

5:76 (80)	do you serve, apart from God, that which cannot hurt or profit you?
6:17 (17)	if God visits thee with affliction none can remove it but He
7:188 (188)	I have no power to profit for myself, or hurt, but as God will
10:12 (13)	when affliction visits a man, he calls Us
10:12 (13)	when We have removed his affliction from him, he passes on
10:12 (13)	he passes on, as if he never called Us to an affliction that visited him
10:49 (50)	I have no power to profit for myself, or hurt
10:107 (107)	if God visits thee with affliction, none can remove it but He
12:88 (88)	O mighty prince, affliction has visited us
13:16 (17)	such as have no power to profit or hurt themselves
16:53 (55)	when affliction visits you it is unto Him that you groan
16:54 (56)	then, when He removes the affliction from you
17:56 (58)	they have no power to remove affliction from you
17:67 (69)	when affliction visits you upon the sea, then there go astray those on whom you call
20:89 (91)	neither had any power to hurt or profit them
21:83 (83)	behold, affliction has visited me
21:84 (84)	We answered him, and removed the affliction that was upon him
22:13 (13)	he calls upon him who is likelier to hurt him
23:75 (77)	did We have mercy on them, and remove the affliction that is upon them
25:3 (4)	and have no power to hurt or profit
30:33 (32)	when some affliction visits mankind, they call unto their Lord
34:42 (41)	today none of you shall have power to profit or hurt another
36:23 (22)	if the All-merciful desires affliction for me
39:8 (11)	when some affliction visits a man, he calls upon his Lord
39:38 (39)	if God desires affliction for me
39:38 (39)	shall they remove His affliction?
39:49 (50)	when some affliction visits a man, he calls unto Us
48:11 (11)	aught against God, if He desires hurt for you
72:21 (21)	I possess no power over you, either for hurt or for rectitude

g) pcple. act. (*ḍārr*)

2:102 (96)	they did not hurt any man thereby, save by the leave of God
58:10 (11)	he will not hurt them anything

ḌARAR n.m.~injury, hurt

4:95 (97)	such believers as sit at home — unless they have an injury — are not the equals

ḌARRĀʾ n.f.~hardship, tribulation, adversity; (frequently used together with either its synonym, *baʾsāʾ*, or antonym, *sarrāʾ*)

2:177 (172)	and endure with fortitude misfortune, hardship and peril
2:214 (210)	they were afflicted by misery and hardship

3:134 (128)	who expend in prosperity and adversity
6:42 (42)	We seized them with misery and hardship
7:94 (92)	We seized its people with misery and hardship
7:95 (93)	hardship and happiness visited our fathers
10:21 (22)	We let the people taste mercy after hardship has visited them
11:10 (13)	if We let him taste prosperity after hardship that has visited him
41:50 (50)	if We let him taste mercy from Us after hardship that has visited him

ḌĀRRA vb. (III)~to press or be pressed, to force or be forced, be made to suffer. (n.vb.) injury, hurt (using force), opposition. (pcple. act.) one who injures; one who is prejudicial

e) impf. pass. (*yuḍārru*)

2:233 (233)	a mother shall not be pressed for her child
2:282 (282)	let not either writer or witness be pressed
65:6 (6)	do not press them, so as to straiten their circumstances

f) n.vb. (*ḍirār*)

2:231 (231)	do not retain them by force, to transgress
9:107 (108)	those who have taken a mosque in opposition

g) pcple. act. (*muḍārr*)

4:12 (16)	not prejudicial; a charge from God

IḌṬARRA vb. (VIII)~to compel, to force. (pcple. pass.) one who is forced, compelled or constrained

b) impf. act. (*yaḍṭarru*)

2:126 (120)	then I shall compel him to the chastisement of the Fire
31:24 (23)	We compel them to a harsh chastisement

d) perf. pass. (*iḍṭurra*)

2:173 (168)	whoso is constrained, not desiring nor transgressing, no sin shall be on him
5:3 (5)	whosoever is constrained in emptiness
6:119 (119)	He has forbidden you, unless you are constrained to it
6:145 (146)	whoso is constrained, not desiring nor transgressing
16:115 (116)	whoso is constrained, not desiring nor transgressing

h) pcple. pass. (*muḍṭarr*)

27:62 (63)	He who answers the constrained, when he calls unto Him

*Ḍ W ʾ

ḌIYĀʾ n.m.~radiance, illumination, light

10:5 (5)	it is He who made the sun a radiance
21:48 (49)	We gave Moses and Aaron the Salvation and a Radiance
28:71 (71)	what god other than God shall bring you illumination?

AḌĀʾA vb. (IV)~to light, give light, shine, illuminate, enlighten

a) perf. act.

2:17 (16)	when it lit all about him God took away their light
2:20 (19)	whensoever it gives them light, they walk in it

b) impf. act. (*yuḍīʾu*)

24:35 (35)	whose oil wellnigh would shine, even if no fire touched it

*Ḍ Y ʿ

AḌĀʿA vb. (IV)~to waste, cause to be lost, neglect

a) perf. act.

19:59 (60)	who wasted the prayer, and followed lusts

b) impf. act. (*yuḍīʿu*)

2:143 (138)	God would never leave your faith to waste
3:171 (165)	God leaves not to waste the wage of the believers
3:195 (193)	I waste not the labour of any that labours among you
7:170 (169)	We leave not to waste the wage of those who set aright
9:120 (121)	God leaves not to waste the wage of the good-doers
11:115 (117)	God will not leave to waste the wage of the good-doers
12:56 (56)	We leave not to waste the wage of the good-doers
12:90 (90)	God leaves not to waste the wage of the good-doers
18:30 (29)	We leave not to waste the wage of him who does good works

*Ḍ Y F

ḌAYF n.m.~a guest

11:78 (80)	and do not degrade me in my guests
15:51 (51)	tell them of the guests of Abraham
15:68 (68)	these are my guests; put me not to shame
51:24 (24)	hast thou received the story of the honoured guests of Abraham?
54:37 (37)	even his guests they had solicited of him

ḌAYYAFA vb. (II)~to receive as guest (hospitably)

b) impf. act. (*yuḍayyifu*)

18:77 (76)	but they refused to receive them hospitably

*Ḍ Y Q

ḌĀQA vb. (I)~to be straitened, narrow; (*ḍāqa dharʿan*) to be distressed. (pcple. act.) that which is narrow or straitened

a) perf. act.

9:25 (25) the land for all its breadth was strait for you
9:118 (119) when the earth became strait for them
9:118 (119) and their souls became strait for them
11:77 (79) he was troubled on their account and distressed for them
29:33 (32) he was troubled on their account and distressed for them

b) impf. act. (*yaḍīqu*)

15:97 (97) We know indeed thy breast is straitened by the things they say
26:13 (12) and my breast will be straitened

g) pcple. act. (*ḍāʾiq*)

11:12 (15) thy breast is straitened by it

ḌAYQ n.m. (adj)~narrow, close, strait

6:125 (125) He makes his breast narrow, tight
16:127 (128) nor be thou straitened for what they devise
25:13 (14) when they are cast, coupled in fetters, into a narrow place
27:70 (72) nor be thou straitened for what they devise

ḌAYYAQA vb. (II)~to make narrow, to straiten (with prep. *ʿalá*)

b) impf. act. (*yuḍayyiqu*)

65:6 (6) do not press them, so as to straiten their circumstances

*Ḍ Y R

ḌĀRA vb. (I)~(n.vb.) harm, injury

f) n.vb. (*ḍayr*)

26:50 (50) There is no harm; surely unto our Lord we are turning

*Ḍ Y Z

ḌĪZÁ n.f. (adj)~unfair, unjust

53:22 (22) that were indeed an unjust division

FĀ

*F ʾ D

FUʾĀD n.m. (pl. *afʾidah*)~heart

6:110 (110)	We shall turn about their hearts and their eyes
6:113 (113)	the hearts of those who believe not in the world to come
11:120 (121)	the tidings of the Messengers is that whereby We strengthen thy heart
14:37 (40)	perform the prayer, and make hearts of men yearn towards them
14:43 (44)	their glances never returned on themselves, their hearts void
16:78 (80)	He appointed for you hearing, and sight, and hearts
17:36 (38)	the sight, the heart — all of those shall be questioned of
23:78 (80)	He who produced for you hearing, and eyes, and hearts
25:32 (34)	that We may strengthen thy heart thereby
28:10 (9)	on the morrow the heart of Moses' mother became empty
32:9 (8)	He appointed for you hearing, and sight, and hearts
46:26 (25)	We appointed for them hearing, and sight, and hearts
46:26 (25)	their sight and their hearts availed them nothing
53:11 (11)	his heart lies not of what he saw
67:23 (23)	He who produced you, and appointed for you hearing and sight and hearts
104:7 (7)	roaring over the hearts

*F ʾ W

FIʾAH n.f.~party, company, host

2:249 (250)	how often a little company has overcome a numerous (company)
2:249 (250)	how often a little (company) has overcome a numerous company
3:13 (11)	there has already been a sign for you in the two companies
3:13 (11)	one company fighting in the way of God
4:88 (90)	how is it with you, that you are two parties
8:16 (16)	unless withdrawing to fight again or removing to join another host
8:19 (19)	and your host will avail you nothing
8:45 (47)	O believers, whensoever you encounter a host, then stand firm
8:48 (50)	when the two hosts sighted each other, he withdrew upon his heels
18:43 (41)	there was no host to help him
28:81 (81)	there was no host to help him, apart from God

*F ʿ L

FAʿALA vb. (I)~to do, commit, act. (pcple. act.) one who does, is active. (pcple. pass.) done, perfomed

a) perf. act.

2:234 (234)	it is no fault in you what they may do with themselves
2:240 (241)	there is no fault in you what they may do with themselves
3:135 (129)	when they commit an indecency or wrong themselves

3:135 (129)	and do not persevere in the things they did
4:66 (69)	they would not have done it, save a few of them
4:66 (69)	yet if they had done as they were admonished
5:79 (82)	they forbade not one another any dishonour that they committed
6:112 (112)	had thy Lord willed, they would never have done it
6:137 (138)	had God willed, they would not have done so
7:28 (27)	whenever they commit an indecency they say
7:155 (154)	wilt Thou destroy us for what the foolish ones of us have done?
7:173 (172)	wilt Thou then destroy us for the deeds of the vain-doers?
10:106 (106)	for if thou dost, then thou wilt surely be of the evildoers
12:89 (89)	are you aware of what you did with Joseph and his brother
14:45 (47)	it became clear to you how We did with them
16:33 (35)	so did those before them
16:35 (37)	so did those before them
18:82 (81)	I did it not of my own bidding
21:59 (60)	who has done this with our gods?
21:62 (63)	art thou the man who did this unto our gods
21:63 (64)	it was this great one of them that did it
26:19 (18)	and thou didst the deed thou (didst)
26:19 (18)	and thou (didst) the deed thou didst
26:20 (19)	I did it then, being one of those that stray
49:6 (6)	and then repent of what you have done
54:52 (52)	every thing that they have done is in the Scrolls
89:6 (5)	hast thou not seen how thy Lord did with Ad
105:1 (1)	hast thou not seen how thy Lord did with the Men of the Elephant?

b) impf. act. (*yafʿalu*)

2:24 (22)	and if you do not — and you will not — then fear the Fire
2:24 (22)	and if you (do) not — and you will not [do] — then fear the Fire
2:71 (66)	therefore they sacrificed her, a thing they had scarcely done
2:85 (79)	what shall be the recompense of those of you who do that
2:197 (193)	whatever good you do, God knows it
2:215 (211)	whatever good you may do, God has knowledge of it
2:231 (231)	whoever does that has wronged himself
2:253 (254)	God does whatsoever He desires
2:279 (279)	but if you do not, then take notice
2:282 (282)	or if you do, that is ungodliness in you
3:28 (27)	for whoso does that belongs not to God in anything
3:40 (35)	God does what He will
3:115 (111)	and whatsoever good you do
3:188 (185)	they have brought, and love to be praised for what they have not done
4:30 (34)	whosoever does that in transgression and wrongfully
4:114 (114)	whoso does that, seeking God's good pleasure
4:127 (126)	whatever good you do, God knows of it
4:147 (146)	what would God do with chastising you
5:67 (71)	for if thou dost not, thou wilt not have delivered His Message
5:79 (82)	surely evil were the things they did
6:159 (160)	He will tell them what they have been doing
8:73 (74)	unless you do this, there will be persecution in the land
10:36 (37)	surely God knows the things they do
10:46 (47)	then God is witness of the things they do
11:36 (38)	be thou not distressed by that they may be doing
11:87 (89)	or to do as we will with our goods
12:32 (32)	yet if he will not do what I command him

14:27 (32)	and God does what He will
16:50 (52)	and they do what they are commanded
16:91 (93)	surely God knows the things you do
21:23 (23)	He shall not be questioned as to what He does
22:14 (14)	surely God does that He desires
22:18 (19)	God does whatsoever He will
24:41 (41)	God knows the things they do
25:68 (68)	whosoever does that shall meet the price of sin
26:74 (74)	we found our fathers so doing
26:226 (226)	and how they say that which they do not
27:34 (34)	even so they too will do
27:88 (90)	he is aware of the things you do
30:40 (39)	is there any of your associates does aught of that?
33:6 (6)	nevertheless you should act towards your friends honourably
37:34 (33)	even so We do with the sinners
39:70 (70)	He knows very well what they do
42:25 (24)	He knows the things you do
58:13 (14)	if you do not so, and God turns again unto
60:1 (1)	whosoever of you does that, has gone astray
61:2 (2)	wherefore do you say what you do not?
61:3 (3)	very hateful is it to God, that you say what you do not
63:9 (9)	whoso does that, they are the losers
66:6 (6)	disobey not God in what He commands them and do what they are commanded
77:18 (18)	so We serve the sinners
82:12 (12)	who know whatever you do
83:36 (36)	have the unbelievers been rewarded what they were doing?
85:7 (7)	and were themselves witnesses of what they did with the believers

c) impv. (*ifʿal*)

2:68 (63)	so do that you are bidden
22:77 (76)	and serve your Lord, and do good
37:102 (102)	my father, do as thou art bidden

d) perf. pass. (*fuʿila*)

34:54 (54)	as was done with the likes of them aforetime

e) impf. pass. (*yufʿalu*)

46:9 (8)	I know not what shall be done with me or with you
75:25 (25)	thou mightest think the Calamity has been wreaked on them

g) pcple. act. (*fāʿil*)

12:10 (10)	and some traveller will pick him out, if you do aught
12:61 (61)	we will solicit him of our father; that we will do
15:71 (71)	these are my daughters, if you would be doing
18:23 (23)	'I am going to do that tomorrow'
21:17 (17)	We would have taken it to Us from Ourselves, had We done aught
21:68 (68)	burn him, and help your gods, if you would do aught
21:79 (79)	the mountains to give glory, and the birds, and We were doers
21:104 (104)	We shall bring it back again — a promise binding on Us; so We shall do
23:4 (4)	and at almsgiving are active

h) pcple. pass. (*mafʿūl*)

4:47 (50)	God's command is done
8:42 (43)	but that God might determine a matter that was done

8:44 (46)	that God might determine a matter that was done
17:5 (5)	and it was a promise performed
17:108 (108)	glory be to our Lord! Our Lord's promise is performed
33:37 (37)	God's commandment must be performed
73:18 (18)	heaven shall be split, and its promise shall be performed

FAʿʿĀL n.m. (adj)~one who accomplishes, performer

11:107 (109)	surely thy Lord accomplishes what He desires
85:16 (16)	Performer of what He desires

FIʿL n.m. (alt. *faʿl*)~deed, action

21:73 (73)	We revealed to them the doing of good deeds
26:19 (18)	thou didst the deed thou didst

*F D Y

FADÁ vb. (I)~to ransom, redeem. (n.vb.) a ransom

a) perf. act.

37:107 (107)	We ransomed him with a mighty sacrifice

f) n.vb. (*fidāʾ*)

47:4 (5)	then set them free, either by grace or ransom

FIDYAH n.f.~ransom, redemption

2:184 (180)	who are able to fast, a redemption by feeding a poor man
2:196 (192)	then redemption by fast, or freewill offering
57:15 (14)	no ransom shall be taken from you

FĀDÁ vb. (III)~to ransom

b) impf. act. (*yufādī*)

2:85 (79)	if they come to you as captives, you ransom them

IFTADÁ vb. (VIII)~to redeem, offer for ransom

a) perf. act.

2:229 (229)	it is no fault in them for her to redeem herself
3:91 (85)	the whole earth full of gold, if he would ransom himself
10:54 (55)	he would offer it for his ransom
13:18 (18)	the like of it with it, they would offer it for their ransom
39:47 (48)	the like of it with it, they would offer it to ransom themselves

b) impf. act. (*yaftadī*)

5:36 (40)	the like of it with it, to ransom themselves
70:11 (11)	the sinner will wish that he might ransom himself from the chastisement

*F Ḍ Ḍ

FIḌḌAH n.f.~silver

3:14 (12)	women, children, heaped-up heaps of gold and silver
9:34 (34)	those who treasure up gold and silver, and do not expend them
43:33 (32)	roofs of silver to their houses, and stairs whereon to mount
76:15 (15)	there shall be passed around them vessels of silver
76:16 (16)	crystal of silver that they have measured
76:21 (21)	they are adorned with bracelets of silver

INFAḌḌA vb. (VII)~to be dispersed, separated, scattered

a) perf. act.

3:159 (153)	they would have scattered from about thee
62:11 (11)	when they see merchandise or diversion they scatter off to it

b) impf. act. (*yanfaḍḍu*)

63:7 (7)	do not expend on them that are with God's Messenger until they scatter off

*F Ḍ Ḥ

FAḌAḤA vb. (I)~to put to shame

b) impf. act. (*yafḍaḥu*)

15:68 (68)	these are my guests; put me not to shame

*F Ḍ L

FAḌL n.m.~bounty, favour, grace

2:64 (61)	but for the bounty and mercy of God towards you
2:90 (84)	grudging that God should send down of His bounty on whomsoever He will
2:105 (99)	God is of bounty abounding
2:198 (194)	it is no fault in you, that you should seek bounty from your Lord
2:237 (238)	forget not to be bountiful one towards another
2:243 (244)	truly God is bounteous to the people
2:251 (252)	but God is bounteous unto all beings
2:268 (271)	God promises you His pardon and His bounty
3:73 (66)	surely bounty is in the hand of God
3:74 (67)	God is of bounty abounding
3:152 (146)	God is bounteous to the believers
3:170 (164)	rejoicing in the bounty that God has given
3:171 (165)	joyful in blessing and bounty from God
3:174 (168)	they returned with blessing and bounty from God
3:174 (168)	God is of bounty abounding
3:180 (175)	as for those who are niggardly with the bounty God has given them
4:32 (36)	do not covet that whereby God in bounty has preferred one of you above another
4:37 (41)	and themselves conceal the bounty that God has given them

4:54 (57)	are they jealous of the people for the bounty that God has given them?
4:70 (72)	that is the bounty from God
4:73 (75)	if a bounty from God visits you
4:83 (85)	but for the bounty of God to you, and His mercy
4:113 (113)	but for God's bounty to thee and His mercy
4:113 (113)	God's bounty to thee is ever great
4:173 (172)	He will give them more, of His bounty
4:175 (174)	He will surely admit them to mercy from Him, and bounty
5:2 (2)	nor those repairing to the Holy House seeking from their Lord bounty
5:54 (59)	that is God's bounty
7:39 (37)	of them, 'You have no superiority over us, then
8:29 (29)	God is of bounty abounding
9:28 (28)	God shall surely enrich you of His bounty
9:59 (59)	God will bring us of His bounty, and His Messenger
9:74 (75)	only that God enriched them, and His Messenger, of His bounty
9:75 (76)	if He gives us of His bounty, we will make offerings
9:76 (77)	when He gave them of His bounty they were niggardly of it
10:58 (59)	in the bounty of God, and His mercy
10:60 (61)	God is bountiful to men
10:107 (107)	none can repel His bounty
11:3 (3)	He will give of His bounty
11:3 (3)	to every man of grace
11:27 (29)	we do not see you have over us any superiority
12:38 (38)	that is of God's bounty to us, and to men
16:14 (14)	that you may seek of His bounty, and so haply you will be thankful
17:12 (13)	that you may seek bounty from your Lord
17:66 (68)	that you may seek His bounty
17:87 (89)	surely His favour to thee is great
24:10 (10)	but for God's bounty to you and His mercy
24:14 (14)	but for God's bounty to you and His mercy
24:20 (20)	but for God's bounty to you and His mercy
24:21 (21)	but for God's bounty to you and His mercy
24:22 (22)	let not those of you who possess bounty and plenty
24:32 (32)	if they are poor, God will enrich them of His bounty
24:33 (33)	be abstinent till God enriches them of His bounty
24:38 (38)	and give them increase of His bounty
27:16 (16)	this is indeed the manifest bounty
27:40 (40)	he said, 'This is of my Lord's bounty'
27:73 (75)	surely thy Lord is bountiful to men
28:73 (73)	night and day, for you to repose in and seek after His bounty
30:23 (22)	and your seeking after His bounty
30:45 (44)	those who believe and do righteous deeds of His bounty
30:46 (45)	and that you may seek His bounty
33:47 (46)	there awaits them with God great bounty
34:10 (10)	We gave David bounty from Us
35:12 (13)	that you may seek of His bounty
35:30 (27)	and enrich them of His bounty
35:32 (29)	that is the great bounty
35:35 (32)	who of His bounty has made us to dwell in the abode of everlasting life
40:61 (63)	surely God is bountiful to men
42:22 (21)	that is the great bounty
42:26 (25)	He gives them increase of His bounty
44:57 (57)	a bounty from thy Lord
45:12 (11)	and that you may seek His bounty
48:29 (29)	thou seest them bowing, prostrating, seeking bounty from God

49:8 (8)	by God's favour and blessing
57:21 (21)	that is the bounty of God
57:21 (21)	God is of bounty abounding
57:29 (29)	they have no power over anything of God's bounty
57:29 (29)	and that bounty is in the hand of God
57:29 (29)	God is of bounty abounding
59:8 (8)	expelled from their habitations and their possessions, seeking bounty from God
62:4 (4)	that is the bounty of God
62:4 (4)	God is of bounty abounding
62:10 (10)	and seek God's bounty, and remember God frequently
73:20 (20)	and others journeying in the land, seeking the bounty of God

FAḌḌALA vb. (II)~to favour, prefer. (n.vb.) preferment; excellence

a) perf. act.

2:47 (44)	I have preferred you above all beings
2:122 (116)	I have preferred you above all beings
2:253 (254)	some We have preferred above others
4:32 (36)	do not covet that whereby God in bounty has preferred one
4:34 (38)	for that God has preferred in bounty one of them over another
4:95 (97)	God has preferred in rank those who struggle
4:95 (97)	God has preferred those who struggle over the ones who sit
6:86 (86)	each one We preferred above all beings
7:140 (136)	other than God, who has preferred you above all beings
16:71 (73)	God has preferred some of you over others
17:21 (22)	behold, how We prefer some of them over others
17:55 (57)	We have preferred some Prophets over others
17:70 (72)	and preferred them greatly over many of those We created
27:15 (15)	praise belongs to God who has preferred us over many
45:16 (15)	and We preferred them above all beings

b) impf. act. (*yufaḍḍilu*)

13:4 (4)	some of them We prefer in produce above others

d) perf. pass. (*fuḍḍila*)

16:71 (73)	those that were preferred shall not give over their provision

f) n.vb. (*tafḍīl*)

17:21 (22)	surely the world to come is greater in ranks, greater in preferment
17:70 (72)	and preferred them <greatly> over many of those We created

TAFAḌḌALA vb. (V)~to gain superiority

b) impf. act. (*yatafaḍḍalu*)

23:24 (24)	a mortal like yourselves, who desires to gain superiority over you

*F Ḍ Y

AFḌÁ vb. (IV)~to be privy with

a) perf. act.

4:21 (25) how shall you take it, when each of you has been privily with the other

*F H M

FAHHAMA vb. (II)~to cause to understand

a) perf. act.

21:79 (79) and We made Solomon to understand it

*F Ḥ SH

FĀḤISHAH n.f. (pl. *fawāḥish*; see also *faḥshā'*)~indecency, iniquity, abomination, scandalous act

3:135 (129) who, when they commit an indecency or wrong themselves, remember God
4:15 (19) such of your women as commit indecency
4:19 (23) except when they commit a flagrant indecency
4:22 (26) surely that is indecent and hateful
4:25 (30) when they are in wedlock, if they commit indecency
6:151 (152) and that you approach not any indecency outward or inward
7:28 (27) and whenever they commit an indecency they say
7:33 (31) My Lord has only forbidden indecencies, the inward and the outward
7:80 (78) what, do you commit such indecency
17:32 (34) approach not fornication; surely it is an indecency
24:19 (18) those who love that indecency should be spread abroad
27:54 (55) do you commit indecency with your eyes open?
29:28 (27) surely you commit such indecency
33:30 (30) Wives of the Prophet, whosoever among you commits a flagrant indecency
42:37 (35) those who avoid the heinous sins and indecencies
53:32 (33) those who avoid the heinous sins and indecencies
65:1 (1) except when they commit a flagrant indecency

FAḤSHĀ' n.f. (see also *fāḥishah*)~indecency, abomination, etc.

2:169 (164) He only commands you to evil and indecency
2:268 (271) Satan promises you poverty, and bids you unto indecency
7:28 (27) say: 'God does not command indecency'
12:24 (24) that We might turn away from him evil and abomination
16:90 (92) He forbids indecency, dishonour, and insolence
24:21 (21) assuredly he bids to indecency and dishonour
29:45 (44) prayer forbids indecency and dishonour

*F J J

FAJJ n.m. (pl. *fijāj*)~ravine

21:31 (32) We set in it ravines to serve as ways
22:27 (28) upon every lean beast, they shall come from every deep ravine
71:20 (19) that thereof you may thread ways, ravines

*F J R

FAJARA (1) vb. (I)~to act wickedly, be a libertine. (n.vb.) wickedness, lewdness. (pcple. act.) wicked, transgressor, libertine

b) impf. act. (*yafjuru*)

75:5 (5)	man desires to continue on as a libertine

f) n.vb. (*fujūr*)

91:8 (8)	and inspired it to lewdness and godfearing

g) pcple. act. (*fājir*, pl. *fajarah* or *fujjār*)

38:28 (27)	shall We make the godfearing as the transgressors?
71:27 (28)	will beget none but unbelieving libertines
80:42 (42)	those — they are the unbelievers, the libertines
82:14 (14)	and the libertines shall be in a fiery furnace
83:7 (7)	no indeed; the Book of the libertines is in Sijjin

FAJARA (2) vb. (I)~to gush forth

b) impf. act. (*yafjuru*)

17:90 (92)	thou makest a spring to gush forth from the earth for us

FAJR n.m.~dawn

2:187 (183)	until the white thread shows clearly to you from the black thread at the dawn
17:78 (80)	to the darkening of the night and the recital of dawn
17:78 (80)	surely the recital of dawn is witnessed
24:58 (57)	ask leave of you three times — before the prayer of dawn
89:1 (1)	by the dawn
97:5 (5)	peace it is, till the rising of dawn

FAJJARA vb. (II)~to cause to gush forth. (n.vb.) the act of causing to gush forth

a) perf. act.

18:33 (32)	and We caused to gush amidst them a river
36:34 (34)	and therein We caused fountains to gush forth
54:12 (12)	and made the earth to gush with fountains

b) impf. act. (*yufajjiru*)

17:91 (93)	thou makest rivers to gush forth abundantly
76:6 (6)	making it to gush forth plenteously

d) perf. pass. (*fujjira*)

2:3 (3)	when the seas swarm over

f) n.vb. (*tafjīr*)

17:91 (93)	thou makest rivers to gush forth <abundantly>
76:6 (6)	making it to gush forth <plenteously>

TAFAJJARA vb. (V)~to flow, to gush forth

b) impf. act. (*yatafajjaru*)

2:74 (69) there are stones from which rivers come gushing

INFAJARA vb. (VII)~to gush forth, to flow

a) perf. act.

2:60 (57) there gushed forth from it twelve fountains

*F J W

FAJWAH n.f.~a fissure

18:17 (16) while they were in a broad fissure of the Cave

*F K H

FAKIHA vb. (I)~(pcple. act.) one who is joyful, rejoicing

g) pcple. act. (*fākih*)

36:55 (55) the inhabitants of Paradise today are busy in their rejoicing
44:27 (26) and what prosperity they had rejoiced in
52:18 (18) rejoicing in that their Lord has given them

FAKIH n.m.~a jester, one who acts blithely

83:31 (31) when they returned to their people they returned blithely

FĀKIHAH n.f. (pl. *fawākih*)~fruit(s)

23:19 (19) gardens of palms and vines wherein are many fruits
36:57 (57) therein they have fruits, and they have all that they call for
37:42 (41) fruits — and they high-honoured
38:51 (51) they call for fruits abundant
43:73 (73) therein you have abundant fruits, whereof you may eat
44:55 (55) therein calling for every fruit, secure
52:22 (22) We shall succour them with fruits and flesh
55:11 (10) therein fruits, and palm-trees with sheaths
55:52 (52) therein of every fruit two kinds
55:68 (68) therein fruits, and palm-trees, and pomegranates
56:20 (20) and such fruits as they shall choose
56:32 (31) and fruits abounding
77:42 (42) and such fruits as their hearts desire
80:31 (31) and fruits, and pastures

TAFAKKAHA vb. (V)~to exclaim, wonder; jest

b) impf. act. (*yatafakkahu*)

56:65 (65) and you would remain bitterly jesting

*F K K

FAKKA vb. (I)~(n.vb.) setting free

f) n.vb. (*fakk*)

90:13 (13)	the freeing of a slave

INFAKKA vb. (VII)~(pcple. act.) one who leaves off

g) pcple. act. (*munfakk*)

98:1 (1)	the idolaters would never leave off

*F K R

FAKKARA vb. (II)~to reflect

a) perf. act.

74:18 (18)	Lo! He reflected, and determined

TAFAKKARA vb. (V)~to reflect

b) impf. act. (*yatafakkaru*)

2:219 (217)	God makes clear His signs to you; haply you will reflect
2:266 (268)	God makes clear the signs to you; haply you will reflect
3:191 (188)	and reflect upon the creation of the heavens and the earth
6:50 (50)	are the blind and the seeing man equal? Will you not reflect?
7:176 (175)	so relate the story; haply they will reflect
7:184 (183)	have they not reflected?
10:24 (25)	We distinguish the signs for a people who reflect
13:3 (3)	surely in that are signs for a people who reflect
16:11 (11)	surely in that is a sign for a people who reflect
16:44 (46)	what was sent down to them; and so haply they will reflect
16:69 (71)	surely in that is a sign for a people who reflect
30:8 (7)	what, have they not considered within themselves?
30:21 (20)	surely in that are signs for a people who consider
34:46 (45)	stand unto God, two by two and one by one, and then reflect
39:42 (43)	surely in that are signs for a people who reflect
45:13 (12)	surely in that are signs for a people who reflect
59:21 (21)	We strike them for men; haply they will reflect

*F KH R

FAKHKHĀR n.m.~earthenware, potter's clay

55:14 (13)	He created man of a clay like the potter's

FAKHŪR n.m. (adj)~boastful

4:36 (40)	God loves not the proud and boastful
11:10 (13)	behold, he is joyous, boastful
31:18 (17)	God loves not any man proud and boastful
57:23 (23)	God loves not any man proud and boastful

TAFĀKHARA vb. (VI)~(n.vb.) mutual boasting

f) n.vb. (*tafākhur*)

57:20 (19)	and a cause for boasting among you

*F L Ḥ

AFLAḤA vb. (IV)~to prosper, to gain the upper hand. (pcple. act.) one who prospers, a prosperer

a) perf. act.

20:64 (67)	whoever today gains the upper hand shall surely prosper
23:1 (1)	prosperous are the believers
87:14 (14)	prosperous is he who has cleansed himself
91:9 (9)	prosperous is he who purifies it

b) impf. act. (*yufliḥu*)

2:189 (185)	come to the houses by their doors, and fear God; haply so you will prosper
3:130 (125)	and fear you God; haply so you will prosper
3:200 (200)	be steadfast; fear God; haply so you will prosper
5:35 (39)	and struggle in His way; haply you will prosper
5:90 (92)	some of Satan's work; so avoid it; haply so you will prosper
5:100 (100)	fear God, O men possessed of minds; haply so you will prosper
6:21 (21)	they shall not prosper, the evildoers
6:135 (136)	surely the evildoers will not prosper
7:69 (67)	remember God's bounties; haply you will prosper
8:45 (47)	remember God frequently; haply so you will prosper
10:17 (18)	surely the sinners do not prosper
10:69 (70)	those who forge against God falsehood shall not prosper
10:77 (78)	is this a sorcery? But sorcerers do not prosper
12:23 (23)	surely the evildoers do not prosper
16:116 (117)	those who forge against God falsehood shall not prosper
18:20 (19)	or restore you to their creed, then you will not prosper ever
20:69 (72)	the sorcerer prospers not, wherever he goes
22:77 (76)	and do good; haply so you shall prosper
23:117 (117)	surely the unbelievers shall not prosper
24:31 (31)	turn all together to God, O you believers; haply so you will prosper
28:37 (37)	surely the evildoers will not prosper
28:82 (82)	the unbelievers do not prosper
62:10 (10)	and remember God frequently; haply you will prosper

g) pcple. act. (*mufliḥ*)

2:5 (4)	those are upon guidance from their Lord, those are the ones who prosper
3:104 (100)	bidding to honour, and forbidding dishonour; those are the prosperers
7:8 (7)	he whose scales are heavy — they are the prosperers

7:157 (156)	they are the prosperers
9:88 (89)	for them await the good things; those — they are the prosperers
23:102 (104)	he whose scales are heavy — they are the prosperers
24:51 (50)	those — they are the prosperers
28:67 (67)	haply he shall be among the prosperers
30:38 (37)	those who desire God's Face; those — they are the prosperers
31:5 (4)	those are upon guidance from their Lord; those are the prosperers
58:22 (22)	why, surely God's party — they are the prosperers
59:9 (9)	those — they are the prosperers
64:16 (16)	those — they are the prosperers

*F L K

FALAK n.m.~orbit, a sky

21:33 (34)	the sun and the moon, each swimming in a sky
36:40 (40)	does the night outstrip the day, each swimming in a sky

FULK n.com.~ship(s); Ark

2:164 (159)	the ship that runs in the sea with profit to men
7:64 (62)	so We delivered him, and those with him, in the Ark
10:22 (23)	He who conveys you on the land and the sea; and when you are in the ship
10:73 (74)	We delivered him, and those with him, in the Ark
11:37 (39)	make thou the Ark under Our eyes
11:38 (40)	so he was making the Ark
14:32 (37)	He subjected to you the ships to run upon the sea
16:14 (14)	and thou mayest see the ships cleaving through it
17:66 (68)	your Lord it is who drives for you the ships on the sea
22:65 (64)	and the ships to run upon the sea at His commandment
23:22 (22)	and upon them, and on the ships, you are borne
23:27 (27)	then We said to him, 'Make thou the Ark'
23:28 (29)	then, when thou art seated in the Ark
26:119 (119)	We delivered him, and those with him, in the laden ship
29:65 (65)	when they embark in the ships, they call on God
30:46 (45)	and that the ships may run at His commandment
31:31 (30)	hast thou not seen how that the ships run upon the sea
35:12 (13)	and thou mayest see the ships cleaving through it
36:41 (41)	a sign for them is that We carried their seed in the laden ship
37:140 (140)	when he ran away to the laden ship
40:80 (80)	and upon them and on the ships you are carried
43:12 (11)	and appointed for you ships and cattle such as you ride
45:12 (11)	God is He who has subjected to you the sea, that the ships may run on it

*F L N

FULĀN n.m.~so-and-so (reference to a nameless person)

25:28 (30)	would that I had not taken So-and-so for a friend

*F L Q

FALAQA vb. (I)~(pcple. act.) one who splits or causes to break forth

g) pcple. act. (*fāliq*)

6:95 (95) it is God who splits the grain and the date-stone
6:96 (96) He splits the sky into dawn

FALAQ n.m.~daybreak

113:1 (1) say: 'I take refuge with the Lord of the Daybreak'

INFALAQA vb. (VII)~to be split open, divided, to cleave

a) perf. act.

26:63 (63) it clave, and each part was as a mighty mount

*F N D

FANNADA vb. (II)~to regard as a dotard, to make a dotard of

b) impf. act. (*yufannidu*)

12:94 (94) I perceive Joseph's scent, unless you think me doting

*F N N

AFNĀN n.m. (pl. of *fanan* or *fann*)~(*fanan*) a branch; (*fann*) a species

55:48 (48) abounding in branches

*F N Y

FANÁ vb. (I)~(pcple. act.) one who perishes, perishing

g) pcple. act. (*fānī*)

55:26 (26) all that dwells upon the earth is perishing

*F Q ᶜ

FAQAᶜA vb. (I)~(pcple. act.) that which is bright in colour

g) pcple. act. (*fāqiᶜ*)

2:69 (64) she shall be a golden cow, bright her colour

*F Q D

FAQADA vb. (I)~to miss something, to look for something missing

b) impf. act. (*yafqidu*)

12:71 (71)	what is it that you are missing?
12:72 (72)	we are missing the king's goblet

TAFAQQADA vb. (V)~to make an inquisition into, to review

a) perf. act.

27:20 (20)	and he reviewed the birds; then he said

*F Q H

FAQIHA vb. (I)~to understand

b) impf. act. (*yafqahu*)

4:78 (80)	how is it with this people? They scarcely understand any tiding
6:25 (25)	We lay veils upon their hearts lest they understand it
6:65 (65)	behold how We turn about the signs; haply they will understand
6:98 (98)	We have distinguished the signs for a people who understand
7:179 (178)	they have hearts, but understand not with them
8:65 (66)	they are a people who understand not
9:81 (82)	Gehenna's fire is hotter, did they but understand
9:87 (88)	a seal has been set upon their hearts, so they understand not
9:127 (128)	for that they are a people who do not understand
11:91 (93)	Shuaib, we do not understand much of what thou sayest
17:44 (46)	you do not understand their extolling
17:46 (48)	We lay veils upon their hearts lest they understand it
18:57 (55)	We have laid veils on their hearts lest they understand it
18:93 (92)	he found this side of them a people scarcely able to understand speech
20:28 (29)	that they may understand my words
48:15 (15)	they have not understood except a little
59:13 (13)	that is because they are a people who understand not
63:3 (3)	a seal has been set on their hearts, and they do not understand
63:7 (7)	the hypocrites do not understand

TAFAQQAHA vb. (V)~to become learned

b) impf. act. (*yatafaqqahu*)

9:122 (123)	why should not a party of every section of them go forth, to become learned in religion

*F Q R

FAQARA vb. (I)~(n.vb.) poverty

f) n.vb. (*faqr*)

2:268 (271) Satan promises you poverty

FAQĪR n.m. (pl. *fuqarā'*)~the poor, the needy

2:271 (273) if you conceal them, and give them to the poor, that is better for you
2:273 (274) the poor who are restrained in the way of God
3:181 (177) surely God is poor, and we are rich'
4:6 (6) if poor, let him consume in reason
4:135 (134) whether the man be rich or poor; God stands closest to either
9:60 (60) the freewill offerings are for the poor and needy
22:28 (29) so eat thereof, and feed the wretched poor
24:32 (32) if they are poor, God will enrich them of His bounty
28:24 (24) I have need of whatever good Thou shalt have sent down upon me
35:15 (16) O men, you are the ones that have need of God
47:38 (40) you are the needy ones
59:8 (8) it is for the poor emigrants, who were expelled

FĀQIRAH n.f.~a calamity

75:25 (25) thou mightest think the Calamity has been wreaked on them

*F R ᶜ

FARᶜ n.m.~a branch or top of a tree

14:24 (29) its roots are firm, and its branches are in heaven

*F R ᶜ N

FIRᶜAWN n.prop.~Pharaoh

2:49 (46) when We delivered you from the folk of Pharaoh
2:50 (47) and delivered you, and drowned Pharaoh's folk
3:11 (9) like Pharaoh's folk, and the people before them
7:103 (101) We sent, after them, Moses with Our signs to Pharaoh
7:104 (102) Pharaoh, I am a Messenger from the Lord of all Being
7:109 (106) said the Council of the people of Pharaoh
7:113 (110) the sorcerers came to Pharaoh, saying
7:123 (120) said Pharaoh, 'You have believed in Him'
7:127 (124) then said the Council of the people of Pharaoh
7:130 (127) then seized We Pharaoh's people with years of dearth
7:137 (133) We destroyed utterly the works of Pharaoh and his people
7:141 (137) when We delivered you from the folk of Pharaoh
8:52 (54) like Pharaoh's folk, and the people before him
8:54 (56) like Pharaoh's folk, and the people before him
8:54 (56) and We drowned the folk of Pharaoh
10:75 (76) We sent forth, after them, Moses and Aaron to Pharaoh
10:79 (80) Pharaoh said, 'Bring me every cunning sorcerer'
10:83 (83) for fear of Pharaoh and their Council
10:83 (83) Pharaoh was high in the land, and he was one of the prodigals
10:88 (88) Thou hast given to Pharaoh and his Council adornment
10:90 (90) Pharaoh and his hosts followed them insolently and impetuously

11:97 (99)	to Pharaoh and his Council
11:97 (99)	they followed Pharaoh's command
11:97 (99)	and Pharaoh's command was not right-minded
14:6 (6)	when He delivered you from the folk of Pharaoh
17:101 (103)	Pharaoh said to him, 'Moses, I think thou art bewitched'
17:102 (104)	and, Pharaoh, I think thou art accursed
20:24 (25)	go to Pharaoh; he has waxed insolent
20:43 (45)	go to Pharaoh, for he has waxed insolent
20:60 (62)	Pharaoh then withdrew, and gathered his guile
20:78 (81)	Pharaoh followed them with his hosts
20:79 (81)	so Pharaoh had led his people astray
23:46 (48)	unto Pharaoh and his Council; but they waxed proud
26:11 (10)	the people of Pharaoh; will they not be godfearing?
26:16 (15)	so go you to Pharaoh, and say
26:23 (22)	Pharaoh said, 'And what is the Lord of all Being?'
26:41 (40)	then, when the sorcerers came, they said to Pharaoh
26:44 (43)	by the might of Pharaoh we shall be the victors
26:53 (53)	then Pharaoh sent among the cities musterers
27:12 (12)	among nine signs to Pharaoh and his people
28:3 (2)	We will recite to thee something of the tiding of Moses and Pharaoh
28:4 (3)	now Pharaoh had exalted himself in the land
28:6 (5)	to show Pharaoh and Haman, and their hosts
28:8 (7)	so then the folk of Pharaoh picked him out
28:8 (7)	Pharaoh and Haman, and their hosts, were of the sinners
28:9 (8)	said Pharaoh's wife, 'He will be a comfort'
28:32 (32)	two proofs from thy Lord to Pharaoh and his Council
28:38 (38)	and Pharaoh said, 'Council, I know not that you ...'
29:39 (38)	and Korah, and Pharaoh, and Haman
38:12 (11)	the people of Noah, and Ad, and Pharaoh
40:24 (25)	to Pharaoh, Haman and Korah; they said
40:26 (27)	and Pharaoh said, 'Let me slay Moses'
40:28 (29)	then said a certain man, a believer of Pharaoh's folk
40:29 (30)	said Pharaoh, 'I only let you see'
40:36 (38)	Pharaoh said, 'Haman, build for me a tower'
40:37 (40)	the evil of his deeds was decked out fair to Pharaoh
40:37 (40)	Pharaoh's guile came only to ruin
40:45 (48)	and there encompassed the folk of Pharaoh the evil
40:46 (49)	when the Hour is come: Admit the folk of Pharaoh
43:46 (45)	We also sent Moses with Our signs to Pharaoh
43:51 (50)	and Pharaoh proclaimed among his people
44:17 (16)	already before them We tried the people of Pharaoh
44:31 (30)	from Pharaoh; surely he was a high one
50:13 (13)	and Ad and Pharaoh, the brothers of Lot
51:38 (38)	and also in Moses, when We sent him unto Pharaoh
54:41 (41)	the warnings came also to Pharaoh's folk
66:11 (11)	the wife of Pharaoh, when she said
66:11 (11)	deliver me from Pharaoh and his work
69:9 (9)	Pharaoh likewise, and those before him
73:15 (15)	even as We sent to Pharaoh a Messenger
73:16 (16)	but Pharaoh rebelled against the Messenger
79:17 (17)	go to Pharaoh; he has waxed insolent
85:18 (18)	Pharaoh and Thamood
89:10 (9)	and Pharaoh, he of the tent-pegs

*F R D

FARD n.m. (pl. *furādá*)~alone, solitary; (pl) one by one

6:94 (94)	you have come to Us one by one, as We created you
19:80 (83)	and he shall come to Us alone
19:95 (95)	every one of them shall come to Him upon the Day of Resurrection, all alone
21:89 (89)	O my Lord, leave me not solitary
34:46 (45)	that you stand unto God, two by two and one by one

*F R D S

FIRDAWS n.m.~Paradise

18:107 (107)	the Gardens of Paradise shall be their hospitality
23:11 (11)	who shall inherit Paradise therein dwelling forever

*F R Ḍ

FARAḌA vb. (I)~to appoint, impose, ordain, undertake a duty. (pcple. pass.) that which is apportioned or appointed

a) perf. act.

2:197 (193)	whoso undertakes the duty of Pilgrimage
2:237 (238)	you have already appointed for them a marriage-portion
2:237 (238)	for them a marriage-portion, then one-half of what you have appointed
24:1 (1)	a sura that We have sent down and appointed
28:85 (85)	He who imposed the Recitation upon thee
33:38 (38)	there is no fault in the Prophet, touching what God has ordained for him
33:50 (50)	We know what We have imposed upon them
66:2 (2)	God has ordained for you the absolution of your oaths

b) impf. act. (*yafriḍu*)

2:236 (237)	as yet you have not touched them nor appointed any marriage-portion

h) pcple. pass. (*mafrūḍ*)

4:7 (8)	whether it be little or much, a share apportioned
4:118 (118)	I will take unto myself a portion appointed of Thy servants

FĀRIḌ n.f.~old cow

2:68 (63)	he says she is a cow neither old, nor virgin

FARĪḌAH n.f.~an ordinance, a settled portion; dowry, marriage-portion

2:236 (237)	nor appointed any marriage-portion for them
2:237 (238)	and you have already appointed for them a marriage-portion
4:11 (12)	so God apportions; surely God is All-knowing
4:24 (28)	such wives as you enjoy thereby, give them their wages apportionate
4:24 (28)	after the due apportionate
9:60 (60)	God's way, and the traveller; so God ordains

*F R GH

FARAGHA vb. (I)~to become empty; (with prep. *li-*) to dispose of, attend to at leisure. (pcple. act.) empty

a) perf. act.

94:7 (7)	so when thou art empty, labour

b) impf. act. (*yafrughu*)

55:31 (31)	We shall surely attend to you at leisure

g) pcple. act. (*fārigh*)

28:10 (9)	on the morrow the heart of Moses' mother became empty

AFRAGHA vb. (IV)~to pour out

b) impf. act. (*yufrighu*)

18:96 (95)	bring me, that I may pour molten brass on it

c) impv. (*afrigh*)

2:250 (251)	our Lord, pour out upon us patience
7:126 (123)	our Lord, pour out upon us patience

*F R H

FARIHA vb. (I)~(pcple. act.) one who is skilful, clever, insolent

g) pcple. act. (*fārih*)

26:149 (149)	will you still skilfully hew houses out of the mountains?

*F R Ḥ

FARIḤA vb. (I)~to rejoice, to be glad, joyful

a) perf. act.

6:44 (44)	when they rejoiced in what they were given, We seized them
9:81 (82)	those who were left behind rejoiced in tarrying
10:22 (23)	and they rejoice in it
13:26 (26)	they rejoice in this present life
30:36 (35)	when We let men taste mercy, they rejoice in it
40:83 (83)	they rejoiced in what knowledge they had
42:48 (47)	when We let man taste mercy from Us, he rejoices in it

b) impf. act. (*yafraḥu*)

3:120 (116)	but if you are smitten by evil, they rejoice at it
3:188 (185)	those who rejoice in what they have brought

10:58 (59)	in the bounty of God, and His mercy — in that let them rejoice
13:36 (36)	rejoice in what is sent down unto thee
27:36 (36)	nay, but instead you rejoice in your gift
28:76 (76)	do not exult; God loves not those that exult
30:4 (3)	on that day the believers shall rejoice
40:75 (75)	that is because you rejoiced in the earth without right
57:23 (23)	nor rejoice in what He has come to you

FARIḤ n.m. (adj)~joyful, rejoicing, one who exults

3:170 (164)	rejoicing in the bounty that God has given
9:50 (50)	[they] turn away, rejoicing
11:10 (13)	behold, he is joyous, boastful
23:53 (55)	each party rejoicing in what is with them
28:76 (76)	God loves not those that exult
30:32(31)	each several party rejoicing in what is theirs

*F R J

FARAJA vb. (I)~to split, cleave asunder

d) perf. pass. (*furija*)

77:9 (9)	when heaven shall be split

FARJ n.m. (pl. *furūj*)~opening, gap; the private parts (of males or females)

21:91 (91)	and she who guarded her virginity
23:5 (5)	and guard their private parts
24:30 (30)	that they cast down their eyes and guard their private parts
24:31 (31)	and guard their private parts, and reveal not their adornment
33:35 (35)	men and women who guard their private parts
50:6 (6)	and it has no cracks
66:12 (12)	Mary, Imran's daughter, who guarded her virginity
70:29 (29)	and guard their private parts

*F R Q

FARAQA vb. (I)~to split, divide, sever, separate; to determine, make clear, distinguish. (n.vb.) the act of severing, distinguishing, separating. (pcple. act.) severing; ones who sever, split, separate, etc.; ones who winnow; (there are several interpretations of 77:4)

a) perf. act.

2:50 (47)	and when We divided for you the sea
17:106 (107)	and a Koran We have divided, for thee to recite it

c) impv. (*ufruq*)

5:25 (28)	divide between us and the people of the ungodly

e) impf. pass. (*yufraqu*)

44:4 (3)	therein every wise bidding determined

f) n.vb. (*farq*)

77:4 (4)	and the <severally> severing

g) pcple. act. f. pl. (*fāriqāt*)

77:4 (4)	and the severally severing

FARIQA vb. (I)~to be afraid

b) impf. act. (*yafraqu*)

9:56 (56)	they are a people that are afraid

FARĪQ n.m.~a group or party of people, section or sect, some

2:75 (70)	seeing there is a party of them that heard
2:85 (79)	killing one another, and expelling a party of you
2:87 (81)	and some cry lies to, and (some) slay
2:87 (81)	and (some) cry lies to, and some slay
2:100 (94)	whensoever they have made a covenant, does a party of them reject it?
2:101 (95)	a party of them that were given the Book reject the Book
2:146 (141)	there is a party of them conceal the truth
2:188 (184)	that you may sinfully consume a portion of other men's goods
3:23 (22)	then a party of them turned away, swerving aside
3:78 (72)	and there is a sect of them twist their tongues
3:100 (95)	if you obey a sect of those who have been given the Book
4:77 (79)	there is a party of them fearing the people as they would
5:70 (74)	some they cried lies to
5:70 (74)	and some they slew
6:81 (81)	which of the two parties has better title to security
7:30 (28)	a part He guided
7:30 (28)	and a part justly disposed to error
8:5 (5)	a part of the believers were averse to it
9:117 (118)	after the hearts of a part of them wellnigh swerved aside
11:24 (26)	the likeness of the two parties is as the man blind and deaf
16:54 (56)	a party of you assign associates to their Lord
19:73 (74)	which of the two parties is better in station
23:109 (111)	there is a party of My servants who said
24:47 (46)	then after that a party of them turn away
24:48 (47)	lo, a party of them are swerving aside
27:45 (46)	and behold, they were two parties
30:33 (32)	a party of them assign associates to their Lord
33:13 (13)	and when a party of them said
33:26 (26)	some you slew
33:26 (26)	some you made captive
34:20 (19)	they followed him, except a party of the believers
42:7 (5)	wherein is no doubt — a party in Paradise
42:7 (5)	and a party in the Blaze

FIRQ n.m.~a separate part, heap, hillock

26:63 (63)	and it clave, and each part was as a mighty mount

FIRQAH n.f.~a group, band or section of people

9:122 (123)	why should not a party of every section of them go forth

FURQĀN n.m.~Salvation [Ar, Bl]; Judgment [Ali]; Distinction, Criterion (between right and wrong) [Pk]

2:53 (50)	when We gave to Moses the Book and the Salvation
2:185 (181)	as clear signs of the Guidance and the Salvation

3:4 (2)	and He sent down the Salvation
8:29 (29)	if you fear God, He will assign you a salvation
8:41 (42)	sent down upon Our servant on the day of salvation
21:48 (49)	We gave Moses and Aaron the Salvation
25:1 (1)	blessed be He who has sent down the Salvation

FARRAQA vb. (II)~to divide and separate. (n.vb.) the act of dividing and separating

a) perf. act.

6:159 (160)	those who have made divisions in their religion
20:94 (95)	Thou hast divided the Children of Israel
30:32 (31)	even of those who have divided up their religion

b) impf. act. (*yufarriqu*)

2:102 (96)	from them they learned how they might divide a man and his wife
2:136 (130)	we make no division between any of them
2:285 (285)	we make no division between any one of His Messengers
3:84 (78)	we make no division between any of them
4:150 (149)	and desire to make division between God and His Messengers
4:152 (151)	and make no division between any of them

f) n.vb. (*tafrīq*)

9:107 (108)	those who have taken a mosque in opposition and unbelief, and to divide the believers

FĀRAQA vb. (III)~to part from, leave. (n.vb.) departure, parting

c) impv. (*fāriq*)

65:2 (2)	retain them honourably, or part from them honourably

f) n.vb. (*firāq*)

18:78 (77)	this is the parting between me and thee
75:28 (28)	and he thinks that it is the parting

TAFARRAQA vb. (V)~to scatter, separate, be divided, split up. (pcple. act.) ones at variance, separate

a) perf. act.

3:105 (101)	be not as those who scattered and fell into variance
42:14 (13)	they scattered not, save after knowledge had come to them
98:4 (3)	they scattered not, those that were given the Book

b) impf. act. (*yatafarraqu*)

3:103 (98)	hold you fast to God's bond, together, and do not scatter
4:130 (129)	if they separate, God will enrich each of them
6:153 (154)	follow not diverse paths lest they scatter you from His path
30:14 (13)	the day when the Hour is come, that day they shall be divided
42:13 (11)	perform the religion, and scatter not regarding it

g) pcple. act. (*mutafarriq*)

12:39 (39) many lords at variance, or God the One, the Omnipotent
12:67 (67) enter not by one door; enter by separate doors

*F R R

FARRA vb. (I)~to flee. (n.vb.) flight, the act of fleeing

a) perf. act.

26:21 (20) so I fled from you, fearing you
33:16 (16) flight will not profit you, if you flee from death or slaying
74:51 (51) fleeing before a lion

b) impf. act. (*yafirru*)

62:8 (8) death, from which you flee, shall encounter you
80:34 (34) upon the day when a man shall flee from his brother

c) impv. (*firr*)

51:50 (50) therefore flee unto God

f) n.vb. (*firār*)

18:18 (17) thou wouldst have turned thy back on them in flight
33:13 (13) yet they were not exposed; they desired only to flee
33:16 (16) say: 'Flight will not profit you'
71:6 (5) my calling has only increased them in flight

MAFARR n.m.~a place whither to flee

75:10 (10) upon that day man shall say, 'Whither to flee?'

*F R SH

FARASHA vb. (I)~to spread forth. (n.vb.) slaughter

a) perf. act.

51:48 (48) and the earth — We spread it forth

f) n.vb. (*farsh*)

6:142 (143) and of the cattle, for burthen and for slaughter

FARĀSH n.m.~moth

101:4 (3) the day that men shall be like scattered moths

FIRĀSH n.m. (pl. *furush*)~couch, carpet, a resting place

2:22 (20) who assigned to you the earth for a couch
55:54 (54) reclining upon couches lined with brocade
56:34 (33) and upraised couches

*F R T

FURĀT n.m. (adj)~sweet (water)

25:53 (55)	He who let forth the two seas, this one sweet
35:12 (13)	not equal are the two seas; this is sweet
77:27 (27)	sated you with sweetest water

*F R TH

FARTH n.m.~filth, foeces

16:66 (68)	between filth and blood, pure milk, sweet to drinkers

*F R Ṭ

FARAṬA vb. (I)~to exceed against (with prep. ʿ*alá*)

b) impf. act. (*yafruṭu*)

20:45 (47)	truly we fear he may exceed against us

FURUṬ n.m. (adv)~all excess, in advance of

18:28 (27)	his affair has become all excess

FARRAṬA vb. (II)~to neglect, fail regarding someone or something

a) perf. act.

6:31 (31)	alas for us, that we neglected it
6:38 (38)	We have neglected nothing in the Book
12:80 (80)	and aforetime you failed regarding Joseph
39:56 (57)	alas for me, in that I neglected my duty to God

b) impf. act. (*yufarriṭu*)

6:61 (61)	Our Messengers take him and they neglect not

AFRAṬA vb. (IV)~(pcple. pass.) made to hasten

h) pcple. pass. (*mufraṭ*)

16:62 (64)	theirs shall be the Fire, and they are hastened in

*F R Y

FARĪY n.m. (adj)~monstrous, amazing, strange

19:27 (28)	thou hast surely committed a monstrous thing

IFTARÁ vb. (VIII)~to feign, invent, forge. (n.vb.) the act of feigning, inventing or forging. (pcple. act.) one who feigns, invents or forges. (pcple. pass.) forged

a) perf. act.

3:94 (88)	whoso forges falsehood against God
4:48 (51)	whoso associates with God anything, has indeed forged a mighty sin
6:21 (21)	who does greater evil than he who forges against God a lie
6:93 (93)	who does greater evil than he who forges against God a lie
6:144 (145)	who does greater evil than he who forges against God a lie
7:37 (35)	who does greater evil than he who forges against God a lie
7:89 (87)	we should have forged against God a lie
10:17 (18)	who does greater evil than he who forges against God a lie
10:38 (39)	or do they say, 'Why, he has forged it?'
11:13 (16)	or do they say, 'He has forged it?'
11:18 (21)	who does greater evil than he who forges against God a lie?
11:35 (37)	or do they say, 'He has forged it?'
11:35 (37)	if I have forged it, upon me falls my sin
18:15 (14)	who does greater evil than he who forges against God a lie?
20:61 (64)	whoso forges has ever failed
21:5 (5)	nay, he has forged it; nay, he is a poet
23:38 (40)	he is naught but a man who has forged against God a lie
25:4 (5)	this is naught but a calumny he has forged
29:68 (68)	who does greater evil than he who forges against God a lie
32:3 (2)	or do they say, 'He has forged it?'
34:8 (8)	what, has he forged against God a lie
42:24 (23)	he has forged against God a lie
46:8 (7)	or do they say, 'He has forged it?'
46:8 (7)	if I have forged it, you have no power to help me against God
61:7 (7)	who does greater evil than he who forges against God falsehood

b) impf. act. (*yaftarī*)

3:24 (23)	the lies they forged has deluded them in their religion
4:50 (53)	consider how they forge falsehood against God
5:103 (102)	the unbelievers forge against God falsehood
6:24 (24)	that which they were forging has gone astray from them
6:112 (112)	so leave them to their forging
6:137 (138)	so leave them to their forging
6:138 (139)	He will assuredly recompense them for what they were forging
7:53 (51)	that which they were forging has gone astray from them
10:30 (31)	there shall go astray from them that they were forging
10:59 (60)	has God given you leave, or do you forge against God?
10:60 (61)	what will they think, who forge falsehood against God
10:69 (70)	those who forge against God falsehood shall not prosper
11:21 (23)	that they forged has gone astray from them
16:56 (58)	you shall be questioned as to that you forged
16:87 (89)	there shall go astray from them that they were forging
16:105 (107)	they only forge falsehood, who believe not
16:116 (117)	so that you may forge against God falsehood
16:116 (117)	those who forge against God falsehood shall not prosper
17:73 (75)	that thou mightest forge against Us another
20:61 (63)	forge not a lie against God
28:75 (75)	there shall go astray from them that they were forging
29:13 (12)	they shall surely be questioned concerning that they were forging
46:28 (27)	that was their calumny, and what they had been forging
60:12 (12)	nor bring a calumny they forge between their hands and their feet

e) impf. pass. (*yuftará*)

10:37 (38) this Koran could not have been forged apart from God
12:111 (111) it is not a tale forged, but a confirmation

f) n.vb. (*iftirā'*)

6:138 (139) al that they say, forging against God
6:140 (141) and have forbidden what God has provided them, forging against God

g) pcple. act. (*muftarī*)

7:152 (151) We recompense those who are forgers
11:50 (52) you have no god other than He; you are but forgers
16:101 (103) thou art a mere forger

h) pcple. pass. (*muftará*)

11:13 (16) bring you ten suras the like of it, forged
28:36 (36) this is nothing but a forged sorcery
34:43 (42) this is nothing but a forged calumny

*F S D

FASADA vb. (I)~to be corrupted, to go into ruin

a) perf. act.

2:251 (252) had God not driven back the people...the earth had surely corrupted
21:22 (22) gods in earth and heaven other than God, they would surely go to ruin
23:71 (73) the heavens and the earth and whosoever in them is had surely corrupted

FASĀD n.m.~corruption, mischief

2:205 (201) God loves not corruption
5:32 (35) for a soul slain, nor for corruption done in the land
5:33 (37) and hasten about the earth, to do corruption there
5:64 (69) God loves not the workers of corruption
8:73 (74) there will be persecution in the land and great corruption
11:116 (118) you, men of a remainder forbidding corruption in the earth
28:77 (77) God loves not the workers of corruption
28:83 (83) for those who desire not exorbitance in the earth, nor corruption
30:41 (40) corruption has appeared in the land and sea
40:26 (27) that he may cause corruption to appear in the land
89:12 (11) and worked much corruption therein

AFSADA vb. (IV)~to disorder, do corruption. (pcple. act.) one who does corruption or mischief

a) perf. act.

27:34 (34) kings, when they enter a city, disorder it

b) impf. act. (*yufsidu*)

2:11 (10) do not corruption in the land
2:27 (25) and such as do corruption in the land
2:30 (28) wilt Thou set therein one who will do corruption there

2:205 (201)	he hastens about the earth, to do corruption there
7:56 (54)	do not corruption in the land
7:85 (83)	do not corruption in the land
7:127 (124)	wilt thou leave Moses and his people to work corruption
12:73 (73)	you know well that we came not to work corruption in the land
13:25 (25)	who work corruption in the earth — theirs shall be the curse
16:88 (90)	chastisement upon chastisement, for that they were doing corruption
17:4 (4)	you shall do corruption in the earth twice
26:152 (152)	who do corruption in the earth, and set not things aright
27:48 (49)	in the city there were nine persons who did corruption
47:22 (24)	would you then haply work corruption in the land

g) pcple. act. (*mufsid*)

2:12 (11)	truly, they are the workers of corruption
2:60 (57)	mischief not in the earth, doing corruption
2:220 (219)	god knows well him who works corruption from him
3:63 (56)	assuredly God knows the workers of corruption
5:64 (69)	God loves not the workers of corruption
7:74 (72)	do not mischief in the earth, working corruption
7:86 (84)	behold, how was the end of the workers of corruption
7:103 (101)	behold thou, how was the end of the workers of corruption
7:142 (138)	do not follow the way of the workers of corruption
10:40 (41)	thy Lord knows very well those who do corruption
10:81 (81)	God sets not right the work of those who do corruption
10:91 (91)	before thou didst rebel, being of those that did corruption
11:85 (86)	do not mischief in the land, working corruption
18:94 (93)	Gog and Magog are doing corruption in the earth
26:183 (183)	do not mischief in the earth, working corruption
27:14 (14)	behold, how was the end of the workers of corruption
28:4 (3)	he was of the workers of corruption
28:77 (77)	God loves not the workers of corruption
29:30 (29)	help me against the people that work corruption
29:36 (35)	do not mischief in the land, working corruption
38:28 (27)	shall We make those who believe and do righteous deeds as the workers of corruption

*F S Ḥ

FASAḤA vb. (I)~to make room

b) impf. act. (*yafsaḥu*)

58:11 (12)	God will make room for you

c) impv. (*ifsaḥ*)

58:11 (12)	make room in the assemblies

TAFASSAḤA vb. (V)~to make room

c) impv. (*taffasaḥ*)

58:11 (12)	then make room

*F S Q

FASAQA vb. (I)~to be ungodly, to commit ungodliness, disobey God's commandment. (n.vb.) ungodliness. (pcple. act.) one who is ungodly [Ar]; reprobate [Bl]; rebellious, wicked, one who forsakes the path [Ali]; miscreant, lewd [Pk]

a) perf. act.

10:33 (34)	the word of thy Lord is realized against the ungodly
17:16 (17)	and they commit ungodliness therein
18:50 (48)	and committed ungodliness against his Lord's command
32:20 (20)	as for the ungodly, their refuge shall be the Fire

b) impf. act. (*yafsuqu*)

2:59 (56)	We sent down upon the evildoers wrath out of heaven of their ungodliness
6:49 (49)	the chastisement shall visit, for that they were ungodly
7:163 (163)	We were trying them for their ungodliness
7:165 (165)	We seized the evildoers with evil chastisement for their ungodliness
29:34 (33)	upon the people of this city wrath out of heaven for their ungodliness
46:20 (19)	and for your ungodliness

f) n.vb. (*fisq*)

5:3 (4)	that is ungodliness
6:121 (121)	it is ungodliness
6:145 (146)	an ungodly thing that has been hallowed to other than God

f) n.vb. (*fusūq*)

2:197 (193)	nor indulge in ungodliness and disputing in the Pilgrimage
2:282 (282)	if you do, that is ungodliness in you
49:7 (7)	He has made detestable to you unbelief and ungodliness
49:11 (11)	an evil name is ungodliness after belief

g) pcple. act. (*fāsiq*)

2:26 (24)	He leads none astray save the ungodly
2:99 (93)	and none disbelieves in them except the ungodly
3:82 (76)	whosoever turns his back after that — they are the ungodly
3:110 (106)	but the most of them are ungodly
5:25 (28)	divide between us and the people of the ungodly
5:26 (29)	grieve not for the people of the ungodly
5:47 (51)	whosoever judges not according to what God has sent down — they are the ungodly
5:49 (54)	surely, many men are ungodly
5:59 (64)	and that most of you are ungodly
5:81 (84)	but many of them are ungodly
5:108 (107)	God guides not the people of the ungodly
7:102 (100)	We found the most part of them ungodly
7:145 (142)	I shall show you the habitation of the ungodly
9:8 (8)	the most of them are ungodly
9:24 (24)	God guides not the people of the ungodly
9:53 (53)	you are surely a people ungodly
9:67 (68)	the hypocrites — they are the ungodly
9:80 (81)	God guides not the people of the ungodly
9:84 (85)	and died while they were ungodly
9:96 (97)	God will surely not be well-pleased with the people of the ungodly

21:74 (74)	they were an evil people, truly ungodly
24:4 (4)	those — they are the ungodly
24:55 (54)	whoso disbelieves after that, those — they are the ungodly
27:12 (12)	they are an ungodly people
28:32 (32)	for surely they are an ungodly people
32:18 (18)	is he who has been a believer like unto him who has been ungodly?
43:54 (54)	surely they were an ungodly people
46:35 (35)	shall any be destroyed but the people of the ungodly?
49:6 (6)	if an ungodly man comes to you with a tiding
51:46 (46)	surely they were an ungodly people
57:16 (15)	have become hard, and many of them are ungodly
57:26 (26)	some of them are guided, and many of them are ungodly
57:27 (27)	and many of them are ungodly
59:5 (5)	and that He might degrade the ungodly
59:19 (19)	those — they are the ungodly
61:5 (5)	God guides never the people of the ungodly
63:6 (6)	God guides not the people of the ungodly

*F S R

FASSARA vb. (II)~(n.vb.) exposition, explanation, interpretation

f) n.vb. (*tafsīr*)

25:33 (35)	We bring thee the truth, and better in exposition

*F SH L

FASHILA vb. (I)~to lose heart

a) perf. act.

3:152 (145)	until you lost heart, and quarrelled about the matter
8:43 (45)	had He shown them as many you would have lost heart

b) impf. act. (*yafshalu*)

3:122 (118)	when two parties of you were about to lose heart
8:46 (48)	do not quarrel together, and so lose heart

*F Ṣ Ḥ

FAṢĪḤ n.m. (adj)~eloquent

28:34 (34)	my brother Aaron is more eloquent than I

*F Ṣ L

FAṢALA vb. (I)~to set or go forth; to distinguish. (n.vb.) decision, decisiveness [Ar]; distinction [Bl] separation [Pk]; sorting [Ali]. (pcple. act.) decider (between truth and falsehood)

a) perf. act.

2:249 (250)	when Saul went forth with the hosts
12:94 (94)	when the caravan set forth

b) impf. act. (*yafṣilu*)

22:17 (17)	God shall distinguish between them on the Day of Resurrection
32:25 (25)	thy Lord will distinguish between them on the Resurrection Day
60:3 (3)	He shall distinguish between you

f) n.vb. (*faṣl*)

37:21 (21)	this is the Day of Decision
38:20 (19)	We strengthened his kingdom, and gave him wisdom and speech decisive
42:21 (20)	but for the Word of Decision, it had been decided
44:40 (40)	the Day of Decision shall be their appointed time
77:13 (13)	to the Day of Decision
77:14 (14)	what shall teach thee what is the Day of Decision?
77:38 (38)	this is the Day of Decision
78:17 (17)	surely the Day of Decision is an appointed time
86:13 (13)	surely it is a decisive word

g) pcple. act. (*fāṣil*)

6:57 (57)	He is the Best of deciders

FAṢĪLAH n.f.~kin, family

70:13 (13)	his kin who sheltered him

FIṢĀL n.m.~weaning

2:233 (233)	desire by mutual consent and consultation to wean
31:14 (13)	his weaning was in two years
46:15 (14)	his bearing and his weaning are thirty months

FAṢṢALA vb. (II)~to distinguish, explain distinctly. (n.vb.) distinguishing, explaining. (pcple. pass.) well-distinguished, distinct

a) perf. act.

6:97 (97)	We have distinguished the signs for a people who know
6:98 (98)	We have distinguished the signs for a people who understand
6:119 (119)	He has distinguished for you that He has forbidden you
6:126 (126)	We have distinguished the signs to a people who remember
7:52 (50)	We have brought to them a Book that We have well distinguished
17:12 (13)	everything We have distinguished very distinctly

b) impf. act. (*yufaṣṣilu*)

6:55 (55)	We distinguish Our signs, that the sinners' way may be manifest
7:32 (30)	We distinguish the signs for a people who know

7:174 (173) We distinguish the signs; and haply they will return
9:11 (11) We distinguish the signs for a people who know
10:5 (5) distinguishing the signs to a people who know
10:24 (25) We distinguish the signs for a people who reflect
13:2 (2) He distinguishes the signs
30:28 (27) We distinguish the signs for a people who understand

d) perf. pass. (*fuṣṣila*)

11:1 (1) Alif Lam Ra A Book whose verses are set clear
41:3 (2) a Book whose signs have been distinguished
41:44 (44) why are its signs not distinguished?

f) n.vb. (*tafṣīl*)

6:154 (155) for him who does good, and distinguishing every thing
7:145 (142) an admonition, and a distinguishing of everything
10:37 (38) it is a confirmation of what is before it, and a distinguishing of the Book
12:111 (111) a confirmation of what is before it, and a distinguishing of every thing
17:12 (13) everything We have distinguished <very distinctly>

h) pcple. pass. (*mufaṣṣal*)

6:114 (114) He who sent down to you the Book well-distinguished
7:133 (130) the lice and the frogs, the blood, distinct signs

*F Ṣ M

INFAṢAMA vb. (VII)~(n.vb.) the act of being broken

f) n.vb. (*infiṣām*)

2:256 (257) and believes in God, has laid hold of the most firm handle, unbreaking

*F T ʾ

FATA'A vb. (I)~to cease

a) perf. act.

12:85 (85) thou wilt never cease mentioning Joseph till thou art consumed

*F T Ḥ

FATAḤA vb. (I)~to open, reveal; give (victory), deliver (with prep. *li-*), give deliverance. (n.vb.) victory, deliverance. (pcple. act.) deliverer, one who opens

a) perf. act.

2:76 (71) do you speak to them of what God has revealed to you
6:44 (44) We opened unto them the gates of everything

7:96 (94)	We would have opened upon them blessings from heaven and earth
12:65 (65)	when they opened their things, they found their merchandise, restored to them
15:14 (14)	We opened to them a gate in heaven, and still they mounted through it
23:77 (79)	when We open against them a door of terrible chastisement
48:1 (1)	surely We have given thee a manifest victory
54:11 (11)	We opened the gates of heaven unto water torrential

b) impf. act. (*yaftaḥu*)

34:26 (25)	our Lord will bring us together, then make deliverance between us
35:2 (2)	whatsoever mercy God opens to men

c) impv. (*iftaḥ*)

7:89 (87)	our Lord, give true deliverance between us and our people
26:118 (118)	give true deliverance between me and them

d) perf. pass. (*futiḥa*)

21:96 (96)	when Gog and Magog are unloosed, and they slide down out of every slope
39:71 (71)	when they have come thither, then its gates will be opened
39:73 (73)	when they have come thither, and its gates are opened
78:19 (19)	and heaven is opened

f) n.vb. (*fatḥ*)

4:141 (140)	if a victory comes to you from God, say
5:52 (57)	it may be that God will bring the victory, or some commandment
8:19 (19)	victory has already come upon you
26:118 (118)	give <true> deliverance between me and them
32:28 (28)	they also say, 'When shall be this Victory?'
32:29 (29)	on the Day of Victory their faith shall not profit the unbelievers
48:1 (1)	We have given thee a manifest victory
48:18 (18)	and rewarded them with a nigh victory
48:27 (27)	He knew what you knew not, and appointed ere that a nigh victory
57:10 (10)	among you who spent, and who fought before the victory
61:13 (13)	and other things you love, help from God and a nigh victory
110:1 (1)	when comes the help of God, and victory

g) pcple. act. (*fātiḥ*)

7:89 (87)	Thou art the best of deliverers

FATTĀḤ n.m.~Deliverer (Divine attribute)

34:26 (25)	He is the Deliverer, the All-knowing

MAFĀTIḤ n.m. (pl. of *miftāḥ*)~key(s)

6:59 (59)	with Him are the keys of the Unseen
24:61 (60)	maternal, or that whereof you own the keys
28:76 (76)	treasures such that the very keys of them were too heavy

FATTAḤA vb. (II)~to open. (pcple. pass.) opened

e) impf. pass. (*yufattaḥu*)

7:40 (38)	the gates of heaven shall not be opened to them

h) pcple. pass. f. (*mufattaḥah*)

38:50 (50)	Gardens of Eden, whereof the gates are open to them

ISTAFTAḤA vb. (X)~seek judgment, ask for victory

a) perf. act.

14:15 (18)	they sought a judgment; then was disappointed every froward tyrant

b) impf. act. (*yastaftiḥu*)

2:89 (83)	they aforetimes prayed for victory over the unbelievers
8:19 (19)	if victory you are seeking, victory has already come upon you

*F T L

FATĪL n.m.~date-thread

4:49 (52)	they shall not be wronged a single date-thread
4:77 (79)	you shall not be wronged a single date-thread
17:71 (73)	they shall not be wronged a single date-thread

*F T N

FATANA vb. (I)~to tempt, try, seduce; persecute, afflict. (n.vb.) a trial. (pcple. act.) tempter. (pcple. pass.) one who is demented

a) perf. act.

6:53 (53)	even so We have tried some of them by others
20:40 (41)	and We tried thee with many trials
20:85 (87)	We have tempted thy people since thou didst leave them
29:3 (2)	We certainly tried those that were before them
38:24 (23)	and David thought that We had only tried him
38:34 (33)	certainly We tried Solomon
44:17 (16)	already before them We tried the people of Pharaoh
57:14 (13)	yes indeed; but you tempted yourselves
85:10 (10)	those who persecute the believers, men and women

b) impf. act. (*yaftinu*)

4:101 (102)	if you fear the unbelievers may afflict you
5:49 (54)	lest they tempt thee away from any of what God has sent down
7:27 (26)	let not Satan tempt you
9:49 (49)	give me leave and do not tempt me
10:83 (83)	for fear of Pharaoh and their Council, that they would persecute them
17:73 (75)	they were near to seducing thee from that We revealed to thee
20:131 (131)	that We may try them therein
72:17 (17)	that We might try them therein

d) perf. pass. (*futina*)

16:110 (111)	who have emigrated after persecution, then struggled and were patient
20:90 (92)	you have been tempted by this thing, no more

e) impf. pass. (*yuftanu*)

9:126 (127)	do they not see that they are tried every year
27:47 (48)	nay, but you are a people being proved
29:2 (1)	that they will be left...and will not be tried
51:13 (13)	upon the day when they shall be tried at the Fire

f) n.vb. (*futūn*)

20:40 (41) We tried thee <with many trials>

g) pcple. act. (*fātin*)

37:162 (162) you shall not tempt any against Him

h) pcple. pass. (*maftūn*)

68:6 (6) which of you is the demented

FITNAH n.f.~trial, temptation, sedition, testing, apostasy; persecution; treachery [Pk]; dissension [Bl]

2:102 (96) We are but a temptation; do not disbelieve
2:191 (187) persecution is more grievous than slaying
2:193 (189) fight them, till there is no persecution and the religion is God's
2:217 (214) and persecution is more heinous than slaying
3:7 (5) they follow the ambiguous part, desiring dissension
4:91 (93) whenever they are returned to temptation, they are overthrown in it
5:41 (45) whomsoever God desires to try, thou canst not avail him anything with God
5:71 (75) they supposed there should be no trial
6:23 (23) then they shall have no proving, but to say
7:155 (154) it is only Thy trial, whereby Thou leadest astray whom Thou wilt
8:25 (25) and fear a trial which shall surely not smite
8:28 (28) know that your wealth and your children are a trial
8:39 (40) fight them, till there is no persecution and the religion is God's
8:73 (74) there will be persecution in the land and great corruption
9:47 (47) seeking to stir up sedition between you
9:48 (48) they sought to stir up sedition already
9:49 (49) have not such men fallen into temptation?
10:85 (85) Lord, make us not a temptation to the people of the evildoers
17:60 (62) and the tree cursed in the Koran to be only a trial for men
21:35 (36) We try you with evil and good for a testing
21:111 (111) I know not; haply it is a trial for you
22:11 (11) but if a trial befalls him he turns completely over
22:53 (52) that He may make what Satan casts a trial for those
24:63 (63) let those who go against His command beware, lest a trial befall them
25:20 (22) We appointed some of you to be a trial for others
29:10 (9) he makes the persecution of men as it were God's chastisement
33:14 (14) then they had been asked to apostatise
37:63 (61) We have appointed it as a trial for the evildoers
39:49 (50) it is a trial, but most of them do not know it
51:14 (14) taste your trial! This is that you were seeking to hasten
54:27 (27) We shall send the She-camel as a trial for them
60:5 (5) make us not a temptation to those who disbelieve
64:15 (15) your wealth and your children are only a trial
74:31 (31) and their number We have appointed only as a trial

*F T Q

FATAQA vb. (I)~to unstitch

a) perf. act.

21:30 (31) the heavens and the earth were a mass all sewn up, and then We unstitched them

*F T R

FATARA vb. (I)~to desist, fail

b) impf. act. (*yafturu*)

21:20 (20)	glorifying Him by night and in the daytime and never failing

FATRAH n.f.~interval

5:19 (22)	making things clear to you, upon an interval between the Messengers

FATTARA vb. (II)~to weaken, diminish; (pass) abate

e) impf. pass. (*yufattaru*)

43:75 (75)	that is not abated for them and therein they are sore confounded

*F T Y

FATÁ n.m. (pl. *fityān*)~young man, youth, page

12:30 (30)	the Governor's wife has been soliciting her page
12:36 (36)	and there entered the prison with him two youths
12:62 (62)	he said to his pages, 'Put their merchandise ...'
18:10 (9)	when the youths took refuge in the Cave saying
18:13 (12)	they were youths who believed in their Lord
18:60 (59)	when Moses said to his page
18:62 (61)	when they had passed over, he said to his page
21:60 (61)	we heard a young man making mention of them

FATAYĀT n.f. (pl. of *fatāt*)~young woman, handmaid, slavegirl

4:25 (29)	let him take believing handmaids
24:33 (33)	constrain not your slavegirls to prostitution

AFTÁ vb. (IV)~to advise, give an opinion, pronounce concerning an issue

b) impf. act. (*yuftī*)

4:127 (126)	God pronounces to you concerning them, and what is recited
4:176 (175)	God pronounces to you concerning the indirect heirs

c) impv. (*afti*)

12:43 (43)	pronounce to me upon my dream, if you are expounders of dreams
12:46 (46)	pronounce to us regarding seven fat kine
27:32 (32)	O Council, pronounce to me concerning my affair

ISTAFTÁ vb. (X)~ask for advice or pronouncement concerning an issue, to enquire

b) impf. act. (*yastaftī*)

4:127 (126)	they will ask thee for a pronouncement concerning women
4:176 (175)	they will ask thee for a pronouncement
12:41 (41)	the matter is decided whereon you enquire
18:22 (22)	ask not any of them for a pronouncement

c) impv. (*istafti*)

37:11 (11) so ask them for a pronouncement
37:149 (149) so ask them for a pronouncement

*F Ṭ R

FAṬARA vb. (I)~to originate, to create. (pcple. act.) Originator, Creator (Divine attribute)

a) perf. act.

6:79 (79) Him who originated the heavens and the earth
11:51 (53) my wage falls only upon Him who did originate me
17:51 (53) He who originated you the first time
20:72 (75) nor over Him who originated us
21:56 (57) the Lord of the heavens and the earth who originated them
30:30 (29) God's original upon which He originated mankind
36:22 (21) why should I not serve Him who originated me
43:27 (26) except Him who originated me

g) pcple. act. (*fāṭir*)

6:14 (14) other than God, the Originator of the heavens and of the earth
12:101 (102) O Thou, the Originator of the heavens and earth
14:10 (11) regarding God, the Originator of the heavens
35:1 (1) praise belongs to God, Originator of the heavens
39:46 (47) O God, Thou originator of the heavens
42:11 (9) the Originator of the heavens and the earth; He has appointed for you

FIṬRAH n.f.~creation, that which is original

30:30 (29) a man of pure faith — God's original

FUṬŪR n.m.~a rent, fissure, flaw

67:3 (3) return thy gaze; seest thou any fissure?

TAFAṬṬARA vb. (V)~to be rent assunder

b) impf. act. (*yataṭaṭṭaru*)

19:90 (92) the heavens are wellnigh rent of it and the earth split asunder
42:5 (3) the heavens wellnigh are rent above them

INFAṬARA vb. (VII)~to be split open, be cloven assunder. (pcple. act.) that which is cloven or split assunder

a) perf. act.

82:1 (1) when heaven is split open

g) pcple. act. (*munfaṭir*)

73:18 (18) whereby heaven shall be split, and its promise shall be performed

*F W Ḍ

FAWWAḌA vb. (II)~to commit a matter to someone for judgment

b) impf. act. (*yufawwiḍu*)

40:44 (47)	I commit my affair to God

*F W H

FĀH n.m. (pl. *afwāh*)~mouth

3:118 (114)	hatred has already shown itself of their mouths
3:167 (161)	saying with their mouths that which never was in their hearts
5:41 (45)	such men as say with their mouths
9:8 (8)	giving you satisfaction with their mouths
9:30 (30)	that is the utterance of their mouths
9:32 (32)	desiring to extinguish with their mouths God's light
13:14 (15)	a man who stretches out his hands to water that it may reach his mouth
14:9 (10)	thrust their hands into their mouths saying
18:5 (4)	a monstrous word it is, issuing out of their mouths
24:15 (14)	and were speaking with your mouths that whereof you had no knowledge
33:4 (4)	that is your own saying, the words of your mouths
36:65 (65)	today We set a seal on their mouths
61:8 (8)	they desire to extinguish with their mouths the light of God

*F W J

FAWJ n.m. (pl. *afwāj*)~a troop, company

27:83 (85)	upon the day when We shall muster out of every nation a troop
38:59 (59)	this is a troop rushing in with you
67:8 (8)	often as a troop is cast into it
78:18 (18)	the day the Trumpet is blown, and you shall come in troops
110:2 (2)	thou seest men entering God's religion in throngs

*F W M

FŪM n.m.~corn; garlic

2:61 (58)	green herbs, cucumbers, corn, lentils, onions

*F W Q

FAWĀQ n.m.~a delay

38:15 (14)	these are only awaiting for a single Cry, to which there is no delay

AFĀQA vb. (IV)~to awake, recover

a) perf. act.

7:143 (140) when he awoke, he said

*F W R

FĀRA vb. (I)~to boil, boil up or over. (n.vb.) haste; (adv) instantly, immediately

a) perf. act.

11:40 (42) until, when Our command came, and the Oven boiled
23:27 (27) when Our command comes and the Oven boils

b) impf. act. (*yafūru*)

67:7 (7) when they are cast into it they will hear it sighing, the while it boils

f) n.vb. (*fawr*)

3:125 (121) if you are patient and godfearing, and the foe come against you instantly

*F W T

FĀTA vb. (I)~to escape (tr); pass away from. (n.vb.) an escape, the act of escaping

a) perf. act.

3:153 (147) that you might not sorrow for what escaped you neither for what smote you
57:23 (23) that you may not grieve for what escapes you
60:11 (11) if any of your wives slips away from you to the unbelievers

f) n.vb. (*fawt*)

34:51 (50) if thou couldst see when they are terrified, and there is no escape

TAFĀWATA vb. (VI)~(n.vb.) a disparity, imperfection

f) n.vb. (*tafāwut*)

67:3 (3) thou seest not in the creation of the All-merciful any imperfection

*F W Z

FĀZA vb. (I)~to win or attain a triumph. (n.vb.) triumph, victory. (pcple. act.) one who is triumphant, victorious

a) perf. act.

3:185 (182) whosoever is removed from the Fire and admitted to Paradise, shall win the triumph
33:71 (71) whosoever obeys God and His Messenger has won a mighty triumph

b) impf. act. (*yafūzu*)

4:73 (75) would that I had been with them, to attain a mighty triumph

f) n.vb. (*fawz*)

4:13 (17) therein dwelling forever; that is the mighty triumph
4:73 (75) would that I had been with them, to attain a mighty triumph
5:119 (119) they well-pleased with Him; that is the mighty triumph
6:16 (16) He will have mercy on him; that is the manifest triumph
9:72 (73) and greater, God's good pleasure; that is the mighty triumph
9:89 (90) therein to dwell forever; that is the mighty triumph
9:100 (101) therein to dwell forever and ever; that is the mighty triumph
9:111 (112) bargain you have made with Him; that is the mighty triumph
10:64 (65) no changing the words of God; that is the mighty triumph
33:71 (71) obeys God and His Messenger has won a mighty triumph
37:60 (58) this is indeed the mighty triumph
40:9 (9) that is indeed the mighty triumph
44:57 (57) a bounty from thy Lord; that is the mighty triumph
45:30 (29) that is the manifest triumph
48:5 (5) that is in God's sight a mighty triumph
57:12 (12) that is indeed the mighty triumph
61:12 (12) goodly in Gardens of Eden; that is the mighty triumph
64:9 (9) therein to dwell for ever and ever; that is the mighty triumph
85:11 (11) gardens underneath which rivers flow; that is the great triumph

g) pcple. act. (*fā'iz*)

9:20 (20) and those — they are the triumphant
23:111 (113) they are the triumphant
24:52 (51) those — they are the triumphant
59:20 (20) the inhabitants of Paradise — they are the triumphant

MAFĀZ n.m.~a place of safety or security

78:31 (31) for the godfearing awaits a place of security

MAFĀZAH n.f.~security

3:188 (185) do not reckon them secure from chastisement
39:61 (62) God shall deliver those that were godfearing in their security

*F Y ʾ

FĀʾA vb. (I)~to revert, return, go back

a) perf. act.

2:226 (226) a wait of four months; if they revert
49:9 (9) if it reverts, set things right between them equitably

b) impf. act. (*yafīʾu*)

49:9 (9) fight the insolent one till it reverts to God's commandment

AFĀʾA vb. (IV)~to give as spoils of war

33:50 (49)	spoils of war that God has given thee
59:6 (6)	whatever spoils of war God has given unto His Messenger
59:7 (7)	whatsoever spoils of war God has given to His Messenger

TAFAYYAʾA vb. (V)~to turn about as to cast one's shadow to one side or another

b) impf. act. (*yatafayyaʾu*)

16:48 (50)	have they not regarded all things that God has created casting their shadows to the right and to the left

*F Y Ḍ

FĀḌA vb. (I)~to overflow

b) impf. act. (*yafīḍu*)

5:83 (86)	thou seest their eyes overflow with tears because of the truth
9:92 (93)	their eyes overflowing with tears of sorrow

AFĀḌA vb. (IV)~to pour out; to press on, rush impetuously; to mutter, dilate, amplify in speech

a) perf. act.

2:198 (194)	when you press on from Arafat, then remember God
2:199 (195)	(then press on) from where the people press on
24:14 (14)	there would have visited you for your mutterings

b) impf. act. (*yufīḍu*)

10:61 (62)	without that We are witnesses over you when you press on it
46:8 (7)	He knows very well what you are pressing upon

c) impv. (*afiḍ*)

2:199 (195)	then press on (from where the people press on)
7:50 (48)	pour on us water, or of that God has provided you

*F Y L

FĪL n.m.~elephant

105:1 (1)	hast thou not seen how thy Lord did with the Men of the Elephant?

*F Z ʿ

FAZIʿA vb. (I)~to be terrified, take fright. (n.vb.) terror, fear

a) perf. act.

27:87 (89)	and terrified is whosoever is in the heavens and earth
34:51 (50)	if thou couldst see when they are terrified
38:22 (21)	when they entered upon David, and he took fright at them

f) n.vb. (*fazaʿ*)

21:103 (103)	the greatest terror shall not grieve them
27:89 (91)	they shall be secure from terror that day

FAZZAʿA vb. (II)~(with prep. *ʿan*) to free from fear or terror, to lift terror

d) perf. pass. (*fuzziʿa*)

34:23 (22)	when terror is lifted from their hearts

*F Z Z

ISTAFAZZA vb. (X)~to startle

b) impf. act. (*yastafizzu*)

17:76 (78)	they were near to startling thee from the land
17:103 (105)	He desired to startle them from the land

c) impv. (*istafziz*)

17:64 (66)	startle whomsoever of them thou canst with thy voice

*F Ẓ Ẓ

FAẒẒ n.m. (adj)~harsh, severe

3:159 (153)	hadst thou been harsh and hard of heart

GHAYN

*GH B N

TAGHĀBANA vb. (V)~(n.vb.) mutual fraud

f) n.vb. (*taghābun*)

64:9 (9) that shall be the Day of Mutual Fraud

*GH B R

GHABARA vb. (I)~(pcple. act.) one who tarries

g) pcple. act. (*ghābir*)

7:83 (81) his wife; she was one of those that tarried
15:60 (60) she shall surely be of those that tarry
26:171 (171) save an old woman among those that tarried
27:57 (58) We decreed she should be of those that tarried
29:32 (31) she has become of those that tarry
29:33 (32) she has become of those that tarry
37:135 (135) save an old woman among those that tarried

GHABARAH n.f.~dust

80:40 (40) some faces on that day shall be dusty

*GH D Q

GHADAQ n.m. (adj)~copious

72:16 (16) We would give them to drink of water copious

*GH D R

GHĀDARA vb. (I)~leave behind

b) impf. act. (*yughādiru*)

18:47 (45) so that We leave not so much as one of them behind
18:49 (47) how is it with this Book, that it leaves nothing behind, small or great

*GH D W

GHADĀ vb. (I)~go forth

a) perf. act.

3:121 (117) when thou wentest forth at dawn from thy people to lodge
68:25 (25) they went forth early, determined upon their purpose

c) impv. (*ughdu*)

68:22 (22) come forth betimes upon your tillage, if you would pluck

GHAD n.m.~the morrow, (adv.), tomorrow

12:12 (12)	send him forth with us tomorrow
18:23 (23)	I am going to do that tomorrow
31:34 (34)	no soul knows what it shall earn tomorrow
54:26 (26)	they shall surely know tomorrow who is the impudent liar
59:18 (18)	let every soul consider what it has forwarded for the morrow

GHADĀ' n.m.~early meal, breakfast

18:62 (61)	he said to his page, 'Bring us our breakfast'

GHADĀT n.f.~morning

6:52 (52)	do not drive away those who call upon their Lord at morning
18:28 (27)	restrain thyself with those who call upon their Lord at morning

GHUDW n.m.~morning

7:205 (204)	not loud of voice, at morn and eventide
13:15 (16)	as do their shadows also in the mornings and the evenings
24:36 (36)	therein glorifying Him, in the mornings and the evenings
34:12 (11)	its morning course was a month's journey
40:46 (49)	the Fire, to which they shall be exposed morning and evening

*GH Ḍ B

GHAḌIBA vb. (I)~be wroth, angry. (n.vb.) anger, wrath. (pcple. pass.) (with prep. *ʿalá*) against whom one is wrathful

a) perf. act.

4:93 (95)	God will be wroth with him and will curse him
5:60 (65)	and with whom He is wroth
42:37 (35)	those who avoid the heinous sins and indecencies and when they are angry forgive
48:6 (6)	God is wroth with them, and has cursed them
58:14 (15)	a people against whom God is wrathful
60:13 (13)	take not for friends a people against whom God is wrathful

f) n.vb. (*ghaḍab*)

2:61 (58)	they were laden with the burden of God's anger
2:90 (84)	they were laden with anger upon (anger)
2:90 (84)	they were laden with (anger) upon anger
3:112 (108)	they will be laden with the burden of God's anger
7:71 (69)	anger and wrath from your Lord have fallen upon you
7:152 (151)	anger shall overtake them from their Lord
7:154 (153)	when Moses' anger abated in him
8:16 (16)	he is laden with the burden of God's anger
16:106 (108)	upon them shall rest anger from God
20:81 (83)	exceed not therein, or My anger shall alight on you
20:81 (83)	on whomsoever My anger alights, that man is hurled to ruin
20:86 (89)	did you desire that anger should alight on you from you Lord
24:9 (9)	and a fifth time, that the wrath of God shall be upon her
42:16 (15)	anger shall rest upon them

h) pcple. pass. (*maghḍūb*)

1:7 (7)	not of those against whom Thou art wrathful

GHAḌBĀN n.m. (adj)~angry

7:150 (149) when Moses returned to his people, angry and sorrowful
20:86 (88) then Moses returned very angry and sorrowful to his people

GHĀḌABA vb. (III)~(pcple. act.) being angry, enraged

g) pcple. act. (*mughāḍib*)

21:87 (87) and Dhul Nun — when he went forth enraged

*GH Ḍ Ḍ

GHAḌḌA vb. (I)~cast down, lower

b) impf. act. (*yaghuḍḍu*)

24:30 (30) say to the believers, that they cast down their eyes
24:31 (31) say to the believing women, that they cast down their eyes
49:3 (3) those who lower their voices in the presence of God's Messenger

c) impv. (*ughḍuḍ*)

31:19 (18) be modest in thy walk, and lower thy voice

*GH F L

GHAFALA vb. (I)~be heedless. (pcple. act.) heedless

b) impf. act. (*yaghfulu*)

4:102 (103) the unbelievers wish that you should be heedless of your weapons

g) pcple. act. (*ghāfil*)

2:74 (69) God is not heedless of the things you do
2:85 (79) God is not heedless of the things you do
2:140 (134) God is not heedless of the things you do
2:144 (139) God is not heedless of the things they do
2:149 (144) God is not heedless of the things you do
3:99 (94) God is not heedless of the things you do
6:131 (131) thy Lord would never destroy the cities unjustly, while their inhabitants were heedless
6:132 (132) thy Lord is not heedless of the things they do
6:156 (157) we have indeed been heedless of their study'
7:136 (132) they cried lies to Our signs and heeded them not
7:146 (144) they have cried lies to Our signs and heeded them not
7:172 (171) as for us, we were heedless of this
7:179 (178) those — they are the heedless
7:205 (204) be not thou among the heedless
10:7 (7) those who are heedless of Our signs
10:29 (30) assuredly we were heedless of your service
10:92 (92) many men are heedless of Our signs
11:123 (123) thy Lord is not heedless of the things you do
12:3 (3) though before it thou wast one of the heedless
12:13 (13) I fear the wolf may eat him, while you are heedless of him
14:42 (43) deem not that God is heedless of what the evildoers work

16:108 (110)	those — they are the heedless ones
23:17 (17)	We were not heedless of creation
24:23 (23)	those who cast it up on women in wedlock that are heedless
27:93 (95)	thy Lord is not heedless of the things you do
30:7 (6)	but of the Hereafter they are heedless
36:6 (5)	so they are heedless
46:5 (4)	such as are heedless of their calling

GHAFLAH n.f.~heedlessness; (with prep. *fī*) heedless

19:39 (40)	when the matter shall be determined, and they yet heedless
21:1 (1)	while they in heedlessness are yet turning away
21:97 (97)	alas for us! We were heedless of this
28:15 (14)	he entered the city, at a time when its people were unheeding
50:22 (21)	thou wast heedless of this

AGHFALA vb. (IV)~make neglectful

a) perf. act.

18:28 (27)	obey not him whose heart We have made neglectful of Our remembrance

*GH F R

GHAFARA vb. (I)~forgive, pardon. (pcple. act.) forgiver

a) perf. act.

28:16 (15)	so God forgave him, for He is the All-forgiving
36:27 (26)	that my Lord has forgiven me
38:25 (24)	accordingly We forgave him that
42:43 (41)	he who bears patiently and is forgiving

b) impf. act. (*yaghfiru*)

2:58 (55)	We will forgive you your transgressions
2:284 (284)	He will forgive whom He will, and chastise whom He will
3:31 (29)	and God will love you, and forgive you your sins
3:129 (124)	He forgives whom He will, and chastises whom He will
3:135 (129)	who shall forgive sins but God?
4:48 (51)	God forgives not that aught should be with Him associated
4:48 (51)	less than that He forgives to whomsoever He will
4:116 (116)	God forgives not that aught should be with Him associated
4:116 (116)	less than that He forgives to whomsoever He will
4:137 (136)	God is not likely to forgive them, neither to guide them
4:168 (166)	God would not forgive them, neither guide them
5:18 (21)	He forgives whom He will, and He chastises whom He will
5:40 (44)	He chastises whom He will, and forgives whom He will
5:118 (118)	if Thou forgivest them, Thou art the All-mighty
7:23 (22)	if Thou dost not forgive us, and have mercy upon us
7:149 (148)	if our Lord has not mercy on us, and forgives us not
7:161 (161)	We will forgive you your transgressions
8:29 (29)	and acquit you of your evil deeds, and forgive you
8:70 (71)	and He will forgive you
9:80 (81)	if thou askest pardon for them seventy times, God will not pardon them
11:47 (49)	if Thou forgivest me not, and hast not mercy on me
12:92 (92)	God will forgive you; He is the most merciful

14:10 (11)	He may forgive you your sins, and defer you to a term
20:73 (75)	We believe in our Lord, that He may pardon us our offences
24:22 (22)	do you not wish that God should forgive you?
26:51 (51)	we are eager that our Lord should forgive us our offences
26:82 (82)	who I am eager shall forgive me my offence on the Day of Doom
33:71 (71)	He will set right your deeds for you and will forgive you your sins
39:53 (54)	surely God forgives sins altogether
42:37 (35)	and indecencies and when they are angry forgive
45:14 (13)	say unto those who believe, that they forgive
46:31 (30)	believe in Him, and He will forgive you
47:34 (36)	and then die disbelieving, them God will not forgive
48:2 (2)	that God may forgive thee thy former and thy latter sins
48:14 (14)	whomsoever He will He forgives
57:28 (28)	He will appoint for you a light whereby you shall walk, and forgive you
61:12 (12)	He will forgive you your sins and admit you into gardens
63:6 (6)	God will never forgive them
64:14 (14)	if you pardon, and overlook, and if you forgive
64:17 (17)	will multiply it for you, and will forgive you
71:4 (4)	He will forgive you your sins, and defer you to a stated term
71:7 (6)	whenever I called them, that Thou mightest forgive them

c) impv. (*ighfir*)

2:286 (286)	and forgive us, and have mercy on us
3:16 (14)	our Lord, we believe; forgive us our sins, and guard us
3:147 (141)	Lord, forgive us our sins
3:193 (191)	forgive Thou us our sins and acquit us
7:151 (150)	O my Lord, forgive me and my brother
7:155 (154)	forgive us, and have mercy on us
14:41 (42)	our Lord, forgive Thou me and my parents
23:109 (111)	forgive us, and have mercy on us
23:118 (118)	my Lord, forgive and have mercy
26:86 (86)	forgive my father, for he is one of those astray
28:16 (15)	my Lord, I have wronged myself. Forgive me
38:35 (34)	my Lord, forgive me, and give me a kingdom
40:7 (7)	therefore forgive those who have repented, and follow Thy way
59:10 (10)	forgive us and our brothers, who preceded us in belief
60:5 (5)	make us not a temptation to those who disbelieve; and forgive us
66:8 (8)	our Lord, perfect for us our light, and forgive us
71:28 (29)	my Lord, forgive me and my parents

e) impf. pass. (*yughfaru*)

7:169 (168)	it will be forgiven us
8:38 (39)	if they give over He will forgive them what is past

g) pcple. act. (*ghāfir*)

7:155 (154)	have mercy on us, for Thou art the best of forgivers
40:3 (2)	Forgiver of sins, Accepter of penitence

GHAFFĀR n.m.~All-forgiving, Forgiver (Divine attribute)

20:82 (84)	I am All-forgiving to him who repents
38:66 (66)	the All-mighty, the All-forgiving
39:5 (7)	is not He the All-mighty, the All-forgiving?
40:42 (45)	while I call you to the All-mighty, the All-forgiving
71:10 (9)	surely He is ever All-forgiving

GHAFŪR n.m. (adj)~All-forgiving (Divine attribute), forgiver, indulgent

2:173 (168)	God is All-forgiving, All-compassionate
2:182 (178)	surely God is All-forgiving, All-compassionate
2:192 (188)	surely God is All-forgiving, All-compassionate
2:199 (195)	God is All-forgiving, All-compassionate
2:218 (215)	God is All-forgiving, All-compassionate
2:225 (225)	God is All-forgiving, All-clement
2:226 (226)	God is All-forgiving, All-compassionate
2:235 (236)	know that God is All-forgiving, All-clement
3:31 (29)	God is All-forgiving, All-compassionate
3:89 (83)	God is All-forgiving, All-compassionate
3:129 (124)	God is All-forgiving, All-compassionate
3:155 (149)	God is All-forgiving, All-clement
4:23 (27)	God is All-forgiving, All-compassionate
4:25 (30)	God is All-forgiving All-compassionate
4:43 (46)	God is All-pardoning, All-forgiving
4:96 (98)	surely God is All-forgiving, All-compassionate
4:99 (100)	God is All-pardoning, All-forgiving
4:100 (101)	God is All-forgiving, All-compassionate
4:106 (106)	surely God is All-forgiving, All-compassionate
4:110 (110)	he shall find God is All-forgiving, All-compassionate
4:129 (128)	God is All-forgiving, All-compassionate
4:152 (151)	God is All-forgiving, All-compassionate
5:3 (5)	God is All-forgiving, All-compassionate
5:34 (38)	know you that God is All-forgiving, All-compassionate
5:39 (43)	God is All-forgiving, All-compassionate
5:74 (78)	God is All-forgiving, All-compassionate
5:98 (98)	God is All-forgiving, All-compassionate
5:101 (101)	for God is All-forgiving, All-clement
6:54 (54)	He is All-forgiving, All-compassionate
6:145 (146)	surely thy Lord is All-forgiving, All-compassionate
6:165 (165)	surely He is All-forgiving, All-compassionate
7:153 (152)	thy Lord is All-forgiving, All-compassionate
7:167 (166)	He is All-forgiving, All-compassionate
8:69 (70)	God is All-forgiving, All-compassionate
8:70 (71)	God is All-forgiving, All-compassionate
9:5 (5)	God is All-forgiving, All-compassionate
9:27 (27)	God is All-forgiving, All-compassionate
9:91 (92)	God is All-forgiving, All-compassionate
9:99 (100)	God is All-forgiving, All-compassionate
9:102 (103)	God is All-forgiving, All-compassionate
10:107 (107)	He is the All-forgiving, the All-compassionate
11:41 (43)	my Lord is All-forgiving, All-compassionate
12:53 (53)	truly my Lord is All-forgiving, All-compassionate
12:98 (99)	He is the All-forgiving, the All-compassionate
14:36 (39)	Thou art All-forgiving, All-compassionate
15:49 (49)	I am the All-forgiving, the All-compassionate
16:18 (18)	surely God is All-forgiving, All-compassionate
16:110 (111)	thy Lord thereafter is All-forgiving
16:115 (116)	God is All-forgiving, All-compassionate
16:119 (120)	thy Lord thereafter is All-forgiving
17:25 (27)	He is All-forgiving to those who are penitent
17:44 (46)	surely He is All-clement, All-forgiving
18:58 (57)	thy Lord is the All-forgiving, full of mercy
22:60 (59)	surely God is All-pardoning, All-forgiving

24:5 (5)	surely God is All-forgiving, All-compassionate
24:22 (22)	God is All-forgiving, All-compassionate
24:33 (33)	surely God, after their being constrained, is All-forgiving
24:62 (62)	surely God is All-forgiving, All-compassionate
25:6 (7)	He is All-forgiving, All-compassionate
25:70 (70)	God is ever All-forgiving, All-compassionate
27:11 (11)	All-forgiving am I, All-compassionate
28:16 (15)	He is the All-forgiving, the All-compassionate
33:5 (5)	God is All-forgiving, All-compassionate
33:24 (24)	surely God is All-forgiving, All-compassionate
33:50 (50)	God is All-forgiving, All-compassionate
33:59 (59)	God is All-forgiving, All-compassionate
33:73 (73)	God is All-forgiving, All-compassionate
34:2 (2)	He is the All-compassionate, the All-forgiving
34:15 (14)	a good land, and a Lord All-forgiving
35:28 (25)	surely God is All-mighty, All-forgiving
35:30 (27)	surely He is All-forgiving, All-thankful
35:34 (31)	our Lord is All-forgiving, All-thankful
35:41 (39)	surely He is All-clement, All-forgiving
39:53 (54)	surely He is the All-forgiving, the All-compassionate
41:32 (32)	as hospitality from One All-forgiving
42:5 (3)	He is the All-forgiving, the All-compassionate
42:23 (22)	surely God is All-forgiving, All-thankful
46:8 (7)	He is the All-forgiving, the All-compassionate
48:14 (14)	God is All-forgiving, All-compassionate
49:5 (5)	God is All-forgiving, All-compassionate
49:14 (14)	God is All-forgiving, All-compassionate
57:28 (28)	God is All-forgiving, All-compassionate
58:2 (3)	surely God is All-pardoning, All-forgiving
58:12 (13)	God is All-forgiving, All-compassionate
60:7 (7)	God is All-powerful; God is All-forgiving
60:12 (12)	God is All-forgiving, All-compassionate
64:14 (14)	surely God is All-forgiving, All-compassionate
66:1 (1)	God is All-forgiving, All-compassionate
67:2 (2)	He is the All-mighty, the All-forgiving
73:20 (20)	God is All-forgiving, All-compassionate
85:14 (14)	He is the All-forgiving, the All-loving

GHUFRĀN n.m.~forgiveness, pardon

2:285 (285)	our Lord, grant us Thy forgiveness

MAGHFIRAH n.f.~forgiveness, pardon

2:175 (170)	the price of guidance, and chastisement at the price of pardon
2:221 (221)	God calls unto Paradise, and pardon
2:263 (265)	honourable words, and forgiveness, are better than a freewill offering
2:268 (271)	God promises you His pardon and His bounty
3:133 (127)	vie with one another, hastening to forgiveness from your Lord
3:136 (130)	their recompense is forgiveness from their Lord
3:157 (151)	forgiveness and mercy from God are a better thing
4:96 (98)	in ranks standing before Him, forgiveness and mercy
5:9 (12)	they shall have forgiveness and a mighty wage
8:4 (4)	degrees with their Lord, and forgiveness, and generous provision
8:74 (75)	theirs shall be forgiveness and generous provision
11:11 (14)	for them awaits forgiveness and a mighty wage
13:6 (7)	thy Lord is forgiving to men, for all their evil-doing

22:50 (49)	theirs shall be forgiveness and generous provision
24:26 (26)	theirs shall be forgiveness and generous provision
33:35 (35)	for them God has prepared forgiveness and a mighty wage
34:4 (4)	theirs shall be forgiveness and generous provision
35:7 (8)	theirs shall be forgiveness and a great wage
36:11 (10)	give him the good tidings of forgiveness and a generous wage
41:43 (43)	thy Lord is a Lord of forgiveness and of painful retribution
47:15 (17)	therein for them is every fruit, and forgiveness from their Lord
48:29 (29)	those of them who believe and do deeds of righteousness forgiveness and a mighty wage
49:3 (3)	they shall have forgiveness and a mighty wage
53:32 (33)	surely thy Lord is wide in His forgiveness
57:20 (20)	and forgiveness from God and good pleasure
57:21 (21)	race to forgiveness from your Lord
67:12 (12)	there awaits them forgiveness and a great wage
74:56 (55)	He is worthy to be feared, worthy to forgive

ISTAGHFARA vb. (X)~pray forgiveness, ask pardon. (n.vb.) the act of asking forgiveness. (pcple. act.) one who asks pardon or forgiveness

a) perf. act.

3:135 (129)	themselves, remember God, and pray forgiveness for their sins
4:64 (67)	they had come to thee, and prayed forgiveness of God
4:64 (67)	the Messenger had prayed forgiveness for them
38:24 (23)	therefore he sought forgiveness of his Lord
63:6 (6)	whether thou askest forgiveness for them or thou askest not

b) impf. act. (*yastaghfiru*)

4:110 (110)	and then prays God's forgiveness, he shall find God is All-forgiving
5:74 (78)	will they not turn to God and pray His forgiveness?
8:33 (33)	God would never chastise them as they begged forgiveness
9:80 (81)	ask pardon for them, or ask not pardon for them
9:80 (81)	if thou askest pardon for them seventy times
9:113 (114)	it is not for the Prophet and the believers to ask pardon for the idolaters
12:98 (99)	I will ask my Lord to forgive you
18:55 (53)	when the guidance came unto them, and seeking their Lord's forgiveness
19:47 (48)	I will ask my Lord to forgive thee
27:46 (47)	why do you not ask forgiveness of God?
40:7 (7)	they ask forgiveness for those who believe
42:5 (3)	and ask forgiveness for those on earth
51:18 (18)	in the mornings they would ask for forgiveness
60:4 (4)	certainly I shall ask pardon for thee
63:5 (5)	God's Messenger will ask forgiveness for you
63:6 (6)	or thou askest not forgiveness for them

c) impv. (*istaghfir*)

2:199 (195)	press on from where the people press on, and pray for God's forgiveness
3:159 (153)	pardon them, and pray forgiveness for them
4:106 (106)	and pray forgiveness of God
9:80 (81)	ask pardon for them, or ask not pardon for them
11:3 (3)	ask forgiveness of your Lord, then repent to Him
11:52 (54)	ask forgiveness of your Lord, then repent to Him
11:61 (64)	ask forgiveness of Him, then repent to Him
11:90 (92)	ask forgiveness of your Lord, then repent to Him

12:29 (29) thou, woman, ask forgiveness of thy crime
12:97 (98) our father, ask forgiveness of our crimes for us
24:62 (62) and ask God's forgiveness for them
40:55 (57) and ask forgiveness for thy sin
41:6 (5) go straight with Him, and ask for His forgiveness
47:19 (21) ask forgiveness for thy sin, and for the believers
48:11 (11) so ask forgiveness for us
60:12 (12) and ask God's forgiveness for them
71:10 (9) ask you forgiveness of your Lord
73:20 (20) and ask God's forgiveness
110:3 (3) proclaim the praise of thy Lord, and seek His forgiveness

f) n.vb. (*istaghfār*)

9:114 (115) Abraham asked not pardon for his father except because of a promise

g) pcple. act. (*mustaghfir*)

3:17 (15) men who are patient, truthful, obedient, expenders in alms, imploring God's pardon

*GH L B

GHALABA vb. (I)~overcome, prevail, conquer. (n.vb.) vanquishing, victory. (pcple. act.) victor, helper. (pcple. pass.) vanquished

a) perf. act.

2:249 (250) how often a little company has overcome a numerous company
18:21 (20) said those who prevailed over their affair
23:106 (108) our adversity prevailed over us

b) impf. act. (*yaghlibu*)

4:74 (76) whosoever fights in the way of God and is slain, or conquers
8:65 (66) if there be twenty of you, patient men, they will overcome two hundred
8:65 (66) a hundred of you, they will overcome a thousand unbelievers
8:66 (67) a hundred of you, patient men, they will overcome two hundred
8:66 (67) a thousand, they will overcome two thousand
30:3 (2) after their vanquishing, they shall be the victors
41:26 (25) haply you will overcome
58:21 (21) I shall assuredly be the victor

d) perf. pass. (*ghuliba*)

7:119 (116) so they were vanquished there
30:2 (1) the Greeks have been vanquished

e) impf. pass. (*yughlabu*)

3:12 (10) you shall be overthrown, and mustered into Gehenna
8:36 (36) expend it, till it is an anguish for them, then be overthrown

f) n.vb. (*ghalab*)

30:3 (2) in the nearer part of the land; and, after their vanquishing

g) pcple. act. (*ghālib*)

3:160 (154) if God helps you, none can overcome you
5:23 (26) when you enter it, you will be victors

5:56 (61)	the believers — the party of God, they are the victors
7:113 (110)	we shall surely have a wage, if we should be the victors
8:48 (50)	today no man shall overcome you
12:21 (21)	God prevails in His purpose, but most men know not
21:44 (45)	or are they the victors?
26:40 (39)	we shall follow the sorcerers if it should be they are the victors
26:41 (40)	shall we indeed have a wage, if we should be the victors?
26:44 (43)	by the might of Pharaoh we shall be the victors
28:35 (35)	you, and whoso follows you, shall be the victors
37:116 (116)	We helped them, so that they were the victors
37:173 (173)	and Our host — they are the victors

h) pcple. pass. (*maghlūb*)

54:10 (10)	I am vanquished; do Thou succour me

GHULB n.m. (pl. of *aghlab*)~dense

80:30 (30)	and dense-tree'd gardens

*GH L F

GHULF n.m. (pl. of *aghlaf*)~uncircumcised

2:88 (82)	they say, 'Our hearts are uncircumcised'
4:155 (154)	their saying, 'Our hearts are uncircumcised'

*GH L L

GHALLA vb. (I)~defraud; fetter, bind. (pcple. pass.) fettered, chained

a) perf. act.

3:161 (155)	whoso defrauds shall bring the fruits

b) impf. act. (*yaghullu*)

3:161 (155)	it is not for a Prophet to be fraudulent
3:161 (155)	whoso defrauds shall bring the fruits

c) impv. (*ghull*)

69:30 (30)	take him, and fetter him

d) perf. pass. (*ghulla*)

5:64 (69)	fettered are their hands, and they are cursed

h) pcple. pass. (*maghlūl*)

5:64 (69)	the Jews have said, 'God's hand is fettered'
17:29 (31)	keep not thy hand chained to thy neck

AGHLĀL n.m. (pl. of *ghull*)~ fetters, yoke

7:157 (156)	relieving them of their loads, and the fetters that were upon them
13:5 (6)	those — on their necks are fetters
34:33 (32)	We put fetters on the necks of the unbelievers
36:8 (7)	surely We have put on their necks fetters
40:71 (73)	when the fetters and chains are on their necks
76:4 (4)	We have prepared for the unbelievers chains, fetters

GHILL n.m.~rancour, grudge, enmity

7:43 (41)	We shall strip away all rancour that is in their breasts
15:47 (47)	We shall strip away all rancour that is in their breasts
59:10 (10)	put Thou not into our hearts any rancour towards those who believe

*GH L M

GHULĀM n.m.~son, young man, lad, boy, youth

3:40 (35)	how shall I have a son, seeing I am an old man?
12:19 (19)	'Good news!' he said. 'Here is a young man'
15:53 (53)	we give thee good tidings of a cunning boy
18:74 (73)	when they met a lad, he slew him
18:80 (79)	as for the lad, his parents were believers
18:82 (81)	as for the wall, it belonged to two orphan lads
19:7 (7)	We give thee good tidings of a boy
19:8 (9)	O my Lord, how shall I have a son
19:19 (19)	a messenger come from thy Lord, to give thee a boy most pure
19:20 (20)	how shall I have a son whom no mortal has touched
37:101 (99)	We gave him the good tidings of a prudent boy
51:28 (28)	they gave him good tidings of a cunning boy
52:24 (24)	and there go round them youths, their own

*GH L Q

GHALLAQA vb. (II)~close, shut

a) perf. act.

12:23 (23)	the woman in whose house he was solicited him, and closed the doors

*GH L W

GHALĀ vb. (I)~go beyond the bounds

b) impf. act. (*yaghlū*)

4:171 (169)	go not beyond the bounds in your religion
5:77 (81)	go not beyond the bounds in your religion

*GH L Y

GHALÁ vb. (I)~boil, bubble. (n.vb.) the act of boiling

b) impf. act. (*yaghlī*)

44:45 (45)	like molten copper, bubbling in the belly

f) n.vb. (*ghaly*)

44:46 (46)	as boiling water bubbles

*GH L Ẓ

GHALUẒA vb. (I)~to be harsh

c) impv. (*ughluẓ*)

9:73 (74) — and be thou harsh with them
66:9 (9) — and be thou harsh with them

GHALĪẒ n.m. (adj)~harsh, severe, solemn

3:159 (153) — hadst thou been harsh and hard of heart
4:21 (25) — they have taken from you a solemn compact
4:154 (153) — We took from them a solemn compact
11:58 (61) — and delivered them from a harsh chastisement
14:17 (20) — and still beyond him is a harsh chastisement
31:24 (23) — then We compel them to a harsh chastisement
33:7 (7) — We took from them a solemn compact
41:50 (50) — We shall let them taste a harsh chastisement
66:6 (6) — over which are harsh, terrible angels

GHILẒAH n.f.~harshness, severity

9:123 (124) — let them find in you a harshness

ISTAGHLAẒA vb. (X)~to be strong, stout

a) perf. act.

48:29 (29) — and it grows stout and rises straight

*GH M Ḍ

AGHMAḌA vb. (IV)~close an eye; desdain

b) impf. act. (*yughmiḍu*)

2:267 (270) — you would never take it yourselves, except you closed an eye on it

*GH M M

GHAMMA vb. (I)~(n.vb.) anguish, grief

f) n.vb. (*ghamm*)

3:153 (147) — He rewarded you with grief on (grief)
3:153 (147) — He rewarded you with (grief) on grief
3:154 (148) — He sent down upon you, after grief, security
20:40 (41) — and We delivered thee out of grief
21:88 (88) — We answered him, and delivered him out of grief
22:22 (22) — as often as they desire in their anguish to come forth from it

GHAMĀM n.m.~cloud(s)

2:57 (54) — We outspread the cloud to overshadow you
2:210 (206) — God shall come to them in the cloud-shadows
7:160 (160) — We outspread the cloud to overshadow them
25:25 (27) — the day that heaven is split asunder with the clouds

GHUMMAH n.f.~darkness; cause of doubt or worry

10:71 (72) — then let not your affair be a worry to you

*GH M R

GHAMRAH n.f.~agony, perplexity

6:93 (93)	see when the evildoers are in the agonies of death
23:54 (56)	leave thou them in their perplexity for a time
23:63 (65)	their hearts are in perplexity as to this
51:11 (11)	who are dazed in perplexity

*GH M Z

TAGHĀMAZA vb. (VI)~wink at one another

b) impf. act. (*yataghāmazu*)

83:30 (30)	when they passed them by winking at one another

*GH N M

GHANIMA vb. (I)~gain as booty

a) perf. act.

8:41 (42)	whatever booty you take, the fifth of it is God's
8:69 (70)	eat of what you have taken as booty

GHANAM n.coll.~sheep

6:146 (147)	of oxen and sheep We have forbidden them the fat of them
20:18 (19)	with it I beat down leaves to feed my sheep
21:78 (78)	judgment concerning the tillage, when the sheep of the people strayed there

MAGHNAM n.m. (pl. *maghānim*)~booty, spoils, plunder

4:94 (96)	with God are spoils abundant
48:15 (15)	when you set forth after spoils, to take them
48:19 (19)	and many spoils to take
48:20 (20)	God has promised you many spoils to take

*GH N Y

GHANIYA vb. (I)~be rich, flourish; dwell in (with prep. *fī*)

b) impf. act. (*yaghná*)

7:92 (90)	they dwelt there; those who cried lies to Shuaib
10:24 (25)	We make it stubble, as though yesterday it flourished not
11:68 (71)	as if they never dwelt there
11:95 (98)	as if they had never dwelt there

GHANĪY n.m. (adj)~rich, sufficient; All-sufficient (Divine attribute); independent of (with prep. *ʿan*)

2:263 (265)	God is All-sufficient, All-clement
2:267 (270)	know that God is All-sufficient, All-laudable
2:273 (274)	the ignorant man supposes them rich
3:97 (92)	God is All-sufficient nor needs any being
3:181 (177)	surely God is poor, and we are rich'
4:6 (6)	if any man is rich, let him be abstinent

4:131 (130)	God is All-sufficient
4:135 (134)	whether the man be rich or poor; God stands closest to either
6:133 (133)	thy Lord is All-sufficient, Merciful
9:93 (94)	the way is open only against those who ask leave of thee, being rich
10:68 (69)	glory be to Him! He is All-sufficient
14:8 (8)	yet assuredly God is All-sufficient
22:64 (63)	He is the All-sufficient, the All-laudable
27:40 (40)	my Lord is surely All-sufficient, All-generous
29:6 (5)	God is All-sufficient nor needs any being
31:12 (11)	surely God is All-sufficient, All-laudable
31:26 (25)	He is the All-sufficient, the All-laudable
35:15 (16)	He is the All-sufficient, the All-laudable
39:7 (9)	if you are unthankful, God is independent of you
47:38 (40)	God is the All-sufficient; you are the needy ones
57:24 (24)	God is the All-sufficient, the All-laudable
59:7 (7)	it be not a thing taken in turns among the rich of you
60:6 (6)	surely God is the All-sufficient
64:6 (6)	God was in no need of them. And God is All-sufficient

AGHNÁ vb. (IV)~enrich, suffice; (with prep. *ʿan*) avail. (pcple. act.) one who avails or enriches

a) perf. act.

7:48 (46)	your amassing has not availed you
9:74 (75)	they took revenge only that God enriched them
11:101 (103)	their gods availed them not that they called upon
15:84 (84)	that they earned did not avail them
26:207 (207)	what will it then avail them
39:50 (51)	but that they earned did not avail them
40:82 (82)	yet that they earned did not avail them
46:26 (25)	their sight and their hearts availed them nothing
53:48 (49)	it is He who gives wealth and riches
69:28 (28)	my wealth has not availed me
93:8 (8)	did He not find thee needy, and suffice thee?
111:2 (2)	his wealth avails him not, neither what he has earned

b) impf. act. (*yughnī*)

3:10 (8)	as for the unbelievers, their riches will not avail them
3:116 (112)	as for the unbelievers, their riches shall not avail them
4:130 (129)	God will enrich each of them of His plenty
8:19 (19)	your host will avail you nothing though it be numerous
9:25 (25)	your multitude was pleasing to you, but it availed you naught
9:28 (28)	God shall surely enrich you of His bounty
10:36 (37)	most of them follow only surmise, and surmise avails naught
10:101 (101)	neither signs nor warnings avail a people
12:67 (67)	I cannot avail you anything against God
12:68 (68)	it availed them nothing against God
19:42 (43)	that which neither hears nor sees, nor avails thee anything
24:32 (32)	God will enrich them of His bounty
24:33 (33)	let those who find not the means to marry be abstinent till God enriches them
36:23 (22)	if the All-merciful desires affliction for me, shall not avail me anything
44:41 (41)	the day a master shall avail nothing
45:10 (9)	that they have earned shall not avail them aught
45:19 (18)	they will not avail thee aught against God
52:46 (46)	the day when their guile shall avail them naught

53:26 (26) how many an angel there is in the heavens whose intercession avails not anything
53:28 (29) only surmise, and surmise avails naught against truth
54:5 (5) a Wisdom far-reaching; yet warnings do not avail
58:17 (18) nor their children shall avail them anything against God
66:10 (10) so they availed them nothing whatsoever against God
77:31 (31) unshading against the blazing flame
80:37 (37) every man that day shall have business to suffice him
88:7 (7) unfattening, unappeasing hunger
92:11 (11) his wealth shall not avail him when he perishes

g) pcple. act. (*mughnī*)

14:21 (24) will you avail us against the chastisement of God anything?
40:47 (50) will you avail us now against any part of the Fire?

ISTAGHNÁ vb. (X)~be self-sufficient, become rich; to be All-sufficient (Divine attribute)

a) perf. act.

64:6 (6) God is All-sufficient
80:5 (5) but the self-sufficient
92:8 (8) as for him who is a miser, and self-sufficient
96:7 (7) for he thinks himself self-sufficient

*GH R B

GHARABA vb. (I)~to set

a) perf. act.

18:17 (16) towards the right, and, when it set, passing them by

b) impf. act. (*yaghrubu*)

18:86 (84) the sun, he found it setting in a muddy spring

GHARABĪB n.m. (adj., pl. of *ghirbīb*)~pitch-black, raven-black

35:27 (25) streaks white and red, of diverse hues, and pitchy black

GHARBĪY n.m. (adj)~western

24:35 (35) an olive that is neither of the East nor of the West
28:44 (44) thou wast not upon the western side when We decreed to Moses

GHURĀB n.m.~raven

5:31 (34) God sent forth a raven, scratching into the earth
5:31 (34) woe is me! Am I unable to be as this raven

GHURŪB n.m.~sunset

20:130 (130) before the rising of the sun, and before its setting
50:39 (38) before the rising of the sun, and before its setting

MAGHRIB n.m. (pl. *maghārib*)~west, setting of the sun

2:115 (109) to God belong the East and the West
2:142 (136) to God belong the East and the West
2:177 (172) it is not piety, that you turn your faces to the East and to the West

2:258 (260)	God brings the sun from the east; so bring thou it from the west
7:137 (133)	We bequeathed upon the people that were abased all the east and the west
18:86 (84)	when he reached the setting of the sun, he found it setting
26:28 (27)	the Lord of the East and West, and what between them is
55:17 (17)	Lord of the Two Wests
70:40 (40)	I swear by the Lord of the Easts and the Wests
73:9 (9)	Lord of the East and the West

*GH R F

GHURFAH (1) n.f. (pl. *ghuraf* or *ghurufāt*)~upper or lofty chamber (symbolically, the highest chambers of Heaven)

25:75 (75)	those shall be recompensed with the highest heaven
29:58 (58)	We shall surely lodge them in lofty chambers of Paradise
34:37 (36)	they shall be in the lofty chambers in security
39:20 (21)	those who fear their Lord — for them await lofty chambers
39:20 (21)	above which are built lofty chambers

GHURFAH (2) n.f.~a scoop with the hand

2:249 (250)	he is of me, saving him who scoops up with his hand

IGHTARAFA vb. (VIII)~to scoop up with the hand

a) perf. act.

2:249 (250)	he is of me, saving him who scoops up with his hand

*GH R M

GHARIMA vb. (I)~(pcple. act.) debtor

g) pcple. act. (*ghārim*)

9:60 (60)	those whose hearts are brought together, the ransoming of slaves, debtors

GHARĀM n.m.~continuous torment

25:65 (66)	its chastisement is torment most terrible

MAGHRAM n.m.~debt, loss

9:98 (99)	some of the Bedouins take what they expend for a fine
52:40 (40)	and so they are weighed down with debt
68:46 (46)	and so they are weighed down with debt

AGHRAMA vb. (IV)~(pcple. pass.) one who is debt-loaded

h) pcple. pass. (*mughram*)

56:66 (66)	we are debt-loaded

*GH R Q

GHARIQA vb. (I)~(n.vb.) drowning

f) n.vb. (*gharq*)

10:90 (90)	till, when the drowning overtook him, he said

GHARQ n.m. (adv)~violently, vehemently

79:1 (1) by those that pluck out vehemently

AGHRAQA vb. (IV)~to drown (tr). (pcple. pass.) one who is drowned

a) perf. act.

2:50 (47) and delivered you, and drowned Pharaoh's folk
7:64 (62) We drowned those who cried lies to Our signs
7:136 (132) We took vengeance on them, and drowned them
8:54 (56) We drowned the folk of Pharaoh
10:73 (74) We drowned those who cried lies to Our signs
17:103 (105) We drowned him and those with him, all together
21:77 (77) they were an evil people, so We drowned them
25:37 (39) We drowned them, and made them to be a sign
26:66 (66) then We drowned the others
26:120 (120) then afterwards We drowned the rest
29:40 (39) We made the earth to swallow, and some We drowned
37:82 (80) then afterwards We drowned the rest
43:55 (55) We took vengenace on them, and We drowned them

b) impf. act. (*yughriqu*)

17:69 (71) and drown you for your thanklessness
18:71 (70) hast thou made a hole in it so as to drown its passengers?
36:43 (43) and if We will, We drown them

d) perf. pass. (*ughriqa*)

71:25 (25) because of their transgressions they were drowned

h) pcple. pass. (*mughraq*)

11:37 (39) those who have done evil; they shall be drowned
11:43 (45) the waves came between them, and he was among the drowned
23:27 (28) those who have done evil; they shall be drowned
44:24 (23) leave the sea becalmed; they are a drowned host

*GH R R

GHARRA vb. (I)~to deceive, delude

a) perf. act.

3:24 (23) the lies they forged has deluded them
6:70 (69) for a sport and a diversion, and whom the present life has deluded
6:130 (130) they were deluded by the present life
7:51 (49) a diversion and a sport, and whom the present life has deluded
8:49 (51) their religion has deluded them
45:35 (34) and the present life deluded you
57:14 (13) and you were in doubt, and fancies deluded you
57:14 (13) until God's commandment came, and the Deluder deluded you
82:6 (6) what deceived thee as to thy generous Lord

b) impf. act. (*yaghurru*)

3:196 (196)	let it not delude thee, that the unbelievers go to and fro
31:33 (33)	let not the present life delude you
31:33 (33)	and let not the Deluder delude you
35:5 (5)	let not the present life delude you
35:5 (5)	and let not the Deluder delude you
40:4 (4)	let not their going to and fro in the land delude thee

GHARŪR n.m.~deceiver, deluder, the Devil

31:33 (33)	let not the Deluder delude you concerning God
35:5 (5)	let not the Deluder delude you concerning God
57:14 (13)	and the Deluder deluded you concerning God

GHURŪR n.m.~delusion, deception

3:185 (182)	the present life is but the joy of delusion
4:120 (119)	there is nothing Satan promises them except delusion
6:112 (112)	revealing tawdry speech to each other, all as a delusion
7:22 (21)	so he led them on by delusion
17:64 (66)	Satan promises them naught, except delusion
33:12 (12)	God and His Messenger promised us only delusion
35:40 (38)	the evildoers promise one another naught but delusion
57:20 (20)	the present life is but the joy of delusion
67:20 (20)	the unbelievers are only in delusion

*GH R W

AGHRÁ vb. (IV)~stir up, incite against, cause enmity

a) perf. act.

5:14 (17)	We have stirred up among them enmity and hatred

b) impf. act. (*yughrī*)

33:60 (60)	We shall assuredly urge thee against them

*GH S L

GHASALA vb. (I)~wash

c) impv. (*ighsil*)

5:6 (8)	O believers, when you stand up to pray wash your faces

GHISLĪN n.m.~foul pus, filth

69:36 (36)	neither any food saving foul pus

MUGHTASAL n.m.~place of washing, laving-place

38:42 (41)	this is a laving-place cool, and a drink

IGHTASALA vb. (VIII)~wash oneself

b) impf. act. (*yaghtasilu*)

4:43 (46)	you are traversing a way — until you have washed yourselves

*GH S Q

GHASAQA vb. (I)~(n.vb.) darkening of the night

f) n.vb. (*ghasaq*)

17:78 (80)	perform the prayer at the sinking of the sun to the darkening of the night

GHĀSIQ n.m.~darkness

113:3 (3)	from the evil of darkness when it gathers

GHASSĀQ n.m.~pus, filth

38:57 (57)	so let them taste it — boiling water and pus
78:25 (25)	save boiling water and pus

*GH SH Y

GHASHIYA vb. (I)~overcome, overwhelm; to be overwhelmed. (pcple. pass.) one in a swoon

a) perf. act.

20:78 (81)	but they were overwhelmed by the sea
20:78 (81)	but they (were overwhelmed) by the sea however they were overwhelmed
31:32 (31)	when the waves cover them like shadows they call upon God

b) impf. act. (*yaghsha*)

3:154 (148)	after grief, security — a slumber overcoming a party
14:50 (51)	their faces enveloped by the Fire
24:40 (40)	they are as shadows upon a sea obscure covered by a billow
29:55 (55)	upon the day the chastisement shall overwhelm them
44:11 (10)	covering the people; this is a painful chastisement
53:16 (16)	when there covered the Lote-Tree that which (covered)
53:16 (16)	when there (covered) the Lote-Tree that which covered
91:4 (4)	and by the night when it enshrouds him
92:1 (1)	by the night enshrouding

e) impf. pass. (*yughshá*)

33:19 (19)	thou seest them looking at thee, their eyes rolling like one who swoons of death

h) pcple. pass. (*maghshī*)

47:20 (22)	thou seest those in whose hearts is sickness looking at thee as one who swoons of death

GHĀSHIYAH n.f.~covering, enveloping

7:41 (39)	Gehenna shall be their cradle, above them coverings
12:107 (107)	there shall come upon them no enveloping of the chastisement of God
88:1 (1)	hast thou received the story of the Enveloper?

GHISHĀWAH n.f.~veil, covering

2:7 (6)	a seal on their hearts and on their hearing, and on their eyes is a covering
45:23 (22)	a seal upon his hearing and his heart, and laid a covering on his eyes

GHASHSHÁ vb. (II)~cover, overcome

a) perf. act.

53:54 (55) so that there covered it that which (covered)
53:54 (55) so that there (covered) it that which covered

b) impf. act. (*yughashshi*)

8:11 (11) when He was causing slumber to overcome you as a security from Him

AGHSHÁ vb. (IV)~cover

a) perf. act.

36:9 (8) We have covered them, so they do not see

b) impf. act. (*yughshī*)

7:54 (52) then sat Himself upon the Throne, covering the day with the night
13:3 (3) He placed there two kinds, covering the day with the night

d) perf. pass. (*ughshiya*)

10:27 (28) as if their faces were covered with strips of night shadowy

TAGHASHSHÁ vb. (V)~cover

a) perf. act.

7:189 (189) when he covered her, she bore a light burden

ISTAGHSHÁ vb. (X)~cover or wrap with a garment

a) perf. act.

71:7 (6) they put their fingers in their ears, and wrapped them in their garments

b) impf. act. (*yastaghshī*)

11:5 (6) they wrap themselves in their garments

*GH Ṣ B

GHAṢB n.m. (adv)~by force
18:79 (78) there was a king who was seizing every ship by brutal force

*GH Ṣ Ṣ

GHUṢṢAH n.f.~that which sticks in the throat and chokes
73:13 (13) food that chokes, and a painful chastisement

*GH TH W

GHUTHĀʾ n.m.~scum, refuse, wrack
23:41 (43) the Cry seized them justly, and We made them as scum
87:5 (5) then made it a blackening wrack

*GH Ṭ SH

AGHṬASHA vb. (IV)~to make dark

a) perf. act.

79:29 (29) and darkened its night, and brought forth its forenoon

*GH Ṭ Y

GHIṬĀʾ n.m.~veil, covering

18:101 (101) whose eyes were covered against My remembrance
50:22 (21) We have now removed from thee thy covering

*GH W L

GHAWL n.m.~sickness, headache, inebriation

37:47 (46) wherein no sickness is, neither intoxication

*GH W R

GHĀRA vb. (I)~(n.vb.) the of sinking in the ground

f) n.vb. (*ghawr*)

18:41 (39) in the morning the water of it will be sunk into the earth
67:30 (30) what think you? If in the morning your water should have vanished into the earth

GHĀR n.m.~cave, cavern

9:40 (40) the second of two, when the two were in the Cave

MAGHĀRAH n.f.~cavern, cave

9:57 (57) if they could find a shelter, or some caverns

AGHĀRA vb. (IV)~(pcple. act.) raider

g) pcple. act. (*mughīr*)

100:3 (3) by the dawn-raiders

*GH W Ṣ

GHĀṢA vb. (I)~to dive

b) impf. act. (*yaghūṣu*)

21:82 (82) and of the Satans some dived for him

GHAWWĀṢ n.m.~diver

38:37 (36) and the Satans, every builder and diver

*GH W TH

YAGHŪTH n.prop.~Yaghuth

71:23 (23) Yaghuth, Ya'uq, neither Nasr

ISTAGHĀTHA vb. (X)~call or cry for aid or succour

a) perf. act.

28:15 (14)	then the one that was of his party cried to him to aid him

b) impf. act. (*yastagīthu*)

8:9 (9)	when you were calling upon your Lord for succour
18:29 (28)	if they call for succour, they will be (succoured) with water
46:17 (16)	while they call upon God for succour

*GH W Ṭ

GHĀʾIṬ n.m.~a privy

4:43 (46)	or if any of you comes from the privy
5:6 (9)	or if any of you comes from the privy

*GH W Y

GHAWÁ vb. (I)~to err. (n.vb.) error. (pcple. act.) one who is in error or pervert

a) perf. act.

20:121 (119)	Adam disobeyed his Lord, and so he erred
28:63 (63)	we perverted them even as we ourselves erred
53:2 (2)	your comrade is not astray, neither errs

f) n.vb. (*ghay*)

2:256 (257)	rectitude has become clear from error
7:146 (143)	they see the way of error, they will take it for a way
7:202 (201)	and their brothers they lead on into error
19:59 (60)	so they shall encounter error

g) pcple. act. (*ghāwī*)

7:175 (174)	Satan followed after him, and he became one of the perverts
15:42 (42)	except those that follow thee, being perverse
26:91 (91)	and Hell advanced for the perverse
26:94 (94)	they shall be pitched into it, they and the perverse
26:224 (224)	and the poets — the perverse follow them
37:32 (31)	therefore we perverted you, and we ourselves were perverts

GHAWĪY n.m.~one who is in error, a quarreller

28:18 (17)	Moses said to him, 'Clearly thou art a quarreller'

AGHWÁ vb. (IV)~to pervert, lead astray

a) perf. act.

7:16 (15)	for Thy perverting me, I shall surely sit in ambush for them
15:39 (39)	my Lord, for Thy perverting me I shall deck all fair
28:63 (63)	our Lord, those whom we perverted
28:63 (63)	we perverted them even as we ourselves erred
37:32 (31)	therefore we perverted you

b) impf. act. (*yughwī*)

11:34 (36)	if God desires to pervert you; He is your Lord
15:39 (39)	I shall pervert them, all together
38:82 (83)	I shall pervert them all together

*GH Y B

GHĀBA vb. (I)~(n.vb.) secret, unseen. (pcple. act.) that which is absent or hidden

f) n.vb. (*ghayb*)

2:3 (2)	who believe in the Unseen, and perform the prayer
2:33 (31)	did I not tell you I know the unseen things of the heavens
3:44 (39)	that is of the tidings of the Unseen, that We reveal to thee
3:179 (174)	and God will not inform you of the Unseen
4:34 (38)	righteous women are therefore obedient, guarding the secret
5:94 (95)	that God may know who fears Him in the Unseen
5:109 (108)	Thou art the Knower of the things unseen
5:116 (116)	Thou knowest the things unseen
6:50 (50)	I know not the Unseen
6:59 (59)	with Him are the keys of the Unseen
6:73 (73)	He is Knower of the Unseen and the visible
7:188 (188)	had I knowledge of the Unseen I would have acquired much good
9:78 (79)	and that God knows the things unseen
9:94 (95)	you will be returned to Him who knows the unseen
9:105 (106)	you will be returned to Him who knows the unseen
10:20 (21)	the Unseen belongs only to God
11:31 (33)	I know not the Unseen
11:49 (51)	that is 34the tidings of the Unseen, that We reveal to thee
11:123 (123)	to God belongs the Unseen in the heavens
12:52 (52)	so that he may know I betrayed him not secretly
12:81 (81)	we were no guardians of the Unseen
12:102 (103)	that is of the tidings of the Unseen that We reveal
13:9 (10)	the Knower of the unseen and the visible
16:77 (79)	to God belongs the Unseen in the heavens
18:22 (21)	they will say...guessing at the Unseen
18:26 (25)	to Him belongs the Unseen in the heavens
19:61 (62)	Gardens of Eden that the All-merciful promised His servants in the Unseen
19:78 (81)	what, has he observed the Unseen
21:49 (50)	such as fear their Lord in the Unseen, trembling
23:92 (94)	who has knowledge of the Unseen and the Visible
27:65 (66)	none knows the Unseen in the heavens and earth except God
32:6 (5)	He is the knower of the Unseen and the Visible
34:3 (3)	it shall come to you, by Him who knows the Unseen
34:14 (13)	had they only known the Unseen, they would not have continued
34:48 (47)	my Lord hurls the truth — the Knower of the Unseen
34:53 (52)	seeing they disbelieved in it before, guessing at the Unseen
35:18 (19)	who fear their Lord in the Unseen and perform the prayer
35:38 (36)	God knows the Unseen in the heavens and the earth
36:11 (10)	and who fears the All-merciful in the Unseen
39:46 (47)	who knowest the Unseen and the Visible
49:18 (18)	God knows the Unseen of the heavens and of the earth
50:33 (32)	whosoever fears the All-merciful in the Unseen
52:41 (41)	or is the Unseen in their keeping, and so they are writing it down?
53:35 (36)	does he possess the knowledge of the Unseen

57:25 (25)	so that God might know who helps Him, and His Messengers, in the Unseen
59:22 (22)	He is the knower of the Unseen and the Visible
62:8 (8)	then you shall be returned to the Knower of the Unseen
64:18 (18)	Knower He of the Unseen and the Visible
67:12 (12)	those who fear their Lord in the Unseen
68:47 (47)	or is the Unseen in their keeping
72:26 (26)	Knower He of the Unseen
72:26 (26)	He discloses not His Unseen to anyone
81:24 (24)	he is not niggardly of the Unseen

g) pcple. act. (*ghāʾib*)

7:7 (6)	assuredly We were not absent
27:20 (20)	I do not see the hoopoe? Or is he among the absent?
27:75 (77)	not a thing is there hidden in heaven and earth
82:16 (16)	nor shall they ever be absent from it

GHAYĀBAH n.f.~the bottom (of a well or pit)

12:10 (10)	kill not Joseph, but cast him into the bottom of the pit
12:15 (15)	when they went with him, and agreed to put him in the bottom of the well

IGHTĀBA vb. (VIII)~to backbite

b) impf. act. (*yaghtābu*)

49:12 (12)	do not spy, neither backbite one another

*GH Y Ḍ

GHĀḌA vb. (I)~to shrink, abate, diminish, subside

b) impf. act. (*yaghīḍu*)

13:8 (9)	God knows what every female bears, and the wombs' shrinking and swelling

d) perf. pass. (*ghīḍa*)

11:44 (46)	and the waters subsided

*GH Y R

GHAYYARA vb. (II)~to alter, to change. (pcple. act.) one who causes to change

b) impf. act. (*yughayyiru*)

4:119 (118)	I will command them and they will alter God's creation
8:53 (55)	He conferred on a people until they changed what was within themselves
13:11 (12)	God changes not what is in a people
13:11 (12)	until they change what is in themselves

g) pcple. act. (*mughayyir*)

8:53 (55)	God would never change His favour that He conferred on a people

TAGHAYYARA vb. (V)~to be changed

b) impf. act. (*yataghayyaru*)

47:15 (16)	rivers of water unstaling, rivers of milk unchanging in flavour

*GH Y TH

GHĀTHA vb.~to succour, to aid (with rain)

e) impf. pass. (*yughāthu*)

12:49 (49)	thereafter there shall come a year wherein the people will be succoured
18:29 (28)	they will be succoured with water like molten copper

GHAYTH n.m.~rain

31:34 (34)	He sends down the rain
42:28 (27)	it is He who sends down the rain
57:20 (19)	it is as a rain whose vegetation pleases the unbelievers

ISTAGHĀTHA vb. (X)~to call for succour; to ask for rain

18:29 (28)	if they call for succour they will (be succoured) with water like molten copper

*GH Y Ẓ

GHĀẒA vb. (I)~to enrage, irritate, anger. (n.vb.) rage, anger, irritation. (pcple. act.) enraging

b) impf. act. (*yaghīẓu*)

9:120 (121)	neither tread they any tread enraging the unbelievers
22:15 (15)	behold whether his guile does away with what enrages him
48:29 (29)	that through them He may enrage the unbelievers

f) n.vb. (*ghayẓ*)

3:119 (115)	they bite at you their fingers, *enraged*
3:119 (115)	die in your rage
3:134 (128)	who expend in prosperity and adversity in almsgiving, and restrain their rage
9:15 (15)	He will remove the rage within their hearts
33:25 (25)	God sent back those that were unbelievers in their rage
67:8 (8)	and wellnigh bursts asunder with rage

g) pcple. act. (*ghāʾiẓ*)

26:55 (55)	and indeed they are enraging us

TAGHAYYAẒA vb. (V)~(n.vb.) a raging furiously, bubbling

f) n.vb. (*taghayyuẓ*)

25:12 (13)	they shall hear its bubbling and sighing

*GH Z L

GHAZALA vb. (I)~(n.vb.) the act of spinning, that which is spun (thread) *f*) n.vb. (*ghazl*)

16:92 (94) be not as a woman who breaks her thread, after it is firmly spun

*GH Z W

GHAZĀ vb. (I)~(pcple. act.) (pl) raiders, combatants

g) pcple. act. (*ghāzī*)

3:156 (150) their brothers, when they journey in the land, or are upon expeditions

HĀ

*H ʾ T

HĀTI vb. (?)~bring, produce

c) impv. (*hāti*)

2:111 (105)	produce your proof, if you speak truly
21:24 (24)	bring your proof! This is the Remembrance
27:64 (65)	produce your proof, if you speak truly
28:75 (75)	produce your proof! Then will they know

*H B Ṭ

HABAṬA vb. (I)~to get down, descend, crash down

b) impf. act. (*yahbiṭu*)

2:74 (69)	others crash down in the fear of God

c) impv. (*ihbiṭ*)

2:36 (34)	get you all down, each of you an enemy of each
2:38 (36)	get you down out of it, all together
2:61 (58)	get you down to Egypt
7:13 (12)	get thee down out of it
7:24 (23)	get you down, each of you an enemy to each
11:48 (50)	Noah, get thee down in peace from Us
20:123 (121)	get you down, both of you together

*H B W

HABĀʾ n.m.~dust

25:23 (25)	what work they have done, and make it a scattered dust
56:6 (6)	and become a dust scattered

*H D D

HADDA vb. (I)~(n.vb.) demolition, crashing

f) n.vb. (*hadd*)

19:90 (92)	the mountains wellnigh fall down crashing

*H D M

HADDAMA vb. (II)~to destroy, demolish

d) perf. pass. (*huddima*)

22:40 (41)	there had been destroyed cloisters and churches

*H D H D

HUD.HUD n.m.~hoopoe (bird)

27:20 (20)	how is it with me, that I do not see the hoopoe?

*H D Y

HADÁ (1) vb. (I)~(n.vb.) offering, gift, sacrifice

f) n.vb. (*hady*)

2:196 (192)	such offering as may be feasible
2:196 (192)	shave not your heads, till the offering reaches its place
2:196 (192)	let his offering be such as may be feasible
5:2 (2)	profane not God's waymarks ... neither the offering
5:95 (96)	an offering to reach the Kaaba
5:97 (98)	an establishment for men, and the holy month, the offering
48:25 (25)	and barred you from the Holy Mosque and the offering

HADÁ (2) vb. (I)~to guide, lead in the right way, direct aright. (n.vb.) guidance. (pcple. act.) a guide, one who guides; Guide (Divine attribute)

a) perf. act.

2:143 (138)	save for those whom God has guided
2:185 (181)	magnify God that He has guided you
2:198 (194)	remember Him as He has guided you
2:213 (209)	then God guided those who believed to the truth
3:8 (6)	after that Thou hast guided us
4:68 (70)	and guided them on a straight path
6:71 (70)	after that God has guided us
6:80 (80)	and He has guided me
6:84 (84)	each one We guided
6:84 (84)	and Noah We guided before
6:87 (87)	We guided them to a straight path
6:90 (90)	those are they whom God has guided
6:149 (150)	He would have guided you all
6:161 (162)	my Lord has guided me to a straight path
7:30 (28)	a part He guided
7:43 (41)	praise belongs to God, who guided us
7:43 (41)	had God not guided us, we had surely never been guided
9:115 (116)	after that He has guided them

13:31 (30)	He would have guided men all together
14:12 (15)	seeing that He has guided us
14:21 (25)	if God had guided us
14:21 (25)	we would have guided you
16:9 (9)	He would have guided you all together
16:36 (38)	then some of them God guided
16:121 (122)	He chose him, and He guided him
19:58 (59)	of those We guided and chose
20:50 (52)	who gave everything its creation then guided it
20:79 (81)	and was no guide to them
20:122 (120)	and He guided him
22:37 (38)	for that He has guided you
37:118 (118)	and guided them in the straight path
39:18 (19)	those are they whom God has guided
39:57 (58)	if only God had guided me
41:17 (16)	as for Thamood, We guided them
49:17 (17)	He has guided you to belief
76:3 (3)	surely We guided him upon the way
87:3 (3)	who determined and guided
90:10 (10)	and guided him on the two highways
93:7 (7)	did He not find thee erring, and guide thee?

b) impf. act. (*yahdī*)

2:26 (24)	thereby He guides many
2:142 (136)	He guides whomsoever He will
2:213 (209)	God guides whomsoever He will
2:258 (260)	God guides not the people of the evildoers
2:264 (266)	God guides not the people of the unbelievers
2:272 (274)	but God guides whomsoever He will
3:86 (80)	how shall God guide a people who have disbelieved
3:86 (80)	God guides not the people of the evildoers
4:26 (31)	and to guide you in the institutions
4:88 (90)	do you desire to guide him
4:137 (136)	God is not likely to forgive them, neither to guide them
4:168 (166)	God would not forgive them, neither guide them
4:175 (174)	and will guide them to Him
5:16 (18)	God guides whosoever follows His good pleasure
5:16 (18)	He guides them to a straight path
5:51 (56)	God guides not the people of the evildoers
5:67 (71)	God guides not the people of the unbelievers
5:108 (107)	God guides not the people of the ungodly
6:77 (77)	if my Lord does not guide me
6:88 (88)	He guides by it whom He will of His servants
6:125 (125)	whomsoever God desires to guide
6:144 (145)	God guides not the people of the evildoers
7:100 (98)	is it not a guidance to those who inherit the earth
7:148 (146)	neither guided them upon any way
7:155 (154)	and guidest whom Thou wilt
7:159 (159)	there is a nation who guide by the truth
7:178 (177)	whomsoever God guides, he is rightly guided
7:181 (180)	of those We created are a nation who guide by the truth
9:19 (19)	God guides not the people of the evildoers
9:24 (24)	God guides not the people of the ungodly
9:37 (37)	God guides not the people of the unbelievers
9:80 (81)	God guides not the people of the ungodly

9:109 (110)	God guides not the people of the evildoers
10:9 (9)	their Lord will guide them
10:25 (26)	He guides whomsoever He will
10:35 (36)	is there any of your associates who guides to the truth?
10:35 (36)	God — He guides to the truth
10:35 (36)	which is worthier to be followed — He who guides to the truth
10:35 (36)	or he who guides not unless he is guided
10:43 (44)	wilt thou then guide the blind
12:52 (52)	God guides not the guile of the treacherous
13:27 (27)	He guides to Him all who are penitent
14:4 (4)	He guides whomsoever He will
16:37 (39)	God guides not those whom He leads astray
16:93 (95)	He leads astray whom He will, and guides whom He will
16:104 (106)	those that believe not in the signs of God God will not guide
16:107 (109)	God guides not the people of the unbelievers
17:9 (9)	this Koran guides to the way that is straightest
17:97 (99)	whomsoever God guides, he is rightly guided
18:17 (16)	whomsoever God guides, he is rightly guided
18:24 (23)	my Lord will guide me unto something nearer to rectitude
19:43 (44)	so follow me, and I will guide thee
20:128 (128)	is it not a guidance to them
21:73 (73)	and appointed them to be leaders guiding by Our command
22:4 (4)	he guides him to the chastisement of the burning
22:16 (16)	God guides whom He desires
24:35 (35)	God guides to His Light whom He will
24:46 (45)	God guides whomsoever He will
26:62 (62)	my Lord is with me; He will guide me
26:78 (78)	who created me, and Himself guides me
27:63 (64)	He who guides you in the shadows
28:22 (21)	my Lord will guide me on the right way
28:50 (50)	God guides not the people of the evildoers
28:56 (56)	thou guidest not whom thou likest
28:56 (56)	but God guides whom He wills
29:69 (69)	We shall guide them in Our ways
30:29 (28)	who shall guide those whom God has led astray?
32:24 (24)	We appointed from among them leaders guiding by Our command
32:26 (26)	is it not a guidance to them?
33:4 (4)	God speaks the truth, and guides on the way
34:6 (6)	[it] guides to the path of the All-mighty
35:8 (9)	whomsoever He will He guides
37:99 (97)	I am going to my Lord; He will guide me
39:3 (5)	surely God guides not him who is a liar
39:23 (24)	that is God's guidance, whereby He guides whomsoever He will
39:37 (38)	whomso God guides, none shall lead him astray
40:28 (29)	God guides not him who is prodigal
40:29 (30)	I only guide you in the way of rectitude
40:38 (41)	I will guide you in the way of rectitude
42:13 (12)	He guides to Himself whosoever turns
42:52 (52)	whereby We guide whom We will of Our servants
42:52 (52)	thou shalt guide unto a straight path
43:27 (26)	and He will guide me
43:40 (39)	shalt thou guide the blind
45:23 (22)	who shall guide him after God?
46:10 (9)	God guides not the people of the evildoers
46:30 (29)	what was before it, guiding to the truth

47:5 (6)	He will guide them, and dispose their minds aright
48:2 (2)	and guide thee on a straight path
48:20 (20)	and to guide you on a straight path
61:5 (5)	God guides never the people of the ungodly
61:7 (7)	God guides never the people of the evildoers
62:5 (5)	god guides never the people of the evildoers
63:6 (6)	God guides not the people of the ungodly
64:6 (6)	shall mortals be our guides?
64:11 (11)	He will guide his heart
72:2 (2)	guiding to rectitude. We believe in it
74:31 (34)	He guides whomsoever He will
79:19 (19)	and that I should guide thee to thy Lord

c) impv. (*ihdi*)

1:6 (5)	guide us in the straight path
37:23 (23)	and guide them unto the path of Hell
38:22 (21)	and guide us to the right path

d) perf. pass. (*hudiya*)

3:101 (96)	he is guided to a straight path
22:24 (24)	they shall be guided unto goodly speech
22:24 (24)	they shall be guided unto the path of the All-laudable

e) impf. pass. (*yuhdá*)

10:35 (36)	unless he is guided

f) n.vb. (*hudá*)

2:2 (1)	a guidance to the godfearing
2:5 (4)	those are upon guidance from their Lord
2:16 (15)	those are they that have bought error at the price of guidance
2:38 (36)	yet there shall come to you guidance from Me
2:38 (36)	whosoever follows My guidance, no fear shall be on them
2:97 (91)	for a guidance and good tidings to the believers
2:120 (114)	God's guidance is the true (guidance)
2:120 (114)	God's (guidance) is the true guidance
2:159 (154)	those who conceal the clear signs and the guidance
2:175 (170)	those are they that have bought error at the price of guidance
2:185 (181)	wherein the Koran was sent down to be a guidance
2:185 (181)	clear signs of the Guidance and the Salvation
2:272 (274)	thou art not responsible for guiding them
3:4 (2)	aforetime, as guidance to the people
3:73 (66)	the true guidance is God's (guidance)
3:73 (66)	the true (guidance) is God's guidance
3:96 (90)	a place holy, and a guidance to all beings
3:138 (132)	this is an exposition for mankind, and a guidance
4:115 (115)	after the guidance has become clear to him
5:44 (48)	the Torah, wherein is guidance and light
5:46 (50)	the Gospel, wherein is guidance and light
5:46 (50)	a guidance and an admonition
6:35 (35)	He would have gathered them to the guidance
6:71 (70)	though he has friends who call him to guidance
6:71 (70)	God's guidance is the true (guidance)
6:71 (70)	God's (guidance) is the true guidance

6:88 (88)	that is God's guidance; He guides by it
6:90 (90)	so follow their guidance
6:91 (91)	that Moses brought as a light and a guidance
6:154 (155)	a guidance and a mercy
6:157 (158)	a clear sign has come to you from your Lord, and a guidance
7:52 (50)	a guidance and a mercy unto a people that believe
7:154 (153)	in the inscription of them was guidance
7:193 (192)	if you call them to guidance they will not follow you
7:198 (197)	if you call them to the guidance they do not hear
7:203 (202)	clear testimony from your Lord, guidance, and mercy
9:33 (33)	He who has sent His Messenger with the guidance
10:57 (58)	a healing for what is in the breasts, and a guidance
12:111 (111)	a distinguishing of every thing, and a guidance
16:37 (39)	though thou art ever so eager to guide them
16:64 (66)	and as a guidance
16:89 (91)	the Book making clear everything, and as a guidance
16:102 (104)	a guidance and good tidings to those who surrender
17:2 (2)	We gave Moses the Book, and made it a guidance
17:94 (96)	naught prevented men from believing when the guidance came to them
18:13 (12)	We increased them in guidance
18:55 (53)	naught prevented men from believing when the guidance came unto them
18:57 (56)	though thou callest them to the guidance
19:76 (78)	God shall increase those who were guided in guidance
20:10 (10)	or I shall find at the fire guidance
20:47 (49)	peace be upon him who follows the guidance
20:123 (121)	if there comes to you from Me guidance
20:123 (122)	whosoever follows My guidance shall not go astray
22:8 (8)	that disputes concerning God without knowledge or guidance
22:67 (66)	thou art upon a straight guidance
27:2 (2)	a guidance, and good tidings unto the believers
27:77 (79)	it is a guidance, and a mercy unto the believers
28:37 (37)	My Lord knows very well who comes with the guidance from Him
28:43 (43)	to be examples and a guidance
28:50 (50)	he who follows his caprice without guidance
28:57 (57)	should we follow the guidance with thee
28:85 (85)	my Lord knows very well who comes with guidance
31:3 (2)	for a guidance and a mercy to the good-doers
31:5 (4)	those are upon guidance from their Lord
31:20 (19)	that disputes concerning God without knowledge or guidance
32:13 (13)	We could have given every soul its guidance
32:23 (23)	We appointed it for a guidance
34:24 (23)	either we or you are upon right guidance
34:32 (31)	did we bar you from the guidance after it came to you?
39:23 (24)	that is God's guidance
40:53 (56)	We also gave Moses the guidance
40:54 (56)	for a guidance and for a reminder
41:17 (16)	they preferred blindness above guidance
41:44 (44)	to the believers it is a guidance
45:11 (10)	this is guidance
45:20 (19)	this is clear proofs for men, and a guidance
47:17 (19)	them He increases in guidance
47:25 (27)	those who have turned back in their traces after the guidance
47:32 (34)	and make a breach with the Messenger after the guidance
48:28 (28)	He who has sent His Messenger with the guidance
53:23 (23)	yet guidance has come to them from their Lord

61:9 (9)	He who has sent His Messenger with the guidance
72:13 (13)	when we heard the guidance, we believed in it
92:12 (12)	surely upon Us rests the guidance
96:11 (11)	what thinkest thou? If he were upon guidance

g) pcple. act. (*hādī*)

7:186 (185)	no guide he has
13:7 (8)	thou art only a warner, and a guide
13:33 (33)	whomsoever God leads astray, no guide has he
22:54 (53)	God ever guides those who believe to a straight path
25:31 (33)	thy Lord suffices as a guide and as a helper
27:81 (83)	thou shalt not guide the blind out of their error
30:53 (52)	thou shalt not guide the blind out of their error
39:23 (24)	whomsoever God leads astray, no guide has he
39:36 (37)	whomsoever God leads astray, no guide has he
40:33 (35)	whomsoever God leads astray, no guide has he

AHDÁ n.m. (comp. adj.)~more or better guided

4:51 (54)	these are more rightly guided on the way than the believers
6:157 (158)	we had surely been more rightly guided than they
17:84 (86)	your Lord knows very well what man is best guided
28:49 (49)	bring a Book from God that gives better guidance than these
35:42 (40)	they would be more rightly guided than any one of the nations
43:24 (23)	though I should bring you a better guidance
67:22 (22)	is he who walks prone upon his face better guided

HADĪYAH n.f.~a gift, present

27:35 (35)	now I will send them a present
27:36 (36)	nay, but instead you rejoice in your gift

IHTADÁ vb. (VIII)~to be truly guided. (pcple. act.) one who is right-guided

a) perf. act.

2:137 (131)	then they are truly guided
3:20 (19)	if they have surrendered, they are right guided
5:105 (104)	he who is astray cannot hurt you, if you are rightly guided
10:108 (108)	whosoever is guided, is (guided) only to his own gain
17:15 (16)	whosoever is guided, is only (guided) to his own gain
19:76 (78)	God shall increase those who were guided in guidance
20:82 (84)	and at last is guided
20:135 (135)	and who is guided
27:92 (94)	whosoever is guided, is only (guided) to his own gain
34:50 (49)	if I am guided, it is by what my Lord reveals to me
39:41 (42)	whosoever is guided, is only (guided) to his own gain
47:17 (19)	those who are guided aright
53:30 (31)	He knows very well those who are guided

b) impf. act. (*yahtadī*)

2:53 (50)	that haply you should be guided
2:135 (129)	be Jews or Christians and you shall be guided
2:150 (145)	that haply so you may be guided
2:170 (165)	and if they were not guided?
3:103 (99)	so haply you will be guided

4:98 (100)	can devise nothing and are not guided to a way
5:104 (103)	even if their fathers had knowledge of naught and were not guided
6:97 (97)	by them you might be guided in the shadows
7:43 (41)	had God not (guided) us we had surely never been guided
7:158 (158)	haply so you will be guided
10:108 (108)	whosoever (is guided) is guided only to his own gain
16:15 (15)	so haply you will be guided
16:16 (16)	by the stars they are guided
17:15 (16)	whosoever (is guided), is only guided to his own gain
18:57 (56)	yet they will not be guided
21:31 (32)	that haply so they may be guided
23:49 (51)	that haply they would be guided
24:54 (53)	if you obey him, you will be guided
27:24 (24)	and therefore they are not guided
27:41 (41)	and we shall behold whether she is guided
27:41 (41)	if she is of those that are not guided
27:92 (94)	whosoever (is guided), is only guided to his own gain
28:64 (64)	ah, if they had been guided
32:3 (2)	that haply so they may be guided
43:10 (9)	that haply you may be guided
46:11 (10)	since they are not guided by it

g) pcple. act. (*muhtadī*)

2:16 (15)	and they are not right-guided
2:70 (65)	if God will, we shall then be guided
2:157 (152)	those — they are the truly guided
6:56 (56)	and would not be of the right-guided
6:82 (82)	they are rightly guided
6:117 (117)	He knows very well the right-guided
6:140 (141)	they have gone astray, and are not right-guided
7:30 (28)	and [they] think them guided
7:178 (177)	whomsoever God guides, he is rightly guided
9:18 (18)	it may be that those will be among the guided
10:45 (46)	lost will be those who ... were not guided
16:125 (126)	He knows very well those who are guided
17:97 (99)	whomsoever God guides, he is rightly guided
18:17 (16)	whomsoever God guides, he is rightly guided
28:56 (56)	and knows very well those that are guided
36:21 (20)	such as ask no wage of you, that are right-guided
43:22 (21)	and we are guided upon their traces
43:37 (36)	they think they are guided
43:49 (48)	surely we shall be right-guided
57:26 (26)	some of them are guided
68:7 (7)	He knows very well those who are guided

*H Ḍ M

HAḌAMA vb. (I)~(n.vb.) injustice

f) n.vb. (*haḍm*)

20:112 (111)	shall fear neither wrong nor injustice

HAḌĪM n.m. (adj)~thin, slender

26:148 (148) sown fields, and palms with slender spathes

*H J ᶜ

HAJAᶜA vb. (I)~to slumber

b) impf. act. (*yahjaᶜu*)

51:17 (17) little of the night would they slumber

*H J D

TAHAJJADA vb. (V)~to keep vigil, to watch

c) impv. (*tahajjad*)

17:79 (81) as for the night, keep vigil a part of it

*H J R

HAJARA vb. (I)~to forsake, flee from, leave off, abstain from, abandon; to talk foolishly. (n.vb.) the act of forsaking, abandoning, leaving, etc. (pcple. pass.) that which is abandoned, shunned, forsaken

b) impf. act. (*yahjuru*)

23:67 (69) talking foolish talk by night

c) impv. (*uhjur*)

4:34 (38) banish them to their couches, and beat them
19:46 (47) so forsake me now for some while
73:10 (10) bear thou patiently what they say, and forsake them graciously
74:5 (5) and defilement flee

f) n.vb. (*hajr*)

73:10 (10) bear thou patiently what they say, and forsake them <...> graciously

h) pcple. pass. (*mahjūr*)

25:30 (32) my people have taken this Koran as a thing to be shunned

HĀJARA vb. (III)~to emigrate. (pcple. act.) one who emigrates, an emigrant

a) perf. act.

2:218 (215) those who emigrate and struggle in God's way
3:195 (194) those who emigrated, and were expelled from their habitations
8:72 (73) those who believe, and have emigrated

8:74 (75)	those who believe, and have emigrated
8:75 (76)	those who have believed afterwards and emigrated
9:20 (20)	those who believe, and have emigrated
16:41 (43)	those that emigrated in God's cause
16:110 (111)	who have emigrated after persecution, then struggled
22:58 (57)	those who emigrated in God's way and were slain
33:50 (49)	and aunts maternal, who have emigrated with thee
59:9 (9)	love whosoever has emigrated to them

b) impf. act. (*yuhājiru*)

4:89 (91)	take not to yourselves friends of them, until they emigrate in
4:97 (99)	so that you might have emigrated in it
4:100 (101)	whoso emigrates in the way of God
8:72 (73)	those who believe, but have not emigrated
8:72 (73)	towards them till they emigrate

g) pcple. act. (*muhājir*)

4:100 (101)	whoso goes forth from his house an emigrant to God
9:100 (101)	the first of the Emigrants and the Helpers
9:117 (118)	God has turned towards the Prophet and the Emigrants
24:22 (22)	and the poor and those who emigrate
29:26 (25)	I will flee to my Lord
33:6 (6)	nearer to one another in the Book of God than the believers and the emigrants
59:8 (8)	it is for the poor emigrants
60:10 (10)	when believing women come to you as emigrants

*H L ᶜ

HALŪᶜ n.m. (adj)~fretful

70:19 (19)	surely man was created fretful

*H L K

HALAKA vb. (I)~to perish. (pcple. act.) one perishes, perishing

a) perf. act.

4:176 (175)	if a man perishes having no children
8:42 (44)	that whosoever perished might perish by a clear sign
40:34 (36)	when he perished, you said
69:29 (29)	my authority is gone from me

b) impf. act. (*yahliku*)

8:42 (44)	that whosoever perished might perish by a clear sign

g) pcple. act. (*hālik*)

12:85 (85)	till thou art consumed, or among the perishing
28:88 (88)	all things perish, except His Face

MAHLIK n.m.~destruction

18:59 (58)	and appointed for their destruction a tryst
27:49 (50)	We were not witnesses of the destruction of his family

TAHLUKAH n.f.~perdition, destruction

2:195 (191)	cast not yourselves by your own hands into destruction

AHLAKA vb. (IV)~to destroy, cause to perish. (pcple. act.) one who destroys or causes to perish. (pcple. pass.) one who is destroyed or made to perish

a) perf. act.

3:117 (113)	and it destroyed that; God wronged them not
6:6 (6)	have they not regarded how We destroyed before them many a generation
6:6 (6)	We destroyed them because of their sins
7:4 (3)	how many a city We have destroyed
7:155 (154)	Thou wouldst have destroyed them before, and me
8:54 (56)	We destroyed them because of their sins
10:13 (14)	We destroyed the generations before you
15:4 (4)	never a city have We destroyed, but it had a known decree
17:17 (18)	how many generations We have destroyed after Noah
18:59 (58)	We destroyed them when they did evil
19:74 (75)	how may a generation We destroyed before them
19:98 (98)	how many a generation We destroyed before them
20:128 (128)	how many generations We destroyed before them
20:134 (134)	We destroyed them with a chastisement aforetime
21:6 (6)	not one city that We destroyed before them believed
21:9 (9)	and We destroyed the prodigal
21:95 (95)	there is a ban upon any city that We have destroyed
22:45 (44)	how many a city We have destroyed in its evildoing
26:139 (139)	they cried him lies; then We destroyed them
26:208 (208)	never a city We destroyed, but it had warners
28:43 (43)	after that We had destroyed the former generations
28:58 (58)	how many a city We have destroyed that flourished in insolent ease
28:78 (78)	did he not know that God had destroyed before him generations
32:26 (26)	how many generations We destroyed before them
36:31 (30)	have they not seen how many generations We have destroyed
38:3 (2)	how many a generation We destroyed before them
43:8 (7)	We destroyed men stronger in valour than they
44:37 (37)	and those before them whom We destroyed
46:27 (26)	We destroyed the cities about you
47:13 (14)	(how many a city) have We destroyed
50:36 (35)	how many a generation We destroyed before them
53:50 (51)	and that He destroyed Ad, the ancient
54:51 (51)	We have destroyed the likes of you
67:28 (28)	what think you? If God destroys me and those with me
90:6 (6)	I have consumed wealth abundant

b) impf. act. (*yuhliku*)

2:205 (201)	to do corruption there and to destroy the tillage
5:17 (19)	if He desires to destroy the Messiah
6:26 (26)	it is only themselves they destroy
7:129 (126)	perchance your Lord will destroy your enemy
7:155 (154)	wilt Thou destroy us for what the foolish ones of us have done?

7:173 (172)	wilt Thou then destroy us for the deeds of the vain-doers?
9:42 (42)	so destroying their souls
11:117 (119)	thy Lord would never destroy the cities unjustly
14:13 (16)	We will surely destroy the evildoers
17:16 (17)	when We desire to destroy a city
45:24 (23)	we die, and we live, and nothing but Time destroys us
77:16 (16)	did We not destroy the ancients

d) perf. pass. (*uhlika*)

69:5 (5)	they were destroyed by the Screamer
69:6 (6)	they were destroyed by a wind clamorous

e) impf. pass. (*yuhlaku*)

6:47 (47)	shall any be destroyed, except the people
46:35 (35)	shall any be destroyed but the people

g) pcple. act. (*muhlik*)

6:131 (131)	thy Lord would never destroy the cities unjustly
7:164 (164)	why do you admonish a people God is about to destroy
17:58 (60)	We shall destroy it before the Day of Resurrection
28:59 (59)	thy Lord never destroyed the cities until He sent in their mother-city
28:59 (59)	and We never destroyed the cities
29:31 (30)	we shall destroy the people of this city

h) pcple. pass. (*muhlak*)

23:48 (50)	they were among the destroyed

*H L L

AHALLA vb. (IV)~to hallow, to invoke the Name of God (at the time of the slaughter of an animal)

d) perf. pass. (*uhilla*)

2:173 (168)	what has been hallowed to other than God
5:3 (4)	what has been hallowed to other than God
6:145 (146)	an ungodly thing that has been hallowed to other than God
16:115 (116)	what has been hallowed to other than God

AHILLAH n.m. (pl. of *hilāl*)~a new moon

2:189 (185)	they will question thee concerning the new moons

*H L M

HALUMMA vb. (?)~Come! Produce! Bring!

c) impv. (*halumma*)

6:150 (151)	produce your witnesses, those who testify
33:18 (18)	come to us, and come to battle but little

*H M D

HAMADA vb. (I)~(pcple. act.) blackened, barren, lifeless

g) pcple. act. f. (*hāmidah*)

22:5 (5)	thou beholdest the earth blackened

*H M M

HAMMA vb. (I)~to purpose, to be about to do something, to think about, to design; (with prep. *bi-*) to desire someone, to take someone (sexually)

a) perf. act.

3:122 (118)	when two parties of you were about to lose heart
4:113 (113)	a party of them purposed to lead thee astray
5:11 (14)	when a certain people purposed to stretch against you
9:13 (13)	a people who broke their oaths and purposed to expel the Messenger
9:74 (75)	they purposed what they never attained to
12:24 (24)	she desired him; (and he would have taken her)
12:24 (24)	(she desired him) and he would have taken her
40:5 (5)	every nation purposed against their Messenger to seize him

AHAMMA vb. (IV)~to cause anxiety or grief

a) perf. act.

3:154 (148)	and a party themselves had grieved

*H M N

HĀMĀN n.prop.~Haman

28:6 (5)	to show Pharaoh and Haman, and their hosts
28:8 (7)	Pharaoh and Haman, and their hosts, were of the sinners
28:38 (38)	kindle me, Haman, a fire upon the clay
29:39 (38)	and Korah, and Pharaoh, and Haman
40:24 (25)	to Pharaoh, Haman and Korah
40:36 (38)	Pharaoh said, 'Haman, build for me a tower' a tower

*H M R

INHAMARA vb. (VII)~(pcple. act.) pouring forth, torrential

g) pcple. act. (*munhamir*)

54:11 (11)	We opened the gates of heaven unto water torrential

*H M S

HAMASA vb. (I)~(n.vb.) a shuffling noise, murmuring, whispering

f) n.vb. (*hams*)

20:108 (107)	so that thou hearest naught but a murmuring

*H M Z

HAMAZĀT n.f.~evil suggestions of the Devil

23:97 (99)	I take refuge in Thee from the evil suggestions of the Satans

HAMMĀZ n.m.~a slanderer, backbiter

68:11 (11)	backbiter, going about with slander

HUMAZAH n.com.~a backbiter

104:1 (1)	woe unto every backbiter, slanderer

*H N ʾ

HANĪʾ n.m. (adv)~wholesome, with wholesome appetite

4:4 (3)	consume it with wholesome appetite
52:19 (19)	eat and drink, with wholesome appetite
69:24 (24)	eat and drink with wholesome appetite
77:43 (43)	eat and drink, with wholesome appetite

*H R ʿ

HARAʿA vb. (I)~to run towards

e) impf. pass. (*yuhraʿu*)

11:78 (80)	his people came to him, running towards him
37:70 (68)	and they run in their footsteps

*H R B

HARABA vb. (I)~(n.vb.) flight

f) n.vb. (*harab*)

72:12 (12)	neither be able to frustrate Him by flight

*H R N

HĀRŪN n.prop.~Aaron

2:248 (249)	what the folk of Moses and Aaron's folk left behind
4:163 (161)	Jonah and Aaron and Solomon
6:84 (84)	Job and Joseph, Moses and Aaron
7:122 (119)	the Lord of Moses and Aaron
7:142 (138)	and Moses said to his brother Aaron
10:75 (76)	then We sent forth, after them, Moses and Aaron
19:28 (29)	Sister of Aaron, thy father was not a wicked man
19:53 (54)	We gave him his brother Aaron
20:30 (31)	Aaron, my brother
20:70 (73)	'We believe,' they said, 'in the Lord of Aaron and Moses.'
20:90 (92)	yet Aaron had aforetime said to them
20:92 (94)	what prevented thee, Aaron, when thou sawest them in error
21:48 (49)	We gave Moses and Aaron the Salvation and a Radiance
23:45 (47)	We sent Moses and his brother Aaron with Our signs
25:35 (37)	and appointed with him his brother Aaron as minister
26:13 (12)	and my tongue will not be loosed; so send to Aaron
26:48 (47)	the Lord of Moses and Aaron
28:34 (34)	moreover my brother Aaron is more eloquent than I
37:114 (114)	We also favoured Moses and Aaron
37:120 (120)	peace be upon Moses and Aaron

*H R T

HĀRŪT n.prop.~Harut

2:102 (96)	upon Babylon's two angels, Harut and Marut

*H SH M

HASHĪM n.m.~stubble, straw

18:45 (43)	in the morning it is straw the winds scatter
54:31 (31)	and they were as the wattles of a pen-builder

*H SH SH

HASHSHA vb. (I)~to beat down leaves from a tree

b) impf. act. (*yahushshu*)

20:18 (19)	with it I beat down leaves to feed my sheep

*H Ṭ ᶜ

AHṬAᶜA vb. (IV)~(pcple. act.) one who runs with outstretched neck

g) pcple. act. (*muhṭiᶜ*)

14:43 (44)	when they shall run with necks outstretched
54:8 (8)	running with outstretched necks to the Caller
70:36 (36)	what ails the unbelievers, running with outstretched necks

*H W

HUWA pron. m~he (not listed here); He (the pronominal depiction of the Divine Name)

2:29 (27)	it is He who created for you all that is in the earth
2:29 (27)	and He has knowledge of everything
2:37 (35)	truly He turns, and is All-compassionate
2:54 (51)	truly He turns, and is All-compassionate
2:137 (131)	He is the All-hearing, the All-knowing
2:139 (133)	Would you then dispute with us concerning God, [He] who is our Lord
2:163 (158)	Your God is One God; there is no god but He
2:255 (256)	God, there is no god but He
2:255 (256)	He is the All-high, the All-glorious
3:2 (1)	God, there is no god but He
3:6 (4)	it is He who forms you in the womb
3:6 (4)	there is no god but He
3:7 (5)	It is He who sent down upon thee the Book
3:18 (16)	God bears witness that there is no god but He
3:18 (16)	there is no god but He, the All-mighty, the All-wise
3:62 (55)	and assuredly God [He] is the All-mighty, the All-wise
3:150 (143)	God is your Protector, and He is the best of helpers
4:87 (89)	God — there is no god but He
4:108 (108)	He is with them while they meditate at night discourse
4:142 (141)	The hypocrites seek to trick God, but God [He] is tricking them
5:17 (19)	they are unbelievers who say, 'God [He] is the Messiah, Mary's son.'
5:72 (76)	they are unbelievers who say, 'God [He] is the Messiah, Mary's son.'
5:76 (80)	God [He] is the All-hearing, the All-knowing
5:120 (120)	and He is powerful over everything
6:2 (2)	it is He who created you of clay
6:3 (3)	He is God in the heavens and the earth
6:13 (13)	and He is the All-hearing, the All-knowing
6:14 (14)	He who feeds and is not fed
6:17 (17)	and if God visits thee with affliction none can remove it but He
6:17 (17)	He is powerful over everything
6:18 (18)	He is Omnipotent over His servants
6:18 (18)	and He is the All-wise, the All-aware
6:19 (19)	He is only One God, and I am quit of that you associate
6:57 (57)	and He is the Best of deciders
6:59 (59)	With Him are the keys of the Unseen; none knows them but He
6:60 (60)	It is He who recalls you by night
6:61 (61)	He is the Omnipotent over His servants
6:62 (62)	He is the swiftest of reckoners
6:65 (65)	He is able to send forth upon you chastisement

6:72 (71)	it is [He] unto Him you shall be mustered
6:73 (72)	It is He who created the heavens and the earth in truth
6:73 (73)	He is the All-wise, the All-aware
6:97 (97)	It is He who has appointed for you the stars
6:98 (98)	It is He who produced you from one living soul
6:99 (99)	It is He who sent down out of heaven water
6:101 (101)	and He has knowledge of everthing
6:102 (102)	that then is God your Lord; there is no god but He
6:102 (102)	for He is Guardian over everything
6:103 (103)	but He attains the eyes
6:103 (103)	He is the All-subtle, the All-aware
6:106 (106)	there is no god but He
6:114 (114)	For it is He who sent down to you the Book well-distinguished
6:115 (115)	He is the All-hearing, the All-knowing
6:117 (117)	Thy Lord [He] knows very well who goes astray from His path
6:117 (117)	He knows very well the right-guided
6:119 (119)	thy Lord [He] knows very well the transgressors
6:127 (127)	and He is their Protector for that they were doing
6:141 (142)	It is He who produces gardens trellised, and untrellised
6:165 (165)	It is He who has appointed you viceroys in the earth
7:57 (55)	It is He who looses the winds, bearing good tidings before His mercy
7:87 (85)	He is the best of judges
7:140 (136)	God, [He] who has preferred you above all beings
7:158 (158)	There is no god but He
7:187 (186)	none shall reveal it at its proper time, but He
7:189 (189)	It is He who created you out of one living soul
7:196 (195)	and He takes into His protection the righteous
8:61 (63)	He is the All-hearing, the All-knowing
8:62 (64)	He has confirmed thee with His help
9:31 (31)	there is no god but He
9:33 (33)	It is He who has sent His Messenger with the guidance
9:51 (51)	He is our Protector
9:104 (105)	God is He who accepts repentance from His servants
9:104 (105)	God — He turns, and is All-compassionate
9:118 (119)	surely God turns, and [He] is All-compassionate
9:129 (130)	there is no god but He
9:129 (130)	He is the Lord of the Mighty Throne
10:5 (5)	it is He who made the sun a radiance
10:22 (23)	it is He who conveys you on the land and the sea
10:56 (57)	He gives life, and makes to die
10:65 (66)	He is the All-hearing, the All-knowing
10:67 (68)	It is He who made for you the night to repose in it
10:68 (69)	Glory be to Him! He is All-sufficient
10:107 (107)	if God visits thee with affliction, none can remove it but He
10:107 (107)	He is the All-forgiving, the All-compassionate
10:109 (109)	and He is the best of judges
11:4 (4)	to He is powerful over everything
11:7 (9)	And it is He who created the heavens and the earth in six days
11:14 (17)	there is no god but He
11:34 (36)	He is your Lord, and unto Him you shall be returned
11:56 (59)	there is no creature that crawls, but He takes it by the forelock
11:61 (64)	It is He who produced you from the earth
11:66 (69)	thy Lord [He] is the All-strong, the All-mighty
12:34 (34)	surely He is the All-hearing, the All-knowing
12:64 (64)	He is the most merciful of the merciful

12:80 (80)	He is the best of judges
12:83 (83)	He is the All-knowing, the All-wise
12:92 (92)	He is the most merciful of the merciful
12:98 (99)	He is the All-forgiving, the All-compassionate
12:100 (101)	He is the All-knowing, the All-wise
13:3 (3)	It is He who stretched out the earth
13:12 (13)	It is He who shows you the lightning, for fear and hope
13:13 (14)	yet they dispute about God, [He] who is mighty in power
13:16 (17)	and He is the One, the Omnipotent
13:30 (29)	He is my Lord
13:30 (29)	there is no god but He
13:33 (33)	He who stands over every soul for what it has earned
13:41 (41)	He is swift at the reckoning
14:4 (4)	He is the All-mighty, the All-wise
14:52 (52)	that they may know that He is One God
15:25 (25)	it is thy Lord [He] shall muster them
15:86 (86)	surely thy Lord, He is the All-creator, the All-knowing
16:10 (10)	it is He who sends down to you out of heaven water
16:14 (14)	it is He who subjected to you the sea
16:51 (53)	He is only One God
16:60 (62)	He is the All-mighty, the All-wise
16:125 (126)	surely thy Lord [He] Knows very well those who have gone astray from His way
16:125 (126)	and He knows very well those who are guided
17:1 (1)	He is the All-hearing, the All-seeing
18:38 (36)	But lo, He is God, my Lord
18:44 (42)	He is best rewarding, best in the issue
20:8 (7)	God — there is no god but He
20:98 (98)	there is no god, but He alone
21:4 (4)	and He is the All-hearing, the All-knowing
21:33 (34)	It is He who created the night and the day
22:6 (6)	That is because God — He is the Truth
22:58 (57)	surely God [He] is the best of providers
22:62 (61)	that is because God — He is the Truth
22:62 (61)	God [He] is the All-high, the All-great
22:64 (63)	surely God — He is the All-sufficient, the All-laudable
22:66 (65)	it is He who gave you life
22:78 (77)	for He has chosen you
22:78 (77)	He named you Muslims
22:78 (78)	He is your Protector — an excellent Protector
23:72 (74)	and He is the best of providers
23:78 (80)	it is He who produced for you hearing, and eyes, and hearts
23:79 (81)	it is He who scattered you in the earth
23:80 (82)	it is He who gives life, and makes to die
23:88 (90)	[He is] protecting and Himself unprotected
23:116 (117)	there is no god but He
24:25 (25)	they shall know that God [He] is the manifest Truth
25:47 (49)	it is He who appointed the night for you to be garment
25:48 (50)	and it is He who has loosed the winds
25:53 (55)	and it is He who let forth the two seas
25:54 (56)	and it is He who created of water a mortal
25:62 (63)	and it is He who made the night and day a succession
26:9 (8)	surely thy Lord, He is the All-mighty, the All-compassionate
26:68 (68)	surely thy Lord, He is the All-mighty, the All-compassionate
26:78 (78)	who created me, and [He] Himself guides me
26:79 (79)	and [He] Himself gives me to eat and drink

26:80 (80)	and, whenever I am sick, [He] heals me
26:104 (104)	Surely thy Lord, He is the All-mighty, the All-compassionate
26:122 (122)	Surely thy Lord, He is the All-mighty, the All-compassionate
26:140 (140)	Surely thy Lord, He is the All-mighty, the All-compassionate
26:159 (159)	Surely thy Lord, He is the All-mighty, the All-compassionate
26:175 (175)	Surely thy Lord, He is the All-mighty, the All-compassionate
26:191 (191)	Surely thy Lord, He is the All-mighty, the All-compassionate
26:220 (220)	Surely He is the All-hearing, the All-knowing
27:26 (26)	God: there is no god but He
28:16 (15)	for He is the All-forgiving, the All-compassionate
28:56 (56)	and [He] knows very well those that are guided
28:70 (70)	and He is God
28:70 (70)	there is no god but He
28:88 (88)	there is no god but He
29:5 (4)	He is the All-hearing, the All-knowing
29:26 (25)	He is the All-mighty, the All-wise
29:42 (41)	He is the All-mighty, the All-wise
29:60 (60)	He is the All-hearer, the All-knower
30:5 (4)	He is the All-mighty, the All-compassionate
30:27 (26)	it is He who originates creation, then brings it back again
30:27 (26)	He is the All-mighty, the All-wise
30:50 (49)	and He is powerful over everything
30:54 (53)	He is the All-knowing, the All-powerful
31:9 (8)	and He is the All-mighty, the All-wise
31:26 (25)	God — He is the All-sufficient, the All-laudable
31:30 (29)	that is because God — He is the Truth
31:30 (29)	and for that God is the All-high, the All-great
32:25 (25)	thy Lord [He] will distinguish between them on the Resurrection Day
33:4 (4)	God speaks the truth, and [He] guides on the way
33:43 (42)	It is He who blesses you, and His angels
34:1 (1)	He is the All-wise, the All-aware
34:2 (2)	He is the All-compassionate, the All-forgiving
34:23 (22)	He is the All-high, the All-great
34:26 (25)	He is the Deliverer, the All-knowing
34:27 (26)	rather He is God, the All-mighty, the All-wise
34:39 (38)	whatever thing you shall expend, He will replace it
34:39 (38)	He is the best of providers
34:47 (46)	He is witness over everything
35:2 (2)	He is the All-mighty, the All-wise
35:3 (3)	There is no god but He
35:15 (16)	He is the All-sufficient, the All-laudable
35:39 (37)	It is He who appointed you viceroys in the earth
36:79 (79)	He knows all creation
36:81 (81)	He is the All-creator, the All-knowing
39:4 (6)	He is God, the One, the Omnipotent
39:5 (7)	Is not He the All-mighty, the All-forgiving?
39:6 (8)	there is no god but He
39:53 (54)	He is the All-forgiving, the All-compassionate
39:62 (63)	He is Guardian over every thing
39:70 (70)	He knows very well what they do
40:3 (3)	the Bountiful; there is no god but He
40:13 (13)	It is He who shows you His signs
40:20 (21)	Surely God is the All-hearing, the All-seeing
40:56 (58)	surely He is the All-hearing, the All-seeing
40:62 (64)	there is no god but He

40:65 (67)	He is the Living One
40:65 (67)	there is no god but He
40:67 (69)	It is He who created you of dust
40:68 (70)	It is He who gives life, and makes to die
41:15 (14)	God, who created them, [He] was stronger than they in might
41:21 (20)	He created you the first time
41:36 (36)	He is the All-hearing, the All-knowing
42:4 (2)	He is the All-high, the All-glorious
42:9 (7)	but God — He is the Protector
42:9 (7)	He quickens the dead
42:9 (7)	and He is powerful over everything
42:11 (9)	He is the All-hearing, the All-seeing
42:19 (18)	He is the All-strong, the All-mighty
42:25 (24)	It is He who accepts repentance from His servants
42:28 (27)	it is He who sends down the rain after they have despaired
42:28 (27)	He is the Protector, the All-laudable
42:29 (28)	and He is able to gather them whenever (He) will
42:39 (37)	and who, when insolence visits them, do help themselves
43:64 (64)	assuredly God — [He] Is my Lord and your Lord
43:84 (84)	and it is He who in heaven is God
43:84 (84)	He is the All-wise, the All-knowing
44:6 (5)	surely He is the All-hearing, the All-knowing
44:8 (7)	there is no god but He
44:42 (42)	He is the All-mighty, the All-compassionate
45:37 (36)	He is the All-mighty, the All-wise
46:8 (7)	He knows very well what you are pressing upon
46:8 (7)	He is the All-forgiving, the All-compassionate
48:4 (4)	It is He who sent down the Shechina into the hearts of the believers
48:24 (24)	It is He who restrained their hands from you
48:28 (28)	It is He who has sent His Messenger with the guidance
51:30 (30)	He is the All-wise, the All-knowing
51:58 (58)	God is the All-provider, the Possessor of Strength
52:28 (28)	He is the All-benign, the All-compassionate
53:30 (31)	thy Lord — [He] knows very well those who have gone astray
53:30 (31)	and He knows very well those who are guided
53:32 (33)	very well He knows you
53:32 (33)	God [He] knows very well him who is godfearing
53:43 (44)	it is He who makes to laugh, and that makes to weep
53:44 (45)	it is He who makes to die, and that makes to live
53:48 (49)	and that it is He who gives wealth and riches
53:49 (50)	it is He who is the Lord of Sirius
55:29 (29)	every day He is upon some labour
57:1 (1)	He is the All-mighty, the All-wise
57:2 (2)	He is powerful over everything
57:3 (3)	He is the First and the Last
57:3 (3)	He has knowledge of everything
57:4 (4)	it is He that created the heavens and the earth in six days
57:4 (4)	He is with you wherever you are
57:6 (6)	He knows the thoughts within the breasts
57:9 (9)	it is He who sends down upon His servant signs
57:24 (24)	God — [He] is the All-sufficient, the All-laudable
58:7 (8)	three men conspire not secretly together, but He is the fourth of them
58:7 (8)	neither five men, but He is the sixth of them
58:7 (8)	neither fewer than that, neither more, but He is with them

59:1 (1)	He is the All-mighty, the All-wise
59:2 (2)	it is He who expelled from their habitations the unbelievers
59:22 (22)	He is God
59:22 (22)	there is no god but He
59:22 (22)	He is the All-merciful, the All-compassionate
59:23 (23)	He is God
59:23 (23)	there is no god but He
59:24 (24)	He is God, the Creator, the Maker, the Shaper
59:24 (24)	He is the All-mighty, the All-wise
60:6 (6)	God — [He] is the All-sufficient, the All-laudable
61:1 (1)	He is the All-mighty, the All-wise
61:9 (9)	It is He who has sent His Messenger with the guidance
62:2 (2)	It is He who has raised up from among the common people a Messenger from among them
62:3 (3)	He is the All-mighty, the All-wise
64:1 (1)	He is powerful over everything
64:2 (2)	It is He who created you
64:13 (13)	God — there is no god but He
65:3 (3)	whosoever puts his trust in God, He shall suffice him
66:2 (2)	He is the All-knowing, the All-wise
66:4 (4)	God — [He] is his Protector
67:1 (1)	He is powerful over everything
67:2 (2)	He is the All-mighty, the All-forgiving
67:14 (14)	He is the All-subtle, the All-aware
67:15 (15)	It is He who made the earth submissive to you
67:23 (23)	it is He who produced you
67:24 (24)	it is He who scattered you in the earth
67:29 (29)	He is the All-merciful. We believe in Him
68:7 (7)	surely thy Lord — [He] Knows very well those who have gone astray
68:7 (7)	and He knows very well those who are guided
73:9 (9)	there is no god but He
74:31 (34)	none knows the hosts of thy Lord but He
74:56 (55)	He is worthy to be feared, worthy to forgive
85:13 (13)	surely it is He who originates, and brings again
85:14 (14)	and He is the All-forgiving, the All-loving
112:1 (1)	He is God, One

*H W D

HĀDA vb. (I)~to repent; to be or become a Jew; to judaise [Bl]. (pcple. act.) one who is or becomes a Jew

a) perf. act.

2:62 (59)	surely they that believe, and those of Jewry
4:46 (48)	some of the Jews pervert words from their meanings
4:160 (158)	for the evildoing of those of Jewry
5:41 (45)	the Jews who listen to falsehood, listen to other folk
5:44 (48)	who had surrendered themselves gave judgment for those of Jewry
5:69 (73)	surely they that believe, and those of Jewry
6:146 (147)	to those of Jewry We have forbidden every beast with claws
7:156 (155)	we have repented unto Thee

16:118 (119)	and those of Jewry
22:17 (17)	they that believe, and those of Jewry
62:6 (6)	you of Jewry, if you assert that you are the friends of God

g) pcple. act. (*hā'id*, pl., *hūd*)

2:111 (105)	none shall enter Paradise except that they be Jews
2:135 (129)	be Jews or Christians and you shall be guided
2:140 (134)	Isaac and Jacob, and the Tribes — they were Jews

HŪD n.prop.~Hood (a Prophet)

7:65 (63)	to Ad their brother Hood; he said
11:50 (52)	to Ad their brother Hood; he said
11:53 (56)	Hood, thou hast not brought us a clear sign
11:58 (61)	when Our command came, We delivered Hood
11:60 (63)	away with Ad, the people of Hood
11:89 (91)	of what smote the people of Noah, or the people of Hood
26:124 (124)	when their brother Hood said to them

*H W N

HĀNA vb. (I)~(n.vb.1) meekness, modesty, quietness; (n.vb.2) contempt, humiliation, ignominy

f) n.vb. (1) (*hawn*)

25:63 (64)	those who walk in the earth modestly

f) n.vb. (2) (*hūn*)

6:93 (93)	you shall be recompensed with the chastisement of humiliation
16:59 (61)	whether he shall preserve it in humiliation, or trample it into the dust
41:17 (16)	the chastisement of humiliation seized them
46:20 (19)	you shall be recompensed with the chastisement of humiliation

HAYYIN n.m. (adj)~easy, light

19:9 (10)	easy is that for Me
19:21 (21)	easy is that for Me
24:15 (14)	that whereof you had no knowledge, and reckoned it a light thing
30:27 (26)	it is very easy for Him

AHĀNA vb. (IV)~to despise, abase (pcple. act.) one that humbles; humbling. (pcple. pass.) one who is humbled

a) perf. act.

89:16 (17)	my Lord has despised me

b) impf. act. (*yuhīnu*)

22:18 (19)	whom God abases, there is none to honour him

g) pcple. act. (*muhīn*)

2:90 (84)	for unbelievers awaits a humbling chastisement
3:178 (172)	there awaits them a humbling chastisement
4:14 (18)	for him there awaits a humbling chastisement

4:37 (41)	We have prepared for the unbelievers a humbling chastisement
4:102 (103)	God has prepared for the unbelievers a humbling chastisement
4:151 (150)	We have prepared for the unbelievers a humbling chastisement
22:57 (56)	for them awaits a humbling chastisement
31:6 (5)	there awaits them a humbling chastisement
33:57 (57)	and has prepared for them a humbling chastisement
34:14 (13)	they would not have continued in the humbling chastisement
44:30 (29)	We delivered the Children of Israel from the humbling chastisement
45:9 (8)	for them awaits a humbling chastisement
58:5 (6)	for the unbelievers awaits a humbling chastisement
58:16 (17)	there awaits them a humbling chastisement

h) pcple. pass. (*muhān*)

25:69 (69)	he shall dwell therein humbled forever

*H W R

HĀR n.m. (adj)~weak, infirm, crumbling, tottering

9:109 (110)	who founded his building upon the brink of a crumbling bank

INHĀRA vb. (VII)~to tumble, to fall in ruin

a) perf. act.

9:109 (110)	a crumbling bank that has tumbled with him

*H W Y

HAWÁ vb. (I)~to plunge, be hurled to ruin

a) perf. act.

20:81 (83)	on whomsoever My anger alights, that man is hurled to ruin
53:1 (1)	by the Star when it plunges

b) impf. act. (*yahwī*)

22:31 (32)	the wind sweeps him headlong into a place far away

HAWIYA vb. (I)~to desire, yearn for

b) impf. act. (*yahwá* or *yahwī*)

2:87 (81)	a Messenger with that your souls had not desire for
5:70 (74)	a Messenger with that their souls had not desire for
14:37 (40)	make hearts of men yearn towards them
53:23 (23)	they follow only surmise, and what the souls desire

HAWÁ n.m. (pl. *ahwā'*)~desire, caprice, lust, inclination

2:120 (114)	if thou followest their caprices
2:145 (140)	if thou followest their caprices

4:135 (134)	then follow not caprice, so as to swerve
5:48 (52)	do not follow their caprices, to forsake the truth
5:49 (54)	do not follow their caprices, and beware of them
5:77 (81)	follow not the caprices of a people who went astray
6:56 (56)	I do not follow your caprices
6:119 (119)	many lead astray by their caprices
6:150 (151)	do not thou follow the caprices of those who cried lies
7:176 (175)	he inclined towards the earth and followed his lust
13:37 (37)	if thou dost follow their caprices
18:28 (27)	he follows his own lust, and his affair has become all excess
20:16 (17)	but follows after his own caprice
23:71 (73)	had the truth followed their caprices
25:43 (45)	him who has taken his caprice to be his god
28:50 (50)	know that they are only following their caprices
28:50 (50)	who is further astray than he who follows his caprice
30:29 (28)	the evildoers follow their own caprices
38:26 (25)	judge between men justly, and follow not caprice
42:15 (14)	do not follow their caprices
45:18 (17)	follow not the caprices of those who do not know
45:23 (22)	him who has taken his caprice to be his god
47:14 (15)	they have followed their caprices
47:16 (18)	they have followed their caprices
53:3 (3)	nor speaks he out of caprice
54:3 (3)	they have cried lies, and followed their caprices
79:40 (40)	and forbade the soul its caprice

HAWĀʾ n.m. (adj)~void

14:43 (44)	their glances never returned on themselves, their hearts void

HĀWIYAH n.prop..~the Pit

101:9 (6)	shall plunge in the womb of the Pit

AHWÁ vb. (IV)~to overthrow, to cause to fall

a) perf. act.

53:53 (54)	and the Subverted City He also overthrew

ISTAHWÁ vb. (X)~to lure, infatuate

a) perf. act.

6:71 (70)	like one lured to bewilderment in the earth

*H Y ʾ

HAYʾAH n.f.~likeness

3:49 (43)	I will create for you out of clay as the likeness of a bird
5:110 (110)	when thou createst out of clay, by My leave, as the likeness

HAYYAʾA vb. (II)~to furnish with

b) impf. act. (*yuhayyiʾu*)

18:16 (15)	and will furnish you with a gentle issue

c) impv. (*hayyi'*)

18:10 (9) give us mercy from Thee, and furnish us with rectitude

*H Y H T

HAYHĀT vb. (?)~away!

23:36 (38) away, (away) with that you are promised
23:36 (38) (away) away with that you are promised

*H Y J

HĀJA vb. (I)~to wither

b) impf. act. (*yahīju*)

39:21 (22) then they wither, and thou seest them turning yellow
57:20 (19) then it withers, and thou seest it turning

*H Y L

HĀLA vb. (I)~(pcple. pass.) poured out

h) pcple. pass. (*mahīl*)

73:14 (14) and the mountains become a slipping heap of sand

*H Y M

HĀMA vb. (I)~to wander

b) impf. act. (*yahīmu*)

26:225 (225) hast thou not seen how they wander in every valley

HĪM n.f. (pl. of *haymā'*)~a thirsty camel

56:55 (55) lapping it down like thirsty camels

*H Y M N

HAYMANA vb. (quad I)~(pcple. act.) assuring; All-preserving (Divine attribute)

g) pcple. act. (*muhaymin*)

5:48 (52)	confirming the Book that was before it, and assuring it
59:23 (23)	the All-faithful, the All-preserver

*H Y T

HAYTA vb. (?)~Come!

c) impv. (*hayta*)

12:23 (23)	'Come,' she said, 'take me!'

*H Z ʾ

HAZIʾA vb. (I)~(n.vb.) mockery, derision, ridicule

f) n.vb. (*huzuʾ*)

2:67 (63)	dost thou take us in mockery?
2:231 (231)	take not God's signs in mockery
5:57 (62)	the unbelievers, who take your religion in mockery
5:58 (63)	take it in mockery and as a sport
18:56 (54)	they have taken My signs, and what they are warned of, in mockery
18:106 (106)	and took My signs and My messengers in mockery
21:36 (37)	they take thee only for mockery
25:41 (43)	they take thee in mockery only
31:6 (5)	and to take it in mockery
45:9 (8)	he takes them in mockery
45:35 (34)	that is for that you took God's signs in mockery

ISTAHZAʾA vb. (X)~to mock, scoff, ridicule, laugh at. (pcple. act.) mocker, scoffer; mocking, scoffing

b) impf. act. (*yastahziʾu*)

2:15 (14)	God shall mock them, and shall lead them on
6:5 (5)	there shall come to them news of that they were mocking
6:10 (10)	those that scoffed at them were encompassed
9:65 (66)	were you mocking God, and His signs
11:8 (11)	they shall be encompassed by that they mocked at
15:11 (11)	not a single Messenger came to them, but they mocked at him
16:34 (36)	they were encompassed by that they mocked at
21:41 (42)	those that scoffed at them were encompassed by that they mocked at
26:6 (5)	tidings will come to them of that they mocked at
30:10 (9)	they cried lies to the signs of God and mocked at them
36:30 (29)	unto them a Messenger, but they mock at him
39:48 (49)	they would be encompassed by that they mocked at
40:83 (83)	and were encompassed by that they mocked at
43:7 (6)	not a Prophet came to them, without they mocked at him
45:33 (32)	they shall be encompassed by that they mocked at
46:26 (25)	they were encompassed by that they mocked at

c) impv. (*istahziʾ*)

9:64 (65)	mock on; God will bring forth what you fear

d) perf. pass. (*istuhzi'a*)

6:10 (10) Messengers indeed were mocked at before thee
13:32 (32) Messengers indeed were scoffed at before thee
21:41 (42) Messengers indeed were mocked at before thee

e) impf. pass. (*yustahza'u*)

4:140 (139) when you hear God's signs being disbelieved and made mock of

g) pcple. act. (*mustahzi'*)

2:14 (13) we are with you; we were only mocking
15:95 (95) We suffice thee against the mockers

*H Z L

HAZILA vb. (I)~(n.vb.) merriment

f) n.vb. (*hazl*)

86:14 (14) it is no merriment

*H Z M

HAZAMA vb. (I)~to route, put to flight. (pcple. pass.) routed, one who is put to flight

a) perf. act.

2:251 (252) and they routed them, by the leave of God

e) impf. pass. (*yuhzamu*)

54:45 (45) certainly the host shall be routed

h) pcple. pass. (*mahzūm*)

38:11 (10) a very host of parties is routed there

*H Z Z

HAZZA vb. (I)~to shake

c) impv. (*huzz*)

19:25 (25) shake also to thee the palm-trunk

IHTAZZA vb. (VIII)~to quiver

a) perf. act.

22:5 (5) when We send down water upon it, it quivers
41:39 (39) when We send down water upon it, it quivers

b) impf. act. (*yahtazzu*)

27:10 (10)	when he saw it quivering like a serpent
28:31 (31)	when he saw it quivering like a serpent

ḤĀ

*Ḥ B B

AḤIBBĀʾ n.m. (pl. of *ḥabīb*)~beloved

5:18 (21)	we are the sons of God, and His beloved ones

ḤABBAH n.f. (pl. *ḥabb*)~grain

2:261 (263)	as the likeness of a grain of corn
2:261 (263)	in every ear a hundred grains
6:59 (59)	not a grain in the earth's shadows
6:95 (95)	it is God who splits the grain and the date-stone
6:99 (99)	bringing forth from it close-compounded grain
21:47 (48)	the weight of one grain of mustard-seed
31:16 (15)	the weight of one grain of mustard-seed
36:33 (33)	and brought forth from it grain
50:9 (9)	gardens and grain of harvest
55:12 (11)	and grain in the blade, and fragrant herbs
78:15 (15)	We may bring forth thereby grain and plants
80:27 (27)	and therein made the grains to grow

ḤUBB n.m.~love

2:165 (160)	loving them as God is loved
2:165 (160)	those that believe love God more ardently
2:177 (172)	to give of one's substance, however cherished
3:14 (12)	decked out fair to men is the love of lusts
12:30 (30)	he smote her heart with love
38:32 (31)	I have loved the love of good things
76:8 (8)	they give food, for the love of Him
89:20 (21)	and you love wealth with an ardent love
100:8 (8)	he is passionate in his love for good things

MAḤABBAH n.f.~love

20:39 (39)	I loaded on thee love from Me

AḤABB n.com. (adj)~more beloved, dearer

9:24 (24)	if these are dearer to you than God
12:8 (8)	Joseph and his brother are dearer to our father
12:33 (33)	prison is dearer to me than that they call me to

ḤABBABA vb. (II)~to endear

a) perf. act.

49:7 (7)	God has endeared to you belief

AḤABBA vb. (IV)~to like, love, long for

a) perf. act.

28:56 (56)	Thou guidest not whom thou likest
38:32 (31)	I have loved the love of good things

b) impf. act. (*yuḥibbu*)

2:165 (160)	who take to themselves compeers apart from God, loving them
2:190 (186)	God loves not the aggressors
2:195 (191)	God loves the good-doers
2:205 (201)	God loves not corruption
2:216 (213)	it may happen that you will love a thing
2:222 (222)	God loves those who repent
2:222 (222)	and He loves those who cleanse themselves
2:276 (277)	god loves not any guilty ingrate
3:31 (29)	if you love God, follow me
3:31 (29)	and God will love you, and forgive you
3:32 (29)	God loves not the unbelievers
3:57 (50)	deeds of righteousness, He will pay them God loves not the evildoers
3:76 (70)	God loves the godfearing
3:92 (86)	until you expend of what you love
3:119 (115)	you love them
3:119 (115)	and they love you not
3:134 (128)	God loves the good-doers
3:140 (134)	God loves not the evildoers
3:146 (140)	God loves the patient
3:148 (141)	God loves the good-doers
3:152 (145)	after He had shown you that you longed for
3:159 (153)	God loves those who put their trust
3:188 (185)	what they have brought, and love to be praised
4:36 (40)	God loves not the proud and boastful
4:107 (107)	God loves not the guilty traitor
4:148 (147)	God likes not the shouting of evil words
5:13 (16)	God loves the good-doers
5:42 (46)	God loves the just
5:54 (59)	God will assuredly bring a people He loves
5:54 (59)	a people He (loves) and who love Him
5:64 (69)	God loves not the workers of corruption
5:87 (89)	God loves not transgressors
5:93 (94)	God loves the good-doers
6:76 (76)	I love not the setters
6:141 (142)	God loves not the prodigal
7:31 (29)	He loves not the prodigal
7:55 (53)	He loves not transgressors
7:79 (77)	you do not love sincere advisers
8:58 (60)	God loves not the treacherous
9:4 (4)	God loves the godfearing
9:7 (7)	God loves the godfearing
9:108 (109)	men who love to cleanse themselves
9:108 (109)	and God loves those who cleanse themselves
16:23 (25)	He loves not those that wax proud
22:38 (39)	God loves not any ungrateful traitor
24:19 (18)	those who love that indecency
24:22 (22)	do you not wish that God should forgive you?
28:76 (76)	God loves not those that exult
28:77 (77)	God loves not the workers of corruption
30:45 (44)	He loves not the unbelievers
31:18 (17)	God loves not any man proud and boastful
42:40 (38)	He loves not the evildoers
49:9 (9)	God loves the just
49:12 (12)	would any of you like to eat the flesh

57:23 (23)	God loves not any man proud and boastful
59:9 (9)	love whosoever has emigrated to them
60:8 (8)	God loves the just
61:4 (4)	God loves those who fight in His way
61:13 (13)	and other things you love
75:20 (20)	but you love the hasty world
76:27 (27)	these men love the hasty world
89:20 (21)	and you love wealth with an ardent love

ISTAḤABBA vb. (X)~to prefer

a) perf. act.

9:23 (23)	if they prefer unbelief to belief
16:107 (109)	because they have preferred the present life
41:17 (16)	they preferred blindness above guidance

b) impf. act. (*yastaḥibbu*)

14:3 (3)	such as prefer the present life

*Ḥ B K

ḤUBUK n.m. (pl. of *ḥibāk*)~a track, way

51:7 (7)	by heaven with all its tracks

*Ḥ B L

ḤABL n.m. (pl. *ḥibāl*)~a rope, cord, bond; jugular vein (*ḥabl al-warīd*)

3:103 (98)	hold you fast to God's bond
3:112 (108)	except they be in a bond of God
3:112 (108)	(a bond) of God and a bond of the people
20:66 (69)	their ropes and their staffs were sliding
26:44 (43)	they cast their ropes and their staffs
50:16 (15)	We are nearer to him than the jugular vein
111:5 (5)	upon her neck a rope of palm-fibre

*Ḥ B R

ḤABARA vb. (I)~to make joyful; (pass) to walk with joy

e) impf. pass. (*yuḥbaru*)

30:15 (14)	they shall walk with joy in a green meadow
43:70 (70)	enter Paradise, you and your wives, walking with joy

ḤABR n.m. (pl. of *ḥabr*)~a learned man or doctor of religion, a master of religion (esp. in Judaism), a rabbi

5:44 (48)	as did the masters and the rabbis
5:63 (68)	why do the masters and the rabbis not forbid them

9:31 (31)	they have taken their rabbis and their monks as lords
9:34 (34)	many of the rabbis and monks indeed consume the goods

*Ḥ B S

ḤABASA vb. (I)~to detain

b) impf. act. (*yaḥbisu*)

5:106 (105)	them you shall detain after the prayer
11:8 (11)	what is detaining it?

*Ḥ B Ṭ

ḤABIṬA vb. (I)~to be fruitless, to fail

a) perf. act.

2:217 (214)	their works have failed in this world
3:22 (21)	their works have failed in this world
5:5 (7)	whoso disbelieves in the faith, his work has failed
5:53 (58)	their works have failed; now they are losers
6:88 (88)	it would have failed them, the things they did
7:147 (145)	their works have failed
9:17 (17)	their works have failed them, and in the Fire
9:69 (70)	their works have failed in this world
11:16 (19)	their deeds there will have failed
18:105 (105)	their works have failed

b) impf. act. (*yaḥbaṭu*)

39:65 (65)	thy work shall surely fail
49:2 (2)	lest your works fail while you are not aware

AḤBAṬA vb. (IV)~to make or cause to fail

a) perf. act.

33:19 (19)	God has made their works to fail
47:9 (10)	He has made their works to fail
47:28 (30)	He has made their works to fail

b) impf. act. (*yuḥbiṭu*)

47:32 (34)	He will make their works to fail

*Ḥ D B

ḤADAB n.m.~an elevation in the ground, a slope

21:96 (96)	they slide down out of every slope

*Ḥ D D

ḤADĪD (1) n.m.~iron

17:50 (53)	let you be stones, or iron
18:96 (95)	bring me ingots of iron
22:21 (21)	for them await hooked iron rods
34:10 (10)	We softened for him iron
57:25 (25)	We sent down iron, wherein is great might

ḤADĪD (2) n.m. (adj.; pl. *ḥidād*)~sharp, piercing

33:19 (19)	they flay you with sharp tongues
50:22 (21)	so thy sight today is piercing

ḤUDŪD n.m. (pl. of *ḥadd*)~bounds, ordinances

2:187 (183)	those are God's bounds; keep well within them
2:229 (229)	unless the couple fear they may not maintain God's bounds
2:229 (229)	if you fear they may not maintain God's bounds
2:229 (229)	those are God's bounds; do not transgress them
2:229 (229)	whosoever transgresses the bounds of God
2:230 (230)	if they suppose that they will maintain God's bounds
2:230 (230)	those are God's bounds
4:13 (17)	those are God's bounds
4:14 (18)	and transgresses His bounds
9:97 (98)	not to know the bounds of what God has sent down
9:112 (113)	those who keep God's bounds
58:4 (5)	those are God's bounds
65:1 (1)	those are God's bounds
65:1 (1)	whosoever trespasses the bounds of God

ḤĀDDA vb. (III)~to oppose

a) perf. act.

58:22 (22)	anyone who opposes God and His Messenger

b) impf. act. (*yuḥāddu*)

9:63 (64)	whosoever opposes God and His Messenger
58:5 (6)	those who oppose God and His Messenger
58:20 (21)	those who oppose God and His Messenger

*Ḥ D Q

ḤADĀʾIQ n.f. (pl. of *ḥadīqah*)~garden

27:60 (61)	We caused to grow therewith gardens
78:32 (32)	gardens and vineyards
80:30 (30)	and dense-tree'd gardens

*Ḥ D TH

ḤADĪTH n.m. (pl. *aḥādīth*)~tiding, talk, discourse, tale, story

4:42 (45)	they will not conceal from God one tiding
4:78 (80)	they scarcely understand any tiding
4:87 (89)	who is truer in tidings than God?
4:140 (139)	until they plunge into some other talk
6:68 (67)	until they plunge into some other talk
7:185 (184)	in what manner of discourse
12:6 (6)	and teach thee the interpretation of tales
12:21 (21)	that We might teach him the interpretation of tales
12:101 (102)	Thou hast taught me the interpretation of tales
12:111 (111)	it is not a tale forged
18:6 (5)	if they believe not in this tiding
20:9 (8)	hast thou received the story of Moses?
23:44 (46)	We made them as but tales
31:6 (5)	some men there are who buy diverting talk
33:53 (53)	disperse, neither lingering for idle talk
34:19 (18)	We made them as but tales
39:23 (24)	God has sent down the fairest discourse as a Book
45:6 (5)	in what manner of discourse
51:24 (24)	hast thou received the story of the honoured guests
52:34 (34)	then let them bring a discourse like it
53:59 (59)	do you then marvel at this discourse
56:81 (80)	do you hold this discourse in disdain
66:3 (3)	the Prophet confided to one of his wives a certain matter
68:44 (44)	leave Me with him who cries lies to this discourse
77:50 (50)	in what discourse after this will they believe?
79:15 (15)	hast thou received the story of Moses?
85:17 (17)	hast thou received the story of the hosts
88:1 (1)	hast thou received the story of the Enveloper?

ḤADDATHA vb. (II)~to speak to, to tell, to declare

b) impf. act. (*yuḥaddithu*)

2:76 (71)	do you speak to them of what God has revealed
99:4 (4)	upon that day she shall tell her tidings

c) impv. (*ḥaddith*)

93:11 (11)	as for thy Lord's blessing, declare it

AḤDATHA vb. (IV)~to cause to occur, bring something new to pass, introduce, arouse. (pcple. pass.) that which is lately remembered or renewed

b) impf. act. (*yuḥdithu*)

18:70 (69)	until I myself introduce the mention of it
20:113 (112)	or it may arouse in them remembrance
65:1 (1)	after that God will bring something new to pass

h) pcple. pass. (*muḥdath*)

21:2 (2)	no Remembrance from their Lord comes to them lately renewed
26:5 (4)	never fresh remembrance comes to them

*Ḥ DH R

ḤADHIRA vb. (I)~to fear, beware, dread, be afraid, take heed of. (n.vb.) fear, precaution; (adj) fearful; (adv) fearfully. (pcple. act.) one who is cautious, on his guard. (pcple. pass.) that of which one is cautious or one bewares

b) impf. act. (*yaḥdharu*)

9:64 (65)	the hypocrites are afraid
9:64 (65)	God will bring forth what you fear
9:122 (123)	that haply they may beware
24:63 (63)	let those who go against His command beware
28:6 (5)	what they were dreading from them
39:9 (12)	he being afraid of the world to come

c) impv. (*iḥdhar*)

2:235 (236)	be fearful of Him
5:41 (45)	if you are not given it, beware
5:49 (54)	beware of them lest they tempt thee
5:92 (93)	and obey the Messenger, and beware
63:4 (4)	so beware of them
64:14 (14)	so beware of them

f) n.vb. (*ḥadhar*)

2:19 (18)	they put their fingers in their ears ... fearful of death
2:243 (244)	who went forth ... in their thousands fearful of death

g) pcple. act. (*ḥādhir*)

26:56 (56)	we are a host on our guard

h) pcple. pass. (*maḥdhūr*)

17:57 (59)	thy Lord's chastisement is a thing to beware of

ḤIDHR n.m.~precaution

4:71 (73)	O believers, take your precautions
4:102 (103)	taking their precautions and their weapons
4:102 (103)	lay aside your weapons; but take your precautions

ḤADHDHARA vb. (II)~to warn

b) impf. act. (*yuḥadhdhiru*)

3:28 (27)	God warns you that you beware of Him
3:30 (28)	God warns you that you beware of Him

*Ḥ Ḍ Ḍ

ḤAḌḌA vb. (I)~to urge

b) impf. act. (*yaḥuḍḍu*)

69:34 (34)	he never urged the feeding of the needy
107:3 (3)	and urges not the feeding of the needy

TAḤĀḌḌA vb. (VI)~to urge one another

a) perf. act.

89:18 (19) you urge not the feeding of the needy

*Ḥ Ḍ R

ḤAḌARA vb. (I)~to come, attend, be in the presence of; be visited by. (pcple. act.) one who is present, bordering on

a) perf. act.

k0 2:133 (127) were you witnesses, when death came to Jacob?
2:180 (176) when any of you is visited by death
4:8 (9) when the division is attended by kinsmen and orphans
4:18 (22) when one of them is visited by death
5:106 (105) when any of you is visited by death
46:29 (28) when they were in its presence they said

b) impf. act. (*yaḥḍuru*)

23:98 (100) I take refuge in Thee, O my Lord, lest they attend me

g) pcple. act. (*ḥāḍir*)

2:196 (192) him whose family are not present at the Holy Mosque
2:282 (282) unless it be merchandise present that you give and take
7:163 (163) the township which was bordering the sea
18:49 (47) they shall find all they wrought present

AḤḌARA vb. (IV)~to produce, parade (tr), be prone to. (pcple. pass.) that which is arraigned [Ar], that which is brought up [Ali], haled [Pk]

a) perf. act.

81:14 (14) then shall a soul know what it has produced

b) impf. act. (*yuḥḍiru*)

19:68 (69) We shall parade them about Gehenna

d) perf. pass. (*uḥḍira*)

4:128 (127) souls are very prone to avarice

h) pcple. pass. (*muḥḍar*)

3:30 (28) what it has done of good brought forward
28:61 (61) on the Resurrection Day shall be of those that are arraigned
30:16 (15) they shall be arraigned into the chastisement
34:38 (37) those shall be arraigned into the chastisement
36:32 (32) they shall every one of them be arraigned
36:53 (53) they are all arraigned before Us
36:75 (75) though they be hosts made ready for them
37:57 (55) but for my Lord's blessing, I were one of the arraigned

37:127 (127) they will be among the arraigned
37:158 (158) the jinn know that they shall be arraigned

IḤTAḌARA vb. (VIII)~(pcple. pass.) be divided in turn [Ar], be witnessed [Pk], brought forward [Ali]

h) pcple. pass. (*muḥtaḍar*)

54:28 (28) water is to be divided between them, each drink for each in turn

*Ḥ F D

ḤAFADAH n.m. (pl. of *ḥafīd*)~grandchild

16:72 (74) your wives sons and grandsons

*Ḥ F F

ḤAFFA vb. (I)~to surround, encircle. (pcple. act.) surrounding, encircling

a) perf. act.

18:32 (31) We assigned two gardens of vines, and surrounded them

g) pcple. act. (*ḥāff*)

39:75 (75) thou shalt see the angels encircling about the Throne

*Ḥ F R

ḤĀFIRAH n.f~former condition [Ar]; original or first state [Pk]

79:10 (10) are we being restored as we were before?

ḤUFRAH n.f.~a pit

3:103 (99) you were upon the brink of a pit of Fire

*Ḥ F Y

ḤAFĪY n.m.~one who is well-informed; one who is gracious

7:187 (187) they will question thee, as though thou art well-informed of it
19:47 (48) I will ask my Lord to forgive thee; surely He is ever gracious to me

AḤFÁ vb. (IV)~to press [Ar]; to be importune [Ali]

b) impf. act. (*yuḥfī*)

47:37 (39) if He asks you for them, and presses you

*Ḥ F Ẓ

ḤAFIẒA vb. (I)~to guard, preserve, keep. (n.vb.) guarding, preserving. (pcple. act.) one who guards, preserves or keeps; guarding, preserving, keeping. (pcple. pass.) well-protected, guarded

a) perf. act.

4:34 (38)	guarding the secret for God's guarding
15:17 (17)	and guarded them from every accursed Satan

b) impf. act. (*yaḥfaẓu*)

12:65 (65)	we shall be watching over our brother
13:11 (12)	(angels) watching over him by God's command
24:30 (30)	that they cast down their eyes and guard their private parts
24:31 (31)	cast down their eyes and guard their private parts

c) impv. (*iḥfaẓ*)

5:89 (91)	but keep your oaths

f) n.vb. (*ḥifẓ*)

2:255 (256)	the preserving of them oppresses Him not
37:7 (7)	and to preserve against every rebel Satan
41:12 (11)	We adorned the lower heaven with lamps, and to preserve

g) pcple. act. (*ḥāfiẓ*)

4:34 (38)	righteous women are therefore obedient, guarding the secret
9:112 (113)	those who keep God's bounds
12:12 (12)	surely we shall be watching over him
12:63 (63)	we shall be watching over him
12:64 (64)	God is the best guardian
12:81 (81)	we were no guardians of the Unseen
15:9 (9)	and We watch over it
21:82 (82)	We were watching over them
23:5 (5)	and guard their private parts
33:35 (35)	men (and women) who guard their private parts
33:35 (35)	(men) and women who guard their private parts
70:29 (29)	and guard their private parts
82:10 (10)	yet there are over you watchers
83:33 (33)	they were not sent as watchers over them
86:4 (4)	over every soul there is a watcher

h) pcple. pass. (*maḥfūẓ*)

21:32 (33)	We set up the heaven as a roof well-protected
85:22 (22)	in a guarded tablet

ḤAFAẒAH n.m. (pl. of *ḥāfiẓ*)~recorders [Ar]; guardian-angels

6:61 (61)	He sends recorders over you

ḤAFĪẒ n.m.~watcher, guardian; Guardian (Divine attribute); warden, mindful [Ar]; preserver [Ali]; recording or note-taking [Ar, Ali]

4:80 (82)	We have not sent thee to be a watcher over them
6:104 (104)	I am not a watcher over you

6:107 (107)	We have not appointed thee a watcher over them
11:57 (60)	my Lord is Guardian over everything
11:86 (88)	I am not a guardian over you
12:55 (55)	I am a knowing guardian
34:21 (20)	thy Lord is Guardian over everything
42:6 (4)	God is Warden over them
42:48 (47)	We sent thee not to be a guardian over them
50:4 (4)	with Us is a book recording
50:32 (31)	it is for every mindful penitent

ḤĀFAẒA vb. (III)~to be watchful, watch over, observe

b) impf. act. (*yuḥāfiẓu*)

6:92 (92)	[those who] watch over their prayers
23:9 (9)	and who observe their prayers
70:34 (34)	and who observe their prayers

c) impv. (*ḥāfiẓ*)

2:238 (239)	be you watchful over the prayers

ISTAḤFAẒA vb. (X)~to commit to one's keeping (or memory)

d) perf. pass. (*istuḥfiẓa*)

5:44 (48)	such portion of God's Book as they were given to keep

*Ḥ J B

ḤAJABA vb. (I)~(pcple. pass.) veiled

h) pcple. pass. (*maḥjūb*)

83:15 (15)	upon that day they shall be veiled

ḤIJĀB n.m.~veil, curtain

7:46 (44)	between them is a veil
17:45 (47)	between thee, and those who do not believe in the world to come, a curtain
19:17 (17)	she took a veil apart from them
33:53 (53)	ask them from behind a curtain
38:32 (31)	until the sun was hidden behind the veil
41:5 (4)	between us and thee there is a veil
42:51 (50)	God should speak to him, except by revelation, or from behind a veil

*Ḥ J J

ḤAJJA vb. (I)~to make the Pilgrimage (to Mecca). (n.vb.) Pilgrimage (to Mecca). (pcple. act.) a pilgrim

a) perf. act.

2:158 (153)	whosoever makes the Pilgrimage to the House

f) n.vb. (*ḥajj*, or *ḥijj*)

2:189 (185) they are appointed times for the people, and the Pilgrimage
2:196 (192) fulfil the Pilgrimage and the Visitation
2:196 (192) whosoever enjoys the Visitation until the Pilgrimage
2:196 (192) a fast of three days in the Pilgrimage
2:197 (193) the Pilgrimage is in months well-known
2:197 (193) whoso undertakes the duty of Pilgrimage
2:197 (193) nor indulge in ungodliness and disputing in the Pilgrimage
3:97 (91) it is the duty of all men towards God to come to the House a pilgrim
9:3 (3) unto mankind on the day of the Greater Pilgrimage
22:27 (28) proclaim among men the Pilgrimage

g) pcple. act. (*ḥājj*)

9:19 (19) do you reckon the giving of water to pilgrims

ḤIJAJ n.f. (pl. of *ḥijjah*)~a year

28:27 (27) on condition that thou hirest thyself to me for eight years

ḤUJJAH n.f.~argument, disputation, ground for dispute

2:150 (145) that the people may not have any argument against you
4:165 (163) so that mankind might have no argument against God
6:83 (83) that is Our argument, which We bestowed upon Abraham
6:149 (150) to God belongs the argument conclusive
42:15 (14) there is no argument between us and you
42:16 (15) their argument is null and void
45:25 (24) their only argument is that they say

ḤĀJJA vb. (III)~to dispute about, to argue

a) perf. act.

2:258 (260) hast thou not regarded him who disputed with Abraham
3:20 (18) if they dispute with thee
3:61 (54) whoso disputes with thee concerning him
3:66 (59) you are the ones who dispute on what you know
6:80 (80) His people disputed with him

b) impf. act. (*yuḥājju*)

2:76 (71) that they may thereby dispute with you
2:139 (133) would you then dispute with us concerning God
3:65 (58) People of the Book! Why do you dispute
3:66 (59) why then dispute you touching a matter of which you know not anything?
3:73 (66) or dispute with you before your Lord
6:80 (80) do you dispute with me concerning God
42:16 (15) those who argue concerning God

TAḤĀJJA vb. (VI)~to dispute or argue with one another

b) impf. act. (*yataḥājju*)

40:47 (50) when they argue one with the other in the Fire

*Ḥ J R

ḤAJARA vb. (I)~(pcple. pass.) forbidden

h) pcple. pass. (*maḥjūr*)

25:22 (24)	they shall say, 'A ban forbidden'
25:53 (55)	between them a barrier, and a ban forbidden

ḤAJAR n.m. (pl. *ḥijārah*)~a stone, rock

2:24 (22)	fear the Fire, whose fuel is men and stones
2:60 (57)	strike with thy staff the rock'
2:74 (69)	your hearts became hardened thereafter and are like stones
2:74 (69)	for there are stones from which rivers come gushing
7:160 (160)	strike with thy staff the rock
8:32 (32)	then rain down upon us stones out of heaven
11:82 (84)	and rained on it stones of baked clay
15:74 (74)	and rained on it stones of baked clay
17:50 (53)	let you be stones, or iron
51:33 (33)	to loose upon them stones of clay
66:6 (6)	against a Fire whose fuel is men and stones
105:4 (4)	hurling against them stones of baked clay

ḤIJR (1) n.m.~anything unlawful, taboo, sacrosanct, a ban; (*dhū ḥijr*) one who is mindful, intelligent

6:138 (139)	these are cattle and tillage sacrosanct
25:22 (24)	they shall say, 'A ban forbidden!'
25:53 (55)	He set between them a barrier, and a ban forbidden
89:5 (4)	is there in that an oath for a mindful man?

ḤIJR (2) n.prop.~el-Hijr

15:80 (80)	the dwellers n El-Hijr cried lies

ḤUJŪR n.m. (pl. of *ḥajr* or *ḥijr*)~a bosom; guardianship, care

4:23 (27)	your stepdaughters who are in your care

ḤUJURĀT n.f. (pl. of *ḥujrah*)~apartment, chamber

49:4 (4)	those who call unto thee from behind the apartments

*Ḥ J Z

ḤAJAZA vb. (I)~(pcple. act.) that which bars, hinders; one who witholds or defends; a partition

g) pcple. act. (*ḥājiz*)

27:61 (62)	and placed a partition between the two seas
69:47 (47)	and not one of you could have defended him

*Ḥ K M

ḤAKAMA vb. (I)~to judge, give judgment, decide between, decree. (n.vb.) judgment [Ar]; verdict [Ali, Pk]. (pcple. act.) judge; Judge (Divine attribute)

a) perf. act.

4:58 (61)	and when you judge between the people
5:42 (46)	and if thou judgest, judge justly between them
40:48 (51)	God already has passed judgment between His servants

b) impf. act. (*yaḥkumu*)

2:113 (107)	God shall decide between them
2:213 (209)	that He might decide between the people
3:23 (22)	that it might decide between them
3:55 (48)	return, and I will decide between you
4:58 (61)	that you judge with justice
4:105 (106)	so that thou mayest judge between the people
4:141 (140)	God will judge between you
5:1 (1)	God decrees whatsoever He desires
5:44 (48)	the Prophets who had surrendered themselves gave judgment
5:44 (48)	whoso judges not according to what God has sent down
5:45 (49)	whoso judges not according to what God has sent down
5:47 (51)	let the People of the Gospel judge
5:47 (51)	whosoever judges not according to what God has sent down
5:95 (96)	as shall be judged by two men of equity
6:136 (137)	evil is their judgment
7:87 (85)	be patient till God shall judge between us
10:35 (36)	what then ails you, how you judge?
10:109 (109)	be thou patient until God shall judge
12:80 (80)	or God judges in my favour
13:41 (41)	God judges; none repels His judgment
16:59 (61)	evil is that they judge
16:124 (125)	thy Lord will decide between them
21:78 (78)	when they gave judgment concerning the tillage
22:56 (55)	He shall judge between them
22:69 (68)	God shall judge between you
24:48 (47)	that he may judge between them
24:51 (50)	that he may judge between them
29:4 (3)	ill they judge
37:154 (154)	what ails you then, how you judge?
39:3 (4)	God shall judge between them
39:46 (47)	Thou shalt judge between Thy servants
45:21 (20)	how ill they judge
60:10 (10)	He judges between you
68:36 (36)	what ails you then, how you judge?
68:39 (39)	you shall have whatever you judge

c) impv. (*uḥkum*)

5:42 (46)	if they come to thee, judge thou between them
5:42 (46)	and if thou judgest, judge justly between them
5:48 (52)	judge between them according to what God has sent down
5:49 (54)	judge between them according to what God has sent down
21:112 (112)	my Lord, judge Thou with truth
38:22 (21)	judge between us justly
38:26 (25)	therefore judge between men justly

f) n.vb. (*ḥukm*)

3:79 (73)	that God should give him the Book, the Judgment
5:43 (47)	the Torah, wherein is God's judgment

5:50 (55)	is it the judgment of pagandom then that they are seeking?
5:50 (55)	who is fairer in judgment than God
6:57 (57)	the judgment is God's alone
6:62 (62)	His is the judgment
6:89 (89)	they to whom We gave the Book, the Judgment
12:22 (22)	We gave him judgment and knowledge
12:40 (40)	judgment belongs only to God
12:67 (67)	judgment belongs not to any but God
13:37 (37)	We have sent it down as an Arabic judgment
13:41 (41)	none repels His judgment
18:26 (25)	He associates in His government no one
19:12 (13)	We gave him judgment, yet a little child
21:74 (74)	Lot — to him We gave judgment and knowledge
21:78 (78)	We bore witness to their judgment
21:79 (79)	unto each gave We judgment and knowledge
26:21 (20)	my Lord gave me Judgment
26:83 (83)	my Lord, give me Judgment
27:78 (80)	thy Lord will decide between them by His Judgment
28:14 (13)	We gave him judgment and knowledge
28:70 (70)	His too is the Judgment
28:88 (88)	His is the Judgment
40:12 (12)	judgment belongs to God
42:10 (8)	the judgment thereof belongs to God
45:16 (15)	We gave the Children of Israel the Book, the Judgment
52:48 (48)	be thou patient under the judgment of thy Lord
60:10 (10)	That is God's judgment
68:48 (48)	be thou patient under the judgement of thy Lord
76:24 (24)	be thou patient under the judgment of thy Lord

g) pcple. act. (*ḥākim*)

2:188 (184)	neither proffer it to the judges
7:87 (85)	He is the best of judges
10:109 (109)	He is the best of judges
11:45 (47)	thou art the justest of those that judge
12:80 (80)	He is the best of judges
95:8 (8)	is not God the justest of judges?

AḤKAM n.m. (comp. adj.)~justest

11:45 (47)	thou art the justest of those that judge
95:8 (8)	is not God the justest of judges?

ḤAKAM n.m.~arbiter, judge

4:35 (39)	bring forth an arbiter from his people
4:35 (39)	and from her people an arbiter
6:114 (114)	shall I seek after any judge but God?

ḤAKĪM n.m. (adj)~wise, knowing; All-wise (Divine attribute)

2:32 (30)	surely Thou art the All-knowing, the All-wise
2:129 (123)	Thou art the All-mighty, the All-wise
2:209 (205)	know then that God is All-mighty, All-wise
2:220 (219)	God is All-mighty, All-wise
2:228 (228)	God is All-mighty, All-wise
2:240 (241)	God is All-mighty, All-wise
2:260 (262)	do thou know that God is All-mighty, All-wise
3:6 (4)	there is no god but He, the All-mighty, the All-wise

3:18 (16)	there is no god but He, the All-mighty, the All-wise
3:58 (51)	We recite to thee of signs and wise remembrance
3:62 (55)	God is the All-mighty, the All-wise
3:126 (122)	help comes only from God the All-mighty, the All-wise
4:11 (12)	God is All-knowing, All-wise
4:17 (21)	God is All-knowing, All-wise
4:24 (28)	God is All-knowing, All-wise
4:26 (31)	God is All-knowing, All-wise
4:56 (59)	God is All-mighty, All-wise
4:92 (94)	God is All-knowing, All-wise
4:104 (105)	God is All-knowing, All-wise
4:111 (111)	God is ever All-knowing, All-wise
4:130 (129)	God is All-embracing, All-wise
4:158 (156)	God is All-mighty, All-wise
4:165 (163)	God is All-mighty, All-wise
4:170 (168)	God is All-knowing, All-wise
5:38 (42)	God is All-mighty, All-wise
5:118 (118)	Thou art the All-mighty, the All-wise
6:18 (18)	He is the All-wise, the All-aware
6:73 (73)	He is the All-wise, the All-aware
6:83 (83)	thy Lord is All-wise, All-knowing
6:128 (128)	thy Lord is All-wise, All-knowing
6:139 (140)	He is All-wise, All-knowing
8:10 (10)	God is All-mighty, All-wise
8:49 (51)	God is All-mighty, All-wise
8:63 (64)	He is All-mighty, All-wise
8:67 (68)	God is All-mighty, All-wise
8:71 (72)	God is All-knowing, All-wise
9:15 (15)	God is All-knowing, All-wise
9:28 (28)	God is All-knowing, All-wise
9:40 (40)	God is All-mighty, All-wise
9:60 (60)	God is All-knowing, All-wise
9:71 (72)	God is All-mighty, All-wise
9:97 (98)	God is All-knowing, All-wise
9:106 (107)	God is All-knowing, All-wise
9:110 (111)	God is All-knowing, All-wise
10:1 (1)	those are the signs of the Wise Book
11:1 (1)	a Book ... from One All-wise, All-aware
12:6 (6)	thy Lord is All-knowing, All-wise
12:83 (83)	He is the All-knowing, the All-wise
12:100 (101)	He is the All-knowing, the All-wise
14:4 (4)	He is the All-mighty, the All-wise
15:25 (25)	He is All-wise, All-knowing
16:60 (62)	He is the All-mighty, the All-wise
22:52 (51)	God is All-knowing, All-wise
24:10 (10)	and that God turns, and is All-wise
24:18 (17)	God is All-knowing, All-wise
24:58 (57)	God is All-knowing, All-wise
24:59 (58)	God is All-knowing, All-wise
27:6 (6)	the Koran from One All-wise, All-knowing
27:9 (9)	it is I, God, the All-mighty, the All-wise
29:26 (25)	He is the All-mighty, the All-wise
29:42 (41)	He is the All-mighty, the All-wise
30:27 (26)	He is the All-mighty, the All-wise
31:2 (1)	those are the signs of the Wise Book

31:9 (8)	He is the All-mighty, the All-wise
31:27 (26)	God is All-mighty, All-wise
33:1 (1)	god is All-knowing, All-wise
34:1 (1)	He is the All-wise, the All-aware
34:27 (26)	rather He is God, the All-mighty, the All-wise
35:2 (2)	He is the All-mighty, the All-wise
36:2 (1)	by the Wise Koran
39:1 (1)	the Book is from God the All-mighty, the All-wise
40:8 (8)	Thou art the All-mighty, the All-wise
41:42 (42)	a sending down from One All-wise, All-laudable
42:3 (1)	God, the All-mighty, the All-wise
42:51 (51)	He is All-high, All-wise
43:4 (3)	sublime indeed, wise
43:84 (84)	He is the All-wise, the All-knowing
44:4 (3)	therein every wise bidding determined
45:2 (1)	the Book is from God, the All-mighty, the All-wise
45:37 (36)	He is the All-mighty, the All-wise
46:2 (1)	the Book is from God, the All-mighty, the All-wise
48:4 (4)	God is All-knowing, All-wise
48:7 (7)	God is All-mighty, All-wise
48:19 (19)	God is ever All-mighty, All-wise
49:8 (8)	God is All-knowing, All-wise
51:30 (30)	He is the All-wise, the All-knowing
57:1 (1)	He is the All-mighty, the All-wise
59:1 (1)	He is the All-mighty, the All-wise
59:24 (24)	He is the All-mighty, the All-wise
60:5 (5)	Thou art the All-mighty, the All-wise
60:10 (10)	God is All-knowing, All-wise
61:1 (1)	He is the All-mighty, the All-wise
62:1 (1)	the King, the All-holy, the All-mighty, the All-wise
62:3 (3)	He is the All-mighty, the All-wise
64:18 (18)	the All-mighty, the All-wise
66:2 (2)	He is the All-knowing, the All-wise
76:30 (30)	God is ever All-knowing, All-wise

ḤIKMAH n.f.~wisdom (often in conjunction with "the Book")

2:129 (123)	teach them the Book and the Wisdom
2:151 (146)	and to teach you the Book and the Wisdom
2:231 (231)	the Book and the Wisdom He has sent down on you
2:251 (252)	God gave him the kingship, and Wisdom
2:269 (272)	He gives the Wisdom to whomsoever He will
2:269 (272)	whoso is given the Wisdom, has been given much good
3:48 (43)	He will teach him the Book, the Wisdom
3:81 (75)	that I have given you of Book and Wisdom
3:164 (158)	and to teach them the Book and the Wisdom
4:54 (57)	We gave the people of Abraham the Book and the Wisdom
4:113 (113)	God has sent down on thee the Book and the Wisdom
5:110 (110)	I taught thee the Book, the Wisdom
16:125 (126)	call thou to the way of thy Lord with wisdom
17:39 (41)	that is of the wisdom thy Lord has revealed to thee
31:12 (11)	indeed, We gave Lokman wisdom
33:34 (34)	the signs of God and the wisdom
38:20 (19)	We strengthened his kingdom, and gave him wisdom
43:63 (63)	I have come to you with wisdom
54:5 (5)	a Wisdom far-reaching
62:2 (2)	and to teach them the Book and the Wisdom

ḤAKKAMA vb. (II)~to make one a judge

b) impf. act. (*yuḥakkimu*)

4:65 (68)	till they make thee the judge regarding the disagreement
5:43 (47)	how will they make thee their judge

AḤKAMA vb. (IV)~to confirm, set clear. (pcple. pass.) clear, unabrogated

b) impf. act. (*yuḥkimu*)

22:52 (51)	then God confirms His signs

d) perf. pass. (*uḥkima*)

11:1 (1)	Alif Lam Ra a Book whose verses are set clear

h) pcple. pass. (*muḥkam*)

3:7 (5)	wherein are verses clear
47:20 (22)	when a clear sura is sent down

TAḤĀKAMA vb. (VI)~to take one's dispute with another for judgment

b) impf. act. (*yataḥākamu*)

4:60 (63)	desiring to take their disputes to idols

*Ḥ L F

ḤALAFA vb. (I)~to swear

a) perf. act.

5:89 (91)	that is the expiation of your oaths when you have sworn

b) impf. act. (*yaḥlifu*)

4:62 (65)	then they come to thee swearing by God
9:42 (42)	still they will swear by God
9:56 (56)	they swear by God that they belong with you
9:62 (63)	they swear to you by God, to please you
9:74 (75)	they swear by God that they said nothing
9:95 (96)	they will swear to you by God
9:96 (97)	they will swear to you, that you may be well-pleased
9:107 (108)	they will swear, We desired nothing
58:14 (15)	they swear upon falsehood, and that wittingly
58:18 (19)	and they will swear to Him
58:18 (19)	as they swear to you

ḤALLĀF n.m.~a swearer

68:10 (10)	obey thou not every mean swearer

*Ḥ L L

ḤALLA (1) vb. (I)~to untie, unloose

c) impv. (*uḥlul*)

20:27 (28)	unloose the knot upon my tongue

ḤALLA (2) vb. (I)~to be lawful, permitted; to complete the Pilgrimage and quit pilgrim sanctity

a) perf. act.

5:2 (3)	when you have quit your pilgrim sanctity

b) impf. act. (*yaḥillu*)

2:228 (228)	it is not lawful for them to hide
2:229 (229)	it is not lawful for you to take of what you have given
2:230 (230)	she shall not be lawful to him after that
4:19 (23)	it is not lawful for you to inherit women
33:52 (52)	thereafter women are not lawful to thee
60:10 (10)	nor are the unbelievers permitted to them

ḤALLA (3) vb. (I)~to alight

b) impf. act. (*yaḥullu*)

11:39 (41)	upon whom there shall alight a lasting chastisement
13:31 (31)	or it alights nigh their habitation
20:81 (83)	or My anger shall alight on you
20:81 (83)	on whomsoever My anger alights
20:86 (89)	did you desire that anger should alight on you
39:40 (41)	and upon whom lights a lasting chastisement

ḤALĀ'IL n.f. (pl. of *ḥalīl*)~a wife

4:23 (27)	the spouses of your sons who are of your loins

ḤALĀL n.m.~lawful

2:168 (163)	eat of what is in the earth lawful and good
5:88 (90)	eat of what God has provided you lawful and good
8:69 (70)	such as is lawful and good
10:59 (60)	you have made some of it unlawful, and some lawful
16:114 (115)	eat of what God has provided you lawful and good
16:116 (117)	this is lawful, and this is forbidden

ḤILL n.m.~anything lawful, permitted; lodger, inhabitant

3:93 (87)	all food was lawful to the Children of Israel
5:5 (7)	the food of those who were given the Book is permitted to you
5:5 (7)	and permitted to them is your food
60:10 (10)	they are not permitted to the unbelievers
90:2 (2)	and thou art a lodger in this land

MAḤILL n.m.~a place of sacrifice

2:196 (192)	till the offering reaches its place of sacrifice
22:33 (34)	their lawful place of sacrifice is by the Ancient House
48:25 (25)	the offering, detained so as not to reach its place of sacrifice

TAḤILLAH n.f.~dissolution, absolution

66:2 (2) God has ordained for you the absolution of your oaths

AḤALLA (2) vb. (IV)~to permit, make lawful. (pcple. act.) one who permits

a) perf. act.

2:275 (276) God has permitted trafficking, and forbidden usury
5:87 (89) forbid not such good things as God has permitted you
33:50 (49) We have made lawful for thee thy wives
66:1 (1) why forbiddest thou what God has made lawful to thee

b) impf. act. (*yuḥillu*)

3:50 (44) and to make lawful to you certain things
5:2 (2) profane not God's waymarks nor the holy month
7:157 (156) making lawful for them the good things
9:37 (37) one year they make it profane, and hallow it another
9:37 (37) the number that God has hallowed

d) perf. pass. (*uḥilla*)

2:187 (183) permitted to you, upon the night of the Fast
4:24 (28) lawful for you, beyond all that, is that you may seek
4:160 (158) We have forbidden them certain good things that were permitted to them
5:1 (1) permitted to you is the beast of the flocks
5:4 (6) they will question thee what is permitted them
5:4 (6) the good things are permitted you
5:5 (7) today the good things are permitted you
5:96 (97) permitted to you is the game of the sea
22:30 (31) and permitted to you are the flocks

g) pcple. act. (*muḥill*)

5:1 (1) so that you deem not game permitted to be hunted

AḤALLA (3) vb. (IV)~to cause to dwell

a) perf. act.

14:28 (33) and caused their people to dwell in the abode of ruin
35:35 (32) has made us to dwell in the abode of everlasting life

*Ḥ L M

ḤALAM n.m. (pl. *aḥlām*)~intellect [Ar], mind [Pk], faculties of understanding [Ali]

52:32 (32) do their intellects bid them do this?

ḤALĪM n.m. (adj)~prudent, clement [Ar]; ready to suffer, forbearing [Ali]; gentle, mild [Pk]; All-clement (Divine attribute)

2:225 (225) God is All-forgiving, All-clement
2:235 (236) know that God is All-forgiving, All-clement
2:263 (265) God is All-sufficient, All-clement
3:155 (149) God is All-forgiving, All-clement

4:12 (16)	God is All-knowing, All-clement
5:101 (101)	God is All-forgiving, All-clement
9:114 (115)	Abraham was compassionate, clement
11:75 (77)	Abraham was clement, compassionate, penitent
11:87 (89)	Thou art the clement one, the right-minded
17:44 (46)	He is All-clement, All-forgiving
22:59 (58)	God is All-knowing, All-clement
33:51 (51)	God is All-knowing, All-clement
35:41 (39)	He is All-clement, All-forgiving
37:101 (99)	We gave him the good tidings of a prudent boy
64:17 (17)	God is All-thankful, All-clement

ḤULM n.m. (pl. *aḥlām*)~dream, nightmare

12:44 (44)	a hotchpotch of nightmares
12:44 (44)	we know nothing of the interpretation of nightmares
21:5 (5)	a hotchpotch of nightmares

ḤULUM n.m.~puberty

24:58 (57)	those of you who have not reached puberty
24:59 (58)	when your children reach puberty

*Ḥ L Q

ḤALAQA vb. (I)~to shave

b) impf. act. (*yaḥliqu*)

2:196 (192)	shave not your heads

ḤALLAQA vb. (II)~(pcple. act.) one who is shaved

g) pcple. act. (*muḥalliq*)

48:27 (27)	your heads shaved, your hair cut short

*Ḥ L Q M

ḤULQŪM n.m.~throat

56:83 (82)	when the soul leaps to the throat of the dying

*Ḥ L Y

ḤILYAH n.f. (coll)~ornaments

7:148 (146)	took to them, after him, of their ornaments a Calf
13:17 (18)	being desirous of ornament or ware
16:14 (14)	and bring forth out of it ornaments for you to wear
35:12 (13)	and bring forth out of it ornaments for you to wear
43:18 (17)	one who is reared amid ornaments

ḤALLÁ vb. (II)~to adorn

d) perf. pass. (*ḥulliya*)

76:21 (21)	they are adorned with bracelets of silver

e) impf. pass. (*yuḥallá*)

18:31 (30)	therein they shall be adorned with bracelets of gold
22:23 (23)	therein they shall be adorned with bracelets of gold
35:33 (30)	they shall be adorned with bracelets of gold

*Ḥ M

ḤĀ MĪM~ml

40:1 (1)	Ha Mim
41:1 (1)	Ha Mim
42:1 (1)	Ha Mim
43:1 (1)	Ha Mim
44:1 (1)	Ha Mim
45:1 (1)	Ha Mim
46:1 (1)	Ha Mim

*Ḥ M ʾ

ḤAMAʾ n.m.~moulded mud [Ar], altered mud [Pk]

15:26 (26)	We created man of a clay of mud moulded
15:28 (28)	I am creating a mortal of a clay of mud moulded
15:33 (33)	a mortal whom Thou hast created of a clay of mud moulded

ḤAMIʾ n.m. (adj)~muddy

18:86 (84)	he found it setting in a muddy spring

*Ḥ M D

ḤAMIDA vb. (I)~to praise. (n.vb.) praise. (pcple. act.) one who prays or praises. (pcple. pass.) praised, laudable

e) impf. pass. (*yuḥmadu*)

3:188 (185)	and love to be praised for what they have not done

f) n.vb. (*ḥamd*)

1:2 (1)	Praise belongs to God the Lord of all Being
2:30 (28)	while We proclaim Thy praise and call Thee Holy
6:1 (1)	praise belongs to God
6:45 (45)	praise belongs to God the Lord of all Being
7:43 (41)	praise belongs to God, who guided us unto this
10:10 (11)	praise belongs to God, the Lord of all Being

13:13 (14)	the thunder proclaims His praise
14:39 (41)	praise be to God
15:98 (98)	proclaim thy Lord's praise, and be of those that bow
16:75 (77)	praise belongs to God
17:44 (46)	nothing is, that does not proclaim His praise
17:52 (54)	He will call you, and you will answer praising Him
17:111 (111)	praise belongs to God, who has not taken to Him a son
18:1 (1)	praise belongs to God who has sent down upon His servant
20:130 (130)	proclaim thy Lord's praise
23:28 (29)	praise belongs to God, who has delivered us
25:58 (60)	and proclaim His praise
27:15 (15)	praise belongs to God who has preferred us
27:59 (60)	praise belongs to God, and peace be on His servants
27:93 (95)	praise belongs to God
28:70 (70)	His is the praise in the former as in the latter
29:63 (63)	praise belongs to God
30:18 (17)	His is the praise in the heavens and earth
31:25 (24)	praise belongs to God
32:15 (15)	and proclaim the praise of their Lord
34:1 (1)	praise belongs to God to whom belongs whatsoever is in the heavens
34:1 (1)	to Him belongs praise also in the Hereafter
35:1 (1)	praise belongs to God, Originator of the heavens and earth
35:34 (31)	praise belongs to God who has put away all sorrow
37:182 (182)	praise belongs to God, the Lord of all Being
39:29 (30)	praise belongs to God
39:74 (74)	praise belongs to God, who has been true
39:75 (75)	about the Throne proclaiming the praise of their Lord
39:75 (75)	praise belongs to God, the Lord of all Being
40:7 (7)	those round about it proclaim the praise of their Lord
40:55 (57)	proclaim the praise of thy Lord at evening and dawn
40:65 (67)	praise belongs to God, the Lord of all Being
42:5 (3)	when the angels proclaim the praise of their Lord
45:36 (35)	to God belongs praise, the Lord of the heavens
50:39 (38)	and proclaim thy Lord's praise
52:48 (48)	proclaim the praise of thy Lord when thou arisest
64:1 (1)	His is the Kingdom, and His is the praise
110:3 (3)	then proclaim the praise of thy Lord

g) pcple. act. (*ḥāmid*)

9:112 (113)	those who repent, those who serve, those who pray

h) pcple. pass. (*maḥmūd*)

17:79 (81)	it may be that thy Lord will raise thee up to a laudable station

AḤMAD n.prop.~Ahmad (a name of the Prophet)

61:6 (6)	a Messenger who shall come after me, whose name shall be Ahmad

ḤAMĪD n.m. (adj)~worthy of praise; (Divine attribute) All-laudable [Ar], Worthy of praise [Pk, Ali]

2:267 (270)	know that God is All-sufficient, All-laudable
4:131 (130)	God is All-sufficient, All-laudable
11:73 (76)	He is All-laudable, All-glorious
14:1 (1)	the path of the All-mighty, the All-laudable
14:8 (8)	God is All-sufficient, All-laudable

22:24 (24)	they shall be guided unto the path of the All-laudable
22:64 (63)	He is the All-sufficient, the All-laudable
31:12 (11)	surely God is All-sufficient, All-laudable
31:26 (25)	He is the All-sufficient, the All-laudable
34:6 (6)	the path of the All-mighty, the All-laudable
35:15 (16)	He is the All-sufficient, the All-laudable
41:42 (42)	a sending down from One All-wise, All-laudable
42:28 (27)	He is the Protector, the All-laudable
57:24 (24)	God is the All-sufficient, the All-laudable
60:6 (6)	God is the All-sufficient, the All-laudable
64:6 (6)	God is All-sufficient, All-laudable
85:8 (8)	they believed in God the All-mighty, the All-laudable

MUḤAMMAD n.prop.~Muhammad

3:144 (138)	Muhammad is naught but a Messenger
33:40 (40)	Muhammad is not the father of any one of your men
47:2 (2)	and believe in what is sent down to Muhammad
48:29 (29)	Muhammad is the Messenger of God

*Ḥ M L

ḤAMALA vb. (I)~to carry, lift up, bear; conceive; load, lay something upon someone; mount, embark [Ar]; (with prep. ʿ*alá*) to attack; to charge someone with a load. (n.vb.) burden, burthen; foetus; time of pregnancy; (*dhāt ḥaml*, pl. *ūlāt al- aḥmāl*) pregnant woman, woman with child (lit. "one with burden"). (pcple. act.) one who carries

a) perf. act.

2:286 (286)	such as Thou didst lay upon those before us
6:146 (147)	save what their backs carry, or their entrails
7:189 (189)	she bore a light burden and passed by with it
17:3 (3)	the seed of those We bore with Noah
17:70 (72)	We have honoured the Children of Adam and carried them on land
19:22 (22)	she conceived him, and withdrew with him to a distant place
19:58 (59)	and of those We bore with Noah
20:111 (110)	He will have failed whose burden is of evildoing
31:14 (13)	We have charged man concerning his parents — his mother bore him in weakness
33:72 (72)	and man carried it
36:41 (41)	We carried their seed in the laden ship
46:15 (14)	his mother bore him painfully
54:13 (13)	We bore him upon a well-planked vessel
69:11 (11)	We bore you in the running ship

b) impf. act. (*yaḥmilu*)

2:248 (249)	what the folk of Moses and Aaron's folk left behind, the angels bearing it
2:286 (286)	charge us not with a load
6:31 (31)	on their backs they shall be bearing their loads
7:176 (175)	if thou attackest it it lolls its tongue out
9:92 (93)	when they came to thee, for thee to mount them
9:92 (93)	I find not whereon to mount you
12:36 (36)	I dreamed that I was carrying on my head bread
13:8 (9)	God knows what every female bears

16:7 (7)	they bear your loads unto a land that you never would reach
16:25 (27)	that they may bear their loads complete
19:27 (28)	then she brought the child to her folk carrying him
20:100 (100)	upon the Day of Resurrection he shall bear a fardel
29:12 (11)	let us carry your offences
29:13 (12)	they shall certainly carry their loads
29:60 (60)	how many a beast that bears not its own provision
33:72 (72)	they refused to carry it and were afraid of it
35:11 (12)	no female bears or brings forth, save with His knowledge
40:7 (7)	those who bear the Throne, and those round about it
41:47 (47)	no female bears or brings forth, save with His knowledge
62:5 (5)	then they have not carried it
62:5 (5)	the likeness of an ass carrying books
69:17 (17)	eight shall carry above them the Throne of thy Lord

c) impv. (*iḥmil*)

11:40 (42)	embark in it two of every kind

d) perf. pass. (*ḥumila*)

69:14 (14)	the earth and the mountains are lifted up

e) impf. pass. (*yuḥmalu*)

23:22 (22)	and upon them, and on the ships, you are borne
35:18 (19)	not a thing of it will be carried
40:80 (80)	and upon them and on the ships you are carried

f) n.vb. (*ḥaml*, pl. *aḥmāl*)

7:189 (189)	when he covered her, she bore a light burden
22:2 (2)	every pregnant woman shall deposit her (burden)
22:2 (2)	every (pregnant woman) shall deposit her burden
46:15 (14)	his bearing and his weaning are thirty months
65:4 (4)	and those who are with child
65:4 (4)	their term is when they bring forth their burden
65:6 (6)	if they are with child expend upon them
65:6 (6)	expend upon them until they bring forth their burden

g) pcple. act. (*ḥāmil*)

29:12 (11)	yet they cannot carry anything, even of their own offences
51:2 (2)	and the burden-bearers

ḤAMMĀLAH n.f.~carrier

111:4 (4)	and his wife, the carrier of the firewood

ḤAMŪLAH n.f.~a beast of burden

6:142 (143)	and of the cattle, for burthen and for slaughter

ḤIML n.m.~a load, a burden

12:72 (72)	whoever brings it shall receive a camel's load
20:101 (101)	how evil upon the Day of Resurrection that burden for them
35:18 (19)	and if one heavy-burdened calls for its load to be carried

ḤAMMALA vb. (II)~to burden, load someone with something, to lay something on someone

b) impf. act. (*yuḥammilu*)

2:286 (286)	do Thou not burden us beyond what we have the strength to bear

d) perf. pass. (*ḥummila*)

20:87 (90)	we were loaded with fardels
24:54 (53)	only upon him rests what is laid on him
24:54 (53)	upon you rests what is laid on you
62:5 (5)	those who have been loaded with the Torah

IḤTAMALA vb. (VIII)~to lay a burden upon oneself, to carry

a) perf. act.

4:112 (112)	thereby has laid upon himself calumny and manifest sin
13:17 (18)	and the torrent carries a swelling scum
33:58 (58)	have laid upon themselves calumny and manifest sin

*Ḥ M M

ḤAMĪM n.m. (adj)~boiling water; loyal, close (friend or relative)

6:70 (69)	for them awaits a draught of boiling water
10:4 (4)	for them awaits a draught of boiling water
22:19 (20)	there shall be poured over their heads boiling water
26:101 (101)	no loyal friend
37:67 (65)	then on top of it they have a brew of boiling water
38:57 (57)	let them taste it — boiling water and pus
40:18 (19)	the evildoers have not one loyal friend
40:72 (73)	into the boiling water, then into the Fire they are poured
41:34 (34)	shall be as if he were a loyal friend
44:46 (46)	as boiling water bubbles
44:48 (48)	then pour over his head the chastisement of boiling water
47:15 (17)	such as are given to drink boiling water
55:44 (44)	they shall go round between it and between hot, boiling water
56:42 (41)	mid burning winds and boiling waters
56:54 (54)	and drink on top of that boiling water
56:93 (93)	there shall be a hospitality of boiling water
69:35 (35)	therefore he today has not here one loyal friend
70:10 (10)	no loyal friend shall question (loyal friend)
70:10 (10)	no (loyal friend) shall question loyal friend
78:25 (25)	save boiling water and pus

YAḤMŪM n.m.~black smoke

56:43 (42)	and the shadow of a smoking blaze

*Ḥ M R

ḤIMĀR n.m. (pl. *ḥamīr* and *ḥumur*)~ass, donkey

2:259 (261)	and look at thy ass
16:8 (8)	and mules, and asses, for you to ride
31:19 (18)	the most hideous of voices is the ass's
62:5 (5)	as the likeness of an ass carrying books
74:50 (51)	as if they were startled asses

ḤUMR n.m. (adj) (pl. of *aḥmar*)~red

35:27 (25)	in the mountains are streaks white and red

*Ḥ M Y

ḤAMIYA vb. (I)~to be hot. (pcple. act.) scorching, blazing

e) impf. pass. (*yuḥmá*)

9:35 (35)	the day they shall be heated in the fire of Gehenna

g) pcple. act. (*ḥāmī*)

88:4 (4)	roasting at a scorching fire
101:11 (8)	a blazing Fire

ḤĀMI n.prop.~Hami, name given to an animal (prob. a camel) dedicated to deities of pagan Arabia

5:103 (102)	to idols, such as Bahira, Sa'iba, Wasila, Hami

ḤAMĪYAH n.f.~fierceness [Ar], disdain [Ali], zealotry [Ali]

48:26 (26)	unbelievers set in their hearts fierceness (the fierceness) of pagandom
48:26 (26)	unbelievers set in their hearts (fierceness) the fierceness of pagandom

*Ḥ N DH

ḤANĪDH n.m. (adj)~roasted

11:69 (72)	and presently he brought a roasted calf

*Ḥ N F

ḤANĪF n.m. (pl. *ḥunafā'*)~one of pure faith [Ar], upright [Pk], true [Ali]

2:135 (129)	Abraham, a man of pure faith
3:67 (60)	he was a Muslim and one pure of faith
3:95 (89)	follow the creed of Abraham, a man of pure faith
4:125 (124)	Abraham, a man of pure faith
6:79 (79)	a man of pure faith
6:161 (162)	the creed of Abraham, a man of pure faith
10:105 (105)	set thy face to the religion, a man of pure faith
16:120 (121)	a man of pure faith and no idolater
16:123 (124)	Abraham, a man of pure faith
22:31 (32)	being men pure of faith unto God
30:30 (29)	set thy face to the religion, a man of pure faith
98:5 (4)	making the religion His sincerely, men of pure faith

*Ḥ N J R

ḤANĀJIR n.f. (pl. of *ḥanjarah*)~throat

33:10 (10)	when your eyes swerved and your hearts reached your throats
40:18 (18)	when, choking with anguish, the hearts are in the throats

*Ḥ N K

IḤTANAKA vb. (VIII)~to master, bring under full control

b) impf. act. (*yaḥtaniku*)

17:62 (64)	I shall assuredly master his seed

*Ḥ N N

ḤANĀN n.m.~tenderness, mercy

19:13 (14)	a tenderness from Us, and purity

ḤUNAYN n.prop.~Hunain (a valley near Mecca)

9:25 (25)	and on the day of Hunain

*Ḥ N TH

ḤANATHA vb. (I)~to fail an oath

b) impf. act. (*yaḥnathu*)

38:44 (43)	do not fail in thy oath

ḤINTH n.m.~wickedness, sinfulness

56:46 (45)	and persisted in the Great Sin

*Ḥ Q B

ḤUQUB n.m. (pl. *aḥqāb*)~a long time, many years, ages

18:60 (59)	though I go on for many years
78:23 (23)	therein to tarry for ages

*Ḥ Q F

AḤQĀF n.m. (pl. of *ḥiqf*)~sand-dunes, winding sand-tracts

46:21 (20)	when he warned his people beside the sand-dunes

*Ḥ Q Q

ḤAQQA vb. (I)~to be realized, come true, be just [Ar], be justified [Pk], be proved true [Ali]; be justly or fitly disposed to, to merit (with prep. *ʿalá*)

a) perf. act.

7:30 (28)	a part He guided, and a part justly disposed to error
10:33 (34)	the word of thy Lord is realized against the ungodly
10:96 (96)	those against whom thy Lord's word is realized
16:36 (38)	some of them God guided, and some were justly disposed to error
17:16 (17)	then the Word is realized against it
22:18 (18)	and many merit the chastisement
28:63 (63)	those against whom the Word is realized
32:13 (13)	but now My Word is realized
36:7 (6)	the Word has been realised against most of them
37:31 (30)	our Lord's Word is realised against us
38:14 (13)	so My retribution was just
39:19 (20)	he against whom the word of chastisement is realized
39:71 (71)	the word of the chastisement has been realized
40:6 (6)	the Word of thy Lord was realised
41:25 (24)	against them has been realized the Word
46:18 (17)	against whom has been realized the Word
50:14 (13)	and My threat came true

b) impf. act. (*yaḥiqqu*)

36:70 (70)	that the Word may be realized against the unbelievers

d) perf. pass. (*ḥuqqa*)

84:2 (2)	and is fitly disposed
84:5 (5)	and is fitly disposed

AḤAQQ n.m. (comp. adj. of *ḥaqq* and *ḥaqīq*)~having better right, truer, worthier

2:228 (228)	their mates have better right to restore them
2:247 (248)	who have better right than he to kingship
5:107 (106)	our testimony is truer than their testimony
6:81 (81)	which of the two parties has better title to security
9:13 (13)	you would do better to be afraid of God
9:62 (63)	more right is it they should please Him
9:108 (109)	a mosque that was founded upon godfearing... is worthier for thee to stand in
10:35 (36)	which is worthier to be followed
33:37 (37)	God has better right for thee to fear Him
48:26 (26)	the word of godfearing to which they have better right

ḤAQĪQ n.m. (adj)~worthy [Ar], approved upon condition [Pk], right [Ali]

7:105 (103)	worthy to say nothing regarding God

ḤAQQ n.m.~(n) truth; that which is right; that which is honourable; that which is due; (with prep. *ʿalá*) an obligation; (*alladhī ʿalayhi al-ḥaqq*) debtor; (adj) true; Truth, the True (Divine attribute); (adv) rightfully, (*bi-ghayr ḥaqq*) without right, unrightfully; (*ḥaqqa tuqātihi*) "as He should be feared"

2:26 (24)	they know it is the truth from their Lord
2:42 (39)	do not confound the truth with vanity
2:42 (39)	do not conceal the truth wittingly
2:61 (58)	that, because they had... slain the Prophets unrightfully
2:71 (66)	now thou hast brought the truth

2:91 (85)	yet it is the truth confirming what is with them
2:109 (103)	after the truth has become clear to them
2:119 (113)	We have sent thee with the truth, good tidings to bear
2:121 (115)	and who recite it with true recitation
2:144 (139)	those who have been given the Book know it is the truth from their Lord
2:146 (141)	there is a party of them conceal the truth and that wittingly
2:147 (142)	the truth comes from thy Lord
2:149 (144)	it is the truth from thy Lord
2:176 (171)	because God has sent down the Book with the truth
2:180 (176)	an obligation on the godfearing
2:213 (209)	He sent down with them the Book with the truth
2:213 (209)	then God guided those who believed to the truth
2:236 (237)	an obligation on the good-doers
2:241 (242)	an obligation on the godfearing
2:252 (253)	these are the signs of God We recite to thee in truth
2:282 (282)	so let him write, and let the debtor dictate
2:282 (282)	if the debtor be a fool, or weak, or unable to dictate
3:3 (2)	He has sent down upon thee the Book with the truth
3:21 (20)	and slay the Prophets without right
3:60 (53)	the truth is of your Lord; be not of the doubters
3:62 (55)	this is the true story. There is no god but God
3:71 (64)	why do you confound the truth with vanity
3:71 (64)	and conceal the truth and that wittingly
3:86 (80)	they believed, and bore witness that the Messenger is true
3:102 (97)	fear God as He should be feared, and see you do not die
3:108 (104)	these are the signs of God We recite to thee in truth
3:112 (108)	they disbelieved in God's signs, and slew the Prophets without right
3:154 (148)	thinking of God thoughts that were not true
3:181 (177)	their slaying the Prophets without right
4:105 (106)	We have sent down to thee the Book with the truth
4:122 (121)	God's promise in truth; and who is truer in speech than God?
4:151 (150)	those in truth are the unbelievers
4:155 (154)	disbelieving in the signs of God, and slaying the Prophets without right
4:170 (168)	the Messenger has now come to you with the truth
4:171 (169)	say not as to God but the truth
5:27 (30)	recite thou to them the story of the two sons of Adam truthfully
5:48 (52)	We have sent down to thee the Book with the truth
5:48 (52)	do not follow their caprices, to forsake the truth
5:77 (81)	go not beyond the bounds in your religion, other than the truth
5:83 (86)	thou seest their eyes overflow with tears because of the truth
5:84 (87)	why should we not believe in God and the truth
5:116 (116)	it is not mine to say what I have no right to
6:5 (5)	they cried lies to the truth when it came to them
6:30 (30)	is not this the truth
6:57 (57)	He relates the truth, and He is the Best of deciders
6:62 (62)	then they are restored to God their Protector, the True
6:66 (66)	Thy people have cried it lies; yet it is the truth
6:73 (72)	it is He who created the heavens and the earth in truth
6:73 (73)	His saying is true, and His is the Kingdom
6:91 (91)	they measured not God with His true measure
6:93 (93)	for what you said untruly about God, waxing proud against His signs
6:114 (114)	it is sent down from thy Lord with the truth
6:141 (142)	pay the due thereof on the day of its harvest
6:151 (152)	slay not the soul God has forbidden, except by right
7:8 (7)	the weighing that day is true

7:33 (31)	indecencies, the inward and the outward, and sin, and unjust insolence
7:43 (41)	indeed, our Lord's Messengers came with the truth
7:44 (42)	we have found that which our Lord promised us true
7:44 (42)	have you found what your Lord promised you true?
7:53 (51)	indeed, our Lord's Messengers came with the truth
7:89 (87)	our Lord, give true deliverance between us and our people
7:105 (103)	worthy to say nothing regarding God except the truth
7:118 (115)	the truth came to pass, and false was proved what they were doing
7:146 (143)	those who wax proud in the earth unjustly
7:159 (159)	there is a nation who guide by the truth
7:169 (168)	that they should say concerning God nothing but the truth
7:181 (180)	of those We created are a nation who guide by the truth
8:4 (4)	those in truth are the believers
8:5 (5)	as thy Lord brought thee forth from thy house with the truth
8:6 (6)	disputing with thee concerning the truth after it had become clear
8:7 (7)	God was desiring to verify the truth by His words
8:8 (8)	that He might verify the truth and prove untrue the untrue
8:32 (32)	if this be indeed the truth from Thee, then rain down upon us stones
8:74 (75)	those in truth are the believers
9:29 (29)	such men as practise not the religion of truth
9:33 (33)	He who has sent His Messenger with the guidance and the religion of truth
9:48 (48)	and turned things upside down for thee, until the truth came
9:111 (112)	that is a promise binding upon God in the Torah
10:4 (4)	to Him shall you return, all together — God's promise, in truth
10:5 (5)	God created that not save with the truth, distinguishing the signs
10:23 (24)	behold, they are insolent in the earth, wrongfully
10:30 (31)	they shall be restored to God, their Protector, the True
10:32 (33)	that then is God, your Lord, the True
10:32 (33)	what is there, after truth, but error
10:35 (36)	is there any of your associates who guides to the truth?
10:35 (36)	God — He guides to the truth
10:35 (36)	which is worthier to be followed — He who guides to the truth
10:36 (37)	surmise avails naught against truth
10:53 (54)	is it true
10:53 (54)	yes, by my Lord! It is true
10:55 (56)	God's promise is true; but the most of them have no knowledge
10:76 (77)	when the truth came to them from Us, they said
10:77 (78)	do you say this to the truth, when it has come to you?
10:82 (82)	God verifies the truth by His words
10:94 (94)	the truth has come to thee from thy Lord
10:103 (103)	as is Our bounden duty, We shall deliver the believers
10:108 (108)	O men, the truth has come to you from you Lord
11:17 (20)	it is the truth from thy Lord, but most men do not believe
11:45 (47)	my son is of my family, and Thy promise is surely the truth
11:79 (81)	thou knowest we have no right to thy daughters
11:120 (121)	there has come to thee the truth and an admonition
12:51 (51)	now the truth is at last discovered
12:100 (101)	my Lord has made it true
13:1 (1)	that which has been sent down to thee from thy Lord is the truth
13:14 (15)	to Him is the call of truth
13:17 (18)	so God strikes both the true and the false
13:19 (19)	what is sent down to thee from thy Lord is the truth
14:19 (22)	God created the heavens and the earth in truth
14:22 (26)	God surely promised you a true promise
15:8 (8)	We send not down the angels, save with truth

15:55 (55)	We give thee good tidings of truth
15:64 (64)	We have come to thee with the truth
15:85 (85)	We created not the heavens and the earth... save in truth
16:3 (3)	He created the heavens and the earth in truth
16:38 (40)	it is a promise binding upon Him, but most men know not
16:102 (104)	the Holy Spirit sent it down from thy Lord in truth
17:26 (28)	and give the kinsman his right
17:33 (35)	slay not the soul God has forbidden, except by right
17:81 (83)	the truth has come, and falsehood has vanished away
17:105 (106)	with the truth We have sent it down
17:105 (106)	and with the truth it has come down
18:13 (12)	We will relate to thee their tidings truly
18:21 (20)	that they might know that God's promise is true
18:29 (28)	the truth is from your Lord
18:44 (42)	protection belongs only to God the True
18:56 (54)	that they may rebut thereby the truth
18:98 (98)	my Lord's promise is ever true
19:34 (35)	that is Jesus, son of Mary, in word of truth
20:114 (113)	so high exalted be God, the true King
21:18 (18)	We hurl the truth against falsehood and it prevails over it
21:24 (24)	the most part of them know not the truth
21:55 (56)	what, hast thou come to us with the truth
21:97 (97)	nigh has drawn the true promise, and behold, the eyes of the unbelievers
21:112 (112)	my Lord, judge Thou with truth
22:6 (6)	He is the Truth, and brings the dead to life
22:40 (41)	who were expelled from their habitations without right
22:54 (53)	that they... may know that it is the truth from thy Lord
22:62 (61)	God — He is the Truth
22:74 (73)	they measure not God with His true measure
22:78 (77)	and struggle for God as is His due
23:41 (43)	the Cry seized them justly
23:62 (64)	with Us is a Book speaking truth
23:70 (72)	he has brought them the truth
23:70 (72)	but most of them are averse from the truth
23:71 (73)	had the truth followed their caprices
23:90 (92)	We brought them the truth, and they are truly liars
23:116 (117)	then high exalted be God, the King, the True
24:25 (25)	upon that day God will pay them in full their just due
24:25 (25)	they shall know that God is the manifest Truth
24:49 (48)	if they are in the right, they will come to him submissively
25:26 (28)	that day, the true Kingdom, shall belong to the All-merciful
25:33 (35)	We bring thee the truth, and better
25:68 (68)	nor slay the soul God has forbidden except by right
27:79 (81)	put thy trust in God; thou art upon the manifest truth
28:3 (2)	We will recite to thee something of the tiding of Moses and Pharaoh truthfully
28:13 (12)	that she might know that the promise of God is true
28:39 (39)	he waxed proud in the land, he and his hosts, wrongfully
28:48 (48)	when the truth came to them from Ourselves, they said
28:53 (53)	we believe in it; surely it is the truth from our Lord
28:75 (75)	then will they know that Truth is God's
29:44 (43)	God created the heavens and the earth with the truth
29:68 (68)	or cries lies to the truth when it comes to him
30:8 (7)	God created not the heavens and the earth... save with the truth
30:38 (37)	give the kinsman his right, and the needy
30:47 (46)	it was ever a duty incumbent upon Us, to help the believers

30:60 (60)	be thou patient; surely God's promise is true
31:9 (8)	therein to dwell forever — God's promise in truth
31:30 (29)	God — He is the Truth
31:33 (33)	surely God's promise is true
32:3 (2)	it is the truth from thy Lord that thou mayest warn a people
33:4 (4)	God speaks the truth, and guides on the way
33:53 (53)	God is not ashamed before the truth
34:6 (6)	what has been sent down to thee from thy Lord is the truth
34:23 (22)	the truth; and He is the All-high, the All-great
34:26 (25)	our Lord will bring us together, then make deliverance between us by the truth
34:43 (42)	the unbelievers say to the truth, when it has come to them
34:48 (47)	my Lord hurls the truth — the Knower of the Unseen
34:49 (48)	truth has come; falsehood originates not, nor brings again
35:5 (5)	God's promise is true; so let not the present life delude you
35:24 (22)	We have sent thee with the truth good tidings to bear
35:31 (28)	and that We have revealed to thee of the Book is the truth
37:37 (36)	he brought the truth, and confirmed the Envoys
38:22 (21)	so judge between us justly, and transgress not
38:26 (25)	judge between men justly, and follow not caprice
38:64 (64)	surely that is true — the disputing of the inhabitants of the Fire
38:84 (85)	this is the truth
38:84 (85)	and the truth I say
39:2 (2)	We have sent down to thee the Book with the truth
39:5 (7)	He created the heavens and the earth in truth
39:41 (42)	We have sent down upon thee the Book for mankind with the truth
39:67 (67)	they measure not God with His true measure
39:69 (69)	and justly the issue be decided between them
39:75 (75)	justly the issue shall be decided between them
40:5 (5)	that they might rebut thereby the truth
40:20 (21)	God shall decide justly
40:25 (26)	when he brought them the truth from Us, they said
40:55 (57)	be thou patient; surely God's promise is true
40:75 (75)	that is because you rejoiced in the earth without right
40:77 (77)	be thou patient; surely God's promise is true
40:78 (78)	when God's command comes, justly the issue shall be decided
41:15 (14)	as for Ad, they waxed proud in the earth without right
41:53 (53)	till it is clear to them that it is the truth
42:17 (16)	God it is who has sent down the Book with the truth
42:18 (17)	those who believe in it go in fear of it, knowing that it is the truth
42:24 (23)	God blots out falsehood and verifies the truth
42:42 (40)	those who do wrong to the people, and are insolent in the earth wrongfully
43:29 (28)	until the truth came unto them, and a manifest Messenger
43:30 (29)	when the truth came to them, they said
43:78 (78)	We brought you the truth
43:78 (78)	but most of you were averse to the truth
43:86 (86)	save such as have testified to the truth
44:39 (39)	We created them not save in truth
45:6 (5)	those are the signs of God that We recite to thee in truth
45:22 (21)	God created the heavens and the earth in truth
45:29 (28)	this is Our Book, that speaks against you the truth
45:32 (31)	God's promise is true, and the Hour, there is no doubt of it
46:3 (2)	We have not created the heavens and the earth… save with the truth
46:7 (6)	the unbelievers say to the truth when it has come to them
46:17 (16)	believe; surely God's promise is true
46:20 (19)	for that you waxed proud in the earth without right

46:30 (29)	guiding to the truth and to a straight path
46:34 (33)	is not this the truth
47:2 (2)	it is the truth from their Lord
47:3 (3)	those who believe follow the truth from their Lord
48:27 (27)	God has indeed fulfilled the vision He vouchsafed to His Messenger truly
48:28 (28)	He who has sent His Messenger with the guidance and the religion of truth
50:5 (5)	they cried lies to the truth when it came to them
50:19 (18)	death's agony comes in truth
50:42 (41)	on the day they hear the Cry in truth
51:19 (19)	and the beggar and the outcast had a share in their wealth
51:23 (23)	it is as surely true as that you have speech
53:28 (29)	surmise avails naught against truth
56:95 (95)	surely this is the truth of certainty
57:16 (15)	who believe should be humbled to the Remembrance of God and the Truth
57:27 (27)	they observed it not as it should be observed
60:1 (1)	offering them love, though they have disbelieved in the truth
61:9 (9)	He who has sent His Messenger with the guidance and the religion of truth
64:3 (3)	He created the heavens and the earth with the truth
69:51 (51)	yet indeed it is the truth of certainty
70:24 (24)	those in whose wealth is a right known
78:39 (39)	that is the true day
103:3 (3)	and do righteous deeds, and counsel each other unto the truth

ḤĀQQAH n.f.~The Indubitable [Ar], Reality [Pk], Sure Reality [Ali], The Inevitable

69:1 (1)	the Indubitable
69:2 (2)	what is the Indubitable?
69:3 (3)	what will teach thee what is the Indubitable?

AḤAQQA vb. (IV)~to verify

b) impf. act. (*yuḥiqqu*)

8:7 (7)	but God was desiring to verify the truth
8:8 (8)	that He might verify the truth
10:82 (82)	God verifies the truth by His words
42:24 (23)	God blots out falsehood and verifies the truth

ISTAḤAQQA vb. (X)~to merit, be near concerned

a) perf. act.

5:107 (106)	if it be discovered that both of them have merited the accusation
5:107 (106)	these being the nearest of those most concerned

*Ḥ R B

ḤARABA vb. (I)~(n.vb.) war

f) n.vb. (*ḥarb*)

2:279 (279)	God shall war with you, and His Messenger
5:64 (69)	as often as they light a fire for war
8:57 (59)	if thou comest upon them anywhere in the war
47:4 (5)	till the war lays down its loads

MIḤRĀB n.m.~sanctuary [Ar], chamber [Pk, Ali]

3:37 (32)	whenever Zachariah went in to her in the Sanctuary
3:39 (33)	angels called to him, standing in the Sanctuary
19:11 (12)	he came forth unto his people from the Sanctuary
34:13 (12)	places of worship, statues, porringers
38:21 (20)	when they scaled the Sanctuary

ḤĀRABA vb. (III)~to fight

a) perf. act.

9:107 (108)	a place of ambush for those who fought God

b) impf. act. (*yuḥāribu*)

5:33 (37)	this is the recompense of those who fight against God

*Ḥ R D

ḤARADA vb. (I)~(n.vb.) purpose

f) n.vb. (*ḥard*)

68:25 (25)	they went forth early, determined upon their purpose

*Ḥ R Ḍ

ḤARAḌ n.m. (adj)~perishing, of ruined health

12:85 (85)	till thou art consumed, or among the perishing

ḤARRAḌA vb. (II)~to urge

c) impv. (*ḥarriḍ*)

4:84 (86)	urge on the believers
8:65 (66)	O Prophet, urge on the believers to fight

*Ḥ R F

ḤARF n.m.~edge, margin

22:11 (11)	such a one as serves God upon the very edge

ḤARRAFA vb. (II)~to pervert, tamper with

b) impf. act. (*yuḥarrifu*)

2:75 (70)	that heard God's word, and then tampered with it
4:46 (48)	some of the Jews pervert words from their meanings
5:13 (16)	perverting words from their meanings
5:41 (45)	perverting words from their meanings

TAḤARRAFA vb. (V)~(pcple. act.) one who withdraws or turns aside; withdrawing

g) pcple. act. (*mutaḥarrif*)

8:16 (16)	unless withdrawing to fight again

*Ḥ R J

ḤARIJA vb. (I)~(n.vb.) impediment, difficulty, fault; (adj) narrow, tight

f) n.vb. (*ḥaraj*)

4:65 (68)	they shall find in themselves no impediment
5:6 (9)	God does not desire to make any impediment for you
6:125 (125)	He makes his breast narrow, tight
7:2 (1)	let there be no impediment in thy breast
9:91 (92)	there is no fault in the weak and the sick
22:78 (77)	and has laid on you no impediment in your religion
24:61 (60)	there is no fault in the blind
24:61 (60)	and there is no fault in the lame
24:61 (60)	and there is no fault in the sick
33:37 (37)	there should not be any fault in the believers
33:38 (38)	there is no fault in the Prophet
33:50 (50)	that there may be no fault in thee
48:17 (17)	there is no fault in the blind
48:17 (17)	and there is no fault in the lame
48:17 (17)	and there is no fault in the sick

*Ḥ R K

ḤARRAKA vb. (II)~to move

b) impf. act. (*yuḥarriku*)

75:16 (16)	move not thy tongue with it to hasten it

*Ḥ R M

ḤARAMA vb. (I)~(pcple. pass.) one who is robbed, deprived; an outcast

h) pcple. pass. (*maḥrūm*)

51:19 (19)	the beggar and the outcast had a share in their wealth
56:67 (66)	nay, we have been robbed
68:27 (27)	nay, rather we have been robbed
70:25 (25)	for the beggar and the outcast

ḤARAM n.m.~holy place, sanctuary, asylum

28:57 (57)	have We not established for them a sanctuary
29:67 (67)	We have appointed a sanctuary secure

ḤARĀM n.m. (see *ḥurum*, below)~holy [Ar]; sacred, forbidden, prohibited [Pk, Ali]

2:144 (139)	turn thy face towards the Holy Mosque
2:149 (144)	turn thy face towards the Holy Mosque
2:150 (145)	turn thy face towards the Holy Mosque
2:191 (187)	fight them not by the Holy Mosque
2:194 (190)	the holy month for the [holy] Month
2:194 (190)	the [holy] Month for the holy month
2:196 (192)	him whose family are not present at the Holy Mosque
2:198 (194)	then remember God at the Holy Waymark
2:217 (214)	they will question thee concerning the holy month
2:217 (214)	disbelief in Him, and the Holy Mosque
5:2 (2)	profane not God's waymarks nor the holy month
5:2 (2)	nor those repairing to the Holy House
5:2 (3)	a people who barred you from the Holy Mosque
5:97 (98)	God has appointed the Kaaba, the Holy House
5:97 (98)	and the holy month
8:34 (34)	when they are barring from the Holy Mosque
9:7 (7)	those with whom you made covenant at the Holy Mosque
9:19 (19)	water to pilgrims and the inhabiting of the Holy Mosque
9:28 (28)	let them not come near the Holy Mosque
10:59 (60)	you have made some of it unlawful, and some lawful
16:116 (117)	this is lawful, and this is forbidden
17:1 (1)	who carried His servant by night from the Holy Mosque
21:95 (95)	there is a ban upon any city that We have destroyed
22:25 (25)	and bar from God's way and the Holy Mosque
48:25 (25)	the ones who disbelieved, and barred you from the Holy Mosque
48:27 (27)	you shall enter the Holy Mosque

ḤURUM n.m. (pl. of *ḥarām*)~sanctified (tech. term pertaining to the Pilgrimage); being in pilgrim sanctity [Ar]; on pilgrimage [Pk]; in the Sacred Precinct or in Pilgrim garb [Ali]

5:1 (1)	when you are in pilgrim sanctity
5:95 (96)	while you are in pilgrim sanctity
5:96 (97)	so long as you remain in pilgrim sanctity
9:5 (5)	when the sacred months are drawn away
9:36 (36)	four of them are sacred

ḤURUMĀT n.f. (pl. of *ḥurmah*)~holy or sacred things [Ar]; prohibited or forbidden things [Pk, Ali]

2:194 (190)	holy things demand retaliation
22:30 (31)	whosoever venerates the sacred things of God

ḤARRAMA vb. (II)~to forbid, to prohibit; to hallow, to make sacred. (pcple. pass.) forbidden; holy

a) perf. act.

2:173 (168)	these things only has He forbidden you
2:275 (276)	God has permitted trafficking, and forbidden usury
3:93 (87)	save what Israel forbade for himself
4:160 (158)	We have forbidden them certain good things
5:72 (76)	God shall prohibit him
6:119 (119)	He has distinguished for you that He has forbidden you
6:140 (141)	and have forbidden what God has provided them
6:143 (144)	is it the two males He has forbidden
6:144 (145)	is it the two males He has forbidden
6:146 (147)	We have forbidden every beast with claws
6:146 (147)	We have forbidden them the fat of them
6:148 (149)	nor would we have forbidden aught

6:150 (151)	those who testify God has forbidden this
6:151 (152)	I will recite what your Lord has forbidden you
6:151 (152)	slay not the soul God has forbidden
7:32 (30)	who has forbidden the ornament of God
7:33 (31)	my Lord has only forbidden indecencies
7:50 (48)	God has forbidden them to the unbelievers
9:29 (29)	what God and His Messenger have forbidden
9:37 (37)	to agree with the number that God has hallowed
9:37 (37)	and so profane what God has hallowed
16:35 (37)	nor would we have forbidden, apart from Him, anything
16:115 (116)	these things only He has forbidden you
16:118 (119)	We have forbidden them what We related to thee before
17:33 (35)	slay not the soul God has forbidden
25:68 (68)	nor slay the soul God has forbidden
27:91 (93)	this territory which He has made sacred
28:12 (11)	We had forbidden to him aforetime to be suckled

b) impf. act. (*yuḥarrimu*)

5:87 (89)	forbid not such good things as God has permitted you
7:157 (156)	bidding them to honour, and forbidding them dishonour
9:29 (29)	do not forbid what God and His Messenger have forbidden
9:37 (37)	one year they make it profane, and hallow it another
66:1 (1)	why forbiddest thou what God has made lawful

d) perf. pass. (*ḥurrima*)

3:50 (44)	and to make lawful to you certain things
4:23 (27)	forbidden to you are your mothers and daughters
5:3 (4)	forbidden to you are carrion, blood
5:96 (97)	forbidden to you is the game of the land
6:138 (139)	cattle whose backs have been forbidden
24:3 (3)	that is forbidden to the believers

h) pcple. pass. (*muḥarram*)

2:85 (79)	yet their expulsion was forbidden you
5:26 (29)	then it shall be forbidden them for forty years
6:139 (140)	reserved for our males and forbidden to our spouses
6:145 (146)	aught forbidden to him who eats thereof
14:37 (40)	a valley where is no sown land by Thy Holy House

*Ḥ R Q

ḤARĪQ n.m.~burning

3:181 (177)	taste the chastisement of the burning
8:50 (52)	taste the chastisement of the burning
22:9 (9)	We shall let him taste the chastisement of the burning
22:22 (22)	taste the chastisement of the burning
85:10 (10)	there awaits them the chastisement of the burning

ḤARRAQA vb. (II)~to burn (tr)

b) impf. act. (*yuḥarriqu*)

20:97 (97)	We will surely burn it and scatter its ashes

c) impv. (*ḥarriq*)

21:68 (68) burn him, and help your gods
29:24 (23) slay him, or burn him

IḤTARAQA vb. (VIII)~to burn, to be consumed by fire

a) perf. act.

2:266 (268) a whirlwind with fire smites it, and it is consumed

*Ḥ R R

ḤARR n.m.~heat; fire

9:81 (82) go not forth in the heat
9:81 (82) Gehenna's fire is hotter, did they but understand
16:81 (83) He has appointed for you shirts to protect you from the heat

ḤARŪR n.f.~torrid heat

35:21 (20) the shade and the torrid heat

ḤARĪR n.m.~silk

22:23 (23) their apparel there shall be of silk
35:33 (30) their apparel there shall be of silk
76:12 (12) and recompensed them for their patience with a Garden, and silk

ḤURR n.m.~a freeman

2:178 (173) freeman for (freeman), slave for slave
2:178 (173) (freeman) for freeman, slave for slave

ḤARRARA vb. (II)~(n.vb.) the act of setting free. (pcple. pass.) set free; dedicated; (adv) in dedication

f) n.vb. (*taḥrīr*)

4:92 (94) let him set free a believing slave
4:92 (94) let the slayer set free a believing slave
4:92 (94) the slayer shall set free a believing slave
5:89 (91) or to set free a slave
58:3 (4) they shall set free a slave

h) pcple. pass. (*muḥarrar*)

3:35 (31) I have vowed to Thee, in dedication, what is within my womb

*Ḥ R S

ḤARAS n.m. (coll)~guards

72:8 (8) but we found it filled with terrible guards

*Ḥ R Ṣ

ḤARAṢA vb. (I)~to be eager, to be anxious; to wish or desire (to do something) ardently

a) perf. act.

4:129 (128)	you will not be able to be equitable between your wives, be you ever so eager
12:103 (103)	be thou ever so eager, the most part of men believe not

b) impf. act. (*yaḥriṣu*)

16:37 (39)	though thou art ever so eager to guide them

ḤARĪṢ n.m. (adj.; comp. *aḥraṣ*)~eager, anxious

2:96 (90)	thou shalt find them the eagerest of men for life
9:128 (129)	anxious is he over you

*Ḥ R TH

ḤARATHA vb. (I)~to till (the soil). (n.vb.) tillage, tilth

b) impf. act. (*yaḥruthu*)

56:63 (63)	have you considered the soil you till?

f) n.vb. (*ḥarth*)

2:71 (66)	a cow not broken to plough the earth or to water the tillage
2:205 (201)	to do corruption there and to destroy the tillage
2:223 (223)	your women are a tillage for you
2:223 (223)	so come unto your tillage as you wish
3:14 (12)	horses of mark, cattle and tillage
3:117 (113)	a freezing blast that smites the tillage
6:136 (137)	they appoint to God, of the tillage and cattle that He multiplied, a portion
6:138 (139)	these are cattle and tillage sacrosanct
21:78 (78)	David and Solomon — when they gave judgment concerning the tillage
42:20 (19)	whoso desires the tillage of the world to come
42:20 (19)	We shall give him increase in his tillage
42:20 (19)	whoso desires the tillage of this world
68:22 (22)	come forth betimes upon your tillage, if you would pluck

*Ḥ R Y

TAḤARRÁ vb. (V)~to seek

a) perf. act.

72:14 (14)	those who have surrendered sought rectitude

*Ḥ S B

ḤASIBA vb. (I)~to suppose, to think, to reckon, to count, to deem. (n.vb.) reckoning, thinking; sufficiency (*ḥasbu* "A" "B", means "B" is sufficient or enough for "A"; for example, *ḥasbunā Allāh*, "God is enough or sufficient for us"). (pcple. act.) a reckoner

a) perf. act.

2:214 (210)	or did you suppose you should enter Paradise
3:142 (136)	or did you suppose you should enter Paradise
5:71 (75)	they supposed there should be no trial
9:16 (16)	or did you suppose you would be left in peace
18:9 (8)	dost thou think the Men of the Cave and Er-Rakeem were among Our signs
18:102 (102)	do the unbelievers reckon that they may take My servants as friends
23:115 (117)	did you think that We created you only for sport
27:44 (44)	when she saw it, she supposed it was a spreading water
29:2 (1)	do the people reckon that they will be left to say
29:4 (3)	do they reckon, those who do evil deeds, that they will outstrip Us
45:21 (20)	do those who commit evil deeds think that We shall make them as those
47:29 (31)	did those in whose hearts is sickness think that God would not bring to light
76:19 (19)	when thou seest them, thou supposest them scattered pearls

b) impf. act. (*yaḥsabu*)

2:273 (274)	the ignorant man supposes them rich because of their abstinence
3:78 (72)	you may suppose it part of the Book, yet it is not part of the Book
3:169 (163)	count not those who were slain in God's way as dead
3:178 (172)	let not the unbelievers suppose that the indulgence We grant them is better
3:180 (175)	let them not suppose it is better for them
3:188 (185)	reckon not that those who rejoice in what they have brought
3:188 (185)	do not reckon them secure from chastisement
7:30 (28)	they have taken Satans for friends instead of God, and think them guided
8:59 (61)	thou art not to suppose that they who disbelieve have outstripped Me
14:42 (43)	deem not that God is heedless of what the evildoers work
14:47 (48)	do not deem that God will fail in His promise to His Messengers
18:18 (17)	thou wouldst have thought them awake, as they lay sleeping
18:104 (104)	while they think that they are working good deeds
23:55 (57)	do they think that We succour them with of wealth and children
24:11 (11)	do not reckon it evil for you; rather it is good
24:15 (14)	that whereof you had no knowledge, and reckoned it a light thing
24:39 (39)	a mirage in a spacious plain which the man athirst supposes to be water
24:57 (56)	think not the unbelievers able to frustrate God in the earth
25:44 (46)	or deemest thou that most of them hear or understand
27:88 (90)	thou shalt see the mountains, that thou supposest fixed, passing by like clouds
33:20 (20)	they think the Confederates have not departed
43:37 (36)	they bar them from the way, and they think they are guided
43:80 (80)	do they think We hear not their secret and what they conspire
58:18 (19)	they will swear to Him, as they swear to you, and think they are on something
59:14 (14)	you think of them as a host
63:4 (4)	they think every cry is against them
75:3 (3)	does man reckon We shall not gather his bones
75:36 (36)	does man reckon he shall be left to roam at will
90:5 (5)	does he think none has power over him
90:7 (7)	does he think none has seen him
104:3 (3)	thinking his riches have made him immortal

f) n.vb. (*ḥasb*)

2:206 (202)	so Gehenna shall be enough for him
3:173 (167)	God is sufficient for us; an excellent Guardian
5:104 (103)	enough for us is what we found our fathers doing
8:62 (64)	God is sufficient for thee; He has confirmed thee
8:64 (65)	O Prophet, God suffices thee, and the believers
9:59 (59)	enough for us is God
9:68 (69)	that is enough for them
9:129 (130)	God is enough for me
39:38 (39)	God is enough for me
58:8 (9)	sufficient for them shall be Gehenna
65:3 (3)	whosoever puts his trust in God, He shall suffice him

g) pcple. act. (*ḥāsib*)

6:62 (62)	He is the swiftest of reckoners
21:47 (48)	sufficient are We for reckoners

ḤASĪB n.m. (adj)~one who reckons or keeps count; Reckoner (Divine attribute)

4:6 (7)	God suffices for a reckoner
4:86 (88)	God keeps a watchful count over everything
17:14 (15)	a reckoner against thee
33:39 (39)	God suffices as a reckoner

ḤISĀB n.m. (see also *ḥusbān*)~reckoning; account

2:202 (198)	God is swift at the reckoning
2:212 (208)	God provides whomsoever He will without reckoning
3:19 (17)	God is swift at the reckoning
3:27 (26)	Thou providest whomsoever Thou wilt without reckoning
3:37 (32)	God provisions whomsoever He will without reckoning
3:199 (199)	God is swift at the reckoning
5:4 (6)	God is swift at the reckoning
6:52 (52)	nothing of their account falls upon thee
6:52 (52)	and nothing of thy account falls upon them
6:69 (68)	nothing of their account falls upon those that are godfearing
10:5 (5)	that you might know the number of the years and the reckoning
13:18 (18)	theirs shall be the evil reckoning
13:21 (21)	and fear their Lord, and dread the evil reckoning
13:40 (40)	and Ours the reckoning
13:41 (41)	He is swift at the reckoning
14:41 (42)	upon the day when the reckoning shall come to pass
14:51 (51)	surely God is swift at the reckoning
17:12 (13)	that you may know the number of the years, and the reckoning
21:1 (1)	nigh unto men has drawn their reckoning
23:117 (117)	his reckoning is with his Lord
24:38 (38)	God provides whomsoever He will, without reckoning
24:39 (39)	He pays him his account in full
24:39 (39)	and God is swift at the reckoning
26:113 (113)	their account falls only upon my Lord
38:16 (15)	hasten to us our share before the Day of Reckoning
38:26 (25)	they have forgotten the Day of Reckoning
38:39 (38)	bestow or withhold without reckoning
38:53 (53)	what you were promised for the Day of Reckoning
39:10 (13)	their wages in full without reckoning
40:17 (17)	surely God is swift at the reckoning

40:27 (28)	and believes not in the Day of Reckoning
40:40 (43)	therein provided without reckoning
65:8 (8)	We made with it a terrible reckoning and chastised it
69:20 (20)	I thought that I should encounter my reckoning
69:26 (26)	and not known my reckoning
78:27 (27)	they indeed hoped not for a reckoning
78:36 (36)	a recompense from thy Lord, a gift, a reckoning
84:8 (8)	he shall surely receive an easy reckoning
88:26 (26)	then upon Us shall rest their reckoning

ḤUSBĀN n.m.~a reckoning; (coll) a thunderbolt

6:96 (96)	and the sun and moon for a reckoning
18:40 (38)	and loose on it a thunderbolt out of heaven
55:5 (4)	the sun and the moon to a reckoning

ḤĀSABA vb. (III)~to reckon, to make a reckoning

a) perf. act.

65:8 (8)	then We made with it a terrible reckoning

b) impf. act. (*yuḥāsibu*)

2:284 (284)	God shall make reckoning with you for it

e) impf. pass. (*yuḥāsabu*)

84:8 (8)	he shall surely receive an easy reckoning

IḤTASABA vb. (VIII)~to reckon, expect

b) impf. act. (*yaḥtasibu*)

39:47 (48)	there would appear to them from God that they never reckoned with
59:2 (2)	God came upon them from whence they had not reckoned
65:3 (2)	He will provide for him from whence he never reckoned

*Ḥ S D

ḤASADA vb. (I)~to be jealous of

b) impf. act. (*yaḥsudu*)

113:5 (5)	from the evil of an envier when he envies
4:54 (57)	are they jealous of the people for the bounty
48:15 (15)	nay, but you are jealous of us

f) n.vb. (*ḥasad*) jealousy

2:109 (103)	the jealousy of their souls

g) pcple. act. (*ḥāsid*) one who envies, envier

113:5 (5)	from the evil of an envier when he envies

*Ḥ S M

ḤUSŪM n.m. (adj)~uninterrupted [Ar]; long [Pk]; in succession [Ali]

69:7 (7)	He compelled against them seven nights and eight days, uninterruptedly

*Ḥ S N

ḤASUNA vb. (I)~to be good, beautiful or fair (this verb is used in a manner similar to the other "verbs of blame and praise" such as *niʿma* and *biʾsa*). (n.vb.) goodness, fairness, beauty, excellence

a) perf. act.

4:69 (71)	good companions they
18:31 (30)	O, how fair a resting-place
25:76 (76)	fair it is as a lodging-place and an abode

f) n.vb. (*ḥusn*)

2:83 (77)	and speak good to men, and perform the prayer
3:14 (12)	with Him is the fairest resort
3:148 (141)	the fairest reward of the world to come
3:195 (195)	with Him is the fairest reward
13:29 (28)	theirs is blessedness and a fair resort
18:86 (85)	or thou shalt take towards them a way of kindness
27:11 (11)	then, after evil, has changed into good
29:8 (7)	that he be kind to his parents
33:52 (52)	though their beauty please thee
38:25 (24)	a near place in Our presence and a fair resort
38:40 (39)	a near place in Our presence and a fair resort
38:49 (49)	for the godfearing is a fair resort
42:23 (22)	whosoever gains a good deed, We shall give him increase of good in respect of it

ḤASAN n.m. (comp. adj.) ***aḥsan*****; (f)** ***ḥasanah*****, (comp. adj.)** ***ḥusná*** **(s),** ***ḥisān*** **(pl)**~good, fair, beautiful, kind

2:138 (132)	who is there that baptizes fairer than God?
2:245 (246)	who is he that will lend God a good loan
3:37 (32)	her Lord received the child with gracious favour
3:37 (32)	by His goodness she grew up comely
4:59 (62)	that is better, and fairer in the issue
4:86 (88)	greet with a fairer than it, or return it
4:95 (97)	to each God has promised the reward most fair
4:125 (124)	who is there that has a fairer religion
5:12 (15)	lend to God a good loan
5:50 (55)	who is fairer in judgment than God
6:152 (153)	approach not the property of the orphan, save in the fairer manner
7:137 (133)	perfectly was fulfilled the most fair word of thy Lord
7:145 (142)	command thy people to take the fairest of it
7:180 (179)	to God belong the Names Most Beautiful
8:17 (17)	that He might confer on the believers a fair benefit
9:52 (52)	one of the two rewards most fair
9:107 (108)	we desired nothing but good
9:121 (122)	God may recompense them the best of what they were doing

10:26 (27)	to the good-doers the reward most fair
11:3 (3)	He will give you fair enjoyment
11:7 (9)	which one of you is fairer in works
11:88 (90)	He has provided me with fair provision from Him
12:3 (3)	We will relate to thee the fairest of stories
13:18 (18)	for those who answer their Lord, the reward most fair
16:62 (64)	that the reward most fair shall be theirs
16:67 (69)	you take therefrom an intoxicant and a provision fair
16:75 (77)	one whom We have provided of Ourselves with a provision fair
16:96 (98)	according to the best of what they did
16:97 (99)	according to the best of what they did
16:125 (126)	with wisdom and good admonition
16:125 (126)	dispute with them in the better way
17:34 (36)	do not approach the property of the orphan save in the fairest manner
17:35 (37)	that is better and fairer in the issue
17:53 (55)	that they say words that are kindlier
17:110 (110)	to Him belong the Names Most Beautiful
18:2 (2)	theirs shall be a goodly wage
18:7 (6)	We may try which of them is fairest in works
18:88 (87)	he shall receive as recompense the reward most fair
19:73 (74)	which of the two parties is better in station, fairer in assembly?
19:74 (75)	who were fairer in furnishing and outward show
20:8 (7)	to Him belong the Names Most Beautiful
20:86 (89)	did your Lord not promise a fair promise to you?
21:101 (101)	unto whom already the reward most fair has gone
22:58 (57)	God shall provide them with a fair provision
23:14 (14)	blessed be God, the fairest of creators
23:96 (98)	repel thou the evil with that which is fairer
24:38 (38)	that God may recompense them for their fairest works
25:24 (26)	better shall be their lodging, fairer their resting-place
25:33 (35)	We bring thee the truth, and better in exposition
28:61 (61)	he to whom We have promised a fair promise
29:7 (6)	the best of what they were doing
29:46 (45)	dispute not with the People of the Book save in the fairer manner
33:21 (21)	you have had a good example in God's Messenger
35:8 (9)	so that he thinks it is good
37:125 (125)	and abandon the Best of creators
39:18 (19)	who give ear to the Word and follow the fairest of it
39:23 (24)	God has sent down the fairest discourse as a Book
39:35 (36)	the fairest of what they were doing
39:55 (56)	follow the fairest of what has been sent down to you
41:33 (33)	who speaks fairer than he who calls unto God
41:34 (34)	repel with that which is fairer
41:50 (50)	the reward most fair with Him will be mine
46:16 (15)	We shall accept the best of what they have done
48:16 (16)	God will give you a goodly wage
53:31 (32)	those who have done good with the reward most fair
55:70 (70)	therein maidens good and comely
55:76 (76)	reclining upon green cushions and lovely druggets
57:10 (10)	God has promised the reward most fair
57:11 (11)	who is he that will lend to God a good loan
57:18 (17)	and have lent to God a good loan
59:24 (24)	to Him belong the Names Most Beautiful
60:4 (4)	you have had a good example in Abraham
60:6 (6)	you have had a good example in them

64:17 (17)	if you lend to God a good loan
67:2 (2)	that He might try you which of you is fairest in works
73:20 (20)	and lend to God a good loan
92:6 (6)	and confirms the reward most fair
92:9 (9)	and cries lies to the reward most fair
95:4 (4)	We indeed created Man in the fairest stature

ḤASANAH n.f.~that which is good, a good thing

2:201 (197)	give to us in this world good
2:201 (197)	and [give us] good in the world to come
3:120 (116)	if you are visited by good fortune
4:40 (44)	if it be a good deed He will double it
4:78 (80)	if a good thing visits them
4:79 (81)	whatever good visits thee, it is of God
4:85 (87)	whoso intercedes with a good intercession
6:160 (161)	whoso brings a good deed
7:95 (93)	We gave them in the place of evil good
7:131 (128)	when good came to them, they said
7:156 (155)	prescribe for us in this world good
7:168 (167)	We tried them with good things and evil
9:50 (50)	if good fortune befalls thee, it vexes them
11:114 (116)	the good deeds will drive away the evil deeds
13:6 (7)	they would have thee hasten the evil ere the good
13:22 (22)	who avert evil with good
16:30 (32)	for those who do (good) in this world good
16:41 (43)	We shall surely lodge them in this world in a goodly lodging
16:122 (123)	We gave him in this world good
25:70 (70)	God will change their evil deeds into good deeds
27:46 (47)	why do you seek to hasten evil before good?
27:89 (91)	whosoever comes with a good deed
28:54 (54)	and avert evil with good
28:84 (84)	whoso brings a good deed shall have better
39:10 (13)	for those who do good in this world good
41:34 (34)	not equal are the good deed and the evil deed
42:23 (22)	whosoever gains a good deed, We shall give him increase of good

AḤSANA vb. (IV)~to do good or right, act with kindness, do something uprightly; to give something goodly; (*alladhīna aḥsanū*) the good-doers. (n.vb.) goodness, kindliness. (pcple. act.) good-doer, righteous man

a) perf. act.

3:172 (166)	to all those of them who did good and feared God
5:93 (94)	there is no fault in those who believe and do deeds of righteousness
6:154 (155)	the Book, complete for him who does good
10:26 (27)	to the good-doers the reward most fair
12:23 (23)	my lord has given me a goodly lodging
12:100 (101)	He was good to me when He brought me forth
16:30 (32)	For those who do good in this world good
17:7 (7)	if you do good it is your own souls you do (good) to
17:7 (7)	if you do (good) it is your own souls you do good to
18:30 (29)	the wage of him who does good works
28:77 (77)	do good, as God has been good to thee
32:7 (6)	who has created all things well
39:10 (13)	for those who do good in this world good

40:64 (66)	He shaped you, and shaped you well
53:31 (32)	those who have done good with the reward most fair
64:3 (3)	He shaped you, and shaped you well
65:11 (11)	God has made for him a goodly provision

b) impf. act. (*yuḥsinu*)

4:128 (127)	if you do good and are godfearing
18:104 (104)	while they think that they are working good deeds

c) impv. (*aḥsin*)

2:195 (191)	be good-doers; God loves the good-doers
28:77 (77)	do good, as God has been good to thee

f) n.vb. (*iḥsān*)

2:83 (77)	and to be good to parents, and the near kinsman
2:178 (173)	let the payment be with kindliness
2:229 (229)	then honourable retention or setting free kindly
4:36 (40)	be kind to parents, and the near kinsman
4:62 (65)	we sought only kindness and conciliation
6:151 (152)	and to be good to your parents
9:100 (101)	those who followed them in doing-good
16:90 (92)	God bids to justice and good-doing and giving to kinsmen
17:23 (24)	Thy Lord has decreed you shall not serve any but Him, and to be good to parents
46:15 (14)	We have charged man, that he be kind to his parents
55:60 (60)	shall the recompense of goodness be other than (goodness)?
55:60 (60)	shall the recompense of (goodness) be other than goodness?

g) pcple. act. (*muḥsin*)

2:58 (55)	We will forgive you your transgressions, and increase the good-doers
2:112 (106)	whosoever submits his will to God, being a good-doer
2:195 (191)	but be good-doers; God loves the good-doers
2:236 (237)	an obligation on the good-doers
3:134 (128)	God loves the good-doers
3:148 (141)	God loves the good-doers
4:125 (124)	he who submits his will to God being a good-doer
5:13 (16)	surely God loves the good-doers
5:85 (88)	that is the recompense of the good-doers
5:93 (94)	God loves the good-doers
6:84 (84)	even so We recompense the good-doers
7:56 (54)	the mercy of God is nigh to the good-doers
7:161 (161)	We will forgive you your transgressions, and increase the good-doers
9:91 (92)	there is no way against the good-doers
9:120 (121)	God leaves not to waste the wage of the good-doers
11:115 (117)	God will not leave to waste the wage of the good-doers
12:22 (22)	even so We recompense the good-doers
12:36 (36)	we see that thou art of the good-doers
12:56 (56)	We leave not to waste the wage of the good-doers
12:78 (78)	we see that thou art one of the good-doers
12:90 (90)	God leaves not to waste the wage of the good-doers
16:128 (128)	those who are godfearing, and those who are good-doers
22:37 (38)	give thou good tidings unto the good-doers
28:14 (13)	even so do We recompense the good-doers
29:69 (69)	God is with the good-doers

31:3 (2)	a guidance and a mercy to the good-doers
31:22 (21)	whosoever submits his will to God, being a good-doer
33:29 (29)	for those amongst you such as do good
37:80 (78)	even so We recompense the good-doers
37:105 (105)	even so We recompense the good-doers
37:110 (110)	even so We recompense the good-doers
37:113 (113)	of their seed some are good-doers
37:121 (121)	even so We recompense the good-doers
37:131 (131)	even so We recompense the good-doers
39:34 (35)	that is the recompense of the good-doers
39:58 (59)	that I might return again, and be among the good-doers
46:12 (11)	good tidings to the good-doers
51:16 (16)	they were good-doers before that
77:44 (44)	even so do We recompense the good-doers

*Ḥ S R

ḤASARA vb. (I)~(pcple. pass.) denuded

h) pcple. pass. (*maḥsūr*)

17:29 (31)	or thou wilt sit reproached and denuded

ḤASĪR n.m. (adj)~weary, fatigued

67:4 (4)	thy gaze comes back to thee dazzled, aweary

ḤASRAH n.f.~sighing, anguish, regret, sorrow; (*yā ḥasrah*) Alas for, O bitter

2:167 (162)	O bitter regrets for them
3:156 (150)	God may make that an anguish in their hearts
6:31 (31)	Alas for us, that we neglected it
8:36 (36)	till it is an anguish for them
19:39 (40)	warn thou them of the day of anguish
35:8 (9)	let not thy soul be wasted in regrets for them
36:30 (29)	Ah, woe for those servants
39:56 (57)	Alas for me, in that I neglected my duty to God
69:50 (50)	surely it is a sorrow to the unbelievers

ISTAḤSARA vb. (X)~to grow weary

b) impf. act. (*yastaḥsiru*)

21:19 (19)	wax not too proud to do Him service neither grow weary

*Ḥ S S

ḤASSA vb. (I)~to blast, destroy

b) impf. act. (*yaḥussu*)

3:152 (145)	when you blasted them by His leave

ḤASĪS n.m.~whisper, hissing sound

21:102 (102)	neither shall they hear any whisper of it

AḤASSA vb. (IV)~to perceive [Ar], be conscious of [Pk], feel, find [Ali]

a) perf. act.

3:52 (45)	when Jesus perceived their unbelief, he said
21:12 (12)	then, when they perceived Our might

b) impf. act. (*yuḥissu*)

19:98 (98)	dost thou perceive so much as one of them

TAḤASSASA vb. (V)~to search out [Ar], ascertain [Pk], enquire [Ali]

c) impv. (*taḥassas*)

12:87 (87)	depart, my sons, and search out tidings of Joseph

*Ḥ SH R

ḤASHARA vb. (I)~to muster, gather, assemble; raise. (n.vb.) mustering. (pcple. act.) musterer. (pcple. pass.) mustered, gathered, assembled

a) perf. act.

6:111 (111)	had We mustered against them every thing
18:47 (45)	and We muster them so that We leave not so much as one
20:125 (125)	why hast thou raised me blind
79:23 (23)	then he mustered and proclaimed

b) impf. act. (*yaḥshuru*)

4:172 (171)	He will assuredly muster them to Him
6:22 (22)	on the day when We shall muster them all together
6:128 (128)	on the day when He shall muster them all together
10:28 (29)	and the day We shall muster them all
10:45 (46)	and the day He shall muster them
15:25 (25)	it is thy Lord shall muster them
17:97 (99)	We shall muster them on the Resurrection Day
19:68 (69)	We shall surely muster them, and the Satans
19:85 (88)	on the day that We shall muster the godfearing
20:102 (102)	We shall muster the sinners
20:124 (124)	on the Resurrection Day We shall raise him blind
25:17 (18)	upon the day when He shall muster them and that they serve
27:83 (85)	We shall muster out of every nation
34:40 (39)	He shall muster them all together

c) impv. (*uḥshur*)

37:22 (22)	muster those who did evil, their wives

d) perf. pass. (*ḥushira*)

27:17 (17) his hosts were mustered to Solomon
46:6 (5) when mankind are mustered
81:5 (5) when the savage beasts shall be mustered

e) impf. pass. (*yuḥsharu*)

2:203 (199) unto Him you shall be mustered
3:12 (10) you shall be overthrown, and mustered into Gehenna
3:158 (152) it is unto God you shall be mustered
5:96 (97) fear God, unto whom you shall be mustered
6:38 (38) then to their Lord they shall be mustered
6:51 (51) those who fear they shall be mustered to their Lord
6:72 (71) it is unto Him you shall be mustered
8:24 (24) to Him you shall be mustered
8:36 (37) the unbelievers will be mustered into Gehenna
20:59 (61) let the people be mustered at the high noon
23:79 (81) to Him you shall be mustered
25:34 (36) those who shall be mustered to Gehenna
41:19 (18) upon the day when God's enemies are mustered to the Fire
58:9 (10) fear God, unto whom you shall be mustered
67:24 (24) unto Him you shall be mustered

f) n.vb. (*ḥashr*)

50:44 (43) that is a mustering easy for Us
59:2 (2) among the People of the Book at the first mustering

g) pcple. act. (*ḥāshir*)

7:111 (108) and send among the cities musterers
26:36 (35) send among the cities musterers
26:53 (53) then Pharaoh sent among the cities musterers

h) pcple. pass. (*maḥshūr*)

38:19 (18) the birds, duly mustered, every one to him reverting

*Ḥ Ṣ B

ḤAṢAB n.m.~fuel

21:98 (98) you, and that you were serving apart from God, are fuel for Gehenna

ḤĀṢIB n.m.~squall of stones or pebbles [Ar], sand-storm [Pk], tornedo with a shower of stones [Ali]

17:68 (70) cause the shore to swallow you up, or loose against you a squall of pebbles
29:40 (39) against some We loosed a squall of pebbles
54:34 (34) We loosed against them a squall of pebbles
67:17 (17) He who is in heaven will not loose against you a squall of pebbles

*Ḥ Ṣ D

ḤAṢADA vb. (I)~to harvest. (n.vb.) a harvest, reaping

a) perf. act.

12:47 (47) what you have harvested leave in the ear

f) n.vb. (*ḥaṣād*)

6:141 (142) pay the due thereof on the day of its harvest

ḤAṢĪD n.m.~stubble; harvest, reaped corn (wheat)

10:24 (25) by night or day, and We make it stubble
11:100 (102) some of them are standing and some stubble
21:15 (15) they ceased not to cry, until We made them stubble
50:9 (9) gardens and grain of harvest

*Ḥ Ṣ Ḥ Ṣ

ḤAṢḤAṢA vb. (quad I)~to be discovered, become manifest

a) perf. act.

12:51 (51) now the truth is at last discovered

*Ḥ Ṣ L

ḤAṢṢALA vb. (II)~to bring out, make manifest

d) perf. pass. (*ḥuṣṣila*)

100:10 (10) that which is in the breasts is brought out

*Ḥ Ṣ N

ḤUṢŪN n.m. (pl. of *ḥuṣn*)~fortress

59:2 (2) they thought that their fortresses would defend them

ḤAṢṢANA vb. (II)~(pcple. pass.) fortified

h) pcple. pass. (*muḥaṣṣan*)

59:14 (14) except in fortified cities, or from behind walls

AḤṢANA vb. (IV)~to guard, (the phrase *allatī aḥṣanat farjahā* means "she who guarded her virginity" or "she who was chaste," a reference to the Virgin Mary); to be married, to be in wedlock; to fortify; keep in store. (pcple. act.) one (m) who is in wedlock. (pcple. pass.) one (f) who is wedded

a) perf. act.

21:91 (91) and she who guarded her virginity
66:12 (12) Mary, Imran's daughter, who guarded her virginity

b) impf. act. (*yuḥṣinu*)

12:48 (48)	all but a little you keep in store
21:80 (80)	to fortify you against your violence

e) impf. pass. (*uḥṣina*)

4:25 (30)	but when they are in wedlock, if they commit indecency

g) pcple. act. (*muḥṣin*)

4:24 (28)	using your wealth, in wedlock and not in licence
5:5 (7)	give them their wages, in wedlock and not in licence

h) pcple. pass. f. (*muḥṣanah*)

4:24 (28)	and wedded women, save what your right hands own
4:25 (29)	to be able to marry believing freewomen in wedlock
4:25 (29)	give them their wages honourably as women in wedlock
4:25 (30)	when they are in wedlock, if they commit indecency
5:5 (7)	likewise believing women in wedlock
5:5 (7)	and in wedlock women of them who were given the Book
24:4 (4)	those who cast it up on women in wedlock
24:23 (23)	those who cast it up on women in wedlock

TAḤAṢṢANA vb. (V)~(n.vb.) chastity

f) n.vb. (*taḥaṣṣun*)

24:33 (33)	if they desire to live in chastity

*Ḥ Ṣ R

ḤAṢARA vb. (I)~to confine

c) impv. (*uḥṣur*)

9:5 (5)	and take them, and confine them, and lie in wait

ḤAṢIRA vb. (I)~to be constricted

a) perf. act.

4:90 (92)	or come to you with breasts constricted

ḤAṢĪR n.m.~prison

17:8 (8)	We have made Gehenna a prison for the unbelievers

ḤAṢŪR n.m. (adj)~chaste

3:39 (34)	who shall confirm a Word of God, a chief, and chaste

AḤṢARA vb. (IV)~to prevent, restrain

d) perf. pass. (*uḥṣira*)

2:196 (192)	but if you are prevented
2:273 (274)	the poor who are restrained in the way of God

*Ḥ Ṣ Y

AḤṢÁ n.m. (comp. adj.)~better in calculating

18:12 (11)	which of the two parties would better calculate the while

AḤṢÁ vb. (IV)~to number, count

a) perf. act.

18:49 (47)	nothing behind, small or great, but it has numbered it
19:94 (94)	He has indeed counted them, and He has numbered them
36:12 (11)	everything We have numbered in a clear register
58:6 (7)	God has numbered it, and they have forgotten it
72:28 (28)	He has numbered everything in numbers
78:29 (29)	everything We have numbered in a Book

b) impf. act. (*yuḥṣī*)

14:34 (37)	if you count God's blessing, you will never number it
16:18 (18)	if you count God's blessing, you will never number it
73:20 (20)	He knows that you will not number it

c) impv. (*aḥṣi*)

65:1 (1)	count the period, and fear God your Lord

*Ḥ T M

ḤATAMA vb. (I)~(n.vb.) a thing decreed

f) n.vb. (*ḥatm*)

19:71 (72)	that for thy Lord is a thing decreed, determined

*Ḥ TH TH

ḤATHĪTH n.m. (adv)~urgently, quickly

7:54 (52)	covering the day with the night it pursues urgently

*Ḥ Ṭ B

ḤAṬAB n.m.~firewood, fuel

72:15 (15)	they have become firewood for Gehenna
111:4 (4)	and his wife, the carrier of the firewood

*Ḥ Ṭ M

ḤAṬAMA vb. (I)~to crush

b) impf. act. (*yaḥṭimu*)

27:18 (18) lest Solomon and his hosts crush you, being unaware

ḤUṬĀM n.m.~broken orts, chaff, straw

39:21 (22) then He makes them broken orts
56:65 (65) We would make it broken orts, and you would remain bitterly
57:20 (19) then it becomes broken orts

ḤUṬAMAH n.f.~The Crusher [Ar]; The Consuming One [Pk]; That which Breaks to Pieces [Ali]; (a name of Hell)

104:4 (4) he shall be thrust into the Crusher
104:5 (5) what shall teach thee what is the Crusher?

*Ḥ Ṭ Ṭ

ḤIṬṬAH n.f.~unburdening [Ar]; repentance [Pk]; humility [Ali] (according to Tradition the word is said to imply submission to God)

2:58 (55) say, Unburdening; We will forgive you
7:161 (161) say, Unburdening; and enter in at the gate, prostrating

*Ḥ W B

ḤĀBA vb. (I)~(n.vb.) sin, crime

f) n.vb. (*ḥūb*)

4:2 (2) surely that is a great crime

*Ḥ W DH

ISTAḤWADHA vb. (X)~to gain mastery

a) perf. act.

58:19 (20) Satan has gained the mastery over them

b) impf. act. (*yastaḥwidhu*)

4:141 (140) did we not gain the mastery over you

*Ḥ W J

ḤĀJAH n.f.~a need, wish

12:68 (68)	it was a need in Jacob's soul that he so satisfied
40:80 (80)	on them you may attain a need in your breasts
59:9 (9)	not finding in their breasts any need

*Ḥ W L

ḤĀLA vb. (I)~to come or stand between

a) perf. act.

11:43 (45)	the waves came between them

b) impf. act. (*yaḥūlu*)

8:24 (24)	know that God stands between a man and his heart

d) perf. pass. (*ḥīla*)

34:54 (53)	a barrier is set between them

ḤAWL (1) n.m.~a year

2:233 (233)	mothers shall suckle their children two years
2:240 (241)	provision for a year without expulsion

ḤAWL (2) n.m.~neighbourhood, precincts; (adv) about, around

2:17 (16)	when it lit all about him God took away their light
3:159 (153)	they would have scattered from about thee
6:92 (92)	to warn the Mother of Cities and those about her
9:101 (102)	some of the Bedouins who dwell around you are hypocrites
9:120 (121)	and for the Bedouins who dwell around them
17:1 (1)	to the Further Mosque the precincts of which We have blessed
19:68 (69)	We shall parade them about Gehenna
26:25 (24)	said he to those about him
26:34 (33)	said he to the Council about him
27:8 (8)	blessed is He who is in the fire, and He who is about it
29:67 (67)	while all about them the people are snatched away
39:75 (75)	thou shalt see the angels encircling about the Throne
40:7 (7)	those who bear the Throne, and those round about it
42:7 (5)	the Mother of Cities and those who dwell about it
46:27 (26)	We destroyed the cities about you

ḤĪLAH n.f.~device, means, plan, strategem

4:98 (100)	who, being abased, can devise nothing

ḤIWAL n.m.~change, removal

18:108 (108)	desiring no removal out of them

ḤAWWALA vb. (II)~(n.vb.) change, altering, removal, variableness

f) n.vb. (*taḥwīl*)

17:56 (58)	they have no power to remove affliction from you, or to transfer it
17:77 (79)	thou wilt find no change to Our wont
35:43 (42)	thou shalt never find any altering the wont of God

*Ḥ W R

ḤĀRA vb. (I)~to revert

b) impf. act. (*yaḥūru*)

84:14 (14)	he surely thought he would never revert

ḤAWĀRĪY n.m. (pl. *ḥawārīyūn*)~Disciple or Apostle (of Christ)

3:52 (45)	the Apostles said, 'We will be helpers of God'
5:111 (111)	when I inspired the Apostles
5:112 (112)	when the Apostles said, 'O Jesus son of Mary'
61:14 (14)	as Jesus, Mary's son, said to the Apostles
61:14 (14)	the Apostles said, 'We will be helpers of God.'

ḤŪR n.f. (pl. of *ḥawrā'*)~houris (maids of Paradise who possess eyes with blackness similar to those of gazelles)

44:54 (54)	We shall espouse them to wide-eyed houris
52:20 (20)	We shall espouse them to wide-eyed houris
55:72 (72)	houris, cloistered in cool pavilions
56:22 (22)	and wide-eyed houris

ḤĀWARA vb. (III)~to converse with

b) impf. act. (*yuḥāwiru*)

18:34 (32)	he said to his fellow, as he was conversing with him
18:37 (35)	said his fellow, as he was conversing with him
58:1 (1)	God hears the two of you conversing together

*Ḥ W SH

ḤĀSHA vb. (I)~(*ḥāsha li-Allāh*) far be it from God, God forbid; God save us [Ar], Allah Blameless [Pk]; God preserve us [Ali]

a) perf. act.

12:31 (31)	they cut their hands, saying, 'God save us!'
12:51 (51)	God save us

*Ḥ W T

ḤŪT n.m. (pl. *ḥītān*)~a fish

7:163 (163)	the Sabbath, when their fish came to them
18:61 (60)	when they reached their meeting, they forgot their fish

18:63 (62)	when we took refuge in the rock, then I forgot the fish
37:142 (142)	then the whale swallowed him down
68:48 (48)	be not as the Man of the Fish

*Ḥ W Ṭ

AḤĀṬA vb. (IV)~(with prep. *bi-*) to encompass, comprehend. (pcple. act.) one who encompasses or comprehends; encompassing, comprehending

a) perf. act.

2:81 (75)	whoso earns evil, and is encompassed by his transgression
17:60 (62)	surely thy Lord encompasses men
18:29 (28)	whose pavilion encompasses them
18:91 (90)	We encompassed in knowledge what was with him
27:22 (22)	I have comprehended that which thou hast not (comprehended)
48:21 (21)	God had encompassed them already
65:12 (12)	God encompasses everything in knowledge
72:28 (28)	He encompasses all that is with them

b) impf. act. (*yuḥīṭu*)

2:255 (256)	they comprehend not anything of His knowledge
10:39 (40)	to that whereof they comprehended not the knowledge
18:68 (67)	thou hast never encompassed in thy knowledge
20:110 (109)	they comprehend Him not in knowledge
27:22 (22)	I have (comprehended) that which thou hast not comprehended
27:84 (86)	My signs, not comprehending them in knowledge

d) perf. pass. (*uḥīṭa*)

10:22 (23)	and they think they are encompassed
18:42 (40)	his fruit was all encompassed

e) impf. pass. (*yuḥāṭu*)

12:66 (66)	unless it be that you are encompassed

g) pcple. act. (*muḥīṭ*)

2:19 (18)	God encompasses the unbelievers
3:120 (116)	God encompasses the things they do
4:108 (108)	God encompasses the things they do
4:126 (125)	God encompasses everything
8:47 (49)	God encompasses the things they do
9:49 (49)	surely Gehenna encompasses the unbelievers
11:84 (85)	I fear for you the chastisement of an encompassing day
11:92 (94)	My Lord encompasses the things you do
29:54 (54)	Gehenna encompasses the unbelievers
41:54 (54)	does He not encompass everything?
85:20 (20)	God is behind them, encompassing

*Ḥ W Y

AḤWÁ n.m. (comp. adj.)~dark-coloured, blackening

87:5 (5) then made it a blackening wrack

ḤAWĀYĀ n.f. (pl. of *ḥawīyah*)~intestines, entrails

6:146 (147) save what their backs carry, or their entrails

*Ḥ W Z

TAḤAYYAZA vb. (V)~(pcple. act.) moving (from one position) and intending to join another; going aside

g) pcple. act. (*mutaḥayyiz*)

8:16 (16) unless withdrawing to fight again or removing to join another host

*Ḥ Y D

ḤĀDA vb. (I)~to shun, avert

b) impf. act. (*yaḥīdu*)

50:19 (18) that is what thou wast shunning

*Ḥ Y Ḍ

ḤĀḌA vb. (I)~to menstruate

b) impf. act. (*yaḥīḍu*)

65:4 (4) those who have not menstruated as yet

MAḤĪḌ n.m.~menstruating, monthly course (of women)

2:222 (222) they will question thee concerning the monthly course
2:222 (222) go apart from women during the monthly course
65:4 (4) as for your women who have despaired of further menstruating

*Ḥ Y F

ḤĀFA vb. (I)~to be unjust

b) impf. act. (*yaḥīfu*)

24:50 (49) do they fear that God may be unjust towards them

*Ḥ Y N

ḤĪN n.m.~a time, a while; a season; (adv) when, at, at the time of (examples not listed); (*ḥīnaʾidhin*) at that hour (56:84)

2:36 (34)	a sojourn shall be yours, and enjoyment for a time
7:24 (23)	a sojourn shall be yours, and enjoyment for a time
10:98 (98)	We gave unto them enjoyment for a time
12:35 (35)	that they should imprison him for a while
14:25 (30)	it gives its produce every season
16:80 (82)	furnishing and an enjoyment for a while
21:111 (111)	a trial for you and an enjoyment for a time
23:25 (25)	so wait on him for a time
23:54 (56)	leave thou them in their perplexity for a time
36:44 (44)	a mercy from Us, and enjoyment for a while
37:148 (148)	so We gave them enjoyment for a while
37:174 (174)	so turn thou from them for a while
37:178 (178)	so turn thou from them for a while
38:3 (2)	and they called, but time was none to escape
38:88 (88)	you shall surely know its tiding after a while
51:43 (43)	take your enjoyment for a while
56:84 (83)	and that hour you are watching
76:1 (1)	has there come on man a while of time

*Ḥ Y Q

ḤĀQA vb. (I)~(with prep. *bi-*) to encompass, surround, hem in

a) perf. act.

6:10 (10)	those that scoffed at them were encompassed
11:8 (11)	they shall be encompassed by that they mocked at
16:34 (36)	they were encompassed by that they mocked at
21:41 (42)	those that scoffed at them were encompassed
39:48 (49)	they would be encompassed by that they mocked at
40:45 (48)	and there encompassed the folk of Pharaoh
40:83 (83)	and were encompassed by that they mocked at
45:33 (32)	they shall be encompassed by that they mocked at
46:26 (25)	they were encompassed by that they mocked at

b) impf. act. (*yaḥīqu*)

35:43 (41)	evil devising encompasses only those who do it

*Ḥ Y R

ḤAYRĀN n.m. (adj)~distracted, bewildered

6:71 (70)	like one lured to bewilderment in the earth

*Ḥ Y Ṣ

MAḤĪṢ n.m.~an asylum, a way of place of escape

4:121 (120)	they shall find no asylum from it
14:21 (25)	we have no asylum,'
41:48 (48)	they will think that they have no asylum
42:35 (33)	those who dispute concerning Our signs may know they have no asylum
50:36 (35)	they searched about in the land; was there any asylum?

*Ḥ Y Y

ḤAYYA vb. (I)~to live

a) perf. act.

8:42 (44)	by a clear sign he might live who lived

b) impf. act. (*yaḥyā*)

7:25 (24)	therein you shall live, and therein you shall die
8:42 (44)	by a clear sign he might live who lived
20:74 (76)	wherein he shall neither die nor live
23:37 (39)	we die, and we live
45:24 (23)	we die, and we live
87:13 (13)	then he shall neither die therein, nor live

ḤAYĀT n.f.~life; (*al-ḥayāt al-dunyā*) the present life, the present world

2:85 (79)	but degradation in the present life
2:86 (80)	those who have purchased the present life
2:96 (90)	thou shalt find them the eagerest of men for life
2:179 (175)	in retaliation there is life for you
2:204 (200)	some men there are whose saying upon the present world pleases thee
2:212 (208)	decked out fair to the unbelievers is the present life
3:14 (12)	that is the enjoyment of the present life
3:117 (113)	the likeness of that they expend in this present life
3:185 (182)	the present life is but the joy of delusion
4:74 (76)	who sell the present life for the world to come
4:94 (96)	seeking the chance goods of the present life
4:109 (109)	you have disputed on their behalf in the present life
6:29 (29)	there is only our present life
6:32 (32)	the present life is naught but a sport
6:70 (69)	and whom the present life has deluded
6:130 (130)	they were deluded by the present life
7:32 (30)	exclusively for those who believed in this present life
7:51 (49)	and whom the present life has deluded
7:152 (151)	and abasement in this present life
9:38 (38)	are you so content with this present life
9:38 (38)	yet the enjoyment of this present life
9:55 (55)	to chastise them in this present life
10:7 (7)	are well-pleased with the present life
10:23 (24)	the enjoyment of this present life

10:24 (25)	the likeness of this present life
10:64 (65)	for them is good tidings in the present life
10:88 (88)	adornment and possessions in this present life
10:98 (98)	the chastisement of degradation in this present life
11:15 (18)	whoso desires the present life and its adornment
13:26 (26)	they rejoice in this present life
13:26 (26)	and this present life, beside the world to come
13:34 (34)	for them is chastisement in the present life
14:3 (3)	such as prefer the present life over the world to come
14:27 (32)	those who believe with the firm word, in the present life
16:97 (99)	We shall assuredly give him to live a goodly life
16:107 (109)	they have preferred the present life
17:75 (77)	then would We have let thee taste the double of life
18:28 (27)	desiring the adornment of the present life
18:45 (43)	strike for them the similitude of the present life
18:46 (44)	wealth and sons are the adornment of the present world
18:104 (104)	those whose striving goes astray in the present life
20:72 (75)	thou canst only decide touching this present life
20:97 (97)	it shall be thine all this life to cry
20:131 (131)	the flower of the present life
23:33 (34)	to whom We had given ease in the present life
23:37 (39)	there is nothing but our present life
24:33 (33)	seek the chance goods of the present life
25:3 (4)	no power of death or life or raising up
28:60 (60)	the enjoyment of the present life and its adornment
28:61 (61)	to whom We have given the enjoyment of the present life
28:79 (79)	those who desired the present life
29:25 (24)	a mark of mutual love between you in the present life
29:64 (64)	this present life is naught but a diversion
30:7 (6)	they know an outward part of the present life
31:33 (33)	let not the present life delude you
33:28 (28)	if you desire the present life and its adornment
35:5 (5)	let not the present life delude you
39:26 (27)	God let them taste degradation in this present life
40:39 (42)	surely this present life is but a passing enjoyment
40:51 (54)	those who have believed, in the present life
41:16 (15)	the chastisement of degradation in the present life
41:31 (31)	We are your friends in the present life
42:36 (34)	the enjoyment of the present life
43:32 (31)	them their livelihood in the present life
43:35 (34)	all this is but the enjoyment of the present life
45:24 (23)	there is nothing but our present life
45:35 (34)	and the present life deluded you
46:20 (19)	you dissipated your good things in your present life
47:36 (38)	the present life is naught but a sport
53:29 (30)	and desires only the present life
57:20 (19)	know that the present life is but a sport
57:20 (20)	the present life is but the joy of delusion
67:2 (2)	who created death and life, that He might try you
79:38 (38)	and preferred the present life
87:16 (16)	nay, but you prefer the present life
89:24 (25)	O would that I had forwarded for my life

ḤAYAWĀN n.m.~Life (eternal)

29:64 (64)	surely the Last Abode is Life

ḤAYY n.m. (adj)~alive, living; the Living (Divine attribute)

2:154 (149)	rather they are living
2:255 (256)	there is no god but He, the Living, the Everlasting
3:2 (1)	there is no god but He, the Living, the Everlasting
3:27 (26)	Thou bringest forth the living from the dead
3:27 (26)	Thou bringest forth the dead from the living
3:169 (163)	but rather living with their Lord
6:95 (95)	brings forth the living from the dead
6:95 (95)	brings forth the dead too from the living
10:31 (32)	who brings forth the living from the dead
10:31 (32)	and brings forth the dead from the living
16:21 (21)	dead, not alive, and are not aware
19:15 (15)	the day he dies, and the day he is raised up alive
19:31 (32)	to pray, and to give the alms, so long as I live
19:33 (34)	and the day I die, and the day I am raised up alive
19:66 (67)	when I am dead shall I then be brought forth alive?
20:111 (110)	faces shall be humbled unto the Living, the Eternal
21:30 (31)	and of water fashioned every living thing
25:58 (60)	put thy trust in the Living God, the Undying
30:19 (18)	He brings forth the living from the dead
30:19 (18)	and brings forth the dead from the living
35:22 (21)	not equal are the living and the dead
36:70 (70)	that he may warn whosoever is living
40:65 (67)	He is the Living One; there is no god but He
77:26 (26)	for the living and for the dead

ḤAYYAH n.f.~serpent

20:20 (21)	he cast it down, and behold it was a serpent sliding

MAḤYÁ n.m.~life, living

6:162 (163)	my living, my dying — all belongs to God
45:21 (20)	equal their living and their dying

YAḤYÁ n.prop.~John

3:39 (34)	God gives thee good tidings of John
6:85 (85)	John, Jesus and Elias; each was of the righteous
19:7 (7)	We give thee good tidings of a boy, whose name is John
19:12 (13)	O John, take the Book forcefully
21:90 (90)	We answered him, and bestowed on him John

ḤAYYÁ vb. (II)~to greet, salute. (n.vb.) greeting, salutation

a) perf. act.

58:8 (9)	they greet thee with a greeting God never (greeted) thee withal

b) impf. act. (*yuḥayyī*)

58:8 (9)	they (greet) thee with a greeting God never greeted thee withal

c) impv. (*ḥayyi*)

4:86 (88)	greet with a fairer than it

d) perf. pass. (*ḥuyyī*)

4:86 (88)	when you are greeted with a greeting

f) n.vb. (*taḥīyah*)

4:86 (88)	when you are greeted with a greeting
10:10 (10)	glory to Thee, O God,' their greeting
14:23 (28)	their greeting therein: Peace
24:61 (61)	greet one another with a greeting from God
25:75 (75)	they shall receive therein a greeting
33:44 (43)	their greeting, on the day when they shall meet Him

AḤYĀ vb. (IV)~to cause to live, give life, quicken, revive. (pcple. act.) one who gives life; Quickener (Divine attribute)

a) perf. act.

2:28 (26)	seeing you were dead and He gave you life
2:164 (159)	the water God sends down from heaven therewith reviving the earth
2:243 (244)	then He gave them life. Truly God is bounteous
5:32 (35)	whoso gives life to a soul
5:32 (35)	shall be as if he had given life to mankind
6:122 (122)	We gave him life, and appointed for him a light
16:65 (67)	and therewith revives the earth after it is dead
22:66 (65)	it is He who gave you life
29:63 (63)	and therewith revives the earth after it is dead
35:9 (10)	We drive it to a dead land and therewith revive the earth
36:33 (33)	that We quickened and brought forth from it grain
40:11 (11)	and Thou hast given us twice to live
41:39 (39)	He who quickens it is He who quickens the dead
45:5 (4)	and therewith revives the earth after it is dead
50:11 (11)	and thereby We revived a land that was dead
53:44 (45)	He who makes to die, and that makes to live

b) impf. act. (*yuḥyī*)

2:28 (26)	then He shall give you life
2:73 (68)	God brings to life the dead
2:258 (260)	my Lord is He who gives life
2:258 (260)	I give life, and make to die
2:259 (261)	how shall God give life to this now it is dead?
2:260 (262)	show me how Thou wilt give life to the dead
3:49 (43)	and bring to life the dead, by the leave of God
3:156 (150)	God gives life, and He makes to die
7:158 (158)	He gives life, and makes to die
8:24 (24)	when He calls you unto that which will give you life
9:116 (117)	He gives life, and makes to die
10:56 (57)	He gives life, and makes to die
15:23 (23)	it is We who give life, and make to die
16:97 (99)	We shall assuredly give him to live a goodly life
22:6 (6)	He is the Truth, and brings the dead to life
22:66 (65)	then He shall give you life
23:80 (82)	it is He who gives life, and makes to die
25:49 (51)	so that We might revive a dead land
26:81 (81)	who makes me to die, then gives me life
30:19 (18)	and He revives the earth after it is dead
30:24 (23)	and He revives the earth after it is dead
30:40 (39)	then He shall give you life
30:50 (49)	how He quickens the earth after it was dead
36:12 (11)	it is We who bring the dead to life
36:78 (78)	who shall quicken the bones when they are decayed?

36:79 (79)	He shall quicken them, who originated them
40:68 (70)	it is He who gives life, and makes to die
42:9 (7)	He quickens the dead, and He is powerful
44:8 (7)	He gives life and makes to die
45:26 (25)	God gives you life, then makes you die
46:33 (32)	is able to give life to the dead
50:43 (42)	it is We who give life, and make to die
57:2 (2)	He gives life, and He makes to die
57:17 (16)	know that God revives the earth after it was dead
75:40 (40)	is He not able to quicken the dead?

g) pcple. act. (*muḥyī*)

30:50 (49)	surely He is the quickener of the dead
41:39 (39)	He who quickens it is He who quickens the dead

ISTAḤÁ vb. (X)~to be ashamed. (n.vb.) modesty, bashfulness

b) impf. act. (*yastaḥī*)

2:26 (24)	God is not ashamed to strike a similitude
33:53 (53)	he is ashamed before you
33:53 (53)	but God is not ashamed before the truth

f) n.vb. (*istiḥyā'*)

28:25 (25)	then came one of the two women to him, walking modestly

ISTAḤYĀ vb. (X)~to save alive, to spare

b) impf. act. (*yastaḥyī*)

2:49 (46)	slaughtering your sons, and sparing your women
7:127 (124)	we shall slaughter their sons and spare their women
7:141 (137)	slaying your sons, and sparing your women
14:6 (6)	slaughtering your sons, and sparing your women
28:4 (3)	slaughtering their sons, and sparing their women

c) impv. (*istaḥyi*)

40:25 (26)	and spare their women

*Ḥ Z B

ḤIZB n.m. (pl. *aḥzāb*)~party, partisan, Confederates [Ar]; ally [Ali]; faction [Pk]

5:56 (61)	the believers — the party of God
11:17 (20)	whosoever disbelieves in it, being one of the partisans
13:36 (36)	and of the parties some reject some of it
18:12 (11)	We might know which of the two parties
19:37 (38)	the parties have fallen into variance among themselves
23:53 (55)	into sects, each party rejoicing in what is with them
30:32 (31)	each several party rejoicing in what is theirs
33:20 (20)	they think the Confederates have not departed
33:20 (20)	if the Confederates come, they will wish that they were desert-dwellers
33:22 (22)	when the believers saw the Confederates

35:6 (6)	He calls his party only that they may be among the inhabitants
38:11 (10)	a very host of parties is routed there
38:13 (12)	and the men of the Thicket — those were the parties
40:5 (5)	and the parties after them
40:30 (31)	truly I fear for you the like of the day of the parties
43:65 (65)	but the parties among them fell into variance
58:19 (20)	those are Satan's party
58:19 (20)	Satan's party, surely, they are the losers
58:22 (22)	those are God's party
58:22 (22)	surely God's party — they are the prosperers

*Ḥ Z N

ḤAZANA vb. (I)~to grieve (tr). (n.vb.) grief, sorrow

b) impf. act. (*yaḥzunu*)

3:176 (170)	let them not grieve thee that vie with one another
5:41 (45)	let them not grieve thee that vie with one another
6:33 (33)	We know indeed that it grieves thee
10:65 (66)	do not let their saying grieve thee
12:13 (13)	it grieves me that you should go with him
21:103 (103)	the greatest terror shall not grieve them
31:23 (22)	let not his disbelief grieve thee
36:76 (76)	do not let their saying grieve thee
58:10 (11)	that the believers may sorrow

f) n.vb. (*ḥazan*)

9:92 (93)	their eyes overflowing with tears of sorrow
28:8 (7)	the folk of Pharaoh picked him out to be an enemy and a sorrow to them
35:34 (31)	praise belongs to God who has put away all sorrow

ḤAZINA vb. (I)~to sorrow, be sad. (n.vb.) sorrow, grief

b) impf. act. (*yaḥzanu*)

2:38 (36)	no fear shall be on them, neither shall they sorrow
2:62 (59)	no fear shall be on them, neither shall they sorrow
2:112 (106)	no fear shall be on them, neither shall they sorrow
2:262 (264)	no fear shall be on them, neither shall they sorrow
2:274 (275)	no fear shall be on them, neither shall they sorrow
2:277 (277)	no fear shall be on them, neither shall they sorrow
3:139 (133)	faint not, neither sorrow; you shall be the upper ones
3:153 (147)	that you might not sorrow for what escaped you
3:170 (164)	no fear shall be on them, neither shall they sorrow
5:69 (73)	no fear shall be on them, neither shall they sorrow
6:48 (48)	no fear shall be on them, neither shall they sorrow
7:35 (33)	no fear shall be on them, neither shall they sorrow
7:49 (47)	no fear upon you, nor shall you sorrow
9:40 (40)	sorrow not; surely God is with us
10:62 (63)	no fear shall be on them, neither shall they sorrow
15:88 (88)	do not sorrow for them
16:127 (128)	do not sorrow for them

19:24 (24)	nay, do not sorrow
20:40 (41)	that she might rejoice, and not sorrow
27:70 (72)	do not sorrow for them, for what they devise
28:7 (6)	do not fear, neither sorrow
28:13 (12)	that she might be comforted and not sorrow
29:33 (32)	fear not, neither sorrow
33:51 (51)	it is likelier they will be comforted, and not sorrow
39:61 (62)	evil shall not visit them, neither shall they sorrow
41:30 (30)	fear not, neither sorrow
43:68 (68)	today no fear is on you, neither do you sorrow
46:13 (12)	no fear shall be on them, neither shall they sorrow

f) n.vb. (*ḥuzn*)

12:84 (84)	his eyes turned white because of the sorrow
12:86 (86)	I make complaint of my anguish and my sorrow unto God

*Ḥ Ẓ R

ḤAẒARA vb. (I)~(pcple. pass.) confined

h) pcple. pass. (*maḥẓūr*)

17:20 (21)	thy Lord's gift is not confined

IḤTAẒARA vb. (VIII)~(pcple. act.) one who builds a pen for cattle, pen-builder

g) pcple. act. (*muḥtaẓir*)

54:31 (31)	and they were as the wattles of a pen-builder

*Ḥ Ẓ Ẓ

ḤAẒẒ n.m.~part, portion, good fortune

3:176 (170)	God desires not to appoint for them a portion
4:11 (12)	to the male the like of the portion of two females
4:176 (175)	the male shall receive the portion of two females
5:13 (16)	they have forgotten a portion of that they were reminded of
5:14 (17)	they have forgotten a portion of that they were reminded of
28:79 (79)	surely he is a man of mighty fortune
41:35 (35)	none shall receive it, except a man of mighty fortune

JĪM

*J ʾ R

JAʾARA vb. (I)~to groan

b) impf. act. (*yajʾaru*)

16:53 (55)	when affliction visits you it is unto Him that you groan
23:64 (66)	the ones of them that live at ease, behold, they groan
23:65 (67)	groan not today; surely you shall not be helped

*J ʿ L

JAʿALA vb. (I)~to make; (with prep. *li-*) to appoint, assign, give to, set, put; (with prep. *ʿalá*) to lay on, place; to reckon, count; to turn (tr), to make into, hence, to break (into fragments), to turn (upside down), to keep (one's hand chained). (pcple. act.) one who makes, sets, appoints, etc.; making, setting, etc.

a) perf. act.

2:22 (20)	who assigned to you the earth for a couch, and heaven for an edifice
2:66 (62)	We made it a punishment exemplary for all the former times
2:125 (119)	when We appointed the House to be a place of visitation
2:143 (137)	thus We appointed you a midmost nation
2:143 (138)	We did not appoint the direction thou wast facing
3:126 (122)	God wrought this not, save as good tiding to you
4:5 (4)	do not give to fools their property that God has assigned to you
4:33 (37)	to everyone We have appointed heirs
4:90 (92)	God assigns not any way to you against them
4:91 (93)	against them We have given you a clear authority
5:13 (16)	so for their breaking their compact
5:20 (23)	remember God's blessing upon you, when He appointed among you Prophets
5:20 (23)	and [He] appointed you kings
5:48 (52)	to every one of you We have appointed a right way
5:48 (53)	if God had willed, He would have made you one nation
5:60 (65)	with whom He is wroth, and made some of them apes and swine
5:97 (98)	God has appointed the Kaaba, the Holy House
5:103 (102)	God has not appointed cattle dedicated to idols
6:1 (1)	who created the heavens and the earth and appointed the shadows
6:6 (6)	how We loosed heaven upon them in torrents, and made the rivers to flow
6:9 (9)	and had We made him an angel
6:9 (9)	We would have made him a man
6:25 (25)	We lay veils upon their hearts lest they understand it
6:96 (96)	and has made the night for a repose
6:97 (97)	it is He who has appointed for you the stars
6:100 (100)	they ascribe to God, as associates, the jinn
6:107 (107)	We have not appointed thee a watcher over them
6:112 (112)	We have appointed to every Prophet an enemy
6:122 (122)	and appointed for him a light to walk by
6:123 (123)	We appointed in every city great ones among its sinners

6:136 (137)	they appoint to God, of the tillage and cattle that He multiplied
6:165 (165)	He who has appointed you viceroys in the earth
7:10 (9)	in the earth and there appointed for you livelihood
7:27 (26)	We have made the Satans the friends of those who do not believe
7:69 (67)	remember when He appointed you as successors
7:74 (72)	remember when He appointed you successors after Ad
7:143 (139)	He made it crumble to dust
7:189 (189)	and made of him his spouse
7:190 (190)	when He gave them a righteous son, they assigned Him associates
8:10 (10)	God wrought this not, save as good tidings
9:19 (19)	do you reckon the giving of water to pilgrims
9:40 (40)	He made the word of the unbelievers the lowest
10:5 (5)	it is He who made the sun a radiance
10:14 (15)	We appointed you viceroys in the earth after them
10:24 (25)	Our command comes upon it by night or day, and We make it stubble
10:59 (60)	you have made some of it unlawful, and some lawful
10:67 (68)	it is He who made for you the night
10:73 (74)	and We appointed them as viceroys
11:82 (84)	so when Our command came, We turned it uppermost nethermost
11:118 (120)	He would have made mankind one nation
12:70 (70)	he put his drinking-cup into the saddlebag of his brother
12:100 (101)	my Lord has made it true
13:3 (3)	and set therein firm mountains and rivers
13:3 (3)	of every fruit He placed there two kinds
13:16 (17)	have they ascribed to God associates who created as He created
13:33 (33)	and yet they ascribe to God associates
13:38 (38)	and We assigned to them wives, and seed
14:30 (35)	they set up compeers to God
15:16 (16)	We have set in heaven constellations
15:20 (20)	and there appointed for you livelihood
15:74 (74)	We turned it uppermost nethermost and rained on it stones
15:91 (91)	who have broken the Koran into fragments
16:72 (74)	God has appointed for you of yourselves wives
16:72 (74)	He has appointed for you of your wives sons and grandsons
16:78 (80)	He appointed for you hearing, and sight, and hearts
16:80 (82)	it is God who has appointed a place of rest
16:80 (82)	appointed for you of the skins of the cattle houses
16:81 (83)	it is God who has appointed for you coverings
16:81 (83)	He has appointed for you of the mountains refuges
16:81 (83)	and He has appointed for you shirts to protect you
16:91 (93)	and you have made God your surety
16:93 (95)	He would have made you one nation
17:2 (2)	We gave Moses the Book, and made it a guidance
17:6 (6)	and We made you a greater host
17:8 (8)	and We have made Gehenna a prison
17:12 (13)	We have appointed the night and the day as two signs
17:12 (13)	and made the sign of the day to see
17:18 (19)	We appoint for him Gehenna wherein he shall roast
17:33 (35)	We have appointed to his next-of-kin authority
17:45 (47)	We place between thee, and those who do not believe
17:46 (48)	We lay veils upon their hearts lest they understand it
17:60 (62)	We made the vision that We showed thee
17:99 (101)	He has appointed for them a term
18:7 (6)	We have appointed all that is on the earth
18:32 (31)	to one of them We assigned two gardens

18:32 (31)	and between them We set a sown field
18:52 (50)	We shall set a gulf between them
18:57 (55)	We have laid veils on their hearts lest they understand it
18:59 (58)	We destroyed them when they did evil, and appointed for their destruction
18:96 (95)	when he had made it a fire, he said
18:98 (98)	He will make it into powder
19:24 (24)	see, thy Lord has set below thee a rivulet
19:30 (31)	God has given me the Book, and made me a Prophet
19:31 (32)	Blessed He has made me, wherever I may be
19:49 (50)	We gave him Isaac and Jacob
19:50 (51)	We gave them of Our mercy, and We appointed unto them a tongue
20:53 (55)	He who appointed the earth to be a cradle for you
21:8 (8)	nor did We fashion them as bodies that ate not food
21:15 (15)	they ceased not to cry, until We made them stubble
21:30 (31)	and of water fashioned every living thing
21:31 (32)	We set in the earth firm mountains
21:31 (32)	and We set in it ravines to serve as ways
21:32 (33)	We set up the heaven as a roof well-protected
21:34 (35)	We have not assigned to any mortal before thee to live forever
21:58 (59)	he broke them into fragments, all but a great one they had
21:70 (70)	so We made them the worse losers
21:72 (72)	and every one made We righteous
21:73 (73)	and appointed them to be leaders guiding by Our command
21:91 (91)	and appointed her and her son to be a sign
22:25 (25)	the Holy Mosque that We have appointed equal unto men
22:34 (35)	We have appointed for every nation a holy rite
22:36 (37)	We have appointed them for you as among God's waymarks
22:67 (66)	We have appointed for every nation a holy rite
22:78 (77)	and has laid on you no impediment in your religion
23:13 (13)	then We set him, a drop, in a receptacle secure
23:41 (43)	and We made them as scum
23:44 (46)	and We made them as but tales
23:50 (52)	We made Mary's son, and his mother, to be a sign
25:10 (11)	He who, if He will, shall assign to thee better than that
25:20 (22)	We appointed some of you to be a trial for others
25:23 (25)	and make it a scattered dust
25:31 (33)	We have appointed to every Prophet an enemy among the sinners
25:35 (37)	We gave Moses the Book, and appointed with him his brother
25:37 (39)	We drowned them, and made them to be a sign
25:45 (47)	had He willed, He would have made it still
25:45 (47)	then We appointed the sun, to be a guide to it
25:47 (49)	it is He who appointed the night for you
25:47 (49)	and day He appointed for a rising
25:53 (55)	He set between them a barrier, and a ban forbidden
25:54 (56)	He who created of water a mortal, and made him kindred of blood
25:61 (62)	He who has set in heaven constellations
25:61 (62)	and [He] has set among them a lamp
25:62 (63)	He who made the night and day a succession
26:21 (20)	my Lord gave me Judgment and made me one of the Envoys
27:34 (34)	disorder it and make the mighty ones of its inhabitants abased
27:61 (62)	He who made the earth a fixed place
27:61 (62)	and set amidst it rivers
27:61 (62)	and appointed for it firm mountains
27:61 (62)	and placed a partition between the two seas
27:86 (88)	have they not seen how We made the night for them

28:4 (3)	Pharaoh had exalted himself in the land
28:41 (41)	We appointed them leaders, calling to the Fire
28:71 (71)	what think you? If God should make the night unceasing over you
28:72 (72)	what think you? If God should make the day unceasing over you
28:73 (73)	of His mercy He has appointed for you night and day
29:10 (9)	he makes the persecution of men as it were God's chastisement
29:15 (14)	and appointed it for a sign unto all beings
29:27 (26)	and We appointed the Prophecy and the Book to be among his seed
29:67 (67)	have they not seen that We have appointed a sanctuary secure
30:21 (20)	He has set between you love and mercy
30:54 (53)	then He appointed after weakness strength
30:54 (53)	then after strength He appointed weakness and grey hairs
32:8 (7)	He fashioned his progeny of an extraction of mean water
32:9 (8)	He appointed for you hearing, and sight
32:23 (23)	We appointed it for a guidance to the Children of Israel
32:24 (24)	We appointed from among them leaders
33:4 (4)	God has not assigned to any man two hearts
33:4 (4)	nor has He made your wives, when you divorce
33:4 (4)	neither has He made your adopted sons your sons in fact
34:18 (17)	We set, between them and the cities
34:19 (18)	We made them as but tales
34:33 (32)	We put fetters on the necks of the unbelievers
35:11 (12)	then He made you pairs
35:39 (37)	it is He who appointed you viceroys in the earth
36:8 (7)	We have put on their necks fetters up to the chin
36:9 (8)	We have put before them a barrier and behind them a barrier
36:27 (26)	and that He has placed me among the honoured
36:34 (34)	We made therein gardens of palms and vines
36:80 (80)	who has made for you out of the green tree fire
37:63 (61)	We have appointed it as a trial for the evildoers
37:77 (75)	We made his seed the survivors
37:98 (96)	so We made them the lower ones
37:158 (158)	they have set up a kinship between Him and the jinn
38:5 (4)	what, has he made the gods One God?
38:26 (25)	We have appointed thee a viceroy in the earth
39:6 (8)	a single soul, then from it He appointed its mate
39:8 (11)	and sets up compeers to God, to lead
40:61 (63)	it is God who made for you the night
40:64 (66)	it is God who made for you the earth a fixed place
40:79 (79)	it is God who appointed for you the cattle
41:10 (9)	He set therein firm mountains over it
41:44 (44)	if We had made it a barbarous Koran
42:8 (6)	if God had willed, He would have made them one nation
42:11 (9)	He has appointed for you, of yourselves, pairs
42:52 (52)	We made it a light, whereby We guide whom We will
43:3 (2)	behold, We have made it an Arabic Koran
43:10 (9)	He who appointed the earth to be a cradle for you
43:10 (9)	and [He] appointed ways for you therein
43:12 (11)	and appointed for you ships and cattle
43:15 (14)	they have assigned to Him a part of His own servants
43:19 (18)	and they have made the angels, who are themselves servants
43:28 (27)	he made it a word enduring among his posterity
43:33 (32)	We would have appointed for those who disbelieve
43:45 (44)	have We appointed, apart from the All-merciful, gods to be served?
43:56 (56)	We made them a thing past, and We appointed them for an example to later folk

43:59 (59)	We made him to be an example to the Children of Israel
43:60 (60)	had We willed, We would have appointed angels among you
45:18 (17)	then We set thee upon an open way of the Command
45:23 (22)	and set a seal upon his hearing and his heart, and laid a covering on his eyes
46:26 (25)	We appointed for them hearing, and sight
48:26 (26)	when the unbelievers set in their hearts fierceness
48:27 (27)	He knew what you knew not, and appointed ere that a nigh victory
49:13 (13)	male and female, and appointed you races and tribes
50:26 (25)	who set up with God another god
51:42 (42)	but made it as stuff decayed
56:36 (35)	and We made them spotless virgins
56:65 (65)	did We will, We would make it broken orts
56:70 (69)	did We will, We would make it bitter
56:73 (72)	We Ourselves made it for a reminder
57:7 (7)	that unto which He has made you successors
57:26 (26)	We appointed the Prophecy and the Book to be among their seed
57:27 (27)	We set in the hearts of those who followed him tenderness
65:3 (3)	God has appointed a measure for everything
67:5 (5)	We adorned the lower heaven with lamps, and made them things to stone Satans
67:15 (15)	it is He who made the earth submissive to you
67:23 (23)	it is He who produced you, and appointed for you hearing
68:50 (50)	his Lord had chosen him, and He placed him among the righteous
71:7 (6)	they put their fingers in their ears
71:16 (15)	and set the moon therein for a light
71:16 (15)	and the sun for a lamp
71:19 (18)	God has laid the earth for you as a carpet
74:12 (12)	and appointed for him ample wealth
74:31 (31)	We have appointed only angels to be masters of the Fire
74:31 (31)	their number We have appointed only as a trial for the unbelievers
75:39 (39)	He made of him two kinds, male and female
76:2 (2)	and We made him hearing, seeing
77:21 (21)	that We laid within a sure lodging
77:27 (27)	set We not therein soaring mountains?
78:9 (9)	and We appointed your sleep for a rest
78:10 (10)	and We appointed night for a garment
78:11 (11)	and We appointed day for a livelihood
78:13 (13)	and We appointed a blazing lamp
87:5 (5)	then made it a blackening wrack
105:5 (5)	and He made them like green blades devoured

b) impf. act. (*yajʿalu*)

2:19 (18)	they put their fingers in their ears against the thunderclaps
2:22 (20)	so set not up compeers to God wittingly
2:30 (28)	wilt Thou set therein one who will do corruption there
2:224 (224)	do not make God a hindrance, through your oaths
2:259 (261)	so We would make thee a sign for the people
3:61 (54)	let us humbly pray and so lay God's curse upon the ones who lie
3:156 (150)	that God may make that an anguish in their hearts
3:176 (170)	God desires not to appoint for them a portion in the world to come
4:15 (19)	until death takes them or God appoints for them a way
4:19 (23)	you may be averse to a thing, and God set in it much good
4:141 (140)	God will not grant the unbelievers any way over the believers
4:144 (143)	do you desire to give God over you a clear authority?
5:6 (9)	God does not desire to make any impediment for you
6:39 (39)	whomsoever He will, He sets him on a straight path

6:91 (91)	you put it into parchments, revealing them, and hiding much
6:124 (124)	God knows very well where to place His Message
6:125 (125)	whomsoever He desires to lead astray, He makes his breast narrow
6:125 (125)	God lays abomination upon those who believe not
7:47 (45)	do not Thou assign us with the people of the evildoers
7:150 (149)	and put me not among the people of the evildoers
8:29 (29)	if you fear God, He will assign you a salvation
8:37 (38)	and place the corrupt one upon another
8:37 (38)	and so heap them up all together, and put them in Gehenna
10:85 (85)	Lord, make us not a temptation to the people
10:100 (100)	He lays abomination upon those who have no understanding
12:15 (15)	and [they] agreed to put him in the bottom of the well
15:96 (96)	those who set up with God another god
16:56 (58)	they appoint a share of that We have provided them
16:57 (59)	they assign to God daughters
16:62 (64)	they assign to God that they themselves dislike
17:22 (23)	set not up with God another god
17:29 (31)	keep not thy hand chained to thy neck, nor outspread it
17:39 (41)	set not up with God another god
18:1 (1)	and has not assigned unto it any crookedness
18:48 (46)	you asserted We should not appoint for you a tryst
18:90 (89)	upon a people for whom We had not appointed any veil
18:94 (93)	so shall we assign to thee a tribute
18:94 (93)	against thy setting up a barrier between us and between them
18:95 (94)	aid me forcefully, and I will set up a rampart
19:7 (8)	no namesake have We given him aforetime
19:21 (21)	and that We may appoint him a sign unto men
19:32 (33)	He has not made me arrogant, unprosperous
19:96 (96)	unto them the All-merciful shall assign love
22:53 (52)	that He may make what Satan casts a trial
23:94 (96)	put me not among the people of the evildoers
24:40 (40)	to whomsoever God assigns no light, no light has he
24:43 (43)	hast thou not seen how God drives the clouds, then composes them
24:63 (63)	make not the calling of the Messenger among yourselves like your calling
25:10 (11)	He who, if He will, shall assign to thee better than that
26:29 (28)	if thou takest a god other than me, I shall surely make thee one
27:62 (63)	and removes the evil and appoints you to be successors
28:5 (4)	We desired to ... make them leaders
28:5 (4)	and to make them the inheritors
28:35 (35)	We shall appoint to you an authority
28:83 (83)	We appoint it for those who desire not exorbitance in the earth
30:48 (47)	He spreads them in heaven how He will, and shatters them
34:33 (32)	when you were ordering us to disbelieve in God, and to set up compeers to Him
38:28 (27)	shall We make those who believe and do righteous deeds as the workers of corruption
38:28 (27)	or shall We make the godfearing as the transgressors?
39:21 (22)	then He makes them broken orts
41:9 (8)	do you set up compeers to Him?
41:29 (29)	we shall set them underneath our feet
42:50 (49)	He makes whom He will barren
45:21 (20)	do those who commit evil deeds think that We shall make them as those who believe
51:51 (51)	and set not up with God another god

56:82 (81)	do you make it your living to cry lies?
57:28 (28)	He will appoint for you a light whereby you shall walk
59:10 (10)	and put Thou not into our hearts any rancour
60:5 (5)	make us not a temptation to those who disbelieve
60:7 (7)	it may be God will yet establish between you and those of them with whom you are at enmity
65:2 (2)	whosoever fears God, He will appoint for him a way out
65:4 (4)	God will appoint for him, of His command, easiness
65:7 (7)	God will assuredly appoint, after difficulty, easiness
68:35 (35)	shall we make those who have surrendered like to the sinners?
69:12 (12)	that We might make it a reminder for you
71:12 (11)	and will appoint for you gardens
71:12 (11)	and will appoint for you rivers
72:25 (26)	whether my Lord will appoint for it a space
73:17 (17)	guard yourselves against a day that shall make the children grey-headed
77:25 (25)	made We not the earth to be a housing
78:6 (6)	have We not made the earth as a cradle
90:8 (8)	have We not appointed to him two eyes
105:2 (2)	did He not make their guile to go astray?

c) impv. (*ijʿal*)

2:126 (120)	my Lord, make this a land secure
2:128 (122)	and our Lord, make us submissive to Thee
2:260 (262)	then set a part of them on every hill
3:41 (36)	appoint to me a sign
4:75 (77)	and appoint to us a protector from Thee
4:75 (77)	and appoint to us from Thee a helper
7:138 (134)	Moses, make for us a god, as they have gods
10:87 (87)	make your houses a direction for men to pray to
12:55 (55)	set me over the land's storehouses; I am a knowing guardian
12:62 (62)	put their merchandise in their saddlebags
14:35 (38)	my Lord, make this land secure
14:37 (40)	let them perform the prayer, and make hearts of men yearn towards them
14:40 (42)	my Lord, make me a performer of the prayer
17:80 (82)	grant me authority from Thee, to help me
19:6 (6)	and make him, my Lord, well-pleasing
19:10 (11)	Lord, appoint to me some sign
20:29 (30)	appoint for me of my folk a familiar
20:58 (60)	therefore appoint a tryst between us
25:74 (74)	and make us a model to the godfearing
26:84 (84)	and appoint me a tongue of truthfulness among the others
26:85 (85)	make me one of the inheritors of the Garden of Bliss
28:38 (38)	make me a tower, that I may mount up to Moses' God

d) perf. pass. (*juʿila*)

16:124 (125)	the Sabbath was only appointed for those who were at variance thereon

g) pcple. act. (*jāʿil*)

2:30 (28)	I am setting in the earth a viceroy
2:124 (118)	behold, I make you a leader for the people
3:55 (48)	I will set thy followers above the unbelievers
18:8 (7)	We shall surely make all that is on it barren dust
28:7 (6)	and shall appoint him one of the Envoys
35:1 (1)	who appointed the angels to be messengers having wings two, three and four

*J B B

JUBB n.m.~pit, well, cistern

12:10 (10)	but cast him into the bottom of the pit
12:15 (15)	[they] agreed to put him in the bottom of the well

*J B H

JIBĀH n.f. (pl. of *jabhah*)~forehead

9:35 (35)	their foreheads and their sides and their backs shall be branded

*J B L

JABAL n.m. (pl. *jibāl*)~mountain, hill

2:260 (262)	then set a part of them on every hill
7:74 (72)	hewing its mountains into houses
7:143 (139)	behold the mountain
7:143 (139)	when his Lord revealed Him to the mountain
7:171 (170)	when We shook the mountain above them
11:42 (44)	so it ran with them amid waves like mountains
11:43 (45)	I will take refuge in a mountain
13:31 (30)	if only a Koran whereby the mountains were set in motion
14:46 (47)	though their devising were such as to remove mountains
15:82 (82)	they were hewing the mountains into houses
16:68 (70)	take unto yourselves, of the mountains, houses
16:81 (83)	He has appointed for you of the mountains refuges
17:37 (39)	thou wilt never tear the earth open, nor attain the mountains in height
18:47 (45)	on the day We shall set the mountains in motion
19:90 (92)	the mountains wellnigh fall down crashing
20:105 (105)	they will question thee concerning the mountains
21:79 (79)	with David We subjected the mountains to give glory
22:18 (18)	the sun and the moon, the stars and the mountains
24:43 (43)	He sends down out of heaven mountains
26:149 (149)	will you still skilfully hew houses out of the mountains?
27:88 (90)	thou shalt see the mountains, that thou supposest fixed
33:72 (72)	We offered the trust to the heavens and the earth and the mountains
34:10 (10)	O you mountains, echo God's praises
35:27 (25)	in the mountains are streaks white and red
38:18 (17)	with him We subjected the mountains to give glory
52:10 (10)	and the mountains are in motion
56:5 (5)	and the mountains crumbled
59:21 (21)	if We had sent down this Koran upon a mountain
69:14 (14)	and the earth and the mountains are lifted up and crushed
70:9 (9)	and the mountains shall be as plucked wool-tufts
73:14 (14)	upon the day when the earth and the mountains shall quake
73:14 (14)	and the mountains become a slipping heap of sand
77:10 (10)	when the mountains shall be scattered
78:7 (7)	and the mountains as pegs

78:20 (20)	and the mountains are set in motion, and become a vapour
79:32 (32)	and the mountains He set firm
81:3 (3)	when the mountains shall be set moving
88:19 (19)	how the mountains were hoisted
101:5 (4)	and the mountains shall be like plucked wool-tufts

JIBILLAH n.f.~crowd, throng, generation

26:184 (184)	who created you, and the generatons of the ancients
36:62 (62)	He led astray many a throng of you

*J B N

JABĪN n.m.~brow

37:103 (103)	and he flung him upon his brow

*J B R

JABBĀR n.m. (adj)~arrogant [Ar]; haughty [Ali]; disdainful [Pk]; All-compeller [Ar, Pk]; Irresistible [Ali] (Divine attribute)

5:22 (25)	Moses, there are people in it very arrogant
11:59 (62)	and followed the command of every froward tyrant
14:15 (18)	then was disappointed every froward tyrant
19:14 (14)	and cherishing his parents, not arrogant, rebellious
19:32 (33)	He has not made me arrogant, unprosperous
26:130 (130)	when you assault, you assault like tyrants
28:19 (18)	thou only desirest to be a tyrant in the land
40:35 (37)	God sets a seal on every heart proud, arrogant
50:45 (44)	thou art not a tyrant over them
59:23 (23)	the All-mighty, the All-compeller

JIBRĪL n.prop.~Gabriel (the Archangel)

2:97 (91)	whosoever is an enemy to Gabriel
2:98 (92)	an enemy to God and His angels and His Messengers, and Gabriel
66:4 (4)	God is his Protector, and Gabriel, and the righteous

*J B T

JIBT n.m.~an idol, false deity; Jibt [Bl]

4:51 (54)	those who were given a share of the Book believing in demons and idols

*J B Y

JABĀ vb. (I)~to collect or gather

e) impf. pass. (*yujbá*)

28:57 (57) a sanctuary secure, to which are collected the fruits of everything

JAWĀBĪ n.f. (pl. of *jābiyah*)~cistern, water-trough

34:13 (12) porringers like water-troughs, and anchored cooking-pots

IJTABÁ vb. (VIII)~to elect, choose

a) perf. act.

6:87 (87) We elected them, and We guided them to a straight path
7:203 (202) why hast thou not chosen one?
16:121 (122) He chose him, and He guided him to a straight path
19:58 (59) the seed of Abraham and Israel, and of those We guided and chose
20:122 (120) therafter his Lord chose him, and turned again unto him
22:78 (77) He has chosen you, and has laid on you no impediment
68:50 (50) his Lord had chosen him, and He placed him among the righteous

b) impf. act. (*yajtabī*)

3:179 (174) God chooses out of His Messengers whom He will
12:6 (6) so will thy Lord choose thee, and teach thee the interpretation of tales
42:13 (12) god chooses unto Himself whomsoever He will

*J D D

JADD n.m.~majesty

72:3 (3) He — exalted be our Lord's majesty

JADĪD n.m. (adj)~new

13:5 (5) shall we indeed then be raised up again in new creation?
14:19 (22) if He will, He can put you away and bring a new creation
17:49 (52) shall we really be raised up again in a new creation?
17:98 (100) shall we really be raised up again in a new creation?
32:10 (9) shall we indeed be in a new creation?
34:7 (7) when you have been utterly torn to pieces, then you shall be in a new creation
35:16 (17) if He will, He can put you away and bring a new creation
50:15 (14) they are in uncertainty as to the new creation

JUDAD n.f. (pl. of *juddah*)~a track, way, streak

35:27 (25) in the mountains are streaks white and red

*J D L

JADAL n.m.~a dispute; (adj) disputatious

18:54 (52) man is the most disputatious of things
43:58 (58) they cite not him to thee, save to dispute

JĀDALA vb. (III)~to dispute, argue. (n.vb.) a dispute, disputation

a) perf. act.

4:109 (109)	you have disputed on their behalf in the present life
11:32 (34)	Noah, thou hast disputed with us
22:68 (67)	if they should dispute with thee, do thou say
40:5 (5)	and disputed with falsehood that they might rebut thereby the truth

b) impf. act. (*yujādilu*)

4:107 (107)	do not dispute on behalf of those who betray themselves
4:109 (109)	who will dispute with God on their behalf
6:25 (25)	when they come to thee they dispute with thee
6:121 (121)	the Satans inspire their friends to dispute with you
7:71 (69)	do you dispute with me regarding names you have named
8:6 (6)	disputing with thee concerning the truth after it had become clear
11:74 (77)	he was disputing with Us concerning the people of Lot
13:13 (14)	yet they dispute about God, who is mighty in power
16:111 (112)	the day that every soul shall come disputing in its own behalf
18:56 (54)	yet do the unbelievers dispute with falsehood
22:3 (3)	there is such a one that disputes concerning God without knowledge
22:8 (8)	there is such a one that disputes concerning God without knowledge
29:46 (45)	dispute not with the People of the Book
31:20 (19)	there is such a one that disputes concerning God without knowledge
40:4 (4)	none but the unbelievers dispute concerning the signs of God
40:35 (37)	those who dispute concerning the signs of God
40:56 (58)	Those who dispute concerning the signs of God
40:69 (71)	hast thou not regarded those who dispute concerning the signs of God
42:35 (33)	those who dispute concerning Our signs may know they have no asylum
58:1 (1)	God has heard the words of her that disputes with thee

c) impv. (*jādil*)

16:125 (126)	and dispute with them in the better way

f) n.vb. (*jidāl*)

2:197 (193)	nor indulge in ungodliness and disputing in the Pilgrimage
11:32 (34)	thou hast disputed with us and make much disputation with us

*J D R

JADĪR n.m. (comp. adj. *ajdar*)~fitting, apt

9:97 (98)	and apter not to know the bounds of what God has sent down on His Messenger

JIDĀR n.m. (pl. *judur*)~a wall

18:77 (76)	there they found a wall about to tumble down
18:82 (81)	as for the wall, it belonged to two orphan lads
59:14 (14)	except in fortified cities, or from behind walls

*J D TH

AJDĀTH n.m. (pl. of *jadath*)~tomb, sepulchre

36:51 (51) behold, they are sliding down from their tombs unto their Lord
54:7 (7) they shall come forth from the tombs as if they were scattered grasshoppers
70:43 (43) they shall come forth from the tombs hastily

*J DH ʿ

JIDHʿ n.m. (pl. *judhūʿ*)~trunk (of a tree)

19:23 (23) the birthpangs surprised her by the trunk of the palm-tree
19:25 (25) shake also to thee the palm-trunk
20:71 (74) then I shall crucify you upon the trunks of palm-trees

*J DH DH

JADHDHA vb. (I)~(pcple. pass.) broken

h) pcple. pass. (*majdhūdh*)

11:108 (110) save as thy Lord will — for a gift unbroken

JUDHĀDH n.m.~broken piece(s), fragments

21:58 (59) so he broke them into fragments

*J DH W

JADHWAH n.f.~a faggot

28:29 (29) perhaps I shall bring you news of it, or a faggot from the fire

*J F ʾ

JUFĀʾ n.m.~froth, jetsam

13:17 (18) as for the scum, it vanishes as jetsam

*J F N

JIFĀN n.f. (pl. of *jafnah*)~porringers

34:13 (12) places of worship, statues, porringers like water-troughs

*J F W

TAJĀFÁ vb. (VI)~to avoid, to shun

a) perf. act.

32:16 (16)	their sides shun their couches as they call on their Lord

*J H D

JAHADA vb. (I)~(n.vb.) striving, endeavour; (adj) most earnest (as in *jahda aymānihim*, "their most earnest oaths")

f) n.vb. (*jahd*)

5:53 (58)	are these the ones who swore by God most earnest oaths
6:109 (109)	they have sworn by God the most earnest oaths
16:38 (40)	they have sworn by God the most earnest oaths
24:53 (52)	they have sworn by God the most earnest oaths
35:42 (40)	they have sworn by God the most earnest oaths

JUHD n.m.~ability, power, endeavour

9:79 (80)	those who find nothing but their endeavour they deride

JĀHADA vb. (III)~to struggle [Ar]; strive [Pk, Bl]; fight for the faith [Ali]. (n.vb.) struggle [Ar]; striving [Pk, Bl]; fighting for the faith [Ali]; Jihad. (pcple. act.) one who struggles, strives or fights (for the faith)

2:218 (215)	those who emigrate and struggle in God's way
3:142 (136)	without God know who of you have struggled and who are patient
8:72 (73)	and struggled with their possessions and their selves
8:74 (75)	those who believe, and have emigrated and struggled in the way of God
8:75 (76)	those who have believed afterwards and emigrated, and struggled with you
9:16 (16)	God knows not as yet those of you who have struggled
9:19 (19)	one who believes in God and the Last Day and struggles in the way of God
9:20 (20)	those who believe, and have emigrated, and have struggled
9:88 (89)	the Messenger, and the believers with him, have struggled
16:110 (111)	who have emigrated after persecution, then struggled
29:6 (5)	whosoever struggles, (struggles) only to his own gain
29:8 (7)	if they strive with thee to make thee associate with Me
29:69 (69)	but those who struggle in Our cause, surely We shall guide them
31:15 (14)	if they strive with thee to make thee associate with Me
49:15 (15)	not doubted, and have struggled with their possessions

b) impf. act. (*yujāhidu*)

5:54 (59)	men who struggle in the path of God, not fearing the reproach
9:44 (44)	ask not leave of thee, that they may struggle with their possessions
9:81 (82)	and were averse to struggle with their possessions
29:6 (5)	whosoever (struggles), struggles only to his own gain
61:11 (11)	you shall believe in God and His Messenger, and struggle in the way

c) impv. (*jāhid*)

5:35 (39)	seek the means to come to Him, and struggle in His way
9:41 (41)	struggle in God's way with your possessions and your selves
9:73 (74)	O Prophet, struggle with the unbelievers and hypocrites
9:86 (87)	believe in God, and struggle with His Messenger
22:78 (77)	and struggle for God as is His due, for He has chosen you
25:52 (54)	obey not the unbelievers, but struggle with them
66:9 (9)	O Prophet, struggle with the unbelievers and the hypocrites

f) n.vb. (*jihād*)

9:24 (24)	if these are dearer to you than God and His Messenger, and to struggle in His way
22:78 (77)	and struggle for God as is His due, for He has chosen you
25:52 (54)	obey not the unbelievers, but struggle with them <thereby mightily>
60:1 (1)	if you go forth to struggle in My way and seek My good pleasure

g) pcple. act. (*mujāhid*)

4:95 (97)	are not the equals of those who struggle in the path of God
4:95 (97)	God has preferred in rank those who struggle
4:95 (97)	and God has preferred those who struggle
47:31 (33)	until We know those of you who struggle and are steadfast

*J H L

JAHILA vb. (I)~to be ignorant. (pcple. act.) one who is ignorant

b) impf. act. (*yajhalu*)

6:111 (111)	but most of them are ignorant
7:138 (134)	you are surely a people who are ignorant
11:29 (31)	but I see you are an ignorant people
27:55 (56)	no, you are a people that are ignorant
46:23 (22)	but I see you are an ignorant people

g) pcple. act. (*jāhil*)

2:67 (63)	I take refuge with God, lest I should be one of the ignorant
2:273 (274)	the ignorant man supposes them rich because of their abstinence
6:35 (35)	so be not thou one of the ignorant
7:199 (198)	bid to what is honourable, and turn away from the ignorant
11:46 (48)	lest thou shouldst be among the ignorant
12:33 (33)	I shall yearn towards them, and so become one of the ignorant
12:89 (89)	are you aware of what you did ... when you were ignorant?
25:63 (64)	and who, when the ignorant address them, say
28:55 (55)	We desire not the ignorant
39:64 (64)	is it other than God you bid me serve, you ignorant ones?

JAHĀLAH n.f.~ignorance; (adv) unwittingly

4:17 (21)	God shall turn only towards those who do evil in ignorance
6:54 (54)	whosoever of you does evil in ignorance
16:119 (120)	unto those who did evil in ignorance, then repented
49:6 (6)	lest you afflict a people unwittingly, and then repent

JĀHILĪYAH n.f.~pagandom, pagans [Ar]; ignorance, pagan ignorance, Time or Age of Ignorance [Pk, Ali]; Jahiliyah

3:154 (148)	thoughts that were not true such as the pagans thought
5:50 (55)	is it the judgment of pagandom then that they are seeking?
33:33 (33)	display not your finery, as did the pagans of old
48:26 (26)	the unbelievers set in their hearts fierceness, the fierceness of pagandom

JAHŪL n.m. (adj)~foolish, very ignorant

33:72 (72)	surely he is sinful, very foolish

*J H N M

JAHANNAM n.f.~Gehenna [Ar, Bl]; Hell [Pk, Ali]

2:206 (202)	so Gehenna shall be enough for him
3:12 (10)	you shall be overthrown, and mustered into Gehenna
3:162 (156)	him who is laden with the burden of God's anger, whose refuge is Gehenna
3:197 (196)	a little enjoyment, then their refuge is Gehenna
4:55 (58)	Gehenna suffices for a Blaze
4:93 (95)	whoso slays a believer wilfully, his recompense is Gehenna
4:97 (99)	such men, their refuge shall be Gehenna
4:115 (115)	We shall roast him in Gehenna
4:121 (120)	such men — their refuge shall be Gehenna
4:140 (139)	God will gather the hypocrites and the unbelievers all in Gehenna
4:169 (167)	the road to Gehenna, therein dwelling forever and ever
7:18 (17)	I shall assuredly fill Gehenna with all of you
7:41 (39)	Gehenna shall be their cradle
7:179 (178)	We have created for Gehenna many jinn and men
8:16 (16)	his refuge is Gehenna
8:36 (37)	and the unbelievers will be mustered into Gehenna
8:37 (38)	and so heap them up all together, and put them in Gehenna
9:35 (35)	the day they shall be heated in the fire of Gehenna
9:49 (49)	surely Gehenna encompasses the unbelievers
9:63 (64)	for him awaits the fire of Gehenna
9:68 (69)	and the unbelievers, the fire of Gehenna, therein to dwell forever
9:73 (74)	their refuge is Gehenna — an evil homecoming
9:81 (82)	Gehenna's fire is hotter, did they but understand
9:95 (96)	their refuge is Gehenna — a recompese
9:109 (110)	that has tumbled with him into the fire of Gehenna
11:119 (120)	I shall assuredly fill Gehenna with jinn and men
13:18 (18)	and their refuge shall be Gehenna
14:16 (19)	beyond him Gehenna, and he is given to drink of oozing pus
14:29 (34)	Gehenna, wherein they are roasted
15:43 (43)	Gehenna shall be their promised land
16:29 (31)	so enter the gates of Gehenna, there to dwell forever
17:8 (8)	We have made Gehenna a prison for the unbelievers
17:18 (19)	We appoint for him Gehenna wherein he shall roast
17:39 (41)	or thou wilt be cast into Gehenna, reproached
17:63 (65)	surely Gehenna shall be your recompense
17:97 (99)	their refuge shall be Gehenna
18:100 (100)	upon that day We shall present Gehenna to the unbelievers
18:102 (102)	We have prepared Gehenna for the unbelievers' hospitality
18:106 (106)	that is their recompense — Gehenna
19:68 (69)	We shall parade them about Gehenna hobbling on their knees
19:86 (89)	and drive the evildoers into Gehenna herding
20:74 (76)	for him awaits Gehenna
21:29 (30)	such a one We recompense with Gehenna
21:98 (98)	you, and that you were serving apart from God, are fuel for Gehenna
23:103 (105)	they have lost their souls in Gehenna dwelling forever
25:34 (36)	those who shall be mustered to Gehenna upon their faces
25:65 (66)	turn Thou from us the chastisement of Gehenna
29:54 (54)	lo, Gehenna encompasses the unbelievers
29:68 (68)	is there not in Gehenna a lodging for the unbelievers?
32:13 (13)	I shall fill Gehenna with jinn and men all together
35:36 (33)	for the unbelievers, theirs shall be the fire of Gehenna

36:63 (63)	this is Gehenna, then, the same that you were promised
38:56 (56)	Gehenna, wherein they are roasted
38:85 (85)	I shall assuredly fill Gehenna with thee
39:32 (33)	is there not in Gehenna a lodging for the unbelievers?
39:60 (61)	is there not in Gehenna a lodging for those that are proud?
39:71 (71)	the unbelievers shall be driven in companies into Gehenna
39:72 (72)	enter the gates of Gehenna, to dwell therein
40:49 (52)	those who are in the Fire will say to the keepers of Gehenna
40:60 (62)	who wax too proud to do Me service shall enter Gehenna
40:76 (76)	enter the gates of Gehenna, to dwell therein
43:74 (74)	the evildoers dwell forever in the chastisement of Gehenna
45:10 (9)	behind them Gehenna; and that they have earned
48:6 (6)	and has cursed them, and has prepared for them Gehenna
50:24 (23)	cast, you twain, into Gehenna every froward unbeliever
50:30 (29)	upon the day We shall say unto Gehenna
52:13 (13)	the day when they shall be pitched into the fire of Gehenna
55:43 (43)	this is Gehenna, that sinners cried lies to
58:8 (9)	sufficient for them shall be Gehenna
66:9 (9)	their refuge shall be Gehenna
67:6 (6)	the chastisement of Gehenna — an evil homecoming
72:15 (15)	those who have deviated, they have become firewood for Gehenna
72:23 (24)	for him there awaits the Fire of Gehenna
78:21 (21)	behold, Gehenna has become an ambush
85:10 (10)	there awaits them the chastisement of Gehenna
89:23 (24)	and Gehenna is brought out, upon that day man will remember
98:6 (5)	the idolaters shall be in the Fire of Gehenna

*J H R

JAHARA vb. (I)~to proclaim, publish, be loud (in speech, prayer, etc.). (n.vb.) being loud or manifest, shouting, publishing; (adv) openly, publicly

a) perf. act.

13:10 (11)	he who conceals his saying, and he who proclaims it

b) impf. act. (*yajharu*)

17:110 (110)	be thou not loud in thy prayer, nor hushed
20:7 (6)	be thou loud in thy speech
49:2 (2)	and be not loud in your speech to him

c) impv. (*ijhar*)

67:13 (13)	be secret in your speech, or proclaim it

f) n.vb. (*jahr*)

4:148 (147)	God likes not the shouting of evil words
6:3 (3)	He knows your secrets, and what you publish
7:205 (204)	humbly and fearfully, not loud of voice
16:75 (77)	and he expends of it secretly and openly
21:110 (110)	surely He knows what is spoken aloud
49:2 (2)	as you are loud one to another
87:7 (7)	He knows what is spoken aloud and what is hidden

JAHRAH n.f. (adv)~openly, publicly, manifestly

2:55 (52)	we will not believe thee till we see God openly
4:153 (152)	show us God openly
6:47 (47)	if God's chastisement comes upon you, suddenly or openly

JĀHARA vb. (III)~(n.vb.) (adv) openly

f) n.vb. (*jihār*)

71:8 (7)	then indeed I called them openly

*J H Z

JIHĀZ n.m.~equipment, paraphernalia

12:59 (59)	when he had equipped them with their equipment
12:70 (70)	when he had equipped them with their equipment

JAHHAZA vb. (II)~to equip

a) perf. act.

12:59 (59)	when he had equipped them
12:70 (70)	when he had equipped them with

*J Ḥ D

JAḤADA vb. (I)~(with prep. *bi-*) to deny

a) perf. act.

11:59 (62)	they denied the signs of their Lord
27:14 (14)	and they denied them, though their souls acknowledged them

b) impf. act. (*yajḥadu*)

6:33 (33)	it is the signs of God that they deny
7:51 (49)	and that they denied Our signs
16:71 (73)	what, and do they deny God's blessing?
29:47 (46)	none denies Our signs but the unbelievers
29:49 (48)	none denies Our signs but the evildoers
31:32 (31)	none denies Our signs, except every ungrateful traitor
40:63 (65)	perverted are they who deny the signs of God
41:15 (14)	and they denied Our signs
41:28 (28)	for that they denied Our signs
46:26 (25)	and their hearts availed them nothing, since they denied the signs

*J Ḥ M

JAḤĪM n.f.~Hell; Blaze [Bl]

2:119 (113)	thou shalt not be questioned touching the inhabitants of Hell
5:10 (13)	they shall be the inhabitants of Hell
5:86 (88)	they are the inhabitants of Hell
9:113 (114)	it has become clear to them that they will be the inhabitants of Hell
22:51 (50)	they shall be the inhabitants of Hell
26:91 (91)	and Hell advanced for the perverse
37:23 (23)	and guide them unto the path of Hell
37:55 (53)	then he looks, and sees him in the midst of Hell
37:64 (62)	it is a tree that comes forth in the root of Hell
37:68 (66)	then their return is unto Hell
37:97 (95)	build him a building, and cast him into the furnace
37:163 (163)	except him who shall roast in Hell
40:7 (7)	and guard them against the chastisement of Hell
44:47 (47)	take him, and thrust him into the midst of Hell
44:56 (56)	He shall guard them against the chastisement of Hell
52:18 (18)	their Lord shall guard them against the chastisement of Hell
56:94 (94)	and the roasting in Hell
57:19 (18)	they are the inhabitants of Hell
69:31 (31)	and then roast him in Hell
73:12 (12)	for with Us there are fetters, and a furnace
79:36 (36)	and Hell is advanced for whoever sees
79:39 (39)	surely Hell shall be the refuge
81:12 (12)	when Hell shall be set blazing
82:14 (14)	and the libertines shall be in a fiery furnace
83:16 (16)	then they shall roast in Hell
102:6 (6)	you shall surely see Hell

*J L B

AJLABA vb. (IV)~to rally against, assault

c) impv. (*ajlib*)

17:64 (66)	rally against them thy horsemen and thy foot

*J L B B

JALĀBĪB n.m. (pl. of *jilbāb*)~veil

33:59 (59)	and the believing women, that they draw their veils

*J L D

JALADA vb. (I)~to scourge. (n.vb.) a flogging, stripe

c) impv. (*ijlid*)

24:2 (2)	scourge each one of them a hundred stripes
24:4 (4)	scourge them with eighty stripes

f) n.vb. (*jaldah*)

24:2 (2)	scourge each one of them a hundred stripes
24:4 (4)	scourge them with eighty stripes

JULŪD n.m. (pl. of *jild*)~skin, hide

4:56 (59)	as often as their skins are wholly burned
4:56 (59)	We shall give them in exchange other skins
16:80 (82)	He has appointed for you of the skins of the cattle
22:20 (21)	and their skins shall be melted
39:23 (24)	whereat shiver the skins of those who fear their Lord
39:23 (24)	their skins and their hearts soften to the remembrance of God
41:20 (19)	their eyes and their skins bear witness against them
41:21 (20)	and they will say to their skins
41:22 (21)	and your skins should not bear witness against you

*J L L

JALĀL n.m.~majesty [Ar]; glory [Ali, Bl]; might [Pk]; (*dhū al-jalāl*) Majestic (Divine attribute)

55:27 (27)	abides the Face of thy Lord, majestic
55:78 (78)	blessed be the Name of thy Lord, majestic

*J L S

MAJĀLIS n.m. (pl. of *majlis*)~assemblies

58:11 (12)	make room in the assemblies

*J L Y

JALĀʾ n.m.~dispersal, banishment

59:3 (3)	had God not prescribed dispersal for them

JĀLŪT n.prop.~Goliath

2:249 (250)	we have no power today against Goliath
2:250 (251)	when they went forth against Goliath and his hosts
2:251 (252)	they routed them, by the leave of God, and David slew Goliath

JALLÁ vb. (II)~to display, reveal

a) perf. act.

91:3 (3)	and by the day when it displays him

b) impf. act. (*yujallī*)

7:187 (186)	none shall reveal it at its proper time, but He

TAJALLÁ vb. (V)~to reveal oneself, to appear (in glory)

a) perf. act.

7:143 (139)	when his Lord revealed Him to the mountain
92:2 (2)	and the day in splendour

*J M ᶜ

JAMAʿA vb. (I)~to gather, amass, take or bring together. (n.vb.) amassing, gathering. (pcple. act.) one who gathers, Gatherer (Divine attribute); (adj) common. (pcple. pass.) gathered, assembled

a) perf. act.

3:25 (24)	when We gather them for a day whereon is no doubt
3:173 (167)	the people have gathered against you; therefore fear them'
6:35 (35)	He would have gathered them to the guidance
18:99 (99)	the Trumpet shall be blown, and We shall gather them together
20:60 (62)	Pharaoh then withdrew, and gathered his guile
70:18 (18)	who amassed and hoarded
77:38 (38)	We have joined you with the ancients
104:2 (2)	who has gathered riches and counted them over

b) impf. act. (*yajmaʿu*)

3:157 (151)	and mercy from God are a better thing than that you amass
4:23 (27)	and that you should take to you two sisters together
4:87 (89)	He will surely gather you to the Resurrection Day
5:109 (108)	the day when God shall gather the Messengers, and say
6:12 (12)	He will surely gather you to the Resurrection Day
10:58 (59)	it is better than that they amass
34:26 (25)	our Lord will bring us together
42:15 (14)	God shall bring us together
43:32 (31)	the mercy of thy Lord is better than that they amass
45:26 (25)	He shall gather you to the Day of Resurrection
64:9 (9)	the day when He shall gather you for the Day of Gathering
75:3 (3)	does man reckon We shall not gather his bones?

d) perf. pass. (*jumiʿa*)

26:38 (37)	so the sorcerers were assembled for the appointed time
75:9 (9)	and the sun and moon are brought together

f) n.vb. (*jamʿ*)

7:48 (46)	your amassing has not availed you
18:99 (99)	the Trumpet shall be blown, and We shall gather them <together>
42:7 (5)	that thou mayest warn of the Day of Gathering
42:29 (28)	He is able to gather them whenever He will
64:9 (9)	the day when He shall gather you for the Day of Gathering
75:17 (17)	ours it is to gather it, and to recite it

g) pcple. act. (*jāmiʿ*)

3:9 (7)	it is Thou that shall gather mankind for a day whereon is no doubt
4:140 (139)	God will gather the hypocrites and the unbelievers
24:62 (62)	and who, when they are with him upon a common matter

h) pcple. pass. (*majmū*ᶜ)

11:103 (105)	that is a day mankind are to be gathered to
56:50 (50)	shall be gathered to the appointed time of a known day

AJMAᶜŪN n.com. (pl. of *ajma*ᶜ)~all, altogether, entire, whole

2:161 (156)	and the angels, and of men altogether
3:87 (81)	and of the angels and of men, altogether
6:149 (150)	for had He willed, He would have guided you all
7:18 (17)	I shall assuredly fill Gehenna with all of you
7:124 (121)	then I shall crucify you all together
11:119 (120)	I shall assuredly fill Gehenna with jinn and men all together
12:93 (93)	then bring me your family all together
15:30 (30)	then the angels bowed themselves all together
15:39 (39)	and I shall pervert them, all together
15:43 (43)	Gehenna shall be their promised land all together
15:59 (59)	the folk of Lot; them we shall deliver all together
15:92 (92)	We shall surely question them all together
16:9 (9)	if He willed, He would have guided you all together
21:77 (77)	so We drowned them all together
26:49 (49)	then I shall crucify you all together
26:65 (65)	We delivered Moses and those with him all together
26:95 (95)	and the hosts of Iblis, all together
26:170 (170)	We delivered him and his people all together
27:51 (52)	We destroyed them and their people all together
32:13 (13)	I shall fill Gehenna with jinn and men all together
37:134 (134)	We delivered him and his people all together
38:73 (73)	then the angels bowed themselves all together
38:82 (83)	I shall pervert them all together
38:85 (85)	and with whosoever of them follows thee, all together
43:55 (55)	and We drowned them all together
44:40 (40)	the Day of Decision shall be their appointed time, all together

JAMᶜ n.m.~host, multitude

3:155 (149)	those of you who turned away the day the two hosts encountered
3:166 (160)	and what visited you, the day the two hosts encountered
8:41 (42)	the day of salvation, the day the two hosts encountered
26:61 (61)	when the two hosts sighted each other
28:78 (78)	generations of men stronger than he in might, and more numerous in multitude
54:45 (45)	certainly the host shall be routed, and turn their backs
100:5 (5)	cleaving there with a host

JAMĪᶜ n.m.~host, congregation; all, together, altogether

2:29 (27)	it is He who created for you all that is in the earth
2:38 (36)	get you down out of it, all together
2:148 (143)	God will bring you all together
2:165 (160)	the power altogether belongs to God
3:103 (98)	hold you fast to God's bond, together
4:71 (73)	move forward in companies, or move forward all together
4:139 (138)	but glory altogether belongs to God
4:140 (139)	God will gather the hypocrites and the unbelievers all in Gehenna
4:172 (171)	He will assuredly muster them to Him, all of them
5:17 (19)	Mary's son, and his mother, and all those who are on earth
5:32 (35)	shall be as if he had slain mankind altogether
5:32 (35)	shall be as if he had given life to mankind altogether

5:36 (40)	though they possessed all that is in the earth
5:48 (53)	unto God shall you return, all together
5:105 (104)	unto God shall you return, all together
6:22 (22)	the day when We shall muster them all together
6:128 (128)	on the day when He shall muster them all together
7:38 (36)	till, when they have all successively come there
7:158 (157)	O mankind, I am the Messenger of God to you all
8:37 (38)	one upon another, and so heap them up all together
8:63 (64)	hadst thou expended all that is in the earth
10:4 (4)	to Him shall you return, all together
10:28 (29)	and the day We shall muster them all
10:65 (66)	the glory belongs altogether to God
10:99 (99)	all of them, all together
11:55 (58)	so try your guile on me, all together
12:83 (83)	haply God will bring them all to me
13:18 (18)	if they possessed all that is in the earth
13:31 (30)	nay, but God's is the affair altogether
13:31 (30)	if God had willed, He would have guided men all together
13:42 (42)	but God's is the devising altogether
14:8 (8)	you and whoso is on earth, all together
14:21 (24)	they sally forth unto God, all together
17:103 (105)	We drowned him and those with him, all together
20:123 (121)	get you down, both of you together, out of it
24:31 (31)	turn all together to God, O you believers
24:61 (60)	there is no fault in you that you eat all together
26:56 (56)	and we are a host on our guard
34:40 (39)	upon the day when He shall muster them all together
35:10 (11)	the glory altogether belongs to God
36:32 (32)	they shall every one of them be arraigned before Us
36:53 (53)	then behold, they are all arraigned before Us
39:44 (45)	to God belongs intercession altogether
39:47 (48)	if the evildoers possessed all that is in the earth
39:53 (54)	surely God forgives sins altogether
39:67 (67)	the earth altogether shall be His handful
45:13 (12)	He has subjected to you what is in the heavens and what is in the earth
54:44 (44)	we are a congregation that shall be succoured
58:6 (7)	upon the day when God shall raise them up all together
58:18 (19)	upon the day when God shall raise them up all together
59:14 (14)	they will not fight against you all together
59:14 (14)	you think of them as a host
70:14 (14)	whosoever is in the earth, all together

JUMUᶜAH n.f.~congregation; (*yawm al-jumuᶜah*) Friday, the Day of Congregation; the day of the assembly [Bl]

62:9 (9)	when proclamation is made for prayer on the Day of Congregation

MAJMAᶜ n.m.~meeting, place of meeting

18:60 (59)	I will not give up until I reach the meeting of the two seas
18:61 (60)	when they reached their meeting, they forgot their fish

AJMAᶜA vb. (IV)~to agree, resolve, gather

a) perf. act.

12:15 (15)	when they went with him, and agreed to put him in the bottom of the well
12:102 (103)	thou wast not with them when they agreed upon their plan

c) impv. (*ajmiᶜ*)

10:71 (72) so resolve on your affair, with your associates
20:64 (67) so gather your guile; then come in battle-line

IJTAMAᶜA vb. (VIII)~to band together, be gathered together. (pcple. act.) assembling, gathering together

a) perf. act.

17:88 (90) if men and jinn banded together to produce the like of this Koran
22:73 (72) shall never create a fly, though they banded together to do it

g) pcple. act. (*mujtamiᶜ*)

26:39 (38) will you assemble?

*J M D

JAMADA vb. (I)~(pcple. act.) that which is fixed

g) pcple. act. (*jāmid*)

27:88 (90) thou shalt see the mountains, that thou supposest fixed

*J M Ḥ

JAMAḤA vb. (I)~to be refractory, turn about

b) impf. act. (*yajmaḥu*)

9:57 (57) they would turn about and bolt away to it

*J M L

JAMAL n.m.~camel

7:40 (38) until the camel passes through the eye of the needle
77:33 (33) sparks like to golden herds

JAMĀL n.m.~beauty

16:6 (6) and there is beauty in them for you

JAMĪL n.m. (adj)~sweet, comely, gracious, fair; kind, kindly

12:18 (18) but come, sweet patience
12:83 (83) but come, sweet patience
15:85 (85) so pardon thou, with a gracious pardoning
33:28 (28) I will make you provision, and set you free with kindliness
33:49 (48) make provision for them, and set them free with kindliness
70:5 (5) be thou patient with a sweet patience
73:10 (10) bear thou patiently what they say, and forsake them graciously

JUMLAH n.f.~(adv) all at once

25:32 (34) why has the Koran not been sent down upon him all at once?

*J M M

JAMM n.m. (adj)~ardent, abounding

89:20 (21)	and you love wealth with an ardent love

*J N B

JANABA vb. (I)~to cause to turn away from

c) impv. (*ujnub*)

14:35 (38)	turn me and my sons away from serving idols

JANB n.m. (pl. *junūb*)~side, flank; (*janb allāh*) duty to God [Ar]; (duty) towards God [Ali]; of God [Pk]

3:191 (188)	who remember God, standing and sitting and on their sides
4:36 (40)	and to the companion at your side
4:103 (104)	remember God, standing and sitting and on your sides
9:35 (35)	their foreheads and their sides and their backs shall be branded
10:12 (13)	when affliction visits a man, he calls Us on his side
22:36 (37)	when their flanks collapse, eat of them and feed the beggar
32:16 (16)	their sides shun their couches as they call on their Lord
39:56 (57)	alas for me, in that I neglected my duty to God

JĀNIB n.m.~side; (*jānib al-barr*) shore; (adv) aside

17:68 (70)	do you feel secure that He will not cause the shore to swallow you up
17:83 (85)	when We bless man, he turns away, and withdraws aside
19:52 (53)	We called to him from the right side of the Mount
20:80 (82)	We made covenant with you upon the right side of the Mount
28:29 (29)	he observed on the side of the Mount a fire
28:44 (44)	thou wast not upon the western side when We decreed to Moses
28:46 (46)	thou wast not upon the side of the Mount when We called
37:8 (8)	they are pelted from every side
41:51 (51)	when We bless man, he turns away and withdraws aside

JUNUB n.m.~stranger; (adj) defiled; (with prep. *ʿan*) from afar

4:36 (40)	and to the neighbour who is a stranger
4:43 (46)	when you are drunken ... or defiled
5:6 (9)	if you are defiled, purify yourselves
28:11 (10)	and she perceived him from afar

JANNABA vb. (II)~to remove, cause to turn aside

e) impf. pass. (*yujannabu*)

92:17 (17)	and from which the most godfearing shall be removed

TAJANNABA vb. (V)~to flout, turn away from

b) impf. act. (*yatajannabu*)

87:11 (11)	but the most wretched shall flout it

IJTANABA vb. (VIII)~to eschew, avoid

a) perf. act.

39:17 (19) those who eschew the serving of idols and turn penitent

b) impf. act. (*yajtanibu*)

4:31 (35) if you avoid the heinous sins that are forbidden you
42:37 (35) those who avoid the heinous sins and indecencies
53:32 (33) those who avoid the heinous sins and indecencies

c) impv. (*ijtanib*)

5:90 (92) so avoid it; haply so you will prosper
16:36 (38) serve you God, and eschew idols
22:30 (31) eschew the abomination of idols
22:30 (31) and eschew the speaking of falsehood
49:12 (12) O believers, eschew much suspicion

*J N D

JUND n.m. (pl. *junūd*)~host, legion, army, troops

2:249 (250) when Saul went forth with the hosts he said
2:249 (250) we have no power today against Goliath and his hosts
2:250 (251) when they went forth against Goliath and his hosts
9:26 (26) He sent down legions you did not see
9:40 (40) God sent down on him His Shechina, and confirmed him with legions
10:90 (90) and Pharaoh and his hosts followed them
19:75 (77) who is worse in place, and who is weaker in hosts
20:78 (81) Pharaoh followed them with his hosts
26:95 (95) and the hosts of Iblis, all together
27:17 (17) his hosts were mustered to Solomon
27:18 (18) enter your dwelling-places, lest Solomon and his hosts crush you
27:37 (37) we shall assuredly come against them with hosts
28:6 (5) and to show Pharaoh and Haman, and their hosts
28:8 (7) Pharaoh and Haman, and their hosts, were of the sinners
28:39 (39) he waxed proud in the land, he and his hosts
28:40 (40) We seized him and his hosts, and cast them into the sea
33:9 (9) remember God's blessing upon you when hosts came against you
33:9 (9) and We loosed against them a wind, and hosts you saw not
36:28 (27) We sent not down upon his people, after him, any host out of heaven
36:75 (75) they cannot help them, though they be hosts made ready
37:173 (173) and Our host — they are the victors
38:11 (10) a very host of parties is routed there
44:24 (23) leave the sea becalmed; they are a drowned host
48:4 (4) to God belong the hosts of the heavens and the earth
48:7 (7) to God belong the hosts of the heavens and the earth
51:40 (40) We seized him and his hosts, and We cast them into the sea
67:20 (20) who is this that shall be a host for you to help you
74:31 (34) none knows the hosts of thy Lord but He
85:17 (17) hast thou received the story of the hosts

*J N F

JANIFA vb. (I)~(n.vb.) a swerving from the right path, injustice

f) n.vb. (*janaf*)

2:182 (178) if any man fears injustice or sin

TAJĀNAFA vb. (VI)~(pcple. act.) inclining to sin

g) pcple. act. (*mutajānif*)

5:3 (5) whosoever is constrained in emptiness and not inclining purposely to sin

*J N Ḥ

JANAḤA vb. (I)~to incline

a) perf. act.

8:61 (63) and if they incline to peace

c) impv. (*ijnaḥ*)

8:61 (63) do thou incline to it; and put thy trust in God

JANĀḤ n.com. (pl. *ajniḥah*)~wing, arm-pit

6:38 (38)	no bird flying with its wings
15:88 (88)	do not sorrow for them, and lower thy wing unto the believers
17:24 (25)	and lower to them the wing of humbleness
20:22 (23)	now clasp thy hand to thy arm-pit
26:215 (215)	lower thy wing to those who follow thee
28:32 (32)	press to thee thy arm, that thou be not afraid
35:1 (1)	angels to be messengers having wings two, three and four

JUNĀḤ n.m.~fault [Ar, Bl]; sin [Pk]; blame [Ali]

2:158 (153)	it is no fault in him to circumambulate them
2:198 (194)	it is no fault in you, that you should seek bounty
2:229 (229)	it is no fault in them for her to redeem herself
2:230 (230)	it is no fault in them to return to each other
2:233 (233)	then it is no fault in them
2:233 (233)	it is no fault in you provide you hand over what you have given
2:234 (234)	then it is no fault in you what they may do
2:235 (235)	there is no fault in you touching the proposal to women you offer
2:236 (237)	there is no fault in you, if you divorce women
2:240 (241)	there is no fault in you what they may do with themselves
2:282 (282)	it shall be no fault in you if you do not write it down
4:23 (27)	if you have not yet been in to them it is no fault in you
4:24 (28)	it is no fault in you in your agreeing together
4:101 (102)	there is no fault in you that you shorten the prayer
4:102 (103)	there is no fault in you, if rain molests you
4:128 (127)	there is no fault in them if the couple set things right
5:93 (94)	there is no fault in those who believe and do deeds

24:29 (29)	there is no fault in you that you enter houses
24:58 (57)	there is no fault in you or them, apart from these
24:60 (59)	there is no fault in them that they put off their clothes
24:61 (60)	there is no fault in you that you eat all together
33:5 (5)	there is no fault in you if you make mistakes
33:51 (51)	if thou seekest any thou hast set aside there is no fault in thee
33:55 (55)	there is no fault in the Prophet's wives touching their fathers
60:10 (10)	there is no fault in you to marry them

*J N N

JANNA vb. (I)~to cover, outspread. (pcple. act.) jinn. (pcple. pass.) one possessed, mad

a) perf. act.

6:76 (76)	when night outspread over him he saw a star

g) pcple. act. (*jānn*)

15:27 (27)	the jinn created We before of fire flaming
55:15 (14)	He created the jinn of a smokeless fire
55:39 (39)	none shall be questioned about his sin, neither man nor jinn
55:56 (56)	untouched before them by any man or jinn
55:74 (74)	untouched before them by any man or jinn

h) pcple. pass. (*majnūn*)

15:6 (6)	thou art assuredly possessed
26:27 (26)	surely your Messenger who was sent to you is possessed
37:36 (35)	shall we forsake our gods for a poet possessed
44:14 (13)	a man tutored, possessed
51:39 (39)	a sorcerer, or a man possessed
51:52 (52)	a sorcerer, or a man possessed
52:29 (29)	thou art not a soothsayer neither possessed
54:9 (9)	a man possessed
68:2 (2)	thou art not, by the blessing of thy Lord, a man possessed
68:51 (51)	surely he is a man possessed
81:22 (22)	your companion is not possessed

AJINNAH n.m. (pl. of *janīn*)~a foetus, embryo, unborn child

53:32 (33)	and when you were yet unborn in your mothers' wombs

JĀNN n.m.~serpent

27:10 (10)	when he saw it quivering like a serpent he turned about
28:31 (31)	when he saw it quivering like a serpent, he turned about

JANNAH n.f.~garden; the Garden (of Eden), Paradise

2:25 (23)	for them await gardens underneath which rivers flow
2:35 (33)	Adam, dwell thou, and thy wife, in the Garden
2:82 (76)	those are the inhabitants of Paradise
2:111 (105)	none shall enter Paradise except that they be Jews or Christians
2:214 (210)	did you suppose you should enter Paradise
2:221 (221)	God calls unto Paradise, and pardon, by His leave

2:265 (267)	is as the likeness of a garden upon a hill
2:266 (268)	would any of you wish to have a garden of palms and vines
3:15 (13)	with their Lord are gardens underneath which rivers flow
3:133 (127)	to a garden whose breadth is as the heavens and earth
3:136 (130)	their recompense is forgiveness from their Lord, and gardens
3:142 (136)	did you suppose you should enter Paradise
3:185 (182)	whosoever is removed from the Fire and admitted to Paradise
3:195 (194)	I shall admit them to gardens underneath which rivers flow
3:198 (197)	for them shall be gardens underneath which rivers flow
4:13 (17)	He will admit him to gardens underneath which rivers flow
4:57 (60)	them We shall admit to gardens underneath which rivers flow
4:122 (121)	them We shall admit to gardens underneath which rivers flow
4:124 (123)	they shall enter Paradise, and not be wronged
5:12 (15)	I will admit you to gardens underneath which rivers flow
5:65 (70)	and admitted them to Gardens of Bliss
5:72 (76)	God shall prohibit him entrance to Paradise
5:85 (88)	God rewards them for what they say with gardens
5:119 (119)	for them await gardens underneath which rivers flow
6:99 (99)	gardens of vines, olives, pomegranates
6:141 (142)	it is He who produces gardens trellised, and untrellised
7:19 (18)	O Adam, dwell, thou and thy wife, in the Garden
7:22 (21)	so they took to stitching upon themselves leaves of the Garden
7:27 (26)	let not Satan tempt you as he brought your parents out of the Garden
7:40 (38)	nor shall they enter Paradise
7:42 (40)	those are the inhabitants of Paradise
7:43 (41)	this is your Paradise; you have been given it as your inheritance
7:44 (42)	the inhabitants of Paradise will call to the inhabitants of the Fire
7:46 (44)	who shall call to the inhabitants of Paradise
7:49 (47)	enter Paradise; no fear upon you
7:50 (48)	the inhabitants of the Fire shall call to the inhabitants of Paradise
9:21 (21)	for them await gardens wherein is lasting bliss
9:72 (73)	God has promised the believers, men and women, gardens
9:72 (73)	and goodly dwelling-places in the Gardens of Eden
9:89 (90)	God has prepared for them gardens underneath which rivers flow
9:100 (101)	and He has prepared for them gardens
9:111 (112)	their selves and their possessions against the gift of Paradise
10:9 (9)	beneath them rivers flowing in gardens of bliss
10:26 (27)	those are the inhabitants of Paradise
11:23 (25)	they shall be the inhabitants of Paradise
11:108 (110)	as for the happy, they shall be in Paradise
13:4 (4)	on the earth are tracts neighbouring each to each, and gardens of vines
13:23 (23)	Gardens of Eden which they shall enter
13:35 (35)	the likeness of Paradise, that is promised to the godfearing
14:23 (28)	they shall be admitted to gardens underneath which rivers flow
15:45 (45)	the godfearing shall be amidst gardens and fountains
16:31 (33)	Gardens of Eden they shall enter
16:32 (34)	enter Paradise for that you were doing
17:91 (93)	or till thou possessest a garden of palms and vines
18:31 (30)	those — theirs shall be Gardens of Eden
18:32 (31)	to one of them We assigned two gardens of vines
18:33 (31)	each of the two gardens yielded its produce
18:35 (33)	and he entered his garden, wronging himself
18:39 (37)	why, when thou wentest into thy garden, didst thou not say
18:40 (38)	it may be that my Lord will give me better than thy garden
18:107 (107)	the Gardens of Paradise shall be their hospitality

19:60 (61)	those — they shall enter Paradise
19:61 (62)	Gardens of Eden that the All-merciful promised His servants
19:63 (64)	that is Paradise which We shall give as an inheritance
20:76 (78)	Gardens of Eden, underneath which rivers flow
20:117 (115)	let him not expel you both from the Garden
20:121 (119)	they took to stitching upon themselves leaves of the Garden
22:14 (14)	God shall surely admit those who believe and do righteous deeds into gardens
22:23 (23)	God shall surely admit those who believe and do righteous deeds into gardens
22:56 (55)	they shall be in Gardens of Bliss
23:19 (19)	We produced for you therewith gardens of palms and vines
25:8 (9)	why is not a treasure thrown to him, or why has he not a Garden
25:10 (11)	better than that — gardens underneath which rivers flow
25:15 (16)	is that better, or the Garden of Eternity
25:24 (26)	the inhabitants of Paradise that day, better shall be their lodging
26:57 (57)	We expelled them from gardens and fountains
26:85 (85)	make me one of the inheritors of the Garden of Bliss
26:90 (90)	Paradise shall be brought forward for the godfearing
26:134 (134)	gardens and fountains
26:147 (147)	among gardens and fountains
29:58 (58)	We shall surely lodge them in lofty chambers of Paradise
31:8 (7)	there awaits them Gardens of Bliss
32:19 (19)	there await them the Gardens of the Refuge
34:15 (14)	there was a sign in their dwelling-place — two gardens
34:16 (15)	and We gave them, in exchange for their two gardens
34:16 (15)	two gardens bearing bitter produce and tamarisk-bushes
35:33 (30)	Gardens of Eden they shall enter
36:26 (25)	enter Paradise
36:34 (34)	We made therein gardens of palms and vines
36:55 (55)	the inhabitants of Paradise today are busy in their rejoicing
37:43 (42)	in the Gardens of Bliss
38:50 (50)	Gardens of Eden, whereof the gates are open to them
39:73 (73)	those that feared their Lord shall be driven in companies into Paradise
39:74 (74)	for us to make our dwelling wheresoever we will in Paradise
40:8 (8)	admit them to the Gardens of Eden that Thou hast promised
40:40 (43)	be it male or female, believing — those shall enter Paradise
41:30 (30)	fear not, neither sorrow; rejoice in Paradise
42:7 (5)	a party in Paradise, and a party in the Blaze
42:22 (21)	those who believe and do righteous deeds are in Meadows of the Gardens
43:70 (70)	enter Paradise, you and your wives, walking with joy
43:72 (72)	this is the Paradise that you have been given for an inheritance
44:25 (24)	they left how many gardens and foutains
44:52 (52)	among gardens and fountains
46:14 (13)	those are the inhabitants of Paradise
46:16 (15)	they are among the inhabitants of Paradise
47:6 (7)	and He will admit them to Paradise
47:12 (13)	God shall surely admit those who believe and do righteous deeds into gardens
47:15 (16)	this is the similitude of Paradise
48:5 (5)	He may admit the believers, men and women alike, into gardens
48:17 (17)	He will admit him into gardens underneath which rivers flow
50:9 (9)	and caused to grow thereby gardens and grain of harvest
50:31 (30)	and Paradise shall be brought forward to the godfearing
51:15 (15)	surely the godfearing shall be among gardens and fountains
52:17 (17)	surely the godfearing shall be in gardens and bliss
53:15 (15)	nigh which is the Garden of the Refuge
54:54 (54)	surely the godfearing shall dwell amid gardens and a river

55:46 (46)	but such as fears the Station of his Lord, for them shall be two gardens
55:54 (54)	the fruits of the gardens nigh to gather
55:62 (62)	and besides these shall be two gardens
56:12 (12)	in the Gardens of Delight
56:89 (88)	there shall be repose and ease, and a Garden of Delight
57:12 (12)	Gardens underneath which rivers flow, therein to dwell for ever
57:21 (21)	a Garden the breadth whereof is as the breadth of heaven and earth
58:22 (22)	He shall admit them into gardens underneath which rivers flow
59:20 (20)	not equal are the inhabitants of the Fire and the inhabitants of Paradise
59:20 (20)	the inhabitants of Paradise — they are the triumphant
61:12 (12)	He will forgive you your sins and admit you into gardens
61:12 (12)	and to dwelling-places goodly in Gardens of Eden
64:9 (9)	and admit him into gardens underneath which rivers flow
65:11 (11)	admit him to gardens underneath which rivers flow
66:8 (8)	and will admit you into gardens underneath which rivers flow
66:11 (11)	my Lord, build for me a house in Paradise, in Thy presence
68:17 (17)	Now We have tried them, even as We tried the owners of the garden when they swore
68:34 (34)	for the godfearing shall be Gardens of Bliss
69:22 (22)	in a lofty Garden
70:35 (35)	those shall be in Gardens, high-honoured
70:38 (38)	is every man of them eager to be admitted to a Garden of Bliss?
71:12 (11)	and will appoint for you gardens, and will appoint for you rivers
74:40 (42)	in Gardens they will question
76:12 (12)	and recompensed them for their patience with a Garden, and silk
78:16 (16)	and gardens luxuriant
79:41 (41)	surely Paradise shall be the refuge
81:13 (13)	when Paradise shall be brought nigh
85:11 (11)	for them await gardens underneath which rivers flow
88:10 (10)	in a sublime Garden
89:30 (30)	enter thou My Paradise
98:8 (7)	Gardens of Eden, underneath which rivers flow

JINN n.m. (coll)~jinn

6:100 (100)	yet they ascribe to God, as associates, the jinn
6:112 (112)	to every Prophet an enemy — Satans of men and jinn
6:128 (128)	company of jinn, you have made much of mankind
6:130 (130)	company of jinn and mankind, did not Messengers come to you
7:38 (36)	enter among nations that passed away before you, jinn and mankind, into the Fire
7:179 (178)	We have created for Gehenna many jinn and men
17:88 (90)	if men and jinn banded together to produce the like of this Koran
18:50 (48)	he was one of the jinn, and committed ungodliness
27:17 (17)	his hosts were mustered to Solomon, jinn, men and birds
27:39 (39)	an efreet of the jinns said
34:12 (11)	of the jinn, some worked before him
34:14 (13)	the jinn saw clearly that, had they only known the Unseen
34:41 (40)	nay rather, they were serving the jinn
41:25 (24)	concerning nations that passed away before them, men and jinn alike
41:29 (29)	show us those that led us astray, both jinn and men
46:18 (17)	concerning nations that passed away before them, men and jinn alike
46:29 (28)	We turned to thee a company of jinn giving ear to the Koran
51:56 (56)	I have not created jinn and mankind except to serve Me
55:33 (33)	O company of jinn and of men, if you are able
72:1 (1)	it has been revealed to me that a company of the jinn gave ear
72:5 (5)	we had thought that men and jinn would never speak against God a lie
72:6 (6)	certain men of mankind who would take refuge with certain men of the jinn

JINNAH (1) n.f.~jinn

11:119 (120)	I shall assuredly fill Gehenna with jinn
32:13 (13)	I shall fill Gehenna with jinn and men
37:158 (158)	they have set up a kinship between Him and the jinn
37:158 (158)	the jinn know that they shall be arraigned
114:6 (6)	of jinn and men

JINNAH (2) n.f.~madness; (with prep. *bi-*) bedevilled

7:184 (183)	no madness is in their comrade
23:25 (25)	he is naught but a man bedevilled
23:70 (72)	or do they say, 'He is bedevilled'?
34:8 (8)	has he forged against God a lie, or is he possessed?
34:46 (45)	no madness is in your comrade

JUNNAH n.f.~a covering, cloak

58:16 (17)	they have taken their oaths as a covering
63:2 (2)	they have taken their oaths as a covering

*J N Y

JANÁ n.m.~fruit

55:54 (54)	the fruits of the gardens nigh to gather

JANĪY n.m. (adj)~ripe

19:25 (25)	there shall come tumbling upon thee dates fresh and ripe

*J R ᶜ

TAJARRAᶜA vb. (V)~to gulp, sip

b) impf. act. (*yatajarraᶜu*)

14:17 (20)	the which he gulps, and can scarce swallow

*J R D

JARĀD n.com.~locusts, grasshoppers

7:133 (130)	We let loose upon them the flood and the locusts
54:7 (7)	they shall come forth from the tombs as if they were scattered grasshoppers

*J R F

JURUF n.m.~a crumbling bank (of a river)

9:109 (110)	who founded his building upon the brink of a crumbling bank

*J R Ḥ

JARAḤA vb. (I)~to work, do, commit

a) perf. act.

6:60 (60) and He knows what you work by day

JAWĀRIḤ n.f. (pl. of *jāriḥah*)~hunting creatures [Ar, Ali]; beasts and birds of prey [Pk, Bl]

5:4 (6) the good things are permitted you; and such hunting creatures as you teach

JURŪḤ n.m. (pl. of *juruḥ*)~a wound

5:45 (49) a tooth for a tooth, and for wounds retaliation

IJTARAḤA vb. (VIII)~to commit, seek to do

a) perf. act.

45:21 (20) do those who commit evil deeds think that We shall make them as those

*J R M

JARAMA vb. (I)~to drive one into, move, seduce

b) impf. act. (*yajrimu*)

5:2 (3) let not detestation for a people who barred you from the Holy Mosque move you to

5:8 (11) let not detestation for a people move you not to be equitable
11:89 (91) O my people, let not the breach with me move you

JARAM n.m.~sin; (*lā jaram*) without a doubt

11:22 (24) they without doubt will be the greatest losers
16:23 (24) without a doubt God knows what they keep secret
16:62 (64) without any doubt theirs shall be the Fire
16:109 (110) without a doubt, in the world to come they will be the losers
40:43 (46) no doubt that what you call me to has no call heard

AJRAMA vb. (IV)~to sin. (n.vb.) a sin, sinning. (pcple. act.) a sinner, a guilty one

a) perf. act.

6:124 (124) and humiliation in God's sight shall befall the sinners
30:47 (46) then We took vengeance upon those who sinned
34:25 (24) you will not be questioned concerning our sins
83:29 (29) Behold, the sinners were laughing at the believers

b) impf. act. (*yujrimu*)

11:35 (37) and I am quit of the sins you do

f) n.vb. (*ijrām*)

11:35 (37) if I have forged it, upon me falls my sin

g) pcple. act. (*mujrim*)

6:55 (55)	We distinguish Our signs, that the sinners' way may be manifest
6:123 (123)	We appointed in every city great ones among its sinners
6:147 (148)	His might will never be turned back from the people of the sinners
7:40 (38)	even so We recompense the sinners
7:84 (82)	behold thou, how was the end of the sinners
7:133 (130)	they waxed proud and were a sinful people
8:8 (8)	and prove untrue the untrue, though the sinners were averse to it
9:66 (67)	We will chastise another party for that they were sinners
10:13 (14)	so We recompense the people of the sinners
10:17 (18)	surely the sinners do not prosper
10:50 (51)	what part of it will the sinners seek to hasten?
10:75 (76)	they waxed proud, and were a sinful people
10:82 (82)	God verifies the truth by His words, though sinners be averse
11:52 (55)	turn not your backs as sinners
11:116 (118)	the evildoers followed the ease they were given to exult in and became sinners
12:110 (110)	Our might will never be turned back from the people of the sinners
14:49 (50)	thou shalt see the sinners that day coupled in fetters
15:12 (12)	even so We cause it to enter into the hearts of the sinners
15:58 (58)	We have been sent unto a people of sinners
18:49 (47)	thou wilt see the sinners fearful at what is in it
18:53 (51)	then the evildoers will see the Fire
19:86 (89)	and drive the evildoers into Gehenna herding
20:74 (76)	whosoever comes unto his Lord a sinner
20:102 (102)	We shall muster the sinners upon that day with eyes staring
25:22 (24)	no good tidings that day for the sinners
25:31 (33)	We have appointed to every Prophet an enemy among the sinners
26:99 (99)	it was naught but the sinners that led us astray
26:200 (200)	We have caused it to enter into the hearts of the sinners
27:69 (71)	journey in the land, then behold how was the end of the sinners
28:17 (16)	I will never be a partisan of the sinners
28:78 (78)	yet the sinners shall not be questioned concerning their sins
30:12 (11)	upon the day when the Hour is come, the sinners shall be confounded
30:55 (54)	upon the day when the Hour is come, the sinners shall swear
32:12 (12)	if thou couldst see the guilty hanging their heads
32:22 (22)	we shall take vengeance upon the sinners
34:32 (31)	nay, rather you were sinners
36:59 (59)	keep yourselves apart, you sinners, upon this day
37:34 (33)	even so We do with the sinners
43:74 (74)	the evildoers dwell forever in the chastisement of Gehenna
44:22 (21)	these are a sinful people
44:37 (37)	they were surely sinners
45:31 (30)	and you waxed proud, and were a sinful people
46:25 (24)	even so do We recompense the people of the sinners
51:32 (32)	we have been sent to a people of sinners
54:47 (47)	surely the sinners are in error and insanity
55:41 (41)	the sinners shall be known by their mark
55:43 (43)	this is Gehenna, that sinners cried lies to
68:35 (35)	shall we make those who have surrendered like to the sinners?
70:11 (11)	the sinner will wish that he might ransom himself
74:41 (42)	concerning the sinners
77:18 (18)	so We serve the sinners
77:46 (46)	eat and take your joy a little; you are sinners

*J R R

JARRA vb. (I)~to drag

b) impf. act. (*yajurru*)

7:150 (149)	and laid hold of his brother's head, dragging him to him

*J R Y

JARÁ vb. (I)~to run, flow. (pcple. act.) one that runs; a ship

a) perf. act.

10:22 (23)	the ships run with them with a fair breeze

b) impf. act. (*yajrī*)

2:25 (23)	gardens underneath which rivers flow
2:164 (159)	and the ship that runs in the sea with profit
2:266 (268)	a garden of palms and vines, with rivers flowing
3:15 (13)	gardens underneath which rivers flow
3:136 (130)	and gardens beneath which rivers flow
3:195 (194)	I shall admit them to gardens underneath which rivers flow
3:198 (197)	gardens underneath which rivers flow
4:13 (17)	to gardens underneath which rivers flow
4:57 (60)	gardens underneath which rivers flow
4:122 (121)	gardens underneath which rivers flow
5:12 (15)	gardens underneath which rivers flow
5:85 (88)	with gardens underneath which rivers flow
5:119 (119)	for them await gardens underneath which rivers flow
6:6 (6)	and made the rivers to flowbeneath them
7:43 (41)	and underneath them rivers flowing
9:72 (73)	gardens underneath which rivers flow
9:89 (90)	gardens underneath which rivers flow
9:100 (101)	gardens underneath which rivers flow
10:9 (9)	beneath them rivers flowing in gardens of bliss
11:42 (44)	so it ran with them amid waves like mountains
13:2 (2)	He subjected the sun and the moon, each one running to a term stated
13:35 (35)	beneath it rivers flow, its produce is eternal
14:23 (28)	to gardens underneath which rivers flow
14:32 (37)	He subjected to you the ships to run upon the sea
16:31 (33)	Gardens of Eden they shall enter, underneath which rivers flow
18:31 (30)	Gardens of Eden, underneath which rivers flow
20:76 (78)	Gardens of Eden, underneath which rivers flow
21:81 (81)	to Solomon the wind, strongly blowing, that ran at his command
22:14 (14)	gardens underneath which rivers flow
22:23 (23)	gardens underneath which rivers flow
22:65 (64)	and the ships to run upon the sea at His commandment
25:10 (11)	gardens underneath which rivers flow
29:58 (58)	chambers of Paradise, underneath which rivers flow
30:46 (45)	and that the ships may run at His commandment
31:29 (28)	the sun and the moon, each of them running to a stated term

31:31 (30)	hast thou not seen how that the ships run upon the sea
35:13 (14)	the sun and the moon, each of them running to a stated term
36:38 (38)	the sun — it runs to a fixed resting-place
38:36 (35)	We subjected to him the wind, that ran at his commandment
39:5 (7)	the sun and the moon, each of them running to a stated term
39:20 (21)	lofty chambers, underneath which rivers flow
43:51 (50)	do I not possess the kingdom of Egypt, and these rivers flowing beneath me?
45:12 (11)	the sea, that the ships may run on it at His commandment
47:12 (13)	gardens underneath which rivers flow
48:5 (5)	gardens underneath which rivers flow
48:17 (17)	gardens underneath which rivers flow
54:14 (14)	running before Our eyes — a recompense for him denied
55:50 (50)	therein two fountains of running water
57:12 (12)	the believers, men and women, their light running before them
58:22 (22)	gardens underneath which rivers flow
61:12 (12)	gardens underneath which rivers flow
64:9 (9)	gardens underneath which rivers flow
65:11 (11)	gardens underneath which rivers flow
66:8 (8)	gardens underneath which rivers flow
85:11 (11)	gardens underneath which rivers flow
98:8 (7)	Gardens of Eden, underneath which rivers flow

g) pcple. act. f. (*jāriyah*, pl. *jāriyāt* or *jawārī*)

42:32 (31)	and of His signs are the ships that run on the sea
51:3 (3)	and the smooth runners
55:24 (24)	His too are the ships that run
69:11 (11)	when the waters rose, We bore you in the running ship
81:16 (16)	the runners, the sinkers
88:12 (12)	therein a running fountain

MAJRÁ n.m.~a course (of a ship)

11:41 (43)	in God's Name shall be its course and its berthing

*J R Z

JURUZ n.m.~dry land, barren dust

18:8 (7)	We shall surely make all that is on it barren dust
32:27 (27)	have they not seen how We drive the water to the dry land

*J S D

JASAD n.m.~a body

7:148 (146)	of their ornaments a Calf — a mere body that lowed
20:88 (90)	then he brought out for them a Calf, a mere body that lowed
21:8 (8)	nor did We fashion them as bodies that ate not food
38:34 (33)	We tried Solomon, and We cast upon his throne a mere body

*J S M

JISM n.m. (pl. *ajsām*)~a body

2:247 (248)	and has increased him broadly in knowledge and body
63:4 (4)	when thou seest them, their bodies please thee

*J S S

TAJASSASA vb. (V)~to spy

b) impf. act. (*yatajassasu*)

49:12 (12)	do not spy, neither backbite one another

*J TH M

JATHAMA vb. (I)~(pcple. act.) one fallen prostrate

g) pcple. act. (*jāthim*)

7:78 (76)	morning found them in their habitation fallen prostrate
7:91 (89)	morning found them in their habitation fallen prostrate
11:67 (70)	morning found them in their habitations fallen prostrate
11:94 (97)	morning found them in their habitations fallen prostrate
29:37 (36)	morning found them in their habitation fallen prostrate

*J TH TH

IJTATHTHA vb. (VIII)~to uproot

d) perf. pass. (*ijtuththa*)

14:26 (31)	the likeness of a corrupt word is as a corrupt tree — uprooted

*J TH W

JATHĀ vb. (I)~(pcple. act.) one who hobbles on his knees, kneeling

g) pcple. act. (*jāthī*, pl. *jithīy*)

19:68 (69)	then We shall parade them about Gehenna hobbling on their knees
19:72 (73)	the evildoers We shall leave there, hobbling on their knees
45:28 (27)	thou shalt see every nation hobbling on their knees

*J W ᶜ

JĀᶜA vb. (I)~to hunger. (n.vb.) hunger

b) impf. act. (*yajūʿu*)

20:118 (116) it is assuredly given to thee neither to hunger therein, nor to go naked

f) n.vb. (*jūʿ*)

2:155 (150) We will try you with something of fear and hunger
16:112 (113) God let it taste the garment of hunger and of fear
88:7 (7) unfattening, unappeasing hunger
106:4 (3) [He] who has fed them against hunger

*J W B

JĀBA vb. (I)~to hollow, cleave

a) perf. act.

89:9 (8) Thamood, who hollowed the rocks in the valley

JAWĀB n.m.~an answer

7:82 (80) the only answer of his people was that they said
27:56 (57) the only answer of his people was that they said
29:24 (23) the only answer of his people was that they said
29:29 (28) the only answer of his people was that they said

AJĀBA vb. (IV)~to answer, give answer. (pcple. act.) one who answers; Answerer (Divine attribute)

a) perf. act.

28:65 (65) what answer gave you to the Envoys?

b) impf. act. (*yujību*)

2:186 (182) I am near to answer the call of the caller
14:44 (46) and we will answer Thy call, and follow
27:62 (63) He who answers the constrained, when he calls unto Him
46:32 (31) whosoever answers not God's summoner

c) impv. (*ajib*)

46:31 (30) O our people, answer God's summoner

d) perf. pass. (*ujība*)

5:109 (108) what answer were you given?
10:89 (89) your prayer is answered

g) pcple. act. (*mujīb*)

11:61 (64) my Lord is nigh, and answers prayer
37:75 (73) and how excellent were the Answerers

ISTAJĀBA vb. (X)~(with prep. *li-*) to answer, respond, hearken

a) perf. act.

3:172 (166) those who answered God and the Messenger
3:195 (193) and their Lord answers them
8:9 (9) when you were calling upon your Lord for succour, and He answered you
12:34 (34) so his Lord answered him, and He turned away from him their guile
13:18 (18) for those who answer their Lord, the reward most fair
14:22 (27) that I called you, and you answered me
21:76 (76) when he called before, and We answered him
21:84 (84) so We answered him, and removed the affliction
21:88 (88) We answered him, and delivered him out of grief
21:90 (90) so We answered him, and bestowed on him John
35:14 (15) if they heard, they would not answer you
42:38 (36) those who answer their Lord, and perform the prayer

b) impf. act. (*yastajību*)

2:186 (182) let them respond to Me, and let them believe in Me
6:36 (36) answer only will those who hear
7:194 (193) call them and let them answer you
11:14 (17) if they do not answer you
13:14 (15) those upon whom they call, apart from Him, answer them nothing
13:18 (18) those who answer Him not ... theirs shall be the evil reckoning
17:52 (54) on the day when He will call you, and you will answer praising Him
18:52 (50) then they shall call on them, but they will not answer them
28:50 (50) then if they do not answer thee
28:64 (64) they will call upon them, but they shall not answer them
40:60 (62) call upon Me and I will answer you
42:26 (25) He answers those who believe and do righteous deeds
46:5 (4) such a one as shall not answer him till the Day of Resurrection?

c) impv. (*istajib*)

8:24 (24) respond to God and the Messenger when He calls you
42:47 (46) answer your Lord, before there comes a day

d) perf. pass. (*istujība*)

42:16 (15) those who argue concerning God after that answer has been made to Him

*J W D

JIYĀD n.m. (pl. of *jawād*)~swift coursers, steeds

38:31 (30) in the evening were presented to him the standing steeds

JŪDĪ n.prop.~El-Judi (a name for Mount Ararat)

11:44 (46) and the Ark settled on El-Judi

*J W F

JAWF n.m.~a belly, interior, breast

33:4 (4)	God has not assigned to any man two hearts within his breast

*J W J

MA'JŪJ n.prop.~Magog

18:94 (93)	Gog and Magog are doing corruption
21:96 (96)	when Gog and Magog are unloosed

*J W R

JĀRA vb. (I)~(pcple. act.) one who turns aside, one who swerves

g) pcple. act. (*jā'ir*)

16:9 (9)	God's it is to show the way; and some do swerve from it

JĀR n.m.~a neighbour

4:36 (40)	and to the neighbour who is of kin
4:36 (40)	and to the neighbour who is a stranger
8:48 (50)	no man shall overcome you, for I shall be your neighbour

JĀWARA vb. (III)~to be or become a neighbour

b) impf. act. (*yujāwiru*)

33:60 (60)	then they will be thy neighbours there only a little

AJĀRA vb. (IV)~to protect, deliver (from punishment)

b) impf. act. (*yujīru*)

23:88 (90)	in whose hand is the dominion of everything, protecting and Himself unprotected
46:31 (30)	He will forgive you some of your sins, and protect you
67:28 (28)	then who will protect the unbelievers from a painful chastisement?
72:22 (22)	from God shall protect me not anyone

c) impv. (*ajir*)

9:6 (6)	grant him protection till he hears the words of God

e) impf. pass. (*yujāru*)

23:88 (90)	in whose hand is the dominion of everything, protecting and Himself unprotected

TAJĀWARA vb. (VI)~(pcple. act.) neighbouring, being near to one another *g*) pcple. act. (*mutajāwir*)

13:4 (4) on the earth are tracts neighbouring each to each

ISTAJĀRA vb. (X)~to seek protection

a) perf. act.

9:6 (6) if any of the idolaters seeks of thee protection

*J W S

JĀSA vb. (I)~to search, go through, explore

a) perf. act.

17:5 (5) men of great might, and they went through the habitations

*J W W

JAW n.m.~air, space, firmament

16:79 (81) have they not regarded the birds, that are subjected in the air of heaven?

*J W Z

JĀWAZA vb. (III)~to cross, pass on or over; (with prep. *bi-*) to bring over

a) perf. act.

2:249 (250) and when he crossed it, and those who believed with him
7:138 (134) We brought the Children of Israel over the sea
10:90 (90) We brought the Children of Israel over the sea
18:62 (61) when they had passed over, he said to his page

TAJĀWAZA vb. (VI)~to pass over

b) impf. act. (*yatajāwazu*)

46:16 (15) and We shall pass over their evil deeds

*J Y ʾ

JĀʾA vb. (I)~to come; to do, commit; (with prep. *bi-*) to bring, produce; (2:275) to receive [Ar]

a) perf. act.

2:71 (66) now thou hast brought the truth
2:87 (81) and whensoever there came to you a Messenger

2:89 (83)	when there came to them a Book from God
2:89 (83)	when there came to them that they recognized
2:92 (86)	Moses came to you with the clear signs
2:101 (95)	when there has come to them a Messenger from God
2:120 (114)	if thou followest their caprices, after the knowledge that has come to thee
2:145 (140)	if thou followest their caprices, after the knowledge that has come to thee
2:209 (205)	if you slip, after the clear signs have come to you
2:211 (207)	whoso changes God's blessing after it has come to him
2:213 (209)	after the clear signs had come to them
2:253 (254)	after the clear signs had come to them
2:275 (276)	whosoever receives an admonition from his Lord and gives over
3:19 (17)	except after the knowledge came to them
3:49 (43)	I have come to you with a sign from your Lord
3:50 (44)	I have come to you with a sign from your Lord
3:61 (54)	whoso disputes with thee concerning him, after the knowledge that has come to thee
3:81 (75)	then there shall come to you a Messenger
3:86 (80)	and the clear signs came to them
3:105 (101)	those who scattered and fell into variance after the clear signs came to them
3:183 (180)	Messengers have come to you before me bearing clear signs
3:184 (181)	Messengers before thee, who came bearing clear signs
4:41 (45)	when We bring forward from every nation a witness
4:41 (45)	and [when We] bring thee to witness against those
4:43 (46)	if any of you comes from the privy
4:62 (65)	then they come to thee swearing by God
4:64 (67)	if, when they wronged themselves, they had come to thee
4:83 (85)	when there comes to them a matter, be it of security or fear
4:90 (92)	or come to you with breasts constricted from fighting
4:153 (152)	to themselves the Calf, after the clear signs had come to them
4:170 (168)	the Messenger has now come to you with the truth
4:174 (174)	a proof has now come to you from your Lord
5:6 (9)	if any of you comes from the privy
5:15 (18)	People of the Book, now there has come to you Our Messenger
5:15 (18)	there has come to you from God a light
5:19 (22)	now there has come to you Our Messenger
5:19 (22)	there has not come to us any bearer of good tidings
5:19 (22)	there has come to you a bearer of good tidings and a warner
5:32 (36)	our Messengers have already come to them
5:42 (46)	if they come to thee, judge thou between them
5:48 (52)	do not follow their caprices, to forsake the truth that has come to thee
5:61 (66)	when they come to you, they say
5:70 (74)	whensoever there came to them a Messenger
5:84 (87)	should we not believe in God and the truth that has come to us
5:110 (110)	when thou camest unto them
6:5 (5)	they cried lies to the truth when it came to them
6:25 (25)	when they come to thee they dispute with thee
6:31 (31)	when the Hour comes to them suddenly they shall say
6:34 (34)	there has already come to thee some tiding of the Envoys
6:43 (43)	when Our might came upon them, they had been humble
6:54 (54)	when those who believe in Our signs come to thee
6:61 (61)	when any one of you is visited by death
6:91 (91)	who sent down the Book that Moses brought as a light
6:94 (94)	now you have come to Us one by one
6:104 (104)	clear proofs have come to you from your Lord
6:109 (109)	if a sign comes to them they will believe in it
6:109 (109)	what will make you realize that, when it comes
6:124 (124)	and when a sign came to them, they said
6:157 (158)	yet indeed a clear sign has come to you from your Lord

6:160 (161)	whoso brings a good deed shall have ten the like of it
6:160 (161)	and whoso brings an evil deed shall only be recompensed the like of it
7:4 (3)	Our might came upon it at night
7:5 (4)	and they but cried, when Our might came upon them
7:34 (32)	when their term comes they shall not put it back
7:37 (35)	when Our messengers come to them, to take them away
7:43 (41)	our Lord's Messengers came with the truth
7:52 (50)	We have brought to them a Book that We have well distinguished
7:53 (51)	our Lord's Messengers came with the truth
7:63 (61)	do you wonder that a reminder from your Lord should come to you
7:69 (67)	do you wonder that a reminder from your Lord should come to you
7:70 (68)	hast thou come to us that we may serve God alone
7:73 (71)	there has now come to you a clear sign from your Lord
7:85 (83)	there has now come to you a clear sign from your Lord
7:101 (99)	their Messengers came to them with the clear signs
7:105 (103)	I have brought a clear sign to you from your Lord
7:106 (103)	if thou hast brought a sign, produce it
7:113 (110)	and the sorcerers came to Pharaoh, saying
7:116 (113)	and called forth fear of them, and produced a mighty sorcery
7:126 (123)	we have believed in the signs of our Lord when they came to us
7:129 (126)	and after thou camest to us
7:131 (128)	so, when good came to them, they said
7:143 (139)	when Moses came to Our appointed time
8:19 (19)	victory has already come upon you
9:48 (48)	and turned things upside down for thee, until the truth came
9:90 (91)	the Bedouins came with their excuses, asking for leave
9:128 (129)	there has come to you a Messenger from among yourselves
10:13 (14)	when they did evil, and their Messengers came to them with the clear signs
10:22 (23)	there comes upon them a strong wind
10:22 (23)	and waves come on them from every side
10:47 (48)	when their Messenger comes, justly the issue is decided
10:49 (50)	when their term comes they shall not put it back
10:57 (58)	now there has come to you an admonition from your Lord
10:74 (75)	and they brought them the clear signs
10:76 (77)	when the truth came to them from Us, they said
10:77 (78)	do you say this to the truth, when it has come to you?
10:78 (79)	art thou come to us to turn us from that we found our fathers practising
10:80 (80)	when the sorcerers came, Moses said to them
10:81 (81)	what you have brought is sorcery
10:93 (93)	so they differed not until the knowledge came to them
10:94 (94)	the truth has come to thee from thy Lord
10:97 (97)	though every sign come to them, till they see
10:108 (108)	the truth has come to you from you Lord
11:12 (15)	a treasure not been sent down upon him, or an angel not come with him
11:40 (42)	when Our command came, and the Oven boiled
11:53 (56)	Hood, thou hast not brought us a clear sign
11:58 (61)	when Our command came, We delivered Hood
11:66 (69)	when Our command came, We delivered Salih
11:69 (72)	Our messengers came to Abraham with the good tidings
11:69 (72)	and presently he brought a roasted calf
11:74 (77)	when the awe departed from Abraham and the good tidings came to him
11:76 (78)	thy Lord's command has surely come
11:77 (79)	when Our messengers came to Lot
11:78 (80)	and his people came to him, running towards him
11:82 (84)	when Our command came, We turned it uppermost nethermost

11:94 (97)	when Our command came, We delivered Shuaib
11:101 (103)	when the command of thy Lord came; and they increased them not
11:120 (121)	in these there has come to thee the truth
12:16 (16)	they came to their father in the evening
12:18 (18)	they brought his shirt with false blood on it
12:19 (19)	then came travellers, and they sent one of them
12:50 (50)	when the messenger came to him, he said
12:58 (58)	the brethren of Joseph came, and entered unto him
12:72 (72)	whoever brings it shall receive a camel's load
12:73 (73)	you know well that we came not to work corruption in the land
12:88 (88)	We come with merchandise of scant worth
12:96 (96)	when the bearer of good tidings came to him
12:100 (101)	and again when He brought you out of the desert
12:110 (110)	Our help came to them and whosoever We willed was delivered
13:37 (37)	if thou dost follow their caprices, after the knowledge that has come to thee
14:9 (10)	their Messengers came to them with the clear signs
15:61 (61)	when the envoys came to the folk of Lot
15:63 (63)	we have brought thee that concerning which they were doubting
15:67 (67)	the people of the city came rejoicing
16:61 (63)	when their term is come they shall not put it back
16:89 (91)	We shall bring thee as a witness against those
16:113 (114)	there came indeed to them a Messenger from amongst them
17:5 (5)	when the promise of the first of these came to pass
17:7 (7)	when the promise of the second came to pass
17:81 (83)	the truth has come, and falsehood has vanished away
17:94 (96)	naught prevented men from believing when the guidance came to them
17:101 (103)	ask the Children of Israel when he came to them
17:104 (106)	when the promise of the world to come comes to pass
17:104 (106)	We shall bring you a rabble
18:48 (46)	you have come to Us, as We created you upon the first time
18:55 (53)	naught prevented men from believing when the guidance came unto them
18:71 (70)	thou hast indeed done a grievous thing
18:74 (73)	thou hast indeed done a horrible thing
18:98 (98)	when the promise of my Lord comes to pass
18:109 (109)	though We brought replenishment the like of it
19:27 (28)	Mary, thou hast surely committed a monstrous thing
19:43 (44)	father, there has come to me knowledge
19:89 (91)	you have indeed advanced something hideous
20:40 (42)	among the people of Midian thou didst sojourn, then camest hither
20:47 (49)	we have brought thee a sign from thy Lord
20:57 (59)	hast thou come, Moses
20:72 (75)	we will not prefer thee over the clear signs that have come to us
21:55 (56)	hast thou come to us with the truth
23:27 (27)	when Our command comes and the Oven boils
23:44 (46)	whenever its Messenger came to a nation they cried him lies
23:68 (70)	have they not pondered the saying, or came there upon them
23:70 (72)	nay, he has brought them the truth
23:99 (101)	when death comes to one of them, he says
24:11 (11)	those who came with the slander are a band of you
24:13 (13)	why did they not bring four witnesses against it?
24:39 (39)	when he comes to it, he finds it is nothing
25:4 (5)	so they have committed wrong and falsehood
25:29 (31)	He indeed led me astray from the Remembrance, after it had come to me
25:33 (35)	We bring thee the truth, and better in exposition
26:30 (29)	even though I brought thee something manifest

26:41 (40)	when the sorcerers came, they said to Pharaoh
26:206 (206)	then there comes on them that they were promised
27:8 (8)	when he came to it, he was called
27:13 (13)	when Our signs came to them visibly, they said
27:22 (22)	I have come from Sheba to thee with a sure tiding
27:36 (36)	but when he came to Solomon he said
27:42 (42)	when she came, it was said
27:84 (86)	when they are come, He shall say
27:89 (91)	whosoever comes with a good deed, he shall have better than it
27:90 (92)	whosoever comes with an evil deed
28:20 (19)	then came a man from the furthest part of the city
28:25 (25)	then came one of the two women to him
28:25 (25)	when he came to him and had related to him the story
28:36 (36)	when Moses came to them with Our signs
28:37 (37)	my Lord knows very well who comes with the guidance
28:48 (48)	when the truth came to them from Ourselves, they said
28:84 (84)	whoso brings a good deed shall have better than it
28:84 (84)	whoso brings an evil deed
28:85 (85)	my Lord knows very well who comes with guidance
29:10 (9)	then if help comes from thy Lord
29:31 (30)	when Our messengers came to Abraham with the good tidings
29:33 (32)	when that Our messengers came to Lot
29:39 (38)	Moses came to them with the clear signs
29:53 (53)	but for a stated term the chastisement would have come upon them
29:68 (68)	or cries lies to the truth when it comes to him
30:9 (8)	and their Messengers came to them with the clear signs
30:47 (46)	unto their people, and they brought them the clear signs
30:58 (58)	if thou bringest them a sign, those who are unbelievers will certainly say
33:9 (9)	remember God's blessing upon you when hosts came against you
33:10 (10)	when they came against you from above you
33:19 (19)	when fear comes upon them, thou seest them looking at thee
34:32 (31)	did we bar you from the guidance after it came to you?
34:43 (42)	the unbelievers say to the truth, when it has come to them
34:49 (48)	truth has come; falsehood originates not, nor brings again
35:25 (23)	their Messengers came to them with the clear signs
35:37 (34)	to you the warner came
35:42 (40)	that if a warner came to them, they would be more rightly guided
35:42 (40)	when a warner came to them, it increased them only in aversion
35:45 (45)	when their term is come — surely God sees His servants
36:13 (12)	the city, when the Envoys came to it
36:20 (19)	then came a man from the furthest part of the city
37:37 (36)	but he brought the truth, and confirmed the Envoys
37:84 (82)	when he came unto his Lord with a pure heart
38:4 (3)	they marvel that a warner has come to them from among them
39:32 (33)	and cries lies to the very truth, when it comes to him
39:33 (34)	he who has come with the very truth and confirms it
39:59 (60)	My signs did come to thee, but thou hast cried them lies
39:71 (71)	when they have come thither, then its gates will be opened
39:73 (73)	when they have come thither, and its gates are opened
40:25 (26)	when he brought them the truth from Us
40:28 (29)	he has brought you the clear signs from your Lord
40:29 (30)	who will help us against the might of God, if it comes upon us?
40:34 (36)	Joseph brought you the clear signs before
40:34 (36)	you continued in doubt concerning that he brought you
40:66 (68)	since the clear signs came to me from my Lord

40:78 (78)	when God's command comes, justly the issue shall be decided
40:83 (83)	when their Messengers brought them the clear signs
41:14 (13)	when the Messengers came unto them from before them
41:20 (19)	till when they are come to it
41:41 (41)	those who disbelieve in the Remembrance when it comes to them
42:14 (13)	they scattered not, save after knowledge had come to them
43:24 (23)	though I should bring you a better guidance than you found
43:29 (28)	until the truth came unto them, and a manifest Messenger
43:30 (29)	when the truth came to them, they said
43:38 (37)	till, when he comes to Us, he says
43:47 (46)	but when he brought them Our signs, lo, they laughed at them
43:53 (53)	or angels not come with him conjoined
43:63 (63)	when Jesus came with the clear signs he said
43:63 (63)	I have come to you with wisdom
43:78 (78)	We brought you the truth, but most of you were averse to the truth
44:13 (12)	how should they have the Reminder, seeing a clear Messenger already came to them
44:17 (16)	and a noble Messenger came unto them
45:17 (16)	they differed not, except after the knowledge had come to them
46:7 (6)	the unbelievers say to the truth when it has come to them
46:22 (21)	hast thou come to pervert us from our gods?
47:18 (20)	already its tokens have come
47:18 (20)	so, when it has come to them, how shall they have their Reminder?
49:6 (6)	if an ungodly man comes to you with a tiding
50:2 (2)	they marvel that a warner has come to them from among them
50:5 (5)	they cried lies to the truth when it came to them
50:19 (18)	death's agony comes in truth; that is what thou wast shunning
50:21 (20)	every soul shall come, and with it a driver and a witness
50:33 (32)	whosoever fears the All-merciful in the Unseen, and comes with a penitent heart
51:26 (26)	then he turned to his household and brought a fattened calf
53:23 (23)	and yet guidance has come to them from their Lord
54:4 (4)	there have come to them such tidings as contain a deterrent
54:41 (41)	the warnings came also to Pharaoh's folk
57:14 (13)	fancies deluded you, until God's commandment came
58:8 (9)	when they come to thee, they greet thee with a greeting
59:10 (10)	as for those who came after them, they say
60:1 (1)	though they have disbelieved in the truth that has come to you
60:10 (10)	when believing women come to you as emigrants, test them
60:12 (12)	when believing women come to thee, swearing fealty
61:6 (6)	when he brought them the clear signs, they said
63:1 (1)	when the hypocrites come to thee they say
63:11 (11)	God will never defer any soul when its term comes
67:9 (9)	yes indeed, a warner came to us; but we cried lies
69:9 (9)	the Subverted Cities — they committed error
71:4 (4)	God's term, when it comes, cannot be deferred
79:34 (34)	then, when the Great Catastrophe comes
80:2 (2)	that the blind man came to him
80:8 (8)	and he who comes to thee eagerly
80:33 (33)	and when the Blast shall sound
89:22 (23)	and thy Lord comes, and the angels rank on rank
98:4 (3)	those that were given the Book, excepting after the Clear Sign came to them
110:1 (1)	when comes the help of God, and victory

d) perf. pass. (*jīʾa*)

39:69 (69)	and the Prophets and witnesses shall be brought
89:23 (24)	and Gehenna is brought out, upon that day man will remember

AJĀʾA vb. (IV)~to cause to come, to drive [Pk, Ali, Bl]; to surprise [Ar]

a) perf. act.

19:23 (23) and the birthpangs surprised her by the trunk of the palm-tree

*J Y B

JAYB n.m. (pl. *juyūb*)~a bosom

24:31 (31) and let them cast their veils over their bosoms
27:12 (12) thrust thy hand in thy bosom and it will come forth white
28:32 (32) insert thy hand into thy bosom, and it will come forth white

*J Y D

JĪD n.m.~a neck

111:5 (5) upon her neck a rope of palm-fibre

*J Z ʾ

JUZʾ n.m.~a part, portion

2:260 (262) then set a part of them on every hill
15:44 (44) seven gates it has, and unto each gate a set portion
43:15 (14) they have assigned to Him a part of His own servants

*J Z ʿ

JAZIʿA vb. (I)~to be impatient, be unable to endure

a) perf. act.

14:21 (25) whether we cannot endure, or whether we are patient

JUZŪʿ n.m. (adj)~impatient

70:20 (20) when evil visits him, impatient

*J Z Y

JAZÁ vb. (I)~to recompense, give satisfaction [Ar, Bl]; award [Pk]; give requital [Ali]. (n.vb.) recompense [Ar, Bl], reward [Pk, Ali]. (pcple. act.) one who gives satisfaction for another

a) perf. act.

6:146 (147)	that We recompensed them for their insolence
23:111 (113)	now today I have recompensed them for their patient endurance
34:17 (16)	thus We recompensed them for their unbelief
76:12 (12)	and recompensed them for their patience with a Garden

b) impf. act. (*yajzī*)

2:48 (45)	beware of a day when no soul for another shall give satisfaction
2:123 (117)	beware a day when no soul for another shall give satisfaction
3:144 (138)	God will recompense the thankful
3:145 (139)	We will recompense the thankful
6:84 (84)	even so We recompense the good-doers
6:138 (139)	He will assuredly recompense them for what they were forging
6:139 (140)	He will assuredly recompense them for their describing
6:157 (158)	We shall surely recompense those who turn away from Our signs
7:40 (38)	even so We recompense the sinners
7:41 (39)	even so We recompense the evildoers
7:152 (151)	so We recompense those who are forgers
9:121 (122)	God may recompense them the best of what they were doing
10:4 (4)	He may recompense those who believe and do deeds of righteousness
10:13 (14)	so We recompense the people of the sinners
12:22 (22)	even so We recompense the good-doers
12:75 (75)	so we recompense the evildoers
12:88 (88)	God recompenses the charitable
14:51 (51)	that God may recompense every soul for its earnings
16:31 (33)	so God recompenses the godfearing
16:96 (98)	We shall recompense those who were patient their wage
16:97 (99)	We shall recompense them their wage
20:127 (127)	We recompense him who is prodigal and believes not in the signs
21:29 (30)	such a one We recompense with Gehenna
21:29 (30)	even so We recompense the evildoers
24:38 (38)	God may recompense them for their fairest works
28:14 (13)	even so do We recompense the good-doers
28:25 (25)	that he may recompense thee with the wage of thy drawing water for us
29:7 (6)	and shall recompense them the best of what they were doing
30:45 (44)	that He may recompense those who believe and do righteous deeds
31:33 (32)	and dread a day when no father shall give satisfaction for his child
33:24 (24)	that God may recompense the truthful ones for their truthfulness
34:4 (4)	that He may recompense those who believe, and do righteous deeds
35:36 (33)	even so We recompense every ungrateful one
37:80 (78)	even so We recompense the good-doers
37:105 (105)	even so We recompense the good-doers
37:110 (110)	even so We recompense the good-doers
37:121 (121)	even so We recompense the good-doers
37:131 (131)	even so We recompense the good-doers
39:35 (36)	and recompense them with the wages of the fairest of what they were doing
41:27 (27)	and shall recompense them with the worst of what they were working
45:14 (13)	that He may recompense a people for that they have been earning
46:25 (24)	even so do We recompense the people of the sinners
53:31 (32)	that He may recompense those who do evil for what they have done
53:31 (32)	and recompense those who have done good with the reward most fair
54:35 (35)	even so We recompense him who is thankful
77:44 (44)	even so do We recompense the good-doers

e) impf. pass. (*yujzá*)

4:123 (122)	whosoever does evil shall be recompensed for it
6:93 (93)	today you shall be recompensed with the chastisement
6:120 (120)	surely the earners of sin shall be recompensed
6:160 (161)	whoso brings an evil deed shall only be recompensed the like of it
7:147 (145)	shall they be recompensed, except according to the things they have done?
7:180 (179)	they shall assuredly be recompensed
10:52 (53)	are you recompensed for aught but that you have been earning?
20:15 (16)	that every soul may be recompensed for its labours
25:75 (75)	those shall be recompensed with the highest heaven
27:90 (92)	are you recompensed but for what you did?
28:84 (84)	those who have done evil deeds shall only be recompensed for that they were doing
34:33 (32)	shall they be recompensed except for what they were doing?
36:54 (54)	you shall not be recompensed, except according to what you have been doing
37:39 (38)	and not be recompensed, except according to what you were doing
40:17 (17)	today each soul shall be recompensed for that it has earned
40:40 (43)	whosoever does an evil deed shall be recompensed
45:22 (21)	every soul may be recompensed for what it has earned
45:28 (27)	today you shall be recompensed for that you were doing
46:20 (19)	today you shall be recompensed with the chastisement
52:16 (16)	you are only being recompensed for that you were working
53:41 (42)	then he shall be recompensed for it with the fullest recompense
66:7 (7)	you are only being recompensed for what you were doing
92:19 (19)	and confers no favour on any man for recompense

f) n.vb. (*jazā'*)

2:85 (79)	what shall be the recompense of those of you who do that
2:191 (187)	such is the recompense of unbelievers
3:87 (81)	their recompense is that there shall rest on them the curse
3:136 (130)	their recompense is forgiveness from their Lord
4:93 (95)	whoso slays a believer wilfully, his recompense is Gehenna
5:29 (32)	that is the recompense of the evildoers
5:33 (37)	this is the recompense of those who fight against God
5:38 (42)	cut off the hands of both, as a recompense for what they have earned
5:85 (88)	that is the recompense of the good-doers
5:95 (96)	whosoever of you slays it wilfully, there shall be recompense
9:26 (26)	that is the recompense of the unbelievers
9:82 (83)	let them laugh little, and weep much, in recompense
9:95 (96)	their refuge is Gehenna — a recompese for what they have been earning
10:27 (28)	the recompense of an evil deed shall be the like of it
12:25 (25)	what is the recompense of him who purposes evil against thy folk
12:74 (74)	what shall be its recompense if you are liars"'
12:75 (75)	this shall be its recompense
12:75 (75)	in whoever's saddlebag the goblet is found, he shall be its recompense
17:63 (65)	surely Gehenna shall be your recompense
17:63 (65)	an ample recompense!
17:98 (100)	that is their recompense because they disbelieved in Our signs
18:88 (87)	he shall receive as recompense the reward most fair
18:106 (106)	that is their recompense — Gehenna
20:76 (78)	that is the recompense of the self-purified
25:15 (16)	that is promised to the godfearing, and is their recompense and homecoming
32:17 (17)	no soul knows what comfort is laid up for them secretly, as a recompense
34:37 (36)	there awaits them the double recompense for that they did
39:34 (35)	that is the recompense of the good-doers

41:28 (28)	that is the recompense of God's enemies
41:28 (28)	wherein they shall have the Abode of Eternity as a recompense
42:40 (38)	and the recompense of evil is evil
46:14 (13)	therein dwelling forever, as a recompense for that they have been doing
53:41 (42)	he shall be recompensed for it with the fullest recompense
54:14 (14)	running before Our eyes — a recompense for him denied
55:60 (60)	shall the recompense of goodness be other than goodness?
56:24 (23)	a recompense for that they laboured
59:17 (17)	that is the recompense of the evildoers
76:9 (9)	we desire no recompense from you
76:22 (22)	this is a recompense for you, and your striving is thanked
78:26 (26)	for a suitable recompense
78:36 (36)	for a recompense from thy Lord, a gift, a reckoning
98:8 (7)	their recompense is with their Lord

g) pcple. act. (*jāzī*)

31:33 (32)	and no child shall give satisfaction for his father whatever

JIZYAH n.f.~a tribute

9:29 (29)	until they pay the tribute out of hand and have been humbled

JĀZĀ vb. (III)~to recompense

b) impf. act. (*yujāzī*)

34:17 (16)	do We ever recompense any but the unbeliever?

KĀF

*K ʾ S

KAʾS n.f.~a cup

37:45 (44)	a cup from a spring being passed round to them
52:23 (23)	while they pass therein a cup one to another
56:18 (18)	with goblets, and ewers, and a cup from a spring
76:5 (5)	surely the pious shall drink of a cup
76:17 (17)	they shall be given to drink a cup whose mixture is ginger
78:34 (34)	and a cup overflowing

*K ʿ B

KAʿB n.m.~an ankle

5:6 (8)	and wipe your heads, and your feet up to the ankles

KAʿBAH n.prop.~The Kaʿbah (In Mecca)

5:95 (96)	as shall be judged by two men of equity among you, an offering to reach the Kaaba
5:97 (98)	God has appointed the Kaaba, the Holy House

KAWĀʿIB n.f. (pl. of *kāʿib*)~well-developed, full-breasted, with swelling breasts [Ar, Bl]; *(kawāʿiba atrāban)* maidens for companions [Pk]; companions of equal age [Ali]

78:33 (33)	and maidens with swelling breasts, like of age

*K B B

KABBA vb. (I)~to thrust or throw

d) perf. pass. (*kubba*)

27:90 (92)	their faces shall be thrust into the Fire

AKABBA vb. (IV)~(pcple. act.) grovelling, prone

g) pcple. act. (*mukibb*)

67:22 (22)	is he who walks prone upon his face better guided

*K B K B

KABKABA vb. (quad I)~to throw down into, to pitch into

d) perf. pass. (*kubkiba*)

26:94 (94)	then they shall be pitched into it

KABĪR n.m. (adj; pl. *kubarāʾ*; comp. adj., m. *akbar*; f. *kubrá*)~great, large, big; grave, grievous, heinous (sin);

*K B D

KABAD n.m.~trouble

90:4 (4)	indeed, We created man in trouble

*K B R

KABIRA vb. (I)~to grow, be aged. (n.vb.) old age, being an old person

b) impf. act. (*yakbaru*)

4:6 (6)	ere they are grown

f) n.vb. (*kibar*)

2:266 (268)	then old age smites him, and he has seed
3:40 (35)	how shall I have a son, [when I have reached old age]
14:39 (41)	praise be to God, who has given me, though I am old
15:54 (54)	do you give me good tidings, though old age has smitten me?
17:23 (24)	be good to parents, whether one or both of them attains old age
19:8 (9)	I have attained to the declining of old age

KABURA vb. (I)~to be grievous, distressful, hateful, monstrous. (n.vb.) pride; greater part of something

a) perf. act.

6:35 (35)	if their turning away is distressful for thee
10:71 (72)	if my standing here is grievous to you
18:5 (4)	a monstrous word it is, issuing out of their mouths
40:35 (37)	very hateful is that in the sight of God
42:13 (11)	very hateful is that for the idolaters
61:3 (3)	very hateful is it to God

b) impf. act. (*yakburu*)

17:51 (53)	or some creation yet more monstrous in your minds

f) n.vb. (*kibr*)

24:11 (11)	whosoever of them took upon himself the greater part of it
40:56 (58)	in their breasts is only pride

KABĀʾIR n.f. (pl. of *kabīrah*)~heinous or grievous sins

4:31 (35)	if you avoid the heinous sins that are forbidden you
42:37 (35)	those who avoid the heinous sins and indecencies
53:32 (33)	those who avoid the heinous sins and indecencies

KABĪR n.m. (adj; pl. *kubarāʾ*; comp. adj., m. *akbar*; f. *kubrá*)~great, large, big; grave, grievous, heinous (sin); old, eldest (among others), aged; chief (among others), lord; Great, All-great (Divine attribute)

Divine attribute

4:34 (38)	God is All-high, All-great
13:9 (10)	the All-great, the All-exalted
22:62 (61)	for that God is the All-high, the All-great

31:30 (29)	for that God is the All-high, the All-great
34:23 (22)	He is the All-high, the All-great
40:12 (12)	judgment belongs to God, the All-high, the All-great

Other usages

2:45 (42)	seek you help in patience and prayer, for grievous it is
2:143 (138)	though it were a grave thing save for those whom God has guided
2:217 (214)	fighting in it is a heinous thing
2:217 (214)	that is more heinous in God's sight
2:217 (214)	and persecution is more heinous than slaying
2:219 (216)	in both is heinous sin, and uses for men
2:219 (216)	the sin in them is more heinous than the usefulness
2:282 (282)	be not loth to write it down, whether it be small or great
3:118 (114)	and what their breasts conceal is yet greater
4:2 (2)	that is a great crime
4:153 (152)	and they asked Moses for greater than that
6:19 (19)	what thing is greatest in testimony
6:78 (78)	this is my Lord; this is greater
6:123 (123)	We appointed in every city great ones among its sinners
8:73 (74)	there will be persecution in the land and great corruption
9:3 (3)	the day of the Greater Pilgrimage
9:72 (73)	goodly dwelling-places in the Gardens of Eden; and greater, God's good pleasure
9:121 (122)	nor do they expend any sum, small or great
10:61 (62)	neither is aught smaller than that, or greater
11:3 (3)	I fear for you the chastisement of a mighty day
11:11 (14)	for them awaits forgiveness and a mighty wage
12:78 (78)	he has a father, aged and great with years
12:80 (80)	said the eldest of them, Do you not know
16:41 (43)	and the wage of the world to come is greater
17:4 (4)	and you shall ascend exceeding high
17:9 (10)	theirs shall be a great wage
17:21 (22)	surely the world to come is greater in ranks
17:21 (22)	(greater) in ranks greater in preferment
17:31 (33)	the slaying of them is a grievous sin
17:43 (45)	high indeed be He exalted above that they say
17:60 (62)	it only increases them in great insolence
17:87 (89)	surely His favour to thee is great
18:49 (47)	it leaves nothing behind, small or great
20:23 (24)	We would show thee some of Our greatest signs
20:71 (74)	he is the chief of you, the same that taught you sorcery
21:58 (59)	he broke them into fragments, all but a great one they had
21:63 (64)	it was this great one of them that did it
21:103 (103)	the greatest terror shall not grieve them
25:19 (21)	We shall let him taste a great chastisement
25:21 (23)	waxed proud they have within them, and become greatly disdainful
25:52 (54)	obey not the unbelievers, but struggle with them thereby mightily
26:49 (48)	he is the chief of you, the same that taught you sorcery
28:23 (23)	and our father is passing old
29:45 (44)	God's remembrance is greater
32:21 (21)	We shall surely let them taste the nearer chastisement, before the greater
33:47 (46)	there awaits them with God great bounty
33:67 (67)	we obeyed our chiefs and great ones
33:68 (68)	give them chastisement twofold, and curse them with a mighty curse
34:3 (3)	neither is aught smaller than that, or greater
35:7 (8)	theirs shall be forgiveness and a great wage

35:32 (29)	that is the great bounty
39:26 (27)	the chastisement of the world to come is assuredly greater
40:10 (10)	God's hatred is greater than your hatred
40:57 (59)	the creation of the heavens and earth is greater
42:22 (21)	that is the great bounty
43:48 (47)	not a sign We showed them, but it was greater than its sister sign
44:16 (15)	upon the day when We shall assault most mightily
53:18 (18)	he saw one of the greatest signs of his Lord
54:53 (53)	everything, great and small, is inscribed
57:7 (7)	those of you who believe and expend shall have a mighty wage
67:9 (9)	you are only in great error'
67:12 (12)	there awaits them forgiveness and a great wage
68:33 (33)	the chastisement of the world to come is assuredly greater
74:35 (38)	surely it is one of the greatest things
76:20 (20)	when thou seest them then thou seest bliss and a great kingdom
79:20 (20)	so he showed him the great sign
79:34 (34)	then, when the Great Catastrophe comes
85:11 (11)	that is the great triumph
87:12 (12)	even he who shall roast in the Great Fire
88:24 (24)	God shall chastise him with the greatest chastisement

KIBRIYĀ' n.f.~domination [Ar]; majesty [Pk]; greatness [Ali]

10:78 (79)	and that the domination in the land might belong to you two
45:37 (36)	His is the Domination in the heavens and the earth

KUBBĀR n.m. (adj)~mighty, magnificent

71:22 (21)	and have devised a mighty device

KABBARA vb. (II)~to magnify [Ar, Pk, Bl]; to glorify [Ali]; (throughout in reference to God, usually by saying *Allāhu akbar*). (n.vb.) magnificat [Ar]; all magnificence [Pk]; greatness and glory [Ali]

b) impf. act. (*yukabbiru*)

2:185 (181)	[that you] magnify God that He has guided you
22:37 (38)	He has subjected them to you, that you may magnify God

c) impv. (*kabbir*)

17:111 (111)	and magnify Him with repeated magnificats
74:3 (3)	thy Lord magnify

f) n.vb. (*takbīr*)

17:111 (111)	and magnify Him <with repeated magnificats>

AKBARA vb. (IV)~to extol, admire

a) perf. act.

12:31 (31)	they so admired him that they cut their hands

TAKABBARA vb. (V)~to wax proud. (pcple. act.) one who is or waxes proud; All-sublime [Ar]; Superb [Pk]; Supreme [Ali]; Majestic [Bl] (Divine attribute)

b) impf. act. (*yatakabbaru*)

7:146 (143)	I shall turn from My signs those who wax proud

g) pcple. act. (*mutakabbir*)

16:29 (31) evil is the lodging of those that wax proud
39:60 (61) is there not in Gehenna a lodging for those that are proud?
39:72 (72) how evil is the lodging of those that are proud
40:27 (28) I take refuge in my Lord and your Lord from every man who is proud
40:35 (37) God sets a seal on every heart proud, arrogant.)
40:76 (76) how evil is the lodging of those that are proud
59:23 (23) the All-mighty, the All-compeller, the All-sublime

ISTAKBARA vb. (X)~to wax proud, become arrogant. (n.vb.) waxing proud. (pcple. act.) one who is or waxes proud a) perf. act.

2:34 (32) save Iblis; he refused, and waxed proud
2:87 (81) that your souls had not desire for, did you become arrogant
4:173 (172) as for them who disdain, and wax proud
7:36 (34) those that cry lies to Our signs, and wax proud against them
7:40 (38) those that cry lies to Our signs and wax proud against them
7:75 (73) the Council of those of his people who waxed proud
7:76 (74) said the ones who waxed proud
7:88 (86) said the Council of those of his people who waxed proud
7:133 (130) but they waxed proud and were a sinful people
10:75 (76) but they waxed proud, and were a sinful people
14:21 (24) then say the weak to those who waxed proud
23:46 (48) but they waxed proud, and they were a lofty people
25:21 (23) waxed proud they have within them, and become greatly disdainful
28:39 (39) he waxed proud in the land, he and his hosts
29:39 (38) they waxed proud in the earth, yet they outstripped Us not
34:31 (30) those that were abased will say to those that waxed proud
34:32 (31) those that waxed proud will say to those that were abased
34:33 (32) those that were abased will say to those that waxed proud
38:74 (74) save Iblis; he waxed proud, and was one of the unbelievers
38:75 (76) hast thou waxed proud, or art thou of the lofty ones?
39:59 (60) thou hast cried them lies, and thou hast waxed proud
40:47 (50) say unto those who waxed proud
40:48 (51) then those who waxed proud shall say
41:15 (14) as for Ad, they waxed proud in the earth without right
41:38 (38) and if they wax proud
45:31 (30) were not My signs recited to you, and you waxed proud
46:10 (9) and you wax proud, God guides not the people of the evildoers
71:7 (6) and persisted, and waxed very proud
74:23 (23) then he retreated, and waxed proud

b) impf. act. (*yastakbiru*)

4:172 (171) whosoever disdains to serve Him, and waxes proud
5:82 (85) some of them are priests and monks, and they wax not proud
6:93 (93) for what you said untruly about God, waxing proud against His signs
7:48 (46) your amassing has not availed you, neither your waxing proud
7:206 (205) those who are with thy Lord wax not too proud
16:49 (51) they have not waxed proud
21:19 (19) those who are with Him wax not too proud
32:15 (15) and proclaim the praise of their Lord, not waxing proud
37:35 (34) they were ever waxing proud
40:60 (62) those who wax too proud to do Me service shall enter Gehenna
46:20 (19) you waxed proud in the earth without right

f) n.vb. (*istikbār*)

35:43 (41) waxing proud in the land, and devising evil
71:7 (6) and persisted, and waxed <very> proud

g) pcple. act. (*mustakbir*)

16:22 (23) they who believe not in the world to come, their hearts deny, and they have waxed proud
16:23 (25) He loves not those that wax proud
23:67 (69) waxing proud against it, talking foolish talk by night
31:7 (6) when Our signs are recited to such a man he turns away, waxing proud
45:8 (7) who hears the signs of God being recited to him, then perseveres in waxing proud
63:5 (5) thou seest them turning their faces away, waxing proud

*K B T

KABATA vb. (I)~to frustrate

b) impf. act. (*yakbitu*)

3:127 (122) or frustrate them, so that they turned in their tracks

d) perf. pass. (*kubita*)

58:5 (6) those who oppose God and His Messenger shall be frustrated
58:5 (6) as those before them were frustrated

*K D Ḥ

KADAḤA vb. (I) (n.vb.)~labouring, (adv) laboriously. (pcple. act.) one who labours, labouring

f) n.vb. (*kadḥ*)

84:6 (6) thou art labouring unto thy Lord laboriously

g) pcple. act. (*kādiḥ*)

84:6 (6) thou art labouring unto thy Lord laboriously

*K D R

INKADARA vb. (VII)~to be thrown down, to fall

a) perf. act.

81:2 (2) when the stars shall be thrown down

*K D Y

KADÁ vb. (IV)~to be niggardly, give grudgingly

a) perf. act.

53:34 (35) and gives a little, and then grudgingly

*K DH B

KADHABA vb. (I)~to lie against, forge a lie, be a liar. (n.vb.) falsehood, a lie. (pcple. act.) one who lies against, who forges a falsehood, who denies (the Truth); a liar. (pcple. pass.) belied

a) perf. act.

6:24 (24) behold how they lie against themselves
9:90 (91) those who lied to God and His Messenger tarried
11:18 (21) those are they who lied against their Lord
12:27 (27) if it be that his shirt has been torn from behind, then she has lied
39:32 (33) who does greater evil than he who lies against God
39:60 (61) upon the Day of Resurrection thou shalt see those who lied against God
53:11 (11) His heart lies not of what he saw

b) impf. act. (*yakdhibu*)

2:10 (9) there awaits them a painful chastisement for that they have cried lies
9:77 (78) they failed God in that they promised Him and they were liars
36:15 (14) you are speaking only lies

d) perf. pass. (*kudhiba*)

12:110 (110) when the Messengers despaired, deeming they were counted liars

f) n.vb. (*kadhib*)

3:75 (69) they speak falsehood against God and that wittingly
3:78 (72) they speak falsehood against God, and that wittingly
3:94 (88) whoso forges falsehood against God after that
4:50 (53) consider how they forge falsehood against God
5:41 (45) the Jews who listen to falsehood, listen to other folk
5:42 (46) who listen to falsehood, and consume the unlawful
5:103 (102) the unbelievers forge against God falsehood
6:21 (21) who does greater evil than he who forges against God a lie
6:93 (93) who does greater evil than he who forges against God a lie
6:144 (145) who does greater evil than he who forges against God a lie
7:37 (35) who does greater evil than he who forges against God a lie
7:89 (87) we should have forged against God a lie
10:17 (18) who does greater evil than he who forges against God a lie
10:60 (61) what will they think, who forge falsehood against God
10:69 (70) those who forge against God falsehood shall not prosper
11:18 (21) who does greater evil than he who forges against God a lie?
12:18 (18) they brought his shirt with false blood on it
16:62 (64) and their tongues describe falsehood
16:105 (107) they only forge falsehood, who believe not in the signs of God

16:116 (117)	do not say, as to what your tongues falsely describe
16:116 (117)	so that you may forge against God falsehood
16:116 (117)	those who forge against God falsehood shall not prosper
18:5 (4)	they say nothing but a lie
18:15 (14)	who does greater evil than he who forges against God a lie?
20:61 (63)	O beware! Forge not a lie against God
23:38 (40)	he is naught but a man who has forged against God a lie
29:68 (68)	who does greater evil than he who forges against God a lie
34:8 (8)	has he forged against God a lie, or is he possessed?
40:28 (29)	if he is a liar, his lying is upon his own head
42:24 (23)	he has forged against God a lie?
58:14 (15)	they swear upon falsehood, and that wittingly
61:7 (7)	who does greater evil than he who forges against God falsehood
72:5 (5)	we had thought that men and jinn would never speak against God a lie

g) pcple. act. (*kādhib*)

3:61 (54)	and so lay God's curse upon the ones who lie
6:28 (28)	they are truly liars
7:66 (64)	we think that thou art one of the liars
9:42 (42)	God knows that they are truly liars
9:43 (43)	which of them spoke the truth, and thou knewest the liars
9:107 (108)	God testifies they are truly liars
11:27 (29)	rather we think you are liars
11:93 (96)	to whom will come the chastisement degrading him, and who is a liar
12:26 (26)	then she has spoken truly, and he is one of the liars
12:74 (74)	what shall be its recompense if you are liars"'
16:39 (41)	the unbelievers may know that they were truly liars
16:86 (88)	surely, you are truly liars
16:105 (107)	those — they are the liars
23:90 (92)	We brought them the truth, and they are truly liars
24:7 (7)	the curse of God shall be upon him, if he should be of the liars
24:8 (8)	if she testify by God four times that he is of the liars
24:13 (13)	in God's sight they are the liars
26:186 (186)	we think that thou art one of the liars
26:223 (223)	they give ear, but most of them are liars
27:27 (27)	or whether thou art amongst those that lie
28:38 (38)	I think that he is one of the liars
29:3 (2)	God knows those who speak truly, and assuredly He knows the liars
29:12 (11)	they are truly liars
37:152 (152)	they are truly liars
39:3 (5)	surely God guides not him who is a liar
40:28 (29)	if he is a liar, his lying is upon his own head
40:37 (39)	I think that he is a liar
56:2 (2)	and none denies its descending
58:18 (19)	surely, they are the liars
59:11 (11)	God bears witness that they are truly liars
63:1 (1)	God bears witness that the hypocrites are truly liars
96:16 (16)	a lying, sinful forelock

h) pcple. pass. (*makdhūb*)

11:65 (68)	that is a promise not to be belied

KADHDHĀB n.m. (adj)~a liar

38:4 (3)	this is a lying sorcerer
40:24 (25)	to Pharaoh, Haman and Korah; they said, A lying sorcerer

40:28 (29)	God guides not him who is prodigal and a liar
54:25 (25)	rather he is an impudent liar
54:26 (26)	they shall surely know tomorrow who is the impudent liar

KADHDHABA vb. (II)~to cry lies to [Ar]; deny [Pk]; belie [Ali]. (n.vb.1) crying a lie. (n.vb.2) a falsehood, lying, crying a lie. (pcple. act) one who cries lies [Ar]; who denies [Pk]; who rejects the Truth [Ali]

a) perf. act.

2:39 (37)	as for the unbelievers who cry lies to Our signs
2:87 (81)	and some cry lies to, and some slay
3:11 (9)	and the people before them, who cried lies to Our signs
3:184 (181)	if they cry lies to thee, lies were cried to Messengers before thee
5:10 (13)	the unbelievers, who cried lies to Our signs
5:70 (74)	some they cried lies to, and some they slew
5:86 (88)	those who disbelieve, and cry lies to Our signs
6:5 (5)	they cried lies to the truth when it came to them
6:21 (21)	he who forges against God a lie, or cries lies to His signs
6:31 (31)	lost indeed are they that cried lies to the encounter with God
6:39 (39)	those who cry lies to Our signs are deaf and dumb
6:49 (49)	those who cry lies to Our signs, them the chastisement shall visit
6:57 (57)	I stand upon a clear sign from my Lord, and you have cried lies to it
6:66 (66)	thy people have cried it lies
6:147 (148)	so, if they cry thee lies, say
6:148 (149)	even so the people before them cried lies
6:150 (151)	do not thou follow the caprices of those who cried lies to Our signs
6:157 (158)	he who cries lies to God's signs
7:36 (34)	those that cry lies to Our signs
7:37 (35)	he who forges against God a lie, or cries lies to His signs
7:40 (38)	those that cry lies to Our signs
7:64 (62)	but they cried him lies; so We delivered him
7:64 (62)	We drowned those who cried lies to Our signs
7:72 (70)	We cut off the last remnant of those who cried lies to Our signs
7:92 (90)	those who cried lies to Shuaib, as if never they dwelt there
7:92 (90)	those who cried lies to Shuaib, they were the losers
7:96 (94)	but they cried lies, and so We seized them
7:101 (99)	they were not the ones to believe in that they had cried lies before
7:136 (132)	they cried lies to Our signs and heeded them not
7:146 (144)	because they have cried lies to Our signs
7:147 (145)	those who cry lies to Our signs, and the encounter in the world to come
7:176 (175)	that is that people's likeness who cried lies to Our signs
7:177 (176)	the likeness of the people who cried lies to Our signs
7:182 (181)	those who cry lies to Our signs We will draw them on little by little
8:54 (56)	and the people before him, who cried lies to the signs
10:17 (18)	he who forges against God a lie, or cries lies to His signs
10:39 (40)	they have cried lies to that whereof they comprehended not the knowledge
10:39 (40)	those that were before them cried lies
10:41 (42)	if they cry lies to thee, then do thou say
10:45 (46)	lost will be those who cried lies to the encounter with God
10:73 (74)	but they cried him lies; so We delivered him
10:73 (74)	We drowned those who cried lies to Our signs
10:74 (75)	they were not men to believe in that they had cried lies to before
10:95 (95)	nor be of those who cry lies to God's signs
15:80 (80)	the dwellers in El-Hijr cried lies to the Envoys
16:113 (114)	but they cried him lies

17:59 (61)	but that the ancients cried lies to them
20:48 (50)	chastisement shall light upon him who cries lies and turns his back'
20:56 (58)	We showed Pharaoh all Our signs, but he cried lies
21:77 (77)	We helped him against the people who cried lies to Our signs
22:42 (43)	the people of Noah cried lies
22:57 (56)	as for the unbelievers, who cried lies to Our signs
23:26 (26)	O my Lord, help me, for that they cry me lies
23:33 (34)	of his people, who cried lies to the encounter of the world to come
23:39 (41)	O my Lord, help me, for that they cry me lies
23:44 (46)	whenever its Messenger came to a nation they cried him lies
23:48 (50)	so they cried them lies, and they were among the destroyed
25:11 (12)	nay, but they cry lies to the Hour
25:11 (12)	We have prepared for him who cries lies to the Hour a Blaze
25:19 (20)	so they cried you lies touching the things you say
25:36 (38)	go to the people who have cried lies to Our signs'
25:37 (39)	the people of Noah, when they cried lies to the Messengers
25:77 (77)	for you have cried lies, and it shall surely be fastened
26:6 (5)	so they have cried lies
26:105 (105)	the people of Noah cried lies to the Envoys
26:117 (117)	my Lord, my people have cried me lies
26:123 (123)	Ad cried lies to the Envoys
26:139 (139)	so they cried him lies; then We destroyed them
26:141 (141)	Thamood cried lies to the Envoys
26:160 (160)	the people of Lot cried lies to the Envoys
26:176 (176)	the men of the Thicket cried lies to the Envoys
26:189 (189)	but they cried him lies; then there seized them the chastisement
27:84 (86)	did you cry lies to My signs, not comprehending them
29:18 (17)	if you cry me lies, nations cried lies before you
29:37 (36)	they cried lies to him; so the earthquake seized them
29:68 (68)	he who forges against God a lie, or cries lies to the truth
30:10 (9)	they cried lies to the signs of God and mocked at them
30:16 (15)	as for those who disbelieved, and cried lies to Our signs
34:45 (44)	those that were before them also cried lies
34:45 (44)	they cried lies to My Messengers, and how was My horror
35:25 (23)	if they cry thee lies, those before them also cried lies
36:14 (13)	We sent unto them two men, but they cried them lies
37:127 (127)	they cried him lies; so they will be among the arraigned
38:12 (11)	cried lies before them the people of Noah
38:14 (13)	not one, that cried not lies to the Messengers
39:25 (26)	those that were before them cried lies
39:32 (33)	he who lies against God and cries lies to the very truth
39:59 (60)	My signs did come to thee, but thou hast cried them lies
40:5 (5)	the people of Noah before them also cried lies
40:70 (72)	those who cry lies to the Book
50:5 (5)	they cried lies to the truth when it came to them
50:12 (12)	cried lies before them the people of Noah
50:14 (13)	every one cried lies to the Messengers
54:3 (3)	they have cried lies, and followed their caprices
54:9 (9)	the people of Noah cried lies before them
54:9 (9)	they cried lies to Our servant, and said
54:18 (18)	Ad cried lies
54:23 (23)	Thamood cried lies to the warnings
54:33 (33)	the people of Lot cried lies to the warnings
54:42 (42)	they cried lies to Our signs, all of them
57:19 (18)	the unbelievers, who have cried lies to Our signs

62:5 (5)	evil is the likeness of the people who have cried lies to God's signs
64:10 (10)	those who disbelieved and cried lies to Our signs
67:9 (9)	but we cried lies, saying, 'God has not sent down anything'
67:18 (18)	those that were before them also cried lies
69:4 (4)	Thamood and Ad cried lies to the Clatterer
75:32 (32)	but he cried it lies, and he turned away
78:28 (28)	and they cried loud lies to Our signs
79:21 (21)	but he cried lies, and rebelled
91:11 (11)	Thamood cried lies in their insolence
91:14 (14)	but they cried him lies, and hamstrung her
92:9 (9)	and cries lies to the reward most fair
92:16 (16)	even he who cried lies, and turned away
96:13 (13)	what thinkest thou? If he cries lies, and turns away

b) impf. act. (*yukadhdhibu*)

6:27 (27)	and then not cry lies to the signs of our Lord
6:33 (33)	it is not thee they cry lies to, but the evildoers
22:42 (43)	if they cry lies to thee, so too before them the people of Noah cried lies
23:105 (107)	were My signs not recited to you, and you cried them lies
26:12 (11)	my Lord, I fear they will cry me lies
27:83 (85)	a troop of those that cried lies to Our signs
28:34 (34)	I fear they will cry me lies
29:18 (17)	if you cry me lies, nations cried lies before you
32:20 (20)	taste the chastisement of the Fire, which you cried lies to
34:42 (41)	taste the chastisement of the Fire, which you cried lies to
35:4 (4)	if they cry lies to thee, Messengers before thee were cried lies to
35:25 (23)	if they cry thee lies, those before them also cried lies
37:21 (21)	this is the Day of Decision, even that you cried lies to
52:14 (14)	this is the fire that you cried lies to
55:13 (12)	O which of your Lord's bounties will you and you deny?
55:16 (15)	O which of your Lord's bounties will you and you deny?
55:18 (18)	O which of your Lord's bounties will you and you deny?
55:21 (21)	O which of your Lord's bounties will you and you deny?
55:23 (23)	O which of your Lord's bounties will you and you deny?
55:25 (25)	O which of your Lord's bounties will you and you deny?
55:28 (28)	O which of your Lord's bounties will you and you deny?
55:30 (30)	O which of your Lord's bounties will you and you deny?
55:32 (32)	O which of your Lord's bounties will you and you deny?
55:34 (34)	O which of your Lord's bounties will you and you deny?
55:36 (36)	O which of your Lord's bounties will you and you deny?
55:38 (38)	O which of your Lord's bounties will you and you deny?
55:40 (40)	O which of your Lord's bounties will you and you deny?
55:42 (42)	O which of your Lord's bounties will you and you deny?
55:43 (43)	this is Gehenna, that sinners cried lies to
55:45 (45)	O which of your Lord's bounties will you and you deny?
55:47 (47)	O which of your Lord's bounties will you and you deny?
55:49 (49)	O which of your Lord's bounties will you and you deny?
55:51 (51)	O which of your Lord's bounties will you and you deny?
55:53 (53)	O which of your Lord's bounties will you and you deny?
55:55 (55)	O which of your Lord's bounties will you and you deny?
55:57 (57)	O which of your Lord's bounties will you and you deny?
55:59 (59)	O which of your Lord's bounties will you and you deny?
55:61 (61)	O which of your Lord's bounties will you and you deny?
55:63 (63)	O which of your Lord's bounties will you and you deny?
55:65 (65)	O which of your Lord's bounties will you and you deny?

55:67 (67)	O which of your Lord's bounties will you and you deny?
55:69 (69)	O which of your Lord's bounties will you and you deny?
55:71 (71)	O which of your Lord's bounties will you and you deny?
55:73 (73)	O which of your Lord's bounties will you and you deny?
55:75 (75)	O which of your Lord's bounties will you and you deny?
55:77 (77)	O which of your Lord's bounties will you and you deny?
56:82 (81)	do you make it your living to cry lies?
68:44 (44)	leave Me with him who cries lies to this discourse
74:46 (47)	and we cried lies to the Day of Doom
77:29 (29)	depart to that you cried was lies
82:9 (9)	no indeed; but you cry lies to the Doom
83:11 (11)	who cry lies to the Day of Doom
83:12 (12)	none cries lies to it but every guilty aggressor
83:17 (17)	this is that you cried lies to
84:22 (22)	nay, but the unbelievers are crying lies
95:7 (7)	what then shall cry thee lies as to the Doom?
107:1 (1)	hast thou seen him who cries lies to the Doom?

d) perf. pass. (*kudhdhiba*)

3:184 (181)	if they cry lies to thee, lies were cried to Messengers before thee
6:34 (34)	Messengers indeed were cried lies to before thee
6:34 (34)	they endured patiently that they were cried lies to
22:44 (43)	to Moses also they cried lies
35:4 (4)	if they cry lies to thee, Messengers before thee were cried lies to

f) n.vb. (1) (*takdhīb*)

85:19 (19)	nay, but the unbelievers still cry lies

f) n.vb. (2) (*kidhdhāb*)

78:28 (28)	and they cried loud lies to Our signs <...>
78:35 (35)	therein they shall hear no idle talk, no cry of lies

g) pcple. act. (*mukadhdhib*)

3:137 (131)	behold how was the end of those that cried lies
6:11 (11)	then behold how was the end of them that cried lies
16:36 (38)	behold how was the end of them that cried lies
43:25 (24)	behold how was the end of them that cried lies
52:11 (11)	woe that day unto those that cry lies
56:51 (51)	then you erring ones, you that cried lies
56:92 (91)	if he be of them that cried lies
68:8 (8)	obey thou not those who cry lies
69:49 (49)	We know that some of you will cry lies
73:11 (11)	leave Me to those who cry lies
77:15 (15)	woe that day unto those who cry it lies
77:19 (19)	woe that day unto those who cry it lies
77:24 (24)	woe that day unto those who cry it lies
77:28 (28)	woe that day unto those who cry it lies
77:34 (34)	woe that day unto those who cry it lies
77:37 (37)	woe that day unto those who cry it lies
77:40 (40)	woe that day unto those who cry it lies
77:45 (45)	woe that day unto those who cry it lies
77:47 (47)	woe that day unto those who cry it lies
77:49 (49)	woe that day unto those who cry it lies
83:10 (10)	woe that day unto those who cry it lies

*K F ʾ

KUFUʾ n.m.~equal, comparable

112:4 (4)	and equal to Him is not any one

*K F F

KAFFA vb. (I)~to restrain, withhold

a) perf. act.

5:11 (14)	and He restrained their hands from you
5:110 (110)	when I restrained from thee the Children of Israel
48:20 (20)	and has restrained the hands of men from you
48:24 (24)	He who restrained their hands from you

b) impf. act. (*yakuffu*)

4:84 (86)	haply God will restrain the unbelievers' might
4:91 (93)	if they withdraw not from you, and offer you peace, and restrain their hands
21:39 (40)	they shall not ward off the Fire from their faces

c) impv. (*kuff*)

4:77 (79)	restrain your hands, and perform the prayer

KAFF n.f.~a hand

13:14 (15)	it is as a man who stretches out his hands to water
18:42 (40)	in the morning he was wringing his hands for that he had expended

KĀFFAH n.f. (adj. and adv)~all, entire; totally, entirely

2:208 (204)	O believers, enter the peace, all of you
9:36 (36)	and fight the unbelievers totally
9:36 (36)	even as they fight you totally
9:122 (123)	it is not for the believers to go forth totally
34:28 (27)	We have sent thee not, except to mankind entire

*K F L

KAFALA vb. (I)~to take charge of

b) impf. act. (*yakfulu*)

3:44 (39)	which of them should have charge of Mary
20:40 (41)	shall I point you to one to have charge of him?
28:12 (11)	the people of a household who will take charge of him for you

KAFĪL n.m.~a surety, bail

16:91 (93)	after they have been confirmed, and you have made God your surety

KIFL n.m.~a like part, portion

4:85 (87)	whosoever intercedes with a bad intercession, he shall receive the like of it
57:28 (28)	He will give you a twofold portion of His mercy

DHŪ AL-KIFL n.prop.~Dhul Kifl (a Prophet who is identified with one of several Biblical names, Ezekiel and Elijah in particular)

21:85 (85)	Idris, Dhul Kifl — each was of the patient
38:48 (48)	remember also Our servants Ishmael, Elisha, and Dhul Kifl

KAFFALA vb. (II)~to take charge of

a) perf. act.

3:37 (32)	by His goodness she grew up comely, Zachariah taking charge of her

AKFALA vb. (IV)~to place into one's charge, to make one responsible for

c) impv. (*akfil*)

38:23 (22)	give her into my charge

*K F R

KAFARA vb. (I)~to disbelieve, to be thankless, unthankful, ungrateful; to disown, deny; (*alladhīna kafarū*) those who disbelieve, the unbelievers. (n.vb.1) unbelief, disbelief; rejection [Pk]; faithlessness [Ali]. (n.vb.2) unbelief, disbelief. (pcple. act.) unbeliever; (57:20) unbelievers [Ar, Bl]; husbandman [Pk]; tillers [Ali]

a) perf. act.

2:6 (5)	as for the unbelievers, alike it is to them whether thou hast warned them
2:26 (24)	as for unbelievers, they say, 'What did God desireby this'
2:39 (37)	as for the unbelievers who cry lies to Our signs
2:89 (83)	they aforetimes prayed for victory over the unbelievers
2:89 (83)	and the curse of God is on the unbelievers
2:102 (96)	Solomon disbelieved not
2:102 (96)	but the Satans disbelieved, teaching the people sorcery
2:105 (99)	those unbelievers of the People of the Book and the idolaters
2:126 (120)	whoso disbelieves, to him I shall give enjoyment a little
2:161 (156)	but those who disbelieve, and die disbelieving
2:171 (166)	the likeness of those who disbelieve is as the likeness of one who shouts
2:212 (208)	decked out fair to the unbelievers is the present life
2:253 (254)	some of them believed, and some disbelieved
2:257 (259)	the unbelievers — their protectors are idols
2:258 (260)	then the unbeliever was confounded
3:4 (3)	as for those who disbelieve in God's signs
3:10 (8)	as for the unbelievers, their riches will not avail them
3:12 (10)	say to the unbelievers: 'You shall be overthrown'
3:55 (48)	I will purify thee of those who believe not
3:55 (48)	I will set thy followers above the unbelievers
3:56 (49)	as for the unbelievers, I will chastise them
3:86 (80)	how shall God guide a people who have disbelieved after they believed
3:90 (84)	surely those who disbelieve after they have believed
3:91 (85)	surely those who disbelieve, and die disbelieving
3:97 (92)	as for the unbeliever, God is All-sufficient

3:106 (102)	did you disbelieve after you had believed?
3:116 (112)	as for the unbelievers, their riches shall not avail them
3:127 (122)	and that He might cut off a part of the unbelievers or frustrate them
3:149 (142)	if you obey the unbelievers they will turn you upon your heels
3:151 (144)	We will cast into the hearts of the unbelievers terror
3:156 (150)	O believers, be not as the unbelievers
3:178 (172)	let not the unbelievers suppose that the indulgence We grant them is better
3:196 (196)	let it not delude thee, that the unbelievers go to and fro
4:42 (45)	upon that day the unbelievers, those who have disobeyed the Messenger
4:51 (54)	believing in demons and idols, and saying to the unbelievers
4:56 (59)	those who disbelieve in Our signs
4:76 (78)	and the unbelievers fight in the idols' way
4:84 (86)	haply God will restrain the unbelievers' might
4:89 (91)	they wish that you should disbelieve as they disbelieve
4:101 (102)	if you fear the unbelievers may afflict you
4:102 (103)	the unbelievers wish that you should be heedless of your weapons
4:137 (136)	those who believe, and then disbelieve
4:137 (136)	and then believe, and then disbelieve
4:167 (165)	those who disbelieve, and bar from the way of God
4:168 (166)	surely the unbelievers, who have done evil
5:3 (4)	today the unbelievers have despaired of your religion
5:10 (13)	the unbelievers, who cried lies to Our signs
5:12 (15)	whosoever of you thereafter disbelieves
5:17 (19)	they are unbelievers who say, 'God is the Messiah'
5:36 (40)	the unbelievers, though they possessed all that is in the earth
5:72 (76)	they are unbelievers who say, 'God is the Messiah'
5:73 (77)	they are unbelievers who say, 'God is the Third of Three'
5:73 (77)	there shall afflict those of them that disbelieve a painful chastisement
5:78 (82)	cursed were the unbelievers of the Children of Israel by the tongue of David
5:80 (83)	thou seest many of them making unbelievers their friends
5:86 (88)	those who disbelieve, and cry lies to Our signs
5:103 (102)	but the unbelievers forge against God falsehood
5:110 (110)	and the unbelievers among them said
6:1 (1)	then the unbelievers ascribe equals to their Lord
6:7 (7)	the unbelievers would have said, 'This is naught but manifest sorcery'
6:25 (25)	the unbelievers saying, 'This is naught but the fairy-tales'
7:66 (64)	said the Council of the unbelievers of his people
7:90 (88)	said the Council of those of his people who disbelieved
8:12 (12)	I shall cast into the unbelievers' hearts terror
8:15 (15)	O believers, when you encounter the unbelievers marching to battle
8:30 (30)	when the unbelievers were devising against thee
8:36 (36)	the unbelievers expend their wealth to bar from God's way
8:36 (37)	and the unbelievers will be mustered into Gehenna
8:38 (39)	say to the unbelievers, if they give over
8:50 (52)	if thou couldst only see when the angels take the unbelievers
8:52 (54)	and the people before him, who disbelieved in God's signs
8:55 (57)	the worst of beasts in God's sight are the unbelievers
8:59 (61)	thou art not to suppose that they who disbelieve have outstripped Me
8:65 (66)	if there be a hundred of you, they will overcome a thousand unbelievers
8:73 (74)	as for the unbelievers, they are friends one of another
9:3 (3)	give thou good tidings to the unbelievers of a painful chastisement
9:26 (26)	He sent down legions you did not see, and He chastised the unbelievers
9:30 (30)	that is the utterance of their mouths, conforming with the unbelievers before them
9:37 (37)	the month postponed is an increase of unbelief whereby the unbelievers go astray
9:40 (40)	God has helped him already, when the unbelievers drove him forth

9:40 (40)	He made the word of the unbelievers the lowest
9:54 (54)	but that they believe not in God and His Messenger
9:66 (67)	you have disbelieved after your believing
9:74 (75)	they indeed said the word of unbelief and disbelieved
9:80 (81)	that, because they disbelieved in God and His Messenger
9:84 (85)	they disbelieved in God and His Messenger
9:90 (91)	there shall befall the unbelievers of them a painful chastisement
10:4 (4)	those who disbelieve — for them awaits a draught of boiling water
11:7 (10)	the unbelievers will say, 'This is naught but a manifest sorcery'
11:27 (29)	said the Council of the unbelievers of his people
11:60 (63)	surely Ad disbelieved in their Lord
11:68 (71)	surely Thamood disbelieved in their Lord
13:5 (6)	those are they that disbelieve in their Lord
13:7 (8)	the unbelievers say, 'Why has a sign not been sent down'
13:27 (27)	the unbelievers say, 'Why has a sign not been sent down'
13:31 (31)	the unbelievers are smitten by a shattering for what they wrought
13:32 (32)	I respited the unbelievers; then I seized them
13:33 (33)	decked out fair to the unbelievers is their devising
13:43 (43)	the unbelievers say, 'Thou art not an Envoy'
14:7 (7)	if you are thankless My chastisement is surely terrible
14:9 (10)	we certainly disbelieve in the Message you have been sent with
14:13 (16)	the unbelievers said to their Messengers
14:18 (21)	the likeness of those who disbelieve in their Lord
14:22 (27)	I disbelieved in your associating me with God aforetime
15:2 (2)	perchance the unbelievers will wish that they had surrendered
16:39 (41)	the unbelievers may know that they were truly liars
16:84 (86)	to the unbelievers no leave shall be given
16:88 (90)	those that disbelieve and bar from the way of God
16:106 (108)	whoso disbelieves in God, after he has believed
16:112 (113)	then it was unthankful for the blessings of God
17:69 (71)	and drown you for your thanklessness
17:98 (100)	that is their recompense because they disbelieved in Our signs
18:37 (35)	disbelievest thou in Him who created thee of dust
18:56 (54)	do the unbelievers dispute with falsehood
18:102 (102)	do the unbelievers reckon that they may take My servants as friends
18:105 (105)	those are they that disbelieve in the signs of their Lord
18:106 (106)	their recompense — Gehenna for that they were unbelievers
19:37 (38)	woe to those who disbelieve for the scene of a dreadful day
19:73 (74)	the unbelievers say to the believers, 'Which of the two parties is better in station'
19:77 (80)	hast thou seen him who disbelieves in Our signs
21:30 (31)	have not the unbelievers then beheld that the heavens and the earth were a mass
21:36 (37)	when the unbelievers behold thee, they take thee only for mockery
21:39 (40)	if the unbelievers but knew when that they shall not ward off the Fire
21:97 (97)	and behold, the eyes of the unbelievers staring
22:19 (20)	as for the unbelievers, for them garments of fire shall be cut
22:25 (25)	those who disbelieve, and bar from God's way
22:55 (54)	the unbelievers will not cease to be in doubt of it
22:57 (56)	as for the unbelievers, who cried lies to Our signs
22:72 (71)	thou recognisest in the faces of the unbelievers denial
22:72 (71)	The Fire — God has promised it to the unbelievers
23:24 (24)	said the Council of the unbelievers of his people
23:33 (34)	said the Council of the unbelievers of his people
24:39 (39)	as for the unbelievers, their works are as a mirage in a spacious plain
24:55 (54)	whoso disbelieves after that, those — they are the ungodly

24:57 (56)	think not the unbelievers able to frustrate God in the earth
25:4 (5)	the unbelievers say, 'This is naught but a calumny'
25:32 (34)	the unbelievers say, 'Why has the Koran not been sent down'
27:40 (40)	and whosoever is ungrateful — my Lord is surely All-sufficient
27:67 (69)	the unbelievers say, 'What, when we are dust'
29:12 (11)	the unbelievers say to the believers, 'Follow our path'
29:23 (22)	those who disbelieve in God's signs and the encounter with Him
29:52 (52)	those who believe in vanity and disbelieve in God
30:16 (15)	as for those who disbelieved, and cried lies to Our signs
30:44 (43)	whoso disbelieves, his unbelief shall be charged against him
30:58 (58)	those who are unbelievers will certainly say
31:12 (11)	and whosoever is ungrateful — surely God is All-sufficient
31:23 (22)	whoso disbelieves, let not his disbelief grieve thee
32:29 (29)	on the Day of Victory their faith shall not profit the unbelievers
33:25 (25)	God sent back those that were unbelievers
34:3 (3)	the unbelievers say, 'The Hour will never come to us'
34:7 (7)	the unbelievers say, 'Shall we point you to a man'
34:17 (16)	thus We recompensed them for their unbelief
34:31 (30)	the unbelievers say, 'We will not believe in this Koran'
34:33 (32)	We put fetters on the necks of the unbelievers
34:43 (42)	the unbelievers say to the truth, when it has come to them
34:53 (52)	seeing they disbelieved in it before, guessing at the Unseen
35:7 (7)	those who disbelieve — there awaits them a terrible chastisement
35:26 (24)	then I seized the unbelievers, and how was My horror
35:36 (33)	as for the unbelievers, theirs shall be the fire of Gehenna
35:39 (37)	whosoever disbelieves, his unbelief shall be charged against him
36:47 (47)	the unbelievers say to the believers, What, shall we feed such a one
37:170 (170)	but they disbelieved in it; soon they shall know
38:2 (1)	nay, but the unbelievers glory in their schism
38:27 (26)	such is the thought of the unbelievers
38:27 (26)	woe unto the unbelievers because of the Fire
39:63 (63)	those who disbelieve in the signs of God, those — they are the losers
39:71 (71)	then the unbelievers shall be driven in companies into Gehenna
40:4 (4)	none but the unbelievers dispute concerning the signs of God
40:6 (6)	the Word of thy Lord was realised against the unbelievers
40:10 (10)	it shall be proclaimed to the unbelievers, Surely God's hatred is greater
40:12 (12)	when God was called to alone, you disbelieved
40:22 (23)	but they disbelieved, so God seized them
40:84 (84)	We believe in God alone, and we disbelieve in that we were associating with Him
41:26 (25)	the unbelievers say, 'Do not give ear to this Koran'
41:27 (26)	We shall let the unbelievers taste a terrible chastisement
41:29 (29)	the unbelievers shall say, 'Our Lord, show us those that led us astray'
41:41 (41)	those who disbelieve in the Remembrance when it comes to them
41:50 (50)	then We shall tell the unbelievers the things they have done
41:52 (52)	what think you? if it is from God, then you disbelieve in it
45:11 (10)	those who disbelieve in the signs of their Lord
45:31 (30)	but as for those who have disbelieved
46:3 (2)	the unbelievers are turning away from that they were warned of
46:7 (6)	the unbelievers say to the truth when it has come to them
46:10 (9)	have you considered? If it be from God, and you disbelieve in it
46:11 (10)	the unbelievers say, as regards the believers
46:20 (19)	upon the day when the unbelievers are exposed to the Fire
46:34 (33)	upon the day when the unbelievers are exposed to the Fire
47:1 (1)	those who disbelieve and bar from God's way

47:3 (3)	that is because those who disbelieve follow falsehood
47:4 (4)	when you meet the unbelievers, smite their necks
47:8 (9)	as for the unbelievers, ill chance shall befall them
47:12 (13)	as for the unbelievers, they take their enjoyment and eat as cattle eat
47:32 (34)	those who disbelieve and bar from God's way
47:34 (36)	those who disbelieve and bar from God's way
48:22 (22)	if the unbelievers had fought you, they would have turned their backs
48:25 (25)	they are the ones who disbelieved
48:25 (25)	then We would have chastised the unbelievers
48:26 (26)	when the unbelievers set in their hearts fierceness
51:60 (60)	woe to the unbelievers, for that day of theirs that they are promised
52:42 (42)	the unbelievers, they are the outwitted
57:15 (14)	no ransom shall be taken from you, neither from those who disbelieved
57:19 (18)	the unbelievers, who have cried lies to Our signs, they are the inhabitants of Hell
59:2 (2)	He who expelled from their habitations the unbelievers
59:11 (11)	hast thou not regarded the hypocrites, saying to their brothers of the People of the Book who disbelieve
59:16 (16)	then, when he disbelieved, he said
60:1 (1)	though they have disbelieved in the truth that has come to you
60:4 (4)	we disbelieve in you, and between us and you enmity has shown itself
60:5 (5)	make us not a temptation to those who disbelieve
61:14 (14)	a party of the Children of Israel believed, and a party disbelieved
63:3 (3)	that is because they have believed, then they have disbelieved
64:5 (5)	has there not come to you the tidings of those that disbelieved before
64:6 (6)	therefore they disbelieved, and turned away
64:7 (7)	the unbelievers assert that they will never be raised up
64:10 (10)	those who disbelieved and cried lies to Our signs
66:7 (7)	O you unbelievers, do not excuse yourselves
66:10 (10)	God has struck a similitude for the unbelievers
67:6 (6)	for those who disbelieve in their Lord there awaits the chastisement
67:27 (27)	when they see it nigh at hand, the faces of the unbelievers will be vexed
68:51 (51)	the unbelievers wellnigh strike thee down with their glances
70:36 (36)	what ails the unbelievers, running with outstretched necks towards thee
73:17 (17)	if therefore you disbelieve, how will you guard yourselves
74:31 (31)	We have appointed only as a trial for the unbelievers
84:22 (22)	nay, but the unbelievers are crying lies
85:19 (19)	nay, but the unbelievers still cry lies
88:23 (23)	he who turns his back, and disbelieves
90:19 (19)	those who disbelieve in Our signs
98:1 (1)	the unbelievers of the People of the Book and the idolaters
98:6 (5)	the unbelievers of the People of the Book and the idolaters

b) impf. act. (*yakfuru*)

2:28 (26)	how do you disbelieve in God, seeing you were dead and He gave you life
2:61 (58)	that, because they had disbelieved the signs of God
2:85 (79)	do you believe in part of the Book, and disbelieve in part?
2:90 (84)	disbelieving in that which God sent down
2:91 (85)	they disbelieve in what is beyond that, yet it is the truth
2:99 (93)	and none disbelieves in them except the ungodly
2:102 (96)	we are but a temptation; do not disbelieve
2:121 (115)	whoso disbelieves in it, they shall be the losers
2:152 (147)	be thankful to Me; and be you not ungrateful towards Me
2:256 (257)	so whosoever disbelieves in idols
3:19 (17)	whoso disbelieves in God's signs

3:21 (20)	those who disbelieve in the signs of God and slay the Prophets
3:70 (63)	why do you disbelieve in God's signs, which you yourselves witness?
3:98 (93)	People of the Book, why do you disbelieve in the signs of God?
3:101 (96)	how can you disbelieve, seeing you have God's signs recited to you
3:106 (102)	then taste the chastisement for that you disbelieved
3:112 (108)	that, because they disbelieved in God's signs
4:60 (63)	yet they have been commanded to disbelieve in them
4:89 (91)	they wish that you should disbelieve
4:131 (130)	if you disbelieve, to God belongs all that is in the heavens
4:136 (135)	whoso disbelieves in God and His angels and His Books
4:150 (149)	those who disbelieve in God and His Messengers
4:150 (149)	we believe in part, and disbelieve in part
4:170 (168)	if you disbelieve, to God belongs all that is in the heavens
5:5 (7)	whoso disbelieves in the faith, his work has failed
5:115 (115)	whoso of you hereafter disbelieves, verily I shall chastise him
6:30 (30)	then taste the chastisement for your unbelief
6:70 (69)	and a painful chastisement, for that they were unbelievers
6:89 (89)	so if these disbelieve in it
8:35 (35)	therefore taste you now the chastisement for your unbelief
10:4 (4)	and a painful chastisement, for their disbelieving
10:70 (71)	taste the terrible chastisement, for that they were unbelievers
11:17 (20)	whosoever disbelieves in it, being one of the partisans
13:30 (29)	and yet they disbelieve in the All-merciful
14:8 (8)	if you are thankless, you and whoso is on earth
16:55 (57)	that they may show unthankfulness for that We have given them
16:72 (74)	do they believe in vanity, and do they disbelieve in God's blessing?
18:29 (28)	let whosoever will believe, and let whosoever will disbelieve
19:82 (85)	they shall deny their service, and they shall be against them
27:40 (40)	He may try me, whether I am thankful or ungrateful
28:48 (48)	did they not disbelieve also in what Moses was given aforetime?
29:25 (24)	upon the Day of Resurrection you will deny one another
29:66 (66)	that they may be ungrateful for what We have given them
29:67 (67)	do they believe in vanity, and do they disbelieve in God's blessing?
30:34 (33)	that they may be ungrateful for what We have given them
30:51 (50)	they remain after that unbelievers
34:33 (32)	when you were ordering us to disbelieve in God
35:14 (15)	on the Day of Resurrection they will disown your partnership
36:64 (64)	roast well in it today, for that you were unbelievers
39:7 (9)	if you are unthankful, God is independent of you
40:10 (10)	when you were called unto belief, and disbelieved
40:42 (45)	you call me to disbelieve in God
41:9 (8)	do you disbelieve in Him who created the earth in two days
43:33 (32)	We would have appointed for those who disbelieve in the All-merciful
46:34 (33)	then taste the chastisement of your unbelief
60:2 (2)	and they wish that you may disbelieve

c) impv. (*ukfur*)

3:72 (65)	and disbelieve at the end of it
59:16 (16)	like Satan, when he said to man, 'Disbelieve'

d) perf. pass. (*kufira*)

54:14 (14)	a recompense for him denied

e) impf. pass. (*yukfaru*)

3:115 (111) whatsoever good you do, you shall not be denied the just reward of it
4:140 (139) when you hear God's signs being disbelieved and made mock of

f) n.vb. (1) (*kufr*)

2:88 (82) God has cursed them for their unbelief
2:93 (87) they were made to drink the Calf in their hearts for their unbelief
2:108 (102) whoso exchanges belief for unbelief
2:217 (214) but to bar from God's way, and disbelief in Him
3:52 (45) when Jesus perceived their unbelief, he said
3:80 (74) would He order you to disbelieve, after you have surrendered?
3:90 (84) then increase in unbelief — their repentance shall not be accepted
3:167 (160) they that day were nearer to unbelief than to belief
3:176 (170) let them not grieve thee that vie with one another in unbelief
3:177 (171) those who buy unbelief at the price of faith
4:46 (49) God has cursed them for their unbelief
4:137 (136) then increase in unbelief — God is not likely to forgive them
4:155 (154) for their breaking the compact, and disbelieving in the signs of God
4:155 (154) God sealed them for their unbelief, so they believe not
4:156 (155) for their unbelief, and their uttering against Mary
5:41 (45) let them not grieve thee that vie with one another in unbelief
5:61 (66) they have entered in unbelief, and so they have departed in it
5:64 (69) will surely increase many of them in insolence and unbelief
5:68 (72) surely increase many of them in insolence and unbelief
9:12 (12) then fight the leaders of unbelief; they have no sacred oaths
9:17 (17) witnessing against themselves unbelief
9:23 (23) take not your fathers and brothers to be your friends, if they prefer unbelief
9:37 (37) the month postponed is an increase of unbelief
9:74 (75) but they indeed said the word of unbelief
9:97 (98) the Bedouins are more stubborn in unbelief and hypocrisy
9:107 (108) those who have taken a mosque in opposition and unbelief
14:28 (33) hast thou not seen those who exchanged the bounty of God with unthankfulness
16:106 (108) whosoever's breast is expanded in unbelief
18:80 (79) we were afraid he would impose on them insolence and unbelief
30:44 (43) whoso disbelieves, his unbelief shall be charged against him
31:23 (22) whoso disbelieves, let not his disbelief grieve thee
35:39 (37) whosoever disbelieves, his unbelief shall be charged against him
35:39 (37) their unbelief increases the disbelievers only in hate in their Lord's sight
35:39 (37) their unbelief increases the disbelievers only in loss
39:7 (9) He approves not unthankfulness in His servants
39:8 (11) enjoy thy unbelief a little
49:7 (7) He has made detestable to you unbelief and ungodliness

f) n.vb. (2) (*kufūr*)

17:89 (91) most men refuse all but unbelief
17:99 (101) yet the evildoers refuse all but unbelief
25:50 (52) most men refuse all but unbelief

g) pcple. act. (*kāfir*, pl. *kāfirūn*, *kafarah*, *kuffār*, and f. *kawāfir*)

2:19 (18) and God encompasses the unbelievers
2:24 (22) the Fire, whose fuel is men and stones, prepared for unbelievers

2:34 (32)	and so he became one of the unbelievers
2:41 (38)	be not the first to disbelieve in it
2:89 (83)	the curse of God is on the unbelievers
2:90 (84)	for unbelievers awaits a humbling chastisement
2:98 (92)	surely God is an enemy to the unbelievers
2:104 (98)	for unbelievers awaits a painful chastisement
2:109 (103)	many of the People of the Book wish they might restore you as unbelievers
2:161 (156)	but those who disbelieve, and die disbelieving
2:191 (187)	slay them — such is the recompense of unbelievers
2:217 (214)	whosoever of you turns from his religion, and dies disbelieving
2:250 (251)	give us aid against the people of the unbelievers
2:254 (255)	the unbelievers — they are the evildoers
2:264 (266)	god guides not the people of the unbelievers
2:286 (286)	help us against the people of the unbelievers
3:13 (11)	one company fighting in the way of God and another unbelieving
3:28 (27)	let not the believers take the unbelievers for friends
3:32 (29)	God loves not the unbelievers
3:91 (85)	surely those who disbelieve, and die disbelieving
3:100 (95)	they will turn you, after you have believed, into unbelievers
3:131 (126)	fear the Fire prepared for the unbelievers
3:141 (135)	God may prove the believers, and blot out the unbelievers
3:147 (141)	help us against the people of the unbelievers
4:18 (22)	neither to those who die disbelieving
4:37 (41)	We have prepared for the unbelievers a humbling chastisement
4:101 (102)	the unbelievers are for you a manifest foe
4:102 (103)	God has prepared for the unbelievers a humbling chastisement
4:139 (138)	those who take unbelievers for their friends instead of believers
4:140 (139)	God will gather the hypocrites and the unbelievers all in Gehenna
4:141 (140)	but if the unbelievers get a share, they say
4:141 (140)	God will not grant the unbelievers any way over the believers
4:144 (143)	take not the unbelievers as friends instead of the believers
4:151 (150)	those in truth are the unbelievers
4:151 (150)	We have prepared for the unbelievers a humbling chastisement
4:161 (159)	We have prepared for the unbelievers among them a painful chastisement
5:44 (48)	whoso judges not according to what God has sent down — they are the unbelievers
5:54 (59)	humble towards the believers, disdainful towards the unbelievers
5:57 (62)	the unbelievers, who take your religion in mockery and as a sport
5:67 (71)	God guides not the people of the unbelievers
5:68 (72)	grieve not for the people of the unbelievers
5:102 (101)	a people before you questioned concerning them, then disbelieved in them
6:89 (89)	entrusted it to a people who do not disbelieve in it
6:122 (122)	it is decked out fair to the unbelievers the things they have done
6:130 (130)	they bear witness against themselves that they were unbelievers
7:37 (35)	they will bear witness against themselves that they were unbelievers
7:45 (43)	to make it crooked, disbelieving in the world to come
7:50 (48)	God has forbidden them to the unbelievers
7:76 (74)	we are unbelievers in the thing in which you believe
7:93 (91)	how should I grieve for a people of unbelievers?
7:101 (99)	God seals the hearts of the unbelievers
8:7 (7)	and to cut off the unbelievers to the last remnant
8:14 (14)	the chastisement of the Fire is for the unbelievers
8:18 (18)	God weakens the unbelievers' guile
9:2 (2)	God degrades the unbelievers
9:26 (26)	that is the recompense of the unbelievers
9:32 (32)	God refuses but to perfect His light, though the unbelievers be averse

9:37 (37)	God guides not the people of the unbelievers
9:49 (49)	surely Gehenna encompasses the unbelievers
9:55 (55)	and that their souls should depart while they are unbelievers
9:68 (69)	God has promised the hypocrites, men and women, and the unbelievers, the fire
9:73 (74)	O Prophet, struggle with the unbelievers and hypocrites
9:85 (86)	and that their souls should depart while they are unbelievers
9:120 (121)	neither tread they any tread enraging the unbelievers
9:123 (124)	O believers, fight the unbelievers who are near to you
9:125 (126)	and they have died while they were unbelievers
10:2 (2)	the unbelievers say, 'This is a manifest sorcerer'
10:86 (86)	deliver us by Thy mercy from the people of the unbelievers
11:19 (22)	they disbelieve in the world to come
11:42 (44)	be thou not with the unbelievers
12:37 (37)	who moreover are unbelievers in the world to come
12:87 (87)	of God's comfort no man despairs, excepting the people of the unbelievers
13:14 (15)	the prayer of the unbelievers goes only astray
13:35 (35)	the requital of the unbelievers is — the Fire
13:42 (42)	the unbelievers shall assuredly know whose will be the Ultimate Abode
14:2 (2)	woe to the unbelievers for a terrible chastisement
16:27 (29)	degradation today and evil are on the unbelievers
16:83 (85)	and the most of them are the unthankful
16:107 (109)	God guides not the people of the unbelievers
17:8 (8)	We have made Gehenna a prison for the unbelievers
18:100 (100)	upon that day We shall present Gehenna to the unbelievers
18:102 (102)	We have prepared Gehenna for the unbelievers' hospitality
19:83 (86)	hast thou not seen how We sent the Satans against the unbelievers
21:36 (37)	they in the Remembrance of the All-merciful are unbelievers
22:44 (43)	I respited the unbelievers, then I seized them
23:117 (117)	surely the unbelievers shall not prosper
25:26 (28)	and it shall be a day harsh for the unbelievers
25:52 (54)	obey not the unbelievers, but struggle with them thereby mightily
25:55 (57)	the unbeliever is ever a partisan against his Lord
26:19 (18)	thou didst the deed thou didst, being one of the ungrateful
27:43 (43)	for she was of a people of unbelievers
28:48 (48)	they said, 'We disbelieve both'
28:82 (82)	ah, the unbelievers do not prosper
28:86 (86)	so be thou not a partisan of the unbelievers
29:47 (46)	none denies Our signs but the unbelievers
29:54 (54)	lo, Gehenna encompasses the unbelievers
29:68 (68)	is there not in Gehenna a lodging for the unbelievers?
30:8 (7)	most men disbelieve in the encounter with their Lord
30:13 (12)	and they shall disbelieve in their associates
30:45 (44)	He loves not the unbelievers
32:10 (10)	they disbelieve in the encounter with their Lord
33:1 (1)	obey not the unbelievers and the hypocrites
33:8 (8)	He has prepared for the unbelievers a painful chastisement
33:48 (47)	obey not the unbelievers and the hypocrites
33:64 (64)	God has cursed the unbelievers, and prepared for them a Blaze
34:34 (33)	we disbelieve in the Message you have been sent with
35:39 (37)	their unbelief increases the disbelievers only in hate in their Lord's sight
35:39 (37)	their unbelief increases the disbelievers only in loss
36:70 (70)	and that the Word may be realized against the unbelievers
38:4 (3)	the unbelievers say, 'This is a lying sorcerer'
38:74 (74)	save Iblis; he waxed proud, and was one of the unbelievers
39:32 (33)	is there not in Gehenna a lodging for the unbelievers?

39:59 (60)	thou hast waxed proud, and become one of the unbelievers
39:71 (71)	the word of the chastisement has been realized against the unbelievers
40:14 (14)	making your religion His sincerely, though the unbelievers be averse
40:25 (26)	the guile of the unbelievers is ever in error
40:50 (53)	the calling of the unbelievers is only in error
40:74 (74)	even so God leads astray the unbelievers
40:85 (85)	the unbelievers shall be lost
41:7 (6)	who pay not the alms, and disbelieve in the world to come
41:14 (13)	so we disbelieve in the Message you were sent with
42:26 (25)	the unbelievers — for them awaits a terrible chastisement
43:24 (23)	we disbelieve in that you were sent with
43:30 (29)	this is a sorcery, and in it we are unbelievers
46:6 (5)	shall be enemies to them, and shall deny their service
47:10 (11)	God destroyed them; the unbelievers shall have the likes thereof
47:11 (12)	and that the unbelievers have no protector
47:34 (36)	then die disbelieving, them God will not forgive
48:13 (13)	We have prepared for the unbelievers a Blaze
48:29 (29)	those who are with him are hard against the unbelievers
48:29 (29)	that through them He may enrage the unbelievers
50:2 (2)	the unbelievers say, 'This is a marvellous thing'
54:8 (8)	the unbelievers shall say, 'This is a hard day!'
54:43 (43)	what, are your unbelievers better than those?
57:20 (19)	it is as a rain whose vegetation pleases the unbelievers
58:4 (5)	for the unbelievers there awaits yet a painful chastisement
58:5 (6)	for the unbelievers awaits a humbling chastisement
60:10 (10)	if you know them to be believers, return them not to the unbelievers
60:10 (10)	do not hold fast to the ties of unbelieving women
60:11 (11)	if any of your wives slips away from you to the unbelievers
60:13 (13)	even as the unbelievers have despaired of the inhabitants of the tombs
61:8 (8)	God will perfect His light, though the unbelievers be averse
64:2 (2)	one of you is an unbeliever, and one of you a believer
66:9 (9)	O Prophet, struggle with the unbelievers and the hypocrites
67:20 (20)	the unbelievers are only in delusion
67:28 (28)	who will protect the unbelievers from a painful chastisement?
69:50 (50)	surely it is a sorrow to the unbelievers
70:2 (2)	for the unbelievers, which none may avert
71:26 (27)	leave not upon the earth of the unbelievers even one
74:10 (10)	for the unbelievers not easy
74:31 (33)	the unbelievers, may say, 'What did God intend by this as a similitude?'
76:4 (4)	We have prepared for the unbelievers chains, fetters, and a Blaze
78:40 (41)	the unbeliever shall say, 'O would that I were dust!'
80:42 (42)	those — they are the unbelievers, the libertines
83:34 (34)	today the believers are laughing at the unbelievers
83:36 (36)	have the unbelievers been rewarded what they were doing?
86:17 (17)	so respite the unbelievers; delay with them awhile
109:1 (1)	say: 'O unbelievers'

KAFFĀR n.m. (adj)~ingrate, a froward unbeliever, unthankful, impious

2:276 (277)	god loves not any guilty ingrate
14:34 (37)	surely man is sinful, unthankful
39:3 (5)	God guides not him who is a liar, unthankful
50:24 (23)	cast, you twain, into Gehenna every froward unbeliever
71:27 (28)	they will lead Thy servants astray, and will beget none but unbelieving

KAFFĀRAH n.f.~expiation

5:45 (49)	whosoever forgoes it as a freewill offering, that shall be for him an expiation
5:89 (91)	the expiation is to feed ten poor persons with the average of the food
5:89 (91)	that is the expiation of your oaths when you have sworn
5:95 (96)	or expiation — food for poor persons

KAFŪR n.m. (adj)~ungrateful, unthankful, thankless

11:9 (12)	he is desperate, ungrateful
17:27 (29)	and Satan is unthankful to his Lord
17:67 (69)	to land, you turn away; man is ever unthankful
22:38 (39)	God loves not any ungrateful traitor
22:66 (65)	surely man is ungrateful
31:32 (31)	none denies Our signs, except every ungrateful traitor
34:17 (16)	do We ever recompense any but the unbeliever?
35:36 (33)	even so We recompense every ungrateful one
42:48 (47)	then surely man is unthankful
43:15 (14)	man is clearly unthankful
76:3 (3)	We guided him upon the way whether he be thankful or unthankful
76:24 (24)	obey not one of them, sinner or unbeliever
80:17 (16)	Perish Man! How unthankful he is

KĀFŪR n.m.~camphor [Ar, Bl]; water of Kafur [Pk]; Kafur (a fountain in the Realm of Bliss) [Ali]

76:5 (5)	the pious shall drink of a cup whose mixture is camphor

KUFRĀN n.m.~unthankfulness

21:94 (94)	no unthankfulness shall befall his endeavour

KAFFARA vb. (II)~(with prep. *ʿan*) to acquit [Ar]; remit, atone [Pk]; blot out, remove [Ali]; to absolve [Bl]

a) perf. act.

5:65 (70)	We would have acquitted them of their evil deeds
47:2 (2)	He will acquit them of their evil deeds

b) impf. act. (*yukaffiru*)

2:271 (273)	and will acquit you of your evil deeds
3:195 (194)	them I shall surely acquit of their evil deeds
4:31 (35)	We will acquit you of your evil deeds
5:12 (15)	I will acquit you of your evil deeds
8:29 (29)	He will assign you a salvation, and acquit you of your evil deeds
29:7 (6)	We shall surely acquit them of their evil deeds
39:35 (36)	God may acquit them of the worst of what they did
48:5 (5)	to dwell forever, and acquit them of their evil deeds
64:9 (9)	God will acquit him of his evil deeds, and admit him into gardens
65:5 (5)	whosoever fears God, He will acquit him of his evil deeds
66:8 (8)	it may be that your Lord will acquit you of your evil deeds

c) impv. (*kaffir*)

3:193 (191)	forgive Thou us our sins and acquit us of our evil deeds

*K F T

KIFĀT n.m.~(meaning uncertain) a housing [Ar]; receptacle [Pk]; a place to draw together [Ali]; inclusive [Bl]

77:25 (25)	made We not the earth to be a housing

*K F Y

KAFÁ vb. (I)~(with prep. *bi-*) to suffice, be all-sufficient; to spare someone something. (pcple. act.) one who suffices; All-sufficient (Divine attribute)

a) perf. act.

4:6 (7)	God suffices for a reckoner
4:45 (47)	God suffices as a protector
4:45 (47)	God suffices as a helper
4:50 (53)	and that suffices for a manifest sin
4:55 (58)	Gehenna suffices for a Blaze
4:70 (72)	God suffices as One who knows
4:79 (81)	God suffices for a witness
4:81 (83)	God suffices for a guardian
4:132 (131)	God suffices for a guardian
4:166 (164)	God suffices for a witness
4:171 (169)	God suffices for a guardian
10:29 (30)	God is a sufficient witness between us and you
13:43 (43)	God suffices as a witness between me and you
15:95 (95)	We suffice thee against the mockers
17:14 (15)	thy soul suffices thee this day as a reckoner against thee
17:17 (18)	thy Lord suffices as one who is aware of and sees the sins of His servants
17:65 (67)	thy Lord suffices as a guardian
17:96 (98)	God suffices as a witness between me and you
21:47 (48)	We shall produce it, and sufficient are We for reckoners
25:31 (33)	thy Lord suffices as a guide and as a helper
25:58 (60)	sufficiently is He aware of His servants' sins
29:52 (51)	God suffices as a witness between me and you
33:3 (3)	God suffices as a guardian
33:25 (25)	God spared the believers of fighting
33:39 (39)	God suffices as a reckoner
33:48 (47)	God suffices as a guardian
46:8 (7)	He suffices as a witness between me and you
48:28 (28)	God suffices as a witness

b) impf. act. (*yakfī*)

2:137 (131)	God will suffice you for them
3:124 (120)	is it not enough for you that your Lord should reinforce you
29:51 (50)	is it not sufficient for them that We have sent down upon thee the Book
41:53 (53)	suffices it not as to thy Lord, that He is witness over everything?

g) pcple. act. (*kāfī*)

39:36 (37)	shall not God suffice His servant

*K H F

KAHF n.m.~a cave; (*aṣḥāb al-kahf*) People of the Cave

18:9 (8)	dost thou think the Men of the Cave and Er-Rakeem were among Our signs a wonder?
18:10 (9)	when the youths took refuge in the Cave
18:11 (10)	then We smote their ears many years in the Cave
18:16 (15)	take refuge in the Cave
18:17 (16)	thou mightest have seen the sun, when it rose, inclining from their Cave
18:25 (24)	they tarried in the Cave three hundred years

*K H L

KAHL n.m.~man of age

3:46 (41)	He shall speak to men in the cradle, and of age
5:110 (109)	to speak to men in the cradle, and of age

*K H N

KĀHIN n.m.~a soothsayer

52:29 (29)	by thy Lord's blessing thou art not a soothsayer neither possessed
69:42 (42)	nor the speech of a soothsayer

*K H Y ʿ Ṣ

KĀF HĀ YĀ ʿAYN ṢĀD~ml

19:1 (1)	Kaf Ha Ya Ain Sad

*K L ʾ

KALAʾA vb. (I)~to guard from

b) impf. act. (*yaklaʾu*)

21:42 (43)	who shall guard you by night and in the daytime from the All-merciful?

*K L B

KALB n.m.~a dog

7:176 (175)	the likeness of him is as the likeness of a dog
18:18 (17)	and their dog stretching its paws on the threshold
18:22 (21)	they will say, 'Three; and their dog was the fourth of them'
18:22 (21)	five; and their dog was the sixth of them
18:22 (21)	seven; and their dog was the eighth of them

KALLABA vb. (IV)~(pcple. act.) training dogs as hounds (for hunting) *g*) pcple. act. (*mukallib*)

5:4 (6) such hunting creatures as you teach, training them as hounds

*K L F

KALLAFA vb. (II)~to charge [Ar]; tax [Pk]; place a burden [Ali]

b) impf. act. (*yukallifu*)

2:233 (233)	no soul is charged save to its capacity
2:286 (286)	God charges no soul save to its capacity
4:84 (86)	thou art charged only with thyself
6:152 (153)	we charge not any soul save to its capacity
7:42 (40)	We charge not any soul, save according to its capacity
23:62 (64)	We charge not any soul save to its capacity
65:7 (7)	God charges no soul save with what He has given him

TAKALLAFA vb. (V)~(pcple. act.) one who takes things upon himself

g) pcple. act. (*mutakallif*)

38:86 (86) neither am I of those who take things upon themselves

*K L Ḥ

KALAḤA vb. (I)~(pcple. act.) one who glowers [Ar]; one who is glum [Pk]; one who grins while his lips are displaced [Ali]

g) pcple. act. (*kāliḥ*)

23:104 (106) the Fire smiting their faces the while they glower there

*K L L

KALLA vb. (I)~(n.vb.) a heavy burden

f) n.vb. (*kall*)

16:76 (78) he is a burden upon his master

KALĀLAH n.f.~a distant relative, indirect heir

4:12 (15)	if a man or a woman have no heir direct, but have a brother or a sister
4:176 (175)	God pronounces to you concerning the indirect heirs

*K L M

KALĀM n.m.~Word; also utterance [Ar]; verdict [Pk]; decree [Ali]

2:75 (70)	there is a party of them that heard God's word, and then tampered with it
7:144 (141)	Moses, I have chosen thee above all men for My Messages and My Utterance

9:6 (6)	grant him protection till he hears the words of God
48:15 (15)	desiring to change God's words

KALIMAH n.f. (pl. *kalimāt*, and *kalim*)~a word, a command; revelation [Pk]; word of inspiration [Ali]. (*kalimatu sawā'*) a common word [Ar]; agreement [Pk]; common terms [Ali]

2:37 (35)	thereafter Adam received certain words from his Lord
2:124 (118)	when his Lord tested Abraham with certain words, and he fulfilled them
3:39 (34)	God gives thee good tidings of John, who shall confirm a Word of God
3:45 (40)	God gives thee good tidings of a Word from Him whose name is Messiah
3:64 (57)	come now to a word common between us and you
4:46 (48)	some of the Jews pervert words from their meanings
4:171 (169)	Jesus son of Mary, was only the Messenger of God, and His Word
5:13 (16)	they perverting words from their meanings
5:41 (45)	who have not come to thee, perverting words from their meanings
6:34 (34)	no man can change the words of God
6:115 (115)	perfect are the words of thy Lord in truthfulness
6:115 (115)	no man can change His words
7:137 (133)	perfectly was fulfilled the most fair word of thy Lord
7:158 (158)	who believes in God and His words
8:7 (7)	God was desiring to verify the truth by His words
9:40 (40)	He made the word of the unbelievers the lowest
9:40 (40)	God's word is the uppermost
9:74 (75)	they indeed said the word of unbelief
10:19 (20)	but for a word that preceded from thy Lord
10:33 (34)	thus the word of thy Lord is realized
10:64 (65)	there is no changing the words of God
10:82 (82)	God verifies the truth by His words
10:96 (96)	those against whom thy Lord's word is realized
11:110 (112)	but for a word that preceded from thy Lord
11:119 (120)	perfectly is fulfilled the word of thy Lord
14:24 (29)	a good word is as a good tree — its roots are firm
14:26 (31)	the likeness of a corrupt word is as a corrupt tree
18:5 (4)	a monstrous word it is, issuing out of their mouths
18:27 (26)	no man can change His words
18:109 (109)	if the sea were ink for the Words of my Lord
18:109 (109)	the sea would be spent before the Words of my Lord are spent
20:129 (129)	but for a word that preceded from thy Lord
23:100 (102)	it is but a word he speaks
31:27 (26)	yet would the Words of God not be spent
35:10 (11)	to Him good words go up
37:171 (171)	already Our Word has preceded to Our servants
39:19 (20)	He against whom the word of chastisement is realized
39:71 (71)	the word of the chastisement has been realized against the unbelievers
40:6 (6)	the Word of thy Lord was realised against the unbelievers
41:45 (45)	but for a Word that preceded from thy Lord
42:14 (13)	but for a Word that preceded from thy Lord until a stated term
42:21 (20)	but for the Word of Decision
42:24 (23)	God blots out falsehood and verifies the truth by His words
43:28 (27)	he made it a word enduring among his posterity
48:26 (26)	and fastened to them the word of godfearing
66:12 (12)	she confirmed the Words of her Lord and His Books

KALLAMA vb. (II)~to speak to or with. (n.vb.) the act of speaking to; (adv) directly

a) perf. act.

2:253 (254) some there are to whom God spoke, and some He raised in rank
4:164 (162) and unto Moses God spoke directly
6:111 (111) We had sent down the angels to them, and the dead had spoken with them
7:143 (139) when Moses came to Our appointed time and his Lord spoke with him
12:54 (54) then, when he had spoken with him, he said

b) impf. act. (*yukallimu*)

2:118 (112) why does God not speak to us?
2:174 (169) God shall not speak to them on the Day of Resurrection
3:41 (36) 'Thy sign,' God said, 'is that thou shalt not speak, save by tokens'
3:46 (41) He shall speak to men in the cradle, and of age
3:77 (71) God shall not speak to them neither look on them on the Resurrection Day
5:110 (109) when I confirmed thee with the Holy Spirit, to speak to men
7:148 (146) did they not see it spoke not to them, neither guided them upon any way?
19:10 (11) thy sign is that thou shalt not speak to men
19:26 (27) I have vowed to the All-merciful a fast, and today I will not speak to any man
19:29 (30) how shall we speak to one who is still in the cradle, a little child?
23:108 (110) He shall say, 'and do not speak to Me'
27:82 (84) out of the earth a beast that shall speak unto them
36:65 (65) today We set a seal on their mouths, and their hands speak to Us
42:51 (50) it belongs not to any mortal that God should speak to him

d) perf. pass. (*kullima*)

13:31 (30) or the earth were cleft, or the dead were spoken to

f) n.vb. (*taklīm*)

4:164 (162) and unto Moses God spoke <directly>

TAKALLAMA vb. (V)~to speak

b) impf. act. (*yatakallamu*)

11:105 (107) no soul shall speak save by His leave
24:16 (15) it is not for us to speak about this; glory be to Thee
30:35 (34) such as speaks of that they associate with Him
78:38 (38) him to whom the All-merciful has given leave, and who speaks aright

*K M H

AKMAH n.m. (adj)~one who is blind from birth

3:49 (43) I will also heal the blind and the leper
5:110 (110) thou healest the blind and the leper by My leave

*K M L

KAMALA vb. (I)~(pcple. act.) complete; (adv) completely, in total, in all *g*) pcple. act. (*kāmil*)

2:196 (192) a fast of three days in the Pilgrimage, and of seven when you return, that is ten completely
2:233 (233) mothers shall suckle their children two years completely
16:25 (27) that they may bear their loads complete on the Day of Resurrection

AKMALA vb. (IV)~to perfect, fulfil, complete

a) perf. act.

5:3 (5) today I have perfected your religion for you, and I have completed My blessing upon you

b) impf. act. (*yukmilu*)

2:185 (181) and that you fulfil the number, and magnify God

*K M M

AKMĀM n.m. (pl. of *kimm*)~sheaths (of a fruit tree)

41:47 (47) not a fruit comes forth from its sheath
55:11 (10) therein fruits, and palm-trees with sheaths

*K N D

KANŪD n.com. (adj)~ungrateful

100:6 (6) surely Man is ungrateful to his Lord

*K N N

KANNA vb. (I)~(pcple. pass.) hidden

h) pcple. pass. (*maknūn*)

37:49 (47) as if they were hidden pearls
52:24 (24) there go round them youths, their own, as if they were hidden pearls
56:23 (22) as the likeness of hidden pearls
56:78 (77) in a hidden Book

AKNĀN n.m. (pl. of *kinn*)~a refuge

16:81 (83) and He has appointed for you of the mountains refuges

AKINNAH n.m. (pl. of *kinn*)~veils, coverings

6:25 (25) We lay veils upon their hearts lest they understand it
17:46 (48) We lay veils upon their hearts lest they understand it
18:57 (55) We have laid veils on their hearts lest they understand it
41:5 (4) our hearts are veiled from what thou callest us to

AKANNA vb. (IV)~to hide (tr)

a) perf. act.

2:235 (235) the proposal to women you offer, or hide in your hearts

b) impf. act. (*yukinnu*)

27:74 (76) thy Lord knows what their hearts conceal, and what they publish
28:69 (69) thy Lord knows what their breasts conceal and what they publish

*K N S

KUNNAS n.m.~the sinkers [Ar]; the setting stars [Pk]; the planets that hide [Ali]; those that fade away [Bl]

81:16 (16) the runners, the sinkers

*K N Z

KANAZA vb. (I)~to treasure up. (n.vb.) a treasure a) perf. act.

9:35 (35) this is the thing you have treasured up for yourselves

b) impf. act. (*yaknizu*)

9:34 (34) those who treasure up gold and silver, and do not expend them
9:35 (35) therefore taste you now what you were treasuring

f) n.vb. (*kanz*, pl. *kunūz*)

11:12 (15) why has a treasure not been sent down upon him
18:82 (81) and under it was a treasure belonging to them
18:82 (81) then bring forth their treasure as a mercy from thy Lord
25:8 (9) why is not a treasure thrown to him
26:58 (58) and treasures and a noble station
28:76 (76) We had given him treasures such that the very keys of them were too heavy a burden

*K R B

KARABA vb. (I)~(n.vb.) grief, distress

f) n.vb. (*karb*)

6:64 (64) God delivers you from them and from every distress
21:76 (76) and delivered him and his people from the great distress
37:76 (74) We delivered him and his people from the great distress
37:115 (115) We delivered them and their people from the great distress

*K R H

KARIHA vb. (I)~to dislike, be averse to, to hate. (n.vb.) being hateful; (adv) unwillingly, forcibly, reluctantly, painfully. (pcple. act.) one who hates, who detests, who is averse. (pcple. pass.) that which is hateful or detested

a) perf. act.

4:19 (23)	or if you are averse to them
8:8 (8)	prove untrue the untrue, though the sinners were averse to it
9:32 (32)	God refuses but to perfect His light, though the unbelievers be averse
9:33 (33)	He may uplift it above every religion, though the unbelievers be averse
9:46 (46)	God was averse that they should be aroused
9:81 (82)	and were averse to struggle with their possessions and their selves
10:82 (82)	God verifies the truth by His words, though sinners be averse
40:14 (14)	making your religion His sincerely, though the unbelievers be averse
47:9 (10)	that is because they have been averse to what God has sent down
47:26 (28)	that is because they said to those who were averse to what God sent down
47:28 (30)	they have followed what angers God, and have been averse to His good pleasure
49:12 (12)	you would abominate it
61:8 (8)	God will perfect His light, though the unbelievers be averse
61:9 (9)	He may uplift it above every religion, though the unbelievers be averse

b) impf. act. (*yakrahu*)

2:216 (213)	it may happen that you will hate a thing which is better for you
4:19 (23)	you may be averse to a thing, and God set in it much good
16:62 (64)	they assign to God that they themselves dislike

f) n.vb. (*karh*)

2:216 (212)	prescribed for you is fighting, though it be hateful to you
3:83 (77)	to Him has surrendered whoso is in the heavens and the earth, willingly or
4:19 (23)	it is not lawful for you to inherit women against their will
9:53 (53)	expend willingly, or unwillingly, it shall not be accepted from you
13:15 (16)	to God bow all who are in the heavens and the earth, willingly or unwillingly
41:11 (10)	come willingly, or unwillingly
46:15 (14)	his mother bore him painfully
46:15 (14)	painfully she gave birth to him

g) pcple. act. (*kārih*)

7:88 (86)	what, even though we detest it?
8:5 (5)	a part of the believers were averse to it
9:48 (48)	until the truth came, and God's command appeared, though they were averse
9:54 (54)	and that they expend not without they are averse
11:28 (30)	shall we compel you to it while you are averse to it?
23:70 (72)	most of them are averse from the truth
43:78 (78)	most of you were averse to the truth

h) pcple. pass. (*makrūh*)

17:38 (40)	the wickedness of it is hateful in the sight of thy Lord

KARRAHA vb. (II)~to cause to be hateful or detestable

a) perf. act.

49:7 (7)	He has made detestable to you unbelief and ungodliness

AKRAHA vb. (IV)~to constrain, to compel one to do something against his will. (n.vb.) compulsion, the act of constraining

a) perf. act.

20:73 (75)	He may pardon us our offences, and the sorcery thou hast constrained us to practise

b) impf. act. (*yukrihu*)

10:99 (99)	wouldst thou then constrain the people, until they are believers?
24:33 (33)	constrain not your slavegirls to prostitution
24:33 (33)	whosoever constrains them, surely God, after their being constrained, is All-forgiving

d) perf. pass. (*ukriha*)

16:106 (108)	he has believed — excepting him who has been compelled

f) n.vb. (*ikrāh*)

2:256 (257)	no compulsion is there in religion
24:33 (33)	whosoever constrains them, surely God, after their being constrained, is All-forgiving

*K R M

KARĪM n.m. (comp. adj. *Akram*)~generous, noble, honourable; All-generous, Most Generous (Divine attribute)

4:31 (35)	We will acquit you of your evil deeds, and admit you by the gate of honour
8:4 (4)	they have degrees with their Lord, and forgiveness, and generous provision
8:74 (75)	theirs shall be forgiveness and generous provision
12:31 (31)	this is no mortal; he is no other but a noble angel
17:23 (24)	speak unto them words respectful
22:50 (49)	theirs shall be forgiveness and generous provision
23:116 (117)	there is no god but He, the Lord of the noble Throne
24:26 (26)	theirs shall be forgiveness and generous provision
25:72 (72)	when they pass by idle talk, pass by with dignity
26:7 (6)	We have caused to grow of every generous kind
26:58 (58)	and treasures and a noble station
27:29 (29)	O Council, see, a letter honourable has been cast unto me
27:40 (40)	my Lord is surely All-sufficient, All-generous
31:10 (9)	and caused to grow in it of every generous kind
33:31 (31)	We have prepared for her a generous provision
33:44 (43)	He has prepared for them a generous wage
34:4 (4)	theirs shall be forgiveness and generous provision
36:11 (10)	give him the good tidings of forgiveness and a generous wage
44:17 (16)	and a noble Messenger came unto them
44:26 (25)	sown fields, and how noble a station
44:49 (49)	surely thou art the mighty, the noble
49:13 (13)	the noblest among you in the sight of God is the most godfearing of you
56:44 (43)	neither cool, neither goodly
56:77 (76)	it is surely a noble Koran
57:11 (11)	He will multiply it for him, and his shall be a generous wage
57:18 (17)	it shall be multiplied for them, and theirs shall be a generous wage
69:40 (40)	it is the speech of a noble Messenger

80:16 (15) noble, pious
81:19 (19) truly this is the word of a noble Messenger
82:6 (6) O Man! What deceived thee as to thy generous Lord
82:11 (11) noble, writers
96:3 (3) thy Lord is the Most Generous

KARRAMA vb. (II)~to honour. (pcple. pass.) one who is honoured

a) perf. act.

17:62 (64) this whom Thou hast honoured above me
17:70 (72) We have honoured the Children of Adam and carried them on land and sea

h) pcple. pass. (*mukarram*)

80:13 (13) upon pages high-honoured

AKRAMA vb. (IV)~to honour; to honour a guest, to give a goodly lodging. (n.vb.) honour, glory; (*dhūl ikrām*) splendid [Ar]; one of Glory [Pk]; full of Bounty and Honour [Ali]; full of honour [Bl]. (pcple. act.) one who honours. (pcple. pass.) one who is honoured

a) perf. act.

89:15 (14) whenever his Lord tries him, and honours him, and blesses him
89:15 (15) then he says, 'My Lord has honoured me'

b) impf. act. (*yukrimu*)

89:17 (18) you honour not the orphan

c) impv. (*akrim*)

12:21 (21) he that bought him, being of Egypt, said to his wife, 'Give him goodly lodging'

f) n.vb. (*ikrām*)

55:27 (27) abides the Face of thy Lord, majestic, splendid
55:78 (78) blessed be the Name of thy Lord, majestic, splendid

g) pcple. act. (*mukrim*)

22:18 (19) and whom God abases, there is none to honour him

h) pcple. pass. (*mukram*)

21:26 (26) nay, but they are honoured servants
36:27 (26) that my Lord has forgiven me and that He has placed me among the honoured
37:42 (41) fruits — and they high-honoured
51:24 (24) hast thou received the story of the honoured guests of Abraham?
70:35 (35) those shall be in Gardens, high-honoured

*K R R

KARRAH n.f.~a return, a turn (of luck); again; (with prep. *li-*) to have another turn, to return again

2:167 (162) if only we might return again and disown them
17:6 (6) then We gave back to you the turn to prevail over them
26:102 (102) O that we might return again, and be among the believers

39:58 (59)	O that I might return again, and be among the good-doers
67:4 (4)	then return thy gaze again, and again
79:12 (12)	they shall say, 'That then were a losing return!'

*K R S

KURSĪY n.m.~a throne

2:255 (256)	His Throne comprises the heavens and earth
38:34 (33)	We tried Solomon, and We cast upon his throne a mere body

*K S B

KASABA vb. (I)~to earn; (*mā yaksibū*) earnings ("that which they earn")

a) perf. act.

2:81 (75)	whoso earns evil, and is encompassed by his transgression
2:134 (128)	there awaits them that they have earned
2:134 (128)	and there awaits you that you have earned
2:141 (135)	there awaits them that they have earned
2:141 (135)	and there awaits you that you have earned
2:202 (198)	those — they shall have a portion from what they have earned
2:225 (225)	He will take you to task for what your hearts have earned
2:264 (266)	they have no power over anything that they have earned
2:267 (269)	expend of the good things you have earned
2:281 (281)	every soul shall be paid in full what it has earned
2:286 (286)	standing to its account is what it has earned
3:25 (24)	every soul shall be paid in full what it has earned
3:155 (149)	Satan made them slip for somewhat they had earned
3:161 (155)	then every soul shall be paid in full what it has earned
4:88 (90)	God has overthrown them for what they earned
5:38 (42)	cut off the hands of both, as a recompense for what they have earned
6:70 (69)	lest a soul should be given up to destruction for what it has earned
6:70 (69)	those are they who are given up to destruction for what they have earned
6:158 (159)	it shall not profit a soul to believe that never believed before, or earned some good
10:27 (28)	for those who have earned evil deeds the recompense of an evil deed
13:33 (33)	He who stands over every soul for what it has earned
14:18 (21)	they have no power over that they have earned
14:51 (51)	God may recompense every soul for its earnings
18:58 (57)	if He should take them to task for that they have earned
30:41 (40)	corruption has appeared in the land and sea, for that men's own hands have earned
35:45 (44)	if God should take men to task for what they have earned
39:48 (49)	and there would appear to them the evils of that they have earned
39:51 (52)	in that the evils of that they earned smote them
39:51 (52)	they too shall be smitten by the evils of that they earned
40:17 (17)	today each soul shall be recompensed for that it has earned
42:22 (21)	thou seest the evildoers going in fear of that they have earned
42:30 (29)	whatever affliction may visit you is for what your own hands have earned

42:34 (32)	He wrecks them for what they have earned
45:10 (9)	and that they have earned shall not avail them aught
45:22 (21)	and that every soul may be recompensed for what it has earned
52:21 (21)	every man shall be pledged for what he earned
74:38 (41)	every soul shall be pledged for what it has earned
111:2 (2)	his wealth avails him not, neither what he has earned

b) impf. act. (*yaksibu*)

2:79 (73)	woe to them for what their hands have written, and woe to them for their earnings
4:111 (111)	whosoever earns a sin, (earns) it against himself only
4:111 (111)	whosoever (earns) a sin, earns it against himself only
4:112 (112)	whosoever earns a fault or a sin and then casts it upon the innocent
6:3 (3)	He knows what you are earning
6:120 (120)	surely the earners of sin shall be recompensed
6:129 (129)	We make the evildoers friends of each other for what they have earned
6:164 (164)	every soul earns only to its own account
7:39 (37)	taste the chastisement for what you have been earning
7:96 (94)	they cried lies, and so We seized them for what they earned
9:82 (83)	let them laugh little, and weep much, in recompense for what they have been earning
9:95 (96)	their refuge is Gehenna — a recompese for what they have been earning
10:8 (8)	those — their refuge is the Fire, for that they have been earning
10:52 (53)	are you recompensed for aught but that you have been earning?
13:42 (42)	He knows what every soul earns
15:84 (84)	that they earned did not avail them
31:34 (34)	no soul knows what it shall earn tomorrow
36:65 (65)	and their feet bear witness as to what they have been earning
39:24 (25)	taste now that you were earning
39:50 (51)	but that they earned did not avail them
40:82 (82)	that they earned did not avail them
41:17 (16)	the thunderbolt of the chastisement of humiliation seized them for that they were earning
45:14 (13)	that He may recompense a people for that they have been earning
83:14 (14)	but that they were earning has rusted upon their hearts

IKTASABA vb. (VIII)~to earn, to merit, to deserve

a) perf. act.

2:286 (286)	and against its account what it has merited
4:32 (36)	to the men a share from what they have earned
4:32 (36)	to the women a share from what they have earned
24:11 (11)	every man of them shall have the sin that he has earned charged to him
33:58 (58)	those who hurt believing men and believing women, without that they have earned it

*K S D

KASADA vb. (I)~(n.vb.) a slackening (of commerce)

f) n.vb. (*kasād*)

9:24 (24)	commerce you fear may slacken, dwellings you love

*K S F

KISF n.m.~fragments, pieces, lumps; (*jaʿala kisfan*) to shatter ("to make into fragments")

17:92 (94)	or till thou makest heaven to fall, as thou assertest, on us in fragments
26:187 (187)	then drop down on us lumps from heaven, if thou art one of the truthful
30:48 (47)	He spreads them in heaven how He will, and shatters them
34:9 (9)	or We would drop down on them lumps from heaven
52:44 (44)	even if they saw lumps falling from heaven

*K S L

KUSĀLÁ n.m. (pl. of *kaslān*)~lazy; (adv) lazily

4:142 (141)	when they stand up to pray they stand up lazily
9:54 (54)	and perform not the prayer save lazily

*K S W

KASĀ vb. (I)~to garment, to clothe

a) perf. act.

23:14 (14)	then We garmented the bones in flesh

b) impf. act. (*yaksū*)

2:259 (261)	look at the bones, how We shall set them up, and then clothe them with flesh

c) impv. (*uksu*)

4:5 (4)	provide for them and clothe them out of it

KISWAH n.f.~clothing

2:233 (233)	it is for the father to provide them and clothe them honourably
5:89 (91)	or to clothe them, or to set free a slave

*K SH F

KASHAFA vb. (I)~to remove, uncover, take off, bare, disclose. (n.vb.) removal. (pcple. act.) one who removes, uncovers, takes off, discloses

a) perf. act.

7:134 (131)	if thou removest from us the wrath, surely we will believe thee
7:135 (131)	but when We removed from them the wrath
10:12 (13)	but when We have removed his affliction from him, he passes on
10:98 (98)	when they believed, We removed from them the chastisement of degradation
16:54 (56)	when He removes the affliction from you
21:84 (84)	We answered him, and removed the affliction that was upon him

23:75 (77)	did We have mercy on them, and remove the affliction that is upon them
27:44 (44)	she supposed it was a spreading water, and she bared her legs
43:50 (49)	when We removed from them the chastisement, behold, they broke their troth
50:22 (21)	therefore We have now removed from thee thy covering

b) impf. act. (*yakshifu*)

6:41 (41)	He will remove that for which you call upon Him
27:62 (63)	He who answers the constrained, when he calls unto Him, and removes the evil

c) impv. (*ikshif*)

44:12 (11)	O our Lord, remove Thou from us the chastisement

e) impf. pass. (*yukshafu*)

68:42 (42)	upon the day when the leg shall be bared, and they shall be summoned

f) n.vb. (*kashf*)

17:56 (58)	they have no power to remove affliction from you

g) pcple. act. (*kāshif*)

6:17 (17)	if God visits thee with affliction none can remove it but He
10:107 (107)	if God visits thee with affliction, none can remove it but He
39:38 (39)	if God desires affliction for me, shall they remove His affliction?
44:15 (14)	behold, We are removing the chastisement a little
53:58 (58)	apart from God none can disclose it

*K SH Ṭ

KASHAṬA vb. (I)~to strip off

d) perf. pass. (*kushiṭa*)

81:11 (11)	when heaven shall be stripped off

*K T B

KATABA vb. (I)~to write; (with prep. *li-* or *ʿalá*) to prescribe [Ar, Bl]; to ordain, to decree, to order [Pk, Ali]. (pcple. act.) a writer, a scribe. (pcple. pass.) that which is written [Ar]; described [Pk]; mentioned [Ali]

a) perf. act.

2:79 (73)	woe to them for what their hands have written
2:187 (183)	seek what God has prescribed for you
4:66 (69)	but had We prescribed for them, saying, Slay yourselves
4:77 (79)	our Lord, why hast thou prescribed fighting for us?
5:21 (24)	enter the Holy Land which God has prescribed for you
5:32 (35)	We prescribed for the Children of Israel that whoso slays a soul not to retaliate
5:45 (49)	therein We prescribed for them: A life for a life
6:12 (12)	He has prescribed for Himself mercy
6:54 (54)	your Lord has prescribed for Himself mercy

7:145 (142)	We wrote for him on the Tablets of everything an admonition
9:51 (51)	naught shall visit us but what God has prescribed for us
21:105 (105)	We have written in the Psalms, after the Remembrance
57:27 (27)	monasticism they invented — We did not prescribe it for them
58:21 (21)	God has written, I shall assuredly be the victor
58:22 (22)	He has written faith upon their hearts
59:3 (3)	had God not prescribed dispersal for them

b) impf. act. (*yaktubu*)

2:79 (73)	woe to those who write the Book with their hands
2:282 (282)	let a writer write it down between you justly
2:282 (282)	let not any writer refuse to write it down
2:282 (282)	let him write, and let the debtor dictate
2:282 (282)	be not loth to write it down, whether it be small or great
2:282 (282)	then it shall be no fault in you if you do not write it down
3:181 (177)	We shall write down what they have said
4:81 (83)	God writes down their meditations
7:156 (155)	I shall prescribe it for those who are godfearing
10:21 (22)	surely Our messengers are writing down what you are devising
19:79 (82)	We shall assuredly write down all that he says
36:12 (11)	it is We who bring the dead to life and write down what they have forwarded
43:80 (80)	Our messengers are present with them writing it down
52:41 (41)	is the Unseen in their keeping, and so they are writing it down?
68:47 (47)	is the Unseen in their keeping, and so they are writing it down?

c) impv. (*uktub*)

2:282 (282)	when you contract a debt one upon another for a stated term, write it down
3:53 (46)	inscribe us therefore with those who bear witness
5:83 (86)	so do Thou write us down among the witnesses
7:156 (155)	prescribe for us in this world good, and in the world to come

d) perf. pass. (*kutiba*)

2:178 (173)	O believers, prescribed for you is retaliation
2:180 (176)	prescribed for you, when any of you is visited by death
2:183 (179)	O believers, prescribed for you is the Fast
2:183 (179)	even as it was prescribed for those that were before you
2:216 (212)	prescribed for you is fighting, though it be hateful to you
2:246 (247)	might it be that, if fighting is prescribed for you, you will not fight?
2:246 (247)	yet when fighting was prescribed for them, they turned their backs
3:154 (148)	those for whom slaying was appointed would have sallied forth unto their last couches
4:77 (79)	as soon as fighting is prescribed for them, there is a party
4:127 (126)	to you in the Book concerning the orphan women to whom you give not what is prescribed for them
9:120 (121)	a righteous deed is thereby written to their account
9:121 (122)	nor do they traverse any valley, but it is written to their account
22:4 (4)	against whom it is written down that whosoever takes him for a friend, him he leads astray

e) impf. pass. (*yuktabu*)

43:19 (18)	their witness shall be written down, and they shall be questioned

g) pcple. act. (*kātib*)

2:282 (282)	let a writer write it down between you justly
2:282 (282)	let not any writer refuse to write it down
2:282 (282)	let not either writer or witness be pressed
2:283 (283)	if you are upon a journey, and you do not find a writer, then a pledge in hand
21:94 (94)	We Ourselves write it down for him
82:11 (11)	noble, writers

h) pcple. pass. (*maktūb*)

7:157 (156)	whom they find written down with them in the Torah and the Gospel

KITĀB n.m. (pl. *kutub*)~a letter; a book, the Book, the Scriptures; (*ahl al-kitāb*) People of the Book; appointed time or term; a decree [Ar]; an account [Pk]; a record [Ali]; (24:33) emancipation [Ar, Pk]; writing (of manumission) [Bl]; a deed (of earned freedom) [Ali]

2:2 (1)	that is the Book, wherein is no doubt
2:44 (41)	will you bid others to piety, and forget yourselves while you recite the Book?
2:53 (50)	when We gave to Moses the Book and the Salvation
2:78 (73)	some there are of them that are common folk not knowing the Book
2:79 (73)	woe to those who write the Book with their hands
2:85 (79)	do you believe in part of the Book, and disbelieve in part?
2:87 (81)	We gave to Moses the Book, and after him
2:89 (83)	there came to them a Book from God, confirming what was with them
2:101 (95)	a party of them that were given the Book reject (the Book) of God
2:101 (95)	a party of them that were given (the Book) reject the Book of God
2:105 (99)	those unbelievers of the People of the Book and the idolaters
2:109 (103)	many of the People of the Book wish they might restore you as unbelievers
2:113 (107)	yet they recite the Book
2:121 (115)	those to whom We have given the Book and who recite it with true recitation
2:129 (123)	and teach them the Book and the Wisdom, and purify them
2:144 (139)	those who have been given the Book know it is the truth
2:145 (140)	if thou shouldst bring to those that have been given the Book every sign
2:146 (141)	whom We have given the Book, and they recognize it
2:151 (146)	and to purify you, and to teach you the Book and the Wisdom
2:159 (154)	after We have shown them clearly in the Book
2:174 (169)	those who conceal what of the Book God has sent down on them
2:176 (171)	that, because God has sent down the Book with the truth
2:176 (171)	those that are at variance regarding the Book are in wide schism
2:177 (172)	to believe in God, and the Last Day, the angels, the Book
2:213 (209)	He sent down with them the Book with the truth
2:231 (231)	and the Book and the Wisdom He has sent down on you, to admonish you
2:235 (236)	do not resolve on the knot of marriage until the book has reached its term
2:285 (285)	each one believes in God and His angels, and in His Books
3:3 (2)	He has sent down upon thee the Book with the truth
3:7 (5)	it is He who sent down upon thee the Book
3:7 (5)	wherein are verses clear that are the Essence of the Book
3:19 (17)	those who were given the Book were not at variance
3:20 (19)	say to those who have been given the Book and to the common folk
3:23 (22)	hast thou not regarded those who were given a portion of the Book
3:23 (22)	being called to the Book of God, that it might decide between them
3:48 (43)	He will teach him the Book, the Wisdom, the Torah
3:64 (57)	People of the Book! Come now to a word common between us and you
3:65 (58)	People of the Book! Why do you dispute concerning Abraham?
3:69 (62)	there is a party of the People of the Book yearn to make you go astray

3:70 (63)	People of the Book! Why do you disbelieve in God's signs
3:71 (64)	People of the Book! Why do you confound the truth with vanity
3:72 (65)	there is a party of the People of the Book
3:75 (68)	of the People of the Book is he who, if thou trust him with a hundredweight, will restore it
3:78 (72)	there is a sect of them twist their tongues with the Book
3:78 (72)	that you may suppose it part of the Book
3:78 (72)	yet it is not part of the Book
3:79 (73)	it belongs not to any mortal that God should give him the Book
3:79 (73)	be you masters in that you know the Book, and in that you study
3:81 (75)	that I have given you of Book and Wisdom
3:98 (93)	People of the Book, why do you disbelieve in the signs of God?
3:99 (94)	People of the Book, why do you bar from God's way the believer
3:100 (95)	if you obey a sect of those who have been given the Book, they will turn you
3:110 (106)	had the People of the Book believed, it were better for them
3:113 (109)	some of the People of the Book are a nation upstanding
3:119 (115)	you believe in the Book, all of it
3:145 (139)	it is not given to any soul to die, save by the leave of God, at an appointed time
3:164 (158)	and to purify them, and to teach them the Book and the Wisdom
3:184 (181)	Messengers before thee, who came bearing clear signs, and the Psalms, and the Book Illuminating
3:186 (183)	you shall hear from those who were given the Book before you
3:187 (184)	when God took compact with those who had been given the Book
3:199 (198)	some there are of the People of the Book who believe in God
4:24 (28)	so God prescribes for you
4:44 (47)	hast thou not regarded those who were given a share of the Book purchasing error
4:47 (50)	you who have been given the Book, believe in what We have sent down
4:51 (54)	hast thou not regarded those who were given a share of the Book believing in demons
4:54 (57)	We gave the people of Abraham the Book and the Wisdom
4:103 (104)	surely the prayer is a timed prescription for the believers
4:105 (106)	We have sent down to thee the Book with the truth
4:113 (113)	God has sent down on thee the Book and the Wisdom
4:123 (122)	it is not your fancies, nor the fancies of the People of the Book
4:127 (126)	what is recited to you in the Book concerning the orphan women
4:131 (130)	We have charged those who were given the Book before you
4:136 (135)	O believers, believe in God and His Messenger and the Book
4:136 (135)	and the Book which He sent down before
4:136 (135)	whoso disbelieves in God and His angels and His Books
4:140 (139)	He has sent down upon you in the Book
4:153 (152)	the People of the Book will ask thee to bring down
4:153 (152)	[they] will ask thee to bring down upon them a Book from heaven
4:159 (157)	there is not one of the People of the Book but will assuredly believe in him
4:171 (169)	People of the Book, go not beyond the bounds in your religion
5:5 (7)	the food of those who were given the Book is permitted to you
5:5 (7)	and in wedlock women of them who were given the Book before you
5:15 (18)	People of the Book, now there has come to you Our Messenger
5:15 (18)	making clear to you many things you have been concealing of the Book
5:15 (18)	there has come to you from God a light, and a Book Manifest
5:19 (22)	People of the Book, now there has come to you Our Messenger
5:44 (48)	and the rabbis, following such portion of God's Book as they were given to keep
5:48 (52)	We have sent down to thee the Book with the truth

5:48 (52)	confirming the Book that was before it, and assuring it
5:57 (62)	take not as your friends those of them, who were given the Book before you
5:59 (64)	say: 'People of the Book, do you blame us'
5:65 (70)	but had the People of the Book believed and been godfearing
5:68 (72)	People of the Book, you do not stand on anything
5:77 (81)	People of the Book, go not beyond the bounds in your religion
5:110 (110)	and when I taught thee the Book, the Wisdom, the Torah
6:7 (7)	had We sent down on thee a Book on parchment
6:20 (20)	those to whom We have given the Book recognize it
6:38 (38)	We have neglected nothing in the Book
6:59 (59)	not a thing, fresh or withered, but it is in a Book Manifest
6:89 (89)	those are they to whom We gave the Book
6:91 (91)	who sent down the Book that Moses brought as a light and a guidance
6:92 (92)	this is a Book We have sent down, blessed
6:114 (114)	it is He who sent down to you the Book well-distinguished
6:114 (114)	those whom We have given the Book know it is sent down from thy Lord
6:154 (155)	then We gave Moses the Book, complete for him who does good
6:155 (156)	this is a Book We have sent down, blessed
6:156 (157)	the Book was sent down only upon two parties before us
6:157 (158)	if the Book had been sent down upon us, we had surely been more rightly guided than they
7:2 (1)	a Book sent down to thee
7:37 (35)	those — their portion of the Book shall reach them
7:52 (50)	We have brought to them a Book that We have well distinguished
7:169 (168)	there succeeded after them a succession who inherited the Book
7:169 (168)	has not the compact of the Book been taken touching them
7:170 (169)	those who hold fast to the Book, and perform the prayer
7:196 (195)	my protector is God who sent down the Book
8:68 (69)	had it not been for a prior prescription from God
8:75 (76)	those related by blood are nearer to one another in the Book of God
9:29 (29)	such men as practise not the religion of truth, being of those who have been given the Book
9:36 (36)	the number of the months, with God, is twelve in the Book of God
10:1 (1)	those are the signs of the Wise Book
10:37 (38)	and a distinguishing of the Book, wherein is no doubt
10:61 (62)	neither is aught smaller than that, or greater, but in a Manifest Book
10:94 (94)	ask those who recite the Book before thee
11:1 (1)	A Book whose verses are set clear
11:6 (8)	all is in a Manifest Book
11:17 (20)	before him is the Book of Moses for an ensample and a mercy
11:110 (112)	We gave Moses the Book
12:1 (1)	those are the signs of the Manifest Book
13:1 (1)	those are the signs of the Book
13:36 (36)	those to whom We have given the Book rejoice in what is sent down unto thee
13:38 (38)	every term has a Book
13:39 (39)	with Him is the Essence of the Book
13:43 (43)	and whosoever possesses knowledge of the Book
14:1 (1)	a Book We have sent down to thee
15:1 (1)	those are the signs of the Book and of a manifest Koran
15:4 (4)	never a city have We destroyed, but it had a known decree
16:64 (66)	We have not sent down upon thee the Book except that thou mayest make clear to them
16:89 (91)	We have sent down on thee the Book making clear everything

17:2 (2)	We gave Moses the Book, and made it a guidance
17:4 (4)	We decreed for the Children of Israel in the Book
17:13 (14)	on the Day of Resurrection, a book he shall find spread wide open
17:14 (15)	Read thy book! Thy soul suffices thee
17:58 (60)	chastisement; that is in the Book inscribed
17:71 (73)	whoso is given his book in his right hand
17:71 (73)	those shall read their book, and they shall not be wronged
17:93 (95)	we will not believe thy going up till thou bringest down on us a book that we may read
18:1 (1)	praise belongs to God who has sent down upon His servant the Book
18:27 (26)	recite what has been revealed to thee of the Book of thy Lord
18:49 (47)	and the Book shall be set in place
18:49 (47)	how is it with this Book, that it leaves nothing behind
19:12 (13)	O John, take the Book forcefully'
19:16 (16)	and mention in the Book Mary
19:30 (31)	lo, I am God's servant; God has given me the Book
19:41 (42)	and mention in the Book Abraham
19:51 (52)	and mention in the Book Moses
19:54 (55)	and mention in the Book Ishmael
19:56 (57)	and mention in the Book Idris
20:52 (54)	the knowledge of them is with my Lord, in a Book
21:10 (10)	We have sent down to you a Book wherein is your Remembrance
21:104 (104)	on the day when We shall roll up heaven as a scroll is rolled for the writings
22:8 (8)	that disputes concerning God without knowledge or guidance, or an illuminating Book
22:70 (69)	surely that is in a Book
23:49 (51)	We gave Moses the Book, that haply they would be guided
23:62 (64)	and with Us is a Book speaking truth
24:33 (33)	those your right hands own who seek emancipation, contract with them accordingly
25:35 (37)	We gave Moses the Book, and appointed with him his brother Aaron
26:2 (1)	those are the signs of the Manifest Book
27:1 (1)	those are the signs of the Koran and a Manifest Book
27:28 (28)	take this letter of mine, and cast it unto them
27:29 (29)	O Council, see, a letter honourable has been cast unto me
27:40 (40)	said he who possessed knowledge of the Book
27:75 (77)	not a thing is there hidden in heaven and earth but it is in a Manifest Book
28:2 (1)	those are the signs of the Manifest Book
28:43 (43)	We gave Moses the Book, after that We had destroyed the former generations
28:49 (49)	bring a Book from God that gives better guidance than these
28:52 (52)	those to whom We gave the Book before this believe in it
28:86 (86)	thou didst not hope that the Book should be cast unto thee
29:27 (26)	We appointed the Prophecy and the Book to be among his seed
29:45 (44)	recite what has been revealed to thee of the Book
29:46 (45)	dispute not with the People of the Book save in the fairer manner
29:47 (46)	even so We have sent down to thee the Book
29:47 (46)	those to whom We have given the Book believe in it
29:48 (47)	not before this didst thou recite any Book
29:51 (50)	is it not sufficient for them that We have sent down upon thee the Book
30:56 (56)	you have tarried in God's Book till the Day of the Upraising
31:2 (1)	those are the signs of the Wise Book
31:20 (19)	that disputes concerning God without knowledge or guidance, or an illuminating Book
32:2 (1)	the sending down of the Book, wherein no doubt is
32:23 (23)	indeed, We gave Moses the Book

33:6 (6)	those who are bound by blood are nearer to one another in the Book of God
33:6 (6)	that stands inscribed in the Book
33:26 (26)	He brought down those of the People of the Book who supported them from their fortresses
34:3 (3)	it is in a Manifest Book
34:44 (43)	We have not given them any Books to study
35:11 (12)	neither is any diminished in his life, but it is in a Book
35:25 (23)	their Messengers came to them with the clear signs, the Psalms, the Illuminating Book
35:29 (26)	those who recite the Book of God and perform the prayer
35:31 (28)	that We have revealed to thee of the Book is the truth
35:32 (29)	We bequeathed the Book on those of Our servants We chose
35:40 (38)	or have We given them a Book so that they are upon a clear sign from it?
37:117 (117)	and We gave them the Manifesting Book
37:157 (157)	bring your Book, if you speak truly
38:29 (28)	a Book We have sent down to thee, blessed
39:1 (1)	the sending down of the Book is from God
39:2 (2)	We have sent down to thee the Book with the truth
39:23 (24)	God has sent down the fairest discourse as a Book
39:41 (42)	We have sent down upon thee the Book for mankind with the truth
39:69 (69)	and the Book shall be set in place
40:2 (1)	the sending down of the Book is from God
40:53 (56)	We bequeathed upon the Children of Israel the Book
40:70 (72)	those who cry lies to the Book
41:3 (2)	a Book whose signs have been distinguished as an Arabic Koran
41:41 (41)	surely it is a Book Sublime
41:45 (45)	and We gave Moses the Book
42:14 (13)	those to whom the Book has been given as an inheritance
42:15 (14)	I believe in whatever Book God has sent down
42:17 (16)	God it is who has sent down the Book with the truth
42:52 (52)	thou knewest not what the Book was, nor belief
43:2 (1)	by the Clear Book
43:4 (3)	behold, it is in the Essence of the Book, with Us
43:21 (20)	did We bring them a Book aforetime to which they hold?
44:2 (1)	by the Clear Book
45:2 (1)	the sending down of the Book is from God
45:16 (15)	indeed, We gave the Children of Israel the Book
45:28 (27)	every nation being summoned unto its Book
45:29 (28)	this is Our Book, that speaks against you the truth
46:2 (1)	the sending down of the Book is from God
46:4 (3)	bring me a Book before this, or some remnant of a knowledge
46:12 (11)	before it was the Book of Moses for a model and a mercy
46:12 (11)	this is a Book confirming, in Arabic tongue, to warn the evildoers
46:30 (29)	we have heard a Book that was sent down after Moses
50:4 (4)	with Us is a book recording
52:2 (2)	and a Book inscribed
56:78 (77)	in a hidden Book
57:16 (15)	that they should not be as those to whom the Book was given aforetime
57:22 (22)	no affliction befalls in the earth or in yourselves, but it is in a Book
57:25 (25)	We sent down with them the Book and the Balance
57:26 (26)	We appointed the Prophecy and the Book to be among their seed
57:29 (29)	that the People of the Book may know that they have no power over anything
59:2 (2)	it is He who expelled from their habitations the unbelievers among the People of the Book
59:11 (11)	saying to their brothers of the People of the Book who disbelieve

62:2 (2)	to purify them, and to teach them the Book and the Wisdom
66:12 (12)	she confirmed the Words of her Lord and His Books
68:37 (37)	or have you a Book wherein you study?
69:19 (19)	as for him who is given his book in his right hand
69:19 (19)	he shall say, 'Here, take and read my book'
69:25 (25)	as for him who is given his book in his left hand
69:25 (25)	he shall say, 'Would that I had not been given my book'
74:31 (31)	that those who were given the Book may have certainty
74:31 (32)	that those who were given the Book and those who believe may not be in doubt
78:29 (29)	and everything We have numbered in a Book
83:7 (7)	no indeed; the Book of the libertines is in Sijjin
83:9 (9)	a book inscribed
83:18 (18)	no indeed; the book of the pious is in Illiyun
83:20 (20)	a book inscribed
84:7 (7)	as for him who is given his book in his right hand
84:10 (10)	as for him who is given his book behind his back
98:1 (1)	the unbelievers of the People of the Book and the idolaters
98:3 (2)	therein true Books
98:4 (3)	they scattered not, those that were given the Book
98:6 (5)	the unbelievers of the People of the Book and the idolaters

KĀTABA vb. (III)~to contract [Ar]; write (a writing of emancipation or manumission) [Pk, Bl]; give a deed [Ali]

c) impv. (*kātib*)

24:33 (33)	those your right hands own who seek emancipation, contract with them

IKTATABA vb. (VIII)~to write down, cause to be written down

a) perf. act.

25:5 (6)	fairy-tales of the ancients that he has had written down

*K T M

KATAMA vb. (I)~to conceal, hide; keep back evidence

a) perf. act.

2:140 (134)	who does greater evil than he who conceals a testimony received from God?

b) impf. act. (*yaktumu*)

2:33 (31)	I know what things you reveal, and what you were hiding
2:42 (39)	do not conceal the truth wittingly
2:72 (67)	and God disclosed what you were hiding
2:146 (141)	there is a party of them conceal the truth
2:159 (154)	those who conceal the clear signs and the guidance
2:174 (169)	those who conceal what of the Book God has sent down
2:228 (228)	it is not lawful for them to hide what God has created in their wombs
2:283 (283)	do not conceal the testimony
2:283 (283)	whoso conceals it, his heart is sinful
3:71 (64)	why do you confound the truth with vanity, and conceal the truth

3:167 (161)	God knows very well the things they hide
3:187 (184)	you shall make it clear unto the people, and not conceal it
4:37 (41)	and themselves conceal the bounty that God has given them
4:42 (45)	they will not conceal from God one tiding
5:61 (66)	God knows very well what they were hiding
5:99 (99)	God knows what you reveal and what you hide
5:106 (105)	nor will we hide the testimony of God
21:110 (110)	He knows what is spoken aloud and He knows what you hide
24:29 (29)	God knows what you reveal and what you hide
40:28 (29)	a believer of Pharaoh's folk that kept hidden his belief

*K TH B

KATHĪB n.m.~a heap of sand

73:14 (14)	and the mountains become a slipping heap of sand

*K TH R

KATHURA vb. (I)~to be much or numerous

a) perf. act.

4:7 (8)	to the women a share of what parents and kinsmen leave, whether it be little or much
8:19 (19)	your host will avail you nothing though it be numerous

KATHĪR n.m.~a host; (adj) many, manifold, much, (comp. adj. *akthar*) most; (adv) oft, frequently, abundantly

2:26 (24)	thereby He leads many astray
2:26 (24)	and thereby He guides many
2:100 (94)	nay, but the most of them are unbelievers
2:109 (103)	many of the People of the Book wish they might restore you as unbelievers
2:243 (244)	God is bounteous to the people, but most of the people are not thankful
2:245 (246)	and He will multiply it for him manifold
2:249 (250)	how often a little company has overcome a numerous company
2:269 (272)	whoso is given the Wisdom, has been given much good
3:41 (36)	mention thy Lord oft, and give glory
3:110 (106)	some of them are believers, but the most of them are ungodly
3:146 (140)	many a Prophet there has been, with whom thousands manifold have fought
3:186 (183)	and from those who are idolaters, much hurt
4:1 (1)	from the pair of them scattered abroad many men and women
4:12 (15)	but if they are more numerous than that
4:19 (23)	you may be averse to a thing, and God set in it much good
4:82 (84)	surely they would have found in it much inconsistency
4:94 (96)	with God are spoils abundant
4:100 (101)	whoso emigrates in the way of God will find in the earth many refuges and plenty
4:114 (114)	no good is there in much of their conspiring
4:160 (158)	and for their barring from God's way many
5:15 (18)	making clear to you many things you have been concealing of the Book

5:15 (18)	and effacing many things
5:32 (36)	many of them thereafter commit excesses in the earth
5:49 (54)	surely, many men are ungodly
5:59 (64)	and that most of you are ungodly
5:62 (67)	thou seest many of them vying in sin and enmity
5:64 (69)	thy Lord will surely increase many of them in insolence and unbelief
5:66 (70)	but many of them — evil are the things they do
5:68 (72)	sent down to thee from thy Lord will surely increase many of them in insolence
5:71 (75)	then again blind they were, many of them, and deaf
5:77 (81)	follow not the caprices of a people who went astray before, and led astray many
5:80 (83)	thou seest many of them making unbelievers their friends
5:81 (84)	but many of them are ungodly
5:103 (102)	the unbelievers forge against God falsehood, and most of them have no understanding
6:37 (37)	God is able to send down a sign, but most of them know not
6:91 (91)	you put it into parchments, revealing them, and hiding much
6:111 (111)	but most of them are ignorant
6:116 (116)	if thou obeyest the most part of those on earth
6:119 (119)	but surely, many lead astray by their caprices
6:137 (138)	those associates of theirs have decked out fair to many idolaters to slay their children
7:17 (16)	thou wilt not find most of them thankful
7:102 (100)	We found no covenant in the most part of them
7:102 (100)	indeed, We found the most part of them ungodly
7:131 (128)	but the most of them knew not
7:179 (178)	We have created for Gehenna many jinn and men
7:187 (187)	the knowledge of it is only with God, but most men know not
8:34 (34)	its only protectors are the godfearing; but most of them know not
8:43 (45)	and had He shown them as many you would have lost heart
8:45 (47)	stand firm, and remember God frequently
9:8 (8)	the most of them are ungodly
9:25 (25)	God has already helped you on many fields
9:34 (34)	many of the rabbis and monks indeed consume the goods of the people
9:69 (70)	those before you, who were stronger than you in might, and more abundant in wealth
9:82 (83)	let them laugh little, and weep much
10:36 (37)	the most of them follow only surmise
10:55 (56)	God's promise is true; but the most of them have no knowledge
10:60 (61)	God is bountiful to men; but most of them are not thankful
10:92 (92)	surely many men are heedless of Our signs
11:17 (20)	it is the truth from thy Lord, but most men do not believe
11:91 (93)	Shuaib, we do not understand much of what thou sayest
12:21 (21)	God prevails in His purpose, but most men know not
12:38 (38)	but most men are not thankful
12:40 (40)	that is the right religion; but most men know not
12:68 (68)	for that We had taught him; but most men know not
12:103 (103)	be thou ever so eager, the most part of men believe not
12:106 (106)	and the most part of them believe not in God
13:1 (1)	but most men do not believe
14:36 (39)	my Lord, they have led astray many men
16:38 (40)	it is a promise binding upon Him, but most men know not
16:75 (77)	praise belongs to God! Nay, most of them know not
16:83 (85)	they recognize the blessing of God, then they deny it
16:101 (103)	nay, but the most of them have no knowledge
17:6 (6)	We succoured you with wealth and children, and We made you a greater host
17:70 (72)	and preferred them greatly over many of those We created

17:74 (76)	thou wert near to inclining unto them a very little
17:89 (91)	yet most men refuse all but unbelief
18:34 (32)	I have more abundance of wealth than thou
18:54 (52)	man is the most disputatious of things
20:33 (34)	so shall we glorify Thee [abundantly]
20:34 (34)	and remember Thee abundantly
21:24 (24)	nay, but the most part of them know not the truth
22:18 (18)	the trees and the beasts, and many of mankind
22:18 (18)	and many merit the chastisement
22:40 (41)	oratories and mosques, wherein God's Name is much mentioned
23:19 (19)	gardens of palms and vines wherein are many fruits
23:21 (21)	and many uses there are in them for you
23:70 (72)	but most of them are averse from the truth
25:14 (15)	call not out today for one destruction, but call for many
25:38 (40)	and Thamood, and the men of Er-Rass, and between that generations a many
25:44 (46)	or deemest thou that most of them hear or understand?
25:49 (51)	cattle and men a many
25:50 (52)	yet most men refuse all but unbelief
26:8 (7)	in that is a sign, yet most of them are not believers
26:67 (67)	in that is a sign, yet most of them are not believers
26:103 (103)	in that is a sign, yet most of them are not believers
26:121 (121)	in that is a sign, yet most of them are not believers
26:139 (139)	in that is a sign, yet most of them are not believers
26:158 (158)	in that is a sign, yet most of them are not believers
26:174 (174)	in that is a sign, yet most of them are not believers
26:190 (190)	in that is a sign, yet most of them are not believers
26:223 (223)	they give ear, but most of them are liars
26:227 (227)	those that believe, and do righteous deeds, and remember God oft
27:15 (15)	who has preferred us over many of His believing servants
27:61 (62)	nay, but the most of them have no knowledge
27:73 (75)	thy Lord is bountiful to men; but most of them are not thankful
27:76 (78)	this Koran relates to the Children of Israel most of that concerning which they are at variance
28:13 (12)	the promise of God is true; but most of them do not know
28:57 (57)	but most of them know not
28:78 (78)	generations of men stronger than he in might, and more numerous in multitude
29:63 (63)	but most of them have no understanding
30:6 (5)	God fails not His promise, but most men do not know it
30:8 (7)	most men disbelieve in the encounter with their Lord
30:9 (8)	they ploughed up the earth and cultivated it more than they themselves have cultivated it
30:30 (29)	that is the right religion; but most men know it not
30:42 (41)	most of them were idolaters
31:25 (24)	nay, but most of them have no knowledge
33:21 (21)	whosoever hopes for God and the Last Day, and remembers God oft
33:35 (35)	men and women who remember God oft
33:41 (41)	O believers, remember God oft
34:28 (27)	but most men do not know it
34:35 (34)	we are more abundant in wealth and children
34:36 (35)	but most men do not know it
34:41 (40)	rather, they were serving the jinn; most of them believed in them
36:7 (6)	the Word has been realised against most of them
36:62 (62)	He led astray many a throng of you
37:71 (69)	before them erred most of the ancients
38:24 (23)	indeed many intermixers do injury one against the other
38:51 (51)	they call for fruits abundant, and sweet potions

39:29 (30)	praise belongs to God! Nay, but most of them do not know
39:49 (50)	it is a trial, but most of them do not know it
40:57 (59)	but most men know it not
40:59 (61)	the Hour is coming, no doubt of it, but most men do not believe
40:61 (63)	God is bountiful to men, but most men are not thankful
40:82 (82)	they were stronger than themselves in might and left firmer traces in the earth
41:4 (3)	most of them have turned away, and do not give ear
41:22 (21)	that God would never know much of the things that you were working
42:30 (29)	for what your own hands have earned; and He pardons much
42:34 (32)	He wrecks them for what they have earned; and He pardons much
43:73 (73)	therein you have abundant fruits, whereof you may eat
43:78 (78)	We brought you the truth, but most of you were averse to the truth
44:39 (39)	We created them not save in truth; but most of them know it not
45:26 (25)	the Day of Resurrection, wherein is no doubt, but most men do not know
48:19 (19)	and many spoils to take
48:20 (20)	God has promised you many spoils to take
49:4 (4)	those who call unto thee from behind the apartments, the most of them do not understand
49:7 (7)	if he obeyed you in much of the affair, you would suffer
49:12 (12)	O believers, eschew much suspicion
52:47 (47)	there surely awaits the evildoers a chastisement beyond even that, but most of them know it not
56:32 (31)	and fruits abounding
57:16 (15)	their hearts have become hard, and many of them are ungodly
57:26 (26)	some of them are guided, and many of them are ungodly
57:27 (27)	and many of them are ungodly
58:7 (8)	neither fewer than that, neither more
62:10 (10)	and seek God's bounty, and remember God frequently
71:24 (24)	and they have led many astray

KATHRAH n.f.~abundance, multitude

5:100 (100)	the corrupt and the good are not equal, though the abundance of the corrupt please thee
9:25 (25)	on the day of Hunain, when your multitude was pleasing to you

KAWTHAR n.m.~abundance; the Fount of Abundance [Ali]

108:1 (1)	surely We have given thee abundance

KATHTHARA vb. (II)~to multiply

a) perf. act.

7:86 (84)	remember when you were few, and He multiplied you

AKTHARA vb. (IV)~to make much, to multiply

a) perf. act.

11:32 (34)	thou hast disputed with us and make much disputation with us
89:12 (11)	and worked much corruption therein

TAKĀTHARA vb. (VI)~(n.vb.) rivalry

f) n.vb. (*takāthur*)

57:20 (19)	a cause for boasting among you, and a rivalry in wealth and children
102:1 (1)	gross rivalry diverts you

ISTAKTHARA vb. (X)~to acquire or have an abundance (of wealth), to think of great gain; (*istakthara min al-insi*) to make much of mankind [Ar]; to seduce many of humankind [Pk]; to take much toll of mankind [Ali]; to ask much of mankind [Bl]

a) perf. act.

6:128 (128)	company of jinn, you have made much of mankind
7:188 (188)	had I knowledge of the Unseen I would have acquired much good

b) impf. act. (*yastakthiru*)

74:6 (6)	give not, thinking to gain greater

*K W B

AKWĀB n.m. (pl. of *kūb*)~cups, goblets

43:71 (71)	there shall be passed around them platters of gold, and cups
56:18 (18)	with goblets, and ewers, and a cup from a spring
76:15 (15)	there shall be passed around them vessels of silver, and goblets of crystal
88:14 (14)	and goblets set forth

*K W K B

KAWKAB n.m. (pl. *kawākib*)~a star

6:76 (76)	when night outspread over him he saw a star
12:4 (4)	I saw eleven stars, and the sun and the moon
24:35 (35)	the glass as it were a glittering star
37:6 (6)	We have adorned the lower heaven with the adornment of the stars
82:2 (2)	when the stars are scattered

*K W N

KĀNA vb. (I) (also an auxiliary verb; impf. act. *yakūnu*)~to be, become, happen, exist (listed below are only the passages where the impv. is a Divine command)

c) impv. (*kun*)

2:65 (61)	be you apes, miserably slinking
2:117 (111)	when He decrees a thing, He but says to it 'Be'
3:47 (42)	when He decrees a thing He does but say to it 'Be'
3:59 (52)	then said He unto him, 'Be,' and he was
3:79 (73)	be you masters in that you know the Book
4:135 (134)	O believers, be you securers of justice, witnesses for God
5:8 (11)	O believers, be you steadfast before God, witnesses for justice
6:73 (72)	the day He says 'Be,' and it is
7:144 (141)	take what I have given thee, and be of the thankful
7:166 (166)	be you apes, miserably slinking
9:119 (120)	O believers, fear God, and be with the truthful ones
15:98 (98)	proclaim thy Lord's praise, and be of those that bow
16:40 (42)	the only words We say to a thing, when We desire it, is that We say to it 'Be'

17:50 (53)	let you be stones, or iron
19:35 (36)	when He decrees a thing, He but says to it 'Be'
21:69 (69)	O fire, be coolness and safety for Abraham
36:82 (82)	when He desires a thing, is to say to it 'Be'
39:66 (66)	but God do thou serve; and be thou among the thankful
40:68 (70)	when He decrees a thing, He but says to it 'Be'
61:14 (14)	O believers, be you God's helpers

MAKĀN n.m.~a place, side; (*sharru makān*) worse situated, worse case

4:20 (24)	if you desire to exchange a wife in place of another
5:60 (65)	they are worse situated, and have gone further astray
7:95 (93)	We gave them in the place of evil good, till they multiplied
7:143 (139)	behold the mountain — if it stays fast in its place, then thou shalt see Me
10:22 (23)	and waves come on them from every side
10:28 (29)	get you to your place, you and your associates
12:77 (77)	you are in a worse case; God knows very well
12:78 (78)	so take one of us in his place
14:17 (20)	and death comes upon him from every side
16:101 (103)	when We exchange a verse in the place of another verse
16:112 (113)	its provision coming to it easefully from every place
19:16 (16)	when she withdrew from her people to an eastern place
19:22 (22)	she conceived him, and withdrew with him to a distant place
19:57 (58)	We raised him up to a high place
19:75 (77)	then they shall surely know who is worse in place
20:58 (60)	therefore appoint a tryst between us and thee, a place mutually agreeable
22:26 (27)	when We settled for Abraham the place of the House
22:31 (32)	or the wind sweeps him headlong into a place far away
25:12 (13)	when it sees them from a far place, they shall hear its bubbling
25:13 (14)	when they are cast, coupled in fetters, into a narrow place of that Fire
25:34 (36)	they shall be worse in place, and gone further astray from the way
28:82 (82)	in the morning those who had longed to be in his place the day before were saying
34:51 (50)	and they are seized from a place near at hand
34:52 (51)	but how can they reach from a place far away
34:53 (52)	seeing they disbelieved in it before, guessing at the Unseen from a place far away
41:44 (44)	those — they are called from a far place
50:41 (40)	listen thou for the day when the caller shall call from a near place

MAKĀNAH n.f.~a place, a station; a position (where one is)

6:135 (135)	O my people, act according to your station
11:93 (95)	O my people, act according to your station
11:121 (122)	act you according to your station
36:67 (67)	We would have changed them where they were
39:39 (40)	my people, act according to your station

*K W R

KAWWARA vb. (II)~to wrap one about another [Ar]; make one to succeed another [Pk]; make to overlap [Ali]; (pass) to be darkened [Ar]; be overthrown [Pk]; be folded up [Ali]

b) impf. act. (*yukawwiru*)

39:5 (7)	wrapping night about the day
39:5 (7)	wrapping the day about the night

d) perf. pass. (*kuwwira*)

81:1 (1) when the sun shall be darkened

*K W Y

KAWÁ vb. (I)~to brand

e) impf. pass. (*yukwá*)

9:35 (35) therewith their foreheads and their sides and their backs shall be branded

*K Y D

KĀDA vb. (I)~to contrive, devise, outwit, try a trick or a guile [Ar]; to plot, circumvent, outwit, contrive [Pk]; to scheme against, concoct a plot, have a plan for, use a trick (or plot), to plot or plan a scheme [Ali]. (n.vb.) guile, outwitting [Ar]; scheme, plan, plot, snare, strategy, guile, strength, artifice, wit, cunning, stratagem, trick [Pk, Ali]; cunning [Bl]. (pcple. pass.) outwitted [Ar]; ensnared [Pk]; one involved in a plot [Ali]

a) perf. act.

12:76 (76) so We contrived for Joseph's sake; he could not have taken his

b) impf. act. (*yakīdu*)

12:5 (5) relate not thy vision to thy brothers, lest they devise against thee
21:57 (58) by God, I shall assuredly outwit your idols, after you have gone away
86:15 (15) they are devising guile
86:16 (16) and I am devising guile

c) impv. (*kid*)

7:195 (194) call you then to your associates; then try your guile on me
11:55 (58) so try your guile on me, all together
77:39 (39) if you have a trick, try you now to trick Me

f) n.vb. (*kayd*)

3:120 (116) if you are patient and godfearing, their guile will hurt you nothing
4:76 (78) surely the guile of Satan is ever feeble
7:183 (182) My guile is sure
8:18 (18) and that God weakens the unbelievers' guile
12:5 (5) to thy brothers, lest they devise against thee some guile
12:28 (28) this is of your women's guile
12:28 (28) your guile is great
12:33 (33) if Thou turnest not from me their guile
12:34 (34) his Lord answered him, and He turned away from him their guile
12:50 (50) surely my Lord has knowledge of their guile
12:52 (52) God guides not the guile of the treacherous
20:60 (62) Pharaoh then withdrew, and gathered his guile
20:64 (67) so gather your guile; then come in battle-line
20:69 (72) for they have fashioned only the guile of a sorcerer
21:70 (70) they desired to outwit him
22:15 (15) whether his guile does away with what enrages him

37:98 (96)	they desired to outwit him; so We made them the lower ones
40:25 (26)	but the guile of the unbelievers
40:37 (40)	and Pharaoh's guile came only to ruin
52:42 (42)	or desire they to outwit
52:46 (46)	the day when their guile shall avail them naught
68:45 (45)	My guile is sure
77:39 (39)	if you have a trick, try you now to trick Me
86:15 (15)	they are devising guile
86:16 (16)	and I am devising guile
105:2 (2)	did He not make their guile to go astray?

h) pcple. pass. (*makīd*)

52:42 (42)	they are the outwitted

*K Y L

KĀLA vb. (I)~to measure. (n.vb.) a measure, load

a) perf. act.

17:35 (37)	and fill up the measure when you measure
83:3 (3)	but, when they measure for them or weigh for them, do skimp

f) n.vb. (*kayl*)

6:152 (153)	and fill up the measure and the balance with justice
7:85 (83)	fill up the measure and the balance, and diminish not the goods of the people
12:59 (59)	do you not see that I fill up the measure, and am the best of hosts?
12:60 (60)	if you bring him not to me, there shall be no measure for you with me
12:63 (63)	the measure was denied to us; so send with us our brother
12:65 (65)	we shall obtain an extra camel's load
12:65 (65)	(an extra camel's load) — that is an easy measure
12:88 (88)	fill up to us the measure, and be charitable to us
17:35 (37)	and fill up the measure when you measure
26:181 (181)	fill up the measure, and be not cheaters

MIKYĀL n.m.~a measure (a measuring vessel)

11:84 (85)	diminish not the measure and the balance
11:85 (86)	fill up the measure and the balance justly

IKTĀLA vb. (VIII)~to measure, obtain a measure

a) perf. act.

83:2 (2)	who, when they measure against the people, take full measure

b) impf. act. (*yaktālu*)

12:63 (63)	so send with us our brother, that we may obtain the measure

*K Y N

ISTAKĀNA vb. (X)~to humble or abase oneself; also, to be brought low [Pk]; to give in [Ali]

a) perf. act.

3:146 (140)	they fainted not for what smote them in God's way, neither weakened, nor did they
23:76 (78)	yet they abased not themselves to their Lord

*K Ẓ M

KAẒAMA vb. (I)~(pcple. act.) one who restrains or chokes. (pcple. pass.) that which is choked or suppressed

g) pcple. act. (*kāẓim*)

3:134 (128)	who expend in prosperity and adversity in almsgiving, and restrain their rage
40:18 (18)	when, choking with anguish, the hearts are in the throats

h) pcple. pass. (*makẓūm*)

68:48 (48)	be not as the Man of the Fish, when he called, choking inwardly

KAẒĪM n.m. (adj)~one who chokes (tr) or suppresses

12:84 (84)	his eyes turned white because of the sorrow that he choked within him
16:58 (60)	his face is darkened and he chokes inwardly
43:17 (16)	his face is darkened, and he chokes inwardly

KHĀ

*KH B ʾ

KHABA'A vb. (I)~(n.vb.) that which is hidden

f) n.vb. (*khabʾ*)

27:25 (25) to God, who brings forth what is hidden in the heavens and earth

*KH B L

KHABĀL n.m.~the act of ruining, trouble

3:118 (114) such men spare nothing to ruin you; they yearn for you to suffer
9:47 (47) had they gone forth among you, they would only have increased you in trouble

*KH B R

KHABARA vb. (I)~(n.vb.) knowledge, understanding

f) n.vb. (*khubr*)

18:68 (67) how shouldst thou bear patiently that thou hast never encompassed in thy

18:91 (90) We encompassed in knowledge what was with him

KHABAR n.m. (pl. *akhbār*)~tidings, news, report

9:94 (95) God has already told us tidings of you
27:7 (7) I observe a fire, and will bring you news of it
28:29 (29) I observe a fire. Perhaps I shall bring you news of it
47:31 (33) until We know those of you who struggle and are steadfast, and try your tidings
99:4 (4) upon that day she shall tell her tidings

KHABĪR n.m. (adj)~one who is infomed; One who knows, One who is aware (Divine attribute, in all cases except 25:59)

2:234 (234) God is aware of the things you do
2:271 (273) God is aware of the things you do
3:153 (147) and God is aware of the things you do
3:180 (176) and God is aware of the things you do
4:35 (39) surely God is All-knowing, All-aware
4:94 (96) surely God is aware of the things you do
4:128 (127) surely God is aware of the things you do
4:135 (134) God is aware of the things you do
5:8 (11) surely God is aware of the things you do
6:18 (18) and He is the All-wise, the All-aware
6:73 (73) He is the All-wise, the All-aware
6:103 (103) He is the All-subtle, the All-aware

9:16 (16)	God is aware of what you do
11:1 (1)	a Book ... from One All-wise, All-aware
11:111 (113)	He is aware of the things they do
17:17 (18)	thy Lord suffices as one who is aware of and sees the sins of His servants
17:30 (32)	surely He is aware of and sees His servants
17:96 (98)	surely He is aware of and sees His servants
22:63 (62)	God is All-subtle, All-aware
24:30 (30)	God is aware of the things they work
24:53 (52)	surely God is aware of the things you do
25:58 (60)	sufficiently is He aware of His servants' sins
25:59 (60)	the All-compassionate: ask any informed of Him
27:88 (90)	He is aware of the things you do
31:16 (15)	surely God is All-subtle, All-aware
31:29 (28)	and that God is aware of what you do
31:34 (34)	surely God is All-knowing, All-aware
33:2 (2)	surely God is aware of the things you do
33:34 (34)	God is All-subtle, All-aware
34:1 (1)	He is the All-wise, the All-aware
35:14 (15)	none can tell thee like One who is aware
35:31 (28)	God is aware of and sees His servants
42:27 (26)	surely He is aware of and sees His servants
48:11 (11)	God is ever aware of the things you do
49:13 (13)	God is All-knowing, All-aware
57:10 (10)	God is aware of the things you do
58:3 (4)	God is aware of the things you do
58:11 (12)	God is aware of the things you do
58:13 (14)	God is aware of the things you do
59:18 (18)	fear God; God is aware of the things you do
63:11 (11)	God is aware of the things you do
64:8 (8)	God is aware of the things you do
66:3 (3)	I was told of it by the All-knowing, the All-aware
67:14 (14)	He is the All-subtle, the All-aware
100:11 (11)	surely on that day their Lord shall be aware of them

*KH B T

AKHBATA vb. (IV)~to acquiesce, to humble oneself. (pcple. act.) one who humbles himself

a) perf. act.

11:23 (25) those who believe, and do righteous deeds, and have humbled themselves

b) impf. act. (*yukhbitu*)

22:54 (53) and believe in it, and so their hearts be humble unto Him

g) pcple. act. (*mukhbit*)

22:34 (35) give thou good tidings unto the humble

*KH B TH

KHABUTHA vb. (I)~to be corrupt [Ar], to be bad

a) perf. act.

7:58 (56) and the corrupt — it comes forth but scantily

KHABĀ'ITH n.f. (pl. of *khabīthah*)~corrupt things, deeds of corruption [Ar]; foul things, abominations [Pk]; bad and impure things, abominations [Ali]

7:157 (156) and making unlawful for them the corrupt things
21:74 (74) We delivered him from the city that had been doing deeds of corruption

KHABĪTH n.m. (adj)~corrupt [Ar]; bad, wicked, vile, evil [Pk]; bad, worthless, impure, evil [Ali]

2:267 (269) intend not the corrupt of it for your expending
3:179 (173) till He shall distinguish the corrupt from the good
4:2 (2) do not exchange the corrupt for the good
5:100 (100) the corrupt and the good are not equal
5:100 (100) though the abundance of the corrupt please thee
8:37 (38) that God may distinguish the corrupt from the good
8:37 (38) and [that He may] place the corrupt one upon another
14:26 (31) and the likeness of a corrupt word is as a (corrupt) tree
14:26 (31) and the likeness of a (corrupt) word is as a corrupt tree
24:26 (26) corrupt women for (corrupt men)
24:26 (26) (corrupt women) for corrupt men
24:26 (26) and corrupt men for (corrupt women)
24:26 (26) and (corrupt men) for corrupt women

*KH B Ṭ

TAKHABBAṬA vb. (V)~to prostrate (tr) by a satanic touch

a) perf. act.

2:275 (276) except as he rises, whom Satan of the touch prostrates

*KH B W

KHABĀ vb. (I)~to abate

a) perf. act.

17:97 (99) whensoever it abates We shall increase for them the Blaze

*KH B Z

KHUBZ n.m.~bread

12:36 (36) I dreamed that I was carrying on my head bread

*KH D ʿ

KHADAʿA vb. (I)~to deceive; to trick [Ar]; to beguile [Pk]. (pcple. act.) one who tricks [Ar]; who beguiles [Pk]; who over-reaches [Ali]

b) impf. act. (*yakhdaʿu*)

2:9 (8) only themselves they deceive, and they are not aware
8:62 (64) if they desire to trick thee, God is sufficient for thee

g) pcple. act. (*khādiʿ*)

4:142 (141) the hypocrites seek (to trick) God but God is tricking them

KHĀDAʿA vb. (III)~to seek to trick [Ar]; to seek to beguile [Pk]; to over-reach, to deceive [Ali]; to outwit [Bl]

b) impf. act. (*yukhādiʿu*)

2:9 (8) they would trick God and the believers
4:142 (141) the hypocrites seek to trick God

*KH D D

KHADD n.m.~a cheek

31:18 (17) turn not thy cheek away from men in scorn

UKHDŪD n.m.~pit, ditch; (*aṣḥāb al-ukhdūd*) Men of the Pit [Ar, Bl]; owners of the ditch [Pk]; makers of the pit (of fire) [Ali]

85:4 (4) slain were the Men of the Pit

*KH D N

AKHDĀN n.m. (pl. of *khidn*)~lovers

4:25 (29) not as in licence or taking lovers
5:5 (7) in wedlock and not in licence, or as taking lovers

*KH DH L

KHADHALA vb. (I)~to forsake [Ar, Ali]; to withdraw one's help [Pk]. (pcple. pass.) forsaken [Ar, Pk]; one who is in destitution [Ali]

b) impf. act. (*yakhdhulu*)

3:160 (154) if He forsakes you, who then can help you after Him?

h) pcple. pass. (*makhdhūl*)

17:22 (23) set not up with God another god, or thou wilt sit condemned

KHADHŪL n.m.~one who forsakes others [Ar]; deserter [Pk]; traitor [Ali]; betrayer [Bl]

25:29 (31) Satan is ever a forsaker of men

*KH Ḍ ᶜ

KHAḌAᶜA vb. (I)~to be abject [Ar]; to be soft [Pk]; to be complaisant [Ali]; to wheedle [Bl]. (pcple. act.) one who is humbled [Ar]; one who is bowed [Pk]; who bends in humility [Ali]; submissive [Bl]

b) impf. act. (*yakhḍaᶜu*)

33:32 (32)	if you are godfearing, be not abject in your speech

g) pcple. act. (*khāḍiᶜ*)

26:4 (3)	so their necks will stay humbled to it

*KH Ḍ D

KHAḌADA vb. (I)~(pcple. pass.) thornless

h) pcple. pass. (*makhḍūd*)

56:28 (27)	mid thornless lote-trees

*KH Ḍ R

AKHḌAR n.m. (pl. *khuḍr*)~green

12:43 (43)	likewise seven green ears of corn, and seven withered
12:46 (46)	seven green ears of corn, and seven withered
18:31 (30)	they shall be robed in green garments of silk
36:80 (80)	who has made for you out of the green tree fire
55:76 (76)	reclining upon green cushions and lovely druggets
76:21 (21)	upon them shall be green garments of silk

KHAḌIR n.m.~green leaf, herb

6:99 (99)	and then We have brought forth the green leaf of it

IKHḌARRA vb. (IX)~(pcple. act.) becoming green

g) pcple. act. (*mukhḍarr*)

22:63 (62)	and in the morning the earth becomes green

*KH F Ḍ

KHAFAḌA vb. (I)~to lower. (pcple. act.) abasing

c) impv. (*ikhfiḍ*)

15:88 (88)	do not sorrow for them, and lower thy wing unto the believers
17:24 (25)	lower to them the wing of humbleness out of mercy and say
26:215 (215)	lower thy wing to those who follow thee, being believers

g) pcple. act. (*khāfiḍ*)

56:3 (3)	abasing, exalting

*KH F F

KHAFFA vb. (I)~to be or weigh light

a) perf. act.

7:9 (8)	he whose scales are light — they have lost their souls
23:103 (105)	he whose scales are light — they have lost their souls
101:8 (6)	but he whose deeds weigh light in the Balance

KHAFĪF n.m. (adj; pl. *khifāf*)~light

7:189 (189)	then, when he covered her, she bore a light burden
9:41 (41)	go forth, light and heavy! Struggle in God's way

KHAFFAFA vb. (II)~to lighten. (n.vb.) making light, lightening

a) perf. act.

8:66 (67)	God has lightened it for you, knowing that there is weakness in you

b) impf. act. (*yukhaffifu*)

4:28 (32)	God desires to lighten things for you
40:49 (52)	call on your Lord, to lighten for us one day of the chastisement

e) impf. pass. (*yukhaffafu*)

2:86 (80)	for them the chastisement shall not be lightened
2:162 (157)	the chastisement shall not be lightened for them
3:88 (82)	the chastisement shall not be lightened for them
16:85 (87)	when the evildoers behold the chastisement, it shall not be lightened for them
35:36 (33)	nor shall its chastisement be lightened for them

f) n.vb. (*takhfīf*)

2:178 (174)	that is a lightening granted you by your Lord

ISTAKHAFFA vb. (X)~to think or find light or easy; to make unsteady [Ar]; to make impatient [Pk]; to shake one's firmness [Ali]; to rush [Bl]

a) perf. act.

43:54 (54)	so he made his people unsteady, and they obeyed him

b) impf. act. (*yastakhiffu*)

16:80 (82)	[He] appointed for you of the skins of the cattle houses you find light
30:60 (60)	let not those who have not sure faith make thee unsteady

*KH F T

KHĀFATA vb. (III)~(with prep. *bi-*) to be hushed, to be silent, to speak in a low tone

b) impf. act. (*yukhāfitu*)

17:110 (110)	be thou not loud in thy prayer, nor hushed therein

TAKHĀFATA vb. (VI)~to whisper

b) impf. act. (*yatakhāfatu*)

20:103 (103)	whispering one to another, 'You have tarried only ten nights'
68:23 (23)	so they departed, whispering together

*KH F Y

KHAFÁ vb. (I)~to be hidden, to be concealed

b) impf. act. (*yakhfá*)

3:5 (4)	from God nothing whatever is hidden in heaven and earth
14:38 (41)	from God nothing whatever is hidden in earth and heaven
40:16 (16)	and naught of theirs is hidden from God
41:40 (40)	those who blaspheme Our signs are not hidden from Us
69:18 (18)	on that day you shall be exposed, not one secret of yours concealed
87:7 (7)	surely He knows what is spoken aloud and what is hidden

KHAFĪY n.m.~(adj) furitive [Ar]; veiled [Pk]; stealthy [Ali]; (comp. adj. *akhfá*) more hidden; (adv) secretly; (Bl reads as vb.; see Form IV, below)

19:3 (2)	when he called upon his Lord secretly
20:7 (6)	surely He knows the secret and that yet more hidden
42:45 (44)	abject in humbleness, looking with furitive glance

KHĀFIYAH n.f.~a secret

69:18 (18)	on that day you shall be exposed, not one secret of yours concealed

KHUFYAH n.f. (adv)~secretly

6:63 (63)	you call upon Him humbly and secretly
7:55 (53)	call on your Lord, humbly and secretly

AKHFÁ vb. (IV)~to conceal, to hide, to do in secret

a) perf. act.

60:1 (1)	yet I know very well what you conceal and what you publish

b) impf. act. (*yukhfī*)

2:271 (273)	if you conceal them, and give them to the poor, that is better for you
2:284 (284)	whether you publish what is in your hearts or hide it
3:29 (27)	whether you hide what is in your breasts or publish it
3:118 (114)	and what their breasts conceal is yet greater
3:154 (148)	they were concealing in their hearts that they show not to thee
4:149 (148)	if you do good openly or in secret or pardon an evil
5:15 (18)	making clear to you many things you have been concealing of the Book
6:28 (28)	that which they were concealing before has now appeared to them
6:91 (91)	you put it into parchments, revealing them, and hiding much
14:38 (41)	thou knowest what we keep secret and what we publish
20:15 (15)	the Hour is coming; I would conceal it
24:31 (31)	nor let them stamp their feet, so that their hidden ornament may be known
27:25 (25)	He knows what you conceal and what you publish

33:37 (37)	thou wast concealing within thyself what God should reveal
33:54 (54)	whether you reveal anything, or whether you conceal it
40:19 (20)	He knows the treachery of the eyes and what the breasts conceal

d) perf. pass. (*ukhfiya*)

32:17 (17)	no soul knows what comfort is laid up for them secretly

ISTAKHFÁ vb. (X)~to hide oneself. (pcple. act.) one who hides himself

b) impf. act. (*yastakhfī*)

4:108 (108)	they hide themselves from men
4:108 (108)	but hide not themselves from God
11:5 (5)	behold, they fold their breasts, to hide them from Him

g) pcple. act. (*mustakhfī*)

13:10 (11)	who hides himself in the night, and he who sallies by day

*KH L ᶜ

KHALAᶜA vb. (I)~to put off, to take off

c) impv. (*ikhlaᶜ*)

20:12 (12)	put off thy shoes; thou art in the holy valley, Towa

*KH L D

KHALADA vb. (I)~to dwell or abide forever, to be eternal. (n.vb.) eternity. (pcple. act.) dwelling forever, abiding forever; living forever, immortal

b) impf. act. (*yakhludu*)

25:69 (69)	and he shall dwell therein humbled forever
26:129 (129)	do you take to you castles, haply to dwell forever?

f) n.vb. (*khulūd*)

50:34 (33)	this is the Day of Eternity

g) pcple. act. (*khālid*)

2:25 (23)	therein they shall dwell forever
2:39 (37)	those shall be the inhabitants of the Fire, therein dwelling forever
2:81 (75)	those are the inhabitants of the Fire; there they shall dwell forever
2:82 (76)	those are the inhabitants of Paradise; there they shall dwell forever
2:162 (157)	therein dwelling forever
2:217 (214)	those are the inhabitants of the Fire; therein they shall dwell forever
2:257 (259)	those are the inhabitants of the Fire, therein dwelling forever
2:275 (276)	those are the inhabitants of the Fire, therein dwelling forever
3:15 (13)	gardens underneath which rivers flow, therein dwelling forever
3:88 (82)	therein dwelling forever

3:107 (103)	they shall be in God's mercy, therein dwelling forever
3:116 (112)	those are the inhabitants of the Fire, therein dwelling forever
3:136 (130)	gardens beneath which rivers flow, therein dwelling forever
3:198 (197)	gardens underneath which rivers flow, therein dwelling forever
4:13 (17)	gardens underneath which rivers flow, therein dwelling forever
4:14 (18)	him He will admit to a Fire, therein dwelling forever
4:57 (60)	gardens underneath which rivers flow, therein dwelling forever and ever
4:93 (95)	his recompense is Gehenna, therein dwelling forever
4:122 (121)	gardens underneath which rivers flow, therein dwelling for ever and ever
4:169 (167)	the road to Gehenna, therein dwelling forever and ever
5:80 (83)	in the chastisement they shall dwell forever
5:85 (88)	gardens underneath which rivers flow, therein dwelling forever
5:119 (119)	gardens underneath which rivers flow, therein dwelling forever
6:128 (128)	the Fire is your lodging, therein to dwell forever
7:20 (19)	lest you become angels, or lest you become immortals
7:36 (34)	those shall be the inhabitants of the Fire, therein dwelling forever
7:42 (40)	those are the inhabitants of Paradise, therein dwelling forever
9:17 (17)	and in the Fire they shall dwell forever
9:22 (22)	therein to dwell forever and ever
9:63 (64)	for him awaits the fire of Gehenna, therein to dwell forever
9:68 (69)	and the unbelievers, the fire of Gehenna, therein to dwell forever
9:72 (73)	gardens underneath which rivers flow, forever therein to dwell
9:89 (90)	gardens underneath which rivers flow, therein to dwell forever
9:100 (101)	gardens underneath which rivers flow, therein to dwell forever and ever
10:26 (27)	those are the inhabitants of Paradise, therein dwelling forever
10:27 (28)	those are the inhabitants of the Fire, therein dwelling forever
11:23 (25)	they shall be the inhabitants of Paradise, therein dwelling forever
11:107 (109)	therein dwelling forever, so long as the heavens and earth abide
11:108 (110)	for the happy, they shall be in Paradise, therein dwelling forever
13:5 (6)	those shall be the inhabitants of the Fire, therein dwelling forever
14:23 (28)	gardens underneath which rivers flow, therein dwelling forever
16:29 (31)	so enter the gates of Gehenna, there to dwell forever
18:108 (108)	therein to dwell forever, desiring no removal out of them
20:76 (78)	Gardens of Eden, underneath which rivers flow, therein dwelling forever
20:101 (101)	therein abiding forever
21:8 (8)	nor did We fashion them as bodies that ate not food, neither were they immortal
21:34 (35)	if thou diest, will they live forever?
21:99 (99)	yet every one of them shall therein abide forever
21:102 (102)	and they shall dwell forever in that their souls desired
23:11 (11)	who shall inherit Paradise therein dwelling forever
23:103 (105)	he whose scales are light — they have lost their souls in Gehenna dwelling forever
25:16 (17)	therein they shall have what they will dwelling forever
25:76 (76)	therein they shall dwell forever; fair it is as a lodging-place
29:58 (58)	chambers of Paradise, underneath which rivers flow, therein dwelling forever
31:9 (8)	therein to dwell forever — God's promise in truth
33:65 (65)	therein to dwell for ever; they shall find neither protector nor helper
39:72 (72)	enter the gates of Gehenna, to dwell therein forever
39:73 (73)	well you have fared; enter in, to dwell forever
40:76 (76)	enter the gates of Gehenna, to dwell therein forever
43:71 (71)	and therein you shall dwell forever
43:74 (74)	but the evildoers dwell forever in the chastisement of Gehenna
46:14 (13)	those are the inhabitants of Paradise, therein dwelling forever
47:15 (17)	are they as he who dwells forever in the Fire
48:5 (5)	gardens underneath which rivers flow, therein to dwell forever
57:12 (12)	gardens underneath which rivers flow, therein to dwell for ever

58:17 (18)	those — they are the inhabitants of the Fire, therein dwelling forever
58:22 (22)	gardens underneath which rivers flow, therein to dwell forever
59:17 (17)	their end is, both are in the Fire, there dwelling forever
64:9 (9)	gardens underneath which rivers flow, therein to dwell for ever and ever
64:10 (10)	those shall be the inhabitants of the Fire, therein to dwell forever
65:11 (11)	gardens underneath which rivers flow; therein they shall dwell for ever and ever
72:23 (24)	for him there awaits the Fire of Gehenna; therein they shall dwell forever
98:6 (5)	the idolaters shall be in the Fire of Gehenna, therein dwelling forever
98:8 (7)	Gardens of Eden, underneath which rivers flow, therein dwelling for ever and ever

KHULD n.m.~eternity

10:52 (53)	taste the chastisement of eternity
20:120 (118)	Adam, shall I point thee to the Tree of Eternity
21:34 (35)	We have not assigned to any mortal before thee to live forever
25:15 (16)	is that better, or the Garden of Eternity
32:14 (14)	taste the chastisement of eternity for that you were doing
41:28 (28)	wherein they shall have the Abode of Eternity as a recompense

KHALLADA vb. (II)~(pcple. pass.) immortal

h) pcple. pass. (*mukhallad*)

56:17 (17)	immortal youths going round about them
76:19 (19)	immortal youths shall go about them

AKHLADA vb. (IV)~to make immortal; to incline towards

a) perf. act.

7:176 (175)	but he inclined towards the earth and followed his lust
104:3 (3)	thinking his riches have made him immortal

*KH L F

KHALAFA vb. (I)~to succeed (tr), to be a successor, to come after, to do in someone else's place (or after one leaves). (pcple. act.) one who stays behind

a) perf. act.

7:150 (149)	evilly have you done in my place, after me
7:169 (168)	there succeeded after them a succession who inherited the Book
19:59 (60)	there succeeded after them a succession who wasted the prayer

b) impf. act. (*yakhlufu*)

43:60 (60)	We would have appointed angels among you to be successors

c) impv. (*ukhluf*)

7:142 (138)	be my successor among my people, and put things right

g) pcple. act. (*khālif*)

9:83 (84)	you were well-pleased to tarry the first time, so now tarry with those behind

KHALF n.m.~a succession, succeeding generation; (with prep. *min*) behind, from behind, after; (adv) after, behind

2:66 (62)	We made it a punishment exemplary for all the former times and for the latter
2:255 (256)	He knows what lies before them and what is after them
3:170 (164)	and joyful in those who remain behind and have not joined them
4:9 (10)	let those fear who, if they left behind them weak seed, would be afraid
7:17 (16)	then I shall come on them from before them and from behind them
7:169 (168)	there succeeded after them a succession who inherited the Book
8:57 (59)	deal with them in such wise as to scatter the ones behind them
10:92 (92)	that thou mayest be a sign to those after thee
13:11 (12)	he has attendant angels, before him and behind him
19:59 (60)	then there succeeded after them a succession who wasted the prayer
19:64 (65)	to Him belongs all that is before us, and all that is behind us
20:110 (109)	He knows what is before them and behind them
21:28 (28)	He knows what is before them and behind them
22:76 (75)	He knows whatsoever is before them and behind them
34:9 (9)	have they not regarded what lies before them and what lies behind them
36:9 (8)	We have put before them a barrier and behind them a barrier
36:45 (45)	fear what is before you and what is behind you
41:14 (13)	the Messengers came unto them from before them and from behind them, saying
41:25 (24)	they have decked out fair to them that which is before them and behind them
41:42 (42)	falsehood comes not to it from before it nor from behind it
46:21 (20)	already warners had passed away alike before him and behind him
72:27 (27)	then He despatches before him and behind him watchers

KHALĪFAH n.m. (pl. *khalā'if*)~a viceroy, successor

2:30 (28)	I am setting in the earth a viceroy
6:165 (165)	it is He who has appointed you viceroys in the earth
7:69 (67)	when He appointed you as successors after the people of Noah
7:74 (72)	remember when He appointed you successors after Ad
10:14 (15)	then We appointed you viceroys in the earth
10:73 (74)	those with him, in the Ark, and We appointed them as viceroys
27:62 (63)	and appoints you to be successors in the earth
35:39 (37)	it is He who appointed you viceroys in the earth
38:26 (25)	David, behold, We have appointed thee a viceroy

KHAWĀLIF n.f. (pl. of *khālifah*)~those who stay behind [Ar, Bl]; the useless [Pk]; (the women) who stay behind (at home) [Ali]

9:87 (88)	they are well-pleased to be with those behind
9:93 (94)	they are well-pleased to be with those behind

KHILĀF n.m.~after, behind; (with prep. *min*) alternately, on opposite or alternate sides

5:33 (37)	or their hands and feet shall alternately be struck off
7:124 (121)	I shall assuredly cut off alternately your hands and feet
9:81 (82)	(those who were left behind) rejoiced in tarrying behind the Messenger of God
17:76 (78)	then they would have tarried after thee only a little
20:71 (74)	I shall assuredly cut off alternately your hands and feet
26:49 (49)	I shall assuredly cut off alternately your hands and feet

KHILFAH n.f.~a succession

25:62 (63)	it is He who made the night and day a succession

KHALLAFA vb. (II)~to leave behind. (pcple. pass.) one who is left behind *d*) perf. pass. (*khullifa*)

9:118 (119) and to the three who were left behind

h) pcple. pass. (*mukhallaf*)

9:81 (82) those who were left behind rejoiced in tarrying
48:11 (11) the Bedouins who were left behind will say to thee
48:15 (15) the Bedouins who were left behind will say
48:16 (16) say to the Bedouins who were left behind

KHĀLAFA vb. (III)~to come behind another, to do something behind another's back; to oppose or go against

b) impf. act. (*yukhālifu*)

11:88 (90) I desire not to come behind you, betaking me to that I forbid you
24:63 (63) let those who go against His command beware

AKHLAFA vb. (IV)~to fail, to break one's word. (pcple. act.) one who fails or breaks his word

a) perf. act.

9:77 (78) for that they failed God in that they promised Him
14:22 (26) and I promised you, then I failed you
20:86 (89) so that you failed in your tryst with me
20:87 (90) we have not failed in our tryst with thee

b) impf. act. (*yukhlifu*)

2:80 (74) God will not fail in His covenant
3:9 (7) verily God will not fail the tryst
3:194 (192) Thou wilt not fail the tryst
13:31 (31) God will not fail the tryst
20:58 (60) and we shall not fail it, neither thou
22:47 (46) God will not fail His promise
30:6 (5) the promise of God! God fails not His promise
34:39 (38) whatever thing you shall expend, He will replace it
39:20 (21) God fails not the tryst

e) impf. pass. (*yukhlafu*)

20:97 (97) thereafter a tryst awaits thee thou canst not fail to keep

g) pcple. act. (*mukhlif*)

14:47 (48) do not deem that God will fail in His promise to His Messengers

TAKHALLAFA vb. (V)~to stay behind

b) impf. act. (*yatakhallafu*)

9:120 (121) for the Bedouins who dwell around them to stay behind God's Messenger

IKHTALAFA vb. (VIII)~to be at variance [Ar]; to find cause for disagreement, to differ [Pk]; to seek causes of dispute, to differ [Ali]. (n.vb.) alternation; difference [Pk]. (pcple. act.) that which is different, diverse, one who is at variance

a) perf. act.

2:176 (171)	those that are at variance regarding the Book are in wide schism
2:213 (209)	that He might decide between the people touching their differences
2:213 (209)	only those who had been given it were at variance upon it
2:213 (209)	then God guided those who believed to the truth, touching which they were at variance
2:253 (254)	but they fell into variance, and some of them believed
3:19 (17)	those who were given the Book were not at variance except after the knowledge came to them
3:105 (101)	be not as those who scattered and fell into variance
4:157 (156)	those who are at variance concerning him surely are in doubt regarding him
8:42 (43)	had you made tryst together, you would have surely failed the tryst
10:19 (20)	Mankind were only one nation, then they fell into variance
10:93 (93)	so they differed not until the knowledge came to them
16:64 (66)	thou mayest make clear to them that whereon they were at variance
16:124 (125)	the Sabbath was only appointed for those who were at variance thereon
19:37 (38)	the parties have fallen into variance among themselves
42:10 (8)	whatever you are at variance on, the judgment thereof belongs to God
43:65 (65)	the parties among them fell into variance
45:17 (16)	so they differed not, except after the knowledge had come to them

b) impf. act. (*yakhtalifu*)

2:113 (107)	on the Day of Resurrection touching their differences
3:55 (48)	I will decide between you, as to what you were at variance on
5:48 (53)	He will tell you of that whereon you were at variance
6:164 (164)	He will tell you of that whereon you were at variance
10:19 (20)	it had been decided between them already touching their differences
10:93 (93)	on the Day of Resurrection touching their differences
16:39 (41)	He may make clear to them that whereon they were at variance
16:92 (94)	upon the Day of Resurrection that whereon you were at variance
16:124 (125)	on the Day of Resurrection, touching their differences
22:69 (68)	on the Day of Resurrection touching that whereon you were at variance
27:76 (78)	this Koran relates to the Children of Israel most of that concerning which they are at variance
32:25 (25)	on the Resurrection Day, touching that whereon they were at variance
39:3 (4)	God shall judge between them touching that whereon they are at variance
39:46 (47)	Thou shalt judge between Thy servants touching that whereon they are at variance
43:63 (63)	I may make clear to you some of that whereon you are at variance
45:17 (16)	on the Day of Resurrection touching their differences

d) perf. pass. (*ikhtulifa*)

11:110 (112)	We gave Moses the Book; and there was difference regarding it
41:45 (45)	We gave Moses the Book; and there was difference concerning it

f) n.vb. (*ikhtilāf*)

2:164 (159)	in the creation of the heavens and the earth and the alternation of night and day
3:190 (187)	in the alternation of night and day there are signs
4:82 (84)	surely they would have found in it much inconsistency
10:6 (6)	in the alternation of night and day
23:80 (82)	to Him belongs the alternation of night and day
30:22 (21)	of His signs is the creation of the heavens and earth and the variety of your tongues and hues
45:5 (4)	in the alternation of night and day, and the provision God sends down from heaven

g) pcple. act. (*mukhtalif*)

6:141 (142) it is He who produces gardens trellised, and untrellised, palm-trees, and crops diverse
11:118 (120) He would have made mankind one nation; but they continue in their differences
16:13 (13) that which He has multiplied for you in the earth of diverse hues
16:69 (71) then comes there forth out of their bellies a drink of diverse hues
35:27 (25) and therewith We bring forth fruits of diverse hues
35:27 (25) in the mountains are streaks white and red, of diverse hues
35:28 (25) men too, and beasts and cattle — diverse are their hues
39:21 (22) then He brings forth therewith crops of diverse hues
51:8 (8) surely you speak at variance
78:3 (3) whereon they are at variance

ISTAKHLAFA vb. (X)~to make one a successor. (pcple. pass.) one who is made a successor or inheritor

a) perf. act.

24:55 (54) even as He made those who were before them successors

b) impf. act. (*yastakhlifu*)

6:133 (133) He can put you away, and leave after you, to succeed you, what He will
7:129 (126) perchance your Lord will destroy your enemy, and will make you successors
11:57 (60) my Lord will make a people other than you successors
24:55 (54) that He will surely make you successors in the land

h) pcple. pass. (*mustakhlaf*)

57:7 (7) and expend of that unto which He has made you successors

*KH L L

KHALĪL n.m. (pl. *akhillā*ʾ)~a friend

4:125 (124) and God took Abraham for a friend
17:73 (75) then they would surely have taken thee as a friend
25:28 (30) alas, would that I had not taken So-and-so for a friend
43:67 (67) friends on that day shall be foes to one another

KHILĀL n.m. (pl. of *khalal*)~the inner parts, midst; amongst, through

9:47 (47) and run to and fro in your midst, seeking to stir up sedition between you
17:5 (5) they went through the habitations, and it was a promise performed
17:91 (93) Thou makest rivers to gush forth abundantly all amongst it
18:33 (32) We caused to gush amidst them a river
24:43 (43) then thou seest the rain issuing out of the midst of them
27:61 (62) He who made the earth a fixed place and set amidst it rivers
30:48 (47) then thou seest the rain issuing out of the midst of them

KHULLAH n.f.~friendship

2:254 (255) there comes a day wherein shall be neither traffick, nor friendship

KHĀLLA vb. (III)~(n.vb.) friendship, befriending

f) n.vb. (*khilāl*)

14:31 (36) a day comes wherein shall be neither bargaining nor befriending

*KH L Q

KHALAQA vb. (I)~to create. (n.vb.) creating, creation; stature, constitution (pcple. act.) creator, creating; Creator (Divine attribute)

a) perf. act.

2:21 (19)	O you men, serve your Lord Who created you
2:29 (27)	it is He who created for you all that is in the earth
2:228 (228)	it is not lawful for them to hide what God has created in their wombs
3:59 (52)	He created him of dust, then said He unto him
3:191 (188)	our Lord, Thou hast not created this for vanity
4:1 (1)	Mankind, fear your Lord, who created you of a single soul
4:1 (1)	and from it [He] created its mate
5:18 (21)	no; you are mortals, of His creating
6:1 (1)	praise belongs to God who created the heavens and the earth
6:2 (2)	it is He who created you of clay
6:73 (72)	it is He who created the heavens and the earth in truth
6:94 (94)	you have come to Us one by one, as We created you upon the first time
6:100 (100)	they ascribe to God, as associates, the jinn, though He created them
6:101 (101)	seeing that He has no consort, and He created all things
7:11 (10)	We created you, then We shaped you
7:12 (11)	I am better than he; Thou createdst me of fire
7:12 (11)	and him Thou createdst of clay
7:54 (52)	your Lord is God, who created the heavens and the earth
7:181 (180)	of those We created are a nation who guide by the truth
7:185 (184)	and what things God has created
7:189 (189)	it is He who created you out of one living soul
9:36 (36)	the day that He created the heavens and the earth
10:3 (3)	your Lord is God, who created the heavens and the earth
10:5 (5)	God created that not save with the truth
10:6 (6)	and what God has created in the heavens and the earth
11:7 (9)	it is He who created the heavens and the earth in six days
11:119 (120)	to that end He created them, and perfectly is fulfilled the word of thy Lord
13:16 (17)	have they ascribed to God associates who created as He created
14:19 (22)	hast thou not seen that God created the heavens and the earth in truth?
14:32 (37)	it is God who created the heavens and the earth
15:26 (26)	surely We created man of a clay
15:27 (27)	and the jinn created We before of fire flaming
15:33 (33)	I would never bow myself before a mortal whom Thou hast created of a clay
15:85 (85)	We created not the heavens and the earth, and all that is between them
16:3 (3)	He created the heavens and the earth in truth
16:4 (4)	He created man of a sperm-drop
16:5 (5)	He created them for you
16:48 (50)	have they not regarded all things that God has created
16:70 (72)	God created you; then He will gather you
16:81 (83)	it is God who has appointed for you coverings of the things He created
17:61 (63)	shall I bow myself unto one Thou hast created of clay?
17:70 (72)	and preferred them greatly over many of those We created
17:99 (101)	have they not seen that God, who created the heavens and earth, is powerful
18:37 (35)	disbelievest thou in Him who created thee of dust
18:48 (46)	you have come to Us, as We created you upon the first time
19:9 (10)	easy is that for Me, seeing that I created thee aforetime
19:67 (68)	will not man remember that We created him aforetime
20:4 (3)	a revelation from Him who created the earth

20:55 (57)	out of the earth We created you
21:16 (16)	We created not the heaven and the earth
21:33 (34)	it is He who created the night and the day
22:5 (5)	We created you of dust then of a sperm-drop
23:12 (12)	We created man of an extraction of clay
23:14 (14)	then We created of the drop a clot
23:14 (14)	then We created of the clot a tissue
23:14 (14)	then We created of the tissue bones
23:17 (17)	We created above you seven ways
23:91 (93)	each god would have taken off that he created
23:115 (117)	did you think that We created you only for sport
24:45 (44)	God has created every beast of water
25:2 (2)	He created every thing, then He ordained it very exactly
25:49 (51)	We might revive a dead land, and give to drink of it, of that We created
25:54 (56)	it is He who created of water a mortal
25:59 (60)	who created the heavens and the earth, and what between them is, in six days
26:78 (78)	who created me, and Himself guides me
26:166 (166)	leaving your wives that your Lord created for you
26:184 (184)	fear Him who created you, and the generations of the ancients
27:60 (61)	He who created the heavens and earth, and sent down for you out of heaven water
29:44 (43)	God created the heavens and the earth with the truth
29:61 (61)	who created the heavens and the earth and subjected the sun and the moon?
30:8 (7)	God created not the heavens and the earth ... save with the truth
30:20 (19)	of His signs is that He created you of dust
30:21 (20)	of His signs is that He created for you
30:40 (39)	God is He that created you, then He provided for you
30:54 (53)	God is He that created you of weakness
31:10 (9)	He created the heavens without pillars you can see
31:11 (10)	now show me what those have created that are apart
31:25 (24)	who created the heavens and the earth?
32:4 (3)	God is He that created the heavens and the earth
32:7 (6)	who has created all things well
35:11 (12)	God created you of dust then of a sperm-drop
35:40 (38)	show me what they have created in the earth
36:36 (36)	glory be to Him, who created all the pairs of what the earth produces
36:42 (42)	We have created for them the like of it whereon they ride
36:71 (71)	have they not seen how that We have created for them of that Our hands wrought cattle that they own?
36:77 (77)	has not man regarded how that We created him of a sperm-drop?
36:81 (81)	is not He, who created the heavens and earth
37:11 (11)	are they stronger in constitution, or those We created?
37:11 (11)	We created them of clinging clay
37:96 (94)	and God created you and what you make
37:150 (150)	or did We create the angels females, while they were witnesses?
38:27 (26)	We have not created the heavens and earth, and what between them is, for vanity
38:75 (75)	Iblis, what prevented thee to bow thyself before that I created with My own hands?
38:76 (77)	Thou createdst me of fire
38:76 (77)	and him Thou createdst of clay
39:5 (7)	He created the heavens and the earth in truth
39:6 (8)	He created you of a single soul
39:38 (39)	who created the heavens and the earth?
40:67 (69)	it is He who created you of dust then of a sperm-drop
41:9 (8)	do you disbelieve in Him who created the earth in two days
41:15 (14)	did they not see that God, who created them, was stronger
41:21 (20)	He created you the first time, and unto Him you shall be returned

41:37 (37)	but bow yourselves to God who created them
43:9 (8)	if thou askest them, 'Who created the heavens and earth?'
43:9 (8)	the All-mighty, the All-knowing created them
43:12 (11)	and who created the pairs, all of them
43:87 (87)	if thou askest them, 'Who created you?'
44:38 (38)	We created not the heavens and earth
44:39 (39)	We created them not save in truth
45:22 (21)	God created the heavens and the earth in truth
46:3 (2)	We have not created the heavens and the earth
46:4 (3)	show me what they have created of the earth
46:33 (32)	have they not seen that God who created the heavens and earth
49:13 (13)	O mankind, We have created you male and female
50:16 (15)	We indeed created man
50:38 (37)	We created the heavens and the earth, and what between them is
51:49 (49)	of everything created We two kinds
51:56 (56)	I have not created jinn and mankind except to serve Me
52:36 (36)	or did they create the heavens and earth?
53:45 (46)	He Himself created the two kinds, male and female
54:49 (49)	surely We have created everything in measure
55:3 (2)	He created man
55:14 (13)	He created man of a clay like the potter's
55:15 (14)	He created the jinn of a smokeless fire
56:57 (57)	We created you; therefore why will you not believe?
57:4 (4)	it is He that created the heavens and the earth in six days
64:2 (2)	it is He who created you. One of you is an unbeliever
64:3 (3)	He created the heavens and the earth with the truth
65:12 (12)	it is God who created seven heavens, and of earth their like
67:2 (2)	who created death and life, that He might try you
67:3 (3)	who created seven heavens one upon another
67:14 (14)	shall He not know, who created?
70:39 (39)	We have created them of what they know
71:14 (13)	seeing He created you by stages
71:15 (14)	have you not regarded how God created seven heavens one upon another
74:11 (11)	leave Me with him whom I created alone
75:38 (38)	then he was a blood-clot, and He created and formed
76:2 (2)	We created man of a sperm-drop, a mingling, trying him
76:28 (28)	We created them, and We strengthened their joints
78:8 (8)	and We created you in pairs
80:18 (17)	of what did He create him?
80:19 (19)	He created him, and determined him
82:7 (7)	who created thee and shaped thee and wrought thee in symmetry
87:2 (2)	who created and shaped
90:4 (4)	indeed, We created man in trouble
92:3 (3)	and That which created the male and the female
95:4 (4)	We indeed created Man in the fairest stature
96:1 (1)	recite: In the Name of thy Lord who created
96:2 (2)	created Man of a blood-clot
113:2 (2)	from the evil of what He has created

b) impf. act. (*yakhluqu*)

3:47 (42)	God said, 'God creates what He will'
3:49 (43)	I will create for you out of clay as the likeness of a bird
5:17 (20)	creating what He will. God is powerful over everything
5:110 (110)	and when thou createst out of clay, by My leave

7:191 (191)	what, do they associate that which creates nothing
16:8 (8)	and as an adornment; and He creates what you know not
16:17 (17)	is He who creates as he who does not (create?)
16:17 (17)	is He who (creates) as he who does not create?
16:20 (20)	those they call upon, apart from God, created nothing
17:99 (101)	is powerful to create the like of them
22:73 (72)	those upon whom you call, apart from God, shall never create a fly
24:45 (44)	God creates whatever He will
25:3 (3)	they have taken to them gods, apart from Him, that create nothing
28:68 (68)	thy Lord creates whatsoever He will
29:17 (16)	you only serve, apart from God, idols and you create a calumny
30:54 (53)	He creates what He will
36:81 (81)	is not He... Able to create the like of them?
39:4 (6)	He would have chosen whatever He willed of that He has created
39:6 (8)	He creates you in your mothers' wombs
42:49 (48)	He creates what He will
43:16 (15)	has He taken to Himself, from that He creates, daughters
56:59 (59)	do you yourselves create it
77:20 (20)	did We not create you of a mean water

d) perf. pass. (*khuliqa*)

4:28 (32)	God desires to lighten things for you, for man was created a weakling
21:37 (38)	man was created of haste
52:35 (35)	or were they created out of nothing?
70:19 (19)	surely man was created fretful
86:5 (5)	so let man consider of what he was created
86:6 (6)	he was created of gushing water
88:17 (17)	do they not consider how the camel was created

e) impf. pass. (*yukhlaqu*)

7:191 (191)	do they associate that which creates nothing and themselves are created
16:20 (20)	those they call upon, apart from God, created nothing
25:3 (3)	they have taken to them gods, apart from Him, that create nothing
89:8 (7)	the like of which was never created in the land

f) n.vb. (*khalq*)

Creating, Creation

2:164 (159)	in the creation of the heavens and the earth
3:190 (187)	in the creation of the heavens and earth
3:191 (188)	reflect upon the creation of the heavens and the earth
4:119 (118)	I will command them and they will alter God's creation
7:54 (52)	verily, His are the creation and the command
10:4 (4)	He originates creation, then He brings it back again
10:34 (35)	is there any of your associates who originates creation
10:34 (35)	God — He originates creation, then brings it back again
13:5 (5)	shall we indeed then be raised up again in new creation?
13:16 (17)	associates who created as <He created>
13:16 (17)	so that creation is all alike to them
14:19 (22)	if He will, He can put you away and bring a new creation
17:49 (52)	shall we really be raised up again in a new creation?
17:51 (53)	or some creation yet more monstrous in your minds
17:98 (100)	shall we really be raised up again in a new creation?
18:51 (49)	I made them not witnesses of the creation of the heavens and earth

18:51 (49)	neither of the creation of themselves
20:50 (52)	our Lord is He who gave everything its creation then guided it
21:104 (104)	as We originated the first creation, so We shall bring it back again
23:14 (14)	thereafter We produced him as another creature
23:17 (17)	and We were not heedless of creation
27:64 (65)	who originates creation, then brings it back again
29:19 (18)	have they not seen how God originates creation, then brings it back again?
29:20 (19)	journey in the land, then behold how He originated creation
30:11 (10)	God originates creation, then brings it back again
30:22 (21)	of His signs is the creation of the heavens and earth
30:27 (26)	it is He who originates creation, then brings it back again
30:30 (29)	there is no changing God's creation
31:11 (10)	this is God's creation
31:28 (27)	your creation and your upraising are as but as a single soul
32:7 (6)	He originated the creation of man out of clay
32:10 (9)	when we have gone astray in the earth, shall we indeed be in a new creation?
34:7 (7)	when you have been utterly torn to pieces, then you shall be in a new creation
35:1 (1)	increasing creation as He wills
35:16 (17)	if He will, He can put you away and bring a new creation
36:78 (78)	He has struck for Us a similitude and forgotten his creation
36:79 (79)	He knows all creation
39:6 (8)	He creates you in your mothers' wombs creation after (creation)
39:6 (8)	He creates you in your mothers' wombs (creation) after creation
40:57 (59)	the creation of the heavens and earth is greater
40:57 (59)	than the creation of men
42:29 (28)	of His signs is the creation of the heavens and earth
43:19 (18)	did they witness their creation?
45:4 (3)	in your creation, and the crawling things He scatters abroad, there are signs
46:33 (32)	who created the heavens and earth, not being wearied by creating them
50:15 (14)	were We wearied by the first creation?
50:15 (14)	they are in uncertainty as to the new creation
67:3 (3)	thou seest not in the creation of the All-merciful any imperfection

Stature, Constitution

7:69 (67)	after the people of Noah, and increased you in stature broadly
36:68 (68)	to whomsoever We give long life, We bend him over in His constitution
37:11 (11)	are they stronger in constitution, or those We created?
79:27 (27)	are you stronger in constitution or the heaven He built?

g) pcple. act. (*khāliq*)

6:102 (102)	there is no god but He, the Creator of everything
13:16 (17)	God is the Creator of everything
15:28 (28)	see, I am creating a mortal of a clay
23:14 (14)	blessed be God, the fairest of creators
35:3 (3)	is there any creator, apart from God, who provides for you
37:125 (125)	do you call on Baal, and abandon the Best of creators?
38:71 (71)	see, I am creating a mortal of a clay
39:62 (63)	God is the Creator of every thing
40:62 (64)	that then is God, your Lord, the Creator of everything
52:35 (35)	or are they the creators?
56:59 (59)	do you yourselves create it, or are We the Creators?
59:24 (24)	He is God, the Creator, the Maker, the Shaper

KHALĀQ n.m.~a share, portion, part

2:102 (96)	knowing well that whoso buys it shall have no share in the world to come
2:200 (196)	such men shall have no part in the world to come
3:77 (71)	there shall be no share for them in the world to come
9:69 (70)	they took enjoyment in their share
9:69 (70)	so do you take enjoyment in your share
9:69 (70)	as those before you took enjoyment in their share

KHALLĀQ n.m. (adj)~All-creator (Divine attribute)

15:86 (86)	surely thy Lord, He is the All-creator
36:81 (81)	He is the All-creator, the All-knowing

KHULUQ n.m.~a habit, morality [Ar]; nature, fable; a customary device, character [Ali]; invention, custom [Bl]

26:137 (137)	this is nothing but the habit of the ancients
68:4 (4)	surely thou art upon a mighty morality

KHALLAQA vb. (II)~(pcple. pass.) formed; shapely [Pk]

h) pcple. pass. f. (*mukhallaqah*)

22:5 (5)	then of a blood clot, then of a lump of flesh, formed and (unformed)
22:5 (5)	then of a blood clot, then of a lump of flesh, (formed) and unformed

IKHTALAQA vb. (VIII)~(n.vb.) an invention [Ar, Pk]; a made-up tale [Ali]; fiction [Bl]

38:7 (6)	We have not heard of this in the last religion; this is surely an invention

*KH L Ṣ

KHALAṢA vb. (I)~to confer with. (pcple. act.) (adj) sincere, pure; (adv) exclusively, only (for someone rather than another), reserved

a) perf. act.

12:80 (80)	when they despaired of moving him, they conferred privily apart

g) pcple. act. (*khāliṣ*)

2:94 (88)	if the Last Abode with God is yours exclusively, and not for other people
6:139 (140)	what is within the bellies of these cattle is reserved for our males
7:32 (30)	these... shall be exclusively for those who believed in this present life
16:66 (68)	between filth and blood, pure milk, sweet to drinkers
33:50 (49)	if the Prophet desire to take her in marriage, for thee exclusively
38:46 (46)	assuredly We purified them with a quality most pure
39:3 (3)	belongs not sincere religion to God?

AKHLAṢA vb. (IV)~to purify, make sincere. (pcple. act.) sincere; (adv) sincerely [Ar, Ali]; one who makes (something) pure [Pk]; exclusively, entirely [Bl]. (pcple. pass.) devoted, sincere [Ar]; chosen, devoted, single-minded [Pk]; sincere and purified, sincere and devoted [Ali]; single-hearted [Bl]

a) perf. act.

4:146 (145)	hold fast to God, and make their religion sincerely God's
38:46 (46)	assuredly We purified them with a quality most pure

g) pcple. act. (*mukhliṣ*)

2:139 (133) to you belong your deeds; Him we serve sincerely
7:29 (28) call on Him, making your religion sincerely His
10:22 (23) they call upon God, making their religion His sincerely
29:65 (65) they call on God, making their religion sincerely His
31:32 (31) they call upon God, making their religion sincerely His
39:2 (2) so worship God, making thy religion His sincerely
39:11 (14) I have been commanded to serve God making my religion His sincerely
39:14 (16) God I serve, making my religion His sincerely
40:14 (14) call unto God, making your religion His sincerely
40:65 (67) call upon Him, making your religion His sincerely
98:5 (4) they were commanded only to serve God, making the religion His sincerely

h) pcple. pass. (*mukhlaṣ*)

12:24 (24) he was one of Our devoted servants
15:40 (40) excepting those Thy servants among them that are devoted
19:51 (52) mention in the Book Moses; he was devoted
37:40 (39) except for God's sincere servants
37:74 (72) except for God's sincere servants
37:128 (128) except for God's sincere servants
37:160 (160) except for God's sincere servants
37:169 (169) then were we God's sincere servants
38:83 (84) excepting those Thy servants among them that are sincere

ISTAKHLAṢA vb. (X)~to attach to oneself

b) impf. act. (*yastakhliṣu*)

12:54 (54) bring him to me! I would attach him to my person

*KH L Ṭ

KHALAṬA vb. (I)~to mix

a) perf. act.

9:102 (103) they have mixed a righteous deed with another evil

KHULAṬĀ' n.m. (pl. of *khalīṭ*)~intermixers [Ar]; partners (in business) [Pk, Ali]; ones whose interests are
38:24 (23) indeed many intermixers do injury one against the other

KHĀLAṬA vb. (III)~to intermix with others

b) impf. act. (*yukhāliṭu*)

2:220 (219) if you intermix with them, they are your brothers

IKHTALAṬA vb. (VIII)~to mingle

a) perf. act.

6:146 (147) or what is mingled with bone
10:24 (25) and the plants of the earth mingle with it
18:45 (43) and the plants of the earth mingle with it

*KH L W

KHALĀ vb. (I)~to be free, to go privily; to pass away; (40:85 and 48:23) to have been in force before. (pcple. act.) that which has gone by

a) perf. act.

2:14 (13) but when they go privily to their Satans, they say
2:76 (71) and when they go privily one to another, they say
2:134 (128) that is a nation that has passed away
2:141 (135) that is a nation that has passed away
2:214 (210) without there had come upon you the like of those who passed away before you
3:119 (115) when they go privily, they bite at you their fingers, enraged
3:137 (131) diverse institutions have passed away before you
3:144 (138) Messengers have passed away before him
5:75 (79) Messengers before him passed away
7:38 (36) enter among nations that passed away before you
10:102 (102) but the like of the days of those who passed away before them
13:6 (7) yet there have passed away before them examples
13:30 (29) We have sent thee among a nation before which other nations have passed away
15:13 (13) they believe not in it, though the wont of the ancients is already gone
24:34 (34) making all clear, and an example of those who passed away before you
33:38 (38) God's wont with those who passed away before
33:62 (62) God's wont with those who passed away before
35:24 (22) there has passed away in it a warner
40:85 (85) the wont of God, as in the past, touching His servants
41:25 (24) against them has been realized the Word concerning nations that passed away before them
46:17 (16) I shall be brought forth, when already generations have passed away before me
46:18 (17) such men are they against whom has been realized the Word concerning nations that passed away before them
46:21 (20) already warners had passed away alike before him and behind him
48:23 (23) the wont of God, as in the past before

b) impf. act. (*yakhlū*)

12:9 (9) your father's face may be free for you

g) pcple. act. f. (*khāliyah*)

69:24 (24) eat and drink with wholesome appetite for that you did long ago, in the days gone by

KHALLÁ vb. (II)~to make clear; (*khallá sabīl*) to let one go his way

c) impv. (*khalli*)

9:5 (5) perform the prayer, and pay the alms, then let them go their way

TAKHALLÁ vb. (V)~to void oneself, to be empty

a) perf. act.

84:4 (4) and casts forth what is in it, and voids itself

*KH M D

KHAMADA vb. (I)~(pcple. act.) silent and still [Ar]; extinct [Pk]; quenched [Ali]

g) pcple. act. (*khāmid*)

21:15 (15)	they ceased not to cry, until We made them stubble, silent and still
36:29 (28)	it was only one Cry and lo, they were silent and still

*KH M R

KHAMR n.f.~wine

2:219 (216)	they will question thee concerning wine, and arrow-shuffling
5:90 (92)	wine and arrow-shuffling, idols and divining-arrows are an abomination
5:91 (93)	Satan only desires to precipitate enmity and hatred between you in regard to wine and arrow-shuffling
12:36 (36)	said one of them, 'I dreamed that I was pressing grapes'
12:41 (41)	fellow-prisoners, as for one of you, he shall pour wine for his lord
47:15 (16)	rivers of wine — a delight to the drinkers

KHUMUR n.m. (pl. of *khimār*)~veils

24:31 (31)	let them cast their veils over their bosoms

*KH M S

KHĀMISAH n.f. (num)~fifth (ordinal)

24:7 (7)	and a fifth time, that the curse of God shall be upon him
24:9 (9)	and a fifth time, that the wrath of God shall be upon her

KHAMSAH n.f. (num)~five

3:125 (121)	your Lord will reinforce you with five thousand swooping angels
18:22 (21)	five; and their dog was the sixth of them
58:7 (8)	He is the fourth of them, neither five men, but He is the sixth of them

KHAMSŪN n.m. (num)~fifty

29:14 (13)	he tarried among them a thousand years, all but fifty
70:4 (4)	whereof the measure is fifty thousand years

KHUMS n.m. (num)~one fifth (fraction)

8:41 (42)	know that, whatever booty you take, the fifth of it is God's

*KH M Ṣ

MAKHMAṢAH n.f.~emptiness [Ar]; hunger [Pk, Ali]; famine [Bl]

5:3 (5)	whosoever is constrained in emptiness and not inclining purposely to sin
9:120 (121)	neither by thirst, nor fatigue, nor emptiness in the way of God

*KH M Ṭ

KHAMAṬA vb. (I)~(n.vb.) bitter

f) n.vb. (*khamṭ*)

34:16 (15)	two gardens bearing bitter produce

*KH N Q

INKHANAQA vb. (VII)~(pcple. pass.) a strangled (beast)

g) pcple. act. f. (*munkhaniqah*)

5:3 (4)	what has been hallowed to other than God, the beast strangled, the beast beaten down

*KH N S

KHANNĀS n.m.~slinking one [Ar]; sneaking one [Pk]; (Evil) who withdraws (after his whisper) [Ali]; lurking one [Bl]

114:4 (4)	from the evil of the slinking whisperer

KHUNNAS n.f.~the slinkers [Ar]; the planets [Pk]; the planets that recede [Ali]; stars that lag [Bl]

81:15 (15)	no! I swear by the slinkers

*KH N Z R

KHINZĪR n.m.~swine

2:173 (168)	carrion, blood, the flesh of swine
5:3 (4)	carrion, blood, the flesh of swine
5:60 (65)	with whom He is wroth, and made some of them apes and swine
6:145 (146)	except it be carrion, or blood outpoured, or the flesh of swine
16:115 (116)	carrion, blood, the flesh of swine

*KH R B

KHARABA vb. (I)~(n.vb.) destruction, desolation

f) n.vb. (*kharāb*)

2:114 (108)	God's places of worship, so that His Name be not rehearsed in them, and strives to destroy them

AKHRABA vb. (IV)~to destroy

b) impf. act. (*yukhribu*)

59:2 (2)	He cast terror into their hearts as they destroyed their houses with their own hands

*KH R D L

KHARDAL n.m.~mustard-seed

21:47 (48)	not one soul shall be wronged anything; even if it be the weight of one grain of
31:16 (15)	if it should be but the weight of one grain of mustard-seed

*KH R J

KHARAJA vb. (I)~to go forth, to issue, to go out, to depart. (n.vb.) going forth, going out. (pcple. act.) one who issues, goes out, comes forth

a) perf. act.

2:149 (144)	from whatsoever place thou issuest, turn thy face towards the Holy Mosque
2:150 (145)	from whatsoever place thou issuest, turn thy face towards the Holy Mosque
2:240 (241)	if they go forth, there is no fault in you what they may do with themselves
2:243 (244)	hast thou not regarded those who went forth from their habitations
5:61 (66)	they have entered in unbelief, and so they have departed in it
8:47 (49)	be not as those who went forth from their habitations
9:42 (42)	had we been able, we would have gone out with you
9:47 (47)	had they gone forth among you, they would only have increased you in trouble
19:11 (12)	so he came forth unto his people from the Sanctuary
28:21 (20)	so he departed therefrom, fearful and vigilant
28:79 (79)	so he went forth unto his people in his adornment
47:16 (18)	some of them there are give ear to thee, till, when they go forth from thee
60:1 (1)	if you go forth to struggle in My way and seek My good pleasure

b) impf. act. (*yakhruju*)

2:74 (69)	and others split, so that water issues from them
4:100 (101)	whoso goes forth from his house an emigrant to God
5:22 (25)	we will not enter it until they depart from it
5:22 (25)	if they depart from it then we will enter
5:37 (41)	they will desire to come forth from the Fire
7:58 (56)	the good land — its vegetation comes forth by the leave of its Lord
7:58 (56)	it comes forth but scantily
9:83 (84)	you shall not go forth with me ever
16:69 (71)	then comes there forth out of their bellies a drink
18:5 (4)	a monstrous word it is, issuing out of their mouths
20:22 (23)	clasp thy hand to thy arm-pit; it shall come forth white
22:22 (22)	as often as they desire in their anguish to come forth from it
23:20 (20)	a tree issuing from the Mount of Sinai that bears oil and seasoning

24:43 (43)	then thou seest the rain issuing out of the midst of them
24:53 (52)	if thou commandest them they will go forth
27:12 (12)	thrust thy hand in thy bosom and it will come forth white
28:32 (32)	insert thy hand into thy bosom, and it will come forth white
30:25 (24)	when He calls you once and suddenly, out of the earth, lo you shall come forth
30:48 (47)	then thou seest the rain issuing out of the midst of them
32:20 (20)	as often as they desire to come forth from it, they shall be restored into it
34:2 (2)	He knows what penetrates into the earth, and what comes forth from it
37:64 (62)	it is a tree that comes forth in the root of Hell
41:47 (47)	not a fruit comes forth from its sheath
49:5 (5)	if they had patience, until thou comest out to them, that would be better
54:7 (7)	abasing their eyes, they shall come forth from the tombs
55:22 (22)	from them come forth the pearl and the coral
57:4 (4)	He knows what penetrates into the earth, and what comes forth from it
59:2 (2)	you did not think that they would go forth
59:11 (11)	if you are expelled, we will go forth with you
59:12 (12)	if those are expelled, they will not go forth with them
65:1 (1)	do not expel them from their houses, nor let them go forth
70:43 (43)	the day they shall come forth from the tombs hastily
86:7 (7)	issuing between the loins and the breast-bones

c) impv. (*ukhruj*)

4:66 (69)	leave your habitations,'
7:13 (12)	it is not for thee to wax proud here, so go thou forth
7:18 (17)	go thou forth from it, despised and banished
12:31 (31)	come forth, attend to them
15:34 (34)	go thou forth hence; thou art accursed
28:20 (19)	depart; I am one of thy sincere advisers
38:77 (78)	then go thou forth hence; thou art accursed

f) n.vb. (*khurūj*)

9:46 (46)	if they had desired to go forth, they would have made some preparation for it
9:83 (84)	and they ask leave of thee to go forth
40:11 (11)	is there any way to go forth?
50:11 (11)	even so is the coming forth
50:42 (41)	on the day they hear the Cry in truth, that is the day of coming forth

g) pcple. act. (*khārij*)

2:167 (162)	never shall they issue from the Fire
5:37 (41)	they will not come forth from it
6:122 (122)	as one whose likeness is in the shadows, and comes not forth from them

KHARĀJ n.m.~a tribute [Ar]; bounty [Pk]; recompense [Ali]; revenue [Bl]

23:72 (74)	yet the tribute of thy Lord is better

KHARJ n.m.~a tribute

18:94 (93)	so shall we assign to thee a tribute
23:72 (74)	or dost thou ask them for tribute?

MAKHRAJ n.m.~a way out

65:2 (2)	whosoever fears God, He will appoint for him a way out

AKHRAJA vb. (IV)~to bring forth, to bring out, to drive out, to expel. (n.vb.) expulsion, driving out; bringing forth. (pcple. act.) one who brings out, who brings forth, who discloses. (pcple. pass.) one who is expelled, driven out, brought forth; outgoing

a) perf. act.

2:22 (20)	out of heaven water, wherewith He brought forth fruits
2:36 (34)	Satan caused them to slip therefrom and brought them out of that they were in
2:191 (187)	and expel them from where they expelled you
2:267 (269)	and of that We have produced for you from the earth
6:99 (99)	thereby We have brought forth the shoot of every plant
6:99 (99)	then We have brought forth the green leaf of it
7:27 (26)	let not Satan tempt you as he brought your parents out of the Garden
7:32 (30)	who has forbidden the ornament of God which He brought forth for His servants
7:57 (55)	therewith send down water, and bring forth therewith all the fruits
8:5 (5)	as thy Lord brought thee forth from thy house with the truth
9:40 (40)	when the unbelievers drove him forth the second of two
12:100 (101)	He was good to me when He brought me forth from the prison
14:32 (37)	wherewith He brought forth fruits to be your sustenance
16:78 (80)	it is God who brought you forth, knowing nothing
20:53 (55)	We have brought forth divers kinds of plants
20:88 (90)	then he brought out for them a Calf
24:40 (40)	when he puts forth his hand, wellnigh he cannot see it
26:57 (57)	so We expelled them from gardens and fountains
27:82 (84)	We shall bring forth for them out of the earth a beast
35:27 (25)	and therewith We bring forth fruits of diverse hues
36:33 (33)	and brought forth from it grain, whereof they eat
47:13 (14)	how many a city that was stronger in might than thy city which has expelled thee
48:29 (29)	as a seed that puts forth its shoot, and strengthens it
51:35 (35)	so We brought forth such believers as were in it
59:2 (2)	it is He who expelled from their habitations the unbelievers
60:9 (9)	those who have fought you in religion's cause, and expelled you from your habitations
79:29 (29)	and darkened its night, and brought forth its forenoon
79:31 (31)	therefrom brought forth its waters and its pastures
87:4 (4)	who brought forth the pasturage
99:2 (2)	and earth brings forth her burdens

b) impf. act. (*yukhriju*)

2:61 (58)	pray to thy Lord for us, that He may bring forth for us of that the earth produces
2:84 (78)	you shall not shed your own blood, neither expel your own from your habitations
2:85 (79)	killing one another, and expelling a party of you from their habitations
2:257 (258)	He brings them forth from the shadows into the light
2:257 (259)	their protectors are idols, that bring them forth from the light into the shadows
3:27 (26)	Thou bringest forth the living from the dead
3:27 (26)	and Thou bringest forth the dead from the living
5:16 (18)	and brings them forth from the shadows into the light by His leave
5:110 (110)	and thou bringest the dead forth by My leave
6:95 (95)	it is God who splits the grain and the date-stone, brings forth the living from the dead
6:99 (99)	bringing forth from it close-compounded grain
6:148 (149)	have you any knowledge, for you to bring forth for us?
7:57 (55)	even so We shall bring forth the dead
7:88 (86)	We will surely expel thee, O Shuaib, and those who believe with thee
7:110 (107)	who desires to expel you from your land
7:123 (120)	this is a device you have devised in the city that you may expel its people from it

8:30 (30)	when the unbelievers were devising against thee, to confine thee, or slay thee, or to expel thee
10:31 (32)	who brings forth the living from the dead
10:31 (32)	and brings forth the dead from the living
14:1 (1)	that thou mayest bring forth mankind from the shadows to the light
14:13 (16)	we will assuredly expel you from our land
17:13 (14)	We shall bring forth for him, on the Day of Resurrection, a book
17:76 (78)	they were near to startling thee from the land, to expel thee from it
20:55 (57)	and bring you forth from it a second time
20:57 (59)	'Hast thou come, Moses,' he said, 'to expel us out of our land'
20:63 (66)	their purpose is to expel you out of your land by their sorcery
20:117 (115)	let him not expel you both from the Garden
22:5 (5)	We establish in the wombs what We will, till a stated term, then We deliver you as infants
26:35 (34)	who desires to expel you from your land by his sorcery
27:25 (25)	to God, who brings forth what is hidden in the heavens and earth
27:37 (37)	we shall expel them from there, abased and utterly humbled
30:19 (18)	He brings forth the living from the dead
30:19 (18)	and brings forth the dead from the living
32:27 (27)	have they not seen how We drive the water to the dry land and bring forth crops therewith
33:43 (42)	to bring you forth from the shadows into the light
39:21 (22)	then He brings forth therewith crops of diverse hues
40:67 (69)	then He delivers you as infants
47:29 (31)	those in whose hearts is sickness think that God would not bring to light their rancour
47:37 (39)	you are niggardly, and He brings to light your rancour
57:9 (9)	clear signs, that He may bring you forth from the shadows into the light
60:1 (1)	expelling the Messenger and you because you believe in God your Lord
60:8 (8)	those who have not fought you in religion's cause, nor expelled you from your habitations
63:8 (8)	the mightier ones of it will expel the more abased
65:1 (1)	do not expel them from their houses, nor let them go forth
65:11 (11)	He may bring forth those who believe and do righteous deeds from the shadows
71:18 (17)	then He shall return you into it, and bring you forth
78:15 (15)	that We may bring forth thereby grain and plants

c) impv. (*akhrij*)

2:191 (187)	and expel them from where they expelled you
4:75 (77)	our Lord, bring us forth from this city
6:93 (93)	give up your souls! Today you shall be recompensed
7:82 (80)	expel them from your city
14:5 (5)	bring forth thy people from the shadows to the light
17:80 (82)	lead me in with a just ingoing, and lead me out with a just outgoing
23:107 (109)	our Lord, bring us forth out of it
27:56 (57)	expel the folk of Lot from your city
35:37 (34)	bring us forth, and we will do righteousness

d) perf. pass. (*ukhrija*)

2:246 (247)	who have been expelled from our habitations
3:110 (106)	you are the best nation ever brought forth to men
3:195 (194)	those who emigrated, and were expelled from their habitations
22:40 (41)	who were expelled from their habitations without right

59:8 (8)	it is for the poor emigrants, who were expelled from their habitations
59:11 (11)	if you are expelled, we will go forth with you
59:12 (12)	if those are expelled, they will not go forth with them

e) impf. pass. (*yukhraju*)

7:25 (24)	therein you shall die, and from there you shall be brought forth
19:66 (67)	when I am dead shall I then be brought forth alive?
30:19 (18)	even so you shall be brought forth
43:11 (10)	even so you shall be brought forth
45:35 (34)	so today they shall not be brought forth from it
46:17 (16)	do you promise me that I shall be brought forth

f) n.vb. (*ikhrāj*)

2:85 (79)	you ransom them; yet their expulsion was forbidden you
2:217 (214)	the Holy Mosque, and to expel its people from it — that is more heinous in God's
2:240 (241)	provision for a year without expulsion
9:13 (13)	and purposed to expel the Messenger
60:9 (9)	and have supported in your expulsion, that you should take them for friends
71:18 (17)	then He shall return you into it, and bring you forth

g) pcple. act. (*mukhrij*)

2:72 (67)	and God disclosed what you were hiding
6:95 (95)	brings forth the living from the dead; He brings forth the dead too from the
9:64 (65)	mock on; God will bring forth what you fear

h) pcple. pass. (*mukhraj*)

15:48 (48)	neither shall they ever be driven forth from there
17:80 (82)	lead me in with a just ingoing, and lead me out with a just outgoing
23:35 (37)	when you are dead, and become dust and bones, you shall be brought forth
26:167 (167)	if thou givest not over, Lot, thou shalt assuredly be one of the expelled
27:67 (69)	when we are dust, and our fathers, shall we indeed be brought forth?

ISTAKHRAJA vb. (X)~to pull out, bring forth, take out

a) perf. act.

12:76 (76)	then he pulled it out of his brother's sack

b) impf. act. (*yastakhriju*)

16:14 (14)	and bring forth out of it ornaments for you to wear
18:82 (81)	thy Lord desired that they should come of age and then bring forth their treasure
35:12 (13)	yet of both you eat fresh flesh, and bring forth out of it ornaments

*KH R Q

KHARAQA vb. (I)~to make a hole, to rend or tear open; to falsely attribute, to impute

a) perf. act.

6:100 (100)	and they impute to Him sons and daughters without any knowledge

18:71 (70) when they embarked upon the ship, he made a hole in it
18:71 (70) hast thou made a hole in it so as to drown its passengers?

b) impf. act. (*yakhriqu*)

17:37 (39) thou wilt never tear the earth open, nor attain the mountains in height

*KH R R

KHARRA vb. (I)~to fall down

a) perf. act.

7:143 (139) He made it crumble to dust; and Moses fell down swooning
12:100 (101) and the others fell down prostrate before him
16:26 (28) and the roof fell down on them from over them
19:58 (59) when the signs of the All-merciful were recited to them, they fell down
22:31 (32) it is as though he has fallen from heaven and the birds snatch him away
32:15 (15) those believe in Our signs who, when they are reminded of them, fall down prostrate
34:14 (13) when he fell down, the jinn saw clearly
38:24 (23) he sought forgiveness of his Lord, and he fell down, bowing

b) impf. act. (*yakhurru*)

17:107 (108) when it is recited to them, fall down upon their faces prostrating
17:109 (109) and they fall down upon their faces weeping
19:90 (92) the mountains wellnigh fall down crashing
25:73 (73) who, when they are reminded of the signs of their Lord, fall not down thereat

*KH R Ṣ

KHARAṢA vb. (I)~to conjecture, to guess

b) impf. act. (*yakhruṣu*)

6:116 (116) they follow only surmise, merely conjecturing
6:148 (149) you follow only surmise, merely conjecturing
10:66 (67) they follow nothing but surmise, merely conjecturing
43:20 (19) they have no knowledge of that; they are only conjecturing

51:10 (10) perish the conjecturers

*KH R Ṭ M

KHURṬŪM n.m.~a muzzle [Ar]; a nose [Pk]; a snout [Ali]

68:16 (16) We shall brand him upon the muzzle

*KH S ʾ

KHASAʾA vb. (I)~to slink, to be driven away, to begone. (pcple. act.) slinking, aweary [Ar]; loathed, weakened and made dim [Pk]; rejected [Ali]

c) impv. (*ikhsaʾ*)

23:108 (110) ‘Slink you into it,’ He shall say

g) pcple. act. (*khāsiʾ*)

2:65 (61) be you apes, miserably slinking
7:166 (166) be you apes, miserably slinking
67:4 (4) return thy gaze again, and again, and thy gaze comes back to thee dazzled, aweary

*KH S F

KHASAFA vb. (I)~to cause (the earth) to swallow

a) perf. act.

28:81 (81) We made the earth to swallow him and his dwelling
28:82 (82) had God not been gracious to us, He would have made us to be swallowed too
29:40 (39) some were seized by the Cry, and some We made the earth to swallow
75:8 (8) and the moon is eclipsed

b) impf. act. (*yakhsifu*)

16:45 (47) do they feel secure... that God will not cause the earth to swallow them?
17:68 (70) do you feel secure that He will not cause the shore to swallow you up?
34:9 (9) did We will, We would make the earth to swallow them
67:16 (16) do you feel secure that He who is in heaven will not cause the earth to swallow you?

*KH S R

KHASIRA vb. (I)~to lose, to be lost, to suffer a loss, to be a loser. (n.vb.) a loss. (pcple. act.) a loser, losing

a) perf. act.

4:119 (118) whoso takes Satan to him for a friend, instead of God, has surely suffered a manifest loss
6:12 (12) those who have lost their souls, they do not believe
6:20 (20) those who have lost their own souls, they do not believe
6:31 (31) lost indeed are they that cried lies to the encounter with God
6:140 (141) losers are they who slay their children in folly, without knowledge
7:9 (8) he whose scales are light — they have lost their souls for wronging Our signs
7:53 (51) they have indeed lost their souls
10:45 (46) lost will be those who cried lies to the encounter with God
11:21 (23) those are they that have lost their souls
22:11 (11) he loses this world and the world to come

23:103 (105)	he whose scales are light — they have lost their souls
39:15 (17)	the losers are they who lose themselves and their families on the Day of Resurrection
40:78 (78)	justly the issue shall be decided; then the vain-doers shall be lost
40:85 (85)	the unbelievers shall be lost
42:45 (44)	the losers are they who lose themselves and their families on the Day of Resurrection

b) impf. act. (*yakhsaru*)

45:27 (26)	upon that day the vain-doers shall lose

f) n.vb. (1) (*khusr*)

65:9 (9)	the end of its affair was loss
103:2 (2)	surely Man is in the way of loss

f) n.vb. (2) (*khasār*)

17:82 (84)	and the evildoers it increases not, except in loss
35:39 (37)	their unbelief increases the disbelievers only in loss
71:21 (20)	him whose wealth and children increase him only in loss

f) n.vb. (3) (*khusrān*)

4:119 (118)	whoso takes Satan to him for a friend, instead of God, has surely suffered a manifest loss <...>
22:11 (11)	that is indeed the manifest loss
39:15 (17)	is not that the manifest loss?

g) pcple. act. (*khāsir*; comp. adj. *akhsar*)

2:27 (25)	and such as do corruption in the land — they shall be the losers
2:64 (61)	but for the bounty and mercy of God towards you, you had been of the losers
2:121 (115)	whoso disbelieves in it, they shall be the losers
3:85 (79)	in the next world he shall be among the losers
3:149 (142)	they will turn you upon your heels, and you will turn about, losers
5:5 (7)	in the world to come he shall be among the losers
5:21 (24)	turn not back in your traces, to turn about losers
5:30 (33)	and he slew him, and became one of the losers
5:53 (58)	their works have failed; now they are losers
7:23 (22)	if Thou dost not forgive us, and have mercy upon us, we shall surely be among the lost
7:90 (88)	if you follow Shuaib, assuredly in that case you will be losers
7:92 (90)	those who cried lies to Shuaib, they were the losers
7:99 (97)	none feels secure against God's devising but the people of the lost
7:149 (148)	if our Lord has not mercy on us, and forgives us not, surely we shall be of the lost
7:178 (177)	whom He leads astray — they are the losers
8:37 (38)	and put them in Gehenna; those are the losers
9:69 (70)	those — they are the losers
10:95 (95)	nor be of those who cry lies to God's signs so as to be of the losers
11:22 (24)	they without doubt will be the greatest losers in the world to come
11:47 (49)	if Thou forgivest me not, and hast not mercy on me, I shall be among the losers
12:14 (14)	if the wolf eats him, and we a band, then are we losers
16:109 (110)	in the world to come they will be the losers

18:103 (103)	shall We tell you who will be the greatest losers in their works?
21:70 (70)	they desired to outwit him; so We made them the worse losers
23:34 (36)	if you obey a mortal like yourselves, then you will be losers
27:5 (5)	and they will be the greatest losers in the Hereafter
29:52 (52)	those who believe in vanity and disbelieve in God — those, they are the losers
39:15 (17)	the losers are they who lose themselves and their families on the Day of Resurrection
39:63 (63)	those who disbelieve in the signs of God, those — they are the losers
39:65 (65)	thy work shall surely fail and thou wilt be among the losers
41:23 (22)	therefore you find yourselves this morning among the losers
41:25 (24)	before them, men and jinn alike; surely they were losers
42:45 (44)	the losers are they who lose themselves and their families on the Day of Resurrection
46:18 (17)	passed away before them, men and jinn alike; they were losers
58:19 (20)	why, Satan's party, surely, they are the losers
63:9 (9)	whoso does that, they are the losers
79:12 (12)	they shall say, 'That then were a losing return!'

KHASSARA vb. (II)~(n.vb.) a loss

f) n.vb. (*takhsīr*)

11:63 (66)	you would do nothing for me, except increase my loss

AKHSARA vb. (IV)~to skimp [Ar]; to fall short (in weighing), to cause a loss [Pk]; to give less than due [Ali]; to scant [Bl]. (pcple. act.) a cheater [Ar]; one who gives less (than the due) [Pk]; one who causes loss (to others by fraud) [Ali]

b) impf. act. (*yukhsiru*)

55:9 (8)	weigh with justice, and skimp not in the Balance
83:3 (3)	but, when they measure for them or weigh for them, do skimp

g) pcple. act. (*mukhsir*)

26:181 (181)	fill up the measure, and be not cheaters

*KH SH ᶜ

KHASHAᶜA vb. (I)~to be hushed or humbled. (n.vb.) humility. (pcple. act.) one who is humble; abasing, humbling

a) perf. act.

20:108 (107)	voices will be hushed to the All-merciful, so that thou hearest

b) impf. act. (*yakhshaᶜu*)

57:16 (15)	is it not time that the hearts of those who believe should be humbled

f) n.vb. (*khushūᶜ*)

17:109 (109)	they fall down upon their faces weeping; and it increases them in humility

g) pcple. act. (*khāshi*ᶜ)

2:45 (42)	for grievous it is, save to the humble
3:199 (198)	men humble to God, not selling the signs of God for a small price
21:90 (90)	and they were humble to Us
23:2 (2)	who in their prayers are humble
33:35 (35)	humble men and (humble women)
33:35 (35)	(humble men) and humble women
41:39 (39)	of His signs is that thou seest the earth humble
42:45 (44)	thou shalt see them, as they are exposed to it, abject in humbleness
54:7 (7)	abasing their eyes, they shall come forth from the tombs
59:21 (21)	thou wouldst have seen it humbled, split asunder out of the fear of God
68:43 (43)	humbled shall be their eyes, and abasement shall overspread them
70:44 (44)	humbled their eyes, overspreading them abasement
79:9 (9)	and their eyes shall be humbled
88:2 (2)	faces on that day humbled

*KH SH B

KHUSHUB n.m. (pl. of *khashab*)~timber, wood

63:4 (4)	thou listenest to their speech, and it is as they were propped-up timbers

*KH SH Y

KHASHIYA vb. (I)~to fear. (n.vb.) fear

a) perf. act.

4:25 (30)	that provision is for those of you who fear sin (fornication)
18:80 (79)	we were afraid he would impose on them insolence and unbelief
20:94 (95)	I was fearful that thou wouldst say
36:11 (10)	Thou only warnest him who follows the Remembrance and who fears the All-merciful
50:33 (32)	whosoever fears the All-merciful in the Unseen
98:8 (8)	that is for him who fears his Lord

b) impf. act. (*yakhshá*)

2:150 (145)	the evildoers of them; and fear you them not
4:9 (10)	let those fear who, if they left behind them weak seed, would be afraid
4:77 (79)	there is a party of them fearing the people as they would
5:3 (4)	today the unbelievers have despaired of your religion; therefore fear them not
5:44 (48)	so fear not men
5:52 (57)	we fear lest a turn of fortune should smite us
9:13 (13)	are you afraid of them?
9:13 (13)	you would do better to be afraid of God
9:18 (18)	performs the prayer, and pays the alms, and fears none but God alone
9:24 (24)	commerce you fear may slacken
13:21 (21)	who join what God has commanded shall be joined, and fear their Lord

20:3 (2)	but only as a reminder to him who fears
20:44 (46)	speak gently to him, that haply he may be mindful, or perchance fear
20:77 (80)	fearing not overtaking, neither afraid
21:49 (50)	such as fear their Lord in the Unseen, trembling
24:52 (51)	whoso obeys God and His Messenger, and fears God
33:37 (37)	concealing within thyself what God should reveal, fearing other men
33:37 (37)	God has better right for thee to fear Him
33:39 (39)	who were delivering the Messages of God, and were fearing Him
33:39 (39)	and fearing not any one except Him
35:18 (19)	Thou warnest only those who fear their Lord in the Unseen
35:28 (25)	only those of His servants fear God who have knowledge
39:23 (24)	whereat shiver the skins of those who fear their Lord
67:12 (12)	those who fear their Lord in the Unseen — there awaits them forgiveness
79:19 (19)	and that I should guide thee to thy Lord, then thou shalt fear
79:26 (26)	surely in that is a lesson for him who fears
79:45 (45)	Thou art only the warner of him who fears it
80:9 (9)	and fearfully
87:10 (10)	and he who fears shall remember

c) impv. (*ikhsha*)

2:150 (145)	but fear you Me; and that I may perfect
3:173 (167)	the people have gathered against you, therefore fear them'
5:3 (4)	but fear you Me
5:44 (48)	but fear you Me; and sell not My signs
31:33 (32)	O men, fear your Lord, and dread a day

f) n.vb. (*khashyah*)

2:74 (69)	and others crash down in the fear of God
4:77 (79)	as they would fear God
4:77 (79)	or with a greater fear
17:31 (33)	slay not your children for fear of poverty
17:100 (102)	yet would you hold back for fear of expending
21:28 (29)	they tremble in awe of Him
23:57 (59)	surely those who tremble in fear of their Lord
59:21 (21)	thou wouldst have seen it humbled, split asunder out of the fear of God

*KH Ṣ F

KHAṢAFA vb. (I)~to stitch together, to sew together

b) impf. act. (*yakhṣifu*)

7:22 (21)	they took to stitching upon themselves leaves of the Garden
20:121 (119)	they took to stitching upon themselves leaves of the Garden

*KH Ṣ M

KHAṢIM n.m. (adj)~contentious

43:58 (58)	nay, but they are a people contentious

KHAṢĪM n.m.~an adversary, opponent; a pleader, advocate

4:105 (106)	so be not an advocate for the traitors
16:4 (4)	and, behold, he is a manifest adversary
36:77 (77)	then lo, he is a manifest adversary

KHAṢM n.m.~a disputant; a dispute; enemy [Ali]; a wrangler [Bl]

22:19 (20)	these are two disputants who have disputed concerning their Lord
38:21 (20)	has the tiding of the dispute come to thee?
38:22 (21)	two disputants we are — one of us has injured the other

KHĀṢAMA vb. (III)~(n.vb.) an altercation, a dispute, contention

f) n.vb. (*khiṣām*)

2:204 (200)	yet he is most stubborn in altercation
43:18 (17)	and, when the time of altercation comes, is not to be seen

TAKHĀṢAMA vb. (VI)~(n.vb.) disputing

f) n.vb. (*takhāṣum*)

38:64 (64)	surely that is true — the disputing of the inhabitants of the Fire

IKHTAṢAMA vb. (VIII)~to dispute, to strive together

a) perf. act.

22:19 (20)	these are two disputants who have disputed concerning their Lord

b) impf. act. (*yakhtaṣimu*)

3:44 (39)	thou wast not with them, when they were disputing.)
26:96 (96)	they shall say, as they dispute there one with another
27:45 (46)	they were two parties, that were disputing one with another
36:49 (49)	they are awaiting only for one Cry to seize them while they are yet disputing
38:69 (69)	I had no knowledge of the High Council when they disputed
39:31 (32)	on the Day of Resurrection before your Lord you shall dispute
50:28 (27)	dispute not before Me! For I sent you beforehand the threat

*KH Ṣ Ṣ

KHAṢṢA vb. (I)~(n.vb.) poverty

f) n.vb. (*khaṣāṣah*)

59:9 (9)	preferring others above themselves, even though poverty be their portion

KHĀṢṢAH n.f.~(adv) particularly, in particular

8:25 (25)	and fear a trial which shall surely not smite in particular the evildoers

IKHTAṢṢA vb. (VIII)~to single out [Ar]; to choose, select [Pk, Ali]

b) impf. act. (*yakhtaṣṣu*)

2:105 (99) God singles out for His mercy whom He will
3:74 (67) He singles out for His mercy whom He will

*KH T M

KHATAMA vb. (I)~to set a seal, to seal. (pcple. pass.) sealed

a) perf. act.

2:7 (6) God has set a seal on their hearts and on their hearing
6:46 (46) what think you? If God seizes your hearing and sight, and sets a seal upon your

45:23 (22) and set a seal upon his hearing and his heart

b) impf. act. (*yakhtimu*)

36:65 (65) today We set a seal on their mouths, and their hands speak to Us
42:24 (23) if God wills, He will set a seal on thy heart

h) pcple. pass. (*makhtūm*)

83:25 (25) as they are given to drink of a wine sealed

KHĀTAM n.m.~a seal

33:40 (40) Muhammad is not the father of any one of your men, but the Messenger of God, and the Seal of the Prophets

KHITĀM n.m.~a seal

83:26 (26) whose seal is musk — so after that let the strivers strive

*KH T R

KHATTĀR n.m~a perfidious man, a traitor

31:32 (31) none denies Our signs, except every ungrateful traitor

*KH Ṭ ʾ

KHAṬIʾA vb. (I)~(n.vb.) a sin. (pcple. act.) a sinner, one who is sinful, one who commits an error

f) n.vb. (*khiṭʾ*)

17:31 (33) surely the slaying of them is a grievous sin

g) pcple. act. (*khāṭiʾ*)

12:29 (29) surely thou art one of the sinners
12:91 (91) God has indeed preferred thee above us, and certainly we have been sinful

12:97 (98)	ask forgiveness of our crimes for us; for certainly we have been sinful
28:8 (7)	certainly Pharaoh and Haman, and their hosts, were of the sinners
69:9 (9)	and the Subverted Cities — they committed error
69:37 (37)	that none excepting the sinners eat
96:16 (16)	a lying, sinful forelock

KHAṬĀʾ n.m.~(adv) by error

4:92 (94)	it belongs not to a believer to slay a believer, except it be by error
4:92 (94)	if any slays a believer by error

KHAṬĪʾAH n.f. (pl. *khaṭīʾāt*, and *khaṭāyā*)~transgression, fault, offence [Ar, Bl]; sin, delinquency, fault [Pk, Ali]

2:58 (55)	We will forgive you your transgressions, and increase the good-doers
2:81 (75)	whoso earns evil, and is encompassed by his transgression
4:112 (112)	whosoever earns a fault or a sin and then casts it upon the innocent
7:161 (161)	We will forgive you your transgressions
20:73 (75)	We believe in our Lord, that He may pardon us our offences
26:51 (51)	We are eager that our Lord should forgive us our offences
26:82 (82)	who I am eager shall forgive me my offence on the Day of Doom
29:12 (11)	follow our path, and let us carry your offences
29:12 (11)	yet they cannot carry anything, even of their own offences
71:25 (25)	because of their transgressions they were drowned

AKHṬAʾA vb. (IV)~to make a mistake; to miss the mark [Pk]; to fall into error [Ali]

a) perf. act.

2:286 (286)	take us not to task if we forget, or make mistake
33:5 (5)	there is no fault in you if you make mistakes

*KH Ṭ B

KHAṬABA vb. (I)~(n.vb.) a matter, business; (*mā khaṭbuka*) what is your business? what happened?

f) n.vb. (*khaṭb*)

12:51 (51)	'What was your business, women,' he said
15:57 (57)	and what is your business, envoys?
20:95 (96)	thou, Samaritan, what was thy business?
28:23 (23)	holding back their flocks. He said, 'What is your business?'
51:31 (31)	and what is your business, envoys?

KHUṬBAH n.f.~proposal [Ar, Bl]; troth [Pk]; betrothal [Ali]

2:235 (235)	there is no fault in you touching the proposal to women you offer

KHĀṬABA vb. (III)~to address, to speak to. (n.vb.) a speech, argument, discourse

a) perf. act.

25:63 (64)	and who, when the ignorant address them, say

b) impf. act. (*yukhāṭibu*)

11:37 (39) address Me not concerning those who have done evil
23:27 (28) address Me not concerning those who have done evil

f) n.vb. (*khiṭāb*)

38:20 (19) We strengthened his kingdom, and gave him wisdom and speech decisive
38:23 (22) and he overcame me in the argument
78:37 (37) the All-merciful of whom they have no power to speak

*KH Ṭ F

KHAṬIFA vb. (I)~to snatch, to snatch away

a) perf. act.

37:10 (10) except such as snatches a fragment

b) impf. act. (*yakhṭafu*)

2:20 (19) the lightning wellnigh snatches away their sight
22:31 (32) it is as though he has fallen from heaven and the birds snatch him away

KHAṬFAH n.f.~a fragment

37:10 (10) except such as snatches a fragment

TAKHAṬṬAFA vb. (V)~to snatch away

b) impf. act. (*yatakhaṭṭafu*)

8:26 (26) and were fearful that the people would snatch you away

e) impf. pass. (*yutakhaṭṭafu*)

28:57 (57) should we follow the guidance with thee, we shall be snatched from our land
29:67 (67) a sanctuary secure, while all about them the people are snatched away

*KH Ṭ Ṭ

KHAṬṬA vb. (I)~to inscribe, to write

b) impf. act. (*yakhuṭṭu*)

29:48 (47) not before this didst thou recite any Book, or inscribe it with thy right hand

*KH Ṭ W

KHUṬWAH n.f.~a step

2:168 (163) follow not the steps of Satan; he is a manifest foe to you
2:208 (204) enter the peace, all of you, and follow not the steps of Satan

6:142 (143)	and follow not the steps of Satan
24:21 (21)	follow not the steps of Satan
24:21 (21)	for whosoever follows the steps of Satan, assuredly he bids to indecency and dishonour

*KH W Ḍ

KHĀḌA vb. (I)~to plunge into [Ar, Bl]; to meddle in, engage in, to talk, to flounder (in talk), to chat, to wade (in vain dispute) [Pk]; to turn (to another subject), to engage in, to talk idly, to babble, to plunge in vain talk [Ali]. (n.vb.) plunging. (pcple. act.) one who plunges (in vain or idle talk)

a) perf. act.

9:69 (70)	you have plunged as they (plunged)
9:69 (70)	you have (plunged) as they plunged

b) impf. act. (*yakhūḍu*)

4:140 (139)	do not sit with them until they plunge into some other talk
6:68 (67)	when thou seest those who plunge into Our signs
6:68 (67)	turn away from them until they plunge into some other talk
9:65 (66)	we were only plunging and playing
43:83 (83)	then leave them alone to plunge and play
70:42 (42)	then leave them alone to plunge and play
74:45 (46)	and we plunged along with the plungers

f) n.vb. (*khawḍ*)

6:91 (91)	then leave them alone, playing their game of plunging
52:12 (12)	such as play at plunging

g) pcple. act. (*khāʾiḍ*)

74:45 (46)	and we plunged along with the plungers

*KH W F

KHĀFA vb. (I)~to fear, to be afraid. (n.vb.) fear. (pcple. act.) one who is in fear, fearful

a) perf. act.

2:182 (178)	if any man fears injustice or sin from one making testament
2:229 (229)	if you fear they may not maintain God's bounds
2:239 (240)	if you are in fear, then afoot or mounted
4:3 (3)	if you fear that you will not act justly towards the orphans
4:3 (3)	if you fear you will not be equitable, then only one
4:9 (10)	behind them weak seed, would be afraid on their account
4:35 (39)	if you fear a breach between the two, bring forth an arbiter
4:101 (102)	there is no fault in you that you shorten the prayer, if you fear the unbelievers may afflict you
4:128 (127)	if a woman fear rebelliousness or aversion in her husband
9:28 (28)	if you fear poverty, God shall surely enrich you of His bounty
11:103 (105)	in that is a sign for him who fears the chastisement
14:14 (17)	that, for him who fears My station
14:14 (17)	and fears My threat
19:5 (5)	now I fear my kinsfolk after I am gone
26:21 (20)	so I fled from you, fearing you

28:7 (6)	then, when thou fearest for him, cast him into the sea
55:46 (46)	but such as fears the Station of his Lord, for them shall be two gardens
79:40 (40)	as for him who feared the Station of his Lord and forbade the soul its caprice

b) impf. act. (*yakhāfu*)

2:229 (229)	unless the couple fear they may not maintain God's bounds
3:175 (169)	that is Satan frightening his friends, therefore do not fear them
4:34 (38)	and those you fear may be rebellious admonish
5:23 (26)	said two men of those that feared God
5:28 (31)	I will not stretch out my hand against thee, to slay thee; I fear God
5:54 (59)	men who struggle in the path of God, not fearing the reproach of any reproacher
5:94 (95)	that God may know who fears Him in the Unseen
5:108 (107)	or else they will be afraid that after their oaths oaths may be rebutted
6:15 (15)	I fear, if I should rebel against my Lord, the chastisement
6:51 (51)	warn therewith those who fear they shall be mustered to their Lord
6:80 (80)	I fear not what you associate with Him
6:81 (81)	how should I fear what you have associated
6:81 (81)	seeing you fear not that you have associated
7:59 (57)	I fear for you the chastisement of a dreadful day
8:26 (26)	and were fearful that the people would snatch you away
8:48 (50)	I fear God; and God is terrible in retribution
8:58 (60)	if thou fearest treachery any way at the hands of a people, dissolve it
10:15 (16)	I fear, if I should rebel against my Lord, the chastisement
11:3 (3)	if you should turn your backs I fear for you the chastisement
11:26 (28)	I fear for you the chastisement of a painful day
11:70 (73)	fear not; we have been sent to the people of Lot
11:84 (85)	I fear for you the chastisement of an encompassing day
12:13 (13)	I fear the wolf may eat him, while you are heedless of him
13:21 (21)	and fear their Lord, and dread the evil reckoning
16:50 (52)	they fear their Lord above them, and they do what they are commanded
17:57 (59)	they hope for His mercy, and fear His chastisement
19:45 (46)	I fear that some chastisement from the All-merciful will smite thee
20:21 (22)	said He, 'Take it, and fear not'
20:45 (47)	truly we fear he may exceed against us, or wax insolent
20:46 (48)	'Fear not,' said He. 'Surely I shall be with you'
20:68 (71)	fear not; surely thou art the uppermost
20:77 (80)	fearing not overtaking, neither afraid
20:112 (111)	whosoever does deeds of righteousness, being a believer, shall fear neither wrong nor injustice
24:37 (37)	fearing a day when hearts and eyes shall be turned about
24:50 (49)	are they in doubt, or do they fear that God may be unjust towards them
26:12 (11)	my Lord, I fear they will cry me lies
26:14 (13)	they also have a sin against me, and I fear they will slay me
26:135 (135)	I fear for you the chastisement of a dreadful day
27:10 (10)	Moses, fear not
27:10 (10)	surely the Envoys do not fear in My presence
28:7 (6)	and do not fear, neither sorrow
28:25 (25)	be not afraid; thou hast escaped from the people of the evildoers
28:31 (31)	Moses, come forward, and fear not
28:33 (33)	I fear that they will slay me
28:34 (34)	I fear they will cry me lies
29:33 (32)	fear not, neither sorrow, for surely we shall deliver thee
30:28 (27)	you are equal in regard to it, you fearing them as you fear each other
38:22 (21)	fear not; two disputants we are
39:13 (15)	I fear, if I should rebel against my Lord

40:26 (27)	I fear that he may change your religion
40:30 (31)	I fear for you the like of the day of the parties
40:32 (34)	I fear for you the Day of Invocation
41:30 (30)	fear not, neither sorrow; rejoice in Paradise
46:21 (20)	I fear for you the chastisement of a dreadful day
48:27 (27)	heads shaved, your hair cut short, not fearing
50:45 (45)	therefore remind by the Koran him who fears My threat
51:28 (28)	be not afraid
51:37 (37)	therein We left a sign to those who fear the painful chastisement
59:16 (16)	surely I fear God, the Lord of all Being
72:13 (13)	whosoever believes in his Lord, he shall fear neither paltriness nor vileness
74:53 (53)	but they do not fear the Hereafter
76:7 (7)	they fulfil their vows, and fear a day whose evil is upon the wing
76:10 (10)	we fear from our Lord a frowning day, inauspicious
91:15 (15)	He fears not the issue thereof

c) impv. (*khaf*)

3:175 (169)	but fear you Me, if you are believers

f) n.vb. (*khawf*)

2:38 (36)	no fear shall be on them, neither shall they sorrow
2:62 (59)	and no fear shall be on them, neither shall they sorrow
2:112 (106)	and no fear shall be on them, neither shall they sorrow
2:155 (150)	surely We will try you with something of fear and hunger
2:262 (264)	no fear shall be on them, neither shall they sorrow
2:274 (275)	no fear shall be on them, neither shall they sorrow
2:277 (277)	no fear shall be on them, neither shall they sorrow
3:170 (164)	no fear shall be on them, neither shall they sorrow
4:83 (85)	when there comes to them a matter, be it of security or fear, they broadcast it
5:69 (73)	no fear shall be on them, neither shall they sorrow
6:48 (48)	no fear shall be on them, neither shall they sorrow
7:35 (33)	no fear shall be on them, neither shall they sorrow
7:49 (47)	enter Paradise; no fear upon you, nor shall you sorrow
7:56 (54)	and call on Him fearfully, eagerly
10:62 (63)	no fear shall be on them, neither shall they sorrow
10:83 (83)	for fear of Pharaoh and their Council, that they would persecute them
13:12 (13)	it is He who shows you the lightning, for fear and hope
16:112 (113)	so God let it taste the garment of hunger and of fear
24:55 (54)	and will give them in exchange, after their fear, security
30:24 (23)	He shows you lightning, for fear and hope
32:16 (16)	their sides shun their couches as they call on their Lord in fear and hope
33:19 (19)	when fear comes upon them, thou seest them looking at thee
33:19 (19)	but when the fear departs, they flay you with sharp tongues
43:68 (68)	O My servants, today no fear is on you
46:13 (12)	no fear shall be on them, neither shall they sorrow
106:4 (4)	and secured them from fear

g) pcple. act. (*khā'if*)

2:114 (108)	such men might never enter them, save in fear
28:18 (17)	in the morning he was in the city, fearful and vigilant
28:21 (20)	he departed therefrom, fearful and vigilant

KHĪFAH n.f.~fear, awe; (adv) fearfully, in fear

7:205 (204)	remember thy Lord in thy soul, humbly and fearfully

11:70 (73)	he was suspicious of them and conceived a fear of them
13:13 (14)	the thunder proclaims His praise, and the angels, in awe of Him
20:67 (70)	and Moses conceived a fear within him
30:28 (27)	you fearing them as you fear each other
51:28 (28)	then he conceived a fear of them

KHAWWAFA vb. (II)~to frighten, to terrify. (n.vb.) frightening; (adv) in order to frighten

b) impf. act. (*yukhawwifu*)

3:175 (169)	that is Satan frightening his friends
17:60 (62)	We frighten them, but it only increases them in great insolence
39:16 (18)	that it is wherewith God frightens His servants
39:36 (37)	they frighten thee with those apart from Him

f) n.vb. (*takhwīf*)

17:59 (61)	We do not send the signs, except to frighten

TAKHAWWAFA vb. (V)~(n.vb.) diminishing or destroying little by little

f) n.vb. (*takhawwuf*)

16:47 (49)	He will not seize them, little by little destroying them

*KH W L

KHĀL n.m. (pl. *akhwāl*)~uncle (maternal)

24:61 (60)	the houses of your uncles or your aunts maternal
33:50 (49)	uncles maternal and aunts maternal

KHĀLĀT n.f. (pl. of *khālah*)~aunt (maternal)

4:23 (27)	your sisters, your aunts paternal and maternal
24:61 (60)	the houses of your uncles or your aunts maternal
33:50 (49)	uncles maternal and aunts maternal

KHAWWALA vb. (II)~to confer on, to grant

a) perf. act.

6:94 (94)	you have left what We conferred on you behind your backs
39:8 (11)	when He confers on him a blessing from Him he forgets that he was calling to before
39:49 (50)	then, when We confer on him a blessing from Us, he says

*KH W N

KHĀNA vb. (I)~to betray, to be in treason against; to trick. (n.vb.) treachery. (pcple. act.) a traitor; (adj) treacherous

a) perf. act.

8:71 (72) they have tricked God before
66:10 (10) they were under two of Our righteous servants, but they betrayed them

b) impf. act. (*yakhūnu*)

8:27 (27) O believers, betray not God and the Messenger
8:27 (27) and betray not your trusts and that wittingly
12:52 (52) so that he may know I betrayed him not secretly

f) n.vb. (*khiyānah*)

8:58 (60) if thou fearest treachery any way at the hands of a people
8:71 (72) if they desire treachery against thee, they have tricked God before

g) pcple. act. (*khā'in*)

4:105 (106) so be not an advocate for the traitors
5:13 (16) thou wilt never cease to light upon some act of treachery on their part
8:58 (60) surely God loves not the treacherous
12:52 (52) God guides not the guile of the treacherous
40:19 (20) He knows the treachery of the eyes and what the breasts conceal

KHAWWĀN n.m.~one who betrays, a traitor

4:107 (107) surely God loves not the guilty traitor
22:38 (39) surely God loves not any ungrateful traitor

IKHTĀNA vb. (VIII)~to deceive, to defraud, to betray

b) impf. act. (*yakhtānu*)

2:187 (183) God knows that you have been betraying yourselves
4:107 (107) do not dispute on behalf of those who betray themselves

*KH W R

KHĀRA vb. (I)~(n.vb.) the lowing (of cattle)

f) n.vb. (*khuwār*)

7:148 (146) the people of Moses took to them, after him, of their ornaments a Calf — a mere body that lowed
20:88 (90) then he brought out for them a Calf, a mere body that lowed

*KH W Y

KHAWÁ vb. (I)~(pcple. act.) that which is fallen down

g) pcple. act. f. (*khāwiyah*)

2:259 (261) a city that was fallen down upon its turrets
18:42 (40) and it was fallen down upon its trellises

22:45 (44)	and now it is fallen down upon its turrets
27:52 (53)	those are their houses, all fallen down because of the evil they committed
69:7 (7)	as if they were the stumps of fallen down palm-trees

*KH Y B

KHĀBA vb. (I)~to fail, to be disappointed. (pcple. act.) one who is disappointed

a) perf. act.

14:15 (18)	they sought a judgment; then was disappointed every froward tyrant
20:61 (64)	whoso forges has ever failed
20:111 (110)	he will have failed whose burden is of evildoing
91:10 (10)	and failed has he who seduces it

g) pcple. act. (*khāʾib*)

3:127 (122)	they turned in their tracks, disappointed

*KH Y L

KHAYL n.f. (coll)~horses

3:14 (12)	heaped-up heaps of gold and silver, horses of mark
8:60 (62)	make ready for them whatever force and strings of horses you can
16:8 (8)	and horses, and mules, and asses, for you to ride
17:64 (66)	rally against them thy horsemen and thy foot
59:6 (6)	against that you pricked neither horse nor camel

MUKHTĀL n.m.~proud

4:36 (40)	God loves not the proud and boastful
31:18 (17)	God loves not any man proud and boastful
57:23 (23)	God loves not any man proud and boastful

KHAYYALA vb. (I)~to make to appear; to seem

e) impf. pass. (*yukhayyalu*)

20:66 (69)	and lo, it seemed to him, by their sorcery

*KH Y M

KHIYĀM n.f. (pl. of *khaymah*)~a pavilion

55:72 (72)	houris, cloistered in cool pavilions

*KH Y R

KHAYR n.m.~(n) that which is good, wealth, prosperity, goods; (pl. *akhyār*) excellent (ones); (adj) good; (with prep. *min*) better than, best

2:54 (51)	that will be better for you in your Creator's sight
2:61 (58)	would you have in exchange what is meaner for what is better?
2:103 (97)	a recompense from God had been better, if they had but known
2:105 (99)	and the idolaters wish not that any good should be sent down upon you from your Lord
2:106 (100)	for whatever verse We abrogate or cast into oblivion, We bring a better or the like of it
2:110 (104)	whatever good you shall forward to your souls' account, you shall find it with God
2:158 (153)	and whoso volunteers good, God is All-grateful, All-knowing
2:180 (176)	when any of you is visited by death, and he leaves behind some goods
2:184 (180)	yet better it is for him who volunteers good
2:184 (180)	yet better it is for him who volunteers good
2:184 (180)	that you should fast is better for you, if you but know
2:197 (193)	whatever good you do, God knows it
2:197 (193)	but the best provision is godfearing
2:215 (211)	whatsoever good you expend is for parents and kinsmen
2:215 (211)	and whatever good you may do, God has knowledge of it
2:216 (213)	it may happen that you will hate a thing which is better for you
2:220 (218)	to set their affairs aright is good
2:221 (220)	a believing slavegirl is better than an idolatress
2:221 (220)	a believing slave is better than an idolater
2:263 (265)	honourable words, and forgiveness, are better than a freewill offering followed by injury
2:269 (272)	whoso is given the Wisdom, has been given much good
2:271 (273)	if you conceal them, and give them to the poor, that is better for you
2:272 (274)	whatever good you expend is for yourselves
2:272 (274)	whatever good you expend shall be repaid to you in full
2:273 (274)	whatever good you expend, surely God has knowledge of it
2:280 (280)	that you should give freewill offerings is better for you
3:15 (13)	shall I tell you of a better than that?
3:26 (25)	in Thy hand is the good; Thou art powerful
3:30 (28)	the day every soul shall find what it has done of good brought forward
3:54 (47)	God is the best of devisers
3:104 (100)	let there be one nation of you, calling to good
3:110 (106)	you are the best nation ever brought forth to men, bidding to honour
3:110 (106)	had the People of the Book believed, it were better for them
3:115 (111)	whatsoever good you do, you shall not be denied the just reward of it
3:150 (143)	God is your Protector, and He is the best of helpers
3:157 (151)	forgiveness and mercy from God are a better thing than that you amass
3:178 (172)	let not the unbelievers suppose that the indulgence We grant them is better for them
3:180 (175)	let them not suppose it is better for them
3:198 (197)	that which is with God is better for the pious
4:19 (23)	you may be averse to a thing, and God set in it much good
4:25 (30)	yet it is better for you to be patient
4:46 (49)	it would have been better for them, and more upright
4:59 (62)	that is better, and fairer in the issue
4:66 (69)	if they had done as they were admonished it would have been better for them
4:77 (79)	the world to come is better for him who fears God
4:114 (114)	no good is there in much of their conspiring
4:127 (126)	whatever good you do, God knows of it
4:128 (127)	right settlement is better
4:149 (148)	if you do good openly or in secret or pardon an evil
4:170 (168)	so believe; better is it for you
4:171 (169)	say not, 'Three.' Refrain; better is it for you
5:114 (114)	Thou art the best of providers

6:17 (17)	if He visits thee with good, He is powerful over everything
6:32 (32)	the Last Abode is better for those that are godfearing
6:57 (57)	He is the Best of deciders
6:158 (159)	it shall not profit a soul to believe that never believed before, or earned some good
7:12 (11)	said he, 'I am better than he'
7:26 (25)	the garment of godfearing — that is better
7:85 (83)	that is better for you, if you are believers
7:87 (85)	He is the best of judges
7:89 (87)	Thou art the best of deliverers
7:155 (154)	Thou art the best of forgivers
7:169 (168)	the Last Abode is better for those who are godfearing
7:188 (188)	had I knowledge of the Unseen I would have acquired much good
8:19 (19)	if you give over, it is better for you
8:23 (23)	if God had known of any good in them He would have made them hear
8:30 (30)	God is the best of devisers
8:70 (71)	if God knows of any good in your hearts
8:70 (71)	He will give you better than what has been taken
9:3 (3)	if you repent, that will be better for you
9:41 (41)	struggle in God's way with your possessions and your selves; that is better for you
9:61 (61)	say: 'An ear of good for you'
9:74 (75)	if they repent it will be better for them
9:109 (110)	is he better who founded his building upon the fear of God
10:11 (12)	if God should hasten unto men evil as they would hasten good
10:58 (59)	it is better than that they amass
10:107 (107)	if He desires any good for thee, none can repel His bounty
10:109 (109)	He is the best of judges
11:31 (33)	God will not give them any good
11:84 (85)	I see you are prospering
11:86 (87)	God's remainder is better for you, if you are believers
12:39 (39)	say, which is better, my fellow-prisoners
12:57 (57)	yet is the wage of the world to come better for those who believe
12:59 (59)	do you not see that I fill up the measure, and am the best of hosts?
12:64 (64)	God is the best guardian, and He is the most merciful
12:80 (80)	He is the best of judges
12:109 (109)	the abode of the world to come is better for those that are godfearing
16:30 (32)	they will say, 'Good'
16:30 (32)	surely the abode of the world to come is better
16:76 (78)	wherever he despatches him, he brings no good
16:95 (97)	what is with God — that is better for you
16:126 (127)	better it is for those patient
17:11 (12)	Man prays for evil, as he prays for good
17:35 (37)	weigh with the straight balance; that is better and fairer in the issue
18:36 (34)	if I am indeed returned to my Lord, I shall surely find a better resort
18:40 (38)	it may be that my Lord will give me better than thy garden
18:44 (42)	He is best rewarding (best) in the issue
18:44 (42)	He is (best) rewarding best in the issue
18:46 (44)	the deeds of righteousness, are better with God in reward
18:46 (44)	(better) with God in reward and better in hope
18:81 (80)	in exchange one better than he in purity, and nearer in tenderness
18:95 (94)	that wherein my Lord has established me is better
19:73 (74)	which of the two parties is better in station
19:76 (79)	the deeds of righteousness, are better with thy Lord in reward
19:76 (79)	(better) with thy Lord in reward and better in return
20:73 (75)	God is better, and more abiding

20:131 (131)	thy Lord's provision is better, and more enduring
21:35 (36)	We try you with evil and good for a testing
21:89 (89)	leave me not solitary; though Thou art the best of inheritors
22:11 (11)	if good befalls him he is at rest in it
22:30 (31)	it shall be better for him with his Lord
22:36 (37)	We have appointed them for you as among God's waymarks; therein is good for you
22:58 (57)	surely God is the best of providers
22:77 (76)	serve your Lord, and do good
23:29 (30)	Thou art the best of harbourers
23:72 (74)	the tribute of thy Lord is better
23:72 (74)	and He is the best of providers
23:109 (111)	have mercy on us, for Thou art the best of the merciful
23:118 (118)	have mercy, for Thou art the best of the merciful
24:11 (11)	do not reckon it evil for you; rather it is good for you
24:12 (12)	did the believing men and women not of their own account think good thoughts
24:27 (27)	ask leave and salute the people thereof; that is better for you
24:33 (33)	contract with them accordingly, if you know some good in them
24:60 (59)	but to abstain is better for them
25:10 (11)	blessed be He who, if He will, shall assign to thee better than that
25:15 (16)	is that better, or the Garden of Eternity
25:24 (26)	better shall be their lodging, fairer their resting-place
27:36 (36)	what God gave me is better than what He has given you
27:59 (60)	what, is God better, or that they associate?
27:89 (91)	whosoever comes with a good deed, he shall have better than it
28:24 (24)	I have need of whatever good Thou shalt have sent down upon me
28:26 (26)	surely the best man thou canst hire is the one strong and trusty
28:60 (60)	what is with God is better and more enduring
28:80 (80)	the reward of God is better for him who believes
28:84 (84)	whoso brings a good deed shall have better than it
29:16 (15)	serve God, and fear Him; that is better for you
30:38 (37)	that is better for those who desire God's Face
33:19 (19)	they flay you with sharp tongues, being niggardly to possess the good things
33:25 (25)	God sent back those that were unbelievers in their rage, and they attained no good
34:39 (38)	He is the best of providers
37:62 (60)	is that better as a hospitality, or the Tree of Ez-Zakkoum?
38:32 (31)	I have loved the love of good things better than the remembrance of my Lord
38:47 (47)	in Our sight they are of the chosen, the excellent
38:48 (48)	Our servants Ishmael, Elisha, and Dhul Kifl; each is among the excellent
38:76 (77)	said he, 'I am better than he'
41:40 (40)	is he who shall be cast into the Fire better
41:49 (49)	Man wearies not of praying for good
42:36 (34)	what is with God is better and more enduring for those who believe
43:32 (31)	the mercy of thy Lord is better than that they amass
43:52 (51)	am I better than this man, who is contemptible
43:58 (58)	what, are our gods better, or he?
44:37 (36)	are they better, or the people of Tubba
46:11 (10)	if it had been aught good, they had not outstripped us to it
47:21 (23)	if they were true to God, it would be better for them
49:5 (5)	if they had patience, until thou comest out to them, that would be better for them
49:11 (11)	let not any people scoff at another people who may be better
49:11 (11)	neither let women scoff at women who may be better
50:25 (24)	every hinderer of the good, transgressor, disquieter
54:43 (43)	what, are your unbelievers better than those?

58:12 (13)	advance a freewill offering; that is better for you and purer
61:11 (11)	that is better for you, did you but know
62:9 (9)	leave trafficking aside; that is better for you
62:11 (11)	what is with God is better than diversion and merchandise
62:11 (11)	God is the best of providers
64:16 (16)	give ear, and obey, and expend well for yourselves
66:5 (5)	his Lord will give him in exchange wives better than you
68:12 (12)	hinderer of good, guilty aggressor
68:32 (32)	it may be that our Lord will give us in exchange a better than it
70:21 (21)	when good visits him, grudging
70:41 (41)	to substitute a better than they; We shall not be outstripped
73:20 (20)	whatever good you shall forward to your souls' account
73:20 (20)	you shall find it with God as better, and mightier a wage
87:17 (17)	the world to come is better, and more enduring
93:4 (4)	the Last shall be better for thee than the First
97:3 (3)	the Night of Power is better than a thousand months
98:7 (6)	those who believe, and do righteous deeds, those are the best of creatures
99:7 (7)	whoso has done an atom's weight of good shall see it
100:8 (8)	surely he is passionate in his love for good things

KHAYRĀT n.f. (pl)~good works, good deeds

2:148 (143)	so be you forward in good works
3:114 (110)	vying one with the other in good works
5:48 (53)	so be you forward in good works
9:88 (89)	those — for them await the good things
21:73 (73)	We revealed to them the doing of good deeds
21:90 (90)	truly they vied with one another, hastening to good works
23:56 (58)	We vie in good works for them
23:61 (63)	those vie in good works, outracing to them
35:32 (29)	some are outstrippers in good works
55:70 (70)	therein maidens good and comely

KHĪRAH n.f.~a choice

28:68 (68)	He chooses; they have not the choice
33:36 (36)	when God and His Messenger have decreed a matter, to have the choice

TAKHAYYARA vb. (V)~to choose

b) impf. act. (*yatakhayyaru*)

56:20 (20)	and such fruits as they shall choose
68:38 (38)	therein you shall have whatever you choose

IKHTĀRA vb. (VIII)~to choose

a) perf. act.

7:155 (154)	and Moses chose of his people seventy men
20:13 (13)	I Myself have chosen thee
44:32 (31)	We chose them, out of a knowledge

b) impf. act. (*yakhtāru*)

28:68 (68)	thy Lord creates whatsoever He will and He chooses

*KH Y Ṭ

KHAYṬ n.m.~a thread

2:187 (183)	eat and drink, until the white thread
2:187 (183)	shows clearly to you from the black thread

KHIYĀṬ n.m.~a needle

7:40 (38)	until the camel passes through the eye of the needle

*KH Z N

KHAZANA vb. (I)~(pcple. act.) treasurer; (pl. *khazanah*) keeper, warder

g) pcple. act. (*khāzin*)

15:22 (22)	We give it to you to drink, and you are not its treasurers
39:71 (71)	then its gates will be opened and its keepers will say to them
39:73 (73)	its keepers will say to them, 'Peace be upon you'
40:49 (52)	those who are in the Fire will say to the keepers of Gehenna
67:8 (8)	as often as a troop is cast into it, its keepers ask them

KHAZĀ'IN n.f. (pl. of *khazānah*)~treasures, treasuries

6:50 (50)	I possess the treasuries of God
11:31 (33)	I do not say to you, 'I possess the treasuries of God'
12:55 (55)	he said, 'Set me over the land's storehouses'
15:21 (21)	naught is there, but its treasuries are with Us
17:100 (102)	if you possessed the treasuries of my Lord's mercy
38:9 (8)	have they the treasuries of thy Lord's mercy
52:37 (37)	are thy Lord's treasuries in their keeping?
63:7 (7)	unto God belong the treasuries of the heavens

*KH Z Y

KHAZIYA vb. (I)~to be degraded, to be disgraced. (n.vb.) shame, degradation, abasement, disgrace

b) impf. act. (*yakhzá*)

20:134 (134)	we might have followed Thy signs before that we were humiliated and degraded

f) n.vb. (*khizy*)

2:85 (79)	what shall be the recompense of those of you who do that, but degradation
2:114 (108)	for them is degradation in the present world
5:33 (37)	that is a degradation for them in this world
5:41 (45)	for them is degradation in this world
9:63 (64)	that is the mighty degradation
10:98 (98)	We removed from them the chastisement of degradation
11:66 (69)	by a mercy from Us, and from the degradation of that day

16:27 (29)	degradation today and evil are on the unbelievers
22:9 (9)	for him is degradation in this world, and on the Resurrection Day
39:26 (27)	God let them taste degradation in this present life
41:16 (15)	We might let them taste the chastisement of degradation

AKHZÁ n.m. (comp. adj.)~more degrading, more disgraceful

41:16 (15)	the chastisement of the world to come is even more degrading

AKHZÁ vb. (IV)~to abase [Ar, Bl]; to confound [Pk]; to put to shame or to cover with shame [Ali]. (pcple. act.) one who degrades or abases, one who puts to shame

a) perf. act.

3:192 (189)	whomsoever Thou admittest into the Fire, Thou wilt have abased

b) impf. act. (*yukhzī*)

3:194 (192)	abase us not on the Day of Resurrection
9:14 (14)	God will chastise them at your hands and degrade them
11:39 (41)	to whom will come a chastisement degrading him
11:78 (80)	fear God, and do not degrade me in my guests
11:93 (96)	to whom will come the chastisement degrading him
15:69 (69)	fear God, and do not degrade me
16:27 (29)	on the Day of Resurrection He will degrade them
26:87 (87)	degrade me not upon the day when they are raised up
39:40 (41)	to whom will come a chastisement degrading him
59:5 (5)	that was by God's leave, and that He might degrade the ungodly
66:8 (8)	upon the day when God will not degrade the Prophet

g) pcple. act. (*mukhzī*)

9:2 (2)	God degrades the unbelievers

LĀM

*L ʾ K

MALĀK n.m. (pl. *malāʾikah*), see also *malak* (*m l k)~an angel

2:30 (28)	when thy Lord said to the angels, 'I am setting in the earth'
2:31 (29)	then He presented them unto the angels
2:34 (32)	when We said to the angels, 'Bow yourselves to Adam'
2:98 (92)	whosoever is an enemy to God and His angels and His Messengers
2:161 (156)	upon them shall rest the curse of God and the angels
2:177 (172)	to believe in God, and the Last Day, the angels
2:210 (206)	but that God shall come to them in the cloud-shadows, and the angels
2:248 (249)	a remnant of what the folk of Moses and Aaron's folk left behind, the angels bearing it
2:285 (285)	each one believes in God and His angels
3:18 (16)	God bears witness that there is no god but He — and the angels
3:39 (33)	the angels called to him, standing in the Sanctuary
3:42 (37)	and when the angels said, 'Mary, God has chosen thee'
3:45 (40)	when the angels said, 'Mary, God gives thee good tidings'
3:80 (74)	He would never order you to take the angels and the Prophets as Lords
3:87 (81)	there shall rest on them the curse of God and of the angels
3:124 (120)	your Lord should reinforce you with three thousand angels sent down upon you
3:125 (121)	your Lord will reinforce you with five thousand swooping angels
4:97 (99)	those the angels take, while still they are wronging themselves
4:136 (135)	whoso disbelieves in God and His angels and His Books
4:166 (164)	the angels also bear witness
4:172 (170)	neither the angels who are near stationed to Him
6:93 (93)	and the angels are stretching out their hands
6:111 (111)	though We had sent down the angels to them
6:158 (159)	do they look for the angels to come to them
7:11 (10)	then We said to the angels: 'Bow yourselves to Adam'
8:9 (9)	I shall reinforce you with a thousand angels riding behind you
8:12 (12)	when thy Lord was revealing to the angels, 'I am with you'
8:50 (52)	if thou couldst only see when the angels take the unbelievers
13:13 (14)	the thunder proclaims His praise, and the angels
13:23 (23)	the angels shall enter unto them from every gate
15:7 (7)	why dost thou not bring the angels unto us, if thou speakest truly?
15:8 (8)	We send not down the angels, save with truth
15:28 (28)	when thy Lord said to the angels, 'See, I am creating a mortal'
15:30 (30)	then the angels bowed themselves all together
16:2 (2)	He sends down the angels with the Spirit of His command
16:28 (30)	whom the angels take while still they are wronging themselves
16:32 (34)	whom the angels take while they are goodly
16:33 (35)	do they look for aught but that the angels shall come to them
16:49 (51)	and every creature crawling on the earth, and the angels
17:40 (42)	has your Lord favoured you with sons and taken to Himself from the angels females?
17:61 (63)	when We said to the angels, 'Bow yourselves to Adam'
17:92 (94)	or thou bringest God and the angels as a surety
17:95 (97)	had there been in the earth angels walking at peace
18:50 (48)	when We said to the angels, 'Bow yourselves to Adam'
20:116 (115)	when We said to the angels, 'Bow yourselves to Adam'

21:103 (103)	the greatest terror shall not grieve them, and the angels shall receive them
22:75 (74)	God chooses of the angels Messengers and of mankind
23:24 (24)	if God willed, He would have sent down angels
25:21 (23)	why have the angels not been sent down on us
25:22 (24)	upon the day that they see the angels
25:25 (27)	the day that heaven is split asunder with the clouds and the angels are sent down
33:43 (42)	it is He who blesses you, and His angels
33:56 (56)	God and His angels bless the Prophet
34:40 (39)	He shall say to the angels, 'Was it you these were serving?'
35.1 (1)	who appointed the angels to be messengers having wings
37:150 (150)	did We create the angels females, while they were witnesses?
38:71 (71)	when thy Lord said to the angels, See, I am creating a mortal
38:73 (73)	then the angels bowed themselves all together
39:75 (75)	thou shalt see the angels encircling about the Throne
41:14 (13)	surely He would have sent down angels
41:30 (30)	upon them the angels descend, saying, 'Fear not'
42:5 (3)	when the angels proclaim the praise of their Lord, and ask forgiveness
43:19 (18)	they have made the angels, who are themselves servants of the All-merciful, females
43:53 (53)	why then have bracelets of gold not been cast on him, or angels not come with him conjoined?
43:60 (60)	We would have appointed angels among you to be successors in the earth
47:27 (29)	when the angels take them, beating their faces and their backs
53:27 (28)	those who do not believe in the world to come name the angels
66:4 (4)	and, after that, the angels are his supporters
66:6 (6)	over which are harsh, terrible angels who disobey not God
70:4 (4)	to Him the angels and the Spirit mount up in a day
74:31 (31)	We have appointed only angels to be masters of the Fire
78:38 (38)	upon the day when the Spirit and the angels stand in ranks
97:4 (4)	in it the angels and the Spirit descend

*L ʾ L ʾ

LUʾLUʾ n.m. (coll)~pearls

22:23 (23)	they shall be adorned with bracelets of gold and with pearls
35:33 (30)	they shall be adorned with bracelets of gold and with pearls
52:24 (24)	there go round them youths, their own, as if they were hidden pearls
55:22 (22)	from them come forth the pearl and the coral
56:23 (22)	as the likeness of hidden pearls
76:19 (19)	when thou seest them, thou supposest them scattered pearls

*L ʿ B

LAʿIBA vb. (I)~to play. (n.vb.) playing, a sport, a passtime. (pcple. act.) one who plays; playing

b) impf. act. (*yalʿabu*)

6:91 (91)	then leave them alone, playing their game of plunging
7:98 (96)	Our might shall not come upon them in daylight while they are playing

9:65 (66)	they will say, 'We were only plunging and playing'
12:12 (12)	send him forth with us tomorrow, to frolic and play
21:2 (2)	but they listen to it yet playing
43:83 (83)	then leave them alone to plunge and play
44:9 (8)	nay, but they are in doubt, playing
52:12 (12)	such as play at plunging
70:42 (42)	then leave them alone to plunge and play

f) n.vb. (*laᶜib*)

5:57 (62)	the unbelievers, who take your religion in mockery and as a sport
5:58 (63)	and when you call to prayer, take it in mockery and as a sport
6:32 (32)	the present life is naught but a sport and a diversion
6:70 (69)	leave alone those who take their religion for a sport
7:51 (49)	who have taken their religion as a diversion and a sport
29:64 (64)	this present life is naught but a diversion and a sport
47:36 (38)	the present life is naught but a sport
57:20 (19)	know that the present life is but a sport and a diversion

g) pcple. act. (*lāᶜib*)

21:16 (16)	We created not the heaven and the earth, and whatsoever between them is, as playing
21:55 (56)	hast thou come to us with the truth, or art thou one of those that play?
44:38 (38)	We created not the heavens and earth, and all that between them is, in play

*L ᶜ N

LAᶜANA vb. (I)~to curse. (n.vb.) the act of cursing; a curse. (pcple. act.) one who curses, a curser. (pcple. pass.) one who is cursed

a) perf. act.

2:88 (82)	God has cursed them for their unbelief
4:46 (49)	God has cursed them for their unbelief
4:47 (50)	curse them as We cursed the Sabbath-men
4:52 (55)	those are they whom God has cursed
4:93 (95)	God will be wroth with him and will curse him
4:118 (118)	accursed by God. He said, 'Assuredly I will take unto myselfa portion'
5:13 (16)	for their breaking their compact We cursed them
5:60 (65)	whomsoever God has cursed, and with whom He is wroth
7:38 (36)	whenever any nation enters, it curses its sister-nation
9:68 (69)	God has cursed them; and there awaits them a lasting chastisement
33:57 (57)	them God has cursed in the present world
33:64 (64)	God has cursed the unbelievers, and prepared for them a Blaze
47:23 (25)	those are they whom God has cursed, and so made them deaf
48:6 (6)	God is wroth with them, and has cursed them

b) impf. act. (*yalᶜanu*)

2:159 (154)	they shall be cursed by God
2:159 (154)	and [they shall be cursed by] the cursers
4:47 (50)	as We cursed the Sabbath-men
4:52 (55)	he whom God has cursed, thou wilt not find for him
29:25 (24)	and you will curse one another

c) impv. (*il^can*)

33:68 (68) give them chastisement twofold, and curse them with a mighty curse

d) perf. pass. (*luʿina*)

5:64 (69) fettered are their hands, and they are cursed for what they have said
5:78 (82) cursed were the unbelievers of the Children of Israel
24:23 (23) that are heedless but believing shall be accursed in the present world

f) n.vb. (*laʿn*)

33:68 (68) give them chastisement twofold, and curse them with a mighty curse

g) pcple. act. (*lāʿin*)

2:159 (154) they shall be cursed by God and the cursers

h) pcple. pass. (*malʿūn*)

17:60 (62) the vision that We showed thee and the tree cursed in the Koran
33:61 (61) cursed they shall be

LAʿNAH n.f.~a curse

2:89 (83) and the curse of God is on the unbelievers
2:161 (156) upon them shall rest the curse of God
3:61 (54) so lay God's curse upon the ones who lie
3:87 (81) their recompense is that there shall rest on them the curse of God
7:44 (42) God's curse is on the evildoers
11:18 (21) the curse of God shall rest upon the evildoers
11:60 (63) there was sent following after them in this world a curse
11:99 (101) there was sent following after them in this world a curse
13:25 (25) who work corruption in the earth — theirs shall be the curse
15:35 (35) upon thee shall rest the curse, till the Day of Doom
24:7 (7) and a fifth time, that the curse of God shall be upon him
28:42 (42) We pursued them in this world with a curse
38:78 (79) upon thee shall rest My curse, till the Day of Doom
40:52 (55) theirs shall be the curse, and theirs the evil abode

*L B B

ALBĀB n.m. (pl. of *lubb*)~mind, heart, understanding, intellect, insight (*ulū al- albāb*) men possessed of minds [Ar]; men of understanding [Pk, Ali]; those that are wise [Ali]; men of insight [Bl]

2:179 (175) in retaliation there is life for you, men possessed of minds
2:197 (193) so fear you Me, men possessed of minds
2:269 (272) yet none remembers but men possessed of minds
3:7 (5) yet none remembers, but men possessed of minds
3:190 (187) in the alternation of night and day there are signs for men possessed of minds
5:100 (100) so fear God, O men possessed of minds
12:111 (111) in their stories is surely a lesson to men possessed of minds
13:19 (19) only men possessed of minds remember
14:52 (52) and that all possessed of minds may remember
38:29 (28) that men possessed of minds may ponder its signs
38:43 (42) and a reminder unto men possessed of minds
39:9 (12) only men possessed of minds remember

39:18 (19) those — they are men possessed of minds
39:21 (22) in that is a reminder for men possessed of minds
40:54 (56) for a guidance and for a reminder to men possessed of minds
65:10 (10) so fear God, O men possessed of minds

*L B D

LIBAD n.f. (pl. of *libdah*)~(that which is packed densely; a mane); swarms, a stifling crowd

72:19 (19) they were wellnigh upon him in swarms

LUBAD n.m. (adj)~abundant, much

90:6 (6) I have consumed wealth abundant

*L B N

LABAN n.m.~milk

16:66 (68) between filth and blood, pure milk, sweet to drinkers
47:15 (16) rivers of water unstaling, rivers of milk unchanging in flavour

*L B S

LABASA vb. (I)~to confuse, to confound. (n.vb.) confusion, uncertainty

a) perf. act.

6:9 (9) We would have made him a man, and confused for them

b) impf. act. (*yalbisu*)

2:42 (39) do not confound the truth with vanity
3:71 (64) why do you confound the truth with vanity
6:9 (9) the thing which they themselves are confusing
6:65 (65) or to confuse you in sects and to make you taste the violence
6:82 (82) those who believe, and have not confounded their belief with evildoing
6:137 (138) to destroy them, and to confuse their religion

f) n.vb. (*labs*)

50:15 (14) they are in uncertainty as to the new creation

LABISA vb. (I)~to wear, to be robed

b) impf. act. (*yalbasu*)

16:14 (14) and bring forth out of it ornaments for you to wear
18:31 (30) they shall be robed in green garments of silk and brocade
35:12 (13) and bring forth out of it ornaments for you to wear
44:53 (53) robed in silk and brocade, set face to face

LABŪS n.m.~a garment (of mail)

21:80 (80)	We taught him the fashioning of garments for you, to fortify you

LIBĀS n.m.~vestment, garment, apparel, clothing

2:187 (183)	they are a vestment for you
2:187 (183)	and you are a vestment for them
7:26 (25)	We have sent down on you a garment to cover your shameful parts
7:26 (25)	the garment of godfearing — that is better
7:27 (26)	stripping them of their garments to show them their shameful parts
16:112 (113)	so God let it taste the garment of hunger
22:23 (23)	and their apparel there shall be of silk
25:47 (49)	it is He who appointed the night for you to be garment and sleep for a rest
35:33 (30)	and their apparel there shall be of silk
78:10 (10)	and We appointed night for a garment

*L B TH

LABITHA vb. (I)~to tarry, to abide, to continue (to abide); (*mā labitha an*) presently. (pcple. act.) one who tarries; tarrying

a) perf. act.

2:259 (261)	how long hast thou tarried?
2:259 (261)	I have tarried a day, or part of a day
2:259 (261)	nay; thou hast tarried a hundred years
10:16 (17)	I abode among you a lifetime before it
11:69 (72)	and presently he brought a roasted calf
12:42 (42)	so that he continued in the prison for certain years
17:52 (54)	you will think you have but tarried a little
18:12 (11)	which of the two parties would better calculate the while they had tarried
18:19 (18)	how long have you tarried?
18:19 (18)	we have tarried a day, or part of a day
18:19 (18)	your Lord knows very well how long you have tarried
18:25 (24)	they tarried in the Cave three hundred years
18:26 (25)	God knows very well how long they tarried
20:40 (42)	many years among the people of Midian thou didst sojourn
20:103 (103)	you have tarried only ten nights
20:104 (104)	you have tarried only a day
23:112 (114)	how long have you tarried in the earth, by number of years?
23:113 (115)	we have tarried a day, or part of a day
23:114 (116)	you have tarried but a little, did you know
26:18 (17)	didst thou not tarry among us years of thy life?
29:14 (13)	We sent Noah to his people, and he tarried among them a thousand years
30:55 (55)	they have not tarried above an hour
30:56 (56)	you have tarried in God's Book till the Day of the Upraising
34:14 (13)	they would not have continued in the humbling chastisement
37:144 (144)	he would have tarried in its belly until the day they shall be raised

b) impf. act. (*yalbathu*)

10:45 (46)	He shall muster them, as if they had not tarried but an hour of the day
17:76 (78)	then they would have tarried after thee only a little
46:35 (35)	they had not tarried but for an hour of a single day
79:46 (46)	they have but tarried for an evening, or its forenoon

g) pcple. act. (*lābith*)

78:23 (23)	therein to tarry for ages

TALABBATHA vb. (V)~to remain, to tarry

a) perf. act.

33:14 (14)	they would have done so, and but tarried about it briefly

*L D D

ALADD n.m. (comp. adj; pl. *ludd*)~most stubborn [Ar]; most rigid,froward [Pk]; most contentious, given to contention [Ali]; most persistent [Bl]

2:204 (200)	yet he is most stubborn in altercation
19:97 (97)	that thou mayest bear good tidings thereby to the godfearing, and warn a people stubborn

*L D N

LADUN n.m.~(with prep. *min*) that which proceeds from the presence of, on one's part, from before (often translated as "from")

3:8 (6)	after that Thou hast guided us; and give us mercy from Thee
3:38 (33)	Lord, give me of Thy goodness a goodly offspring
4:40 (44)	He will double it, and give from Himself a mighty wage
4:67 (70)	We surely would have given them from Us a mighty wage
4:75 (77)	and appoint to us a protector from Thee
4:75 (77)	and appoint to us from Thee a helper
11:1 (1)	Alif Lam Ra a Book whose verses are set clear, and then distinguished
17:80 (82)	grant me authority from Thee, to help me
18:2 (2)	to warn of great violence from Him
18:10 (9)	our Lord, give us mercy from Thee
18:65 (64)	and We had taught him knowledge proceeding from Us
18:76 (75)	thou hast already experienced excuse sufficient on my part
19:5 (5)	so give me, from Thee, a kinsman
19:13 (14)	and a tenderness from Us
20:99 (99)	and We have given thee a remembrance from Us
21:17 (17)	We would have taken it to Us from Ourselves
27:6 (6)	thou receivest the Koran from One All-wise
28:57 (57)	to which are collected the fruits of everything, as a provision from Us

*L DH DH

LADHDHA vb. (I)~to delight in, to take pleasure in

b) impf. act. (*yaladhdhu*)

43:71 (71)	whatever the souls desire, and the eyes delight in

LADHDHAH n.f.~delight, pleasure

37:46 (45)	a delight to the drinkers
47:15 (16)	and rivers of wine — a delight to the drinkers

*L F F

ALFĀF n.m. (pl. of *liff*)~luxuriant (growth); thick foliage

78:16 (16)	and gardens luxuriant
17:104 (106)	We shall bring you a rabble

ILTAFFA vb. (VIII)~to be intertwined

a) perf. act.

75:29 (29)	and leg is intertwined with leg

*L F Ḥ

LAFAḤA vb. (I)~to burn, to scorch; to smite

b) impf. act. (*yalfaḥu*)

23:104 (106)	the Fire smiting their faces

*L F T

LAFATA vb. (I)~to turn someone from

b) impf. act. (*yalfitu*)

10:78 (79)	art thou come to us to turn us from that we found our fathers practising

ILTAFATA vb. (VIII)~to turn round, to look back

b) impf. act. (*yaltafitu*)

11:81 (83)	let not any one of you turn round, excepting thy wife
15:65 (65)	let not any one of you turn round

*L F W

ALFÁ vb. (IV)~to find, to encounter

a) perf. act.

2:170 (165)	we will follow such things as we found our fathers doing
12:25 (25)	they encountered her master by the door
37:69 (67)	they found their fathers erring

*L F Ẓ

LAFAẒA vb. (I)~to utter

b) impf. act. (*yalfiẓu*)

50:18 (17)	not a word he utters, but by him is an observer ready

*L GH B

LAGHABA vb. (I)~(n.vb.) weariness, fatigue

f) n.vb. (*lughūb*)

35:35 (32)	wherein no weariness assails us neither fatigue
50:38 (37)	and no weariness touched Us

*L GH Y

LAGHIYA vb. (I)~to talk idly. (n.vb.) idle talk, a slip (in talk), unintentional (talk)

c) impv. (*ulghu*)

41:26 (25)	do not give ear to this Koran, and talk idly about it

f) n.vb. (*laghw*)

2:225 (225)	God will not take you to task for a slip in your oaths
5:89 (91)	God will not take you to task for a slip in your oaths
19:62 (63)	there they shall hear no idle talk
23:3 (3)	and from idle talk turn away
25:72 (72)	when they pass by idle talk, pass by with dignity
28:55 (55)	when they hear idle talk, they turn away
52:23 (23)	a cup one to another wherein is no idle talk
56:25 (24)	therein they shall hear no idle talk, no cause of sin
78:35 (35)	therein they shall hear no idle talk, no cry of lies

LĀGHIYAH n.f.~vain talk, babble

88:11 (11)	hearing there no babble

*L H B

ABŪ LAHAB n.prop.~Abu Lahab (uncle of the Prophet)

111:1 (1)	perish the hands of Abu Lahab, and perish he

LAHAB n.m.~a flame; (adj) flaming

77:31 (31)	unshading against the blazing flame
111:3 (3)	he shall roast at a flaming fire

*L H M

ALHAMA vb. (IV)~to inspire with

a) perf. act.

91:8 (8)	and inspired it to lewdness and godfearing

*L H TH

LAHATHA vb. (I)~to loll or pant its (a dog's) tongue

b) impf. act. (*yalhathu*)

7:176 (175)	if thou attackest it it lolls its tongue out
7:176 (175)	or if thou leavest it it lolls its tongue out

*L H W

LAHĀ vb. (I)~(n.vb.) a diversion, a sport. (pcple. act.) one who is diverted

f) n.vb. (*lahw*)

6:32 (32)	the present life is naught but a sport and a diversion
6:70 (69)	leave alone those who take their religion for a sport and a diversion
7:51 (49)	who have taken their religion as a diversion and a sport
21:17 (17)	had We desired to take to Us a diversion
29:64 (64)	this present life is naught but a diversion and a sport
31:6 (5)	some men there are who buy diverting talk
47:36 (38)	the present life is naught but a sport and a diversion
57:20 (19)	know that the present life is but a sport and a diversion
62:11 (11)	when they see merchandise or diversion they scatter off to it
62:11 (11)	what is with God is better than diversion and merchandise

g) pcple. act. (*lāhī*)

21:3 (3)	diverted their hearts

ALHÁ vb. (IV)~to divert, to beguile, to bemuse

a) perf. act.

102:1 (1) gross rivalry diverts you

b) impf. act. (*yulhī*)

15:3 (3) and to take their joy, and to be bemused by hope
24:37 (37) men whom neither commerce nor trafficking diverts from the remembrance of God
63:9 (9) let not your possessions neither your children divert you from God's remembrance

TALAHHÁ vb. (V)~(with prep. *ʿan*) to pay no heed to

b) impf. act. (*yatalahhá*)

80:10 (10) to him thou payest no heed

*L Ḥ D

ALḤADA vb. (IV)~(with prep. *fī*) to blaspheme [Ar, Pk]; to make covert hints, to decry [Bl]; to use profanity, to pervert [Ali]; to distort [Pk]; (with prep. *ilá*) to hint at, to point to. (n.vb.) the act of violating [Ar]; partiality [Pk]; profanity [Ali]

b) impf. act. (*yulḥidu*)

7:180 (179) and leave those who blaspheme His Names
16:103 (105) the speech of him at whom they hint is barbarous
41:40 (40) those who blaspheme Our signs are not hidden from Us

f) n.vb. (*ilḥād*)

22:25 (26) whosoever purposes to violate it wrongfully

ILTAḤADA vb. (VIII)~(pcple. pass.) (used as a noun) a refuge

h) pcple. pass. (*multaḥad*)

18:27 (26) apart from Him, thou wilt find no refuge
72:22 (23) I shall find, apart from Him, no refuge

*L Ḥ F

ALḤAFA vb. (IV)~(n.vb.) importunity; (adv) importunately

f) n.vb. (*ilḥāf*)

2:273 (274) they do not beg of men importunately

*L Ḥ M

LAḤM n.m. (pl. *luḥūm*)~flesh

2:173 (168)	carrion, blood, the flesh of swine
2:259 (261)	look at the bones, how We shall set them up, and then clothe them with flesh
5:3 (4)	carrion, blood, the flesh of swine
6:145 (146)	except it be carrion, or blood outpoured, or the flesh of swine
16:14 (14)	it is He who subjected to you the sea, that you may eat of it fresh flesh
16:115 (116)	carrion, blood, the flesh of swine
22:37 (38)	the flesh of them shall not reach God
23:14 (14)	then We garmented the bones in flesh
35:12 (13)	yet of both you eat fresh flesh
49:12 (12)	would any of you like to eat the flesh of his brother dead?
52:22 (22)	We shall succour them with fruits and flesh
56:21 (21)	and such flesh of fowl as they desire

*L Ḥ N

LAḤANA vb. (I)~(n.vb.) twisting (of speech) [Ar]; burden (of talk) [Pk]; tone (of speech) [Ali]; evasive (speech) [Bl]

f) n.vb. (*laḥn*)

47:30 (32)	thou shalt certainly know them in the twisting of their speech

*L Ḥ Q

LAḤIQA vb. (I)~to join

b) impf. act. (*yalḥaqu*)

3:170 (164)	and joyful in those who remain behind and have not joined them
62:3 (3)	and others of them who have not yet joined them

ALḤAQA vb. (IV)~to cause to join

a) perf. act.

34:27 (26)	show me those you have joined to Him as associates
52:21 (21)	in belief, We shall join their seed with them

c) impv. (*alḥiq*)

12:101 (102)	receive me to Thee in true submission, and join me with the righteous
26:83 (83)	give me Judgment, and join me with the righteous

*L Ḥ Y

LIḤYAH n.f.~a beard

20:94 (95)	take me not by the beard, or the head

*L J ʾ

MALJAʾ n.m.~a shelter

9:57 (57)	if they could find a shelter, or some caverns
9:118 (119)	they thought that there was no shelter from God except in Him
42:47 (46)	upon that day you shall have no shelter, no denial

*L J J

LAJJA vb. (I)~to persist

a) perf. act.

23:75 (77)	they would persist in their insolence wandering blindly
67:21 (21)	they persist in disdain and aversion

LUJJAH n.f.~a spreading water, a pool

27:44 (44)	when she saw it, she supposed it was a spreading water

LUJJĪ n.m. (adj)~obscure [Ar]; vast and abysmal [Pk, Ali]; roaring [Bl]

24:40 (40)	or they are as shadows upon a sea obscure

*L M Ḥ

LAMAḤA vb. (I)~(n.vb.) twinkling (of an eye)

f) n.vb. (*lamḥ*)

16:77 (79)	the matter of the Hour is as a twinkling of the eye, or nearer
54:50 (50)	Our commandment is but one word, as the twinkling of an eye

*L M M

LAMAM n.m.~lesser offences [Ar]; unwilled offences [Pk]; small faults [Ali]; inadvertent sins [Bl]

53:32 (33)	those who avoid the heinous sins and indecencies, save lesser offences

LAMM n.m. (adv)~greedily

89:19 (20)	and you devour the inheritance greedily

*L M S

LAMASA vb. (I)~to stretch towards, to touch [Ar]; to seek, to feel [Pk]; to pry into, to touch [Ali]; to reach up [Bl]

a) perf. act.

6:7 (7) a Book on parchment and so they touched it with their hands
72:8 (8) we stretched towards heaven, but we found it filled with terrible guards

LĀMASA vb. (III)~to touch

a) perf. act.

4:43 (46) or you have touched women, and you can find no water
5:6 (9) or you have touched women, and you can find no water

ILTAMASA vb. (VIII)~to seek, to look for

c) impv. (*iltamis*)

57:13 (13) return you back behind, and seek for a light

*L M Z

LAMAZA vb. (I)~to find fault

b) impf. act. (*yalmizu*)

9:58 (58) some of them find fault with thee touching the freewill offerings
9:79 (80) those who find fault with the believers who volunteer their freewill offerings
49:11 (11) find not fault with one another

LUMAZAH n.com.~a slanderer

104:1 (1) woe unto every backbiter, slanderer

*L Q B

ALQĀB n.m. (pl. of *laqab*)~nicknames

49:11 (11) neither revile one another by nicknames

*L Q F

LAQIFA vb. (I)~to swallow

b) impf. act. (*yalqafu*)

7:117 (114) and lo, it forthwith swallowed up their lying invention
20:69 (72) cast down what is in thy right hand, and it shall swallow what they have fashioned
26:45 (44) and lo, it forthwith swallowed up their lying invention

*L Q Ḥ

LAQAḤA vb. (I)~(pcple. act.) that which fertilizes; fertilising

g) pcple. act. (*lawāqiḥ*, pl. of *lāqiḥ*)

15:22 (22) and We loose the winds fertilising

*L Q M

LUQMĀN n.prop.~Lokman

31:12 (11) indeed, We gave Lokman wisdom
31:13 (12) and when Lokman said to his son, admonishing him

ILTAQAMA vb. (VIII)~to swallow

a) perf. act.

37:142 (142) then the whale swallowed him down, and he blameworthy

*L Q Ṭ

ILTAQAṬA vb. (VIII)~to pick out, to take up

a) perf. act.

28:8 (7) then the folk of Pharaoh picked him out to be an enemy

b) impf. act. (*yaltaqiṭu*)

12:10 (10) and some traveller will pick him out, if you do aught

*L Q Y

LAQIYA vb. (I)~to meet, to encounter, to find; to fall in with [Pk]; to suffer from [Ali]. (n.vb.) an encounter, meeting. (pcple. act.) one who receives [Ar], who finds [Pk], who reaches (a fulfilment) [Ali]; one who meets [Bl]

a) perf. act.

2:14 (13) when they meet those who believe, they say
2:76 (71) when they meet those who believe, they say
3:119 (115) and when they meet you they say
8:15 (15) O believers, when you encounter the unbelievers marching to battle
8:45 (47) O believers, whensoever you encounter a host, then stand firm
18:62 (61) indeed, we have encountered weariness from this our journey
18:74 (73) so they departed; until, when they met a lad, he slew him
47:4 (4) when you meet the unbelievers, smite their necks

b) impf. act. (*yalqá*)

3:143 (137) you were longing for death before you met it
9:77 (78) He put hypocrisy into their hearts, until the day they meet Him

17:13 (14)	on the Day of Resurrection, a book he shall find
19:59 (60)	they shall encounter error
25:68 (68)	for whosoever does that shall meet the price of sin
33:44 (43)	their greeting, on the day when they shall meet Him, will be Peace

f) n.vb. (*liqā'*)

6:31 (31)	lost indeed are they that cried lies to the encounter with God
6:130 (130)	and warning you of the encounter of this your day
6:154 (155)	haply they would believe in the encounter with their Lord
7:51 (49)	today We forget them as they forgot the encounter of this their day
7:147 (145)	those who cry lies to Our signs, and the encounter in the world to come
10:7 (7)	those who look not to encounter Us and are well-pleased with the present life
10:11 (12)	We leave those, who look not to encounter Us, in their insolence
10:15 (16)	those who look not to encounter Us say
10:45 (46)	lost will be those who cried lies to the encounter with God
13:2 (2)	haply you will have faith in the encounter with your Lord
18:105 (105)	those are they that disbelieve in the signs of their Lord and the encounter with Him
18:110 (110)	him, who hopes for the encounter with his Lord
23:33 (34)	who cried lies to the encounter of the world to come
25:21 (23)	say those who look not to encounter Us
29:5 (4)	whoso looks to encounter God, God's term is coming
29:23 (22)	those who disbelieve in God's signs and the encounter with Him
30:8 (7)	yet most men disbelieve in the encounter with their Lord
30:16 (15)	and cried lies to Our signs and the encounter of the Hereafter
32:10 (10)	they disbelieve in the encounter with their Lord
32:14 (14)	now taste, for that you forgot the encounter of this your day
32:23 (23)	so be not in doubt concerning the encounter with him
39:71 (71)	and warning you against the encounter of this your day
41:54 (54)	are they not in doubt touching the encounter with their Lord?
45:34 (33)	today We do forget you, even as you forgot the encounter of this your day

g) pcple. act. (*lāqī*)

28:61 (61)	what, is he to whom We have promised a fair promise, and he receives it

TILQĀ' n.m.~towards; (*min tilqā'i nafsihi*) of his own accord

7:47 (45)	when their eyes are turned towards the inhabitants of the Fire
10:15 (16)	it is not for me to alter it of my own accord
28:22 (21)	and when he turned his face towards Midian

LAQQÁ vb. (II)~to procure (something for someone) [Ar]; to make one to find [Pk]; to shed over someone [Ali]; to meet [Bl]. (impf. pass) to receive

a) perf. act.

76:11 (11)	God has guarded them from the evil of that day, and has procured them radiancy

e) impf. pass. (*yulaqqá*)

25:75 (75)	and they shall receive therein a greeting
27:6 (6)	thou receivest the Koran from One All-wise
28:80 (80)	none shall receive it except the steadfast
41:35 (35)	none shall receive it, except the steadfast
41:35 (35)	none shall receive it, except a man of mighty fortune

LĀQÁ vb. (III)~to meet, to encounter. (pcple. act.) one who encounters, who meets

b) impf. act. (*yulāqī*)

43:83 (83) until they encounter that day of theirs which they are promised
52:45 (45) then leave them, till they encounter their day
70:42 (42) leave them alone to plunge and play until they encounter that day of theirs

g) pcple. act. (*mulāqī*)

2:46 (43) who reckon that they shall meet their Lord
2:223 (223) fear God, and know that you shall meet Him
2:249 (250) said those who reckoned they should meet God
11:29 (31) those who believe; they shall surely meet their Lord
62:8 (8) surely death, from which you flee, shall encounter you
69:20 (20) I thought that I should encounter my reckoning
84:6 (6) thou art labouring unto thy Lord laboriously, and thou shalt encounter Him

ALQÁ vb. (IV)~to cast, to throw, to lay (tr), to fling; to offer; to commit, to convey; (*alqá al-sam*ᶜ) to give ear. (pcple. act.) one who casts; hurling

a) perf. act.

4:90 (92) if they withdraw from you, and do not fight you, and offer you peace
4:94 (96) do not say to him who offers you a greeting
4:171 (169) and His Word that He committed to Mary
5:64 (69) We have cast between them enmity and hatred, till the Day of Resurrection
7:107 (104) so he cast his staff; and behold, it was a serpent manifest
7:116 (113) and when they cast they put a spell upon the people's eyes
7:150 (149) he cast down the Tablets, and laid hold of his brother's head
10:81 (81) then, when they had cast, Moses said
12:96 (96) but when the bearer of good tidings came to him, and laid it on his face
15:19 (19) We stretched it forth, and cast on it firm mountains
16:15 (15) He cast on the earth firm mountains, lest it shake with you
16:28 (30) then they will offer surrender: We were doing nothing evil
16:86 (88) they will fling back at them the saying
16:87 (89) they will offer God surrender that day
20:20 (21) he cast it down, and behold it was a serpent sliding
20:39 (39) I loaded on thee love from Me
20:65 (68) or we shall be the first to cast
20:87 (90) we cast them, as the Samaritan also threw them, into the fire
22:52 (51) but that Satan cast into his fancy, when he was fancying
26:32 (31) he cast his staff, and behold, it was a serpent manifest
26:44 (43) they cast their ropes and their staffs, and said
26:45 (44) then Moses cast his staff
31:10 (9) He cast on the earth firm mountains, lest it shake with you
38:34 (33) We tried Solomon, and We cast upon his throne a mere body
50:7 (7) We stretched it forth, and cast on it firm mountains
50:37 (36) in that there is a reminder to him who has a heart, or will give ear
75:15 (15) even though he offer his excuses
84:4 (4) and casts forth what is in it, and voids itself

b) impf. act. (*yulqī*)

2:195 (191) cast not yourselves by your own hands into destruction
3:44 (39) wast not with them, when they were casting quills

3:151 (144)	We will cast into the hearts of the unbelievers terror
4:91 (93)	if they withdraw not from you, and offer you peace
7:115 (112)	they said, 'Moses, wilt thou castor shall we be the casters?'
8:12 (12)	I shall cast into the unbelievers' hearts terror
20:39 (39)	and let the river throw him up on the shore
20:65 (68)	they said, 'Moses, either thou wilt cast, or we shall be the first to cast'
22:52 (51)	but God annuls what Satan casts
22:53 (52)	that He may make what Satan casts a trial
26:223 (223)	they give ear, but most of them are liars
40:15 (15)	casting the Spirit of His bidding upon whomever He will
60:1 (1)	take not My enemy and your enemy for friends, offering them love
73:5 (5)	behold, We shall cast upon thee a weighty word

c) impv. (*alqi*)

7:116 (113)	he said, 'You cast'
7:117 (114)	and We revealed to Moses: 'Cast thy staff'
10:80 (80)	Moses said to them, 'Cast you down what you will cast'
12:10 (10)	kill not Joseph, but cast him into the bottom of the pit
12:93 (93)	go, take this shirt, and do you cast it on my father's face
20:19 (20)	said He, 'Cast it down, Moses!'
20:66 (69)	'No,' said Moses. 'Do you cast!'
20:69 (72)	cast down what is in thy right hand
26:43 (42)	Moses said to them, 'Cast you down what you will cast'
27:10 (10)	cast down thy staff
27:28 (28)	take this letter of mine, and cast it unto them
28:7 (6)	cast him into the sea, and do not fear, neither sorrow
28:31 (31)	cast down thy staff
37:97 (95)	build him a building, and cast him into the furnace
50:24 (23)	cast, you twain, into Gehenna every froward unbeliever
50:26 (25)	therefore, you twain, cast him into the terrible chastisement

d) perf. pass. (*ulqiya*)

7:120 (117)	and the sorcerers were cast down, bowing themselves
20:70 (73)	and the sorcerers cast themselves down prostrating
25:13 (14)	and when they are cast, coupled in fetters, into a narrow place
26:46 (45)	so the sorcerers were cast down, bowing themselves
27:29 (29)	O Council, see, a letter honourable has been cast unto me
43:53 (53)	why then have bracelets of gold not been cast on him
54:25 (25)	has the Reminder been cast upon him alone among us?
67:7 (7)	when they are cast into it they will hear it sighing
67:8 (8)	as often as a troop is cast into it, its keepers ask them

e) impf. pass. (*yulqá*)

17:39 (41)	set not up with God another god, or thou wilt be cast
25:8 (9)	or why is not a treasure thrown to him
28:86 (86)	thou didst not hope that the Book should be cast unto thee, except it be as a mercy
41:40 (40)	what, is he who shall be cast into the Fire better

g) pcple. act. (*mulqī*)

7:115 (112)	Moses, wilt thou cast, or shall we be the casters?
10:80 (80)	Moses said to them, 'Cast you down what you will cast'
26:43 (42)	Moses said to them, 'Cast you down what you will cast'
77:5 (5)	and those hurling a reminder

TALAQQÁ vb. (V)~to receive; to meet. (pcple. act.) angel [Ar]; Receiver [Pk]; guardian angel [Ali]

a) perf. act.

2:37 (35) thereafter Adam received certain words from his Lord
24:15 (14) when you received it on your tongues, and were speaking with your mouths

b) impf. act. (*yatalaqqá*)

21:103 (103) and the angels shall receive them
50:17 (16) when the two angels meet together, sitting one on the right

g) pcple. act. (*mutalaqqī*)

50:17 (16) when the two angels meet together, sitting one on the right

TALĀQÁ vb. (VI)~(n.vb.) encounter, meeting; (*yawm at-talāqi*) Day of Encounter, Day of Judgment

f) n.vb. (*talāqī*)

40:15 (15) that he may warn them of the Day of Encounter

ILTAQÁ vb. (VIII)~to meet one another, to encounter

a) perf. act.

3:13 (11) there has already been a sign for you in the two companies that encountered
3:155 (149) those of you who turned away the day the two hosts encountered
3:166 (160) and what visited you, the day the two hosts encountered, was by God's leave
8:41 (42) sent down upon Our servant on the day of salvation, the day the two hosts

8:44 (46) when God showed you them in your eyes as few, when you encountered
54:12 (12) and the waters met for a matter decreed

b) impf. act. (*yaltaqī*)

55:19 (19) He let forth the two seas that meet together

*L S N

LISĀN n.com. (pl. *alsinah*)~a tongue, language; (*afṣaḥu lisānan*) more eloquent

3:78 (72) there is a sect of them twist their tongues with the Book
4:46 (48) twisting with their tongues and traducing religion
5:78 (82) cursed were the unbelievers of the Children of Israel by the tongue of David
14:4 (4) We have sent no Messenger save with the tongue of his people
16:62 (64) and their tongues describe falsehood
16:103 (105) the speech of him at whom they hint is barbarous
16:103 (105) and this is speech Arabic, manifest
16:116 (117) do not say, as to what your tongues falsely describe
19:50 (51) We appointed unto them a tongue of truthfulness
19:97 (97) We have made it easy by thy tongue that thou mayest bear good tidings
20:27 (28) unloose the knot upon my tongue
24:15 (14) when you received it on your tongues, and were speaking with your mouths
24:24 (24) the day when their tongues, their hands and their feet shall testify against them
26:13 (12) my breast will be straitened, and my tongue will not be loosed
26:84 (84) and appoint me a tongue of truthfulness
26:195 (195) in a clear, Arabic tongue

28:34 (34)	moreover my brother Aaron is more eloquent than I
30:22 (21)	and the variety of your tongues and hues
33:19 (19)	when the fear departs, they flay you with sharp tongues
44:58 (58)	We have made it easy by thy tongue
46:12 (11)	this is a Book confirming, in Arabic tongue
48:11 (11)	they say with their tongues what is not in their hearts
60:2 (2)	and stretch against you their hands and their tongues
75:16 (16)	move not thy tongue with it to hasten it
90:9 (9)	and a tongue, and two lips

*L Ṭ F

LAṬĪF n.m. (adj)~All-subtle, All-gentle [Ar]; Tender, Subtile, Gracious [Pk]; Gentle [Bl]; One who is above all comprehension, One who understands the finest mysteries, Gracious (42:19) [Ali] (Divine attribute)

6:103 (103)	He is the All-subtle, the All-aware
12:100 (101)	My Lord is gentle to what He will
22:63 (62)	God is All-subtle, All-aware
31:16 (15)	surely God is All-subtle, All-aware
33:34 (34)	God is All-subtle, All-aware
42:19 (18)	God is All-gentle to His servants
67:14 (14)	He is the All-subtle, the All-aware

TALAṬṬAFA vb. (V)~to be courteous

b) impf. act. (*yatalaṭṭafu*)

18:19 (18)	let him be courteous, and apprise no man

*L W DH

LĀDHA vb. (I)~(n.vb.) the act of hiding oneself; (adv) surreptitiously

f) n.vb. (*liwādh*)

24:63 (63)	God knows those of you who slip away surreptitiously

*L W Ḥ

LAWḤ n.m. (pl. *alwāḥ*)~tablet; plank

7:145 (142)	We wrote for him on the Tablets of everything an admonition
7:150 (149)	he cast down the Tablets, and laid hold of his brother's head
7:154 (153)	when Moses' anger abated in him, he took the Tablets
54:13 (13)	We bore him upon a well-planked vessel well-caulked
85:22 (22)	in a guarded tablet

LAWWĀḤ n.m. (adj)~scorching [Ar, Bl]; shrivelling [Pk]; darkening and changing [Ali]

74:29 (29)	scorching the flesh

*L W M

LĀMA vb. (I)~to blame. (pcple. act.) a reproacher [Ar]; blamer [Pk, Bl]; one who finds fault [Ali]. (pcple. pass.) reproached, blameworthy, rebuked

a) perf. act.

12:32 (32) this is he you blamed me for

b) impf. act. (*yalūmu*)

14:22 (27) do not blame me but (blame) yourselves

c) impv. (*lum*)

14:22 (27) do not (blame) me but blame yourselves

g) pcple. act. (*lāʾim*)

5:54 (59) in the path of God, not fearing the reproach of any reproacher

h) pcple. pass. (*malūm*)

17:29 (31) or thou wilt sit reproached and denuded
17:39 (41) or thou wilt be cast into Gehenna, reproached
23:6 (6) save from their wives and what their right hands own then being not blameworthy
51:54 (54) so turn thou from them; thou wilt not be reproached
70:30 (30) save from their wives and what their right hands own, then not being blameworthy

LAWMAH n.f.~a reproach, a blame

5:54 (59) men who struggle in the path of God, not fearing the reproach of any reproacher

LAWWĀM n.m. (f. *lawwāmah*)~(adj) reproachful, accusing; self reproaching [Ali]; blame- casting [Bl]

75:2 (2) no! I swear by the reproachful soul

ALĀMA vb. (IV)~(pcple. act.) blameworthy

g) pcple. act. (*mulīm*)

37:142 (142) then the whale swallowed him down, and he blameworthy
51:40 (40) We seized him and his hosts, and We cast them into the sea, and he blameworthy

TALĀWAMA vb. (VI)~to blame each other

b) impf. act. (*yatalāwamu*)

68:30 (30) they advanced one upon another, blaming each other

*L W N

LAWN n.m. (pl. *alwān*)~colour, hue

2:69 (64) pray to thy Lord for us, that He make clear to us what her colour may be
2:69 (64) she shall be a golden cow, bright her colour
16:13 (13) that which He has multiplied for you in the earth of diverse hues

16:69 (71)	then comes there forth out of their bellies a drink of diverse hues
30:22 (21)	and the variety of your tongues and hues
35:27 (25)	therewith We bring forth fruits of diverse hues
35:27 (25)	in the mountains are streaks white and red, of diverse hues
35:28 (25)	men too, and beasts and cattle — diverse are their hues
39:21 (22)	He brings forth therewith crops of diverse hues

*L W T

LĀTA vb. (I)~it is not; (*lāta ḥīna manāṣ*) time was none to escape

a) perf. act.

38:3 (2)	and they called, but time was none to escape

*L W Ṭ

LŪṬ n.prop.~Lot

6:86 (86)	Jonah and Lot — each one We preferred above all beings
7:80 (78)	and Lot, when he said to his people
11:70 (73)	fear not; we have been sent to the people of Lot
11:74 (77)	he was disputing with Us concerning the people of Lot
11:77 (79)	when Our messengers came to Lot, he was troubled on their account
11:81 (83)	Lot, we are messengers of thy Lord
11:89 (91)	Salih; and the people of Lot are not far away from you
15:59 (59)	excepting the folk of Lot; them we shall deliver
15:61 (61)	so, when the envoys came to the folk of Lot
21:71 (71)	We delivered him, and Lot, unto the land that We had blessed
21:74 (74)	and Lot — to him We gave judgment and knowledge
22:43 (43)	and the people of Abraham, the people of Lot
26:160 (160)	the people of Lot cried lies to the Envoys
26:161 (161)	when their brother Lot said to them, 'Will you not be godfearing?'
26:167 (167)	if thou givest not over, Lot, thou shalt assuredly be one of the expelled
27:54 (55)	and Lot, when he said to his people
27:56 (57)	expel the folk of Lot from your city
29:26 (25)	but Lot believed him; and he said, 'I will flee to my Lord'
29:28 (27)	and Lot, when he said to his people
29:32 (31)	he said, 'Lot is in it'
29:33 (32)	when that Our messengers came to Lot he was troubled on their account
37:133 (133)	Lot too was one of the Envoys
38:13 (12)	and the people of Lot, and the men of the Thicket
50:13 (13)	and Ad and Pharaoh, the brothers of Lot
54:33 (33)	the people of Lot cried lies to the warnings
54:34 (34)	We loosed against them a squall of pebbles except the folk of Lot
66:10 (10)	the wife of Noah, and the wife of Lot

*L W Y

LAWĀ vb. (I)~to twist, to twist about, to pervert, to distort (i.e. to twist one's tongue). (n.vb.) twisting, distorting *b*) impf. act. (*yalwī*)

3:78 (72) there is a sect of them twist their tongues with the Book
3153 (147) when you were going up, not twisting about for anyone
4:135 (134) for if you twist or turn, God is aware of the things you do

f) n.vb. (*layy*)

4:46 (48) twisting with their tongues

LAWWA vb. (II)~to twist, to avert

a) perf. act.

63:5 (5) they twist their heads, and thou seest them turning their faces away

*L Y L

LAYL n.m. (f. *laylah*, pl. *layālī*)~(f) a night, (m) night, night-time, (adv) by night; (*laylat al-qadar*) The Night of Power

2:51 (48) and when We appointed with Moses forty nights
2:164 (159) in the creation of the heavens and the earth and the alternation of night and day
2:187 (183) permitted to you, upon the night of the Fast, is to go in to your wives
2:187 (183) then complete the Fast unto the night
2:274 (275) those who expend their wealth night and day, secretly and in public
3:27 (26) Thou makest the night to enter into the day
3:27 (26) Thou makest the day to enter into the night
3:113 (109) a nation upstanding, that recite God's signs in the watches of the night
3:190 (187) in the alternation of night and day there are signs
6:13 (13) to Him belongs whatsoever inhabits the night and the day
6:60 (60) it is He who recalls you by night
6:76 (76) when night outspread over him he saw a star
6:96 (96) He splits the sky into dawn, and has made the night for a repose
7:54 (52) covering the day with the night it pursues urgently
7:142 (138) We appointed with Moses thirty nights and We completed them with ten
7:142 (138) so the appointed time of his Lord was forty nights
10:6 (6) in the alternation of night and day
10:24 (25) Our command comes upon it by night or day
10:27 (28) as if their faces were covered with strips of night shadowy
10:67 (68) it is He who made for you the night to repose in it
11:81 (83) so set forth, thou with thy family, in a watch of the night
11:114 (116) perform the prayer at the two ends of the day and nigh of the night
13:3 (3) of every fruit He placed there two kinds, covering the day with the night
13:10 (11) he who hides himself in the night, and he who sallies by day
14:33 (37) He subjected to you the night and day
15:65 (65) so set forth, thou with thy family, in a watch of the night
16:12 (12) He subjected to you the night and day
17:1 (1) Glory be to Him, who carried His servant by night
17:12 (13) We have appointed the night and the day as two signs
17:12 (13) then We have blotted out the sign of the night, and made the sign of the day to see
17:78 (80) perform the prayer at the sinking of the sun to the darkening of the night
17:79 (81) and as for the night, keep vigil a part of it
19:10 (11) thou shalt not speak to men, though being without fault, three nights
20:130 (130) proclaim thy Lord's praise in the watches of the night

21:20 (20)	glorifying Him by night and in the daytime
21:33 (34)	it is He who created the night and the day
21:42 (43)	who shall guard you by night and in the daytime from the All-merciful?
22:61 (60)	that is because God makes the night to enter into the day
22:61 (60)	and makes the day to enter into the night
23:80 (82)	to Him belongs the alternation of night and day
24:44 (44)	God turns about the day and the night
25:47 (49)	it is He who appointed the night for you to be garment
25:62 (63)	it is He who made the night and day a succession
27:86 (88)	have they not seen how We made the night for them, to repose in it
28:71 (71)	what think you? if God should make the night unceasing over you
28:72 (72)	what god other than God shall bring you night to repose in?
28:73 (73)	of His mercy He has appointed for you night and day
30:23 (22)	of His signs is your slumbering by night and day
31:29 (28)	hast thou not seen how that God makes the night to enter into the day
31:29 (28)	and makes the day to enter into the night
34:18 (17)	journey among them by night and day in security
34:33 (32)	but devising night and day, when you were ordering us to disbelieve in God
35:13 (14)	He makes the night to enter into the day
35:13 (14)	and makes the day to enter into the night
36:37 (37)	and a sign for them is the night
36:40 (40)	it behoves not the sun to overtake the moon, neither does the night outstrip the day
37:138 (138)	and in the night; will you not understand?
39:5 (7)	wrapping night about the day
39:5 (7)	wrapping the day about the night
39:9 (12)	is he who is obedient in the watches of the night, bowing himself and standing
40:61 (63)	it is God who made for you the night, to repose in it
41:37 (37)	of His signs are the night and the day, the sun and the moon
41:38 (38)	those who are with thy Lord do glorify Him by night and day
44:3 (2)	We have sent it down in a blessed night
44:23 (22)	then set thou forth with My servants in a watch of the night
45:5 (4)	in the alternation of night and day
50:40 (39)	proclaim thy Lord's praise in the night, and at the ends of the prostrations
51:17 (17)	little of the night would they slumber
52:49 (49)	proclaim the praise of thy Lord in the night, and at the declining of the stars
57:6 (6)	He makes the night to enter into the day
57:6 (6)	and makes the day to enter into the night
69:7 (7)	He compelled against them seven nights and eight days
71:5 (5)	my Lord, I have called my people by night and by day
73:2 (2)	keep vigil the night, except a little
73:6 (6)	the first part of the night is heavier in tread, more upright in speech
73:20 (20)	thy Lord knows that thou keepest vigil nearly two-thirds of the night
73:20 (20)	God determines the night and the day
74:33 (36)	and the night when it retreats
76:26 (26)	and part of the night
76:26 (26)	and magnify Him through the long night
78:10 (10)	and We appointed night for a garment
79:29 (29)	and darkened its night, and brought forth its forenoon
81:17 (17)	by the night swarming
84:17 (17)	and the night and what it envelops
89:2 (1)	and ten nights
89:4 (3)	by the night when it journeys on
91:4 (4)	and by the night when it enshrouds him
92:1 (1)	by the night enshrouding

93:2 (2)	and the brooding night
97:1 (1)	behold, We sent it down on the Night of Power
97:2 (2)	what shall teach thee what is the Night of Power
97:3 (3)	the Night of Power is better than a thousand months

*L Y N

LĀNA vb. (I)~to be gentle, to be lenient, to soften

a) perf. act.

3:159 (153) it was by some mercy of God that thou wast gentle to them

b) impf. act. (*yalīnu*)

39:23 (24) their skins and their hearts soften to the remembrance of God

LAYYIN n.m. (adj)~soft, gentle

20:44 (46) speak gently to him, that haply he may be mindful

LĪNAH n.f.~a palm-tree

59:5 (5) whatever palm-trees you cut down, or left standing upon their roots

ALĀNA vb. (IV)~to soften (tr)

a) perf. act.

34:10 (10) and We softened for him iron

*L Y T

LĀTA vb. (I)~to diminish (tr), to withhold

b) impf. act. (*yalītu*)

49:14 (14) if you obey God and His Messenger, He will not diminish you anything of your works

AL-LĀT n.prop.~Al-Lat (a goddess of pre-Islamic Arabia)

53:19 (19) Have you considered Al-Lat and Al-'Uzza

*L Z B

LAZABA vb. (I)~(pcple. act.) (adj) clinging, plastic, sticky

g) pcple. act. (*lāzib*)

37:11 (11) We created them of clinging clay

*L Z M

LAZIMA vb. (III)~(n.vb.) fastening [Ar]; inevitable (punishment or judgment) [Bl, pk, Ali]; close at hand [Bl]; (adv) necessarily [Ali]

f) n.vb. (*lizām*)

20:129 (129)	for a word that preceded from thy Lord, and a stated term, it had been fastened
25:77 (77)	for you have cried lies, and it shall surely be fastened

ALZAMA vb. (IV)~to fasten to; to compel

a) perf. act.

17:13 (14)	We have fastened to him his bird of omen upon his neck
48:26 (26)	His Messenger and the believers, and fastened to them the word of godfearing

b) impf. act. (*yulzimu*)

11:28 (30)	shall we compel you to it while you are averse to it?

*L Ẓ Y

LAẒÁ n.f.~a furnace [Ar]; fire of hell [Pk, Ali]; flame [Bl]

70:15 (15)	nay, verily it is a furnace

TALAẒẒÁ vb. (V)~to flame [Ar, Pk]; to blaze fiercely [Ali, Bl]

b) impf. act. (*yatalaẓẓa*)

92:14 (14)	now I have warned you of a Fire that flames

MĪM

*M ʾ Y

MIʾAH n.f.~a hundred

2:259 (261)	God made him die a hundred years, then He raised him up
2:259 (261)	nay; thou hast tarried a hundred years
2:261 (263)	of a grain of corn that sprouts seven ears, in every ear a hundred grains
8:65 (66)	if there be twenty of you, patient men, they will overcome two hundred
8:65 (66)	if there be a hundred of you, they will overcome a thousand unbelievers
8:66 (67)	if there be a hundred of you, patient men, they will overcome two (hundred)
8:66 (67)	if there be a (hundred) of you, patient men, they will overcome two hundred
18:25 (24)	they tarried in the Cave three hundred years
24:2 (2)	scourge each one of them a hundred stripes
37:147 (147)	then We sent him unto a hundred thousand, or more

*M ʿ N

MĀʿŪN n.m.~charity [Ar]; small kindness [Pk]; neighbourly needs [Ali]; succour [Bl]

107:7 (7)	and refuse charity

*M ʿ Y

AMʿĀʾ n.com. (pl. of *maʿy*)~bowels, intestines

47:15 (17)	boiling water, that tears their bowels asunder

*M ʿ Z

MAʿZ n.m.~goat(s)

6:143 (144)	eight couples: two of sheep, of goats two

*M D D

MADDA vb. (I)~to stretch out, stretch forth, to extend, to spread out; to prolong; to lead on, to cause to increase; to replenish, to reinforce with, to support. (n.vb.) the act of extending or prolonging. (pcple. pass.) that which is spread out, extended; (adj) ample

a) perf. act.

13:3 (3)	it is He who stretched out the earth
15:19 (19)	We stretched it forth, and cast on it firm mountains

25:45 (47)	hast thou not regarded thy Lord, how He has stretched out the shadow?
50:7 (7)	We stretched it forth, and cast on it firm mountains

b) impf. act. (*yamuddu*)

2:15 (14)	God shall mock them, and shall lead them on
7:202 (201)	and their brothers they lead on into error
15:88 (88)	stretch not thine eyes to that We have given pairs of them to enjoy
19:75 (76)	whosoever is in error, let the All-merciful prolong his term for him
19:79 (82)	We shall prolong for him the chastisement
20:131 (131)	stretch not thine eyes to that We have given pairs of them to enjoy
22:15 (15)	let him stretch up a rope to heaven, then let him sever it
31:27 (26)	seven seas after it to replenish it

c) impv. (*mudda*)

84:3 (3)	when earth is stretched out

f) n.vb. (*madd*)

19:75 (76)	whosoever is in error, let the All-merciful prolong his term for him <...>
19:79 (82)	We shall prolong for him the chastisement <...>

h) pcple. pass. (*mamdūd*)

56:30 (29)	and spreading shade
74:12 (12)	and appointed for him ample wealth

MADAD n.m.~replenishment, support

18:109 (109)	though We brought replenishment the like of it

MIDĀD n.m.~ink

18:109 (109)	if the sea were ink for the Words of my Lord

MUDDAH n.f.~a period, a term, a space of time

9:4 (4)	with them fulfil your covenant till their term

MADDADA vb. (II)~(pcple. pass.) outstretched

h) pcple. pass. (*mumaddad*)

104:9 (9)	in columns outstretched

AMADDA vb. (IV)~to succour, to reinforce. (pcple. act.) one who succours or reinforces

a) perf. act.

17:6 (6)	We succoured you with wealth and children
26:132 (132)	fear Him who has succoured you with what you know
26:133 (133)	succoured you with flocks and sons
52:22 (22)	We shall succour them with fruits and flesh

b) impf. act. (*yumiddu*)

3:124 (120)	your Lord should reinforce you with three thousand angels
3:125 (121)	your Lord will reinforce you with five thousand swooping angels
17:20 (21)	each We succour, these and those, from thy Lord's gift

23:55 (57)	what do they think that We succour them with of wealth and children?
27:36 (36)	would you succour me with wealth?
71:12 (11)	and will succour you with wealth and sons

g) pcple. act. (*mumidd*)

8:9 (9)	I shall reinforce you with a thousand angels

*M D N

MADĪNAH n.f. (pl. *madā'in*)~a city, the City (Medina)

7:111 (108)	and send among the cities musterers
7:123 (120)	surely this is a device you have devised in the city
9:101 (102)	some of the people of the City are grown bold
9:120 (121)	it is not for the people of the City
12:30 (30)	certain women that were in the city said
15:67 (67)	the people of the city came rejoicing
18:19 (18)	now send one of you forth with this silver to the city
18:82 (81)	as for the wall, it belonged to two orphan lads in the city
26:36 (35)	send among the cities musterers
26:53 (53)	then Pharaoh sent among the cities musterers
27:48 (49)	in the city there were nine persons
28:15 (14)	he entered the city, at a time when its people were unheeding
28:18 (17)	now in the morning he was in the city, fearful and vigilant
28:20 (19)	then came a man from the furthest part of the city, running
33:60 (60)	they that make commotion in the city
36:20 (19)	then came a man from the furthest part of the city, running
63:8 (8)	if we return to the City, the mightier ones of it will expel the more abased

MADYAN n.prop.~Midian

7:85 (83)	to Midian their brother Shuaib; he said
9:70 (71)	Thamood, the people of Abraham, the men of Midian
11:84 (85)	to Midian their brother Shuaib; he said
11:95 (98)	so away with Midian, even as Thamood was done away
20:40 (42)	many years among the people of Midian thou didst sojourn
22:44 (43)	and the men of Midian; to Moses also they cried lies
28:22 (21)	when he turned his face towards Midian he said
28:23 (22)	when he came to the waters of Midian he found a company of the people
28:45 (45)	neither wast thou a dweller among the Midianites
29:36 (35)	to Midian their brother Shuaib; he said

*M Ḍ GH

MUḌGHAH n.f.~tissue, a lump of flesh (the size of a morsel)

22:5 (5)	then of a lump of flesh, formed and unformed
23:14 (14)	then We created of the clot a tissue
23:14 (14)	then We created of the tissue bones

*M Ḍ Y

MAḌÁ vb. (I)~to pass away, to be past, to go away, to depart. (n.vb.) the act of going away

a) perf. act.

8:38 (39) He will forgive them what is past
43:8 (7) the example of the ancients passed away

b) impf. act. (*yamḍī*)

18:60 (59) I will not give up until I reach the meeting of the two seas, though I go on for many years

c) impv. (*imḍi*)

15:65 (65) depart unto the place you are commanded

f) n.vb. (*muḍīy*)

36:67 (67) then they could not go on, nor could they return

*M H D

MAHADA vb. (I)~to make provision. (pcple. act.) one who spreads or smooths (a bed or cradle)

b) impf. act. (*yamhadu*)

30:44 (43) whosoever does righteousness — for themselves they are making provision

g) pcple. act. (*māhid*)

51:48 (48) and the earth — We spread it forth

MAHD n.m.~a cradle

3:46 (41) He shall speak to men in the cradle, and of age
5:110 (109) to speak to men in the cradle, and of age
19:29 (30) how shall we speak to one who is still in the cradle
20:53 (55) He who appointed the earth to be a cradle for you
43:10 (9) He who appointed the earth to be a cradle for you

MIHĀD n.m.~a cradle, cradling

2:206 (202) Gehenna shall be enough for him — how evil a cradling
3:12 (10) overthrown, and mustered into Gehenna — an evil cradling
3:197 (196) their refuge is Gehenna — an evil cradling
7:41 (39) Gehenna shall be their cradle
13:18 (18) their refuge shall be Gehenna — an evil cradling
38:56 (56) Gehenna, wherein they are roasted — an evil cradling
78:6 (6) have We not made the earth as a cradle

MAHHADA vb. (II)~to make smooth. (n.vb.) the act of making smooth

a) perf. act.

74:14 (14) — and made all things smooth for him

f) n.vb. (*tamhīd*)

74:14 (14) — and made all things smooth for him <...>

*M H L

MUHL n.m.~molten copper

18:29 (28) — they will be succoured with water like molten copper
44:45 (45) — like molten copper, bubbling in the belly
70:8 (8) — upon the day when heaven shall be as molten copper

MAHHALA vb. (II)~to respite

c) impv. (*mahhil*)

73:11 (11) — leave Me to those who cry lies, those prosperous ones, and respite them a little
86:17 (17) — so respite the unbelievers; delay with them awhile

AMHALA vb. (IV)~to delay

c) impv. (*amhil*)

86:17 (17) — so respite the unbelievers; delay with them awhile

*M H N

MAHĪN n.m. (adj)~mean, contemptible, despicable

32:8 (7) — He fashioned his progeny of an extraction of mean water
43:52 (51) — or am I better than this man, who is contemptible
68:10 (10) — and obey thou not every mean swearer
77:20 (20) — did We not create you of a mean water

*M Ḥ L

MAḤALA vb. (I)~(n.vb.) power

f) n.vb. (*miḥāl*)

13:13 (14) — yet they dispute about God, who is mighty in power

*M Ḥ N

IMTAḤANA vb. (VIII)~to test, to try

a) perf. act.

49:3 (3) those are they whose hearts God has tested for godfearing

c) impv. (*imtaḥin*)

60:10 (10) when believing women come to you as emigrants, test them

*M Ḥ Q

MAḤAQA vb. (I)~to blot out

b) impf. act. (*yamḥaqu*)

2:276 (277) God blots out usury, but freewill offerings He augments
3:141 (135) that God may prove the believers, and blot out the unbelievers

*M Ḥ Ṣ

MAḤḤAṢA vb. (II)~to prove, to try

b) impf. act. (*yumaḥḥiṣu*)

3:141 (135) and that God may prove the believers
3:154 (148) that He might prove what was in your hearts

*M Ḥ W

MAḤĀ vb. (I)~to blot out, to obliterate

a) perf. act.

17:12 (13) We have blotted out the sign of the night

b) impf. act. (*yamḥū*)

13:39 (39) God blots out, and He establishes whatsoever He will
42:24 (23) God blots out falsehood and verifies the truth

*M J D

MAJĪD n.m. (adj)~glorious; All-glorious (Divine attribute)

11:73 (76) surely He is All-laudable, All-glorious
50:1 (1) by the glorious Koran
85:15 (15) Lord of the Throne, the All-glorious
85:21 (21) nay, but it is a glorious Koran

*M J S

MAJŪS n.prop.~the Magians

22:17 (17)	the Sabaeans, the Christians, the Magians and the idolaters

*M K K

MAKKAH n.prop.~Mecca

48:24 (24)	He who restrained their hands from you, and your hands from them, in the hollow of Mecca

*M K L

MĪKĀL n.prop.~Michael (the Archangel)

2:98 (92)	His angels and His Messengers, and Gabriel, and Michael

*M K N

MAKĪN n.m. (adj)~sure, firm, secure

12:54 (54)	thou art established firmly in our favour and in our trust
23:13 (13)	then We set him, a drop, in a receptacle secure
77:21 (21)	that We laid within a sure lodging
81:20 (20)	having power, with the Lord of the Throne secure

MAKKANA vb. (II)~to establish firmly

a) perf. act.

6:6 (6)	many a generation We established in the earth
7:10 (9)	We have established you in the earth
12:21 (21)	so We established Joseph in the land
12:56 (56)	so We established Joseph in the land
18:84 (83)	We established him in the land
18:95 (94)	that wherein my Lord has established me is better
22:41 (42)	who, if We establish them in the land, perform the prayer
46:26 (25)	and We had established them in that
46:26 (25)	wherein We have not established you

b) impf. act. (*yumakkinu*)

6:6 (6)	as We never established you
24:55 (54)	He will surely establish their religion for them
28:6 (5)	and to establish them in the land
28:57 (57)	have We not established for them a sanctuary secure

AMKANA vb. (IV)~to give one power over someone or something

a) perf. act.

8:71 (72)	they have tricked God before; but He has given thee power over them

*M K R

MAKARA vb. (I)~to devise, to scheme, to plot, to plan. (n.vb.) devising, a device; a plot; sly whispers or talk. (pcple. act.) a planner, deviser, plotter

a) perf. act.

3:54 (47)	and they devised and God (devised)
3:54 (47)	and they (devised) and God devised
7:123 (120)	surely this is a device you have devised in the city
13:42 (42)	Those that were before them devised; but God's
14:46 (47)	they devised their devising, and their devising is known to God
16:26 (28)	those that were before them contrived
16:45 (47)	do they feel secure, those who devise evil things
27:50 (51)	and they devised a device
27:50 (51)	and We likewise devised a device
40:45 (48)	God guarded him against the evil things of their devising
71:22 (21)	and have devised a mighty device

b) impf. act. (*yamkuru*)

6:123 (123)	We appointed in every city great ones among its sinners, to devise there
6:123 (123)	they devised only against themselves, and they were not aware
6:124 (124)	a terrible chastisement, for what they devised
8:30 (30)	when the unbelievers were devising against thee, to confine thee
8:30 (30)	or to expel thee, and were devising
8:30 (30)	and God was devising
10:21 (22)	Our messengers are writing down what you are devising
12:102 (103)	thou wast not with them when they agreed upon their plan, devising
16:127 (128)	nor be thou straitened for what they devise
27:70 (72)	nor be thou straitened for what they devise
35:10 (11)	those who devise evil deeds — theirs shall be a terrible chastisement

f) n.vb. (*makr*)

7:99 (97)	do they feel secure against God's devising?
7:99 (97)	none feels secure against God's devising
7:123 (120)	surely this is a device you have devised in the city
10:21 (22)	they have a device concerning Our signs
10:21 (22)	say: 'God is swifter at devising'
12:31 (31)	when she heard their sly whispers, she sent to them
13:33 (33)	decked out fair to the unbelievers is their devising
13:42 (42)	but God's is the devising altogether
14:46 (47)	they devised their devising
14:46 (47)	and their devising is known to God
14:46 (47)	though their devising were such as to remove mountains
27:50 (51)	and they devised a device

27:50 (51)	and We likewise devised a device
27:51 (52)	and behold, how was the end of their device
34:33 (32)	but devising night and day, when you were ordering us to disbelieve in God
35:10 (11)	and their devising shall come to naught
35:43 (41)	waxing proud in the land, and devising evil
35:43 (41)	but evil devising encompasses only those who do it
71:22 (21)	and have devised a mighty device

g) pcple. act. (*mākir*)

3:54 (47)	God is the best of devisers
8:30 (30)	God was devising; and God is the best of devisers

*M K TH

MAKATHA vb. (I)~to tarry, to abide. (n.vb.) the act of tarrying; (with prep. *ʿalá*) at intervals. (pcple. act.) one who abides or tarries

a) perf. act.

27:22 (22) but he tarried not long, and said

b) impf. act. (*yamkuthu*)

13:17 (18) and what profits men abides in the earth

c) impv. (*umkuth*)

20:10 (9)	tarry you here; I observe a fire
28:29 (29)	tarry you here; I observe a fire

f) n.vb. (*mukth*)

17:106 (107) a Koran We have divided, for thee to recite it to mankind at intervals

g) pcple. act. (*mākith*)

18:3 (2)	therein to abide for ever
43:77 (77)	He will say, 'You will surely tarry'

*M K W

MAKĀ vb. (I)~(n.vb.) whistling

f) n.vb. (*mukāʾ*)

8:35 (35) their prayer at the House is nothing but a whistling

*M KH Ḍ

MAKHĀḌ n.m. (coll)~birthpangs, pains of childbirth

19:23 (23) the birthpangs surprised her by the trunk of the palm-tree

*M KH R

MAKHARA vb. (I)~(pcple. act.) that which ploughs or cleaves through the waves

g) pcple. act. f. (*mawākhir*, pl. of *mākhirah*)

16:14 (14)	and thou mayest see the ships cleaving through it
35:12 (13)	and thou mayest see the ships cleaving through it

*M L ʾ

MALAʾA vb. (I)~to fill. (pcple. act.) one who fills

b) impf. act. (*yamlaʾu*)

7:18 (17)	I shall assuredly fill Gehenna with all of you
11:119 (120)	I shall assuredly fill Gehenna with jinn and men
32:13 (13)	assuredly I shall fill Gehenna with jinn and men
38:85 (85)	I shall assuredly fill Gehenna with thee

d) perf. pass. (*muliʾa*)

18:18 (17)	thou wouldst have turned thy back on them in flight, and been filled with terror
72:8 (8)	we stretched towards heaven, but we found it filled with terrible guards

g) pcple. act. (*māliʾ*)

37:66 (64)	they eat of it, and of it fill their bellies
56:53 (53)	and you shall fill therewith your bellies

MALAʾ n.m.~council [Ar]; chiefs, leaders [Pk, Ali]; assembly [Bl]

2:246 (247)	hast thou not regarded the Council of the Children of Israel
7:60 (58)	said the Council of his people, 'We see thee'
7:66 (64)	said the Council of the unbelievers of his people
7:75 (73)	said the Council of those of his people who waxed proud
7:88 (86)	said the Council of those of his people who waxed proud
7:90 (88)	said the Council of those of his people who disbelieved
7:103 (101)	We sent, after them, Moses with Our signs to Pharaoh and his Council
7:109 (106)	said the Council of the people of Pharaoh
7:127 (124)	then said the Council of the people of Pharaoh
10:75 (76)	We sent forth, after them, Moses and Aaron to Pharaoh and his Council
10:83 (83)	for fear of Pharaoh and their Council
10:88 (88)	Thou hast given to Pharaoh and his Council adornment
11:27 (29)	said the Council of the unbelievers of his people
11:38 (40)	whenever a council of his people passed by him they scoffed at him
11:97 (99)	to Pharaoh and his Council
12:43 (43)	my counsellors, pronounce to me upon my dream
23:24 (24)	said the Council of the unbelievers of his people
23:33 (34)	said the Council of the unbelievers of his people
23:46 (48)	unto Pharaoh and his Council
26:34 (33)	said he to the Council about him
27:29 (29)	O Council, see, a letter honourable has been cast unto me
27:32 (32)	O Council, pronounce to me concerning my affair

27:38 (38)	O Council, which one of you will bring me her throne
28:20 (19)	Moses, the Council are conspiring to slay thee
28:32 (32)	these shall be two proofs from thy Lord to Pharaoh and his Council
28:38 (38)	Council, I know not that you have any god but me
37:8 (8)	they listen not to the High Council
38:6 (5)	and the Council of them depart, saying
38:69 (69)	I had no knowledge of the High Council when they disputed
43:46 (45)	We also sent Moses with Our signs to Pharaoh and his Council

MIL' n.m.~a quantity that fills anything; (*mil' al-arḍ*) the earth full

3:91 (85)	there shall not be accepted from any one of them the whole earth full of gold

IMTALA'A vb. (VIII)~to be full

a) perf. act.

50:30 (29)	upon the day We shall say unto Gehenna, 'Art thou filled?'

*M L Ḥ

MILḤ n.com.~salt

25:53 (55)	He who let forth the two seas, this one sweet, grateful to taste, and this salt
35:12 (13)	this is sweet, grateful to taste, delicious to drink, and that is salt

*M L K

MALAKA vb. (I)~to own, to possess; to have power or dominion over, to rule; (*malaka min Allāh*) to avail with or against God, to overrule God. (n.vb.1) volition, that which is in one's power. (n.vb.2) dominion, kingship, kingdom. (pcple. act.) one who has dominion or power, who owns or possesses; Master (Divine attribute). (pcple. pass.) one who is owned or possessed by someone else, a slave

a) perf. act.

4:3 (3)	then only one, or what your right hands own
4:24 (28)	and wedded women, save what your right hands own
4:25 (29)	let him take believing handmaids that your right hands own
4:36 (40)	to the traveller, and to that your right hands own
16:71 (73)	shall not give over their provision to that their right hands possess
23:6 (6)	save from their wives and what their right hands own
24:31 (31)	or their women, or what their right hands own
24:33 (33)	those your right hands own who seek emancipation, contract with them accordingly
24:58 (57)	let those your right hands own and those of you who have not reached puberty ask leave of you three times
24:61 (60)	the houses of your uncles or your aunts maternal, or that whereof you own the keys
30:28 (27)	do you have, among that your right hands own, associates
33:50 (49)	thy wives whom thou hast given their wages and what thy right hand owns
33:50 (50)	We know what We have imposed upon them touching their wives and what their right hands own
33:52 (52)	though their beauty please thee, except what thy right hand owns

33:55 (55)	their women, and what their right hands own
70:30 (30)	save from their wives and what their right hands own

b) impf. act. (*yamliku*)

5:17 (19)	who then shall overrule God in any way
5:25 (28)	I rule no one except myself and my brother
5:41 (45)	whomsoever God desires to try, thou canst not avail him anything with God
5:76 (80)	do you serve, apart from God, that which cannot hurt or profit you?
7:188 (188)	I have no power to profit for myself, or hurt, but as God will
10:31 (32)	or who possesses hearing and sight
10:49 (50)	I have no power to profit for myself, or hurt, but as God will
13:16 (17)	such as have no power to profit or hurt themselves
16:73 (75)	that which has no power to provide them anything from the heavens
17:56 (58)	they have no power to remove affliction from you
17:100 (102)	if you possessed the treasuries of my Lord's mercy
19:87 (90)	having no power of intercession, save
20:89 (91)	neither had any power to hurt or profit them
25:3 (4)	and have no power to hurt or profit themselves
25:3 (4)	no power of death or life or raising up
27:23 (23)	I found a woman ruling over them
29:17 (16)	those you serve, apart from God, have no power to provide for you
34:22 (21)	they possess not so much as the weight of an ant in the heavens
34:42 (41)	today none of you shall have power to profit or hurt another
35:13 (14)	those you call upon, apart from Him, possess not so much as the skin of a date-stone
39:43 (44)	even though they have no power whatever and no understanding
43:86 (86)	those they call upon, apart from Him, have no power of intercession
46:8 (7)	if I have forged it, you have no power to help me against God
48:11 (11)	who can avail you aught against God, if He desires hurt for you
60:4 (4)	I have no power to do aught for thee against God
72:21 (21)	I possess no power over you, either for hurt or for rectitude
78:37 (37)	the All-merciful of whom they have no power to speak
82:19 (19)	a day when no soul shall possess aught to succour another soul

f) n.vb. (1) (*malk*)

20:87 (90)	'We have not failed in our tryst with thee,' they said, 'of our volition'

f) n.vb. (2) (*mulk*)

2:102 (96)	they follow what the Satans recited over Solomon's kingdom
2:107 (101)	to God belongs the kingdom of the heavens and the earth
2:247 (248)	they said, 'How should he be king over us'
2:247 (248)	who have better right than he to kingship
2:247 (248)	God gives the kingship to whom He will
2:248 (249)	the sign of his kingship is that the Ark will come to you
2:251 (252)	and God gave him the kingship, and Wisdom
2:258 (260)	that God had given him the kingship
3:26 (25)	O God, Master of the Kingdom
3:26 (25)	Thou givest the Kingdom to whom Thou wilt
3:26 (25)	and seizest the Kingdom from whom Thou wilt
3:189 (186)	to God belongs the Kingdom of the heavens and of the earth
4:53 (56)	or have they a share in the Kingdom?
4:54 (57)	We gave them a mighty kingdom
5:17 (20)	to God belongs the kingdom of the heavens and of the earth
5:18 (21)	to God belongs the kingdom of the heavens and of the earth

5:40 (44)	knowest thou not that to God belongs the kingdom of the heavens and the earth?
5:120 (120)	to God belongs the kingdom of the heavens and of the earth
6:73 (73)	His saying is true, and His is the Kingdom
7:158 (158)	Him to whom belongs the kingdom of the heavens and of the earth
9:116 (117)	to God belongs the kingdom of the heavens and of the earth
12:101 (102)	O my Lord, Thou hast given me to rule
17:111 (111)	and who has not any associate in the Kingdom
20:120 (118)	shall I point thee to the Tree of Eternity, and a Kingdom that decays not?
22:56 (55)	the Kingdom upon that day shall belong to God
24:42 (42)	to God belongs the Kingdom of the heavens and the earth
25:2 (2)	to whom belongs the Kingdom of the heavens and the earth
25:2 (2)	He has no associate in the Kingdom
25:26 (28)	the Kingdom that day, the true Kingdom, shall belong to the All-merciful
35:13 (14)	that is God, your Lord; to Him belongs the Kingdom
38:10 (9)	or is theirs the kingdom of the heavens and earth
38:20 (19)	We strengthened his kingdom, and gave him wisdom
38:35 (34)	forgive me, and give me a kingdom such as may not befall anyone after me
39:6 (8)	that then is God, your Lord; to Him belongs the Kingdom
39:44 (45)	His is the kingdom of the heavens and the earth
40:16 (16)	'Whose is the Kingdom today?' 'God's, the One, the Omnipotent'
40:29 (30)	O my people, today the kingdom is yours, who are masters in the land
42:49 (48)	to God belongs the Kingdom of the heavens and the earth
43:51 (50)	O my people, do I not possess the kingdom of Egypt
43:85 (85)	blessed be He, to whom belongs the Kingdom of the heavens and the earth
45:27 (26)	to God belongs the Kingdom of the heavens and the earth
48:14 (14)	to God belongs the kingdom of the heavens and of the earth
57:2 (2)	to Him belongs the Kingdom of the heavens and the earth
57:5 (5)	to Him belongs the Kingdom of the heavens and the earth
64:1 (1)	His is the Kingdom, and His is the praise
67:1 (1)	blessed be He in whose hand is the Kingdom
76:20 (20)	when thou seest them then thou seest bliss and a great kingdom
85:9 (9)	to whom belongs the Kingdom of the heavens and the earth

g) pcple. act. (*mālik*)

1:4 (3)	the Master of the Day of Doom
3:26 (25)	say: 'O God, Master of the Kingdom'
36:71 (71)	of that Our hands wrought cattle that they own

h) pcple. pass. (*mamlūk*)

16:75 (77)	God has struck a similitude: a servant possessed by his master, having no power

MALAK n.m.~angel(s)

2:102 (96)	that which was sent down upon Babylon's two angels, Harut and Marut
6:8 (8)	why has an angel not been sent down on him?
6:8 (8)	yet had We sent down an angel, the matter would have been determined
6:9 (9)	had We made him an angel, yet assuredly We would have made him a man
6:50 (50)	I say not to you, 'I am an angel'
7:20 (19)	your Lord has only prohibited you from this tree lest you become angels
11:12 (15)	why has a treasure not been sent down upon him, or an angel not come with him?
11:31 (33)	I do not say, 'I am an angel'
12:31 (31)	this is no mortal; he is no other but a noble angel
17:95 (97)	We would have sent down upon them out of heaven an angel as Messenger
25:7 (8)	why has an angel not been sent down to him, to be a warner with him?
32:11 (11)	death's angel, who has been charged with you, shall gather you

53:26 (26)	how many an angel there is in the heavens whose intercession avails not anything
69:17 (17)	the angels shall stand upon its borders
89:22 (23)	thy Lord comes, and the angels rank on rank

MALAKŪT n.m.~kingdom, dominion

6:75 (75)	We were showing Abraham the kingdom of the heavens and earth
7:185 (184)	have they not considered the dominion of the heaven and of the earth
23:88 (90)	in whose hand is the dominion of everything, protecting and Himself unprotected
36:83 (83)	glory be to Him, in whose hand is the dominion of everything

MALIK n.m. (pl. *mulūk*)~king; King (Divine attribute)

2:246 (247)	raise up for us a king, and we will fight in God's way
2:247 (248)	God has raised up Saul for you as king
5:20 (23)	when He appointed among you Prophets, and appointed you kings
12:43 (43)	the king said, 'I saw in a dream seven fat kine'
12:50 (50)	the king said, 'Bring him to me'
12:54 (54)	the king said, 'Bring him to me'
12:72 (72)	they said, 'We are missing the king's goblet'
12:76 (76)	he could not have taken his brother, according to the king's doom
18:79 (78)	there was a king who was seizing every ship by brutal force
20:114 (113)	so high exalted be God, the true King
23:116 (117)	then high exalted be God, the King, the True
27:34 (34)	kings, when they enter a city, disorder it
59:23 (23)	He is the King, the All-holy, the All-peaceable
62:1 (1)	all that is in the heavens and the earth magnifies God, the King
114:2 (2)	the King of men

MALĪK n.m.~King (Divine attribute)

54:55 (55)	in a sure abode, in the presence of a King Omnipotent

MĀLIK n.prop.~Malik (an angel)

43:77 (77)	O Malik, let thy Lord have done with us

*M L L

MILLAH n.f.~religion, faith, creed

2:120 (114)	neither the Christians, not till thou followest their religion
2:130 (124)	who therefore shrinks from the religion of Abraham, except he be foolish-minded?
2:135 (129)	nay, rather the creed of Abraham, a man of pure faith
3:95 (89)	God has spoken the truth; therefore follow the creed of Abraham
4:125 (124)	who is there that has a fairer religion than he who submits his will to God
6:161 (162)	the creed of Abraham, a man of pure faith
7:88 (86)	unless you return into our creed
7:89 (87)	we should have forged against God a lie if we returned into your creed
12:37 (37)	I have forsaken the creed of a people who believe not in God
12:38 (38)	I have followed the creed of my fathers, Abraham, Isaac and Jacob
14:13 (16)	or you will surely return into our creed
16:123 (124)	follow thou the creed of Abraham, a man of pure faith
18:20 (19)	they will stone you, or restore you to their creed
22:78 (77)	being the creed of your father Abraham
38:7 (6)	we have not heard of this in the last religion

AMALLA vb. (IV)~to dictate

b) impf. act. (*yumillu*)

2:282 (282) let him write, and let the debtor dictate
2:282 (282) if the debtor be a fool, or weak, or unable to dictate himself
2:282 (282) then let his guardian dictate justly

*M L Q

AMLAQA vb. (IV)~(n.vb.) poverty, penury, want

f) n.vb. (*imlāq*)

6:151 (152) and not to slay your children because of poverty
17:31 (33) slay not your children for fear of poverty

*M L Y

MALĪY n.m.~(adv) for a while

19:46 (47) so forsake me now for some while

AMLÁ vb. (IV)~(with prep. *li-*) to respite, to grant indulgence; (with prep. *ʿalá*) to recite

a) perf. act.

13:32 (32) Messengers indeed were scoffed at before thee, and I respited the unbelievers
22:44 (43) I respited the unbelievers, then I seized them
22:48 (47) how many a city I have respited in its evildoing
47:25 (27) Satan it was that tempted them, and God respited them

b) impf. act. (*yumlī*)

3:178 (172) let not the unbelievers suppose that the indulgence We grant them is better
3:178 (172) We grant them indulgence only that they may increase in sin
7:183 (182) I respite them — assuredly My guile is sure
68:45 (45) I shall respite them — assuredly My guile is sure

e) impf. pass. (*yumlá*)

25:5 (6) they are recited to him at the dawn and in the evening

*M N ʿ

MANAʿA vb. (I)~to bar from, to prevent, to deny someone something; to defend or protect from. (pcple. act.) one who protects or defends. (pcple. pass.) forbidden

a) perf. act.

2:114 (108) who does greater evil than he who bars God's places of worship

7:12 (11) what prevented thee to bow thyself, when I commanded thee?
9:54 (54) naught prevents that their expendings should be accepted from them
17:59 (61) naught prevented Us from sending the signs
17:94 (96) naught prevented men from believing when the guidance came to them
18:55 (53) naught prevented men from believing when the guidance came unto them
20:92 (94) what prevented thee, Aaron, when thou sawest them in error
38:75 (75) Iblis, what prevented thee to bow thyself before that I created

b) impf. act. (*yamnaʿu*)

4:141 (140) did we not defend you from the believers?
21:43 (44) have they gods that shall defend them apart from Us?
107:7 (7) and refuse charity

d) perf. pass. (*muniʿa*)

12:63 (63) they said, 'Father, the measure was denied to us'

g) pcple. act. f. (*māniʿah*)

59:2 (2) they thought that their fortresses would defend them against God

h) pcple. pass. (*mamnūʿ*)

56:33 (32) unfailing, unforbidden

MANNĀʿ n.m.~one who hinders, hinderer

50:25 (24) every hinderer of the good, transgressor, disquieter
68:12 (12) hinderer of good, guilty aggressor

MANŪʿ n.m. (adj)~grudging

70:21 (21) when good visits him, grudging

*M N N

MANNA vb. (I) (with prep. *ʿalá*)~to be gracious to, to show grace to, to favour, to bestow, to give (liberally); to reproach. (n.vb.) reproach; grace. (pcple. pass.) failing, diminished

a) perf. act.

3:164 (158) God was gracious to the believers when He raised up among them a Messenger
4:94 (96) God has been gracious to you
6:53 (53) are these the ones God has been gracious to among us?
12:90 (90) God has indeed been gracious unto us
20:37 (37) already another time We favoured thee
28:82 (82) had God not been gracious to us, He would have made us to be swallowed too
37:114 (114) We also favoured Moses and Aaron
52:27 (27) God was gracious to us, and guarded us

b) impf. act. (*yamunnu*)

14:11 (13) God is gracious unto whomsoever He will of His servants
26:22 (21) that is a blessing thou reproachest me with
28:5 (4) We desired to be gracious to those that were abased in the land
49:17 (17) they count it as a favour to thee that they have surrendered

49:17 (17)	do not count your surrendering as a favour to me
49:17 (17)	God confers a favour upon you, in that He has guided you to belief
74:6 (6)	give not, thinking to gain greater

c) impv. (*umnun*)

38:39 (38)	this is Our gift; bestow or withhold without reckoning

f) n.vb. (*mann*)

2:262 (264)	then follow not up what they have expended with reproach and injury
2:264 (266)	void not your freewill offerings with reproach and injury
47:4 (5)	then set them free, either by grace or ransom

h) pcple. pass. (*mamnūn*)

41:8 (7)	those who believe, and do righteous deeds shall have a wage unfailing
68:3 (3)	surely thou shalt have a wage unfailing
84:25 (25)	theirs shall be a wage unfailing
95:6 (6)	they shall have a wage unfailing

MANN n.m.~manna

2:57 (54)	We sent down manna and quails upon you
7:160 (160)	We sent down manna and quails upon them
20:80 (82)	and sent down on you manna and quails

MANŪN n.m.~Fate [Ar, Bl]; time [Pk, Ali]

52:30 (30)	he is a poet for whom we await Fate's uncertainty

*M N Y

MANĀT n.prop.~Manat (a goddess of pre-Islamic Arabia)

53:20 (20)	and Manat the third, the other

MANĪ n.m.~a sperm-drop

75:37 (37)	was he not a sperm-drop spilled?

UMNĪYAH n.f. (pl. *amānī*)~a fancy [Ar]; hearsay, desire [Pk]; desire [Ali]; a thing taken on trust, dogma, formulation [Bl]

2:78 (73)	some there are of them that are common folk not knowing the Book, but only fancies
2:111 (105)	such are their fancies
4:123 (122)	it is not your fancies
4:123 (122)	nor the fancies of the People of the Book
22:52 (51)	but that Satan cast into his fancy, when he was fancying
57:14 (13)	you awaited, and you were in doubt, and fancies deluded you

MANNÁ vb. (II)~to fill with fancies [Ar]; to arouse or fill with (false) desires [Ali, Bl, Pk]

b) impf. act. (*yumannī*)

4:119 (118)	I will lead them astray, and fill them with fancies
4:120 (119)	He promises them and fills them with fancies

AMNÁ vb. (IV)~to cast forth, to spill

b) impf. act. (*yumnī*)

56:58 (58) have you considered the seed you spill?

e) impf. pass. (*yumná*)

53:46 (47) of a sperm-drop, when it was cast forth
75:37 (37) was he not a sperm-drop spilled?

TAMANNÁ vb. (V)~to fancy, to long for, to covet

a) perf. act.

22:52 (51) but that Satan cast into his fancy, when he was fancying
28:82 (82) in the morning those who had longed to be in his place the day before were saying
53:24 (24) shall man have whatever he fancies?

b) impf. act. (*yatamanná*)

2:95 (89) they will never long for it, because of that their hands have forwarded
3:143 (137) you were longing for death before you met it
4:32 (36) do not covet that whereby God in bounty has preferred one of you above another
62:7 (7) they will never long for it, because of that their hands have forwarded

c) impv. (*tamanna*)

2:94 (88) then long for death — if you speak truly
62:6 (6) then do you long for death

*M Q T

MAQATA vb. (I)~(n.vb.) hate, hatred, [Ar]; abhorrence, abomination, [Pk, Bl]; aversion, odium [Ali]; (adj) hateful [Ar, Pk]; odious [Ali]; abhorrent [Bl]

f) n.vb. (*maqt*)

4:22 (26) surely that is indecent and hateful, an evil way
35:39 (37) their unbelief increases the disbelievers only in hate in their Lord's sight
40:10 (10) surely God's hatred is greater than your (hatred) one of another
40:10 (10) surely God's (hatred) is greater than your hatred one of another
40:35 (37) very hateful is that in the sight of God and the believers
61:3 (3) very hateful is it to God, that you say what you do not

*M R ʾ

IMRAʾAH n.f.~a woman, a wife

2:282 (282) or if the two be not men, then one man and two women
3:35 (31) the wife of Imran said, 'Lord, I have vowed to Thee'
3:40 (35) how shall I have a son, seeing I am an old man and my wife is barren?
4:12 (15) if a man or a woman have no heir direct

4:128 (127)	if a woman fear rebelliousness or aversion in her husband
7:83 (81)	We delivered him and his family, except his wife
11:71 (74)	and his wife was standing by
11:81 (83)	let not any one of you turn round, excepting thy wife
12:21 (21)	he that bought him, being of Egypt, said to his wife
12:30 (30)	the Governor's wife has been soliciting her page
12:51 (51)	the Governor's wife said, 'Now the truth is at last discovered'
15:60 (60)	excepting his wife — we have decreed, she shall surely be of those that tarry
19:5 (5)	I fear my kinsfolk after I am gone; and my wife is barren
19:8 (9)	how shall I have a son, seeing my wife is barren
27:23 (23)	I found a woman ruling over them
27:57 (58)	We delivered him and his family, except his wife
28:9 (8)	said Pharaoh's wife, 'He will be a comfort to me and thee'
28:23 (23)	he found, apart from them, two women holding back their flocks
29:32 (31)	We shall deliver him and his family, except his wife
29:33 (32)	we shall deliver thee and thy family, except thy wife
33:50 (49)	and any woman believer, if she give herself to the Prophet
51:29 (29)	then came forward his wife, clamouring
66:10 (10)	the wife of Noah and the (wife) of Lot
66:10 (10)	the (wife) of Noah and the wife of Lot
66:11 (11)	God has struck a similitude for the believers — the wife of Pharaoh
111:4 (4)	and his wife, the carrier of the firewood

IMRUʾ n.m. (with definite article, *al-marʾ*)~a man

2:102 (96)	they learned how they might divide a man and his wife
4:176 (175)	if a man perishes having no children
8:24 (24)	know that God stands between a man and his heart
19:28 (29)	Sister of Aaron, thy father was not a wicked man
24:11 (11)	every man of them shall have the sin that he has earned charged to him
52:21 (21)	every man shall be pledged for what he earned
70:38 (38)	is every man of them eager to be admitted to a Garden of Bliss?
74:52 (52)	every man of them desires to be given scrolls unrolled
78:40 (41)	upon the day when a man shall behold what his hands have forwarded
80:34 (34)	upon the day when a man shall flee from his brother
80:37 (37)	every man that day shall have business to suffice him

MARĪʾ n.m. (adj)~wholesome, easy to digest

4:4 (3)	if they are pleased to offer you any of it, consume it with wholesome appetite

*M R D

MARADA vb. (I)~to grow bold, to persist (rebelliously). (pcple. act.) one who is rebellious

a) perf. act.

9:101 (102)	some of the people of the City are grown bold in hypocrisy

g) pcple. act. (*mārid*)

37:7 (7)	and to preserve against every rebel Satan

MARĪD n.m.~a rebel

4:117 (117)	they pray not except to a rebel Satan
22:3 (3)	that disputes concerning God without knowledge and follows every rebel Satan

MARRADA vb. (II)~(pcple. pass.) that which is rendered smooth

h) pcple. pass. (*mumarrad*)

27:44 (44)	it is a pavilion smoothed of crystal

*M R Ḍ

MARIḌA vb. (I)~to be sick. (n.vb.) sickness, disease, illness

a) perf. act.

26:80 (80)	and, whenever I am sick, heals me

f) n.vb. (*maraḍ*)

2:10 (9)	in their hearts is a sickness
2:10 (9)	and God has increased their sickness
5:52 (57)	thou seest those in whose hearts is sickness vying with one another
8:49 (51)	when the hypocrites, and those in whose hearts was sickness, said
9:125 (126)	but as for those in whose heart is sickness
22:53 (52)	He may make what Satan casts a trial for those in whose hearts is sickness
24:50 (49)	is there sickness in their hearts, or are they in doubt
33:12 (12)	when the hypocrites, and those in whose hearts is sickness, said
33:32 (32)	so that he in whose heart is sickness may be lustful
33:60 (60)	if the hypocrites do not give over, and those in whose hearts there is sickness
47:20 (22)	thou seest those in whose hearts is sickness looking at thee as one who swoons
47:29 (31)	did those in whose hearts is sickness think that God would not bring to light their rancour?
74:31 (33)	those in whose hearts there is sickness, and the unbelievers, may say

MARĪḌ n.m. (pl. *marḍá*)~sick, ill

2:184 (180)	and if any of you be sick, or if he be on a journey
2:185 (181)	and if any of you be sick, or if he be on a journey
2:196 (192)	if any of you is sick, or injured in his head
4:43 (46)	but if you are sick, or on a journey
4:102 (103)	there is no fault in you, if rain molests you, or you are sick
5:6 (9)	but if you are sick or on a journey
9:91 (92)	there is no fault in the weak and the sick
24:61 (60)	there is no fault in the sick, neither in yourselves
48:17 (17)	there is no fault in the lame, and there is no fault in the sick
73:20 (20)	He knows that some of you are sick

*M R Ḥ

MARIḤA vb. (I)~to be exultant, to be petulant. (n.vb.) exultantly (adv).

a) perf. act.

40:75 (75)	that is because you rejoiced in the earth without right, and were exultant

f) n.vb. (*maraḥ*)

17:37 (39)	and walk not in the earth exultantly
31:18 (17)	and walk not in the earth exultantly

*M R J

MARAJA vb. (I)~to let forth [Ar]; to loose, to give independence to [Pk]; to let free [Ali]; to pour out, to mingle [Bl]

a) perf. act.

25:53 (55)	it is He who let forth the two seas, this one sweet
55:19 (19)	He let forth the two seas that meet together

MĀRIJ n.m.~a smokeless fire

55:15 (14)	He created the jinn of a smokeless fire

MARĪJ n.m. (adj)~confused, troubled

50:5 (5)	when it came to them, and so they are in a case confused

MARJĀN n.m.~coral

55:22 (22)	from them come forth the pearl and the coral
55:58 (58)	lovely as rubies, beautiful as coral

*M R R

MARRA vb. (I)~(with prep. *ʿalá* or *bi-*) to pass, to pass by, to pass on. (n.vb.) the act of passing

a) perf. act.

2:259 (261)	or such as he who passed by a city that was fallen
7:189 (189)	she bore a light burden and passed by with it
10:12 (13)	when We have removed his affliction from him, he passes on
11:38 (40)	whenever a council of his people passed by him they scoffed at him
25:72 (72)	when they pass by idle talk
25:72 (72)	pass by with dignity
83:30 (30)	when they passed them by winking at one another

b) impf. act. (*yamurru*)

12:105 (105)	how many a sign there is in the heavens and in the earth that they pass by
27:88 (90)	thou shalt see the mountains, that thou supposest fixed, passing by like clouds
37:137 (137)	and you pass by them in the morning

f) n.vb. (*marr*)

27:88 (90)	thou shalt see the mountains, that thou supposest fixed, passing by like [the passing of the] clouds

AMARR n.m. (comp. adj. of *murr*)~bitter

54:46 (46)	the Hour is very calamitous and bitter

MARRAH n.f.~one time, one turn; (adv) once, twice (du)

2:229 (229)	divorce is twice; then honourable retention
6:94 (94)	you have come to Us one by one, as We created you upon the first time
6:110 (110)	even as they believed not in it the first time
8:56 (58)	then they break their compact every time
9:13 (13)	and purposed to expel the Messenger, beginning the first time against you
9:80 (81)	if thou askest pardon for them seventy times
9:83 (84)	you were well-pleased to tarry the first time
9:101 (102)	We know them, and We shall chastise them twice
9:126 (127)	do they not see that they are tried every year once or (twice?)
9:126 (127)	do they not see that they are tried every year (once) or twice?
17:4 (4)	you shall do corruption in the earth twice
17:7 (7)	and to enter the Temple, as they entered it the first time
17:51 (53)	say: 'He who originated you the first time'
18:48 (46)	you have come to Us, as We created you upon the first time
20:37 (37)	already another time We favoured thee
24:58 (57)	those of you who have not reached puberty ask leave of you three times
28:54 (54)	these shall be given their wage twice over
33:31 (31)	We shall pay her her wage twice over
36:79 (79)	He shall quicken them, who originated them the first time
41:21 (20)	He created you the first time

MIRRAH n.f.~(*dhū mirrah*) very strong [Ar]; vigorous [Pk]; wise [Ali]; forceful [Bl]

53:6 (6)	very strong; he stood poised

ISTAMARRA vb. (X)~(pcple. act.) continuous

g) pcple. act. (*mustamirr*)

54:2 (2)	they turn away, and they say, 'A continuous sorcery'
54:19 (19)	clamorous in a day of ill fortune continuous

*M R T

MĀRŪT n.prop.~Marut (a rebellious angel)

2:102 (96)	Babylon's two angels, Harut and Marut

*M R W

MARWAH n.prop.~Marwa (a mountain near Mecca)

2:158 (153)	Safa and Marwa are among the waymarks of God

*M R Y

MIRYAH n.f.~a doubt

11:17 (20)	his promised land is the Fire. So be thou not in doubt of it
11:109 (111)	be thou not in doubt concerning what these men serve

22:55 (54)	the unbelievers will not cease to be in doubt of it
32:23 (23)	be not in doubt concerning the encounter with him
41:54 (54)	are they not in doubt touching the encounter with their Lord?

MĀRÁ vb. (III)~to dispute, to contend; to doubt. (n.vb.) disputation, contenting

b) impf. act. (*yumārī*)

18:22 (22)	do not dispute with them, except in outward disputation
42:18 (17)	those who are in doubt concerning the Hour are indeed in far error
53:12 (12)	what, will you dispute with him what he sees?

f) n.vb. (*mirā'*)

18:22 (22)	do not dispute with them, except in outward disputation

TAMĀRÁ vb. (VI)~to dispute; (also) to doubt [Pk]

a) perf. act.

54:36 (36)	He had warned them of Our assault, but they disputed the warnings

b) impf. act. (*yatamārá*)

53:55 (56)	then which of thy Lord's bounties disputest thou?

IMTARÁ vb. (VIII)~to doubt; to dispute [Pk]. (pcple. act.) one who doubts

b) impf. act. (*yamtarī*)

6:2 (2)	a term is stated with Him; yet thereafter you doubt
15:63 (63)	we have brought thee that concerning which they were doubting
19:34 (35)	that is Jesus, son of Mary, in word of truth, concerning which they are doubting
43:61 (61)	doubt not concerning it, and follow me
44:50 (50)	this is that concerning which you were doubting

g) pcple. act. (*mumtarī*)

2:147 (142)	then be not among the doubters
3:60 (53)	the truth is of your Lord; be not of the doubters
6:114 (114)	so be not thou of the doubters
10:94 (94)	so be not of the doubters

*M R Y M

MARYAM n.prop.~Mary

2:87 (81)	We gave Jesus son of Mary the clear signs
2:253 (254)	We gave Jesus son of Mary the clear signs
3:36 (31)	I have named her Mary, and commend her to Thee
3:37 (32)	'Mary,' he said. 'how comes this to thee?'
3:42 (37)	Mary, God has chosen thee, and purified thee
3:43 (38)	Mary, be obedient to thy Lord, prostrating and bowing before Him
3:44 (39)	they were casting quills which of them should have charge of Mary
3:45 (40)	Mary, God gives thee good tidings of a Word from Him whose name is Messiah
3:45 (40)	whose name is Messiah, Jesus, son of Mary
4:156 (155)	for their unbelief, and their uttering against Mary a mighty calummy

4:157 (156)	we slew the Messiah, Jesus son of Mary, the Messenger of God
4:171 (169)	the Messiah, Jesus son of Mary, was only the Messenger of God
4:171 (169)	[Jesus] was only the Messenger of God, and His Word that He committed to Mary
5:17 (19)	they are unbelievers who say, 'God is the Messiah, Mary's son'
5:17 (19)	if He desires to destroy the Messiah, Mary's son
5:46 (50)	We sent, following in their footsteps, Jesus son of Mary
5:72 (76)	God is the Messiah, Mary's son
5:75 (79)	the Messiah, son of Mary, was only a Messenger
5:78 (82)	by the tongue of David, and Jesus, Mary's son
5:110 (109)	Jesus Son of Mary, remember My blessing upon thee
5:112 (112)	O Jesus son of Mary, is thy Lord able to send down on us
5:114 (114)	said Jesus son of Mary
5:116 (116)	Jesus son of Mary, didst thou say unto men
9:31 (31)	as lords apart from God, and the Messiah, Mary's son
19:16 (16)	mention in the Book Mary when she withdrew from her people
19:27 (28)	Mary, thou hast surely committed a monstrous thing
19:34 (35)	that is Jesus, son of Mary, in word of truth
23:50 (52)	We made Mary's son, and his mother, to be a sign
33:7 (7)	from Noah, and Abraham, Moses, and Jesus, Mary's son
43:57 (57)	when the son of Mary is cited as an example, behold, thy people turn away from it
57:27 (27)	We sent, following, Jesus son of Mary
61:6 (6)	when Jesus son of Mary said
61:14 (14)	be you God's helpers, as Jesus, Mary's son, said to the Apostles
66:12 (12)	Mary, Imran's daughter, who guarded her virginity

*M S D

MASAD n.m.~palm-fibre

111:5 (5)	upon her neck a rope of palm-fibre

*M S Ḥ

MASAḤA vb. (I)~to wipe [Ar]; to rub. (n.vb.) the act of stroking [Ar, Bl], slashing (with a sword) [Pk] or passing one's hand over something [Ali]

c) impv. (*imsaḥ*)

4:43 (46)	then have recourse to wholesome dust and wipe your faces
5:6 (8)	and wipe your heads, and your feet up to the ankles
5:6 (9)	then have recourse to wholesome dust and wipe your faces

f) n.vb. (*masḥ*)

38:33 (32)	and he began to stroke their shanks and necks

MASĪḤ n.prop. (always with the definite article)~The Messiah; Christ [Ali]

3:45 (40)	whose name is Messiah, Jesus, son of Mary
4:157 (156)	we slew the Messiah, Jesus son of Mary
4:171 (169)	the Messiah, Jesus son of Mary, was only the Messenger of God
4:172 (170)	the Messiah will not disdain to be a servant of God

5:17 (19)	they are unbelievers who say, 'God is the Messiah, Mary's son'
5:17 (19)	who then shall overrule God in any way if He desires to destroy the Messiah
5:72 (76)	they are unbelievers who say, 'God is the Messiah, Mary's son'
5:72 (76)	for the Messiah said, 'Children of Israel, serve God'
5:75 (79)	the Messiah, son of Mary, was only a Messenger
9:30 (30)	the Christians say, 'The Messiah is the Son of God'
9:31 (31)	and their monks as lords apart from God, and the Messiah, Mary's son

*M S K

MISK n.com.~musk

83:26 (26)	whose seal is musk

MASSAKA vb. (II)~(with prep. *bi-*) to hold fast to [Ar, Ali]; to make one keep something [Pk]

b) impf. act. (*yumassiku*)

7:170 (169)	those who hold fast to the Book, and perform the prayer

AMSAKA vb. (IV)~to hold, to detain, to retain, to withhold, to hold back; (with prep. *ʿalá*) to seize for someone, to keep; (with prep. *bi-*) to hold fast. (n.vb.) retention. (pcple. act.) one who withholds or retains

a) perf. act.

5:4 (6)	eat what they seize for you
17:100 (102)	yet would you hold back for fear of expending
35:41 (39)	did they remove, none would hold them after Him
67:21 (21)	who is this that shall provide for you if He withholds His provision?

b) impf. act. (*yumsiku*)

2:231 (231)	do not retain them by force, to transgress
16:59 (61)	whether he shall preserve it in humiliation, or trample it into the dust
16:79 (81)	naught holds them but God
22:65 (64)	He holds back heaven lest it should fall
35:2 (2)	whatsoever He withholds, none can loose after Him
35:41 (39)	God holds the heavens and the earth, lest they remove
39:42 (43)	He withholds that against which He has decreed death
60:10 (10)	do not hold fast to the ties of unbelieving women
67:19 (19)	naught holds them but the All-merciful

c) impv. (*amsik*)

2:231 (231)	and they have reached their term, then retain them honourably
4:15 (19)	if they witness, then detain them in their houses
33:37 (37)	keep thy wife to thyself, and fear God
38:39 (38)	this is Our gift; bestow or withhold without reckoning
65:2 (2)	when they have reached their term, retain them honourably

f) n.vb. (*imsāk*)

2:229 (229)	divorce is twice; then honourable retention

g) pcple. act. (*mumsik*)

35:2 (2)	whatsoever mercy God opens to men, none can withhold

39:38 (39)	if He desires mercy for me, shall they withhold His mercy?

ISTAMSAKA vb. (X)~to lay hold of, to hold fast unto. (pcple. act.) one who lays hold of, who holds fast unto

a) perf. act.

2:256 (257)	whosoever disbelieves in idols and believes in God, has laid hold of the most firm handle
31:22 (21)	whosoever submits his will to God, being a good-doer, has laid hold of the most firm handle

c) impv. (*istamsik*)

43:43 (42)	hold thou fast unto that which has been revealed unto thee

g) pcple. act. (*mustamsik*)

43:21 (20)	or did We bring them a Book aforetime to which they hold?

*M S KH

MASAKHA vb. (I)~to change, to transform

a) perf. act.

36:67 (67)	did We will, We would have changed them where they were

*M S S

MASSA vb. (I)~to touch, to befall, to visit (with affliction), to afflict. (n.vb.) a touch

a) perf. act.

2:214 (210)	they were afflicted by misery and hardship
3:140 (134)	if a wound touches you, a like wound already has touched the heathen
7:95 (93)	hardship and happiness visited our fathers
7:188 (188)	I would have acquired much good, and evil would not have touched me
7:201 (200)	the godfearing, when a visitation of Satan troubles them
8:68 (69)	God, there had afflicted you, for what you took, a mighty chastisement
10:12 (13)	when affliction visits a man, he calls Us
10:12 (13)	as if he never called Us to an affliction that visited him
10:21 (22)	We let the people taste mercy after hardship has visited them
11:10 (13)	if We let him taste prosperity after hardship that has visited him
12:88 (88)	O mighty prince, affliction has visited us
15:54 (54)	do you give me good tidings, though old age has smitten me?
16:53 (55)	when affliction visits you it is unto Him that you groan
17:67 (69)	when affliction visits you upon the sea
17:83 (85)	but when evil visits him, he is in despair
21:46 (47)	if but a breath of thy Lord's chastisement touched them
21:83 (83)	behold, affliction has visited me

24:14 (14)	there would have visited you for your mutterings a mighty chastisement
30:33 (32)	when some affliction visits mankind, they call unto their Lord
38:41 (40)	Satan has visited me with weariness
39:8 (11)	when some affliction visits a man, he calls upon his Lord
39:49 (50)	when some affliction visits a man, he calls unto Us
41:49 (49)	when evil visits him, then he is cast down and desperate
41:50 (50)	if We let him taste mercy from Us after hardship that has visited him
41:51 (51)	when evil visits him, he is full of endless prayers
50:38 (37)	what between them is, in six days, and no weariness touched Us
70:20 (20)	when evil visits him, impatient
70:21 (21)	when good visits him, grudging

b) impf. act. (*yamassu*)

2:80 (74)	and they say, 'The Fire shall not touch us'
2:236 (237)	if you divorce women while as yet you have not touched them
2:237 (238)	if you divorce them before you have touched them
3:24 (23)	the Fire shall not touch us, except for a number 34days
3:47 (42)	how shall I have a son seeing no mortal has touched me?
3:120 (116)	if you are visited by good fortune, it vexes them
3:140 (134)	if a wound touches you, a like wound already
3:174 (168)	they returned with blessing and bounty from God, untouched by evil
5:73 (77)	there shall afflict those of them that disbelieve a painful chastisement
6:17 (17)	if God visits thee with affliction none can remove it
6:17 (17)	if He visits thee with good, He is powerful over everything
6:49 (49)	those who cry lies to Our signs, them the chastisement shall visit
7:73 (71)	do not touch her with evil, lest you be seized
10:107 (107)	if God visits thee with affliction, none can remove it
11:48 (50)	then there shall visit them from Us a painful chastisement
11:64 (67)	touch her not with evil, lest you be seized
11:113 (115)	lean not on the evildoers, so that the Fire touches you
15:48 (48)	no fatigue there shall smite them
19:20 (20)	how shall I have a son whom no mortal has touched
19:45 (46)	I fear that some chastisement from the All-merciful will smite thee
24:35 (35)	whose oil wellnigh would shine, even if no fire touched it
26:156 (156)	and do not touch her with malice
33:49 (48)	then divorce them before you touch them
35:35 (32)	wherein no weariness assails us
35:35 (32)	neither fatigue
36:18 (17)	there shall visit you from us a painful chastisement
39:61 (62)	evil shall not visit them, neither shall they sorrow
56:79 (78)	none but the purified shall touch

f) n.vb. (*mass*)

2:275 (276)	except as he rises, whom Satan of the touch prostrates
54:48 (48)	taste now the touch of Sakar

MĀSSA vb. (III)~(n.vb.) mutual touch; (*lā misās*) untouchable

f) n.vb. (*misās*)

20:97 (97)	it shall be thine all this life to cry, 'Untouchable!'

TAMĀSSA vb. (VI)~to touch one another

b) impf. act. (*yatamāssu*)

58:3 (4) they shall set free a slave, before the two of them touch one another
58:4 (5) let him fast two successive months, before the two of them touch one another

*M S W

AMSÁ vb. (IV)~to be or do (something) in the evening hour

b) impf. act. (*yumsī*)

30:17 (16) glory be to God both in your evening hour and in your morning hour

*M SH J

AMSHĀJ n.m. (pl. of *mashīj*)~a mingling

76:2 (2) We created man of a sperm-drop, a mingling

*M SH Y

MASHÁ vb. (I)~to walk, to go. (n.vb.) the act of walking, a walk

a) perf. act.

2:20 (19) whensoever it gives them light, they walk in it

b) impf. act. (*yamshī*)

6:122 (122) We gave him life, and appointed for him a light to walk by
7:195 (194) what, have they feet wherewith they walk
17:37 (39) and walk not in the earth exultantly
17:95 (97) had there been in the earth angels walking at peace
20:40 (41) when thy sister went out, saying
20:128 (128) how many generations We destroyed before them in whose dwelling-places they walk
24:45 (44) and some of them go upon their bellies
24:45 (44) and some of them go upon two feet
24:45 (44) and some of them go upon four
25:7 (8) that he eats food, and goes in the markets
25:20 (22) they ate food, and went in the markets
25:63 (64) the servants of the All-merciful are those who walk in the earth modestly
28:25 (25) then came one of the two women to him, walking modestly
31:18 (17) and walk not in the earth exultantly
32:26 (26) how many generations We destroyed before them in whose dwelling-places they walk
57:28 (28) He will appoint for you a light whereby you shall walk
67:22 (22) what, is he who walks prone upon his face
67:22 (22) better guided than he who walks upright

c) impv. (*imshi*)

38:6 (5) Go! Be steadfast to your gods
67:15 (15) walk in its tracts, and eat of His provision

f) n.vb. (*mashy*)

31:19 (18) be modest in thy walk, and lower thy voice

MASHSHĀʾ n.m.~one who goes about with slander

68:11 (11) backbiter, going about with slander

*M Ṣ R

MIṢR n.prop.~Egypt

2:61 (58) get you down to Egypt; you shall have there that you demanded
10:87 (87) take you, for your people, in Egypt certain houses
12:21 (21) he that bought him, being of Egypt, said to his wife
12:99 (100) enter you into Egypt, if God will, in security
43:51 (50) O my people, do I not possess the kingdom of Egypt

*M T ᶜ

MATĀᶜ n.m. (pl. *amtiᶜah*)~provision, baggage, things, belongings; enjoyment, joy

2:36 (34) in the earth a sojourn shall be yours, and enjoyment for a time
2:236 (237) yet make provision for them, the affluent man according to his means
2:240 (241) for their wives, provision for a year without expulsion
2:241 (242) there shall be for divorced women provision honourable
3:14 (12) that is the enjoyment of the present life
3:185 (182) the present life is but the joy of delusion
3:197 (196) a little enjoyment, then their refuge is Gehenna
4:77 (79) say: 'The enjoyment of this world is little'
4:102 (103) the unbelievers wish that you should be heedless of your weapons and your baggage
5:96 (97) permitted to you is the game of the sea and the food of it, as a provision
7:24 (23) in the earth a sojourn shall be yours, and enjoyment for a time
9:38 (38) the enjoyment of this present life, compared with the world to come
10:23 (24) the enjoyment of this present life, then unto Us you shall return
10:70 (71) some enjoyment in this world; then unto Us they shall return
11:3 (3) He will give you fair enjoyment unto a term stated
12:17 (17) we went running races, and left Joseph behind with our things
12:65 (65) when they opened their things, they found their merchandise
12:79 (79) any other but him in whose possession we found the goods
13:17 (18) fire, being desirous of ornament or ware
13:26 (26) this present life, beside the world to come, is naught but passing enjoyment
16:80 (82) of their hair furnishing and an enjoyment for a while
16:117 (118) a little enjoyment, then for them awaits a painful chastisement
21:111 (111) haply it is a trial for you and an enjoyment for a time
24:29 (29) there is no fault in you that you enter houses uninhabited wherein enjoyment is for you
28:60 (60) whatever thing you have been given is the enjoyment of the present life

28:61 (61)	him to whom We have given the enjoyment of the present life
33:53 (53)	when you ask his wives for any object, ask them from behind a curtain
36:44 (44)	save as a mercy from Us, and enjoyment for a while
40:39 (42)	surely this present life is but a passing enjoyment
42:36 (34)	whatever thing you have been given is the enjoyment of the present life
43:35 (34)	surely all this is but the enjoyment of the present life
56:73 (72)	We Ourselves made it for a reminder, and a boon to the desert-dwellers
57:20 (20)	the present life is but the joy of delusion
79:33 (33)	an enjoyment for you and your flocks
80:32 (32)	an enjoyment for you and your flocks

MATTAʿA vb. (II)~to give enjoyment; to make provision

a) perf. act.

10:98 (98)	We gave unto them enjoyment for a time
15:88 (88)	stretch not thine eyes to that We have given pairs of them to enjoy
20:131 (131)	stretch not thine eyes to that We have given pairs of them to enjoy
21:44 (45)	nay, but Ourselves gave these and their fathers enjoyment of days
25:18 (19)	Thou gavest them and their fathers enjoyment of days
26:205 (205)	what thinkest thou? If We give them enjoyment of days
28:61 (61)	like him to whom We have given the enjoyment of the present life
37:148 (148)	so We gave them enjoyment for a while
43:29 (28)	I gave these and their fathers enjoyment of days

b) impf. act. (*yumattiʿu*)

2:126 (120)	whoso disbelieves, to him I shall give enjoyment a little
11:3 (3)	repent to Him, and He will give you fair enjoyment
11:48 (50)	We shall give them enjoyment, then there shall visit them from Us a painful chastisement
31:24 (23)	to them We give enjoyment a little
33:28 (28)	I will make you provision, and set you free with kindliness

c) impv. (*mattiʿ*)

2:236 (237)	yet make provision for them, the affluent man
33:49 (48)	so make provision for them, and set them free

e) impf. pass. (*yumattaʿu*)

26:207 (207)	what will it then avail them, the enjoyment of days they were given
33:16 (16)	you will be given enjoyment of days then but little

TAMATTAʿA vb. (V)~to enjoy, to take joy

a) perf. act.

2:196 (192)	whosoever enjoys the Visitation until the Pilgrimage

b) impf. act. (*yatamattaʿu*)

15:3 (3)	leave them to eat, and to take their joy
29:66 (66)	they may be ungrateful for what We have given them, and take their enjoyment
47:12 (13)	as for the unbelievers, they take their enjoyment and eat as cattle eat

c) impv. (*tamatta*ᶜ)

11:65 (68)	take your joy in your habitation three days
14:30 (35)	take your joy! Your homecoming shall be — the Fire
16:55 (57)	so take your joy; certainly you will soon know
30:34 (33)	take your enjoyment; certainly you will soon know
39:8 (11)	enjoy thy unbelief a little
51:43 (43)	take your enjoyment for a while
77:46 (46)	eat and take your joy a little; you are sinners

ISTAMTAᶜA vb. (X)~to enjoy; to profit one from the other [Ar]

a) perf. act.

4:24 (28)	such wives as you enjoy thereby, give them their wages apportionate
6:128 (128)	we have profited each of the other
9:69 (70)	they took enjoyment in their share
9:69 (70)	so do you take enjoyment in your share
9:69 (70)	as those before you took enjoyment in their share
46:20 (19)	and you took your enjoyment in them

*M T N

MATĪN n.m. (adj)~sure, strong, powerful; Ever-sure (Divine attribute)

7:183 (182)	I respite them — assuredly My guile is sure
51:58 (58)	God is the All-provider, the Possessor of Strength, the Ever-Sure
68:45 (45)	I shall respite them — assuredly My guile is sure

*M TH L

AMTHAL n.m. (comp. adj.; f. *muthlá*)~justest, best

20:63 (66)	and to extirpate your justest way
20:104 (104)	what they will say, when the justest of them in the way will say

MATHAL n.m. (pl. *amthāl*)~likeness, similitude, example

2:17 (16)	the likeness of them is as the (likeness) of a man
2:17 (16)	the (likeness) of them is as the likeness of a man
2:26 (24)	God is not ashamed to strike a similitude even of a gnat
2:26 (24)	what did God desire by this for a similitude?
2:171 (166)	the likeness of those who disbelieve
2:171 (166)	the likeness of one who shouts to that which hears nothing
2:214 (210)	without there had come upon you the like of those who passed away
2:261 (263)	the likeness of those who expend their wealth in the way of God
2:261 (263)	is as the likeness of a grain of corn that sprouts seven ears
2:264 (266)	the likeness of him
2:264 (266)	is as the likeness of a smooth rock on which is soil
2:265 (267)	the likeness of those who expend their wealth

2:265 (267)	is as the likeness of a garden upon a hill
3:59 (52)	truly, the likeness of Jesus, in God's sight
3:59 (52)	is as Adam's likeness
3:117 (113)	the likeness of that they expend in this present life
3:117 (113)	is as the likeness of a freezing blast that smites
6:122 (122)	among the people as one whose likeness is in the shadows
7:176 (175)	so the likeness of him
7:176 (175)	is as the likeness of a dog
7:176 (175)	that is that people's likeness who cried lies to Our signs
7:177 (176)	an evil likeness is the (likeness) of the people who cried lies to Our signs
10:24 (25)	the likeness of this present life is as water
11:24 (26)	the likeness of the two parties is as the man blind and deaf
11:24 (26)	are they equal in likeness?
13:17 (18)	even so God strikes His similitudes
13:35 (35)	the likeness of Paradise, that is promised to the godfearing
14:18 (21)	the likeness of those who disbelieve in their Lord
14:24 (29)	hast thou not seen how God has struck a similitude?
14:25 (30)	so God strikes similitudes for men
14:26 (31)	the likeness of a corrupt word is as a corrupt tree
14:45 (47)	how We struck similitudes for you
16:60 (62)	those who believe not in the world to come, theirs is the evil likeness
16:60 (62)	God's is the loftiest likeness
16:74 (76)	so strike not any similitudes for God
16:75 (77)	God has struck a similitude: a servant possessed by his master
16:76 (78)	God has struck a similitude: two men, one of them dumb
16:112 (113)	God has struck a similitude: a city that was secure
17:48 (51)	behold, how they strike similitudes for thee
17:89 (91)	We have indeed turned about for men in this Koran every manner of similitude
18:32 (31)	and strike for them a similitude: two men
18:45 (43)	and strike for them the similitude of the present life
18:54 (52)	We have indeed turned about for men in this Koran every manner of similitude
22:73 (72)	a similitude is struck; so give you ear to it
24:34 (34)	and an example of those who passed away before you
24:35 (35)	the likeness of His Light is as a niche wherein is a lamp
24:35 (35)	God strikes similitudes for men
25:9 (10)	behold, how they strike similitudes for thee
25:33 (35)	they bring not to thee any similitude but that We bring thee the truth
25:39 (41)	for each We struck similitudes, and each We ruined utterly
29:41 (40)	the likeness of those who have taken to them protectors
29:41 (40)	is as the likeness of the spider that takes to itself a house
29:43 (42)	and those similitudes — We strike them for the people
30:27 (26)	His is the loftiest likeness in the heavens and the earth
30:28 (27)	He has struck for you a similitude from yourselves
30:58 (58)	We have struck for the people in this Koran every manner of similitude
36:13 (12)	strike for them a similitude — the inhabitants of the city
36:78 (78)	he has struck for Us a similitude and forgotten his creation
39:27 (28)	We have struck for the people in this Koran every manner of similitude
39:29 (30)	God has struck a similitude — a man in whom partners disagreeing share
39:29 (30)	are the two equal in likeness?
43:8 (7)	the example of the ancients passed away
43:17 (16)	tidings of that he has likened to the All-merciful
43:56 (56)	We appointed them for an example to later folk
43:57 (57)	when the son of Mary is cited as an example, behold
43:59 (59)	He is only a servant We blessed, and We made him to be an example
47:3 (3)	even so God strikes their similitudes for men

47:15 (16)	this is the similitude of Paradise which the godfearing have been promised
48:29 (29)	that is their likeness in the Torah
48:29 (29)	and their likeness in the Gospel
56:23 (22)	as the likeness of hidden pearls
57:20 (19)	it is as a rain whose vegetation pleases the unbelievers
59:15 (15)	like those who a short time before them tasted the mischief of their action
59:16 (16)	like Satan, when he said to man, 'Disbelieve'
59:21 (21)	those similitudes — We strike them for men
62:5 (5)	the likeness of those who have been loaded with the Torah
62:5 (5)	the likeness of an ass carrying books
62:5 (5)	evil is the likeness of the people who have cried lies to God's signs
66:10 (10)	God has struck a similitude for the unbelievers — the wife of Noah
66:11 (11)	God has struck a similitude for the believers — the wife of Pharaoh
74:31 (33)	what did God intend by this as a similitude?

MATHULĀT n.f. (pl. of *mathulah*)~an example [Ar, Bl]; exemplary punishment [Pk, Ali]

13:6 (7)	yet there have passed away before them examples

MITHL n.m. (pl. *amthāl*)~likeness; like, as, similar

2:23 (21)	then bring a sura like it, and call your witnesses
2:106 (100)	We bring a better or the like of it
2:113 (107)	so too the ignorant say the like of them
2:118 (112)	so spoke those before them as these men say
2:137 (131)	if they believe in the like of that you believe in
2:194 (190)	do you commit aggression against him like as he has committed against you
2:228 (228)	women have such honourable rights as obligations
2:233 (233)	the heir has a like duty
2:275 (276)	trafficking is like usury
3:13 (11)	they saw them twice the like of them
3:73 (66)	that anyone should be given the like of what you have been given
3:140 (134)	if a wound touches you, a like wound already has touched the heathen
3:165 (159)	when an affliction visited you, and you had visited twice over the like of it
4:11 (12)	to the male the like of the portion of two females
4:140 (139)	else you will surely be like to them
4:176 (175)	the male shall receive the portion of two females
5:31 (34)	am I unable to be as this raven
5:36 (40)	though they possessed all that is in the earth, and the like of it with it
5:95 (96)	there shall be recompense — the like of what he has slain
6:38 (38)	but they are nations like unto yourselves
6:93 (93)	I will send down the like of what God has sent down
6:124 (124)	we will not believe until we are given the like of what God's Messengers were given
6:160 (161)	whoso brings a good deed shall have ten the like of it
6:160 (161)	whoso brings an evil deed shall only be recompensed the like of it
7:169 (168)	if chance goods the like of them come to them, they will take them
7:194 (193)	those on whom you call apart from God, are servants the likes of you
8:31 (31)	if we wished, we could say the like of this
10:27 (28)	the recompense of an evil deed shall be the like of it
10:38 (39)	say: 'Then produce a sura like it'
10:102 (102)	so do they watch and wait for aught but the like of the days of those who passed away
11:13 (16)	then bring you ten suras the like of it, forged
11:27 (29)	we see thee not other than a mortal like ourselves
11:89 (91)	so that theresmite you the like of what smote the people of Noah

13:17 (18)	out of that rises a scum the like of it
13:18 (18)	if they possessed all that is in the earth, and the like of it with it
14:10 (12)	you are nothing but mortals, like us
14:11 (13)	we are nothing but mortals, like you
16:126 (127)	if you chastise, chastise even as you have been chastised
17:88 (90)	if men and jinn banded together to produce the like of this Koran
17:88 (90)	they would never produce its like
17:99 (101)	who created the heavens and earth, is powerful to create the like of them
18:109 (109)	though We brought replenishment the like of it
18:110 (110)	I am only a mortal the like of you
20:58 (60)	We shall assuredly bring thee sorcery the like of it
21:3 (3)	is this aught but a mortal like to yourselves?
21:84 (84)	We gave his people, and the like of them with them, mercy
22:60 (59)	whosoever chastises after the manner that he was chastised
23:24 (24)	this is naught but a mortal like yourselves
23:33 (34)	this is naught but a mortal like yourselves
23:34 (36)	if you obey a mortal like yourselves, then you will be losers
23:47 (49)	shall we believe two mortals like ourselves
23:81 (83)	they said the like of what the ancients said
24:17 (16)	God admonishes you, that you shall never repeat the like of it again
26:154 (154)	thou art naught but a mortal, like us
26:186 (186)	thou art naught but a mortal, like us
28:48 (48)	why has he not been given the like of that Moses was given?
28:79 (79)	would that we possessed the like of that Korah has been given
35:14 (15)	none can tell thee like One who is aware
36:15 (14)	you are naught but mortals like us
36:42 (42)	We have created for them the like of it whereon they ride
36:81 (81)	is not He, who created the heavens and earth, able to create the like of them?
37:61 (59)	and for the like of this let the workers work
38:43 (42)	We gave to him his family, and the like of them with them
39:47 (48)	if the evildoers possessed all that is in the earth, and the like of it with it
40:30 (31)	truly I fear for you the like of the day of the parties
40:31 (32)	the like of the case of Noah's people, Ad, Thamood
40:40 (43)	whosoever does an evil deed shall be recompensed only with the like of it
41:6 (5)	I am only a mortal, like you are
41:13 (12)	I warn you of a thunderbolt like to the thunderbolt of Ad and Thamood
42:11 (9)	like Him there is naught
42:40 (38)	the recompense of evil is evil the like of it
46:10 (9)	a witness from among the Children of Israel bears witness to its like
47:10 (11)	the unbelievers shall have the likes thereof
47:38 (40)	another people instead of you, then they will not be your likes
51:23 (23)	it is as surely true as that you have speech
51:59 (59)	the evildoers shall have their portion, like the portion of their fellows
52:34 (34)	then let them bring a discourse like it
56:61 (61)	that We may exchange the likes of you
60:11 (11)	give those whose wives have gone away the like of what they have expended
65:12 (12)	it is God who created seven heavens, and of earth their like
76:28 (28)	when We will, We shall exchange their likes
89:8 (7)	the like of which was never created in the land

TAMĀTHĪL n.m. (pl. of *timthāl*)~statues, images

21:52 (53)	what are these statues unto which you are cleaving?
34:13 (12)	fashioning for him whatsoever he would — places of worship, statues

TAMATHTHALA vb. (V)~to present oneself [Ar]; to assume a likeness [Pk]; to appear as someone else [Ali]; to take the form of (someone else) [Bl]

a) perf. act.

19:17 (17)	then We sent unto her Our Spirit that presented himself to her a man without fault

*M Ṭ R

MAṬARA vb. (I)~(n.vb.) rain

f) n.vb. (*maṭar*)

4:102 (103)	there is no fault in you, if rain molests you
7:84 (82)	and We rained down upon them a rain
25:40 (42)	they have come by the city that was rained on by an evil rain
26:173 (173)	We rained on them a rain
26:173 (173)	and evil is the rain of them that are warned
27:58 (59)	and We rained on them a rain
27:58 (59)	and evil indeed is the rain of them that are warned

AMṬARA vb. (IV)~to rain down. (pcple. act.) that which gives rain

a) perf. act.

7:84 (82)	and We rained down upon them a rain
11:82 (84)	uppermost nethermost, and rained on it stones of baked clay
15:74 (74)	and rained on it stones of baked clay
26:173 (173)	and We rained on them a rain
27:58 (59)	and We rained on them a rain

c) impv. (*amṭir*)

8:32 (32)	if this be indeed the truth from Thee, then rain down upon us stones

d) perf. pass. (*umṭira*)

25:40 (42)	they have come by the city that was rained on by an evil rain

g) pcple. act. (*mumṭir*)

46:24 (23)	this is a cloud, that shall give us rain

*M Ṭ W

TAMAṬṬÁ vb. (V)~to go or walk arrogantly or haughtily

b) impf. act. (*yatamaṭṭá*)

75:33 (33)	then he went to his household arrogantly

*M W H

MĀʾ n.m.~water; (80:25) rain

2:22 (20)	and sent down out of heaven water, wherewith He brought forth fruits
2:74 (69)	and others split, so that water issues from them
2:164 (159)	the water God sends down from heaven therewith reviving the earth
4:43 (46)	and you can find no water, then have recourse to wholesome dust
5:6 (9)	and you can find no water, then have recourse to wholesome dust
6:99 (99)	it is He who sent down out of heaven water
7:50 (48)	pour on us water, or of that God has provided you
7:57 (55)	and therewith send down water, and bring forth therewith all the fruits
8:11 (11)	and sending down on you water from heaven, to purify you thereby
10:24 (25)	the likeness of this present life is as water that We send down out of heaven
11:7 (9)	and His Throne was upon the waters
11:43 (45)	I will take refuge in a mountain, that shall defend me from the water
11:44 (46)	earth, swallow thy waters; and, heaven, abate
11:44 (46)	and the waters subsided
13:4 (4)	palms in pairs, and palms single, watered with one water
13:14 (15)	it is as a man who stretches out his hands to water
13:17 (18)	He sends down out of heaven water
14:16 (19)	and he is given to drink of oozing pus
14:32 (37)	and sent down out of heaven water
15:22 (22)	and We send down out of heaven water
16:10 (10)	it is He who sends down to you out of heaven water
16:65 (67)	and it is God who sends down out of heaven water
18:29 (28)	they will be succoured with water like molten copper
18:41 (39)	in the morning the water of it will be sunk into the earth
18:45 (43)	it is as water that We send down out of heaven
20:53 (55)	threaded roads for you, and sent down water out of heaven
21:30 (31)	and of water fashioned every living thing
22:5 (5)	then, when We send down water upon it, it quivers
22:63 (62)	hast thou not seen how that God has sent down out of heaven water
23:18 (18)	We sent down out of heaven water in measure
24:39 (39)	their works are as a mirage in a spacious plain which the man athirst supposes to be water
24:45 (44)	God has created every beast of water
25:48 (50)	We sent down from heaven pure water
25:54 (56)	it is He who created of water a mortal
27:60 (61)	He who created the heavens and earth, and sent down for you out of heaven water
28:23 (22)	when he came to the waters of Midian he found a company of the people there
29:63 (63)	who sends down out of heaven water, and therewith revives the earth
30:24 (23)	and that He sends down out of heaven water
31:10 (9)	We sent down out of heaven water
32:8 (7)	then He fashioned his progeny of an extraction of mean water
32:27 (27)	have they not seen how We drive the water to the dry land
35:27 (25)	hast thou not seen how that God sends down out of heaven water
39:21 (22)	hast thou not seen how that God has sent down out of heaven water
41:39 (39)	then, when We send down water upon it, it quivers
43:11 (10)	who sent down out of heaven water in measure
47:15 (16)	therein are rivers of water unstaling
47:15 (17)	such as are given to drink boiling water
50:9 (9)	We sent down out of heaven water blessed
54:11 (11)	then We opened the gates of heaven unto water torrential

54:12 (12)	and the waters met for a matter decreed
54:28 (28)	tell them that the water is to be divided between them
56:31 (30)	and outpoured waters
56:68 (67)	have you considered the water you drink?
67:30 (30)	what think you? If in the morning your water should have vanished
67:30 (30)	then who would bring you running water?
69:11 (11)	when the waters rose, We bore you in the running ship
72:16 (16)	We would give them to drink of water copious
77:20 (20)	did We not create you of a mean water
77:27 (27)	sated you with sweetest water
78:14 (14)	and have sent down out of the rain-clouds water cascading
79:31 (31)	therefrom brought forth its waters and its pastures
80:25 (25)	We poured out the rains abundantly
86:6 (6)	he was created of gushing water

*M W J

MĀJA vb. (I)~to surge

b) impf. act. (*yamūju*)

18:99 (99)	upon that day We shall leave them surging on one another

MAWJ n.m. (coll)~wave(s), billow(s)

10:22 (23)	and waves come on them from every side
11:42 (44)	so it ran with them amid waves like mountains
11:43 (45)	the waves came between them, and he was among the drowned
24:40 (40)	or they are as shadows upon a sea obscure covered by a billow
24:40 (40)	above which is a billow
31:32 (31)	when the waves cover them like shadows they call upon God

*M W L

MĀL n.m. (pl. *amwāl*)~goods, wealth, property, substance, possessions, riches; (*ra'ṣ al-māl*) principal

2:155 (150)	We will try you with something of fear and hunger, and diminution of goods
2:177 (172)	to give of one's substance, however cherished, to kinsmen, and orphans
2:188 (184)	consume not your goods between you in vanity
2:188 (184)	that you may sinfully consume a portion of other men's goods
2:247 (248)	seeing he has not been given amplitude of wealth
2:261 (263)	the likeness of those who expend their wealth in the way of God
2:262 (264)	those who expend their wealth in the way of God
2:264 (266)	as one who expends of his substance to show off to men
2:265 (267)	but the likeness of those who expend their wealth, seeking God's good pleasure
2:274 (275)	those who expend their wealth night and day, secretly and in public
2:279 (279)	if you repent, you shall have your principal
3:10 (8)	as for the unbelievers, their riches will not avail them
3:116 (112)	as for the unbelievers, their riches shall not avail them
3:186 (183)	you shall surely be tried in your possessions and your selves
4:2 (2)	give the orphans their property
4:2 (2)	and devour not their property with your (property)

4:2 (2)	and devour not their (property) with your property
4:5 (4)	do not give to fools their property that God has assigned to you to manage
4:6 (5)	if you perceive in them right judgment, deliver to them their property
4:6 (7)	when you deliver to them their property, take witnesses over them
4:10 (11)	those who devour the property of orphans unjustly
4:24 (28)	lawful for you, beyond all that, is that you may seek, using your wealth
4:29 (33)	O believers, consume not your goods between you in vanity
4:34 (38)	one of them over another, and for that they have expended of their property
4:38 (42)	such as expend of their substance to show off to men
4:95 (97)	those who struggle in the path of God with their possessions and their selves
4:95 (97)	God has preferred in rank those who struggle with their possessions
4:161 (159)	and consuming the wealth of the people in vanity
6:152 (153)	and that you approach not the property of the orphan
8:28 (28)	know that your wealth and your children are a trial
8:36 (36)	the unbelievers expend their wealth to bar from God's way
8:72 (73)	and struggled with their possessions and their selves in the way of God
9:20 (20)	those who believe, and have emigrated, and have struggled in the way of God with their possessions
9:24 (24)	your possessions that you have gained
9:34 (34)	many of the rabbis and monks indeed consume the goods of the people
9:41 (41)	struggle in God's way with your possessions and your selves
9:44 (44)	ask not leave of thee, that they may struggle with their possessions
9:55 (55)	let not their possessions or their children please thee
9:69 (70)	those before you, who were stronger than you in might, and more abundant in wealth
9:81 (82)	and were averse to struggle with their possessions and their selves
9:85 (86)	let not their possessions and their children please thee
9:88 (89)	the Messenger, and the believers with him, have struggled with their possessions
9:103 (104)	take of their wealth a freewill offering, to purify
9:111 (112)	God has bought from the believers their selves and their possessions
10:88 (88)	Thou hast given to Pharaoh and his Council adornment and possessions
10:88 (88)	Our Lord, obliterate their possessions
11:29 (31)	O my people, I do not ask of you wealth for this
11:87 (89)	or to do as we will with our goods
17:6 (6)	We succoured you with wealth and children
17:34 (36)	do not approach the property of the orphan save in the fairest manner
17:64 (66)	share with them in their wealth and their children
18:34 (32)	I have more abundance of wealth than thou
18:39 (37)	if thou seest me, that I am less than thou in wealth and children
18:46 (44)	wealth and sons are the adornment of the present world
19:77 (80)	I shall be given wealth and children
23:55 (57)	do they think that We succour them with of wealth and children
24:33 (33)	give them of the wealth of God that He has given you
26:88 (88)	the day when neither wealth nor sons shall profit
27:36 (36)	what, would you succour me with wealth
30:39 (38)	that it may increase upon the people's wealth
33:27 (27)	He bequeathed upon you their lands, their habitations, and their possessions
34:35 (34)	we are more abundant in wealth and children
34:37 (36)	it is not your wealth nor your children that shall bring you nigh in nearness to Us
47:36 (38)	He will give you your wages, and will not ask of you your goods
48:11 (11)	we were occupied by our possessions and our families
49:15 (15)	and have struggled with their possessions and their selves in the way of God
51:19 (19)	and the beggar and the outcast had a share in their wealth
57:20 (19)	a cause for boasting among you, and a rivalry in wealth and children

58:17 (18)	neither their riches nor their children shall avail them anything
59:8 (8)	it is for the poor emigrants, who were expelled from their habitations and their possessions
61:11 (11)	struggle in the way of God with your possessions and your selves
63:9 (9)	let not your possessions neither your children divert you from God's remembrance
64:15 (15)	your wealth and your children are only a trial
68:14 (14)	because he has wealth and sons
69:28 (28)	my wealth has not availed me
70:24 (24)	those in whose wealth is a right known
71:12 (11)	and will succour you with wealth and sons
71:21 (20)	him whose wealth and children increase him only in loss
74:12 (12)	and appointed for him ample wealth
89:20 (21)	and you love wealth with an ardent love
90:6 (6)	I have consumed wealth abundant
92:11 (11)	his wealth shall not avail him when he perishes
92:18 (18)	even he who gives his wealth to purify himself
104:2 (2)	who has gathered riches and counted them over
104:3 (3)	thinking his riches have made him immortal
111:2 (2)	his wealth avails him not, neither what he has earned

*M W R

MĀRA vb. (I)~to rock, to heave, to spin. (n.vb.) the act of heaving, rocking or spinning

b) impf. act. (*yamūru*)

52:9 (9)	upon the day when heaven spins dizzily
67:16 (16)	will not cause the earth to swallow you, the while it rocks

f) n.vb. (*mawr*)

52:9 (9)	upon the day when heaven spins <dizzily>

*M W S

MŪSÁ n.prop.~Moses

2:51 (48)	when We appointed with Moses forty nights
2:53 (50)	when We gave to Moses the Book and the Salvation
2:54 (51)	when Moses said to his people, My people, you have done wrong
2:55 (52)	Moses, we will not believe thee
2:60 (57)	when Moses sought water for his people
2:61 (58)	Moses, we will not endure one sort of food
2:67 (63)	when Moses said to his people, God commands you to sacrifice a cow
2:87 (81)	We gave to Moses the Book
2:92 (86)	and Moses came to you with the clear signs
2:108 (102)	do you desire to question your Messenger as Moses was questioned
2:136 (130)	and that which was given to Moses and Jesus
2:246 (247)	hast thou not regarded the Council of the Children of Israel, after Moses
2:248 (249)	a remnant of what the folk of Moses and Aaron's folk left behind
3:84 (78)	in that which was given to Moses and Jesus, and the Prophets

4:153 (152)	and they asked Moses for greater than that
4:153 (152)	and We bestowed upon Moses a clear authority
4:164 (162)	and unto Moses God spoke directly
5:20 (23)	when Moses said to his people, O my people, remember God's blessing
5:22 (25)	Moses, there are people in it
5:24 (27)	Moses, we will never enter it
6:84 (84)	of his seed David and Solomon, Job and Joseph, Moses
6:91 (91)	who sent down the Book that Moses brought as a light and a guidance
6:154 (155)	then We gave Moses the Book, complete
7:103 (101)	then We sent, after them, Moses with Our signs to Pharaoh
7:104 (102)	Moses said, 'Pharaoh, I am a Messenger from the Lord of all Being'
7:115 (112)	they said, 'Moses, wilt thou cast, or shall we be the casters?'
7:117 (114)	and We revealed to Moses: 'Cast thy staff'
7:122 (119)	the Lord of Moses and Aaron
7:127 (124)	wilt thou leave Moses and his people to work corruption in the land
7:128 (125)	said Moses to his people, 'Pray for succour to God'
7:131 (128)	if any evil smote them, they would augur ill by Moses and those with him
7:134 (131)	Moses, pray to thy Lord for us by the covenant
7:138 (134)	Moses, make for us a god, as they have gods
7:142 (138)	We appointed with Moses thirty nights and We completed them with ten
7:142 (138)	Moses said to his brother Aaron, 'Be my successor'
7:143 (139)	when Moses came to Our appointed time
7:143 (139)	He made it crumble to dust; and Moses fell down swooning
7:144 (141)	Moses, I have chosen thee above all men for My Messages
7:148 (146)	the people of Moses took to them, after him, of their ornaments a Calf
7:150 (149)	when Moses returned to his people, angry and sorrowful
7:154 (153)	when Moses' anger abated in him, he took the Tablets
7:155 (154)	Moses chose of his people seventy men for Our appointed time
7:159 (159)	of the people of Moses there is a nation who guide by the truth
7:160 (160)	We revealed to Moses, when his people asked him for water
10:75 (76)	We sent forth, after them, Moses and Aaron to Pharaoh
10:77 (78)	Moses said, 'What, do you say this to the truth'
10:80 (80)	then, when the sorcerers came, Moses said to them
10:81 (81)	Moses said, 'What you have brought is sorcery'
10:83 (83)	so none believed in Moses, save a seed of his people
10:84 (84)	Moses said, 'O my people, if you believe in God'
10:87 (87)	and We revealed to Moses and his brother
10:88 (88)	Moses said, 'Our Lord, Thou hast given to Pharaoh and his Council adornment'
11:17 (20)	before him is the Book of Moses for an ensample
11:96 (99)	We sent Moses with Our signs, and a manifest authority
11:110 (112)	and We gave Moses the Book
14:5 (5)	and We sent Moses with Our signs
14:6 (6)	when Moses said to his people, Remember God's blessing
14:8 (8)	Moses said, 'If you are thankless, you and whoso is on earth'
17:2 (2)	We gave Moses the Book, and made it a guidance
17:101 (103)	and We gave Moses nine signs
17:101 (103)	Pharaoh said to him, 'Moses, I think thou art bewitched'
18:60 (59)	when Moses said to his page, I will not give up
18:66 (65)	Moses said to him, 'Shall I follow thee so that thou teachest me'
19:51 (52)	and mention in the Book Moses
20:9 (8)	hast thou received the story of Moses?
20:11 (11)	when he came to it, a voice cried, 'Moses'
20:17 (18)	what is that, Moses, thou hast in thy right hand?
20:19 (20)	said He, 'Cast it down, Moses!'
20:36 (36)	said He, 'Thou art granted, Moses, thy petition'

20:40 (42)	thou didst sojourn, then camest hither, Moses
20:49 (51)	Pharaoh said, 'Who is your Lord, Moses?'
20:57 (59)	'Hast thou come, Moses,' he said, 'to expel us'
20:61 (63)	Moses said to them, 'O beware! Forge not a lie'
20:65 (68)	Moses, either thou wilt cast, or we shall be the first to cast
20:67 (70)	and Moses conceived a fear within him
20:70 (73)	'We believe,' they said, 'in the Lord of Aaron and Moses'
20:77 (79)	We revealed unto Moses, Go with My servants by night
20:83 (85)	what has sped thee far from thy people, Moses?
20:86 (88)	then Moses returned very angry and sorrowful to his people
20:88 (90)	this is your god, and the god of Moses
20:91 (93)	'We will not cease,' they said, 'to cleave to it, until Moses returns to us'
21:48 (49)	We gave Moses and Aaron the Salvation and a Radiance
22:44 (43)	and the men of Midian; to Moses also they cried lies
23:45 (47)	We sent Moses and his brother Aaron with Our signs
23:49 (51)	and We gave Moses the Book
25:35 (37)	We gave Moses the Book
26:10 (9)	when thy Lord called to Moses, Go to the people of the evildoers
26:43 (42)	Moses said to them, 'Cast you down what you will cast'
26:45 (44)	then Moses cast his staff
26:48 (47)	the Lord of Moses and Aaron
26:52 (52)	We revealed unto Moses, Go with My servants by night
26:61 (61)	the companions of Moses said, 'We are overtaken!'
26:63 (63)	then We revealed to Moses, Strike with thy staff the sea
26:65 (65)	We delivered Moses and those with him all together
27:7 (7)	when Moses said to his people I observe a fire
27:9 (9)	Moses, behold, it is I, God, the All-mighty
27:10 (10)	Moses, fear not
28:3 (2)	We will recite to thee something of the tiding of Moses and Pharaoh
28:7 (6)	so We revealed to Moses' mother, 'Suckle him'
28:10 (9)	on the morrow the heart of Moses' mother became empty
28:15 (14)	Moses struck him, and despatched him, and said
28:18 (17)	Moses said to him, 'Clearly thou art a quarreller'
28:19 (18)	the man said, 'Moses, dost thou desire to slay me'
28:20 (19)	Moses, the Council are conspiring to slay thee
28:29 (29)	when Moses had accomplished the term and departed with his household
28:30 (30)	Moses, I am God, the Lord of all Being
28:31 (31)	Moses, come forward, and fear not
28:36 (36)	when Moses came to them with Our signs, clear signs
28:37 (37)	Moses said, 'My Lord knows very well who comes with the guidance'
28:38 (38)	make me a tower, that I may mount up to Moses' God
28:43 (43)	and We gave Moses the Book
28:44 (44)	thou wast not upon the western side when We decreed to Moses the commandment
28:48 (48)	why has he not been given the like of that Moses was given?
28:48 (48)	did they not disbelieve also in what Moses was given aforetime?
28:76 (76)	now Korah was of the people of Moses
29:39 (38)	Moses came to them with the clear signs
32:23 (23)	indeed, We gave Moses the Book
33:7 (7)	Moses, and Jesus, Mary's son; We took from them a solemn compact
33:69 (69)	O believers, be not as those who hurt Moses
37:114 (114)	We also favoured Moses and Aaron
37:120 (120)	Peace be upon Moses and Aaron
40:23 (24)	We also sent Moses with Our signs
40:26 (27)	let me slay Moses, and let him call to his Lord
40:27 (28)	Moses said, 'I take refuge in my Lord and your Lord'

40:37 (39)	and look upon Moses' God
40:53 (56)	We also gave Moses the guidance
41:45 (45)	and We gave Moses the Book
42:13 (11)	We have revealed to thee, and that We charged Abraham with, Moses and Jesus
43:46 (45)	We also sent Moses with Our signs to Pharaoh and his Council
46:12 (11)	yet before it was the Book of Moses for a model and a mercy
46:30 (29)	we have heard a Book that was sent down after Moses
51:38 (38)	and also in Moses, when We sent him unto Pharaoh, with a clear authority
53:36 (37)	has he not been told of what is in the scrolls of Moses
61:5 (5)	when Moses said to his people, O my people, why do you hurt me
79:15 (15)	hast thou received the story of Moses?
87:19 (19)	the scrolls of Abraham and Moses

*M W T

MĀTA vb. (I)~to die, to be dead. (n.vb.) death

a) perf. act.

2:161 (156)	those who disbelieve, and die disbelieving
3:91 (85)	those who disbelieve, and die disbelieving
3:144 (138)	if he should die or is slain, will you turn about on your heels?
3:156 (150)	they had been with us, they would not have died
3:157 (151)	if you are slain or die in God's way
3:158 (152)	if you die or are slain, it is unto God you shall be mustered
9:84 (85)	pray thou never over any one of them when he is dead
9:84 (85)	they disbelieved in God and His Messenger, and died while they were ungodly
9:125 (126)	they have died while they were unbelievers
19:23 (23)	would I had died ere this, and become a thing forgotten
19:66 (67)	when I am dead shall I then be brought forth alive?
21:34 (35)	therefore, if thou diest, will they live forever?
22:58 (57)	those who emigrated in God's way and were slain, or died
23:35 (37)	does he promise you that when you are dead, and become dust and bones
23:82 (84)	when we are dead and become dust and bones, shall we be indeed raised up?
37:16 (16)	when we are dead and become dust and bones, shall we indeed be raised up?
37:53 (51)	when we are dead and become dust and bones, shall we indeed be requited?
47:34 (36)	and then die disbelieving, them God will not forgive
50:3 (3)	when we are dead and become dust? That is a far returning
56:47 (47)	when we are dead and become dust and bones, shall we indeed be raised up?

b) impf. act. (*yamūtu*)

2:132 (126)	see that you die not save in surrender
2:217 (214)	whosoever of you turns from his religion, and dies disbelieving
3:102 (97)	and see you do not die, save in surrender
3:145 (139)	it is not given to any soul to die, save by the leave of God
4:18 (22)	neither to those who die disbelieving
7:25 (24)	therein you shall live, and therein you shall die
16:38 (40)	God will never raise up him who dies
19:15 (15)	peace be upon him, the day he was born, and the day he dies
19:33 (34)	peace be upon me, the day I was born, and the day I die
20:74 (76)	for him awaits Gehenna wherein he shall neither die nor live
23:37 (39)	we die, and we live, and we shall not be raised up

25:58 (60)	put thy trust in the Living God, the Undying
31:34 (34)	no soul knows in what land it shall die
35:36 (33)	they shall neither be done with and die, nor shall its chastisement be lightened
39:42 (43)	and that which has not died, in its sleep
45:24 (23)	there is nothing but our present life; we die, and we live
87:13 (13)	then he shall neither die therein, nor live

c) impv. (*mut*)

2:243 (244)	God said to them, 'Die!' Then He gave them life
3:119 (115)	die in your rage; God knows the thoughts in the breasts

f) n.vb. (*mawt*)

2:19 (18)	they put their fingers in their ears against the thunderclaps, fearful of death
2:56 (53)	then We raised you up after you were dead
2:94 (88)	then long for death — if you speak truly
2:133 (127)	why, were you witnesses, when death came to Jacob?
2:164 (159)	therewith reviving the earth after it is dead
2:180 (176)	prescribed for you, when any of you is visited by death
2:243 (244)	those who went forth from their habitations in their thousands fearful of death
2:259 (261)	how shall God give life to this now it is dead?
3:143 (137)	you were longing for death before you met it
3:168 (162)	then avert death from yourselves, if you speak truly
3:185 (182)	every soul shall taste of death
4:15 (19)	then detain them in their houses until death takes them
4:18 (22)	when one of them is visited by death, he says, 'Indeed now I repent'
4:78 (80)	wherever you may be, death will overtake you
4:100 (101)	then death overtakes him, his wage shall have fallen on God
4:159 (157)	but will assuredly believe in him before his death
5:106 (105)	the testimony between you when any of you is visited by death
5:106 (105)	and the affliction of death befalls you
6:61 (61)	when any one of you is visited by death
6:93 (93)	if thou couldst only see when the evildoers are in the agonies of death
8:6 (6)	they were being driven into death with their eyes wide open
11:7 (10)	you shall surely be raised up after death
14:17 (20)	and death comes upon him from every side
16:65 (67)	and therewith revives the earth after it is dead
21:35 (36)	every soul shall taste of death
23:99 (101)	till, when death comes to one of them, he says
25:3 (4)	no power of death or life or raising up
29:57 (57)	every soul shall taste of death
29:63 (63)	therewith revives the earth after it is dead
30:19 (18)	and He revives the earth after it is dead
30:24 (23)	and He revives the earth after it is dead
30:50 (49)	how He quickens the earth after it was dead
32:11 (11)	death's angel, who has been charged with you, shall gather you
33:16 (16)	flight will not profit you, if you flee from death
33:19 (19)	thou seest them looking at thee, their eyes rolling like one who swoons of death
34:14 (13)	and when We decreed that he should die
34:14 (13)	naught indicated to them that he was dead
35:9 (10)	and therewith revive the earth, after it is dead
39:42 (43)	God takes the souls at the time of their death
39:42 (43)	He withholds that against which He has decreed death
44:56 (56)	they shall not taste therein of death
45:5 (4)	and therewith revives the earth after it is dead

47:20 (22)	looking at thee as one who swoons of death
50:19 (18)	death's agony comes in truth; that is what thou wast shunning
56:60 (60)	We have decreed among you Death
57:17 (16)	know that God revives the earth after it was dead
62:6 (6)	then do you long for death, if you speak truly
62:8 (8)	surely death, from which you flee, shall encounter you
63:10 (10)	expend of what We have provided you before that death comes upon one of you
67:2 (2)	who created death and life, that He might try you

MAMĀT n.m.~the act of dying, death

6:162 (163)	my living, my dying — all belongs to God
17:75 (77)	then would We have let thee taste the double of life and the double of death
45:21 (20)	equal their living and their dying

MAWTAH n.f.~a single death

37:59 (57)	except for our first death, and are we not chastised?
44:35 (34)	there is nothing but our first death
44:56 (56)	save the first death

MAYT n.m. (pl. *amwāt*)~dead

2:28 (26)	seeing you were dead and He gave you life
2:154 (149)	say not of those slain in God's way, 'They are dead'
3:169 (163)	count not those who were slain in God's way as dead
6:122 (122)	why, is he who was dead, and We gave him life
16:21 (21)	dead, not alive, and are not aware
25:49 (51)	so that We might revive a dead land
35:22 (21)	not equal are the living and the dead
43:11 (10)	We revived thereby a land that was dead
49:12 (12)	would any of you like to eat the flesh of his brother dead?
50:11 (11)	and thereby We revived a land that was dead
77:26 (26)	for the living and for the dead

MAYTAH n.f.~a dead body, carrion

2:173 (168)	these things only has He forbidden you: carrion, blood
5:3 (4)	forbidden to you are carrion, blood
6:139 (140)	but if it be dead, then they all shall be partners in it
6:145 (146)	except it be carrion, or blood outpoured
16:115 (116)	these things only He has forbidden you: carrion, blood
36:33 (33)	a sign for them is the dead land

MAYYIT n.m. (pl. *mawtá* and *mayyitūn*)~dead, mortal

2:73 (68)	God brings to life the dead
2:260 (262)	my Lord, show me how Thou wilt give life to the dead
3:27 (26)	Thou bringest forth the living from the dead
3:27 (26)	Thou bringest forth the dead from the living
3:49 (43)	and [I will also] bring to life the dead, by the leave of God
5:110 (110)	thou bringest the dead forth by My leave
6:36 (36)	as for the dead, God will raise them up
6:95 (95)	it is God who splits the grain and the date-stone, brings forth the living from the dead
6:95 (95)	He brings forth the dead too from the living
6:111 (111)	and the dead had spoken with them
7:57 (55)	when they are charged with heavy clouds, We drive it to a dead land
7:57 (55)	even so We shall bring forth the dead

10:31 (32)	who brings forth the living from the dead
10:31 (32)	and brings forth the dead from the living
13:31 (30)	the dead were spoken to
14:17 (20)	yet he cannot die
22:6 (6)	He is the Truth, and brings the dead to life
23:15 (15)	then after that you shall surely die
27:80 (82)	thou shalt not make the dead to hear
30:19 (18)	He brings forth the living from the dead
30:19 (18)	and brings forth the dead from the living
30:50 (49)	surely He is the quickener of the dead
30:52 (51)	thou shalt not make the dead to hear
35:9 (10)	then We drive it to a dead land
36:12 (11)	surely it is We who bring the dead to life
37:58 (56)	what, do we then not die
39:30 (31)	thou art mortal and they are (mortal)
39:30 (31)	thou art (mortal) and they are mortal
41:39 (39)	He who quickens it is He who quickens the dead
42:9 (7)	He quickens the dead, and He is powerful over everything
46:33 (32)	not being wearied by creating them, is able to give life to the dead
75:40 (40)	is He not able to quicken the dead?

AMĀTA vb. (IV)~to cause or make to die

a) perf. act.

2:259 (261)	so God made him die a hundred years
40:11 (11)	our Lord, Thou hast caused us to die two deaths
53:44 (45)	it is He who makes to die, and that makes to live
80:21 (21)	then makes him to die, and buries him

b) impf. act. (*yumītu*)

2:28 (26)	He gave you life, then He shall make you dead
2:258 (260)	my Lord is He who gives life, and makes to die
2:258 (260)	he said, 'I give life, and make to die'
3:156 (150)	for God gives life, and He makes to die
7:158 (158)	He gives life, and makes to die
9:116 (117)	He gives life, and makes to die
10:56 (57)	He gives life, and makes to die
15:23 (23)	it is We who give life, and make to die
22:66 (65)	it is He who gave you life, then He shall make you dead
23:80 (82)	it is He who gives life, and makes to die
26:81 (81)	who makes me to die, then gives me life
30:40 (39)	then He shall make you dead, then He shall give you life
40:68 (70)	it is He who gives life, and makes to die
44:8 (7)	there is no god but He; He gives life and makes to die
45:26 (25)	God gives you life, then makes you die
50:43 (42)	it is We who give life, and make to die
57:2 (2)	He gives life, and He makes to die

*M Y D

MĀDA vb. (I)~to shake, to quake

b) impf. act. (*yamīdu*)

16:15 (15) He cast on the earth firm mountains, lest it shake with you
21:31 (32) We set in the earth firm mountains lest it should shake with them
31:10 (9) He cast on the earth firm mountains, lest it shake with you

MĀʾIDAH n.f.~a table (set out with food)

5:112 (112) is thy Lord able to send down on us a Table out of heaven?
5:114 (114) send down upon us a Table out of heaven

*M Y L

MĀLA vb. (I)~to swerve; to be partial; (with prep. *ʿalá*) to wheel on, to turn against, to attack. (n.vb.) the act of swerving, turning or being partial

b) impf. act. (*yamīlu*)

4:27 (32) those who follow their lusts desire you to swerve away mightily
4:102 (103) then they would wheel on you all at once
4:129 (128) do not be altogether partial so that you leave her as it were suspended

f) n.vb. (*mayl*)

4:27 (32) those who follow their lusts desire you to swerve away <mightily>
4:129 (128) yet do not be altogether partial

MAYLAH n.f.~a single act of turning, wheeling on

4:102 (103) then they would wheel on you <all at once>

*M Y R

MĀRA vb. (I)~to get provision

b) impf. act. (*yamīru*)

12:65 (65) we shall get provision for our family

*M Y Z

MĀZA vb. (I)~to distinguish, to separate the one from the other

b) impf. act. (*yamīzu*)

3:179 (173) till He shall distinguish the corrupt from the good
8:37 (38) that God may distinguish the corrupt from the good

TAMAYYAZA vb. (V)~to burst

b) impf. act. (*yatamayyazu*)

67:8 (8) and wellnigh bursts asunder with rage

IMTĀZA vb. (VIII)~to be separated

c) impv. (*imtaz*)

36:59 (59) keep yourselves apart, you sinners, upon this day

*M Z J

MIZĀJ n.m.~a mixture

76:5 (5) the pious shall drink of a cup whose mixture is camphor
76:17 (17) they shall be given to drink a cup whose mixture is ginger
83:27 (27) and whose mixture is Tasnim

*M Z N

MUZN n.m.~a cloud

56:69 (68) did you send it down from the clouds, or did We send it?

*M Z Q

MAZZAQA vb. (II)~to tear to pieces. (pcple. pass.) that which is torn to pieces

a) perf. act.

34:19 (18) and We tore them utterly to pieces

d) perf. pass. (*muzziqa*)

34:7 (7) when you have been utterly torn to pieces

h) pcple. pass. (*mumazzaq*)

34:7 (7) when you have been utterly torn to pieces
34:19 (18) and We tore them utterly to pieces

NŪN

*N

NŪN~ml

68:1 (1) Nun. By the Pen, and what they inscribe

*N ʾ Y

NAʾÁ vb. (I)~to withdraw aside, to keep afar

a) perf. act.

17:83 (85) when We bless man, he turns away, and withdraws aside
41:51 (51) when We bless man, he turns away and withdraws aside

b) impf. act. (*yanʾá*)

6:26 (26) and they forbid it, and keep afar from it

*N ʿ J

NAʿJAH n.f. (pl. *niʿāj*)~a ewe, (pl) sheep

38:23 (22) behold, this my brother has ninety-nine ewes
38:23 (22) and I have one ewe
38:24 (23) he has wronged thee in asking for thy ewe
38:24 (23) in addition to his sheep

*N ʿ L

NAʿL n.f.~a shoe

20:12 (12) I am thy Lord; put off thy shoes

*N ʿ M

NAʿIMA vb. (I)~(pcple. act.) jocund [Ar]; calm [Pk]; joyful [Ali]; pleasant [Bl]

g) pcple. act. f. (*nāʿimah*)

88:8 (8) faces on that day jocund

NIʿMA vb. (I) an irregular verb that appears only in the 3rd pers. s. described as "a verb of praise." It is the antonym of *biʾsa* (*b ʾ s) . Occasionally it is suffixed by *mā* and is read *niʿimmā*~how excellent, how bountiful

2:271 (273) if you publish your freewill offerings, it is excellent
3:136 (130) how excellent is the wage of those who labour

3:173 (167)	God is sufficient for us; an excellent Guardian is He
4:58 (61)	good is the admonition God gives you
8:40 (41)	know that God is your Protector — an excellent Protector
8:40 (41)	an excellent Helper
13:24 (24)	fair is the Ultimate Abode
16:30 (32)	excellent is the abode of the godfearing
18:31 (30)	O, how excellent a reward
22:78 (78)	He is your Protector — an excellent Protector
22:78 (78)	an excellent Helper
29:58 (58)	and excellent is the wage of those who labour
37:75 (73)	Noah called to Us; and how excellent were the Answerers
38:30 (29)	how excellent a servant he was
38:44 (44)	how excellent a servant he was
39:74 (74)	how excellent is the wage of those that labour
51:48 (48)	O excellent Smoothers
77:23 (23)	We determined; excellent determiners are We

NAʿAM n.m. (pl. *anʿām*)~cattle, flocks

3:14 (12)	heaped-up heaps of gold and silver, horses of mark, cattle and tillage
4:119 (118)	I will command them and they will cut off the cattle's ears
5:1 (1)	permitted to you is the beast of the flocks
5:95 (96)	there shall be recompense — the like of what he has slain, in flocks
6:136 (137)	they appoint to God, of the tillage and cattle that He multiplied
6:138 (139)	these are cattle and tillage sacrosanct
6:138 (139)	cattle whose backs have been forbidden
6:138 (139)	and cattle over which they mention not the Name of God
6:139 (140)	what is within the bellies of these cattle is reserved for our males
6:142 (143)	of the cattle, for burthen and for slaughter, eat of what God has provided you
7:179 (178)	they are like cattle; nay, rather they are further astray
10:24 (25)	the plants of the earth mingle with it whereof men and cattle eat
16:5 (5)	and the cattle — He created them for you
16:66 (68)	surely in the cattle there is a lesson for you
16:80 (82)	He has appointed for you of the skins of the cattle houses
20:54 (56)	do you eat, and pasture your cattle
22:28 (29)	mention God's Name on days well-known over such beasts of the flocks
22:30 (31)	permitted to you are the flocks, except that which is recited to you
22:34 (35)	that they may mention God's Name over such beasts of the flocks
23:21 (21)	surely in the cattle there is a lesson for you
25:44 (46)	they are but as the cattle
25:49 (51)	of that We created, cattle and men a many
26:133 (133)	succoured you with flocks and sons
32:27 (27)	and bring forth crops therewith whereof their cattle and themselves eat
35:28 (25)	men too, and beasts and cattle — diverse are their hues
36:71 (71)	have they not seen how that We have created for them of that Our hands wrought cattle that they own?
39:6 (8)	He sent down to you of the cattle eight couples
40:79 (79)	it is God who appointed for you the cattle
42:11 (9)	He has appointed for you, of yourselves, pairs, and pairs also of the cattle
43:12 (11)	and appointed for you ships and cattle such as you ride
47:12 (13)	they take their enjoyment and eat as cattle eat
79:33 (33)	an enjoyment for you and your flocks
80:32 (32)	an enjoyment for you and your flocks

NAʿMĀʾ n.f.~prosperity [Ar]; grace [Pk]; favour [Ali]

11:10 (13)	if We let him taste prosperity after hardship

NAʿĪM n.m.~bliss, delight, pleasure

5:65 (70)	We would have acquitted them of their evil deeds, and admitted them to Gardens of Bliss
9:21 (21)	for them await gardens wherein is lasting bliss
10:9 (9)	beneath them rivers flowing in gardens of bliss
22:56 (55)	they shall be in Gardens of Bliss
26:85 (85)	make me one of the inheritors of the Garden of Bliss
31:8 (7)	those who believe, and do deeds of righteousness, there awaits them Gardens of Bliss
37:43 (42)	in the Gardens of Bliss
52:17 (17)	surely the godfearing shall be in gardens and bliss
56:12 (12)	in the Gardens of Delight
56:89 (88)	there shall be repose and ease, and a Garden of Delight
68:34 (34)	for the godfearing shall be Gardens of Bliss with their Lord
70:38 (38)	is every man of them eager to be admitted to a Garden of Bliss?
76:20 (20)	when thou seest them then thou seest bliss and a great kingdom
82:13 (13)	surely the pious shall be in bliss
83:22 (22)	surely the pious shall be in bliss
83:24 (24)	thou knowest in their faces the radiancy of bliss
102:8 (8)	then you shall be questioned that day concerning true bliss

NAʿMAH n.f.~prosperity [Ar]; pleasant things, ease and comfort [Pk]; wealth and conveniences of life [Ali]

44:27 (26)	and what prosperity they had rejoiced in
73:11 (11)	leave Me to those who cry lies, those prosperous ones

NIʿMAH n.f. (pl. *anʿum*)~blessing [Ar]; grace [Pk, Ali]; (also) favour [Ar, Pk]

2:40 (38)	Children of Israel, remember My blessing wherewith I blessed you
2:47 (44)	Children of Israel, remember My blessing wherewith I blessed you
2:122 (116)	Children of Israel, remember My blessing wherewith I blessed you
2:150 (145)	and that I may perfect My blessing upon you
2:211 (207)	whoso changes God's blessing after it has come to him
2:231 (231)	remember God's blessing upon you
3:103 (98)	remember God's blessing upon you when you were enemies
3:103 (98)	so that by His blessing you became brothers
3:171 (165)	joyful in blessing and bounty from God
3:174 (168)	they returned with blessing and bounty from God, untouched by evil
5:3 (5)	I have perfected your religion for you, and I have completed My blessing upon you
5:6 (9)	that He may complete His blessing upon you
5:7 (10)	remember God's blessing upon you, and His compact which He made with you
5:11 (14)	O believers, remember God's blessing upon you
5:20 (23)	O my people, remember God's blessing upon you
5:110 (109)	Jesus Son of Mary, remember My blessing upon thee
8:53 (55)	God would never change His favour that He conferred on a people
12:6 (6)	and perfect His blessing upon thee and upon the House of Jacob
14:6 (6)	remember God's blessing upon you when He delivered you
14:28 (33)	hast thou not seen those who exchanged the bounty of God with unthankfulness
14:34 (37)	if you count God's blessing, you will never number it
16:18 (18)	if you count God's blessing, you will never number it
16:53 (55)	whatsoever blessing you have, it comes from God
16:71 (73)	what, and do they deny God's blessing?

16:72 (74)	do they believe in vanity, and do they disbelieve in God's blessing?
16:81 (83)	even so He perfects His blessing upon you
16:83 (85)	they recognize the blessing of God
16:112 (113)	then it was unthankful for the blessings of God
16:114 (115)	be you thankful for the blessing of God
16:121 (122)	showing thankfulness for His blessings
26:22 (21)	that is a blessing thou reproachest me with
27:19 (19)	dispose me that I may be thankful for Thy blessing
29:67 (67)	do they believe in vanity, and do they disbelieve in God's blessing?
31:20 (19)	He has lavished on you His blessings, outward and inward?
31:31 (30)	hast thou not seen how that the ships run upon the sea by the blessing of God
33:9 (9)	O believers, remember God's blessing upon you
35:3 (3)	O men, remember God's blessing upon you
37:57 (55)	but for my Lord's blessing, I were one of the arraigned
39:8 (11)	when He confers on him a blessing from Him
39:49 (50)	when We confer on him a blessing from Us, he says
43:13 (12)	and then remember your Lord's blessing
46:15 (14)	that I may be thankful for Thy blessing wherewith Thou hast blessed me
48:2 (2)	that God may forgive thee thy former and thy latter sins, and complete His blessing upon thee
49:8 (8)	by God's favour and blessing
52:29 (29)	by thy Lord's blessing thou art not a soothsayer neither possessed
54:35 (35)	a blessing from Us; even so We recompense him who is thankful
68:2 (2)	thou art not, by the blessing of thy Lord, a man possessed
68:49 (49)	had there not overtaken him a blessing from his Lord
92:19 (19)	and confers no favour on any man for recompense
93:11 (11)	as for thy Lord's blessing, declare it

NAʿʿAMA vb. (II)~to bless, to be gracious

a) perf. act.

89:15 (14)	whenever his Lord tries him, and honours him, and blesses him

ANʿAMA vb. (IV)~(with prep. *ʿalá*) to bless, to be gracious toward, to favour

a) perf. act.

1:7 (6)	the path of those whom Thou hast blessed
2:40 (38)	remember My blessing wherewith I blessed you
2:47 (44)	remember My blessing wherewith I blessed you
2:122 (116)	remember My blessing wherewith I blessed you
4:69 (71)	they are with those whom God has blessed
4:72 (74)	God has blessed me, in that I was not a martyr with them
5:23 (26)	said two men of those that feared God whom God had blessed
8:53 (55)	that is because God would never change His favour
17:83 (85)	when We bless man, he turns away, and withdraws aside
19:58 (59)	these are they whom God has blessed among the Prophets
27:19 (19)	that I may be thankful for Thy blessing wherewith Thou hast blessed me
28:17 (16)	forasmuch as Thou hast blessed me, I will never be a partisan of the sinners
33:37 (37)	when thou saidst to him whom God had blessed
33:37 (37)	and thou hadst favoured, 'Keep thy wife to thyself'
41:51 (51)	when We bless man, he turns away and withdraws aside
43:59 (59)	he is only a servant We blessed
46:15 (14)	that I may be thankful for Thy blessing wherewith Thou hast blessed me

*N ᶜ Q

NAᶜAQA vb. (I)~to shout, to call aloud (this verb is usually used for the calling of the crow)

b) impf. act. (*yanᶜaqu*)

2:171 (166)	the likeness of one who shouts to that which hears nothing

*N ᶜ S

NAᶜASA vb. (I)~(n.vb.) slumber, sleepiness

f) n.vb. (*nuᶜās*)

3:154 (148)	then He sent down upon you, after grief, security — a slumber overcoming a party
8:11 (11)	when He was causing slumber to overcome you as a security from Him

*N B ᵓ

NABAᵓ n.m. (pl. *anbāᵓ*)~news, tiding, story, tale

3:44 (39)	that is of the tidings of the Unseen, that We reveal to thee
5:27 (30)	recite thou to them the story of the two sons of Adam truthfully
6:5 (5)	there shall come to them news of that they were mocking
6:34 (34)	there has already come to thee some tiding of the Envoys
6:67 (66)	every tiding has its time appointed
7:101 (99)	those cities We relate to thee tidings of
7:175 (174)	recite to them the tiding of him to whom We gave Our signs
9:70 (71)	has there not come to you the tidings of those who were before you
10:71 (72)	recite to them the story of Noah when he said to his people
11:49 (51)	that is of the tidings of the Unseen
11:100 (102)	that is of the tidings of the cities We relate to thee
11:120 (121)	all that We relate to thee of the tidings of the Messengers
12:102 (103)	that is of the tidings of the Unseen that We reveal to thee
14:9 (9)	has there not come to you the tidings of those who were before you
18:13 (12)	We will relate to thee their tidings truly
20:99 (99)	We relate to thee stories of what has gone before
26:6 (5)	tidings will come to them of that they mocked at
26:69 (69)	recite to them the tiding of Abraham
27:22 (22)	I have come from Sheba to thee with a sure tiding
28:3 (2)	We will recite to thee something of the tiding of Moses
28:66 (66)	the tidings will be darkened for them
33:20 (20)	they will wish that they were desert-dwellers among the Bedouins asking for news of you
38:21 (20)	has the tiding of the dispute come to thee?
38:67 (67)	say: 'It is a mighty tiding'
38:88 (88)	you shall surely know its tiding after a while
49:6 (6)	if an ungodly man comes to you with a tiding
54:4 (4)	there have come to them such tidings as contain a deterrent

64:5 (5)	has there not come to you the tidings of those that disbelieved before
78:2 (2)	of the mighty tiding

NABĪY n.m. (pl. *nabīyūn* and *anbiyā'*)~a prophet, The Prophet (*al-nabīy*)

2:61 (58)	they had disbelieved the signs of God and slain the Prophets
2:91 (85)	why then were you slaying the Prophets of God
2:136 (130)	that which was given to Moses and Jesus and the Prophets
2:177 (172)	to believe in God, and the Last Day, the angels, the Book, and the Prophets
2:213 (209)	then God sent forth the Prophets, good tidings to bear
2:246 (247)	when they said to a Prophet of theirs
2:247 (248)	then their Prophet said to them, 'Verily God has raised up Saul
2:248 (249)	their Prophet said to them, 'The sign of his kingship is that the Ark will come to you'
3:21 (20)	those who disbelieve in the signs of God and slay the Prophets without right
3:39 (34)	a Word of God, a chief, and chaste, a Prophet, righteous
3:68 (61)	the people standing closest to Abraham are those who followed him, and this Prophet
3:80 (74)	He would never order you to take the angels and the Prophets as Lords
3:81 (75)	when God took compact with the Prophets
3:84 (78)	that which was given to Moses and Jesus, and the Prophets
3:112 (108)	they disbelieved in God's signs, and slew the Prophets
3:146 (140)	many a Prophet there has been, with whom thousands manifold have fought
3:161 (155)	it is not for a Prophet to be fraudulent
3:181 (177)	their slaying the Prophets without right
4:69 (71)	they are with those whom God has blessed, Prophets, just men, martyrs
4:155 (154)	disbelieving in the signs of God, and slaying the Prophets without right
4:163 (161)	We have revealed to thee as We revealed to Noah, and the Prophets after him
5:20 (23)	when He appointed among you Prophets, and appointed you kings
5:44 (48)	thereby the Prophets who had surrendered themselves gave judgment
5:81 (84)	had they believed in God and the Prophet and what has been sent down
6:112 (112)	We have appointed to every Prophet an enemy
7:94 (92)	We have sent no Prophet to any city but that We seized its people with misery
7:157 (156)	those who follow the Messenger, the Prophet of the common folk
7:158 (158)	believe then in God, and in His Messenger, the Prophet of the common folk
8:64 (65)	O Prophet, God suffices thee, and the believers who follow thee
8:65 (66)	O Prophet, urge on the believers to fight
8:67 (68)	it is not for any Prophet to have prisoners
8:70 (71)	O Prophet, say to the prisoners in your hands
9:61 (61)	some of them hurt the Prophet, saying
9:73 (74)	O Prophet, struggle with the unbelievers and hypocrites
9:113 (114)	it is not for the Prophet and the believers to ask pardon for the idolaters
9:117 (118)	God has turned towards the Prophet and the Emigrants
17:55 (57)	We have preferred some Prophets over others
19:30 (31)	God has given me the Book, and made me a Prophet
19:41 (42)	mention in the Book Abraham; surely he was a true man, a Prophet
19:49 (50)	We gave him Isaac and Jacob, and each We made a Prophet
19:51 (52)	he was devoted, and he was a Messenger, a Prophet
19:53 (54)	We gave him his brother Aaron, of Our mercy, a Prophet
19:54 (55)	he was true to his promise, and he was a Messenger, a Prophet
19:56 (57)	mention in the Book Idris; he was a true man, a Prophet
19:58 (59)	these are they whom God has blessed among the Prophets
22:52 (51)	We sent not ever any Messenger or Prophet before thee
25:31 (33)	We have appointed to every Prophet an enemy among the sinners
33:1 (1)	O Prophet, fear God, and obey not the unbelievers

33:6 (6)	the Prophet is nearer to the believers than their selves
33:7 (7)	when We took compact from the Prophets, and from thee
33:13 (13)	a part of them were asking leave of the Prophet, saying
33:28 (28)	O Prophet, say to thy wives: 'If you desire the present life'
33:30 (30)	Wives of the Prophet, whosoever among you commits a flagrant indecency
33:32 (32)	Wives of the Prophet, you are not as other women
33:38 (38)	there is no fault in the Prophet, touching what God has ordained for him
33:40 (40)	the Messenger of God, and the Seal of the Prophets
33:45 (44)	O Prophet, We have sent thee as a witness
33:50 (49)	O Prophet, We have made lawful for thee thy wives
33:50 (49)	any woman believer, if she give herself to the Prophet
33:50 (49)	if the Prophet desire to take her in marriage
33:53 (53)	O believers, enter not the houses of the Prophet
33:53 (53)	neither lingering for idle talk; that is hurtful to the Prophet
33:56 (56)	God and His angels bless the Prophet
33:59 (59)	O Prophet, say to thy wives and daughters and the believing women
37:112 (112)	We gave him the good tidings of Isaac, a Prophet, one of the righteous
39:69 (69)	and the Prophets and witnesses shall be brought
43:6 (5)	how many a Prophet We sent among the ancients
43:7 (6)	not a Prophet came to them, without they mocked at him
49:2 (2)	O believers, raise not your voices above the Prophet's voice
60:12 (12)	O Prophet, when believing women come to thee
65:1 (1)	O Prophet, when you divorce women
66:1 (1)	O Prophet, why forbiddest thou what God has made lawful to thee
66:3 (3)	when the Prophet confided to one of his wives a certain matter
66:8 (8)	upon the day when God will not degrade the Prophet
66:9 (9)	O Prophet, struggle with the unbelievers and the hypocrites

NUBŪWAH n.f.~prophecy, prophethood

3:79 (73)	it belongs not to any mortal that God should give him the Book, the Judgment, the Prophethood
6:89 (89)	those are they to whom We gave the Book, the Judgment, the Prophethood
29:27 (26)	We appointed the Prophecy and the Book to be among his seed
45:16 (15)	We gave the Children of Israel the Book, the Judgment, and the Prophethood
57:26 (26)	We appointed the Prophecy and the Book to be among their seed

NABBA'A vb. (II)~to tell

a) perf. act.

9:94 (95)	God has already told us tidings of you
12:37 (37)	ere it comes to you I shall tell you its interpretation
66:3 (3)	then, when she told of it, and God disclosed that to him
66:3 (3)	then, when he told her of it
66:3 (3)	I was told of it by the All-knowing, the All-aware

b) impf. act. (*yunabbi'u*)

3:15 (13)	say: 'Shall I tell you of a better than that?'
3:49 (43)	I will inform you too of what things you eat
5:14 (17)	God will assuredly tell them of the things they wrought
5:48 (53)	He will tell you of that whereon you were at variance
5:60 (65)	shall I tell you of a recompense with God, worse than that?
5:105 (104)	He will tell you what you were doing
6:60 (60)	He will tell you of what you have been doing

6:108 (108)	He will tell them what they have been doing
6:159 (160)	He will tell them what they have been doing
6:164 (164)	He will tell you of that whereon you were at variance
9:64 (65)	lest a sura should be sent down against them, telling thee what is in their hearts
9:94 (95)	He will tell you what you were doing
9:105 (106)	He will tell you what you were doing
10:18 (19)	will you tell God what He knows not either in the heavens or in the earth?
10:23 (24)	then We shall tell you what you were doing
12:15 (15)	thou shalt tell them of this their doing when they are unaware
12:45 (45)	I will myself tell you its interpretation
13:33 (33)	wll you tell Him what He knows not in the earth?
18:78 (77)	now I will tell thee the interpretation of that thou couldst not bear patiently
18:103 (103)	shall We tell you who will be the greatest losers in their works?
22:72 (71)	shall I tell you of something worse than that?
24:64 (64)	then He will tell them of what they did
26:221 (221)	shall I tell you on whom the Satans come down?
29:8 (7)	I shall tell you what you were doing
31:15 (14)	I shall tell you what you were doing
31:23 (22)	We shall tell them what they did
34:7 (7)	shall we point you to a man who will tell you
35:14 (15)	none can tell thee like One who is aware
39:7 (9)	He will tell you what you have been doing
41:50 (50)	then We shall tell the unbelievers the things they have done
58:6 (7)	then He shall tell them what they did
58:7 (8)	then He shall tell them what they have done
62:8 (8)	He will tell you that you have been doing

c) impv. (*nabbiʾ*)

6:143 (144)	tell me the knowledge, if you speak truly
12:36 (36)	tell us its interpretation; we see that thou art of the good-doers
15:49 (49)	tell My servants I am the All-forgiving
15:51 (51)	and tell them of the guests of Abraham
54:28 (28)	tell them that the water is to be divided between them

e) impf. pass. (*yunabbaʾu*)

53:36 (37)	has he not been told of what is in the scrolls of Moses
64:7 (7)	then you shall be told the things you did
75:13 (13)	upon that day man shall be told his former deeds and his latter

ANBAʾA vb. (IV)~to tell

a) perf. act.

2:33 (31)	and when he had told them their names
66:3 (3)	she said, 'Who told thee this?'

c) impv. (*anbiʾ*)

2:31 (29)	now tell Me the names of these, if you speak truly
2:33 (31)	He said, 'Adam, tell them their names'

ISTANBAʾA vb. (X)~to ask to be told

b) impf. act. (*yastanbiʾu*)

10:53 (54)	they ask thee to tell them, 'Is it true?'

*N B ᶜ

YANBŪᶜ n.m. (pl. *yanābīᶜ*)~a spring

17:90 (92)	we will not believe thee till thou makest a spring to gush forth
39:21 (22)	hast thou not seen how that God has sent down out of heaven water and threaded it as springs in the earth

*N B DH

NABADHA vb. (I)~to reject, to cast, to set aside, to throw; (with prep. *ilá*) to dissolve (a relationship)

a) perf. act.

2:100 (94)	whensoever they have made a covenant, does a party of them reject it?
2:101 (95)	a party of them that were given the Book reject the Book of God
3:187 (184)	but they rejected it behind their backs
20:96 (96)	I seized a handful of dust from the messenger's track, and cast it into the thing
28:40 (40)	We seized him and his hosts, and cast them into the sea
37:145 (145)	We cast him upon the wilderness, and he was sick
51:40 (40)	We seized him and his hosts, and We cast them into the sea

c) impv. (*inbidh*)

8:58 (60)	if thou fearest treachery any way at the hands of a people, dissolve it with them equally

d) perf. pass. (*nubidha*)

68:49 (49)	he would have been cast upon the wilderness, being condemned

e) impf. pass. (*yunbadhu*)

104:4 (4)	no indeed; he shall be thrust into the Crusher

INTABADHA vb. (VIII)~to withdraw

a) perf. act.

19:16 (16)	when she withdrew from her people to an eastern place
19:22 (22)	so she conceived him, and withdrew with him to a distant place

*N B T

NABATA vb. (I)~(with prep. *bi-*) to bear (fruit), to produce. (n.vb.) the act of bringing forth fruit; (n) plant(s), vegetation

b) impf. act. (*yanbutu*)

23:20 (20)	a tree issuing from the Mount of Sinai that bears oil

f) n.vb. (*nabāt*)

3:37 (32)	by His goodness she grew up <comely>
6:99 (99)	thereby We have brought forth the shoot of every plant
7:58 (56)	its vegetation comes forth by the leave of its Lord
10:24 (25)	and the plants of the earth mingle with it
18:45 (43)	and the plants of the earth mingle with it
20:53 (55)	We have brought forth divers kinds of plants
57:20 (19)	it is as a rain whose vegetation pleases the unbelievers
71:17 (16)	God caused you to grow out of the earth <...>
78:15 (15)	that We may bring forth thereby grain and plants

ANBATA vb. (IV)~to sprout, to cause to grow, to put forth (fruit), to produce

a) perf. act.

2:261 (263)	the way of God is as the likeness of a grain of corn that sprouts seven ears
3:37 (32)	by His goodness she grew up comely
15:19 (19)	We caused to grow therein of every thing justly weighed
22:5 (5)	it quivers, and swells, and puts forth herbs of every joyous kind
26:7 (6)	how many therein We have caused to grow of every generous kind?
27:60 (61)	We caused to grow therewith gardens full of loveliness
31:10 (9)	and caused to grow in it of every generous kind
37:146 (146)	We caused to grow over him a tree of gourds
50:7 (7)	We caused to grow therein of every joyous kind
50:9 (9)	and caused to grow thereby gardens and grain of harvest
71:17 (16)	and God caused you to grow out of the earth
80:27 (27)	and therein made the grains to grow

b) impf. act. (*yunbitu*)

2:61 (58)	that He may bring forth for us of that the earth produces
16:11 (11)	thereby He brings forth for you crops, and olives
27:60 (61)	whose trees you could never grow
36:36 (36)	glory be to Him, who created all the pairs of what the earth produces

*N B Ṭ

ISTANBAṬA vb. (X)~to investigate or think out a matter

b) impf. act. (*yastanbiṭu*)

4:83 (85)	those of them whose task it is to investigate would have known the matter

*N B Z

TANĀBAZA vb. (VI)~to revile or insult one another

b) impf. act. (*yatanābazu*)

49:11 (11)	find not fault with one another, neither revile one another

*N D D

ANDĀD n.m. (pl. of *nidd*)~compeer [Ar]; rival [Pk]; an equal [Ali]; peer [Bl]

2:22 (20)	so set not up compeers to God wittingly
2:165 (160)	there be men who take to themselves compeers apart from God
14:30 (35)	they set up compeers to God, that they might lead astray from His way
34:33 (32)	when you were ordering us to disbelieve in God, and to set up compeers to Him
39:8 (11)	he forgets that he was calling to before and sets up compeers to God
41:9 (8)	do you set up compeers to Him?

*N D M

NADIMA vb. (I)~(n.vb.) remorse, repentance. (pcple. act.) one who is remorseful, one who repents

f) n.vb. (*nadāmah*)

10:54 (55)	they will be secretly remorseful when they see the chastisement
34:33 (32)	they will be secretly remorseful when they see the chastisement

g) pcple. act. (*nādim*)

5:31 (34)	and he became one of the remorseful
5:52 (57)	then they will find themselves, for that they kept secret within them, remorseful
23:40 (42)	in a little they will be remorseful
26:157 (157)	but they hamstrung her, and in the morning they were remorseful
49:6 (6)	lest you afflict a people unwittingly, and then repent of what you have done

*N D W

NĀDĪ n.m.~assembly [Ar, Bl]; concourse [Ar]; meeting, henchmen [Pk]; council [Ali, Bl]

29:29 (28)	and commit in your assembly dishonour
96:17 (17)	so let him call on his concourse

NADĪY n.m.~an assembly [Ar, Bl]; army [Pk]; council [Ali]

19:73 (74)	which of the two parties is better in station, fairer in assembly?

NĀDÁ vb. (III)~to call, to cry; (with prep. *fī*) to proclaim. (n.vb.) the act of calling, a call, a shout, a cry. (pcple. act.) a caller, a crier

a) perf. act.

3:39 (33)	the angels called to him, standing in the Sanctuary
5:58 (63)	and when you call to prayer, take it in mockery
7:22 (21)	their Lord called to them, 'Did not I prohibit you'
7:44 (42)	the inhabitants of Paradise will call to the inhabitants of the Fire
7:46 (44)	who shall call to the inhabitants of Paradise: 'Peace be upon you'
7:48 (46)	the dwellers on the Battlements shall call to certain men they know
7:50 (48)	the inhabitants of the Fire shall call to the inhabitants of Paradise
11:42 (44)	Noah called to his son, who was standing apart
11:45 (47)	Noah called unto his Lord, and said, 'O my Lord'
19:3 (2)	when he called upon his Lord secretly
19:24 (24)	but the one that was below her called to her

19:52 (53)	We called to him from the right side of the Mount
21:76 (76)	and Noah — when he called before, and We answered him
21:83 (83)	and Job — when he called unto his Lord
21:87 (87)	then he called out in the darkness, There is no god but Thou
21:89 (89)	and Zachariah — when he called unto his Lord
26:10 (9)	and when thy Lord called to Moses
28:46 (46)	thou wast not upon the side of the Mount when We called
37:75 (73)	Noah called to Us; and how excellent were the Answerers
37:104 (104)	We called unto him, Abraham
38:3 (2)	and they called, but time was none to escape
38:41 (40)	remember also Our servant Job; when he called to his Lord
43:51 (50)	and Pharaoh proclaimed among his people
43:77 (77)	they shall call, 'O Malik, let thy Lord have done with us!'
54:29 (29)	then they called their comrade
68:48 (48)	be not as the Man of the Fish, when he called, choking inwardly
79:16 (16)	when his Lord called to him in the holy valley, Towa
79:23 (23)	then he mustered and proclaimed

b) impf. act. (*yunādī*)

3:193 (190)	our Lord, we have heard a caller calling us to belief
28:62 (62)	upon the day when He shall call to them, and He shall say
28:65 (65)	upon the day when He shall call to them, and He shall say
28:74 (74)	upon the day when He shall call to them, and He shall say
41:47 (47)	upon the day when He shall call to them, 'Where now are My associates?'
49:4 (4)	those who call unto thee from behind the apartments
50:41 (40)	listen thou for the day when the caller shall call from a near place
57:14 (13)	they shall be calling unto them, 'Were we not with you?'

c) impv. (*nādi*)

18:52 (50)	call on My associates whom you asserted

d) perf. pass. (*nūdiya*)

7:43 (41)	it will be proclaimed: 'This is your Paradise'
20:11 (11)	when he came to it, a voice cried, 'Moses'
27:8 (8)	when he came to it, he was called: 'Blessed is He who is in the fire'
28:30 (30)	when he came to it, a voice cried from the right bank of the watercourse
62:9 (9)	when proclamation is made for prayer on the Day of Congregation

e) impf. pass. (*yunādá*)

40:10 (10)	it shall be proclaimed to the unbelievers, Surely God's hatred is greater
41:44 (44)	those — they are called from a far place

f) n.vb. (*nidā'*)

2:171 (166)	one who shouts to that which hears nothing, save (a call) and a cry
19:3 (2)	when he called upon his Lord <secretly>

g) pcple. act. (*munādī*)

3:193 (190)	we have heard a caller calling us to belief
50:41 (40)	listen thou for the day when the caller shall call

TANĀDÁ vb. (VI)~to call one another. (n.vb.) invocation [Ar]; summoning [Pk]; mutual calling (and wailing) [Ali, Bl]

a) perf. act.

68:21 (21) in the morning they called to one another

40:32 (34) O my people, I fear for you the Day of Invocation

*N DH R

NADHARA vb. (I)~to vow (in dedication or consecration). (n.vb.) a vow

a) perf. act.

2:270 (273) whatever vow you vow, surely God knows it
3:35 (31) I have vowed to Thee, in dedication, what is within my womb
19:26 (27) I have vowed to the All-merciful a fast

f) n.vb. (*nadhr*)

2:270 (273) whatever vow you vow, surely God knows it
22:29 (30) let them fulfil their vows, and go about
76:7 (7) they fulfil their vows, and fear a day whose evil is upon the wing

NADHĪR n.m. (pl. *nudhur*)~a warner

2:119 (113) We have sent thee with the truth, good tidings to bear, and warning
5:19 (22) there has not come to us any bearer of good tidings, neither any warner
5:19 (22) there has come to you a bearer of good tidings and a warner
7:184 (183) he is naught but a plain warner
7:188 (188) I am only a warner, and a bearer of good tidings
11:2 (2) I am to you a warner from Him and a bearer of good tidings
11:12 (15) thou art only a warner; and God is a Guardian over everything
11:25 (27) I am for you a warner, and a bearer of good tidings
15:89 (89) and say, 'Surely, I am the manifest warner'
17:105 (106) We have sent thee not, except good tidings to bear, and warning
22:49 (48) say: 'O men, I am only for you a plain warner'
25:1 (1) who has sent down the Salvation upon His servant, that he may be a warner
25:7 (8) why has an angel not been sent down to him, to be a warner with him?
25:51 (53) if We had willed, We would have raised up in every city a warner
25:56 (58) We have sent thee not, except good tidings to bear, and warning
26:115 (115) I am naught but a plain warner
28:46 (46) that thou mayest warn a people to whom no warner came before thee
29:50 (49) the signs are only with God, and I am only a plain warner
32:3 (2) that thou mayest warn a people to whom no warner came before thee
33:45 (44) We have sent thee as a witness, and good tidings to bear and warning
34:28 (27) We have sent thee not, except to mankind entire, good tidings to bear, and warning
34:34 (33) We sent no warner into any city
34:44 (43) nor have We sent them before thee any warner
34:46 (45) he is naught but a warner unto you, before a terrible chastisement
35:23 (21) thou art naught but a warner
35:24 (22) We have sent thee with the truth good tidings to bear, and warning
35:24 (22) not a nation there is, but there has passed away in it a warner
35:37 (34) to you the warner came

35:42 (40)	if a warner came to them, they would be more rightly guided
35:42 (40)	when a warner came to them, it increased them only in aversion
38:70 (70)	this alone is revealed to me, that I am only a clear warner
41:4 (3)	good tidings to bear, and warning
43:23 (22)	We sent never before thee any warner into any city
46:9 (8)	I am only a clear warner
48:8 (8)	We have sent thee as a witness, good tidings to bear, and warning
51:50 (50)	I am a clear warner from Him to you
51:51 (51)	I am a clear warner from Him to you
53:56 (57)	this is a warner of (the warners) of old
67:8 (8)	came there no warner to you?
67:9 (9)	yes indeed, a warner came to us; but we cried lies
67:17 (17)	then you shall know how My warning is?
67:26 (26)	the knowledge is with God; I am only a clear warner
71:2 (2)	O my people, I am unto you a clear warner
74:36 (39)	as a warner to mortals

NUDHR n.m.~a warning

77:6 (6)	excusing or warning

NUDHUR n.m.~warning(s); (pl. of *nadhīr*, above) warners

10:101 (101)	neither signs nor warnings avail a people who do not believe
46:21 (20)	already warners had passed away alike before him and behind him
53:56 (57)	this is (a warner) of the warners of old
54:5 (5)	a Wisdom far-reaching; yet warnings do not avail
54:16 (16)	how then were My chastisement and My warnings?
54:18 (18)	how then were My chastisement and My warnings?
54:21 (21)	how then were My chastisement and My warnings?
54:23 (23)	Thamood cried lies to the warnings
54:30 (30)	how then were My chastisement and My warnings?
54:33 (33)	the people of Lot cried lies to the warnings
54:36 (36)	they disputed the warnings
54:37 (37)	taste now My chastisement and My warnings
54:39 (39)	taste now My chastisement and My warnings
54:41 (41)	the warnings came also to Pharaoh's folk

ANDHARA vb. (IV)~to warn. (pcple. act.) a warner; warning. (pcple. pass.) one who is warned

a) perf. act.

2:6 (5)	alike it is to them whether thou hast warned them or hast not warned them
36:10 (9)	alike it is to them whether thou hast warned them
41:13 (12)	I warn you of a thunderbolt like to the thunderbolt of Ad
46:21 (20)	remember the brother of Ad, when he warned his people beside the sand-dunes
54:36 (36)	he had warned them of Our assault
78:40 (40)	lo, We have warned you of a nigh chastisement
92:14 (14)	now I have warned you of a Fire that flames

b) impf. act. (*yundhiru*)

2:6 (5)	whether thou hast warned them or hast not warned them
6:19 (19)	this Koran has been revealed to me that I may warn you thereby
6:92 (92)	for thee to warn the Mother of Cities and those about her
6:130 (130)	and warning you of the encounter of this your day
7:2 (1)	to warn thereby, and as a reminder to believers
7:63 (61)	that he may warn you, and you be godfearing

7:69 (67)	that he may warn you; and remember
9:122 (123)	to become learned in religion, and to warn their people
18:2 (2)	to warn of great violence from Him
18:4 (3)	to warn those who say, 'God has taken to Himself a son'
19:97 (97)	thereby to the godfearing, and warn a people stubborn
21:45 (46)	say: 'I warn you only by the Revelation'
28:46 (46)	that thou mayest warn a people to whom no warner came before thee
32:3 (2)	that thou mayest warn a people to whom no warner came before thee
35:18 (19)	thou warnest only those who fear their Lord
36:6 (5)	that thou mayest warn a people whose fathers were never warned
36:10 (9)	or thou hast not warned them, they do not believe
36:11 (10)	thou only warnest him who follows the Remembrance
36:70 (70)	that he may warn whosoever is living
39:71 (71)	and warning you against the encounter of this your day
40:15 (15)	that he may warn them of the Day of Encounter
42:7 (5)	that thou mayest warn the Mother of Cities
42:7 (5)	and that thou mayest warn of the Day of Gathering
46:12 (11)	a Book confirming, in Arabic tongue, to warn the evildoers

c) impv. (*andhir*)

6:51 (51)	and warn therewith those who fear they shall be mustered
10:2 (2)	warn the people, and give thou good tidings to the believers
14:44 (44)	and warn mankind of the day when the chastisement comes on them
16:2 (2)	give you warning that there is no god but I
19:39 (40)	warn thou them of the day of anguish, when the matter shall be determined
26:214 (214)	and warn thy clan, thy nearest kin
40:18 (18)	and warn them against the Day of the Imminent
71:1 (1)	warn thy people, ere there come on them a painful chastisement
74:2 (2)	arise, and warn

d) perf. pass. (*undhira*)

18:56 (54)	they have taken My signs, and what they are warned of, in mockery
36:6 (5)	that thou mayest warn a people whose fathers were never warned
46:3 (2)	the unbelievers are turning away from that they were warned of

e) impf. pass. (*yundharu*)

14:52 (52)	this is a Message to be delivered to mankind that they may be warned by it
21:45 (46)	they that are deaf do not hear the call when they are warned

g) pcple. act. (*mundhir*)

2:213 (209)	then God sent forth the Prophets, good tidings to bear and warning
4:165 (163)	Messengers bearing good tidings, and warning
6:48 (48)	We do not send the Envoys, except good tidings to bear, and warning
13:7 (8)	thou art only a warner, and a guide to every people
18:56 (54)	We send not the Envoys, but good tidings to bear, and warning
26:194 (194)	upon thy heart, that thou mayest be one of the warners
26:208 (208)	never a city We destroyed, but it had warners
27:92 (94)	say: 'I am naught but a warner'
37:72 (70)	and We sent among them warners
38:4 (3)	they marvel that a warner has come to them from among them
38:65 (65)	say: 'I am only a warner'
44:3 (2)	We are ever warning
46:29 (28)	when it was finished, they turned back to their people, warning

50:2 (2) they marvel that a warner has come to them from among them
79:45 (45) thou art only the warner of him who fears it

h) pcple. pass. (*mundhar*)

10:73 (74) behold how was the end of them that were warned
26:173 (173) evil is the rain of them that are warned
27:58 (59) evil indeed is the rain of them that are warned
37:73 (71) behold, how was the end of them that were warned
37:177 (177) how evil will be the morning of them that are warned

*N Ḍ D

NAḌADA vb. (I)~(pcple. pass.) one on another, serried [Ar]; piled up [Bl]; (arranged) one after the other, clustered [Pk]; spread layer on layer, overspread with piles of flowers [Ali]

h) pcple. pass. (*manḍūd*)

11:82 (84) and rained on it stones of baked clay
56:29 (28) and serried acacias

NAḌĪD n.m. (adj)~compact, ranged

50:10 (10) and tall palm-trees with spathes compact

*N Ḍ J

NAḌIJA vb. (I)~to be wholly burned [Ar]; to be consumed [Pk]; to be roasted through [Ali]

a) perf. act.

4:56 (59) as often as their skins are wholly burned

*N Ḍ KH

NAḌḌĀKH n.m. (adj)~gushing, abundant

55:66 (66) therein two fountains of gushing water

*N Ḍ R

NAḌARA vb. (I)~(pcple. act.) radiant, bright, beaming

g) pcple. act. f. (*nāḍirah*)

75:22 (22) upon that day faces shall be radiant

NAḌRAH n.f.~radiancy [Ar]; brightness [Pk]; a light of beauty [Ali]

76:11 (11) and has procured them radiancy and gladness
83:24 (24) thou knowest in their faces the radiancy of bliss

*N F ᶜ

NAFAᶜA vb. (I)~to profit (tr), to be profitable, to be useful; to avail. (n.vb.) usefulness, profit

a) perf. act.

10:98 (98)	was there never a city that believed, and its belief profited it?
87:9 (9)	therefore remind, if the Reminder profits

b) impf. act. (*yanfaᶜu*)

2:102 (96)	they learned what hurt them, and did not profit them
2:123 (117)	nor any intercession shall be profitable to it
2:164 (159)	the ship that runs in the sea with profit to men
5:119 (119)	this is the day the truthful shall be profited by their truthfulness
6:71 (70)	shall we call, apart from God, on that which neither profits nor hurts us
6:158 (159)	it shall not profit a soul to believe that never believed before
10:18 (19)	they serve, apart from God, what hurts them not neither profits them
10:106 (106)	do not call, apart from God, on that which neither profits nor hurts thee
11:34 (36)	my sincere counsel will not profit you, if I desire to counsel you
12:21 (21)	give him goodly lodging, and it may be that he will profit us
13:17 (18)	and what profits men abides in the earth
20:109 (108)	upon that day the intercession will not profit
21:66 (67)	do you serve, apart from God, that which profits you nothing
22:12 (12)	he calls, apart from God, upon that which hurts him not, and which neither profits him anything
25:55 (57)	they serve, apart from God, what neither profits them nor hurts them
26:73 (73)	or do they profit you, or harm?
26:88 (88)	the day when neither wealth nor sons shall profit
28:9 (8)	slay him not; perchance he will profit us
30:57 (57)	so that day their excuses will not profit the evildoers
32:29 (29)	on the Day of Victory their faith shall not profit the unbelievers
33:16 (16)	flight will not profit you, if you flee from death or slaying
34:23 (22)	intercession will not avail with Him save for him to whom He gives leave
40:52 (55)	upon the day when their excuses shall not profit the evildoers
40:85 (85)	their belief when they saw Our might did not profit them
43:39 (38)	it shall not profit you today, since you did evil
51:55 (55)	the Reminder profits the believers
60:3 (3)	nor your children shall profit you upon the Day of Resurrection
74:48 (49)	then the intercession of the intercessors shall not profit them
80:4 (4)	or yet remember, and the Reminder profit him

f) n.vb. (*nafᶜ*)

2:219 (216)	the sin in them is more heinous than the usefulness
4:11 (12)	you know not which out of them is nearer in profit to you
5:76 (80)	do you serve, apart from God, that which cannot hurt or profit you?
7:188 (188)	I have no power to profit for myself, or hurt, but as God will
10:49 (50)	I have no power to profit for myself, or hurt, but as God will
13:16 (17)	such as have no power to profit or hurt themselves
20:89 (91)	returned no speech unto them, neither had any power to hurt or profit them
22:13 (13)	he calls upon him who is likelier to hurt him, rather than to profit him
25:3 (4)	and have no power to hurt or profit themselves
34:42 (41)	today none of you shall have power to profit or hurt another
48:11 (11)	if He desires hurt for you, or desires profit for you

MANĀFIʿ n.f. (pl. of *manfaʿah*)~uses, that which is profitable [Ar, Bl]; utility [Pk]; profit [Ali]

2:219 (216)	in both is heinous sin, and uses for men
16:5 (5)	He created them for you; in them is warmth, and uses various
22:28 (29)	that they may witness things profitable to them
22:33 (34)	there are things therein profitable to you unto a stated term
23:21 (21)	and many uses there are in them for you
36:73 (73)	other uses also they have in them, and beverages
40:80 (80)	other uses also you have in them
57:25 (25)	We sent down iron, wherein is great might, and many uses for men

*N F D

NAFIDA vb. (I)~to be spent, to come to an end [Ar]; to be used up [Pk]; to be exhausted [Ali]; to give out [Bl]. (n.vb.) an end, the act of wasting away

a) perf. act.

18:109 (109)	the sea would be spent before the Words of my Lord are spent
31:27 (26)	yet would the Words of God not be spent

b) impf. act. (*yanfadu*)

16:96 (98)	what is with you comes to an end, but what is with God abides
18:109 (109)	the sea would be spent before the Words of my Lord are spent

f) n.vb. (*nafād*)

38:54 (54)	this is Our provision unto which there is no end

*N F DH

NAFADHA vb. (I)~to pass through

b) impf. act. (*yanfudhu*)

55:33 (33)	if you are able to pass through the confines of heaven and earth
55:33 (33)	you shall not pass through except with an authority

c) impv. (*unfudh*)

55:33 (33)	pass through them!

*N F Ḥ

NAFḤAH n.f.~a breath

21:46 (47)	if but a breath of thy Lord's chastisement touched them

*N F KH

NAFAKHA vb. (I)~to blow; (with prep. *fī*) to breathe

a) perf. act.

15:29 (29) when I have shaped him, and breathed My spirit in him, fall you down
21:91 (91) so We breathed into her of Our spirit
32:9 (8) then He shaped him, and breathed His spirit in him
38:72 (72) when I have shaped him, and breathed My spirit in him, fall you down
66:12 (12) so We breathed into her of Our Spirit

b) impf. act. (*yanfukhu*)

3:49 (43) then I will breathe into it, and it will be a bird
5:110 (110) and thou breathest into it, and it is a bird

c) impv. (*unfukh*)

18:96 (95) he said, 'Blow!'

d) perf. pass. (*nufikha*)

18:99 (99) the Trumpet shall be blown, and We shall gather them together
23:101 (103) when the Trumpet is blown, that day there shall be no kinship
36:51 (51) the Trumpet shall be blown; then behold, they are sliding down
39:68 (68) the Trumpet shall be blown, and whosoever is in the heavens ... Shall swoon
39:68 (68) then it shall be blown again, and lo, they shall stand
50:20 (19) the Trumpet shall be blown; that is the Day of the Threat
69:13 (13) so, when the Trumpet is blown with a single blast

e) impf. pass. (*yunfakhu*)

6:73 (73) His is the Kingdom the day the Trumpet is blown
20:102 (102) on the day the Trumpet is blown; and We shall muster the sinners
27:87 (89) on the day the Trumpet is blown, and terrified is whosoever is in the heavens
78:18 (18) the day the Trumpet is blown, and you shall come in troops

NAFKHAH n.f.~blast

69:13 (13) when the Trumpet is blown with a single blast

*N F L

ANFĀL n.m. (pl. of *nafal*)~spoils (of war)

8:1 (1) they will question thee concerning the spoils
8:1 (1) the spoils belong to God and the Messenger

NĀFILAH n.f.~a work of supererogation or superfluity [Ar]; largess, a grandson (i.e. in addition to a son) [Pk]; additional act, additional gift [Ali]; (something) extra, over and above [Bl]

17:79 (81) as for the night, keep vigil a part of it, as a work of supererogation for thee
21:72 (72) We gave him Isaac and Jacob in superfluity

*N F Q

NAFAQ n.m.~a hole in the ground (with another exit)

6:35 (35)	if thou canst seek out a hole in the earth

NAFAQAH n.f.~an expenditure, an expending, a sum expended

2:270 (273)	and whatever expenditure you expend
9:54 (54)	naught prevents that their expendings should be accepted from them
9:121 (122)	nor do they expend any sum, small or great

NĀFAQA vb. (III)~to be a hypocrite; (*alladhīna nāfaqū*) the hypocrites. (n.vb.) hypocrisy. (pcple. act.) the hypocrites

a) perf. act.

3:167 (160)	that He might also know the hypocrites when it was said of them
59:11 (11)	hast thou not regarded the hypocrites, saying to their brothers

f) n.vb. (*nifāq*)

9:77 (78)	as a consequence He put hypocrisy into their hearts
9:97 (98)	the Bedouins are more stubborn in unbelief and hypocrisy
9:101 (102)	some of the people of the City are grown bold in hypocrisy

g) pcple. act. (*munāfiq*)

4:61 (64)	then thou seest the hypocrites barring the way to thee
4:88 (90)	how is it with you, that you are two parties touching the hypocrites
4:138 (137)	give thou good tidings to the hypocrites that for them awaits a painful chastisement
4:140 (139)	God will gather the hypocrites and the unbelievers all in Gehenna
4:142 (141)	the hypocrites seek to trick God, but God is tricking them
4:145 (144)	the hypocrites will be in the lowest reach of the Fire
8:49 (51)	when the hypocrites, and those in whose hearts was sickness, said
9:64 (65)	the hypocrites are afraid, lest a sura should be sent down against them
9:67 (68)	the hypocrites, the men and (the women) are as one another
9:67 (68)	the hypocrites (the men) and the women, are as one another
9:67 (68)	the hypocrites — they are the ungodly
9:68 (69)	God has promised the hypocrites, men and (women) and the unbelievers, the fire of Gehenna
9:68 (69)	God has promised the hypocrites (men) and women, and the unbelievers, the fire of Gehenna
9:73 (74)	O Prophet, struggle with the unbelievers and hypocrites
9:101 (102)	some of the Bedouins who dwell around you are hypocrites
29:11 (10)	God surely knows the believers, and He knows the hypocrites
33:1 (1)	obey not the unbelievers and the hypocrites
33:12 (12)	when the hypocrites, and those in whose hearts is sickness, said
33:24 (24)	and chastise the hypocrites, if He will, or turn again unto them
33:48 (47)	obey not the unbelievers and the hypocrites
33:60 (60)	now, if the hypocrites do not give over
33:73 (73)	that God may chastise the hypocrites, men (and women) alike, and the idolaters
33:73 (73)	that God may chastise the hypocrites, (men) and women alike, and the idolaters

48:6 (6)	He may chastise the hypocrites, men (and women) alike, and the idolaters
48:6 (6)	He may chastise the hypocrites, (men) and women alike, and the idolaters
57:13 (13)	upon the day when the hypocrites, men (and women) shall say to those who have believed
57:13 (13)	upon the day when the hypocrites (men) and women, shall say to those who have believed
63:1 (1)	when the hypocrites come to thee they say
63:1 (1)	God bears witness that the hypocrites are truly liars
63:7 (7)	but the hypocrites do not understand
63:8 (8)	but the hypocrites do not know it
66:9 (9)	O Prophet, struggle with the unbelievers and the hypocrites

ANFAQA vb. (IV)~to expend, to spend. (n.vb.) the act of expending or spending. (pcple. act.) an expender

a) perf. act.

2:215 (211)	whatsoever good you expend is for parents and kinsmen
2:262 (264)	those who expend their wealth in the way of God
2:270 (273)	whatever expenditure you expend, and whatever vow you vow
4:34 (38)	and for that they have expended of their property
4:39 (43)	believed in God and the Last Day, and expended of that God has provided them
8:63 (64)	hadst thou expended all that is in the earth
13:22 (22)	who perform the prayer, and expend of that We have provided them
18:42 (40)	in the morning he was wringing his hands for that he had expended upon it
25:67 (67)	who, when they expend, are neither prodigal nor parsimonious
34:39 (38)	whatever thing you shall expend, He will replace it
35:29 (26)	perform the prayer, and expend of that We have provided them
57:7 (7)	and expend of that unto which He has made you successors
57:10 (10)	not equal is he among you who spent, and who fought before the victory
57:10 (10)	those are mightier in rank than they who spent and fought afterwards
60:10 (10)	give the unbelievers what they have expended
60:10 (10)	hold fast to the ties of unbelieving women, and ask what you have expended
60:10 (10)	and let them ask what they have expended
60:11 (11)	give those whose wives have gone away the like of what they have expended

b) impf. act. (*yunfiqu*)

2:3 (2)	and expend of that We have provided them
2:215 (211)	they will question thee concerning what they should expend
2:219 (216)	they will question thee concerning what they should expend
2:261 (263)	the likeness of those who expend their wealth in the way of God
2:262 (264)	those who expend their wealth in the way of God
2:264 (266)	as one who expends of his substance to show off to men
2:265 (267)	the likeness of those who expend their wealth, seeking God's good pleasure
2:267 (269)	and intend not the corrupt of it for your expending
2:272 (274)	whatever good you expend is for yourselves
2:272 (274)	for then you are expending, being desirous only of God's Face
2:272 (274)	whatever good you expend shall be repaid to you in full
2:273 (274)	whatever good you expend, surely God has knowledge of it
2:274 (275)	those who expend their wealth night and day, secretly and in public
3:92 (86)	you will not attain piety until you expend of what you love
3:92 (86)	and whatever thing you expend, God knows of it
3:117 (113)	the likeness of that they expend in this present life
3:134 (128)	who expend in prosperity and adversity in almsgiving, and restrain their rage

4:38 (42) and such as expend of their substance to show off to men
5:64 (69) nay, but His hands are outspread; He expends how He will
8:3 (3) those who perform the prayer, and expend of what We have provided them
8:36 (36) the unbelievers expend their wealth to bar from God's way
8:36 (36) still they will expend it, till it is an anguish for them
8:60 (62) whatsoever you expend in the way of God shall be repaid you in full
9:34 (34) those who treasure up gold and silver, and do not expend them in the way of God
9:54 (54) and that they expend not without they are averse
9:91 (92) there is no fault in the weak and the sick and those who find nothing to expend
9:92 (93) their eyes overflowing with tears of sorrow, because they found nothing to expend
9:98 (99) some of the Bedouins take what they expend for a fine
9:99 (100) and take what they expend for offerings bringing them near to God
9:121 (122) nor do they expend any sum, small or great
14:31 (36) and expend of that We have provided them, secretly
16:75 (77) with a provision fair, and he expends of it secretly and openly
22:35 (36) who perform the prayer, and expend of what We have provided them
28:54 (54) and expend of that We have provided them
32:16 (16) they expend of that We have provided them
42:38 (36) they expend of that We have provided them
47:38 (40) you are called upon to expend in God's way
57:10 (10) how it is with you, that you expend not in the way of God
63:7 (7) do not expend on them that are with God's Messenger
65:7 (7) let the man of plenty expend out of his plenty
65:7 (7) let him expend of what God has given him

c) impv. (*anfiq*)

2:195 (191) and expend in the way of God
2:254 (255) O believers, expend of that wherewith We have provided you
2:267 (269) O believers, expend of the good things you have earned
9:53 (53) expend willingly, or unwillingly, it shall not be accepted from you
36:47 (47) expend of that God has provided you
57:7 (7) believe in God and His Messenger, and expend of that unto which He has made you successors
63:10 (10) expend of what We have provided you before that death comes upon one of you
64:16 (16) give ear, and obey, and expend well for yourselves
65:6 (6) if they are with child, expend upon them until they bring forth their burden

f) n.vb. (*infāq*)

17:100 (102) yet would you hold back for fear of expending

g) pcple. act. (*munfiq*)

3:17 (15) men who are patient, truthful, obedient, expenders in alms

*N F R

NAFARA vb. (I)~to go forth, to move forward. (n.vb.) aversion

a) perf. act.

9:122 (123) why should not a party of every section of them go forth *b*) impf. act. (*yanfiru*)

9:39 (39) if you go not forth, He will chastise you with a painful chastisement
9:81 (82) go not forth in the heat
9:122 (123) it is not for the believers to go forth totally

c) impv. (*infir*)

4:71 (73) move forward in companies
4:71 (73) or move forward all together
9:38 (38) go forth in the way of God
9:41 (41) go forth, light and heavy

f) n.vb. (*nufūr*)

17:41 (43) it increases them only in aversion
17:46 (49) they turn in their traces in aversion
25:60 (61) it increases them in aversion
35:42 (40) when a warner came to them, it increased them only in aversion
67:21 (21) no, but they persist in disdain and aversion

NAFAR n.m.~a group or company of men (or jinn)

18:34 (32) I have more abundance of wealth than thou and am mightier in respect of men
46:29 (28) and when We turned to thee a company of jinn
72:1 (1) it has been revealed to me that a company of the jinn gave ear

NAFĪR n.m.~a host, group or company of men

17:6 (6) and We made you a greater host

ISTANFARA vb. (X)~(pcple. act.) one who is startled or frightened

g) pcple. act. (*mustanfir*)

74:50 (51) as if they were startled asses

*N F S

NAFS n.f. (pl. *anfus* and *nufūs*)~soul, self, life, person; heart [Ar, Ali, Bl]; mind [Pk]; (used as a reflexive when followed by a pronominal suffix) -self, -selves, own, own behalf; each other, one another (as in 2:54). Several phrases employ *nafs* such as (*min tilqāʾ nafsī*) of my own accord; (*rāwada ʿan nafsihi*) to solicit; (*shaqq al-nafs*) great distress or trouble (for oneself); (*ṭāba nafsan*) to be pleased to do something

2:9 (8) they would trick God and the believers, and only themselves they deceive
2:44 (41) will you bid others to piety, and forget yourselves
2:48 (45) a day when no soul for (another) shall give satisfaction
2:48 (45) a day when no (soul) for another [soul] shall give satisfaction
2:54 (51) you have done wrong against yourselves by your taking the Calf
2:54 (51) now turn to your Creator and slay one another
2:57 (54) they worked no wrong upon Us, but themselves they wronged
2:72 (67) when you killed a living soul, and disputed thereon
2:84 (78) then you confirmed it and yourselves bore witness
2:85 (79) then there you are killing one another, and expelling a party of you
2:87 (81) whensoever there came to you a Messenger with that your souls had not desire for
2:90 (84) evil is the thing they have sold themselves for
2:102 (96) evil then was that they sold themselves for

2:109 (103)	restore you as unbelievers, after you have believed, in the jealousy of their souls
2:110 (104)	whatever good you shall forward to your souls' account, you shall find it with God
2:123 (117)	beware a day when no soul for (another [soul]) shall give satisfaction
2:123 (117)	beware a day when no (soul) for another [soul] shall give satisfaction
2:130 (124)	who therefore shrinks from the religion of Abraham, except he be foolish-minded?
2:155 (150)	We will try you with something of fear and hunger, and diminution of goods and lives
2:187 (183)	God knows that you have been betraying yourselves
2:207 (203)	but other men there are that sell themselves
2:223 (223)	so come unto your tillage as you wish, and forward for your souls
2:228 (228)	divorced women shall wait by themselves for three periods
2:231 (231)	whoever does that has wronged himself
2:233 (233)	no soul is charged save to its capacity
2:234 (234)	they shall wait by themselves for four months and ten nights
2:234 (234)	then it is no fault in you what they may do with themselves honourably
2:235 (235)	touching the proposal to women you offer, or hide in your hearts
2:235 (236)	and know that God knows what is in your hearts
2:240 (241)	there is no fault in you what they may do with themselves honourably
2:265 (267)	seeking God's good pleasure, and to confirm themselves
2:272 (274)	whatever good you expend is for yourselves
2:281 (281)	every soul shall be paid in full what it has earned
2:284 (284)	whether you publish what is in your hearts or hide it
2:286 (286)	God charges no soul save to its capacity
3:25 (24)	every soul shall be paid in full what it has earned
3:28 (27)	God warns you that you beware of Him
3:30 (28)	the day every soul shall find what it has done of good brought forward
3:30 (28)	God warns you that you beware of Him [Himself]
3:61 (54)	our selves and your (selves)
3:61 (54)	our (selves) and your selves
3:69 (62)	yet none they make to stray, except themselves
3:93 (87)	all food was lawful to the Children of Israel save what Israel forbade for himself
3:117 (113)	the tillage of a people who wronged themselves
3:117 (113)	God wronged them not, but themselves they wronged
3:135 (129)	who, when they commit an indecency or wrong themselves, remember God
3:145 (139)	it is not given to any soul to die, save by the leave of God
3:154 (148)	a party themselves had grieved, thinking of God thoughts that were not true
3:154 (148)	they were concealing in their hearts that they show not to thee
3:161 (155)	then every soul shall be paid in full what it has earned
3:164 (158)	when He raised up among them a Messenger from themselves
3:165 (159)	this is from your own selves; surely God is powerful
3:168 (162)	then avert death from yourselves, if you speak truly
3:178 (172)	let not the unbelievers suppose that the indulgence We grant them is better for them [themselves]
3:185 (182)	every soul shall taste of death
3:186 (183)	you shall surely be tried in your possessions and your selves
4:1 (1)	fear your Lord, who created you of a single soul
4:4 (3)	if they are pleased to offer you any of it, consume it with wholesome appetite
4:29 (33)	kill not one another [yourselves]
4:49 (52)	hast thou not regarded those who purify themselves?
4:63 (66)	and say to them penetrating words about themselves
4:64 (67)	if, when they wronged themselves, they had come to thee
4:65 (68)	then they shall find in themselves no impediment touching thy verdict
4:66 (69)	had We prescribed for them, saying, 'Slay yourselves'
4:79 (81)	whatever evil visits thee is of thyself

4:84 (86)	thou art charged only with thyself
4:95 (97)	those who struggle in the path of God with their possessions and their selves
4:95 (97)	God has preferred in rank those who struggle with their possessions and their selves
4:97 (99)	those the angels take, while still they are wronging themselves
4:107 (107)	do not dispute on behalf of those who betray themselves
4:110 (110)	whosoever does evil, or wrongs himself, and then prays God's forgiveness
4:111 (111)	whosoever earns a sin, earns it against himself only
4:113 (113)	but they lead only themselves astray
4:128 (127)	souls are very prone to avarice
4:135 (134)	witnesses for God, even though it be against yourselves
5:25 (28)	I rule no one except myself and my brother
5:30 (33)	then his soul prompted him to slay his brother
5:32 (35)	that whoso slays a soul not to retaliate for a (soul) slain
5:32 (35)	that whoso slays a (soul) not to retaliate for a soul slain
5:45 (49)	a life for a (life) an eye for an eye
5:45 (49)	a (life) for a life, an eye for an eye
5:52 (57)	then they will find themselves, for that they kept secret within them
5:70 (74)	whensoever there came to them a Messenger with that their souls had not desire for
5:80 (83)	evil is that they have forwarded to their account [their selves]
5:105 (104)	O believers, look after your own souls
5:116 (116)	thou knowest it, knowing what is within my soul
5:116 (116)	I know not what is within Thy soul
6:12 (12)	He has prescribed for Himself mercy
6:12 (12)	those who have lost their souls, they do not believe
6:20 (20)	those who have lost their own souls, they do not believe
6:24 (24)	behold how they lie against themselves
6:26 (26)	it is only themselves they destroy
6:54 (54)	your Lord has prescribed for Himself mercy
6:70 (69)	remind hereby, lest a soul should be given up to destruction
6:93 (93)	give up your souls! Today you shall be recompensed
6:98 (98)	it is He who produced you from one living soul
6:104 (104)	whoso sees clearly, it is to his own gain
6:123 (123)	but they devised only against themselves
6:130 (130)	they shall say, 'We bear witness against ourselves'
6:130 (130)	they were deluded by the present life, and they bear witness against themselves
6:151 (152)	slay not the soul God has forbidden, except by right
6:152 (153)	We charge not any soul save to its capacity
6:158 (159)	it shall not profit a soul to believe that never believed before
6:164 (164)	every soul earns only to its own account
7:9 (8)	they have lost their souls for wronging Our signs
7:23 (22)	they said, 'Lord, we have wronged ourselves'
7:37 (35)	they will bear witness against themselves that they were unbelievers
7:42 (40)	We charge not any sou, save according to its capacity
7:53 (51)	they have indeed lost their souls
7:160 (160)	they worked no wrong upon Us, but themselves they wronged
7:172 (171)	from their loins, their seed, and made them testify touching themselves
7:177 (176)	the people who cried lies to Our signs, and themselves were wronging
7:188 (188)	say: 'I have no power to profit for myself'
7:189 (189)	it is He who created you out of one living soul
7:192 (191)	and that have no power to help them, neither they help themselves
7:197 (196)	have no power to help you, neither they help themselves
7:205 (204)	remember thy Lord in thy soul, humbly and fearfully
8:53 (55)	God would never change His favour that He conferred on a people until they changed what was within themselves

8:72 (73)	and struggled with their possessions and their selves
9:17 (17)	witnessing against themselves unbelief
9:20 (20)	[those who] have struggled in the way of God with their possessions and their selves
9:35 (35)	this is the thing you have treasured up for yourselves
9:36 (36)	so wrong not each other during them
9:41 (41)	struggle in God's way with your possessions and your selves
9:42 (42)	so destroying their souls
9:44 (44)	that they may struggle with their possessions and their selves
9:55 (55)	and that their souls should depart while they are unbelievers
9:70 (71)	God would not wrong them, but themselves they wronged
9:81 (82)	and were averse to struggle with their possessions and their selves
9:85 (86)	and that their souls should depart while they are unbelievers
9:88 (89)	and the believers with him, have struggled with their possessions and their selves
9:111 (112)	God has bought from the believers their selves and their possessions
9:118 (119)	and their souls became strait for them
9:120 (121)	and to prefer their lives to (his [life])
9:120 (121)	and to prefer their (lives) to his [life]
9:128 (129)	there has come to you a Messenger from among yourselves
10:15 (16)	it is not for me to alter it of my own accord
10:23 (24)	O men, your insolence is only against yourselves
10:30 (31)	there every soul shall prove its past deeds
10:44 (45)	God wrongs not men anything, but themselves men wrong
10:49 (50)	I have no power to profit for myself, or hurt, but as God will
10:54 (55)	if every soul that has done evil possessed all that is in the earth
10:100 (100)	it is not for any soul to believe save by the leave of God
10:108 (108)	whosoever is guided is guided only to his own gain
11:21 (23)	those are they that have lost their souls
11:31 (33)	God knows best what is in their hearts
11:101 (103)	We wronged them not, but they wronged themselves
11:105 (107)	the day it comes, no soul shall speak save by His leave
12:18 (18)	no; but your spirits tempted you to do somewhat
12:23 (23)	now the woman in whose house he was solicited him
12:26 (26)	it was she that solicited me
12:30 (30)	the Governor's wife has been soliciting her page
12:32 (32)	yes, I solicited him, but he abstained
12:51 (51)	what was your business, women, when you solicited Joseph?
12:51 (51)	I solicited him; he is a truthful man
12:53 (53)	yet I claim not that my soul was innocent
12:53 (53)	surely the soul of man incites to evil
12:54 (54)	bring him to me! I would attach him to my person
12:68 (68)	it was a need in Jacob's soul that he so satisfied
12:77 (77)	but Joseph secreted it in his soul and disclosed it not to them
12:83 (83)	'No!' he said. 'But your spirits tempted you to do somewhat'
13:11 (12)	God changes not what is in a people, until they change what is in themselves
13:16 (17)	such as have no power to profit or hurt themselves
13:33 (33)	He who stands over every soul for what it has earned
13:42 (42)	He knows what every soul earns
14:22 (27)	so do not blame me, but blame yourselves
14:45 (47)	you dwelt in the dwelling-places of those who wronged themselves
14:51 (51)	that God may recompense every soul for its earnings
16:7 (7)	they bear your loads unto a land that you never would reach, excepting with great distress
16:28 (30)	whom the angels take while still they are wronging themselves
16:33 (35)	God wronged them not, but themselves they wronged

16:72 (74)	God has appointed for you of yourselves wives
16:89 (91)	the day We shall raise up from every nation a witness against them from amongst them
16:111 (112)	the day that every soul shall come disputing
16:111 (112)	every (soul) shall come disputing in its own behalf
16:111 (112)	every soul shall be paid in full for what it wrought
16:118 (119)	We wronged them not, but they wronged themselves
17:7 (7)	if you do good, it is your own souls you do good to
17:14 (15)	thy soul suffices thee this day as a reckoner against thee
17:15 (16)	whosoever is guided, is only guided to his own gain
17:25 (26)	your Lord knows very well what is in your hearts
17:33 (35)	slay not the soul God has forbidden, except by right
18:6 (5)	if they believe not in this tiding, thou wilt consume thyself
18:28 (27)	restrain thyself with those who call upon their Lord
18:35 (33)	and he entered his garden, wronging himself
18:51 (49)	neither of the creation of themselves
18:74 (73)	hast thou slain a soul innocent
18:74 (73)	and that not to retaliate for a soul slain
20:15 (16)	that every soul may be recompensed for its labours
20:40 (41)	then thou slewest a living soul
20:41 (43)	I have chosen thee for My service
20:67 (70)	Moses conceived a fear within him
20:96 (96)	so my soul prompted me
21:35 (36)	every soul shall taste of death
21:43 (44)	they are not able to help themselves
21:47 (48)	not one soul shall be wronged anything
21:64 (65)	so they returned one to another
21:102 (102)	they shall dwell forever in that their souls desired
23:62 (64)	We charge not any soul save to its capacity
23:103 (105)	they have lost their souls in Gehenna dwelling forever
24:6 (6)	those who cast it up on their wives having no witnesses except themselves
24:12 (12)	did the believing men and women not of their own account think good thoughts
24:61 (60)	there is no fault in the sick, neither in yourselves
24:61 (61)	greet one another with a greeting from God, blessed and good
25:3 (4)	and have no power to hurt or profit themselves
25:21 (23)	waxed proud they have within them, and become greatly disdainful
25:68 (68)	nor slay the soul God has forbidden except by right
26:3 (2)	perchance thou consumest thyself that they are not believers
27:14 (14)	they denied them, though their souls acknowledged them
27:40 (40)	whosoever gives thanks gives thanks only for his own soul's good
27:44 (45)	my Lord, indeed I have wronged myself
27:92 (94)	whosoever is guided, is only guided to his own gain
28:16 (15)	my Lord, I have wronged myself. Forgive me
28:19 (18)	dost thou desire to slay me, even as thou slewest a living soul yesterday?
28:33 (33)	my Lord, I have indeed slain a living soul among them
29:6 (5)	whosoever struggles, struggles only to his own gain
29:40 (39)	God would never wrong them, but they wronged themselves
29:57 (57)	every soul shall taste of death
30:8 (7)	have they not considered within themselves?
30:9 (8)	they were stronger than themselves in might
30:21 (20)	of His signs is that He created for you, of yourselves, spouses
30:28 (27)	He has struck for you a similitude from yourselves
30:28 (27)	you fearing them as you fear each other
30:44 (43)	whosoever does righteousness — for themselves they are making provision
31:12 (11)	whosoever gives thanks gives thanks only for his own soul's good

31:28 (27)	your creation and your upraising are as but as a single soul
31:34 (34)	no soul knows what it shall earn tomorrow
31:34 (34)	no soul knows in what land it shall die
32:13 (13)	if We had so willed, We could have given every soul its guidance
32:17 (17)	no soul knows what comfort is laid up for them secretly
32:27 (27)	and bring forth crops therewith whereof their cattle and themselves eat
33:6 (6)	the Prophet is nearer to the believers than their selves
33:37 (37)	thou wast concealing within thyself what God should reveal
33:50 (49)	and any woman believer, if she give herself to the Prophet
34:19 (18)	they wronged themselves, so We made them as but tales
34:50 (49)	if I go astray, I go astray only to my own loss
35:8 (9)	so let not thy soul be wasted in regrets for them
35:18 (19)	whosoever purifies himself, purifies himself only for his own soul's good
35:32 (29)	but of them some wrong themselves, some of them are lukewarm
36:36 (36)	who created all the pairs of what the earth produces, and of themselves
36:54 (54)	today no soul shall be wronged anything
37:113 (113)	of their seed some are good-doers, and some manifest self-wrongers
39:6 (8)	He created you of a single soul
39:15 (17)	surely the losers are they who lose themselves and their families
39:41 (42)	whosoever is guided, is only guided to his own gain
39:42 (43)	God takes the souls at the time of their death
39:53 (54)	O my people who have been prodigal against yourselves
39:56 (57)	lest any soul should say, 'Alas for me'
39:70 (70)	every soul shall be paid in full for what it has wrought
40:10 (10)	God's hatred is greater than your hatred one of another
40:17 (17)	today each soul shall be recompensed for that it has earned
41:31 (31)	therein you shall have all that your souls desire
41:46 (46)	whoso does righteousness, it is to his own gain
41:53 (53)	We shall show them Our signs in the horizons and in themselves
42:11 (9)	He has appointed for you, of yourselves, pairs
42:45 (44)	the losers are they who lose themselves and their families
43:71 (71)	therein being whatever the souls desire, and the eyes delight in
45:15 (14)	whoso does righteousness, it is to his own gain
45:22 (21)	and that every soul may be recompensed for what it has earned
47:38 (40)	whoso is niggardly is niggardly only to his own soul
48:10 (10)	whosoever breaks his oath breaks it but to his own hurt
49:11 (11)	and find not fault with one another
49:15 (15)	and have struggled with their possessions and their selves
50:16 (15)	We know what his soul whispers within him
50:21 (20)	every soul shall come, and with it a driver and a witness
51:21 (21)	and in your selves; what, do you not see?
53:23 (23)	they follow only surmise, and what the souls desire
53:32 (33)	therefore hold not yourselves purified
57:14 (13)	yes indeed; but you tempted yourselves, and you awaited
57:22 (22)	no affliction befalls in the earth or in yourselves
58:8 (9)	they say within themselves, 'Why does God not chastise us for what we say?'
59:9 (9)	preferring others above themselves, even though poverty be their portion
59:9 (9)	whoso is guarded against the avarice of his own soul
59:18 (18)	let every soul consider what it has forwarded for the morrow
59:19 (19)	be not as those who forgot God, and so He caused them to forget their souls
61:11 (11)	struggle in the way of God with your possessions and your selves
63:11 (11)	God will never defer any soul when its term comes
64:16 (16)	give ear, and obey, and expend well for yourselves
64:16 (16)	whosoever is guarded against the avarice of his own soul
65:1 (1)	whosoever trespasses the bounds of God has done wrong to himself

65:7 (7)	God charges no soul save with what He has given him
66:6 (6)	guard yourselves and your families against a Fire whose fuel is men and stones
73:20 (20)	whatever good you shall forward to your souls' account
74:38 (41)	every soul shall be pledged for what it has earned
75:2 (2)	no! I swear by the reproachful soul
75:14 (14)	nay, man shall be a clear proof against himself
79:40 (40)	and forbade the soul its caprice
81:7 (7)	when the souls shall be coupled
81:14 (14)	then shall a soul know what it has produced
82:5 (5)	then a soul shall know its works, the former and the latter
82:19 (19)	a day when no soul shall possess aught
82:19 (19)	to succour another soul
86:4 (4)	over every soul there is a watcher
89:27 (27)	O soul at peace
91:7 (7)	by the soul, and That which shaped it

TANAFFASA vb. (V)~to breathe, to sigh

a) perf. act.

81:18 (18) by the dawn sighing

TANĀFASA vb. (VI)~to strive for, to aspire after. (pcple. act.) one who strives, an aspirer

b) impf. act. (*yatanāfasu*)

83:26 (26) so after that let the strivers strive

g) pcple. act. (*mutanāfis*)

83:26 (26) so after that let the strivers strive

*N F SH

NAFASHA vb. (I)~to stray. (pcple. pass.) plucked, carded

a) perf. act.

21:78 (78) judgment concerning the tillage, when the sheep of the people strayed there

h) pcple. pass. (*manfūsh*)

101:5 (4) and the mountains shall be like plucked wool-tufts

*N F TH

NAFFĀTHAH n.f.~one who blows

113:4 (4) from the evil of the women who blow on knots

*N F Y

NAFÁ vb. (I)~to banish, to expel

e) impf. pass. (*yunfá*)

5:33 (37) or they shall be banished from the land. That is a degradation for them

*N GH Ḍ

ANGHAḌA vb. (IV)~to shake (tr)

b) impf. act. (*yunghiḍu*)

17:51 (53) then they will shake their heads at thee

*N H J

MINHĀJ n.m.~an open road

5:48 (52) to every one of you We have appointed a right way and an open road

*N H R

NAHARA vb. (I)~to chide, to scold [Ar, Bl]; to repulse, to drive away [Pk]; to repel [Ali]

b) impf. act. (*yanharu*)

17:23 (24) say not to them 'Fie' neither chide them
93:10 (10) and as for the beggar, scold him not

NAHAR n.m. (pl. *anhār*)~a river

2:25 (23) for them await gardens underneath which rivers flow
2:74 (69) there are stones from which rivers come gushing
2:249 (250) he said, 'God will try you with a river'
2:266 (268) a garden of palms and vines, with rivers flowing beneath it
3:15 (13) are gardens underneath which rivers flow
3:136 (130) and gardens beneath which rivers flow
3:195 (194) I shall admit them to gardens underneath which rivers flow
3:198 (197) gardens underneath which rivers flow
4:13 (17) to gardens underneath which rivers flow
4:57 (60) them We shall admit to gardens underneath which rivers flow
4:122 (121) them We shall admit to gardens underneath which rivers flow
5:12 (15) to gardens underneath which rivers flow
5:85 (88) with gardens underneath which rivers flow
5:119 (119) for them await gardens underneath which rivers flow
6:6 (6) and made the rivers to flow beneath them
7:43 (41) and underneath them rivers flowing
9:72 (73) gardens underneath which rivers flow
9:89 (90) God has prepared for them gardens underneath which rivers flow
9:100 (101) for them gardens underneath which rivers flow

10:9 (9)	beneath them rivers flowing in gardens of bliss
13:3 (3)	He who stretched out the earth and set therein firm mountains and rivers
13:35 (35)	beneath it rivers flow
14:23 (28)	to gardens underneath which rivers flow
14:32 (37)	He subjected to you the rivers
16:15 (15)	He cast on the earth firm mountains, lest it shake with you, and rivers
16:31 (33)	Gardens of Eden they shall enter, underneath which rivers flow
17:91 (93)	thou makest rivers to gush forth abundantly all amongst it
18:31 (30)	theirs shall be Gardens of Eden, underneath which rivers flow
18:33 (32)	and We caused to gush amidst them a river
20:76 (78)	Gardens of Eden, underneath which rivers flow
22:14 (14)	into gardens underneath which rivers flow
22:23 (23)	into gardens underneath which rivers flow
25:10 (11)	gardens underneath which rivers flow
27:61 (62)	He who made the earth a fixed place and set amidst it rivers
29:58 (58)	chambers of Paradise, underneath which rivers flow
39:20 (21)	lofty chambers, underneath which rivers flow
43:51 (50)	do I not possess the kingdom of Egypt, and these rivers flowing beneath me?
47:12 (13)	into gardens underneath which rivers flow
47:15 (16)	therein are rivers of water unstaling
47:15 (16)	rivers of milk unchanging in flavour
47:15 (16)	and rivers of wine — a delight to the drinkers
47:15 (17)	rivers, too, of honey purified
48:5 (5)	men and women alike, into gardens underneath which rivers flow
48:17 (17)	into gardens underneath which rivers flow
54:54 (54)	the godfearing shall dwell amid gardens and a river
57:12 (12)	gardens underneath which rivers flow, therein to dwell for ever
58:22 (22)	gardens underneath which rivers flow
61:12 (12)	into gardens underneath which rivers flow, and to dwelling-places
64:9 (9)	into gardens underneath which rivers flow
65:11 (11)	admit him to gardens underneath which rivers flow
66:8 (8)	into gardens underneath which rivers flow
71:12 (11)	gardens, and will appoint for you rivers
85:11 (11)	await gardens underneath which rivers flow
98:8 (7)	Gardens of Eden, underneath which rivers flow

NAHĀR n.m.~a day, daytime (from sunrise to sunset)

2:164 (159)	and the alternation of night and day
2:274 (275)	those who expend their wealth night and day
3:27 (26)	Thou makest the night to enter into the day
3:27 (26)	and Thou makest the day to enter into the night
3:72 (65)	those who believe at the beginning of the day, and disbelieve at the end of it
3:190 (187)	in the alternation of night and day there are signs
6:13 (13)	to Him belongs whatsoever inhabits the night and the day
6:60 (60)	and He knows what you work by day
7:54 (52)	covering the day with the night it pursues urgently
10:6 (6)	in the alternation of night and day
10:24 (25)	Our command comes upon it by night or day
10:45 (46)	as if they had not tarried but an hour of the day
10:50 (51)	if His chastisement comes upon you by night or day
10:67 (68)	He who made for you the night to repose in it, and the day, to see
11:114 (116)	and perform the prayer at the two ends of the day
13:3 (3)	of every fruit He placed there two kinds, covering the day with the night
13:10 (11)	he who hides himself in the night, and he who sallies by day
14:33 (37)	and He subjected to you the night and day

16:12 (12)	and He subjected to you the night and day
17:12 (13)	We have appointed the night and the day as two signs
17:12 (13)	then We have blotted out the sign of the night, and made the sign of the day to see
20:130 (130)	in the watches of the night, and at the ends of the day
21:20 (20)	glorifying Him by night and in the daytime
21:33 (34)	it is He who created the night and the day
21:42 (43)	who shall guard you by night and in the daytime from the All-merciful?
22:61 (60)	that is because God makes the night to enter into the day
22:61 (60)	and makes the day to enter into the night
23:80 (82)	to Him belongs the alternation of night and day
24:44 (44)	God turns about the day and the night
25:47 (49)	and sleep for a rest, and day He appointed for a rising
25:62 (63)	it is He who made the night and day a succession
27:86 (88)	have they not seen how We made the night for them, to repose in it, and the day, to see?
28:72 (72)	what think you? if God should make the day unceasing over you
28:73 (73)	of His mercy He has appointed for you night and day
30:23 (22)	of His signs is your slumbering by night and day
31:29 (28)	hast thou not seen how that God makes the night to enter into the day
31:29 (28)	and makes the day to enter into the night
34:33 (32)	but devising night and day, when you were ordering us to disbelieve in God
35:13 (14)	He makes the night to enter into the day
35:13 (14)	and makes the day to enter into the night
36:37 (37)	We strip it of the day and lo, they are in darkness
36:40 (40)	neither does the night outstrip the day
39:5 (7)	wrapping night about the day
39:5 (7)	and wrapping the day about the night
40:61 (63)	it is God who made for you the night, to repose in it, and the day, to see
41:37 (37)	and of His signs are the night and the day
41:38 (38)	those who are with thy Lord do glorify Him by night and day
45:5 (4)	and in the alternation of night and day
46:35 (35)	they had not tarried but for an hour of a single day
57:6 (6)	He makes the night to enter into the day
57:6 (6)	and makes the day to enter into the night
71:5 (5)	my Lord, I have called my people by night and by day
73:7 (7)	surely in the day thou hast long business
73:20 (20)	God determines the night and the day
78:11 (11)	and We appointed day for a livelihood
91:3 (3)	and by the day when it displays him
92:2 (2)	and the day in splendour

*N H W

NAHÁ vb. (I)~to forbid, to prohibit. (pcple. act.) one who forbids

a) perf. act.

7:20 (19)	your Lord has only prohibited you from this tree
22:41 (42)	and bid to honour, and forbid dishonour
59:7 (7)	whatever he forbids you, give over
79:40 (40)	and forbade the soul its caprice

b) impf. act. (*yanhá*)

3:104 (100)	calling to good, and bidding to honour, and forbidding dishonour
3:110 (106)	bidding to honour, and forbidding dishonour
3:114 (110)	bidding to honour and forbidding dishonour
5:63 (68)	why do the masters and the rabbis not forbid them to utter sin
6:26 (26)	and they forbid it, and keep afar from it
7:22 (21)	did not I prohibit you from this tree
7:157 (156)	bidding them to honour, and forbidding them dishonour
7:165 (165)	We delivered those who were forbidding wickedness
9:67 (68)	they bid to dishonour, and forbid honour
9:71 (72)	they bid to honour, and forbid dishonour
11:62 (65)	dost thou forbid us to serve that our fathers served?
11:88 (90)	I desire not to come behind you, betaking me to that I forbid you
11:116 (118)	men of a remainder forbidding corruption in the earth
15:70 (70)	have we not forbidden thee all beings?
16:90 (92)	He forbids indecency, dishonour, and insolence
29:45 (44)	prayer forbids indecency and dishonour
60:8 (8)	God forbids you not, as regards those who have not fought you in religion's cause
60:9 (9)	God only forbids you as to those who have fought you in religion's cause
96:9 (9)	what thinkest thou? He who forbids

c) impv. (*inha*)

31:17 (16)	perform the prayer, and bid unto honour, and forbid dishonour

d) perf. pass. (*nuhiya*)

4:161 (159)	for their taking usury, that they were prohibited
6:28 (28)	they would again commit the very thing they were prohibited
6:56 (56)	I am forbidden to serve those you call on apart from God
7:166 (166)	and when they turned in disdain from that forbidding
40:66 (68)	I am forbidden to serve those you call on apart from God
58:8 (9)	hast thou not regarded those who were forbidden to converse secretly together
58:8 (9)	then they return to that they were forbidden, and they converse

e) impf. pass. (*yunhá*)

4:31 (35)	if you avoid the heinous sins that are forbidden you, We will acquit you

g) pcple. act. (*nāhī*)

9:112 (113)	those who bid to honour and forbid dishonour

MUNTAHÁ n.m.~final end, goal, boundary

53:14 (14)	by the Lote-Tree of the Boundary
53:42 (43)	and that the final end is unto thy Lord
79:44 (44)	unto thy Lord is the final end of it

NUHÁ n.m.~understanding, reason

20:54 (56)	surely in that are signs for men possessing reason
20:128 (128)	surely in that are signs for men possessing reason

TANĀHÁ vb. (VI)~to forbid one another

b) impf. act. (*yatanāhá*)

5:79 (82)	they forbade not one another any dishonour that they committed

INTAHÁ vb. (VIII)~to refrain oneself, to give over, to desist. (pcple. act.) one who desists, who gives over

a) perf. act.

2:192 (188) but if they give over, surely God is All-forgiving
2:193 (189) then if they give over, there shall be no enmity
2:275 (276) whosoever receives an admonition from his Lord and gives over
8:39 (40) then if they give over, surely God sees the things they do

b) impf. act. (*yantahī*)

5:73 (77) if they refrain not from what they say
8:19 (19) if you give over, it is better for you
8:38 (39) if they give over He will forgive them what is past
9:12 (12) they have no sacred oaths; haply they will give over
19:46 (47) surely, if thou givest not over, I shall stone thee
26:116 (116) if thou givest not over, Noah, thou shalt assuredly be one of the stoned
26:167 (167) if thou givest not over, Lot, thou shalt assuredly be one of the expelled
33:60 (60) if the hypocrites do not give over
36:18 (17) we augur ill of you. If you give not over, we will stone you
96:15 (15) if he gives not over, We shall seize him by the forelock

c) impv. (*intahi*)

4:171 (169) refrain; better is it for you. God is only One God
59:7 (7) whatever the Messenger gives you, take; whatever he forbids you, give over

g) pcple. act. (*muntahī*)

5:91 (93) to bar you from the remembrance of God, and from prayer. Will you then desist?

*N Ḥ B

NAḤABA vb. (I)~(n.vb.) a vow; (*qaḍá naḥbahu*) to die, to fulfill one's vow by death

f) n.vb. (*naḥb*)

33:23 (23) some of them have fulfilled their vow by death

*N Ḥ L

NAḤL n.com.~bees

16:68 (70) and thy Lord revealed unto the bees, saying

NIḤLAH n.f.~a spontaneous gift (usually in relation to dowry)

4:4 (3) give the women their dowries as a gift spontaneous

*N Ḥ R

NAḤARA vb. (I)~to sacrifice

c) impv. (*inḥar*)

108:2 (2) so pray unto thy Lord and sacrifice

*N Ḥ S

NAḤS n.m.~bad luck, ill fortune

41:16 (15) We loosed against them a wind clamorous in days of ill fortune
54:19 (19) We loosed against them a wind clamorous in a day of ill fortune continuous

NUḤĀS n.m.~molten brass [Ar, Pk]; smoke [Ali, Bl]

55:35 (35) against you shall be loosed a flame of fire, and molten brass

*N Ḥ T

NAḤATA vb. (I)~to hew, to carve

b) impf. act. (*yanḥitu*)

7:74 (72) and hewing its mountains into houses
15:82 (82) they were hewing the mountains into houses
26:149 (149) will you still skilfully hew houses out of the mountains?
37:95 (93) he said, 'Do you serve what you hew'

*N J D

NAJD n.m.~an open highway

90:10 (10) and guided him on the two highways

*N J L

INJĪL n.com.~The Gospel

3:3 (2) and He sent down the Torah and the Gospel
3:48 (43) He will teach him the Book, the Wisdom, the Torah, the Gospel
3:65 (58) The Torah was not sent down, neither the Gospel, but after him
5:46 (50) We gave to him the Gospel, wherein is guidance and light
5:47 (51) let the People of the Gospel judge according to what God has sent down
5:66 (70) had they performed the Torah and the Gospel
5:68 (72) you do not stand on anything, until you perform the Torah and the Gospel
5:110 (110) when I taught thee the Book, the Wisdom, the Torah, the Gospel
7:157 (156) whom they find written down with them in the Torah and the Gospel
9:111 (112) that is a promise binding upon God in the Torah, and the Gospel
48:29 (29) that is their likeness in the Torah, and their likeness in the Gospel
57:27 (27) and We sent, following, Jesus son of Mary, and gave unto him the Gospel

*N J M

NAJM n.m. (pl. *nujūm*)~a star

6:97 (97)	it is He who has appointed for you the stars
7:54 (52)	the sun, and the moon, and the stars subservient, by His command
16:12 (12)	and the stars are subjected by His command
16:16 (16)	and by the stars they are guided
22:18 (18)	the sun and the moon, the stars and the mountains
37:88 (86)	and he cast a glance at the stars
52:49 (49)	proclaim the praise of thy Lord in the night, and at the declining of the stars
53:1 (1)	by the Star when it plunges
55:6 (5)	and the stars and the trees bow themselves
56:75 (74)	no! I swear by the fallings of the stars
77:8 (8)	when the stars shall be extinguished
81:2 (2)	when the stars shall be thrown down
86:3 (3)	the piercing star

*N J S

NAJISA vb. (I)~(n.vb.) uncleanness, (adj) unclean

f) n.vb. (*najas*)

9:28 (28)	O believers, the idolaters are indeed unclean

*N J W

NAJĀ vb. (I)~to escape, to be delivered. (n.vb.1) salvation, deliverence. (n.vb.2) conspiring, the act of conversing secretly. (pcple. act.) one who is saved

a) perf. act.

12:45 (45)	then said the one who had been delivered, remembering after a time
28:25 (25)	be not afraid; thou hast escaped from the people of the evildoers

f) n.vb. (1) (*najāt*)

40:41 (44)	I call you to salvation, and you call me to the Fire

f) n.vb. (2) (*najwá*)

4:114 (114)	no good is there in much of their conspiring
9:78 (79)	God knows their secret and what they conspire together
17:47 (50)	when they listen to thee, and when they conspire
20:62 (65)	they disputed upon their plan between them, and communed secretly
21:3 (3)	the evildoers whisper one to another
43:80 (80)	do they think We hear not their secret and what they conspire together?
58:7 (8)	three men conspire not secretly together, but He is the fourth of them
58:8 (9)	hast thou not regarded those who were forbidden to converse secretly together
58:10 (11)	conspiring secretly together is of Satan
58:12 (13)	before your conspiring advance a freewill offering
58:13 (14)	are you afraid, before your conspiring, to advance freewill offerings?

g) pcple. act. (*nājī*)

12:42 (42)	then he said to the one he deemed should be saved of the two

NAJĪY n.m.~(adv) privately, secretly, in communion

12:80 (80)	when they despaired of moving him, they conferred privily apart
19:52 (53)	and We brought him near in communion

NAJJÁ vb. (II)~to deliver, to rescue, to save. (pcple. act.) one who delivers, who rescues

a) perf. act.

2:49 (46)	and when We delivered you from the folk of Pharaoh
7:89 (87)	if we returned into your creed, after God delivered us from it
10:73 (74)	but they cried him lies; so We delivered him
11:58 (61)	We delivered Hood and those who believed with him
11:58 (61)	and delivered them from a harsh chastisement
11:66 (69)	We delivered Salih and those who believed with him
11:94 (97)	We delivered Shuaib and those who believed with him
17:67 (69)	when He delivers you to land, you turn away
20:40 (41)	and We delivered thee out of grief
21:71 (71)	We delivered him, and Lot, unto the land that We had blessed
21:74 (74)	We delivered him from the city that had been doing deeds of corruption
21:76 (76)	and We answered him, and delivered him and his people
21:88 (88)	so We answered him, and delivered him out of grief
23:28 (29)	God, who has delivered us from the people of the evildoers
26:170 (170)	so We delivered him and his people all together
29:65 (65)	when He has delivered them to the land, they associate others with Him
31:32 (31)	when He has delivered them to the land, some of them are lukewarm
37:76 (74)	We delivered him and his people from the great distress
37:115 (115)	We delivered them and their people from the great distress
37:134 (134)	when We delivered him and his people all together
41:18 (17)	We delivered those who believed and were godfearing
44:30 (29)	We delivered the Children of Israel from the humbling chastisement
54:34 (34)	We delivered them at the dawn

b) impf. act. (*yunajjī*)

6:63 (63)	who delivers you from the shadows of land and sea?
6:64 (64)	God delivers you from them and from every distress
10:92 (92)	today We shall deliver thee with thy body
10:103 (103)	then We shall deliver Our Messengers and the believers
19:72 (73)	then We shall deliver those that were godfearing
29:32 (31)	We shall deliver him and his family, except his wife
39:61 (62)	but God shall deliver those that were godfearing

c) impv. (*najji*)

10:86 (86)	deliver us by Thy mercy from the people of the unbelievers
26:118 (118)	and deliver me and the believers that are with me
26:169 (169)	my Lord, deliver me and my people from that they do
28:21 (20)	my Lord, deliver me from the people of the evildoers
66:11 (11)	deliver me from Pharaoh and his work
66:11 (11)	and do Thou deliver me from the people of the evildoers

d) perf. pass. (*nujjiya*)

12:110 (110)	Our help came to them and whosoever We willed was delivered

g) pcple. act. (*munajjī*)

15:59 (59) excepting the folk of Lot; them we shall deliver
29:33 (32) surely we shall deliver thee and thy family, except thy wife

NĀJÁ vb. (III)~to conspire [Ar]; to confer with [Pk]; to consult in private [Ali, Bl]

a) perf. act.

58:12 (13) O believers, when you conspire with the Messenger

ANJÁ vb. (IV)~to deliver, to rescue,

a) perf. act.

2:50 (47) and when We divided for you the sea and delivered you
6:63 (63) if Thou deliverest from these, we shall be among the thankful
7:64 (62) so We delivered him, and those with him, in the Ark
7:72 (70) so We delivered him, and those with him, by a mercy from Us
7:83 (81) so We delivered him and his family, except his wife
7:141 (137) and when We delivered you from the folk of Pharaoh
7:165 (165) We delivered those who were forbidding wickedness
10:22 (23) if Thou deliverest us from these, surely we shall be among the thankful
10:23 (24) nevertheless when He has delivered them behold, they are insolent
11:116 (118) except a few of those whom We delivered of them
14:6 (6) remember God's blessing upon you when He delivered you from the folk of Pharaoh
20:80 (82) Children of Israel, We delivered you from your enemy
21:9 (9) then We made true the promise We gave them and We delivered them
26:65 (65) and We delivered Moses and those with him all together
26:119 (119) so We delivered him, and those with him, in the laden ship
27:53 (54) and We delivered those who believed and were godfearing
27:57 (58) so We delivered him and his family, except his wife
29:15 (14) yet We delivered him, and those who were in the ship
29:24 (23) then God delivered him from the fire

b) impf. act. (*yunjī*)

10:103 (103) even so, as is Our bounden duty, We shall deliver the believers
21:88 (88) even so do We deliver the believers
61:10 (10) shall I direct you to a commerce that shall deliver you from a painful chastisement?
70:14 (14) so that then it might deliver him

TANĀJÁ vb. (VI)~to conspire or converse secretly, to hold secret counsel

a) perf. act.

58:9 (10) O believers, when you conspire secretly

b) impf. act. (*yatanājá*)

58:8 (9) they converse secretly together in sin and enmity
58:9 (10) conspire not together in sin and enmity and disobedience to the Messenger

c) impv. (*tanāja*)

58:9 (10) but conspire in piety and godfearing

*N K B

NAKABA vb. (I)~(pcple. act.) one who deviates, who is astray

g) pcple. act. (*nākib*)

23:74 (76) surely they that believe not in the world to come are deviating from the path

MANĀKIB n.m. (pl. of *mankib*)~tracts, paths

67:15 (15) it is He who made the earth submissive to you; therefore walk in its tracts

*N K D

NAKID n.m.~(adv) scantily

7:58 (56) and the corrupt — it comes forth but scantily

*N K F

ISTANKAFA vb. (X)~to disdain

a) perf. act.

4:173 (172) and as for them who disdain, and wax proud

b) impf. act. (*yastankifu*)

4:172 (170) the Messiah will not disdain to be a servant of God
4:172 (171) whosoever disdains to serve Him, and waxes proud

*N K Ḥ

NAKAḤA vb. (I)~to marry. (n.vb.) marriage

a) perf. act.

4:22 (26) do not marry women that your fathers married
33:49 (48) when you marry believing women and then divorce them before you touch them

b) impf. act. (*yankiḥu*)

2:221 (220) do not marry idolatresses, until they believe
2:230 (230) she shall not be lawful to him after that, until she marries another husband
2:232 (232) do not debar them from marrying their husbands
4:22 (26) do not marry women that your fathers married
4:25 (29) any one of you who has not the affluence to be able to marry believing freewomen
4:127 (126) women to whom you give not what is prescribed for them, and yet desire to marry them
24:3 (3) the fornicator shall marry none but a fornicatress or an idolatress

24:3 (3)	and the fornicatress — none shall marry her but a fornicator or an idolator
33:53 (53)	it is not for you to hurt God's Messenger, neither to marry his wives after him
60:10 (10)	there is no fault in you to marry them when you have given them their wages

c) impv. (*inkiḥ*)

4:3 (3)	marry such women as seem good to you, two, three, four
4:25 (29)	so marry them, with their people's leave

f) n.vb. (*nikāḥ*)

2:235 (236)	do not resolve on the knot of marriage until the book has reached its term
2:237 (238)	they make remission, or he makes remission in whose hand is the knot of marriage
4:6 (5)	test well the orphans, until they reach the age of marrying
24:33 (33)	let those who find not the means to marry be abstinent till God enriches them
24:60 (59)	such women as are past child-bearing and have no hope of marriage

ANKAḤA vb. (IV)~to marry, to wed

b) impf. act. (*yunkiḥu*)

2:221 (220)	do not marry idolaters, until they believe
28:27 (27)	I desire to marry thee to one of these my two daughters

c) impv. (*ankiḥ*)

24:32 (32)	marry the spouseless among you, and your slaves and handmaidens that are righteous

ISTANKAḤA vb. (X)~to take in marriage

b) impf. act. (*yastankiḥu*)

33:50 (49)	and if the Prophet desire to take her in marriage

*N K L

ANKĀL n.m. (pl. of *nikl*)~fetters

73:12 (12)	for with Us there are fetters, and a furnace

NAKĀL n.m.~chastisement, an exemplary punishment

2:66 (62)	We made it a punishment exemplary for all the former times and for the latter
5:38 (42)	as a recompense for what they have earned, and a punishment exemplary from God
79:25 (25)	God seized him with the chastisement of the Last World and the First

NAKKALA vb. (II)~(n.vb.) the act of punishing

f) n.vb. (*tankīl*)

4:84 (86)	God is stronger in might, more terrible in punishing

*N K R

NAKIRA vb. (I)~to be suspicious of, to mistrust

a) perf. act.

11:70 (73) he was suspicious of them and conceived a fear of them

NAKĪR n.m.~horror [Ar]; abhorrence [Pk]; rejection [Ali]; disapproval [Bl]

22:44 (43) the unbelievers, then I seized them; and how was My horror
34:45 (44) they cried lies to My Messengers, and how was My horror
35:26 (24) then I seized the unbelievers, and how was My horror
42:47 (46) upon that day you shall have no shelter, no denial
67:18 (18) those that were before them also cried lies; then how was My horror

NUKR n.m. (*nukur*, in 54:6)~horrible, horrid; (comp.adj. *ankar*) hideous

18:74 (73) thou hast indeed done a horrible thing
18:87 (86) He shall chastise him with a horrible chastisement
31:19 (18) the most hideous of voices is the ass's
54:6 (6) upon the day when the Caller shall call unto a horrible thing
65:8 (8) and chastised it with a horrible chastisement

NAKKARA vb. (II)~to disguise

c) impv. (*nakkir*)

27:41 (41) he said, 'Disguise her throne for her'

ANKARA vb. (IV)~to deny, to reject. (pcple. act.) one who does not know, who denies. (pcple. pass.) unknown (opp. *maʿrūf*), denial; that which is denied or is dishonourable [Ar]; that which is wrong, an abomination [Pk]; that which is wrong, evil, injustice [Ali]; disreputable [Bl]

b) impf. act. (*yunkiru*)

13:36 (36) and of the parties some reject some of it
16:83 (85) they recognize the blessing of God, then they deny it
40:81 (81) He shows you His signs; then which of God's signs do you reject?

g) pcple. act. (*munkir*)

12:58 (58) and he knew them, but they knew him not
16:22 (23) their hearts deny, and they have waxed proud
21:50 (51) this is a blessed Remembrance that We have sent down; so are you now denying it?
23:69 (71) or did they not recognise their Messenger and so denied him?

h) pcple. pass. (*munkar*)

3:104 (100) and bidding to honour, and forbidding dishonour
3:110 (106) bidding to honour, and forbidding dishonour
3:114 (110) bidding to honour and forbidding dishonour
5:79 (82) they forbade not one another any dishonour that they committed
7:157 (156) bidding them to honour, and forbidding them dishonour
9:67 (68) they bid to dishonour, and forbid honour
9:71 (72) they bid to honour, and forbid dishonour
9:112 (113) those who bid to honour and forbid dishonour
15:62 (62) surely you are a people unknown to me
16:90 (92) He forbids indecency, dishonour, and insolence
22:41 (42) and bid to honour, and forbid dishonour
22:72 (71) thou recognisest in the faces of the unbelievers denial
24:21 (21) the steps of Satan, assuredly he bids to indecency and dishonour
29:29 (28) do you approach men, and cut the way, and commit in your assembly dishonour?

29:45 (44)	prayer forbids indecency and dishonour
31:17 (16)	perform the prayer, and bid unto honour, and forbid dishonour
51:25 (25)	you are a people unknown to me
58:2 (2)	they are surely saying a dishonourable saying

*N K S

NAKASA vb. (I)~to be in confusion, to be confounded. (pcple. act.) one who bends down, who hangs (tr)

d) perf. pass. (*nukisa*)

21:65 (66)	then they were utterly put to confusion

g) pcple. act. (*nākis*)

32:12 (12)	if thou couldst see the guilty hanging their heads before their Lord

NAKKASA vb. (II)~to bend over (tr)

b) impf. act. (*yunakkisu*)

36:68 (68)	to whomsoever We give long life, We bend him over in His constitution

*N K Ṣ

NAKAṢA vb. (I)~to withdraw

a) perf. act.

8:48 (50)	when the two hosts sighted each other, he withdrew upon his heels

b) impf. act. (*yankiṣu*)

23:66 (68)	My signs were recited to you, but upon your heels you withdrew

*N K TH

NAKATHA vb. (I)~to break (an oath)

a) perf. act.

9:12 (12)	but if they break their oaths after their covenant
9:13 (13)	will you not fight a people who broke their oaths
48:10 (10)	whosoever breaks his oath breaks it but to his own hurt

b) impf. act. (*yankuthu*)

7:135 (131)	they broke their troth
43:50 (49)	chastisement, behold, they broke their troth
48:10 (10)	whosoever breaks his oath breaks it but to his own hurt

ANKĀTH n.m. (pl. of *nikth*)~fibres (of a rope or string)

16:92 (94)	be not as a woman who breaks her thread, after it is firmly spun, into fibres

*N KH L

NAKHLAH n.f. (pl. *nakhl*, and *nakhīl*)~a palm, palm-tree

2:266 (268)	would any of you wish to have a garden of palms and vines
6:99 (99)	and out of the palm-tree, from the spathe of it, dates thick-clustered
6:141 (142)	it is He who produces gardens trellised, and untrellised, palm-trees
13:4 (4)	and palms in pairs, and palms single, watered with one water
16:11 (11)	thereby He brings forth for you crops, and olives, and palms
16:67 (69)	of the fruits of the palms and the vines, you take therefrom an intoxicant
17:91 (93)	or till thou possessest a garden of palms and vines
18:32 (31)	to one of them We assigned two gardens of vines, and surrounded them with palm-trees
19:23 (23)	the birthpangs surprised her by the trunk of the palm-tree
19:25 (25)	shake also to thee the palm-trunk
20:71 (74)	then I shall crucify you upon the trunks of palm-trees
23:19 (19)	then We produced for you therewith gardens of palms and vines
26:148 (148)	sown fields, and palms with slender spathes
36:34 (34)	and We made therein gardens of palms and vines
50:10 (10)	and tall palm-trees with spathes compact
54:20 (20)	plucking up men as if they were stumps of uprooted palm-trees
55:11 (10)	therein fruits, and palm-trees with sheaths
55:68 (68)	therein fruits, and palm-trees, and pomegranates
69:7 (7)	as if they were the stumps of fallen down palm-trees
80:29 (29)	and olives, and palms

*N KH R

NAKHIRAH n.f. (adj)~old and wasted, crumbled, rotten

79:11 (11)	what, when we are bones old and wasted?

*N M L

ANĀMIL n.f. (pl. of *anmulah*)~fingers

3:119 (115)	but when they go privily, they bite at you their fingers

NAMLAH n.f. (pl. *naml*)~an ant

27:18 (18)	till, when they came on the Valley of Ants
27:18 (18)	an ant said
27:18 (18)	Ants, enter your dwelling-places

*N M M

NAMĪM n.m.~slander

68:11 (11) backbiter, going about with slander

*N M R Q

NAMĀRIQ n.m. (pl. of *namraq*)~cushions

88:15 (15) and cushions arrayed

*N Q ᶜ

NAQAᶜA vb. (I)~(n.vb.) a trail of dust

f) n.vb. (*naqᶜ*)

100:4 (4) blazing a trail of dust

*N Q B

NAQABA vb. (I)~(n.vb.) the act of piercing or digging through

f) n.vb. (*naqb*)

18:97 (96) so they were unable either to scale it or pierce it

NAQĪB n.m.~a chieftain

5:12 (15) We raised up from among them twelve chieftains

NAQQABA vb. (II)~(with prep. *fī*) to search about

a) perf. act.

50:36 (35) they searched about in the land; was there any asylum?

*N Q DH

ANQADHA vb. (IV)~to deliver, to save

a) perf. act.

3:103 (99) you were upon the brink of a pit of Fire, and He delivered you from it

b) impf. act. (*yunqidhu*)

36:23 (22) shall not avail me anything, and who will never deliver me

39:19 (20) shalt thou deliver him out of the Fire?

e) impf. pass. (*yunqadhu*)

36:43 (43) then none have they to cry to, neither are they delivered

ISTANQADHA vb. (X)~to seek to deliver, to rescue

b) impf. act. (*yastanqidhu*)

22:73 (72) if a fly should rob them of aught, they would never rescue it from him

*N Q Ḍ

NAQAḌA vb. (I)~to break, to violate. (n.vb.) the act of breaking or violating

a) perf. act.

16:92 (94) be not as a woman who breaks her thread, after it is firmly spun

b) impf. act. (*yanquḍu*)

2:27 (25) such as break the covenant of God after its solemn binding
8:56 (58) then they break their compact every time
13:20 (20) who fulfil God's covenant, and break not the compact
13:25 (25) those who break the covenant of God after His compact
16:91 (93) and break not the oaths after they have been confirmed

f) n.vb. (*naqḍ*)

4:155 (154) so, for their breaking the compact, and disbelieving
5:13 (16) so for their breaking their compact We cursed them

ANQAḌA vb. (IV)~to weigh down (tr)

a) perf. act.

94:3 (3) the burden that weighed down thy back

*N Q M

NAQAMA vb. (I)~to seek or take revenge, to blame

a) perf. act.

9:74 (75) they took revenge only that God enriched them
85:8 (8) they took revenge on them only because they believed in God

b) impf. act. (*yanqimu*)

5:59 (64) do you blame us for any other cause than that we believe in God
7:126 (123) Thou takest vengeance upon us only because we have believed in the signs

INTAQAMA vb. (VIII)~to take vengeance [Ar, Bl]; to requite, to punish, [Pk]; to exact retribution [Ali]. (n.vb.) the act of taking vengeance; *(dhū intiqām)* Vengeful [Ar]; Able to Requite [Pk]; Lord of Retribution [Ali]; Wielder of vengeance [Bl] (Divine attribute). (pcple. act.) one who takes vengeance [Ar, Bl]; one who requites, who punishes [Pk]; one who exacts retribution [Ali]

a) perf. act.

7:136 (132) so We took vengeance on them, and drowned them
15:79 (79) and We took vengeance on them
30:47 (46) then We took vengeance upon those who sinned
43:25 (24) so We took vengeance upon them
43:55 (55) when they had angered Us, We took vengenace on them

b) impf. act. (*yantaqimu*)

5:95 (96) whoever offends again, God will take vengeance on him

f) n.vb. (*intiqām*)

3:4 (3) God is All-mighty, Vengeful
5:95 (96) God will take vengeance on him; God is All-mighty, Vengeful
14:47 (48) surely God is All-mighty, Vengeful
39:37 (38) is not God All-mighty, All-vengeful?

g) pcple. act. (*muntaqim*)

32:22 (22) We shall take vengeance upon the sinners
43:41 (40) We shall take vengenace upon them
44:16 (15) then We shall take Our vengeance

*N Q R

NAQARA vb. (I)~to sound

d) perf. pass. (*nuqira*)

74:8 (8) for when the Trump is sounded

NAQĪR n.m.~a date-spot; a speck, dint or groove on the date-stone

4:53 (56) they do not give the people a single date-spot
4:124 (123) they shall enter Paradise, and not be wronged a single date-spot

NĀQŪR n.m.~a trumpet

74:8 (8) for when the Trump is sounded

*N Q Ṣ

NAQAṢA vb. (I)~to diminish; to abate, to reduce, to fail. (n.vb.) diminution, scarcity, loss. (pcple. pass.) that which is diminished, abated

b) impf. act. (*yanquṣu*)

9:4 (4) then they failed you naught neither lent support to any man against you
11:84 (85) diminish not the measure and the balance
13:41 (41) have they not seen how We come to the land diminishing it in its extremities?
21:44 (45) how We come to the land, diminishing it in its extremities
50:4 (4) We know what the earth diminishes of them

c) impv. (*unquṣ*)

73:3 (3) a half of it, or diminish a little

e) impf. pass. (*yunqaṣu*)

35:11 (12) neither is any diminished in his life, but it is in a Book

f) n.vb. (*naqṣ*)

2:155 (150) We will try you with something of fear and hunger, and diminution of goods
7:130 (127) then seized We Pharaoh's people with years of dearth, and scarcity of fruits

h) pcple. pass. (*manqūṣ*)

11:109 (111) We shall surely pay them in full their portion undiminished

*N S ʾ

MINSAʾAH n.f.~a staff

34:14 (13) but the Beast of the Earth devouring his staff

NASĪʾ n.m.~the act of postponing a (sacred) month

9:37 (37) the month postponed is an increase of unbelief

*N S B

NASABA vb. (I)~(n.vb.) kinship, kindred

f) n.vb. (*nasab*, pl. *ansāb*)

23:101 (103) that day there shall be no kinship any more between them
25:54 (56) it is He who created of water a mortal, and made him kindred of blood
37:158 (158) they have set up a kinship between Him and the jinn

*N S F

NASAFA vb. (I)~to scatter. (n.vb.) the act of scattering

b) impf. act. (*yansifu*)

20:97 (97) We will surely burn it and scatter its ashes into the sea
20:105 (105) say: 'My Lord will scatter them as ashes'

d) perf. pass. (*nusifa*)

77:10 (10) when the mountains shall be scattered

f) n.vb. (*nasf*)

20:97 (97) We will surely burn it and scatter its ashes into the sea <...>
20:105 (105) say: 'My Lord will scatter them as ashes <...>'

*N S K

NASAKA vb. (I)~(n.vb.) a ritual sacrifice, sacrificial offering. (pcple. act.) one who performs a rite

f) n.vb. (*nuśuk*)

2:196 (192)	then redemption by fast, or freewill offering, or ritual sacrifice
6:162 (163)	my ritual sacrifice, my living, my dying — all belongs to God

g) pcple. act. (*nāsik*)

22:67 (66)	We have appointed for every nation a holy rite that they shall perform

MANSAK n.m. (pl. *manāsik*)~a holy rite, a devotional act; (2:128 and 2:200) a place for the celebration of the holy rites [Ali]

2:128 (122)	and show us our holy rites
2:200 (196)	when you have performed your holy rites remember God
22:34 (35)	We have appointed for every nation a holy rite
22:67 (66)	We have appointed for every nation a holy rite that they shall perform

*N S KH

NASAKHA vb. (I)~to abrogate, to annul

b) impf. act. (*yansakhu*)

2:106 (100)	for whatever verse We abrogate or cast into oblivion, We bring a better
22:52 (51)	God annuls what Satan casts, then God confirms His signs

NUSKHAH n.f.~inscription

7:154 (153)	in the inscription of them was guidance, and mercy unto all

ISTANSAKHA vb. (X)~to register, to record

b) impf. act. (*yastansikhu*)

45:29 (28)	We have been registering all that you were doing

*N S L

NASALA vb. (I)~to slide down [Ar]; to hasten, to hie [Pk]; to swarm swiftly, to rush forth [Ali]; to trickle down [Bl]

b) impf. act. (*yansilu*)

21:96 (96)	when Gog and Magog are unloosed, and they slide down out of every slope
36:51 (51)	then behold, they are sliding down from their tombs unto their Lord

NASL n.m.~stock, progeny

2:205 (201)	to do corruption there and to destroy the tillage and the stock
32:8 (7)	then He fashioned his progeny of an extraction of mean water

*N S R

NASR n.prop.~Nasr (an idol)

71:23 (23)	Yaghuth, Ya'uq, neither Nasr

*N S W

NISĀʾ n.f. (pl; see also *niswah*, below)~women, wives

2:49 (46)	slaughtering your sons, and sparing your women
2:187 (183)	permitted to you, upon the night of the Fast, is to go in to your wives
2:222 (222)	go apart from women during the monthly course
2:223 (223)	your women are a tillage for you
2:226 (226)	for those who forswear their women a wait of four months
2:231 (231)	when you divorce women, and they have reached their term
2:232 (232)	when you divorce women, and they have reached their term
2:235 (235)	there is no fault in you touching the proposal to women you offer
2:236 (237)	if you divorce women while as yet you have not touched them
3:14 (12)	women, children, heaped-up heaps of gold
3:42 (37)	He has chosen thee above all women
3:61 (54)	our wives and your (wives)
3:61 (54)	our (wives) and your wives
4:1 (1)	from the pair of them scattered abroad many men and women
4:3 (3)	marry such women as seem good to you, two, three, four
4:4 (3)	give the women their dowries as a gift spontaneous
4:7 (8)	to the women a share of what parents and kinsmen leave
4:11 (12)	if they be women above two, then for them two-thirds
4:15 (19)	such of your women as commit indecency
4:19 (23)	it is not lawful for you to inherit women against their will
4:22 (26)	do not marry women that your fathers married
4:23 (27)	your suckling sisters, your wives' mothers
4:23 (27)	being born of your wives you have been in to
4:24 (28)	and wedded women, save what your right hands own
4:32 (36)	to the women a share from what they have earned
4:34 (38)	men are the managers of the affairs of women
4:43 (46)	or you have touched women, and you can find no water
4:75 (77)	for the men, women, and children who, being abased, say
4:98 (100)	except the men, women, and children who, being abased
4:127 (126)	they will ask thee for a pronouncement concerning women
4:127 (126)	to you in the Book concerning the orphan women
4:129 (128)	you will not be able to be equitable between your wives
4:176 (175)	the male shall receive the portion of two females
5:6 (9)	or you have touched women, and you can find no water
7:81 (79)	see, you approach men lustfully instead of women
7:127 (124)	we shall slaughter their sons and spare their women
7:141 (137)	slaying your sons, and sparing your women
14:6 (6)	slaughtering your sons, and sparing your women
24:31 (31)	say to the believing women, that they cast down their eyes
24:31 (31)	or their sisters' sons, or their women
24:60 (59)	such women as are past child-bearing and have no hope of marriage
27:55 (56)	what, do you approach men lustfully instead of women?
28:4 (3)	slaughtering their sons, and sparing their women

33:30 (30)	Wives of the Prophet, whosoever among you commits a flagrant indecency
33:32 (32)	Wives of the Prophet, you are not as other (women)
33:32 (32)	(Wives) of the Prophet you are not as other women
33:52 (52)	thereafter women are not lawful to thee
33:55 (55)	their women, and what their right hands own
33:59 (59)	say to thy (wives) and daughters and the believing women
40:25 (26)	slay the sons of those who believe with him, and spare their women
48:25 (25)	if it had not been for certain men believers and certain women believers
49:11 (11)	neither let women scoff at (women) who may be better than themselves
49:11 (11)	neither let (women) scoff at women who may be better than themselves
58:2 (2)	those of you who say, regarding their wives
58:3 (4)	and those who say, regarding their wives
65:1 (1)	when you divorce women, divorce them when they have reached their period
65:4 (4)	as for your women who have despaired of further menstruating

NISWAH n.f. (pl.; see *nisā*ʾ, above)~women

12:30 (30)	certain women that were in the city said
12:50 (50)	what of the women who cut their hands?

*N S Y

NASIYA vb. (I)~to forget. (pcple. pass.) forgotten

a) perf. act.

2:286 (286)	our Lord, take us not to task if we forget
5:13 (16)	they have forgotten a portion of that they were reminded of
5:14 (17)	they have forgotten a portion of that they were reminded of
6:44 (44)	when they forgot what they were reminded of
7:51 (49)	as they forgot the encounter of this their day
7:53 (51)	the day its interpretation comes, those who before forgot it shall say
7:165 (165)	when they forgot that they were reminded of
9:67 (68)	they have forgotten God
9:67 (68)	and He has forgotten them
18:24 (23)	mention thy Lord, when thou forgettest
18:57 (55)	turns away from them and forgets what his hands have forwarded
18:61 (60)	when they reached their meeting, they forgot their fish
18:63 (62)	then I forgot the fish
18:73 (72)	do not take me to task that I forgot, neither constrain me
20:88 (90)	this is your god, and the god of Moses, whom he has forgotten
20:115 (114)	We made covenant with Adam before, but he forgot
20:126 (126)	Our signs came unto thee, and thou didst forget them
25:18 (19)	until they forgot the Remembrance, and were a people corrupt
32:14 (14)	now taste, for that you forgot the encounter of this your day
32:14 (14)	We indeed have forgotten you
36:78 (78)	he has struck for Us a similitude and forgotten his creation
38:26 (25)	for that they have forgotten the Day of Reckoning
39:8 (11)	He confers on him a blessing from Him he forgets that he was calling to before
45:34 (33)	as you forgot the encounter of this your day
58:6 (7)	God has numbered it, and they have forgotten it
59:19 (19)	be not as those who forgot God

b) impf. act. (*yansá*)

2:44 (41) will you bid others to piety, and forget yourselves
2:237 (238) forget not to be bountiful one towards another
6:41 (41) and you will forget that you associate with Him
7:51 (49) therefore today We forget them
20:52 (54) my Lord goes not astray, nor forgets
28:77 (77) forget not thy portion of the present world
45:34 (33) it shall be said, 'Today We do forget you'
87:6 (6) We shall make thee recite, to forget not

e) impf. pass. (*yunsá*)

20:126 (126) didst forget them; and so today thou art forgotten

h) pcple. pass. (*mansīy*)

19:23 (23) would I had died ere this, and become a thing forgotten

NASĪY n.m. (adj)~forgetful

19:64 (65) thy Lord is never forgetful

NASY n.m.~a forgotten thing

19:23 (23) would I had died ere this, and become a thing forgotten

ANSÁ vb. (IV)~to cause to forget, to cast into oblivion

a) perf. act.

12:42 (42) Satan caused him to forget to mention him to his master
18:63 (62) it was Satan himself that made me forget it
23:110 (112) till they made you forget My remembrance, mocking at them
58:19 (20) Satan has gained the mastery over them, and caused them to forget God's Remembrance
59:19 (19) be not as those who forgot God, and so He caused them to forget their souls

b) impf. act. (*yunsī*)

2:106 (100) for whatever verse We abrogate or cast into oblivion, We bring a better
6:68 (67) if Satan should make thee forget, do not sit

*N SH ʾ

NASHAʾA vb. (I)~(pcple. act.) first part, beginning [Ar, Bl]; vigil [Pk]; (the act of) rising by night [Ali]

g) pcple. act. f. (*nāshiʾah*)

73:6 (6) the first part of the night is heavier in tread, more upright in speech

NASHʾAH n.f.~growth

29:20 (19) then God causes the second growth to grow
53:47 (48) and that upon Him rests the second growth
56:62 (62) you have known the first growth

NASHSHA'A vb. (II)~to rear, to bring up

e) impf. pass. (*yunashsha'u*)

43:18 (17) one who is reared amid ornaments

ANSHA'A vb. (IV)~to produce, to cause to grow, to set up, to raise up, to form, to originate. (n.vb.) the act of forming, creating. (pcple. act.) one who makes, who creates. (pcple. pass.) that which is raised up [Ar]; that which is displayed [Pk]; sailing smoothly [Ali]; towering [Bl]

a) perf. act.

6:6 (6) We destroyed them because of their sins, and raised up after them another generation
6:98 (98) it is He who produced you from one living soul
6:133 (133) succeed you, what He will, as He produced you from the seed of another people
6:141 (142) it is He who produces gardens trellised, and untrellised
11:61 (64) it is He who produced you from the earth
21:11 (11) how many a city that was evildoing We have shattered, and set up after it another people
23:14 (14) thereafter We produced him as another creature
23:19 (19) We produced for you therewith gardens of palms and vines
23:31 (32) thereafter, after them, We produced another generation
23:42 (44) thereafter, after them, We produced other generations
23:78 (80) it is He who produced for you hearing, and eyes, and hearts
28:45 (45) We raised up generations, and long their lives continued
36:79 (79) He shall quicken them, who originated them the first time
53:32 (33) very well He knows you, when He produced you from the earth
56:35 (34) perfectly We formed them, perfect
56:72 (71) did you make its timber to grow
67:23 (23) it is He who produced you, and appointed for you hearing

b) impf. act. (*yunshi'u*)

13:12 (13) it is He who shows you the lightning, for fear and hope, and produces the heavy

29:20 (19) He originated creation; then God causes the second growth to grow

f) n.vb. (*inshā'*)

56:35 (34) perfectly We formed them, <perfect>

g) pcple. act. (*munshi'*)

56:72 (71) did you make its timber to grow, or did We make it?

h) pcple. pass. (*munsha'*)

55:24 (24) His too are the ships that run, raised up in the sea like land-marks

*N SH R

NASHARA vb. (I)~to unfold, to unroll, to spread. (n.vb.1) scattering; reviving [Pk]. (n.vb.2) raising up, rising, uprising. (pcple. act.) (pl) scatterers; ones who cause vegetation to revive [Pk]. (pcple. pass.) unrolled, spread *b*) impf. act. (*yanshuru*)

18:16 (15) your Lord will unfold to you of His mercy
42:28 (27) and He unfolds His mercy

d) perf. pass. (*nushira*)

81:10 (10) when the scrolls shall be unrolled

f) n.vb. (1) (*nashr*)

77:3 (3) by the scatterers <scattering>

f) n.vb. (2) (*nushūr*)

25:3 (4) and have no power to hurt or profit themselves, no power of death or life or raising up
25:40 (42) but they look for no uprising
25:47 (49) and sleep for a rest, and day He appointed for a rising
35:9 (10) even so is the Uprising
67:15 (15) eat of His provision; to Him is the Uprising

g) pcple. act. f. (*nāshirah*)

77:3 (3) by the scatterers scattering

h) pcple. pass. (*manshūr*)

17:13 (14) on the Day of Resurrection, a book he shall find spread wide open
52:3 (3) in a parchment unrolled

NASHSHARA vb. (II)~(pcple. pass.) unrolled, spread

h) pcple. pass. (*munashshar*)

74:52 (52) every man of them desires to be given scrolls unrolled

ANSHARA vb. (IV)~to revive, to raise up. (pcple. pass.) that which is revived

a) perf. act.

43:11 (10) We revived thereby a land that was dead
80:22 (22) then, when He wills, He raises him

b) impf. act. (*yunshiru*)

21:21 (21) have they taken gods out of the earth who raise the dead?

h) pcple. pass. (*munshar*)

44:35 (34) there is nothing but our first death; we shall not be revived

INTASHARA vb. (VIII)~to be scattered abroad, to disperse. (pcple. act.) scattered, dispersed

b) impf. act. (*yantashiru*)

30:20 (19) He created you of dust; then lo, you are mortals, all scattered abroad

c) impv. (*intashir*)

33:53 (53) when you have had the meal, disperse
62:10 (10) when the prayer is finished, scatter in the land

g) pcple. act. (*muntashir*)

54:7 (7) they shall come forth from the tombs as if they were scattered grasshoppers

*N SH Ṭ

NASHAṬA vb. (I)~(n.vb.) the act of drawing out [Ar]; hustling and bustling [Bl]; rushing [Pk]; the act of drawing out gently [Ali]. (pcple. act.) (pl) those who draw out violently [Ar]; meteors [Pk]; those who draw out (the souls of the blessed) [Ali]; those who hustle and bustle [Bl]

f) n.vb. (*nashṭ*)

79:2 (2) and those that draw out <violently>

g) pcple. act. f. (*nāshiṭah*)

79:2 (2) and those that draw out violently

*N SH Z

NASHAZA vb. (I)~to move up. (n.vb.) rebelliousness [Ar]; ill-treatment, rebellion [Pk]; disloyalty and ill-conduct [Ali]; refractoriness [Bl]

c) impv. (*unshuz*)

58:11 (12) and when it is said, 'Move up'
58:11 (12) and God will raise up in rank those of you who believe

f) n.vb. (*nushūz*)

4:34 (38) and those you fear may be rebellious admonish
4:128 (127) if a woman fear rebelliousness or aversion in her husband

ANSHAZA vb. (IV)~to set up, to raise

b) impf. act. (*yunshizu*)

2:259 (261) look at the bones, how We shall set them up

*N Ṣ B

NAṢABA vb. (I)~to hoist, to set up d) perf. pass. (*nuṣiba*)

88:19 (19) how the mountains were hoisted

NAṢIBA vb. (I)~to labour, to toil. (n.vb.) weariness, fatigue. (pcple. act.) toilworn, weary

c) impv. (*inṣab*)

94:7 (7) so when thou art empty, labour

f) n.vb. (1) (*nuṣb*)

38:41 (40) Satan has visited me with weariness and chastisement

f) n.vb. (2) (*naṣab*)

9:120 (121) that is because they are smitten neither by thirst, nor fatigue
15:48 (48) no fatigue there shall smite them
18:62 (61) indeed, we have encountered weariness from this our journey
35:35 (32) wherein no weariness assails us neither fatigue

g) pcple. act. f. (*nāṣibah*)

88:3 (3) labouring, toilworn

NAṢĪB n.m.~a portion, a share

2:202 (198) they shall have a portion from what they have earned
3:23 (22) hast thou not regarded those who were given a portion of the Book
4:7 (8) to the men a share of what parents and kinsmen leave
4:7 (8) and to the women a share of what parents and kinsmen leave
4:7 (8) whether it be little or much, a share apportioned
4:32 (36) to the men a share from what they have earned
4:32 (36) and to the women a share from what they have earned
4:33 (37) so give to them their share
4:44 (47) hast thou not regarded those who were given a share of the Book purchasing error
4:51 (54) hast thou not regarded those who were given a share of the Book believing in demons
4:53 (56) or have they a share in the Kingdom?
4:85 (87) whoso intercedes with a good intercession shall receive a share of it
4:118 (118) I will take unto myself a portion appointed of Thy servants
4:141 (140) but if the unbelievers get a share, they say
6:136 (137) they appoint to God, of the tillage and cattle that He multiplied, a portion
7:37 (35) those — their portion of the Book shall reach them
11:109 (111) We shall surely pay them in full their portion undiminished
16:56 (58) they appoint a share of that We have provided them to what they know not
28:77 (77) forget not thy portion of the present world
40:47 (50) will you avail us now against any part of the Fire?
42:20 (19) in the world to come he will have no share

NUṢUB n.m. (pl. *anṣāb*)~idol; stone (altar) [Bl]; (70:43) waymark [Ar]; standard [Bl]; goal [Pk]; goal-post [Ali]

5:3 (4) as also things sacrificed to idols
5:90 (92) wine and arrow-shuffling, idols and divining-arrows are an abomination
70:43 (43) as if they were hurrying unto a waymark

*N Ṣ F

NIṢF n.m.~a half

2:237 (238) for them a marriage-portion, then one-half of what you have appointed
4:11 (12) but if she be one then to her a half
4:12 (13) for you a half of what your wives leave, if they have no children
4:25 (30) they shall be liable to half the chastisement of freewomen
4:176 (175) she shall receive a half of what he leaves
73:3 (3) a half of it, or diminish a little
73:20 (20) thy Lord knows that thou keepest vigil nearly two-thirds of the night, or a half of it

*N Ṣ Ḥ

NAṢAḤA vb. (I)~to advise, to counsel; (with prep. *li-*) to be true, to be faithful. (n.vb.) counsel, advice. (pcple. act.) one who advises, who counsels, who looks after someone

a) perf. act.

7:79 (77)	I have delivered to you the Message of my Lord, and advised you sincerely
7:93 (91)	I have delivered to you the Messages of my Lord, and advised you sincerely
9:91 (92)	those who find nothing to expend, if they are true to God

b) impf. act. (*yanṣaḥu*)

7:62 (60)	I deliver to you the Messages of my Lord, and I advise you sincerely
11:34 (36)	if I desire to counsel you sincerely

f) n.vb. (*nuṣḥ*)

11:34 (36)	my sincere counsel will not profit you

g) pcple. act. (*nāṣiḥ*)

7:21 (20)	truly, I am for you a sincere adviser
7:68 (66)	I am your adviser sincere, faithful
7:79 (77)	but you do not love sincere advisers
12:11 (11)	surely we are his sincere well-wishers
28:12 (11)	who will take charge of him for you and look after him?
28:20 (19)	I am one of thy sincere advisers

NAṢŪḤ n.f. (adj)~sincere, true

66:8 (8)	Believers, turn to God in sincere repentance

*N Ṣ R

NAṢARA vb. (I)~to help, to aid, to succour. (n.vb.) help, aid, succour; victory. (pcple. act.) a helper. (pcple. pass.) one who is helped

a) perf. act.

3:123 (119)	God most surely helped you at Badr, when you were utterly abject
7:157 (156)	those who believe in him and succour him and help him
8:72 (73)	those who have given refuge and help — those are friends one of another
8:74 (75)	those who have given refuge and help — those in truth are the believers
9:25 (25)	God has already helped you on many fields, and on the day of Hunain
9:40 (40)	if you do not help him, yet God has helped him already
21:77 (77)	We helped him against the people who cried lies to Our signs
37:116 (116)	We helped them, so that they were the victors
46:28 (27)	why did those not help them that they had taken to themselves as mediators
59:12 (12)	even if they helped them, they would surely turn their backs

b) impf. act. (*yanṣuru*)

3:81 (75)	you shall believe in him and you shall help him
3:160 (154)	if God helps you, none can overcome you
3:160 (154)	if He forsakes you, who then can help you after Him?
7:192 (191)	neither they help themselves

7:197 (196)	neither they help themselves
9:14 (14)	He will help you against them, and bring healing
9:40 (40)	if you do not help him, yet God has helped him
11:30 (32)	who would help me against God, if I drive them away?
11:63 (66)	who shall help me against God if I rebel against Him?
18:43 (41)	but there was no host to help him
22:15 (15)	whosoever thinks God will not help him in the present world
22:40 (41)	assuredly God will help him who (helps) Him
22:40 (41)	assuredly God will (help) him who helps Him
22:60 (59)	God will help him
26:93 (93)	do they help you
28:81 (81)	there was no host to help him, apart from God
30:5 (4)	God helps whomsoever He will
40:29 (30)	who will help us against the might of God
40:51 (54)	We shall help Our Messengers and those who have believed
42:46 (45)	they have no protectors to help them, apart from God
47:7 (8)	O believers, if you help God, He will (help) you
47:7 (8)	O believers, if you (help) God, He will help you
48:3 (3)	and that God may help thee
57:25 (25)	so that God might know who helps Him, and His Messengers
59:8 (8)	and good pleasure, and helping God and His Messenger
59:11 (11)	if you are fought against, we will help you
59:12 (12)	if they are fought against, they will not help them
67:20 (20)	who is this that shall be a host for you to help you

c) impv. (*unṣur*)

2:250 (251)	give us aid against the people of the unbelievers
2:286 (286)	help us against the people of the unbelievers
3:147 (141)	help us against the people of the unbelievers
21:68 (68)	burn him, and help your gods, if you would do aught
23:26 (26)	O my Lord, help me, for that they cry me lies
23:39 (41)	O my Lord, help me, for that they cry me lies
29:30 (29)	my Lord, help me against the people that work corruption

e) impf. pass. (*yunṣaru*)

2:48 (45)	be taken, neither shall they be helped
2:86 (80)	shall not be lightened, neither shall they be helped
2:123 (117)	neither shall they be helped
3:111 (107)	then they will not be helped
11:113 (115)	and then you will not be helped
21:39 (40)	nor from their backs, neither shall they be helped
23:65 (67)	surely you shall not be helped from Us
28:41 (41)	on the Day of Resurrection they shall not be helped
36:74 (74)	haply they might be helped
39:54 (55)	you will not be helped
41:16 (15)	and they shall not be helped
44:41 (41)	and they shall not be helped
52:46 (46)	and they shall not be helped
59:12 (12)	they would surely turn their backs, then they would not be helped

f) n.vb. (*naṣr*)

2:214 (210)	when comes God's help?
2:214 (210)	God's help is nigh
3:13 (11)	God confirms with His help whom He will

3:126 (122)	help comes only from God
6:34 (34)	that they were cried lies to, and were hurt, until Our help came unto them
7:192 (191)	and that have no power to help them
7:197 (196)	those on whom you call, apart from God, have no power to help you
8:10 (10)	help comes only from God
8:26 (26)	He gave you refuge, and confirmed you with His help
8:62 (64)	He has confirmed thee with His help, and with the believers
8:72 (73)	it is your duty to help them
12:110 (110)	Our help came to them and whosoever We willed was delivered
21:43 (44)	they are not able to help themselves, nor shall they be guarded
22:39 (40)	surely God is able to help them
25:19 (20)	you can neither turn it aside, nor find any help
29:10 (9)	then if help comes from thy Lord, he will say
30:5 (4)	in God's help
30:47 (46)	it was ever a duty incumbent upon Us, to help the believers
36:75 (75)	they cannot help them, though they be hosts
48:3 (3)	and that God may help thee with mighty help
61:13 (13)	other things you love, help from God and a nigh victory
110:1 (1)	when comes the help of God, and victory

g) pcple. act. (*nāṣir*)

3:22 (21)	they have no helpers
3:56 (49)	they shall have no helpers
3:91 (85)	they shall have no helpers
3:150 (143)	God is your Protector, and He is the best of helpers
16:37 (39)	they have no helpers
29:25 (24)	your refuge will be the Fire, and you will have no helpers
30:29 (28)	they have no helpers
45:34 (33)	your refuge is the Fire, and you shall have no helpers
47:13 (14)	there was no helper for them
72:24 (25)	then they will know who is weaker in helpers and fewer in numbers
86:10 (10)	and he shall have no strength, no helper

h) pcple. pass. (*manṣūr*)

17:33 (35)	let him not exceed in slaying; he shall be helped
37:172 (172)	assuredly they shall be helped

NAṢĪR n.m. (pl. *anṣār*)~helper; (pl) Helpers, Ansar (the people of Medina who helped the Prophet)

2:107 (101)	and that you have none, apart from God, neither protector nor helper
2:120 (114)	thou shalt have against God neither protector nor helper
2:270 (273)	no helpers have the evildoers
3:52 (45)	who will be my helpers unto God?
3:52 (45)	we will be helpers of God; we believe in God
3:192 (189)	and the evildoers shall have no helpers
4:45 (47)	God suffices as a protector, God suffices as a helper
4:52 (55)	he whom God has cursed, thou wilt not find for him any helper
4:75 (77)	a protector from Thee, and appoint to us from Thee a helper
4:89 (91)	take not to yourselves any one of them as friend or helper
4:123 (122)	and will not find for him, apart from God, a friend or helper
4:145 (144)	thou wilt not find for them any helper
4:173 (173)	and they shall not find for them, apart from God, a friend or helper
5:72 (76)	and wrongdoers shall have no helpers
8:40 (41)	God is your Protector — an excellent Protector, an excellent Helper
9:74 (75)	on the earth they have no protector or helper

9:100 (101)	the first of the Emigrants and the Helpers, and those who followed them
9:116 (117)	you have not, apart from God, either protector or helper
9:117 (118)	God has turned towards the Prophet and the Emigrants and the Helpers who followed him
17:75 (77)	thou wouldst have found none to help thee against Us
17:80 (82)	grant me authority from Thee, to help me
22:71 (70)	and for the evildoers there shall be no helper
22:78 (78)	He is your Protector — an excellent Protector, an excellent Helper
25:31 (33)	thy Lord suffices as a guide and as a helper
29:22 (21)	you have not, apart from God, either protector or helper
33:17 (17)	they shall find for themselves, apart from God, neither protector nor helper
33:65 (65)	they shall find neither protector nor helper
35:37 (35)	the evildoers shall have no helper
42:8 (6)	the evildoers shall have neither protector nor helper
42:31 (30)	apart from God, you have neither protector nor helper
48:22 (22)	would have turned their backs, and then found neither protector nor helper
61:14 (14)	be you God's helpers, as Jesus, Mary's son, said to the Apostles
61:14 (14)	who will be my helpers unto God?
61:14 (14)	the Apostles said, 'We will be helpers of God'
71:25 (26)	they found not, apart from God, any to help them

NAṢRĀNĪ n.m. (pl. *naṣārá*)~a Christian

2:62 (59)	they that believe, and those of Jewry, and the Christians
2:111 (105)	they say, 'None shall enter Paradise except that they be Jews or Christians'
2:113 (107)	the Jews say, 'The Christians stand not on anything'
2:113 (107)	the Christians say, 'The Jews stand not on anything'
2:120 (114)	never will the Jews be satisfied with thee, neither the Christians
2:135 (129)	they say, 'Be Jews or Christians and you shall be guided'
2:140 (134)	they were Jews, or they were Christians
3:67 (60)	Abraham in truth was not a Jew, neither a Christian
5:14 (17)	with those who say, 'We are Christians,' We took compact
5:18 (21)	say the Jews and Christians, 'We are the sons of God'
5:51 (56)	O believers, take not Jews and Christians as friends
5:69 (73)	and the Sabaeans, and those Christians
5:82 (85)	the nearest of them in love to the believers are those who say, 'We are Christians'
9:30 (30)	the Christians say, 'The Messiah is the Son of God'
22:17 (17)	the Sabaeans, the Christians, the Magians

TANĀṢARA vb. (VI)~to help one another

b) impf. act. (*yatanāṣaru*)

37:25 (25)	why help you not one another?

INTAṢARA vb. (VIII)~to help oneself; (54:10) to help. (pcple. act.) one who is helped, who is succoured; (*mā kāna muntaṣiran*) helpless

a) perf. act.

26:227 (228)	and help themselves after being wronged
42:41 (39)	whosoever helps himself after he has been wronged
47:4 (5)	if God had willed, He would have avenged Himself upon them

b) impf. act. (*yantaṣiru*)

26:93 (93) or help themselves
42:39 (37) who, when insolence visits them, do help themselves
55:35 (35) and you shall not be helped

c) impv. (*intaṣir*)

54:10 (10) I am vanquished; do Thou succour me

g) pcple. act. (*muntaṣir*)

18:43 (41) apart from God, and he was helpless
28:81 (81) and he was helpless
51:45 (45) they were not able to stand upright, and were not helped
54:44 (44) do they say, 'We are a congregation that shall be succoured?'

ISTANṢARA vb. (X)~to ask for help, to seek succour

a) perf. act.

8:72 (73) yet if they ask you for help, for religion's sake
28:18 (17) the man who had sought his succour on the day before cried out to him again

*N Ṣ T

ANṢATA vb. (IV)~to be silent, to pay heed

c) impv. (*anṣit*)

7:204 (203) when the Koran is recited, give you ear to it and be silent
46:29 (28) when they were in its presence they said, 'Be silent!'

*N Ṣ W

NĀṢIYAH n.f. (pl. *nawāṣī*)~a forelock

11:56 (59) there is no creature that crawls, but He takes it by the forelock
55:41 (41) they shall be seized by their forelocks and their feet
96:15 (15) if he gives not over, We shall seize him by the forelock
96:16 (16) a lying, sinful forelock

*N T Q

NATAQA vb. (I)~to shake (tr)

a) perf. act.

7:171 (170) when We shook the mountain above them as if it were a canopy

*N TH R

NATHARA vb. (I)~(pcple. pass.) scattered

h) pcple. pass. (*manthūr*)

25:23 (25) We shall advance upon what work they have done, and make it a scattered dust
76:19 (19) when thou seest them, thou supposest them scattered pearls

INTATHARA vb. (VIII)~to be scattered

a) perf. act.

82:2 (2) when the stars are scattered

*N Ṭ F

NUṬFAH n.f.~a sperm-drop

16:4 (4) He created man of a sperm-drop
18:37 (35) disbelievest thou in Him who created thee of dust, then of a sperm-drop
22:5 (5) surely We created you of dust then of a sperm-drop
23:13 (13) then We set him, a drop, in a receptacle secure
23:14 (14) then We created of the drop a clot
35:11 (12) God created you of dust then of a sperm-drop
36:77 (77) has not man regarded how that We created him of a sperm-drop?
40:67 (69) it is He who created you of dust then of a sperm-drop
53:46 (47) of a sperm-drop, when it was cast forth
75:37 (37) was he not a sperm-drop spilled?
76:2 (2) We created man of a sperm-drop, a mingling, trying him
80:19 (18) of a sperm-drop

*N Ṭ Ḥ

NAṬĪḤAH n.f.~an animal gored to death

5:3 (4) the beast fallen to death, the beast gored

*N Ṭ Q

NAṬAQA vb. (I)~to speak. (n.vb.) speech

b) impf. act. (*yanṭiqu*)

21:63 (64) question them, if they are able to speak
21:65 (66) very well indeed thou knowest these do not speak
23:62 (64) with Us is a Book speaking truth
27:85 (87) because of the evil they committed, while they speak naught
37:92 (90) what ails you, that you speak not?

45:29 (28)	this is Our Book, that speaks against you the truth
51:23 (23)	by the Lord of heaven and earth, it is as surely true as that you have speech
53:3 (3)	nor speaks he out of caprice
77:35 (35)	this is the day they shall not speak

f) n.vb. (*manṭiq*)

27:16 (16)	men, we have been taught the speech of the birds

ANṬAQA vb. (IV)~to give speech

a) perf. act.

41:21 (20)	God gave us speech, as He gave everything (speech)
41:21 (20)	God gave us (speech) as He gave everything speech

*N W ʾ

NĀʾA vb. (I)~to be a heavy burden

b) impf. act. (*yanūʾu*)

28:76 (76)	treasures such that the very keys of them were too heavy a burden

*N W B

ANĀBA vb. (IV)~to be penitent, to turn (in repentance), to repent: (pcple. act.) one who turns (in repentance), penitent

a) perf. act.

13:27 (27)	and He guides to Him all who are penitent
31:15 (14)	follow the way of him who turns to Me
38:24 (23)	he fell down, bowing, and he repented
38:34 (33)	We cast upon his throne a mere body; then he repented
39:17 (19)	those who eschew the serving of idols and turn penitent to God
60:4 (4)	our Lord, in Thee we trust; to Thee we turn

b) impf. act. (*yunību*)

11:88 (90)	in Him I have put my trust, and to Him I turn, penitent
40:13 (13)	yet none remembers but he who repents
42:10 (8)	in Him I have put my trust, and to Him I turn, penitent
42:13 (12)	He guides to Himself whosoever turns, penitent

c) impv. (*anib*)

39:54 (55)	turn unto your Lord and surrender to Him

g) pcple. act. (*munīb*)

11:75 (77)	Abraham was clement, compassionate, penitent
30:31 (30)	turning to Him. And fear you Him

30:33 (32)	when some affliction visits mankind, they call unto their Lord, turning to Him
34:9 (9)	in that is a sign to every penitent servant
39:8 (11)	when some affliction visits a man, he calls upon his Lord, turning to Him
50:8 (8)	for an insight and a reminder to every penitent servant
50:33 (32)	whosoever fears the All-merciful in the Unseen, and comes with a penitent heart

*N W Ḥ

NŪḤ n.prop.~Noah

3:33 (30)	God chose Adam and Noah and the House of Abraham
4:163 (161)	We have revealed to thee as We revealed to Noah
6:84 (84)	and Noah We guided before; and of his seed
7:59 (57)	and We sent Noah to his people
7:69 (67)	when He appointed you as successors after the people of Noah
9:70 (71)	those who were before you — the people of Noah, Ad
10:71 (72)	and recite to them the story of Noah
11:25 (27)	and We sent Noah to his people
11:32 (34)	Noah, thou hast disputed with us and make much disputation with us
11:36 (38)	and it was revealed to Noah, saying
11:42 (44)	Noah called to his son, who was standing apart
11:45 (47)	and Noah called unto his Lord
11:46 (48)	Noah, he is not of thy family
11:48 (50)	Noah, get thee down in peace from Us
11:89 (91)	so that there smite you the like of what smote the people of Noah
14:9 (9)	those who were before you — the people of Noah
17:3 (3)	the seed of those We bore with Noah
17:17 (18)	how many generations We have destroyed after Noah
19:58 (59)	among the Prophets of the seed of Adam, and of those We bore with Noah
21:76 (76)	and Noah — when he called before, and We answered him
22:42 (43)	the people of Noah cried lies, and Ad
23:23 (23)	and We sent Noah to his people
25:37 (39)	the people of Noah, when they cried lies to the Messengers
26:105 (105)	the people of Noah cried lies to the Envoys
26:106 (106)	when their brother Noah said to them
26:116 (116)	if thou givest not over, Noah, thou shalt assuredly be one of the stoned
29:14 (13)	indeed, We sent Noah to his people
33:7 (7)	when We took compact from the Prophets, and from thee, and from Noah
37:75 (73)	Noah called to Us
37:79 (77)	peace be upon Noah among all beings
38:12 (11)	cried lies before them the people of Noah
40:5 (5)	the people of Noah before them also cried lies, and the parties after them
40:31 (32)	the like of the case of Noah's people
42:13 (11)	He has laid down for you as religion that He charged Noah with
50:12 (12)	cried lies before them the people of Noah
51:46 (46)	the people of Noah before; surely they were an ungodly people
53:52 (53)	the people of Noah before — certainly they did exceeding evil
54:9 (9)	the people of Noah cried lies before them
57:26 (26)	and We sent Noah, and Abraham
66:10 (10)	a similitude for the unbelievers — the wife of Noah
71:1 (1)	We sent Noah to his people, saying
71:21 (20)	Noah said, 'My Lord, they have rebelled against me'
71:26 (27)	and Noah said, 'My Lord, leave not upon the earth of the unbelievers'

*N W M

NĀMA vb. (I)~(n.vb.) sleep, slumber. (pcple. act.) sleeper, sleeping

f) n.vb. (*nawm*)

2:255 (256)	slumber seizes Him not, neither sleep
25:47 (49)	it is He who appointed the night for you to be garment and sleep for a rest
78:9 (9)	and We appointed your sleep for a rest

g) pcple. act. (*nāʾim*)

7:97 (95)	Our might shall not come upon them at night while they are sleeping
68:19 (19)	then a visitation from thy Lord visited it, while they were sleeping

MANĀM n.m.~slumbering, sleep; dream

8:43 (45)	when God showed thee them in thy dream as few
30:23 (22)	and of His signs is your slumbering by night and day
37:102 (101)	my son, I see in a dream that I shall sacrifice thee
39:42 (43)	and that which has not died, in its sleep

*N W N

NŪN n.prop.~Dhul Nun (lit. "lord of the fish," i.e. Jonah)

21:87 (87)	and Dhul Nun — when he went forth enraged

*N W Q

NĀQAH n.f.~a she-camel

7:73 (71)	this is the She-camel of God, to be a sign for you
7:77 (75)	so they hamstrung the She-camel
11:64 (67)	this is the She-camel of God, to be a sign for you
17:59 (61)	We brought Thamood the She-camel visible, but they did her wrong
26:155 (155)	this is a she-camel; to her a draught and to you a draught
54:27 (27)	We shall send the She-camel as a trial for them
91:13 (13)	the She-camel of God; let her drink

*N W R

NĀR n.f.~a fire

2:17 (16)	the likeness of them is as the likeness of a man who kindled a fire
2:24 (22)	fear the Fire, whose fuel is men and stones
2:39 (37)	those shall be the inhabitants of the Fire
2:80 (74)	the Fire shall not touch us save a number of days
2:81 (75)	those are the inhabitants of the Fire
2:126 (120)	then I shall compel him to the chastisement of the Fire

2:167 (162)	O bitter regrets for them! Never shall they issue from the Fire
2:174 (169)	they shall eat naught but the Fire in their bellies
2:175 (170)	how patiently they shall endure the Fire
2:201 (197)	guard us against the chastisement of the Fire
2:217 (214)	those are the inhabitants of the Fire
2:221 (221)	those call unto the Fire; and God calls unto Paradise
2:257 (259)	those are the inhabitants of the Fire
2:266 (268)	then a whirlwind with fire smites it, and it is consumed
2:275 (276)	those are the inhabitants of the Fire
3:10 (8)	those — they shall be fuel for the Fire
3:16 (14)	and guard us against the chastisement of the Fire
3:24 (23)	the Fire shall not touch us, except for a number of days
3:103 (99)	you were upon the brink of a pit of Fire
3:116 (112)	those are the inhabitants of the Fire
3:131 (126)	and fear the Fire prepared for the unbelievers
3:151 (144)	their lodging shall be the Fire
3:183 (179)	we believe not any Messenger until he brings to us a sacrifice devoured by fire
3:185 (182)	whosoever is removed from the Fire and admitted to Paradise
3:191 (188)	guard us against the chastisement of the Fire
3:192 (189)	whomsoever Thou admittest into the Fire, Thou wilt have abased
4:10 (11)	those who devour the property of orphans unjustly, devour Fire in their bellies
4:14 (18)	and transgresses His bounds, him He will admit to a Fire
4:30 (34)	him We shall certainly roast at a Fire
4:56 (59)	those who disbelieve in Our signs — We shall certainly roast them at a Fire
4:145 (144)	the hypocrites will be in the lowest reach of the Fire
5:29 (32)	I desire that thou shouldest be laden with my sin and thy sin, and so become an inhabitant of the Fire
5:37 (41)	they will desire to come forth from the Fire
5:64 (69)	as often as they light a fire for war, God will extinguish it
5:72 (76)	and his refuge shall be the Fire
6:27 (27)	if thou couldst see when they are stationed before the Fire
6:128 (128)	the Fire is your lodging, therein to dwell
7:12 (11)	I am better than he; Thou createdst me of fire
7:36 (34)	those shall be the inhabitants of the Fire
7:38 (36)	enter among nations that passed away before you, jinn and mankind, into the Fire
7:38 (36)	so give them a double chastisement of the Fire
7:44 (42)	the inhabitants of Paradise will call to the inhabitants of the Fire
7:47 (45)	when their eyes are turned towards the inhabitants of the Fire they shall say
7:50 (48)	the inhabitants of the Fire shall call to the inhabitants of Paradise
8:14 (14)	the chastisement of the Fire is for the unbelievers
9:17 (17)	their works have failed them, and in the Fire they shall dwell forever
9:35 (35)	the day they shall be heated in the fire of Gehenna
9:63 (64)	whosoever opposes God and His Messenger — for him awaits the fire of Gehenna
9:68 (69)	and the unbelievers, the fire of Gehenna, therein to dwell forever
9:81 (82)	say: 'Gehenna's fire is hotter, did they but understand'
9:109 (110)	crumbling bank that has tumbled with him into the fire of Gehenna
10:8 (8)	those — their refuge is the Fire
10:27 (28)	those are the inhabitants of the Fire
11:16 (19)	those are they for whom in the world to come there is only the Fire
11:17 (20)	his promised land is the Fire
11:98 (100)	and will have led them down to the Fire — evil the watering-place to be led down to
11:106 (108)	as for the wretched, they shall be in the Fire

11:113 (115)	lean not on the evildoers, so that the Fire touches you
13:5 (6)	those shall be the inhabitants of the Fire
13:17 (18)	and out of that over which they kindle fire, being desirous of ornament or ware
13:35 (35)	and the requital of the unbelievers is — the Fire
14:30 (35)	take your joy! Your homecoming shall be — the Fire
14:50 (51)	of pitch their shirts, their faces enveloped by the Fire
15:27 (27)	and the jinn created We before of fire flaming
16:62 (64)	without any doubt theirs shall be the Fire
18:29 (28)	We have prepared for the evildoers a fire, whose pavilion encompasses them
18:53 (51)	then the evildoers will see the Fire
18:96 (95)	when he had made it a fire, he said
20:10 (9)	when he saw a fire, and said to his family
20:10 (9)	tarry you here; I observe a fire
20:10 (10)	or I shall find at the fire guidance
21:39 (40)	if the unbelievers but knew when that they shall not ward off the Fire from their faces
21:69 (69)	O fire, be coolness and safety for Abraham
22:19 (20)	for them garments of fire shall be cut
22:72 (71)	the Fire — God has promised it to the unbelievers
23:104 (106)	the Fire smiting their faces the while they glower there
24:35 (35)	whose oil wellnigh would shine, even if no fire touched it
24:57 (56)	their refuge is the Fire — an evil homecoming
27:7 (7)	I observe a fire, and will bring you news of it
27:8 (8)	blessed is He who is in the fire
27:90 (92)	whosoever comes with an evil deed, their faces shall be thrust into the Fire
28:29 (29)	he observed on the side of the Mount a fire
28:29 (29)	tarry you here; I observe a fire
28:29 (29)	perhaps I shall bring you news of it, or a faggot from the fire
28:41 (41)	We appointed them leaders, calling to the Fire
29:24 (23)	then God delivered him from the fire
29:25 (24)	and your refuge will be the Fire
32:20 (20)	as for the ungodly, their refuge shall be the Fire
32:20 (20)	taste the chastisement of the Fire
33:66 (66)	upon the day when their faces are turned about in the Fire they shall say
34:42 (41)	taste the chastisement of the Fire, which you cried lies to
35:36 (33)	as for the unbelievers, theirs shall be the fire of Gehenna
36:80 (80)	who has made for you out of the green tree fire and lo, from it you kindle
38:27 (26)	wherefore woe unto the unbelievers because of the Fire
38:59 (59)	they shall roast in the Fire
38:61 (61)	whoso forwarded this for us, give him a double chastisement in the Fire
38:64 (64)	surely that is true — the disputing of the inhabitants of the Fire
38:76 (77)	Thou createdst me of fire, and him Thou createdst of clay
39:8 (11)	thou shalt be among the inhabitants of the Fire
39:16 (18)	above them ey shall have overshadowings of the Fire
39:19 (20)	shalt thou deliver him out of the Fire?
40:6 (6)	that they are the inhabitants of the Fire
40:41 (44)	I call you to salvation, and you call me to the Fire
40:43 (46)	and that the prodigal are the inhabitants of the Fire
40:46 (49)	the Fire, to which they shall be exposed morning and evening
40:47 (50)	when they argue one with the other in the Fire
40:47 (50)	will you avail us now against any part of the Fire?
40:49 (52)	those who are in the Fire will say to the keepers of Gehenna
40:72 (73)	into the boiling water, then into the Fire they are poured
41:19 (18)	upon the day when God's enemies are mustered to the Fire

41:24 (23)	then if they persist, the Fire shall be a lodging for them
41:28 (28)	that is the recompense of God's enemies — the Fire
41:40 (40)	what, is he who shall be cast into the Fire better
45:34 (33)	your refuge is the Fire, and you shall have no helpers
46:20 (19)	upon the day when the unbelievers are exposed to the Fire
46:34 (33)	upon the day when the unbelievers are exposed to the Fire
47:12 (13)	and the Fire shall be their lodging
47:15 (17)	are they as he who dwells forever in the Fire
51:13 (13)	upon the day when they shall be tried at the Fire
52:13 (13)	the day when they shall be pitched into the fire of Gehenna
52:14 (14)	this is the fire hat you cried lies to
54:48 (48)	the day when they are dragged on their faces into the Fire
55:15 (14)	and He created the jinn of a smokeless fire
55:35 (35)	against you shall be loosed a flame of fire
56:71 (70)	have you considered the fire you kindle?
57:15 (14)	your refuge is the Fire, that is your master — an evil homecoming
58:17 (18)	those — they are the inhabitants of the Fire
59:3 (3)	there awaits them in the world to come the chastisement of the Fire
59:17 (17)	their end is, both are in the Fire, there dwelling forever
59:20 (20)	not equal are the inhabitants of the Fire and the inhabitants of Paradise
64:10 (10)	those shall be the inhabitants of the Fire
66:6 (6)	guard yourselves and your families against a Fire whose fuel is men and stones
66:10 (10)	enter, you two, the Fire with those who enter
71:25 (25)	they were drowned, and admitted into a Fire
72:23 (24)	for him there awaits the Fire of Gehenna
74:31 (31)	We have appointed only angels to be masters of the Fire
85:5 (5)	the fire abounding in fuel
87:12 (12)	even he who shall roast in the Great Fire
88:4 (4)	roasting at a scorching fire
90:20 (20)	over them is a Fire covered down
92:14 (14)	now I have warned you of a Fire that flames
98:6 (5)	and the idolaters shall be in the Fire of Gehenna
101:11 (8)	a blazing Fire
104:6 (6)	the Fire of God kindled
111:3 (3)	he shall roast at a flaming fire

NŪR n.m.~light; Light (Divine attribute)

2:17 (16)	God took away their light, and left them in darkness
2:257 (258)	He brings them forth from the shadows into the light
2:257 (259)	idols, that bring them forth from the light into the shadows
4:174 (174)	We have sent down to you a manifest light
5:15 (18)	there has come to you from God a light, and a Book Manifest
5:16 (18)	and brings them forth from the shadows into the light by His leave
5:44 (48)	We sent down the Torah, wherein is guidance and light
5:46 (50)	We gave to him the Gospel, wherein is guidance and light
6:1 (1)	who created the heavens and the earth and appointed the shadows and light
6:91 (91)	who sent down the Book that Moses brought as a light and a guidance
6:122 (122)	We gave him life, and appointed for him a light to walk by
7:157 (156)	and follow the light that has been sent down with him
9:32 (32)	desiring to extinguish with their mouths God's light
9:32 (32)	and God refuses but to perfect His light
10:5 (5)	it is He who made the sun a radiance, and the moon a light
13:16 (17)	or are the shadows and the light equal?
14:1 (1)	that thou mayest bring forth mankind from the shadows to the light
14:5 (5)	bring forth thy people from the shadows to the light

24:35 (35)	God is the Light of the heavens and the earth
24:35 (35)	the likeness of His Light is as a niche wherein is a lamp
24:35 (35)	Light upon (Light)
24:35 (35)	(Light) upon Light
24:35 (35)	God guides to His Light whom He will
24:40 (40)	to whomsoever God assigns no light
24:40 (40)	no light has he
33:43 (42)	to bring you forth from the shadows into the light
35:20 (20)	the shadows and the light
39:22 (23)	so he walks in a light from his Lord
39:69 (69)	the earth shall shine with the light of its Lord
42:52 (52)	but We made it a light, whereby We guide whom We will of Our servants
57:9 (9)	that He may bring you forth from the shadows into the light
57:12 (12)	their light running before them, and on their right hands
57:13 (13)	wait for us, so that we may borrow your light
57:13 (13)	it shall be said, 'Return you back behind, and seek for a light'
57:19 (18)	they have their wage, and their light
57:28 (28)	He will appoint for you a light whereby you shall walk, and forgive you
61:8 (8)	they desire to extinguish with their mouths the light of God
61:8 (8)	but God will perfect His light
64:8 (8)	believe in God and His Messenger, and in the Light which We have sent down
65:11 (11)	He may bring forth those who believe and do righteous deeds from the shadows into the light
66:8 (8)	those who believe with him, their light running before them
66:8 (8)	our Lord, perfect for us our light, and forgive us
71:16 (15)	and set the moon therein for a light

ANĀRA vb. (IV)~(pcple. act.) illuminating, that which gives light

g) pcple. act. (*munīr*)

3:184 (181)	who came bearing clear signs, and the Psalms, and the Book Illuminating
22:8 (8)	that disputes concerning God without knowledge or guidance, or an illuminating Book
25:61 (62)	and has set among them a lamp, and an illuminating moon
31:20 (19)	
33:46 (45)	calling unto God by His leave, and as a light-giving lamp
35:25 (23)	their Messengers came to them with the clear signs, the Psalms, the Illuminating Book

*N W S

NĀS n.m. (pl. of *insān* (*a n s*)~mankind, men, people, others

2:8 (7)	and some men there are who say
2:13 (12)	when it is said to them, 'Believe as the people believe'
2:21 (19)	O you men, serve your Lord Who created you
2:24 (22)	fear the Fire, whose fuel is men and stones
2:44 (41)	will you bid others to piety, and forget yourselves
2:83 (77)	and speak good to men, and perform the prayer
2:94 (88)	if the Last Abode with God is yours exclusively, and not for other people
2:96 (90)	thou shalt find them the eagerest of men for life

2:102 (96)	but the Satans disbelieved, teaching the people sorcery
2:124 (118)	behold, I make you a leader for the people
2:125 (119)	when We appointed the House to be a place of visitation for the people
2:142 (136)	the fools among the people will say
2:143 (137)	We appointed you a midmost nation that you might be witnesses to the people
2:143 (138)	truly, God is All-gentle with the people
2:150 (145)	turn your faces towards it, that the people may not have any argument against you
2:159 (154)	after We have shown them clearly in the Book — they shall be cursed
2:161 (156)	upon them shall rest the curse of God and the angels, and of men altogether
2:164 (159)	and the ship that runs in the sea with profit to men
2:165 (160)	yet there be men who take to themselves compeers apart from God
2:168 (163)	O men, eat of what is in the earth lawful and good
2:185 (181)	wherein the Koran was sent down to be a guidance to the people
2:187 (183)	so God makes clear His signs to men
2:188 (184)	that you may sinfully consume a portion of other men's goods
2:189 (185)	they are appointed times for the people, and the Pilgrimage
2:199 (195)	then press on from where the people press on
2:200 (196)	now some men there are who say
2:204 (200)	and some men there are whose saying upon the present world pleases thee
2:207 (203)	but other men there are that sell themselves
2:213 (209)	the people were one nation
2:213 (209)	that He might decide between the people touching their differences
2:219 (216)	in both is heinous sin, and uses for men
2:221 (221)	He makes clear His signs to the people
2:224 (224)	to being pious and godfearing, and putting things right between men
2:243 (244)	truly God is bounteous to the people
2:243 (244)	but most of the people are not thankful
2:251 (252)	had God not driven back the people, some by the means of others
2:259 (261)	so We would make thee a sign for the people
2:264 (266)	as one who expends of his substance to show off to men
2:273 (274)	they do not beg of men importunately
3:4 (2)	aforetime, as guidance to the people
3:9 (7)	it is Thou that shall gather mankind for a day whereon is no doubt
3:14 (12)	decked out fair to men is the love of lusts
3:21 (20)	and slay such men as bid to justice
3:41 (36)	thou shalt not speak, save by tokens, to men for three days
3:46 (41)	He shall speak to men in the cradle, and of age
3:68 (61)	the people standing closest to Abraham are those who followed him
3:79 (73)	then he should say to men, 'Be you servants to me'
3:87 (81)	there shall rest on them the curse of God and of the angels and of men, altogether
3:96 (90)	the first House established for the people was that at Bekka
3:97 (91)	it is the duty of all men towards God to come to the House a pilgrim
3:110 (106)	you are the best nation ever brought forth to men
3:112 (108)	except they be in a bond of God, and a bond of the people
3:134 (128)	restrain their rage, and pardon the offences of their fellowmen
3:138 (132)	this is an exposition for mankind, and a guidance
3:140 (134)	such days We deal out in turn among men
3:173 (167)	those to whom the people said, 'The (people)'
3:173 (167)	'the people have gathered against you'
3:187 (184)	you shall make it clear unto the people, and not conceal it
4:1 (1)	Mankind, fear your Lord, who created you of a single soul
4:37 (41)	such as are niggardly, and bid other men to be niggardly
4:38 (42)	such as expend of their substance to show off to men
4:53 (56)	if that is so, they do not give the people a single date-spot
4:54 (57)	are they jealous of the people for the bounty that God has given them?

4:58 (61)	when you judge between the people, that you judge with justice
4:77 (79)	there is a party of them fearing the people as they would fear God
4:79 (81)	and We have sent thee to men a Messenger
4:105 (106)	so that thou mayest judge between the people by that God has shown thee
4:108 (108)	they hide themselves from men
4:114 (114)	him who bids to freewill offering, or honour, or setting things right between the people
4:133 (132)	if He will, He can put you away, O men
4:142 (141)	they stand up lazily, showing off to the people
4:161 (159)	and consuming the wealth of the people in vanity
4:165 (163)	so that mankind might have no argument against God, after the Messengers
4:170 (168)	O men, the Messenger has now come to you with the truth
4:174 (174)	O men, a proof has now come to you from your Lord
5:32 (35)	whoso slays a soul ... Shall be as if he had slain mankind altogether
5:32 (35)	whoso gives life to a soul, shall be as if he had given life to mankind altogether
5:44 (48)	so fear not men, but fear you Me
5:49 (54)	surely, many men are ungodly
5:67 (71)	God will protect thee from men
5:82 (85)	thou wilt surely find the most hostile of men to the believers are the Jews
5:97 (98)	God has appointed the Kaaba, the Holy House, as an establishment for men
5:110 (109)	to speak to men in the cradle, and of age
5:116 (116)	Jesus son of Mary, didst thou say unto men
6:91 (91)	who sent down the Book that Moses brought as a light and a guidance to men?
6:122 (122)	and appointed for him a light to walk by among the people
6:144 (145)	who forges against God a lie, in order that he may lead mankind astray
7:85 (83)	and diminish not the goods of the people
7:116 (113)	and when they cast they put a spell upon the people's eyes
7:144 (141)	Moses, I have chosen thee above all men for My Messages and My Utterance
7:158 (157)	O mankind, I am the Messenger of God to you all
7:187 (187)	the knowledge of it is only with God, but most men know not
8:26 (26)	and were fearful that the people would snatch you away
8:47 (49)	be not as those who went forth from their habitations swaggering boastfully to show off to men
8:48 (50)	today no man shall overcome you
9:3 (3)	a proclamation, from God and His Messenger, unto mankind
9:34 (34)	many of the rabbis and monks indeed consume the goods of the people
10:2 (2)	was it a wonder to the people that We revealed to a man from among them
10:2 (2)	warn the people, and give thou good tidings to the believers
10:11 (12)	if God should hasten unto men evil as they would hasten good
10:19 (20)	mankind were only one nation, then they fell into variance
10:21 (22)	when We let the people taste mercy after hardship has visited them
10:23 (24)	O men, your insolence is only against yourselves
10:24 (25)	the plants of the earth mingle with it whereof men and cattle eat
10:44 (45)	surely God wrongs not men anything
10:44 (45)	but themselves men wrong
10:57 (58)	O men, now there has come to you an admonition from your Lord
10:60 (61)	God is bountiful to men
10:92 (92)	surely many men are heedless of Our signs
10:99 (99)	wouldst thou then constrain the people, until they are believers?
10:104 (104)	O men, if you are in doubt regarding my religion
10:108 (108)	O men, the truth has come to you from your Lord
11:17 (20)	it is the truth from thy Lord, but most men do not believe
11:85 (86)	do not diminish the goods of the people
11:103 (105)	that is a day mankind are to be gathered to
11:118 (120)	had thy Lord willed, He would have made mankind one nation
11:119 (120)	I shall assuredly fill Gehenna with jinn and men all together

12:21 (21)	God prevails in His purpose, but most men know not
12:38 (38)	that is of God's bounty to us, and to men
12:38 (38)	but most men are not thankful
12:40 (40)	that is the right religion; but most men know not
12:46 (46)	haply I shall return to the men, haply they will know
12:49 (49)	then thereafter there shall come a year wherein the people will be succoured
12:68 (68)	for that We had taught him; but most men know not
12:103 (103)	be thou ever so eager, the most part of men believe not
13:1 (1)	from thy Lord is the truth, but most men do not believe
13:6 (7)	thy Lord is forgiving to men, for all their evil-doing
13:17 (18)	and what profits men abides in the earth
13:31 (30)	if God had willed, He would have guided men all together
14:1 (1)	that thou mayest bring forth mankind from the shadows to the light
14:25 (30)	so God strikes similitudes for men
14:36 (39)	my Lord, they have led astray many men
14:37 (40)	perform the prayer, and make hearts of men yearn towards them
14:44 (44)	and warn mankind of the day when the chastisement comes on them
14:52 (52)	this is a Message to be delivered to mankind
16:38 (40)	it is a promise binding upon Him, but most men know not
16:44 (46)	that thou mayest make clear to mankind what was sent down to them
16:61 (63)	if God should take men to task for their evildoing
16:69 (71)	out of their bellies a drink of diverse hues wherein is healing for men
17:60 (62)	surely thy Lord encompasses men
17:60 (62)	and the tree cursed in the Koran to be only a trial for men
17:89 (91)	We have indeed turned about for men in this Koran every manner of similitude
17:89 (91)	yet most men refuse all but unbelief
17:94 (96)	naught prevented men from believing when the guidance came to them
17:106 (107)	a Koran We have divided, for thee to recite it to mankind at intervals
18:54 (52)	We have indeed turned about for men in this Koran every manner of similitude
18:55 (53)	naught prevented men from believing when the guidance came unto them
19:10 (11)	thy sign is that thou shalt not speak to men
19:21 (21)	We may appoint him a sign unto men
20:59 (61)	let the people be mustered at the high noon
21:1 (1)	nigh unto men has drawn their reckoning
21:61 (62)	they said, 'Bring him before the people's eyes'
22:1 (1)	O men, fear your Lord
22:2 (2)	shall deposit her burden, and thou shalt see mankind drunk
22:3 (3)	among men there is such a one that disputes concerning God without knowledge
22:5 (5)	O men, if you are in doubt as to the Upraising
22:8 (8)	among men there is such a one that disputes concerning God without knowledge
22:11 (11)	among men there is such a one as serves God upon the very edge
22:18 (18)	the trees and the beasts, and many of mankind
22:25 (25)	and the Holy Mosque that We have appointed equal unto men
22:27 (28)	and proclaim among men the Pilgrimage
22:40 (41)	had God not driven back the people, some by the means of others
22:49 (48)	O men, I am only for you a plain warner
22:65 (64)	surely God is All-gentle to men, All-compassionate
22:73 (72)	O men, a similitude is struck
22:75 (74)	God chooses of the angels Messengers and of mankind
22:78 (78)	and that you might be witnesses against mankind
24:35 (35)	and God strikes similitudes for men
25:37 (39)	We drowned them, and made them to be a sign to mankind
25:50 (52)	yet most men refuse all but unbelief
26:39 (38)	the people were asked, 'Will you assemble?'
26:183 (183)	and diminish not the goods of the people

27:16 (16)	men, we have been taught the speech of the birds
27:73 (75)	surely thy Lord is bountiful to men
27:82 (84)	mankind had no faith in Our signs
28:23 (22)	he found a company of the people there drawing water
28:43 (43)	after that We had destroyed the former generations, to be examples and a guidance and a mercy
29:2 (1)	do the people reckon that they will be left to say, 'We believe'
29:10 (9)	some men there are who say, 'We believe in God'
29:10 (9)	he makes the persecution of men as it were God's chastisement
29:43 (42)	those similitudes — We strike them for the people
29:67 (67)	a sanctuary secure, while all about them the people are snatched away
30:6 (5)	God fails not His promise, but most men do not know it
30:8 (7)	yet most men disbelieve in the encounter with their Lord
30:30 (29)	a man of pure faith — God's original upon which He originated mankind
30:30 (29)	that is the right religion; but most men know it not
30:33 (32)	when some affliction visits mankind, they call unto their Lord
30:36 (35)	when We let men taste mercy, they rejoice in it
30:39 (38)	that it may increase upon the people's wealth
30:41 (40)	corruption has appeared in the land and sea, for that men's own hands have earned
30:58 (58)	We have struck for the people in this Koran every manner of similitude
31:6 (5)	some men there are who buy diverting talk to lead astray from the way of God
31:18 (17)	turn not thy cheek away from men in scorn
31:20 (19)	among men there is such a one that disputes concerning God without knowledge
31:33 (32)	O men, fear your Lord, and dread a day when no father shall give satisfaction
32:13 (13)	assuredly I shall fill Gehenna with jinn and men all together
33:37 (37)	thou wast concealing within thyself what God should reveal, fearing other men
33:63 (63)	the people will question thee concerning the Hour
34:28 (27)	We have sent thee not, except to mankind entire
34:28 (27)	but most men do not know it
34:36 (35)	but most men do not know it
35:2 (2)	whatsoever mercy God opens to men
35:3 (3)	O men, remember God's blessing upon you
35:5 (5)	O men, God's promise is true
35:15 (16)	O men, you are the ones that have need of God
35:28 (25)	men too, and beasts and cattle — diverse are their hues
35:45 (44)	if God should take men to task for what they have earned
38:26 (25)	therefore judge between men justly, and follow not caprice
39:27 (28)	indeed We have struck for the people in this Koran every manner of similitude
39:41 (42)	We have sent down upon thee the Book for mankind with the truth
40:57 (59)	the creation of the heavens and earth is greater than the creation of men
40:57 (59)	but most men know it not
40:59 (61)	the Hour is coming, no doubt of it, but most men do not believe
40:61 (63)	surely God is bountiful to men
40:61 (63)	but most men are not thankful
42:42 (40)	the way is only open against those who do wrong to the people
43:33 (32)	were it not that mankind would be one nation
44:11 (10)	covering the people; this is a painful chastisement
45:20 (19)	this is clear proofs for men, and a guidance, and a mercy
45:26 (25)	but most men do not know
46:6 (5)	when mankind are mustered, shall be enemies to them
47:3 (3)	even so God strikes their similitudes for men
48:20 (20)	and has restrained the hands of men from you
49:13 (13)	O mankind, We have created you male and female
54:20 (20)	plucking up men as if they were stumps of uprooted palm-trees

57:24 (24)	such as are niggardly, and bid men to be niggardly
57:25 (25)	We sent down with them the Book and the Balance so that men might uphold justice
57:25 (25)	We sent down iron, wherein is great might, and many uses for men
59:21 (21)	and those similitudes — We strike them for men
62:6 (6)	if you assert that you are the friends of God, apart from other men
66:6 (6)	guard yourselves and your families against a Fire whose fuel is men and stones
83:2 (2)	who, when they measure against the people, take full measure
83:6 (6)	a day when mankind shall stand before the Lord of all Being
99:6 (6)	upon that day men shall issue in scatterings to see their works
101:4 (3)	the day that men shall be like scattered moths
110:2 (2)	thou seest men entering God's religion in throngs
114:1 (1)	say: 'I take refuge with the Lord of men'
114:2 (2)	the King of men
114:3 (3)	the God of men
114:5 (5)	who whispers in the breasts of men
114:6 (6)	of jinn and men

*N W SH

TANĀWASHA vb. (VI)~(n.vb.) the act of reaching

f) n.vb. (*tanāwush*)

34:52 (51)	but how can they reach from a place far away

*N W Ṣ

MANĀṢ n.m.~a time for escape

38:3 (2)	and they called, but time was none to escape

*N W Y

NAWĀ n.m.~a date-stone

6:95 (95)	it is God who splits the grain and the date-stone

*N Y L

NĀLA vb. (I)~to reach, to attain, to overtake; (with prep. *min*) to gain, to obtain. (n.vb.) that which one obtains or gains

b) impf. act. (*yanālu*)

2:124 (118)	my covenant shall not reach the evildoers
3:92 (86)	you will not attain piety until you expend of what you love

5:94 (95)	God will surely try you with something of the game that your hands and lances attain
7:37 (35)	those — their portion of the Book shall reach them
7:49 (47)	are these the ones that you swore God would never reach with mercy?
7:152 (151)	anger shall overtake them from their Lord
9:74 (75)	they purposed what they never attained to
9:120 (121)	nor gain [they] any gain from any enemy
22:37 (38)	the flesh of them shall not reach God
22:37 (38)	but godliness from you shall reach Him
33:25 (25)	and they attained no good

f) n.vb. (*nayl*)

9:120 (121)	nor gain [they] any gain from any enemy

*N Z ᶜ

NAZAᶜA vb. (I)~to strip, to wrest, to draw out, to seize, to pluck. (pcple. act. pl.) those who pluck, who tear out

a) perf. act.

7:43 (41)	We shall strip away all rancour that is in their breasts
7:108 (105)	he drew forth his hand, and lo, it was white to the beholders
11:9 (12)	if We let a man taste mercy from Us, and then We wrest it from him
15:47 (47)	We shall strip away all rancour that is in their breasts
26:33 (32)	he drew forth his hand, and lo, it was white to the beholders
28:75 (75)	We shall draw out from every nation a witness, and say

b) impf. act. (*yanziᶜu*)

3:26 (25)	and seizest the Kingdom from whom Thou wilt
7:27 (26)	stripping them of their garments to show them their shameful parts
19:69 (70)	then We shall pluck forth from every party
54:20 (20)	plucking up men as if they were stumps of uprooted palm-trees

g) pcple. act. f. (*nāziᶜah*)

79:1 (1)	by those that pluck out vehemently

NAZZĀᶜAH n.f. (adj)~snatching [Ar]; removing [Bl]; plucking out [Ali]; eager [Pk]

70:16 (16)	snatching away the scalp

NĀZAᶜA vb. (III)~to wrangle, to dispute

b) impf. act. (*yunāziᶜu*)

22:67 (66)	let them not therefore wrangle with thee upon the matter

TANĀZAᶜA vb. (VI)~to dispute, to quarrel, to contend with one another; to pass something from one to another

a) perf. act.

3:152 (145)	you lost heart, and quarrelled about the matter
4:59 (62)	if you should quarrel on anything, refer it to God

8:43 (45) had He shown them as many you would have lost heart, and quarrelled about the matter
20:62 (65) and they disputed upon their plan between them

b) impf. act. (*yatanāzaʿu*)

8:46 (48) do not quarrel together
18:21 (20) when they were contending among themselves of their affair
52:23 (23) while they pass therein a cup one to another

*N Z F

NAZAFA vb. (I)~to exhaust, to intoxicate, to make mad

e) impf. pass. (*yunzafu*)

37:47 (46) wherein no sickness is, neither intoxication
56:19 (19) no brows throbbing, no intoxication)

*N Z GH

NAZAGHA vb. (I)~to provoke, to set two people at variance. (n.vb.) provocation

a) perf. act.

12:100 (101) after that Satan set at variance me and my brethren

b) impf. act. (*yanzaghu*)

7:200 (199) if a provocation from Satan should provoke thee
17:53 (55) Satan provokes strife between them
41:36 (36) if a provocation from Satan should provoke thee

f) n.vb. (*nazgh*)

7:200 (199) if a provocation from Satan should provoke thee
41:36 (36) if a provocation from Satan should provoke thee

*N Z L

NAZALA vb. (I)~to come down, to light (descend); (with prep. *bi-*) to bring down

a) perf. act.

17:105 (106) and with the truth it has come down
26:193 (193) brought down by the Faithful Spirit
37:177 (177) when it lights in their courtyard, how evil will be the morning
57:16 (15) remembrance of God and the Truth which has come down

b) impf. act. (*yanzilu*)

34:2 (2) what comes down from heaven, and what goes up to it
57:4 (4) what comes down from heaven, and what goes up unto it

MANĀZIL n.f. (pl. of *manzil*)~(a mansion), a station

10:5 (5) it is He who made the sun a radiance, and the moon a light, and determined it by stations
36:39 (39) and the moon — We have determined it by stations

NAZLAH n.f.~once, one time

53:13 (13) indeed, he saw him another time

NUZUL n.m. (pl. of *nazl*)~that which is prepared for a guest, a hospitality, a welcome

3:198 (197) a hospitality God Himself offers
18:102 (102) We have prepared Gehenna for the unbelievers' hospitality
18:107 (107) the Gardens of Paradise shall be their hospitality
32:19 (19) there await them the Gardens of the Refuge, in hospitality for that they were doing
37:62 (60) is that better as a hospitality
41:32 (32) as hospitality from One All-forgiving
56:56 (56) this shall be their hospitality on the Day of Doom
56:93 (93) there shall be a hospitality of boiling water

NAZZALA vb. (II)~to send down, to reveal. (n.vb.) the act of sending down, a revelation. (pcple. act.) one who sends down. (pcple. pass.) that which is sent down

a) perf. act.

2:23 (21) if you are in doubt concerning that We have sent down on Our servant
2:97 (91) he it was that brought it down upon thy heart by the leave of God
2:176 (171) that, because God has sent down the Book with the truth
3:3 (2) He has sent down upon thee the Book with the truth
4:47 (50) you who have been given the Book, believe in what We have sent down
4:136 (135) and the Book He has sent down on His Messenger
4:140 (139) He has sent down upon you in the Book
6:7 (7) had We sent down on thee a Book on parchment
6:111 (111) though We had sent down the angels to them
7:71 (69) you and your fathers, touching which God has sent down never authority
7:196 (195) my protector is God who sent down the Book
15:9 (9) it is We who have sent down the Remembrance
16:89 (91) and We have sent down on thee the Book
16:102 (104) the Holy Spirit sent it down from thy Lord in truth
17:95 (97) We would have sent down upon them out of heaven an angel as Messenger
17:106 (107) We have sent it down successively
20:80 (82) and sent down on you manna and quails
25:1 (1) blessed be He who has sent down the Salvation upon His servant
26:198 (198) if We had sent it down on a barbarian
29:63 (63) who sends down out of heaven water
39:23 (24) God has sent down the fairest discourse as a Book
43:11 (10) and who sent down out of heaven water in measure
47:26 (28) that is because they said to those who were averse to what God sent down
50:9 (9) and We sent down out of heaven water blessed
67:9 (9) God has not sent down anything; you are only in great error
76:23 (23) surely We have sent down the Koran on thee

b) impf. act. (*yunazzilu*)

2:90 (84)	grudging that God should send down of His bounty
3:151 (144)	for that they have associated with God that for which He sent down never authority
4:153 (152)	the People of the Book will ask thee to bring down upon them a Book from heaven
5:112 (112)	Mary, is thy Lord able to send down on us a Table out of heaven?
6:37 (37)	God is able to send down a sign, but most of them know not
6:81 (81)	that whereon He has not sent down on you any authority
7:33 (31)	and that you associate with God that for which He sent down never authority
8:11 (11)	and sending down on you water from heaven, to purify you thereby
15:8 (8)	We send not down the angels, save with truth
15:21 (21)	We send it not down but in a known measure
16:2 (2)	He sends down the angels with the Spirit of His command
16:101 (103)	God knows very well what He is sending down
17:82 (84)	We send down, of the Koran, that which is a healing and a mercy
17:93 (95)	we will not believe thy going up till thou bringest down on us a book that we may read
22:71 (70)	they serve, apart from God, that whereon He has sent down never authority
24:43 (43)	He sends down out of heaven mountains, wherein is hail
26:4 (3)	if We will, We shall send down on them out of heaven a sign
30:24 (23)	and that He sends down out of heaven water
31:34 (34)	He sends down the rain
40:13 (13)	it is He who shows you His signs and sends down to you out of heaven provision
42:27 (26)	He sends down in measure whatsoever He will
42:28 (27)	it is He who sends down the rain after they have despaired
57:9 (9)	it is He who sends down upon His servant signs

d) perf. pass. (*nuzzila*)

6:37 (37)	why has no sign been sent down upon him from his Lord?
15:6 (6)	thou, upon whom the Remembrance is sent down
16:44 (46)	that thou mayest make clear to mankind what was sent down to them
25:25 (27)	and the angels are sent down in majesty
25:32 (34)	why has the Koran not been sent down upon him all at once?
43:31 (30)	why was this Koran not sent down upon some man of moment
47:2 (2)	and believe in what is sent down to Muhammad
47:20 (22)	why has a sura not been sent down?

e) impf. pass. (*yunazzalu*)

2:105 (99)	the idolaters wish not that any good should be sent down upon you from your Lord
3:93 (87)	save what Israel forbade for himself before the Torah was sent down
5:101 (101)	if you question concerning them when the Koran is being sent down
9:64 (65)	the hypocrites are afraid, lest a sura should be sent down against them
30:49 (48)	although before it was sent down on them before that they had been in despair

f) n.vb. (*tanzīl*)

17:106 (107)	and We have sent it down <successively>
20:4 (3)	a revelation from Him who created the earth and the high heavens
25:25 (27)	and the angels are sent down <in majesty>
26:192 (192)	truly it is the revelation of the Lord of all Being
32:2 (1)	the sending down of the Book, wherein no doubt is, from the Lord of all Being
36:5 (4)	the sending down of the All-mighty, the All-compassionate
39:1 (1)	the sending down of the Book is from God the All-mighty
40:2 (1)	the sending down of the Book is from God the All-mighty

41:2 (1) a sending down from the All-merciful, the All-compassionate
41:42 (42) a sending down from One All-wise, All-laudable
45:2 (1) the sending down of the Book is from God, the All-mighty
46:2 (1) the sending down of the Book is from God, the All-mighty
56:80 (79) a sending down from the Lord of all Being
69:43 (43) a sending down from the Lord of all Being
76:23 (23) surely We have sent down the Koran on thee, <a sending down>

g) pcple. act. (*munazzil*)

5:115 (115) verily I do send it down on you

h) pcple. pass. (*munazzal*)

6:114 (114) those whom We have given the Book know it is sent down from thy Lord with the truth

ANZALA (1) vb. (IV)~to harbour (as a guest). (pcple. act.) a host, a harbourer, one who brings to land. (pcple. pass.) a harbour, a landing-place

c) impv. (*anzil*)

23:29 (30) O my Lord, do Thou harbour me in a blessed harbour

g) pcple. act. (*munzil*)

12:59 (59) do you not see that I fill up the measure, and am the best of hosts?
23:29 (30) for Thou art the best of harbourers

h) pcple. pass. (*munzal*)

23:29 (30) do Thou harbour me in a blessed harbour

ANZALA (2) vb. (IV)~to send down. (pcple. act.) one who sends down. (pcple. pass.) that which is sent down

a) perf. act.

2:22 (20) and sent down out of heaven water, wherewith He brought forth fruits
2:41 (38) and believe in that I have sent down
2:57 (54) and We sent down manna and quails upon you
2:59 (56) We sent down upon the evildoers wrath out of heaven of their ungodliness
2:90 (84) disbelieving in that which God sent down
2:91 (85) believe in that God has sent down
2:99 (93) We have sent down unto thee signs, clear signs
2:159 (154) those who conceal the clear signs and the guidance that We have sent down
2:164 (159) and the water God sends down from heaven therewith reviving the earth after it is dead
2:170 (165) follow what God has sent down
2:174 (169) those who conceal what of the Book God has sent down on them
2:213 (209) He sent down with them the Book with the truth
2:231 (231) remember God's blessing upon you, and the Book and the Wisdom He has sent down on you
3:3 (2) and He sent down the Torah and the Gospel
3:4 (2) and He sent down the Salvation
3:7 (5) it is He who sent down upon thee the Book
3:53 (46) Lord, we believe in that Thou hast sent down
3:154 (148) then He sent down upon you, after grief, security

4:61 (64)	come now to what God has sent down, and the Messenger
4:105 (106)	surely We have sent down to thee the Book
4:113 (113)	God has sent down on thee the Book and the Wisdom
4:136 (135)	and the Book which He sent down before
4:166 (164)	God bears witness to that He has sent down to thee
4:166 (164)	He has sent it down with His knowledge
4:174 (174)	We have sent down to you a manifest light
5:44 (48)	We sent down the Torah, wherein is guidance and light
5:44 (48)	whoso judges not according to what God has sent down
5:45 (49)	whoso judges not according to what God has sent down
5:47 (51)	let the People of the Gospel judge according to what God has sent down therein
5:47 (51)	whosoever judges not according to what God has sent down
5:48 (52)	We have sent down to thee the Book with the truth
5:48 (52)	so judge between them according to what God has sent down
5:49 (54)	judge between them according to what God has sent down
5:49 (54)	lest they tempt thee away from any of what God has sent down to thee
5:104 (103)	come now to what God has sent down, and the Messenger
6:8 (8)	yet had We sent down an angel, the matter would have been determined
6:91 (91)	God has not sent down aught on any mortal
6:91 (91)	who sent down the Book that Moses brought as a light and a guidance
6:92 (92)	this is a Book We have sent down, blessed and confirming that which was before it
6:93 (93)	I will (send down) the like of what God has sent down
6:99 (99)	it is He who sent down out of heaven water
6:114 (114)	for it is He who sent down to you the Book
6:155 (156)	this is a Book We have sent down, blessed
7:26 (25)	We have sent down on you a garment to cover your shameful parts
7:57 (55)	and therewith send down water, and bring forth therewith all the fruits
7:160 (160)	and We sent down manna and quails upon them
8:41 (42)	if you believe in God and that We sent down upon Our servant on the day of salvation
9:26 (26)	then God sent down upon His Messenger His Shechina
9:26 (26)	and He sent down legions you did not see
9:40 (40)	then God sent down on him His Shechina
9:97 (98)	and apter not to know the bounds of what God has sent down on His Messenger
10:24 (25)	the likeness of this present life is as water that We send down out of heaven
10:59 (60)	have you considered the provision God has sent down for you
10:94 (94)	if thou art in doubt regarding what We have sent down to thee
12:2 (2)	We have sent it down as an Arabic Koran
12:40 (40)	God has sent down no authority touching them
13:17 (18)	He sends down out of heaven water
13:37 (37)	even so We have sent it down as an Arabic judgment
14:1 (1)	a Book We have sent down to thee
14:32 (37)	it is God who created the heavens and the earth, and sent down out of heaven water
15:22 (22)	and We send down out of heaven water
15:90 (90)	so We sent it down to the partitioners
16:10 (10)	it is He who sends down to you out of heaven water
16:24 (26)	what has your Lord sent down?
16:30 (32)	What has your Lord sent down?
16:44 (46)	We have sent down to thee the Remembrance
16:64 (66)	We have not sent down upon thee the Book except that thou mayest make clear to them
16:65 (67)	it is God who sends down out of heaven water

17:102 (104)	indeed thou knowest that none sent these down, except the Lord
17:105 (106)	with the truth We have sent it down
18:1 (1)	praise belongs to God who has sent down upon His servant the Book
18:45 (43)	it is as water that We send down out of heaven
20:2 (1)	We have not sent down the Koran upon thee for thee to be unprosperous
20:53 (55)	threaded roads for you, and sent down water out of heaven
20:113 (112)	even so We have sent it down as an Arabic Koran
21:10 (10)	now We have sent down to you a Book wherein is your Remembrance
21:50 (51)	and this is a blessed Remembrance that We have sent down
22:5 (5)	then, when We send down water upon it, it quivers
22:16 (16)	even so We have sent it down as signs
22:63 (62)	hast thou not seen how that God has sent down out of heaven water
23:18 (18)	We sent down out of heaven water in measure
23:24 (24)	if God willed, He would have sent down angels
24:1 (1)	a sura that We have sent down and appointed
24:1 (1)	and We have sent down in it signs, clear signs
24:34 (34)	now We have sent down to you signs making all clear
24:46 (45)	now We have sent down signs making all clear
25:6 (7)	He sent it down, who knows the secret
25:48 (50)	We sent down from heaven pure water
27:60 (61)	He who created the heavens and earth, and sent down for you out of heaven water
28:24 (24)	I have need of whatever good Thou shalt have sent down upon me
29:47 (46)	even so We have sent down to thee the Book
29:51 (50)	is it not sufficient for them that We have sent down upon thee the Book
30:35 (34)	have We sent down any authority upon them
31:10 (9)	We sent down out of heaven water
31:21 (20)	follow what God has sent down
33:26 (26)	He brought down those of the People of the Book who supported them from their fortresses
35:27 (25)	hast thou not seen how that God sends down out of heaven water
36:15 (14)	the All-merciful has not sent down anything
36:28 (27)	We sent not down upon his people, after him, any host out of heaven
38:29 (28)	a Book We have sent down to thee, blessed
39:2 (2)	We have sent down to thee the Book with the truth
39:6 (8)	and He sent down to you of the cattle eight couples
39:21 (22)	hast thou not seen how that God has sent down out of heaven water
39:41 (42)	We have sent down upon thee the Book for mankind with the truth
41:14 (13)	had our Lord willed, surely He would have sent down angels
41:39 (39)	then, when We send down water upon it, it quivers
42:15 (14)	I believe in whatever Book God has sent down
42:17 (16)	God it is who has sent down the Book with the truth
44:3 (2)	We have sent it down in a blessed night
45:5 (4)	and the provision God sends down from heaven
47:9 (10)	that is because they have been averse to what God has sent down
48:4 (4)	it is He who sent down the Shechina into the hearts of the believers
48:18 (18)	so He sent down the Shechina upon them, and rewarded them
48:26 (26)	then God sent down His Shechina upon His Messenger
53:23 (23)	God has sent down no authority touching them
56:69 (68)	did you send it down from the clouds
57:25 (25)	We sent down with them the Book and the Balance
57:25 (25)	We sent down iron, wherein is great might, and many uses for men
58:5 (6)	now We have sent down signs, clear signs
59:21 (21)	if We had sent down this Koran upon a mountain, thou wouldst have seen it humbled

64:8 (8)	believe in God and His Messenger, and in the Light which We have sent down
65:5 (5)	that is God's command, that He has sent down unto you
65:10 (11)	Believers, God has sent down to you for a remembrance
78:14 (14)	and have sent down out of the rain-clouds water cascading
97:1 (1)	behold, We sent it down on the Night of Power

b) impf. act. (*yunzilu*)

6:93 (93)	I will send down the like of what God has (sent down)

c) impv. (*anzil*)

5:114 (114)	send down upon us a Table out of heaven

d) perf. pass. (*unzila*)

2:4 (3)	who believe in what has been sent down to thee
2:4 (3)	and what has been sent down before thee
2:91 (85)	we believe in what was sent down on us
2:102 (96)	and that which was sent down upon Babylon's two angels, Harut and Marut
2:136 (130)	we believe in God, and in that which has been sent down on us
2:136 (130)	and sent down on Abraham, Ishmael, Isaac and Jacob
2:185 (181)	the month of Ramadan, wherein the Koran was sent down to be a guidance
2:285 (285)	the Messenger believes in what was sent down to him from his Lord
3:65 (58)	the Torah was not sent down, neither the Gospel, but after him
3:72 (65)	believe in what has been sent down upon those who believe
3:84 (78)	we believe in God, and that which has been sent down on us
3:84 (78)	and sent down on Abraham and Ishmael, Isaac and Jacob
3:199 (198)	and what has been sent down unto you
3:199 (198)	and what has been sent down unto them
4:60 (63)	that they believe in what has been sent down to thee
4:60 (63)	and what was sent down before thee
4:162 (160)	and the believers believing in what has been sent down to thee
4:162 (160)	and what was sent down before thee
5:59 (64)	for any other cause than that we believe in God, and what has been sent down to us
5:59 (64)	and what was sent down before
5:64 (69)	and what has been sent down to thee from thy Lord will surely increase many of them
5:66 (70)	the Torah and the Gospel, and what was sent down to them from their Lord
5:67 (71)	O Messenger, deliver that which has been sent down to thee from thy Lord
5:68 (72)	until you perform the Torah and the Gospel, and what was sent down to you from your Lord
5:68 (72)	and what has been sent down to thee from thy Lord will surely increase many of them in insolence
5:81 (84)	yet had they believed in God and the Prophet and what has been sent down to him
5:83 (86)	when they hear what has been sent down to the Messenger
6:8 (8)	why has an angel not been sent down on him?
6:156 (157)	the Book was sent down only upon two parties before us
6:157 (158)	if the Book had been sent down upon us, we had surely been more rightly guided than they
7:2 (1)	a Book sent down to thee
7:3 (2)	follow what has been sent down to you from your Lord
7:157 (156)	succour him and help him, and follow the light that has been sent down with him

9:86 (87)	when a sura is sent down, saying
9:124 (125)	whenever a sura is sent down to thee, some of them say
9:127 (128)	whenever a sura is sent down, they look one at another
10:20 (21)	why has a sign not been sent down upon him from his Lord?
11:12 (15)	why has a treasure not been sent down upon him, or an angel not come with him?
11:14 (17)	if they do not answer you, know that it has been sent down with God's knowledge
13:1 (1)	that which has been sent down to thee from thy Lord is the truth
13:7 (8)	why has a sign not been sent down upon him from his Lord?
13:19 (19)	is he who knows what is sent down to thee from thy Lord is the truth, like him who is blind?
13:27 (27)	why has a sign not been sent down upon him from his Lord?
13:36 (36)	those to whom We have given the Book rejoice in what is sent down unto thee
25:7 (8)	why has an angel not been sent down to him, to be a warner with him?
25:21 (23)	why have the angels not been sent down on us
28:87 (87)	let them not bar thee from the signs of God, after that they have been sent down to thee
29:46 (45)	we believe in what has been sent down to us
29:46 (45)	and what has been sent down to you
29:50 (49)	why have signs not been sent down upon him from his Lord?
34:6 (6)	that what has been sent down to thee from thy Lord is the truth
38:8 (7)	has the Remembrance been sent down on him out of us all?
39:55 (56)	follow the fairest of what has been sent down to you from your Lord
46:30 (29)	we have heard a Book that was sent down after Moses, confirming what was before it
47:20 (22)	when a clear sura is sent down, and therein fighting is mentioned

g) pcple. act. (*munzil*)

29:34 (33)	We shall send down upon the people of this city wrath out of heaven
36:28 (27)	neither would We send any down
56:69 (68)	did We send it?

h) pcple. pass. (*munzal*)

3:124 (120)	for you that your Lord should reinforce you with three thousand angels sent down upon you

TANAZZALA vb. (V)~to come down, to descend; (with prep. *bi-*) to bring down

a) perf. act.

26:210 (210)	not by the Satans has it been brought down

b) impf. act. (*yatanazzalu*)

19:64 (65)	We come not down, save at the commandment of thy Lord
26:221 (221)	shall I tell you on whom the Satans come down?
26:222 (222)	they come down on every guilty impostor
41:30 (30)	upon them the angels descend, saying, 'Fear not'
65:12 (12)	between them the Command descending, that you may know that God is powerful over everything
97:4 (4)	in it the angels and the Spirit descend, by the leave of their Lord

*N Ẓ R

NAẒARA vb. (I)~to look, to behold, to cast a glance, to have one's eyes wide open, to watch, to regard; (with prep. *fī*) to consider; to expect, to await. (n.vb.) the act of looking, a look. (pcple. act.) one who looks, who beholds, who gazes, who watches, who sees

a) perf. act.

9:127 (128)	whenever a sura is sent down, they look one at another
37:88 (86)	and he cast a glance at the stars
74:21 (21)	then he beheld

b) impf. act. (*yanẓuru*)

2:50 (47)	and delivered you, and drowned Pharaoh's folk while you were beholding
2:55 (52)	and the thunderbolt took you while you were beholding
2:210 (206)	what do they look for, but that God shall come to them in the cloud-shadows
3:77 (71)	God shall not speak to them neither look on them on the Resurrection Day
3:143 (137)	now you have seen it, while you were beholding
6:158 (159)	do they look for the angels to come to them, nothing less, or that thy Lord should come
7:53 (51)	do they look for aught else but its interpretation?
7:129 (126)	and will make you successors in the land, so that He may behold how you shall do
7:143 (139)	oh my Lord, show me, that I may behold Thee
7:185 (184)	have they not considered the dominion of the heaven and of the earth
7:198 (197)	thou seest them looking at thee, unperceiving
8:6 (6)	after it had become clear, as though they were being driven into death with their eyes wide open
10:14 (15)	that We might behold how you would do
10:43 (44)	and some of them look unto thee
12:109 (109)	have they not beheld how was the end of those before them?
16:33 (35)	do they look for aught but that the angels shall come to them
18:19 (18)	and let him look for which of them has purest food
22:15 (15)	let him sever it, and behold whether his guile does away with what enrages him
27:27 (27)	now we will see whether thou hast spoken truly
27:41 (41)	and we shall behold whether she is guided
30:9 (8)	have they not journeyed in the land and beheld how was the end of those before them?
33:19 (19)	thou seest them looking at thee, their eyes rolling like one who swoons of death
35:43 (41)	do they expect anything but the wont of the ancients?
35:44 (43)	have they not journeyed in the land and beheld how was the end of those before them?
36:49 (49)	they are awaiting only for one Cry to seize them while they are yet disputing
37:19 (19)	for it is only a single scaring, then behold, they are watching
38:15 (14)	these are only awaiting for a single Cry, to which there is no delay
39:68 (68)	then it shall be blown again, and lo, they shall stand, beholding
40:21 (22)	have they not journeyed in the land and beheld how was the end of those before them?
40:82 (82)	have they not journeyed in the land and beheld how was the end of those before them?
42:45 (44)	thou shalt see them, as they are exposed to it, abject in humbleness, looking with furitive glance
43:66 (66)	are they looking for aught but the Hour, that it shall come upon them suddenly
47:10 (11)	have they not journeyed in the land and beheld how was the end of those before them?

47:18 (20)	are they looking for aught but the Hour, that it shall come upon them suddenly?
47:20 (22)	thou seest those in whose hearts is sickness looking at thee as one who swoons of death
50:6 (6)	what, have they not beheld heaven above them
51:44 (44)	and the thunderbolt took them and they themselves beholding
56:84 (83)	and that hour you are watching
59:18 (18)	let every soul consider what it has forwarded for the morrow
78:40 (41)	upon the day when a man shall behold what his hands have forwarded
80:24 (24)	let Man consider his nourishment
83:23 (23)	upon couches gazing
83:35 (35)	upon couches gazing
86:5 (5)	so let man consider of what he was created
88:17 (17)	do they not consider how the camel was created

c) impv. (*unẓur*)

2:104 (98)	but say, 'Regard us'; and give ear
2:259 (261)	look at thy food and drink — it has not spoiled
2:259 (261)	and look at thy ass
2:259 (261)	and look at the bones, how We shall set them up
3:137 (131)	journey in the land, and behold how was the end of those that cried lies
4:46 (49)	if they had said, 'We have heard and obey', and, 'Hear', and, 'Regard us'
4:50 (53)	consider how they forge falsehood against God
5:75 (79)	behold, how We make clear the signs to them
5:75 (79)	then behold, how they perverted are
6:11 (11)	journey in the land, then behold how was the end of them that cried lies
6:24 (24)	behold how they lie against themselves
6:46 (46)	behold how We turn about the signs
6:65 (65)	behold how We turn about the signs
6:99 (99)	look upon their fruits when they fructify and ripen
7:84 (82)	so behold thou, how was the end of the sinners
7:86 (84)	behold, how was the end of the workers of corruption
7:103 (101)	so behold thou, how was the end of the workers of corruption
7:143 (139)	but behold the mountain — if it stays fast in its place
10:39 (40)	then behold how was the end of the evildoers
10:73 (74)	then behold how was the end of them that were warned
10:101 (101)	behold what is in the heavens and in the earth
16:36 (38)	journey in the land, and behold how was the end of them that cried lies
17:21 (22)	behold, how We prefer some of them over others
17:48 (51)	behold, how they strike similitudes for thee, and go astray
20:97 (97)	behold thy god, to whom all the day thou wast cleaving
25:9 (10)	behold, how they strike similitudes for thee, and go astray
27:14 (14)	behold, how was the end of the workers of corruption
27:28 (28)	then turn back from them and see what they shall return
27:33 (33)	the affair rests with thee; so consider what thou wilt command
27:51 (52)	and behold, how was the end of their device
27:69 (71)	journey in the land, then behold how was the end of the sinners
28:40 (40)	so behold how was the end of the evildoers
29:20 (19)	journey in the land, then behold how He originated creation
30:42 (41)	journey in the land, then behold how was the end of those that were before
30:50 (49)	so behold the marks of God's mercy
37:73 (71)	behold, how was the end of them that were warned
37:102 (101)	I see in a dream that I shall sacrifice thee; consider, what thinkest thou?
43:25 (24)	and behold how was the end of them that cried lies
57:13 (13)	wait for us, so that we may borrow your light

f) n.vb. (*naẓar*)

47:20 (22)	hearts is sickness looking at thee <as> one who swoons of death

g) pcple. act. (*nāẓir*)

2:69 (64)	she shall be a golden cow, bright her colour, gladdening the beholders
7:108 (105)	he drew forth his hand, and lo, it was white to the beholders
15:16 (16)	and decked them out fair to the beholders
26:33 (32)	he drew forth his hand, and lo, it was white to the beholders
27:35 (35)	I will send them a present, and see what the envoys bring back
33:53 (53)	the Prophet, except leave is given you for a meal, without watching for its hour
75:23 (23)	gazing upon their Lord

NAẒIRAH n.f.~a respite

2:280 (280)	let him have respite till things are easier

NAẒRAH n.f.~a look, a glance

37:88 (86)	and he cast a glance at the stars

ANẒARA vb. (IV)~to give respite. (pcple. pass.) one who is respited

b) impf. act. (*yunẓiru*)

7:195 (194)	then try your guile on me, and give me no respite
10:71 (72)	make decision unto me, and respite me not
11:55 (58)	try your guile on me, all together, then you shall give me no respite

c) impv. (*anẓir*)

7:14 (13)	respite me till the day they shall be raised
15:36 (36)	my Lord, respite me till the day they shall be raised
38:79 (80)	my Lord, respite me till the day they shall be raised

e) impf. pass. (*yunẓaru*)

2:162 (157)	the chastisement shall not be lightened for them; no respite shall be given them
3:88 (82)	the chastisement shall not be lightened for them; no respite shall be given them
6:8 (8)	the matter would have been determined, and then no respite would be given them
16:85 (87)	it shall not be lightened for them, and no respite shall be given them
21:40 (41)	they shall not be able to repel it, nor shall they be respited
32:29 (29)	on the Day of Victory their faith shall not profit the unbelievers, nor shall they be respited

h) pcple. pass. (*munẓar*)

7:15 (14)	thou art among the ones that are respited
15:8 (8)	then they would not be respited
15:37 (37)	thou art among the ones that are respited
26:203 (203)	and they will say, 'Shall we be respited?'
38:80 (81)	thou art among the ones that are respited
44:29 (28)	neither heaven nor earth wept for them, nor were they respited

INTAẒARA vb. (VIII)~to watch and wait, to wait. (pcple. act.) one who is waiting, who is watching and waiting

b) impf. act. (*yantaẓiru*)

10:102 (102)	so do they watch and wait for aught but the like of the days of those who passed away before them?
33:23 (23)	and some are still awaiting, and they have not changed in the least

c) impv. (*intaẓir*)

6:158 (159)	say: 'Watch and wait'
7:71 (69)	then watch and wait
10:20 (21)	then watch and wait
10:102 (102)	then watch and wait
11:122 (122)	and watch and wait
32:30 (30)	so turn thou away from them, and wait

g) pcple. act. (*muntaẓir*)

6:158 (159)	We too are waiting
7:71 (69)	I shall be with you watching and waiting
10:20 (21)	I shall be with you watching and waiting
10:102 (102)	I shall be with you watching and waiting
11:122 (122)	we are also watching and waiting
32:30 (30)	they too are waiting

QĀF

*Q

QĀF~ml

50:1 (1)	Qaf. By the glorious Koran!

*Q ʿ D

QAʿADA vb. (I)~to hold back, to tarry, to wait, to sit. (n.vb.) sitting, tarrying. (pcple. act.) one who sits at home [Ar, Ali], one who sits still [Pk, Bl]

a) perf. act.

3:168 (162)	who said of their brothers and they themselves (held back)
9:90 (91)	those who lied to God and His Messenger tarried

b) impf. act. (*yaqʿudu*)

4:140 (139)	do not sit with them until they plunge into some other talk
6:68 (67)	do not sit, after the reminding, with the people of the evildoers
7:16 (15)	I shall surely sit in ambush for them on Thy straight path
7:86 (84)	do not sit in every path, threatening and barring from God's way
17:22 (23)	set not up with God another god
17:29 (31)	or thou wilt sit reproached and denuded
72:9 (9)	We would sit there on seats to hear

c) impv. (*uqʿud*)

9:5 (5)	confine them, and lie in wait for them at every place of ambush
9:46 (46)	it was said to them, 'Tarry you with the tarriers'
9:83 (84)	so now tarry with those behind

f) n.vb. (*quʿūd*)

3:191 (188)	who remember God, standing and sitting and on their sides
4:103 (104)	remember God, standing and sitting and on your sides
9:83 (84)	you were well-pleased to tarry the first time

g) pcple. act. (*qāʿid*, pl. *quʿūd*)

4:95 (97)	such believers as sit at home — unless they have an injury
4:95 (97)	over the ones who sit at home
4:95 (97)	God has preferred those who struggle over the ones who sit at home
5:24 (27)	go forth, thou and thy Lord, and do battle; we will be sitting here
9:46 (46)	it was said to them, 'Tarry you with the tarriers'
9:86 (87)	the affluent among them ask leave of thee, saying, 'Let us be with the tarriers'
10:12 (13)	when affliction visits a man, he calls Us on his side, or sitting, or standing
85:6 (6)	when they were seated over it

MAQʿAD n.m. (pl. *maqāʿid*)~pitches, positions; abode; seat; sitting, tarrying

3:121 (117)	to lodge the believers in their pitches for the battle
9:81 (82)	those who were left behind rejoiced in tarrying behind the Messenger of God

54:55 (55)	in a sure abode, in the presence of a King Omnipotent
72:9 (9)	We would sit there on seats to hear

QAʿĪD n.com. (adj)~sitting

50:17 (16)	when the two angels meet together, sitting one on the right, and one on the left

QAWĀʿID n.f. (pl. of *qāʿidah*)~foundations; women who are past child-bearing

2:127 (121)	when Abraham, and Ishmael with him, raised up the foundations of the House
16:26 (28)	then God came upon their building from the foundations
24:60 (59)	such women as are past child-bearing and have no hope of marriage

*Q ʿ R

INQAʿARA vb. (VII)~(pcple. act.) uprooted

g) pcple. act. (*munqaʿir*)

54:20 (20)	plucking up men as if they were stumps of uprooted palm-trees

*Q B Ḍ

QABAḌA vb. (I)~to seize , to grasp; to close, to shut (esp. one's hand). (n.vb.) the act of seizing, drawing. (pcple. pass.) that which is held in hand

a) perf. act.

20:96 (96)	I seized a handful of dust from the messenger's track
25:46 (48)	thereafter We seize it to Ourselves, drawing it gently

b) impf. act. (*yaqbiḍu*)

2:245 (246)	God grasps, and outspreads
9:67 (68)	they keep their hands shut; they have forgotten
67:19 (19)	have they not regarded the birds above them spreading their wings, and closing them?

f) n.vb. (*qabḍ*)

25:46 (48)	thereafter We seize it to Ourselves, <drawing> it gently

h) pcple. pass. (*maqbūḍ*)

2:283 (283)	if you are upon a journey, and you do not find a writer, then a pledge in hand

QABḌAH n.f.~handful

20:96 (96)	I seized a handful of dust from the messenger's track
39:67 (67)	the earth altogether shall be His handful on the Day of Resurrection

*Q B Ḥ

QABAḤA vb. (I)~(pcple. pass.) one who is spurned, who is hateful, who is loathed

h) pcple. pass. (*maqbūḥ*)

28:42 (42) on the Day of Resurrection they shall be among the spurned

*Q B L

QABILA vb. (I)~to accept. (n.vb.) acceptance; favour. (pcple. act.) one who accepts

b) impf. act. (*yaqbalu*)

9:104 (105) do they not know that God is He who accepts repentance from His servants
24:4 (4) and do not accept any testimony of theirs ever
42:25 (24) it is He who accepts repentance from His servants

e) impf. pass. (*yuqbalu*)

2:48 (45) no intercession shall be accepted from it, nor any counterpoise
2:123 (117) and no counterpoise shall be accepted from it
3:85 (79) whoso desires another religion than Islam, it shall not be accepted of him
3:90 (84) their repentance shall not be accepted; those are the ones who stray
3:91 (85) there shall not be accepted from any one of them the whole earth full of gold
9:54 (54) naught prevents that their expendings should be accepted from them

f) n.vb. (*qabūl*)

3:37 (32) her Lord received the child with gracious favour

g) pcple. act. (*qābil*)

40:3 (2) Forgiver of sins, Accepter of penitence

QABĪL (1) n.f. (pl. *qabā'il*)~a tribe

7:27 (26) he sees you, he and his tribe, from where you see them not
49:13 (13) and appointed you races and tribes, that you may know one another

QABĪL (2) n.m.~a surety, a warranty

17:92 (94) or thou bringest God and the angels as a surety

QIBAL n.m. or prep.~(n) power; (prep) to, towards, against

2:177 (172) it is not piety, that you turn your faces to the East and to the West
27:37 (37) we shall assuredly come (against) them with hosts they have not power to resist
57:13 (13) a door in the inward whereof is mercy, and against the outward thereof is chastisement
70:36 (36) what ails the unbelievers, running with outstretched necks towards thee

QIBLAH n.f.~direction of prayer [Ar]; Qiblah; (10:87) oratories [Pk]; places of prayer [Ali]; qibla [Bl]

2:142 (136) what has turned them from the direction they were facing in their prayers aforetime?
2:143 (138) We did not appoint the direction thou wast facing

2:144 (139)	We will surely turn thee to a direction that shall satisfy thee
2:145 (140)	if thou shouldst bring to those that have been given the Book every sign, they will not follow thy direction
2:145 (140)	thou art not a follower of their direction
2:145 (140)	neither are they followers of one another's direction
10:87 (87)	make your houses a direction for men to pray to

QUBUL n.m.~front part, face; (*min qubul*) from before, from the front; (adv) face to face, in array

6:111 (111)	had We mustered against them every thing, face to face
12:26 (26)	if his shirt has been torn from before then she has spoken truly
18:55 (53)	or that the chastisement should come upon them face to face

AQBALA vb. (IV)~to come forward, to advance, to approach, to turn to

a) perf. act.

12:71 (71)	they said, turning to them, 'What is it that you are missing?'
12:82 (82)	enquire of the city wherein we were, and the caravan in which we approached
37:27 (27)	advance one upon another, asking each other questions
37:50 (48)	they advance one upon another, asking each other questions
37:94 (92)	then came the others to him hastening
51:29 (29)	then came forward his wife, clamouring
52:25 (25)	they advance one upon another, asking each other questions
68:30 (30)	and they advanced one upon another, blaming each other

c) impv. (*aqbil*)

28:31 (31)	Moses, come forward, and fear not

TAQABBALA vb. (V)~to receive, to accept

a) perf. act.

3:37 (32)	her Lord received the child with gracious favour

b) impf. act. (*yataqabbalu*)

5:27 (30)	God accepts only of the godfearing
46:16 (15)	those are they from whom We shall accept the best of what they have done

c) impv. (*taqabbal*)

2:127 (121)	our Lord, receive this from us
3:35 (31)	receive Thou this from me; Thou hearest, and knowest
14:40 (42)	our Lord, and receive my petition

d) perf. pass. (*tuqubbila*)

5:27 (30)	when they offered a sacrifice, and it was accepted of one of them
5:36 (40)	it would not be accepted of them

e) impf. pass. (*yutaqabbalu*)

5:27 (30)	and [it was] not accepted of the other
9:53 (53)	expend willingly, or unwillingly, it shall not be accepted from you

TAQĀBALA vb. (VI)~(pcple. act.) facing one another, face to face

g) pcple. act. (*mutaqābil*)

15:47 (47) as brothers they shall be upon couches set face to face
37:44 (43) upon couches, set face to face
44:53 (53) robed in silk and brocade, set face to face
56:16 (16) reclining upon them, set face to face

ISTAQBALA vb. (X)~(pcple. act.) coming or proceeding towards

g) pcple. act. (*mustaqbil*)

46:24 (23) when they saw it as a sudden cloud coming towards their valleys, they said

*Q B R

MAQĀBIR n.f. (pl. of *maqbarah*)~a cemetery

102:2 (2) even till you visit the tombs

QABR n.m. (pl. *qubūr*)~a grave

9:84 (85) pray thou never over any one of them when he is dead, nor stand over his grave
22:7 (7) God shall raise up whosoever is within the tombs
35:22 (21) thou canst not make those in their tombs to hear
60:13 (13) even as the unbelievers have despaired of the inhabitants of the tombs
82:4 (4) when the tombs are overthrown
100:9 (9) knows he not that when that which is in the tombs is overthrown

AQBARA vb. (IV)~to bury

a) perf. act.

80:21 (21) then makes him to die, and buries him

*Q B S

QABAS n.m.~a firebrand

20:10 (10) perhaps I shall bring you a brand from it
27:7 (7) I observe a fire, and will bring you news of it, or I will bring you a flaming brand

IQTABASA vb. (VIII)~to borrow (a light)

a) perf. act.

57:13 (13) wait for us, so that we may borrow your light

*Q D D

QADDA vb. (I)~to tear, to rend

a) perf. act.

12:25 (25) they raced to the door; and she tore his shirt from behind

d) perf. pass. (*qudda*)

12:26 (26) if his shirt has been torn from before
12:27 (27) if it be that his shirt has been torn from behind
12:28 (28) when he saw his shirt was torn from behind he said

QIDAD n.f. (adj.; pl. of *qiddah*)~ones differing from one another

72:11 (11) some of us are otherwise; we are sects differing

*Q D H

QADAḤA vb. (I)~(n.vb.) the act of striking fire

f) n.vb. (*qadḥ*)

100:2 (2) by the strikers of fire

*Q D M

QADIMA vb. (I)~to go before; (with prep. *ilá*) to advance upon

a) perf. act.

25:23 (25) We shall advance upon what work they have done, and make it a scattered dust

b) impf. act. (*yaqdumu*)

11:98 (100) he shall go before his people on the Day of Resurrection, and will have led them down

QADAM n.f. (pl. *aqdām*)~a foot

2:250 (251) upon us patience, and make firm our feet
3:147 (141) make firm our feet, and help us against the people of the unbelievers
8:11 (11) and to strengthen your hearts, and to confirm your feet
10:2 (2) give thou good tidings to the believers that they have a sure footing with their Lord
16:94 (96) lest any foot should slip after it has stood firm
41:29 (29) we shall set them underneath our feet, that they may be among the lower ones
47:7 (8) if you help God, He will help you, and confirm your feet
55:41 (41) and they shall be seized by their forelocks and their feet

QADĪM n.m. (comp.; *aqdam*)~ancient, old, aged

12:95 (95) by God, thou art certainly in thy ancient error
26:76 (76) you and your fathers, the elders
36:39 (39) till it returns like an aged palm-bough
46:11 (10) certainly they will say, 'This is an old calumny!'

QADDAMA vb. (II)~to forward, to advance; to lay up for; to send or do beforehand

a) perf. act.

2:95 (89)	they will never long for it, because of that their hands have forwarded
3:182 (178)	for what your hands have forwarded, and for that God is never unjust
4:62 (65)	when they are visited by an affliction for what their own hands have forwarded
5:80 (83)	evil is that they have forwarded to their account
8:51 (53)	that, for what your hands have forwarded, and for that God is never unjust
12:48 (48)	seven hard years, that shall devour what you have laid up for them
18:57 (55)	turns away from them and forgets what his hands have forwarded
22:10 (10)	that is for what thy hands have forwarded and for that God is never unjust
28:47 (47)	else, did an affliction visit them for that their own hands have forwarded
30:36 (35)	if some evil befalls them for that their own hands have forwarded, behold, they despair
36:12 (11)	write down what they have forwarded and what they have left behind
38:60 (60)	no, it is you have no Welcome; you forwarded it for us
38:61 (61)	whoso forwarded this for us, give him a double chastisement in the Fire
42:48 (47)	if some evil befalls him for that his own hands have forwarded
50:28 (27)	dispute not before Me! For I sent you beforehand the threat
59:18 (18)	let every soul consider what it has forwarded for the morrow
62:7 (7)	they will never long for it, because of that their hands have forwarded
75:13 (13)	upon that day man shall be told his former deeds and his latter
78:40 (41)	upon the day when a man shall behold what his hands have forwarded
82:5 (5)	then a soul shall know its works, the former and the latter
89:24 (25)	O would that I had forwarded for my life

b) impf. act. (*yuqaddimu*)

2:110 (104)	whatever good you shall forward to your souls' account, you shall find it with God
49:1 (1)	O believers, advance not before God and His Messenger
58:13 (14)	are you afraid, before your conspiring, to advance freewill offerings?
73:20 (20)	whatever good you shall forward to your souls' account

c) impv. (*qaddim*)

2:223 (223)	come unto your tillage as you wish, and forward for your souls
58:12 (13)	before your conspiring advance a freewill offering

TAQADDAMA vb. (V)~to go forward, to be former or foremost

a) perf. act.

48:2 (2)	that God may forgive thee thy former and thy latter sins

b) impf. act. (*yataqaddamu*)

74:37 (40)	to whoever of you desires to go forward or lag behind

ISTAQDAMA vb. (X)~to put forward. (pcple. act.) one who presses forward

b) impf. act. (*yastaqdimu*)

7:34 (32)	they shall not put it back by a single hour nor put it forward
10:49 (50)	they shall not put it back by a single hour nor put it forward
16:61 (63)	they shall not put it back by a single hour nor put it forward
34:30 (29)	you have the tryst of a day that you shall not put back by a single hour nor put it forward

g) pcple. act. (*mustaqdim*)

15:24 (24) We know the ones of you who press forward, and We know the laggards

*Q D R

QADA/IRA vb. (I)~to measure, to decree, to determine, to stint, to straiten; to have power, to be able. (n.vb.) a measure; means, ability, power, (*laylat al-qadr*) the Night of Power; a term; decree, doom, destiny, Divine pre-ordainment, providence. (pcple. act.) one who is able, who has power; one who determines; Able, Powerful (Divine attribute). (pcple. pass.) measured, decreed

a) perf. act.

6:91 (91) they measured not God with His true measure
22:74 (73) they measure not God with His true measure
39:67 (67) they measure not God with His true measure
77:23 (23) We determined; excellent determiners are We
89:16 (16) but when he tries him and stints for him his provision

b) impf. act. (*yaqdiru*)

2:264 (266) they have no power over anything that they have earned
5:34 (38) except for such as repent, before you have power over them
13:26 (26) God outspreads and straitens His provision unto whomsoever He will
14:18 (21) they have no power over that they have earned
16:75 (77) a servant possessed by his master, having no power over anything
16:76 (78) two men, one of them dumb, having no power over anything
17:30 (32) thy Lord outspreads and straitens His provision unto whom He will
21:87 (87) and thought that We would have no power over him
28:82 (82) God outspreads and straitens His provision to whomsoever He will of His servants
29:62 (62) God outspreads and straitens His provision to whomsoever He will of his servants
30:37 (36) have they not seen that God outspreads and straitens His provision to whom He will?
34:36 (35) my Lord outspreads and straitens His provision to whomsoever He will
34:39 (38) my lord outspreads and straitens His provision to whomsoever He will
39:52 (53) do they know that God outspreads and straitens His provision to whomsoever He will?
42:12 (10) He outspreads and straitens His provision to whom He will
48:21 (21) and other spoils you were not able to take
57:29 (29) that the People of the Book may know that they have no power over anything of God's bounty
90:5 (5) what, does he think none has power over him

d) perf. pass. (*qudira*)

54:12 (12) and the waters met for a matter decreed
65:7 (7) as for him whose provision is stinted to him

f) n.vb. (1) (*qadar*)

2:236 (237) make provision for them, the affluent man according to his means
2:236 (237) and according to his means the needy man, honourably
13:17 (18) He sends down out of heaven water, and the wadis flow each in its measure
15:21 (21) We send it not down but in a known measure

20:40 (42)	thou didst sojourn, then camest hither, Moses, according to a decree
23:18 (18)	We sent down out of heaven water in measure and lodged it in the earth
33:38 (38)	God's commandment is doom decreed
42:27 (26)	He sends down in measure whatsoever He will
43:11 (10)	who sent down out of heaven water in measure
54:49 (49)	surely We have created everything in measure
77:22 (22)	till a known term decreed

f) n.vb. (2) (*qadr*)

6:91 (91)	they measured not God with His true measure
22:74 (73)	they measure not God with His true measure
39:67 (67)	they measure not God with His true measure
65:3 (3)	God has appointed a measure for everything
97:1 (1)	behold, We sent it down on the Night of Power
97:2 (2)	what shall teach thee what is the Night of Power
97:3 (3)	the Night of Power is better than a thousand months

g) pcple. act. (*qādir*)

6:37 (37)	God is able to send down a sign, but most of them know not
6:65 (65)	He is able to send forth upon you chastisement
10:24 (25)	its inhabitants think they have power over it
17:99 (101)	have they not seen that God, who created the heavens and earth, is powerful
23:18 (18)	and We are able to take it away
23:95 (97)	We are able to show thee that We promise them
36:81 (81)	is not He, who created the heavens and earth, able to create the like of them?
46:33 (32)	is able to give life to the dead
68:25 (25)	they went forth early, determined upon their purpose
70:40 (40)	I swear by the Lord of the Easts and the Wests, surely We are able
75:4 (4)	We are able to shape again his fingers
75:40 (40)	is He not able to quicken the dead?
77:23 (23)	We determined; excellent determiners are We
86:8 (8)	surely He is able to bring him back

h) pcple. pass. (*maqdūr*)

33:38 (38)	God's commandment is doom decreed

MIQDĀR n.m.~a measure

13:8 (9)	everything with Him has its measure
32:5 (4)	whose measure is a thousand years of your counting
70:4 (4)	to Him the angels and the Spirit mount up in a day whereof the measure is fifty thousand years

QADĪR n.m. (adj)~Powerful, Able, Omnipotent (Divine attribute)

2:20 (19)	truly, God is powerful over everything
2:106 (100)	knowest thou not that God is powerful over everything?
2:109 (103)	truly God is powerful over everything
2:148 (143)	surely God is powerful over everything
2:259 (261)	I know that God is powerful over everything
2:284 (284)	God is powerful over everything
3:26 (25)	Thou art powerful over everything
3:29 (27)	God is powerful over everything
3:165 (159)	surely God is powerful over everything

3:189 (186)	God is powerful over everything
4:133 (132)	surely God is powerful over that
4:149 (148)	surely God is All-pardoning, All-powerful
5:17 (20)	God is powerful over everything
5:19 (22)	God is powerful over everything
5:40 (44)	and God is powerful over everything
5:120 (120)	and He is powerful over everything
6:17 (17)	visits thee with good, He is powerful over everything
8:41 (42)	and God is powerful over everything
9:39 (39)	will not hurt Him anything, for God is powerful over everything
11:4 (4)	He is powerful over everything
16:70 (72)	God is All-knowing, All-powerful
16:77 (79)	surely God is powerful over everything
22:6 (6)	He is the Truth, and brings the dead to life, and is powerful over everything
22:39 (40)	they were wronged — surely God is able to help them
24:45 (44)	God is powerful over everything
25:54 (56)	kindred of blood and marriage; thy Lord is All-powerful
29:20 (19)	God is powerful over everything
30:50 (49)	and He is powerful over everything
30:54 (53)	He is the All-knowing, the All-powerful
33:27 (27)	a land you never trod, God is powerful over everything
35:1 (1)	surely God is powerful over everything
35:44 (43)	surely He is All-knowing, All-powerful
41:39 (39)	surely He is powerful over everything
42:9 (7)	He quickens the dead, and He is powerful over everything
42:29 (28)	He is able to gather them whenever He will
42:50 (49)	surely He is All-knowing, All-powerful
46:33 (32)	yes indeed; He is powerful over everything
48:21 (21)	God is powerful over everything
57:2 (2)	He gives life, and He makes to die, and He is powerful over everything
59:6 (6)	God is powerful over everything
60:7 (7)	God is All-powerful; God is All-forgiving, All-compassionate
64:1 (1)	and He is powerful over everything
65:12 (12)	that you may know that God is powerful over everything
66:8 (8)	surely Thou art powerful over everything
67:1 (1)	He is powerful over everything

QUDŪR n.com. (pl. of *qidr*)~cooking pots

34:13 (12)	statues, porringers like water-troughs, and anchored cooking-pots

QADDARA vb. (II)~to determine, to decree, to ordain; to measure. (n.vb.) the act of ordaining, decreeing

a) perf. act.

10:5 (5)	it is He who made the sun a radiance, and the moon a light, and determined it by stations
15:60 (60)	we have decreed, she shall surely be of those that tarry
25:2 (2)	He created every thing, then He ordained it very exactly
27:57 (58)	We decreed she should be of those that tarried
34:18 (17)	and well We measured the journey between them
36:39 (39)	and the moon — We have determined it by stations
41:10 (9)	He blessed it, and He ordained therein its diverse sustenance in four days
56:60 (60)	We have decreed among you Death
74:18 (18)	lo! He reflected, and determined

74:19 (19)	death seize him, how he determined
74:20 (20)	again, death seize him, how he determined
76:16 (16)	crystal of silver that they have measured very exactly
80:19 (19)	He created him, and determined him
87:3 (3)	who determined and guided

b) impf. act. (*yuqaddiru*)

73:20 (20)	God determines the night and the day

c) impv. (*qaddir*)

34:11 (10)	fashion wide coats of mail, and measure well the links

f) n.vb. (*taqdīr*)

6:96 (96)	that is the ordaining of the All-mighty, the All-knowing
25:2 (2)	then He ordained it <very exactly>
36:38 (38)	that is the ordaining of the All-mighty, the All-knowing
41:12 (11)	that is the ordaining of the All-mighty, the All-knowing
76:16 (16)	crystal of silver that they have measured <very exactly>

IQTADARA vb. (VIII)~(pcple. act.) one who has power; Omnipotent (Divine attribute)

g) pcple. act. (*muqtadir*)

18:45 (43)	God is omnipotent over everything
43:42 (41)	of that We promised them, surely We have power over them
54:42 (42)	We seized them with the seizing of One Mighty, Omnipotent
54:55 (55)	in a sure abode, in the presence of a King Omnipotent

*Q D S

QUDDŪS n.m. (adj)~holy, All-holy (Divine attribute)

59:23 (23)	He is the King, the All-holy, the All-peaceable
62:1 (1)	all that is in the heavens and the earth magnifies God, the King, the All-holy

QUDUS n.m.~holy; (*rūḥ al-qudus*) the Holy Spirit

2:87 (81)	We gave Jesus son of Mary the clear signs, and confirmed him with the Holy Spirit
2:253 (254)	We gave Jesus son of Mary the clear signs, and confirmed him with the Holy Spirit
5:110 (109)	when I confirmed thee with the Holy Spirit, to speak to men
16:102 (104)	the Holy Spirit sent it down from thy Lord in truth

QADDASA vb. (II)~to sanctify, to proclaim holy. (pcple. pass.) sanctified, holy

b) impf. act. (*yuqaddisu*)

2:30 (28)	while We proclaim Thy praise and call Thee Holy

h) pcple. pass. f. (*muqaddasah*)

5:21 (24)	O my people, enter the Holy Land
20:12 (12)	put off thy shoes; thou art in the holy valley, Towa
79:16 (16)	when his Lord called to him in the holy valley, Towa

*Q D W

IQTADÁ vb. (VIII)~to imitate, to follow (as an example). (pcple. act.) one who follows

c) impv. (*iqtadi(h)*)

6:90 (90) those are they whom God has guided; so follow their guidance

g) pcple. act. (*muqtadī*)

43:23 (22) we indeed found our fathers upon a community, and we are following

*Q DH F

QADHAFA vb. (I)~to cast, to hurl, to pelt; to guess

a) perf. act.

20:87 (90) we cast them, as the Samaritan also threw them, into the fire
33:26 (26) and cast terror in their hearts; some you slew
59:2 (2) whence they had not reckoned, and He cast terror into their hearts

b) impf. act. (*yaqdhifu*)

21:18 (18) nay, but We hurl the truth against falsehood
34:48 (47) my Lord hurls the truth — the Knower of the Unseen
34:53 (52) seeing they disbelieved in it before, guessing at the Unseen from a place far away

c) impv. (*iqdhif*)

20:39 (39) cast him into the ark
20:39 (39) and cast him into the river

e) impf. pass. (*yuqdhafu*)

37:8 (8) for they are pelted from every side

*Q Ḍ B

QAḌABA vb. (I)~(n.vb.) reeds, green fodder

f) n.vb. (*qaḍb*)

80:28 (28) and vines, and reeds

*Q Ḍ Ḍ

INQAḌḌA vb. (VII)~to tumble down

b) impf. act. (*yanqaḍḍu*)

18:77 (76)	there they found a wall about to tumble down

*Q Ḍ Y

QAḌÁ vb. (I)~to decree, to issue a verdict, to determine, to decide; to create; to perform, to accomplish, to satisfy, to fulfil; (with prep. *ʿalá*) to dispatch, to do someone in, to terminate, to kill. (pcple. act.) one who decides, who decrees, who judges. (pcple. pass.) that which is determined, decreed

a) perf. act.

2:117 (111)	when He decrees a thing, He but says to it 'Be'
2:200 (196)	when you have performed your holy rites remember God
3:47 (42)	when He decrees a thing He does but say to it 'Be'
4:65 (68)	then they shall find in themselves no impediment touching thy verdict
4:103 (104)	when you have performed the prayer, remember God
6:2 (2)	it is He who created you of clay, then determined a term
12:68 (68)	it was a need in Jacob's soul that he so satisfied
15:66 (66)	We decreed for him that commandment
17:4 (4)	We decreed for the Children of Israel in the Book
17:23 (24)	thy Lord has decreed you shall not serve any but Him
19:35 (36)	when He decrees a thing, He but says to it 'Be'
28:15 (14)	Moses struck him, and despatched him, and said
28:28 (28)	whichever of the two terms I fulfil, it shall be no injustice to me
28:29 (29)	so when Moses had accomplished the term
28:44 (44)	thou wast not upon the western side when We decreed to Moses the commandment
33:23 (23)	some of them have fulfilled their vow by death
33:36 (36)	when God and His Messenger have decreed a matter
33:37 (37)	when Zaid had accomplished what he would of her, then We gave her in marriage to thee
33:37 (37)	when they have accomplished what they would of them
34:14 (13)	when We decreed that he should die, naught indicated to them that he was dead
39:42 (43)	He withholds that against which He has decreed death
40:68 (70)	when He decrees a thing, He but says to it 'Be'
41:12 (11)	He determined them as seven heavens in two days

b) impf. act. (*yaqḍī*)

8:42 (43)	but that God might determine a matter that was done
8:44 (46)	that God might determine a matter that was done
10:93 (93)	thy Lord will decide between them on the Day of Resurrection touching their differences
20:72 (75)	thou canst only decide touching this present life
22:29 (30)	let them then finish with their self-neglect
27:78 (80)	thy Lord will decide between them by His Judgment
40:20 (21)	God shall decide justly
40:20 (21)	and those they call on, apart from Him, shall not decide by any means
43:77 (77)	they shall call, 'O Malik, let thy Lord have done with us!'
45:17 (16)	thy Lord will decide between them on the Day of Resurrection
80:23 (23)	no indeed! Man has not accomplished His bidding

c) impv. (*iqḍi*)

10:71 (72)	but make decision unto me, and respite me not
20:72 (75)	decide then what thou wilt decide

d) perf. pass. (*quḍiya*)

2:210 (206) the matter is determined, and unto God all matters are returned
6:8 (8) yet had We sent down an angel, the matter would have been determined
6:58 (58) the matter between you and me would be decided
10:11 (12) as they would hasten good, their term would be already decided for them
10:19 (20) it had been decided between them already touching their differences
10:47 (48) when their Messenger comes, justly the issue is decided between them
10:54 (55) justly the issue is decided between them, and they are not wronged
11:44 (46) the affair was accomplished, and the Ark settled on El-Judi
11:110 (112) but for a word that preceded from thy Lord, it had been decided between them
12:41 (41) the matter is decided whereon you enquire
14:22 (26) and Satan says, when the issue is decided
19:39 (40) warn thou them of the day of anguish, when the matter shall be determined
39:69 (69) and justly the issue be decided between them, and they not wronged
39:75 (75) and justly the issue shall be decided between them
40:78 (78) when God's command comes, justly the issue shall be decided
41:45 (45) but for a Word that preceded from thy Lord, it had been decided between them
42:14 (13) but for a Word that preceded from thy Lord until a stated term, it had been decided
42:21 (20) but for the Word of Decision, it had been decided between them
46:29 (28) when it was finished, they turned back to their people, warning
62:10 (10) then, when the prayer is finished, scatter in the land

e) impf. pass. (*yuqḍá*)

6:60 (60) then He raises you up therein, that a stated term may be determined
20:114 (113) hasten not with the Koran ere its revelation is accomplished
35:36 (33) they shall neither be done with and die, nor shall its chastisement be lightened for them

g) pcple. act. (*qāḍī*)

20:72 (75) decide then what thou wilt decide

h) pcple. pass. (*maqḍī*)

19:21 (21) and a mercy from Us; it is a thing decreed
19:71 (72) that for thy Lord is a thing decreed, determined

QĀḌIYAH n.f.~the end, death

69:27 (27) would it had been the end

*Q F L

AQFĀL n.m. (pl. of *qufl*)~locks

47:24 (26) or is it that there are locks upon their hearts?

*Q F Y

QAFĀ vb. (I)~to pursue

b) impf. act. (*yaqfū*)

17:36 (38) pursue not that thou hast no knowledge of

QAFFÁ vb. (II)~to send following or after a) perf. act.

2:87 (81) We gave to Moses the Book, and after him sent succeeding Messengers
5:46 (50) We sent, following in their footsteps, Jesus son of Mary
57:27 (27) then We sent, following in their footsteps, Our Messengers
57:27 (27) and We sent, following, Jesus son of Mary

*Q H R

QAHARA vb. (I)~to overcome, to oppress. (pcple. act.) triumphant; Omnipotent (Divine attribute)

b) impf. act. (*yaqharu*)

93:9 (9) as for the orphan, do not oppress him

g) pcple. act. (*qāhir*)

6:18 (18) He is Omnipotent over His servants
6:61 (61) He is the Omnipotent over His servants
7:127 (124) surely we are triumphant over them

QAHHĀR n.m. (adj)~Omnipotent (Divine attribute)

12:39 (39) many lords at variance, or God the One, the Omnipotent
13:16 (17) God is the Creator of everything, and He is the One, the Omnipotent
14:48 (49) they sally forth unto God, the One, the Omnipotent
38:65 (65) there is not any god but God, the One, the Omnipotent
39:4 (6) glory be to Him! He is God, the One, the Omnipotent
40:16 (16) whose is the Kingdom today? God's, the One, the Omnipotent

*Q Ḥ M

IQTAḤAMA vb. (VIII)~to assault. (pcple. act.) one who assaults, who rushes in

a) perf. act.

90:11 (11) yet he has not assaulted the steep

g) pcple. act. (*muqtaḥim*)

38:59 (59) this is a troop rushing in with you; there is no Welcome for them

*Q L ᶜ

AQLAᶜA vb. (IV)~to abate, to desist

c) impv. (*aqliᶜ*)

11:44 (46) it was said, 'Earth, swallow thy waters; and, heaven, abate!'

*Q L B

QALABA vb. (I)~to turn, to overturn

e) impf. pass. (*yuqlabu*)

29:21 (20)	on whomsoever He will, and unto Him you shall be turned

MUNQALAB n.m.~resort; overturning

18:36 (34)	I shall surely find a better resort than this
26:227 (228)	those who do wrong shall surely know by what overturning they will be overturned

MUTAQALLAB n.m.~going to and fro

47:19 (21)	God knows your going to and fro, and your lodging

QALB n.m. (pl. *qulūb*)~a heart

2:7 (6)	God has set a seal on their hearts and on their hearing
2:10 (9)	in their hearts is a sickness, and God has increased their sickness
2:74 (69)	then your hearts became hardened thereafter
2:88 (82)	and they say, 'Our hearts are uncircumcised'
2:93 (87)	they were made to drink the Calf in their hearts for their unbelief
2:97 (91)	he it was that brought it down upon thy heart by the leave of God
2:118 (112)	so spoke those before them as these men say; their hearts are much alike
2:204 (200)	such a one calls on God to witness what is in his heart
2:225 (225)	He will take you to task for what your hearts have earned
2:260 (262)	'Yes,' he said, 'but that my heart may be at rest'
2:283 (283)	conceal the testimony; whoso conceals it, his heart is sinful
3:7 (5)	as for those in whose hearts is swerving, they follow the ambiguous part
3:8 (6)	make not our hearts to swerve after that Thou hast guided us
3:103 (98)	He brought your hearts together, so that by His blessing you became brothers
3:126 (122)	this not, save as good tiding to you, and that your hearts might be at rest
3:151 (144)	We will cast into the hearts of the unbelievers terror
3:154 (148)	they were concealing in their hearts that they show not to thee
3:156 (150)	that God may make that an anguish in their hearts
3:159 (153)	hadst thou been harsh and hard of heart, they would have scattered from about thee
3:167 (161)	saying with their mouths that which never was in their hearts
4:63 (66)	those — God knows what is in their hearts
4:155 (154)	and for their saying, 'Our hearts are uncircumcised'
5:13 (16)	for their breaking their compact We cursed them and made their hearts hard
5:41 (45)	such men as say with their mouths, 'We believe,' but their hearts believe not
5:41 (45)	those are they whose hearts God desired not to purify
5:52 (57)	thou seest those in whose hearts is sickness vying with one another
5:113 (113)	We desire that we should eat of it and our hearts be at rest
6:25 (25)	We lay veils upon their hearts lest they understand it
6:43 (43)	but their hearts were hard, and Satan decked out fair to them
6:46 (46)	what think you? if God seizes your hearing and sight, and sets a seal upon your hearts
7:100 (98)	did We will, We would smite them because of their sins, sealing their hearts
7:101 (99)	so God seals the hearts of the unbelievers
7:179 (178)	they have hearts, but understand not with them
8:2 (2)	those only are believers who, when God is mentioned, their hearts quake
8:10 (10)	and that your hearts thereby might be at rest
8:11 (11)	and to put away from you the defilement of Satan, and to strengthen your hearts

8:12 (12)	I shall cast into the unbelievers' hearts terror
8:24 (24)	know that God stands between a man and his heart
8:49 (51)	when the hypocrites, and those in whose hearts was sickness, said
8:63 (64)	and brought their hearts together
8:63 (64)	thou couldst not have brought their hearts together
8:70 (71)	if God knows of any good in your hearts He will give you better
9:8 (8)	giving you satisfaction with their mouths but in their hearts refusing
9:15 (15)	and He will remove the rage within their hearts
9:45 (45)	those whose hearts are filled with doubt, so that in their doubt they go
9:60 (60)	those who work to collect them, those whose hearts are brought together
9:64 (65)	the hypocrites are afraid, lest a sura should be sent down against them, telling thee what is in their hearts
9:77 (78)	as a consequence He put hypocrisy into their hearts
9:87 (88)	and a seal has been set upon their hearts
9:93 (94)	God has set a seal on their hearts
9:110 (111)	the buildings they have built will not cease to be a point of doubt within their hearts
9:110 (111)	unless it be that their hearts are cut into pieces
9:117 (118)	after the hearts of a part of them wellnigh swerved aside
9:125 (126)	but as for those in whose heart is sickness
9:127 (128)	God has turned away their hearts
10:74 (75)	so We seal the hearts of the transgressors
10:88 (88)	our Lord, obliterate their possessions, and harden their hearts
13:28 (28)	those who believe, their hearts being at rest in God's remembrance
13:28 (28)	in God's remembrance are at rest the hearts
15:12 (12)	even so We cause it to enter into the hearts of the sinners
16:22 (23)	they who believe not in the world to come, their hearts deny, and they have waxed proud
16:106 (108)	who has been compelled, and his heart is still at rest in his belief
16:108 (110)	those — God has set a seal on their hearts
17:46 (48)	We lay veils upon their hearts lest they understand it
18:14 (13)	We strengthened their hearts, when they stood up and said
18:28 (27)	obey not him whose heart We have made neglectful of Our remembrance
18:57 (55)	We have laid veils on their hearts lest they understand it
21:3 (3)	diverted their hearts. The evildoers whisper
22:32 (33)	whosoever venerates God's waymarks, that is of the godliness of the hearts
22:35 (36)	who, when God is mentioned, their hearts quake
22:46 (45)	so that they have hearts to understand with
22:46 (45)	it is not the eyes that are blind, but blind are the hearts
22:53 (52)	that He may make what Satan casts a trial for those in whose hearts is sickness
22:53 (52)	and those whose hearts are hard
22:54 (53)	and believe in it, and so their hearts be humble unto Him
23:60 (62)	those who give what they give, their hearts quaking that they are returning to their Lord
23:63 (65)	nay, but their hearts are in perplexity as to this
24:37 (37)	fearing a day when hearts and eyes shall be turned about
24:50 (49)	what, is there sickness in their hearts
26:89 (89)	except for him who comes to God with a pure heart
26:194 (194)	upon thy heart, that thou mayest be one of the warners
26:200 (200)	even so We have caused it to enter into the hearts of the sinners
28:10 (9)	she wellnigh disclosed him had We not strengthened her heart
30:59 (59)	even so God seals the hearts of those that know not
33:4 (4)	God has not assigned to any man two hearts within his breast
33:5 (5)	there is no fault in you if you make mistakes, but only in what your hearts premeditate
33:10 (10)	when your eyes swerved and your hearts reached your throats

33:12 (12)	when the hypocrites, and those in whose hearts is sickness, said
33:26 (26)	and cast terror in their hearts; some you slew
33:32 (32)	abject in your speech, so that he in whose heart is sickness may be lustful
33:51 (51)	God knows what is in your hearts; God is All-knowing
33:53 (53)	that is cleaner for your hearts and (theirs)
33:53 (53)	that is cleaner for your (hearts) and their [hearts]
33:60 (60)	if the hypocrites do not give over, and those in whose hearts there is sickness
34:23 (22)	when terror is lifted from their hearts, they will say
37:84 (82)	when he came unto his Lord with a pure heart
39:22 (23)	woe to those whose hearts are hardened against the remembrance of God
39:23 (24)	then their skins and their hearts soften to the remembrance of God
39:45 (46)	when God is mentioned alone, then shudder the hearts of those who believe not in the Hereafter
40:18 (18)	when, choking with anguish, the hearts are in the throats
40:35 (37)	so God sets a seal on every heart proud, arrogant.)
41:5 (4)	our hearts are veiled from what thou callest us to
42:24 (23)	if God wills, He will set a seal on thy heart
45:23 (22)	and set a seal upon his hearing and his heart
47:16 (18)	those are they upon whose hearts God has set a seal
47:20 (22)	thou seest those in whose hearts is sickness looking at thee
47:24 (26)	or is it that there are locks upon their hearts?
47:29 (31)	did those in whose hearts is sickness think that God would not bring to light their rancour?
48:4 (4)	it is He who sent down the Shechina into the hearts of the believers
48:11 (11)	they say with their tongues what is not in their hearts
48:12 (12)	that was decked out fair in your hearts
48:18 (18)	He knew what was in their hearts
48:26 (26)	when the unbelievers set in their hearts fierceness
49:3 (3)	those are they whose hearts God has tested for godfearing
49:7 (7)	but God has endeared to you belief, decking it fair in your hearts
49:14 (14)	say, 'We surrender'; for belief has not yet entered your hearts
50:33 (32)	whosoever fears the All-merciful in the Unseen, and comes with a penitent heart
50:37 (36)	surely in that there is a reminder to him who has a heart
57:16 (15)	is it not time that the hearts of those who believe should be humbled
57:16 (15)	the term seemed over long to them, so that their hearts have become hard
57:27 (27)	We set in the hearts of those who followed him tenderness and mercy
58:22 (22)	He has written faith upon their hearts
59:2 (2)	He cast terror into their hearts as they destroyed their houses with their own hands
59:10 (10)	put Thou not into our hearts any rancour towards those who believe
59:14 (14)	you think of them as a host; but their hearts are scattered
61:5 (5)	when they swerved, God caused their hearts to swerve
63:3 (3)	therefore a seal has been set on their hearts
64:11 (11)	whosoever believes in God, He will guide his heart
66:4 (4)	if you two repent to God, yet your hearts certainly inclined
74:31 (33)	those in whose hearts there is sickness
79:8 (8)	hearts upon that day shall be athrob
83:14 (14)	but that they were earning has rusted upon their hearts

QALLABA vb. (II)~to turn something upside down, to turn about, to wring (one's hands); to confound [Pk]

a) perf. act.

9:48 (48)	they sought to stir up sedition already before, and turned things upside down for thee

b) impf. act. (*yuqallibu*)

6:110 (110) We shall turn about their hearts and their eyes
18:18 (17) while We turned them now to the right, now to the left
18:42 (40) in the morning he was wringing his hands for that he had expended
24:44 (44) God turns about the day and the night

e) impf. pass. (*yuqallabu*)

33:66 (66) upon the day when their faces are turned about in the Fire

TAQALLABA vb. (V)~to turn about. (n.vb.) the act of turning about, going to and fro

b) impf. act. (*yataqallabu*)

24:37 (37) fearing a day when hearts and eyes shall be turned about

f) n.vb. (*taqallub*)

2:144 (139) We have seen thee turning thy face about in the heaven
3:196 (196) let it not delude thee, that the unbelievers go to and fro in the land
16:46 (48) He will not seize them in their going to and fro
26:219 (219) and when thou turnest about among those who bow
40:4 (4) let not their going to and fro in the land delude thee

INQALABA vb. (VII)~to turn about, to turn back, to return, to come back. (pcple. act.) turning, one who returns

a) perf. act.

3:144 (138) if he should die or is slain, will you turn about on your heels?
3:174 (168) so they returned with blessing and bounty from God
7:119 (116) so they were vanquished there, and they turned about, humbled
9:95 (96) they will swear to you by God, when you turn back to them, that you may turn aside from them
12:62 (62) haply they will recognize it when they have turned to their people
22:11 (11) if a trial befalls him he turns completely over
83:31 (31) when they returned to their people
83:31 (31) they returned blithely

b) impf. act. (*yanqalibu*)

2:143 (138) except that We might know who followed the Messenger from him who turned on his heels
3:127 (122) so that they turned in their tracks, disappointed
3:144 (138) if any man should turn about on his heels, he will not harm God in any way
3:149 (142) they will turn you upon your heels, and you will turn about, losers
5:21 (24) turn not back in your traces, to turn about losers
26:227 (228) those who do wrong shall surely know by what overturning they will be overturned
48:12 (12) you thought that the Messenger and the believers would never return to their families
67:4 (4) then return thy gaze again, and again, and thy gaze comes back to thee dazzled
84:9 (9) and he will return to his family joyfully

g) pcple. act. (*munqalib*)

7:125 (122) surely unto our Lord we are turning
26:50 (50) there is no harm; surely unto our Lord we are turning
43:14 (13) surely unto our Lord we are turning

*Q L D

QALĀ'ID n.f. (pl. of *qilādah*)~a necklace

5:2 (2)	profane not God's waymarks nor the holy month, neither the offering, nor the necklaces
5:97 (98)	the holy month, the offering, and the necklaces

MAQĀLĪD n.m. (pl. of *miqlād*)~a key

39:63 (63)	unto Him belong the keys of the heavens and the earth
42:12 (10)	to Him belong the keys of the heavens and the earth

*Q L L

QALLA vb. (I)~to be little

a) perf. act.

4:7 (8)	to the women a share of what parents and kinsmen leave, whether it be little or much

QALĪL n.m. (adj.; comp. *aqall*)~little, few, small

2:41 (38)	sell not My signs for a little price
2:79 (73)	that they may sell it for a little price
2:83 (77)	then you turned away, all but a few of you, swerving aside
2:88 (82)	little will they believe
2:126 (120)	whoso disbelieves, to him I shall give enjoyment a little
2:174 (169)	those who conceal what of the Book God has sent down on them, and sell it for a little price
2:246 (247)	when fighting was prescribed for them, they turned their backs except a few of them
2:249 (250)	they drank of it, except a few of them
2:249 (250)	how often a little company has overcome a numerous company
3:77 (71)	those that sell God's covenant, and their oaths, for a little price
3:187 (184)	they rejected it behind their backs and sold it for a small price
3:197 (196)	a little enjoyment, then their refuge is Gehenna
3:199 (198)	men humble to God, not selling the signs of God for a small price
4:46 (49)	God has cursed them for their unbelief, so they believe not except a few
4:66 (69)	they would not have done it, save a few of them
4:77 (79)	the enjoyment of this world is little
4:83 (85)	you would surely have followed Satan, except a few
4:142 (141)	and not remembering God save a little
4:155 (154)	for their unbelief, so they believe not, except a few
5:13 (16)	some act of treachery on their part, except a few of them
5:44 (48)	sell not My signs for a little price
7:3 (2)	little do you remember
7:10 (9)	little thanks you show
7:86 (84)	remember when you were few, and He multiplied you
8:26 (26)	remember when you were few and abased in the land
8:43 (45)	when God showed thee them in thy dream as few
8:44 (46)	when God showed you them in your eyes as few
9:9 (9)	they have sold the signs of God for a small price
9:38 (38)	the enjoyment of this present life, compared with the world to come, is a little thing
9:82 (83)	therefore let them laugh little, and weep much

11:40 (42)	there believed not with him except a few
11:116 (118)	except a few of those whom We delivered of them
12:47 (47)	what you have harvested leave in the ear, excepting a little whereof you eat
12:48 (48)	that shall devour what you have laid up for them, all but a little you keep in store
16:95 (97)	do not sell the covenant of God for a small price
16:117 (118)	a little enjoyment, then for them awaits a painful chastisement
17:52 (54)	you will think you have but tarried a little
17:62 (64)	I shall assuredly master his seed, save a few
17:74 (76)	thou wert near to inclining unto them a very little
17:76 (78)	then they would have tarried after thee only a little
17:85 (87)	you have been given of knowledge nothing except a little
18:22 (21)	my Lord knows very well their number, and none knows them, except a few
18:39 (37)	if thou seest me, that I am less than thou in wealth and children
23:40 (42)	in a little they will be remorseful
23:78 (80)	little thanks you show
23:114 (116)	you have tarried but a little, did you know
26:54 (54)	behold, these are a small troop
27:62 (63)	little indeed do you remember
28:58 (58)	their dwelling-places, undwelt in after them, except a little
31:24 (23)	to them We give enjoyment a little
32:9 (8)	little thanks you show
33:16 (16)	you will be given enjoyment of days then but little
33:18 (18)	those who say to their brothers, 'Come to us,' and come to battle but little
33:20 (20)	if they were among you, they would fight but little
33:60 (60)	then they will be thy neighbours there only a little
34:13 (12)	few indeed are those that are thankful among My servants
34:16 (15)	and here and there a few lote-trees
38:24 (23)	those who believe, and do deeds of righteousness — and how few they are
39:8 (11)	enjoy thy unbelief a little; thou shalt be among the inhabitants of the Fire
40:58 (60)	little do you reflect
44:15 (14)	behold, We are removing the chastisement a little
48:15 (15)	nay, but they have not understood except a little
51:17 (17)	little of the night would they slumber
53:34 (35)	and gives a little, and then grudgingly
56:14 (14)	and how few of the later folk)
67:23 (23)	little thanks you show
69:41 (41)	little do you believe
69:42 (42)	little do you remember
72:24 (25)	then they will know who is weaker in helpers and fewer in numbers
73:2 (2)	keep vigil the night, except a little
73:3 (3)	a half of it, or diminish a little
73:11 (11)	leave Me to those who cry lies, those prosperous ones, and respite them a little
77:46 (46)	eat and take your joy a little; you are sinners

QALLALA vb. (II)~to make few, to lessen

b) impf. act. (*yuqallilu*)

8:44 (46)	and made you few in their eyes

AQALLA vb. (IV)~to carry, to be charged with

a) perf. act.

7:57 (55)	when they are charged with heavy clouds, We drive it to a dead land

*Q L M

QALAM n.m. (pl. *aqlām*)~a pen, a quill

3:44 (39)	they were casting quills which of them should have charge of Mary
31:27 (26)	though all the trees in the earth were pens
68:1 (1)	by the Pen, and what they inscribe
96:4 (4)	who taught by the Pen

*Q L Y

QALÁ vb. (I)~to hate. (pcple. act.) a detester

a) perf. act.

93:3 (3) thy Lord has neither forsaken thee nor hates thee

g) pcple. act. (*qālī*)

26:168 (168) truly I am a detester of what you do

*Q M ᶜ

MAQĀMIᶜ n.f. (pl. of *miqmaᶜah*)~a mace, a hooked iron rod

22:21 (21) for them await hooked iron rods

*Q M Ḥ

AQMAḤA vb. (IV)~(pcple. pass.) one whose head is raised; one who is stiff-necked

h) pcple. pass. (*muqmaḥ*)

36:8 (7) up to the chin, so their heads are raised

*Q M L

QUMMAL n.m.~lice

7:133 (130) We let loose upon them the flood and the locusts, the lice and the frogs

*Q M R

QAMAR n.m.~moon

6:77 (77) when he saw the moon rising, he said, This is my Lord

6:96 (96)	and has made the night for a repose, and the sun and moon for a reckoning
7:54 (52)	the sun, and the moon, and the stars subservient, by His command
10:5 (5)	it is He who made the sun a radiance, and the moon a light
12:4 (4)	Father, I saw eleven stars, and the sun and the moon
13:2 (2)	he subjected the sun and the moon
14:33 (37)	He subjected to you the sun and moon constant upon their courses
16:12 (12)	He subjected to you the night and day, and the sun and moon
21:33 (34)	it is He who created the night and the day, the sun and the moon
22:18 (18)	the sun and the moon, the stars and the mountains
25:61 (62)	and has set among them a lamp, and an illuminating moon
29:61 (61)	who created the heavens and the earth and subjected the sun and the moon?
31:29 (28)	He has subjected the sun and the moon, each of them running to a stated term
35:13 (14)	He has subjected the sun and the moon, each of them running to a stated term
36:39 (39)	and the moon — We have determined it by stations
36:40 (40)	it behoves not the sun to overtake the moon
39:5 (7)	He has subjected the sun and the moon, each of them running to a stated term
41:37 (37)	of His signs are the night and the day, the sun and the moon
41:37 (37)	bow not yourselves to the sun and moon
54:1 (1)	the Hour has drawn nigh: the moon is split
55:5 (4)	the sun and the moon to a reckoning
71:16 (15)	and set the moon therein for a light
74:32 (35)	nay! By the moon
75:8 (8)	and the moon is eclipsed
75:9 (9)	and the sun and moon are brought together
84:18 (18)	and the moon when it is at the full
91:2 (2)	and by the moon when she follows him

*Q M Ṣ

QAMĪṢ n.m.~a shirt

12:18 (18)	they brought his shirt with false blood on it
12:25 (25)	they raced to the door; and she tore his shirt from behind
12:26 (26)	if his shirt has been torn from before
12:27 (27)	if it be that his shirt has been torn
12:28 (28)	when he saw his shirt was torn from behind he said
12:93 (93)	go, take this shirt, and do you cast it on my father's face

*Q M Ṭ R

QAMṬARĪR n.m. (adj)~inauspicious

76:10 (10)	we fear from our Lord a frowning day, inauspicious

*Q N ᶜ

QANAʿA vb. (I)~(pcple. act.) a beggar

g) pcple. act. (*qāniᶜ*)

22:36 (37)	when their flanks collapse, eat of them and feed the beggar and the suppliant

AQNAʿA vb. (IV)~(pcple. act.) one whose head is erect

g) pcple. act. (*muqniʿ*)

14:43 (44) when they shall run with necks outstretched and heads erect

*Q N T

QANATA vb. (I)~to be obedient. (pcple. act.) one who obeys, obedient

b) impf. act. (*yaqnutu*)

33:31 (31) whosoever of you is obedient to God and His Messenger

c) impv. (*uqnut*)

3:43 (38) Mary, be obedient to thy Lord, prostrating and bowing before Him

g) pcple. act. (*qānit*)

2:116 (110) all that is in the heavens and the earth; all obey His will
2:238 (239) and do you stand obedient to God
3:17 (15) men who are patient, truthful, obedient, expenders in alms
4:34 (38) righteous women are therefore obedient
16:120 (121) surely, Abraham was a nation obedient unto God
30:26 (25) to Him belongs whosoever is in the heavens and the earth; all obey His will
33:35 (35) obedient men and (obedient women)
33:35 (35) (obedient men) and obedient women
39:9 (12) is he who is obedient in the watches of the night, bowing himself and standing
66:5 (5) women who have surrendered, believing, obedient, penitent, devout
66:12 (12) she confirmed the Words of her Lord and His Books, and became one of the obedient

*Q N Ṭ

QANAṬA vb. (I)~to despair. (pcple. act.) one who despairs

a) perf. act.

42:28 (27) it is He who sends down the rain after they have despaired

b) impf. act. (*yaqnaṭu*)

15:56 (56) who despairs of the mercy of his Lord, excepting those that are astray?
30:36 (35) if some evil befalls them for that their own hands have forwarded, behold, they

39:53 (54) do not despair of God's mercy; surely God forgives sins

g) pcple. act. (*qāniṭ*)

15:55 (55) We give thee good tidings of truth. Be not of those that despair

QANŪṬ n.m. (adj)~desperate

41:49 (49) when evil visits him, then he is cast down and desperate

*Q N Ṭ R

QANṬARA vb. (quad I)~(pcple. pass.) heaped-up

h) pcple. pass. f. (*muqanṭarah*)

3:14 (12) women, children, heaped-up heaps of gold and silver

QINṬĀR n.m.~a hundredweight, heaps

3:14 (12) women, children, heaped-up heaps of gold
3:75 (68) he who, if thou trust him with a hundredweight, will restore it thee
4:20 (24) you have given to one a hundredweight, take of it nothing

*Q N W

QINWĀN n.m. (pl. of *qinā*)~a thick cluster of dates

6:99 (99) from the spathe of it, dates thick-clustered, ready to the hand

*Q N Y

AQNÁ vb. (IV)~to cause to acquire, to make rich

a) perf. act.

53:48 (49) it is He who gives wealth and riches

*Q R ʾ

QARAʾA vb. (I)~to recite, to read

a) perf. act.

16:98 (100) when thou recitest the Koran, seek refuge in God from the accursed Satan
17:45 (47) when thou recitest the Koran, We place between thee, and those ... a curtain
26:199 (199) and he had recited it to them, they would not have believed in it
75:18 (18) when We recite it, follow thou its recitation

b) impf. act. (*yaqraʾu*)

10:94 (94) what We have sent down to thee, ask those who recite the Book before thee
17:71 (73) whoso is given his book in his right hand — those shall read their book
17:93 (95) we will not believe thy going up till thou bringest down on us a book that we may read
17:106 (107) a Koran We have divided, for thee to recite it to mankind

c) impv. (*iqraʾ*)

17:14 (15) read thy book

69:19 (19)	he shall say, 'Here, take and read my book'
73:20 (20)	therefore recite of the Koran so much as is feasible
73:20 (20)	recite of it so much as is feasible
96:1 (1)	recite: In the Name of thy Lord who created
96:3 (3)	recite: And thy Lord is the Most Generous

d) perf. pass. (*quriʾa*)

7:204 (203)	when the Koran is recited, give you ear to it and be silent
84:21 (21)	when the Koran is recited to them they do not bow

QURʾĀN n.m.~a recitation, a reading; the Koran (English spellings vary)

2:185 (181)	the Koran was sent down to be a guidance to the people
4:82 (84)	what, do they not ponder the Koran?
5:101 (101)	if you question concerning them when the Koran is being sent down
6:19 (19)	God is witness between me and you, and this Koran has been revealed to me
7:204 (203)	when the Koran is recited, give you ear to it and be silent
9:111 (112)	that is a promise binding upon God in the Torah, and the Gospel, and the Koran
10:15 (16)	bring a Koran other than this, or alter it
10:37 (38)	this Koran could not have been forged apart from God
10:61 (62)	neither recitest thou any Koran of it, nor do you any work
12:2 (2)	We have sent it down as an Arabic Koran
12:3 (3)	We will relate to thee the fairest of stories in that We have revealed to thee this Koran
13:31 (30)	if only a Koran whereby the mountains were set in motion
15:1 (1)	those are the signs of the Book and of a manifest Koran
15:87 (87)	We have given thee seven of the oft-repeated, and the mighty Koran
15:91 (91)	who have broken the Koran into fragments
16:98 (100)	when thou recitest the Koran, seek refuge in God from the accursed Satan
17:9 (9)	surely this Koran guides to the way that is straightest
17:41 (43)	We have turned about in this Koran, that they may remember
17:45 (47)	when thou recitest the Koran, We place between thee, and those ... a curtain
17:46 (49)	when thou mentionest thy Lord only in the Koran, they turn in their traces in aversion
17:60 (62)	the vision that We showed thee and the tree cursed in the Koran to be only a trial
17:78 (80)	perform the prayer at the sinking of the sun to the darkening of the night and the recital of dawn
17:78 (80)	surely the recital of dawn is witnessed
17:82 (84)	We send down, of the Koran, that which is a healing and a mercy
17:88 (90)	if men and jinn banded together to produce the like of this Koran
17:89 (91)	We have indeed turned about for men in this Koran every manner of similitude
17:106 (107)	a Koran We have divided, for thee to recite it to mankind
18:54 (52)	We have indeed turned about for men in this Koran every manner of similitude
20:2 (1)	We have not sent down the Koran upon thee for thee to be unprosperous
20:113 (112)	even so We have sent it down as an Arabic Koran
20:114 (113)	hasten not with the Koran ere its revelation is accomplished unto thee
25:30 (32)	my people have taken this Koran as a thing to be shunned
25:32 (34)	why has the Koran not been sent down upon him all at once?
27:1 (1)	those are the signs of the Koran and a Manifest Book
27:6 (6)	thou receivest the Koran from One All-wise, All-knowing
27:76 (78)	surely this Koran relates to the Children of Israel most of that
27:92 (94)	and to recite the Koran
28:85 (85)	He who imposed the Recitation upon thee shall surely restore thee
30:58 (58)	We have struck for the people in this Koran every manner of similitude

34:31 (30)	we will not believe in this Koran, nor in that before it
36:2 (1)	by the Wise Koran
36:69 (69)	it is only a Remembrance and a Clear Koran
38:1 (1)	by the Koran, containing the Remembrance
39:27 (28)	We have struck for the people in this Koran every manner of similitude
39:28 (29)	an Arabic Koran, wherein there is no crookedness
41:3 (2)	a Book whose signs have been distinguished as an Arabic Koran for a people having knowledge
41:26 (25)	do not give ear to this Koran, and talk idly about it
41:44 (44)	if We had made it a barbarous Koran, they would have said
42:7 (5)	and so We have revealed to thee an Arabic Koran
43:3 (2)	behold, We have made it an Arabic Koran
43:31 (30)	why was this Koran not sent down upon some man of moment
46:29 (28)	and when We turned to thee a company of jinn giving ear to the Koran
47:24 (26)	what, do they not ponder the Koran?
50:1 (1)	by the glorious Koran
50:45 (45)	therefore remind by the Koran him who fears My threat
54:17 (17)	now We have made the Koran easy for Remembrance
54:22 (22)	now We have made the Koran easy for Remembrance
54:32 (32)	now We have made the Koran easy for Remembrance
54:40 (40)	now We have made the Koran easy for Remembrance
55:2 (1)	has taught the Koran
56:77 (76)	it is surely a noble Koran
59:21 (21)	if We had sent down this Koran upon a mountain, thou wouldst have seen it humbled
72:1 (1)	we have indeed heard a Koran wonderful
73:4 (4)	and chant the Koran very distinctly
73:20 (20)	therefore recite of the Koran so much as is feasible
75:17 (17)	ours it is to gather it, and to recite it
75:18 (18)	so, when We recite it, follow thou its recitation
76:23 (23)	surely We have sent down the Koran on thee
84:21 (21)	when the Koran is recited to them they do not bow
85:21 (21)	nay, but it is a glorious Koran

QURŪʾ n.m.~a menstrual period

2:228 (228)	divorced women shall wait by themselves for three periods

AQRAʾA vb. (IV)~to cause to read, to make someone recite

b) impf. act. (*yuqriʾu*)

87:6 (6)	We shall make thee recite, to forget not

*Q R ʿ

QĀRIʿAH n.f.~a shattering; the Clatterer [Ar]; judgment, disaster, Calamity [Pk]; Noise and Clamour [Ali]; a striking (calamity) [Bl]

13:31 (31)	still the unbelievers are smitten by a shattering for what they wrought
69:4 (4)	Thamood and Ad cried lies to the Clatterer
101:1 (1)	the Clatterer
101:2 (1)	what is the Clatterer?
101:3 (2)	what shall teach thee what is the Clatterer?

*Q R B

QARIBA vb. (I)~to draw nigh, to keep well within, to approach, to come near

b) impf. act. (*yaqrabu*)

2:35 (33)	but draw not nigh this tree, lest you be evildoers
2:187 (183)	those are God's bounds; keep well within them
2:222 (222)	go apart from women during the monthly course, and do not approach them
4:43 (46)	draw not near to prayer when you are drunken
6:151 (152)	and that you approach not any indecency
6:152 (153)	and that you approach not the property of the orphan
7:19 (18)	but come not nigh this tree, lest you be of the evildoers
9:28 (28)	let them not come near the Holy Mosque after this
12:60 (60)	there shall be no measure for you with me, neither shall you come nigh me
17:32 (34)	and approach not fornication
17:34 (36)	do not approach the property of the orphan save in the fairest manner

AQRABŪN n.m. (pl)~kinsmen, nearest kin

2:180 (176)	to make testament in favour of his parents and kinsmen honourably
2:215 (211)	whatsoever good you expend is for parents and kinsmen
4:7 (8)	to the men a share of what parents and kinsmen leave
4:7 (8)	and to the women a share of what parents and kinsmen leave
4:33 (37)	to everyone We have appointed heirs of that which parents and kinsmen leave
4:135 (134)	even though it be against yourselves, or your parents and kinsmen
26:214 (214)	and warn thy clan, thy nearest kin

MAQRABAH n.f.~(with *dhū*) kinsman, near of kin

90:15 (15)	to an orphan near of kin

QARĪB n.m.~(adj.; comp. *aqrab*) near, nigh; (adv) shortly

2:186 (182)	I am near to answer the call of the caller
2:214 (210)	ah, but surely God's help is nigh
2:237 (238)	yet that you should remit is nearer to godfearing
3:167 (160)	they that day were nearer to unbelief than to belief
4:11 (12)	you know not which out of them is nearer in profit to you
4:17 (21)	God shall turn only towards those who do evil in ignorance, then shortly repent
4:77 (79)	why not defer us to a near term?
5:8 (11)	be equitable — that is nearer to godfearing
5:82 (85)	the nearest of them in love to the believers are those who say
7:56 (54)	surely the mercy of God is nigh to the good-doers
9:42 (42)	were it a gain near at hand, and an easy journey
11:61 (64)	surely my Lord is nigh, and answers prayer
11:64 (67)	touch her not with evil, lest you be seized by a nigh chastisement
11:81 (83)	their promised time is the morning; is the morning not nigh?
13:31 (31)	or it alights nigh their habitation, until God's promise comes
14:44 (45)	our Lord, defer us to a near term
16:77 (79)	the matter of the Hour is as a twinkling of the eye, or nearer
17:51 (53)	it is possible that it may be nigh
17:57 (59)	seeking the means to come to their Lord, which of them shall be nearer
18:24 (23)	it may be that my Lord will guide me unto something nearer to rectitude
18:81 (80)	in exchange one better than he in purity, and nearer in tenderness
21:109 (109)	even though I know not whether near or far is that you are promised
22:13 (13)	He calls upon him who is likelier to hurt him, rather than to profit him

33:63 (63)	what shall make thee know? Haply the Hour is nigh
34:50 (49)	He is All-hearing, Ever-nigh
34:51 (50)	they are seized from a place near at hand
42:17 (16)	what shall make thee know? Haply the Hour is nigh
48:18 (18)	He sent down the Shechina upon them, and rewarded them with a nigh victory
48:27 (27)	He knew what you knew not, and appointed ere that a nigh victory
50:16 (15)	We are nearer to him than the jugular vein
50:41 (40)	listen thou for the day when the caller shall call from a near place
56:85 (84)	We are nigher him than you, but you do not see Us)
59:15 (15)	like those who a short time before them tasted the mischief of their action
61:13 (13)	other things you love, help from God and a nigh victory
63:10 (10)	if only Thou wouldst defer me unto a near term
70:7 (7)	but We see it is nigh
72:25 (26)	I do not know whether that which you are promised is nigh
78:40 (40)	We have warned you of a nigh chastisement

QURBÁ n.f.~kinship; (with *dhū* or *ulū*) kinsmen, kin

2:83 (77)	and to be good to parents, and the near kinsman
2:177 (172)	to give of one's substance, however cherished, to kinsmen, and orphans
4:8 (9)	when the division is attended by kinsmen and orphans and the poor
4:36 (40)	be kind to parents, and the near kinsman
4:36 (40)	and to the neighbour who is of kin
5:106 (105)	we will not sell it for a price, even though it were a near kinsman
6:152 (153)	when you speak, be just, even if it should be to a near kinsman
8:41 (42)	whatever booty you take, the fifth of it is God's, and the Messenger's, and the near kinsman's
9:113 (114)	to ask pardon for the idolaters, even though they be near kinsmen
16:90 (92)	surely God bids to justice and good-doing and giving to kinsmen
17:26 (28)	give the kinsman his right, and the needy
24:22 (22)	let not those of you who possess bounty and plenty swear off giving kinsmen
30:38 (37)	give the kinsman his right, and the needy, and the traveller
35:18 (19)	not a thing of it will be carried, though he be a near kinsman
42:23 (22)	I do not ask of you a wage for this, except love for the kinsfolk
59:7 (7)	belongs to God, and His Messenger, and the near kinsman

QURBAH n.f. (pl. *qurubāt*)~an offering

9:99 (100)	take what they expend for offerings bringing them near to God
9:99 (100)	surely they are an offering for them

QURBĀN n.m.~a sacrifice; a mediator, a way of approach

3:183 (179)	we believe not any Messenger until he brings to us a sacrifice
5:27 (30)	recite thou to them the story of the two sons of Adam truthfully, when they offered a sacrifice
46:28 (27)	that they had taken to themselves as mediators, gods apart from God

QARRABA vb. (II)~to offer, to bring near, to lay or set something (as offering) before someone. (pcple. pass.) that which is brought nigh, which is near stationed

a) perf. act.

5:27 (30)	recite thou to them the story of the two sons of Adam truthfully, when they offered a sacrifice
19:52 (53)	and We brought him near in communion
51:27 (27)	and he laid it before them saying

b) impf. act. (*yuqarribu*)

34:37 (36) it is not your wealth nor your children that shall bring you nigh in nearness to Us
39:3 (4) we only serve them that they may bring us nigh in nearness to God

h) pcple. pass. (*muqarrab*)

3:45 (40) Jesus, son of Mary; high honoured shall he be in this world and the next
4:172 (170) neither the angels who are near stationed to Him
7:114 (111) yes, indeed; and you shall be among the near-stationed
26:42 (41) yes indeed; and you shall then be among the near-stationed
56:11 (11) those are they brought nigh the Throne
56:88 (87) if he be of those brought nigh the Throne
83:21 (21) witnessed by those brought nigh
83:28 (28) a fountain at which do drink those brought nigh

IQTARABA vb. (VIII)~to draw or be nigh

a) perf. act.

7:185 (184) and that it may be their term is already nigh
21:1 (1) nigh unto men has drawn their reckoning
21:97 (97) and nigh has drawn the true promise, and behold
54:1 (1) the Hour has drawn nigh: the moon is split

c) impv. (*iqtarib*)

96:19 (19) do thou not obey him, and bow thyself, and draw nigh

*Q R D

QIRADAH n.m. (pl. of *qird*)~apes

2:65 (61) be you apes, miserably slinking
5:60 (65) and made some of them apes and swine
7:166 (166) be you apes, miserably slinking

*Q R Ḍ

QARAḌA vb. (I)~to pass someone or something, to turn away from. (n.vb.) a loan

b) impf. act. (*yaqriḍu*)

18:17 (16) and, when it set, passing them by on the left

f) n.vb. (*qarḍ*)

2:245 (246) who is he that will lend God a good loan
5:12 (15) believe in My Messengers and succour them, and lend to God a good loan
57:11 (11) who is he that will lend to God a good loan
57:18 (17) who make freewill offerings and have lent to God a good loan
64:17 (17) if you lend to God a good loan, He will multiply it for you
73:20 (20) perform the prayer, and pay the alms, and lend to God a good loan

AQRAḌA vb. (IV)~to lend

a) perf. act.

5:12 (15) believe in My Messengers and succour them, and lend to God a good loan
57:18 (17) who make freewill offerings and have lent to God a good loan

b) impf. act. (*yuqriḍu*)

2:245 (246) who is he that will lend God a good loan
57:11 (11) who is he that will lend to God a good loan
64:17 (17) if you lend to God a good loan, He will multiply it for you

c) impv. (*aqriḍ*)

73:20 (20) perform the prayer, and pay the alms, and lend to God a good loan

*Q R F

IQTARAFA vb. (VIII)~to gain, to earn. (pcple. act.) one who gains

a) perf. act.

9:24 (24) your clan, your possessions that you have gained

b) impf. act. (*yaqtarifu*)

6:113 (113) and that they may gain what they are gaining
6:120 (120) the earners of sin shall be recompensed for what they have earned
42:23 (22) whosoever gains a good deed, We shall give him increase of good in respect of it

g) pcple. act. (*muqtarif*)

6:113 (113) and that they may gain what they are gaining

*Q R Ḥ

QARAḤA vb. (I)~(n.vb.) a wound, an ulcer

f) n.vb. (*qarḥ*)

3:140 (134) if a wound touches you
3:140 (134) a like wound already has touched the heathen
3:172 (166) those who answered God and the Messenger after the wound had smitten them

*Q R N

QARN n.m. (pl. *qurūn*)~a generation; a horn

6:6 (6) have they not regarded how We destroyed before them many a generation
6:6 (6) We destroyed them because of their sins, and raised up after them another generation

10:13 (14)	We destroyed the generations before you when they did evil
11:116 (118)	if there had been, of the generations before you, men of a remainder
17:17 (18)	how many generations We have destroyed after Noah
19:74 (75)	and how many a generation We destroyed before them
19:98 (98)	and how many a generation We destroyed before them
20:51 (53)	and what of the former generations?
20:128 (128)	is it not a guidance to them, how many generations We destroyed before them
23:31 (32)	thereafter, after them, We produced another generation
23:42 (44)	thereafter, after them, We produced other generations
25:38 (40)	Ad, and Thamood, and the men of Er-Rass, and between that generations a many
28:43 (43)	We gave Moses the Book, after that We had destroyed the former generations
28:45 (45)	but We raised up generations, and long their lives continued
28:78 (78)	did he not know that God had destroyed before him generations of men stronger than he
32:26 (26)	is it not a guidance to them, how many generations We destroyed before them
36:31 (30)	have they not seen how many generations We have destroyed before them
38:3 (2)	how many a generation We destroyed before them
46:17 (16)	I shall be brought forth, when already generations have passed away before me
50:36 (35)	how many a generation We destroyed before them that was stronger in valour

DHUL-QARNAYN n.prop.~Dhool Qarnain (Alexander the Great)

18:83 (82)	they will question thee concerning Dhool Karnain
18:86 (85)	O Dhool Karnain, either thou shalt chastise them
18:94 (93)	O Dhool Karnain, behold

QARĪN n.m. (pl. *qoranā'*)~a comrade

4:38 (42)	whosoever has Satan for a comrade
4:38 (42)	an evil comrade is he
37:51 (49)	one of them says, 'I had a comrade'
41:25 (24)	We have allotted them comrades
43:36 (35)	to him We assign a Satan for comrade
43:38 (37)	an evil comrade
50:23 (22)	his comrade shall say, 'This is what I have, made ready'
50:27 (26)	his comrade shall say, 'Our Lord, I made him not insolent'

QĀRŪN n.prop.~Korah

28:76 (76)	now Korah was of the people of Moses
28:79 (79)	would that we possessed the like of that Korah has been given
29:39 (38)	and Korah, and Pharaoh, and Haman
40:24 (25)	to Pharaoh, Haman and Korah; they said

QARRANA vb. (II)~(pcple. pass.) one who is coupled, one who is bound

h) pcple. pass. (*muqarran*)

14:49 (50)	thou shalt see the sinners that day coupled in fetters
25:13 (14)	when they are cast, coupled in fetters, into a narrow place
38:38 (37)	and others also, coupled in fetters

AQRANA vb. (IV)~(pcple. act.) one who is equal to another, who is a peer, a match

g) pcple. act. (*muqrin*)

43:13 (12)	and we ourselves were not equal to it

IQTARANA vb. (VIII)~(pcple. act.) one who is conjoined or connected with another

g) pcple. act. (*muqtarin*)

43:53 (53) why then have bracelets of gold not been cast on him, or angels not come with him conjoined?

*Q R R

QARRA vb. (I)~to remain in one place, to settle down; (*qarra ʿaynan*) to rejoice, be comforted. (n.vb.) stability; establishment, lodging, fixed place, receptacle, a hollow

b) impf. act. (*yaqarru*)

20:40 (41) We returned thee to thy mother that she might rejoice
28:13 (12) We returned him to his mother, that she might be comforted
33:51 (51) it is likelier they will be comforted, and not sorrow

c) impv. (*qarra*)

9:26 (26) eat therefore, and drink, and be comforted
33:33 (33) remain in your houses; and display not your finery

f) n.vb. (*qarār*)

14:26 (31) a corrupt tree — uprooted from the earth, having no stablishment
14:29 (34) Gehenna, wherein they are roasted; an evil stablishment
23:13 (13) then We set him, a drop, in a receptacle secure
23:50 (52) and gave them refuge upon a height, where was a hollow and a spring
27:61 (62) He who made the earth a fixed place and set amidst it rivers
38:60 (60) you forwarded it for us how evil a stablishment
40:39 (42) the world to come is the abode of stability
40:64 (66) it is God who made for you the earth a fixed place
77:21 (21) that We laid within a sure lodging

MUSTAQARR n.m.~a sojourn, a lodging place, a resting place; a recourse, a time appointed

2:36 (34) in the earth a sojourn shall be yours, and enjoyment for a time
6:67 (66) every tiding has its time appointed
6:98 (98) it is He who produced you from one living soul, and then a lodging-place
7:24 (23) in the earth a sojourn shall be yours, and enjoyment
11:6 (8) He knows its lodging-place and its repository
25:24 (26) better shall be their lodging, fairer their resting-place
25:66 (66) evil it is as a lodging-place and an abode
25:76 (76) fair it is as a lodging-place and an abode
36:38 (38) the sun — it runs to a fixed resting-place
75:12 (12) upon that day the recourse shall be to thy Lord

QAWĀRĪR n.f. (pl. of *qārūrah*)~crystal

27:44 (44) it is a pavilion smoothed of crystal
76:15 (15) there shall be passed around them vessels of silver, and goblets of crystal
76:16 (16) crystal of silver that they have measured very exactly

QURRAH n.f.~coolness; (*qurrat ʿayn*) a refreshment, comfort, consolation

25:74 (74) our Lord, give us refreshment of our wives and seed
28:9 (8) he will be a comfort to me and thee. Slay him not
32:17 (17) no soul knows what comfort is laid up for them secretly

AQARRA vb. (IV)~to confirm, to agree, to establish

a) perf. act.

2:84 (78) then you confirmed it and yourselves bore witness
3:81 (75) and you shall help him; do you agree?
3:81 (75) they said, 'We do agree'

b) impf. act. (*yuqirru*)

22:5 (5) We establish in the wombs what We will, till a stated term

ISTAQARRA vb. (X)~to stay fast, to settle. (pcple. act.) that which has settled

a) perf. act.

7:143 (139) behold the mountain — if it stays fast in its place

g) pcple. act. (*mustaqirr*)

27:40 (40) then, when he saw it settled before him, he said
54:3 (3) they have cried lies, and followed their caprices; but every matter is settled
54:38 (38) in the morning early there came upon them a settled chastisement

*Q R SH

QURAYSH n.prop.~Koraish (various spellings)

106:1 (1) for the composing of Koraish

*Q R Ṭ S

6:7 (7) had We sent down on thee a Book on parchment
6:91 (91) you put it into parchments, revealing them, and hiding much

*Q R Y

QARYAH n.f. (pl. *qurá*)~city, town

2:58 (55) enter this township, and eat easefully of it wherever you will
2:259 (261) such as he who passed by a city that was fallen down upon its turrets
4:75 (77) bring us forth from this city whose people are evildoers
6:92 (92) and for thee to warn the Mother of Cities and those about her
6:123 (123) even so We appointed in every city great ones among its sinners
6:131 (131) that is because thy Lord would never destroy the cities unjustly
7:4 (3) how many a city We have destroyed
7:82 (80) expel them from your city
7:88 (86) we will surely expel thee, O Shuaib, and those who believe with thee, from our city
7:94 (92) We have sent no Prophet to any city but that We seized its people with misery
7:96 (94) yet had the peoples of the cities believed and been godfearing

7:97 (95)	do the people of the cities feel secure Our might shall not come upon them
7:98 (96)	do the people of the cities feel secure Our might shall not come upon them
7:101 (99)	those cities We relate to thee tidings of
7:161 (161)	dwell in this township and eat of it wherever you will
7:163 (163)	question them concerning the township which was bordering the sea
10:98 (98)	why was there never a city that believed, and its belief profited it?
11:100 (102)	that is of the tidings of the cities We relate to thee
11:102 (104)	such is the seizing of thy Lord, when He seizes the cities that are evildoing
11:117 (119)	yet thy Lord would never destroy the cities unjustly
12:82 (82)	enquire of the city wherein we were, and the caravan in which we approached
12:109 (109)	We sent not forth any before thee, but men We revealed to of the people living in the cities
15:4 (4)	never a city have We destroyed, but it had a known decree
16:112 (113)	God has struck a similitude: a city that was secure
17:16 (17)	when We desire to destroy a city
17:58 (60)	no city is there, but We shall destroy it before the Day of Resurrection
18:59 (58)	and those cities, We destroyed them when they did evil
18:77 (76)	when they reached the people of a city, they asked the people for food
21:6 (6)	not one city that We destroyed before them believed
21:11 (11)	how many a city that was evildoing We have shattered
21:74 (74)	we delivered him from the city that had been doing deeds of corruption
21:95 (95)	there is a ban upon any city that We have destroyed
22:45 (44)	how many a city We have destroyed in its evildoing
22:48 (47)	how many a city I have respited in its evildoing
25:40 (42)	they have come by the city that was rained on by an evil rain
25:51 (53)	if We had willed, We would have raised up in every city a warner
26:208 (208)	never a city We destroyed, but it had warners
27:34 (34)	kings, when they enter a city, disorder it
27:56 (57)	expel the folk of Lot from your city
28:58 (58)	how many a city We have destroyed that flourished in insolent ease
28:59 (59)	yet thy Lord never destroyed the cities
28:59 (59)	We never destroyed the cities, save that their inhabitants were evildoers
29:31 (30)	We shall destroy the people of this city
29:34 (33)	We shall send down upon the people of this city wrath out of heaven
34:18 (17)	We set, between them and the cities that We have blessed
34:18 (17)	cities apparent and well We measured the journey between them
34:34 (33)	We sent no warner into any city except its men who lived at ease said
36:13 (12)	a similitude — the inhabitants of the city, when the Envoys came to it
42:7 (5)	that thou mayest warn the Mother of Cities and those who dwell about it
43:23 (22)	We sent never before thee any warner into any city
43:31 (30)	why was this Koran not sent down upon some man of moment in the two cities?
46:27 (26)	and We destroyed the cities about you
47:13 (14)	how many a city that was stronger in might
47:13 (14)	than thy city which has expelled thee have We destroyed
59:7 (7)	whatsoever spoils of war God has given to His Messenger from the people of the cities
59:14 (14)	they will not fight against you all together except in fortified cities
65:8 (8)	how many a city turned in disdain from the commandment of its Lord

*Q S M

QASAMA vb. (I)~to divide. (pcple. pass.) that which is set or appointed

a) perf. act.

43:32 (31) We have divided between them their livelihood in the present life

b) impf. act. (*yaqsimu*)

43:32 (31) is it they who divide the mercy of thy Lord?

h) pcple. pass. (*maqsūm*)

15:44 (44) seven gates it has, and unto each gate a set portion of them belongs

QASAM n.m.~an oath

56:76 (75) that is indeed a mighty oath, did you but know it)
89:5 (4) is there in that an oath for a mindful man?

QISMAH n.f.~division

4:8 (9) when the division is attended by kinsmen and orphans and the poor
53:22 (22) that were indeed an unjust division
54:28 (28) tell them that the water is to be divided between them

QASSAMA vb. (II)~(pcple. act.) a partitioner

g) pcple. act. (*muqassim*)

51:4 (4) and the partitioners [by command]

QĀSAMA vb. (III)~to swear (an oath) to someone

a) perf. act.

7:21 (20) he swore to them, 'Truly, I am for you a sincere adviser'

AQSAMA vb. (IV)~to swear (an oath)

a) perf. act.

5:53 (58) are these the ones who swore by God most earnest oaths
6:109 (109) they have sworn by God the most earnest oaths
7:49 (47) are these the ones that you swore God would never reach with mercy?
14:44 (46) did you not swear aforetime there should be no removing for you?
16:38 (40) they have sworn by God the most earnest oaths
24:53 (52) they have sworn by God the most earnest oaths
35:42 (40) they have sworn by God the most earnest oaths
68:17 (17) even as We tried the owners of the garden when they swore they would pluck in the morning

b) impf. act. (*yuqsimu*)

5:106 (105) they shall swear by God, if you are doubtful
5:107 (106) they shall swear by God, Our testimony is truer
24:53 (52) do not swear; honourable obedience is sufficient
30:55 (54) upon the day when the Hour is come, the sinners shall swear
56:75 (74) No! I swear by the fallings of the stars
69:38 (38) No! I swear by that you see
70:40 (40) No! I swear by the Lord of the Easts and the Wests
75:1 (1) No! I swear by the Day of Resurrection
75:2 (2) No! I swear by the reproachful soul

81:15 (15) No! I swear by the slinkers
84:16 (16) No! I swear by the twilight
90:1 (1) No! I swear by this land

TAQĀSAMA vb. (VI)~to swear to one another

c) impv. (*taqāsam*)

27:49 (50) they said, 'Swear you, one to another, by God'

IQTASAMA vb. (VIII)~(pcple. act.) a partitioner

g) pcple. act. (*muqtasim*)

15:90 (90) so We sent it down to the partitioners

ISTAQSAMA vb. (X)~to partition

b) impf. act. (*yastaqsimu*)

5:3 (4) and partition by the divining arrows

*Q S R

QASWARAH n.m.~a lion

74:51 (51) fleeing before a lion

*Q S S

QISSĪS n.m.~a (Christian) priest

5:82 (85) because some of them are priests and monks, and they wax not proud

*Q S Ṭ

QASAṬA vb. (I)~(pcple. act.) one who swerves from justice, one who deviates

g) pcple. act. (*qāsiṭ*)

72:14 (14) some of us have surrendered, and some of us have deviated
72:15 (15) as for those who have deviated, they have become firewood for Gehenna

AQSAṬ n.m. (comp. adj)~more equitable

2:282 (282) that is more equitable in God's sight, more upright for testimony
33:5 (5) call them after their true fathers; that is more equitable in the sight of God

QISṬ n.m.~justice

3:18 (16) upholding justice; there is no god but He
3:21 (20) slay such men as bid to justice

4:127 (126)	and the oppressed children, and that you secure justice for orphans
4:135 (134)	O believers, be you securers of justice, witnesses for God
5:8 (11)	O believers, be you steadfast before God, witnesses for justice
5:42 (46)	and if thou judgest, judge justly between them
6:152 (153)	and fill up the measure and the balance with justice
7:29 (28)	say: 'My Lord has commanded justice'
10:4 (4)	that He may recompense those who believe and do deeds of righteousness, justly
10:47 (48)	when their Messenger comes, justly the issue is decided between them
10:54 (55)	when they see the chastisement, and justly the issue is decided between them
11:85 (86)	O my people, fill up the measure and the balance justly
21:47 (48)	We shall set up the just balances for the Resurrection Day
55:9 (8)	and weigh with justice, and skimp not in the Balance.)
57:25 (25)	We sent down with them the Book and the Balance so that men might uphold justice

AQSAṬA vb. (IV)~to act justly, to be just. (pcple. act.) one who is just

b) impf. act. (*yuqsiṭu*)

4:3 (3)	if you fear that you will not act justly towards the orphans
60:8 (8)	you should be kindly to them, and act justly towards them

c) impv. (*aqsiṭ*)

49:9 (9)	set things right between them equitably, and be just

g) pcple. act. (*muqsiṭ*)

5:42 (46)	God loves the just
49:9 (9)	God loves the just
60:8 (8)	God loves the just

*Q S Ṭ S

QISṬĀS n.m.~a balance

17:35 (37)	weigh with the straight balance; that is better
26:182 (182)	and weigh with the straight balance

*Q S W

QASĀ vb. (I)~to be or become hard. (n.vb.) hardness; (*ashadd qaswah*) harder. (pcple. act.) one who is hard

a) perf. act.

2:74 (69)	then your hearts became hardened thereafter and are like stones
6:43 (43)	their hearts were hard, and Satan decked out fair to them what they were doing
57:16 (15)	so that their hearts have become hard, and many of them are ungodly

f) n.vb. (*qaswah*)

2:74 (69)	and are like stones, or even yet harder

g) pcple. act. (*qāsī*)

5:13 (16) for their breaking their compact We cursed them and made their hearts hard
22:53 (52) a trial for those in whose hearts is sickness, and those whose hearts are hard
39:22 (23) woe to those whose hearts are hardened against the remembrance of God

*Q SH ʿ R

IQSHAʿARRA vb. (quad IV)~to shiver

b) impf. act. (*yaqshaʿirru*)

39:23 (24) a Book, consimilar in its oft-repeated, whereat shiver the skins of those who fear their Lord

*Q Ṣ D

QAṢADA vb. (I)~to be modest. (n.vb.) the act of showing, direction. (pcple. act.) easy, moderate

c) impv. (*iqṣid*)

31:19 (18) be modest in thy walk, and lower thy voice

f) n.vb. (*qaṣd*)

16:9 (9) God's it is to show the way

g) pcple. act. (*qāṣid*)

9:42 (42) were it a gain near at hand, and an easy journey, they would have followed thee

IQTAṢADA vb. (VIII)~(pcple. act.) just; lukewarm

g) pcple. act. (*muqtaṣid*)

5:66 (70) some of them are a just nation
31:32 (31) but when He has delivered them to the land, some of them are lukewarm
35:32 (29) but of them some wrong themselves, some of them are lukewarm

*Q Ṣ F

QĀṢIF n.m.~a hurricane

17:69 (71) and loose against you a hurricane of wind

*Q Ṣ M

QAṢAMA vb. (I)~to shatter

a) perf. act.

21:11 (11) how many a city that was evildoing We have shattered

*Q Ṣ R

QAṢARA vb. (I)~to shorten. (pcple. act.) restraining, one who restrains. (pcple. pass.) cloistered

b) impf. act. (*yaqṣuru*)

4:101 (102) there is no fault in you that you shorten the prayer

g) pcple. act. (*qāṣir*)

37:48 (47) with them wide-eyed maidens restraining their glances
38:52 (52) and with them maidens restraining their glances
55:56 (56) therein maidens restraining their glances

h) pcple. pass. (*maqṣūr*)

55:72 (72) houris, cloistered in cool pavilions

QAṢR n.m. (pl. *quṣūr*)~a castle, a palace; (77:32) dry faggots [Ar]

7:74 (72) taking to yourselves castles of its plains
22:45 (44) how many a ruined well, a tall palace
25:10 (11) and He shall assign to thee palaces
77:32 (32) that shoots sparks like dry faggots

QAṢṢARA vb. (II)~(pcple. act.) one who cuts short

g) pcple. act. (*muqaṣṣir*)

48:27 (27) you shall enter the Holy Mosque, if God wills, in security, your heads shaved, your hair cut short

AQṢARA vb. (IV)~to stop short, to desist

b) impf. act. (*yuqṣiru*)

7:202 (201) their brothers they lead on into error, then they stop not short

*Q Ṣ Ṣ

QAṢṢA vb. (I)~to relate, to narrate, to tell; to follow. (n.vb.) a story; the act of following

a) perf. act.

4:164 (162) Messengers We have already told thee of before
16:118 (119) those of Jewry — We have forbidden them what We related to thee before
28:25 (25) when he came to him and had related to him the story
40:78 (78) We sent Messengers before thee; of some We have related to thee

b) impf. act. (*yaquṣṣu*)

4:164 (162) and Messengers We have not told thee of
6:57 (57) He relates the truth, and He is the Best of deciders
6:130 (130) did not Messengers come to you from among you, relating to you My signs
7:7 (6) and We shall relate to them with knowledge
7:35 (33) if there should come to you Messengers from among you, relating to you My signs
7:101 (99) those cities We relate to thee tidings of
11:100 (102) that is of the tidings of the cities We relate to thee
11:120 (121) all that We relate to thee of the tidings of the Messengers is that whereby We strengthen thy heart
12:3 (3) We will relate to thee the fairest of stories
12:5 (5) O my son, relate not thy vision to thy brothers
18:13 (12) We will relate to thee their tidings truly
20:99 (99) so We relate to thee stories of what has gone before
27:76 (78) surely this Koran relates to the Children of Israel most of that
40:78 (78) and some We have not related to thee

c) impv. (*quṣṣ* or *uqṣuṣ*)

7:176 (175) who cried lies to Our signs. So relate the story
28:11 (10) and she said to his sister, 'Follow him'

f) n.vb. (*qaṣaṣ*)

3:62 (55) this is the true story
7:176 (175) so relate the story; haply they will reflect
12:3 (3) We will relate to thee the fairest of stories
12:111 (111) in their stories is surely a lesson to men possessed of minds
18:64 (63) so they returned upon their tracks, retracing them
28:25 (25) when he came to him and had related to him the story, he said

QIṢĀṢ n.m.~retaliation

2:178 (173) prescribed for you is retaliation, touching the slain
2:179 (175) in retaliation there is life for you
2:194 (190) holy things demand retaliation
5:45 (49) a tooth for a tooth, and for wounds retaliation

*Q Ṣ W

QAṢĪY n.m. (adj)~distant, far; (comp., *aqṣá*) farther, further

8:42 (43) when you were on the nearer bank, and they were on the farther bank
17:1 (1) who carried His servant by night from the Holy Mosque to the Further Mosque
19:22 (22) so she conceived him, and withdrew with him to a distant place
28:20 (19) then came a man from the furthest part of the city, running
36:20 (19) then came a man from the furthest part of the city, running

*Q T L

QATALA vb. (I)~to kill, to slay; (perf. pass.) May he be slain, Perish he, May death sieze him. (n.vb.) the act of killing, slaying

a) perf. act.

2:72 (67)	when you killed a living soul, and disputed thereon
2:251 (252)	they routed them, by the leave of God, and David slew Goliath
3:183 (180)	why therefore did you slay them, if you speak truly?
4:92 (94)	if any slays a believer by error, then let him set free a believing slave
4:157 (156)	we slew the Messiah, Jesus son of Mary, the Messenger of God
4:157 (156)	yet they did not slay him, neither crucified him
4:157 (156)	they slew him not of a certainty
5:30 (33)	and he slew him, and became one of the losers
5:32 (35)	whoso slays a soul not to retaliate for a soul slain
5:32 (35)	shall be as if he had slain mankind altogether
5:95 (96)	whosoever of you slays it wilfully, there shall be recompense
5:95 (96)	the like of what he has slain, in flocks
6:140 (141)	losers are they who slay their children in folly, without knowledge
8:17 (17)	you did not (slay) them but God slew them
18:74 (73)	they departed; until, when they met a lad, he slew him
18:74 (73)	hast thou slain a soul innocent, and that not to retaliate for a soul slain?
20:40 (41)	then thou slewest a living soul
28:19 (18)	dost thou desire to slay me, even as thou slewest a living soul yesterday?
28:33 (33)	my Lord, I have indeed slain a living soul among them

b) impf. act. (*yaqtulu*)

2:61 (58)	that, because they had disbelieved the signs of God and slain the Prophets unrightfully
2:85 (79)	then there you are killing one another, and expelling a party of you
2:87 (81)	did you become arrogant, and some cry lies to, and some slay?
2:91 (85)	why then were you slaying the Prophets of God
3:21 (20)	those who disbelieve in the signs of God and slay the Prophets without right
3:21 (20)	and slay such men as bid to justice
3:112 (108)	that, because they disbelieved in God's signs, and slew the Prophets without right
4:29 (33)	kill not one another
4:92 (94)	it belongs not to a believer to slay a believer, except it be by error
4:93 (95)	whoso slays a believer wilfully, his recompense is Gehenna
5:27 (30)	'I will surely slay thee,' said one
5:28 (31)	if thou stretchest out thy hand against me, to slay me
5:28 (31)	I will not stretch out my hand against thee, to slay thee
5:70 (74)	some they cried lies to, and some they slew
5:95 (96)	O believers, slay not the game while you are in pilgrim sanctity
6:151 (152)	to be good to your parents, and not to slay your children because of poverty
6:151 (152)	and that you slay not the soul God has forbidden, except by right
7:150 (149)	surely the people have abased me, and wellnigh slain me
8:17 (17)	you did not slay them but God (slew) them
8:30 (30)	when the unbelievers were devising against thee, to confine thee, or slay thee
9:111 (112)	they fight in the way of God; they kill
12:10 (10)	one of them said, 'No, kill not Joseph'
17:31 (33)	slay not your children for fear of poverty
17:33 (35)	slay not the soul God has forbidden, except by right
25:68 (68)	nor slay the soul God has forbidden except by right
26:14 (13)	I fear they will slay me
28:9 (8)	slay him not; perchance he will profit us
28:19 (18)	dost thou desire to slay me
28:20 (19)	Moses, the Council are conspiring to slay thee
28:33 (33)	a living soul among them, and I fear that they will slay me

33:26 (26)	some you slew, some you made captive
40:26 (27)	let me slay Moses, and let him call to his Lord
40:28 (29)	will you slay a man because he says, 'My Lord is God'
60:12 (12)	and will not steal, neither commit adultery, nor slay their children

c) impv. (*uqtul*)

2:54 (51)	now turn to your Creator and slay one another
2:191 (187)	and slay them wherever you come upon them
2:191 (187)	then, if they fight you, slay them
4:66 (69)	had We prescribed for them, saying, 'Slay yourselves'
4:89 (91)	if they turn their backs, take them, and slay them wherever you find them
4:91 (93)	take them, and slay them wherever you come on them
9:5 (5)	slay the idolaters wherever you find them
12:9 (9)	kill you Joseph, or cast him forth into some land
29:24 (23)	the only answer of his people was that they said, 'Slay him, or burn him'
40:25 (26)	slay the sons of those who believe with him

d) perf. pass. (*qutila*)

3:144 (138)	if he should die or is slain, will you turn about on your heels?
3:154 (148)	if we had had a part in the affair, never would we have been slain here
3:156 (150)	if they had been with us, they would not have died and not been slain
3:157 (151)	if you are slain or die in God's way, forgiveness and mercy from God are a better thing
3:158 (152)	if you die or are slain, it is unto God you shall be mustered
3:168 (162)	had they obeyed us, they would not have been slain
3:169 (163)	count not those who were slain in God's way as dead
3:195 (194)	those who suffered hurt in My way, and fought, and were slain
17:33 (35)	whosoever is slain unjustly, We have appointed to his next-of-kin authority
22:58 (57)	those who emigrated in God's way and were slain
47:4 (5)	those who are slain in the way of God, He will not send their works astray
51:10 (10)	perish the conjecturers
74:19 (19)	death seize him, how he determined
74:20 (20)	again, death seize him, how he determined
80:17 (16)	perish Man! How unthankful he is
81:9 (9)	for what sin she was slain
85:4 (4)	slain were the Men of the Pit

e) impf. pass. (*yuqtalu*)

2:154 (149)	say not of those slain in God's way, 'They are dead'
4:74 (76)	whosoever fights in the way of God and is slain
9:111 (112)	they fight in the way of God; they kill and are killed

f) n.vb. (*qatl*)

2:191 (187)	persecution is more grievous than slaying
2:217 (214)	and persecution is more heinous than slaying
3:154 (148)	those for whom slaying was appointed would have sallied forth
3:181 (177)	We shall write down what they have said, and their slaying the Prophets without right
4:155 (154)	in the signs of God, and slaying the Prophets without right
5:30 (33)	then his soul prompted him to slay his brother
6:137 (138)	thus those associates of theirs have decked out fair to many idolaters to slay their children
17:31 (33)	surely the slaying of them is a grievous sin
17:33 (35)	but let him not exceed in slaying; he shall be helped
33:16 (16)	flight will not profit you, if you flee from death or slaying

QATLÁ n.m. (pl. of *qatīl*)~the slain

2:178 (173) O believers, prescribed for you is retaliation, touching the slain

QATTALA vb. (II)~to slaughter. (n.vb.) the act of slaughtering

b) impf. act. (*yuqattilu*)

7:127 (124) we shall slaughter their sons and spare their women
7:141 (137) who were visiting you with evil chastisement, slaying your sons, and sparing your women

d) perf. pass. (*quttila*)

33:61 (61) wheresoever they are come upon they shall be seized and slaughtered all

e) impf. pass. (*yuqattalu*)

5:33 (37) they shall be slaughtered, or crucified

f) n.vb. (*taqtīl*)

33:61 (61) they are come upon they shall be seized and slaughtered <all>

QĀTALA vb. (III)~to fight; (*qātalahum Allāh*) God assail them. (n.vb.) the act of fighting

a) perf. act.

2:191 (187) then, if they fight you, slay them
3:146 (140) many a Prophet there has been, with whom thousands manifold have fought
3:195 (194) those who suffered hurt in My way, and fought, and were slain
4:90 (92) then certainly they would have fought you
9:30 (30) God assail them! How they are perverted
33:20 (20) if they were among you, they would fight but little
48:22 (22) if the unbelievers had fought you, they would have turned their backs
57:10 (10) not equal is he among you who spent, and who fought before the victory
57:10 (10) those are mightier in rank than they who spent and fought afterwards
60:9 (9) God only forbids you as to those who have fought you in religion's cause
63:4 (4) God assail them! How they are perverted

b) impf. act. (*yuqātilu*)

2:190 (186) fight in the way of God with those who fight with you
2:191 (187) but fight them not by the Holy Mosque
2:191 (187) until they should fight you there
2:217 (214) they will not cease to fight with you, till they turn you from your religion
2:246 (247) raise up for us a king, and we will fight in God's way
2:246 (247) that, if fighting is prescribed for you, you will not fight
2:246 (247) they said, 'Why should we not fight in God's way'
3:13 (11) one company fighting in the way of God and another unbelieving
3:111 (107) if they fight with you, they will turn on you
4:74 (76) let them fight in the way of God who sell the present life for the world to come
4:74 (76) whosoever fights in the way of God and is slain
4:75 (77) how is it with you, that you do not fight in the way of God
4:76 (78) the believers fight in the way of God
4:76 (78) the unbelievers fight in the idols' way
4:90 (92) or come to you with breasts constricted from fighting with you
4:90 (92) or fighting their people

4:90 (92) if they withdraw from you, and do not fight you
9:13 (13) will you not fight a people who broke their oaths
9:36 (36) fight the unbelievers totally even as they fight you totally
9:83 (84) you shall not fight with me any enemy
9:111 (112) they fight in the way of God; they kill
48:16 (16) you shall be called against a people possessed of great might to fight them
59:14 (14) they will not fight against you all together except in fortified cities
60:8 (8) God forbids you not, as regards those who have not fought you in religion's cause
61:4 (4) God loves those who fight in His way in ranks
73:20 (20) and others fighting in the way of God

c) impv. (*qātil*)

2:190 (186) and fight in the way of God
2:193 (189) fight them, till there is no persecution
2:244 (245) so fight in God's way
3:167 (160) come now, fight in the way of God, or repel
4:76 (78) fight you therefore against the friends of Satan
4:84 (86) so do thou fight in the way of God
5:24 (27) go forth, thou and thy Lord, and do battle
8:39 (40) fight them, till there is no persecution
9:12 (12) then fight the leaders of unbelief
9:14 (14) fight them, and God will chastise them at your hands
9:29 (29) fight those who believe not in God and the Last Day
9:36 (36) and fight the unbelievers totally
9:123 (124) O believers, fight the unbelievers who are near to you
49:9 (9) if one of them is insolent against the other, fight the insolent one

d) perf. pass. (*qūtila*)

59:11 (11) if you are fought against, we will help you
59:12 (12) and if they are fought against, they will not help them

e) impf. pass. (*yuqātalu*)

22:39 (40) leave is given to those who fight because they were wronged

f) n.vb. (*qitāl*)

2:216 (212) prescribed for you is fighting, though it be hateful to you
2:217 (214) they will question thee concerning the holy month, and fighting in it
2:217 (214) say: 'Fighting in it is a heinous thing'
2:246 (247) might it be that, if fighting is prescribed for you, you will not fight?
2:246 (247) when fighting was prescribed for them, they turned their backs
3:121 (117) when thou wentest forth at dawn from thy people to lodge the believers in their pitches for the battle
3:167 (160) if only we knew how to fight, we would follow you
4:77 (79) as soon as fighting is prescribed for them, there is a party
4:77 (79) our Lord, why hast thou prescribed fighting for us?
8:16 (16) whoso turns his back that day to them, unless withdrawing to fight again
8:65 (66) O Prophet, urge on the believers to fight
33:25 (25) God spared the believers of fighting
47:20 (22) when a clear sura is sent down, and therein fighting is mentioned

IQTATALA vb. (VIII)~to fight one against the other

a) perf. act.

2:253 (254) those who came after him would not have fought one against the other

2:253 (254)	had God willed they would not have fought one against the other
49:9 (9)	if two parties of the believers fight, put things right between them

b) impf. act. (*yaqtatilu*)

28:15 (14)	and found there two men fighting

*Q T R

QATARA vb. (I)~to be parsimonious

b) impf. act. (*yaqturu*)

25:67 (67)	who, when they expend, are neither prodigal nor parsimonious

QATAR n.m. (f. *qatarah*)~(m) dust; (f) darkness

10:26 (27)	neither dust nor abasement shall overspread their faces
80:41 (41)	o'erspread with darkness

QATŪR n.m. (adj)~niggardly

17:100 (102)	man is ever niggardly

AQTARA vb. (IV)~(pcple. act.) one who is needy

g) pcple. act. (*muqtir*)

2:236 (237)	and according to his means the needy man, honourably

*Q TH ʾ

QITHTHĀʾ n.m.~cucumbers

2:61 (58)	green herbs, cucumbers, corn, lentils, onions

*Q Ṭ ʿ

QAṬAʿA vb. (I)~to cut off, to break, to sever, to traverse. (pcple. act.) one who decides. (pcple. pass.) that which is cut off; unfailing; out of reach

a) perf. act.

7:72 (70)	We cut off the last remnant of those who cried lies to Our signs
59:5 (5)	whatever palm-trees you cut down, or left standing upon their roots
69:46 (46)	then We would surely have cut his life-vein

b) impf. act. (*yaqṭaʿu*)

2:27 (25)	such as break the covenant of God after its solemn binding
3:127 (122)	He might cut off a part of the unbelievers or frustrate them
8:7 (7)	God was desiring to verify the truth by His words, and to cut off the unbelievers
9:121 (122)	nor do they expend any sum, small or great, nor do they traverse any valley

13:25 (25) those who break the covenant of God after His compact
22:15 (15) let him stretch up a rope to heaven, then let him sever it
29:29 (28) what, do you approach men, and cut the way

c) impv. (*iqṭaᶜ*)

5:38 (42) the thief, male and female: cut off the hands of both

d) perf. pass. (*quṭiᶜa*)

6:45 (45) the last remnant of the people who did evil was cut off

g) pcple. act. (*qāṭiᶜ*)

27:32 (32) I am not used to decide an affair until you bear me witness

h) pcple. pass. (*maqṭūᶜ*)

15:66 (66) that the last remnant of those should be cut off in the morning
56:33 (32) unfailing, unforbidden

QIṬᶜ n.m.~a part, a watch of the night

11:81 (83) set forth, thou with thy family, in a watch of the night
15:65 (65) set forth, thou with thy family, in a watch of the night

QIṬAᶜ n.f. (pl. of *qiṭᶜah*)~parts, strips, tracts

10:27 (28) as if their faces were covered with strips of night shadowy
13:4 (4) on the earth are tracts neighbouring each to each

QAṬṬAᶜA vb. (II)~to cut, to cut up, to cut off, to strike off, to break, to cleave

a) perf. act.

7:160 (160) We cut them up into twelve tribes, nations
7:168 (167) We cut them up into nations in the earth
12:31 (31) when they saw him, they so admired him that they cut their hands
12:50 (50) what of the women who cut their hands?
47:15 (17) such as are given to drink boiling water, that tears their bowels asunder

b) impf. act. (*yuqaṭṭiᶜu*)

7:124 (121) I shall assuredly cut off alternately your hands and feet
20:71 (74) I shall assuredly cut off alternately your hands and feet
26:49 (49) I shall assuredly cut off alternately your hands and feet
47:22 (24) would you then haply work corruption in the land, and break your bonds of kin?

d) perf. pass. (*quṭṭiᶜa*)

13:31 (30) a Koran whereby the mountains were set in motion, or the earth were cleft
22:19 (20) for the unbelievers, for them garments of fire shall be cut

e) impf. pass. (*yuqaṭṭiᶜu*)

5:33 (37) their hands and feet shall alternately be struck off

TAQAṬṬAᶜA vb. (V)~to be cut asunder, to be broken

a) perf. act.

2:166 (161) they see the chastisement, and their cords are cut asunder

6:94 (94) the bond between you is now broken
21:93 (93) but they split up their affair between them
23:53 (55) but they split in their affair between them into sects

b) impf. act. (*yataqaṭṭaʿu*)

9:110 (111) unless it be that their hearts are cut into pieces

*Q Ṭ F

QUṬŪF n.m. (pl. of *qiṭf*)~clusters

69:23 (23) its clusters nigh to gather
76:14 (14) near them shall be its shades, and its clusters hung meekly down

*Q Ṭ M R

QIṬMĪR n.m.~the skin of a date-stone

35:13 (14) those you call upon, apart from Him, possess not so much as the skin of a date-stone

*Q Ṭ N

YAQṬĪN n.m.~gourds

37:146 (146) We caused to grow over him a tree of gourds

*Q Ṭ R

AQṬĀR n.m. (pl. of *quṭr*)~quarters, confines

33:14 (14) if entrance had been forced against them from those quarters
55:33 (33) if you are able to pass through the confines of heaven and earth

QAṬIRĀN n.m.~pitch

14:50 (51) of pitch their shirts, their faces enveloped by the Fire

QIṬR n.m.~molten brass

18:96 (95) bring me, that I may pour molten brass on it
34:12 (11) We made the Fount of Molten Brass to flow for him

*Q Ṭ Ṭ

QIṬṬ n.m.~a share; a judge's sentence

38:16 (15) hasten to us our share before the Day of Reckoning

*Q W ʿ

QĀʿ n.m. (pl. *qīʿah*)~a level or spacious plain, a hollow

20:106 (106)	then He will leave them a level hollow
24:39 (39)	their works are as a mirage in a spacious plain

*Q W B

QĀB n.m.~a length, a distance

53:9 (9)	two bows'-length away, or nearer

*Q W L

QĀLA vb. (I)~to say, to speak; (with prep. *li-*, usually after the pass. form) to be called, to be named. (n.vb.) word, speech, saying, utterance, a thing said, discourse; argument; greeting; (pl. *aqāwīl*, occurs in 69:44) (pcple. act.) one who says, who speaks

a) perf. act. (not listed)

2:11 (10)	they say, 'We are only ones that put things right'

b) impf. act. (*yaqūlu*, not listed)

2:8 (7)	some men there are who say

c) impv. (*qul*)

2:58 (55)	and enter in at the gate, prostrating, and say, 'Unburdening'
2:80 (74)	Say: 'Have you taken with God a covenant?'
2:83 (77)	and speak good to men, and perform the prayer, and pay the alms
2:91 (85)	Say: 'Why then were you slaying the Prophets of God in former time, if you were believers?'
2:93 (87)	Say: 'Evil is the thing your faith bids you to, if you are believers'
2:94 (88)	Say: 'If the Last Abode with God is yours exclusively'
2:97 (91)	Say: 'Whosoever is an enemy to Gabriel'
2:104 (98)	but say, 'Regard us'; and give ear
2:111 (105)	Such are their fancies. Say: 'Produce your proof, if you speak truly'
2:120 (114)	Say: 'God's guidance is the true guidance'
2:135 (129)	Say thou: 'Nay, rather the creed of Abraham, a man of pure faith'
2:136 (130)	Say you: 'We believe in God, and in that which has been sent down on us'
2:139 (133)	Say: 'Would you then dispute with us concerning God, who is our Lord and your Lord?'
2:140 (134)	Say: 'Have you then greater knowledge, or God?'
2:142 (136)	Say: 'To God belong the East and the West'
2:189 (185)	Say: 'They are appointed times for the people, and the Pilgrimage'
2:215 (211)	Say: 'Whatsoever good you expend is for parents and kinsmen'
2:217 (214)	Say: 'Fighting in it is a heinous thing'
2:219 (216)	Say: 'In both is heinous sin, and uses for men'
2:219 (217)	Say: 'The abundance'
2:220 (218)	Say: 'To set their affairs aright is good'

2:222 (222)	Say: 'It is hurt; so go apart from women during the monthly course'
3:12 (10)	Say to the unbelievers: 'You shall be overthrown, and mustered into Gehenna'
3:15 (13)	Say: 'Shall I tell you of a better than that?'
3:20 (18)	So if they dispute with thee, say: 'I have surrendered my will to God'
3:20 (19)	say to those who have been given the Book and to the common folk: 'Have you surrendered?'
3:26 (25)	Say: 'O God, Master of the Kingdom, Thou givest the Kingdom to whom Thou wilt'
3:29 (27)	Say: 'Whether you hide what is in your breasts or publish it, God knows it'
3:31 (29)	Say: 'If you love God, follow me'
3:32 (29)	Say: 'Obey God, and the Messenger'
3:61 (54)	Say: 'Come now, let us call our sons and your sons, our wives and your wives'
3:64 (57)	Say: 'People of the Book! Come now to a word common between us and you'
3:64 (57)	say: 'Bear witness that we are Muslims'
3:73 (66)	Say: 'The true guidance is God's guidance'
3:73 (66)	Say: 'Surely bounty is in the hand of God'
3:84 (78)	Say: 'We believe in God, and that which has been sent down on us'
3:93 (87)	Say: 'Bring you the Torah now, and recite it'
3:95 (89)	Say: 'God has spoken the truth; therefore follow the creed of Abraham'
3:98 (93)	Say: 'People of the Book, why do you disbelieve in the signs of God?'
3:99 (94)	Say: 'People of the Book, why do you bar from God's way the believer?'
3:119 (115)	Say: 'Die in your rage; God knows the thoughts in the breasts'
3:154 (148)	Say: 'The affair belongs to God entirely'
3:154 (148)	Say: 'Even if you had been in your houses, those for whom slaying was appointed would have sallied forth'
3:165 (159)	Say: 'This is from your own selves'
3:168 (162)	Say: 'Then avert death from yourselves, if you speak truly'
3:183 (180)	Say: 'Messengers have come to you before me bearing clear signs'
4:5 (4)	provide for them and clothe them out of it, and speak to them honourable words
4:8 (9)	make provision for them out of it, and speak to them honourable words
4:63 (66)	and say to them penetrating words about themselves
4:77 (79)	Say: 'The enjoyment of this world is little; the world to come is better for him who fears God'
4:78 (80)	Say: 'Everything is from God'
4:127 (126)	Say: 'God pronounces to you concerning them'
4:176 (175)	Say: 'God pronounces to you concerning the indirect heirs'
5:4 (6)	Say: 'The good things are permitted you'
5:17 (19)	Say: 'Who then shall overrule God in any way?'
5:18 (21)	Say: 'Why then does He chastise you for your sins?'
5:59 (64)	Say: 'People of the Book, do you blame us for any other cause than that we believe in God?'
5:60 (65)	Say: 'Shall I tell you of a recompense with God, worse than that?'
5:68 (72)	Say: 'People of the Book, you do not stand on anything, until you perform the Torah and the Gospel'
5:76 (80)	Say: 'Do you serve, apart from God, that which cannot hurt or profit you?'
5:77 (81)	Say: 'People of the Book, go not beyond the bounds in your religion, other than the truth'
5:100 (100)	Say: 'The corrupt and the good are not equal'
6:11 (11)	Say: 'Journey in the land, then behold how was the end of them that cried lies'
6:12 (12)	Say: 'To whom belongs what is in the heavens and in the earth?'
6:12 (12)	Say: 'It is God's. He has prescribed for Himself mercy'
6:14 (14)	Say: 'Shall I take to myself as protector other than God?'
6:14 (14)	Say: 'I have been commanded to be the first of them that surrender'
6:15 (15)	Say: 'Indeed I fear, if I should rebel against my Lord, the chastisement of a dreadful day'

6:19 (19)	Say: 'What thing is greatest in testimony?'
6:19 (19)	Say: 'God is witness between me and you'
6:19 (19)	Say: 'I do not testify'
6:19 (19)	Say: 'He is only One God, and I am quit of that you associate'
6:37 (37)	Say: 'Surely God is able to send down a sign, but most of them know not'
6:40 (40)	Say: 'What think you? If God's chastisement comes upon you?'
6:46 (46)	Say: 'What think you? If God seizes your hearing and sight?'
6:47 (47)	Say: 'What think you? If God's chastisement comes upon you, suddenly or openly?'
6:50 (50)	Say: 'I do not say to you, "I possess
6:50 (50)	Say: 'Are the blind and the seeing man equal?'
6:54 (54)	say, 'Peace be upon you. Your Lord has prescribed for Himself mercy'
6:56 (56)	Say: 'I am forbidden to serve those you call on apart from God'
6:56 (56)	Say: 'I do not follow your caprices, or else I had gone astray'
6:57 (57)	Say: 'I stand upon a clear sign from my Lord'
6:58 (58)	Say: 'If what you seek to hasten were with me, the matter between you and me would be decided'
6:63 (63)	Say: 'Who delivers you from the shadows of land and sea?'
6:64 (64)	Say: 'God delivers you from them and from every distress'
6:65 (65)	Say: 'He is able to send forth upon you chastisement'
6:66 (66)	Say: 'I am not a guardian over you'
6:71 (70)	Say: 'Shall we call, apart from God, on that which neither profits nor hurts us?'
6:71 (70)	Say: 'God's guidance is the true guidance'
6:90 (90)	Say: 'I ask of you no wage for it; it is but a reminder unto all beings'
6:91 (91)	Say: 'Who sent down the Book that Moses brought as a light and a guidance to men?'
6:91 (91)	Say: 'God' Then leave them alone, playing their game of plunging
6:109 (109)	Say: 'Signs are only with God'
6:135 (135)	Say: 'O my people, act according to your station'
6:143 (144)	Say: 'Is it the two males He has forbidden or the two females?'
6:144 (145)	Say: 'Is it the two males He has forbidden or the two females?'
6:145 (146)	Say: 'I do not find, in what is revealed to me, aught forbidden to him who eats thereof'
6:147 (148)	say: 'Your Lord is of mercy all-embracing'
6:148 (149)	Say: 'Have you any knowledge, for you to bring forth for us?'
6:149 (150)	Say: 'To God belongs the argument conclusive'
6:150 (151)	Say: 'Produce your witnesses, those who testify God has forbidden this'
6:151 (152)	Say: 'Come, I will recite what your Lord has forbidden you'
6:158 (159)	Say: 'Watch and wait; We too are waiting'
6:161 (162)	Say: 'As for me, my Lord has guided me to a straight path, a right religion'
6:162 (163)	Say: 'My prayer, my ritual sacrifice, my living, my dying — all belongs to God'
6:164 (164)	Say: 'Shall I seek after a Lord other than God, who is the Lord of all things?'
7:28 (27)	Say: 'God does not command indecency'
7:29 (28)	Say: 'My Lord has commanded justice'
7:32 (30)	Say: 'Who has forbidden the ornament of God which He brought forth for His servants?'
7:32 (30)	Say: 'These, on the Day of Resurrection, shall be exclusively for those who believed in this present life'
7:33 (31)	Say: 'My Lord has only forbidden indecencies'
7:158 (157)	Say: 'O mankind, I am the Messenger of God to you all'
7:161 (161)	and say, Unburdening; and enter in at the gate, prostrating
7:187 (186)	Say: 'The knowledge of it is only with my Lord'
7:187 (187)	Say: 'The knowledge of it is only with God, but most men know not'
7:188 (188)	Say: 'I have no power to profit for myself, or hurt, but as God will'
7:195 (194)	Say: 'Call you then to your associates; then try your guile on me'

7:203 (202)	Say: 'I follow only what is revealed to me from my Lord'
8:1 (1)	Say: 'The spoils belong to God and the Messenger'
8:38 (39)	Say to the unbelievers, if they give over He will forgive them what is past
8:70 (71)	O Prophet, say to the prisoners in your hands:
9:24 (24)	Say: 'If your fathers, your sons, your brothers, your wives'
9:51 (51)	Say: 'Naught shall visit us but what God has prescribed for us'
9:52 (52)	Say: 'Are you awaiting for aught to come to us but one of the two rewards most fair?'
9:53 (53)	Say: 'Expend willingly, or unwillingly, it shall not be accepted from you'
9:61 (61)	Say: 'An ear of good for you; he believes in God, and believes the believers'
9:64 (65)	Say: 'Mock on; God will bring forth what you fear'
9:65 (66)	Say: 'What, then were you mocking God, and His signs, and His Messenger?'
9:81 (82)	Say: 'Gehenna's fire is hotter, did they but understand'
9:83 (84)	say: 'You shall not go forth with me ever'
9:94 (95)	Say: 'Do not excuse yourselves; we will not believe you'
9:105 (106)	Say: 'Work; and God will surely see your work'
9:129 (130)	So if they turn their backs, say: 'God is enough for me'
10:15 (16)	Say: 'It is not for me to alter it of my own accord'
10:16 (17)	Say: 'Had God willed I would not have recited it to you'
10:18 (19)	Say: 'Will you tell God what He knows not either in the heavens or in the earth?'
10:20 (21)	Say: 'The Unseen belongs only to God'
10:21 (22)	Say: 'God is swifter at devising'
10:31 (32)	Say: 'Who provides you out of heaven and earth?'
10:31 (32)	then say: 'Will you not be godfearing?'
10:34 (35)	Say: 'Is there any of your associates who originates creation, then brings it back again?'
10:34 (35)	Say: 'God — He originates creation, then brings it back again'
10:35 (36)	Say: 'Is there any of your associates who guides to the truth?'
10:35 (36)	Say: 'God — He guides to the truth'
10:38 (39)	Say: 'Then produce a sura like it'
10:41 (42)	If they cry lies to thee, then do thou say: 'I have my work, and you have your work'
10:49 (50)	Say: 'I have no power to profit for myself, or hurt, but as God will'
10:50 (51)	Say: 'Have you considered?'
10:53 (54)	Say: 'Yes, by my Lord! It is true'
10:58 (59)	Say: 'In the bounty of God, and His mercy — in that let them rejoice'
10:59 (60)	Say: 'Have you considered the provision God has sent down for you?'
10:59 (60)	Say: 'Has God given you leave, or do you forge against God?'
10:69 (70)	Say: 'Those who forge against God falsehood shall not prosper'
10:101 (101)	Say: 'Behold what is in the heavens and in the earth!'
10:102 (102)	Say: 'Then watch and wait; I shall be with you watching and waiting'
10:104 (104)	Say: 'O men, if you are in doubt regarding my religion'
10:108 (108)	Say: 'O men, the truth has come to you from you Lord'
11:13 (16)	Say: 'Then bring you ten suras the like of it, forged'
11:35 (37)	Say: 'If I have forged it, upon me falls my sin'
11:121 (122)	And say to the unbelievers: 'Act you according to your station; we are acting'
12:81 (81)	Return you all to your father, and say, 'Father, thy son stole'
12:108 (108)	Say: 'This is my way'
13:16 (17)	Say: 'Who is the Lord of the heavens and of the earth?'
13:16 (17)	Say: 'God'
13:16 (17)	Say: 'Then have you taken unto you others beside Him?'
13:16 (17)	Say: 'Are the blind and the seeing man equal, or are the shadows and the light equal?'
13:16 (17)	Say: 'God is the Creator of everything, and He is the One, the Omnipotent'

13:27 (27)	Say: 'God leads astray whomsoever He will, and He guides to Him all who are penitent'
13:30 (29)	Say: 'He is my Lord — there is no god but He. In Him I have put my trust'
13:33 (33)	Say: 'Name them! Or will you tell Him what He knows not in the earth?'
13:36 (36)	Say: 'I have only been commanded to serve God, and not to associate aught with Him'
13:43 (43)	Say: 'God suffices as a witness between me and you'
14:30 (35)	Say: 'Take your joy! Your homecoming shall be — the Fire!'
14:31 (36)	Say to My servants who believe, that they perform the prayer
15:89 (89)	and say, 'Surely, I am the manifest warner'
16:102 (104)	Say: 'The Holy Spirit sent it down from thy Lord in truth'
17:23 (24)	speak unto them words respectful
17:24 (25)	and say, 'My Lord, have mercy upon them, as they raised me up when I was little'
17:28 (30)	then speak unto them gentle words
17:42 (44)	Say: 'If there had been other gods with Him'
17:50 (53)	Say: 'Let you be stones, or iron,
17:51 (53)	'Who will bring us back?' Say: 'He who originated you the first time'
17:51 (53)	'When will it be?' Say: 'It is possible that it may be nigh'
17:53 (55)	And say to My servants, that they (say) words that are kindlier
17:56 (58)	Say: 'Call on those you asserted apart from Him'
17:80 (82)	say: 'My Lord, lead me in with a just ingoing, and lead me out with a just outgoing'
17:81 (83)	And say: 'The truth has come, and falsehood has vanished away'
17:84 (86)	Say: 'Every man works according to his own manner'
17:85 (87)	Say: 'The Spirit is of the bidding of my Lord'
17:88 (90)	Say: 'If men and jinn banded together to produce the like of this Koran ...'
17:93 (95)	Say: 'Glory be to my Lord! Am I aught but a mortal, a Messenger?'
17:95 (97)	Say: 'Had there been in the earth angels walking at peace ...'
17:96 (98)	Say: 'God suffices as a witness between me and you'
17:100 (102)	Say: 'If you possessed the treasuries of my Lord's mercy ...'
17:107 (108)	Say: 'Believe in it, or believe not'
17:110 (110)	Say: 'Call upon God, or call upon the Merciful'
17:111 (111)	And say: 'Praise belongs to God, who has not taken to Him a son'
18:22 (21)	Say: 'My Lord knows very well their number'
18:24 (23)	say 'It may be that my Lord will guide me unto something nearer to rectitude'
18:26 (25)	Say: 'God knows very well how long they tarried'
18:29 (28)	Say: 'The truth is from your Lord'
18:83 (82)	Say: 'I will recite to you a mention of him'
18:103 (103)	Say: 'Shall We tell you who will be the greatest losers in their works?'
18:109 (109)	Say: 'If the sea were ink for the Words of my Lord ...'
18:110 (110)	Say: 'I am only a mortal the like of you'
19:26 (27)	say, 'I have vowed to the All-merciful a fast'
19:75 (76)	Say: 'Whosoever is in error, let the All-merciful prolong his term for him'
20:44 (46)	yet speak gently to him, that haply he may be mindful
20:47 (49)	go you both to Pharaoh, and say, 'We are the Messengers of thy Lord'
20:105 (105)	Say: 'My Lord will scatter them as ashes'
20:114 (113)	say, 'O my Lord, increase me in knowledge'
20:135 (135)	Say: 'Everyone is waiting; so wait'
21:24 (24)	Say: 'Bring your proof! This is the Remembrance of him who is with me'
21:42 (43)	Say: 'Who shall guard you by night and in the daytime from the All-merciful?'
21:45 (46)	Say: 'I warn you only by the Revelation'
21:108 (108)	Say: 'It is revealed unto me only that your God is One God'
21:109 (109)	say: 'I have proclaimed to you all equally'
22:49 (48)	Say: 'O men, I am only for you a plain warner'

22:68 (67)	say, 'God knows very well what you are doing'
22:72 (71)	Say: 'Shall I tell you of something worse than that?'
23:28 (29)	say, 'Praise belongs to God, who has delivered us'
23:29 (30)	say, 'O my Lord, do Thou harbour me in a blessed harbour'
23:84 (86)	Say: 'Whose is the earth, and whoso is in it?'
23:85 (87)	Say: 'Will you not then remember?'
23:86 (88)	Say: 'Who is the Lord of the seven heavens and the Lord of the mighty Throne?'
23:87 (89)	Say: 'Will you not then be godfearing?'
23:88 (90)	Say: 'In whose hand is the dominion of everything?'
23:89 (91)	Say: 'How then are you bewitched?'
23:93 (95)	Say: 'O my Lord, if Thou shouldst show me that they are promised'
23:97 (99)	say: 'O my Lord, I take refuge in Thee from the evil suggestions of the Satans'
23:118 (118)	say: 'My Lord, forgive and have mercy, for Thou art the best of the merciful'
24:30 (30)	Say to the believers, that they cast down their eyes and guard their private parts
24:31 (31)	say to the believing women, that they cast down their eyes and guard their private parts
24:53 (52)	Say: 'Do not swear; honourable obedience is sufficient'
24:54 (53)	Say: 'Obey God, and obey the Messenger'
25:6 (7)	Say: 'He sent it down, who knows the secret in the heavens and earth'
25:15 (16)	Say: 'Is that better, or the Garden of Eternity?'
25:57 (59)	Say: 'I do not ask of you a wage for this'
25:77 (77)	Say: 'My Lord esteems you not at all were it not for your prayer'
26:16 (15)	say, 'Verily, I am the Messenger of the Lord of all Being'
26:216 (216)	say, 'I am quit of that you do'
27:59 (60)	Say: 'Praise belongs to God, and peace be on His servants whom He has chosen'
27:64 (65)	Say: 'Produce your proof, if you speak truly'
27:65 (66)	Say: 'None knows the Unseen in the heavens and earth except God'
27:69 (71)	Say: 'Journey in the land, then behold how was the end of the sinners'
27:72 (74)	Say: 'It may be that riding behind you already is some part of that you seek to hasten on'
27:92 (94)	say: 'I am naught but a warner'
27:93 (95)	And say: 'Praise belongs to God. He shall show you His signs'
28:49 (49)	Say: 'Bring a Book from God that gives better guidance than these'
28:71 (71)	Say: 'What think you? If God should make the night unceasing over you?'
28:72 (72)	Say: 'What think you? If God should make the day unceasing over you?'
28:85 (85)	Say: 'My Lord knows very well who comes with guidance, and who is in manifest error'
29:20 (19)	Say: 'Journey in the land, then behold how He originated creation'
29:46 (45)	say, 'We believe in what has been sent down to us, and what has been sent down to you'
29:50 (49)	Say: 'The signs are only with God, and I am only a plain warner'
29:52 (51)	Say: 'God suffices as a witness between me and you'
29:63 (63)	Say: 'Praise belongs to God'
30:42 (41)	Say: 'Journey in the land, then behold how was the end of those that were before'
31:25 (24)	Say: 'Praise belongs to God'
32:11 (11)	Say: 'Death's angel, who has been charged with you, shall gather you'
32:29 (29)	Say: 'On the Day of Victory their faith shall not profit the unbelievers'
33:16 (16)	Say: 'Flight will not profit you, if you flee from death or slaying'
33:17 (17)	Say: 'Who is he that shall defend you from God, if He desires evil for you?'
33:28 (28)	say to thy wives: 'If you desire the present life and its adornment, come now, I will make you provision'
33:32 (32)	be not abject in your speech ... but speak honourable words

33:59 (59)	say to thy wives and daughters and the believing women, that they draw their veils close to them
33:63 (63)	Say: 'The knowledge of it is only with God'
33:70 (70)	O believers, fear God, and speak words hitting the mark
34:3 (3)	Say: 'Yes indeed, by my Lord, it shall come to you, by Him who knows the Unseen'
34:22 (21)	Say: 'Call on those you have asserted apart from God'
34:24 (23)	Say: 'Who provides for you out of the heavens and the earth?'
34:24 (23)	(Say): 'Who provides for you out of the heavens and the earth?' Say: 'God'
34:25 (24)	Say: 'You will not be questioned concerning our sins'
34:26 (25)	Say: 'Our Lord will bring us together, then make deliverance between us by the truth'
34:27 (26)	Say: 'Show me those you have joined to Him as associates'
34:30 (29)	Say: 'You have the tryst of a day that you shall not put back by a single hour'
34:36 (35)	Say: 'My Lord outspreads and straitens His provision to whomsoever He will'
34:39 (38)	Say: 'My lord outspreads and straitens His provision to whomsoever He will'
34:46 (45)	Say: 'I give you but one admonition, that you stand unto God, two by two and one by one, and then reflect'
34:47 (46)	Say: 'I have asked no wage of you; that shall be yours'
34:48 (47)	Say: 'My Lord hurls the truth — the Knower of the Unseen'
34:49 (48)	Say: 'Truth has come; falsehood originates not, nor brings again'
34:50 (49)	Say: 'If I go astray, I go astray only to my own loss'
35:40 (38)	Say: 'Have you considered your associates on whom you call, apart from God?'
36:79 (79)	Say: 'He shall quicken them, who originated them the first time'
37:18 (18)	Say: 'Yes, and in all lowliness'
38:65 (65)	Say: 'I am only a warner. There is not any god but God, the One, the Omnipotent'
38:67 (67)	Say: 'It is a mighty tiding'
38:86 (86)	Say: 'I ask of you no wage for it, neither am I of those who take things upon themselves'
39:8 (11)	Say: 'Enjoy thy unbelief a little; thou shalt be among the inhabitants of the Fire'
39:9 (12)	Say: 'Are they equal — those who know and those who know not?'
39:10 (13)	Say: 'My servants who believe, fear your Lord'
39:11 (14)	Say: 'I have been commanded to serve God making my religion His sincerely'
39:13 (15)	Say: 'Truly I fear, if I should rebel against my Lord, the chastisement of a dreadful day'
39:14 (16)	Say: 'God I serve, making my religion His sincerely'
39:15 (17)	Say: 'Surely the losers are they who lose themselves and their families on the Day of Resurrection'
39:38 (39)	Say; 'What think you? That you call upon apart from God?'
39:38 (39)	Say: 'God is enough for me; in Him all those put their trust who put their trust'
39:39 (40)	Say: 'My people, act according to your station; I am acting'
39:43 (44)	Say: 'What, even though they have no power whatever and no understanding?'
39:44 (45)	Say: 'To God belongs intercession altogether'
39:46 (47)	Say: 'O God, Thou originator of the heavens and the earth'
39:53 (54)	Say: 'O my people who have been prodigal against yourselves, do not despair of God's mercy'
39:64 (64)	Say: 'Is it other than God you bid me serve, you ignorant ones?'
40:66 (68)	Say: 'I am forbidden to serve those you call on apart from God'
41:6 (5)	Say: 'I am only a mortal, like you are'
41:9 (8)	Say: 'What, do you disbelieve in Him who created the earth in two days?'
41:13 (12)	say, 'I warn you of a thunderbolt like to the thunderbolt of Ad and Thamood'
41:44 (44)	Say: 'To the believers it is a guidance, and a healing'

41:52 (52)	Say: 'What think you? If it is from God, then you disbelieve in it'
42:15 (14)	And say: 'I believe in whatever Book God has sent down'
42:23 (22)	Say: 'I do not ask of you a wage for this, except love for the kinsfolk'
43:24 (23)	Say: 'What, though I should bring you a better guidance than you found your fathers upon?'
43:81 (81)	Say: 'If the All-merciful has a son, then I am the first to serve him'
43:89 (89)	yet pardon them, and say, 'Peace!'
45:14 (13)	Say unto those who believe, that they forgive those who do not look for the days of God
45:26 (25)	Say: 'God gives you life, then makes you die'
46:4 (3)	Say: 'Have you considered that you call upon apart from God?'
46:8 (7)	Say: 'If I have forged it, you have no power to help me against God'
46:9 (8)	Say: 'I am not an innovation among the Messengers'
46:10 (9)	Say: 'Have you considered? If it be from God, and you disbelieve in it'
48:11 (11)	Say: 'Who can avail you aught against God, if He desires hurt for you?'
48:15 (15)	Say: 'You shall not follow us; so God said before'
48:16 (16)	Say to the Bedouins who were left behind: 'You shall be called against a people possessed of great might'
49:14 (14)	Say: 'You do not believe'
49:14 (14)	rather say, "We surrender"; for belief has not yet entered your hearts
49:16 (16)	Say: 'What, would you teach God what your religion is?'
49:17 (17)	Say: 'Do not count your surrendering as a favour to me'
52:31 (31)	Say: 'Await! I shall be awaiting with you'
56:49 (49)	Say: 'The ancients, and the later folk'
62:6 (6)	Say: 'You of Jewry, if you assert that you are the friends of God ...'
62:8 (8)	Say: 'Surely death, from which you flee, shall encounter you'
62:11 (11)	Say: 'What is with God is better than diversion and merchandise'
64:7 (7)	Say: 'Yes indeed, by my Lord! You shall be raised up'
67:23 (23)	Say: 'It is He who produced you, and appointed for you hearing and sight and hearts'
67:24 (24)	Say: 'It is He who scattered you in the earth, and unto Him you shall be mustered'
67:26 (26)	Say: 'The knowledge is with God; I am only a clear warner'
67:28 (28)	Say: 'What think you? If God destroys me and those with me?'
67:29 (29)	Say: 'He is the All-merciful. We believe in Him, and in Him we put all our trust'
67:30 (30)	Say: 'What think you? If in the morning your water should have vanished into the earth?'
72:1 (1)	Say: 'It has been revealed to me that a company of the jinn gave ear'
72:20 (20)	Say: 'I call only upon my Lord, and I do not associate with Him anyone'
72:21 (21)	Say: 'Surely I possess no power over you, either for hurt or for rectitude'
72:22 (22)	Say: 'From God shall protect me not anyone'
72:25 (26)	Say: 'I do not know whether that which you are promised is nigh'
79:18 (18)	And say, 'Hast thou the will to purify thyself?'
109:1 (1)	Say: 'O unbelievers'
112:1 (1)	Say: 'He is God, One'
113:1 (1)	Say: 'I take refuge with the Lord of the Daybreak'
114:1 (1)	Say: 'I take refuge with the Lord of men'

d) perf. pass. (*qīla*, not listed)

2:11 (10)	when it is said to them, 'Do not corruption in the land'

e) impf. pass. (*yuqālu*)

21:60 (61)	making mention of them, and he was called Abraham

41:43 (43)	naught is said to thee but what already was said to the Messengers
83:17 (17)	then it shall be said to them, 'This is that you cried lies to'

f) n.vb. (*qawl*)

2:59 (56)	then the evildoers substituted a saying
2:113 (107)	so too the ignorant say the like [saying] of them
2:118 (112)	so spoke those before them as [these men say]
2:204 (200)	some men there are whose saying upon the present world pleases thee
2:235 (235)	do not make troth with them secretly without you speak honourable words
2:263 (265)	honourable words, and forgiveness, are better than a freewill offering
3:147 (141)	nothing else they said but [their saying], 'Lord, forgive us our sins'
3:181 (177)	God has heard the saying of those who said
4:5 (4)	and speak to them honourable words
4:8 (9)	and speak to them honourable words
4:9 (10)	let them fear God, and speak words hitting the mark
4:63 (66)	admonish them and say to them penetrating words about themselves
4:108 (108)	while they meditate at night discourse unpleasing to Him
4:148 (147)	God likes not the shouting of evil words unless a man has been wronged
4:155 (154)	and for their saying, 'Our hearts are uncircumcised'
4:156 (155)	and for their unbelief, and their uttering against Mary a mighty calummy
4:157 (156)	and for their saying, 'We slew the Messiah, Jesus son of Mary'
5:63 (68)	why do the masters and the rabbis not forbid them to utter sin?
6:73 (73)	His saying is true, and His is the Kingdom
6:112 (112)	revealing tawdry speech to each other, all as a delusion
7:162 (162)	then the evildoers of them substituted a saying
7:205 (204)	remember thy Lord in thy soul, humbly and fearfully, not loud of voice
9:30 (30)	that is the utterance of their mouths
9:30 (30)	conforming with [the saying of] the unbelievers before them
10:65 (66)	and do not let their saying grieve thee
11:40 (42)	except for him against whom the word has already been spoken
11:53 (56)	we will not leave our gods for what thou sayest
13:5 (5)	surely wonderful is their saying
13:10 (11)	alike of you is he who conceals his saying, and he who proclaims it
13:33 (33)	or in apparent words
14:27 (32)	God confirms those who believe with the firm word
16:40 (42)	the only words We say to a thing, when We desire it
16:86 (88)	they will fling back at them the saying, 'Surely, you are truly liars'
17:16 (17)	then the Word is realized against it, and We destroy it utterly
17:23 (24)	speak unto them words respectful
17:28 (30)	then speak unto them gentle words
17:40 (42)	it is a monstrous thing you are saying
18:93 (92)	he found this side of them a people scarcely able to understand speech
19:34 (35)	Jesus, son of Mary, in word of truth, concerning which they are doubting
20:7 (6)	Be thou loud in thy speech
20:28 (29)	that they may understand my words
20:44 (46)	speak <gently> to him
20:89 (91)	did they not see that thing returned no speech unto them?
20:94 (95)	and thou hast not observed my word
20:109 (108)	him to whom the All-merciful gives leave, and whose speech He approves
21:4 (4)	My Lord knows what is said in the heavens and the earth
21:27 (27)	that outstrip Him not in speech
21:110 (110)	surely He knows what is spoken aloud
22:24 (24)	and they shall be guided unto goodly speech
22:30 (31)	and eschew the speaking of falsehood
23:27 (28)	except for him against whom the word already has been spoken

23:68 (70)	have they not pondered the saying?
24:51 (50)	all that the believers say, when they are called to God
27:19 (19)	but he smiled, laughing at its words
27:82 (84)	when the Word falls on them
27:85 (87)	the Word shall fall upon them because of the evil they committed
28:51 (51)	now We have brought them the Word
28:63 (63)	those against whom the Word is realized
32:13 (13)	but now My Word is realized
33:4 (4)	that is your own saying
33:32 (32)	if you are godfearing, be not abject in your speech
33:32 (32)	but speak honourable words
33:70 (70)	O believers, fear God, and speak words hitting the mark
34:31 (30)	bandying argument the one against the other
36:7 (6)	the Word has been realised against most of them
36:58 (58)	'Peace!' — such is the greeting, from a Lord All-compassionate
36:70 (70)	and that the Word may be realized against
36:76 (76)	So do not let their saying grieve thee
37:31 (30)	So our Lord's Word is realised against us
39:18 (19)	who give ear to the Word and follow the fairest of it
41:25 (24)	so against them has been realized the Word concerning nations that passed away
41:33 (33)	and who speaks fairer than he who calls unto God
46:18 (17)	against whom has been realized the Word concerning nations that passed away
47:21 (22)	obedience, and words honourable
47:30 (32)	thou shalt certainly know them in the twisting of their speech
49:2 (2)	and be not loud in your speech to him
50:18 (17)	not a word he utters, but by him is an observer ready
50:29 (28)	the Word is not changed with Me
51:8 (8)	surely you speak at variance
58:1 (1)	God has heard the words of her that disputes with thee concerning her husband
58:2 (2)	they are surely saying a dishonourable saying, and a falsehood
60:4 (4)	except that Abraham said unto his father
63:4 (4)	but when they speak, thou listenest to their speech
67:13 (13)	Be secret in your speech, or proclaim it
69:40 (40)	it is the speech of a noble Messenger
69:41 (41)	it is not the speech of a poet
69:42 (42)	nor the speech of a soothsayer
69:44 (44)	had he invented against Us any sayings
73:5 (5)	Behold, We shall cast upon thee a weighty word
74:25 (25)	this is nothing but mortal speech
81:19 (19)	truly this is the word of a noble Messenger
81:25 (25)	it is not the word of an accursed Satan
86:13 (13)	surely it is a decisive word

g) pcple. act. (*qā'il*)

12:10 (10)	one [sayer] of them said, 'No, kill not Joseph'
18:19 (18)	one [sayer] of them said, 'How long have you tarried?'
23:100 (102)	nay, it is but a word he speaks
33:18 (18)	those who say to their brothers, 'Come to us'
37:51 (49)	one [sayer] of them says, 'I had a comrade'

QĪL n.m.~speech, saying, discourse

4:122 (121)	God's promise in truth; and who is truer in speech than God?
43:88 (88)	and for his saying, 'My Lord, surely these are a peoplewho believe not'
56:26 (25)	only the saying 'Peace, Peace!'
73:6 (6)	the first part of the night is heavier in tread, more upright in speech

TAQAWWALA vb. (V)~to invent, to fabricate

a) perf. act.

52:33 (33) or do they say, 'He has invented it?'
69:44 (44) had he invented against Us any sayings

*Q W M

QĀMA vb. (I)~to keep vigil, to arise, to rise; to halt, to stand up, to stand over; to come to pass; (with prep. *li-*) to secure something for someone; (with prep. *bi-*) to uphold. (n.vb.) the act of standing, rising. (pcple. act.) one who is standing; coming to pass; (with prep. *bi-*) one who is upholding, one who performs (a duty)

a) perf. act.

2:20 (19) when the darkness is over them, they halt
4:142 (141) when they stand up to pray
4:142 (141) they stand up lazily, showing off to the people
5:6 (8) when you stand up to pray wash your faces
18:14 (13) We strengthened their hearts, when they stood up and said
72:19 (19) when the servant of God stood calling on Him

b) impf. act. (*yaqūmu*)

2:275 (276) those who devour usury shall not rse again
2:275 (276) except as he rises, whom Satan of the touch prostrates
4:102 (103) let a party of them stand with thee
4:127 (126) and that you secure justice for orphans
5:107 (106) then two others shall stand in their place
9:84 (85) pray thou never over any one of them when he is dead, nor stand over his grave
9:108 (109) stand there never
9:108 (109) a mosque that was founded upon godfearing from the first day is worthier for thee to stand in
14:41 (42) upon the day when the reckoning shall come to pass
26:218 (218) who sees thee when thou standest
27:39 (39) I will bring it to thee, before thou risest from thy place
30:12 (11) upon the day when the Hour is come, the sinners shall be confounded
30:14 (13) upon the day when the Hour is come, that day they shall be divided
30:25 (24) of His signs is that the heaven and earth stand firm
30:55 (54) upon the day when the Hour is come, the sinners shall swear
34:46 (45) I give you but one admonition, that you stand unto God
40:46 (49) on the day when the Hour is come: Admit the folk
40:51 (54) upon the day when the witnesses arise
45:27 (26) on the day when the Hour is come, upon that day the vain-doers shall lose
52:48 (48) proclaim the praise of thy Lord when thou arisest
57:25 (25) so that men might uphold justice
73:20 (20) thy Lord knows that thou keepest vigil nearly two-thirds of the night
78:38 (38) upon the day when the Spirit and the angels stand in ranks
83:6 (6) a day when mankind shall stand before the Lord of all Being

c) impv. (*qum*)

2:238 (239) and do you stand obedient to God
73:2 (2) keep vigil the night, except a little
74:2 (2) arise, and warn

f) n.vb. (*qiyām*)

51:45 (45)	they were not able to stand upright, and were not helped

g) pcple. act. (*qā'im*)

3:18 (16)	upholding justice; there is no god but He
3:39 (33)	the angels called to him, standing in the Sanctuary
3:75 (68)	one pound, will not restore it thee, unless ever thou standest over him
3:113 (109)	some of the People of the Book are a nation upstanding
10:12 (13)	he calls Us on his side, or sitting, or standing
11:71 (74)	and his wife was standing by
11:100 (102)	some of them are standing and some stubble
13:33 (33)	He who stands over every soul for what it has earned
18:36 (34)	I do not think that the Hour is coming
22:26 (27)	do thou purify My House for those that shall go about it and those that stand
39:9 (12)	is he who is obedient in the watches of the night, bowing himself and standing
41:50 (50)	this is mine; I think not the Hour is coming
59:5 (5)	whatever palm-trees you cut down, or left standing upon their roots
62:11 (11)	they scatter off to it, and they leave thee standing
70:33 (33)	and perform their witnessings

MAQĀM n.m.~a place, a station; the act of standing

2:125 (119)	take to yourselves Abraham's station for a place of prayer
3:97 (91)	therein are clear signs — the station of Abraham
5:107 (106)	then two others shall stand in their place
10:71 (72)	if my standing here is grievous to you
14:14 (17)	that, for him who fears My station and fears My threat
17:79 (81)	it may be that thy Lord will raise thee up to a laudable station
19:73 (74)	which of the two parties is better in station, fairer in assembly?
26:58 (58)	and treasures and a noble station
27:39 (39)	I will bring it to thee, before thou risest from thy place
37:164 (164)	none of us is there, but has a known station
44:26 (25)	sown fields, and how noble a station
44:51 (51)	surely the godfearing shall be in a station secure
55:46 (46)	such as fears the Station of his Lord, for them shall be two gardens
79:40 (40)	but as for him who feared the Station of his Lord

MUQĀM n.m.~an abode

25:66 (66)	evil it is as a lodging-place and an abode
25:76 (76)	fair it is as a lodging-place and an abode
33:13 (13)	people of Yathrib, there is no abiding here for you
35:35 (32)	who of His bounty has made us to dwell in the abode of everlasting life

QAWĀM n.m.~a just stand

25:67 (67)	neither prodigal nor parsimonious, but between that is a just stand

QAWĪM n.m. (adj.; comp. *aqwam*; pl. *qiyām*)~standing, upright, erect, straight

2:282 (282)	that is more equitable in God's sight, more upright for testimony
3:191 (188)	who remember God, standing and sitting and on their sides
4:46 (49)	it would have been better for them, and more upright
4:103 (104)	remember God, standing and sitting and on your sides
17:9 (9)	surely this Koran guides to the way that is straightest
25:64 (65)	who pass the night prostrate to their Lord and standing
39:68 (68)	then it shall be blown again, and lo, they shall stand, beholding
73:6 (6)	the first part of the night is heavier in tread, more upright in speech

QAWM n.m.~people, folk; (3:140 and 4:104) heathen [Ar]; enemy [Bl]

2:54 (51)	and when Moses said to his people
2:54 (51)	My people, you have done wrong against yourselves
2:60 (57)	and when Moses sought water for his people
2:67 (63)	and when Moses said to his people
2:118 (112)	We have made clear the signs unto a people who are sure
2:164 (159)	surely there are signs for a people having understanding
2:230 (230)	He makes them clear unto a people that have knowledge
2:258 (260)	God guides not the people of the evildoers
2:264 (266)	God guides not the people of the unbelievers
2:286 (286)	help us against the people of the unbelievers
3:86 (80)	how shall God guide a people who have disbelieved after they believed
3:86 (80)	God guides not the people of the evildoers
3:117 (113)	a freezing blast that smites the tillage of a people who wronged themselves
3:140 (134)	if a wound touches you, a like wound already has touched the heathen
3:147 (141)	help us against the people of the unbelievers
4:78 (80)	how is it with this people? They scarcely understand any tiding
4:90 (92)	those that betake themselves to a people who are joined with you
4:90 (92)	with breasts constricted from fighting with you or fighting their people
4:91 (93)	you will find others desiring to be secure from you, and secure from their people
4:92 (94)	if he belong to a people at enmity with you and is a believer
4:92 (94)	if he belong to a people joined with you by a compact
4:104 (105)	faint not in seeking the heathen
5:2 (3)	let not detestation for a people who barred you from the Holy Mosque
5:8 (11)	let not detestation for a people move you not to be equitable
5:11 (14)	when a certain people purposed to stretch against you their hands
5:20 (23)	and when Moses said to his people
5:20 (23)	O my people, remember God's blessing
5:21 (24)	O my people, enter the Holy Land
5:22 (25)	Moses, there are people in it very arrogant
5:25 (28)	so do Thou divide between us and the people of the ungodly
5:26 (29)	so grieve not for the people of the ungodly
5:41 (45)	who listen to falsehood, listen to other folk
5:50 (55)	who is fairer in judgment than God, for a people having sure faith?
5:51 (56)	God guides not the people of the evildoers
5:54 (59)	God will assuredly bring a people He loves
5:58 (63)	that is because they are a people who have no understanding
5:67 (71)	God guides not the people of the unbelievers
5:68 (72)	grieve not for the people of the unbelievers
5:77 (81)	follow not the caprices of a people who went astray before
5:84 (87)	and be eager that our Lord should admit us with the righteous people
5:102 (101)	a people before you questioned concerning them
5:108 (107)	God guides not the people of the ungodly
6:45 (45)	the last remnant of the people who did evil was cut off
6:47 (47)	shall any be destroyed, except the people of the evildoers?
6:66 (66)	Thy people have cried it lies
6:68 (67)	do not sit, after the reminding, with the people of the evildoers
6:74 (74)	I see thee, and thy people, in manifest error
6:77 (77)	if my Lord does not guide me I shall surely be of the people gone astray
6:78 (78)	O my people, surely I am quit of that you associate
6:80 (80)	his people disputed with him
6:83 (83)	that is Our argument, which We bestowed upon Abraham as against his people
6:89 (89)	We have already entrusted it to a people who do not disbelieve in it
6:97 (97)	We have distinguished the signs for a people who know
6:98 (98)	We have distinguished the signs for a people who understand

6:99 (99)	in all this are signs for a people who do believe
6:105 (105)	We may make it clear to a people having knowledge
6:126 (126)	We have distinguished the signs to a people who remember
6:133 (133)	He produced you from the seed of another people
6:135 (135)	O my people, act according to your station
6:144 (145)	God guides not the people of the evildoers
6:147 (148)	His might will never be turned back from the people of the sinners
7:32 (30)	so We distinguish the signs for a people who know
7:47 (45)	do not Thou assign us with the people of the evildoers
7:52 (50)	a guidance and a mercy unto a people that believe
7:58 (56)	We turn about the signs for a people that are thankful
7:59 (57)	and We sent Noah to his people
7:59 (57)	he said, 'O my people, serve God'
7:60 (58)	said the Council of his people, 'We see thee in manifest error'
7:61 (59)	my people, there is no error in me; but I am a Messenger
7:64 (62)	assuredly they were a blind people
7:65 (63)	he said, 'O my people, serve God'
7:66 (64)	said the Council of the unbelievers of his people, 'We see thee in folly'
7:67 (65)	my people, there is no folly in me; but I am a Messenger
7:69 (67)	remember when He appointed you as successors after the people of Noah
7:73 (71)	he said, 'O my people, serve God'
7:75 (73)	said the Council of those of his people who waxed proud
7:79 (77)	O my people, I have delivered to you the Message of my Lord
7:80 (78)	and Lot, when he said to his people
7:81 (79)	no, you are a people that do exceed
7:82 (80)	the only answer of his people was that they said
7:85 (83)	he said, 'O my people, serve God'
7:88 (86)	said the Council of those of his people who waxed proud
7:89 (87)	give true deliverance between us and our people
7:90 (88)	said the Council of those of his people who disbelieved
7:93 (91)	O my people, I have delivered to you the Messages of my Lord
7:93 (91)	how should I grieve for a people of unbelievers?
7:99 (97)	none feels secure against God's devising but the people of the lost
7:109 (106)	said the Council of the people of Pharaoh
7:127 (124)	then said the Council of the people of Pharaoh
7:127 (124)	wilt thou leave Moses and his people to work corruption in the land
7:128 (125)	Said Moses to his people, 'Pray for succour'
7:133 (130)	but they waxed proud and were a sinful people
7:137 (133)	We bequeathed upon the people that were abased all the east and the west
7:137 (133)	We destroyed utterly the works of Pharaoh and his people
7:138 (134)	they came upon a people cleaving to idols they had
7:138 (134)	you are surely a people who are ignorant
7:142 (138)	be my successor among my people
7:145 (142)	take it forcefully, and command thy people to take the fairest
7:148 (146)	the people of Moses took to them, after him, of their ornaments a Calf
7:150 (149)	when Moses returned to his people, angry and sorrowful
7:150 (149)	surely the people have abased me
7:150 (149)	put me not among the people of the evildoers
7:155 (154)	Moses chose of his people seventy men for Our appointed time
7:159 (159)	of the people of Moses there is a nation who guide by the truth
7:160 (160)	We revealed to Moses, when his people asked him for water
7:164 (164)	why do you admonish a people God is about to destroy
7:176 (175)	that is that people's likeness who cried lies to Our signs
7:177 (176)	the likeness of the people who cried lies to Our signs
7:188 (188)	I am only a warner, and a bearer of good tidings, to a people believing

7:203 (202)	guidance, and mercy for a people of believers
8:53 (55)	God would never change His favour that He conferred on a people
8:58 (60)	if thou fearest treachery any way at the hands of a people
8:65 (66)	they are a people who understand not
8:72 (73)	except against a people between whom and you there is a compact
9:6 (6)	that, because they are a people who do not know
9:11 (11)	We distinguish the signs for a people who know
9:13 (13)	will you not fight a people who broke their oaths
9:14 (14)	and bring healing to the breasts of a people who believe
9:19 (19)	God guides not the people of the evildoers
9:24 (24)	God guides not the people of the ungodly
9:37 (37)	God guides not the people of the unbelievers
9:39 (39)	instead of you He will substitute another people
9:53 (53)	you are surely a people ungodly
9:56 (56)	they are not of you; they are a people that are afraid
9:70 (71)	those who were before you — the people of Noah, Ad
9:70 (71)	the people of Abraham, the men of Midian and the subverted cities
9:80 (81)	God guides not the people of the ungodly
9:96 (97)	God will surely not be well-pleased with the people of the ungodly
9:109 (110)	God guides not the people of the evildoers
9:115 (116)	God would never lead a people astray after that He has guided them
9:122 (123)	and to warn their people when they return to them
9:127 (128)	God has turned away their hearts, for that they are a people who do not understand
10:5 (5)	distinguishing the signs to a people who know
10:6 (6)	surely there are signs for a godfearing people
10:13 (14)	so We recompense the people of the sinners
10:24 (25)	even so We distinguish the signs for a people who reflect
10:67 (68)	in that are signs for a people who have ears
10:71 (72)	recite to them the story of Noah when he said to his people
10:71 (72)	my people, if my standing here is grievous to you
10:74 (75)	then We sent forth, after him, Messengers to their people
10:75 (76)	but they waxed proud, and were a sinful people
10:83 (83)	none believed in Moses, save a seed of his people
10:84 (84)	O my people, if you believe in God, in Him put your trust
10:85 (85)	make us not a temptation to the people of the evildoers
10:86 (86)	deliver us by Thy mercy from the people of the unbelievers
10:87 (87)	take you, for your people, in Egypt certain houses
10:98 (98)	except the people of Jonah; when they believed
10:101 (101)	neither signs nor warnings avail a people who do not believe
11:25 (27)	and We sent Noah to his people
11:27 (29)	said the Council of the unbelievers of his people
11:28 (30)	he said, 'O my people, what think you?'
11:29 (31)	O my people, I do not ask of you wealth for this
11:29 (31)	I see you are an ignorant people
11:30 (32)	O my people, who would help me against God, if I drive them away?
11:36 (38)	none of thy people shall believe but he who has already believed
11:38 (40)	whenever a council of his people passed by him they scoffed at him
11:44 (46)	away with the people of the evildoers
11:49 (51)	thou didst not know it, neither thy people, before this
11:50 (52)	he said, 'O my people, serve God'
11:51 (53)	O my people, I do not ask of you a wage for this
11:52 (54)	O my people, ask forgiveness of your Lord, then repent to Him
11:57 (60)	my Lord will make a people other than you successors
11:60 (63)	so away with Ad, the people of Hood
11:61 (64)	he said, 'O my people, serve God'

11:63 (66)	he said, 'O my people, what think you?'
11:64 (67)	O my people, this is the She-camel of God
11:70 (73)	fear not; we have been sent to the people of Lot
11:74 (77)	he was disputing with Us concerning the people of Lot
11:78 (80)	and his people came to him, running towards him
11:78 (80)	O my people, these are my daughters
11:84 (85)	he said, 'O my people, serve God'
11:85 (86)	O my people, fill up the measure and the balance justly
11:88 (90)	He said, 'O my people, what think you?'
11:89 (91)	O my people, let not the breach with me move you
11:89 (91)	so that there smite you the like of what smote the people of Noah
11:89 (91)	or the people of Hood
11:89 (91)	or the people of Salih
11:89 (91)	and the people of Lot are not far away from you
11:92 (94)	he said, 'O my people, is my tribe stronger against you than God?'
11:93 (95)	O my people, act according to your station
11:98 (100)	he shall go before his people on the Day of Resurrection
12:9 (9)	free for you, and thereafter you may be a righteous people
12:37 (37)	I have forsaken the creed of a people who believe not in God
12:87 (87)	of God's comfort no man despairs, excepting the people of the unbelievers
12:110 (110)	Our might will never be turned back from the people of the sinners
12:111 (111)	and a guidance, and a mercy to a people who believe
13:3 (3)	surely in that are signs for a people who reflect
13:4 (4)	surely in that are signs for a people who understand
13:7 (8)	Thou art only a warner, and a guide to every people
13:11 (12)	God changes not what is in a people, until they change what is in themselves
13:11 (12)	whensoever God desires evil for a people, there is no turning it back
14:4 (4)	We have sent no Messenger save with the tongue of his people
14:5 (5)	bring forth thy people from the shadows to the light
14:6 (6)	and when Moses said to his people, Remember God's blessing upon you
14:9 (9)	the people of Noah, Ad, Thamood
14:28 (33)	and caused their people to dwell in the abode of ruin
15:15 (15)	nay, we are a people bewitched
15:58 (58)	they said, 'We have been sent unto a people of sinners'
15:62 (62)	surely you are a people unknown to me
16:11 (11)	surely in that is a sign for a people who reflect
16:12 (12)	surely in that are signs for a people who understand
16:13 (13)	surely in that is a sign for a people who remember
16:59 (61)	as he hides him from the people because of the evil
16:64 (66)	as a guidance and as a mercy to a people who believe
16:65 (67)	surely in that is a sign for a people who have ears
16:67 (69)	surely in that is a sign for a people who understand
16:69 (71)	surely in that is a sign for a people who reflect
16:79 (81)	surely in that are signs for a people who believe
16:107 (109)	God guides not the people of the unbelievers
18:15 (14)	these our people have taken to them other gods
18:86 (84)	he found it setting in a muddy spring, and he found nearby a people
18:90 (89)	he found it rising upon a people for whom We had not appointed any veil
18:93 (92)	he found this side of them a people scarcely able to understand speech
19:11 (12)	so he came forth unto his people from the Sanctuary
19:27 (28)	then she brought the child to her folk carrying him
19:97 (97)	bear good tidings thereby to the godfearing, and warn a people stubborn
20:79 (81)	so Pharaoh had led his people astray, and was no guide to them
20:83 (85)	what has sped thee far from thy people, Moses?
20:85 (87)	We have tempted thy people since thou didst leave them

20:86 (88)	then Moses returned very angry and sorrowful to his people
20:86 (89)	my people, did your Lord not promise a fair promise to you?
20:87 (90)	we were loaded with fardels, even the ornaments of the people
20:90 (92)	my people, you have been tempted by this thing, no more
21:11 (11)	how many a city that was evildoing We have shattered, and set up after it another people
21:52 (53)	when he said to his father and his people
21:74 (74)	they were an evil people, truly ungodly
21:77 (77)	We helped him against the people who cried lies to Our signs
21:77 (77)	they were an evil people, so We drowned them all together
21:78 (78)	judgment concerning the tillage, when the sheep of the people strayed there
21:106 (106)	in this is a Message delivered unto a people who serve
22:42 (43)	the people of Noah cried lies, and Ad and Thamood
22:43 (43)	and the people of Abraham
22:43 (43)	the people of Lot
23:23 (23)	and We sent Noah to his people
23:23 (23)	and he said, 'O my people, serve God'
23:24 (24)	said the Council of the unbelievers of his people
23:28 (29)	praise belongs to God, who has delivered us from the people of the evildoers
23:33 (34)	said the Council of the unbelievers of his people
23:41 (43)	so away with the people of the evildoers
23:44 (46)	so away with a people who do not believe
23:46 (48)	they waxed proud, and they were a lofty people
23:47 (49)	two mortals like ourselves, whose people are our servants
23:94 (96)	O my Lord, put me not among the people of the evildoers
23:106 (108)	our adversity prevailed over us; we were an erring people
25:4 (5)	this is naught but a calumny he has forged, and other folk have helped him to it
25:18 (19)	and were a people corrupt
25:30 (32)	my people have taken this Koran as a thing to be shunned
25:36 (38)	go to the people who have cried lies to Our signs
25:37 (39)	the people of Noah, when they cried lies to the Messengers
26:10 (9)	go to the people of the evildoers
26:11 (10)	the people of Pharaoh; will they not be godfearing?
26:70 (70)	when he said to his father and his people, 'What do you serve?'
26:105 (105)	the people of Noah cried lies to the Envoys
26:117 (117)	he said, 'My Lord, my people have cried me lies'
26:160 (160)	the people of Lot cried lies to the Envoys
26:166 (166)	nay, but you are a people of transgressors
27:12 (12)	among nine signs to Pharaoh and his people
27:12 (12)	they are an ungodly people
27:24 (24)	I found her and her people prostrating to the sun, apart from God
27:43 (43)	for she was of a people of unbelievers
27:46 (47)	O my people, why do you seek to hasten evil before good?
27:47 (48)	nay, but you are a people being proved
27:51 (52)	We destroyed them and their people all together
27:52 (53)	surely in that is a sign for a people who have knowledge
27:54 (55)	and Lot, when he said to his people, 'What, do you commit indecency'
27:55 (56)	no, you are a people that are ignorant
27:56 (57)	the only answer of his people was that they said
27:60 (61)	nay, but they are a people who assign to Him equals
27:86 (88)	surely in that is a sign for a people who are believers
28:3 (2)	We will recite to thee something of the tiding of Moses and Pharaoh truthfully, for a people who believe
28:21 (20)	my Lord, deliver me from the people of the evildoers
28:25 (25)	thou hast escaped from the people of the evildoers

28:32 (32)	for surely they are an ungodly people
28:46 (46)	that thou mayest warn a people to whom no warner came before thee
28:50 (50)	surely God guides not the people of the evildoers
28:76 (76)	now Korah was of the people of Moses
28:76 (76)	when his people said to him, 'Do not exult'
28:79 (79)	so he went forth unto his people in his adornment
29:14 (13)	indeed, We sent Noah to his people
29:16 (15)	and Abraham, when he said to his people, 'Serve God'
29:24 (23)	the only answer of his people was that they said
29:24 (23)	surely in that are signs for a people who believe
29:28 (27)	and Lot, when he said to his people
29:29 (28)	the only answer of his people was that they said
29:30 (29)	he said, 'My Lord, help me against the people that work corruption'
29:35 (34)	We have left thereof a sign, a clear sign, unto a people who understand
29:36 (35)	he said, 'O my people, serve God, and look you for the Last Day'
29:51 (50)	in that is a mercy, and a reminder to a people who believe
30:21 (20)	surely in that are signs for a people who consider
30:23 (22)	surely in that are signs for a people who hear
30:24 (23)	surely in that are signs for a people who understand
30:28 (27)	so We distinguish the signs for a people who understand
30:37 (36)	surely in that are signs for a people who believe
30:47 (46)	We sent before thee Messengers unto their people
32:3 (2)	that thou mayest warn a people to whom no warner came before thee
36:6 (5)	that thou mayest warn a people whose fathers were never warned
36:19 (18)	but you are a prodigal people
36:20 (19)	he said, 'My people, follow the Envoys'
36:26 (25)	ah, would that my people had knowledge
36:28 (27)	We sent not down upon his people, after him, any host out of heaven
37:30 (29)	we had no authority over you; no, you were an insolent people
37:85 (83)	when he said to his father and his folk, 'What do you serve?'
37:115 (115)	We delivered them and their people from the great distress
37:124 (124)	when he said to his people, 'Will you not be godfearing?'
38:12 (11)	cried lies before them the people of Noah, and Ad, and Pharaoh
38:13 (12)	and Thamood, and the people of Lot
39:39 (40)	my people, act according to your station; I am acting
39:42 (43)	surely in that are signs for a people who reflect
39:52 (53)	surely in that are signs for a people who believe
40:5 (5)	the people of Noah before them also cried lies
40:29 (30)	O my people, today the kingdom is yours
40:30 (31)	my people, truly I fear for you the like of the day of the parties
40:31 (32)	the like of the case of Noah's people
40:32 (34)	O my people, I fear for you the Day of Invocation
40:38 (41)	my people, follow me, and I will guide you
40:39 (42)	O my people, surely this present life is but a passing enjoyment
40:41 (44)	O my people, how is it with me, that I call you to salvation
41:3 (2)	an Arabic Koran for a people having knowledge
43:5 (4)	shall We turn away the Remembrance from you, for that you are a prodigal people?
43:26 (25)	and when Abraham said to his father and his people
43:44 (43)	surely it is a Reminder to thee and to thy people
43:51 (50)	and Pharaoh proclaimed among his people
43:51 (50)	O my people, do I not possess the kingdom of Egypt
43:54 (54)	so he made his people unsteady
43:54 (54)	surely they were an ungodly people
43:57 (57)	behold, thy people turn away from it

43:58 (58)	nay, but they are a people contentious
43:88 (88)	these are a people who believe not
44:17 (16)	already before them We tried the people of Pharaoh
44:22 (21)	these are a sinful people
44:28 (27)	We bequeathed them upon another people
44:37 (36)	are they better, or the people of Tubba'
45:4 (3)	there are signs for a people having sure faith
45:5 (4)	there are signs for a people who understand
45:13 (12)	surely in that are signs for a people who reflect
45:14 (13)	that He may recompense a people for that they have been earning
45:20 (19)	a guidance, and a mercy to a people having sure faith
45:31 (30)	you waxed proud, and were a sinful people
46:10 (9)	you wax proud, God guides not the people of the evildoers
46:21 (20)	remember the brother of Ad, when he warned his people beside the sand-dunes
46:23 (22)	but I see you are an ignorant people
46:25 (24)	even so do We recompense the people of the sinners
46:29 (28)	then, when it was finished, they turned back to their people, warning
46:30 (29)	our people, we have heard a Book that was sent down after Moses
46:31 (30)	O our people, answer God's summoner
46:35 (35)	shall any be destroyed but the people of the ungodly?
47:38 (40)	if you turn away, He will substitute another people instead of you
48:12 (12)	you thought evil thoughts, and you were a people corrupt
48:16 (16)	you shall be called against a people possessed of great might
49:6 (6)	make clear, lest you afflict a people unwittingly
49:11 (11)	let not any people scoff at another (people)
49:11 (11)	let not any (people) scoff at another people
50:12 (12)	cried lies before them the people of Noah
50:14 (13)	the men of the Thicket, the people of Tubba
51:25 (25)	peace! You are a people unknown to me
51:32 (32)	we have been sent to a people of sinners
51:46 (46)	and the people of Noah before
51:46 (46)	they were an ungodly people
51:53 (53)	nay, but they are an insolent people
52:32 (32)	or are they an insolent people?
53:52 (53)	the people of Noah before — certainly they did exceeding evil
54:9 (9)	the people of Noah cried lies before them
54:33 (33)	the people of Lot cried lies to the warnings
58:14 (15)	for friends a people against whom God is wrathful
58:22 (22)	thou shalt not find any people who believe in God and the Last Day
59:13 (13)	that is because they are a people who understand not
59:14 (14)	that is because they are a people who have no sense
60:4 (4)	when they said to their people, 'We are quit of you'
60:13 (13)	take not for friends a people against whom God is wrathful
61:5 (5)	and when Moses said to his people
61:5 (5)	O my people, why do you hurt me
61:5 (5)	God guides never the people of the ungodly
61:7 (7)	God guides never the people of the evildoers
62:5 (5)	evil is the likeness of the people who have cried lies to God's signs
62:5 (5)	God guides never the people of the evildoers
63:6 (6)	God guides not the people of the ungodly
66:11 (11)	and do Thou deliver me from the people of the evildoers
69:7 (7)	and thou mightest see the people laid prostrate in it
71:1 (1)	We sent Noah to his people, saying
71:1 (1)	Warn thy people, ere there come on them a painful chastisement
71:2 (2)	O my people, I am unto you a clear warner
71:5 (5)	my Lord, I have called my people by night and by day

QAWWĀM n.m.~a manager; (with prep. *bi-*) a secorer, one who is staunch

4:34 (38)	men are the managers of the affairs of women
4:135 (134)	be you securers of justice, witnesses for God
5:8 (11)	O believers, be you steadfast before God, witnesses for justice

QAYYIM n.m. (*qiyam*, in 6:161; f. *qayyimah*, in 98:5)~right, true

6:161 (162)	my Lord has guided me to a straight path, a right religion
9:36 (36)	that is the right religion. So wrong not each other
12:40 (40)	that is the right religion
18:2 (2)	right, to warn of great violence from Him
30:30 (29)	that is the right religion
30:43 (42)	so set thy face to the true religion
98:3 (2)	therein true Books
98:5 (4)	that is the religion of the True

QAYYŪM n.m. (adj)~Everlasting, Eternal (Divine attribute)

2:255 (256)	God there is no god but He, the Living, the Everlasting
3:2 (1)	God there is no god but He, the Living, the Everlasting
20:111 (110)	faces shall be humbled unto the Living, the Eternal

QIYĀM n.m.~the act of maintining or managing; an establishment, a standard; an asylum

4:5 (4)	do not give to fools their property that God has assigned to you to manage
5:97 (98)	God has appointed the Kaaba, the Holy House, as an establishment for men

QIYĀMAH n.f.~resurrection; (*yawm al-qiyāmah*) Resurrection Day

2:85 (79)	on the Day of Resurrection to be returned unto the most terrible of chastisement
2:113 (107)	God shall decide between them on the Day of Resurrection
2:174 (169)	God shall not speak to them on the Day of Resurrection
2:212 (208)	those who were godfearing shall be above them on the Resurrection Day
3:55 (48)	I will set thy followers above the unbelievers till the Resurrection Day
3:77 (71)	neither look on them on the Resurrection Day
3:161 (155)	whoso defrauds shall bring the fruits of his fraud on the Day of Resurrection
3:180 (176)	that they were niggardly with they shall have hung about their necks on the Resurrection Day
3:185 (182)	you shall surely be paid in full your wages on the Day of Resurrection
3:194 (192)	abase us not on the Day of Resurrection
4:87 (89)	He will surely gather you to the Resurrection Day
4:109 (109)	who will dispute with God on their behalf on the Resurrection Day
4:141 (140)	God will judge between you on the Resurrection Day
4:159 (157)	on the Resurrection Day he will be a witness against them
5:14 (17)	We have stirred up among them enmity and hatred, till the Day of Resurrection
5:36 (40)	to ransom themselves from the chastisement of the Day of Resurrection thereby
5:64 (69)	between them enmity and hatred, till the Day of Resurrection
6:12 (12)	He will surely gather you to the Resurrection Day
7:32 (30)	these, on the Day of Resurrection, shall be exclusively for those
7:167 (166)	when thy Lord proclaimed He would send forth against them, unto the Day of Resurrection
7:172 (171)	lest you should say on the Day of Resurrection
10:60 (61)	what will they think, who forge falsehood against God, on the Day of Resurrection?
10:93 (93)	thy Lord will decide between them on the Day of Resurrection
11:60 (63)	after them in this world a curse, and upon the Day of Resurrection
11:98 (100)	He shall go before his people on the Day of Resurrection
11:99 (101)	after them in this world a curse, and upon the Day of Resurrection
16:25 (27)	that they may bear their loads complete on the Day of Resurrection

16:27 (29)	then on the Day of Resurrection He will degrade them
16:92 (94)	He will make clear to you upon the Day of Resurrection
16:124 (125)	thy Lord will decide between them on the Day of Resurrection
17:13 (14)	We shall bring forth for him, on the Day of Resurrection
17:58 (60)	but We shall destroy it before the Day of Resurrection
17:62 (64)	if Thou deferrest me to the Day of Resurrection
17:97 (99)	We shall muster them on the Resurrection Day upon their faces
18:105 (105)	on the Day of Resurrection We shall not assign to them any weight
19:95 (95)	every one of them shall come to Him upon the Day of Resurrection
20:100 (100)	upon the Day of Resurrection he shall bear a fardel
20:101 (101)	how evil upon the Day of Resurrection that burden for them
20:124 (124)	on the Resurrection Day We shall raise him blind
21:47 (48)	We shall set up the just balances for the Resurrection Day
22:9 (9)	on the Resurrection Day We shall let him taste the chastisement
22:17 (17)	God shall distinguish between them on the Day of Resurrection
22:69 (68)	God shall judge between you on the Day of Resurrection
23:16 (16)	then on the Day of Resurrection you shall surely be raised up
25:69 (69)	doubled shall be the chastisement for him on the Resurrection Day
28:41 (41)	on the Day of Resurrection they shall not be helped
28:42 (42)	on the Day of Resurrection they shall be among the spurned
28:61 (61)	then he on the Resurrection Day shall be of those that are arraigned
28:71 (71)	what think you? if God should make the night unceasing over you, until the Day of Resurrection
28:72 (72)	what think you? if God should make the day unceasing over you, until the Day of Resurrection
29:13 (12)	upon the Day of Resurrection they shall surely be questioned
29:25 (24)	then upon the Day of Resurrection you will deny one another
32:25 (25)	thy Lord will distinguish between them on the Resurrection Day
35:14 (15)	on the Day of Resurrection they will disown your partnership
39:15 (17)	the losers are they who lose themselves and their families on the Day of Resurrection
39:24 (25)	is he who guards himself with his face against the evil of the chastisement on the Day of Resurrection
39:31 (32)	on the Day of Resurrection before your Lord you shall dispute
39:47 (48)	ransom themselves from the evil of the chastisement on the Day of Resurrection
39:60 (61)	upon the Day of Resurrection thou shalt see those who lied against God
39:67 (67)	the earth altogether shall be His handful on the Day of Resurrection
41:40 (40)	he who comes on the Day of Resurrection in security
42:45 (44)	they who lose themselves and their families on the Day of Resurrection
45:17 (16)	thy Lord will decide between them on the Day of Resurrection
45:26 (25)	He shall gather you to the Day of Resurrection
46:5 (4)	such a one as shall not answer him till the Day of Resurrection
58:7 (8)	He shall tell them what they have done, on the Day of Resurrection
60:3 (3)	nor your children shall profit you upon the Day of Resurrection
68:39 (39)	have you oaths from Us, reaching to the Day of Resurrection?
75:1 (1)	no! I swear by the Day of Resurrection
75:6 (6)	when shall be the Day of Resurrection?

QAWWAMA vb. (II)~(n.vb.) symmetry, stature

f) n.vb. (*taqwīm*)

95:4 (4)	We indeed created Man in the fairest stature

AQĀMA vb. (IV)~to abide; to set or set up; to perform (*aqāma al-ṣalāt*, "to perform the prayer"); to maintain; to assign; (*aqāma al-wazn*, in 55:9, "to set up the balance," hence "to weigh with justice"). (n.vb.) the act of performing (the prayer); the act of abiding. (pcple. act.) one who performs (the prayer); that which remains, lasting

a) perf. act.

2:177 (172)	to perform the prayer, to pay the alms
2:277 (277)	those who ... perform the prayer, and pay the alms
4:102 (103)	when thou art amongst them, and performest for them the prayer
5:12 (15)	if you perform the prayer, and pay the alms, and believe in My Messengers
5:66 (70)	had they performed the Torah and the Gospel
7:170 (169)	those who hold fast to the Book, and perform the prayer
9:5 (5)	if they repent, and perform the prayer, and pay the alms
9:11 (11)	if they repent, and perform the prayer, and pay the alms
9:18 (18)	who believes in God and the Last Day, and performs the prayer, and pays the alms
13:22 (22)	patient men, desirous of the Face of their Lord, who perform the prayer
18:77 (76)	they found a wall about to tumble down, and so he set it up
22:41 (42)	who, if We establish them in the land, perform the prayer, and pay the alms
35:18 (19)	who fear their Lord in the Unseen and perform the prayer
35:29 (26)	those who recite the Book of God and perform the prayer
42:38 (36)	those who answer their Lord, and perform the prayer

b) impf. act. (*yuqīmu*)

2:3 (2)	who believe in the Unseen, and perform the prayer
2:229 (229)	unless the couple fear they may not maintain God's bounds
2:229 (229)	if you fear they may not maintain God's bounds
2:230 (230)	if they suppose that they will maintain God's bounds
5:55 (60)	and the believers who perform the prayer
5:68 (72)	you do not stand on anything, until you perform the Torah and the Gospel
8:3 (3)	those who perform the prayer, and expend of what We have provided them
9:71 (72)	they perform the prayer, and pay the alms
14:31 (36)	Say to My servants who believe, that they perform the prayer
14:37 (40)	Our Lord, let them perform the prayer
18:105 (105)	and on the Day of Resurrection We shall not assign to them any weight
27:3 (3)	who perform the prayer, and pay the alms
31:4 (3)	who perform the prayer, and pay the alms
98:5 (4)	and to perform the prayer, and pay the alms

c) impv. (*aqim*)

2:43 (40)	And perform the prayer, and pay the alms
2:83 (77)	speak good to men, and perform the prayer, and pay the alms
2:110 (104)	perform the prayer, and pay the alms
4:77 (79)	restrain your hands, and perform the prayer, and pay the alms
4:103 (104)	then, when you are secure, perform the prayer
6:72 (71)	Perform the prayer, and fear Him
7:29 (28)	Set your faces in every place of worship
10:87 (87)	and perform the prayer
10:105 (105)	Set thy face to the religion, a man of pure faith
11:114 (116)	and perform the prayer at the two ends of the day
17:78 (80)	Perform the prayer at the sinking of the sun to the darkening of the night
20:14 (14)	and perform the prayer of My remembrance
22:78 (78)	So perform the prayer, and pay the alms
24:56 (55)	Perform the prayer, and pay the alms
29:45 (44)	Recite what has been revealed to thee of the Book, and perform the prayer
30:30 (29)	So set thy face to the religion, a man of pure faith
30:31 (30)	and perform the prayer, and be not of the idolaters
30:43 (42)	So set thy face to the true religion
31:17 (16)	O my son, perform the prayer, and bid unto honour, and forbid dishonour
33:33 (33)	And perform the prayer, and pay the alms
42:13 (11)	Perform the religion, and scatter not regarding it

55:9 (8)	and weigh with justice, and skimp not in the Balance
58:13 (14)	you, then perform the prayer, and pay the alms, and obey God
65:2 (2)	and perform the witnessing to God Himself
73:20 (20)	and perform the prayer, and pay the alms

f) n.vb. (*iqām* or *iqāmah*)

16:80 (82)	you find light on the day that you journey, and on the day you abide
21:73 (73)	to perform the prayer, and to pay the alms
24:37 (37)	and to perform the prayer, and to pay the alms

g) pcple. act. (*muqīm*)

4:162 (160)	[those] that perform the prayer and pay the alms
5:37 (41)	for them awaits a lasting chastisement
9:21 (21)	for them await gardens wherein is lasting bliss
9:68 (69)	and there awaits them a lasting chastisement
11:39 (41)	upon whom there shall alight a lasting chastisement
14:40 (42)	My Lord, make me a performer of the prayer, and of my seed
15:76 (76)	surely it is on a way yet remaining
22:35 (36)	[those] who perform the prayer, and expend of what We have
39:40 (41)	upon whom lights a lasting chastisement
42:45 (44)	surely the evildoers are in lasting chastisement

ISTAQĀMA vb. (X)~to go straight. (pcple. act.) straight

a) perf. act.

9:7 (7)	so long as they go straight with you
41:30 (30)	then have gone straight, upon them the angels descend
46:13 (12)	[those who] go straight, no fear shall be on them
72:16 (16)	Would they but go straight on the way,

b) impf. act. (*yastaqīmu*)

81:28 (28)	for whosoever of you who would go straight

c) impv. (*istaqim*)

9:7 (7)	do you go straight with them
10:89 (89)	go you straight, and follow not the way of those that know not
11:112 (114)	go thou straight, as thou hast been commanded
41:6 (5)	so go straight with Him, and ask for His forgiveness
42:15 (14)	therefore call thou, and go straight as thou hast been commanded

g) pcple. act. (*mustaqīm*)

1:6 (5)	Guide us in the straight path
2:142 (136)	He guides whomsoever He will to a straight path
2:213 (209)	and God guides whomsoever He will to a straight path
3:51 (44)	so serve Him. This is a straight path
3:101 (96)	whosoever holds fast to God, he is guided to a straight path
4:68 (70)	and guided them on a straight path
4:175 (174)	and will guide them to Him on a straight path
5:16 (18)	and He guides them to a straight path
6:39 (39)	and whomsoever He will, He sets him on a straight path
6:87 (87)	and We elected them, and We guided them to a straight path
6:126 (126)	This is the path of thy Lord, straight

6:153 (154)	And that this is My path, straight
6:161 (162)	my Lord has guided me to a straight path, a right religion
7:16 (15)	I shall surely sit in ambush for them on Thy straight path
10:25 (26)	and He guides whomsoever He will to a straight path
11:56 (59)	surely my Lord is on a straight path
15:41 (41)	this is for Me a straight path
16:76 (78)	is he equal to him who bids to justice, and is on a straight path?
16:121 (122)	He chose him, and He guided him to a straight path
17:35 (37)	and weigh with the straight balance
19:36 (37)	so serve you Him. This is a straight path
22:54 (53)	God ever guides those who believe to a straight path
22:67 (66)	surely thou art upon a straight guidance
23:73 (75)	assuredly thou art calling them to a straight path
24:46 (45)	God guides whomsoever He will to a straight path
26:182 (182)	and weigh with the straight balance
36:4 (3)	on a straight path
36:61 (61)	this is a straight path
37:118 (118)	and guided them in the straight path
42:52 (52)	surely thou shalt guide unto a straight path
43:43 (42)	surely thou art upon a straight path
43:61 (61)	this is a straight path
43:64 (64)	therefore serve Him; this is a straight path
46:30 (29)	guiding to the truth and to a straight path
48:2 (2)	and guide thee on a straight path
48:20 (20)	and to guide you on a straight path
67:22 (22)	he who walks upright on a straight path

*Q W S

QAWS n.m.~a bow

53:9 (9)	two bows'-length away, or nearer

*Q W T

AQWĀT n.m. (pl. of *qūt*)~sustenance

41:10 (9)	He ordained therein its diverse sustenance in four days

AQĀTA vb. (IV)~(pcple. act.) one who has power; Overseer (Divine attribute)

g) pcple. act. (*muqīt*)

4:85 (87)	God has power over everything

*Q W Y

QAWĪY n.m. (adj)~one having strength (27:39), strong; All-strong (Divine attribute)

8:52 (54)	God is strong, terrible in retribution

11:66 (69)	thy Lord is the All-strong, the All-mighty
22:40 (41)	surely God is All-strong, All-mighty
22:74 (73)	surely God is All-strong, All-mighty
27:39 (39)	I have strength for it and I am trusty
28:26 (26)	the best man thou canst hire is the one strong and trusty
33:25 (25)	surely God is All-strong, All-mighty
40:22 (23)	surely He is All-strong, terrible in retribution
42:19 (18)	He is the All-strong, the All-mighty
57:25 (25)	surely God is All-strong, All-mighty
58:21 (21)	surely God is All-strong, All-mighty

QŪWAH n.f. (pl. *quwá*)~force, power, strength, might; (with prep. *bi*) forcefully; (adv) firmly

2:63 (60)	take forcefully what We have given you
2:93 (87)	take forcefully what We have given you
2:165 (160)	the power altogether belongs to God
7:145 (142)	so take it forcefully,
7:171 (170)	take forcefully what We have given you
8:60 (62)	make ready for them whatever force and strings of horses you can
9:69 (70)	those before you, who were stronger than you in might
11:52 (55)	He will increase you in strength
11:52 (55)	He will increase you in (strength) unto your strength
11:80 (82)	O would that I had power against you
16:92 (94)	be not as a woman who breaks her thread, after it is firmly spun
18:39 (37)	there is no power except in God
18:95 (94)	so aid me forcefully
19:12 (13)	O John, take the Book forcefully
27:33 (33)	we possess force and we possess great (might)
28:76 (76)	a burden for a company of men endowed with strength
28:78 (78)	God had destroyed before him generations of men stronger than he in might
30:9 (8)	they were stronger than themselves in might
30:54 (53)	then He appointed after weakness strength
30:54 (53)	then after strength He appointed weakness and grey hairs
35:44 (43)	they were stronger than themselves in might
40:21 (22)	they were stronger than themselves in might
40:82 (82)	they were stronger than themselves in might
41:15 (14)	who is stronger than we in might?
41:15 (14)	God, who created them, was stronger than they in might
47:13 (14)	how many a city that was stronger in might than thy city ...?
51:58 (58)	God is the All-provider, the Possessor of Strength
53:5 (5)	taught him by one terrible in power
81:20 (20)	having power, with the Lord of the Throne secure
86:10 (10)	and he shall have no strength, no helper

AQWÁ vb. (IV)~(pcple. act.) a desert dweller

g) pcple. act. (*muqwī*)

56:73 (72)	We Ourselves made it for a reminder, and a boon to the desert-dwellers

*Q Y Ḍ

QAYYAḌA vb. (II)~to allot, to assign

a) perf. act.

41:25 (24) We have allotted them comrades

b) impf. act. (*yuqayyiḍu*)

43:36 (35) to him We assign a Satan for comrade

*Q Y L

QĀLA vb. (I)~(pcple. act.) one who sleeps at noon

g) pcple. act. (*qāʾil*)

7:4 (3) while they took their ease in the noontide

MAQĪL n.m.~a resting-place

25:24 (26) better shall be their lodging, fairer their resting-place

RĀ

*R ʾ F

RAʾFAH n.f.~tenderness

24:2 (2)	let no tenderness for them seize you
57:27 (27)	We set in the hearts of those who followed him tenderness

RAʾŪF n.m. (adj)~gentle; All-gentle, All-clement [Ar, Bl]; full of pity [Pk]; full of kindness, Most Kind [Ali] (Divine attribute)

2:143 (138)	truly, God is All-gentle with the people
2:207 (203)	desiring God's good pleasure; and God is gentle with His servants
3:30 (28)	beware of Him; and God is gentle with His servants
9:117 (118)	surely He is Gentle to them, and All-compassionate
9:128 (129)	anxious is he over you, gentle to the believers
16:7 (7)	surely your Lord is All-clement, All-compassionate
16:47 (49)	surely thy Lord is All-clement, All-compassionate
22:65 (64)	surely God is All-gentle to men, All-compassionate
24:20 (20)	and that God is All-gentle, All-compassionate
57:9 (9)	God is to you All-gentle, All-compassionate
59:10 (10)	surely Thou art the All-gentle, the All-compassionate

*R ʾ S

RAʾS n.m. (pl. *ruʾūs*)~a head; (*raʾs māl*) principal, capital sum; (*nukisa ʿalá raʾsihi*) to be put to confusion

2:196 (192)	shave not your heads, till the offering reaches its place of sacrifice
2:196 (192)	if any of you is sick, or injured in his head
2:279 (279)	if you repent, you shall have your principal
5:6 (8)	wipe your heads, and your feet
7:150 (149)	he cast down the Tablets, and laid hold of his brother's head
12:36 (36)	I dreamed that I was carrying on my head bread
12:41 (41)	he shall be crucified, and birds will eat of his head
14:43 (44)	when they shall run with necks outstretched and heads erect
17:51 (53)	then they will shake their heads at thee
19:4 (3)	the bones within me are feeble and my head is all aflame with hoariness
20:94 (95)	take me not by the beard, or the head
21:65 (66)	then they were utterly put to confusion
22:19 (20)	there shall be poured over their heads boiling water
32:12 (12)	if thou couldst see the guilty hanging their heads before their Lord
37:65 (63)	its spathes are as the heads of Satans
44:48 (48)	then pour over his head the chastisement of boiling water
48:27 (27)	you shall enter the Holy Mosque, if God wills, in security, your heads shaved
63:5 (5)	they twist their heads, and thou seest them turning their faces away

*R ʾ Y

RAʾÁ vb. (I)~to see, to behold, to regard; to dream; to think, to consider

a) perf. act.

2:166 (161)	they see the chastisement, and their cords are cut asunder
3:143 (137)	now you have seen it, while you were beholding
4:61 (64)	then thou seest the hypocrites barring the way to thee
6:40 (40)	what think you? If God's chastisement comes upon you
6:46 (46)	what think you? If God seizes your hearing and sight
6:47 (47)	what think you? If God's chastisement comes upon you
6:68 (67)	when thou seest those who plunge into Our signs, turn away from them
6:76 (76)	when night outspread over him he saw a star and said
6:77 (77)	when he saw the moon rising, he said
6:78 (78)	when he saw the sun rising, he said
7:149 (148)	when they smote their hands, and saw that they had gone astray
10:50 (51)	have you considered? If His chastisement comes upon you by night
10:54 (55)	they will be secretly remorseful when they see the chastisement
10:59 (60)	have you considered the provision God has sent down for you
11:28 (30)	what think you? If I stand upon a clear sign from my Lord
11:63 (66)	what think you? If I stand upon a clear sign from my Lord
11:70 (73)	when he saw their hands not reaching towards it
11:88 (90)	what think you? If I stand upon a clear sign from my Lord
12:4 (4)	Father, I saw eleven stars, and the sun and the moon
12:4 (4)	I saw them bowing down before me
12:24 (24)	he would have taken her, but that he saw the proof of his Lord
12:28 (28)	when he saw his shirt was torn from behind he said
12:31 (31)	when they saw him, they so admired him
12:35 (35)	then it seemed good to them, after they had seen the signs
16:85 (87)	when the evildoers behold the chastisement, it shall not be lightened for them
16:86 (88)	when the idolaters behold their associates, they shall say
17:62 (64)	what thinkest Thou? This whom Thou hast honoured above me
18:53 (51)	then the evildoers will see the Fire
18:63 (62)	what thinkest thou? When we took refuge in the rock
19:75 (77)	till, when they see that they were threatened
19:77 (80)	hast thou seen him who disbelieves in Our signs
20:10 (9)	when he saw a fire, and said to his family
20:92 (94)	what prevented thee, Aaron, when thou sawest them in error
21:36 (37)	when the unbelievers behold thee, they take thee only for mockery
25:12 (13)	when it sees them from a far place, they shall hear its bubbling
25:41 (43)	when they see thee, they take thee in mockery only
25:43 (45)	hast thou seen him who has taken his caprice to be his god?
26:75 (75)	have you considered what you have been serving
26:205 (205)	what thinkest thou? If We give them enjoyment of days
27:10 (10)	when he saw it quivering like a serpent he turned about
27:40 (40)	then, when he saw it settled before him
27:44 (44)	when she saw it, she supposed it was a spreading water
28:31 (31)	when he saw it quivering like a serpent, he turned about
28:64 (64)	they shall see the chastisement — ah, if they had been guided
28:71 (71)	what think you? If God should make the night unceasing over you
28:72 (72)	what think you? If God should make the day unceasing over you
30:51 (50)	if We loose a wind, and they see it growing yellow
33:19 (19)	thou seest them looking at thee, their eyes rolling like one who swoons
33:22 (22)	when the believers saw the Confederates they said
34:33 (32)	they will be secretly remorseful when they see the chastisement
35:8 (9)	the evil of whose deeds has been decked out fair to him, so that he thinks it is good
35:40 (38)	have you considered your associates on whom you call, apart from God
37:14 (14)	when they see a sign, would scoff
37:55 (53)	then he looks, and sees him in the midst of Hell

39:38 (39)	what think you? That you call upon apart from God
40:84 (84)	then, when they saw Our might, they said
40:85 (85)	their belief when they saw Our might did not profit them
41:52 (52)	what think you? If it is from God, then you disbelieve in it
42:44 (43)	when they see the chastisement
45:23 (22)	hast thou seen him who has taken his caprice to be his god
46:4 (3)	have you considered that you call upon apart from God
46:10 (9)	have you considered? If it be from God, and you disbelieve in it
46:24 (23)	when they saw it as a sudden cloud coming towards their valleys
47:20 (22)	thou seest those in whose hearts is sickness looking at thee
53:11 (11)	his heart lies not of what he saw
53:13 (13)	indeed, he saw him another time
53:18 (18)	he saw one of the greatest signs of his Lord
53:19 (19)	have you considered El-Lat and El-'Uzza
53:33 (34)	hast thou considered him who turns his back
56:58 (58)	have you considered the seed you spill?
56:63 (63)	have you considered the soil you till?
56:68 (67)	have you considered the water you drink?
56:71 (70)	have you considered the fire you kindle?
59:21 (21)	thou wouldst have seen it humbled, split asunder
62:11 (11)	when they see merchandise or diversion they scatter off to it
63:4 (4)	when thou seest them, their bodies please thee
63:5 (5)	they twist their heads, and thou seest them turning their faces away
67:27 (27)	when they see it nigh at hand, the faces of the unbelievers will be vexed
67:28 (28)	what think you? If God destroys me and those with me
67:30 (30)	what think you? If in the morning your water should have vanished
68:26 (26)	but when they saw it, they said
72:24 (25)	when they see that which they are promised, then they will know who is weaker
76:19 (19)	when thou seest them, thou supposest them scattered pearls
76:20 (20)	when thou seest them
76:20 (20)	then thou seest bliss and a great kingdom
81:23 (23)	he truly saw him on the clear horizon
83:32 (32)	when they saw them they said
96:7 (7)	for he thinks himself self-sufficient
96:9 (9)	what thinkest thou? He who forbids
96:11 (11)	what thinkest thou? If he were upon guidance
96:13 (13)	what thinkest thou? If he cries lies, and turns away
107:1 (1)	hast thou seen him who cries lies to the Doom?
110:2 (2)	thou seest men entering God's religion in throngs

b) impf. act. (*yará*)

2:55 (52)	we will not believe thee till we see God openly
2:144 (139)	We have seen thee turning thy face about in the heaven
2:165 (160)	O if the evildoers might see
2:165 (160)	when they see the chastisement
2:243 (244)	hast thou not regarded those who went forth from their habitations
2:246 (247)	hast thou not regarded the Council of the Children of Israel
2:258 (260)	hast thou not regarded him who disputed with Abraham
3:13 (11)	they saw them twice the like of them
3:23 (22)	hast thou not regarded those who were given a portion of the Book
4:44 (47)	hast thou not regarded those who were given a share of the Book
4:49 (52)	hast thou not regarded those who purify themselves
4:51 (54)	hast thou not regarded those who were given a share of the Book
4:60 (63)	hast thou not regarded those who assert that they believe

4:77 (79)	hast thou not regarded those to whom it was said
5:52 (57)	thou seest those in whose hearts is sickness vying with one another
5:62 (67)	thou seest many of them vying in sin and enmity
5:80 (83)	thou seest many of them making unbelievers their friends
5:83 (86)	thou seest their eyes overflow with tears because of the truth
6:6 (6)	have they not regarded how We destroyed before them many a generation
6:25 (25)	if they see any sign whatever, they do not believe in it
6:27 (27)	if thou couldst see when they are stationed before the Fire
6:30 (30)	if thou couldst see when they are stationed before their Lord
6:74 (74)	I see thee, and thy people, in manifest error
6:93 (93)	if thou couldst only see when the evildoers are in the agonies of death
6:94 (94)	we do not see with you your intercessors
7:27 (26)	surely he sees you, he and his tribe
7:27 (26)	from where you see them not
7:60 (58)	we see thee in manifest error
7:66 (64)	we see thee in folly
7:143 (139)	thou shalt not see Me; but behold the mountain
7:143 (139)	if it stays fast in its place, then thou shalt see Me
7:146 (143)	though they see every sign, they will not believe in it
7:146 (143)	though they see the way of rectitude they will not take it for a way
7:146 (143)	though they see the way of error, they will take it for a way
7:148 (146)	did they not see it spoke not to them, neither guided them upon any way?
7:198 (197)	thou seest them looking at thee, unperceiving
8:48 (50)	I am quit of you; for I see what you do not (see)
8:48 (50)	for I (see) what you do not see
8:50 (52)	if thou couldst only see when the angels take the unbelievers
9:26 (26)	He sent down legions you did not see
9:40 (40)	and confirmed him with legions you did not see
9:94 (95)	God will surely see your work, and His Messenger
9:105 (106)	work; and God will surely see your work
9:126 (127)	do they not see that they are tried every year
9:127 (128)	does anyone see you?
10:88 (88)	they do not believe, till they see the painful chastisement
10:97 (97)	though every sign come to them, till they see the painful chastisement
11:27 (29)	we see thee not other than a mortal like ourselves
11:27 (29)	we see not any following thee but the vilest of us
11:27 (29)	we do not see you have over us any superiority
11:29 (31)	but I see you are an ignorant people
11:84 (85)	I see you are prospering
11:91 (93)	truly we see thee weak among us
12:30 (30)	we see her in manifest error
12:36 (36)	I dreamed that I was pressing grapes
12:36 (36)	I dreamed that I was carrying on my head bread
12:36 (36)	we see that thou art of the good-doers
12:43 (43)	I saw in a dream seven fat kine, and seven lean ones
12:59 (59)	do you not see that I fill up the measure
12:78 (78)	we see that thou art one of the good-doers
13:2 (2)	God is He who raised up the heavens without pillars you can see
13:41 (41)	have they not seen how We come to the land diminishing it
14:19 (22)	hast thou not seen that God created the heavens
14:24 (29)	hast thou not seen how God has struck a similitude
14:28 (33)	hast thou not seen those who exchanged the bounty of God
14:49 (50)	thou shalt see the sinners that day coupled in fetters
16:14 (14)	thou mayest see the ships cleaving through it
16:48 (50)	have they not regarded all things that God has created

16:79 (81)	have they not regarded the birds, that are subjected in the air of heaven?
17:99 (101)	have they not seen that God, who created the heavens and earth, is powerful
18:17 (16)	and thou mightest have seen the sun
18:39 (37)	if thou seest me, that I am less than thou in wealth
18:47 (45)	thou seest the earth coming forth, and We muster them
18:49 (47)	thou wilt see the sinners fearful at what is in it
19:26 (26)	if thou shouldst see any mortal
19:83 (86)	hast thou not seen how We sent the Satans against the unbelievers
20:46 (48)	surely I shall be with you, hearing and seeing
20:89 (91)	did they not see that thing returned no speech unto them
20:107 (106)	wherein thou wilt see no crookedness neither any curving
21:30 (31)	have not the unbelievers then beheld that the heavens and the earth were a mass
21:44 (45)	do they not see how We come to the land, diminishing it
22:2 (2)	on the day when you behold it, every suckling woman shall neglect the child
22:2 (2)	thou shalt see mankind drunk, yet they are not drunk
22:5 (5)	and thou beholdest the earth blackened
22:18 (18)	hast thou not seen how to God bow all who are in the heavens
22:63 (62)	hast thou not seen how that God has sent down out of heaven water
22:65 (64)	hast thou not seen how that God has subjected to you all that is in the earth
24:40 (40)	when he puts forth his hand, wellnigh he cannot see it
24:41 (41)	hast thou not seen how that whatsoever is in the heavens and in the earth extols God
24:43 (43)	hast thou not seen how God drives the clouds, then composes them
24:43 (43)	then thou seest the rain issuing out of the midst of them
25:21 (23)	why see we not our Lord?
25:22 (24)	upon the day that they see the angels
25:40 (42)	what, have they not seen it
25:42 (44)	assuredly they shall know, when they see the chastisement
25:45 (47)	hast thou not regarded thy Lord, how He has stretched out the shadow
26:7 (6)	what, have they not regarded the earth
26:201 (201)	who will not believe in it, until they see the painful chastisement
26:218 (218)	who sees thee when thou standest
26:225 (225)	hast thou not seen how they wander in every valley
27:20 (20)	how is it with me, that I do not see the hoopoe
27:86 (88)	have they not seen how We made the night for them
27:88 (90)	thou shalt see the mountains, that thou supposest fixed, passing by
29:19 (18)	have they not seen how God originates creation
29:67 (67)	have they not seen that We have appointed a sanctuary secure
30:37 (36)	have they not seen that God outspreads and straitens His provision
30:48 (47)	then thou seest the rain issuing out of the midst of them
31:10 (9)	He created the heavens without pillars you can see
31:20 (19)	have you not seen how that God has subjected to you whatsoever is in the heavens
31:29 (28)	hast thou not seen how that God makes the night to enter into the day
31:31 (30)	hast thou not seen how that the ships run upon the sea
32:12 (12)	if thou couldst see the guilty hanging their heads before their Lord
32:27 (27)	have they not seen how We drive the water to the dry land
33:9 (9)	We loosed against them a wind, and hosts you saw not
34:6 (6)	those who have been given the knowledge see that what has been sent down
34:9 (9)	have they not regarded what lies before them and what lies behind
34:31 (30)	if thou couldst see when the evildoers are stationed before their Lord
34:51 (50)	if thou couldst see when they are terrified
35:12 (13)	thou mayest see the ships cleaving through it
35:27 (25)	hast thou not seen how that God sends down out of heaven water
36:31 (30)	have they not seen how many generations We have destroyed
36:71 (71)	have they not seen how that We have created for them

36:77 (77)	has not man regarded how that We created him of a sperm-drop?
37:102 (101)	I see in a dream that I shall sacrifice thee
37:102 (101)	consider, what thinkest thou?
38:62 (62)	how is it with us, that we do not see men here that we counted among the wicked?
39:21 (22)	hast thou not seen how that God has sent down out of heaven water
39:21 (22)	then they wither, and thou seest them turning yellow
39:58 (59)	lest it should say, when it sees the chastisement
39:60 (61)	upon the Day of Resurrection thou shalt see those who lied against God
39:75 (75)	thou shalt see the angels encircling about the Throne
40:29 (30)	I only let you see what I see
40:69 (71)	hast thou not regarded those who dispute concerning the signs of God
41:15 (14)	did they not see that God, who created them, was stronger
41:39 (39)	of His signs is that thou seest the earth humble
42:22 (21)	thou seest the evildoers going in fear
42:44 (42)	thou shalt see the evildoers
42:45 (44)	thou shalt see them, as they are exposed to it
45:28 (27)	thou shalt see every nation hobbling on their knees
46:23 (22)	but I see you are an ignorant people
46:33 (32)	have they not seen that God who created the heavens
46:35 (34)	it shall be as if, on the day they see that they are promised
48:29 (29)	thou seest them bowing, prostrating, seeking bounty
52:44 (44)	even if they saw lumps falling from heaven, they would say
53:12 (12)	what, will you dispute with him what he sees?
53:35 (36)	does he possess the knowledge of the Unseen, and therefore he sees?
54:2 (2)	yet if they see a sign they turn away
57:12 (12)	upon the day when thou seest the believers, men and women
57:20 (19)	thou seest it turning yellow, then it becomes broken orts
58:7 (8)	hast thou not seen that God knows whatsoever is in the heavens
58:8 (9)	hast thou not regarded those who were forbidden to converse secretly
58:14 (15)	hast thou not regarded those who have taken for friends
59:11 (11)	hast thou not regarded the hypocrites, saying to their brothers
67:3 (3)	thou seest not in the creation of the All-merciful any imperfection
67:3 (3)	return thy gaze; seest thou any fissure?
67:19 (19)	have they not regarded the birds above them spreading their wings
69:7 (7)	thou mightest see the people laid prostrate in it
69:8 (8)	now dost thou see any remnant of them?
70:6 (6)	behold, they see it as if far off
70:7 (7)	but We see it is nigh
71:15 (14)	have you not regarded how God created seven heavens
76:13 (13)	therein they shall see neither sun nor bitter cold
79:36 (36)	Hell is advanced for whoever sees
79:46 (46)	it shall be as if, on the day they see it, they have but tarried
89:6 (5)	hast thou not seen how thy Lord did with Ad
90:7 (7)	what, does he think none has seen him?
96:14 (14)	did he not know that God sees?
99:7 (7)	whoso has done an atom's weight of good shall see it
99:8 (8)	whoso has done an atom's weight of evil shall see it
102:6 (6)	you shall surely see Hell
102:7 (7)	you shall surely see it with the eye of certainty
105:1 (1)	hast thou not seen how thy Lord did with the Men of the Elephant

d) perf. pass. (*yurá*)

46:25 (24)	in the morning there was naught to be seen but their dwelling-places
53:40 (41)	and that his labouring shall surely be seen

RAʾY n.m.~the act of seeing; judgment, opinion, consideration

3:13 (11)	they saw them twice the like of them, as the eye sees
11:27 (29)	we see not any following thee but the vilest of us

RIʾĀʾ n.m.~the act of showing off, the act of being seen

2:264 (266)	as one who expends of his substance to show off to men
4:38 (42)	such as expend of their substance to show off to men
8:47 (49)	those who went forth from their habitations swaggering boastfully to show off to men

RIʾY n.m.~outward show

19:74 (75)	who were fairer in furnishing and outward show

RUʾYĀ n.f.~a vision, a dream

12:5 (5)	O my son, relate not thy vision to thy brothers
12:43 (43)	my counsellors, pronounce to me upon my dream
12:43 (43)	if you are expounders of dreams
12:100 (101)	this is the interpretation of my vision
17:60 (62)	We made the vision that We showed thee
37:105 (105)	thou hast confirmed the vision
48:27 (27)	God has indeed fulfilled the vision He vouchsafed to His Messenger truly

RĀʾÁ vb. (III)~to show off, to make display

b) impf. act. (*yurāʾī*)

4:142 (141)	they stand up lazily, showing off to the people
107:6 (6)	to those who make display

ARÁ vb. (IV)~to show, to cause to see

a) perf. act.

3:152 (145)	after He had shown you that you longed for
4:105 (106)	that thou mayest judge between the people by that God has shown thee
8:43 (45)	had He shown them as many you would have lost heart
17:60 (62)	We made the vision that We showed thee
20:56 (58)	We showed Pharaoh all Our signs
47:30 (32)	did We will, We would show them to thee
79:20 (20)	so he showed him the great sign

b) impf. act. (*yurī*)

2:73 (68)	God brings to life the dead, and He shows you His signs
2:167 (162)	even so God shall show them their works
5:31 (34)	God sent forth a raven, scratching into the earth, to show him how he might conceal the vile body
6:75 (75)	We were showing Abraham the kingdom of the heavens and earth
7:27 (26)	stripping them of their garments to show them their shameful parts
7:145 (142)	I shall show you the habitation of the ungodly
8:43 (45)	when God showed thee them in thy dream as few
8:44 (46)	when God showed you them in your eyes as few
10:46 (47)	whether We show thee a part of that We promise them, or We call thee
13:12 (13)	it is He who shows you the lightning, for fear and hope
13:40 (40)	whether We show thee a part of that We promise them, or We call thee

17:1 (1)	that We might show him some of Our signs
20:23 (24)	so We would show thee some of Our greatest signs
21:37 (38)	I shall show you My signs
23:93 (95)	if Thou shouldst show me that they are promised
23:95 (97)	We are able to show thee that We promise them
27:93 (95)	He shall show you His signs
28:6 (5)	to show Pharaoh and Haman, and their hosts, what they were dreading
30:24 (23)	of His signs He shows you lightning, for fear and hope
31:31 (30)	that He may show you some of His signs
40:13 (13)	it is He who shows you His signs
40:29 (30)	I only let you see what I see
40:77 (77)	whether We show thee a part of that We promise them, or We call thee
40:81 (81)	He shows you His signs
41:53 (53)	We shall show them Our signs in the horizons and in themselves
43:42 (41)	We show thee a part of that We promised them
43:48 (47)	not a sign We showed them, but it was greater than its sister sign

c) impv. (*ari*)

2:128 (122)	show us our holy rites, and turn towards us
2:260 (262)	show me how Thou wilt give life to the dead
4:153 (152)	show us God openly
7:143 (139)	oh my Lord, show me, that I may behold Thee
31:11 (10)	now show me what those have created that are apart from Him
34:27 (26)	show me those you have joined to Him as associates
35:40 (38)	show me what they have created in the earth
41:29 (29)	our Lord, show us those that led us astray
46:4 (3)	show me what they have created of the earth

e) impf. pass. (*yurá*)

99:6 (6)	upon that day men shall issue in scatterings to see their works

TARĀ'Á vb. (VI)~to sight one another a) perf. act.

8:48 (50)	when the two hosts sighted each other, he withdrew upon his heels
26:61 (61)	when the two hosts sighted each other

*R ᶜ B

RAᶜABA vb. (I)~(n.vb.) terror, fear

f) n.vb. (*ruᶜb*)

3:151 (144)	We will cast into the hearts of the unbelievers terror
8:12 (12)	I shall cast into the unbelievers' hearts terror
18:18 (17)	thou wouldst have turned thy back on them in flight, and been filled with terror
33:26 (26)	and cast terror in their hearts
59:2 (2)	He cast terror into their hearts as they destroyed their houses

*R ᶜ D

RAᶜD n.m.~thunder

2:19 (18) a cloudburst out of heaven in which is darkness, and thunder
13:13 (14) the thunder proclaims His praise, and the angels, in awe of Him

*R ᶜ Y

RAᶜĀ vb. (I)~to pasture (tr), to feed (cattle); to observe. (n.vb.) the act of observing. (pcple. act.) one who pastures (cattle), a shepherd; one who preserves

a) perf. act.

57:27 (27) they observed it not as it should be observed

c) impv. (*irᶜa*)

20:54 (56) do you eat, and pasture your cattle

f) n.vb. (*riᶜāyah*)

57:27 (27) they (observed) it not as it should be observed

g) pcple. act. (*rāᶜī*)

23:8 (8) and who preserve their trusts and their covenant
28:23 (23) we may not draw water until the shepherds drive off
70:32 (32) and who preserve their trusts and their covenant

MARᶜĀ n.m.~pasture

79:31 (31) therefrom brought forth its waters and its pastures
87:4 (4) who brought forth the pasturage

RĀᶜĀ vb. (III)~to observe, to look at

c) impv. (*rāᶜi*)

2:104 (98) O believers, do not say, 'Observe us'
4:46 (48) observe us

*R B ᶜ

ARBAᶜ n.num.~four

2:226 (226) for those who forswear their women a wait of four months
2:234 (234) those of you who die, leaving wives, they shall wait by themselves for four months
2:260 (262) take four birds, and twist them to thee
4:15 (19) such of your women as commit indecency, call four of you to witness
9:2 (2) journey freely in the land for four months
9:36 (36) four of them are sacred
24:4 (4) those who cast it up on women in wedlock, and then bring not four witnesses
24:6 (6) the testimony of one of them shall be to testify by God four times
24:8 (8) if she testify by God four times that he is of the liars
24:13 (13) why did they not bring four witnesses against it
24:45 (44) some of them go upon four
41:10 (9) He ordained therein its diverse sustenance in four days

ARBAʿŪN n.num.~forty

2:51 (48)	when We appointed with Moses forty nights
5:26 (29)	then it shall be forbidden them for forty years, while they are wandering
7:142 (138)	so the appointed time of his Lord was forty nights
46:15 (14)	when he is fully grown, and reaches forty years

RĀBIʿ n.num.~the fourth

18:22 (21)	three; and their dog was the fourth of them
58:7 (8)	three men conspire not secretly together, but He is the fourth

RUBĀʿ n.num.~four

4:3 (3)	marry such women as seem good to you, two, three, four
35:1 (1)	who appointed the angels to be messengers having wings two, three and four

RUBUʿ n.num.~a fourth

4:12 (13)	if they have children, then for you of what they leave a fourth
4:12 (14)	for them a fourth of what you leave

*R B B

RABB n.m. (pl. *arbāb*)~master, lord; the Lord (God)

1:2 (1)	praise belongs to God, the Lord of all Being
2:5 (4)	those are upon guidance from their Lord
2:21 (19)	O you men, serve your Lord Who created you
2:26 (24)	as for the believers, they know it is the truth from their Lord
2:30 (28)	when thy Lord said to the angels
2:37 (35)	thereafter Adam received certain words from his Lord
2:46 (43)	who reckon that they shall meet their Lord
2:49 (46)	in that was a grievous trial from your Lord
2:61 (58)	pray to thy Lord for us
2:62 (59)	their wage awaits them with their Lord
2:68 (63)	pray to thy Lord for us, that He may make clear to us
2:69 (64)	pray to thy Lord for us, that He make clear
2:70 (65)	pray to thy Lord for us, that He make clear to us
2:76 (71)	that they may thereby dispute with you before your Lord
2:105 (99)	the idolaters wish not that any good should be sent down upon you from your Lord
2:112 (106)	whosoever submits his will to God, being a good-doer, his wage is with his Lord
2:124 (118)	when his Lord tested Abraham with certain words
2:126 (120)	my Lord, make this a land secure
2:127 (121)	our Lord, receive this from us
2:128 (122)	our Lord, make us submissive to Thee
2:129 (123)	our Lord, do Thou send among them a Messenger
2:131 (125)	when his Lord said to him
2:131 (125)	I have surrendered me to the Lord of all Being
2:136 (130)	that which was given to Moses and Jesus and the Prophets, of their Lord
2:139 (133)	would you then dispute with us concerning God, who is our Lord
2:139 (133)	and your Lord
2:144 (139)	those who have been given the Book know it is the truth from their Lord
2:147 (142)	the truth comes from thy Lord
2:149 (144)	it is the truth from thy Lord
2:157 (152)	upon those rest blessings and mercy from their Lord
2:178 (174)	that is a lightening granted you by your Lord
2:198 (194)	it is no fault in you, that you should seek bounty from your Lord

2:200 (196)	our Lord, give to us in this world
2:201 (197)	our Lord, give to us in this world good
2:248 (249)	the Ark will come to you, in it a Shechina from your Lord
2:250 (251)	our Lord, pour out upon us patience, and make firm our feet
2:258 (260)	hast thou not regarded him who disputed with Abraham, concerning his Lord
2:258 (260)	my Lord is He who gives life, and makes to die
2:260 (262)	my Lord, show me how Thou wilt give life to the dead
2:262 (264)	their wage is with their Lord
2:274 (275)	their wage awaits them with their Lord
2:275 (276)	whosoever receives an admonition from his Lord and gives over
2:277 (277)	their wage awaits them with their Lord
2:282 (282)	let him fear God his Lord
2:283 (283)	let him fear God his Lord
2:285 (285)	the Messenger believes in what was sent down to him from his Lord
2:285 (285)	our Lord, grant us Thy forgiveness
2:286 (286)	our Lord, take us not to task if we forget
2:286 (286)	our Lord, charge us not with a load
2:286 (286)	our Lord, do Thou not burden us
3:7 (5)	we believe in it; all is from our Lord
3:8 (6)	our Lord, make not our hearts to swerve
3:9 (7)	our Lord, it is Thou that shall gather mankind
3:15 (13)	with their Lord are gardens underneath which rivers flow
3:16 (14)	our Lord, we believe; forgive us our sins
3:35 (31)	Lord, I have vowed to Thee, in dedication
3:36 (31)	Lord, I have given birth to her, a female
3:37 (32)	her Lord received the child with gracious favour
3:38 (33)	then Zachariah prayed to his Lord
3:38 (33)	Lord, give me of Thy goodness a goodly offspring
3:40 (35)	'Lord,' said Zachariah, 'how shall I have a son'
3:41 (36)	'Lord,' said Zachariah, 'appoint to me a sign'
3:41 (36)	mention thy Lord oft, and give glory at evening
3:43 (38)	Mary, be obedient to thy Lord, prostrating and bowing before Him
3:47 (42)	'Lord,' said Mary, 'how shall I have a son'
3:49 (43)	I have come to you with a sign from your Lord
3:50 (44)	I have come to you with a sign from your Lord
3:51 (44)	God is my Lord
3:51 (44)	and your Lord; so serve Him
3:53 (46)	Lord, we believe in that Thou hast sent down
3:60 (53)	the truth is of your Lord
3:64 (57)	do not some of us take others as Lords, apart from God
3:73 (66)	or dispute with you before your Lord
3:80 (74)	He would never order you to take the angels and the Prophets as Lords
3:84 (78)	that which was given to Moses and Jesus, and the Prophets, of their Lord
3:124 (120)	is it not enough for you that your Lord should reinforce you
3:125 (121)	your Lord will reinforce you with five thousand swooping angels
3:133 (127)	vie with one another, hastening to forgiveness from your Lord
3:136 (130)	those — their recompense is forgiveness from their Lord
3:147 (141)	Lord, forgive us our sins, and that we exceeded in our affair
3:169 (163)	but rather living with their Lord
3:191 (188)	our Lord, Thou hast not created this for vanity
3:192 (189)	our Lord, whomsoever Thou admittest into the Fire
3:193 (190)	our Lord, we have heard a caller calling us to belief
3:193 (190)	believe you in your Lord
3:193 (191)	our Lord, forgive Thou us our sins and acquit us
3:194 (192)	our Lord, give us what Thou hast promised us by Thy Messengers

3:195 (193)	and their Lord answers them
3:198 (197)	those who fear their Lord — for them shall be gardens
3:199 (199)	those — their wage is with their Lord
4:1 (1)	mankind, fear your Lord, who created you of a single soul
4:65 (68)	but no, by thy Lord! They will not believe
4:75 (77)	our Lord, bring us forth from this city whose people are evildoers
4:77 (79)	our Lord, why hast thou prescribed fighting for us?
4:170 (168)	the Messenger has now come to you with the truth from your Lord
4:174 (174)	a proof has now come to you from your Lord
5:2 (2)	nor those repairing to the Holy House seeking from their Lord bounty
5:24 (27)	go forth, thou and thy Lord, and do battle
5:25 (28)	O my Lord, I rule no one except myself and my brother
5:28 (31)	I fear God, the Lord of all Being
5:64 (69)	what has been sent down to thee from thy Lord will surely increase many of them
5:66 (70)	what was sent down to them from their Lord
5:67 (71)	deliver that which has been sent down to thee from thy Lord
5:68 (72)	what was sent down to you from your Lord
5:68 (72)	what has been sent down to thee from thy Lord
5:72 (76)	Children of Israel, serve God, my Lord
5:72 (76)	and your Lord
5:83 (86)	our Lord, we believe; so do Thou write us down
5:84 (87)	that our Lord should admit us with the righteous people
5:112 (112)	O Jesus son of Mary, is thy Lord able to send down on us
5:114 (114)	O God, our Lord, send down upon us a Table
5:117 (117)	serve God, my Lord
5:117 (117)	and your Lord
6:1 (1)	then the unbelievers ascribe equals to their Lord
6:4 (4)	not a sign of their Lord comes to them, but they turn away from it
6:15 (15)	indeed I fear, if I should rebel against my Lord
6:23 (23)	by God our Lord, we never associated other gods with Thee
6:27 (27)	and then not cry lies to the signs of our Lord
6:30 (30)	if thou couldst see when they are stationed before their Lord
6:30 (30)	yes indeed, by our Lord
6:37 (37)	why has no sign been sent down upon him from his Lord
6:38 (38)	then to their Lord they shall be mustered
6:45 (45)	praise belongs to God the Lord of all Being
6:51 (51)	warn therewith those who fear they shall be mustered to their Lord
6:52 (52)	do not drive away those who call upon their Lord at morning
6:54 (54)	peace be upon you. Your Lord has prescribed for Himself mercy
6:57 (57)	I stand upon a clear sign from my Lord
6:71 (70)	we are commanded to surrender to the Lord of all Being
6:76 (76)	this is my Lord
6:77 (77)	this is my Lord
6:77 (77)	if my Lord does not guide me I shall surely be of the people gone astray
6:78 (78)	this is my Lord; this is greater
6:80 (80)	I fear not what you associate with Him, except my Lord will aught
6:80 (80)	my Lord embraces all things in His knowledge
6:83 (83)	surely thy Lord is All-wise, All-knowing
6:102 (102)	that then is God your Lord
6:104 (104)	clear proofs have come to you from your Lord
6:106 (106)	follow thou what has been revealed to thee from thy Lord
6:108 (108)	then to their Lord they shall return
6:112 (112)	had thy Lord willed, they would never have done it
6:114 (114)	those whom We have given the Book know it is sent down from thy Lord
6:115 (115)	perfect are the words of thy Lord in truthfulness and justice

6:117 (117)	thy Lord knows very well who goes astray from His path
6:119 (119)	thy Lord knows very well the transgressors
6:126 (126)	this is the path of thy Lord; straight
6:127 (127)	theirs is the abode of peace with their Lord
6:128 (128)	our Lord, we have profited each of the other
6:128 (128)	surely thy Lord is All-wise, All-knowing
6:131 (131)	that is because thy Lord would never destroy the cities unjustly
6:132 (132)	thy Lord is not heedless of the things they do
6:133 (133)	thy Lord is All-sufficient, Merciful
6:145 (146)	surely thy Lord is All-forgiving, All-compassionate
6:147 (148)	your Lord is of mercy all-embracing
6:150 (151)	who believe not in the world to come, and ascribe equals to their Lord
6:151 (152)	come, I will recite what your Lord has forbidden you
6:154 (155)	haply they would believe in the encounter with their Lord
6:157 (158)	yet indeed a clear sign has come to you from your Lord
6:158 (159)	nothing less, or that thy Lord should come
6:158 (159)	or that one of thy Lord's signs should come
6:158 (159)	on the day that one of thy Lord's signs comes
6:161 (162)	as for me, my Lord has guided me to a straight path
6:162 (163)	all belongs to God, the Lord of all Being
6:164 (164)	shall I seek after a Lord other than God
6:164 (164)	who is the Lord of all things?
6:164 (164)	then to your Lord shall you return
6:165 (165)	surely thy Lord is swift in retribution
7:3 (2)	follow what has been sent down to you from your Lord
7:20 (19)	your Lord has only prohibited you from this tree
7:22 (21)	and their Lord called to them
7:23 (22)	Lord, we have wronged ourselves
7:29 (28)	my Lord has commanded justice
7:33 (31)	my Lord has only forbidden indecencies
7:38 (36)	O our Lord, these led us astray
7:43 (41)	indeed, our Lord's Messengers came with the truth
7:44 (42)	we have found that which our Lord promised us true
7:44 (42)	have you found what your Lord promised you true?
7:47 (45)	our Lord, do not Thou assign us with the people of the evildoers
7:53 (51)	indeed, our Lord's Messengers came with the truth
7:54 (52)	surely your Lord is God, who created the heavens
7:54 (52)	blessed be God, the Lord of all Being
7:55 (53)	call on your Lord, humbly and secretly
7:58 (56)	its vegetation comes forth by the leave of its Lord
7:61 (59)	I am a Messenger from the Lord of all Being
7:62 (60)	I deliver to you the Messages of my Lord
7:63 (61)	do you wonder that a reminder from your Lord should come to you
7:67 (65)	but I am a Messenger from the Lord of all Being
7:68 (66)	I deliver to you the Messages of my Lord
7:69 (67)	do you wonder that a reminder from your Lord should come to you
7:71 (69)	anger and wrath from your Lord have fallen upon you
7:73 (71)	there has now come to you a clear sign from your Lord
7:75 (73)	do you know that Salih is an Envoy from his Lord?
7:77 (75)	and turned in disdain from the commandment of their Lord
7:79 (77)	I have delivered to you the Message of my Lord
7:85 (83)	there has now come to you a clear sign from your Lord
7:89 (87)	it is not for us to return into it, unless God our Lord so will
7:89 (87)	our Lord embraces all things in His knowledge
7:89 (87)	our Lord, give true deliverance

7:93 (91)	I have delivered to you the Messages of my Lord
7:104 (102)	Pharaoh, I am a Messenger from the Lord of all Being
7:105 (103)	I have brought a clear sign to you from your Lord
7:121 (118)	we believe in the Lord of all Being
7:122 (119)	the Lord of Moses and Aaron
7:125 (122)	surely unto our Lord we are turning
7:126 (123)	because we have believed in the signs of our Lord
7:126 (123)	our Lord, pour out upon us patience
7:129 (126)	perchance your Lord will destroy your enemy
7:134 (131)	Moses, pray to thy Lord for us by the covenant
7:137 (133)	perfectly was fulfilled the most fair word of thy Lord
7:141 (137)	in that was a grievous trial from your Lord
7:142 (138)	so the appointed time of his Lord was forty nights
7:143 (139)	when Moses came to Our appointed time and his Lord spoke with him
7:143 (139)	oh my Lord, show me, that I may behold Thee
7:143 (139)	when his Lord revealed Him to the mountain He made it crumble to dust
7:149 (148)	if our Lord has not mercy on us, and forgives us not
7:150 (149)	what, have you outstripped your Lord's commandment
7:151 (150)	O my Lord, forgive me and my brother and enter us into Thy mercy
7:152 (151)	anger shall overtake them from their Lord
7:153 (152)	thy Lord is All-forgiving, All-compassionate
7:154 (153)	guidance, and mercy unto all those who hold their Lord in awe
7:155 (154)	my Lord, hadst Thou willed Thou wouldst have destroyed them before
7:164 (164)	as an excuse to your Lord; and haply they will be godfearing
7:167 (166)	when thy Lord proclaimed He would send forth against them, unto the Day of Resurrection
7:167 (166)	surely thy Lord is swift in retribution
7:172 (171)	when thy Lord took from the Children of Adam, from their loins, their seed
7:172 (171)	am I not your Lord?
7:187 (186)	the knowledge of it is only with my Lord
7:189 (189)	when it became heavy they cried to God their Lord
7:203 (202)	I follow only what is revealed to me from my Lord
7:203 (202)	this is clear testimony from your Lord
7:205 (204)	remember thy Lord in thy soul, humbly and fearfully
7:206 (205)	surely those who are with thy Lord wax not too proud
8:2 (2)	and in their Lord they put their trust
8:4 (4)	they have degrees with their Lord, and forgiveness
8:5 (5)	as thy Lord brought thee forth from thy house with the truth
8:9 (9)	when you were calling upon your Lord for succour
8:12 (12)	when thy Lord was revealing to the angels
8:54 (56)	the people before him, who cried lies to the signs of their Lord
9:21 (21)	their Lord gives them good tidings of mercy from Him and good pleasure
9:31 (31)	they have taken their rabbis and their monks as lords apart from God
9:129 (130)	He is the Lord of the Mighty Throne
10:2 (2)	give thou good tidings to the believers that they have a sure footing with their Lord
10:3 (3)	surely your Lord is God, who created the heavens
10:9 (9)	their Lord will guide them for their belief
10:10 (11)	praise belongs to God, the Lord of all Being
10:15 (16)	truly I fear, if I should rebel against my Lord
10:19 (20)	but for a word that preceded from thy Lord, it had been decided
10:20 (21)	why has a sign not been sent down upon him from his Lord
10:32 (33)	that then is God, your Lord, the True
10:33 (34)	thus the word of thy Lord is realized against the ungodly
10:37 (38)	a distinguishing of the Book, wherein is no doubt, from the Lord of all Being

10:40 (41)	thy Lord knows very well those who do corruption
10:53 (54)	yes, by my Lord! It is true; you cannot frustrate Him
10:57 (58)	now there has come to you an admonition from your Lord
10:61 (62)	not so much as the weight of an ant in earth or heaven escapes from thy Lord
10:85 (85)	our Lord, make us not a temptation to the people
10:88 (88)	our Lord, Thou hast given to Pharaoh and his Council adornment
10:88 (88)	our Lord, let them go astray from Thy way
10:88 (88)	our Lord, obliterate their possessions, and harden their hearts
10:93 (93)	surely thy Lord will decide between them
10:94 (94)	the truth has come to thee from thy Lord
10:96 (96)	those against whom thy Lord's word is realized will not believe
10:99 (99)	if thy Lord had willed, whoever is in the earth would have believed
10:108 (108)	the truth has come to you from you Lord
11:3 (3)	ask forgiveness of your Lord, then repent to Him
11:17 (20)	what of him who stands upon a clear sign from his Lord
11:17 (20)	it is the truth from thy Lord, but most men do not believe
11:18 (21)	those shall be presented before their Lord
11:18 (21)	those are they who lied against their Lord
11:23 (25)	and have humbled themselves unto their Lord
11:28 (30)	if I stand upon a clear sign from my Lord
11:29 (31)	those who believe; they shall surely meet their Lord
11:34 (36)	He is your Lord, and unto Him you shall be returned
11:41 (43)	surely my Lord is All-forgiving, All-compassionate
11:45 (47)	and Noah called unto his Lord
11:45 (47)	O my Lord, my son is of my family, and Thy promise is surely the truth
11:47 (49)	my Lord, I take refuge with Thee
11:52 (54)	O my people, ask forgiveness of your Lord, then repent to Him
11:56 (59)	truly, I have put my trust in God, my Lord
11:56 (59)	and your Lord
11:56 (59)	surely my Lord is on a straight path
11:57 (60)	my Lord will make a people other than you successors
11:57 (60)	my Lord is Guardian over everything
11:59 (62)	that was Ad; they denied the signs of their Lord
11:60 (63)	surely Ad disbelieved in their Lord: so away with Ad
11:61 (64)	surely my Lord is nigh, and answers prayer
11:63 (66)	if I stand upon a clear sign from my Lord
11:66 (69)	thy Lord is the All-strong, the All-mighty
11:68 (71)	surely Thamood disbelieved in their Lord
11:76 (78)	turn away from this; thy Lord's command has surely come
11:81 (83)	Lot, we are messengers of thy Lord
11:83 (84)	one on another, marked with thy Lord
11:88 (90)	if I stand upon a clear sign from my Lord
11:90 (92)	ask forgiveness of your Lord, then repent to Him
11:90 (92)	surely my Lord is All-compassionate, All-loving
11:92 (94)	my Lord encompasses the things you do
11:101 (103)	that they called upon, apart from God, anything, when the command of thy Lord came
11:102 (104)	such is the seizing of thy Lord, when He seizes the cities that are evildoing
11:107 (109)	so long as the heavens and earth abide, save as thy Lord will
11:107 (109)	surely thy Lord accomplishes what He desires
11:108 (110)	so long as the heavens and earth abide, save as thy Lord will
11:110 (112)	there was difference regarding it, and but for a word that preceded from thy Lord
11:111 (113)	each one of them — thy Lord will pay them in full for their works
11:117 (119)	thy Lord would never destroy the cities unjustly

11:118 (120)	had thy Lord willed, He would have made mankind one nation
11:119 (120)	excepting those on whom thy Lord has mercy
11:119 (120)	to that end He created them, and perfectly is fulfilled the word of thy Lord
11:123 (123)	thy Lord is not heedless of the things you do
12:6 (6)	so will thy Lord choose thee, and teach thee the interpretation of tales
12:6 (6)	surely thy Lord is All-knowing, All-wise
12:23 (23)	surely my lord has given me a goodly lodging
12:24 (24)	he would have taken her, but that he saw the proof of his Lord
12:33 (33)	my Lord, prison is dearer to me than that they call me to
12:34 (34)	his Lord answered him, and He turned away from him their guile
12:37 (37)	that I shall tell you is of what my Lord has taught me
12:39 (39)	which is better, my fellow-prisoners — many lords at variance, or God the One
12:41 (41)	fellow-prisoners, as for one of you, he shall pour wine for his lord
12:42 (42)	mention me in thy lord's presence
12:42 (42)	but Satan caused him to forget to mention him to his master
12:50 (50)	return unto thy lord, and ask of him
12:50 (50)	surely my Lord has knowledge of their guile
12:53 (53)	except inasmuch as my Lord had mercy
12:53 (53)	truly my Lord is All-forgiving, All-compassionate
12:98 (99)	assuredly I will ask my Lord to forgive you
12:100 (101)	this is the interpretation of my vision of long ago; my Lord has made it true
12:100 (101)	my Lord is gentle to what He will
12:101 (102)	O my Lord, Thou hast given me to rule
13:1 (1)	that which has been sent down to thee from thy Lord is the truth
13:2 (2)	haply you will have faith in the encounter with your Lord
13:5 (6)	those are they that disbelieve in their Lord
13:6 (7)	thy Lord is forgiving to men, for all their evil-doing
13:6 (7)	thy Lord is terrible in retribution
13:7 (8)	why has a sign not been sent down upon him from his Lord
13:16 (17)	who is the Lord of the heavens and of the earth?
13:18 (18)	for those who answer their Lord, the reward most fair
13:19 (19)	is he who knows what is sent down to thee from thy Lord is the truth, like him who is blind?
13:21 (21)	and fear their Lord, and dread the evil reckoning
13:22 (22)	patient men, desirous of the Face of their Lord
13:27 (27)	why has a sign not been sent down upon him from his Lord?
13:30 (29)	He is my Lord — there is no god but He
14:1 (1)	thou mayest bring forth mankind from the shadows to the light by the leave of their Lord
14:6 (6)	in that was a grievous trial from your Lord
14:7 (7)	and when your Lord proclaimed
14:13 (16)	then did their Lord reveal unto them
14:18 (21)	the likeness of those who disbelieve in their Lord: their works are as ashes
14:23 (28)	therein dwelling forever, by the leave of their Lord
14:25 (30)	it gives its produce every season by the leave of its Lord
14:35 (38)	my Lord, make this land secure
14:36 (39)	my Lord, they have led astray many men
14:37 (40)	our Lord, I have made some of my seed to dwell in a valley
14:37 (40)	our Lord, let them perform the prayer
14:38 (41)	our Lord, Thou knowest what we keep secret
14:39 (41)	surely my Lord hears the petition
14:40 (42)	my Lord, make me a performer of the prayer
14:40 (42)	our Lord, and receive my petition
14:41 (42)	our Lord, forgive Thou me and my parents
14:44 (45)	our Lord, defer us to a near term
15:25 (25)	it is thy Lord shall muster them

15:28 (28)	and when thy Lord said to the angels
15:36 (36)	my Lord, respite me till the day they shall be raised
15:39 (39)	my Lord, for Thy perverting me I shall deck all fair to them in the earth
15:56 (56)	who despairs of the mercy of his Lord, excepting those that are astray?
15:86 (86)	surely thy Lord, He is the All-creator, the All-knowing
15:92 (92)	now by thy Lord, We shall surely question them all together
15:98 (98)	proclaim thy Lord's praise
15:99 (99)	serve thy Lord, until the Certain comes to thee
16:7 (7)	surely your Lord is All-clement, All-compassionate
16:24 (26)	what has your Lord sent down
16:30 (32)	what has your Lord sent down
16:33 (35)	but that the angels shall come to them, or thy Lord's command shall come
16:42 (44)	even such men as are patient, and put their trust in their Lord
16:47 (49)	surely thy Lord is All-clement, All-compassionate
16:50 (52)	they fear their Lord above them
16:54 (56)	lo, a party of you assign associates to their Lord
16:68 (70)	and thy Lord revealed unto the bees, saying
16:69 (71)	then eat of all manner of fruit, and follow the ways of your Lord
16:86 (88)	our Lord, these are our associates on whom we called apart from Thee
16:99 (101)	he has no authority over those who believe and trust in their Lord
16:102 (104)	the Holy Spirit sent it down from thy Lord in truth
16:110 (111)	then, surely thy Lord
16:110 (111)	thy Lord thereafter is All-forgiving, All-compassionate
16:119 (120)	then, surely thy Lord
16:119 (120)	thy Lord thereafter is All-forgiving, All-compassionate
16:124 (125)	thy Lord will decide between them on the Day of Resurrection
16:125 (126)	call thou to the way of thy Lord with wisdom
16:125 (126)	thy Lord knows very well those who have gone astray
17:8 (8)	perchance your Lord will have mercy upon you
17:12 (13)	that you may seek bounty from your Lord
17:17 (18)	thy Lord suffices as one who is aware of and sees the sins of His servants
17:20 (21)	each We succour, these and those, from thy Lord's gift
17:20 (21)	thy Lord's gift is not confined
17:23 (24)	thy Lord has decreed you shall not serve any but Him
17:24 (25)	my Lord, have mercy upon them, as they raised me up
17:25 (26)	your Lord knows very well what is in your hearts
17:27 (29)	Satan is unthankful to his Lord
17:28 (30)	seeking mercy from thy Lord that thou hopest for
17:30 (32)	thy Lord outspreads and straitens His provision unto whom He will
17:38 (40)	the wickedness of it is hateful in the sight of thy Lord
17:39 (41)	that is of the wisdom thy Lord has revealed to thee
17:40 (42)	has your Lord favoured you with sons
17:46 (49)	when thou mentionest thy Lord only in the Koran
17:54 (56)	your Lord knows you very well
17:55 (57)	thy Lord knows very well all who are in the heavens
17:57 (59)	those they call upon are themselves seeking the means to come to their Lord
17:57 (59)	thy Lord's chastisement is a thing to beware of
17:60 (62)	thy Lord encompasses men
17:65 (67)	thy Lord suffices as a guardian
17:66 (68)	your Lord it is who drives for you the ships on the sea
17:79 (81)	it may be that thy Lord will raise thee up to a laudable station
17:80 (82)	my Lord, lead me in with a just ingoing
17:84 (86)	your Lord knows very well what man is best guided as to the way
17:85 (87)	the Spirit is of the bidding of my Lord
17:87 (89)	excepting by some mercy of thy Lord

17:93 (95)	glory be to my Lord
17:100 (102)	if you possessed the treasuries of my Lord's mercy
17:102 (104)	thou knowest that none sent these down, except the Lord of the heavens
17:108 (108)	glory be to our Lord
17:108 (108)	our Lord's promise is performed
18:10 (9)	our Lord, give us mercy from Thee
18:13 (12)	they were youths who believed in their Lord
18:14 (13)	our Lord is the (Lord) of the heavens and earth
18:14 (13)	our (Lord) is the Lord of the heavens and earth
18:16 (15)	your Lord will unfold to you of His mercy
18:19 (18)	your Lord knows very well how long you have tarried
18:21 (20)	their Lord knows of them very well
18:22 (21)	my Lord knows very well their number
18:24 (23)	mention thy Lord, when thou forgettest
18:24 (23)	it may be that my Lord will guide me unto something nearer to rectitude
18:27 (26)	recite what has been revealed to thee of the Book of thy Lord
18:28 (27)	restrain thyself with those who call upon their Lord at morning
18:29 (28)	the truth is from your Lord
18:36 (34)	if I am indeed returned to my Lord, I shall surely find a better resort
18:38 (36)	He is God, my Lord
18:38 (36)	I will not associate with my Lord any one
18:40 (38)	it may be that my Lord will give me better than thy garden
18:42 (40)	would I had not associated with my Lord any one
18:46 (44)	the deeds of righteousness, are better with your Lord in reward
18:48 (46)	they shall be presented before their Lord in ranks
18:49 (47)	they shall find all they wrought present, and thy Lord shall not wrong anyone
18:50 (48)	and committed ungodliness against his Lord's command
18:55 (53)	and seeking their Lord's forgiveness
18:57 (55)	who, being reminded of the signs of his Lord, turns away from them
18:58 (57)	thy Lord is the All-forgiving, full of mercy
18:82 (81)	thy Lord desired that they should come of age
18:82 (81)	then bring forth their treasure as a mercy from thy Lord
18:87 (86)	then he shall be returned to his Lord and He shall chastise him
18:95 (94)	that wherein my Lord has established me is better
18:98 (97)	this is a mercy from my Lord
18:98 (98)	when the promise of my Lord comes to pass, He will make it into powder
18:98 (98)	my Lord's promise is ever true
18:105 (105)	those are they that disbelieve in the signs of their Lord
18:109 (109)	if the sea were ink for the Words of my Lord
18:109 (109)	the sea would be spent before the Words of my Lord are spent
18:110 (110)	so let him, who hopes for the encounter with his Lord
18:110 (110)	and not associate with his Lord's service anyone
19:2 (1)	the mention of thy Lord's mercy unto His servant Zachariah
19:3 (2)	when he called upon his Lord secretly
19:4 (3)	O my Lord, behold the bones within me are feeble
19:4 (4)	in calling on Thee, my Lord, I have never been hitherto unprosperous
19:6 (6)	make him, my Lord, well-pleasing
19:8 (9)	O my Lord, how shall I have a son
19:9 (10)	thy Lord says, 'Easy is that for me'
19:10 (11)	Lord, appoint to me some sign
19:19 (19)	I am but a messenger come from thy Lord
19:21 (21)	even so thy Lord has said
19:24 (24)	see, thy Lord has set below thee a rivulet
19:36 (37)	surely God is my Lord
19:36 (37)	and your Lord; so serve you Him

19:47 (48)	I will ask my Lord to forgive thee
19:48 (49)	I will call upon my Lord
19:48 (49)	haply I shall not be, in calling upon my Lord, unprosperous
19:55 (56)	and he was pleasing to his Lord
19:64 (65)	we come not down, save at the commandment of thy Lord
19:64 (65)	thy Lord is never forgetful
19:65 (66)	Lord He of the heavens and earth and all that is between them
19:68 (69)	now, by thy Lord, We shall surely muster them
19:71 (72)	that for thy Lord is a thing decreed, determined
19:76 (79)	the deeds of righteousness, are better with thy Lord in reward
20:12 (12)	I am thy Lord; put off thy shoes
20:25 (26)	Lord, open my breast
20:45 (47)	O our Lord
20:47 (49)	We are the Messengers of thy Lord
20:47 (49)	we have brought thee a sign from thy Lord
20:49 (51)	who is your Lord, Moses?
20:52 (54)	the knowledge of them is with my Lord, in a Book
20:52 (54)	my Lord goes not astray, nor forgets
20:70 (73)	'We believe,' they said, 'in the Lord of Aaron and Moses'
20:73 (75)	we believe in our Lord, that He may pardon us
20:74 (76)	whosoever comes unto his Lord a sinner, for him awaits Gehenna
20:84 (86)	I have hastened, Lord, only that I may please Thee
20:86 (89)	my people, did your Lord not promise a fair promise to you
20:86 (89)	or did you desire that anger should alight on you from you Lord
20:90 (92)	your Lord is the All-merciful
20:105 (105)	my Lord will scatter them as ashes
20:114 (113)	O my Lord, increase me in knowledge
20:121 (119)	Adam disobeyed his Lord, and so he erred
20:122 (120)	therafter his Lord chose him
20:125 (125)	O my Lord, why hast thou raised me blind
20:127 (127)	We recompense him who is prodigal and believes not in the signs of his Lord
20:129 (129)	but for a word that preceded from thy Lord, and a stated term
20:130 (130)	proclaim thy Lord's praise before the rising of the sun
20:131 (131)	thy Lord's provision is better, and more enduring
20:133 (133)	why does he not bring us a sign from his Lord
20:134 (134)	our Lord, why didst Thou not send us a Messenger
21:2 (2)	no Remembrance from their Lord comes to them lately renewed
21:4 (4)	my Lord knows what is said in the heavens and the earth
21:22 (22)	glory be to God, the Lord of the Throne
21:42 (43)	but from the Remembrance of their Lord they are turning away
21:46 (47)	if but a breath of thy Lord's chastisement touched them
21:49 (50)	such as fear their Lord in the Unseen, trembling because of the Hour
21:56 (57)	nay, but your Lord
21:56 (57)	is the Lord of the heavens and the earth
21:83 (83)	and Job — when he called unto his Lord
21:89 (89)	and Zachariah — when he called unto his Lord
21:89 (89)	O my Lord, leave me not solitary; though Thou art the best
21:92 (92)	this community of yours is one community, and I am your Lord
21:112 (112)	my Lord, judge Thou with truth
21:112 (112)	our Lord is the All-merciful
22:1 (1)	O men, fear your Lord
22:19 (20)	these are two disputants who have disputed concerning their Lord
22:30 (31)	whosoever venerates the sacred things of God, it shall be better for him with his Lord
22:40 (41)	our Lord is God

22:47 (46)	a day with thy Lord is as a thousand years of your counting
22:54 (53)	they who have been given knowledge may know that it is the truth from thy Lord
22:67 (66)	and do thou summon unto thy Lord
22:77 (76)	O men bow you down and prostrate yourselves, and serve your Lord
23:26 (26)	O my Lord, help me, for that they cry me lies
23:29 (30)	O my Lord, do Thou harbour me in a blessed harbour
23:39 (41)	O my Lord, help me, for that they cry me lies
23:52 (54)	this community of yours is one community, and I am your Lord
23:57 (59)	surely those who tremble in fear of their Lord
23:58 (60)	those who believe in the signs of their Lord
23:59 (61)	those who associate naught with their Lord
23:60 (62)	their hearts quaking that they are returning to their Lord
23:72 (74)	yet the tribute of thy Lord is better
23:86 (88)	who is the Lord of the seven heavens
23:86 (88)	and the Lord of the mighty Throne
23:93 (95)	O my Lord, if Thou shouldst show me that they are promised
23:94 (96)	O my Lord, put me not among the people of the evildoers
23:97 (99)	O my Lord, I take refuge in Thee from the evil suggestions of the Satans
23:98 (100)	I take refuge in Thee, O my Lord, lest they attend me
23:99 (101)	my Lord, return me
23:106 (108)	our Lord, our adversity prevailed over us; we were an erring people
23:107 (109)	our Lord, bring us forth out of it
23:109 (111)	our Lord, we believe; therefore forgive us, and have mercy on us
23:116 (117)	there is no god but He, the Lord of the noble Throne
23:117 (117)	whosoever calls upon another god with God, whereof he has no proof, his reckoning is with his Lord
23:118 (118)	my Lord, forgive and have mercy, for Thou art the best
25:16 (17)	it is a promise binding upon thy Lord
25:20 (22)	thy Lord is ever All-seeing
25:21 (23)	or why see we not our Lord?
25:30 (32)	O my Lord, behold, my people have taken this Koran
25:31 (33)	but thy Lord suffices as a guide and as a helper
25:45 (47)	hast thou not regarded thy Lord, how He has stretched out the shadow
25:54 (56)	kindred of blood and marriage; thy Lord is All-powerful
25:55 (57)	the unbeliever is ever a partisan against his Lord
25:57 (59)	except for him who wishes to take to his Lord a way
25:64 (65)	who pass the night prostrate to their Lord and standing
25:65 (66)	our Lord, turn Thou from us the chastisement of Gehenna
25:73 (73)	who, when they are reminded of the signs of their Lord, fall not down thereat
25:74 (74)	our Lord, give us refreshment of our wives and seed
25:77 (77)	my Lord esteems you not at all were it not for your prayer
26:9 (8)	thy Lord, He is the All-mighty, the All-compassionate
26:10 (9)	and when thy Lord called to Moses
26:12 (11)	my Lord, I fear they will cry me lies
26:16 (15)	verily, I am the Messenger of the Lord of all Being
26:21 (20)	but my Lord gave me Judgment
26:23 (22)	and what is the Lord of all Being?
26:24 (23)	the Lord of the heavens and earth, and what between them is
26:26 (25)	your Lord
26:26 (25)	and the Lord of your fathers, the ancients
26:28 (27)	the Lord of the East and West, and what between them is
26:47 (46)	we believe in the Lord of all Being
26:48 (47)	the Lord of Moses and Aaron
26:50 (50)	unto our Lord we are turning

26:51 (51)	we are eager that our Lord should forgive us our offences
26:62 (62)	surely my Lord is with me; He will guide me
26:68 (68)	thy Lord, He is the All-mighty, the All-compassionate
26:77 (77)	they are an enemy to me, except the Lord of all Being
26:83 (83)	my Lord, give me Judgment, and join me
26:98 (98)	when we made you equal with the Lord of all Being
26:104 (104)	thy Lord, He is the All-mighty, the All-compassionate
26:109 (109)	my wage falls only upon the Lord of all Being
26:113 (113)	their account falls only upon my Lord
26:117 (117)	my Lord, my people have cried me lies
26:122 (122)	thy Lord, He is the All-mighty, the All-compassionate
26:127 (127)	my wage falls only upon the Lord of all Being
26:140 (140)	thy Lord, He is the All-mighty, the All-compassionate
26:145 (145)	my wage falls only upon the Lord of all Being
26:159 (159)	thy Lord, He is the All-mighty, the All-compassionate
26:164 (164)	my wage falls only upon the Lord of all Being
26:166 (166)	leaving your wives that your Lord created for you
26:169 (169)	my Lord, deliver me and my people from that they do
26:175 (175)	thy Lord, He is the All-mighty, the All-compassionate
26:180 (180)	my wage falls only upon the Lord of all Being
26:188 (188)	my Lord knows very well what you are doing
26:191 (191)	thy Lord, He is the All-mighty, the All-compassionate
26:192 (192)	truly it is the revelation of the Lord of all Being
27:8 (8)	glory be to God, the Lord of all Being
27:19 (19)	my Lord, dispose me that I may be thankful for Thy blessing
27:26 (26)	there is no god but He, the Lord of the Mighty Throne
27:40 (40)	this is of my Lord's bounty that He may try me
27:40 (40)	my Lord is surely All-sufficient, All-generous
27:44 (45)	my Lord, indeed I have wronged myself
27:44 (45)	I surrender with Solomon to God, the Lord of all Being
27:73 (75)	surely thy Lord is bountiful to men
27:74 (76)	surely thy Lord knows what their hearts conceal
27:78 (80)	surely thy Lord will decide between them by His Judgment
27:91 (93)	I have only been commanded to serve the Lord of this territory
27:93 (95)	thy Lord is not heedless of the things you do
28:16 (15)	my Lord, I have wronged myself. Forgive me
28:17 (16)	my Lord, forasmuch as Thou hast blessed me, I will never be a partisan
28:21 (20)	my Lord, deliver me from the people of the evildoers
28:22 (21)	it may be that my Lord will guide me on the right way
28:24 (24)	O my Lord, surely I have need of whatever good Thou shalt have sent down upon me
28:30 (30)	Moses, I am God, the Lord of all Being
28:32 (32)	so these shall be two proofs from thy Lord to Pharaoh
28:33 (33)	my Lord, I have indeed slain a living soul among them
28:37 (37)	my Lord knows very well who comes with the guidance from Him
28:46 (46)	but for a mercy from thy Lord, that thou mayest warn a people
28:47 (47)	our Lord, why didst Thou not send a Messenger to us
28:53 (53)	we believe in it; surely it is the truth from our Lord
28:59 (59)	yet thy Lord never destroyed the cities until He sent in their mother-city a Messenger
28:63 (63)	our Lord, those whom we perverted, we perverted them even as we ourselves erred
28:68 (68)	thy Lord creates whatsoever He will and He chooses
28:69 (69)	thy Lord knows what their breasts conceal and what they publish
28:85 (85)	my Lord knows very well who comes with guidance

28:86 (86)	cast unto thee, except it be as a mercy from thy Lord
28:87 (87)	call upon thy Lord, and be thou not of the idolaters
29:10 (9)	then if help comes from thy Lord, he will say
29:26 (25)	I will flee to my Lord; He is the All-mighty
29:30 (29)	my Lord, help me against the people that work corruption
29:50 (49)	why have signs not been sent down upon him from his Lord
29:59 (59)	such men as are patient, and put their trust in their Lord
30:8 (7)	most men disbelieve in the encounter with their Lord
30:33 (32)	when some affliction visits mankind, they call unto their Lord
30:33 (32)	a party of them assign associates to their Lord
31:5 (4)	those are upon guidance from their Lord
31:33 (32)	O men, fear your Lord, and dread a day
32:2 (1)	the Book, wherein no doubt is, from the Lord of all Being
32:3 (2)	not so; it is the truth from thy Lord
32:10 (10)	they disbelieve in the encounter with their Lord
32:11 (11)	then to your Lord you shall be returned
32:12 (12)	the guilty hanging their heads before their Lord
32:12 (12)	our Lord, we have seen and heard; now return us
32:15 (15)	and proclaim the praise of their Lord
32:16 (16)	their sides shun their couches as they call on their Lord
32:22 (22)	he who is reminded of the signs of his Lord
32:25 (25)	thy Lord will distinguish between them on the Resurrection Day
33:2 (2)	follow what is revealed to thee from thy Lord
33:67 (67)	our Lord, we obeyed our chiefs and great ones
33:68 (68)	our Lord, give them chastisement twofold
34:3 (3)	yes indeed, by my Lord, it shall come to you
34:6 (6)	that what has been sent down to thee from thy Lord
34:12 (11)	by the leave of his Lord
34:15 (14)	eat of your Lord's provision, and give thanks
34:15 (14)	a good land, and a Lord All-forgiving
34:19 (18)	our Lord, prolong the stages of our travel
34:21 (20)	thy Lord is Guardian over everything
34:23 (22)	what said your Lord?
34:26 (25)	our Lord will bring us together
34:31 (30)	when the evildoers are stationed before their Lord, bandying argument
34:36 (35)	my Lord outspreads and straitens His provision
34:39 (38)	my lord outspreads and straitens His provision
34:48 (47)	my Lord hurls the truth — the Knower of the Unseen
34:50 (49)	if I am guided, it is by what my Lord reveals to me
35:13 (14)	that is God, your Lord; to Him belongs the Kingdom
35:18 (19)	thou warnest only those who fear their Lord
35:34 (31)	our Lord is All-forgiving, All-thankful
35:37 (34)	our Lord, bring us forth, and we will do righteousness
35:39 (37)	their unbelief increases the disbelievers only in hate in their Lord's sight
36:16 (15)	our Lord knows we are Envoys unto you
36:25 (24)	I believe in your Lord; therefore hear me
36:27 (26)	that my Lord has forgiven me
36:46 (46)	never any sign of the signs of their Lord comes to them
36:51 (51)	behold, they are sliding down from their tombs unto their Lord
36:58 (58)	such is the greeting, from a Lord All-compassionate
37:5 (5)	Lord of the heavens and the earth
37:5 (5)	Lord of the Easts
37:31 (30)	so our Lord's Word is realised against us
37:57 (55)	but for my Lord's blessing, I were one of the arraigned
37:84 (82)	when he came unto his Lord with a pure heart

37:87 (85)	what think you then of the Lord of all Being?
37:99 (97)	I am going to my Lord
37:100 (98)	my Lord, give me one of the righteous
37:126 (126)	God, your Lord
37:126 (126)	the Lord of your fathers, the ancients
37:149 (149)	has thy Lord daughters, and they sons?
37:180 (180)	glory be to thy Lord
37:180 (180)	the Lord of Glory, above that they describe
37:182 (182)	praise belongs to God, the Lord of all Being
38:9 (8)	have they the treasuries of thy Lord's mercy
38:16 (15)	our Lord, hasten to us our share before the Day of Reckoning
38:24 (23)	therefore he sought forgiveness of his Lord
38:32 (31)	the love of good things better than the remembrance of my Lord
38:35 (34)	my Lord, forgive me
38:41 (40)	remember also Our servant Job; when he called to his Lord
38:61 (61)	our Lord, whoso forwarded this for us, give him a double chastisement
38:66 (66)	Lord of the heavens and earth
38:71 (71)	when thy Lord said to the angels
39:6 (8)	that then is God, your Lord
39:7 (9)	to your Lord shall you return
39:8 (11)	when some affliction visits a man, he calls upon his Lord
39:9 (12)	and hoping for the mercy of his Lord
39:10 (13)	My servants who believe, fear your Lord
39:13 (15)	truly I fear, if I should rebel against my Lord
39:20 (21)	those who fear their Lord — for them await lofty chambers
39:22 (23)	so he walks in a light from his Lord
39:23 (24)	whereat shiver the skins of those who fear their Lord
39:31 (32)	on the Day of Resurrection before your Lord you shall dispute
39:34 (35)	they shall have whatsoever they will with their Lord
39:54 (55)	turn unto your Lord and surrender to Him
39:55 (56)	the fairest of what has been sent down to you from your Lord
39:69 (69)	the earth shall shine with the light of its Lord
39:71 (71)	reciting to you the signs of your Lord
39:73 (73)	those that feared their lord shall be driven in companies
39:75 (75)	encircling about the Throne proclaiming the praise of their Lord
39:75 (75)	praise belongs to God, the Lord of all Being
40:6 (6)	even so the Word of thy Lord was realised against the unbelievers
40:7 (7)	those round about it proclaim the praise of their Lord
40:7 (7)	our Lord, Thou embracest every thing in mercy and knowledge
40:8 (8)	our Lord, and admit them to the Gardens of Eden
40:11 (11)	our Lord, Thou hast caused us to die two deaths
40:26 (27)	let me slay Moses, and let him call to his Lord
40:27 (28)	I take refuge in my Lord
40:27 (28)	and your Lord from every man who is proud
40:28 (29)	my Lord is God
40:28 (29)	he has brought you the clear signs from your Lord
40:49 (52)	call on your Lord, to lighten for us one day of the chastisement
40:55 (57)	proclaim the praise of thy Lord at evening and dawn
40:60 (62)	your Lord has said
40:62 (64)	that then is God, your Lord, the Creator of everything
40:64 (66)	that then is God, your Lord, so blessed be God
40:64 (66)	that then is God, your Lord, so blessed be God
40:65 (67)	praise belongs to God, the Lord of all Being
40:66 (68)	since the clear signs came to me from my Lord
40:66 (68)	I am commanded to surrender to the Lord of all Being

41:9 (8)	that is the Lord of all Being
41:14 (13)	had our Lord willed, surely He would have sent down angels
41:23 (22)	the thought you thought about your Lord, has destroyed you
41:29 (29)	our Lord, show us those that led us astray
41:30 (30)	our Lord is God
41:38 (38)	those who are with thy Lord do glorify Him
41:43 (43)	thy Lord is a Lord of forgiveness and of painful retribution
41:45 (45)	but for a Word that preceded from thy Lord
41:46 (46)	thy Lord wrongs not His servants
41:50 (50)	if I am returned to my Lord
41:53 (53)	suffices it not as to thy Lord, that He is witness over everything?
41:54 (54)	are they not in doubt touching the encounter with their Lord
42:5 (3)	the angels proclaim the praise of their Lord
42:10 (8)	that then is God, my Lord
42:14 (13)	but for a Word that preceded from thy Lord until a stated term
42:15 (14)	God is our Lord
42:15 (14)	and your Lord
42:16 (15)	their argument is null and void in the sight of their Lord
42:22 (21)	whatsoever they will they shall have with their Lord
42:36 (34)	those who believe and put their trust in their Lord
42:38 (36)	those who answer their Lord, and perform the prayer
42:47 (46)	answer your Lord, before there comes a day from God
43:13 (12)	then remember your Lord's blessing
43:14 (13)	surely unto our Lord we are turning
43:32 (31)	is it they who divide the mercy of thy Lord
43:32 (31)	the mercy of thy Lord is better than that they amass
43:35 (34)	the world to come with thy Lord is for the godfearing
43:46 (45)	surely I am the Messenger of the Lord of all Being
43:49 (48)	pray to thy Lord for us by the covenant He has made with thee
43:64 (64)	God is my Lord
43:64 (64)	and your Lord
43:77 (77)	O Malik, let thy Lord have done with us
43:82 (82)	glory be to the Lord of the heavens and the earth
43:82 (82)	the Lord of the Throne
43:88 (88)	my Lord, surely these are a people who believe not
44:6 (5)	as a mercy from thy Lord
44:7 (6)	Lord of the heavens and earth
44:8 (7)	your Lord
44:8 (7)	and the Lord of your fathers, the ancients
44:12 (11)	O our Lord, remove Thou from us the chastisement
44:20 (19)	I take refuge in my Lord
44:20 (19)	and your Lord, lest you should stone me
44:22 (21)	he called to his Lord, saying
44:57 (57)	a bounty from thy Lord; that is the mighty triumph
45:11 (10)	those who disbelieve in the signs of their Lord
45:15 (14)	to your Lord you shall be returned
45:17 (16)	thy Lord will decide between them on the Day of Resurrection
45:30 (29)	their Lord shall admit them into His mercy
45:36 (35)	the Lord of the heavens
45:36 (35)	and the Lord of the earth
45:36 (35)	Lord of all Being
46:13 (12)	our Lord is God
46:15 (14)	O my Lord, dispose me that I may be thankful
46:25 (24)	destroying everything by the commandment of its Lord
46:34 (33)	yes, by our Lord

47:2 (2)	it is the truth from their Lord
47:3 (3)	those who believe follow the truth from their Lord
47:14 (15)	he who is upon a clear sign from his Lord
47:15 (17)	for them is every fruit, and forgiveness from their Lord
50:27 (26)	our Lord, I made him not insolent, but he was in far error
50:39 (38)	proclaim thy Lord's praise
51:16 (16)	taking whatsoever their Lord has given them
51:23 (23)	by the Lord of heaven and earth, it is as surely true
51:30 (30)	so says thy Lord; He is the All-wise
51:34 (34)	marked with thy Lord for the prodigal
51:44 (44)	they turned in disdain from the commandment of their Lord
52:7 (7)	surely thy Lord's chastisement is about to fall
52:18 (18)	rejoicing in that their Lord has given them
52:18 (18)	their Lord shall guard them against the chastisement
52:29 (29)	by thy Lord's blessing thou art not a soothsayer
52:37 (37)	or are thy Lord's treasuries in their keeping?
52:48 (48)	be thou patient under the judgment of thy Lord
52:48 (48)	proclaim the praise of thy Lord when thou arisest
53:18 (18)	indeed, he saw one of the greatest signs of his Lord
53:23 (23)	yet guidance has come to them from their Lord
53:30 (31)	thy Lord knows very well those who have gone astray
53:32 (33)	surely thy Lord is wide in His forgiveness
53:42 (43)	the final end is unto thy Lord
53:49 (50)	it is He who is the Lord of Sirius
53:55 (56)	which of thy Lord's bounties disputest thou?
54:10 (10)	so he called unto his Lord, saying
55:13 (12)	O which of your Lord's bounties will you and you deny?
55:16 (15)	O which of your Lord's bounties will you and you deny?
55:17 (16)	Lord of the Two Easts
55:17 (17)	Lord of the Two Wests
55:18 (18)	O which of your Lord's bounties will you and you deny?
55:21 (21)	O which of your Lord's bounties will you and you deny?
55:23 (23)	O which of your Lord's bounties will you and you deny?
55:25 (25)	O which of your Lord's bounties will you and you deny?
55:27 (27)	the Face of thy Lord, majestic, splendid
55:28 (28)	O which of your Lord's bounties will you and you deny?
55:30 (30)	O which of your Lord's bounties will you and you deny?
55:32 (32)	O which of your Lord's bounties will you and you deny?
55:34 (34)	O which of your Lord's bounties will you and you deny?
55:36 (36)	O which of your Lord's bounties will you and you deny?
55:38 (38)	O which of your Lord's bounties will you and you deny?
55:40 (40)	O which of your Lord's bounties will you and you deny?
55:42 (42)	O which of your Lord's bounties will you and you deny?
55:45 (45)	O which of your Lord's bounties will you and you deny?
55:46 (46)	such as fears the Station of his Lord
55:47 (47)	O which of your Lord's bounties will you and you deny?
55:49 (49)	O which of your Lord's bounties will you and you deny?
55:51 (51)	O which of your Lord's bounties will you and you deny?
55:53 (53)	O which of your Lord's bounties will you and you deny?
55:55 (55)	O which of your Lord's bounties will you and you deny?
55:57 (57)	O which of your Lord's bounties will you and you deny?
55:59 (59)	O which of your Lord's bounties will you and you deny?
55:61 (61)	O which of your Lord's bounties will you and you deny?
55:63 (63)	O which of your Lord's bounties will you and you deny?
55:65 (65)	O which of your Lord's bounties will you and you deny?

55:67 (67)	O which of your Lord's bounties will you and you deny?
55:69 (69)	O which of your Lord's bounties will you and you deny?
55:71 (71)	O which of your Lord's bounties will you and you deny?
55:73 (73)	O which of your Lord's bounties will you and you deny?
55:75 (75)	O which of your Lord's bounties will you and you deny?
55:77 (77)	O which of your Lord's bounties will you and you deny?
55:78 (78)	blessed be the Name of thy Lord, majestic, splendid
56:74 (73)	then magnify the Name of thy Lord, the All-mighty
56:80 (79)	a sending down from the Lord of all Being
56:96 (96)	then magnify the Name of thy Lord, the All-mighty
57:8 (8)	the Messenger is calling you to believe in your Lord
57:19 (18)	they are the just men and the martyrs in their Lord's sight
57:21 (21)	race to forgiveness from your Lord
59:10 (10)	our Lord, forgive us and our brothers, who preceded us
59:10 (10)	our Lord, surely Thou art the All-gentle
59:16 (16)	surely I fear God, the Lord of all Being
60:1 (1)	and you because you believe in God your Lord
60:4 (4)	our Lord, in Thee we trust; to Thee we turn
60:5 (5)	our Lord, make us not a temptation to those who disbelieve
60:5 (5)	our Lord, Thou art the All-mighty, the All-wise
63:10 (10)	O my Lord, if only Thou wouldst defer me unto a near term
64:7 (7)	by my Lord! You shall be raised up
65:1 (1)	count the period, and fear God your Lord
65:8 (8)	how many a city turned in disdain from the commandment of its Lord
66:5 (5)	his Lord will give him in exchange wives better than you
66:8 (8)	it may be that your Lord will acquit you of your evil deeds
66:8 (8)	our Lord, perfect for us our light, and forgive us
66:11 (11)	my Lord, build for me a house in Paradise
66:12 (12)	she confirmed the Words of her Lord and His Books
67:6 (6)	for those who disbelieve in their Lord there awaits the chastisement
67:12 (12)	those who fear their Lord in the Unseen
68:2 (2)	thou art not, by the blessing of thy Lord, a man possessed
68:7 (7)	thy Lord knows very well those who have gone astray
68:19 (19)	then a visitation from thy Lord visited it
68:29 (29)	glory be to God, our Lord
68:32 (32)	it may be that our Lord will give us in exchange a better than it
68:32 (32)	to our Lord we humbly turn
68:34 (34)	for the godfearing shall be Gardens of Bliss with their Lord
68:48 (48)	be thou patient under the judgement of thy Lord
68:49 (49)	had there not overtaken him a blessing from his Lord
68:50 (50)	but his Lord had chosen him
69:10 (10)	they rebelled against the Messenger of their Lord
69:17 (17)	upon that day eight shall carry above them the Throne of thy Lord
69:43 (43)	a sending down from the Lord of all Being
69:52 (52)	then magnify the Name of thy Lord, the All-mighty
70:27 (27)	go in fear of the chastisement of their Lord
70:28 (28)	from their Lord's chastisement none feels secure
70:40 (40)	I swear by the Lord of the Easts and the Wests
71:5 (5)	my Lord, I have called my people by night and by day
71:10 (9)	ask you forgiveness of your Lord
71:21 (20)	my Lord, they have rebelled against me
71:26 (27)	my Lord, leave not upon the earth of the unbelievers even one
71:28 (29)	my Lord, forgive me and my parents
72:2 (2)	we will not associate with our Lord anyone
72:3 (3)	exalted be our Lord's majesty

72:10 (10)	whether their Lord intends for them rectitude
72:13 (13)	whosoever believes in his Lord, he shall fear neither paltriness
72:17 (17)	whosoever turns away from the Remembrance of his Lord
72:20 (20)	I call only upon my Lord
72:25 (26)	whether my Lord will appoint for it a space
72:28 (28)	they have delivered the Messages of their Lord
73:8 (8)	remember the Name of thy Lord, and devote thyself unto Him
73:9 (9)	Lord of the East and the West
73:19 (19)	so let him who will take unto his Lord a way
73:20 (20)	thy Lord knows that thou keepest vigil nearly two-thirds of the night
74:3 (3)	thy Lord magnify
74:7 (7)	be patient unto thy Lord
74:31 (34)	none knows the hosts of thy Lord but He
75:12 (12)	upon that day the recourse shall be to thy Lord
75:23 (23)	gazing upon their Lord
75:30 (30)	upon that day unto thy Lord shall be the driving
76:10 (10)	for we fear from our Lord a frowning day, inauspicious
76:21 (21)	their Lord shall give them to drink a pure draught
76:24 (24)	be thou patient under the judgment of thy Lord
76:25 (25)	remember the Name of thy Lord at dawn and in the evening
76:29 (29)	he who will, takes unto his Lord a way
78:36 (36)	for a recompense from thy Lord, a gift, a reckoning
78:37 (37)	Lord of the heavens and earth
78:39 (39)	whosoever wills takes unto his Lord a resort
79:16 (16)	when his Lord called to him in the holy valley, Towa
79:19 (19)	that I should guide thee to thy Lord
79:24 (24)	I am your Lord, the Most High
79:40 (40)	as for him who feared the Station of his Lord
79:44 (44)	unto thy Lord is the final end of it
81:29 (29)	will you shall not, unless God wills, the Lord of all Being
82:6 (6)	O Man! What deceived thee as to thy generous Lord
83:6 (6)	a day when mankind shall stand before the Lord of all Being
83:15 (15)	upon that day they shall be veiled from their Lord
84:2 (2)	and gives ear to its Lord, and is fitly disposed
84:5 (5)	and gives ear to its Lord, and is fitly disposed
84:6 (6)	thou art labouring unto thy Lord laboriously
84:15 (15)	yes indeed; his Lord had sight of him
85:12 (12)	surely thy Lord's assault is terrible
87:1 (1)	magnify the Name of thy Lord the Most High
87:15 (15)	and mentions the Name of his Lord, and prays
89:6 (5)	hast thou not seen how thy Lord did with Ad
89:13 (12)	thy Lord unloosed on them a scourge of chastisement
89:14 (13)	surely thy Lord is ever on the watch
89:15 (14)	as for man, whenever his Lord tries him
89:15 (15)	my Lord has honoured me
89:16 (17)	my Lord has despised me
89:22 (23)	thy Lord comes, and the angels rank on rank
89:28 (28)	return unto thy Lord, well-pleased, well-pleasing
91:14 (14)	their Lord crushed them for their sin, and levelled them
92:20 (20)	only seeking the Face of his Lord the Most High
93:3 (3)	thy Lord has neither forsaken thee nor hates thee
93:5 (5)	thy Lord shall give thee, and thou shalt be satisfied
93:11 (11)	as for thy Lord's blessing, declare it
94:8 (8)	let thy Lord be thy Quest
96:1 (1)	recite: In the Name of thy Lord who created

96:3 (3)	recite: And thy Lord is the Most Generous
96:8 (8)	surely unto thy Lord is the Returning
97:4 (4)	the angels and the Spirit descend, by the leave of their Lord
98:8 (7)	their recompense is with their Lord
98:8 (8)	that is for him who fears his Lord
99:5 (5)	for that her Lord has inspired her
100:6 (6)	surely Man is ungrateful to his Lord
100:11 (11)	on that day their Lord shall be aware of them
105:1 (1)	how thy Lord did with the Men of the Elephant
106:3 (3)	so let them serve the Lord of this House
108:2 (2)	so pray unto thy Lord and sacrifice
110:3 (3)	proclaim the praise of thy Lord, and seek His forgiveness
113:1 (1)	I take refuge with the Lord of the Daybreak
114:1 (1)	I take refuge with the Lord of men

RABĀʾIB n.f. (pl. of *rabībah*)~stepdaughters

4:23 (27)	your stepdaughters who are in your care

RABBĀNĪ n.m.~master, rabbi

3:79 (73)	be you masters in that you know the Book
5:44 (48)	gave judgment for those of Jewry, as did the masters and the rabbis
5:63 (68)	why do the masters and the rabbis not forbid them to utter sin

RIBBĪYŪN n.m. (pl. of *ribīy*)~thousands; manifold, myriads

3:146 (140)	many a Prophet there has been, with whom thousands manifold have fought

*R B Ḥ

RABIḤA vb. (I)~to profit

a) perf. act.

2:16 (15)	their commerce has not profited them

*R B Ṣ

TARABBAṢA vb. (V)~to await, to wait. (n.vb.) a wait. (pcple. act.) awaiting

a) perf. act.

57:14 (13)	you awaited, and you were in doubt

b) impf. act. (*yatarabbaṣu*)

2:228 (228)	divorced women shall wait by themselves for three periods
2:234 (234)	they shall wait by themselves for four months
4:141 (140)	those who wait upon you
9:52 (52)	are you awaiting for aught to come to us but one of the two rewards
9:52 (52)	we are awaiting in your case too
9:98 (99)	take what they expend for a fine, and await the turns of fortune
52:30 (30)	he is a poet for whom we await Fate's uncertainty

c) impv. (*tarabbaṣ*)

9:24 (24)	then wait till God brings His command
9:52 (52)	so await; we are awaiting with you
20:135 (135)	everyone is waiting; so wait, and assuredly you shall know
23:25 (25)	he is naught but a man bedevilled; so wait on him for a time
52:31 (31)	await! I shall be awaiting with you

f) n.vb. (*tarabbuṣ*)

2:226 (226)	those who forswear their women a wait of four months

g) pcple. act. (*mutarabbiṣ*)

9:52 (52)	we are awaiting with you
20:135 (135)	everyone is waiting
52:31 (31)	I shall be awaiting with you

*R B Ṭ

RABAṬA vb. (I)~(with prep. *ʿalá*) to strengthen, to confirm

a) perf. act.

18:14 (13)	We strengthened their hearts, when they stood up
28:10 (9)	she wellnigh disclosed him had We not strengthened her heart

b) impf. act. (*yarbiṭu*)

8:11 (11)	to strengthen your hearts, and to confirm your feet

RIBĀṬ n.m.~a string of horses

8:60 (62)	make ready for them whatever force and strings of horses you can

RĀBAṬA vb. (III)~to be firm, to be steadfast

b) impf. act. (*yurābiṭu*)

3:200 (200)	be patient, and vie you in patience; be steadfast

*R B W

RABĀ vb. (I)~to increase, to swell. (pcple. act.) numerous, swelling, increasing

a) perf. act.

22:5 (5)	when We send down water upon it, it quivers, and swells
41:39 (39)	when We send down water upon it, it quivers, and swells

b) impf. act. (*yarbū*)

30:39 (38)	what you give in usury, that it may increase upon the people's wealth
30:39 (38)	increases not with God

g) pcple. act. (*rābī*, comp. *arbá*)

13:17 (18) the torrent carries a swelling scum
16:92 (94) one nation being more numerous than another nation
69:10 (10) He seized them with a surpassing grip

RABWAH n.f.~a hill, a height

2:265 (267) the likeness of a garden upon a hill
23:50 (52) and gave them refuge upon a height, where was a hollow and a spring

RIBĀ n.m.~usury

2:275 (276) those who devour usury shall not rise again
2:275 (276) trafficking is like usury
2:275 (276) God has permitted trafficking, and forbidden usury
2:276 (277) God blots out usury, but freewill offerings He augments
2:278 (278) give up the usury that is outstanding, if you are believers
3:130 (125) devour not usury, doubled and redoubled
4:161 (159) for their taking usury, that they were prohibited
30:39 (38) what you give in usury, that it may increase

RABBÁ vb. (II)~to raise up

a) perf. act.

17:24 (25) have mercy upon them, as they raised me up

b) impf. act. (*yurabbī*)

26:18 (17) did we not raise thee amongst us as a child

ARBÁ vb. (IV)~to cause to increase; to augment with interest

b) impf. act. (*yurbī*)

2:276 (277) but freewill offerings He augments with interest

*R D ʾ

RIDʾ n.m.~a helper

28:34 (34) send him with me as a helper

*R D D

RADDA vb. (I)~to return something to someone, to give back, to restore, to send back; (with prep. *ilá* or *li-*) to refer something to someone; to rebut, to keep back; to turn upon, to turn from, to turn someone away, to repel, to thrust. (n.vb.) the act of restoring; the act of repelling. (pcple. act.) one who repels; one who returns or restores (tr); one who gives over (tr). (pcple. pass.) that which is turned back or restored

a) perf. act.

4:83 (85) if they had referred it to the Messenger and to those in authority
14:9 (10) they thrust their hands into their mouths saying
17:6 (6) We gave back to you the turn to prevail over them

21:40 (41)	they shall not be able to repel it, nor shall they be respited
28:13 (12)	We returned him to his mother, that she might be comforted
33:25 (25)	God sent back those that were unbelievers in their rage
95:5 (5)	then We restored him the lowest of the low

b) impf. act. (*yaruddu*)

2:109 (103)	many of the People of the Book wish they might restore you as unbelievers
2:217 (214)	till they turn you from your religion
3:100 (95)	they will turn you, after you have believed, into unbelievers
3:149 (142)	they will turn you upon your heels
4:47 (50)	before We obliterate faces, and turn them upon their backs

c) impv. (*rudda*)

4:59 (62)	if you should quarrel on anything, refer it to God
4:86 (88)	greet with a fairer than it, or return it
38:33 (32)	return them to me

d) perf. pass. (*rudda*)

4:91 (93)	whenever they are returned to temptation, they are overthrown in it
6:28 (28)	even if they were returned, they would again commit the very thing
6:62 (62)	then they are restored to God their Protector
10:30 (31)	they shall be restored to God, their Protector, the True
12:65 (65)	they found their merchandise, restored to them
12:65 (65)	see, our merchandise here is restored to us
18:36 (34)	if I am indeed returned to my Lord

e) impf. pass. (*yuraddu*)

2:85 (79)	on the Day of Resurrection to be returned unto the most terrible of chastisement
5:108 (107)	they will be afraid that after their oaths oaths may be rebutted
6:27 (27)	would that we might be returned
6:71 (70)	shall we be turned back on our heels after that God has guided us
6:147 (148)	His might will never be turned back from the people of the sinners
7:53 (51)	shall we be returned, to do other than that we have done?
9:94 (95)	then you will be returned to Him who knows the unseen
9:101 (102)	then they will be returned to a mighty chastisement
9:105 (106)	you will be returned to Him who knows the unseen
12:110 (110)	Our might will never be turned back from the people of the sinners
16:70 (72)	some of you will be kept back unto the vilest state of life
18:87 (86)	then he shall be returned to his Lord
22:5 (5)	some of you are kept back unto the vilest state of life
41:47 (47)	to Him is referred the knowledge of the Hour
62:8 (8)	then you shall be returned to the Knower of the Unseen

f) n.vb. (*radd*)

2:228 (228)	in such time their mates have better right to restore them
21:40 (41)	they shall not be able to repel it, nor shall they be respited

g) pcple. act. (*rādd*)

10:107 (107)	none can repel His bounty
16:71 (73)	those that were preferred shall not give over their provision
28:7 (6)	We shall return him to thee, and shall appoint him
28:85 (85)	He who imposed the Recitation upon thee shall surely restore thee

h) pcple. pass. (*mardūd*)

11:76 (78) there is coming upon them a chastisement not to be turned back
79:10 (10) what, are we being restored as we were before?

MARADD n.m.~the act of turning back, a return

13:11 (12) whensoever God desires evil for a people, there is no turning it back
19:76 (79) the deeds of righteousness, are better with thy Lord in reward, and better in return
30:43 (42) before there comes a day from God that cannot be turned back
40:43 (46) to God we return
42:44 (43) is there any way to be sent back?
42:47 (46) before there comes a day from God that cannot be turned back

TARADDADA vb. (V)~to hesitate, to go this way and that

b) impf. act. (*yataraddadu*)

9:45 (45) in their doubt they go this way and that

IRTADDA vb. (VIII)~to return, to turn back, to go back to an earlier state or condition (thus, "once again" in 12:96); to apostatize ("to turn from one's religion"); to become a renegade [Pk]

a) perf. act.

12:96 (96) and laid it on his face, forthwith he saw once again
18:64 (63) so they returned upon their tracks, retracing them
47:25 (27) those who have turned back in their traces after the guidance

b) impf. act. (*yartaddu*)

2:217 (214) whosoever of you turns from his religion
5:21 (24) turn not back in your traces, to turn about losers
5:54 (59) whosoever of you turns from his religion
14:43 (44) their glances never returned on themselves, their hearts void
27:40 (40) I will bring it to thee, before ever thy glance returns to thee

*R D F

RADIFA vb. (I)~to come behind, to follow. (pcple. act.) that which follows

a) perf. act.

27:72 (74) it may be that riding behind you already is some part of that you seek to hasten on

g) pcple. act. f. (*rādifah*)

79:7 (7) the second blast follows it

ARDAFA vb. (IV)~(pcple.act.) that which follows, which comes behind another

g) pcple. act. (*murdif*)

8:9 (9) I shall reinforce you with a thousand angels riding behind you

*R D M

RADAMA vb. (I)~(n.vb.) filling up; a rampart; debris

f) n.vb. (*radm*)

18:95 (94) I will set up a rampart between you and between them

*R D Y

RADÁ vb. (I)~to perish, to be destroyed

b) impf. act. (*yardá*)

20:16 (17) but follows after his own caprice, or thou wilt perish

ARDÁ vb. (IV)~to cause to perish, to destroy

a) perf. act.

41:23 (22) the thought you thought about your Lord, has destroyed you

b) impf. act. (*yurdī*)

6:137 (138) to many idolaters to slay their children, to destroy them
37:56 (54) by God, wellnigh thou didst destroy me

TARADDÁ vb. (V)~to fall, to perish. (pcple. act.) that (animal) which is fallen to death

a) perf. act.

92:11 (11) his wealth shall not avail him when he perishes

g) pcple. act. f. (*mutaraddiyah*)

5:3 (4) the beast fallen to death, the beast gored

*R DH L

RADHĪL n.m. (comp. adj. *ardhal*)~vile, base, low

11:27 (29) we see not any following thee but the vilest of us
16:70 (72) some of you will be kept back unto the vilest state of life
22:5 (5) some of you are kept back unto the vilest state of life
26:111 (111) shall we believe thee, whom the vilest follow?

*R Ḍ ᶜ

RAḌIᶜA vb. (I)~(n.vb.) suckling

48:29 (29) bowing, prostrating, seeking bounty from God and good pleasure
57:20 (20) forgiveness from God and good pleasure
57:27 (27) only seeking the good pleasure of God
59:8 (8) seeking bounty from God and good pleasure

ARḌÁ vb. (IV)~to give satisfaction, to please

b) impf. act. (*yurḍī*)

9:8 (8) giving you satisfaction with their mouths but in their hearts refusing
9:62 (63) they swear to you by God, to please you
9:62 (63) more right is it they should please Him, if they are believers

TARĀḌÁ vb. (VI)~to agree together. (n.vb.) the act of agreeing together, mutual consent

a) perf. act.

2:232 (232) do not debar them from marrying their husbands, when they have agreed together
4:24 (28) it is no fault in you in your agreeing together

f) n.vb. (*tarāḍī*)

2:233 (233) if the couple desire by mutual consent and consultation to wean
4:29 (33) except there be trading, by your agreeing together

IRTAḌÁ vb. (VIII)~to be well-pleased, to approve

a) perf. act.

21:28 (29) save for him with whom He is well-pleased
24:55 (54) He will surely establish their religion for them that He has approved
72:27 (27) save only to such a Messenger as He is well-pleased with

*R F ʿ

RAFAʿA vb. (I)~to raise, to lift, to exalt. (pcple. act.) one who raises or exalts. (pcple. pass.) uplifted, upraised

a) perf. act.

2:63 (60) when We took compact with you, and raised above you the Mount
2:93 (87) when We took compact with you, and raised over you the Mount
2:253 (254) some there are to whom God spoke, and some He raised in rank
4:154 (153) We raised above them the Mount
4:158 (156) God raised him up to Him
6:165 (165) and has raised some of you in rank above others
7:176 (175) had We willed, We would have raised him up thereby
12:100 (101) he lifted his father and mother upon the throne
13:2 (2) God is He who raised up the heavens without pillars
19:57 (58) We raised him up to a high place
43:32 (31) and raised some of them above others in rank
55:7 (6) He raised it up, and set the Balance
79:28 (28) He lifted up its vault, and levelled it
94:4 (4) did We not exalt thy fame?

b) impf. act. (*yarfaᶜu*)

2:127 (121)	Abraham, and Ishmael with him, raised up the foundations
6:83 (83)	We raise up in degrees whom We will
12:76 (76)	whomsoever We will, We raise in rank
35:10 (11)	the righteous deed — He uplifts it
49:2 (2)	raise not your voices above the Prophet's voice
58:11 (12)	God will raise up in rank those of you who believe

d) perf. pass. (*rufiᶜa*)

88:18 (18)	how heaven was lifted up

e) impf. pass. (*yurfaᶜu*)

24:36 (36)	in temples God has allowed to be raised up

g) pcple. act. (*rāfiᶜ*)

3:55 (48)	I will take thee to Me and will raise thee to Me
56:3 (3)	abasing, exalting

h) pcple. pass. (*marfūᶜ*)

52:5 (5)	and the roof uplifted
56:34 (33)	and upraised couches
80:14 (14)	uplifted, purified
88:13 (13)	therein uplifted couches

RAFĪᶜ n.m. (adj)~high, exalted; Exalter (Divine attribute)

40:15 (15)	Exalter of ranks is He, Possessor of the Throne

*R F D

RAFADA vb. (I)~(pcple. pass.) that which is offered

h) pcple. pass. (*marfūd*)

11:99 (101)	evil the offering to be offered

RIFD n.m.~an offering

11:99 (101)	evil the offering to be offered

*R F Q

MARĀFIQ n.m. (pl. of *mirfaq*)~elbows

5:6 (8)	wash your faces, and your hands up to the elbows

MIRFAQ n.m.~ease, comfort, a gentle issue

18:16 (15)	and will furnish you with a gentle issue of your affair

MURTAFAQ n.m.~a resting place

18:29 (28)	how evil a potion, and how evil a resting-place
18:31 (30)	how excellent a reward! And O, how fair a resting-place

RAFĪQ n.m.~a companion

4:69 (71)	just men, martyrs, the righteous; good companions they

*R F R F

RAFRAF n.m.~a cushion

55:76 (76)	reclining upon green cushions and lovely druggets

*R F T

RUFĀT n.m.~broken bits, dust

17:49 (52)	when we are bones and broken bits, shall we really be raised up
17:98 (100)	when we are bones and broken bits, shall we really be raised up

*R F TH

RAFATH n.m.~obscenity, casual intercourse, going in to (a woman)

2:187 (183)	permitted to you, upon the night of the Fast, is to go in to your wives
2:197 (193)	whoso undertakes the duty of Pilgrimage in them shall not go in to his womenfolk

*R GH B

RAGHIBA vb. (I)~to desire; (with prep. *ʿan*) to shrink from; to prefer (*raghiba bi-* "a" *ʿan* "b", to prefer "a" to "b"); (with prep. *ilá*) to have as a quest; to turn to. (n.vb.) yearning. (pcple. act.) (with prep. *ilá*) one who turns to, who quests; (with prep. *ʿan*) one who shrinks from, who turns away from

b) impf. act. (*yarghabu*)

2:130 (124)	who therefore shrinks from the religion of Abraham
4:127 (126)	and yet desire to marry them
9:120 (121)	to stay behind God's Messenger, and to prefer their lives to his

c) impv. (*irghab*)

94:8 (8)	let thy Lord be thy Quest

f) n.vb. (*raghab*)

21:90 (90)	and called upon Us out of yearning and awe

g) pcple. act. (*rāghib*)

9:59 (59) to God we humbly turn
19:46 (47) what, art thou shrinking from my gods, Abraham
68:32 (32) to our Lord we humbly turn

*R GH D

RAGHAD n.m.~ease; (adv) easefully

2:35 (33) dwell thou, and thy wife, in the Garden, and eat thereof easefully
2:58 (55) enter this township, and eat easefully of it wherever you will
16:112 (113) a city that was secure, at rest, its provision coming to it easefully

*R GH M

MURĀGHAM n.m.~a refuge

4:100 (101) whoso emigrates in the way of God will find in the earth many refuges

*R H B

RAHIBA vb. (I)~to have awe of, to hold in awe. (n.vb.) awe, fear

b) impf. act. (*yarhabu*)

7:154 (153) mercy unto all those who hold their Lord in awe

c) impv. (*irhab*)

2:40 (38) have awe of Me
16:51 (53) He is only One God; so have awe of Me

f) n.vb. (*rahb*, *rahab* or *rahbah*)

21:90 (90) and called upon Us out of yearning and awe
28:32 (32) press to thee thy arm, that thou be not afraid
59:13 (13) you arouse greater fear in their hearts than God

RAHBĀNĪYAH n.f.~monasticism

57:27 (27) monasticism they invented — We did not prescribe it for them

RUHBĀN n.m. (pl. of *rāhib*)~monks

5:82 (85) some of them are priests and monks, and they wax not proud
9:31 (31) they have taken their rabbis and their monks as lords
9:34 (34) many of the rabbis and monks indeed consume the goods of the people

ARHABA vb. (IV)~to terrify

b) impf. act. (*yurhibu*)

8:60 (62) to terrify thereby the enemy of God and your enemy

ISTARHABA vb. (X)~to call forth fear, to terrify

a) perf. act.

7:116 (113) they put a spell upon the people's eyes, and called forth fear of them

*R H N

RAHĪN n.m.~that which is pledged

52:21 (21) every man shall be pledged for what he earned
74:38 (41) every soul shall be pledged for what it has earned

RIHĀN n.m. (pl. of *rahn*)~a pledge

2:283 (283) if you are upon a journey, and you do not find a writer, then a pledge in hand

*R H Q

RAHIQA vb. (I)~to overspread, to come over. (n.vb.) vileness

b) impf. act. (*yarhaqu*)

10:26 (27) neither dust nor abasement shall overspread their faces
10:27 (28) abasement shall overspread them
68:43 (43) humbled shall be their eyes, and abasement shall overspread them
70:44 (44) humbled their eyes, overspreading them abasement
80:41 (41) o'erspread with darkness

f) n.vb. (*rahaq*)

72:6 (6) they increased them in vileness
72:13 (13) he shall fear neither paltriness nor vileness

ARHAQA vb. (IV)~to constrain, to impose something on someone

b) impf. act. (*yurhiqu*)

18:73 (72) neither constrain me to do a thing too difficult
18:80 (79) we were afraid he would impose on them insolence and unbelief
74:17 (17) I shall constrain him to a hard ascent

*R H Ṭ

RAHṬ n.m.~a group (of persons), a band, a tribe

11:91 (93) but for thy tribe we would have stoned thee

11:92 (94)	is my tribe stronger against you than God
27:48 (49)	in the city there were nine persons who did corruption

*R H W

RAHĀ vb. (I)~(n.vb.) calm, tranquility; (adv) becalmed

f) n.vb. (*rahw*)

44:24 (23)	leave the sea becalmed; they are a drowned host

*R Ḥ B

RAḤUBA vb. (I)~to be wide or spacious; (*bimā raḥubat*) for all its breadth

a) perf. act

9:25 (25)	the land for all its breadth was strait for you
9:118 (119)	when the earth became strait for them, for all its breadth

MARḤABAN n.m.~Welcome! (a salutation)

38:59 (59)	this is a troop rushing in with you; there is no Welcome for them
38:60 (60)	it is you have no Welcome; you forwarded it for us

*R Ḥ L

RAḤL n.m: (pl. *riḥāl*)~saddlebag

12:62 (62)	put their merchandise in their saddlebags
12:70 (70)	he put his drinking-cup into the saddlebag of his brother
12:75 (75)	in whoever's saddlebag the goblet is found, he shall be its recompense

RIḤLAH n.f.~a journey; a caravan

106:2 (2)	their composing for the winter and summer caravan

*R Ḥ M

RAḤIMA vb. (I)~to have mercy on someone, to be compassionate. (n.vb.) mercy, compassion. (pcple. act.) merciful, compassionate

a) perf. act.

6:16 (16)	He will have mercy on him
11:43 (45)	there is no defender from God's command but for him on whom He has mercy
11:119 (120)	excepting those on whom thy Lord has mercy
12:53 (53)	except inasmuch as my Lord had mercy

23:75 (77)	did We have mercy on them, and remove the affliction that is upon them
40:9 (9)	on him Thou hast had mercy
44:42 (42)	save him upon whom God has mercy
67:28 (28)	if God destroys me and those with me, or has mercy on us

b) impf. act. (*yarḥamu*)

7:23 (22)	if Thou dost not forgive us, and have mercy upon us
7:149 (148)	if our Lord has not mercy on us, and forgives us not
9:71 (72)	those — upon them God will have mercy
11:47 (49)	if Thou forgivest me not, and hast not mercy on me
17:8 (8)	perchance your Lord will have mercy upon you
17:54 (56)	if He will, He will have mercy on you
29:21 (20)	chastising whom He will, and having mercy on whomsoever He will

c) impv. (*irḥam*)

2:286 (286)	pardon us, and forgive us, and have mercy on us
7:155 (154)	have mercy on us, for Thou art the best of forgivers
17:24 (25)	have mercy upon them, as they raised me up
23:109 (111)	forgive us, and have mercy on us, for Thou art the best of the merciful
23:118 (118)	forgive and have mercy, for Thou art the best of the merciful

e) impf. pass. (*yurḥamu*)

3:132 (126)	obey God and the Messenger; haply so you will find mercy
6:155 (156)	be godfearing; haply so you will find mercy
7:63 (61)	that he may warn you, and you be godfearing, haply to find mercy
7:204 (203)	give you ear to it and be silent; haply so you will find mercy
24:56 (55)	and obey the Messenger — haply so you will find mercy
27:46 (47)	haply so you will find mercy
36:45 (45)	fear what is before you and what is behind you; haply you will find mercy
49:10 (10)	and fear God; haply so you will find mercy

f) n.vb. (*raḥmah*)

2:64 (61)	but for the bounty and mercy of God towards you
2:105 (99)	God singles out for His mercy whom He will
2:157 (152)	upon those rest blessings and mercy from their Lord
2:178 (174)	that is a lightening granted you by your Lord, and a mercy
2:218 (215)	and struggle in God's way — those have hope of God's compassion
3:8 (6)	Thou hast guided us; and give us mercy from Thee
3:74 (67)	He singles out for His mercy whom He will
3:107 (103)	they shall be in God's mercy, therein dwelling forever
3:157 (151)	forgiveness and mercy from God are a better thing than that you amass
3:159 (153)	it was by some mercy of God that thou wast gentle to them
4:83 (85)	but for the bounty of God to you, and His mercy
4:96 (98)	in ranks standing before Him, forgiveness and mercy
4:113 (113)	but for God's bounty to thee and His mercy
4:175 (174)	He will surely admit them to mercy from Him, and bounty
6:12 (12)	He has prescribed for Himself mercy
6:54 (54)	your Lord has prescribed for Himself mercy
6:133 (133)	thy Lord is All-sufficient, Merciful
6:147 (148)	your Lord is of mercy all-embracing
6:154 (155)	and as a guidance and a mercy
6:157 (158)	a clear sign has come to you from your Lord, and a guidance and a mercy
7:49 (47)	are these the ones that you swore God would never reach with mercy?

7:52 (50)	a guidance and a mercy unto a people that believe
7:56 (54)	the mercy of God is nigh to the good-doers
7:57 (55)	it is He who looses the winds, bearing good tidings before His mercy
7:72 (70)	We delivered him, and those with him, by a mercy from Us
7:151 (150)	forgive me and my brother and enter us into Thy mercy
7:154 (153)	guidance, and mercy unto all those who hold their Lord in awe
7:156 (155)	My mercy embraces all things
7:203 (202)	this is clear testimony from your Lord, guidance, and mercy
9:21 (21)	their Lord gives them good tidings of mercy from Him and good pleasure
9:61 (62)	he is a mercy to the believers among you
9:99 (100)	they are an offering for them, and God will admit them into His mercy
10:21 (22)	We let the people taste mercy after hardship has visited them
10:57 (58)	a guidance, and a mercy to the believers
10:58 (59)	in the bounty of God, and His mercy — in that let them rejoice
10:86 (86)	deliver us by Thy mercy from the people of the unbelievers
11:9 (12)	if We let a man taste mercy from Us
11:17 (20)	before him is the Book of Moses for an ensample and a mercy
11:28 (30)	and He has given me mercy from Him
11:58 (61)	We delivered Hood and those who believed with him by a mercy from Us
11:63 (66)	and He has given me mercy from Him
11:66 (69)	We delivered Salih and those who believed with him by a mercy from Us
11:73 (76)	the mercy of God and His blessings be upon you
11:94 (97)	We delivered Shuaib and those who believed with him by a mercy from Us
12:56 (56)	We visit with Our mercy whomsoever We will
12:111 (111)	a guidance, and a mercy to a people who believe
15:56 (56)	who despairs of the mercy of his Lord
16:64 (66)	as a guidance and as a mercy to a people who believe
16:89 (91)	the Book making clear everything, and as a guidance and a mercy
17:24 (25)	lower to them the wing of humbleness out of mercy
17:28 (30)	if thou turnest from them, seeking mercy from thy Lord
17:57 (59)	they hope for His mercy, and fear His chastisement
17:82 (84)	that which is a healing and a mercy to the believers
17:87 (89)	excepting by some mercy of thy Lord
17:100 (102)	if you possessed the treasuries of my Lord's mercy
18:10 (9)	our Lord, give us mercy from Thee
18:16 (15)	your Lord will unfold to you of His mercy
18:58 (57)	thy Lord is the All-forgiving, full of mercy
18:65 (64)	they found one of Our servants unto whom We had given mercy
18:82 (81)	then bring forth their treasure as a mercy from thy Lord
18:98 (97)	this is a mercy from my Lord
19:2 (1)	the mention of thy Lord's mercy unto His servant Zachariah
19:21 (21)	that We may appoint him a sign unto men and a mercy from Us
19:50 (51)	We gave them of Our mercy
19:53 (54)	We gave him his brother Aaron, of Our mercy, a Prophet
21:75 (75)	We admitted him into Our mercy
21:84 (84)	We gave his people, and the like of them with them, mercy from Us
21:86 (86)	We admitted them into Our mercy
21:107 (107)	We have not sent thee, save as a mercy unto all beings
24:10 (10)	but for God's bounty to you and His mercy
24:14 (14)	m28but for God's bounty to you and His mercy
24:20 (20)	but for God's bounty to you and His mercy
24:21 (21)	but for God's bounty to you and His mercy
25:48 (50)	He who has loosed the winds, bearing good tidings before His mercy
27:19 (19)	do Thou admit me, by Thy mercy, amongst Thy righteous servants
27:63 (64)	and looses the winds, bearing good tidings before His mercy

27:77 (79) it is a guidance, and a mercy unto the believers
28:43 (43) We had destroyed the former generations, to be examples and a guidance and a mercy
28:46 (46) but for a mercy from thy Lord, that thou mayest warn a people
28:73 (73) of His mercy He has appointed for you night and day
28:86 (86) except it be as a mercy from thy Lord
29:23 (22) they despair of My mercy, and there awaits them a painful chastisement
29:51 (50) in that is a mercy, and a reminder to a people who believe
30:21 (20) He has set between you love and mercy
30:33 (32) when He lets them taste mercy from Him, lo, a party of them assign associates
30:36 (35) when We let men taste mercy, they rejoice in it
30:46 (45) that He may let you taste of His mercy
30:50 (49) so behold the marks of God's mercy
31:3 (2) for a guidance and a mercy to the good-doers
33:17 (17) if He desires evil for you, or desires mercy for you
35:2 (2) whatsoever mercy God opens to men
36:44 (44) save as a mercy from Us, and enjoyment for a while
38:9 (8) or have they the treasuries of thy Lord's mercy
38:43 (42) the like of them with them, as a mercy from us
39:9 (12) being afraid of the world to come and hoping for the mercy of his Lord
39:38 (39) or if He desires mercy for me
39:38 (39) shall they withhold His mercy
39:53 (54) do not despair of God's mercy
40:7 (7) Thou embracest every thing in mercy and knowledge
41:50 (50) if We let him taste mercy from Us after hardship
42:8 (6) He admits whomsoever He will into His mercy
42:28 (27) and He unfolds His mercy
42:48 (47) when We let man taste mercy from Us, he rejoices in it
43:32 (31) is it they who divide the mercy of thy Lord
43:32 (31) the mercy of thy Lord is better than that they amass
44:6 (5) as a mercy from thy Lord
45:20 (19) a guidance, and a mercy to a people having sure faith
45:30 (29) their Lord shall admit them into His mercy
46:12 (11) before it was the Book of Moses for a model and a mercy
48:25 (25) God may admit into His mercy whom He will
57:13 (13) a wall shall be set up between them, having a door in the inward whereof is mercy
57:27 (27) We set in the hearts of those who followed him tenderness and mercy
57:28 (28) He will give you a twofold portion of His mercy
76:31 (31) He admits into His mercy whomsoever He will

g) pcple. act. (*rāḥim*; comp. *arḥam*)

7:151 (150) Thou art the most merciful of the (merciful)
7:151 (150) Thou art the (most merciful) of the merciful
12:64 (64) and He is the most merciful of the (merciful)
12:64 (64) and He is the (most merciful) of the merciful
12:92 (92) He is the most merciful of the (merciful)
12:92 (92) He is the (most merciful) of the merciful
21:83 (83) Thou art the most merciful of the (merciful)
21:83 (83) Thou art the (most merciful) of the merciful
23:109 (111) have mercy us, for Thou art the best of the merciful
23:118 (118) have mercy, for Thou art the best of the merciful

ARḤĀM n.m. (pl. of *raḥim* or *riḥm*)~womb; (*ūlū al-arḥām*) ones related by blood

2:228 (228) it is not lawful for them to hide what God has created in their wombs
3:6 (4) it is He who forms you in the womb as He will

4:1 (1) fear God by whom you demand one of another, and the wombs
6:143 (144) or what the wombs of the two females contain
6:144 (145) or what the wombs of the two females contain
8:75 (76) those related by blood are nearer to one another in the Book
13:8 (9) what every female bears, and the wombs' shrinking and swelling
22:5 (5) We establish in the wombs what We will
31:34 (34) He sends down the rain; He knows what is in the wombs
33:6 (6) those who are bound by blood are nearer to one another in the Book
47:22 (24) work corruption in the land, and break your bonds of kin
60:3 (3) neither your blood-kindred nor your children shall profit you

MARḤAMAH n.f.~mercy, compassion

90:17 (17) and counsel each other to be merciful

RAḤĪM n.m. (pl. *ruḥamā'*)~merciful, compassionate; the All-compassionate (Divine attribute, used frequently after *ar-raḥmān*, below)

1:1 (1) in the Name of God, the Merciful, the Compassionate
1:3 (2) the All-merciful, the All-compassionate
2:37 (35) truly He turns, and is All-compassionate
2:54 (51) truly He turns, and is All-compassionate
2:128 (122) surely Thou turnest, and art All-compassionate
2:143 (138) God is All-gentle with the people, All-compassionate
2:160 (155) towards them I shall turn; I turn, All-compassionate
2:163 (158) there is no god but He, the All-merciful, the All-compassionate
2:173 (168) God is All-forgiving, All-compassionate
2:182 (178) surely God is All-forgiving, All-compassionate
2:192 (188) surely God is All-forgiving, All-compassionate
2:199 (195) God is All-forgiving, All-compassionate
2:218 (215) God is All-forgiving, All-compassionate
2:226 (226) God is All-forgiving, All-compassionate
3:31 (29) God is All-forgiving, All-compassionate
3:89 (83) God is All-forgiving, All-compassionate
3:129 (124) God is All-forgiving, All-compassionate
4:16 (20) God turns, and is All-compassionate
4:23 (27) God is All-forgiving, All-compassionate
4:25 (30) God is All-forgiving All-compassionate
4:29 (33) surely God is compassionate to you
4:64 (67) they would have found God turns, All-compassionate
4:96 (98) God is All-forgiving, All-compassionate
4:100 (101) God is All-forgiving, All-compassionate
4:106 (106) God is All-forgiving, All-compassionate
4:110 (110) he shall find God is All-forgiving, All-compassionate
4:129 (128) God is All-forgiving, All-compassionate
4:152 (151) God is All-forgiving, All-compassionate
5:3 (5) God is All-forgiving, All-compassionate
5:34 (38) know you that God is All-forgiving, All-compassionate
5:39 (43) God is All-forgiving, All-compassionate
5:74 (78) God is All-forgiving, All-compassionate
5:98 (98) God is All-forgiving, All-compassionate
6:54 (54) He is All-forgiving, All-compassionate
6:145 (146) thy Lord is All-forgiving, All-compassionate
6:165 (165) surely He is All-forgiving, All-compassionate
7:153 (152) thy Lord is All-forgiving, All-compassionate
7:167 (166) surely He is All-forgiving, All-compassionate
8:69 (70) God is All-forgiving, All-compassionate

8:70 (71)	God is All-forgiving, All-compassionate
9:5 (5)	God is All-forgiving, All-compassionate
9:27 (27)	God is All-forgiving, All-compassionate
9:91 (92)	God is All-forgiving, All-compassionate
9:99 (100)	God is All-forgiving, All-compassionate
9:102 (103)	God is All-forgiving, All-compassionate
9:104 (105)	He turns, and is All-compassionate
9:117 (118)	surely He is Gentle to them, and All-compassionate
9:118 (119)	surely God turns, and is All-compassionate
9:128 (129)	anxious is he over you, gentle to the believers, compassionate
10:107 (107)	He is the All-forgiving, the All-compassionate
11:41 (43)	my Lord is All-forgiving, All-compassionate
11:90 (92)	my Lord is All-compassionate, All-loving
12:53 (53)	my Lord is All-forgiving, All-compassionate
12:98 (99)	He is the All-forgiving, the All-compassionate
14:36 (39)	surely Thou art All-forgiving, All-compassionate
15:49 (49)	I am the All-forgiving, the All-compassionate
16:7 (7)	surely your Lord is All-clement, All-compassionate
16:18 (18)	surely God is All-forgiving, All-compassionate
16:47 (49)	surely thy Lord is All-clement, All-compassionate
16:110 (111)	thy Lord thereafter is All-forgiving, All-compassionate
16:115 (116)	God is All-forgiving, All-compassionate
16:119 (120)	thy Lord thereafter is All-forgiving, All-compassionate
17:66 (68)	He is All-compassionate towards you
22:65 (64)	surely God is All-gentle to men, All-compassionate
24:5 (5)	surely God is All-forgiving, All-compassionate
24:20 (20)	and that God is All-gentle, All-compassionate
24:22 (22)	God is All-forgiving, All-compassionate
24:33 (33)	God, after their being constrained, is All-forgiving, All-compassionate
24:62 (62)	surely God is All-forgiving, All-compassionate
25:6 (7)	He is All-forgiving, All-compassionate
25:70 (70)	God is ever All-forgiving, All-compassionate
26:9 (8)	thy Lord, He is the All-mighty, the All-compassionate
26:68 (68)	thy Lord, He is the All-mighty, the All-compassionate
26:104 (104)	thy Lord, He is the All-mighty, the All-compassionate
26:122 (122)	thy Lord, He is the All-mighty, the All-compassionate
26:140 (140)	thy Lord, He is the All-mighty, the All-compassionate
26:159 (159)	thy Lord, He is the All-mighty, the All-compassionate
26:175 (175)	thy Lord, He is the All-mighty, the All-compassionate
26:191 (191)	thy Lord, He is the All-mighty, the All-compassionate
26:217 (217)	put thy trust in the All-mighty, the All-compassionate
27:11 (11)	All-forgiving am I, All-compassionate
27:30 (30)	in the Name of God, the Merciful, the Compassionate
28:16 (15)	God forgave him, for He is the All-forgiving, the All-compassionate
30:5 (4)	He is the All-mighty, the All-compassionate
32:6 (5)	the Visible, the All-mighty, the All-compassionate
33:5 (5)	God is All-forgiving, All-compassionate
33:24 (24)	surely God is All-forgiving, All-compassionate
33:43 (42)	He is All-compassionate to the believers
33:50 (50)	God is All-forgiving, All-compassionate
33:59 (59)	God is All-forgiving, All-compassionate
33:73 (73)	God is All-forgiving, All-compassionate
34:2 (2)	He is the All-compassionate, the All-forgiving
36:5 (4)	the sending down of the All-mighty, the All-compassionate
36:58 (58)	such is the greeting, from a Lord All-compassionate

39:53 (54)	surely He is the All-forgiving, the All-compassionate
41:2 (1)	a sending down from the All-merciful, the All-compassionate
41:32 (32)	as hospitality from One All-forgiving, One All-compassionate
42:5 (3)	surely God — He is the All-forgiving, the All-compassionate
44:42 (42)	He is the All-mighty, the All-compassionate
46:8 (7)	He is the All-forgiving, the All-compassionate
48:14 (14)	God is All-forgiving, All-compassionate
48:29 (29)	those who are with him are hard against the unbelievers, merciful one to another
49:5 (5)	God is All-forgiving, All-compassionate
49:12 (12)	God turns, and He is All-compassionate
49:14 (14)	God is All-forgiving, All-compassionate
52:28 (28)	He is the All-benign, the All-compassionate
57:9 (9)	surely God is to you All-gentle, All-compassionate
57:28 (28)	God is All-forgiving, All-compassionate
58:12 (13)	if you find not means, God is All-forgiving, All-compassionate
59:10 (10)	surely Thou art the All-gentle, the All-compassionate
59:22 (22)	He is the All-merciful, the All-compassionate
60:7 (7)	God is All-forgiving, All-compassionate
60:12 (12)	God is All-forgiving, All-compassionate
64:14 (14)	surely God is All-forgiving, All-compassionate
66:1 (1)	God is All-forgiving, All-compassionate
73:20 (20)	God is All-forgiving, All-compassionate

RAḤMĀN n.m. (always with the definite article and very often with *ar-raḥīm*, above)~the All-merciful [Ar, Bl]; Beneficent [Pk]; Most Gracious [Ali] (Divine attribute)

1:1 (1)	in the Name of God, the Merciful, the Compassionate
1:3 (2)	the All-merciful, the All-compassionate
2:163 (158)	the All-merciful, the All-compassionate
13:30 (29)	yet they disbelieve in the All-merciful
17:110 (110)	call upon God, or call upon the Merciful
19:18 (18)	I take refuge in the All-merciful from thee
19:26 (27)	I have vowed to the All-merciful a fast
19:44 (45)	surely Satan is a rebel against the All-merciful
19:45 (46)	some chastisement from the All-merciful will smite thee
19:58 (59)	when the signs of the All-merciful were recited to them
19:61 (62)	Gardens of Eden that the All-merciful promised His servants
19:69 (70)	whichever of them was the most hardened in disdain of the All-merciful
19:75 (76)	let the All-merciful prolong his term for him
19:78 (81)	or taken a covenant with the All-merciful
19:85 (88)	We shall muster the godfearing to the All-merciful
19:87 (90)	those who have taken with the All-merciful covenant
19:88 (91)	the All-merciful has taken unto Himself a son
19:91 (93)	they have attributed to the All-merciful a son
19:92 (93)	it behoves not the All-merciful to take a son
19:93 (94)	but he comes to the All-merciful as a servant
19:96 (96)	unto them the All-merciful shall assign love
20:5 (4)	the All-merciful sat Himself upon the Throne
20:90 (92)	surely your Lord is the All-merciful
20:108 (107)	voices will be hushed to the All-merciful
20:109 (108)	save for him to whom the All-merciful gives leave
21:26 (26)	the All-merciful has taken to Him a son
21:36 (37)	they in the Remembrance of the All-merciful are unbelievers
21:42 (43)	who shall guard you by night and in the daytime from the All-merciful
21:112 (112)	and our Lord is the All-merciful

25:26 (28) that day, the true Kingdom, shall belong to the All-merciful
25:59 (60) the All-compassionate: ask any informed of Him
25:60 (61) bow yourselves to the All-merciful
25:60 (61) what is the All-merciful
25:63 (64) the servants of the All-merciful are those who walk in the earth
26:5 (4) never fresh remembrance comes to them from the All-merciful
27:30 (30) in the Name of God, the Merciful, the Compassionate
36:11 (10) him who follows the Remembrance and who fears the All-merciful
36:15 (14) the All-merciful has not sent down anything
36:23 (22) if the All-merciful desires affliction for me
36:52 (52) this is what the All-merciful promised
41:2 (1) a sending down from the All-merciful, the All-compassionate
43:17 (16) the good tidings of that he has likened to the All-merciful
43:19 (18) who are themselves servants of the All-merciful
43:20 (19) had the All-merciful so willed, we would not have served them
43:33 (32) We would have appointed for those who disbelieve in the All-merciful
43:36 (35) whoso blinds himself to the Remembrance of the All-merciful
43:45 (44) have We appointed, apart from the All-merciful, gods
43:81 (81) if the All-merciful has a son, then I am the first to serve him
50:33 (32) whosoever fears the All-merciful in the Unseen
55:1 (1) the All-merciful
59:22 (22) He is the All-merciful, the All-compassionate
67:3 (3) thou seest not in the creation of the All-merciful any imperfection
67:19 (19) naught holds them but the All-merciful
67:20 (20) a host for you to help you, apart from the All-merciful
67:29 (29) He is the All-merciful. We believe in Him
78:37 (37) the All-merciful of whom they have no power to speak
78:38 (38) save him to whom the All-merciful has given leave

RUḤM n.m.~tenderness

18:81 (80) one better than he in purity, and nearer in tenderness

*R Ḥ Q

RAḤĪQ n.m.~exquisite wine

83:25 (25) as they are given to drink of a wine sealed

*R J ʿ

RAJAʿA vb. (I)~to return; (34:31) to bandy against [Ar]; to engage in (altercation). (n.vb.) the act of returning, of coming back. (pcple. act.) one who returns; returning

a) perf. act.

2:196 (192) a fast of three days in the Pilgrimage, and of seven when you return
7:150 (149) when Moses returned to his people, angry and sorrowful
9:83 (84) so, if God returns thee to a party of them
9:94 (95) they will excuse themselves to you, when you return to them
9:122 (123) and to warn their people when they return to them
12:63 (63) when they had returned to their father, they said

20:40 (41)	We returned thee to thy mother that she might rejoice
20:86 (88)	then Moses returned very angry and sorrowful to his people
21:64 (65)	so they returned one to another
63:8 (8)	if we return to the City, the mightier ones of it will expel the more abased

b) impf. act. (*yarjiᶜu*)

2:18 (17)	deaf, dumb, blind — so they shall not return
3:72 (65)	they will then return
7:168 (167)	that haply they should return
7:174 (173)	We distinguish the signs; and haply they will return
12:46 (46)	haply I shall return to the men, haply they will know
12:62 (62)	when they have turned to their people; haply they will return
20:89 (91)	did they not see that thing returned no speech unto them
20:91 (93)	until Moses returns to us
21:58 (59)	all but a great one they had, for haply they would return to it
21:95 (95)	they shall not return
27:28 (28)	then turn back from them and see what they shall return
27:35 (35)	I will send them a present, and see what the envoys bring back
30:41 (40)	that haply so they may return
32:21 (21)	haply so they will return
34:31 (30)	stationed before their Lord, bandying argument the one against the other
36:31 (31)	it is not unto them that they return
36:50 (50)	nor will they return to their people
36:67 (67)	then they could not go on, nor could they return
43:28 (27)	haply so they would return
43:48 (47)	We seized them with chastisement, that haply they should return
46:27 (26)	We turned about the signs, that haply they would return
56:87 (86)	do you not bring back his soul, if you speak truly?
60:10 (10)	if you know them to be believers, return them not to the unbelievers

c) impv. (*irjiᶜ*)

12:50 (50)	return unto thy lord, and ask of him
12:81 (81)	return you all to your father, and say
21:13 (13)	return you unto the luxury that you exulted in
23:99 (101)	my Lord, return me
24:28 (28)	and if you are told, 'Return'
24:28 (28)	return; that is purer for you
27:37 (37)	return thou to them
32:12 (12)	now return us, that we may do righteousness
33:13 (13)	there is no abiding here for you, therefore return
57:13 (13)	return you back behind, and seek for a light
67:3 (3)	return thy gaze; seest thou any fissure?
67:4 (4)	then return thy gaze again, and again
89:28 (28)	return unto thy Lord, well-pleased, well-pleasing

d) perf. pass. (*rujiᶜa*)

41:50 (50)	if I am returned to my Lord

e) impf. pass. (*yurjaᶜu*)

2:28 (26)	He shall give you life, then unto Him you shall be returned
2:210 (206)	and unto God all matters are returned
2:245 (246)	God grasps, and outspreads; and unto Him you shall be returned
2:281 (281)	fear a day wherein you shall be returned to God

3:83 (77)	willingly or unwillingly, and to Him they shall be returned
3:109 (105)	in the earth, and unto Him all matters are returned
6:36 (36)	God will raise them up, then unto Him they will be returned
8:44 (46)	unto God all matters are returned
10:56 (57)	He gives life, and makes to die, and to Him you shall be returned
11:34 (36)	He is your Lord, and unto Him you shall be returned
11:123 (123)	to Him the whole matter shall be returned; so serve Him
19:40 (41)	unto Us they shall be returned
21:35 (36)	with evil and good for a testing, then unto Us you shall be returned
22:76 (75)	unto God all matters are returned
23:115 (117)	and that you would not be returned to Us
24:64 (64)	the day when they shall be returned to Him
28:39 (39)	they thought they should not be returned to Us
28:70 (70)	His too is the Judgment, and unto Him you shall be returned
28:88 (88)	His is the Judgment, and unto Him you shall be returned
29:17 (16)	be thankful to Him; unto Him you shall be returned
29:57 (57)	every soul shall taste of death; then unto Us you shall be returned
30:11 (10)	then unto Him you shall be returned
32:11 (11)	then to your Lord you shall be returned
35:4 (4)	unto God all matters are returned
36:22 (21)	Him who originated me, and unto whom you shall be returned
36:83 (83)	and unto whom you shall be returned
39:44 (45)	then unto Him you will be returned
40:77 (77)	to Us they shall be returned
41:21 (20)	He created you the first time, and unto Him you shall be returned
43:85 (85)	with Him is the knowledge of the Hour, and to Him you shall be returned
45:15 (14)	to your Lord you shall be returned
57:5 (5)	and unto Him all matters are returned

f) n.vb. (1) (*raj*ᶜ)

50:3 (3)	when we are dead and become dust? That is a far returning
86:8 (8)	surely He is able to bring him back
86:11 (11)	by heaven of the returning rain

f) n.vb. (2) (*ruj*ᶜ*á*)

96:8 (8)	surely unto thy Lord is the Returning

g) pcple. act. (*rājì*ᶜ)

2:46 (43)	and that unto Him they are returning
2:156 (151)	surely we belong to God, and to Him we return
21:93 (93)	all shall return to Us
23:60 (62)	their hearts quaking that they are returning to their Lord

MARJIᶜ **n.m.**~a return

3:55 (48)	then unto Me shall you return, and I will decide between you
5:48 (53)	unto God shall you return, all together
5:105 (104)	unto God shall you return, all together
6:60 (60)	unto Him shall you return
6:108 (108)	to their Lord they shall return
6:164 (164)	to your Lord shall you return, and
10:4 (4)	to Him shall you return, all together
10:23 (24)	then unto Us you shall return
10:46 (47)	We call thee unto Us, to Us they shall return

10:70 (71)	some enjoyment in this world; then unto Us they shall return
11:4 (4)	to God shall you return; He is powerful over everything
29:8 (7)	unto Me you shall return
31:15 (14)	then unto Me you shall return
31:23 (22)	unto Us they shall return
37:68 (66)	then their return is unto Hell
39:7 (9)	your Lord shall you return

TARĀJAʿA vb. (VI)~to return to one another; to back off

b) impf. act. (*yatarājaʿu*)

2:230 (230)	then it is no fault in them to return to each other

*R J F

RAJAFA vb. (I)~to quake, to shiver

b) impf. act. (*yarjufu*)

73:14 (14)	upon the day when the earth and the mountains shall quake
79:6 (6)	upon the day when the first blast shivers

RAJFAH n.f.~an earthquake

7:78 (76)	so the earthquake seized them
7:91 (89)	so the earthquake seized them
7:155 (154)	when the earthquake seized them, he said
29:37 (36)	the earthquake seized them

RĀJIFAH n.f.~a blast (the first blast of the trumpet on the Day of Resurrection)

79:6 (6)	upon the day when the first blast shivers

ARJAFA vb. (IV)~(pcple. act.) one who makes a commotion

g) pcple. act. (*murjif*)

33:60 (60)	they that make commotion in the city, We assuredly urge thee against them

*R J J

RAJJA vb. (I)~to rock, to shake. (n.vb.) the act of rocking, shaking

d) perf. pass. (*rujja*)

56:4 (4)	when the earth shall be rocked

f) n.vb. (*rajj*)

56:4 (4)	when the earth shall be rocked <...>

*R J L

RAJIL n.m. (pl. *rijāl*)~foot, foot-soldier; (adv) on foot, walking

2:239 (240)	if you are in fear, then afoot or mounted
17:64 (66)	rally against them thy horsemen and thy foot
22:27 (28)	they shall come unto thee on foot and upon every lean beast

RAJUL n.m. (pl. *rijāl*)~a man

2:228 (228)	but their men have a degree above them
2:282 (282)	call in to witness two witnesses, men
2:282 (282)	or if the two be not men
2:282 (282)	then one man and two women, such witnesses as you approve of
4:1 (1)	from the pair of them scattered abroad many men and women
4:7 (8)	to the men a share of what parents and kinsmen leave
4:12 (15)	if a man or a woman have no heir direct
4:32 (36)	to the men a share from what they have earned
4:34 (38)	men are the managers of the affairs of women
4:75 (77)	for the men, women, and children who, being abased
4:98 (100)	except the men, women, and children
4:176 (175)	if a man perishes having no children
5:23 (26)	said two men of those that feared God
6:9 (9)	We would have made him a man
7:46 (44)	on the Ramparts are men knowing each by their mark
7:48 (46)	the dwellers on the Battlements shall call to certain men they know
7:63 (61)	by the lips of a man from among you
7:69 (67)	by the lips of a man from among you
7:81 (79)	you approach men lustfully instead of women
7:155 (154)	Moses chose of his people seventy men
9:108 (109)	therein are men who love to cleanse themselves
10:2 (2)	was it a wonder to the people that We revealed to a man from among them
11:78 (80)	is there not one man among you of a right mind?
12:109 (109)	We sent not forth any before thee, but men We revealed to
16:43 (45)	We sent not any before thee, except men to whom We revealed
16:76 (78)	God has struck a similitude: two men, one of them dumb
17:47 (50)	you are only following a man bewitched
18:32 (31)	strike for them a similitude: two men
18:37 (35)	Him who created thee of dust, then of a sperm-drop, then shaped thee as a man
21:7 (7)	We sent none before thee, but men to whom We made revelation
23:25 (25)	he is naught but a man bedevilled
23:38 (40)	he is naught but a man who has forged against God a lie
24:31 (31)	such men as attend them, not having sexual desire
24:37 (37)	men whom neither commerce nor trafficking diverts from the remembrance of God
25:8 (9)	you are only following a man bewitched
27:55 (56)	do you approach men lustfully instead of women
28:15 (14)	and found there two men fighting; the one was of his own party
28:20 (19)	then came a man from the furthest part of the city, running
29:29 (28)	do you approach men, and cut the way, and commit in your assembly dishonour
33:4 (4)	God has not assigned to any man two hearts within his breast
33:23 (23)	among the believers are men who were true to their covenant
33:40 (40)	Muhammad is not the father of any one of your men
34:7 (7)	shall we point you to a man who will tell you
34:43 (42)	this is naught but a man who desires to bar you
36:20 (19)	then came a man from the furthest part of the city, running
38:62 (62)	how is it with us, that we do not see men here

39:29 (30)	God has struck a similitude — a man in whom partners disagreeing share
39:29 (30)	and a man the property of one (man)
39:29 (30)	and a (man) the property of one man
40:28 (29)	then said a certain man, a believer of Pharaoh's folk
40:28 (29)	will you slay a man because he says
43:31 (30)	why was this Koran not sent down upon some man of moment
48:25 (25)	if it had not been for certain men believers
72:6 (6)	but there were certain men of mankind
72:6 (6)	who would take refuge with certain men of the jinn

RIJL n.f. (pl. *arjul*)~a foot

5:6 (8)	wipe your heads, and your feet up to the ankles
5:33 (37)	or their hands and feet shall alternately be struck off
5:66 (70)	what was above them, and what was beneath their feet
6:65 (65)	He is able to send forth upon you chastisement, from above you or from under your feet
7:124 (121)	I shall assuredly cut off alternately your hands and feet
7:195 (194)	what, have they feet wherewith they walk
20:71 (74)	I shall assuredly cut off alternately your hands and feet
24:24 (24)	their hands and their feet shall testify against them
24:31 (31)	nor let them stamp their feet, so that their hidden ornament may be known
24:45 (44)	and some of them go upon two feet
26:49 (49)	I shall assuredly cut off alternately your hands and feet
29:55 (55)	the chastisement shall overwhelm them from above them and from under their feet
36:65 (65)	their feet bear witness as to what they have been earning
38:42 (41)	stamp thy foot! This is a laving-place cool, and a drink
60:12 (12)	nor bring a calumny they forge between their hands and their feet

*R J M

RAJAMA vb. (I)~to stone. (n.vb.) the act of stoning; a missile, something to stone with; guesswork, guessing. (pcple. pass.) stoned

a) perf. act.

11:91 (93)	but for thy tribe we would have stoned thee

b) impf. act. (*yarjumu*)

18:20 (19)	if they should get knowledge of you they will stone you
19:46 (47)	surely, if thou givest not over, I shall stone thee
36:18 (17)	if you give not over, we will stone you
44:20 (19)	I take refuge in my Lord and your Lord, lest you should stone me

f) n.vb. (*rajm* pl. *rujūm*)

18:22 (21)	they will say, 'Five; and their dog was the sixth of them;' guessing at the Unseen
67:5 (5)	We adorned the lower heaven with lamps, and made them things to stone Satans

h) pcple. pass. (*marjūm*)

26:116 (116)	if thou givest not over, Noah, thou shalt assuredly be one of the stoned

RAJĪM n.m. (adj)~stoned; accursed, damned (an epithet of Satan)

3:36 (31)	commend her to Thee with her seed, to protect them from the accursed Satan
15:17 (17)	and guarded them from every accursed Satan
15:34 (34)	then go thou forth hence; thou art accursed
16:98 (100)	when thou recitest the Koran, seek refuge in God from the accursed Satan
38:77 (78)	then go thou forth hence; thou art accursed
81:25 (25)	and it is not the word of an accursed Satan

*R J S

RIJS n.m.~an abomination; anger [Ar]; wrath [Bl]; infamy, ignominy; terror [Pk]; penalty, punishment [Ali]

5:90 (92)	wine and arrow-shuffling, idols and divining-arrows are an abomination
6:125 (125)	so God lays abomination upon those who believe not
6:145 (146)	or the flesh of swine — that is an abomination — or an ungodly thing
7:71 (69)	anger and wrath from your Lord have fallen upon you
9:95 (96)	turn aside from them, for they are an abomination
9:125 (126)	them it has increased in abomination
9:125 (126)	added to their abomination, and they have died
10:100 (100)	He lays abomination upon those who have no understanding
22:30 (31)	eschew the abomination of idols
33:33 (33)	God only desires to put away from you abomination

*R J W

RAJĀ vb. (I)~to hope for, to look for. (pcple. pass.) source of hope

b) impf. act. (*yarjū*)

2:218 (215)	those have hope of God's compassion; and God is All-forgiving
4:104 (105)	you are hoping from God
4:104 (105)	for that for which they cannot hope
10:7 (7)	those who look not to encounter Us and are well-pleased with the present life
10:11 (12)	We leave those, who look not to encounter Us, in their insolence
10:15 (16)	those who look not to encounter Us say
17:28 (30)	seeking mercy from thy Lord that thou hopest for
17:57 (59)	they hope for His mercy, and fear His chastisement
18:110 (110)	let him, who hopes for the encounter with his Lord, work righteousness
24:60 (59)	such women as are past child-bearing and have no hope of marriage
25:21 (23)	say those who look not to encounter Us
25:40 (42)	have they not seen it? Nay, but they look for no upraising
28:86 (86)	thou didst not hope that the Book should be cast unto thee
29:5 (4)	whoso looks to encounter God, God's term is coming
33:21 (21)	for whosoever hopes for God and the Last Day
35:29 (26)	look for a commerce that comes not to naught
39:9 (12)	he being afraid of the world to come and hoping for the mercy
45:14 (13)	those who do not look for the days of God
60:6 (6)	a good example in them for whoever hopes for God and the Last Day
71:13 (12)	what ails you, that you look not for majesty in God
78:27 (27)	they indeed hoped not for a reckoning

c) impv. (*urju*)

29:36 (35) O my people, serve God, and look you for the Last Day

h) pcple. pass. (*marjū*)

11:62 (65) Salih, thou hast hitherto been a source of hope among us

ARJĀʾ n.m. (pl. of *rajā*)~borders, sides

69:17 (17) and the angels shall stand upon its borders

ARJÁ vb. (IV)~to put off, to defer, to postpone. (pcple. pass.) someone or something that is deferred

b) impf. act. (*yurjī*)

33:51 (51) thou mayest put off whom thou wilt of them

c) impv. (*arji*)

7:111 (108) put him and his brother off a while
26:36 (35) put him and his brother off a while

h) pcple. pass. (*murjá*)

9:106 (107) and others are deferred to God's commandment

*R J Z

RIJZ n.m.~wrath, punishment; defilement [Ar]; pollution [Bl]; terror [Pk]; plague, penalty [Ali]

2:59 (56) We sent down upon the evildoers wrath out of heaven
7:134 (131) when the wrath fell upon them, they said
7:134 (131) if thou removest from us the wrath, surely we will believe thee
7:135 (131) when We removed from them the wrath unto a term
7:162 (162) We sent down upon them wrath out of heaven
8:11 (11) to put away from you the defilement of Satan
29:34 (33) We shall send down upon the people of this city wrath out of heaven
34:5 (5) theirs shall be a chastisement of painful wrath
45:11 (10) there awaits them a painful chastisement of wrath

RUJZ~defilement

74:5 (5) and defilement flee

*R K ᶜ

RAKAᶜA vb. (I)~to prostrate oneself, to bow, to bow down. (pcple. act.) one who bows, who prostrates himself

b) impf. act. (*yarkaᶜu*)

77:48 (48) when it is said to them, ('Prostrate) yourselves!' they prostrate not *c*) impv. (*irka*ᶜ)

2:43 (40) pay the alms, and bow with those that (bow)
3:43 (38) be obedient to thy Lord, (prostrating) and bowing before Him
22:77 (76) O men bow you down and (prostrate) yourselves
77:48 (48) when it is said to them, 'Prostrate yourselves!' they (prostrate) not

g) pcple. act. (*rāki*ᶜ; pl. *rāki*ᶜ*ūn* and *rukka*ᶜ)

2:43 (40) pay the alms, and (bow) with those that bow
2:125 (119) to those who bow and (prostrate) themselves
3:43 (38) and (bowing) before Him with those that bow
5:55 (60) who perform the prayer and pay the alms, and bow them down
9:112 (113) those who journey, those who bow
22:26 (27) those that stand, for those that bow and (prostrate) themselves
38:24 (23) he fell down, bowing, and he repented
48:29 (29) thou seest them bowing, (prostrating,) seeking bounty

*R K B

RAKIBA vb. (I)~to ride, to mount, to embark (upon a ship). (pcple. act.) one who is mounted

a) perf. act.

18:71 (70) when they embarked upon the ship, he made a hole in it
29:65 (65) when they embark in the ships, they call on God

b) impf. act. (*yarkabu*)

16:8 (8) horses, and mules, and asses, for you to ride
36:42 (42) We have created for them the like of it whereon they ride
40:79 (79) it is God who appointed for you the cattle, some of them to ride
43:12 (11) and appointed for you ships and cattle such as you ride
84:19 (19) you shall surely ride stage after stage

c) impv. (*irkab*)

11:41 (43) embark in it! In God's Name shall be its course and its berthing
11:42 (44) embark with us, my son, and be thou not with the unbelievers

g) pcple. act. (*rākib*, pl. *rukbān*)

2:239 (240) if you are in fear, then afoot or mounted

RAKB n.m.~a cavalcade

8:42 (43) they were on the farther bank, and the cavalcade was below you

RAKŪB n.m.~mount; a riding animal

36:72 (72) We have subdued them to them, and some of them they ride

RIKĀB n.m. (coll)~camels

59:6 (6) against that you pricked neither horse nor camel

RAKKABA vb. (II)~to compose, to put together

a) perf. act.

82:8 (8) and composed thee after what form He would

TARĀKABA vb. (VI)~(pcple. act.) close-compounded, thick-clustered

g) pcple. act. (*mutarākib*)

6:99 (99) bringing forth from it close-compounded grain

*R K D

RAKADA vb. (I)~(pcple. act.) motionless

g) pcple. act. f. (*rākidah*, pl. *rawākid*)

42:33 (31) He stills the wind, and they remain motionless on its back

*R K Ḍ

RAKAḌA vb. (I)~to run; to stamp (one's foot)

b) impf. act. (*yarkuḍu*)

21:12 (12) when they perceived Our might, behold, they ran headlong out of it
21:13 (13) run not

c) impv. (*urkuḍ*)

38:42 (41) stamp thy foot

*R K M

RAKAMA vb. (I)~to heap up, to amass. (pcple. pass.) heaped-up, amassed

b) impf. act. (*yarkumu*)

8:37 (38) so heap them up all together, and put them in Gehenna

h) pcple. pass. (*markūm*)

52:44 (44) a massed cloud

RUKĀM n.m.~a mass, a heap

24:43 (43) how God drives the clouds, then composes them, then converts them into a mass

*R K N

RAKINA vb. (I)~to lean on, to incline unto

b) impf. act. (*yarkanu*)

11:113 (115) lean not on the evildoers, so that the Fire touches you
17:74 (76) thou wert near to inclining unto them a very little

RUKN n.m.~a pillar, a support; a court

11:80 (82) would that I had power against you, or might take refuge in a strong pillar
51:39 (39) but he turned his back, with his court

*R K S

ARKASA vb. (IV)~to overthrow

a) perf. act.

4:88 (90) God has overthrown them for what they earned

d) perf. pass. (*urkisa*)

4:91 (93) whenever they are returned to temptation, they are overthrown in it

*R K Z

RIKZ n.m.~a whisper

19:98 (98) dost thou perceive so much as one of them, or hear of them a whisper?

*R KH W

RUKHĀʾ n.m.~a gentle or soft wind

38:36 (35) We subjected to him the wind, that ran at his commandment, softly

*R M D

RAMĀD n.m.~ashes

14:18 (21) their works are as ashes, whereon the wind blows strong

*R M Ḍ

RAMAḌĀN n.prop.~Ramadan (the ninth month of the Muslim calendar)

2:185 (181) the month of Ramadan, wherein the Koran was sent down to be a guidance

*R M Ḥ

RIMĀḤ n.m. (pl. of *rumḥ*)~lances

5:94 (95)	with something of the game that your hands and lances attain

*R ʿM M

RAMĪM n.com. (adj)~rotten, decayed

36:78 (78)	who shall quicken the bones when they are decayed?
51:42 (42)	that left nothing it came upon, but made it as stuff decayed

*R M N

RUMMĀN n.m.~pomegranates

6:99 (99)	gardens of vines, olives, pomegranates
6:141 (142)	olives, pomegranates, like each to each
55:68 (68)	therein fruits, and palm-trees, and pomegranates

*R M Y

RAMÁ vb. (I)~to throw, to hurl, to shoot, to cast; to accuse, to cast up on someone

a) perf. act.

8:17 (17)	and when thou threwest
8:17 (17)	it was not thyself that threw
8:17 (17)	but God threw

b) impf. act. (*yarmī*)

4:112 (112)	whosoever earns a fault or a sin and then casts it upon the innocent
24:4 (4)	those who cast it up on women in wedlock
24:6 (6)	those who cast it up on their wives having no witnesses
24:23 (23)	those who cast it up on women in wedlock that are heedless but believing
77:32 (32)	that shoots sparks like dry faggots
105:4 (4)	hurling against them stones of baked clay

*R M Z

RAMZ n.m.~a token, a sign

3:41 (36)	thou shalt not speak, save by tokens, to men for three days

*R Q B

RAQABA vb. (I)~to observe, to watch, to regard; to respect

b) impf. act. (*yarqubu*)

9:8 (8)	they will not observe towards you any bond or treaty
9:10 (10)	observing neither bond nor treaty towards a believer
20:94 (95)	thou hast divided the Children of Israel, and thou hast not observed my word

RAQABAH n.f. (pl. *riqāb*)~a neck; a slave

2:177 (172)	to ransom the slave, to perform the prayer
4:92 (94)	then let him set free a believing slave
4:92 (94)	let the slayer set free a believing slave
4:92 (94)	and the slayer shall set free a believing slave
5:89 (91)	or to clothe them, or to set free a slave
9:60 (60)	those whose hearts are brought together, the ransoming of slaves, debtors
47:4 (4)	when you meet the unbelievers, smite their necks
58:3 (4)	they shall set free a slave, before the two of them touch one another
90:13 (13)	the freeing of a slave

RAQĪB n.m.~an observer, a watcher; watchful, watching; sentinel [Ali]; regardful [Bl]; Watcher (Divine attribute)

4:1 (1)	surely God ever watches over you
5:117 (117)	when Thou didst take me to Thyself, Thou wast Thyself the watcher
11:93 (96)	I shall be with you, watching
33:52 (52)	God is watchful over everything
50:18 (17)	not a word he utters, but by him is an observer ready

TARAQQABA vb. (V)~to look about oneself, to be vigilant

b) impf. act. (*yataraqqabu*)

28:18 (17)	now in the morning he was in the city, fearful and vigilant
28:21 (20)	so he departed therefrom, fearful and vigilant

IRTAQABA vb. (VIII)~to observe, to watch, to be on the watch. (pcple. act. pl) ones who are on the watch

c) impv. (*irtaqib*)

11:93 (96)	be upon the watch
44:10 (9)	be on the watch for a day when heaven shall bring a manifest smoke
44:59 (59)	so be on the watch
54:27 (27)	so watch thou them and keep patience

g) pcple. act. (*murtaqib*)

44:59 (59)	so be on the watch; they too are on the watch

*R Q D

RAQADA vb. (I)~(pcple. act.) sleeping, slumbering

g) pcple. act. (*rāqid*, pl. *ruqūd*)

18:18 (17) thou wouldst have thought them awake, as they lay sleeping

MARQAD n.m.~a sleeping-place, a bed

36:52 (52) who roused us out of our sleeping-place?

*R Q M

RAQAMA vb. (I)~(pcple. pass.) inscribed, written

h) pcple. pass. (*marqūm*)

83:9 (9) a book inscribed
83:20 (20) a book inscribed

RAQĪM n.prop.~Er-Rakeem

18:9 (8) dost thou think the Men of the Cave and Er-Rakeem were among Our signs a wonder?

*R Q Q

RAQQ n.m.~a scroll of parchment

52:3 (3) in a parchment unrolled

*R Q Y

RAQIYA vb. (I)~to go up, to mount. (n.vb.) an ascent; going up. (pcple. act.) an enchanter

b) impf. act. (*yarqá*)

17:93 (95) till thou possessest a house of gold ornament, or till thou goest up into heaven

f) n.vb. (*ruqīy*)

17:93 (95) we will not believe thy going up till thou bringest down on us a book

g) pcple. act. (*rāqī*)

75:27 (27) who is an enchanter?

TARĀQĪ n.f. (pl. of *tarquwah*)~clavicles; throat

75:26 (26) when it reaches the clavicles

IRTAQÁ vb. (VIII)~to ascend

b) impf. act. (*yartaqī*)

38:10 (9) why, then let them ascend the cords

*R S KH

RASAKHA vb. (I) (pcple. act. pl)~ones who are firmly rooted

g) pcple. act. (*rāsikh*)

3:7 (5)	those firmly rooted in knowledge say
4:162 (160)	those of them that are firmly rooted in knowledge

*R S L

RASŪL n.m. (see pl. *rusul*, below)~Messenger; Apostle [Ali]

2:87 (81)	whensoever there came to you a Messenger with that your souls had not desire for
2:101 (95)	when there has come to them a Messenger from God confirming what was with them
2:108 (102)	do you desire to question your Messenger as Moses was questioned
2:129 (123)	our Lord, do Thou send among them a Messenger
2:143 (137)	and that the Messenger might be a witness to you
2:143 (138)	We might know who followed the Messenger from him who turned on his heels
2:151 (146)	as also We have sent among you, of yourselves, a Messenger
2:214 (210)	that the Messenger and those who believed with him said
2:279 (279)	God shall war with you, and His Messenger
2:285 (285)	the Messenger believes in what was sent down to him from his Lord
3:32 (29)	obey God, and the Messenger
3:49 (43)	to be a Messenger to the Children of Israel saying
3:53 (46)	we believe in that Thou hast sent down, and we follow the Messenger
3:81 (75)	there shall come to you a Messenger confirming what is with you
3:86 (80)	after they believed, and bore witness that the Messenger is true
3:101 (96)	seeing you have God's signs recited to you, and His Messenger among you
3:132 (126)	and obey God and the Messenger
3:144 (138)	Muhammad is naught but a Messenger
3:153 (147)	the Messenger was calling you in your rear
3:164 (158)	when He raised up among them a Messenger from themselves
3:172 (166)	those who answered God and the Messenger after the wound had smitten them
3:183 (179)	that we believe not any Messenger until he brings to us a sacrifice
4:13 (17)	whoso obeys God and His Messenger, He will admit him to gardens
4:14 (18)	whoso disobeys God, and His Messenger, and transgresses His bounds
4:42 (45)	those who have disobeyed the Messenger, will wish that the earth might be levelled
4:59 (62)	O believers, obey God, and obey the Messenger
4:59 (62)	if you should quarrel on anything, refer it to God and the Messenger
4:61 (64)	come now to what God has sent down, and the Messenger
4:64 (67)	We sent not ever any Messenger, but that he should be obeyed
4:64 (67)	and the Messenger had prayed forgiveness for them
4:69 (71)	whosoever obeys God, and the Messenger
4:79 (81)	and We have sent thee to men a Messenger
4:80 (82)	whosoever obeys the Messenger, thereby obeys God
4:83 (85)	if they had referred it to the Messenger and to those in authority
4:100 (101)	whoso goes forth from his house an emigrant to God and His Messenger
4:115 (115)	whoso makes a breach with the Messenger
4:136 (135)	O believers, believe in God and His Messenger
4:136 (135)	and the Book He has sent down on His Messenger
4:157 (156)	Jesus son of Mary, the Messenger of God

4:170 (168)	the Messenger has now come to you with the truth
4:171 (169)	the Messiah, Jesus son of Mary, was only the Messenger of God
5:15 (18)	now there has come to you Our Messenger, making clear to you many things
5:19 (22)	now there has come to you Our Messenger, making things clear to you
5:33 (37)	those who fight against God and His Messenger
5:41 (45)	O Messenger, let them not grieve thee
5:55 (60)	your friend is only God, and His Messenger
5:56 (61)	whoso makes God his friend , and His Messenger, and the believers
5:67 (71)	O Messenger, deliver that which has been sent down
5:70 (74)	whensover there came to them a Messenger
5:75 (79)	the Messiah, son of Mary, was only a Messenger
5:83 (86)	when they hear what has been sent down to the Messenger
5:92 (93)	obey God and obey the Messenger, and beware
5:92 (93)	it is only for Our Messenger to deliver the Message Manifest
5:99 (99)	it is only for the Messenger to deliver the Message
5:104 (103)	come now to what God has sent down, and the Messenger
5:111 (111)	believe in Me and My Messenger
7:61 (59)	I am a Messenger from the Lord of all Being
7:67 (65)	I am a Messenger from the Lord of all Being
7:104 (102)	Pharaoh, I am a Messenger from the Lord of all Being
7:157 (156)	those who follow the Messenger, the Prophet of the common folk
7:158 (157)	O mankind, I am the Messenger of God to you all
7:158 (158)	believe then in God, and in His Messenger
8:1 (1)	the spoils belong to God and the Messenger
8:1 (1)	obey you God and His Messenger, if you are believers
8:13 (13)	because they had made a breach with God and with His Messenger
8:13 (13)	whosoever makes a breach with God and with His Messenger
8:20 (20)	O believers, obey God and His Messenger
8:24 (24)	O believers, respond to God and the Messenger
8:27 (27)	O believers, betray not God and the Messenger
8:41 (42)	whatever booty you take, the fifth of it is God's, and the Messenger's
8:46 (48)	and obey God, and His Messenger
9:1 (1)	an acquittal, from God and His Messenger
9:3 (3)	a proclamation, from God and His Messenger
9:3 (3)	God is quit, and His Messenger, of the idolaters
9:7 (7)	how should the idolaters have a covenant with God and His Messenger
9:13 (13)	a people who broke their oaths and purposed to expel the Messenger
9:16 (16)	and taken not — apart from God and His Messenger and the believers — any intimate
9:24 (24)	if these are dearer to you than God and His Messenger
9:26 (26)	then God sent down upon His Messenger His Shechina
9:29 (29)	do not forbid what God and His Messenger have forbidden
9:33 (33)	it is He who has sent His Messenger with the guidance
9:54 (54)	but that they believe not in God and His Messenger
9:59 (59)	O were they well-pleased with what God and His Messenger have brought them
9:59 (59)	God will bring us of His bounty, and His Messenger
9:61 (62)	those who hurt God's Messenger — for them awaits a painful chastisement
9:62 (63)	God and His Messenger — more right is it they should please Him
9:63 (64)	whosoever opposes God and His Messenger
9:65 (66)	what, then were you mocking God, and His signs, and His Messenger?
9:71 (72)	and they obey God and His Messenger
9:74 (75)	they took revenge only that God enriched them, and His Messenger, of His bounty
9:80 (81)	that, because they disbelieved in God and His Messenger
9:81 (82)	those who were left behind rejoiced in tarrying behind the Messenger of God

9:84 (85)	they disbelieved in God and His Messenger, and died
9:86 (87)	believe in God, and struggle with His Messenger
9:88 (89)	but the Messenger, and the believers with him, have struggled
9:90 (91)	those who lied to God and His Messenger tarried
9:91 (92)	those who find nothing to expend, if they are true to God and to His Messenger
9:94 (95)	God will surely see your work, and His Messenger
9:97 (98)	apter not to know the bounds of what God has sent down on His Messenger
9:99 (100)	bringing them near to God, and the prayers of the Messenger
9:105 (106)	work; and God will surely see your work, and His Messenger
9:107 (108)	a place of ambush for those who fought God and His Messenger aforetime
9:120 (121)	to stay behind God's Messenger, and to prefer their lives to his
9:128 (129)	now there has come to you a Messenger from among yourselves
10:47 (48)	every nation has its Messenger
10:47 (48)	when their Messenger comes, justly the issue is decided between them
12:50 (50)	when the messenger came to him, he said
13:38 (38)	it was not for any Messenger to bring a sign
14:4 (4)	We have sent no Messenger save with the tongue of his people
15:11 (11)	not a single Messenger came to them, but they mocked at him
16:36 (38)	indeed, We sent forth among every nation a Messenger
16:113 (114)	there came indeed to them a Messenger from amongst them
17:15 (16)	We never chastise, until We send forth a Messenger
17:93 (95)	am I aught but a mortal, a Messenger?
17:94 (96)	has God sent forth a mortal as Messenger?
17:95 (97)	We would have sent down upon them out of heaven an angel as Messenger
19:19 (19)	I am but a messenger come from thy Lord
19:51 (52)	mention in the Book Moses; he was devoted, and he was a Messenger
19:54 (55)	he was true to his promise, and he was a Messenger
20:96 (96)	I seized a handful of dust from the messenger's track
20:134 (134)	our Lord, why didst Thou not send us a Messenger
21:25 (25)	We sent never a Messenger before thee except that We revealed to him
22:52 (51)	We sent not ever any Messenger or Prophet before thee
22:78 (78)	aforetime and in this, that the Messenger might be a witness against you
23:32 (33)	We sent amongst them a Messenger of themselves
23:44 (46)	whenever its Messenger came to a nation they cried him lies
23:69 (71)	did they not recognise their Messenger and so denied him?
24:47 (46)	we believe in God and the Messenger, and we obey
24:48 (47)	when they are called to God and His Messenger that he may judge between them
24:50 (49)	do they fear that God may be unjust towards them and His Messenger
24:51 (50)	when they are called to God and His Messenger
24:52 (51)	whoso obeys God and His Messenger, and fears God
24:54 (53)	obey God, and obey the Messenger
24:54 (53)	it is only for the Messenger to deliver the manifest Message
24:56 (55)	perform the prayer, and pay the alms, and obey the Messenger
24:62 (62)	those only are believers, who believe in God and His Messenger
24:62 (62)	those are they that believe in God and His Messenger
24:63 (63)	make not the calling of the Messenger among yourselves like your calling one of another
25:7 (8)	what ails this Messenger that he eats food, and goes in the markets?
25:27 (29)	would that I had taken a way along with the Messenger
25:30 (32)	the Messenger says, 'O my Lord, behold'
25:41 (43)	what, is this he whom God sent forth as a Messenger?
26:16 (15)	verily, I am the Messenger of the Lord of all Being
26:27 (26)	surely your Messenger who was sent to you is possessed
26:107 (107)	I am for you a faithful Messenger

26:125 (125)	I am for you a faithful Messenger
26:143 (143)	I am for you a faithful Messenger
26:162 (162)	I am for you a faithful Messenger
26:178 (178)	I am for you a faithful Messenger
28:47 (47)	why didst Thou not send a Messenger to us
28:59 (59)	thy Lord never destroyed the cities until He sent in their mother-city a Messenger
29:18 (17)	it is only for the Messenger to deliver the Manifest Message
33:12 (12)	God and His Messenger promised us only delusion
33:21 (21)	you have had a good example in God's Messenger
33:22 (22)	this is what God and His Messenger promised us
33:22 (22)	and God and His Messenger have spoken truly
33:29 (29)	but if you desire God and His Messenger and the Last Abode
33:31 (31)	whosoever of you is obedient to God and His Messenger
33:33 (33)	and obey God and His Messenger
33:36 (36)	when God and His Messenger have decreed a matter
33:36 (36)	whosoever disobeys God and His Messenger has gone astray
33:40 (40)	Muhammad is not the father of any one of your men, but the Messenger of God
33:53 (53)	it is not for you to hurt God's Messenger
33:57 (57)	those who hurt God and His Messenger — them God has cursed
33:66 (66)	ah, would we had obeyed God and the Messenger
33:71 (71)	whosoever obeys God and His Messenger has won a mighty triumph
36:30 (29)	never comes unto them a Messenger, but they mock at him
40:5 (5)	every nation purposed against their Messenger to seize him
40:34 (36)	God will never send forth a Messenger after him
40:78 (78)	it was not for any Messenger to bring a sign, save by God's leave
42:51 (51)	or that He should send a Messenger and he reveal whatsoever He will
43:29 (28)	until the truth came unto them, and a manifest Messenger
43:46 (45)	I am the Messenger of the Lord of all Being
44:13 (12)	seeing a clear Messenger already came to them
44:17 (16)	and a noble Messenger came unto them
44:18 (17)	I am for you a faithful Messenger,'
47:32 (34)	and bar from God's way and make a breach with the Messenger
47:33 (35)	O believers, obey God, and obey the Messenger
48:9 (9)	that you may believe in God and His Messenger
48:12 (12)	you thought that the Messenger and the believers would never return
48:13 (13)	whoso believes not in God and His Messenger
48:17 (17)	whosoever obeys God and His Messenger, He will admit him into gardens
48:26 (26)	then God sent down His Shechina upon His Messenger
48:27 (27)	God has indeed fulfilled the vision He vouchsafed to His Messenger truly
48:28 (28)	it is He who has sent His Messenger with the guidance
48:29 (29)	Muhammad is the Messenger of God
49:1 (1)	O believers, advance not before God and His Messenger
49:3 (3)	those who lower their voices in the presence of God's Messenger
49:7 (7)	know that the Messenger of God is among you
49:14 (14)	if you obey God and His Messenger, He will not diminish you anything
49:15 (15)	the believers are those who believe in God and His Messenger
51:52 (52)	even so not a Messenger came to those before them
57:7 (7)	believe in God and His Messenger
57:8 (8)	seeing that the Messenger is calling you to believe in your Lord
57:28 (28)	O believers, fear God, and believe in His Messenger
58:4 (5)	tat, that you may believe in God and His Messenger
58:5 (6)	those who oppose God and His Messenger shall be frustrated
58:8 (9)	they converse secretly together in sin and enmity, and in disobedience to the Messenger

58:9 (10)	conspire not together in sin and enmity and disobedience to the Messenger
58:12 (13)	when you conspire with the Messenger, before your conspiring advance a freewill offering
58:13 (14)	pay the alms, and obey God and His Messenger
58:20 (21)	those who oppose God and His Messenger, those are among the most abject
58:22 (22)	who are loving to anyone who opposes God and His Messenger
59:4 (4)	that is because they made a breach with God and His Messenger
59:6 (6)	whatever spoils of war God has given unto His Messenger from them
59:7 (7)	whatsoever spoils of war God has given to His Messenger from the people
59:7 (7)	belongs to God, and His Messenger, and the near kinsman
59:7 (7)	whatever the Messenger gives you, take
59:8 (8)	and helping God and His Messenger
60:1 (1)	expelling the Messenger and you because you believe in God
61:5 (5)	why do you hurt me, though you know I am the Messenger of God
61:6 (6)	Children of Israel, I am indeed the Messenger of God to you
61:6 (6)	giving good tidings of a Messenger who shall come after me
61:9 (9)	it is He who has sent His Messenger with the guidance
61:11 (11)	you shall believe in God and His Messenger
62:2 (2)	it is He who has raised up from among the common people a Messenger
63:1 (1)	we bear witness that thou art indeed the Messenger of God
63:1 (1)	God knows that thou art indeed His Messenger
63:5 (5)	God's Messenger will ask forgiveness for you
63:7 (7)	do not expend on them that are with God's Messenger
63:8 (8)	yet glory belongs unto God, and unto His Messenger
64:8 (8)	therefore believe in God and His Messenger
64:12 (12)	obey God, and obey the Messenger
64:12 (12)	it is only for the Messenger to deliver the Manifest Message
65:11 (11)	a Messenger reciting to you the signs of God
69:10 (10)	they rebelled against the Messenger of their Lord
69:40 (40)	it is the speech of a noble Messenger
72:23 (24)	whoso rebels against God and His Messenger
72:27 (27)	save only to such a Messenger as He is well-pleased with
73:15 (15)	We have sent unto you a Messenger as a witness over you
73:15 (15)	even as We sent to Pharaoh a Messenger
73:16 (16)	but Pharaoh rebelled against the Messenger
81:19 (19)	truly this is the word of a noble Messenger
91:13 (13)	then the Messenger of God said to them
98:2 (2)	a Messenger from God, reciting pages purified

RISĀLAH n.f.~a message

5:67 (71)	thou wilt not have delivered His Message
6:124 (124)	God knows very well where to place His Message
7:62 (60)	I deliver to you the Messages of my Lord
7:68 (66)	I deliver to you the Messages of my Lord
7:79 (77)	I have delivered to you the Message of my Lord
7:93 (91)	I have delivered to you the Messages of my Lord
7:144 (141)	Moses, I have chosen thee above all men for My Messages
33:39 (39)	who were delivering the Messages of God, and were fearing Him
72:23 (24)	excepting a Deliverance from God and His Messages
72:28 (28)	that He may know they have delivered the Messages of their Lord

RUSUL n.m. (pl. of *rasūl*, above)~Messengers

2:87 (81)	We gave to Moses the Book, and after him sent succeeding Messengers
2:98 (92)	whosoever is an enemy to God and His angels and His Messengers

2:253 (254)	those Messengers, some We have preferred above others
2:285 (285)	each one believes in God and His angels, and in His Books and His Messengers
2:285 (285)	we make no division between any one of His Messengers
3:144 (138)	Messengers have passed away before him
3:179 (174)	God chooses out of His Messengers whom He will
3:179 (174)	believe you then in God and His Messengers
3:183 (180)	Messengers have come to you before me bearing clear signs
3:184 (181)	if they cry lies to thee, lies were cried to Messengers before thee
3:194 (192)	give us what Thou hast promised us by Thy Messengers
4:136 (135)	whoso disbelieves in God and His angels and His Books, and His Messengers
4:150 (149)	those who disbelieve in God and His Messengers
4:150 (149)	and desire to make division between God and His Messengers
4:152 (151)	those who believe in God and His Messengers
4:164 (162)	Messengers We have already told thee of before
4:164 (162)	and Messengers We have not told thee of
4:165 (163)	Messengers bearing good tidings, and warning
4:165 (163)	so that mankind might have no argument against God, after the Messengers
4:171 (169)	so believe in God and His Messengers
5:12 (15)	and believe in My Messengers and succour them
5:19 (22)	upon an interval between the Messengers
5:32 (36)	Our Messengers have already come to them with the clear signs
5:70 (74)	We took compact with the Children of Israel, and We sent Messengers to them
5:75 (79)	Messengers before him passed away
5:109 (108)	the day when God shall gather the Messengers, and say
6:10 (10)	Messengers indeed were mocked at before thee
6:34 (34)	Messengers indeed were cried lies to before thee
6:61 (61)	by death, Our messengers take him and they neglect not
6:124 (124)	until we are given the like of what God's Messengers were given
6:130 (130)	did not Messengers come to you from among you, relating to you My signs
7:35 (33)	if there should come to you Messengers from among you, relating to you
7:37 (35)	till, when Our messengers come to them, to take them away
7:43 (41)	indeed, our Lord's Messengers came
7:53 (51)	indeed, our Lord's Messengers came with the truth
7:101 (99)	their Messengers came to them with the clear signs
9:70 (71)	their Messengers came to them with the clear signs
10:13 (14)	their Messengers came to them with the clear signs, but they would not believe
10:21 (22)	Our messengers are writing down what you are devising
10:74 (75)	We sent forth, after him, Messengers to their people
10:103 (103)	then We shall deliver Our Messengers and the believers
11:59 (62)	they denied the signs of their Lord, and rebelled against His Messengers
11:69 (72)	Our messengers came to Abraham with the good tidings
11:77 (79)	when Our messengers came to Lot, he was troubled
11:81 (83)	Lot, we are messengers of thy Lord
11:120 (121)	all that We relate to thee of the tidings of the Messengers
12:110 (110)	when the Messengers despaired, deeming they were counted liars
13:32 (32)	Messengers indeed were scoffed at before thee
13:38 (38)	We sent Messengers before thee, and We assigned to them wives
14:9 (10)	their Messengers came to them with the clear signs
14:10 (11)	their Messengers said
14:11 (13)	their Messengers said to them
14:13 (16)	the unbelievers said to their Messengers
14:44 (46)	we will answer Thy call, and follow the Messengers
14:47 (48)	do not deem that God will fail in His promise to His Messengers
16:35 (37)	is aught for the Messengers, but to deliver the manifest Message?
17:77 (79)	the wont of those We sent before thee of Our Messengers

18:106 (106)	they were unbelievers and took My signs and My messengers in mockery
20:47 (49)	we are the Messengers of thy Lord
21:41 (42)	Messengers indeed were mocked at before thee
22:75 (74)	God chooses of the angels Messengers and of mankind
23:44 (46)	then sent We Our Messengers successively
23:51 (53)	O Messengers, eat of the good things and do righteousness
25:37 (39)	the people of Noah, when they cried lies to the Messengers
29:31 (30)	when Our messengers came to Abraham with the good tidings
29:33 (32)	when that Our messengers came to Lot he was troubled
30:9 (8)	their Messengers came to them with the clear signs
30:47 (46)	We sent before thee Messengers unto their people
34:45 (44)	they cried lies to My Messengers, and how was My horror
35:1 (1)	[He] who appointed the angels to be Messengers
35:4 (4)	Messengers before thee were cried lies to
35:25 (23)	their Messengers came to them with the clear signs
38:14 (13)	not one, that cried not lies to the Messengers
39:71 (71)	did not Messengers come to you from among yourselves
40:22 (23)	that was because their Messengers came to them with the clear signs
40:50 (53)	did not your Messengers bring you the clear signs?
40:51 (54)	surely We shall help Our Messengers
40:70 (72)	those who cry lies to the Book and that wherewith We sent Our Messengers
40:78 (78)	We sent Messengers before thee
40:83 (83)	when their Messengers brought them the clear signs
41:14 (13)	when the Messengers came unto them from before them
41:43 (43)	naught is said to thee but what already was said to the Messengers before thee
43:45 (44)	ask those of Our Messengers We sent before thee
43:80 (80)	Our messengers are present with them writing it down
46:9 (8)	I am not an innovation among the Messengers
46:35 (34)	be thou patient, as the Messengers possessed of constancy were also patient
50:14 (13)	every one cried lies to the Messengers, and My threat came true
57:19 (18)	those who believe in God and His Messengers — they are the just men
57:21 (21)	made ready for those who believe in God and His Messengers
57:25 (25)	indeed, We sent Our Messengers with the clear signs
57:25 (25)	that God might know who helps Him, and His Messengers, in the Unseen
57:27 (27)	then We sent, following in their footsteps, Our Messengers
58:21 (21)	I shall assuredly be the victor, I and My Messengers
59:6 (6)	God gives authority to His Messengers over whomsoever He will
64:6 (6)	that is because their Messengers came to them with the clear signs
65:8 (8)	how many a city turned in disdain from the commandment of its Lord and His Messengers
77:11 (11)	and when the Messengers' time is set

ARSALA vb. (IV)~to send; to loose. (pcple. act.) one who sends; sending. (pcple. pass.) one who is sent, an envoy; one that is loosed

a) perf. act.

2:119 (113)	We have sent thee with the truth, good tidings to bear
2:151 (146)	as also We have sent among you, of yourselves, a Messenger
4:64 (67)	We sent not ever any Messenger, but that he should be obeyed
4:79 (81)	We have sent thee to men a Messenger
4:80 (82)	We have not sent thee to be a watcher over them
5:70 (74)	We took compact with the Children of Israel, and We sent Messengers to them
6:6 (6)	and how We loosed heaven upon them in torrents
6:42 (42)	indeed We sent to nations before thee
7:59 (57)	and We sent Noah to his people

7:94 (92)	We have sent no Prophet to any city but that We seized its people with misery
7:133 (130)	We let loose upon them the flood and the locusts
7:162 (162)	We sent down upon them wrath out of heaven
9:33 (33)	it is He who has sent His Messenger with the guidance
11:25 (27)	and We sent Noah to his people
11:96 (99)	and We sent Moses with Our signs
12:19 (19)	then came travellers, and they sent one of them, a water-drawer
12:31 (31)	when she heard their sly whispers, she sent to them
12:109 (109)	We sent not forth any before thee, but men We revealed to
13:30 (29)	thus We have sent thee among a nation
13:38 (38)	We sent Messengers before thee
14:4 (4)	We have sent no Messenger save with the tongue of his people
14:5 (5)	We sent Moses with Our signs
15:10 (10)	indeed, We sent Messengers before thee
15:22 (22)	We loose the winds fertilising
16:43 (45)	We sent not any before thee, except men to whom We revealed
16:63 (65)	assuredly We sent Messengers to nations before thee
17:54 (56)	We sent thee not to be a guardian over them
17:77 (79)	the wont of those We sent before thee of Our Messengers
17:105 (106)	We have sent thee not, except good tidings to bear
19:17 (17)	We sent unto her Our Spirit that presented himself to her
19:83 (86)	hast thou not seen how We sent the Satans against the unbelievers
20:134 (134)	our Lord, why didst Thou not send us a Messenger
21:7 (7)	We sent none before thee, but men to whom We made revelation
21:25 (25)	We sent never a Messenger before thee except that We revealed to him
21:107 (107)	We have not sent thee, save as a mercy unto all beings
22:52 (51)	We sent not ever any Messenger or Prophet before thee
23:23 (23)	We sent Noah to his people
23:32 (33)	We sent amongst them a Messenger of themselves
23:44 (46)	then sent We Our Messengers successively
23:45 (47)	then We sent Moses and his brother Aaron with Our signs
25:20 (22)	We sent not before thee any Envoys
25:48 (50)	it is He who has loosed the winds, bearing good tidings
25:56 (58)	We have sent thee not, except good tidings to bear
26:53 (53)	then Pharaoh sent among the cities musterers
27:45 (46)	We sent to Thamood their brother Salih
28:47 (47)	why didst Thou not send a Messenger to us
29:14 (13)	indeed, We sent Noah to his people
29:40 (39)	of them against some We loosed a squall of pebbles
30:47 (46)	indeed, We sent before thee Messengers unto their people
30:51 (50)	but if We loose a wind, and they see it growing yellow
33:9 (9)	when hosts came against you, and We loosed against them a wind
33:45 (44)	O Prophet, We have sent thee as a witness
34:16 (15)	they turned away; so We loosed on them the Flood of Arim
34:28 (27)	We have sent thee not, except to mankind entire
34:34 (33)	We sent no warner into any city
34:44 (43)	nor have We sent them before thee any warner
35:9 (10)	God is He that looses the winds, that stir up cloud
35:24 (22)	We have sent thee with the truth good tidings to bear
36:14 (13)	when We sent unto them two men, but they cried them lies
37:72 (70)	and We sent among them warners
37:147 (147)	then We sent him unto a hundred thousand, or more
40:23 (24)	We also sent Moses with Our signs and a clear authority
40:70 (72)	those who cry lies to the Book and that wherewith We sent Our Messengers
40:78 (78)	We sent Messengers before thee

41:16 (15)	then We loosed against them a wind clamorous in days of ill fortune
42:48 (47)	We sent thee not to be a guardian over them
43:6 (5)	how many a Prophet We sent among the ancients
43:23 (22)	even so We sent never before the any warner into any city
43:45 (44)	ask those of Our Messengers We sent before thee
43:46 (45)	We also sent Moses with Our signs to Pharaoh and his Council
48:8 (8)	surely We have sent thee as a witness
48:28 (28)	it is He who has sent His Messenger with the guidance
51:38 (38)	also in Moses, when We sent him unto Pharaoh
51:41 (41)	also in Ad, when We loosed against them the withering wind
54:19 (19)	We loosed against them a wind clamorous
54:31 (31)	We loosed against them one Cry
54:34 (34)	We loosed against them a squall of pebbles
57:25 (25)	We sent Our Messengers with the clear signs
57:26 (26)	and We sent Noah, and Abraham
61:9 (9)	it is He who has sent His Messenger with the guidance
71:1 (1)	We sent Noah to his people, saying
73:15 (15)	We have sent unto you a Messenger as a witness over you
73:15 (15)	We have sent unto you a Messenger as a witness over you
105:3 (3)	He loosed upon them birds in flights

b) impf. act. (*yursilu*)

6:48 (48)	We do not send the Envoys, except good tidings to bear
6:61 (61)	He sends recorders over you
7:57 (55)	it is He who looses the winds, bearing good tidings before His mercy
7:134 (131)	we will believe thee, and send forth with thee the Children of Israel
11:52 (54)	then repent to Him, and He will loose heaven in torrents upon you
12:66 (66)	never will I send him with you until you bring me a solemn pledge
13:13 (14)	He looses the thunderbolts, and smites with them whomsoever He will
17:59 (61)	naught prevented Us from sending the signs
17:59 (61)	We do not send the signs, except to frighten
17:68 (70)	or loose against you a squall of pebbles
17:69 (71)	[that He will] loose against you a hurricane of wind
18:40 (38)	better than thy garden, and loose on it a thunderbolt out of heaven
18:56 (54)	We send not the Envoys, but good tidings to bear
27:63 (64)	He who guides you in the shadows of the land and the sea and looses the winds
30:46 (45)	of His signs is that He looses the winds
30:48 (47)	God is He that looses the winds, that stir up clouds
39:42 (43)	but looses the other till a stated term
42:51 (51)	or that He should send a messenger and he reveal whatsoever He will
51:33 (33)	to loose upon them stones of clay
67:17 (17)	do you feel secure that He who is in heaven will not loose against you a squall of pebbles
71:11 (10)	He will loose heaven upon you in torrents

c) impv. (*arsil*)

7:105 (103)	so send forth with me the Children of Israel
7:111 (108)	put him and his brother off a while, and send among the cities musterers
12:12 (12)	send him forth with us tomorrow, to frolic and play
12:45 (45)	I will myself tell you its interpretation; so send me forth
12:63 (63)	send with us our brother, that we may obtain the measure
20:47 (49)	so send forth with us the Children of Israel
26:13 (12)	my tongue will not be loosed; so send to Aaron
26:17 (16)	so send forth with us the Children of Israel
28:34 (34)	send him with me as a helper and to confirm I speak truly

d) perf. pass. (*ursila*)

7:6 (5) so We shall question those unto whom a Message was sent
7:75 (73) in the Message he has been sent with we are believers
7:87 (85) if there is a party of you who believe in the Message I have been sent with
11:57 (60) I have delivered to you that I was sent with unto you
11:70 (73) fear not; we have been sent to the people of Lot
14:9 (10) we certainly disbelieve in the Message you have been sent with
15:58 (58) we have been sent unto a people of sinners
21:5 (5) even as the ancient ones were sent as Messengers
26:27 (26) surely your Messenger who was sent to you is possessed
34:34 (33) we disbelieve in the Message you have been sent with
41:14 (13) so we disbelieve in the Message you were sent with
43:24 (23) we disbelieve in that you were sent with
46:23 (22) I deliver to you the Message with which I was sent
51:32 (32) we have been sent to a people of sinners
83:33 (33) yet they were not sent as watchers over them

e) impf. pass. (*yursalu*)

55:35 (35) against you shall be loosed a flame of fire, and molten brass

g) pcple. act. (*mursil*)

27:35 (35) I will send them a present, and see what the envoys bring back
28:45 (45) but We were sending Messengers
35:2 (2) whatsoever He withholds, none can loose after Him
44:5 (4) We are ever sending
54:27 (27) We shall send the She-camel as a trial for them

h) pcple. pass. (*mursal*)

2:252 (253) assuredly thou art of the number of the Envoys
6:34 (34) there has already come to thee some tiding of the Envoys
6:48 (48) We do not send the Envoys, except good tidings to bear
7:6 (5) We shall question the Envoys
7:75 (73) do you know that Salih is an Envoy from his Lord?
7:77 (75) O Salih, bring us that thou promisest us, if thou art an Envoy
13:43 (43) thou art not an Envoy
15:57 (57) and what is your business, envoys?
15:61 (61) when the envoys came to the folk of Lot
15:80 (80) the dwellers in El-Hijr cried lies to the Envoys
18:56 (54) We send not the Envoys, but good tidings to bear
25:20 (22) We sent not before thee any Envoys, but that they ate food
26:21 (20) my Lord gave me Judgment and made me one of the Envoys
26:105 (105) the people of Noah cried lies to the Envoys
26:123 (123) Ad cried lies to the Envoys
26:141 (141) Thamood cried lies to the Envoys
26:160 (160) the people of Lot cried lies to the Envoys
26:176 (176) the men of the Thicket cried lies to the Envoys
27:10 (10) surely the Envoys do not fear in My presence
27:35 (35) now I will send them a present, and see what the envoys bring back
28:7 (6) We shall return him to thee, and shall appoint him one of the Envoys
28:65 (65) what answer gave you to the Envoys?
36:3 (2) thou art truly among the Envoys
36:13 (12) strike for them a similitude — the inhabitants of the city, when the Envoys came to it

36:14 (13)	we are assuredly Envoys unto you
36:16 (15)	our Lord knows we are Envoys unto you
36:20 (19)	my people, follow the Envoys
36:52 (52)	this is what the All-merciful promised, and the Envoys spoke truly
37:37 (36)	he brought the truth, and confirmed the Envoys
37:123 (123)	Elias too was one of the Envoys
37:133 (133)	Lot too was one of the Envoys
37:139 (139)	Jonah too was one of the Envoys
37:171 (171)	already Our Word has preceded to Our servants, the Envoys
37:181 (181)	peace be upon the Envoys
51:31 (31)	what is your business, envoys?
77:1 (1)	by the loosed ones successively

*R S S

RASS n.prop.~Er-Rass (name of a well near Midian or near Antioch)

25:38 (40)	Ad, and Thamood, and the men of Er-Rass
50:12 (12)	cried lies before them the people of Noah and the men of Er-Rass

*R S Y

RASĀ vb. (I)~(pcple. act.) that which is anchored, which is firmly fixed

g) pcple. act. f. (*rāsiyah*, pl. *rāsiyāt*)

34:13 (12)	porringers like water-troughs, and anchored cooking-pots

MURSÁ n.f.~a berth, a harbour

7:187 (186)	they will question thee concerning the Hour, when it shall berth
11:41 (43)	in God's Name shall be its course and its berthing
79:42 (42)	they will question thee concerning the Hour, when it shall berth

RAWĀSĪ n.f. (pl. of *rāsiyah*)~mountains

13:3 (3)	it is He who stretched out the earth and set therein firm mountains
15:19 (19)	We stretched it forth, and cast on it firm mountains
16:15 (15)	He cast on the earth firm mountains, lest it shake with you
21:31 (32)	We set in the earth firm mountains
27:61 (62)	and set amidst it rivers and appointed for it firm mountains
31:10 (9)	He cast on the earth firm mountains
41:10 (9)	He set therein firm mountains over it
50:7 (7)	We stretched it forth, and cast on it firm mountains
77:27 (27)	set We not therein soaring mountains?

ARSÁ vb. (IV)~to set firm

a) perf. act.

79:32 (32)	and the mountains He set firm

*R SH D

RASHADA vb. (I)~to go aright, to be on the right way. (n.vb.) rectitude, right judgment. (pcple. act.) one who is rightly minded

b) impf. act. (*yarshudu*)

2:186 (182) let them believe in Me; haply so they will go aright

f) n.vb. (*rushd*)

2:256 (257) rectitude has become clear from error
4:6 (5) if you perceive in them right judgment, deliver to them their property
7:146 (143) though they see the way of rectitude they will not take it for a way
18:66 (65) so that thou teachest me, of what thou hast been taught, right judgment
21:51 (52) We gave Abraham aforetime his rectitude
72:2 (2) guiding to rectitude. We believe in it

g) pcple. act. (*rāshid*)

49:7 (7) those — they are the right-minded

RASHAD n.m.~rectitude

18:10 (9) and furnish us with rectitude in our affair
18:24 (23) it may be that my Lord will guide me unto something nearer to rectitude
72:10 (10) whether their Lord intends for them rectitude
72:14 (14) those who have surrendered sought rectitude
72:21 (21) I possess no power over you, either for hurt or for rectitude

RASHĀD n.m.~rectitude

40:29 (30) I only guide you in the way of rectitude
40:38 (41) follow me, and I will guide you in the way of rectitude

RASHĪD n.m. (adj)~one who is right-minded

11:78 (80) is there not one man among you of a right mind?
11:87 (89) thou art the clement one, the right-minded
11:97 (99) Pharaoh's command was not right-minded

ARSHADA vb. (IV)~(pcple. act.) one who guides or directs

g) pcple. act. (*murshid*)

18:17 (16) thou wilt not find for him a protector to direct

*R Ṣ D

IRṢĀD n.m.~a place of ambush

9:107 (108) as a place of ambush for those who fought God and His Messenger

MARṢAD n.m.~a place of ambush

9:5 (5) confine them, and lie in wait for them at every place of ambush

MIRṢĀD n.m.~an ambush; a watch

78:21 (21)	behold, Gehenna has become an ambush
89:14 (13)	surely thy Lord is ever on the watch

RAṢAD n.m.~a meteor; (coll) a band of watchers

72:9 (9)	but any listening now finds a meteor in wait for him
72:27 (27)	then He despatches before him and behind him watchers

*R Ṣ Ṣ

RAṢṢA vb. (I)~(pcple. pass.) that which is well-compacted

h) pcple. pass. (*marṣūṣ*)

61:4 (4)	as though they were a building well-compacted

*R T ᶜ

RATAᶜA vb. (I)~to frolic

b) impf. act. (*yartaᶜu*)

12:12 (12)	send him forth with us tomorrow, to frolic and play

*R T L

RATTALA vb. (II)~to chant; to arrange [Pk], to rehearse in well-arranged stages [Ali]. (n.vb.) the act of chanting; the act of arranging

a) perf. act.

25:32 (34)	We have chanted it very distinctly

c) impv. (*rattil*)

73:4 (4)	chant the Koran very distinctly

f) n.vb. (*tartīl*)

25:32 (34)	We have chanted it <very distinctly>
73:4 (4)	chant the Koran <very distinctly>

*R T Q

RATAQA vb. (I)~(n.vb.) the act of sewing up, joining together *f*) n.vb. (*ratq*)

21:30 (31) the heavens and the earth were a mass all sewn up

*R Ṭ B

RAṬB n.m. (adj)~fresh

6:59 (59) not a thing, fresh or withered, but it is in a Book Manifest

RUṬAB n.m.~fresh dates

19:25 (25) there shall come tumbling upon thee dates fresh and ripe

*R W ͑

RĀ͑A vb. (I)~(n.vb.) awe, fear, fright

f) n.vb. (*raw͑*)

11:74 (77) when the awe departed from Abraham and the good tidings came to him

*R W D

RUWAYDAN n.m. (adv)~slowly, gently, leisurely, awhile

86:17 (17) so respite the unbelievers; delay with them awhile

RĀWADA vb. (III)~(with prep. *͑an*) to solicit, to seduce, to seek, to tempt

a) perf. act.

12:23 (23) the woman in whose house he was solicited him
12:26 (26) it was she that solicited me'
12:32 (32) yes, I solicited him, but he abstained
12:51 (51) 'What was your business, women,' he said, 'when you solicited Joseph?'
12:51 (51) I solicited him; he is a truthful man
54:37 (37) even his guests they had solicited of him

b) impf. act. (*yurāwidu*)

12:30 (30) the Governor's wife has been soliciting her page
12:61 (61) we will solicit him of our father

ARĀDA vb. (IV)~to want, to desire, to wish, to seek, to purpose, to intend

a) perf. act.

2:26 (24) what did God desire by this for a similitude
2:228 (228) their mates have better right to restore them, if they desire to set things right
2:233 (233) for such as desire to fulfil the suckling

2:233 (233) if the couple desire by mutual consent and consultation to wean
2:233 (233) if you desire to seek nursing for your children
4:20 (24) if you desire to exchange a wife in place of another
4:62 (65) we sought only kindness and conciliation
5:17 (19) who then shall overrule God in any way if He desires to destroy the Messiah
9:46 (46) if they had desired to go forth, they would have made some preparation
9:107 (108) we desired nothing but good
11:34 (36) my sincere counsel will not profit you, if I desire to counsel you sincerely
12:25 (25) what is the recompense of him who purposes evil against thy folk
13:11 (12) whensoever God desires evil for a people, there is no turning it back
16:40 (42) the only words We say to a thing, when We desire it
17:16 (17) when We desire to destroy a city
17:19 (20) whosoever desires the world to come and strives after it
17:103 (105) He desired to startle them from the land
18:79 (78) I desired to damage it
18:81 (80) we desired that their Lord should give to them in exchange one better
18:82 (81) thy Lord desired that they should come of age
20:86 (89) did you desire that anger should alight on you from your Lord
21:17 (17) had We desired to take to Us a diversion
21:70 (70) they desired to outwit him
22:22 (22) as often as they desire in their anguish to come forth from it
24:33 (33) constrain not your slavegirls to prostitution, if they desire to live in chastity
25:62 (63) it is He who made the night and day a succession for whom He desires to remember
25:62 (63) or He desires to be thankful
28:19 (18) Moses, dost thou desire to slay me
32:20 (20) as often as they desire to come forth from it
33:17 (17) who is he that shall defend you from God, if He desires evil for you
33:17 (17) or desires mercy for you
33:50 (49) if the Prophet desire to take her in marriage
36:82 (82) His command, when He desires a thing, is to say to it
37:98 (96) they desired to outwit him
39:4 (6) had God desired to take to Him a son
39:38 (39) if God desires affliction for me, shall they remove His affliction
39:38 (39) or if He desires mercy for me, shall they withhold His mercy
48:11 (11) who can avail you aught against God, if He desires hurt for you
48:11 (11) or desires profit for you
72:10 (10) whether their Lord intends for them rectitude
74:31 (33) what did God intend by this as a similitude?

b) impf. act. (*yurīdu*)

2:108 (102) do you desire to question your Messenger
2:185 (181) God desires ease for you
2:185 (181) and desires not hardship for you
2:253 (254) but God does whatsoever He desires
3:108 (104) God desires not any injustice to living beings
3:145 (139) whoso desires the reward of this world, We will give him of this
3:145 (139) whoso desires the reward of the other world, We will give him of that
3:152 (146) some of you there are that desire this world
3:152 (146) and some of you there are desire the next world
3:176 (170) God desires not to appoint for them a portion in the world to come
4:26 (31) God desires to make clear to you
4:27 (32) God desires to turn towards you
4:27 (32) those who follow their lusts desire you to swerve away mightily
4:28 (32) God desires to lighten things for you
4:35 (39) from her people an arbiter, if they desire to set things right
4:44 (47) and desiring that you should also err from the way

4:60 (63)	desiring to take their disputes to idols
4:60 (63)	but Satan desires to lead them astray into far error
4:88 (90)	do you desire to guide him whom God has led astray?
4:91 (93)	you will find others desiring to be secure from you
4:134 (133)	whoso desires the reward of this world
4:144 (143)	do you desire to give God over you a clear authority?
4:150 (149)	and desire to make division between God and His Messengers
4:150 (149)	desiring to take between this and that a way
5:1 (1)	God decrees whatsoever He desires
5:6 (9)	God does not desire to make any impediment for you
5:6 (9)	but He desires to purify you
5:29 (32)	I desire that thou shouldest be laden with my sin
5:37 (41)	they will desire to come forth from the Fire
5:41 (45)	whomsoever God desires to try, thou canst not avail him anything with God
5:41 (45)	those are they whose hearts God desired not to purify
5:49 (54)	know that God desires only to smite them for some sin
5:91 (93)	Satan only desires to precipitate enmity and hatred between you
5:113 (113)	we desire that we should eat of it and our hearts be at rest
6:52 (52)	those who call upon their Lord at morning and evening desiring His countenance
6:125 (125)	whomsoever God desires to guide, He expands his breast to Islam
6:125 (125)	whomsoever He desires to lead astray, He makes his breast narrow
7:110 (107)	who desires to expel you from your land
8:7 (7)	but God was desiring to verify the truth
8:62 (64)	if they desire to trick thee, God is sufficient for thee
8:67 (68)	you desire the chance goods of the present world
8:67 (68)	and God desires the world to come
8:71 (72)	if they desire treachery against thee, they have tricked God before
9:32 (32)	desiring to extinguish with their mouths God's light
9:55 (55)	God only desires thereby to chastise them in this present life
9:85 (86)	God only desires thereby to chastise them in this present world
10:107 (107)	if He desires any good for thee, none can repel His bounty
11:15 (18)	whoso desires the present life and its adornment, We will pay them in full
11:34 (36)	if God desires to pervert you; He is your Lord
11:79 (81)	thou well knowest what we desire
11:88 (90)	I desire not to come behind you
11:88 (90)	I desire only to set things right, so far as I am able
11:107 (109)	surely thy Lord accomplishes what He desires
14:10 (12)	you desire to bar us from that our fathers served
17:18 (19)	whosoever desires this hasty world
17:18 (19)	We hasten for him therein what We will unto whomsoever We desire
18:28 (27)	those who call upon their Lord at morning and evening, desiring His countenance
18:28 (27)	let not thine eyes turn away from them, desiring the adornment of the present life
18:77 (76)	there they found a wall about to tumble down
20:63 (66)	these two men are sorcerers and their purpose is to expel you
22:14 (14)	surely God does that He desires
22:16 (16)	for that God guides whom He desires
22:25 (26)	whosoever purposes to violate it wrongfully
23:24 (24)	this is naught but a mortal like yourselves, who desires to gain superiority
26:35 (34)	who desires to expel you from your land by his sorcery
28:5 (4)	We desired to be gracious to those that were abased in the land
28:19 (18)	Moses, dost thou desire to slay me
28:19 (18)	thou only desirest to be a tyrant in the land
28:19 (18)	thou desirest not to be of them that put things right

28:27 (27)	I desire to marry thee to one of these my two daughters
28:27 (27)	I do not desire to press hard upon thee
28:79 (79)	those who desired the present life said
28:83 (83)	We appoint it for those who desire not exorbitance in the earth
30:38 (37)	that is better for those who desire God's Face
30:39 (38)	but what you give in alms, desiring God's Face
33:13 (13)	yet they were not exposed; they desired only to flee
33:28 (28)	if you desire the present life and its adornment, come now
33:29 (29)	if you desire God and His Messenger and the Last Abode
33:33 (33)	God only desires to put away from you abomination
34:43 (42)	a man who desires to bar you from that your fathers served
35:10 (11)	whosoever desires glory, the glory altogether belongs to God
36:23 (22)	if the All-merciful desires affliction for me
37:86 (84)	gods apart from God, that you desire
40:31 (33)	God desires not wrong for His servants
42:20 (19)	whoso desires the tillage of the world to come
42:20 (19)	whoso desires the tillage of this world, We shall give him of it
48:15 (15)	desiring to change God's words
51:57 (57)	I desire of them no provision
51:57 (57)	neither do I desire that they should feed Me
52:42 (42)	or desire they to outwit
53:29 (30)	him who turns away from Our Remembrance, and desires only the present life
61:8 (8)	they desire to extinguish with their mouths the light of God
74:52 (52)	every man of them desires to be given scrolls unrolled
75:5 (5)	nay, but man desires to continue on as a libertine
76:9 (9)	we desire no recompense from you, no thankfulness
85:16 (16)	performer of what He desires

d) perf. pass. (*urīda*)

72:10 (10)	so we know not whether evil is intended for those in the earth

e) impf. pass. (*yurādu*)

38:6 (5)	be steadfast to your gods; this is a thing to be desired

*R W Ḍ

RAWḌAH n.f.~a (well-watered) meadow

30:15 (14)	they shall walk with joy in a green meadow
42:22 (21)	those who believe and do righteous deeds are in Meadows of the Gardens

*R W GH

RĀGHA vb. (I)~to turn

a) perf. act.

37:91 (89)	then he turned to their gods, and said
37:93 (91)	he turned upon them smiting them with his right hand
51:26 (26)	then he turned to his household and brought a fattened calf

*R W Ḥ

RĀḤA vb. (I)~(n.vb.1) departure, going, leaving; evening course. (n.vb.2) repose, comfort, refreshment

f) n.vb. (1) (*rawāḥ*)

34:12 (11)	and its evening course was a month's journey

f) n.vb. (2) (*rawḥ*)

12:87 (87)	do not despair of God's comfort
12:87 (87)	of God's comfort no man despairs
56:89 (88)	there shall be repose and ease, and a Garden of Delight

RĪḤ n.m. (pl. *aryāḥ*)~wind; power; scent

2:164 (159)	the turning about of the winds and the clouds compelled between heaven and earth
3:117 (113)	the likeness of a freezing blast that smites the tillage of a people
7:57 (55)	it is He who looses the winds, bearing good tidings before His mercy
8:46 (48)	do not quarrel together, and so lose heart, and your power depart
10:22 (23)	the ships run with them with a fair breeze, and they rejoice in it
10:22 (23)	there comes upon them a strong wind
12:94 (94)	surely I perceive Joseph's scent, unless you think me doting
14:18 (21)	their works are as ashes, whereon the wind blows strong
15:22 (22)	We loose the winds fertilising
17:69 (71)	and loose against you a hurricane of wind and drown you for your thanklessness
18:45 (43)	in the morning it is straw the winds scatter
21:81 (81)	and to Solomon the wind, strongly blowing
22:31 (32)	the birds snatch him away, or the wind sweeps him headlong into a place far away
25:48 (50)	it is He who has loosed the winds, bearing good tidings before His mercy
27:63 (64)	He who guides you in the shadows of the land and the sea and looses the winds
30:46 (45)	of His signs is that He looses the winds, bearing good tidings
30:48 (47)	God is He that looses the winds, that stir up clouds
30:51 (50)	if We loose a wind, and they see it growing yellow, they remain after that unbelievers
33:9 (9)	when hosts came against you, and We loosed against them a wind
34:12 (11)	and to Solomon the wind
35:9 (10)	God is He that looses the winds, that stir up cloud
38:36 (35)	We subjected to him the wind, that ran at his commandment, softly
41:16 (15)	then We loosed against them a wind clamorous in days of ill fortune
42:33 (31)	and if He wills, He stills the wind
45:5 (4)	the turning about of the winds, there are signs for a people who understand
46:24 (23)	a wind, wherein is a painful chastisement
51:41 (41)	also in Ad, when We loosed against them the withering wind
54:19 (19)	We loosed against them a wind clamorous in a day of ill fortune
69:6 (6)	as for Ad, they were destroyed by a wind clamorous, violent

RAYḤĀN n.m.~ease; fragrant herb

55:12 (11)	grain in the blade, and fragrant herbs
56:89 (88)	there shall be repose and ease, and a Garden of Delight

RŪḤ n.m.~spirit; (*rūḥ al-quds*) the Holy Spirit

2:87 (81)	We gave Jesus son of Mary the clear signs, and confirmed him with the Holy Spirit
2:253 (254)	We gave Jesus son of Mary the clear signs, and confirmed him with the Holy Spirit

4:171 (169)	His Word that He committed to Mary, and a Spirit from Him
5:110 (109)	when I confirmed thee with the Holy Spirit, to speak to men
15:29 (29)	when I have shaped him, and breathed My spirit in him
16:2 (2)	He sends down the angels with the Spirit of His command upon whomsoever He will
16:102 (104)	the Holy Spirit sent it down from thy Lord in truth
17:85 (87)	they will question thee concerning the Spirit
17:85 (87)	the Spirit is of the bidding of my Lord
19:17 (17)	then We sent unto her Our Spirit that presented himself to her
21:91 (91)	We breathed into her of Our spirit and appointed her and her son to be a sign
26:193 (193)	brought down by the Faithful Spirit
32:9 (8)	then He shaped him, and breathed His spirit in him
38:72 (72)	I have shaped him, and breathed My spirit in him
40:15 (15)	casting the Spirit of His bidding upon whomever He will of His servants
42:52 (52)	even so We have revealed to thee a Spirit of Our bidding
58:22 (22)	He has confirmed them with a Spirit from Himself
66:12 (12)	so We breathed into her of Our Spirit
70:4 (4)	to Him the angels and the Spirit mount up in a day
78:38 (38)	upon the day when the Spirit and the angels stand in ranks
97:4 (4)	in it the angels and the Spirit descend

ARĀḤA vb. (IV)~to give rest

b) impf. act. (*yurīḥu*)

16:6 (6)	there is beauty in them for you, when you bring them home to rest

*R W M

RŪM n.prop.~Greeks [Ar]; Romans [Pk, Bl]; Roman Empire [Ali]

30:2 (1)	the Greeks have been vanquished

*R Y ᶜ

RĪᶜ n.m.~a prominence, a high hill

26:128 (128)	do you build on every prominence a sign, sporting

*R Y B

RĀBA vb. (I)~(n.vb.) a doubt, suspicion, uncertainty

f) n.vb. (*rayb*)

2:2 (1)	that is the Book, wherein is no doubt
2:23 (21)	if you are in doubt concerning that We have sent down on Our servant
3:9 (7)	it is Thou that shall gather mankind for a day whereon is no doubt
3:25 (24)	how will it be, when We gather them for a day whereon is no doubt
4:87 (89)	He will surely gather you to the Resurrection Day, no doubt of it

6:12 (12)	He will surely gather you to the Resurrection Day, of which is no doubt
9:45 (45)	so that in their doubt they go this way and that
10:37 (38)	a distinguishing of the Book, wherein is no doubt
17:99 (101)	He has appointed for them a term, no doubt of it
18:21 (20)	God's promise is true, and that the Hour — there is no doubt of it
22:5 (5)	if you are in doubt as to the Upraising
22:7 (7)	because the Hour is coming, no doubt of it
32:2 (1)	the sending down of the Book, wherein no doubt is
40:59 (61)	the Hour is coming, no doubt of it, but most men do not believe
42:7 (5)	that thou mayest warn of the Day of Gathering, wherein is no doubt
45:26 (25)	then He shall gather you to the Day of Resurrection, wherein is no doubt
45:32 (31)	God's promise is true, and the Hour, there is no doubt of it
52:30 (30)	he is a poet for whom we await Fate's uncertainty

RĪBAH n.f.~a doubt

9:110 (111)	the buildings they have built will not cease to be a point of doubt within their hearts

ARĀBA vb. (IV)~(pcple. act.) disquieting, arousing suspicion

g) pcple. act. (*murīb*)

11:62 (65)	truly we are in doubt, concerning what thou callest us to, disquieting
11:110 (112)	they are in doubt of it disquieting
14:9 (10)	we are in doubt, concerning that you call us unto, disquieting
34:54 (54)	they were in doubt disquieting
41:45 (45)	they are in doubt of it disquieting
42:14 (13)	behold, they are in doubt of it disquieting
50:25 (24)	every hinderer of the good, transgressor, disquieter

IRTĀBA vb. (VIII)~to be doubtful, to be in doubt. (pcple. act.) a doubter

a) perf. act.

5:106 (105)	they shall swear by God, if you are doubtful
9:45 (45)	those whose hearts are filled with doubt
24:50 (49)	is there sickness in their hearts, or are they in doubt
29:48 (47)	for then those who follow falsehood would have doubted
57:14 (13)	you awaited, and you were in doubt, and fancies deluded you
65:4 (4)	if you are in doubt, their period shall be three months

b) impf. act. (*yartābu*)

2:282 (282)	more upright for testimony, and likelier that you will not be in doubt
49:15 (15)	those who believe in God and His Messenger, then have not doubted
74:31 (32)	those who were given the Book and those who believe may not be in doubt

g) pcple. act. (*murtāb*)

40:34 (36)	even so God leads astray the prodigal and the doubter

*R Y N

RĀNA vb. (I)~to overcome (with rust)

a) perf. act.

83:14 (14) that they were earning has rusted upon their hearts

*R Y SH

RĪSH n.m. (coll)~feathers

7:26 (25) a garment to cover your shameful parts, and feathers

*R Z Q

RAZAQA vb. (I)~to provide, to endow, to make provision for, to give for sustenance; to bless. (n.vb.) provision, providing, living, livelihood, blessing; (*lā yamliku rizqan*) to have no power to provide. (pcple. act.) a provider

a) perf. act.

2:3 (2) expend of that We have provided them
2:57 (54) eat of the good things wherewith We have provided you
2:172 (167) eat of the good things wherewith We have provided you
2:254 (255) expend of that wherewith We have provided you
4:39 (43) and expended of that God has provided them
5:88 (90) eat of what God has provided you lawful and good
6:140 (141) and have forbidden what God has provided them, forging against God
6:142 (143) eat of what God has provided you
7:50 (48) pour on us water, or of that God has provided you
7:160 (160) eat of the good things wherewith We have supplied you
8:3 (3) those who perform the prayer, and expend of what We have provided them
8:26 (26) confirmed you with His help, and provided you with the good things
10:93 (93) and We provided them with good things
11:88 (90) He has provided me with fair provision from Him
13:22 (22) and expend of that We have provided them, secretly and in public
14:31 (36) that they perform the prayer, and expend of that We have provided them
16:56 (58) they appoint a share of that We have provided them to what they know not
16:72 (74) He has provided you of the good things
16:75 (77) one whom We have provided of Ourselves with a provision fair
16:114 (115) so eat of what God has provided you lawful and good
17:70 (72) and carried them on land and sea, and provided them with good things
20:81 (83) eat of the good things wherewith We have provided you
22:28 (29) over such beasts of the flocks as He has provided them
22:34 (35) that they may mention God's Name over such beasts of the flocks as He has provided them
22:35 (36) who perform the prayer, and expend of what We have provided them
28:54 (54) and avert evil with good, and expend of that We have provided them
30:28 (27) associates in what We have provided for you
30:40 (39) God is He that created you, then He provided for you
32:16 (16) they expend of that We have provided them
35:29 (26) and expend of that We have provided them, secretly and in public
36:47 (47) expend of that God has provided you
40:64 (66) and provided you with the good things
42:38 (36) they expend of that We have provided them
45:16 (15) and We provided them with good things
63:10 (10) expend of what We have provided you

b) impf. act. (*yarziqu*)

2:212 (208)	God provides whomsoever He will without reckoning
3:27 (26)	Thou providest whomsoever Thou wilt without reckoning
3:37 (32)	God provisions whomsoever He will without reckoning
6:151 (152)	We will provide you and them
10:31 (32)	who provides you out of heaven and earth
17:31 (33)	We will provide for you and them
20:132 (132)	We ask of thee no provision, but it is We who provide thee
22:58 (57)	God shall provide them with a fair provision
24:38 (38)	God provides whomsoever He will, without reckoning
27:64 (65)	and provides you out of heaven and earth
29:60 (60)	but God provides for it and you
34:24 (23)	who provides for you out of the heavens and the earth?
35:3 (3)	is there any creator, apart from God, who provides for you
42:19 (18)	God is All-gentle to His servants, providing for whomsoever He will
65:3 (2)	He will provide for him from whence he never reckoned
67:21 (21)	who is this that shall provide for you if He withholds His provision

c) impv. (*irziq*)

2:126 (120)	make this a land secure, and provide its people with fruits
4:5 (4)	provide for them and clothe them out of it
4:8 (9)	make provision for them out of it
5:114 (114)	provide for us; Thou art the best of providers
14:37 (40)	make hearts of men yearn towards them, and provide them with fruits

d) perf. pass. (*ruziqa*)

2:25 (23)	whensoever they are provided with fruits therefrom they shall say
2:25 (23)	this is that wherewithal we were provided before

e) impf. pass. (*yurzaqu*)

3:169 (163)	but rather living with their Lord, by Him provided
12:37 (37)	no food shall come to you for your sustenance, but ere it comes to you
40:40 (43)	those shall enter Paradise, therein provided without reckoning

f) n.vb. (*rizq*)

2:22 (20)	out of heaven water, wherewith He brought forth fruits for your provision
2:25 (23)	whensoever they are provided with fruits <...> therefrom they shall say
2:60 (57)	eat and drink of God's providing
2:233 (233)	it is for the father to provide them and clothe them honourably
3:37 (32)	whenever Zachariah went in to her in the Sanctuary, he found her provisioned
7:32 (30)	which He brought forth for His servants, and the good things of His providing
8:4 (4)	degrees with their Lord, and forgiveness, and generous provision
8:74 (75)	theirs shall be forgiveness and generous provision
10:59 (60)	have you considered the provision God has sent down for you
11:6 (8)	no creature is there crawling on the earth, but its provision rests on God
11:88 (90)	He has provided me with fair provision from Him
13:26 (26)	God outspreads and straitens His provision unto whomsoever He will
14:32 (37)	wherewith He brought forth fruits to be your sustenance
16:67 (69)	you take therefrom an intoxicant and a provision fair
16:71 (73)	God has preferred some of you over others in provision
16:71 (73)	but those that were preferred shall not give over their provision
16:73 (75)	do they serve, apart from God, that which has no power to provide them anything
16:75 (77)	one whom We have provided of Ourselves with a provision fair

16:112 (113)	a city that was secure, at rest, its provision coming to it easefully from every place
17:30 (32)	thy Lord outspreads and straitens His provision unto whom He will
18:19 (18)	let him look for which of them has purest food, and bring you provision thereof
19:62 (63)	there they shall have their provision at dawn and evening
20:131 (131)	thy Lord's provision is better, and more enduring
20:132 (132)	We ask of thee no provision, but it is We who provide thee
22:50 (49)	theirs shall be forgiveness and generous provision
22:58 (57)	God shall provide them with a fair provision
24:26 (26)	theirs shall be forgiveness and generous provision
28:57 (57)	to which are collected the fruits of everything, as a provision from Us
28:82 (82)	God outspreads and straitens His provision to whomsoever He will of His servants
29:17 (16)	those you serve, apart from God, have no power to provide for you
29:17 (16)	so seek after your provision with God, and serve Him
29:60 (60)	how many a beast that bears not its own provision, but God provides for it
29:62 (62)	God outspreads and straitens His provision to whomsoever He will
30:37 (36)	God outspreads and straitens His provision to whom He will
33:31 (31)	We have prepared for her a generous provision
34:4 (4)	theirs shall be forgiveness and generous provision
34:15 (14)	eat of your Lord's provision, and give thanks to Him
34:36 (35)	my Lord outspreads and straitens His provision to whomsoever He will
34:39 (38)	my lord outspreads and straitens His provision to whomsoever He will
37:41 (40)	for them awaits a known provision
38:54 (54)	this is Our provision unto which there is no end
39:52 (53)	do they know that God outspreads and straitens His provision to whomsoever He will?
40:13 (13)	it is He who shows you His signs and sends down to you out of heaven provision
42:12 (10)	He outspreads and straitens His provision to whom He will
42:27 (26)	had God expanded His provision to His servants, they would have been insolent
45:5 (4)	and the provision God sends down from heaven
50:11 (11)	a provision for the servants, and thereby We revived a land that was dead
51:22 (22)	in heaven is your provision, and that you are promised
51:57 (57)	I desire of them no provision
56:82 (81)	do you make it your living to cry lies?
65:7 (7)	as for him whose provision is stinted to him
65:11 (11)	God has made for him a goodly provision
67:15 (15)	therefore walk in its tracts, and eat of His provision
67:21 (21)	who is this that shall provide for you if He withholds His provision
89:16 (16)	when he tries him and stints for him his provision

g) pcple. act. (*rāziq*)

5:114 (114)	Thou art the best of providers
15:20 (20)	there appointed for you livelihood, and for those you provide not for
22:58 (57)	surely God is the best of providers
23:72 (74)	the tribute of thy Lord is better, and He is the best of providers
34:39 (38)	He is the best of providers
62:11 (11)	God is the best of providers

RAZZĀQ n.m.~All-provider (Divine attribute)

51:58 (58)	surely God is the All-provider

SĪN

*S ʾ L

SA'ALA vb. (I)~to ask, to question, to demand. (n.vb.) asking, demanding, questioning. (pcple. act.) one who asks, a questioner; a beggar. (pcple. pass.) questioned

a) perf. act.

2:61 (58)	get you down to Egypt; you shall have there that you demanded
2:186 (182)	when My servants question thee concerning Me — I am near to answer the call
4:153 (152)	the People of the Book will ask thee to bring down upon them a Book from heaven
5:102 (101)	a people before you questioned concerning them, then disbelieved in them
9:65 (66)	if thou questionest them, then assuredly they will say
10:72 (73)	then if you turn your backs, I have not asked you for any wage
14:34 (37)	and gave you of all you asked Him
18:76 (75)	if I question thee on anything after this, then keep me company no more
29:61 (61)	if thou askest them, 'Who created the heavens and the earth'
29:63 (63)	if thou askest them, 'Who sends down out of heaven water'
31:25 (24)	if thou askest them, 'Who created the heavens and the earth?'
33:53 (53)	when you ask his wives for any object
34:47 (46)	say: 'I have asked no wage of you'
39:38 (39)	if thou askest them, 'Who created the heavens and the earth?'
43:9 (8)	if thou askest them, 'Who created the heavens and earth?'
43:87 (87)	if thou askest them, 'Who created you?'
67:8 (8)	often as a troop is cast into it, its keepers ask them
70:1 (1)	a questioner asked of a chastisement about to fall

b) impf. act. (*yasʾalu*)

2:108 (102)	or do you desire to question your Messenger
2:189 (185)	they will question thee concerning the new moons
2:215 (211)	they will question thee concerning what they should expend
2:217 (214)	they will question thee concerning the holy month, and fighting in it
2:219 (216)	they will question thee concerning wine, and arrow-shuffling
2:219 (216)	they will question thee concerning what they should expend
2:220 (218)	they will question thee concerning the orphans
2:222 (222)	they will question thee concerning the monthly course
2:273 (274)	they do not beg of men importunately
4:153 (152)	the People of the Book will ask thee to bring down upon them a Book from heaven
5:4 (6)	they will question thee what is permitted them
5:101 (101)	question not concerning things which, if they were revealed to you, would vex you
5:101 (101)	if you question concerning them when the Koran is being sent down
6:90 (90)	I ask of you no wage for it; it is but a reminder
7:6 (5)	so We shall question those unto whom a Message was sent
7:6 (5)	and We shall question the Envoys
7:187 (186)	they will question thee concerning the Hour, when it shall berth
7:187 (187)	they will question thee, as though thou art well-informed of it
8:1 (1)	they will question thee concerning the spoils
11:29 (31)	O my people, I do not ask of you wealth for this
11:46 (48)	Do not ask of Me that whereof thou hast no knowledge
11:47 (49)	I take refuge with Thee, lest I should ask of Thee that whereof I have no knowledge
11:51 (53)	O my people, I do not ask of you a wage for this

12:104 (104)	thou askest of them no wage for it
15:92 (92)	by thy Lord, We shall surely question them all together
17:85 (87)	they will question thee concerning the Spirit
18:70 (69)	question me not on anything until I myself introduce the mention of it to thee
18:83 (82)	they will question thee concerning Dhool Karnain
20:105 (105)	they will question thee concerning the mountains
20:132 (132)	We ask of thee no provision, but it is We who provide thee
23:72 (74)	or dost thou ask them for tribute?
25:57 (59)	say: 'I do not ask of you a wage for this'
26:109 (109)	I ask of you no wage for this
26:127 (127)	I ask of you no wage for this
26:145 (145)	I ask of you no wage for this
26:164 (164)	I ask of you no wage for this
26:180 (180)	I ask of you no wage for this
33:8 (8)	that He might question the truthful concerning their truthfulness
33:20 (20)	they will wish that they were desert-dwellers among the Bedouins asking for news of you
33:63 (63)	the people will question thee concerning the Hour
36:21 (20)	follow such as ask no wage of you, that are right-guided
38:86 (86)	say: 'I ask of you no wage for it'
42:23 (22)	I do not ask of you a wage for this, except love for the kinsfolk
47:36 (38)	He will give you your wages, and will not ask of you your goods
47:37 (39)	if He asks you for them, and presses you, you are niggardly
51:12 (12)	asking, 'When shall be the Day of Doom?'
52:40 (40)	or askest thou them for a wage, and so they are weighed down with debt?
55:29 (29)	whatsoever is in the heavens and the earth implore Him
60:10 (10)	let them ask what they have expended
68:46 (46)	or askest thou them for a wage, and so they are weighed down with debt?
70:10 (10)	no loyal friend shall question loyal friend
75:6 (6)	asking, 'When shall be the Day of Resurrection?'
79:42 (42)	they will question thee concerning the Hour

c) impv. (*is'al* or *sal*)

2:211 (207)	ask the Children of Israel how many a clear sign We gave them
4:32 (36)	and ask God of His bounty
7:163 (163)	and question them concerning the township which was bordering the sea
10:94 (94)	ask those who recite the Book before thee
12:50 (50)	return unto thy lord, and ask of him
12:82 (82)	enquire of the city wherein we were, and the caravan in which we approached
16:43 (45)	question the people of the Remembrance, if it should be that you do not know
17:101 (103)	ask the Children of Israel when he came to them, and Pharaoh
21:7 (7)	question the People of the Remembrance, if you do not know
21:63 (64)	question them, if they are able to speak
23:113 (115)	we have tarried a day, or part of a day; ask the numberers
25:59 (60)	the All-compassionate: ask any informed of Him
33:53 (53)	ask them from behind a curtain
43:45 (44)	ask those of Our Messengers We sent before thee
60:10 (10)	ask what you have expended
68:40 (40)	ask them, which of them will guarantee that

d) perf. pass. (*su'ila*)

2:108 (102)	as Moses was questioned in former time
33:14 (14)	then they had been asked to apostatise, they would have done so
81:8 (8)	when the buried infant shall be asked

e) impf. pass. (*yus'alu*)

2:119 (113) thou shalt not be questioned touching the inhabitants of Hell
2:134 (128) you shall not be questioned concerning the things they did
2:141 (135) you shall not be questioned concerning the things they did
16:56 (58) by God, you shall be questioned as to that you forged
16:93 (95) you will surely be questioned about the things you wrought
21:13 (13) haply you shall be questioned
21:23 (23) He shall not be questioned as to what He does
21:23 (23) but they shall be questioned
28:78 (78) yet the sinners shall not be questioned concerning their sins
29:13 (12) they shall surely be questioned concerning that they were forging
34:25 (24) you will not be questioned concerning our sins
34:25 (24) neither shall we be questioned as to what you do
43:19 (18) their witness shall be written down, and they shall be questioned
43:44 (43) assuredly you will be questioned
55:39 (39) on that day none shall be questioned about his sin
102:8 (8) then you shall be questioned that day concerning true bliss

f) n.vb. (*su'āl*)

38:24 (23) he has wronged thee in asking for thy ewe in addition to his sheep

g) pcple. act. (*sā'il*)

2:177 (172) and orphans, the needy, the traveller, beggars
12:7 (7) in Joseph and his brethren were signs for those who ask questions.)
41:10 (9) He odained therein its diverse sustenance in four days, equal to those who ask
51:19 (19) the beggar and the outcast had a share in their wealth
70:1 (1) a questioner asked of a chastisement about to fall
70:25 (25) for the beggar and the outcast
93:10 (10) and as for the beggar, scold him not

h) pcple. pass. (*mas'ūl*)

17:34 (36) fulfil the covenant; surely the covenant shall be questioned of
17:36 (38) the sight, the heart — all of those shall be questioned of
25:16 (17) it is a promise binding upon thy Lord, and of Him to be required
33:15 (15) covenants with God shall be questioned of
37:24 (24) and halt them, to be questioned

SU'L n.m.~a petition

20:36 (36) thou art granted, Moses, thy petition

TASĀ'ALA vb. (VI)~to question one another, to demand of one another

b) impf. act. (*yatasā'alu*)

4:1 (1) fear God by whom you demand one of another
18:19 (18) We raised them up again that they might question one another
23:101 (103) there shall be no kinship any more between them, neither will they question one another
28:66 (66) the tidings will be darkened for them, nor will they ask each other
37:27 (27) and advance one upon another, asking each other questions
37:50 (48) they advance one upon another, asking each other questions
52:25 (25) they advance one upon another, asking each other questions
74:40 (42) in Gardens they will question
78:1 (1) of what do they question one another?

*S ʾ M

SAʾIMA vb. (I)~to disdain, to dislike, to grow weary, to be loth

b) impf. act. (*yasʾamu*)

2:282 (282)	be not loth to write it down, whether it be small or great
41:38 (38)	those who are with thy Lord do glorify Him by night and day, and grow not weary
41:49 (49)	man wearies not of praying for good

*S ʿ D

SAʿIDA vb. (I)~to be happy

d) perf. pass. (*suʿida*)

11:108 (110)	as for the happy, they shall be in Paradise

SAʿĪD n.m. (adj)~happy

11:105 (107)	by His leave; some of them shall be wretched and some happy

*S ʿ R

SAʿĪR n.f.~fire, burning; Hell, the Blaze

4:10 (11)	and shall assuredly roast in a Blaze
4:55 (58)	Gehenna suffices for a Blaze
17:97 (99)	whensoever it abates We shall increase for them the Blaze
22:4 (4)	he guides him to the chastisement of the burning
25:11 (12)	We have prepared for him who cries lies to the Hour a Blaze
31:21 (20)	even though Satan were calling them to the chastisement of the burning
33:64 (64)	God has cursed the unbelievers, and prepared for them a Blaze
34:12 (11)	We would let them taste the chastisement of the Blaze
35:6 (6)	only that they may be among the inhabitants of the Blaze
42:7 (5)	a party in Paradise, and a party in the Blaze
48:13 (13)	We have prepared for the unbelievers a Blaze
67:5 (5)	We have prepared for them the chastisement of the Blaze
67:10 (10)	we would not have been of the inhabitants of the Blaze
67:11 (11)	so they confess their sins. Curse the inhabitants of the Blaze
76:4 (4)	We have prepared for the unbelievers chains, fetters, and a Blaze
84:12 (12)	and he shall roast at a Blaze

SUʿUR n.m.~madness, insanity

54:24 (24)	then indeed we should be in error and insanity
54:47 (47)	surely the sinners are in error and insanity

SAʿʿARA vb. (II)~to set blazing, to cause to burn fiercely

d) perf. pass. (*suʿʿira*)

81:12 (12)	when Hell shall be set blazing

*S ᶜ Y

SAᶜÁ vb. (I)~to endeavour, to strive, to labour; to hasten about; to run, to slide (as with a serpent); (*jāʾa yasᶜá*) to come eagerly. (n.vb.) running; striving, labouring; endeavour

a) perf. act.

2:114 (108)	so that His Name be not rehearsed in them, and strives to destroy them
2:205 (201)	he hastens about the earth, to do corruption there
17:19 (20)	whosoever desires the world to come and strives after it as he should
22:51 (50)	those who strive against Our signs to void them
34:5 (5)	those who strive against Our signs to void them
53:39 (40)	a man shall have to his account only as he has laboured
79:35 (35)	upon the day when man shall remember what he has striven

b) impf. act. (*yasᶜá*)

5:33 (37)	and hasten about the earth, to do corruption there
5:64 (69)	they hasten about the earth, to do corruption there
20:15 (16)	that every soul may be recompensed for its labours
20:20 (21)	he cast it down, and behold it was a serpent sliding
20:66 (69)	their ropes and their staffs were sliding
28:20 (19)	then came a man from the furthest part of the city, running
34:38 (37)	those who strive against Our signs to void them
36:20 (19)	then came a man from the furthest part of the city, running
57:12 (12)	men and women, their light running before them
66:8 (8)	those who believe with him, their light running before them
79:22 (22)	then he turned away hastily
80:8 (8)	he who comes to thee eagerly

c) impv. (*isᶜa*)

62:9 (9)	hasten to God's remembrance and leave trafficking aside

f) n.vb. (*saᶜy*)

2:260 (262)	then summon them, and they will come to thee running
17:19 (20)	whosoever desires the world to come and strives after it as he should
17:19 (20)	being a believer — those, their striving shall be thanked
18:104 (104)	those whose striving goes astray in the present life
21:94 (94)	no unthankfulness shall befall his endeavour
37:102 (100)	when he had reached the age of running with him
53:40 (41)	and that his labouring shall surely be seen
76:22 (22)	this is a recompense for you, and your striving is thanked
88:9 (9)	with their striving well-pleased
92:4 (4)	surely your striving is to diverse ends

*S B ʾ

SABAʾ n.prop.~Sheba

27:22 (22)	I have come from Sheba to thee with a sure tiding
34:15 (14)	for Sheba also there was a sign in their dwelling-place

*S B ᶜ

SABᶜAH n.num.~seven

2:29 (27)	He lifted Himself to heaven and levelled them seven heavens
2:196 (192)	a fast of three days in the Pilgrimage, and of seven when you return
2:261 (263)	the way of God is as the likeness of a grain of corn that sprouts seven ears
12:43 (43)	I saw in a dream seven fat kine
12:43 (43)	and seven lean ones devouring them
12:43 (43)	likewise seven green ears of corn, and seven withered
12:46 (46)	pronounce to us regarding seven fat kine
12:46 (46)	that seven lean ones were devouring
12:46 (46)	seven green ears of corn
12:47 (47)	you shall sow seven years after your wont
12:48 (48)	thereafter there shall come upon you seven hard years
15:44 (44)	seven gates it has, and unto each gate a set portion
15:87 (87)	We have given thee seven of the oft-repeated
17:44 (46)	the seven heavens and the earth, and whosoever in them is, extol Him
18:22 (21)	seven; and their dog was the eighth of them
23:17 (17)	and We created above you seven ways
23:86 (88)	say: 'Who is the Lord of the seven heavens'
31:27 (26)	and the sea — seven seas after it to replenish it
41:12 (11)	so He determined them as seven heavens in two days
65:12 (12)	it is God who created seven heavens, and of earth their like
67:3 (3)	who created seven heavens one upon another
69:7 (7)	He compelled against them seven nights and eight days
71:15 (14)	have you not regarded how God created seven heavens
78:12 (12)	We have built above you seven strong ones

SABᶜŪN n.num.~seventy

7:155 (154)	Moses chose of his people seventy men for Our appointed time
9:80 (81)	if thou askest pardon for them seventy times
69:32 (32)	then in a chain of seventy cubits' length insert him

SABUᶜ n.m.~a beast of prey

5:3 (4)	and that devoured by beasts of prey

*S B B

SABBA vb. (I)~to abuse, to revile

b) impf. act. (*yasubbu*)

6:108 (108)	abuse not those to whom they pray, apart from God
6:108 (108)	or they will abuse God in revenge without knowledge

SABAB n.m. (pl. *asbāb*)~a rope, a cord; a way

2:166 (161)	and their cords are cut asunder
18:84 (83)	and We gave him a way to everything
18:85 (83)	and he followed a way
18:89 (88)	then he followed a way

18:92 (91)	then he followed a way
22:15 (15)	let him stretch up a rope to heaven
38:10 (9)	why, then let them ascend the cords
40:36 (38)	build for me a tower, that haply so I may reach the cords
40:37 (39)	the cords of the heavens, and look upon Moses' God

*S B GH

SĀBIGHAH n.f. (pl)~a coat of mail

34:11 (10)	fashion wide coats of mail

ASBAGHA vb. (IV)~to lavish

a) perf. act.

31:20 (19)	He has lavished on you His blessings, outward and inward

*S B Ḥ

SABAḤA vb. (I)~to swim. (n.vb.) the act of swimming; business. (pcple. act.) swimmer

b) impf. act. (*yasbaḥu*)

21:33 (34)	the sun and the moon, each swimming in a sky
36:40 (40)	neither does the night outstrip the day, each swimming in a sky

f) n.vb. (*sabḥ*)

73:7 (7)	surely in the day thou hast long business
79:3 (3)	by those that swim <serenely>

g) pcple. act. f. (*sābiḥah*)

79:3 (3)	by those that swim serenely

SUBḤĀN n.m.~praise, glory (*subḥān Allāh*) glory be to God, God be praised

2:32 (30)	glory be to Thee! We know not save what Thou hast taught us
2:116 (110)	glory be to Him! Nay, to Him belongs all
3:191 (188)	glory be to Thee! Guard us against the chastisement
4:171 (169)	God is only One God. Glory be to Him
5:116 (116)	to Thee be glory! It is not mine to say what I have no right
6:100 (100)	glory be to Him! High be He exalted
7:143 (140)	glory be to Thee! I repent to Thee
9:31 (31)	there is no god but He; glory be to Him
10:10 (10)	their cry therein, 'Glory to Thee, O God'
10:18 (19)	glory be to Him! High be He exalted
10:68 (69)	glory be to Him! He is All-sufficient
12:108 (108)	to God be glory! And I am not among the idolaters
16:1 (1)	glory be to Him! High be He exalted
16:57 (59)	they assign to God daughters; glory be to Him
17:1 (1)	glory be to Him, who carried His servant by night

17:43 (45)	glory be to Him! High indeed be He exalted
17:93 (95)	glory be to my Lord! Am I aught but a mortal
17:108 (108)	glory be to our Lord! Our Lord's promise is
19:35 (36)	it is not for God to take a son unto Him. Glory be to Him
21:22 (22)	glory be to God, the Lord of the Throne
21:26 (26)	glory be to Him! Nay, but they are honoured servants
21:87 (87)	there is no god but Thou. Glory be to Thee
23:91 (93)	glory be to God, beyond that they describe
24:16 (15)	it is not for us to speak about this; glory be to Thee
25:18 (19)	glory be to Thee! It did not behove us to take
27:8 (8)	glory be to God, the Lord of all Being
28:68 (68)	glory be to God! High be He exalted
30:17 (16)	glory be to God both in your evening hour and in your morning hour
30:40 (39)	glory be to Him! High be He exalted
34:41 (40)	glory be to Thee! Thou art our Protector
36:36 (36)	glory be to Him, who created all the pairs
36:83 (83)	glory be to Him, in whose hand is the dominion
37:159 (159)	glory be to God above that they describe
37:180 (180)	glory be to thy Lord, the Lord of Glory
39:4 (6)	glory be to Him! He is God, the One, the Omnipotent
39:67 (67)	glory be to Him! High be He exalted
43:13 (12)	glory be to Him, who has subjected this to us
43:82 (82)	glory be to the Lord of the heavens and the earth
52:43 (43)	glory be to God, above that which they associate
59:23 (23)	glory be to God, above that they associate
68:29 (29)	glory be to God, our Lord; truly, we were evildoers

SABBAḤA vb. (II)~to praise, to proclaim (God's) praise, to extol, to glorify, to magnify. (n.vb.) praise, extolling, glorification. (pcple. act.) one who glorifies, who praises

a) perf. act.

32:15 (15)	fall down prostrate and proclaim the praise of their Lord
57:1 (1)	all that is in the heavens and the earth magnifies God
59:1 (1)	all that is in the heavens and the earth magnifies God
61:1 (1)	all that is in the heavens and the earth magnifies God

b) impf. act. (*yusabbiḥu*)

2:30 (28)	while We proclaim Thy praise and call Thee Holy
7:206 (205)	they chant His praise, and to Him they bow
13:13 (14)	the thunder proclaims His praise, and the angels, in awe of Him
17:44 (46)	the seven heavens and the earth, and whosoever in them is, extol Him
17:44 (46)	nothing is, that does not proclaim His praise
20:33 (34)	so shall we glorify Thee
21:20 (20)	glorifying Him by night and in the daytime and never failing
21:79 (79)	with David We subjected the mountains to give glory
24:36 (36)	therein glorifying Him, in the mornings and the evenings
24:41 (41)	hast thou not seen how that whatsoever is in the heavens and in the earth extols God
38:18 (17)	with him We subjected the mountains to give glory at evening and sunrise
39:75 (75)	thou shalt see the angels encircling about the Throne proclaiming the praise of their Lord
40:7 (7)	and those round about it proclaim the praise of their Lord, and believe in Him
41:38 (38)	those who are with thy Lord do glorify Him by night and day
42:5 (3)	when the angels proclaim the praise of their Lord

48:9 (9)	that you may give Him glory at the dawn and in the evening
59:24 (24)	all that is in the heavens and the earth magnifies Him
62:1 (1)	all that is in the heavens and the earth magnifies God
64:1 (1)	all that is in the heavens and the earth magnifies God
68:28 (28)	did I not say to you, 'Why do you not give glory?'

c) impv. (*sabbiḥ*)

3:41 (36)	mention thy Lord oft, and give glory at evening and dawn
15:98 (98)	proclaim thy Lord's praise, and be of those that bow
19:11 (12)	give you glory at dawn and evening
20:130 (130)	proclaim thy Lord's praise before the rising of the sun
20:130 (130)	proclaim thy Lord's praise in the watches of the night
25:58 (60)	put thy trust in the Living God, the Undying, and proclaim His praise
33:42 (41)	give Him glory at the dawn and in the evening
40:55 (57)	ask forgiveness for thy sin, and proclaim the praise of thy Lord
50:39 (38)	proclaim thy Lord's praise before the rising of the sun
50:40 (39)	proclaim thy Lord's praise in the night
52:48 (48)	proclaim the praise of thy Lord when thou arisest
52:49 (49)	proclaim the praise of thy Lord in the night
56:74 (73)	then magnify the Name of thy Lord, the All-mighty
56:96 (96)	then magnify the Name of thy Lord, the All-mighty
69:52 (52)	then magnify the Name of thy Lord, the All-mighty
76:26 (26)	bow down before Him and magnify Him through the long night
87:1 (1)	magnify the Name of thy Lord the Most High
110:3 (3)	then proclaim the praise of thy Lord, and seek His forgiveness

f) n.vb. (*tasbīḥ*)

17:44 (46)	but you do not understand their extolling
24:41 (41)	each — He knows its prayer and its extolling

g) pcple. act. (*musabbiḥ*)

37:143 (143)	had he not been of those that glorify God
37:166 (166)	we are they that give glory

*S B L

SABĪL n.com. (pl. *subul*)~a way, a road, a path; (*ibn al-sabīl*) traveller

2:108 (102)	whoso exchanges belief for unbelief has surely strayed from the right way
2:154 (149)	say not of those slain in God's way, 'They are dead'
2:177 (172)	and orphans, the needy, the traveller, beggars
2:190 (186)	fight in the way of God with those who fight with you
2:195 (191)	and expend in the way of God
2:215 (211)	parents and kinsmen, orphans, the needy, and the traveller
2:217 (214)	fighting in it is a heinous thing, but to bar from God's way
2:218 (215)	the believers, and those who emigrate and struggle in God's way
2:244 (245)	so fight in God's way, and know that God is All-hearing
2:246 (247)	raise up for us a king, and we will fight in God's way
2:246 (247)	why should we not fight in God's way, who have been expelled
2:261 (263)	the likeness of those who expend their wealth in the way of God
2:262 (264)	those who expend their wealth in the way of God
2:273 (274)	the poor who are restrained in the way of God

3:13 (11)	one company fighting in the way of God and another unbelieving
3:75 (69)	there is no way over us as to the common people
3:97 (91)	to come to the House a pilgrim, if he is able to make his way there
3:99 (94)	why do you bar from God's way the believer
3:146 (140)	they fainted not for what smote them in God's way
3:157 (151)	if you are slain or die in God's way
3:167 (160)	come now, fight in the way of God, or repel
3:169 (163)	count not those who were slain in God's way as dead
3:195 (194)	those who suffered hurt in My way, and fought, and were slain
4:15 (19)	detain them in their houses until death takes them or God appoints for them a way
4:22 (26)	surely that is indecent and hateful, an evil way
4:34 (38)	if they then obey you, look not for any way against them
4:36 (40)	to the companion at your side, and to the traveller
4:43 (46)	unless you are traversing a way — until you have washed yourselves
4:44 (47)	and desiring that you should also err from the way
4:51 (54)	these are more rightly guided on the way than the believers
4:74 (76)	let them fight in the way of God who sell the present life for the world to come
4:74 (76)	whosoever fights in the way of God and is slain
4:75 (77)	how is it with you, that you do not fight in the way of God
4:76 (78)	the believers fight in the way of God
4:76 (78)	and the unbelievers fight in the idols' way
4:84 (86)	so do thou fight in the way of God
4:88 (90)	whom God leads astray, thou wilt not find for him a way
4:89 (91)	take not to yourselves friends of them, until they emigrate in the way of God
4:90 (92)	then God assigns not any way to you against them
4:94 (96)	O believers, when you are journeying in the path of God
4:95 (97)	those who struggle in the path of God with their possessions
4:98 (100)	who, being abased, can devise nothing and are not guided to a way
4:100 (101)	whoso emigrates in the way of God
4:115 (115)	and follows a way other than the believers'
4:137 (136)	God is not likely to forgive them, neither to guide them on any way
4:141 (140)	God will not grant the unbelievers any way over the believers
4:143 (142)	whom God leads astray, thou wilt not find for him a way
4:150 (149)	desiring to take between this and that a way
4:160 (158)	and for their barring from God's way many
4:167 (165)	those who disbelieve, and bar from the way of God
5:12 (15)	surely he has gone astray from the right way
5:16 (18)	God guides whosoever follows His good pleasure in the ways of peace
5:35 (39)	seek the means to come to Him, and struggle in His way
5:54 (59)	men who struggle in the path of God, not fearing the reproach
5:60 (65)	they are worse situated, and have gone further astray from the right way
5:77 (81)	and now again have gone astray from the right way
6:55 (55)	We distinguish Our signs, that the sinners' way may be manifest
6:116 (116)	they will lead thee astray from the path of God
6:117 (117)	thy Lord knows very well who goes astray from His path
6:153 (154)	follow it, and follow not diverse paths
6:153 (154)	lest they scatter you from His path
7:45 (43)	who bar from God's way, desiring to make it crooked
7:86 (84)	and barring from God's way those who believe in Him
7:142 (138)	do not follow the way of the workers of corruption
7:146 (143)	and though they see the way of rectitude
7:146 (143)	they will not take it for a way
7:146 (143)	and though they see the way of error
7:146 (143)	they will take it for a way
7:148 (146)	did they not see it spoke not to them, neither guided them upon any way?

8:36 (36)	the unbelievers expend their wealth to bar from God's way
8:41 (42)	and the orphans', and for the needy, and the traveller
8:47 (49)	to show off to men, and barring from God's way
8:60 (62)	whatsoever you expend in the way of God shall be repaid you in full
8:72 (73)	and struggled with their possessions and their selves in the way of God
8:74 (75)	those who believe, and have emigrated and struggled in the way of God
9:5 (5)	if they repent, and perform the prayer, and pay the alms, then let them go their way
9:9 (9)	they have sold the signs of God for a small price, and have barred from His way
9:19 (19)	one who believes in God and the Last Day and struggles in the way of God
9:20 (20)	those who believe, and have emigrated, and have struggled in the way of God
9:24 (24)	if these are dearer to you than God and His Messenger, and to struggle in His way
9:34 (34)	consume the goods of the people in vanity and bar from God's way
9:34 (34)	those who treasure up gold and silver, and do not expend them in the way of God
9:38 (38)	when it is said to you, 'Go forth in the way of God,' you sink down heavily
9:41 (41)	struggle in God's way with your possessions and your selves
9:60 (60)	the ransoming of slaves, debtors, in God's way
9:60 (60)	and the traveller; so God ordains
9:81 (82)	and were averse to struggle with their possessions and their selves in the way of God
9:91 (92)	there is no way against the good-doers
9:93 (94)	the way is open only against those who ask leave of thee
9:111 (112)	they fight in the way of God
9:120 (121)	they are smitten neither by thirst, nor fatigue, nor emptiness in the way of God
10:88 (88)	our Lord, let them go astray from Thy way
10:89 (89)	go you straight, and follow not the way of those that know not
11:19 (22)	who bar from God's way, desiring to make it crooked
12:108 (108)	say: 'This is my way'
13:33 (33)	and they are barred from the way
14:3 (3)	such as prefer the present life over the world to come, and bar from God's way
14:12 (15)	why should we not put our trust in God, seeing that He has guided us in our ways?
14:30 (35)	they set up compeers to God, that they might lead astray from His way
15:76 (76)	surely it is on a way yet remaining
16:9 (9)	God's it is to show the way
16:15 (15)	He cast on the earth firm mountains, lest it shake with you, and rivers and ways
16:69 (71)	follow the ways of your Lord easy to go upon
16:88 (90)	those that disbelieve and bar from the way of God
16:94 (96)	for that you barred from the way of God
16:125 (126)	call thou to the way of thy Lord with wisdom and good admonition
16:125 (126)	thy Lord knows very well those who have gone astray from His way
17:26 (28)	give the kinsman his right, and the needy, and the traveller
17:32 (34)	surely it is an indecency, and evil as a way
17:42 (44)	they would have sought a way unto the Lord of the Throne
17:48 (51)	behold, how they strike similitudes for thee, and go astray, and cannot find a way
17:72 (74)	he shall be even further astray from the way
17:84 (86)	your Lord knows very well what man is best guided as to the way
17:110 (110)	be thou not loud in thy prayer, nor hushed therein, but seek thou for a way between that
18:61 (60)	they forgot their fish, and it took its way into the sea
18:63 (62)	so it took its way into the sea in a manner marvellous
20:53 (55)	He who appointed the earth to be a cradle for you, and therein threaded roads for you
21:31 (32)	We set in it ravines to serve as ways
22:9 (9)	turning his side to lead astray from God's way

22:25 (25)	those who disbelieve, and bar from God's way
22:58 (57)	those who emigrated in God's way and were slain
24:22 (22)	the poor and those who emigrate in the way of God
25:9 (10)	and go astray, and are unable to find a way
25:17 (18)	or did they themselves err from the way?
25:27 (29)	would that I had taken a way along with the Messenger
25:34 (36)	they shall be worse in place, and gone further astray from the way
25:42 (44)	they shall know, when they see the chastisement, who is further astray from the way
25:44 (46)	nay, they are further astray from the way
25:57 (59)	except for him who wishes to take to his Lord a way
27:24 (24)	and he has barred them from the way
28:22 (21)	it may be that my Lord will guide me on the right way
29:12 (11)	follow our path, and let us carry your offences
29:29 (28)	do you approach men, and cut the way, and commit in your assembly dishonour?
29:38 (37)	Satan decked out fair to them their works, and barred them from the way
29:69 (69)	surely We shall guide them in Our ways
30:38 (37)	give the kinsman his right, and the needy, and the traveller
31:6 (5)	some men there are who buy diverting talk to lead astray from the way of God
31:15 (14)	but follow the way of him who turns to Me
33:4 (4)	but God speaks the truth, and guides on the way
33:67 (67)	we obeyed our chiefs and great ones, and they led us astray from the way
38:26 (25)	follow not caprice, lest it lead thee astray from the way of God
38:26 (25)	those who go astray from the way of God
39:8 (11)	and sets up compeers to God, to lead astray from His way
40:7 (7)	therefore forgive those who have repented, and follow Thy way
40:11 (11)	is there any way to go forth?
40:29 (30)	I see; I only guide you in the way of rectitude
40:37 (40)	he was barred from the way, and Pharaoh's guile came only
40:38 (41)	follow me, and I will guide you in the way of rectitude
42:41 (39)	whosoever helps himself after he has been wronged — against them there is no way
42:42 (40)	the way is only open against those who do wrong to the people
42:44 (43)	is there any way to be sent back?
42:46 (45)	whomsoever God leads astray, no way has he
43:10 (9)	He who appointed the earth to be a cradle for you, and appointed ways for you therein
43:37 (36)	they bar them from the way, and they think they are guided
47:1 (1)	those who disbelieve and bar from God's way
47:4 (5)	those who are slain in the way of God, He will not send their works astray
47:32 (34)	those who disbelieve and bar from God's way
47:34 (36)	those who disbelieve and bar from God's way and then die
47:38 (40)	you are called upon to expend in God's way
49:15 (15)	and have struggled with their possessions and their selves in the way of God
53:30 (31)	thy Lord knows very well those who have gone astray from His way
57:10 (10)	how it is with you, that you expend not in the way of God
58:16 (17)	they have taken their oaths as a covering, and barred from God's way
59:7 (7)	near kinsman, orphans, the needy and the traveller
60:1 (1)	if you go forth to struggle in My way and seek My good pleasure
60:1 (1)	whosoever of you does that, has gone astray from the right way
61:4 (4)	God loves those who fight in His way in ranks
61:11 (11)	struggle in the way of God with your possessions and your selves
63:2 (2)	then they have barred from the way of God
68:7 (7)	thy Lord knows very well those who have gone astray from His way

71:20 (19)	that thereof you may thread ways, ravines
73:19 (19)	so let him who will take unto his Lord a way
73:20 (20)	and others fighting in the way of God
76:3 (3)	We guided him upon the way whether he be thankful or unthankful
76:29 (29)	this is a Reminder; so he who will, takes unto his Lord a way
80:20 (20)	then the way eased for him

SALSABĪL n.prop.~Salsabil (a name of a spring in Paradise)

76:18 (18)	therein a fountain whose name is called Salsabil

*S B Q

SABAQA vb. (I)~to precede, to go before, to be prior, to outstrip; also the sense of "already", "before". (n.vb.) the act of outstripping, of going before. (pcple. act.) outstripper; outracing. (pcple. pass.) outstripped

a) perf. act.

7:80 (78)	do you commit such indecency as never any being in all the world committed before you?
8:59 (61)	thou art not to suppose that they who disbelieve have outstripped Me
8:68 (69)	had it not been for a prior prescription from God
10:19 (20)	but for a word that preceded from thy Lord, it had been decided
11:40 (42)	except for him against whom the word has already been spoken
11:110 (112)	but for a word that preceded from thy Lord, it had been decided
20:99 (99)	We relate to thee stories of what has gone before
20:129 (129)	but for a word that preceded from thy Lord, and a stated term
21:101 (101)	as for those unto whom already the reward most fair has gone forth
23:27 (28)	except for him against whom the word already has been spoken
29:28 (27)	you commit such indecency as never any being in all the world committed before you
37:171 (171)	already Our Word has preceded to Our servants, the Envoys
41:45 (45)	but for a Word that preceded from thy Lord, it had been decided
42:14 (13)	but for a Word that preceded from thy Lord until a stated term
46:11 (10)	if it had been aught good, they had not outstripped us to it
59:10 (10)	forgive us and our brothers, who preceded us in belief

b) impf. act. (*yasbiqu*)

15:5 (5)	no nation outstrips its term, nor do they put it back
21:27 (27)	that outstrip Him not in speech, and perform as He commands
23:43 (45)	no nation outstrips its term, nor do they put it back
29:4 (3)	or do they reckon, those who do evil deeds, that they will outstrip Us?

f) n.vb. (*sabq*)

79:4 (4)	and those that outstrip <suddenly>

g) pcple. act. (*sābiq*)

9:100 (101)	and the Outstrippers, the first of the Emigrants
23:61 (63)	those vie in good works, outracing to them
29:39 (38)	they waxed proud in the earth, yet they outstripped Us not
35:32 (29)	some are outstrippers in good works by the leave of God
36:40 (40)	it behoves not the sun to overtake the moon, neither does the night outstrip the day

56:10 (10)	and the Outstrippers: (the Outstrippers)
56:10 (10)	and the (Outstrippers): the Outstrippers
79:4 (4)	and those that outstrip suddenly

h) pcple. pass. (*masbūq*)

56:60 (60)	We have decreed among you Death; We shall not be outstripped
70:41 (41)	to substitute a better than they; We shall not be outstripped

SĀBAQA vb. (III)~to race

c) impv. (*sābiq*)

57:21 (21)	race to forgiveness from your Lord

ISTABAQA vb. (VIII)~to race; to be forward

a) perf. act.

12:25 (25)	they raced to the door; and she tore his shirt from behind
36:66 (66)	We would have obliterated their eyes, then they would race to the path

b) impf. act. (*yastabiqu*)

12:17 (17)	we went running races, and left Joseph behind with our things

c) impv. (*istabiq*)

2:148 (143)	so be you forward in good works
5:48 (53)	so be you forward in good works

*S B T

SABATA vb. (I)~to keep the Sabbath

b) impf. act. (*yasbitu*)

7:163 (163)	on the day they kept not Sabbath, they came not unto them

SABT n.prop.~the Sabbath

2:65 (61)	well you know there were those among you that transgressed the Sabbath
4:47 (50)	or curse them as We cursed the Sabbath-men
4:154 (153)	transgress not the Sabbath
7:163 (163)	the township which was bordering the sea, when they transgressed the Sabbath
7:163 (163)	when their fish came to them on the day of their Sabbath
16:124 (125)	the Sabbath was only appointed for those who were at variance thereon

SUBĀT n.m.~rest

25:47 (49)	it is He who appointed the night for you to be garment and sleep for a rest
78:9 (9)	and We appointed your sleep for a rest

*S B Ṭ

ASBĀṬ n.m. (pl. of *sibṭ*)~tribes (of the Children of Israel)

2:136 (130)	and sent down on Abraham, Ishmael, Isaac and Jacob, and the Tribes
2:140 (134)	Isaac and Jacob, and the Tribes — they were Jews
3:84 (78)	and sent down on Abraham and Ishmael, Isaac and Jacob, and the Tribes
4:163 (161)	We revealed to Abraham, Ishmael, Isaac, Jacob, and the Tribes
7:160 (160)	We cut them up into twelve tribes, nations

*S D D

SADD n.m.~a barrier, a rampart

18:93 (92)	when he reached between the two barriers, he found this side
18:94 (93)	so shall we assign to thee a tribute, against thy setting up a barrier
36:9 (8)	We have put before them a barrier
36:9 (8)	and behind them a barrier

SADĪD n.m. (adj)~hitting the mark

4:9 (10)	let them fear God, and speak words hitting the mark
33:70 (70)	fear God, and speak words hitting the mark

*S D R

SIDRAH n.f. (pl. *sidr*)~lote-tree

34:16 (15)	and tamarisk-bushes, and here and there a few lote-trees
53:14 (14)	by the Lote-Tree of the Boundary
53:16 (16)	when there covered the Lote-Tree that which covered
56:28 (27)	mid thornless lote-trees

*S D S

SĀDIS n.num.~the sixth

18:22 (21)	five; and their dog was the sixth of them;'
58:7 (8)	but He is the sixth of them, neither fewer than that

SUDS n.num.~a sixth

4:11 (12)	to his parents to each one of the two the sixth of what he leaves
4:11 (12)	if he has brothers, to his mother a sixth
4:12 (15)	if a man or a woman have no heir direct, but have a brother or a sister, to each of the two a sixth

*S D Y

SUDÁ n.m. (adv)~at will; in vain

75:36 (36)	does man reckon he shall be left to roam at will?

*S F ʿ

SAFAʿA vb. (I)~to drag, to seize

b) impf. act. (*yasfuʿu*)

96:15 (15) if he gives not over, We shall seize him by the forelock

*S F H

SAFIHA vb. (I)~to be foolish, to be stupid. (n.vb.) folly, stupidity

a) perf. act.

2:130 (124) who therefore shrinks from the religion of Abraham, except he be foolish-minded?

f) n.vb. (*safah*)

6:140 (141) losers are they who slay their children in folly, without knowledge

f) n.vb. (*safāhah*)

7:66 (64) we see thee in folly
7:67 (65) my people, there is no folly in me; but I am a Messenger

SAFĪH n.m. (pl. *sufahāʾ*)~a fool; (adj) foolish, stupid

2:13 (12) they say, 'Shall we believe, as fools believe?'
2:13 (12) truly, they are the foolish ones, but they do not know
2:142 (136) the fools among the people will say
2:282 (282) if the debtor be a fool, or weak, or unable
4:5 (4) do not give to fools their property that God has assigned to you to manage
7:155 (154) wilt Thou destroy us for what the foolish ones of us have done?
72:4 (4) the fool among us spoke against God outrage

*S F Ḥ

SAFAḤA vb. (I)~(pcple. pass.) outpoured, spilled, shed

h) pcple. pass. (*masfūḥ*)

6:145 (146) except it be carrion, or blood outpoured

SĀFAḤA vb. (III)~(pcple. act.) fornicator, one who is licentious; (adv) in licence

g) pcple. act. (*musāfiḥ*)

4:24 (28) that you may seek, using your wealth, in wedlock and not in licence
4:25 (29) give them their wages honourably as women in wedlock, not as in licence
5:5 (7) if you give them their wages, in wedlock and not in licence

*S F K

SAFAKA vb. (I)~to shed (blood)

b) impf. act. (*yasfiku*)

2:30 (28)	wilt Thou set therein one who will do corruption there, and shed blood
2:84 (78)	you shall not shed your own blood, neither expel your own

*S F L

SĀFIL n.m. (adj; comp. *asfal*)~low, nethermost; below

95:5 (5)	then We restored him the lowest of the low
4:145 (144)	the hypocrites will be in the lowest reach of the Fire
8:42 (43)	were on the farther bank, and the cavalcade was below you
9:40 (40)	He made the word of the unbelievers the lowest
11:82 (84)	when Our command came, We turned it uppermost nethermost
15:74 (74)	and We turned it uppermost nethermost
33:10 (10)	when they came against you from above you and from below you
37:98 (96)	they desired to outwit him; so We made them the lower ones
41:29 (29)	we shall set them underneath our feet, that they may be among the lower ones
95:5 (5)	then We restored him the lowest of the low

*S F N

SAFĪNAH n.f.~ship, boat

18:71 (70)	when they embarked upon the ship, he made a hole in it
18:79 (78)	as for the ship, it belonged to certain poor men
18:79 (78)	there was a king who was seizing every ship by brutal force
29:15 (14)	yet We delivered him, and those who were in the ship

*S F R

ASFĀR n.m. (pl. of *sifr*)~a book

62:5 (5)	the likeness of an ass carrying books

SAFAR n.m. (pl. *asfār*)~journey, travel, trip

2:184 (180)	if any of you be sick, or if he be on a journey
2:185 (181)	if any of you be sick, or if he be on a journey
2:283 (283)	if you are upon a journey, and you do not find a writer
4:43 (46)	if you are sick, or on a journey, or if any of you comes from the privy
5:6 (9)	if you are sick or on a journey, or if any of you comes from the privy
9:42 (42)	were it a gain near at hand, and an easy journey, they would have followed thee
18:62 (61)	indeed, we have encountered weariness from this our journey
34:19 (18)	our Lord, prolong the stages of our travel

SAFARAH n.m. (pl. of *sāfir*)~a scribe

80:15 (15) by the hands of scribes

ASFARA vb. (IV)~to shine, to glow; to be white (with brightness). (pcple. act.) that which shines

a) perf. act.

74:34 (37) and the dawn when it is white

g) pcple. act. (*musfir*)

80:38 (38) some faces on that day shall shine

*S GH B

MASGHABAH n.f.~famine, hunger

90:14 (14) or giving food upon a day of hunger

*S H L

SAHL n.m. (pl. *suhūl*)~a plain

7:74 (72) taking to yourselves castles of its plains, and hewing its mountains

*S H M

SĀHAMA vb. (III)~to cast lots

a) perf. act.

37:141 (141) and cast lots, and was of the rebutted

*S H R

SĀHIRAH n.f.~awakening

79:14 (14) and behold, they are awakened

*S H W

SAHĀ vb. (I)~(pcple. act.) dazed, heedless, inattentive, negligent

g) pcple. act. (*sāhī*)

51:11 (11) who are dazed in perplexity
107:5 (5) and are heedless of their prayers

*S Ḥ B

SAḤABA vb. (I)~to drag

e) impf. pass. (*yus.ḥabu*)

40:71 (73)	when the fetters and chains are on their necks, and they dragged
54:48 (48)	the day when they are dragged on their faces into the Fire

SAḤĀB n.m (coll)~clouds

2:164 (159)	the clouds compelled between heaven and earth
7:57 (55)	till, when they are charged with heavy clouds, We drive it to a dead land
13:12 (13)	it is He who shows you the lightning, for fear and hope, and produces the heavy clouds
24:40 (40)	above which is a billow above which are clouds
24:43 (43)	hast thou not seen how God drives the clouds, then composes them
27:88 (90)	thou shalt see the mountains, that thou supposest fixed, passing by like clouds
30:48 (47)	God is He that looses the winds, that stir up clouds
35:9 (10)	God is He that looses the winds, that stir up cloud
52:44 (44)	even if they saw lumps falling from heaven, they would say, 'A massed cloud!'

*S Ḥ L

SĀḤIL n.m.~shore

20:39 (39)	cast him into the river, and let the river throw him up on the shore

*S Ḥ Q

SAḤUQA vb. (I)~(n.vb.) distance, remoteness; (*suḥqan lahu*) To hell with him, Away with him, Curse him

f) n.vb. (*suḥq*)

67:11 (11)	so they confess their sins. Curse the inhabitants of the Blaze

IS.ḤĀQ n.prop.~Isaac

2:133 (127)	the God of thy fathers Abraham, Ishmael and Isaac, One God
2:136 (130)	and sent down on Abraham, Ishmael, Isaac
2:140 (134)	or do you say, 'Abraham, Ishmael, Isaac'
3:84 (78)	and sent down on Abraham and Ishmael, Isaac
4:163 (161)	We revealed to Abraham, Ishmael, Isaac
6:84 (84)	and We gave to him Isaac and Jacob
11:71 (74)	therefore We gave her the glad tidings of Isaac
11:71 (74)	and, after Isaac, of Jacob
12:6 (6)	as He perfected it formerly on thy fathers Abraham and Isaac
12:38 (38)	I have followed the creed of my fathers, Abraham, Isaac
14:39 (41)	praise be to God, who has given me, though I am old, Ishmael and Isaac
19:49 (50)	We gave him Isaac and Jacob, and each We made a Prophet
21:72 (72)	and We gave him Isaac and Jacob
29:27 (26)	and We gave him Isaac and Jacob

37:112 (112)	then We gave him the good tidings of Isaac, a Prophet
37:113 (113)	and We blessed him, and Isaac
38:45 (45)	remember also Our servants Abraham, Isaac and Jacob

SAḤĪQ n.m. (adj)~distant, far away

22:31 (32)	or the wind sweeps him headlong into a place far away

*S Ḥ R

SAḤARA vb. (I)~to cast a spell, to bewitch, to enchant. (n.vb.) sorcery. (pcple. act.) sorcerer. (pcple. pass.) bewitched

a) perf. act.

7:116 (113)	and when they cast they put a spell upon the people's eyes
7:132 (129)	whatsoever sign thou bringest to us, to cast a spell upon us

b) impf. act. (*yas.ḥaru*)

23:89 (91)	say: 'How then are you bewitched?'

f) n.vb. (*siḥr*)

2:102 (96)	but the Satans disbelieved, teaching the people sorcery
5:110 (110)	the unbelievers among them said, 'This is nothing but sorcery'
6:7 (7)	the unbelievers would have said, 'This is naught but manifest sorcery'
7:116 (113)	and called forth fear of them, and produced a mighty sorcery
10:76 (77)	they said, 'Surely this is a manifest sorcery'
10:77 (78)	do you say this to the truth, when it has come to you? 'Is this a sorcery?'
10:81 (81)	Moses said, 'What you have brought is sorcery'
11:7 (10)	the unbelievers will say, 'This is naught but a manifest sorcery'
20:57 (59)	'Hast thou come, Moses,' he said, 'to expel us out of our land by thy sorcery?'
20:58 (60)	We shall assuredly bring thee sorcery the like of it
20:63 (66)	their purpose is to expel you out of your land by their sorcery
20:66 (69)	it seemed to him, by their sorcery, their ropes and their staffs were sliding
20:71 (74)	he is the chief of you, the same that taught you sorcery
20:73 (75)	He may pardon us our offences, and the sorcery thou hast constrained us to practise
21:3 (3)	what, will you take to sorcery with your eyes open?
26:35 (34)	who desires to expel you from your land by his sorcery
26:49 (48)	he is the chief of you, the same that taught you sorcery
27:13 (13)	they said, 'This is a manifest sorcery'
28:36 (36)	this is nothing but a forged sorcery
28:48 (48)	a pair of sorceries mutually supporting each other
34:43 (42)	this is nothing but manifest sorcery
37:15 (15)	this is nothing but manifest sorcery
43:30 (29)	this is a sorcery, and in it we are unbelievers
46:7 (6)	this is manifest sorcery
52:15 (15)	what, is this magic, or is it you that do not see?
54:2 (2)	if they see a sign they turn away, and they say, 'A continuous sorcery!'
61:6 (6)	when he brought them the clear signs, they said, 'This is a manifest sorcery'
74:24 (24)	this is naught but a trumped-up sorcery

g) pcple. act. (*sāḥir*, pl. *saḥarah* and *sāḥirūn*)

7:109 (106)	surely this man is a cunning sorcerer
7:112 (109)	to bring thee every cunning sorcerer
7:113 (110)	and the sorcerers came to Pharaoh, saying
7:120 (117)	and the sorcerers were cast down, bowing themselves
10:2 (2)	the unbelievers say, 'This is a manifest sorcerer'
10:77 (78)	is this a sorcery? But sorcerers do not prosper
10:79 (80)	Pharaoh said, 'Bring me every cunning sorcerer'
10:80 (80)	then, when the sorcerers came, Moses said to them
20:63 (66)	these two men are sorcerers
20:69 (72)	they have fashioned only the guile of a sorcerer
20:69 (72)	and the sorcerer prospers not, wherever he goes
20:70 (73)	the sorcerers cast themselves down prostrating
26:34 (33)	surely this man is a cunning sorcerer
26:38 (37)	the sorcerers were assembled for the appointed time of a fixed day
26:40 (39)	haply we shall follow the sorcerers if it should be they are the victors
26:41 (40)	then, when the sorcerers came, they said to Pharaoh
26:46 (45)	so the sorcerers were cast down, bowing themselves
38:4 (3)	the unbelievers say, 'This is a lying sorcerer'
40:24 (25)	to Pharaoh, Haman and Korah; they said, 'A lying sorcerer!'
43:49 (48)	Sorcerer, pray to thy Lord for us by the covenant He has made with thee
51:39 (39)	a sorcerer, or a man possessed
51:52 (52)	not a Messenger came to those before them but they said, 'A sorcerer, or a man possessed!'

h) pcple. pass. (*mas.ḥūr*)

15:15 (15)	nay, we are a people bewitched
17:47 (50)	say, 'You are only following a man bewitched!'
17:101 (103)	Pharaoh said to him, 'Moses, I think thou art bewitched'
25:8 (9)	the evildoers say, 'You are only following a man bewitched!'

SAḤAR n.m. (pl. *as.ḥār*)~morning, daybreak

3:17 (15)	expenders in alms, imploring God's pardon at the daybreak
51:18 (18)	and in the mornings they would ask for forgiveness
54:34 (34)	except the folk of Lot; We delivered them at the dawn

SAḤḤĀR n.m.~sorcerer

26:37 (36)	to bring thee every cunning sorcerer

SAḤḤARA vb. (II)~(pcple. pass.) bewitched

h) pcple. pass. (*musaḥḥar*)

26:153 (153)	thou art merely one of those that are bewitched
26:185 (185)	thou art merely one of those that are bewitched

*S Ḥ T

SUḤT n.m.~unlawful, forbidden, banned

5:42 (46)	who listen to falsehood, and consume the unlawful
5:62 (67)	thou seest many of them vying in sin and enmity, and how they consume the unlawful
5:63 (68)	why do the masters and the rabbis not forbid them to utter sin, and consume the unlawful?

AS.ḤATA vb. (IV)~to destroy

b) impf. act. (*yus.ḥitu*)

20:61 (64) lest He destroy you with a chastisement

*S J D

SAJADA vb. (I)~to bow down, to bow in worship, to prostrate oneself. (n.vb.) prostration, bowing down (in worship). (pcple. act.) one who bows down, who prostrates himself

a) perf. act.

2:34 (32) so they bowed themselves, save Iblis; he refused
4:102 (103) when they bow themselves, let them be behind you
7:11 (10) so they bowed themselves, save Iblis
15:30 (30) then the angels bowed themselves all together
17:61 (63) so they bowed themselves, save Iblis
18:50 (48) so they bowed themselves, save Iblis
20:116 (115) so they bowed themselves, save Iblis; he refused
38:73 (73) then the angels bowed themselves all together

b) impf. act. (*yasjudu*)

3:113 (109) a nation upstanding, that recite God's signs in the watches of the night, bowing themselves
7:12 (11) what prevented thee to bow thyself, when I commanded thee?
7:206 (205) they chant His praise, and to Him they bow
13:15 (16) to God bow all who are in the heavens and the earth
15:33 (33) I would never bow myself before a mortal whom Thou hast created of a clay
16:49 (51) to God bows everything in the heavens, and every creature crawling
17:61 (63) shall I bow myself unto one Thou hast created of clay?
22:18 (18) hast thou not seen how to God bow all who are in the heavens
25:60 (61) shall we bow ourselves to what thou biddest us?
27:24 (24) I found her and her people prostrating to the sun, apart from God
27:25 (25) so that they prostrate not themselves to God
38:75 (75) Iblis, what prevented thee to bow thyself before that I created
41:37 (37) bow not yourselves to the sun and moon
55:6 (5) and the stars and the trees bow themselves
84:21 (21) and when the Koran is recited to them they do not bow

c) impv. (*usjud*)

2:34 (32) when We said to the angels, 'Bow yourselves to Adam'
3:43 (38) Mary, be obedient to thy Lord, prostrating and bowing before Him
7:11 (10) We said to the angels: 'Bow yourselves to Adam'
17:61 (63) when We said to the angels, 'Bow yourselves to Adam'
18:50 (48) when We said to the angels, 'Bow yourselves to Adam'
20:116 (115) when We said to the angels, 'Bow yourselves to Adam'
22:77 (76) O men bow you down and prostrate yourselves
25:60 (61) bow yourselves to the All-merciful
41:37 (37) but bow yourselves to God who created them
53:62 (62) so bow yourselves before God, and serve Him
76:26 (26) bow down before Him and magnify Him through the long night
96:19 (19) do thou not obey him, and bow thyself, and draw nigh

f) n.vb. (*sujūd*)

48:29 (29)	their mark is on their faces, the trace of prostration
50:40 (39)	proclaim thy Lord's praise in the night, and at the ends of the prostrations
68:42 (42)	the day when the leg shall be bared, and they shall be summoned to bow themselves
68:43 (43)	for they had been summoned to bow themselves while they were whole

g) pcple. act. (*sājid*, pl. *sājidūn*, *sujjad* or *sujūd*)

2:58 (55)	and enter in at the gate, prostrating
2:125 (119)	those that cleave to it, to those who bow and prostrate themselves
4:154 (153)	enter in at the gate, prostrating
7:11 (10)	save Iblis — he was not of those that bowed themselves
7:120 (117)	the sorcerers were cast down, bowing themselves
7:161 (161)	and enter in at the gate, prostrating
9:112 (113)	those who bow, those who prostrate themselves
12:4 (4)	eleven stars, and the sun and the moon; I saw them bowing down before me
12:100 (101)	the others fell down prostrate before him
15:29 (29)	when I have shaped him, and breathed My spirit in him, fall you down, bowing before him
15:31 (31)	save Iblis; he refused to be among those bowing
15:32 (32)	what ails thee, Iblis, that thou art not among those bowing?
15:98 (98)	proclaim thy Lord's praise, and be of those that bow
16:48 (50)	bowing themselves before God in all lowliness
17:107 (108)	when it is recited to them, fall down upon their faces prostrating
19:58 (59)	when the signs of the All-merciful were recited to them, they fell down prostrate, weeping
20:70 (73)	and the sorcerers cast themselves down prostrating
22:26 (27)	those that stand, for those that bow and prostrate themselves
25:64 (65)	who pass the night prostrate to their Lord and standing
26:46 (45)	so the sorcerers were cast down, bowing themselves
26:219 (219)	and when thou turnest about among those who bow
32:15 (15)	only those believe in Our signs who, when they are reminded of them, fall down prostrate
38:72 (72)	when I have shaped him, and breathed My spirit in him, fall you down, bowing before him
39:9 (12)	is he who is obedient in the watches of the night, bowing himself and standing
48:29 (29)	thou seest them bowing, prostrating, seeking bounty

MASJID n.m. (pl. *masājid*)~a place of worship, mosque; (*al-masjid al-ḥarām*) the Holy Mosque (in Mecca); (*al-masjid al-aqṣā*) the Further Mosque (in Jerusalem)

2:114 (108)	who does greater evil than he who bars God's places of worship
2:144 (139)	turn thy face towards the Holy Mosque
2:149 (144)	from whatsoever place thou issuest, turn thy face towards the Holy Mosque
2:150 (145)	from whatsoever place thou issuest, turn thy face towards the Holy Mosque
2:187 (183)	do not lie with them while you cleave to the mosques
2:191 (187)	fight them not by the Holy Mosque until they should fight you there
2:196 (192)	that is for him whose family are not present at the Holy Mosque
2:217 (214)	but to bar from God's way, and disbelief in Him, and the Holy Mosque
5:2 (3)	let not detestation for a people who barred you from the Holy Mosque
7:29 (28)	set your faces in every place of worship and call on Him
7:31 (29)	Children of Adam! Take your adornment at every place of worship
8:34 (34)	that God should not chastise them, when they are barring from the Holy Mosque
9:7 (7)	excepting those with whom you made covenant at the Holy Mosque

9:17 (17) it is not for the idolaters to inhabit God's places of worship
9:18 (18) only he shall inhabit God's places of worship who believes in God
9:19 (19) the inhabiting of the Holy Mosque as the same as one who believes in God
9:28 (28) let them not come near the Holy Mosque after this year of theirs
9:107 (108) those who have taken a mosque in opposition and unbelief
9:108 (109) a mosque that was founded upon godfearing from the first day is worthier for thee to stand in
17:1 (1) glory be to Him, who carried His servant by night from the Holy Mosque
17:1 (1) to the Further Mosque the precincts of which We have blessed
17:7 (7) and to enter the Temple, as they entered it the first time
18:21 (20) we will raise over them a place of worship
22:25 (25) the Holy Mosque that We have appointed equal unto men
22:40 (41) there had been destroyed cloisters and churches, oratories and mosques
48:25 (25) they are the ones who disbelieved, and barred you from the Holy Mosque
48:27 (27) you shall enter the Holy Mosque, if God wills, in security
72:18 (18) the places of worship belong to God

*S J L

SIJILL n.m.~a scroll; a recorder [Pk]

21:104 (104) on the day when We shall roll up heaven as a scroll is rolled for the writings

SIJJĪL n.m.~baked clay

11:82 (84) We turned it uppermost nethermost, and rained on it stones of baked clay
15:74 (74) We turned it uppermost nethermost and rained on it stones of baked clay
105:4 (4) hurling against them stones of baked clay

*S J N

SAJANA vb. (I)~to imprison, to jail. (pcple. pass.) imprisoned

b) impf. act. (*yasjunu*)

12:35 (35) it seemed good to them, after they had seen the signs, that they should imprison him

e) impf. pass. (*yusjanu*)

12:25 (25) what is the recompense of him who purposes evil against thy folk, but that he

12:32 (32) yet if he will not do what I command him, he shall be imprisoned

h) pcple. pass. (*masjūn*)

26:29 (28) I shall surely make thee one of the imprisoned

SIJJĪN n.prop.~Sijjin (a record of wicked actions)

83:7 (7) the Book of the libertines is in Sijjin
83:8 (8) and what shall teach thee what is Sijjin?

SIJN n.m.~a prison; (*ṣāḥib al-sijn*) fellow-prisoner

12:33 (33)	prison is dearer to me than that they call me to
12:36 (36)	and there entered the prison with him two youths
12:39 (39)	which is better, my fellow-prisoners — many lords at variance, or God the One
12:41 (41)	fellow-prisoners, as for one of you, he shall pour wine for his lord
12:42 (42)	so that he continued in the prison for certain years
12:100 (101)	He was good to me when He brought me forth from the prison

*S J R

SAJARA vb. (I)~to fire up, to burn; to pour (into fire as fuel). (pcple. pass.) poured over, overflowing, swarming

e) impf. pass. (*yusjaru*)

40:72 (73) into the boiling water, then into the Fire they are poured

h) pcple. pass. (*masjūr*)

52:6 (6) and the sea swarming

SAJJARA vb. (II)~to cause to overflow; to boil over d) perf. pass. (*sujjira*)

81:6 (6) when the seas shall be set boiling

*S J Y

SAJÁ vb. (I)~to brood; to be quiet

a) perf. act.

93:2 (2) and the brooding night

*S K B

SAKABA vb. (I)~(pcple. pass.) outpoured

h) pcple. pass. (*maskūb*)

56:31 (30) and outpoured waters

*S K N

SAKANA vb. (I)~to inhabit, to lodge, to dwell; to repose, to rest; to be still, to be tranquil. (n.vb.) repose, comfort; a place of rest; dwelling, abode. (pcple. act.) calm, still. (pcple. pass.) inhabited

a) perf. act.

6:13 (13) to Him belongs whatsoever inhabits the night and the day
14:45 (47) you dwelt in the dwelling-places of those who wronged themselves
65:6 (6) lodge them where you are lodging, according to your means

b) impf. act. (*yaskunu*)

7:189 (189) and made of him his spouse that he might rest in her
10:67 (68) it is He who made for you the night to repose in it
27:86 (88) have they not seen how We made the night for them, to repose in it
28:72 (72) what god other than God shall bring you night to repose in?
28:73 (73) He has appointed for you night and day, for you to repose in
30:21 (20) He created for you, of yourselves, spouses, that you might repose in them
40:61 (63) it is God who made for you the night, to repose in it

c) impv. (*uskun*)

2:35 (33) Adam, dwell thou, and thy wife, in the Garden, and eat thereof easefully
7:19 (18) O Adam, dwell, thou and thy wife, in the Garden
7:161 (161) dwell in this township and eat of it wherever you will
17:104 (106) We said to the Children of Israel after him, 'Dwell in the land'

e) impf. pass. (*yuskanu*)

28:58 (58) those are their dwelling-places, undwelt in after them

f) n.vb. (*sakan*)

6:96 (96) He splits the sky into dawn, and has made the night for a repose
9:103 (104) thy prayers are a comfort for them
16:80 (82) it is God who has appointed a place of rest for you of your houses

g) pcple. act. (*sākin*)

25:45 (47) had He willed, He would have made it still

h) pcple. pass. f. (*maskūnah*)

24:29 (29) there is no fault in you that you enter houses uninhabited

MASKAN n.m. (pl. *masākin*)~a dwelling, a dwelling-place, abode; house

9:24 (24) dwellings you love — if these are dearer to you than God
9:72 (73) therein to dwell, and goodly dwelling-places in the Gardens of Eden
14:45 (47) and you dwelt in the dwelling-places of those who wronged themselves
20:128 (128) how many generations We destroyed before them in whose dwelling-places they walk
21:13 (13) return you unto the luxury that you exulted in, and your dwelling-places
27:18 (18) ants, enter your dwelling-places, lest Solomon and his hosts crush you
28:58 (58) those are their dwelling-places, undwelt in after them
29:38 (37) it has become clear to you from their dwelling-places
32:26 (26) how many generations We destroyed before them in whose dwelling-places they walk
34:15 (14) for Sheba also there was a sign in their dwelling-place
46:25 (24) in the morning there was naught to be seen but their dwelling-places
61:12 (12) and admit you into gardens underneath which rivers flow, and to dwelling-places

MASKANAH n.f.~poverty

2:61 (58)	and abasement and poverty were pitched upon them
3:112 (108)	they will be laden with the burden of God's anger, and poverty shall be pitched on them

MISKĪN n.com. (pl. *masākīn*)~needy, poor

2:83 (77)	to be good to parents, and the near kinsman, and to orphans, and to the needy
2:177 (172)	to give of one's substance, however cherished, to kinsmen, and orphans, the needy
2:184 (180)	for those who are able to fast, a redemption by feeding a poor man
2:215 (211)	whatsoever good you expend is for parents and kinsmen, orphans, the needy
4:8 (9)	when the division is attended by kinsmen and orphans and the poor
4:36 (40)	be kind to parents, and the near kinsman, and to orphans, and to the needy
5:89 (91)	whereof the expiation is to feed ten poor persons with the average
5:95 (96)	food for poor persons or the equivalent of that in fasting
8:41 (42)	and for the needy, and the traveller, if you believe in God
9:60 (60)	the freewill offerings are for the poor and needy
17:26 (28)	give the kinsman his right, and the needy, and the traveller
18:79 (78)	as for the ship, it belonged to certain poor men
24:22 (22)	let not those of you who possess bounty and plenty swear off giving kinsmen and the poor
30:38 (37)	give the kinsman his right, and the needy, and the traveller
58:4 (5)	if any man is not able to, then let him feed sixty poor persons
59:7 (7)	belongs to God, and His Messenger, and the near kinsman, orphans, the needy
68:24 (24)	no needy man shall enter it today against your will
69:34 (34)	he never urged the feeding of the needy
74:44 (45)	we fed not the needy
76:8 (8)	they give food, for the love of Him, to the needy
89:18 (19)	and you urge not the feeding of the needy
90:16 (16)	or a needy man in misery
107:3 (3)	and urges not the feeding of the needy

SAKĪNAH n.f.~God-inspired peace; Shechina [Ar]; peace of reassurance [Pk]; calm, assurance of security [Ali]; Sakina, assurance [Bl]

2:248 (249)	the Ark will come to you, in it a Shechina from your Lord
9:26 (26)	then God sent down upon His Messenger His Shechina
9:40 (40)	then God sent down on him His Shechina, and confirmed him with legions
48:4 (4)	it is He who sent down the Shechina into the hearts of the believers
48:18 (18)	so He sent down the Shechina upon them, and rewarded them
48:26 (26)	then God sent down His Shechina upon His Messenger and the believers

SIKKĪN n.com.~a knife

12:31 (31)	then she gave to each one of them a knife

ASKANA vb. (IV)~to lodge someone, to make to dwell; to still, to make calm

a) perf. act.

14:37 (40)	I have made some of my seed to dwell in a valley where is no sown land
23:18 (18)	We sent down out of heaven water in measure and lodged it in the earth

b) impf. act. (*yuskinu*)

14:14 (17)	We will surely make you to dwell in the land after them
42:33 (31)	and if He wills, He stills the wind

c) impv. (*askin*)

65:6 (6) lodge them where you are lodging

*S K R

SAKAR n.m.~an intoxicant

16:67 (69) of the fruits of the palms and the vines, you take therefrom an intoxicant

SAKRAH n.f.~dazzlement; inebriety; (*sakrat al-mawt*) the agony of death

15:72 (72) by thy life, they wandered blindly in their dazzlement
50:19 (18) death's agony comes in truth; that is what thou wast shunning

SUKĀRÁ n.m. (pl. of *sakrān*)~drunken, intoxicated

4:43 (46) draw not near to prayer when you are drunken until you know what you are saying
22:2 (2) shall deposit her burden, and thou shalt see mankind drunk
22:2 (2) yet they are not drunk, but God's chastisement is terrible

SAKKARA vb. (II)~to dazzle; to make drunken

d) perf. pass. (*sukkira*)

15:15 (15) yet would they say, 'Our eyes have been dazzled'

*S K T

SAKATA vb. (I)~to calm down, to abate, to subside

a) perf. act.

7:154 (153) when Moses' anger abated in him, he took the Tablets

*S KH R

SAKHIRA vb. (I)~(with prep. *min*) to scoff, to deride. (pcple. act.) a scoffer

a) perf. act.

6:10 (10) those that scoffed at them were encompassed by that they mocked at
9:79 (80) God derides them; for them awaits a painful chastisement
11:38 (40) whenever a council of his people passed by him they scoffed at him
21:41 (42) those that scoffed at them were encompassed by that they mocked at

b) impf. act. (*yaskharu*)

2:212 (208) decked out fair to the unbelievers is the present life, and they deride the believers
9:79 (80) those who find nothing but their endeavour they deride

11:38 (40)	if you scoff at us
11:38 (40)	we shall surely scoff at you
11:38 (40)	as you scoff
37:12 (12)	nay, thou marvellest; and they scoff
49:11 (11)	let not any people scoff at another people who may be better

g) pcple. act. (*sākhir*)

39:56 (57)	I neglected my duty to God, and was a scoffer

SIKHRĪ n.m.~laughing-stock, ridicule

23:110 (112)	you took them for a laughing-stock, till they made you forget My remembrance
38:63 (63)	what, did we take them for a laughing-stock?

SUKHRĪ n.m.~servitude, forced labour

43:32 (31)	that some of them may take others in servitude

SAKHKHARA vb. (II)~to subject, to make subservient; (with prep. *ʿalá*) to compel against (pcple. pass.) compelled, subjected, subservient

a) perf. act.

13:2 (2)	He subjected the sun and the moon, each one running to a term stated
14:32 (37)	He subjected to you the ships to run upon the sea at His commandment
14:32 (37)	and He subjected to you the rivers
14:33 (37)	He subjected to you the sun and moon constant upon their courses
14:33 (37)	and He subjected to you the night and day
16:12 (12)	He subjected to you the night and day
16:14 (14)	it is He who subjected to you the sea, that you may eat of it
21:79 (79)	with David We subjected the mountains to give glory
22:36 (37)	so We have subjected them to you
22:37 (38)	He has subjected them to you, that you may magnify God for that
22:65 (64)	hast thou not seen how that God has subjected to you all that is in the earth
29:61 (61)	who created the heavens and the earth and subjected the sun and the moon?
31:20 (19)	have you not seen how that God has subjected to you whatsoever is in the heavens and earth
31:29 (28)	He has subjected the sun and the moon, each of them running to a stated term
35:13 (14)	He has subjected the sun and the moon, each of them running to a stated term
38:18 (17)	with him We subjected the mountains to give glory
38:36 (35)	We subjected to him the wind, that ran at his commandment
39:5 (7)	He has subjected the sun and the moon, each of them running to a stated term
43:13 (12)	glory be to Him, who has subjected this to us
45:12 (11)	God is He who has subjected to you the sea
45:13 (12)	He has subjected to you what is in the heavens and what is in the earth
69:7 (7)	that He compelled against them seven nights and eight days

h) pcple. pass. (*musakhkhar*)

2:164 (159)	the clouds compelled between heaven and earth
7:54 (52)	the sun, and the moon, and the stars subservient, by His command
16:12 (12)	the sun and moon; and the stars are subjected by His command
16:79 (81)	have they not regarded the birds, that are subjected in the air of heaven?

ISTASKHARA vb. (X)~to scoff

b) impf. act. (*yastaskhiru*)

37:14 (14)	and, when they see a sign, would scoff

*S KH Ṭ

SAKHIṬA vb. (I)~(with prep. *ʿalá*) to be angry, to be displeased. (n.vb.) anger, wrath

a) perf. act.

5:80 (83) evil is that they have forwarded to their account, that God is angered against them

b) impf. act. (*yaskhaṭu*)

9:58 (58) they are well-pleased, but if they are given none then they are angry

f) n.vb. (*sakhaṭ*)

3:162 (156) like him who is laden with the burden of God's anger

ASKHAṬA vb. (IV)~to anger, to enrage

a) perf. act.

47:28 (30) that is because they have followed what angers God

*S L B

SALABA vb. (I)~to rob, to take away,

b) impf. act. (*yaslubu*)

22:73 (72) if a fly should rob them of aught, they would never rescue it from him

*S L F

SALAFA vb. (I)~to be past, to be bygone; to precede. (n.vb.) a precedent; a thing past

a) perf. act.

2:275 (276) whosoever receives an admonition from his Lord and gives over, he shall have his past gains
4:22 (26) do not marry women that your fathers married, unless it be a thing of the past
4:23 (27) you should take to you two sisters together, unless it be a thing of the past
5:95 (96) God has pardoned what is past; but whoever offends
8:38 (39) if they give over He will forgive them what is past

f) n.vb. (*salaf*)

43:56 (56) and We made them a thing past

ASLAFA vb. (IV)~to make precede; to have done in the past

a) perf. act.

10:30 (31) there every soul shall prove its past deeds
69:24 (24) eat and drink with wholesome appetite for that you did long ago, in the days gone by

*S L Ḥ

ASLIḤAH n.m. (pl. of *silāḥ*)~weapons, arms

4:102 (103)	let a party of them stand with thee, and let them take their weapons
4:102 (103)	come and pray with thee, taking their precautions and their weapons
4:102 (103)	the unbelievers wish that you should be heedless of your weapons and your baggage
4:102 (103)	there is no fault in you, if rain molests you, or you are sick, to lay aside your weapons

*S L K

SALAKA vb. (I)~to thread; to thrust; to cause to enter, to insert; to follow (a path); to dispatch

a) perf . act.

20:53 (55)	He who appointed the earth to be a cradle for you, and therein threaded roads for you
26:200 (200)	even so We have caused it to enter into the hearts of the sinners
39:21 (22)	hast thou not seen how that God has sent down out of heaven water and threaded it as springs in the earth
74:42 (43)	what thrusted you into Sakar?

b) impf. act. (*yasluku*)

15:12 (12)	even so We cause it to enter into the hearts of the sinners
71:20 (19)	that thereof you may thread ways, ravines
72:17 (17)	He will thrust him into chastisement rigorous
72:27 (27)	then He despatches before him and behind him watchers

c) impv. (*usluk*)

16:69 (71)	then eat of all manner of fruit, and follow the ways of your Lord
23:27 (28)	insert in it two of every kind and thy family
28:32 (32)	insert thy hand into thy bosom, and it will come forth white
69:32 (32)	then in a chain of seventy cubits' length insert him

*S L KH

SALAKHA vb. (I)~to strip off

b) impf. act. (*yaslakhu*)

36:37 (37)	We strip it of the day and lo, they are in darkness

INSALAKHA vb. (VII)~to be drawn away; (with prep. *min*) to cast off

a) perf. act.

7:175 (174)	recite to them the tiding of him to whom We gave Our signs, but he cast them off
9:5 (5)	when the sacred months are drawn away, slay the idolaters wherever you find them

*S L L

SULĀLAH n.f.~extraction

23:12 (12)	We created man of an extraction of clay
32:8 (7)	then He fashioned his progeny of an extraction of mean water

TASALLALA vb. (V)~to slip away

b) impf. act. (*yatasallalu*)

24:63 (63)	God knows those of you who slip away surreptitiously

*S L M

SALIMA vb. (I)~(pcple. act.) safe, secure; whole, complete; healthy, unblemished

g) pcple. act. (*sālim*)

68:43 (43)	they had been summoned to bow themselves while they were whole

SALAM n.m.~peace; surrender, submission; a captive, a man belonging to another

4:90 (92)	if they withdraw from you, and do not fight you, and offer you peace
4:91 (93)	if they withdraw not from you, and offer you peace
16:28 (30)	then they will offer surrender: We were doing nothing evil
16:87 (89)	they will offer God surrender that day
39:29 (30)	a man in whom partners disagreeing share, and a man the property of one man

SALĀM n.m.~soundness, well-being, unimpairedness; peace; security, safety; a greeting; (*al-salām*) the All-peaceable [Ar]; Perfect [Bl] (Divine attribute, in 59:23)

4:94 (96)	do not say to him who offers you a greeting, 'Thou art not a believer'
5:16 (18)	God guides whosoever follows His good pleasure in the ways of peace
6:54 (54)	peace be upon you. Your Lord has prescribed for Himself mercy
6:127 (127)	theirs is the abode of peace with their Lord
7:46 (44)	who shall call to the inhabitants of Paradise: Peace be upon you
10:10 (10)	their cry therein, 'Glory to Thee, O God,' their greeting, 'Peace'
10:25 (26)	and God summons to the Abode of Peace
11:48 (50)	Noah, get thee down in peace from Us, and blessings upon thee
11:69 (72)	Our messengers came to Abraham with the good tidings; they said, 'Peace!'
11:69 (72)	'Peace,' he said; and presently he brought a roasted calf
13:24 (24)	peace be upon you, for that you were patient
14:23 (28)	by the leave of their Lord, their greeting therein: 'Peace!'
15:46 (46)	enter you them, in peace and security
15:52 (52)	when they entered unto him, saying, 'Peace!' He said
16:32 (34)	peace be on you! Enter Paradise for that you were doing
19:15 (15)	peace be upon him, the day he was born, and the day he dies
19:33 (34)	peace be upon me, the day I was born, and the day I die
19:47 (48)	he said, 'Peace be upon thee'
19:62 (63)	there they shall hear no idle talk, but only 'Peace'
20:47 (49)	a sign from thy Lord; and peace be upon him who follows the guidance
21:69 (69)	We said, 'O fire, be coolness and safety for Abraham!'
25:63 (64)	and who, when the ignorant address them, say, 'Peace'

25:75 (75)	they shall receive therein a greeting and — 'Peace!'
27:59 (60)	praise belongs to God, and peace be on His servants
28:55 (55)	we have our deeds, and you your deeds. Peace be upon you
33:44 (43)	their greeting, on the day when they shall meet Him, will be, 'Peace'
36:58 (58)	'Peace!' — such is the greeting, from a Lord All-compassionate
37:79 (77)	peace be upon Noah among all beings
37:109 (109)	peace be upon Abraham
37:120 (120)	peace be upon Moses and Aaron
37:130 (130)	peace be upon Elias
37:181 (181)	and peace be upon the Envoys
39:73 (73)	and its keepers will say to them, 'Peace be upon you!'
43:89 (89)	yet pardon them, and say, 'Peace!'
50:34 (33)	enter it in peace
51:25 (25)	when they entered unto him, saying 'Peace'
51:25 (25)	he said, 'Peace! You are a people unknown to me'
56:26 (25)	only the saying 'Peace, (Peace!')
56:26 (25)	only the saying, ('Peace), Peace!'
56:91 (90)	peace be upon thee, Companion of the Right
59:23 (23)	He is the King, the All-holy, the All-peaceable
97:5 (5)	peace it is, till the rising of dawn

SALĪM n.m. (adj)~pure; safe, secure; whole, unblemished, unimpaired; sound

26:89 (89)	except for him who comes to God with a pure heart
37:84 (82)	when he came unto his Lord with a pure heart

SALM n.m.~peace

8:61 (63)	if they incline to peace, do thou incline to it
47:35 (37)	so do not faint and call for peace

SILM n.com.~peace [Ar, Bl]; submission [Pk]; Islam [Ali]

2:208 (204)	O believers, enter the peace, all of you

SULAYMĀN n.prop.~Solomon

2:102 (96)	they follow what the Satans recited over Solomon's kingdom
2:102 (96)	Solomon disbelieved not, but the Satans disbelieved
4:163 (161)	Jesus and Job, Jonah and Aaron and Solomon
6:84 (84)	Noah We guided before; and of his seed David and Solomon
21:78 (78)	David and Solomon — when they gave judgment concerning the tillage
21:79 (79)	and We made Solomon to understand it
21:81 (81)	to Solomon the wind, strongly blowing, that ran at his command unto the land
27:15 (15)	We gave David and Solomon knowledge
27:16 (16)	and Solomon was David's heir
27:17 (17)	his hosts were mustered to Solomon, jinn, men and birds, duly disposed
27:18 (18)	ants, enter your dwelling-places, lest Solomon and his hosts crush you
27:30 (30)	it is from Solomon, and it is 'In the Name of God
27:36 (36)	but when he came to Solomon he said
27:44 (45)	I surrender with Solomon to God, the Lord of all Being
34:12 (11)	to Solomon the wind; its morning course was a month's journey
38:30 (29)	We gave unto David Solomon; how excellent a servant he was
38:34 (33)	We tried Solomon, and We cast upon his throne a mere body

SULLAM n.m.~a ladder

6:35 (35)	if thou canst seek out a hole in the earth, or a ladder in heaven
52:38 (38)	or have they a ladder whereon they listen?

SALLAMA vb. (II)~to save, to preserve; to hand over intact; to surrender, to hand over; to salute, to greet; (with prep. *ʿalá*) to pray someone peace. (n.vb.) submission, surrender; greeting; peace. (pcple. pass.) secure; handed over, paid

a) perf. act.

2:233 (233)	it is no fault in you provide you hand over what you have given honourably
8:43 (45)	but God saved; He knows the thoughts in the breasts

b) impf. act. (*yusallimu*)

4:65 (68)	but shall surrender in full submission
24:27 (27)	until you first ask leave and salute the people thereof

c) impv. (*sallim*)

24:61 (61)	when you enter houses, greet one another with a greeting from God
33:56 (56)	O believers, do you also bless him, and pray him peace

f) n.vb. (*taslīm*)

4:65 (68)	touching thy verdict, but shall surrender in <full submission>
33:22 (22)	it only increased them in faith and surrender
33:56 (56)	O believers, do you also bless him, and pray him peace <...>

h) pcple. pass. f. (*musallamah*)

2:71 (66)	to plough the earth or to water the tillage, one kept secure
4:92 (94)	let him set free a believing slave
4:92 (94)	then bloodwit is to be paid to his family

ASLAMA vb. (IV)~to submit, to surrender. (n.vb.) surrender, submission; Islam. (pcple. act.) submissive, one who surrenders (to God); Muslim (Moslem)

a) perf. act.

2:112 (106)	whosoever submits his will to God, being a good-doer
2:131 (125)	I have surrendered me to the Lord of all Being
3:20 (18)	I have surrendered my will to God, and whosoever follows me
3:20 (19)	and to the common folk: 'Have you surrendered?'
3:20 (19)	if they have surrendered, they are right guided
3:83 (77)	to Him has surrendered whoso is in the heavens and the earth
4:125 (124)	who is there that has a fairer religion than he who submits his will to God
5:44 (48)	thereby the Prophets who had surrendered themselves gave judgment
6:14 (14)	I have been commanded to be the first of them that surrender
27:44 (45)	I surrender with Solomon to God, the Lord of all Being
37:103 (103)	when they had surrendered, and he flung him upon his brow
49:14 (14)	rather say, 'We surrender'
49:17 (17)	they count it as a favour to thee that they have surrendered
72:14 (14)	those who have surrendered sought rectitude

b) impf. act. (*yuslimu*)

6:71 (70)	we are commanded to surrender to the Lord of all Being
16:81 (83)	He perfects His blessing upon you, that haply you will surrender
31:22 (21)	whosoever submits his will to God, being a good-doer
40:66 (68)	I am commanded to surrender to the Lord of all Being
48:16 (16)	you shall be called against a people possessed of great might to fight them, or they surrender

c) impv. (*aslim*)

2:131 (125)	when his Lord said to him, 'Surrender,'
22:34 (35)	your God is One God, so to Him surrender
39:54 (55)	turn unto your Lord and surrender to Him

f) n.vb. (*islām*)

3:19 (17)	the true religion with God is Islam
3:85 (79)	whoso desires another religion than Islam, it shall not be accepted of him
5:3 (5)	I have completed My blessing upon you, and I have approved Islam
6:125 (125)	whomsoever God desires to guide, He expands his breast to Islam
9:74 (75)	they indeed said the word of unbelief and disbelieved, after they had surrendered
39:22 (23)	is he whose breast God has expanded unto Islam
49:17 (17)	do not count your surrendering as a favour to me
61:7 (7)	he who forges against God falsehood, when he is being called unto surrender

g) pcple. act. (*muslim*)

2:128 (122)	and our Lord, make us submissive to Thee
2:128 (122)	and of our seed a nation submissive to Thee
2:132 (126)	see that you die not save in surrender
2:133 (127)	the God of thy fathers Abraham, Ishmael and Isaac, One God; to Him we surrender
2:136 (130)	make no division between any of them, and to Him we surrender
3:52 (45)	we believe in God; witness thou our submission
3:64 (57)	if they turn their backs, say: 'Bear witness that we are Muslims'
3:67 (60)	Abraham in truth was not a Jew, neither a Christian; but he was a Muslim
3:80 (74)	would He order you to disbelieve, after you have surrendered?
3:84 (78)	we make no division between any of them, and to Him we surrender
3:102 (97)	fear God as He should be feared, and see you do not die, save in surrender
5:111 (111)	we believe; witness Thou our submission
6:163 (163)	I have been commanded, and I am the first of those that surrender
7:126 (123)	pour out upon us patience, and gather us unto Thee surrendering
10:72 (73)	and I have been commanded to be of those that surrender
10:84 (84)	in Him put your trust, if you have surrendered
10:90 (90)	the Children of Israel believe; I am of those that surrender
11:14 (17)	there is no god but He. So have you surrendered?
12:101 (102)	receive me to Thee in true submission, and join me with the righteous
15:2 (2)	perchance the unbelievers will wish that they had surrendered
16:89 (91)	as a guidance and a mercy, and as good tidings to those who surrender
16:102 (104)	to be a guidance and good tidings to those who surrender
21:108 (108)	your God is One God; do you then surrender?
22:78 (77)	being the creed of your father Abraham; He named you Muslims
27:31 (31)	rise not up against me, but come to me in surrender
27:38 (38)	which one of you will bring me her throne, before they come to me in surrender?
27:42 (42)	we were given the knowledge before her, and we were in surrender
27:81 (83)	save such as believe in Our signs, and so surrender
27:91 (93)	I have been commanded to be of those that surrender
28:53 (53)	indeed, even before it we had surrendered
29:46 (45)	our God and your God is One, and to Him we have surrendered
30:53 (52)	except for such as believe in Our signs, and so surrender
33:35 (35)	men and (women) who have surrendered
33:35 (35)	(men) and women who have surrendered
39:12 (14)	I have been commanded to be the first of those that surrender
41:33 (33)	surely I am of them that surrender
43:69 (69)	even those who believed in Our signs, and had surrendered themselves
46:15 (14)	I repent to Thee, and am among those that surrender

51:36 (36)	We found not therein except one house of those that have surrendered themselves
66:5 (5)	wives better than you, women who have surrendered
68:35 (35)	shall we make those who have surrendered like to the sinners?
72:14 (14)	and some of us have surrendered

ISTASLAMA vb. (X)~(pcple. act.) one who resigns himself in submission

g) pcple. act. (*mustaslim*)

37:26 (26)	but today they resign themselves in submission

*S L Q

SALAQA vb. (I)~to flay, to abuse

a) perf. act.

33:19 (19)	but when the fear departs, they flay you with sharp tongues

*S L S L

SILSILAH n.f. (pl. *salāsil*)~chain

40:71 (73)	when the fetters and chains are on their necks
69:32 (32)	then in a chain of seventy cubits' length insert him
76:4 (4)	We have prepared for the unbelievers chains, fetters, and a Blaze

*S L Ṭ

SULṬĀN n.com.~authority; power

3:151 (144)	for that they have associated with God that for which He sent down never authority
4:91 (93)	against them We have given you a clear authority
4:144 (143)	do you desire to give God over you a clear authority?
4:153 (152)	We bestowed upon Moses a clear authority
6:81 (81)	that whereon He has not sent down on you any authority
7:33 (31)	that for which He sent down never authority
7:71 (69)	you and your fathers, touching which God has sent down never authority
10:68 (69)	and in the earth; you have no authority for this
11:96 (99)	We sent Moses with Our signs, and a manifest authority
12:40 (40)	you and your fathers; God has sent down no authority touching them
14:10 (12)	then bring us a manifest authority
14:11 (13)	it is not for us to bring you an authority
14:22 (26)	I promised you, then I failed you, for I had no authority over you
15:42 (42)	over My servants thou shalt have no authority
16:99 (101)	he has no authority over those who believe and trust in their Lord
16:100 (102)	his authority is over those who take him for their friend
17:33 (35)	whosoever is slain unjustly, We have appointed to his next-of-kin authority
17:65 (67)	surely over My servants thou shalt have no authority
17:80 (82)	grant me authority from Thee, to help me

18:15 (14)	if only they would bring some clear authority regarding them
22:71 (70)	they serve, apart from God, that whereon He has sent down never authority
23:45 (47)	We sent Moses and his brother Aaron with Our signs and a manifest authority
27:21 (21)	or I will slaughter him, or he bring me a clear authority
28:35 (35)	We shall appoint to you an authority, so that they shall not reach you
30:35 (34)	have We sent down any authority upon them
34:21 (20)	yet he had no authority over them
37:30 (29)	we had no authority over you; no, you were an insolent people
37:156 (156)	or have you a clear authority?
40:23 (24)	We also sent Moses with Our signs and a clear authority
40:35 (37)	those who dispute concerning the signs of God, without any authority
40:56 (58)	those who dispute concerning the signs of God, without any authority
44:19 (18)	rise not up against God; behold, I come to you with a clear authority
51:38 (38)	also in Moses, when We sent him unto Pharaoh, with a clear authority
52:38 (38)	let any of them that has listened bring a clear authority
53:23 (23)	God has sent down no authority touching them
55:33 (33)	you shall not pass through except with an authority
69:29 (29)	my authority is gone from me

SALLAṬA vb. (II)~to give authority

a) perf. act.

4:90 (92)	had God willed, He would have given them authority over you

b) impf. act. (*yusalliṭu*)

59:6 (6)	God gives authority to His Messengers over whomsoever He will

*S L W

SALWÁ n.f.~quails

2:57 (54)	and We sent down manna and quails upon you
7:160 (160)	and We sent down manna and quails upon them
20:80 (82)	and sent down on you manna and quails

*S M ᶜ

SAMIᶜA vb. (I)~to hear, to give ear; to listen, to hearken; to learn. (n.vb.) hearing, listening, giving ear

a) perf. act.

2:93 (87)	they said, 'We hear, and rebel'
2:181 (177)	if any man changes it after hearing it, the sin shall rest upon those who change it
2:285 (285)	we hear, and obey. Our Lord, grant us Thy forgiveness
3:181 (177)	God has heard the saying of those who said, 'Surely God is poor'
3:193 (190)	our Lord, we have heard a caller calling us to belief
4:46 (48)	saying, 'We have heard and we disobey'
4:46 (49)	if they had said, 'We have heard and obey'
4:140 (139)	when you hear God's signs being disbelieved and made mock of

5:7 (10)	when you said, 'We have heard and we obey'
5:83 (86)	when they hear what has been sent down to the Messenger
8:21 (21)	be not as those who say, 'We hear'
8:31 (31)	when Our signs were being recited to them, they said, 'We have already heard'
12:31 (31)	when she heard their sly whispers, she sent to them
21:60 (61)	we heard a young man making mention of them, and he was called Abraham
23:24 (24)	we never heard of this among our fathers, the ancients
24:12 (12)	when you heard it, did the believing men and women not of their own account think good thoughts
24:16 (15)	why, when you heard it, did you not say, 'It is not for us to speak'
24:51 (50)	we hear, and we obey
25:12 (13)	when it sees them from a far place, they shall hear its bubbling and sighing
28:36 (36)	we never heard of this among our fathers, the ancients
28:55 (55)	when they hear idle talk, they turn away from it and say
32:12 (12)	our Lord, we have seen and heard; now return us
35:14 (15)	and if they heard, they would not answer you
38:7 (6)	we have not heard of this in the last religion
46:30 (29)	we have heard a Book that was sent down after Moses, confirming
58:1 (1)	God has heard the words of her that disputes with thee
67:7 (7)	when they are cast into it they will hear it sighing, the while it boils
68:51 (51)	when they hear the Reminder, and they say, 'Surely he is a man possessed!'
72:1 (1)	we have indeed heard a Koran wonderful
72:13 (13)	when we heard the guidance, we believed in it

b) impf. act. (*yasmaʿu*)

2:75 (70)	seeing there is a party of them that heard God's word, and then tampered with it
2:171 (166)	the likeness of one who shouts to that which hears nothing
3:186 (183)	you shall hear from those who were given the Book before you
6:36 (36)	answer only will those who hear; as for the dead
7:100 (98)	We would smite them because of their sins, sealing their hearts so they do not hear
7:179 (178)	they have ears, but they hear not with them
7:195 (194)	or have they ears wherewith they give ear?
7:198 (197)	if you call them to the guidance they do not hear
8:20 (20)	do not turn away from Him, even as you are listening
8:21 (21)	and they hear not
9:6 (6)	grant him protection till he hears the words of God
10:67 (68)	surely in that are signs for a people who have ears
16:65 (67)	surely in that is a sign for a people who have ears
19:42 (43)	why worshippest thou that which neither hears nor sees
19:62 (63)	there they shall hear no idle talk, but only, Peace
19:98 (98)	dost thou perceive so much as one of them, or hear of them a whisper?
20:46 (48)	surely I shall be with you, hearing and seeing
20:108 (107)	voices will be hushed to the All-merciful, so that thou hearest naught but a murmuring
21:45 (46)	but they that are deaf do not hear the call when they are warned
21:100 (100)	there shall be sighing for them therein, and naught they shall hear
21:102 (102)	neither shall they hear any whisper of it
22:46 (45)	so that they have hearts to understand with or ears to hear with
25:44 (46)	or deemest thou that most of them hear or understand?
26:72 (72)	do they hear you when you call
28:71 (71)	will you not hear?
30:23 (22)	surely in that are signs for a people who hear
31:7 (6)	a man he turns away, waxing proud, as though he heard them not

32:26 (26)	surely in that are signs; what, will they not hear?
35:14 (15)	if you call upon them, they will not hear your prayer
41:4 (3)	most of them have turned away, and do not give ear
41:26 (25)	do not give ear to this Koran, and talk idly about it
43:80 (80)	or do they think We hear not their secret
45:8 (7)	who hears the signs of God being recited to him
45:8 (7)	then perseveres in waxing proud, as if he has not heard them
50:42 (41)	on the day they hear the Cry in truth, that is the day of coming forth
56:25 (24)	therein they shall hear no idle talk, no cause of sin
58:1 (1)	God hears the two of you conversing together
63:4 (4)	when they speak, thou listenest to their speech
67:10 (10)	if we had only heard, or had understood
78:35 (35)	therein they shall hear no idle talk, no cry of lies
88:11 (11)	hearing there no babble

c) impv. (*isma*ᶜ)

2:93 (87)	take forcefully what We have given you and give ear
2:104 (98)	but say, 'Regard us'; and give ear
4:46 (48)	hear, and be thou not given to hear
4:46 (49)	and, 'Hear', and, 'Regard us'
5:108 (107)	fear God, and hearken; God guides not the people of the ungodly
36:25 (24)	behold, I believe in your Lord; therefore hear me
64:16 (16)	fear God as far as you are able, and give ear, and obey

f) n.vb. (*sam*ᶜ)

2:7 (6)	God has set a seal on their hearts and on their hearing
2:20 (19)	had God willed, He would have taken away their hearing
6:46 (46)	what think you? If God seizes your hearing and sight
10:31 (32)	or who possesses hearing and sight
11:20 (22)	they could not hear, neither did they see
15:18 (18)	excepting such as listens by stealth
16:78 (80)	He appointed for you hearing, and sight, and hearts
16:108 (110)	God has set a seal on their hearts, and their hearing
17:36 (38)	the hearing, the sight, the heart — all of those shall be questioned of
18:101 (101)	whose eyes were covered against My remembrance, and they were not able to hear
23:78 (80)	it is He who produced for you hearing, and eyes
26:212 (212)	truly, they are expelled from hearing
26:223 (223)	they give ear, but most of them are liars
32:9 (8)	He appointed for you hearing, and sight, and hearts
41:20 (19)	their hearing, their eyes and their skins bear witness against them
41:22 (21)	not so did you cover yourselves, that your hearing, your eyes and your skins should not bear witness against you
45:23 (22)	and set a seal upon his hearing and his heart
46:26 (25)	We appointed for them hearing, and sight, and hearts
46:26 (25)	and yet their hearing, their sight and their hearts availed them nothing
50:37 (36)	in that there is a reminder to him who has a heart, or will give ear with a present mind
67:23 (23)	it is He who produced you, and appointed for you hearing and sight and hearts
72:9 (9)	we would sit there on seats to hear

SAMĪᶜ n.m. (adj)~one who hears; All-hearing (Divine attribute)

2:127 (121)	receive this from us; Thou art the All-hearing
2:137 (131)	God will suffice you for them; He is the All-hearing
2:181 (177)	those who change it; surely God is All-hearing

2:224 (224)	things right between men. Surely God is All-hearing
2:227 (227)	if they resolve on divorce, surely God is All-hearing
2:244 (245)	fight in God's way, and know that God is All-hearing
2:256 (257)	the most firm handle, unbreaking; God is All-hearing
3:34 (30)	the seed of one another; God hears, and knows
3:35 (31)	receive Thou this from me; Thou hearest, and knowest
3:38 (33)	yea, Thou hearest prayer
3:121 (117)	God is All-hearing
4:58 (61)	good is the admonition God gives you; God is All-hearing
4:134 (133)	God is All-hearing
4:148 (147)	unless a man has been wronged; God is All-hearing
5:76 (80)	God is the All-hearing
6:13 (13)	and He is the All-hearing
6:115 (115)	no man can change His words; He is the All-hearing
7:200 (199)	He is All-hearing, All-knowing
8:17 (17)	surely God is All-hearing
8:42 (44)	and surely God is All-hearing
8:53 (55)	and that God is All-hearing
8:61 (63)	put thy trust in God; He is the All-hearing
9:98 (99)	theirs shall be the evil turn; God is All-hearing
9:103 (104)	thy prayers are a comfort for them; God is All-hearing
10:65 (66)	the glory belongs altogether to God; He is the All-hearing
11:24 (26)	is as the man blind and deaf, and the man who sees and hears; are they equal in likeness?
12:34 (34)	away from him their guile; surely He is the All-hearing
14:39 (41)	surely my Lord hears the petition
17:1 (1)	He is the All-hearing, the All-seeing
21:4 (4)	and the earth, and He is the All-hearing
22:61 (60)	and makes the day to enter into the night; and that God is All-hearing
22:75 (74)	and of mankind; surely God is All-hearing
24:21 (21)	God purifies whom He will; and God is All-hearing
24:60 (59)	to abstain is better for them; and God is All-hearing
26:220 (220)	surely He is the All-hearing, the All-knowing
29:5 (4)	He is the All-hearing, the All-knowing
29:60 (60)	He is the All-hearer, the All-knower
31:28 (27)	God is All-hearing, All-seeing
34:50 (49)	He is All-hearing, Ever-nigh
40:20 (21)	surely God is the All-hearing, the All-seeing
40:56 (58)	surely He is the All-hearing, the All-seeing
41:36 (36)	He is the All-hearing, the All-knowing
42:11 (9)	He is the All-hearing, the All-seeing
44:6 (5)	surely He is the All-hearing, the All-knowing
49:1 (1)	fear God. God is All-hearing, All-knowing
58:1 (1)	God hears the two of you conversing together; surely God is All-hearing
76:2 (2)	and We made him hearing, seeing

SAMMĀʿ n.m.~one who listens, who hearkens

5:41 (45)	the Jews who listen to falsehood
5:41 (45)	listen to other folk
5:42 (46)	who listen to falsehood, and consume the unlawful
9:47 (47)	and some of you would listen to them

ASMAʿA vb. (IV)~to make someone hear; (*asmiʿ bihi*) How well he hears. (pcple. act.) one who makes to hear. (pcple. pass.) one who is made to hear

a) perf. act.

8:23 (23)	if God had known of any good in them He would have made them hear
8:23 (23)	and if He had made them hear, they would have turned away

b) impf. act. (*yusmiʿu*)

10:42 (43)	wilt thou make the deaf to hear, though they understand not?
27:80 (82)	thou shalt not make the dead to hear
27:80 (82)	neither shalt thou make the deaf to hear the call
27:81 (83)	neither shalt thou make any to hear, save such as believe in Our signs
30:52 (51)	thou shalt not make the dead to hear
30:52 (51)	neither shalt thou make the deaf to hear the call
30:53 (52)	neither shalt thou make any to hear except for such as believe in Our signs
35:22 (21)	God makes to hear whomsoever He will
43:40 (39)	what, shalt thou make the deaf to hear

c) impv. (*asmiʿ*)

18:26 (25)	how well He sees! How well He hears
19:38 (39)	how well they will hear and see on the day they come to Us

g) pcple. act. (*musmiʿ*)

35:22 (21)	thou canst not make those in their tombs to hear

h) pcple. pass. (*musmaʿ*)

4:46 (48)	hear, and be thou not given to hear

TASAMMAʿA vb. (V)~to listen to

b) impf. act. (*yassammaʿu*)

37:8 (8)	they listen not to the High Council, for they are pelted from every side

ISTAMAʿA vb. (VIII)~to listen, to give ear; to hear; to overhear, to eavesdrop. (pcple. act.) listening; one who listens

a) perf. act.

21:2 (2)	no Remembrance from their Lord comes to them lately renewed, but they listen to it yet playing
72:1 (1)	it has been revealed to me that a company of the jinn gave ear

b) impf. act. (*yastamiʿu*)

6:25 (25)	some of them there are that listen to thee, and We lay veils upon their hearts
10:42 (43)	and some of them give ear to thee
17:47 (50)	We know very well how they listen
17:47 (50)	when they listen to thee
26:25 (24)	said he to those about him, 'Do you not hear?'
39:18 (19)	who give ear to the Word and follow the fairest of it
46:29 (28)	when We turned to thee a company of jinn giving ear to the Koran
47:16 (18)	some of them there are give ear to thee, till, when they go forth
52:38 (38)	or have they a ladder whereon they listen?
72:9 (9)	We would sit there on seats to hear; but any listening now finds a meteor in wait for him

c) impv. (*istamiᶜ*)

7:204 (203)	when the Koran is recited, give you ear to it
20:13 (13)	I Myself have chosen thee; therefore give thou ear to this revelation
22:73 (72)	O men, a similitude is struck; so give you ear to it
50:41 (40)	listen thou for the day when the caller shall call from a near place

g) pcple. act. (*mustamiᶜ*)

26:15 (14)	We assuredly shall be with you, listening
52:38 (38)	then let any of them that has listened bring a clear authority

*S M D

SAMADA vb. (I)~(pcple. act.) one who passes his life in merriment

g) pcple. act. (*sāmid*)

53:61 (61)	while you make merry

*S M K

SAMK n.m.~ceiling, roof, vault

79:28 (28)	He lifted up its vault, and levelled it

*S M M

SAMM n.m.~hole, eye (of a needle)

7:40 (38)	until the camel passes through the eye of the needle

SAMŪM n.f.~hot or burning wind, burning (like the hot wind)

15:27 (27)	and the jinn created We before of fire flaming
52:27 (27)	God was gracious to us, and guarded us against the chastisement of the burning wind
56:42 (41)	mid burning winds and boiling waters

*S M N

SAMĪN n.m. (pl. *simān*)~fat, fattened

12:43 (43)	I saw in a dream seven fat kine, and seven lean ones
12:46 (46)	pronounce to us regarding seven fat kine
51:26 (26)	then he turned to his household and brought a fattened calf

ASMANA vb. (IV)~to fatten

b) impf. act. (*yusminu*)

88:7 (7) unfattening, unappeasing hunger

*S M R

SAMARA vb. (I)~(pcple. act.) one who chats or talks idly (at night)

g) pcple. act. (*sāmir*)

23:67 (69) waxing proud against it, talking foolish talk by night

SĀMIRĪ n.prop.~The Samaritan, the Samiri

20:85 (87) the Samaritan has misled them into error
20:87 (90) we cast them, as the Samaritan also threw them, into the fire
20:95 (96) Moses said, 'And thou, Samaritan, what was thy business?'

*S M W

ISM n.m. (pl. *asmā'*)~a name; (*bism Allāh al-raḥmān al-raḥīm*) In the Name of God the Merciful, the Compassionate (this invocation opens every Sura of the Qur'an except Sura 9. It is also found at 27:30)

1:1 (1) In the Name of God, the Merciful, the Compassionate
2:31 (29) He taught Adam the names, all of them
2:31 (29) now tell Me the names of these, if you speak truly
2:33 (31) He said, 'Adam, tell them their names'
2:33 (31) when he had told them their names He said
2:114 (108) God's places of worship, so that His Name be not rehearsed in them
3:45 (40) God gives thee good tidings of a Word from Him whose name is Messiah
5:4 (6) eat what they seize for you, and mention God's Name over it
6:118 (118) eat of that over which God's Name has been mentioned
6:119 (119) how is it with you, that you do not eat of that over which God's Name has been mentioned
6:121 (121) eat not of that over which God's Name has not been mentioned
6:138 (139) and cattle over which they mention not the Name of God
7:71 (69) do you dispute with me regarding names you have named
7:180 (179) to God belong the Names Most Beautiful
7:180 (179) leave those who blaspheme His Names — they shall assuredly be recompensed
11:41 (43) embark in it! In God's Name shall be its course and its berthing
12:40 (40) that which you serve, apart from Him, is nothing but namesyourselves have named
17:110 (110) whichsoever you call upon, to Him belong the Names Most Beautiful
19:7 (7) We give thee good tidings of a boy, whose name is John
20:8 (7) to Him belong the Names Most Beautiful
22:28 (29) mention God's Name on days well-known over such beasts of the flocks
22:34 (35) that they may mention God's Name over such beasts of the flocks
22:36 (37) so mention God's Name over them, standing in ranks
22:40 (41) oratories and mosques, wherein God's Name is much mentioned
24:36 (36) in temples God has allowed to be raised up, and His Name to be commemorated therein
27:30 (30) it is 'In the Name of God, the Merciful, the Compassionate'
49:11 (11) an evil name is ungodliness after belief

53:23 (23)	they are naught but names yourselves have named
55:78 (78)	blessed be the Name of thy Lord, majestic, splendid
56:74 (73)	then magnify the Name of thy Lord, the All-mighty
56:96 (96)	then magnify the Name of thy Lord, the All-mighty
59:24 (24)	to Him belong the Names Most Beautiful
61:6 (6)	giving good tidings of a Messenger who shall come after me
69:52 (52)	then magnify the Name of thy Lord, the All-mighty
73:8 (8)	remember the Name of thy Lord, and devote thyself unto Him very devoutly
76:25 (25)	remember the Name of thy Lord at dawn and in the evening
87:1 (1)	magnify the Name of thy Lord the Most High
87:15 (15)	and mentions the Name of his Lord, and prays
96:1 (1)	recite: In the Name of thy Lord who created

SAMĀʾ n.com. (pl. *samāwāt*)~heaven, the heavens, sky; firmament

2:19 (18)	or as a cloudburst out of heaven in which is darkness
2:22 (20)	who assigned to you the earth for a couch, and heaven for an edifice
2:22 (20)	and sent down out of heaven water, wherewith He brought forth fruits
2:29 (27)	then He lifted Himself to heaven
2:29 (27)	and levelled them seven heavens
2:33 (31)	did I not tell you I know the unseen things of the heavens and earth?
2:59 (56)	We sent down upon the evildoers wrath out of heaven of their ungodliness
2:107 (101)	knowest thou not that to God belongs the kingdom of the heavens and the earth
2:116 (110)	nay, to Him belongs all that is in the heavens and the earth
2:117 (111)	the Creator of the heavens and the earth
2:144 (139)	We have seen thee turning thy face about in the heaven
2:164 (159)	surely in the creation of the heavens and the earth
2:164 (159)	to men, and the water God sends down from heaven
2:164 (159)	and the clouds compelled between heaven and earth
2:255 (256)	to Him belongs all that is in the heavens and the earth
2:255 (256)	His Throne comprises the heavens and earth
2:284 (284)	to God belongs all that is in the heavens and the earth
3:5 (4)	from God nothing whatever is hidden in heaven and earth
3:29 (27)	God knows what is in the heavens and what is in the earth
3:83 (7)	to Him has surrendered whoso is in the heavens and the earth
3:109 (105)	to God belongs all that is in the heavens and in the earth
3:129 (124)	to God belongs all that is in the heavens and earth
3:133 (127)	a garden whose breadth is as the heavens and earth
3:180 (176)	to God belongs the inheritance of the heavens and earth
3:189 (186)	to God belongs the Kingdom of the heavens and of the earth
3:190 (187)	surely in the creation of the heavens and earth
3:191 (188)	and reflect upon the creation of the heavens and the earth
4:126 (125)	to God belongs all that is in the heavens and in the earth
4:131 (130)	to God belongs all that is in the heavens and in the earth
4:131 (130)	to God belongs all that is in the heavens and in the earth
4:132 (131)	to God belongs all that is in the heavens and in the earth
4:153 (152)	the People of the Book will ask thee to bring down upon them a Book from heaven
4:170 (168)	to God belongs all that is in the heavens and in the earth
4:171 (169)	to Him belongs all that is in the heavens and in the earth
5:17 (20)	to God belongs the kingdom of the heavens and of the earth
5:18 (21)	to God belongs the kingdom of the heavens and of the earth
5:40 (44)	knowest thou not that to God belongs the kingdom of the heavens and the earth?
5:97 (98)	that you may know that God knows all that is in the heavens

5:112 (112)	is thy Lord able to send down on us a Table out of heaven?
5:114 (114)	send down upon us a Table out of heaven
5:120 (120)	to God belongs the kingdom of the heavens and of the earth
6:1 (1)	praise belongs to God who created the heavens and the earth
6:3 (3)	He is God in the heavens and the earth
6:6 (6)	and how We loosed heaven upon them in torrents
6:12 (12)	to whom belongs what is in the heavens and in the earth?
6:14 (14)	shall I take to myself as protector other than God, the Originator of the heavens
6:35 (35)	if thou canst seek out a hole in the earth, or a ladder in heaven
6:73 (72)	it is He who created the heavens and the earth in truth
6:75 (75)	so We were showing Abraham the kingdom of the heavens and earth
6:79 (79)	I have turned my face to Him who originated the heavens and the earth
6:99 (99)	it is He who sent down out of heaven water
6:101 (101)	the Creator of the heavens and the earth
6:125 (125)	He makes his breast narrow, tight, as if he were climbing to heaven
7:40 (38)	the gates of heaven shall not be opened to them
7:54 (52)	surely your Lord is God, who created the heavens
7:96 (94)	We would have opened upon them blessings from heaven and earth
7:158 (158)	Him to whom belongs the kingdom of the heavens and of the earth
7:162 (162)	so We sent down upon them wrath out of heaven for their evildoing
7:185 (184)	have they not considered the dominion of the heaven and of the earth
7:187 (186)	heavy is it in the heavens and the earth
8:11 (11)	and sending down on you water from heaven, to purify you thereby
8:32 (32)	if this be indeed the truth from Thee, then rain down upon us stones out of heaven
9:36 (36)	the day that He created the heavens and the earth; four of them are sacred
9:116 (117)	surely to God belongs the kingdom of the heavens
10:3 (3)	your Lord is God, who created the heavens and the earth in six days
10:6 (6)	in the alternation of night and day, and what God has created in the heavens and the earth
10:18 (19)	will you tell God what He knows not either in the heavens or in the earth?
10:24 (25)	the likeness of this present life is as water that We send down out of heaven
10:31 (32)	say: 'Who provides you out of heaven and earth'
10:55 (56)	to God belongs everything that is in the heavens and earth
10:61 (62)	not so much as the weight of an ant in earth or heaven escapes from thy Lord
10:66 (67)	to God belongs everyone that is in the heavens and in the earth
10:68 (69)	to Him belongs all that is in the heavens and in the earth
10:101 (101)	behold what is in the heavens and in the earth
11:7 (9)	it is He who created the heavens and the earth in six days
11:44 (46)	earth, swallow thy waters; and, heaven, abate
11:52 (54)	He will loose heaven in torrents upon you
11:107 (109)	therein dwelling forever, so long as the heavens and earth abide
11:108 (110)	Paradise, therein dwelling forever, so long as the heavens and earth abide
11:123 (123)	to God belongs the Unseen in the heavens and the earth
12:101 (102)	O Thou, the Originator of the heavens and earth, Thou art my Protector
12:105 (105)	how many a sign there is in the heavens and in the earth that they pass by
13:2 (2)	God is He who raised up the heavens without pillars you can see
13:15 (16)	to God bow all who are in the heavens and the earth
13:16 (17)	who is the Lord of the heavens and of the earth?
13:17 (18)	He sends down out of heaven water
14:2 (2)	God, to whom belongs all that is in the heavens and all that is in the earth
14:10 (11)	is there any doubt regarding God, the Originator of the heavens and the earth
14:19 (22)	hast thou not seen that God created the heavens and the earth in truth?
14:24 (29)	its roots are firm, and its branches are in heaven
14:32 (37)	it is God who created the heavens and the earth

14:32 (37)	and sent down out of heaven water wherewith He brought forth fruits
14:38 (41)	from God nothing whatever is hidden in earth and heaven
14:48 (49)	and the heavens and they sally forth unto God
15:14 (14)	though We opened to them a gate in heaven, and still they mounted through it
15:16 (16)	We have set in heaven constellations and decked them out fair to the beholders
15:22 (22)	and We send down out of heaven water
15:85 (85)	We created not the heavens and the earth, and all that is between them
16:3 (3)	He created the heavens and the earth in truth
16:10 (10)	it is He who sends down to you out of heaven water of which you have to drink
16:49 (51)	to God bows everything in the heavens, and every creature crawling
16:52 (54)	to Him belongs all that is in the heavens and earth
16:65 (67)	it is God who sends down out of heaven water
16:73 (75)	that which has no power to provide them anything from the heavens
16:77 (79)	to God belongs the Unseen in the heavens and in the earth
16:79 (81)	have they not regarded the birds, that are subjected in the air of heaven?
17:44 (46)	the seven heavens and the earth, and whosoever in them is, extol Him
17:55 (57)	thy Lord knows very well all who are in the heavens and the earth
17:92 (94)	or till thou makest heaven to fall, as thou assertest
17:93 (95)	or till thou goest up into heaven
17:95 (97)	We would have sent down upon them out of heaven an angel as Messenger
17:99 (101)	have they not seen that God, who created the heavens and earth, is powerful
17:102 (104)	indeed thou knowest that none sent these down, except the Lord of the heavens
18:14 (13)	our Lord is the Lord of the heavens and earth
18:26 (25)	to Him belongs the Unseen in the heavens and in the earth
18:40 (38)	better than thy garden, and loose on it a thunderbolt out of heaven
18:45 (43)	it is as water that We send down out of heaven
18:51 (49)	I made them not witnesses of the creation of the heavens and earth
19:65 (66)	Lord He of the heavens and earth and all that is between them
19:90 (92)	the heavens are wellnigh rent of it and the earth split asunder
19:93 (94)	none is there in the heavens and earth but he comes to the All-merciful as a servant
20:4 (3)	a revelation from Him who created the earth and the high heavens
20:6 (5)	to Him belongs all that is in the heavens and the earth
20:53 (55)	threaded roads for you, and sent down water out of heaven
21:4 (4)	my Lord knows what is said in the heavens and the earth
21:16 (16)	We created not the heaven and the earth, and whatsoever between them is, as playing
21:19 (19)	to Him belongs whosoever is in the heavens and the earth
21:30 (31)	have not the unbelievers then beheld that the heavens and the earth were a mass all sewn up
21:32 (33)	and We set up the heaven as a roof well-protected
21:56 (57)	nay, but your Lord is the Lord of the heavens and the earth
21:104 (104)	on the day when We shall roll up heaven as a scroll is rolled
22:15 (15)	let him stretch up a rope to heaven, then let him sever it
22:18 (18)	hast thou not seen how to God bow all who are in the heavens
22:31 (32)	it is as though he has fallen from heaven and the birds snatch him away
22:63 (62)	hast thou not seen how that God has sent down out of heaven water
22:64 (63)	to Him belongs all that is in the heavens and in the earth
22:65 (64)	He holds back heaven lest it should fall upon the earth
22:70 (69)	didst thou not know that God knows all that is in heaven
23:18 (18)	We sent down out of heaven water in measure and lodged it in the earth
23:71 (73)	the heavens and the earth and whosoever in them is had surely corrupted
23:86 (88)	say: 'Who is the Lord of the seven heavens'
24:35 (35)	God is the Light of the heavens and the earth

24:41 (41)	hast thou not seen how that whatsoever is in the heavens and in the earth extols God
24:42 (42)	to God belongs the Kingdom of the heavens and the earth
24:43 (43)	He sends down out of heaven mountains, wherein is hail
24:64 (64)	to God belongs whatsoever is in the heavens and the earth
25:2 (2)	to whom belongs the Kingdom of the heavens and the earth
25:6 (7)	He sent it down, who knows the secret in the heavens and earth
25:25 (27)	upon the day that heaven is split asunder with the clouds
25:48 (50)	We sent down from heaven pure water
25:59 (60)	who created the heavens and the earth, and what between them is
25:61 (62)	blessed be He who has set in heaven constellations
26:4 (3)	if We will, We shall send down on them out of heaven a sign
26:24 (23)	he said, 'The Lord of the heavens and earth'
26:187 (187)	then drop down on us lumps from heaven, if thou art one of the truthful
27:25 (25)	to God, who brings forth what is hidden in the heavens and earth
27:60 (61)	He who created the heavens and earth
27:60 (61)	and sent down for you out of heaven water
27:64 (65)	and provides you out of heaven and earth
27:65 (66)	none knows the Unseen in the heavens and earth except God
27:75 (77)	not a thing is there hidden in heaven and earth but it is in a Manifest Book
27:87 (89)	on the day the Trumpet is blown, and terrified is whosoever is in the heavens
29:22 (21)	you are not able to frustrate Him either in the earth or in heaven
29:34 (33)	We shall send down upon the people of this city wrath out of heaven
29:44 (43)	God created the heavens and the earth with the truth
29:52 (52)	He knows whatsoever is in the heavens and earth
29:61 (61)	who created the heavens and the earth and subjected the sun and the moon?
29:63 (63)	who sends down out of heaven water, and therewith revives the earth
30:8 (7)	God created not the heavens and the earth, and what between them is
30:18 (17)	His is the praise in the heavens and earth
30:22 (21)	of His signs is the creation of the heavens and earth
30:24 (23)	and that He sends down out of heaven water
30:25 (24)	of His signs is that the heaven and earth stand firm by His command
30:26 (25)	to Him belongs whosoever is in the heavens and the earth
30:27 (26)	His is the loftiest likeness in the heavens and the earth
30:48 (47)	He spreads them in heaven how He will, and shatters them
31:10 (9)	He created the heavens without pillars you can see
31:10 (9)	We sent down out of heaven water, and caused to grow in itof every generous kind
31:16 (15)	though it be in a rock, or in the heavens, or in the earth
31:20 (19)	have you not seen how that God has subjected to you whatsoever is in the heavens
31:25 (24)	if thou askest them, 'Who created the heavens and the earth?'
31:26 (25)	to God belongs all that is in the heavens and the earth
32:4 (3)	God is He that created the heavens and the earth
32:5 (4)	He directs the affair from heaven to earth
33:72 (72)	We offered the trust to the heavens and the earth and the mountains
34:1 (1)	praise belongs to God to whom belongs whatsoever is in the heavens
34:2 (2)	what comes down from heaven, and what goes up to it
34:3 (3)	not so much as the weight of an ant in heaven and earth escapes from Him
34:9 (9)	what lies before them and what lies behind them of heaven and earth?
34:9 (9)	or We would drop down on them lumps from heaven. Surely in that is a sign
34:22 (21)	they possess not so much as the weight of an ant in the heavens nor in the earth
34:24 (23)	who provides for you out of the heavens and the earth?
35:1 (1)	praise belongs to God, Originator of the heavens and earth
35:3 (3)	is there any creator, apart from God, who provides for you out of heaven and earth?
35:27 (25)	hast thou not seen how that God sends down out of heaven water
35:38 (36)	God knows the Unseen in the heavens and the earth

35:40 (38)	or have they a partnership in the heavens? Or have We given them a Book
35:41 (39)	God holds the heavens and the earth, lest they remove
35:44 (43)	there is naught in the heavens or the earth that can frustrate Him
36:28 (27)	We sent not down upon his people, after him, any host out of heaven
36:81 (81)	is not He, who created the heavens and earth, able to create the like of them?
37:5 (5)	Lord of the heavens and the earth, and of what between them is
37:6 (6)	We have adorned the lower heaven with the adornment of the stars
38:10 (9)	is theirs the kingdom of the heavens and earth and of what between them is?
38:27 (26)	We have not created the heavens and earth, and what between them is
38:66 (66)	Lord of the heavens and earth, and of what between them is
39:5 (7)	He created the heavens and the earth in truth
39:21 (22)	hast thou not seen how that God has sent down out of heaven water
39:38 (39)	who created the heavens and the earth?
39:44 (45)	His is the kingdom of the heavens and the earth
39:46 (47)	O God, Thou originator of the heavens and the earth
39:63 (63)	unto Him belong the keys of the heavens and the earth
39:67 (67)	on the Day of Resurrection, and the heavens shall be rolled up in His right hand
39:68 (68)	whosoever is in the heavens and whosoever is in the earth shall swoon
40:13 (13)	it is He who shows you His signs and sends down to you out of heaven provision
40:37 (39)	the cords of the heavens, and look upon Moses' God
40:57 (59)	the creation of the heavens and earth is greater than the creation of men
40:64 (66)	it is God who made for you the earth a fixed place and heaven for an edifice
41:11 (10)	then He lifted Himself to heaven when it was smoke
41:12 (11)	so He determined them as seven heavens in two days
41:12 (11)	and revealed its commandment in every heaven
41:12 (11)	We adorned the lower heaven with lamps
42:4 (2)	to Him belongs whatsoever is in the heavens and whatsoever is in the earth
42:5 (3)	the heavens wellnigh are rent above them
42:11 (9)	the Originator of the heavens and the earth
42:12 (10)	to Him belong the keys of the heavens and the earth
42:29 (28)	of His signs is the creation of the heavens and earth
42:49 (48)	to God belongs the Kingdom of the heavens and the earth
42:53 (53)	the path of God, to whom belongs whatsoever is in the heavens
43:9 (8)	if thou askest them, 'Who created the heavens and earth?'
43:11 (10)	and who sent down out of heaven water in measure
43:82 (82)	glory be to the Lord of the heavens and the earth
43:84 (84)	it is He who in heaven is God and in earth is God
43:85 (85)	blessed be He, to whom belongs the Kingdom of the heavens and the earth
44:7 (6)	Lord of the heavens and earth, and all that between them is
44:10 (9)	be on the watch for a day when heaven shall bring a manifest smoke
44:29 (28)	neither heaven nor earth wept for them, nor were they respited
44:38 (38)	We created not the heavens and earth, and all that between them is, in play
45:3 (2)	in the heavens and earth there are signs for the believers
45:5 (4)	and the provision God sends down from heaven
45:13 (12)	He has subjected to you what is in the heavens and what is in the earth
45:22 (21)	God created the heavens and the earth in truth
45:27 (26)	to God belongs the Kingdom of the heavens and the earth
45:36 (35)	to God belongs praise, the Lord of the heavens and the Lord of the earth
45:37 (36)	His is the Domination in the heavens and the earth
46:3 (2)	We have not created the heavens and the earth, and what between them is
46:4 (3)	or have they a partnership in the heavens?
46:33 (32)	have they not seen that God who created the heavens and earth, not being wearied by creating them
48:4 (4)	to God belong the hosts of the heavens and the earth

48:7 (7)	to God belong the hosts of the heavens and the earth
48:14 (14)	to God belongs the kingdom of the heavens and of the earth
49:16 (16)	God knows what is in the heavens and what is in the earth
49:18 (18)	God knows the Unseen of the heavens and of the earth
50:6 (6)	what, have they not beheld heaven above them
50:9 (9)	We sent down out of heaven water blessed
50:38 (37)	We created the heavens and the earth, and what between them is
51:7 (7)	by heaven with all its tracks
51:22 (22)	in heaven is your provision, and that you are promised
51:23 (23)	by the Lord of heaven and earth, it is as surely true as that you have speech
51:47 (47)	and heaven — We built it with might
52:9 (9)	upon the day when heaven spins dizzily
52:36 (36)	did they create the heavens and earth?
52:44 (44)	even if they saw lumps falling from heaven, they would say
53:26 (26)	how many an angel there is in the heavens whose intercession avails not anything
53:31 (32)	to God belongs whatsoever is in the heavens and whatsoever is in the earth
54:11 (11)	We opened the gates of heaven unto water torrential
55:7 (6)	and heaven — He raised it up, and set the Balance
55:29 (29)	whatsoever is in the heavens and the earth implore Him
55:33 (33)	if you are able to pass through the confines of heaven and earth
55:37 (37)	and when heaven is split asunder
57:1 (1)	all that is in the heavens and the earth magnifies God
57:2 (2)	to Him belongs the Kingdom of the heavens and the earth
57:4 (4)	it is He that created the heavens and the earth in six days
57:4 (4)	what comes down from heaven, and what goes up unto it
57:5 (5)	to Him belongs the Kingdom of the heavens and the earth
57:10 (10)	and to God belongs the inheritance of the heavens and the earth
57:21 (21)	a Garden the breadth whereof is as the breadth of heaven and earth
58:7 (8)	hast thou not seen that God knows whatsoever is in the heavens
59:1 (1)	all that is in the heavens and the earth magnifies God
59:24 (24)	all that is in the heavens and the earth magnifies Him
61:1 (1)	all that is in the heavens and the earth magnifies God
62:1 (1)	all that is in the heavens and the earth magnifies God
63:7 (7)	unto God belong the treasuries of the heavens and of the earth
64:1 (1)	all that is in the heavens and the earth magnifies God
64:3 (3)	He created the heavens and the earth with the truth
64:4 (4)	He knows whatever is in the heavens and the earth
65:12 (12)	it is God who created seven heavens, and of earth their like
67:3 (3)	who created seven heavens one upon another
67:5 (5)	and We adorned the lower heaven with lamps
67:16 (16)	do you feel secure that He who is in heaven will not cause the earth to swallow you
67:17 (17)	do you feel secure that He who is in heaven will not loose against you a squall of pebbles
69:16 (16)	heaven shall be split, for upon that day it shall be very frail
70:8 (8)	upon the day when heaven shall be as molten copper
71:11 (10)	He will loose heaven upon you in torrents
71:15 (14)	have you not regarded how God created seven heavens one upon another
72:8 (8)	we stretched towards heaven, but we found it filled with terrible guards
73:18 (18)	heaven shall be split, and its promise shall be performed
77:9 (9)	when heaven shall be split
78:19 (19)	and heaven is opened, and become gates
78:37 (37)	Lord of the heavens and earth, and all that between them is
79:27 (27)	are you stronger in constitution or the heaven He built?

81:11 (11)	when heaven shall be stripped off
82:1 (1)	when heaven is split open
84:1 (1)	when heaven is rent asunder
85:1 (1)	by heaven of the constellations
85:9 (9)	to whom belongs the Kingdom of the heavens and the earth
86:1 (1)	by heaven and the night-star
86:11 (11)	by heaven of the returning rain
88:18 (18)	how heaven was lifted up
91:5 (5)	by the heaven and That which built it

SAMĪY n.m.~namesake

19:7 (8)	no namesake have We given him aforetime
19:65 (66)	knowest thou any that can be named with His Name?

SAMMÁ vb. (II)~to name. (n.vb.) the act of naming. (pcple. pass.) named, stated, determined

a) perf. act.

3:36 (31)	and I have named her Mary
7:71 (69)	do you dispute with me regarding names you have named
12:40 (40)	that which you serve, apart from Him, is nothing but names yourselves have named
22:78 (77)	being the creed of your father Abraham; He named you Muslims
53:23 (23)	they are naught but names yourselves have named

b) impf. act. (*yusammī*)

53:27 (28)	those who do not believe in the world to come name the angels

c) impv. (*sammi*)

13:33 (33)	yet they ascribe to God associates. Say: 'Name them'

e) impf. pass. (*yusammá*)

76:18 (18)	therein a fountain whose name is called Salsabil

f) n.vb. (*tasmiyah*)

53:27 (28)	those who do not believe ... name the angels <with the names> of females

h) pcple. pass. (*musammá*)

2:282 (282)	when you contract a debt one upon another for a stated term
6:2 (2)	then determined a term and a term is stated with Him
6:60 (60)	then He raises you up therein, that a stated term may be determined
11:3 (3)	He will give you fair enjoyment unto a term stated
13:2 (2)	He subjected the sun and the moon, each one running to a term stated
14:10 (11)	He may forgive you your sins, and defer you to a term stated
16:61 (63)	but He is deferring them to a term stated
20:129 (129)	but for a word that preceded from thy Lord, and a stated term
22:5 (5)	We establish in the wombs what We will, till a stated term
22:33 (34)	there are things therein profitable to you unto a stated term
29:53 (53)	but for a stated term the chastisement would have come upon them
30:8 (7)	save with the truth and a stated term
31:29 (28)	He has subjected the sun and the moon, each of them running to a stated term
35:13 (14)	He has subjected the sun and the moon, each of them running to a stated term
35:45 (44)	but he is deferring them to a stated term

39:5 (7)	He has subjected the sun and the moon, each of them running to a stated term
39:42 (43)	He withholds that against which He has decreed death, but looses the other till a stated term
40:67 (69)	and that you may reach a stated term
42:14 (13)	but for a Word that preceded from thy Lord until a stated term
46:3 (2)	save with the truth and a stated term
71:4 (4)	He will forgive you your sins, and defer you to a stated term

*S N B L

SUNBULAH n.f. (pl. *sanābil* and *sunbulāt*)~ear of corn (wheat or grain)

2:261 (263)	the way of God is as the likeness of a grain of corn that sprouts seven ears
2:261 (263)	in every ear a hundred grains
12:43 (43)	likewise seven green ears of corn, and seven withered
12:46 (46)	seven green ears of corn, and seven withered
12:47 (47)	what you have harvested leave in the ear, excepting a little

*S N D

SANNADA vb. (II)~(pcple. pass.) propped-up

h) pcple. pass. (*musannad*)

63:4 (4)	thou listenest to their speech, and it is as they were propped-up timbers

*S N D S

SUNDUS n.m.~silk

18:31 (30)	they shall be robed in green garments of silk and brocade
44:53 (53)	robed in silk and brocade, set face to face
76:21 (21)	upon them shall be green garments of silk and brocade

*S N H

TASANNAHA vb. (V)~to be spoiled, to be mouldy through age

b) impf. act. (*yatasannahu*)

2:259 (261)	look at thy food and drink — it has not spoiled

*S N M

TASNĪM n.prop.~Tasnim (name of a fountain in Paradise)

83:27 (27)	and whose mixture is Tasnim

*S N N

SANNA vb. (I)~(pcple. pass.) moulded, formed

h) pcple. pass. (*masnūn*)

15:26 (26) surely We created man of a clay of mud moulded
15:28 (28) see, I am creating a mortal of a clay of mud moulded
15:33 (33) I would never bow myself before a mortal whom Thou hast created of a clay

SINN n.f.~a tooth

5:45 (49) an ear for an ear, a tooth for a (tooth)
5:45 (49) an ear for an ear, a (tooth) for a tooth

SUNNAH n.f. (pl. *sunan*)~institution, customary action, wont

3:137 (131) diverse institutions have passed away before you
4:26 (31) God desires to make clear to you, and to guide you in the institutions
8:38 (39) but if they return, the wont of the ancients is already gone
15:13 (13) they believe not in it, though the wont of the ancients is already gone
17:77 (79) the wont of those We sent before thee of Our Messengers
17:77 (79) thou wilt find no change to Our wont
18:55 (53) but that the wont of the ancients should come upon them
33:38 (38) God has ordained for him — God's wont with those who passed away before
33:62 (62) God's wont with those who passed away before
33:62 (62) thou shalt find no changing the wont of God
35:43 (41) do they expect anything but the wont of the ancients?
35:43 (41) thou shalt never find any changing the wont of God
35:43 (42) thou shalt never find any altering the wont of God
40:85 (85) the wont of God, as in the past, touching His servants
48:23 (23) the wont of God, as in the past before
48:23 (23) thou shalt never find any changing the wont of God

*S N W

SANĀ n.m.~brilliance, splendour, gleam

24:43 (43) wellnigh the gleam of His lightning snatches away the sight

SANAH n.f. (pl. *sinīn*)~a year

2:96 (90) there is one of them wishes if he might be spared a thousand years
5:26 (29) it shall be forbidden them for forty years, while they are wandering
7:130 (127) then seized We Pharaoh's people with years of dearth
10:5 (5) and determined it by stations, that you might know the number of the years
12:42 (42) he continued in the prison for certain years
12:47 (47) you shall sow seven years after your wont
17:12 (13) that you may know the number of the years, and the reckoning
18:11 (10) then We smote their ears many years in the Cave
18:25 (24) they tarried in the Cave three hundred years
20:40 (42) many years among the people of Midian thou didst sojourn
22:47 (46) surely a day with thy Lord is as a thousand years
23:112 (114) how long have you tarried in the earth, by number of years?
26:18 (17) didst thou not tarry among us years of thy life?
26:205 (205) what thinkest thou? If We give them enjoyment of days for many years

29:14 (13)	he tarried among them a thousand years
30:4 (3)	in a few years
32:5 (4)	it goes up to Him in one day, whose measure is a thousand years of your counting
46:15 (14)	when he is fully grown, and reaches forty years, he says
70:4 (4)	a day whereof the measure is fifty thousand years

*S Q F

SAQF n.m. (pl. *suquf*)~a roof

16:26 (28)	and the roof fell down on them from over them
21:32 (33)	We set up the heaven as a roof well-protected
43:33 (32)	for those who disbelieve in the All-merciful roofs of silver to their houses
52:5 (5)	and the roof uplifted

*S Q M

SAQĪM n.m. (adj)~sick, ill

37:89 (87)	and he said, 'Surely I am sick'
37:145 (145)	but We cast him upon the wilderness, and he was sick

*S Q R

SAQAR n.f. (prop)~Sakar; hell-fire

54:48 (48)	taste now the touch of Sakar
74:26 (26)	I shall surely roast him in Sakar
74:27 (27)	and what will teach thee what is Sakar?
74:42 (43)	what thrusted you into Sakar?

*S Q Ṭ

SAQAṬA vb. (I)~to fall; (*suqiṭa fī aydīhim*, 7:149) they smote their hands. (pcple. act.) falling

a) perf. act.

9:49 (49)	have not such men fallen into temptation?

b) impf. act. (*yasquṭu*)

6:59 (59)	not a leaf falls, but He knows it

d) perf. pass. (*suqiṭa*)

7:149 (148)	when they smote their hands, and saw that they had gone astray

g) pcple. act. (*sāqiṭ*)

52:44 (44)	even if they saw lumps falling from heaven, they would say

SĀQAṬA vb. (III)~to let fall; to cause tumbling

b) impf. act. (*yusāqiṭu*)

19:25 (25) there shall come tumbling upon thee dates fresh and ripe

ASQAṬA vb. (IV)~to cause to fall, to drop

a) perf. act.

17:92 (94) till thou makest heaven to fall, as thou assertest
34:9 (9) or We would drop down on them lumps from heaven

c) impv. (*asqiṭ*)

26:187 (187) then drop down on us lumps from heaven, if thou art one of the truthful

*S Q Y

SAQÁ vb. (I)~to draw water; to give to drink; to water; to pour wine

a) perf. act.

28:24 (24) so he drew water for them; then he turned away
28:25 (25) that he may recompense thee with the wage of thy drawing water for us
76:21 (21) and their Lord shall give them to drink a pure draught

b) impf. act. (*yasqī*)

2:71 (66) a cow not broken to plough the earth or to water the tillage
12:41 (41) as for one of you, he shall pour wine for his lord
26:79 (79) and Himself gives me to eat and drink
28:23 (22) he found a company of the people there drawing water
28:23 (23) We may not draw water until the shepherds drive off

d) perf. pass. (*suqiya*)

47:15 (17) such as are given to drink boiling water, that tears their bowels asunder

e) impf. pass. (*yusqá*)

13:4 (4) palms in pairs, and palms single, watered with one water
14:16 (19) beyond him Gehenna, and he is given to drink of oozing pus
76:17 (17) therein they shall be given to drink a cup whose mixture is ginger
83:25 (25) as they are given to drink of a wine sealed
88:5 (5) watered at a boiling fountain

SIQĀYAH n.f.~giving water to drink; watering; a drinking cup

9:19 (19) do you reckon the giving of water to pilgrims and the inhabiting of the Holy

12:70 (70) he put his drinking-cup into the saddlebag of his brother

SUQYĀ n.m.~watering; giving to drink

91:13 (13) the She-camel of God; let her drink

ASQÁ vb. (IV)~to give to drink; to sate, to saturate

a) perf. act.

15:22 (22)	We send down out of heaven water, then We give it to you to drink
72:16 (16)	We would give them to drink of water copious
77:27 (27)	set We not therein soaring mountains? Sated you with sweetest water?

b) impf. act. (*yusqī*)

16:66 (68)	We give you to drink of what is in their bellies
23:21 (21)	We give you to drink of what is in their bellies
25:49 (51)	so that We might revive a dead land, and give to drink of it

ISTASQÁ vb. (X)~to seek or ask for water to drink; to pray for rain

a) perf. act.

2:60 (57)	and when Moses sought water for his people
7:160 (160)	We revealed to Moses, when his people asked him for water

*S R ᶜ

SARĪᶜ n.m. (pl. *sirāᶜ*, comp. adj. *asraᶜ*)~swift, quick, prompt; (adv) hastily, hastening forth

2:202 (198)	God is swift at the reckoning
3:19 (17)	whoso disbelieves in God's signs, God is swift at the reckoning
3:199 (199)	their wage is with their Lord; God is swift at the reckoning
5:4 (6)	fear God; God is swift at the reckoning
6:62 (62)	His is the judgment; He is the swiftest of reckoners
6:165 (165)	surely thy Lord is swift in retribution
7:167 (166)	surely thy Lord is swift in retribution
10:21 (22)	say: 'God is swifter at devising'
13:41 (41)	none repels His judgment; He is swift at the reckoning
14:51 (51)	God may recompense every soul for its earnings; surely God is swift at the reckoning
24:39 (39)	and God is swift at the reckoning
40:17 (17)	surely God is swift at the reckoning
50:44 (43)	upon the day when the earth is split asunder from about them as they hasten forth
70:43 (43)	the day they shall come forth from the tombs hastily

SĀRAᶜA vb. (III)~to vie with one another; to hasten

b) impf. act. (*yusāriᶜu*)

3:114 (110)	vying one with the other in good works; those are of the righteous
3:176 (170)	let them not grieve thee that vie with one another in unbelief
5:41 (45)	let them not grieve thee that vie with one another in unbelief
5:52 (57)	thou seest those in whose hearts is sickness vying with one another to come to them
5:62 (67)	thou seest many of them vying in sin and enmity
21:90 (90)	truly they vied with one another, hastening to good works
23:56 (58)	we vie in good works for them? Nay
23:61 (63)	those vie in good works, outracing to them

c) impv. (*sāriᶜ*)

3:133 (127)	vie with one another, hastening to forgiveness

*S R B

SARIBA vb. (I)~(pcple. act.) one who sallies; one who is visible; one who goes about carelessly

g) pcple. act. (*sārib*)

13:10 (11) he who hides himself in the night, and he who sallies by day

SARAB n.m.~a burrow; tunnel, conduit; (adv) burrowing

18:61 (60) they forgot their fish, and it took its way into the sea, burrowing

SARĀB n.m.~mirage; phantom; vapour

24:39 (39) their works are as a mirage in a spacious plain
78:20 (20) the mountains are set in motion, and become a vapour

*S R B L

SARĀBĪL n.m. (pl. of *sirbāl*)~a shirt, a garment

14:50 (51) of pitch their shirts, their faces enveloped by the Fire
16:81 (83) He has appointed for you shirts to protect you from the heat
16:81 (83) and shirts to protect you from your own violence

*S R D

SARD n.m.~links

34:11 (10) fashion wide coats of mail, and measure well the links

*S R D Q

SURĀDIQ n.m.~large tent, pavilion

18:29 (28) We have prepared for the evildoers a fire, whose pavilion encompasses them

*S R F

ASRAFA vb. (IV)~to exceed all bounds, to be extravagant; to waste; to be prodigal. (n.vb.) the act of exceeding, of being wasteful; being prodigal. (pcple. act.) prodigal; one who is excessive

a) perf. act.

20:127 (127) We recompense him who is prodigal and believes not in the signs
39:53 (54) O my people who have been prodigal against yourselves, do not despair

b) impf. act. (*yusrifu*)

6:141 (142) and be not prodigal; God loves not the prodigal

7:31 (29) and eat and drink, but be you not prodigal
17:33 (35) let him not exceed in slaying; he shall be helped
25:67 (67) who, when they expend, are neither prodigal nor parsimonious

f) n.vb. (*isrāf*)

3:147 (141) forgive us our sins, and that we exceeded in our affair
4:6 (5) deliver to them their property; consume it not wastefully and hastily

g) pcple. act. (*musrif*)

5:32 (36) many of them thereafter commit excesses in the earth
6:141 (142) and be not prodigal; God loves not the prodigal
7:31 (29) be you not prodigal; He loves not the prodigal
7:81 (79) instead of women; no, you are a people that do exceed
10:12 (13) so decked out fair to the prodigal is that they have been doing
10:83 (83) Pharaoh was high in the land, and he was one of the prodigals
21:9 (9) We delivered them, and whomsoever We would; and We destroyed the prodigal
26:151 (151) obey not the commandment of the prodigal
36:19 (18) your augury is with you; if you are reminded? But you are a prodigal people
40:28 (29) God guides not him who is prodigal and a liar
40:34 (36) even so God leads astray the prodigal and the doubter
40:43 (46) and that the prodigal are the inhabitants of the Fire
43:5 (4) shall We turn away the Remembrance from you, for that you are a prodigal people?
44:31 (30) surely he was a high one, of the prodigals
51:34 (34) marked with thy Lord for the prodigal

*S R Ḥ

SARAḤA vb. (I)~to graze freely, to drive (cattle) forth to pasture. (n.vb.) release, setting free

b) impf. act. (*yasraḥu*)

16:6 (6) when you bring them home to rest and when you drive them forth abroad to pasture

f) n.vb. (*sarāḥ*)

33:28 (28) I will make you provision, and set you free <with kindliness>
33:49 (48) so make provision for them, and set them free <with kindliness>

SARRAḤA vb. (II)~to set free, to release. (n.vb.) setting free, release

b) impf. act. (*yusarriḥu*)

33:28 (28) I will make you provision, and set you free with kindliness

c) impv. (*sarriḥ*)

2:231 (231) then retain them honourably or set them free honourably
33:49 (48) make provision for them, and set them free with kindliness

f) n.vb. (*tasrīḥ*)

2:229 (229) divorce is twice; then honourable retention or setting free kindly

*S R J

SIRĀJ n.m.~a lamp

25:61 (62)	and has set among them a lamp, and an illuminating moon
33:46 (45)	calling unto God by His leave, and as a light-giving lamp
71:16 (15)	and set the moon therein for a light and the sun for a lamp
78:13 (13)	and We appointed a blazing lamp

*S R M D

SARMAD n.m.~endless duration; (adj) unceasing, endless

28:71 (71)	what think you? If God should make the night unceasing over you
28:72 (72)	what think you? If God should make the day unceasing over you

*S R Q

SARAQA vb. (I)~to steal, to rob, to be a thief. (pcple. act.) a thief, a robber

a) perf. act.

12:77 (77)	a brother of his was a thief before
12:81 (81)	Father, thy son stole

b) impf. act. (*yasriqu*)

12:77 (77)	if he is a thief a brother of his (was a thief) before
60:12 (12)	they will not associate with God anything, and will not steal

g) pcple. act. (*sāriq*)

5:38 (42)	and the thief, male and (female): cut off the hands of both
5:38 (42)	and the thief (male) and female: cut off the hands of both
12:70 (70)	ho, cameleers, you are robbers
12:73 (73)	we are not robbers

ISTARAQA vb. (VIII)~to steal; (*istaraqa al-sama*ᶜ) to eavesdrop, to listen by stealth

a) perf. act.

15:18 (18)	excepting such as listens by stealth

*S R R

SARRA vb. (I)~to make happy, to gladden. (n.vb.) joy, happiness, gladness. (pcple. pass.) joyful, gladdened; (adv) joyfully

b) impf. act. (*yasurru*)

2:69 (64)	she shall be a golden cow, bright her colour, gladdening the beholders

f) n.vb. (*surūr*)

76:11 (11) — and has procured them radiancy and gladness

h) pcple. pass. (*masrūr*)

84:9 (9) — and he will return to his family joyfully
84:13 (13) — he once lived among his family joyfully

SARĀ'IR n.f. (pl. of *sarīrah*)~secret; secret thoughts

86:9 (9) — upon the day when the secrets are tried

SARRĀ' n.m.~happiness; prosperity

3:134 (128) — who expend in prosperity and adversity in almsgiving
7:95 (93) — hardship and happiness visited our fathers

SIRR n.m.~secret; secret thought; (adv) secretly

2:235 (235) — do not make troth with them secretly without you speak honourable words
2:274 (275) — those who expend their wealth night and day, secretly and in public
6:3 (3) — He knows your secrets, and what you publish
9:78 (79) — did they not know that God knows their secret
13:22 (22) — and expend of that We have provided them, secretly and in public
14:31 (36) — and expend of that We have provided them, secretly and in public
16:75 (77) — and he expends of it secretly and openly
20:7 (6) — surely He knows the secret and that yet more hidden
25:6 (7) — He sent it down, who knows the secret in the heavens and earth
35:29 (26) — and expend of that We have provided them, secretly and in public
43:80 (80) — do they think We hear not their secret

SURUR n.m. (pl. of *sarīr*)~couch, bed

15:47 (47) — as brothers they shall be upon couches set face to face
37:44 (43) — upon couches, set face to face
43:34 (33) — and doors to their houses, and couches whereon to recline
52:20 (20) — reclining upon couches ranged in rows
56:15 (15) — upon close-wrought couches
88:13 (13) — therein uplifted couches

ASARRA vb. (IV)~to keep secret, to secrete, to hide, to conceal; to speak or commune secretly; to confide; to whisper. (n.vb.) secret; (adv) secretly

a) perf. act.

5:52 (57) — then they will find themselves, for that they kept secret within them, remorseful
10:54 (55) — they will be secretly remorseful when they see the chastisement
12:19 (19) — they hid him as merchandise; but God knew what they were doing
12:77 (77) — but Joseph secreted it in his soul and disclosed it not to them
13:10 (11) — alike of you is he who conceals his saying
20:62 (65) — they disputed upon their plan between them, and communed secretly
21:3 (3) — the evildoers whisper one to another, Is this aught but a mortal
34:33 (32) — they will be secretly remorseful when they see the chastisement
66:3 (3) — when the Prophet confided to one of his wives a certain matter
71:9 (8) — then indeed I spoke publicly unto them, and I spoke unto them secretly

b) impf. act. (*yusirru*)

2:77 (72) — know they not that God knows what they keep secret

11:5 (6)	their garments He knows what they secrete and what they publish
16:19 (19)	God knows what you keep secret and what you publish
16:23 (24)	without a doubt God knows what they keep secret
36:76 (76)	We know what they keep secret and what they publish
60:1 (1)	if you go forth to struggle in My way and seek My good pleasure, secretly loving them
64:4 (4)	He knows what you conceal and what you publish

c) impv. (*asirra*)

67:13 (13)	be secret in your speech, or proclaim it

f) n.vb. (*isrār*)

47:26 (28)	and God knows their secrets
71:9 (8)	and I spoke unto them <secretly>

*S R Y

SARÁ vb. (I)~to travel by night; to journey, to set out

b) impf. act. (*yasrī*)

89:4 (3)	by the night when it journeys on

SARĪY n.m.~a little creek, a brook, a rivulet

19:24 (24)	see, thy Lord has set below thee a rivulet

ASRÁ vb. (IV)~to travel by night, to set forth by night; (with prep. *bi-*) to make someone travel by night

a) perf. act.

17:1 (1)	glory be to Him, who carried His servant by night

c) impv. (*asri*)

11:81 (83)	so set forth, thou with thy family, in a watch of the night
15:65 (65)	so set forth, thou with thy family, in a watch of the night
20:77 (79)	go with My servants by night
26:52 (52)	go with My servants by night
44:23 (22)	then set thou forth with My servants in a watch of the night

*S T R

SATARA vb. (I)~(pcple. pass.) spread over as a veil; obstructing (vision)

h) pcple. pass. (*mastūr*)

17:45 (47)	We place between thee, and those who do not believe in the world to come, a curtain

SITR n.m.~a veil

18:90 (89)	he found it rising upon a people for whom We had not appointed any veil

ISTATARA vb. (VIII)~to cover oneself

b) impf. act. (*yastatiru*)

41:22 (21) not so did you cover yourselves, that your hearing, your eyes

*S T T

SITTAH n.num.~six

7:54 (52) your Lord is God, who created the heavens and the earth in six days
10:3 (3) your Lord is God, who created the heavens and the earth in six days
11:7 (9) it is He who created the heavens and the earth in six days
25:59 (60) who created the heavens and the earth, and what between them is, in six days
32:4 (3) God is He that created the heavens and the earth, and what between them is, in six days
50:38 (37) We created the heavens and the earth, and what between them is, in six days
57:4 (4) it is He that created the heavens and the earth in six days

SITTŪN n.num.~sixty

58:4 (5) then let him feed sixty poor persons

*S Ṭ Ḥ

SAṬAḤA vb. (I)~to stretch out, to spread out

d) perf. pass. (*suṭiḥa*)

88:20 (20) how the earth was outstretched

*S Ṭ R

SAṬARA vb. (I)~to write; to inscribe. (pcple. pass.) written; inscribed

b) impf. act. (*yasṭuru*)

68:1 (1) by the Pen, and what they inscribe

h) pcple. pass. (*masṭūr*)

17:58 (60) a terrible chastisement; that is in the Book inscribed
33:6 (6) you should act towards your friends honourably; that stands inscribed
52:2 (2) and a Book inscribed

ASĀṬĪR n.f. (pl. of *usṭūrah*)~fairy-tale, fable, legend

6:25 (25) this is naught but the fairy-tales of the ancient ones
8:31 (31) this is naught but the fairy-tales of the ancients
16:24 (26) what has your Lord sent down? They say, 'Fairy-tales of the ancients'
23:83 (85) this is naught but the fairy-tales of the ancients

25:5 (6) fairy-tales of the ancients that he has had written down
27:68 (70) this is naught but the fairy-tales of the ancients
46:17 (16) this is naught but the fairy-tales of the ancients
68:15 (15) when Our signs are recited to him, he says, 'Fairy-tales of the ancients!'
83:13 (13) when our signs are recited to him, he says, 'Fairy-tales of the ancients!'

ISTAṬARA vb. (VIII)~(pcple. pass.) inscribed, written

h) pcple. pass. (*mustaṭar*)

54:53 (53) everything, great and small, is inscribed

*S Ṭ W

SAṬĀ vb. (I)~to rush upon, to assail, to attack

b) impf. act. (*yasṭū*)

22:72 (71) wellnigh they rush upon those who recite to them Our signs

*S W ʾ

SĀʾA vb. (I)~to be or become evil, wicked or bad; how evil, how wicked; to grieve, to sadden, to vex, to discountenance, to trouble. (n.vb.) evil, wickedness

a) perf. act.

4:22 (26) surely that is indecent and hateful, an evil way
4:38 (42) whosoever has Satan for a comrade, an evil comrade is he
4:97 (99) their refuge shall be Gehenna — an evil homecoming
4:115 (115) We shall roast him in Gehenna — an evil homecoming
5:66 (70) but many of them — evil are the things they do
6:31 (31) on their backs they shall be bearing their loads; O how evil the loads they bear
6:136 (137) what is for God reaches their associates. Evil is their judgment
7:177 (176) an evil likeness is the likeness of the people who cried lies to Our signs
9:9 (9) truly evil is that they have been doing
16:25 (27) O evil the load they bear
16:59 (61) ah, evil is that they judge
17:32 (34) approach not fornication; surely it is an indecency, and evil as a way
18:29 (28) how evil a potion, and how evil a resting-place
20:101 (101) how evil upon the Day of Resurrection that burden for them
25:66 (66) evil it is as a lodging-place and an abode'
26:173 (173) and evil is the rain of them that are warned
27:58 (59) and evil indeed is the rain of them that are warned
29:4 (3) they will outstrip Us? Ill they judge
37:177 (177) how evil will be the morning of them that are warned
45:21 (20) how ill they judge
48:6 (6) and has prepared for them Gehenna — an evil homecoming
58:15 (16) evil are the things they have been doing
63:2 (2) evil are the things they have been doing

b) impf. act. (*yasū'*)

3:120 (116) — if you are visited by good fortune, it vexes them
5:101 (101) — question not concerning things which, if they were revealed to you, would vex you
9:50 (50) — if good fortune befalls thee, it vexes them
17:7 (7) — We sent against you Our servants to discountenance you

d) perf. pass. (*sī'a*)

11:77 (79) — he was troubled on their account and distressed for them
29:33 (32) — he was troubled on their account and distressed for them
67:27 (27) — when they see it nigh at hand, the faces of the unbelievers will be vexed

f) n.vb. (*saw'*)

9:98 (99) — theirs shall be the evil turn
16:60 (62) — those who believe not in the world to come, theirs is the evil likeness
19:28 (29) — Sister of Aaron, thy father was not a wicked man
21:74 (74) — they were an evil people, truly ungodly
21:77 (77) — they were an evil people, so We drowned them all together
25:40 (42) — they have come by the city that was rained on by an evil rain
48:6 (6) — men and women alike, and those who think evil thoughts of God
48:6 (6) — against them shall be the evil turn of fortune
48:12 (12) — you thought evil thoughts, and you were a people corrupt

SAW'AH n.f.~shame, disgrace, vileness; (adj) shameful, disgraceful, vile

5:31 (34) — to show him how he might conceal the vile body of his brother
5:31 (34) — am I unable to be as this raven, and so conceal my brother's vile body?
7:20 (19) — Satan whispered to them, to reveal to them that which was hidden from them of their shameful parts
7:22 (21) — and when they tasted the tree, their shameful parts revealed to them
7:26 (25) — We have sent down on you a garment to cover your shameful parts
7:27 (26) — stripping them of their garments to show them their shameful parts
20:121 (119) — so the two of them ate of it, and their shameful parts revealed to them

SAYYI' n.m.~(adj.; comp. *aswa'*) bad, evil, wicked; (n) wickedness

4:85 (87) — whosoever intercedes with a bad intercession, he shall receive the like of it
9:102 (103) — they have mixed a righteous deed with another evil
17:38 (40) — the wickedness of it is hateful in the sight of thy Lord
35:43 (41) — waxing proud in the land, and devising evil
35:43 (41) — but evil devising encompasses only those who do it
39:35 (36) — that God may acquit them of the worst of what they did
41:27 (27) — and shall recompense them with the worst of what they were working

SAYYI'AH n.f.~evil, evil deed, sin

2:81 (75) — whoso earns evil, and is encompassed by his transgression
2:271 (273) — that is better for you, and will acquit you of your evil deeds
3:120 (116) — if you are smitten by evil, they rejoice at it
3:193 (191) — forgive Thou us our sins and acquit us of our evil deeds
3:195 (194) — them I shall surely acquit of their evil deeds
4:18 (22) — God shall not turn towards those who do evil deeds
4:31 (35) — We will acquit you of your evil deeds
4:78 (80) — but if an evil thing visits them, they say
4:79 (81) — whatever evil visits thee is of thyself
5:12 (15) — I will acquit you of your evil deeds
5:65 (70) — We would have acquitted them of their evil deeds

6:160 (161)	whoso brings an evil deed shall only be recompensed the like of it
7:95 (93)	then We gave them in the place of evil good
7:131 (128)	if any evil smote them, they would augur ill by Moses
7:153 (152)	those who do evil deeds, then repent thereafter and believe
7:168 (167)	and We tried them with good things and evil
8:29 (29)	He will assign you a salvation, and acquit you of your evil deeds
10:27 (28)	and for those who have earned evil deeds
10:27 (28)	the recompense of an evil deed shall be the like of it
11:10 (13)	the evils have gone from me
11:78 (80)	erstwhile they had been doing evil deeds
11:114 (116)	surely the good deeds will drive away the evil deeds
13:6 (7)	they would have thee hasten the evil ere the good
13:22 (22)	who avert evil with good — theirs shall be the Ultimate Abode
16:34 (36)	so the evil things that they wrought smote them
16:45 (47)	do they feel secure, those who devise evil things
23:96 (98)	repel thou the evil with that which is fairer
25:70 (70)	those, God will change their evil deeds into good deeds
27:46 (47)	O my people, why do you seek to hasten evil before good?
27:90 (92)	whosoever comes with an evil deed, their faces shall be thrust into the Fire
28:54 (54)	for that they patiently endured, and avert evil with good
28:84 (84)	whoso brings an evil deed
28:84 (84)	those who have done evil deeds shall only be recompensed for that they were doing
29:4 (3)	do they reckon, those who do evil deeds, that they will outstrip Us?
29:7 (6)	We shall surely acquit them of their evil deeds
30:36 (35)	if some evil befalls them for that their own hands have forwarded
35:10 (11)	those who devise evil deeds — theirs shall be a terrible chastisement
39:48 (49)	there would appear to them the evils of that they have earned
39:51 (52)	in that the evils of that they earned smote them
39:51 (52)	they too shall be smitten by the evils of that they earned
40:9 (9)	and guard them against evil deeds
40:9 (9)	whomsoever Thou guardest against evil deeds on that day
40:40 (43)	whosoever does an evil deed shall be recompensed only with the like of it
40:45 (48)	so God guarded him against the evil things of their devising
41:34 (34)	not equal are the good deed and the evil deed
42:25 (24)	it is He who accepts repentance from His servants, and pardons evil deeds
42:40 (38)	and the recompense of evil is (evil)the like of it
42:40 (38)	and the recompense of (evil) is evil the like of it
42:48 (47)	if some evil befalls him for that his own hands have forwarded
45:21 (20)	do those who commit evil deeds think that We shall make them as those who believe
45:33 (32)	the evil deeds that they have done shall appear to them
46:16 (15)	and We shall pass over their evil deeds
47:2 (2)	He will acquit them of their evil deeds
48:5 (5)	to dwell forever, and acquit them of their evil deeds
64:9 (9)	God will acquit him of his evil deeds
65:5 (5)	whosoever fears God, He will acquit him of his evil deeds
66:8 (8)	it may be that your Lord will acquit you of your evil deeds

SŪʾ n.m.~evil, iniquity, malice

2:49 (46)	We delivered you from the folk of Pharaoh who were visiting you with evil chastisement
2:169 (164)	He only commands you to evil and indecency
3:30 (28)	what it has done of good brought forward, and what it has done of evil
3:174 (168)	they returned with blessing and bounty from God, untouched by evil

4:17 (21)	God shall turn only towards those who do evil in ignorance
4:110 (110)	whosoever does evil, or wrongs himself, and then prays God's forgiveness
4:123 (122)	whosoever does evil shall be recompensed for it
4:148 (147)	God likes not the shouting of evil words unless a man has been wronged
4:149 (148)	if you do good openly or in secret or pardon an evil
6:54 (54)	whosoever of you does evil in ignorance, and thereafter repents
6:157 (158)	We shall surely recompense those who turn away from Our signs with an evil chastisement
7:73 (71)	do not touch her with evil, lest you be seized by a painful chastisement
7:141 (137)	the folk of Pharaoh who were visiting you with evil chastisement
7:165 (165)	We seized the evildoers with evil chastisement for their ungodliness
7:167 (166)	those who should visit them with evil chastisement
7:188 (188)	I would have acquired much good, and evil would not have touched me
9:37 (37)	decked out fair to them are their evil deeds
11:54 (57)	we say nothing, but that one of our gods has smitten thee with some evil
11:64 (67)	touch her not with evil, lest you be seized by a nigh chastisement
12:24 (24)	so was it, that We might turn away from him evil
12:25 (25)	what is the recompense of him who purposes evil against thy folk
12:51 (51)	we know no evil against him
12:53 (53)	surely the soul of man incites to evil
13:11 (12)	whensoever God desires evil for a people, there is no turning it back
13:18 (18)	theirs shall be the evil reckoning
13:21 (21)	and fear their Lord, and dread the evil reckoning
13:25 (25)	theirs shall be the curse, and theirs the Evil Abode
14:6 (6)	when He delivered you from the folk of Pharaoh, who were visiting you with evil chastisement
16:27 (29)	degradation today and evil are on the unbelievers
16:28 (30)	we were doing nothing evil
16:59 (61)	he hides him from the people because of the evil of the good tidings
16:94 (96)	it has stood firm, and you should taste evil
16:119 (120)	unto those who did evil in ignorance, then repented
20:22 (23)	now clasp thy hand to thy arm-pit; it shall come forth white, without evil
26:156 (156)	and do not touch her with malice
27:5 (5)	those are they whom an evil chastisement awaits
27:11 (11)	then, after evil, has changed into good
27:12 (12)	thrust thy hand in thy bosom and it will come forth white without evil
27:62 (63)	when he calls unto Him, and removes the evil
28:32 (32)	insert thy hand into thy bosom, and it will come forth white without evil
33:17 (17)	who is he that shall defend you from God, if He desires evil for you
35:8 (9)	what of him, the evil of whose deeds has been decked out fair to him
39:24 (25)	is he who guards himself with his face against the evil of the chastisement
39:47 (48)	they would offer it to ransom themselves from the evil of the chastisement
39:61 (62)	evil shall not visit them, neither shall they sorrow
40:37 (40)	so the evil of his deeds was decked out fair to Pharaoh
40:45 (48)	and there encompassed the folk of Pharaoh the evil chastisement
40:52 (55)	theirs shall be the curse, and theirs the evil abode
47:14 (15)	like unto such a one unto whom his evil deeds have been decked out fair
60:2 (2)	and stretch against you their hands and their tongues, to do you evil

SŪ'Á n.f.~evil

30:10 (9)	then the end of those that did evil was evil

ASĀ'A vb. (IV)~to do evil. (pcple. act.) wrongdoer

a) perf. act.

17:7 (7)	it is your own souls you do good to, and if you do evil it is to them likewise
30:10 (9)	then the end of those that did evil was evil
41:46 (46)	whoso does evil, it is to his own loss
45:15 (14)	whoso does evil, it is to his own loss
53:31 (32)	that He may recompense those who do evil for what they have done

g) pcple. act. (*musīʾ*)

40:58 (60)	not equal are ... those who believe and do deeds of righteousness, and the wrongdoer

*S W ʿ

SĀʿAH n.f.~hour; the Hour; time

6:31 (31)	so that when the Hour comes to them suddenly they shall say
6:40 (40)	what think you? If God's chastisement comes upon you, or the Hour comes upon you
7:34 (32)	when their term comes they shall not put it back by a single hour
7:187 (186)	they will question thee concerning the Hour, when it shall berth
9:117 (118)	the Helpers who followed him in the hour of difficulty
10:45 (46)	the day He shall muster them, as if they had not tarried but an hour of the day
10:49 (50)	when their term comes they shall not put it back by a single hour
12:107 (107)	or that the Hour shall not come upon them suddenly
15:85 (85)	the Hour is coming; so pardon thou, with a gracious pardoning
16:61 (63)	when their term is come they shall not put it back by a single hour
16:77 (79)	the matter of the Hour is as a twinkling of the eye, or nearer
18:21 (20)	promise is true, and that the Hour — there is no doubt of it
18:36 (34)	I do not think that the Hour is coming
19:75 (77)	when they see that they were threatened, whether the chastisement, or the Hour
20:15 (15)	the Hour is coming; I would conceal it
21:49 (50)	such as fear their Lord in the Unseen, trembling because of the Hour
22:1 (1)	surely the earthquake of the Hour is a mighty thing
22:7 (7)	because the Hour is coming, no doubt of it
22:55 (54)	the unbelievers will not cease to be in doubt of it, until the Hour comes on them suddenly
25:11 (12)	nay, but they cry lies to the Hour
25:11 (12)	and We have prepared for him who cries lies to the Hour a Blaze
30:12 (11)	upon the day when the Hour is come, the sinners shall be confounded
30:14 (13)	upon the day when the Hour is come, that day they shall be divided
30:55 (54)	upon the day when the Hour is come, the sinners shall swear
30:55 (55)	they have not tarried above an hour; so they were perverted
31:34 (34)	surely God — He has knowledge of the Hour
33:63 (63)	the people will question thee concerning the Hour
33:63 (63)	haply the Hour is nigh
34:3 (3)	the Hour will never come to us
34:30 (29)	you have the tryst of a day that you shall not put back by a single hour
40:46 (49)	and on the day when the Hour is come: 'Admit the folk of Pharaoh'
40:59 (61)	the Hour is coming, no doubt of it
41:47 (47)	to Him is referred the knowledge of the Hour
41:50 (50)	this is mine; I think not the Hour is coming
42:17 (16)	what shall make thee know? Haply the Hour is nigh

42:18 (17)	those who are in doubt concerning the Hour are indeed in far error
43:61 (61)	it is knowledge of the Hour; doubt not concerning it
43:66 (66)	are they looking for aught but the Hour
43:85 (85)	with Him is the knowledge of the Hour
45:27 (26)	on the day when the Hour is come, upon that day the vain-doers shall lose
45:32 (31)	God's promise is true, and the Hour, there is no doubt of it
45:32 (31)	we know not what the Hour may be
46:35 (35)	they had not tarried but for an hour of a single day
47:18 (20)	are they looking for aught but the Hour
54:1 (1)	the Hour has drawn nigh: the moon is split
54:46 (46)	nay, but the Hour is their tryst
54:46 (46)	and the Hour is very calamitous and bitter
79:42 (42)	they will question thee concerning the Hour, when it shall berth

SUWĀʿ n.prop.~Suwaʿ (a pagan deity)

71:23 (22)	do not leave your gods, and do not leave Wadd, nor Suwa'

*S W D

ASWAD n.m. (adj.; pl. *sūd*)~black

2:187 (183)	until the white thread shows clearly to you from the black thread
35:27 (25)	streaks white and red, of diverse hues, and pitchy black

SAYYID n.m. (pl. *sādah*)~chief, master, lord

3:39 (34)	John, who shall confirm a Word of God, a chief
12:25 (25)	they encountered her master by the door
33:67 (67)	we obeyed our chiefs and great ones, and they led us astray

ISWADDA vb. (IX)~to become black, to be blackened. (pcple. act.) blackened, darkened

a) perf. act.

3:106 (102)	as for those whose faces are blackened

b) impf. act. (*yaswaddu*)

3:106 (102)	the day when some faces are blackened, and some faces whitened

g) pcple. act. (*muswadd*)

16:58 (60)	his face is darkened and he chokes inwardly
39:60 (61)	thou shalt see those who lied against God, their faces blackened
43:17 (16)	his face is darkened, and he chokes inwardly

*S W GH

SĀGHA vb. (I)~(pcple. act.) easy to swallow; tasty, delicious; sweet

g) pcple. act. (*sāʾigh*)

16:66 (68)	between filth and blood, pure milk, sweet to drinkers
35:12 (13)	this is sweet, grateful to taste, delicious to drink

ASĀGHA vb. (IV)~to swallow easily

b) impf. act. (*yusīghu*)

14:17 (20) the which he gulps, and can scarce swallow

*S W Ḥ

SĀḤAH n.f.~courtyard

37:177 (177) when it lights in their courtyard, how evil will be the morning

*S W L

SAWWALA vb. (II)~(with prep. *la-*) to prompt, to tempt, to entice, to seduce

a) perf. act.

12:18 (18) your spirits tempted you to do somewhat
12:83 (83) your spirits tempted you to do somewhat
20:96 (96) I seized a handful of dust from the messenger's track, and cast it into the thing. So my soul prompted me
47:25 (27) Satan it was that tempted them, and God respited them

*S W M

SĀMA vb. (I)~to afflict, to impose, to visit someone with (a calamity)

b) impf. act. (*yasūmu*)

2:49 (46) the folk of Pharaoh who were visiting you with evil chastisement
7:141 (137) the folk of Pharaoh who were visiting you with evil chastisement
7:167 (166) those who should visit them with evil chastisement
14:6 (6) He delivered you from the folk of Pharaoh, who were visiting you with evil chastisement

SĪMĀ n.m.~mark, sign

2:273 (274) but thou shalt know them by their mark
7:46 (44) on the Ramparts are men knowing each by their mark
7:48 (46) the dwellers on the Battlements shall call to certain men they know by their sign
47:30 (32) then thou wouldst know them by their mark
48:29 (29) their mark is on their faces, the trace of prostration
55:41 (41) the sinners shall be known by their mark

SAWWAMA vb. (II)~(pcple. act.) swooping; sweeping on; making a terrific onslaught. (pcple. pass.) marked, distinguished

g) pcple. act. (*musawwim*)

3:125 (121) your Lord will reinforce you with five thousand swooping angels

h) pcple. pass. (*musawwam*)

3:14 (12)	heaped-up heaps of gold and silver, horses of mark
11:83 (84)	marked with thy Lord, and never far from the evildoers
51:34 (34)	marked with thy Lord for the prodigal

ASĀMA vb. (IV)~to let cattle graze freely; to pasture herds

b) impf. act. (*yusīmu*)

16:10 (10)	and of which trees, for you to pasture your herds

*S W Q

SĀQA vb. (I)~to drive, to herd, to urge on. (pcple. act.) driver

a) perf. act.

7:57 (55)	when they are charged with heavy clouds, We drive it to a dead land
35:9 (10)	then We drive it to a dead land and therewith revive the earth

b) impf. act. (*yasūqu*)

19:86 (89)	and drive the evildoers into Gehenna herding
32:27 (27)	have they not seen how We drive the water to the dry land

d) perf. pass. (*sīqa*)

39:71 (71)	then the unbelievers shall be driven in companies into Gehenna
39:73 (73)	those that feared their Lord shall be driven in companies into Paradise

e) impf. pass. (*yusāqu*)

8:6 (6)	as though they were being driven into death with their eyes wide open

g) pcple. act. (*sā'iq*)

50:21 (20)	every soul shall come, and with it a driver and a witness

ASWĀQ n.f. (pl. of *sūq*)~market(s)

25:7 (8)	what ails this Messenger that he eats food, and goes in the markets?
25:20 (22)	but that they ate food, and went in the markets

MASĀQ n.m.~driving, herding, urging on

75:30 (30)	upon that day unto thy Lord shall be the driving

SĀQ n.f. (pl. *sūq*)~leg; shank; stem, stalk (of a plant)

27:44 (44)	she supposed it was a spreading water, and she bared her legs
38:33 (32)	he began to stroke their shanks and necks
48:29 (29)	it grows stout and rises straight upon its stalk, pleasing the sowers
68:42 (42)	upon the day when the leg shall be bared, and they shall be summoned
75:29 (29)	and leg is intertwined with (leg)
75:29 (29)	and (leg) is intertwined with leg

*S W R

ASWIRAH n.f. (pl. *asāwir*)~a bracelet

18:31 (30)	therein they shall be adorned with bracelets of gold
22:23 (23)	therein they shall be adorned with bracelets of gold
35:33 (30)	therein they shall be adorned with bracelets of gold
43:53 (53)	why then have bracelets of gold not been cast on him
76:21 (21)	they are adorned with bracelets of silver

SŪR n.m.~a wall; enclosure, fence

57:13 (13)	a wall shall be set up between them, having a door in the inward

SŪRAH n.f. (pl. *suwar*)~a sura, a chapter of the Koran

2:23 (21)	then bring a sura like it, and call your witnesses
9:64 (65)	the hypocrites are afraid, lest a sura should be sent down against them
9:86 (87)	and when a sura is sent down, saying, 'Believe in God'
9:124 (125)	whenever a sura is sent down to thee, some of them say
9:127 (128)	whenever a sura is sent down, they look one at another
10:38 (39)	then produce a sura like it, and call on whom you can
11:13 (16)	then bring you ten suras the like of it, forged
24:1 (1)	a sura that We have sent down and appointed
47:20 (22)	those who believe say, 'Why has a sura not been sent down?'
47:20 (22)	when a clear sura is sent down, and therein fighting is mentioned

TASAWWARA vb. (V)~to climb over a wall, to scale a wall

a) perf. act.

38:21 (20)	has the tiding of the dispute come to thee? When they scaled the Sanctuary

*S W Ṭ

SAWṬ n.m.~a scourge, a whip

89:13 (12)	thy Lord unloosed on them a scourge of chastisement

*S W Y

SAWĀʾ n.m.~equal; alike; midst, depth; (adv) equally; right, straight; (*sawāʾ as-sabīl*) the right path

2:6 (5)	alike it is to them whether thou hast warned them or hast not warned them
2:108 (102)	strayed from the right way
3:64 (57)	come now to a word common between us and you
3:113 (109)	yet they are not all alike; some of the People
4:89 (91)	they wish that you should disbelieve as they disbelieve, and then you would be equal
5:12 (15)	surely he has gone astray from the right way
5:60 (65)	they are worse situated, and have gone further astray from the right way
5:77 (81)	and now again have gone astray from the right way

7:193 (192)	equal it is to you whether you call them, or whether you are silent
8:58 (60)	if thou fearest treachery any way at the hands of a people, dissolve it with them equally
13:10 (11)	alike of you is he who conceals his saying, and he who proclaims it
14:21 (25)	alike it is for us whether we cannot endure, or whether we are patient
16:71 (73)	to that their right hands possess, so that they may be equal therein
21:109 (109)	I have proclaimed to you all equally
22:25 (25)	the Holy Mosque that We have appointed equal unto men
26:136 (136)	alike it is to us, whether thou admonishest, or art not one of the admonishers
28:22 (21)	it may be that my Lord will guide me on the right way
30:28 (27)	so that you are equal in regard to it, you fearing them as you fear each other
36:10 (9)	alike it is to them whether thou hast warned them or thou hast not warned them
37:55 (53)	then he looks, and sees him in the midst of Hell
38:22 (21)	judge between us justly, and transgress not, and guide us to the right path
41:10 (9)	He ordained therein its diverse sustenance in four days, equal to those who ask
44:47 (47)	take him, and thrust him into the midst of Hell
45:21 (20)	equal their living and their dying
52:16 (16)	bear you patiently, or bear not patiently, equal it is to you
60:1 (1)	whosoever of you does that, has gone astray from the right way
63:6 (6)	equal it is for them, whether thou askest forgiveness for them or thou askest not forgiveness for them

SAWĪY n.m. (adj)~even, level; upright, without fault

19:10 (11)	thou shalt not speak to men, though being without fault, three nights
19:17 (17)	Our Spirit that presented himself to her a man without fault
19:43 (44)	follow me, and I will guide thee on a level path
20:135 (135)	you shall know who are the travellers on the even path
67:22 (22)	is he who walks prone upon his face better guided than he who walks upright

SUWÁ n.m. (adj)~mutually agreeable, convenient to both

20:58 (60)	appoint a tryst between us and thee, a place mutually agreeable

SAWWÁ vb. (II)~to level; to shape, to form; to make equal

a) perf. act.

2:29 (27)	He lifted Himself to heaven and levelled them seven heavens
15:29 (29)	when I have shaped him, and breathed My spirit in him
18:37 (35)	disbelievest thou in Him who created thee of dust, then of a sperm-drop, then shaped thee as a man?
32:9 (8)	then He shaped him, and breathed His spirit in him
38:72 (72)	when I have shaped him, and breathed My spirit in him
75:38 (38)	then he was a blood-clot, and He created and formed
79:28 (28)	He lifted up its vault, and levelled it
82:7 (7)	who created thee and shaped thee and wrought thee in symmetry
87:2 (2)	who created and shaped
91:7 (7)	by the soul, and That which shaped it
91:14 (14)	so their Lord crushed them for their sin, and levelled them

b) impf. act. (*yusawwī*)

26:98 (98)	when we made you equal with the Lord of all Being
75:4 (4)	yes indeed; We are able to shape again his fingers

e) impf. pass. (*yusawwá*)

4:42 (45) those who have disobeyed the Messenger, will wish that the earth might be levelled

SĀWÁ vb. (III)~to equalize; to make level

a) perf. act.

18:96 (95) when he had made all level between the two cliffs, he said

ISTAWÁ vb. (VIII)~to be equal, to be on the same level; (with prep. *ʿalá*) to sit down on, to mount; to sit firmly, to be seated; to settle on; to lift oneself up, to straighten up, to rise straight, to be poised

a) perf. act.

2:29 (27)	then He lifted Himself to heaven and levelled them seven heavens
7:54 (52)	then sat Himself upon the Throne
10:3 (3)	then sat Himself upon the Throne
11:44 (46)	accomplished, and the Ark settled on El-Judi
13:2 (2)	then He sat Himself upon the Throne
20:5 (4)	the All-merciful sat Himself upon the Throne
23:28 (29)	when thou art seated in the Ark and those with thee, say
25:59 (60)	then sat Himself upon the Throne
28:14 (13)	when he was fully grown and in the perfection of his strength, We gave him judgment
32:4 (3)	then seated Himself upon the Throne
41:11 (10)	He lifted Himself to heaven when it was smoke, and said to it
43:13 (12)	remember your Lord's blessing when you are seated on them
48:29 (29)	it grows stout and rises straight upon its stalk, pleasing the sowers
53:6 (6)	very strong; he stood poised
57:4 (4)	then seated Himself upon the Throne

b) impf. act. (*yastawī*)

4:95 (97)	are not the equals of those who struggle in the path of God
5:100 (100)	say: 'The corrupt and the good are not equal'
6:50 (50)	say: 'Are the blind and the seeing man equal?'
9:19 (19)	not equal are they in God's sight; and God guides not the people
11:24 (26)	the man blind and deaf, and the man who sees and hears; are they equal in likeness?
13:16 (17)	say: 'Are the blind and the seeing man equal'
13:16 (17)	or are the shadows and the light equal?
16:75 (77)	are they equal? Praise belongs to God
16:76 (78)	is he equal to him who bids to justice, and is on a straight path?
32:18 (18)	is he who has been a believer like unto him who has been ungodly? They are not equal
35:12 (13)	not equal are the two seas; this is sweet, grateful to taste
35:19 (20)	not equal are the blind and the seeing man
35:22 (21)	not equal are the living and the dead
39:9 (12)	are they equal — those who know and those who know not?
39:29 (30)	are the two equal in likeness? Praise belongs to God
40:58 (60)	not equal are the blind and the seeing man
41:34 (34)	not equal are the good deed and the evil deed
43:13 (12)	that you may be seated on their backs and then remember your Lord's blessing
57:10 (10)	not equal is he among you who spent, and who fought before the victory
59:20 (20)	not equal are the inhabitants of the Fire and the inhabitants of Paradise

*S Y B

SĀ'IBAH n.prop.~Sa'iba (a she-camel associated with paganism)

5:103 (102) God has not appointed cattle dedicated to idols, such as Bahira, Sa'iba

*S Y Ḥ

SĀḤA vb. (I)~to journey, to roam about. (pcple. act.) one who journeys; one who is inclined to fasting

c) impv. (*siḥ*)

9:2 (2) journey freely in the land for four months

g) pcple. act. (*sā'iḥ*)

9:112 (113) those who serve, those who pray, those who journey
66:5 (5) women who have surrendered, believing, obedient, penitent, devout, given to fasting

*S Y L

SĀLA vb. (I)~to flow

a) perf. act.

13:17 (18) He sends down out of heaven water, and the wadis flow each in its measure

SAYL n.m.~torrent; flood, inundation

13:17 (18) and the torrent carries a swelling scum
34:16 (15) they turned away; so We loosed on them the Flood of Arim

ASĀLA vb. (IV)~to cause to flow

a) perf. act.

34:12 (11) We made the Fount of Molten Brass to flow for him

*S Y N

SAYNĀ' n.prop.~Sinai, (*ṭūr saynā'*) Mount Sinai

23:20 (20) a tree issuing from the Mount of Sinai that bears oil and seasoning

SĪNĪN n.prop.~Sinai, (*ṭūr sīnīn*) Mount Sinai

95:2 (2) and the Mount Sinai

*S Y R

SĀRA vb. (I)~to journey, to travel; to move, to be in motion. (n.vb.) journeying, travel; motion

a) perf. act.

28:29 (29) when Moses had accomplished the term and departed with his household

b) impf. act. (*yasīru*)

12:109 (109) have they not journeyed in the land?
22:46 (45) have they not journeyed in the land so that they have hearts to understand with
30:9 (8) have they not journeyed in the land and beheld how was the end of those before them?
35:44 (43) have they not journeyed in the land and beheld how was the end of those before them?
40:21 (22) have they not journeyed in the land and beheld how was the end of those before them?
40:82 (82) have they not journeyed in the land and beheld how was the end of those before them?
47:10 (11) have they not journeyed in the land and beheld how was the end of those before them?
52:10 (10) and the mountains are in motion

c) impv. (*sir*)

3:137 (131) journey in the land, and behold how was the end of those that cried lies
6:11 (11) journey in the land, then behold how was the end of them that cried lies
16:36 (38) journey in the land, and behold how was the end of them that cried lies
27:69 (71) journey in the land, then behold how was the end of the sinners
29:20 (19) journey in the land, then behold how He originated creation
30:42 (41) journey in the land, then behold how was the end of those that were before
34:18 (17) journey among them by night and day in security

f) n.vb. (*sayr*)

34:18 (17) and well We measured the journey between them
52:10 (10) and [when] the mountains are in motion <...>

SAYYĀRAH n.f.~company of travellers; companions

5:96 (97) permitted to you is the game of the sea and the food of it, as a provision for you

12:10 (10) but cast him into the bottom of the pit and some traveller will pick him out
12:19 (19) then came travellers, and they sent one of them, a water-drawer

SĪRAH n.f.~state, condition; way of life

20:21 (22) We will restore it to its first state

SAYYARA vb. (II)~to set in motion, to set moving; to convey

b) impf. act. (*yusayyiru*)

10:22 (23) it is He who conveys you on the land and the sea
18:47 (45) and on the day We shall set the mountains in motion

d) perf. pass. (*suyyira*)

13:31 (30) if only a Koran whereby the mountains were set in motion
78:20 (20) and the mountains are set in motion, and become a vapour
81:3 (3) when the mountains shall be set moving

*S Y Ṭ R

SAYṬARA vb. (quad I)~(pcple. act.) ruler; overseer; registrar

g) pcple. act. (*muṣayṭir*)

52:37 (37)	or are they the registrars?
88:22 (22)	thou art not charged to oversee them

SHĪN

*SH ʾ M

MASHʾAMAH n.f.~the left (hand)

56:9 (9)	Companions of the Left
56:9 (9)	O Companions of the Left
90:19 (19)	they are the Companions of the Left Hand

*SH ʾ N

SHAʾN n.m.~matter, affair, business, occupation, labour

10:61 (62)	Thou art not upon any occupation, neither recitest thou any Koran of it
24:62 (62)	when they ask thy leave for some affair of their own
55:29 (29)	every day He is upon some labour
80:37 (37)	every man that day shall have business to suffice him

*SH ʿ B

SHUʿAB n.f. (pl. of *shuʿbah*)~a branch; prong; -fold, -massing

77:30 (30)	depart to a triple-massing shadow

SHUʿAYB n.prop.~Shuaib

7:85 (83)	and to Midian their brother Shuaib; he said
7:88 (86)	We will surely expel thee, O Shuaib, and those who believe with thee
7:90 (88)	if you follow Shuaib, assuredly in that case you will be losers
7:92 (90)	those who cried lies to Shuaib, as if never they dwelt there
7:92 (90)	those who cried lies to Shuaib, they were the losers
11:84 (85)	and to Midian their brother Shuaib; he said
11:87 (89)	Shuaib, does thy prayer command thee that we should leave that our fathers served
11:91 (93)	Shuaib, we do not understand much of what thou sayest
11:94 (97)	when Our command came, We delivered Shuaib and those who believed with him
26:177 (177)	when Shuaib said to them, 'Will you not be godfearing?'
29:36 (35)	and to Midian their brother Shuaib; he said

SHUʿŪB n.m. (pl. of *shaʿb*)~race; nation; people

49:13 (13)	We have created you male and female, and appointed you races and tribes

*SH ʿ L

ISHTAʿALA vb. (VIII)~to be lighted, to be aflame

a) perf. act.

19:4 (3)	and my head is all aflame with hoariness

*SH ʿ R

SHAʿARA vb. (I)~to be aware, to sense; to know

b) impf. act. (*yashʿuru*)

2:9 (8)	only themselves they deceive, and they are not aware
2:12 (11)	they are the workers of corruption but they are not aware
2:154 (149)	rather they are living, but you are not aware
3:69 (62)	yet none they make to stray, except themselves, but they are not aware
6:26 (26)	it is only themselves they destroy, but they are not aware
6:123 (123)	they devised only against themselves, and they were not aware
7:95 (93)	so We seized them suddenly, unawares
12:15 (15)	thou shalt tell them of this their doing when they are unaware
12:107 (107)	the Hour shall not come upon them suddenly when they are unaware
16:21 (21)	dead, not alive, and are not aware
16:26 (28)	the chastisement came upon them from whence they were not aware
16:45 (47)	the chastisement will not come upon them, from whence they are not aware
23:56 (58)	nay, but they are not aware
26:113 (113)	their account falls only upon my Lord, were you but aware
26:202 (202)	so that it will come upon them suddenly, while they are not aware
27:18 (18)	lest Solomon and his hosts crush you, being unaware
27:50 (51)	We likewise devised a device, while they were not aware
27:65 (66)	none knows the Unseen in the heavens and earth except God. And they are not aware
28:9 (8)	and they were not aware
28:11 (10)	she perceived him from afar, even while they were not aware
29:53 (53)	it shall come upon them suddenly, when they are not aware
39:25 (26)	the chastisement came upon them from whence they were not aware
39:55 (56)	ere the chastisement comes upon you suddenly while you are unaware
43:66 (66)	that it shall come upon them suddenly, when they are not aware
49:2 (2)	lest your works fail while you are not aware

ASHʿĀR n.m. (pl. of *shaʿr*)~hair

16:80 (82)	and of their hair furnishing and an enjoyment for a while

MASHʿAR n.m.~waymark, sacred monument

2:198 (194)	then remember God at the Holy Waymark

SHAʿĀʾIR n.f. (pl. of *shiʿārah*)~waymark, indication

2:158 (153)	Safa and Marwa are among the waymarks of God
5:2 (2)	O believers, profane not God's waymarks
22:32 (33)	whosoever venerates God's waymarks, that is of the godliness of the hearts
22:36 (37)	We have appointed them for you as among God's waymarks

SHĀʿIR n.m. (pl. *shuʿarāʾ*)~a poet

21:5 (5)	nay, he has forged it; nay, he is a poet
26:224 (224)	and the poets — the perverse follow them
37:36 (35)	what, shall we forsake our gods for a poet possessed?
52:30 (30)	he is a poet for whom we await Fate's uncertainty
69:41 (41)	it is not the speech of a poet

SHIʿR n.m.~poetry

36:69 (69)	We have not taught him poetry; it is not seemly for him

SHIʿRÁ n.prop.~Sirius, Dog Star

53:49 (50)	and that it is He who is the Lord of Sirius

ASHʿARA vb. (IV)~to make one realize; (with prep. *bi-*) to make known, to appraise

b) impf. act . (*yushʿiru*)

6:109 (109)	what will make you realize that, when it comes, they will not believe?
18:19 (18)	let him be courteous, and apprise no man of you

*SH B H

SHABBAHA vb. (II)~(with prep. *li-*) to show someone a likeness of another or of something; to cause to appear to someone

d) perf. pass. (*shubbiha*)

4:157 (156)	only a likeness of that was shown to them

TASHĀBAHA vb. (VI)~to be alike, to resemble one another; to be ambiguous. (pcple. act.) ambiguous; alike, in perfect semblance, consimilar

a) perf. act.

2:70 (65)	cows are much alike to us
2:118 (112)	their hearts are much alike
3:7 (5)	for those in whose hearts is swerving, they follow the ambiguous part
13:16 (17)	have they ascribed to God associates who created as He created, so that creation is all alike to them?

g) pcple. act. (*mutashābih*)

2:25 (23)	that they shall be given in perfect semblance
3:7 (5)	wherein are verses clear that are the Essence of the Book, and others ambiguous
6:99 (99)	olives, pomegranates, (like) each to each, and each unlike to each
6:141 (142)	olives, pomegranates, like each to each, and each (unlike) to each
6:141 (142)	olives, pomegranates, (like) each to each, and each unlike to each
39:23 (24)	a Book, consimilar in its oft-repeated

ISHTABAHA vb. (VIII)~(pcple. act.) alike

g) pcple. act. (*mushtabih*)

6:99 (99)	olives, pomegranates, like each to each

*SH D D

SHADDA vb. (I)~to strengthen, to confirm; to tie fast; (with prep. *ʿala*) to harden

a) perf. act.

38:20 (19)	We strengthened his kingdom, and gave him wisdom
76:28 (28)	We created them, and We strengthened their joints

b) impf. act. (*yashuddu*)

28:35 (35)	We will strengthen thy arm by means of thy brother

c) impv. (*shudda* and *ushdud*)

10:88 (88)	our Lord, obliterate their possessions, and harden their hearts
20:31 (32)	by him confirm my strength
47:4 (4)	tie fast the bonds

ASHUDD n.m.~physical maturity, coming of age; (*balagha ashuddahu*) to come of age, to be fully grown

6:152 (153)	approach not the property of the orphan, save in the fairer manner, until he is of age
12:22 (22)	when he was fully grown, We gave him judgment and knowledge
17:34 (36)	do not approach the property of the orphan save in the fairest manner, until he is of age
18:82 (81)	thy Lord desired that they should come of age
22:5 (5)	We deliver you as infants, then that you may come of age
28:14 (13)	when he was fully grown and in the perfection of his strength
40:67 (69)	He delivers you as infants, then that you may come of age
46:15 (14)	when he is fully grown, and reaches forty years, he says

SHADĪD n.m. (adj.; pl. *ashiddā'* and *shidād*)~terrible; strong, mighty, powerful, great; hard; (comp. adj. of *ashadd*) harder, etc.; (when followed by indefinite substantives) more — , very —

2:74 (69)	your hearts became hardened thereafter and are like stones, or even yet harder
2:85 (79)	on the Day of Resurrection to be returned unto the most terrible of chastisement
2:165 (160)	but those that believe love God more ardently
2:165 (160)	God is terrible in chastisement
2:191 (187)	persecution is more grievous than slaying
2:196 (192)	know that God is terrible in retribution
2:200 (196)	remember God, as you remember your fathers or yet more devoutly
2:211 (207)	whoso changes God's blessing after it has come to him, God is terrible in retribution
3:4 (3)	those who disbelieve in God's signs, for them awaits a terrible chastisement
3:11 (9)	because of their sins; God is terrible in retribution
3:56 (49)	as for the unbelievers, I will chastise them with a terrible chastisement
4:66 (69)	it would have been better for them, and stronger confirming them
4:77 (79)	fearing the people as they would fear God, or with a greater fear
4:84 (86)	God is stronger in might, more terrible
4:84 (86)	God is stronger in might, more terrible in punishing
5:2 (3)	fear God; surely God is terrible in retribution
5:82 (85)	thou wilt surely find the most hostile of men to the believers are the Jews
5:98 (98)	know God is terrible in retribution
6:124 (124)	humiliation in God's sight shall befall the sinners, and a terrible chastisement
7:164 (164)	a people God is about to destroy or to chastise with a terrible chastisement
8:13 (13)	surely God is terrible in retribution
8:25 (25)	know that God is terrible in retribution
8:48 (50)	God is terrible in retribution
8:52 (54)	God is strong, terrible in retribution
9:69 (70)	who were stronger than you in might, and more abundant in wealth and children
9:81 (82)	say: 'Gehenna's fire is hotter'
9:97 (98)	the Bedouins are more stubborn in unbelief and hypocrisy
10:70 (71)	then We shall let them taste the terrible chastisement
11:80 (82)	would that I had power against you, or might take refuge in a strong pillar
11:102 (104)	surely His seizing is painful, terrible
12:48 (48)	thereafter there shall come upon you seven hard years
13:6 (7)	thy Lord is terrible in retribution
13:13 (14)	yet they dispute about God, who is mighty in power

14:2 (2)	woe to the unbelievers for a terrible chastisement
14:7 (7)	My chastisement is surely terrible
17:5 (5)	We sent against you servants of Ours, men of great might
17:58 (60)	We shall chastise it with a terrible chastisement
18:2 (2)	to warn of great violence from Him, and to give good tidings
19:69 (70)	We shall pluck forth from every party whichever of them was the most hardened in disdain
20:71 (74)	you shall know of a certainty which of us is more terrible in chastisement
20:127 (127)	the chastisement of the world to come is more terrible
22:2 (2)	they are not drunk, but God's chastisement is terrible
23:77 (79)	when We open against them a door of terrible chastisement
27:21 (21)	I will chastise him with a terrible chastisement
27:33 (33)	we possess force and we possess great might
28:78 (78)	God had destroyed before him generations of men stronger than he
30:9 (8)	they were stronger than themselves in might
33:11 (11)	there it was that the believers were tried, and shaken most mightily
34:46 (45)	he is naught but a warner unto you, before a terrible chastisement
35:7 (7)	those who disbelieve — there awaits them a terrible chastisement
35:10 (11)	those who devise evil deeds — theirs shall be a terrible chastisement
35:44 (43)	they were stronger than themselves in might
37:11 (11)	are they stronger in constitution, or those We created?
38:26 (25)	there awaits them a terrible chastisement, for that they have forgotten
40:3 (2)	Forgiver of sins, Accepter of penitence, Terrible in retribution
40:21 (22)	they were stronger than themselves in might
40:22 (23)	surely He is All-strong, terrible in retribution
40:46 (49)	admit the folk of Pharaoh into the most terrible chastisement
40:82 (82)	they were stronger than themselves in might
41:15 (14)	who is stronger than we in might?
41:15 (14)	God, who created them, was stronger than they in might
41:27 (26)	We shall let the unbelievers taste a terrible chastisement
42:16 (15)	there awaits them a terrible chastisement
42:26 (25)	the unbelievers — for them awaits a terrible chastisement
43:8 (7)	We destroyed men stronger in valour than they
47:13 (14)	how many a city that was stronger in might than thy city
48:16 (16)	He will chastise you with a painful chastisement
48:29 (29)	those who are with him are hard against the unbelievers
50:26 (25)	cast him into the terrible chastisement
50:36 (35)	how many a generation We destroyed before them that was stronger in valour
53:5 (5)	taught him by one terrible in power
57:20 (19)	in the world to come there is a terrible chastisement
57:25 (25)	We sent down iron, wherein is great might, and many uses for men
58:15 (16)	God has made ready for them a chastisement terrible
59:4 (4)	whosoever makes a breach with God, God is terrible in retribution
59:7 (7)	fear God; surely God is terrible in retribution
59:13 (13)	you arouse greater fear in their hearts than God
59:14 (14)	their valour is great, among themselves
65:8 (8)	then We made with it a terrible reckoning
65:10 (10)	God prepared for them a terrible chastisement
66:6 (6)	and over which are harsh, terrible angels
72:8 (8)	we found it filled with terrible guards and meteors
73:6 (6)	surely the first part of the night is heavier in tread
78:12 (12)	We have built above you seven strong ones
79:27 (27)	what, are you stronger in constitution
85:12 (12)	surely thy Lord's assault is terrible
100:8 (8)	surely he is passionate in his love for good things

ISHTADDA vb. (VIII)~(with prep. *bi-*) to blow strong

a) perf. act.

14:18 (21)	their works are as ashes, whereon the wind blows strong

*SH F ᶜ

SHAFAᶜA vb. (I)~to intercede, to plead. (n.vb.) intercession, mediation. (pcple. act.) intercessor

b) impf. act. (*yashfaᶜu*)

2:255 (256)	who is there that shall intercede with Him save by His leave?
4:85 (87)	whoso intercedes with a good intercession shall receive a share of it
4:85 (87)	whosoever intercedes with a bad intercession, he shall receive the like of it
7:53 (51)	have we then any intercessors to intercede for us
21:28 (28)	and they intercede not

f) n.vb.f. (*shafāᶜah*)

2:48 (45)	no intercession shall be accepted from it, nor any counterpoise
2:123 (117)	nor any intercession shall be profitable to it
2:254 (255)	there comes a day wherein shall be neither traffick, nor friendship, nor intercession
4:85 (87)	whoso intercedes with a good intercession shall receive a share of it
4:85 (87)	whosoever intercedes with a bad intercession, he shall receive the like of it
19:87 (90)	having no power of intercession
20:109 (108)	upon that day the intercession will not profit
34:23 (22)	intercession will not avail with Him
36:23 (22)	shall I take, apart from Him, gods whose intercession
39:44 (45)	say: 'To God belongs intercession altogether'
43:86 (86)	those they call upon, apart from Him, have no power of intercession
53:26 (26)	how many an angel there is in the heavens whose intercession avails not anything
74:48 (49)	then the intercession of the intercessors shall not profit them

g) pcple. act. (*shāfiᶜ*)

26:100 (100)	so now we have no intercessors
74:48 (49)	then the intercession of the intercessors shall not profit them

SHAFᶜ n.m.~even number

89:3 (2)	by the even and the odd

SHAFĪᶜ n.m. (pl. *shufaᶜāʾ*)~intercessor, mediator

6:51 (51)	they have, apart from God, no protector and no intercessor
6:70 (69)	it has no protector and no intercessor
6:94 (94)	we do not see with you your intercessors
7:53 (51)	have we then any intercessors to intercede for us
10:3 (3)	intercessor there is none, save after His leave
10:18 (19)	these are our intercessors with God
30:13 (12)	no intercessors shall they have amongst their associates
32:4 (3)	apart from Him, you have no protector neither intercessor
39:43 (44)	or have they taken intercessors apart from God?
40:18 (19)	the evildoers have not one loyal friend, no intercessor to be heeded

*SH F H

SHAFAH n.f.~(du) lips

90:9 (9) — and a tongue, and two lips

*SH F Q

SHAFAQ n.m.~twilight

84:16 (16) — No! I swear by the twilight

ASHFAQA vb. (IV)~to be afraid, to be apprehensive. (pcple. act.) fearful, going in fear, apprehensive, one who trembles (in fear)

a) perf. act.

33:72 (72) — they refused to carry it and were afraid of it
58:13 (14) — are you afraid, before your conspiring, to advance freewill offerings?

g) pcple. act. (*mushfiq*)

18:49 (47) — thou wilt see the sinners fearful at what is in it
21:28 (29) — they tremble in awe of Him
21:49 (50) — such as fear their Lord in the Unseen, trembling because of the Hour
23:57 (59) — surely those who tremble in fear of their Lord
42:18 (17) — those who believe in it go in fear of it
42:22 (21) — thou seest the evildoers going in fear of that they have earned
52:26 (26) — we were before among our people, ever going in fear
70:27 (27) — and go in fear of the chastisement of their Lord

*SH F W

SHAFĀ n.m.~edge, brink

3:103 (99) — you were upon the brink of a pit of Fire
9:109 (110) — who founded his building upon the brink of a crumbling bank

*SH F Y

SHAFÁ vb. (I)~to heal, to cure. (n.vb.) healing, cure

b) impf. act. (*yashfī*)

9:14 (14) — and bring healing to the breasts of a people who believe
26:80 (80) — and, whenever I am sick, heals me

f) n.vb. (*shifā'*)

10:57 (58) — there has come to you an admonition from your Lord, and a healing for what is in the breasts
16:69 (71) — a drink of diverse hues wherein is healing for men

17:82 (84)	We send down, of the Koran, that which is a healing and a mercy
41:44 (44)	to the believers it is a guidance, and a healing

*SH GH F

SHAGHAFA vb. (I)~to infatuate, to smite the heart (with love)

a) perf. act.

12:30 (30)	he smote her heart with love

*SH GH L

SHAGHALA vb. (I)~to occupy, to busy. (n.vb.) occupancey, being busy; (*fī shughul*) busy

a) perf. act.

48:11 (11)	we were occupied by our possessions and our families

f) n.vb. (*shughul*)

36:55 (55)	the inhabitants of Paradise today are busy in their rejoicing

*SH H B

SHIHĀB n.m. (pl. *shuhub*)~flame, fire; meteor, shooting star

15:18 (18)	and he is pursued by a manifest flame
27:7 (7)	or I will bring you a flaming brand
37:10 (10)	and he is pursued by a piercing flame
72:8 (8)	found it filled with terrible guards and meteors
72:9 (9)	any listening now finds a meteor in wait for him

*SH H D

SHAHIDA vb. (I)~to witness; to be present; to bear witness, to testify. (n.vb.) testimony, witnessing; that which is visible. (pcple. act.) a witness; (adv) witnessing, standing before. (pcple. pass.) witnessed; memorable (day)

a) perf. act.

2:185 (181)	let those of you, who are present at the month, fast it
3:18 (16)	God bears witness that there is no god but He
3:86 (80)	after they believed, and bore witness that the Messenger is true
4:15 (19)	and if they witness, then detain them
6:130 (130)	they shall say, 'We bear witness against ourselves'
6:130 (130)	they bear witness against themselves that they were unbelievers
6:150 (151)	then if they testify, bear not witness with them

7:37 (35)	and they will bear witness against themselves
7:172 (171)	they said, 'Yes, we testify'
12:26 (26)	and a witness of her folk bore witness
12:81 (81)	we do not testify except that we know
27:49 (50)	we were not witnesses of the destruction of his family
41:20 (19)	their eyes and their skins bear witness against them
41:21 (20)	they will say to their skins, 'Why bore you witness against us?'
43:19 (18)	what, did they witness their creation?
43:86 (86)	such as have testified to the truth
46:10 (9)	a witness from among the Children of Israel bears witness to its like

b) impf. act. (*yash.hadu*)

2:84 (78)	then you confirmed it and yourselves bore witness
3:70 (63)	why do you disbelieve in God's signs, which you yourselves witness?
4:166 (164)	but God bears witness to that He has sent down to thee
4:166 (164)	and the angels also bear witness
6:19 (19)	do you indeed testify that there are other gods with God?
6:19 (19)	say: 'I do not testify'
6:150 (151)	produce your witnesses, those who testify God has forbidden this
6:150 (151)	then if they testify, bear not witness with them
9:107 (108)	God testifies they are truly liars
21:61 (62)	haply they shall bear witness
22:28 (29)	that they may witness things profitable to them
24:2 (2)	let a party of the believers witness their chastisement
24:8 (8)	if she testify by God four times that he is of the liars
24:24 (24)	their feet shall testify against them touching that they were doing
25:72 (72)	those who bear not false witness
27:32 (32)	I am not used to decide an affair until you bear me witness
36:65 (65)	their feet bear witness as to what they have been earning
41:22 (21)	your skins should not bear witness against you
59:11 (11)	God bears witness that they are truly liars
63:1 (1)	we bear witness that thou art indeed the Messenger of God
63:1 (1)	God bears witness that the hypocrites are truly liars
83:21 (21)	witnessed by those brought nigh

c) impv. (*ish.had*)

3:52 (45)	we believe in God; witness thou our submission
3:64 (57)	bear witness that we are Muslims
3:81 (75)	they said, 'We do agree.' God said, 'Bear witness so'
5:111 (111)	we believe; witness Thou our submission
11:54 (57)	and witness you, that I am quit of that you associate

f) n.vb. (*shahādah*)

2:140 (134)	who does greater evil than he who conceals a testimony received from God?
2:282 (282)	that is more equitable in God's sight, more upright for testimony
2:283 (283)	do not conceal the testimony
5:106 (105)	the testimony between you when any of you is visited by death
5:106 (105)	nor will we hide the testimony of God
5:107 (106)	they shall swear by God, Our testimony
5:107 (106)	is truer than their testimony
5:108 (107)	it is likelier that they will bear testimony in proper form
6:19 (19)	say: 'What thing is greatest in testimony?'
6:73 (73)	He is Knower of the Unseen and the visible
9:94 (95)	you will be returned to Him who knows the unseen and the visible

9:105 (106)	you will be returned to Him who knows the unseen and the visible
13:9 (10)	the Knower of the unseen and the visible
23:92 (94)	who has knowledge of the Unseen and the Visible
24:4 (4)	do not accept any testimony of theirs ever
24:6 (6)	the testimony of one of them shall be
24:6 (6)	to testify by God four times
24:8 (8)	if she testify by God four times
32:6 (5)	He is the knower of the Unseen and the Visible
39:46 (47)	who knowest the Unseen and the Visible
43:19 (18)	their witness shall be written down, and they shall be questioned
59:22 (22)	He is the knower of the Unseen and the Visible
62:8 (8)	then you shall be returned to the Knower of the Unseen and the Visible
64:18 (18)	Knower He of the Unseen and the Visible
65:2 (2)	perform the witnessing to God Himself
70:33 (33)	and perform their witnessings

g) pcple. act. (*shāhid*; pl. *shuhūd* and *shāhidūn*)

3:53 (46)	inscribe us therefore with those who bear witness
3:81 (75)	I shall be with you among the witnesses
5:83 (86)	so do Thou write us down among the witnesses
5:113 (113)	that we may be among its witnesses
9:17 (17)	worship, witnessing against themselves unbelief
10:61 (62)	without that We are witnesses over you when you press on it
11:17 (20)	a witness from Him recites it
11:18 (21)	the witnesses will say, 'Those are they who lied'
12:26 (26)	a witness of her folk bore witness
21:56 (57)	I am one of those that bear witness
21:78 (78)	We bore witness to their judgment
28:44 (44)	nor wast thou of those witnessing
33:45 (44)	We have sent thee as a witness, and good tidings to bear
37:150 (150)	or did We create the angels females, while they were witnesses?
40:51 (54)	upon the day when the witnesses arise
46:10 (9)	a witness from among the Children of Israel bears witness to its like
48:8 (8)	surely We have sent thee as a witness
73:15 (15)	surely We have sent unto you a Messenger as a witness over you
74:13 (13)	and sons standing before him
85:3 (3)	by the witness and the witnessed
85:7 (7)	and were themselves witnesses of what they did with the believers

h) pcple. pass. (*mash.hūd*)

11:103 (105)	that is a day mankind are to be gathered to, a day to witness
17:78 (80)	surely the recital of dawn is witnessed
85:3 (3)	by the witness and the witnessed

MASH.HAD n.m.~scene

19:37 (38)	woe to those who disbelieve for the scene of a dreadful day

SHAHĪD n.m. (pl. *shuhadā'*)~a witness; Witness (Divine attribute); martyr; one with a present mind, with full intelligence

2:23 (21)	call your witnesses, apart from God, if you are truthful
2:133 (127)	were you witnesses, when death came to Jacob?
2:143 (137)	that you might be witnesses to the people

2:143 (137)	and that the Messenger might be a witness to you
2:282 (282)	call in to witness two witnesses, men
2:282 (282)	then one man and two women, such witnesses as you approve of
2:282 (282)	let the witnesses not refuse, whenever they are summoned
2:282 (282)	let not either writer or witness be pressed
3:98 (93)	surely God is witness of the things you do
3:99 (94)	desiring to make it crooked, yourselves being witnesses
3:140 (134)	He may take witnesses from among you
4:33 (37)	give to them their share; God is witness over everything
4:41 (45)	how then shall it be, when We bring forward from every nation a witness
4:41 (45)	and bring thee to witness against those
4:69 (71)	Prophets, just men, martyrs, the righteous; good companions they
4:72 (74)	God has blessed me, in that I was not a martyr with them
4:79 (81)	We have sent thee to men a Messenger; God suffices for a witness
4:135 (134)	O believers, be you securers of justice, witnesses for God
4:159 (157)	on the Resurrection Day he will be a witness against them
4:166 (164)	the angels also bear witness; and God suffices for a witness
5:8 (11)	O believers, be you steadfast before God, witnesses for justice
5:44 (48)	following such portion of God's Book as they were given to keep and were witnesses to
5:117 (117)	I was a witness over them, while I remained among them
5:117 (117)	Thou Thyself art witness of everything
6:19 (19)	say: 'God is witness between me and you'
6:144 (145)	or were you witnesses when God charged you with this?
6:150 (151)	produce your witnesses, those who testify God has forbidden this
10:29 (30)	God is a sufficient witness between us and you
10:46 (47)	then God is witness of the things they do
13:43 (43)	God suffices as a witness between me and you
16:84 (86)	and the day We shall raise up from every nation a witness
16:89 (91)	We shall raise up from every nation a witness against them from amongst them
16:89 (91)	and We shall bring thee as a witness against those
17:96 (98)	God suffices as a witness between me and you
22:17 (17)	assuredly God is witness over everything
22:78 (78)	that the Messenger might be a witness against you
22:78 (78)	and that you might be witnesses against mankind
24:4 (4)	those who cast it up on women in wedlock, and then bring not four witnesses
24:6 (6)	those who cast it up on their wives having no witnesses
24:13 (13)	why did they not bring four witnesses against it?
24:13 (13)	since they did not bring the witnesses, in God's sight they are the liars
28:75 (75)	We shall draw out from every nation a witness, and say
29:52 (51)	God suffices as a witness between me and you
33:55 (55)	fear you God; surely God is witness of everything
34:47 (46)	He is witness over everything
39:69 (69)	the Prophets and witnesses shall be brought
41:47 (47)	we proclaim to Thee, there is not a witness among us
41:53 (53)	suffices it not as to thy Lord, that He is witness over everything?
46:8 (7)	He suffices as a witness between me and you
48:28 (28)	God suffices as a witness
50:21 (20)	every soul shall come, and with it a driver and a witness
50:37 (36)	who has a heart, or will give ear with a present mind
57:19 (18)	Messengers — they are the just men and the martyrs in their Lord's sight
58:6 (7)	God is witness over everything
85:9 (9)	God is Witness over everything
100:7 (7)	surely he is a witness against that

ASH.HADA vb. (IV)~to make one testify, to call to witness

a) perf. act.

7:172 (171) from their loins, their seed, and made them testify touching themselves
18:51 (49) I made them not witnesses of the creation of the heavens and earth

b) impf. act. (*yush.hidu*)

2:204 (200) such a one calls on God to witness what is in his heart
11:54 (57) he said, 'I call God to witness'

c) impv. (*ash.hid*)

2:282 (282) take witnesses when you are trafficking one with another
4:6 (7) when you deliver to them their property, take witnesses over them
65:2 (2) call in to witness two men of equity from among yourselves

ISTASH.HADA vb. (X)~to call to witness

c) impv. (*istash.hid*)

2:282 (282) call in to witness two witnesses, men
4:15 (19) such of your women as commit indecency, call four of you to witness against them

*SH H Q

SHAHAQA vb. (I)~(n.vb.) sighing

f) n.vb. (*shahīq*)

11:106 (108) Fire, wherein there shall be for them sighing and moaning
67:7 (7) when they are cast into it they will hear it sighing

*SH H R

SHAHR n.m. (pl. *shuhūr* and *ash.hur*)~a month

2:185 (181) the month of Ramadan, wherein the Koran was sent down to be a guidance
2:185 (181) let those of you, who are present at the month, fast it
2:194 (190) the holy month for the holy (month)
2:194 (190) the holy (month) for the holy month
2:197 (193) the Pilgrimage is in months well-known
2:217 (214) they will question thee concerning the holy month, and fighting in it
2:226 (226) for those who forswear their women a wait of four months
2:234 (234) they shall wait by themselves for four months and ten nights
4:92 (94) if he finds not the means, let him fast two successive months
5:2 (2) O believers, profane not God's waymarks nor the holy month
5:97 (98) God has appointed the Kaaba, the Holy House, as an establishment for men, and the holy month
9:2 (2) journey freely in the land for four months
9:5 (5) when the sacred months are drawn away, slay the idolaters
9:36 (36) the number of the months, with God, is twelve ([months])
9:36 (36) the number of the (months), with God, is twelve [months] in the Book of God
34:12 (11) its morning course was a month's journey

34:12 (11)	and its evening course was a month's journey
46:15 (14)	his bearing and his weaning are thirty months
58:4 (5)	whosoever finds not the means, then let him fast two successive months
65:4 (4)	if you are in doubt, their period shall be three months
97:3 (3)	the Night of Power is better than a thousand months

*SH H Y

SHAHWAH n.f. (pl. *shahawāt*)~lust, desire

3:14 (12)	decked out fair to men is the love of lusts
4:27 (32)	those who follow their lusts desire you to swerve away mightily
7:81 (79)	see, you approach men lustfully instead of women
19:59 (60)	there succeeded after them a succession who wasted the prayer, and followed lusts
27:55 (56)	do you approach men lustfully instead of women?

ISHTAHÁ vb. (VIII)~to desire

a) perf. act.

21:102 (102)	they shall dwell forever in that their souls desired

b) impf. act. (*yashtahī*)

16:57 (59)	and they have their desire
34:54 (53)	a barrier is set between them and that they desire
41:31 (31)	the world to come; therein you shall have all that your souls desire
43:71 (71)	therein being whatever the souls desire, and the eyes delight in
52:22 (22)	We shall succour them with fruits and flesh such as they desire
56:21 (21)	and such flesh of fowl as they desire
77:42 (42)	and such fruits as their hearts desire

*SH Ḥ Ḥ

ASHIḤḤAH n.m. (pl. of *shaḥīḥ*)~niggardly, stingy, avaricious

33:19 (19)	being niggardly towards you
33:19 (19)	they flay you with sharp tongues, being niggardly to possess the good things

SHUḤḤ n.m.~avarice, niggardliness, stinginess

4:128 (127)	souls are very prone to avarice
59:9 (9)	whoso is guarded against the avarice of his own soul
64:16 (16)	whosoever is guarded against the avarice of his own soul

*SH Ḥ M

SHUḤŪM n.m. (pl. of *shaḥm*)~fat

6:146 (147)	of oxen and sheep We have forbidden them the fat of them

*SH Ḥ N

SHAḤANA vb. (I)~(pcple. pass.) laden, loaded, filled up

h) pcple. pass. (*mash.ḥūn*)

26:119 (119)	We delivered him, and those with him, in the laden ship
36:41 (41)	a sign for them is that We carried their seed in the laden ship
37:140 (140)	when he ran away to the laden ship

*SH J R

SHAJARA vb. (I)~to be a matter of disagreement

a) perf. act.

4:65 (68)	till they make thee the judge regarding the disagreement between them

SHAJARAH n.f.~a tree

2:35 (33)	but draw not nigh this tree
7:19 (18)	but come not nigh this tree
7:20 (19)	your Lord has only prohibited you from this tree
7:22 (21)	when they tasted the tree, their shameful parts revealed to them
7:22 (21)	did not I prohibit you from this tree
14:24 (29)	a good word is as a good tree
14:26 (31)	the likeness of a corrupt word is as a corrupt tree
16:10 (10)	and of which trees, for you to pasture your herds
16:68 (70)	and of the trees, and of what they are building
17:60 (62)	the vision that We showed thee and the tree cursed in the Koran
20:120 (118)	Adam, shall I point thee to the Tree of Eternity
22:18 (18)	the stars and the mountains, the trees and the beasts
23:20 (20)	and a tree issuing from the Mount of Sinai
24:35 (35)	kindled from a Blessed Tree
27:60 (61)	gardens full of loveliness whose trees you could never grow
28:30 (30)	a voice cried from the right bank of the watercourse, in the sacred hollow, coming from the tree
31:27 (26)	though all the trees in the earth were pens
36:80 (80)	who has made for you out of the green tree fire and lo, from it you kindle
37:62 (60)	is that better as a hospitality, or the Tree of Ez-Zakkoum?
37:64 (62)	it is a tree that comes forth in the root of Hell
37:146 (146)	We caused to grow over him a tree of gourds
44:43 (43)	lo, the Tree of Ez-Zakkoum
48:18 (18)	when they were swearing fealty to thee under the tree
55:6 (5)	and the stars and the trees bow themselves
56:52 (52)	you shall eat of a tree called Zakkoum
56:72 (71)	did you make its timber to grow

*SH K K

SHAKK n.m.~a doubt, suspicion, uncertainty

4:157 (156)	those who are at variance concerning him surely are in doubt regarding him
10:94 (94)	if thou art in doubt regarding what We have sent down to thee
10:104 (104)	O men, if you are in doubt regarding my religion
11:62 (65)	truly we are in doubt, concerning what thou callest us to
11:110 (112)	they are in doubt of it disquieting
14:9 (10)	we are in doubt, concerning that you call us unto
14:10 (11)	is there any doubt regarding God
27:66 (68)	nay, they are in doubt of it
34:21 (20)	We might know him who believed in the Hereafter from him who was in doubt thereof
34:54 (54)	they were in doubt disquieting
38:8 (7)	nay, but they are in doubt of My Remembrance
40:34 (36)	you continued in doubt concerning that he brought you
41:45 (45)	they are in doubt of it disquieting
42:14 (13)	behold, they are in doubt of it disquieting
44:9 (8)	nay, but they are in doubt, playing

*SH K L

SHĀKILAH n.f.~same manner, likeness

17:84 (86)	every man works according to his own manner

SHAKL n.m.~a likeness, like kind

38:58 (58)	and other torments of the like kind coupled together

*SH K R

SHAKARA vb. (I)~to thank, to be thankful, to give thanks; to praise, to laud, to extol. (n.vb.) thankfulness; praise (pcple. act.) thankful, grateful; All-thankful, All-grateful (Divine attribute). (pcple. pass.) thanked, worthy of thanks, praiseworthy

a) perf. act.

4:147 (146)	what would God do with chastising you if you are thankful
14:7 (7)	if you are thankful, surely I will increase you
27:40 (40)	whosoever gives thanks gives thanks only for his own soul's good
54:35 (35)	even so We recompense him who is thankful

b) impf. act. (*yashkuru*)

2:52 (49)	We pardoned you after that, that haply you should be thankful
2:56 (53)	We raised you up after you were dead, that haply you should be thankful
2:185 (181)	magnify God that He has guided you, and haply you will be thankful
2:243 (244)	but most of the people are not thankful
3:123 (119)	fear God, and haply you will be thankful
5:6 (9)	that He may complete His blessing upon you; haply you will be thankful
5:89 (91)	God makes clear to you His signs; haply you will be thankful
7:10 (9)	little thanks you show
7:58 (56)	We turn about the signs for a people that are thankful
8:26 (26)	and provided you with the good things, that haply you might be thankful
10:60 (61)	God is bountiful to men; but most of them are not thankful

12:38 (38)	bounty to us, and to men; but most men are not thankful
14:37 (40)	and provide them with fruits; haply they will be thankful
16:14 (14)	that you may seek of His bounty, and so haply you will be thankful
16:78 (80)	He appointed for you hearing, and sight, and hearts, that haply so you will be thankful
22:36 (37)	We have subjected them to you; haply you will be thankful
23:78 (80)	little thanks you show
27:19 (19)	dispose me that I may be thankful for Thy blessing
27:40 (40)	that He may try me, whether I am thankful or ungrateful
27:40 (40)	whosoever gives thanks gives thanks only for his own soul's good
27:73 (75)	thy Lord is bountiful to men; but most of them are not thankful
28:73 (73)	seek after His bounty, that haply you will be thankful
30:46 (45)	you may seek His bounty; haply so you will be thankful
31:12 (11)	whosoever gives thanks (gives thanks) only for his own soul's good
31:12 (11)	whosoever (gives thanks) gives thanks only for his own soul's good
32:9 (8)	little thanks you show
35:12 (13)	that you may seek of His bounty, and so haply you will be thankful
36:35 (35)	what, will they not be thankful?
36:73 (73)	what, will they not be thankful?
39:7 (9)	but if you are thankful, He will approve it in you
40:61 (63)	God is bountiful to men, but most men are not thankful
45:12 (11)	that you may seek His bounty; haply so you will be thankful
46:15 (14)	dispose me that I may be thankful for Thy blessing
56:70 (69)	why are you not thankful?
67:23 (23)	little thanks you show

c) impv. (*ushkur*)

2:152 (147)	be thankful to Me; and be you not ungrateful towards Me
2:172 (167)	give thanks to God, if it be Him that you serve
16:114 (115)	be you thankful for the blessing of God, if it be Him that you serve
29:17 (16)	serve Him, and be thankful to Him
31:12 (11)	give thanks to God
31:14 (13)	be thankful to Me, and to thy parents
34:15 (14)	eat of your Lord's provision, and give thanks to Him

f) n.vb. (*shukr*, pl. *shukūr*)

25:62 (63)	for whom He desires to remember or He desires to be thankful
34:13 (12)	labour, O House of David, in thankfulness
76:9 (9)	we desire no recompense from you, no thankfulness

g) pcple. act. (*shākir*)

2:158 (153)	whoso volunteers good, God is All-grateful, All-knowing
3:144 (138)	God will recompense the thankful
3:145 (139)	We will give him of that; and We will recompense the thankful
4:147 (146)	God is All-thankful
6:53 (53)	knows not God very well the thankful?
6:63 (63)	if Thou deliverest from these, we shall be among the thankful
7:17 (16)	Thou wilt not find most of them thankful
7:144 (141)	take what I have given thee, and be of the thankful
7:189 (189)	if Thou givest us a righteous son, we indeed shall be of the thankful
10:22 (23)	if Thou deliverest us from these, surely we shall be among the thankful
16:121 (122)	showing thankfulness for His blessings
21:80 (80)	then are you thankful?
39:66 (66)	nay, but God do thou serve; and be thou among the thankful

76:3 (3)	whether he be thankful or unthankful
17:19 (20)	being a believer — those, their striving shall be thanked

h) pcple. pass. (*mashkūr*)

76:22 (22)	your striving is thanked

SHAKŪR n.m. (adj)~thankful; All-thankful (Divine attribute)

14:5 (5)	in that are signs for every man enduring, thankful
17:3 (3)	Noah; he was a thankful servant
31:31 (30)	in that are signs for every man enduring, thankful
34:13 (12)	few indeed are those that are thankful among My servants
34:19 (18)	in that are signs for every man enduring, thankful
35:30 (27)	surely He is All-forgiving, All-thankful
35:34 (31)	our Lord is All-forgiving, All-thankful
42:23 (22)	surely God is All-forgiving, All-thankful
42:33 (31)	in that are signs for every man enduring, thankful
64:17 (17)	God is All-thankful, All-clement

*SH K S

TASHĀKASA vb. (VI)~(pcple. act.) disagreeing, quarrelling

g) pcple. act. (*mutashākis*)

39:29 (30)	God has struck a similitude — a man in whom partners disagreeing share

*SH K W

SHAKĀ vb. (I)~to complain, to make complaint

b) impf. act. (*yashkū*)

12:86 (86)	I make complaint of my anguish and my sorrow unto God

MISHKĀT n.f.~a niche

24:35 (35)	the likeness of His Light is as a niche wherein is a lamp

ISHTAKÁ vb. (VIII)~to make complaint

b) impf. act. (*yashtakī*)

58:1 (1)	the words of her that disputes with thee concerning her husband, and makes complaint unto God

*SH KH Ṣ

SHAKHAṢA vb. (I)~to stare, to gaze. (pcple. act.) staring, gazing

b) impf. act. (*yashkhaṣu*)

14:42 (43) He is only deferring them to a day when eyes shall stare

g) pcple. act. f. (*shākhiṣah*)

21:97 (97) behold, the eyes of the unbelievers staring: Alas for us

*SH M KH

SHAMAKHA vb. (I)~(pcple. act.) soaring, lofty, towering

g) pcple. act. (*shāmikh*)

77:27 (27) set We not therein soaring mountains?

*SH M L

SHAMĀ'IL n.f. (pl)~left, left hand

7:17 (16) from behind them, from their right hands and their left hands
16:48 (50) casting their shadows to the right and to the left

SHIMĀL n.m.~left

18:17 (16) and, when it set, passing them by on the left
18:18 (17) while We turned them now to the right, now to the left
34:15 (14) two gardens, one on the right and one on the left
50:17 (16) when the two angels meet together, sitting one on the right, and one on the left
56:41 (40) the Companions of the Left
56:41 (40) O Companions of the Left
69:25 (25) as for him who is given his book in his left hand
70:37 (37) on the right hand and on the left hand in knots

ISHTAMALA vb. (VIII)~(with prep. *ʿalá*) to contain

a) perf. act.

6:143 (144) or what the wombs of the two females contain
6:144 (145) or what the wombs of the two females contain

*SH M S

SHAMS n.f.~the sun

2:258 (260) said Abraham, 'God brings the sun from the east'
6:78 (78) when he saw the sun rising, he said
6:96 (96) the night for a repose, and the sun and moon for a reckoning
7:54 (52) the sun, and the moon, and the stars subservient
10:5 (5) it is He who made the sun a radiance
12:4 (4) Father, I saw eleven stars, and the sun and the moon

13:2 (2)	He subjected the sun and the moon
14:33 (37)	and He subjected to you the sun and moon
16:12 (12)	He subjected to you the night and day, and the sun and moon
17:78 (80)	perform the prayer at the sinking of the sun to the darkening of the night
18:17 (16)	and thou mightest have seen the sun
18:86 (84)	when he reached the setting of the sun, he found it setting in a muddy spring
18:90 (89)	when he reached the rising of the sun, he found it rising
20:130 (130)	proclaim thy Lord's praise before the rising of the sun
21:33 (34)	it is He who created the night and the day, the sun and the moon
22:18 (18)	the sun and the moon, the stars and the mountains
25:45 (47)	then We appointed the sun, to be a guide to it
27:24 (24)	I found her and her people prostrating to the sun, apart from God
29:61 (61)	who created the heavens and the earth and subjected the sun and the moon?
31:29 (28)	He has subjected the sun and the moon, each of them running
35:13 (14)	He has subjected the sun and the moon, each of them running
36:38 (38)	the sun — it runs to a fixed resting-place
36:40 (40)	it behoves not the sun to overtake the moon
39:5 (7)	He has subjected the sun and the moon, each of them running
41:37 (37)	of His signs are the night and the day, the sun and the moon
41:37 (37)	bow not yourselves to the sun and moon
50:39 (38)	proclaim thy Lord's praise before the rising of the sun
55:5 (4)	the sun and the moon to a reckoning
71:16 (15)	and set the moon therein for a light and the sun for a lamp
75:9 (9)	and the sun and moon are brought together
76:13 (13)	therein they shall see neither sun nor bitter cold
81:1 (1)	when the sun shall be darkened
91:1 (1)	by the sun and his morning brightness

*SH M T

SHAMITA vb. (I)~(with prep. *bi-*) to gloat over

b) impf. act. (*yashmatu*)

7:150 (149)	make not my enemies to gloat over me

*SH M ʾ Z

ISHMA'AZZA vb. (quad IV)~to shudder, to feel disgust

a) perf. act.

39:45 (46)	when God is mentioned alone, then shudder the hearts of those who believe not

*SH N ʾ

SHANA'A vb. (I)~(n.vb.) hate, detestation. (pcple. act.) one who hates, who detests *f*) n.vb. (*shana'ān*)

5:2 (3) let not detestation for a people who barred you from the Holy Mosque
5:8 (11) let not detestation for a people move you not to be equitable

g) pcple. act. (*shāni'*)

108:3 (3) he that hates thee, he is the one cut off

*SH Q Q

SHAQQA vb. (I)~to split, to cleave; (with prep. *'alá*) to be opperssive, to press hard, to be heavy. (n.vb.) the act of splitting. (pcple. act.) grievous, troublesome

a) perf. act.

80:26 (26) then We split the earth in fissures

b) impf. act. (*yashuqqu*)

28:27 (27) I do not desire to press hard upon thee

f) n.vb. (*shaqq*)

80:26 (26) then We split the earth <in fissures>

g) pcple. act. (*shāqq*; comp. *ashaqq*)

13:34 (34) the chastisement of the world to come is yet more grievous

SHIQQ n.m.~difficulty, hardship; (*bi-shiqq al-anfus*) with great distress, with great difficulty

16:7 (7) they bear your loads unto a land that you never would reach, excepting with great distress

SHUQQAH n.f.~destination of a journey, distance

9:42 (42) they would have followed thee; but the distance was too far for them

SHĀQQA vb. (III)~to make a breach with someone; to contend with. (n.vb.) schism, variance, breach; discord, dissension

a) perf. act.

8:13 (13) that, because they had made a breach with God and with His Messenger
47:32 (34) those who disbelieve and bar from God's way and make a breach with the Messenger
59:4 (4) that is because they made a breach with God and His Messenger

b) impf. act. (*yushāqqu* or *yushāqiqu*)

4:115 (115) whoso makes a breach with the Messenger
8:13 (13) that, because they had made a breach with God and with His Messenger
16:27 (29) where are My associates concerning which you made a breach together?
59:4 (4) that is because they made a breach with God and His Messenger

f) n.vb. (*shiqāq*)

2:137 (131) if they turn away, then they are clearly in schism
2:176 (171) those that are at variance regarding the Book are in wide schism

4:35 (39)	if you fear a breach between the two
11:89 (91)	let not the breach with me move you
22:53 (52)	surely the evildoers are in wide schism
38:2 (1)	nay, but the unbelievers glory in their schism
41:52 (52)	who is further astray than he who is in wide schism?

TASHAQQAQA vb. (V)~to be split, to be cleft

b) impf. act. (*yatashaqqaqu*, *yashshaqqaqu* and *yashaqqaqu*)

2:74 (69)	and others split, so that water issues from them
25:25 (27)	upon the day that heaven is split asunder with the clouds
50:44 (43)	upon the day when the earth is split asunder from about them

INSHAQQA vb. (VII)~to be split, to be cleft; to split, to crack

a) perf. act.

54:1 (1)	the Hour has drawn nigh: the moon is split
55:37 (37)	and when heaven is split asunder
69:16 (16)	and heaven shall be split
84:1 (1)	when heaven is rent asunder

b) impf. act. (*yanshaqqu*)

19:90 (92)	and the earth split asunder

*SH Q Y

SHAQIYA vb. (I)~to be wretched, to be unprosperous, to be miserable

a) perf. act.

11:106 (108)	as for the wretched, they shall be in the Fire

b) impf. act. (*yashqá*)

20:2 (1)	We have not sent down the Koran upon thee for thee to be unprosperous
20:117 (115)	let him not expel you both from the Garden, so that thou art unprosperous
20:123 (122)	shall not go astray, neither shall he be unprosperous

SHAQĪY n.m. (adj; comp. *ashqá*)~wretched, unprosperous, miserable

11:105 (107)	some of them shall be wretched and some happy
19:4 (4)	I have never been hitherto unprosperous
19:32 (33)	He has not made me arrogant, unprosperous
19:48 (49)	haply I shall not be, in calling upon my Lord, unprosperous
87:11 (11)	but the most wretched shall flout it
91:12 (12)	when the most wretched of them uprose
92:15 (15)	whereat none but the most wretched shall be roasted

SHIQWAH n.f.~adversity, misery

23:106 (108)	they shall say, 'Our Lord, our adversity prevailed over us'

*SH R ͨ

SHARAͨA vb. (I)~to lay down law, to ordain, to enact (a law). (pcple. act.) swimming shorewards [Ar]; visibly [Pk]; openly holding up their heads [Ali]; right to the shore [Bl]

a) perf. act.

42:13 (11) He has laid down for you as religion that He charged Noah with
42:21 (20) have they associates who have laid down for them as religion that for which God gave not leave?

g) pcple. act. (*shurraͨ*, pl. of *shāriͨ*)

7:163 (163) the Sabbath, when their fish came to them on the day of their Sabbath, swimming shorewards

SHARĪͨAH n.f.~an open way, a clear way, a right way

45:18 (17) then We set thee upon an open way of the Command

SHIRͨAH n.f.~a right way [Ar]; a Divine law [Pk, Ali]; an access [Bl]

5:48 (52) to every one of you We have appointed a right way and an open road

*SH R B

SHARIBA vb. (I)~to drink. (n.vb.) the act of drinking; a drink, a draught. (pcple. act.) drinker; drinking, lapping

a) perf. act.

2:249 (250) whosoever drinks of it is not of me
2:249 (250) but they drank of it, except a few of them

b) impf. act. (*yashrabu*)

23:33 (35) and drinks of what you (drink)
23:33 (35) and (drinks) of what you drink
56:68 (67) have you considered the water you drink?
76:5 (5) the pious shall drink of a cup whose mixture is camphor
76:6 (6) a fountain whereat drink the servants of God
83:28 (28) a fountain at which do drink those brought nigh

c) impv. (*ishrab*)

2:60 (57) eat and drink of God's providing
2:187 (183) eat and drink, until the white thread shows clearly to you from the black thread
7:31 (29) eat and drink, but be you not prodigal
19:26 (26) eat therefore, and drink, and be comforted
52:19 (19) eat and drink, with wholesome appetite
69:24 (24) eat and drink with wholesome appetite for that you did
77:43 (43) eat and drink, with wholesome appetite

f) n.vb. (1) (*shirb*)

26:155 (155) this is a she-camel; to her a draught
26:155 (155) and to you a draught, on a day appointed
54:28 (28) the water is to be divided between them, each drink for each in turn

f) n.vb. (2) (*shurb*)

56:55 (55) lapping it down <like> thirsty camels

g) pcple. act. (*shārib*)

16:66 (68) between filth and blood, pure milk, sweet to drinkers
37:46 (45) white, a delight to the drinkers
47:15 (16) rivers of wine — a delight to the drinkers
56:54 (54) and drink on top of that boiling water
56:55 (55) lapping it down like thirsty camels

MASHRAB n.m.~a drinking place; a drink, a beverage

2:60 (57) all the people knew now their drinking-place
7:160 (160) all the people knew now their drinking-place
36:73 (73) other uses also they have in them, and beverages

SHARĀB n.m.~a drink, a draught, a potion

2:259 (261) look at thy food and drink — it has not spoiled
6:70 (69) for them awaits a draught of boiling water
10:4 (4) for them awaits a draught of boiling water, and a painful chastisement
16:10 (10) it is He who sends down to you out of heaven water of which you have to drink
16:69 (71) out of their bellies a drink of diverse hues wherein
18:29 (28) how evil a potion, and how evil a resting-place
35:12 (13) not equal are the two seas; this is sweet, grateful to taste, delicious to drink
38:42 (41) stamp thy foot! This is a laving-place cool, and a drink
38:51 (51) they call for fruits abundant, and sweet potions
76:21 (21) their Lord shall give them to drink a pure draught
78:24 (24) tasting therein neither coolness nor any drink

ASHRABA vb. (IV)~to make to drink

d) perf. pass. (*ushriba*)

2:93 (87) they were made to drink the Calf in their hearts

*SH R D

SHARRADA vb. (II)~to scatter, to disperse

c) impv. (*sharrid*)

8:57 (59) deal with them in such wise as to scatter the ones behind them

*SH R DH M

SHIRDHIMAH n.m.~a troop, a band

26:54 (54) behold, these are a small troop

*SH R Ḥ

SHARAḤA vb. (I)~to open, to expand

a) perf. act.

16:106 (108)	whosoever's breast is expanded in unbelief
39:22 (23)	is he whose breast God has expanded unto Islam

b) impf. act. (*yashraḥu*)

6:125 (125)	whomsoever God desires to guide, He expands his breast to Islam
94:1 (1)	did We not expand thy breast for thee

c) impv. (*ishraḥ*)

20:25 (26)	'Lord, open my breast,' said Moses

*SH R K

SHARIKA vb. (I)~(n.vb.) the act of associating, ascribing partners; partnership

f) n.vb. (*shirk*)

31:13 (12)	to associate others with God is a mighty wrong
34:22 (21)	they have no partnership in either of them
35:14 (15)	on the Day of Resurrection they will disown your partnership
35:40 (38)	or have they a partnership in the heavens?
46:4 (3)	or have they a partnership in the heavens?

SHARĪK n.m. (pl. *shurakā'*)~one who shares, an associate, a partner

4:12 (15)	if they are more numerous than that, they share equally a third
6:22 (22)	where are your associates whom you were asserting?
6:94 (94)	we do not see with you your intercessors, those you asserted to be associates
6:100 (100)	yet they ascribe to God, as associates, the jinn
6:136 (137)	this is for God — so they assert — and this is for our associates
6:136 (137)	so what is for their associates reaches not God
6:136 (137)	what is for God reaches their associates
6:137 (138)	those associates of theirs have decked out fair to many idolaters to slay their children
6:139 (140)	if it be dead, then they all shall be partners in it
6:163 (163)	no associate has He
7:190 (190)	when He gave them a righteous son, they assigned Him associates
7:195 (194)	say: 'Call you then to your associates'
10:28 (29)	get you to your place, you and your associates
10:28 (29)	their associates will say, 'Not us you were serving'
10:34 (35)	is there any of your associates who originates creation
10:35 (36)	is there any of your associates who guides to the truth?
10:66 (67)	they follow, who call upon associates, apart from God
10:71 (72)	so resolve on your affair, with your associates
13:16 (17)	or have they ascribed to God associates who created as He created
13:33 (33)	and yet they ascribe to God associates
16:27 (29)	where are My associates concerning which you made a breach together?

16:86 (88)	when the idolaters behold their associates, they shall say
16:86 (88)	our Lord, these are our associates on whom we called apart from Thee
17:111 (111)	and who has not any associate in the Kingdom
18:52 (50)	on the day He shall say, 'Call on My associates whom you asserted'
25:2 (2)	He has no associate in the Kingdom
28:62 (62)	where now are My associates whom you were asserting?
28:64 (64)	it shall be said, 'Call you now upon your associates!'
28:74 (74)	where now are My associates whom you were asserting?
30:13 (12)	no intercessors shall they have amongst their associates
30:13 (12)	they shall disbelieve in their associates
30:28 (27)	do you have, among that your right hands own, associates
30:40 (39)	is there any of your associates does aught of that?
34:27 (26)	show me those you have joined to Him as associates
35:40 (38)	have you considered your associates on whom you call, apart from God?
39:29 (30)	God has struck a similitude — a man in whom partners disagreeing share
41:47 (47)	the day when He shall call to them, 'Where now are My associates?'
42:21 (20)	or have they associates who have laid down for them as religion that for which God gave not leave?
68:41 (41)	or do they have associates?
68:41 (41)	let them bring their associates

SHĀRAKA vb. (III)~to share

c) impv. (*shārik*)

17:64 (66)	and share with them in their wealth

ASHRAKA vb. (IV)~(with prep. *bi-*) to make someone a partner or associate; (*ashraka bi-Allāh*) to associate someone or something with God, to ascribe partners unto God, to be idolatrous; (*alladhīna ashrakū*) those who have associated with God, the idolaters, the polytheists. (pcple. act.) idolater, polytheist

a) perf. act.

2:96 (90)	and of the idolaters; there is one of them
3:151 (144)	they have associated with God that for which He sent down never authority
3:186 (183)	who were given the Book before you, and from those who are idolaters, much hurt
5:82 (85)	the most hostile of men to the believers are the Jews and the idolaters
6:22 (22)	We shall say unto those who associated other gods with God
6:81 (81)	how should I fear what you have associated
6:81 (81)	seeing you fear not that you have associated with God
6:88 (88)	had they been idolaters, it would have failed them
6:107 (107)	had God willed, they were not idolaters
6:148 (149)	the idolaters will say, 'Had God willed'
6:148 (149)	'we would not have been idolaters'
7:173 (172)	our fathers were idolaters aforetime, and we were seed after them
10:28 (29)	then We shall say to those who associate other gods with God
14:22 (27)	I disbelieved in your associating me with God aforetime
16:35 (37)	the idolators say, 'If God had willed we would not have served'
16:86 (88)	when the idolaters behold their associates, they shall say
22:17 (17)	the Sabaeans, the Christians, the Magians and the idolaters
39:65 (65)	if thou associatest other gods with God, thy work shall surely fail

b) impf. act. (*yushriku*)

3:64 (57)	we serve none but God, and that we associate not aught with Him
4:36 (40)	serve God, and associate naught with Him

4:48 (51)	whoso associates with God anything, has indeed forged a mighty sin
4:116 (116)	whoso associates with God anything, has gone astray into far error
5:72 (76)	whoso associates with God anything, God shall prohibit him
6:19 (19)	He is only One God, and I am quit of that you associate
6:41 (41)	if He will, and you will forget that you associate with Him
6:64 (64)	then you assign Him associates
6:78 (78)	O my people, surely I am quit of that you associate
6:80 (80)	I fear not what you associate with Him, except my Lord will aught
6:151 (152)	that you associate not anything with Him
7:33 (31)	that you associate with God that for which He sent down never authority
7:190 (190)	when He gave them a righteous son, they assigned Him associates in that He had given them
7:191 (191)	do they associate that which creates nothing
9:31 (31)	there is no god but He; glory be to Him, above that they associate
10:18 (19)	glory be to Him! High be He exalted above that they associate
11:54 (57)	witness you, that I am quit of that you associate
12:38 (38)	not ours is it to associate aught with God
13:36 (36)	I have only been commanded to serve God, and not to associate aught with Him
16:1 (1)	high be He exalted above that they associate with Him
16:3 (3)	high be He exalted above that they associate with Him
16:54 (56)	a party of you assign associates to their Lord
18:26 (25)	He associates in His government no one
18:38 (36)	I will not associate with my Lord any one
18:42 (40)	would I had not associated with my Lord any one
18:110 (110)	and not associate with his Lord's service anyone
22:26 (27)	thou shall not associate with Me anything
22:31 (32)	whosoever associates with God anything, it is as though he has fallen from heaven
23:59 (61)	those who associate naught with their Lord
23:92 (94)	high exalted be He, above that they associate
24:55 (54)	they shall serve Me, not associating with Me anything
27:59 (60)	what, is God better, or that they associate?
27:63 (64)	high exalted be God, above that which they associate
28:68 (68)	glory be to God! High be He exalted above that they associate
29:8 (7)	if they strive with thee to make thee associate with Me
29:65 (65)	they associate others with Him
30:33 (32)	a party of them assign associates to their Lord
30:35 (34)	such as speaks of that they associate with Him
30:40 (39)	glory be to Him! High be He exalted above that they associate
31:13 (12)	O my son, do not associate others with God
31:15 (14)	if they strive with thee to make thee associate with Me
39:67 (67)	glory be to Him! High be He exalted above that they associate
40:42 (45)	you call me to disbelieve in God, and to associate with Him that
40:73 (74)	then it is said to them, 'Where are those you associated'
52:43 (43)	glory be to God, above that which they associate
59:23 (23)	glory be to God, above that they associate
60:12 (12)	they will not associate with God anything
72:2 (2)	we will not associate with our Lord anyone
72:20 (20)	I do not associate with Him anyone

c) impv. (*ashrik*)

20:32 (33)	and associate him with me in my task

e) impf. pass. (*yushraku*)

4:48 (51)	God forgives not that aught should be with Him associated

4:116 (116)	God forgives not that aught should be with Him associated
40:12 (12)	but if others are associated with Him, then you believe

g) pcple. act. (*mushrik*)

2:105 (99)	those unbelievers of the People of the Book and the idolaters
2:135 (129)	the creed of Abraham, a man of pure faith; he was no idolater
2:221 (220)	do not marry idolatresses, until they believe
2:221 (220)	a believing slavegirl is better than an idolatress
2:221 (220)	do not marry idolaters, until they believe
2:221 (220)	a believing slave is better than an idolater
3:67 (60)	certainly he was never of the idolaters
3:95 (89)	the creed of Abraham, a man of pure faith and no idolater
6:14 (14)	be not thou of the idolaters
6:23 (23)	by God our Lord, we never associated other gods with Thee
6:79 (79)	I am not of the idolaters
6:106 (106)	and turn thou away from the idolaters
6:121 (121)	if you obey them, you are idolaters
6:137 (138)	those associates of theirs have decked out fair to many idolaters to slay their children
6:161 (162)	the creed of Abraham, a man of pure faith; he was no idolater
9:1 (1)	an acquittal, from God and His Messenger, unto the idolaters with whom you made covenant
9:3 (3)	God is quit, and His Messenger, of the idolaters
9:4 (4)	excepting those of the idolaters with whom you made covenant
9:5 (5)	slay the idolaters wherever you find them
9:6 (6)	if any of the idolaters seeks of thee protection, grant him protection
9:7 (7)	how should the idolaters have a covenant with God and His Messenger?
9:17 (17)	it is not for the idolaters to inhabit God's places of worship
9:28 (28)	O believers, the idolaters are indeed unclean
9:33 (33)	He may uplift it above every religion, though the unbelievers be averse
9:36 (36)	fight the unbelievers totally even as they fight you totally
9:113 (114)	it is not for the Prophet and the believers to ask pardon for the idolaters
10:105 (105)	a man of pure faith, and be thou not of the idolaters
12:106 (106)	but they associate other gods with Him
12:108 (108)	I am not among the idolaters
15:94 (94)	turn thou away from the idolaters
16:100 (102)	those who take him for their friend and ascribe associates to God
16:120 (121)	a man of pure faith and no idolater
16:123 (124)	the creed of Abraham, a man of pure faith and no idolater
22:31 (32)	being men pure of faith unto God, not associating with Him anything
24:3 (3)	the fornicator shall marry none but a fornicatress or an idolatress
24:3 (3)	none shall marry her but a fornicator or an idolator
28:87 (87)	and be thou not of the idolaters
30:31 (30)	perform the prayer, and be not of the idolaters
30:42 (41)	most of them were idolaters
33:73 (73)	God may chastise the ... idolaters, men and (women) alike
33:73 (73)	God may chastise the ... idolaters, (men) and women alike
40:84 (84)	we disbelieve in that we were associating with Him
41:6 (5)	and woe to the idolaters
42:13 (11)	very hateful is that for the idolaters
48:6 (6)	He may chastise ... the idolaters, men and (women) alike
48:6 (6)	He may chastise ... the idolaters, (men) and women alike
61:9 (9)	He may uplift it above every religion, though the unbelievers be averse
98:1 (1)	the idolaters would never leave off
98:6 (5)	the idolaters shall be in the Fire of Gehenna

ISHTARAKA vb. (VIII)~(pcple. act.) (with prep. *fī*) a partner, a sharer

g) pcple. act. (*mushtarik*)

37:33 (32) all of them on that day are sharers in the chastisement
43:39 (38) you are partners in the chastisement

*SH R Q

MASHRIQ n.m. (pl. *mashāriq*)~the east, the place of sunrise

2:115 (109) to God belong the East and the West
2:142 (136) to God belong the East and the West
2:177 (172) it is not piety, that you turn your faces to the East and to the West
2:258 (260) God brings the sun from the east
7:137 (133) We bequeathed upon the people that were abased all the east and the west
26:28 (27) the Lord of the East and West
37:5 (5) Lord of the Easts
43:38 (37) would there had been between me and thee the distance of the two Easts
55:17 (16) Lord of the Two Easts
70:40 (40) I swear by the Lord of the Easts and the Wests
73:9 (9) Lord of the East and the West; there is no god but He

SHARQĪ n.m. (adj)~eastern, of the east

19:16 (16) when she withdrew from her people to an eastern place
24:35 (35) an olive that is neither of the East nor of the West

ASHRAQA vb. (IV)~to shine; to rise (the sun). (n.vb.) radiance; rising (of the sun); illumination. (pcple. act.) radiant, resplendent, shining; (adv) at sunrise

a) perf. act.

39:69 (69) the earth shall shine with the light of its Lord, and the Book

f) n.vb. (*ishrāq*)

38:18 (17) We subjected the mountains to give glory at evening and sunrise

g) pcple. act. (*mushriq*)

15:73 (73) and the Cry seized them at the sunrise
26:60 (60) then they followed them at the sunrise

*SH R R

SHARAR n.m. (coll)~sparks (of fire)

77:32 (32) that shoots sparks like dry faggots

SHARR n.m.~evil, ill, calamity; (pl. *ashrār*) evil, wicked; (as elative) worse, more evil

2:216 (213) it may happen that you will love a thing which is worse for you
3:180 (175) suppose it is better for them; nay, it is worse for them
5:60 (65) shall I tell you of a recompense with God, worse than that?

5:60 (65)	worshippers of idols — they are worse situated
8:22 (22)	the worst of beasts in God's sight are those that are deaf
8:55 (57)	the worst of beasts in God's sight are the unbelievers
10:11 (12)	if God should hasten unto men evil as they would hasten good
12:77 (77)	you are in a worse case
17:11 (12)	man prays for evil, as he prays for good
17:83 (85)	but when evil visits him, he is in despair
19:75 (77)	then they shall surely know who is worse in place
21:35 (36)	We try you with evil and good for a testing
22:72 (71)	shall I tell you of something worse than that?
24:11 (11)	do not reckon it evil for you
25:34 (36)	they shall be worse in place, and gone further astray from the way
38:55 (55)	for the insolent awaits an ill resort
38:62 (62)	how is it with us, that we do not see men here that we counted among the wicked?
41:49 (49)	when evil visits him, then he is cast down and desperate
41:51 (51)	when evil visits him, he is full of endless prayers
70:20 (20)	when evil visits him, impatient
72:10 (10)	we know not whether evil is intended for those in the earth
76:7 (7)	they fulfil their vows, and fear a day whose evil is upon the wing
76:11 (11)	God has guarded them from the evil of that day
98:6 (5)	those are the worst of creatures
99:8 (8)	whoso has done an atom's weight of evil shall see it
113:2 (2)	from the evil of what He has created
113:3 (3)	from the evil of darkness when it gathers
113:4 (4)	from the evil of the women who blow on knots
113:5 (5)	from the evil of an envier when he envies
114:4 (4)	from the evil of the slinking whisperer

*SH R Ṭ

ASHRĀṬ n.m. (pl. of *sharaṭ*)~tokens

47:18 (20)	already its tokens have come

*SH R Y

SHARÁ vb. (I)~to sell, to barter

a) perf. act.

2:102 (96)	evil then was that they sold themselves for
12:20 (20)	then they sold him for a paltry price

b) impf. act. (*yashrī*)

2:207 (203)	other men there are that sell themselves desiring God's good pleasure
4:74 (76)	let them fight in the way of God who sell the present life for the world to come

ISHTARÁ vb. (VIII)~to buy, to purchase; to barter; to sell

a) perf. act.

2:16 (15)	those are they that have bought error at the price of guidance

2:86 (80) those who have purchased the present life at the price of the world to come
2:90 (84) evil is the thing they have sold themselves for
2:102 (96) knowing well that whoso buys it shall have no share in the world to come
2:175 (170) those are they that have bought error at the price of guidance
3:177 (171) those who buy unbelief at the price of faith
3:187 (184) they rejected it behind their backs and sold it for a small price
9:9 (9) they have sold the signs of God for a small price
9:111 (112) God has bought from the believers their selves and their possessions
12:21 (21) he that bought him, being of Egypt, said to his wife

b) impf. act. (*yashtarī*)

2:41 (38) sell not My signs for a little price; and fear you Me
2:79 (73) that they may sell it for a little price
2:174 (169) and sell it for a little price
3:77 (71) those that sell God's covenant, and their oaths, for a little price
3:187 (184) and sold it for a small price — how evil was that their selling
3:199 (198) men humble to God, not selling the signs of God for a small price
4:44 (47) hast thou not regarded those who were given a share of the Book purchasing error
5:44 (48) fear you Me; and sell not My signs for a little price
5:106 (105) we will not sell it for a price
16:95 (97) do not sell the covenant of God for a small price
31:6 (5) some men there are who buy diverting talk to lead astray from the way of God

*SH T T

ASHTĀT n.m. (pl. of *shatt*)~(adv) separately, dispersed, scattered, in scatterings

24:61 (60) there is no fault in you that you eat all together, or in groups separately
99:6 (6) upon that day men shall issue in scatterings to see their works

SHATTÁ n.m. (pl. of *shatīt*)~diverse, various; dispersed, scattered

20:53 (55) We have brought forth diverse kinds of plants
59:14 (14) but their hearts are scattered
92:4 (4) surely your striving is to diverse ends

*SH T W

SHITĀʾ n.m.~winter

106:2 (2) their composing for the winter and summer caravan

*SH Ṭ ʾ

SHAṬʾ n.m.~a shoot; stalk (of a plant)

48:29 (29) as a seed that puts forth its shoot, and strengthens it

SHĀṬIʾ n.m.~shore; bank

28:30 (30) when he came to it, a voice cried from the right bank of the watercourse

*SH Ṭ N

SHAYṬĀN n.m. (pl. *shayāṭīn*)~a satan; (with definite article) Satan

2:14 (13)	when they go privily to their Satans, they say
2:36 (34)	then Satan caused them to slip therefrom
2:102 (96)	they follow what the Satans recited over Solomon's kingdom
2:102 (96)	Solomon disbelieved not, but the Satans disbelieved
2:168 (163)	follow not the steps of Satan; he is a manifest foe to you
2:208 (204)	enter the peace, all of you, and follow not the steps of Satan
2:268 (271)	Satan promises you poverty, and bids you unto indecency
2:275 (276)	except as he rises, whom Satan of the touch prostrates
3:36 (31)	commend her to Thee with her seed, to protect them from the accursed Satan
3:155 (149)	Satan made them slip for somewhat they had earned
3:175 (169)	that is Satan frightening his friends
4:38 (42)	whosoever has Satan for a comrade
4:60 (63)	Satan desires to lead them astray into far error
4:76 (78)	fight you therefore against the friends of Satan
4:76 (78)	surely the guile of Satan is ever feeble
4:83 (85)	you would surely have followed Satan
4:117 (117)	they pray not except to a rebel Satan
4:119 (118)	whoso takes Satan to him for a friend, instead of God
4:120 (119)	there is nothing Satan promises them except delusion
5:90 (92)	idols and divining-arrows are an abomination, some of Satan's work
5:91 (93)	Satan only desires to precipitate enmity and hatred between you
6:43 (43)	Satan decked out fair to them what they were doing
6:68 (67)	if Satan should make thee forget, do not sit, after the reminding
6:71 (70)	like one lured to bewilderment in the earth by Satans
6:112 (112)	Satans of men and jinn, revealing tawdry speech to each other
6:121 (121)	the Satans inspire their friends to dispute with you
6:142 (143)	and follow not the steps of Satan
7:20 (19)	then Satan whispered to them, to reveal to them that which was hidden
7:22 (21)	verily Satan is for you a manifest foe
7:27 (26)	Children of Adam! Let not Satan tempt you
7:27 (26)	We have made the Satans the friends of those who do not believe
7:30 (28)	they have taken Satans for friends instead of God
7:175 (174)	Satan followed after him, and he became one of the perverts
7:200 (199)	if a provocation from Satan should provoke thee, seek refuge in God
7:201 (200)	the godfearing, when a visitation of Satan troubles them
8:11 (11)	and to put away from you the defilement of Satan
8:48 (50)	when Satan decked out their deeds fair to them, and said
12:5 (5)	surely Satan is to man a manifest enemy
12:42 (42)	Satan caused him to forget to mention him to his master
12:100 (101)	Satan set at variance me and my brethren
14:22 (26)	and Satan says, when the issue is decided
15:17 (17)	and guarded them from every accursed Satan
16:63 (65)	but Satan decked out fair to them their deeds
16:98 (100)	when thou recitest the Koran, seek refuge in God from the accursed Satan
17:27 (29)	the squanderers are brothers of Satan
17:27 (29)	and Satan is unthankful to his Lord
17:53 (55)	Satan provokes strife between them
17:53 (55)	Satan is ever a manifest foe to man
17:64 (66)	but Satan promises them naught, except delusion
18:63 (62)	it was Satan himself that made me forget it
19:44 (45)	Father, serve not Satan

19:44 (45)	surely Satan is a rebel against the All-merciful
19:45 (46)	so that thou becomest a friend to Satan
19:68 (69)	by thy Lord, We shall surely muster them, and the Satans
19:83 (86)	hast thou not seen how We sent the Satans against the unbelievers
20:120 (118)	then Satan whispered to him saying, 'Adam, shall I point thee to the Tree of Eternity'
21:82 (82)	and of the Satans some dived for him
22:3 (3)	and follows every rebel Satan
22:52 (51)	but that Satan cast into his fancy, when he was fancying
22:52 (51)	but God annuls what Satan casts
22:53 (52)	He may make what Satan casts a trial for those in whose hearts is sickness
23:97 (99)	I take refuge in Thee from the evil suggestions of the Satans
24:21 (21)	O believers, follow not the steps of Satan
24:21 (21)	for whosoever follows the steps of Satan, assuredly he bids to indecency
25:29 (31)	Satan is ever a forsaker of men
26:210 (210)	not by the Satans has it been brought down
26:221 (221)	shall I tell you on whom the Satans come down?
27:24 (24)	Satan has decked out fair their deeds to them
28:15 (14)	this is of Satan's doing; he is surely an enemy
29:38 (37)	Satan decked out fair to them their works, and barred them from the way
31:21 (20)	even though Satan were calling them to the chastisement of the burning
35:6 (6)	surely Satan is an enemy to you
36:60 (60)	made I not covenant with you, Children of Adam, that you should not serve Satan
37:7 (7)	and to preserve against every rebel Satan
37:65 (63)	its spathes are as the heads of Satans
38:37 (36)	and the Satans, every builder and diver
38:41 (40)	Satan has visited me with weariness and chastisement
41:36 (36)	if a provocation from Satan should provoke thee, seek refuge in God
43:36 (35)	to him We assign a Satan for comrade
43:62 (62)	let not Satan bar you; he is for you a manifest foe
47:25 (27)	Satan it was that tempted them
58:10 (11)	conspiring secretly together is of Satan
58:19 (20)	Satan has gained the mastery over them
58:19 (20)	those are Satan's party
58:19 (20)	why, Satan's party, surely, they are the losers
59:16 (16)	like Satan, when he said to man, 'Disbelieve'
67:5 (5)	We adorned the lower heaven with lamps, and made them things to stone Satans
81:25 (25)	it is not the word of an accursed Satan

*SH Ṭ R

SHAṬR n.m.~direction; (adv) in the direction of, towards

2:144 (139)	turn thy face towards the Holy Mosque
2:144 (139)	wherever you are, turn your faces towards it
2:149 (144)	from whatsoever place thou issuest, turn thy face towards the Holy Mosque
2:150 (145)	from whatsoever place thou issuest, turn thy face towards the Holy Mosque
2:150 (145)	wherever you may be, turn your faces towards it

*SH Ṭ Ṭ

SHAṬAṬ n.m.~outrage; that which exceeds proper bounds, excess; enormity

18:14 (13) from Him, or then we had spoken outrage
72:4 (4) the fool among us spoke against God outrage

ASHAṬṬA vb. (IV)~to transgress, to act unjustly

b) impf. act. (*yushṭiṭu*)

38:22 (21) so judge between us justly, and transgress not

*SH W B

SHAWB n.m.~a (cooked) mixture, a brew, a blend; a drink

37:67 (65) then on top of it they have a brew of boiling water

*SH W K

SHAWKAH n.f.~a thorn; weapon; might, power, verve; (*dhāt al-shawkah*) accoutred; armed

8:7 (7) you were wishing that the one not accoutred should be yours

*SH W R

SHŪRÁ n.f.~consultation, counsel

42:38 (36) perform the prayer, their affair being counsel between them

SHĀWARA vb. (III)~to take counsel, to consult

c) impv. (*shāwir*)

3:159 (153) forgiveness for them, and take counsel with them in the affair

ASHĀRA vb. (IV)~to point

a) perf. act.

19:29 (30) Mary pointed to the child then

TASHĀWARA vb. (VI)~(n.vb.) counsel, consultation

f) n.vb. (*tashāwur*)

2:233 (233) if the couple desire by mutual consent and consultation to wean

*SH W Y

SHAWÁ (1) vb. (I)~to roast; to scald

b) impf. act. (*yashwī*)

18:29 (28) succoured with water like molten copper, that shall scald their faces

SHAWÁ (2) n.m. (pl. of *shawāt*)~a scalp

70:16 (16) snatching away the scalp

*SH W Ẓ

SHUWĀẒ n.m.~a flame, fire

55:35 (35) against you shall be loosed a flame of fire, and molten brass

*SH Y ʾ

SHĀʾA vb. (I)~to will; to wish, to desire; to want; (*in shāʾa Allāh*) if God wills, God willing

a) perf. act.

2:20 (19) had God willed, He would have taken away their hearing and their sight
2:35 (33) in the Garden, and eat thereof easefully where you desire
2:58 (55) and eat easefully of it wherever you will
2:70 (65) and, if God will, we shall then be guided
2:220 (219) had He willed He would have harassed you
2:223 (223) your women are a tillage for you; so come unto your tillage as you wish
2:253 (254) had God willed, those who came after him would not have fought
2:253 (254) had God willed they would not have fought one against the other
2:255 (256) they comprehend not anything of His knowledge save such as He wills
4:90 (92) had God willed, He would have given them authority over you
5:48 (53) if God had willed, He would have made you one nation
6:35 (35) but had God willed, He would have gathered them to the guidance
6:41 (41) He will remove that for which you call upon Him if He will
6:107 (107) had God willed, they were not idolaters
6:112 (112) had thy Lord willed, they would never have done it
6:128 (128) the Fire is your lodging, therein to dwell forever' — except as God will
6:137 (138) had God willed, they would not have done so
6:148 (149) had God willed, we would not have been idolaters
6:149 (150) for had He willed, He would have guided you all
7:19 (18) dwell, thou and thy wife, in the Garden, and eat of where you will
7:155 (154) hadst Thou willed Thou wouldst have destroyed them before, and me
7:161 (161) and eat of it wherever you will
7:176 (175) had We willed, We would have raised him up
7:188 (188) I have no power to profit for myself, or hurt, but as God will
9:28 (28) God shall surely enrich you of His bounty, if He will
10:16 (17) had God willed I would not have recited it to you
10:49 (50) I have no power to profit for myself, or hurt, but as God will
10:99 (99) if thy Lord had willed, whoever is in the earth would have believed
11:33 (35) God will bring you it if He will
11:107 (109) so long as the heavens and earth abide, save as thy Lord will
11:108 (110) so long as the heavens and earth abide, save as thy Lord will
11:118 (120) had thy Lord willed, He would have made mankind one nation

12:99 (100)	enter you into Egypt, if God will, in security
16:9 (9)	if He willed, He would have guided you all together
16:35 (37)	if God had willed we would not have served, apart from Him
16:93 (95)	if God had willed, He would have made you one nation
17:86 (88)	if We willed, We could take away that We have revealed to thee
18:29 (28)	the truth is from your Lord; so let whosoever will believe
18:29 (28)	and let whosoever will disbelieve
18:39 (37)	as God will; there is no power except in God
18:69 (68)	yet thou shalt find me, if God will, patient
18:77 (76)	if thou hadst wished, thou couldst have taken a wage for that
23:24 (24)	if God willed, He would have sent down angels
24:62 (62)	give leave to whom thou wilt of them, and ask God's forgiveness
25:10 (11)	blessed be He who, if He will, shall assign to thee better
25:45 (47)	had He willed, He would have made it still
25:51 (53)	if We had willed, We would have raised up in every city a warner
25:57 (59)	except for him who wishes to take to his Lord a way
27:87 (89)	terrified is whosoever is in the heavens and earth, excepting whom God wills
28:27 (27)	thou shalt assuredly find me, if God wills, one of the righteous
32:13 (13)	if We had so willed, We could have given every soul its guidance
33:24 (24)	and chastise the hypocrites, if He will, or turn again unto them
37:102 (102)	thou shalt find me, God willing, one of the steadfast
39:15 (17)	so serve what you will apart from Him
39:68 (68)	whosoever is in the earth shall swoon, save whom God wills
41:14 (13)	had our Lord willed, surely He would have sent down angels
41:40 (40)	do what you will; surely He sees
42:8 (6)	if God have willed, He would have made them one nation
43:20 (19)	had the All-merciful so willed, we would not have served them
48:27 (27)	you shall enter the Holy Mosque, if God wills, in security
73:19 (19)	this is a Reminder; so let him who will take unto his Lord a way
74:37 (40)	to whoever of you desires to go forward or lag behind
74:55 (54)	whoever wills shall remember it
76:28 (28)	when We will, We shall exchange their likes
76:29 (29)	this is a Reminder; so he who will, takes unto his Lord a way
78:39 (39)	so whosoever wills takes unto his Lord a resort
80:12 (12)	whoso wills, shall remember it)
80:22 (22)	then, when He wills, He raises him
81:28 (28)	for whosoever of you who would go straight
82:8 (8)	and composed thee after what form He would
87:7 (7)	save what God wills

b) impf. act. (*yashāʾu*)

2:90 (84)	grudging that God should send down of His bounty on whomsoever He will
2:105 (99)	God singles out for His mercy whom He will
2:142 (136)	He guides whomsoever He will to a straight path
2:212 (208)	God provides whomsoever He will without reckoning
2:213 (209)	God guides whomsoever He will to a straight path
2:247 (248)	God gives the kingship to whom He will
2:251 (252)	the kingship, and Wisdom, and He taught him such as He willed
2:261 (263)	so God multiplies unto whom He will
2:269 (272)	He gives the Wisdom to whomsoever He will
2:272 (274)	but God guides whomsoever He will
2:284 (284)	He will forgive whom He will
2:284 (284)	and chastise whom He will; God is powerful
3:6 (4)	it is He who forms you in the womb as He will
3:13 (11)	God confirms with His help whom He will

3:26 (25)	Thou givest the Kingdom to whom Thou wilt
3:26 (25)	and seizest the Kingdom from whom Thou wilt
3:26 (25)	Thou exaltest whom Thou wilt, and
3:26 (25)	Thou abasest whom Thou wilt
3:27 (26)	Thou providest whomsoever Thou wilt without reckoning
3:37 (32)	truly God provisions whomsoever He will
3:40 (35)	God does what He will
3:47 (42)	God said, 'God creates what He will'
3:73 (66)	He gives it unto whomsoever He will
3:74 (67)	He singles out for His mercy whom He will
3:129 (124)	He forgives whom He will
3:129 (124)	and chastises whom He will
3:179 (174)	God chooses out of His Messengers whom He will
4:48 (51)	less than that He forgives to whomsoever He will
4:49 (52)	nay; only God purifies whom He will
4:116 (116)	less than that He forgives to whomsoever He will
4:133 (132)	if He will, He can put you away, O men
5:17 (20)	creating what He will. God is powerful
5:18 (21)	He forgives whom He will
5:18 (21)	and He chastises whom He will
5:40 (44)	He chastises whom He will
5:40 (44)	and forgives whom He will
5:54 (59)	that is God's bounty; He gives it unto whom He will
5:64 (69)	He expends how He will
6:39 (39)	whomsoever God will, He leads astray
6:39 (39)	and whomsoever He will, He sets him on a straight path
6:80 (80)	I fear not what you associate with Him, except my Lord will aught
6:83 (83)	We raise up in degrees whom We will
6:88 (88)	He guides by it whom He will of His servants
6:111 (111)	they would not have been the ones to believe, unless God willed
6:133 (133)	if He will, He can put you away
6:133 (133)	and leave after you, to succeed you, what He will
6:138 (139)	none shall eat them, but whom we will
7:89 (87)	it is not for us to return into it, unless God our Lord so will
7:100 (98)	did We will, We would smite them because of their sins
7:128 (125)	the earth is God's and He bequeaths it to whom He will
7:155 (154)	it is only Thy trial, whereby Thou leadest astray whom Thou wilt
7:155 (154)	and guidest whom Thou wilt. Thou art our Protector
7:156 (155)	My chastisement — I smite with it whom I will
8:31 (31)	if we wished, we could say the like of this
9:15 (15)	God turns towards whomsoever He will
9:27 (27)	then God thereafter turns towards whom He will
10:25 (26)	He guides whomsoever He will to a straight path
10:107 (107)	He causes it to fall upon whomsoever He will of His servants
11:87 (89)	or to do as we will with our goods? Thou art the clement one
12:56 (56)	make his dwelling there wherever he would
12:56 (56)	We visit with Our mercy whomsoever We will
12:76 (76)	he could not have taken his brother, according to the king's doom, except that God willed
12:76 (76)	whomsoever We will, We raise in rank
12:100 (101)	my Lord is gentle to what He will
12:110 (110)	whosoever We willed was delivered
13:13 (14)	He looses the thunderbolts, and smites with them whomsoever He will
13:26 (26)	God outspreads and straitens His provision unto whomsoever He will
13:27 (27)	say: 'God leads astray whomsoever He will'

13:31 (30)	believers know that, if God had willed, He would have guided men all together
13:39 (39)	God blots out, and He establishes whatsoever He will
14:4 (4)	then God leads astray whomsoever He will
14:4 (4)	and He guides whomsoever He will
14:11 (13)	God is gracious unto whomsoever He will of His servants
14:19 (22)	if He will, He can put you away and bring a new creation
14:27 (32)	and God does what He will
16:2 (2)	He sends down the angels with the Spirit of His command upon whomsoever He will
16:31 (33)	underneath which rivers flow, wherein they shall have all they will
16:93 (95)	He leads astray whom He will, and
16:93 (95)	guides whom He will
17:18 (19)	We hasten for him therein what We will unto whomsoever We desire
17:30 (32)	thy Lord outspreads and straitens His provision unto whom He will
17:54 (56)	if He will, He will have mercy on you
17:54 (56)	or, if He will, He will chastise you
18:24 (23)	but only, 'If God will'; and mention
21:9 (9)	We delivered them, and whomsoever We would
22:5 (5)	We establish in the wombs what We will, till a stated term
22:18 (19)	God does whatsoever He will
24:21 (21)	but God purifies whom He will
24:35 (35)	God guides to His Light whom He will
24:38 (38)	God provides whomsoever He will, without reckoning
24:43 (43)	He smites whom He will with it
24:43 (43)	and turns it aside from whom He will
24:45 (44)	God creates whatever He will
24:46 (45)	God guides whomsoever He will to a straight path
25:16 (17)	therein they shall have what they will dwelling forever
26:4 (3)	if We will, We shall send down on them out of heaven a sign
28:56 (56)	thou guidest not whom thou likest, but God guides whom He wills
28:68 (68)	thy Lord creates whatsoever He will and He chooses
28:82 (82)	God outspreads and straitens His provision to whomsoever He will
29:21 (20)	chastising whom He will
29:21 (20)	and having mercy on whomsoever He will
29:62 (62)	God outspreads and straitens His provision to whomsoever He will
30:5 (4)	God helps whomsoever He will
30:37 (36)	have they not seen that God outspreads and straitens His provision to whom He will?
30:48 (47)	He spreads them in heaven how He will, and shatters them
30:48 (47)	when He smites with it whomsoever of His servants He will, lo, they rejoice
30:54 (53)	weakness and grey hairs; He creates what He will
33:51 (51)	thou mayest put off whom thou wilt of them
33:51 (51)	and whom thou wilt thou mayest take to thee
34:9 (9)	did We will, We would make the earth to swallow them
34:13 (12)	fashioning for him whatsoever he would
34:36 (35)	my Lord outspreads and straitens His provision to whomsoever He will
34:39 (38)	my lord outspreads and straitens His provision to whomsoever He will
35:1 (1)	having wings two, three and four, increasing creation as He wills
35:8 (9)	God leads astray whomsoever He will
35:8 (9)	and whomsoever He will He guides
35:16 (17)	if He will, He can put you away and bring a new creation
35:22 (21)	God makes to hear whomsoever He will
36:43 (43)	if We will, We drown them
36:47 (47)	shall we feed such a one whom, if God willed, He would feed?
36:66 (66)	did We will, We would have obliterated their eyes

36:67 (67)	did We will, We would have changed them where they were
39:4 (6)	He would have chosen whatever He willed of that He has created
39:23 (24)	He guides whomsoever He will
39:34 (35)	they shall have whatsoever they will with their Lord
39:52 (53)	do they know that God outspreads and straitens His provision to whomsoever He will?
39:74 (74)	for us to make our dwelling wheresoever we will in Paradise
40:15 (15)	casting the Spirit of His bidding upon whomever He will
42:8 (6)	but He admits whomsoever He will into His mercy
42:12 (10)	He outspreads and straitens His provision to whom He will
42:13 (12)	God chooses unto Himself whomsoever He will
42:19 (18)	God is All-gentle to His servants, providing for whomsoever He will
42:22 (21)	whatsoever they will they shall have with their Lord
42:24 (23)	if God wills, He will set a seal on thy heart
42:27 (26)	He sends down in measure whatsoever He will
42:29 (28)	He is able to gather them whenever He will
42:33 (31)	if He wills, He stills the wind
42:49 (48)	He creates what He will
42:49 (48)	He gives to whom He will females
42:49 (48)	and He gives to whom He will males
42:50 (49)	He makes whom He will barren
42:51 (51)	or that He should send a messenger and he reveal whatsoever He will
42:52 (52)	We made it a light, whereby We guide whom We will of Our servants
43:60 (60)	had We willed, We would have appointed angels among you to be successors
47:4 (5)	if God had willed, He would have avenged Himself upon them
47:30 (32)	did We will, We would show them to thee
48:14 (14)	whomsoever He will He forgives
48:14 (14)	and whomsoever He will He chastises
48:25 (25)	that God may admit into His mercy whom He will
50:35 (34)	therein they shall have whatever they will
53:26 (27)	that God gives leave to whomsoever He wills
56:65 (65)	did We will, We would make it broken orts
56:70 (69)	did We will, We would make it bitter
57:21 (21)	bounty of God; He gives it unto whomsoever He will
57:29 (29)	the hand of God; He gives it unto whomsoever He will
59:6 (6)	God gives authority to His Messengers over whomsoever He will
62:4 (4)	that is the bounty of God; He gives it to whom He will
74:31 (34)	so God leads astray whomsoever He will
74:31 (34)	and He guides whomsoever He will
74:56 (55)	they will not remember, except that God wills
76:30 (30)	but you will not unless God (wills)
76:30 (30)	but you (will) not unless God wills
76:31 (31)	He admits into His mercy whomsoever He will
81:29 (29)	but will you shall not
81:29 (29)	unless God wills, the Lord of all Being

SHAY' n.m. (pl. *ashyā'*)~a matter, an affair, a thing, anything, something; (*kullu shay'*) everything; (with prep. *min*) here and there, some; (with neg) nothing, naught; (adv) at all, in any way

2:20 (19)	truly, God is powerful over everything
2:29 (27)	He has knowledge of everything
2:48 (45)	beware of a day when no soul for another shall give satisfaction
2:106 (100)	knowest thou not that God is powerful over everything?
2:109 (103)	truly God is powerful over everything
2:113 (107)	the Jews say, 'The Christians stand not on anything'

2:113 (107)	the Christians say, 'The Jews stand not on anything'
2:123 (117)	beware a day when no soul for another shall give satisfaction
2:148 (143)	surely God is powerful over everything
2:155 (150)	We will try you with something of fear
2:170 (165)	what? And if their fathers had no understanding of anything
2:178 (173)	but if aught is pardoned a man by his brother
2:216 (213)	it may happen that you will hate a thing which is better for you
2:216 (213)	and it may happen that you will love a thing which is worse for you
2:229 (229)	it is not lawful for you to take of what you have given them
2:231 (231)	fear God, and know that God has knowledge of everything
2:255 (256)	they comprehend not anything of His knowledge
2:259 (261)	I know that God is powerful over everything
2:264 (266)	they have no power over anything that they have earned
2:282 (282)	let him fear God his Lord and not diminish aught of it
2:282 (282)	God teaches you, and God has knowledge of everything
2:284 (284)	and chastise whom He will; God is powerful over everything
3:5 (4)	from God nothing whatever is hidden in heaven and earth
3:10 (8)	their riches will not avail them, neither their children, aught against God
3:26 (25)	Thou art powerful over everything
3:28 (27)	whoso does that belongs not to God in anything
3:29 (27)	God is powerful over everything
3:64 (57)	and that we associate not aught with Him
3:92 (86)	whatever thing you expend, God knows of it
3:116 (112)	their riches shall not avail them, neither their children, against God
3:120 (116)	if you are patient and godfearing, their guile will hurt you nothing
3:128 (123)	no part of the matter is thine
3:144 (138)	if any man should turn about on his heels, he will not harm God in any way
3:154 (148)	have we any part whatever in the affair?
3:154 (148)	if we had had a part in the affair, never would we have been slain here
3:165 (159)	surely God is powerful over everything
3:176 (170)	they will nothing hurt God
3:177 (171)	those who buy unbelief at the price of faith, they will nothing hurt God
3:189 (186)	God is powerful over everything
4:4 (3)	if they are pleased to offer you any of it, consume it
4:19 (23)	you may be averse to a thing, and God set in it much good
4:20 (24)	you have given to one a hundredweight, take of it nothing
4:32 (36)	God knows everything
4:33 (37)	give to them their share; God is witness over everything
4:36 (40)	serve God, and associate naught with Him
4:59 (62)	if you should quarrel on anything, refer it to God
4:85 (87)	God has power over everything
4:86 (88)	God keeps a watchful count over everything
4:113 (113)	they do not hurt thee in anything
4:126 (125)	God encompasses everything
4:176 (175)	lest you go astray; God has knowledge of everything
5:17 (19)	who then shall overrule God in any way if He desires to destroy the Messiah
5:17 (20)	creating what He will. God is powerful over everything
5:19 (22)	God is powerful over everything
5:40 (44)	God is powerful over everything
5:41 (45)	whomsoever God desires to try, thou canst not avail him anything with God
5:42 (46)	if thou turnest away from them, they will hurt thee nothing
5:68 (72)	you do not stand on anything, until you perform the Torah and the Gospel
5:94 (95)	O believers, God will surely try you
5:97 (98)	God has knowledge of everything
5:101 (101)	question not concerning things which, if they were revealed to you, would vex you

5:104 (103)	What, even if their fathers had knowledge of naught
5:117 (117)	Thou Thyself art witness of everything
5:120 (120)	and He is powerful over everything
6:17 (17)	He is powerful over everything
6:19 (19)	say: 'What thing is greatest in testimony?'
6:38 (38)	We have neglected nothing in the Book
6:44 (44)	We opened unto them the gates of everything
6:52 (52)	nothing of their account falls upon thee
6:52 (52)	and nothing of thy account falls upon them
6:69 (68)	nothing of their account falls upon those that are godfearing
6:80 (80)	I fear not what you associate with Him, except my Lord will aught
6:80 (80)	my Lord embraces all things in His knowledge
6:91 (91)	God has not sent down aught on any mortal
6:93 (93)	or says, 'To me it has been revealed', when naught has been revealed to him
6:99 (99)	thereby We have brought forth the shoot of every plant
6:101 (101)	He has no consort, and He created all things
6:101 (101)	and He has knowledge of everthing
6:102 (102)	there is no god but He, the Creator of everything
6:102 (102)	for He is Guardian over everything
6:111 (111)	had We mustered against them every thing, face to face
6:148 (149)	nor would we have forbidden aught
6:151 (152)	forbidden you: that you associate not anything with Him
6:154 (155)	We gave Moses the Book, complete for him who does good, and distinguishing every thing
6:159 (160)	thou art not of them in anything
6:164 (164)	shall I seek after a Lord other than God, who is the Lord of all things?
7:85 (83)	diminish not the goods of the people
7:89 (87)	our Lord embraces all things in His knowledge
7:145 (142)	We wrote for him on the Tablets of everything an admonition
7:145 (142)	and a distinguishing of everything
7:156 (155)	My mercy embraces all things
7:185 (184)	have they not considered the dominion of the heaven and of the earth, and what things
7:191 (191)	what, do they associate that which creates nothing
8:19 (19)	and your host will avail you nothing
8:41 (42)	whatever booty you take, the fifth of it is God's, and the Messenger's
8:41 (42)	God is powerful over everything
8:60 (62)	whatsoever you expend in the way of God shall be repaid you in full
8:72 (73)	you have no duty of friendship towards them till they emigrate
8:75 (76)	surely God has knowledge of everything
9:4 (4)	you made covenant, then they failed you naught
9:25 (25)	when your multitude was pleasing to you, but it availed you naught
9:39 (39)	He will substitute another people; and you will not hurt Him anything
9:39 (39)	for God is powerful over everything
9:115 (116)	surely God knows everything
10:36 (37)	and surmise avails naught against truth
10:44 (45)	surely God wrongs not men anything
11:4 (4)	He is powerful over everything
11:12 (15)	thou art only a warner; and God is a Guardian over everything
11:57 (60)	you will not hurt Him anything
11:57 (60)	my Lord is Guardian over everything
11:72 (75)	this assuredly is a strange thing
11:85 (86)	do not diminish the goods of the people
11:101 (103)	their gods availed them not that they called upon, apart from God, anything
12:38 (38)	not ours is it to associate aught with God

12:67 (67)	I cannot avail you anything against God
12:68 (68)	their father commanded them, it availed them nothing against God
12:111 (111)	a confirmation of what is before it, and a distinguishing of every thing
13:8 (9)	everything with Him has its measure
13:14 (15)	those upon whom they call, apart from Him, answer them nothing
13:16 (17)	say: 'God is the Creator of everything'
14:18 (21)	they have no power over that they have earned
14:21 (24)	will you avail us against the chastisement of God anything?
14:38 (41)	from God nothing whatever is hidden in earth and heaven
15:19 (19)	We caused to grow therein of every thing justly weighed
15:21 (21)	naught is there, but its treasuries are with Us
16:20 (20)	those they call upon, apart from God, created nothing
16:35 (37)	we would not have served, apart from Him, anything
16:35 (37)	nor would we have forbidden, apart from Him, anything
16:40 (42)	the only words We say to a thing, when We desire it
16:48 (50)	have theynot regarded all things that God has created
16:70 (72)	that after knowing somewhat, they may know nothing
16:73 (75)	do they serve, apart from God, that which has no power to provide them anything
16:75 (77)	a servant possessed by his master, having no power over anything
16:76 (78)	two men, one of them dumb, having no power over anything
16:77 (79)	surely God is powerful over everything
16:78 (80)	it is God who brought you forth, knowing nothing
16:89 (91)	We have sent down on thee the Book making clear everything
17:12 (13)	and everything We have distinguished very distinctly
17:44 (46)	nothing is, that does not proclaim His praise
17:74 (76)	thou wert near to inclining unto them a very little
18:23 (23)	do not say, regarding anything, 'I am going to do that tomorrow'
18:33 (31)	each of the two gardens yielded its produce and failed naught in any wise
18:45 (43)	God is omnipotent over everything
18:54 (52)	man is the most disputatious of things
18:70 (69)	question me not on anything until I myself introduce
18:71 (70)	thou hast indeed done a grievous thing
18:74 (73)	thou hast indeed done a horrible thing
18:76 (75)	if I question thee on anything after this, then keep me company no more
18:84 (83)	and We gave him a way to everything
19:9 (10)	seeing that I created thee aforetime, when thou wast nothing
19:27 (28)	Mary, thou hast surely committed a monstrous thing
19:42 (43)	why worshippest thou that which neither hears nor sees, nor avails thee anything?
19:60 (61)	enter Paradise, and they shall not be wronged anything
19:67 (68)	will not man remember that We created him aforetime, when he was nothing?
19:89 (91)	you have indeed advanced something hideous
20:50 (52)	our Lord is He who gave everything its creation
20:98 (98)	there is no god, but He alone who in His knowledge embraces everything
21:30 (31)	then We unstitched them and of water fashioned every living thing
21:47 (48)	so that not one soul shall be wronged anything
21:66 (67)	do you serve, apart from God, that which profits you nothing
21:81 (81)	that We had blessed; and We had knowledge of everything
22:1 (1)	surely the earthquake of the Hour is a mighty thing
22:5 (5)	that after knowing somewhat, they may know nothing
22:6 (6)	He is the Truth, and brings the dead to life, and is powerful over everything
22:17 (17)	assuredly God is witness over everything
22:26 (27)	thou shall not associate with Me anything
22:73 (72)	if a fly should rob them of aught, they would never rescue it from him

23:88 (90)	in whose hand is the dominion of everything, protecting and Himself unprotected
24:35 (35)	and God has knowledge of everything.)
24:39 (39)	till, when he comes to it, he finds it is nothing
24:45 (44)	creates whatever He will; God is powerful over everything
24:55 (54)	they shall serve Me, not associating with Me anything
24:64 (64)	will tell them of what they did; and God knows everything
25:2 (2)	He created every thing, then He ordained it
25:3 (3)	they have taken to them gods, apart from Him, that create nothing
26:30 (29)	even though I brought thee something manifest
26:183 (183)	and diminish not the goods of the people
27:16 (16)	and we have been given of everything
27:23 (23)	and she has been given of everything
27:88 (90)	passing by like clouds — God's handiwork, who has created everything very well
27:91 (93)	to Him belongs everything
28:57 (57)	to which are collected the fruits of everything, as a provision from Us
28:60 (60)	whatever thing you have been given is the enjoyment of the present life
28:88 (88)	all things perish, except His Face
29:12 (11)	yet they cannot carry anything, even of their own offences
29:20 (19)	God is powerful over everything
29:42 (41)	God knows whatever thing they call upon apart from Him
29:62 (62)	God has knowledge of everything
30:40 (39)	is there any of your associates does aught of that?
30:50 (49)	and He is powerful over everything
31:33 (32)	no child shall give satisfaction for his father whatever
32:7 (6)	who has created all things well
33:27 (27)	and a land you never trod, God is powerful over everything
33:40 (40)	and the Seal of the Prophets; God has knowledge of everything
33:52 (52)	God is watchful over everything
33:54 (54)	whether you reveal anything, or whether you conceal it
33:54 (54)	surely God has knowledge of everything
33:55 (55)	fear you God; surely God is witness of everything
34:16 (15)	tamarisk-bushes, and here and there a few lote-trees
34:21 (20)	thy Lord is Guardian over everything
34:39 (38)	whatever thing you shall expend, He will replace it
34:47 (46)	He is witness over everything
35:1 (1)	surely God is powerful over everything
35:18 (19)	not a thing of it will be carried, though he be a near
35:44 (43)	there is naught in the heavens or the earth that can frustrate Him
36:12 (11)	everything We have numbered in a clear register
36:15 (14)	the All-merciful has not sent down anything
36:23 (22)	whose intercession, if the All-merciful desires affliction for me, shall not avail me anything
36:54 (54)	today no soul shall be wronged anything
36:82 (82)	His command, when He desires a thing, is to say to it, 'Be'
36:83 (83)	glory be to Him, in whose hand is the dominion of everything
38:5 (4)	has he made the gods One God? This is indeed a marvellous thing
38:6 (5)	be steadfast to your gods; this is a thing to be desired
39:43 (44)	even though they have no power whatever and no understanding
39:62 (63)	God is the Creator of every thing
39:62 (63)	He is Guardian over every thing
40:7 (7)	Thou embracest every thing in mercy and knowledge
40:16 (16)	the day they sally forth, and naught of theirs is hidden from God
40:20 (21)	those they call on, apart from Him, shall not decide by any means
40:62 (64)	that then is God, your Lord, the Creator of everything

40:74 (74)	it was nothing at all that we called upon aforetime
41:21 (20)	God gave us speech, as He gave everything speech
41:39 (39)	surely He is powerful over everything
41:53 (53)	as to thy Lord, that He is witness over everything
41:54 (54)	does He not encompass everything?
42:9 (7)	He quickens the dead, and He is powerful over everything
42:10 (8)	whatever you are at variance on, the judgment thereof belongs to God
42:11 (9)	like Him there is naught
42:12 (10)	surely He has knowledge of everything
42:36 (34)	whatever thing you have been given is the enjoyment of the present life
44:41 (41)	the day a master shall avail nothing a client, and they shall not be helped
45:9 (8)	when he knows anything of Our signs, he takes them in mockery
45:10 (9)	that they have earned shall not avail them aught
45:19 (18)	surely they will not avail thee aught against God
46:8 (7)	if I have forged it, you have no power to help me against God
46:25 (24)	destroying everything by the commandment of its Lord
46:26 (25)	their sight and their hearts availed them nothing, since they denied the signs
46:33 (32)	yes indeed; He is powerful over everything
47:32 (34)	they will nothing hurt God, and He will make their works to fail
48:11 (11)	who can avail you aught against God
48:21 (21)	God is powerful over everything
48:26 (26)	and God has knowledge of everything
49:14 (14)	He will not diminish you anything of your works
49:16 (16)	and God has knowledge of everything
50:2 (2)	this is a marvellous thing
51:42 (42)	that left nothing it came upon, but made it as stuff decayed
51:49 (49)	and of everything created We two kinds
52:21 (21)	We shall join their seed with them, and We shall not defraud them of aught of their work
52:35 (35)	or were they created out of nothing?
52:46 (46)	the day when their guile shall avail them naught
53:26 (26)	how many an angel there is in the heavens whose intercession avails not anything
53:28 (29)	only surmise, and surmise avails naught against truth
54:6 (6)	the day when the Caller shall call unto a horrible thing
54:49 (49)	surely We have created everything in measure
54:52 (52)	every thing that they have done is in the Scrolls
57:2 (2)	He gives life, and He makes to die, and He is powerful over everything
57:3 (3)	He has knowledge of everything
57:29 (29)	they have no power over anything of God's bounty
58:6 (7)	God is witness over everything
58:7 (8)	surely God has knowledge of everything
58:10 (11)	he will not hurt them anything
58:17 (18)	neither their riches nor their children shall avail them anything against God
58:18 (19)	they will swear to Him, as they swear to you, and think they are on something
59:6 (6)	God is powerful over everything
60:4 (4)	I have no power to do aught for thee against God
60:11 (11)	if any of your wives slips away from you to the unbelievers, and then you retaliate
60:12 (12)	swearing fealty to thee upon the terms that they will not associate with God anything
64:1 (1)	and He is powerful over everything
64:11 (11)	and God has knowledge of everything
65:3 (3)	God has appointed a measure for everything
65:12 (12)	that you may know that God is powerful over everything

65:12 (12)	and that God encompasses everything in knowledge
66:8 (8)	surely Thou art powerful over everything
66:10 (10)	so they availed them nothing whatsoever against God
67:1 (1)	He is powerful over everything
67:9 (9)	God has not sent down anything; you are only in great error
67:19 (19)	He sees everything
72:28 (28)	and He has numbered everything in numbers
76:1 (1)	has there come on man a while of time when he was a thing unremembered?
78:29 (29)	and everything We have numbered in a Book
80:18 (17)	of what did He create him?
82:19 (19)	a day when no soul shall possess aught to succour another soul
85:9 (9)	and God is Witness over everything

*SH Y ᶜ

SHĀᶜA vb. (I)~to be spread, to be published abroad

b) impf. act. (*yashīᶜu*)

24:19 (18)	those who love that indecency should be spread abroad concerning them that believe

SHĪᶜAH n.f. (pl. *shiyaᶜ* and *ashyāᶜ*)~a sect, a faction, party; (pl) ones of the same persuasion, the likes of someone

6:65 (65)	or to confuse you in sects and to make you taste the violence of one another
6:159 (160)	those who have made divisions in their religion and become sects
15:10 (10)	We sent Messengers before thee, among the factions of the ancients
19:69 (70)	We shall pluck forth from every party whichever of them was the most hardened in disdain
28:4 (3)	Pharaoh had exalted himself in the land and had divided its inhabitants into sects
28:15 (14)	and found there two men fighting; the one was of his own party
28:15 (14)	then the one that was of his party cried to him to aid him
30:32 (31)	even of those who have divided up their religion, and become sects
34:54 (54)	as was done with the likes of them aforetime
37:83 (81)	of his party was also Abraham
54:51 (51)	We have destroyed the likes of you

*SH Y B

SHĀBA vb. (I)~(n.vb.) hoariness, greyness of hair; old age

f) n.vb. (*shayb* or *shaybah*)

19:4 (3)	and my head is all aflame with hoariness
30:54 (53)	then after strength He appointed weakness and grey hairs

SHĪB n.m. (pl. of *ashyab*)~grey-headed; old

73:17 (17)	how will you guard yourselves against a day that shall make the children grey-headed?

*SH Y D

SHĀDA vb. (I)~(pcple. pass.) plastered; set up, constructed; lofty, tall, high

h) pcple. pass. (*mashīd*)

22:45 (44)	how many a ruined well, a tall palace

SHAYYADA vb. (II)~(pcple. pass.) raised-up, constructed; lofty, imposing, high

h) pcple. pass. (*mushayyad*)

4:78 (80)	wherever you may be, death will overtake you, though you should be in raised-up towers

*SH Y KH

SHAYKH n.m. (pl. *shuyūkh*)~old man, an elderly, one who is passing old, aged

11:72 (75)	being an old woman, and this my husband is an old man
12:78 (78)	mighty prince, he has a father, aged and great with years
28:23 (23)	water until the shepherds drive off, and our father is passing old
40:67 (69)	then that you may be old men

ṢĀD

*Ṣ

ṢĀD~ml

38:1 (1)	Sad. By the Koran, containing the Remembrance —

*Ṣ ᶜ D

ṢAᶜIDA vb. (I)~to ascend, to go up

b) impf. act. (*yaṣᶜadu*)

35:10 (11)	to Him good words go up

ṢAᶜAD n.m. (adj)~sever, rigorous

72:17 (17)	He will thrust him into chastisement rigorous

ṢAᶜĪD n.m.~earth, dust

4:43 (46)	then have recourse to wholesome dust and wipe your faces
5:6 (9)	then have recourse to wholesome dust and wipe your faces
18:8 (7)	We shall surely make all that is on it barren dust
18:40 (38)	in the morning it will be a slope of dust

ṢAᶜŪD n.m.~severe torment; a mountain of fire (or in Hell); a hard ascent

74:17 (17)	I shall constrain him to a hard ascent

AṢᶜADA vb. (IV)~to mount up, to go up

b) impf. act. (*yuṣᶜidu*)

3:153 (147)	when you were going up, not twisting about for anyone

TAṢAᶜᶜADA vb. (V)~to climb up

b) impf. act. (*yaṣṣaᶜᶜadu* for *yataṣaᶜᶜadu*)

6:125 (125)	He makes his breast narrow, tight, as if he were climbing to heaven

*Ṣ ᶜ Q

ṢAᶜIQA vb. (I)~to swoon, to expire; to be thunderstruck

a) perf. act.

39:68 (68)	whosoever is in the earth shall swoon, save whom God wills

e) impf. pass. (*yuṣʿaqu*)

52:45 (45) their day wherein they shall be thunderstruck

ṢAʿIQ n.m.~(adv) swooning, dumbfounded, thunderstruck

7:143 (139) Moses fell down swooning

ṢĀʿIQAH n.f. (pl. *ṣawāʿiq*)~thunderbolt, thunderclap

2:19 (18) they put their fingers in their ears against the thunderclaps
2:55 (52) the thunderbolt took you while you were beholding
4:153 (152) the thunderbolt took them for their evildoing
13:13 (14) He looses the thunderbolts, and smites with them whomsoever He will
41:13 (12) I warn you of a thunderbolt like to the (thunderbolt)
41:13 (12) a (thunderbolt) like to the thunderbolt of Ad and Thamood
41:17 (16) the thunderbolt of the chastisement of humiliation seized them
51:44 (44) the thunderbolt took them and they themselves beholding

*Ṣ ʿ R

ṢAʿʿARA vb. (II)~to turn (one's cheek) away; to put on a contempteous look

b) impf. act. (*yuṣaʿʿir u*)

31:18 (17) turn not thy cheek away from men in scorn

*Ṣ B ʾ

ṢĀBIʾŪN n.prop.~the Sabaeans

2:62 (59) the Christians, and those Sabaeans, whoso believes in God
5:69 (73) the Sabaeans, and those Christians, whosoever believes in God
22:17 (17) they that believe, and those of Jewry, the Sabaeans

*Ṣ B ʿ

AṢĀBIʿ n.m. (pl. of *iṣbaʿ*)~finger

2:19 (18) they put their fingers in their ears against the thunderclaps
71:7 (6) they put their fingers in their ears, and wrapped them in their garments

*Ṣ B B

ṢABBA vb. (I)~to pour out; to unloose, to empty. (n.vb.) the act of pouring out

a) perf. act.

80:25 (25) We poured out the rains abundantly
89:13 (12) thy Lord unloosed on them a scourge of chastisement

c) impv. (*ṣubb*)

44:48 (48) then pour over his head the chastisement of boiling water

e) impf. pass. (*yuṣabbu*)

22:19 (20) there shall be poured over their heads boiling water

f) n.vb. (*ṣabb*)

80:25 (25) We poured out the rains <abundantly>

*Ṣ B GH

ṢIBGH n.m.~seasoning, relish

23:20 (20) a tree issuing from the Mount of Sinai that bears oil and seasoning

ṢIBGHAH n.f.~baptism [Ar, Ali]; colour [Pk]; savour [Bl]

2:138 (132) the baptism of God
2:138 (132) who is there that baptizes fairer than God?

*Ṣ B Ḥ

IṢBĀḤ n.m.~dawn, morning

6:96 (96) He splits the sky into dawn

MIṢBĀḤ n.m. (pl. *maṣābīḥ*)~lamp

24:35 (35) the likeness of His Light is as a niche wherein is a lamp
24:35 (35) the lamp in a glass
41:12 (11) We adorned the lower heaven with lamps
67:5 (5) We adorned the lower heaven with lamps

ṢABĀḤ n.m.~morning

37:177 (177) how evil will be the morning of them that are warned

ṢUBḤ n.m.~morning, dawn

11:81 (83) their promised time is the morning
11:81 (83) is the morning not nigh?
74:34 (37) and the dawn when it is white
81:18 (18) by the dawn sighing
100:3 (3) by the dawn-raiders

ṢABBAḤA vb. (II)~to come in the morning

a) perf. act.

54:38 (38) in the morning early there came upon them a settled chastisement

AṢBAḤA vb. (IV)~to become; to come to be in the morning or the morrow. (pcple. act.) happening in the morning

a) perf. act.

3:103 (98)	so that by His blessing you became brothers
5:30 (33)	he slew him, and became one of the losers
5:31 (34)	he became one of the remorseful
5:53 (58)	their works have failed; now they are losers
5:102 (101)	a people before you questioned concerning them, then disbelieved in them
7:78 (76)	morning found them in their habitation fallen prostrate
7:91 (89)	morning found them in their habitation fallen prostrate
11:67 (70)	morning found them in their habitations fallen prostrate
11:94 (97)	morning found them in their habitations fallen prostrate
18:42 (40)	in the morning he was wringing his hands for that he had expended
18:45 (43)	in the morning it is straw the winds scatter
26:157 (157)	they hamstrung her, and in the morning they were remorseful
28:10 (9)	on the morrow the heart of Moses' mother became empty
28:18 (17)	now in the morning he was in the city
28:82 (82)	in the morning those who had longed to be in his place the day before were saying
29:37 (36)	morning found them in their habitation fallen prostrate
41:23 (22)	therefore you find yourselves this morning among the losers
46:25 (24)	in the morning there was naught to be seen but their dwelling-places
61:14 (14)	We confirmed those who believed against their enemy, and they became masters
67:30 (30)	in the morning your water should have vanished into the earth
68:20 (20)	in the morning it was as if it were a garden plucked

b) impf. act. (*yuṣbiḥu*)

5:52 (57)	then they will find themselves, for that they kept secret within them, remorseful
18:40 (38)	in the morning it will be a slope of dust
18:41 (39)	in the morning the water of it will be sunk into the earth
22:63 (62)	in the morning the earth becomes green
23:40 (42)	in a little they will be remorseful
30:17 (16)	glory be to God both in your evening hour and in your morning hour
49:6 (6)	lest you afflict a people unwittingly, and then repent

g) pcple. act. (*muṣbiḥ*)

15:66 (66)	the last remnant of those should be cut off in the morning
15:83 (83)	the Cry seized them in the morning
37:137 (137)	you pass by them in the morning
68:17 (17)	the owners of the garden when they swore they would pluck in the morning
68:21 (21)	in the morning they called to one another

*Ṣ B R

ṢABARA vb. (I)~to be patient, to endure patiently; to keep steadfastly, to persist; to restrain oneself. (n.vb.) patience, forbearance; steadfastness, firmness; endurance, perseverance (pcple. act.) patient, enduring, long-suffering, steadfast; (*mā aṣbara*) how patiently he shall endure!

a) perf. act.

6:34 (34)	yet they endured patiently that they were cried lies to
7:137 (133)	upon the Children of Israel, for that they endured patiently
11:11 (14)	save such as are patient, and do deeds of righteousness
13:22 (22)	patient men, desirous of the Face of their Lord

13:24 (24)	peace be upon you, for that you were patient
14:21 (25)	whether we cannot endure, or whether we are patient
16:42 (44)	even such men as are patient, and put their trust in their Lord
16:96 (98)	We shall recompense those who were patient
16:110 (111)	those who have emigrated after persecution, then struggled and were patient
16:126 (127)	yet assuredly if you are patient
23:111 (113)	today I have recompensed them for their patient endurance
25:42 (44)	wellnigh he had led us astray from our gods, but that we kept steadfast to them
25:75 (75)	those shall be recompensed with the highest heaven, for that they endured patiently
28:54 (54)	these shall be given their wage twice over for that they patiently endured
29:59 (59)	such men as are patient, and put their trust in their Lord
32:24 (24)	when they endured patiently, and had sure faith
41:35 (35)	yet none shall receive it, except the steadfast
42:43 (41)	surely he who bears patiently and is forgiving
46:35 (34)	as the Messengers possessed of constancy were also patient
49:5 (5)	if they had patience, until thou comest out to them, that would be better for them
76:12 (12)	and recompensed them for their patience with a Garden

b) impf. act. (*yaṣbiru*)

2:61 (58)	Moses, we will not endure one sort of food
3:120 (116)	if you are patient and godfearing, their guile will hurt you nothing
3:125 (121)	if you are patient and godfearing, and the foe come against you
3:186 (183)	if you are patient and godfearing — surely that is true constancy
4:25 (30)	yet it is better for you to be patient
12:90 (90)	whosoever fears God, and is patient
14:12 (15)	we will surely endure patiently, whatever you hurt us
18:68 (67)	how shouldst thou bear patiently that thou hast never encompassed
25:20 (22)	will you endure
41:24 (23)	if they persist, the Fire shall be a lodging for them
52:16 (16)	bear you patiently, or bear not patiently, equal it is to you

f) n.vb. (*ṣabr*)

3:200 (200)	O believers, be patient, and vie you in patience
7:87 (85)	be patient till God shall judge between us
7:128 (125)	pray for succour to God, and be patient
8:46 (48)	be patient; surely God is with the patient
10:109 (109)	be thou patient until God shall judge
11:49 (51)	so be patient; the issue ultimate is to the godfearing.)
11:115 (117)	be thou patient; God will not leave to waste the wage of the good-doers
16:127 (128)	yet is thy patience only with the help of God
18:28 (27)	restrain thyself with those who call upon their Lord at morning and evening
20:130 (130)	so be thou patient under what they say
30:60 (60)	be thou patient; surely God's promise is true
31:17 (16)	bear patiently whatever may befall thee
38:6 (5)	be steadfast to your gods
38:17 (16)	bear patiently what they say, and remember
40:55 (57)	be thou patient; surely God's promise is true
40:77 (77)	be thou patient; surely God's promise is true
46:35 (34)	be thou patient, as the Messengers possessed of constancy were also patient
50:39 (38)	so be thou patient under what they say
52:16 (16)	bear you patiently, or bear not patiently
52:48 (48)	be thou patient under the judgment of thy Lord

68:48 (48)	be thou patient under the judgement of thy Lord
70:5 (5)	so be thou patient with a sweet patience
73:10 (10)	and bear thou patiently what they say
74:7 (7)	and be patient unto thy Lord
76:24 (24)	be thou patient under the judgment of thy Lord
2:45 (42)	seek you help in patience and prayer
2:153 (148)	O all you who believe, seek you help in patience and prayer
2:250 (251)	pour out upon us patience, and make firm our feet
7:126 (123)	pour out upon us patience, and gather us unto Thee
12:18 (18)	but come, sweet patience
12:83 (83)	but come, sweet patience
16:127 (128)	yet is thy patience only with the help of God
18:67 (66)	assuredly thou wilt not be able to bear with me patiently
18:72 (71)	did I not say that thou couldst never bear with me patiently?
18:75 (74)	did I not say that thou couldst never bear with me patiently?
18:78 (77)	the interpretation of that thou couldst not bear patiently
18:82 (81)	this is the interpretation of that thou couldst not bear patiently
70:5 (5)	so be thou patient with a sweet patience
90:17 (17)	and counsel each other to be steadfast
103:3 (3)	and counsel each other to be steadfast

g) pcple. act. (*ṣābir*)

2:153 (148)	surely God is with the patient
2:155 (150)	give thou good tidings unto the patient
2:175 (170)	how patiently they shall endure the Fire
2:177 (172)	endure with fortitude misfortune, hardship and peril
2:249 (250)	God is with the patient
3:17 (15)	men who are patient, truthful, obedient
3:142 (136)	who of you have struggled and who are patient
3:146 (140)	God loves the patient
8:46 (48)	surely God is with the patient
8:65 (66)	if there be twenty of you, patient men, they will overcome two hundred
8:66 (67)	if there be a hundred of you, patient men, they will overcome two hundred
8:66 (67)	God is with the patient
16:126 (127)	better it is for those patient
18:69 (68)	thou shalt find me, if God will, patient
21:85 (85)	Ishmael, Idris, Dhul Kifl — each was of the patient
22:35 (36)	such as endure patiently whatever visits them
28:80 (80)	none shall receive it except the steadfast
33:35 (35)	enduring men and (enduring women)
33:35 (35)	(enduring men) and enduring women
37:102 (102)	thou shalt find me, God willing, one of the steadfast
38:44 (43)	surely We found him a steadfast man
39:10 (13)	the patient will be paid their wages in full
47:31 (33)	until We know those of you who struggle and are steadfast

ṢABBĀR n.m.~enduring, patient, steadfast

14:5 (5)	in that are signs for every man enduring, thankful
31:31 (30)	in that are signs for every man enduring, thankful
34:19 (18)	in that are signs for every man enduring, thankful
42:33 (31)	in that are signs for every man enduring, thankful

ṢĀBARA vb. (III)~to excel or vie in patience

c) impv. (*ṣābir*)

3:200 (200) O believers, be patient, and vie you in patience

IṢṬABARA vb. (VIII)~to be patient, to have or keep patience, to be forbearing

c) impv. (*iṣṭabir*)

19:65 (66) be thou patient in His service
20:132 (132) bid thy family to pray, and be thou patient in it
54:27 (27) so watch thou them and keep patience

*Ṣ B Y

ṢABĀ vb. (I)~(with prep. *ilá*) to yearn towards; to incline to

b) impf. act. (*yaṣbū*)

12:33 (33) turnest not from me their guile, then I shall yearn towards them

ṢABĪY n.m.~a child; a boy, a lad, a youth

19:12 (13) We gave him judgment, yet a little child
19:29 (30) one who is still in the cradle, a little child

*Ṣ D ᶜ

ṢADAᶜA vb. (I)~to cleave, to split; to shout; to proclaim, to say openly. (n.vb.) splitting (with verdure)

c) impv. (*iṣdaᶜ*)

15:94 (94) so shout that thou art commanded

f) n.vb. (*ṣadᶜ*)

86:12 (12) by earth splitting with verdure

ṢADDAᶜA vb. (II)~to cause a headache, to suffer from a headache

e) impf. pass. (*yuṣaddaᶜu*)

56:19 (19) no brows throbbing, no intoxication

TAṢADDAᶜA vb. (V)~to be split up, to be sundered apart, to break. (pcple. act.) split asunder, rent asunder

b) impf. act. (*yaṣṣaddaᶜu* for *yataṣaddaᶜu*)

30:43 (42) on that day they shall be sundered apart

g) pcple. act. (*mutaṣaddiᶜ*)

59:21 (21) thou wouldst have seen it humbled, split asunder out of the fear of God

*Ṣ D D

ṢADDA vb. (I)~to bar, to debar, to prevent, to hinder; to dissuade; to turn away from; to disbelieve. (n.vb.) stopping; prevention, barring

a) perf. act.

4:55 (58) some of them there are that believe, and some of them that bar from it
4:167 (165) those who disbelieve, and bar from the way of God
5:2 (3) a people who barred you from the Holy Mosque
9:9 (9) they have sold the signs of God for a small price, and have barred from His way
16:88 (90) those that disbelieve and bar from the way of God
16:94 (96) for that you barred from the way of God
27:24 (24) he has barred them from the way
27:43 (43) but that she served, apart from God, barred her
29:38 (37) Satan decked out fair to them their works, and barred them from the way
34:32 (31) did we bar you from the guidance after it came to you?
47:1 (1) those who disbelieve and bar from God's way
47:32 (34) those who disbelieve and bar from God's way
47:34 (36) those who disbelieve and bar from God's way
48:25 (25) they are the ones who disbelieved, and barred you from the Holy Mosque
58:16 (17) they have taken their oaths as a covering, and barred from God's way
63:2 (2) then they have barred from the way of God

b) impf. act. (*yaṣuddu*)

3:99 (94) People of the Book, why do you bar from God's way the believer
4:61 (64) then thou seest the hypocrites barring the way to thee
5:91 (93) and to bar you from the remembrance of God, and from prayer
7:45 (43) who bar from God's way, desiring to make it crooked
7:86 (84) threatening and barring from God's way those who believe
8:34 (34) when they are barring from the Holy Mosque
8:36 (36) the unbelievers expend their wealth to bar from God's way
8:47 (49) to show off to men, and barring from God's way
9:34 (34) consume the goods of the people in vanity and bar from God's way
11:19 (22) who bar from God's way, desiring to make it crooked
14:3 (3) and bar from God's way, desiring to make it crooked
14:10 (12) you desire to bar us from that our fathers served
20:16 (17) let none bar thee from it, that believes not in it
22:25 (25) those who disbelieve, and bar from God's way
28:87 (87) let them not bar thee from the signs of God
34:43 (42) this is naught but a man who desires to bar you from that your fathers served
43:37 (36) and they bar them from the way
43:57 (57) when the son of Mary is cited as an example, behold, thy people turn away from it
43:62 (62) let not Satan bar you; he is for you a manifest foe
63:5 (5) thou seest them turning their faces away, waxing proud

d) perf. pass. (*ṣudda*)

13:33 (33) and they are barred from the way
40:37 (40) Pharaoh, and he was barred from the way

f) n.vb. (1) (*ṣadd*)

2:217 (214) but to bar from God's way, and disbelief in Him
4:160 (158) and for their barring from God's way many

f) n.vb. (2) (*ṣudūd*)

4:61 (64) then thou seest the hypocrites barring the way to thee <...>

ṢADĪD n.m.~pus

14:16 (19) he is given to drink of oozing pus

*Ṣ D F

ṢADAFA vb. (I)~(with prep. *ʿan*) to turn away from

6:157 (158) he who cries lies to God's signs, and turns away from them

b) impf. act. (*yaṣdifu*)

6:46 (46) yet thereafter they are turning away
6:157 (158) We shall surely recompense those who turn away from Our signs
6:157 (158) with an evil chastisement for their turning away

ṢADAF n.m.~cliff

18:96 (95) when he had made all level between the two cliffs

*Ṣ D Q

ṢADAQA vb. (I)~to be true, to be sincere; to speak truly; to be right. (n.vb.) truth, truthfulness; sincerity; correctness, veracity; (adj) sure, just. (pcple. act.) truthful, one who speaks truly; sincere

a) perf. act.

2:177 (172) these are they who are true in their faith
3:95 (89) God has spoken the truth
3:152 (145) God has been true in His promise towards you
5:113 (113) that we may know that thou hast spoken true to us
9:43 (43) till it was clear to thee which of them spoke the truth
12:26 (26) if his shirt has been torn from before then she has spoken truly
21:9 (9) then We made true the promise We gave them
27:27 (27) now we will see whether thou hast spoken truly
29:3 (2) assuredly God knows those who speak truly
33:22 (22) God and His Messenger have spoken truly
33:23 (23) among the believers are men who were true to their covenant
36:52 (52) the Envoys spoke truly
39:74 (74) praise belongs to God, who has been true in His promise to us
47:21 (23) if they were true to God, it would be better for them
48:27 (27) God has indeed fulfilled the vision He vouchsafed to His Messenger truly

f) n.vb. (*ṣidq*)

5:119 (119) this is the day the truthful shall be profited by their truthfulness
6:115 (115) Perfect are the words of thy Lord in truthfulness
10:2 (2) they have a sure footing with their Lord
10:93 (93) We settled the Children of Israel in a sure settlement
17:80 (82) my Lord, lead me in with a just ingoing

17:80 (82)	and lead me out with a just outgoing
19:50 (51)	We appointed unto them a tongue of truthfulness
26:84 (84)	appoint me a tongue of truthfulness among the others
33:8 (8)	that He might question the truthful concerning their truthfulness
33:24 (24)	that God may recompense the truthful ones for their truthfulness
39:32 (33)	lies against God and cries lies to the very truth
39:33 (34)	he who has come with the very truth and confirms it
46:16 (15)	the promise of the very truth, which they were promised
54:55 (55)	in a sure abode, in the presence of a King Omnipotent

g) pcple. act. (*ṣādiq*; comp. *aṣdaq*)

2:23 (21)	call your witnesses, apart from God, if you are truthful
2:31 (29)	now tell Me the names of these, if you speak truly
2:94 (88)	then long for death — if you speak truly
2:111 (105)	produce your proof, if you speak truly
3:17 (15)	men who are patient, truthful, obedient
3:93 (87)	bring you the Torah now, and recite it, if you are truthful
3:168 (162)	then avert death from yourselves, if you speak truly
3:183 (180)	why therefore did you slay them, if you speak truly?
4:87 (89)	who is truer in tidings than God?
4:122 (121)	God's promise in truth; and who is truer in speech than God?
5:119 (119)	this is the day the truthful shall be profited
6:40 (40)	will you call upon any other than God if you speak truly?
6:143 (144)	tell me the knowledge, if you speak truly
6:146 (147)	surely We speak truly
7:70 (68)	then bring us that thou promisest us, if thou speakest truly
7:106 (103)	if thou hast brought a sign, produce it, if thou speakest truly
7:194 (193)	call them and let them answer you, if you speak truly
9:119 (120)	O believers, fear God, and be with the truthful ones
10:38 (39)	call on whom you can, apart from God, if you speak truly
10:48 (49)	when will this promise be, if you speak truly?
11:13 (16)	call upon whom you are able, apart from God, if you speak truly
11:32 (34)	then bring us that thou promisest us, if thou speakest truly
12:17 (17)	thou wouldst never believe us, though we spoke truly
12:27 (27)	then she has lied, and he is one of the truthful
12:51 (51)	I solicited him; he is a truthful man
12:82 (82)	we are truthful men
15:7 (7)	why dost thou not bring the angels unto us, if thou speakest truly?
15:64 (64)	assuredly we speak truly
19:54 (55)	he was true to his promise, and he was a Messenger
21:38 (39)	when shall the promise come to pass, if you speak truly?
24:6 (6)	to testify by God four times that he is of the truthful
24:9 (9)	the wrath of God shall be upon her, if he should be of the truthful
26:31 (30)	bring it then, if thou art of the truthful
26:154 (154)	then produce a sign, if thou art one of the truthful
26:187 (187)	then drop down on us lumps from heaven, if thou art one of the truthful
27:49 (50)	assuredly we are truthful men
27:64 (65)	produce your proof, if you speak truly
27:71 (73)	when shall this promise come to pass, if you speak the truth?
28:49 (49)	better guidance than these, and follow it, if you speak truly
29:29 (28)	then bring us the chastisement of God, if thou speakest truly
32:28 (28)	when shall be this Victory, if you speak truly?
33:8 (8)	that He might question the truthful concerning their truthfulness
33:24 (24)	that God may recompense the truthful ones for their truthfulness
33:35 (35)	truthful men and (truthful women)

33:35 (35) (truthful men) and truthful women
34:29 (28) when shall this promise come to pass, if you speak the truth?
36:48 (48) when shall this promise come to pass, if you speak truly?
37:157 (157) bring your Book, if you speak truly
40:28 (29) if he is truthful, somewhat of that he promises you will smite you
44:36 (35) bring us our fathers, if you speak truly
45:25 (24) bring us our fathers, if you speak truly
46:4 (3) or some remnant of a knowledge, if you speak truly
46:22 (21) bring us that thou promisest us, if indeed thou speakest truly
49:15 (15) those — they are the truthful ones
49:17 (17) if it be that you are truthful
51:5 (5) surely that you are promised is true
52:34 (34) let them bring a discourse like it, if they speak truly
56:87 (86) do you not bring back his soul, if you speak truly?
59:8 (8) those — they are the truthful ones
62:6 (6) then do you long for death, if you speak truly
67:25 (25) when shall this promise come to pass, if you speak truly?
68:41 (41) let them bring their associates, if they speak truly

ṢADAQAH n.f.~freewill offering, charity, almsgiving, alms

2:196 (192) then redemption by fast, or freewill offering
2:263 (265) honourable words, and forgiveness, are better than a freewill offering
2:264 (266) void not your freewill offerings with reproach and injury
2:271 (273) if you publish your freewill offerings, it is excellent
2:276 (277) freewill offerings He augments with interest
4:114 (114) except for him who bids to freewill offering, or honour
9:58 (58) some of them find fault with thee touching the freewill offerings
9:60 (60) the freewill offerings are for the poor and needy
9:79 (80) those who find fault with the believers who volunteer their freewill offerings
9:103 (104) take of their wealth a freewill offering, to purify
9:104 (105) God is He who accepts repentance from His servants, and takes the freewill offerings
58:12 (13) before your conspiring advance a freewill offering
58:13 (14) are you afraid, before your conspiring, to advance freewill offerings

ṢADĪQ n.m.~a friend

24:61 (60) or that whereof you own the keys, or of your friend
26:101 (101) no loyal friend

ṢADUQĀT n.f. (pl. of *ṣaduqah*)~dowry

4:4 (3) give the women their dowries as a gift spontaneous

ṢIDDĪQ n.m.~a true (person), a just (person); righteous, upright

4:69 (71) those whom God has blessed, Prophets, just men, martyrs
5:75 (79) his mother was a just woman
12:46 (46) Joseph, thou true man, pronounce to us regarding seven fat kine
19:41 (42) mention in the Book Abraham; surely he was a true man
19:56 (57) mention in the Book Idris; he was a true man
57:19 (18) Messengers — they are the just men and the martyrs in their Lord's sight

ṢADDAQA vb. (II)~to confirm, to give credence; to believe; to accept as true. (n.vb.) confirmation; accepting as true, belief. (pcple. act.) confirming; establishing as true

a) perf. act.

34:20 (19)	Iblis proved true his opinion of them
37:37 (36)	he brought the truth, and confirmed the Envoys
37:105 (105)	thou hast confirmed the vision
39:33 (34)	he who has come with the very truth and confirms it
66:12 (12)	she confirmed the Words of her Lord and His Books
75:31 (31)	he confirmed it not, and did not pray
92:6 (6)	and confirms the reward most fair

b) impf. act. (*yuṣaddiqu*)

28:34 (34)	send him with me as a helper and to confirm I speak truly
56:57 (57)	We created you; therefore why will you not believe?
70:26 (26)	who confirm the Day of Doom

f) n.vb. (*taṣdīq*)

10:37 (38)	but it is a confirmation of what is before it
12:111 (111)	it is not a tale forged, but a confirmation of what is before it

g) pcple. act. (*muṣaddiq*)

2:41 (38)	that I have sent down, confirming that which is with you
2:89 (83)	a Book from God, confirming what was with them
2:91 (85)	it is the truth confirming what is with them
2:97 (91)	he it was that brought it down upon thy heart by the leave of God, confirming what was before it
2:101 (95)	when there has come to them a Messenger from God confirming what was with them
3:3 (2)	He has sent down upon thee the Book with the truth, confirming what was before it
3:39 (34)	God gives thee good tidings of John, who shall confirm
3:50 (44)	likewise confirming the truth of the Torah that is before me
3:81 (75)	then there shall come to you a Messenger confirming what is with you
4:47 (50)	believe in what We have sent down, confirming what is with you
5:46 (50)	We sent ... Jesus son of Mary, confirming the Torah before him
5:46 (50)	wherein is guidance and light, and confirming the Torah before it
5:48 (52)	We have sent down to thee the Book with the truth, confirming the Book that was before it
6:92 (92)	a Book We have sent down, blessed and confirming that which was before it
35:31 (28)	that We have revealed to thee of the Book is the truth, confirming what is before it
37:52 (50)	are you a confirmer?
46:12 (11)	this is a Book confirming, in Arabic tongue
46:30 (29)	we have heard a Book that was sent down after Moses, confirming what was before it
61:6 (6)	Israel, I am indeed the Messenger of God to you, confirming the Torah

TAṢADDAQA vb. (V)~to give a freewill offering, to give alms, to donate; to be charitable. (pcple. act.) charitable; one who gives in charity, who makes freewill offerings

a) perf. act.

2:280 (280)	that you should give freewill offerings is better for you
5:45 (49)	whosoever forgoes it as a freewill offering, that shall be for him an expiation

b) impf. act. (*yataṣaddaqu* or *yaṣṣaddaqu*)

4:92 (94)	bloodwit is to be paid to his family unless they forgo it as a freewill offering
9:75 (76)	if He gives us of His bounty, we will make offerings

c) impv. (*taṣaddaq*)

63:10 (10)	Thou wouldst defer me unto a near term, so that I may make freewill offering
12:88 (88)	fill up to us the measure, and be charitable to us

g) pcple. act. (*mutaṣaddiq* or *muṣṣaddiq*)

12:88 (88)	surely God recompenses the charitable
33:35 (35)	men and (women) who give in charity
33:35 (35)	(men) and women who give in charity
57:18 (17)	those, the men and (the women) who make freewill offerings
57:18 (17)	those, (the men) and the women, who make freewill offerings

*Ṣ D R

ṢADARA vb. (I)~to issue, to go out

b) impf. act. (*yaṣduru*)

99:6 (6)	upon that day men shall issue in scatterings to see their works

ṢADR n.m. (pl. *ṣudūr*)~breast, chest; heart; mind

3:29 (27)	whether you hide what is in your breasts or publish it
3:118 (114)	what their breasts conceal is yet greater
3:119 (115)	die in your rage; God knows the thoughts in the breasts
3:154 (148)	that God might try what was in your breasts
3:154 (148)	God knows the thoughts in the breasts
4:90 (92)	or come to you with breasts constricted from fighting with you
5:7 (10)	surely God knows the thoughts in the breasts
6:125 (125)	whomsoever God desires to guide, He expands his breast to Islam
6:125 (125)	whomsoever He desires to lead astray, He makes his breast narrow
7:2 (1)	let there be no impediment in thy breast because of it
7:43 (41)	We shall strip away all rancour that is in their breasts
8:43 (45)	He knows the thoughts in the breasts
9:14 (14)	and bring healing to the breasts of a people who believe
10:57 (58)	an admonition from your Lord, and a healing for what is in the breasts
11:5 (5)	they fold their breasts, to hide them from Him
11:5 (7)	surely He knows all the thoughts within the breasts
11:12 (15)	thou art leaving part of what is revealed to thee, and thy breast is straitened by it
15:47 (47)	We shall strip away all rancour that is in their breasts
15:97 (97)	thy breast is straitened by the things they say
16:106 (108)	whosoever's breast is expanded in unbelief
17:51 (53)	or some creation yet more monstrous in your minds
20:25 (26)	Lord, open my breast
22:46 (45)	but blind are the hearts within the breasts
26:13 (12)	and my breast will be straitened
27:74 (76)	thy Lord knows what their hearts conceal, and what they publish
28:69 (69)	thy Lord knows what their breasts conceal and what they publish

29:10 (9)	does not God know very well what is in the breasts
29:49 (48)	it is signs, clear signs in the breasts of those who have been given knowledge
31:23 (22)	surely God knows all the thoughts within the breasts
35:38 (36)	He knows the thoughts within the breasts
39:7 (10)	He knows the thoughts within the breasts
39:22 (23)	he whose breast God has expanded unto Islam
40:19 (20)	He knows the treachery of the eyes and what the breasts conceal
40:56 (58)	in their breasts is only pride, that they shall never attain
40:80 (80)	that on them you may attain a need in your breasts
42:24 (23)	He knows the thoughts within the breasts
57:6 (6)	He knows the thoughts within the breasts
59:9 (9)	not finding in their breasts any need for what they have been given
59:13 (13)	why, you arouse greater fear in their hearts than God
64:4 (4)	God knows the thoughts within the breasts
67:13 (13)	He knows the thoughts within the breasts
94:1 (1)	did We not expand thy breast for thee
100:10 (10)	that which is in the breasts is brought out
114:5 (5)	who whispers in the breasts of men

AṢDARA vb. (IV)~to send, to send out, to dispatch; to drive off

b) impf. act. (*yuṣdiru*)

28:23 (23)	we may not draw water until the shepherds drive off

*Ṣ D Y

ṢADDÁ vb. (II)~(n.vb.) clapping of hands

f) n.vb. (*taṣdiyah*)

8:35 (35)	their prayer at the House is nothing but a whistling and a clapping of hands

TAṢADDÁ vb. (V)~to pay regard, to attend to someone b) impf. act. (*yataṣaddá*)

80:6 (6)	to him thou attendest

*Ṣ F D

AṢFĀD n.m. (pl. of *ṣafad*)~fetters, bonds

14:49 (50)	thou shalt see the sinners that day coupled in fetters
38:38 (37)	others also, coupled in fetters

*Ṣ F F

ṢAFFA vb. (I)~(pcple. act.) spreading the wings; ranger; standing in ranks; setting the ranks in battle order. (pcple. pass.) arrayed, ranged in rows *g*) pcple. act. (*ṣāff*)

22:36 (37)	mention God's Name over them, standing in ranks
24:41 (41)	and the birds spreading their wings
37:1 (1)	by the rangers ranging
37:165 (165)	we are the rangers
67:19 (19)	have they not regarded the birds above them spreading their wings

h) pcple. pass. f. (*maṣfūfah*)

52:20 (20)	reclining upon couches ranged in rows
88:15 (15)	and cushions arrayed

ṢAFF n.m.~rank, battle-line; ranging, ranking

18:48 (46)	they shall be presented before their Lord in ranks
20:64 (67)	gather your guile; then come in battle-line
37:1 (1)	by the rangers ranging
61:4 (4)	God loves those who fight in His way in ranks
78:38 (38)	upon the day when the Spirit and the angels stand in ranks
89:22 (23)	thy Lord comes, and the angels rank on (rank)
89:22 (23)	thy Lord comes, and the angels (rank) on rank

*Ṣ F Ḥ

ṢAFAḤA vb. (I)~to forgive, to pardon; to overlook. (n.vb.) pardoning; (*ḍaraba ʿanhu ṣafḥan*) to turn away from someone or something

b) impf. act. (*yaṣfaḥu*)

24:22 (22)	let them pardon and forgive
64:14 (14)	but if you pardon, and overlook, and if you forgive

c) impv. (*iṣfaḥ*)

2:109 (103)	yet do you pardon and be forgiving, till God brings His command
5:13 (16)	yet pardon them, and forgive
15:85 (85)	so pardon thou, with a gracious pardoning
43:89 (89)	yet pardon them

f) n.vb. (*ṣafḥ*)

15:85 (85)	so pardon thou, with a gracious pardoning
43:5 (4)	shall We turn away the Remembrance from you

*Ṣ F N

ṢAFANA vb. (I)~(pcple. act.) standing with one foot slightly raised

g) pcple. act. f. (*ṣāfinah*)

38:31 (30)	when in the evening were presented to him the standing steeds

*Ṣ F R

ṢAFRĀ' n.f. (adj; pl. *ṣufr*)~golden; yellow

2:69 (64)	she shall be a golden cow, bright her colour
77:33 (33)	sparks like to golden herds

IṢFARRA vb. (IX)~(pcple. pass.) growing yellow

h) pcple. pass. (*muṣfarr*)

30:51 (50)	if We loose a wind, and they see it growing yellow
39:21 (22)	then they wither, and thou seest them turning yellow
57:20 (19)	then it withers, and thou seest it turning yellow

*Ṣ F Ṣ F

ṢAFṢAF n.m. (adj)~level, even; desolate, barren

20:106 (106)	then He will leave them a level hollow

*Ṣ F W

ṢAFĀ n.prop.~Safa (a mountain near Mecca)

2:158 (153)	Safa and Marwa are among the waymarks of God

ṢAFWĀN n.m.~a hard or smooth rock, a stone

2:264 (266)	the likeness of him is as the likeness of a smooth rock on which is soil

ṢAFFÁ vb. (II)~(pcple. pass.) clarified, filtered, purified

h) pcple. pass. (*muṣaffá*)

47:15 (17)	rivers, too, of honey purified

AṢFÁ vb. (IV)~to choose, to select, to favour

17:40 (42)	has your Lord favoured you with sons and taken to Himself from the angels females
43:16 (15)	or has He taken to Himself, from that He creates, daughters

IṢṬAFÁ vb. (VIII)~to choose, to select. (pcple. pass.) chosen, select

a) perf. act.

2:130 (124)	indeed, We chose him in the present world
2:132 (126)	my sons, God has chosen for you the religion
2:247 (248)	God has chosen him over you, and has increased him
3:33 (30)	God chose Adam and Noah and the House of Abraham
3:42 (37)	Mary, God has chosen thee, and purified thee
3:42 (37)	He has chosen thee above all women
7:144 (141)	Moses, I have chosen thee above all men for My Messages
27:59 (60)	peace be on His servants whom He has chosen

35:32 (29)	then We bequeathed the Book on those of Our servants We chose
37:153 (153)	has He chosen daughters above sons?
39:4 (6)	He would have chosen whatever He willed of that He has created

b) impf. act. (*yaṣṭafī*)

22:75 (74)	God chooses of the angels Messengers and of mankind

h) pcple. pass. (*muṣṭafá*)

38:47 (47)	in Our sight they are of the chosen, the excellent

*Ṣ GH R

ṢAGHARA vb. (I)~(pcple. act.) one who is small, humbled, contemptible

g) pcple. act. (*ṣāghir*)

7:13 (12)	surely thou art among the humbled
7:119 (116)	they were vanquished there, and they turned about, humbled
9:29 (29)	until they pay the tribute out of hand and have been humbled
12:32 (32)	he shall be imprisoned, and be one of the humbled
27:37 (37)	we shall expel them from there, abased and utterly humbled

ṢAGHĀR n.m.~humiliation, contempt

6:124 (124)	humiliation in God's sight shall befall the sinners

ṢAGHĪR n.m. (adj; comp. *aṣghar*)~small, little

2:282 (282)	be not loth to write it down, whether it be small or great
9:121 (122)	nor do they expend any sum, small or great
10:61 (62)	neither is aught smaller than that, or greater
17:24 (25)	have mercy upon them, as they raised me up when I was little
18:49 (47)	how is it with this Book, that it leaves nothing behind, small or great
34:3 (3)	neither is aught smaller than that, or greater
54:53 (53)	everything, great and small, is inscribed

*Ṣ GH Y

ṢAGHIYA vb. (I)~to incline, to bend toward, to lean

a) perf. act.

66:4 (4)	yet your hearts certainly inclined

b) impf. act. (*yaṣghá*)

6:113 (113)	that the hearts of those who believe not in the world to come may incline to it

*Ṣ H R

ṢAHARA vb. (I)~to melt, to dissolve

e) impf. pass. (*yuṣharu*)

22:20 (21)	whatsoever is in their bellies and their skins shall be melted

ṢIHR n.m.~kin by marriage

25:54 (56)	He who created of water a mortal, and made him kindred of blood and marriage

*Ṣ Ḥ B

ṢĀḤIB n.m. (pl. *aṣḥāb*)~companion, comrade, associate, fellow, friend; (*ṣāḥib al-ḥūt* , in 68:48) the Man of the Fish, Jonah; (f) consort, companion, wife; (pl) lords, possessors, masters, men of, owners; dwellers, inhabitants; (*aṣḥāb al-jannah*) Inhabitants of Paradise, (*aṣḥāb al-nār*) Inhabitants of the Fire, (*aṣḥāb al- maymanah*) Companions of the Right, (*aṣḥāb al-mash'amah*) Companions of the Left

2:39 (37)	those shall be the inhabitants of the Fire
2:81 (75)	those are the inhabitants of the Fire
2:82 (76)	those are the inhabitants of Paradise
2:119 (113)	thou shalt not be questioned touching the inhabitants of Hell
2:217 (214)	those are the inhabitants of the Fire
2:257 (259)	those are the inhabitants of the Fire
2:275 (276)	those are the inhabitants of the Fire
3:116 (112)	those are the inhabitants of the Fire
4:36 (40)	and to the companion at your side
4:47 (50)	turn them upon their backs, or curse them as We cursed the Sabbath-men
5:10 (13)	they shall be the inhabitants of Hell
5:29 (32)	and so become an inhabitant of the Fire
5:86 (88)	they are the inhabitants of Hell
6:71 (70)	though he has friends who call him to guidance
6:101 (101)	how should He have a son, seeing that He has no consort
7:36 (34)	those shall be the inhabitants of the Fire
7:42 (40)	those are the inhabitants of Paradise
7:44 (42)	the inhabitants of Paradise will call
7:44 (42)	to the inhabitants of the Fire
7:46 (44)	who shall call to the inhabitants of Paradise
7:47 (45)	when their eyes are turned towards the inhabitants of the Fire
7:48 (46)	the dwellers on the Battlements shall call to certain men they know
7:50 (48)	the inhabitants of the Fire shall call
7:50 (48)	to the inhabitants of Paradise
7:184 (183)	no madness is in their comrade
9:40 (40)	when he said to his companion
9:70 (71)	the people of Abraham, the men of Midian and the subverted cities
9:113 (114)	after that it has become clear to them that they will be the inhabitants of Hell
10:26 (27)	those are the inhabitants of Paradise
10:27 (28)	those are the inhabitants of the Fire
11:23 (25)	they shall be the inhabitants of Paradise
12:39 (39)	say, which is better, my fellow-prisoners
12:41 (41)	fellow-prisoners, as for one of you, he shall pour wine for his lord
13:5 (6)	those shall be the inhabitants of the Fire
15:78 (78)	certainly the dwellers in the Thicket were evildoers
15:80 (80)	the dwellers in El-Hijr cried lies to the Envoys
18:9 (8)	dost thou think the Men of the Cave and Er-Rakeem were among Our signs a wonder?
18:34 (32)	he said to his fellow, as he was conversing with him
18:37 (35)	said his fellow, as he was conversing with him

20:135 (135)	assuredly you shall know who are the travellers on the even path
22:44 (43)	the men of Midian; to Moses also they cried lies
22:51 (50)	they shall be the inhabitants of Hell
25:24 (26)	the inhabitants of Paradise that day, better shall be their lodging
25:38 (40)	Ad, and Thamood, and the men of Er-Rass
26:61 (61)	when the two hosts sighted each other, the companions of Moses said
26:176 (176)	the men of the Thicket cried lies to the Envoys
29:15 (14)	We delivered him, and those who were in the ship
34:46 (45)	no madness is in your comrade
35:6 (6)	only that they may be among the inhabitants of the Blaze
36:13 (12)	the inhabitants of the city, when the Envoys came to it
36:55 (55)	the inhabitants of Paradise today are busy in their rejoicing
38:13 (12)	the men of the Thicket — those were the parties
39:8 (11)	thou shalt be among the inhabitants of the Fire
40:6 (6)	that they are the inhabitants of the Fire
40:43 (46)	the prodigal are the inhabitants of the Fire
46:14 (13)	those are the inhabitants of Paradise
46:16 (15)	they are among the inhabitants of Paradise
50:12 (12)	cried lies before them the people of Noah and the men of Er-Rass
50:14 (13)	the men of the Thicket, the people of Tubba'
51:59 (59)	the evildoers shall have their portion, like the portion of their fellows
53:2 (2)	your comrade is not astray, neither errs
54:29 (29)	then they called their comrade
56:8 (8)	Companions of the Right
56:8 (8)	O Companions of the Right
56:9 (9)	Companions of the Left
56:9 (9)	O Companions of the Left
56:27 (26)	the Companions of the Right
56:27 (26)	O Companions of the Right
56:38 (37)	for the Companions of the Right
56:41 (40)	the Companions of the Left
56:41 (40)	O Companions of the Left
56:90 (89)	if he be a Companion of the Right
56:91 (90)	peace be upon thee, Companion of the Right
57:19 (18)	they are the inhabitants of Hell
58:17 (18)	those — they are the inhabitants of the Fire
59:20 (20)	not equal are the inhabitants of the Fire
59:20 (20)	and the inhabitants of Paradise
59:20 (20)	the inhabitants of Paradise — they are the triumphant
60:13 (13)	the unbelievers have despaired of the inhabitants of the tombs
64:10 (10)	those shall be the inhabitants of the Fire
67:10 (10)	we would not have been of the inhabitants of the Blaze
67:11 (11)	so they confess their sins. Curse the inhabitants of the Blaze
68:17 (17)	We have tried them, even as We tried the owners of the garden
68:48 (48)	be not as the Man of the Fish, when he called, choking inwardly
70:12 (12)	his companion wife, his brother
72:3 (3)	has not taken to Himself either consort or a son
74:31 (31)	We have appointed only angels to be masters of the Fire
74:39 (41)	save the Companions of the Right
80:36 (36)	his consort, his sons
81:22 (22)	your companion is not possessed
85:4 (4)	slain were the Men of the Pit
90:18 (18)	those are the Companions of the Right Hand
90:19 (19)	those who disbelieve in Our signs, they are the Companions of the Left Hand
105:1 (1)	hast thou not seen how thy Lord did with the Men of the Elephant

ṢĀḤABA vb. (III)~to keep company

b) impf. act. (*yuṣāḥibu*)

18:76 (75)	if I question thee on anything after this, then keep me company no more

c) impv. (*ṣāḥib*)

31:15 (14)	keep them company honourable in this world

AṢḤABA vb. (IV)~to preserve, to guard

e) impf. pass. (*yuṣḥabu*)

21:43 (44)	nor shall they be guarded in safety from Us

*Ṣ Ḥ F

ṢIḤĀF n.f. (pl. of *ṣaḥfah*)~platter

43:71 (71)	there shall be passed around them platters of gold

ṢUḤUF n.f. (pl. of *ṣaḥīfah*)~scrolls, scriptures

20:133 (133)	has there not come to them the clear sign of what is in the former scrolls?
53:36 (37)	or has he not been told of what is in the scrolls of Moses
74:52 (52)	every man of them desires to be given scrolls unrolled
80:13 (13)	upon pages high-honoured
81:10 (10)	when the scrolls shall be unrolled
87:18 (18)	surely this is in the ancient scrolls
87:19 (19)	the scrolls of Abraham and Moses
98:2 (2)	a Messenger from God, reciting pages purified

*Ṣ K K

ṢAKKA vb. (I)~to smite, to strike

a) perf. act.

51:29 (29)	then came forward his wife, clamouring, and she smote her face

*Ṣ KH KH

ṢĀKHKHAH n.f.~a blast; a shout

80:33 (33)	when the Blast shall sound

*Ṣ KH R

ṢAKHR n.m.~rocks; (f.s) a rock

18:63 (62)	what thinkest thou? When we took refuge in the rock
31:16 (15)	though it be in a rock, or in the heavens, or in the earth
89:9 (8)	and Thamood, who hollowed the rocks in the valley

*Ṣ L B

ṢALABA vb. (I)~to crucify

a) perf. act.

4:157 (156)	yet they did not slay him, neither crucified him

e) impf. pass. (*yuṣlabu*)

12:41 (41)	as for the other, he shall be crucified

ṢULB n.m. (pl. *aṣlāb*)~loins, backbone

4:23 (27)	the spouses of your sons who are of your loins
86:7 (7)	issuing between the loins and the breast-bones

ṢALLABA vb. (II)~to crucify

b) impf. act. (*yuṣallibu*)

7:124 (121)	then I shall crucify you all together
20:71 (74)	then I shall crucify you upon the trunks of palm-trees
26:49 (49)	then I shall crucify you all together

e) impf. pass. (*yuṣallabu*)

5:33 (37)	they shall be slaughtered, or crucified

*Ṣ L D

ṢALD n.m. (adj)~hard; barren

2:264 (266)	a torrent smites it, and leaves it barren

*Ṣ L Ḥ

ṢALAḤA vb. (I)~to be righteous, to be good, to do right, to do a deed of righteousness. (pcple. act.) one who does deeds or works of righteousness; (n) righteousness; (adj) righteous, good, right

a) perf. act.

13:23 (23)	those who were righteous of their fathers
40:8 (8)	those who were righteous of their fathers, and their wives

g) pcple. act. (*ṣāliḥ*)

2:25 (23)	give thou good tidings to those who believe and do deeds of righteousness

2:62 (59)	whoso believes in God and the Last Day, and works righteousness
2:82 (76)	those that believe, and do deeds of righteousness
2:130 (124)	in the world to come he shall be among the righteous
2:277 (277)	those who believe and do deeds of righteousness
3:39 (34)	a chief, and chaste, a Prophet, righteous
3:46 (41)	and righteous he shall be
3:57 (50)	as for the believers, who do deeds of righteousness
3:114 (110)	those are of the righteous
4:34 (38)	righteous women are therefore obedient
4:57 (60)	those that believe, and do deeds of righteousness
4:69 (71)	Prophets, just men, martyrs, the righteous; good companions they
4:122 (121)	those that believe, and do deeds of righteousness
4:124 (123)	whosoever does deeds of righteousness, be it male or female
4:173 (172)	as for the believers, who do deeds of righteousness
5:9 (12)	God has promised those that believe, and do deeds of righteousness
5:69 (73)	whosoever believes in God and the Last Day, and works righteousness
5:84 (87)	that our Lord should admit us with the righteous people
5:93 (94)	there is no fault in those who believe and do deeds of righteousness what they may eat
5:93 (94)	they are godfearing, and believe, and do deeds of righteousness
6:85 (85)	Zachariah and John, Jesus and Elias; each was of the righteous
7:42 (40)	those who believe, and do deeds of righteousness
7:168 (167)	some of them righteous, and some of them otherwise
7:189 (189)	if Thou givest us a righteous son, we indeed shall be of the thankful
7:190 (190)	when He gave them a righteous son, they assigned Him associates
7:196 (195)	He takes into His protection the righteous
9:75 (76)	we will make offerings and be of the righteous
9:102 (103)	they have mixed a righteous deed with another evil
9:120 (121)	a righteous deed is thereby written to their account
10:4 (4)	He may recompense those who believe and do deeds of righteousness
10:9 (9)	those who believe, and do deeds of righteousness
11:11 (14)	such as are patient, and do deeds of righteousness
11:23 (25)	those who believe, and do righteous deeds
11:46 (48)	it is a deed not righteous
12:9 (9)	thereafter you may be a righteous people
12:101 (102)	receive me to Thee in true submission, and join me with the righteous
13:29 (28)	those who believe and do righteous deeds
14:23 (28)	but as for those who believe, and do deeds of righteousness
16:97 (99)	whosoever does a righteous deed, be it male or female
16:122 (123)	in the world to come he shall be among the righteous
17:9 (10)	who do deeds of righteousness, that theirs shall be a great wage
17:25 (26)	your Lord knows very well what is in your hearts if you are righteous
18:2 (2)	to give good tidings unto the believers, who do righteous deeds
18:30 (29)	those who believe, and do deeds of righteousness
18:46 (44)	the abiding things, the deeds of righteousness, are better with God in reward
18:82 (81)	their father was a righteous man
18:88 (87)	as for him who believes, and does righteousness
18:107 (107)	those who believe, and do deeds of righteousness
18:110 (110)	let him, who hopes for the encounter with his Lord, work righteousness
19:60 (61)	save him who repents, and believes, and does a righteous deed
19:76 (79)	the abiding things, the deeds of righteousness, are better with thy Lord in reward
19:96 (96)	those who believe and do deeds of righteousness
20:75 (77)	whoso comes unto Him a believer having done deeds of righteousness
20:82 (84)	I am All-forgiving to him who repents and believes, and does righteousness

20:112 (111)	whosoever does deeds of righteousness, being a believer
21:72 (72)	every one made We righteous
21:75 (75)	We admitted him into Our mercy; he was of the righteous
21:86 (86)	We admitted them into Our mercy; they were of the righteous
21:94 (94)	whosoever does deeds of righteousness, being a believer
21:105 (105)	the earth shall be the inheritance of My righteous servants
22:14 (14)	God shall surely admit those who believe and do righteous deeds into gardens
22:23 (23)	God shall surely admit those who believe and do righteous deeds into gardens
22:50 (49)	those who believe, and do deeds of righteousness
22:56 (55)	as for those who believe, and do deeds of righteousness
23:51 (53)	O Messengers, eat of the good things and do righteousness
23:100 (102)	haply I shall do righteousness in that I forsook
24:32 (32)	marry the spouseless among you, and your slaves and handmaidens that are righteous
24:55 (54)	God has promised those of you who believe and do righteous deeds
25:70 (70)	save him who repents, and believes, and does righteous work
25:71 (71)	whosoever repents, and does righteousness, he truly turns to God in repentance
26:83 (83)	my Lord, give me Judgment, and join me with the righteous
26:227 (227)	save those that believe, and do righteous deeds
27:19 (19)	and that I may do righteousness well-pleasing to Thee
27:19 (19)	do Thou admit me, by Thy mercy, amongst Thy righteous servants
28:27 (27)	thou shalt assuredly find me, if God wills, one of the righteous
28:67 (67)	but as for him who repents, and believes, and works righteousness
28:80 (80)	the reward of God is better for him who believes, and works righteousness
29:7 (6)	those who believe, and do righteous deeds
29:9 (8)	those who believe, and do righteous deeds
29:9 (8)	assuredly We shall admit them among the righteous
29:27 (26)	and in the world to come he shall be among the righteous
29:58 (58)	those who believe, and do righteous deeds
30:15 (14)	as for those who believed, and did deeds of righteousness
30:44 (43)	whosoever does righteousness — for themselves they are making provision
30:45 (44)	He may recompense those who believe and do righteous deeds of His bounty
31:8 (7)	those who believe, and do deeds of righteousness, there awaits them Gardens
32:12 (12)	we have seen and heard; now return us, that we may do righteousness
32:19 (19)	as for those who believe, and do deeds of righteousness, there await them the Gardens
33:31 (31)	whosoever of you is obedient to God and His Messenger, and does righteousness
34:4 (4)	that He may recompense those who believe, and do righteous deeds
34:11 (10)	do ye righteousness, for surely I see the things you do
34:37 (36)	except for him who believes, and does righteousness
35:7 (8)	but those who believe, and do deeds of righteousness
35:10 (11)	to Him good words go up, and the righteous deed
35:37 (34)	we will do righteousness, other than what we have done
37:100 (98)	my Lord, give me one of the righteous
37:112 (112)	We gave him the good tidings of Isaac, a Prophet, one of the righteous
38:24 (23)	save those who believe, and do deeds of righteousness
38:28 (27)	shall We make those who believe and do righteous deeds as the workers of corruption
40:40 (43)	whosoever does a righteous deed, be it male or female
40:58 (60)	those who believe and do deeds of righteousness, and the wrongdoer
41:8 (7)	those who believe, and do righteous deeds shall have a wage unfailing
41:33 (33)	who speaks fairer than he who calls unto God and does righteousness
41:46 (46)	whoso does righteousness, it is to his own gain
42:22 (21)	those who believe and do righteous deeds are in Meadows
42:23 (22)	that is the good tidings God gives to His servants who believe and do righteous deeds
42:26 (25)	He answers those who believe and do righteous deeds

45:15 (14)	whoso does righteousness, it is to his own gain
45:21 (20)	We shall make them as those who believe and do righteous deeds
45:30 (29)	as for those who have believed and done deeds of righteousness
46:15 (14)	that I may do righteousness well-pleasing to Thee
47:2 (2)	those who believe and do righteous deeds and believe in what is sent down
47:12 (13)	God shall surely admit those who believe and do righteous deeds into gardens
48:29 (29)	those of them who believe and do deeds of righteousness
63:10 (10)	and so I may become one of the righteous
64:9 (9)	whosoever believes in God, and does righteousness
65:11 (11)	He may bring forth those who believe and do righteous deeds
65:11 (11)	whosoever believes in God, and does righteousness
66:4 (4)	God is his Protector, and Gabriel, and the righteous among the believers
66:10 (10)	they were under two of Our righteous servants
68:50 (50)	He placed him among the righteous
72:11 (11)	and some of us are the righteous
84:25 (25)	except those that believe, and do righteous deeds
85:11 (11)	those who believe, and do righteous deeds
95:6 (6)	save those who believe, and do righteous deeds
98:7 (6)	but those who believe, and do righteous deeds
103:3 (3)	save those who believe, and do righteous deeds

ṢĀLIḤ n.prop.~Salih (a prophet sent to the tribe of Thamood)

7:73 (71)	and to Thamood their brother Salih
7:75 (73)	do you know that Salih is an Envoy from his Lord?
7:77 (75)	O Salih, bring us that thou promisest us
11:61 (64)	and to Thamood their brother Salih
11:62 (65)	Salih, thou hast hitherto been a source of hope among us
11:66 (69)	when Our command came, We delivered Salih
11:89 (91)	the people of Hood, or the people of Salih
26:142 (142)	when their brother Salih said to them
27:45 (46)	We sent to Thamood their brother Salih

ṢULḤ n.m.~peace, reconciliation, settlement, compromise

4:128 (127)	there is no fault in them if the couple set things right between them
4:128 (127)	right settlement is better

AṢLAḤA vb. (IV)~to make amends, to make right, to put in order, to settle, to compensate. (n.vb.) the act of setting things right, restoration, restitution, reparation, reconciliation (pcple. act.) one who sets things right

a) perf. act.

2:160 (155)	such as repent and make amends
2:182 (178)	if any man fears injustice or sin from one making testament, and so makes things right between them
3:89 (83)	but those who repent thereafter, and make amends
4:16 (20)	but if they repent and make amends, then suffer them to be
4:146 (145)	such as repent, and make amends, and hold fast to God
5:39 (43)	whoso repents, after his evildoing, and makes amends
6:48 (48)	whoever believes and makes amends — no fear shall be on them
6:54 (54)	whosoever of you does evil in ignorance, and thereafter repents and makes amends
7:35 (33)	whosoever is godfearing and makes amends — no fear shall be on them
16:119 (120)	those who did evil in ignorance, then repented after that and put things right
21:90 (90)	and We set his wife right for him

24:5 (5)	save such as repent thereafter and make amends
42:40 (38)	whoso pardons and puts things right, his wage falls upon God
47:2 (2)	He will acquit them of their evil deeds, and dispose their minds aright

b) impf. act. (*yuṣliḥu*)

2:224 (224)	being pious and godfearing, and putting things right between men
4:128 (127)	there is no fault in them if the couple set things right between them
4:129 (128)	if you set things right, and are godfearing, God is All-forgiving
10:81 (81)	God sets not right the work of those who do corruption
26:152 (152)	who do corruption in the earth, and set not things aright
27:48 (49)	who did corruption in the land, and put not things right
33:71 (71)	He will set right your deeds for you
47:5 (6)	He will guide them, and dispose their minds aright

c) impv. (*aṣliḥ*)

7:142 (138)	be my successor among my people, and put things right
8:1 (1)	fear you God, and set things right between you
46:15 (14)	make me righteous also in my seed
49:9 (9)	if two parties of the believers fight, put things right between them
49:9 (9)	if it reverts, set things right between them equitably
49:10 (10)	so set things right between your two brothers

f) n.vb. (*iṣlāḥ*)

2:220 (218)	to set their affairs aright is good
2:228 (228)	their mates have better right to restore them, if they desire to set things right
4:35 (39)	and from her people an arbiter, if they desire to set things right
4:114 (114)	offering, or honour, or setting things right between the people
7:56 (54)	do not corruption in the land, after it has been set right
7:85 (83)	do not corruption in the land, after it has been set right
11:88 (90)	I desire only to set things right, so far as I am able

g) pcple. act. (*muṣliḥ*)

2:11 (10)	we are only ones that put things right
2:220 (219)	God knows well him who works corruption from him who sets aright
7:170 (169)	We leave not to waste the wage of those who set aright
11:117 (119)	while as yet their people were putting things right
28:19 (18)	thou desirest not to be of them that put things right

*Ṣ L Ṣ L

ṢALṢĀL n.m.~dry clay

15:26 (26)	We created man of a clay of mud moulded
15:28 (28)	see, I am creating a mortal of a clay of mud moulded
15:33 (33)	a mortal whom Thou hast created of a clay of mud moulded
55:14 (13)	He created man of a clay like the potter's

*Ṣ L W

MUṢALLÁ n.m.~a place of prayer

2:125 (119) take to yourselves Abraham's station for a place of prayer

ṢALĀH n.f. (pl. *ṣalawāt*)~a prayer, worship; (pl) oratories (22:40)

2:3 (2)	who believe in the Unseen, and perform the prayer
2:43 (40)	and perform the prayer, and pay the alms
2:45 (42)	seek you help in patience and prayer
2:83 (77)	speak good to men, and perform the prayer
2:110 (104)	perform the prayer, and pay the alms
2:153 (148)	all you who believe, seek you help in patience and prayer
2:157 (152)	upon those rest blessings and mercy from their Lord
2:177 (172)	to perform the prayer, to pay the alms
2:238 (239)	be you watchful over the prayers
2:238 (239)	and the middle prayer
2:277 (277)	perform the prayer, and pay the alms
4:43 (46)	draw not near to prayer when you are drunken
4:77 (79)	restrain your hands, and perform the prayer
4:101 (102)	there is no fault in you that you shorten the prayer
4:102 (103)	when thou art amongst them, and performest for them the prayer
4:103 (104)	when you have performed the prayer, remember God
4:103 (104)	then, when you are secure, perform the prayer
4:103 (104)	the prayer is a timed prescription for the believers
4:142 (141)	when they stand up to pray they stand up lazily
4:162 (160)	that perform the prayer and pay the alms
5:6 (8)	when you stand up to pray wash your faces
5:12 (15)	if you perform the prayer, and pay the alms
5:55 (60)	the believers who perform the prayer and pay the alms
5:58 (63)	and when you call to prayer, take it in mockery
5:91 (93)	to bar you from the remembrance of God, and from prayer
5:106 (105)	them you shall detain after the prayer
6:72 (71)	perform the prayer, and fear Him
6:92 (92)	those who believe in the world to come believe in it, and watch over their prayers
6:162 (163)	my prayer, my ritual sacrifice, my living, my dying — all belongs to God
7:170 (169)	those who hold fast to the Book, and perform the prayer
8:3 (3)	those who perform the prayer, and expend of what We have provided them
8:35 (35)	their prayer at the House is nothing but a whistling
9:5 (5)	but if they repent, and perform the prayer
9:11 (11)	yet if they repent, and perform the prayer
9:18 (18)	who believes in God and the Last Day, and performs the prayer
9:54 (54)	they believe not in God and His Messenger, and perform not the prayer
9:71 (72)	they perform the prayer, and pay the alms
9:99 (100)	bringing them near to God, and the prayers of the Messenger
9:103 (104)	thy prayers are a comfort for them
10:87 (87)	a direction for men to pray to; and perform the prayer
11:87 (89)	Shuaib, does thy prayer command thee that we should leave
11:114 (116)	perform the prayer at the two ends of the day
13:22 (22)	who perform the prayer, and expend of that We have provided them
14:31 (36)	say to My servants who believe, that they perform the prayer
14:37 (40)	our Lord, let them perform the prayer
14:40 (42)	my Lord, make me a performer of the prayer, and of my seed
17:78 (80)	perform the prayer at the sinking of the sun
17:110 (110)	be thou not loud in thy prayer, nor hushed therein
19:31 (32)	He has enjoined me to pray, and to give the alms
19:55 (56)	He bade his people to pray and to give the alms
19:59 (60)	then there succeeded after them a succession who wasted the prayer
20:14 (14)	therefore serve Me, and perform the prayer of My remembrance

20:132 (132)	bid thy family to pray, and be thou patient in it
21:73 (73)	to perform the prayer, and to pay the alms
22:35 (36)	who perform the prayer, and expend of what We have provided them
22:40 (41)	there had been destroyed cloisters and churches, oratories and mosques
22:41 (42)	who, if We establish them in the land, perform the prayer
22:78 (78)	so perform the prayer, and pay the alms
23:2 (2)	who in their prayers are humble
23:9 (9)	and who observe their prayers
24:37 (37)	to perform the prayer, and to pay the alms
24:41 (41)	each — He knows its prayer and its extolling
24:56 (55)	perform the prayer, and pay the alms
24:58 (57)	ask leave of you three times — before the prayer of dawn
24:58 (57)	at the noon, and after the evening prayer
27:3 (3)	who perform the prayer, and pay the alms
29:45 (44)	recite what has been revealed to thee of the Book, and perform the prayer
29:45 (44)	prayer forbids indecency and dishonour
30:31 (30)	perform the prayer, and be not of the idolaters
31:4 (3)	who perform the prayer, and pay the alms
31:17 (16)	O my son, perform the prayer
33:33 (33)	perform the prayer, and pay the alms
35:18 (19)	those who fear their Lord in the Unseen and perform the prayer
35:29 (26)	those who recite the Book of God and perform the prayer
42:38 (36)	those who answer their Lord, and perform the prayer
58:13 (14)	then perform the prayer, and pay the alms
62:9 (9)	when proclamation is made for prayer on the Day of Congregation
62:10 (10)	then, when the prayer is finished, scatter in the land
70:23 (23)	and continue at their prayers
70:34 (34)	and who observe their prayers
73:20 (20)	perform the prayer, and pay the alms
98:5 (4)	to perform the prayer, and pay the alms
107:5 (5)	and are heedless of their prayers

ṢALLÁ vb. (II)~to pray, to worship; (with prep. *ʿalá*) to bless. (pcple. act.) one who prays, worshipper

a) perf. act.

75:31 (31)	for he confirmed it not, and did not pray
87:15 (15)	and mentions the Name of his Lord, and prays
96:10 (10)	a servant when he prays

b) impf. act. (*yuṣallī*)

3:39 (33)	the angels called to him, standing in the Sanctuary
4:102 (103)	let another party who have not prayed
4:102 (103)	come and pray with thee, taking their precautions
9:84 (85)	pray thou never over any one of them when he is dead
33:43 (42)	it is He who blesses you, and His angels
33:56 (56)	God and His angels bless the Prophet

c) impv. (*ṣalli*)

9:103 (104)	to cleanse them thereby, and pray for them
33:56 (56)	O believers, do you also bless him, and (pray) him peace
108:2 (2)	so pray unto thy Lord and sacrifice

g) pcple. act. (*muṣallī*)

70:22 (22) save those that pray
74:43 (44) we were not of those who prayed
107:4 (4) so woe to those that pray

*Ṣ L Y

ṢALÁ vb. (I)~to roast, to broil, to fry. (n.vb.) roasting, burning. (pcple. act.) one who roasts, who burns

b) impf. act. (*yaṣlá*)

4:10 (11) and shall assuredly roast in a Blaze
14:29 (34) Gehenna, wherein they are roasted
17:18 (19) We appoint for him Gehenna wherein he shall roast
38:56 (56) Gehenna, wherein they are roasted
58:8 (9) sufficient for them shall be Gehenna, at which they shall be roasted
82:15 (15) roasting therein on the Day of Doom
84:12 (12) and he shall roast at a Blaze
87:12 (12) even he who shall roast in the Great Fire
88:4 (4) roasting at a scorching fire
92:15 (15) whereat none but the most wretched shall be roasted
111:3 (3) he shall roast at a flaming fire

c) impv. (*iṣla*)

36:64 (64) roast well in it today, for that you were unbelievers
52:16 (16) roast in it

f) n.vb. (*ṣilīy*)

19:70 (71) then We shall know very well those most deserving to burn there

g) pcple. act. (*ṣālī*)

37:163 (163) except him who shall roast in Hell
38:59 (59) they shall roast in the Fire
83:16 (16) then they shall roast in Hell

ṢALLÁ vb. (II)~to roast (tr). (n.vb.) roasting, broiling; burning

c) impv. (*ṣalli*)

69:31 (31) and then roast him in Hell

f) n.vb. (*taṣliyah*)

56:94 (94) and the roasting in Hell

AṢLÁ vb. (IV)~(tr) to roast, to thrust into a fire

b) impf. act. (*yuṣlī*)

4:30 (34) him We shall certainly roast at a Fire
4:56 (59) We shall certainly roast them at a Fire
4:115 (115) and We shall roast him in Gehenna
74:26 (26) I shall surely roast him in Sakar

IṢṬALÁ vb. (VIII)~to warm oneself

b) impf. act. (*yaṣṭalī*)

27:7 (7) I will bring you a flaming brand, that haply you shall warm yourselves
28:29 (29) or a faggot from the fire, that haply you shall warm yourselves

*Ṣ M ʿ

ṢAWĀMIʿ n.f. (pl. of *ṣawmaʿah*)~cloisters

22:40 (41) there had been destroyed cloisters and churches

*Ṣ M D

ṢAMAD n.m. (adj)~(Divine attribute) Everlasting Refuge [Ar]; One eternally Besought by all [Pk]; Eternal [Bl]; Eternal and Absolute [Ali]

112:2 (2) God, the Everlasting Refuge

*Ṣ M M

ṢAMMA vb. (I)~to be or become deaf

5:71 (75) they supposed there should be no trial; but blind they were, and deaf
5:71 (75) then again blind they were, many of them, and deaf

ṢUMM n.m. (pl. of *aṣamm*)~deaf

2:18 (17) deaf, dumb, blind — so they shall not return
2:171 (166) deaf, dumb, blind — they do not understand
6:39 (39) those who cry lies to Our signs are deaf and dumb
8:22 (22) those that are deaf and dumb and do not understand
10:42 (43) wilt thou make the deaf to hear, though they understand not?
11:24 (26) the likeness of the two parties is as the man blind and deaf
17:97 (99) upon their faces, blind, deaf, dumb
21:45 (46) but they that are deaf do not hear the call
25:73 (73) fall not down thereat deaf and blind
27:80 (82) neither shalt thou make the deaf to hear the call
30:52 (51) neither shalt thou make the deaf to hear the call
43:40 (39) what, shalt thou make the deaf to hear

AṢAMMA vb. (IV)~to make deaf

a) perf. act.

47:23 (25) those are they whom God has cursed, and so made them deaf

*Ṣ M T

ṢAMATA vb. (I)~(pcple. act.) silent

ṢAMATA vb. (I)~(pcple. act.) silent

g) pcple. act. (*ṣāmit*)

7:193 (192) equal it is to you whether you call them, or whether you are silent

*Ṣ N ᶜ

ṢANAᶜA vb. (I)~to work, to do, to make, to fashion, to form. (n.vb.) handiwork; working

a) perf. act.

11:16 (19) their deeds there will have failed, and void will be their works
13:31 (31) the unbelievers are smitten by a shattering for what they wrought
20:69 (72) it shall swallow what they have fashioned
20:69 (72) they have fashioned only the guile of a sorcerer

b) impf. act. (*yaṣnaᶜu*)

5:14 (17) God will assuredly tell them of the things they wrought
5:63 (68) evil is the thing they have been working
7:137 (133) We destroyed utterly the works of Pharaoh and his people
11:38 (40) so he was making the Ark
16:112 (113) God let it taste the garment of hunger and of fear, for the things that they were working
24:30 (30) God is aware of the things they work
29:45 (44) God's remembrance is greater; and God knows the things you work
35:8 (9) God has knowledge of the things they work

c) impv. (*iṣnaᶜ*)

11:37 (39) make thou the Ark under Our eyes, and as We reveal
23:27 (27) make thou the Ark under Our eyes and as We reveal

e) impf. pass. (*yuṣnaᶜu*)

20:39 (40) and to be formed in My sight

f) n.vb. (*ṣunᶜ*)

18:104 (104) while they think that they are working good deeds
27:88 (90) God's handiwork, who has created everything very well

MAṢĀNIᶜ n.m. (pl. of *maṣnaᶜ*)~a large structure, a castle, a stronghold

26:129 (129) do you take to you castles, haply to dwell forever?

ṢANᶜAH n.f.~an art; fashioning

21:80 (80) We taught him the fashioning of garments for you

IṢṬANAᶜA vb. (VIII)~to commission, to appoint as agent, to choose for one's service

a) perf. act.

20:41 (43) I have chosen thee for My service

*Ṣ N M

AṢNĀM n.m. (pl. of *ṣanam*)~an idol

6:74 (74)	takest thou idols for gods?
7:138 (134)	they came upon a people cleaving to idols they had
14:35 (38)	turn me and my sons away from serving idols
21:57 (58)	by God, I shall assuredly outwit your idols
26:71 (71)	we serve idols, and continue cleaving to them

*Ṣ N W

ṢINWĀN n.m. (pl. of *ṣinw*)~(s) single; (du) pair, in pairs

13:4 (4)	palms in pairs, and palms (single)
13:4 (4)	palms in (pairs) and palms single

*Ṣ R ᶜ

ṢARᶜÁ n.m. (pl. of *ṣarīᶜ*)~laid prostrate; lying overthrown

69:7 (7)	thou mightest see the people laid prostrate

*Ṣ R F

ṢARAFA vb. (I)~to turn, to turn away, to avert. (n.vb.) turning something away or aside, averting. (pcple. pass.) turned away or aside, averted

a) perf. act.

3:152 (146)	He turned you from them, that He might try you
9:127 (128)	God has turned away their hearts
12:34 (34)	his Lord answered him, and He turned away from him their guile
46:29 (28)	when We turned to thee a company of jinn

b) impf. act. (*yaṣrifu*)

7:146 (143)	I shall turn from My signs those who wax proud in the earth
12:24 (24)	that We might turn away from him evil and abomination
12:33 (33)	if Thou turnest not from me their guile
24:43 (43)	He smites whom He will with it, and turns it aside

c) impv. (*iṣrif*)

25:65 (66)	our Lord, turn Thou from us the chastisement of Gehenna

d) perf. pass. (*ṣurifa*)

7:47 (45)	when their eyes are turned towards the inhabitants of the Fire

e) impf. pass. (*yuṣrafu*)

6:16 (16) from whomsoever it is averted on that day
10:32 (33) how are you turned about?
39:6 (8) so how are you turned about?
40:69 (71) concerning the signs of God, how they are turned about

f) n.vb. (*ṣarf*)

25:19 (20) you can neither turn it aside, nor find any help

h) pcple. pass. (*maṣrūf*)

11:8 (11) the day it shall come to them, it shall not be turned aside from them

MAṢRIF n.m.~an escape; a refuge

18:53 (51) and will find no escape from it

ṢARRAFA vb. (II)~to turn about [Ar, Bl]; to display [Pk]; to explain [Ali]. (n.vb.) turning about [Ar]; ordinance, ordering [Pk]; change [Ali, Bl]

a) perf. act.

17:41 (43) We have turned about in this Koran, that they may remember
17:89 (91) We have indeed turned about for men in this Koran
18:54 (52) We have indeed turned about for men in this Koran
20:113 (112) We have turned about in it something of threats
25:50 (52) We have indeed turned it about amongst them
46:27 (26) We turned about the signs, that haply they would return

b) impf. act. (*yuṣarrifu*)

6:46 (46) behold how We turn about the signs
6:65 (65) behold how We turn about the signs
6:105 (105) We turn about the signs, that they may say
7:58 (56) even so We turn about the signs for a people that are thankful

f) n.vb. (*taṣrīf*)

2:164 (159) and the turning about of the winds
45:5 (4) and the turning about of the winds

INṢARAFA vb. (VII)~to turn away, to depart

a) perf. act.

9:127 (128) then they turn away. God has turned away

*Ṣ R Ḥ

ṢARḤ n.m.~a pavilion, a tower

27:44 (44) enter the pavilion
27:44 (44) it is a pavilion smoothed of crystal
28:38 (38) make me a tower, that I may mount up to Moses' God
40:36 (38) build for me a tower, that haply so I may reach the cords

*Ṣ R KH

ṢARĪKH n.m.~one to whom one cries (for help)

36:43 (43) then none have they to cry to

AṢRAKHA vb. (IV)~(pcple. act.) one who aids or helps

g) pcple. act. (*muṣrikh*)

14:22 (27) I cannot aid you
14:22 (27) neither can you aid me

IṢṬARAKHA vb. (VIII)~to shout, to cry aloud

b) impf. act. (*yaṣṭarikhu*)

35:37 (34) therein they shall shout

ISTAṢRAKHA vb. (X)~to cry out to someone (for help)

b) impf. act. (*yastaṣrikhu*)

28:18 (17) the man who had sought his succour on the day before cried out to him again

*Ṣ R M

ṢARAMA vb. (I)~to pluck (fruit). (pcple. act.) one who plucks (fruit)

b) impf. act. (*yaṣrimu*)

68:17 (17) the owners of the garden when they swore they would pluck in the morning

g) pcple. act. (*ṣārim*)

68:22 (22) come forth betimes upon your tillage, if you would pluck

ṢARĪM n.m.~a plucked garden

68:20 (20) in the morning it was as if it were a garden plucked

*Ṣ R R

ṢARRAH n.f.~clamour; a loud cry

51:29 (29) then came forward his wife, clamouring

ṢIRR n.m.~excessive cold, freezing

3:117 (113) is as the likeness of a freezing blast that smites the tillage

AṢARRA vb. (IV)~to persist, to persevere

a) perf. act.

71:7 (6)	and wrapped them in their garments, and persisted

b) impf. act. (*yuṣirru*)

3:135 (129)	and do not persevere in the things they did
45:8 (7)	who hears the signs of God being recited to him, then perseveres in waxing proud
56:46 (45)	and persisted in the Great Sin

*Ṣ R Ṣ R

ṢARṢAR n.m. (adj)~violent; clamorous, raging (wind)

41:16 (15)	We loosed against them a wind clamorous in days of ill fortune
54:19 (19)	We loosed against them a wind clamorous in a day of ill fortune continuous
69:6 (6)	as for Ad, they were destroyed by a wind clamorous, violent

*Ṣ R Ṭ

ṢIRĀṬ n.m.~a path, a way, a road

1:6 (5)	guide us in the straight path
1:7 (6)	the path of those whom Thou hast blessed
2:142 (136)	He guides whomsoever He will to a straight path
2:213 (209)	God guides whomsoever He will to a straight path
3:51 (44)	this is a straight path
3:101 (96)	whosoever holds fast to God, he is guided to a straight path
4:68 (70)	and guided them on a straight path
4:175 (174)	and will guide them to Him on a straight path
5:16 (18)	He guides them to a straight path
6:39 (39)	whomsoever He will, He sets him on a straight path
6:87 (87)	We elected them, and We guided them to a straight path
6:126 (126)	this is the path of thy Lord; straight
6:153 (154)	this is My path, straight
6:161 (162)	my Lord has guided me to a straight path
7:16 (15)	I shall surely sit in ambush for them on Thy straight path
7:86 (84)	do not sit in every path, threatening and barring from God's way
10:25 (26)	He guides whomsoever He will to a straight path
11:56 (59)	surely my Lord is on a straight path
14:1 (1)	to the path of the All-mighty, the All-laudable
15:41 (41)	this is for Me a straight path
16:76 (78)	is he equal to him who bids to justice, and is on a straight path?
16:121 (122)	He chose him, and He guided him to a straight path
19:36 (37)	so serve you Him. This is a straight path
19:43 (44)	follow me, and I will guide thee on a level path
20:135 (135)	you shall know who are the travellers on the even path
22:24 (24)	they shall be guided unto the path of the All-laudable
22:54 (53)	God ever guides those who believe to a straight path
23:73 (75)	assuredly thou art calling them to a straight path
23:74 (76)	they that believe not in the world to come are deviating from the path
24:46 (45)	God guides whomsoever He will to a straight path

34:6 (6)	and guides to the path of the All-mighty
36:4 (3)	on a straight path
36:61 (61)	this is a straight path
36:66 (66)	then they would race to the path
37:23 (23)	and guide them unto the path of Hell
37:118 (118)	and guided them in the straight path
38:22 (21)	and transgress not, and guide us to the right path
42:52 (52)	surely thou shalt guide unto a straight path
42:53 (53)	the path of God, to whom belongs whatsoever is in the heavens
43:43 (42)	surely thou art upon a straight path
43:61 (61)	and follow me. This is a straight path
43:64 (64)	therefore serve Him; this is a straight path
48:2 (2)	and complete His blessing upon thee, and guide thee on a straight path
48:20 (20)	that it may be a sign to the believers, and to guide you on a straight path
67:22 (22)	he who walks upright on a straight path

*Ṣ W ᶜ

ṢUWĀᶜ n.m.~a goblet, a drinking cup

12:72 (72)	we are missing the king's goblet

*Ṣ W B

MUṢĪBAH n.f.~affliction, calamity

2:156 (151)	who, when they are visited by an affliction, say
3:165 (159)	when an affliction visited you, and you had visited twice over the like of it
4:62 (65)	how shall it be, when they are visited by an affliction
4:72 (74)	then, if an affliction visits you, he says
5:106 (105)	when any of you is visited by death
9:50 (50)	but if thou art visited by an affliction
28:47 (47)	did an affliction visit them for that their own hands have forwarded
42:30 (29)	whatever affliction may visit you is for what your own hands have earned
57:22 (22)	no affliction befalls in the earth or in yourselves
64:11 (11)	no affliction befalls, except it be by the leave of God

ṢAWĀB n.m.~that which is right

78:38 (38)	save him to whom the All-merciful has given leave, and who speaks aright

ṢAYYIB n.m.~a cloudburst, a rain cloud

2:19 (18)	a cloudburst out of heaven in which is darkness

AṢĀBA vb. (IV)~to smite, to hit, to befall, to visit; to light on, to will, to intend; to happen. (pcple. act.) that which smites; smiting; happening

a) perf. act.

2:156 (151)	who, when they are visited by an affliction
2:264 (266)	a torrent smites it, and leaves it barren
2:265 (267)	a torrent smites it and it yields its produce twofold

2:266 (268)	then old age smites him, and he has seed, but weaklings
2:266 (268)	then a whirlwind with fire smites it, and it is consumed
3:117 (113)	the likeness of a freezing blast that smites the tillage
3:146 (140)	they fainted not for what smote them in God's way
3:153 (147)	that you might not sorrow for what escaped you neither for what smote you
3:165 (159)	why, when an affliction visited you
3:165 (159)	and you had visited twice over the like of it
3:166 (160)	what visited you, the day the two hosts encountered, was by God's leave
3:172 (166)	those who answered God and the Messenger after the wound had smitten them
4:62 (65)	how shall it be, when they are visited by an affliction
4:72 (74)	then, if an affliction visits you, he says
4:73 (75)	but if a bounty from God visits you
4:79 (81)	whatever good visits thee, it is of God
4:79 (81)	whatever evil visits thee is of thyself
5:106 (105)	the testimony between you when any of you is visited by death
7:100 (98)	did We will, We would smite them because of their sins
11:81 (83)	surely she shall be smitten
11:89 (91)	so that there smite you the like of what smote the people of Noah
16:34 (36)	so the evil things that they wrought smote them
22:11 (11)	if good befalls him he is at rest in it
22:11 (11)	if a trial befalls him he turns completely over
22:35 (36)	such as endure patiently whatever visits them
30:48 (47)	when He smites with it whomsoever of His servants He will
31:17 (16)	bear patiently whatever may befall thee
38:36 (35)	softly, wherever he might light on
39:51 (52)	in that the evils of that they earned smote them
42:30 (29)	whatever affliction may visit you is for what your own hands have earned
42:39 (37)	who, when insolence visits them, do help themselves
57:22 (22)	no affliction befalls in the earth or in yourselves
64:11 (11)	no affliction befalls, except it be by the leave of God

b) impf. act. (*yuṣību*)

2:265 (267)	it yields its produce twofold; if no torrent smites it
3:120 (116)	but if you are smitten by evil, they rejoice at it
4:78 (80)	if a good thing visits them
4:78 (80)	but if an evil thing visits them
5:49 (54)	God desires only to smite them for some sin
5:52 (57)	we fear lest a turn of fortune should smite us
6:124 (124)	humiliation in God's sight shall befall the sinners
7:131 (128)	if any evil smote them, they would augur ill by Moses
7:156 (155)	My chastisement — I smite with it whom I will
8:25 (25)	a trial which shall surely not smite in particular the evildoers
9:50 (50)	if good fortune befalls thee, it vexes them
9:50 (50)	if thou art visited by an affliction
9:51 (51)	naught shall visit us but what God has prescribed for us
9:52 (52)	we are awaiting in your case too, for God to visit you with chastisement
9:90 (91)	there shall befall the unbelievers of them a painful chastisement
9:120 (121)	that is because they are smitten neither by thirst, nor fatigue
10:107 (107)	He causes it to fall upon whomsoever He will of His servants
11:89 (91)	so that there smite you the like of what smote the people of Noah
12:56 (56)	We visit with Our mercy whomsoever We will
13:13 (14)	He looses the thunderbolts, and smites with them whomsoever He will
13:31 (31)	the unbelievers are smitten by a shattering for what they wrought
24:43 (43)	so that He smites whom He will with it
24:63 (63)	let those who go against His command beware, lest a trial befall them

24:63 (63) or there befall them a painful chastisement
28:47 (47) else, did an affliction visit them
30:36 (35) if some evil befalls them for that their own hands have forwarded
39:51 (52) they too shall be smitten by the evils of that they earned
40:28 (29) if he is truthful, somewhat of that he promises you will smite you
42:48 (47) but if some evil befalls him for that his own hands have forwarded
48:25 (25) and there befall you guilt unwittingly on their account
49:6 (6) make clear, lest you afflict a people unwittingly

g) pcple. act. (*muṣīb*)

11:81 (83) she shall be smitten by that which smites them

*Ṣ W F

AṢWĀF n.m. (pl. of *ṣūf*)~wool

16:80 (82) and of their wool, and of their fur

*Ṣ W M

ṢĀMA vb. (I)~to fast. (n.vb.) fasting, a fast. (pcple. act.) one who fasts

b) impf. act. (*yaṣūmu*)

2:184 (180) that you should fast is better for you
2:185 (181) let those of you, who are present at the month, fast it

f) n.vb. (1) (*ṣawm*)

19:26 (27) I have vowed to the All-merciful a fast

f) n.vb. (2) (*ṣiyām*)

2:183 (179) O believers, prescribed for you is the Fast
2:187 (183) permitted to you, upon the night of the Fast
2:187 (183) then complete the Fast unto the night
2:196 (192) if any of you is sick, or injured in his head, then redemption by fast
2:196 (192) if he finds none, then a fast of three days in the Pilgrimage
4:92 (94) if he finds not the means, let him fast two successive months
5:89 (91) if any finds not the means, let him fast for three days
5:95 (96) or the equivalent of that in fasting
58:4 (5) whosoever finds not the means, then let him fast two successive months

g) pcple. act. (*ṣā'im*)

33:35 (35) men who fast and (women who fast)
33:35 (35) (men who fast) and women who fast

*Ṣ W R

ṢĀRA vb. (I)~to twist or turn something, to cause something to incline *c*) impv. (*ṣur*)

2:260 (262) take four birds, and twist them to thee

ṢŪR n.m.~trumpet

6:73 (73) His is the Kingdom the day the Trumpet is blown
18:99 (99) the Trumpet shall be blown, and We shall gather them together
20:102 (102) on the day the Trumpet is blown; and We shall muster the sinners
23:101 (103) for when the Trumpet is blown, that day there shall be no kinship
27:87 (89) on the day the Trumpet is blown, and terrified is whosoever is in the heavens and earth
36:51 (51) the Trumpet shall be blown; then behold, they are sliding down
39:68 (68) for the Trumpet shall be blown, and whosoever is in the heavens
50:20 (19) the Trumpet shall be blown; that is the Day of the Threat
69:13 (13) when the Trumpet is blow with a single blast
78:18 (18) the day the Trumpet is blown, and you shall come in troops

ṢŪRAH n.f. (pl. *ṣuwar*)~form, fashion; image, likeness; (*aḥsana ṣuwarakum*) He shaped you well

40:64 (66) He shaped you, and shaped you well
64:3 (3) He shaped you, and shaped you well
82:8 (8) and composed thee after what form He would

ṢAWWARA vb. (II)~to shape, to form, to fashion (this verb is used throughout in reference to God). (pcple. act.) Shaper, Fashioner (Divine attribute)

a) perf. act.

7:11 (10) We created you, then We shaped you
40:64 (66) He shaped you, and (shaped) you well
64:3 (3) He shaped you, and (shaped) you well

b) impf. act. (*yuṣawwiru*)

3:6 (4) it is He who forms you in the womb as He will

g) pcple. act. (*muṣawwir*)

59:24 (24) He is God, the Creator, the Maker, the Shaper

*Ṣ W T

ṢĀTA vb. (I)~(n.vb.) voice, sound

f) n.vb. (*ṣawt*, pl. *aṣwāt*)

17:64 (66) startle whomsoever of them thou canst with thy voice
20:108 (107) voices will be hushed to the All-merciful
31:19 (18) be modest in thy walk, and lower thy voice
31:19 (18) the most hideous of voices is the ass's ([voice])
31:19 (18) the most hideous of (voices) is the ass's [voice]
49:2 (2) O believers, raise not your voices
49:2 (2) above the Prophet's voice
49:3 (3) those who lower their voices in the presence of God's Messenger

*Ṣ Y D

ṢĀDA vb. (I)~(n.vb.) hunting; fishing; game (of land or sea)

f) n.vb. (*ṣayd*)

5:1 (1)	so that you deem not game permitted to be hunted
5:94 (95)	the game that your hands and lances attain
5:95 (96)	slay not the game while you are in pilgrim sanctity
5:96 (97)	permitted to you is the game of the sea
5:96 (97)	but forbidden to you is the game of the land

IṢṬĀDA vb. (VIII)~to hunt; to fish

c) impv. (*iṣṭad*)

5:2 (3)	when you have quit your pilgrim sanctity, then hunt for game

*Ṣ Y F

ṢĀFA vb. (I)~(n.vb.) summer

f) n.vb. (*ṣayf*)

106:2 (2)	their composing for the winter and summer caravan

*Ṣ Y Ḥ

ṢAYḤAH n.f.~cry, shout; (the Cry of Gabriel or the Cry of punishment and destruction)

11:67 (70)	the evildoers were seized by the Cry
11:94 (97)	the evildoers were seized by the Cry
15:73 (73)	the Cry seized them at the sunrise
15:83 (83)	the Cry seized them in the morning
23:41 (43)	the Cry seized them justly
29:40 (39)	some were seized by the Cry
36:29 (28)	it was only one Cry and lo, they were silent and still
36:49 (49)	they are awaiting only for one Cry to seize them
36:53 (53)	it was only one Cry
38:15 (14)	these are only awaiting for a single Cry
50:42 (41)	on the day they hear the Cry in truth
54:31 (31)	We loosed against them one Cry
63:4 (4)	they think every cry is against them

*Ṣ Y R

ṢĀRA vb. (I)~to arrive, to reach, to come home. (n.vb.) homecoming, journey's end, journeying

b) impf. act. (*yaṣīru*)

42:53 (53)	surely unto God all things come home

f) n.vb. (*maṣīr*)

2:126 (120)	how evil a homecoming
2:285 (285)	grant us Thy forgiveness; unto Thee is the homecoming
3:28 (27)	and unto God is the homecoming
3:162 (156)	whose refuge is Gehenna? An evil homecoming
4:97 (99)	such men, their refuge shall be Gehenna — an evil homecoming
4:115 (115)	We shall roast him in Gehenna — an evil homecoming
5:18 (21)	to Him is the homecoming
8:16 (16)	his refuge is Gehenna — an evil homecoming
9:73 (74)	their refuge is Gehenna — an evil homecoming
14:30 (35)	your homecoming shall be — the Fire
22:48 (47)	then I seized it, and to Me was the homecoming
22:72 (71)	God has promised it to the unbelievers — an evil homecoming
24:42 (42)	to Him is the homecoming
24:57 (56)	their refuge is the Fire — an evil homecoming
25:15 (16)	or the Garden of Eternity, that is promised to the godfearing
31:14 (13)	be thankful to Me, and to thy parents; to Me is the homecoming
35:18 (19)	to God is the homecoming
40:3 (3)	and unto Him is the homecoming
42:15 (14)	God shall bring us together, and unto Him is the homecoming
48:6 (6)	and has prepared for them Gehenna — an evil homecoming
50:43 (42)	and to Us is the homecoming
57:15 (14)	your refuge is the Fire, that is your master — an evil homecoming
58:8 (9)	Gehenna, at which they shall be roasted — an evil homecoming
60:4 (4)	to Thee we turn; to Thee is the homecoming
64:3 (3)	unto Him is the homecoming
64:10 (10)	therein to dwell forever — an evil homecoming
66:9 (9)	their refuge shall be Gehenna — an evil homecoming
67:6 (6)	there awaits the chastisement of Gehenna — an evil homecoming

*Ṣ Y Ṣ

ṢAYĀṢĪ n.f. (pl. of *ṣīṣah*)~fortress, stronghold

33:26 (26)	those of the People of the Book who supported them from their fortresses

TĀ

*T ʿ S

TAʿS n.m.~ill-chance; perditon

47:8 (9)	as for the unbelievers, ill chance shall befall them

*T B ʿ

TABIʿA vb. (I)~to follow. (pcple. act.) a follower; attendant, servant

a) perf. act.

2:38 (36)	whosoever follows My guidance, no fear shall be on them
2:145 (140)	they will not follow thy direction
3:73 (66)	believe not any but him who follows your religion
7:18 (17)	those of them that follow thee
14:36 (39)	then whoso follows me belongs to me
17:63 (65)	depart! Those of them that follow thee
38:85 (85)	I shall assuredly fill Gehenna with thee, and with whosoever of them follows thee

b) impf. act. (*yatbaʿu*)

2:263 (265)	better than a freewill offering followed by injury
79:7 (7)	and the second blast follows it

g) pcple. act. (*tābiʿ*)

2:145 (140)	thou art not a follower of their direction
2:145 (140)	neither are they followers of one another's direction
24:31 (31)	or such men as attend them, not having sexual desire

TABAʿ n.m.~followers

14:21 (24)	we were your followers
40:47 (50)	we were your followers

TABĪʿ n.m.~a helper; prosecutor; avenger

17:69 (71)	then you will find no prosecutor for you against Us

TUBBAʿ n.prop.~Tubba' (name and title of a king of Himyar)

44:37 (36)	are they better, or the people of Tubba'
50:14 (13)	the men of the Thicket, the people of Tubba'

ATBAʿA vb. (IV)~to follow, to follow up, to pursue; to cause to follow

a) perf. act.

7:175 (174)	Satan followed after him, and he became one of the perverts
10:90 (90)	Pharaoh and his hosts followed them insolently and impetuously
15:18 (18)	excepting such as listens by stealth — and he is pursued by a manifest flame
18:85 (83)	and he followed a way
18:89 (88)	then he followed a way
18:92 (91)	then he followed a way
20:78 (81)	Pharaoh followed them with his hosts

23:44 (46)	they cried him lies, so We caused some of them to follow others
26:60 (60)	then they followed them at the sunrise
28:42 (42)	We pursued them in this world with a curse
37:10 (10)	and he is pursued by a piercing flame

b) impf. act. (*yutbiʿu*)

2:262 (264)	those who expend their wealth in the way of God then follow not up what they have
77:17 (17)	then follow them with the later folk

d) perf. pass. (*utbiʿa*)

11:60 (63)	there was sent following after them in this world a curse
11:99 (101)	there was sent following after them in this world a curse

TATĀBAʿA vb. (VI)~(pcple. act.) successive

g) pcple. act. (*mutatābiʿ*)

4:92 (94)	if he finds not the means, let him fast two successive months
58:4 (5)	whosoever finds not the means, then let him fast two successive months

ITTABAʿA vb. (VIII)~to follow; to obey, to observe, to heed. (n.vb.) pursuing, following. (pcple. pass.) followed

a) perf. act.

2:102 (96)	they follow what the Satans recited over Solomon's kingdom
2:120 (114)	never will the Jews be satisfied with thee, neither the Christians, not till thou followest their religion
2:145 (140)	if thou followest their caprices, after the knowledge that has come to thee
2:166 (161)	when those that were followed disown their followers
2:167 (162)	those that followed say, 'O if only we might return again'
3:20 (18)	I have surrendered my will to God, and whosoever follows me
3:53 (46)	we believe in that Thou hast sent down, and we follow the Messenger
3:55 (48)	I will set thy followers above the unbelievers till the Resurrection Day
3:68 (61)	the people standing closest to Abraham are those who followed him
3:162 (156)	is he who follows God's good pleasure like him who is laden with the burden
3:167 (160)	if only we knew how to fight, we would follow you
3:174 (168)	they followed the good pleasure of God
4:83 (85)	you would surely have followed Satan, except a few
4:125 (124)	being a good-doer, and who follows the creed of Abraham
5:16 (18)	whereby God guides whosoever follows His good pleasure in the ways of peace
7:90 (88)	if you follow Shuaib, assuredly in that case you will be losers
7:157 (156)	those who believe in him and succour him and help him, and follow the light that has been sent down with him
7:176 (175)	but he inclined towards the earth and followed his lust
8:64 (65)	O Prophet, God suffices thee, and the believers who follow thee
9:42 (42)	were it a gain near at hand, and an easy journey, they would have followed thee
9:100 (101)	the first of the Emigrants and the Helpers, and those who followed them in doing-good
9:117 (118)	the Helpers who followed him in the hour of difficulty
11:27 (29)	we see not any following thee but the vilest of us, inconsiderately
11:59 (62)	and followed the command of every froward tyrant
11:97 (99)	but they followed Pharaoh's command
11:116 (118)	but the evildoers followed the ease they were given to exult in

12:38 (38)	I have followed the creed of my fathers, Abraham, Isaac and Jacob
12:108 (108)	I call to God with sure knowledge, I and whoever follows after me
13:37 (37)	and if thou dost follow their caprices
15:42 (42)	over My servants thou shalt have no authority, except those that follow thee
18:28 (27)	so that he follows his own lust, and his affair has become all excess
18:70 (69)	then if thou followest me, question me not on anything
19:59 (60)	there succeeded after them a succession who wasted the prayer, and followed lusts
20:16 (17)	that believes not in it but follows after his own caprice
20:47 (49)	and peace be upon him who follows the guidance
20:123 (122)	whosoever follows My guidance shall not go astray
23:71 (73)	had the truth followed their caprices
26:111 (111)	shall we believe thee, whom the vilest follow?
26:215 (215)	lower thy wing to those who follow thee, being believers
28:35 (35)	you, and whoso follows you, shall be the victors
28:50 (50)	who is further astray than he who follows his caprice without guidance
30:29 (28)	the evildoers follow their own caprices, without knowledge
34:20 (19)	they followed him, except a party of the believers
36:11 (10)	Thou only warnest him who follows the Remembrance
40:7 (7)	forgive those who have repented, and follow Thy way
47:3 (3)	that is because those who disbelieve follow falsehood
47:3 (3)	those who believe follow the truth from their Lord
47:14 (15)	and they have followed their caprices
47:16 (18)	has set a seal, and they have followed their caprices
47:28 (30)	that is because they have followed what angers God
52:21 (21)	those who believed, and their seed followed them in belief
54:3 (3)	they have cried lies, and followed their caprices
57:27 (27)	We set in the hearts of those who followed him tenderness and mercy
71:21 (20)	they have rebelled against me, and followed him whose wealth and children increase him

b) impf. act. (*yattabiᶜu*)

2:120 (114)	never will the Jews be satisfied with thee, neither the Christians, not till thou followest their religion
2:143 (138)	except that We might know who followed the Messenger from him who turned
2:168 (163)	follow not the steps of Satan; he is a manifest foe to you
2:170 (165)	we will follow such things as we found our fathers doing
2:208 (204)	enter the peace, all of you, and follow not the steps of Satan
3:7 (5)	as for those in whose hearts is swerving, they follow the ambiguous part
4:27 (32)	those who follow their lusts desire you to swerve away mightily
4:115 (115)	and follows a way other than the believers', him We shall turn over to what he has turned to
4:135 (134)	then follow not caprice, so as to swerve
5:48 (52)	and do not follow their caprices, to forsake the truth
5:49 (54)	and do not follow their caprices, and beware of them
5:77 (81)	follow not the caprices of a people who went astray before
6:50 (50)	I only follow what is revealed to me
6:56 (56)	I do not follow your caprices, or else I had gone astray
6:116 (116)	they follow only surmise, merely conjecturing
6:142 (143)	and follow not the steps of Satan
6:148 (149)	you follow only surmise, merely conjecturing
6:150 (151)	do not thou follow the caprices of those who cried lies
6:153 (154)	follow not diverse paths lest they scatter you from His path
7:3 (2)	follow no friends other than He

7:142 (138)	do not follow the way of the workers of corruption
7:157 (156)	those who follow the Messenger, the Prophet of the common folk
7:193 (192)	if you call them to guidance they will not follow you
7:203 (202)	I follow only what is revealed to me from my Lord
10:15 (16)	I follow nothing, except what is revealed to me
10:36 (37)	and the most of them follow only surmise
10:66 (67)	they follow, who call upon associates, apart from God
10:66 (67)	they follow nothing but surmise, merely conjecturing
10:89 (89)	follow not the way of those that know not
14:44 (46)	and we will answer Thy call, and follow the Messengers
17:47 (50)	you are only following a man bewitched
18:66 (65)	shall I follow thee so that thou teachest me
20:93 (94)	so that thou didst not follow after me
20:108 (107)	on that day they will follow the Summoner in whom is no crookedness
20:134 (134)	so that we might have followed Thy signs
22:3 (3)	and follows every rebel Satan
24:21 (21)	O believers, follow not the steps of Satan
24:21 (21)	whosoever follows the steps of Satan, assuredly he bids to indecency
25:8 (9)	you are only following a man bewitched
26:40 (39)	haply we shall follow the sorcerers
26:224 (224)	and the poets — the perverse follow them
28:47 (47)	that we might follow Thy signs and so be among the believers
28:49 (49)	bring a Book from God that gives better guidance than these, and follow it
28:50 (50)	if they do not answer thee, know that they are only following their caprices
28:57 (57)	should we follow the guidance with thee, we shall be snatched
31:21 (20)	we will follow such things as we found our fathers doing
38:26 (25)	therefore judge between men justly, and follow not caprice
39:18 (19)	who give ear to the Word and follow the fairest of it
42:15 (14)	thou hast been commanded; do not follow their caprices
45:18 (17)	follow not the caprices of those who do not know
46:9 (8)	I only follow what is revealed to me
48:15 (15)	let us follow you
48:15 (15)	you shall not follow us
53:23 (23)	they follow only surmise, and what the souls desire
53:28 (29)	they follow only surmise, and surmise avails naught against truth
54:24 (24)	shall we follow a mortal, one out of ourselves?

c) impv. (*ittabi*ᶜ)

2:170 (165)	follow what God has sent down
3:31 (29)	if you love God, follow me, and God will love you
3:95 (89)	God has spoken the truth; therefore follow the creed of Abraham
6:106 (106)	follow thou what has been revealed to thee from thy Lord
6:153 (154)	this is My path, straight; so do you follow it
6:155 (156)	this is a Book We have sent down, blessed; so follow it
7:3 (2)	follow what has been sent down to you from your Lord
7:158 (158)	the Prophet of the common folk, who believes in God and His words, and follow him
10:109 (109)	and follow thou what is revealed to thee
15:65 (65)	in a watch of the night, and follow after the backs of them
16:123 (124)	follow thou the creed of Abraham, a man of pure faith
19:43 (44)	so follow me, and I will guide thee on a level path
20:90 (92)	therefore follow me, and obey my commandment
29:12 (11)	follow our path, and let us carry your offences
31:15 (14)	but follow the way of him who turns to Me
31:21 (20)	follow what God has sent down

33:2 (2)	follow what is revealed to thee from thy Lord
36:20 (19)	my people, follow the Envoys
36:21 (20)	follow such as ask no wage of you
39:55 (56)	follow the fairest of what has been sent down to you
40:38 (41)	follow me, and I will guide you in the way of rectitude
43:61 (61)	it is knowledge of the Hour; doubt not concerning it, and follow me
45:18 (17)	We set thee upon an open way of the Command; therefore follow it
75:18 (18)	so, when We recite it, follow thou its recitation

d) perf. pass. (*ittubiʿa*)

2:166 (161)	when those that were followed disown their followers

e) impf. pass. (*yuttabaʿu*)

10:35 (36)	He guides to the truth; and which is worthier to be followed

f) n.vb. (*ittibāʿ*)

2:178 (173)	let the pursuing be honourable
4:157 (156)	they have no knowledge of him, except the following of surmise

h) pcple. pass. (*muttabaʿ*)

26:52 (52)	surely you will be followed
44:23 (22)	surely you will be followed

*T B B

TABBA vb. (I)~to perish, to be destroyed. (n.vb.) loss, ruin

a) perf. act.

111:1 (1)	perish the hands of Abu Lahab and (perish) he
111:1 (1)	(perish) the hands of Abu Lahab and perish he

f) n.vb. (*tabāb*)

40:37 (40)	Pharaoh's guile came only to ruin

TABBABA vb. (II)~(n.vb.) destruction, ruin

f) n.vb. (*tatbīb*)

11:101 (103)	they increased them not, save in destruction

*T B R

TABĀR n.m.~ruin, destruction

71:28 (29)	do Thou not increase the evildoers save in ruin

TABBARA vb. (II)~to destroy, to ruin, to shatter. (n.vb.) destruction, ruin. (pcple. pass.) shattered, destroyed

a) perf. act.

25:39 (41)	We struck similitudes, and each We ruined utterly

b) impf. act. (*yutabbiru*)

17:7 (7) — and to destroy utterly that which they ascended to

f) n.vb. (*tatbīr*)

17:7 (7) — and to destroy <utterly> that which they ascended to
25:39 (41) — We struck similitudes, and each We ruined <utterly>

h) pcple. pass. (*mutabbar*)

7:139 (135) — surely this they are engaged upon shall be shattered

*T B T

TĀBŪT n.m.~box, chest, ark; the Ark (of the Covenant)

2:248 (249) — the sign of his kingship is that the Ark will come to you
20:39 (39) — cast him into the ark, and cast him into the river

*T F TH

TAFATH n.m.~self-neglect, unkemptness [Ar, Pk]; prescribed rites [Ali]; (ritual) uncleanness [Bl]

22:29 (30) — let them then finish with their self-neglect

*T J R

TIJĀRAH n.f.~commerce; merchandise; trading, trade

2:16 (15) — and their commerce has not profited them
2:282 (282) — unless it be merchandise present that you give and take between you
4:29 (33) — except there be trading, by your agreeing together
9:24 (24) — commerce you fear may slacken, dwellings you love
24:37 (37) — men whom neither commerce nor trafficking diverts from the remembrance of God
35:29 (26) — look for a commerce that comes not to naught
61:10 (10) — shall I direct you to a commerce that shall deliver you
62:11 (11) — when they see merchandise or diversion they scatter off to it
62:11 (11) — what is with God is better than diversion and merchandise

*T L L

TALLA vb. (I)~(with prep. *li-*) to fling someone, to lay someone prostrate

a) perf. act.

37:103 (103) — when they had surrendered, and he flung him upon his brow

*T L W

TALĀ vb. (I)~to recite, to read; to relate; (91:2) to follow. (n.vb.) recitation, reading. (pcple. act.) a reader, reciter

a) perf. act.

10:16 (17) — had God willed I would not have recited it to you
91:2 (2) — and by the moon when she follows him

b) impf. act. (*yatlū*)

2:44 (41) — and forget yourselves while you recite the Book
2:102 (96) — they follow what the Satans recited over Solomon's kingdom

2:113 (107)	yet they recite the Book
2:121 (115)	and who recite it with true recitation
2:129 (123)	a Messenger, one of them, who shall recite to them Thy signs
2:151 (146)	a Messenger, to recite Our signs to you
2:252 (253)	these are the signs of God We recite to thee in truth
3:58 (51)	this We recite to thee of signs and wise remembrance
3:108 (104)	these are the signs of God We recite to thee in truth
3:113 (109)	a nation upstanding, that recite God's signs in the watches of the night
3:164 (158)	He raised up among them a Messenger from themselves, to recite to them His signs
6:151 (152)	come, I will recite what your Lord has forbidden you
10:61 (62)	neither recitest thou any Koran of it
11:17 (20)	and a witness from Him recites it
13:30 (29)	to recite to them that We have revealed to thee
18:83 (82)	I will recite to you a mention of him
22:72 (71)	and when Our signs are recited to them, clear signs
27:92 (94)	and to recite the Koran
28:3 (2)	We will recite to thee something of the tiding of Moses and Pharaoh
28:45 (45)	neither wast thou a dweller among the Midianites, reciting to them Our signs
28:59 (59)	a Messenger, to recite Our signs unto them
29:48 (47)	not before this didst thou recite any Book
35:29 (26)	those who recite the Book of God and perform the prayer
39:71 (71)	did not Messengers come to you from among yourselves, reciting to you
45:6 (5)	those are the signs of God that We recite to thee in truth
62:2 (2)	a Messenger from among them, to recite His signs to them
65:11 (11)	a Messenger reciting to you the signs of God
98:2 (2)	a Messenger from God, reciting pages purified

c) impv. (*uṭlu*)

3:93 (87)	bring you the Torah now, and recite it
5:27 (30)	recite thou to them the story of the two sons of Adam
7:175 (174)	recite to them the tiding of him to whom We gave Our signs
10:71 (72)	recite to them the story of Noah
18:27 (26)	recite what has been revealed to thee of the Book of thy Lord
26:69 (69)	recite to them the tiding of Abraham
29:45 (44)	recite what has been revealed to thee of the Book

d) perf. pass. (*tuliya*)

8:2 (2)	when His signs are recited to them, it increases them in faith

e) impf. pass. (*yutlá*)

3:101 (96)	how can you disbelieve, seeing you have God's signs recited to you
4:127 (126)	and what is recited to you in the Book concerning the orphan
5:1 (1)	permitted to you is the beast of the flocks, except that which is now recited to you
8:31 (31)	when Our signs were being recited to them, they said
10:15 (16)	when Our signs are recited to them, clear signs
17:107 (108)	those who were given the knowledge before it when it is recited to them
19:58 (59)	when the signs of the All-merciful were recited to them
19:73 (74)	when Our signs are recited to them as clear signs
22:30 (31)	permitted to you are the flocks, except that which is recited to you
22:72 (71)	when Our signs are recited to them, clear signs
23:66 (68)	My signs were recited to you, but upon your heels you withdrew
23:105 (107)	what, were My signs not recited to you
28:53 (53)	when it is recited to them, they say

29:51 (50)	We have sent down upon thee the Book that is recited to them
31:7 (6)	when Our signs are recited to such a man he turns away
33:34 (34)	remember that which is recited in your houses
34:43 (42)	when Our signs are recited to them, clear signs
45:8 (7)	who hears the signs of God being recited to him
45:25 (24)	when Our signs are recited to them, clear signs
45:31 (30)	were not My signs recited to you, and you waxed proud
46:7 (6)	when Our signs are recited to them, clear signs
68:15 (15)	when Our signs are recited to him
83:13 (13)	when Our signs are recited to him

f) n.vb. (*tilāwah*)

2:121 (115)	those to whom We have given the Book and who recite it with true recitation

g) pcple. act. f. (*tāliyāt*, pl. of *tāliyah*)

37:3 (3)	and the reciters of a Remembrance

*T M M

TAMMA vb. (I)~to be perfect; to be fulfilled, to be or become complete. (n.vb.) completion; complete

a) perf. act.

6:115 (115)	perfect are the words of thy Lord in truthfulness and justice
7:137 (133)	and perfectly was fulfilled the most fair word of thy Lord
7:142 (138)	We completed them with ten, so the appointed time of his Lord was forty nights
11:119 (120)	to that end He created them, and perfectly is fulfilled the word of thy Lord

f) n.vb. (*tamām*)

6:154 (155)	We gave Moses the Book, complete for him who does good

ATAMMA vb. (IV)~to fulfil, to complete; to perfect. (pcple. act.) one who completes, perfects or fulfils

a) perf. act.

2:124 (118)	when his Lord tested Abraham with certain words, and he fulfilled them
5:3 (5)	I have completed My blessing upon you, and I have approved Islam
7:142 (138)	We appointed with Moses thirty nights and We completed them with ten
12:6 (6)	as He perfected it formerly on thy fathers Abraham and Isaac
28:27 (27)	if thou completest ten, that shall be of thy own accord

b) impf. act. (*yutimmu*)

2:150 (145)	but fear you Me; and that I may perfect My blessing upon you
2:233 (233)	for such as desire to fulfil the suckling
5:6 (9)	that He may complete His blessing upon you
9:32 (32)	and God refuses but to perfect His light
12:6 (6)	and perfect His blessing upon thee and upon the House of Jacob
16:81 (83)	even so He perfects His blessing upon you
48:2 (2)	and complete His blessing upon thee, and guide thee

c) impv. (*atmim*)

2:187 (183)	then complete the Fast unto the night
2:196 (192)	fulfil the Pilgrimage and the Visitation unto God

9:4 (4) — with them fulfil your covenant till their term
66:8 (8) — our Lord, perfect for us our light, and forgive us

g) pcple. act. (*mutimm*)

61:8 (8) — but God will perfect His light

*T N R

TANNŪR n.m.~an oven, furnace

11:40 (42) — when Our command came, and the Oven boiled, We said
23:27 (27) — then, when Our command comes and the Oven boils

*T Q N

ATQANA vb. (IV)~to perfect; to create very well

a) perf. act.

27:88 (90) — God's handiwork, who has created everything very well

*T R B

ATRĀB n.m. (pl. of *tirb*)~person of the same age

38:52 (52) — with them maidens restraining their glances of equal age
56:37 (36) — chastely amorous, like of age
78:33 (33) — and maidens with swelling breasts, like of age

MATRABAH n.f.~misery, poverty

90:16 (16) — or a needy man in misery

TARĀ'IB n.f. (pl. of *tarībah*)~chest, thorax, breast-bone

86:7 (7) — issuing between the loins and the breast-bones

TURĀB n.m.~soil, earth, dust

2:264 (266) — the likeness of him is as the likeness of a smooth rock on which is soil
3:59 (52) — He created him of dust
13:5 (5) — when we are dust shall we indeed then be raised up again
16:59 (61) — whether he shall preserve it in humiliation, or trample it into the dust
18:37 (35) — disbelievest thou in Him who created thee of dust
22:5 (5) — surely We created you of dust
23:35 (37) — does he promise you that when you are dead, and become dust
23:82 (84) — when we are dead and become dust and bones
27:67 (69) — when we are dust, and our fathers
30:20 (19) — and of His signs is that He created you of dust
35:11 (12) — God created you of dust
37:16 (16) — when we are dead and become dust and bones
37:53 (51) — when we are dead and become dust and bones
40:67 (69) — it is He who created you of dust
50:3 (3) — when we are dead and become dust
56:47 (47) — when we are dead and become dust and bones
78:40 (41) — O would that I were dust

*T R F

ATRAFA vb. (IV)~to give ease or opulence, to surround with luxury. (pcple. pass.) living in ease and luxury

a) perf. act.

23:33 (34) and to whom We had given ease in the present life

d) perf. pass. (*utrifa*)

11:116 (118) the evildoers followed the ease they were given to exult in
21:13 (13) return you unto the luxury that you exulted in

h) pcple. pass. (*mutraf*)

17:16 (17) We command its men who live at ease, and they commit ungodliness
23:64 (66) when We seize with the chastisement the ones of them that live at ease
34:34 (33) except its men who lived at ease said
43:23 (22) except that its men who lived at ease said
56:45 (44) and before that they lived at ease

*T R K

TARAKA vb. (I)~to leave, to leave behind; to abandon; to forsake. (pcple. act.) one who leaves; leaving

a) perf. act.

2:17 (16) God took away their light, and left them in darkness unseeing
2:180 (176) when any of you is visited by death, and he leaves behind some goods
2:248 (249) a remnant of what the folk of Moses and Aaron's folk left behind
2:264 (266) and a torrent smites it, and leaves it barren
4:7 (8) to the men a share of what parents and kinsmen leave
4:7 (8) and to the women a share of what parents and kinsmen leave
4:9 (10) let those fear who, if they left behind them weak seed, would be afraid
4:11 (12) then for them two-thirds of what he leaves
4:11 (12) to his parents to each one of the two the sixth of what he leaves
4:12 (13) and for you a half of what your wives leave, if they have no children
4:12 (13) if they have children, then for you of what they leave a fourth
4:12 (14) and for them a fourth of what you leave
4:12 (14) then for them of what you leave an eighth
4:33 (37) to everyone We have appointed heirs of that which parents and kinsmen leave
4:176 (175) she shall receive a half of what he leaves
4:176 (175) if there be two sisters, they shall receive two-thirds of what he leaves
6:94 (94) and you have left what We conferred on you behind your backs
12:17 (17) we went running races, and left Joseph behind with our things
12:37 (37) I have forsaken the creed of a people who believe not in God
16:61 (63) He would not leave on the earth one creature that crawls
18:99 (99) upon that day We shall leave them surging on one another
23:100 (102) haply I shall do righteousness in that I forsook
29:35 (34) We have left thereof a sign, a clear sign
35:45 (44) He would not leave upon the face of the earth one creature that crawls
37:78 (76) and left for him among the later folk
37:108 (108) and left for him among the later folk
37:119 (119) and left them among the later folk
37:129 (129) and We left for him among the later folk
44:25 (24) they left how many gardens and foutains
51:37 (37) therein We left a sign to those who fear the painful chastisement
54:15 (15) and We left it for a sign
59:5 (5) whatever palm-trees you cut down, or left standing upon their roots
62:11 (11) they scatter off to it, and they leave thee standing

b) impf. act. (*yatruku*)

7:176 (175) or if thou leavest it it lolls its tongue out
11:87 (89) does thy prayer command thee that we should leave that our fathers served

c) impv. (*utruk*)

44:24 (23) and leave the sea becalmed

e) impf. pass. (*yutraku*)

9:16 (16) or did you suppose you would be left in peace
26:146 (146) will you be left secure in this here
29:2 (1) do the people reckon that they will be left to say
75:36 (36) does man reckon he shall be left to roam at will?

g) pcple. act. (*tārik*)

11:12 (15) perchance thou art leaving part of what is revealed to thee
11:53 (56) we will not leave our gods for what thou sayest
37:36 (35) shall we forsake our gods for a poet possessed?

*T S ᶜ

TISᶜAH n.num.~nine

17:101 (103) We gave Moses nine signs, clear signs
18:25 (24) hundred years, and to that they added nine more
27:12 (12) among nine signs to Pharaoh and his people
27:48 (49) in the city there were nine persons who did corruption
38:23 (22) this my brother has ninety-nine ewes, and I have one ewe

TISᶜATA-ᶜASHARA n.num.~nineteen

74:30 (30) over it are nineteen

TISᶜŪN n.num.~ninety

38:23 (22) this my brother has ninety-nine ewes, and I have one ewe

*T W B

TĀBA vb. (I)~to repent, to be penitent, to do penance; (with prep. *ᶜalá*) to turn towards someone (in forgiveness); (with prep. *ilá*) to turn towards someone (in penance). (n.vb.) repentance, penitence. (pcple. act.) one who repents, penitent

a) perf. act.

2:37 (35) from his Lord, and He turned towards him
2:54 (51) that will be better for you in your Creator's sight, and He will turn to you
2:160 (155) save such as repent and make amends
2:187 (183) and has turned to you and pardoned you
2:279 (279) if you repent, you shall have your principal
3:89 (83) but those who repent thereafter, and make amends
4:16 (20) but if they repent and make amends
4:18 (22) indeed now I repent
4:146 (145) save such as repent, and make amends, and hold fast to God
5:34 (38) except for such as repent, before you have power over them
5:39 (43) whoso repents, after his evildoing, and makes amends

5:71 (75)	then God turned towards them; then again blind they were
6:54 (54)	whosoever of you does evil in ignorance, and thereafter repents
7:143 (140)	I repent to Thee; I am the first of the believers
7:153 (152)	those who do evil deeds, then repent thereafter and believe
9:3 (3)	so if you repent, that will be better for you
9:5 (5)	but if they repent, and perform the prayer, and pay the alms
9:11 (11)	yet if they repent, and perform the prayer
9:117 (118)	God has turned towards the Prophet and the Emigrants
9:117 (118)	then He turned towards them
9:118 (119)	then He turned towards them
11:112 (114)	go thou straight, as thou hast been commanded, and whoso repents with thee
16:119 (120)	unto those who did evil in ignorance, then repented
19:60 (61)	save him who repents, and believes, and does a righteous deed
20:82 (84)	I am All-forgiving to him who repents and believes
20:122 (120)	therafter his Lord chose him, and turned again unto him
24:5 (5)	save such as repent thereafter and make amends
25:70 (70)	save him who repents, and believes, and does righteous work
25:71 (71)	whosoever repents, and does righteousness
28:67 (67)	as for him who repents, and believes, and works righteousness
40:7 (7)	therefore forgive those who have repented, and follow Thy way
46:15 (14)	I repent to Thee, and am among those that surrender
58:13 (14)	if you do not so, and God turns again unto you
73:20 (20)	will not number it, and He has turned towards you

b) impf. act. (*yatūbu*)

2:160 (155)	clearly — towards them I shall turn
3:128 (123)	whether He turns towards them again, or chastises them
4:17 (21)	God shall turn only towards those who do evil in ignorance, then shortly repent
4:17 (21)	God will return towards those
4:26 (31)	before you, and to turn towards you
4:27 (32)	and God desires to turn towards you
5:39 (43)	God will turn towards him
5:74 (78)	will they not turn to God and pray His forgiveness?
9:15 (15)	and God turns towards whomsoever He will
9:27 (27)	then God thereafter turns towards whom He will
9:74 (75)	so if they repent it will be better for them
9:102 (103)	it may be that God will turn towards them
9:106 (107)	whether He chastises them, or turns towards them
9:118 (119)	He (turned) towards them, that they might also turn
9:126 (127)	yet still they do not repent, nor do they remember
25:71 (71)	he truly turns to God in repentance
33:24 (24)	and chastise the hypocrites, if He will, or turn again unto them
33:73 (73)	that God may turn again unto the believers, men and women alike
49:11 (11)	whoso repents not, those — they are the evildoers
66:4 (4)	if you two repent to God, yet your hearts certainly inclined
85:10 (10)	those who persecute the believers, men and women, and then have not repented

c) impv. (*tub*)

2:54 (51)	now turn to your Creator and slay one another
2:128 (122)	show us our holy rites, and turn towards us
11:3 (3)	ask forgiveness of your Lord, then repent to Him
11:52 (54)	O my people, ask forgiveness of your Lord, then repent to Him
11:61 (64)	so ask forgiveness of Him, then repent to Him
11:90 (92)	ask forgiveness of your Lord, then repent to Him

24:31 (31) turn all together to God, O you believers
66:8 (8) believers, turn to God in sincere repentance

f) n.vb. (*tawbah*)

3:90 (84) their repentance shall not be accepted; those are the ones who stray
4:17 (21) God shall turn only towards those who do evil in ignorance, then shortly repent
4:18 (22) God shall not turn towards those who do evil deeds
4:92 (94) if he finds not the means, let him fast two successive months — God's turning
9:104 (105) do they not know that God is He who accepts repentance from His servants
40:3 (2) Forgiver of sins, Accepter of penitence
42:25 (24) it is He who accepts repentance from His servants, and pardons evil deeds
66:8 (8) believers, turn to God in sincere repentance

g) pcple. act. (*tā'ib*)

9:112 (113) those who repent, those who serve, those who pray
66:5 (5) women who have surrendered, believing, obedient, penitent

MATĀB n.m.~turning in repentance; recourse

13:30 (29) in Him I have put my trust, and to Him I turn
25:71 (71) he truly turns to God in repentance

TAWWĀB n.m.~One who turns (Divine attribute); (pl) ones who repent (2:222)

2:37 (35) truly He turns, and is All-compassionate
2:54 (51) truly He turns, and is All-compassionate
2:128 (122) surely Thou turnest, and art All-compassionate
2:160 (155) I turn, All-compassionate
2:222 (222) truly, God loves those who repent
4:16 (20) God turns, and is All-compassionate
4:64 (67) they would have found God turns, All-compassionate
9:104 (105) God — He turns, and is All-compassionate
9:118 (119) surely God turns, and is All-compassionate
24:10 (10) and that God turns, and is All-wise
49:12 (12) assuredly God turns, and He is All-compassionate
110:3 (3) for He turns again unto men

*T W R

TĀRAH n.f.~a time

17:69 (71) do you feel secure that He will not send you back into it a second time
20:55 (57) and bring you forth from it a second time

TAWRĀT n.prop.~the Torah, the Pentateuch

3:3 (2) He sent down the Torah and the Gospel
3:48 (43) He will teach him the Book, the Wisdom, the Torah
3:50 (44) likewise confirming the truth of the Torah that is before me
3:65 (58) the Torah was not sent down, neither the Gospel, but after him
3:93 (87) save what Israel forbade for himself before the Torah was sent down
3:93 (87) bring you the Torah now, and recite it
5:43 (47) seeing they have the Torah, wherein is God's judgment
5:44 (48) surely We sent down the Torah, wherein is guidance
5:46 (50) We sent ... Jesus son of Mary, confirming the Torah before him
5:46 (50) confirming the Torah before it, as a guidance
5:66 (70) had they performed the Torah and the Gospel

5:68 (72)	you do not stand on anything, until you perform the Torah
5:110 (110)	when I taught thee the Book, the Wisdom, the Torah
7:157 (156)	whom they find written down with them in the Torah
9:111 (112)	that is a promise binding upon God in the Torah
48:29 (29)	that is their likeness in the Torah
61:6 (6)	Israel, I am indeed the Messenger of God to you, confirming the Torah
62:5 (5)	the likeness of those who have been loaded with the Torah

*T Y H

TĀHA vb. (I)~to wander about

b) impf. act. (*yatīhu*)

5:26 (29)	while they are wandering in the earth

*T Y N

TĪN n.m.~fig

95:1 (1)	by the fig and the olive

THĀ

*TH ᶜ B

THUᶜBĀN n.m.~a serpent

7:107 (104)	he cast his staff; and behold, it was a serpent manifest
26:32 (31)	he cast his staff, and behold, it was a serpent manifest

*TH B R

THABARA vb. (I)~(n.vb.) destruction, ruin. (pcple. pass.) accursed; destroyed

f) n.vb. (*thubūr*)

25:13 (14)	of that Fire, they will call out there for destruction
25:14 (15)	call not out today for one destruction
25:14 (15)	but call for many [destructions]
84:11 (11)	he shall call for destruction

h) pcple. pass. (*mathbūr*)

17:102 (104)	Pharaoh, I think thou art accursed

*TH B T

THABATA vb. (I)~to stand firm, to be stable. (n.vb.) constancy; sureness, standing firm. (pcple. act.) firm

c) impv. (*uthbut*)

8:45 (47)	O believers, whensoever you encounter a host, then stand firm

f) n.vb. (*thubūt*)

16:94 (96)	lest any foot should slip after it has stood firm

g) pcple. act. (*thābit*)

14:24 (29)	its roots are firm, and its branches are in heaven
14:27 (32)	God confirms those who believe with the firm word

THABBATA vb. (II)~to confirm, to make firm; to strengthen. (n.vb.) confirmation, strengthening

a) perf. act.

17:74 (76)	had We not confirmed thee, surely thou wert near to inclining unto them

b) impf. act. (*yuthabbitu*)

8:11 (11)	and to strengthen your hearts, and to confirm your feet
11:120 (121)	the tidings of the Messengers is that whereby We strengthen thy heart
14:27 (32)	God confirms those who believe with the firm word
16:102 (104)	the Holy Spirit sent it down from thy Lord in truth, and to confirm
25:32 (34)	even so, that We may strengthen thy heart thereby
47:7 (8)	if you help God, He will help you, and confirm your feet

c) impv. (*thabbit*)

2:250 (251) pour out upon us patience, and make firm our feet
3:147 (141) make firm our feet, and help us against the people of the unbelievers
8:12 (12) I am with you; so confirm the believers

f) n.vb. (*tathbīt*)

2:265 (267) seeking God's good pleasure, and to confirm themselves
4:66 (69) it would have been better for them, and stronger confirming them

ATHBATA vb. (IV)~to confirm, to establish; (8:30) to confine [Ar]; to wound fatally [Pk]; to keep in bonds [Ali]; to bring to a stand [Bl]

b) impf. act. (*yuthbitu*)

8:30 (30) when the unbelievers were devising against thee, to confine thee, or slay thee
13:39 (39) God blots out, and He establishes whatsoever He will

*TH B Ṭ

THABBAṬA vb. (II)~to make someone pause, to hold back, to hinder

a) perf. act.

9:46 (46) God was averse that they should be aroused, so He made them pause

*TH B Y

THUBĀT n.f. (pl. of *thubah*)~a group, a company of men; (adv) in companies

4:71 (73) move forward in companies, or move forward all together

*TH J J

THAJJĀJ n.m. (adj)~streaming, cascading

78:14 (14) and have sent down out of the rain-clouds water cascading

*TH KH N

ATHKHANA vb. (IV)~to slay in great numbers, to make a wide slaughter, to massacre (the enemy)

a) perf. act.

47:4 (4) when you have made wide slaughter among them, tie fast the bonds

b) impf. act. (*yuthkhinu*)

8:67 (68) it is not for any Prophet to have prisoners until he make wide slaughter in the land

*TH L L

THULLAH n.f.~a throng, a group, a band, a party

56:13 (13) a throng of the ancients
56:39 (38) a throng of the ancients
56:40 (39) and a throng of the later folk

*TH L TH

THALĀTHAH n.num.~three

2:196 (192)	if he finds none, then a fast of three days in the Pilgrimage
2:228 (228)	divorced women shall wait by themselves for three periods
3:41 (36)	thou shalt not speak, save by tokens, to men for three days
3:124 (120)	that your Lord should reinforce you with three thousand angels
4:171 (169)	believe in God and His Messengers, and say not, 'Three'
5:73 (77)	they are unbelievers who say, 'God is the Third of Three'
5:89 (91)	if any finds not the means, let him fast for three days
9:118 (119)	and to the three who were left behind
11:65 (68)	take your joy in your habitation three days
18:22 (21)	they will say, 'Three; and their dog was the fourth'
18:25 (24)	they tarried in the Cave three hundred years
19:10 (11)	thou shalt not speak to men, though being without fault, three nights
24:58 (57)	[let] those of you who have not reached puberty ask leave of you three times
24:58 (57)	three times of nakedness for you
39:6 (8)	He creates you in your mothers' wombs creation after creation in threefold shadows
56:7 (7)	and you shall be three bands
58:7 (8)	three men conspire not secretly together, but He is the fourth
65:4 (4)	if you are in doubt, their period shall be three months
77:30 (30)	depart to a triple-massing shadow

THALĀTHŪN n.num.~thirty

7:142 (138)	We appointed with Moses thirty nights and We completed them with ten
46:15 (14)	his bearing and his weaning are thirty months

THĀLITH n.num.~third

5:73 (77)	who say, 'God is the Third of Three'
36:14 (13)	they cried them lies, so We sent a third as reinforcement
53:20 (20)	El-Lat and El-'Uzza and Manat the third

THULĀTH n.num.~in threes, three by three

4:3 (3)	marry such women as seem good to you, two, three, four
35:1 (1)	who appointed the angels to be messengers having wings two, three and four

THULTH n.num.~a third

4:11 (12)	if they be women above two, then for them two-thirds
4:11 (12)	[if] his heirs are his parents, a third to his mother
4:12 (15)	if they are more numerous than that, they share equally a third
4:176 (175)	if there be two sisters, they shall receive two-thirds of what he leaves
73:20 (20)	thy Lord knows that thou keepest vigil nearly two-thirds of the night
73:20 (20)	or a half of it, or a third of it

*TH M D

THAMŪD n.prop.~Thamood (a pre-Islamic tribe)

7:73 (71)	and to Thamood their brother Salih
9:70 (71)	who were before you — the people of Noah, Ad, Thamood
11:61 (64)	and to Thamood their brother Salih
11:68 (71)	surely Thamood disbelieved in their Lord, so away with (Thamood)
11:68 (71)	surely (Thamood) disbelieved in their Lord, so away with Thamood
11:95 (98)	away with Midian, even as Thamood was done away

14:9 (9)	who were before you — the people of Noah, Ad, Thamood
17:59 (61)	and We brought Thamood the She-camel
22:42 (43)	the people of Noah cried lies, and Ad and Thamood
25:38 (40)	and Ad, and Thamood, and the men of Er-Rass
26:141 (141)	Thamood cried lies to the Envoys
27:45 (46)	We sent to Thamood their brother Salih
29:38 (37)	and Ad, and Thamood — it has become clear to you from their dwelling-places
38:13 (12)	and Thamood, and the people of Lot
40:31 (32)	the like of the case of Noah's people, Ad, Thamood
41:13 (12)	a thunderbolt like to the thunderbolt of Ad and Thamood
41:17 (16)	as for Thamood, We guided them
50:12 (12)	cried lies before them the people of Noah and the men of Er-Rass, and Thamood
51:43 (43)	and also in Thamood, when it was said to them
53:51 (52)	and Thamood, and He did not spare them
54:23 (23)	Thamood cried lies to the warnings
69:4 (4)	Thamood and Ad cried lies to the Clatterer
69:5 (5)	as for Thamood, they were destroyed by the Screamer
85:18 (18)	Pharaoh and Thamood
89:9 (8)	and Thamood, who hollowed the rocks in the valley
91:11 (11)	Thamood cried lies in their insolence

*TH M N

THAMAN n.m.~a price, cost; value

2:41 (38)	sell not My signs for a little price
2:79 (73)	'This is from God,' that they may sell it for a little price
2:174 (169)	those who conceal what of the Book God has sent down on them, and sell it for a little price
3:77 (71)	those that sell God's covenant, and their oaths, for a little price
3:187 (184)	they rejected it behind their backs and sold it for a small price
3:199 (198)	men humble to God, not selling the signs of God for a small price
5:44 (48)	but fear you Me; and sell not My signs for a little price
5:106 (105)	we will not sell it for a price
9:9 (9)	they have sold the signs of God for a small price
12:20 (20)	then they sold him for a paltry price
16:95 (97)	do not sell the covenant of God for a small price

THAMĀNIYAH n.num.~eight

6:143 (144)	eight couples: two of sheep, of goats two
28:27 (27)	these my two daughters, on condition that thou hirest thyself to me for eight years
39:6 (8)	He sent down to you of the cattle eight couples
69:7 (7)	He compelled against them seven nights and eight days
69:17 (17)	upon that day eight shall carry above them the Throne of thy Lord

THAMĀNŪN n.num.~eighty

24:4 (4)	scourge them with eighty stripes

THĀMIN n.num.~the eighth

18:22 (21)	seven; and their dog was the eighth of them

THUMN n.num.~an eighth

4:12 (14)	if you have children, then for them of what you leave an eighth

*TH M R

THAMARAH n.f. (pl. *thamar*)~(f) a fruit; (pl) fruits

2:22 (20)	out of heaven water, wherewith He brought forth fruits
2:25 (23)	whensoever they are provided with fruits therefrom
2:126 (120)	a land secure, and provide its people with fruits
2:155 (150)	and hunger, and diminution of goods and lives and fruits
2:266 (268)	and all manner of fruit there for him
6:99 (99)	look upon their fruits when they fructify and ripen
6:141 (142)	eat of their fruits when they fructify
7:57 (55)	and therewith send down water, and bring forth therewith all the fruits
7:130 (127)	then seized We Pharaoh's people with years of dearth, and scarcity of fruits
13:3 (3)	and of every fruit He placed there two kinds
14:32 (37)	wherewith He brought forth fruits to be your sustenance
14:37 (40)	men yearn towards them, and provide them with fruits
16:11 (11)	for you crops, and olives, and palms, and vines, and all manner of fruit
16:67 (69)	of the fruits of the palms and the vines, you take therefrom an intoxicant
16:69 (71)	then eat of all manner of fruit
18:34 (32)	so he had fruit
18:42 (40)	and his fruit was all encompassed
28:57 (57)	to which are collected the fruits of everything
35:27 (25)	therewith We bring forth fruits of diverse hues
36:35 (35)	that they might eat of its fruits and their hands' labour
41:47 (47)	not a fruit comes forth from its sheath
47:15 (17)	and therein for them is every fruit

ATHMARA vb. (IV)~to bear fruit, to fructify

a) perf. act.

6:99 (99)	look upon their fruits when they fructify and ripen
6:141 (142)	eat of their fruits when they fructify

*TH N Y

THANÁ vb. (I)~to fold; to turn away. (pcple. act.) one who folds; one who turns away

b) impf. act. (*yathnī*)

11:5 (5)	behold, they fold their breasts, to hide them from Him

g) pcple. act. (*thānī*)

22:9 (9)	turning his side to lead astray

ITHNĀ-ʿASHARA n.num.~twelve

2:60 (57)	and there gushed forth from it twelve fountains
5:12 (15)	We raised up from among them twelve chieftains
7:160 (160)	and We cut them up into twelve tribes, nations
7:160 (160)	there gushed forth from it twelve fountains
9:36 (36)	the number of the months, with God, is twelve

ITHNĀN n.num.~two

4:11 (12)	if they be women above two, then for them two-thirds
4:176 (175)	if there be two sisters, they shall receive two-thirds of what he leaves

5:106 (105)	at the bequeathing, shall be two men of equity among you
6:143 (144)	eight couples: two of sheep, of goats (two)
6:143 (144)	eight couples: (two) of sheep, of goats two
6:144 (145)	of camels two, of oxen (two)
6:144 (145)	of camels (two), of oxen two
9:40 (40)	when the unbelievers drove him forth the second of two
11:40 (42)	embark in it two of every kind, and thy family
13:3 (3)	and of every fruit He placed there two kinds
16:51 (53)	take not to you two gods
23:27 (28)	insert in it two of every kind and thy family
36:14 (13)	when We sent unto them two men, but they cried them lies
40:11 (11)	Thou hast caused us to die two deaths
40:11 (11)	Thou hast given us twice to live; now we confess our sins

MATHĀNĪ n.f.~repetitions; oft-repeated (parts or stories of the Koran)

15:87 (87)	We have given thee seven of the oft-repeated, and the mighty Koran
39:23 (24)	a Book, consimilar in its oft-repeated

MATHNÁ n.num.~by twos, in pairs, two by two

4:3 (3)	marry such women as seem good to you, two, three, four
34:46 (45)	that you stand unto God, two by two and one by one
35:1 (1)	who appointed the angels to be messengers having wings two, three and four

THĀNI n.num.~the second

9:40 (40)	when the unbelievers drove him forth the second of two

ISTATHNÁ vb. (X)~to add the saving words [Ar]; to make an exception (by saying "If God wills") [Pk, Ali, Bl]

b) impf. act. (*yastathnī*)

68:18 (18)	and they added not the saving words

*TH Q B

THAQABA vb. (I)~(pcple. act.) piercing

g) pcple. act. (*thāqib*)

37:10 (10)	and he is pursued by a piercing flame
86:3 (3)	the piercing star

*TH Q F

THAQIFA vb. (I)~to come upon someone, to find, to meet

a) perf. act.

2:191 (187)	and slay them wherever you come upon them
4:91 (93)	take them, and slay them wherever you come on them

b) impf. act. (*yathqafu*)

8:57 (59)	if thou comest upon them anywhere in the war, deal with them in such wise
60:2 (2)	if they come on you, they will be enemies to you

d) perf. pass. (*thuqifa*)

3:112 (108) abasement shall be pitched on them, wherever they are come upon
33:61 (61) wheresoever they are come upon they shall be seized

*TH Q L

THAQULA vb. (I)~to be heavy

a) perf. act.

7:8 (7) he whose scales are heavy — they are the prosperers
7:187 (186) heavy is it in the heavens and the earth
23:102 (104) then he whose scales are heavy — they are the prosperers
101:6 (5) then he whose deeds weigh heavy in the Balance

ATHQĀL n.m. (pl. of *thiql*)~load, burden

16:7 (7) they bear your loads unto a land that you never would reach
29:13 (12) they shall certainly carry their loads
29:13 (12) and other loads along with their (loads)
29:13 (12) and other (loads) along with their loads
99:2 (2) and earth brings forth her burdens

MITHQĀL n.m.~a weight, an equivalent in weight

4:40 (44) God shall not wrong so much as the weight of an ant
10:61 (62) not so much as the weight of an ant in earth or heaven escapes from thy Lord
21:47 (48) even if it be the weight of one grain of mustard-seed
31:16 (15) if it should be but the weight of one grain of mustard-seed
34:3 (3) not so much as the weight of an ant in heaven and earth escapes from Him
34:22 (21) they possess not so much as the weight of an ant in the heavens
99:7 (7) whoso has done an atom's weight of good shall see it
99:8 (8) whoso has done an atom's weight of evil shall see it

THAQAL n.m. (only the dual *thaqalān*, occurs)~weight [Ar]; dependent (man and jinn) [Pk]; world (of man and jinn) [Ali]; burdensome companies [Bl]

55:31 (31) We shall surely attend to you at leisure, you weight and you weight

THAQĪL n.m. (pl. *thiqāl*)~heavy, weighty

7:57 (55) when they are charged with heavy clouds, We drive it to a dead land
9:41 (41) go forth, light and heavy
13:12 (13) it is He who shows you the lightning, for fear and hope, and produces the heavy clouds
73:5 (5) behold, We shall cast upon thee a weighty word
76:27 (27) these men love the hasty world, and leave behind them a heavy day

ATHQALA vb. (IV)~to become heavy, to weigh down. (pcple. pass.) heavy-burdened, weighed down

7:189 (189) when it became heavy they cried to God their Lord

h) pcple. pass. (*muthqal*)

35:18 (19) if one heavy-burdened calls for its load to be carried
52:40 (40) and so they are weighed down with debt
68:46 (46) and so they are weighed down with debt

ITHTHĀQALA vb. (VI)~to incline heavily downwards, to sink down heavily

a) perf. act.

9:38 (38) you sink down heavily to the ground

*TH R B

THARRABA vb. (II)~(n.vb.) reproach, blame

f) n.vb. (*tathrīb*)

12:92 (92) no reproach this day shall be on you

*TH R Y

THARÁ n.m.~soil, ground, moist earth

20:6 (5) all that is between them, and all that is underneath the soil

*TH W B

MATHĀBAH n.f.~a place of visitation, a resort

2:125 (119) when We appointed the House to be a place of visitation for the people

MATHŪBAH n.f.~a recompense, reward (from God)

2:103 (97) a recompense from God had been better
5:60 (65) shall I tell you of a recompense with God

THAWĀB n.m.~reward (for good deeds), requital

3:145 (139) whoso desires the reward of this world, We will give him of this
3:145 (139) whoso desires the reward of the other world, We will give him of that
3:148 (141) God gave them the reward of this world
3:148 (141) and [God gave them] the fairest reward of the world to come
3:195 (195) a reward from God. And God — with Him is the fairest (reward)
3:195 (195) a (reward) from God. And God — with Him is the fairest reward
4:134 (133) whoso desires the reward of this world
4:134 (133) with God is the reward of this world and of the world to come
18:31 (30) O, how excellent a reward
18:44 (42) He is best rewarding
18:46 (44) the deeds of righteousness, are better with God in reward
19:76 (79) the deeds of righteousness, are better with thy Lord in reward
28:80 (80) the reward of God is better for him who believes

THIYĀB n.m. (pl. of *thawb*)~garments, clothes, robes

11:5 (6) they wrap themselves in their garments
18:31 (30) they shall be robed in green garments of silk and brocade
22:19 (20) for them garments of fire shall be cut
24:58 (57) and when you put off your garments at the noon
24:60 (59) there is no fault in them that they put off their clothes
71:7 (6) they put their fingers in their ears, and wrapped them in their garments
74:4 (4) thy robes purify
76:21 (21) upon them shall be green garments of silk and brocade

THAWWABA vb. (II)~to reward

d) perf. pass. (*thuwwiba*)

83:36 (36) have the unbelievers been rewarded what they were doing?

ATHĀBA vb. (IV)~to reward, to repay, to requite

a) perf. act.

3:153 (147) so He rewarded you with grief on grief
5:85 (88) God rewards them for what they say with gardens
48:18 (18) He sent down the Shechina upon them, and rewarded them with a nigh victory

*TH W R

ATHĀRA vb. (IV)~to plough, to break up the ground; to stir up, to blaze (dust)

a) perf. act.

30:9 (8) they ploughed up the earth and cultivated it
100:4 (4) blazing a trail of dust

b) impf. act. (*yuthīru*)

2:71 (66) she shall be a cow not broken to plough the earth
30:48 (47) God is He that looses the winds, that stir up clouds
35:9 (10) God is He that looses the winds, that stir up cloud

*TH W Y

THAWÁ vb. (I)~(pcple. act.) a dweller

g) pcple. act. (*thāwī*)

28:45 (45) neither wast thou a dweller among the Midianites

MATHWÁ n.m.~a dwelling, an abode, lodging

3:151 (144) evil is the lodging of the evildoers
6:128 (128) the Fire is your lodging, therein to dwell
12:21 (21) give him goodly lodging
12:23 (23) surely my lord has given me a goodly lodging
16:29 (31) evil is the lodging of those that wax proud
29:68 (68) is there not in Gehenna a lodging for the unbelievers?
39:32 (33) is there not in Gehenna a lodging for the unbelievers?
39:60 (61) is there not in Gehenna a lodging for those that are proud?
39:72 (72) how evil is the lodging of those that are proud
40:76 (76) how evil is the lodging of those that are proud
41:24 (23) if they persist, the Fire shall be a lodging for them
47:12 (13) and eat as cattle eat; and the Fire shall be their lodging
47:19 (21) God knows your going to and fro, and your lodging

*TH Y B

THAYYIBĀT n.f. (pl. of *thayyib*)~women who have been previously married, widows

66:5 (5) given to fasting, who have been married and virgins too

ṬĀ

*Ṭ ᶜ M

ṬAᶜIMA vb. (I)~to eat, to have a meal; to taste. (n.vb.) flavour, taste. (pcple. act.) one who eats, eater

a) perf. act.

5:93 (94) what they may eat
33:53 (53) when you have had the meal, disperse

b) impf. act. (*yaṭᶜamu*)

2:249 (250) whoso tastes it not, he is of me
6:138 (139) none shall eat them, but whom we will
6:145 (146) aught forbidden to him who eats thereof

f) n.vb. (*ṭaᶜm*)

47:15 (16) rivers of milk unchanging in flavour

g) pcple. act. (*ṭāᶜim*)

6:145 (146) aught forbidden to him who eats thereof

ṬAᶜĀM n.m.~food; feeding

2:61 (58) Moses, we will not endure one sort of food
2:184 (180) for those who are able to fast, a redemption by feeding a poor man
2:259 (261) look at thy food and drink — it has not spoiled
3:93 (87) all food was lawful to the Children of Israel
5:5 (7) the food of those who were given the Book is permitted to you
5:5 (7) and permitted to them is your food
5:75 (79) they both ate food
5:95 (96) food for poor persons
5:96 (97) permitted to you is the game of the sea and the food of it
12:37 (37) no food shall come to you for your sustenance
18:19 (18) let him look for which of them has purest food
21:8 (8) nor did We fashion them as bodies that ate not food
25:7 (8) what ails this Messenger that he eats food
25:20 (22) We sent not before thee any Envoys, but that they ate food
33:53 (53) except leave is given you for a meal
44:44 (44) is the food of the guilty
69:34 (34) he never urged the feeding of the needy
69:36 (36) neither any food saving foul pus
73:13 (13) food that chokes, and a painful chastisement
76:8 (8) they give food, for the love of Him, to the needy
80:24 (24) let Man consider his nourishment
88:6 (6) no food for them but cactus thorn
89:18 (19) and you urge not the feeding of the needy
107:3 (3) and urges not the feeding of the needy

AṬᶜAMA vb.~to feed, to give to eat; to serve food. (n.vb.) the act of feeding, giving food

a) perf. act.

36:47 (47) such a one whom, if God willed, He would feed
106:4 (3) who has fed them against hunger

b) impf. act. (*yuṭʿimu*)

5:89 (91)	the average of the food you serve to your families
6:14 (14)	He who feeds and is not fed
26:79 (79)	and Himself gives me to eat and drink
36:47 (47)	shall we feed such a one whom, if God willed
51:57 (57)	neither do I desire that they should feed Me
74:44 (45)	we fed not the needy
76:8 (8)	they give food, for the love of Him, to the needy
76:9 (9)	we feed you only for the Face of God

c) impv. (*aṭʿim*)

22:28 (29)	so eat thereof, and feed the wretched poor
22:36 (37)	when their flanks collapse, eat of them and feed the beggar

e) impf. pass. (*yuṭʿamu*)

6:14 (14)	He who feeds and is not fed

f) n.vb. (*iṭʿām*)

5:89 (91)	the expiation is to feed ten poor persons
58:4 (5)	then let him feed sixty poor persons
90:14 (14)	or giving food upon a day of hunger

ISTAṬʿAMA vb. (X)~to ask for food

a) perf. act.

18:77 (76)	they asked the people for food

*Ṭ ʿ N

ṬAʿANA vb. (I)~(with prep. *fī*) to thrust; to defame, to discredit, to speak ill of someone. (n.vb.) speaking ill of someone, traducing, defaming

a) perf. act.

9:12 (12)	if they break their oaths after their covenant and thrust at your religion

f) n.vb. (*ṭaʿn*)

4:46 (48)	twisting with their tongues and traducing religion

*Ṭ B ʿ

ṬABAʿA vb. (I)~to seal, to stamp, to set a seal

a) perf. act.

4:155 (154)	nay, but God sealed them for their unbelief
9:93 (94)	God has set a seal on their hearts
16:108 (110)	God has set a seal on their
47:16 (18)	those are they upon whose hearts God has set a seal

b) impf. act. (*yaṭbaʿu*)

7:100 (98)	We would smite them because of their sins, sealing their hearts

7:101 (99)	so God seals the hearts of the unbelievers
10:74 (75)	so We seal the hearts of the transgressors
30:59 (59)	God seals the hearts of those that know not
40:35 (37)	God sets a seal on every heart proud, arrogant

d) perf. pass. (*ṭubiʿa*)

9:87 (88)	a seal has been set upon their hearts
63:3 (3)	therefore a seal has been set on their hearts

*Ṭ B Q

ṬABAQ n.m.~stage, plane

84:19 (19)	you shall surely ride stage after (stage)
84:19 (19)	you shall surely ride (stage) after stage

ṬIBĀQ n.f. (pl. of *ṭabaqah*)~stratum, floor; (adv) one upon another [Ar, Ali]; in harmony [Pk]

67:3 (3)	who created seven heavens one upon another
71:15 (14)	have you not regarded how God created seven heavens one upon another

*Ṭ F ʾ

AṬFA'A vb. (IV)~to extinguish

a) perf. act.

5:64 (69)	as often as they light a fire for war, God will extinguish it

b) impf. act. (*yuṭfiʾu*)

9:32 (32)	desiring to extinguish with their mouths God's light
61:8 (8)	they desire to extinguish with their mouths the light of God

*Ṭ F F

ṬAFFAFA vb. (II)~(pcple. act.) stinter, one who gives short measure

g) pcple. act. (*muṭaffif*)

83:1 (1)	woe to the stinters

*Ṭ F L

ṬIFL n.m. (pl. *aṭfāl*)~infant, child

22:5 (5)	then We deliver you as infants
24:31 (31)	or children who have not yet attained knowledge of women's private parts
24:59 (58)	when your children reach puberty, let them ask leave
40:67 (69)	then He delivers you as infants

*Ṭ F Q

ṬAFIQA vb. (I)~to begin to do something, to take to doing something

a) perf. act.

7:22 (21)	they took to stitching upon themselves leaves of the Garden
20:121 (119)	they took to stitching upon themselves leaves of the Garden
38:33 (32)	he began to stroke their shanks and necks

*Ṭ GH Y

ṬAGHIYA vb. (I)~to be insolent, to be overbold; to transgress, to exceed proper bounds; to rage, to rise, to overflow; to go astray. (n.vb.) insolence, contumacy. (pcple. act.) insolent, wayward, wicked

a) perf. act.

20:24 (25)	go to Pharaoh; he has waxed insolent
20:43 (45)	go to Pharaoh, for he has waxed insolent
53:17 (17)	his eye swerved not, nor swept astray
69:11 (11)	when the waters rose, We bore you in the running ship
79:17 (17)	go to Pharaoh; he has waxed insolent
79:37 (37)	then as for him who was insolent
89:11 (10)	who all were insolent in the land

b) impf. act. (*yaṭghá*)

11:112 (114)	and be you not insolent
20:45 (47)	truly we fear he may exceed against us, or wax insolent
20:81 (83)	exceed not therein, or My anger shall alight on you
55:8 (7)	transgress not in the Balance
96:6 (6)	surely Man waxes insolent

f) n.vb. (*ṭughyān*)

2:15 (14)	and shall lead them on blindly wandering in their insolence
5:64 (69)	what has been sent down to thee from thy Lord will surely increase many of them in insolence
5:68 (72)	sent down to thee from thy Lord will surely increase many of them in insolence
6:110 (110)	We shall leave them in their insolence wandering blindly
7:186 (185)	He leaves them in their insolence blindly wandering
10:11 (12)	We leave those, who look not to encounter Us, in their insolence
17:60 (62)	but it only increases them in great insolence
18:80 (79)	we were afraid he would impose on them insolence
23:75 (77)	they would persist in their insolence wandering blindly

g) pcple. act. (*ṭāghī*; comp. adj. *aṭghá*)

37:30 (29)	no, you were an insolent people
38:55 (55)	but for the insolent awaits an ill resort
51:53 (53)	nay, but they are an insolent people
52:32 (32)	or are they an insolent people?
53:52 (53)	certainly they did exceeding evil, and were insolent
68:31 (31)	alas for us! Truly, we were insolent
78:22 (22)	for the insolent a resort

ṬĀGHIYAH n.f.~screamer [Ar]; lightning [Pk]; a storm of thunder and lightning [Ali]; Outburst [Bl]

69:5 (5)	as for Thamood, they were destroyed by the Screamer

ṬĀGHŪT n.m.~idol(s); demon(s); sorcerer or any other source of wickedness

2:256 (257)	whosoever disbelieves in idols and believes in God

2:257 (259)	the unbelievers — their protectors are idols
4:51 (54)	hast thou not regarded those who were given a share of the Book believing in demons and idols
4:60 (63)	desiring to take their disputes to idols
4:76 (78)	the unbelievers fight in the idols' way
5:60 (65)	and made some of them apes and swine, and worshippers of idols
16:36 (38)	serve you God, and eschew idols
39:17 (19)	those who eschew the serving of idols and turn penitent

ṬAGHWÁ n.f.~insolence, wickedness

91:11 (11)	Thamood cried lies in their insolence

AṬGHÁ vb. (IV)~to make someone insolent or wicked

a) perf. act.

50:27 (26)	I made him not insolent, but he was in far error

*Ṭ H

ṬĀ HĀ~ml

20:1 (1)	Ta Ha

*Ṭ H R

ṬAHARA vb. (I)~to be or become clean or pure

b) impf. act. (*yaṭhuru*)

2:222 (222)	do not approach them till they are clean

AṬHAR n.m. (comp.adj. of *ṭāhir*)~purer, cleaner

2:232 (232)	that is cleaner and purer for you
11:78 (80)	these are my daughters; they are cleaner for you
33:53 (53)	that is cleaner for your hearts and theirs
58:12 (13)	that is better for you and purer

ṬAHŪR n.m. (adj)~pure; purifying

25:48 (50)	We sent down from heaven pure water
76:21 (21)	their Lord shall give them to drink a pure draught

ṬAHHARA vb. (II)~to purify, to cleanse. (n.vb.) purification, cleansing. (pcple. act.) one who purifies or cleanses. (pcple. pass.) purified, clean

a) perf. act.

3:42 (37)	Mary, God has chosen thee, and purified thee

b) impf. act. (*yuṭahhiru*)

5:6 (9)	but He desires to purify you
5:41 (45)	those are they whose hearts God desired not to purify
8:11 (11)	sending down on you water from heaven, to purify you
9:103 (104)	a freewill offering, to purify them and to cleanse them thereby
33:33 (33)	God only desires to put away from you abomination and to cleanse you

c) impv. (*ṭahhir*)

2:125 (119) purify My House for those that shall go about it
22:26 (27) do thou purify My House for those that shall go about it
74:4 (4) thy robes purify

f) n.vb. (*taṭhīr*)

33:33 (33) to put away from you abomination and to cleanse you <...>

g) pcple. act. (*muṭahhir*)

3:55 (48) I will purify thee of those who believe not

h) pcple. pass. (*muṭahhar*)

2:25 (23) for them shall be spouses purified
3:15 (13) therein dwelling forever, and spouses purified
4:57 (60) therein for them shall be spouses purified
56:79 (78) none but the purified shall touch
80:14 (14) uplifted, purified
98:2 (2) a Messenger from God, reciting pages purified

TAṬAHHARA vb. (V)~to be purified; to cleanse oneself, to keep oneself clean. (pcple. act.) one who cleanses himself

a) perf. act.

2:222 (222) when they have cleansed themselves, then come unto them as God

b) impf. act. (*yataṭahharu*)

7:82 (80)
9:108 (109) therein are men who love to cleanse themselves
27:56 (57) they are men that keep themselves clean

c) impv. (*iṭṭahar* for *taṭahhar*)

5:6 (9) if you are defiled, purify yourselves

g) pcple. act. (*mutaṭahhir* and *muṭṭahir*)

2:222 (222) He loves those who cleanse themselves
9:108 (109) God loves those who cleanse themselves

*Ṭ Ḥ Y

ṬAḤÁ vb. (I)~to extend, to spread out

a) perf. act.

91:6 (6) by the earth and That which extended it

*Ṭ L ʿ

ṬALAʿA vb. (I)~to ascend, to rise, to come up (used with celestial bodies). (n.vb.) rising, coming up

a) perf. act.

18:17 (16) thou mightest have seen the sun, when it rose

b) impf. act. (*yaṭluʿu*)

18:90 (89) the sun, he found it rising upon a people

f) n.vb. (*ṭulūʿ*)

20:130 (130) proclaim thy Lord's praise before the rising of the sun
50:39 (38) proclaim thy Lord's praise before the rising of the sun

MAṬLAʿ n.m.~rising

18:90 (89) when he reached the rising of the sun

MAṬLIʿ n.m.~place of rising (of the celestial body)

97:5 (5) peace it is, till the rising of dawn

ṬALʿ n.m.~a spathe

6:99 (99) and out of the palm-tree, from the spathe of it
26:148 (148) sown fields, and palms with slender spathes
37:65 (63) its spathes are as the heads of Satans
50:10 (10) and tall palm-trees with spathes compact

AṬLAʿA vb. (IV)~to inform, to tell

b) impf. act. (*yuṭliʿu*)

3:179 (174) God will not inform you of the Unseen

IṬṬALAʿA vb. (VIII)~to observe, to look; to survey; to peruse; to light upon, to discover; to mount up; to roar over, to leap up over. (pcple. act.) one who observes, who looks down upon

a) perf. act.

18:18 (17) hadst thou observed them surely thou wouldst have turned thy back
19:78 (81) what, has he observed the Unseen
37:55 (53) then he looks, and sees him in the midst of Hell

b) impf. act. (*yaṭṭaliʿu*)

5:13 (16) thou wilt never cease to light upon some act of treachery
28:38 (38) make me a tower, that I may mount up to Moses' God
40:37 (39) and look upon Moses' God
104:7 (7) roaring over the hearts

g) pcple. act. (*muṭṭaliʿ*)

37:54 (52) are you looking down?

*Ṭ L B

ṬALABA vb. (I)~to seek out, to pursue, to search for. (n.vb.) seeking out, search. (pcple. act.) seeker. (pcple. pass.) sought

b) impf. act. (*yaṭlubu*)

7:54 (52) covering the day with the night it pursues urgently

f) n.vb. (*ṭalab*)

18:41 (39) so that thou wilt not be able to seek it out

g) pcple. act. (*ṭālib*)

22:73 (72) feeble indeed alike are the seeker and the sought

h) pcple. pass. (*maṭlūb*)

22:73 (72) feeble indeed alike are the seeker and the sought

*Ṭ L Ḥ

ṬALḤ n.f. (pl. of *ṭalḥah*)~acacias; plaintains; banana trees

56:29 (28) and serried acacias

*Ṭ L L

ṬALL n.m.~dew, light moisture; shower

2:265 (267) if no torrent smites it, yet dew

*Ṭ L Q

ṬALAQA vb. (I)~(n.vb.) divorce; setting free

f) n.vb. (*ṭalāq*)

2:227 (227) if they resolve on divorce, surely God is All-hearing
2:229 (229) divorce is twice; then honourable retention

ṬALLAQA vb. (II)~to divorce. (pcple. pass.) a divorced woman

a) perf. act.

2:230 (230) if he divorces her finally, she shall not be lawful to him after that
2:230 (230) if he divorces her, then it is no fault in them to return to each other
2:231 (231) when you divorce women, and they have reached their term
2:232 (232) when you divorce women, and they have reached their term
2:236 (237) if you divorce women while as yet you have not touched them
2:237 (238) if you divorce them before you have touched them
33:49 (48) when you marry believing women and then divorce them
65:1 (1) O Prophet, when you divorce women
66:5 (5) if he divorces you, his Lord will give him in exchange wives

c) impv. (*ṭalliq*)

65:1 (1) divorce them when they have reached their period

h) pcple. pass. f. (*muṭallaqah*)

2:228 (228) divorced women shall wait by themselves for three periods
2:241 (242) there shall be for divorced women provision honourable

INṬALAQA vb. (VII)~to depart, to set forth; to be loosed

a) perf. act.

18:71 (70) so they departed; until, when they embarked upon the ship
18:74 (73) so they departed; until, when they met a lad
18:77 (76) so they departed; until, when they reached the people
38:6 (5) and the Council of them depart, saying
48:15 (15) will say, when you set forth after spoils, to take them
68:23 (23) so they departed, whispering together

b) impf. act. (*yanṭaliqu*)

26:13 (12) and my tongue will not be loosed

c) impv. (*inṭaliq*)

77:29 (29) depart to that you cried was lies
77:30 (30) depart to a triple-massing shadow

*Ṭ L T

ṬĀLŪT n.prop.~Saul [Ar, Pk]; Talut [Ali, Bl]

2:247 (248) God has raised up Saul for you as king
2:249 (250) when Saul went forth with the hosts

*Ṭ M ᶜ

ṬAMIᶜA vb. (I)~to be eager, to desire, to hope for; to be lustful. (n.vb.) eagerness; hope

b) impf. act. (*yaṭmaᶜu*)

2:75 (70) are you then so eager that they should believe you
5:84 (87) and be eager that our Lord should admit us
7:46 (44) they have not entered it, for all their eagerness
26:51 (51) We are eager that our Lord should forgive us our offences
26:82 (82) and who I am eager shall forgive me my offence
33:32 (32) so that he in whose heart is sickness may be lustful
70:38 (38) is every man of them eager to be admitted to a Garden of Bliss?
74:15 (15) then he is eager that I should do more

f) n.vb. (*ṭamaᶜ*)

7:56 (54) and call on Him fearfully, eagerly
13:12 (13) it is He who shows you the lightning, for fear and hope
30:24 (23) He shows you lightning, for fear and hope
32:16 (16) their sides shun their couches as they call on their Lord in fear and hope

*Ṭ M M

ṬĀMMAH n.f.~calamity, catastrophe

79:34 (34) then, when the Great Catastrophe comes

*Ṭ M ᵓ N

IṬMAᵓANNA vb. (quad IV)~to be at rest, to be secure, to be tranquil, to be at peace. (pcple. act.) one who is at peace, at rest

a) perf. act.

4:103 (104) then, when you are secure, perform the prayer
10:7 (7) well-pleased with the present life and are at rest in it
22:11 (11) if good befalls him he is at rest in it

b) impf. act. (*yaṭma'innu*)

2:260 (262) but that my heart may be at rest
3:126 (122) good tiding to you, and that your hearts might be at rest
5:113 (113) we desire that we should eat of it and our hearts be at rest
8:10 (10) and that your hearts thereby might be at rest
13:28 (28) those who believe, their hearts being at rest in God's remembrance
13:28 (28) in God's remembrance are at rest the hearts of those who believe

g) pcple. act. (*muṭma'inn*)

16:106 (108) his heart is still at rest in his belief
16:112 (113) God has struck a similitude: a city that was secure, at rest
17:95 (97) had there been in the earth angels walking at peace
89:27 (27) O soul at peace

*Ṭ M S

ṬAMASA vb. (I)~(with prep. *ʿalá*) to obliterate, to efface; to extinguish

a) perf. act.

36:66 (66) did We will, We would have obliterated their eyes
54:37 (37) so We obliterated their eyes, saying

b) impf. act. (*yaṭmisu*)

4:47 (50) confirming what is with you, before We obliterate faces

c) impv. (*iṭmis*)

10:88 (88) obliterate their possessions, and harden their hearts

d) perf. pass. (*ṭumisa*)

77:8 (8) when the stars shall be extinguished

*Ṭ M TH

ṬAMATHA vb. (I)~to touch (a female sexually), to deflower

b) impf. act. (*yaṭmithu*)

55:56 (56) untouched before them by any man or jinn
55:74 (74) untouched before them by any man or jinn

*Ṭ R D

ṬARADA vb. (I)~to drive away, to repel. (pcple. act.) one who drives away, who repels

a) perf. act.

11:30 (32) who would help me against God, if I drive them away?

b) impf. act. (*yaṭrudu*)

6:52 (52) do not drive away those who call upon their Lord at morning
6:52 (52) thy account falls upon them, that thou shouldst drive them away

g) pcple. act. (*ṭārid*)

11:29 (31) I will not drive away those who believe
26:114 (114) I would not drive away the believers

*Ṭ R F

ṬARAFA vb. (I)~(n.vb.) a glance, a look, a gaze

f) n.vb. (*ṭarf*)

14:43 (44) their glances never returned on themselves, their hearts void
27:40 (40) I will bring it to thee, before ever thy glance returns to thee
37:48 (47) and with them wide-eyed maidens restraining their glances
38:52 (52) and with them maidens restraining their glances
42:45 (44) abject in humbleness, looking with furitive glance
55:56 (56) therein maidens restraining their glances

ṬARAF n.m. (pl. *aṭrāf*)~section, part; end, extremity

3:127 (122) that He might cut off a part of the unbelievers
11:114 (116) perform the prayer at the two ends of the day
13:41 (41) how We come to the land diminishing it in its extremities
20:130 (130) in the watches of the night, and at the ends of the day
21:44 (45) how We come to the land, diminishing it in its extremities

*Ṭ R Ḥ

ṬARAḤA vb. (I)~to cast, to throw

b) impf. act. (*yaṭraḥu*)

12:9 (9) kill you Joseph, or cast him forth into some land

*Ṭ R Q

ṬĀRIQ n.m.~a nocturnal visitor; night-star [Ar]; morning-star [Pk]; Night-Visitant [Ali]; Meteor [Bl]

86:1 (1) by heaven and the night-star
86:2 (2) what shall teach thee what is the night-star?

ṬARĪQ n.com.~way, road, path

4:168 (166) God would not forgive them, neither guide them on any road
4:169 (167) but the road to Gehenna, therein dwelling forever
20:77 (79) strike for them a dry path in the sea
46:30 (29) guiding to the truth and to a straight path

ṬARĪQAH n.f. (pl. *ṭarāʾiq*)~way, procedure, mode of conduct, tradition; sect; tract, path (for the passage of the celestial luminaries)

20:63 (66) and to extirpate your justest way
20:104 (104) when the justest of them in the way will say
23:17 (17) We created above you seven ways

72:11 (11) some of us are otherwise; we are sects differing
72:16 (16) would they but go straight on the way, We would give them to drink

*Ṭ R Y

ṬARĪY n.m. (adj)~fresh, succulent

16:14 (14) He who subjected to you the sea, that you may eat of it fresh flesh
35:12 (13) yet of both you eat fresh flesh

*Ṭ S

ṬĀ SĪN~ml

27:1 (1) Ta Sin. Those are the signs of the Koran

*Ṭ S M

ṬĀ SĪN MĪM~ml

26:1 (1) Ta Sin Mim
28:1 (1) Ta Sin Mim

*Ṭ W ᶜ

ṬĀᶜA vb. (I)~(n.vb.) obedience; willingness, voluntariness; (adv) willingly, voluntarily. (pcple. act.) one who is obedient, willing

f) n.vb. (*ṭawᶜ*)

3:83 (77) to Him has surrendered whoso is in the heavens and the earth, willingly or unwillingly
9:53 (53) expend willingly, or unwillingly, it shall not be accepted from you
13:15 (16) to God bow all who are in the heavens and the earth, willingly or unwillingly
41:11 (10) come willingly, or unwillingly

g) pcple. act. (*ṭāʾiᶜ*)

41:11 (10) we come willingly

ṬĀᶜAH n.f.~obedience, compliance

4:81 (83) they say, 'Obedience'
24:53 (52) do not swear; honourable obedience is sufficient
47:21 (22) obedience, and words honourable

ṬAWWAᶜA vb. (II)~to prompt; to impose

a) perf. act.

5:30 (33) then his soul prompted him to slay his brother

AṬĀᶜA vb. (IV)~to obey, to submit. (pcple. pass.) obeyed

a) perf. act.

2:285 (285) we hear, and obey
3:168 (162) had they obeyed us, they would not have been slain
4:34 (38) if they then obey you, look not for any way against them
4:46 (49) we have heard and obey
4:80 (82) whosoever (obeys) the Messenger, thereby obeys God

5:7 (10)	we have heard and we obey
6:121 (121)	if you obey them, you are idolaters
23:34 (36)	if you obey a mortal like yourselves, then you will be losers
24:47 (46)	we believe in God and the Messenger, and we obey
24:51 (50)	we hear, and we obey
33:66 (66)	would we had obeyed God and ([obeyed]) the Messenger
33:66 (66)	would we had (obeyed) God and [obeyed] the Messenger
33:67 (67)	our Lord, we obeyed our chiefs and great ones
43:54 (54)	he made his people unsteady, and they obeyed him

b) impf. act. (*yuṭīʿu*)

3:100 (95)	if you obey a sect of those who have been given the Book
3:149 (142)	O believers, if you obey the unbelievers
4:13 (17)	whoso obeys God and His Messenger
4:69 (71)	whosoever obeys God, and the Messenger
4:80 (82)	whosoever obeys the Messenger
6:116 (116)	if thou obeyest the most part of those on earth
9:71 (72)	and they obey God and His Messenger
18:28 (27)	obey not him whose heart We have made neglectful
24:52 (51)	whoso obeys God and His Messenger
24:54 (53)	if you obey him, you will be guided
25:52 (54)	so obey not the unbelievers
26:151 (151)	obey not the commandment of the prodigal
29:8 (7)	then do not obey them
31:15 (14)	then do not obey them
33:1 (1)	fear God, and obey not the unbelievers
33:48 (47)	obey not the unbelievers and the hypocrites
33:71 (71)	whosoever obeys God and His Messenger has won a mighty triumph
47:26 (28)	we will obey you in some of the affair
48:16 (16)	if you obey, God will give you a goodly wage
48:17 (17)	whosoever obeys God and His Messenger
49:7 (7)	if he obeyed you in much of the affair, you would suffer
49:14 (14)	if you obey God and His Messenger, He will not diminish you anything
59:11 (11)	we will never obey anyone in regard to you
68:8 (8)	so obey thou not those who cry lies
68:10 (10)	obey thou not every mean swearer
76:24 (24)	and obey not one of them, sinner or unbeliever
96:19 (19)	no indeed; do thou not obey him

c) impv. (*aṭiʿ*)

3:32 (29)	obey God, and the Messenger
3:50 (44)	so fear you God, and obey you me
3:132 (126)	and obey God and the Messenger
4:59 (62)	O believers, obey God and (obey) the Messenger
4:59 (62)	O believers, (obey) God and obey the Messenger
5:92 (93)	and obey God
5:92 (93)	and obey the Messenger, and beware
8:1 (1)	obey you God and His Messenger
8:20 (20)	O believers, obey God and His Messenger
8:46 (48)	and obey God, and His Messenger
20:90 (92)	follow me, and obey my commandment
24:54 (53)	obey God, and (obey) the Messenger
24:54 (53)	(obey) God, and obey the Messenger
24:56 (55)	pay the alms, and obey the Messenger

26:108 (108)	so fear you God, and obey you me
26:110 (110)	so fear you God, and obey you me
26:126 (126)	so fear you God, and obey you me
26:131 (131)	so fear you God, and obey you me
26:144 (144)	so fear you God, and obey you me
26:150 (150)	so fear you God, and obey you me
26:163 (163)	so fear you God, and obey you me
26:179 (179)	so fear you God, and obey you me
33:33 (33)	and obey God and His Messenger
43:63 (63)	so fear you God and obey you me
47:33 (35)	O believers, obey God and (obey) the Messenger
47:33 (35)	O believers, (obey) God and obey the Messenger
58:13 (14)	pay the alms, and obey God and His Messenger
64:12 (12)	obey God, and (obey) the Messenger
64:12 (12)	(obey) God, and obey the Messenger
64:16 (16)	fear God as far as you are able, and give ear, and obey
71:3 (3)	serve God, and fear Him, and obey you me

e) impf. pass. (*yuṭāʿu*)

4:64 (67)	We sent not ever any Messenger, but that he should be obeyed
40:18 (19)	the evildoers have not one loyal friend, no intercessor to be heeded

h) pcple. pass. (*muṭāʿ*)

81:21 (21)	obeyed, moreover trusty

TAṬAWWAʿA vb. (V)~to volunteer, to do voluntarily. (pcple. act.) a volunteer

a) perf. act.

2:158 (153)	whoso volunteers good, God is All-grateful, All-knowing
2:184 (180)	yet better it is for him who volunteers good

g) pcple. act. (*muṭṭawwiʿ* for *mutaṭawwiʿ*)

9:79 (80)	the believers who volunteer their freewill offerings

ISTAṬĀʿA vb. (X)~to be able; can, could

a) perf. act.

2:217 (214)	till they turn you from your religion, if they are able
3:97 (91)	if he is able to make his way there
6:35 (35)	if thou canst seek out a hole in the earth
8:60 (62)	make ready for them whatever force and strings of horses you can
9:42 (42)	had we been able, we would have gone out with you,'
10:38 (39)	then produce a sura like it, and call on whom you can
11:13 (16)	call upon whom you are able, apart from God
11:88 (90)	I desire only to set things right, so far as I am able
17:64 (66)	startle whomsoever of them thou canst with thy voice
18:97 (96)	they were unable either to scale it or ([able]) to pierce it
18:97 (96)	they (were unable) either to scale it or [able] to pierce it
36:67 (67)	then they could not go on
51:45 (45)	they were not able to stand upright
55:33 (33)	if you are able to pass through the confines of heaven
64:16 (16)	so fear God as far as you are able

b) impf. act. (*yastaṭīʿu* or *yasṭīʿu*)

2:273 (274)	and are unable to journey in the land
2:282 (282)	if the debtor be a fool, or weak, or unable to dictate himself
4:25 (29)	any one of you who has not the affluence to be able to marry
4:98 (100)	who, being abased, can devise nothing
4:129 (128)	you will not be able to be equitable between your wives
5:112 (112)	is thy Lord able to send down on us a Table out of heaven?
7:192 (191)	that have no power to help them, neither they help themselves
7:197 (196)	those on whom you call, apart from God, have no power to help you
11:20 (22)	they are unable to frustrate Him on earth
16:73 (75)	do they serve, apart from God, that which has no power to provide them
17:48 (51)	and go astray, and cannot find a way
18:41 (39)	so that thou wilt not be able to seek it out
18:67 (66)	thou wilt not be able to bear with me patiently
18:72 (71)	did I not say that thou couldst never bear with me patiently?
18:75 (74)	did I not say that thou couldst never bear with me patiently?
18:78 (77)	the interpretation of that thou couldst not bear patiently
18:82 (81)	this is the interpretation of that thou couldst not bear patiently
18:101 (101)	and they were not able to hear
21:40 (41)	they shall not be able to repel it
21:43 (44)	apart from Us? Why, they are not able to help themselves
25:9 (10)	and go astray, and are unable to find a way
25:19 (20)	you can neither turn it aside, nor find any help
26:211 (211)	it behoves them not, neither are they able
36:50 (50)	then they will not be able to make any testament
36:75 (75)	they cannot help them, though they be hosts
58:4 (5)	if any man is not able to, then let him feed sixty
68:42 (42)	they shall be summoned to bow themselves, but they cannot

*Ṭ W D

ṬAWD n.m.~a (high) mountain

26:63 (63)	and each part was as a mighty mount

*Ṭ W F

ṬĀFA vb. (I)~to go round, to go or wander about; (with prep. *bi-*) to pass something around; circumambulate. (pcple. act.) one who goes about or around, who circumambulates the Kaaba (performing the rite of *ṭawāf*)

b) impf. act. (*yaṭūfu*)

52:24 (24)	there go round them youths, their own
55:44 (44)	they shall go round between it and between hot, boiling water
56:17 (17)	immortal youths going round about them
76:19 (19)	immortal youths shall go about them

e) impf. pass. (*yuṭāfu*)

37:45 (44)	a cup from a spring being passed round to them
43:71 (71)	there shall be passed around them platters of gold
76:15 (15)	there shall be passed around them vessels of silver

g) pcple. act. (*ṭāʾif*)

2:125 (119)	purify My House for those that shall go about it
22:26 (27)	purify My House for those that shall go about it

ṬĀ'IFAH n.f.~a party, a section

3:69 (62)	there is a party of the People of the Book
3:72 (65)	there is a party of the People of the Book
3:122 (118)	when two parties of you were about to lose heart
3:154 (148)	a slumber overcoming a party of you
3:154 (148)	and a party themselves had grieved
4:81 (83)	a party of them meditate all night on other than what thou sayest
4:102 (103)	let a party of them stand with thee
4:102 (103)	let another party who have not prayed come and pray
4:113 (113)	a party of them purposed to lead thee astray
6:156 (157)	the Book was sent down only upon two parties before us
7:87 (85)	if there is a party of you who believe in the Message
7:87 (85)	and a party who believe not
8:7 (7)	when God promised you one of the two parties should be yours
9:66 (67)	if We forgive one party of you
9:66 (67)	We will chastise another party
9:83 (84)	if God returns thee to a party of them
9:122 (123)	why should not a party of every section of them go forth
24:2 (2)	let a party of the believers witness their chastisement
28:4 (3)	abasing one party of them, slaughtering their sons
33:13 (13)	and when a party of them said
49:9 (9)	if two parties of the believers fight
61:14 (14)	a party of the Children of Israel believed
61:14 (14)	and a party disbelieved
73:20 (20)	or a third of it, and a party of those with thee

ṬAWWĀF n.m.~one who goes about or around

24:58 (57)	there is no fault in you or them, apart from these, that you go about one to the other

ṬŪFĀN n.m.~flood, inundation, deluge

7:133 (130)	We let loose upon them the flood and the locusts
29:14 (13)	the Flood seized them, while they were evildoers

TAṬAWWAFA vb. (V)~to circumambulate, to go about (the Kaaba)

b) impf. act. (*yaṭṭawwafu*, for *yataṭawwafu*)

2:158 (153)	it is no fault in him to circumambulate them
22:29 (30)	let them fulfil their vows, and go about the Ancient House

*Ṭ W L

ṬĀLA vb. (I)~to be long, to last long. (n.vb.) length; height

a) perf. act.

20:86 (89)	did the time of the covenant seem so long to you
21:44 (45)	until their life had lasted long while upon them
57:16 (15)	the term seemed over long to them

f) n.vb. (*ṭūl*)

17:37 (39)	thou wilt never tear the earth open, nor attain the mountains in height

ṬAWĪL n.m. (adj)~long

73:7 (7)	surely in the day thou hast long business
76:26 (26)	and magnify Him through the long night

ṬAWL n.m.~affluence, bounty, might, power; (*dhū al-ṭawl*) the Bountiful (Divine attribute)

4:25 (29)	any one of you who has not the affluence to be able to marry
9:86 (87)	the affluent among them ask leave of thee
40:3 (3)	the Bountiful; there is no god but He

TAṬĀWALA vb. (VI)~to be prolonged, to continue to be long

a) perf. act.

28:45 (45)	and long their lives continued

*Ṭ W Q

ṬĀQAH n.f.~power, strength

2:249 (250)	we have no power today against Goliath and his hosts
2:286 (286)	do Thou not burden us beyond what we have the strength to bear

ṬAWWAQA vb. (II)~to hang something around a neck, to twist a collar

e) impf. pass. (*yuṭawwaqu*)

3:180 (176)	that they were niggardly with they shall have hung about their necks

AṬĀQA vb. (IV)~to be able to, to afford

b) impf. act. (*yuṭīqu*)

2:184 (180)	for those who are able to fast, a redemption by feeding

*Ṭ W R

AṬWĀR n.m. (pl. of *ṭawr*)~a stage, a state

71:14 (13)	seeing He created you by stages

ṬŪR n.m.~a mountain; the Mount

2:63 (60)	when We took compact with you, and raised above you the Mount
2:93 (87)	when We took compact with you, and raised over you the Mount
4:154 (153)	We raised above them the Mount, taking compact with them
19:52 (53)	We called to him from the right side of the Mount
20:80 (82)	We made covenant with you upon the right side of the Mount
23:20 (20)	a tree issuing from the Mount of Sinai
28:29 (29)	he observed on the side of the Mount a fire
28:46 (46)	thou wast not upon the side of the Mount when We called
52:1 (1)	by the Mount
95:2 (2)	and the Mount Sinai

*Ṭ W Y

ṬAWÁ vb. (I)~to roll up, to fold. (n.vb.) rolling up, folding. (pcple. pass.) rolled up, folded up

b) impf. act. (*yaṭwī*)

21:104 (104)	on the day when We shall roll up heaven as a scroll

f) n.vb. (*ṭayy*)

21:104 (104) when We shall roll up heaven as a scroll <is rolled> for the writing

h) pcple. pass. (*maṭwīy*)

39:67 (67) the heavens shall be rolled up in His right hand

ṬUWÁ n.prop.~Towa (a valley near Mt. Sinai)

20:12 (12) thou art in the holy valley, Towa
79:16 (16) when his Lord called to him in the holy valley, Towa

*Ṭ Y B

ṬĀBA vb. (I)~to seem good, to fare well; (with prep. *ʿan*) to give up gladly, to be pleased to offer

a) perf. act.

4:3 (3) marry such women as seem good to you
4:4 (3) if they are pleased to offer you any of it, consume it
39:73 (73) well you have fared; enter in, to dwell forever

ṬAYYIB n.m. (fs, *ṭayyibah*; pl. *ṭayyibāt*)~(n) good things, good men or women; (adj) good, wholesome, pleasant, fair

2:57 (54) eat of the good things wherewith We have provided you
2:168 (163) eat of what is in the earth lawful and good
2:172 (167) eat of the good things wherewith We have provided you
2:267 (269) expend of the good things you have earned
3:38 (33) Lord, give me of Thy goodness a goodly offspring
3:179 (173) till He shall distinguish the corrupt from the good
4:2 (2) do not exchange the corrupt for the good
4:43 (46) then have recourse to wholesome dust
4:160 (158) We have forbidden them certain good things that were permitted to them
5:4 (6) the good things are permitted you
5:5 (7) today the good things are permitted you
5:6 (9) then have recourse to wholesome dust
5:87 (89) forbid not such good things as God has permitted you
5:88 (90) eat of what God has provided you lawful and good
5:100 (100) the corrupt and the good are not equal
7:32 (30) the good things of His providing
7:58 (56) the good land — its vegetation comes forth by the leave of its Lord
7:157 (156) making lawful for them the good things
7:160 (160) eat of the good things wherewith We have supplied you
8:26 (26) with His help, and provided you with the good things
8:37 (38) that God may distinguish the corrupt from the good
8:69 (70) eat of what you have taken as booty, such as is lawful and good
9:72 (73) therein to dwell, and goodly dwelling-places in the Gardens of Eden
10:22 (23) the ships run with them with a fair breeze
10:93 (93) We provided them with good things; so they differed not
14:24 (29) a good word is as a (good) tree — its roots are firm
14:24 (29) a (good) word is as a good tree — its roots are firm
16:32 (34) whom the angels take while they are goodly, saying
16:72 (74) sons and grandsons, and He has provided you of the good things
16:97 (99) We shall assuredly give him to live a goodly life
16:114 (115) eat of what God has provided you lawful and good

17:70 (72)	and provided them with good things
20:81 (83)	eat of the good things wherewith We have provided you
22:24 (24)	they shall be guided unto goodly speech
23:51 (53)	O Messengers, eat of the good things and do righteousness
24:26 (26)	and good men for (good women)
24:26 (26)	and (good men) for good women
24:26 (26)	good women for (good men)
24:26 (26)	(good women) for good men
24:61 (61)	greet one another with a greeting from God, blessed and good
34:15 (14)	a good land, and a Lord All-forgiving
35:10 (11)	to Him good words go up
40:64 (66)	and provided you with the good things
45:16 (15)	We provided them with good things
46:20 (19)	you dissipated your good things in your present life
61:12 (12)	and to dwelling-places goodly in Gardens of Eden

ṬŪBÁ n.f.~blessedness; happiness, joy

13:29 (28)	theirs is blessedness and a fair resort

*Ṭ Y F

ṬĀFA vb. (I)~to visit (in one's sleep); to appear (as a spectre). (pcple. act.) a visitation, a spectre

a) perf. act.

68:19 (19)	then a visitation from thy Lord visited it

g) pcple. act. (*ṭā'if*)

7:201 (200)	when a visitation of Satan troubles them
68:19 (19)	then a visitation from thy Lord visited it

*Ṭ Y N

ṬĪN n.m.~clay

3:49 (43)	I will create for you out of clay as the likeness of a bird
5:110 (110)	when thou createst out of clay, by My leave
6:2 (2)	it is He who created you of clay
7:12 (11)	Thou createdst me of fire, and him Thou createdst of clay
17:61 (63)	shall I bow myself unto one Thou hast created of clay?
23:12 (12)	We created man of an extraction of clay
28:38 (38)	kindle me, Haman, a fire upon the clay
32:7 (6)	He originated the creation of man out of clay
37:11 (11)	We created them of clinging clay
38:71 (71)	see, I am creating a mortal of a clay
38:76 (77)	Thou createdst me of fire, and him Thou createdst of clay
51:33 (33)	to loose upon them stones of clay

*Ṭ Y R

ṬĀRA vb. (I)~to fly. (pcple. act.) a bird; bird of omen, augury

b) impf. act. (*yaṭīru*)

6:38 (38)	no creature is there crawling on the earth, no bird flying with its wings

g) pcple. act. (*ṭāʾir*)

6:38 (38)	no bird flying with its wings
7:131 (128)	their ill augury was with God; but the most of them knew not
17:13 (14)	We have fastened to him his bird of omen upon his neck
27:47 (48)	your augury is with God
36:19 (18)	your augury is with you

ṬAYR n.m. (coll)~bird, birds, fowl; (pl. of *ṭāʾir*, above) omens, auguries

2:260 (262)	take four birds, and twist them to thee
3:49 (43)	I will create for you out of clay as the likeness of a bird
3:49 (43)	then I will breathe into it, and it will be a bird
5:110 (110)	when thou createst out of clay, by My leave, as the likeness of a bird
5:110 (110)	thou breathest into it, and it is a bird
12:36 (36)	I dreamed that I was carrying on my head bread, that birds were eating of
12:41 (41)	he shall be crucified, and birds will eat of his head
16:79 (81)	have they not regarded the birds
21:79 (79)	with David We subjected the mountains to give glory, and the birds
22:31 (32)	it is as though he has fallen from heaven and the birds snatch him away
24:41 (41)	and the birds spreading their wings
27:16 (16)	we have been taught the speech of the birds
27:17 (17)	jinn, men and birds, duly disposed
27:20 (20)	he reviewed the birds; then he said
34:10 (10)	O you mountains, echo God's praises with him, and you birds
38:19 (18)	and the birds, duly mustered, every one to him reverting
56:21 (21)	and such flesh of fowl as they desire
67:19 (19)	have they not regarded the birds above them spreading their wings
105:3 (3)	He loosed upon them birds in flights

IṬṬAYYARA vb. (V)~to augur ill

a) perf. act.

27:47 (48)	we augur ill of thee and of those that are with thee
36:18 (17)	we augur ill of you

b) impf. act. (*yaṭṭayyaru* for *yataṭayyaru*)

7:131 (128)	if any evil smote them, they would augur ill by Moses

ISTAṬĀRA vb. (X)~(pcple. act.) that which is upon a wing [Ar]; widespread [Pk]; that which flies far and wide [Ali]; ready to fly [Bl]

g) pcple. act. (*mustaṭīr*)

76:7 (7)	they fulfil their vows, and fear a day whose evil is upon the wing

WAW

*W ʾ D

WAʾADA vb. (I)~(pcple. pass.) buried infant (girl)

h) pcple. pass. f. (*mawʾūdah*)

81:8 (8)	when the buried infant shall be asked

*W ʾ L

MAWʾIL n.m.~an escape, a refuge

18:58 (57)	but they have a tryst, from which they will find no escape

*W ʿ D

WAʿADA vb. (I)~to promise, to make a promise; to threaten. (n.vb.) a promise. (pcple. pass.) promised

a) perf. act.

3:194 (192)	our Lord, give us what Thou hast promised us
4:95 (97)	yet to each God has promised the reward most fair
5:9 (12)	God has promised those that believe, and do deeds of righteousness
7:44 (42)	we have found that which our Lord promised us true
7:44 (42)	have you found what your Lord promised you true?
9:68 (69)	God has promised the hypocrites, men and women, and the unbelievers, the fire of Gehenna
9:72 (73)	God has promised the believers, men and women, gardens underneath which rivers flow
9:77 (78)	for that they failed God in that they promised Him and they were liars
9:114 (115)	because of a promise he had made to him
14:22 (26)	God surely promised you a true promise
14:22 (26)	and I promised you, then I failed you
19:61 (62)	Gardens of Eden that the All-merciful promised His servants in the Unseen
22:72 (71)	the Fire — God has promised it to the unbelievers
24:55 (54)	God has promised those of you who believe
28:61 (61)	is he to whom We have promised a fair promise, and he receives it
33:12 (12)	God and His Messenger promised us only delusion
33:22 (22)	they said, 'This is what God and His Messenger promised us'
36:52 (52)	this is what the All-merciful promised, and the Envoys spoke truly
40:8 (8)	admit them to the Gardens of Eden that Thou hast promised them
43:42 (41)	or We show thee a part of that We promised them
48:20 (20)	God has promised you many spoils to take
48:29 (29)	God has promised those of them who believe and do deeds
57:10 (10)	unto each God has promised the reward most fair

b) impf. act. (*yaʿidu*)

2:268 (271)	Satan promises you poverty, and bids you unto indecency
2:268 (271)	but God promises you His pardon and His bounty
4:120 (119)	He promises them and fills them with fancies
4:120 (119)	but there is nothing Satan promises them except delusion

7:70 (68)	then bring us that thou promisest us
7:77 (75)	O Salih, bring us that thou promisest us
8:7 (7)	when God promised you one of the two parties should be yours
10:46 (47)	whether We show thee a part of that We promise them, or We call thee unto Us
11:32 (34)	then bring us that thou promisest us
13:40 (40)	whether We show thee a part of that We promise them, or We call thee to Us
17:64 (66)	but Satan promises them naught, except delusion
20:86 (89)	did your Lord not promise a fair promise to you?
23:35 (37)	does he promise you that when you are dead, and become dust and bones
23:95 (97)	assuredly, We are able to show thee that We promise them
35:40 (38)	the evildoers promise one another naught but delusion
40:28 (29)	somewhat of that he promises you will smite you
40:77 (77)	whether We show thee a part of that We promise them, or We call thee unto Us
46:17 (16)	fie upon you! Do you promise me that I shall be brought forth
46:22 (21)	pervert us from our gods? Then bring us that thou promisest us

c) impv. (*ᶜid*)

17:64 (66)	share with them in their wealth and their children, and promise them

d) perf. pass. (*wuᶜida*)

13:35 (35)	the likeness of Paradise, that is promised to the godfearing
23:83 (85)	we and our fathers have been promised this before
25:15 (16)	is that better, or the Garden of Eternity, that is promised
27:68 (70)	we have been promised this, and our fathers before
47:15 (16)	this is the similitude of Paradise which the godfearing have been promised

e) impf. pass. (*yūᶜadu*)

6:134 (134)	the thing you are promised, that will surely come
19:75 (77)	till, when they see that they were threatened
21:103 (103)	the angels shall receive them: 'This is your day that you were promised'
21:109 (109)	even though I know not whether near or far is that you are promised
23:36 (38)	away, away with that you are promised
23:93 (95)	O my Lord, if Thou shouldst show me that they are promised
26:206 (206)	then there comes on them that they were promised
36:63 (63)	this is Gehenna, then, the same that you were promised
38:53 (53)	this is what you were promised
41:30 (30)	rejoice in Paradise that you were promised
43:83 (83)	until they encounter that day of theirs which they are promised
46:16 (15)	the promise of the very truth, which they were promised
46:35 (34)	it shall be as if, on the day they see that they are promised
50:32 (31)	this is that you were promised; it is for every mindful penitent
51:5 (5)	surely that you are promised is true
51:22 (22)	in heaven is your provision, and that you are promised
51:60 (60)	woe to the unbelievers, for that day of theirs that they are promised
70:42 (42)	until they encounter that day of theirs which they are promised
70:44 (44)	that is the day which they were promised
72:24 (25)	when they see that which they are promised, then they will know
72:25 (26)	I do not know whether that which you are promised is nigh
77:7 (7)	surely that which you are promised is about to fall

f) n.vb. (*waᶜd*)

3:152 (145)	God has been true in His promise towards you
4:122 (121)	God's promise in truth; and who is truer
9:111 (112)	that is a promise binding upon God

10:4 (4)	God's promise, in truth. He originates
10:48 (49)	they say, 'When will this promise be'
10:55 (56)	God's promise is true
11:45 (47)	and Thy promise is surely the truth. Thou art the justest
11:65 (68)	three days — that is a promise not to be belied
13:31 (31)	until God's promise comes; and God will not fail the tryst
14:22 (26)	God surely promised you a true promise
14:47 (48)	do not deem that God will fail in His promise to His Messengers
16:38 (40)	it is a promise binding upon Him
17:5 (5)	when the promise of the first of these came to pass
17:5 (5)	and it was a promise performed
17:7 (7)	when the promise of the second came to pass
17:104 (106)	when the promise of the world to come comes to pass
17:108 (108)	glory be to our Lord! Our Lord's promise is performed
18:21 (20)	that they might know that God's promise is true
18:98 (98)	when the promise of my Lord comes to pass
18:98 (98)	and my Lord's promise is ever true
19:54 (55)	mention in the Book Ishmael; he was true to his promise
19:61 (62)	His promise is ever performed
20:86 (89)	my people, did your Lord not promise a fair promise to you?
21:9 (9)	then We made true the promise We gave them
21:38 (39)	they say, 'And when shall the promise come to pass'
21:97 (97)	nigh has drawn the true promise, and behold, the eyes
21:104 (104)	We shall bring it back again — a promise binding on Us
22:47 (46)	God will not fail His promise
25:16 (17)	it is a promise binding upon thy Lord
27:71 (73)	when shall this promise come to pass, if you speak the truth?
28:13 (12)	that she might know that the promise of God is true
28:61 (61)	is he to whom We have promised a fair promise
30:6 (5)	the promise of God
30:6 (5)	God fails not His promise
30:60 (60)	surely God's promise is true
31:9 (8)	therein to dwell forever — God's promise in truth
31:33 (33)	surely God's promise is true
34:29 (28)	when shall this promise come to pass, if you speak the truth?
35:5 (5)	O men, God's promise is true
36:48 (48)	when shall this promise come to pass, if you speak truly?
39:20 (21)	God's promise; God fails not the tryst
39:74 (74)	praise belongs to God, who has been true in His promise to us
40:55 (57)	surely God's promise is true
40:77 (77)	surely God's promise is true
45:32 (31)	when it was said, 'God's promise is true'
46:16 (15)	the promise of the very truth, which they were promised
46:17 (16)	woe upon thee! Believe; surely God's promise is true
67:25 (25)	they say, 'When shall this promise come to pass'
73:18 (18)	whereby heaven shall be split, and its promise shall be performed

h) pcple. pass. (*mawʿūd*)

85:2 (2)	by the promised day

MAWʿID n.m. (f. in 9:114)~a promise, a tryst; time or place of realizing a promise or a threat; a promised land

9:114 (115)	Abraham asked not pardon for his father except because of a promise he had made to him
11:17 (20)	whosoever disbelieves in it, being one of the partisans, his promised land is the Fire
11:81 (83)	their promised time is the morning

15:43 (43)	Gehenna shall be their promised land
18:48 (46)	nay, you asserted We should not appoint for you a tryst
18:58 (57)	they have a tryst, from which they will find no escape
18:59 (58)	We destroyed them when they did evil, and appointed for their destruction a tryst
20:58 (60)	therefore appoint a tryst between us and thee
20:59 (61)	your tryst shall be upon the Feast Day
20:86 (89)	so that you failed in your tryst with me
20:87 (90)	we have not failed in our tryst with thee
20:97 (97)	thereafter a tryst awaits thee thou canst not fail to keep
54:46 (46)	nay, but the Hour is their tryst

MĪʿĀD n.m.~a tryst, a promise

3:9 (7)	verily God will not fail the tryst
3:194 (192)	Thou wilt not fail the tryst
8:42 (43)	together, you would have surely failed the tryst
13:31 (31)	and God will not fail the tryst
34:30 (29)	you have the tryst of a day that you shall not put back by a single hour
39:20 (21)	God's promise; God fails not the tryst

WAʿĪD n.m.~a threat

14:14 (17)	that, for him who fears My station and fears My threat
20:113 (112)	We have turned about in it something of threats
50:14 (13)	and My threat came true
50:20 (19)	the Trumpet shall be blown; that is the Day of the Threat
50:28 (27)	dispute not before Me! For I sent you beforehand the threat
50:45 (45)	therefore remind by the Koran him who fears My threat

WĀʿADA vb. (III)~to arrange for a meeting, to appoint with someone, to make covenant with someone, to make troth with someone

a) perf. act.

2:51 (48)	and when We appointed with Moses forty nights
7:142 (138)	We appointed with Moses thirty nights and We completed them with ten
20:80 (82)	We made covenant with you upon the right side of the Mount

b) impf. act. (*yuwāʿidu*)

2:235 (235)	but do not make troth with them secretly

AWʿADA vb. (IV)~to threaten

b) impf. act. (*yūʿidu*)

7:86 (84)	and do not sit in every path, threatening

TAWĀʿADA vb. (VI)~to make tryst together

a) perf. act.

8:42 (43)	had you made tryst together, you would have surely failed

*W ʿ Y

WAʿÁ vb. (I)~to hold; to remember, to retain in one's memory; to heed. (pcple. act.) heeding *b*) impf. act. (*yaʿī*)

69:12 (12) that We might make it a reminder for you and for heeding ears to hold

g) pcple. act. f. (*wāʿiyah*)

69:12 (12) and for heeding ears to hold

WIʿĀʾ n.m. (pl. *awʿiyah*)~a bag, a sack, a vessel, a container

12:76 (76) so he made beginning with their sacks
12:76 (76) before his brother's sack
12:76 (76) then he pulled it out of his brother's sack

AWʿÁ vb. (IV)~to hold in a container, to amass; to secrete, to conceal, to hide

a) perf. act.

70:18 (18) who amassed and hoarded

b) impf. act. (*yūʿī*)

84:23 (23) and God knows very well what they are secreting

*W ʿ Ẓ

WAʿAẒA vb. (I)~to admonish, to give admonition, to exhort; to warn. (pcple. act.) admonisher

a) perf. act.

26:136 (136) alike it is to us, whether thou admonishest, or art not one of the admonishers

b) impf. act. (*yaʿiẓu*)

2:231 (231) and the Wisdom He has sent down on you, to admonish you
4:58 (61) good is the admonition God gives you
7:164 (164) why do you admonish a people God is about to destroy
11:46 (48) I admonish thee, lest thou shouldst be among the ignorant
16:90 (92) He forbids indecency, dishonour, and insolence, admonishing you
24:17 (16) God admonishes you, that you shall never repeat the like of it again
31:13 (12) when Lokman said to his son, admonishing him, 'O my son'
34:46 (45) I give you but one admonition, that you stand unto God

c) impv. (*ʿiẓ*)

4:34 (38) those you fear may be rebellious admonish; banish them to their couches
4:63 (66) so turn away from them, and admonish them

e) impf. pass. (*yūʿaẓu*)

2:232 (232) [by this then is admonished] whoso of you believes in God
4:66 (69) if they had done as they were admonished it would have been better for them
58:3 (4) by that you are admonished
65:2 (2) by this then is admonished whosoever believes in God

g) pcple. act. (*wāʿiẓ*)

26:136 (136) thou admonishest, or art not one of the admonishers

MAWʿIẒAH n.f.~admonition, exhortation

2:66 (62)	and an admonition to such as are godfearing
2:275 (276)	whosoever receives an admonition from his Lord and gives over
3:138 (132)	and an admonition for such as are godfearing
5:46 (50)	confirming the Torah before it, as a guidance and an admonition
7:145 (142)	We wrote for him on the Tablets of everything an admonition
10:57 (58)	now there has come to you an admonition from your Lord
11:120 (121)	in these there has come to thee the truth and an admonition
16:125 (126)	call thou to the way of thy Lord with wisdom and good admonition
24:34 (34)	and an admonition for the godfearing

*W B L

WABĀL n.m.~mischief, harm; evil consequence of an action

5:95 (96)	so that he may taste the mischief of his action
59:15 (15)	those who a short time before them tasted the mischief of their action
64:5 (5)	that disbelieved before, then tasted the mischief of their action
65:9 (9)	so it tasted the mischief of its action

WĀBIL n.m.~a torrent, a heavy downpour

2:264 (266)	a torrent smites it, and leaves it barren
2:265 (267)	a torrent smites it and it yields its produce twofold
2:265 (267)	if no torrent smites it, yet dew

WABĪL n.m.~remorseful; calamitous; hurtful

73:16 (16)	so We seized him remorselessly

*W B Q

MAWBIQ n.m.~a place of destruction; a gulf (of doom)

18:52 (50)	We shall set a gulf between them

AWBAQA vb. (IV)~to wreck, to ruin

b) impf. act. (*yūbiqu*)

42:34 (32)	or He wrecks them for what they have earned

*W B R

AWBĀR n.m. (pl. of *wabar*)~fur (of goats or camels)

16:80 (82)	and of their fur, and of their hair furnishing and an enjoyment for a while

*W D ʿ

WADAʿA vb. (I)~to let, to leave, to heed not

c) impv. (*daʿ*)

33:48 (47)	heed not their hurt

MUSTAWADAʿ n.m.~repository

6:98 (98)	then a lodging-place, and then a repository
11:6 (8)	He knows its lodging-place and its repository

WADDAʿA vb. (II)~to forsake

a) perf. act.

93:3 (3) thy Lord has neither forsaken thee nor hates thee

*W D D

WADDA vb. (I)~to wish, to want; to yearn; to like, to love. (n.vb.) love

a) perf. act.

2:109 (103) many of the People of the Book wish they might restore you as unbelievers
3:69 (62) there is a party of the People of the Book yearn to make you go astray
3:118 (114) they yearn for you to suffer
4:89 (91) they wish that you should disbelieve as they disbelieve
4:102 (103) the unbelievers wish that you should be heedless of your weapons
60:2 (2) and they wish that you may disbelieve
68:9 (9) they wish that thou shouldst compromise

b) impf. act. (*yawaddu*)

2:96 (90) there is one of them wishes if he might be spared a thousand years
2:105 (99) the idolaters wish not that any good should be sent down upon you
2:266 (268) would any of you wish to have a garden of palms and vines
3:30 (28) it will wish if there were only a far space between it and that day
4:42 (45) those who have disobeyed the Messenger, will wish that the earth might be levelled
8:7 (7) you were wishing that the one not accoutred should be yours
15:2 (2) perchance the unbelievers will wish that they had surrendered
33:20 (20) they will wish that they were desert-dwellers among the Bedouins
70:11 (11) the sinner will wish that he might ransom himself

f) n.vb. (*wudd*)

19:96 (96) unto them the All-merciful shall assign love

MAWADDAH n.f.~affection, love

4:73 (75) as if there had never been any affection between you and him
5:82 (85) thou wilt surely find the nearest of them in love to the believers
29:25 (24) as a mark of mutual love between you
30:21 (20) He has set between you love and mercy
42:23 (22) I do not ask of you a wage for this, except love for the kinsfolk
60:1 (1) take not My enemy and your enemy for friends, offering them love
60:1 (1) if you go forth to struggle in My way and seek My good pleasure, secretly loving them
60:7 (7) it may be God will yet establish between you and those of them with whom you are at enmity love

WADD n.prop.~Wadd (an idol)

71:23 (22) do not leave Wadd, nor Suwa'

WADŪD n.m.~All-loving (Divine attribute)

11:90 (92) surely my Lord is All-compassionate, All-loving
85:14 (14) He is the All-forgiving, the All-loving

WĀDDA vb. (III)~to love, to make friends

b) impf. act. (*yuwāddu*)

58:22 (22)	who are loving to anyone who opposes God and His Messenger

*W D Q

WADQ n.m.~rain

24:43 (43)	then thou seest the rain issuing out of the midst of them
30:48 (47)	then thou seest the rain issuing out of the midst of them

*W D Y

DIYAH n.f.~bloodwit, indemnity

4:92 (94)	and bloodwit is to be paid to his family
4:92 (94)	then bloodwit is to be paid to his family

WĀDĪ n.m. (pl. *awdiyah*)~valley, river, river bed

9:121 (122)	nor do they traverse any valley, but it is written to their account
13:17 (18)	and the wadis flow each in its measure
14:37 (40)	I have made some of my seed to dwell in a valley where is no sown land
20:12 (12)	thou art in the holy valley, Towa
26:225 (225)	hast thou not seen how they wander in every valley
27:18 (18)	till, when they came on the Valley of Ants
28:30 (30)	a voice cried from the right bank of the watercourse, in the sacred hollow
46:24 (23)	when they saw it as a sudden cloud coming towards their valleys
79:16 (16)	when his Lord called to him in the holy valley, Towa
89:9 (8)	and Thamood, who hollowed the rocks in the valley

*W DH R

WADHARA vb. (I)~to leave, to let, to forsake, to let go, to abandon; to give up

b) impf. act. (*yadharu*)

2:234 (234)	those of you who die, leaving wives
2:240 (241)	those of you who die, leaving wives
3:179 (173)	God will not leave the believers in the state in which you are
4:129 (128)	so that you leave her as it were suspended
6:110 (110)	We shall leave them in their insolence wandering blindly
7:70 (68)	that we may serve God alone, and forsake that our fathers served
7:127 (124)	wilt thou leave Moses and his people to work corruption in the land
7:127 (124)	and leave thee and thy gods
7:186 (185)	He leaves them in their insolence blindly wandering
10:11 (12)	We leave those, who look not to encounter Us
19:72 (73)	the evildoers We shall leave there, hobbling on their knees
20:106 (106)	then He will leave them a level hollow
21:89 (89)	O my Lord, leave me not solitary
26:166 (166)	leaving your wives that your Lord created for you
37:125 (125)	do you call on Baal, and abandon the Best of creators?
51:42 (42)	that left nothing it came upon
71:23 (22)	do not leave your gods
71:23 (22)	and do not leave Wadd, nor Suwa

71:26 (27)	leave not upon the earth of the unbelievers even one
71:27 (28)	if Thou leavest them, they will lead Thy servants astray
74:28 (28)	it spares not, neither leaves alone
75:21 (21)	and leave behind the Hereafter
76:27 (27)	these men love the hasty world, and leave behind them a heavy day

c) impv. (*dhar*)

2:278 (278)	give up the usury that is outstanding
6:70 (69)	leave alone those who take their religion for a sport
6:91 (91)	then leave them alone, playing their game of plunging
6:112 (112)	so leave them to their forging
6:120 (120)	forsake the outward sin, and the inward
6:137 (138)	so leave them to their forging
7:73 (71)	leave her that she may eat in God's earth
7:180 (179)	and leave those who blaspheme His Names
9:86 (87)	let us be with the tarriers
11:64 (67)	leave her that she may eat in God's earth
12:47 (47)	what you have harvested leave in the ear, excepting a little
15:3 (3)	leave them to eat, and to take their joy
23:54 (56)	so leave thou them in their perplexity
40:26 (27)	let me slay Moses
43:83 (83)	then leave them alone to plunge and play
48:15 (15)	let us follow you
52:45 (45)	then leave them, till they encounter their day
62:9 (9)	leave trafficking aside; that is better for you
68:44 (44)	so leave Me with him who cries lies to this discourse
70:42 (42)	then leave them alone to plunge and play
73:11 (11)	leave Me to those who cry lies
74:11 (11)	leave Me with him whom I created alone

*W Ḍ ᶜ

WAḌAᶜA vb. (I)~to set, to set down; to set up, to establish; to lay aside, to put something off; to lay something down, to deposit; to give birth, to bring forth (a baby); (with prep. *ᶜan*) to take away, to rid, to lift (a burden), to relieve. (pcple. pass.) set forth

a) perf. act.

3:36 (31)	and when she gave birth to her
3:36 (31)	Lord, I have given birth to her, a female
3:36 (31)	God knew very well what she had given birth to
46:15 (14)	painfully she gave birth to him
55:7 (6)	heaven — He raised it up, and set the Balance
55:10 (9)	earth — He set it down for all beings
94:2 (2)	and lift from thee thy burden

b) impf. act. (*yaḍaᶜu*)

4:102 (103)	if rain molests you, or you are sick, to lay aside your weapons
7:157 (156)	and relieving them of their loads, and the fetters
21:47 (48)	We shall set up the just balances
22:2 (2)	every pregnant woman shall deposit her burden
24:58 (57)	when you put off your garments at the noon
24:60 (59)	there is no fault in them that they put off their clothes
35:11 (12)	no female bears or brings forth, save with His knowledge

41:47 (47)	no female bears or brings forth, save with His knowledge
47:4 (5)	till the war lays down its loads
65:4 (4)	their term is when they bring forth their burden
65:6 (6)	expend upon them until they bring forth their burden

d) perf. pass. (*wuḍiᶜa*)

3:96 (90)	the first House established for the people was that at Bekka
18:49 (47)	the Book shall be set in place; and thou wilt see
39:69 (69)	the earth shall shine with the light of its Lord, and the Book shall be set in place

h) pcple. pass. (*mawḍūᶜ*)

88:14 (14)	and goblets set forth

MAWĀḌIᶜ n.m. (pl. of *mawḍiᶜ*)~meaning [Ar]; context [Pk]; right places [Ali]; position [Bl]

4:46 (48)	some of the Jews pervert words from their meanings
5:13 (16)	they perverting words from their meanings
5:41 (45)	who have not come to thee, perverting words from their meanings

AWḌAᶜA vb. (IV)~to run or hurry to and fro

a) perf. act.

9:47 (47)	they would only have increased you in trouble, and run to and fro in your midst

*W Ḍ N

WAḌANA vb. (I)~(pcple. pass.) close-wrought [Ar]; lined [Pk]; encrusted (with gold and precious stones) [Ali]; set with jewels [Bl]

h) pcple. pass. (*mawḍūn*)

56:15 (15)	upon close-wrought couches

*W F D

WAFADA vb. (I)~(n.vb.) coming with pomp [Ar]; coming as a goodly company [Pk]; coming as before royalty [Ali]; embassy [Bl]

f) n.vb. (*wafd*)

19:85 (88)	the day that We shall muster the godfearing to the All-merciful with pomp

*W F Ḍ

AWFAḌA vb. (IV)~to hasten, to hurry

b) impf. act. (*yūfiḍu*)

70:43 (43)	as if they were hurrying unto a waymark

*W F Q

WAFFAQA vb. (II)~(with prep. *bayn*) to reconcile, to compose the differences between parties. (n.vb.) conciliation; succour *b*) impf. act. (*yuwaffiqu*)

4:35 (39) God will compose their differences

f) n.vb. (*tawfīq*)

4:62 (65) we sought only kindness and conciliation
11:88 (90) my succour is only with God

WĀFAQA vb. (III)~(n.vb.) accordance, suitability

f) n.vb. (*wifāq*)

78:26 (26) for a suitable recompense

*W F R

WAFARA vb. (I)~(pcple. pass.) ample, abundant

h) pcple. pass. (*mawfūr*)

17:63 (65) Gehenna shall be your recompense, an ample recompense

*W F Y

WAFĪY n.m. (adj.; comp. *awfá*)~true, faithful; complete; fulfilling; full

9:111 (112) who fulfils his covenant truer than God?
53:41 (42) then he shall be recompensed for it with the fullest recompense

WAFFÁ vb. (II)~to pay an account in full, to pay what is due. (pcple. act.) one who pays in full

a) perf. act.

24:39 (39) He pays him his account in full
53:37 (38) and Abraham, he who paid his debt in full

b) impf. act. (*yuwaffī*)

3:57 (50) He will pay them in full their wages
4:173 (172) He will pay them in full their wages
11:15 (18) We will pay them in full for their works therein
11:111 (113) thy Lord will pay them in full for their works
24:25 (25) upon that day God will pay them in full their just due
35:30 (27) that He may pay them in full their wages
46:19 (18) that He may pay them in full for their works

d) perf. pass. (*wuffiya*)

3:25 (24) every soul shall be paid in full what it has earned
39:70 (70) every soul shall be paid in full for what it has wrought

e) impf. pass. (*yuwaffá*)

2:272 (274) whatever good you expend shall be repaid to you in full
2:281 (281) every soul shall be paid in full what it has earned
3:161 (155) then every soul shall be paid in full what it has earned
3:185 (182) you shall surely be paid in full your wages on the Day of Resurrection
8:60 (62) whatsoever you expend in the way of God shall be repaid you in full

16:111 (112) every soul shall be paid in full for what it wrought
39:10 (13) the patient will be paid their wages in full without reckoning

g) pcple. act. (*muwaffī*)

11:109 (111) We shall surely pay them in full their portion

AWFÁ vb. (IV)~to fulfil, to live up to; to fill up, to give to the full. (pcple. act.) one who fulfils

a) perf. act.

3:76 (70) whoso fulfils his covenant and fears God
48:10 (10) whoso fulfils his covenant made with God, God will give him a mighty wage

b) impf. act. (*yūfī*)

2:40 (38) I shall fulfil your covenant
12:59 (59) do you not see that I fill up the measure
13:20 (20) who fulfil God's covenant, and break not the compact
22:29 (30) let them fulfil their vows, and go about
76:7 (7) they fulfil their vows, and fear a day whose evil is upon the wing

c) impv. (*awfi*)

2:40 (38) wherewith I blessed you, and fulfil My covenant
5:1 (1) O believers, fulfil your bonds
6:152 (153) fill up the measure and the balance with justice
6:152 (153) and fulfil God's covenant
7:85 (83) so fill up the measure and the balance
11:85 (86) O my people, fill up the measure and the balance justly
12:88 (88) fill up to us the measure
16:91 (93) fulfil God's covenant, when you make covenant
17:34 (36) and fulfil the covenant
17:35 (37) and fill up the measure when you measure
26:181 (181) fill up the measure, and be not cheaters

g) pcple. act. (*mūfī*)

2:177 (172) and they who fulfil their covenant

TAWAFFÁ vb. (V)~to take to oneself, to receive, to recall, to call to oneself, to gather unto oneself. (pcple. act.) one who takes unto himself

a) perf. act.

4:97 (99) those the angels take, while still they are wronging themselves
5:117 (117) when Thou didst take me to Thyself
6:61 (61) Our messengers take him and they neglect not
47:27 (29) how shall it be, when the angels take them, beating their faces

b) impf. act. (*yatawaffá*)

4:15 (19) then detain them in their houses until death takes them
6:60 (60) it is He who recalls you by night
7:37 (35) when Our messengers come to them, to take them away
8:50 (52) if thou couldst only see when the angels take the unbelievers
10:46 (47) whether We show thee a part of that We promise them, or We call thee unto Us
10:104 (104) I serve God, who will gather you to Him
13:40 (40) whether We show thee a part of that We promise them, or We call thee to Us

16:28 (30)	whom the angels take while still they are wronging themselves
16:32 (34)	whom the angels take while they are goodly
16:70 (72)	God created you; then He will gather you to Him
32:11 (11)	death's angel, who has been charged with you, shall gather you
39:42 (43)	God takes the souls at the time of their death
40:77 (77)	whether We show thee a part of that We promise them, or We call thee unto Us

c) impv. (*tawaffa*)

3:193 (191)	take us to Thee with the pious
7:126 (123)	gather us unto Thee surrendering
12:101 (102)	O receive me to Thee in true submission

e) impf. pass. (*yutawaffá*)

2:234 (234)	those of you who die, leaving wives
2:240 (241)	those of you who die, leaving wives
22:5 (5)	and some of you die
40:67 (69)	though some of you there are who die before it

g) pcple. act. (*mutawaffī*)

3:55 (48)	Jesus, I will take thee to Me and will raise thee to Me

ISTAWFÁ vb. (X)~to take full measure, to receive in full

b) impf. act. (*yastawfī*)

83:2 (2)	who, when they measure against the people, take full measure

*W H B

WAHABA vb. (I)~to give, to donate, to grant, to bestow

a) perf. act.

6:84 (84)	We gave to him Isaac and Jacob
14:39 (41)	praise be to God, who has given me, though I am old, Ishmael
19:49 (50)	We gave him Isaac and Jacob, and each We made a Prophet
19:50 (51)	and We gave them of Our mercy
19:53 (54)	We gave him his brother Aaron
21:72 (72)	We gave him Isaac and Jacob in superfluity
21:90 (90)	so We answered him, and bestowed on him John
26:21 (20)	but my Lord gave me Judgment
29:27 (26)	We gave him Isaac and Jacob
33:50 (49)	spoils of war that God has given thee
38:30 (29)	We gave unto David Solomon
38:43 (42)	We gave to him his family

b) impf. act. (*yahabu*)

19:19 (19)	I am but a messenger come from thy Lord, to give thee a boy most pure
42:49 (48)	He gives to whom He will females
42:49 (48)	and He gives to whom He will males

c) impv. (*hab*)

3:8 (6)	and give us mercy from Thee
3:38 (33)	give me of Thy goodness a goodly offspring

19:5 (5)	so give me, from Thee, a kinsman
25:74 (74)	give us refreshment of our wives and seed, and make us a model
26:83 (83)	give me Judgment, and join me with the righteous
37:100 (98)	my Lord, give me one of the righteous
38:35 (34)	give me a kingdom such as may not befall anyone after me

WAHHĀB n.m.~Giver, All-giving, All-giver, Bestower (Divine attribute)

3:8 (6)	Thou art the Giver
38:9 (8)	the All-mighty, the All-giving
38:35 (34)	surely Thou art the All-giver

*W H J

WAHHĀJ n.m. (adj)~blazing, brightly burning, glowing

78:13 (13)	We appointed a blazing lamp

*W H N

WAHANA vb. (I)~to faint, to be feeble, to be weak, to be frail. (n.vb.) weakness, feebleness

a) perf. act.

3:146 (140)	they fainted not for what smote them in God's way
19:4 (3)	O my Lord, behold the bones within me are feeble

b) impf. act. (*yahinu*)

3:139 (133)	faint not, neither sorrow; you shall be the upper ones
4:104 (105)	
47:35 (37)	so do not faint and call for peace

f) n.vb. (*wahn*)

31:14 (13)	his mother bore him in weakness upon (weakness)
31:14 (13)	his mother bore him in (weakness) upon weakness

AWHAN n.m. (comp. adj. of *wahn*)~weakest, frailest

29:41 (40)	the frailest of houses is the house of the spider

AWHANA vb. (IV)~(pcple. act.) one who weakens, who makes someone frail or feeble

g) pcple. act. (*mūhin*)

8:18 (18)	God weakens the unbelievers' guile

*W H Y

WAHÁ vb. (I)~(pcple. act.) frail, fragile, weak

g) pcple. act. f. (*wāhiyah*)

69:16 (16)	heaven shall be split, for upon that day it shall be very frail

*W Ḥ D

WAḤD n.m. (adv)~(*waḥdahu*) alone, only

7:70 (68)	hast thou come to us that we may serve God alone
17:46 (49)	when thou mentionest thy Lord only in the Koran
39:45 (46)	when God is mentioned alone, then shudder the hearts
40:12 (12)	that is because, when God was called to alone, you disbelieved
40:84 (84)	we believe in God alone
60:4 (4)	hatred for ever, until you believe in God alone

WĀḤID n.num.~one; the One (Divine attribute)

2:61 (58)	Moses, we will not endure one sort of food
2:133 (127)	the God of thy fathers Abraham, Ishmael and Isaac, One God
2:163 (158)	your God is One God
2:213 (209)	the people were one nation
4:1 (1)	fear your Lord, who created you of a single soul
4:3 (3)	if you fear you will not be equitable, then only one
4:11 (12)	but if she be one then to her a half
4:11 (12)	to his parents to each one of the two the sixth
4:12 (15)	but have a brother or a sister, to each of the two a sixth
4:102 (103)	then they would wheel on you all at once
4:171 (169)	God is only One God
5:48 (53)	if God had willed, He would have made you one nation
5:73 (77)	no god is there but One God
6:19 (19)	He is only One God
6:98 (98)	it is He who produced you from one living soul
7:189 (189)	it is He who created you out of one living soul
9:31 (31)	they were commanded to serve but One God
10:19 (20)	mankind were only one nation
11:118 (120)	had thy Lord willed, He would have made mankind one nation
12:31 (31)	then she gave to each one of them a knife
12:39 (39)	which is better, my fellow-prisoners — many lords at variance, or God the One
12:67 (67)	enter not by one door; enter by separate doors
13:4 (4)	palms in pairs, and palms single, watered with one water
13:16 (17)	He is the One, the Omnipotent
14:48 (49)	they sally forth unto God, the One, the Omnipotent
14:52 (52)	that they may know that He is One God
16:22 (23)	your God is One God
16:51 (53)	take not to you two gods. He is only One God
16:93 (95)	if God had willed, He would have made you one nation
18:110 (110)	it is revealed to me that your God is One God
21:92 (92)	surely this community of yours is one community
21:108 (108)	it is revealed unto me only that your God is One God
22:34 (35)	your God is One God, so to Him surrender
23:52 (54)	surely this community of yours is one community
24:2 (2)	scourge each one of them a hundred stripes
25:14 (15)	call not out today for one destruction, but call for many
25:32 (34)	why has the Koran not been sent down upon him all at once?
29:46 (45)	our God and your God is One
31:28 (27)	your creation and your upraising are as but as a single soul
34:46 (45)	I give you but one admonition
36:29 (28)	it was only one Cry and lo, they were silent and still
36:49 (49)	they are awaiting only for one Cry to seize them
36:53 (53)	it was only one Cry
37:4 (4)	surely your God is One
37:19 (19)	for it is only a single scaring, then behold, they are watching
38:5 (4)	what, has he made the gods One God
38:15 (14)	these are only awaiting for a single Cry

38:23 (22)	this my brother has ninety-nine ewes, and I have one ewe
38:65 (65)	there is not any god but God, the One
39:4 (6)	glory be to Him! He is God, the One, the Omnipotent
39:6 (8)	He created you of a single soul
40:16 (16)	God's, the One, the Omnipotent
41:6 (5)	to me it has been revealed that your God is One God
42:8 (6)	if God have willed, He would have made them one nation
43:33 (32)	and were it not that mankind would be one nation
54:24 (24)	shall we follow a mortal, one out of ourselves?
54:31 (31)	We loosed against them one Cry
54:50 (50)	Our commandment is but one word
69:13 (13)	when the Trumpet is blown with a single blast
69:14 (14)	the earth and the mountains are lifted up and crushed with a single blow
79:13 (13)	it shall be only a single scare

WAḤĪD n.m. (adv)~alone

74:11 (11)	leave Me with him whom I created alone

*W Ḥ SH

WUḤŪSH n.m. (pl. of *waḥsh*)~savage beasts

81:5 (5)	when the savage beasts shall be mustered

*W Ḥ Y

WAḤÁ vb. (I)~(n.vb.) a revelation

f) n.vb. (*waḥy*)

11:37 (39)	make thou the Ark under Our eyes, and as We reveal
20:114 (113)	hasten not with the Koran ere its revelation is accomplished
21:45 (46)	I warn you only by the Revelation'
23:27 (27)	make thou the Ark under Our eyes and as We reveal
42:51 (50)	that God should speak to him, except by revelation
53:4 (4)	this is naught but a revelation revealed

AWḤÁ vb. (IV)~to reveal; to inspire; to make a signal, to signify

a) perf. act.

4:163 (161)	We have revealed to thee
4:163 (161)	as We revealed to Noah, and the Prophets after him
4:163 (161)	We revealed to Abraham, Ishmael, Isaac, Jacob
5:111 (111)	when I inspired the Apostles
7:117 (114)	and We revealed to Moses
7:160 (160)	We revealed to Moses, when his people asked him
10:2 (2)	was it a wonder to the people that We revealed to a man from among them
10:87 (87)	We revealed to Moses and his brother
12:3 (3)	in that We have revealed to thee this Koran
12:15 (15)	in the bottom of the well, and We revealed to him
13:30 (29)	recite to them that We have revealed to thee
14:13 (16)	then did their Lord reveal unto them
16:68 (70)	thy Lord revealed unto the bees, saying
16:123 (124)	then We revealed to thee

17:39 (41) that is of the wisdom thy Lord has revealed to thee
17:73 (75) indeed they were near to seducing thee from that We revealed to thee
17:86 (88) We could take away that We have revealed to thee
19:11 (12) he came forth unto his people from the Sanctuary, then he made signal to them
20:38 (38) when We revealed what was revealed unto thy mother
20:77 (79) also We revealed unto Moses
21:73 (73) We revealed to them the doing of good deeds
23:27 (27) make thou the Ark under Our eyes and as We reveal
26:52 (52) also We revealed unto Moses
26:63 (63) then We revealed to Moses
28:7 (6) so We revealed to Moses' mother
35:31 (28) that We have revealed to thee of the Book is the truth
41:12 (11) in two days, and revealed its commandment in every heaven
42:7 (5) so We have revealed to thee an Arabic Koran
42:13 (11) and that We have revealed to thee
42:52 (52) even so We have revealed to thee a Spirit of Our bidding
53:10 (10) then revealed to his servant that he (revealed)
53:10 (10) then (revealed) to his servant that he revealed
99:5 (5) for that her Lord has inspired her

b) impf. act. (*yūḥī*)

3:44 (39) that is of the tidings of the Unseen, that We reveal to thee
6:112 (112) Satans of men and jinn, revealing tawdry speech to each other
6:121 (121) the Satans inspire their friends to dispute with you
8:12 (12) when thy Lord was revealing to the angels
11:49 (51) that is of the tidings of the Unseen, that We reveal to thee
12:102 (103) that is of the tidings of the Unseen that We reveal to thee
12:109 (109) We sent not forth any before thee, but men We revealed to
16:43 (45) We sent not any before thee, except men to whom We revealed
21:7 (7) We sent none before thee, but men to whom We made revelation
21:25 (25) We sent never a Messenger before thee except that We revealed to him
34:50 (49) if I am guided, it is by what my Lord reveals to me
42:3 (1) so reveals to thee, and to those before thee
42:51 (51) He should send a messenger and he reveal whatsoever He will

d) perf. pass. (*ūḥiya*)

6:19 (19) this Koran has been revealed to me
6:93 (93) to me it has been revealed
6:106 (106) follow thou what has been revealed to thee from thy Lord
6:145 (146) I do not find, in what is revealed to me, aught forbidden to him who eats thereof
11:36 (38) and it was revealed to Noah
18:27 (26) recite what has been revealed to thee of the Book of thy Lord
20:48 (50) it has been revealed to us that chastisement shall light upon him
29:45 (44) recite what has been revealed to thee of the Book
39:65 (65) it has been revealed to thee, and to those before thee
43:43 (42) hold thou fast unto that which has been revealed unto thee
72:1 (1) it has been revealed to me that a company of the jinn gave ear

e) impf. pass. (*yūḥá*)

6:50 (50) I only follow what is revealed to me
6:93 (93) when naught has been revealed to him
7:203 (202) I follow only what is revealed to me from my Lord
10:15 (16) I follow nothing, except what is revealed to me
10:109 (109) follow thou what is revealed to thee

11:12 (15)	perchance thou art leaving part of what is revealed to thee
18:110 (110)	it is revealed to me that your God is One God
20:13 (13)	give thou ear to this revelation
20:38 (38)	what was revealed unto thy mother
21:108 (108)	it is revealed unto me only that your God is One God
33:2 (2)	follow what is revealed to thee from thy Lord
38:70 (70)	this alone is revealed to me, that I am only a clear warner
41:6 (5)	to me it has been revealed that your God is One God
46:9 (8)	I only follow what is revealed to me
53:4 (4)	this is naught but a revelation revealed

*W J B

WAJABA vb. (I)~to collapse, to fall (dead)

a) perf. act.

22:36 (37)	then, when their flanks collapse, eat of them

*W J D

WAJADA vb. (I)~to find, to discover; to perceive

a) perf. act.

3:37 (32)	whenever Zachariah went in to her in the Sanctuary
4:64 (67)	for them, they would have found God turns
4:82 (84)	surely they would have found in it much inconsistency
4:89 (91)	take them, and slay them wherever you find them
5:104 (103)	enough for us is what we found our fathers doing
7:28 (27)	we found our fathers practising it
7:44 (42)	we have found that which our Lord promised us true
7:44 (42)	have you found what your Lord promised you true?
7:102 (100)	We found no covenant in the most part of them
7:102 (100)	indeed, We found the most part of them ungodly
9:5 (5)	slay the idolaters wherever you find them
10:78 (79)	art thou come to us to turn us from that we found our fathers practising
12:65 (65)	when they opened their things, they found their merchandise
12:79 (79)	any other but him in whose possession we found the goods
18:49 (47)	they shall find all they wrought present
18:65 (64)	then they found one of Our servants
18:77 (76)	there they found a wall about to tumble down
18:86 (84)	he found it setting in a muddy spring
18:86 (84)	and he found nearby a people
18:90 (89)	he found it rising upon a people
18:93 (92)	he found this side of them a people scarcely able to understand speech
21:53 (54)	we found our fathers serving them
24:39 (39)	there indeed he finds God
26:74 (74)	nay, but we found our fathers so doing
27:23 (23)	I found a woman ruling over them
27:24 (24)	I found her and her people prostrating to the sun
28:15 (14)	and found there two men fighting
28:23 (22)	he found a company of the people there drawing water
28:23 (23)	he found, apart from them, two women
31:21 (20)	we will follow such things as we found our fathers doing

38:44 (43)	surely We found him a steadfast man
43:22 (21)	we found our fathers upon a community
43:23 (22)	we indeed found our fathers upon a community
43:24 (23)	a better guidance than you found your fathers upon
51:36 (36)	We found not therein except one house of those
72:8 (8)	we found it filled with terrible guards
93:7 (7)	did He not find thee erring, and guide thee?
93:8 (8)	did He not find thee needy, and suffice thee?

b) impf. act. (*yajidu*)

2:96 (90)	thou shalt find them the eagerest of men for life
2:110 (104)	good you shall forward to your souls' account, you shall find it with God
2:196 (192)	or if he finds none, then a fast of three days
2:283 (283)	if you are upon a journey, and you do not find a writer
3:30 (28)	the day every soul shall find what it has done of good
4:43 (46)	and you can find no water
4:52 (55)	thou wilt not find for him any helper
4:65 (68)	then they shall find in themselves no impediment
4:88 (90)	whom God leads astray, thou wilt not find for him a way
4:91 (93)	you will find others desiring to be secure from you
4:92 (94)	but if he finds not the means, let him fast
4:100 (101)	whoso emigrates in the way of God will find in the earth many refuges
4:110 (110)	he shall find God is All-forgiving, All-compassionate
4:121 (120)	their refuge shall be Gehenna, and they shall find no asylum from it
4:123 (122)	and will not find for him, apart from God, a friend or helper
4:143 (142)	whom God leads astray, thou wilt not find for him a way
4:145 (144)	thou wilt not find for them any helper
4:173 (173)	they shall not find for them, apart from God, a friend or helper
5:6 (9)	and you can find no water, then have recourse to wholesome dust
5:82 (85)	thou wilt surely find the most hostile of men to the believers
5:82 (85)	thou wilt surely find the nearest of them in love to the believers
5:89 (91)	if any finds not the means, let him fast for three days
6:145 (146)	I do not find, in what is revealed to me, aught forbidden to him who eats thereof
7:17 (16)	Thou wilt not find most of them thankful
7:157 (156)	whom they find written down with them in the Torah
9:57 (57)	if they could find a shelter, or some caverns
9:79 (80)	those who find nothing but their endeavour they deride
9:91 (92)	the weak and the sick and those who find nothing to expend
9:92 (93)	I find not whereon to mount you
9:92 (93)	overflowing with tears of sorrow, because they found nothing to expend
9:123 (124)	let them find in you a harshness
12:94 (94)	surely I perceive Joseph's scent
17:68 (70)	you will find no guardian for you
17:69 (71)	then you will find no prosecutor for you against Us
17:75 (77)	thou wouldst have found none to help thee against Us
17:77 (79)	thou wilt find no change to Our wont
17:86 (88)	then thou wouldst find none thereover to guard thee
17:97 (99)	thou wilt not find for them protectors, apart from Him
18:17 (16)	thou wilt not find for him a protector to direct
18:27 (26)	apart from Him, thou wilt find no refuge
18:36 (34)	I shall surely find a better resort than this
18:53 (51)	and will find no escape from it
18:58 (57)	they have a tryst, from which they will find no escape
18:69 (68)	thou shalt find me, if God will, patient
20:10 (10)	or I shall find at the fire guidance

20:115 (114)	but he forgot, and We found in him no constancy
24:28 (28)	if you find not anyone therein, enter it not until leave is given
24:33 (33)	let those who find not the means to marry be abstinent
24:39 (39)	till, when he comes to it, he finds it is nothing
28:27 (27)	thou shalt assuredly find me, if God wills, one of the righteous
33:17 (17)	they shall find for themselves, apart from God, neither protector nor helper
33:62 (62)	thou shalt find no changing the wont of God
33:65 (65)	they shall find neither protector nor helper
35:43 (41)	thou shalt never find any changing the wont of God
35:43 (42)	thou shalt never find any altering the wont of God
37:102 (102)	thou shalt find me, God willing, one of the steadfast
48:22 (22)	and then found neither protector nor helper
48:23 (23)	thou shalt never find any changing the wont of God
58:4 (5)	whosoever finds not the means, then let him fast
58:12 (13)	yet if you find not means, God is All-forgiving
58:22 (22)	thou shalt not find any people who believe
59:9 (9)	not finding in their breasts any need for what they have been given
71:25 (26)	for they found not, apart from God, any to help them
72:9 (9)	any listening now finds a meteor in wait for him
72:22 (23)	I shall find, apart from Him, no refuge
73:20 (20)	you shall find it with God as better, and mightier a wage
93:6 (6)	did He not find thee an orphan, and shelter thee?

d) perf. pass. (*wujida*)

12:75 (75)	in whoever's saddlebag the goblet is found

WUJD n.m.~wealth, means

65:6 (6)	lodge them where you are lodging, according to your means

*W J F

WAJAFA vb. (I)~(pcple. act.) being athrob, (a heart) beating painfully

g) pcple. act. (*wājif*)

79:8 (8)	hearts upon that day shall be athrob

AWJAFA vb. (IV)~to urge, to prick (an animal to make it move faster)

a) perf. act.

59:6 (6)	against that you pricked neither horse nor camel

*W J H

WAJH n.m. (pl. *wujūh*)~a face, countenance; a will; a beginning; proper form, true form; favour, honour; (with prep. *li-*) for the sake of; (*inqalaba ʿala wajhihi*) to turn completely over, to fall away utterly

2:112 (106)	but whosoever submits his will to God
2:115 (109)	whithersoever you turn, there is the Face of God
2:144 (139)	We have seen thee turning thy face about in the heaven
2:144 (139)	turn thy face towards the Holy Mosque
2:144 (139)	wherever you are, turn your faces towards it
2:149 (144)	from whatsoever place thou issuest, turn thy face towards the Holy Mosque
2:150 (145)	from whatsoever place thou issuest, turn thy face towards the Holy Mosque
2:150 (145)	wherever you may be, turn your faces towards it
2:177 (172)	it is not piety, that you turn your faces to the East
2:272 (274)	for then you are expending, being desirous only of God's Face

3:20 (18)	I have surrendered my will to God
3:72 (65)	those who believe at the beginning of the day
3:106 (102)	the day when some faces are blackened
3:106 (102)	and some faces whitened
3:106 (102)	as for those whose faces are blackened
3:107 (103)	but as for those whose faces are whitened
4:43 (46)	wipe your faces and your hands
4:47 (50)	before We obliterate faces, and turn them upon their backs
4:125 (124)	who is there that has a fairer religion than he who submits his will to God
5:6 (8)	when you stand up to pray wash your faces
5:6 (9)	wipe your faces and your hands with it
5:108 (107)	it is likelier that they will bear testimony in proper form
6:52 (52)	those who call upon their Lord at morning and evening desiring His countenance
6:79 (79)	I have turned my face to Him who originated the heavens
7:29 (28)	set your faces in every place of worship
8:50 (52)	if thou couldst only see when the angels take the unbelievers, beating their faces
10:26 (27)	neither dust nor abasement shall overspread their faces
10:27 (28)	as if their faces were covered with strips of night shadowy
10:105 (105)	set thy face to the religion, a man of pure faith
12:9 (9)	that your father's face may be free for you
12:93 (93)	take this shirt, and do you cast it on my father's face
12:96 (96)	when the bearer of good tidings came to him, and laid it on his face
13:22 (22)	patient men, desirous of the Face of their Lord
14:50 (51)	their faces enveloped by the Fire
16:58 (60)	his face is darkened and he chokes inwardly
17:7 (7)	We sent against you Our servants to discountenance you
17:97 (99)	We shall muster them on the Resurrection Day upon their faces
18:28 (27)	those who call upon their Lord at morning and evening, desiring His countenance
18:29 (28)	succoured with water like molten copper, that shall scald their faces
20:111 (110)	faces shall be humbled unto the Living
21:39 (40)	they shall not ward off the Fire from their faces
22:11 (11)	if a trial befalls him he turns completely over
22:72 (71)	thou recognisest in the faces of the unbelievers denial
23:104 (106)	the Fire smiting their faces the while they glower there
25:34 (36)	those who shall be mustered to Gehenna upon their faces
27:90 (92)	whosoever comes with an evil deed, their faces shall be thrust into the Fire
28:88 (88)	all things perish, except His Face
30:30 (29)	so set thy face to the religion
30:38 (37)	that is better for those who desire God's Face
30:39 (38)	what you give in alms, desiring God's Face
30:43 (42)	so set thy face to the true religion
31:22 (21)	whosoever submits his will to God
33:66 (66)	upon the day when their faces are turned about in the Fire
39:24 (25)	he who guards himself with his face against the evil
39:60 (61)	thou shalt see those who lied against God, their faces blackened
43:17 (16)	his face is darkened, and he chokes inwardly
47:27 (29)	how shall it be, when the angels take them, beating their faces
48:29 (29)	their mark is on their faces, the trace of prostration
51:29 (29)	then came forward his wife, clamouring, and she smote her face
54:48 (48)	the day when they are dragged on their faces into the Fire
55:27 (27)	abides the Face of thy Lord, majestic, splendid
67:22 (22)	is he who walks prone upon his face better guided
67:27 (27)	when they see it nigh at hand, the faces of the unbelievers will be vexed
75:22 (22)	upon that day faces shall be radiant
75:24 (24)	upon that day faces shall be scowling

76:9 (9)	we feed you only for the Face of God
80:38 (38)	some faces on that day shall shine
80:40 (40)	some faces on that day shall be dusty
83:24 (24)	thou knowest in their faces the radiancy of bliss
88:2 (2)	faces on that day humbled
88:8 (8)	faces on that day jocund
92:20 (20)	only seeking the Face of his Lord the Most High

WAJĪH n.m. (adj)~high honoured, illustrious, well-esteemed

3:45 (40)	high honoured shall he be in this world and the next
33:69 (69)	he was high honoured with God

WIJHAH n.f.~direction; a goal

2:148 (143)	every man has his direction to which he turns

WAJJAHA vb. (II)~to turn (one's face); to direct or dispatch someone

a) perf. act.

6:79 (79)	I have turned my face to Him who originated the heavens

b) impf. act. (*yuwajjihu*)

16:76 (78)	wherever he despatches him, he brings no good

TAWAJJAHA vb. (V)~to turn one's face towards

a) perf. act.

28:22 (21)	when he turned his face towards Midian

*W J L

WAJILA vb. (I)~to quake, to be afraid

a) perf. act.

8:2 (2)	when God is mentioned, their hearts quake
22:35 (36)	when God is mentioned, their hearts quake

b) impf. act. (*yawjalu*)

15:53 (53)	be not afraid; behold, we give thee good tidings

WAJIL n.m. (adj)~afraid, quaking

15:52 (52)	behold, we are afraid of you
23:60 (62)	those who give what they give, their hearts quaking

*W J S

AWJASA vb. (IV)~to sense, to feel, to conceive, to have a sensation of (fear)

a) perf. act.

11:70 (73)	he was suspicious of them and conceived a fear of them
20:67 (70)	Moses conceived a fear within him
51:28 (28)	then he conceived a fear of them

*W K ʾ

MUTTAKAʾ n.m.~a place of reclining; a repast, a banquet

12:31 (31) and made ready for them a repast

TAWAKKAʾA vb. (V)~to lean

b) impf. act. (*yatawakkaʾu*)

20:18 (19) I lean upon it

ITTAKAʾA vb. (VIII)~to recline. (pcple. act.) reclining

b) impf. act. (*yattakiʾu*)

43:34 (33) couches whereon to recline

g) pcple. act. (*muttakiʾ*)

18:31 (30) therein reclining upon couches
36:56 (56) they and their spouses, reclining upon couches in the shade
38:51 (51) wherein they recline
52:20 (20) reclining upon couches ranged in rows
55:54 (54) reclining upon couches lined with brocade
55:76 (76) reclining upon green cushions and lovely druggets
56:16 (16) reclining upon them, set face to face
76:13 (13) therein they shall recline upon couches

*W K D

WAKKADA vb. (II)~(n.vb.) confirmation, ratification

f) n.vb. (*tawkīd*)

16:91 (93) break not the oaths after they have been confirmed

*W K L

WAKĪL n.m.~guardian, someone in whom one trusts, trustee; Guardian [Ar], Trustee [Pk, Bl]; Disposer of affairs [Ali] (Divine attribute)

3:173 (167) God is sufficient for us; an excellent Guardian is He
4:81 (83) put thy trust in God; God suffices for a guardian
4:109 (109) who will be a guardian for them?
4:132 (131) God suffices for a guardian
4:171 (169) God suffices for a guardian
6:66 (66) I am not a guardian over you
6:102 (102) so serve Him, for He is Guardian over everything
6:107 (107) neither art thou their guardian
10:108 (108) I am not a guardian over you
11:12 (15) thou art only a warner; and God is a Guardian over everything
12:66 (66) God shall be Guardian over what we say
17:2 (2) take not unto yourselves any guardian apart from Me
17:54 (56) We sent thee not to be a guardian over them
17:65 (67) thy Lord suffices as a guardian
17:68 (70) you will find no guardian for you
17:86 (88) then thou wouldst find none thereover to guard thee

25:43 (45)	wilt thou be a guardian over them?
28:28 (28)	God is guardian of what we say
33:3 (3)	put thy trust in God; God suffices as a guardian
33:48 (47)	put thy trust in God; God suffices as a guardian
39:41 (42)	thou art not a guardian over them
39:62 (63)	He is Guardian over every thing
42:6 (4)	thou art not a guardian over them
73:9 (9)	so take Him for a Guardian

WAKKALA vb. (II)~to entrust, to charge someone with

a) perf. act.

6:89 (89)	We have already entrusted it to a people who do not disbelieve in it

d) perf. pass. (*wukkila*)

32:11 (11)	death's angel, who has been charged with you, shall gather you

TAWAKKALA vb. (V)~(with prep. *ʿalá*) to put one's trust in (God), to trust. (pcple. act.) one who trusts, who puts his trust in (God)

a) perf. act.

7:89 (87)	in God we have put our trust
9:129 (130)	there is no god but He. In Him I have put my trust
10:71 (72)	in God have I put my trust
10:85 (85)	in God we have put our trust
11:56 (59)	truly, I have put my trust in God
11:88 (90)	my succour is only with God; in Him I have put my trust
12:67 (67)	in Him I have put my trust
13:30 (29)	there is no god but He. In Him I have put my trust
42:10 (8)	that then is God, my Lord; in Him I have put my trust
60:4 (4)	our Lord, in Thee we trust; to Thee we turn
67:29 (29)	we believe in Him, and in Him we put all our trust

b) impf. act. (*yatawakkalu*)

3:122 (118)	in God let the believers put all their trust
3:160 (154)	therefore in God let the believers put all their trust
5:11 (14)	in God let the believers put all their trust
8:2 (2)	and in their Lord they put their trust
8:49 (51)	whosoever puts his trust in God
9:51 (51)	in God let the believers put all their trust
12:67 (67)	in Him let all put their trust
14:11 (14)	in God let the believers put all their trust
14:12 (15)	why should we not put our trust in God, seeing that He has guided us
14:12 (15)	in God let all put their trust who put their trust
16:42 (44)	even such men as are patient, and put their trust in their Lord
16:99 (101)	he has no authority over those who believe and trust in their Lord
29:59 (59)	such men as are patient, and put their trust in their Lord
39:38 (39)	in Him all those put their trust who put their trust
42:36 (34)	those who believe and put their trust in their Lord
58:10 (11)	in God let the believers put all their trust
64:13 (13)	in God let the believers put their trust
65:3 (3)	whosoever puts his trust in God, He shall suffice him

c) impv. (*tawakkal*)

3:159 (153)	when thou art resolved, put thy trust in God
4:81 (83)	so turn away from them, and put thy trust in God
5:23 (26)	put you all your trust in God, if you are believers
8:61 (63)	put thy trust in God
10:84 (84)	if you believe in God, in Him put your trust
11:123 (123)	so serve Him, and put thy trust in Him
25:58 (60)	put thy trust in the Living God, the Undying
26:217 (217)	put thy trust in the All-mighty, the All-compassionate
27:79 (81)	so put thy trust in God
33:3 (3)	put thy trust in God
33:48 (47)	put thy trust in God

g) pcple. act. (*mutawakkil*)

3:159 (153)	surely God loves those who put their trust
12:67 (67)	in Him let all put their trust who put their trust
14:12 (15)	in God let all put their trust who put their trust
39:38 (39)	in Him all those put their trust who put their trust

*W K Z

WAKAZA vb. (I)~to strike (with the fist)

a) perf. act.

28:15 (14)	Moses struck him, and despatched him

*W L D

WALADA vb. (I)~to bear, to give birth; to beget. (pcple. act.) (m) progenitor, begetter, father; (f) mother; (du) parents, father and mother. (pcple. pass.) a child; (with prep. *lahu*) a father (the one to whom a child is born)

a) perf. act.

37:152 (152)	'God has begotten?' They are truly liars
58:2 (2)	their mothers are only those who gave them birth
90:3 (3)	and that he begot

b) impf. act. (*yalidu*)

11:72 (75)	shall I bear, being an old woman
71:27 (28)	they will lead Thy servants astray, and will beget none but unbelieving
112:3 (3)	[He] who has not begotten

d) perf. pass. (*wulida*)

19:15 (15)	peace be upon him, the day he was born
19:33 (34)	peace be upon me, the day I was born

e) impf. pass. (*yūladu*)

112:3 (3)	and [who] has not been begotten

g) pcple. act. (*wālid*; f. *wālidah*; du. *wālidān*)

2:83 (77)	to be good to parents, and the near kinsman

2:180 (176)	to make testament in favour of his parents and kinsmen
2:215 (211)	whatsoever good you expend is for parents and kinsmen
2:233 (233)	mothers shall suckle their children two years
2:233 (233)	a mother shall not be pressed for her child
4:7 (8)	to the men a share of what parents and kinsmen leave
4:7 (8)	to the women a share of what parents and kinsmen leave
4:33 (37)	to everyone We have appointed heirs of that which parents and kinsmen leave
4:36 (40)	be kind to parents, and the near kinsman
4:135 (134)	even though it be against yourselves, or your parents
5:110 (109)	remember My blessing upon thee and upon thy mother
6:151 (152)	to be good to your parents, and not to slay your children
14:41 (42)	our Lord, forgive Thou me and my parents
17:23 (24)	you shall not serve any but Him, and to be good to parents
19:14 (14)	cherishing his parents, not arrogant, rebellious
19:32 (33)	and likewise to cherish my mother
27:19 (19)	wherewith Thou hast blessed me and my father and mother
29:8 (7)	We have charged man, that he be kind to his parents
31:14 (13)	We have charged man concerning his parents
31:14 (13)	be thankful to Me, and to thy parents
31:33 (32)	dread a day when no father shall give satisfaction for his child
31:33 (32)	and no child shall give satisfaction for his father
46:15 (14)	We have charged man, that he be kind to his parents
46:15 (14)	Thou hast blessed me and my father and mother
46:17 (16)	he who says to his father and his mother
71:28 (29)	my Lord, forgive me and my parents
90:3 (3)	by the begetter, and that he begot

h) pcple. pass. (*mawlūd*)

2:233 (233)	it is for the father to provide them
2:233 (233)	a mother shall not be pressed for her child, neither a father for his child
31:33 (32)	and no child shall give satisfaction for his father

WALAD n.m. (pl. *awlād*)~a child; a son

2:116 (110)	they say, 'God has taken to Him a son'
2:233 (233)	mothers shall suckle their children two years
2:233 (233)	a mother shall not be pressed for her child
2:233 (233)	neither a father for his child
2:233 (233)	if you desire to seek nursing for your children
3:10 (8)	their riches will not avail them, neither their children
3:47 (42)	how shall I have a son seeing no mortal has touched me
3:116 (112)	their riches shall not avail them, neither their children
4:11 (12)	God charges you, concerning your children
4:11 (12)	to each one of the two the sixth of what he leaves, if he has children
4:11 (12)	if he has no children, and his heirs are his parents
4:12 (13)	for you a half of what your wives leave, if they have no children
4:12 (13)	if they have children, then for you of what they leave a fourth
4:12 (14)	for them a fourth of what you leave, if you have no children
4:12 (14)	but if you have children, then for them of what you leave an eighth
4:171 (169)	glory be to Him — that He should have a son
4:176 (175)	if a man perishes having no children
4:176 (175)	he is her heir if she has no children
6:101 (101)	the Creator of the heavens and the earth — how should He have a son
6:137 (138)	those associates of theirs have decked out fair to many idolaters to slay their children
6:140 (141)	losers are they who slay their children in folly

6:151 (152)	and not to slay your children because of poverty
8:28 (28)	know that your wealth and your children are a trial
9:55 (55)	let not their possessions or their children please thee
9:69 (70)	more abundant in wealth and children
9:85 (86)	let not their possessions and their children please thee
10:68 (69)	they say, 'God has taken to Him a son'
12:21 (21)	or we may take him for our own son
17:31 (33)	slay not your children for fear of poverty
17:64 (66)	share with them in their wealth and their children
17:111 (111)	praise belongs to God, who has not taken to Him a son
18:4 (3)	those who say, 'God has taken to Himself a son'
18:39 (37)	if thou seest me, that I am less than thou in wealth and children
19:35 (36)	it is not for God to take a son unto Him
19:77 (80)	I shall be given wealth and children
19:88 (91)	the All-merciful has taken unto Himself a son
19:91 (93)	for that they have attributed to the All-merciful a son
19:92 (93)	behoves not the All-merciful to take a son
21:26 (26)	the All-merciful has taken to Him a son
23:91 (93)	God has not taken to Himself any son
25:2 (2)	He has not taken to Him a son
28:9 (8)	perchance he will profit us, or we will take him for a son
31:33 (32)	when no father shall give satisfaction for his child
34:35 (34)	we are more abundant in wealth and children
34:37 (36)	nor your children that shall bring you nigh in nearness to Us
39:4 (6)	had God desired to take to Him a son
43:81 (81)	if the All-merciful has a son, then I am the first to serve him
57:20 (19)	a rivalry in wealth and children
58:17 (18)	nor their children shall avail them anything against God
60:3 (3)	nor your children shall profit you upon the Day of Resurrection
60:12 (12)	neither commit adultery, nor slay their children
63:9 (9)	neither your children divert you from God's remembrance
64:14 (14)	among your wives and children there is an enemy to you
64:15 (15)	your wealth and your children are only a trial
71:21 (20)	him whose wealth and children increase him only in loss
72:3 (3)	has not taken to Himself either consort or a son

WALĪD n.m. (pl. *wildān*)~a child

4:75 (77)	the men, women, and children who, being abased
4:98 (100)	except the men, women, and children who, being abased
4:127 (126)	the oppressed children, and that you secure justice for orphans
26:18 (17)	did we not raise thee amongst us as a child
56:17 (17)	immortal youths going round about them
73:17 (17)	a day that shall make the children grey-headed
76:19 (19)	immortal youths shall go about them

*W L J

WALAJA vb. (I)~to pass through, to penetrate, to enter

b) impf. act. (*yaliju*)

7:40 (38)	until the camel passes through the eye of the needle
34:2 (2)	He knows what penetrates into the earth
57:4 (4)	He knows what penetrates into the earth

WALĪJAH n.f.~intimate friend, confidant

9:16 (16)	and taken not — apart from God and His Messenger and the believers — any intimate

AWLAJA vb. (IV)~to cause to enter, to insert

b) impf. act. (*yūliju*)

3:27 (26)	Thou makest the night to enter into the day
3:27 (26)	Thou makest the day to enter into the night
22:61 (60)	that is because God makes the night to enter into the day
22:61 (60)	and makes the day to enter into the night
31:29 (28)	that God makes the night to enter into the day
31:29 (28)	and makes the day to enter into the night
35:13 (14)	He makes the night to enter into the day
35:13 (14)	and makes the day to enter into the night
57:6 (6)	He makes the night to enter into the day
57:6 (6)	and makes the day to enter into the night

*W L Y

WALÁ vb. (I)~to be near; (*alladhī yalīka*) your kindred, ones who are near to you. (n.vb.) duty of friendship, of nearness or kinship; protection. (pcple. act.) protector

b) impf. act. (*yalī*)

9:123 (124)	fight the unbelievers who are near to you

f) n.vb. (*walāyah*)

8:72 (73)	you have no duty of friendship towards them till they emigrate
18:44 (42)	thereover protection belongs only to God the True

g) pcple. act. (*wālī*)

13:11 (12)	apart from Him, they have no protector

AWLÁ n.m. (adj)~closest, nearest; (with prep. *bi*-) most deserving, more entitled

3:68 (61)	the people standing closest to Abraham are those who followed him
4:135 (134)	whether the man be rich or poor; God stands closest to either
5:107 (106)	these being the nearest of those most concerned
8:75 (76)	those related by blood are nearer to one another in the Book of God
19:70 (71)	We shall know very well those most deserving to burn there
33:6 (6)	the Prophet is nearer to the believers than their selves
33:6 (6)	those who are bound by blood are nearer to one another
47:20 (22)	but better for them would be
75:34 (34)	nearer to thee
75:34 (34)	and nearer
75:35 (35)	then nearer to thee
75:35 (35)	and nearer

MAWLÁ n.m. (pl. *mawālī*)~master, lord; patron; Protector (Divine attribute); a client, a charge; an heir

2:286 (286)	have mercy on us; Thou art our Protector
3:150 (143)	no; but God is your Protector
4:33 (37)	to everyone We have appointed heirs

6:62 (62)	then they are restored to God their Protector
8:40 (41)	know that God is your Protector
8:40 (41)	an excellent Protector, an excellent Helper
9:51 (51)	He is our Protector
10:30 (31)	they shall be restored to God, their Protector
16:76 (78)	he is a burden upon his master
19:5 (5)	now I fear my kinsfolk after I am gone
22:13 (13)	an evil protector indeed, he, an evil friend
22:78 (78)	hold you fast to God; He is your Protector
22:78 (78)	an excellent Protector, an excellent Helper
33:5 (5)	then they are your brothers in religion, and your clients
44:41 (41)	the day a master shall avail nothing (a client)
44:41 (41)	the day a (master) shall avail nothing a client
47:11 (12)	that is because God is the Protector of the believers
47:11 (12)	and that the unbelievers have no protector
57:15 (14)	your refuge is the Fire, that is your master
66:2 (2)	God is your Protector, and He is the All-knowing, the All-wise
66:4 (4)	if you support one another against him, God is his Protector

WALĪY n.m. (pl. *awliyā'*)~a protector, a guardian; a friend; next-of-kin, kinsman; Protector, Guardian (Divine attribute)

2:107 (101)	you have none, apart from God, neither protector nor helper?
2:120 (114)	thou shalt have against God neither protector nor helper
2:257 (258)	God is the Protector of the believers
2:257 (259)	the unbelievers — their protectors are idols
2:282 (282)	then let his guardian dictate justly
3:28 (27)	let not the believers take the unbelievers for friends
3:68 (61)	God is the Protector of the believers
3:122 (118)	when two parties of you were about to lose heart, though God was their Protector
3:175 (169)	that is Satan frightening his friends
4:45 (47)	God suffices as a protector
4:75 (77)	appoint to us a protector from Thee
4:76 (78)	fight you therefore against the friends of Satan
4:89 (91)	take not to yourselves friends of them
4:89 (91)	take not to yourselves any one of them as friend or helper
4:119 (118)	whoso takes Satan to him for a friend, instead of God
4:123 (122)	and will not find for him, apart from God, a friend or helper
4:139 (138)	those who take unbelievers for their friends instead of believers
4:144 (143)	take not the unbelievers as friends instead of the believers
4:173 (173)	they shall not find for them, apart from God, a friend or helper
5:51 (56)	take not Jews and Christians as friends
5:51 (56)	they are friends of each other
5:55 (60)	your friend is only God, and His Messenger
5:57 (62)	take not as your friends those of them, who were given the Book
5:81 (84)	they would not have taken them as friends
6:14 (14)	shall I take to myself as protector other than God
6:51 (51)	they have, apart from God, no protector and no intercessor
6:70 (69)	apart from God, it has no protector and no intercessor
6:121 (121)	the Satans inspire their friends to dispute with you
6:127 (127)	He is their Protector for that they were doing
6:128 (128)	then their friends among mankind will say
7:3 (2)	and follow no friends other than He
7:27 (26)	We have made the Satans the friends of those who do not believe
7:30 (28)	they have taken Satans for friends instead of God
7:155 (154)	Thou art our Protector; so forgive us

7:196 (195)	my protector is God who sent down the Book
8:34 (34)	when they are barring from the Holy Mosque, not being its protectors
8:34 (34)	Its only protectors are the godfearing
8:72 (73)	those who have given refuge and help — those are friends one of another
8:73 (74)	as for the unbelievers, they are friends one of another
9:23 (23)	take not your fathers and brothers to be your friends
9:71 (72)	the men and the women, are friends one of the other
9:74 (75)	on the earth they have no protector or helper
9:116 (117)	you have not, apart from God, either protector or helper
10:62 (63)	surely God's friends — no fear shall be on them
11:20 (22)	they have no protectors, apart from God
11:113 (115)	you have no protectors apart from God
12:101 (102)	Thou art my Protector in this world and the next
13:16 (17)	then have you taken unto you others beside Him to be your protectors
13:37 (37)	thou shalt have no protector against God, and no defender
16:63 (65)	he is their protector today
17:33 (35)	whosoever is slain unjustly, We have appointed to his next-of-kin authority
17:97 (99)	thou wilt not find for them protectors, apart from Him
17:111 (111)	not any associate in the Kingdom, nor any protector out of humbleness
18:17 (16)	thou wilt not find for him a protector to direct
18:26 (25)	they have no protector, apart from Him
18:50 (48)	do you take him and his seed to be your friends
18:102 (102)	do the unbelievers reckon that they may take My servants as friends
19:5 (5)	so give me, from Thee, a kinsman
19:45 (46)	so that thou becomest a friend to Satan
25:18 (19)	it did not behove us to take unto ourselves protectors
27:49 (50)	then we will tell his protector
29:22 (21)	you have not, apart from God, either protector or helper
29:41 (40)	the likeness of those who have taken to them protectors
32:4 (3)	apart from Him, you have no protector neither intercessor
33:6 (6)	nevertheless you should act towards your friends honourably
33:17 (17)	they shall find for themselves, apart from God, neither protector nor helper
33:65 (65)	they shall find neither protector nor helper
34:41 (40)	Thou art our Protector, apart from them
39:3 (4)	those who take protectors, apart from Him
41:31 (31)	We are your friends in the present life and in the world to come
41:34 (34)	he between whom and thee there is enmity shall be as if he were a loyal friend
42:6 (4)	those who have taken to them protectors apart from Him
42:8 (6)	the evildoers shall have neither protector nor helper
42:9 (7)	have they taken to them protectors apart from Him
42:9 (7)	but God — He is the Protector
42:28 (27)	He is the Protector, the All-laudable
42:31 (30)	apart from God, you have neither protector nor helper
42:44 (42)	whomsoever God leads astray, he has no protector after him
42:46 (45)	they have no protectors to help them, apart from God
45:10 (9)	nor those they took as protectors, apart from God
45:19 (18)	surely the evildoers are friends one of the other
45:19 (18)	God is the friend of the godfearing
46:32 (31)	he has no protectors apart from Him
48:22 (22)	and then found neither protector nor helper
60:1 (1)	take not My enemy and your enemy for friends
62:6 (6)	you of Jewry, if you assert that you are the friends of God

WALLÁ vb. (II)~to turn, to turn about, to turn back from, to turn away; (6:129) to make friends with each other [Ar]; to have power over others [Pk], to turn to each other [Ali]; to make one a patron and client of another [Bl]. (pcple. act.) one who turns

a) perf. act.

2:142 (136)	what has turned them from the direction they were facing
9:25 (25)	all its breadth was strait for you, and you turned about, retreating
9:57 (57)	they would turn about and bolt away to it
17:46 (49)	when thou mentionest thy Lord only in the Koran, they turn in their traces in aversion
18:18 (17)	while We turned them now to the right, now to the left
27:10 (10)	when he saw it quivering like a serpent he turned about
27:80 (82)	neither shalt thou make the deaf to hear the call when they turn about
28:31 (31)	when he saw it quivering like a serpent, he turned about
30:52 (51)	neither shalt thou make the deaf to hear the call when they turn about
31:7 (6)	when Our signs are recited to such a man he turns away
46:29 (28)	then, when it was finished, they turned back to their people
48:22 (22)	if the unbelievers had fought you, they would have turned their backs

b) impf. act. (*yuwallī*)

2:115 (109)	whithersoever you turn, there is the Face of God
2:144 (139)	now We will surely turn thee to a direction that shall satisfy thee
2:177 (172)	it is not piety, that you turn your faces to the East
3:111 (107)	they will turn on you their backs; then they will not be helped
4:115 (115)	him We shall turn over to what he has turned to
6:129 (129)	so We make the evildoers friends of each other
8:15 (15)	when you encounter the unbelievers marching to battle, turn not your backs to them
8:16 (16)	whoso turns his back that day to them
21:57 (58)	I shall assuredly outwit your idols, after you have gone away turning your backs
33:15 (15)	they would not turn their backs
40:33 (35)	the day you turn about, retreating
54:45 (45)	certainly the host shall be routed, and turn their backs
59:12 (12)	they would surely turn their backs

c) impv. (*walli*)

2:144 (139)	turn thy face towards the Holy Mosque
2:144 (139)	wherever you are, turn your faces towards it
2:149 (144)	from whatsoever place thou issuest, turn thy face towards the Holy Mosque
2:150 (145)	from whatsoever place thou issuest, turn thy face towards the Holy Mosque
2:150 (145)	wherever you may be, turn your faces towards it

g) pcple. act. (*muwallī*)

2:148 (143)	every man has his direction to which he turns

TAWALLÁ vb. (V)~to turn, to turn away, to turn one's back; to take upon oneself; to take charge of, to take into one's protection; to take as friend

a) perf. act.

2:64 (61)	then you turned away thereafter
2:83 (77)	then you turned away, all but a few of you, swerving aside
2:137 (131)	but if they turn away, then they are clearly in schism
2:205 (201)	when he turns his back, he hastens about the earth
2:246 (247)	when fighting was prescribed for them, they turned their backs
3:20 (19)	if they turn their backs, thine it is only to deliver the Message
3:32 (29)	but if they turn their backs
3:63 (56)	if they turn their backs, assuredly God knows
3:64 (57)	and if they turn their backs, say

3:82 (76)	whosoever turns his back after that — they are the ungodly
3:155 (149)	those of you who turned away the day the two hosts encountered
4:80 (82)	whosoever turns his back — We have not sent thee to be a watcher over them
4:89 (91)	then, if they turn their backs, take them
4:115 (115)	him We shall turn over to what he has turned to
5:49 (54)	if they turn their backs, know that God desires only to smite them
5:92 (93)	if you turn your backs, then know that it is only for Our Messenger to deliver
7:79 (77)	so he turned his back on them, and said
7:93 (91)	so he turned his back on them, and said
8:23 (23)	if He had made them hear, they would have turned away, swerving aside
8:40 (41)	if they turn away, know that God is your Protector
9:3 (3)	if you turn your backs, know that you cannot frustrate the will of God
9:76 (77)	they were niggardly of it, and turned away, swerving aside
9:92 (93)	they turned away, their eyes overflowing with tears of sorrow
9:129 (130)	so if they turn their backs, say
10:72 (73)	then if you turn your backs, I have not asked you for any wage
12:84 (84)	and he turned away from them, and said
16:82 (84)	if they turn their backs, thine it is only to deliver
20:48 (50)	chastisement shall light upon him who cries lies and turns his back
20:60 (62)	Pharaoh then withdrew, and gathered his guile
21:109 (109)	then, if they should turn their backs, say
22:4 (4)	whosoever takes him for a friend, him he leads astray
24:11 (11)	whosoever of them took upon himself the greater part of it
28:24 (24)	he drew water for them; then he turned away to the shade
37:90 (88)	they went away from him, turning their backs
44:14 (13)	then they turned away from him
47:22 (24)	if you turned away, would you then haply work corruption
48:16 (16)	as you turned your backs before
51:39 (39)	but he turned his back, with his court
53:29 (30)	turn thou from him who turns away from Our Remembrance
53:33 (34)	hast thou considered him who turns his back
58:14 (15)	those who have taken for friends a people against whom God is wrathful
64:6 (6)	therefore they disbelieved, and turned away
64:12 (12)	but if you turn your backs, it is only for the Messenger to deliver
70:17 (17)	calling him who drew back and turned away
75:32 (32)	but he cried it lies, and he turned away
80:1 (1)	he frowned and turned away
88:23 (23)	but he who turns his back, and disbelieves
92:16 (16)	even he who cried lies, and turned away
96:13 (13)	what thinkest thou? If he cries lies, and turns away

b) impf. act. (*yatawallá*)

3:23 (22)	then a party of them turned away, swerving aside
5:43 (47)	then thereafter turn their backs
5:51 (56)	whoso of you makes them his friends is one of them
5:56 (61)	whoso makes God his friend, and His Messenger, and the believers
5:80 (83)	thou seest many of them making unbelievers their friends
7:196 (195)	He takes into His protection the righteous
8:20 (20)	obey God and His Messenger, and do not turn away from Him
9:23 (23)	whosoever of you takes them for friends, those — they are the evildoers
9:50 (50)	and turn away, rejoicing
9:74 (75)	if they turn away God will chastise them with a painful chastisement
11:3 (3)	if you should turn your backs I fear for you the chastisement
11:52 (55)	and turn not your backs as sinners
11:57 (60)	if you turn your backs, I have delivered to you that I was sent with

16:100 (102) his authority is over those who take him for their friend
24:47 (46) then after that a party of them turn away
24:54 (53) if you turn away, only upon him rests what is laid on him
47:38 (40) if you turn away, He will substitute
48:16 (16) but if you turn your backs
48:17 (17) whosoever turns his back, him He will chastise
57:24 (24) whosoever turns away, God is the All-sufficient
60:6 (6) whosoever turns away, surely God is the All-sufficient
60:9 (9) that you should take them for friends
60:9 (9) whosoever takes them for friends, those — they are the evildoers
60:13 (13) take not for friends a people against whom God is wrathful

c) impv. (*tawalla*)

27:28 (28) then turn back from them and see what they shall return
37:174 (174) so turn thou from them for a while
37:178 (178) so turn thou from them for a while
51:54 (54) so turn thou from them
54:6 (6) so turn thou away from them

*W N Y

WANÁ vb. (I)~to neglect

b) impf. act. (*yanī*)

20:42 (44) neglect not to remember Me

*W Q ᶜ

WAQAᶜA vb. (I)~to fall; to descend; to come to pass, to happen. (pcple. act.) that which falls; about to fall

a) perf. act.

4:100 (101) then death overtakes him, his wage shall have fallen on God
7:71 (69) anger and wrath from your Lord have fallen upon you
7:118 (115) the truth came to pass, and false was proved what they were doing
7:134 (131) when the wrath fell upon them, they said
10:51 (52) what, when it has come to pass, will you then believe in it
27:82 (84) when the Word falls on them, We shall bring forth for them
27:85 (87) the Word shall fall upon them because of the evil they committed
56:1 (1) when the Terror descends
69:15 (15) then, on that day, the Terror shall come to pass

b) impf. act. (*yaqaᶜu*)

22:65 (64) He holds back heaven lest it should fall upon the earth

c) impv. (*qaᶜ*)

15:29 (29) fall you down, bowing before him
38:72 (72) fall you down, bowing before him

g) pcple. act. (*wāqiᶜ*)

7:171 (170) as if it were a canopy, and they supposed it was about to fall on them
42:22 (21) thou seest the evildoers going in fear of that they have earned, that is about to fall on them

51:6 (6)	surely the Doom is about to fall
52:7 (7)	surely thy Lord's chastisement is about to fall
70:1 (1)	a questioner asked of a chastisement about to fall
77:7 (7)	surely that which you are promised is about to fall

MAWĀQIʿ n.m. (pl. of *mawqiʿ*)~a place, a place of falling; orbit (of a star)

56:75 (74)	No! I swear by the fallings of the stars

WAQʿAH n.f.~descent, descending, a fall

56:2 (2)	none denies its descending

WĀQIʿAH n.f.~the inevitable, Doom, the Terror, the Event

56:1 (1)	when the Terror descends
69:15 (15)	then, on that day, the Terror shall come to pass

WĀQAʿA vb. (III)~(pcple. act.) one who is about to fall

g) pcple. act. (*muwāqiʿ*)

18:53 (51)	the evildoers will see the Fire, and think that they are about to fall into it

AWQAʿA vb. (IV)~to precipitate, to bring about

b) impf. act. (*yūqiʿu*)

5:91 (93)	Satan only desires to precipitate enmity and hatred between you

*W Q B

WAQABA vb. (I)~to become dark with intensity

a) perf. act.

113:3 (3)	from the evil of darkness when it gathers

*W Q D

WAQŪD n.m.~fuel

2:24 (22)	fear the Fire, whose fuel is men and stones
3:10 (8)	those — they shall be fuel for the Fire
66:6 (6)	against a Fire whose fuel is men and stones
85:5 (5)	the fire abounding in fuel

AWQADA vb. (IV)~to kindle, to light a fire. (pcple. pass.) kindled

a) perf. act.

5:64 (69)	as often as they light a fire for war, God will extinguish it

b) impf. act. (*yūqidu*)

13:17 (18)	out of that over which they kindle fire, being desirous of ornament
36:80 (80)	out of the green tree fire and lo, from it you kindle

c) impv. (*awqid*)

28:38 (38) kindle me, Haman, a fire upon the clay

e) impf. pass. (*yūqadu*)

24:35 (35) a glittering star kindled from a Blessed Tree

h) pcple. pass. f. (*mūqadah*)

104:6 (6) the Fire of God kindled

ISTAWQADA vb. (X)~to light or kindle a fire

a) perf. act.

2:17 (16) the likeness of them is as the likeness of a man who kindled a fire

*W Q DH

WAQADHA vb. (I)~(pcple. pass.) beaten to death

h) pcple. pass. f. (*mawqūdhah*)

5:3 (4) the beast strangled, the beast beaten down

*W Q F

WAQAFA vb. (I)~to stand, to be stationed, to halt, to stop; to stop or halt someone. (pcple. pass.) stationed, brought up (standing) before someone

c) impv. (*qif*)

37:24 (24) and halt them, to be questioned

d) perf. pass. (*wuqifa*)

6:27 (27) if thou couldst see when they are stationed before the Fire
6:30 (30) if thou couldst see when they are stationed before their Lord

h) pcple. pass. (*mawqūf*)

34:31 (30) if thou couldst see when the evildoers are stationed before their Lord

*W Q R

WAQARA vb. (I)~(n.vb.) heaviness (in the ear), deafness

f) n.vb. (*waqr*)

6:25 (25) veils upon their hearts lest they understand it, and in their ears heaviness
17:46 (48) veils upon their hearts lest they understand it, and in their ears heaviness
18:57 (55) veils on their hearts lest they understand it, and in their ears heaviness
31:7 (6) though he heard them not, and in his ears were heaviness
41:5 (4) and in our ears is a heaviness
41:44 (44) those who believe not, in their ears is a heaviness

WAQĀR n.m.~majesty, dignity

71:13 (12) what ails you, that you look not for majesty in God

WIQR n.m.~burden, heavy load

51:2 (2) and the burden-bearers

WAQQARA vb. (II)~to reverence, to revere

b) impf. act. (*yuwaqqiru*)

48:9 (9) you may believe in God and His Messenger and succour Him, and reverence Him

*W Q T

WAQATA vb. (I)~(n.vb.) time. (pcple. pass.) timed, appointed, fixed

f) n.vb. (*waqt*)

7:187 (186) none shall reveal it at its proper time, but He
15:38 (38) unto the day of a known time
38:81 (82) until the day of the known time

h) pcple. pass. (*mawqūt*)

4:103 (104) surely the prayer is a timed prescription for the believers

MĪQĀT n.m. (pl. *mawāqīt*)~appointed time

2:189 (185) they are appointed times for the people, and the Pilgrimage
7:142 (138) so the appointed time of his Lord was forty nights
7:143 (139) and when Moses came to Our appointed time
7:155 (154) Moses chose of his people seventy men for Our appointed time
26:38 (37) so the sorcerers were assembled for the appointed time
44:40 (40) surely the Day of Decision shall be their appointed time
56:50 (50) shall be gathered to the appointed time of a known day
78:17 (17) surely the Day of Decision is an appointed time

WAQQATA vb. (II)~to set the time for, to schedule for a given time

d) perf. pass. (*uqqita*)

77:11 (11) and when the Messengers' time is set

*W Q Y

WAQÁ vb. (I)~to protect, to guard, to defend, to preserve. (pcple. act.) defender, protector, one who guards

a) perf. act.

40:45 (48) God guarded him against the evil things of their devising
44:56 (56) He shall guard them against the chastisement of Hell
52:18 (18) their Lord shall guard them against the chastisement of Hell
52:27 (27) God was gracious to us, and guarded us against the chastisement
76:11 (11) God has guarded them from the evil of that day

b) impf. act. (*yaqī*)

16:81 (83) He has appointed for you shirts to protect you from the heat
16:81 (83) and shirts to protect you from your own violence
40:9 (9) whomsoever Thou guardest against evil deeds on that day

c) impv. (*qi*)

2:201 (197) guard us against the chastisement of the Fire
3:16 (14) guard us against the chastisement of the Fire
3:191 (188) guard us against the chastisement
40:7 (7) follow Thy way, and guard them against the chastisement of Hell
40:9 (9) guard them against evil deeds
66:6 (6) guard yourselves and your families against a Fire

e) impf. pass. (*yūqá*)

59:9 (9) whoso is guarded against the avarice of his own soul
64:16 (16) whosoever is guarded against the avarice of his own soul

g) pcple. act. (*wāqī*)

13:34 (34) they have none to defend them from God
13:37 (37) thou shalt have no protector against God, and no defender
40:21 (22) they had none to defend them from God

TAQĪY n.m. (adj; comp. *atqá*)~godfearing, devout

19:13 (14) and he was godfearing
19:18 (18) if thou fearest God
19:63 (64) as an inheritance to those of Our servants who are godfearing
49:13 (13) the noblest among you in the sight of God is the most godfearing
92:17 (17) from which the most godfearing shall be removed

TAQWÁ n.f.~godfearing, godliness; fear [Ar]; warding off evil, pious duty, right conduct, righteousness [Pk, Ali]; piety [Bl]

2:197 (193) but the best provision is godfearing
2:237 (238) that you should remit is nearer to godfearing
5:2 (3) help one another to piety and godfearing
5:8 (11) be equitable — that is nearer to godfearing
7:26 (25) the garment of godfearing — that is better
9:108 (109) a mosque that was founded upon godfearing from the first day is worthier
9:109 (110) is he better who founded his building upon the fear of God
20:132 (132) the issue ultimate is to godfearing
22:32 (33) whosoever venerates God's waymarks, that is of the godliness of the hearts
22:37 (38) neither their blood, but godliness from you shall reach Him
47:17 (19) He increases in guidance, and gives them their godfearing
48:26 (26) fastened to them the word of godfearing to which they have better right
49:3 (3) those are they whose hearts God has tested for godfearing
58:9 (10) but conspire in piety and godfearing
74:56 (55) He is worthy to be feared, worthy to forgive
91:8 (8) and inspired it to lewdness and godfearing
96:12 (12) or bade to godfearing

TUQĀT n.f.~fear; security, precaution; (*ḥaqqa tuqātihi*) as He should be feared

3:28 (27) unless you have a fear of them
3:102 (97) O believers, fear God as He should be feared

ITTAQÁ vb. (VIII)~to fear (God), to be godfearing; to ward off evil, to guard oneself against evil [Pk, Ali]; to act piously [Bl]<; (*alladhīna ittaqū*) the godfearing [Ar]; those who act piously [Bl]. (pcple. act.) godfearing, one who wards off evil, who guards himself against evil, who act piously

a) perf. act.

2:103 (97)	had they believed, and been godfearing
2:189 (185)	but piety is to be godfearing
2:203 (199)	if any delays, it is not a sin in him, if he be godfearing
2:212 (208)	those who were godfearing shall be above them on the Resurrection Day
3:15 (13)	for those that are godfearing, with their Lord are gardens
3:76 (70)	whoso fulfils his covenant and fears God, God loves the godfearing
3:172 (166)	to all those of them who did good and feared God, shall be a mighty wage
3:198 (197)	those who fear their Lord — for them shall be gardens
4:77 (79)	the world to come is better for him who fears God
5:65 (70)	had the People of the Book believed and been godfearing
5:93 (94)	what they may eat, if they are godfearing, and believe
5:93 (94)	then are godfearing and believe
5:93 (94)	then are godfearing and do good
7:35 (33)	whosoever is godfearing and makes amends
7:96 (94)	had the peoples of the cities believed and been godfearing
7:201 (200)	the godfearing, when a visitation of Satan troubles them
12:109 (109)	the abode of the world to come is better for those that are godfearing
13:35 (35)	that is the requital of the godfearing
16:30 (32)	it shall be said to the godfearing
16:128 (128)	God is with those who are godfearing
19:72 (73)	then We shall deliver those that were godfearing
33:32 (32)	if you are godfearing, be not abject in your speech
39:20 (21)	but those who fear their Lord — for them await lofty chambers
39:61 (62)	God shall deliver those that were godfearing in their security
39:73 (73)	those that feared their Lord shall be driven in companies into Paradise
53:32 (33)	God knows very well him who is godfearing
92:5 (5)	as for him who gives and is godfearing

b) impf. act. (*yattaqī*)

2:21 (19)	haply so you will be godfearing
2:63 (60)	remember what is in it; haply you shall be godfearing
2:179 (175)	haply you will be godfearing
2:183 (179)	haply you will be godfearing
2:187 (183)	God makes clear His signs to men; haply they will be godfearing
2:224 (224)	do not make God a hindrance, through your oaths, to being pious and godfearing
2:282 (282)	let him fear God his Lord
2:283 (283)	let him fear God his Lord
3:28 (27)	unless you have a fear of them
3:120 (116)	yet if you are patient and godfearing
3:125 (121)	yea; if you are patient and godfearing
3:179 (174)	if you believe and are godfearing, there shall be for you a mighty wage
3:186 (183)	if you are patient and godfearing — surely that is true constancy
4:9 (10)	let them fear God, and speak words hitting the mark
4:128 (127)	if you do good and are godfearing, surely God is aware of the things you do
4:129 (128)	if you set things right, and are godfearing
6:32 (32)	the Last Abode is better for those that are godfearing
6:51 (51)	no protector and no intercessor; haply they will be godfearing
6:69 (68)	nothing of their account falls upon those that are godfearing; but a reminding

6:69 (68)	haply they will be godfearing
6:153 (154)	that then He has charged you with; haply you will be godfearing
7:63 (61)	that he may warn you, and you be godfearing
7:65 (63)	will you not be godfearing?
7:156 (155)	I shall prescribe it for those who are godfearing
7:164 (164)	as an excuse to your Lord; and haply they will be godfearing
7:169 (168)	the Last Abode is better for those who are godfearing
7:171 (170)	haply you will be godfearing
8:29 (29)	if you fear God, He will assign you a salvation
8:56 (58)	then they break their compact every time, not being godfearing
9:115 (116)	until He makes clear to them as to what they should be godfearing
10:6 (6)	surely there are signs for a godfearing people
10:31 (32)	will you not be godfearing?
10:63 (64)	those who believe, and are godfearing
12:57 (57)	yet is the wage of the world to come better for those who believe, and are godfearing
12:90 (90)	whosoever fears God, and is patient
16:52 (54)	will you fear other than God?
20:113 (112)	that haply they may be godfearing
23:23 (23)	will you not be godfearing?
23:32 (33)	will you not be godfearing?
23:87 (89)	will you not then be godfearing?
24:52 (51)	whoso obeys God and His Messenger, and fears God
26:11 (10)	the people of Pharaoh; will they not be godfearing?
26:106 (106)	will you not be godfearing?
26:124 (124)	will you not be godfearing?
26:142 (142)	will you not be godfearing?
26:161 (161)	will you not be godfearing?
26:177 (177)	will you not be godfearing?
27:53 (54)	We delivered those who believed and were godfearing
37:124 (124)	will you not be godfearing?
39:24 (25)	is he who guards himself with his face
39:28 (29)	haply they will be godfearing
41:18 (17)	We delivered those who believed and were godfearing
47:36 (38)	if you believe and are godfearing, He will give you your wages
65:2 (2)	whosoever fears God, He will appoint for him a way out
65:4 (4)	whoso fears God, God will appoint for him, of His command, easiness
65:5 (5)	whosoever fears God, He will acquit him of his evil deeds
73:17 (17)	how will you guard yourselves against a day that shall make the children grey-headed?

c) impv. (*ittaqi*)

2:24 (22)	fear the Fire, whose fuel is men and stones
2:41 (38)	fear you Me
2:48 (45)	beware of a day when no soul for another shall give satisfaction
2:123 (117)	beware a day when no soul for another shall give satisfaction
2:189 (185)	come to the houses by their doors, and fear God
2:194 (190)	fear you God, and know that God is with the godfearing
2:196 (192)	fear God, and know that God is terrible in retribution
2:197 (193)	so fear you Me, men possessed of minds
2:203 (199)	fear you God, and know that unto Him you shall be mustered
2:206 (202)	fear God
2:223 (223)	fear God, and know that you shall meet Him
2:231 (231)	fear God, and know that God has knowledge of everything
2:233 (233)	fear God, and know that God sees the things you do
2:278 (278)	O believers, fear you God
2:281 (281)	fear a day wherein you shall be returned to God

2:282 (282)	fear God; God teaches you
3:50 (44)	so fear you God, and obey you me
3:102 (97)	O believers, fear God as He should be feared
3:123 (119)	so fear God, and haply you will be thankful
3:130 (125)	fear you God; haply so you will prosper
3:131 (126)	fear the Fire prepared for the unbelievers
3:200 (200)	be steadfast; fear God; haply so you will prosper
4:1 (1)	mankind, fear your Lord, who created you
4:1 (1)	fear God by whom you demand one of another
4:131 (130)	fear God
5:2 (3)	fear God; surely God is terrible in retribution
5:4 (6)	fear God; God is swift at the reckoning
5:7 (10)	fear you God; surely God knows the thoughts in the breasts
5:8 (11)	fear God; surely God is aware of the things you do
5:11 (14)	and fear God
5:35 (39)	fear God, and seek the means to come to Him
5:57 (62)	fear God, if you are believers
5:88 (90)	fear God, in whom you are believers
5:96 (97)	fear God, unto whom you shall be mustered
5:100 (100)	so fear God, O men possessed of minds
5:108 (107)	fear God, and hearken
5:112 (112)	fear you God, if you are believers
6:72 (71)	perform the prayer, and fear Him
6:155 (156)	so follow it, and be godfearing
8:1 (1)	so fear you God, and set things right between you
8:25 (25)	fear a trial which shall surely not smite in particular the evildoers
8:69 (70)	fear you God
9:119 (120)	O believers, fear God, and be with the truthful ones
11:78 (80)	so fear God, and do not degrade me in my guests
15:69 (69)	fear God, and do not degrade me
16:2 (2)	that there is no god but I; so fear you Me
22:1 (1)	O men, fear your Lord
23:52 (54)	I am your Lord; so fear Me
26:108 (108)	so fear you God, and obey you me
26:110 (110)	so fear you God, and obey you me
26:126 (126)	so fear you God, and obey you me
26:131 (131)	so fear you God, and obey you me
26:132 (132)	and fear Him who has succoured you
26:144 (144)	so fear you God, and obey you me
26:150 (150)	so fear you God, and obey you me
26:163 (163)	so fear you God, and obey you me
26:179 (179)	so fear you God, and obey you me
26:184 (184)	fear Him who created you, and the generations
29:16 (15)	serve God, and fear Him
30:31 (30)	fear you Him, and perform the prayer
31:33 (32)	O men, fear your Lord, and dread a day
33:1 (1)	fear God, and obey not the unbelievers
33:37 (37)	keep thy wife to thyself, and fear God
33:55 (55)	fear you God; surely God is witness of everything
33:70 (70)	fear God, and speak words hitting the mark
36:45 (45)	fear what is before you and what is behind you
39:10 (13)	My servants who believe, fear your Lord
39:16 (18)	O My servants, so fear you Me
43:63 (63)	so fear you God and obey you me
49:1 (1)	fear God. God is All-hearing, All-knowing

49:10 (10) set things right between your two brothers, and fear God
49:12 (12) fear you God; assuredly God turns
57:28 (28) fear God, and believe in His Messenger
58:9 (10) fear God, unto whom you shall be mustered
59:7 (7) fear God; surely God is terrible in retribution
59:18 (18) O believers, fear God
59:18 (18) fear God; God is aware of the things you do
60:11 (11) fear God, in whom you believe
64:16 (16) so fear God as far as you are able
65:1 (1) count the period, and fear God your Lord
65:10 (10) so fear God, O men possessed of minds
71:3 (3) serve God, and fear Him, and obey you me

g) pcple. act. (*muttaqī*)

2:2 (1) a guidance to the godfearing
2:66 (62) and an admonition to such as are godfearing
2:177 (172) these are the truly godfearing
2:180 (176) an obligation on the godfearing
2:194 (190) fear you God, and know that God is with the godfearing
2:241 (242) an obligation on the godfearing
3:76 (70) whoso fulfils his covenant and fears God, God loves the godfearing
3:115 (111) God knows the godfearing
3:133 (127) is as the heavens and earth, prepared for the godfearing
3:138 (132) an admonition for such as are godfearing
5:27 (30) God accepts only of the godfearing,'
5:46 (50) a guidance and an admonition unto the godfearing
7:128 (125) the issue ultimate is to the godfearing
8:34 (34) its only protectors are the godfearing
9:4 (4) God loves the godfearing
9:7 (7) God loves the godfearing
9:36 (36) know that God is with the godfearing
9:44 (44) God knows the godfearing
9:123 (124) let them find in you a harshness; and know that God is with the godfearing
11:49 (51) be patient; the issue ultimate is to the godfearing
13:35 (35) that is the requital of the godfearing
15:45 (45) but the godfearing shall be amidst gardens
16:30 (32) excellent is the abode of the godfearing
16:31 (33) so God recompenses the godfearing
19:85 (88) the day that We shall muster the godfearing to the All-merciful with pomp
19:97 (97) that thou mayest bear good tidings thereby to the godfearing
21:48 (49) a Radiance, and a Remembrance for the godfearing
24:34 (34) an admonition for the godfearing
25:15 (16) that is promised to the godfearing, and is their recompense
25:74 (74) make us a model to the godfearing
26:90 (90) Paradise shall be brought forward for the godfearing
28:83 (83) the issue ultimate is to the godfearing
38:28 (27) shall We make the godfearing as the transgressors?
38:49 (49) this is a Remembrance; and for the godfearing is a fair resort
39:33 (34) those — they are the godfearing
39:57 (58) I should have been among the godfearing
43:35 (34) the world to come with thy Lord is for the godfearing
43:67 (67) friends on that day shall be foes to one another, but the godfearing
44:51 (51) surely the godfearing shall be in a station secure
45:19 (18) friends one of the other; God is the friend of the godfearing
47:15 (16) this is the similitude of Paradise which the godfearing have been promised

50:31 (30)	Paradise shall be brought forward to the godfearing
51:15 (15)	the godfearing shall be among gardens and fountains
52:17 (17)	surely the godfearing shall be in gardens and bliss
54:54 (54)	surely the godfearing shall dwell amid gardens
68:34 (34)	surely for the godfearing shall be Gardens
69:48 (48)	surely it is a Reminder to the godfearing
77:41 (41)	truly the godfearing shall dwell amid shades
78:31 (31)	surely for the godfearing awaits a place of security

*W R D

WARADA vb. (I)~to come, to arrive, to go down. (pcple. act.) one who goes down; water-drawer. (pcple. pass.) that which is led down to

a) perf. act.

21:99 (99)	if those had been gods, they would never have gone down to it
28:23 (22)	when he came to the waters of Midian

g) pcple. act. (*wārid*)

12:19 (19)	they sent one of them, a water-drawer, who let down his bucket
19:71 (72)	not one of you there is, but he shall go down to it
21:98 (98)	Gehenna; you shall go down to it

h) pcple. pass. (*mawrūd*)

11:98 (100)	the Fire — evil the watering-place to be led down to

WARDAH n.f.~(adj) crimson, rosy

55:37 (37)	when heaven is split asunder, and turns crimson

WARĪD n.m.~jugular vein

50:16 (15)	We are nearer to him than the jugular vein

WIRD n.m.~a watering place; (adv) herding, as a weary herd

11:98 (100)	evil the watering-place to be led down to
19:86 (89)	and drive the evildoers into Gehenna herding

AWRADA vb. (IV)~to let down, to lead down

a) perf. act.

11:98 (100)	and will have led them down to the Fire

*W R Q

WARAQ n.m. (coll)~leaves; (f.s. *waraqah*) a leaf

6:59 (59)	not a leaf falls, but He knows it
7:22 (21)	they took to stitching upon themselves leaves of the Garden
20:121 (119)	they took to stitching upon themselves leaves of the Garden

WARIQ n.m.~money, silver

18:19 (18)	now send one of you forth with this silver to the city

*W R TH

WARITHA vb. (I)~to inherit, to be an heir. (n.vb.) inheritance. (pcple. act.) heir, inheritor; Inheritor (Divine attribute)

a) perf. act.

4:11 (12)	if he has no children, and his heirs are his parents
7:169 (168)	there succeeded after them a succession who inherited the Book
27:16 (16)	and Solomon was David's heir

b) impf. act. (*yarithu*)

4:19 (23)	it is not lawful for you to inherit women against their will
4:176 (175)	he is her heir if she has no children
7:100 (98)	is it not a guidance to those who inherit the earth
19:6 (6)	who shall be my inheritor
19:6 (6)	the inheritor of the House
19:40 (41)	We shall inherit the earth and all that are upon it
19:80 (83)	and We shall inherit from him that
21:105 (105)	the earth shall be the inheritance of My righteous servants
23:11 (11)	who shall inherit Paradise therein dwelling forever

f) n.vb. (*turāth*)

89:19 (20)	and you devour the inheritance greedily

g) pcple. act. (*wārith*, pl. *wārithūn* and *warathah*)

2:233 (233)	the heir has a like duty
15:23 (23)	it is We who are the inheritors
21:89 (89)	though Thou art the best of inheritors
23:10 (10)	those are the inheritors
26:85 (85)	make me one of the inheritors of the Garden of Bliss
28:5 (4)	make them the inheritors
28:58 (58)	Ourselves are the inheritors

MĪRĀTH n.m.~inheritance

3:180 (176)	to God belongs the inheritance of the heavens and earth
57:10 (10)	to God belongs the inheritance of the heavens and the earth

AWRATHA vb. (IV)~to bequeath, to give as inheritance

a) perf. act.

7:137 (133)	We bequeathed upon the people that were abased all the east
26:59 (59)	even so, and We bequeathed them upon the Children of Israel
33:27 (27)	He bequeathed upon you their lands
35:32 (29)	then We bequeathed the Book on those of Our servants We chose
39:74 (74)	who has been true in His promise to us, and has bequeathed upon us the earth
40:53 (56)	We bequeathed upon the Children of Israel the Book
44:28 (27)	We bequeathed them upon another people

b) impf. act. (*yūrithu*)

7:128 (125)	the earth is God's and He bequeaths it to whom He will
19:63 (64)	that is Paradise which We shall give as an inheritance

d) perf. pass. (*ūritha*)

7:43 (41) you have been given it as your inheritance for what you did
42:14 (13) those to whom the Book has been given as an inheritance after them
43:72 (72) this is the Paradise that you have been given for an inheritance

e) impf. pass. (*yūrathu*)

4:12 (15) if a man or a woman have no heir direct

*W R Y

WARĀʾ n.m. (adv)~beyond, behind, after

2:91 (85) they disbelieve in what is beyond that
2:101 (95) a party of them that were given the Book reject the Book of God behind their backs
3:187 (184) but they rejected it behind their backs
4:24 (28) lawful for you, beyond all that, is that you may seek
4:102 (103) when they bow themselves, let them be behind you
6:94 (94) you have left what We conferred on you behind your backs
11:71 (74) We gave her the glad tidings of Isaac, and, after Isaac, of Jacob
11:92 (94) have you taken Him as something to be thrust behind you
14:16 (19) beyond him Gehenna
14:17 (20) he cannot die; and still beyond him is a harsh chastisement
18:79 (78) for behind them there was a king who was seizing
19:5 (5) now I fear my kinsfolk after I am gone
23:7 (7) whosoever seeks after more than that
23:100 (102) there, behind them, is a barrier until the day
33:53 (53) ask them from behind a curtain; that is cleaner
42:51 (50) except by revelation, or from behind a veil
45:10 (9) behind them Gehenna; and that they have earned
49:4 (4) those who call unto thee from behind the apartments
57:13 (13) return you back behind, and seek for a light
59:14 (14) except in fortified cities, or from behind walls
70:31 (31) whoso seeks after more than that
76:27 (27) leave behind them a heavy day
84:10 (10) as for him who is given his book behind his back
85:20 (20) God is behind them, encompassing

WĀRÁ vb. (III)~to conceal, to cover, to hide

b) impf. act. (*yuwārī*)

5:31 (34) to show him how he might conceal the vile body of his brother
5:31 (34) am I unable to be as this raven, and so conceal my brother's vile body
7:26 (25) We have sent down on you a garment to cover your shameful parts

d) perf. pass. (*wūriya*)

7:20 (19) to reveal to them that which was hidden from them of their shameful parts

TAWĀRÁ vb. (III)~to hide; to be hidden, to be concealed

a) perf. act.

38:32 (31) until the sun was hidden behind the veil

b) impf. act. (*yatawārá*)

16:59 (61) as he hides him from the people because of the evil

AWRÁ vb. (IV)~to strike a fire, to kindle. (pcple. act.) striker of fire

b) impf. act. (*yūrī*)

56:71 (70) have you considered the fire you kindle?

g) pcple. act. f. (*mūriyah*)

100:2 (2) by the strikers of fire

*W S ᶜ

WASIᶜA vb. (I)~to embrace, to comprise. (n.vb.1) amplitude, plenty; affluence, wealth. (n.vb.2) capacity, scope. (pcple. act.) wide; All-embracing (Divine attribute)

a) perf. act.

2:255 (256) His Throne comprises the heavens and earth
6:80 (80) my Lord embraces all things in His knowledge
7:89 (87) our Lord embraces all things in His knowledge
7:156 (155) My mercy embraces all things
20:98 (98) who in His knowledge embraces everything
40:7 (7) Thou embracest every thing in mercy and knowledge

f) n.vb. (1) (*saᶜah*)

2:247 (248) seeing he has not been given amplitude of wealth
4:100 (101) whoso emigrates in the way of God will find in the earth many refuges and plenty
4:130 (129) God will enrich each of them of His plenty
24:22 (22) let not those of you who possess bounty and plenty swear off giving kinsmen
65:7 (7) let the man of plenty expend out of his (plenty)
65:7 (7) let the man of (plenty) expend out of his plenty

f) n.vb. (2) (*wusᶜ*)

2:233 (233) no soul is charged save to its capacity
2:286 (286) God charges no soul save to its capacity
6:152 (153) We charge not any soul save to its capacity
7:42 (40) We charge not any soul, save according to its capacity
23:62 (64) We charge not any soul save to its capacity

g) pcple. act. (*wāsiᶜ*)

2:115 (109) God is All-embracing, All-knowing
2:247 (248) God is All-embracing, All-knowing
2:261 (263) God is All-embracing, All-knowing
2:268 (271) God is All-embracing, All-knowing
3:73 (66) God is All-embracing, All-knowing
4:97 (99) but was not God's earth wide
4:130 (129) God is All-embracing, All-wise
5:54 (59) God is All-embracing, All-knowing
6:147 (148) your Lord is of mercy all-embracing, and His might
24:32 (32) God is All-embracing, All-knowing
29:56 (56) O My servants who believe, surely My earth is wide

39:10 (13)	God's earth is wide
53:32 (33)	surely thy Lord is wide in His forgiveness

AWSAʿA vb. (IV)~(pcple. act.) one who extends something wide; affluent, rich, wealthy

g) pcple. act. (*mūsiʿ*)

2:236 (237)	make provision for them, the affluent man according to his means
51:47 (47)	We built it with might, and We extend it wide

*W S L

WASĪLAH n.f.~means, way

5:35 (39)	fear God, and seek the means to come to Him
17:57 (59)	those they call upon are themselves seeking the means to come to their Lord

*W S M

WASAMA vb. (I)~to brand, to mark

b) impf. act. (*yasimu*)

68:16 (16)	We shall brand him upon the muzzle

TAWASSAMA vb. (V)~(pcple. act.) one who marks [Ar, Bl]; one who reads a mark [Pk]; one who understands by tokens [Ali]

g) pcple. act. (*mutawassim*)

15:75 (75)	surely in that are signs for such as mark

*W S N

SINAH n.f.~slumber

2:255 (256)	slumber seizes Him not, neither sleep

*W S Q

WASAQA vb. (I)~to envelop, to enshroud

a) perf. act.

84:17 (17)	the night and what it envelops

ITTASAQA vb. (VIII)~to be in good order, to be at the full (the moon)

a) perf. act.

84:18 (18)	the moon when it is at the full

*W S Ṭ

WASAṬA vb. (I)~to cleave (the centre) [Ar, Pk]; to penetrate into or move in the midst [Ali, Bl]

a) perf. act.

100:5 (5)	cleaving there with a host

WASAṬ n.m. (adj)~midmost, middle (f. *wusṭá*; comp. *awsaṭ*) average; most moderate

2:143 (137)	thus We appointed you a midmost nation
2:238 (239)	be you watchful over the prayers, and the middle prayer
5:89 (91)	the expiation is to feed ten poor persons with the average of the food
68:28 (28)	said the most moderate of them

*W S W S

WASWASA vb. (quad I)~to whisper (evil)

a) perf. act.

7:20 (19)	then Satan whispered to them, to reveal
20:120 (118)	then Satan whispered to him

b) impf. act. (*yuwaswisu*)

50:16 (15)	We know what his soul whispers within him
114:5 (5)	who whispers in the breasts of men

WASWĀS n.m.~whisperer (of evil), the Tempter (Satan)

114:4 (4)	from the evil of the slinking whisperer

*W SH Y

SHIYAH n.f.~blotch, blemish, spot

2:71 (66)	one kept secure, with no blemish on her

*W Ṣ B

WAṢABA vb. (I)~(pcple. act.) everlasting; (adv) for ever

g) pcple. act. (*wāṣib*)

16:52 (54)	His is the religion for ever
37:9 (9)	theirs is an everlasting chastisement

*W Ṣ D

WAṢĪD n.m.~threshold

18:18 (17)	their dog stretching its paws on the threshold

AWṢADA vb. (IV)~(pcple. pass.) covered

h) pcple. pass. f. (*mu'ṣadah* for *mūṣadah*)

90:20 (20)	over them is a Fire covered down
104:8 (8)	covered down upon them

*W Ṣ F

WAṢAFA vb. (I)~to describe, to depict, to portray. (n.vb.) describing, portrayal, depiction *b*) impf. act. (*yaṣifu*)

6:100 (100)	high be He exalted above what they describe
12:18 (18)	whose succour is ever there to seek against that you describe
12:77 (77)	God knows very well what you are describing
16:62 (64)	their tongues describe falsehood
16:116 (117)	do not say, as to what your tongues falsely describe
21:18 (18)	then woe to you for that you describe
21:22 (22)	glory be to God, the Lord of the Throne, above that they describe
21:112 (112)	His succour is ever to be sought against that you describe
23:91 (93)	glory be to God, beyond that they describe
23:96 (98)	We Ourselves know very well that they describe
37:159 (159)	glory be to God above that they describe
37:180 (180)	glory be to thy Lord, the Lord of Glory, above that they describe
43:82 (82)	the Lord of the Throne, above that they describe

f) n.vb. (*waṣf*)

6:139 (140)	He will assuredly recompense them for their describing

*W Ṣ L

WAṢALA vb. (I)~to reach; to join; to betake oneself; to take refuge with

b) impf. act. (*yaṣilu*)

4:90 (92)	a people who are joined with you by a compact
6:136 (137)	so what is for their associates reaches not God
6:136 (137)	what is for God reaches their associates
11:70 (73)	when he saw their hands not reaching towards it, he was suspicious of them
11:81 (83)	they shall not reach thee
13:21 (21)	who join what God has commanded shall (be joined)
28:35 (35)	so that they shall not reach you because of Our signs

e) impf. pass. (*yūṣalu*)

2:27 (25)	such as cut what God has commanded should be joined
13:21 (21)	who (join) what God has commanded shall be joined
13:25 (25)	who snap what God has commanded to be joined

WAṢĪLAH n.prop.~Wasila (a she-camel consecrated to idols)

5:103 (102)	idols, such as Bahira, Sa'iba, Wasila, Hami

WAṢṢALA vb. (II)~to bring; to cause to reach

a) perf. act.

28:51 (51)	now We have brought them the Word

*W Ṣ Y

WAṢĪYAH n.f.~testament, bequest, bequeathing

2:180 (176)	to make testament in favour of his parents and kinsmen
2:240 (241)	let them make testament for their wives
4:11 (12)	to his mother a sixth, after any bequest he may bequeath
4:12 (13)	for you of what they leave a fourth, after any bequest they may bequeath

4:12 (14)	for them of what you leave an eighth, after any bequest you may bequeath
4:12 (15)	they share equally a third, after any bequest he may bequeath
4:12 (16)	a charge from God
5:106 (105)	when any of you is visited by death, at the bequeathing

WAṢṢÁ vb. (II)~to charge, to commend, to entrust, to enjoin. (n.vb.) a testament, a bequest

a) perf. act.

2:132 (126)	Abraham charged his sons with this
4:131 (130)	We have charged those who were given the Book before you
6:144 (145)	were you witnesses when God charged you with this
6:151 (152)	that then He has charged you with
6:152 (153)	that then He has charged you with
6:153 (154)	that then He has charged you with
29:8 (7)	We have charged man, that he be kind to his parents
31:14 (13)	We have charged man concerning his parents
42:13 (11)	He has laid down for you as religion that He charged Noah with
42:13 (11)	We have revealed to thee, and that We charged Abraham with
46:15 (14)	We have charged man, that he be kind to his parents

f) n.vb. (*tawṣiyah*)

36:50 (50)	then they will not be able to make any testament

AWṢÁ vb. (IV)~to enjoin, to charge; to bequeath. (pcple. act.) one who makes a testament, a testator

a) perf. act.

19:31 (32)	He has enjoined me to pray, and to give the alms

b) impf. act. (*yūṣī*)

4:11 (12)	God charges you, concerning your children
4:11 (12)	to his mother a sixth, after any bequest he may bequeath
4:12 (13)	for you of what they leave a fourth, after any bequest they may bequeath
4:12 (14)	for them of what you leave an eighth, after any bequest you may bequeath

e) impf. pass. (*yūṣá*)

4:12 (15)	they share equally a third, after any bequest he may bequeath

g) pcple. act. (*mūṣī*)

2:182 (178)	if any man fears injustice or sin from one making testament

TAWĀṢÁ vb. (VI)~to bequeath to one another; to counsel one another, to enjoin each other

a) perf. act.

51:53 (53)	what, have they bequeathed it one to another?
90:17 (17)	and counsel each other to be steadfast
90:17 (17)	and counsel each other to be merciful
103:3 (3)	and counsel each other unto the truth
103:3 (3)	and counsel each other to be steadfast

*W T D

AWTĀD n.m. (pl. of *watad*)~a peg, a tent-peg; stake [Bl]; (*dhū al-awtād*) he of the tent-pegs [Ar]; firmly planted [Pk]; Lord of the Stakes [Ali, Bl]

38:12 (11)	Ad, and Pharaoh, he of the tent-pegs
78:7 (7)	and the mountains as pegs
89:10 (9)	Pharaoh, he of the tent-pegs

*W T N

WATĪN n.m.~life-vein, life-artery

69:46 (46)	then We would surely have cut his life-vein

*W T R

WATARA vb. (I)~to deprive, to cheat someone out of something

b) impf. act. (*yatiru*)

47:35 (37)	God is with you, and will not deprive you of your works

WATR n.m.~odd (number); (*tatrā*) one by one, one after another, successively

23:44 (46)	then sent We Our Messengers successively
89:3 (2)	by the even and the odd

*W TH N

AWTHĀN n.m. (pl. of *wathan*)~idols

22:30 (31)	eschew the abomination of idols, and eschew the speaking
29:17 (16)	you only serve, apart from God, idols
29:25 (24)	you have only taken to yourselves idols, apart from God

*W TH Q

MAWTHIQ n.m.~covenant, agreement, pledge

12:66 (66)	never will I send him with you until you bring me a solemn pledge by God
12:66 (66)	when they had brought him their solemn pledge he said
12:80 (80)	do you not know how your father has taken a solemn pledge from you by God

MĪTHĀQ n.m.~a compact, a covenant, solemn binding, a treaty

2:27 (25)	such as break the covenant of God after its solemn binding
2:63 (60)	when We took compact with you, and raised above you
2:83 (77)	when We took compact with the Children of Israel
2:84 (78)	when We took compact with you
2:93 (87)	when We took compact with you, and raised over you
3:81 (75)	when God took compact with the Prophets
3:187 (184)	when God took compact with those who had been given the Book
4:21 (25)	and they have taken from you a solemn compact
4:90 (92)	a people who are joined with you by a compact
4:92 (94)	if he belong to a people joined with you by a compact
4:154 (153)	We raised above them the Mount, taking compact with them
4:154 (153)	We took from them a solemn compact
4:155 (154)	for their breaking the compact, and disbelieving in the signs of God

5:7 (10)	remember God's blessing upon you, and His compact which He made with you
5:12 (15)	God took compact with the Children of Israel
5:13 (16)	so for their breaking their compact We cursed them
5:14 (17)	with those who say 'We are Christians' We took compact
5:70 (74)	We took compact with the Children of Israel
7:169 (168)	has not the compact of the Book been taken touching them
8:72 (73)	except against a people between whom and you there is a compact
13:20 (20)	who fulfil God's covenant, and break not the compact
13:25 (25)	those who break the covenant of God after His compact
33:7 (7)	when We took compact from the Prophets
33:7 (7)	We took from them a solemn compact
57:8 (8)	He has taken compact with you, if you are believers

WATHĀQ n.m.~bond, fetter, shackle

47:4 (4)	when you have made wide slaughter among them, tie fast the bonds
89:26 (26)	none shall bind as He binds

WUTHQÁ n.f. (comp. adj. of *wathīqah*)~most firm

2:256 (257)	has laid hold of the most firm handle, unbreaking
31:22 (21)	whosoever submits his will to God, being a good-doer, has laid hold of the most firm handle

WĀTHAQA vb. (III)~to make a compact, to make a covenant

a) perf. act.

5:7 (10)	remember God's blessing upon you, and His compact which He made with you

AWTHAQA vb. (IV)~to bind, to tie up, to fetter

b) impf. act. (*yūthiqu*)

89:26 (26)	none shall bind as He binds

*W Ṭ ʾ

WAṬIʾA vb. (I)~to tread, to trample on. a tread; (*ashaddu waṭʾan*) heavier in tread [Ar]; more keen [Pk]; most potent (for governing the soul) [Ali]; strongest in impression [Bl] b) impf. act. (*yaṭaʾu*)

9:120 (121)	neither tread they any tread enraging the unbelievers
33:27 (27)	their habitations, and their possessions, and a land you never trod
48:25 (25)	whom you knew not, lest you should trample them

f) n.vb. (*waṭʾ*)

73:6 (6)	the first part of the night is heavier in tread

MAWṬIʾ n.m.~a tread, a step

9:120 (121)	neither tread they any tread enraging the unbelievers

WĀṬAʾA vb. (III)~to agree with, to make

b) impf. act. (*yuwāṭiʾu*)

9:37 (37)	hallow it another, to agree with the number that God has hallowed

*W Ṭ N

MAWĀṬIN n.m. (pl. of *mawṭin*)~battle-field

9:25 (25)	God has already helped you on many fields

*W Ṭ R

WAṬAR n.m.~a wish, a desire, what one would like (to accomplish)

33:37 (37)	when Zaid had accomplished what he would of her
33:37 (37)	when they have accomplished what they would of them

*W Y L

WAYL n.m.~woe; (exclamation) Woe! Alas! O beware!

2:79 (73)	woe to those who write the Book with their hands
2:79 (73)	woe to them for what their hands have written
2:79 (73)	woe to them for their earnings
5:31 (34)	woe is me! Am I unable to be as this raven
11:72 (75)	woe is me! Shall I bear, being an old woman
14:2 (2)	woe to the unbelievers for a terrible chastisement
18:49 (47)	alas for us! How is it with this Book, that it leaves nothing behind
19:37 (38)	then woe to those who disbelieve for the scene of a dreadful day
20:61 (63)	O beware! Forge not a lie against God
21:14 (14)	alas for us! We have been evildoers
21:18 (18)	then woe to you for that you describe
21:46 (47)	alas for us! We were evildoers
21:97 (97)	alas for us! We were heedless of this; nay, we were evildoers
25:28 (30)	alas, would that I had not taken So-and-so for a friend
28:80 (80)	woe upon you
36:52 (52)	alas for us! Who roused us out of our sleeping-place?
37:20 (20)	woe, alas for us! This is the Day of Doom
38:27 (26)	wherefore woe unto the unbelievers because of the Fire
39:22 (23)	woe to those whose hearts are hardened
41:6 (5)	and woe to the idolaters
43:65 (65)	woe unto those who did evil
45:7 (6)	woe to every guilty impostor
46:17 (16)	woe upon thee
51:60 (60)	so woe to the unbelievers, for that day of theirs
52:11 (11)	woe that day unto those that cry lies
68:31 (31)	woe, alas for us! Truly, we were insolent
77:15 (15)	woe that day unto those who cry it lies
77:19 (19)	woe that day unto those who cry it lies
77:24 (24)	woe that day unto those who cry it lies
77:28 (28)	woe that day unto those who cry it lies
77:34 (34)	woe that day unto those who cry it lies
77:37 (37)	woe that day unto those who cry it lies
77:40 (40)	woe that day unto those who cry it lies
77:45 (45)	woe that day unto those who cry it lies
77:47 (47)	woe that day unto those who cry it lies
77:49 (49)	woe that day unto those who cry it lies
83:1 (1)	woe to the stinters
83:10 (10)	woe that day unto those who cry it lies
104:1 (1)	woe unto every backbiter, slanderer
107:4 (4)	so woe to those that pray

*W Z ᶜ

WAZAᶜA vb. (I)~to drive on (in ranks), to set in battle order, to set in array; to dispose duly

e) impf. pass. (*yūzaᶜu*)

27:17 (17)	his hosts were mustered to Solomon, jinn, men and birds, duly disposed
27:83 (85)	a troop of those that cried lies to Our signs, duly disposed
41:19 (18)	the day when God's enemies are mustered to the Fire, duly disposed

AWZAᶜA vb. (IV)~to dispose [Ar]; to arouse [Pk]; to order, to grant [Ali]; to constrain, to hold [Bl]

c) impv. (*awziᶜ*)

27:19 (19)	dispose me that I may be thankful for Thy blessing
46:15 (14)	dispose me that I may be thankful for Thy blessing

*W Z N

WAZANA vb. (I)~to weigh. (n.vb.) weighing; weight, measure; (*aqāma al-wazn*) to weigh with justice. (pcple. pass.) weighed, measured

a) perf. act.

83:3 (3)	but, when they measure for them or weigh for them, do skimp

c) impv. (*zin*)

17:35 (37)	weigh with the straight balance; that is better
26:182 (182)	weigh with the straight balance

f) n.vb. (*wazn*)

7:8 (7)	the weighing that day is true
18:105 (105)	on the Day of Resurrection We shall not assign to them any weight
55:9 (8)	weigh with justice, and skimp not in the Balance

h) pcple. pass. (*mawzūn*)

15:19 (19)	We caused to grow therein of every thing justly weighed

MĪZĀN n.m. (pl. *mawāzīn*)~balance, scales

6:152 (153)	fill up the measure and the balance with justice
7:8 (7)	he whose scales are heavy — they are the prosperers
7:9 (8)	he whose scales are light — they have lost their souls
7:85 (83)	so fill up the measure and the balance, and diminish not
11:84 (85)	diminish not the measure and the balance
11:85 (86)	O my people, fill up the measure and the balance justly
21:47 (48)	We shall set up the just balances for the Resurrection Day
23:102 (104)	then he whose scales are heavy — they are the prosperers
23:103 (105)	he whose scales are light — they have lost their souls
42:17 (16)	God it is who has sent down the Book with the truth, and also the Balance
55:7 (6)	He raised it up, and set the Balance
55:8 (7)	transgress not in the Balance
55:9 (8)	weigh with justice, and skimp not in the Balance
57:25 (25)	We sent down with them the Book and the Balance
101:6 (5)	then he whose deeds weigh heavy in the Balance
101:8 (6)	but he whose deeds weigh light in the Balance

*W Z R

WAZARA vb. (I)~to carry, to bear (a load or burden); to sin. (n.vb.) heavy load, burden; encumberance; fardel; sin. (pcple. act.) a soul laden, a bearer of burdens; a sinner

b) impf. act. (*yaziru*)

6:31 (31)	O how evil the loads they bear
6:164 (164)	no soul laden bears the load of another
16:25 (27)	O evil the load they bear
17:15 (16)	no soul laden bears the load of another
35:18 (19)	no soul laden bears the load of another
39:7 (9)	no soul laden bears the load of another
53:38 (39)	that no soul laden bears the load of another

f) n.vb. (*wizr*, pl. *awzār*)

6:31 (31)	on their backs they shall be bearing their loads
6:164 (164)	no soul laden bears the load of another
16:25 (27)	that they may bear their loads complete
16:25 (27)	and some of the loads of those that they lead astray
17:15 (16)	no soul laden bears the load of another
20:87 (90)	but we were loaded with fardels
20:100 (100)	upon the Day of Resurrection he shall bear a fardel
35:18 (19)	no soul laden bears the load of another
39:7 (9)	no soul laden bears the load of another
47:4 (5)	till the war lays down its loads
53:38 (39)	that no soul laden bears the load of another
94:2 (2)	and lift from thee thy burden

g) pcple. act. f. (*wāzirah*)

6:164 (164)	no soul laden bears the load of another
17:15 (16)	no soul laden bears the load of another
35:18 (19)	no soul laden bears the load of another
39:7 (9)	no soul laden bears the load of another
53:38 (39)	that no soul laden bears the load of another

WAZAR n.m.~a refuge, a place of safety

75:11 (11)	no indeed; not a refuge

WAZĪR n.m.~a minister; a henchman [Pk]; a familiar [Ar]; wazir [Bl]

20:29 (30)	appoint for me of my folk a familiar
25:35 (37)	and appointed with him his brother Aaron as minister

YĀ

*Y ʾ S

YA'ISA vb. (I)~to despair, to give up hope; to know (13:31)

a) perf. act.

5:3 (4)	today the unbelievers have despaired of your religion
29:23 (22)	they despair of My mercy
60:13 (13)	and who have despaired of the world to come
60:13 (13)	even as the unbelievers have despaired of the inhabitants of the tombs
65:4 (4)	as for your women who have despaired of further menstruating

b) impf. act. (*yayʾasu*)

12:87 (87)	do not despair of God's comfort
12:87 (87)	of God's comfort no man despairs
13:31 (30)	did not the believers know that, if God had willed

YA'US n.m. (adj)~desperate, in despair

11:9 (12)	then We wrest it from him, he is desperate, ungrateful
17:83 (85)	when evil visits him, he is in despair
41:49 (49)	when evil visits him, then he is cast down and desperate

ISTAY'ASA vb. (X)~to despair

a) perf. act.

12:80 (80)	when they despaired of moving him, they conferred privily apart
12:110 (110)	when the Messengers despaired, deeming they were counted liars

*Y ʿ Q

YAʿŪQ n.prop.~Ya'uq (idol)

71:23 (23)	Yaghuth, Ya'uq, neither Nasr

*Y ʿ Q B

YAʿQŪB n.prop.~Jacob

2:132 (126)	Abraham charged his sons with this and Jacob likewise
2:133 (127)	were you witnesses, when death came to Jacob?
2:136 (130)	Abraham, Ishmael, Isaac and Jacob
2:140 (134)	Abraham, Ishmael, Isaac and Jacob
3:84 (78)	Abraham and Ishmael, Isaac and Jacob
4:163 (161)	Abraham, Ishmael, Isaac, Jacob
6:84 (84)	We gave to him Isaac and Jacob
11:71 (74)	We gave her the glad tidings of Isaac, and, after Isaac, of Jacob
12:6 (6)	blessing upon thee and upon the House of Jacob,
12:38 (38)	the creed of my fathers, Abraham, Isaac and Jacob
12:68 (68)	it was a need in Jacob's soul that he so satisfied.
19:6 (6)	the inheritor of the House of Jacob
19:49 (50)	We gave him Isaac and Jacob

21:72 (72)	We gave him Isaac and Jacob
29:27 (26)	We gave him Isaac and Jacob
38:45 (45)	Our servants Abraham, Isaac and Jacob

*Y B S

YABISA vb. (I)~(pcple. act.) withered, dry

g) pcple. act. (*yābis*)

6:59 (59)	not a thing, fresh or withered, but it is in a Book Manifest
12:43 (43)	likewise seven green ears of corn, and seven withered
12:46 (46)	seven green ears of corn, and seven withered

YABAS n.m.~a dry path

20:77 (79)	strike for them a dry path in the sea

*Y D Y

YAD n.f. (du. *yadān*; pl. *aydī*)~hand; (*bayna yaday*) before, in front of

2:66 (62)	We made it a punishment exemplary for all the former times
2:79 (73)	woe to those who write the Book with their hands
2:79 (73)	woe to them for what their hands have written
2:95 (89)	they will never long for it, because of that their hands have forwarded
2:97 (91)	by the leave of God, confirming what was before it
2:195 (191)	cast not yourselves by your own hands into destruction
2:237 (238)	in whose hand is the knot of marriage
2:249 (250)	saving him who scoops up with his hand
2:255 (256)	He knows what lies before them and what is after them
3:3 (2)	He has sent down upon thee the Book with the truth, confirming what was before it
3:26 (25)	in Thy hand is the good
3:50 (44)	likewise confirming the truth of the Torah that is before me
3:73 (66)	surely bounty is in the hand of God
3:182 (178)	that, for what your hands have forwarded
4:43 (46)	and wipe your faces and your hands
4:62 (65)	when they are visited by an affliction for what their own hands have forwarded
4:77 (79)	restrain your hands, and perform the prayer
4:91 (93)	and offer you peace, and restrain their hands
5:6 (8)	wash your faces, and your hands up to the elbows
5:6 (9)	and wipe your faces and your hands with it
5:11 (14)	when a certain people purposed to stretch against you their hands
5:11 (14)	and He restrained their hands from you
5:28 (31)	yet if thou stretchest out thy hand against me, to slay me
5:28 (31)	I will not stretch out my hand
5:33 (37)	or their hands and feet shall alternately be struck off
5:38 (42)	the thief, male and female: cut off the hands of both
5:46 (50)	We sent ... Jesus son of Mary, confirming the Torah before him
5:46 (50)	wherein is guidance and light, and confirming the Torah before it
5:48 (52)	confirming the Book that was before it, and assuring it
5:64 (69)	God's hand is fettered
5:64 (69)	fettered are their hands, and they are cursed
5:64 (69)	nay, but His hands are outspread; He expends how He will
5:94 (95)	God will surely try you with something of the game that your hands and lances attain
6:7 (7)	so they touched it with their hands

6:92 (92)	a Book We have sent down, blessed and confirming that which was before it
6:93 (93)	the angels are stretching out their hands
7:17 (16)	then I shall come on them from before them
7:57 (55)	He who looses the winds, bearing good tidings before His mercy
7:108 (105)	he drew forth his hand, and lo, it was white
7:124 (121)	I shall assuredly cut off alternately your hands and feet
7:149 (148)	when they smote their hands
7:195 (194)	or have they hands wherewith they lay hold
8:51 (53)	that, for what your hands have forwarded
8:70 (71)	O Prophet, say to the prisoners in your hands
9:14 (14)	fight them, and God will chastise them at your hands
9:29 (29)	until they pay the tribute out of hand
9:52 (52)	with chastisement from Him, or at our hands
9:67 (68)	they keep their hands shut; they have forgotten
10:37 (38)	it is a confirmation of what is before it
11:70 (73)	when he saw their hands not reaching towards it
12:31 (31)	when they saw him, they so admired him that they cut their hands
12:50 (50)	what of the women who cut their hands
12:111 (111)	it is not a tale forged, but a confirmation of what is before it
13:11 (12)	he has attendant angels, before him and behind him
14:9 (10)	but they thrust their hands into their mouths saying
17:29 (31)	keep not thy hand chained to thy neck
18:57 (55)	turns away from them and forgets what his hands have forwarded
19:64 (65)	to Him belongs all that is before us
20:22 (23)	now clasp thy hand to thy arm-pit
20:71 (74)	I shall assuredly cut off alternately your hands and feet
20:110 (109)	He knows what is before them and behind them
21:28 (28)	He knows what is before them and behind them
22:10 (10)	that is for what thy hands have forwarded
22:76 (75)	He knows whatsoever is before them and behind them
23:88 (90)	in whose hand is the dominion of everything
24:24 (24)	the day when their tongues, their hands and their feet shall testify
24:40 (40)	when he puts forth his hand, wellnigh he cannot see it
25:27 (29)	upon the day the evildoer shall bite his hands
25:48 (50)	it is He who has loosed the winds, bearing good tidings before His mercy
26:33 (32)	he drew forth his hand, and lo, it was white
26:49 (49)	I shall assuredly cut off alternately your hands and feet
27:12 (12)	thrust thy hand in thy bosom
27:63 (64)	and looses the winds, bearing good tidings before His mercy
28:32 (32)	insert thy hand into thy bosom
28:47 (47)	for that their own hands have forwarded
30:36 (35)	if some evil befalls them for that their own hands have forwarded
30:41 (40)	corruption has appeared in the land and sea, for that men's own hands have earned
34:9 (9)	have they not regarded what lies before them
34:12 (11)	of the jinn, some worked before him
34:31 (30)	we will not believe in this Koran, nor in that before it
34:46 (45)	he is naught but a warner unto you, before a terrible chastisement
35:31 (28)	that We have revealed to thee of the Book is the truth, confirming what is before it
36:9 (8)	We have put before them a barrier
36:35 (35)	that they might eat of its fruits and their hands' labour
36:45 (45)	fear what is before you
36:65 (65)	today We set a seal on their mouths, and their hands speak to Us
36:71 (71)	of that Our hands wrought cattle that they own

36:83 (83)	glory be to Him, in whose hand is the dominion of everything
38:44 (43)	take in thy hand a bundle of rushes
38:75 (75)	to bow thyself before that I created with My own hands
41:14 (13)	when the Messengers came unto them from before them and from behind them
41:25 (24)	that which is before them and behind them
41:42 (42)	falsehood comes not to it from before it nor from behind it
42:30 (29)	whatever affliction may visit you is for what your own hands have earned
42:48 (47)	evil befalls him for that his own hands have forwarded
46:21 (20)	already warners had passed away alike before him and behind him
46:30 (29)	that was sent down after Moses, confirming what was before it
48:10 (10)	God's hand is over their (hands)
48:10 (10)	God's (hand) is over their hands
48:20 (20)	and has restrained the hands of men from you
48:24 (24)	it is He who restrained their hands from you
48:24 (24)	and your hands from them
49:1 (1)	O believers, advance not before God and His Messenger
57:12 (12)	their light running before them
57:29 (29)	and that bounty is in the hand of God
58:12 (13)	before your conspiring advance a freewill offering
58:13 (14)	are you afraid, before your conspiring, to advance freewill offerings?
59:2 (2)	as they destroyed their houses with their own hands
59:2 (2)	and the hands of the believers
60:2 (2)	and stretch against you their hands and their tongues, to do you evil
60:12 (12)	nor bring a calumny they forge between their hands and their feet
61:6 (6)	confirming the Torah that is before me
62:7 (7)	they will never long for it, because of that their hands have forwarded
66:8 (8)	their light running before them
67:1 (1)	blessed be He in whose hand is the Kingdom
72:27 (27)	then He despatches before him and behind him watchers
78:40 (41)	the day when a man shall behold what his hands have forwarded
80:15 (15)	by the hands of scribes
111:1 (1)	perish the hands of Abu Lahab, and perish he

*Y H D

YAHŪDĪ n.prop. (pl. *yahūd*)~Jews

2:113 (107)	the Jews say, 'The Christians stand not on anything'
2:113 (107)	the Jews stand not on anything
2:120 (114)	never will the Jews be satisfied with thee
3:67 (60)	Abraham in truth was not a Jew
5:18 (21)	say the Jews and Christians, 'We are the sons of God'
5:51 (56)	take not Jews and Christians as friends
5:64 (69)	the Jews have said, 'God's hand is fettered'
5:82 (85)	most hostile of men to the believers are the Jews
9:30 (30)	the Jews say, 'Ezra is the Son of God'

*Y J J

YA'JŪJ n.prop.~Gog

18:94 (93)	Gog and Magog are doing corruption
21:96 (96)	when Gog and Magog are unloosed, and they slide down out of every slope

*Y M M

YAMM n.m.~sea; river

7:136 (132)	We took vengeance on them, and drowned them in the sea
20:39 (39)	cast him into the ark, and cast him into the river
20:39 (39)	and let the river throw him up on the shore
20:78 (81)	but they were overwhelmed by the sea
20:97 (97)	We will surely burn it and scatter its ashes into the sea
28:7 (6)	when thou fearest for him, cast him into the sea
28:40 (40)	We seized him and his hosts, and cast them into the sea
51:40 (40)	We seized him and his hosts, and We cast them into the sea

TAYAMMAMA vb. (V)~to aim at getting, to intend; to have recourse to, to resort to, to head for

b) impf. act. (*tayammama*)

2:267 (269)	intend not the corrupt of it for your expending

c) impv. (*tayammam*)

4:43 (46)	then have recourse to wholesome dust
5:6 (9)	then have recourse to wholesome dust

*Y M N

AYMAN n.m.~right side, right

19:52 (53)	We called to him from the right side of the Mount
20:80 (82)	We made covenant with you upon the right side of the Mount
28:30 (30)	a voice cried from the right bank of the watercourse

MAYMANAH n.f.~right, right hand

56:8 (8)	Companions of the Right
56:8 (8)	O Companions of the Right
90:18 (18)	those are the Companions of the Right Hand

YAMĪN n.f. (pl. *aymān*)~right side, right hand; oath

2:224 (224)	do not make God a hindrance, through your oaths
2:225 (225)	God will not take you to task for a slip in your oaths
3:77 (71)	those that sell God's covenant, and their oaths, for a little price
4:3 (3)	then only one, or what your right hands own
4:24 (28)	and wedded women, save what your right hands own
4:25 (29)	let him take believing handmaids that your right hands own
4:33 (37)	and those with whom you have sworn compact
4:36 (40)	and to the traveller, and to that your right hands own
5:53 (58)	the ones who swore by God most earnest oaths
5:89 (91)	God will not take you to task for a slip in your oaths
5:89 (91)	but He will take you to task for such bonds as you have made by oaths
5:89 (91)	that is the expiation of your oaths when you have sworn
5:89 (91)	but keep your oaths
5:108 (107)	or else they will be afraid that after their oaths
5:108 (107)	oaths may be rebutted
6:109 (109)	they have sworn by God the most earnest oaths
7:17 (16)	from behind them, from their right hands and their left hands
9:12 (12)	but if they break their oaths after their covenant
9:12 (12)	they have no sacred oaths
9:13 (13)	will you not fight a people who broke their oaths

16:38 (40)	they have sworn by God the most earnest oaths
16:48 (50)	casting their shadows to the right and to the left
16:71 (73)	shall not give over their provision to that their right hands possess
16:91 (93)	break not the oaths after they have been confirmed
16:92 (94)	by taking your oaths as mere mutual deceit
16:94 (96)	take not your oaths as mere mutual deceit
17:71 (73)	whoso is given his book in his right hand
18:17 (16)	when it rose, inclining from their Cave towards the right
18:18 (17)	while We turned them now to the right, now to the left
20:17 (18)	what is that, Moses, thou hast in thy right hand?
20:69 (72)	cast down what is in thy right hand
23:6 (6)	save from their wives and what their right hands own
24:31 (31)	or what their right hands own
24:33 (33)	those your right hands own who seek emancipation
24:53 (52)	they have sworn by God the most earnest oaths
24:58 (57)	O believers, let those your right hands own
29:48 (47)	not before this didst thou recite any Book, or inscribe it with thy right hand
30:28 (27)	do you have, among that your right hands own, associates
33:50 (49)	and what thy right hand owns, spoils of war
33:50 (50)	touching their wives and what their right hands own
33:52 (52)	though their beauty please thee, except what thy right hand owns
33:55 (55)	their women, and what their right hands own
34:15 (14)	two gardens, one on the right and one on the left
35:42 (40)	they have sworn by God the most earnest oaths
37:28 (28)	you of old would come to us from the right hand
37:93 (91)	he turned upon them smiting them with his right hand
39:67 (67)	and the heavens shall be rolled up in His right hand
50:17 (16)	sitting one on the right, and one on the left
56:27 (26)	the Companions of the Right
56:27 (26)	O Companions of the Right
56:38 (37)	for the Companions of the Right
56:90 (89)	and if he be a Companion of the Right
56:91 (90)	peace be upon thee, Companion of the Right
57:12 (12)	their light running before them, and on their right hands
58:16 (17)	they have taken their oaths as a covering
63:2 (2)	they have taken their oaths as a covering
66:2 (2)	God has ordained for you the absolution of your oaths
66:8 (8)	their light running before them, and on their right hands
68:39 (39)	or have you oaths from Us
69:19 (19)	then as for him who is given his book in his right hand
69:45 (45)	We would have seized him by the right hand
70:30 (30)	save from their wives and what their right hands own
70:37 (37)	on the right hand and on the left hand in knots
74:39 (41)	save the Companions of the Right
84:7 (7)	as for him who is given his book in his right hand

*Y N ᶜ

YANAᶜA vb. (I)~(n.vb.) ripeness

f) n.vb. (*yanᶜ*)

6:99 (99)	look upon their fruits when they fructify and ripen

*Y Q N

YAQĪN n.m.~certainty; the Certain; (adv) surely, certainly, of a certainty

4:157 (156)	they slew him not of a certainty
15:99 (99)	serve thy Lord, until the Certain comes to thee
27:22 (22)	I have come from Sheba to thee with a sure tiding
56:95 (95)	surely this is the truth of certainty
69:51 (51)	yet indeed it is the truth of certainty
74:47 (48)	till the Certain came to us
102:5 (5)	did you know with the knowledge of certainty
102:7 (7)	you shall surely see it with the eye of certainty

AYQANA vb. (IV)~to be sure, to be certain, to ascertain; to have sure faith. (pcple. act.) one who has sure faith, one who is certain

b) impf. act. (*yūqinu*)

2:4 (3)	and have faith in the Hereafter
2:118 (112)	We have made clear the signs unto a people who are sure
5:50 (55)	who is fairer in judgment than God, for a people having sure faith?
13:2 (2)	haply you will have faith in the encounter with your Lord
27:3 (3)	who perform the prayer, and pay the alms, and have sure faith
27:82 (84)	mankind had no faith in Our signs
30:60 (60)	let not those who have not sure faith make thee unsteady
31:4 (3)	who perform the prayer, and pay the alms, and have sure faith
32:24 (24)	and had sure faith in Our signs
45:4 (3)	there are signs for a people having sure faith
45:20 (19)	a guidance, and a mercy to a people having sure faith
52:36 (36)	nay, but they have not sure faith

g) pcple. act. (*mūqin*)

6:75 (75)	that he might be of those having sure faith
26:24 (23)	the Lord of the heavens and earth, and what between them is, if you have faith
32:12 (12)	now return us, that we may do righteousness, for we have sure faith
44:7 (6)	Lord of the heavens and earth, and all that between them is, if you have faith
51:20 (20)	in the earth are signs for those having sure faith

ISTAYQANA vb. (X)~to ascertain, to have certainty; to acknowledge. (pcple. act.) one who is certain

a) perf. act.

27:14 (14)	they denied them, though their souls acknowledged them

b) impf. act. (*yastayqinu*)

74:31 (31)	that those who were given the Book may have certainty

g) pcple. act. (*mustayqin*)

45:32 (31)	we have only a surmise, and are by no means certain

*Y Q T

YĀQŪT n.m. (coll)~rubies

55:58 (58)	lovely as rubies, beautiful as coral

*Y Q Ẓ

AYQĀẒ n.m. (pl. of *yaquẓ*)~awake

18:18 (17)	thou wouldst have thought them awake

*Y S

YĀ SĪN~ml

36:1 (1)	Ya Sin

*Y S ᶜ

ALYASAᶜ n.prop.~Elisha

6:86 (86)	Ishmael and Elisha, Jonah and Lot
38:48 (48)	remember also Our servants Ishmael, Elisha, and Dhul Kifl

*Y S F

YŪSUF n.prop.~Joseph

6:84 (84)	and of his seed David and Solomon, Job and Joseph
12:4 (4)	when Joseph said to his father
12:7 (7)	in Joseph and his brethren were signs for those who ask questions
12:8 (8)	surely Joseph and his brother are dearer to our father than we
12:9 (9)	kill you Joseph, or cast him forth into some land
12:10 (10)	kill not Joseph, but cast him into the bottom of the pit
12:11 (11)	what ails thee, that thou trustest us not with Joseph?
12:17 (17)	we went running races, and left Joseph behind with our things
12:21 (21)	so We established Joseph in the land
12:29 (29)	Joseph, turn away from this
12:46 (46)	Joseph, thou true man, pronounce to us regarding seven fat kine
12:51 (51)	what was your business, women, when you solicited Joseph
12:56 (56)	so We established Joseph in the land
12:58 (58)	the brethren of Joseph came, and entered unto him
12:69 (69)	when they entered unto Joseph
12:76 (76)	so We contrived for Joseph's sake
12:77 (77)	Joseph secreted it in his soul and disclosed it not to them
12:80 (80)	and aforetime you failed regarding Joseph
12:84 (84)	ah, woe is me for Joseph
12:85 (85)	thou wilt never cease mentioning Joseph till thou art consumed
12:87 (87)	depart, my sons, and search out tidings of Joseph and his brother
12:89 (89)	are you aware of what you did with Joseph and his brother
12:90 (90)	why, art thou indeed Joseph?
12:90 (90)	I am Joseph
12:94 (94)	surely I perceive Joseph's scent
12:99 (100)	when they entered unto Joseph, he took his father and mother into his arms
40:34 (36)	Joseph brought you the clear signs before

*Y S R

YASURA vb. (I)~(n.vb.) ease, easiness; prosperity; (adv) smoothly, easily. (pcple. pass.) easy, gentle, kind

f) n.vb. (*yusr*)

2:185 (181)	God desires ease for you, and desires not hardship

18:88 (87)	we shall speak to him, of our command, easiness
51:3 (3)	and the smooth runners
65:4 (4)	whoso fears God, God will appoint for him, of His command, easiness
65:7 (7)	God will assuredly appoint, after difficulty, easiness
94:5 (5)	so truly with hardship comes ease
94:6 (6)	truly with hardship comes ease

h) pcple. pass. (*maysūr*)

17:28 (30)	then speak unto them gentle words

MAYSARAH n.f.~time of ease and prosperity

2:280 (280)	let him have respite till things are easier

MAYSIR n.m.~arrow-shuffling (a game of chance)

2:219 (216)	they will question thee concerning wine, and arrow-shuffling
5:90 (92)	arrow-shuffling, idols and divining-arrows are an abomination
5:91 (93)	Satan only desires to precipitate enmity and hatred between you in regard to wine and arrow-shuffling

YASĪR n.m.~(adj) easy; gentle; small; (adv) briefly, for a little while

4:30 (34)	and that for God is an easy matter
4:169 (167)	and that for God is an easy matter
12:65 (65)	we shall obtain an extra camel's load — that is an easy measure
22:70 (69)	surely that for God is an easy matter
25:46 (48)	thereafter We seize it to Ourselves, drawing it gently
29:19 (18)	that is an easy matter for God
33:14 (14)	they would have done so, and but tarried about it briefly
33:19 (19)	God has made their works to fail; and that is easy for God
33:30 (30)	the chastisement shall be doubled; that is easy for God
35:11 (12)	surely that is easy for God
50:44 (43)	that is a mustering easy for Us
57:22 (22)	that is easy for God
64:7 (7)	that is easy for God
74:10 (10)	for the unbelievers not easy
84:8 (8)	he shall surely receive an easy reckoning

YUSRÁ n.f.~easing, state of ease

87:8 (8)	We shall ease thee unto the Easing
92:7 (7)	We shall surely ease him to the Easing

YASSARA vb. (II)~to make easy, to ease, to facilitate

a) perf. act.

19:97 (97)	now We have made it easy by thy tongue
44:58 (58)	now We have made it easy by thy tongue
54:17 (17)	now We have made the Koran easy for Remembrance
54:22 (22)	now We have made the Koran easy for Remembrance
54:32 (32)	now We have made the Koran easy for Remembrance
54:40 (40)	now We have made the Koran easy for Remembrance
80:20 (20)	then the way eased for him

b) impf. act. (*yuyassiru*)

87:8 (8)	We shall ease thee unto the Easing
92:7 (7)	We shall surely ease him to the Easing
92:10 (10)	We shall surely ease him to the Hardship

c) impv. (*yassir*)

20:26 (27)	and do Thou ease for me my task

TAYASSARA vb. (V)~to be easy; to be feasible

a) perf. act.

73:20 (20)	recite of the Koran so much as is feasible
73:20 (20)	recite of it so much as is feasible

ISTAYSARA vb. (X)~to be easy; to be feasible

a) perf. act.

2:196 (192)	but if you are prevented, then such offering as may be feasible
2:196 (192)	let his offering be such as may be feasible

*Y T M

YATĪM n.m. (pl. *yatāmá*)~orphan

2:83 (77)	to be good to parents, and the near kinsman, and to orphans
2:177 (172)	to give of one's substance, however cherished, to kinsmen, and orphans
2:215 (211)	whatsoever good you expend is for parents and kinsmen, orphans
2:220 (218)	they will question thee concerning the orphans
4:2 (2)	give the orphans their property
4:3 (3)	if you fear that you will not act justly towards the orphans
4:6 (5)	test well the orphans, until they reach the age of marrying
4:8 (9)	when the division is attended by kinsmen and orphans and the poor
4:10 (11)	those who devour the property of orphans unjustly
4:36 (40)	be kind to parents, and the near kinsman, and to orphans
4:127 (126)	what is recited to you in the Book concerning the orphan women
4:127 (126)	and that you secure justice for orphans
6:152 (153)	that you approach not the property of the orphan
8:41 (42)	fifth of it is God's, and the Messenger's, and the near kinsman's, and the orphans'
17:34 (36)	do not approach the property of the orphan
18:82 (81)	as for the wall, it belonged to two orphan lads in the city
59:7 (7)	belongs to God, and His Messenger, and the near kinsman, orphans
76:8 (8)	they give food, for the love of Him, to the needy, the orphan
89:17 (18)	but you honour not the orphan
90:15 (15)	to an orphan near of kin
93:6 (6)	did He not find thee an orphan, and shelter thee?
93:9 (9)	as for the orphan, do not oppress him
107:2 (2)	that is he who repulses the orphan

*Y TH R B

YATHRIB n.prop.~Yathrib (the earlier name for Medina)

33:13 (13)	O people of Yathrib, there is no abiding here for you

*Y W M

YAWM n.m. (pl. *ayyām*)~a day; (*al-yawm*) today, this day; (*yawmaʾidhin*) that day, then

1:4 (3)	the Master of the Day of Doom
2:8 (7)	we believe in God and the Last Day'
2:48 (45)	beware of a day when no soul for another shall give satisfaction
2:62 (59)	whoso believes in God and the Last Day
2:80 (74)	the Fire shall not touch us save a number of days
2:85 (79)	and on the Day of Resurrection to be returned
2:113 (107)	God shall decide between them on the Day of Resurrection
2:123 (117)	beware a day when no soul for another shall give satisfaction
2:126 (120)	such of them as believe in God and the Last Day
2:174 (169)	God shall not speak to them on the Day of Resurrection
2:177 (172)	to believe in God, and the Last Day
2:184 (180)	for days numbered
2:184 (180)	or if he be on a journey, then a number of other days
2:185 (181)	or if he be on a journey, then a number of other days
2:196 (192)	if he finds none, then a fast of three days in the Pilgrimage
2:203 (199)	remember God during certain days numbered
2:203 (199)	if any man hastens on in two days, that is no sin in him
2:212 (208)	those who were godfearing shall be above them on the Resurrection Day
2:228 (228)	if they believe in God and the Last Day
2:232 (232)	whoso of you believes in God and the Last Day
2:249 (250)	we have no power today against Goliath and his hosts
2:254 (255)	there comes a day wherein shall be neither traffick, nor friendship
2:259 (261)	I have tarried a day
2:259 (261)	or part of a day
2:264 (266)	and believes not in God and the Last Day
2:281 (281)	and fear a day wherein you shall be returned to God
3:9 (7)	it is Thou that shall gather mankind for a day whereon is no doubt
3:24 (23)	the Fire shall not touch us, except for a number of days'
3:25 (24)	how will it be, when We gather them for a day whereon is no doubt
3:30 (28)	the day every soul shall find what it has done of good
3:41 (36)	thou shalt not speak, save by tokens, to men for three days
3:55 (48)	I will set thy followers above the unbelievers till the Resurrection Day
3:77 (71)	God shall not speak to them neither look on them on the Resurrection Day
3:106 (102)	the day when some faces are blackened, and some faces whitened
3:114 (110)	believing in God and in the Last Day
3:140 (134)	such days We deal out in turn among men
3:155 (149)	those of you who turned away the day the two hosts encountered
3:161 (155)	whoso defrauds shall bring the fruits of his fraud on the Day of Resurrection
3:166 (160)	what visited you, the day the two hosts encountered, was by God's leave
3:167 (160)	they that day were nearer to unbelief than to belief
3:180 (176)	hung about their necks on the Resurrection Day
3:185 (182)	you shall surely be paid in full your wages on the Day of Resurrection
3:194 (192)	abase us not on the Day of Resurrection
4:38 (42)	believe not in God and the Last Day
4:39 (43)	what would it harm them, if they believed in God and the Last Day
4:42 (45)	upon that day the unbelievers, those who have disobeyed the Messenger, will wish
4:59 (62)	if you believe in God and the Last Day; that is better
4:87 (89)	He will surely gather you to the Resurrection Day
4:109 (109)	who will dispute with God on their behalf on the Resurrection Day
4:136 (135)	His Books, and His Messengers, and the Last Day
4:141 (140)	God will judge between you on the Resurrection Day
4:159 (157)	on the Resurrection Day he will be a witness against them

4:162 (160)	those who believe in God and the Last Day
5:3 (4)	today the unbelievers have despaired of your religion
5:3 (5)	today I have perfected your religion for you
5:5 (7)	today the good things are permitted you
5:14 (17)	We have stirred up among them enmity and hatred, till the Day of Resurrection
5:36 (40)	to ransom themselves from the chastisement of the Day of Resurrection
5:64 (69)	We have cast between them enmity and hatred, till the Day of Resurrection
5:69 (73)	whosoever believes in God and the Last Day
5:89 (91)	if any finds not the means, let him fast for three days
5:109 (108)	the day when God shall gather the Messengers
5:119 (119)	this is the day the truthful shall be profited
6:12 (12)	He will surely gather you to the Resurrection Day
6:15 (15)	I fear, if I should rebel against my Lord, the chastisement of a dreadful day
6:16 (16)	from whomsoever it is averted on that day
6:22 (22)	on the day when We shall muster them all together
6:73 (72)	the day He says 'Be', and it is
6:73 (73)	His saying is true, and His is the Kingdom the day the Trumpet is blown
6:93 (93)	today you shall be recompensed with the chastisement of humiliation
6:128 (128)	on the day when He shall muster them all together
6:130 (130)	and warning you of the encounter of this your day
6:141 (142)	pay the due thereof on the day of its harvest
6:158 (159)	on the day that one of thy Lord's signs comes
7:8 (7)	the weighing that day is true
7:14 (13)	respite me till the day they shall be raised
7:32 (30)	these, on the Day of Resurrection, shall be exclusively for those who believed
7:51 (49)	therefore today We forget them
7:51 (49)	as they forgot the encounter of this their day
7:53 (51)	the day its interpretation comes, those who before forgot it shall say
7:54 (52)	your Lord is God, who created the heavens and the earth in six days
7:59 (57)	I fear for you the chastisement of a dreadful day
7:163 (163)	when their fish came to them on the day of their Sabbath
7:163 (163)	but on the day they kept not Sabbath
7:167 (166)	thy Lord proclaimed He would send forth against them, unto the Day of Resurrection
7:172 (171)	lest you should say on the Day of Resurrection
8:16 (16)	whoso turns his back that day to them
8:41 (42)	if you believe in God and that We sent down upon Our servant on the day of salvation
8:41 (42)	the day the two hosts encountered
8:48 (50)	today no man shall overcome you
9:3 (3)	unto mankind on the day of the Greater Pilgrimage
9:18 (18)	who believes in God and the Last Day
9:19 (19)	as one who believes in God and the Last Day
9:25 (25)	God has already helped you on many fields, and on the day of Hunain
9:29 (29)	fight those who believe not in God and the Last Day
9:35 (35)	the day they shall be heated in the fire of Gehenna
9:36 (36)	the day that He created the heavens and the earth
9:44 (44)	those who believe in God and the Last Day ask not leave of thee
9:45 (45)	they only ask leave of thee who believe not in God and the Last Day
9:77 (78)	He put hypocrisy into their hearts, until the day they meet Him
9:99 (100)	some of the Bedouins believe in God and the Last Day
9:108 (109)	a mosque that was founded upon godfearing from the first day
10:3 (3)	your Lord is God, who created the heavens and the earth in six days
10:15 (16)	I fear, if I should rebel against my Lord, the chastisement of a dreadful day
10:28 (29)	the day We shall muster them all
10:45 (46)	the day He shall muster them, as if they had not tarried

10:60 (61)	what will they think, who forge falsehood against God, on the Day of Resurrection?
10:92 (92)	today We shall deliver thee with thy body
10:93 (93)	thy Lord will decide between them on the Day of Resurrection
10:102 (102)	but the like of the days of those who passed away before them
11:3 (3)	I fear for you the chastisement of a mighty day
11:7 (9)	it is He who created the heavens and the earth in six days
11:8 (11)	the day it shall come to them, it shall not be turned aside
11:26 (28)	I fear for you the chastisement of a painful day
11:43 (45)	today there is no defender from God's command
11:60 (63)	there was sent following after them in this world a curse, and upon the Day of Resurrection
11:65 (68)	take your joy in your habitation three days
11:66 (69)	mercy from Us, and from the degradation of that day
11:77 (79)	this is a fierce day
11:84 (85)	I fear for you the chastisement of an encompassing day
11:98 (100)	He shall go before his people on the Day of Resurrection
11:99 (101)	there was sent following after them in this world a curse, and upon the Day of Resurrection
11:103 (105)	that is a day mankind are to be gathered to
11:103 (105)	a day to witness
11:105 (107)	the day it comes, no soul shall speak save by His leave
12:54 (54)	today thou art established firmly in our favour
12:92 (92)	no reproach this day shall be on you
14:5 (5)	and remind thou them of the Days of God
14:18 (21)	whereon the wind blows strong upon a tempestuous day
14:31 (36)	a day comes wherein shall be neither bargaining
14:41 (42)	upon the day when the reckoning shall come to pass
14:42 (43)	He is only deferring them to a day when eyes shall stare
14:44 (44)	warn mankind of the day when the chastisement comes on them
14:48 (49)	upon the day the earth shall be changed to other than the earth
14:49 (50)	thou shalt see the sinners that day coupled in fetters
15:35 (35)	upon thee shall rest the curse, till the Day of Doom
15:36 (36)	respite me till the day they shall be raised
15:38 (38)	unto the day of a known time
16:25 (27)	that they may bear their loads complete on the Day of Resurrection
16:27 (29)	then on the Day of Resurrection He will degrade them
16:27 (29)	degradation today and evil are on the unbelievers
16:63 (65)	he is their protector today
16:80 (82)	you find light on the day that you journey
16:80 (82)	and on the day you abide
16:84 (86)	the day We shall raise up from every nation a witness
16:87 (89)	they will offer God surrender that day
16:89 (91)	the day We shall raise up from every nation a witness
16:92 (94)	He will make clear to you upon the Day of Resurrection
16:111 (112)	the day that every soul shall come disputing
16:124 (125)	thy Lord will decide between them on the Day of Resurrection
17:13 (14)	We shall bring forth for him, on the Day of Resurrection, a book
17:14 (15)	thy soul suffices thee this day as a reckoner against thee
17:52 (54)	on the day when He will call you
17:58 (60)	no city is there, but We shall destroy it before the Day of Resurrection
17:62 (64)	if Thou deferrest me to the Day of Resurrection
17:71 (73)	on the day when We shall call all men
17:97 (99)	We shall muster them on the Resurrection Day
18:19 (18)	we have tarried a day

18:19 (18)	or part of a day
18:47 (45)	on the day We shall set the mountains in motion
18:52 (50)	on the day He shall say, 'Call on My associates'
18:99 (99)	upon that day We shall leave them surging on one another
18:100 (100)	upon that day We shall present Gehenna to the unbelievers
18:105 (105)	on the Day of Resurrection We shall not assign to them any weight
19:15 (15)	peace be upon him, the day he was born
19:15 (15)	and the day he dies
19:15 (15)	and the day he is raised up alive
19:26 (27)	today I will not speak to any man
19:33 (34)	peace be upon me, the day I was born
19:33 (34)	and the day I die
19:33 (34)	and the day I am raised up alive
19:37 (38)	woe to those who disbelieve for the scene of a dreadful day
19:38 (39)	how well they will hear and see on the day they come to Us
19:38 (39)	the evildoers even today are in error manifest
19:39 (40)	warn thou them of the day of anguish
19:85 (88)	on the day that We shall muster the godfearing to the All-merciful
19:95 (95)	every one of them shall come to Him upon the Day of Resurrection
20:59 (61)	your tryst shall be upon the Feast Day
20:64 (67)	whoever today gains the upper hand shall surely prosper
20:100 (100)	whosoever turns away from it, upon the Day of Resurrection
20:101 (101)	how evil upon the Day of Resurrection that burden for them
20:102 (102)	on the day the Trumpet is blown
20:102 (102)	We shall muster the sinners upon that day with eyes staring
20:104 (104)	you have tarried only a day
20:108 (107)	on that day they will follow the Summoner
20:109 (108)	upon that day the intercession will not profit
20:124 (124)	on the Resurrection Day We shall raise him blind
20:126 (126)	so today thou art forgotten
21:47 (48)	We shall set up the just balances for the Resurrection Day
21:103 (103)	this is your day that you were promised
21:104 (104)	on the day when We shall roll up heaven as a scroll
22:2 (2)	on the day when you behold it
22:9 (9)	on the Resurrection Day We shall let him taste the chastisement
22:17 (17)	God shall distinguish between them on the Day of Resurrection
22:28 (29)	mention God's Name on days well-known
22:47 (46)	a day with thy Lord is as a thousand years of your counting
22:55 (54)	or there shall come upon them the chastisement of a barren day
22:56 (55)	the Kingdom upon that day shall belong to God
22:69 (68)	God shall judge between you on the Day of Resurrection
23:16 (16)	on the Day of Resurrection you shall surely be raised up
23:65 (67)	groan not today
23:100 (102)	behind them, is a barrier until the day that they shall be raised up
23:101 (103)	when the Trumpet is blown, that day there shall be no kinship
23:111 (113)	today I have recompensed them for their patient endurance
23:113 (115)	we have tarried a day
23:113 (115)	or part of a day; ask the numberers
24:2 (2)	if you believe in God and the Last Day
24:24 (24)	on the day when their tongues, their hands and their feet shall testify
24:25 (25)	upon that day God will pay them in full their just due
24:37 (37)	fearing a day when hearts and eyes shall be turned about
24:64 (64)	the day when they shall be returned to Him
25:14 (15)	call not out today for one destruction
25:17 (18)	upon the day when He shall muster them and that they serve

25:22 (24)	upon the day that they see the angels
25:22 (24)	no good tidings that day for the sinners
25:24 (26)	the inhabitants of Paradise that day
25:25 (27)	upon the day that heaven is split asunder with the clouds
25:26 (28)	that day, the true Kingdom, shall belong to the All-merciful
25:26 (28)	it shall be a day harsh for the unbelievers
25:27 (29)	upon the day the evildoer shall bite his hands
25:59 (60)	who created the heavens and the earth, and what between them is, in six days
25:69 (69)	doubled shall be the chastisement for him on the Resurrection Day
26:38 (37)	the sorcerers were assembled for the appointed time of a fixed day
26:82 (82)	who I am eager shall forgive me my offence on the Day of Doom
26:87 (87)	degrade me not upon the day when they are raised up
26:88 (88)	the day when neither wealth nor sons shall profit
26:135 (135)	I fear for you the chastisement of a dreadful day
26:155 (155)	to her a draught and to you a draught, on a day appointed
26:156 (156)	so that there seize you the chastisement of a dreadful day
26:189 (189)	then there seized them the chastisement of the Day of Shadow
26:189 (189)	assuredly it was the chastisement of a dreadful day
27:83 (85)	upon the day when We shall muster out of every nation a troop
27:87 (89)	on the day the Trumpet is blown
27:89 (91)	they shall be secure from terror that day
28:41 (41)	on the Day of Resurrection they shall not be helped
28:42 (42)	on the Day of Resurrection they shall be among the spurned
28:61 (61)	he on the Resurrection Day shall be of those that are arraigned
28:62 (62)	upon the day when He shall call to them
28:65 (65)	upon the day when He shall call to them
28:66 (66)	upon that day the tidings will be darkened for them
28:71 (71)	the night unceasing over you, until the Day of Resurrection
28:72 (72)	the day unceasing over you, until the Day of Resurrection
28:74 (74)	upon the day when He shall call to them
29:13 (12)	upon the Day of Resurrection they shall surely be questioned
29:25 (24)	upon the Day of Resurrection you will deny one another
29:36 (35)	serve God, and look you for the Last Day
29:55 (55)	upon the day the chastisement shall overwhelm them
30:4 (3)	on that day the believers shall rejoice
30:12 (11)	upon the day when the Hour is come, the sinners shall be confounded
30:14 (13)	upon the day when the Hour is come
30:14 (13)	that day they shall be divided
30:43 (42)	before there comes a day from God that cannot be turned back
30:43 (42)	on that day they shall be sundered apart
30:55 (54)	upon the day when the Hour is come, the sinners shall swear
30:56 (56)	you have tarried in God's Book till the Day of the Upraising
30:56 (56)	this is the Day of the Upraising, but you did not know
30:57 (57)	that day their excuses will not profit the evildoers
31:33 (32)	dread a day when no father shall give satisfaction for his child
32:4 (3)	God is He that created the heavens and the earth, and what between them is, in six days
32:5 (4)	then it goes up to Him in one day
32:14 (14)	so now taste, for that you forgot the encounter of this your day
32:25 (25)	thy Lord will distinguish between them on the Resurrection Day
32:29 (29)	on the Day of Victory their faith shall not profit the unbelievers
33:21 (21)	whosoever hopes for God and the Last Day, and remembers God oft
33:44 (43)	on the day when they shall meet Him
33:66 (66)	upon the day when their faces are turned about in the Fire

34:18 (17)	journey among them by night and day in security
34:30 (29)	you have the tryst of a day
34:40 (39)	upon the day when He shall muster them all together
34:42 (41)	today none of you shall have power to profit
35:14 (15)	on the Day of Resurrection they will disown your partnership
36:54 (54)	today no soul shall be wronged anything
36:55 (55)	the inhabitants of Paradise today are busy in their rejoicing
36:59 (59)	now keep yourselves apart, you sinners, upon this day
36:64 (64)	roast well in it today, for that you were unbelievers
36:65 (65)	today We set a seal on their mouths, and their hands speak to Us
37:20 (20)	woe, alas for us! This is the Day of Doom
37:21 (21)	this is the Day of Decision, even that you cried lies to
37:26 (26)	today they resign themselves in submission
37:33 (32)	all of them on that day are sharers in the chastisement
37:144 (144)	he would have tarried in its belly until the day they shall be raised
38:16 (15)	hasten to us our share before the Day of Reckoning
38:26 (25)	for that they have forgotten the Day of Reckoning
38:53 (53)	this is what you were promised for the Day of Reckoning
38:78 (79)	upon thee shall rest My curse, till the Day of Doom
38:79 (80)	respite me till the day they shall be raised
38:81 (82)	until the day of the known time
39:13 (15)	I fear, if I should rebel against my Lord, the chastisement of a dreadful day
39:15 (17)	lose themselves and their families on the Day of Resurrection
39:24 (25)	against the evil of the chastisement on the Day of Resurrection
39:31 (32)	then on the Day of Resurrection before your Lord you shall dispute
39:47 (48)	ransom themselves from the evil of the chastisement on the Day of Resurrection
39:60 (61)	upon the Day of Resurrection thou shalt see those who lied against God
39:67 (67)	the earth altogether shall be His handful on the Day of Resurrection
39:71 (71)	and warning you against the encounter of this your day
40:9 (9)	whomsoever Thou guardest against evil deeds on that day
40:15 (15)	that he may warn them of the Day of Encounter
40:16 (16)	the day they sally forth, and naught of theirs is hidden
40:16 (16)	whose is the Kingdom today
40:17 (17)	today each soul shall be recompensed for that it has earned
40:17 (17)	no wrong today
40:18 (18)	warn them against the Day of the Imminent
40:27 (28)	who is proud, and believes not in the Day of Reckoning
40:29 (30)	today the kingdom is yours, who are masters in the land
40:30 (31)	I fear for you the like of the day of the parties
40:32 (34)	O my people, I fear for you the Day of Invocation
40:33 (35)	the day you turn about, retreating
40:46 (49)	and on the day when the Hour is come
40:49 (52)	call on your Lord, to lighten for us one day of the chastisement
40:51 (54)	upon the day when the witnesses arise
40:52 (55)	upon the day when their excuses shall not profit the evildoers
41:9 (8)	do you disbelieve in Him who created the earth in two days
41:10 (9)	He ordained therein its diverse sustenance in four days
41:12 (11)	He determined them as seven heavens in two days
41:16 (15)	then We loosed against them a wind clamorous in days of ill fortune
41:19 (18)	upon the day when God's enemies are mustered to the Fire
41:40 (40)	he who comes on the Day of Resurrection in security
41:47 (47)	upon the day when He shall call to them
42:7 (5)	that thou mayest warn of the Day of Gathering
42:45 (44)	they who lose themselves and their families on the Day of Resurrection
42:47 (46)	answer your Lord, before there comes a day from God that cannot be turned back

42:47 (46)	upon that day you shall have no shelter, no denial
43:39 (38)	it shall not profit you today, since you did evil
43:65 (65)	woe unto those who did evil, because of the chastisement of a painful day
43:67 (67)	friends on that day shall be foes to one another
43:68 (68)	O My servants, today no fear is on you
43:83 (83)	until they encounter that day of theirs
44:10 (9)	be on the watch for a day when heaven shall bring a manifest smoke
44:16 (15)	upon the day when We shall assault most mightily
44:40 (40)	the Day of Decision shall be their appointed time
44:41 (41)	the day a master shall avail nothing a client
45:14 (13)	those who do not look for the days of God
45:17 (16)	thy Lord will decide between them on the Day of Resurrection
45:26 (25)	He shall gather you to the Day of Resurrection
45:27 (26)	on the day when the Hour is come
45:27 (26)	upon that day the vain-doers shall lose
45:28 (27)	today you shall be recompensed for that you were doing
45:34 (33)	today We do forget you
45:34 (33)	even as you forgot the encounter of this your day
45:35 (34)	today they shall not be brought forth from it
46:5 (4)	upon such a one as shall not answer him till the Day of Resurrection
46:20 (19)	upon the day when the unbelievers are exposed to the Fire
46:20 (19)	today you shall be recompensed with the chastisement of humiliation
46:21 (20)	I fear for you the chastisement of a dreadful day
46:34 (33)	upon the day when the unbelievers are exposed to the Fire
46:35 (34)	on the day they see that they are promised
50:20 (19)	the Trumpet shall be blown; that is the Day of the Threat
50:22 (21)	so thy sight today is piercing
50:30 (29)	upon the day We shall say unto Gehenna
50:34 (33)	this is the Day of Eternity
50:38 (37)	We created the heavens and the earth, and what between them is, in six days
50:41 (40)	listen thou for the day when the caller shall call from a near place
50:42 (41)	on the day they hear the Cry in truth
50:42 (41)	that is the day of coming forth
50:44 (43)	upon the day when the earth is split asunder from about them
51:12 (12)	when shall be the Day of Doom?
51:13 (13)	upon the day when they shall be tried at the Fire
51:60 (60)	woe to the unbelievers, for that day of theirs that they are promised
52:9 (9)	upon the day when heaven spins dizzily
52:11 (11)	woe that day unto those that cry lies
52:13 (13)	the day when they shall be pitched into the fire of Gehenna
52:45 (45)	then leave them, till they encounter their day
52:46 (46)	the day when their guile shall avail them naught
54:6 (6)	upon the day when the Caller shall call unto a horrible thing
54:8 (8)	this is a hard day
54:19 (19)	We loosed against them a wind clamorous in a day of ill fortune continuous
54:48 (48)	the day when they are dragged on their faces into the Fire
55:29 (29)	every day He is upon some labour
55:39 (39)	on that day none shall be questioned about his sin
56:50 (50)	shall be gathered to the appointed time of a known day
56:56 (56)	this shall be their hospitality on the Day of Doom
57:4 (4)	it is He that created the heavens and the earth in six days
57:12 (12)	upon the day when thou seest the believers, men and women
57:12 (12)	good tidings for you today
57:13 (13)	upon the day when the hypocrites, men and women, shall say
57:15 (14)	today no ransom shall be taken from you

58:6 (7)	upon the day when God shall raise them up all
58:7 (8)	then He shall tell them what they have done, on the Day of Resurrection
58:18 (19)	upon the day when God shall raise them up all
58:22 (22)	thou shalt not find any people who believe in God and the Last Day
60:3 (3)	nor your children shall profit you upon the Day of Resurrection
60:6 (6)	whoever hopes for God and the Last Day
62:9 (9)	when proclamation is made for prayer on the Day of Congregation
64:9 (9)	upon the day when He shall gather you
64:9 (9)	for the Day of Gathering
64:9 (9)	that shall be the Day of Mutual Fraud
65:2 (2)	by this then is admonished whosoever believes in God and the Last Day
66:7 (7)	O you unbelievers, do not excuse yourselves today
66:8 (8)	upon the day when God will not degrade the Prophet
68:24 (24)	no needy man shall enter it today against your will
68:39 (39)	have you oaths from Us, reaching to the Day of Resurrection
68:42 (42)	upon the day when the leg shall be bared
69:7 (7)	He compelled against them seven nights and eight days
69:15 (15)	on that day, the Terror shall come to pass
69:16 (16)	heaven shall be split, for upon that day it shall be very frail
69:17 (17)	upon that day eight shall carry above them the Throne of thy Lord
69:18 (18)	on that day you shall be exposed
69:24 (24)	for that you did long ago, in the days gone by
69:35 (35)	therefore he today has not here one loyal friend
70:4 (4)	to Him the angels and the Spirit mount up in a day
70:8 (8)	upon the day when heaven shall be as molten copper
70:11 (11)	might ransom himself from the chastisement of that day even by his sons
70:26 (26)	who confirm the Day of Doom
70:42 (42)	until they encounter that day of theirs
70:43 (43)	the day they shall come forth from the tombs hastily
70:44 (44)	that is the day which they were promised
73:14 (14)	upon the day when the earth and the mountains shall quake
73:17 (17)	how will you guard yourselves against a day that shall make the children grey-headed?
74:9 (9)	that day will be a harsh (day)
74:9 (9)	that (day) will be a harsh day
74:46 (47)	we cried lies to the Day of Doom
75:1 (1)	no! I swear by the Day of Resurrection
75:6 (6)	when shall be the Day of Resurrection?
75:10 (10)	upon that day man shall say, 'Whither to flee?'
75:12 (12)	upon that day the recourse shall be to thy Lord
75:13 (13)	upon that day man shall be told his former deeds and his latter
75:22 (22)	upon that day faces shall be radiant
75:24 (24)	upon that day faces shall be scowling
75:30 (30)	upon that day unto thy Lord shall be the driving
76:7 (7)	they fulfil their vows, and fear a day whose evil is upon the wing
76:10 (10)	for we fear from our Lord a frowning day
76:11 (11)	God has guarded them from the evil of that day
76:27 (27)	these men love the hasty world, and leave behind them a heavy day
77:12 (12)	to what day shall they be delayed?
77:13 (13)	to the Day of Decision
77:14 (14)	what shall teach thee what is the Day of Decision?
77:15 (15)	woe that day unto those who cry it lies
77:19 (19)	woe that day unto those who cry it lies
77:24 (24)	woe that day unto those who cry it lies
77:28 (28)	woe that day unto those who cry it lies

77:34 (34)	woe that day unto those who cry it lies
77:35 (35)	this is the day they shall not speak
77:37 (37)	woe that day unto those who cry it lies
77:38 (38)	this is the Day of Decision
77:40 (40)	woe that day unto those who cry it lies
77:45 (45)	woe that day unto those who cry it lies
77:47 (47)	woe that day unto those who cry it lies
77:49 (49)	woe that day unto those who cry it lies
78:17 (17)	surely the Day of Decision is an appointed time
78:18 (18)	the day the Trumpet is blown, and you shall come in troops
78:38 (38)	upon the day when the Spirit and the angels stand in ranks
78:39 (39)	that is the true day
78:40 (41)	upon the day when a man shall behold what his hands have forwarded
79:6 (6)	upon the day when the first blast shivers
79:8 (8)	hearts upon that day shall be athrob
79:35 (35)	upon the day when man shall remember what he has striven
79:46 (46)	it shall be as if, on the day they see it
80:34 (34)	upon the day when a man shall flee from his brother
80:37 (37)	every man that day shall have business to suffice him
80:38 (38)	some faces on that day shall shine
80:40 (40)	some faces on that day shall be dusty
82:15 (15)	roasting therein on the Day of Doom
82:17 (17)	what shall teach thee what is the Day of Doom?
82:18 (18)	what shall teach thee what is the Day of Doom?
82:19 (19)	a day when no soul shall possess aught to succour another soul
82:19 (19)	that day the Command shall belong unto God
83:5 (5)	unto a mighty day
83:6 (6)	a day when mankind shall stand before the Lord of all Being
83:10 (10)	woe that day unto those who cry it lies
83:11 (11)	who cry lies to the Day of Doom
83:15 (15)	upon that day they shall be veiled from their Lord
83:34 (34)	today the believers are laughing at the unbelievers
85:2 (2)	by the promised day
86:9 (9)	upon the day when the secrets are tried
88:2 (2)	faces on that day humbled
88:8 (8)	Faces on that day jocund
89:23 (24)	[upon that day] Gehenna is brought out
89:23 (24)	upon that day man will remember
89:25 (25)	upon that day none shall chastise as He chastises
90:14 (14)	or giving food upon a day of hunger
99:4 (4)	upon that day she shall tell her tidings
99:6 (6)	upon that day men shall issue in scatterings to see their works
100:11 (11)	on that day their Lord shall be aware of them
101:4 (3)	the day that men shall be like scattered moths
102:8 (8)	then you shall be questioned that day concerning true bliss

*Y W N

YŪNUS n.prop.~Jonah

4:163 (161)	Jesus and Job, Jonah and Aaron
6:86 (86)	Jonah and Lot — each one We preferred above all beings
10:98 (98)	except the people of Jonah; when they believed
37:139 (139)	Jonah too was one of the Envoys

ZAYN

*Z ᶜ M

ZAᶜAMA vb. (I)~to assert; to allege, to claim. (n.vb.) assertion; claim

a) perf. act.

6:94 (94)	we do not see with you your intercessors, those you asserted to be associates in you
17:56 (58)	call on those you asserted apart from Him
17:92 (94)	or till thou makest heaven to fall, as thou assertest
18:48 (46)	you asserted We should not appoint for you a tryst
18:52 (50)	call on My associates whom you asserted
34:22 (21)	call on those you have asserted apart from God
62:6 (6)	you of Jewry, if you assert that you are the friends of God
64:7 (7)	the unbelievers assert that they will never be raised up

b) impf. act. (*yazᶜamu*)

4:60 (63)	hast thou not regarded those who assert that they believe in what has been sent down
6:22 (22)	where are your associates whom you were asserting?
6:94 (94)	that which you ever asserted has now gone astray from you
28:62 (62)	where now are My associates whom you were asserting?
28:74 (74)	where now are My associates whom you were asserting?

f) n.vb. (*zaᶜm*)

6:136 (137)	a portion, saying, 'This is for God' — so they assert
6:138 (139)	'none shall eat them, but whom we will' — so they assert

ZAᶜĪM n.m.~a guarantor

12:72 (72)	that I guarantee
68:40 (40)	ask them, which of them will guarantee that

*Z B D

ZABAD n.m.~scum, froth

13:17 (18)	and the torrent carries a swelling scum
13:17 (18)	out of that rises a scum the like of it
13:17 (18)	as for the scum, it vanishes as jetsam

*Z B N

ZABĀNIYAH n.m. (pl. of *zabānī*, or *zābin* or *zibniyah*)~guards of Hell

96:18 (18)	We shall call on the guards of Hell

*Z B R

ZABŪR n.m. (pl. *zubur*)~book, scroll; Scriptures, Book of David, hence the Psalms

3:184 (181)	Messengers before thee, who came bearing clear signs, and the Psalms
4:163 (161)	and We gave to David Psalms

16:44 (46)	with the clear signs, and the Psalms
17:55 (57)	and We gave to David Psalms
21:105 (105)	We have written in the Psalms, after the Remembrance
26:196 (196)	truly it is in the Scriptures of the ancients
35:25 (23)	their Messengers came to them with the clear signs, the Psalms
54:43 (43)	or have you an immunity in the Scrolls?
54:52 (52)	every thing that they have done is in the Scrolls

ZUBAR n.f. (pl. of *zubrah*)~ingot, piece, large lump

18:96 (95)	bring me ingots of iron

ZUBUR n.f. (pl. of *zubrah*)~a sect

23:53 (55)	but they split in their affair between them into sects

*Z F F

ZAFFA vb. (I)~to hasten

b) impf. act. (*yaziffu*)

37:94 (92)	then came the others to him hastening

*Z F R

ZAFĪR n.m.~a sigh, a sob; (adv) sighing, sobbing

11:106 (108)	Fire, wherein there shall be for them sighing and moaning
21:100 (100)	there shall be sighing for them therein
25:12 (13)	from a far place, they shall hear its bubbling and sighing

*Z H D

ZAHADA vb. (I)~(pcple. act.) (with prep. *fī*) one who holds someone in low esteem, who sets small store for someone

g) pcple. act. (*zāhid*)

12:20 (20)	handful of counted dirhams; for they set small store by him

*Z H Q

ZAHAQA vb. (I)~to vanish away, to perish; (*zahaqat nafsuhu*) his soul departed. (pcple. act.) that which vanishes away

a) perf. act.

17:81 (83)	the truth has come, and falsehood has vanished away

b) impf. act. (*yazhaqu*)

9:55 (55)	and that their souls should depart while they are unbelievers
9:85 (86)	and that their souls should depart while they are unbelievers

g) pcple. act. (*zāhiq*)

21:18 (18)	then behold, falsehood vanishes away

ZAHŪQ n.m. (adj)~perishable, vanishing, passing

17:81 (83)	surely falsehood is ever certain to vanish

*Z H R

ZAHRAH n.f.~a flower

20:131 (131) the flower of the present life, that We may try them therein

*Z Ḥ F

ZAḤAFA vb. (I)~(n.vb.) crawling; marching to battle

f) n.vb. (*zaḥf*)

8:15 (15) O believers, when you encounter the unbelievers marching to battle

*Z Ḥ Z Ḥ

ZAḤZAḤA vb. (quad I)~to remove. (pcple. act.) one who removes

d) perf. pass. (*zuḥziḥa*)

3:185 (182) whosoever is removed from the Fire and admitted to Paradise

g) pcple. act. (*muzaḥziḥ*)

2:96 (90) yet his being spared alive shall not remove him from the chastisement

*Z J J

ZUJĀJAH n.f.~a glass

24:35 (35) the lamp in a glass
24:35 (35) the glass as it were a glittering star

*Z J R

ZAJARA vb. (I)~(n.vb.) scaring [Ar]; reproof [Pk]; repelling [Ali]; shouting [Bl]. (pcple. act.) (pl) scarers [Ar, Bl]; ones who drive someone or something away [Pk]; ones who repel [Ali]

f) n.vb. (*zajr*)

37:2 (2) and the scarers scaring

g) pcple. act. f. (*zājirah*)

37:2 (2) and the scarers scaring

ZAJRAH n.f.~a scare [Ar]; a shout [Pk]; a compelling cry [Ali]; a scaring shout [Bl]

37:19 (19) for it is only a single scaring, then behold, they are watching
79:13 (13) but it shall be only a single scare

IZDAJARA vb. (VIII)~to drive away; to reject. (pcple. pass.) a deterrent

d) perf. pass. (*izdujira*)

54:9 (9) and he was rejected

h) pcple. pass. (*muzdajar*)

54:4 (4) there have come to them such tidings as contain a deterrent

*Z J W

AZJÁ vb. (IV)~to drive, to urge on

b) impf. act. (*yuzjī*)

17:66 (68)	your Lord it is who drives for you the ships on the sea
24:43 (43)	hast thou not seen how God drives the clouds, then composes them

MUZJĀT n.f.~of scant worth

12:88 (88)	we come with merchandise of scant worth

*Z K R

ZAKARĪYĀ n.prop.~Zachariah

3:37 (32)	Zachariah taking charge of her
3:37 (32)	whenever Zachariah went in to her in the Sanctuary
3:38 (33)	then Zachariah prayed to his Lord
6:85 (85)	Zachariah and John, Jesus and Elias
19:2 (1)	the mention of thy Lord's mercy unto His servant Zachariah
19:7 (7)	O Zachariah, We give thee good tidings of a boy
21:89 (89)	and Zachariah — when he called unto his Lord

*Z K W

ZAKĀ vb. (I)~to be pure in heart, to be righteous

a) perf. act.

24:21 (21)	not one of you would have been pure ever

ZAKĀT n.f.~alms [Ar]; poor-due [Pk]; charity [Ali]; Zakat [Bl]

2:43 (40)	and perform the prayer, and pay the alms
2:83 (77)	speak good to men, and perform the prayer, and pay the alms
2:110 (104)	perform the prayer, and pay the alms
2:177 (172)	to perform the prayer, to pay the alms
2:277 (277)	and perform the prayer, and pay the alms
4:77 (79)	and perform the prayer, and pay the alms
4:162 (160)	sent down before thee, that perform the prayer and pay the alms
5:12 (15)	if you perform the prayer, and pay the alms
5:55 (60)	the believers who perform the prayer and pay the alms
7:156 (155)	I shall prescribe it for those who are godfearing and pay the alms
9:5 (5)	repent, and perform the prayer, and pay the alms
9:11 (11)	if they repent, and perform the prayer, and pay the alms
9:18 (18)	performs the prayer, and pays the alms, and fears
9:71 (72)	they perform the prayer, and pay the alms
18:81 (80)	their Lord should give to them in exchange one better than he in purity
19:13 (14)	and a tenderness from Us, and purity

19:31 (32)	He has enjoined me to pray, and to give the alms
19:55 (56)	He bade his people to pray and to give the alms
21:73 (73)	to perform the prayer, and to pay the alms
22:41 (42)	perform the prayer, and pay the alms
22:78 (78)	so perform the prayer, and pay the alms
23:4 (4)	and at almsgiving are active
24:37 (37)	and to perform the prayer, and to pay the alms
24:56 (55)	perform the prayer, and pay the alms
27:3 (3)	who perform the prayer, and pay the alms
30:39 (38)	but what you give in alms, desiring God's Face
31:4 (3)	who perform the prayer, and pay the alms
33:33 (33)	and perform the prayer, and pay the alms
41:7 (6)	who pay not the alms, and disbelieve in the world to come
58:13 (14)	then perform the prayer, and pay the alms
73:20 (20)	and perform the prayer, and pay the alms
98:5 (4)	and to perform the prayer, and pay the alms

ZAKĪY n.m. (adj.; comp. *azká*)~innocent, pure, clean, faultless

2:232 (232)	that is cleaner and purer for you; God knows
18:19 (18)	and let him look for which of them has purest food
18:74 (73)	what, hast thou slain a soul innocent
19:19 (19)	I am but a messenger come from thy Lord, to give thee a boy most pure
24:28 (28)	that is purer for you; and God knows
24:30 (30)	and guard their private parts; that is purer for them

ZAKKÁ vb. (II)~to purify, to cleanse

a) perf. act.

91:9 (9)	prosperous is he who purifies it

b) impf. act. (*yuzakkī*)

2:129 (123)	teach them the Book and the Wisdom, and purify them
2:151 (146)	a Messenger, to recite Our signs to you and to purify you
2:174 (169)	God shall not speak to them on the Day of Resurrection neither purify them
3:77 (71)	neither will He purify them
3:164 (158)	to recite to them His signs and to purify them
4:49 (52)	hast thou not regarded those who purify themselves?
4:49 (52)	nay; only God purifies whom He will
9:103 (104)	take of their wealth a freewill offering, to purify them and to cleanse them thereby
24:21 (21)	but God purifies whom He will
53:32 (33)	therefore hold not yourselves purified
62:2 (2)	a Messenger from among them, to recite His signs to them and to purify them

TAZAKKÁ vb. (V)~to purify or cleanse oneself

a) perf. act.

20:76 (78)	that is the recompense of the self-purified
35:18 (19)	and perform the prayer; and whosoever purifies himself
79:18 (18)	hast thou the will to purify thyself
87:14 (14)	prosperous is he who has cleansed himself

b) impf. act. (*yatazakká* or *yazzakká*)

35:18 (19)	purifies himself only for his own soul's good
80:3 (3)	what should teach thee? Perchance he would cleanse him
80:7 (7)	though it is not thy concern, if he does not cleanse himself

92:18 (18)	even he who gives his wealth to purify himself

*Z KH R F

ZUKHRUF n.m.~glitter, ornament; tawdriness

6:112 (112)	Satans of men and jinn, revealing tawdry speech to each other
10:24 (25)	till, when the earth has taken on its glitter
17:93 (95)	or till thou possessest a house of gold ornament
43:35 (34)	and ornaments; surely all this is but the enjoyment of the present life

*Z L F

ZULFÁ n.f. (pl. *zulaf*)~nearness, proximity, near place, nigh

11:114 (116)	perform the prayer at the two ends of the day and nigh of the night
34:37 (36)	it is not your wealth nor your children that shall bring you (nigh) in nearness to Us
38:25 (24)	and he has a near place in Our presence
38:40 (39)	and he had a near place in Our presence
39:3 (4)	we only serve them that they may bring us (nigh) in nearness to God

ZULFAH n.f (adv)~nigh or near at hand

67:27 (27)	then, when they see it nigh at hand

AZLAFA vb. (IV)~to bring near, to bring close

a) perf. act.

26:64 (64)	and there We brought the others on

d) perf. pass. (*uzlifa*)

26:90 (90)	Paradise shall be brought forward for the godfearing
50:31 (30)	Paradise shall be brought forward to the godfearing, not afar
81:13 (13)	when Paradise shall be brought nigh

*Z L L

ZALLA vb. (I)~to slip, to slide back

a) perf. act.

2:209 (205)	but if you slip, after the clear signs have come to you

b) impf. act. (*yazillu*)

16:94 (96)	lest any foot should slip after it has stood firm

AZALLA vb. (IV)~to cause someone to slip or slide back

a) perf. act.

2:36 (34)	then Satan caused them to slip therefrom

ISTAZALLA vb. (X)~to cause someone to slip or slide back

a) perf. act.

3:155 (149)	Satan made them slip for somewhat they had earned

*Z L M

AZLĀM n.m. (pl. of *zalam*)~arrow without head or feathers used in divination, divining-arrow

5:3 (4)	and partition by the divining arrows; that is ungodliness
5:90 (92)	idols and divining-arrows are an abomination

*Z L Q

ZALIQA vb. (I)~(n.vb.) a slippery place; a smooth hillside, a slope

f) n.vb. (*zalaq*)

18:40 (38)	in the morning it will be a slope of dust

AZLAQA vb. (IV)~to cause someone to slide; (*zalaqahu bi-baṣarihi*) to look at someone sternly, to strike someone down with his glances; to disconcert someone with his eyes

b) impf. act. (*yuzliqu*)

68:51 (51)	the unbelievers wellnigh strike thee down with their glances

*Z L Z L

ZALZALA vb. (quad I)~to convulse, to shake. (n.vb.) shaking, convulsion; earthquake

d) perf. pass. (*zulzila*)

2:214 (210)	they were afflicted by misery and hardship and were so convulsed
33:11 (11)	there it was that the believers were tried, and shaken most mightily
99:1 (1)	when earth is shaken with a mighty shaking

f) n.vb. (*zilzāl*)

33:11 (11)	there it was that the believers were tried, and shaken most *mightily*
99:1 (1)	when earth is shaken with *a mighty shaking*

ZALZALAH n.f.~earthquake

22:1 (1)	surely the earthquake of the Hour is a mighty thing

*Z M H R

ZAMHARĪR n.m.~bitter cold; moon's excessive cold (contrasted with the sun's excessive heat)

76:13 (13)	therein they shall see neither sun nor bitter cold

*Z M L

IZZAMMALA vb. (V)~(pcple. act.) enwrapped, wrapped, folded

g) pcple. act. (*muzzammil* for *mutazammil*)

73:1 (1)	O thou enwrapped in thy robes

*Z M R

ZUMAR n.f. (pl. of *zumrah*)~a company (of men), a crowd

39:71 (71) then the unbelievers shall be driven in companies into Gehenna
39:73 (73) then those that feared their Lord shall be driven in companies into Paradise

*Z N J B L

ZANJABĪL n.m.~ginger

76:17 (17) therein they shall be given to drink a cup whose mixture is ginger

*Z N M

ZANĪM n.m. (adj)~ignoble, base-born; intrusive

68:13 (13) coarse-grained, moreover ignoble

*Z N Y

ZANÁ vb. (I)~to fornicate, to commit adultery. (n.vb.) fornication, adultery. (pcple. act.) fornicator, fornicatress, adulterer, adulteress

b) impf. act. (*yaznī*)

25:68 (68) nor slay the soul God has forbidden except by right, neither fornicate
60:12 (12) and will not steal, neither commit adultery

f) n.vb. (*ziná*)

17:32 (34) and approach not fornication

g) pcple. act. (*zānī*; f., *zāniyah*)

24:2 (2) the fornicatress and the (fornicator) — scourge each of them a hundred stripes
24:2 (2) the (fornicatress) and the fornicator — scourge each of them a hundred stripes
24:3 (3) the fornicator shall marry none but a (fornicatress)
24:3 (3) the (fornicator) shall marry none but a fornicatress
24:3 (3) the fornicatress — none shall marry her but a (fornicator)
24:3 (3) the (fornicatress) — none shall marry her but a fornicator

*Z Q M

ZAQQŪM n.prop.~Zakkoum (a tree growing in the midst of Hell, see 37:64)

37:62 (60) is that better as a hospitality, or the Tree of Ez-Zakkoum?
44:43 (43) lo, the Tree of Ez-Zakkoum
56:52 (52) you shall eat of a tree called Zakkoum

*Z R ᶜ

ZARAᶜA vb. (I)~to sow, to plant, to grow. (n.vb.) the act of sowing, planting, growing; (n) crops; a shoot (of a seed); sown land or field. (pcple. act.) sower

b) impf. act. (*yazraᶜu*)

12:47 (47) you shall sow seven years after your wont
56:64 (64) do you yourselves sow it, or are We

f) n.vb. (*zarᶜ*, pl. *zurūᶜ*)

6:141 (142) palm-trees, and crops diverse in produce

13:4 (4)	and gardens of vines, and fields sown
14:37 (40)	dwell in a valley where is no sown land by Thy Holy House
16:11 (11)	thereby He brings forth for you crops, and olives
18:32 (31)	and between them We set a sown field
26:148 (148)	sown fields, and palms with slender spathes
32:27 (27)	have they not seen how We drive the water to the dry land and bring forth crops
39:21 (22)	then He brings forth therewith crops of diverse hues
44:26 (25)	sown fields, and how noble a station
48:29 (29)	and their likeness in the Gospel: as a seed that puts forth its shoot

g) pcple. act. (*zāri*ᶜ; pl., *zāri*ᶜ*ūn* and *zurrā*ᶜ)

48:29 (29)	it grows stout and rises straight upon its stalk, pleasing the sowers
56:64 (64)	do you yourselves sow it, or are We the Sowers?

*Z R B

ZARĀBĪ n.f. (pl. of *zurbīyah*)~carpet, rug

88:16 (16)	and carpets outspread

*Z R Q

ZURQ n.m. (adj., pl. of *azraq*)~staring [Ar]; white-eyed (with terror) [Pk]; blear-eyed (with terror) [Ali]; blue [Bl]

20:102 (102)	We shall muster the sinners upon that day with eyes staring

*Z R Y

IZDARÁ vb. (VIII)~to despise, to slight

b) impf. act. (*yazdarī*)

11:31 (33)	nor do I say to those your eyes despise

*Z W D

ZĀD n.m.~provision

2:197 (193)	but the best provision is godfearing

TAZAWWADA vb. (V)~to take provision

c) impv. (*tazawwad*)

2:197 (193)	God knows it. And take provision

*Z W J

ZAWJ n.com. (pl. *azwāj*)~spouse, husband, wife, mate; a couple, a pair; each party in a pair; (du) a couple (pl., in addition to above) bands, divers kinds

2:25 (23)	for them shall be spouses purified
2:35 (33)	Adam, dwell thou, and thy wife, in the Garden
2:102 (96)	from them they learned how they might divide a man and his wife
2:230 (230)	be lawful to him after that, until she marries another husband
2:232 (232)	do not debar them from marrying their husbands
2:234 (234)	and those of you who die, leaving wives
2:240 (241)	and those of you who die, leaving wives

2:240 (241)	let them make testament for their wives
3:15 (13)	therein dwelling forever, and spouses purified, and God's good pleasure
4:1 (1)	and from it [He] created its mate
4:12 (13)	for you a half of what your wives leave, if they have no children
4:20 (24)	and if you desire to exchange a wife in place of another ([wife])
4:20 (24)	and if you desire to exchange a (wife) in place of another [wife]
4:57 (60)	therein for them shall be spouses purified
6:139 (140)	of these cattle is reserved for our males and forbidden to our spouses
6:143 (144)	eight couples: two of sheep, of goats two
7:19 (18)	O Adam, dwell, thou and thy wife, in the Garden
7:189 (189)	and made of him his spouse
9:24 (24)	if your fathers, your sons, your brothers, your wives
11:40 (42)	the Oven boiled, We said, 'Embark in it two of every kind'
13:3 (3)	and of every fruit He placed there two kinds
13:23 (23)	those who were righteous of their fathers, and their wives
13:38 (38)	We sent Messengers before thee, and We assigned to them wives
15:88 (88)	stretch not thine eyes to that We have given pairs of them to enjoy
16:72 (74)	God has appointed for you of yourselves wives
16:72 (74)	He has appointed for you of your wives sons and grandsons
20:53 (55)	and therewith We have brought forth divers kinds of plants
20:117 (115)	Adam, surely this is an enemy to thee and thy wife
20:131 (131)	stretch not thine eyes to that We have given pairs of them to enjoy
21:90 (90)	John, and We set his wife right for him
22:5 (5)	it quivers, and swells, and puts forth herbs of every joyous kind
23:6 (6)	save from their wives and what their right hands own
23:27 (28)	insert in it two of every kind
24:6 (6)	and those who cast it up on their wives
25:74 (74)	our Lord, give us refreshment of our wives and seed
26:7 (6)	We have caused to grow of every generous kind
26:166 (166)	leaving your wives that your Lord created
30:21 (20)	He created for you, of yourselves, spouses
31:10 (9)	and caused to grow in it of every generous kind
33:4 (4)	nor has He made your wives, when you divorce, saying
33:6 (6)	his wives are their mothers
33:28 (28)	O Prophet, say to thy wives: 'If you desire the present life'
33:37 (37)	keep thy wife to thyself, and fear God
33:37 (37)	so that there should not be any fault in the believers, touching the wives of their adopted sons
33:50 (49)	We have made lawful for thee thy wives whom thou hast given their wages
33:50 (50)	We know what We have imposed upon them touching their wives and what their right hands own
33:52 (52)	neither for thee to take other wives in exchange for them
33:53 (53)	neither to marry his wives after him, ever
33:59 (59)	O Prophet, say to thy wives and daughters
35:11 (12)	then He made you pairs
36:36 (36)	glory be to Him, who created all the pairs of what the earth produces
36:56 (56)	they and their spouses, reclining upon couches in the shade
37:22 (22)	muster those who did evil, their wives, and that they were serving
38:58 (58)	and other torments of the like kind coupled together
39:6 (8)	He created you of a single soul, then from it He appointed its mate
39:6 (8)	He sent down to you of the cattle eight couples
40:8 (8)	those who were righteous of their fathers, and their wives, and their seed
42:11 (9)	He has appointed for you, of yourselves, pairs
42:11 (9)	and pairs also of the cattle
43:12 (11)	and who created the pairs, all of them
43:70 (70)	enter Paradise, you and your wives, walking with joy
50:7 (7)	and We caused to grow therein of every joyous kind

51:49 (49)	and of everything created We two kinds
53:45 (46)	He Himself created the two kinds, male and female
55:52 (52)	therein of every fruit two kinds
56:7 (7)	and you shall be three bands
58:1 (1)	God has heard the words of her that disputes with thee concerning her husband
60:11 (11)	if any of your wives slips away from you to the unbelievers
60:11 (11)	give those whose wives have gone away the like of what they have expended
64:14 (14)	O believers, among your wives and children there is an enemy to you
66:1 (1)	made lawful to thee, seeking the good pleasure of thy wives
66:3 (3)	when the Prophet confided to one of his wives a certain matter
66:5 (5)	his Lord will give him in exchange wives better than you
70:30 (30)	save from their wives and what their right hands own
75:39 (39)	He made of him two kinds, male and female
78:8 (8)	and We created you in pairs

ZAWWAJA vb. (II)~to give in marriage, to espouse, to couple

a) perf. act.

33:37 (37)	then We gave her in marriage to thee, so that there should not be any fault
44:54 (54)	We shall espouse them to wide-eyed houris
52:20 (20)	and We shall espouse them to wide-eyed houris

b) impf. act. (*yuzawwiju*)

42:50 (49)	or He couples them, both males and females

d) perf. pass. (*zuwwija*)

81:7 (7)	when the souls shall be coupled

*Z W L

ZĀLA vb. (I)~to go away; to deviate; to remove. (n.vb.) removing [Ar]; end [Pk]; decline [Ali, Bl]

a) perf. act.

35:41 (39)	did they remove, none would hold them after Him

b) impf. act. (*yazūlu*)

14:46 (47)	though their devising were such as to remove mountains
35:41 (39)	God holds the heavens and the earth, lest they remove

f) n.vb. (*zawāl*)

14:44 (46)	there should be no removing for you

*Z W R

ZĀRA vb. (I)~to visit

a) perf. act.

102:2 (2) even till you visit the tombs

ZŪR n.m.~falsehood; lie, untruth

22:30 (31) and eschew the speaking of falsehood
25:4 (5) so they have committed wrong and falsehood
25:72 (72) and those who bear not false witness
58:2 (2) they are surely saying a dishonourable saying, and a falsehood

TAZĀWARA vb. (VI)~to incline [Ar, Bl]; move away [Pk]; to decline [Ali]

b) impf. act. (*tazāwaru* for *tatazāwaru*)

18:17 (16) when it rose, inclining from their Cave

*Z Y D

ZĀDA vb. (I)~to increase, to give double or more, to add; to enrich; (*aw yazīd*) to exceed in number, or more. (n.vb.) increase, surplus, excess a) perf. act.

2:10 (9) and God has increased their sickness
2:247 (248) God has chosen him over you, and has increased him broadly in knowledge
3:173 (167) but it increased them in faith, and they said
7:69 (67) when He appointed you as successors after the people of Noah, and increased you in stature broadly
8:2 (2) when His signs are recited to them, it increases them in faith
9:47 (47) had they gone forth among you, they would only have increased you in trouble
9:124 (125) say, 'Which of you has this increased in belief?'
9:124 (125) as for the believers, them it has increased in belief
9:125 (126) them it has increased in abomination added
11:101 (103) and they increased them not, save in destruction
16:88 (90) them We shall give increase of chastisement upon chastisement
17:97 (99) We shall increase for them the Blaze
18:13 (12) and We increased them in guidance
25:60 (61) and it increases them in aversion
33:22 (22) it only increased them in faith and surrender
35:42 (40) when a warner came to them, it increased them only in aversion
47:17 (19) those who are guided aright, them He increases in guidance
72:6 (6) and they increased them in vileness

b) impf. act. (*yazīdu*)

2:58 (55) We will forgive you your transgressions, and increase the good-doers
4:173 (172) and He will give them more, of His bounty
5:64 (69) what has been sent down to thee from thy Lord will surely increase many of them in insolence
5:68 (72) what has been sent down to thee from thy Lord will surely increase many of them in insolence
7:161 (161) We will forgive you your transgressions, and increase the good-doers
11:52 (55) He will increase you in strength unto your strength
11:63 (66) you would do nothing for me, except increase my loss

14:7 (7)	if you are thankful, surely I will increase you
17:41 (43)	and it increases them only in aversion
17:60 (62)	but it only increases them in great insolence
17:82 (84)	and the evildoers it increases not, except in loss
17:109 (109)	and it increases them in humility
19:76 (78)	and God shall increase those who were guided in guidance
24:38 (38)	and give them increase of His bounty
35:1 (1)	increasing creation as He wills
35:30 (27)	that He may pay them in full their wages and enrich them of His bounty
35:39 (37)	their unbelief increases the disbelievers only in hate in their Lord's sight
35:39 (37)	their unbelief increases the disbelievers only in loss
37:147 (147)	then We sent him unto a hundred thousand, or more
42:20 (19)	We shall give him increase in his tillage
42:23 (22)	We shall give him increase of good in respect of it
42:26 (25)	and He gives them increase of His bounty
71:6 (5)	my calling has only increased them in flight
71:21 (20)	whose wealth and children increase him only in loss
71:24 (24)	increase Thou not the evildoers save in error
71:28 (29)	do Thou not increase the evildoers save in ruin
74:15 (15)	then he is eager that I should do more
78:30 (30)	taste! We shall increase you not save in chastisement

c) impv. (*zid*)

20:114 (113)	O my Lord, increase me in knowledge
38:61 (61)	our Lord, whoso forwarded this for us, give him a double chastisement in the Fire
73:4 (4)	or add a little, and chant the Koran very distinctly

f) n.vb. (*ziyādah*)

9:37 (37)	the month postponed is an increase of unbelief
10:26 (27)	to the good-doers the reward most fair and a surplus

MAZĪD n.m.~an increase, an addition; more

50:30 (29)	it shall say, 'Are there any more to come?'
50:35 (34)	and with Us there is yet more

ZAYD n.prop.~Zaid (the Prophet's freed man and adopted son)

33:37 (37)	when Zaid had accomplished what he would of her, then We gave her in marriage

IZDĀDA vb. (VIII)~to grow, to swell, to increase; to add, to obtain more

a) perf. act.

3:90 (84)	those who disbelieve after they have believed and then increase in unbelief
4:137 (136)	then believe, and then disbelieve, and then increase in unbelief
18:25 (24)	hundred years, and to that they added nine more

b) impf. act. (*yazdādu*)

3:178 (172)	We grant them indulgence only that they may increase in sin
12:65 (65)	we shall obtain an extra camel's load
13:8 (9)	and the wombs' shrinking and swelling
48:4 (4)	into the hearts of the believers, that they might add faith to their faith
74:31 (31)	and that those who believe may increase in belief

*Z Y GH

ZĀGHA vb. (I)~to swerve, to turn away (from), to deviate. (n.vb.) swerving, deviation, a turning away *a)* perf. act.

33:10 (10)	when your eyes swerved and your hearts reached your throats
38:63 (63)	did we take them for a laughing-stock? Or have our eyes swerved away from them?
53:17 (17)	his eye swerved not, nor swept astray
61:5 (5)	when they swerved

b) impf. act. (*yazīghu*)

9:117 (118)	after the hearts of a part of them wellnigh swerved aside
34:12 (11)	and such of them as swerved away from Our commandment

f) n.vb. (*zaygh*)

3:7 (5)	as for those in whose hearts is swerving, they follow the ambiguous part

AZĀGHA vb. (IV)~to cause someone to swerve, to cause to deviate

a) perf. act.

61:5 (5)	God caused their hearts to swerve

b) impf. act. (*yuzīghu*)

3:8 (6)	our Lord, make not our hearts to swerve

*Z Y L

ZĀLA vb. (I)~(with negatives *mā*, *lā* or *lam*) does not cease, to continue; still yet

a) perf. act.

21:15 (15)	so they ceased not to cry, until We made them
40:34 (36)	yet you continued in doubt concerning that he brought you

b) impf. act. (*yazālu*)

2:217 (214)	they will not cease to fight with you
5:13 (16)	thou wilt never cease to light upon some act of treachery on their part
9:110 (111)	the buildings they have built will not cease to be a point of doubt
11:118 (120)	one nation; but they continue in their differences
13:31 (31)	the unbelievers are smitten by a shattering for what they wrought
22:55 (54)	the unbelievers will not cease to be in doubt of it

ZAYYALA vb. (II)~(with prep. *bayna*) to separate, to set apart, to set a space between

a) perf. act.

10:28 (29)	then We shall set a space between them, and their associates

TAZAYYALA vb. (V)~to be separated

a) perf. act.

48:25 (25)	had they been separated clearly, then We would have chastised the unbelievers among them

*Z Y N

ZĪNAH n.f.~adornment, ornament, embellishment; finery; (*yawm al-zīnah*) the Feast Day

7:31 (29)	take your adornment at every place of worship

7:32 (30)	who has forbidden the ornament of God which He brought forth
10:88 (88)	Thou hast given to Pharaoh and his Council adornment
11:15 (18)	whoso desires the present life and its adornment
16:8 (8)	horses, and mules, and asses, for you to ride, and as an adornment
18:7 (6)	We have appointed all that is on the earth for an adornment for it
18:28 (27)	let not thine eyes turn away from them, desiring the adornment of the present life
18:46 (44)	wealth and sons are the adornment of the present world
20:59 (61)	your tryst shall be upon the Feast Day
20:87 (90)	but we were loaded with fardels, even the ornaments of the people
24:31 (31)	and reveal not their adornment save such as is outward
24:31 (31)	and not reveal their adornment save to their husbands
24:31 (31)	so that their hidden ornament may be known
24:60 (59)	so be it that they flaunt no ornament
28:60 (60)	whatever thing you have been given is the enjoyment of the present life and its adornment
28:79 (79)	so he went forth unto his people in his adornment
33:28 (28)	if you desire the present life and its adornment, come now
37:6 (6)	We have adorned the lower heaven with the adornment of the stars
57:20 (19)	know that the present life is but a sport and a diversion, an adornment

ZAYYANA vb. (II)~to deck out fair, to make something appear pleasing; to beautify; to adorn

a) perf. act.

6:43 (43)	Satan decked out fair to them what they were doing
6:108 (108)	We have decked out fair to every nation their deeds
6:137 (138)	those associates of theirs have decked out fair to many idolaters to slay their children
8:48 (50)	when Satan decked out their deeds fair to them, and said
15:16 (16)	We have set in heaven constellations and decked them out fair to the beholders
16:63 (65)	but Satan decked out fair to them their deeds
27:4 (4)	We have decked out fair for them their works
27:24 (24)	Satan has decked out fair their deeds to them
29:38 (37)	Satan decked out fair to them their works
37:6 (6)	We have adorned the lower heaven with the adornment of the stars
41:12 (11)	We adorned the lower heaven with lamps, and to preserve
41:25 (24)	they have decked out fair to them that which is before them and behind them
49:7 (7)	but God has endeared to you belief, decking it fair in your hearts
50:6 (6)	how We have built it, and decked it out fair
67:5 (5)	We adorned the lower heaven with lamps

b) impf. act. (*yuzayyinu*)

15:39 (39)	I shall deck all fair to them in the earth

d) perf. pass. (*zuyyina*)

2:212 (208)	decked out fair to the unbelievers is the present life
3:14 (12)	decked out fair to men is the love of lusts
6:122 (122)	so it is decked out fair to the unbelievers the things they have done
9:37 (37)	decked out fair to them are their evil deeds
10:12 (13)	so decked out fair to the prodigal is that they have been doing
13:33 (33)	decked out fair to the unbelievers is their devising
35:8 (9)	what of him, the evil of whose deeds has been decked out fair to him
40:37 (40)	the evil of his deeds was decked out fair to Pharaoh
47:14 (15)	unto whom his evil deeds have been decked out fair
48:12 (12)	and that was decked out fair in your hearts

IZZAYYANA vb. (V)~to be adorned, to be decked fair

a) perf. act.

10:24 (25) when the earth has taken on its glitter and has decked itself fair

*Z Y T

ZAYT n.m.~oil

24:35 (35) whose oil wellnigh would shine, even if no fire touched it

ZAYTŪNAH n.f. (pl. m. *zaytūn*)~(f.s) olive-tree; (pl) olives; olive-trees

6:99 (99) gardens of vines, olives, pomegranates
6:141 (142) crops diverse in produce, olives, pomegranates
16:11 (11) thereby He brings forth for you crops, and olives
24:35 (35) an olive that is neither of the East nor of the West
80:29 (29) and olives, and palms
95:1 (1) by the fig and the olive

ẒĀ

*Ẓ ʿ N

ẒAʿANA vb. (I)~(n.vb.) departure, migration, journey (in caravan)

f) n.vb. (*ẓaʿn*)

16:80 (82) you find light on the day that you journey

*Ẓ F R

ẒUFUR n.m.~claw, talon, nail; (*dhū ẓufur*) with claws

6:146 (147) to those of Jewry We have forbidden every beast with claws

AẒFARA vb. (IV)~to make someone a victor

a) perf. act.

48:24 (24) the hollow of Mecca, after that He made you victors over them

*Ẓ H R

ẒAHARA vb. (I)~to appear, to be or become manifest; (with prep. *ʿalá*) to get the better of, to gain the upper hand, to gain knowledge of someone; to mount, to scale; (*mā ẓahara*) that which is outward, which appears, which is apparent. (pcple. act.) outward, apparent; having mastery, master; Outward, Evident (Divine attribute)

a) perf. act.

6:151 (152) and that you approach not any indecency outward or inward
7:33 (31) my Lord has only forbidden indecencies, the inward and the outward
9:48 (48) until the truth came, and God's command appeared
24:31 (31) and reveal not their adornment save such as is outward
30:41 (40) corruption has appeared in the land and sea

b) impf. act. (*yaẓharu*)

9:8 (8) how? If they get the better of you
18:20 (19) if they should get knowledge of you they will stone you
18:97 (96) so they were unable either to scale it
24:31 (31) children who have not yet attained knowledge of women's private parts
43:33 (32) roofs of silver to their houses, and stairs whereon to mount

g) pcple. act. (*ẓāhir*)

6:120 (120) forsake the outward sin, and the inward
13:33 (33) will you tell Him what He knows not in the earth? Or in apparent words?
18:22 (22) do not dispute with them, except in outward disputation
30:7 (6) they know an outward part of the present life
31:20 (19) and He has lavished on you His blessings, outward and inward
34:18 (17) We set, between them and the cities that We have blessed, cities apparent
40:29 (30) O my people, today the kingdom is yours, who are masters in the land
57:3 (3) He is the First and the Last, the Outward and the Inward
57:13 (13) and against the outward thereof is chastisement
61:14 (14) We confirmed those who believed against their enemy, and they became masters

ẒAHĪR n.m.~helper, supporter, partisan, one who backs another

17:88 (90)	they would never produce its like, not though they backed one another
25:55 (57)	the unbeliever is ever a partisan against his Lord
28:17 (16)	I will never be a partisan of the sinners
28:86 (86)	so be thou not a partisan of the unbelievers
34:22 (21)	nor has He in them any supporter
66:4 (4)	and, after that, the angels are his supporters

ẒAHĪRAH n.f.~noon, midday

24:58 (57)	and when you put off your garments at the noon

ẒAHR n.m. (pl. *ẓuhūr*)~back; loins; upper part, surface, face (of the earth)

2:101 (95)	that were given the Book reject the Book of God behind their backs
2:189 (185)	it is not piety to come to the houses from the backs of them
3:187 (184)	but they rejected it behind their backs
6:31 (31)	on their backs they shall be bearing their loads
6:94 (94)	you have left what We conferred on you behind your backs
6:138 (139)	and cattle whose backs have been forbidden
6:146 (147)	We have forbidden them the fat of them, save what their backs carry
7:172 (171)	when thy Lord took from the Children of Adam, from their loins, their seed
9:35 (35)	their foreheads and their sides and their backs shall be branded
21:39 (40)	they shall not ward off the Fire from their faces nor from their backs
35:45 (44)	He would not leave upon the face of the earth one creature that crawls
42:33 (31)	they remain motionless on its back
43:13 (12)	that you may be seated on their backs
84:10 (10)	but as for him who is given his book behind his back
94:3 (3)	the burden that weighed down thy back

ẒIHRĪ n.m.~that which is disregarded, that which is thrust behind the back

11:92 (94)	have you taken Him as something to be thrust behind you?

ẒĀHARA vb. (III)~to support, to help; to divorce, to be as one's mother's back (a pre-Islamic custom of divorce whereby a man declared to his wife, "You are to me as my mother's back"; the declaration is known as *ẓihār*)

a) perf. act.

33:26 (26)	He brought down those of the People of the Book who supported them
60:9 (9)	and have supported in your expulsion, that you should take them for friends

b) impf. act. (*yuẓāhiru*)

9:4 (4)	then they failed you naught neither lent support to any man against you
33:4 (4)	nor has He made your wives, when you divorce, saying, 'Be as my mother's back'
58:2 (2)	those of you who say, regarding their wives, 'Be as my mother's back'
58:3 (4)	those who say, regarding their wives, 'Be as my mother's back'

AẒHARA vb. (IV)~to disclose, to cause to appear; (with prep. *ʿalá*) to uplift [Ar], to cause someone or something to prevail [Pk], to proclaim over [Ali]; to set above [Bl]; to enter on the period of noon (30:18)

a) perf. act.

66:3 (3)	when she told of it, and God disclosed that to him

b) impf. act. (*yuẓhiru*)

9:33 (33)	He may uplift it above every religion
30:18 (17)	alike at the setting sun and in your noontide hour
40:26 (27)	that he may cause corruption to appear in the land

48:28 (28)	He may uplift it above every religion
61:9 (9)	He may uplift it above every religion
72:26 (26)	He discloses not His Unseen to anyone

TAẒĀHARA vb. (VI)~to support one another; (with prep. *ʿalá*) to help one another against, to conspire against

a) perf. act.

28:48 (48)	they said, 'A pair of sorceries mutually supporting each other'
66:4 (4)	if you support one another against him, God is his Protector

b) impf. act. (*yataẓāharu*)

2:85 (79)	from their habitations, conspiring against them in sin and enmity

*Ẓ L L

ẒALLA vb. (I)~to be; to stay, to remain; to continue doing something

a) perf. act.

15:14 (14)	still they mounted through it
16:58 (60)	a girl, his face is darkened
20:97 (97)	behold thy god, to whom all the day thou wast cleaving
26:4 (3)	out of heaven a sign, so their necks will stay humbled to it
30:51 (50)	they remain after that unbelievers
43:17 (16)	All-merciful, his face is darkened
56:65 (65)	and you would remain bitterly jesting

b) impf. act. (*yaẓallu*)

26:71 (71)	We serve idols, and continue cleaving to them
42:33 (31)	they remain motionless on its back

ẒALĪL n.m. (adj)~shading; (*ẓill ẓalīl*) plenteous shade

4:57 (60)	We shall admit them to a shelter of plenteous shade
77:31 (31)	unshading against the blazing flame

ẒILL n.m. (pl. *ẓilāl*)~shade, shadow; covering, shelter

4:57 (60)	We shall admit them to a shelter of plenteous shade
13:15 (16)	as do their shadows also in the mornings and the evenings
13:35 (35)	its produce is eternal, and its shade
16:48 (50)	casting their shadows to the right and to the left
16:81 (83)	it is God who has appointed for you coverings of the things He created
25:45 (47)	hast thou not regarded thy Lord, how He has stretched out the shadow?
28:24 (24)	he drew water for them; then he turned away to the shade
35:21 (20)	the shade and the torrid heat
36:56 (56)	they and their spouses, reclining upon couches in the shade
56:30 (29)	and spreading shade
56:43 (42)	and the shadow of a smoking blaze
76:14 (14)	near them shall be its shades, and its clusters hung
77:30 (30)	depart to a triple-massing shadow
77:41 (41)	truly the godfearing shall dwell amid shades and fountains

ẒULLAH n.f. (pl. *ẓulal*)~shadow, cloud-shadows, a canopy; sheltering tent, overshadowing, covering, awning; (*yawm al-ẓullah*) the Day of the Shadow [Ar, Bl]; the day of gloom [Pk]; the day of overshadowing gloom [Ali]

2:210 (206)	God shall come to them in the cloud-shadows
7:171 (170)	when We shook the mountain above them as if it were a canopy

26:189 (189)	then there seized them the chastisement of the Day of Shadow
31:32 (31)	when the waves cover them like shadows they call upon God
39:16 (18)	above them they shall have overshadowings of the Fire
39:16 (18)	and underneath them overshadowings

ẒALLALA vb. (II)~to shade, to cast a shadow, to outspread (a cloud), to overshade

a) perf. act.

2:57 (54)	and We outspread the cloud to overshadow you
7:160 (160)	and We outspread the cloud to overshadow them

*Ẓ L M

ẒALAMA vb. (I)~to do or work wrong, to wrong, to do evil, to act unjustly, to oppress, to be oppressive; (*alladhīna ẓalamū*) those who do wrong, the evildoers; (*mā ẓalama shay'an min*) to fail naught, to withhold naught (16:33). (n.vb.) wrong, iniquity, wrongdoing, evildoing; injustice, oppression, inequity; (adv) wrongfully, unjustly. (pcple. act.) evildoer, sinner, offender, wrongdoer; oppressor, unjust; evildoing, dealing unjustly, wrongdoing (pcple. pass.) oppressed, one treated unjustly, wronged

a) perf. act.

2:54 (51)	you have done wrong against yourselves by your taking the Calf
2:57 (54)	and they worked no wrong upon Us
2:59 (56)	then the evildoers substituted a saying
2:59 (56)	We sent down upon the evildoers wrath out of heaven
2:150 (145)	excepting the evildoers of them; and fear you them not
2:165 (160)	O if the evildoers might see, when they see the chastisement
2:231 (231)	whoever does that has wronged himself
3:117 (113)	the tillage of a people who wronged themselves
3:117 (113)	God wronged them not
3:135 (129)	who, when they commit an indecency or wrong themselves, remember God
4:64 (67)	if, when they wronged themselves, they had come to thee
4:168 (166)	the unbelievers, who have done evil, God would not forgive them
6:45 (45)	the last remnant of the people who did evil was cut off
7:23 (22)	they said, 'Lord, we have wronged ourselves'
7:103 (101)	but they did them wrong
7:160 (160)	and they worked no wrong upon Us
7:162 (162)	then the evildoers of them substituted a saying
7:165 (165)	We seized the evildoers with evil chastisement
8:25 (25)	and fear a trial which shall surely not smite in particular the evildoers
10:13 (14)	We destroyed the generations before you when they did evil
10:52 (53)	then it will be said to the evildoers
10:54 (55)	if every soul that has done evil possessed all that is in the earth
11:37 (39)	address Me not concerning those who have done evil
11:67 (70)	and the evildoers were seized by the Cry
11:94 (97)	and the evildoers were seized by the Cry
11:101 (103)	and We wronged them not
11:101 (103)	but they wronged themselves
11:113 (115)	and lean not on the evildoers
11:116 (118)	the evildoers followed the ease they were given to exult in
14:44 (45)	those who did evil shall say, 'Our Lord, defer us to a near term'
14:45 (47)	you dwelt in the dwelling-places of those who wronged themselves
16:33 (35)	God wronged them not, but themselves they (wronged)
16:85 (87)	when the evildoers behold the chastisement, it shall not be lightened
16:118 (119)	and We wronged them not
17:59 (61)	but they did her wrong
18:59 (58)	those cities, We destroyed them when they did evil
18:87 (86)	as for the evildoer, him we shall chastise

21:3 (3)	the evildoers whisper one to another, Is this aught but a mortal
23:27 (28)	address Me not concerning those who have done evil
26:227 (228)	those who do wrong shall surely know
27:11 (11)	save him who has done evil, then, after evil, has changed into good
27:44 (45)	indeed I have wronged myself, and I surrender
27:52 (53)	those are their houses, all fallen down because of the evil they committed
27:85 (87)	the Word shall fall upon them because of the evil they committed
28:16 (15)	my Lord, I have wronged myself. Forgive me
29:46 (45)	save in the fairer manner, except for those of them that do wrong
30:29 (28)	the evildoers follow their own caprices, without knowledge
30:57 (57)	that day their excuses will not profit the evildoers
34:19 (18)	they wronged themselves, so We made them as but tales
34:42 (41)	and We shall say to the evildoers
37:22 (22)	muster those who did evil, their wives, and that they were serving
38:24 (23)	assuredly he has wronged thee in asking for thy ewe
39:47 (48)	if the evildoers possessed all that is in the earth
39:51 (52)	the evildoers of these men, they too shall be smitten by the evils
43:39 (38)	it shall not profit you today, since you did evil
43:65 (65)	so woe unto those who did evil, because of the chastisement
43:76 (76)	We never wronged them, but they themselves did the wrong
46:12 (11)	this is a Book confirming, in Arabic tongue, to warn the evildoers
51:59 (59)	the evildoers shall have their portion
52:47 (47)	there surely awaits the evildoers a chastisement beyond even that
65:1 (1)	whosoever trespasses the bounds of God has done wrong to himself

b) impf. act. (*yaẓlimu*)

2:57 (54)	they (worked no wrong) upon Us, but themselves they wronged
2:279 (279)	you shall have your principal, unwronging and unwronged
3:117 (113)	God (wronged) them not, but themselves they wronged
4:40 (44)	God shall not wrong so much as the weight of an ant
4:110 (110)	whosoever does evil, or wrongs himself, and then prays God's forgiveness
7:9 (8)	they have lost their souls for wronging Our signs
7:160 (160)	they (worked no wrong) upon Us but themselves they wronged
7:162 (162)	We sent down upon them wrath out of heaven for their evildoing
7:177 (176)	the people who cried lies to Our signs, and themselves were wronging
9:36 (36)	so wrong not each other during them
9:70 (71)	God would not wrong them
9:70 (71)	but themselves they wronged
10:44 (45)	surely God wrongs not men anything
10:44 (45)	but themselves men wrong
16:33 (35)	God God (wronged) them not, but themselves they wronged
16:118 (119)	We (wronged) them not, but they wronged themselves
18:33 (31)	each of the two gardens yielded its produce and failed naught in any wise
18:49 (47)	they shall find all they wrought present, and thy Lord shall not wrong anyone
25:19 (21)	whosoever of you does evil, We shall let him taste a great chastisement
29:40 (39)	God would never wrong them
29:40 (39)	but they wronged themselves
30:9 (8)	and God would never wrong them
30:9 (8)	but themselves they wronged
42:42 (40)	the way is only open against those who do wrong to the people

d) perf. pass. (*ẓulima*)

4:148 (147)	God likes not the shouting of evil words unless a man has been wronged
16:41 (43)	those that emigrated in God's cause after they were wronged
22:39 (40)	leave is given to those who fight because they were wronged
26:227 (228)	and help themselves after being wronged

e) impf. pass. (*yuẓlamu*)

2:272 (274)	and you will not be wronged
2:279 (279)	you shall have your principal, unwronging and unwronged
2:281 (281)	and they shall not be wronged
3:25 (24)	and they shall not be wronged
3:161 (155)	and they shall not be wronged
4:49 (52)	they shall not be wronged a single date-thread
4:77 (79)	you shall not be wronged a single date-thread
4:124 (123)	they shall enter Paradise, and not be wronged a single date-spot
6:160 (161)	whoso brings an evil deed shall only be recompensed the like of it; they shall not be wronged
8:60 (62)	whatsoever you expend in the way of God shall be repaid you in full; you will not be wronged
10:47 (48)	justly the issue is decided between them, and they are not wronged
10:54 (55)	justly the issue is decided between them, and they are not wronged
16:111 (112)	every soul shall be paid in full for what it wrought, and they shall not be wronged
17:71 (73)	those shall read their book, and they shall not be wronged a single date-thread
19:60 (61)	they shall enter Paradise, and they shall not be wronged anything
21:47 (48)	not one soul shall be wronged anything
23:62 (64)	with Us is a Book speaking truth, and they shall not be wronged
36:54 (54)	so today no soul shall be wronged anything
39:69 (69)	justly the issue be decided between them, and they not wronged
45:22 (21)	that every soul may be recompensed for what it has earned; they shall not be wronged
46:19 (18)	that He may pay them in full for their works, and they not being wronged

f) n.vb. (*ẓulm*)

3:108 (104)	God desires not any injustice to living beings
4:10 (11)	those who devour the property of orphans unjustly, devour Fire
4:30 (34)	whosoever does that in transgression and wrongfully, him We shall certainly roast
4:153 (152)	and the thunderbolt took them for their evildoing
4:160 (158)	for the evildoing of those of Jewry, We have forbidden them certain good things
5:39 (43)	whoso repents, after his evildoing, and makes amends
6:82 (82)	those who believe, and have not confounded their belief with evildoing
6:131 (131)	that is because thy Lord would never destroy the cities unjustly
11:117 (119)	thy Lord would never destroy the cities unjustly
13:6 (7)	thy Lord is forgiving to men, for all their evil-doing
16:61 (63)	if God should take men to task for their evildoing
20:111 (110)	He will have failed whose burden is of evildoing
20:112 (111)	whosoever does deeds of righteousness, being a believer, shall fear neither wrong nor injustice
22:25 (26)	whosoever purposes to violate it wrongfully, We shall let him taste a painful chastisement
25:4 (5)	so they have committed wrong and falsehood
27:14 (14)	their souls acknowledged them, wrongfully and out of pride
31:13 (12)	to associate others with God is a mighty wrong
40:17 (17)	no wrong today
40:31 (33)	God desires not wrong for His servants
42:41 (39)	whosoever helps himself after he has been wronged

g) pcple. act. (*ẓālim*)

2:35 (33)	draw not nigh this tree, lest you be evildoers
2:51 (48)	then you took to yourselves the Calf after him and you were evildoers
2:92 (86)	then you took to yourselves the Calf after him and you were evildoers
2:95 (89)	their hands have forwarded; God knows the evildoers
2:124 (118)	My covenant shall not reach the evildoers
2:145 (140)	then thou wilt surely be among the evildoers

2:193 (189)	there shall be no enmity save for evildoers
2:229 (229)	whosoever transgresses the bounds of God — those are the evildoers
2:246 (247)	and God has knowledge of the evildoers
2:254 (255)	the unbelievers — they are the evildoers
2:258 (260)	God guides not the people of the evildoers
2:270 (273)	no helpers have the evildoers
3:57 (50)	God loves not the evildoers
3:86 (80)	God guides not the people of the evildoers
3:94 (88)	those are the evildoers
3:128 (123)	they are evildoers
3:140 (134)	and God loves not the evildoers
3:151 (144)	evil is the lodging of the evildoers
3:192 (189)	the evildoers shall have no helpers
4:75 (77)	bring us forth from this city whose people are evildoers
4:97 (99)	those the angels take, while still they are wronging themselves
5:29 (32)	an inhabitant of the Fire; that is the recompense of the evildoers
5:45 (49)	they are the evildoers
5:51 (56)	God guides not the people of the evildoers
5:72 (76)	and wrongdoers shall have no helpers
5:107 (106)	for then we would assuredly be among the evildoers
6:21 (21)	they shall not prosper, the evildoers
6:33 (33)	yet it is not thee they cry lies to, but the evildoers
6:47 (47)	shall any be destroyed, except the people of the evildoers?
6:52 (52)	shouldst drive them away, and so become one of the evildoers
6:58 (58)	God knows very well the evildoers
6:68 (67)	do not sit, after the reminding, with the people of the evildoers
6:93 (93)	if thou couldst only see when the evildoers are in the agonies of death
6:129 (129)	so We make the evildoers friends of each other
6:135 (136)	surely the evildoers will not prosper
6:144 (145)	surely God guides not the people of the evildoers
7:5 (4)	we were evildoers
7:19 (18)	come not nigh this tree, lest you be of the evildoers
7:41 (39)	even so We recompense the evildoers
7:44 (42)	God's curse is on the evildoers
7:47 (45)	Thou assign us with the people of the evildoers
7:148 (147)	yet they took it to them, and were evildoers
7:150 (149)	put me not among the people of the evildoers
8:54 (56)	all were evildoers
9:19 (19)	God guides not the people of the evildoers
9:23 (23)	whosoever of you takes them for friends, those — they are the evildoers
9:47 (47)	some of you would listen to them; and God knows the evildoers
9:109 (110)	God guides not the people of the evildoers
10:39 (40)	then behold how was the end of the evildoers
10:85 (85)	make us not a temptation to the people of the evildoers
10:106 (106)	if thou dost, then thou wilt surely be of the evildoers
11:18 (21)	the curse of God shall rest upon the evildoers
11:31 (33)	in that case I should be among the evildoers
11:44 (46)	it was said: 'Away with the people of the evildoers!'
11:83 (84)	marked with thy Lord, and never far from the evildoers
11:102 (104)	such is the seizing of thy Lord, when He seizes the cities that are evildoing
12:23 (23)	surely the evildoers do not prosper
12:75 (75)	so we recompense the evildoers
12:79 (79)	for if we did so, we would be evildoers
14:13 (16)	We will surely destroy the evildoers
14:22 (27)	as for the evildoers, for them awaits a painful chastisement
14:27 (32)	and God leads astray the evildoers
14:42 (43)	deem not that God is heedless of what the evildoers work
15:78 (78)	certainly the dwellers in the Thicket were evildoers

16:28 (30)	whom the angels take while still they are wronging themselves
16:113 (114)	they were seized by the chastisement while they were evildoers
17:47 (50)	they conspire, when the evildoers say, 'You are only following a man bewitched!'
17:82 (84)	the evildoers it increases not, except in loss
17:99 (101)	yet the evildoers refuse all but unbelief
18:29 (28)	surely We have prepared for the evildoers a fire
18:35 (33)	and he entered his garden, wronging himself
18:50 (48)	how evil is that exchange for the evildoers
19:38 (39)	but the evildoers even today are in error manifest
19:72 (73)	the evildoers We shall leave there, hobbling on their knees
21:11 (11)	how many a city that was evildoing We have shattered
21:14 (14)	they said, 'Alas for us! We have been evildoers'
21:29 (30)	even so We recompense the evildoers
21:46 (47)	they would surely say, 'Alas for us! We were evildoers'
21:59 (60)	surely he is one of the evildoers
21:64 (65)	they said, 'Surely it is you who are the evildoers'
21:87 (87)	glory be to Thee! I was one of the evildoers
21:97 (97)	nay, we were evildoers
22:45 (44)	how many a city We have destroyed in its evildoing
22:48 (47)	how many a city I have respited in its evildoing
22:53 (52)	surely the evildoers are in wide schism
22:71 (70)	for the evildoers there shall be no helper
23:28 (29)	God, who has delivered us from the people of the evildoers
23:41 (43)	so away with the people of the evildoers
23:94 (96)	O my Lord, put me not among the people of the evildoers
23:107 (109)	we shall be evildoers indeed
24:50 (49)	they are the evildoers
25:8 (9)	the evildoers say, 'You are only following a man bewitched!'
25:27 (29)	upon the day the evildoer shall bite his hands, saying
25:37 (39)	We have prepared for the evildoers a painful chastisement
26:10 (9)	go to the people of the evildoers
26:209 (209)	and never did We wrong
28:21 (20)	my Lord, deliver me from the people of the evildoers
28:25 (25)	be not afraid; thou hast escaped from the people of the evildoers
28:37 (37)	surely the evildoers will not prosper
28:40 (40)	so behold how was the end of the evildoers
28:50 (50)	surely God guides not the people of the evildoers
28:59 (59)	save that their inhabitants were evildoers
29:14 (13)	so the Flood seized them, while they were evildoers
29:31 (30)	we shall destroy the people of this city, for its people are evildoers
29:49 (48)	and none denies Our signs but the evildoers
31:11 (10)	nay, but the evildoers are in manifest error
34:31 (30)	if thou couldst see when the evildoers are stationed before their Lord
35:32 (29)	but of them some wrong themselves, some of them are lukewarm
35:37 (35)	the evildoers shall have no helper
35:40 (38)	the evildoers promise one another naught but delusion
37:63 (61)	We have appointed it as a trial for the evildoers
37:113 (113)	of their seed some are good-doers, and some manifest self-wrongers
39:24 (25)	and it is said to the evildoers, 'Taste now that you were earning!'
40:18 (19)	and the evildoers have not one loyal friend
40:52 (55)	upon the day when their excuses shall not profit the evildoers
42:8 (6)	and the evildoers shall have neither protector nor helper
42:21 (20)	for the evildoers there awaits a painful chastisement
42:22 (21)	thou seest the evildoers going in fear of that they have earned
42:40 (38)	surely He loves not the evildoers
42:44 (42)	and thou shalt see the evildoers
42:45 (44)	surely the evildoers are in lasting chastisement
43:76 (76)	We never (wronged) them, but they themselves did the wrong

45:19 (18)	the evildoers are friends one of the other
46:10 (9)	God guides not the people of the evildoers
49:11 (11)	whoso repents not, those — they are the evildoers
59:17 (17)	that is the recompense of the evildoers
60:9 (9)	whosoever takes them for friends, those — they are the evildoers
61:7 (7)	God guides never the people of the evildoers
62:5 (5)	God guides never the people of the evildoers
62:7 (7)	God knows the evildoers
66:11 (11)	deliver me from the people of the evildoers
68:29 (29)	truly, we were evildoers
71:24 (24)	increase Thou not the evildoers save in error
71:28 (29)	and do Thou not increase the evildoers save in ruin
76:31 (31)	as for the evildoers, He has prepared for them a painful chastisement

h) pcple. pass. (*maẓlūm*)

17:33 (35)	whosoever is slain unjustly

AẒLAM n.m. (comp. adj)~one who does greater wrong or evil

2:114 (108)	who does greater evil than he who bars God's places of worship
2:140 (134)	who does greater evil than he who conceals a testimony received from God?
6:21 (21)	who does greater evil than he who forges against God a lie
6:93 (93)	who does greater evil than he who forges against God a lie
6:144 (145)	who does greater evil than he who forges against God a lie
6:157 (158)	who does greater evil than he who cries lies to God's signs
7:37 (35)	who does greater evil than he who forges against God a lie
10:17 (18)	who does greater evil than he who forges against God a lie
11:18 (21)	who does greater evil than he who forges against God a lie?
18:15 (14)	who does greater evil than he who forges against God a lie?
18:57 (55)	who does greater evil than he who, being reminded of the signs of his Lord, turns away from them
29:68 (68)	who does greater evil than he who forges against God a lie
32:22 (22)	who does greater evil than he who is reminded of the signs of his Lord
39:32 (33)	who does greater evil than he who lies against God
53:52 (53)	the people of Noah before — certainly they did exceeding evil
61:7 (7)	who does greater evil than he who forges against God falsehood

ẒALLĀM n.m. (adj)~unjust, one who wrongs, oppressor

3:182 (178)	for that God is never unjust unto His servants
8:51 (53)	for that God is never unjust unto His servants
22:10 (10)	for that God is never unjust unto His servants
41:46 (46)	thy Lord wrongs not His servants
50:29 (28)	the Word is not changed with Me; I wrong not My servants

ẒALŪM n.m. (adj)~sinful, wrongdoing, evildoing

14:34 (37)	surely man is sinful, unthankful
33:72 (72)	surely he is sinful, very foolish

ẒULUMĀT n.f. (pl.of *ẓulmah*)~darkness; shadows

2:17 (16)	God took away their light, and left them in darkness
2:19 (18)	as a cloudburst out of heaven in which is darkness, and thunder
2:257 (258)	He brings them forth from the shadows into the light
2:257 (259)	idols, that bring them forth from the light into the shadows
5:16 (18)	and brings them forth from the shadows into the light by His leave
6:1 (1)	who created the heavens and the earth and appointed the shadows and light
6:39 (39)	those who cry lies to Our signs are deaf and dumb, dwelling in the shadows
6:59 (59)	not a grain in the earth's shadows
6:63 (63)	who delivers you from the shadows of land and sea?

6:97 (97) by them you might be guided in the shadows of land and sea
6:122 (122) as one whose likeness is in the shadows, and comes not forth from them
13:16 (17) or are the shadows and the light equal?
14:1 (1) that thou mayest bring forth mankind from the shadows to the light
14:5 (5) bring forth thy people from the shadows to the light
21:87 (87) then he called out in the darkness
24:40 (40) or they are as shadows upon a sea obscure
24:40 (40) shadows piled one upon another
27:63 (64) He who guides you in the shadows of the land and the sea
33:43 (42) to bring you forth from the shadows into the light
35:20 (20) the shadows and the light
39:6 (8) creation after creation in threefold shadows
57:9 (9) that He may bring you forth from the shadows into the light
65:11 (11) He may bring forth those who believe and do righteous deeds from the shadows

AẒLAMA vb. (IV)~to darken, to be or grow dark. (pcple. act.) shadowy, dark; being in darkness

a) perf. act.

2:20 (19) and when the darkness is over them, they halt

g) pcple. act. (*muẓlim*)

10:27 (28) as if their faces were covered with strips of night shadowy
36:37 (37) We strip it of the day and lo, they are in darkness

*Ẓ M ʾ

ẒAMIʾA vb. (I)~to thirst. (n.vb.) thirst

b) impf. act. (*yaẓmaʾu*)

20:119 (117) neither to thirst therein, nor to suffer the sun

f) n.vb. (*ẓamaʾ*)

9:120 (121) that is because they are smitten neither by thirst, nor fatigue

ẒAMʾĀN n.m.~thirsty, a man athirst

24:39 (39) which the man athirst supposes to be water

*Ẓ N N

ẒANNA vb. (I)~to suppose, to think (without certain knowledge), to deem, to reckon, to assume, to surmise; to suspect (n.vb.) a surmise, opinion, thought (without certain knowledge); suspicion (pcple. act.) one who thinks (evil thoughts), who surmises, who assumes

a) perf. act.

2:230 (230) if they suppose that they will maintain God's bounds
7:171 (170) as if it were a canopy, and they supposed it was about to fall on them
9:118 (119) they thought that there was no shelter from God
10:22 (23) and they think they are encompassed
10:24 (25) and its inhabitants think they have power over it
12:42 (42) then he said to the one he deemed should be saved of the two
12:110 (110) when the Messengers despaired, deeming they were counted liars
18:53 (51) the evildoers will see the Fire, and think that they are about to fall into it
21:87 (87) when he went forth enraged and thought that We would have no power
24:12 (12) did the believing men and women not of their own account think good thoughts

28:39 (39)	and they thought they should not be returned to Us
38:24 (23)	and David thought that We had only tried him
41:22 (21)	but you thought that God would never know much of the things that you were working
41:23 (22)	the thought you thought about your Lord, has destroyed you
41:48 (48)	and they will think that they have no asylum
48:12 (12)	you thought that the Messenger and the believers would never return
48:12 (12)	that was decked out fair in your hearts, and you thought evil thoughts
59:2 (2)	you did not think that they would go forth
59:2 (2)	and they thought that their fortresses would defend them against God
69:20 (20)	I thought that I should encounter my reckoning
72:5 (5)	we had thought that men and jinn would never speak against God a lie
72:7 (7)	and they thought, even as you also (thought), that God would never raise up anyone
72:7 (7)	and they (thought), even as you also thought, that God would never raise up anyone
72:12 (12)	we thought that we should never be able to frustrate God in the earth
75:28 (28)	and he thinks that it is the parting
84:14 (14)	he surely thought he would never revert

b) impf. act. (*yaẓunnu*)

2:46 (43)	who reckon that they shall meet their Lord
2:78 (73)	not knowing the Book, but only fancies and mere conjectures
2:249 (250)	said those who reckoned they should meet God
3:154 (148)	a party themselves had grieved, thinking of God thoughts that were not true
7:66 (64)	we think that thou art one of the liars
11:27 (29)	no, rather we think you are liars
17:52 (54)	you will think you have but tarried a little
17:101 (103)	Moses, I think thou art bewitched
17:102 (104)	Pharaoh, I think thou art accursed
18:35 (33)	I do not think that this will ever perish
18:36 (34)	I do not think that the Hour is coming
22:15 (15)	whosoever thinks God will not help him in the present world
26:186 (186)	indeed, we think that thou art one of the liars
28:38 (38)	for I think that he is one of the liars
33:10 (10)	your hearts reached your throats, while you thought thoughts about God
40:37 (39)	for I think that he is a liar
41:50 (50)	this is mine; I think not the Hour is coming
45:24 (23)	of that they have no knowledge; they merely conjecture
45:32 (31)	we have only a surmise, and are by no means
75:25 (25)	thou mightest think the Calamity has been wreaked on them
83:4 (4)	do those not think that they shall be raised up

f) n.vb. (*ẓann*, pl. *ẓunūn*)

3:154 (148)	such as the pagans thought, saying
4:157 (156)	they have no knowledge of him, except the following of surmise
6:116 (116)	they follow only surmise, merely conjecturing
6:148 (149)	you follow only surmise, merely conjecturing
10:36 (37)	the most of them follow only surmise
10:36 (37)	and surmise avails naught against truth
10:60 (61)	what will they think, who forge falsehood against God
10:66 (67)	they follow nothing but surmise
33:10 (10)	your hearts reached your throats, while you thought thoughts about God
34:20 (19)	Iblis proved true his opinion of them
37:87 (85)	what think you then of the Lord of all Being?
38:27 (26)	such is the thought of the unbelievers
41:23 (22)	the thought you thought about your Lord, has destroyed you
45:32 (31)	we have only a surmise, and are by no means certain
48:6 (6)	men and women alike, and those who think evil thoughts of God

48:12 (12)	fair in your hearts, and you thought evil thoughts
49:12 (12)	O believers, eschew much suspicion
49:12 (12)	some suspicion is a sin
53:23 (23)	they follow only surmise
53:28 (29)	they have not any knowledge thereof; they follow only surmise
53:28 (29)	and surmise avails naught against truth

g) pcple. act. (*ẓānn*)

48:6 (6)	men and women alike, and those who think evil thoughts

I. TERMS ASSOCIATED WITH THE DIVINE NAME

abase
  ahāna (*h w n)
able
  qadīr (*q d r)
abuse
  sabba (*s b b)
acquit
  kaffara (*k f r)
  barraʾa (*b r ʾ)
acquittal
  barāʾah (*b r ʾ)
admit
  adkhala (*d kh l)
admonish
  waʿaẓa (*w ʿ ẓ)
affair
  amara (*a m r)
afraid, to be
  khashiya (*kh sh y)
allow
  adhina (*a dh n)
anger (n)
  ghaḍiba (*gh ḍ b)
  sakhiṭa (*s kh ṭ)
anger (v)
  askhaṭa (*s kh ṭ)
angry, to be
  ghaḍiba (*gh ḍ b)
  sakhiṭa (*s kh ṭ)
annul
  nasakha (*n s kh)
answer (v)
  istajāba (*j w b)
apart (from God)
  allāh (*a l h)
appear
  badā (*b d w)
appoint
  jaʿala (*j ʿ l)
apportioned, that which is
  farīḍah (*f r ḍ)
argue
  ḥājja (*ḥ j j)
argument
  ḥujjah (*ḥ j j)
ashamed, to be
  istaḥá (*ḥ y y)
assail
  qātala (*q t l)
assign
  jaʿala (*j ʿ l)
associate (n)
  sharīk (*sh r k)
associate (v)
  ashraka (*sh r k)
avail against (God)
  aghná (*gh n y)
  malaka (*m l k)
averse, to be
  kariha (*k r h)
aware
  khabīr (*kh b r)

baptism
  ṣibghah (*ṣ b gh)
before (God)
  yad (*y d y)
beget
  walada (*w l d)
believe, belief, believer
  āmana (*a m n)
betray
  khāna (*kh w n)
better
  khayr (*kh y r)
bid (v)
  amara (*a m r)
bless
  anʿama (*n ʿ m)
  ṣallá (*ṣ l w)
blessed, to be
  tabāraka (*b r k)
blessing
  niʿmah (*n ʿ m)
blot out
  maḥā (*m ḥ w)
  maḥaqa (*m ḥ q)
bond
  ḥabl (*ḥ b l)
book
  kitāb (*k t b)
bounds
  ḥudūd (*ḥ d d)
bounty, bounteous
  ālāʾ (*a l w)
  faḍl (*f ḍ l)
bow (v)
  sajada (*s j d)
breach, to make
  shāqqa (*sh q q)
bring
  ātá (*a t y)
bring forth
  akhraja (*kh r j)
bring to light
  akhraja (*kh r j)
bring to naught
  abṭala (*b ṭ l)
bring together
  jamaʿa (*j m ʿ)
  allafa (*a l f)
buy
  ishtará (*sh r y)

call
  daʿā (*d ʿ w)
camel, she-
  nāqah (*n w q)
change (v)
  ghayyara (*gh y r)
  baddala (*b d l)
charge (n)
  waṣīyah (*w ṣ y)
charge (v)
  kallafa (*k l f)
  awṣá (*w ṣ y)
  waṣṣá (*w ṣ y)
chastise
  ʿadhdhaba (*ʿ dh b)
chastisement
  ʿadhāb (*ʿ dh b)
choose
  ijtabā (*j b y)
  iṣṭafá (*ṣ f w)
clear, to make
  bayyana (*b y n)
close (adj)
  awlá (*w l y)
come
  atá (*a t y)
comfort (n)

rāḥa (*r w ḥ)
command
amara (*a m r)
compact
mīthāq (*w th q)
compeers
andād (*n d d)
complaint, to make
ishtaká (*sh k w)
shakā (*sh k w)
compose differences
waffaqa (*w f q)
conceal
katama (*k t m)
confirm
aḥkama (*ḥ k m)
count, one who keeps
ḥasīb (*ḥ s b)
covenant (n)
ʿahd (*ʿ h d)
covenant, to make
ʿāhada (*ʿ h d)
ʿahida (*ʿ h d)
create, creation, creator
khalaqa (*kh l q)
cry to
daʿā (*d ʿ w)
curse (n)
laʿnah (*l ʿ n)
curse (v)
laʿana (*l ʿ n)

day
yawm (*y w m)
decide
qaḍá (*q ḍ y)
ḥakama (*ḥ k m)
defend
ʿaṣama (*ʿ ṣ m)
dāfaʿa (*d f ʿ)
manaʿa (*m n ʿ)
defender
waqá (*w q y)
defer
akhkhara (*a kh r)
deliver
anjá (*n j w)
najjá (*n j w)
deliverance
balagha (*b l gh)
delude
gharra (*gh r r)
deride
sakhira (*s kh r)
desire (v)
arāda (*r w d)
destroy
dammara (*d m r)
ahlaka (*h l k)
determine
qaddara (*q d r)
devise, devising, deviser
makara (*m k r)
die, to cause
amāta (*m w t)
disbelieve
kafara (*k f r)
disclose
akhraja (*kh r j)
aẓhara (*ẓ h r)
disobey
ʿaṣá (*ʿ ṣ w)
dispute (v)
ḥājaja (*ḥ j j)
jādala (*j d l)
distinguish
faṣala (*f ṣ l)
māza (*m y z)
division, to make
farraqa (*f r q)
do (v)
faʿala (*f ʿ l)
doubt (n)
shakk (*sh k k)
drive (v)
azjá (*z j w)
drive back
dafaʿa (*d f ʿ)

earth
arḍ (*a r ḍ)
easy
yasīr (*y s r)
efface
ʿafā (*ʿ f w)
emigrate, emigrant
hājara (*h j r)
encompass
aḥāṭa (*ḥ w ṭ)
encounter (n)
laqiya (*l q y)
enemy
ʿadūw (*ʿ d w)
enough
ḥasiba (*ḥ s b)
enrich
aghná (*gh n y)
enter, to make to
awlaja (*w l j)
equitable
aqsaṭ (*q s ṭ)
establish
jaʿala (*j ʿ l)
exalted
taʿālá (*ʿ l w)
expand
sharaḥa (*sh r ḥ)
extinguish
aṭfaʾa (*ṭ f ʾ)
extol
sabbaḥa (*s b ḥ)

face (n)
wajh (*w j h)
fail
akhlafa (*kh l f)
fail, cause to
aḥbaṭa (*ḥ b ṭ)
faith
āmana (*a m n)
faith, pure of
ḥanīf (*ḥ n f)
favour, to confer a
manna (*m n n)
fear (n)
khashiya (*kh sh y)
rahiba (*r h b)
taqwá (*w q y)
fear (v)
khāfa (*kh w f)
ittaqá (*w q y)
khashiya (*kh sh y)
fight (v)
ḥāraba (*ḥ r b)
find
wajada (*w j d)
fire
nār (*n w r)
flee
farra (*f r r)
forbid
ḥarrama (*ḥ r m)
nahá (*n h y)
maʿādh (*ʿ w dh)
forge (against God)
iftará (*f r y)

qāla (*q w l)
forget
nasiya (*n s y)
forgive
ghafara (*gh f r)
forgiveness
maghfirah (*gh f r)
forgiveness, pray
istaghfara (*gh f r)
forgiving
ghafūr (*gh f r)
friend
walīy (*w l y)
friend, to make a
tawallá (*w l y)
frighten
khawwafa (*kh w f)
from (God)
Allāh (*a l h)
frustrate
aʿjaza (*ʿ j z)

gather
jamaʿa (*j m ʿ)
gentle
raʾūf (*r ʾ f)
give
afāʾa (*f y ʾ)
ātá (*a t y)
jaʿala (*j ʿ l)
glory
ʿizzah (*ʿ z z)
glory be (to God)
subḥān (*s b ḥ)
godfearing
ittaqá (*w q y)
good-doer
muḥsin (*ḥ s n)
good, to do someone
aḥsana (*ḥ s n)
gracious, to be
manna (*m n n)
grasp (v)
qabaḍa (*q b ḍ)
grateful
shakara (*sh k r)
great
ʿazīz (*ʿ z z)
greet
ḥayyā (*ḥ y y)
grow, cause to
anbata (*n b t)
anshaʾa (*n sh ʾ)
guard (v)
ḥafiẓa (*ḥ f ẓ)
waqá (*w q y)
guardian
ḥafiẓa (*ḥ f ẓ)
wakīl (*w k l)
guide, guidance
hadá (*h d y)

hallow
ḥarrama (*ḥ r m)
hand (n)
yad (*y d y)
handiwork
ṣanaʿa (*ṣ n ʿ)
harm (v)
ḍarra (*ḍ r r)
hasten
ʿajjala (*ʿ j l)
hatred
maqata (*m q t)
hear
samiʿa (*s m ʿ)
hear, to make to
asmaʿa (*s m ʿ)
hearing
samīʿ (*s m ʿ)
heedless
ghafala (*gh f l)
help
naṣara (*n ṣ r)
helper
naṣīr (*n ṣ r)
hidden, to be
khafá (*kh f y)
hide
istakhfá (*kh f y)
hold (v)
amsaka (*m s k)
iʿtaṣama (*ʿ ṣ m)
homecoming
ṣāra (*ṣ y r)
hope for
rajā (*r j w)
humble
khashaʿa (*kh sh ʿ)
hurt (n)
ādhá (*a dh y)
hurt (v)
ḍarra (*ḍ r r)
increase (v)
zāda (*z y d)
independent
ghanīy (*gh n y)
inform
aṭlaʿa (*ṭ l ʿ)
innocent
barīʾ (*b r ʾ)
intercession
shafaʿa (*sh f ʿ)
intercessor
shafīʿ (*sh f ʿ)
issue
amara (*a m r)

judge, judgment
ḥakama (*ḥ k m)

kingdom
malaka (*m l k)
know
ʿalima (*ʿ l m)
knowledge
ʿilm (*ʿ l m)
knowledgeable
ʿalīm (*ʿ l m)

lawful, to make
aḥalla (*ḥ l l)
lead astray
aḍalla (*ḍ l l)
leave (of God)
adhina (*a dh n)
leave, to give
adhina (*a dh n)
lend
aqraḍa (*q r ḍ)
lie (v)
kadhaba (*k dh b)
life, to bring to
aḥyā (*ḥ y y)
light (n)
nūr (*n w r)
lighten
khaffafa (*kh f f)
like (v)
aḥabba (*ḥ b b)
likeness
mathal (*m th l)
look for
rajā (*r j w)
loose

arsala (*r s l)
love (n)
ḥubb (*ḥ b b)
love (v)
aḥabba (*ḥ b b)

magnify
kabbara (*k b r)
sabbaḥa (*s b ḥ)
make
jaʿala (*j ʿ l)
matter
amara (*a m r)
measure (v)
qadara (*q d r)
meet
lāqá (*l q y)
mention
dhakara (*dh k r)
mercy
maghfirah (*gh f r)
raḥima (*r ḥ m)
mercy, to have
raḥima (*r ḥ m)
message
risālah (*r s l)
messenger(s), Messenger
rasūl (*r s l)
rusul (*r s l)
Messiah
masīḥ (*m s ḥ)
might
baʾs (*b ʾ s)
mock
istahzaʾa (*h z ʾ)
mosque
masjid (*s j d)
multiply
ḍāʿafa (*ḍ ʿ f)
muster
ḥashara (*ḥ sh r)

name (n)
ism (*s m w)
near, to bring
qarraba (*q r b)
need, one in
faqīr (*f q r)
need, to be in no
istaghná (*gh n y)
neglect
farraṭa (*f r ṭ)
number (v)
aḥṣá (*ḥ ṣ y)

O God
allāhumma (*a l h)
obedient, to be
qanata (*q n t)
obey
aṭāʿa (*ṭ w ʿ)
omnipotent
iqtadara (*q d r)
one
aḥad (*a ḥ d)
wāḥid (*w ḥ d)
open
fataḥa (*f t ḥ)
oppose
ḥādda (*ḥ d d)
ordain
faraḍa (*f r ḍ)
ordained, that which is
farīḍah (*f r ḍ)
original
fiṭrah (*f ṭ r)
ornament
zīnah (*z y n)
other (than God)
allāh (*a l h)
overthrow
arkasa (*r k s)

pardon
ʿafā (*ʿ f w)
ghafara (*gh f r)
party
ḥizb (*ḥ z b)
path
ṣirāṭ (*ṣ r ṭ)
patience, patient
ṣabara (*ṣ b r)
pay in full
waffá (*w f y)
penitent, to turn
anāba (*n w b)
permit (v)
aḥalla (*ḥ l l)
pilgrimage
ḥajja (*ḥ j j)
place (v)
jaʿala (*j ʿ l)
please (v)
arḍá (*r ḍ y)
pleased, to be well-
raḍiya (*r ḍ y)
pleasure
marḍāt (*r ḍ y)
riḍwān (*r ḍ y)
pledge, a solemn
mawthiq (*w th q)
poor
faqīr (*f q r)
power
qūwah (*q w y)
power, to have
malaka (*m l k)
powerful
qadīr (*q d r)
aqāta (*q w t)
praise (n)
ḥamida (*ḥ m d)
prefer
āthara (*a th r)
faḍḍala (*f ḍ l)
prepare
aʿadda (*ʿ d d)
prescribe
kataba (*k t b)
kitāb (*k t b)
proclamation
adhān (*a dh n)
balāgh (*b l gh)
prohibit
ḥarrama (*ḥ r m)
promise
waʿada (*w ʿ d)
pronounce (judgment)
afatá (*f t y)
prophet
nabīy (*n b ʾ)
prostrate oneself
sajada (*s j d)
protect
ajāra (*j y r)
ʿaṣama (*ʿ ṣ m)
protection
walá (*w l y)
protector
ʿaṣama (*ʿ ṣ m)
mawlá (*w l y)
walīy (*w l y)
prove
maḥḥaṣa (*m ḥ ṣ)
provide
razaqa (*r z q)

provider
rāziq (*r z q)
razzāq (*r z q)
providing
rizq (*r z q)
provision (n)
rizq (*r z q)
provision (v)
razaqa (*r z q)
punishment
nakāl (*n k l)
pure of faith
ḥanīf (*ḥ n f)
purify
zakká (*z k w)
purpose
amara (*a m r)

quit
barīʾ (*b r ʾ)

raise
rafaʿa (*r f ʿ)
baʿatha (*b ʿ th)
reach (v)
nāla (*n y l)
waṣala (*w ṣ l)
reckoner
ḥasīb (*ḥ s b)
reckoning
ḥisāb (*ḥ s b)
reckoning, to make
ḥāsaba (*ḥ s b)
recompense (n)
mathūbah (*th w b)
recompense (v)
jazā (*j z y)
refer
radda (*r d d)
refuge, everlasting
ṣamad (*ṣ m d)
refuge, to seek
istaʿādha (*ʿ w dh)
refuge, to take
ʿādha (*ʿ w dh)
maʿādh (*ʿ w dh)
religion
dīn (*d y n)
remainder
baqīyah (*b q y)
remember, remembrance
dhakara (*dh k r)
restore
radda (*r d d)
restrain
kaffa (*k f f)
retribution
ʿiqāb (*ʿ q b)
return (n)
maradd (*r d d)
marjiʿ (*r j ʿ)
tāba (*t w b)
return (v)
rajaʿa (*r j ʿ)
tāba (*t w b)
reveal
abdá (*b d y)
fataḥa (*f t ḥ)
revive
aḥyā (*ḥ y y)
reward (n)
thawāb (*th w b)
reward (v)
athāba (*th w b)
rich
ghanīy (*gh n y)
right, to set
aṣlaḥa (*ṣ l ḥ)
rise up
ʿalā (*ʿ l w)
room, to make
fasaḥa (*f s ḥ)

sacred things
ḥurumāt (*ḥ r m)
sally forth
baraza (*b r z)
save
ḥāsha (*ḥ w sh)
sallama (*s l m)
say (v)
qāla (*q w l)
seal (v)
ṭabaʿa (*ṭ b ʿ)
seal, to set a
khatama (*kh t m)
see
raʾá (*r ʾ y)
sees, one who
baṣīr (*b ṣ r)
seize
akhadha (*a kh dh)
send
arsala (*r s l)
baʿatha (*b ʿ th)
send back
radda (*r d d)
send down
anzala (*n z l)
nazzala (*n z l)
servant
ʿabd (*ʿ b d)
serve
ʿabada (*ʿ b d)
set (v)
jaʿala (*j ʿ l)
she-camel
nāqah (*n w q)
shelter (n)
maljaʾ (*l j ʾ)
show (v)
ará (*r ʾ y)
signs
āyāt (*a y w)
similitude
mathal (*m th l)
slay
qatala (*q t l)
son
ibn (*b n w)
spare (v)
kafá (*k f y)
speak
kallama (*k l m)
qāla (*q w l)
speech
kalām (*k l m)
speech, to give
anṭaqa (*n ṭ q)
split
falaqa (*f l q)
stand (v)
qāma (*q w m)
ḥāla (*ḥ w l)
staunch
qawwām (*q w m)
steadfast
qawwām (*q w m)
strong
qawīy (*q w y)
struggle (v)
jāhada (*j h d)
subject (v)
sakhkhara (*s kh r)
submit
aslama (*s l m)

succour
waffaqa (*w f q)
succour, to call for
istaᶜāna (*ᶜ w n)
mustaᶜān (*ᶜ w n)
istaghātha (*gh w th)
suffice
kafá (*k f y)
suffices, one who
kāfī (*k f y)
sufficient
ḥasiba (*ḥ s b)
summon
daᶜā (*d ᶜ w)
surrender (n)
salam (*s l m)
surrender (v)
aslama (*s l m)
swallow, to cause to
khasafa (*kh s f)
swear
ḥalafa (*ḥ l f)
aqsama (*q s m)
taqāsama (*q s m)
swear fealty
bāyaᶜa (*b y ᶜ)
swerve, to cause
azāgha (*z y gh)

take
ittakhadha (*a kh dh)
tawaffá (*w f y)
take away
dhahaba (*dh h b)
take to task
ākhadha (*a kh dh)
taste, to let someone
adhāqa (*dh w q)
teach
ᶜallama (*ᶜ l m)
tell
nabbaʾa (*n b ʾ)
term
ajal (*a j l)
test (v)
balā (*b l w)
imtaḥana (*m ḥ n)
testify, testimony
shahida (*sh h d)
thankful
shakara (*sh k r)
shakūr (*sh k r)
thanks, to give
shakara (*sh k r)
think (evil thoughts)
ẓanna (*ẓ n n)
third (ord)
thālith (*th l th)
throw
ramá (*r m y)
tiding
bushrá (*b sh r)
tidings, to give
bashshara (*b sh r)
touch (v)
massa (*m s s)
treasuries
khazāʾin (*kh z n)
trick (v)
khādaᶜa (*kh d ᶜ)
khāna (*kh w n)
true, to be
naṣaḥa (*n ṣ ḥ)
ṣadaqa (*ṣ d q)
trust, to put one's
tawakkala (*w k l)
truth
ḥaqq (*ḥ q q)
truth, to speak the
ṣadaqa (*ṣ d q)
try
balā (*b l w)
ibtalá (*b l w)
turn humbly
raghiba (*r gh b)
turn something about
qallaba (*q l b)
turn something away
ṣarafa (*ṣ r f)
turn towards
tāba (*t w b)
turning back
maradd (*r d d)
turns, one who
tawwāb (*t w b)

unbeliever
kafara (*k f r)
unjust, to be
ḥāfa (*ḥ y f)
unseen
ghāba (*gh y b)

vengeance, to take
intaqama (*n q m)
verify
aḥaqqa (*ḥ q q)
victory
fataḥa (*f t ḥ)
visit (with affliction)
massa (*m s s)

wage
ajr (*a j r)
war
ḥaraba (*ḥ r b)
warden
ḥafīẓ (*ḥ f ẓ)
warn
ḥadhdhara (*ḥ dh r)
watchful
raqīb (*r q b)
way
sabīl (*s b l)
waymarks
shaᶜāʾir (*sh ᶜ r)
wealth
māl (*m w l)
will (v)
shāʾa (*sh y ʾ)
with (God)
Allāh (*a l h)
witness (n)
shahida (*sh h d)
shahīd (*sh h d)
witness, to bear
shahida (*sh h d)
witness, to call to
ash.hada (*sh h d)
wont
sunnah (*s n n)
word
kalām (*k l m)
kalimah (*k l m)
worship (v)
ᶜabada (*ᶜ b d)
worship, a place of
masjid (*s j d)
wrath
ghaḍiba (*gh ḍ b)
write
kataba (*k t b)
wrong (v)
ẓalama (*ẓ l m)
wroth, to be
ghaḍiba (*gh ḍ b)

II. (A) DIVINE NAME AND ATTRIBUTES

Able
  qadira (*q d r)
Absolute
  ṣamad (*ṣ m d)
Answerer
  ajāba (*j w b)
Aware
  khabīr (*kh b r)

Beneficent
  raḥmān (*r ḥ m)
Benign
  barr (1) (*b r r)
Bestower
  wahhāb (*w h b)
Blameless
  ḥāsha (*ḥ w sh)
Bountiful
  akrama (*k r m)
  ṭawl (*ṭ w l)

Clement
  ʿafūw (*ʿ f w)
  ḥalīm (*ḥ l m)
  raʾūf (*r ʾ f)
Compassionate
  raḥīm (*r ḥ m)
Compeller
  jabbār (*j b r)
Creator
  badīʿ (*b d ʿ)
  baraʾa (*b r ʾ)
  faṭara (*f ṭ r)
  khalaqa (*kh l q)
  khallāq (*kh l q)

Deliverer
  fattāḥ (*f t ḥ)
Disposer (of affairs)
  wakīl (*w k l)

Embracing
  wasiʿa (*w s ʿ)
Eternal
  qayyūm (*q w m)
  ṣamad (*ṣ m d)
Everlasting
  qayyūm (*q w m)
Everlasting Refuge
  ṣamad (*ṣ m d)
Evident
  ẓahara (*ẓ h r)
Exalted
  taʿālá (*ʿ l w)
Exalter
  rafīʿ (*r f ʿ)

Faithful
  āmana (*a m n)
Fashioner
  ṣawwara (*ṣ w r)
First
  awwal (*a w l)
Forgiver
  ghaffār (*gh f r)
  ghafūr (*gh f r)

Gatherer
  jamaʿa (*j m ʿ)
Generous
  karīm (*k r m)
Gentle
  laṭīf (*l ṭ f)
  raʾūf (*r ʾ f)
Giver
  wahhāb (*w h b)
Glorious
  ʿaẓīm (*ʿ ẓ m)
  akrama (*k r m)
  majīd (*m j d)
God
  Allāh (Allāh)
  ilāh (*a l h)
Gracious
  laṭīf (*l ṭ f)
  raḥmān (*r ḥ m)
Grateful
  shakara (*sh k r)
Great
  kabīr (*k b r)
Guardian
  ḥafīẓ (*ḥ f ẓ)
  wakīl (*w k l)
  walīy (*w l y)
Guide
  hadá (2) (*h d y)

He
  huwa (*h w)
Hearing
  samīʿ (*s m ʿ)
High
  ʿalīy (*ʿ l w)
Holy
  quddūs (*q d s)
Honourable
  akrama (*k r m)

Informed
  khabīr (*kh b r)
Inheritor
  waritha (*w r th)
Inward
  baṭana (*b ṭ n)
Irresistible
  jabbār (*j b r)

Judge
  ḥakama (*ḥ k m)

Kind
  laṭīf (*l ṭ f)
  raʾūf (*r ʾ f)
King
  malik (*m l k)
  malīk (*m l k)
Knower
  ʿalīm (*ʿ l m)
  ʿalima (*ʿ l m)
  khabīr (*kh b r)

Last
  ākhir (*a kh r)
Laudable
  ḥamīd (*ḥ m d)
Light
  nūr (*n w r)
Living
  ḥayy (*ḥ y y)
Lord
  rabb (*r b b)

Loving
wadūd (*w d d)

Majestic
jalāl (*j l l)
takabbara (*k b r)
Master of the Kingdom
malaka (*m l k)
Merciful
raḥmān (*r ḥ m)
Mighty
ʿazīz (*ʿ z z)
ʿaẓīm (*ʿ ẓ m)

Omnipotent
iqtadara (*q d r)
qadīr (*q d r)
qahara (*q h r)
qahhār (*q h r)
One
aḥad (*a ḥ d)
wāḥid (*w ḥ d)
Originator
faṭara (*f ṭ r)
Outward
ẓahara (*ẓ h r)
Overseer
aqāta (*q w t)

Pardoner
ʿafūw (*ʿ f w)
Peaceable
salām (*s l m)
Powerful
qadira (*q d r)
qadīr (*q d r)
aqāta (*q w t)
Praiseworthy
ḥamīd (*ḥ m d)
Preserver
haymana (*h y m n)
Protector
mawlá (*w l y)
walá (*w l y)
walīy (*w l y)
Provider
razzāq (*r z q)

Quickener
aḥyā (*ḥ y y)

Reckoner
ḥasīb (*ḥ s b)

Sagacious
khabīr (*kh b r)
Seeing
baṣīr (*b ṣ r)
Shaper
ṣawwara (*ṣ w r)
Splendid
akrama (*k r m)
Strong
qawīy (*q w y)
Sublime
takabbara (*k b r)
Subtle, Subtile
laṭīf (*l ṭ f)
Sufficient
ghanīy (*gh n y)
istaghná (*gh n y)
kafá (*k f y)
Superb
takabbara (*k b r)
Supreme
takabbara (*k b r)
Sure
matīn (*m t n)

Tender
laṭīf (*l ṭ f)
Thankful
shakara (*sh k r)
shakūr (*sh k r)
True
ḥaqq (*ḥ q q)
Trustee
wakīl (*w k l)
Turns, One who
tawwāb (*t w b)

Watcher
raqīb (*r q b)
Wise
ḥakīm (*ḥ k m)
Witness
shahīd (*sh h d)

II. (B) PROPER NOUNS

- Aaron
  - hārūn (*h r n)
- Abode, the
  - dār (*d w r)
- Abraham
  - ibrāhīm (*a b r)
- Abu Lahab
  - abu (*l h b)
  - lahab (*a b w)
- Ad
  - ʿād (*ʿ w d)
- Adam
  - ādam (*a d m)
- Ahmad
  - aḥmad (*ḥ m d)
- Al-Uzza
  - ʿuzzá (*ʿ z z)
- Al-Lat
  - al-lāt (*l y t)
- Alexander
  - dhul-qarnayn (*q r n)
- All-being
  - ʿālamīn (*ʿ l m)
- Ansar
  - naṣīr (*n ṣ r)
- Apostle(s)
  - ḥawārīyūn (*ḥ w r)
  - rasūl (*r s l)
  - rusul (*r s l)
- Aqsa (Mosque)
  - masjid (*s j d)
  - aqṣā (*q ṣ y)
- Arab, non-
  - aʿjamīy (*ʿ j m)
- Arabic
  - ʿarabīy (*ʿ r b)
- Arafat
  - ʿarafāt (*ʿ r f)
- Ararat
  - jūdī (*j w d)
- Arim (flood)
  - ʿarim (*ʿ r m)
- Ark
  - fulk (*f l k)
  - tābūt (*t b t)
- Ayah
  - āyah (*a y w)
- Azar
  - āzar (*a z r)

- Baal
  - baʿl (*b ʿ l)
- Babylon
  - bābil (*b b l)
- Badr
  - badr (*b d r)
- Bahira
  - baḥīrah (*b ḥ r)
- Bekka
  - bakkah (*b k k)
- Blaze
  - saʿīr (*s ʿ r)
  - jaḥīm (*j ḥ m)
- Book
  - kitāb (*k t b)
- Book of David
  - zabūr (*z b r)

- Certain, the
  - yaqīn (*y q n)
- Christ
  - masīḥ (*m s ḥ)
- Christian
  - naṣrānī (*n ṣ r)
- Clatterer, the
  - qāriʿah (*q r ʿ)
- Confederates
  - ḥizb (*ḥ z b)
- Consuming One
  - ḥuṭamah (*ḥ ṭ m)
- Criterion
  - furqān (*f r q)
- Crusher
  - ḥuṭamah (*ḥ ṭ m)
- Cry (of Gabriel)
  - ṣayḥah (*ṣ y ḥ)

- David
  - dāwūd (*d w d)
- Devil
  - iblīs (*b l s)
  - gharūr (*gh r r)
  - khannās (*kh n s)
  - shayṭān (*sh ṭ n)
  - waswās (*w s w s)
- Dhikr
  - dhakara (*dh k r)
- Dhul Karnain
  - dhul-qarnayn (*q r n)
- Dhul Kifl
  - kifl (*k f l)
- Dhul Nun
  - nūn (*n w n)
- Disciples
  - ḥawārīyūn (*ḥ w r)
- Distinction
  - furqān (*f r q)
- Dog Star
  - shiʿrá (*sh ʿ r)
- Doom
  - wāqiʿah (*w q ʿ)

- Eden
  - ʿadn (*ʿ d n)
  - jannah (*j n n)
- Efreet
  - ʿifrīt (*ʿ f r)
- Egypt
  - miṣr (*m ṣ r)
- Elias
  - ilyās (*a l s)
- Elijah
  - ilyās (*a l s)
  - kifl (*k f l)
- Elisha
  - alyasaʿ (*y s ʿ)
- Enoch
  - idrīs (*d r s)
- Event
  - wāqiʿah (*w q ʿ)
- Evident
  - ẓahara (*ẓ h r)
- Ezekiel
  - kifl (*k f l)
- Ezra
  - ʿuzayr (*ʿ z r)

- Fate
  - manūn (*m n n)
- Fount of Abundance
  - kawthar (*k th r)

Friday
jumuʿah (*j m ʿ)

Gabriel
jibrīl (*j b r)
Garden
jannah (*j n n)
Gehenna
jahannam (*j h n m)
Gog
yaʾjūj (*y j j)
Goliath
jālūt (*j l y)
Gospel
injīl (*n j l)
Greeks
rūm (*r w m)

Haman
hāmān (*h m n)
Hami
ḥāmi (*ḥ m y)
Harut
hārūt (*h r t)
Heaven
samāʾ (*s m w)
Heaven, highest place in
ʿillīyūn (*ʿ l w)
ghurfah (*gh r f)
Hell
ḥuṭamah (*ḥ ṭ m)
jahannam (*j h n m)
jaḥīm (*j ḥ m)
saʿīr (*s ʿ r)
Hell, guards of
zabāniyah (*z b n)
Hell, mountain in
ṣaʿūd (*ṣ ʿ d)
Hell, plant of
ḍarīʿ (*ḍ r ʿ)
Helpers
naṣīr (*n ṣ r)
Hereafter
ākhirah (*a kh r)
dār (*d w r)
Hijr (Thamood's habitat)
ḥijr (*ḥ j r)
Holy Spirit
qudus (*q d s)
rūḥ (*r w ḥ)
Hood
hūd (*h w d)
Hour
āzifah (*a z f)
sāʿah (*s w ʿ)
House, the
bayt (*b y t)
Hunain (Hunayn)
ḥunayn (*ḥ n n)

Iblis
iblīs (*b l s)
Idris
idrīs (*d r s)
Ignorance
jāhilīyah (*j h l)
Illiyun
ʿillīyūn (*ʿ l w)
Imran
ʿimrān (*ʿ m r)
Indubitable
ḥāqqah (*ḥ q q)
Inevitable
ḥāqqah (*ḥ q q)
Iram
iram (*a r m)
Isaac
is.ḥāq (*s ḥ q)
Ishmael
ismāʿīl (*s m ʿ)
Islam
aslama (*s l m)
silm (*s l m)
Israel
isrāʾīl (*s r y)

Jacob
yaʿqūb (*y ʿ q b)
Jahiliyah
jāhilīyah (*j h l)
Jesus
ʿīsá (*ʿ y s)
Jews
hāda (*h w d)
yahūd (*y h d)
Jibt
jibt (*j b t)
Jihad
jāhada (*j h d)
Job
ayyūb (*a y b)
John
yaḥyá (*ḥ y y)
Jonah
ḥūt (*ḥ w t)
nūn (*n w n)
ṣāḥib (*ṣ ḥ b)
yūnus (*y w n)
Joseph
yūsuf (*y s f)
Judgment
furqān (*f r q)
Judi
jūdī (*j w d)

Kaaba
bayt (*b y t)
kaʿbah (*k ʿ b)
masjid (*s j d)
Kafur (fountain in Paradise)
kāfūr (*k f r)
Korah
qārūn (*q r n)
Koraish (Quraish)
quraysh (*q r sh)
Koran (Qur'an)
furqān (*f r q)
kitāb (*k t b)
qurʾān (*q r ʾ)
mathānī (*th n y)

Law
shirʿah (*sh r ʿ)
Life (eternal)
ḥayawān (*ḥ y y)
Lokman
luqmān (*l q m)
Lot
lūṭ (*l w ṭ)

Magians
majūs (*m j s)
Magog
maʾjūj (*j w j)
Malik (angel)
mālik (*m l k)
Manat
manāt (*m n y)
Manna
mann (*m n n)
Marut
mārūt (*m r t)
Marwa
marwah (*m r w)
Mary
farj (*f r j)

aḥṣana (*ḥ ṣ n)
maryam (*m r y m)
Mecca
bakkah (*b k k)
makkah (*m k k)
Mecca, to visit
iʿtamara (*ʿ m r)
Meccans
ummīy (*a m m)
Medina
madīnah (*m d n)
yathrib (*y th r b)
Men of the Pit
ukhdūd (*kh d d)
Messenger(s)
rasūl (*r s l)
rusul (*r s l)
Messiah
masīḥ (*m s ḥ)
Michael
mīkāl (*m k l)
Midian
aykah (*a y k)
madyan (*m d n)
Moses
mūsá (*m w s)
Mosque (Jerusalem)
masjid (*s j d)
aqṣā (*q ṣ y)
Mosque (Kaaba)
bayt (*b y t)
masjid (*s j d)
Mount Ararat
jūdī (*j w d)
Mount Sinai
saynāʾ (*s y n)
Mount, the
ṭūr (*ṭ w r)
Muhammad
aḥmad (*ḥ m d)
muḥammad (*ḥ m d)
nabīy (*n b ʾ)
rasūl (*r s l)
Muslim (Moslem)
aslama (*s l m)
Mysterious Letters
alif.lām.mīm (*a l m)
alif.lām.mīm.rā (*a l m r)
alif.lām.mīm.ṣād (*a l m ṣ)
alif.lām.rā (*a l r)
ʿayn.sīn.qāf (*ʿ s q)
ḥā.mīm (*ḥ m)
kāf.hā.yā.ʿayn.ṣād (*k h y ṣ)
nūn (*n)
qāf (*q)
ṣād (*ṣ)
ṭā.hā (*ṭ h)
ṭā.sīn (*ṭ s)
ṭā.sīn.mīm (*ṭ s m)
yā.sīn (*y s)

Name of God, to invoke
ahalla (*h l l)
Nasr
nasr (*n s r)
Noah
nūḥ (*n w ḥ)

Outburst
ṭāghiyah (*ṭ gh y)
Outward
ẓahara (*ẓ h r)

Paradise
firdaws (*f r d s)
jannah (*j n n)
Paradise, fountain in
kāfūr (*k f r)
kawthar (*k th r)
Pentateuch
tawrāt (*t w r)
Pharaoh
firʿawn (*f r ʿ n)
Pilgrim garb, in
ḥurum (*ḥ r m)
Pilgrimage
ḥajja (*ḥ j j)
ḥalla (*ḥ l l)
Pit
hāwiyah (*h w y)
Power
qadar (*q d r)
Prophet
nabīy (*n b ʾ)
Psalms
zabūr (*z b r)

Qadar
qadar (*q d r)
Qiblah
qiblah (*q b l)

Rakeem
raqīm (*r q m)
Ramadan
ramaḍān (*r m ḍ)
Rass
rass (*r s s)
Reality
ḥāqqah (*ḥ q q)
Receiver
talaqqá (*l q y)
Romans
rūm (*r w m)

Sa'iba
sāʾibah (*s y b)
Sabaeans
ṣābiʾūn (*ṣ b ʾ)
Sabbath
sabt (*s b t)
Sabbath, to keep the
sabata (*s b t)
Sacred Precinct, in
ḥurum (*ḥ r m)
Safa
ṣafā (*ṣ f w)
Sakar
saqar (*s q r)
Sakina
sakīnah (*s k n)
Salih
ṣāliḥ (*ṣ l ḥ)
Salsabil
salsabīl (*s b l)
Salvation
furqān (*f r q)
Samaritan
sāmirī (*s m r)
Satan
iblīs (*b l s)
gharūr (*gh r r)
khannās (*kh n s)
shayṭān (*sh ṭ n)
waswās (*w s w s)
Saul
ṭālūt (*ṭ l t)
Scriptures
kitāb (*k t b)
zabūr (*z b r)
Sheba
ʿarim (*ʿ r m)
sabaʾ (*s b ʾ)
Shechina
sakīnah (*s k n)
Shuaib

shuʿayb (*sh ʿ b)
Sijjin
sijjīn (*s j n)
Sinai
saynāʾ (*s y n)
sīnīn (*s y n)
Sirius
shiʿrá (*sh ʿ r)
Solomon
sulaymān (*s l m)
Striking
qāriʿah (*q r ʿ)
Sura
sūrah (*s w r)
Suwa
suwāʿ (*s w ʿ)

Talut
ṭālūt (*ṭ l t)
Tasnim
tasnīm (*s n m)
Tempter, the
waswās (*w s w s)
Terror
wāqiʿah (*w q ʿ)
Thamood
thamūd (*th m d)
Torah
tawrāt (*t w r)
Towa
ṭuwá (*ṭ w y)
Tubba'
tubbaʿ (*t b ʿ)

Wadd
wadd (*w d d)
Wall (between Heaven and Hell)
aʿrāf (*ʿ r f)
Wasila
waṣīlah (*w ṣ l)
Whisperer
khannās (*kh n s)
Word
kalām (*k l m)
World to Come
ākhirah (*a kh r)

Ya'uq
yaʿūq (*y ʿ q)
Yaghuth
yaghūth (*gh w th)
Yathrib
yathrib (*y thr b)

Zachariah
zakarīya (*z k r)
Zaid
zayd (*z y d)
Zakat
zakāt (*z k w)
Zakkoum
zaqqūm (*z q m)

II. (C) GENERAL INDEX

abandon
hajara (*h j r)
taraka (*t r k)
wadhara (*w dh r)
abase
adhalla (*dh l l)
istaḍʿafa (*ḍ ʿ f)
ahāna (*h w n)
istakāna (*k y n)
akhbata (*kh b t)
khafaḍa (*kh f ḍ)
khashaʿa (*kh sh ʿ)
akhzá (*kh z y)
khaziya (*kh z y)
abased
dhalīl (*dh l l)
abasement
dhillah (*dh l l)
abate
fattara (*f t r)
ghāḍa (*gh y ḍ)
khabā (*kh b w)
naqaṣa (*n q ṣ)
aqlaʿa (*q l ʿ)
sakata (*s k t)
abhorrence
maqata (*m q t)
nakīr (*n k r)
abide
baqiya (*b q y)
labitha (*l b th)
makatha (*m k th)
aqāma (*q w m)
abide forever
khalada (*kh l d)
ability
juhd (*j h d)
abject
dakhara (*d kh r)
dhalīl (*dh l l)
khaḍaʿa (*kh ḍ ʿ)
able
qadīr (*q d r)
able, to be
qadara (*q d r)
istaṭāʿa (*ṭ w ʿ)
aṭāqa (*ṭ w q)
abode
umm (*a m m)
bayt (*b y t)
dār (*d w r)
maqʿad (*q ʿ d)
muqām (*q w m)
maskan (*s k n)
sakana (*s k n)
mathwá (*th w y)
abomination
fāḥishah (*f ḥ sh)
faḥshāʾ (*f ḥ sh)
khabāʾith (*kh b th)
maqata (*m q t)
rijs (*r j s)
abounding
ʿarīḍ (*ʿ r ḍ)
jamm (*j m m)
about
ḥawl (*ḥ w l)
abrogate
nasakha (*n s kh)
absolution
taḥillah (*ḥ l l)
absolve
barraʾa (*b r ʾ)
kaffara (*k f r)
abstain
istaʿṣama (*ʿ ṣ m)
hajara (*h j r)
abstinence
taʿaffafa (*ʿ f f)
abstinent, to be
istaʿaffa (*ʿ f f)
abundance
ʿafā (*ʿ f w)
kathrah (*k th r)
kawthar (*k th r)
abundant
kathīr (*k th r)
lubad (*l b d)
naḍḍākh (*n ḍ kh)
wafara (*w f r)
abuse
sabba (*s b b)
salaqa (*s l q)
acacias
ṭalḥ (*ṭ l ḥ)
accept
qabila (*q b l)
taqabbala (*q b l)
raḍiya (*r ḍ y)
acceptance
qabila (*q b l)
riḍwān (*r ḍ y)
access
shirʿah (*sh r ʿ)
accomplish
faʿʿāl (*f ʿ l)
qaḍá (*q ḍ y)
waṭar (*w ṭ r)
accordance
wāfaqa (*w f q)
account
ḥisāb (*ḥ s b)
kitāb (*k t b)
accoutre
shawkah (*sh w k)
accursed
rajīm (*r j m)
thabara (*th b r)
accuse
ramá (*r m y)
accusing
lawwām (*l w m)
acknowledge
istayqana (*y q n)
acquaint
ʿarrafa (*ʿ r f)
acquiesce
akhbata (*kh b t)
acquire (wealth)
istakthara (*k th r)
acquire, to cause to
aqná (*q n y)
acquit
barraʾa (*b r ʾ)
kaffara (*k f r)
acquittal
barāʾah (*b r ʾ)
act (v)
ʿamila (*ʿ m l)
faʿala (*f ʿ l)
act (n)

nāfilah (*n f l)
act blithely
fakih (*f k h)
act justly
aqsaṭa (*q s ṭ)
act unjustly
ashaṭṭa (*sh ṭ ṭ)
ẓalama (*ẓ l m)
act wickedly
fajara (*f j r)
act with kindness
aḥsana (*ḥ s n)
action
ʿamila (*ʿ m l)
fiʿl (*f ʿ l)
action, customary
sunnah (*s n n)
active, to be
faʿala (*f ʿ l)
add
izdāda (*z y d)
zāda (*z y d)
add the saving words
istathná (*th n y)
addition
mazīd (*z y d)
address
khāṭaba (*kh ṭ b)
admire
aʿjaba (*ʿ j b)
akbara (*k b r)
admit
adkhala (*d kh l)
admonish
waʿaẓa (*w ʿ ẓ)
admonition
tadhkirah (*dh k r)
mawʿiẓah (*w ʿ ẓ)
adopted son
adʿiyāʾ (*d ʿ w)
adorn
ḥallá (*ḥ l y)
zayyana (*z y n)
adorned, to be
izzayyana (*z y n)
adornment
zīnah (*z y n)
adultery
zaná (*z n y)
advance (v)
barraza (*b r z)
furuṭ (*f r ṭ)
aqbala (*q b l)
qaddama (*q d m)
advantage
ʿaraḍ (*ʿ r ḍ)
adversary
khaṣīm (*kh ṣ m)
adversity
ḍarrāʾ (*ḍ r r)
shiqwah (*sh q y)
advice
naṣaḥa (*n ṣ ḥ)
advise
aftá (*f t y)
naṣaḥa (*n ṣ ḥ)
advocate
khaṣīm (*kh ṣ m)
afar, from
junub (*j n b)
afar, to keep
naʾá (*n ʾ y)
affair
amara (*a m r)
shaʾn (*sh ʾ n)
shayʾ (*sh y ʾ)
affection
mawaddah (*w d d)
afflict
iʿtarā (*ʿ r w)
fatana (*f t n)
massa (*m s s)
sāma (*s w m)
affliction
ḍarra (*ḍ r r)
muṣībah (*ṣ w b)
affluence
ṭawl (*ṭ w l)
wasiʿa (*w s ʿ)
affluent
awsaʿa (*w s ʿ)
afford
aṭāqa (*ṭ w q)
aflame, be
ishtaʿala (*sh ʿ l)
afraid
wajil (*w j l)
afraid, be
fariqa (*f r q)
ḥadhira (*ḥ dh r)
khāfa (*kh w f)
ashfaqa (*sh f q)
wajila (*w j l)
after
athar (*a th r)
khalf (*kh l f)
khilāf (*kh l f)
warāʾ (*w r y)
afternoon
ʿaṣr (*ʿ ṣ r)
again
karrah (*k r r)
against
ḍidd (*ḍ d d)
qibal (*q b l)
age
ʿumur (*ʿ m r)
ḥuqub (*ḥ q b)
age, to come of
balagha (*b l gh)
ashudd (*sh d d)
aged
kabīr (*k b r)
kabira (*k b r)
qadīm (*q d m)
shaykh (*sh y kh)
aggressor, to be an
iʿtadá (*ʿ d w)
agony
ghamrah (*gh m r)
agony (of death)
sakrah (*s k r)
agree
ajmaʿa (*j m ʿ)
aqarra (*q r r)
tarāḍá (*r ḍ y)
wāṭaʾa (*w ṭ ʾ)
agreeable
suwá (*s w y)
agreement
kalimah (*k l m)
mawthiq (*w th q)
ahead
amām (*a m m)
aid
ghātha (*gh y th)
naṣara (*n ṣ r)
aṣrakha (*ṣ r kh)
aid, to call for
istaghātha (*gh y th)
ailment
adhá (*a dh y)
aim at getting
tayammama (*y m m)
air
jaw (*j w w)

Alas!
wayl (*w y l)
alight
ḥalla (*ḥ l l)
alike
kufuʾ (*k f ʾ)
sawāʾ (*s w y)
ishtabaha (*sh b h)
tashābaha (*sh b h)
alive
ḥayy (*ḥ y y)
all
ajmaʿūn (*j m ʿ)
jamīʿ (*j m ʿ)
kāffah (*k f f)
all at once
jumlah (*j m l)
allege
zaʿama (*z ʿ m)
allegiance
bāyaʿa (*b y ʿ)
allot
qayyaḍa (*q y ḍ)
allow
adhina (*a dh n)
ally
ḥizb (*ḥ z b)
alms
ṣadaqah (*ṣ d q)
zakāt (*z k w)
alms, to give
taṣaddaqa (*ṣ d q)
alone
fard (*f r d)
waḥd (*w ḥ d)
waḥīd (*w ḥ d)
already
sabaqa (*s b q)
altar
nuṣub (*n ṣ b)
alter
baddala (*b d l)
ghayyara (*gh y r)
ḥawwala (*ḥ w l)
altercation
khāṣama (*kh ṣ m)
alternate
dāwala (*d w l)
ikhtalafa (*kh l f)
alternately
khilāf (*kh l f)
altogether
jamīʿ (*j m ʿ)
ajmaʿūn (*j m ʿ)
amass
jamaʿa (*j m ʿ)
rakama (*r k m)
awʿá (*w ʿ y)
amazing
farīy (*f r y)
ambiguous
tashābaha (*sh b h)
ambush
irṣād (*r ṣ d)
marṣad (*r ṣ d)
mirṣād (*r ṣ d)
amends, to make
aʿtaba (*ʿ t b)
aṣlaḥa (*ṣ l ḥ)
amongst
khilāl (*kh l l)
amorous
ʿurub (*ʿ r b)
ample
madda (*m d d)
wafara (*w f r)
amplify in speech
afāḍa (*f y ḍ)
amplitude
wasiʿa (*w s ʿ)
anchor (v)
rasā (*r s y)
ancient
ʿatīq (*ʿ t q)
qadīm (*q d m)
ancient ones
awwalūn (*a w l)
angel
ʿaqqaba (*ʿ q b)
ḥafaẓah (*ḥ f ẓ)
talaqqá (*l q y)
malak (*m l k)
malāk (*l ʾ k)
anger
āsafa (*a s f)
ghaḍiba (*gh ḍ b)
ghāẓa (*gh y ẓ)
askhaṭa (*s kh ṭ)
sakhiṭa (*s kh ṭ)
rijs (*r j s)
angry
ghāḍaba (*gh ḍ b)
ghaḍbān (*gh ḍ b)
ghaḍiba (*gh ḍ b)
sakhiṭa (*s kh ṭ)
anguish
baththa (*b th th)
ghamma (*gh m m)
ḥasrah (*ḥ s r)
animal
bahīmah (*b h m)
dābbah (*d b b)
animal gored to death
naṭīḥah (*n ṭ ḥ)
animal, riding
rakūb (*r k b)
ankle
kaʿb (*k ʿ b)
announce
aʿlana (*ʿ l n)
announce one's presence
istaʾnasa (*a n s)
annul
nasakha (*n s kh)
another
ākhar (*a kh r)
answer (n)
jawāb (*j w b)
answer (v)
ajāba (*j w b)
istajāba (*j w b)
ant
namlah (*n m l)
ant-weight
dharrah (*dh r r)
anxiety, to cause
ahamma (*h m m)
anxious
ḥarīṣ (*ḥ r ṣ)
anxious, to be
ḥaraṣa (*ḥ r ṣ)
anyone
aḥad (*a ḥ d)
dayyār (*d w r)
anything
shayʾ (*sh y ʾ)
anything lawful
ḥill (*ḥ l l)
anything unlawful
ḥijr (*ḥ j r)
apart, to set
zayyala (*z y l)
apartment
ḥujurāt (*ḥ j r)
apes
qiradah (*q r d)

apostasy
fitnah (*f t n)
apostatize
irtadda (*r d d)
apparel
libās (*l b s)
apparent
ẓahara (*ẓ h r)
appear
badā (*b d w)
ẓahara (*ẓ h r)
appear (as someone else)
tamaththala (*m th l)
appear (as spectre)
ṭāfa (*ṭ y f)
appear (in glory)
tajallá (*j l y)
appear, cause to
khayyala (*kh y l)
shabbaha (*sh b h)
aẓhara (*ẓ h r)
appetite
hanī' (*h n ')
appoint
ajjala (*a j l)
faraḍa (*f r ḍ)
jaᶜala (*j ᶜ l)
qasama (*q s m)
waqata (*w q t)
appoint as agent
iṣṭanaᶜa (*ṣ n ᶜ)
appoint with someone
wāᶜada (*w ᶜ d)
apportion
faraḍa (*f r ḍ)
appraise
ashᶜara (*sh ᶜ r)
apprehensive
ashfaqa (*sh f q)
approach (n)
qurbān (*q r b)
approach (v)
atá (*a t y)
azifa (*a z f)
aqbala (*q b l)
qariba (*q r b)
approve
irtaḍá (*r ḍ y)
raḍiya (*r ḍ y)
approved
ḥaqīq (*ḥ q q)
apraising
inbaᶜatha (*b ᶜ th)
apt
jadīr (*j d r)
arbiter
ḥakam (*ḥ k m)
architect
bannā' (*b n y)
ardent
jamm (*j m m)
argue
ḥājja (*ḥ j j)
jādala (*j d l)
argument
abāna (*b y n)
ḥujjah (*ḥ j j)
khāṭaba (*kh ṭ b)
qāla (*q w l)
arise
qāma (*q w m)
ark
tābūt (*t b t)
arm
ᶜaḍud (*ᶜ ḍ d)
dhirāᶜ (*dh r ᶜ)
arm-pit
janāḥ (*j n ḥ)
arm, length of
dharᶜ (*dh r ᶜ)
dhirāᶜ (*dh r ᶜ)
armed
shawkah (*sh w k)
arms
asliḥah (*s l ḥ)
arms, take in
āwá (*a w y)
army
jund (*j n d)
nadīy (*n d w)
around
ḥawl (*ḥ w l)
arouse
inbaᶜatha (*b ᶜ th)
aḥdatha (*ḥ d th)
awzaᶜa (*w z ᶜ)
arouse a desire
manná (*m n y)
arouse suspicion
arāba (*r y b)
arraign
aḥḍara (*ḥ ḍ r)
arrange
ᶜaddada (*ᶜ d d)
rattala (*r t l)
arrange for a meeting
wāᶜada (*w ᶜ d)
array, in
qubul (*q b l)
array, to set it
wazaᶜa (*w z ᶜ)
arrayed
ṣaffa (*ṣ f f)
arrive
ṣāra (*ṣ y r)
warada (*w r d)
arrogant
baṭira (*b ṭ r)
jabbār (*j b r)
istakbara (*k b r)
arrogantly, to walk
tamaṭṭá (*m ṭ w)
arrow (of divination)
azlām (*z l m)
arrow-shuffling
maysir (*y s r)
art
ṣanᶜah (*ṣ n ᶜ)
artifice
kāda (*k y d)
as
mithl (*m th l)
ascend
ᶜalā (*ᶜ l w)
ᶜaraja (*ᶜ r j)
irtaqá (*r q y)
ṣaᶜida (*ṣ ᶜ d)
ṭalaᶜa (*ṭ l ᶜ)
ascent
ᶜalā (*ᶜ l w)
ᶜaqabah (*ᶜ q b)
raqiya (*r q y)
ṣaᶜūd (*ṣ ᶜ d)
ascertain
taḥassasa (*ḥ s s)
ayqana (*y q n)
istayqana (*y q n)
ascribe (partners to God)
ᶜadala (*ᶜ d l)
ashraka (*sh r k)
sharika (*sh r k)
ashamed, to be
istaḥá (*ḥ y y)
ashes
ramād (*r m d)
aside

jānib (*j n b)
aside, to set
ʿazala (*ʿ z l)
nabadha (*n b dh)
ask
saʾala (*s ʾ l)
ask (for favour)
istaʿtaba (*ʿ t b)
ask (for food)
istaṭʿama (*ṭ ʿ m)
ask (for help)
istanṣara (*n ṣ r)
ask (for pardon)
istaghfara (*gh f r)
ask (for pronouncement)
istaftá (*f t y)
ask (for rain)
istaghātha (*gh y th)
ask (for victory)
istaftaḥa (*f t ḥ)
ask (leave)
istaʾnasa (*a n s)
ask (permission)
istaʾdhana (*a dh n)
ask to be told
istanbaʾa (*n b ʾ)
aspire
tanāfasa (*n f s)
ass
ḥimār (*ḥ m r)
assail
saṭā (*s ṭ w)
assault
baṭasha (*b ṭ sh)
baṭshah (*b ṭ sh)
ajlaba (*j l b)
iqtaḥama (*q ḥ m)
assemble
ḥashara (*ḥ sh r)
jamaʿa (*j m ʿ)
ijtamaʿa (*j m ʿ)
assembly
maʿshar (*ʿ sh r)
majālis (*j l s)
malaʾ (*m l ʾ)
nādī (*n d w)
nadīy (*n d w)
assert
zaʿama (*z ʿ m)
assign
jaʿala (*j ʿ l)
aqāma (*q w m)
qayyaḍa (*q y ḍ)
assist
aʿāna (*ʿ w n)
ʿazzara (*ʿ z r)
associate (n)
sharīk (*sh r k)
ṣāḥib (*ṣ ḥ b)
associate (v)
ashraka (*sh r k)
sharika (*sh r k)
assume
ẓanna (*ẓ n n)
assurance
sakīnah (*s k n)
assure
haymana (*h y m n)
astonished, to be
bariqa (*b r q)
astray
ḍalla (*ḍ l l)
nakaba (*n k b)
astray, to lead
aḍalla (*ḍ l l)
aghwá (*gh w y)
asylum
ḥaram (*ḥ r m)
maḥīṣ (*ḥ y ṣ)
qiyām (*q w m)
athrob
wajafa (*w j f)
atom
dharrah (*dh r r)
atone
kaffara (*k f r)
attach to oneself
istakhlaṣa (*kh l ṣ)
attack (v)
ḥamala (*ḥ m l)
māla (*m y l)
saṭā (*s ṭ w)
attack by night
bayyata (*b y t)
attain
balagha (*b l gh)
adraka (*d r k)
nāla (*n y l)
attainment
mablagh (*b l gh)
attend
ḥaḍara (*ḥ ḍ r)
faragha (*f r gh)
taṣaddá (*ṣ d y)
attendant
tabiʿa (*t b ʿ)
attribute
daʿā (*d ʿ w)
augment (with interest)
arbá (*r b w)
augur ill
iṭṭayyara (*ṭ y r)
augury
ṭāra (*ṭ y r)
ṭayr (*ṭ y r)
aunt maternal
khālāt (*kh w l)
aunt paternal
ʿammah (*ʿ m m)
authority
sulṭān (*s l ṭ)
authority, to give
sallaṭa (*s l ṭ)
avail
aghná (*gh n y)
malaka (*m l k)
nafaʿa (*n f ʿ)
avarice
bakhila (*b kh l)
shuḥḥ (*sh ḥ ḥ)
avaricious
ḍanīn (*ḍ n n)
ashiḥḥah (*sh ḥ ḥ)
avenge
intaqama (*n q m)
avenger
tabīʿ (*t b ʿ)
average
wasaṭ (*w s ṭ)
averse, aversion
aʿraḍa (*ʿ r ḍ)
kariha (*k r h)
maqata (*m q t)
naʾá (*n ʾ y)
nafara (*n f r)
avert
dafaʿa (*d f ʿ)
daraʾa (*d r ʾ)
ḥāda (*ḥ y d)
lawwa (*l w y)
ṣarafa (*ṣ r f)
avid
ḍanīn (*ḍ n n)
avoid
tajāfá (*j f w)
ijtanaba (*j n b)

await
nazara (*n z r)
tarabbaṣa (*r b ṣ)
awake
afāqa (*f w q)
ayqāẓ (*y q ẓ)
awakening
sāhirah (*s h r)
award
jazá (*j z y)
aware, to be
shaʿara (*sh ʿ r)
awe
khīfah (*kh w f)
rahiba (*r h b)
rāʿa (*r w ʿ)
aweary
khasaʾa (*kh s ʾ)
awhile
ruwaydan (*r w d)
awning
ẓullah (*ẓ l l)

babble
khāḍa (*kh w ḍ)
lāghiyah (*l gh y)
back
dubur (*d b r)
ẓahr (*ẓ h r)
ẓahīr (*ẓ h r)
back off
tarājaʿa (*r j ʿ)
back, to keep
radda (*r d d)
backbite
ightāba (*gh y b)
backbiter
hammāz (*h m z)
humazah (*h m z)
backbone
ṣulb (*ṣ l b)
bad luck
naḥs (*n ḥ s)
bad, bad things
khabāʾith (*kh b th)
sharr (*sh r r)
bad, be
khabutha (*kh b th)
sāʾa (*s w ʾ)
baffle
ʿājaza (*ʿ j z)
bag
wiʿāʾ (*w ʿ y)
baggage
matāʿ (*m t ʿ)
bail
kafīl (*k f l)
baked clay
sijjīl (*s j l)
balance (n)
mīzān (*w z n)
qisṭās (*q s ṭ s)
ban
ḥijr (*ḥ j r)
banana tree
ṭalḥ (*ṭ l ḥ)
band
ʿuṣbah (*ʿ ṣ b)
firqah (*f r q)
rahṭ (*r h ṭ)
shirdhimah (*sh r dh m)
thullah (*th l l)
zawj (*z w j)
band of watchers
raṣad (*r ṣ d)
band together
ijtamaʿa (*j m ʿ)
bandy
rajaʿa (*r j ʿ)
banish
daḥara (*d ḥ r)
nafá (*n f y)
banishment
jalāʾ (*j l y)
bank (of a river)
juruf (*j r f)
shāṭiʾ (*sh ṭ ʾ)
bank (of valley)
ʿudwah (*ʿ d w)
banned
suḥt (*s ḥ t)
banquet
muttakaʾ (*w k ʾ)
baptism
ṣibghah (*ṣ b gh)
bar (v)
ḥajaza (*ḥ j z)
manaʿa (*m n ʿ)
ṣadda (*ṣ d d)
barbarous
aʿjamīy (*ʿ j m)
bare
kashafa (*k sh f)
bargain, to make a
bāyaʿa (*b y ʿ)
barren
ʿaqīm (*ʿ q m)
ʿāqir (*ʿ q r)
hamada (*h m d)
ṣafṣaf (*ṣ f ṣ f)
ṣald (*ṣ l d)
barren dust
juruz (*j r z)
barrier
barzakh (*b r z kh)
sadd (*s d d)
barter
shará (*sh r y)
ishtará (*sh r y)
base
radhīl (*r dh l)
base-born
zanīm (*z n m)
bashfulness
istaḥá (*ḥ y y)
battle
baʾs (*b ʾ s)
battle order, to set in
wazaʿa (*w z ʿ)
battle-field
mawāṭin (*w ṭ n)
battle-line
ṣaff (*ṣ f f)
battlements
aʿrāf (*ʿ r f)
be
kāna (*k w n)
ẓalla (*ẓ l l)
bear (burden)
wazara (*w z r)
bear (child)
ḥamala (*ḥ m l)
walada (*w l d)
bear (fruit)
nabata (*n b t)
athmara (*th m r)
bear (good tidings)
bashīr (*b sh r)
bashshara (*b sh r)
bear (witness)
shahida (*sh h d)
beard
liḥyah (*l ḥ y)
beast
bahīmah (*b h m)
dābbah (*d b b)

beast of burden
  ḥamūlah (*ḥ m l)
beast of prey
  jawāriḥ (*j r ḥ)
  sabuᶜ (*s b ᶜ)
beast of sacrifice
  budn (*b d n)
beat
  ḍaraba (*ḍ r b)
beat down (leaves)
  hashsha (*h sh sh)
beaten to death
  waqadha (*w q dh)
beautiful
  ḥasan (*ḥ s n)
beautiful, to be
  ḥasuna (*ḥ s n)
beautify
  zayyana (*z y n)
beauty
  ḥasuna (*ḥ s n)
  jamāl (*j m l)
beauty, light of
  naḍrah (*n ḍ r)
becalmed
  rahā (*r h w)
become
  kāna (*k w n)
  aṣbaḥa (*ṣ b ḥ)
bed
  marqad (*r q d)
  surur (*s r r)
bedevilled
  jinnah (*j n n)
bedouins
  aᶜrāb (*ᶜ r b)
bees
  naḥl (*n ḥ l)
befall
  inbaghá (*b gh y)
  massa (*m s s)
  aṣāba (*ṣ w b)
before
  amām (*a m m)
  yad (*y d y)
befriend
  khālla (*kh l l)
  wallá (*w l y)
beget
  walada (*w l d)
beggar
  qanaᶜa (*q n ᶜ)
  saʾala (*s ʾ l)
begin
  badaʾa (*b d ʾ)
  ṭafiqa (*ṭ f q)
begin, to cause to
  abdaʾa (*b d ʾ)
beginning
  wajh (*w j h)
begone, be
  khasaʾa (*kh s ʾ)
beguile
  alhá (*l h w)
beguile
  khadaᶜa (*kh d ᶜ)
  khādaᶜa (*kh d ᶜ)
behind
  khalf (*kh l f)
  khilāf (*kh l f)
  warāʾ (*w r y)
behold
  baṣura (*b ṣ r)
  naẓara (*n ẓ r)
  raʾá (*r ʾ y)
behove
  inbaghá (*b gh y)
beings
  anām (*a n m)
  ᶜālamīn (*ᶜ l m)
  ᶜalima (*ᶜ l m)
belie
  kadhaba (*k dh b)
  kadhdhaba (*k dh b)
belief
  āmana (*a m n)
  kafara (*k f r)
  ṣaddaqa (*ṣ d q)
believe
  āmana (*a m n)
  ṣaddaqa (*ṣ d q)
believer
  āmana (*a m n)
believer, un-
  kafara (*k f r)
  kaffār (*k f r)
belly
  baṭn (*b ṭ n)
  jawf (*j w f)
belongings
  matāᶜ (*m t ᶜ)
beloved
  ᶜurub (*ᶜ r b)
  aḥabb (*ḥ b b)
  aḥibbāʾ (*ḥ b b)
below
  sāfil (*s f l)
bemuse
  alhá (*l h w)
bend down
  nakasa (*n k s)
  nakkasa (*n k s)
beneficent
  barr (*b r r)
benefit
  alá (*a l w)
  balā (*b l w)
benefitial
  ᶜurf (*ᶜ r f)
bequeath
  awratha (*w r th)
  awṣá (*w ṣ y)
  tawāṣá (*w ṣ y)
bequeathing
  waṣīyah (*w ṣ y)
bequest
  waṣṣá (*w ṣ y)
  waṣīyah (*w ṣ y)
berth
  mursá (*r s y)
beseech
  ibtahala (*b h l)
best
  khayr (*kh y r)
  amthal (*m th l)
bestow
  wahaba (*w h b)
betake oneself
  waṣala (*w ṣ l)
betray
  khadhūl (*kh dh l)
  ikhtāna (*kh w n)
  khāna (*kh w n)
  khawwān (*kh w n)
betrothal
  khuṭbah (*kh ṭ b)
beverage
  mashrab (*sh r b)
beware
  ḥadhira (*ḥ dh r)
  wayl (*w y l)
bewildered
  ḥayrān (*ḥ y r)
bewitch
  saḥara (*s ḥ r)
  saḥḥara (*s ḥ r)

beyond
warā' (*w r y)
bid
amara (*a m r)
bidding
amara (*a m r)
big
kabīr (*k b r)
billow
mawj (*m w j)
bind
ghalla (*gh l l)
awthaqa (*w th q)
binding, solemn
mīthāq (*w th q)
bird
ṭāra (*ṭ y r)
ṭayr (*ṭ y r)
bird of omen
ṭāra (*ṭ y r)
birds of prey
jawāriḥ (*j r ḥ)
birth, to give
waḍaʿa (*w ḍ ʿ)
walada (*w l d)
birthpangs
makhāḍ (*m kh ḍ)
bite
ʿaḍḍa (*ʿ ḍ ḍ)
bits, broken
rufāt (*r f t)
bitter
ujāj (*a j j)
ḥasrah (*ḥ s r)
khamaṭa (*kh m ṭ)
amarr (*m r r)
bitter cold
zamharīr (*z m h r)
black
gharabīb (*gh r b)
aswad (*s w d)
black smoke
yaḥmūm (*ḥ m m)
black, to become
hamada (*h m d)
aḥwá (*ḥ w y)
iswadda (*s w d)
blame (n)
junāḥ (*j n ḥ)
lawmah (*l w m)
tharraba (*th r b)
blame (v)
lāma (*l w m)
talāwama (*l w m)
naqama (*n q m)
blame-casting
lawwām (*l w m)
blameworthy
alāma (*l w m)
lāma (*l w m)
blaspheme
alḥada (*l ḥ d)
blast
ḥassa (*ḥ s s)
nafkhah (*n f kh)
rājifah (*r j f)
ṣākhkhah (*ṣ kh kh)
blaze (n)
athāra (*th w r)
wahhāj (*w h j)
blaze (v)
ḥamiya (*ḥ m y)
saʿʿara (*s ʿ r)
talaẓẓá (*l ẓ y)
blear-eyed (with terror)
zurq (*z r q)
blemish
shiyah (*w sh y)
blemished, un-
salīm (*s l m)
blend
shawb (*sh w b)
bless
bāraka (*b r k)
anʿama (*n ʿ m)
naʿʿama (*n ʿ m)
razaqa (*r z q)
ṣallá (*ṣ l w)
blessed, to be
tabāraka (*b r k)
blessedness
ṭūbá (*ṭ y b)
blessing
barakah (*b r k)
niʿmah (*n ʿ m)
rizq (*r z q)
blind (n)
ʿami (*ʿ m y)
aʿmá (*ʿ m y)
akmah (*k m h)
blind (v)
ʿammá (*ʿ m y)
aʿmá (*ʿ m y)
ʿashā (*ʿ sh w)
blind, to be
ʿamiya (*ʿ m y)
blindness
ʿamá (*ʿ m y)
bliss
naʿīm (*n ʿ m)
blood
dam (*d m m)
blood-clot
ʿalaqah (*ʿ l q)
blood-relations
arḥām (*r ḥ m)
bloodwit
diyah (*w d y)
blot out
kaffara (*k f r)
maḥaqa (*m ḥ q)
maḥā (*m ḥ w)
blotch
shiyah (*w sh y)
blow
dakkah (*d k k)
nafakha (*n f kh)
naffāthah (*n f th)
blue
zurq (*z r q)
boast
baṭira (*b ṭ r)
tafākhara (*f kh r)
boastful
fakhūr (*f kh r)
boat
safīnah (*s f n)
body
badan (*b d n)
jasad (*j s d)
jism (*j s m)
boil
fāra (*f w r)
ghalá (*gh l y)
sajjara (*s j r)
boiling
aná (*a n y)
boiling water
ḥamīm (*ḥ m m)
bold, to grow
marada (*m r d)
bolt of lightening
ṣāʿiqah (*ṣ ʿ q)
bond
ill (*a l l)
ʿaqd (*ʿ q d)

ḥabl (*ḥ b l)
aṣfād (*ṣ f d)
wathāq (*w th q)
bonds, to keep in
athbata (*th b t)
bone
ʿaẓm (*ʿ ẓ m)
book
kitāb (*k t b)
asfār (*s f r)
zabūr (*z b r)
booty
maghnam (*gh n m)
border (v)
ḥaḍara (*ḥ ḍ r)
borders
arjāʾ (*r j w)
borrow
iqtabasa (*q b s)
bosom
ḥujūr (*ḥ j r)
jayb (*j y b)
bottom
ghayābah (*gh y b)
boundary
muntahá (*n h w)
bounds
ḥudūd (*ḥ d d)
bountiful
niʿma (*n ʿ m)
bounty
alá (*a l w)
faḍl (*f ḍ l)
kharāj (*kh r j)
ṭawl (*ṭ w l)
bow (n)
qaws (*q w s)
bow (v)
khaḍaʿa (*kh ḍ ʿ)
rakaʿa (*r k ʿ)
sajada (*s j d)
bowels
amʿāʾ (*m ʿ y)
box
tābūt (*t b t)
boy
ghulām (*gh l m)
ṣabīy (*ṣ b y)
bracelet
aswirah (*s w r)
brain (v)
damagha (*d m gh)
branch
ḍighth (*ḍ gh th)
afnān (*f n n)
farʿ (*f r ʿ)
shuʿab (*sh ʿ b)
brand
kawá (*k w y)
wasama (*w s m)
brass, molten
nuḥās (*n ḥ s)
qiṭr (*q ṭ r)
breach
shāqqa (*sh q q)
bread
khubz (*kh b z)
breadth
ʿaraḍa (*ʿ r ḍ)
raḥuba (*r ḥ b)
break
jadhdha (*j dh dh)
naqaḍa (*n q ḍ)
qaṭaʿa (*q ṭ ʿ)
qaṭṭaʿa (*q ṭ ʿ)
taṣaddaʿa (*ṣ d ʿ)
break (an oath)
nakatha (*n k th)
break (into fragments)
jaʿala (*j ʿ l)
break (one's word)
akhlafa (*kh l f)
break forth, to cause to
falaqa (*f l q)
break the head
damagha (*d m gh)
break to pieces
ḥuṭamah (*ḥ ṭ m)
break up the ground
athāra (*th w r)
breakfast
ghadāʾ (*gh d w)
breast
jawf (*j w f)
ṣadr (*ṣ d r)
breast-bone
tarāʾib (*t r b)
breasts, swelling
kawāʿib (*k ʿ b)
breath
nafḥah (*n f ḥ)
breathe
nafakha (*n f kh)
tanaffasa (*n f s)
brew
shawb (*sh w b)
briefly
yasīr (*y s r)
bright
faqaʿa (*f q ʿ)
naḍara (*n ḍ r)
brightly burning
wahhāj (*w h j)
brightness
naḍrah (*n ḍ r)
brilliance
sanā (*s n w)
bring
atá (*a t y)
ātá (*a t y)
jāʾa (*j y ʾ)
waṣṣala (*w ṣ l)
bring about
awqaʿa (*w q ʿ)
bring back
aʿāda (*ʿ w d)
bāʾa (*b w ʾ)
bring close
azlafa (*z l f)
bring down
bāʾa (*b w ʾ)
nazala (*n z l)
tanazzala (*n z l)
bring forth
akhraja (*kh r j)
istakhraja (*kh r j)
bring forth (a baby)
waḍaʿa (*w ḍ ʿ)
bring low
dhallala (*dh l l)
bring near
adná (*d n w)
qarraba (*q r b)
azlafa (*z l f)
bring out
akhraja (*kh r j)
ḥaṣṣala (*ḥ ṣ l)
bring over
jāwaza (*j w z)
bring to land
anzala (*n z l)
bring to naught
abṭala (*b ṭ l)
bring to pass
aḥdatha (*ḥ d th)
bring together

allafa (*a l f)
jamaʿa (*j m ʿ)
bring under control
iḥtanaka (*ḥ n k)
bring up
aḥḍara (*ḥ ḍ r)
nashshaʾa (*n sh ʾ)
brink
shafā (*sh f w)
broadcast
adhāʿa (*dh y ʿ)
brocade
istabraq (*b r q)
broil
ṣalá (*ṣ l y)
ṣallá (*ṣ l y)
broken
dhalūl (*dh l l)
broken bits
rufāt (*r f t)
broken orts
ḥuṭām (*ḥ ṭ m)
broken piece(s)
judhādh (*j dh dh)
broken, to be
infaṣama (*f ṣ m)
taqaṭṭaʿa (*q ṭ ʿ)
brood
sajá (*s j y)
brook
sarīy (*s r y)
brother
akh (*a kh w)
brought forward
iḥtaḍara (*ḥ ḍ r)
brought together
allafa (*a l f)
brow
jabīn (*j b n)
bubble
ghalá (*gh l y)
taghayyaẓa (*gh y ẓ)
bucket
dalw (*d l w)
build
ʿarasha (*ʿ r sh)
ʿamara (*ʿ m r)
baná (*b n y)
iḥtaẓara (*ḥ ẓ r)
builder
bannāʾ (*b n y)
building
baná (*b n y)
bunyān (*b n y)
building (the act)
baná (*b n y)
bunch
lafīf (*l f f)
bundle of grass
ḍighth (*ḍ gh th)
burden
iṣr (*a ṣ r)
ḥammala (*ḥ m l)
ḥiml (*ḥ m l)
kalla (*k l l)
athqāl (*th q l)
wiqr (*w q r)
wazara (*w z r)
burden (of talk)
laḥana (*l ḥ n)
burden, to be a
nāʾa (*n w ʾ)
burdened, heavy-
athqala (*th q l)
burdening, un-
ḥiṭṭah (*ḥ ṭ ṭ)
burdensome company
thaqal (*th q l)
buried infant (girl)
waʾada (*w ʾ d)
burn (v)
iḥtaraqa (*ḥ r q)
ḥarraqa (*ḥ r q)
lafaḥa (*l f ḥ)
naḍija (*n ḍ j)
saʿʿara (*s ʿ r)
sajara (*s j r)
ṣalá (*ṣ l y)
ṣallá (*ṣ l y)
burning
ḥarīq (*ḥ r q)
saʿīr (*s ʿ r)
samūm (*s m m)
burrow
sarab (*s r b)
burst
tamayyaza (*m y z)
burst forth
inbajasa (*b j s)
burthen
ḥamala (*ḥ m l)
bury
dassa (*d s s)
aqbara (*q b r)
business
khaṭaba (*kh ṭ b)
sabaḥa (*s b ḥ)
shaʾn (*sh ʾ n)
busy
shaghala (*sh gh l)
butter
duhn (*d h n)
buxom
kawāʿib (*k ʿ b)
buy
ishtará (*sh r y)
bygone, to be
salafa (*s l f)

calamitous
ad.há (*d h y)
wabīl (*w b l)
calamity
fāqirah (*f q r)
qāriʿah (*q r ʿ)
sharr (*sh r r)
muṣībah (*ṣ w b)
ṭāmmah (*ṭ m m)
calculate
aḥṣá (*ḥ ṣ y)
calf
ʿijl (*ʿ j l)
call (n)
daʿwah (*d ʿ w)
daʿwá (*d ʿ w)
nādá (*n d w)
call (v)
daʿā (*d ʿ w)
naʿaqa (*n ʿ q)
nādá (*n d w)
tanādá (*n d w)
qāla (*q w l)
call for
iddaʿá (*d ʿ w)
call for aid
istaghātha (*gh w th)
call for succour
istaghātha (*gh y th)
call forth fear
istarhaba (*r h b)
call to account
ḥāsaba (*ḥ s b)
call to oneself
tawaffá (*w f y)
call to witness
ash.hada (*sh h d)

istash.hada (*sh h d)
calm
niᶜma (*n ᶜ m)
rahā (*r h w)
sakana (*s k n)
sakīnah (*s k n)
calm down
sakata (*s k t)
askana (*s k n)
calumny
ifk (*a f k)
buhtān (*b h t)
camel
ibil (*a b l)
baᶜīr (*b ᶜ r)
jamal (*j m l)
rikāb (*r k b)
camel, fur of
awbār (*w b r)
camel, pregnant
ᶜishār (*ᶜ sh r)
camel, thirsty
hīm (*h y m)
cameleers
ᶜīr (*ᶜ y r)
camphor
kāfūr (*k f r)
can
istaṭāᶜa (*ṭ w ᶜ)
canopy
ẓullah (*ẓ l l)
capacity
wasiᶜa (*w s ᶜ)
capital
raʾs māl
raʾs (*r ʾ s)
māl (*m w l)
caprice
hawá (*h w y)
captive
asīr (*a s r)
salam (*s l m)
captive, to make
asara (*a s r)
caravan
ᶜīr (*ᶜ y r)
riḥlah (*r ḥ l)
card (v)
nafasha (*n f sh)
care
ḥujūr (*ḥ j r)
careless, to be
sariba (*s r b)
carpet
ᶜabqarīy (*ᶜ b q r)
bisāṭ (*b s ṭ)
firāsh (*f r sh)
zarābī (*z r b)
carrier
ḥammālah (*ḥ m l)
carrion
maytah (*m w t)
carry
ḥamala (*ḥ m l)
iḥtamala (*ḥ m l)
aqalla (*q l l)
wazara (*w z r)
carve
naḥata (*n ḥ t)
cascading
thajjāj (*th j j)
case
makān (*k w n)
cast
alqá (*l q y)
nabadha (*n b dh)
qadhafa (*q dh f)
ramá (*r m y)
ṭaraḥa (*ṭ r ḥ)
awqaᶜa (*w q ᶜ)
cast (a glance)
naẓara (*n ẓ r)
cast (a shadow)
ẓallala (*ẓ l l)
cast (a spell)
saḥara (*s ḥ r)
cast (a veil)
ḍaraba (*ḍ r b)
cast down
ghaḍḍa (*gh ḍ ḍ)
cast forth
amná (*m n y)
cast into oblivion
ansá (*n s y)
cast lots
sāhama (*s h m)
cast off
insalakha (*s l kh)
cast up
ramá (*r m y)
castle
maṣāniᶜ (*ṣ n ᶜ)
catastrophe
ṭāmmah (*ṭ m m)
cattle
naᶜam (*n ᶜ m)
cattle, to feed
raᶜá (*r ᶜ y)
cause tumbling
sāqaṭa (*s q ṭ)
cautious
ḥadhira (*ḥ dh r)
cavalcade
rakb (*r k b)
cave
ghār (*gh w r)
maghārah (*gh w r)
kahf (*k h f)
cease
baraḥa (*b r ḥ)
fataʾa (*f t ʾ)
ceasing, un-
sarmad (*s r m d)
ceiling
samk (*s m k)
cemetery
maqābir (*q b r)
certain, a
biḍᶜ (*b ḍ ᶜ)
certain, to be
ayqana (*y q n)
istayqana (*y q n)
certainty
yaqīn (*y q n)
certainty, to have
istayqana (*y q n)
certainty, un-
labasa (*l b s)
rāba (*r y b)
shakk (*sh k k)
chaff
ḥuṭām (*ḥ ṭ m)
chain (n)
silsilah (*s l s l)
chain (v)
ghalla (*gh l l)
chamber
ghurfah (*gh r f)
ḥujurāt (*ḥ j r)
miḥrāb (*ḥ r b)
change
abdala (*b d l)
baddala (*b d l)
ghayyara (*gh y r)
ḥawwala (*ḥ w l)
masakha (*m s kh)

ṣarrafa (*ṣ r f)
change (n)
ḥiwal (*ḥ w l)
changed, to be
taghayyara (*gh y r)
changing
lawwāḥ (*l w ḥ)
chant (v)
rattala (*r t l)
chapter (of the Koran)
sūrah (*s w r)
character
khuluq (*kh l q)
charge (v)
ḥamala (*ḥ m l)
kallafa (*k l f)
aqalla (*q l l)
wakkala (*w k l)
awṣá (*w ṣ y)
waṣṣá (*w ṣ y)
charge (n)
mawlá (*w l y)
charge, place in one's
akfala (*k f l)
charge, take
tawallá (*w l y)
charger
ʿādiyah (*ʿ d w)
charitable, to be
taṣaddaqa (*ṣ d q)
charity
māʿūn (*m ʿ n)
ṣadaqah (*ṣ d q)
zakāt (*z k w)
charity, to give in
taṣaddaqa (*ṣ d q)
chaste
ḥaṣūr (*ḥ ṣ r)
taḥaṣṣana (*ḥ ṣ n)
chastise
ʿadhdhaba (*ʿ dh b)
ʿāqaba (*ʿ q b)
chastisement
ʿadhāb (*ʿ dh b)
nakāl (*n k l)
chastity
taḥaṣṣana (*ḥ ṣ n)
chat
khāḍa (*kh w ḍ)
samara (*s m r)
cheat
akhsara (*kh s r)
watara (*w t r)
cheek
khadd (*kh d d)
cheek, to turn away
ṣaʿʿara (*ṣ ʿ r)
chest
tābūt (*t b t)
tarāʾib (*t r b)
ṣadr (*ṣ d r)
chide
nahara (*n h r)
chief
kabīr (*k b r)
malaʾ (*m l ʾ)
naqīb (*n q b)
sayyid (*s w d)
child
ibn (*b n y)
ṣabīy (*ṣ b y)
ṭifl (*ṭ f l)
walad (*w l d)
walīd (*w l d)
child, unborn
ajinnah (*j n n)
childbirth, pain of
makhāḍ (*m kh ḍ)
childless
abtar (*b t r)
chin
adhqān (*dh q n)
choice
khīrah (*kh y r)
choke
kaẓama (*k ẓ m)
kaẓīm (*k ẓ m)
chokes, that which
ghuṣṣah (*gh ṣ ṣ)
choose
ijtabá (*j b y)
akhlaṣa (*kh l ṣ)
ikhtaṣṣa (*kh ṣ ṣ)
ikhtāra (*kh y r)
takhayyara (*kh y r)
aṣfá (*ṣ f w)
iṣṭafá (*ṣ f w)
iṣṭanaʿa (*ṣ n ʿ)
church
biyaʿ (*b y ʿ)
circumambulate
ṭāfa (*ṭ w f)
taṭawwafa (*ṭ w f)
circumcised, un-
ghulf (*gh l f)
circumvent
kāda (*k y d)
cistern
biʾr (*b ʾ r)
jubb (*j b b)
jawābī (*j b y)
cite
ḍaraba (*ḍ r b)
city
madīnah (*m d n)
qaryah (*q r y)
city, subverted
iʾtafaka (*a f k)
claim
iddaʿá (*d ʿ w)
zaʿama (*z ʿ m)
clamorous
ṣarṣar (*ṣ r ṣ r)
clamour
qāriʿah (*q r ʿ)
ṣarrah (*ṣ r r)
clan
ʿashīrah (*ʿ sh r)
clap (v)
ṣaddá (*ṣ d y)
clarify
ṣaffá (*ṣ f w)
clasp (v)
ḍamma (*ḍ m m)
clavicle
tarāqī (*r q y)
claw
ẓufur (*ẓ f r)
clay
ṭīn (*ṭ y n)
clay, baked
sijjīl (*s j l)
clay, dry
ṣalṣāl (*ṣ l ṣ l)
clay, potter's
fakhkhār (*f kh r)
clean (n)
zakīy (*z k w)
aṭhar (*ṭ h r)
clean, to be
taṭahhara (*ṭ h r)
ṭahara (*ṭ h r)
clean, un-
najisa (*n j s)
cleanse
ṭahhara (*ṭ h r)

taṭahhara (*ṭ h r)
tazakká (*z k w)
zakká (*z k w)
clear
istabāna (*b y n)
aḥkama (*ḥ k m)
clear oneself
tabarraʾa (*b r ʾ)
clear proof
bayyinah (*b y n)
clear, to make
abāna (*b y n)
bayyana (*b y n)
istabāna (*b y n)
tabayyana (*b y n)
faraqa (*f r q)
khallá (*kh l w)
clear, to set
aḥkama (*ḥ k m)
cleave
infalaqa (*f l q)
faraja (*f r j)
infaṭara (*f ṭ r)
qaṭṭaʿa (*q ṭ ʿ)
inshaqqa (*sh q q)
shaqqa (*sh q q)
tashaqqaqa (*sh q q)
ṣadaʿa (*ṣ d ʿ)
wasaṭa (*w s ṭ)
cleave to
ʿakafa (*ʿ k f)
iʿtaṣama (*ʿ ṣ m)
jāba (*j w b)
cleave through the waves
makhara (*m kh r)
clement
ḥalīm (*ḥ l m)
clever
fariha (*f r h)
client
mawlá (*w l y)
cliff
ṣadaf (*ṣ d f)
climb (a wall)
tasawwara (*s w r)
taṣaʿʿada (*ṣ ʿ d)
cling
lazaba (*l z b)
cloak
junnah (*j n n)
cloistered
qaṣara (*q ṣ r)
cloisters
ṣawāmiʿ (*ṣ m ʿ)
close (v)
ʿasʿasa (*ʿ s s)
ghallaqa (*gh l q)
qabaḍa (*q b ḍ)
close (n)
ḍayq (*ḍ y q)
ḥamīm (*ḥ m m)
awlá (*w l y)
close an eye
aghmaḍa (*gh m ḍ)
close-compounded
tarākaba (*r k b)
close-wrought
waḍana (*w ḍ n)
clot
ʿalaqah (*ʿ l q)
clothe
kasā (*k s w)
clothes
kiswah (*k s w)
libās (*l b s)
thiyāb (*th w b)
cloud-shadow
ẓullah (*ẓ l l)
cloud, rain
ṣayyib (*ṣ w b)
cloud, sudden
ʿāriḍ (*ʿ r ḍ)
cloudburst
ṣayyib (*ṣ w b)
clouds
ghamām (*gh m m)
muzn (*m z n)
saḥāb (*s ḥ b)
aʿṣara (*ʿ ṣ r)
cloven assunder, to be
infaṭara (*f ṭ r)
cluster
quṭūf (*q ṭ f)
coarse-grained
ʿutull (*ʿ t l)
coat of mail
sābighah (*s b gh)
codex
imām (*a m m)
cold, excessive
ṣirr (*ṣ r r)
zamharīr (*z m h r)
collapse
wajaba (*w j b)
collar, to twist a
ṭawwaqa (*ṭ w q)
collect
jabā (*j b y)
colour
lawn (*l w n)
ṣibghah (*ṣ b gh)
column
ʿimād (*ʿ m d)
combatants
ghazā (*gh z w)
come
atá (*a t y)
ḥaḍara (*ḥ ḍ r)
jāʾa (*j y ʾ)
istaqbala (*q b l)
wafada (*w f d)
warada (*w r d)
come after, behind
khalafa (*kh l f)
khālafa (*kh l f)
radifa (*r d f)
come back
inqalaba (*q l b)
rajaʿa (*r j ʿ)
come between
ḥāla (*ḥ w l)
come down
nazala (*n z l)
tanazzala (*n z l)
come forth
kharaja (*kh r j)
come forward
aqbala (*q b l)
come home
ṣāra (*ṣ y r)
come in the morning
ṣabbaḥa (*ṣ b ḥ)
come later
taʾakhkhara (*a kh r)
come near
qariba (*q r b)
come over
rahiqa (*r h q)
come successively
tadāraka (*d r k)
come to an end
nafida (*n f d)
come to naught
bāra (*b w r)
come to pass
qāma (*q w m)

waqaʿa (*w q ʿ)
come true
ḥaqqa (*ḥ q q)
come up
ṭalaʿa (*ṭ l ʿ)
come upon
atá (*a t y)
thaqifa (*th q f)
come with pomp
wafada (*w f d)
come!
taʿālá (*ʿ l w)
come, to cause to
ajāʾa (*j y ʾ)
comely
jamīl (*j m l)
comfort (n)
mirfaq (*r f q)
naʿmah (*n ʿ m)
qurrah (*q r r)
comfort (v)
rāḥa (*r w ḥ)
sakana (*s k n)
comforted, to be
qarra (*q r r)
command, commandment
amara (*a m r)
kalimah (*k l m)
commemorate
dhakara (*dh k r)
commend
waṣṣá (*w ṣ y)
commerce
tijārah (*t j r)
commission
iṣṭanaʿa (*ṣ n ʿ)
commit
atá (*a t y)
faʿala (*f ʿ l)
ijtaraḥa (*j r ḥ)
jaraḥa (*j r ḥ)
jāʾa (*j y ʾ)
alqá (*l q y)
commit adultery
zaná (*z n y)
commit aggression
iʿtadá (*ʿ d w)
commit an error
khaṭiʾa (*kh ṭ ʾ)
commit for judgment
fawwaḍa (*f w ḍ)
commit to memory
istaḥfaẓa (*ḥ f ẓ)
commit ungodliness
fasaqa (*f s q)
commodity
dūlah (*d w l)
common
jamaʿa (*j m ʿ)
common folk, one of
ummīy (*a m m)
commotion, to make a
arjafa (*r j f)
communication (from God)
āyah (*a y w)
communion, in
najīy (*n j w)
compact (n)
ʿaqd (*ʿ q d)
mīthāq (*w th q)
naḍīd (*n ḍ d)
compact (v)
raṣṣa (*r ṣ ṣ)
compact, to make a
ʿaqada (*ʿ q d)
wāthaqa (*w th q)
companion
ʿashīr (*ʿ sh r)
kawāʿib (*k ʿ b)
rafīq (*r f q)
sayyārah (*s y r)
ṣāḥib (*ṣ ḥ b)
company
maʿshar (*ʿ sh r)
ʿuṣbah (*ʿ ṣ b)
fiʾah (*f ʾ w)
fawj (*f w j)
company of men
thubāt (*th b y)
zumar (*z m r)
company of travellers
sayyārah (*s y r)
company, burdensome
thaqal (*th q l)
company, to keep
ṣāḥaba (*ṣ ḥ b)
comparable
kufuʾ (*k f ʾ)
compassion
marḥamah (*r ḥ m)
raḥima (*r ḥ m)
compassionate
awwāh (*a w h)
raḥīm (*r ḥ m)
compassionate, to be
raḥima (*r ḥ m)
compeer
andād (*n d d)
compel
iḍṭarra (*ḍ r r)
akraha (*k r h)
alzama (*l z m)
sakhkhara (*s kh r)
compensate
aṣlaḥa (*ṣ l ḥ)
complain
shakā (*sh k w)
ishtaká (*sh k w)
complaisant, be
khaḍaʿa (*kh ḍ ʿ)
complete
akmala (*k m l)
kamala (*k m l)
salima (*s l m)
atamma (*t m m)
tamma (*t m m)
wafīy (*w f y)
compliance
ṭāʿah (*ṭ w ʿ)
compose
allafa (*a l f)
rakkaba (*r k b)
compose differences
waffaqa (*w f q)
comprehend
ʿaqala (*ʿ q l)
aḥāṭa (*ḥ w ṭ)
comprise
wasiʿa (*w s ʿ)
compromise
ad.hana (*d h n)
ṣulḥ (*ṣ l ḥ)
compulsion
akraha (*k r h)
comrade
qarīn (*q r n)
ṣāḥib (*ṣ ḥ b)
conceal
ʿammá (*ʿ m y)
katama (*k t m)
akhfá (*kh f y)
khafá (*kh f y)
asarra (*s r r)
awʿá (*w ʿ y)
tawārá (*w r y)
wārá (*w r y)

conceive
ḥamala (*ḥ m l)
awjasa (*w j s)
concerned, to be
ʿabaʾa (*ʿ b ʾ)
istaḥaqqa (*ḥ q q)
conciliation
waffaqa (*w f q)
conclusive
balagha (*b l gh)
concoct a plot
kāda (*k y d)
concourse
nādī (*n d w)
condemn
adḥaḍa (*d ḥ ḍ)
condemned, to be
dhamma (*dh m m)
condition
sīrah (*s y r)
condition, former
ḥāfirah (*ḥ f r)
conduct, ill-
nashaza (*n sh z)
conduct, mode of
ṭarīqah (*ṭ r q)
conduct, right
taqwá (*w q y)
conduct, virtuous
birr (*b r r)
conduit
sarab (*s r b)
confer
ablá (*b l w)
khalaṣa (*kh l ṣ)
khawwala (*kh w l)
nājá (*n j w)
confess
iʿtarafa (*ʿ r f)
confidant
walījah (*w l j)
confide
asarra (*s r r)
confine (n)
aqṭār (*q ṭ r)
confine (v)
athbata (*th b t)
ḥaṣara (*ḥ ṣ r)
ḥaẓara (*ḥ ẓ r)
confirm
ayyada (*a y d)
aḥkama (*ḥ k m)
aqarra (*q r r)
rabaṭa (*r b ṭ)
shadda (*sh d d)
ṣaddaqa (*ṣ d q)
athbata (*th b t)
thabbata (*th b t)
wakkada (*w k d)
conform
ḍāhá (*ḍ h y)
confound
bahata (*b h t)
ablasa (*b l s)
akhzá (*kh z y)
labasa (*l b s)
nakasa (*n k s)
qallaba (*q l b)
confuse
labasa (*l b s)
confused
marīj (*m r j)
confusion
aḍghāth (*ḍ gh th)
congregation
jamīʿ (*j m ʿ)
jumuʿah (*j m ʿ)
conjecture
kharaṣa (*kh r ṣ)
conjecturer
kharrāṣ (*kh r ṣ)
conjoined, to be
iqtarana (*q r n)
conquer
ʿazza (*ʿ z z)
ghalaba (*gh l b)
conscious of, to be
aḥassa (*ḥ s s)
consecrate
nadhara (*n dh r)
consent, mutual
tarāḍá (*r ḍ y)
consequence
ʿuqb (*ʿ q b)
consider
abṣara (*b ṣ r)
tadabbara (*d b r)
naẓara (*n ẓ r)
raʾá (*r ʾ y)
consideration
raʾy (*r ʾ y)
consimilar
tashābaha (*sh b h)
consolation
qurrah (*q r r)
consort (n)
ṣāḥib (*ṣ ḥ b)
consort (v)
ʿāshara (*ʿ sh r)
conspire
iʾtamara (*a m r)
nājá (*n j w)
najā (*n j w)
taẓāhara (*ẓ h r)
constancy
ʿazama (*ʿ z m)
thabata (*th b t)
constant
daʾaba (*d ʾ b)
constellation
burūj (*b r j)
constitution
khalaqa (*kh l q)
constrain
iḍṭarra (*ḍ r r)
akraha (*k r h)
arhaqa (*r h q)
awzaʿa (*w z ʿ)
constricted, to be
ḥaṣira (*ḥ ṣ r)
construct
shāda (*sh y d)
shayyada (*sh y d)
constumacious
ʿanīd (*ʿ n d)
consult
iʾtamara (*a m r)
nājá (*n j w)
shāwara (*sh w r)
tashāwara (*sh w r)
consultation
shūrá (*sh w r)
consume
akala (*a k l)
consumed, to be
naḍija (*n ḍ j)
consumer
akkāl (*a k l)
consumption
akala (*a k l)
contain
ishtamala (*sh m l)
awʿá (*w ʿ y)
container
wiʿāʾ (*w ʿ y)
contemplation

tabṣirah (*b ṣ r)
contempt
hāna (*h w n)
ṣaghār (*ṣ gh r)
contempteous
ṣaʿʿara (*ṣ ʿ r)
contemptible
mahīn (*m h n)
contend
khāṣama (*kh ṣ m)
mārá (*m r y)
tanāzaʿa (*n z ʿ)
shāqqa (*sh q q)
content with, to be
raḍiya (*r ḍ y)
contentious
khaṣim (*kh ṣ m)
aladd (*l d d)
contentment
riḍwān (*r ḍ y)
context
mawāḍiʿ (*w ḍ ʿ)
continue
dāma (*d w m)
labitha (*l b th)
istamarra (*m r r)
zāla (*z y l)
ẓalla (*ẓ l l)
contract
bāyaʿa (*b y ʿ)
kātaba (*k t b)
contrary
ḍidd (*ḍ d d)
contrive
abrama (*b r m)
kāda (*k y d)
contumacy
baghy (*b gh y)
ṭaghiya (*ṭ gh y)
convenience
naʿmah (*n ʿ m)
convenient
suwá (*s w y)
converse
ḥāwara (*ḥ w r)
converse secretly
tanājá (*n j w)
convey
ablagha (*b l gh)
adrá (*d r y)
alqá (*l q y)
sayyara (*s y r)
convulse
zalzala (*z l z l)
convulsion
zalzala (*z l z l)
cooking pots
qudūr (*q d r)
cool, coolness
barada (*b r d)
qurrah (*q r r)
cooperate
taʿāwana (*ʿ w n)
copious
ghadaq (*gh d q)
copper, molten
muhl (*m h l)
coral
marjān (*m r j)
cord
ḥabl (*ḥ b l)
sabab (*s b b)
corn
fūm (*f w m)
ḥaṣīd (*ḥ ṣ d)
sunbulah (*s n b l)
corner of ground
buqʿah (*b q ʿ)
correctness
ṣadaqa (*ṣ d q)
corrupt, corruption
būr (*b w r)
dakhal (*d kh l)
dassā (*d s w)
afsada (*f s d)
fasād (*f s d)
fasada (*f s d)
khabāʾith (*kh b th)
khabutha (*kh b th)
cost
thaman (*th m n)
couch
arīkah (*a r k)
maḍājiʿ (*ḍ j ʿ)
firāsh (*f r sh)
surur (*s r r)
council
malaʾ (*m l ʾ)
nādī (*n d w)
nadīy (*n d w)
counsel (n)
shūrá (*sh w r)
counsel (v)
iʾtamara (*a m r)
naṣaḥa (*n ṣ ḥ)
tanājá (*n j w)
shāwara (*sh w r)
tashāwara (*sh w r)
tawāṣá (*w ṣ y)
count
ʿadda (*ʿ d d)
jaʿala (*j ʿ l)
ḥasiba (*ḥ s b)
aḥṣá (*ḥ ṣ y)
count over
ʿaddada (*ʿ d d)
countenance
wajh (*w j h)
counterpoise
ʿadl (*ʿ d l)
couple (n)
zawj (*z w j)
couple (v)
zawwaja (*z w j)
coupled, to be
qarrana (*q r n)
course (of a ship)
majrá (*j r y)
courser
ʿādiyah (*ʿ d w)
jiyād (*j w d)
court
rukn (*r k n)
courteous, to be
talaṭṭafa (*l ṭ f)
courtyard
sāḥah (*s w ḥ)
covenant
ʿahd (*ʿ h d)
mawthiq (*w th q)
mīthāq (*w th q)
covenant, to make a
ʿāhada (*ʿ h d)
ʿahida (*ʿ h d)
wāʿada (*w ʿ d)
wāthaqa (*w th q)
cover
aghshá (*gh sh y)
ghashshá (*gh sh y)
istaghshá (*gh sh y)
taghashshá (*gh sh y)
janna (*j n n)
istatara (*s t r)
wārá (*w r y)
awṣada (*w ṣ d)
cover, un-

kashafa (*k sh f)
covering
ghāshiyah (*gh sh y)
ghishāwah (*gh sh y)
ghiṭā' (*gh ṭ y)
junnah (*j n n)
akinnah (*k n n)
ẓill (*ẓ l l)
ẓullah (*ẓ l l)
covet
tamanná (*m n y)
cow
baqarah (*b q r)
fāriḍ (*f r ḍ)
crack
inshaqqa (*sh q q)
cradle
mahd (*m h d)
mihād (*m h d)
crash (n)
dakkah (*d k k)
crash (v)
habaṭa (*h b ṭ)
hadda (*h d d)
crawl (v)
zaḥafa (*z ḥ f)
crawling creature
dābbah (*d b b)
create
bara'a (*b r ')
dhara'a (*dh r ')
faṭara (*f ṭ r)
khalaqa (*kh l q)
ansha'a (*n sh ')
qaḍá (*q ḍ y)
create false desires
manná (*m n y)
create in symmetry
ʿadala (*ʿ d l)
create very well
atqana (*t q n)
creation
fiṭrah (*f ṭ r)
khalaqa (*kh l q)
creature
anām (*a n m)
barīyah (*b r ')
credence, to give
ṣaddaqa (*ṣ d q)
creed
millah (*m l l)
creek
sarīy (*s r y)
crime
maʿarrah (*ʿ r r)
dhanb (*dh n b)
ḥāba (*ḥ w b)
crimson
wardah (*w r d)
crookedness
ʿiwaj (*ʿ w j)
crops
zaraʿa (*z r ʿ)
cross (v)
jāwaza (*j w z)
crowd
jibillah (*j b l)
libad (*l b d)
lafīf (*l f f)
zumar (*z m r)
crucify
ṣallaba (*ṣ l b)
cruel
ʿutull (*ʿ t l)
crumble
bassa (*b s s)
hāra (*h w r)
crumble to dust
dakka (*d k k)
crumbled
nakhirah (*n kh r)
crumbling bank (of a river)
juruf (*j r f)
crush
dakka (*d k k)
damdama (*d m d m)
ḥaṭama (*ḥ ṭ m)
cry
daʿwá (*d ʿ w)
nādá (*n d w)
ṣayḥah (*ṣ y ḥ)
cry aloud
iṣṭarakha (*ṣ r kh)
cry for help
istaghātha (*gh w th)
istaṣrakha (*ṣ r kh)
ṣarīkh (*ṣ r kh)
cry lies to
kadhdhaba (*k dh b)
cry, compelling
zajrah (*z j r)
cry, loud
ṣarrah (*ṣ r r)
crystal
qawārīr (*q r r)
cubit
dharʿ (*dh r ʿ)
dhirāʿ (*dh r ʿ)
cucumbers
qiththā' (*q th ')
cultivate
ʿamara (*ʿ m r)
cunning
ʿalīm (*ʿ l m)
kāda (*k y d)
cup
ka's (*k ' s)
akwāb (*k w b)
siqāyah (*s q y)
ṣuwāʿ (*ṣ w ʿ)
cure
abra'a (*b r ')
shafá (*sh f y)
curse
laʿana (*l ʿ n)
curtain
ḥijāb (*ḥ j b)
curvature
ʿiwaj (*ʿ w j)
curving
amt (*a m t)
cushions
namāriq (*n m r q)
rafraf (*r f r f)
custom
da'b (*d ' b)
khuluq (*kh l q)
sunnah (*s n n)
customary device
khuluq (*kh l q)
cut asunder, to be
taqaṭṭaʿa (*q ṭ ʿ)
cut off
battaka (*b t k)
qaṭaʿa (*q ṭ ʿ)
qaṭṭaʿa (*q ṭ ʿ)
cut off, to be
abtar (*b t r)
cut short
qaṣṣara (*q ṣ r)
cut up
qaṭṭaʿa (*q ṭ ʿ)

damage
ʿāba (*ʿ y b)
damned

rajīm (*r j m)
dark, darken
a^cmá (*^c m y)
aghṭasha (*gh ṭ sh)
aḥwá (*ḥ w y)
kawwara (*k w r)
lawwāḥ (*l w ḥ)
iswadda (*s w d)
waqaba (*w q b)
aẓlama (*ẓ l m)
dark, to keep in the
ʿammá (*ʿ m y)
darkening of the night
ghasaqa (*gh s q)
darkness
ghummah (*gh m m)
ghāsiq (*gh s q)
qatar (*q t r)
ẓulumāt (*ẓ l m)
darkness, to be in
ʿamiya (*ʿ m y)
aẓlama (*ẓ l m)
date-spot
naqīr (*n q r)
date-stalk, dry
ʿurjūn (*ʿ r j n)
date-stone
nawá (*n w y)
date-stone, dint on
naqīr (*n q r)
date-stone, skin of
qiṭmīr (*q ṭ m r)
date-thread
fatīl (*f t l)
dates, cluster of
qinwān (*q n w)
daughter
ibnah (*b n y)
daughter, step-
rabāʾib (*r b b)
dawn
abkara (*b k r)
bukrah (*b k r)
fajr (*f j r)
iṣbāḥ (*ṣ b ḥ)
ṣubḥ (*ṣ b ḥ)
day
nahār (*n h r)
yawm (*y w m)
day before
ams (*a m s)
day of doom
āzifah (*a z f)
day of gloom
ẓullah (*ẓ l l)
day, declining
ʿaṣr (*ʿ ṣ r)
day, that
yawm (*y w m)
daybreak
falaq (*f l q)
saḥar (*s ḥ r)
daylight
ḍuḥá (*ḍ ḥ y)
daytime
ḍuḥá (*ḍ ḥ y)
nahār (*n h r)
daze
bariqa (*b r q)
sahā (*s h w)
dazzle
sakkara (*s k r)
dazzlement
sakrah (*s k r)
dead
mayt (*m w t)
mayyit (*m w t)
dead body
maytah (*m w t)
dead, to be
māta (*m w t)
deaf
ṣumm (*ṣ m m)
deaf, to be
ṣamma (*ṣ m m)
deaf, to make
aṣamma (*ṣ m m)
deafness
waqara (*w q r)
deal out
dāwala (*d w l)
dearer
aḥabb (*ḥ b b)
death
māta (*m w t)
mamāt (*m w t)
mawtah (*m w t)
qāḍiyah (*q ḍ y)
death, beaten to
waqadha (*w q dh)
death, to fall to
taraddá (*r d y)
debar
ʿaḍala (*ʿ ḍ l)
ṣadda (*ṣ d d)
debris
radama (*r d m)
debt
dayn (*d y n)
maghram (*gh r m)
debt-loaded, to be
aghrama (*gh r m)
debt, to contract a
tadāyana (*d y n)
debtor
gharima (*gh r m)
ḥaqq (*ḥ q q)
decay
baliya (*b l y)
ramīm (*r m m)
deceit
dakhal (*d kh l)
deceive
gharra (*gh r r)
khādaʿa (*kh d ʿ)
khadaʿa (*kh d ʿ)
ikhtāna (*kh w n)
deceiver
gharūr (*gh r r)
deception
ghurūr (*gh r r)
decide
faṣala (*f ṣ l)
ḥakama (*ḥ k m)
qaḍá (*q ḍ y)
qaṭaʿa (*q ṭ ʿ)
decision
faṣala (*f ṣ l)
decisiveness
faṣala (*f ṣ l)
deck oneself
tabarraja (*b r j)
izzayyana (*z y n)
zayyana (*z y n)
declare
bayyana (*b y n)
ḥaddatha (*ḥ d th)
decline (v)
aʿraḍa (*ʿ r ḍ)
tazāwara (*z w r)
zāla (*z w l)
adbara (*d b r)
decree (n)
kalām (*k l m)
kitāb (*k t b)
decree (v)

ḥakama (*ḥ k m)
ḥatama (*ḥ t m)
kataba (*k t b)
qadara (*q d r)
qaddara (*q d r)
qaḍá (*q ḍ y)
decry
alḥada (*l ḥ d)
dedicate
ḥarrara (*ḥ r r)
nadhara (*n dh r)
deed
ʿamila (*ʿ m l)
fiʿl (*f ʿ l)
kitāb (*k t b)
deed, give a
kātaba (*k t b)
deem
ḥasiba (*ḥ s b)
ẓanna (*ẓ n n)
deep
ʿamīq (*ʿ m q)
dark (*d r k)
defame
ṭaʿana (*ṭ ʿ n)
defend
ʿaṣama (*ʿ ṣ m)
dāfaʿa (*d f ʿ)
ḥajaza (*ḥ j z)
manaʿa (*m n ʿ)
waqá (*w q y)
defer
akhkhara (*a kh r)
arjá (*r j w)
defiled
junub (*j n b)
defilement
rujz (*r j z)
deflower
ṭamatha (*ṭ m th)
defraud
alata (*a l t)
bakhasa (*b kh s)
ghalla (*gh l l)
ikhtāna (*kh w n)
degrade
akhzá (*kh z y)
khaziya (*kh z y)
degree
darajah (*d r j)
deity
ilāh (*a l h)
deity, false
jibt (*j b t)
delay
ajjala (*a j l)
taʾakhkhara (*a kh r)
ʿawwaqa (*ʿ w q)
fawāq (*f w q)
amhala (*m h l)
delight
ladhdha (*l dh dh)
ladhdhah (*l dh dh)
naʿīm (*n ʿ m)
delinquency
khaṭīʾah (*kh ṭ ʾ)
deliver (from)
ajāra (*j w r)
anjá (*n j w)
najā (*n j w)
najjá (*n j w)
anqadha (*n q dh)
deliver (to)
addá (*a d y)
ablagha (*b l gh)
ballagha (*b l gh)
dafaʿa (*d f ʿ)
fataḥa (*f t ḥ)
deliver, to seek to
istanqadha (*n q dh)
delude
gharra (*gh r r)
deluder
gharūr (*gh r r)
deluge
ṭūfān (*ṭ w f)
delusion
ghurūr (*gh r r)
demand
saʾala (*s ʾ l)
tasāʾala (*s ʾ l)
demented, to be
fatana (*f t n)
demolish
haddama (*h d m)
demolition
hadda (*h d d)
demon
ʿifrīt (*ʿ f r)
ṭāghūt (*ṭ gh y)
demonstrate
abāna (*b y n)
dense
ghulb (*gh l b)
denude
ḥasara (*ḥ s r)
deny
ankara (*n k r)
jaḥada (*j ḥ d)
kadhaba (*k dh b)
kadhdhaba (*k dh b)
kafara (*k f r)
manaʿa (*m n ʿ)
depart
dhahaba (*dh h b)
fāraqa (*f r q)
kharaja (*kh r j)
maḍá (*m ḍ y)
rāḥa (*r w ḥ)
inṣarafa (*ṣ r f)
inṭalaqa (*ṭ l q)
ẓaʿana (*ẓ ʿ n)
dependent
thaqal (*th q l)
depict
waṣafa (*w ṣ f)
deposit (n)
amānah (*a m n)
deposit (v)
waḍaʿa (*w ḍ ʿ)
depression
buqʿah (*b q ʿ)
deprive
alata (*a l t)
ḥarama (*ḥ r m)
watara (*w t r)
depth
sawāʾ (*s w y)
deride
haziʾa (*h z ʾ)
sakhira (*s kh r)
descend
habaṭa (*h b ṭ)
nazala (*n z l)
tanazzala (*n z l)
waqaʿa (*w q ʿ)
descent
waqʿah (*w q ʿ)
describe
kataba (*k t b)
waṣafa (*w ṣ f)
desdain
aghmaḍa (*gh m ḍ)
desert
badw (*b d w)
desert-dweller

badā (*b d w)
aqwá (*q w y)
deserter
khadhūl (*kh dh l)
deserve
iktasaba (*k s b)
deserving
awlá (*w l y)
design
hamma (*h m m)
desire (n)
umnīyah (*m n y)
shahwah (*sh h y)
waṭar (*w ṭ r)
desire (v)
baghá (*b gh y)
ibtaghá (*b gh y)
hamma (*h m m)
hawá (*h w y)
hawiya (*h w y)
ḥaraṣa (*ḥ r ṣ)
raghiba (*r gh b)
arāda (*r w d)
ishtahá (*sh h y)
shā'a (*sh y ')
ṭami'a (*ṭ m ')
desire, sexual
irbah (*a r b)
desire, to arouse
manná (*m n y)
desist
fatara (*f t r)
intahá (*n h w)
aqla'a (*q l ')
aqṣara (*q ṣ r)
desolate, desolation
kharaba (*kh r b)
ṣafṣaf (*ṣ f ṣ f)
despair
ibta'asa (*b ' s)
ablasa (*b l s)
qanaṭa (*q n ṭ)
istay'asa (*y ' s)
ya'isa (*y ' s)
desperate
qanūṭ (*q n ṭ)
ya'us (*y ' s)
despicable
mahīn (*m h n)
despise
dha'ama (*dh ' m)
ahāna (*h w n)
izdará (*z r y)
destination
shuqqah (*sh q q)
destiny
qadara (*q d r)
destitution
khadhala (*kh dh l)
destroy
a'nata (*' n t)
damdama (*d m d m)
dammara (*d m r)
haddama (*h d m)
ahlaka (*h l k)
ḥassa (*ḥ s s)
akhraba (*kh r b)
takhawwafa (*kh w f)
ardá (*r d y)
radá (*r d y)
as.ḥata (*s ḥ t)
tabba (*t b b)
tabbara (*t b r)
thabara (*th b r)
destruction
absala (*b s l)
dammara (*d m r)
mahlik (*h l k)
tahlukah (*h l k)
kharāb (*kh r b)
tabbaba (*t b b)
tabār (*t b r)
tabbara (*t b r)
thabara (*th b r)
destruction, cry of
ṣayḥah (*ṣ y ḥ)
destruction, place of
mawbiq (*w b q)
detain
ḥabasa (*ḥ b s)
detain
amsaka (*m s k)
detained, to be
'akafa (*' k f)
determine
'azama (*' z m)
ajjala (*a j l)
abrama (*b r m)
faraqa (*f r q)
qadara (*q d r)
qaddara (*q d r)
qaḍá (*q ḍ y)
sammá (*s m w)
deterrent
izdajara (*z j r)
detest
kariha (*k r h)
karraha (*k r h)
qalá (*q l y)
shana'a (*sh n ')
deviate
nakaba (*n k b)
qasaṭa (*q s ṭ)
zāgha (*z y gh)
zāla (*z w l)
deviate, to cause to
azāgha (*z y gh)
device
ḥīlah (*ḥ w l)
makara (*m k r)
devise
kāda (*k y d)
makara (*m k r)
devote, devotion
battala (*b t l)
tabattala (*b t l)
akhlaṣa (*kh l ṣ)
mansak (*n s k)
devour
akala (*a k l)
devout
'abada (*' b d)
battala (*b t l)
taqīy (*w q y)
dew
ṭall (*ṭ l l)
dictate
amalla (*m l l)
die
māta (*m w t)
die, to cause to
amāta (*m w t)
differ
ikhtalafa (*kh l f)
qidad (*q d d)
difficult
'asara (*' s r)
'asīr (*' s r)
difficult, to be
ta'āsara (*' s r)
difficulty
'asara (*' s r)
'usrá (*' s r)
'usrah (*' s r)
ḥarija (*ḥ r j)
shiqq (*sh q q)

dig through
naqaba (*n q b)
digest, easy to
marīʾ (*m r ʾ)
dignity
waqār (*w q r)
dilate
afāḍa (*f y ḍ)
dilatory, to be
baṭṭaʾa (*b ṭ ʾ)
diligent
daʾaba (*d ʾ b)
dim, be
khasaʾa (*kh s ʾ)
diminish
bakhasa (*b kh s)
fattara (*f t r)
ghāḍa (*gh y ḍ)
takhawwafa (*kh w f)
lāta (*l y t)
manna (*m n n)
naqaṣa (*n q ṣ)
dimness, to be in
ʿamiya (*ʿ m y)
dinar
dīnār (*d n r)
direct
dabbara (*d b r)
dalla (*d l l)
arshada (*r sh d)
wajjaha (*w j h)
direct aright
hadá (*h d y)
direction
qaṣada (*q ṣ d)
shaṭr (*sh ṭ r)
wijhah (*w j h)
direction of prayer
qiblah (*q b l)
dirham
darāhim (*d r h m)
disagree
ikhtalafa (*kh l f)
shajara (*sh j r)
tashākasa (*sh k s)
disappoint
khāba (*kh y b)
disapproval
nakīr (*n k r)
disaster
qāriʿah (*q r ʿ)
disbelieve (see also "believe")
kafara (*k f r)
ṣadda (*ṣ d d)
discern
ʿarafa (*ʿ r f)
disclose
kashafa (*k sh f)
akhraja (*kh r j)
aẓhara (*ẓ h r)
disconcert someone with his eyes
azlaqa (*z l q)
discord
shāqqa (*sh q q)
discountenance
sāʾa (*s w ʾ)
discourse
ḥadīth (*ḥ d th)
khāṭaba (*kh ṭ b)
qāla (*q w l)
qīl (*q w l)
discover
ʿathara (*ʿ th r)
ḥaṣḥaṣa (*ḥ ṣ ḥ ṣ)
iṭṭalaʿa (*ṭ l ʿ)
wajada (*w j d)
discredit
ṭaʿana (*ṭ ʿ n)
disdain (n)
ḥamīyah (*ḥ m y)
disdain (v)
ʿatā (*ʿ t w)
ad.hana (*d h n)
istankafa (*n k f)
saʾima (*s ʾ m)
disdainful
ʿazīz (*ʿ z z)
jabbār (*j b r)
disdainful
ʿitīy (*ʿ t w)
disease
mariḍa (*m r ḍ)
disgrace
akhzá (*kh z y)
khaziya (*kh z y)
sawʾah (*s w ʾ)
disguise
nakkara (*n k r)
disgust, to feel
ishmaʾazza (*sh m ʾ z)
dislike
kariha (*k r h)
saʾima (*s ʾ m)
disloyalty
nashaza (*n sh z)
disobedience
ʿaṣīy (*ʿ ṣ y)
baghy (*b gh y)
disobey
ʿaṣá (*ʿ ṣ y)
fasaqa (*f s q)
disorder
afsada (*f s d)
disown
tabarraʾa (*b r ʾ)
kafara (*k f r)
disparity
tafāwata (*f w t)
dispatch (v)
qaḍá (*q ḍ y)
salaka (*s l k)
aṣdara (*ṣ d r)
wajjaha (*w j h)
dispersal
jalāʾ (*j l y)
disperse
baththa (*b th th)
inbaththa (*b th th)
infaḍḍa (*f ḍ ḍ)
intashara (*n sh r)
sharrada (*sh r d)
dispersed
ashtāt (*sh t t)
shattá (*sh t t)
display
jallá (*j l y)
anshaʾa (*n sh ʾ)
ṣarrafa (*ṣ r f)
display one's finery
tabarraja (*b r j)
display, to make
rāʾá (*r ʾ y)
displeased, to be
sakhiṭa (*s kh ṭ)
dispose
faragha (*f r gh)
infaḍḍa (*f ḍ ḍ)
awzaʿa (*w z ʿ)
wazaʿa (*w z ʿ)
disposed, to be
ḥaqqa (*ḥ q q)
dispute
iddāraʾa (*d r ʾ)
ḥājja (*ḥ j j)
ḥujjah (*ḥ j j)
taḥājja (*ḥ j j)

jadal (*j d l)
jādala (*j d l)
ikhtalafa (*kh l f)
ikhtaṣama (*kh ṣ m)
khāṣama (*kh ṣ m)
khaṣm (*kh ṣ m)
takhāṣama (*kh ṣ m)
mārá (*m r y)
imtará (*m r y)
tamārá (*m r y)
nāzaʿa (*n z ʿ)
tanāzaʿa (*n z ʿ)
disquiet
arāba (*r y b)
disregard
ẓihrī (*ẓ h r)
disreputable
ankara (*n k r)
dissension
fitnah (*f t n)
shāqqa (*sh q q)
dissipate
adh.haba (*dh h b)
dissolution
taḥillah (*ḥ l l)
dissolve
nabadha (*n b dh)
ṣahara (*ṣ h r)
dissuade
ṣadda (*ṣ d d)
distance
baʿuda (*b ʿ d)
qāb (*q w b)
saḥuqa (*s ḥ q)
shuqqah (*sh q q)
distance, to cause a
bāʿada (*b ʿ d)
distant
baʿīd (*b ʿ d)
qaṣīy (*q ṣ w)
saḥīq (*s ḥ q)
distant, to be
baʿuda (*b ʿ d)
distinct
faṣṣala (*f ṣ l)
distinguish
faraqa (*f r q)
faṣala (*f ṣ l)
faṣṣala (*f ṣ l)
māza (*m y z)
sawwama (*s w m)
distort
alḥada (*l ḥ d)
lawá (*l w y)
distract
ḥayrān (*ḥ y r)
distress
ibtaʾasa (*b ʾ s)
dharʿ (*dh r ʿ)
ḍāqa (*ḍ y q)
kabura (*k b r)
karaba (*k r b)
ditch
ukhdūd (*kh d d)
dive
ghāṣa (*gh w ṣ)
ghawwāṣ (*gh w ṣ)
diverse
ikhtalafa (*kh l f)
shattá (*sh t t)
zawj (*z w j)
diversion
lahā (*l h w)
alḥada (*l ḥ d)
divert
alhá (*l h w)
diverted, to be
lahā (*l h w)
divide
faraqa (*f r q)
farraqa (*f r q)
iḥtaḍara (*ḥ ḍ r)
qasama (*q s m)
divided, to be
infalaqa (*f l q)
tafarraqa (*f r q)
divining-arrows
azlām (*z l m)
division
qismah (*q s m)
divorce
ṭalaqa (*ṭ l q)
ṭallaqa (*ṭ l q)
ẓāhara (*ẓ h r)
divorced woman
ṭallaqa (*ṭ l q)
do
ātá (*a t y)
ʿamila (*ʿ m l)
faʿala (*f ʿ l)
jaraḥa (*j r ḥ)
jāʾa (*j y ʾ)
ṣanaʿa (*ṣ n ʿ)
do (as consequence)
aʿqaba (*ʿ q b)
do again
ʿāda (*ʿ w d)
do away
baʿuda (*b ʿ d)
do in
qaḍá (*q ḍ y)
do openly
abdá (*b d w)
do uprightly
aḥsana (*ḥ s n)
do voluntarily
taṭawwaʿa (*ṭ w ʿ)
do, to be about to
hamma (*h m m)
do, to seek to
ijtaraḥa (*j r ḥ)
doctor of religion
ḥabr (*ḥ b r)
dog
kalb (*k l b)
dog, to train
kallaba (*k l b)
dogma
umnīyah (*m n y)
domination
kibriyāʾ (*k b r)
dominion
malakūt (*m l k)
dominion, to have
malaka (*m l k)
donate
taṣaddaqa (*ṣ d q)
wahaba (*w h b)
donkey
ḥimār (*ḥ m r)
doom
damdama (*d m d m)
dīn (*d y n)
qadara (*q d r)
doom, day of
āzifah (*a z f)
door
bāb (*b w b)
dotard, to make a
fannada (*f n d)
dotard, to regard as
fannada (*f n d)
double (n)
ḍiʿf (*ḍ ʿ f)
double (v)
aḍʿafa (*ḍ ʿ f)

ḍāʿafa (*ḍ ʿ f)
zāda (*z y d)
doubt (n)
jaram (*j r m)
miryah (*m r y)
rības (*r y b)
doubt (v)
imtará (*m r y)
mārá (*m r y)
tamārá (*m r y)
rāba (*r y b)
shakk (*sh k k)
doubt, to be in
irtāba (*r y b)
doubt, to cause
ghummah (*gh m m)
down, to get
habaṭa (*h b ṭ)
down, to let
adlá (*d l w)
dallá (*d l w)
awrada (*w r d)
downpour, heavy
wābil (*w b l)
dowry
farīḍah (*f r ḍ)
niḥlah (*n ḥ l)
ṣaduqāt (*ṣ d q)
drag
ʿatala (*ʿ t l)
jarra (*j r r)
safaʿa (*s f ʿ)
saḥaba (*s ḥ b)
draught
sharāb (*sh r b)
shariba (*sh r b)
draw (a veil)
ḍaraba (*ḍ r b)
draw back
adbara (*d b r)
draw near
adná (*d n w)
danā (*d n w)
qabaḍa (*q b ḍ)
iqtaraba (*q r b)
qariba (*q r b)
draw on gradually
istadraja (*d r j)
draw out
nashaṭa (*n sh ṭ)
nazaʿa (*n z ʿ)
draw together, a place to
kifāt (*k f t)
draw water
saqá (*s q y)
drawn away, to be
insalakha (*s l kh)
dread (v)
ḥadhira (*ḥ dh r)
dreadful
baʾīs (*b ʾ s)
imr (*a m r)
dream (n)
ḥulm (*ḥ l m)
manām (*n w m)
ruʾyā (*r ʾ y)
dream (v)
raʾá (*r ʾ y)
drink (n)
mashrab (*sh r b)
sharāb (*sh r b)
shawb (*sh w b)
drink (v)
shariba (*sh r b)
drink, giving to
siqāyah (*s q y)
suqyā (*s q y)
drink, to give to
asqá (*s q y)
saqá (*s q y)
ashraba (*sh r b)
drink, to seek a
istasqá (*s q y)
drinking cup
kaʾs (*k ʾ s)
akwāb (*k w b)
siqāyah (*s q y)
ṣuwāʿ (*ṣ w ʿ)
drinking place
mashrab (*sh r b)
drive
jarama (*j r m)
ajāʾa (*j y ʾ)
saraḥa (*s r ḥ)
sāqa (*s w q)
wazaʿa (*w z ʿ)
azjá (*z j w)
drive away, back
daʿʿa (*d ʿ ʿ)
dafaʿa (*d f ʿ)
daraʾa (*d r ʾ)
adh.haba (*dh h b)
akhraja (*kh r j)
khasaʾa (*kh s ʾ)
nahara (*n h r)
aṣdara (*ṣ d r)
ṭarada (*ṭ r d)
izdajara (*z j r)
zajara (*z j r)
driving
masāq (*s w q)
drop
asqaṭa (*s q ṭ)
drown
ghariqa (*gh r q)
drown (tr)
aghraqa (*gh r q)
drugget
ʿabqarīy (*ʿ b q r)
drunken
sukārá (*s k r)
drunken, to make
sakkara (*s k r)
dry (v)
yabisa (*y b s)
dry clay
ṣalṣāl (*ṣ l ṣ l)
dry land
barr (*b r r)
juruz (*j r z)
due, that which is
dayn (*d y n)
ḥaqq (*ḥ q q)
dumb
abkam (*b k m)
dumbfound
bahata (*b h t)
ṣaʿiq (*ṣ ʿ q)
dust
athāra (*th w r)
dakka (*d k k)
dakkāʾ (*d k k)
ghabarah (*gh b r)
habāʾ (*h b w)
juruz (*j r z)
naqaʿa (*n q ʿ)
qatar (*q t r)
rufāt (*r f t)
ṣaʿīd (*ṣ ʿ d)
turāb (*t r b)
dust, crumble to
bassa (*b s s)
dakka (*d k k)
duty
janb (*j n b)
walá (*w l y)

taqwá (*w q y)
duty, to undertake a
faraḍa (*f r ḍ)
dwell
tabawwaʾa (*b w ʾ)
ghaniya (*gh n y)
sakana (*s k n)
thawá (*th w y)
dwell forever
khalada (*kh l d)
dwell, to cause to
aḥalla (*ḥ l l)
askana (*s k n)
dweller
ṣāḥib (*ṣ ḥ b)
dwelling-place
mubawwaʾ (*b w ʾ)
dār (*d w r)
maskan (*s k n)
sakana (*s k n)
mathwá (*th w y)
dwelling, to prepare a
bawwaʾa (*b w ʾ)
dying
mamāt (*m w t)

eager
ḥarīṣ (*ḥ r ṣ)
nazzāʿah (*n z ʿ)
eager, to be
ḥaraṣa (*ḥ r ṣ)
ṭamiʿa (*ṭ m ʿ)
eagerness
ṭamiʿa (*ṭ m ʿ)
ear
udhun (*a dh n)
ear of corn
sunbulah (*s n b l)
ear, to give
adhina (*a dh n)
alqá (*l q y)
istamaʿa (*s m ʿ)
samʿ (*s m ʿ)
samiʿa (*s m ʿ)
early meal
ghadāʾ (*gh d w)
early morning
bukrah (*b k r)
earn
iqtarafa (*q r f)
earn
iktasaba (*k s b)
kasaba (*k s b)
earnest
jahada (*j h d)
earth
arḍ (*a r ḍ)
ṣaʿīd (*ṣ ʿ d)
turāb (*t r b)
earth, face of
ẓahr (*ẓ h r)
earth, moist
thará (*th r y)
earthenware
fakhkhār (*f kh r)
earthquake
rajfah (*r j f)
zalzala (*z l z l)
zalzalah (*z l z l)
ease
naʿmah (*n ʿ m)
mirfaq (*r f q)
raghad (*r gh d)
rayḥān (*r w ḥ)
maysarah (*y s r)
yassara (*y s r)
yasura (*y s r)
yusrá (*y s r)
ease, to give
atrafa (*t r f)
east
mashriq (*sh r q)
eastern
sharqī (*sh r q)
easy
hayyin (*h w n)
istakhaffa (*kh f f)
qaṣada (*q ṣ d)
yasīr (*y s r)
yasura (*y s r)
easy to digest
marīʾ (*m r ʾ)
easy to swallow
sāgha (*s w gh)
easy, to be
istaysara (*y s r)
tayassara (*y s r)
easy, to make
yassara (*y s r)
eat
akala (*a k l)
ṭaʿima (*ṭ ʿ m)
eat, to give to
aṭʿama (*ṭ ʿ m)
eavesdrop
istamaʿa (*s m ʿ)
istaraqa (*s r q)
edge
ḥarf (*ḥ r f)
shafā (*sh f w)
edifice
baná (*b n y)
efface
ʿafā (*ʿ f w)
ṭamasa (*ṭ m s)
eggs
bayḍ (*b y ḍ)
eight
thamāniyah (*th m n)
eighth
thāmin (*th m n)
thumn (*th m n)
eighty
thamānūn (*th m n)
elapse
ʿasʿasa (*ʿ s s)
elbows
marāfiq (*r f q)
elderly
shaykh (*sh y kh)
elect
ijtabá (*j b y)
elephant
fīl (*f y l)
elevation
ḥadab (*ḥ d b)
eleven
aḥada ʿashara (*a ḥ d)
eloquent
balīgh (*b l gh)
faṣīḥ (*f ṣ ḥ)
emancipation
kātaba (*k t b)
kitāb (*k t b)
embark
ḥamala (*ḥ m l)
rakiba (*r k b)
embassy
wafada (*w f d)
embellishment
zīnah (*z y n)
embrace
wasiʿa (*w s ʿ)
embryo
ajinnah (*j n n)
emigrant

hājara (*h j r)
emigrate
hājara (*h j r)
emptiness
makhmaṣah (*kh m ṣ)
empty (n)
faragha (*f r gh)
ṣabba (*ṣ b b)
empty, to be
faragha (*f r gh)
takhallá (*kh l w)
enact (a law)
sharaᶜa (*sh r ᶜ)
enchant
saḥara (*s ḥ r)
enchanter
raqiya (*r q y)
encircle
ḥaffa (*ḥ f f)
enclosure
sūr (*s w r)
encompass
aḥāṭa (*ḥ w ṭ)
ḥāqa (*ḥ y q)
encounter
alfá (*l f w)
iltaqá (*l q y)
lāqá (*l q y)
laqiya (*l q y)
talāqá (*l q y)
encroach
baghá (*b gh y)
encumberance
wazara (*w z r)
end (v)
nafida (*n f d)
zāla (*z w l)
end (n)
ākhir (*a kh r)
ᶜāqibah (*ᶜ q b)
ᶜuqbá (*ᶜ q b)
dubur (*d b r)
muntahá (*n h w)
qāḍiyah (*q ḍ y)
ṭaraf (*ṭ r f)
endear
ḥabbaba (*ḥ b b)
endeavour
jahada (*j h d)
juhd (*j h d)
saᶜá (*s ᶜ y)
endless
sarmad (*s r m d)
endow
razaqa (*r z q)
endure
baqiya (*b q y)
ṣabara (*ṣ b r)
endure, unable to
jaziᶜa (*j z ᶜ)
enduring
ṣabbār (*ṣ b r)
enemy
ᶜadūw (*ᶜ d w)
iᶜtadá (*ᶜ d w)
khaṣm (*kh ṣ m)
qawm (*q w m)
energy
asr (*a s r)
engage in
khāḍa (*kh w ḍ)
enjoin
ammār (*a m r)
awṣá (*w ṣ y)
tawāṣá (*w ṣ y)
waṣṣá (*w ṣ y)
enjoy
istamtaᶜa (*m t ᶜ)
tamattaᶜa (*m t ᶜ)
enjoyment
matāᶜ (*m t ᶜ)
enjoyment, to give
mattaᶜa (*m t ᶜ)
enlighten
aḍāʾa (*ḍ w ʾ)
enmity
ᶜadāwah (*ᶜ d w)
ᶜudwān (*ᶜ d w)
ghill (*gh l l)
enmity, to be at
ᶜādá (*ᶜ d w)
enmity, to cause
aghrá (*gh r w)
enormity
shaṭaṭ (*sh ṭ ṭ)
enquire
istaftá (*f t y)
taḥassasa (*ḥ s s)
enrage
ghāḍaba (*gh ḍ b)
ghāẓa (*gh y ẓ)
askhaṭa (*s kh ṭ)
enrich
aghná (*gh n y)
aqná (*q n y)
zāda (*z y d)
ensample
imām (*a m m)
enshroud
wasaqa (*w s q)
enslave
ᶜabbada (*ᶜ b d)
ensnare
kāda (*k y d)
enter
dakhala (*d kh l)
walaja (*w l j)
enter, to cause to
adkhala (*d kh l)
salaka (*s l k)
awlaja (*w l j)
entice
sawwala (*s w l)
entire
ajmaᶜūn (*j m ᶜ)
kāffah (*k f f)
entitled
awlá (*w l y)
entrails
ḥawāyā (*ḥ w y)
entrust
amina (*a m n)
wakkala (*w k l)
waṣṣá (*w ṣ y)
envelop
wasaqa (*w s q)
enveloping
ghāshiyah (*gh sh y)
envoy
arsala (*r s l)
envy
ḥasada (*ḥ s d)
enwrapped, be
izzammala (*z m l)
eqivalent, to offer an
ᶜadala (*ᶜ d l)
equal
kufuʾ (*k f ʾ)
andād (*n d d)
sawāʾ (*s w y)
equal portion
ḍiᶜf (*ḍ ᶜ f)
equal, make
sāwá (*s w y)
sawwá (*s w y)
equal, to be

aqrana (*q r n)
istawá (*s w y)
equip
jahhaza (*j h z)
equipment
ʿuddah (*ʿ d d)
jihāz (*j h z)
equitable
aqsaṭ (*q s ṭ)
equitable, to be
ʿadala (*ʿ d l)
equity
ʿadl (*ʿ d l)
erect
qawīm (*q w m)
error
ḍalālah (*ḍ l l)
ghawá (*gh w y)
khaṭāʾ (*kh ṭ ʾ)
error, commit an
ḍalla (*ḍ l l)
ghawá (*gh w y)
akhṭaʾa (*kh ṭ ʾ)
khaṭiʾa (*kh ṭ ʾ)
error, one in
ghawīy (*gh w y)
escape (v)
ʿazaba (*ʿ z b)
fāta (*f w t)
najā (*n j w)
escape (n)
manāṣ (*n w ṣ)
maḥīṣ (*ḥ y ṣ)
maṣrif (*ṣ r f)
mawʾil (*w ʾ l)
eschew
ijtanaba (*j n b)
espouse
zawwaja (*z w j)
essence
umm (*a m m)
establish
assasa (*a s s)
makkana (*m k n)
aqarra (*q r r)
ṣaddaqa (*ṣ d q)
athbata (*th b t)
waḍaʿa (*w ḍ ʿ)
establishment
qarra (*q r r)
qiyām (*q w m)
esteem
ʿabaʾa (*ʿ b ʾ)
dhakara (*dh k r)
wajīh (*w j h)
eternal
dāma (*d w m)
khalada (*kh l d)
eternity
khuld (*kh l d)
evasive speech
laḥana (*l ḥ n)
even
sawīy (*s w y)
ṣafṣaf (*ṣ f ṣ f)
even number
shafʿ (*sh f ʿ)
evening
ʿashīy (*ʿ sh w)
ʿishāʾ (*ʿ sh w)
aṣīl (*a ṣ l)
evening course
rāḥa (*r w ḥ)
evening hour, to do in the
amsá (*m s w)
ever
abad (*a b d)
everlasting
waṣaba (*w ṣ b)
everything
shayʾ (*sh y ʾ)
evidence, evident
baṣīrah (*b ṣ r)
abāna (*b y n)
bayyinah (*b y n)
tabayyana (*b y n)
evil
baʾīs (*b ʾ s)
sāʾa (*s w ʾ)
sayyiʾ (*s w ʾ)
sayyiʾah (*s w ʾ)
sūʾ (*s w ʾ)
sūʾá (*s w ʾ)
sharr (*sh r r)
wabāl (*w b l)
evil suggestions
hamazāt (*h m z)
evil, do or be
ʿathā (*ʿ th w)
biʾsa (*b ʾ s)
asāʾa (*s w ʾ)
sāʾa (*s w ʾ)
ẓalama (*ẓ l m)
evil, to think
ẓanna (*ẓ n n)
evil, to ward off
ittaqá (*w q y)
taqwá (*w q y)
evildoer
asāʾa (*s w ʾ)
ẓalama (*ẓ l m)
ẓalūm (*ẓ l m)
evildoing
ẓalama (*ẓ l m)
ewe
naʿjah (*n ʿ j)
ewer
ibrīq (*b r q)
exalt
ʿalā (*ʿ l w)
aʿazza (*ʿ z z)
rafaʿa (*r f ʿ)
exalted
rafīʿ (*r f ʿ)
exalted, to be
taʿālá (*ʿ l w)
example
imām (*a m m)
uswah (*a s w)
mathal (*m th l)
mathulāt (*m th l)
exceed
faraṭa (*f r ṭ)
asrafa (*s r f)
ṭaghiya (*ṭ gh y)
zāda (*z y d)
exceeding proper bounds
shaṭaṭ (*sh ṭ ṭ)
excellence
faḍḍala (*f ḍ l)
ḥasuna (*ḥ s n)
excellent
khayr (*kh y r)
niʿma (*n ʿ m)
exception, to make
istathná (*th n y)
excess
furuṭ (*f r ṭ)
shaṭaṭ (*sh ṭ ṭ)
zāda (*z y d)
excessive, to be
asrafa (*s r f)
exchange (n)
badal (*b d l)
exchange (v)
baddala (*b d l)

tabaddala (*b d l)
istabdala (*b d l)
exclaim
tafakkaha (*f k h)
exclusive
khalaṣa (*kh l ṣ)
excuse (n)
ʿudhr (*ʿ dh r)
maʿdhirah (*ʿ dh r)
excuse, to have
ʿadhdhara (*ʿ dh r)
iʿtadhara (*ʿ dh r)
exemplary punishment
mathulāt (*m th l)
nakāl (*n k l)
exhaust
nazafa (*n z f)
exhausted, to be
nafida (*n f d)
exhort
waʿaẓa (*w ʿ ẓ)
exhortation
mawʿiẓah (*w ʿ ẓ)
exist
kāna (*k w n)
exit
makhraj (*kh r j)
exorbitance
ʿalā (*ʿ l w)
expand
basaṭa (*b s ṭ)
sharaḥa (*sh r ḥ)
expect
iḥtasaba (*ḥ s b)
naẓara (*n ẓ r)
expel
ʿazala (*ʿ z l)
akhraja (*kh r j)
nafá (*n f y)
expend
anfaqa (*n f q)
expenditure
nafaqah (*n f q)
experience (v)
dhāqa (*dh w q)
experience, cause to
ablá (*b l w)
expiation
kaffārah (*k f r)
explain
abāna (*b y n)
fassara (*f s r)
faṣṣala (*f ṣ l)
ṣarrafa (*ṣ r f)
explore
jāsa (*j w s)
exposed
ʿawrah (*ʿ w r)
exposed, to be
ḍaḥiya (*ḍ ḥ y)
exposition
abāna (*b y n)
tibyān (*b y n)
fassara (*f s r)
expound
ʿabara (*ʿ b r)
extend
madda (*m d d)
ṭaḥá (*ṭ ḥ y)
extinct
khamada (*kh m d)
extinguish
aṭfaʾa (*ṭ f ʾ)
ṭamasa (*ṭ m s)
extol
akbara (*k b r)
sabbaḥa (*s b ḥ)
shakara (*sh k r)
extra
nāfilah (*n f l)
extraction
sulālah (*s l l)
extravagant, to be
asrafa (*s r f)
extreme
dābir (*d b r)
ṭaraf (*ṭ r f)
exult
fariḥ (*f r ḥ)
exultant, to be
mariḥa (*m r ḥ)
eye
ʿayn (*ʿ y n)
eye (of needle)
samm (*s m m)
eye-sight
baṣar (*b ṣ r)
eye, to close an
aghmaḍa (*gh m ḍ)
eye, twinkling of
lamaḥa (*l m ḥ)
eyed, wide-
ʿīn (*ʿ y n)
eyes, to have open
abṣara (*b ṣ r)

fable
khuluq (*kh l q)
asāṭīr (*s ṭ r)
fabricate
ikhtalaqa (*kh l q)
taqawwala (*q w l)
face (n)
adhqān (*dh q n)
qubul (*q b l)
wajh (*w j h)
face (of the earth)
ẓahr (*ẓ h r)
face (v)
taqābala (*q b l)
face, to turn one's
wajjaha (*w j h)
facilitate
yassara (*y s r)
faction
ḥizb (*ḥ z b)
shīʿah (*sh y ʿ)
fade away
kunnas (*k n l)
faggot
jadhwah (*j dh w)
fail
farraṭa (*f r ṭ)
fatara (*f t r)
ḥabiṭa (*ḥ b ṭ)
akhlafa (*kh l f)
khāba (*kh y b)
manna (*m n n)
naqaṣa (*n q ṣ)
fail an oath
ḥanatha (*ḥ n th)
fail, to cause to
aḥbaṭa (*ḥ b ṭ)
failing, un-
qaṭaʿa (*q ṭ ʿ)
faint
wahana (*w h n)
fair
ḥasan (*ḥ s n)
jamīl (*j m l)
ṭayyib (*ṭ y b)
fair, to be
ḥasuna (*ḥ s n)
fair, to deck
izzayyana (*z y n)
zayyana (*z y n)

fair, un-
ḍīzá (*ḍ y z)
fairness
ḥasuna (*ḥ s n)
fairy-tale
asāṭīr (*s ṭ r)
faith
āmana (*a m n)
millah (*m l l)
faith, one of pure
ḥanīf (*ḥ n f)
faith, to have sure
ayqana (*y q n)
faithful
amīn (*a m n)
naṣaḥa (*n ṣ ḥ)
wafīy (*w f y)
faithless, be
kafara (*k f r)
fall (n)
waqᶜah (*w q ᶜ)
fall (dead)
wajaba (*w j b)
fall (v)
inkadara (*k d r)
kharra (*kh r r)
khawá (*kh w y)
taraddá (*r d y)
saqaṭa (*s q ṭ)
waqaᶜa (*w q ᶜ)
fall in ruin
inhāra (*h w r)
fall into error
akhṭaʾa (*kh ṭ ʾ)
fall into misfortune
ᶜanita (*ᶜ n t)
fall short
akhsara (*kh s r)
fall to death
taraddá (*r d y)
fall, to be about to
wāqaᶜa (*w q ᶜ)
fall, to cause to
ahwá (*h w y)
asqaṭa (*s q ṭ)
fall, to let
sāqaṭa (*s q ṭ)
falling, place of
mawāqiᶜ (*w q ᶜ)
false
bāṭil (*b ṭ l)
false deity
jibt (*j b t)
falsehood
abṭala (*b ṭ l)
bāṭil (*b ṭ l)
ḍalālah (*ḍ l l)
kadhaba (*k dh b)
kadhdhaba (*k dh b)
kharaqa (*kh r q)
zūr (*z w r)
fame
dhakara (*dh k r)
familiar
wazīr (*w z r)
family
ahl (*a h l)
bayt (*b y t)
faṣīlah (*f ṣ l)
famine
makhmaṣah (*kh m ṣ)
masghabah (*s gh b)
fancies, to fill with
manná (*m n y)
fancy
umnīyah (*m n y)
tamanná (*m n y)
far
baᶜīd (*b ᶜ d)
qaṣīy (*q ṣ w)
saḥīq (*s ḥ q)
fardel
wazara (*w z r)
fare well
ṭāba (*ṭ y b)
fashion (n)
ṣūrah (*ṣ w r)
fashion (v)
ṣawwara (*ṣ w r)
ṣanaᶜa (*ṣ n ᶜ)
fashioning
ṣanᶜah (*ṣ n ᶜ)
fast (v)
ṣāma (*ṣ w m)
fasten
alzama (*l z m)
lazima (*l z m)
fasting
ṣāma (*ṣ w m)
fasting, to be inclined to
sāḥa (*s y ḥ)
fat
samīn (*s m n)
shuḥūm (*sh ḥ m)
father
ab (*a b w)
walada (*w l d)
fatigue
laghaba (*l gh b)
naṣiba (*n ṣ b)
fatigued
ḥasīr (*ḥ s r)
fatten
asmana (*s m n)
fault
dhanb (*dh n b)
ḥarija (*ḥ r j)
junāḥ (*j n ḥ)
khaṭīʾah (*kh ṭ ʾ)
lamam (*l m m)
fault, to find
lamaza (*l m z)
lāma (*l w m)
faultless
sawīy (*s w y)
zakīy (*z k w)
favour (n)
faḍl (*f ḍ l)
naᶜmāʾ (*n ᶜ m)
niᶜmah (*n ᶜ m)
wajh (*w j h)
favour (v)
aᶜtaba (*ᶜ t b)
faḍḍala (*f ḍ l)
anᶜama (*n ᶜ m)
aṣfá (*ṣ f w)
qabila (*q b l)
fealty, to swear
bāyaᶜa (*b y ᶜ)
fear
baʾs (*b ʾ s)
faziᶜa (*f z ᶜ)
ḥadhira (*ḥ dh r)
khāfa (*kh w f)
khīfah (*kh w f)
khashiya (*kh sh y)
raᶜaba (*r ᶜ b)
istarhaba (*r h b)
rahiba (*r h b)
rāᶜa (*r w ᶜ)
ashfaqa (*sh f q)
ittaqá (*w q y)
taqwá (*w q y)
tuqāt (*w q y)
fear, to free from
fazzaᶜa (*f z ᶜ)

feasible, to be
istaysara (*y s r)
tayassara (*y s r)
feast
ʿīd (*ʿ y d)
feathers
rīsh (*r y sh)
feeble, feeblness
ḍaʿīf (*ḍ ʿ f)
awhana (*w h n)
wahana (*w h n)
feed
aṭʿama (*ṭ ʿ m)
feed (cattle)
raʿá (*r ʿ y)
feeding
ṭaʿām (*ṭ ʿ m)
feel
aḥassa (*ḥ s s)
lamasa (*l m s)
awjasa (*w j s)
feel disgust
ishmaʾazza (*sh m ʾ z)
feign
iftará (*f r y)
fellow
ṣāḥib (*ṣ ḥ b)
female
unthá (*a n th)
fence
sūr (*s w r)
fertilize
laqaḥa (*l q ḥ)
festival
ʿīd (*ʿ y d)
fetter (v)
ghalla (*gh l l)
awthaqa (*w th q)
fetters (n)
aghlāl (*gh l l)
ankāl (*n k l)
aṣfād (*ṣ f d)
wathāq (*w th q)
few
biḍʿ (*b ḍ ʿ)
adná (*d n w)
qalīl (*q l l)
few, to make
qallala (*q l l)
fibres
ankāth (*n k th)
fiction
ikhtalaqa (*kh l q)
fie!
affa (*a f f)
fierce, fierceness
ʿaṣīb (*ʿ ṣ b)
ʿatā (*ʿ t w)
ḥamīyah (*ḥ m y)
fifth
khāmisah (*kh m s)
khums (*kh m s)
fifty
khamsūn (*kh m s)
fig
tīn (*t y n)
fight
ḥāraba (*ḥ r b)
jāhada (*j h d)
iqtatala (*q t l)
qātala (*q t l)
fill
malaʾa (*m l ʾ)
radama (*r d m)
shaḥana (*sh ḥ n)
awfá (*w f y)
filter
ṣaffá (*ṣ f w)
filth
farth (*f r th)
ghassāq (*gh s q)
ghislīn (*gh s l)
find
aḥassa (*ḥ s s)
alfá (*l f w)
laqiya (*l q y)
thaqifa (*th q f)
wajada (*w j d)
find fault
lamaza (*l m z)
lāma (*l w m)
find, to cause to
laqqá (*l q y)
finery
zīnah (*z y n)
finery, to display
tabarraja (*b r j)
finger(s)
banān (*b n n)
anāmil (*n m l)
aṣābiʿ (*ṣ b ʿ)
fire
ḥarr (*ḥ r r)
nār (*n w r)
saʿīr (*s ʿ r)
shihāb (*sh h b)
shuwāẓ (*sh w ẓ)
fire of hell
laẓá (*l ẓ y)
fire up
sajara (*s j r)
fire, smokeless
mārij (*m r j)
fire, thrust into a
aṣlá (*ṣ l y)
fire, to be consumed by
iḥtaraqa (*ḥ r q)
fire, to kindle a
istawqada (*w q d)
fire, to strike
qadaḥa (*q d ḥ)
awrá (*w r y)
firebrand
qabas (*q b s)
firewood
ḥaṭab (*ḥ ṭ b)
firm
makīn (*m k n)
wuthqá (*w th q)
firm, to be
rābaṭa (*r b ṭ)
rasakha (*r s kh)
ṣabara (*ṣ b r)
thabata (*th b t)
firm, to make
thabbata (*th b t)
firm, to set
arsá (*r s y)
firmament
jaw (*j w w)
samāʾ (*s m w)
first
awwal (*a w l)
nashaʾa (*n sh ʾ)
first state
ḥāfirah (*ḥ f r)
fish (n)
ḥūt (*ḥ w t)
fish (v)
iṣṭāda (*ṣ y d)
ṣāda (*ṣ y d)
fissure
fajwah (*f j w)
fuṭūr (*f ṭ r)
fit, to be
inbaghá (*b gh y)

fitting
jadīr (*j d r)
five
khamsah (*kh m s)
fix
ʿalima (*ʿ l m)
abrama (*b r m)
rasā (*r s y)
waqata (*w q t)
fixed
jamada (*j m d)
fixed place
qarra (*q r r)
flagrant
bayyana (*b y n)
flame
lahab (*l h b)
laẓá (*l ẓ y)
talaẓẓá (*l ẓ y)
shihāb (*sh h b)
shuwāẓ (*sh w ẓ)
flank
janb (*j n b)
flaunt oneself
tabarraja (*b r j)
flavour
ṭaʿima (*ṭ ʿ m)
flaw
fuṭūr (*f ṭ r)
flay
salaqa (*s l q)
flee
farra (*f r r)
hajara (*h j r)
haraba (*h r b)
flee, to cause to
hazama (*h z m)
flesh
laḥm (*l ḥ m)
flesh, lump of
muḍghah (*m ḍ gh)
flight, to put to
hazama (*h z m)
flights (of birds)
abābīl (*a b l)
fling
alqá (*l q y)
talla (*t l l)
flocks
naʿam (*n ʿ m)
flogging
jalada (*j l d)
flood
sayl (*s y l)
ṭūfān (*ṭ w f)
floor
ṭibāq (*ṭ b q)
flounder (in talk)
khāḍa (*kh w ḍ)
flourish
ghaniya (*gh n y)
flout
tajannaba (*j n b)
flow
infajara (*f j r)
tafajjara (*f j r)
jará (*j r y)
sāla (*s y l)
flow, to cause to
asāla (*s y l)
flower
zahrah (*z h r)
fly (n)
dhubāb (*dh b b)
fly (v)
istaṭāra (*ṭ y r)
ṭāra (*ṭ y r)
fodder
abb (*a b b)
qaḍaba (*q ḍ b)
foe
ʿadūw (*ʿ d w)
foeces
farth (*f r th)
foetus
ḥamala (*ḥ m l)
ajinnah (*j n n)
fold (v)
kawwara (*k w r)
thaná (*th n y)
ṭawá (*ṭ w y)
fold, un-
nashara (*n sh r)
foliage
alfāf (*l f f)
folk
ahl (*a h l)
unās (*a n s)
āl (*a w l)
qawm (*q w m)
folk, of the common
ummīy (*a m m)
follow
tadāraka (*d r k)
iqtadá (*q d w)
qaṣṣa (*q ṣ ṣ)
ardafa (*r d f)
radifa (*r d f)
salaka (*s l k)
atbaʿa (*t b ʿ)
ittabaʿa (*t b ʿ)
tabiʿa (*t b ʿ)
follow up
atbaʿa (*t b ʿ)
follow, to cause to
aʿqaba (*ʿ q b)
atbaʿa (*t b ʿ)
followers
tabaʿ (*t b ʿ)
folly
safiha (*s f h)
food
ṭaʿām (*ṭ ʿ m)
food, to give
aṭʿama (*ṭ ʿ m)
foolish
jahūl (*j h l)
safīh (*s f h)
foolish, to be
safiha (*s f h)
foot
qadam (*q d m)
rajil (*r j l)
rijl (*r j l)
footstep
athar (*a th r)
forbearance
ṣabara (*ṣ b r)
forbearing
ḥalīm (*ḥ l m)
forbearing, to be
iṣṭabara (*ṣ b r)
forbid
ḥajara (*ḥ j r)
ḥarrama (*ḥ r m)
manaʿa (*m n ʿ)
nahá (*n h w)
tanāhá (*n h w)
forbidden
ḥarām (*ḥ r m)
suḥt (*s ḥ t)
force (n)
ghaṣb (*gh ṣ b)
qūwah (*q w y)
force (v)
iḍṭarra (*ḍ r r)

fresh dates
ruṭab (*r ṭ b)
fretful
halūʿ (*h l ʿ)
friend
ʿashīr (*ʿ sh r)
ḥamīm (*ḥ m m)
khalīl (*kh l l)
ṣadīq (*ṣ d q)
ṣāḥib (*ṣ ḥ b)
walīy (*w l y)
friend, take as
tawallá (*w l y)
friends, to make
wādda (*w d d)
wallá (*w l y)
friendship
khālla (*kh l l)
khullah (*kh l l)
fright
faziʿa (*f z ʿ)
rāʿa (*r w ʿ)
frighten
khawwafa (*kh w f)
frog
ḍafādiʿ (*ḍ f d ʿ)
frolic
rataʿa (*r t ʿ)
front, in front
amām (*a m m)
qubul (*q b l)
yad (*y d y)
froth
jufāʾ (*j f ʾ)
zabad (*z b d)
froward
ʿanīd (*ʿ n d)
aladd (*l d d)
frown
ʿabasa (*ʿ b s)
frowning
ʿabūs (*ʿ b s)
fructify
athmara (*th m r)
fruit(s)
fākihah (*f k h)
janá (*j n y)
thamarah (*th m r)
fruit, to bring forth
nabata (*n b t)
fruitless, to be
ḥabiṭa (*ḥ b ṭ)
frustrate
aʿjaza (*ʿ j z)
abṭala (*b ṭ l)
kabata (*k b t)
fry
ṣalá (*ṣ l y)
fuel
ḥaṣab (*ḥ ṣ b)
ḥaṭab (*ḥ ṭ b)
waqūd (*w q d)
fulfil
akmala (*k m l)
qaḍá (*q ḍ y)
atamma (*t m m)
tamma (*t m m)
awfá (*w f y)
fulfilling
wafīy (*w f y)
full
dihāq (*d h q)
wafīy (*w f y)
full moon, to be
ittasaqa (*w s q)
full of
ʿarīḍ (*ʿ r ḍ)
full, to be
imtalaʾa (*m l ʾ)
fullness
milʾ (*m l ʾ)
fur
awbār (*w b r)
furitive
khafīy (*kh f y)
furnace
laẓá (*l ẓ y)
tannūr (*t n r)
furnish
hayyaʾa (*h y ʾ)
furniture
athāth (*a th th)
further
qaṣīy (*q ṣ w)
fury
baʾs (*b ʾ s)

gain (v)
nāla (*n y l)
iqtarafa (*q r f)
gain as booty
ghanima (*gh n m)
gain knowledge
ẓahara (*ẓ h r)
gain mastery
istaḥwadha (*ḥ w dh)
gain superiority
tafaḍḍala (*f ḍ l)
gain the upper hand
istaʿlá (*ʿ l w)
aflaḥa (*f l ḥ)
ẓahara (*ẓ h r)
gain, to seek
adlá (*d l w)
istakthara (*k th r)
game
ṣāda (*ṣ y d)
gap
farj (*f r j)
garden
firdaws (*f r d s)
ḥadāʾiq (*ḥ d q)
jannah (*j n n)
ṣarīm (*ṣ r m)
garlic
fūm (*f w m)
garment(s)
kasā (*k s w)
labūs (*l b s)
libās (*l b s)
sarābīl (*s r b l)
thiyāb (*th w b)
gate
bāb (*b w b)
mudkhal (*d kh l)
gather
ḥashara (*ḥ sh r)
jabā (*j b y)
ajmaʿa (*j m ʿ)
ijtamaʿa (*j m ʿ)
jamaʿa (*j m ʿ)
tawaffá (*w f y)
gaze
shakhaṣa (*sh kh ṣ)
naẓara (*n ẓ r)
ṭarafa (*ṭ r f)
generation
jibillah (*j b l)
qarn (*q r n)
generation, succeeding
khalf (*kh l f)
generous
karīm (*k r m)
genitals
farj (*f r j)
gentle

go in
dakhala (*d kh l)
go in unto (a woman)
bāshara (*b sh r)
rafath (*r f th)
go out
kharaja (*kh r j)
go privily
khalā (*kh l w)
go straight
istaqāma (*q w m)
go this way and that
taraddada (*r d d)
go through
jāsa (*j w s)
go to and fro
mutaqallab (*q l b)
taqallaba (*q l b)
go up
ᶜaraja (*ᶜ r j)
raqiya (*r q y)
raqiya (*r q y)
aṣᶜada (*ṣ ᶜ d)
ṣaᶜida (*ṣ ᶜ d)
go, to let
wadhara (*w dh r)
goal
muntahá (*n h w)
nuṣub (*n ṣ b)
wijhah (*w j h)
goal-post
nuṣub (*n ṣ b)
goat(s)
maᶜz (*m ᶜ z)
goat, fur of
awbār (*w b r)
goblet(s)
akwāb (*k w b)
ṣuwāᶜ (*ṣ w ᶜ)
god
ilāh (*a l h)
godfearing
ittaqá (*w q y)
taqīy (*w q y)
taqwá (*w q y)
godliness, un-
fasaqa (*f s q)
gold
dhahab (*dh h b)
golden
ṣafrāʾ (*ṣ f r)
good
ḥasan (*ḥ s n)
ḥasanah (*ḥ s n)
khayr (*kh y r)
khayrāt (*kh y r)
ṭayyib (*ṭ y b)
good, to be
ḥasuna (*ḥ s n)
ṣalaḥa (*ṣ l ḥ)
good, to do
aḥsana (*ḥ s n)
good, to seem
ṭāba (*ṭ y b)
goods
biḍāᶜah (*b ḍ ᶜ)
māl (*m w l)
goods, temporal
ᶜaraḍ (*ᶜ r ḍ)
goodwill
riḍwān (*r ḍ y)
gourds
yaqṭīn (*q ṭ n)
governor
ᶜazīz (*ᶜ z z)
grace
manna (*m n n)
naᶜmāʾ (*n ᶜ m)
faḍl (*f ḍ l)
niᶜmah (*n ᶜ m)
gracious
jamīl (*j m l)
gracious, to be
ḥafīy (*ḥ f y)
anᶜama (*n ᶜ m)
naᶜᶜama (*n ᶜ m)
grade
darajah (*d r j)
grain
ᶜaṣf (*ᶜ ṣ f)
dharrah (*dh r r)
ḥabbah (*ḥ b b)
sunbulah (*s n b l)
grandchild
ḥafadah (*ḥ f d)
nāfilah (*n f l)
grant
khawwala (*kh w l)
wahaba (*w h b)
awzaᶜa (*w z ᶜ)
grapes
ᶜinab (*ᶜ n b)
grasp
qabaḍa (*q b ḍ)
grass
abb (*a b b)
grass, a bundle of
ḍighth (*ḍ gh th)
grasshoppers
jarād (*j r d)
grateful
shakara (*sh k r)
grateful, un-
kafara (*k f r)
kafūr (*k f r)
kanūd (*k n d)
grave
kabīr (*k b r)
grave (n)
qabr (*q b r)
graze freely
saraḥa (*s r ḥ)
asāma (*s w m)
great
ᶜazīz (*ᶜ z z)
kabīr (*k b r)
shadīd (*sh d d)
great, make
ᶜaẓẓama (*ᶜ ẓ m)
great, be
kabura (*k b r)
greatness
kabbara (*k b r)
kibriyāʾ (*k b r)
greedily
lamm (*l m m)
greedy
akkāl (*a k l)
ḍanīn (*ḍ n n)
green
akhḍar (*kh ḍ r)
green fodder
qaḍaba (*q ḍ b)
green leaf
khaḍir (*kh ḍ r)
green, become
id.hāmma (*d h m)
ikhḍarra (*kh ḍ r)
greet, greeting
ḥayyá (*ḥ y y)
qāla (*q w l)
sallama (*s l m)
salām (*s l m)
grey-headed
shīb (*sh y b)
greyness of hair

shāba (*sh y b)
grief
asifa (*a s f)
bakhaʿa (*b kh ʿ)
ghamma (*gh m m)
ahamma (*h m m)
ḥazana (*ḥ z n)
ḥazina (*ḥ z n)
karaba (*k r b)
grieve
asif (*a s f)
ibtaʾasa (*b ʾ s)
ḥazana (*ḥ z n)
asá (*a s y)
sāʾa (*s w ʾ)
grievous
imr (*a m r)
ʿaṣīb (*ʿ ṣ b)
ʿazīz (*ʿ z z)
ʿaẓīm (*ʿ ẓ m)
kabīr (*k b r)
kabura (*k b r)
ashaqq (*sh q q)
grin (v)
kalaḥa (*k l ḥ)
groan
jaʾara (*j ʾ r)
ground
dakkāʾ (*d k k)
thará (*th r y)
ground for dispute
ḥujjah (*ḥ j j)
ground, a corner of
buqʿah (*b q ʿ)
ground, to break up the
athāra (*th w r)
group
ʿuṣbah (*ʿ ṣ b)
ʿizah (*ʿ z w)
farīq (*f r q)
firqah (*f r q)
nafar (*n f r)
nafīr (*n f r)
rahṭ (*r h ṭ)
thubāt (*th b y)
thullah (*th l l)
grovel
akabba (*k b b)
grow
kabira (*k b r)
zaraʿa (*z r ʿ)
izdāda (*z y d)
grow bold
marada (*m r d)
grow weary
istaḥsara (*ḥ s r)
saʾima (*s ʾ m)
grow yellow
iṣfarra (*ṣ f r)
grow, to cause to
anbata (*n b t)
anshaʾa (*n sh ʾ)
grown, to be fully
balagha (*b l gh)
ashudd (*sh d d)
growth
alfāf (*l f f)
nashʾah (*n sh ʾ)
grudge (n)
ghill (*gh l l)
grudging
baghá (*b gh y)
manūʿ (*m n ʿ)
guarantor
zaʿīm (*z ʿ m)
guard (n)
ḥaras (*ḥ r s)
guard (v)
ḥadhira (*ḥ dh r)
ḥafiẓa (*ḥ f ẓ)
aḥṣana (*ḥ ṣ n)
kalaʾa (*k l ʾ)
aṣḥaba (*ṣ ḥ b)
waqá (*w q y)
guard against evil
ittaqá (*w q y)
guardian
ḥafīẓ (*ḥ f ẓ)
wakīl (*w k l)
walīy (*w l y)
guardian-angel
ḥafaẓah (*ḥ f ẓ)
talaqqá (*l q y)
guardianship
ʿiṣam (*ʿ ṣ m)
ḥujūr (*ḥ j r)
guards of Hell
zabāniyah (*z b n)
guess
kharaṣa (*kh r ṣ)
qadhafa (*q dh f)
rajama (*r j m)
guest
ḍayf (*ḍ y f)
guest, preparation for
nuzul (*n z l)
guest, to receive a
ḍayyafa (*ḍ y f)
guide (n)
imām (*a m m)
dalīl (*d l l)
ahdá (*h d y)
arshada (*r sh d)
guide (v)
hadá (*h d y)
ihtadá (*h d y)
guile
kāda (*k y d)
guilt
maʿarrah (*ʿ r r)
guilt, to free from
barāʾ (*b r ʾ)
barīʾ (*b r ʾ)
guilty
athīm (*a th m)
ajrama (*j r m)
gulf (of doom)
mawbiq (*w b q)
gulp
tajarraʿa (*j r ʿ)
gush forth
inbajasa (*b j s)
dafaqa (*d f q)
fajara (*f j r)
infajara (*f j r)
tafajjara (*f j r)
gush forth, to cause to
fajjara (*f j r)
gushing
naḍḍākh (*n ḍ kh)

habit
khuluq (*kh l q)
habitation
dār (*d w r)
hail
barad (*b r d)
hair
ashʿār (*sh ʿ r)
hale
aḥḍara (*ḥ ḍ r)
half
niṣf (*n ṣ f)
hallow
ahalla (*h l l)
ḥarrama (*ḥ r m)

halt
qāma (*q w m)
waqafa (*w q f)
hampered, to be
ʿanita (*ʿ n t)
hamstring
ʿaqara (*ʿ q r)
hand
kaff (*k f f)
yad (*y d y)
hand over
sallama (*s l m)
hand, left
mashʾamah (*sh ʾ m)
shamāʾil (*sh m l)
shimāl (*sh m l)
hand, right
maymanah (*y m n)
yamīn (*y m n)
hand, take in
taʿāṭá (*ʿ ṭ y)
handful
qabḍah (*q b ḍ)
handhold
ʿurwah (*ʿ r w)
handiwork
ṣanaʿa (*ṣ n ʿ)
handle
ʿurwah (*ʿ r w)
handmaiden
amah (*a m w)
fatayāt (*f t y)
hang
tadallá (*d l w)
nakasa (*n k s)
happen
kāna (*k w n)
aṣāba (*ṣ w b)
waqaʿa (*w q ʿ)
happiness
sarra (*s r r)
sarrāʾ (*s r r)
ṭūbá (*ṭ y b)
happy
saʿīd (*s ʿ d)
happy, to be
saʿida (*s ʿ d)
happy, to make
sarra (*s r r)
harbour (n)
anzala (*n z l)
mursá (*r s y)
harbour (v)
anzala (*n z l)
hard
shadīd (*sh d d)
ṣald (*ṣ l d)
hard, to be
qasā (*q s w)
harden
shadda (*sh d d)
hardship
ʿasara (*ʿ s r)
ʿusrá (*ʿ s r)
baʾsāʾ (*b ʾ s)
ḍarrāʾ (*ḍ r r)
shiqq (*sh q q)
hardship, to cause
aʿnata (*ʿ n t)
harlot
baghīy (*b gh y)
harm (n)
wabāl (*w b l)
harm (v)
ḍāra (*ḍ y r)
ḍarra (*ḍ r r)
harmony
ṭibāq (*ṭ b q)
harsh
ʿasīr (*ʿ s r)
faẓẓ (*f ẓ ẓ)
ghalīẓ (*gh l ẓ)
harsh, to be
ghaluẓa (*gh l ẓ)
harshness
ghilẓah (*gh l ẓ)
harvest (n)
ḥaṣīd (*ḥ ṣ d)
harvest (v)
ḥaṣada (*ḥ ṣ d)
haste
ʿajal (*ʿ j l)
fāra (*f w r)
hasten
ʿajila (*ʿ j l)
ʿajjala (*ʿ j l)
istaʿjala (*ʿ j l)
taʿajjala (*ʿ j l)
nasala (*n s l)
saʿá (*s ʿ y)
sāraʿa (*s r ʿ)
awfaḍa (*w f ḍ)
zaffa (*z f f)
hasten, to cause to
aʿjala (*ʿ j l)
afraṭa (*f r ṭ)
istaʿjala (*ʿ j l)
hastily
bidār (*b d r)
sarīʿ (*s r ʿ)
hasty
ʿajila (*ʿ j l)
ʿajūl (*ʿ j l)
hate
kariha (*k r h)
karraha (*k r h)
maqata (*m q t)
qalá (*q l y)
shanaʾa (*sh n ʾ)
hateful
kabura (*k b r)
hatred
baghḍāʾ (*b gh ḍ)
aḍghān (*ḍ gh n)
maqata (*m q t)
haughtily, to walk
tamaṭṭá (*m ṭ w)
haughty
jabbār (*j b r)
he
huwa (*h w)
head
raʾs (*r ʾ s)
head (v)
tayammama (*y m m)
head, raise one's
aqmaḥa (*q m ḥ)
aqnaʿa (*q n ʿ)
headache
ghawl (*gh w l)
headache, to cause a
ṣaddaʿa (*ṣ d ʿ)
heal
abraʾa (*b r ʾ)
shafá (*sh f y)
health, ruined
ḥaraḍ (*ḥ r ḍ)
heap
firq (*f r q)
rukām (*r k m)
heap of sand
kathīb (*k th b)
heap up
qanṭara (*q n ṭ r)
rakama (*r k m)
heaps

qinṭār (*q n ṭ r)
hear
istamaʿa (*s m ʿ)
hear
samiʿa (*s m ʿ)
hear, to cause to
asmaʿa (*s m ʿ)
hearken
istajāba (*j w b)
samiʿa (*s m ʿ)
sammāʿ (*s m ʿ)
hearsay
umnīyah (*m n y)
heart
fuʾād (*f ʾ d)
albāb (*l b b)
nafs (*n f s)
qalb (*q l b)
ṣadr (*ṣ d r)
wajafa (*w j f)
heart, blindness of
ʿamá (*ʿ m y)
heart, to lose
fashila (*f sh l)
heat
ḥarr (*ḥ r r)
ḥarūr (*ḥ r r)
heathen
qawm (*q w m)
heave
māra (*m w r)
heaven
samāʾ (*s m w)
heavy
ʿaṣīb (*ʿ ṣ b)
thaqīl (*th q l)
heavy, to be
shaqqa (*sh q q)
athqala (*th q l)
thaqula (*th q l)
waqara (*w q r)
heed (v)
iʿtabara (*ʿ b r)
ḥadhira (*ḥ dh r)
anṣata (*n ṣ t)
ittabaʿa (*t b ʿ)
waʿá (*w ʿ y)
heed not
talahhá (*l h w)
wadaʿa (*w d ʿ)
heedless, to be
ghafala (*gh f l)
sahā (*s h w)
heedlessness
ghaflah (*gh f l)
heel
ʿaqib (*ʿ q b)
height
ʿalā (*ʿ l w)
rabwah (*r b w)
ṭāla (*ṭ w l)
heir
mawlá (*w l y)
waritha (*w r th)
heir, be an
waritha (*w r th)
heir, indirect
kalālah (*k l l)
hell, fire of
laẓá (*l ẓ y)
saqar (*s q r)
help
aʿāna (*ʿ w n)
intaṣara (*n ṣ r)
naṣara (*n ṣ r)
aṣrakha (*ṣ r kh)
ẓāhara (*ẓ h r)
help one another
taʿāwana (*ʿ w n)
tanāṣara (*n ṣ r)
taẓāhara (*ẓ h r)
help, to seek
istaʿāna (*ʿ w n)
helped, to be
intaṣara (*n ṣ r)
naṣara (*n ṣ r)
helper
ʿaḍud (*ʿ ḍ d)
ghalaba (*gh l b)
naṣara (*n ṣ r)
naṣīr (*n ṣ r)
ridʾ (*r d ʾ)
ṣarīkh (*ṣ r kh)
tabīʿ (*t b ʿ)
ẓahīr (*ẓ h r)
hem in
ḥāqa (*ḥ y q)
henchman
nādī (*n d w)
wazīr (*w z r)
herald
adhdhana (*a dh n)
herb(s)
baql (*b q l)
khaḍir (*kh ḍ r)
herb, fragrant
rayḥān (*r w ḥ)
herd
sāqa (*s w q)
herd, a weary
wird (*w r d)
herding
masāq (*s w q)
wird (*w r d)
hesitate
taraddada (*r d d)
hew
naḥata (*n ḥ t)
hidden, to be
ʿazaba (*ʿ z b)
baṭana (*b ṭ n)
ghāba (*gh y b)
khafīy (*kh f y)
tawārá (*w r y)
hide (v)
ʿammá (*ʿ m y)
dassa (*d s s)
akanna (*k n n)
kanna (*k n n)
katama (*k t m)
khabaʾa (*kh b ʾ)
akhfá (*kh f y)
istakhfá (*kh f y)
khafá (*kh f y)
lādha (*l w dh)
asarra (*s r r)
awʿá (*w ʿ y)
tawārá (*w r y)
wārá (*w r y)
hide (n)
julūd (*j l d)
hideous
idd (*a d d)
nukr (*n k r)
hie
nasala (*n s l)
high
ʿalīy (*ʿ l w)
rafīʿ (*r f ʿ)
high, to be
ʿalā (*ʿ l w)
taʿālá (*ʿ l w)
highway
najd (*n j d)
hill
jabal (*j b l)

rabwah (*r b w)
rīᶜ (*r y ᶜ)
hillock
firq (*f r q)
hind
dubur (*d b r)
hinder
ᶜawwaqa (*ᶜ w q)
ḥajaza (*ḥ j z)
mannāᶜ (*m n ᶜ)
ṣadda (*ṣ d d)
thabbaṭa (*th b ṭ)
hindrance
ᶜurḍah (*ᶜ r ḍ)
hint
alḥada (*l ḥ d)
hire
ajara (*a j r)
istaʾjara (*a j r)
hissing sound
ḥasīs (*ḥ s s)
hit
aṣāba (*ṣ w b)
hitting the mark
sadīd (*s d d)
hoariness
shāba (*sh y b)
hobble
jathā (*j th w)
hoist (v)
naṣaba (*n ṣ b)
hold
iᶜtaṣama (*ᶜ ṣ m)
amsaka (*m s k)
istamsaka (*m s k)
massaka (*m s k)
qabaḍa (*q b ḍ)
waᶜá (*w ᶜ y)
awzaᶜa (*w z ᶜ)
hold back
dhāda (*dh w d)
amsaka (*m s k)
qaᶜada (*q ᶜ d)
thabbaṭa (*th b ṭ)
hole
nafaq (*n f q)
samm (*s m m)
hole, make a
kharaqa (*kh r q)
hollow
buqᶜah (*b q ᶜ)
baṭn (*b ṭ n)
jāba (*j w b)
qāᶜ (*q w ᶜ)
qarra (*q r r)
holy
bāraka (*b r k)
ḥarrama (*ḥ r m)
qaddasa (*q d s)
quddūs (*q d s)
qudus (*q d s)
ḥarām (*ḥ r m)
holy place
ḥaram (*ḥ r m)
holy rite
mansak (*n s k)
holy things
ḥurumāt (*ḥ r m)
home
maᶜād (*ᶜ w d)
home, to sit at
qaᶜada (*q ᶜ d)
homecoming
ṣāra (*ṣ y r)
honey
ᶜasal (*ᶜ s l)
honour (n)
ᶜizzah (*ᶜ z z)
wajh (*w j h)
honour (v)
ᶜaẓẓama (*ᶜ ẓ m)
akrama (*k r m)
karrama (*k r m)
honourable
ᶜarafa (*ᶜ r f)
ᶜurf (*ᶜ r f)
ḥaqq (*ḥ q q)
karīm (*k r m)
honoured, high
wajīh (*w j h)
hoopoe (bird)
hud.hud (*h d h d)
hope (n)
amal (*a m l)
hope (v)
rajā (*r j w)
ṭamiᶜa (*ṭ m ᶜ)
hope, to give up
yaʾisa (*y ʾ s)
horizon
ufuq (*a f q)
horrible
nukr (*n k r)
horrid
nukr (*n k r)
horror
nakīr (*n k r)
horses
khayl (*kh y l)
ribāṭ (*r b ṭ)
hospitality
nuzul (*n z l)
host (v)
anzala (*n z l)
host (n)
fiʾah (*f ʾ w)
jamᶜ (*j m ᶜ)
jamīᶜ (*j m ᶜ)
jund (*j n d)
kathīr (*k th r)
nafīr (*n f r)
hot, to be
ḥamiya (*ḥ m y)
hotchpotch
aḍghāth (*ḍ gh th)
hound, train as
kallaba (*k l b)
hour
iná (*a n y)
sāᶜah (*s w ᶜ)
houris
ḥūr (*ḥ w r)
house
āl (*a w l)
bayt (*b y t)
maskan (*s k n)
household
ahl (*a h l)
bayt (*b y t)
housing
kifāt (*k f t)
hue
lawn (*l w n)
hug
ḍamma (*ḍ m m)
humble
ᶜanā (*ᶜ n w)
dakhara (*d kh r)
dhalla (*dh l l)
dhallala (*dh l l)
dhalīl (*dh l l)
taḍarraᶜa (*ḍ r ᶜ)
ahāna (*h w n)
hāna (*h w n)
istakāna (*k y n)
akhbata (*kh b t)

khaḍaʿa (*kh ḍ ʿ)
khashaʿa (*kh sh ʿ)
ṣaghara (*ṣ gh r)
humiliation
dhalla (*dh l l)
dhallala (*dh l l)
dhillah (*dh l l)
hāna (*h w n)
ṣaghār (*ṣ gh r)
humility
ḥiṭṭah (*ḥ ṭ ṭ)
khaḍaʿa (*kh ḍ ʿ)
khashaʿa (*kh sh ʿ)
hundred
miʾah (*m ʾ y)
hundredweight
qinṭār (*q n ṭ r)
hunger
jāʿa (*j w ʿ)
makhmaṣah (*kh m ṣ)
masghabah (*s gh b)
hunt
iṣṭāda (*ṣ y d)
ṣāda (*ṣ y d)
hunting creatures
jawāriḥ (*j r ḥ)
hurl
alqá (*l q y)
qadhafa (*q dh f)
ramá (*r m y)
hurricane
qāṣif (*q ṣ f)
hurry
taʿajjala (*ʿ j l)
awḍaʿa (*w ḍ ʿ)
awfaḍa (*w f ḍ)
hurt (n)
adhá (*a dh y)
ḍarar (*ḍ r r)
hurt (v)
adhá (*a dh y)
ādhá (*a dh y)
ḍārra (*ḍ r r)
ḍarra (*ḍ r r)
hurtful
wabīl (*w b l)
husband
baʿl (*b ʿ l)
zawj (*z w j)
husbandman
kafara (*k f r)
hushed, be
khāfata (*kh f t)
khashaʿa (*kh sh ʿ)
hypocrite
nāfaqa (*n f q)

idle talk
istaʾnasa (*a n s)
laghiya (*l gh y)
samara (*s m r)
idol
jibt (*j b t)
tamāthīl (*m th l)
ṣūrah (*ṣ w r)
nuṣub (*n ṣ b)
aṣnām (*ṣ n m)
ṭāghūt (*ṭ gh y)
awthān (*w th n)
idolatrous, to be
ashraka (*sh r k)
ignoble
zanīm (*z n m)
ignominy
hāna (*h w n)
rijs (*r j s)
ignorance
jahālah (*j h l)
jāhilīyah (*j h l)
ignorant
jahila (*j h l)
jahūl (*j h l)
ill
marīḍ (*m r ḍ)
saqīm (*s q m)
sharr (*sh r r)
ill-chance
taʿs (*t ʿ s)
ill-feeling
aḍghān (*ḍ gh n)
ill-fortune
naḥs (*n ḥ s)
ill-treatment
nashaza (*n sh z)
ill, to augur
iṭṭayyara (*ṭ y r)
illiterate
ummīy (*a m m)
illness
mariḍa (*m r ḍ)
illuminate
aḍāʾa (*ḍ w ʾ)
anāra (*n w r)
ashraqa (*sh r q)
illumination
ḍiyāʾ (*ḍ w ʾ)
illustrious
wajīh (*w j h)
image(s)
tamāthīl (*m th l)
ṣūrah (*ṣ w r)
imitate
iqtadá (*q d w)
immediately
fāra (*f w r)
imminent
āzifah (*a z f)
azifa (*a z f)
immortal
akhlada (*kh l d)
khalada (*kh l d)
khallada (*kh l d)
immunity
barāʾah (*b r ʾ)
impaired, un-
salām (*s l m)
salīm (*s l m)
impatient
jaziʿa (*j z ʿ)
juzūʿ (*j z ʿ)
istakhaffa (*kh f f)
impediment
ʿurḍah (*ʿ r ḍ)
ḥarija (*ḥ r j)
imperfection
tafāwata (*f w t)
impetuous, impetuousness
ʿadá (*ʿ d w)
impious
kaffār (*k f r)
importune, be
aḥfá (*ḥ f y)
alḥafa (*l ḥ f)
impose
faraḍa (*f r ḍ)
arhaqa (*r h q)
sāma (*s w m)
ṭawwaʿa (*ṭ w ʿ)
impostor
affāk (*a f k)
imprison
sajana (*s j n)
impudent
ashir (*a sh r)
impure (things)
khabāʾith (*kh b th)

impute
  kharaqa (*kh r q)
inattentive
  sahā (*s h w)
inauspicious
  qamṭarīr (*q m ṭ r)
incite
  ammār (*a m r)
  aghrá (*gh r w)
inclination
  hawá (*h w y)
incline
  janaḥa (*j n ḥ)
  akhlada (*kh l d)
  rakina (*r k n)
  ṣabā (*ṣ b y)
  tazāwara (*z w r)
incline downwards
  iththāqala (*th q l)
incline, to cause to
  ṣāra (*ṣ w r)
inconsiderate
  badā (*b d w)
increase (n)
  mazīd (*z y d)
increase (v)
  aʿẓama (*ʿ ẓ m)
  akthara (*k th r)
  rabā (*r b w)
  izdāda (*z y d)
  zāda (*z y d)
increase, to cause to
  madda (*m d d)
  arbá (*r b w)
indebted, one who is
  madīn (*d y n)
indecency
  fāḥishah (*f ḥ sh)
  faḥshā᾽ (*f ḥ sh)
indemnity
  diyah (*w d y)
independence, to give
  maraja (*m r j)
independent
  ghanīy (*gh n y)
indicate
  dalla (*d l l)
indication
  shaʿā᾽ir (*sh ʿ r)
indulgence, to grant
  amlá (*m l y)
indulgent
  ghafūr (*gh f r)
inebriation
  ghawl (*gh w l)
inebriety
  sakrah (*s k r)
inequity
  ẓalama (*ẓ l m)
inevitable
  wāqiʿah (*w q ʿ)
inevitable judgement
  lazima (*l z m)
infamy
  rijs (*r j s)
infant
  ṭifl (*ṭ f l)
infant girl, buried
  wa᾽ada (*w ᾽ d)
infatuate
  istahwá (*h w y)
  shaghafa (*sh gh f)
infirm
  ʿitīy (*ʿ t w)
  ḍaʿīf (*ḍ ʿ f)
  ḍaʿufa (*ḍ ʿ f)
  hār (*h w r)
inform
  ḥafīy (*ḥ f y)
  aṭlaʿa (*ṭ l ʿ)
informed
  khabīr (*kh b r)
ingoing
  mudkhal (*d kh l)
ingot
  zubar (*z b r)
ingrate
  kaffār (*k f r)
inhabit
  ʿakafa (*ʿ k f)
  ʿamara (*ʿ m r)
  sakana (*s k n)
inhabitant(s)
  ahl (*a h l)
  ḥill (*ḥ l l)
  ṣāḥib (*ṣ ḥ b)
inhabiting
  ʿimārah (*ʿ m r)
inherit
  istakhlafa (*kh l f)
  waritha (*w r th)
inheritance
  mīrāth (*w r th)
inheritance, to give as
  awratha (*w r th)
iniquity
  fāḥishah (*f ḥ sh)
  sū᾽ (*s w ᾽)
  ẓalama (*ẓ l m)
injure
  baghá (*b gh y)
  ḍārra (*ḍ r r)
  ḍarra (*ḍ r r)
injury
  adhá (*a dh y)
  ḍāra (*ḍ y r)
  ḍarar (*ḍ r r)
injustice
  haḍama (*h ḍ m)
  janifa (*j n f)
  ẓalama (*ẓ l m)
ink
  midād (*m d d)
inner linings
  biṭānah (*b ṭ n)
inner parts
  khilāl (*kh l l)
innocent
  barā᾽ (*b r ᾽)
  barī᾽ (*b r ᾽)
  barra (*b r r)
  zakīy (*z k w)
innocent, to declare
  barra᾽a (*b r ᾽)
  tabarra᾽a (*b r ᾽)
innovation
  bidʿ (*b d ʿ)
inquisition, to make an
  tafaqqada (*f q d)
insanity
  suʿur (*s ʿ r)
inscribe
  khaṭṭa (*kh ṭ ṭ)
  raqama (*r q m)
  istaṭara (*s ṭ r)
  saṭara (*s ṭ r)
inscription
  nuskhah (*n s kh)
insert
  salaka (*s l k)
  awlaja (*w l j)
insight
  tabṣirah (*b ṣ r)
  albāb (*l b b)
insolence
  ʿatā (*ʿ t w)

baghá (*b gh y)
baṭira (*b ṭ r)
fariha (*f r h)
ṭaghiya (*ṭ gh y)
ṭaghwá (*ṭ gh y)
insolent, to make someone
aṭghá (*ṭ gh y)
inspiration
kalimah (*k l m)
inspire
alhama (*l h m)
awḥá (*w ḥ y)
instantly
fāra (*f w r)
institution
sunnah (*s n n)
insult (v)
tanābaza (*n b z)
intellect
ḥalam (*ḥ l m)
albāb (*l b b)
intelligent
ḥijr (*ḥ j r)
intend
arāda (*r w d)
aṣāba (*ṣ w b)
tayammama (*y m m)
intercede
shafaʿa (*sh f ʿ)
intercessor
shafīʿ (*sh f ʿ)
intercourse, casual
rafath (*r f th)
interest, to augment with
arbá (*r b w)
interior
jawf (*j w f)
intermix(er)
khālaṭa (*kh l ṭ)
khulaṭāʾ (*kh l ṭ)
interpretation
fassara (*f s r)
awwala (*a w l)
interrupted, un-
ḥusūm (*ḥ s m)
intertwined, to be
iltaffa (*l f f)
interval
fatrah (*f t r)
intestines
ḥawāyā (*ḥ w y)
amʿāʾ (*m ʿ y)
intimate friend
biṭānah (*b ṭ n)
walījah (*w l j)
intoxicant
sakar (*s k r)
intoxicate
nazafa (*n z f)
intoxicated
sukārá (*s k r)
introduce
adkhala (*d kh l)
aḥdatha (*ḥ d th)
intrusive
zanīm (*z n m)
inundation
sayl (*s y l)
ṭūfān (*ṭ w f)
invent
ibtadaʿa (*b d ʿ)
iftará (*f r y)
ikhtalaqa (*kh l q)
taqawwala (*q w l)
invention
khuluq (*kh l q)
investigate
istanbaṭa (*n b ṭ)
invocation
tanādá (*n d w)
invoke (the Name)
ahalla (*h l l)
inward, to be
baṭana (*b ṭ n)
iron
ḥadīd (*ḥ d d)
qalá (*q m ʿ)
iron rod
maqāmiʿ (*q m ʿ)
irritate
ghāẓa (*gh y ẓ)
issue
awwala (*a w l)
ʿāqibah (*ʿ q b)
ʿuqb (*ʿ q b)
ʿuqbá (*ʿ q b)
kharaja (*kh r j)
issue, gentle
mirfaq (*r f q)

jail
sajana (*s j n)
jealousy
ḥasada (*ḥ s d)
jest
tafakkaha (*f k h)
jester
fakih (*f k h)
jetsam
jufāʾ (*j f ʾ)
jewels, set with
waḍana (*w ḍ n)
jinn
janna (*j n n)
jinn (*j n n)
jinnah (*j n n)
thaqal (*th q l)
jocund
niʿma (*n ʿ m)
join
laḥiqa (*l ḥ q)
rataqa (*r t q)
waṣala (*w ṣ l)
join, to cause to
alḥaqa (*l ḥ q)
joint
asr (*a s r)
journey (n)
riḥlah (*r ḥ l)
safar (*s f r)
journey (v)
ḍaraba (*ḍ r b)
sará (*s r y)
sāḥa (*s y ḥ)
sāra (*s y r)
ṣāra (*ṣ y r)
ẓaʿana (*ẓ ʿ n)
journey, destination of
shuqqah (*sh q q)
joy
matāʿ (*m t ʿ)
tamattaʿa (*m t ʿ)
sarra (*s r r)
ṭūbá (*ṭ y b)
joyful, joyous
bahīj (*b h j)
istabshara (*b sh r)
fariḥ (*f r ḥ)
niʿma (*n ʿ m)
sarra (*s r r)
joyful, to be
fakiha (*f k h)
fariḥa (*f r ḥ)
joyful, to make
ḥabara (*ḥ b r)
judaise

hāda (*h w d)
judge
dāna (*d y n)
ḥakam (*ḥ k m)
ḥakama (*ḥ k m)
qaḍá (*q ḍ y)
judge, to make a
ḥakkama (*ḥ k m)
judge's sentence
qiṭṭ (*q ṭ ṭ)
judgment
dīn (*d y n)
ḥakama (*ḥ k m)
taḥākama (*ḥ k m)
lazima (*l z m)
qāriʿah (*q r ʿ)
raʾy (*r ʾ y)
rashada (*r sh d)
judgment, to commit for
fawwaḍa (*f w ḍ)
judgment, to seek
istaftaḥa (*f t ḥ)
jug
ibrīq (*b r q)
jugular vein
warīd (*w r d)
jumble
aḍghāth (*ḍ gh th)
just
barr (*b r r)
aḥkam (*ḥ k m)
amthal (*m th l)
iqtaṣada (*q ṣ d)
ṣadaqa (*ṣ d q)
ṣiddīq (*ṣ d q)
just stand
qawām (*q w m)
just, to be
ʿadala (*ʿ d l)
barra (*b r r)
ḥaqqa (*ḥ q q)
aqsaṭa (*q s ṭ)
just, un-
ḥāfa (*ḥ y f)
ḍīzá (*ḍ y z)
ẓalama (*ẓ l m)
ẓallām (*ẓ l m)
justice
ʿadl (*ʿ d l)
qisṭ (*q s ṭ)
justice, to swerve from
qasaṭa (*q s ṭ)
justice, to weigh with
wazana (*w z n)
justified, to be
ḥaqqa (*ḥ q q)
justly, to act
aqsaṭa (*q s ṭ)
justly, to act un-
ashaṭṭa (*sh ṭ ṭ)
ẓalama (*ẓ l m)

keen
waṭiʾa (*w ṭ ʾ)
keep
ḥafiẓa (*ḥ f ẓ)
khazana (*kh z n)
amsaka (*m s k)
keep back
katama (*k t m)
keep far off
abʿada (*b ʿ d)
keep, to cause to
massaka (*m s k)
kemptness, un-
tafath (*t f th)
key(s)
mafātiḥ (*f t ḥ)
maqālīd (*q l d)
kill
qaḍá (*q ḍ y)
qatala (*q t l)
athbata (*th b t)
kin
faṣīlah (*f ṣ l)
nasaba (*n s b)
qurbá (*q r b)
ṣihr (*ṣ h r)
kin, next-of-
aqrabūn (*q r b)
maqrabah (*q r b)
walīy (*w l y)
kind
barr (*b r r)
ḥasan (*ḥ s n)
jamīl (*j m l)
yasura (*y s r)
kind, to be
aḥsana (*ḥ s n)
kindle
awqada (*w q d)
istawqada (*w q d)
awrá (*w r y)
kindly, to deal
barra (*b r r)
kindness
birr (*b r r)
māʿūn (*m ʿ n)
kindness, full of
raʾūf (*r ʾ f)
kindred
ʿashīrah (*ʿ sh r)
walá (*w l y)
kinds, diverse
zawj (*z w j)
kine
baqarah (*b q r)
king
malik (*m l k)
kingdom
malaka (*m l k)
malakūt (*m l k)
kinship
nasaba (*n s b)
qurbá (*q r b)
walá (*w l y)
kinsmen
aqrabūn (*q r b)
maqrabah (*q r b)
qurbá (*q r b)
walīy (*w l y)
kneel
jathā (*j th w)
knife
sikkīn (*s k n)
knock out
damagha (*d m gh)
knot
ʿuqdah (*ʿ q d)
ʿizīn (*ʿ z w)
knot, to tie a
ʿaqada (*ʿ q d)
know
ʿalima (*ʿ l m)
ʿarafa (*ʿ r f)
taʿārafa (*ʿ r f)
dará (*d r y)
khabara (*kh b r)
shaʿara (*sh ʿ r)
yaʾisa (*y ʾ s)
know, not to
ankara (*n k r)
know, to cause to
adrá (*d r y)
knower, knowledgeable
aʿlam (*ʿ l m)

ʿalīm (*ʿ l m)
ʿallām (*ʿ l m)
ḥakīm (*ḥ k m)
knowledge, sure
basīrah (*b ṣ r)
known, to make
ʿarrafa (*ʿ r f)
ashʿara (*sh ʿ r)
known, un-
ankara (*n k r)

labour (n)
shaʾn (*sh ʾ n)
labour (v)
ʿamila (*ʿ m l)
kadaḥa (*k d ḥ)
naṣiba (*n ṣ b)
saʿá (*s ʿ y)
labour, forced
sukhrī (*s kh r)
lad
ghulām (*gh l m)
ṣabīy (*ṣ b y)
ladder
maʿārij (*ʿ r j)
sullam (*s l m)
lade
shaḥana (*sh ḥ n)
laden with, to be
bāʾa (*b w ʾ)
lag behind
taʾakhkhara (*a kh r)
lag, stars that
khunnas (*kh n s)
laggard, to be a
istaʾkhara (*a kh r)
laid prostrate
ṣarʿá (*ṣ r ʿ)
lame
aʿraj (*ʿ r j)
lamp
sirāj (*s r j)
miṣbāḥ (*ṣ b ḥ)
lance(s)
rimāḥ (*r m ḥ)
land
arḍ (*a r ḍ)
balad (*b l d)
land, dry
barr (*b r r)
juruz (*j r z)
landing-place
anzala (*n z l)
landmark
ʿalam (*ʿ l m)
language
lisān (*l s n)
lap (v)
shariba (*sh r b)
large
kabīr (*k b r)
largess
nāfilah (*n f l)
last
ākhar (*a kh r)
ākhir (*a kh r)
last (v)
aqāma (*q w m)
last long
ṭāla (*ṭ w l)
late(r)
ākhir (*a kh r)
late, to come
taʾakhkhara (*a kh r)
lately
ānif (*a n f)
laud
ḥamida (*ḥ m d)
shakara (*sh k r)
laugh
ḍaḥika (*ḍ ḥ k)
laugh at
istahzaʾa (*h z ʾ)
laugh, to cause to
aḍḥaka (*ḍ ḥ k)
laughing-stock
sikhrī (*s kh r)
laving-place
mughtasal (*gh s l)
lavish
asbagha (*s b gh)
law, Divine
shirʿah (*sh r ʿ)
law, to enact
sharaʿa (*sh r ʿ)
lawful
aḥalla (*ḥ l l)
ḥalāl (*ḥ l l)
ḥalla (*ḥ l l)
lawful, un-
suḥt (*s ḥ t)
lay aside
waḍaʿa (*w ḍ ʿ)
lay down
alqá (*l q y)
waḍaʿa (*w ḍ ʿ)
lay hold of
akhadha (*a kh dh)
baṭasha (*b ṭ sh)
istamsaka (*m s k)
lay something before someone
qaddama (*q d m)
qarraba (*q r b)
lay something on someone
ḥamala (*ḥ m l)
ḥammala (*ḥ m l)
iḥtamala (*ḥ m l)
jaʿala (*j ʿ l)
lazy
kusālá (*k s l)
lead
dallá (*d l w)
lead astray
aḍalla (*ḍ l l)
aghwá (*gh w y)
lead down
awrada (*w r d)
warada (*w r d)
lead in the right way
hadá (*h d y)
lead on
madda (*m d d)
lead someone step by step
istadraja (*d r j)
leader(s)
imām (*a m m)
malaʾ (*m l ʾ)
leaf
khaḍir (*kh ḍ r)
waraq (*w r q)
lean
ʿijāf (*ʿ j f)
ḍāmir (*ḍ m r)
lean on
rakina (*r k n)
tawakkaʾa (*w k ʾ)
leap up over
iṭṭalaʿa (*ṭ l ʿ)
learn
ʿalima (*ʿ l m)
taʿallama (*ʿ l m)
samiʿa (*s m ʿ)
learned man
ḥabr (*ḥ b r)
learned, to become
tafaqqaha (*f q h)

least degree
dharrah (*dh r r)
leather, red
dihān (*d h n)
leave
adhina (*a dh n)
baraḥa (*b r ḥ)
infakka (*f k k)
fāraqa (*f r q)
ghādara (*gh d r)
hajara (*h j r)
rāḥa (*r w ḥ)
taraka (*t r k)
wadaᶜa (*w d ᶜ)
wadhara (*w dh r)
leave behind
khallafa (*kh l f)
leave, to give
adhina (*a dh n)
left behind, that which is
athar (*a th r)
left, left hand
mashʾamah (*sh ʾ m)
shamāʾil (*sh m l)
shimāl (*sh m l)
leg
sāq (*s w q)
legend
asāṭīr (*s ṭ r)
legion
jund (*j n d)
leisurely
ruwaydan (*r w d)
lend
aqraḍa (*q r ḍ)
length
qāb (*q w b)
ṭāla (*ṭ w l)
length of an arm
dharᶜ (*dh r ᶜ)
dhirāᶜ (*dh r ᶜ)
lenient, to be
lāna (*l y n)
lentils
ᶜadas (*ᶜ d s)
leper
abraṣ (*b r ṣ)
lessen
qallala (*q l l)
lesson
ᶜibrah (*ᶜ b r)
let
wadaᶜa (*w d ᶜ)
wadhara (*w dh r)
let down
adlá (*d l w)
dallá (*d l w)
awrada (*w r d)
let fall
sāqaṭa (*s q ṭ)
let forth
maraja (*m r j)
let free
maraja (*m r j)
let go
wadhara (*w dh r)
letter
kitāb (*k t b)
lettered, un-
ummīy (*a m m)
level (n)
sawīy (*s w y)
ṣafṣaf (*ṣ f ṣ f)
level (v)
sawwá (*s w y)
level, to be on the same
istawá (*s w y)
lewd, lewdness
fajara (*f j r)
fasaqa (*f s q)
liar
kadhaba (*k dh b)
kadhdhāb (*k dh b)
libertine
fajara (*f j r)
lice
qummal (*q m l)
licentious
sāfaḥa (*s f ḥ)
lie
afaka (*a f k)
ifk (*a f k)
kadhaba (*k dh b)
kadhdhaba (*k dh b)
zūr (*z w r)
lie hid
baṭana (*b ṭ n)
lie with
bāshara (*b sh r)
life
ᶜamr (*ᶜ m r)
ᶜumur (*ᶜ m r)
ᶜīshah (*ᶜ y sh)
maᶜīshah (*ᶜ y sh)
ḥayāt (*ḥ y y)
maḥyá (*ḥ y y)
nafs (*n f s)
life-artery
watīn (*w t n)
life, to give
aḥyā (*ḥ y y)
life, to give a long
ᶜammara (*ᶜ m r)
life, to pass
samada (*s m d)
life, to spare
ᶜammara (*ᶜ m r)
istaḥyā (*ḥ y y)
life, way of
sīrah (*s y r)
lifeless
hamada (*h m d)
lifetime
ᶜumur (*ᶜ m r)
lift
ḥamala (*ḥ m l)
rafaᶜa (*r f ᶜ)
istawá (*s w y)
waḍaᶜa (*w ḍ ᶜ)
ligament
asr (*a s r)
light (n)
ḍiyāʾ (*ḍ w ʾ)
nūr (*n w r)
light (v)
aḍāʾa (*ḍ w ʾ)
anāra (*n w r)
awqada (*w q d)
istawqada (*w q d)
light, easy
hayyin (*h w n)
khafīf (*kh f f)
lighted, to be
ishtaᶜala (*sh ᶜ l)
lighten
khaffafa (*kh f f)
lightening
ṭāghiyah (*ṭ gh y)
lightning
barq (*b r q)
like (n)
daʾb (*d ʾ b)
ḍiᶜf (*ḍ ᶜ f)
mithl (*m th l)
like (v)
aḥabba (*ḥ b b)

wadda (*w d d)
likely
adná (*d n w)
liken
shabbaha (*sh b h)
likeness
hay'ah (*h y ')
mathal (*m th l)
mithl (*m th l)
shākilah (*sh k l)
shakl (*sh k l)
ṣūrah (*ṣ w r)
likeness, assume a
tamaththala (*m th l)
limits, exceed
iʿtadá (*ʿ d w)
linger for idle talk
ista'nasa (*a n s)
link
sard (*s r d)
lion
qaswarah (*q s r)
lips
shafah (*sh f h)
listen
istamaʿa (*s m ʿ)
samiʿa (*s m ʿ)
tasammaʿa (*s m ʿ)
listen by stealth
istaraqa (*s r q)
listener
sammāʿ (*s m ʿ)
little
qalīl (*q l l)
ṣaghīr (*ṣ gh r)
little, to be
qalla (*q l l)
live
ḥayya (*ḥ y y)
live forever
khalada (*kh l d)
live up to
awfá (*w f y)
live with
ʿāshara (*ʿ sh r)
live, to cause to
istaʿmara (*ʿ m r)
aḥyā (*ḥ y y)
livelihood, living
maʿāsh (*ʿ y sh)
maʿīshah (*ʿ y sh)
maḥyá (*ḥ y y)
rizq (*r z q)
living
ḥayy (*ḥ y y)
load (n)
iṣr (*a ṣ r)
ḥiml (*ḥ m l)
athqāl (*th q l)
wazara (*w z r)
wiqr (*w q r)
load (v)
ḥamala (*ḥ m l)
ḥammala (*ḥ m l)
kāla (*k y l)
shaḥana (*sh ḥ n)
wazara (*w z r)
loan
qaraḍa (*q r ḍ)
loathe
khasa'a (*kh s ')
lock
aqfāl (*q f l)
locusts
jarād (*j r d)
lodge (v)
bawwa'a (*b w ')
qarra (*q r r)
askana (*s k n)
sakana (*s k n)
lodger
ḥill (*ḥ l l)
lodging
ma'wá (*a w y)
mubawwa' (*b w ')
mustaqarr (*q r r)
mathwá (*th w y)
lofty
ʿalā (*ʿ l w)
ʿalīy (*ʿ l w)
shamakha (*sh m kh)
loins
ṣulb (*ṣ l b)
ẓahr (*ẓ h r)
loll the tongue
lahatha (*l h th)
long (n)
baʿīd (*b ʿ d)
ḥusūm (*ḥ s m)
ṭawīl (*ṭ w l)
long for
aḥabba (*ḥ b b)
tamanná (*m n y)
long, continue to be
taṭāwala (*ṭ w l)
long, to be
ṭāla (*ṭ w l)
look (n)
naẓrah (*n ẓ r)
look (v)
naẓara (*n ẓ r)
rāʿá (*r ʿ y)
iṭṭalaʿa (*ṭ l ʿ)
ṭarafa (*ṭ r f)
look about oneself
taraqqaba (*r q b)
look after someone
naṣaḥa (*n ṣ ḥ)
look back
iltafata (*l f t)
look down upon
iṭṭalaʿa (*ṭ l ʿ)
look for
baghá (*b gh y)
faqada (*f q d)
iltamasa (*l m s)
rajā (*r j w)
look sternly
azlaqa (*z l q)
loose (v)
arsala (*r s l)
maraja (*m r j)
inṭalaqa (*ṭ l q)
loose, un-
ḥalla (*ḥ l l)
ṣabba (*ṣ b b)
lord
kabīr (*k b r)
rabb (*r b b)
sayyid (*s w d)
mawlá (*w l y)
lose
aḍāʿa (*ḍ y ʿ)
khasira (*kh s r)
lose heart
fashila (*f sh l)
loss
maghram (*gh r m)
akhsara (*kh s r)
khasira (*kh s r)
khassara (*kh s r)
naqaṣa (*n q ṣ)
tabba (*t b b)
lost, to be
ḍalla (*ḍ l l)
lote-tree

sidrah (*s d r)
loth, to be
sa'ima (*s ' m)
lots, to cast
sāhama (*s h m)
loud
jahara (*j h r)
love (n)
ḥubb (*ḥ b b)
maḥabbah (*ḥ b b)
mawaddah (*w d d)
love (v)
aḥabba (*ḥ b b)
raḍiya (*r ḍ y)
shaghafa (*sh gh f)
wādda (*w d d)
wadda (*w d d)
loveliness
bahjah (*b h j)
lovers
akhdān (*kh d n)
loving
ʿurub (*ʿ r b)
low, be
danā (*d n w)
low, be brought
istakāna (*k y n)
low, lower
adlá (*d l w)
dallá (*d l w)
adná (*d n w)
dunyā (*d n w)
dark (*d r k)
radhīl (*r dh l)
sāfil (*s f l)
lower (v)
ghaḍḍa (*gh ḍ ḍ)
khafaḍa (*kh f ḍ)
lowing (of cattle)
khāra (*kh w r)
lowly, to be
dakhara (*d kh r)
loyal
ḥamīm (*ḥ m m)
luck, bad
naḥs (*n ḥ s)
luck, turn of
karrah (*k r r)
lukewarm
iqtaṣada (*q ṣ d)
lump
kisf (*k s f)
zubar (*z b r)
lump of flesh
muḍghah (*m ḍ gh)
lure
istahwá (*h w y)
lurking
khannās (*kh n s)
lust
hawá (*h w y)
shahwah (*sh h y)
lustful, to be
ṭamiʿa (*ṭ m ʿ)
luxuriant
alfāf (*l f f)
luxury, to live in
atrafa (*t r f)

mace
maqāmiʿ (*q m ʿ)
mad
janna (*j n n)
mad, to make
nazafa (*n z f)
madness
jinnah (*j n n)
suʿur (*s ʿ r)
magnificent
kubbār (*k b r)
magnify
aʿẓama (*ʿ ẓ m)
kabbara (*k b r)
sabbaḥa (*s b ḥ)
maidens
kawāʿib (*k ʿ b)
maintain
aqāma (*q w m)
qiyām (*q w m)
majesty
jadd (*j d d)
jalāl (*j l l)
kibriyā' (*k b r)
waqār (*w q r)
make
ʿamila (*ʿ m l)
jaʿala (*j ʿ l)
ajā'a (*j y ')
ansha'a (*n sh ')
ṣanaʿa (*ṣ n ʿ)
wāṭa'a (*w ṭ ')
male
dhakar (*dh k r)
malice
sū' (*s w ')
man, mankind
insān (*a n s)
insīy (*a n s)
bashar (*b sh r)
imru' (*m r ')
nās (*n w s)
unās (*a n s)
rajul (*r j l)
man, dependent
thaqal (*th q l)
man, good
ṭayyib (*ṭ y b)
man, old
shaykh (*sh y kh)
man, young
fatá (*f t y)
ghulām (*gh l m)
man of age
kahl (*k h l)
man of moment
ʿaẓīm (*ʿ ẓ m)
manage
dabbara (*d b r)
qiyām (*q w m)
manager
qawwām (*q w m)
mane
libad (*l b d)
manifest
abāna (*b y n)
bayyana (*b y n)
jahara (*j h r)
manifest sign
bayyinah (*b y n)
manifest, to be
badā (*b d w)
istabāna (*b y n)
ḥaṣḥaṣa (*ḥ ṣ ḥ ṣ)
ẓahara (*ẓ h r)
manifest, to make
aʿlana (*ʿ l n)
barraza (*b r z)
bayyana (*b y n)
ḥaṣṣala (*ḥ ṣ l)
manifestly
jahrah (*j h r)
manifold
aḍʿafa (*ḍ ʿ f)
kathīr (*k th r)
manner
da'b (*d ' b)

mansion
  manāzil (*n z l)
many
  ʿadad (*ʿ d d)
  kathīr (*k th r)
mar
  ʿāba (*ʿ y b)
march to battle
  zaḥafa (*z ḥ f)
margin
  ḥarf (*ḥ r f)
mark
  athar (*a th r)
  sīmá (*s w m)
mark (v)
  tawassama (*w s m)
  wasama (*w s m)
  sawwama (*s w m)
market
  aswāq (*s w q)
marriage-portion
  farīḍah (*f r ḍ)
married, un-
  ayāmá (*a y m)
marry, marriage
  aḥṣana (*ḥ ṣ n)
  ankaḥa (*n k ḥ)
  istankaḥa (*n k ḥ)
  nakaḥa (*n k ḥ)
  zawwaja (*z w j)
martyr
  shahīd (*sh h d)
marvel
  ʿajiba (*ʿ j b)
marvellous
  ʿajab (*ʿ j b)
  ʿajīb (*ʿ j b)
  ʿujāb (*ʿ j b)
mass
  rukām (*r k m)
massacre
  dhabbaḥa (*dh b ḥ)
  athkhana (*th kh n)
master (v)
  iḥtanaka (*ḥ n k)
  malaka (*m l k)
master (n)
  rabb (*r b b)
  rabbānī (*r b b)
  sayyid (*s w d)
  ṣāḥib (*ṣ ḥ b)
  mawlá (*w l y)
  ẓahara (*ẓ h r)
master of religion
  ḥabr (*ḥ b r)
mastery, to have
  ẓahara (*ẓ h r)
match
  aqrana (*q r n)
mate
  baʿl (*b ʿ l)
  zawj (*z w j)
matter
  amara (*a m r)
  khaṭaba (*kh ṭ b)
  shaʾn (*sh ʾ n)
  shayʾ (*sh y ʾ)
maturity, physical
  ashudd (*sh d d)
meadow, well-watered
  rawḍah (*r w ḍ)
meal, early
  ghadāʾ (*gh d w)
meal, to have a
  ṭaʿima (*ṭ ʿ m)
mean
  dunyā (*d n w)
  mahīn (*m h n)
meaning
  mawāḍiʿ (*w ḍ ʿ)
means
  ḥīlah (*ḥ w l)
  wasīlah (*w s l)
  wujd (*w j d)
measure (n)
  mikyāl (*k y l)
  miqdār (*q d r)
measure (v)
  iktāla (*k y l)
  kāla (*k y l)
  qadara (*q d r)
  qaddara (*q d r)
  wazana (*w z n)
measure, give short
  ṭaffafa (*ṭ f f)
measure, take full
  istawfá (*w f y)
meddle
  khāḍa (*kh w ḍ)
mediation
  shafaʿa (*sh f ʿ)
mediator
  qurbān (*q r b)
  shafīʿ (*sh f ʿ)
meditate
  bayyata (*b y t)
  tadabbara (*d b r)
meek, meekness
  dhallala (*dh l l)
  hāna (*h w n)
meet
  iltaqá (*l q y)
  lāqá (*l q y)
  laqiya (*l q y)
  laqqá (*l q y)
  talāqá (*l q y)
  talaqqá (*l q y)
  thaqifa (*th q f)
meet, arrange to
  wāʿada (*w ʿ d)
meeting
  majmaʿ (*j m ʿ)
  nādī (*n d w)
melt
  ṣahara (*ṣ h r)
memorable
  shahida (*sh h d)
memory, commit to
  istaḥfaẓa (*ḥ f ẓ)
men, company of
  thubāt (*th b y)
  zumar (*z m r)
menstruation
  ḥāḍa (*ḥ y ḍ)
  maḥīḍ (*ḥ y ḍ)
mention
  dhakara (*dh k r)
  kataba (*k t b)
merchandise
  biḍāʿah (*b ḍ ʿ)
  tijārah (*t j r)
merciful
  raḥīm (*r ḥ m)
  raḥima (*r ḥ m)
mercy
  ḥanān (*ḥ n n)
  marḥamah (*r ḥ m)
  raḥima (*r ḥ m)
merit
  istaḥaqqa (*ḥ q q)
  ḥaqqa (*ḥ q q)
  iktasaba (*k s b)
merriment
  hazila (*h z l)
message
  risālah (*r s l)

meteor
nashaṭa (*n sh ṭ)
raṣad (*r ṣ d)
shihāb (*sh h b)
midday
ẓahīrah (*ẓ h r)
middle
wasaṭ (*w s ṭ)
middle-aged
ʿawān (*ʿ w n)
midst
khilāl (*kh l l)
sawāʾ (*s w y)
might
ayd (*a y d)
ʿazza (*ʿ z z)
ʿizzah (*ʿ z z)
baʾs (*b ʾ s)
baṭshah (*b ṭ sh)
jalāl (*j l l)
qūwah (*q w y)
shawkah (*sh w k)
ṭawl (*ṭ w l)
mighty
ʿazīz (*ʿ z z)
ʿaẓīm (*ʿ ẓ m)
kubbār (*k b r)
shadīd (*sh d d)
migration
ẓaʿana (*ẓ ʿ n)
mild
ḥalīm (*ḥ l m)
milk
laban (*l b n)
mind
bāl (*b w l)
ḥalam (*ḥ l m)
albāb (*l b b)
nafs (*n f s)
ṣadr (*ṣ d r)
mind, one with a present
shahīd (*sh h d)
mindful, to be
dhakara (*dh k r)
tadhakkara (*dh k r)
ḥafīẓ (*ḥ f ẓ)
ḥijr (*ḥ j r)
mingle
ikhtalaṭa (*kh l ṭ)
maraja (*m r j)
amshāj (*m sh j)
minister
wazīr (*w z r)
mirage
sarāb (*s r b)
mischief
fasād (*f s d)
wabāl (*w b l)
mischief, to do
ʿathā (*ʿ th w)
afsada (*f s d)
miscreant
fasaqa (*f s q)
miser, to be a
bakhila (*b kh l)
miserable
biʾs (*b ʾ s)
shaqīy (*sh q y)
shaqiya (*sh q y)
misery
matrabah (*t r b)
shiqwah (*sh q y)
misfortune, bodily
baʾsāʾ (*b ʾ s)
misfortune, to fall into
ʿanita (*ʿ n t)
miss (v)
faqada (*f q d)
miss the mark
akhṭaʾa (*kh ṭ ʾ)
missile
rajama (*r j m)
mistake, make a
akhṭaʾa (*kh ṭ ʾ)
mistrust
nakira (*n k r)
mix
khalaṭa (*kh l ṭ)
mixture
mizāj (*m z j)
mixture, cooked
shawb (*sh w b)
mock, mockery
haziʾa (*h z ʾ)
istahzaʾa (*h z ʾ)
mode of conduct
ṭarīqah (*ṭ r q)
model
imām (*a m m)
uswah (*a s w)
moderate
qaṣada (*q ṣ d)
wasaṭ (*w s ṭ)
modesty
taʿaffafa (*ʿ f f)
hāna (*h w n)
istaḥá (*ḥ y y)
qaṣada (*q ṣ d)
moist earth
thará (*th r y)
moisture, light
ṭall (*ṭ l l)
molestation
adhá (*a dh y)
molten brass
qiṭr (*q ṭ r)
monasticism
rahbānīyah (*r h b)
money
darāhim (*d r h m)
wariq (*w r q)
monks
ruhbān (*r h b)
monstrous
farīy (*f r y)
kabura (*k b r)
month
shahr (*sh h r)
month, postponed
nasīʾ (*n s ʾ)
moon
qamar (*q m r)
morality
khuluq (*kh l q)
more
mazīd (*z y d)
morning
bukrah (*b k r)
ghadāt (*gh d w)
ghuduw (*gh d w)
saḥar (*s ḥ r)
iṣbāḥ (*ṣ b ḥ)
ṣabāḥ (*ṣ b ḥ)
ṣubḥ (*ṣ b ḥ)
morning star
ṭāriq (*ṭ r q)
morning, to happen in the
aṣbaḥa (*ṣ b ḥ)
morrow
ghad (*gh d w)
morsel
muḍghah (*m ḍ gh)
mortal
bashar (*b sh r)
mayyit (*m w t)
mosque

masjid (*s j d)
moth
farāsh (*f r sh)
mother
umm (*a m m)
walada (*w l d)
mother, foster
arḍaʿa (*r ḍ ʿ)
motion, to be in
sāra (*s y r)
motion, to set in
sayyara (*s y r)
motionless
rakada (*r k d)
mould
sanna (*s n n)
moulded mud
ḥamaʾ (*ḥ m ʾ)
mouldy, to be
tasannaha (*s n h)
mound, flat
dakkāʾ (*d k k)
mount (n)
rakūb (*r k b)
mount (v)
ʿaraja (*ʿ r j)
ḥamala (*ḥ m l)
rakiba (*r k b)
raqiya (*r q y)
istawá (*s w y)
aṣʿada (*ṣ ʿ d)
iṭṭalaʿa (*ṭ l ʿ)
ẓahara (*ẓ h r)
mountain
jabal (*j b l)
rawāsī (*r s y)
ṭawd (*ṭ w d)
ṭūr (*ṭ w r)
mountain of fire
ṣaʿūd (*ṣ ʿ d)
mouth
fāh (*f w h)
move
ḥarraka (*ḥ r k)
taḥayyaza (*ḥ w z)
jarama (*j r m)
sāra (*s y r)
move away
tazāwara (*z w r)
move forward
nafara (*n f r)
move to and fro
dhabdhaba (*dh b dh b)
move up
nashaza (*n sh z)
much
kathīr (*k th r)
lubad (*l b d)
much, be
kathura (*k th r)
mud, moulded
ḥamaʾ (*ḥ m ʾ)
muddy
ḥamiʾ (*ḥ m ʾ)
mule
baghl (*b gh l)
multiply
ʿafā (*ʿ f w)
dharaʾa (*dh r ʾ)
ḍāʿafa (*ḍ ʿ f)
akthara (*k th r)
kaththara (*k th r)
multitude
jamʿ (*j m ʿ)
kathrah (*k th r)
murmur
hamasa (*h m s)
musk
misk (*m s k)
mustard-seed
khardal (*kh r d l)
muster
ḥashara (*ḥ sh r)
mutter
afāḍa (*f y ḍ)
muzzle
khurṭūm (*kh r ṭ m)

nail
dusur (*d s r)
ẓufur (*ẓ f r)
naked, to be
ʿariya (*ʿ r y)
nakedness
ʿawrah (*ʿ w r)
name (n)
ism (*s m w)
name (v)
sammá (*s m w)
name, nick-
alqāb (*l q b)
named, to be
qāla (*q w l)
namesake
samīy (*s m w)
narrate
qaṣṣa (*q ṣ ṣ)
narrow
ḍayq (*ḍ y q)
narrow, to be
ḍāqa (*ḍ y q)
ḥarija (*ḥ r j)
narrow, to make
ḍayyaqa (*ḍ y q)
narrowness
ḍanuka (*ḍ n k)
nation
ummah (*a m m)
shuʿūb (*sh ʿ b)
nature
khuluq (*kh l q)
naught
bāra (*b w r)
shayʾ (*sh y ʾ)
naught, to go to
ḍallala (*ḍ l l)
near of kin
aqrabūn (*q r b)
maqrabah (*q r b)
near, nearer
adná (*d n w)
dunyā (*d n w)
qarīb (*q r b)
awlá (*w l y)
near, to be
danā (*d n w)
tajāwara (*j w r)
qarraba (*q r b)
walá (*w l y)
nearness
walá (*w l y)
zulfá (*z l f)
necessary
lazima (*l z m)
neck
ʿunuq (*ʿ n q)
jīd (*j y d)
raqabah (*r q b)
neck, hang around
ṭawwaqa (*ṭ w q)
necklace
qalāʾid (*q l d)
need
ḥājah (*ḥ w j)
needle
khiyāṭ (*kh y ṭ)

needle, eye of
samm (*s m m)
needs, neighbourly
māʿūn (*m ʿ n)
needy
ʿāla (*ʿ y l)
baʾisa (*b ʾ s)
faqīr (*f q r)
aqtara (*q t r)
miskīn (*s k n)
neglect
ʿaṭṭala (*ʿ ṭ l)
dhahala (*dh h l)
aḍāʿa (*ḍ y ʿ)
farraṭa (*f r ṭ)
tafath (*t f th)
waná (*w n y)
neglectful, to make
aghfala (*gh f l)
neighbour
jār (*j w r)
jāwara (*j w r)
tajāwara (*j w r)
neighbourhood
ḥawl (*ḥ w l)
neighbourly needs
māʿūn (*m ʿ n)
nethermost
sāfil (*s f l)
never
abad (*a b d)
new
bidʿ (*b d ʿ)
jadīd (*j d d)
new moon
ahillah (*h l l)
news
khabar (*kh b r)
nabaʾ (*n b ʾ)
next-of-kin
aqrabūn (*q r b)
maqrabah (*q r b)
walīy (*w l y)
niche
mishkāt (*sh k w)
nickname
alqāb (*l q b)
niggardliness
shuḥḥ (*sh ḥ ḥ)
niggardly
bakhila (*b kh l)
ḍanīn (*ḍ n n)
qatūr (*q t r)
ashiḥḥah (*sh ḥ ḥ)
niggardly, be
kadá (*k d y)
nigh
qarīb (*q r b)
zulfah (*z l f)
nigh, to draw
azifa (*a z f)
danā (*d n w)
iqtaraba (*q r b)
night
bayāt (*b y t)
layl (*l y l)
night, a watch of
iná (*a n y)
qiṭʿ (*q ṭ ʿ)
night, attack by
bayyata (*b y t)
night, darkening of
ghasaqa (*gh s q)
night, set forth by
asrá (*s r y)
night star
ṭāriq (*ṭ r q)
night visitor
ṭāriq (*ṭ r q)
nightmare
ḥulm (*ḥ l m)
nine
tisʿah (*t s ʿ)
nineteen
tisʿata-ʿashara (*t s ʿ)
ninety
tisʿūn (*t s ʿ)
noble
karīm (*k r m)
nocturnal visitor
ṭāriq (*ṭ r q)
noise
hamasa (*h m s)
adhāʿa (*dh y ʿ)
qāriʿah (*q r ʿ)
nomads
aʿrāb (*ʿ r b)
noon
ḍuḥá (*ḍ ḥ y)
aẓhara (*ẓ h r)
ẓahīrah (*ẓ h r)
noon, sleep at
qāla (*q y l)
nose
anf (*a n f)
khurṭūm (*kh r ṭ m)
nothing
shayʾ (*sh y ʾ)
notice, take
adhina (*a dh n)
now
ānif (*a n f)
null
daḥaḍa (*d ḥ ḍ)
number (n)
ʿadad (*ʿ d d)
ʿiddah (*ʿ d d)
number (v)
ʿadda (*ʿ d d)
aḥṣá (*ḥ ṣ y)
number, even
shafʿ (*sh f ʿ)
number, odd
watr (*w t r)
numerous
kathura (*k th r)
rabā (*r b w)
nurse
arḍaʿa (*r ḍ ʿ)
istarḍaʿa (*r ḍ ʿ)

oakum
dusur (*d s r)
oath
qasam (*q s m)
yamīn (*y m n)
oath, to break an
ḥanatha (*ḥ n th)
nakatha (*n k th)
oath, to swear an
aqsama (*q s m)
qāsama (*q s m)
obedience
ṭāʿah (*ṭ w ʿ)
obey
adhʿana (*dh ʿ n)
qanata (*q n t)
ittabaʿa (*t b ʿ)
aṭāʿa (*ṭ w ʿ)
ṭāʿa (*ṭ w ʿ)
obligation
ḥaqq (*ḥ q q)
obliterate
maḥā (*m ḥ w)
ṭamasa (*ṭ m s)
oblivion, to cast into

ansá (*n s y)
obscenity
rafath (*r f th)
obscure
ʿamiya (*ʿ m y)
lujjī (*l j j)
observe
ānasa (*a n s)
baṣura (*b ṣ r)
ḥāfaẓa (*ḥ f ẓ)
raʿá (*r ʿ y)
rāʿá (*r ʿ y)
irtaqaba (*r q b)
ittabaʿa (*t b ʿ)
iṭṭalaʿa (*ṭ l ʿ)
observer
raqīb (*r q b)
obtain
nāla (*n y l)
obtain more
izdāda (*z y d)
occupation
shaʾn (*sh ʾ n)
occupy
shaghala (*sh gh l)
tabawwaʾa (*b w ʾ)
occur, to cause to
aḥdatha (*ḥ d th)
odd number
watr (*w t r)
odious
maqata (*m q t)
offence
khaṭīʾah (*kh ṭ ʾ)
lamam (*l m m)
offender
ẓalama (*ẓ l m)
offer
ʿadala (*ʿ d l)
ʿaraḍa (*ʿ r ḍ)
ʿarraḍa (*ʿ r ḍ)
alqá (*l q y)
qarraba (*q r b)
rafada (*r f d)
taṣaddaqa (*ṣ d q)
offering
ʿaraḍa (*ʿ r ḍ)
hadá (*h d y)
qurbah (*q r b)
rifd (*r f d)
offering, freewill
ṣadaqah (*ṣ d q)
offspring
dhurrīyah (*dh r r)
oft
kathīr (*k th r)
oil
duhn (*d h n)
zayt (*z y t)
old
ʿatīq (*ʿ t q)
kabīr (*k b r)
kabira (*k b r)
nakhirah (*n kh r)
qadīm (*q d m)
old age
ʿitīy (*ʿ t w)
shāba (*sh y b)
shīb (*sh y b)
old man
shaykh (*sh y kh)
old woman
ʿajūz (*ʿ j z)
olive-tree
zaytūnah (*z y t)
olives
zaytūnah (*z y t)
omen
ṭayr (*ṭ y r)
omnipotent
qadīr (*q d r)
qahara (*q h r)
once
marrah (*m r r)
nazlah (*n z l)
one
aḥad (*a ḥ d)
wāḥid (*w ḥ d)
one by one
fard (*f r d)
watr (*w t r)
one upon another
ṭibāq (*ṭ b q)
onions
baṣal (*b ṣ l)
only
waḥd (*w ḥ d)
open
fataḥa (*f t ḥ)
fattaḥa (*f t ḥ)
sharaḥa (*sh r ḥ)
opening
farj (*f r j)
openly
jāhara (*j h r)
jahara (*j h r)
jahrah (*j h r)
opinion
raʾy (*r ʾ y)
ẓanna (*ẓ n n)
opinion, to give an
aftá (*f t y)
opponent
khaṣīm (*kh ṣ m)
oppose, opposition
ʿaṣá (*ʿ ṣ y)
ḍārra (*ḍ r r)
ḥādda (*ḥ d d)
khālafa (*kh l f)
opposite
khilāf (*kh l f)
oppress, oppression
āda (*a w d)
baghá (*b gh y)
baghy (*b gh y)
istaḍʿafa (*ḍ ʿ f)
qahara (*q h r)
shaqqa (*sh q q)
ẓalama (*ẓ l m)
oppressor
ẓallām (*ẓ l m)
oppulence, to give
atrafa (*t r f)
oratory
qiblah (*q b l)
ṣalāh (*ṣ l w)
orbit
falak (*f l k)
mawāqiʿ (*w q ʿ)
ordain
faraḍa (*f r ḍ)
kataba (*k t b)
qaddara (*q d r)
sharaʿa (*sh r ʿ)
order
amara (*a m r)
kataba (*k t b)
ṣarrafa (*ṣ r f)
awzaʿa (*w z ʿ)
order, to be in
ittasaqa (*w s q)
ordinance
farīḍah (*f r ḍ)
ḥudūd (*ḥ d d)
ṣarrafa (*ṣ r f)
original

fiṭrah (*f ṭ r)
ḥāfirah (*ḥ f r)
originate
abdaʾa (*b d ʾ)
badaʾa (*b d ʾ)
faṭara (*f ṭ r)
anshaʾa (*n sh ʾ)
ornaments
ḥilyah (*ḥ l y)
zukhruf (*z kh r f)
zīnah (*z y n)
orphan
yatīm (*y t m)
orts, broken
ḥuṭām (*ḥ ṭ m)
other(s)
aḥad (*a ḥ d)
ākhar (*a kh r)
nās (*n w s)
out of reach
qaṭaʿa (*q ṭ ʿ)
outcast
daḥara (*d ḥ r)
ḥarama (*ḥ r m)
outgoing
akhraja (*kh r j)
outpour
safaḥa (*s f ḥ)
sakaba (*s k b)
outrace
sabaqa (*s b q)
outrage
shaṭaṭ (*sh ṭ ṭ)
outspread
basaṭa (*b s ṭ)
baththa (*b th th)
janna (*j n n)
ẓallala (*ẓ l l)
outstanding, to be
baqiya (*b q y)
outstretch
maddada (*m d d)
outstrip
ʿajila (*ʿ j l)
sabaqa (*s b q)
outward
ẓahara (*ẓ h r)
outwit
kāda (*k y d)
oven
tannūr (*t n r)
overbold, to be
ṭaghiya (*ṭ gh y)
overburden
aʿnata (*ʿ n t)
overcome
ʿazza (*ʿ z z)
ghalaba (*gh l b)
ghashiya (*gh sh y)
ghashshá (*gh sh y)
qahara (*q h r)
rāna (*r y n)
overflow
fāḍa (*f y ḍ)
sajara (*s j r)
ṭaghiya (*ṭ gh y)
overflow, to cause to
sajjara (*s j r)
overflowing
dihāq (*d h q)
overhear
istamaʿa (*s m ʿ)
overlap, cause to
kawwara (*k w r)
overlook
ṣafaḥa (*ṣ f ḥ)
overpass
baghá (*b gh y)
overreach
khadaʿa (*kh d ʿ)
overrule
malaka (*m l k)
overseer
sayṭara (*s y ṭ r)
overshadow
ẓallala (*ẓ l l)
ẓullah (*ẓ l l)
overspread
rahiqa (*r h q)
overtake
adraka (*d r k)
daraka (*d r k)
tadāraka (*d r k)
nāla (*n y l)
overthrow
baʿthara (*b ʿ th r)
ahwá (*h w y)
kawwara (*k w r)
arkasa (*r k s)
ṣarʿá (*ṣ r ʿ)
overturn
munqalab (*q l b)
qalaba (*q l b)
overwhelm
ghashiya (*gh sh y)
ghāshiyah (*gh sh y)
own
nafs (*n f s)
own (v)
malaka (*m l k)
owner(s)
ahl (*a h l)
ṣāḥib (*ṣ ḥ b)
oxen
baqarah (*b q r)

packed densely
libad (*l b d)
pact
ill (*a l l)
dhimmah (*dh m m)
pagandom
jāhilīyah (*j h l)
page
fatá (*f t y)
pain of childbirth
makhāḍ (*m kh ḍ)
painful
alīm (*a l m)
kariha (*k r h)
pair
mathná (*th n y)
ṣinwān (*ṣ n w)
zawj (*z w j)
palm-bough, aged
ʿurjūn (*ʿ r j n)
palm-tree
līnah (*l y n)
nakhlah (*n kh l)
palm-tree, fibres of
dusur (*d s r)
masad (*m s d)
paltriness
bakhasa (*b kh s)
panic
baʾs (*b ʾ s)
pant (v)
ḍabaḥa (*ḍ b ḥ)
parade (v)
aḥḍara (*ḥ ḍ r)
paraphernalia
jihāz (*j h z)
parchment
qirṭās (*q r ṭ s)
pardon
ʿafā (*ʿ f w)

ghafara (*gh f r)
ghufrān (*gh f r)
maghfirah (*gh f r)
ṣafaḥa (*ṣ f ḥ)
pardon, to ask
istaghfara (*gh f r)
parents
ab (*a b w)
walada (*w l d)
park
firdaws (*f r d s)
parsimonious, to be
qatara (*q t r)
part (n)
ḥaẓẓ (*ḥ ẓ ẓ)
juzʾ (*j z ʾ)
khalāq (*kh l q)
qiṭaʿ (*q ṭ ʿ)
qiṭʿ (*q ṭ ʿ)
ṭaraf (*ṭ r f)
part, on one's
ladun (*l d n)
part (v)
fāraqa (*f r q)
partial, to be
ʿāla (*ʿ w l)
alḥada (*l ḥ d)
māla (*m y l)
particular
khāṣṣah (*kh ṣ ṣ)
partisan
ḥizb (*ḥ z b)
ẓahīr (*ẓ h r)
partition (n)
barzakh (*b r z kh)
ḥajaza (*ḥ j z)
istaqsama (*q s m)
partition (v)
iqtasama (*q s m)
qassama (*q s m)
partner(s)
khulaṭāʾ (*kh l ṭ)
sharīk (*sh r k)
partner, to make a
ashraka (*sh r k)
sharika (*sh r k)
party
fiʾah (*f ʾ w)
ḥizb (*ḥ z b)
shīʿah (*sh y ʿ)
thullah (*th l l)
ṭāʾifah (*ṭ w f)
pass (v)
ʿasʿasa (*ʿ s s)
marra (*m r r)
pass away
fāta (*f w t)
khalā (*kh l w)
maḍá (*m ḍ y)
pass life
samada (*s m d)
pass over
jāwaza (*j w z)
tajāwaza (*j w z)
pass someone
qaraḍa (*q r ḍ)
pass something
tanāzaʿa (*n z ʿ)
ṭāfa (*ṭ w f)
pass the night
bāta (*b y t)
pass through
nafadha (*n f dh)
walaja (*w l j)
passing
zahūq (*z h q)
passtime
laʿiba (*l ʿ b)
past
maḍá (*m ḍ y)
aslafa (*s l f)
salafa (*s l f)
pasture (n)
abb (*a b b)
marʿá (*r ʿ y)
pasture (v)
raʿá (*r ʿ y)
asāma (*s w m)
path
manākib (*n k b)
sabīl (*s b l)
ṣirāṭ (*ṣ r ṭ)
ṭarīq (*ṭ r q)
ṭarīqah (*ṭ r q)
path, dry
yabas (*y b s)
path, right
sawāʾ (*s w y)
sharīʿah (*sh r ʿ)
shirʿah (*sh r ʿ)
path, to be on the right
rashada (*r sh d)
patient
aṣbar (*ṣ b r)
ṣabara (*ṣ b r)
ṣabbār (*ṣ b r)
patient, to be
iṣṭabara (*ṣ b r)
ṣabara (*ṣ b r)
ṣābara (*ṣ b r)
patron
mawlá (*w l y)
pause, to cause to
thabbaṭa (*th b ṭ)
pavilion
khiyām (*kh y m)
surādiq (*s r d q)
ṣarḥ (*ṣ r ḥ)
paw
dhirāʿ (*dh r ʿ)
pay (v)
aʿṭá (*ʿ ṭ y)
sallama (*s l m)
pay in full
waffá (*w f y)
pay over
dafaʿa (*d f ʿ)
payment
adāʾ (*a d y)
peace
sakīnah (*s k n)
salām (*s l m)
salam (*s l m)
sallama (*s l m)
salm (*s l m)
silm (*s l m)
ṣulḥ (*ṣ l ḥ)
peace, to be at
iṭmaʾanna (*ṭ m ʾ n)
peace, to pray someone
sallama (*s l m)
pearls
bayḍ (*b y ḍ)
luʾluʾ (*l ʾ l ʾ)
pebbles, squall of
ḥāṣib (*ḥ ṣ b)
peer
andād (*n d d)
aqrana (*q r n)
peg
awtād (*w t d)
pelt
qadhafa (*q dh f)
pen (writing)
qalam (*q l m)
pen-builder

iḥtaẓara (*ḥ ẓ r)
penalty
rijs (*r j s)
rijz (*r j z)
penance, to do
tāba (*t w b)
penetrate
walaja (*w l j)
wasaṭa (*w s ṭ)
penetrating
balīgh (*b l gh)
penitent
awwāb (*a w b)
anāba (*n w b)
tāba (*t w b)
penury
amlaqa (*m l q)
people
ahl (*a h l)
unās (*a n s)
āl (*a w l)
ʿabd (*ʿ b d)
nās (*n w s)
qawm (*q w m)
shuʿūb (*sh ʿ b)
perceive
ānasa (*a n s)
abṣara (*b ṣ r)
baṣura (*b ṣ r)
aḥassa (*ḥ s s)
wajada (*w j d)
perdition
bāra (*b w r)
tahlukah (*h l k)
taʿs (*t ʿ s)
perfect
akmala (*k m l)
atamma (*t m m)
tamma (*t m m)
atqana (*t q n)
perfidious
khattār (*kh t r)
perform
atá (*a t y)
ātá (*a t y)
nasaka (*n s k)
qaḍá (*q ḍ y)
aqāma (*q w m)
performer
faʿʿāl (*f ʿ l)
peril
baʾs (*b ʾ s)
period
ʿiddah (*ʿ d d)
muddah (*m d d)
perish
bāda (*b y d)
baṭala (*b ṭ l)
faná (*f n y)
halaka (*h l k)
radá (*r d y)
taraddá (*r d y)
tabba (*t b b)
zahaqa (*z h q)
perish, to cause to
ahlaka (*h l k)
ardá (*r d y)
perishable
zahūq (*z h q)
perishing
faná (*f n y)
halaka (*h l k)
ḥaraḍ (*ḥ r ḍ)
permission
adhina (*a dh n)
permit (v)
aḥalla (*ḥ l l)
ḥalla (*ḥ l l)
permitted
ḥill (*ḥ l l)
perplexity
ghamrah (*gh m r)
persecute
fatana (*f t n)
persecution
fitnah (*f t n)
persevere
aṣarra (*ṣ r r)
ṣabara (*ṣ b r)
persist
lajja (*l j j)
marada (*m r d)
ṣabara (*ṣ b r)
aṣarra (*ṣ r r)
persistent
aladd (*l d d)
person
nafs (*n f s)
person of same age
atrāb (*t r b)
persuasion, ones of same
shīʿah (*sh y ʿ)
peruse
iṭṭalaʿa (*ṭ l ʿ)
pervert
afaka (*a f k)
aghwá (*gh w y)
ghawá (*gh w y)
ḥarrafa (*ḥ r f)
alḥada (*l ḥ d)
lawá (*l w y)
petition
daʿā (*d ʿ w)
suʾl (*s ʾ l)
petulant, to be
mariḥa (*m r ḥ)
phantom
sarāb (*s r b)
pick out
iltaqaṭa (*l q ṭ)
piece(s)
ḥuṭamah (*ḥ ṭ m)
judhādh (*j dh dh)
kisf (*k s f)
zubar (*z b r)
pierce
ḥadīd (*ḥ d d)
naqaba (*n q b)
thaqaba (*th q b)
piety
birr (*b r r)
taqwá (*w q y)
pile up
naḍada (*n ḍ d)
pilgrim, pilgrimage
ḥajja (*ḥ j j)
ḥijaj (*ḥ j j)
ḥurum (*ḥ r m)
pillar
ʿimād (*ʿ m d)
rukn (*r k n)
pious
barr (*b r r)
barra (*b r r)
piously, to act
ittaqá (*w q y)
pit
ḥufrah (*ḥ f r)
jubb (*j b b)
ukhdūd (*kh d d)
pit against
ḍidd (*ḍ d d)
pit, bottom of
ghayābah (*gh y b)
pitch
maqʿad (*q ʿ d)

mā l (*m w l)
possessor
ṣāḥib (*ṣ ḥ b)
posterity
ʿaqib (*ʿ q b)
postpone
ʿaqqaba (*ʿ q b)
akhkhara (*a kh r)
arjá (*r j w)
pot, cooking
qudūr (*q d r)
potion
sharāb (*sh r b)
potter's clay
fakhkhār (*f kh r)
pour, pour forth
dafaqa (*d f q)
afragha (*f r gh)
afāḍa (*f y ḍ)
inhamara (*h m r)
hāla (*h y l)
maraja (*m r j)
sajara (*s j r)
saqá (*s q y)
ṣabba (*ṣ b b)
poverty
ʿaylah (*ʿ y l)
maskanah (*s k n)
matrabah (*t r b)
poverty, to be in
faqara (*f q r)
khaṣṣa (*kh ṣ ṣ)
amlaqa (*m l q)
powder
dakkāʾ (*d k k)
dakka (*d k k)
power
ʿazza (*ʿ z z)
ʿizzah (*ʿ z z)
dharʿ (*dh r ʿ)
juhd (*j h d)
maḥala (*m ḥ l)
qibal (*q b l)
qadara (*q d r)
qūwah (*q w y)
rīḥ (*r w ḥ)
sulṭān (*s l ṭ)
shawkah (*sh w k)
ṭawl (*ṭ w l)
ṭāqah (*ṭ w q)
power, to give
aʿazza (*ʿ z z)
amkana (*m k n)
power, to have
malaka (*m l k)
iqtadara (*q d r)
qadara (*q d r)
wallá (*w l y)
powerful
matīn (*m t n)
qadīr (*q d r)
shadīd (*sh d d)
praise
awwaba (*a w b)
ḥamīd (*ḥ m d)
ḥamida (*ḥ m d)
sabbaḥa (*s b ḥ)
subḥān (*s b ḥ)
shakara (*sh k r)
pray
ibtahala (*b h l)
daʿā (*d ʿ w)
ḥamida (*ḥ m d)
ṣallá (*ṣ l w)
pray for rain
istasqá (*s q y)
pray forgiveness
istaghfara (*gh f r)
pray someone peace
sallama (*s l m)
prayer
daʿwá (*d ʿ w)
daʿwah (*d ʿ w)
jahara (*j h r)
ṣalāh (*ṣ l w)
prayer, direction of
qiblah (*q b l)
prayer, place of
muṣallá (*ṣ l w)
pre-ordainment
qadara (*q d r)
precaution
ḥadhira (*ḥ dh r)
ḥidhr (*ḥ dh r)
tuqāt (*w q y)
precede
sabaqa (*s b q)
salafa (*s l f)
precede, to make
aslafa (*s l f)
precincts
ḥawl (*ḥ w l)
precipitate
awqaʿa (*w q ʿ)
prefer
āthara (*a th r)
faḍḍala (*f ḍ l)
istaḥabba (*ḥ b b)
raghiba (*r gh b)
pregnant, pregnancy
ḥamala (*ḥ m l)
prejudicial
ḍārra (*ḍ r r)
premeditate
taʿammada (*ʿ m d)
preparation
ʿuddah (*ʿ d d)
prepare
aʿadda (*ʿ d d)
aʿtada (*ʿ t d)
prescribe
kataba (*k t b)
kitāb (*k t b)
presence
ladun (*l d n)
presence, to announce one's
istaʾnasa (*a n s)
present (n)
hadīyah (*h d y)
present (v)
ʿaraḍa (*ʿ r ḍ)
present oneself
tamaththala (*m th l)
present, to be
ḥaḍara (*ḥ ḍ r)
shahida (*sh h d)
presently
labitha (*l b th)
preserve (v)
istaʿṣama (*ʿ ṣ m)
ḥafiẓa (*ḥ f ẓ)
raʿá (*r ʿ y)
sallama (*s l m)
aṣḥaba (*ṣ ḥ b)
waqá (*w q y)
preserver
ḥafīẓ (*ḥ f ẓ)
press (v)
ʿaṣara (*ʿ ṣ r)
aḥfá (*ḥ f y)
press forward
istaqdama (*q d m)
press hard
shaqqa (*sh q q)
press on
afāḍa (*f y ḍ)

sajada (*s j d)
talla (*t l l)
protect
ʿaṣama (*ʿ ṣ m)
aʿādha (*ʿ w dh)
ḥafiẓa (*ḥ f ẓ)
ajāra (*j w r)
manaʿa (*m n ʿ)
walá (*w l y)
tawallá (*w l y)
waqá (*w q y)
protection, to seek
istajāra (*j w r)
protector
walīy (*w l y)
prove
balā (*b l w)
ibtalá (*b l w)
maḥḥaṣa (*m ḥ ṣ)
prove untrue
abṭala (*b ṭ l)
baṭala (*b ṭ l)
provide
mahada (*m h d)
mattaʿa (*m t ʿ)
razaqa (*r z q)
provision
matāʿ (*m t ʿ)
rizq (*r z q)
zād (*z w d)
provision, to get
māra (*m y r)
tazawwada (*z w d)
provoke
nazagha (*n z gh)
prowess
baʾs (*b ʾ s)
proximity
zulfá (*z l f)
prudent
ʿaqala (*ʿ q l)
ḥalīm (*ḥ l m)
pry into
lamasa (*l m s)
puberty
ḥulum (*ḥ l m)
publicly
ʿalāniyah (*ʿ l n)
jahara (*j h r)
publish
aʿlana (*ʿ l n)
abdá (*b d w)
adhāʿa (*dh y ʿ)
jahara (*j h r)
shāʿa (*sh y ʿ)
pull out
istakhraja (*kh r j)
punish
ādhá (*a dh y)
ʿadhdhaba (*ʿ dh b)
ʿāqaba (*ʿ q b)
nakkala (*n k l)
intaqama (*n q m)
punishment
ʿadhāb (*ʿ dh b)
ʿiqāb (*ʿ q b)
lazima (*l z m)
mathulāt (*m th l)
nakāl (*n k l)
rijs (*r j s)
punishment, cry of
ṣayḥah (*ṣ y ḥ)
purchase
ishtará (*sh r y)
pure
salīm (*s l m)
ṭahūr (*ṭ h r)
zakīy (*z k w)
pure, be
khalaṣa (*kh l ṣ)
zakā (*z k w)
ṭahara (*ṭ h r)
purify
akhlaṣa (*kh l ṣ)
taṭahhara (*ṭ h r)
ṭahhara (*ṭ h r)
tazakká (*z k w)
zakká (*z k w)
purpose (v)
taʿammada (*ʿ m d)
hamma (*h m m)
ḥarada (*ḥ r d)
arāda (*r w d)
pursue
qafā (*q f y)
atbaʿa (*t b ʿ)
ittabaʿa (*t b ʿ)
ṭalaba (*ṭ l b)
pus
ghassāq (*gh s q)
ghislīn (*gh s l)
ṣadīd (*ṣ d d)
push
daʿʿa (*d ʿ ʿ)
dafaʿa (*d f ʿ)
put
jaʿala (*j ʿ l)
put away
adh.haba (*dh h b)
put back
istaʾkhara (*a kh r)
put forth
anbata (*n b t)
put forward
istaqdama (*q d m)
put in order
aṣlaḥa (*ṣ l ḥ)
put off
ʿaqqaba (*ʿ q b)
khalaʿa (*kh l ʿ)
arjá (*r j w)
waḍaʿa (*w ḍ ʿ)
put to flight
hazama (*h z m)
put to shame
faḍaḥa (*f ḍ ḥ)
put together
rakkaba (*r k b)

qiblah
qiblah (*q b l)
quails
salwá (*s l w)
quake
māda (*m y d)
rajafa (*r j f)
wajila (*w j l)
quaking
wajil (*w j l)
quarrel
tanāzaʿa (*n z ʿ)
tashākasa (*sh k s)
quarreller
ghawīy (*gh w y)
quarters
aqṭār (*q ṭ r)
quest, question
raghiba (*r gh b)
saʾala (*s ʾ l)
tasāʾala (*s ʾ l)
quick
sarīʿ (*s r ʿ)
quicken
aḥyā (*ḥ y y)
quickly
ḥathīth (*ḥ th th)

quiet, to be
hāna (*h w n)
sajá (*s j y)
quill
qalam (*q l m)
quit (n)
barīʾ (*b r ʾ)
barāʾ (*b r ʾ)
quit (v)
baraḥa (*b r ḥ)
quit, to declare
barraʾa (*b r ʾ)
quiver
ihtazza (*h z z)

rabbi
ḥabr (*ḥ b r)
rabbānī (*r b b)
rabble
lafīf (*l f f)
race (v)
istabaqa (*s b q)
sābaqa (*s b q)
race(s) (n)
shuʿūb (*sh ʿ b)
radiance
ḍiyāʾ (*ḍ w ʾ)
naḍrah (*n ḍ r)
ashraqa (*sh r q)
radiant, to be
naḍara (*n ḍ r)
ashraqa (*sh r q)
rage
ghāẓa (*gh y ẓ)
taghayyaẓa (*gh y ẓ)
ṭaghiya (*ṭ gh y)
raging wind
ṣarṣar (*ṣ r ṣ r)
raider
aghāra (*gh w r)
ghazā (*gh z w)
rain
midrār (*d r r)
ghayth (*gh y th)
amṭara (*m ṭ r)
maṭara (*m ṭ r)
māʾ (*m w h)
wadq (*w d q)
rain cloud
ṣayyib (*ṣ w b)
raise
baʿatha (*b ʿ th)
ḥashara (*ḥ sh r)
anshaʾa (*n sh ʾ)
anshara (*n sh r)
nashara (*n sh r)
anshaza (*n sh z)
rabbá (*r b w)
rafaʿa (*r f ʿ)
shayyada (*sh y d)
rally against
ajlaba (*j l b)
rampart(s)
aʿrāf (*ʿ r f)
radama (*r d m)
sadd (*s d d)
rancour
aḍghān (*ḍ gh n)
ghill (*gh l l)
range
naḍīd (*n ḍ d)
ṣaffa (*ṣ f f)
ranging
ṣaff (*ṣ f f)
rank
darajah (*d r j)
ṣaff (*ṣ f f)
ransom (n)
fidyah (*f d y)
ransom (v)
fādá (*f d y)
fadá (*f d y)
iftadá (*f d y)
rash
ashir (*a sh r)
ratification
wakkada (*w k d)
raven
ghurāb (*gh r b)
raven-black
gharabīb (*gh r b)
ravine
fajj (*f j j)
reach
balagha (*b l gh)
lamasa (*l m s)
laqiya (*l q y)
tanāwasha (*n w sh)
nāla (*n y l)
ṣāra (*ṣ y r)
waṣala (*w ṣ l)
waṣṣala (*w ṣ l)
read
darasa (*d r s)
qaraʾa (*q r ʾ)
talā (*t l w)
read, to cause to
aqraʾa (*q r ʾ)
reading
dirāsah (*d r s)
qurʾān (*q r ʾ)
talā (*t l w)
ready
ʿatīd (*ʿ t d)
danā (*d n w)
ready, to make
aʿadda (*ʿ d d)
aʿtada (*ʿ t d)
realize, to cause to
ashʿara (*sh ʿ r)
realized, to be
ḥaqqa (*ḥ q q)
reap
ḥaṣada (*ḥ ṣ d)
reaped corn
ḥaṣīd (*ḥ ṣ d)
rear (n)
ukhrá (*a kh r)
rear (v)
nashshaʾa (*n sh ʾ)
reason
ʿarafa (*ʿ r f)
nuhá (*n h w)
reassurance
sakīnah (*s k n)
rebellious
ʿaṣīy (*ʿ ṣ y)
marīd (*m r d)
rebellious, to be
ʿaṣá (*ʿ ṣ y)
fasaqa (*f s q)
marada (*m r d)
nashaza (*n sh z)
rebuke
lāma (*l w m)
rebut
adḥaḍa (*d ḥ ḍ)
radda (*r d d)
recall
tawaffá (*w f y)
receive
jāʾa (*j y ʾ)
laqiya (*l q y)
laqqá (*l q y)
talaqqá (*l q y)
taqabbala (*q b l)

tawaffá (*w f y)
receive a guest
ḍayyafa (*ḍ y f)
receive in full
istawfá (*w f y)
receptacle
kifāt (*k f t)
qarra (*q r r)
recitation
qurʾān (*q r ʾ)
talā (*t l w)
recite
amlá (*m l y)
qaraʾa (*q r ʾ)
talā (*t l w)
recite, to cause to
aqraʾa (*q r ʾ)
recklessness
baṭira (*b ṭ r)
reckon
ʿadda (*ʿ d d)
iʿtadda (*ʿ d d)
ḥasiba (*ḥ s b)
iḥtasaba (*ḥ s b)
jaʿala (*j ʿ l)
ẓanna (*ẓ n n)
reckoner
ḥasīb (*ḥ s b)
reckoning
ḥisāb (*ḥ s b)
ḥusbān (*ḥ s b)
reckoning, to make a
ḥāsaba (*ḥ s b)
recline
ittakaʾa (*w k ʾ)
muttakaʾ (*w k ʾ)
recognize
ʿarafa (*ʿ r f)
taʿārafa (*ʿ r f)
recollect
tadhakkara (*dh k r)
recompense
jāzá (*j z y)
jazá (*j z y)
kharāj (*kh r j)
mathūbah (*th w b)
reconcile
aṣlaḥa (*ṣ l ḥ)
ṣulḥ (*ṣ l ḥ)
waffaqa (*w f q)
record (n)
imām (*a m m)
kitāb (*k t b)
record (v)
istansakha (*n s kh)
recorder(s)
ḥafaẓah (*ḥ f ẓ)
ḥafīẓ (*ḥ f ẓ)
sijill (*s j l)
recount
ʿaddada (*ʿ d d)
recourse
mustaqarr (*q r r)
matāb (*t w b)
recourse, to have
tayammama (*y m m)
recover
afāqa (*f w q)
rectitude
rashād (*r sh d)
rashad (*r sh d)
rashada (*r sh d)
red
ḥumr (*ḥ m r)
redeem
fadá (*f d y)
iftadá (*f d y)
redemption
fidyah (*f d y)
redouble
ḍāʿafa (*ḍ ʿ f)
reduce
naqaṣa (*n q ṣ)
reeds
qaḍaba (*q ḍ b)
refer
radda (*r d d)
reflect
fakkara (*f k r)
tafakkara (*f k r)
refractory, to be
jamaḥa (*j m ḥ)
nashaza (*n sh z)
refrain
intahá (*n h w)
refreshment
qurrah (*q r r)
rāḥa (*r w ḥ)
refuge
maʾwá (*a w y)
maʿādh (*ʿ w dh)
aknān (*k n n)
iltaḥada (*l ḥ d)
murāgham (*r gh m)
maṣrif (*ṣ r f)
mawʾil (*w ʾ l)
wazar (*w z r)
refuge, seek
istaʿādha (*ʿ w dh)
refuge, take
ʿādha (*ʿ w dh)
awá (*a w y)
waṣala (*w ṣ l)
refuge, to give
āwá (*a w y)
refuse (n)
ghuthāʾ (*gh th w)
refuse (v)
abá (*a b y)
refute
adḥaḍa (*d ḥ ḍ)
regard
naẓara (*n ẓ r)
raʾá (*r ʾ y)
raqaba (*r q b)
regard, to pay
taṣaddá (*ṣ d y)
regardful
raqīb (*r q b)
register (n)
imām (*a m m)
register (v)
istansakha (*n s kh)
sayṭara (*s y ṭ r)
regret
ḥasrah (*ḥ s r)
rehearse
rattala (*r t l)
rein, to give
amlá (*m l y)
reinforce
ʿazzaza (*ʿ z z)
amadda (*m d d)
madda (*m d d)
reject
daḥara (*d ḥ r)
khasaʾa (*kh s ʾ)
nabadha (*n b dh)
ankara (*n k r)
izdajara (*z j r)
rejection
kafara (*k f r)
nakīr (*n k r)
rejoice
abshara (*b sh r)
istabshara (*b sh r)

fakiha (*f k h)
fariḥa (*f r ḥ)
rejoicing
fariḥ (*f r ḥ)
relate
qaṣṣa (*q ṣ ṣ)
talā (*t l w)
relative
ḥamīm (*ḥ m m)
kalālah (*k l l)
arḥām (*r ḥ m)
release (n)
saraḥa (*s r ḥ)
release (v)
sarraḥa (*s r ḥ)
relieve
waḍaʿa (*w ḍ ʿ)
religion
ummah (*a m m)
dīn (*d y n)
millah (*m l l)
religion, doctor of
ḥabr (*ḥ b r)
religion, to practise
dāna (*d y n)
relish
ṣibgh (*ṣ b gh)
reluctant
kariha (*k r h)
remain
baqiya (*b q y)
dāma (*d w m)
talabbatha (*l b th)
aqāma (*q w m)
qarra (*q r r)
ẓalla (*ẓ l l)
remain, to cause to
abqá (*b q y)
remainder
baqīyah (*b q y)
remember
iddakara (*d k r)
dhakara (*dh k r)
tadhakkara (*dh k r)
aḥdatha (*ḥ d th)
waʿá (*w ʿ y)
remembrance
dhakara (*dh k r)
remind
dhakkara (*dh k r)
reminder
dhakara (*dh k r)
dhikrá (*dh k r)
tadhkirah (*dh k r)
remit
ʿafā (*ʿ f w)
kaffara (*k f r)
remnant
athārah (*a th r)
baqiya (*b q y)
baqīyah (*b q y)
dābir (*d b r)
remorse
nadima (*n d m)
remorseful
wabīl (*w b l)
remote, to be
saḥuqa (*s ḥ q)
remove
ʿazala (*ʿ z l)
baʿuda (*b ʿ d)
adh.haba (*dh h b)
ḥawwala (*ḥ w l)
ḥiwal (*ḥ w l)
jannaba (*j n b)
kaffara (*k f r)
kashafa (*k sh f)
zaḥzaḥa (*z ḥ z ḥ)
zāla (*z w l)
removing
nazzāʿah (*n z ʿ)
rend, rending
fuṭūr (*f ṭ r)
tafaṭṭara (*f ṭ r)
kharaqa (*kh r q)
qadda (*q d d)
taṣaddaʿa (*ṣ d ʿ)
renegade, to become a
irtadda (*r d d)
renew
aḥdatha (*ḥ d th)
repair to
amma (*a m m)
reparation
aṣlaḥa (*ṣ l ḥ)
repast
muttakaʾ (*w k ʾ)
repay
athāba (*th w b)
repel
ʿaqqaba (*ʿ q b)
dafaʿa (*d f ʿ)
daḥara (*d ḥ r)
nahara (*n h r)
radda (*r d d)
ṭarada (*ṭ r d)
repent
hāda (*h w d)
nadima (*n d m)
anāba (*n w b)
tāba (*t w b)
repentance
ḥiṭṭah (*ḥ ṭ ṭ)
matāb (*t w b)
repentant
tawwāb (*t w b)
replenish
madda (*m d d)
replenishment
madad (*m d d)
report
khabar (*kh b r)
repose
rāḥa (*r w ḥ)
sakana (*s k n)
repository
mustawadaʿ (*w d ʿ)
reproach (n)
lawmah (*l w m)
reproach (v)
lāma (*l w m)
manna (*m n n)
tharraba (*th r b)
reproachful
lawwām (*l w m)
reprobate
fasaqa (*f s q)
reprove
zajara (*z j r)
repulse
daʿʿa (*d ʿ ʿ)
nahara (*n h r)
reputation
dhakara (*dh k r)
requital
ʿiqāb (*ʿ q b)
ʿuqbá (*ʿ q b)
thawāb (*th w b)
requite
jazá (*j z y)
intaqama (*n q m)
athāba (*th w b)
rescue
anjá (*n j w)
najjá (*n j w)
istanqadha (*n q dh)

resemble
ḍāhá (*ḍ h y)
tashābaha (*sh b h)
reserve
khalaṣa (*kh l ṣ)
resign oneself
istaslama (*s l m)
resolve
ʿazama (*ʿ z m)
ajmaʿa (*j m ʿ)
resort (n)
maʾāb (*a w b)
munqalab (*q l b)
mathābah (*th w b)
resort (v)
tayammama (*y m m)
respect
raqaba (*r q b)
respite (n)
naẓirah (*n ẓ r)
respite (v)
mahhala (*m h l)
amlá (*m l y)
anẓara (*n ẓ r)
resplendent
ashraqa (*sh r q)
respond
istajāba (*j w b)
responsible, make
akfala (*k f l)
rest (n)
subāt (*s b t)
rest (v)
baqiya (*b q y)
sakana (*s k n)
iṭmaʾanna (*ṭ m ʾ n)
rest, to give
arāḥa (*r w ḥ)
resting place
maḍājiʿ (*ḍ j ʿ)
firāsh (*f r sh)
mustaqarr (*q r r)
maqīl (*q y l)
murtafaq (*r f q)
sakana (*s k n)
restitution
aṣlaḥa (*ṣ l ḥ)
restoration
aṣlaḥa (*ṣ l ḥ)
restore
addá (*a d y)
radda (*r d d)
restrain
taʿaffafa (*ʿ f f)
aḥṣara (*ḥ ṣ r)
kaffa (*k f f)
kaẓama (*k ẓ m)
qaṣara (*q ṣ r)
ṣabara (*ṣ b r)
result (n)
ʿāqibah (*ʿ q b)
result (v)
awwala (*a w l)
resurrection
qiyāmah (*q w m)
retain
waʿá (*w ʿ y)
amsaka (*m s k)
retaliate
ʿāqaba (*ʿ q b)
retaliation
qiṣāṣ (*q ṣ ṣ)
retard
baṭṭaʾa (*b ṭ ʾ)
retrace one's steps
ʿaqqaba (*ʿ q b)
retract
ʿāda (*ʿ w d)
retreat (n)
muddakhal (*d kh l)
retreat (v)
adbara (*d b r)
retribution
ʿiqāb (*ʿ q b)
retribution, to exact
intaqama (*n q m)
return (v)
āba (*a w b)
ʿāda (*ʿ w d)
fāʾa (*f y ʾ)
inqalaba (*q l b)
irtadda (*r d d)
radda (*r d d)
rajaʿa (*r j ʿ)
tarājaʿa (*r j ʿ)
return (n)
karrah (*k r r)
maradd (*r d d)
marjiʿ (*r j ʿ)
return, cause to
aʿāda (*ʿ w d)
return, place of
maʾāb (*a w b)
maʿād (*ʿ w d)
reveal
abdá (*b d w)
badā (*b d w)
fataḥa (*f t ḥ)
jallá (*j l y)
nazzala (*n z l)
awḥá (*w ḥ y)
waḥá (*w ḥ y)
reveal oneself
tajallá (*j l y)
revelation
āyah (*a y w)
kalimah (*k l m)
revenge
ʿadá (*ʿ d w)
naqama (*n q m)
revenue
kharāj (*kh r j)
revere
waqqara (*w q r)
reverse
ʿaqqaba (*ʿ q b)
revert
ʿāda (*ʿ w d)
fāʾa (*f y ʾ)
ḥāra (*ḥ w r)
reverting
awwāb (*a w b)
review
tafaqqada (*f q d)
revile
tanābaza (*n b z)
sabba (*s b b)
revive
aḥyā (*ḥ y y)
anshara (*n sh r)
nashara (*n sh r)
reward (n)
ajr (*a j r)
ʿuqbá (*ʿ q b)
mathūbah (*th w b)
thawāb (*th w b)
reward (v)
jazá (*j z y)
athāba (*th w b)
thawwaba (*th w b)
rich
ghanīy (*gh n y)
awsaʿa (*w s ʿ)
rich, to be
ghaniya (*gh n y)
istaghná (*gh n y)

rich, to make
aghná (*gh n y)
aqná (*q n y)
zāda (*z y d)
riches
māl (*m w l)
rid
waḍaʿa (*w ḍ ʿ)
ride
rakiba (*r k b)
ridicule
haziʾa (*h z ʾ)
istahzaʾa (*h z ʾ)
sikhrī (*s kh r)
right
ḥaqq (*ḥ q q)
ḥaqīq (*ḥ q q)
qayyim (*q w m)
sawāʾ (*s w y)
ṣawāb (*ṣ w b)
ayman (*y m n)
maymanah (*y m n)
right conduct
taqwá (*w q y)
right hand
maymanah (*y m n)
yamīn (*y m n)
right judgment
rashada (*r sh d)
right path
sawāʾ (*s w y)
right places
mawāḍiʿ (*w ḍ ʿ)
right side
ayman (*y m n)
yamīn (*y m n)
right way
sharīʿah (*sh r ʿ)
shirʿah (*sh r ʿ)
right-guided, to be
ihtadá (*h d y)
right-minded
rashada (*r sh d)
rashīd (*r sh d)
right, be
ṣadaqa (*ṣ d q)
right, do
aḥsana (*ḥ s n)
ṣalaḥa (*ṣ l ḥ)
right, have
aḥaqq (*ḥ q q)
right, make
aṣlaḥa (*ṣ l ḥ)
righteous
aḥsana (*ḥ s n)
ṣiddīq (*ṣ d q)
ṣalaḥa (*ṣ l ḥ)
zakā (*z k w)
righteousness
birr (*b r r)
ṣalaḥa (*ṣ l ḥ)
taqwá (*w q y)
rigid
aladd (*l d d)
rigorous
ṣaʿad (*ṣ ʿ d)
ripe
janīy (*j n y)
yanaʿa (*y n ʿ)
rise
ʿalā (*ʿ l w)
bazagha (*b z gh)
nashara (*n sh r)
qāma (*q w m)
istawá (*s w y)
ashraqa (*sh r q)
ṭaghiya (*ṭ gh y)
ṭalaʿa (*ṭ l ʿ)
rising
maṭlaʿ (*ṭ l ʿ)
maṭliʿ (*ṭ l ʿ)
rite, holy
mansak (*n s k)
rite, perform a
nasaka (*n s k)
rite, prescribed
tafath (*t f th)
rival
andād (*n d d)
rivalry
takāthara (*k th r)
river
nahar (*n h r)
wādī (*w d y)
yamm (*y m m)
rivulet
sarīy (*s r y)
road, roadway
imām (*a m m)
minhāj (*n h j)
sabīl (*s b l)
ṣirāṭ (*ṣ r ṭ)
ṭarīq (*ṭ r q)
roam about
sāḥa (*s y ḥ)
roar over
iṭṭalaʿa (*ṭ l ʿ)
roaring
lujjī (*l j j)
roast (v)
shawá (*sh w y)
aṣlá (*ṣ l y)
ṣalá (*ṣ l y)
ṣallá (*ṣ l y)
roasted
ḥanīdh (*ḥ n dh)
roasted through, to be
naḍija (*n ḍ j)
rob
ḥarama (*ḥ r m)
salaba (*s l b)
saraqa (*s r q)
robber
saraqa (*s r q)
robed, to be
labisa (*l b s)
robes
thiyāb (*th w b)
rock (n)
ḥajar (*ḥ j r)
ṣafwān (*ṣ f w)
ṣakhr (*ṣ kh r)
rock (v)
māra (*m w r)
rajja (*r j j)
rod
ʿaṣā (*ʿ ṣ w)
rod, iron
maqāmiʿ (*q m ʿ)
roll
dāra (*d w r)
roll up
ṭawá (*ṭ w y)
roll, un-
nashara (*n sh r)
nashshara (*n sh r)
roof
samk (*s m k)
saqf (*s q f)
room, to make
fasaḥa (*f s ḥ)
tafassaḥa (*f s ḥ)
root
aṣl (*a ṣ l)
rope
ḥabl (*ḥ b l)

sabab (*s b b)
rope, fibres of
ankāth (*n k th)
rosy
wardah (*w r d)
rotten
nakhirah (*n kh r)
ramīm (*r m m)
route (v)
hazama (*h z m)
rub
masaḥa (*m s ḥ)
ruby
yāqūt (*y q t)
rug
zarābī (*z r b)
ruggedness
amt (*a m t)
ruin
ʿaṭṭala (*ʿ ṭ l)
bāra (*b w r)
khabāl (*kh b l)
tabba (*t b b)
tabbaba (*t b b)
tabār (*t b r)
tabbara (*t b r)
thabara (*th b r)
awbaqa (*w b q)
ruined health
ḥaraḍ (*ḥ r ḍ)
ruined, to be
ʿanita (*ʿ n t)
fasada (*f s d)
hawá (*h w y)
rule
malaka (*m l k)
sayṭara (*s y ṭ r)
run
haraʿa (*h r ʿ)
ahṭaʿa (*h ṭ ʿ)
jará (*j r y)
rakaḍa (*r k ḍ)
saʿá (*s ʿ y)
awḍaʿa (*w ḍ ʿ)
run away
abaqa (*a b q)
rush
afāḍa (*f y ḍ)
istakhaffa (*kh f f)
nasala (*n s l)
rush in
iqtaḥama (*q ḥ m)
rush upon
saṭā (*s ṭ w)
rushes, a bundle of
ḍighth (*ḍ gh th)
rust (v)
rāna (*r y n)

sack
wiʿāʾ (*w ʿ y)
sacred
ḥarām (*ḥ r m)
sacred monument
mashʿar (*sh ʿ r)
sacred things
ḥurumāt (*ḥ r m)
sacred visitation (to Mecca)
ʿamara (*ʿ m r)
sacred, to make
ḥarrama (*ḥ r m)
sacrifice
dhabaḥa (*dh b ḥ)
dhibḥ (*dh b ḥ)
dhakká (*dh k y)
hadá (*h d y)
naḥara (*n ḥ r)
nasaka (*n s k)
qurbān (*q r b)
sacrifice, beast of
budn (*b d n)
sacrifice, place of
maḥill (*ḥ l l)
sacrosanct
ḥijr (*ḥ j r)
sad, to be
ḥazina (*ḥ z n)
sadden
sāʾa (*s w ʾ)
saddlebag
raḥl (*r ḥ l)
safe
salīm (*s l m)
salima (*s l m)
safety
salām (*s l m)
safety, place of
mafāz (*f w z)
wazar (*w z r)
sagacious
ʿaqala (*ʿ q l)
sake
ajl (*a j l)
wajh (*w j h)
sally
baraza (*b r z)
sariba (*s r b)
salt
milḥ (*m l ḥ)
salute
ḥayyá (*ḥ y y)
sallama (*s l m)
salvation
najā (*n j w)
same manner
shākilah (*sh k l)
sanctify
qaddasa (*q d s)
sanctity, pilgrim
ḥurum (*ḥ r m)
sanctuary
bayt (*b y t)
miḥrāb (*ḥ r b)
ḥaram (*ḥ r m)
sand
kathīb (*k th b)
sand-dunes, -tracts
aḥqāf (*ḥ q f)
sand-storm
ḥāṣib (*ḥ ṣ b)
satan
shayṭān (*sh ṭ n)
sate
asqá (*s q y)
satisfaction
marḍāt (*r ḍ y)
riḍwān (*r ḍ y)
satisfaction, to give
jazá (*j z y)
qaḍá (*q ḍ y)
arḍá (*r ḍ y)
satisfied, to be
raḍiya (*r ḍ y)
saturate
asqá (*s q y)
savage beasts
wuḥūsh (*w ḥ sh)
save
ʿaṣama (*ʿ ṣ m)
istaḥyā (*ḥ y y)
najjá (*n j w)
anqadha (*n q dh)
sallama (*s l m)
saved, to be
najā (*n j w)
savour

ṣibghah (*ṣ b gh)
say, saying
qāla (*q w l)
qīl (*q w l)
ṣadaʿa (*ṣ d ʿ)
scald
shawá (*sh w y)
scale
ẓahara (*ẓ h r)
scale a wall
tasawwara (*s w r)
scales
mīzān (*w z n)
scalp
shawá (*sh w y)
scandalous act
fāḥishah (*f ḥ sh)
scant (v)
akhsara (*kh s r)
scant worth
muzjāt (*z j w)
scantily
nakid (*n k d)
scarcity
naqaṣa (*n q ṣ)
scare (n)
zajrah (*z j r)
scare (v)
zajara (*z j r)
scatter
baʿthara (*b ʿ th r)
baththa (*b th th)
inbaththa (*b th th)
dharaʾa (*dh r ʾ)
dharā (*dh r w)
infaḍḍa (*f ḍ ḍ)
tafarraqa (*f r q)
nasafa (*n s f)
intashara (*n sh r)
nashara (*n sh r)
nathara (*n th r)
sharrada (*sh r d)
scattered
ashtāt (*sh t t)
shattá (*sh t t)
scattered, to be
intashara (*n sh r)
intathara (*n th r)
scene
mash.had (*sh h d)
scent
rīḥ (*r w ḥ)
schedule (v)
waqqata (*w q t)
scheme
kāda (*k y d)
makara (*m k r)
schism
shāqqa (*sh q q)
scoff
istahzaʾa (*h z ʾ)
istaskhara (*s kh r)
sakhira (*s kh r)
scold
nahara (*n h r)
scoop (n)
ghurfah (*gh r f)
scoop (v)
ightarafa (*gh r f)
scope
wasiʿa (*w s ʿ)
scorch
ḥamiya (*ḥ m y)
lafaḥa (*l f ḥ)
scorching
lawwāḥ (*l w ḥ)
scorn
ad.hana (*d h n)
scourge (n)
sawṭ (*s w ṭ)
scourge (v)
jalada (*j l d)
scowl
basara (*b s r)
scratch
baḥatha (*b ḥ th)
screamer
ṭāghiyah (*ṭ gh y)
scribe(s)
kataba (*k t b)
safarah (*s f r)
scriptures
ṣuḥuf (*ṣ ḥ f)
scroll
raqq (*r q q)
sijill (*s j l)
ṣuḥuf (*ṣ ḥ f)
zabūr (*z b r)
scum
ghuthāʾ (*gh th w)
zabad (*z b d)
sea
baḥr (*b ḥ r)
yamm (*y m m)
seal
khātam (*kh t m)
khatama (*kh t m)
khitām (*kh t m)
ṭabaʿa (*ṭ b ʿ)
search
taḥassasa (*ḥ s s)
jāsa (*j w s)
naqqaba (*n q b)
ṭalaba (*ṭ l b)
season
iná (*a n y)
ḥīn (*ḥ y n)
seasoning
ṣibgh (*ṣ b gh)
seat
maqʿad (*q ʿ d)
seated, to be
istawá (*s w y)
second
ākhar (*a kh r)
thāni (*th n y)
secret
ghāba (*gh y b)
akhfá (*kh f y)
khāfiyah (*kh f y)
khafīy (*kh f y)
khufyah (*kh f y)
najīy (*n j w)
tanājá (*n j w)
asarra (*s r r)
sarāʾir (*s r r)
sirr (*s r r)
awʿá (*w ʿ y)
secretly, converse
najā (*n j w)
sect, section
farīq (*f r q)
shīʿah (*sh y ʿ)
ṭaraf (*ṭ r f)
ṭarīqah (*ṭ r q)
ṭāʾifah (*ṭ w f)
zubur (*z b r)
secure, security
amanah (*a m n)
amīn (*a m n)
amina (*a m n)
mafāzah (*f w z)
makīn (*m k n)
qāma (*q w m)
sakīnah (*s k n)
salām (*s l m)

salīm (*s l m)
salima (*s l m)
sallama (*s l m)
iṭma'anna (*ṭ m ' n)
tuqāt (*w q y)
securer
qawwām (*q w m)
security, place of
amina (*a m n)
ma'man (*a m n)
mafāz (*f w z)
sedition
fitnah (*f t n)
seduce
dassā (*d s w)
fatana (*f t n)
jarama (*j r m)
istakthara (*k th r)
rāwada (*r w d)
sawwala (*s w l)
see
abṣara (*b ṣ r)
baṣura (*b ṣ r)
istabṣara (*b ṣ r)
naẓara (*n ẓ r)
ra'á (*r ' y)
ra'y (*r ' y)
see, cause to
abāna (*b y n)
ará (*r ' y)
seed
dhurrīyah (*dh r r)
seeing, sense of
baṣar (*b ṣ r)
seek
baghá (*b gh y)
ibtaghá (*b gh y)
taḥarrá (*ḥ r y)
iltamasa (*l m s)
lamasa (*l m s)
arāda (*r w d)
rāwada (*r w d)
ṭalaba (*ṭ l b)
seem
badā (*b d w)
khayyala (*kh y l)
seemly, to be
inbaghá (*b gh y)
seen, being
ri'ā' (*r ' y)
seen, un-
ghāba (*gh y b)
seize
akhadha (*a kh dh)
baṭasha (*b ṭ sh)
amsaka (*m s k)
naza'a (*n z ')
qabaḍa (*q b ḍ)
safa'a (*s f ')
select
ikhtaṣṣa (*kh ṣ ṣ)
aṣfá (*ṣ f w)
iṣṭafá (*ṣ f w)
self
nafs (*n f s)
sell
bā'a (*b y ')
tabāya'a (*b y ')
ishtará (*sh r y)
shará (*sh r y)
semblance
tashābaha (*sh b h)
send
ba'atha (*b ' th)
arsala (*r s l)
aṣdara (*ṣ d r)
send back
radda (*r d d)
send beforehand
qaddama (*q d m)
send down
anzala (*n z l)
nazzala (*n z l)
send following
qaffá (*q f y)
sense (v)
awjasa (*w j s)
sha'ara (*sh ' r)
sent, to be
inba'atha (*b ' th)
arsala (*r s l)
sentinel
raqīb (*r q b)
separate
ḍaraba (*ḍ r b)
infaḍḍa (*f ḍ ḍ)
faraqa (*f r q)
farraqa (*f r q)
tafarraqa (*f r q)
imtāza (*m y z)
māza (*m y z)
tazayyala (*z y l)
zayyala (*z y l)
separate part
firq (*f r q)
separately
ashtāt (*sh t t)
sepulchre
ajdāth (*j d th)
serpent
ḥayyah (*ḥ y y)
jānn (*j n n)
thu'bān (*th ' b)
serried
naḍada (*n ḍ d)
servant
'abd (*' b d)
serve
'abada (*' b d)
tabi'a (*t b ')
servitude
sukhrī (*s kh r)
set (go down)
afala (*a f l)
gharaba (*gh r b)
set (put)
ja'ala (*j ' l)
qasama (*q s m)
aqāma (*q w m)
waḍa'a (*w ḍ ')
set above
aẓhara (*ẓ h r)
set forth
faṣala (*f ṣ l)
inṭalaqa (*ṭ l q)
waḍa'a (*w ḍ ')
set free
ḥarrara (*ḥ r r)
saraḥa (*s r ḥ)
set out
sará (*s r y)
set up
ḍaraba (*ḍ r b)
ansha'a (*n sh ')
anshaza (*n sh z)
naṣaba (*n ṣ b)
shāda (*sh y d)
waḍa'a (*w ḍ ')
setting of the sun
maghrib (*gh r b)
settle
ista'mara (*' m r)
istaqarra (*q r r)
qarra (*q r r)
istawá (*s w y)
settlement

ṣulḥ (*ṣ l ḥ)
seven
sabʿah (*s b ʿ)
seventy
sabʿūn (*s b ʿ)
sever
faraqa (*f r q)
qaṭaʿa (*q ṭ ʿ)
ṣaʿad (*ṣ ʿ d)
severe
faẓẓ (*f ẓ ẓ)
ghalīẓ (*gh l ẓ)
severity
ghilẓah (*gh l ẓ)
sew together
khaṣafa (*kh ṣ f)
rataqa (*r t q)
sexual desire
irbah (*a r b)
shackle
wathāq (*w th q)
shading
ẓalīl (*ẓ l l)
shadow, shade
ẓill (*ẓ l l)
ẓullah (*ẓ l l)
ẓulumāt (*ẓ l m)
shadow, to cast a
ẓallala (*ẓ l l)
shadowy, to be
aẓlama (*ẓ l m)
shake
hazza (*h z z)
istakhaffa (*kh f f)
māda (*m y d)
anghaḍa (*n gh ḍ)
nataqa (*n t q)
rajja (*r j j)
zalzala (*z l z l)
shame
faḍaḥa (*f ḍ ḥ)
akhzá (*kh z y)
khaziya (*kh z y)
sawʾah (*s w ʾ)
shank
sāq (*s w q)
shape
sawwá (*s w y)
ṣawwara (*ṣ w r)
shapely
khallaqa (*kh l q)
share
khalāq (*kh l q)
naṣīb (*n ṣ b)
qiṭṭ (*q ṭ ṭ)
shāraka (*sh r k)
sharīk (*sh r k)
sharp
ḥadīd (*ḥ d d)
shatter
kisf (*k s f)
qāriʿah (*q r ʿ)
qaṣama (*q ṣ m)
tabbara (*t b r)
shave
ḥalaqa (*ḥ l q)
ḥallaqa (*ḥ l q)
she-camel
nāqah (*n w q)
shed
safaḥa (*s f ḥ)
safaka (*s f k)
laqqá (*l q y)
sheep
ḍaʾn (*ḍ ʾ n)
ghanam (*gh n m)
naʿjah (*n ʿ j)
shelter
āwá (*a w y)
maʿādh (*ʿ w dh)
maljaʾ (*l j ʾ)
ẓill (*ẓ l l)
ẓullah (*ẓ l l)
shepherd
raʿá (*r ʿ y)
shine
aḍāʾa (*ḍ w ʾ)
asfara (*s f r)
ashraqa (*sh r q)
shining
durrīy (*d r r)
ship
fulk (*f l k)
jará (*j r y)
safīnah (*s f n)
shirt
qamīṣ (*q m ṣ)
sarābīl (*s r b l)
shiver
iqshaʿarra (*q sh ʿ r)
rajafa (*r j f)
shoe
naʿl (*n ʿ l)
shoot
ramá (*r m y)
shaṭʾ (*sh ṭ ʾ)
shore
sāḥil (*s ḥ l)
shāṭiʾ (*sh ṭ ʾ)
shorten
qaṣara (*q ṣ r)
shortly
qarīb (*q r b)
shout
daʿā (*d ʿ w)
jahara (*j h r)
naʿaqa (*n ʿ q)
nādá (*n d w)
ṣadaʿa (*ṣ d ʿ)
ṣākhkhah (*ṣ kh kh)
iṣṭarakha (*ṣ r kh)
ṣayḥah (*ṣ y ḥ)
zajara (*z j r)
zajrah (*z j r)
show
abdá (*b d w)
badā (*b d w)
bayyana (*b y n)
dalla (*d l l)
qaṣada (*q ṣ d)
ará (*r ʾ y)
show off
rāʾá (*r ʾ y)
riʾāʾ (*r ʾ y)
show, outward
riʾy (*r ʾ y)
shower
ṭall (*ṭ l l)
shrewd
ad.há (*d h y)
shrink
ghāḍa (*gh y ḍ)
raghiba (*r gh b)
shrivelling
lawwāḥ (*l w ḥ)
shroud (v)
daththara (*d th r)
shudder
ishmaʾazza (*sh m ʾ z)
shun
hajara (*h j r)
ḥāda (*ḥ y d)
tajāfá (*j f w)
shut
ghallaqa (*gh l q)
qabaḍa (*q b ḍ)

sick, sickness
ghawl (*gh w l)
marīḍ (*m r ḍ)
mariḍa (*m r ḍ)
saqīm (*s q m)
side
ʿiṭf (*ʿ ṭ f)
jānib (*j n b)
janb (*j n b)
makān (*k w n)
arjāʾ (*r j w)
side, left
mashʾamah (*sh ʾ m)
shamāʾil (*sh m l)
shimāl (*sh m l)
side, right
ayman (*y m n)
yamīn (*y m n)
sigh, sighing
ḥasrah (*ḥ s r)
tanaffasa (*n f s)
shahaqa (*sh h q)
zafīr (*z f r)
sight (n)
ʿayn (*ʿ y n)
baṣar (*b ṣ r)
sight (v)
tarāʾá (*r ʾ y)
sight, to give
baṣṣara (*b ṣ r)
sign
āyah (*a y w)
ʿalam (*ʿ l m)
ramz (*r m z)
sīmá (*s w m)
sign, clear
bayyinah (*b y n)
signal, to make a
awḥá (*w ḥ y)
silent, be
khāfata (*kh f t)
khamada (*kh m d)
anṣata (*n ṣ t)
ṣamata (*ṣ m t)
silk
ḥarīr (*ḥ r r)
sundus (*s n d s)
silver
fiḍḍah (*f ḍ ḍ)
wariq (*w r q)
similar
mithl (*m th l)
similitude
mathal (*m th l)
sin
athām (*a th m)
athima (*a th m)
aththama (*a th m)
ithm (*a th m)
ʿanita (*ʿ n t)
bayyana (*b y n)
dhanb (*dh n b)
ḥinth (*ḥ n th)
ḥāba (*ḥ w b)
tajānafa (*j n f)
junāḥ (*j n ḥ)
ajrama (*j r m)
jaram (*j r m)
khaṭiʾa (*kh ṭ ʾ)
khaṭīʾah (*kh ṭ ʾ)
kabāʾir (*k b r)
kabīr (*k b r)
lamam (*l m m)
sayyiʾah (*s w ʾ)
wazara (*w z r)
ẓalama (*ẓ l m)
ẓalūm (*ẓ l m)
sincere
akhlaṣa (*kh l ṣ)
khalaṣa (*kh l ṣ)
naṣūḥ (*n ṣ ḥ)
ṣadaqa (*ṣ d q)
single
ṣinwān (*ṣ n w)
single out
ikhtaṣṣa (*kh ṣ ṣ)
single-hearted
akhlaṣa (*kh l ṣ)
single-minded
akhlaṣa (*kh l ṣ)
sink
dalaka (*d l k)
ghāra (*gh w r)
iththāqala (*th q l)
sinkers
kunnas (*k n s)
sip
tajarraʿa (*j r ʿ)
sister
ukht (*a kh w)
sit
qaʿada (*q ʿ d)
istawá (*s w y)
sitting
maqʿad (*q ʿ d)
qaʿīd (*q ʿ d)
six
sittah (*s t t)
sixth
sādis (*s d s)
suds (*s d s)
sixty
sittūn (*s t t)
skilful, to be
fariha (*f r h)
skimp
akhsara (*kh s r)
skin
julūd (*j l d)
sky
falak (*f l k)
samāʾ (*s m w)
slackening (of commerce)
kasada (*k s d)
slander
ifk (*a f k)
buhtān (*b h t)
hammāz (*h m z)
lumazah (*l m z)
mashshāʾ (*m sh y)
namīm (*n m m)
slash
masaḥa (*m s ḥ)
slaughter
dhabaḥa (*dh b ḥ)
dhabbaḥa (*dh b ḥ)
dhibḥ (*dh b ḥ)
farasha (*f r sh)
qattala (*q t l)
athkhana (*th kh n)
slave
ʿabd (*ʿ b d)
malaka (*m l k)
raqabah (*r q b)
salam (*s l m)
slavegirl
amah (*a m w)
fatayāt (*f t y)
slay
dhabaḥa (*dh b ḥ)
dhakká (*dh k y)
qatala (*q t l)
qatlá (*q t l)
athkhana (*th kh n)
sleep
manām (*n w m)

nāma (*n w m)
naʿasa (*n ʿ s)
raqada (*r q d)
sleep at noon
qāla (*q y l)
sleeping place
maḍājiʿ (*ḍ j ʿ)
marqad (*r q d)
slender
haḍīm (*h ḍ m)
ḍāmir (*ḍ m r)
slide (v)
saʿá (*s ʿ y)
slide back
zalla (*z l l)
slide down
nasala (*n s l)
slide, to cause to
azlaqa (*z l q)
slight
izdará (*z r y)
slink
khannās (*kh n s)
khunnas (*kh n s)
khasaʾa (*kh s ʾ)
slip
laghiya (*l gh y)
zalla (*z l l)
slip away
tasallala (*s l l)
slip, to cause to
azalla (*z l l)
istazalla (*z l l)
slope
ḥadab (*ḥ d b)
slowly
ruwaydan (*r w d)
slumber
hajaʿa (*h j ʿ)
naʿasa (*n ʿ s)
manām (*n w m)
nāma (*n w m)
raqada (*r q d)
sinah (*w s n)
small
qalīl (*q l l)
ṣaghīr (*ṣ gh r)
yasīr (*y s r)
small, to be
ṣaghara (*ṣ gh r)
smart
ad.há (*d h y)
smile
tabassama (*b s m)
smite
iʿtarā (*ʿ r w)
ḍaraba (*ḍ r b)
lafaḥa (*l f ḥ)
ṣakka (*ṣ k k)
aṣāba (*ṣ w b)
smoke
dukhān (*d kh n)
yaḥmūm (*ḥ m m)
nuḥās (*n ḥ s)
smooth
mahada (*m h d)
mahhada (*m h d)
marrada (*m r d)
snare
kāda (*k y d)
snatch
dhahaba (*dh h b)
khaṭifa (*kh ṭ f)
takhaṭṭafa (*kh ṭ f)
nazzāʿah (*n z ʿ)
sneaking one
khannās (*kh n s)
snort
ḍabaḥa (*ḍ b ḥ)
snout
khurṭūm (*kh r ṭ m)
so-and-so
fulān (*f l n)
soar
shamakha (*sh m kh)
sob
zafīr (*z f r)
soft
layyin (*l y n)
soft, be
khaḍaʿa (*kh ḍ ʿ)
soften
alāna (*l y n)
lāna (*l y n)
soil
turāb (*t r b)
thará (*th r y)
sojourn
mustaqarr (*q r r)
soldier, foot-
rajil (*r j l)
solemn
ghalīẓ (*gh l ẓ)
solicit
rāwada (*r w d)
solitary
fard (*f r d)
some
biḍʿ (*b ḍ ʿ)
farīq (*f r q)
shayʾ (*sh y ʾ)
son
ibn (*b n y)
ghulām (*gh l m)
walad (*w l d)
son, adopted
adʿiyāʾ (*d ʿ w)
soothsayer
kāhin (*k h n)
sorcery
saḥara (*s ḥ r)
saḥḥār (*s ḥ r)
ṭāghūt (*ṭ gh y)
sorrow
asif (*a s f)
ḥazana (*ḥ z n)
ḥazina (*ḥ z n)
ḥasrah (*ḥ s r)
soul
nafs (*n f s)
soul, laden
wazara (*w z r)
sound (v)
naqara (*n q r)
ṣāta (*ṣ w t)
sound, to be
barāʾ (*b r ʾ)
barīʾ (*b r ʾ)
salīm (*s l m)
salām (*s l m)
sow
zaraʿa (*z r ʿ)
space
jaw (*j w w)
space, to set a
zayyala (*z y l)
spacious, to be
raḥuba (*r ḥ b)
spare
alā (*a l w)
abqá (*b q y)
kafá (*k f y)
sparks (of fire)
sharar (*sh r r)
spathe
ṭalʿ (*ṭ l ʿ)

speak
ᶜaᶜlana (*ᶜ l n)
ḥaddatha (*ḥ d th)
kallama (*k l m)
takallama (*k l m)
khāfata (*kh f t)
khāṭaba (*kh ṭ b)
naṭaqa (*n ṭ q)
qāla (*q w l)
speak ill
ṭaᶜana (*ṭ ᶜ n)
speak secretly
asarra (*s r r)
speak truly
ṣadaqa (*ṣ d q)
species
afnān (*f n n)
speck
naqīr (*n q r)
spectre
ṭāfa (*ṭ y f)
speech
qīl (*q w l)
speech, to give
anṭaqa (*n ṭ q)
speech, twisting of
laḥana (*l ḥ n)
speed (v)
aᶜjala (*ᶜ j l)
spell, to cast a
saḥara (*s ḥ r)
spend
anfaqa (*n f q)
spent, to be
nafida (*n f d)
sperm-drop
manī (*m n y)
nuṭfah (*n ṭ f)
spider
ᶜankabūt (*ᶜ n k b)
spill
amná (*m n y)
safaḥa (*s f ḥ)
spin
ghazala (*gh z l)
māra (*m w r)
spirit
rūḥ (*r w ḥ)
splendour
sanā (*s n w)
split
falaqa (*f l q)
infalaqa (*f l q)
faraja (*f r j)
faraqa (*f r q)
tafarraqa (*f r q)
infaṭara (*f ṭ r)
inshaqqa (*sh q q)
shaqqa (*sh q q)
tashaqqaqa (*sh q q)
ṣadaᶜa (*ṣ d ᶜ)
taṣaddaᶜa (*ṣ d ᶜ)
spoiled, to be
tasannaha (*s n h)
spoils
afāʾa (*f y ʾ)
maghnam (*gh n m)
anfāl (*n f l)
sport
ᶜabatha (*ᶜ b th)
laᶜiba (*l ᶜ b)
lahā (*l h w)
spot
shiyah (*w sh y)
spouse
zawj (*z w j)
spread
basaṭa (*b s ṭ)
daḥā (*d ḥ w)
farasha (*f r sh)
madda (*m d d)
mahada (*m h d)
nashara (*n sh r)
nashshara (*n sh r)
satara (*s t r)
saṭaḥa (*s ṭ ḥ)
shāᶜa (*sh y ᶜ)
ṣaffa (*ṣ f f)
ṭaḥá (*ṭ ḥ y)
spring
ᶜayn (*ᶜ y n)
maᶜīn (*ᶜ y n)
yanbūᶜ (*n b ᶜ)
sprout
anbata (*n b t)
spy
tajassasa (*j s s)
squander
badhdhara (*b dh r)
stability
qarra (*q r r)
stable, to be
thabata (*th b t)
staff
ᶜaṣā (*ᶜ ṣ w)
minsaʾah (*n s ʾ)
stage
ṭabaq (*ṭ b q)
aṭwār (*ṭ w r)
stairs
maᶜārij (*ᶜ r j)
stake
awtād (*w t d)
stale
asana (*a s n)
stalk
sāq (*s w q)
shaṭʾ (*sh ṭ ʾ)
stalwart
ᶜifrīt (*ᶜ f r)
stamp
ḍaraba (*ḍ r b)
ṭabaᶜa (*ṭ b ᶜ)
rakaḍa (*r k ḍ)
stand
ḥāla (*ḥ w l)
qāma (*q w m)
qiyām (*q w m)
shahida (*sh h d)
ṣafana (*ṣ f n)
thabata (*th b t)
waqafa (*w q f)
stand, bring to a
athbata (*th b t)
stand, just
qawām (*q w m)
standard
nuṣub (*n ṣ b)
qawīm (*q w m)
standing
maqām (*q w m)
qawīm (*q w m)
star
kawkab (*k w k b)
najm (*n j m)
star, lagging
khunnas (*kh n s)
star, morning or night
ṭāriq (*ṭ r q)
star, orbit of
mawāqiᶜ (*w q ᶜ)
star, setting
kunnas (*k n s)
star, shooting
shihāb (*sh h b)
stare

shakhaṣa (*sh kh ṣ)
zurq (*z r q)
startle
istafazza (*f z z)
istanfara (*n f r)
state (n)
sīrah (*s y r)
ḥāfirah (*ḥ f r)
aṭwār (*ṭ w r)
state (v)
sammá (*s m w)
station
makānah (*k w n)
manāzil (*n z l)
maqām (*q w m)
waqafa (*w q f)
statue
tamāthīl (*m th l)
stature
basṭah (*b s ṭ)
khalaqa (*kh l q)
qawwama (*q w m)
staunch
qawwām (*q w m)
stay
nazila (*n z l)
istaqarra (*q r r)
ẓalla (*ẓ l l)
stay behind
khalafa (*kh l f)
khawālif (*kh l f)
takhallafa (*kh l f)
steadfast
ʿazama (*ʿ z m)
rābaṭa (*r b ṭ)
ṣabara (*ṣ b r)
ṣabbār (*ṣ b r)
steady, be un-
istakhaffa (*kh f f)
steal
istaraqa (*s r q)
saraqa (*s r q)
stealthy
khafiy (*kh f y)
steeds
jiyād (*j w d)
steep
ʿaqabah (*ʿ q b)
stem
sāq (*s w q)
step
darajah (*d r j)
khuṭwah (*kh ṭ w)
mawṭiʾ (*w ṭ ʾ)
stepdaughter
rabāʾib (*r b b)
sticky
lazaba (*l z b)
still
khamada (*kh m d)
askana (*s k n)
sakana (*s k n)
stinginess
bakhila (*b kh l)
ashiḥḥah (*sh ḥ ḥ)
shuḥḥ (*sh ḥ ḥ)
stint
qadara (*q d r)
ṭaffafa (*ṭ f f)
stipulate
ʿahida (*ʿ h d)
stir up
athara (*a th r)
aghrá (*gh r w)
athāra (*th w r)
stitch together
khaṣafa (*kh ṣ f)
stitch, un-
fataqa (*f t q)
stock
nasl (*n s l)
stone (n)
ḥajar (*ḥ j r)
ḥāṣib (*ḥ ṣ b)
ṣafwān (*ṣ f w)
stone altar
nuṣub (*n ṣ b)
stone (v)
rajama (*r j m)
rajīm (*r j m)
stop
ṣadda (*ṣ d d)
waqafa (*w q f)
stop short
aqṣara (*q ṣ r)
store up
idhdhakhara (*dh kh r)
aḥṣana (*ḥ ṣ n)
storm
ṭāghiyah (*ṭ gh y)
story
ḥadīth (*ḥ d th)
nabaʾ (*n b ʾ)
qaṣṣa (*q ṣ ṣ)
stout
istaghlaẓa (*gh l ẓ)
straight
istaqāma (*q w m)
qawīm (*q w m)
sawāʾ (*s w y)
straighten up
istawá (*s w y)
strait
ḍayq (*ḍ y q)
straiten
ḍāqa (*ḍ y q)
ḍayyaqa (*ḍ y q)
qadara (*q d r)
strange
ʿajīb (*ʿ j b)
fariy (*f r y)
stranger
junub (*j n b)
strangled, be
inkhanaqa (*kh n q)
strategem
ḥīlah (*ḥ w l)
kāda (*k y d)
stratum
ṭibāq (*ṭ b q)
straw
hashīm (*h sh m)
ḥuṭām (*ḥ ṭ m)
stray
ḍalla (*ḍ l l)
nafasha (*n f sh)
nakaba (*n k b)
streak
judad (*j d d)
streaming
thajjāj (*th j j)
strength
ayd (*a y d)
azr (*a z r)
dharʿ (*dh r ʿ)
kāda (*k y d)
mirrah (*m r r)
qūwah (*q w y)
ṭāqah (*ṭ w q)
strengthen
āzara (*a z r)
ʿazzaza (*ʿ z z)
rabaṭa (*r b ṭ)
shadda (*sh d d)
thabbata (*th b t)
stress

ba's (*b ' s)
stretch
basaṭa (*b s ṭ)
lamasa (*l m s)
madda (*m d d)
saṭaḥa (*s ṭ ḥ)
strike
ḍaraba (*ḍ r b)
qaṭṭaʿa (*q ṭ ʿ)
ṣakka (*ṣ k k)
wakaza (*w k z)
strike fire
qadaḥa (*q d ḥ)
string, fibres of
ankāth (*n k th)
strip (n)
qiṭaʿ (*q ṭ ʿ)
strip (v)
kashaṭa (*k sh ṭ)
nazaʿa (*n z ʿ)
salakha (*s l kh)
stripe
jalada (*j l d)
strive
iddāra'a (*d r ')
jāhada (*j h d)
jahada (*j h d)
ikhtaṣama (*kh ṣ m)
tanāfasa (*n f s)
saʿá (*s ʿ y)
stroke
masaḥa (*m s ḥ)
strong
ʿazīz (*ʿ z z)
istaghlaẓa (*gh l ẓ)
mirrah (*m r r)
matīn (*m t n)
qawīy (*q w y)
shadīd (*sh d d)
stronghold
maṣāniʿ (*ṣ n ʿ)
ṣayāṣī (*ṣ y ṣ)
structure, large
maṣāniʿ (*ṣ n ʿ)
struggle
jāhada (*j h d)
stubble
hashīm (*h sh m)
ḥaṣīd (*ḥ ṣ d)
stubborn
ʿanīd (*ʿ n d)
aladd (*l d d)
study
ʿallama (*ʿ l m)
darasa (*d r s)
dirāsah (*d r s)
stumble
aʿthara (*ʿ th r)
ʿathara (*ʿ th r)
stumps
aʿjāz (*ʿ j z)
stunt
dassā (*d s w)
stupidity
safīh (*s f h)
safiha (*s f h)
subdue
dhallala (*dh l l)
subject (v)
dhallala (*dh l l)
sakhkhara (*s kh r)
sublime
ʿalā (*ʿ l w)
ʿalīy (*ʿ l w)
ʿazīz (*ʿ z z)
submissive
dhalūl (*dh l l)
khaḍaʿa (*kh ḍ ʿ)
submissive, to render
dhallala (*dh l l)
submit, submission
adhʿana (*dh ʿ n)
khaḍaʿa (*kh ḍ ʿ)
aslama (*s l m)
salam (*s l m)
sallama (*s l m)
silm (*s l m)
aṭāʿa (*ṭ w ʿ)
subservient
sakhkhara (*s kh r)
subside
ghāḍa (*gh y ḍ)
sakata (*s k t)
substance
māl (*m w l)
substitute
baddala (*b d l)
istabdala (*b d l)
subvert
i'tafaka (*a f k)
succeed, cause to
kawwara (*k w r)
succeed, successor, succession
ʿurf (*ʿ r f)
ḥusūm (*ḥ s m)
istakhlafa (*kh l f)
khalafa (*kh l f)
khalf (*kh l f)
khalīfah (*kh l f)
khilfah (*kh l f)
tatābaʿa (*t b ʿ)
watr (*w t r)
success
ʿuqb (*ʿ q b)
successive
watr (*w t r)
succour
istaʿāna (*ʿ w n)
ʿazzara (*ʿ z r)
istaghātha (*gh w th)
ghātha (*gh y th)
māʿūn (*m ʿ n)
amadda (*m d d)
intaṣara (*n ṣ r)
istanṣara (*n ṣ r)
naṣara (*n ṣ r)
waffaqa (*w f q)
succulent
ṭarīy (*ṭ r y)
suckle
arḍaʿa (*r ḍ ʿ)
raḍiʿa (*r ḍ ʿ)
suckling woman
arḍaʿa (*r ḍ ʿ)
suckling, to seek
istarḍaʿa (*r ḍ ʿ)
suddenly
baghtah (*b gh t)
suffer
alima (*a l m)
ʿanita (*ʿ n t)
ḍaḥiya (*ḍ ḥ y)
laqiya (*l q y)
ṣaddaʿa (*ṣ d ʿ)
suffer to be
aʿraḍa (*ʿ r ḍ)
suffer, cause to
ḍārra (*ḍ r r)
suffer, ready to
ḥalīm (*ḥ l m)
suffering, long-
ṣabara (*ṣ b r)
suffice
aghná (*gh n y)
sufficient
ghanīy (*gh n y)

ḥasiba (*ḥ s b)
kafá (*k f y)
sufficient, to be self-
istaghná (*gh n y)
suggestions, evil
hamazāt (*h m z)
suitable
wāfaqa (*w f q)
sum
mablagh (*b l gh)
nafaqah (*n f q)
summer
ṣāfa (*ṣ y f)
summon
daʿā (*d ʿ w)
tanādá (*n d w)
sun
shams (*sh m s)
sunrise
ashraqa (*sh r q)
mashriq (*sh r q)
sunset
ghurūb (*gh r b)
maghrib (*gh r b)
supererogation
nāfilah (*n f l)
superfluous
ʿafā (*ʿ f w)
nāfilah (*n f l)
suppliant
iʿtarra (*ʿ r r)
supplication
daʿā (*d ʿ w)
support
ayyada (*a y d)
ʿaḍud (*ʿ ḍ d)
ʿazzara (*ʿ z r)
madad (*m d d)
madda (*m d d)
rukn (*r k n)
taẓāhara (*ẓ h r)
ẓāhara (*ẓ h r)
ẓahīr (*ẓ h r)
suppose
ḥasiba (*ḥ s b)
ẓanna (*ẓ n n)
suppress
kaẓama (*k ẓ m)
kaẓīm (*k ẓ m)
sure
makīn (*m k n)
matīn (*m t n)
ṣadaqa (*ṣ d q)
thabata (*th b t)
ayqana (*y q n)
yaqīn (*y q n)
surety
kafīl (*k f l)
qabīl (*q b l)
surface
ẓahr (*ẓ h r)
surge
māja (*m w j)
surmise
ẓanna (*ẓ n n)
surplus
zāda (*z y d)
surprise
ajāʾa (*j y ʾ)
surrender
aslama (*s l m)
salam (*s l m)
sallama (*s l m)
surreptitious
lādha (*l w dh)
surround
ḥaffa (*ḥ f f)
ḥāqa (*ḥ y q)
survey
iṭṭalaʿa (*ṭ l ʿ)
suspend
ʿallaqa (*ʿ l q)
suspicion
nakira (*n k r)
arāba (*r y b)
rāba (*r y b)
shakk (*sh k k)
ẓanna (*ẓ n n)
sustenance
aqwāt (*q w t)
razaqa (*r z q)
swallow
balaʿa (*b l ʿ)
khasafa (*kh s f)
laqifa (*l q f)
iltaqama (*l q m)
asāgha (*s w gh)
swallow, easy to
sāgha (*s w gh)
swarm (n)
abābīl (*a b l)
libad (*l b d)
swarm (v)
ʿasʿasa (*ʿ s ʿ s)
nasala (*n s l)
sajara (*s j r)
swear
iʾtalá (*a l w)
ʿaqada (*ʿ q d)
bāyaʿa (*b y ʿ)
ḥalafa (*ḥ l f)
aqsama (*q s m)
qāsama (*q s m)
taqāsama (*q s m)
swearer
ḥallāf (*ḥ l f)
sweep on
sawwama (*s w m)
sweet
ʿadhb (*ʿ dh b)
jamīl (*j m l)
swell
rabā (*r b w)
izdāda (*z y d)
swerve
ʿadala (*ʿ d l)
aʿraḍa (*ʿ r ḍ)
ʿāla (*ʿ w l)
janifa (*j n f)
jāra (*j w r)
māla (*m y l)
qasaṭa (*q s ṭ)
azāgha (*z y gh)
zāgha (*z y gh)
swift
sarīʿ (*s r ʿ)
swim
sabaḥa (*s b ḥ)
sharaʿa (*sh r ʿ)
swine
khinzīr (*kh n z r)
swoon
ghashiya (*gh sh y)
ṣaʿiq (*ṣ ʿ q)
swoop
sawwama (*s w m)
symmetry
qawwama (*q w m)

table
māʾidah (*m y d)
tablet
lawḥ (*l w ḥ)
taboo
ḥijr (*ḥ j r)
take

akhadha (*a kh dh)
ittakhadha (*a kh dh)
tawaffá (*w f y)
take (sexually)
hamma (*h m m)
take away
dhahaba (*dh h b)
salaba (*s l b)
waḍaʿa (*w ḍ ʿ)
take charge of
kafala (*k f l)
kaffala (*k f l)
take counsel
shāwara (*sh w r)
take off
kashafa (*k sh f)
khalaʿa (*kh l ʿ)
take out
istakhraja (*kh r j)
take to task
ākhadha (*a kh dh)
take up
iltaqaṭa (*l q ṭ)
take upon oneself
takallafa (*k l f)
tawallá (*w l y)
tale
ḥadīth (*ḥ d th)
ikhtalaqa (*kh l q)
nabaʾ (*n b ʾ)
talk
istaʾnasa (*a n s)
hajara (*h j r)
ḥadīth (*ḥ d th)
khāḍa (*kh w ḍ)
laghiya (*l gh y)
lāghiyah (*l gh y)
makara (*m k r)
samara (*s m r)
talk, idle
samara (*s m r)
tall
bāsiq (*b s q)
talon
ẓufur (*ẓ f r)
tamarisk-bushes
athl (*a th l)
tamper
ḥarrafa (*ḥ r f)
tarry
baṭṭaʾa (*b ṭ ʾ)
ghabara (*gh b r)
labitha (*l b th)
talabbatha (*l b th)
makatha (*m k th)
maqʿad (*q ʿ d)
qaʿada (*q ʿ d)
task
amara (*a m r)
task, take to
ākhadha (*a kh dh)
taste
dhāqa (*dh w q)
sāgha (*s w gh)
ṭaʿima (*ṭ ʿ m)
taste, to cause to
adhāqa (*dh w q)
tasty
sāgha (*s w gh)
tawdriness
zukhruf (*z kh r f)
tax
kallafa (*k l f)
teach
ʿallama (*ʿ l m)
adrá (*d r y)
tear (v)
kharaqa (*kh r q)
mazzaqa (*m z q)
nazaʿa (*n z ʿ)
qadda (*q d d)
tears
damaʿa (*d m ʿ)
tell
ḥaddatha (*ḥ d th)
anbaʾa (*n b ʾ)
nabbaʾa (*n b ʾ)
qaṣṣa (*q ṣ ṣ)
aṭlaʿa (*ṭ l ʿ)
tempestuous
ʿaṣafa (*ʿ ṣ f)
temple
bayt (*b y t)
temporal goods
ʿaraḍ (*ʿ r ḍ)
tempt
fatana (*f t n)
rāwada (*r w d)
sawwala (*s w l)
temptation
fitnah (*f t n)
ten
ʿashr (*ʿ sh r)
tendance
ʿimārah (*ʿ m r)
tenderness
ḥanān (*ḥ n n)
raʾfah (*r ʾ f)
ruḥm (*r ḥ m)
tent
surādiq (*s r d q)
ẓullah (*ẓ l l)
tent-peg
awtād (*w t d)
tenth
miʿshār (*ʿ sh r)
term
ajal (*a j l)
amad (*a m d)
ḥijaj (*ḥ j j)
kitāb (*k t b)
muddah (*m d d)
qadara (*q d r)
terminate
qaḍá (*q ḍ y)
terrible
shadīd (*sh d d)
terrify
faziʿa (*f z ʿ)
khawwafa (*kh w f)
raʿaba (*r ʿ b)
arhaba (*r h b)
istarhaba (*r h b)
terror
rijs (*r j s)
rijz (*r j z)
terror, to lift
fazzaʿa (*f z ʿ)
test
ablá (*b l w)
balā (*b l w)
ibtalá (*b l w)
fitnah (*f t n)
imtaḥana (*m ḥ n)
testament
waṣīyah (*w ṣ y)
waṣṣá (*w ṣ y)
testament, to make a
awṣá (*w ṣ y)
testimony
ash.hada (*sh h d)
shahida (*sh h d)
thank
shakara (*sh k r)
shakūr (*sh k r)
thankless, thanklessness

kafara (*k f r)
kaffār (*k f r)
kafūr (*k f r)
kufrān (*k f r)
thicket
aykah (*a y k)
thief
saraqa (*s r q)
thin
haḍīm (*h ḍ m)
thing(s)
amara (*a m r)
matāʿ (*m t ʿ)
shayʾ (*sh y ʾ)
thing, good
ḥasanah (*ḥ s n)
ṭayyib (*ṭ y b)
think
hamma (*h m m)
ḥasiba (*ḥ s b)
raʾá (*r ʾ y)
ẓanna (*ẓ n n)
third
thālith (*th l th)
thulth (*th l th)
thirst, thirsty
ẓamʾān (*ẓ m ʾ)
ẓamiʾa (*ẓ m ʾ)
thirty
thalāthūn (*th l th)
thorax
tarāʾib (*t r b)
thorn
shawkah (*sh w k)
thorn-fruit
ḍarīʿ (*ḍ r ʿ)
thornless
khaḍada (*kh ḍ d)
thoughts, evil
ẓanna (*ẓ n n)
thoughts, secret
sarāʾir (*s r r)
thousand
alf (*a l f)
thread (n)
khayṭ (*kh y ṭ)
thread (v)
salaka (*s l k)
threat
waʿīd (*w ʿ d)
threaten
awʿada (*w ʿ d)
waʿada (*w ʿ d)
three
thalāthah (*th l th)
thulāth (*th l th)
threshold
waṣīd (*w ṣ d)
throat
ḥulqūm (*ḥ l q m)
ḥanājir (*ḥ n j r)
tarāqī (*r q y)
throne
ʿarsh (*ʿ r sh)
kursīy (*k r s)
throng
jibillah (*j b l)
thullah (*th l l)
through
khilāl (*kh l l)
throw
kabba (*k b b)
kabkaba (*k b k b)
inkadara (*k d r)
alqá (*l q y)
nabadha (*n b dh)
ramá (*r m y)
ṭaraḥa (*ṭ r ḥ)
thrust
ʿatala (*ʿ t l)
daʿʿa (*d ʿ ʿ)
kabba (*k b b)
radda (*r d d)
salaka (*s l k)
ṭaʿana (*ṭ ʿ n)
ẓihrī (*ẓ h r)
thunder
raʿd (*r ʿ d)
ṭāghiyah (*ṭ gh y)
thunderbolt
ḥusbān (*ḥ s b)
ṣāʿiqah (*ṣ ʿ q)
thunderstruck
ṣaʿiq (*ṣ ʿ q)
tiding
ḥadīth (*ḥ d th)
khabar (*kh b r)
nabaʾ (*n b ʾ)
tidings, good
bashshara (*b sh r)
bushr (*b sh r)
bushrá (*b sh r)
tie (n)
ʿuqdah (*ʿ q d)
ʿiṣam (*ʿ ṣ m)
tie (v)
ʿaqada (*ʿ q d)
shadda (*sh d d)
awthaqa (*w th q)
tie, un-
ḥalla (*ḥ l l)
tight
ḥarija (*ḥ r j)
tillage
ḥaratha (*ḥ r th)
tiller
kafara (*k f r)
timber
khushub (*kh sh b)
time
amad (*a m d)
ummah (*a m m)
iná (*a n y)
dahr (*d h r)
ḥuqub (*ḥ q b)
ḥīn (*ḥ y n)
muddah (*m d d)
manūn (*m n n)
mustaqarr (*q r r)
sāʿah (*s w ʿ)
tārah (*t w r)
mīqāt (*w q t)
waqata (*w q t)
time, to set
waqqata (*w q t)
tissue
muḍghah (*m ḍ gh)
today
yawm (*y w m)
together
jamīʿ (*j m ʿ)
toil
naṣiba (*n ṣ b)
token
ramz (*r m z)
ashrāṭ (*sh r ṭ)
tomb
ajdāth (*j d th)
tomorrow
ghad (*gh d w)
tone (of speech)
laḥana (*l ḥ n)
tongue
lisān (*l s n)
tongue, foreign
aʿjamīy (*ʿ j m)

tooth
sinn (*s n n)
torment
ʿadhāb (*ʿ dh b)
ʿadhdhaba (*ʿ dh b)
gharām (*gh r m)
ṣaʿūd (*ṣ ʿ d)
tornedo
ḥāṣib (*ḥ ṣ b)
torrent
midrār (*d r r)
inhamara (*h m r)
sayl (*s y l)
wābil (*w b l)
torture
ʿadhāb (*ʿ dh b)
ʿadhdhaba (*ʿ dh b)
total
kāffah (*k f f)
kamala (*k m l)
totter
hār (*h w r)
touch
lāmasa (*l m s)
lamasa (*l m s)
massa (*m s s)
māssa (*m s s)
tamāssa (*m s s)
touch (sexually)
ṭamatha (*ṭ m th)
towards
tilqāʾ (*l q y)
qibal (*q b l)
shaṭr (*sh ṭ r)
tower
burūj (*b r j)
anshaʾa (*n sh ʾ)
shamakha (*sh m kh)
ṣarḥ (*ṣ r ḥ)
town
qaryah (*q r y)
trace, track
athar (*a th r)
athārah (*a th r)
ḥubuk (*ḥ b k)
judad (*j d d)
tract
manākib (*n k b)
qiṭaʿ (*q ṭ ʿ)
ṭarīqah (*ṭ r q)
trade
tijārah (*t j r)
tradition
ṭarīqah (*ṭ r q)
traduce
ṭaʿana (*ṭ ʿ n)
traffick
bāʿa (*b y ʿ)
tabāyaʿa (*b y ʿ)
trail
naqaʿa (*n q ʿ)
train
dhalūl (*dh l l)
traitor
khadhūl (*kh dh l)
khattār (*kh t r)
khāna (*kh w n)
khawwān (*kh w n)
trample
dassa (*d s s)
waṭiʾa (*w ṭ ʾ)
tranquility
rahā (*r h w)
sakana (*s k n)
iṭmaʾanna (*ṭ m ʾ n)
transact
adāra (*d w r)
transform
masakha (*m s kh)
transgress, transgression
ʿadá (*ʿ d w)
ʿudwān (*ʿ d w)
iʿtadá (*ʿ d w)
taʿaddá (*ʿ d w)
fajara (*f j r)
khaṭīʾah (*kh ṭ ʾ)
ashaṭṭa (*sh ṭ ṭ)
ṭaghiya (*ṭ gh y)
transitory world
ʿajila (*ʿ j l)
travel
safar (*s f r)
asrá (*s r y)
sará (*s r y)
sāra (*s y r)
traveller
sabīl (*s b l)
sayyārah (*s y r)
traverse
ʿabara (*ʿ b r)
qaṭaʿa (*q ṭ ʿ)
treachery
fitnah (*f t n)
tread
mawṭiʾ (*w ṭ ʾ)
waṭiʾa (*w ṭ ʾ)
treasure (n)
khazāʾin (*kh z n)
treasure (v)
idhdhakhara (*dh kh r)
kanaza (*k n z)
treaty
dhimmah (*dh m m)
mīthāq (*w th q)
tree
shajarah (*sh j r)
ṭalḥ (*ṭ l ḥ)
tree, fig-
tīn (*t y n)
tree, lote-
sidrah (*s d r)
tree, olive-
zaytūnah (*z y t)
tree, palm-
līnah (*l y n)
nakhlah (*n kh l)
tree, sheaths of
akmām (*k m m)
tree, stump of
aʿjāz (*ʿ j z)
tree, trunk of
jidhʿ (*j dh ʿ)
trellise
ʿarasha (*ʿ r sh)
ʿarsh (*ʿ r sh)
tremble
ashfaqa (*sh f q)
trespass
taʿaddá (*ʿ d w)
tribe
ʿashīrah (*ʿ sh r)
qabīl (*q b l)
rahṭ (*r h ṭ)
asbāṭ (*s b ṭ)
tribulation
baʾsāʾ (*b ʾ s)
ḍarrāʾ (*ḍ r r)
tribute
jizyah (*j z y)
kharāj (*kh r j)
kharj (*kh r j)
trick
kāda (*k y d)
khādaʿa (*kh d ʿ)
khadaʿa (*kh d ʿ)
khāna (*kh w n)

trickle down
nasala (*n s l)
trip
safar (*s f r)
triumph
fāza (*f w z)
qahara (*q h r)
troop(s)
fawj (*f w j)
jund (*j n d)
shirdhimah (*sh r dh m)
troth
khuṭbah (*kh ṭ b)
troth, make a
wāᶜada (*w ᶜ d)
trouble
kabad (*k b d)
khabāl (*kh b l)
marīj (*m r j)
sāʾa (*s w ʾ)
shaqqa (*sh q q)
troublesome
ashaqq (*sh q q)
true
ḥanīf (*ḥ n f)
aḥaqq (*ḥ q q)
ḥaqq (*ḥ q q)
naṣūḥ (*n ṣ ḥ)
qayyim (*q w m)
ṣiddīq (*ṣ d q)
wafīy (*w f y)
true, accept as
ṣaddaqa (*ṣ d q)
true, be
naṣaḥa (*n ṣ ḥ)
ṣadaqa (*ṣ d q)
true, be proved
ḥaqqa (*ḥ q q)
true, un-
bāṭil (*b ṭ l)
zūr (*z w r)
trump up
athara (*a th r)
trumpet
nāqūr (*n q r)
ṣūr (*ṣ w r)
trunk (of tree)
jidhᶜ (*j dh ᶜ)
trust
amānah (*a m n)
amina (*a m n)
iʾtamana (*a m n)
tawakkala (*w k l)
trust, thing taken on
umnīyah (*m n y)
trustee
wakīl (*w k l)
trustworthy
amīn (*a m n)
truth
ṣadaqa (*ṣ d q)
ḥaqq (*ḥ q q)
try, trial
balā (*b l w)
ibtalá (*b l w)
fatana (*f t n)
fitnah (*f t n)
imtaḥana (*m ḥ n)
maḥḥaṣa (*m ḥ ṣ)
tryst
mawᶜid (*w ᶜ d)
mīᶜād (*w ᶜ d)
tryst, to make a
tawāᶜada (*w ᶜ d)
tumble
inhāra (*h w r)
inqaḍḍa (*q ḍ ḍ)
tunnel
sarab (*s r b)
turn (n)
dāʾirah (*d w r)
karrah (*k r r)
maylah (*m y l)
turn (v)
ᶜadá (*ᶜ d w)
ᶜaqqaba (*ᶜ q b)
aᶜraḍa (*ᶜ r ḍ)
baᶜthara (*b ᶜ th r)
adbara (*d b r)
dāra (*d w r)
ḍaraba (*ḍ r b)
tafayyaʾa (*f y ʾ)
taḥarrafa (*ḥ r f)
jaᶜala (*j ᶜ l)
jamaḥa (*j m ḥ)
janaba (*j n b)
jannaba (*j n b)
tajannaba (*j n b)
jāra (*j w r)
iltafata (*l f t)
lafata (*l f t)
māla (*m y l)
anāba (*n w b)
aqbala (*q b l)
inqalaba (*q l b)
qalaba (*q l b)
qallaba (*q l b)
taqallaba (*q l b)
qaraḍa (*q r ḍ)
irtadda (*r d d)
radda (*r d d)
raghiba (*r gh b)
rāgha (*r w gh)
ṣaᶜᶜara (*ṣ ᶜ r)
ṣadda (*ṣ d d)
ṣadafa (*ṣ d f)
inṣarafa (*ṣ r f)
ṣarafa (*ṣ r f)
ṣarrafa (*ṣ r f)
ṣāra (*ṣ w r)
tāba (*t w b)
thaná (*th n y)
tawajjaha (*w j h)
wajjaha (*w j h)
tawallá (*w l y)
wallá (*w l y)
zāgha (*z y gh)
turning back
maradd (*r d d)
turret
ᶜarsh (*ᶜ r sh)
tutor (v)
ᶜallama (*ᶜ l m)
twelve
ithnā-ᶜashara (*th n y)
twenty
ᶜishrūn (*ᶜ sh r)
twice
marrah (*m r r)
twilight
shafaq (*sh f q)
twinkle
lamaḥa (*l m ḥ)
twist
laḥana (*l ḥ n)
lawá (*l w y)
lawwa (*l w y)
ṣāra (*ṣ w r)
ṭawwaqa (*ṭ w q)
two
ithnān (*th n y)
two by two
mathná (*th n y)
twofold
ḍiᶜf (*ḍ ᶜ f)
tyrant

jabbār (*j b r)

ulcer
qaraḥa (*q r ḥ)
ultimate
ʿuqbá (*ʿ q b)
uncle (maternal)
khāl (*kh w l)
uncle (paternal)
ʿamm (*ʿ m m)
uncleanness
tafath (*t f th)
understand, to cause to
fahhama (*f h m)
understand, understanding
ʿaqala (*ʿ q l)
baṣīr (*b ṣ r)
faqiha (*f q h)
ḥalam (*ḥ l m)
khabara (*kh b r)
albāb (*l b b)
nuhá (*n h w)
undertake
taʿāṭá (*ʿ ṭ y)
faraḍa (*f r ḍ)
unite
allafa (*a l f)
untouchable
māssa (*m s s)
uphold
qāma (*q w m)
uplift
rafaʿa (*r f ʿ)
aẓhara (*ẓ h r)
upon
ʿalā (*ʿ l w)
upper
ʿalīy (*ʿ l w)
ẓahr (*ẓ h r)
uppermost
ʿalā (*ʿ l w)
istaʿlá (*ʿ l w)
upraise
baʿatha (*b ʿ th)
inbaʿatha (*b ʿ th)
nashara (*n sh r)
rafaʿa (*r f ʿ)
upright
ḥanīf (*ḥ n f)
qawīm (*q w m)
sawīy (*s w y)
ṣiddīq (*ṣ d q)
uproot
ijtaththa (*j th th)
inqaʿara (*q ʿ r)
urge
ḥaḍḍa (*ḥ ḍ ḍ)
taḥāḍḍa (*ḥ ḍ ḍ)
ḥarraḍa (*ḥ r ḍ)
masāq (*s w q)
sāqa (*s w q)
awjafa (*w j f)
azjá (*z j w)
urgent
ḥathīth (*ḥ th th)
use, useful
maʾrab (*a r b)
nafaʿa (*n f ʿ)
manāfiʿ (*n f ʿ)
used up, to be
nafida (*n f d)
useless
khawālif (*kh l f)
usury
ribā (*r b w)
utility
manāfiʿ (*n f ʿ)
utter, utterance
kalām (*k l m)
lafaẓa (*l f ẓ)
qāla (*q w l)

vain talk
lāghiyah (*l gh y)
vain-doer
abṭala (*b ṭ l)
vain, in
sudá (*s d y)
vain, to be in
baṭala (*b ṭ l)
vainglory
ʿizzah (*ʿ z z)
valley
wādī (*w d y)
valour
baṭshah (*b ṭ sh)
value
thaman (*th m n)
vanish
zahaqa (*z h q)
zahūq (*z h q)
vanity
bāṭil (*b ṭ l)
vanquish
ghalaba (*gh l b)
vapour
sarāb (*s r b)
variableness
ḥawwala (*ḥ w l)
variance
tafarraqa (*f r q)
ikhtalafa (*kh l f)
nazagha (*n z gh)
shāqqa (*sh q q)
various
shattá (*sh t t)
vast
lujjī (*l j j)
vault
samk (*s m k)
vegetation
nabata (*n b t)
vehement
gharq (*gh r q)
veil (n)
ḥijāb (*ḥ j b)
ghishāwah (*gh sh y)
ghiṭāʾ (*gh ṭ y)
jalābīb (*j l b b)
akinnah (*k n n)
khafīy (*kh f y)
khumur (*kh m r)
sitr (*s t r)
veil (v)
ḍaraba (*ḍ r b)
ḥajaba (*ḥ j b)
vein, jugular
warīd (*w r d)
venerate
ʿaẓẓama (*ʿ ẓ m)
vengeance, take
intaqama (*n q m)
veracity
ṣadaqa (*ṣ d q)
verdict
ḥakama (*ḥ k m)
kalām (*k l m)
qaḍá (*q ḍ y)
verify
aḥaqqa (*ḥ q q)
verse
āyah (*a y w)
verve
shawkah (*sh w k)
vessel
ināʾ (*a n y)

wiʿāʾ (*w ʿ y)
vestment
libās (*l b s)
vex
sāʾa (*s w ʾ)
vice
dakhal (*d kh l)
viceroy
khalīfah (*kh l f)
victory
fataḥa (*f t ḥ)
fāza (*f w z)
ghalaba (*gh l b)
naṣara (*n ṣ r)
aẓfara (*ẓ f r)
vie
sāraʿa (*s r ʿ)
vigil, to keep
tahajjada (*h j d)
qāma (*q w m)
taraqqaba (*r q b)
vigour
irbah (*a r b)
asr (*a s r)
mirrah (*m r r)
vile, vileness
radhīl (*r dh l)
rahiqa (*r h q)
sawʾah (*s w ʾ)
vine
ʿinab (*ʿ n b)
violate
alḥada (*l ḥ d)
naqaḍa (*n q ḍ)
violent
ʿutull (*ʿ t l)
ʿatā (*ʿ t w)
gharq (*gh r q)
ṣarṣar (*ṣ r ṣ r)
virgin
bikr (*b k r)
virtuous conduct
birr (*b r r)
visible
sariba (*s r b)
sharaʿa (*sh r ʿ)
vision
ruʾyā (*r ʾ y)
visit
ʿamara (*ʿ m r)
ʿimārah (*ʿ m r)
iʿtamara (*ʿ m r)
ḥaḍara (*ḥ ḍ r)
massa (*m s s)
sāma (*s w m)
aṣāba (*ṣ w b)
ṭāfa (*ṭ y f)
zāra (*z w r)
visitation
ʿamara (*ʿ m r)
ʿumrah (*ʿ m r)
mathābah (*th w b)
visitor, nocturnal
ṭāriq (*ṭ r q)
voice
ṣāta (*ṣ w t)
void (n)
bāṭil (*b ṭ l)
hawāʾ (*h w y)
void (v)
ʿājaza (*ʿ j z)
daḥaḍa (*d ḥ ḍ)
takhallá (*kh l w)
volition
malaka (*m l k)
volunteer
ṭāʿa (*ṭ w ʿ)
taṭawwaʿa (*ṭ w ʿ)
taṭawwaʿa (*ṭ w ʿ)
vow
ālá (*a l w)
nadhara (*n dh r)
naḥaba (*n ḥ b)

wade
khāḍa (*kh w ḍ)
wage
ajr (*a j r)
wait
intaẓara (*n ẓ r)
qaʿada (*q ʿ d)
tarabbaṣa (*r b ṣ)
walk
ḥabara (*ḥ b r)
mashá (*m sh y)
tamaṭṭá (*m ṭ w)
walking
rajil (*r j l)
wall
jidār (*j d r)
sūr (*s w r)
wall, to climb over
tasawwara (*s w r)
wander
ʿamaha (*ʿ m h)
ḍalla (*ḍ l l)
hāma (*h y m)
tāha (*t y h)
ṭāfa (*ṭ w f)
want
amlaqa (*m l q)
arāda (*r w d)
shāʾa (*sh y ʾ)
wadda (*w d d)
war
ḥaraba (*ḥ r b)
war, spoils of
afāʾa (*f y ʾ)
maghnam (*gh n m)
anfāl (*n f l)
ward (v)
khazana (*kh z n)
ittaqá (*w q y)
warden
ḥafīẓ (*ḥ f ẓ)
warm
difʾ (*d f ʾ)
iṣṭalá (*ṣ l y)
warn, warning, warner
dhakara (*dh k r)
dhakkara (*dh k r)
dhikrá (*dh k r)
tadhkirah (*dh k r)
ḥadhdhara (*ḥ dh r)
andhara (*n dh r)
nadhara (*n dh r)
nadhīr (*n dh r)
nudhr (*n dh r)
nudhur (*n dh r)
waʿaẓa (*w ʿ ẓ)
warranty
qabīl (*q b l)
wash
ghasala (*gh s l)
ightasala (*gh s l)
washing, place of
mughtasal (*gh s l)
waste
dhahaba (*dh h b)
aḍāʿa (*ḍ y ʿ)
nafida (*n f d)
asrafa (*s r f)
wasted
nakhirah (*n kh r)
watch
baṣura (*b ṣ r)

tahajjada (*h j d)
ḥāfaẓa (*ḥ f ẓ)
intaẓara (*n ẓ r)
naẓara (*n ẓ r)
irtaqaba (*r q b)
raqaba (*r q b)
mirṣād (*r ṣ d)
watch of the night
qiṭʿ (*q ṭ ʿ)
watcher
raṣad (*r ṣ d)
watchful
ḥafīẓ (*ḥ f ẓ)
raqīb (*r q b)
water (v)
istasqá (*s q y)
saqá (*s q y)
water (n)
maʿīn (*ʿ y n)
furāt (*f r t)
lujjah (*l j j)
māʾ (*m w h)
water-drawer
warada (*w r d)
water-trough
jawābī (*j b y)
water, boiling
ḥamīm (*ḥ m m)
watering
siqāyah (*s q y)
suqyā (*s q y)
watering place
wird (*w r d)
wave(s)
mawj (*m w j)
waver
dhabdhaba (*dh b dh b)
wax proud
istakbara (*k b r)
takabbara (*k b r)
way
ḥubuk (*ḥ b k)
judad (*j d d)
sabab (*s b b)
sabīl (*s b l)
sharīʿah (*sh r ʿ)
ṣirāṭ (*ṣ r ṭ)
ṭarīq (*ṭ r q)
ṭarīqah (*ṭ r q)
wasīlah (*w s l)
way of approach
qurbān (*q r b)
way of life
sīrah (*s y r)
way out
makhraj (*kh r j)
way, right
sharīʿah (*sh r ʿ)
shirʿah (*sh r ʿ)
way, to be on the right
rashada (*r sh d)
waymark
ʿalam (*ʿ l m)
nuṣub (*n ṣ b)
mashʿar (*sh ʿ r)
shaʿāʾir (*sh ʿ r)
wayward
ṭaghiya (*ṭ gh y)
wazir
wazīr (*w z r)
weak, weakness
ʿajaza (*ʿ j z)
ḍaʿīf (*ḍ ʿ f)
ḍaʿufa (*ḍ ʿ f)
istaḍʿafa (*ḍ ʿ f)
hār (*h w r)
awhan (*w h n)
wahana (*w h n)
wahá (*w h y)
weaken
aʿjaza (*ʿ j z)
fattara (*f t r)
khasaʾa (*kh s ʾ)
awhana (*w h n)
wealth, wealthy
khayr (*kh y r)
māl (*m w l)
naʿmah (*n ʿ m)
wujd (*w j d)
awsaʿa (*w s ʿ)
wasiʿa (*w s ʿ)
wean
fiṣāl (*f ṣ l)
weapon(s)
asliḥah (*s l ḥ)
shawkah (*sh w k)
wear
labisa (*l b s)
weary, weariness
ʿayá (*ʿ y y)
ḥasīr (*ḥ s r)
istaḥsara (*ḥ s r)
laghaba (*l gh b)
naṣiba (*n ṣ b)
saʾima (*s ʾ m)
wed, wedlock
aḥṣana (*ḥ ṣ n)
ankaḥa (*n k ḥ)
weep, weeping
abká (*b k y)
baká (*b k y)
bukkīy (*b k y)
weigh light
khaffa (*kh f f)
weigh, weight
anqaḍa (*n q ḍ)
athqala (*th q l)
mithqāl (*th q l)
thaqal (*th q l)
thaqīl (*th q l)
wazana (*w z n)
weightless, to be
daḥaḍa (*d ḥ ḍ)
welcome
nuzul (*n z l)
marḥaban (*r ḥ b)
well
biʾr (*b ʾ r)
jubb (*j b b)
well-being
salām (*s l m)
well, bottom of
ghayābah (*gh y b)
west, western
gharbīy (*gh r b)
maghrib (*gh r b)
wet nurse
arḍaʿa (*r ḍ ʿ)
wheat
ʿaṣf (*ʿ ṣ f)
ḥaṣīd (*ḥ ṣ d)
sunbulah (*s n b l)
wheedle (v)
khaḍaʿa (*kh ḍ ʿ)
wheel (v)
māla (*m y l)
when
ḥīn (*ḥ y n)
while
ḥīn (*ḥ y n)
malīy (*m l y)
whip
sawṭ (*s w ṭ)
whirlwind
aʿṣara (*ʿ ṣ r)
whisper

hamasa (*h m s)
ḥasīs (*ḥ s s)
takhāfata (*kh f t)
makara (*m k r)
rikz (*r k z)
asarra (*s r r)
waswās (*w s w s)
waswasa (*w s w s)
whistle
makā (*m k w)
white
abyaḍ (*b y ḍ)
ibyaḍḍa (*b y ḍ)
asfara (*s f r)
whole
ajmaʿūn (*j m ʿ)
salima (*s l m)
wholesome
hanīʾ (*h n ʾ)
marīʾ (*m r ʾ)
ṭayyib (*ṭ y b)
wicked, wickedness
būr (*b w r)
fajara (*f j r)
fasaqa (*f s q)
ḥinth (*ḥ n th)
sāʾa (*s w ʾ)
sayyiʾ (*s w ʾ)
sharr (*sh r r)
aṭghá (*ṭ gh y)
ṭaghiya (*ṭ gh y)
ṭaghwá (*ṭ gh y)
ṭāghūt (*ṭ gh y)
wide
baʿīd (*b ʿ d)
raḥuba (*r ḥ b)
wasiʿa (*w s ʿ)
widow
thayyibāt (*th y b)
wife
ḥalāʾil (*ḥ l l)
imraʾah (*m r ʾ)
nisāʾ (*n s w)
ṣāḥib (*ṣ ḥ b)
zawj (*z w j)
wife, to go in unto
bāshara (*b sh r)
wilderness
ʿarāʾ (*ʿ r y)
wilfull
taʿammada (*ʿ m d)
will
arāda (*r w d)
shāʾa (*sh y ʾ)
aṣāba (*ṣ w b)
wajh (*w j h)
will, at
sudá (*s d y)
willing
ṭāʿa (*ṭ w ʿ)
willing, un-
kariha (*k r h)
win
fāza (*f w z)
wind
rīḥ (*r w ḥ)
wind, gentle
rukhāʾ (*r kh w)
wind, hot
samūm (*s m m)
wind, raging
ṣarṣar (*ṣ r ṣ r)
wind, strong
ʿaṣafa (*ʿ ṣ f)
wine
khamr (*kh m r)
raḥīq (*r ḥ q)
wing
janāḥ (*j n ḥ)
wings, spreading
ṣaffa (*ṣ f f)
wink
taghāmaza (*gh m z)
winnow
dharā (*dh r w)
faraqa (*f r q)
winter
shitāʾ (*sh t w)
wipe
masaḥa (*m s ḥ)
wise, wisdom
ḥakīm (*ḥ k m)
ḥikmah (*ḥ k m)
albāb (*l b b)
mirrah (*m r r)
wish
ḥaraṣa (*ḥ r ṣ)
ḥājah (*ḥ w j)
arāda (*r w d)
shāʾa (*sh y ʾ)
wadda (*w d d)
waṭar (*w ṭ r)
wit
kāda (*k y d)
withdraw
iʿtazala (*ʿ z l)
taḥarrafa (*ḥ r f)
naʾá (*n ʾ y)
intabadha (*n b dh)
nakaṣa (*n k ṣ)
withdraw one's help
khadhala (*kh dh l)
wither
ʿaqīm (*ʿ q m)
hāja (*h y j)
yabisa (*y b s)
withhold
ḥajaza (*ḥ j z)
kaffa (*k f f)
lāta (*l y t)
amsaka (*m s k)
ẓalama (*ẓ l m)
witness
iḥtaḍara (*ḥ ḍ r)
shahīd (*sh h d)
shahida (*sh h d)
wittingly, un-
jahālah (*j h l)
woe
asifa (*a s f)
wayl (*w y l)
wolf
dhiʾb (*dh ʾ b)
woman
imraʾah (*m r ʾ)
nisāʾ (*n s w)
niswah (*n s w)
woman, divorced
ṭallaqa (*ṭ l q)
woman, good
ṭayyib (*ṭ y b)
woman, old
ʿajūz (*ʿ j z)
woman, past child-bearing
qawāʿid (*q ʿ d)
woman, pregnant
ḥamala (*ḥ m l)
woman, previously married
thayyibāt (*th y b)
woman, suckling
arḍaʿa (*r ḍ ʿ)
woman, to go in unto
bāshara (*b sh r)
woman, unchaste
baghīy (*b gh y)
woman, unmarried